ISBN 978-1-5280-1964-4
PIBN 10904013

A

Concise Dictionary

OF THE

ASSYRIAN LANGUAGE

BY

W. Muss-Arnolt.

VOLUME II: MIQQU—TITURRU

PAGES 577—1202

BERLIN,
Reuther & Reichard
1905.

LONDON,
Williams & Norgate

NEW YORK,
Lemcke & Büchner

2) **mu-ug** | MUG | mu-uk-ku; *cf* S[c] 1 *b* 29 (Br 1881) but see maqaqu; AV 5452; 5461.

miqqu. ⊕ 84 iv 41 (II 26 *no* 1 *add*) .... KU = mi-iq-qu, also šup-lum, xu-ub-bu. AV 5347; Br 14404; 2500 & 2502 *ad* II 24 *a-b* 30; 22 *c-d* 10 (mi-ik-ku-u) AV 5283. (√מקק).

mequ (?) DT 71 *R* 6 .... me-iq-šu šu-up-pu-ux his *m* spread out (or scatter); *cf* II 28 *f-g* 63 DUGUD (= kabtu) = mi-iq.... (AV 5286; Br 9229: mik(q)tu).

maqdū some article of wood {ein Holzgegenstand} K 4378 iv 18—19 GIŠ-GAR-KAM-PAL & GIŠ-KU-LAL = ma-aq-du-u (D 88; II 46). AV 4990 (makdū).

maqaddu. H 39, 158; V 26 *a-b* 18 GIŠ (gi-iš-ki-bir) 𒄑 = ma-qad-du (Br 10872) in one group with eš-te-'-u (17) & ki-bir-ru. AV 5108. K 4378 (D 86) i 57 GIŠ-GAN-DAMAL (? or GUŠUR, II 20) = ma-qad-du, Br 3192; II 44, 34—6. — GGN '80, 541 *rm* 1; ZK ii 282—3 & *rm* 4 compares מקטר, thus = stake *etc.* {Scheiterhaufen}; TSBA iv 379. M[S] 84 *a* 3—4 reads II 14 *c-d* 9 (= H 73, 5—6) i-na (iç) ma-qad mu-sa-ri-e (*q. v.*) ušakkak; also MEISSNER, 12 *rm* 3.

maqdadu some vessel {ein Gefäss} K 55 *O* 18 ..... SA = ma-aq-da-du.

maqlū, maqlūtu (§ 65, 31 *a*; Br 10873) ‖ qilūtu (√qalū) burning, consuming by fire {Verbrennung}. IV² 50 *c* 26 ma-aq-lu-u. name of a whole series of incantations, see T[M] introd., *passim* & i 145; iv 128; viii 100; BEZOLD, *Catalogue*, v *pp* xxv & 2056. Šalm. *Mon*, *O* 17 their young men, their maidens a-na ma-aq-lu-te ašrup (KGF 526; HEBR. iii 226). Also maqalūtu (?) 81—2—4, 58 *R* 7 ma-qa-lu-tu aq-tu-lu (HARPER, *Letters*, 361). *Cf* Anp ii 110 & *var* on III 6 ma-aq-lu-te.

muqalpitu (Br 3741 *etc.*) see קלפ.

miqq(gg?)ānu a worm {ein Wurm}. D[S] 84; Br 5814, 8829. II 28 *b-c* 9 MAR = mi-ig-ga-nu (AV 5226); 10—11 MAR-GAL & MAR-ŠA (= LIB)-SUR = iš-kip-pu (BA i 74: Krankheitsname); II 5 *c-d* 42 UX-KU-SAR-DA = mi-iq-qa[-nu], AV 5346; between akšu (moth) & tul'u (worm); V 27 *g-h* 23 (II 31 *g-h* 84) same id = me-iq-qa-a-nu = xar.... (between ri'ašu & ibxu) Br 8329; ZA x 202, 1—2 mi-iq-qa-ni = miq]-qa-nu.

NOTE. — Here belongs perhaps also NE XII ii 30 (see mekkū); orig. = insect, used here metaphorically, to express the gnawing sorrow of Gilgameš over the loss of Eabani, BA i 74; J[I-N] 55, note 106.

maqāçu rack, implement of torture? {Marterbank, Schinderbrett} § 64; BA i 173. II 23 *a-b* 9 na-aṭ-ba-xu = ma-ka-çu, AV 4984; SMITH, *Asurb*, 137, 79 *Dunānu* eli (iç) ma-ka-çi id-du-šum-ma iṭ-bu-xu-uš az-liš, KB ii 256—7; KAT² 557; Z[B] 24, 2; D[H] 29; D[Pr] 75. √קוץ.

maqaççu some instrument of destruction {ein Zerstörungswerk?} √קצץ. V 17 *a-b* 13—14 [ma-xa-çu] ša ma-qaç-çi (Br 14089—90; AV 4915); id in 13 *a* ... GAZ-MAN-DA; 14 *a* ... GAZ-MAN-DU-DU; BA i 173—4.

maqçaru, see makçaru.

maqaqu (or ***magagu?***) perhaps fill up, in; wall in {viell. ein-, auffüllen; einschliessen; einmauern?} AV 4913; PSBA x 299. I 51 *no* 2 *b* 5 e-li te-me-en-ni-šu la-bi-ri eprē ellūti am-ku-uk-ma (KB iii, 2, 59 ich füllte auf). V 56, 44—5 (see makū & KB iii, 1 171). Rm 343 *R* 4 TIK-LAL = šur-rum; 5 TIK-BU = ma-qa-qu (Br 3289); 6 TIK-BU-BU = mi-tan-gu-gu (Br 3291 ✕ AV 5257); II 20 *c-d* 52—3 TIK-BU-I = ma-ga-gu (Br 3290); TIK-BU-BU-I = mi-tan-gu-gu (Br 3292). Also see MEISSNER, *Suppl*, *p* 59 where S[c] 1 *b* 29 is restored to muk-ku-[qu].

𝔍 = 𝔔 (intensive). Anp i 90 the ones (an-nu-te) ina lib-bi ¹/₂-si-te u-ma-gig (*var* gi-gi) *etc.* KB i 66—7; BOUTFLOWER, HEBR., xv 50 some I walled up within the tower; Anp ii 72: 20 people I captured alive, ina dūr ēkalli(-šu) u-ma-gi-gi.

𝔍[t] *ac* mitangugu see 𝔔.

𝔑 II 35 *g-h* 14 + K 2032 na-ma-gu-gu ‖ of mu.....

Derr. probably muqqu & miqqu.

maqarūtu (?) III 50 *no* 1, 5—8: 60 ma-qa-ru-tu + 20 + 20 *ditto* = 100 ma-qur-

ma-qi-ir (!!) Šamši *cf* migru, migir. ∾ maqrū see magrū.

rat^{meš} ŠE in-nu^{meš}. some measure for grain, *etc.* Neb 92, 5 ma-qar-ra-a-tu mentioned in a list of utensils between pa-a-šu (4) & na-al-pa-a-ta (6).

maqatu, imqut (Esh *Sendsch*, *R* 20 beg.), & iqqut (? § 49*a*), imaq(q)ut fall, fall down, tumble {fallen, stürzen} ‖ šaxatu, AV 5110; Br 1432. *a*) literally. *Etana*-legend (Km 2. 454 *R* 30) našru im-qu-ut(-ma) stürzte herab (also *l* 36); III 56 *a* 5 kakkabu rabû RU (= imqu)-ut, Jensen, 157—8; III 4 *no* 4, 50 ul-tu çi-ir sisê qaq-qa-riš im-qu-ut fell from his horse to the ground. S^P III 2 *O* 15 his son ina kakki qâtâšu mux-xa-šu im-qut (-xaç?, or to *b*?). NE 59, 17 ki-ma tar-ta[-xi] im-qut (or xaç?); perhaps NE XII *col* ii 29—30 (end) a-na erçi-tim im-qut(? xaç)-an-ni-ma. — *b*) fall upon one (eli), strike, attack {auf jemanden fallen, überfallen, angreifen}. IV^2 29 *no* 3, 5—6 the asakku ..... im-qut-ma; see xattu (*p* 347 *col* 1, where *l* 4 read *Ann* 29 *o*) & xarbašu (336 *col* 2). Sp II 265 *a* xvii 11 ma-qit bêlê. IV^2 30 *a* 27 ni-iz-za-tu ma-li i-na û-um im-qu-tu-ma ina i-dir-tim (?). — *c*) thrust oneself, jump {sich werfen, stürzen} Asb iv 58 who with their lord had not jumped into the fire (im-qu-tu ina išâti); K 647 *O* 13—14 (= IV^2 45 *no* 3; Pinches, *Texts*, 4) man-ma ma-la a-na pa-ni-ka-nu i-ma-aq-qu-ta (see, above, *p* 331 *col* 1). — ZA iii 364 am-qut I threw myself down. — *d*) in court: to claim {Anspruch erheben gegen} Cyr 332, 27 ta-am-qu-tu (3 *f sg*), see muquttû. KB iv 90 *col* vi 5 i-na kišid-ta ša im-qut-ma (Peiser, KAS 108, mit dem Vermögen, worauf er Anspruch machte). — K 689, 30 i-ma-qu-ut (or -tu); K 177, 49 i-ma-qu-tu(-šu); V 61 vi 54 lim-qut (or xaç?) šal-mat-su-ma; 81, 3—4, 188 *R* 22 lim-qu-ta pa-ša-xi. ● 51 i 32 ma-qa-tum in one group with na-du-u & [n]a-ša-ku. V 24 *c-d* 13 na-du-u = ma-qa-tum (✕ AV 5107).

Q^t = Q *a* & *b*. K 56 iv 24 igaru ša iquppu eli-šu [im]-ta-qu-ut (= IM-MA-AN-RU). *del* 129 (139) urru im-ta-qut eli dûr appija. NE 58, 20 im-taq-qu-tu. K 479, 31 words from the mouth in-da-aq-tu (have proceeded). Knudtzon, 107 *R* 16 (in an omen) im-ta(?)-qa-at(?); K 551 *R* 1 a fox ina bûri i-tu-qut fell into a well (Hr^L 142); Meissner, *Suppl*, 59; but Johnston, JAOS xix 71 = N^t. — K 31 *O* 20 bu-bu-tu u çu-um-mu-u eli-ja in-da-qut.

Q^{tn} fall down {stürzen, fallen}. Barth, ZA ii 383 *rm* 1; *Nominalbildung*, § 100 *b*; Philippi, BA ii 387 *rm* *†. NE 6, 47 (13, 28) im-da-nak-qu-tu (or -ta) e-lu çêri-ja (BA i 103); K 2326, 12 [šimat ul]-tu šame-e in-da-naq-qu-ta-nš-ši. — run hastily {hastig laufen} Šalm *Mon*, *R* 73 many among them a-na ka-a-pe (*q. v.*) ša šadê i-ta-na-qu-tu-ni fled to the rocks of the mountains. Also see Meissner, *Suppl*, 59 *col* 2.

J perhaps V 47 *a* 59 maš-kan ram-ni-ja muq-qu-tu (or ut) še-pa-a-a; maš-kan: bi-ri-tum, into my own fetters have fallen my feet.

Š overthrow, throw down, overpower {niederwerfen, hinstrecken, überwältigen}. TP i 45 u-šam-qi-tu gi-ir A-šur; vi 81: 800 lions i-na pat-tu-te u (*var* lu)-šim-qit (= 1 *sg*); v 71 their warriors u-šim-qit. Asb ix 57 u-šam-qit-su-nu-ti Dibbarra qar-du; also iv 79 (see Girra, *p* 281 *col* 2; ZK i 244 *rm* 1); ix 89 (Nusku) u-šam-qi-tu ga-ri-ja. TP III *Ann* u-šam-qit often (195, 199 *etc.*). ina kakkê u-šam-qit D 113, 11; Sarg *Ann* 85, 94, 362; *Khors* 136; *Ann* 96 u-šam-qit-su-nu-ti (142); Anp iii 36 u-šam-qit; Asb ii 2 u-šam-qi-tu (3 *pl*); Sp III 2 *O* 9 ... ina kakki u-šam-qit. V 64 *b* 18 nap-xar-šu-nu li-šam-qit; 37 za-ma-ni-ja li-ša-am-qit (see zamânu), *c* 50 li-ša-am-qi-ta ga-ri-šu. K 2846, 29 liš-šam-ki-tu ga-ri-šu may fall his enemies. K 2619 iv 1 ša $^{(il)}$ DUN-PA-UD-DU ša-ru-ru-šu lu-šam-qit (I will overthrow). IV^2 48 *a* 13 if Bêl um-mânšu u-šam-ga-tim; *b* 2 (end) u-šam-qat-ma; 34 i *O* 33 um-ma-an-šu-nu rabî-ta u-šam-ki-tu. H 125, 12 (= IV^2 30 *a* 25) tu-šam-qit (see laqatu). K 2867 *O* 28 bu-ul çêri ka-a-a-an u-šam-qa-tu (S 2148, 7). K 8571 *O* 11 šum-qu-ut bu-ul çêri (see mâtu, die); ana šum-qut napšâtišu Šalm. *Mon* ii 100 (KB i 172, see, again, Schеil., *Šalm*, 100). Sarg *Cyl* 7 a-na šum-qut na-ki-ri (AV 8509);

Anns 3; *Nimr* 3. IV² 18, 3 *O* i 36 ana māt nu-kur-ti sa-pa-ni a-a-bi šum-qu-ti. Neb *Bors* (= I 51 *no* 1) ii 21 šu-um-ku-tu na-ki-ri (§ 132; ZA ii 129 *b* 28); V 66 *a* 25 šu-um-qu-ut ma-a-ti a-a-bi-ja. K 3474 i + K 8232 i 26 [šu?]-um-ki-ta er-çi-tu ta-ba-'u ū-me (*var* mi)-šam; III 61 *a* 17. — V 34 *c* 48—9 lu-u šu-um-gu-tu na-ki-re-ja | u sa-pa-nim māt a-a-bi-ja *etc.* ki-be-i. — TP v 65 mu-šim-qit la-a ma-gi-ri; Anp i 7 (34) *Ninib* mu-u-šam-qit tar-gi-gi, iii 130; Sarg *Nimr* 12 Sargon .... mu-šim-qit (māt) Ma-da-a-a ru-qu-u-te (KB ii 38—9); Esh *Sendsch*, *R* 33 mu[-šam]-qit māt nu-kur-ti a-na-ku; 29, mu-šam-qit la ma-gi-ri. K 3197 i B, *R* 13 mu-šam-qit ra-bi-çi lim-ni (= IV² 21). Craig, *Texts*, I 1, 21 mu-šam-ki-tat (amēl) nakru (*cf* 83—1—18, 1847 ii 8, ta-ad, Harper, Hebr. xiv 173—4). AV 5589. — Cyr 338, 8 šu-un-qu-ut-tu it-ti a-xa-meš i-te-ep-šu = have given quit claims mutually {haben einander Entlastung erteilt}; also Nabd 715, 13 (šu-un-qu-tu ep-šu) a *noun*?; 867, 9 the debt of 4 šeqel of silver on such and such a day ina šîmi ša (of 2 slaves) u-ša-an-qa-at (BA i 535 *no* 48; Peiser, KAS 108); 553, 11.

Š̌[t] IV² 23 *no* 4, 2 bu-ul] çe-ri ina ri-ti uš-tam-qit (= RU-RU-TA); V 50 *b* 58 bu-ul çēri ina ri-i-ti uš-tam-qit (H 187, below).

Note. — 1. Asb vii 81 ik-ku-ud (Latrille, ZK ii 340 √maqatu) see ???.

2. *dcl* 69 (end) read am-xaç (see maxaçu, 2).

3. T. A. ana šēpē šarri am-qut (& ku-ut) very often = prostrate oneself, obey. Lo. 12, 5; 13, 6; also im-ku-ut Lo. 74, 7 = 1 *sg*. *cf* Ber. 120, 6; am-ku-kut Lo. 65, 6; 42, 6 ni-am-ku-ut; 14, 43 u-ul ji-ma-ku-ta çābē ka-ra-ši eli-ja may (they) not fall upon me (*cf* Ber. 89, 31); Ber. 61, 12 ma-qa-ti (3 *sg* pm); Lo. 12, 32 ni-ma-ku-ut we will fall (upon Gebal); 21, 36 ni-mu-ku-ut; 16, 10 in order that the troops ti-ma-ku-tu eli (may fall upon); *or* perhaps Lo. 28, 74 iš-tu ma-qa-ti nakrū-tum | i-na mux-xi-ja (since the enemy fell upon me).

Derr. šunqūtu (Nabd 715, 13) & these 6:

maqtu *adj* fallen {gestürzt, gefallen} K 3459 *R* 15 eli ma-aq-tu-ti (taš-ta-kan gi-mil-la) ZA iv 15 to those that are fallen. K 2711 *R* 6 (see labaru 1 (Q), end). Zimm., *Šurp*, iv 17 ma-aq-tu šu-ut-b[u-u] ‖ qā-at en-ši ça-ba[-tu]; 52 (*b*) ma-aq-tu l[it]-bi. King, *Magic*, *no* 6, 44 ma-aq-tum ša ..... K 518, 6 (H[L] 140) a letter to the king about some officers (amēl ma-ak-tu-te), ina muxxi (amēl) ma-ak-tu-te; *R* 5: XV (amēl) ma-ak-tu-te; also *cf* Bu 89—4—26, 163 (*Letters*, 404) *O* 17, 20; *R* 19; 83—1—18, 18 (*Letters*, 343) *O* 18 & *R* 13 (Hebr. xiv 11—12). K 576 (Hr[L] 110) *R* 9—10 see misû (Q) & AJSL xv 141.

maqittu *a*) = miqittu (*q. v.*). 81—6—7, 209 (Dupl. K 6346) 32 ma-qit-ta-šu as-sux; 37 in-na-xu-ma ma-qit-ti i-raš-šu-u aš-ra-ti-šu liš-te-'e-e-ma ma-qit-ta-šu lik-šir may restore its delapidation (BA iii 262 × Hebr. viii 14); *b*) bow, prostration {Vorbeugung *etc.*} T. A. Lo. 83, 5 ma-aq-ti-ti VII (or = pm as KB v, Glossary?); 67, 4—5, *etc.*, see mila = times.

miqtu, *c. st.* miqit, meqit (BA i 6, 163 *no* 5 & *rm* †) AV 5286. *a*) precipice, abyss {Abgrund, Absturz} Asb iii 125 ina mi-qit išāti *etc.*, will I ruin their life (BA i 6; 163, 5); iv 51 Šamaššumukin ina mi-qit (il) GIŠ-BAR (= li'bi?) a-ri-ri id-du-šu (ZK ii 28?, cast him on a glowing pile of fire); IV² 50 *b* 42 a-na mi-qit mē u išāti lid-di-ki may he throw thee into an abyss of water and fire (Jensen, 123; T[M] 136, below). II 49 *e-f* 11 UL-DIR = miq (written RU)-tim išāti; *no* 3, 31 MUL-DIR = me-qit i-šat, preceded by ma-ag-ru-u (= II 51 *no* 2 *O* 29 = *b* 65, Br 3740) BA i 163. III 53 *b* 38 MUL-DIR-RU-tim *i. e.* miqit-tim išāti name of a star (Jensen, 117: Planet Mars). — *b*) low spirit, lowness of spirit, depression of spirit {Niedergeschlagenheit}. miqit ṭēme *cf* ṭēmu (*p* 355 *col* 2); KB ii 180—1; Rost, 115 *etc.* — *c*) debaseness, vileness {Niedrigkeit, Gemeinheit}. II 39 *a-b* 13 + V 39 *a-b* 13 (Br 1433) KA-TA-SUB-BA = mi-qit pi-i (Br 639); also *cf* II 28 *f* 64 (Br 465), 63 (Br 9229); 35 *g-h* 47 mi-iq-tum ‖ tu-uš-šu. K 8204, 3 ša s(s)ul (or dun?)-xa-a u mi-ik-ti ab-bak (PSBA xvii 140 √קוט), Z[B] 73. — *d*) damage {Beschädigung} Sm 26 i (?) 16 mi-ki(= qi)-it tarbaçi. BA iv 84.

Note. — Geo. Hoffmann, ZA xi 365—7 still adheres to the comparison with ???, Lotz, *Quaer-*

stiones, 32, long given up by most Assyriologists; *ibid* he says: Die Winterconstellation des Mercur unter dem Namen miqit me = Nusku; vielleicht wurden auch Nusku u. Gibil in zweiter Hand auf den Planeten Merkur bezogen.

miqittu = maqittu, *a*. BA i 163 & *rm* ††. Neb *Bors* ii 11 mi-ki-it-ta-ša (u-) uš-zi-iz (the tower's) decay I repaired {seinen Verfall stellte ich wieder her}. V 62 *a-b* 56 mi-ki-it-ta-šu (= [BI?]-RI-GA-BI, Br 2595) lu-u uš-ziz, Lehmann, ii 54; *Diss.* 23, 26; — K 185, 17 (Harper, *Letters*, 74) me-qit-ti išāti.

miquttu (?) NE 65, 4 (see katamu Q).

muqut(t)ū claims for damages *etc.* {Ansprüche auf Entschädigung} T^C 97. Peiser, KAS 108, ZA iii 83 *rm* 2 fine, imposed upon one, that had lost a suit in court; Oppert, *ibid*, 179 *rm* 5. Nabd 13, 10 (amēl) da'ānē im-tal-ku-ma 1/2 ma-na 5 šiqli kas-pi ma-la .... mu-qut-te-e-šu in pān (sal) Be-li-li-tum ip-ru-su-ma a-na *NN.* id-di-nu (as much as was her claim); Cyr 332, 26 *fol* mu-qu-tu-u ša in connection with the verb tamqutu.

miqtu in miqti xammu see *p* 536 *col* 1.

muqtablu (Br 6220 *etc.*, AV 5548) warrior {Krieger} see קבל Q^t.

miqtānu. II 53 *no* 2 *O* 2 qabal (al) Ki-nu-a | X GUN a-na mi-iq-ta-ni (in revenue accounts).

muqutānu. II 43 *a-b* 60 (šam) mu-qu-ta-nu = (šam) ki-sa-at çiri (*q. v.*).

maru V 21 *g-h* 39 GIŠ(IÇ) = ma-ru Br 5703.

māru *m*, *c. st.* mar (D 90, 6); *pl* mārē son, child {Sohn, Kind} id usually TUR (§ 9, 130; Br 4081; TP ii 25; Hebr. i 226); H 18, 286 (S^b 305, Br 4070) du-u | TUR | ma-a-ru (II^F 50 *no* 27), preceded by (285) tu-ur | TUR | çi-ix-ru & followed by (287) i-bi-la | TUR-UŠ | ab(p)-lu & 288 TUR-SAL = mar-tu. *pl* TUR-MEŠ nab-ni-it libbišu TP ii 47; Knudtzon, 303. — Also A = ma-ru H 41, 276; § 9, 1; Br 11344; IV² 24 *a* 14—5 (= ma-ru); TP vii 67 *var* TUR; Anp i 28 (ZA i 62 *rm* 1) — ṬU-MU *e. g.* Sm 1366 *O* + ṬU-MU-ZU = ma-ra-ki (ZA i 18, 20; Br 11917), see perh. damu, dumu (above, *p* 252, *col* 2). — S^c 1 *a* i 4 see bīru 2 *a*. II 47 *e-f* 19 BU = ma-a-ru. Usually = child, son in the real sense of the word {Sohn, Kind, im eigentlichen Sinne}. III 35 *b* 26 U-a-a-te-' ma-ru-uš-šu im-xur-šu-ma. Esh *Sendsch*, *R* 45 ri-ix-ti TUR-MEŠ-šu the rest of his sons, so often; IV² 5 *a* 65 AN-MEŠ TUR-MEŠ-šu = ilāni mārēšu; II 67, 17, 21 *etc.* mārē-šu mārāti-šu his sons (and) daughters; Šalm. *Ob* 49, 126; Sn ii 60 *etc.* Bu 88—5—12, 21, 10: mārē ma-la a-ṵa-al-du; 12 u i-ṵa-la-du mārē-ši-na-ma (Meissner, *no* 89). — K 2729 *R* 3 ma(?)-a-ri ni-bi-ri za-ku-u (BA ii 566 *foll*). *Zū*-legend (K 3454) 35 al-ka ma]-ru Rammān (BA ii 409); Creat.-*frg* III 71 AN-ŠAR ma-ru[-ku-nu?]; D 96, 24 li-ša-an-ni-ma a-bu u ma-ri; NE 8, 20 tul-tab-ši ma-a-ri (see bašū Š¹), xii, 1, 40—1. Sp II 265 *a* xvii 3 ma-a-ru ..... šu-par(?ut) max[....]; 5 ma-ar .... šu-ur[...]; 6 ma-ar ka-ti-i; 10 ma-ar kab-ti; xv 10 ma-ra u mar-tum lu-ba-'; xxii 9 li-il-lu ma-ru pa-na-a i-al-lad; xxiv 2 šar-xu (il) zu-lum ma-ru (*var* mar); Strong, PSBA xvii 150 reads mar (*var* ma-ar)-ka ri-çu (*var* -iç) ṭi-iṭ-ṭi-šin (*var* ta-ši-na). V 25 *col* 3, 23—5 šum-ma ma-ru (= TUR) a-na a-bi-šu *etc.* (GGN '80, 524 *rm* 2); 29 šum-ma ma-ri (= TUR) a-na um-mi-šu *etc.* 34—7 šum-ma | a-bu ana ma-ri-šu (TUR-NA-RA) | ul ma-ri at-ta | iq-ta-bi (= D 131, 34 *foll*; § 142); *cf* 40—3 šum-ma um-mu ana ma-ri-šu | ul ma-a-ri at-ta | iq-ta-bi (see Oppert, GGA '78, 1613 *foll*, *ad* H^F; PSBA vii *pt* 2; Hommel, *Sum. Les.*, 109 *foll*); H 76, 10 ṭe-im ma-ri-ja (= TUR-MU); 77, 30 mār ru-bi-e; 76, 26 TUR-šu with *var* ma-ra-šu (II 9, 57); 80, 6 (il) Nin-ib šar-ru ma-ru ša (il) Bēl, 14, 24 (il) Nin-ib be-lum mar (il) Bēl; 81, 6 ma-ru ša ana mu-še-niq-ti la aš-bu; 78 *R* 9 qar-ra-du mar ap-si-i (= TUR-ZU-AB), D 133, 9. IV² 1* iii 5—6 ma-ru-u (= TUR) git-ma-lu-tum ap-lu git-ma-lu-tum šu-nu (§ 67 *b*); 1 i 7 nam-ta-ru ma-ru (= TUR) na-ram (il) Bēl (*Rev. Sém.* iv 344); 7 *a* 32 a-lik ma-ri (= TUR-MU) (il) Marduk (go my son *M.*), *cf* ll 25, 26—7; 22, 1 *R* 8; H 77, 28; IV 22, 1 *R* 4 ma-a-ri mi-na-a la ti-di; 28* 4 *R* 53 ma-ri-mi; K 4870, 9—10 ma-ri-ja; ma-ri = my son also Z^š v/vi 30, 35; vii [48, 53]; T. A. (Ber.) 92, 45 ja-nu-um-ma ma-ri-ja a[-nu ja-ši] I have no son; IV² 27 *no* 5, 13 ma-a-ra (= TUR) ina bīt a-bi-šu u-še-çu-u (IV² 2 v 7 ma-ru *var* ma-a-ra); K 4648, 19—20 ki-ma ma-a-ri (= TUR-RA) la ki-nim (H 178; H *Sintfl.* 26 *rm* 76); *c. st.*, *e. g.* IV² 4 iii 22 mar (il) Sin (+ 23); 21 (ilat) Iš-tar ma-rat (il) Sin; K 321, 35 lim-mu Mar-la-rim *etc.* — Also = the young of an animal (*cf* būru 3, *no b*) *e. g.* mār iç-çu-ri (see admu & lidānu); *del* 117 ki-i TUR-MEŠ nūnē like spawn of fish. — māru çīt libbišu (see libbu), *e. g.* Schell, *Nabd*, i 39 mār çi-it lib-bi-šu. mār la mamāna II 67, 65 (= *R* 15), see mammana. mārmāru: K 4256 *O* 5 (Br 13990; AV 5181) . . . . RI = mar-ma-ru; II 31 *no* 3, 71 (L^T 90) mar-ma-ru = reš-tum; *cf* Hr^L 406 *R* 18 mārmārēšu; K 824, 40; K 595 *R* 6 (Hr^L 1). TUR-TUR I 35 *no* 3, 14; Asb vii 17, 28 & see lipu. Perhaps P. N. Ma-ra-am (Strassm., *Warka*, 36, 19, *etc.*).

II 30 *c-d* 29—49 ma-ar (*d*) ‖ iš(mil)-ku (29), da(or ra?)-du (30), ri-du (31), a-ja-ru(m, 32), se-se-rum (33), pi-ir-xu (34), še-ir-rum (35), mu-u-rum (36),  (pu?)-bu(= sir, AV 7118)-rum (37), ta-xu-u (38), te-ir-du-u (39), a-ta-mu (40), da-du (41), xu-u-ru-u (42), ka-lu-mu (43), ad(t)-mu (44), me-ir (45, AV 5848), te-ir-di-en-nu (46), li-il-li-du (47), pi-it-qu SU (*i. e.* in the country of *Su*, 48), ni-ip(b)-ru (49). AV 5111. — II 36 *c-d* 47—57 has ma-a-ru = li-du (47), zi-e-ru (48), ni-ip(b)-ru (49), bu-u-nu (50), pi-te-e-qu (51), li-da-nu (52), im-me-ru (53), ba-bu (54), li-i-du (55), me-i-ru (56), da-mu (57) AV 5121. V 23 *b-d* 29 TUR-UŠ (Br 4119) *a-c* 30 TUR-ARAD (Br 4090), 31 TUR-SAG (Br 4097, really = māru reštū, Br 4081), 32 TUR-DIŠ = ap-lu = ma-ru & šu-mu (Br 41; V 38 *a-b* 10).

T. A. often written TUR (Lo. 5, 38), māri-ja (3, 41), māri-ka (11, 4), -ka-ma (15, 2), -šu (5, 32); ma-ri-šu (45, 10); TUR-nu (14, 37); *pl* TUR-MEŠ (12, 37); TUR-TUR-MEŠ (27, 21) *etc.* In T. A. equivalent to Hebr (& Arabic) בְּנִי. — **mār ilišu** = a pious, a godfearing man; ZK ii 320 *ad* II 51 *b* 3; IV² 4 *b* 35 TUR-DINGIR-RA-NA = TUR-AN-šu = mār-ili-šu; 22 *b* 15 a-me-lu TUR-AN-šu; 2 *a* 25—6 (Br 430); also 5 *c* 37—8; 13 *a* 60—1; 14 *b* 24—5; 17 *a* 49—50; 2 *a* 47—8 TUR (*var* mar)-AN-šu. — māru kunnū see kānu 1, & kunnū. — mār ṭi-e-mi = Edan II 32 *no* 5 (*add*; AV 5193; Br 5875, 10123, 11451; ZA i 398). — mār ridūtišu (*q. v.*) the son of his begetting (= his own son, Schrader). — **mār reštū** (*q. v.*) firstborn son, crown-prince {erstgeborener, Kronprinz}. Winckler, *Forsch.*, i 517: the son, who during the father's lifetime conducts, or assists in, the goverment; also ii 193 *foll* (see talīmu). H 38, 107 TUR-SAG = mar reš-tu-u, L^T 91; II 18, 57 (il) Marduk mār reš-tu-u ša ap-si-i (H 99); IV² 30* *no* 3 *O* 22 ša (il) Marduk maš-maš EN-KI mār reš-ti-i ša (il) Ê-a mār šip-ri-šu a-na (*var* ana)-ku; — **mār šarru** crownprince {Kronprinz} Lehmann i 34 *foll*, ii 74 (*ad* K 432), 75 (K 501, 25 + 26), 76 (K 628), 78 (K 1118, 7), 109 {es ist nur derjenige von den legitimen Söhnen des Königs, der durch einen feierlichen Akt zur Thronfolge erwählt und bestimmt ist; braucht nicht der älteste zu sein}; Tiele, ZA vii 77; Latrille, ZK ii 349; *id* K 4567, 4 (Br 12478); mār-šarrūtu (§ 73) princely dignity, right of succession to the throne; Asb i 20, 26; x 63. — J. Oppert, ZA xiii 254: Was eigentlich der mār-šarri ist, wissen wir nicht. Ist es *Mann* oder *Sohn* des Königs? — **mār-bānū** & *abstr. n* mār-bānūtu. Pinches, in S. A. Smith, *Asurb*, ii 68—9 = μόθαξ (*cf* ZA v 28—9). Peiser, ZA iii 367 *rm* 3, 369; KAS 87 (ii); *Babyl. Vertr.* 127, 320; KB iv 238 *fol*: adopted son {Adoptivsohn} so T^C; adoption is mārūtu. *Babyl. Vertr.* cxlix 1 (amēl) mar-ba-ni-ja = Adoptionsbeamter. — J. Oppert, ZA iii 21; JA '87 (x) 537 (fils d'ancêtre de tribus); RP² i 156—8; ZA vii 68, *etc.* comparing יְלִיד בַּיִת with mār-bānū; mār-bānūtu = condition of being a free-born citizen {Stand der Edlen}; also see Meissner, *Diss*, 27—8 (ingenuus, freigeborener, Edler); Jensen, ZA vi 348 × T^C 22; 91. Delitzsch, BA iv 79 mār-bāni = Sohnzeuger (= geboren), such is only the *free* man (*cf* also Peiser, OLZ ii *no* 4, *col* 129); BA iv 12, 26 {scheint eine Mittelstufe zwischen gewöhnlichen

Sklaven und Freien gewesen zu sein}. K 894, 7 ša mârê ba-ni-i ša šarru iš-pura. KB ii 246, 81 mârê ba-ni-e ša (mât) Elamti {echte (?) Elamiter}. Nabd 1113, 4 + 15 + 18 mâr-ba-ni-i; 380, 1 bît mâr-ba-ni-i (ZA iii 366; PEISER & KOHLER, *Babyl. Rechtsleben*, ii 7). — mâr-bânûtu (DELITZSCH) Sohnzeugung & = Freilassung, sometimes also only bânûtu (Neb 386, 8); JOHNSTON, JAOS xix 71 mârê bânûti (wr. TUR-KAK-MEŠ) = free-born citizens, nobles (K 10, 16); properly: sons of ancestors; see also PINCHES, *Guide to Nimr. Centr. Saloon*, *p* 94, *no* 49; ZA iii 87; 89; 178 (clientel); JA '87 (x) 538, 16. — VATh 85, 8 [a. ˈl-šarru-u-tu u mar-bânu-u-tu (also VATh 93, 8); VATh 184, 7 mâr-ba-nu-tu; VATh 388, 11 (amêltu) mar-bânu-u-tu. VATh 180, 9 we have (amêl) ban-mâru-u-tu, PEISER, *Babyl. Vertr.*, *passim*, espec. 351. Neb 67, 9 (263, 6) mâr ba-nu-tu (KB iv 187 Adoption; Clientelschaft, T^C 91); Nabd 1113, 16 mâr-ba-nu-tu & mâr-bânu-ut-ka, 19 mâr-ba-nu-ta-a; 892, 8 mâr (amêl) ba-nu-tu; 533, 8 mâr-ba-nu-u-tu. Cyr 332, 20 (amêl) mâr-ba-nu-u-tu (BA iv 32—4 & × *ibid*, 78—9). Nabd 380, 11 lu-u mâru ça-bit qâte-i-ni (ZA iii 369 our adopted son; BA iv 79: er sei unser Hülfssohn).

Often used to indicate profession, *etc.* (= בן, GESENIUS^{12}, 109). mâr ummâni; V 33 ii 22 mârê (= TUR-MEŠ) um-ma-ni; V 13 *a-b* 41 TUR-um-ma-ni; V 65 *a* 36 mârê um-me-a (ZA i 33—4; KB iii, 2, 110—111); mâr here = member of a profession {Mitglied einer Zunft} Br 2144; 2658; but *cf* HAUPT, *Papers of Phil. Or. Club*, i 270 & *rm* 26 ad *del* 86. mâr išpari = weaver {Weber} *c. t.*; mâr ikkari IV 8 *b* 9 = ikkaru. (amêl) mâr u-di-e a title (*cf* udû) Dar 416, 11; Rm 367 + 83, 1—18, 461 *a* *R* 21 GIŠ-LAM-TUR = mâr-ušI (wr. TUR-A-ZU), preceded by (20) GIŠ-LAM-GAL = bu(pu)-ṭu-ut-tum. — **mâr šipri** (*q. v.*) messenger {Bote}. II 31, 84; 39 *g-h* 47 RA-GAB = TUR šip-ri; H 40, 190 LU-KIN-GI-A = TUR šip-ri, Br 10763. PEISER, *Babyl. Vertr.*, 320: secretary. id here also A (so KNUDTZON, 308). Asb ii 27 amêl A-KIN xa-an-ṭu amêl mâr šip-ri; Nabd 22, 13; 55, 14; 80, 2; 362, 4; 298, 2 *etc.* A-KIN Nabd 147, 10; 947, 12. mâr šip-ri-a-tum Nabd 288, 12; mâr šip-ra-a-tum Cyr 44, 4. also see BA i 535 *no* 54 *ad* Nabd 1050 *etc.*; PSBA ix 313. IV^2 5 *a* 28 si-bit-ti šu-nu TUR šip-ri ša (il) A-nim šar-ri-šu-nu (& 25); 6 *b* 42 mâr šip-ri ša (il) Marduk a-na-ku; 30* *no* 3 *O* 20 (22) see (âlik) max-ri. *Adapa*-legend *O* 34—5 ma-ar ši-ip-ri | ša (il) A-ni ik-ta-al-da; *pl* IV^2 1* *c* 7—8 TUR-MEŠ (*cf* 6: ma-ru-u *etc.*) šip-ri ša nam-ta-ri šu-nu. — T. A. (Ber.) 29 *R* 4 itti mârê šiprika; 9 *R* 18 mârê ši-ip-ri; Lo. 82, 3 ma-a-ar ši-i-ip-ri; 82, 11 ma-ar ši-i-ip-ri; 7, 11 TUR ši-ip-ri; 31, 34 TUR-KIN-i, *etc.* *pl* TUR-TUR ši-ip-ri Lo. 49, 18.

descendant {Nachkomme} Anp *Balaw*, *R* 12; Sn *Bav* 24, 57; Sn vi 64; Esh vi 58; Asb x 100 *etc.*

Inhabitants {Einwohner} just as בן (ZK i 244). Šuzub mâr Bâbili (*q. v.*) Sn vi 35; TP III *Ann* 174, 175; II 67, 38; also IV^2 61 (*passim*); mârê âli city-inhabitants Sn i 39; iii 4; mârê Bâbili Sn v 6; Asb iii 82, 90; iv 92; mârê (mât) Aššur Asb ii 24, *etc.* — With mâru connected are the following 6:

mârûtu *abstr noun* condition, status of child, son, daughter {Kindschaft}. AV 5128; Br 4081; II 9 *c-d* 58—60 ma-ru-tu (62 = ap-lu-tu), ma-ru-us-su, ana ma-ru-ti-šu; 61 ana marûtišu iṭ-ru-šu (he brought him to be adopted as a son); *cf* II 9 *b* 13—14; 33 *e-f* 6 NAM-TUR (Br 2169)-A-NI-KU = ana ma-ru-ti-šu. III 4 *no* 7, 9 a-na ma-ru-ti [lû?] u-rab-ban-ni brought me up as his son (KB iii, 1, 100 *fol*; D^{Pa} 208 *fol*; HOMMEL, *Gesch.*, 302 *fol*; WZ iv 306; AV 5128: perhaps -šu instead of lû?). Nabd 356, 20 *B* a-na ma-ru-tu ni-il-qa-am-ma; 20 dup-pi ma-ru-ti-šu niš-ṭur-ma (document of adoption); 380, 10 lu-u mâru-u-a šu-u ina duppi ma-ru-ti-šu ti-ša-ab; 626, 2; 625, 8 mâru-u-tu; Cyr 183, 6 (sal) Na-da-a ma(?)-ru-u-tum a-na....

mârtu *f*, *c. st.* mârat girl, daughter {Mädchen, Tochter} ‖ bintu, *q. v.* id TUR-SAL, often in Z^b; § 9, 139; AV 5193; Br 4082; 4160. IV^2 1 *b* 38—9 mar-ti (il) E-a; 53—4 mar-ti ap-si-i lu-u ta-ma-at (Br 4060; TUR-SAL); 4 iii 21 Iš-tar ma-rat (= TUR) (il) Sin (& 22); 28^{*} *no* 4 *R* 54—5 mar-tum (= TUR) si-xir-tum a-bi-mi. K 41 *b* 18 (end) ma-rat-su iš-kun (he placed it on his daughter), PSBA xvii 65 *foll*; Knudtzon, 80 *R* 3 TUR-SAL šarri ša [bīt ri-dūti]. K 3600 (hymn to goddess Ninā) 17 nu-xi ma-rat (il) Sin. K 257 (H 122 *foll*) 14—5 ul a-na-ku-u mar-ti (= ṬU-MU, Br 11918) [il] MU-UL-LIL-LAL (= Marduk); 18—9 iš-ta-ri-tum ul ana-ku-u mar-tum qa-rit-tum; 20—1 mar-tum a-ša-rit-tum (the first daughter of Bēl, am I not?), 71—2 mar-tum (TUR-MAX?) ša [il] Bēl anāku. *R* 66 ēni-ku (?) mar-ti it-ti um-mi-šu. TUR-SAL also IV 31 *a* 2, 3 *etc*. Ištar mārat (il) Sin; *cf* IV^{2} 4 *b* 21 Ištar ma-rat (= TUR) (il) Sin; Asb ix 10; K 4567, 4 (AV 5122; Jastrow, *Relig. of Babyl. and Assyr.*, 205); NE 8, 28 ma-rat qu-ra-di xi-rat ....; H 213, 9 mar-ti e-mi (214, 10) see emu. H 94—5, 59 la-bar-tu ma-rat (= TUR) [il] A-nim. Banks, *Diss*, 1 (*no* 4) 25 a-mat-su um-ma mar-tu ki-ma bu-ri-e [....]-bar (?); Asb ii 60, 65 mārat-su; *pl* TUR-SAL-MEŠ = mārāti, ii 56, 60; vi 81. Cyr 277, 6 *N* (mār) mar-ti-šu-nu (+ 10) and *N* the son of their daughter; Neb 100, 3 mar-tum 3 šanāti; *cf* Nabd 509, 4 mārat 5 šanāti. KB iv 22 ii 23 (ilat) mar-ta (il) Marduk (the daughter of *M*); 322—3 iii 29 a-na mar-ti-šu; 24 a-na mārti-šu; Br. M. 84, 2—11, 342, 13—4 Esaggil-ramat | mar-ti-šu. II 41 *no* 3 *e-f* 12 (šam) TUR-SAL A-ŠAGA = mārat eqli. V 39 *c-d* 67 TUR-SAL = ma-aš-tum; Jensen, ZA i 388; Bezold, ZA ii 460 maintaining (>< Delitzsch, *ibid*, 101) that Pinches reading is correct; also Bezold, ZA iv 430 *rm* 1; Jensen, ZA vii 180; & *cf* ZK ii 66—7; 355. AV 9001; Br 4160. II 30 *c-d* 50—3 mu-ar-tum (*d*) = me-ir-tum (50 *c*), im-me-ir-tum (51 *c*), ba(!)-na-tum (52 *c*), bi-in(?)-tum (53 *c*); II 47 *c-d* 16 DA-MAR-ZA = ma-rat-ki (Br 6674; AV 5116); II 9 *b* 34 ma-rat-su (ana aš-šūtu iškun); III 66 *col* 7, 30 (ilat) ši-na ma-ra-te ša Suti (= the 2 daughters, PSBA xxi, 124—5). On mārat-erçiti = a daughter of one's own blood (Meissner, 154) *c. t.* see Hommel, *Ancient Hebrew Tradition*, 98.

mēru *a*) child {Kind} me-ir, me-i-ru (AV 5855) ‖ mār(u) *q. v.* Cappad. inscr. Golen. 11, 2 [a-š]a-su u me-ir-e-šu his wife and his children (*cf ibid*, 16); Banks, *Diss*, 18 *foll* (*no* 2, 8—10) 72 mi-ri (*var* -ru) ba-nu-u a-bi Bēl u-šak-ki-ka. — *b*) young of an animal (ox, *etc.*) {Junges eines Tieres (Ochsen, *etc*) ‖ bīru (*q. v.*). 82, 5—22, 1048 *O* 28 lit-tu bu-ur ša me-ru (*cf* littu & laxru) Pinches, JRAS xix 319; xxiii ('91) 400; K 152 iv 22 GUD-LID = mi-i-rum foll. by bi-i-rum. Br 8871; II 22 *no* 1 (*add*); Neb *Grot* (I 66) *c* 12 im-mi-ir mi-ir gu-uk-ka-al-lum (*cf* Ball, PSBA xii, 10); mi-ri Pognon, *Wadi-Bav*, 58 *ad* Neb-Pogn. C vii 18; A vii 6 (says: perhaps corruption for im-mi-ri).

mērtu girl, daughter {Mädchen, Tochter} me-ir-tum ‖ mārtum (*q. v.*) AV 5359. II 32 *c-d* 26 me-ir-tum, me-me-tum (25 *c*) & ši-du-ri ‖ ar[-da-tum]; *cf* Cappad. inscr. 24, 11 his wife and me-ir-a-su (& his daughter).

mūru *m*, *pl* mūrē & mūrāni young of an animal, esp. of ass, wildox; foal, cub {Tier-junges, namentl. das Junge eines Esels oder Wildochsen} Latrille, ZK ii 343; Haupt, KAT^{2} 508; ZDMG 48, 203; §§ 47; 65, 3; AV 5554; Pinches, JRAS (*n. s.*) xix 319; ZA iii 206; ‖ ma-ar (see mūru). T^{M} vii 25 çēnu im-mir-ša çubītu ar-ma-ša atānu mu-ur-ša; I 28 *a* 6 mu-ri *pl* bal-ṭu-te ša rīmāni uçabbita the living young of wildbulls (§ 128). NE 51, 7 i-du-ša mu-ri-ši-na (asses' foals) attanāti (‖ pu-ri-ši-na, 8), *Johns Hopk. Circ.*, iii 29; J^{I-N} 14—5; King, *Magic*, 18, 11—12 ki-i mu-ra-ni (il) Marduk a-la-su-um (*cf* lasamu) ur-ki-[ka]. K 883 (oracle to Asb) 25 ma(?)-a la ta-pal-lax mu-u-ri ša ana-ku u-rab-bu-u-ni (BA ii 633—5); IV^{2} 61 v *R* 69 šul-mu ana mu-ri-ša; 18^{*} *no* 6, *R* 1—2 mu-ur (= IMĒR-ARAD-GUŠUR) ni-ki ši-iz-bi ši-iz-ba ul (S 1708, 17; AV 5563; L^{T} 147; Br 4988); Lay. 44, 15: L (= fifty) mu-ra-ni | nešē (young lions); 16: mu-ra-ni šu-nu (§ 51 *a*) a-na ma-'a-diš u-ša-li-di (KB i 124—5). L⁴ iii 18 ki-ma mu-ri-e an-xu-te like whining young animals. P. N. Murānu AV 5545, D^Pr 203 *rm* 2; KB iv 294—5 *no* i 11 Mu-ra-nu; Strassm., *Stockh. O. C.*, *no* 3, 2 ina eli Mu-ra-nu; Cyr 67, 5; Peiser, *Babyl. Vertr.*, 337. — Contained also in **mūr nisqi** (√nasaqu) of a noble horse, a splendid, spirited horse, originally: young horse (*cf* مُهْر) AV 5564; § 73; a charger; § 9, 244 on ID; Tiele, *Gesch.*, 147 *rm* 4. Sn v 80 see lasmu; vi 55 mur-ni-is-ki parê; *cf* L⁴ i 20; I 44, 66 aš-šu mur-ni-iz-ki-ja šuk-nu-še for the training of my chargers; IV² 48 *a* 32—33 ana mur-ni-is-ki; 83, 1—18, 483, 5 mur-ni-is-qi rab]ûti (Winckler, *Forsch.*, ii 8) a ‖ text of Esh iv 26; 53 ^imêr mur-ni-is-qi (*var* -ki) rabûti; vi 46; III 88 (*no* 2) 62 ^imêr mu-ur-ni-is-ki-ja (= K 2060) my steeds; Winckler, *Sargon*, 191 (bel) mur-ni-iz-ki šu-te-ši-ra | šul-li-ma çi-in-di-šu; K 3600, 22 šul-li-me mur-ni-is-qi çi-in-da-at ni-ri[-šu]. — Cook compares 2 Chron. 9 : 24 סוסים (וּפְרָשִׁים), but see Cheyne, *Expositor*, Apr. '99, 331.

mirānu *m* young dog, pup, cub {junger Hund}. AV 5849; Hebr. i 226; § 65, 35; Hommel, VK 492 *rm* 232. Sn *Bell* 13: Belibni who kîma mi-ra-a-ni ça-ax-ri had grown up in my palace (KB ii 115; Tiele, *Gesch.*, 313; AV 7157); ZDMG 28, 152. II 6 *a-b* 13 LIK-KU = kal-bu, 14, ... TUR = mi-ra-nu (Br 4081; 14054). — To this noun perhaps also: Asb iv 26 mi-ra-nu-uš-šu-un ina eli libbû (*var* lib-bi)-šu-nu | ip(b)-ši-lu-nim-ma, Zimmern, KB ii 189 *rm* † like young dogs {w'e junge Hunde} (L^M 118: bitterness, √מרר, l :t, *p* 75: a *m*-formation from ירא 'fear', *cf* bašalu); Jensen, *ibid*, would prefer some such meaning as: their nakedness {ihre Entblösstheit, *i. e.*, entblösst von allem}, referring also to II 47 *a-b* 21 mâtu me-ri-nu-uš-ša RU (= innadi) = mâtu ina ki-çir-ša RU (= inna)-di; Asb v 112 Ummanaldasi, king of Elam | mi-ra-nu-uš-šu in-na-bit(-ma); IV² 51 *a* 54 mi-ra-nu-uš-šu ed-lu la u-maš-ši-ru (= Z^B ii 51: Gewalt; King, *First Steps in Assyrian*, 259: From his power (?) a man has he not let go free); II 30 *no* 4 *O* 6 BAR = mi-ri-nu (?) AV 5351. Bu 88, 5—12, 75 + 76 vii 26 bušâšunu šallûti utêr, mi-ra-nu-te lu-bu-uš-tu | u-lab-biš the poor (miserable) I have clothed with garments (BA iii 253—4).

marû 1. = מרא. ℑ perhaps Dar 193, 19 gi-šimmaru zarîti ul u-mar-ri. — Š fatten, make luxurious {fett, üppig machen}. IV² 9 *R* 3—4 ka-a-tu a-mat-ka tar-ba-çu u su-pu-ru u-šam-ri thou, thy word, makes luxurious stable and hurdle (Br 6934: PEŠ), see also PSBA xxi 138.

Der.:

marû *2.* *adj* fat {fett, feist} AV 5123; Z^B 16 (above); ZA iii 94 & again, 109 *rm* 1. Sarg *Ann* 311; 432 gu-max-xi bit-ru-ti šu-'-e ma-ru(-u)-ti; (*cf* Lehmann, L⁴ iii 28; i 20); *Khors* 168 (KB ii 78—9); also *Nimr* 19 (ma-ru-ti); Salm *Balaw* vi 3 alpê kab-ru-ti LU-ARAD-MEŠ (= kirrê?) ma-ru-ti ‖ ki-ma šu-u-ri ma-ru-ti Sn v 74. Neb *Grot* (I 65 *a*) i 16 ište-en alpu elli (KB iii, 2, 32) ma-ra-a; ii 26 (‖ bi-it-ru-tim, 27). H 24, 481 lu-gu-ru-uš | AMEL-UŠ | ma-ru-u; II 32 *a-b* 65 (Br 6419); 66 AMEL ^ni-ga ŠE & 67 AMEL ^(ul-lu) ŠE = ma-ru-u (Z^B 16; 115; Br 6423).

marû *3.* a terminus technicus of Assyrian grammar × xa-am-ṭu (3) *q. v.*, & Hommel, *Sum. Les.*, 56: marû indicates a fuller, more complete form as compared with a shorter, reduced, without respect to its position in the first (neo-sumerian), or second (early-sumerian) column. AV 5123; V 11 *d-f* 39 (Br 4183, 4187); Br 7488 *ad* II 6 *c-d* 38; 7429 *ad* II 6 *c-d* 37 (D^S 60; II^OV xxix); Levias, AJSL xv 232 *rm* 2 (end): xamṭu: sign of feminine, must mean womb, woman, or both.

marru *1.* *pl* marrâti some field instrument (of iron, *etc.*) perh. hoe {Hacke} *cf* zabbilu. ZA iv 114 (bel) Nabopol. text: 3 parzillu šul-kat-ka-a-ta | 1 xa-çi-in-ni | 1 ap-pa-tum | 2 ma-rat ^MEŠ. Camb 18, 3 *foll* mar-ri ^MEŠ parzilli ...; 7 mar-ri 7 xal-li-li parzilli (BA iii 479); 330, 4 *foll* iste-en mar-ri [parzilli], BA iii 463: Schaufel; 331, 12; Peiser, KAS 106 (bel) ^(is) mar-ri; *cf* Cyr 26, 5: 4-ta ^(is) mar-re ^MEŠ. Nabd 529, 1 mar-ri-e ša kaspi; 571, 2 mar-ri MEŠ; 752, 4: 3 mar-ri parzilli; 753, 32; 982, 2 mar-ra-a[-ta]; 530, 2 mar-ra-a-tu (810, 2 -ta); also Neb 285, 2: 5²/3 minas of iron KI-LAL 3 mar-ra-a-ta; 433, 9; ZA iv 138: mar-rat-MEŠ K 2711 *R* 3 .... mar-ri (?) xurâçi ru-uš-še-e. STRASSM., *Stockh. O. C.*, 12: AH 492. 83—1—18, 2: 5 AN-BAR (= parzillu) mar-ri ‖ 1: 10 (iç) zab-bi(l)-li. T^C 97 on etymology; BA i 535, 636 (incorrect).

marru 2. *adj* bitter {bitter} V 24 *c-d* 14—6 (K 2036, 8—10) mar-ru ‖ ir-ru-u, ⟨sign⟩ (pir?)-xu, ax-xu (*q. v.*) Br 8326; II 30 (*g*)-*h* 30 mar[-ru?], followed by mara[-ru]; AV 5188; S^a iii 5 ma-ar | MAR | mar-ru. H 84—5 (K 246 i) 37 mu-še-niq-tu ša tu-lu-ša mar-ru (= ŠEŠ-A, Br 6115, 6442), *cf* HOMMEL, *Sum. Les.*, 113. V 31 *e-f* 35 GIG-SI(XAB?)-BA = mar-ru (Br 9244); ZA xii 410—11, 27 GIŠ-GIŠIMMAR-GIG-XAB-BA = mar-ri (bitter date). K 4345 *R* 22 (šam) a-ru-šu mar-ru ‖ (šam) e-zi-zu. *f* see in nâr Marratu. Sm 1316 XI-GIŠ-ŠEŠ-SAR = mar-ru. √mararu (*q. v.*).

murru bitterness {Bitterkeit} K 3812 iii 20 a-na mur-ri pi-i-šu dunnamû išassika ZA iv 11: in the bitterness of his mouth; while others translate: for the food of his mouth (Hebr מרא) the weak cries to thee (see also xarru). ZA ii 61—2 nâr mur-ri; iii 318, 87 (end) nâr mur-ru. — T. A. (Lo.) 63 let my lord, the king send (16) riqqu SAR^pl | mu-ur-ru (myrrh) | for medicinal purposes (KB v 298—99); (Ber.) 25 iv 52: I aban ta-pa-tum šamni mur-ri | 1 t]a-pa-tum šamni (riq) MUR. Rm 367 + 83, 1—18, 461 *a* ii 20 GIŠ-ŠIM-ŠIŠ = mur-ru; 79, 7—8, 19, 13 *fol* (šam) mur-ra = (šam) karân [šêlibi?]; (šam) zûr ŠIM-ŠIŠ (*i. e.* mur-ri) = (šam) zûr karân [šêlibi?]; id ŠIM-ŠIŠ also Nabd 413, 1; 920, 8.

murrû HOMMEL, *Sum. Les.*, *ad* S^b 1 *R*, *col* iv 2 mur(?)-ru-u.

muribu *e. g.* Anp i 20 mu-ri-ib; III 48 *no* 3, 28 amêl mu-ri-ba nakri the fighter, combatter of the enemy {dem Bekämpfer des Feindes} AV 5552; *cf* râbu (רב).

murbašu, BA i 178; ZDMG 43, 95; see xarbašu (Z^B 108). POGNON, *Bav*, 106 √rapašu.

murub (?) II 48 *e* 4 (Br 2938, 10061) mu-ru-ub (AV 5557); II 30 *c-d* 17 sal mu-ru-ub ⟨sign⟩ = u-ru (*q. v.*); perh. √erebu, same id = pu-u (mouth) V 39 *a-b* 3. II 26 *no* 1, *add* (*l* 35 *d*) = xi-iç-bu; S^b 88 mu-ru[-ub] | id | qab-lum (*var* qa-ab-lu; ‖ qirbu (Br 6702, 67?3; H 24, 507); II 39 *e-f* 11 murub-ba = qablîtum; JÄGER, BA ii 303 murub > gurub > qurub = קרב: relative. II 32 *e-f* 67 (V 39 *a-b* 43) SAL mu-ru-ub UŠ-DAM = u-mu [rabû], ZK ii 299; 411 *foll*; ZA i 394, AV 2276; Br 10941; FRIEDRICH, *Kabiren*, 10 *fol* = *pudenda muliebria*. K 4386 i 33 SAL (mu-ru-ub) LA = u-ru-u ša sinništi. III 53 *no* 3 *b* 58 (*cf* ⊕ 51 i 12 EN-NUN-MURUB-BA = qablitum); also ⊕ 59 i 12; Rm 345 *O* 23.

NOTE. — JENSEN, 270 *fol* Ὁμόρ(ω)κα (Sumerian name of kirbiš-Tiâmat) > Sum. murub = kirbiš (approved by LEHMANN, i 126), see, however, Marduk.

mûragu see mušâlu.

mirgu a gardenplant {Gartenpflanze} ZA vi 291 i 4 mi-ir-gu.

margannu; a tree, whose bark, *etc.* is used for perfumery, K 165 *R* 14 (iç riq) mar-gan-nu, AV 5177 (-kan-).

margûnu, margûçu a spice {eine Spezerei}. Rm 367 + 83, 1—18, 461 *a* iii 3 GIŠ-ŠIM-MAR-GU-NU = ŠU *i. e.* mar-gu-nu, followed by GIŠ-ŠIM-MAR-GU-ÇU = ŠU *i. e.* margûçu.

mergirânu K 61, 21 (šam) me-ir-gi-ra-nu, ZK ii 206—7.

maradu (ד, ט, ת?) ג V 45 iv 36 tu-mar-rad (ZDMG 32, 403); Perhaps Rm 67 (Hr^L 348) 9—10 ma-a mar-dak kar-rak | ina libbi ša xu-un-ṭu | šu-u.

NOTE. — RP² v 81 *rm* 6 reads T. A. (Ber.) 115, 30 [uš]-am-ra-ad, but see KB v 322.

mirdu. So BOISSIER (*Rev. Sém.*, vii 133, § 30) proposes for V 11 *d-f* 39 AT-MAR = AT..... GAL = mir (Br 4183 ṭu)-du ma-ru-u, explaining it as "an animal"; A(T)-GAL perhaps √agal > agalu calf.

marab, TIELE, *Gesch.*, 327 *etc.* see MAGAL.

[redacted]

maradû AV 8916, Br 9078 *ad* V 27 *a-b* 28 GUL-MARAD-DA = ma(?)-ra-du(?)-u(?), also see Br 9079.

murradu. Dar 435, 4 ša ina sûqu xurbi mu-ur-ra-du.

murdudû. Sm 8 *a-b* 12 U-MUR-KAK-KAK = mu-ur (*cf* murru?)-du-du-u.

(il) **Marduk** = מְרֹדָךְ Bêl-Merodach, national god of Babylon; son of Êa, Jastrow, *Religion of Babyl.*, 139 *foll*; consort of Çarpanitum. Written AN Mar-duk (Br 5828); III 2, 8 (AV 5124) (il) Ma-ru-duk-šum-ba-ša (a P.N.); II 63, 18 (P.N.) Mar-duk; *cf* K 6, 13; also Mar-du-ku (in Nabd *c. t.*); Sp 12, 10 (P.N.) Mar-duk-ablu. Usually written AN 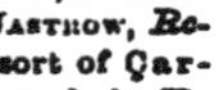 (§ 9, 60) = AN-AMAR (or ZUR, D 29, 45)-UD, IV^{2} 30* *O* 22 (Br 9080 AN-MARAD-DAŠ) = offspring, child of dawn, daybreak, *l* 21 AN-ŠILIG-GAL-ŠAR (BA ii 628); also see Jensen, ZK i 309; ii 403 *fol*, 420; ZA vi 153; Z^{B} 49; AV 564; 3185; Br 924—930; 948; 1082 (= AN-TU-TU K^{M} 18, 11 + 18; 22, 1 + 70; 33, 6); often in Z^{B}, K^{M} & T^{M}. AN-ŠILIG-GAL-ŠAR (?) *cf* T^{M} i 62 (*M* bêl a-ši-pu-ti, also ii 158; vi 58; vii 20), 72; iv 8; *cf* K 2971 ii 18 (= IV^{2} 56) & iii 15 maš-mašu (*q. v.*) a-ši-pu [il] Marduk. Z^{B} ii 193; v/vi 175; K^{M} 12, 85 + 88 + 105 + 114; 62, 25. AN- = AN-ŠILIG-GAL-ŠAR S 28, 37 *R* (AV 5135); C^{a} 161; III 66 *R* 27 *b* (Br 5974); AN 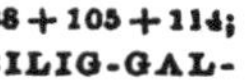 K^{M} 2, 47; 13, 15 *etc.*; V 46 *c-d* 7. 8, 22 (Br 7996); III 66 *R* 9 *a*, AV 4777.

Marduk is called bêlu rabû (Xammurabi, *etc.*); bêl Êsaggila u Êzida (*ibid*); bêl Êsaggila u Bâbili (V 33 i 44); mâr reštû ša (il) Êa (H 97, 5), mâr reštû (*q. v.*) ša apsî (99, 57); ri-mi-nu-u II 54 *h* 53 (= [il] Gudibir) Br 2605; mâr E-ri-du IV^{2} 15 *b* 62—3 *etc.* (AJP v 79); Halévy, *Rev. Hist. Rel.*, xvii 187 = seigneur (not sont) of Eridu; also Br 2649; IV^{2} 4 iii 23; gušri ilâni âšarid šamê u erçitim ZA iv 280, 1; I 27, 6 ab-kal ilâni (D 98 *R* 11) bêl te-ri-e-ti; šar šamê u erçitim, KB iii (2) 66, 45; 78, 4 ba-an ni-me-qi; I 68, 6 a-ša-ri-du ilâni mu-ši-im ši-ma-a-ti; I 67 *a* 35 bêl ilâni; qar-du, Messerschmidt, *Nabuna'id*, 64, 26; bêl mâtâti in Creat.-*frg*, D 96, 13 be-el KUR-KUR šum-šu it-ta-bi a[-bu] Bêl; 26 bêl (?) ilâni (il) Marduk (= AN-AMAR-UD). id MUL-LIL-LA = Marduk Sayce, *Hibbert Lectures*, 143—8; see Halévy, *Rev. Hist. Rel.*, xvii 190. Banks, *Diss*, 14, 1) *no* 4, 101 kab-tu (il) MU-UL-LIL ša çît pîšu la uštepillum; 10, 1) *no* 4, 33 a-mat (il) Marduk; 39 a-mat (il) MU-UL-LI-LA. — Scheil, *Rec. Trav.*, xvii 83 (*no* xxiii) 4 [il] a-kit (= Marduk).

Cf II 57 *a-b* 46 (Br 51; ZA i 260, 410 = Planet Jupiter); II 39 *e-f* 64; V 46 *a-b* 50; II 51 *a-b* 61; 57 *a-b* 45 *cf* Br 9081—2; ZA i 265 *rm* 3 = star of AMAR-UD.

II 54 *g-h* 48 AN-EN-KI-ŠA (*i. e.* ŠI + RU)-DA; 50 AN-SA-AL-I-LA; 51 AN-MI-IL-MA; 52 AN-A-MA (V 46 *c* 38 = )-RU; 53 AN ni-bi-ru (or NI-BI-RU? V 21 *g-h* 49; 46 *d* 34 = ri-mi-nu-u Br 9080; Pognon, *Bav*, 167; ZK i 309; ii 418), all = AN-AMAR-UD (*i. e.* [il] Marduk, = V 46 *c-d* 28—34) *cf* Br 2908, 3129, 5354, 8930; V 46 *c* 28 AN-ŠI-XU (Br 9302); II 54 *g-h* 59 (Br 223).

II 46 *a-b* 46 AN-NIN-BI-DIB-DIB (T^{M} vii 107, 111, 114) Br 11041; *a-b* 47 (Br 11085); 48 (Br 8809); 49 AN . . . . XAR (XIR); *c-d* 46 (Br 8817), 47 (Br 8830), 49 (Br 8827) all = AN-AMAR-UD.

K 2107 *O* 10 AN-KA (du-ut-tu) KA = [il] Marduk mu-tak-kil ilâni (AV 5672, Br 575); 11 AN MU-MU (*i. e.* KA + inserted LI) = [il] Marduk mu-uš-pi-iš ilâni (Br 778, 786); 12 AN 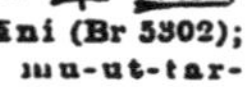 = [il] M. ba-ni (?) ka-la ilâni (Br 5302); 13 AN-DU-DU = [il] M. mu-ut-tar-ru-u ilâni (Br 4917; L^{T} 131); 14 AN 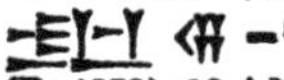 = [il] M. ša ši-pat-su el-lit (Br 4379); 18 AN-ZI-SI = [il] M. na-si-ix ša pu-ti (ša-bu-ti? Br 2354, AV 6068); 19 AN-ŠUD- = [il] M. mu-bal-lu-u a-a-bi (Br 3011, 3016, 3041, AV 5411). Bezold, *Literature*, 285 *foll.* V 44 *c-d* 2—3 *cf* Br 12458; also V 46 *a-b* 9; *c-d* 6 AN-TU-TU = AN-AMAR-UD; & *l* 21, where also AN-TA-GAL (Br 469) = AN-AMAR-UD; Br 1082; K 2107, 9 AN-TU-TU = (il) M. mu-al-lid ilâni = mu-ud-di-iš ilâni (AV 5407) — see also the stars mentioned V 46 *a-b* 6 & 8; II 47 *c-d* 23 (Br 11149); D 88 v 80 GIŠ-MA'-KU-A = elippu AN-AMAR-UD (also see FLEMMING, *Neb*, *ad* ii 48; iii 10; Br 10661); II 48 *a-b* 36 (gu-di-bi-ir) — AN-AMAR-UD (Br 1415); III 68 *b* 7; AV 5135; ZK ii 403, 418. Asb v 50 AN-ŠU, var AMAR-UD; V 65 *b* 50; Br 10884.

Late-Babylonian forms are Maš-tu-ku & Maš-tuk-ku (AV 5280—1); ZA vii 181; Dar 37, 3-4 mâr Maš-tuk-ku; *etc.* On PN. with Marduk see PEISER, *Babyl. Vertr.*, 336—7; AV 5184 *foll*; BEZOLD, *Catalogue*, v 2107—10.

NOTE. — TIELE, *Gesch.*, 531; HOMMEL, *Gesch.*, 62, 223, 276; *Sum. Les.* 51 on II 59 *a-b* 46 *foll*: Marduk > AMAR-UDUG (AMAR = young wild ox); HALÉVY, *Rev. Hist. Rev.*, xvii 187 = mâr uduki (not utukki, as in *Rech. crit.*, 268) fils ou maitre des génies nommés *utuk* (≍ SAYCE, *Hibb. Lect.*, 107 *rm* 1); J. H. WRIGHT, ZA x 71—4. 'Ομερέzα = 'Ο Μερόzα = Marduk. PINCHES, *Trans. Vict. Inst.*, xxviii, 2 *foll* on id for Marduk; believes that gloss a-sa-ri(-ru) V 65, 45; II 55 *c-d* 66 = *Osiris*, of the Egyptians; *ibid*, remarks on development of his worship; although chiefgod among Babylonians yet few Proper Names compounded with his name; *ibid*, *p* 8 quotes 81—11—3, 111 a tablet on the different names of Marduk; also *pp* 221 *foll* — See also HOMMEL, *Anc. Hebr. Tradition*, 63, 144.

JENSEN, 88: originally a solar deity; MUSS-ARNOLT, *Assyro-Babyl. Months*, 28—30; LEHMANN, ii 35, 49, 63 *etc.* originally god of the rising (early) sun: ‖ Gott der Frühsonne; god of prophecy; ii 40: consort of Çarpânit-Erûa. JASTROW, *Religion of Babylonia and Assyria*, 116—21 (originally a solar deity); 190 *foll*; *M.* treated almost as a generic term deity, *cf* 81—11—3, 11; 190 *rm* 1, see remarks on PINCHES' conclusions referred to above; 548 Adapa and Marduk are identical (ZIMMERN). — Above all JEREMIAS' article "Marduk" in ROSCHER'S *Lexikon der Mythologie*, ii, 2340—72.

On Mordecbai of the book of Esther & Marduk see ZIMMERN, ZATW xi 167 *foll*; WILDEBOER, *Kurz. Hand-Commentar z. A. T.*, Abt. xvii, *p* 173.

mardîtu march; way, road {Marsch, Weg} √redû, BEHRT, *Diss*, 13 (= HEBR. xi 185) Rm 2, 1 *R* 7 ku-ri-ru-u-ni mar-di-tu; Rm 77 *O* 4 (Hr[L] 414); Rm 353 *R* 8. — II 22 *a-b* 8? we find among ropes mentioned ša mar-di-it xur-ri. K 4785, 23 egirâte ša bît mar-di-a-te ..... axiš ipaqidu.

mardûtu (?) AV 5172; Br 12804 *ad* II 35 *c* 1 mar-du-tu (but??).

mirdîtu. AV 5356. S 31. 52 *R* 1 ka-ma-rum; 2 mir-di-e-tum; 3 GIŠ-MAX & 4 GIŠ-SU-LAL = mir-di-e-tum (ZA ix 221—22), with this compare mir-di-e-tu V 26 *a-b* 51 same id as mesû (*q. v.*), 52 GIŠ-AM-RI-BI-NI, 53—4 GIŠ-MAX (AV 5356, Br 3260), 55 GIŠ (gi?) LAL, same id in 56 = ka-ma-rum; II 22 *a-b* 8 (= K 242) GIŠ-GAR-ZAK-KU-LAL ša mir-di-it xar (xur)-ri Br 12098; *a-b* 33 GIŠ-TIK-SI-KI-IR = (iç) mir-di-tum, same id in V 26 *a-b* 57 = ka-ma-rum. Br 8245 *ad* II 46 *no* 6 *add* (AV 5356) GIŠ-TIK-ZI-BI-IR-RA (√šibirru?) = mir-di-e-tum, and GIŠ-ŠU-KAT (Br 7097, ZA i 182, same id = paššûru). ZA x 207 ii *O* 1 mi-ir[-di-tum] Br 2750; 3254 *fol.* — Also *cf* redû.

mur(?)-zu-mur-za SAR plant {Gewächs} 81—7—6, 688 S. H. (ZA vi 291 i 14).

murxu clothing, dress for prairie *etc.* {Wüstenkleid, -Anzug} V 28 *c-d* 38 mu-ur-xu = lubâr çêri AV 5450, 5561; perh. II 28 *no* 4 (*add*); √מרח.

ma-ru-xu 82—7—4, 13 *l* 16 napxar 786 ma-ru-xu. BO ii 145 perhaps a mistake for ma-ši-xu (*q. v.*).

marxallu a stone {ein Stein} T. A. (Ber.) 25 ii 49; 26 ii 67 (aban) mar-xal-lu (√רחל). ZIM., *Babyl. Relig.*, 114, 28.

mar-xa-çu *1.* i-nam-din-nu trustworthiness they shall give. PINCHES, *Inscr. Babyl. Tablets*, *p* 38, 8.

marxaçu *2.* BEZOLD, *Catalogue*, 760: ina libî tuballal ina mar-xa-çi taraxaç M[8] 88—9: fat thou shalt pour over it, with irrigation thou shalt water it. ‖

marxuçu 83—1—18, 2, *R* 1—6 (Hr[L] 391) i-su-ur-ri | xu-un-ṭu an-ni-ia-u ultu pa-an | šarri be-ili-ia ip-pa-ṭar | mar-xu-çu šu-u ša šamnê | II šanîtu III šanîtu a-na šarri be-ili-ia e-ta-pa-aš. R. F. HARPER, AJSL xv 140 "lotion". √raxaçu sprinkle, water.

marxašu a stone {ein Stein} T. A. (Ber.) 25 i 52: 25 (aban) mar-xa-ši; V 33 ii 36 (aban) pî mar-xa-ši (KB iii, 1, 140—1, *rm* †), iii 9; called green in ii 36; JENSEN, ZA x 370 & *rm* 1: where a country Marxaši, East of Babylonia, is discussed (II 50 *c* 66; Br 12807; and IV[2] 36 *O* 17; also

ma-ru-um-a-a, AV 5568 see xarruxša (*p* 347, *col* 1). ~ mur-xum-ma-tum AV 5562, see xurxummatum.

II 6 *a-b* 16; Br 12806), *cf* parašū; *ZDMG* 53, 664. Hommel, *Anc. Hebr. Tradition*, 87 (= *Mar'ash* in Northern Syria), 212; but see Jensen, ZA x 370 *rm* 1; Zimmern, *Theol. Qu.*, i 323. ‖ is:

marxušū II 37 *g-h* 66 = II 40 *c-d* 15 TAG-MAR-XU-ŠUM = ŠU-u, AV 5176; Br 12803.

marxītu wife, woman {Weib, Frau} AV 5175. *del* 191, 198 ana mar-xi-ti-šu to his wife; 194, 244 mar-xi-is-su. II 36 *c-d* 44 see xīr(a)tu, *p* 342 *col* 2; *c-d* 46 mar-xi-tum = aš-ša-tu. — Jensen (ZA i 395 *rm* 2): belongs to the same stem as tirxātu (wedding present) & rixū (give a wedding present); Z^B 43, 2 √ rexū love {lieben} but? added; D^S 44, 1; ZA ii 277; BA i 174 & i 4; 14 *rm* 6 √ رخى: be soft, tender.

mērixtu, mīrixtu impudence, insolence {Vermessenheit, Frevel, Frechheit} *pl* mērixēti; Lyon, *Manual*, 175; BA i 174. Smith, *Asurb*, 134, 51 ši-pir me-ri-ix-ti (KB ii 256—7 vermessene Botschaft); 147, 8 it-ti GIŠ-ZU-MEŠ (= zi-e, tablets) ši-pir me-ri-ix-tu; 117, 94 ana eli me-ri-xi-e-ti (but KB ii 248—9 & *rm* 1 me-ri-ix-ti; Smith had -xa- instead of -ri-); 120, 26 šu-par mi-ri-ix-ti an-ni-ti ša iq-bu-u (KB ii 250—1; ✕ Hebr. ix 161). K 2852, 9 šu-par me-ri-xi-e-ti Teumman ..... iš-tap-pa-ra. Asb iv 14 the king of Elam who ..... mi-ri-ix-tu iq-bu-u (KB ii 188—9 & *rm* *; Winckler, *Forsch.*, i 247 on *ll* 12—18; Meissner, ZA x 79 *fol*; Tiele, *Gesch.*, 380 *rm* 1). DT 71, 15 u ana] ilūti-šu çir-tum iq-bu-u me-ri-ix-tu. Tiele, *Gesch.*, 338; Mürdter-Delitzsch[2] 216: e-tap-pa-lu me-ri-ix-tu spoke insolently (Sn-text).

mūraku (?) see for the present mušālu.

murāku (?) K 3456 *R* 10 edlu narkabat (?) mu-ra-ku ti-'-u-ti; perhaps rather: edlu narkabtu šug-mu-ra-ku (Š pm of *g*[*k*, *q*]-*m*-*r*).

markasu. AV 5178. *a*) rope, Pinches, BO i 42 cordage of a ship {Seil, Tau}, or, railing of a ship (Haupt). K 4378 vi 32 GIŠ-DIM-MA' = mar-kas elippi (33 = d(t)im-mu ša elippi, Br 2740, 2748). D^S 137; ZA ix 156. K 3500 + K 4444 + K 10235, 11 šāru limnu ina elippi-ku-nu lu-šat-ba (iç) mar-kas-ši-na lip-ṭu-ur (Winckler, *Forsch.*, ii 10 *fol*). — *b*) *vinculum*, bonds, lock, bolt {Band, Verschluss, Riegel} id SA (D 11, 74); H 10 & 210, 55; 14, 184; ‖ mēdilu & pa-ar-ku, II 23 *c-d* 39 mar-kas dalti = šu-ul-bu-u, also *ibid*, 25. IV[2] 3 *a* 30 it-ta-šu ga-mir-tu mar-ka-as-su (Br 4332) man-ma ul i-di (BO i 130, *rm* 2, wrong); IV[2] 16 *a* 54—55 (Br 3080) see kalū 1 *a* (*p* 380, *col* 1); Bu 88—5—12, 75 + 76 v 14 mar-kas išni] la pa-ṭa-ri (*cf* Bu 88—5—12, 77 vi 1 *foll*; BA iii 246—7). — *c*) = riksu, bond, uniting tie {Band, Verbindung} Flemming, *Neb*, 56; Lhotzky, *Anp*, 26 castle; D^H 28. Neb vii 37—8 the royal palace ma-ar-ka-sa MA-DA (= māti), Tiele, *Gesch.*, 442 *rm* 3; *Grot* iii 28 my royal palace ma-ar-ka-as ni-ši-im ra-bi-a-tim. Anp i 2 *fol* Ninib mu-kil mar-kas šamē (u) erçi-ti(m), Šamš i 3 *fol* (Schrader, *Šalm.*, 102 compares Rabbin. פרוס). Šalm, *Balaw.*, v 5 Bābilu mar-kas šame-e u erçi-te šu-bat ba-la-ṭi; Asb i 24 aš(!)-ru nak-lu mar-kas šarru-u-ti; S^P II 987 *O* 3 .... mar-kas šame-e ša ana ir-bit im-ru[-uç??] the bond (?) of heaven, which to the four regions .... — II 31 *f* 10 .... KU = mar-ka-su (Br 10587); II 47 *e-f* 18 (du-ur) KU = mar-kas (Br 10530); 21 (gu-uz) BU = *idem* (Br 7528; AV 5178).

murākisu some official {ein Beamter} Rm 2, 19, 7 u]piš-ma Šum-lišir amēl mu-ra-ki-s[u] KB iv 104. (√ rakasu, *q. v.*) M^S 89 & mušarkisu.

markītu refuge, place of refuge {Zuflucht, Zufluchtsort} BA i 16 *rm* 18; 168, 13; 174. Lyon, *Manual*, 118 √ רכה; § 65, 31 *a*; AV 5179. Asb iii 2 he fled to his fortress and e-xu-uz mar-ki-tu (and took refuge Smith, *Asurb*, 91, 46 = KB ii 242); iv 60 (ša) li'bi a-ri-ri i-še-tu-u-ni e-xu-zu mar-ki-i-tu (*cf* ix 39); vii 77 the mountain a-šar mar-ki-ti-šu-un (vii 12; ix 41); x 13 ultu šade-e mar-ki-ti-šu ...... a-bar-šu-nu (also Smith, *Sen*, 67, 18). Br 13868 *ad* ⊕ 252 *a-b* 7 mar-ki-tu. Cappadoc. inscr. (*cf* Delitzsch, *Kappad. Keilschrifttafeln*, *p* 51).

marukuttum. Dar 257, 1: 1 alpu bu-uš-tum ma-ra-ku-ut-tum ša mu-ši-in-di-tum perh. √ maraqu (*q. v.*).

marultu see maruštu.

mēriltu request {Bitte} see mērištu 1.

murīm II 28 *d* 5 e-ri-a mu-ri-im, √מרם?

marmaxxu a spice {eine Spezerei} Rm 367 + 83, 1—18, 461 *a*, *R* 15—6 GIŠ-KIB-GAL & GIŠ-KIB-KUR-RA = mar-max-xu (same id in 14 = ka-meš-ša-ru; M[8] 60).

marinnu K 4111 (4602) 5 something made of leather ma-ri-in-[nu] Meissner, 105; *Lit. Centralbl.*, '90, 1549; ZA viii 140.

Murānu see mūru.

murrānu II 23 *e-f* 29 GIŠ-MA-NU = mu-ur-ra-nu = 30 (ic) nu-u (נון); 28 *e* = (ic) e-ni-tum (AV 5566), Z[B] 44 *rm* 3 receptacle {Behältnis}. V 26 *g-h* 2—3 GIŠ-MA-NU-MUR-RA & GIŠ-MA-NU 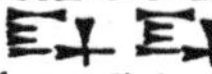 = mur-ra-nu. Jensen, (√מרר?) 1: pedum (shepherd's crook), 2: baculus (Brockelmann, *Lex. Syr.*, 194, *col* 2). ZA vii 217: Stab, Zweig, grüner Zweig. Fränkel, ZA xiii 124 (*no* iii) compares Mishnic מורן cage {Käfig}; but Mishnic borrowed from Assyr.-Babyl.

mirānu, mirēnu see above *p* 584 *col a*.

merīnu? K 2148 iii description of a statue of a deity {Beschreibung eines Gottesbildes}?, 37 pag-ru me]-ri-nu (*cf* dupl.), ZA ix 118—9; *ibid* 118 ii 9 pa-ag-ru (amēltu) me-ri-nu (der Leib eines Weibes??); *cf* II 30 *no* 4 *O* 6, 33 BAR = mi-ri-nu (Br 1769); Rm 279 *O* 9 .... nēši šakin(-in) pag-ru me-ri-in-nu ki-is-su (= kīt-su?) GU; ZA ix 407; Puchstein, *ibid*; vii 76 *foll*; ix 422. ZK ii 301, 1 mi-ri-in-na (Br 13312). M[8] 55 = Hündin(?), thus connecting with mirānu (*q.v.*).

marsu a kind of narṭabu. II 30 *c-d* 77 GUL-ŠU-AK-A = mar-su, AV 5183; Br 8970.

marasu. Jensen-Ball, PSBA xii 277: mix up ingredients into an ointment. IV[2] 13 *b* 59—60 ka-ma-na (see *p* 396) mi-ri-is šam-ni mu-ru-u[s-ma] | mi-ri-is ṭa-ba-a-ti mu-ru [-us-ma?], Br 6017; ZA i 55 *rm* 1. — 3 V 45 iv 34 tu-mar-ra-as(ç?). **Der.:**

mirsu *1.* see marasu, & II 25 *e-f* 41 dux-xu-du ša mir-si (see girsū, where add Br 4438, 5219, 6959, 10423; Sayce, PSBA xviii 175 *no* 5); Cyr 327, 6 so & so much xi-me-tum a-na me-ir-su. Zim., *Babyl. Relig.*, 98—99: Mus (aus Honig & Butter).

mirsu *2.* Nabd 912, 16 a-na mir-su ša bābāni; according to BA i 518 *rm* *: "feststehender Tribut, Pacht der Thorkasse", *cf* Aram מרס: Pächter, *etc.*

mur-pa-lu > mušpalu (*q. v.*), Šalm, *Mon*, *O* 99; AJSL xiv 4.

maraçu 1. pr imraç, imruç, ps imarruç. — *a*) be steep, inaccessible {steil, unzugänglich sein} Anp ii 104 the city GIG (*var* mar-çi) dan-niš (was very inaccessible, § 92; or *adj*?); IV[2] 13 *b* 5—6 rab-bu-ut-ka el çu-ux-xu-ri lim-ra-aç (XEN-GIG) ZA v 73. H 143 & 210: deine Grösse überwältige den Elenden (*cf* מרץ be strong, violent); ZA v 67 (81, 2—4, 188) 15 am-ri-in-ni bēltu ki-i su-ux-xu-ra-ki libbi ardi-ki lim-ra-aç (King, *First Steps*, 251: look upon me, o Lady, that through thy turning to me, the heart of thy servant may become strong; *ibid*, transl. *l* 14 a-na zik-ri-ja šum-ru-çi ka-bit-ta-ki lip-pa-šir: to my speech that is afflicted let thy mind be opened); 68, 20 ga-ma-lu lib-ba-ki eli-ja lim-ra-aç (also *p* 76 perhaps: let mercy overcome thine anger against me; ZA iv 242. — *b*) be difficult, hard, troublesome {schwer, schwierig sein} NR 36 ša Ahuramazda utāmū ina mux-xi-ka la i-mar-ru-uç; IV[2] 49 *a* 7 eli a-me-ri-ja (wr. MU) am-ru-uç (*var* -çu) a-na-ku.

Š perh. TP III *Ann* 113 (= III 9 *no* 2, 12) šum-ru-ça-at. *Rec. Trav.*, xx 127 *fol*, 7 ab-kal-lum ki-bit-su ma-am-man ul u-šam-riç (cannot be infringed); Banks, *Diss*, 12, 1 *no* 4, 73 a-mat-su ni-ši u-šam-ra-aç ni-ši un-na-aš: u-zar-rab (also *l* 75, end). Sp II 265 *a* i 4 .... | ša šum-ru-çu | ka .... | lud-lul-ka.

Št III 4 *no* 4, 41, ana-ku a-di um-mānūtija u-sa (> štn, § 51)-am-ri-iç.

NOTE. — T. A. Ber. 17, 24 ma-ri-iç is difficult; Lo. 13, 50 (the chieftains) ma-ri-iç dan-nis a-na ja-ši; 24, 22; Ber. 77, 49 the garrison which remained with me mar-ça (3 *f pl*) is discontent; 71, 32 qa-ab-šu u mar-xu-u dan-niš are angry and very discontented.

Derr. namraçu 1, šumruçu & these 2:

---

mu-rim read limutti, AV 5553; Br 3641; 11868; mu-rim ba-a-bi see mu-kil, *s. v.* kālu. ~ murrānu read ‖ Weg, see xarrānu.

marçu *1. adj* steep, inaccessible, arduous {steil, unzugänglich; schwierig}, AV 5182; id § 9, 268. II 32 *b* 10 ūmu mar-çu. K 2801 (+ K 221 + 2669) *R* 14 šip-ru mar-çu a difficult work; TP ii 7 šada-a mar-ça u gir-ri-te-šu-nu | pa-aš-qa-te (*cf* Asb vii 70); iv 53 ṭu-ud-di mar-çu-te u ni-ri-bi-te | šup-šu-qa-a-te; vi 51 eqla ṭa-a-ba ..... u mar-ça. Anp i 43 ar-xi pa-aš-qu-te šadē mar-zu (*var* -çu)-te; 45 gi(*var* gir)-ri pa-aš-qu-te šadē GIG ^{MEŠ} (*var* mar-çu-te), 48 šadū mar-çu (= GIG; *cf* ii 74; Sarg *Khors* 41 ina pu-uz-rat šadī mar-çi); ii 104 māxaz marçu (*var* mar-çi) dan-niš. On the top of the mountain *X*, šadi-i mar-çi Sn iii 69; 75 me-li-e mar-çu-ti; *Bav* ^{šad} Ta-as | 13) šadi-i mar-çi; Asb vii 72 šadu-u mar-çu; Esh *Sendsch*, *R* 37 šad-di-e marçūti. Šalm, *Mon*, *O* 19 (*R* 42) arxē pašqūte šadē mar-çu-ti; *Ob* 189 ša-di-i mur(for mar)-çi. Sarg *Khors* 43 birātišu mar-ça-a-ti | 42 dan-na-a-ti; *Ann* 125, 303 šadē mar-çu-ti (also 127), 265 (nāru), 126 (eqla mar-ça). K 3351, 20 i-na nab-li-šu u-tab-ba-šu šadē mar-çu-ti. T. A. Ber. 71, 95 ep-ši mar-zi an-nu-u, that base act.

marçiš *1. adv* with difficulty, sorely *etc.* {beschwerlich, mühevoll, arg} Sn iv 11 mar-çi-iš I mounted the steep mountain peaks; Sn *Kui* 1, 44; 3, 29; Lay 38, 12 ina danāni (*q. v.*) u šupšuqi mar-çi-iš. K 2852 + K 9662 i 37 a-ram-mu ina ši-pik ip-ri-e u abnē mar-çi-iš pa-aš-qi-iš [ušakbis?] Winckler, *Forsch.*, ii 34. H 77, 30 ša ina šamū mar-çi-iš 'i-ad-ru (*cf* 76, 10; he is sorely oppressed).

maraçu 2. be or become sick {krank sein oder werden}, but see note 1; § 84; id GIG, AV 5114; Br 9234. IV² 49 *a* 7 (T^{M} i 7) see maraçu 1. ṗm mariç & maruç PSBA '83—4, 65. K 183, 26 who for many days mar-çu-u-ni ib-tal-ṭu (recovered), ba-ri-u-ti is-sab-bu, ub-bu-lu-ti us-sa-ad-mi-nu (BA ii 304); K 167, 16 liptušu da-an ma-ri-iç a-dan-niš (BA ii 28 & liptu); K 524, 13 ma-ru-uç (AV 5128) he is sick (§ 89 i); K 40 iii 2 (D 82; II 27 *a-b* 50) DUP-TU-RA = ab-na ma-ru-uç (D^{H} 8—9; D^{Pr} 107; Br 3101); II 27 *e-f* 53 see musarū 1. (ZA i 13); 82—5—22, 174 *O* 9—10 (ea ilat) Ba-u-ga-me-lat | mar-ça-at a-dan-niš (AJSL xv 141); K 525, 14 Xu-te-ru ma-ri-çi (*l* 33); S 752 (AV 6912) mar-ça-a-tu; III 38 *b* 11 mar-ça-at abēšunu ēpušu (or *noun*?); perh. NE 71, 12 lu mar-ça-a-ti; Knudtzon, *no* 101 *O* 3 mar-ça-tu-ma; 56, 12 i-mar-ra-çu (= ps); 28, 6 i-m]ar-ra-çu; 20, 2—3; VATh 66, 3 mar-çu-ka I am sick (KB iv 218). II 16 *d* 12—13 (he thine enemy) ana nu-uk-ku-ri-ka ma-ri-iç (D 134 *C* 4; ZK i 129; D^{Pr} 65 *rm* 1 >< RÉJ x 300; Hommel, *Sum. Les.*, 118).

Q¹ = Q V 25 *a-b* 9 when a slave is lost .... owing to sickness (im-ta-ra-çu = TU-RA-AK, Br 1092), WZ iv 303 *no* 2; Meissner, 11; PSBA '85, 150; § 149. — ℑ perh. V 45 iv 34, see marasu. — Š make sick, strike with disease {krank machen, mit Krankheit schlagen}. K 61, 10 u-šam-ra-ça (ZK ii 10); IV² 19 *a* 9—10 ni-iš da-ad-me u-šam-ra-çu (3 *pl*; $Z^{Š}$ vii 10); 81, 7—27, 80 (Creat.-*frg*) *O* 50 .... kat-su-nu la šum-ru-ça. — K 140 *O* 11 ana-ku pulpul mār pulpul mar-çu šum-ru-çu ardi-ka. K 4931 *R* 3—4 šum-ru-ça-at (= GIG-GA-A-AN EME-SAL) ka-bit-ti Hommel, VK 318—19 schmerzbereitend ist meine Seele >< Z^{B} 11 *rm* 4; 44 full of grief is my soul; Sayce, *Hibb. Lect.*, 336; 511—2; J^{L-N} 58—9. KB iv 56 (*no* viii) 25 li-ba-ga o u-ša-am-ri-iç I will not grieve thy heart. K 4648, 16 ili libbu-ka iz-zu ja(?)-a-ti u-šam-ri-ça-an-ni (H 178, 78). BA ii 302 *rm* *.

NOTE. — 1. Oefele, OLZ, ii *no* 1, *cols* 26—7 √ *m-r-ç* not sickness but pain; also *no* 2, *cols* 92—3: the disease of Ištar (in IV 31) was the *Dengue*-fever, which Vambéry explains as extreme weariness, languor.

2. T. A. Ber. 6 *R* 5 if Çalmu m[a-ri-iç]: is sick; 7, 16 should not my brother have heard ki-i ma-ar-ça-ku (ZA v 15; 138); 24 ki-i ma-ar-ça-ta-a that you were sick (ZA v 15; 140); Lo. 40, 22 mur-ça-ku dan-niš I was very sick. Ber. 22 *R* 19 ki-i lib-bi im-ra-çu mi-im-ma; 20 u la-a i-ma-ar-ra-aç (or maraçu, 1?). Lo. 8, 64—66 i-na libbi axi-ja | lu-u la-a im-ma-ra-aç u ad-du-ja lib-bi axi-ja lu-u la-a | u-ša-am-ra-aç (ZA v 162—3). — Q² Ber. 24, 57 am-ta-ra-aç I mourned (or *ad* 1?). — Š Ber. 24 *R* 48 lib-bi-i u-ša-am-ra-aç he will grieve my heart; also 54 + 70; Lo. 11 + Murch, 55 u-ša-am-ra-aç; Ber. 24 *R* 52 libbi axija lū la

u-še-im-ri-iç (*cf* 51, end) & *O* 64; Rostow. *R* 6. — Š3 Bez. 142, 9 lib-pa-ka la du-uš-ma-ra-aç. — Š[t] Lo. 8, 19 ul ul-te-im-ri-iç libbašu I did not grieve his heart (ZA v 156) 24, 23 a-ma-ti ul ul-te]-im-ri-iç (*l* 78).

Derr. namraçu 2 (?) & these:

marçu *2. adj.* — *a*) sick {krank} iD § 9, 263; Br 1074 (TU). 9285 (GIG); ZDMG 29, 24. IV² 4 *a* 31—2 qaq-qa-di mar-çi; *b* 11—12 ša ina zu-um-ri mar-çi (= TU) iš-šak-nu; 1 *b* 7—8 (ana) mar-çi (TU-RA); 3 *a* 45; *b* 9 qaq-qad mar-çi; *a* 46 & *b* 10 ki-šad mar-çi; 21 *b* 29 ina ri-eš mar-çi; 29 *b* 20 ša mar-çi mu-ru-us-su lit-ta-šib. Z[Š] ii 70 ina ikkibi mar-çi (*var* -ça) ša i-ku-lu. K 519 *R* 1 mar-çi. H 82—3, 11 qa-diš-tu ša lib-ba mar-ça (= GIG, Br 9284 mar-ça[-at]); 26 (end) im-šu mar-çu; IV² 17 *a* 37 kasâ uššuru mar-ça (Br 10640); 29* 4 C *R* ii 14 *b* ana i-ni mar-ça-a-ti si-im-me (*l* 11) iš-ta-kan. KB iv 308—9 (*no* ix) 18 e-lat ištēn gišim-maru ša mar-çu-u (foul {faul} ?). — *b*) full of trouble, painful {leidvoll, schmerzlich, schmerzvoll} IV² 26 *b* 61 ta-ni-xa mar-ça-am (= lim-ni, 55); 53 ina qu-ub-bi-e mar-çu-ti; 27 *b* 44—5 ina ți-ix mar-çi); DT 67 (H 119) *a* 13, *b* 11 (of a maiden) ši-ma-tu-ša mar-ça (her fate is full of trouble); 94—5, 42 it-ti mar-çi (TU-RA); IV² 16 *a* 22 lu-u nam-ta-ru lim-nu lu-u a-šak-ku mar-çu lu-u mur-çu la ța-a-bu; H 84—5, 45 + 50; 94—5, 63. S[b] 152 gi-ig GIG | mar-çu; H 12 + 218, 103; 30, 676; Z[Š] iv 16, 78 [amēl] GIG.

marçiš *adv* full of misery, sorrowfully {voll Leids, leidvoll} IV² 20 *a* 53 [(ilat)] Iš-tar e-li-ja is-bu-us-ma mar-çi-iš (= GIG-GA) u-še-man(-an)-ni; 19 *a* 55—6; 17 *a* 51—2 meš-ri-tu-šu mar-çi-iš (= GIG) ip-ša mar-çi-iš ina mur-çi (Br 1075) ni-il; 27 *a* 35 mar-çi-iš uš-tan-na-ax; 29* 4 C *O* ii 18 mar-çi-iš i-bak-ki. K 4931 *R* 1—2 mar-çi-iš (= GIG-GA) a-dam-mu-um (II 110—7). Creat.-*frg* III (K 3473 + 79, 7—8, 296 + Rm 615) 126 [il] Igigi (written: VII) nap-xar-šu-nu i-nu-qu mar-ç[i-iš] lamented, sighed full of misery. a ‖ is:

marçâku. IV² 54 *a* 17 mar-ça-ku i[-bak]-ki-ka; § 80*b*, note: originally an *adj* = marçiš; Z[B] 94 (>< Sayce, *Hibbert Lectures*, 183 *rm* 3); but Jensen, ZDMG 50, 261 (>< Zimmern, Lehmann, *Šamaššumukîn*, 146 *foll* & ZDMG 49, 308; *etc.*) marçaku = I am sick. ZA iii 395, 16 ma-ar-ça-ku.

marçûtu. IV² 17 *b* 2 mar-zu-us-su his sickness {seine Krankheit}.

marçâtu (?) S[P] III *R* 6 . . . . . mar-ça-a-tum i-rat-su-nu (with ?) sickness their breast; perhaps K 4664, 3—4 NAM-GIG-GIG-GA-BI = mar-ça-ti-šu (H 180 *no* ix).

murçu *m* sickness, disease {Krankheit} iD GIG (Br 9286; Knudtzon, 147, 9; § 9, 263, *etc.*) & TU (Br 1075; *cf* IV² 15* i 14—5 TU-RA = GIG, *var* mar-çi). § 65, 3; AV 5565. IV² 16 *a* 21—22 mur-çu la ța-a-bu (= TU--RA-NU-DUG-GA), IV² 29 *b* 31—33; V 50 *b* 6—7 (mur-ça); IV² 1* iii 41—2 mur-çu (TU-RA; *var* mu-ru-uç) di-lip-ti; 3 *b* 53 mu-ru-us-su lu-uk-kiš; 54 *a* 13—14 mur-çu di-xu (*q. v.*); 60* C *R* 12 ul u-ša-pi a-ši-pu ši-kin mur-çi-ja. I 44, 73 šu-tu-qi mur-çu (*cf* țexû); Z[Š] viii 27 xi-țe-it-ka . . . . ni-iš-ka mu-ru-uç-ka; iv 62 GIG[pl]-šu; on Z[Š] iv 59 *cf* mamîtu. IV² 19 *b* 3—4 mu-ru-us-su (= TU-RA, § 51) dan-na (Br 6194) see mandu; 27 *no* 6 *R* 7—8; 31 *O* 70—4 muruç (= GIG) ênâ, *m* a-xi, *m* šêpâ, *m* lib-bi, *m* qaqqadi. II 16 *a-b* 45 mur-çu li-mun; Rm 67 (Hr[L] 348) *R* 6 mu-ru-us-su u-ça (AJSL xv 140); 81, 1—18, 2 (Hr[L] 391) *R* 8 (li-pu-uš-šu-u) mur-çu-um-ma *etc.* (*ibid*, xv 141); 81, 2—4, 188 *R* 21 šu-çi-i mur-çi ‖ šum-si-ki xi-ți-ti (ZA v 68); II 82—3, 23 mu-ru-uç xa-še-e, *m* lib-bi (Br 8065), ki-is lib-bi; mur-çu mu-ru-uç mar-ti (*q. v.*; Z[B] 44—5) mu-ru-uç qaq-qa-di (also 97, 30); 84—5, 55—8 mu-ru-uç (= TU-RA) xa-še-e (*q. v.*) ma-ru-uš-tu; *m* ka-ça-a-ti; *m* la a-çu-u; *m* bi-na-a-ti (*q. v.*); *m* la te-b[u-u mur]-çu lim-nu. muruç daddari (*q. v.*) IV² 3 *b* 30 (Z[B] 97). — muruç qaqqadi (§ 86) & țe'u *cf* Jensen, ZK i 302; ii 201, 204; Bartels, ZA viii, 170 = erysipelas; also Tiele, *Gesch.*, 540 *rm* 1; Haupt, ZA ii 274; Stucken, *Astralmythen*, i 62—3 = {Erynnien, die Wahnsinn bewirken}. IV² 3 *a* 2, 55 (*cf* IV² *add* 9 *a* 62); 3 *b* 18 mu-ru-uç

(= GIG) qaq-qa-di + 28 + 32 + 34 + 36 + 43 + 45 + 49 *etc.*; 22 *no* 1 *R* 24 (*cf* qaqqadu); Br 3513, 3638. — II 47 *a-b* 25 KUR-GAB-LA LU-⊢ = q(g)ab-la mur-çu (Br 10707); 62 *c-d* 51 ni-qil-pu-u (*cf* קלפא) ša mur-çi (Br 6922); xatū ša GIG = murçi (*cf* xatū; Br 2056); II 35 *e-f* 38 (see xatū, *p* 346); V 47 *a* 48 see lu-'-tum; II 48 *d-e* 19 ši-iq-çu = mur-çu. T. A. (Ber.) 71, 29 ši-ma-ti u mur-zu dan-nu a-na ^(šēr) ra-ma-ni-ja, old age and disease press heavily upon me.

maraqu. PEISER, *Babyl. Vertr.*, 260 = Talm מרק *plane solvere*; show, prove a claim to {nachweisen (ein Recht an)} MEISSNER, *Diss*, 31. K 164, 11—12 ^(iç) a-ma-ri | ša irši i-mar-ru-qu (*cf l* 26), 21 (BA ii 636), 31 . . . u-šal-bu-ni (?) i-mar-ru-qu; KB iv 90—1 *no* vi 14 (a-na lib-bi a[-mi-li-ti] im-ru-uq (hatte er Anrecht); perh. also PSBA xviii ('96) 252: 81—11—3, 478 iv 5 dul-la-ka la mar-ku. KB iv 314—5, 18 isqi šu'áti u-mar-raq-ma' they will prove; 19 . . . a-na mur-ru-qu isqi to prove the right of income; PEISER, *Babyl. Vertr.*, lxi 7 mu-ru-qa (ac); lxxiii 8 ummušu u-mar-raq-am-ma (PINCHES, PSBA '83—4; *ibid* 104 quotes u-mar-qa-u-nim-ma, translating: forfeit); lvi 9 u-mar-ra-qa-nim-ma; Dar 379, 68 (-qu-); V 45 iv 35 tu-mar-raq. ℑ (?) Neb 64, 22 kaspu ina çēri ul im-mar-riq-qi. **Der.:**

muruqqū proof {Nachweis} Neb 738, 12 mu-ru-u]q-qu-u-šu.

mararu be bitter {bitter sein}. Ⓢ 59 iv 38—9 ŠEŠ = ma-ra[-ru]; [cuneiform sign]-BI-IB-BA = *m* ša [inbi?]; II 39 *g-h* 31; perh. K 1028, 10 ultu Sippar adī bāb nār mar-rat (said of water). T. A. Ber. 189, 66 šar-ru bēli-ja im-ru-ur-mi; 71 u šu-um-r[i-ir i]ṣ-tu ša-a-šu, *etc.* BA iv 121 *fol.* STRASS., *Warka*, 57, 4 lu-ma-ru-ur-ma. — ℑ V 45 iv 33 tu-mar-ra-ar. — Š embitter, make bitter, let one's weapon do a violent act. Asb ii 46 e-li ^(māt) Mu-çur u ^(māt) Ku-u-si ^(iç) kakkū-ja u-šam-ri-ir (liess ich wüten); iii 50 u-šam-ri-ru (1 *sg*); Sarg *Khors* 150 while I eli ^(māt) la-at-bu-ri u-šam-ra-ru (ps) kakkē-ja; also *Ann* 372. 81—6—7, 209, 35 mux-xi kul-lat na-ki-ri li-šam-ri-ir kakkē-ja (HEBR. viii 14; PAOS, My '91, cxxxii).

NOTE. — 1. T. A. Ber. 77, 30 (and till the king, the sun) ju-ša-am-ri-ir (drives out) the enemy from his land (KB v 170—1); perh. Ber. 158, 18; 81, 24 (in order that the troops) tu-ša-am-ri[-ir the enemy] from the country; 314 *R* 2 ju-ša]-am-ri-ru expels (KB v 414).

2. KNUDTZON *ad* 68 *R* 15 i-mar-ri-ru (ps) = *m-r-r* (Q) be splendid, glorious or the like ‖ herrlich sein, oder dergleichen.

Derr. marru 2, murru, martu, marratu 1, namurratu, namriru (?) but see namāru &:

murāru Sm 1316 ‖ marru 2 (*q. v.*):

marāru a plant {eine Pflanze, Gewächs} K 13577, 9, together with other kinds of xassu we have ^(šam) ma-ra-ru (SAR).

ma-raš (?) K 376, 2: 150 ^(kirru) ma-raš ^(meš) KB iv 128—9.

maršu *1. adj* probably unclean, polluted {unrein, befleckt} Z^B 57; NE 42, 3 after killing Xumbaba Gilgameš put away (iddī) mar-šu-ti-šu ittalbiš(a) zakūtišu (his defiled clothes, put on clean ones).

maršu *2. f* **maruštu** & **marultu**. — *a*) *adj* (Br 12143 *fol*; 9237; id GIG) § 65, 8. — *b*) usually *noun* calamity, misfortune; disaster; sickness {Unglück, Unheil; Elend, Krankheit} AV 5127. LE GAČ, ZA ix 386, 9—10 ar-ra-at ma-ru-uš-ti (*cf* limuttu); TP viii 76 ar-ra-ta ma-ru-uš-ta li-ru-ru-šu (3 *pl*); L^T 186. I 27 *no* 2, 91—2 ir-ri-ta ma-ru-ul-ta; IV² 39 *b* 53 (-uš); 54 *a* 37 šmurma ep-še-ta-šu ma-ru-uš (*var* -ul)-ta; V 52 *R* 43—5 ki-ma bi-tum ma-ru-uš-ti it-ta-šab (& u-qat-tu-šu), also 47. PEISER, KAS 20: 30—1 ar-rat la nap-šu-ru | ma-ru (or -ar-? KB iv 214—5) -uš-tum li-ru-ru-šu. IV² 6 *a* 24 a-šar ma-ru-uš-ti-šu; 16 *b* 53—4 ma-ru-uš-tu (= ŠA-GIG-GA) ša e-mu-ki i-na-aš-ša-ru; *cf* 17 *a* 48 (ma-ru-uš-ta-šu); 22 *no* 2, 13 a-na ma-ru-uš-ti-šu ina çi-in(?)-di ul i-na-ax (also *cf* H 180 *no* vii; K 5267); 5 *a* 6—7 šūnu ēpeš ma-ru-uš-ti (= GIG-GA) šu-nu they are the ones that perpetrate evil; 24 *no* 3, 14—5 ma-ru-uš-tum te-pu-ša-an-ni (H 208); V 59, 59 a-di ū-um bal-ṭu ma-ru-uš-ta li-iš-du-ud (shall he drag along with him misfortune) ZK ii 28 *rm* 2; *cf* Mer.-Balad. stone v 40 liš-du-ud ma-ru-uš-ti (BA ii 265; KB iii, 1, 192—3); Asb vii 123 Ušte'a ma-ru-uš-tu im-xur-šu-u-ma (misfortune befell *U.*). H 84—5, 27 ma-ru-uš-tu nu (or NU? = lā)-ul-la-tu, 55 (see murçu); 90—1, 65 ma-ru-uš-tu up-ša-šu-u la ṭa-bu-ti; also *cf* K 5268, 30 (AV 8555); K 4623 *O* 17 ana ardi-ki ša ma-ru-uš-tum ep-šu ri-e-mu ri-ši-šu (H 122; Z^B 57; Br 4770; also 79—7—8, 24, 20; K 5726 *R* 1). II 8 *c-d* 69—70 (K 245 ii), see maçartu. Banks, *Diss*, 18 *foll* (*no* 2) 8—10 : 4, ša ..... ma-ru-uš-tum i-pu-uš. Cyr 277, 17—18 ar-ra-as-su mar-ru-tu (perh. mistake for mar-ru-uš-tu) li-i-ru-ur (BA iii 428—9); Bu 88—5—12, 75 + 76 ii (= K 192 *O*) 9 .... ar-rat ma-ru-uš-ti iš-ša-kin ina pi-i-šu.

maršu *3.* and **mara(ā?)šu** bed, couch {Bett, Lager} = ma'āltu, mālitu (*q. v.*). AV 5115. II 23 *c-d* 65—6 mar-šum & ma-ra-šum. Z^B 44; BA i 174, same √ as eršu, bed; T. A. (Ber.) 26 i 52 ša i-na mar-ši-šu XVI DIŠ-KU-ŠU, *etc.*

muraš(š)ū some term of relationship. II 32 *a-b* 60; 35 *c-d* 32, mu-ra(-aš)-šu-u; = XAR-KU-DU; AV 5548—50; Br 8592; *cf* mubattitum.

maršītu. § 65, 31 *a*; ZK ii 308—8; AV 3225; 5190; √rašū. — *a*) possessions, goods, property {Besitz, Hab und Gut}; TP v 51 *foll* šal-la-su-nu | bu-ša-šu-nu u mar-ši-su-nu | a-na la(-a)ma-ni-e u-te-ir-ra; also 61 *fol.* L^T 147; Hebr. iii 110, 1; Fränkel, *Aram. Fremdwörter*, 98; III 9 *no* 1, 6; 3, 38 *etc.* (TP III *Ann* 66, 95, 138, 140, 206, 234) a-di mar-ši-ti-šu-nu; II 67, 16 + 18; Sarg *Khors* 45, 71, 75; *Ann* 22, 90, 252, 273. T. A. (Ber.) 71, 74 mar-ši-te *pl* āli the property of the city. — *b*) especially cattle, herds {namentlich Vieh, Herde}. I 28 *a* 21—22 su-gul-la-a-te-šu-nu ik-çur u-ša-lid mar-ši-su-nu | ki-ma mar-ši-it (imēr) çi-e-ni *pl* im-nu; Lay 43—44, 14 mar-ši-si-na ana ma-'-diš u-ša-li-di; Sarg *Ann* 183 mar-šit çēni; Anp i 32 kīma mar-šit (imēr) çe-ni; TP v 6 mar-šit qir-be-te-šu-nu.

mē(ī)rišu *1.* *m* decision, wisdom {Entscheidung, Weisheit} √erešu. Sarg *Cyl* 47 i-na mi-ri-ši-ja pal-ki ša ...... ta-šim-ta xunnunūma malū niklāti (Lyon, *Sargon*, 70; AV 5352); Sn *Kui* 4, 22 i-na me-lik ṭe-me-ja u me-riš ka-bit-ti-ja; Sarg (Winckler, 164), 13 ina me(mi)-ri-ši-ja rapši (*cf* xissatu). Perh. T. A. (Ber.) 85, 32 mi-ri-ši wish {Wunsch}. ‖ is:

mē(ī)rištu *1.* Knudtzon, 71 *a* 7 (K 83, 1—18, 587) mi-riš-ti & see K 11445 *O* 11. KB iii (2) 4—5, ii 14 i-na me-ri-iš-ta with the art of Êa (ZA iv 111); V 52 *b* 49 ša mi-riš-ta-šu ra-pa-aš-tum 'i-xa-ab-tu (Br 3179); also perh. IV^2 23 *no* 1, ii 6—7 ša mi-riš-ti (= GAN) ...

NOTE. — T. A. Ber. 18, 8 u mi-ri-iš-ta ša a-bu-ka e-ri-šu (+ 11 + 20) ZA v 150 *rm* 3; 34, 4—5 mi-ri-iš-tum | ša e-te-ir-ri-iš; 34 a 11 gab-bi mi-ri-iš-te *pl* all the demands; 36, 18 mi-ri-iš-ta-šu; also merištu wish ‖ Wunsch, T. A. Lo. 2, 10 me-ri-el-ta ba-ni-ta ana axāmeš ul iqbū, ZA v 150 & *rm* 3 ohne eine ausdrückliche Bitte gegenseitig auszusprechen; KB v 14 reads ik-lu-u: and they have not refused one another any wish.

mē(ī)rišu *2.* *pl* mīrišūtu (√erešu plant {pflanzen}), AV 5352; T^C 51. planting, plantation {Anpflanzung} BA i 321 *ad* 135; Jensen, *Theol. Litztg.*, '95 *no* 10 *m* = Bewässerungseimer (also ZA xiii 336); aber auch (?) Bewässerung & ein bewässertes Stück Land, √erešu bewässern. KB iii (1) 122 *col* i 20—21 ki-ša-di-ša (of the canal) ki-la-li-en | a-na me-ri-šim lu-u-te-ir. (ZA ii 360 I used for plantation); Sn *Bav* 23 see makaru Š. III 54 *a* 12 (*c* 43) me-ri-šu suluppi date-plantation; 61 *a* 42 me-ri-šu lā iššir (will not prosper); II 32 (*g*)-*h* 75 ina (iç) me-ri-šu bal-ku-tu. K 4148 *R* (AV 3935) SI = me-ri-šu (Br 3394). BOR ii 3, 2 a corn-field zaq-pi (*q. v.*) u me-ri-šu planted and tilled (= 81—6—25, 45); *cf* V 68 *no* 1 *O* 2 (*b*) mi-ri-šu u ki-ru-bu-u šap-la-nu (*l* 20); K 313, 8 see karabxu; III 50 *no* 3, 21; K 400 (= III 50 *no* 2) 8—9: 4 me-ri-še 4 kar-ab-xe ikkal; me-ri-še-šu u-šal-lim (KB iv 126—7; see, however, Oppert, ZA xiii 259: mērišu: Getreideernte, kar-ab-xi lieu kirubū: Wiesengrund). Strassm., *Stockholm*, 23, 1: zēru me-ri-šu; Nabd 116, 24 me-ri-šu (Cyr 161, 1); 1102, 1 bīt me-ri-šu; 116, 2 + 20 mi-ri-šu; 440, 1 (Peiser, KAS 98, *med.*, bīt mi-ri-ši); Cyr 3, 3 mi-ri-eš; ZA iv 13, 11 ana me-ri-eš še-im u-ga-ri to plant the corn of the field. II 23 *e-f* 15 mi-ri-šu = (iç) di-lu-tum (?); mi-ri-šu-tu ku-zip-pe uk-ta-at-ti-mu (*q. v.*) K 183, 29. a ‖ is:

mē(ī)rištu *2.* ZA i 410. Z^{B} iv 80 li-ix-ziz (il) Nin-ger-su ("the Lord of fields") bēl me-riš-ti li-xal-liq mur-çu. III 53 *a* 3 ri-eš me-riš-te šur-ri (*cf* šur-rū), ZA i 409 (below): the harvest has begun; ZA iv 120 *no* 17 ana mi-riš-tum na-din; Neb 361, 5 mi-reš-tu; K 3456 *O* 17 + 32 aš-rat la me(& mi)-riš-ti ir-ri-ša ra-ax-çu (PSBA xxi 38—40); V 21 *e-f* 3 SAR = mi-riš-tu (AV 5353; Br 4320); perhaps II 7 *c-f* 46 BAR-BI-KU-GAR = me-ri-ša-a-tu, Br 1904.

martu gall, bile; bitterness {Galle; Bitterkeit} probably > marratu; id ÇI Br 4196; AV 5193. BA i 10; ‖ daddaru (*q. v.*). S^{b} 194; H 18, 291 çi-i | ÇI | mar-tum. II 16 *f* 22—4 ina ki-ri-i (*q. v.*) tab-ši-ma | su-lu-up-pa-ka | mar-tum (= ÇI) Br 4197; D^{Pr} 137 *rm* 2; Z^{B} 97; BA ii 299—302, *etc.* IV² 1 i 16—17 i-mat mar-ti ša ilāni; 29 *no* 3, 9—10 .... i-šu a-na mar-ti it-tur mu-u eli-šu ul ṭa-a-bu; $Z^{Š}$ vii 26 *b* mar-ta iz-za-ar-qu-šu. H 82—3, 24 *cf* murçu. S^{P} II 987 *O* 12 (end) tab-bi-ik mar-tum which pours out gall; II 37 *g-h* 47 (aban) mar-tu = (aban) da-a[d-da-ri?] gallstone; 82, 8—16, 1 iv 13 ÇI-I | KI-NE | mar-tum (Br 9706).

marratu *1.* *e. g.* in (nâr) mar-ra-ti salt-river {Salzfluss, -wasser} Sarg *Khors* 122 = Persian Gulf {Persischer Meerbusen}. D^{Par} 180 *fol*; Jensen. S 1208, 10 ultu Sippar adi bāb (nâr) mar-rat (Hr^{L} 418); K 1374 *R* 14; Winckler, *Forsch.*, ii, 2, 309: Lagune an der Mündung der Flüsse. Smith, *Sen*, 89, 80 cities, *etc.*, situated e-bir-tan (nâr) mar-ra-ti, on the other side of the Persian Gulf. II 67, 3 ul-tu (nâr)] mar-ra-ti ša Bīt-la-ki-ni, *etc.* (KB ii 10—11); Lay 91, 84; III 12 *no* 2, 5. Pognon, *Bav.*, 33, 102. KB ii 68—9; Schrader, *Abh. der Ak der Wiss.*, Berlin '77 (78), 176; Z^{B} 48 √ Akkadian MAR-TU (MAR = ša-kanu + TU = erebu) = dwelling of the setting sun (*cf* MAR-TU-KI). ZK i 265 *no* 12 √מרר; ZA iii 196; ii 265 *rm* 1 Isa 50, 21; iv 366. Bezold, *Catalog* v, 2110.

Also *cf* Neb vi 40 ki-ma e-bir ti am-ti gal-la-ti ja-ar-ri (*q. v.*) r ar-ti KB iii (2) 22 saltwater {Salzf said of the ocean.

marratu *2.* a bird {ein Vogel} AV 5 II 37 *a-c* 16 + K 4206 *R* 14 ŠEŠ (iš XU = mar-ra-tum = iç-çur tu-ba *ibid* 65 *b-c* mar-ra-tu = iç-çur tu-.. qi D^{S} 100; Br 6445.

marratu *3.* Neb 245, 1: 60 (iç) mar-ri-a-ta parzilli | ša ana li-bi-en ša libnāte Nadin (amēl) rab-bāni .... ittadin; T^{C} 60; BA i 636 tile-mold, brick-mold {Ziegelrahmen}.

marratum *4.* V 28 *a-b* 76 mar-ra-tum = un-qu; & *cf* II 25 *e* 48 mar-ra-tum.

mar-ru-tu SAR a plant {ein Gewächs} 81—7—6, 688 S. H. (ZA vi 291 i 15).

(mât) **MAR-TU**ki often in Asb; K 692, 2; 698, 2, AV 5191; a country usually explained as = (mât) A-mur (xar?)-ri(ru) T. A. (Ber.) 31, 32 *fol* (& *passim*); D^{Par} = Phoenicia; Jensen, ZA x 338 *foll*; xi 304—5 = A murrū not axarrū. Meissner, *no* 42 has ugar A-mu-ur-ri-i ki & 61 ugar MAR-TU. V 14 *c-(d)* 18 ši-pat MAR-TU ki in a list of wool, *etc.* from countries (Br 12801); *cf* V 18, 5. DT 98, 13 mât MAR-TU ki, 14 (mât) A-mur (xar)-ru (Hr^{L} 337); AJSL xv 142: perhaps two different countries.

NOTE. — On mountain Tid(a)num in Mar-tu ki *e. g.* II 50 *col* iii—iv 16 see ZA x 334—7 (Hommel, ZDMG 49 522 *foll*); "according to II 48 *c-d* 12 Tidnu = Axarrū or rather Amurru. *T.* perhaps the Lebanon, more especially the Antilebanon; Mar-tu ki may well be identical with Amur-rū (so first read by Delattre); the exact location and nature of the country not quite certain; whether it is to be read mar-tu or MAR-TU (of course not the same as MAR-TU = abūbu) cannot be decided. In Babylonia there was a city or district Amurrī (id MAR-TU); but whether this name is connected with that of the Amorites (Pinches, *Academy*, 2 Nov. '95, *p* 368) cannot be proved (ZA x 344) nor can it be disproved. It is possible, that MAR-TU indicated originally this Babylonian Amurrū & was later transferred to Amor, the land of the Amorites". See also Scheil, ZA xi 84; Hommel, PSBA xviii 17, § 13 (almost the whole of Palestine in early Babyl. inscr.; Hebr. [illegible], whence [illegible].

ma-ra-a-tu AV 5117 *ad* II 36, 4 read la a-mu-ra-a-tu (*q. v.*)

‑ martu > amartu); SAYCE, *ibid*. 171–2 on (mâti) MAR-TU. Against HOMMEL, *Anc. Hebr. Tradition*, 34, 57–8, 166, 170, 194 *rm*, 222, 237. "Martu also = land of the Amorites, Palestine", see ZIMMERN, *Theol. Rundschau*, i 323. BEZOLD, *Cat.*, v, 1963.

(ilu) **MAR-TU-E** K 4931 *R* 11; K 5332 *R* 5; Z[B] 19; 48; Br 12800, 14291 (ilu) MAR-TU, II 56 *c-d* 42; also 41 ilâni MAR-TU (Br 14292); J[e] 69. VATh 706, 3 (KB iv 40—1); — (ilu) MAR-TU = Adad (HOMMEL, *Sum. Les.*, *ad* II 59 *R* 42; 43—6 the 4 names for his wife: DAM-BI-SAL); III 66 *col* 3, 12; 67 *c-d* 51 (ilu) MAR-TU = AN-IM (= ilu Adad) ša a-bu-bi (*q. v.*); JASTROW, *Religion*, 166—7; 212: the west-god, but see above.

mirtum (?) Br 2750 *ad* D 89 vi 53 *b* mir-[tu]m?

martû V 26 *a-b* 20 GIŠ (gi-iš) KAL = mar-tu-u = e-šu-u & nap-pa-çu (Br 6201, AV 5192); II 44 *a-b* 39—40; also V 26 *g-h* 4—5 GIŠ-MA-NU-TUR-TUR = mar-tu-u, GIŠ-MA-NU-GIŠ-DAN (or KAL) = giš-kal-lu (Br 4104, 6795) ZK ii 205 cedar?

murâtu in name of streets. Cyr 345, 15 sûqu SIQ mu-rat nâri; 161, 20 = mu-ra-at; TALLQVIST, *Schenkungsbriefe*, 13 perhaps √ ירה lead, guide.

mirûtu (?) T. A. (Lo.) 30, 20 pa-ni-ia a-na mi(?)-ru-ti | sa(?)-bu-ti šarri bêlija. KB v 277: for the service {Zum Dienste}.

mirîtu pasture, food, feeding {Weide, Futter, Speise} √ רעה; AV 5354; Xammurabi, *Louvre* 1 ii 5 mi-ri-tu u ma-aš-ki-tu, also *l* 3 (ZA ii 360; KB iii, 1, 122; see mašqîtu). K 3456 *O* 20 mi-rit bu-lim (the cattle's pasture) u-šam-mi-xa, 26 ina ri-eš šatti u ki-it šatti at-ta-ṭa-al mi-ri-ti (PSBA xxi 37—40). D[Pr] 191; BA i 174, *bel.*

murta'imu. Epithet of Adad (Rammân) mur-ta-i-mu (the thunderer, √ רעם), also **mur-ta-as-nu** (√ רסן be hot, burning) JA '89 (xiii) 504; ZA iv 215.

mur-te-'-at, AV 5569 *cf* re'û.

murtiddû ruler {Leiter} § 126; Br 5069; see redû.

martakal see maštakal.

mar-tak-ni-e Sarg *Khors* 177; *Ann* 437 see taknû.

murtaššû VATh 244 i 23 GAL-TI-TI = mu-ur-taš-šu-u; 25 = mur-taš-šu-u (ZA ix 157).

mêš *adv* how? where? {wie? wo?} § 78; K 143 *R* 7 ilî me-e-eš at-ta my God, where art thou?

maši stars *Creat.-frg* V 2 (D 94, 2) LU (or lu?) ma-ši uš-zi-iz he sat up as constellations (ZIMMERN), JASTROW, *Religion*, 434 *rm* 4. JENSEN, 47 *foll* on III 57 *a* 53—6 where the seven maši (LU ma-ši, so read *p* 489, *col* 2) are mentioned. *Cf* LU-BAT = bibbu = planet. Perhaps *cf* S[c] 1 *b* 6 ma-šu-u & laxû = MAŠ-MAŠ (ZA i 300 *rm*: mašû from Sumerian).

mâšu (מאש) Q *pr* imêš, imîš despise, observe not, ignore, do away with {verachten, nicht achten, missachten} D[Pr] 66 *rm* 1; § 116. TP III *Ann* 92 Tu-ta-am-mu-u (mâti) Un-qi a-di-ja e-miš (= III 9 *no* 1); K 2852 + K 9662 i 23 ša e-ti-qu (= *pl*) a-mat šarrû-ti-ka ša a-me-šu; Sarg *Ann* 42 a-di-e ilâni i-miš-ma; *Khors* 73 Urzana who ..... i-mi(-e)-šu ar-du-tu who did not regard his servitude. Asb hymn to Marduk (STRONG, JA, My-Je, '93; WINCKLER, *Forsch.*, i 492—3) 21—22 ni-i[š ilâni] | i-miš la ik-kud-ma zi-kir-ka kab-tu; also MESSERSCHMIDT, *Nabuna'id*, 63—4. SMITH, *Asurb*, 37, 4 danân (ilu) Ašur e-me-iš (36, 6); POGNON, *Bavian*, 110 *rm*. IV² 51 *b* 17 ina gab-bi ilu u (ilu) Ištar ša i-me-šu; 19 ina s(š?)ur-ki šum ili-šu i-me-šu. Of sins: not to look at, overlook, forgive. Sarg *Khors* a-bu-uk a-mi-iš qil-lat-su KB ii 58 (= mašû). — Q[t] = Q IV² 51 *a* 35 see dâçu; *a* 38 a-na ummi im-te-eš a-na axâti rabî-ti uk(q)-tal-lil. — Ƶ Sm 1371 (= NE 93) 6 di-in-ka ul in-nen-ni ul im-meš a[-mat-ka.

NOTE. — KNUDTZON, 206, connects these forms with m-š-', whence also mûšu & (sixu)maštu.

Der. ti-mi-e-šu forgiving ‖ vergebungsvoll, ZA iv 238, 29.

mâšu *2.* name of a mountain {Name eines Berges} NE 60, 1—2 ša ša-di-i še-mu-šu ma-šu .... | ana ša-ad ma-a-ši i-na ka-ša-[di-šu]; on this plate see J[e]; DELITZSCH, *Chald. Gen.*, 211; SAYCE, *Hibb. Lect.*, 363; BO iii 148—9; JASTROW, *Religion*, 488—9; 516 *rm* 4; HOMMEL, *Anc. Hebr. Tradition*, 35, 183 (>< ZIMMERN, *Theol.*

Rundsch., i 323). Perh. NE 62, 40 KUR-MEŠ ma-a-šu. AV 5205. Asb viii 87 *etc.* read mad-bar (see mad-baru) instead of (māt or šad) MAŠ; but, BEZOLD, *Cat.*, v, 2111 reads Māš in Sarg *Cyl* 13, *etc.* = name of the Arabian desert. On the the socalled MAŠ in ki-maš see maššu.

māšu, mašū twin {Zwilling}? AV 5205; ZA i 259: double; Rm 2, 555, 9 ma-a-šu prec. by ši-na; tu-'a-mu & followed by ki-lal-la-an. ZA iv 436; M^S 60 *col* 2, how., reads ma-šo-e, & refers to BEZOLD, *Catalogue*, 432 aššat amēli ma-ša-a-ti ul ikašad. S^c 1 *a* 10 ma-a-šu = ma-šu-u & tu-'-a-mu, see *l* 12 (ZA i 390 *rm* 1; ii 203—4); S^c 1 *b* 4 (Br 1842); also S^c 3 (Br 1770); The seven ma-a-šu stars are mentioned in III 57 *a* 57 *foll* = die sieben Paar-sterne (ZA i 259 *rm*; JENSEN, 57; 144—6) see maši; II 7 *c-d* 28—9 MAŠ-TAB-BA & GIŠ-IK-TAB-BA = tu-'a-[a-mu?]. III 66 iv 24 ^{il} EN-<< ^{il} MAŠ-TAB-BA (*cf* v 11—12 ^{il} EN-<< | ^{il} AK (= Nabū) ^{il} MAŠ-TAB-BA; v 19 ^{il} MAŠ-TAB-BA GI (= çix)-ru, ^{il} PA (= Nabū): vi 17). III 68 *a-b* 68 AN-MAŠ-TAB-BA = ilu kilallān = the 2 gods (ZK ii 307—8); also see V 46 *a-b* 4—5 (ZA i 259 *rm* 1); 6—7 (ZK ii 308—9) = the larger or the smaller constellation of twin-stars (see on this text R. BROWN jr., PSBA xii 137—52; 180—206; ZA iv 170); IV^2 21, 1 B 16—18: II ça-lam ma-a-ši (= MAŠ-TAB-BA) kiççurūti (Br 1895); 30—31 (see ZIMMERN, *Ritualtafeln*, *p* 120 *rm* 7); 32—34 MAŠ-MAŠ = ma-a-ši (mu-un-dax-çe) = a couple of warriors. V 37 i 32 ma-an | MAN | ma-šu-u (Br 9959) same id = kilallān, šina, tap-pu-u, at-xu-u.

māšu, maššū. S^c 1 *a* 2 ma-a-šu = a-ša-ri-du; *cf* also II 47 *a-b* 15 where maš(?)-šu-u = a-ša-ri-du (AV 5227; Br 1930); 14, maš-šu-u = kak-ku (Br 1929; 11884); GUYARD, ZK i 113. SAYCE, *Hibb. Lect.*, √ Accadian = hero; but HALÉVY, *Rev. Hist. Rel.*, xvii 181 √ *mašāh* = retirer. JRAS '92, 342, 8 (= Lay 73) maš-šu-u šakkanak ilāni. S^c 1 *a* 4 ma-a-šu : gaš(?)ru : ma-aš (or -rum?) Br 1768. K 4200 *R* 12 .... LAL = maš-šu-u (Br 14378; AV 7031).

mašū be light, shining {hell sein, scheinen, leuchten}? II 47 *e-f* 59 NI = ma-šu-u (57 ux-xu-ru; 58 na-ma-ru) AV 5206; Br 5316. Perhaps S^c 1 *a* i 9 [ma-aš] MAŠ | a-ma-ru : ma-šu-u; S^c 1 *b* 1; 6 (Br 1771, 1848). With this also compare S^c 3 el-lu : ma-a-šu (HOMMEL, *Sum. Les.*, = double) Br 1770; H 13, 143—6 ma-aš | MAŠ | ma-a-šu, el-lu, na-ma-ru, ša-am-šu, AV 5194. V 24 *c-d* 2—4 še-e-ri = še-xe(?)-ri | na-ma-ru | mu-šu-ma.

ma-a-šu S^c 1 *b* 5 = mul-li-lum (*q. v.*).

mašū, pr imšī, in-ši (SMITH, *Asurb*, 216 *g*); ps imašši forget, disregard, be unmindful of {vergessen, nicht beachten, uneingedenk sein} AV 5206. IV^2 60* B *O* 21; V 47 *a* 42, see maxū; Asb i 56 the power of the great gods im-ši-ma (*cf* māšu); 119 ṭābtu (1, *q. v.*) ēpussunūti im-šu-ma (3 *pl*); iii 78 (v 28) im-ši-ma (3 *sg*); K 2673 + K 228 *O* 35; K 2401 iii 10 ta-maš-ši-a a-di-e an-nu-ti you forget these commands (BA ii 628 *foll*); *del* 155 lu-u .... a-a am-ši; 156 see xasasu; Sarg *Cyl* 23 whose prince had forgotten (im-šu-ma) the gracious favor of S. IV^2 50 *d* 34 ta-maš-ši-i širē[ki?] = T^M iii 140; K^M 6, 66 ša la ma-še-e. Nabd 741, 15 *fol* tax-sis-tum la ma-še-e a P. S. = the notice is not to be forgotten; 562, 15; 557, 12 *l.* ana la maš-še-e. VATh 90, 17 *l.* la maš-še-e (PEISER, *Babyl. Vertr.*, 230); Neb 466, 16 tax-xi-su la maš-ši; Nabd 1006, 11—12 tax-xi-is ša a-na la maš-še-e; 68, 15 (according to KB iv 212) la *ba*-še-e; also 708, 13; Neb 348, 18 (T^C 143); Synchr. Hist. iv 25 (end) a-na la ma-še-e lid[-da-a] KB i 202—3; *ibid*, *l* 26 (?) ma-še. — 27 be or become forgotten {vergessen sein oder werden} IV^2 59 *no* 2 *b* (K 254), 11 lip-paṭ-ru ar-nu-u-a lim-ma-ša-a xi-ṭa-tu-u-a (forgotten be my sins). K 3258 *R* 11 a-a im-ma-ši ta-nit-ti ^{il} Ašur; K 8522 (D 95) 17 a-a im-ma-ša-a a-ma-tu-šu (*ibid* 4 a-a im-ma-ši ina a-pa-a-ti) not be forgotten; Sarg *Khors* 11 the freedom of *A* & *X* which since many days im-ma-šu-ma; Merodach-Baladan-stone iii 19 ki-sur-re-ši-na (see kisurru) im-ma-šu-ma (BA ii 262 *foll*); V 60 i 9 par-çu-šu im-ma-šu-ma; K[M] 60, 10 ki-bit-ka ul im-maš-ši ut-nin-ka ul iš-ša-na-an: thy command is not forgotten, thy intercession is unequalled.

NOTE. — T. A. Lo. 11 + March 23 (end) the friendly relations with him la im-ši (?); 26 itti axi-ka ra-'-mu-ut-ka la ta-ma-aš-ši; 31 [la] I a-ma-aš-ši I will not forget.

Derr. these 2:

mašû 2. *adj* forgotten, neglected {vergessen, vernachlässigt} Sarg *Ann* 165 gi-mir na-gi-šu-nu u-tir-ru a-na ti-li ma-šu-u-ti; *Khors* 136, see kisurru; V 62 *no* 2, 12 *cf* kidudû.

mišu oblivion {Vergessenheit} IV² 39 *b* 18 whosoever my tablet a-na mi(*var* me)-ši i-na-du-u (GGA '89 867 *fol*; ✕ KB i 7; see, however, again AJSL xii 152, 171; also OPPERT, *Adad-Nirar*, 10 *rm* 2).

mašû 3. ג find, locate {finden, ausfindig machen} Sarg *Cyl* 44—46 the place *M* ša ..... a-a-um-ma ina lib-bi-šu-nu a-šar-šu ul u-maš-ši-i-ma (KB ii 292 *ad pp* 46—7); § 53*d*, on accent; Aram מַשֵּׁשׁ: touch. Sarg *Ann* XIV 67 ul u-maš-ši; *Bull* 45 (-ma); Sn *Bav* 54 aš-šu axrât ûmê qaqqar šli šu-a-tu u bîtâte ilâni la muš-ši so that .... could not be found, POGNON, *Bavian*, 40; 94.

Mašû 4. name of a canal KB iv 92 *col* ii *R* 13 (nâr) Ma-še-e.

mašû 5. *f* **mašitum** in zêr-mašîtum (*q. v.*, *p* 297, and *add*: *cf* AV 4527; Z[B] viii 52).

mašŝu 1. shining, bright, brilliant {leuchtend, glänzend} especially in connection with q(k)i-e = qû as q(k)i-e maš-ši; √mašašu (2, *q. v.*). I 44, 80 sal AN-KAL (DAN)[MEŠ] erê ma-ša-a-ti Esh v 52 lamassi erê maš-ša-a-te, MEISSNER & ROST, 59 *rm* 79: cast {gegossen} but JENSEN, ZA ix 120 says: in these 2 passages perh. connected with mâšu (mašû) double (see also ZA i 259); ABEL-PUCHSTEIN translates: brilliant, bright {hellschimmernde} see however ZA ix 129, 131. V 27 *c-d* 43 SIB-TIR-RA-XU = du-ši-maš-šat (Br 5693). T. A. Ber. 21, 33: 1 na-ax-ra ma-aš-ši (KB v: a cast *n*); 28 ii 5 (end) xurâçi maš-ši.

maššu 2. Bu 91—5—9, 2176 *A* 25 maš (or bar?)-šu-še i-te-en-ma u(?)-te-ga(?)-ši(?) PINCHES, JRAS 97, 607—8: her meal she shall grind and shall obey her (?).

maša'u pr imšu'- plunder, rob, keep back {plündern, rauben, zurückhalten}. ZA x 212, 19 ma-ša-'u = xa-ma-lu, Br 7746; II 48 *c-d* 60 𒄑 = ma-ša-'-u; *a-b* 52 —3 KAR = ma-ša-'-u = ša-la-lum = itaššulum AV 5197; K 192 *O* (= Bu 88—5—12, 75 + 76 ii) 5 im-šu-'u bûša-šu. IV² 19 *b* 33—4 a-di ma-tim be-el-ti nak-ru gab-šu muš-tak-ki im-šu-' (= KAR-RA). Z[B] 118; PINCHES, BO, Dec., '86; RP² i 84—5; PSBA xvii. I 33 iii 43 um-ma-na-at | mâti-ja ma-da-ta lu im-šu-' (SCHEIL, *Šamš*, 68). K 13, 57 kurummata-a-ni ma-ša-'a our provisions which have been stolen. Perhaps K 2619 ii 16 (amêl) nakru id-kam-ma ki-i še-im ina pâni mê i-maš-ša-'-. (BA ii 428; but see KB vi, 1, 62, 16); Bu 88—5—12, 75 + 76 v 15—16 si-mat É]-sag-ila la ma-še]-e BA iii 246—7 in order that ... should not be touched). — Q[t] 83—1—18, 6, 15 im-ta-ša-'a. — ג V 45 vi 26 tu-maš-ša-'a; also see M[S] 60 *col* 2; perhaps IV² 55 *a* 38 e-nu-ma AMÊLU-TUR tu-maš-ša-'-u; Š perhaps V 37 *b* 53 EŠ = šum-šu-u. Der.:

maššî'u *adj* IV² 1* iii 17 si-bit ilâni[pl] maš-ši-'u-u-ti, Br 11896.

maššû S 31, 52 *O* 16 GIŠ(-GI-ZI)-ŠUD-ŠUD (or SIR-SIR) = maš-šu-u Apparently ‖ of ga-ši-šu.

maššu'tum II 43 *a-b* 40 ša [maš??]-ut-tum = maš-šu-'-tum AV 5227.

muššu 1. II 35 *no* 4 (S 1081 + K 4355) ar-da-tu ša muš-ši-ša ši-iz-ba la ib-šu-u; whose breast contains no milk, T[M] 128—9; but better read çir-ti-ša (*cf* çirtu).

muššû 2. V 60, 3[d] inscr.: agû il Šamaš | muš-ši (il) Šamaš. SCHEIL, ZA iv 337 invention du disque de Š; JASTROW, PAOS *vol* xiv *p* xcvii *rm* * muššî refers to the stick (so W. H. WARD), √našû = the wand of Šamaš; so also POGNON, *Bavian*, 40; 94 *ad* Sn *Bav* 53—4; 36. BA i 268—9: Gerät (?) des Šamaš; PEISER, KB iii (1) 174 —5 & *rm* 4 reads agû Šamaš | çir pân Šamaš = Mondscheibe, Sonne, Aufleuchten (?) vor Šamaš (*i. e.* Ištar); also *cf* TSBA viii 164 *foll*; PSBA iii 109 *foll*. AV 5628 *ad* N 3554, 21 PAT(SUK)^{MEŠ} (= ku-rummēti?) ša mu-uš-ši šu.

mūšu *m* night {Nacht} >< urru 1 (*q. v.*), often in T. A.; id MI § 9, 50; Br 8920; *cf* S^b 150 gi-e | MI | mu-šu, AV 5586, 5617; H^{CV} xxxii; T^M √מוש; BA ii 298 √אמש; perhaps rather מוש. V 56, 44 ur-ra u mu-ša (see makū 1); K 3474 i 42 ša ur-ra tal-li-ka u mu-ša ta-šam[-mi]; IV^2 5 i 69 mu-ša u ur-ra; V 65 *b* 28 ur-ra u mu-ša. K 891 *R* 12 ur-ra u MI (= mūša) a-na-as-su-us. IV^2 18 *a* 21 ni-gu-ta mu-šu u ur-ra; 26 *b* 57 šu-up-šu-uq mu-ši (*var* -ša) u ur-ri; 27 *a* 31 (end) mu-ša. — In observatory reports: K 15, 2—3 ū-mu u mu-ši šit-qu-lu (were of equal length); V 47 *a* 31 ū-mu šu-ta-nu-xu mu-šu gir-ra-a-ni (*q. v.*); K 3474 i (K 8232) 40 ina mu-ši-im-ma >< ū-me-šam-ma (39). K 3473 + 79, 7—8, 296 + Rm 615 (Creat.-*frg* III) 20 & 78 (end) mu-ša u im-ma (*q. v.*); II 40, 217 UD-MI-GA = mu-šam u ur-ri (H^F 37, 2) = IV^2 19 *no* 3, 49—50. IV^2 24 *no* 1 *R* 42—3 bēl mut-tal-lik mu-ši (MI-A) going around at night (K 1284, 12); Creat.-*frg* V (D 94) 12 mu-ša ip-ti-qa (entrusted to him the night); 13 u-ad-di-šum-ma šu-uk-nat mu-ši. K 4872 i 46 ša e-kim-mu lim-nu ina mu-ši ir-mu-šu (= V 50 *a*). K 1282 *R* 6—7 ina šat mu-ši u-šab-ri-šu-ma ki-i ša ina mu-na-at-[ti e-ru, *cf* KB vi. 1, 70 & *n* 7] a-a-am-ma ul [....]. IV^2 26 *a* 18—19; II 27 *e-f* 4 šat mu-ši (preceded by muttat, *q. v.*, mu-ši); Knudtzon, 108, 16 šat MI, *cf* šattu; K 2852 + K 9662 ii 4 ina zir (= çir)-ti mu-ši: in the height of the night. K 883, 23 ša mu-ši ja-e-rak (*q. v.*) an-çar-ka. K 3444 (IV^2 20 *no* 1) 8 (end) ina ut-lu mu-ši ṭa-a-bu. V 13 *b* 26 maçar mu-u-ši (= MI-A); Cuthean Creat.-legend iii 3 ša-lum-mat ni-ši mu-ši: the pride of the nightly people. (ZA xii 321 *fol*); Asb x 69 ina ma-a-a-al (*q. v.*) mu-ši >< 70 ina ša še-e-ri; *cf* NE 50, 2 *fol*; IV^2 15 ii 53—4. ri-ix-ti mu-ši-šu lil-li-ka K 166, 29: his nocturnal fate = death; Asb ii 21 illik šīmat (written NAM) mu-ši-šu (KB ii 166—7 >< nam-mu-ši-šu, Tiele, *Gesch.*, 358 *rm* 1; Haupt, BA i 20 *no* 29; 315—6); *cf* *Khors* 118 (see mūtu). IV^2 22 *no* 1 *R* 24 (end) ša ki-ma zu-un-ni mu-ši kit-mu-ru; *a* 8 mu-ru-uç mu-ši u ur-ra šu-u; K 3152 *O* 16 (= IV^2 30*) end, ina mu-ši i-du-ul (*var* -dul). IV^2 3 *a* 12 (end) ki-ma mē mu-ši (= MI-A) like as dew (unnoticeably) cometh the muruç qaqqadi; 15* *R* I 21 mu-ši (*var* -šu) = MI-A; also 18—19 ina ka-ra-ri-e mu-ši (*var* šu) u ur-ra; IV^2 30* *no* 3 *O* 6 ni-gi-iç-çi ina mu-ši (MI-A); 8 ... mu-ši a-šar ek-li-ti; 14 alū limnu ša ki-ma mu-ši ni-iṭ-la la ibaššū at-ta; 16 ina mu-ši (*Rev. Sém.*, vi 148 on this text); 19 *no* 3, 50 mu-šam u ur-ri. Sn vi 13 read a-di II kaspu MU (= mūši) il-li-ku (BA i 4, 6; ZA iii 112 >< mi-il-li-ku, KB ii 110 & M^S); *Rec. Trav.*, xx 127—8, 21 kūla] muš-ši-ma elippi-šu u-max-xir. V 31 *no* 3, *e-f* 4 MI = mu-ši; *no* 1 *R* 9 .... MI = kak-kab mu-ši; *no* 3, 13 ka-la mu-ši la u-ta-ad-di; kal mu-ši ul ix-za-zi; II 22 *e-g* 12 ÇIR-MI-A = çi-ir mu-ši = çir çal[-mi?]; çir mu-ši Br 7653, *cf* çīru. 37 *a-c* 31 MI-A-XU = iç-çur mu-ši = ça-lam-du. Marduk is called Sin ša mu-nam-mir mu-ši (81—11—3, 111, 8). **Derr.**: these 4.

mūšiš *adv* = ina mūši at night {in, während der Nacht} §§ 25; 80*b*; Sarg *Khors* 120 ki-ma su-din-ni ip-pa-riš mu-šiš; also *Ann* 290; TP III *Ann* 67. *S* ana šūzub nap-ša-tuš mu-šiš ix-liq-ma; 81, 7—27, 80 (Creat.-*frg*) *O* 54 lu šu-xa-at mu-šiš ib-[......]. ‖ is:

mūšītan TP III *Nimr no* 2, 35 mu-še-tan ix-liq fled at night; NE 59, 8 see ka-ša-du Q^t.

mūšamma *adv* yesterday (properly: yesterday night) {gestern} § 80, 2*a*; D^H 19; Z^B 70; ZA v 45; Prätorius, *Lit. Or. Phil.*, i '99 (*cf* ᵑᵑᵑ); II 194 *no* 170 (mūšu + ma *emphat.*); L^T 118; AV 5479; 5586. II 32 *a-b* 23 mu-šam-ma = ti-ma-li; 21 = am-ša-at (so H 194, or -la? Br 4552).

mūšītu *f* night {Nacht} § 65, 10; BA ii 205 > mūšatu; Anp ii 104 kal mu-ši-ti; *Mon*, *R* 22; AV 5616. Sarg *Ann* 342 III ū-me mu-ši-tu 3 days (&) nights; Asb ix 13—14 mu-ši-ta ka-la-ša | ar-die-ma I marched all night. KB ii 180 *rm*, *l* 8 (= SMITH, *Asurb*, 98) il-li-ka ki-rib mu-ši-ti; perh. NE 13, 26 mu-ši-ti (6, 45 -ja); IV^2 49 *a* 1 ilāni mu-ši-ti (also 20 + 36) the gods of night; 2, mu-ši-tum (see kattumu, *p* 450, *col* 1). T^M introd. § 4, iv & vii (*pp* 21 & 28); *pl del* 121: 6 ur-ra u mu-ša-a-ti (§ 70 *a*, note; so GEO. SMITH; JENSEN, 379, 480; DA i 133; NE 140 *rm* 2); 188: 6 ur-re(u) 7 mu-ša-a-ti; NE 4, 45 (11, 21) 6 ur-ro(u) 7 MI^{MEŠ} (= mu-šāti).

maš'altu spell {Bann} Z^Š 58 *ad* v/vi 67 + 77 ni-šu ma-mit tur-ta maš-al-tu (+ 87 + 97 + 107 + 117 (*var* -ta) + 138); maš-al-ti, 126. IV^2 14 *b* 38 maš-al-tu GIG-ta. √ša'alu.

mūšabu *a*) seat {Sitz} II 23 *c* 72 = kussū (*q. v.*); *b*) dwelling, residence, house {Wohnung, Wohnsitz} √ašabu (*q. v.*) ‖ šubtu; AV 5571; § 65, 31 *a*, *rm*; DA i 7; 178. TP vii 91—2 šu-bat xi-da-te-šu-nu ‖ mu-šab ta-ši-il-ti-šu-nu; Asb v 128 (al) Šu-ša-an .... mu-šab ilāni-šu-nu; 19 *U* al mu-šab bēlūtišu u-maš-šir; i 66 *c* 27 (*cf* xidūtu); SCHEIL, *Nabd*, viii 24 a-na mu-ša-bi-šu; Sn vi 46 mu-šab be-lu-ti-ja (also Sn *Kui* 4, 31 *fol*); i 78 the tents mu-ša-bi-šu-nu; Asb vii 121; V 65 *a* 17 see bēlūtu; *b* 7 a-na mu-ša-bu ilūtiša (*a* 38 mu-šab i-lu-ti-šu); 83, 4—20, 2 *a* 50 bītu šu-a-tim a-na mu-ša-ab (il) Šamši .... u (ilat) Malkatum; also I 69 *a* 59—60 (mu-šab), *a* 27 ēkallu mu-ša-ab šar-ru-ti-ja; ZA iii 317, 84 a-na mu-šab šarrū-ti-ja. TP III *Ann* 9, 21; IV^2 31 *R* 27 as-kup-pa-tu lu mu-ša-bu-u-ka = ana mūšabika (to thee a dwelling place, Z^B 97 bel., § 80 *e*); *O* 4 mu-šab (il) Irkalla (*var* šu-bat) J^{W} 10; ZA iv 10, 46 mu-šab-šu L^3 *O* 6 mu-šab Ištar (LEHMANN ii 83); K 4143 *O* 7 mu-ša-bu.

mušbil Sarg *Cyl* 61 mu-uš-bil (*var* -bi-il), *cf* pēlu, פבל, LYON, *Sargon*, 74.

mu-še-ib-ri TP i 8, *etc.* *cf* eberu (עבר), Š & AJSL xiv, 2.

mušabšū (-ši) *etc.* *cf* bašū, Š.

(amēl) **mu-še-bi-šu** *etc.* see ep(b)ešu, Š.

mušgarru some kind of serpent; then also a precious stone, named after it {eine Schlangenart; dann auch ein nach ihr genannter Edelstein} id MUŠ-GIR belongs to the genus xulālu (*q. v.*). POGNON, *Bavian*, 62 *ad* III 14, 27 (aban) MUŠ-GIR (MEISSNER & ROST, 83); AV 5618; ZA i 178 bel. V 33 ii 37 (aban) ZA-ṬU-MUŠ-GIR; also iii 8; iii 5 (aban) ZA-ṬU-ŠI-MUŠ-GIR (*cf* KB iii, 1, 140—1); V 30 *e-f* 67 aban ZA-ṬU?]-MUŠ-GIR = muš-gar-ru; 68 aban ZA-Ṭ]U-ŠI-MUŠ-GIR = i-ni muš-gar-ri. IV^2 18* *no* 3 *R* iv 5—8, 24—6 aban ZA-ṬU-MUŠ-GIR = (xu-lal i-ni) muš-gar (= ša)-ru. Br 11809 reads çirgarru.

mašgašu see mašqašu.

mašadu, *pr* imšid, press; oppress, throw down, strike {drücken, niederdrücken, niederwerfen, schlagen} IV^2 20 *no* 3, 3—4 the ašakku has struck that man and ba-ma-as-su im-ši-id (BA-AN-PAR) has his height laid low (*i. e.* has felled him); 57 *a* 57 maš-da (*pm*) šunātu-u-a; Z^Š ii 64 maš-da pa-ar-šu šap-ta-šu deceitful, obstreperous are his lips; Babyl. Chron. iii 20 Me-na-nu šar Elamti mi-šid-tum i-mi-šid-su-ma, KB ii 280—1 rührte *M* der Schlag; also *cf* RP^2 i 27 & *rm* 5. III 65 *b* 12—13 when a newborn babe a-bu-ça-at širi (& duppi ša širi) ma-ši-id. II 27 *e-f* 47—48 SA-A = ma-ša-du; SA-SA = muš-šu-du (AV 5195, 5631; Br 3097); = II 48 *e-f* 44—45 (followed by tašrixtu & muš-tarrixu, 46—7); II 36 *g-h* 73; also 82, 9—18, 4159 ii 35; 83, 1—18, 1335 i 7 (M^S 60; Br 3031, 7174). — ℑ oppress violently; crush {heftig drücken; überwältigen} II 86—7, 66 a-ka-lu ša zumur amēli muš-šu-du (= GUŠUR-GUŠUR-RA; ZK i 120; Z^B 40, *cf* kaparu); V 45 *g* 25 tu-maš-šad; see also Q. — ℑ^1 Creat.-*frg* III 28 (86) e-liš um-daš-šad. — 𝔑 V 47 *b* 33 mut-tu-tu am-ma-šid.

NOTE. — KB iii (2) 116 reads V 63 *a* 43 šat-ti-ša-am-ma šu-un-šu-du, but rather šu-ur-šu-du. — Der. these 5:

mašdu, maldu Sn vi 38 ina qaq-qar u-sal-li ša ul-tu mal-di nāri aç-ba-ta and with the earth which I had taken from the bed of the river (but perhaps a mistake for šid-di).

mašdū(-u?) oppressive {erdrückend} IV^2 17 *b* 16 šunāte maš-da-u-ti, & *cf* labaru 2.

mašdū 2. Creat.-*frg* IV 137 he cut down

tiāmat (ix-pi-ši-ma) ki-ma nu-nu (*q.v.*) maš-di-e (ZIMMERN-GUNKEL: like as a flat fish {wie einen platten Fisch}; they propose, however, to read: çalmē: twin-star constellation; *cf* JENSEN, 65; 288—9); IV^2 58 iii 43 .... da-a a-na maš-di-i uš-ta-na .... II 32 *c-d* 76 SI-DU = maš(? [cuneiform])-du-u (Br 3151, 3451, same id = ka-a-nu, V 21 *c* 5); 77 *cf* Br 5055 = UŠ-KU (*i. e.* id for akalu) = mašdū; 78 SA-LAL = mašdū (Br 3158); 79 SA-U (= ši + lu)-LI = mašdū (Br 3151); 80 *cf* Br 7894 same id = parū (*q. v.*); 81 GIL-LA = mašdū; AV 5210.

NOTE. — JENSEN, 288; 342 *ad* Creat.-*frg* IV 130 reads ina miṭišu la maš(?)-di-i, referring to AV 5210; but read pa-di-i.

mišittu see mašadu; M^S 60 *col* 2; and ZA ii 156, 20 mi-šit-tum.

mešdu, mišdu. IV^2 10 *b* 8—9 Gula may grant him recovery ina me-šid (= ŠU-GUŠUR-RA) qa-ti-ša el-li-te (× Br 7175); Esh iii 26 (māt) Ba-a-zu .... mi-šid na-ba-li (also III 16 iv 11); *cf* HARPER, *Cyl. A. of Esh Inscr.*, 1888, *p* 8; HEBR. vii part 2.

ma-šad. II 47 *c-f* 16 kakkab Anim ma-šad ša šamē; JENSEN, 18 *rm* read rabu-u ([cuneiform]) instead of [cuneiform]; *cf* V 46 *a-b* 12.

mašaddu some part of a wagon, chariot: tongue? {Teil eines Wagens: Deichsel?} √šadadu, ZDMG 43, 200; AV 5196; Br 1227; II 47 *c-f* 17 MU = ma-šad-du; ● 287 i 5 GIŠ-MU-BU-[cuneiform] = ma-šad-du followed by ni-i-ru. BEZOLD, *Catalogue*, 448 lu-u (iç) ni-i-ru lū (iç) ma-šad-du lū (iç) as-mar-u (K 2495).

mašdaxu *a*) procession, promenade {Prozession}, AV 5209; √šadaxu; Neb iv 1 see zagmuku. ZA ii 187; FLEMMING, *Neb*, 44; also v 40—41. I 52 *no* 4 ii 7 *foll* a-na ma-aš-da-xa (*var* -ax); SCHEIL, *Nabd*, viii 39 ša maš-da-xu (ilat) Çar-pa-ni-tum. — *b*) street of procession; then: street in general {Prozessionsstrasse; Strasse im allgemeinen} Neb v 19—20 ma-aš-da-xa bēlī rabī (il) Marduk | u-ba-an-na-a ta-al-lak-ti; v 49 *foll*; Sarg *Ann* 304 ana maš-da-ax (il) Nabū (*cf* WINCKLER, *Sargon*, pref. xxxvii *rm* 4). POGNON, *Wadi-Brissa*, (Curs. Inscr.) vi 16 iš-tu ma-aš-da-xu ša kišad (nār) Pu-rattu (*cf pp* 72, 74, 88, 97); II 33 *c-d* 13 E .... SIR = maš-da-xu (same id = sūqu) Br 14158; also see *Rev. Ét. Juives*, xiv 158; HOMMEL in HASTINGS, *Bible Dictionary*, i 217.

muššēzibu *etc.* (AV 5601—5605) see ezebu.

***mašaxu* 1.** *pr* imšux, *ps* imaššux(-šax) measure {messen} D^H 68 : 5; D^{Pr} 178 *rm* 1; *Rev. Ét. Juives*, xiv (27) 157. I 7 *F* 22—3: 66 great-cubits am-šu-ux | ru-pu-us-sa (*i. e.* of the street; *cf* PEISER, KAS ix *rm* 2 on this text; also ZA iv 284 *foll* on duplicate text). Nabd 293, 9 zēri itti axāmeš lā im-šu-xu. Sn *Bav* 79 tamlā umallīma am-šu-ux me-ši-ix-tum (-ta; *Bell* 51) ZA iii 316, 79; Bu 88—5, 12, 75 + 76, iv 17 mi-ši-ix-ta-šu am-šu-ux (+ vi 38—9); 82—7—4, 37, 28 & 30 im-šu-xu-ma & id-di-nu (3 *sg*: measured off). Creat.-*frg* IV *R* 148 im-šu-ux-ma be-lum ša ZU-AB bi-nu-tu-uš-šu (*q. v.*); III 43 i 18 so & so much land (a-na) *X* im-šu-ux-ma a-na ça-ti i-ri-en-šu; iii 16 whosoever says eqlu ul ma-ši-ix the field is not measured off (17 u kunūku ul ka-ni-ki, § 92). KB iv 58 i 21 eqlu šu-a-tum im-šu-xu-ma (= 3 *pl*). STRASSM., *Leyden*, 33, 7 eqlē šu-a-tim i-maš-šu-ux(-ma); 16 i-maš-šax; AV* 87 *col* 2; Cyr 59, 1 *foll* ŠE-BAR ir-bi ša ir-ri-še-e .... ša maš-xa-tum (BA iii 436; 388: shows that noun for ŠE-BAR is *fem*). Neb 19, 8 (beg.) maš-xu; Nabd 350, 3 (beg.); 1049, 2 (end) maš-xa-tum.

ℑ be measured (off) {gemessen werden}; Nabd 293, 10 zēru šu-a-tim im-ma-ši-ix-ma; 477, 32 im-ma-ša-ax(-ma). 1102, 11 im-ma-šax-ma.

DERR. namšuxu (?) & the following 6:

mišxu *1.* Nabd 648, 4—5 a-šar Eṭir-Marduk (amēl) šangū Sippar | mi-iš-xi i-çab-ba-tu; also Dar 9, 6. PEISER, KAS measuring off {Vermessung}.

me(i)šixtu measure, extent of ground, field, building *etc.* {Mass, Ausdehnung *etc.*} D 62, 6; § 30; AV 5361, 5364. TP III in II 67, 69 mi-šix-ti qaq-qa-ri (KB ii 22—3; RP^2 v 115 *foll*); Sarg *Cyl.* 65 so and so many cubits mi-ši-ix-ti dūrišu aškun; also *Ann* XIV 77; I 7 *F* 20 ina mi-šix-ti-šu; ZA iii 317, 83 çi-ir me-ši-ix-ti škalli maxrîti. Peiser, KAS 30 v 1 miš-xa-at; 5 miš-xa-tum; *Babyl. Vertr.* lxxxix (VATh 384) 1 ina mi-iš-xa-tum (bei der Vermessung) + 5; cxvii 14 mi-ši-ix-tum [šu]-a-tim (*cf* xciv 10). Nabd 116, 11 + 16 + 20 mi-ši-ix-ti; 203, 10 end (-tum) + 18 end (-tim); 687, 17 (-ti); Cyr 188, 15 mi-ši-ix-tum eqli šu-a-ti: the extent of this field (ZA iii 15) *c. st.* 320, 8 ša ina meš-xat i-ti-ru {das bei der Vermessung überschüssig war} (BA iii 401—2); 346, 4 ša ina meš-xa-tum (AV 5368) i-ti-ru; 174, 1 miš-xat zêri {Vermessung des Saatfeldes}. Nabd 835, 1 meš-xat-tum ŠE-ZIR ŠE-BAR i-mit-tum (= 1021, 1); Strassm., *Stockholm, VIII. Or. Congr.*, 6, 9: 14 ubâni qanâte mi-šix-ti ištên eqlu; + 15 napxar 6 ammât 9 ubân qanâte mi-šix-tu šani-i eqlu + 18 mi-šix-ti bîti šu-ma-a-ti (= šuqâti = šuâti) also VATh 451, 7 mi-šix-tu bîti šu-a-ti the extent of this property (KB iv 172). V 68 *no* 2, 11 ištêni-it (*l* 20 ša-ni-tu) mi-ši-ix-ti; 21 mi-šix-tu bîti šu-a-ti (see ZA i 87 *foll*, on this text; also AV* 61 *col* 1); *no* 1, 11 + 20 + 21; ZK i 47, 11 & 17; & *p* 58. a ‖ is

mišaxtu. ZA iii 214 (Dar 14—22—2) 7: 275 ammat napxar napxaru 2 GUR 43 QA 5 ŠA-XI-A (= ZUN) zêr mi-ša-xat.

mašxattum, *idem* Dar 351, 5 ina muxxi maš-xat-tum ili'-; 419, 7; 74, 2 ma-aš-xa-tum.

mašîxu *m* measure {Mass}. *a*) in general {im allgemeinen} id PI; Peiser, KAS 101; *Babyl. Vertr.*, 243. Nabd 206, 8 (iç) ma-ši-xu; Camb 358, 7 see makkasu, 2; Nabd 973, 8 ina ma-še-xi. ZA iv 119 *no* 16 ina ma-ši-xu ša Šamaš (Neb 62, 3; 73, 11 -xi); 127 *no* 8 ina (iç) ma-ši-xu ša šarri (Neb 347, 8; 424, 7); Neb 50, 3 ina ma-ši-xi ša il Bêl; 152, 5 ina (iç) ma-ši-xu ša Šullumu. Camb 56, 7 ina ma-ši-xi ša I PI : in PI measures; Neb 273, 17; VATh 78, 12 ina ma-ši-xu ša I PI (1 PI = 36 QA); ZA iv 152, 9 (KB iv 298—99); Nabd 6, 8; 7, 11. — *b*) specific measure of quantity of grain, dates *etc.* {ein bestimmtes Hohlmass für Getreide, Datteln *etc.*} especially in *c. t.*; Peiser, *l. c.*, J. Oppert, ZA vi 277. Nabd 49, 8 so & so many ma-ši-xe sat-tuk ša Addar ša il Adad; 912, 1 (5): 5 ma-ši-xe ša sat-tuk suluppi. Neb 1, 1: 7 ma-ši-xe ša sat-tuk. Camb 281, 12: 1 ma-ši-xi ina pap-pa-su ša bît G; 415, 1: 3 ma-ši-xu la-bi-ri; 62, 1 see makkasu 2. Cyr 66, 1: ište-en ma-ši-xi ina sat-tuk; 50, 1—2 *cf* makkasu 2; 118, 2: 32 ma-ši-xi; Dar 90, 1 *fol*: 50 ma-ši-xe ša sat-tuk ŠE-BAR ina sat-tuk; also 5 *fol*. Strassm., *Stockholm*, 20, 4 ina (iç) ma-ši-xu; 25, 6; 26, 8 (without iç); 19, 1—2: 150 ma-ši-xi ša (amêl) pa . . . | ma-ak-ka-su *etc.* AII 82, 9—18, 519 (ZA iv 145 *fol*; 121 *fol*) 27: 15 ma-ši-xu ša ŠE-BAR.

NOTE. — Nabd 479, 6: amêl mašîxu in name of canal nâr (amêl) ma-še-xu; 483, 3.

mašîxânu. III 41 i 14 ma-ši-xa-an eqli land surveyor {Feldmesser} ZK i 62; III 43 i 26 ma-ši-xa-an(-nu) eqli (KB iv 68 & *rm* 8 & 9; § 72 *b*; BA ii 119).

mašaxu 2. pr imšux rise, shine flash up, said of stars {aufleuchten, von Sternen gesagt}, *cf* çararu 1. III 57 *no* 4, 43 kakkab Dilbat (= Venus-star) muš-xa im-šux, Jensen, 155 *rm* 2; 58 *c* 44 kakkab AN-NA (= šamê?) meš-xa im-šux; 54 *a* 25—6 kakkab šamê a-dir >< *k. š.* miš-xa imšux; 57 *a* 6 & 8 where we have adaru of the Eridu-star as >< to meš-xa im-šux of the same; 50 *a* 19 kakkab Marduk me-iš-xu im-šu-ux (Jensen, 25: entfaltet einen besondern Glanz); 52 *no* 2, 21 the eagle star meš-xa im-šu-ux. V 46 *a* 57 stars of heaven meš-xu imšu (= [cuneiform]) -ux; Jensen, 156 *rm* 1; thus S^c 5 *a* 5 SUR = ma-ša-xu ša . . . . (Br 2972).

NOTE. — IV² 11 *a* 45—6 Hommel reads še-li-bu zib-bat-su im-ta-na-aš-šax (others -šir, *cf* mašaru). Derr. these 5:

mašxu *1.* glittering {leuchtend} V 15 *c-f* 34 KU-BAR-SI = maš-[xu?]; perhaps also T. A. (Lo.) 9, 48 (end) I ma-aš-xu xurâçi (some ornament, precious stone *etc.*).

me(i)šxu *2.* Jensen, ZA ii 86; *Kosmologie*, 155 intense brilliancy of stars {helles Geblitze, von Sternen} AV 5369. K 250 (II 49) *R* iv 15—22: (15) KI-GAL me-šix (šax?) = kakkabâni; (16) ni(or zal)-lum-mu-u = meš-xu ša kakkabi; (18)

ni-lum-mu-u = mi-šix kakkabi; (19) = ça-ra-ar kakkabi; (20) = zi-im (*q. v.*) kakkabi (ZK ii 43 *rm* 2; ZA i 37; Z[B] 104); (21) = ša-lum[-ma-tu?]; (22) me[-lam?]. III 52 *a* 11 *fol* mi-ši-ix-šu kīma nam-maš[-ti aqrabi zibbatu] | ša-kin his brilliancy made a tail like that of a scorpion. V 31 *e-f* 11—12 mi-iš-xi | aš-šu LAL; muš-xi ša ça-ra-ru (AV 2805, 5619; Br 8931).

NOTE. — CHEYNE, *Jew. Quart. Rev.*, x 570—1 connects Hebr [illegible]; Job 38, 36, with mišxu (+ *pl* ending), "a name applied to meteors and shooting stars, with reference to their flaring up", see also meširū.

mušxu, *idem* see mašaxu 2; mišxu & III 57 *b* 24, 26 muš-xa TUK, & III TUK.

maṧxatum (?) Perhaps V 42 *a-b* 14 DUK-AL-UŠ-SA-SUR-RA = maṧ-xa-[tu?] Br 5764.

mašaxu 3. whence **mumaššixu** (*q. v.*)

mašxu *2.* K 2100 *R* iv 14 ma-aš-xu = i[lu] kaš-šu-u; 82, 9—18 *O* 17 ba-aš-xu = i-lu. ZA iii 193—7 (& literature there given); WEISBACH, *Sum. Frage*, 155.

mušixxu = mušīxu, √משׁח. mu-ši-ix-xu, between mu-z(ç)ib-bu & mu-kan-zib-tu, *q. v.*; D 86 i 8; AV 5606; Br 10733.

mašxalu. T. A. (Ber.) 28 ii 44: 1 ma-aš-xa-lum ša kaspi; iii 63: 3 *m* ša abni. Here according to some V 42*a-b* 14, DUK-AL-UŠ-SA-SUR-RA = maṧ-xa[-lum] preceded by karpat ši-ik-ki; *c-d* 21—3: DUK-SI-[sign]-GA-ŠU (= KAT)-TAG-GA; DUK-ŠA (= GAR) [signs]-MA; DUK-MAŠ-XA-LUM = maš[-xa-lum] Br 1956.

mušxalçitum see xalaçu 2.

mušaxxīnu some object, article of bronce; kettle? {bronzener Kessel?} PEISER, *etc.*; K 8676 iii 23 URUDU-ŠUN-BIL-MA = mu-šax[-xi]-nu ZA viii 77 = axe {Axt} mentioned among such instruments as hoe, spade, *etc.* >< ZEHNPFUND, BA i 632; PEISER, *Babyl. Vertr.*, 287; T[C] 132 & TALLQVIST, *Schenkungsbriefe*, 13. 83, 1—18, 1866 *R* vi: 2 shekels of silver for mu-šax-xi-nu (PINCHES, PSBA xviii 254—5: a caldron of copper). 84, 2—11, 136, 5 (end) mu-šax-xi-nu siparri; VATh 51, 10 ki-i . . . amēlu ištēn erū mu-šax-xi-nu ištēn-it erū tik-zi (?). Nabd 258, 11 ište-en mu-šax-xi-nu (241, 1 + 7; 258, 11; 310, 12); 310, 1 + 8 mu-šax-xi-in-nu siparri (910, 8), 10 mu-šax-xi-in; 761, 6 mu-šax-xi-na. Neb 441, 3 ištēn-it siparru mu-ša-xi-nu; 420, 1 (mu-šax-xi-nu ša . . . . gul-gul-lu; 869, 2); Camb 330, 25: 1 mu-šax-xi-nu (831, 11); 331, 3: 2 mu-šax-xi-na-nu siparri ša $7^1/_2$ manē šu-kul-ta-šu-nu (BA iii 463—5). V 23 *c-f* 20 perhaps mu-ša[-xi-nu] ZA viii 76; or [-lu?] *cf* V 27 *e-f* 29. √משׁח₂ ZIMMERN, *etc.*; or, better, √שׁחן, T[C] 132; *etc.*

mišxīru (?) *cf* xinçurru (where read -çur- instead of -çu-).

mašṭaru & **malṭaru** (√šaṭaru). — *a*) tablet, written document {Inschrift, Document} K 4378 (D 86) i 3 GIŠ-MAŠ-DAR = maš-ṭa-ru preceded by lī'ū. Br 1872; AV 5212. — *b*) writing, inscription {Schrift, Aufschrift} Asb iii 121 (*var*) Nebo u-šu-uz-ma iš-ta-na-sa-a mal-ṭa-ru ki-g(k)al-li [(1)] Sin (KB ii 186—7, *rm*). KNUDTZON, 98, 4 k[īm]a . . . . ma-al-ṭa-ra an-na-a li-pu-u-šu. K 552, 6 *foll* ma-al-ṭa-ru [ša] pa-ni Am-mu-ra-pi (WZ xii 364) šarri (Hr[L] 255); K 3312 iii (ZA iv 11) 11 muš-tin-nu-u šap-la-a-ti ina maš-ṭ(d)a-ri ša . . . . & 22 um-mi šal-la maš-ṭ(d)a-ra gi-na-a i-max-xar-ka; ZA iv 238, 26 gi-na-a maš-ṭ(d)a-ri iš-ta-ra-niš (K 2361 *O* ii).

mušaṭru signature, handwriting {Namensschreibung, -zug} see mū 2. & šaṭru.

mašaku. ב *del* 205 (215) šanī-tum muš-šu-kat said of the kurummatu; J[I-N] 38: zum andern wurde sie gehäutet?? **Der.:**

mašku *c. st.* mašak (AV 5198), id SU (Š 9, 67; H 9 & 200, 12); II 36 *a* 37; § 65, 1. Br 167; *a*) skin of human beings {Haut des Menschen} see xalapu ב. Asb x 5 of A-a-mu SU (*var* ma-šak)-šu aš-xu-uṭ; *cf* ii 4; ZA iii 54 *no* 5; Sarg *Cyl* 25 ša ma-šak I-lu(-u)-bi-di . . . . iç-ru-pu na-ba-si-iš; WINCKLER, *Sargon*, 191, 5 ma-šak-šu a-ku-uç I flayed him. II 16 *a-b* 57 ma-ša-ak la ruq[qi ipálal] rubs the skin without oiling it (BA ii 279

muš-ku II 37, 48 *cf* çir ku.

—80); IV² 13 *a* 19 at-ta e-ra-a dan-na ki-ma maš-ki[-im] thou [makest flexible], like a skin, the hard copper; BO i 132. — *b*) skin of animals {Tierhaut} TP vii 73 SU-MEŠ-šu-nu (of elephants, *ibid* 68); also Nabd 1000, 4. TP III *Ann* 89, 154 ma-šak pîri; IV² 15* 3 *B* 11 ana lib-bi ma-šak u-ni-ki la pi-ti-ti. — T. A. (Lo.) 3, 31 ma-aš-ku; 21, 19 u ma-aš-ka; Ber. 23, 57 ir-bi-e-it ma-aš-gu 4 skins. — id SU used as a prefix to indicate something made of leather, or the like *e. g.* Anp iii 33; D 97, 3 *etc*, *etc.* — *c*) some skin disease {Hautausschlag} *del* 231 lid-di maš-ke-šu-ma li-bil tam-tum; 238 id-di SU [-MEŠ-šu-ma] u-bil tam-tum; 228 maš-ku-u uq-[t]a-at-tu-u du-muq šêre-šu. perhaps NE 65, 6 maš-ka la-biš (see, however, labašu); according to some: the dry or indurated ulcer, a distinct feature of the leprous ulcer; others: syphilis; Halévy, ZA iii 189 leprosy; BOR iii 288; Jensen, ZA ii 249, 251 *ad del* 228; J^{P} 90 on *l* 238; J$^{\text{I-M}}$ 39. — *d*) in transferred meaning (perhaps like עֶצֶם Gen 7, 13; Ex 24, 10; גֶּרֶם 2 kings 9, 13) = self {selbst} Sn v 49 pa-an maš-ki-ja çab-tu-ma they placed themselves right in front of me.

mašša(k)ku & muššakku sacrifice {Opfer} Isa 26, 5; BA iii 111 *rm* *: speciell das Versöhnungsopfer beim Totenkultus (Z^{B} 14 *rm* 4; ZA v 87 *fol*; Jensen, 487 *fol*) ‎שׁ‎ׁakaku = pašaxu > maškaku, a libation for the purpose of conciliating the gods; BA ii 292 & *rm* **: vielleicht auch Schlauch des Totenbeschwörers (*Theol. Litbl.*, 1900, *no* 5 *col* 53). *Etana*-legend 11 see gamaru Q^{t}. V 47 *a* 37 see zurqinu, where read maš-šak-ku; (√נשׁק = Hebr נסך, σπένδειν); BA i 174 & again, 280. 282, 325 (massaku); Evetts, PSBA x 478 : 7; IV² 60 B *O* 7 (K 2518, 7) ina ma-aš-šak-ka (u) šâ'ilu (wr. ^{amêl}EN-ME-LI) u u-ša-pi di-i-ni (A *O* 7) BA ii 401. IV² 22 *no* 2, 10—11 ša-i-lu (= ^{amêl} EN-ME-LI) ina mu-uš-ša-ak-ka ul i-pi-te-šu (Br 5877).

mešek(q)u Bu 88—5—12, 679, 9: 6 ŠE-GUR i-na GIŠ-BAR $^{\text{(il)}}$ Šamaš i-na me-še-qu; Bu 88—5—12, 743—44, 12 i-na mi-še-qu (?) | i-na kar Sippar^{ki} (Meissner, 126: im Speicher von *S.*)

mešku (?) II 23 *c-d* 14 mi-eš-ki ‖ dal-tu; *cf* 16 mi-eš-ka-lu-u (AV 5369, 5370).

maškadu ulcer {Geschwür} BA i 174, 325; AV 5213. H 82—3, 20 maš-ka-du (= SA-SAR) ra-pa-du ša-aš-ša-ṭu(-)sa-[at? or -ma-nu, Jensen, ZK ii 275 *rm* 1; ZA i 309]. II 28 *b-c* 13—16 SA-SAR-SA (Br 3116 = šaššaṭu, ZK ii 105) | SA-GA-KAS-SA, Br 3133 | SA-AD-GAL (= ra-pa-du, Br 3107) | SA-GIG (Br 3140) = maš-ka-du; V 21 *a-b* 8 SA-SAR (Br 3114) = maš-ka-du, together with ša-aš-ša-ṭu (7) & šu-'-u (9); Z^{B} 117: perhaps connected with šikdu. K 4360 iii 15 $^{\text{(šam)}}$el-li-b(p)u ‖ $^{\text{(šam)}}$maš-ka-di (II 42 *c-d* 47) Br 1832; V 48 v 32 on the 30th day he will not eat pork or | 33) maš-ka-du iççabat-su *m* will seize him.

mušâkil içi or iççûrê II 31 *c* 60 *fol* (K 4393 iv 1—2) = ag Š of akalu; but ZA iii 120, 5 has also šâkil iççûrê & posits ‎שׂכל‎; Meissner, 138 arborist, birdfancier {Baumzüchter, Vögelfütterer}.

muškallu (?) AV 5621 *ad* II 34 *no* 3, 28 mu-uš-kal-lu = ša maš(= bar)-kal-ša[. . .].

maškânu *1.* pledge {Pfand} esp. in *c. t.* § 65, 31 *a*; AV 5124. — Nabd 668, 12 (*cf* 5, 9) the 4 female slaves mal maš-ka-ni-šu; 344, 7 mal maš-ka-nu max-ru-u (605, 7; 103, 8); Neb 350, 11 maš-kan ša $^{\text{(sal il)}}$ Bi-tin-nam-šar-rat; 91, 7 maš-ka-nu ša ^{sal} Xa-am-ma-a; 72, 9; Cyr 154, 8—9 bît *N.* maš-ka-nu | çab-ta-ta (= צבת with passive meaning); 321, 8—9 bît-su u a-me-lut-su maš-ka-nu çab(*var* ça-ab)-ta-tu (Nabd 390, 7—8); 332, 10—11 . . . a-na maš-ka-nu ina pân *A* iš-ku-nu-ni-šu; 254, 8—9 her slave maš-ka-nu (is a pledge) a-di eli (until) *etc.*; Camb 257, 6 pi-i šul-pu maš-ka-nu çab-tu (*cf* 315, 7); VATh 66, 25 ri-mu-tu ul i-ri-me maš-ka-ru ul i-šak-kan (Peiser, KAS 18; KB iv 214—5); Strassm., *Stockholm. VIII. Or. Congr.*, 31, 7 ša Ar-pa-ta (?) maš-ka-nu ku-u kaspu. (ZK i 88 *no* 2); Br. M. 94, 6—11, 36, 6 mim-mu-šu-nu

---

maš-šik-ku, AV 5639 *cf* dupšikku.

ma-la ba-šu-u maš-ka-nu (ZA x 398) Camb 81, 10. — J. Oppert, JA xv ('80) 547; ZA iv 400 >< Meissner, *ibid*, 78; JA x ('87) 537: 10; ZA i 385; 430; iv 117 *no* 11; BA i 325—6; often in Peiser, KAS (101) & *Babyl. Vertr.*; Barth, *Nominallehre*, 490 √šakanu; as T[C] 134 (where a host of passages for maš-ka-nu & maškan); ZA iii 54 bel. *etc.*, √משך. Der.:

maškanūtu *e.g.* ZA iv 67; 70. ana maška-nu-tu | ṣab-tu Neb 133, 6—7; 420, 4; T[C] 7.

maškanu *2.* fetter {Fessel} Z[B] 59. V 47 *a* 59 see maqatu 3. V 27 *e* 36 [erū] maška-nu (Br 1831), 38 [erū] ab-bu-ut-tum, *cf* xuqakipu; Strassm., *Warka*, 44, 9 ga-du ma-aš-ka-nim in fetters; Meissner, 145.

maškanu *3.* place, dwelling {Stätte, Wohnstätte} √šakanu (*q. v.*) AV 5214; § 65, 31 *a*. Sn vi 37 maš-kan ēkalli maxri-ti (*q. v.*) ēzib; Esh i 13 a-šar maškan-i-šu u-xal-liq (1 *sg*); III 62, 61 (KB ii 252—3, 64); Asb i 113 u-tir-ma a-šar pi-qid-ti-šu-un ina maš-kani-šu-nu ap-qid-su-un-ti (ii 17); x 76 maš-kan ši-kit-ti-šu; K 2675 *O* 62. Bu 88—5—12, 346, 7 i-na ma-aš-kanim (KB iv 8—9); Bu 88—5—12, 75 + 76 vi 32 see maxru, maxar. K 4220, 6 diqaru (?) ša maš-ka-ni = qid-datum nap-ra-xa-tum. H 68, 21 KI [(ki-is-lax)] 𒆠 = maš-ka-nu (II 52 *no* 3 *g-h* 68) in one group with ni-du-tum (22), ti(*var* te)-riq-tum (23), tur (AV 9033 ṭu)-ba-lu-u; S[b] 1 *R* iv 10—11 su-u & su[ ] | id | maš-ka-nu (H 81, 706) = V 38 *O* 2, 10—11; Br 9614, 9787; ZA i 185 *rm* 1. Also see makānu; T. A. (Ber.) 24, 68 i-na (64 iš-tu) ma-aš-ka-ni-šu (64 -ši-ma) in his stead; from its place.

NOTE. — ZA iii 418 reads *del* 34 ina m[aška]-nu-ma; Jensen, ina šil-ku-nu-ma, *etc.*

maškannu, VATh 387, 2 ištēn-it [(iṣ)] ma'šlu ša maš-kan-nu u šu-pa-lu šēpā.

muškīnu *ag* Š3 of kānu 1 (*q. v.*) pauper, wretch {armer, elender} D[Pr] 186 *no* 3. K 3312 iii 21 see xubbulu. T. A. (Lo.) 1, 37 mārat ištēn mu-uš-ki-nu daughter of a miserable (poor) fellow. II 32 *g-h* 34.

muškinūtu. Bezold, *Catalogue*, 1566 muš-ki-nu-tu illak, he will become a beggar. M[B] 44 *col* 1.

NOTE. — Hommel in Hastings, *Dict. of the Bible*, i 217 muškīnu > muškahīnu = מְשְׁתַּחֲוֶה "one who pays homage or whorship"; but see kānu, 1, Note.

muššekiš II 31 *b* 62 an official {ein Beamter} mu-še-kiš √שכש? Br 1307.

maškattum Nabd 251, 8 ŠE-BAR .... ina eli maš-kat (*i. e.* 𒋻)-tum inam-din; 405, 6—7 ŠE-BAR ga-mirtum maš-kat-tum ina eli iṭ(t?)-ridtum | i-nam-din; 497, 7—8 ina eli | iṭ(t?)-rit-tum ina eli | maš-kat-tum i-nam-din; Neb 273, 16; 210, 8 (ina eli maš-kat-tu a-na .... | i-namdin. ZA x 211 ii *R* 8 na-du-u ša maškat-tum. III 4 (*col a*) *no* 4, 40 i-na libbi-šu maš-ka-na-te ar(or ub)-ba? *fem* of maškānu 1, ?

maššiktu. Rm 609 *R* (*cf* II 33 *no* 2 *O* 16) 10 ŠE-BA-LA-GUM = še-im maššik-ti, perhaps same √ as mašša(k)ku.

mašalu be or become alike, equal, resemble {gleich sein oder werden} V 47 *a* 23 maša-lu = e-mu-u; AV 5109; § 77; Z[B] 70; D[H] 54—55; *cf Rev. Ét. Juives*, x 302 deriving muššlum & muššulum from √שלי?, but see D[Pr] 21 *rm* 1; 95 *rm* (on משל = (1) rule & (2) be alike). IV[2] 60* B *O* 22 (end) a-na-ku am-šal; IV[2] 9 *b* 13—14 NU-MU-UN-DA-AB-SIG-SIG-ga = la maš-lu (Br 4414); 34 *no* 2, 2 u a-me-ni dib-bu-ku-nu a-na šaxar-ra-bi-e maš-lu. D 94, 17 i-na ūmi VII a-ga [ma-ša]-la, or [šumšu?]-la ZA ii 81 *rm* 3; Jensen, 288, 359; JAOS xv 12 *fol.* *Adapa*-legend *R* 15 nuni a-ba-ar ta-am-ta i-na mi-še-li in-ši-il-ma (here perhaps = zāzu: make into 2 halves; BA ii 419: das Meer war spiegelglatt) — Winckler & Abel, T. A. *no* 240. K 4704 *R* 8 zēr [(šam)] martakal .... ša lā i-ma-šal-u-ni (Hr[L] 111); K 2652, 25 am-ša-la iš-tin šab-ru-u; NE 9, 50 (end) pa-nu-šu maš-lu (*cf* 14, 18: his face was like unto ....; Z[B] 94); T. A. (Lo.) 8, 77 lu-u ma-aš-lu may remain alike {mögen sich gleich bleiben} ZA v 163; also perhaps Ber. 79 15—16 eqli-ja aššata ša la mu-ta | ma-ši-el *etc.* my field resembles a woman which has no husband (BA iv 117—8 *ad* KB v *no* 79);

also Ber. 6 *R* 8 ša-am-ni ša çi-e-ri ša ana a-xa-mi-iš ma-aš-lu with field plants that are like each other; ZA v 14 bel., KB v 20—21. On lū (& lā) ma-šil *cf* (lū) mān & VAT 244 *O* 9 *a-b*, 18 *c-d*. — $\mathfrak{Q}^1$ perhaps BO iv 132, 17 la-ši (or šil?) in-da-šal ina pāni Bēl-maxar an-na-a, thus it was delivered before this Bēlmaxar. — $\mathfrak{P}$ *a*) make alike, equal {gleich, ähnlich machen, nachahmen} § 77; JENSEN, ZA ii 81 *rm* 3 halve {hälften} also ZA vi 241, 12. IV^2 60^* C *O* 11 ta-na-da-a-ti šarri i-liš (B *O* 31 e-liš?) u-maš-šil the majesty of the king I have made equal to that of god. 83—1—18, 37, 16—18 ištēn a-na ša-ni-e la mu-šu-ul (Hr^L 355); V 47 *b* 19 (end) u-maš-šil. — *b*) form, fashion, mould {abbilden, bilden} *etc.* T^M i 131 bu-un-na-an-ni-ia u-maš-ši-lu ‖ ib-nu-u (*cf* i 96 -lum); vii 66 (u-maš-šil); Sp II 265 *a* ii 8 na-'-du ṭe(?)-en-ka tu-maš-šil la-li-'-ka. — KNUDTZON, 41 *R* 4 ana GIŠ-KU mu-šu-ul (pni?). T. A. (Lo.) 8, 24 (ilat) Ištar (?) u (il) A-ma-nu-um ki-i libbi-šu ša axi-ia li-me-eš-še-el-ši, ZIMMERN (ZA v 156) *I. & A.* may make her in accordance with the wish of my brother. SAYCE, RP^2 iii 76 *rm* 2: may advise [him]; ‖ משל: speak in proverbs. II 67, 64 the king of Tabal a-na ep-šit (mât) Aššur u-maš-šil-ma a-di maxrija lā illika (KB ii 20—21; ROST, 115—6 perhaps: eine gleichgültige Haltung einnehmen; according to WINCKLER, *Alt. Untersuch.*, 179 = משל ridicule, despise = despised the deeds of Assyria). V 45 vi 23 tu-maš-šal. — $\mathfrak{P}^1$ K 3477 *O* 28 *foll* la ut-tak-ka-rum çi-it pi-i-ša (of Ištar) ... la un-daš (wr. 𒁹)-ša-lu dan-nu-u-sa. — $\mathfrak{S}$ make alike, equalize {gleich machen} in connection with zāzu = divide into 2 equal halves. II 65 *a* 22 see zāzu (*p* 276) & D^K 7; RP^2 iv 24 *foll.* V 45 vi 37 tu-ša-an-šal; SCHEIL, *Rec. Trav.*, xvii *p* 84 (*no* xxiii *col* 2, below) lu u-šam-še-lu (je divisais en deux), see makkūru, note. D 96, 6 šum-ša-lu or šum-šu lū (his name be) JENSEN, 128.

Derr. tamšīlu, tanšīlu & these 6 (7?):

mašlu *1. c. st.* mašal totality {Gesammtheit} ilāni ma-šal mātišu Sn iii 55; I 43, 8; ilāni ma-šal māti-šu-un Sn iv 23. Bu 88—5—12, 75 + 76 vi 9 (BA iii 250) ma-šal-šu-nu & SMITH, Sn 88, 27 ilāni nap-xar māti-šu-un = their totality, BA iii 359.

mašlu *2.* middle {Mitte} G § 78; IV^2 13 *no* 3 *b* 58 ina mu-ši ma-ši-il = midnight; 15^* *b* 23 ina mu-ši ma-šil (or -šal?, *var* -aš-li = MI-BAR-A-AN).

NOTE. — On mašlum in kakkab EN-TE-NA-maš-lum V 46 *a*(-*b*) 24 = 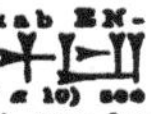 (also II 49 *no* 3, 47; 57 *a-b* 48; III 57 *a* 10) see ZA i 266; Br 2894; SAYCE, *Hibbert Lect.*, 151; for EN-TE-NA see kuççu.

mišlu *c. st.* mišil (AV 5340; 5365) *pl* mišlānu(-i) AV 5371, equal part, half {gleicher Teil, Hälfte} § 77; D^H 54. Esh *Sendsch*, *R* 42 (end) ina me-šil ū-me .... al-me *etc.*; V 34 iii 25, 33 mi-ši-il a-gur-ri tu-ba-lu (half a brick high); V 61 v 12—3 mi-šil šēr kar-ši (& qir-bi); Rm 2, 2 *R* 30 meš-la-šu (half of it); K 583, 24—25 ça-al-mu ša Šamaš šu-u mi-ši-il ǀ ū-me (?) u-ta-da-ar (was darkened) BA i 628; SCHEIL, *Rec. Trav.*, xix, Repr. *p* 25 *no* 3, 2 mi-šil ū-mu. K 358, 5 bītu u at-ru me-šil (iç) Kirī (KB iv 112); Bu 91—5—9, 418, 6 a plantation (was) mi-iš-lum (the portion) ǀ it-ba-al (which he took); 23 mi-ši-il eqli-ia. Creat.-*frg* IV (82, 9—18, 3737) *R* (55) 138 mi-iš-lu-uš-ša (= ina miš-liša): an der einen Hälfte von ihr; JENSEN, 288; JASTROW, *Religion*, 428; TSBA vii 389; PINCHES, *ibid*, viii 287: her end. Nabd 49, 10 mi-šil ma-ši-xi (*q. v.*) = 1/2 *m* (*cf* 662, 12 + 13, beg.) Cyr 118, 3: 18 mi-šil; Dar 7, 8; Nabd 299, 6 a-xi kaspi ina mi-šil šatti & the balance ina ki-it (*q. v.*) šatti inaddin (& T^C 98); Camb 97, 7 i-na mi-ši-el šatti i-nam-din (Camb 184; Cyr 228, 5 *fol*) *cf* ZA v 150, 13 & *rm* 5; D 94, 18 see maxaru $\mathfrak{S}^t$ & ZA ii 81 *rm* 3. II 37 *g-h* 52 TAG-ŠI III GAL-LA = aban mišil (wr. BAR) ma-na stone of half a mine; *cf* also ZA iv 68. *id* V 25, 11—12 BAR (= mišil) manā kaspi *etc.* K 2401 iii 32 BAR (karpat) ma-si-tu; 31 (end) BAR a-kal; S^b 1 *b* 36—7 BAR = meš-lu, meš-la[-nu] Br 1773. V 37 *d-f* 44 ba-a ǀ 𒌍 ǀ mi-iš-lum (ZA ii 81 *rm* 3 = 30 followed by še-la-ša-a; mišlu = 1/2 of

60; also BA i 634 (*ad* 517) Br 9985. V 42 *g-h* 36 IM ^(za-ad(t)-ru)^ ŠIT = meš-la-nu (Br 8438); same id = pi-sa-nu (perhaps here √šalū); also V 40 *c-d* 51 SU-RI-A-AN = meš-la-nu (Br 7136, also Rm II 200, 1 see TSBA vii 289; Z^B 70; ZK ii 273; H 63 *R* 2; 74, 3, *cf* miksu; 71, 25 eqil mi-iš-la-ni perhaps a field worked at half shares) *cf* ZA vii 25 *ad* II 14 *c-d* 15—8. — T. A. (Lo.) 2, 13 mi-ši-el ša ab-bi-ka šu-bi-i-la (ZA v 150—3); 30, 50 i-ša-tum mi-ši-il-šu | i-kul u mi-ši[-il]-šu ia-nu; 35, 42 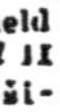 (= mišil)-šu-nu; (Ber.) 28 iii 33 (end) mi-iš-lu ul-lu-u (also 31). a ‖ is:

mešlatu (?) K 96, 18 ina meš-la-te ša arax šabaṭi.

mušālu, muššulum probably some furniture *etc.* mirror? {Spiegel?} D^H: splendor; ZK ii 289 *rm* 1; AV 5570. V 28 *a-b* 90—1 mu-ša-lum & muš-šu-lum ‖ na-ma-rum (AV 5632); 27 *e-f* 29 ^erū^ ŠA-ŠU-UD-KA-BAR (= siparru) = mu-ša-lu (Br 12109); also V 28 *f* 19 UD-KA-BAR = mu-ša[-lu] = namru Br 7816; ZA vi 242, 12 and 82, 9—18, 4159 iv 6. On V 27 *g-h* 43—45 *cf* Br 1205—97. — Jensen, 370, 396, 400 reads *dcl* 25 (end) mu-šal-ša its (the ship's) design, shape; Haupt (H^CV xliii; *Johns Hopk. Circ.*, 69, 18; POOS, Oct. 88; BA i 127; so also J^I-X 33) mu-rag-ša (muragu: height); Delitzsch^W 185, 10 mu-rak-ša (√araku). Perhaps V 33 viii 24 mu[-ša]-lum.

me-ṣu-el IV² 35 *no* 5, 6 he who delivers (me-šu-el) the command (of Eridu). D^Pr 195 *rm* mušālu = מושל: ruler.

mašlū K 64 ii 7—9 E; E-LIBIT; SÉR-RA = maš-lu-u ša igari (II 62 *c-d* 65, Br 6250, 7524); II 62 *no* 3, *c-d* 66 SU-AMĒL (Br 6403); 67 SU-MAŠ-LU-UM (Br 1943) = maš-lu-u ša zumri (or maški? Br 185, 219). ZK ii 328; ZA i 54 *etc.*; *cf* šillū, BA ii 561; perhaps some "skin-like covering", AV 5220. V 32 *a-b* 49 maš-lu-u ‖ maš-lum (= II 32 *g-h* 38); VATh 574, 10 i-na ma-aš-li-i, Meissner, BA ii 561. V 14 *c-d* 36 maš-lu = ṣu-ba-a-tu; 37 KU maš-lu = ku-si-tu (*q. v.*); also see 38 *foll.* II 6 *c-d* 33 ŠAX-MAŠ-LUM = ap-par-ru-u.

mašla'u (√שלא) D 88 iv 8—11 GIŠ 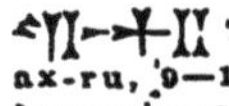 TUR (& NI) = kutū (8) ṣa-ax-ru, 9—10 maš-la-'-u, 11 (ku-ut) šam-ni = a small kutū (*q. v.*) AV 5218; Br 8112, 8116.

mašla'tum. II 43 *a-b* 40 (= Rm 131 *O* 6) ša-par-tum = maš-la-'-tum; ZA x 208 *O* 16 gal-la-bi ma-aš-la-tum = paṭ-ri ša abu bīti. Bezold, *Catalogue*, 1426 pūtu maš-la-'-tum, M^S 94 *col* 2.

mašallu V 42 *a-b* 10 DUK-RAD(T) = ma-šal-lu gutter {Rinne}; followed by karpat šināti; AV 5200, Br 2297; D^Par 142 aqueduct. BA i 174, ‖ rāṭu (*q. v.*).

mušallū Dar 391, 1 *f*: 150 mu-šal-lu-u ša 1 ammat 2 ubān ina 6 ammāt šarri. M^S 9 *col* 2 pictures? mirrors?

mušelū *a*) Br 5287, 5351 *ad* V 13 *a-b* 7 mu-še-lu-u sikkati = GIŠ-KAK (= DU), same id = pi-tu-u ša sikkati (6) porter {Pförtner} √elū. — *b*) = niptū properly lifter {Heber}; key {Schlüssel}. V 26 *a-b* 8—9 mu-še-lu-u ‖ mazūru Br 12006, 1804; 12004; II 23 *c-d* 49—50 mu-še-lu-u = ni-ip-tu-u (49) = up-pu (50 *c*) = nam-za-qu (50 *d*); also in *c. t.* (AV* 40 *col* 1) ištēn mu-še-lu-u parzillu Nabd 258, 36; Cyr 183, 20. — *c*) necromancer, conjurer {Totenbeschwörer}. II 51 *no* 2 *R* 20—21 (49 & 50 *d-g*) mu-še-lu-u (ša) e-kim-mu; mu-še-lu-u ša-pil-ti; Br 3361 *ad l* 51; II 38 *e-f* 3—4 mu-še-lu-u (also V 13 *c-d* 52 = šā'ilu, Br 7034); J^W 53 *rm* 5; 102.

^aban^ **mašeldu** whet-stone {Wetzstein}? KB v 46*; T. A. (Ber.) 28 iii 74: icxvii ^(aban)^ ma-še-el-du ša ^(amēl)^ gallabi; *cf* mašla'tum.

mašlaxu K 4200 *R* 14 maš-la-xu (√שלח?), canal?

muš(šu)laxxu. Sm 54 *R* 5 max-xu, 6 maš-ma-šu, 7—8 a-ši-pu, 9 MUŠ ^muš-la-ax^ LAX = ŠU = mušlaxxu = mu-ši-pu. II 32 *e-f* 13 MUŠ-LAX = muš-šu(?)-la-ax-xu; IV² 50 *a* 43 MUŠ-$\frac{DU}{DU}$-tum (= mušlaxxī-tum) a-gu-gi-il-tum; D^Par 109; Jensen, 410, 421 = rudder {Ruder}, but Zimmern (quoted by Jensen, KB iii, 1, 146) = conjurer {Zauberer}; V 33 v 15 MUŠ-$\frac{DU}{DU}$ (KB iii *loc. cit.*: ein Schlangenbeschwörer, referring to Bezold, ZA iv 430 muš-la-lax-xu. ZK ii 413 mu-ša-lax[-tu?]; T^{M} 136 quotes form muš-šu-lax-xu (Br çir-ma-lax-xu); 80—7—19, 129, *R* (amēl) MUŠ-LA-AX-$\frac{DU}{DU}$ = ŠU-xu. T^{M} iv 106 (sal) kaššapat muš-lax-at ana[-ku pa-ši-ra-ak; vii 95 muš-laxxu^{pl} li-pu-šu-ki.

mušullilu. IV^{2} 23 *a* 12—13 XI-LI (Jensen ŠAR-GUB)-A = mu-šul-li-lu A-GAR (= ugari) Br 8248; perhaps √elolu (Lyon, *Sargon*, 66); same iđ in II 7 *g-h* 6 = xasasu; but Jensen, 236 *rm* 1 √šalalu = let grow, raise {wachsen lassen}; iđ usually = conveying idea of luxury, vigor (= kuzbu); thus > mušallil; BA ii 417.

mušallimu. *a*) arxu mušallimu = a full month (see šalamu), AV 5580; — *b*) $Z^{Š}$ v/vi 198 u mu-šal-li-ma-ta-ma at-ta na-az-za-rak-ka and an avenger by thy sword.

mašlupu (שלף), AV 5221 = kusīpu 1 (*q. v.*).

mušalqiu title of official {Beamtentitel} *e.g.* II 31 *a* 89 amēl ša TUR mu-šal-qi-u, *cf* loqû.

maš-laq-qu (*i. e.* [illegible] [illegible]-qu) II 37 *c-f* 52 ma [illegible] (?) [illegible] la-lu (?) followed by *f* 53 ni-id lib-bi.

mašaltu *cf* maš'altu.

mašmašu conjurer, charmer {Beschwörer} = āšipu; with same iđ (amēl) MAŠ-MAŠ for both. See, however, Zimmern, *Beitr. z. Babyl. Relig.*, 93; *cf* also mušlaxxu. Lehmann, ii 68, 76; *Rev. Critique*, '90, 482. T^{M} i 143; ii 144 *etc.*, & *p* 129: Chiefmagician = Grossmagier; also see BA ii 572. II 32 *c-f* 10 MAŠ]-MAŠ = maš-ma-šu. AV 5222, Br 1844 = mullilu; IV^{2} 60* B *O* 9 (amēl) mašmaš (or āšipu?) ina ki-kit-ṭi-e ki-mil-ti ul ip-ṭur (also A *O* 9); C *R* 10 (end); PSBA '87—8, 478; IV^{2} 57 *R* 25 (beg.) u ana-ku maš-maš; 10 (end) (il) Marduk (wr. AN-ŠILIG-GAL-ŠAR) mašmaš ilāni rabūti (Sayce, *Hibb. Lect.*, 149 *rm* 4); 52 *b* 19 pu-ṭur maš-maš ilāni bēl rem-nu-u (il) Marduk; 56 iii 49 lid-din-ki (amēl) maš-maš a-ši-pu (il) Marduk; 30* *no* 3 *O* 22 ša (il) Marduk maš-maš (il) Ēa mār reš-ti-i ša (il) Ēa (K 3152); K 2711 *O* 8 (amēl) mašmaš-šu ša (BA iii 264; *cf* Nabd 850, 3); K 5258 (il) Marduk mār (al) Eridi mašmaš ilāni; Sn *Bav* 27 (Meissner & Rost: Priesteramt); K 167, 24; $Z^{Š}$ viii 71 ina ki-bit maš-maš ilāni; perhaps V 33 vi 37 maš-maš (KB iii, 1, 148: mullilu); rab-mašmašu K 317 *R* 12 chief of the conjurers. *pl* (amēl) MAŠ-MAŠ^{MEŠ} = mašmašē K 572, 7 (BA i 217—8); III 66 *col* 4, 21 Aššur ^{il} IM (= Adad) ^{il} MAŠ-MAŠ (Hommel, PSBA xxi: *gemini*); 30 (il) Ku-ti bīt maš-maš (also 40); 12, 15 ina pān (il) Maš-maš (PSBA xxi 130 = Nergal, but here perhaps Ninib); on (il) maš-maš K 310 *R* 7 = Nergal (S^{c} 1 *b* 8) *cf* BA ii 572; Nabd 480, 3—5 also = Ninib. *abstr. noun:*

mašmašūtu; ZA vi 243, 39 (amēl) maš-maš-u-tu (perhaps: baru-u-tu?).

mušmaxxu see çirmaxxu.

mušmītu *cf* mâtu die {sterben}.

maššanu some furniture, vessel *etc.* {Gerät, Gefäss *etc.*} √אשן or שאן Tallqvist, *Schenkungsbriefe*, 13—14. Nabd 258, 34: 3 (iç) pa-aš-šu-ru^{pl}, 2 maš-ša[-nu]^{pl}; Camb 330, 6: 1 maš-ša-nu (mentioned among the articles comprising the dowry of Xunnatu); 331, 14: 2 maš-ša-na-nu.

mu-ša-na(u) an-ni-i *etc.* *cf* šanû change, alter {ändern, umstossen}.

mišēnu sandal {Sandale} T. A. (Ber.) 28 i 63: 2 mi-še-nu ša šēpi ša xurâçi; ii 57: 3 mi-še-nu ša še-e-ni ša kaspi. Nabd 506, 8 (end) mi-še-e-nu.

MUŠEN (Lehmann, i 16 *rm b*) iđ for iççuru (*q. v.*). Halévy, *Mélanges*, 301 = ag Š of √'anū: cry; V 38 *a-c* 62; S^{a} i 10 xu-u | XU | mu-še-en-nu, 13 mu-še-en | XU | = *idem* (ZK ii 418—19); H 14, 159—60; AV 5611; also II 30 *c* 44; 37 *a* 57.

mušinditum *cf* marakuttum.

mušēniqtu wet nurse {Amme} *pl* mušēniqēti, √enequ. H^{F} 16; ZDMG 34, 761 *rm*; ZA i 402; Peiser, KAS 87—88. H 84—5, 35—9 mu-še-niq-tu (= UM-ME-GA-LAL, Br 3907); AV 3475; H 81, 6 *cf* māru. II 9 *c-d* 45 a-na mu-še-niq-ti id-din-šu (*cf* K 133 *R* 5); 47 a-na mu-še-niq-ti-šu *etc.* (ZA i 176 *rm* 1 on *ll* 47—50). V 42 *e-f* 65 UM-ME-GA-LAL = mu-še-n[iq-tum]; IV^{2} 61 iii 25 mu-še-niq-ta-ka = I (am) thy nurse; *pl* Asb ix 66 ina eli VII ta-a-an mu-še-ni-qa-a-te (*var* -ti) e-ni-qu-u (of nursing animals).

muša(n)nītum; Nabd 910, 4 ana dullu ša mu-ša-ni-tum ša (nâr) Sumanti; 6, 3; 1002, 6; Cyr 180, 10; also Nabd 770, 2 a list of workmen engaged ša dullu ina eli mu-ša-an-ni-tum ša Gilušu; 784, 3; 1080, 2. AVTh 386, 8—9 ina mux-xi | mu-ša-an-ni-tum. Peiser, *Babyl. Vertr.*, 305—6 √šanū; the word may refer to some kind of construction for purposes of irrigation; T^C 139; Jastrow, Hebr. x 193—4: embankment (√שׁנן); also see Levias, AJSL xv 234 *rm* 4.

muššipu ‖ āšipu, mašmašu, mušlaxxu (*q. v.*); ag ℑ of נשׁף; Z^B 60; II 32 *e-f* 14 (Br 1221; AV 5630); K 2866 *O* 28 = mullilu (*q. v.*); also see Marduk.

mušapū Asb ix 86 Nusku sukkallu na-'i-du mu-ša-pu-u hālu-u-ti. (√apū, אפה, or as Jensen, KB ii 226 *rm* 5 suggests: mu-nam-bu-u, √nabū; while Winckler reads mu-ša[-ar]-bu-u, √rabū).

mašapzirtum ‖ daltu, II 23 *e-f* 69 mu-šap-zi-ir-tum ‖ da-al-tum. √pa-zaru.

mušpalu (also **murpalu**) depth {Tiefe} ‖ šupālu TP vii 81; § 65, 31 *a rm*; Z^B 66, 1; ZK ii 399, 1 (& ≍ Craig, *Diss*, 20, 30: xarpalu, KB i 172); ZA iv 374 *rm* 2; BA i 16 note 14*a*; 174, 178; AV 5624. II 29 *a-b* 67 PÚ (or DUL)-LA(L) = mušpa-lu together with mūlū, šup-lu, a-sur-rak-ku, Br 10113, 10274. Anp ii 132: 120 tik-pi a-na muš-pa-li lu-ṭa-bi; iii 136; perh. III 8, 99 u-šar-di dāmē-šu-nu mur-pa-lu ša na-gu[-u?], I caused their blood to flow down the passes of the district (AJSL xiv, 4); K 196 iii 13—5 see mūlū; M^S 97 *col* 1: Part of a city {Unter-, Vorstadt}, comparing Xenoph. *Anab* iii 4, 10 Μέσπιλα.

mušpīlu *cf* pēlu (פיל).

mašpas(ç)u? Sp II 265 *a* v 7 (end) u-bil maš-pa[-su?].

mušpar(-pir)du(-u) *cf* niperdū.

mušpišu *cf* *p* 586 *col* 2, sect. 5 (K 2107, 11).

mušēpišu Peiser, *Babyl. Vertr.*, 272 structure {Bau}? ag Š epešu (*q. v.*); VATh 374, 7 ina mu-še-pi-šu ša bīt maršarri i-nam-din. — Dar 214, 5 indicating a locality: ina eli nāri ina mu-še-pi-šu ša xubur inaddin.

mašqū watering place, trough {Tränke} √šaqū, BA i 174. NE 8, 40 maš-qa-a i-tip-pir; 11, 4 it-ti bu-lim maš-qa-a i-šat-ti (10, 50); 9, 43 i-na pu-ut maš-ki-i ša-a-šu uštamxiršu (also *p* 9, below, *l* 7); 10, 49; 11, 41 ana] maš-ki-i. V 55, 19 (end) see bataqu ℑ; Reisner, *Hymns*, 15, 21 kibri limnu ša çēnu ina maš-ki-e (= NAK) lā utarri (M^S 97); perhaps VATh 486, 4 ... piš-ša u maš-qa ul-tu (Peiser, *Babyl. Vertr.*, 218); & V 42 *e-f* 28 maš-qa(-)lil[-lu] Br 12030 some vessel.

mašqītu *f* of mašqū, D^Pr 186, 2; 191; Hommel, VK 489; AV 5216, 5223; — *a*) watering {Tränkung} Esh vi 19 a-na maš-qit sisē, *etc.* — *b*) drink {Trank} II 44 *g* 10 (karān) maš-qi-tu ša šarri = (karān) ar-na-ba-ni (Br 12640); H 39, 174 U-A (*cf* V 50 *b* 52) = ri-i-tum u maš-qi-tum (= V 40 *e-f* 5, Br 6089; 11345); Sn i 41—2 šaa-r ri-i-ti | u maš-ki-ti; IV² 9 *a* 62 ri]-i-tu u maš-ki-tum u-da-aš-ša. V 47 *b* 15 *cf* mākalū; also see mirītu.

mašqīmu (? √šaqamu), perhaps S^b 216 ma-aš-ki-im | ID | ra-bi-çu (*q. v.*), between bil-lu-du = bil-lu-du-u & ša-ab-ra = šab-ru-u; *cf* P. N. ša-qi-mu *etc.* H 21, 402; AV 5215; Br 5658 *fol.*

mašqaqqatu (?) V 52 *a* 44 ma-aš-ka-aq-ka-tu.

mašqašu some weapon {ein Mordgerät} *Rec. Trav.*, i ('79) 185; L^T 91; ZK i 124 *fol*; BA i 17; AV 5208; Br 386. V 26 *a-b* 33 (= II 46 *g-h* 62) GIŠ (xa-aš) TAR = maš-ga-šu; V 17 *c-d* 44—5 GIŠ-XAŠ & GIŠ-GAZ (H 39, 140) = maš-ga-šu (*ibid*, 35 *foll*: ša-ka-šum), Br 4726.

***mašaru* 1.** cut, cut to pieces {schneiden, zerschneiden} ag maššru see xutnū & meçu; Boissier, PSBA xx 163 § 1. V 14 *e-f* 61—2 KU-U-GIR-GUŠUR-RA ša ina a-ša̤-gi maš-ru; & ša ina kun-sil-li m/aš-ru, Br 1954; 6033. Perhaps S^c 297 ma-ša-rum (Br 2716). Derr.: muššuru, tamšāru &

mašru *adj* torn {zerrissen} of a garment, *etc.* V 14 *e-f* 59 KU-KA-RA-AX = mašru (Br 691); 60 KU-NU-KA-RA-

AX = la mašru. To this Z^{B} 54 refers also ii 68 (see mašdu).

(māt) **Mašri**, written māt Ma-a-aš-ri (in Mitanni letters) = Miçri (*q. v.*), in T. A., also in same letters written Mi-zi-ir-ri.

mašaru 2. AV 5202; JA viii ('80) 69; G § 54 (but *cf* AJP iv 341); KAT² 266; ZK ii 198. — Q guide, lead; let go, cease {leiten, führen; loslassen, ablassen} T. A. (Lo.) 8, 14 the god li-me-eš-še-ru-šu-nu-ti-ma may the gods give them prosperity, 62 ilâni li-me-eš-še-ru-šu-ma may let it (the gold) pass through without trouble. (ZA v 14; 154—5); 72 xa-mut-ta li-meš-šir-šu-ma (*cf* 76; 9, 48; ZA v 162—3); or 𐎟?; 11, 26 la ta-ma-aš-ši-ra; Ber. 226 *R* 2 li-meš-šir-šu; perhaps also 71, 67 ma-ša-ra-at ālu the city is lost, has ceased?; Rostow. 1, 23 a-nu-ma maš-ša-ru.—Q¹ Asb iii 9 upon the street of his city they threw him dead (ša-lam-ta-šu) and in-du-aš-ša-ru (> imtaššaru) amêl pa-gar-šu and left his corpse there; perhaps K 582, 11 a-ta-šar. — 𐎟 let {lassen} u-maš-šir(-šer) often. Nabd 7, 12; 738, 12 (-šar); 184, 18 (-ša-ar); *cf* T. A. (Ber.) 24 *R* 16, 56, 57. — *a*) forsake, leave, abandon {verlassen, im Stiche lassen}. TP iii 67 their cities lu-maš-še-ru (3 *pl*); u-maš-še-ru Sn vi 17; Šamš iii 9, 30; u-maš-ši-ru ii 45; K 2674, 43 āli-šu u-maš-šir (3 *sg*). TP III *Ann* 28 āl dan-nu-ti-šu u-maš-š[ir]; 71 a-šar-šu-nu lu-maš-še-ru (3 *pl*); 228 edênuš u-maš[-šir]. Esh i 38 who u-maš-šir-u-ma (had forsaken) the gods; Asb ii 134 u-maš-šir Izirtu (3 *sg*); v 19 see mûšabu; vii 90 (-an-ni); K 2852 + K 9662 iii 19 who ..... bêle-šu-nu u-maš-ši-ru (3 *pl*); ZA iv 228, 6 ul u-maš-ša-ru-ka bêlum. *Dibbara*-legend (K 2619) i 12 āl]a tu-maš-šir-ma ta-at-ta-çi a-na a-xa-a-ti; K 509, 26 šarru bêlija la u-maš-šar-an-ni may not abandon me; 80—7—19. 19, 15 (Pinches, *Texts*, 10). K 13 (IV² 45 *no* 2) 20 see kutallu & AV 5638; perh. Anp ii 113 dûrânijšunu (dannûti) u (*var* uš)-še-ru, & fled to the mountains (Lay 84, 9) KB i 90—1. ZA iv 362, 7 mu-šu-ra they have forsaken; Sn vi 11 ši-na muš-šu-ra-ma (3 *pl*) they were forsaken. NE 1, 12 iš-ta-as-sa šip-ta-šu ša la u-maš-ša-ru; 51, 2 bu-la-šu u-maš[-šir]; *del* 20 muš-šir mešrê (Jensen, 395 & IV²) ✕ BA i 123—4, 421. — *b*) leave behind {zurücklassen} Sn iii 58 his brothers ša u-maš(KB ii 96)-še-ru a-xi tâmtim; *Kui* 1, 36. TP III *Ann* 172; Esh iii 32: 20 miles .... a-na arki-ja u-maš-šir-ma (*cf* III 15 iv 15; KB ii 146); K 7599, 5 (end) assemble them et-lu e-du la tu-maš-šir-ma. Br. Mu. 84, 2—11, 165, see mimma. — *c*) let go, set free, let loose {los-, freilassen} *del* 140 u-še-çi-ma summatu u-maš-šir (also 142, 144), Sn vi 20—1 ki-rib (iç) narkabâtišunu | u-maš-še-ru (3 *pl*) ni-zu-šu-un; *cf* I 44, 54; Sn *Bav* 89. *Etana*-legend *frg*, *R* 19 u-maš-šar-ka(-ma) BA iii 366—7 if I release thee. VATh 793, 19 pi(= u)-uš-še-ir-šu-nu-ši-im let them go {lass sie los} pu-uṭ-te-ir-šu-nu-ti (Meissner-Rost, 34); IV² 51 *a* 31 çab-ta la u-maš-ši-ru ka-sa-a la u-ram-mu-u (a question); 54 (see mirânu); 16 *a* 33—4 .... ilâni u-çu-rat šame-e u erçi-tim a-a u-maš-šir-šu (H 138); H 85 i 46 (+ 51) ašakku (or namtâru) ša amêlu la u-maš-ša-ru (Br 1774; 7111); — *d*) send away, dismiss {entlassen, fortsenden} TP v 21 a-na mâtâti-šu-nu u-maš-šir-šu-nu-ti; v 28—9 a-na napiš-ti | u-maš-šir-šu. K 2852 + K 9662 i 17 a-na nap-ša-a-ti muš-šir-an-ni. T. A. Rostow. 2, 21 la u-maš-šir-šu-nu-ti ana alaki not allowed them to go; Ber. 92, 42 tu-ma-šir-an-ni šarru bêli-ja let the king my lord leave me (yet) this year; 22, 20 a-na mu-uš-šu-r[i] to send away; Lo. 12, 60 ju-ua-ši-ra; Ber. 75, 29. — *e*) In T. A. especially, to send out, despatch {senden, aussenden} (ZA vi 255 *rm* 18); Lo. 6, 9—10 why have you not tu-ua-ši-ra your messenger, *l* 48; 9, 49 li-me-eš-šir-šu-nu; 10, 25; (*cf* 8, 72 + 76) Ber. 24 *R* 73; 105 *R* 10 mu-še-ra send! 104, 45 the king lu-ma-še-ru) may send); 24, 52 muš-šir (= ip); 22, 24 whom my brother u-ma-aš-ša-ar-šu-nu; 103, 58 I am not able mu-še-ra girru (to forward the caravans); *ibid* 51 mu-še-ra-an-ni (ZA vi 254) send to me (a garrison); also 52; 53 mu-še-ir-ti I sent (to my lord, the king): — *f*) leave off, desist *etc.* {ablassen, aufgeben} SMITH, *Asurb*, 119, 24 ul u-maš-šar a-di al-la-ku I will not leave off coming; T. A. (Ber.) 23, 21 muš-šir forbear (do not)?; 40, 31 the slanders against me la du-ṵa-aš-šir do not allow; 7 *R* 21 see manma (& ZA v 142). Lo. 2, 25 mu-uš-šo-ir desist {gieb auf} ZA v 17 *rm* 2; 152—3 *R* 1. — Ber. 22 *R* 20 may T., the lord never u-ma-aš-ša-ra-an-ni permit me (to be angry at my brother); Lo. 9, 16 — *g*) cede something {aufgeben, lassen} Neb 240, 9 u-maš-šir (a field to another); VATh 105, 10 the house ina pānišunu tu-maš-šir (3 *f*); also KB iv 202—3, 12 (u-maš-šir); Br. Mu. 84, 2—11, 283, 13 (end); 84, 2—11, 214 la muš-šu-ur ia-a-tu nicht liess er mir (KOHLER & PEISER, ii 63—4). — I 27 *no* 2, 38 ina la ma-a-ri u mu-šu-ri (KB i 118); Sp II 265 *a* xiii 6 (end) lu-maš-šir; V 45 vi 24 tu-maš-šar; DT 81 iii 30 pi(= ṵa)-aš-ša[-ar] BA iii 501—3; T. A. (Ber.) 199, 18 read tu-ma-še-ir (BA iv 127) not tu-ma-'-ir. — ℨ[1] *a*) active: utašir (*i. e.* ūtaššir > uttaššir > umtaššir) KGF 140 *rm* 1 & umdašir (§ 48; POGNON, *Bavian*, 32, 151), unde(i)ššir. Anp ii 16 nine of their cities u-ta-še-ru (they abandoned; KB i 72—3); iii 71 the mountain *X.* a-na šumēli-ia u-ta-šir I left (to my left) Z[B] 57. VATh 66, 4 a-xu-u-a un-da-aš-šir-an-ni my brother forsook me ‖ māru-u-a ix-te-li-iq-an-ni (PEISER, KAS 18; KB iv 212 *foll*). DT 81 vi 5 u-ta-aš-šar he will give {er wird es überlassen}; Šalm, *Ob* 37 his royal city um (KB i 132 in)-da-šir he left (§ 84); K 13, 7 (= IV² 45) the city Madaktu un-𒁹(= daš, LEHMANN, ii 111—2)-šir; L⁴ iii 17 (end) um-𒁹-ši-ra ša-ru-ri; Cyr 183, 10 un-da-aš-šar(šir?); 337, 17 this acre (field) ina pānišu tu-un-da-šir; D 98 *R* 13 im-xul-lu ça-bit ar-ka-ti panuššu um-taš-šir let loose {loslassen}. — T. A. (Ber.) 22, 19 xamutta u[m-ta-aš-š]ir-šu-nu-ti I have sent back speedily. — *b* passive. TP vi 98 the palaces which um-da-še(*var* ši)-ra-ma e-na-xa-ma (had been abandoned and thus gone to decay (§ 84).

muššuru. T. A. (Ber.) 24, 50 ub-ku(-n)-tum muš-šu-ru-tum; *R* 15, 42, 51 (where KAR-KAR-MEŠ ša xurāçi), 68. √mašaru 1 (?).

mašaru 3. Q[m] see zibbatu & mašaxu, 2, note (Br 11897).

mašaru 4. see maššartu.

ma-ša-ri *5.* in qa-an ma-ša-ri Br 2431 *ad* V 32 *d-e* 36; 2179 *ad* II 24 *a-b* 4. AV 5201; see li-ša-ri.

mašāru wheel {Rad} √שור (*q. v.*) L⁴ i 23 I hold the reins ki-ma as-sa-ri ušasxar sixir [iç] ma-ša-re, like a charioteer leading the turning of the wheels (LEHMANN, ii 67 Deichsel); V 55, 26 ša [iç] ma-ša-ra-šu (= charioteer) bīt i-mit-ti | šarri bēli-šu la im-mir-šu-ma ma-ša-ra-šu uk-til-la (also *ll* 36, 37; HILPRECHT, *Diss*, 4—5; KB iii, 1, 166—7). Sn v 82—3 ša narkabāt . . . . 83 da-mu u par(pir?)-šu ri-it-mu-ku ma-ša-ru-uš (HEBR. iii 110; vii 69). Asb iv 30 *T.* man-za-az [iç] ma-ša-re-ia (*var* ma-za-az [iç] man-ša-re-ia, double transposition) iç-bat. BA i 175 ⋊ KB ii 188—9. NE 42, 11 ša ma-ša-ru-ša (*var* šu) namely of the wagon(*l* 10) xurāça-am-ma; perhaps K 8466, 7 . . . m]a-ša-ru i-šax-xi-it; sik-kat ma-ša-ri *cf* sikkatu; some also S^c 298 dub-bi-in | iD | ma-ša-rum = wagon; *cf* 299 ‖ çu-um-bu car {Karren}. — H[F] 72; Z[B] 99; BA i 174 (√אשר?) thus māšaru: wheel, or perhaps the nave. HOMMEL, *Gesch.*, 450 *rm*: war-chariot. BERRY, AJSL xvi 50 reads magarru (√gararu).

maširi (?) V 31 *c-d* 56 NU [la] ŠAT [ša] TI = la ma-ši-ri (or la-ma-ar?) AV 5111; Br 7402.

mašrū (√אשר grow, sprout abundantly, *etc.*) = luxurious growth, thriving {Wachstum, Gedeihen}; JENSEN, ZA i 410 *fol*; ii 89 *rm*; JÄGER, BA ii 297. TP viii 28 ša-na-at nu-ux-še u maš(or bar?)-re-e. Sp II 265 *a* vii 9 see katatu; xxiv 7 šar-ma(-mi) meš (*var* maš)-ru-u (*var* -šu) il-la-ku i-da-a-šu; also vi 8 gi-iç maš-ri-e (PSBA xvii 148; but ZA x 5 gi-ix-bar-ri-e, *q. v.*). A ‖ is:

mešrū BA i 16 *rm* 15; ii 290—7; KING property, wealth; iD ŠA-TUK *e. g. del* 20. Sp II 265 *a* ii 9 na-am-ra-a be-lu meš-ri-e; IV² 5 iii 27—8 ina bīt bal-ti u meš-ri[-e?]; V 65 *b* 31 xarrān šul-lum u meš-ri-e (*cf* mišaru); K 4315,

13; Bu 88—5—12, 75 + 76 iv (K 192 *R*) 16 tam-šil meš-ri-šu (BA iii 246 wie seine Gestalt). K^{M} 8, 13 ša im-nu-uk-ki meš-ra-a lu-uç-çip that which is on thy right hand increase good fortune! On *del* 20 see mašaru, 2 & NE 135, 25 (✕ J^{I-N} 83), Jensen, 395; V 11 *a-c* 47 NAM-TUK (Br 4777) | GAR-TUK (Br 12177) | meš (*var* me?)-ru-u, 48 = bu-šu-u (H 111 & 118, 43; D 127, 45), Jensen, 395: Hab & Gut; BA ii 206: an Frische strotzend (thus an *adj*). II 30 *c-d* 46 (Br 7252 = ŠU-GAR-IK[or GAL]-LA, AV 5373, ZA i 258); also see L^{T} 142 & *rm*; ZA iii 308, 31. — Also figure, form {Gestalt} see above; especially *pl* mešrûti (& u); BA i 175; G § 70 (*p* 67) note 2: members of the body; Pognon, *Wadi-Brissa*, 107, meš-ri-e-ti (Curs. *col* 6, b, 21); Meissner & Rost, 34 note 64 *ad* Sn *Kui* 4, 23; Jäger, BA ii 297 compares Aram. משרא muscles (so called because they are *viridi*). Šamš i 21 Ninib ra-aš e-mu-ki ša šum-mu-xu meš-re-ti (Bezold, *Literature*, 77 reads ►—Ү<Ү), see KB i 174—5; Jensen, 466 *fol*; Scheil, *Šamši R.* 34—5; ZK ii 278; ZA ii 317, bel. RP^{2} i 9—22; R. F. Harper: with well-developed muscles; IV^{2} 60* C *R* 7 meš-re-tu-u-a su-up-pu-xa; K^{M} 10, 4 meš-re-tu-u-a ili-ja; S. A. Smith, *Asurb* III, 3, 61 aṭbuxšu u-par-ri-sa meš-ri-ti-šu (K 2674). H 79 *R* 25 (K 44) ša a-me-li mâr ili-šu meš-ri-ti-šu li-tab-bi-ba (Br 12026); T^{M} vii 67 see minûtu. iD ID-ŠU-NER in IV^{2} 3 *b* 12 meš-ri-ti-šu ruk-kis-ma (Br 6605); 17 *a* 52 (see marçiš); V 50 *a* 49—50 ša ilu lim-nu meš-ri-ti-šu iç-bu-ru (H 187); IV^{2} 9 *a* 20 (see kabbaru) ša meš-ri-ti šuk-lu-lum (Br 6588, where also AV 7996: ša-pa-ku ša meš-ri-e-tum is quoted). K 2971 (IV^{2} 56, *add* 11; K 3377 + K 7078) 1 meš-re-ti tu-çab-bi-ti tu-ab-bi-ti bi-na-a-ti. Sn *Kui* 4, 15 ça-lam meš-re(-e-)ti ^{aban} pa-ru-ti. Merod.-Balad.-Stone v 38—9 ub-bur (paralysis: Lähmung) | meš-ri-e-ti BA ii 265; KB iii (1) 192—3.

kakkab mešrî V 46 *a-b* 51 MUL-KAK-SI-DI (which also = šu-ku-du, tar-ta-xu) = kakkab meš-ri-e (Br 3462) = the greenish-shining star {der grünleuchtende Stern} ✕ kakkab namru, 52, according to Jensen, ZA i 66 *rm*: the reddish-shining star {der rothleuchtende Stern}; but Jäger agrees with Jensen, *Kosmologie*, Nachtrag II: mešrû the powerful, an epithet of Ninib. *k. m.* = the star of the powerful = KAK-SI-DI as star of Ninib. — On the kakkab mešrî, see literature cited in Muss-Arnolt, "The works of Jules Oppert", BA ii 551 *foll*: *nos* 284, 285, 286, 287, 292; Jensen, 49 *no* 4; Br 5278. To these add also Hommel, *Sum. Les.*, 51 *rm*: mišrû = north {nördlich} = [illegible] √ يسر be on the left side; Ideler in Hastings, *Dict. of the Bible*, i 218: Procyon = kakkab mešrî = north star or "Northern weapon" in contradistinction to the "Southern weapon" *viz.* "Sirius" (= bowstar = kakkab qašti). Cheyne, *Jew. Quart. Rev.*, x 570—1, compares שכוי, Job 38, 36 to mišri in *k. m.*, ‖ tartaxu; Z^{B} 55 *ad* ii 181 mešrû = lance. — I 28 *a* 14—15 ina ûma-at ni-pi-ix | kakkab KAK-SI-DI (= mešrê) ša ki-ma eri i-çu-du (L^{T} 176, 196; KB i 124—5). See on this text also RP xi; D^{K} 10 *rm* 9; Tiele, *Gesch.*, 160; KGF 254—6. Oppert reads tam-at for ûma-at (see BA ii 549 *no* 261; also 551 *nos* 282, 283, 286, 287, 296).

mašrû (or *s*?) I 28 *b* 9 dalâte bâbi . . . . maš(s)-ra-a-te u-ni-ki-ir (I changed) dalâte ašûxi çi-ra-a-te ûpuš.

mušîrtu (?) H 98, 26 ina bîti mu-šir-ti â êrubšu.

mašîrru some vessel or instrument {Gefäss oder Gerät}, AV 5204, see maltu.

mušarû, *cf* musarû & 81—6—7, 209, 40 but who (= ša) mu-ša-ru ši-ṭir šumi-ja (see *l* 38) . . . . unakkaru; K 504 *R* 3 muš-ša-ru-u, *O* 19 muš-ša-ra-ni-i (= *pl*), JAOS xix 71; AV 5591; 5596.

muš-ša-ru *cf* mušgarru.

mîšaru, mêšaru, mêšeru *m* justice, righteousness {Recht, Gerechtigkeit} BA i 16, 15; ZA ii 118; AV 5363; Br 4757; § 30; √ישר; ‖ kêttu (*q. v.*), Lyon, *Sargon*, 21 & 77 *ad Cyl* 50; G § 58. KB iv 64 ii *R* 19 šanâte mi-ša-ri (here according to Hilprecht, *Assyriaca*, 47—8 also: "Gedeihung, Segen", *cf* ZA i 258). See K 183, 10 (BA i 617, 622: Jahre der Gerechtigkeit). V

55 i 6 ša di-in mi-ša-ri i-din-nu (ZA iv 10, 45 = K 3474 ii 29 ša di-in me-ša-ri i-di-nu); also IV² 48 *a* 8 tu-da-at mi-ša-ri. ID SI-DI Br 8462. Sp iii 586 + Rm III 1 (hymn to the setting sun) 8 mi-ša-rum su-uk-kal-lum, *etc.* (TSBA viii 167 *foll*; HOMMEL, *Sum. Les.*, 120 *fol*); V 65 *b* 31 *fol*: u-ru-ux ket-ti u mi-ša-ri; *cf a* 5; Asb iii 89 (ZA iii 163 *rm* 6; 163—5); Bu 88—5—12, 75 + 76 viii 14—15 ina ket-ti u mi-ša-ri lu-ur-te-'-u. 81—2—4, 188 (ZA v 66) Prayer to Ištar of Nineveh, 10 a-na il (wr. ►►+)-tim rim-ni-ti ša me-ša-ra i-ra-am-mu; Sn i 4 Sen. na-çir ket-ti (*q. v.*), ra-'i-im mi-ša-ri. I 65 *a* 1 šar mi-ša-ri-im. IV² 28 *no* 1 *a* 13—14 AN-UD (= il Šamaš) mi-ša-ru (= GAR-SI-DI) re-is-su i-na-aš-ši-ik (IV *R* -*rn*); K 4623 (H 123) *R* 13 il Mi-ša-ru (= GAR-SI-DI) ik-ri-bi *etc.* (Br 3462) *cf* Z^{B} viii 9 il Mi-šar[-rum] & *p* 60; K 2096 *O* 25; *R* 22. II 67, 85 bābi me-ša-ri (muš-te-šir di-in malki); S^{P} 158 + S^{P} II 962 *R* 6 i-nu-um la-ša-si (?) mi-ša-ri when (there was) absence (?) of justice (righteousness), PINCHES. Also *cf* ZIM., *Beitr. z. bab. Rel.*, 90.

NOTE. — 1. Also mi-ša-ar-tu (iš-ta-nak-ka-šu) AV *39 *col* 1.

2. S. A. SMITH, *Asurb*, 31 *ad* K 625, 12 ša ina ma-šar-ti iq-bu-u-ni who spoke in righteousness, but read iš-šar-ti (DELITZSCH).

mēšariš (AV 5362), mēšeriš (AV 5366) *adv* justly, righteously {rechtmässig, gerecht} ZA i 258; L^{T} 142. Anp i 22 Anp who me-še(*var* ša)-riš i-tal-la-ku; iii 128; TP iv 47 ša i-na kib-rat arba-'i | me-še-riš ul-tal-li-ṭu-ma who ruleth .... righteously; Šalm, *Mon*, ii 7 me-še-riš šal-ṭi-iš ... lu at-ta-lak.

miširtu due, tribute {Gebühr} perh. IV 20 *ro* 1, 22 instead of mi-xir-ta-šu (see mixirtu, 2); justice, K 704, 4.

mušarbibu TP v 65, √rababu (*q. v.*). AMIAUD (*Rev. d'Assyr.*, ii 12; RP² i 109 *rm* 6), POGNON, *Bav*, 94 √šababu; AV 5593.

mušarbidu II 34 *no* 3 *g-h* 31 mu-šar-bi-du (√רבד) = su-kal-lu, AV 5594; POGNON, *Bav*, 94 √שבש.

mušarkisu an official {Beamter} AV 5595; √rakasu. K 4395 v 3: 4 (amēl) mu-šar-kis (II 31 *b* 63); K 11, 12 (amēl) mu-šar-kis a-bit šarri; Ⅺ 616, 6 ina eli bītāti ša (amēl) mu-šar-ki-sa-a-ni (Hr^{L} 127); K 596, 4 (amēl) mu-šar-kis^{pl} (+ *l* 16; Hr^{L} 190); also see K 558, 8 + 14; K 655, 27; KNUDTZON, *no* 108, 6 (amēl) mu-šar-ki-si^{pl}.

mušruššu see çirruššu (WINCKLER, *etc.*).

mušērišu. III 41 i 32 (end) lu mu-še-ri-šu.

maššartu, *pl* maššarāti; √mašaru, 4, whose exact meaning is not yet determined. T^{C} 98—99 completion (of a month = ša arxi) {Ablauf (des Monats)}, in *c. t.*, *e.g.* Nabd 346, 5 *fol* (1: 20 GUR suluppi) i-na ma-aš-šar-tum ša (arax) Tešrīti | u ma-aš-šar-tum ša (arax) Ṭebēti | i-nam-di-in (ZIMMER, BA iv 66 = von der Besoldung (?) des Monats *T. etc.*, soll er sie (die Datteln) abgeben); *cf* Nabd 630, 5; 219, 4 so & so many tons of dates ina pap-pa-su (3) | ina maš-šar-tum ša (arax) Nisanni inamdin; *cf* Cyr 373, 6; Nabd 115, 5 *fol*; 28, 1 (end) ina maš-šar-tum [ša] (arax) Abi; 237, 24; 111, 5 + 6 (-ti); 311, 4 three of the 4 AŠ owed, the debtor ina ma-aš-šar-tum | ša (arax) Šabāṭi, (arax) Addari (arax) Nisanni i-nam-din. Camb 314, 2: 108 ma-ši-xe ša sat-tuk ŠE-BAR i-na maš-šar-tum (also Lohnrate) ša (arax) Abi a-na *X*. iddin(a); Nabd 28, 1 (BA iii 486, 7). Cyr 374, 10: 100 tons of dates you shall give to *NN*. and with reference to these 100 ina ma-aš-ša-ru-a-ta-šu ti-ni-iṭ-ra-'- (ye shall be paid back with his *m.*), also *cf* PEISER, KAS 92 & 102 (bel.). VATh 106, 13 i-nam-din i-na maš-šir (= šar)-tum ša ... SCHEIL (*Rec. Trav.* xix) Notes d'épigr., *p* 58 *no* 266, 2 i-na libbi maš-šar-ti ra-bi-ti | ša e-bi-ir-ti.

mašaḥu 1. pr imšuš forget {vergessen} II 16 *a-b* 68-9 ša bi-el-šu | im-šu-šu BA ii 279—80 whom his lord forgot. V 47 *b* 28 see mammū 2.

mašaḥu 2. see maššu 1; only in 𒌋. AV 5203; Br 203, 205. K 246 iv (= D 133; H 98—99; II 18 *a-b*) 53—4 amēlu mut-tal-li-ku ina ni-iq ri-e-me | šul-me ki-ma ki-e (= qū bronce {Bronze}) maš-ši lim-ma-šiš (Br 203; 7075; 7814; ZK i 302; ii 410). IV² 4 *b* 42—3 ki-ma ki-e maš-ši (= IM-SU-UB-TA) lim-ma-šiš (= XE-EN-TA-SU-UB) ‖ li-tabbib, littanbiṭ WINCKLER: like as shining copper let it be cleansed; IV² 28 *no* 1 *b* 16—17 ki-ma ki-e ma-aš-ši lim-ma-šiš. HOMMEL, *Sum. Les.*, 125: qû maššu = gegossene Schnur *i. e.* Kette. — Perhaps = balalu, on which see WINCKLER, *Altor. Forsch.*, ii 161 *fol.* u-zak-ki V 47 *b* 27 (end) may have been written with reference to an imšuš > mašašu = purify *etc.* {läutern} a homonym of mašašu 1.

NOTE. — 1. II 16/27 a-ma-ša-as-su-ma BA ii 302—3; I polish it ‖ ich polire ihn, apparently, √mašašu Q.

2. IV² 21 1 B *O* 34 ma-a-ši mu-un-dax-çi ša u-ma-ši-ša id-di-e, WINCKLER, *loc. cit.*: the two warriors, which I have molted out of earth pitch.

3. ki-e maš-ši read by SAYCE kemaššu (AV 4322): copper (RP² I 56 *rm* 2; ZA vi 161 *fol* & note 2, kêmassu; this *k* is derived from the name of the land ki-maš (KI = land + MAŠ, the whole = land of MAŠ *i. e.* northern Arabia); also see SAYCE, *Higher Criticism & the Verdict of the Monuments*, 479; & PSBA xix, ('97) 69—70; *p* 70 he reads UD-KA-✱ (= MAS) = ka-mas, whence the Semites borrowed kemassu. — AMIAUD, RP² ii 81 *rm* 3: From ki-maš (the land of Mash) or Arabia Petraea (= Gen 10, 23) was derived the Assyrian kêmassi = copper. (Amiaud bases his remarks on the Gudea-inscr., see below); WINCKLER, *Forsch.*, i 167—8 KI-MAŠ (Gudea, B. vi 22) = kemaššû: copper ‖ Kupfererz = dem Gebirge von Kupfer eigen >< JENSEN, KB iii, 1, 36—7: dem Gebirge des [Landes] *kimaš*). — See JENSEN, *loc. cit.* & ZA x 363 *foll* where Sayce's etymology is rejected & kemaššu derived as in body of this article (qê + maššu); but he adds: "doch gibt es ein Gebirge kimmaš II 51, 7 Berg (von) kim(?)-maš = Berg des grossen *Lam*-baumes; lammu = aššxu II 23 *e-f* 20: eine Art Ceder. *Ibid*, *pp* 365—6 on location of mountain kimmaš, probably in the Lebanon; or the Hermon; or the country of Damascus. "Ein Land *Maš* wird in den assyrischen Inschriften gar nicht erwähnt; jedoch ist das Land KI-maš in Gudea ein Kupferland, hat aber nichts mit dem Namen qe-maššu zu tun."

4. ZA xi 25 has name of the town KI-maš in Elam = NIM ki-ma-ša-(ki).

Derr. maššu 1. & nimšištu (?).

muššêšibu *etc.*, *cf* ašabu (ישב).

muššêšeru (√ešeru) regent, ruler {Herrscher, Leiter} AV 5615; Z^B 85; V 30 *e-f* 18 SI-SI = mu-še-še-ru ‖ šarru (Br 8431); V 26 *g-h* 50 mu-še-šir (?) mentioned as some part of the giššimmaru tree. AV 5615; also see multarixu.

mašištu. ZK ii 413 (*ad p* 300) K 2051 ii ma-ši-iš[-tu].

mešeštum a small net {ein kleines Netz} SCHEIL, ZA ix 221—22 (S 31—52) *R* 18 GIŠ-SA-TUR = me-še-eš-tum ‖ te-šu-u & pûgu.

maštu in saxmaštu (*q. v.*).

mâštum *1.* daughter {Tochter} see mârtu.

maš-tum *2.* S^c 265, Br 10538, AV 9005 šub(?)-tum.

maštû, maltû (AV 5028) *m* drinkingjar, bowl {Trinkgefäss} √šatû; § 65, 31*a*; HEBR. iii 110; BA i 326 *ad* 175. II 44 *no* 8, 54—55 ma-al-tu-u çixru & rabu-u explanatory to lum-mu & di-qa-ru (*q. v.*); also *e-f* 47 anaqqu = mal-tu-u(?); II 47 (*e*)-*f* 53 mal-tu-u ša-pu-tu (Br 14115); V 20 (*a*-)*b* 36—7 kannu (*q. v.*) ša maš-ti-i.

maštîtu & maltîtu *f* drink, beverage {Getränk} §§ 51; 65, 31*a*; Asb viii 104 water a-na maš-ti-ti-šu-nu; ix 34 maš-ti-tu u-ša-qir a-na pi-i-šu-un; IV 31 *R* 25 see xabanâti; K 4931 *O* 22 (H 117) see dimtu 1 (= U-A-MU-EME-SAL, Br 6090); IV² 49 *a* 11 (= T^M i) see maṭû ℶ; √šatû; to the same √ also:

meštû drunkard, drunk {trunken} BA ii 296—7 *i. e.* der vom maštû überwältigte. II 16 *d* 24 meš-tu-u ul ux-xur-šu (to the strength of the worm) the drunkard is not inferior; AV 5374.

maššitu V 31 *g-h* 30 maš-ši-ti ‖ ni-ši-tim; *cf* AV 5225; perhaps also P. N. Arad (amêl) Ul-maš-ši-tum (PINCHES, PSBA xix 132, 10—11).

maššittum V 27 *e-f* 30 GUL-SIN-GAL-LUM = maš-šit (or laq?)-tum, AV 5226, Br 259; *cf* V 32 *b* 66 šin-gal-lum = ga-an-nu.

mašittu (?) Perhaps K 3364 *O* 17 ma-ši-is-su i-xa-sa [   ] (amêl) Ub-bar(or maš?).

mašêtu Sarg *Ann* 175 (mât) Tabalum ana pâṭ gimrišu uqatti ma-še-ti-iš.

mešêtu Smsk, K 626, 13 that and that ina me-še-ti ša bâbi 'i-i-la (Hr^L i *p* 23).

---

muš-ri-it V 33 vii 14 read çir-ri-it (çirîtu). ∾ maš-tum II 49, 18; AV 5212 see bar-tum. ∾ ma-šit-tum AV 5367 *ad* V 28 *a* 33 read pi-rit-tum (*q. v.*).

muštе'û *e. g.* muš-te-'-u par-çi; I 65 *a* 4 Neb mu-uš-tu-'u-um ba-la-ṭam; also IV^2 1 *a* 45; ZA iv 107, 21, see še'u.

muštabil *e. g.* Sarg *Cyl* 34 *etc.*; V 30 *a-b* 36 KA-XI-XI = muš-ta-bil a-ma-ti; AV 5635; Br 788; see abalu (יבל).

muštabarrû salîmi & mûtânu. ag Š^t of ℶ of barû 4 (see *p* 186 *col* 1); § 85; AV 5634; Br 9543.

muštaxmeṭu D 97, 5 *etc.* ag Š^t of xamaṭu 2 (*q. v.*).

Maštuk & Maštuku (ZA vii 181) see Marduk.

maštaku abode, dwelling, chamber {Stätte, Wohnraum, Kammer}; Z^B *ad* ii 168 sanctuary {Heiligtum}; Lyon, *Sargon*, 81; *Manual*, 119. Asb x 72 maš-ta-ku ša-a-tu mu-šal-li-mu bêli-šu šu-u-ma (*i. e.* the bît-ridûti) Winckler, *Forsch.*, 252. V 35, 33—4 (ilâni) i-na ša-li-im-tim | i-na maš-ta-ke-šu-nu u-še-ši-ib (1 *sg*) šu-ba-at ṭu-ub libbi. KB iii (2) 90 ii 7 kummu darû maš-ta[-ku]; V 65 *b* 10 maš (so instead of the erroneous pa)-ta-ku la-li-e-šu (*cf var* maš-tak-ku, ZA iii 302, 10). IV^2 27 *b* 8—9 ardatu ina maš-ta-ki-ša (= DAMAL-A-NI) u-še-el-lu-u (*i. e.*, the seven evil spirits) make the girl rise up from her abode; 19 *b* 33—4, see maša'u. K 41 *b* 6 (end) ana maš-tak-ki-ja i-ru-ba-am (PSBA xvii 65 *foll*). 85, 4—30, 1 i 42 ki-iç-çi (*q. v.*) ellu ma-aš-ta-ku tak-ni-e (Ball, PSBA xi 320). II 57 *a-b* 11 AN-UD $^{(bu-ri-da)}$ AN-UD = ^{il} A-A (? malkatu?) ša maš-ta-ki (AV 5228); S^b 1 *R* v 14—15 see kiççu; V 38 *col* 2, 15; 41 *e-f* 15; Br 5488; 7808.

NOTE. — T. A. (Lo.) 15, 5 (Bezold, *Dipl*, 109) ma-aš-ta-ka i-na pa-ni favour?, but KB v 130 reads ba-aš-ta-ka.

maš(l)taktu *1.* D 86 i 10—11 GIŠ-LU-LU & GIŠ-KI-LAL = maš-tak-tum (*cf* mušixxu); II 45 *c-d* 14—15; AV 5229; Br 9811, 10731; BA ii 289 treasury {Schatzkammer}; Sarg *Khors* 162: 8 lion-colossusses each of 4610 talents mal-tak-ti erî nam-ri; also *Bull* 71; Sarg *Ann* 424 (BA iii 192—3 *rm* **: product {Produkt}); XIV 74; Pp ii 32; iv 110. Jäger; BA ii 290 restores II 16 *d* 47 *foll* maštaktum kaspi u maçarru xurûçi. Meissner-Rost, *Bît-xilâni*, 8 *rm* 2: *m* something like: Produkt, Machwerk, √šataku.

maštaktu *2.* K 4388 *a* i 11 maštaktu foll. by açarru & içç ur iṣṣûri.

maš(r, l)takal a plant used for magic purposes {eine für magische Zwecke verwendete Pflanze} §§ 51; 106; T^M 29 *rm* 2; PSBA iii ('81) 83; Jensen, ZA vii 179; BA i 168, 13 & 181 *rm* ** (on *p* 182) where much literature is given. Lehmann, i 159 *rm*: original form not known, etymology not yet determined. IV^2 57 *b* 9 bînu ^{šam} IN-NU-UŠ (= maštakal); 26 *b* 35—6 *cf* bînu. maš-ta-kal = ^{šam} IN-NU-UŠ; Z^B 44—5. DT 59 *R* 7—8 bi-nu mar-ta-kal; also K 4704 *R* 2—3 (Hr^L 111) & mašalu Q.

muš(l)tâlu decider {Entscheider} properly ag Q^t of שאל, BA i 278; Z^B 99, bel. ZK i 307; not שלה as G § 90. AV 5636. IV^2 26 *a* 28—9 be-lum muš-ta-lum (= ŠA-KUŠ-U) ma-lik mil-ki (*q. v.*) ša ilâni rabûti (id also *ll* 30 [Br 8049], 31, 32); 60 *a* 31 Šamaš muš-ta-a-lum la da-a-tim (*q. v.*); 48 *a* 26 $^{(il)}$ Marduk ab-kal (= NUN-ME) ilâni rabû muš-ta-lum; *cf* 7 *a* 12—3 $^{(ilat)}$ Iš-tar-šu muš-tal-tum ina a-xa-a-ti it-ta-ziz; I 35 *no* 2, Nabû is called *l* 4 (end) muš-ta-lu; Šalm. *Ob*, 12 Nusku called ilu mul-ta-lu (KB i 130—1; Scheil, *Šalm*, 86); Neb i 7 Neb mu-uš-ta-lam êxiz nî-mêqi (RP^2 v 113: the exalted; PSBA x 88: the mild; Flemming, *Neb*, 24—5, where a wrong etymology); I 65 *a* 4; Sm 1371 *O* 2 (NE 93) O Gilgameš rubû muš-ta-lu rab-bu ša nišê. ZA iv 10, 45 (K 3474 ii 29) da-a-a-na muš-ta-lum, the judge, the decider. *Rec. Trav.* xx (*p* 70. *no* xxxvii *col* 2, 8—9) mu-uš-ta-al uš(?)-ta-na-da-nu (√דין?)-šu-nu-ti. V 29 *a-b* 69 ZAG = muš-tal-ti (or çir-ri-ti?, AV 5627 muš-ri-ti; Br 6488); H 40, 220 ŠA (= LIB)-KUŠ-U (*i. e.* big ŠA) = muš-ṭa-lum; id also V 13 *c* 8—10.

muštamû. II 32 *a-b* 63 KA $^{(i-nim-du-ut-tu)}$ KA-KA-KA = mu-uš-ta-mu-u = a-ma-nu-u (62) talker {Schwätzer} ag Š^3 of אמה; § 104; ZA v 87 *rm*; AV 5637; Br 584.

muštîmu, *etc.* see šâmu (שים).

muštêmiqu used as *adj* & *noun*? suppliant {Fleher} √emequ. Neb mu-uš-te-mi-qu V 34 *a* 8 (KB iii, 2, 38); Sp II 265 *a* vii 5 il tab-ni-i-te bēli-šu (Strong, PSBA xvii 142 *fol* il-tab-ni i-te-en-šu) muš-te-mi-qu ša .....; *pl* muš-te-me-qu-te, ZA iv 232, 7.

muštēmeqūtu ardent prayer, sighing {Gebet, Flehen} ZA v 59, 12 i-giš muš-te-me-qu-ti (draw nigh to my ardent prayer).

maštenū. K 4174 + 4583 iii 17 maš-te-nu-u evidently some plant. M^{8} *Texts*, *p* 8.

muštepištu = epištu witch {Hexe} √ epe-šu bewitch {behexen}. T^{M} 15 note 1; 157. IV^{2} 49 *b* 42 muš-te-piš-tu te-pu-ša-an-ni *etc.*; *a* 74 e-piš-ja u muš-te-piš-ti-ja; ZK ii 34 *fol.*

muštarū Merod.-Balad. ii 8 muš-ta-ru-u Sippar, Nippur u Bābili (; *ag* Š^{1} of arū who leadeth right {der rechtleitet}).

muštarrixu, muš(l)tarxu (*q. v.*) √ ša-raxu. powerful {gewaltig, mächtig}. GGN '80, 510 *rm* 1; AV 5478, 5638; K 4386 ii 57 (II 48 *c-f* 47) EME-XA-MUN-DI-DI (si-lim-sa) = muš-tar-ri-xu (Br 853; ZK ii 347); K 2852 + K 9662 ii 26 ja-a-ti .... mul-tar-xu (Winckler, *Forsch.*, ii 34—5). V 66 *a* 17 (end) muš-tar-xu (see Oppert, *Mélanges Rénier*, 220 *fol.*, Hommel, *Gesch.*, 792—4; PSBA vi 182; ZK ii 233). Neb ix 48; I 51 *no* 2, *a* 8 Marduk bēlu rabū ... mu-uš (*var* muš)-ta-ar(*var* -tar)-xu; ZA iv 107, 2 ilu .... mu-uš-ta-ar-xa (& *cf* KB iii, 2, 2—3 Marduk *m* = dem hehren); Anp i 15, 40; iii 116. TP v 66 ka-liš mul-tar-xi all those who deemed themselves powerful.

muštaškin see šakanu.

muštešmi Xammurabi (KB iii, 1, 222 *col* i 4) AV 5642, see šemū.

muštēšeru (*ag* Š^{1} of ešeru, ישׁר) ruler, leader {Regierer, Leiter}. TP i 1 ^{il} Ašur muš-te-šir kiššat ilāni; Šalm, *Mon*, *O* 3 $^{(il)}$ Šamaš muš-te-šir tēnišēti. Sm 949 *O* 7 $^{(il)}$ Šamaš muš-te-eš-še-ru te-ni-še-e-ti; ZA iv 10, 42 muš-te-še-ru; 8, 32 muš-te-šir (13, 5); II 67, 85 *cf* mīšaru; Sp III 586 + Rm III 1, 12 muš-te-šir-ša at-ta its director art thou. K^{M} *no* 12, 20 (end) muš-te-eš-ru nārē^{pl}. AV 5641. IV^{2} 29* *no* 5 (K 101 *R* = H 105—6) 1—2 e-la ka-a-ti i-lim muš-te-še-ru (= SI-DI) ul i-ši. V 46 *b* 32 $^{(il)}$ muš-te-šir si-lim = AN-XI-UR (ZA i 259 *rm* 1); *var* to I 49 i 5—6 $^{(il)}$ Marduk muš-te-šir kāl gim-ri; *f.* K 4931 *O* 9—10 Ištar muš-te-šir-rat (SI-DI) gi-mir nab-ni-tu (H 116); *cf* Z^{B} 83—51; Sayce, *Hibb. Lect.*, 336; 521—2; Hommel, VK 318—9; J^{1-N} 58—9. — *b*) caretaker, provider {Versorger} Sarg *Cyl* 70 Ēa mu-uš (*var* muš)-te-šir naq-bi-šu (*q. v.*); *bull* inscr. 88; Neb *Babyl*, i 4 Neb mu-uš-te-ši-ir ašrūti ^{il} Nabū.

muštatallu Br 10713 *ad* II 47 *c-d* 22 AN-LU-BAD 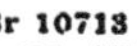 = muš-ta-tal-lu, AV 5639; Lotz, *Quaestiones*, 31: muš-ta-ri-lu, name of a star.

mati, mat (> matū > matai, § 62, 1) *adv* when? {wann?} **adi mat(i)** = until when, how long? {bis wann, wie lange?} §§ 41, 78; H^{P} 15. = עַד־מָתַי. T. A. (Ber.) 58, 38 a-di ma-ti how long? V 47 *b* 6 (end) a-xu-la-ja = a-di ma-ti (Z^{B} 18; 116); Br 10302. IV^{2} 20*$^{+}$ *no* 5 (= H 105) *R* 7—8 a-di ma-ti (= ME-EN-NA EMESAL) be-el-ti suxxuru pāniki ‖ 6 a-xu-lap-ja (= axulāpia, PSBA xix 315); perh. 10 *b* 21—22 ME-EN-NA = a-di-ma-ti(-i?) Br 10407; ME-EN-NA also *ll* 23, 25, 27. (Z^{B} 30, 72, 75); 18 *no* 2 *O* 13—14 ^{il} A-nim .... ma-ti (= ME-NA-KU, Br 10392) nu-ux liq-bi-ka; 15/16, 17/18 (ME-NA = ma-ti), also 19/20, 21/22, 23/24 (ZK i 208); *ibid*, *R* only nu-ux liq-bi(u)-ka. K 5157, 8—+ *foll* ME-NA-KU = a-di ma-tim (nine times); Z^{B} 28; H 181 *no* xii; H^{CV} 38. IV^{2} 23 *no* 1 26—7 a-di-ma-ti (= LI, Br 1100); 28/29; 30/31 (end) a-di mat (= LI-KU EMESAL); 19 *no* 3, 33—34 a-di ma-tim, Z^{B} 75. Often amplified by -ma:

matēma, matīma (AV 5230), *adv indef* whenever {wann nur immer} §§ 30, 78, 79. I 7 F 23 ma-ti-ma; Br. Mu. 84, 2—11, 103, 23; often in *c. t.* (T^{C} 99); II 9 *c-d* 51 šum-ma ma-ti-ma (Br 7050); 81—6—7, 209, 86 ma-ti-ma ina ax-rat ūmē (L^{2} 49; S^{3} 77; L^{2} 22; P^{1} 25; *cf* Lehmann, ii 86). TP viii 50—51 a-na ar-kat ū-um ça-a-te | a-na ma-te-ma. II 27, 58 *g* u-kur-šu | UD-KUR-KU | = a-na ma-ti-ma; *cf* II 48 *a-b* 12 (+ 13); ZK ii

90 *fol*; H^{F} 15; Br 7832; K 1282 *R* 26; V 25 *c-d* 4 (22 where is added a-na ar-ka-nu); KB iv 58 ii 12 ma-ti-ma a-na arkūt ūmē (HILPRECHT, *Assyriaca*, 14—15); III 46 *a* 13, 16 ina ma-te-me(& ma); *no* 3, 14 ina ur-kiš ina ma-te-e-ma; 41 *a* 31 ma-ti-ma i-na ar-kat ū-mi. T.A. Lo. 29, 59 ma-ti-mi; Ber 40 *R* 10 (-ma). — With following lā *etc.* = never {niemals} Asb viii 60 ma-te(*var* -ti)-e-ma . . . . la; SMITH, *Asurb*, 202 *f*.: ma-te-e-ma; 289, 48 ma-ti-ma. NE 67, 21 ul ib-ši Gilgameš ni-bi-ru ma-ti-ma, there never was a crossing (J$^{\mho}$ 86; J^{I-N} 30—1); Nabd 668, 18 aš-šu ma-ti-ma la; VATh 575, 5—6 ma-ti-ma u-ul aq-bi-qu-ma; — also contracted to immatēma (> in(a) matēma) with neg = never (ZA xi 352); NE 65, 26—9 im-ma-ti-ma (§ 73, AV 3739); K 2852 + K 9662 i 29 im-ma-te-ma-a tal-te-me didst thou ever hear? III 44 *no* iii 1; 48 iii 1 im-ma-ti-ma i-na ar-ka-ti ū-mi (ZK ii 16); I 70 ii 1; perh. 82—5—22, 90 *R* 5 im-ma-at sisē . . . . ir-rab-u-ni. T. A. Ber. 24, 17 u-ul . . . . im-ma-ti-i-me (*cf* 20), 28 and im]-ma-ti-i-me(& -e) at last; 49 (= continually); *R* 55, 56, 58; 21, 31 im-ma-ti-ma u-ul a-mur; Lo. 35, 14 im-ma-ti-i-me-e (as soon as).

mātu *1.* (AV 5238) *c. st.* ma-at (AV 5233) *f* land, country {Land, Landschaft}. *pl* mātāte(-i), §§ 30, 70 *b* id usually KUR (§§ 9, 176; 23, Br 7394; NE 67, 22; Behist. 23; TP i 22), prefixed also to names of countries; IV 31 *O* 1 a-na KUR-NU-GI-A = (māt lā târat); UN(= ka-lam)-MA Br 5010, 5014, *etc.*; § 62, 2: entirely unknown as to its original form; ZDMG 23, 857; 37, 757. S^{a} v 15 ma-at = ku-u-ru (see kūru, 5); H 5, 148. TP i 59 eli māt ^{il} Ašur ma-a-ta eli ni-šē-ša nišē lu-rad-di (vii 31); vii 25 i-na KUR-ti-ja (*cf* i 88, iv 38; iii 9—10); i 48 KUR-ti-šu-nu. II 38 *c-d* 11 pāṭu (*q.v.*) ma-a-ti; ZA iv 8, 45 + 46 (-tum); Esh iv 26 (see ṭibu & × WINCKLER, *Forsch.*, ii 9 *rm* 1), *Sendsch*, 34 ma-a-tu (= people); Neb *Senk*, i 9 ma-a-ti u ni-ši land and people; V 65 *b* 42 ma-ti-ja; 66 *a* 25 ma-a-ti a-a-bi-ja; I 67 *a* 12 see gamalu; D 93, 2 *cf* zakaru, Q *b*. *del* 100 (end) ma-a-tum; K 2852 + K 9662 iii 5 (end) ša eli e-ri-bi ma-a-tum; 81—6—7, 209, 41 (end); K 3474 i 45 (end) ilāni ma-a-ti; 46 namuratka ezzitu ma-a-tum sap-xat; 47 [ina] nap-xar mātāti (*cf l* 88); H 78, 27 nap-xar ma-a-ti (IV^{2} 9 *a* 27); Sp II 265 *a* xvii 4 ma-ta . . . . šu-um-[qu-tu?]. Sn ii 29 ma-a-ti my land; K 5157, 22 māt-ka; 24 ma-at-ka (H 181, xii); 26 ni-ši ma-ti-ka; Sn iii 26 māt-su (§ 51, also D 98, 27), 23 māti-šu; IV^{2} 48, 1 māt-su; māti-šu Cuthean Creat.-*frg* 24; *del* 197 a-na ma-ti-šu let him return; 174 KUR-šu (?); *Rec. Trav.* xx, 65 *foll* (*no* xxxv) 11 end [ma]-ti-šu (ZA xii 318); ZA v 144, 31 see kiçru, 1. Sn *Bav* 39 ma-tu-uš-šu-un into their land (§ 80 *e*); I 44, 54 e-diš ip-par-šid-du-ma ma-tu-uš-šu-un (= & escaped alone to their country). — IV^{2} 19 *a* 11—12 ina ali u ma-a-ti (= UN-MA), see S^{b} 247 ka-lam-ma | UN | = ma-a-tu, II 23, 462; same id also IV^{2} 12 *O* 19—20 māt-su; 1 iii 15—6 ma-a-ti ra-pa-aš-ti; 5 ii 71 (H 77, 40), 60 = KUR; 20 *no* 2, 7—8 a-na ma-a-ti; V 44 *a-b* 16 (= ma-a-ti) ZK ii 318. II 19 *b* 28—6 = ma-a-tum; K 4870, 39 a-na ma-a-ti; K 133 *O* 9—10; IV^{2} 11 *a* 1—2 (*cf* 3) ka-la ma-a-tim (= KA-NAG-GA EME-SAL) Br 596; *cf* ZK i 112 (refers to kingi); ZK i 172; IV^{2} 20 *no* 1 16 ib-tar-ra-a ni-ši ma-a-ti; 27 *b* 24—5 ša ma-a-tu(m) i-nar-[ru]-šu-nu (Z^{B} 83 *rm* 1). IV^{2} 29 *no* 1 *a* 9—10 (ma-a-ti be-el ma-ta-a-ti); 13 *b* 32—33 (ki-ma da-a-a-ni ma-ta-a-te šu-te-šir); IV^{2} 28, 1 *R* 7—8 ri-me-nu-u ša ma-ta-a-ti at[-ta], see below for other plurals. — KUR in *e. g.* IV^{2} 24 *no* 3, 13 ma-a-ta u ni-ši; 28 *no* 1, 9—10 KUR-KUR-RA = ma-ta-a-ti (*var* -te); *b* 5—6; S^{b} 302 see kūru 5; also perh. V 39 *a-b* 50; H 26, 552. III 59 *b* 31 = ma-at; V 52 *b* 39—40 = ina ma-a-tim; V 44 *c-d* 5 > (un) = bêl ma-a-ti; Lay 16, 43 ma-a-tu rapaš-tu (*q. v.*); K 3238 i. 13—14 ma-a-tum (= MA-DA, *q. v.*) ra-pa-aš-tum (H 181, x); S 954, 1—2 KI = ina ma-a-tim; H 31, 708 also IV^{2} 1* iv 9 + 11 mu-na-aš-šir ma-a-ti; 12 *a* 19—20 kiš-šat ma-a-ti; 83—1—18, 215, 14 . . . . . (māt) Bît-ma-at-ti. R. 2. 454, 23 *cf* dagalu; 27 ma-a-tum-me-e limid-da šada-a; K 2619 iv 15 ma-a-ta ma-a-ta. *Adapa*-legend 7 (= T. A., Ber., 240) šu-u-t]u a-na ma-a-ti u-ul izigga (+9); 23 i-na ma-a-ti-ni (*cf* 24); *R* 7+8; R. 2. 454+79, 7—8, 180 *R* 22 *cf* musarû, 1; 17 ib-ri nap-li-is ma-a-ti (20, ma-a-tum; 24 -tu), 18 ša ma-a-ti i-xa-am-pu (?). K 112 (Hr^{L}) *R* 6—7 i-sa-al ma-a i-na muxxi ša b(p)al-ku-te | ša ma-a-ti i-du-bu-ub (AJSL xiv 9); Sp III 586 + Rm III 1, 24 (il) Šamaš ša ma-a-ti da-i-nu (*cf* TSBA viii 167 *fol*). — IV^2 39 *a* 21 la-ur-ri u ma-ta-ti-šu-nu, *l* 7 KUR-KUR(*var* ≻— *i. e. pl*-ending)-šu-nu; 40 *no* 1 *O col* 1, 7 KUR-KUR-RA = 8 KUR-KUR-MEŠ (Br 7394). V 35, 11 *b* kul-lat ma-ta-a-ta ka-li-ši-na. T^M i 51 ka-li-ši-na ma-ta-a-ti; ii 21 (end); *Dibbara*-legend (K 1282 *R*) 27 ma-ta-a-ti nap-xar-ši-na (may listen); II 29 *a-b* 62 DIM-KUR-KUR-RA = ri-kis ma-ta-a-ti (Br 2762). *pl* KUR-MEŠ *e. g.* IV^2 27 *a* 20 (*cf* 19); 1* *c* 30 (*var* ma-ta ....; 29 = KUR-KUR-RA) *cf ibid.*, 32+36; KUR-KUR. $Z^{Š}$ ii 132; iv 85; Šalm. *Ob*, 3, 7, 18, 72; V 53 *no* 3 (K 618) *R* 1 ša KUR-KUR dan-na-ti; Beh 7; TP i 10; V 69, 19—20 DAMAL-MEŠ (= rapšâti) | KUR-KUR Na-i-ri (ZK ii 355); II 50 *c-d* 4; KUR-KUR-MEŠ Šalm. *Mon, O* 11; *cf R* 83 ana mâtâti ša-ni-a-ti. TP vii 48; also KUR-KUR-ti (HILPRECHT, *Assyriaca*, 56 *rm*); iv 83, N.B 8; IV^2 2 *no* 2, 10; KB iii (1) 130—1 Samsu-iluna i 18 ma-ta-tim; JRAS '91, 400, 27 ma-ta-a-tum; K 2701 *a* 15 (-ti); ZA iv 13, 20; HILPRECHT, *OBI*, I *no* 41 (& 46) 1—2 a-na (il) Bêl | be-el ma-ti-a-ti; BANKS, *Diss*, 14, 1 *no* 4, 95 kab-tu be-el ma-ta-a-tu. Marduk (*q. v.*) is called bêl mâtâti. šar ma-a-a-ta-ti Cyr 175, 2 *etc.* title of king Cyrus = king of the world. — 81—11—3, 478 ii KI-EN-GI = ma-a-tum. (PSBA xviii 252); H 31, 712; — V 29 *c-f* 45 MA-DA (II 50, 46) = ma-a-tum; 46 MA-DA KI-IN-GI = ma-a-tum Šu-me-ri; 47 MA-DA-KI-IN-GI $\frac{BUR}{BUR}$-KI (HOMMEL, VK 19 AGADE) = mâtum Šu-me-ri u Ak-kad-i (H 25, 580; Br 6828 *fol*); H 40, 201 (Br 6825); 26, 551 (§ 9, 49); KB iii (2) 4—5 ii 3 di-ku-ut MA-DA-ja (AJP xi 496—7; ZA iv 100 *rm* 1); Neb ii 13+26 (KB iii, 2, 66—7 *ad* 12 *col* iii 39); IV^2 27 *no* 5, 6—7 MA-DA MA-DA-BI = ma-a-ta ana ma-a-ti; K 5157 *O* 25—6 (II 181 xii); K 3238 i 13—4;

II 30 *c-d* 4—15 ma-a-tum (*col d*) = 4, KUR (Br 7394); 5 KALAM (Br 5914); 6 XU-KA $^{EME-SAL}$ (Br 2055); 7, ŠI (Br 9275; S^c 3, 14); 8, KI Br 9630); 9, KI-IN-GI (Br 9678; *cf* V 62 *a-b* 40); 10, GI (Br 2394; H^F 51); 11, MA (Br 6774; S^c 98); 12, MA-DA (Br 6825); 13, TIK (Br 3216); 14, DAR (Br 3483); 15, SUX (Br 3017); II 47 *c-d* 26 TAG-DAR = abnu ma-a-tu; *e-f* 15 $^{(ra-bi-ta)}$ EDIN = ma-ta-a-ti (Br 4528). II 30 *g-h* 7 ma-tum e-li-tum (Br 9377: ŠI-NIM which also = elî-tu, E-lam-tum *etc.*) ≍ šaplîtu (Br 9403). *Cf* II 50 *R* 2—4. — ša mâtâte after names of officials designates these offices as imperial (Reichsämter) BA ii 136, 38. — mât (= KI) palê (but *cf* קבל), *m* nukurti, *m* nabalkatti *etc.* see these words. —

plain, valley {Ebene, Thal} ≍ šadû. *Del* 96 illakû guzalê šad-u u ma-a-tum (traversed mountain and dale); SCHEIL, *Nabd* ix 16 i-na i-pat (*cf* V 63 *b* 46 i-pa-at) ma-ti kal || xi-çi-ib šadê; also *cf* Sarg *Cyl* 72; *bull* inscr. 93.

NOTE. — 1. Asb ii 81 e-me-du KUR-šu = mâti-šu, KB ii 172—3; see, however, WINCKLER, *Forsch.*, i 105, 246, 261 *rm* 3. — Sn ii 37; Synchr. Hist. II 30: V 64, 40—41.

2. V 16 *a-b* 13 SIG = ma-a-çu (*q. v.*): tum (≍ Z^B 93); preceded by (12) ša-du-u & foll. by E-lam-tum (14—6); Su-bar-tum (17—9). AV 5100; Br 11872; the ib SIG (= enšu *etc*), perhaps owing to a confusion with mâtu = die (*q. v.*).

3. T. A. (Ber.) 8, 3 ma-t[i-ja]; 7 *R* 31 ina ma-ti-ka ša ma-at ki-iç-ri; *O* 22 ma-tum ru-ga-at (the land is far off); 73, 10 a-na (mât) ma-su; 9 *R* 10 ma-ta-tum ru-qa-tum; — in Lo. written ma-ti (1, 94); ma-a-ti (1, 91); ma-ti-ka (3, 6 & Ber. 2, 5); KUR & KUR-KI-šu (49, 17); KUR-ti-šu (9, 35); KUR-i-šu (7, 7); *pl* (mât) ma-ta-ti (20, 7); KUR-MEŠ (12, 10) KUR-KUR-MEŠ (45, 12); KUR-KUR (10, 13); KUR-XI-A (17, 32); KUR-KUR-XI-A (14, 18); KUR-KUR-KI (12, 35); KUR-MEŠ-KI (24, 47); KUR-KUR-MEŠ-KI (12, 31); KUR-KUR-KI-MEŠ (14, 2); KUR-KI-XI-A (17, 11) *etc.* — Der.:

mâtitan (or -ân?) totality of the country (-ies); all countries {Gesammtheit aller Länder, alle Lande} § 80*d*. Sarg *Ann* 428 tenêšêti (*Khors* 165 dadmê, 177 malkê) ma-ti-tan. Smith, *Asurb*, 138, 88 a-na ta-mar-ti ma-ti-tan throughout the land (KB ii 258—9); Neb viii 26 ki-ir-bi ma-ti-ta-an in all countries; IV² 60* B *O* 10 a-a-i-te ep-še-e-ti ša-na-a-ti ma-ti-tan; V 63 *b* 48 xi-çi-ib ša-di-i u ma-ti-ta-an; 65 *b* 41 bu-še-e ma-ti-tan (ZK ii 351 *rm* 1).

ma-a-at-ta *etc.*; T. A. *cf* ma'du, mâdu.

mâtu 2. (מות) pr imût (*pl* imûtû §§ 27; 31); ps imât; pm mêt, mit die {sterben}, §§ 114 *foll*; AV 5230. II 83, 39 see mixçu & Br 4388; 80, 22 (& K 567, 13) see bûbûtu; 80, 27 (*cf* kibru); 28 ša ina çi-rim u çu-çi-e i-mu-ut ([cuneiform]-GA) Z^B 77. IV² 60* *C* 10 *cf* balaṭu Q pr & add II 194 *no* 179 (§ 150). K 522, 9 i-mu-tu (*cf l* 13); K 96, 17 ina ku-uç-çu i-mut-tu (they die of cold) AV 4585; Jensen, 51; 495; — IV² 59 *no* 1 see ba-laṭu Q pc; II 40 *a-b* 56 a stone called šag-gi li-mut; K 2527 + K 1547 *O* 29 see bûbûtu *a*) end; also *R* 29 (i-mu-ut); K 2660 (= III 38, 2) *R* 5 (end) lu-mut-tam-ma I will die. — ia-mu-tu K 181 *O* 29 *etc.*, see ja-mu-tu (*p* 360 *col* 2) where read Johns & add JAOS xx 250. — NE 59, 3 a-na-ku a-mat-ma ul (I will not die) J^W 82 *foll*; J^{I-K} 28 *foll.* K 517, 26 ina çu-um-me-e la ni-ma-ta; II 16 *f* 42 *foll* see balaṭu Q ps (& BA i 462; ii 305; Hommel, *Sum. Lesest.*, 119; Br 4388; 6122). K 1282 *R* 18 (= *Dibbara*-legend) ul i-ma-ti ina šib-ṭi (BA ii 433); K 646, 21 man-ma ul i-mit-ti; K 31 *R* 20 anâku ina çu-mi ša mê a-ma-a-tu. V 31 *a-b* 60 see kabatu (Br 1517); Strassm., *Liverpool*, 8, 16 ina paṭri parzilli ta-ma-a-tu (= 3 *f sg*) ZA iii 78; BA iv 7 she shall be killed with a dagger. — K 81, 12 ša mi-i-tu a-na-ku because I was dead {weil ich tot war} BA i 198; K 509, 19; Beh 37 (he died); K 79, 10; 81, 2—4, 65, 1 šarru mi-e-ti is dead. K 533, 4—5 mi-tu-u-ni ištu libbišunu | mi-e-tu. Cyr 292, 15 *L* son of *Š* mi-ti. K 11, 22—3: ma-a abu-u-a | lu me-e-ti; *ibid* 15 (AV 5378). — Q^t = Q Sn v 2 Ku-durnaxundi .... ur-ru-xiš im-tu-ut died suddenly. V 25 *c-d* 16 (*cf* xalaqu & maraçu 2, Q^t; Br 1517). Nabd-Ann ii 14 the king's mother im-tu-ut (BA ii 237—8; KB iii, 2, 130); Beh 17 after this Cambyses mi-tu-tu ra-man-ni-šu mi-i-ti (committed suicide) § 55*c*; *ac* Asb iii 6 I, Ištar mi-tu-tu Ax-še-e-ri (the killing of *A*) .... eppuš (BA ii 295); iv 56 ša mi-tu-tu ip-la-xu, who were afraid to die (ZK ii 281). — Q^{tn} K 196 *R* iii 7 the owners of the house im-ta-nu-ut-tu shall die (Pinches, *Texts*, 13). — ŠJ deliver to death, kill, murder {dem Tod überliefern, töten, morden} Z^B 31. IV² 30 *no* 1, *b* 11—12 atûda ..... ina ša-di-i ta-na-ar u tuš-mit (Jensen, 330); Banks, *Diss*, 1 *no* 4, 27 (end) ina šu-uk-li-šu uš-ma-a-at; 18 *no* 2 (8—10); 25 uš-ma-at. *Rec. Trav.* xx 57 *foll* (*no* vii 12) a-na mi-nam tu-uš-mat-ma. Nabd-Ann iii 23 ušmâ-at (Prince, *Diss*, 90; but KB iii, 2, 134 mita-at); K 8571 *O* 10 çal-mat qaqqa-du a-na šu-mut-ti. *Dibbara*-legend iii 21 see xarabu 1; i 20 (K 2619) çi-ix-ru u ra-ba-a iš-te-niš šu-mit-ma (kill {töte}!); H 77, 84 the seven evil spirits .... muš-mi-tu-ti (*var* mi-tu-tu) la a-di-ru-ti šu-nu (= IV² 5 *b* 64—5); V 46 *a-b* 41 MUL-LU-BAD = muš-mit bu-lim (murderer of cattle); S^c 1 *b* 26 muš-mi [-tu?], Jensen, 95 *fol*, D 93, 6. Rm 239, 17 uš-mi-it. — Š^t tuš-ta-mat KB vi, 1, 65 *col* 3, 16—17; 23 *foll.*

Note. — T. A. Ber. 46, 50 If therefore he remains upon his journey and dies (i-nu-ma i(a)-mu-ta); 9 *R* 24 li-mu-ut; 104, 59—60 BA-BAD = ni-mu-tum that we may die (ZA vi 260 *rm* 1); — 22 *R* 28 ul i-ma-a-at (if he does not die); 9 *R* 20 i-na çi-ti i-ma-at-tum so that they die in foreign lands (also // 26; 36) KB v 30—1; 92, 38 by command of the king da-ma-at thou shalt die. — 24, 62 la-a mi-i-it *N*: *N* is not dead, *cf* 58 a-na-ku-ma lu-u mi-i-it (if only I had died); 9 *R* 14 mi-tum (3 *pl*, *m*); 58, 128 mi-ta-tu (and when) I die; 44, 17 šum-ma mi-ta-ti but if I die; 58, 65 BAD: mi-it; 44, 20; 43, 22 (*pl*) mi-it! Lo. 5, 31 (3 *sg*, *m*) + 39 (3 *sg*, *f*); *f* ma-a-ta-at (Lo. 6, 61), ma-'a-ta-at (8, 63), mi-ta-at (1, 14 + 48); me-ja-te (43, 5; = 1 *sg*), *cf* ZA v 19; BA-BAD Lo. 28, 53; 50, 52 *etc.* — 21, 31 ima-at? — J Ber. 219 *R* 12 and you ti-mi-tu-na-nu (give us death); ŠJ Ber. 39, 7 u at-ta du-uš-mi-it-an-ni and you give me death. — Derr.:

mûtu *m* death {Tod} §§ 31; 64; AV 5661; Br 1519; 2132. Šalm. *Ob*, 152 mu-ut šimti-šu il-lik and he went to death of his own choice? (Hommel, *Gesch.*, 676 *rm* 2), *cf* Asb ii 21; iii 124 mu-u-tu lim-nu a-šar-raq-šu-nu-ti. NE 58, 18 iz-za-nun mu-u-tu; 59, 5 mu-ta ap-lax (-ma); 60, 7 (end) im-rat-su-nu mu-tu; 61, 5 mu-ta u TI-LA (= balaṭa); also 66, 38 (see balāṭu), 39 ša mu-ti ul ud-du-u ūmē-šu (ZK ii 342); 66, 34 ša mu-ti ul iç-çi-ru çal-mi (so long no picture is drawn of death); 67, 25 (*cf* barū, 6) + 27; 69, 50; 70, 8 A-MEŠ (= mē) mu-ti & mu-u-ti the waters of death. (Jensen, 214 ocean); *Adapa*-legend *O* 29 me-e mu-u-ti (BA ii 418 *foll*: "here not = Ocean"); 28 a-ka-la ša mu-ti; Hymn to Ninib, 24: ki-ma mu-ti li-duk-ka-ma (Abel & Winckler, *Texte*, 60 *fol*; Hommel, *Sum. Les.*, 123—4); IV^2 3 *a* 26 (end) it-ti mu-u-ti (Br 1519) ra-kis is bound unto death. Sp II 265 *a* ii 5 (end) il-la-ku u-ru-ux mu-u-t[e]; *cf* Sarg *Khors* 118 (-ti); *Ann* 403 (mu-ti); II 120 *R* 8 nap-lu-us mu-tim-ma (Br 1517); Cuthean Creat.-*frg* iii 3 šu-lum-mat ni-ši mu-ši mu-u-tu (ZA xii 321 *fol*) *del* 223 šu-u mu-tum-ma that means death (NE 145, 246); 222 ina bīt ma-a-li-[a] a-šib mu-u-tum. I 67 *a* 27 (end) i-za-an-nu (*q. v.*) i-ma-at mu-u-ti (fear of death); Sarg *Cyl* 29 is-lu-xa i-mat mu-u-ti; *Ann* 338. K 2061 ii 18 (= H 203) mu-u-tum, same id in H 18, 300 = mi-i-tum (Br 4389); V 30 *g-h* 36 É-KUR-BAD = bīt mu-ti (H 23, 467; *ibid* 66 = naqbaru, Br 6259); 37 *cf* Br 1519; H 215, 85 *foll*; V 16 *e-f* 42 E-KUR$^{(a-ra-li)}$-BAD = mi-i-tum (Br 1518, 6257, 6261; AV 5384; KAT^2 610); J^w 63 *no* 10; Jensen, 220. — II 50 *d-e* 10 $^{(11)}$ mu-ti (?) ZA i 185—6; or MU-TI? (*cf l* 11).

mūtānu death, pestilence {Tod, Seuche, Pest}. § 64; AV 5651; Z^B 93; Hommel, *Gesch.*, 643 *rm*; AJP viii 266 *rm* 4; ZA v 117. — Planet Mars is called V 46 *a-b* 42 MUL-NI (= ZAL) ⟼ (Bertin, JRAS xviii 410: mut)-a-nu = muš-tab-bar-ru-u (*q. v.*) mu-ta-nu (see barū, 4; Br 1519; BO i 208; D 8 *no* 42); III 60, 113 (Jensen, 479); III 53 *a* 32; II 49 *no* 3, 33, Schell, *Rec. Trav.*, xvii 178—9, 27 (end) Dibbar-ra mu-ta-ni. Often in Eponym canon mu-ta-nu (KB i 208—9 *ad* 803; 210—11 *ad* 765, 759; II 52 *a-b* 5); II 36 *a-b* 5 NAM-BAD = mu-ta-nu (Br 1510); T. A. (Ber.) 6, 14 i-na] mu-ta-ni mi-ta[-at] died of the plague; 82, 10 mu-ta-nu (there was a plague in Simyra); 12 (mu-ta-nu-u), 14; 115, 32 amīlt i-na mu-ta-a-an; that I shall die the death?

mītu, mētu *adj* dead {tot, toter} *pl* mi-tu-ta-an (V 35, 9) in collective sense, § 80 *d*; see bulluṭu ℷ and balṭu, xar-bidu; §§ 9, 10 id; 64; Br 4390. Cyr 292, 1—2 $^{(amēl)}$ çābē xal-qu-tu u | mītu-u-tu; also *ll* 19, 21; Nabd 208, 2 mit-tu (?); 1130, 10 mi-tu-tu (a *pl*), mit-tu-tu (*l* 1). *Etana*-legend *O* 17 ri[-mu mi-i-tu]; IV 31 *R* 58 mītūte (written BA-BAD-MEŠ) li-lu-nim-ma, ZA vi 260; xii 395. Z^K iii 135 ma-mit $^{(amēl)}$ BAD u $^{(amēl)}$ balṭi (iv 78); K 4870, 33 (mi-tu-ti, *var* -tu); K 684, 37 mi-i-tu. V 16 *c-d* 74 TA ... = mi-i-tum = di-i-ku (75) Br 14044; AV 5384; Br 10688 *ad* II 50 *c-d* 31; V 52 iv 7.

mittu corpse {Leichnam} V 31 *c-d* 38 na-bu-ul-tu mi-it-ti LU (or ṬU?)-NU-UP (= AR?) $^{xi-bi}$, 39 nu-ul-tum = mi-it-tum, AV 5403.

mītūtu condition of death, being dead {Zustand des Totseins} AV 5386; § 64. Asb vii 33 *cf* xašaxu; vii 46 eli ša maxri (*q. v.*) mi-tu-us-su ut-ter. J^w 57 *rm* 1; KB ii 212—8. Cyr 332, 8 ar-ki mītu-u-tu ša Nūr-Šamaš; Nabd 1113, 28 ar-ki mi-tu-tu ša Nabū-axē-iddin (JA '87 x 538); Neb 346, 9 pūt(būd) mi-tu-tu in case of death (of the slave); also Nabd 1048, 5. IV^2 20 *no* 1, 1—2 ki-ma mi-tu-ut (Br 4390); 30 *no* 2 *a* 24—5 ana erçi-tim mi-tu-ti; 60* C *R* 17 a-di la mi-tu-ti-i-ma without finding death (§ 53*d*).

mutu *m* man, especially husband, consort {Mann, namentl. Ehemann, Gemahl} §§ 27; 62, 2; Z^B 49; H 7, 222; 35, 835; AV 5062; Br 11113. *Dibbara*-legend (K 2619) i 7 see manū 1 (Q. NE 42, 9 at-ta lu mu-ti-ma be thou my husband (§ 56 *a*); Bu 88—5—12, 21, 37 u ši-na (and they) a-na *A. Š.* mu-ti-ši-na, 38 u-ul mu-ut-ni at-ta i-qa-bi-i-ma (Meissner, *no* 89);

me-tu AV 5363 *ad* Asb iii 110 see metuqu. — mat-ti-ia-nu AV 4814 *cf* tibnu.

Bu 91—5—9, 2, 474, 7 Sin-na-çir mu-ti (husband of) *A.* KB iv 320—1 *col* iv 1—4 šumma | aš-ša-ta mu-us-su (= DAM-NA) i-zi-ir-ma | ul mu-ti at-ta, *etc.* (= V 25 *a-b* 1—4); 8—9 šumma mu-tu (DAM-E) a-na aššatišu (= V 25 *a-b* 8—9); 322—3 iv 9 a woman whose dowry mu-ut-su il-qu-u, 11—2 u mu-ut-sa ši-im-ti | ub-lu ina nikkasi ša mu-ti-šu *etc.*; 15 šumma mu-ut-su ši-riq-tum | iš-[ša]-raq-šu. V 25 *c-d* 3—4 mu-tu lib-bi-šu. H 89, 30 ardat lilî (*q. v.*) ša mu-ta la i-šu-u; II 35 *g-h* 68—71 ardatu ša ina su-un mu-ti-ša (& 66—7) çu-bat-sa la iš-xu-ṭu. Sp II 265 *a* vii 3 *cf* zikru 2. IV^{2} 28* *b* 48 ša mu-us-sa (= DAM) çi-ix-ru mu-ti-ma i-qab-bi; 35 *a* 27 P. N. Mu-tum-ilu (= מתושאל), also Mu-ut-ilu (Strassm., *Warka*, 38, 31). KB iv 46 i 1 P. N. ^{sal}Mu-ti-ba-aš-ti (see baštu); Nabd 356, 23 mu-ta-a šîmtum ûbil fate (*i. e.* death) took away my husband (5 mu-ti-ja); 375, 9 mu-ti-šu. Cyr 332, 9—10 ša *N* .... Tab-ba-ni-e-a mu-ti-šu ar-ku-u (her later husband); ZA iii 366, 6 mu-ti-šu maxrû. II 32 *c-d* 14 mu-tu ‖ zi-ka-ru, a-ja-lum (15), a-ra-du (16); also S 2052 iii/iv 41 mu]-tu = qar-ra-du (BA iii 276—7); V 12, 3 & 4 DAM = mu-tum, preceded by MU-TIN = zi-ka-rum; AV 5656, § 56 *a.* II 32 *no* 5 (AV 2276, 5628; Br 10937) SAL $^{mu-us-sa}$UD-DA = e-mu (?) çi[-ix-ru] ZA i 394. — T. A. (Lo.) 82, 34 at-ta lu mu-ti-ma; 11 (+ Murch) 8 *M.* mu-ti-i-ka; + 9; + 11 mu-ti-i-ki; + 13; 21 mu-ti; 36, 36 LU-GAL-MEŠ mu-te-MEŠ-šu (?; KB v 28* suggests = מתים priests). Ber. 70 *O* 75 *cf* mašalu; 24, 68 *N* mu-ti-šu. — *abstr noun:*

mutûtum. AV 5663. II 32 *c-d* 7—8 mu-tu-tum & mu-tu-a-tum ‖ me .... preceded by ‖ of ed[lûtum]. Bu 91—5—9, 407, 5 a-na aš-šu-tim u mu-tu-tim | i-di-in (JRAS, '99, 106—7); Bu 91—5—9, 366, 5—6 . . . i-di-ši (JRAS, '97, 605 *fol*).

muttu, properly fronthead, then front (in general) {Stirn, dann Vorderseite, Front} II 36 *e-f* 64 DUB-SAG-GA = mu-ut-tum (Br 3939) in one group with qud-mu (63), rêšu (62), max-ru (65), AV 5674. I 67 *b* 21 a-na mu-ut-tam kišâd $^{(nâr)}$ Puratti fronting the bank of the Euphrates river (AJP xi 501); BA iv 84—5 says: muttu, muttatu in family-laws only: das das Antlitz, die Schläfe umrahmende Haupthaar. Ball, PSBA xii 55, 80, following H^{F} 73 *etc.* hair {Haar}. Derr. these 2:

muttiš, *adv* properly: on or at the front; then with foll *gen*, construed as preposition = before (‖ adi, ana maxar, *etc.*) {eigtl.: in Front; dann mit folg. *gen* als Preposition construiert = vor *etc.*}. Creat.-*frg* III 131 the gods i-ru-bu-ma mut-ti-iš AN-ŠAR (= before *A.*); also II 69 (79, 7—8, 178, 4 . . . mut-tiš ti-âmat i-zix-za at-ta). Rm 2, 200 *a* 3 mu-ut-ti-iš.

muttatu *a*) fronthead, esp. frontlock? {Stirne, namentl. Stirnlocke?} (>< BA 15 *no* 14), see galabu. AV 5673; K 4580, 4—5 gul-lu-bu ša mut-ta-ti (Br 9862); King, *First Steps in Assyrian, ad* V 25 *c-d* 31: his face they shall brand (Br 5039). — *b*) frontside, front {Vorderseite, Front} Nabd 349, 2 so & so many shekels ..... | a-na mu-ut-ta-tum (*cf* 284, 10, end) | ša kib-su a-na | išparê iddin. AJSL xv 79: kibsu here a generic term for "band", of which *m* represents a particular species; *cf* 81, 11—28, 33 *l* 15 ištên mut-ta-tum ša ta-bar-ri one Chaplet of light-purple wool. See also BA i 513; 521. III 65 *a* 18 mut-ta-at mâti: face of the globe; II 27 *e-f* 3 mut-ta-at mu-ši (followed by šat mu-ši); II 61 *b* 55—6 [cuneiform] mut-ta-at šadi-i i-tab-bal, mut-ta-at ^{mât}BAB (= nukur)-tum. S^{b} 1 *R* iv 16 (D 66) ki-ši | [cuneiform] | mut-ta-tum (Br 9861; H^{F} 73) *cf* II 27 *e-f* 4; Hommel, *Sum. Les.*, 30, 365; V 38 *O* 2, 16 = ri-eš-tum; 37 *d-f* 46 ba-a | [cuneiform] | mut-ta-tum (Br 9986; Ball, PSBA xii 214: hair, whiskers??).

$^{(amêl)}$ **MU-u-tu** *e. g.* Cyr 248, 7 *fol.* BA iii 420—1 perh. = puçammu-u-tu, others = b(p)urgul(l)u-u-tu (*q. v.*); Peiser, KAS 74 (ix 1); *Babyl. Vertr.*, xxiii, 1 reads $^{(amêl)}$ mu-u-tu (as BO i 83, 3; ii 119, 7) an officer, *cf* Dar 5, 8. But Zimmern, ZDMG 53, 115—6 has $^{(amêl)}$ MU = baker {Bäcker} = nuxatimmu (*q. v.*).

matû 83, 1—18, 1335 ii 41 ku-rum | TAR |

ma-tu-u; Br 10098 has II 8 *a-b* 27 KA-BA-LAL = ša pi-šu ma-tu[-u] ZA i 177; *cf* maṭû & AV 5240. Perhaps Camb 126, 7: 2 manê ŠIM-LI (= riqqê) a-na ma-te-e ša kiçru. — ℑ ac muttû V 16 *g-h* 26—7 ŠA-BA-GI = mu-ut-tu-u (AV 5674; Br 11096, 7058); also 83, 1—18, 1335 iv 19.

mutta'idu lofty, high {erhaben, hoch} *etc.* √טאו *e. g.* Creat.-*frg* IV 125 a-a-bu mut-ta-'i-du, JENSEN, 286: the terrible adversary. IV 30, 28 ab-nu mut-ta-'i-di ta-bu-ut (Br 4729); ZDMG 27, 698.

mute'imu & muta'imu ruler {Herrscher, Gebieter} ‖ šarru. √ta'amu BEZOLD, *Achaem*, 56. Dar. inscr. vii *O* 10—11 see maxrû *pl*; D 5 ina mu-te-'-e-me ma-du-u-tu; E 7 *fol* iš-ten mu-te-'-e-[me?]-'e; F 11 ina mu-ta-'i-i-me-e max-ru-tu ište-en.

mu-ti-ib for muṭîb, *cf* ṭâbu, 1. (AV 5655).

mitbaku (?) see midbaku.

muttabbilu √abalu ‖ muttarû (*q. v.*); §§ 53; 67*b*; ZA i 403 lit^y: governing. IV^2 14 *no* 3, 7—8 Nebo mut-ta-bel qân nin-da-na-ki; TP i 15 the great gods mu-ut-tab-bi-lu-ut šamê erçiti guardians of heaven and earth (KB i 16—17; AV 5665); Sn i 32 mut-tab-bi-lu-tu (or -ut) êkallu-uš the guardians of his palace (HEBR. vii 59); also *Bell* 9. Asb vi 19 u-nu-tu mut-tab-bil-ti (*var* -tu) êkallâte-šu ka-la-mu (KB ii 204—5). IV^2 58*d* 32 mut-ta-bi-lat mârat [Anim]. II 22*a-b* 16 GIŠ-SA $\frac{\text{DU DU}}{\text{DU DU}}$ = mut-tab-bil-tum ‖ še-e-tum (Br 3124; AV 5666). NE 49, 198—9 Gilgameš a-na mut-tab-pi (*var* tib-pi; tab-bi)-la-ti (*var* car.) ša .... | a-ma-ta i-zak-ra (to the princesses {zu den Fürstinnen}); perhaps V 19 *c-d* 22 *fol* AG-A-KA-GA = mut]-tab-bil-tum foll. by *m* ša ka-la-mu.

mut-tab(p)-ri-tum H 129 (K 257) *R* 16 read muddapritum (*cf* daparu) or muttabrîtum (*cf* barû? fill {füllen}); Br 4611; ZK i 97 *rm*; ZA i 65.

matgigu (?). Esh A vi 6 ṣi-el-lu mat-gi-gu kîma AN-TAR-AN-NA (JENSEN, *Theol. Litztg.* '99 *no* 2: milky way) uš-na-xira gimir bâbâ-ni. BA iii 214 √magagu = maqaqu (?).

mat-gi-ru *cf* kurgîru.

mitgâru *adj* (√magaru) favorable {günstig} *etc.* Esh v 27 ina arxu šêmê û-mu mit-ga-ri a day when prayers are listened to; Sn vi 41; also Sarg *Bull* 50. K 2801 (+K 221 + K 2669) *R* 15 ši-pir te-diš-ti it-ti a-me-lu-ti la še-me-ti la mit-gar-ti.

mitgurtu agreement {Uebereinstimmung} (√magaru). PEISER, KAS 24—5; ZA iii 367, 5; AV 5387. KB iv 20, 46 i-na mi-it-gu-ur-ti-šu-nu is-ga-am (*cf* isqu) i-du-u-ma in mutual agreement they have fixed the income {in Übereinstimmung mit einander haben sie das Einkommen bestimmt}. Warka *c. t.* B 62, 24 mi-im-ma u-ul i-šu-u i-na mi-it-gu-ur-ti-šu-nu iš-du(= ṭu)-ru; 80, 225; 61, 13 i-ša-mu i-na mi-it-gur-ti-šu-nu; *cf* Dar 379, 2 ina mit-gur-ti-šu-nu. The kunuk tamgurti (II 40 *g-h* 52) is the result of the šaṭaru ina mitgurtišunu. V 31 *c-d* 54 KU-[cuneiform sign]-TI = la mit-gur-ti; 55 = la [cuneiform sign]-ti. KB iii (1) 158—9 *col* iii 16 i-na mi-it-gur-ti-šu.

muttag(g)išu (√nagašu, *q.v.*). II 44 *c-d* 5 (amêl) TIN = mut-tag-gi-šu (Br 9855; AV 5668), preceded by TIN = xa-a-a-ṭu = see, go around, inspect. Perhaps title of an officer in charge of tearing down buildings *etc.* (Sm 1034, 15 *foll*) BA i 617. — Z^B iii 83 ma-mit ....]^{MEŠ} mut-tag-gi-šu-ti (Bann durch eilende .... löst er).

mataxu stretch, extend, direct {strecken, ausdehnen, richten auf} *etc.* IV^2 61 *b* 28 see dagalu Q *a.* D^R 48; *Rev. Et. Juiv.*, x 305; D^{Pr} 66 *rm* 1; 177 & again *Rev. Et. Juiv.*, xiv 155. K 125, 15 i-ma-ta-xu-ni-e a-na (al) Bâbilu they took the road toward *B.* (Hr^L 196); K 556 *R* 10, 12 ma-a ki-i ša a-na-ku ina ra-me-ni-ja iš-qar a-ma-tax-u-ni; ma-a šu-u a-na ra-me-ni[-šu] li-in-tu-xu; also K 482 *R* 6 (Hr^L 178); S 1031, 10; 83—1—18, 14 *R* 14—5 šarru be-ili ina bur-ki-šu | li-in-tu-ux (AJSL xiv 179); K 4780 *R* 6 ûm 20 KAN kuzippi .... li-in-tu-ux (Hr^L 26). — Q^t V 53 *no* 3, 7 (K 618) šulmu ana piqitti ša bît ku-talli re-ši-šu in-ta-at-xa; K 556 *O* 9 in-ta-tax; also K 609 *R* 4 (in-ta-at-xu, Hr^L 126). — ℑ perhaps II 44 (*g*-)*h* 66 mut-tu[-xu?] together with ma-xa-ru & na-šu-u; iD ended in -GA (Br 14175). — 𒌑ṭ u-ma-a it-tan-ta-xa (not √מח) it-tax-kim šap-la (kakkab) narkabti *etc.* III 51 *no* 9 (K 480), 25; & it-ta-na-at-xu, Boissier, *Doc*, 40, 17.

muttaxalilum, mutaxlilu *etc.* see xalalu.

mu-tax-çi AV 5644 *ad* Anp i 107 = mun-daxçē, *cf* maxaçu Q[t].

mitxuçu *cf* maxaçu Q[t] = fight, battle {Kampf, Schlacht}. a ‖ is:

mitxuçūtu *e. g.* Smith, *Asurb*, 120 (KB ii 250—51) 25: I will not rest a-di al-la-ku it-ti-šu [ ] e-pu-šu mit-xu-çu-ti; perh. also Knudtzon, 41 *O* 4 mi]-tax-çu-tu li-pu-ši (or *pl* of mitxuçu?; see *ibid*, *p* 304)

mitxāru, *f* mitxartu agreeing, harmonizing, harmonious {übereinstimmend, harmonierend} §§ 65, 40; 77 "one" in the sense of "harmony", "agreed". *Rev. d'Assyr.*, ii 13—14; AV 5391 *ad* II 22 *c* 8 mit-xa-ru ‖ nu-us-xu ..... IV[2] 19 *a* 45—6 li-ša-nu mit-xar-ti (XA-MUN) ki-ma iš-tin šu-me tuš-te-šir (Br 11834). Jensen in Lehmann, ii 66: eine ein Ganzes bildende (organisch zusammenhängende) Sprache (*cf* ātmē lā mitxurti) ordnest du, als wenn es ein Wort wäre (✕ ZA iii 350); V 39 *a* 21 KA-XA-MUN = li-ša-ni m[it-xar-ti]. D 87 ii 53 (= II 48 *no* 4 *c-d* 37) ku-us-si mit-xar-ti (*var* -tum) Br 10345; 11160; *cf* Anp ii 54 ina mit-xar(or xur) sa-an-ti, AV 5389.

mitxu(a?)rtu *1.* ba'ulāt arba'i lišānu (*q. v.*) axītu at-mi(*var* -me) la mit-xa(u)r-ti people of different tongues {Völker fremder Sprachen} .... pa-a ištēn ušaškin Sarg *Cyl* 72; *Ann* XIV 86. Bu 88—5—12, 75 + 76 ii (= K 192 *O*) 10 ša xa-laq mit-xur-tim die Eintracht (*i. e.* das Zusammenwirken der Sterne) zu zerstören. III 52 *b* 30 mit-xur-ti agreement {Eintracht, Übereinstimmung} § 65, 40 *a* & *b*. Perh. H 70, 34—5 mi]t-xu-ur-te.

mitxurtu *2.* door {Türe} K 128 *O* 2 (Jensen, 470) *cf* maxirtu 2. Lehmann, ii 57 *ad* L[5] 2 sa-niq mit-xur-ti quotes K 128 *O* 1 sa-ni-iq mit-xur-ti who closes the door.

mitxariš in harmony, together {zusammen, in eins, in gleicher Weise} ‖ ištēniš *Rev. d'Assyr.*, ii 13—4; AV 5390. Sn i 47 mit-xa-riš ak-šud; vi 12—3 the wagons mit-xa-riš | u-tir-ra (I gathered in one place); *cf* v 44. H 81, 19—20 mit-xa-riš (= UR-BI) šumšu im-bu-u šam-mu ana šar-ru-ti-šu-nu, together (with one accord) the plants called his name to the royal dominion over them, (*cf* IV 13 *b* 1—2. Br 11305; 11261); 70, 39—41 mit-xa-riš i-zu-zu; *cf* D 96, 28. K 193 *O* 12 ... ki mit-xa-riš it-ta-nak-ki-ra i-da-a-ti-ša; *cf* ZA iv 8, 23. V 33 *c* 14—16 u Ē-sag-ila | mit-xa-riš MUŠ-DU-DU (*cf* mušlaxxu) | lu-u-ul-li-lu-ma; 17—18 iš-tu te-lil-ti bi-tim mit-xa-riš | šak[-nat]. K 292 *R* 9—10 ina up-šu-uk-ken (S[b] 266)-na-ki mit-xa-riš xa-diš a-a i-tur, *etc.* Sp II 265 *a* ii 7 na-aṭ(?)-la(?)-ta-ma | nišē | mit-xa-riš | a-pa-a-tu[m]; xxii 5 li-bit (?) qāti (il) A-ru-ru | mit-xa-riš | na-piš-ti. II 66 *no* 1, 3 ša .... mit-xa-ri-iš (*var* -riš) ta-xi-ṭa. H 199, 4 AŠ-AŠ = mi-it-xa-r[i-iš]; ZA vii 118 *O* 17; Br 23, 31, 32. KB iv 40 (iv) 20 mi-it-xa-ri-iš i-zu-uz-zu (√zâzu); also *p* 42 ii 12; Warka *c. t.* 80, 24. D 96, 23 *cf* malaku Q[t]. T. A. Lo. 11, 36 mi-it-xa-ri-iš (also Ber. 23, 42), KB v 23* = by malevolence or *vicissim*.

matkū, see kurkū & Br 10388 *ad* 82—8—16, 1 *O* 28.

mutkū II 34 *no* 3 *e-f* 47 .... bu(or BU?) = mut-ku-u, AV 5430.

mit(mat?)-tak, E. Müller, ZA i 360 √נתק. AV 5402. Anp ii 88, 98; iii 2, 3, 6, 8, 9, 10 *fol*; 12, 14, 15, 16 there and there a-sa-kan mit-tak; iii 6 (a-sa-ka-an); ii 93, 94 (ŠA-an, *var* a-sa-kan); iii 5, 79 (ŠA-an); without place or locality iii 72 a-sa-kan mit-tak; ii 38 a-na uš-ma-ni-ja (ii 44, 65, 75)-ma GUR (= utē)-ra mit-tak. III 65 *a* 11 the enraged gods shall return to the country and mat-tak ne-ix-tu KU-ab (= and it [the land] shall have a peaceful *m.* Peiser: *masc* to metaqtu (*cf* Šamš-R. iv 27 mi-taq-ti-ja) = mētiqu; see, however, BA i 172 *a*.

---

mit-xal-la-ti AV 5398 *cf* ba(i)txallu.

mitkula *cf* makalu and correct AV 5394 accordingly.

matkanū see kurkanū.

mutakpūtum in ūmē mut-tak-pu-tum see nakapu.

matallu a precious stone {Edelstein} belonging to the xulālu species (*q. v.*); AV 5234; Br 11808 *ad* V 30 *e-f* 66.

mut(t)allu, see mudallu & I 27 *a* 7 ilu mu-tal-lu; Asb i 13 ina e-peš pi-i mut-tal-li (KB ii 155 auf den gepriesenen Befehl hin, √דלל); Sarg *Ann* 388 am-nu-u-šu-nu-ti mut-tal-lum (ZA iv 413); 195 P. N. Mut-tal-lu(m) of Qummux. K^{M} 58, 10 ilāni ^{pl} mu-tal-lum (*p* 180 √חלה); Lyon, *Manual*, 68 √אלה be strong; D^{W} 424 √עלה = lofty; also § 104. Lehmann, ii 57; 80 √אלל. AV 5649.

metlu, *c. st.* metil power, might, supremacy, government {Macht, Herrschaft} Sarg *Cyl* 73 whom I i-na mi-til ši-bir-ri-ja (with the power of my club, *i. e.* my weapon) aš-lu-la. Lyon, *Sargon*, 78 (√מתל) >< KB ii 50 *fol*; Sarg *Ann* XIV 88, *Stele* 94. L^{T} 128. Šalm, *Mon O* 9 ša . . . . . i-xi-lu mātāte ina metil qar-du-ti-šu iš-da-ši-na. (Scheil, *Šalm*, 92; Rost, 97 √אתל or עתל; >< KB i 152 & Craig, *Diss*: mēdil iddūti?); II 67, 74 whom I had subjugated ina mi-til qar-ra-du-ti-ja. AV 5250; 5879. Perhaps IV^{2} 34 i *O* 32 illi-ku-ma mit-til-šu-nu im-xa-çu (*q. v.*). ‖ are these 2:

metlūtu. TP vi 78 i-na qit-ru-ub mi-it-lu-ti-ja with my heroic onslaught. I 28 *a* 10 ina qi-it-ru-ub me-it(>< KB i 124)-lu-ti-šu; G § 104 (√etlu); *Rec. Trav.* ii 19 (*no* ii); AV 5395. ZA iv 430 (bel.) *ad* 80—7—19, 126 reads ina I-si-in maxaz >< (= mit)-lu-ti-šu.

metillūtu. TP ii 64 see danānu 2. AV 5379; L^{T} 128; BA i 175 √אתל. I 27 *no* 2, 50 ina li-te kiš-šu[-ti]-ja u me-til-lu-ti. II 43 *a-b* 9 mi-til-lu-tum ‖ ra-pa-aš-tum, preceded by emūqu (*cf* kabartu); also perh. II 47 *c-d* 47 . . . . lum | me-til-lu-tu.

Note. — Delattre, JA '97 Ja.-F., 175: all 3 nouns from √אתל; TP i 37 he reads u-ša-ti-lu = a rendues puissantes (>< u-ša-xi-lu); ti for ti occurring quite often.

muttalliku *adj* (properly *ag* Q^{t} of alaku, (*q. v.*) going about, moving, roaming about; being in anxiety; tossing about {umhergehend; ängstlich seiend; sich umherwälzend} AV 5669. IV^{2} 24 *no* 1 *R* 42—3 (44) Nergal bēlu mut-tal-lik (= DU-DU) mu-ši. ZA iv 230, 14 mut-tal-lik qirib šamāmē. IV^{2} 50 *a* 1 kaššaptu mut-tal-lik-tu ša sūqē (§ 68 note 1). K 252 (III 66) *col* 2, 8 $^{(il)}$ I-šum(-taq?) mu-ut-tal-li-ku ša sūqē. H 99 (= K 246 iv) 53—4 see mašašu; also *cf* amēlu mut-tal-li-ki(-ku) being under the ban of ṭe'u, IV^{2} 3 *a* 13—14 (see mexru); 4 *b* 17—18; 24—25; 15* iii *R* 22—24 (-ka, *var* -ki & ku?) Br 11595, id PAP-XAL-LA; ZK ii 410. RP^{2} ii 183 *rm* 1 (Pinches = "sickness"), *cf* S^{c} 301 [pa-ap]-xa-al | PAP-XAL | i-tal-lu-ku ‖ pušqu *etc.* — II 23 *c-f* 71 mut-tal-lik-tum = dal-tum, lit^{y}: the going to and fro (AV 5670) V 39 *a-b* 57 IM-MA(Br 8461 -ŠU)-NI-GIN-DU-DU = mut-tal-li-ku (ZK i 122; ii 52); V 42 *a-b* 28 IM-ŠU-NIGIN-NA-DU-DU = (ti-nu-ru) mut-tal-li-ku, & 26 KI-NE-DU-DU = (ki-nu-nu) mut-tal-liku (Br 8460, 9716) = a portable oven.

mitluku (√malaku) K 7592 + K 8717 + DT 363, 27 mit-lu-uk mil-ki (ZA v 58) he who would be well counselled (*ag* Q^{t}).

mitluktu consultation, decision {Beratung, Entscheidung} √malaku. § 65, 40; V 65 *a* 34 the sages *etc.* a-na mi-(it)-lu-uk-ti aš-pur-šu-nu-ti (I sent for) ZA i 34; I 67 *a* 5 ilāni rabūti iš-ku-nu mi-it-lu-uk-ti; *cf* III 61 *b* 13; 62 *b* 10 (mit-lu-uk-ta [& -ti] iškunu); 81—11—3, 111, 6 Marduk is called Bēl ša bu(or mit?)-lu-tu u mit-lu-uk-tu.

mutlillū H 81, 12 $^{(il)}$ Nin-ib zi-ka-ru mut-lil-lu-u (= IL-IL-LA) Br 8447. Pinches, in S. A. Smith, *Asurb*, *vol* iii 91 √elū; see ZA v 38, √elēlu.

mu-ti-la-at šik-nat na-piš-ti II 51 *b* 31 name of a river or canal.

mutamū (√amū, speak). II 7 *c-d* 32 KA-BAL-BAL-E = mu-ta-mu-u; also V 39 *c-d* 12 (KA-BAL-BAL); preceded by *c* 11 $^{(amēl)}$ KA-KA-KA = one who speaks. AV 5650; Br 559, 581.

mitk(q)u AV 5397 *etc.*, *cf* batqu & pitqu. ~ mat-lu-ti KAT^{2} 298 *ad* Sn ii 50 but read šad-lu-ti

mutamētu (?) STRASSM., *Stockholm*, *no* 4, 10: 1 ma-na 2 šiqil kaspu ša su-ur-ru mu-ta-me-ti.

matnija *cf* madnija and W. MAX MÜLLER, OLZ ii *col* 75 *rm* 1: Weg(zehrung). Perhaps also Cappad. inscr. (London) 6 ma-ta-nim.

matnu S^b 187; II 15, 214 sa-a | SA | = mat-nu (?) cord, rope {Seil} perh. talm. קִיטְרָא; ‖ riksu. HOMMEL, *Sum. Les.*, 77: nerve {Nerv}. ZA i 178 reads gin-nu; iv 60 *rm* 3: dun-nu; Br 3077 kur-nu.

matinnu (?) V 41 *a-b* 17 [?] ma-tin (*var* -ti)-nu = kab-tum (*q. v.*).

(māt) **Mi-ta-a-ni** *e. g.* TP vi 63 ina xu-rib-te ina (māt) Mi-ta-a-ni; a country or city? {ein Land oder eine Stadt?} AV 5376. I 45 (Sn) *b* 24; III 15 iii 13 *foll* (māt) Me-ta-a-nu (× KB ii 144); T. A. Lo. 9, 3 šar (māt) [Mi-i]-it-ta-an-ni; 8, 8; Ber. 178, 37; Lo. 21, 12 a-na (māt) Mi-ta-na (Ber. 53, 20); Lo. 44, 10. Ber. 26 iv 44 Dušratta ša Mi-i-ta-a-an-ni. See JENSEN, ZA vi 57—9; WINCKLER, *Forsch.*, i 80 *rm* (& JENSEN, *Berl. Philol. Wochenschr.*, 10 F. '94 *no* 7, 214 *b*); MÜLLER, *Asien u. Europa*, 281—90; HILPRECHT, *Assyriaca*, 125 *foll*: Tar-qu-u-tim-me šar māt (al) Me-tan: Reich der Stadt *M.* (also TIELE, ZA x 106—7 & × JENSEN, ZDMG 48, 482); *Berl. Sitzgsber.*, '88, 1355. LEHMANN, i 63, 144, 171; ii 110; & ZDMG 50, 321 *foll.* BELCK, ZDMG 51, 557. ROST, *Untersuchungen*, 36 *foll.*

mutinnu wine {Wein}. AV 5456 *ad* II 25 *a-b* 28 mu-tin = i-nu. Bu 88, 5—12, 75 + 76 iv 12 & Bu 88, 5—12, 103 ii 7 *cf* kurūnu; perh. = mu'tinu with infixed *t* of √יין; BA i 634; iii 224; 274; Bu 88, 5—12, 101 ii 22; K 2801 *R* 46.

mutta(na)anbiṭu see nabaṭu.

mutninnū he who prays, prayerful, pleader, worshiper {fromm; Beter, Fleher} *etc.* AV 5431—2. § 67, 37 *rm* ag ℑ[t] of חנן; HAUPT, HEBR. ii 4—5 √תנן by-form of חנן; ZA v 38. Rm III 105 i 11 ri-du-u mut-nin-nu-u, the prayerful shepherd, WINCKLER, *Forsch.*, i 254—5. Sn *Rass* 1 Sen. rē'um mut-nen-nu-u (*Bell* 1). Asb vii 95 Asurb. (šarru) šangū ellu re-e-šu mut-nen-nu-u (× 9). Neb *Bab* i 11 Nebk. emga mu-ut-ni-en-nu-u; *Senk* i 12; also FLEMMING, *Neb*, 31 *ad* Neb i 18. *Var* to I 49 i 5—6 (end) ri-e-šu mut-nin-nu-u; BA iii 218 *rm* * (das betende Oberhaupt). IV² 20 *no* 1, 5—6 mu t]-nen-nu-u (Z^B 78 *rm* 1); KB iii (2) 76 i 4 Nerigl. e-im-ga-am mu-ut-ni-en-nu-u. Sp II 265 *a* xxv 3 ri-e-šu pal-ku-u mut-nen-nu-u. *Proc. Berl. Acad.*, '88, 756 (above) ri-e-um mut-nin-nu-tu; ZA v 60, 23; ZA iv 232, 18 šax-tu mut-nin-nu-u.

muttaprišu, AV 5671, properly ag ℑℑ[t] of parašu, 1. § 122. Anp i 49 iççur šame-e mut(*var* muš)-tap-ri-šu a winged bird of heaven {ein befiederter Vogel des Himmels}. TP vi 83 iççur šame-e mut-tap-ri-ša (L^T 108); I 28 *a* 31 XU^MEŠ šame-e mut-tap-ri-ša. III 9 *no* 3, 56 iç-çur šame-e mut-tap-ri-šu-ti ša a-gap-pi-šu-nu ana ta-kil-te çarpū (KB ii 30—1 = TP III *Ann* 156); Lay 34, 20; ZA iv 262 *R* 7 (iççur) mut-tap-ri-ši la u-šal-la-mu. V 32 *d-f* 6 . . . . XU = mut-tap-ri-šu (Br 13989; AV 320, 3780, 5503, 5667, 5671).

matqu *a*) sweet, sweet food or drink {süss, Süssigkeit: in Speise oder Trank} ‖ dašpu (*q. v.*). AV 5243. POGNON, *Wadi-Brissa*, 68. V 24 *c-d* 17 da-aš-p[u] = mat]-qu (preceded by marru); K 4150 [ ] [illegible]-pa-nu (*cf* V 24 *c-d* 18) = mat-qu = da-aš-pu ZA iv 156. *Creat.-frg* III 135 ši-ri-sa mat-qu u-sa-an-ni [çur-ra-]šu[-un] (JENSEN, 279 *rm* 2); S^b 230 ku-u [illegible] | mat-qu (*cf* ZA iv 340—1; vi 74 *ad* V 61 iv 33 where Z^B 98 reads ina dišpi karāni, BA i 273; Br 3345). Perhaps also V 12 *a-b* 48 [illegible] = ma[-at-qu?]. V 25 *c-d* 17 *cf* dašpu. — *b*) honey {Honig}. K 2020 *R* 24 ma-at-qu ‖ diš[-pu] as well as pa-ar nu-ub-tu & lal-la-rum (Z^B 94). a ‖ is:

mutqu *1.* ZIM., *Beitr. z. babyl. Religion*, 98, 33 akal mut-ki (*cf* *l* 45); *var* -gi (43); 47 akal mut-ki-i: sweet bread, unleavened bread × akal tumri (*ibid*, *p* 94).

mutāqu or **muttaqu** perhaps: honey {Honig} Neb, POGNON C vii 26 ximēṭu mu-ut-ta-qu šizbi u-lu šam-ni (as sacrificial gifts); also A iv 46; vii 15 (mu-ut-ta-qa POGNON, *Wadi-Brissa*, 67; BA i 635 *ad* 584 *rm* 3: fermentation {Gährung} *cf* Nabd 161, 5; 200, 3; Cyr 282.

mutqu 2. louse {Laus} II 20 *g-h* 20 mut-qu = ub-lu; also *cf* II 5 *c* 28; perhaps V 27 *g-h* 20; Br 8312.

mētiqu, mētequ (√etequ) AV 5882; §§ 32*aγ*; 35; 65, 31 *a*; BA i 6; 175; Pognon, *Bav*, 85. — *a*) progress, advance, passage {Vorwärtskommen, Passage} TP ii 9 xu-la ana me-te-iq (*var* tiq) narkabātelja u ummānātelja: (I constructed) a road for the passage of my chariots and my troops (AJP xix 386); also iv 69 a-na me-ti-iq *etc.* Anp often. Esh Cyl tunnel of Negoub (*Rec. Trav.*, xvii 81—2) 9 ix-za-ti im-ça an (= ana) kib-si me-te[-qi] les bords étaient devenus trop étroits pour y marcher et passer. — *b*) road, way, street {Weg, Strasse} ‖ xarrānu (*q. v.*), Br 8568 *ad* II 38 *c-d* 26; ‖ urxu (II 40, 236); I 27, 61—2 kibis u-ma-mi u me-ti-iq | bu-u-li; Z^B viii 35 itti ma-mit iki palgi ti-tur-ru mi-ti-qu a-lak-ti u xar-ra-ni. — *c*) progress, course {Fortgang, Verlauf} ‖ ina alak (girrija); ina (ana) me(i)tiq girrija Sarg *Ann* 248 (TP v 33); Asb i 68; iv 132; v 93. TP III *Ann* 27, 103 see girru, 1. also Sn i 52; *Bell* 17; *Kui* 1, 7; Sn ii 65; *Kui* 1, 33; Sn iv 47; I 7 F 14 me-ti-iq gir-ri šarri; III 55 *b* 59 xarrāni u mi-te-ki. TP ii 73 see naṭū.

mētaqtu course, advance {Zug, Fortgang} §§ 35; 65, 31 *a*; AV 5377. Šamš iv 27 that city ina mi-taq-ti-ja I took (KB i 186); Anp i 77 ina me-taq-ti-ja; ii 20 ina me(*var* mi)-taq-ti-(i)a. a ‖ is:

mētuqu. Anp iii 110 ša ina šarrāni abēa ma-am-ma kib-su u me-tu-qu ina lib-bi la-a iš-kun-ma (KB i 112) § 65, 31 *a*, note. So correct AV 5883.

mūtaqu path, street {Pfad, Strasse}; T^C 53—4; Peiser, KAS 14, 30; 87 & 115 *col* 1; Pognon, *Wadi-Brissa*, 13 le mu-taq du grand maitre Marduk. Strassm., *Stockholm* (VIII Or. Congr.), 5, 3—4 sūqu rapšu | mu-tak [(1)] .... šarri VATh 475, 3 mu-ta-qu Nabū u Na-na-a; also VATh 447, 2. KB iv 164 *col* iv 30 itu e-sir mu-ta-qu-tu the side of the *M*-street, T^C 7. Dar 82, 4 bīt-su ša itu mu-taq-qa KB iv 305: an der Seite des Pfades. *Cf* sat-tuq mu-ta-qu ša arax Abi, Pinches, *Inscr. Bab. Tablets*, *p* 15, 2.

matrū. T. A. (Ber.) 26 ii 18 ma-at-ru-u-šu (?) ša ta-kil-ti ana II-šu.

maturru see makurru (K 8239 *b-c* 9); and šat dur-ru (*ad* AV 5245) ZK ii 286.

mitru (d, ṭ?) Sm 2052 *R* 12 = dannatum (*q. v.*) power, force {Macht, Gewalt} AV 5401. *adj* in II 31 *no* 3, 31 mi-it-ru = ra-aš-bu (*q. v.*).

mutturu II 22 *no* 2 add (= II 44 *h* 66) .... GA = mut-tu-ru (AV 5676) or mut-tuxu? see mataxu.

mutirru (mutīru). ag ℑ of tāru (*q. v.*) used as *adj* & *noun*, *e. g.* mu-tir gi-mil avenger {Rächer} Creat.-*frg* III 58, 116, 138; *cf* gimillu. AV 5657. — (amēl) GUR (= mutir) pūti (× AV 1745) = satellite, vassal, guardian {Trabant, Leibwächter} Z^B 46 *rm* 2. II 51 *R* 31; K 2852 + K 9662 iii 12 (amēl) narkabti GUR (= mutir) ar(or ub)-te um-ma-ni (amēl) bat-xal GUR ar-te (amēl) šak-nu-te, *etc.* — bolt {Riegel} ⊕ 287 iv 9 GIŠ-ŠAG-KUL-NU(I)M-MA-KI = mu-tir-ru ‖ sik-kur ša-ki-li (*cf* sikkūru, ZA vi 132), lit^y: an Elamite bolt. AV 6055; Br 3546. — net of birdcatcher {Netz des Vogelfängers} K 242 i (II 22 *a-b*) 15 GIŠ-SA-XU-KAK = mu-tir-ru ‖ še-e-tum (4) AV 5659; Br 3094. *f* mu-tir-tum II 34 *no* 3, 29 ‖ šētum ša iççuri (‖ a-xu) AV 5660. — ZA iv 11, 29 mu-tir-ru būli cattlethief; *f pl* **mutērēti,** mu-tirrēti (*sc.* dalāti) = doorwings {Türflügel} Meissner & Rost, *Bīt-xillāni*. 6 *rm.* II 23 *c-d* 24 mu-tir-re-e-tum (AV 5658) = tu-'a-a-ma-ti, Lyon, *Sargon*, 76. bīt mu-tir-re-te Sn *Kui* 4, 4 = house of doorwings (?); portico, vestibule; *cf* bīt-xillāni = doorhouse {Türenhaus} also Jensen, ZA ix 132; Meissner-Rost, 25: Propylaeen. — III 67 *c-d* 58 DINGIR-IG-GAL-LA = god Papsukal as the god ša mu-te-re-ti. See now also Friedrich, BA iv 227—78.

muttarū leader, guide {Leiter, Führer}, √arū, ag Q^t; § 113; I 65 *a* 2 mu-ut-ta-ru-u te-ne-še-ti. K 2107 *O* 13 Marduk mu-ut-tar-ru-u ilāni leader

[1] mut-ru-u AV 5664 see mudrū.

of the gods. IV² 9 a 49—51 Sin mut-tar-ru-u (= DU-DU EMESAL) šik-na-at na-piš-tim. I 43, 3 Sen. mut-ta-ru-u nišē rap-ša-a-ti. AV 5672.

mutarbū? II 42 c 36 (šam) ša mu-tar (xaç, -sil)-bu-u, Br 13816.

mutarrītu crowing {krächzend} K 2051 ii SAL (ga-ga) GA-GA = mu-tar-ri-tu; ZK ii 300; 413 √tarū crow {krächzen}; ZA v 98 = muçapirtu, Br 10944; AV 5652.

ma-a-ti-iš dan-is often in T. A. = ma'a-diš (*q. v.*).

muttašrab(b)iṭu. ag 2t of שרב; § 117; Br 4403. IV² 2 v 4—5; 41—42 šūnu za-ki-qu mut-taš-ra(b)-bi-ṭu (*var* -tu)-ti; Banks, *Diss*, 18 *foll*, *no* 2 (8—10) 39 ā[bu?] Uruk(?)ki rabū mut-taš-rab-bi-iṭ qar-rad ut-ta-'a-ad. H 18, 305; G § 118 reads muttanrabbitu.

muttūtu V 47 *b* 32 see mašadu 2.

נ

-ni (rarely **-nu**) *1.* enclitic particle of emphasis {hervorhebende enclitische Partikel}; especially common with verbal forms in a relative clause, with or without prenominal suffix; it draws the tone to the immediately preceding syllable, § 79β. K 525 *R* 8 (Hr[L] 252) ša il-lik-u-ni-ni a-na te-gir-te-šu (+ 14; relative in both cases). K 2674 i 7 who the head of the king of Xidali na-šu-ni; IV² 61 i 15 (ša) .... ak-kar-ru-u-ni; ii 16 a-na-ku qa-la-ku-u-ni; i 17 ša aq-qa-ba-kan-ni (+ iv 48) what I tell thee; i 20 ša i-ṭi-ba-kan-ni. V 53 *d* 56 ša .... ta-da-nu-u-ni (has granted); V 54 *a* 61—2 see la'u, 1 (*p* 463). TP ii 26 ša .... i-sa-si-u-šu-ni whom they also called. Anp i 82 ub-lu-ni-šu-nu (*var* -ni); i 103 ša ... ušaçbitu-šu-nu-ni; iii 125, 133; I 27 *no* 2, 23 the countries ša a-pi-lu-ši-na-ni. II 67, 10 (end) ša .... i-qab-bu-šu-u-ni. K 5291 *O* 8—10 (Hr[L] 317) mi-i-nu | ša a-ma-ru-ni ša a-šam-mu-ni | ina pa-an šar bēli-ja a-qab-bi whatever I shall see and hear, I will report to the king my lord; K 538 *R* 10 (Hr[L] 114) rēš arxi ṭa-bu-u-ni the beginning of the month was good; thus also Anp i 101 *etc.* us-ba-ku-ni (ich verweilte) Lehmann, ZA xiv 372. — Also added as emphatic particle to nominal suffixes. K 498, 14 di-bi-šu-u-ni his communication; Asb v 32 epšit ilu-ti-šu-(ni); Smith, *Asurb*, 228, 76; Šalm, *Mon*, *O* 4 i-ni-ni my part. — K 2401 ii 25 .... a-ki Ašur bēl ilāni a-na-ku-ni that I am Ašur the lord of gods (BA ii 637). According to some also -ni in D 95, 8 mim-ma-ni i-çu (but see niçu). On -ni & -nu in attūnu *etc.*, see § 56*a*. Bez., *Dipl*, xxxv *rm* on Lo. 5, 25 + 26 comparing Eth. *-ni*; but see KB v 82—3.

-ni *2.* suffix of 1 *pl* (§ 74); K 46 ii 35 it-ti-ni with us; *cf* ⊕ 116 i 45 e-li-ni (Br 10373; 10406); Beh 3 zēr-u-ni our family {unser Geschlecht}; Sn v 25; *del* 181 (pu-ud-ni?). K 991, 13 + 15.

-ni *3.* T. A. for -ani = me (verb. suff. 1 *sgl*) Bez, *Dipl*, xx § 13*a*.

-nu *2.* T. A. for -ni nom. suff. of 1 *pl*, quite common; Bez., *Dipl*, xx § 12*b*; *e.g.* mārinu Lo. 14, 37 *etc.*; but usually -ni Lo. 41, 14 (amēlūti) mār šipri-ni ana šarri be-ili-ni aš-bu-nim.

(ilu) **Ni** (or **Çal?**) III 67 *d* 12 (Br 12685).

nī'u (*ni'ū?*), pr inī turn, repulse {wenden, zurückstossen}, ניא. AV 6202. Lehmann, i 139; ZA iv 239 (K 2301 iii) 14 ul i-ni-'-i i-na-as-sa xušaxka (*q. v.*). Used especially in connection with irtu (breast) as object. Sn v 66 with the weapons of Ašur and with my fierce onslaught i-rat-su-un a-ni-'i-ma sux-xur-ta-šu-nu aš-kun I kept back their advance and brought about their repulse (L[T] 112). Creat.-*frg* III 30 (88) *b* it is said of the monsters, created by Tiāmat la i-ni-'-u i-rat (*var* GAB)-su-un (KB vi, 1, 14—7; & 309). also I 118. IV² 30* *no* 3 *O* 26—7 i-rat-ka ni-'i turn away! 23 *no* 2 *O* 3—4 (ilat) Ištar id-ka la ta-ni-am-ma. BA ii 148: perhaps also III 41 *b* 28 pi-lik-šu li-ni (or √enū, KB iv 78—9). T[M] v 101 šadū li-ni-'-ku-nu-ši: der

Berg erschüttere euch? perh. IV² 31 *R* 50 (šal) u-xa-te li-na-'a-a kab-ta-a[s-sa] (J^W 43; *cf* Ezek 32, 18; Mic 2, 4); *cf* K 3399 + K 8934 ii 82; iii 47, 57 (i-ni-') KB vi (1) 28, 278, 284; Sp II 265 *a* xiii 8 [lu]-ni-' bu-bu-ti. V 21 *c-d* 43—44 TU (= tūru IV² 29 *no* 3, 9—10) = ni-'-u; GAB = ir-tum; Br 1076; V 29 (*g*)-*h* 24; K 10014, 8*fol* (M^S 62). III 48 *no* 6, 22 pān k(q)i-bit ni-e(?). ·· 𐤍 = Q (intens.) V 45 ii 51—4 tu-na-'a, tu-na-'a-an-ni, tu-na-'a-a-šu-nu, tu-na-'a-an-na-ši (§ 56*b*); Sargon mu-ni-'i i-rat (mât) Ka-ak-mi-e Lay 33, 9 (KB ii 36; Winckler, *Sargon*, 170); also K 514 (18+)28 u siparru mu-ni-'-e ša-ṭa-ru i-na mux-xi (Hr^L 268; AV 5448). — 𐤍 K 3454 (*Zū*-legend) Anu spoke to Adad (*l* 35) . . . a-a i-ni-'i qa-bal-ka let not thy attack be repulsed (also *l* 79). BA ii 409—10; KB vi, 1, 48—9. K^M 1. 49 (K 155 *R* 14) lid(ṭ)-d(ṭ)ip-pir (il) Nam-tar li-ni-'i irat-su; 33, 33.

Derr. — nîtu (but see KB vi, 1, 300), nîtiš; (Lenormant i, 128—9 also nûtu & Ni-nu-a, but ?), &:

nu'u wavering, feeble, weak (physically or morally) {schwankend, schwächlich (physisch oder moralisch)}. III 41 ii 9 whosoever sends sak-la sak-ka nu-'-a (*cf* § passage III 43 in KB iv 70 below, i 31—2); Merod.-Balad.-stone v 27 nu-'-a la pa-lix ilāni rabūti lim-niš u-ma-'-a-ru (BA ii 265*foll*; KB iii, 1, 192); Belser, (BA ii 126—7) Strolch. Perh. V 16 *e-f* 33 BAR-NU = nu-'-u (Br 1861, 13954). AV 6404.

(iç) **nu-u** II 23 *e-f* 30 = (iç) ma-nu (?) Br 1994. J^{1-X} 28 reads giš-ma-nu laurel {Lorbeer}? *ad* NE 56, 23. AV 6387.

na'butum (AV 5920) = nābutum *ac* 𐤍 of abatu, BA i 181, 502; H^F 10; II 39, 167; §§ 47 & 84; BA i 181. V 39 *g-h* 51; same iD with (amēlu) prefixed = mun-nabtu (*q. v.*) Br 6036; *cf* II 7 *g-h* 46 (Br 6035); 48 *c-d* 58 (*l* 57 XA-A [= xalaqu, Br 11856] = na-bu-tum, Br 11857; AV 5890). ZA iii 73 *rm* 3; 48 (bel).

na'adu, nādu 1. pr i'ud; ps ina'ad. §§ 84; 100--101; 105; G § 110; AV 5921. ·· *a*) *trans*: uplift, raise, praise {erheben, erhöhen; preisen}. K 2024 *O* 27 see karabu, (*R* 7). ZA ii 133 *a* 18 a-na-dam be-lu-u(t)-su I praise his rule. K 1282 *R* 11 nap-xar-šu-nu i-na-ad-du it-ti-š[u] KB vi, 1, 73 fürchten sich mit ihm; 13 ša . . . . . i-na-du (3 *sgl*); 27 li-na-du qur-di-ja; K^M 11, 29 li-na-du-ka; 82-7-4, 42 (Br. M.) *O* 11 the god who over heaven and earth u-ša-til bēlūtsu i-na-a-du [ilūtsu?]; K 3449a *R* 3 ep-šit e-te-ip-pu-šu i-na-a-du; W-A 235 + B 1617 + W-A 239*β*, 9 . . . ma-li-e a-ni ul ta-na-a[d] BA iv 133; perh IV² 61 *a* 33 (*b* 39) na-i-da-a-ni praise me, honor me (BOR iii 27), § 91 we are exalted (1 *pl* pm); Sp II 265*a* ii 1 na-a-a-du eb-ri ša taq-bu-u i-dir-tum (or *adj?*). — *b*) *intr*: be exalted, lofty, high, glorious {erhaben, hoch, herrlich sein} §§ 9, 2; 20; 89, i. Perhaps Sp II 265*a* ii 8 na-'i-du ṭe-en-ka . . . .; § 92 na(-a)-di he was high. — S^c 126—7 i I na-a-du Br 3980; II 185, 19 (K 4225) UP (or AR) = na-a-du (?) *cf* 17, 281; Br 5783; H 40, 234 IM-TUK na-'-du : pa-la-xu. — Q^t *a*) *trans* = Q raise, praise, glorify. § 84; Asb i 9. K 8522, 10 liq-bu-u lit-ta-'i-du lid-lu-la da-lilišu (*q. v.*). *del* 29 at-']-ta-'-id (KB vi, 1, 232, 34); II 76, 14 (= IV² 5 *b* 44—5) (il) Nusku a-mat be-ili-šu it-ta-'-id-ma (Br 3571); II 40 *a-b* 53 it-ta[-'-id] Br 5783. V 33 ii 1 ak-pu-ud at-ta-id-ma. Šalm, *Balaw*, v 4 it-ta-'-id-ka-ma bēli rabi-e Marduk, he praised thee highly, O Marduk, great lord. Winckler, *Sargon*, 182, 60 šumu ilāni lit-ta-id may he reverence the name of the gods. Asb x 31 see labanu, 1; also ZA ii 141 *a* 27 (= KB iii, 2, 64). V 35, 29 ša ṭūbiš ni-it-ta[-'a-du i-lu-ti-šu] çir-ti (BA ii 212—3 we praised); IV² 57 *b* 20 the word of Ea lu-ut-ta-'i-id (I will honor, K^M 12, 89); K^M 11, 12 lu-ut-ta-id-ma; IV² 59 *no* 2 *R* 27 lut-ta-'-id ilu-ut-ka (see dalalu); V 52, 35 lut-ta-id ilūtika rabīti; also ZA v 68, 26; K^M 5, 8. Sp III 586 + *R* III 1, 18 qar-ra-du et-lum (il) Šamaš li-it-ta-i-du-ka (see Abel & Winckler, *Texte*, 59 *fol*, Hommel, *Sum. Lesest.*, 120 *fol*, TSBA viii 167 *fol*, *Rev. d'Assyr.* i 157; Br 3980, 10458); Esh *Sendsch*, *R* 60 zik-ri Ašūr bēli-ja lu-ta-'-id. *ac* IV² 60* *a* 18 pa-la-xu u it-'u-du la u-šal-me-du nišēšu (*cf* 31). — *b*) *intr*: ab-nu mut-ta-'i-di *etc.* (see above, *p* 621). — Q^{tn} = Q^t

40

Neb i 31/2 ša Marduk epšêtušu na-ak-la-a-ti | e-li-ià at-ta-na-a-du (1 *sgl*) §§ 84; 107 (end) I raise high. — ℑ praise highly {hochpreisen} NE 49, 188 (see kubru) *var* i-na-ad-du. Smith, *Asurb*, 125, 66 (KB ii 252) nu-'i-id ilu-u-ti (§ 107). V 45 ii 48 tu-na-'a-ad. II 35 *a-b* 33—4 [UB]-I & [UB]-RI = nu-'u-du Br 8980, 5702, 5706 (*cf* xittum). — T. A. (Ber.) 22 *R* 26 u-na-'a-du-šu he honors him; Rostow. 1, 36 u nu-id a-na Ri-a-na-ap, but give command to R. (KB v 354—55). — ℑ^1 Banks, *Diss*, 18 *foll*, 2 (8—10) 39 see muttašrab(b)iṭu. K 5268, 4 ^{il} Nergal lut-ta-'-id qar-rad ilâni bi-ru šu-pu-u mâr $^{(il)}$ Bêl. — Š^1 Neb i 35—6 a-lak-ti i-lu-ti-šu çir-ti | ki-ni-iš uš-te-ni-e-du (1 *sgl*); Xammurabi (KB iii, 1, 113) ii 12 ta-na-da-ti-ka ra-bi-a-tim li-iš-ta-ni-da thy glorious deeds may be exalted. ZA iii 318, 80.

Derr. tanattu, tanittu & these 2:

nâ'idu & **nâdu** *2*, & **nu-a-du** (Bu 88—5-12. 80, 8) *adj* lofty, high {erhaben, hoch, hehr} §§ 47 (*cf* ZA vi 808 *fol*); 65, 7; G § 116. id IM-TUK (& I, see above). AV 5921; § 9, 54; Br 8404; Pognon, *Bavian*, 100; ZA i 18. IV^2 12 *a* 9—10 = na-'-du. IM-TUK in K 3473 + 79, 7—8, 296 + Rm 615 *O* 52; also see KB vi 8, 38 & rem 3 & 4 (terrible: furchtbar); 315. Anp i 21; iii 127; IV^2 18 *no* 1 *R* 21 et-lu na-'i-du (= IM-TUK); TP i 31 šíppu na-'i-du; 19 rêi-ja na-a-di. Anp *Mon*, *O* 10 *fol*: Anp. rubu-u na-a-'i-du; *cf* Merod.-Balad.-stone ii 31. V 55, 1 Neb. rubû na-a-du (also *var* to I 49 i 5—6), V 63 *a* 2; Anp i 18 + 38; Šalm, *Mon*, *O* 6 (rubu-u). I 35 *no* 3, 16 Adad-nirari rubû na-'i-du; Asb ix 86 Nusku suk-kallu na-'i-du. Nabopolassar calls himself ru-ba-a-am na-'i-dam (KB iii, 2, 1—2, 13; ZA iv 107): Neb i 3 Neb. ru-ba-a na-a-dam; *Bab* i 2 (*cf* V 34 *a* 2) ru-ba-a-am na-a-dam: I 65 *a* 5 (§ 66); NE 44, 53 na-'i-id qab-li. K 3456 *R* 7 (end) ana sisû na-'i-id qab-li (PSBA xxi 40 *foll*); ZA v 59, 3 Marduk šurbû na-'i-du. Sarg *Cyl* 1 Sargon nisakku na-'i-id $^{(il)}$ Ašur; Anp i 32 na-'i (*var* a)-da-ku. Anp i 40 (ii 41) šadû kîma zi-qip paṭri parzilli še(-e)-su (*cf* ZK ii 289) na-a-di. — Na'id often in P.N. *cf* AV 5922—24; Na-'i-id-Marduk Esh ii 36; Nabû-na-'i-id & Nabû-IM-TUK & Nabû-I = Nabûnâ'id = Nabonidus. Against Latrille's reading ûmu nâ'di V 64 *a* 50 *cf* KB iii (2) 100 *rm* 1.

nâ'idiš *adv* solemnly {feierlich} Sarg *Khors* 178 na-'i-di-iš ak-me-sa; *Ann* 435.

na'duru (AV 5925) & **nanduru**; 27 *ac* √אדר; Z^D 94 oppression, plague, distress; properly: clouded, darkened {Bedrängnis, Not}; §§ 11; 52; BA i 168; 181 *rm* 3. IV^2 5 *b* 32—33 Bêl ša et-li Sin na-an-dur-šu | ina šamê êmur (id SU-MU-UG-GA); *var* K 4870, 31 na-'a-dur-šu (II 76, 2; 77, 82; Br 181). — eclipse {Verfinsterung} or *adj* (§ 65, 31 *b*) V 55, 31 na-'a-du-ru pân $^{(il)}$ Šam-ši (§ 104). — II 49 *c-d* 29 = V 16 *a-b* 82 IM-A-AB-LAL-E = na-'a-du-rum (*cf* H 198 *no* 4, 32) || eklitum & eṭûtum, Br 8498. V 30 *c-f* 23 UD-$^{(GI-DI)}$GAN = û-mu na-'a-du-ru (Br 4042, 7850: ZK ii 42) followed by UD-LAX = ûmu nam-ru. Sch 2, 5 na-'a-du-ru(m) ZA ix 210 *no* 2. û-mu na-an-du-ru Craig, *Rel. texts*, i 37, 2; T^M ii 114 (= furchtbarer Tag); viii 5. V 50 *a* 8 e-ma šamû u erçitum na-an-du-ru (Br 11202); II 38 *g-h* 2.

na'alu 1. ps ine(l)li, pm nîl lie, lie down {sich (nieder)legen} || nâxu, rabaçu Z^B 6 *rm* 1; § 105; AV 5983. Scheil, *Nabd*, ii 39—41 see ma'âlu; vii 11—12 a-na-al; x 47 a-na-la aṭ-ṭa-lu (but Messerschmidt a-na la ba-ṭa-lu) te-ri-e-ti-šu. NE 71, 22 ana-ku ul ki-i ša-šu-ma-a a-ni-el-lam-ma I will not lie down as he has done; ul atebbâ dûr dâr; *cf* 67, 13; 69, 31; 74, 20; 58, 4 ni-il-šu-ma(?) § 106: he lies; 48, 208 ni(or çal)-li. IV^2 17 *a* 51—2 *cf* marçiš & Br 8991; perh. Sp II 265 *a* xxv 3, see mutnenû. V 52 *b* 60—1 *cf* birûš; 80—7—19, 136 *II* 6—8 alpu na-ka-ri šam-me ik-kal alpu ra-ma-ni-šu bi-ri-iš ni-il = the ox of the enemy shall eat weeds, one's own ox shall lie in fat pasture. — Q^1 Craig, *Rel. texts*, i 5, 5 at-te-'-i-la ina šêpê ^{il} Nabû, M^S 62; K 749 *R* 2 i-na ṭâbti an-di-di-il-šu I preserved it in brine, *cf* Thompson, *Reports of the Magicians & Astrologers*, ii p xcl. — ℑ^1 lay down, lie, rest, sleep {sich legen, liegen, ruhen, schlafen} pm ušûl (*cf* above, *p* 130 *col* 1) & naṭalu; in addition also NE 50, 208 see ma'âlu; 209 u-tu-ul-ma (*var* ça-lil) Êabani šu-na-ta (*var* -tu) i-na-aṭ-ṭal. V 31 *no* 5, 46, *cf* kunnu, 2. II 42 *f* 24 a-b(p)ur-riš u-tu-lum. — Š̌^{1} pr ušna'il, ušnîl; ip šuni'il, šunîl (§ 106; Delitzsch in L^{T} 122—3). — *a*) take a rest {sich ausruhen} NE 15, 36 see ma'âlu; 58, 4; IV^{2} 18° (S 1708) *O* 9 a[-šak]-ku ina u-ri-e si-si-i uš-ni-il-ma (AV 5983). T^{M} i 108 mê napišti-ja (wr. MU) ina qab-rim uš-ni-lum {das Wasser meines Lebens haben sie im Grabe zur Ruhe gebracht} *ibid*, *p* 124 comparing IV^{2} 59 *no* 1 *a* 17 ina qab[-rim m]êšu lu-uš-ni-il; or, better = throw down, pour out? — *b*) throw down, overthrow {hinwerfen, niederwerfen} TP ii 20 the hostile armies ki-ma šu(-u)-be(lu-)uš-na-il (I threw down; ZA v 92); *cf* ii 80; vi 5 *etc*. V 47 *a* 50 kum-ti (*q. v.*) rap-ša-tu ur-ba-ti-iš uš-ni-il-lum they have thrown down my high figure like a reed, D^{Pr} 78. IV^{2} 22 *a* 36 ši-i-xu kîma ur-ba-ti uš-na-al; 15" *R* i 16—17 ki-ma (*var* kîma) sa-pa-ri rap-ši ina ša-ri rap-ši šu-ni(-'i)-il (= NÁ-A, Br 8991) i-di-ma, ZK i 358, bel. T^{M} iv 29—30 çalmê-ja it-ti pag-ri tuš-ni-il-la (also 34, 48, 49) ye have thrown down. II 32 *no* 7, 74 še-im ša ina IÇ-PA šu-nu-lu (pm). — *c*) lay down, stretch out {niederlegen, ausstrecken} Asb vii 40 *cf* ṭubtu, 3; K 7856 i 4 *fol* ṭa-biš uš-ni[l-ma]; IV^{2} 27 *b* 44—5 see ṭîxu & Br 5318; Z^{B} 81.

NOTE. — On D^{II} 5 *fol*; D^{Pr} 18—21, *cf* Nöldeke, ZDMG 40, 728; Schrader, ZA i 460; also ZK i 357 *fol*; *Lit. Or. Phil.*, i 193; Cheyne, London *Academy*, Ap. 12, '84; *Deu. Lit. Ztg.*, '86 *col* 1262; ZA v 306 *rm* 1; R. D. Wilson, *Presb. Rev.*, Ap. '88.

Derr. utullu, 2 herd (*q. v.*) & these 3 (?):

ni'lu rest {Ruhe} ZA v 68, 7 ni'lu ul a[ ] rest I do not find.

na'âlu *2.* lowland {Niederung}? KB ii 8, 28 a-na na-al bis zur Niederung (ZA v 306 ✕ KB ii 9; also see BA ii 307, 27), but *cf* Rost I, 46.

na'âlu *3.* K 8204 iii 11 al-ta-pil (√שפל) ina çâbê aq-ta-qur (or -kam?, √קפר) na-a-a-al, PSBA xvii 139; K 1274, 9 (Hr^{L} 220) ša (amêl) bêl pixâti ša bît na-a-a-la-ni.

na'alu (najalu) *4.* hind, roe {Hindin}. II 6 *c-d* 12—3 DARA-MAŠ-KAK & DARA-XAL-XAL-LA = na-a-a-lu, preceded by DARA-MAŠ = a-a-lu & followed by çabîtum & daššu (*q. v.*) § 13. AV 5982; Br 2949, 2954; D^{S} 52: L^{T} 170; II 24 *c-f* 7 na-a-lu = a[-a-lu?]; ZA v 93 (= יָעֵל); BA i 462 *rm* 1. XAL-XAL = gararu (*q. v.*) = run; I 28 *a* 19 ar-me *pl* tu-ra-a-xe *pl* na-a-le *pl* ja-e-le *pl*, *cf* TP vii 5 na-a-le *pl* ajalê *pl* ar-mi *pl* tu-ra(-a)-xe *pl*. V 21 *a-b* 38 na-a-lu = a-a-lu.

ni'lû D 81 (= K 40) ii 58 TIK-LAL = ni-'-lu-u (Z^{B} 103 | אלה; ZA iv 24 *rm* 1; AV 6203); II 26 *no* 2, *add* (Br 3305 & 10086); ZDMG 43, 193—9: fetter(?)

na-el-tum *cf* mummu, 1 (end).

ni'mêlu restlessness {Unruhe} Z^{B} 50 | אמל(?)' *ad* vii 97 šiptu ni-'-mil ni-ix-lu (*var* -li) gu-ux-xu xa-ax-xu ru[-tu] = IV^{2} 19 *b* 22; also see viii 1.

na'apu see nâpu.

nu-a-qu II 35 *e-f* 48 & ***nu-a-su*** (ph = נוש, see nâšu) 50 = alaku (BA ii 39).

na-a-rum V 16 *c-d* 42 = SAG-KI-BU; same id = nikilmû (*q. v.*, *p* 389); Br 3650; AV 5927; Z^{B} 68 splendor {Glanz}, *cf* namaru.

na'ru (= Heb. נער) KB vi (1) 68 *no* 3 *O* 11 ina pi-i lab (*var* la)-bi na-'-ri from the mouth of the roaring lion. — V 46 *a-b* 43 MUL-UD-KA-GAB-A (also II 49 *no* 1 *R* v 14) = û-mu na-'-ri followed by ilu ša-gi-mu (= roaring god), names of stars; the id is that for nimru = panther, and also that for nadru (II 6 *a-b* 8—9); see Jensen 48, 2 (the second star of the seven (lu)-ma-ši), also 65 *fol*, where III 57 *a* 53 (UD-KA-GAB-A) is explained as ûmu na'iri & especially, *p* 488: a wild lion {ein wilder Löwe}. On the other hand see Delitzsch in Z^{B} 117; *Weltschöpfungsepos*, 125, *etc*. ûmu = (1) day, (2) tempest, (3) storm; *cf* again KB vi (1) 310—11; Halévy, *Rev. de l'hist. des Rel.*, xxii 180 & 192 explains na'ri as נער of na'aru (= נער *cf* Jer 51, 38 ✕ § 49 *a*); ℶ in IV^{2} 58 iii 41 the daughter of Anu nu-'-u-rat (§ 101) ki-ma UR[-MAX?]

na'aqu; na-a-qu; na-a-qu *cf* nâqu; naçu; nâqu.

followed by uš-ta-na-al-xab ki-ma UR[-MAX?]; V 45 ii 49 tu-na-'a-ar. A " is

ni'ru Sn *Kui* 4, 23: 12 UR-MAX pl ni-'i-ru-ti a-di 12 ALAD-AN-KAL pl çi-rūte (Lay 41, 27 ni-'i-ru-ut-ti?). Meissner & Rost, 34 *rm* 62: נהר = נמר glänzende Löwen.

(mât) **Na-i-ri** a country to the north of Assyria; often from TP 1 on, *e. g.*, TP iv 83, 97; v 9, 20: viii 13; also III 6 *O* 27; *R* 14, 35, 44, 45 *etc.* (mâtâte) Na-i-rat Asp ii 117 (*var*): *cf* ii 6, 13, 15, 97; (mât) Na-'-i-ri Sarg *Khors* 54; I 35 *no* 2, 8; V 69, 20 (*cf* mâtu, 1, *pl*). See KAT[2] 91; 213; AV 5955: Bezold, *Catalogue*, v 2132 *col* 2; Streck, ZA xiii 57 *foll.*

ni'âru Ner 55, 12—13 a-ki-i ni-'a-a-ri ša ki-na-a çal[-la-ni] u (maðak) du(?)-še-e iṭ-ṭi-ri.

נאשׁ 1. *cf* muna'išu Rm 338 *R* 15 (*see p* 559 *a*).

נאשׁ 2. II 29 *g-h* 39 ..... A = **ni-e-šu** (Br 11450) in a group with nu-ni-nu (36) & na-a-qu (38); Barth, ZA iii 60, 2: howl {heulen}. AV 6365.

Derr. perh. nêšu (*f* nešṭu) lion, *q. v.*

ni-ja-ši & ni-ja-ti (also a-na ni-a-šim) = we, contained in annaši = an + ni-ja-ši, BA i 458, 481 (= to us); § 55 *b* & see nâši.

nabu Sarg *Cyl* 55 the pious words of my mouth u-lu(-u)-ni eli na-bi çirûti bêlê-ja ma-'-diš i-ṭi-ib. Tiele, *Gesch.*, 547 *rm* 5: perhaps "prophets".

nâbu 1. — *a*) some vermin, such as louse, flee, *etc.* {Ungeziefer von der Art der Läuse, Flöhe *etc.*} II 5 *c-d* 23 UX (lam-mu-bi) na-a-bu ‖ ublu, kalmatum (*q. v.*), pur-šu-'-u; S[c] 11 [u-xu?] | UX | na-a-bu, Br 8294; also II 16 *d* 23 (BA ii 296). D[S] 79, 80; *cf* II 49 *no* 4, *a* 6 (*i. e. l* 62) kakkabu ana na-a-bi itûr (64 ana sa-a-si, 65 ana kal-ma-ti, Br 1646). — *b*) II 35 *c-d* 40 UX-TAG-GA = na-a-bu; according to some √נבא = distracted, insane (ZA i 247 *rm* 2) Br 8315. In IV[2] 1* ii 1 we are told that ointments are used against UX-TUK (*var* UX-TAG-GA); perh.: sting of an insect? On this text see *Rev. Sém.*, vi 150; 245; 344.

nâbu 2. II 37 *e-f* 63 *pl* na-a-a-be ‖ a-bul-lum; perh. part of human (animal?) body?

nâb(p)u 3. 83—1—18, 1332 *O* ii 19 *foll*: NAB = na-a-b(p)u, na-a-ri (= river?), Bêl, ti-am-tum (ocean), i-la-an (the 2 ilu). See also KB vi (1) 270 *rm* 2.

nâbu 4. & nûbtum see nâpu, nûptum.

ilu **Na-i-bu** II 54 *c* 48, Br 1606.

nab(p)û 2. name of an insect {Insektenname} K 4373 *d* 3 (M[S] plates, 12) na-bu-u; K 4140 *b*, *R* 4 na-pu[-u] ‖ bukânu, na-pi-lu, *etc.* GGA '98, 821.

nabû 1. call {rufen} *pr* ibbi, im-bi (§ 49 *b*; K 3449 *a*, *R* 6); *ps* inambi, inabi (§ 52); *ip* ibi; § 84. — *a*) call {berufen} TP vii 48 (3 *sg*) *cf* kûniš; Asb vi 111 ina ûme-šuma ši-i u ilâni abêša tab-bu-u (3 *sg f*, exceptional, § 141 *bel*) šu-me (*var* šumi) a-na bêlût mâtâte, called my name to the lordship over the countries; x 109 ša Ašur u Ištar a-na be-lut mâti u niši i-nam-bu-u zi-kir-šu; *cf* Sn vi 65; I 69 *c* 25 when Š. u A. a-na ri'ût mâti šu-um im-bu-u. Schell, *Nabd*, vii 52 (ulì) šarrâni ša tam-bu-ma (2 *sg*); ZA v 67, 27 (ilat) Ištar tab-bi-in-ni thou didst call me; Neb vii 26 since ib-ba-an-ni (il) Marduk ana šarrûti; perh also vii 4, whom *M.* as a blessing of his city Babylon ib-bu-šu; i 57 the king whom thou lovest ta-na-am-bu-u zi-ki-ir-šu ša elika ṭâbu whose name, that pleases thee, thou callest. ZA iii 319, 93 i-nam-bu-u zi-kiršu (Sn *Bav*, 2); K 133 (H 81) *R* 20 see mitxariš; IV[2] 13 *b* 1—2 ina mât nu-kur-ti ina ma-a-ti mit-xa-riš šu-mi lu-u tam-bi; 48 *a* 23 mitxariš ta-nam-bi; 6 *c* 16 ilu A-nu-um u ilu Bêl im-bu-šu-nu-ti (Br 697); 9 *a* 35 na-bu-u (= SA, Br 2200) šar-ru-ti, na-din xaṭ-ṭi ša šim-ti ana û-me ru-qu-ti i-šim-mu. V 62 *no* 2, 7—8 a-na e-nu-ut niše šu-mi ṭa-bi-iš | lu-u ta-am-bi šar-rat ilâni (ilat) E-ru-u-a (Lehmann, ii 7; 34: ZA ii 250); 13 ul-çi-iš lu-u im-bu-in-ni-ma (or to *b*?) Lay 39, 37 Ašur u Ištar na-bu-u šumi-ja ‖ Sn *Kui*, 4, 10 na-bu; KB iii (2) 62 *no* 10 (*col*) 23—4 whom Marduk to do thus and thus šu-ma çi-ra-am ib-be-u. V 64 *c* 11 ab-bi-e-šu I called upon him {ich rief ihn an} § 53 *rm.* —

b) call out, announce, command {ausrufen, ankündigen, befehlen}. KB iii (1) 124 i 10 na-bi-u Anim prophet of Anu. K 8522 *O* 5 im-bu-u they called; *R* 14 zik-ri [il] Igigi im-bu-u na-gab-šu-un (+ 21) S 747 *R* 11 ša im-bu-u u-ša-ti-ru al-kat-su; see V 21 *g-h* 10 KAK = ni-bu-u (9 = ba-nu-u); *c-d* 67 MA = ni-bu (65 = zik-ri); 62 MA = na-bu-u (61 = šu-mu), thus nibû = nabû. II 67, 84 a-na šu-me-ši-in ab-bi I proclaimed as their name. Neb *Bors*, ii 25 i-be a-ra-ku û-mi-ja ⸗ šu-du-ur li-it tu-u-tim (*Bab* ii 28). T[M] ii 19 firegod *etc.* ta-na-bi šum-ka (thou proclaimest). P. N. Na-bi NI-NI (= ili?)-šu. Asb ix 110 ša ni-rib mas-naq-ti ad-na-a-ti na-bu-u zi-kir-ša, see zikru, 1 for passages. KB iv 160—1 (ii) 37 maxIru im-bi-e-ma; (iii) 12 (also 300—1, 11) *etc.* — name the price, offer {den Preis nennen, anbieten} Br 2290; Sp II 265 *a* i 11 a-bi u ba-an-ti i-nam-bu-in-ni-ma. V 43 *c-d* 41 Nabû has the epithet na-bu-u. P. N. I-bi [il] Nu-us-ku (*c. t.*); I-bi-Adad; I-bi-Sin, *etc.* — On i-ba-a ši m-ti (K 4832 *R* + K 292, 6) see KB vi (1) 318. — *c*) with šuma = call somebody by name, name somebody {mit šuma = jemanden mit Namen rufen, nennen}; also without šuma. According to Semitic ideas the name of a thing was regarded as its essence, hence "to bear a name" = "be in existence". pm somebody šuma nabi is called by name (H[F] 51; Z[D] 67). V 65 *b* 23 i-bi šu-mi ana du-ru ûmê. IV[2] 9 *a* 31 .... u ma-a-ta mu-šar-ši-du eš-ri-e-ti na-bu-u šu-me-šu-un (Br 2290). KB iii (2) 76 *a* 20 šu-um ṭa-a-bi lu-u im-ba-an-ni has given me a good name. Creat.-*frg* I 1 e-nu-ma e-liš la na-bu-u ša-ma-mu long since, when above the heaven had not been named. On mala šuma nabû *etc.* see malû, 2 (& Br 2290); also IV[2] 12 *R* 29—30 a-mi-lu-tu ma-lu šu-ma na-bu-u; 20 *no* 1 *a* 43—44 šik-na-at na-piš-ti ma-la šu-ma na-ba-a. K 44 *R* 15 mim-ma ša šu-ma na-bu-u (IV[2] 14 *b* 15); 21 ša [ilat] Nin-kasi tab-bu-šu at-ta; K[M] 11, 8 [a-me-lu]-tum ma-la šu-ma na-bat (*var* be-at). Anp ii 86 Dûr-Ašur šum-šu ab-bi; *cf* iii 50; II 67, 11; also see Šalm, *Mon*, *R* 35; I 27 *no* 2, 7; KB ii 4, 7; Sarg *Cyl* 68 zik-ri abulli .... am-bi; + 59 ša .... na-bu-u šum-šu; II 66 *no* 1, 8 (end). Nabd 697, 1—2 Adad-Bêl ša Rimût šun-šu im-bu-u.

II 7 *g-h* 38 PAD (pa-a) (Br 9414, 9422; H 30, 680; § 9, 264), 37 DIL-BAD (Br 42), 38 KA(gu)DÉ (Br 697; II 10, 59; 211, 59; II 29 *c-d* 18); 39 SA(sa-a) (Br 2290) = na-bu-u: V 30 *g-h* 40 PAD, 41 PAD-DA, 42 DIL-BAD (perh. = herald), 43 KA(gu-du)DÉ, 44 SA(sa-a) = na-bu-u: V 19 *c-d* 39—41 SIM(si-im) = ša-xa-lu (roar, ZK i 98 § 2), SIM-SIM = na-bu-u (Br 2130; ZA i 411) ŠU-SIM = šu-çu-u (proclaim an edict), II 14, 166—7; V 21 *c-d* 62 MA = na-bu-u; 43 *d* 41 AG = na-bu-u; also *cf* xababu. — V 46 *a-b* 40 (= D 93, 4) MUL-DIL-BAD (= Δελέφατ?) = na-ba-at kak-ka-bu (the herald-star) = star Venus (see also Çarpanitu), KAT[2] 178; AV 1970; Br 43. For DIL-BAD(T) see II 48 *a-b* 51 AN-ÇIP = DIL-BAD SAG-UŠ (= NIT?) ZK ii 84, 15; III 57 *a* 66; II 51 *a* 29; 39, 57; 49 *a-b* 49 (*no* 3), ZA i 260 *rm* 1. — IV[2] 27 *a* 23—4 ki-ma kak-kab šamê na-bu-u (= MUL-AN-NA-DIL-BAD-DU) ma-lu-u çi-xa-a-ti, Br 42; 3855; JENSEN, 117 *foll*; LEHMANN, i 125 E., ii 40. — ZA iii 220, 22 im-bi-e-ma (ZK i 48, 24); KB iii (2) 78, 20 ab-bi-e I call (on thee, O Marduk, in prayer). — On nabû = give a holy name to the king (by a god), or to give a name to a god (by the king) = SA (id XU + id for iršu, bed, couch) see HOMMEL, PSBA '08, 291 *foll.*

Q[t] attabi: I called, named; §§ 42; 49 *b*. D 96, 13 be-el mâtâti šum-šu it-ta-bi abu Bêl (K 8522 *R*). V 35, 12 Kuraš šar [al] Anšan it-ta-bi ni-bi-it-su "Cyrus, king of Anšan" he proclaimed (as) his name. Sn ii 26 at (*var* it)-ta-bi ni-bit-su; *Kui* 1, 16; *Bell* 32; *Bav* 12; Esh i 31. IV[2] 61 *a* 27 at-ta-ab-bi u-šab I said: sit down (on the throne)?! KB iii (2) 50 *col* iii 34 Šamaš the lofty judge e-di-eš-ša it-ta-bi (commanded its renovation).

ℑ cry aloud, lament, howl, bewail {laut rufen, wehklagen, heulen, beklagen} ZA ix 274—5; § 84. *del* 111 (118) u-nam-bi (*var* -ba) [ilat] Rubât ṭâbat (*q. v.*) rig-ma, ‖ i-šes-si (§ 52; KB vi (1) 238—9); IV^2 49 *a* 12 (T^M i 12) e-le-li nu-bu-u xi-du-ti si-ip-di my cheering is turned into wailing, my joy into mourning. T. A. (Lo.) 8, 15—16 May *T.*, my lord, and Ammon ki-i ša i-na-an[-na] lu-u li-ni-ib-bi[-u?] ordain (it) eternally as it is now (ZA v 136). II 7 *g-h* 44—5; V 39 *g-h* 49—50 I-LU = nu-bu-u (Br 4021, AV 6302; H 17, 283 qu-ub-bu-u), I-LU-DI = mu-nam-bu-u (II 32 *e-f* 17, see lallaru, 1); II 20 *a-b* 24; 25 *a* 70. — ag munambû name of a priest; Z^B 95; ZA ix 275 Klagepriester; Br 4027; AV 5490; II 38, 105—6 ‖ ça-ri-xu; on Asb ix 86 see mušapû.

ᴝ^1 KB ii 258—9 *ad* III 16 *no* 5, 9 (ša) u-tam-bu who has called (me).

ᴝ perhaps IV^2 6 iv 14 il ma-am-mam ul in-nam-bi; S^P II 987 *O* 22 in-nam-bi was proclaimed; also KB iii (2) 50 *col* 3, 21 it-ti e-eš-ri-e-tim ilâni la in-na-am-bu[-u?] which was not mentioned among the temples of the gods.

Derr. imbû(?), nibîtu 1 & the following 3:

nâbu *5.* Peiser, *Bab. Vertr.*, *p* 38 *no* xxvii 12 na-a-bi ša Esaggilrâmat word, edict of *E.* ¦Ausspruch der *E.*¦; *pp* 56—7, *no* xl, 10 na-a-bi = in accordance with the word of; see *ibid*, *p* 246.

nubû lamentation ¦Wehklage¦ *etc.* & **numbû** ‖ qubbû. K 890, 17 (al) Aššur tal-lak ta-si-si-i nu-bu-u, BA ii 634. Perh. also II 7, 44, V 39, 49 (see above), whence, according to Meissner, *Diss*, Thesis 8 the Mandean נאמביא. K 3428, 6 a-xu-lap (PSBA xix 315) i-na mâti-ja ša ba-ki u sa-pa-du, a-xu-lap ina e-me-ja ša nu-um-bi-e u ba-ki-e how long does wailing and mourning last in my land, how long in my clan lamenting & crying? (*Rev. Sém.*, ii 76).

nîbu (> nibbu > nib'u, § 47), properly: naming ¦Nennung¦ then also: numbering, number § 65, 4. K 1282 *R* 1 ša-na-at la ni-bu (KB vi (1) 70). Sn ii 75 see karû, 1 Q^1 (= a countless army) *Kui* 1, 24; 2, 39; *Konst* (I 43) 32 ša la ni-ba; Sn i 30 (-bi), i 29 ša-ša makkûru la ni-bi. I 65 *a* 26 ki-ma me-e na-a-ri la ni-bi-im; 66 *c* 15 ti-bi-ik se-ra-na la ne-bi (+ 20). Asb ii 130 ša ni-ba la i-šu-u; v 105 ša ni-i-ba la išû; Sn i 75; ZA iii 312, 57; KB ii 240—1, 37; TP III *Ann* often *e. g.* 70; 106 a]-na la ni-bi (-ba, 65), 206 (ni-i-ba). DT 83 (Pinches, *Texts*, 16) *R* 13 bâšû ša ni-bi a-qar-tu. V 35, 16 la u-ta-ad-du-u ni-ba-šu-un. Perhaps V 21 *c-d* 67?

(il) **Nabû** = Nebo, נְבוֹ, Isa 46, 1; AV 5695—6; 5690; written Na-bu-u II 7 *g-h* 40 (Br 2786); (il) Na-bi-um (often), II 23 *a* 55; 21 *a* 31, in colophons *etc.*, I 51 (1) *a* 1; V 65 *b* 49; II 7 *g-h* 41 = il Na-bu-u (V 39 *g-h* 36, Br 1629); II 60 *no* 2 = il AG ša kul-la-ti, AV 5695. Originally a water-deity (Jastrow, *Religion*, 124—5); in pantheon of Xammurabi = chief god of Borsippa (*ibid*, 130 *foll*); Tašmêtum, properly abstr. noun; il tašmîtum = god of revelation = Nabû (II 59 *a-b* 58 taš-me-tum); then also name for a goddess, always mentioned together with Nabû (see, however, Tiele, ZA xiv, 187 & AJSL xvi 210 *rm* 55), 228—30; another title of Nabû was Papsukal; but this was also used of other gods (Jastrow, 130 ✕ Jensen, 77). See also Jeremias in Roscher's *Lexikon der griech. u. röm. Mythologie*, iii 45—69 (an excellent article); Tiele, *Gesch*, 532—38. He is not a god of fire, and therefore not to be identified with Nusku (✕ Lenormant, Hommel, Jensen, *etc.*). He is the son of Marduk and Çarpanit, I 51 *no* 1 *b* 16 (il) Na-bi-um mâr ki-i-nim su-uk-ka-al-lam çi-i-ri | ši-it-lu-ṭu na-ra-am (il) Marduk; also Neb i 24(30) + 33 il Nabû a-bi-el-šu ki-i-nim (*i. e.* of Marduk): IV^2 14 *no* 3 *O* 1—2 a-na (il) Na-bi-um (= AN-AG, 1) suk-kal-li çi-i-ri (a hymn to Nebo); *R*, last line of text, (il) Na-bi-um suk-kal-lum çi[. . . .]. KB iii (1) 46, 11—12 (il) Na-bi-um su-ka-al-lam çi-i-ri | mu-ša-ri-ku ûm balâṭišu. He is the rikis kalâma, he that holds together the world (II 60 *no* 2, 28); the pa-qid kiš-šat šamê u erçiti V 43 *c-d* 27 (Jensen, 2), see kiššatu; the pa-qid (*q. v.*) kiššat nag-bi, supervisor of all & everything. — The god of fertility and of life (Jensen, 239; 325 *rm*). — His consort is either (ilat) Nanâ (*q. v.*) in Babylon, or Tašmêtum. I 63 *b* 34 pa-rakku (il) Na-bi-um u (ilat) Na-na-a bêle-e-a. Neb i 4 + 6 Nebuchadrezzar calls himself mi-gi-ir (il) Marduk & na-ra-am (il) Na-bi-um. KB iii (2) 2, 14 Nabopol. ti-ri-iç ga-at (il) Na-bi-um u (il) Marduk; 4, 16 i-na ṭe[-im] ša (il) Na-bi-um. KB iii (1) 184—5 *col* 2, 1 pa-lix (il) Nabû (written AN-PA) u (il) Marduk | ilâni Ê-sag-gil u Ê-zi-da. At the Newyear's festival (akîtu) the statue of Nebo of Borsippa (Êzida) and that of Marduk (*q. v.*) of Babylon (Êsagila) were carried about in solemn procession.

The chief ideograms are AN-PA & AN-AG. — AN-PA, mainly as the possessor of the writing stylus. D 19, 153; § 9, 60; H 87, 30, H^{OV} xxxi; KAT^{2} 413. Br 5379; II 60 *no* 2, 49; 40 Nabû called ilu muštabarrû šûlimu. Ash vii 47 (Br 2786) *var* to AN-AG. Nabû dup-šar gimri L^{1} i 11; Na-bi-um dup-šar Ê-sag-gil S^{1} 22 (LEHMANN, ii 10—11; 57). II 60 *no* 2 (*add.*, AV 7022) AN-PA-A-TI = AN-AG (Br 5639); *del* 95 (100) AN-PA u il Šarru (= Marduk) il-la-ku ina max-ri; V 46 *a* 20. — AN-AG as wisdom personified (D 11, 67; § 9, 60); I 35 *no* 2, 1 where the inscription on a statue of Nebo recites many of his attributes and doings (KB i 192—3; JEREMIAS in ROSCHER, iii 49); IV^{2} 48 *b* 12 AN-AG TUB-SAR Ê-sag-ila; II 59 *a-b* 56—7; often in colophons *e. g.* Ašurbanipal to whom AN-AG u (ilat) Taš-me-tum have given *etc.* IV^{2} 48 *col* 2 (end). T^{M} i 148, 151 *etc.*; IV^{2} 14 *no* 3 *R* 4; 6 ni-me-iq AN-AG; V 15 *a* 33; 16 *c* 60, 72 ni-me-ki AN-AG; D 49, 29 + 37; K 2711 *R* 6. — V 43 *c-d* 41 (Br 2785); also see IV^{2} 20 *no* 3 *O* 7—8 (21^{3} *no* 2 *R* 16 = AN-IB *cf* Br 1267, 1306, 10228; Z^{B} 50); II 57 *c-d* 28 AN-NIN-IB is called AN-AG (Br 11099). — He is the patron of priests and scribes. — His chief seat of worship was the temple Êzida at Borsippa; his worship came from Babylonia to Assyria, but here he was never very popular. — K 501, 15—16 says AN-PA (ilat) Taš-me-tum ina bît ma'ûlti | e-ru-bu (Hr^{L} 113).

III 57 *a* 57 *etc.* mentions as fifth pair of stars: Nabû & Šarru (*i. e.* Marduk) JENSEN 125; HOMMEL, "Astronomie der alten Chaldäer" (*Ausland*, '91 *no* 19 & 20). JENSEN, 239 *ad* V 43 *c-d* 17 + V 46 *c-d* 52: Der Name "Gott von *Duazag*" des Gottes *Nabû* bezeichnet ihn als den Gott des Wachstums, welcher als aus dem Osten stammend betrachtet wird, weil die Sonne, die das Wachstum bringt, im Osten aufgeht. Dass aber *Nabû* als Ost-Gott aufgefasst wurde, hängt damit zusammen, dass sein Stern, der Mercur, nur im Osten oder Westen sichtbar ist". See also, *pp* 117, 136, 145, 148, 492 *foll*, 506.

The Etymology of the name is not conclusively determined. JEREMIAS says, "certainly not √נבא (*cf* נָבִיא, which, however, may have been borrowed from the Babylonian; *cf* TIELE, *Gesch*, 533 *rm* 2) the interpretation of the id as herald, prophet is probably a popular etymology, as also the reading Na-bi-um" (JEREMIAS). Literature see GESENIUS^{13} *s. v.* נָבִיא; GESENIUS-BROWN, 612 *col* 2. HALÉVY: the prophet god.

On S + 17 (V 67 *no* 3) the name Pa-ni-Nabû-ṭe-e-mu is reproduced in Aramaic characters as: פנבוטם; also see PEISER, *Babyl. Vertr.*, *no* 67 (see plate, 43) & *pp* 266—7. where the name is transcribed נב. On the ram's head hand of Nabû see HOFFMANN, ZA xi 287—88 (§ 22); *ibid*, 263, § 14 on Nabû in Hades.

V 43 *c-d* 13 *foll* = K 104 + ⊕ 61 contains a list of titles of Nebo (also II 60 *no* 2; 54 *no* 5): 13 il Na-bi-um = AN-AG ša k(g)ul-la-ti (of the universe?); 14 AN-AG = AN-AG ša dup[-šar-ru-ti]; 15 AN-EN (za-ag) ZAG = AN-AG bi-e[l] or -l[um?], V 46 *c-d* 47 says here = AN-AG NI-TUK-KI (= Dilmun); 16 AN-PA-A-TI (see above) = V 46 *c-d* 48 AN (mu-u-a-ti) PA, ZA i 182 *rm* 1, which is also = êlat šamê; 17 AN-DU(L)-AZAG-GA, *cf* V 46 *c-d* 52; JENSEN 239 (see above); 18 AN-SE (id = nadanu), see V 46 *c-d* 53; 19 AN-UR (*cf* V 46 *c-d* 54, usually id for išid šamê); 20 AN-MUD + id for rabaçu (D 28, 240; V 46 *c-d* 55; Z^{B} 50 mu-zi-ib-ba-sa-a; also V 43 *c-d* 25); 21 AN-GAN-UL (V 46 *c-d* 56, for GAN-UL see xittu, 1); 22 AN-ŠEG(ZK ii 190)-DA(?, V 46, 57); 24 AN-MU-DUG-GA[-SA-A?] *i. e.*, ša šumu ṭâbu nabû; 26 AN .... BAR (MAŠ) = AN-AG ... par (bir?)-çi; 27 AN-ŠIT-KAK (or DU)-KI-ŠAR (= NI)-RA = AN-AG pa-qid kiš-šat šamē u erçitim (V 46 *c-d* 49, Br 5989); 28 AN (dub-bi-saq) 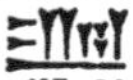 = AN-AG ap-lu (il) Marduk (II 60 *no* 2, 29; L^T 180; same id in S^b 238 = dup-šar-ru, Br 6013); 29 AN-U (= bêl)-ZAG = AN-AG bêl a-ša-ri-du (Br 8823); 30 AN-A-A-UR = AN-AG ri-kis ka-la-ma (Br 11690); 31 AN-AB-BA = AN-AG qa-eš-še ab-bu-ti = awarding decision (Br 3826; ZA i 404), 32 AN-GI-NAL = AN-AG ba-nu-u pi-riš-ti (Br 2410; ZA iv 279); 33 AN-DIM (= DIṢ?)-SAR = AN-AG ba-nu-u ši-iṭ-ri dup-šar-ru-ti (II 48 *a-b* 38; Br 9128, 12254 *fol*); 34 AN-NI-ZU = AN-AG ilu mu-du-u (Br 5340; K 7331; Zimmern, *Beitr. Babyl. Rel.*, 86—7); 35 AN-NI-ZU-ZU = AN-AG ilu te-li-'-u (Br 5341); 36 AN-ME-IR-ME-IR = AN-AG xa-mi-mu (*q. v.*) par-çi (Br 10427; KB iii (1) 194 an inscription abounding in epithets of Nabû); 37 AN-NE-DAR = AN-AG e-muq li-i-ti (Br 4615); 38 AN-UR (TAŠ *etc.*) = AN-AG ilu bu(n)l-ti (Br 11262); 39 AN-DI (= silim) MU-UN-ZAL (or -NI; Z^B 31) = AN-AG ilu mu-uš-ta-bar-ru-u (*q. v.*) sa-li-mi; 45 AN-AG = (il) Na-bi-um; this (il) Na-bi-um is also = 46 ilu ba-nu-u; 47 ilu ša tes-lit-tu i-ma-xa-rum (§ 147); 48 ilu xa-si-su; 49 ilu xa-si-sa-tu; 50 . . . . . en-ši; 51 ilu pi-it ux-ni; 52 ilu rap-ša uz-ni. II 60 *c-f* 49 & 50 see Br 11837 *fol.* K 8522, 5 AN-ZI-AZAG & 9 AN-NIN-IGE-GAL = Nabû. — II 54 *g-h* 66—75 AN-AG-NI-TUK-KI in *h* for 66—75 (corresponding to lines in V 43 *c-d*) see Br 2883, 5579 (*cf* III 66 *O* 6*b*; 19*e*), 5089, 9795, 3082, 9609, 4416, 4834, 2291, 5634 & 7222 (III 69 *g-h* 63; AV 5605). — On Nabû + compounds see Bezold, *Catalogue*, 2118 - 2131; AV 5697—5880, where Nabû is written mostly AN-PA; also Knudtzon, 331. T^M 1, 145 (*var*) Nabû-ba-nu-un-ni; K 481, 2 ardaka Na-bu-u-a; K 551, 2; 603, 2; 513, 14; Neb vii 47 (il) Na-bi-um (i 21; vii 11 id)-aplu-u-çu-ur; I 65 *a* 7; KB iii (2) 1, 9 Na-bi-um-ku-du-ur-ri-u-çu-ur šar Bâbilu a-na-ku (often); I 65 *a* 1; AV 5807; I 51 *no* 1 *b* 29; KB iii (2) 6, 6 (il) Na-bi-um-šu-li-ši-ir.

nâb(p)û II 57 *c-d* 20 na-a-bu-u (Br 1647) = tiz-qa-ru e-lu-u, preceded by (il) Ma-da-nu-nu = (il) Nin-ib(p). AV 2716.

nibû 1. √נבע. well, issue or gush forth {hervorquellen, sprudeln}, TP i 35 *TP.* ša si-kir-šu | eli ma-li-ki ni-bu-u (= pm) whose name is exalted over all the rulers (Haupt); perhaps ZA v 58, 34 (il) Marduk (il) Šam-šu ni-bu-u. — ℶ K 7856 *b* 1 *a* u-nam-ba-a xirâtê, M^S 62*b*.

Derr. namba'u, imbû'u (imbû) &:

nib'u *c. st.* nibi' sprout, offspring, *etc.* {Spross, Sprössling} ZA x 208 *O* 12 (end) ni-bi-'i erçi-tim; K 4216 *b* (šam) ni-bi-i' eqli, followed by (šam) inib eqli; II 11 *c-f* 73 (II 53) ni-pi-'i eqli (Br 2028, 2036); Sm 1071 *O* (iç) ni-bi-i' balti (wr. IÇ-NUM).

nabû 3. pr ibbi'; ag nâbi' destroy, take away, seize {zerstören, wegreissen, ergreifen}. I 49 ii 4—5 eš-ri-e-ti-šu-nu | ib-bi-'-ma | u-šo-me kar-meš; Esh ii 42 na-bi-'i (mât) Bît-Dakkurri ! III 15 iii 19 aš-lu-lu *etc.*; Hebr. vii 90. Sarg *Cyl* 26 na-(-a)bi-' Gar-ga-meš. *etc.* *Bull*-inscr. 24 na-pi-'i (al) Šinuxti; Pp IV 23 na-pi-'i (mât) Kammûni (Winckler, *Sargon*, 148).

Der. perhaps:

nibû *2.* ZA iii 137 (*no* ii) 12 ina bîtu ni-bu-u.

(aban) **ni-bu** a stone {ein Stein} 81, 7—27, 145, 5 followed by xannaxuru & sag-gillimut.

nabbu S^b 3 na-ab | NAB | = nab-bu (between šamû, ilu & kakkabu (Br 3840) Hommel, *Gesch.*, 119 "brilliant, pure"; Idem, *Sum. Les.*, 74: Luftraum. √nababu?

nababu. Abel & Winckler, 60 *fol*, 6 (aban) gišširgal ša zu-mur-šu ki-ma ûmi it-ta-na-an-bi-ib (= ittanabbib).

nibu = nibxu. II 42 *c-f* 67—8 (šam çubât) ni-bu = (šam çubât) ni-ib-xu, which latter = (šam) e-zi-zu; AV 4348; Br 10603—4; II 41 *e-f* 51 . . . . ni-bu = (šam) KU ni-ib[-xu], 52 . . . . ni-ib-xu = (šam) e-zi-zu.

nabadu (?). 83, 1—18, 1335 iv 22 [TAR] = na-ba-du ša narkabti. M[S] 62. Der :

nibdu. CRAIG, *Rel. Texts*, 75, 2 xi-ir-çu u ni-ib(p)-du ana ....

nubazu (?) Neb 168, 5 nu-ba-zu.

nībxu & nībixu. — *a*) sling, loop, snare {Schleife, Schlinge} ? M[S] 2 *col* 1] אבנ; BA i 290. V 28 *g-h* 41 *foll* ni-ib-xu ‖ ab-šu (41), mi-ig-ru (42), iṭ(ṭ?)-ru (43), e-al-u (44), e-nu-u (45). — *b*) frieze, enclosure {Fries, Karnies, Umschliessung}. Esh (A) vi 4 sixirti ēkalli šātu ni-bi-xu (*var* -xa) pa-aš-qu (*q. v.*) ša (aban) KA (aban) uknu u-še-piš-ma (KB ii 138—9); *Nai* 4, 9; Lay 39, 31. K 2675, 29 (aban) uknī ni-bi-xu e-bi-ix-šu (S. A. SMITH, *Asurb*, ii 12 *foll*). V 60 i 18 ni-ib-xa ša pa-an (ilu) Šamši u-šat-ri-ça-am-ma (PINCHES, PSBA viii: curtain, drapery). — *c*) V 61 v 46 we have (çubāt) ni-bi-xu mentioned together with xullānu (*q. v.*) as garments belonging to a god or goddess—given here to the sun-temple; in *c. l.* written KU-EB-LAL which in V 15 *c-f* 52 = ni[-ib (or -bi)-xu] between naxlaptum & xullānu (BA i 531 *fol*). Nabd 78, 20 (çubāt) ni-bi-xu; 547, 4: 22 mana šipāti ana ni-bi-xi ša (ilu) Šamaš u kusītum (*q.v.*) ša (ilat) A-A (BA i 527); 954, 2 ni-ib-xi-šu. - Also see KB vi 129 *rm* 14 *ad* NE 1 *col* v 7 & nibittu, 3. — *d*) ZA vi 291 i 7 mentions a plant {Gartengewächs} (çubāt) ni-ib-xi SAR (K 4398, 8), see nibu.

NOTE. — 1. BA ii 434 *ad* K 2619 *O* 24 reads nap-xat pit-pa-nu za-qip pat-ru: gespannt war der Bogen, gezückt der Dolch; connects with nibxu. KB vi (1) 60—1 nap(b)xat *mit*-pa-nu & leaves untranslated.

2. See MEISSNER & ROST, *pp* 4; 29 *rm* 48; BA iii 213.

nib(p?)xu. S[P] 158 + S[P] II 962 *R* 16 ina ni-ib(p?)-xi Ê-an-na u-sax-xu uçurtašu.

nub(p)uxātu? V 41 *f* 47 nu-bu-xa-tu.

nab(p)atu 1. flare up, shine, rise with splendor, begin (of day, stars, *etc.*) {erglänzen, aufleuchten, scheinen, leuchtend aufgehen oder anbrechen, *etc.*}. Hebr לפד (?); D[Pr] 98. II 47 *c-d* 31 AL-UD-DU = na-pa-ṭu (Br 5769) = II 48 iii 37 na-ba-ṭu ša kakkabi (Br 5768); V 20 *g-h* 9 MUL = na-ba-ṭu = II 48 iii 35; II 17, 268 (Br 8550); II 48 iii 36 KAR-KAR = na-ba-ṭu ša ū-me (Br 3187, same id = ittanpuxu); II 48 ii 22 (dil) RI = na-ba-ṭu (‖ šarūru) II 15, 199; Br 2550, 2564. K 8331, 18 (hymn to Ninib) ina im-xul-lu i-nam-bu-ṭu kakkē-šu; K 851 *O* 1 of a star: i-nam-bu-uṭ (= is brilliant); perhaps KNUDTZON, 41 *O* 6 i-ne-i[b-biṭ-u?], but??; *ibid*, *p* 307 on ubānu ibbiṭ (in omens); also Br 7786. JENSEN, 358—9 (& KB vi (1) 32; ZIMMERN-GUNKEL) *ad* K 3567 *O* 16 qar-ni na-ba-a-ta (for ṭa) that the horns (of the moon) may shine; *cf* 83, 1—18, 1332 ii 20 MUL = na-ba-tu (ZA iv 280); KB iii (1) 148—9 adds also V 33 *col* 7, 16—18 çir-ri-it šame-e | rap-šu-ti li-ib-bi-ta-šu {Strahlen aus dem weiten Himmel mögen ihm leuchten}.

ג IV² 38 ii 16 u-mi-iš nu-ub-bu-ṭi, lit up like daylight.

Š cause to shine {glänzen machen} D[II] 52; § 49*b*. II 67, 82 see būnu (*p* 178 *col* 1). Neb ii 45 Êkua u-ša-an-bi-iṭ (1 *sg*) ša-aš-ša-ni-iš (KB iii, 2, 15); also V 64 *b* 13; V 45 vi 48 tu-ša-an-baṭ; KB iii (2) 108, 33 u-ša-an-na-bi-iṭ; K 2801 *R* 38 ça-al-me .... u-šag(k,q)-li-du u-ša-an-bi-ṭu kima (ilu) Šamši. JASTROW, *Dibbara-frg* 5 šu-kut-ta ša-a-ša u-ša-an-bi-ṭu (3 *sg*); & ana šu-un-bu-uṭ šu-kut-ti (*cf* ZA vi 460); Bu 88—5—12, 77 *col* vi 15 u-ša-an-biṭ çu-bat-su-nu.

גt *pm* its horns nin-bu-ṭa (are brilliant) irat-ça nam-rat, 80—7—19, 55 *R* 6. — גtt IV² 4 *O* 40—1 like purified silver ru-uš-šu-šu lit-tan-biṭ (H 138; Br 8144; §§ 84; 101; also see § 52); V 42 *c-d* 45—7 SAR (mu-mu) SAR = i-tanbu-ṭu (Z[B] 37; § 49*b*; Br 4326, 4361); PA (xu-ud-xu-ud) PA = itanbuṭu ša kakkabē (Z[B] 102, bel; ZA ii 83; Br 5617); KAR (kar-kar) KAR = i-tan-pu-xu. Bu 88—5—12, 79 v mut-tan-bi-ṭu (said of Jupiter) BA iii 243 *rm* ****. — גtn IV² 25 *b* 50—1 šir(?)-tu it-ta-na-an-biṭ (= MUL-MUL, Br 3856); 27 *a*

nibzu see nipxu. — nabaxu see napaxu; nabbaxu *cf* naṭbaxu.

21—22 qar-na-a-šu ki-ma ša-ru-ur (il) Šam-ši it-ta-na-an-bi-ṭu (= MUL-MUL-LA, Br 3856, 7470) had risen in glory; also Rm 194 *R* 6; K^{M} 30, 12; § 101 = Q^{tn}; K 8713 *O* 7 it-tan-na-an-bi-ṭu; Scheil., *Nabd*, iv 9—11 ina aban GIŠ-ŠIR-GAL | ša ki-ma ū-mi | it-ta-na-an-bi-ṭu. Banks, *Diss*, 18 *foll*, *no* 2 (8—10), 63 . . . nu-ri (*var* -ur) mut-ta(-na)-an-bi-ṭu ša ša-me-e, the brilliant light of heaven.

Derr. nambaṭu &:

nab(p)āṭiš *adv* of נבט openly, manifestly, by daylight {öffentlich, am hellen Tage} Sarg *Cyl* 28 the inhabitants of these cities who against the country of Kakme id-bu-bu na-ba-ṭi-iš (see Lyon, *Sargon*, 63); *Ann* 51 na-pa-ṭi-iš; also XIV 46 na[-pa-ṭi-iš].

nibṭu. III 61 (2) *b* 31 šumma (or ana?) ni-ib(p)-ṭu ana na-pa-ax (il) Šam-ši RI-ix; also Rm 194, 3 Sin ina ni-ib-ṭi-e it-ti (il) Šamši innammar (see Thompson, *Reports*).

nabṭu. Ner 41, 1—4 ribū-tu xal-lu-ru | a-na nab-ṭu | a-na (il) Šamaš-uballiṭ | . . . nadin; 83—1—18, 774, 1 . . . . nab-ṭi-e Sin u Šamaš (see Thompson, *l. c.*).

nabaṭu 2. (?) Bezold, *Catalogue*, 1449 šumma ina kišādišu maxiçma libbūšu it-te-nin-bi-ṭu.

nab(p)alu 1. pr ib(b)ul destroy {zerstören} usually in connection with naqaru & šarapu ina išāti. D^{Pr} 33; ZDMG 40, 725 fall {fallen} Hebr נבל. Šalm, *Mon*, i 48 his cities ab-bu-ul aq-qur ina išāti aš-ru-up; a-bul a-qur ina išāti ašru-up III 5 *no* 6, 57 *fol*; D 113, 18; ab-bul aq-qur ina išāti aš-ru-up III 8, 90; *Khors* 70, & often. Their city (-ies) ina NE *pl* aš-ru-up ab-bul aq-qur TP i 94; ii 1, 34 *fol*; iii 11—12; 64—5 (ab-bu-ul); 83—4; iv 3—4; 25—6; v 2—3; 60—1; 72—3: 97—8; Their city (-ies) ab-bul aq-qur ina AN-GIŠ-BAR aq-mu Asb ii 131; Sn iv 33—4 *etc.*; KB ii 242—3, 150 this district ak-šu-ud ab-bul aq-qur ina li'bi(?) aq-mu. — pm na-pi-il was destroyed {ward zerstört} Nabd *Ann* iv 4 (BA ii 224—5); Rm 2. 97 (KB iii, 2, 196—7) *ad* 709: (al) Dūr-Ia-kin na-bil. T. A. (Ber.) 91, 30 ašrāti ša nab-la. 83, 1—18, 1330 iii 7 DAX (du-u) = na-pa-lu ša ēni. K 844, 21 adū (al) Qibi-Bēl ana na-pa-li š[i] and now the city *Q* must be destroyed. TP vi 30 the wall ib-bul ana tili utēr; 28 the wall . . . a-na na-pa-li aq-ba-šu(m-ma). — Q^{t} = Q Šalm, *Ob*, 157 *fol*, 180 their cities at-ta-bal (= bul?) at-ta-qar ina NE a-sa-rap. — ℑ Anp i 117 ša (BA i 398) çābē ma'adūti ēnā-šu-nu u-ni-bil; iii 113 an-nu-te ŠI II *pl*-šu-nu u-na-pil (-bel, KB i 70—1). KB v *23 *col* 1 refers here also T. A. (Lo.) 61, 25 nu-bu-ul-me (which Bezold, *Dipl*, 68 √ abalu). S^{P} 158 + S^{P} II 962 *R* 38 u-nab-bil. — ℑ K 815 *R* 2 šarru, šuātu LIK-KU in-na-bal (or Q ps?).

Note. — On nabalu & נָבַל see D^{Pa} 156; D^{H} 67; D^{Pr} 122; Brown-Gesenius, 620 *col* 1; PSBA '99, Apr., *p* 197; Ball in *Genesis* (SBOT, Polychrome edition), 53; on the other hand, KAT^{2} 66 *rm* 2; Hehn. i 179; also literature in Gesenius[13], *s. v.* — Derr. these 5:

nabultu = mītu corpse {Leichnam} *cf* נְבֵלָה D^{H} 67; D^{Pr} 122. lit^y = what is destroyed; see mittu; nultu of course a dialectic form for nabultu. K 1550, 22: 2 (amēl) qinnāti u na-bul-ti-šu-nu lapani'a ixtabtu; 20: u anāku šammu (?) na-bul-ti 150 na-bul-ti xubussu kī ax-butu.

nabbaltu. K 58 *R* 5—6 IM-BAL = nab-bal-tu; IM-BAL-BAL = nab-bal-la-a-tu D^{H} 67 hurricane; D^{Pr} 156; BA i 182 = Orkan; Hebr. iii 175 *fol*. = storm.

nabb(pp)illu an animal, insect, destroying the young plants {ein den Pflanzenwuchs zerstörendes Insekt} ‖ zirbabu (*q. v.*). AV 5891; D^{S} 77; II 5 *c-d* 19 id *cf* kisimmu & Br 5548; with reading xi-bi-in = nab-bil-lum (H 22, 422); perh also II 5 *c-d* 46—7 (Br 11784, 11787) see mūnu. Perhaps better read nappillu; see na-pi-lu.

nubal(l)ū *1.* sling, net, trap {Schlinge, Netz, Fallstrick} NE 9, 10 ut-ta-as-si-ix (√ nasaxu) nu-bal-li-e ša uš[-par-ri-ru] J^{I-N} 17; KB vi (1) 122—3; 124—5, 37. 83, 1—18, 1330 iii 16 du | DAX | nu-b(p)al-lu.

nabālu(m) *2.* ruin, damage, destruction {Ruin, Zerstörung} KB iii (2) 48—9 *ad* Neb *Ball* ii 20 *var* la na-aš-ku-un na-ba-lum to la na[š-ku-]nu pa-ri-im, that no harm (?) may be done to it. (*cf* also PSBA xi, 323).

nabālu *3.* Esh iii 26 see mišdu. Cheyne, Hebr. iii 26 = √nabalu, destroy: a journey (mi-lik) of desert land.

nablu, *m* fire, flame, glow {Feuer, Feuersglut, Lohe} *etc.*; so first Jensen, ZA i 64 *foll*; WZ i 158 comparing Eth. *nabalbâl* "fire, flame"; also see D^{Pa} 156; D^{Pr} 122 *fol*; ZDMG 40, 732. V 19 *c-d* 48 NI$^{(za-al-za-al)}$ NI = qamū ša nab-li (Br 5359); AV 5898. Asb ix 81 Ištar was clothed in fire . . . eli $^{(māt)}$ A-ri-bi i-za-an-nun nab-li. TP i 42 nab-lu šurruxu; v 42 nab-lu xa-am-ṭu = the glowing flame. Creat.-*frg* IV 40 nab-lu muš-tax-me (*var* -mi)-ṭu, Jensen, 280; Hebr. ix 18—19; KB vi, 1, 22—3; also Esh *Sendsch*, *R* 15. For V 55, 18 see xamaṭu, 2. Anp ii 106 nab-lu elišunu u-ša-za-nin (§ 152); K 2852 + K 9662 i 1 šu-u . . . . ša ki-ma nab-li i-qam-mu-u; K 3351, 20 i-na nab-li-šu u-tab-ba-tu mātāti mar-çu-ti; K 257 (H 129) *R* 15—16 Ištar says: a kindled fire I am ša nab-lu-ša *etc.* (see daparu; Jensen, 484; Br 9486); Šalm, *Mon*, *R* 68 see mulmullu, KB i 169; Scheil, *Šalm*, 96. Also ZA iv 12, 11 mušax-miṭ ki-ma nab-li & v 58, 32. Perhaps IV^2 24 *no* 2, 18—19 u nab-li. AV 6094.

nablū H 98, 20 ina bi]-ti mar $^{(il)}$ Šamaš nab-li-e ā ērubšu. Nabd 429, 5 nab(?)-li-i ša daltu (also *cf* 882, 3).

nabālu *4.* = תֵּבֵל *terra firma*, Haupt, ZK ii 315 (√وبل); Barth, § 179, 1; PSBA xi 323 dyke, riverwall ‖ xalçu, *cf* KB iii (2) 30—1, *col* 3, 17 na-ba-lam ab-ši-im-ma. Hebr. vii 88 *rm* 14. Asb i 69: 22 šarrāni ša a-xi tam-tim qabal tam-tim u na-ba-li; also ii 53. Smith, *Senn*, 93, 70 (= Sn *Kui* 2, 24) anāku ana itēšun na-ba-lu çab-ta-ku I advanced by land {ich nahm den Landweg}. KB iii (2) 126—7 *ad* v 35, 29 a-ši-ib na[-ba-li]. T^M 1, 64 ša na-ba-li (‖ erçitim, 63) ši-ma-a amatsu; II 67, 63 bi-nu-ut tam-tim na-ba-li. III 30 *a* 40 ina tāmtim u na-ba-li gir-re-ti-šu u-çab-bit alaktašu aprus. Banks, *Diss*, 16, 1 *no* 4, 132 ki-ma e-ri (= GIŠ-MA-NU) ina na-ba-li (upon dry land) u-še-man-ni. — KB v 276 *rm* 1 *ad* T. A. (Lo.) 30, 42 suggests reading nabāli for AN-AB-BA. See also tabālu (ZA iv 261, 33; & again, ZA viii 82); Meissner & Rost, 24.

nab(p)āliš, *adv* or = ana nabāli = on dry land, § 80*b*. Sn *Kui* 2, 16 (= Smith, *Senn*, 91, 62) na-ba-liš ušēlušināti, they brought (the ship) up to the dry land; Meissner, ZA viii 82 (*cf* iv 265): auf festem Lande. ZA iii 316, 76 na-ba-liš u-tir = ina tili u karmi utīr. Sarg *Prisma* 39—40 the Tigris and the Euphrates i-na mili kiš-ša-ti e-du-u [gab-šu . . . .] na-pa-liš u-še-tiq I crossed the mighty stream like as on dry land (× Winckler, *Sargon*, 188).

nubalu *2.* TP vii 57 Ninibpalēkur ša nu-ba-lu-šu ki-ma u-ri(-in)-ni eli mātišu šu-b(p)ar-ru-ru-ma whose lightning fire (?) like the light of day was spread over the country; see also ZDMG 43, 197; Sayce, RP^2 i 116: whose might like a sling, *etc.* Hommel, *Gesch.*, 509: whose power (?) like a weapon (‖ šibirru) *etc.*

nubal(l)u *3.* part of an eagle {Teil des Adlers}, *pl* nuballē. Jastrow, Etana-*frg*: the serpent u-nak-ki-is kap-pe-šu ab-re-šu u nu-bal-le-šu (BA iii 366) tore out his wing, his feather, his pinion; KB vi, 1, 106. BA iii 369 Jastrow corrects K 1547 (BA ii 393), 27 çu-up-ra]-šu into nu-bal-li]-šu & connects it with nubalu, 2.

nabalṭū *cf* *b-l-ṭ-'* (*pp* 164—5). Br 5530 *fol*, 10680; AV 6082; PSBA xii 399.

nablaṭu Rm 281 (*med*) see balaṭu (*p* 164 *col* 2, NOTE) & mixçu.

nabalkattu — *a*) desertion, revolt, rebellion {Abfall, Empörung} Jensen, 220—1; Br 270, 3277. Šalm, *Balaw*, i 2 mu-ni-ir nab-al-kat-tu. V 20 *e-f* 44, 48 (= II 38 *g-h* 14, 18) TIK-GIŠ-SAR = na-bal-kat-tum (& -tu) ‖ pirsu; KI-BAL = mātu na-bal-kat-ti (*var* -tu) & māt(u) nu-kur-ti; D 83 iii 58, 60; *Babyl. Chron.* iii 18 nabalkat-tum $^{(māt)}$ Aššur epuš (KB ii 280). Sn *Bav* 53 na-bal(?)-qa-ta-šu u-ša-tir, but Meissner & Rost, 85—6 na-i-qa-ta-šu destruction, ruin, √nāqu, *q. v.* Knudtzon, *nos* 68 *O* 12; 115 *O* 6. — *b*) name for Hades; J^W 65 (but

JENSEN, 221: merely: adjoining land, *i. e.* das Jenseits). II 26 *a-b* 5 KI-BAL-tum (*cf* II 26 *c-f* 42; 38 *g-h* 18); see קבל. — *c*) some siege-instrument, -machine {eine Belagerungsmaschine} M^S 24. S 279, 13 [na]-bal-kat-tu in a list of weapons, followed by sir-ja-am. Esh *Sendsch*, *R* 43 ina pil-ši nik-si u na-bal-kat-ti alme (also see Sn *Bav* 45 ina pil-ši u na-bal-qa-te on which M^S 24, & above, *p* 169 *col* 1). ROST reads na-bal-qat-ti ‌‌√פלק, *cf* pilaqqu, as LYON, *Manual*. — JENSEN: perhaps = ladders {Leitern}, balkātu scale (but adds??). AV 6083.

nabalkattānu rebel {Aufrührer, Empörer} ZA ii 231 *rm* 1; §§ 65, 35; 117, 1. III 15 ii 15 see baranu. In lawsuits also = defendant {Angeklagter} T^C 57; BP^2 i 161 *rm* 3 ✕ paqirānu plaintiff {Ankläger}; BO i 88, 11; ii 123, 125. PEISER, *Babyl. Vertr.*, 320 *col* 2: one who breaks a contract or repudiates it; *e. g.*, *no* xxiii 20; lii 14 na-bal-kat-ta-nu (also cxxxiv 15). Nabd 210, 10; 1030, 10; Cyr 64, 11 na-bal-kat-ta-nu 1/3 manū kaspi i-nam-din.

nabalkūtu rebellion {Aufruhr} see balkatu (*pp* 165, 166), Br 270, 10341.

nabnītu, *f* √banu, 1. AV 5894; Br 7021, 7381. BA i 4—5 > mabnitu; § 65, 31 *a*. — *a*) creation, birth {Schöpfung, Geburt}. TIELE, *Gesch*, 353 *rm* 2: Erzeugnis; ZIMMERN: place of giving birth {Ort des Gebärens} in V 62 *no* 2, 6 a-šar nab-ni-it ummi (alittija), but see LEHMANN, ii 40 *rm* 1; *ibid* 150 *rm* 6 on id ALAM; JENSEN, KB iii (1) 199: an dem Ort [wo ich] ein Gebilde [war] der Mutter. BA ii 261, 54: das Geborenwerden oder das Gebildetwerden im Mutterleibe. IV 56 *b* 10 Bēlit-ilāni .... pa-ti-qat nab-ni-te, *cf* Lay 38, 8. II 58 *no* 5, 4 Ea is called (ilu) NU-DIM-MUD as ša nab-ni-ti. II 66 *no* 1, 2 ina AN-IŠTAR^{MEŠ} (= ištarāte) šu-tu-rat nab-ni-sa. Esh v 23 such & such stones ultu kirib xuršāni a-šar nab-ni-ti-šu-nu. Neb i 25 see banū Q *no* 2. D 94, 7; H 116 *O* 10 *etc.* see gimru (*p* 224 *col* 2); K^M 1, 53; 2, 48; 9, 40. — *b*) creature, offspring (of man or beast) {Geschöpf, Spross (von Mensch oder Tier)} Šalm, *Ob*, 19 nab-ni-tu elli-tu ša Tukulti-Ninib; *Mon*, *O* 11. TP ii 29 (47) mārē nab-ni-it libbi-šu; v 17 (šarrū-ti-šu-nu); vii 18. K 2801 *R* 36 nab-nit a-ra-al-li e-pir šad-di-šu u-šar-ri-xa nab-nit-sun; *O* 4 Ea .... ba-nu-u nab-nit; ZA x 292, 26 nab-nit (ilu) Da-gan. 82—7—4, 82 *R* 4 (end) ip-ti-iq na-ab-ni[-tu]. K 1794, 32 ag-mu-ra nab-nit-sa. Rm 982 we have šam-xat nab-ni-su; K 3464, 28 (ilat) Ištar, mārat (written: TUR-SAL) (ilu) A-nim nab-ni-it ilāni rabūti. T^M 7, 58 u-ç[ab-bi] nab-n[it-ki]; 65 (end) nab-nit-ki u-çab-bi, see BA iv 161—2. — *c*) structure, work {Machwerk} Sn *Kui* 4, 25 the bull-colossusses nab-nit erē; & nšaklila nab-ni-su-un. KB vi, 1, 308: Form, Gestalt & adds here also II 66 *no* 1, 2, see, above, *a*). Sm 747, 2 (end) nab-ni-[tu?]; K 2711 *R* 20 u-ša-tir nab-nit-sa bīt a-ki-it çīri bīt ni-gu-ti.

Sm 2052, 10 li-da-a-tum = na-ab-ni-tum. II 29 *e-f* 71 i-li-it-tum ‖ na-ab-ni-tu(m); 21 *a-b* 25; V 18 *a-b* 32 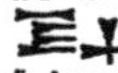 + ALAM = nab-ni-tum ‖ ‖ bunnanū; V 39 *f* 58; ⊕ 253, 1; Z^B 37—8.

nab(p)as(s)u & nabāšu dyed (usually: red) wool {(rot) gefärbte Wolle}. BA i 290 undyed wool; çirpu dyed wool, & id(t)qu "Rohwolle"; Arm. נפש OPPERT, JA vi, 3, 240 *foll* (1864); LYON, *Sargon*, 63. HOMMEL, PSBA xix '97, 78 § 22: red wool, √napašu (*q. v.*) = pick wool: √نفش; true Babylonian form is napašu not nabasu ‖ çirpu. id TUK (often) T^C 143—44. TP iv 20—1 dāmē (qu-ra-de)-šu-nu (šad) Xirixa ki-ma na-ba-si lu(-u) aç-ru-up with their (the warriors') blood I dyed mount X like red wool (L^{TP} 140). Anp i 53 dāmē-šu-nu kīma na-pa(-a)-si šadu-u lu aç-ru-up; ii 17, 18 (na-pa-si); Šalm, *Mon*, *O* 47; *R* 78 (kīma na-pa-a-si); II 67, 48; Asb iii 43 its waters aç-ru-up ki-ma na-ba-as-si. II 89, 45 ki-e na-ba[-si] el-lu-ti pure cords made of wool (= GAN-ME-DA, Br 11150) ZK ii 41 *rm*. Nabd 78, 7 irbit-ta (çubāt) [na-xal]-ap-tum na-ba-su; Cyr 241, 6 irbitta naxlaptum SEG-GAN-ME-DA (= nabāsu); ku-si-tum (*q. v.*) nabāsi often together (wr. SEG-GAN-ME-DA); Cyr 241, 18 see kusītum. IV 23 *no* 2 *R* 4—5 šamû ki-ma na-ba-ši ça-rip. V 14 *c-d* 10 [SEG-GAN-ME-DA] = n]a-ba-su (but ZK ii 264—5 -ti *i. e.* ṭ; § 44). *adv*:

nabasiš like wool dyed red {gleich rotgefärbter Wolle} Sarg *Khors* 130 iç-ru-pu (3 *pl*) na-ba-si-iš; *Cyl* 25 *cf* Nammaʾu (*p* 320 *col* 2) & mašku; Šalm, *Mon*, ii 50 kīma na-pa-si-iš aç-ru-up.

nab(p)urru. Meissner & Rost, 59 *rm* 20: battlement, pinnacle {Zinnen, Stufenabsätze}, perh compare nipru ‖ taxlubu (?). √عبر? Sn vi 61 the palace ul-tu uš-še-ša a-di na-bur-ri-ša ar-çip. I 49 iv 22 temple, city, and walls ul-tu uš-še-šu-un a-di na-bur-ri-šu-un eš-šeš u-še-piš (I built anew). TP uses in such connection tax-lu-bi-šu; Bu 88, 5—12, 103, 21—22 ul-tu uš[-še-šu-un] | a-di na-bur[-ri-šu-un]. *adv*:

naburriš. I 44, 81 female lamassu I made carry the threshold, and placed them between the (sal) lit (?) zazāti na-bur-riš u-še-me (or šib)-ma u-ša-lik as-me-iš.

ibru *1.* Winckler, *Forsch*, i 541—2 *ad* DT 71 *R* 16 tu-xa]l-li-qa ni-ib-ri-šu thou shalt destroy its power {sollst vernichten seine Stärke}, √abaru? *cf* nipru.

ibru. III 66 *R* 23 (il) pat (?) ni-ib-ri (Br 13463).

ibaru, *m*; **nabārtum**, *f* trap (place of catching, locking up) {Käfig, Falle} § 65, 31 *a*; √אבר₃. I 7 (ix) 1 a mighty lion of the desert ištu libbi (iç) na-bar-ti ušēçûni (they let loose from the cage). II 22 *no* 1, 27 GIŠ-AZ-BAL = na-ba-ru = na-bar-tum ša nēši (Br 3871); 28 GIŠ-KAD-AZ = na-ba-ru = na-bar-tum, AV 2086. V 26 *a-b* 39—41 GIŠ-AZ-BAL = ši-ga-ru, na-ba[-ru], e-ri-in[-nu]. BA i 162; 326 *ad* 175. ZA iii 51, 52 compares Aram. נַבְרְקָא.

bburu(pp?) 82—8—16, 1, 14 ni-ib-bu-ru.

biru *1.* — *a*) crossing {Überfahrt} across a river, sea or ocean. § 65, 31 *a*; √עבר. D^Pr 142, 1; Z^B 45, 7; BA i 175. Meissner & Rost, 21, 14: Furt, seichte Stelle. NE 67, 21 (24) see ma-ti-ma; KB vi (1) 217: Übergangsstelle. on *R* 20 *foll*, see J^w 86; J^{I-N} 30, 31. K 823, 16 ina nār A-ba-ni ni-bi-ru. D 88 vi 14 e-lip ni-bi-ri ferryboat (Br 3742). V 21 *g-h* 49 (ni-bi-ru). — *b*) ferry, ferryboat {Fähre, Fährschiff}. *del* 225 (249), but *cf* KB vi, 1, 249: Übergangsstelle. K 2729 *R* 3 ni-bi-ri za-ku-u die Fähre ist frei (KB iv 144—47; BA ii 566 *foll*); D 88 vi 9 GIŠ-MÁ-DIRIG-GA = ni-bi-ru (Br 11515, 3743); T^M 1, 50 ak-la ni-bi-ru, ak-ta-li ka-a-ru. ZA iv 15 (K 2361 + S 389 ii) 9 ni-bir ka-a-ri perh: die seichten Stellen des Ufers. Z^K iii 48 ma-mit ka-a]-ri u ni-bi-ri; viii 36 written id GIŠ-MÁ-DIRIG-GA. 81, 2—4, 219 *O* ii 15 id-du-ku (they kill) ša ni-bi-ri ru-u-a (*Rev. Sém.*, vi *no* 4).

nīburu ferry {Übergangsstelle} Johnston, JAOS xix 72 *ad* K 515, 13 ni-bu-ru tu-pa-aš; *R* 5 ni-bu-ru lu tu-pi-iš; 13 ni-bu-ru u-pu-šu (Hr^L 89). *Cf* Rost, OLZ ii *no* 5, *col* 158. AV 6189.

nībiru *2.* Name of planet Jupiter (?). Jensen, 288—9; 128—9; ZA i 94; 260 *rm* 1; 265 *rm* 3; D^Pr 142; Z^B 45; Lotz, *Quaestiones Sabbat.*, 30. K 3567 (D 94) 6 man-za-az il Ni-bi-ri (KB vi, 1, 30—1); V 46 *c-d* 34 (il) Ni-bi-ru | ri-mi-nu-u; *cf* II 54 (*no* 5 *O*) ii 6 & II 51 *b* 61; III 54 *b* 32, *d* 36; 53 *b* 8. AV 6182.

Nībiru *3.* K 8522 *R* 6 šum-šu lu (il) Ni-bi-ru a-xi-zu [kir-bi(š)]. KB vi 37 may his name be Nibiru (*i. e.*) the seizer of *K.* Jastrow, *Religion of Babylonia*, 434 & *rm* 6.

nībiru *4.* some instrument, comp. Mod. Hebr. מַעְבֵּר fork, used for loading (?) straw. Nabd 429, 2 ni-bi-ri.

nab(p)ramu. II 23 *b* 29 nab-ra-mu (embroidered? ornamented?), 29 *a* KA (?) (iç) sa-ak-ku (?) AV 5896.

nab(p)rarū field, plain {Feld, Ebene} Schell., *Šalm*, 100 (√פרר) *ad* Šalm, *Mon*, *R* 100 nab-ra-ru-u rap-šu a-na qub-bu-ri-šu-nu ix-li-iq the whole wide field

nabsamu see napsamu; nabaçu, nibçu *cf* napaçu, nipçu. — nabbaqu see nappaqu. — u 2. see nipru 1; nubaru see nuparu.

was used up for their burial ground. Against CRAIG, *Diss*, 30 see KB i 172. BA i 177 "flight of an army".

nībirtu — *a*) crossing {Überfahrt} NE 67, 24 pa-aš-qat ni-bir-tum (KB vi, 1, 217: Übergangsort) šup-šu-qat u-ru-ux-ša. TP III *Ann* 134 ni-bir-ti (nār) Za-ba *etc.* ak-ka-çi (KB ii 28—9; ROST, 109: Fuhrt) BA i 5. — *b*) the other, farther, opposite side (of a river or ocean) {das Jenseits eines Stromes, Meeres, *etc.*} Anp iii 134 the city of Çirku ša ni-bir-tu (nār) Purāti. Asb ii 95 (māt) Lu-ud-di na-gu-u ša ni-bir-ti tam-tim (WINCKLER, *Forsch*, i 513 *rm* 1: Küstenland *not* jenseits des Meeres); K 359, 3 ana a-xu-la na-aç-çu-u ni-bir-ti mat .... AV 6183.

nībartu crossing (over a river) {Übergang (über einen Fluss)} § 65, 31 *a*; BA i 175; ZA ii 112. Asb v 96 ip-la-xu a-na ni-ba-ar-te; *cf* city Ni-bar-ti-Aššur Anp iii 50 (on the Euphrates, ZA i 358).

nibirtum (?) Cyr 331, 1: 40 GUR suluppu ša ni-bir-tum ŠE-BAR.

(il) **Nab-ri-iš** III 66 ix 10.

nibrētu, *f* hunger, famine {Hunger, Hungersnot} barū, 2 (*q. v.*) § 65, 31 *a* (*rm*); ROST, 98. Asb iv 43 ni-ib-re(-e)-tu iç-bat-su-nu-ti; *cf* 93 those who had escaped ina .... ni-ib-ri-e-ti (KB ii 192—3). I 70 *d* 17 su-ga-a u ni-ib-re-ta; Sn v 14; SMITH, *Asurb*, 100, 18 su-un-qu ‖ ni-ib-re-tu. I 29, 94 see bubūtu *a*). Cuthean Creat.-*legend* (ZA xii 321 *foll*) iii 4 (end) ni-ib-ri-tu (KB vi 296—7).

nabšaltum something cooked {etwas gekochtes} √bašalu. D^{Pr} 32; Z^{B} 76; § 65, 31 *a*. IV^2 57 *b* 7 (= IV 64) see kānu ℶ *p* 402 *col* 1 (end) where read nab-šal-tum; & see *p* 201 *col* 1. BA i 175; but see also napšaltu.

nabatu 1. ℨ II 7 *g-h* 43 = V 30 *g-h* 48 DA-DA-RA = nin-bu-tum, Br 6677.

nabatu 2. see ***nabaṭu 1.*** (JENSEN, 358 *fol*).

nibiṭtu *1. c. st.* nibit. — *a*) properly: calling; then also called, appointed {Ruf, Berufung; berufen} Anp i 21 Anp i-ši-pu nādu ni-bit (il) Ninib qar-di; 33 ni-bit (il) Sin, *etc.*; iii 127 & see migru. I 68 *no* 2, 2 Nabd ni-bi-it (il) Nabū u (il) Marduk; V 33 i 5' ni-bi-it (il) A-nim. 81—6—7, 209, *o* ni-bit (il) Marduk. V 60 ii 20; Esh *Sendsch*, *R* 22 ni-bit (il) Sin. ‖ ni-šit, nayad, naram, *etc.* — *b*) name {Name} see nabū. Asb ii 97 ni-bit šumi-ja ‖ zi-kir šumi-šu (96); iv 131; x 120. K 3351, 24 apil É-šar-ra zi-kir-šu qar-rad ilāni ni-bit-su (said of Ninib); *Khors* 155 so and so azkura (*cf* zakaru) ni-bit-su (*Ann* 416); Esh vi 26; Sn *Bab* 12; K 2852 + K 9662 iv 7 az-ku-ra ni-bit-sun (= *pl*). III 29 *no* 2, 15 a-na eš-šu-u-te iš-ku-na ni-bi-is-su-un. Sp II 265 *a*, xxii 10 li-'-u qar(-ra)-du ša ša-ni-i ni-bit-su. AV 6185.

nibittu 2. (& **nabbitu?**). *del* 264—5 (295—6) we read Arad-Ea šam-mu an-nu-u šam-mu ni-bit-ti ša amēlu ina lib-bi-šu i-kaš-ša-du nab(p)-bi-su. J^{I-N} nibittu = nibittu 1. Pflanze der Verheissung; nap-bi-su > nappiš-šu perh. *m.*-form of napištu; the lines must contain a description of the wonderful, magic herb. DELITZSCH, *Weltschöpfungsepos*: this plant is the plant of transformation. JENSEN, KB vi (1) 251: UR-NINIM „dies Kraut ist ein Kraut des .... wodurch der Mensch seine *Vollkraft* erlangt", & *ibid* *rm* 13: ni-bit-ti wäre auch = „Name", „Genannter", ni-ḳit-ti = Verfall.

nibittu *3.* √נבא$_4$ rope, fetter, bond {Strick, Band} ZK i 299 (עבט); BA i 175. II 7 *g-h* 42 = V 30 *g-h* 47 KU^{da-ra} IB = ni-bit-tu(m); *cf* V 15 *e-f* 43; 14 *e-f* 53 KU-EB (or TUM)-BAL = ni-bit-tum (Br 4965), 52 na-ax-tum. S^b 220 da-ra IB ni-bit-tum; II 33, 790; S^c 2, 5; Br 10485 *fol*; also see KB vi (1) 129 *rm* 14.

(amēl) **Na-bat-a-a.** Nabatean: Aramean tribe {Nabatäer}. K 502, 3 (Hr^L 305); D^{Pa} 240; KAT^2 117 *rm* 1; 147 (settled in North-Arabia). Asb vii 124 Uāte'a flees alone a-na māt Na-ba-a-a-te (KB ii 217 to Nabatea; § 13); viii 56 Na-ad(t)-nu (*cf* נתן) šar (māt) Na-ba-a-a-ti (to whom Uāte'a fled); 70; also see III 35 *no* 6 *c* 34; IV^2 47 *no* 1, 13 (ul-tu šar Ni-

nabšu *cf* napšu; nibšu see nipšu; nabšsu *cf* nabāsu. ~ nibiš(t)u *cf* nipiš(t)u; nabištu see napištu.

ba-'-a-ti); ZA vi 199 & 207 (amēl) Ni-ba-'-ti. The nation is called in Asb viii 48 the people of (māt) Na-ba-a-a-ta-a-a (95 *var* -ti, see BA i 19 *no* 26; 113); also see III 34 *b* 35; 35 *no* 6 *b* 4, 30, 38. Merodach-Bal.-stone (KB iii, 1, 190) iv 17 a-na tar-çi (al) Na-ba-ti. See Gesenius[13]; & Brown-Gesenius, *p* 614. AV 6178.

(amēl) **Na-ba-tu.** Sn i 42 a subtribe of the Babylonian Arameans. KGF 99—116; D[Pa] 240; KAT[2] 147; 346. II 67, 6 among many tribes is mentioned (amēl) Na-ba-tu & in *l* 8 it defines them as A-ru-mu (Aramean?).

nibittu 4. KB iii (1) 198—9 *ad* Šamaš-šumukīn *Cyl*, 28 (end) i-raš-šu-u ni (or i?)-bit-tu and will go to ruin {und wird zu Grunde gehen}. Jensen, *ibid*, *rm* *: eigtl. Untergang bekommen wird; suggesting reading i-bit-tu. Lehmann, ii 12 i-kaš-šu-u ni-bit-tu and when the inscription (Aufschrift?) becomes unintelligible. AV* 49 *col* 2 reads V 65 *a* 23 (end) ni-bit-ti ar-ši, but ZK ii 340—1 ni-k(q)it-ti, and KB iii (2) 110 ni-qid-ti ar-ši I became frightened {ich bekam Angst}; preceded by ma-'-diš ap-lax-ma. Also see KB vi (1) 296—7 iii 4 ni-*bi-is* (or b(p)il)-su-u, between xar-ba-šu & ni-ib-re-tu.

nu-…-tu (nu-bat, bit, mit, -tu) Lotz, *Quaestiones*, 51 (√ עבר?); Johnston. AJSL xvi 31 *foll* (where most literature) holy day & holiday, rest {Feiertag. Rasttag} Haupt ('84); so also S. A. Smith, ZA iii 101 (see kašapu); Jensen, 107 *fol*, 502; KB vi (1) 162—3; 252—3: Totenklage. — *del* 269, 283 (301, 319); NE 57. 44+45; Haupt, BA i 144 *rm* *; Delitzsch, *ibid*, 231 (237) *ad* K 618, 28 kal ū-me ši-a-ri nu-bat-te a-na sa-ru-ri (V 53 *b* 29); III 66 *O* 10*d* ina ū-me še-ir-ti nu-bat-ti (PSBA xxi 220—1: in the days of work and rest. but adds?y) thou shalt call upon the name of the gods; 67, 4—2, 1 *R* 2—3 nu-bat-ti ina Ninā-ki ul i-kit (& ZA ii 63—4, 12—13). K 1335+80—7—19, 335 *R* 1 i-da-a-ti ina nu-bat-ti; Asb ix 11 ūm III kam nu-bat-tu ša šar ilāni (il) Marduk (KB ii 222—3; BA i 16 *no* 19); K 3445, 15 nu-bat-ta. 16 .... ni-ip-pu[uš]; K 2866, 25 *fol* (S. A. Smith, *Miscell. Texts*, 17); K 1250, 13 emūqu ša bēl šarrāni bēlija adi Dūr-ilu iqṭirba nu-bat-ta ul i-bi; K 1107 *R* 9 (Hr[L] 9) ina nu-bat-ti dullu; K 602, 19 (Hr[L] 23) ina nu-bat-ti Arad-Êa ina gušur ēkalli ippaš (+ *R* 1); K 626 *R* 12 (Hr[L] 24) ši-a-ru nu-bat-tu ip-pa-aš; K 1108 *R* 15 (Hr[L] 49); K 649, 7 (Hr[L] 56), *etc.* Z[B] viii 25 nu-bat-ti ūm AB-AB; T[M] ii 137—8 anā-ku ina qi-bit (il) Marduk bēl nu-bat-ti | u (il) Marduk bēl a-ši-pu-ti (*cf* vii 19—20). II 32 *a-b* 13 [ūm] nu-bat-ti-im = ûm i-dir-ti, perh. a holy day; II 30 *g* 2 nu(?)-bat (zi-li-ba) —(?) Br 1967; ZA i 55 *rm* 1. IV 32 *a* 11, 28; *b* 27: the 3[d], 7th, 16th of Elūl nu-bat-tu(m) ša (il) Marduk (u) (ilat) Çarpanītu. — See also Craig, Hebr. xi 107 (feast?) quoting K 8293, 7 *fol*: (ūm) 2, (ūm) 7, (ūm) 15, ūm nu-bat-ti; Hommel, *Hastings Dictionary*, i 217: a festival, specially connected with the worship of Merodach & Çarpanit; ZDMG 43, 197 proposed also reading nu-zix-tu (√naza-xu): it is the name of a day sacred to a deity and, also, a *new-moon* day.

NOTE. — Nabd 351, 26; 360, 26 ina nu-bat-ta-tum (il) Šamaš; Cyr 372, 12 nu-bat-tum ina ŠI (= maxri?)-ia; Dar 40, 2. According to M[N] 63 of a different meaning.

nubtu bee {Biene}; Eth *nĕ'ĕb*; نُوبٌ; H[F] 6. II 7 *g-h* 48 = V 39 *g-h* 53 NUM (= fly = Fliege) 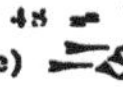 (= dišpu, V 40 *c-f* 51) = nu-ub-tum; V 27 *g-h* 10, with which compare II 5 *a-b* 23 (nu-ub-tum, II 40, 240), 24 xu-um-bi di-iš-pi (*q. v.*); K 2020 *R* 23—5 see matqu, *b*. — Perh. P. N. Nu-ub-ta-a my bee! (BOR i 82); Nabd 356, 21: Cyr 64, 1 (KB iv 266); 130, 1; but see also nuptu. AV 6395.

nubbutum. K 4188 III 8 nu-ub-bu-tum (AV 6447); II 28 *c* 49 (add.. AV 6394; Br 13997 = ... AK-A); Br 3333 quotes same as TUR-TU-LU = šupiltu ša nu-ub-bu-tu (?).

nug (*adr*) see nuk.

nigû be light, bright, shine; then also: be joyful, rejoice {licht, hell sein, glänzen; fröhlich sein, sich freuen} נגה; § 34β; Z[B] 22; 44; 76; D[Pr] 33. K 8522 *R* 26 li-ig-gi-ma a-na (il) Bēl AN-AN (= ilāni) (il) Marduk (KB vi, 1, 39). II 20 *c-d* 27—30 . . .] (xu-ul) XUL (Br 10888); [. . .]-LU (Br 10690); [A?]-ŠA´(= LIB)-GA (Br 14482); . . . . . GA (Br 14178) = ni-gu-u. — $\mathfrak{Q}^1$ K 10485, 5 šum-ma . . . . [i]-te-gi-ma. — ℑ ac *c. st.* nug, properly: making joyful, hilarity (of heart) = xud of xadû ℑ & nummur. *Khors* 194 nu-ug lib-bi; II 20 *c-d* 32—34 ŠA´-GI-[ ] Br 14307; ŠA´-KA-[ ] Br 14306; SU-ŠA[-NI?] Br 248 = nu-ug lib-bi SCHEIL, ZA x 292, 25 nu-ug libbi (il) Bêl; K 8212, 21 nu-ug lib-bi nišê. — $\mathfrak{II}^1$ be made glad }erheitert werden{ K 8522 *R* 15 ka-bit-ta-šu i-te-en-gu (KB vi, 1, 37). AV 6196; 6396.

NOTE. — According to HAUPT, BA i 160 šangû from nigû, but see na(i)qû.

Der. nigûtu.

nagû sound, make noise }schallen, tönen{ ‖ nagagu (*q. v.*); G § 40. II 29 *c-d* 20 [KA-D]E = na-gu-u (Br 14229).

Der. nigûtu.

nagû *m*, *pl* nagê & nagiâni; AV 5905; § 65, 6. — *a*) district, land, circuit; island }Bezirk, Landstrich; Insel{ ZA vi 175 (see *ibid*, 124) Insel, Küstenland; also see ZA viii 236—7 (& bêrûtu, 1). Arm [illegible]. I 48, 15 rap-šu na-gu-u (mât) Ia-u-di the wide country of Judea; the capital and fortress na-gi-e šu-a-tu Sn ii 24 (*cf* dannatu); iv 28 Xupapânu na-gi-e (+ I 43, 20) ša (mât) Elamtu, + 33 alâni ša ki-rib na-gi-e ša-tu-nu (+ I 43, 25); Esh iii 37: 8 kings ša ki-rib na-gi-e šu-a-tu; KB ii 242—3, 50 na-gu-u šu-a-tu ak-šu-ud *etc.*, this district I conquered, + 57 na-gu-u ša (al) Arsiânis, + 63 na-gu-u ša (al) Erištejana. III 8, 99 see mušpalu. Sarg *Bull* 28 la-i na-ge-e ša At-na-nu; *pl* na-gi-e also Sarg *Ann* 264, *Khors* 43 cities ša VIII na-gi-e-šu; + 66; *Ann* 73, 119 (na-gi-i) *etc.*; 165 gi-mir na-gi-šu-nu; *Khors* 70: V na-gi-i ša pa-ṭi-šu; III 9 *no* 3, 30: XIX na-gi-e (= TP III *Ann* 180), TP III *Ann* 209; 170 (*sg*); 230; II 67, 32 na-gi-e ša (mât) Ma-du-a-a (+ 47); K 2852 + K 9662 ii 1 a-di (while) as-na-ku ina ki-rib na-gi-e šu-a-tu at-ta-al-la-ku šal-ṭa-niš; K 667, 11 ina na-gi-i. 83, 1—18, 1330 *O* ii 15 nagû = nadbaku (PSBA '88, Dec.). Asb ii 95 Gyges, king of Lydia na-gu-u ša ni-bir-ti tam-tim; such & such a city a-di na-gi-šu (with its surrounding territory) v 68, 77, 78, 79, 80, 82; + 113 (al) Ba-nu-nu a-di na-gi-e ša (al) Tasarra; vii 111 ina na-gi-e (= *pl*) of *X*.; vi 78; also iii 2 na-gu-u šu-a-tu (*var* -šu). K 619, 5 (mât) Na-gi-u (AV 5902); K 2401 iii 8—9 ina alâni-ku-nu | na-gi-a-ni-ku-nu. See also ZA iv 362 *R* 6, 8 *etc.* *del* 133 (140) i-te-la-a na-gu-u (JENSEN, 435—6; KB vi, 1, 239). Neb 329, 17 na-gi-i ni-su-tu ša kirib tâmtim. II 20 *c-d* 35—6 na-gu-u; 36 same id as S^b 148 na-an-ga | LAL-KIL | na-gu-u (H 32, 749; Br 10143; *cf* II 29, 20). HOMMEL, *Sum. Les.*, 32, 376 × BALL, PSBA xii 68 *rm* 1. — *b*) village, place }Ortschaft{ Sn i 59 na-gu-u šu-a-tu ‖ âla šu-a-tu *Kui* 1, 8. — SCHEIL, 10 *R* 7 na-gi--ga (ZA x 217). — See Nagîtu.

nugu'. K 5494 *a* (BEZOLD, *Catalogue*, 725) (amêl) nu-gu-'u (M^5 63) title of an officer, or, name of a tribe.

NU-GI-A in erçit NU-GI = lâ târi, D 58, 176; IV 31 *a* 1 (KB vi, 1, 80—1 & *rm* 2); Br 1973; NU-GA-A (Br 1996); Br 1998, 7406—7 & târu. Sp II 265 *a* i 10 it(?)-ta-ar KUR-NU-GI.

nagb(p?)u *c. st.* nagab totality }Gesammtheit{ ‖ kullatu & napxaru; so first WINCKLER, *Sargon*, *p* 217; BA ii 435. ROST, 116: Schlupfwinkel, Gebiet. KB vi(1) 318: Das assyr. Wort lautete eigentlich, jedenfalls aber ursprünglich, naqbu: *ad* NE 1 1 ša na]g-[b]a i-mu-r[u] (*cf* NE 50, 218). Sarg Pp II 10; III 13 (I 12) na-gab (amêl) A-ri-mi(-me); *Khors* 149 na-gab (amêl) A-ri-me; 16 u-ra-as-si-ba na-gab ga-re-ja. IV^2 39 *a* 25 see zâ'iru (*p* 293 *col* 2); also zamânu (*p* 284 *col* 1); 82—7—4, 82 *O* 16—17 mu-a-ab-bi-it | na-ga-ab li-im[-nu-ti]; *cf* K 8522, 20 (KB vi 36), *R* 14 see nabû ($\mathfrak{Q}$ *b*). K 2619 iv 18 (end) na-gab-šu-un ‖ nap-xar-šu-nu (18, beg.). K 2660 (III 38 *no* 2) 8 ma-xa]-zi çi-ru-ti na-gab-šu-nu. Creat.-*frg* III 7 ilâ]ni na-gab-šu-un them all }insgesammt{ ‖ 17 ilâni gi-mir-šu-nu; III 69 *e-f* 57 na-gab nu-ux-še ‖ (il) Adad ša me-xi-e;

me-xu-u, *etc.* (Br 2618). V 21 *c-d* 68 UZU = nag-bu (Br 4558). AV 6128.

ni-gab (*i. e.* NI-GAB) see petû.

nagagu, ps inagag, speak, call, cry {sprechen, rufen, schreien} G § 40; Br 530; AV 5898. IV^2 26 *b* 58—9 to his god kîma litti (*q. v.*) i-na-ga-ag (= KA-IM-ME, Br 753) = i-šá-as-si IV^2 27 *a* 33, Br 754; Z^B 85. II 20 *c-d* 24—6 KA (gu-de) DÉ (Br 699; II 29 *c-d* 21); KA-DÉ-DÉ (Br 704; ‖ šagamu, šasû, *etc.*); KA-GE-GE (Br 687) = na-ga-gu. II 29 *c-d* 22; 49 *no* 5, 58 (= H 10 (+211), 58) KA-DÉ; 57 KA-DUB (Br 709 = nabû); 59 KA-RU-RU-TIK (Br 604); ‖ ramamu, xababu, 1 (*q. v.*); also *cf* nagû. H 37, 54 KA-ME = na-ga-gu ‖ ša-su-u (55); 81, 8—18, 4159 i 33 UD = na-gu-g[u] followed by rigmu (Z^B 63). — ℑ ag perh II 32 *a-b* 57 mu-na-gi[-gu] Br 716. — 𝔑 II 20 *c-d* 31 [na?]-an-gi-gu (or √ugagu?).

Der. nuggatu.

nagalu 80—7—19, 55 (Astron. Text) *R* 5 when in the flaming light of Scorpio qarnātišu nin-gu-la its horns are bright (explained, *ibid*, by nin-bu-ṭa √nabaṭu) THOMPSON, *Reports of the Magicians, etc.* II, *pp* lxxii *fol*; 77.

niggallu Rm. fragm.]ṬU-GAL = pa-aš (see pāšu) ni-ig-gal[-lu?].

nigul(l)û best, choice oil {bestes Öl} compound of NI = šamnu + gul(l)û (*q. v.*) > GULA. V 65 *b* 13 ni (or NI? = šamni) gu-la-a (*cf* duxadu); Esh vi 40 where u-ša-qi of First Rawlinson is, no doubt, a mistake for u-ša-aš-qi. Also II 58 *no* 6, 71 ni-gu-la.

naglabu knife, or some other instrument for cutting {Messer, *etc.*}. See above *p* 118 *col* 1 for other suggestions; also ZA iii 231 *no* 20; BA i *pp* 8; 10; 175; § 65, 31*a*; AV 5908; Br 320. II^V 72. WINCKLER, *Sargon*, read also naklabu (*q. v.*), naqlabu. K 2619 ii 11 na-aš paṭ-ri na-aš nag-la-bi qup-pi-e u çur-ti (BA ii 428, 430, 435: Classe von Tempeldienern; KB vi, 1, 62—3). Sarg *Ann* 136 ana Ursâ ....çur-ti nag-la-bi qu-bi-e iç .... ti iškun; 294—5 Merodachbaladan ... nag-la-bu iš-ši-ma u-ša-aç-ri-xa bi-ki-tu; *Stele* i 43 all Urarṭu [u]-ša-aš-ša-a (1 *sg*) nag-la-ba. II 24 *no* 2 *c-d* 60—1 GER (= paṭru)-ŠU-I = nag-la-bu (Br 7148); UZU-BAR-TAR = *n* ša šêri (Br 1835, 4560); K 4580, 6—7.

NOTE. — On root נגלב see also SCHULTHESS, *Homonyme Wurzeln im Syrischen*, (1900) *pp* 8—9: "naglabu, ein 'Messer zum Ritzen der Haut', z. B. um seiner Verzweiflung Ausdruck zu geben".

NU-GIM(or DIM)-MUD(T) = Êa, often *e. g.* Creat.-*frg* III 54; IV 120, 142 ni-is-mat (ilu) NU-GIM-MUD (KB vi 319—20). JASTROW, *Religion of Babylonia*, 230 *rm* 4 on DELITZSCH, *Weltschöpfungsepos*, 99 *rm* (the name is so commonly used, that it applies to more than only Êa and Bêl; I 35 *no* 2, 2 Nabû son of ilu NU-GIM-MUD; see, however, KB vi. 1, 320); & also 424 *rm* 3. II 58 *no* 5, 4 (ilu) Ê-a (= the god) ša nab-ni-ti = AN-NU-GIM-MUD, followed by AN-NA-GIM-MUD = AN-NA-DIM-MUD = ilu Ea ša ku-la-ma (AV 5910); V 44 *c-d* 15 AN-LA-BAR AN-NU-GIM-MUD = arad ilu Ea; II 67, 67; IV^2 5 *b* 48—9; K 2675, 30 ina ep-šit ilu NU-GIM-MUD; also = Bêl (father of Ninib) = bukur AN-NU-GIM-MUD, *cf* Anp i 2; Šamš i 15 = bukur AN-EN-LIL (= Bêl); *cf* Sarg *Nimr*, 6. AV 6401.

nagmir *cf* gamaru 27.

nigiççu *pl* nigiççâte cleft, hollow, cavern {Erdspalte, Erdhöhlung} § 65, 21; Z^B 54—5; G § 116; *cf* giççu. Sn i 17—8 ki-ma su-din-ni XU ‖ ni-gi-iç-çi like a falcon, the bird (living) in the clefts (HEBR. vii 58 & *rm* 8). IV^2 30* *no* 3 *O* 6 see mûšu. II 93, 39—40 ina ni-gi-iç-çi bi-i-ti & ina ni-gi-iç-çi qab-ri (*cf* 37—8), nigiççi = KI-IN-DAR which is found also in IV^2 15* ii 25—6 (the seven evil spirits) ina ni-gi-iç-çi ir-çi-ti it-tanaššabû (√ישב); 39—40 see xalalu 2?(tn); Br 9682; ROST, 105. K 41 iii 4 (end) ina ni-gi-iç-çi (iç DI-DA-AL) eš-te-ri (in a hollow I perch, PSBA xvii 65 *foll*). II 19 *b* 49—50 see xumçiru (Br 9584; and on the iç JENSEN, 235 *rm* 1). V 21 *a-b* 11—12 GIŠ-ZI-DIR (Br 2355;

H 39, 137) = ni-gi-iç-çu (preceded by xurru); KI-IN-DIR (Br 9683) = ni-giççu qaq-qa-ri (H 31, 714). AV 6195.

nagaru 1. K 1285, 10 lišān-ka la ta-at-ta-ni-gi-ir ultu šapti-ka, S. A. STRONG, *IX. Or. Congr.*, ii 207: 2te of נגר: fluere; effudit. **Der.** perh.:

na(n)garu. Tc 100 *ad* Nabd 203, 2 (578, 1) ugār nan(KB iv 222: nam)-ga-ri water ditch {Wassercanal} = נִגְרָא (zur Berieselung des Feldes).

nagaru 3. JENSEN, 394 (& KB vi, 1, 230), JEREMIAS, *etc.* on *del* 20 (24) u-gur bīta ‖ bi-ni elippa (see, above, *p* 173 banū, 1. ip) = prepare, timber {zimmern}. HAUPT, KING, *etc.* read u-qur (√naqaru). To this nagaru belongs, according to JENSEN & AV 5899, also II 15 *b* 32 bītu ša ina ramānišu ig-gur i-pu-uš (but see naqaru, & Br 6202).

Derr. these 3:

naggaru, namgaru = נַגָּרָא carpenter {Zimmermann} Br 11163. S 760, 10 (ABEL & WINCKLER, *Texte*, 60 *foll*, 22) nam-ga-ru ša šip-ra(-ru)du-um-mu-qa (AV 6010; Br 7380. 10768, 11165); ⊕ 51 iv 29 (amēl) GIŠ-ŠU-KAR = nam-ga[-ru] mentioned with gurgurru (*q. v.*), ça-dimmu, & b(p)urk(q)ullu. Berl. Vokab. (ZA ix 159 *foll*) i 18 GIŠ-ŠU-(šu-uk-ra) KAR = na-ag-ga-rum (JENSEN, 293—4, *rm* 2). BA i 283; 534 *no* 42; KB iii (1) 148 *rm* 3 = *faber lignarius.* S[a] iv 4 MUL-NA-GAR = na-an-ga-ru (JENSEN, 394; BA i 534; AV 6057). In Astronomy it means: crab, cancer (EPPING-STRASSM., *Astronom aus Babylon*, Anhang, *p* 7). See also nannaru & p(b)ulukku.

(amel)  = **nagar** AV 6010; see Nabd 416, 4; Neb 107, 10 *etc.* (T[C] 100); STRASSM., *Stockholm*, *no* 2, 1 (iD); K 3456 *O* 38 (PSBA xxi, 38; *ibid*, *p* 44 BOISSIER says: JENSEN, 394, is not convincing, and compares ik-karu = farmer (*cf* en-ga-ar a gloss to ikkaru). K 334 (III 49 *no* 5) 18.

nagargallu = chief naggaru {oberster naggaru}. IV² 18 *no* 3 *O* i 37—8 (39—40) god NIN-IGI-NAGAR-GID (or BU) is called nagar-gal-lum ša (il) Anim (he is commanded to do some work in a forest of high & lofty trees); also V 61 iv 15 ina ši-pir of god NIN-IGI-NAGAR-GID (BA i 283; KB iii, 1, 178—9); II 59 *b-c* 45 it occurs as an epithet of Ēa.

nagaru 4. 83, 1—18, 1335 iii 30 ta-ra | TAR | na-ga-rum. ℑ perh. ZA iv 239, 16 u-nam-ga-ru kar-ra M[S] 63 (but see karru).

nāgiru probably: steward, overseer, prefect, commander {wahrscheinlich: Vogt, Aufseher, Praefekt, Kommandant} AV 5904; DELITZSCH, *Aegypt. Zeitschr.*, Aug.-Sept. '78, 59. D[OG] 309; HOMMEL, VK 393. iD (amēl) LIGIR, Br 6966, 10147; H 28, 527. iD consisting of character for frontlet + inserted KAŠKAL = xarrānu, *i. e.* one that leads the way. IV² 48 *a* 25 il-ki ši-si-it (amēl) na-gi-ri elišu ukannu; IV² 30* *no* 3, *O* 36 a-ri-ba iç-çu-ra na-gi-ir šamē (*Rev. Sém.*, vi 149; ZIMMERN, GGA '98, 822); IV² 1* v 23—4 I-šum (-taq) is called na-gir (*cf* PINCHES, *Texts*, Signlist iii 144; H 175 *no* 7, end) su-ki ša-qu-um-mi; H 99, 47 (il) I-šum na-gi-ru rabu-u ra-bi-çu | çi-ru ša ilāni. IV² 15* i 47—8 (il) I-šum na-gir (*var* gi-ru) rabu-u ra-bi-çi çi-i-ri ša ilāni; *cf* KB vi, 1, 72—3, 10 a-mat (il) I-šum a-lik max-ri-šu; Z[B] 60, 14; H 176, 3; ZK ii 277. K 823, 13 (PINCHES, *Texts*, 7) iD (amēl) nāgir ēkalli, holding a military office; Su v 69 X (amēl) na-gi-ru ša šar (māt) Elamtu the chief commander (KB ii 109) who was mu-ma-'-ir çābē-šu; *Rec. Trav.*, xvi 176 *foll.* (amēl) nāgir ēkalli *cf* KB i 208 *foll* for the years B. C. 808, 778, 751, 741 = prefect of palace {Schlosshauptmann}; Sarg *Ann* 138; SMITH, *Asurb*, 199, 10 (& *p* 140); TP III *Ann* 17; Merodach-Baladan-stone (Berl.) v 7; II 31 *c-d* 39 (Br 6968); 53 *a-b* 19. Cyr 361, 7 (amēl) na-gi-ru iti sūqu qat-nu. V 52 *a* 30 na-gi-ir (see 29 for iD) a-xat bīti. V 16 *e-f* 35 LI-BI-IR = na-gi-rum (AV 1222; Br 1133, 11291) same iD = susap(b)inu & q(g)allū. On LI-BI-IR = nāgiru see Z[B] 60—1; H 118 *R* 9; 183; ZK ii 281; HOMMEL, *Sum. Les.*, 22, 262.

---

nagaru 2. see naqaru.

na-gar-ru-rum (II 27, 13; AV 5900) & **na-gur-ru-ru** (II 34, 67; AV 5907) Br 10213 see garaṛu.

***nagâšu** 1.* throw down, overthrow, overpower, espec. of a bull knocking someone down with his horns {niederwerfen, überwältigen} *etc.* = Hebr נגשׂ; ZA i 59 *rm* 1; AV 5901. II 36 *g-h* 10—12 (+ ⊕ 270) DAG-DAG (Br 5535) = na-ga-šu ša amêli; SI = nagašu ša NE (= išâti) Br 3396; SI-MUL = nagašu ša alpi (Br 3442). IV² 22 *a* 32—33 çi-la-ni kîma e-lip-pi la-bir-ti i-na[-gi-iš] = IN-DAG-DAG[-GI], but see Br 5535—6. In *c. t.* we have P.N. Bel-tum-na-gi-iš. — Q¹ tear down (buildings, *etc.*) see muttagišu. scale; Sn i 60 aš-ru šup-šu-qu i-na šêpe-ja ri-ma-niš at-ta-giš I scaled like a wild bull. *Kui* 1, 10; *Bell* 21. — J¹ = passive of Q¹. Perh NE 65, 5 Gilgameš ut-ta-gi-šam-ma G. ran hither & thither (KB vi, 1, 210—11). H 87 ii 9 e-kim-mu (the departed spirit) la mut-tag-gi-šu (= DAG-DAG-GE). — 𝔗ᵗⁿ II 28 *a* 9 it-ta-na-gi-iš (✕ AV 113).

***nagâšu** 2.* D 142*a* = alaku go {gehen} Hebr נגשׁ approach; ig-gu-uš = il-lik. Perhaps ZA v 59, 12 i-giš muš-te-me-qu-ti draw nigh unto my prayers! — J¹ ZA iv 11, 32 ina sulê çêri mut-tag-gi-šu = walking on the street or field; Z^B iii 83. J. Oppert, ZA x 52 speaks of muttagiš of a field as adjoining {anstossend an}. — 𝔗ᵗⁿ (?) or Qᵗⁿ (?) Bu 88—5—12, 75 + 76 ii 16 . . . id-du-ma it-ta-nam-gi-šu a-xa-a-ti BA iii 248 sie machten sich auf und davon; perhaps = nazazu ina axâti (*q. v.*).

(amêl) **NU-GIŠ-ŠAR (SAR)** = ikkaru (*q. v.*).

Nagîtu *f of* nagû. City in Elam. Sn iv 25 (al) Na-gi-te ša (mât) Elamtu; 27 (al) Na-gi-tu, (al) Na-gi-tu-di-'-bi-na (Jensen, ZA viii 237: Wolfsküste; *cf* Arm דבנין; also Rost, xiii *rm* 3; D^Pa 328); iii 56 (al) Na-gi-(i-)te-ra-aq-qi (ZA viii 237 Schildkröteninsel). K 1376 mentions Nagiatâ'a Inhabitants of Nagîtu (Bezold, *Catalogue*, 278); also na-gi-a-tu for nagîtu, § 68.

nuggatu (√nagagu) roaring, wrath {Toben, Zorn} Z^B 66; BA i 182. IV² 10 *O* 1—2 ša be-lim nu-ug-gat libbi-šu ana ašrišu litûra (iD ŠA'(= LIB)-IB-BA = uggatu, Br 4959); 57 *b* 8 a-a u-qa-ri-bu-ni uz-zu nu-ug-gat ilu.

NOTE. — ZDMG 43, 197 reads nu-uk-kum √nakamu heap up, for nu-ug-gat. Z^B 118: nu-uq-qum; D^W 332, 2 nu-uk-kut.

nigittu *f* light, shine, splendor {Licht, Glanz} √nigû. II 66 *no* 1, 7 see gitmâlu; NE 58, 19 ib-te-li]-im-ma ni-git-tu ‖ ib-te-li i-ša-tu (KB vi, 1, 164); perh also V 31 *no* 3, 9 kukkabê ni-git-ti šaknu (Jensen, 505); see ZK ii 80 (or ni-bu ina pânišunu?).

nigûtu *f*; *pl* nigâti; also **ningûtu** joy, music, merrymaking {Freude, Musik, Jubelfest}. D^Pr 33; Z^B 31 *rm* 2; BA i 182 *rm*; § 65, 9. Sarg *Ann* 439 aš-ta-kan ni-gu-tu (= *Khors* 179); ni-gu-tu aškun, Winckler, *Sargon*, 172, 20; also *Cyl* 20. IV² 18 *no* 1 *O* 20—1 [i-sit]-tu ni-gu-ta mu-šu u ur-ra uš-ta-b[ar-ri] Br 7990; IV² 60* C *O* 7—8 ik-ri-bi šarri ši-i xi-du-ti u ni-gu-ta-šu a-na da-me-iq-ti laputum-ma. Pinches, *Texts*, 15 *no* 4 *O* 7 (DT 83) ar-ax ša bu-la-ṭi i-sin-ni a-ki-ti liš-ša-kin ni-gu-tu (PSBA xvii '95, 133; Jensen, 412); ZA x 293, 47 ina bît arax i-sin-ni ta-ši-la-ti ni-gu-u[-ti]. Smith, *Asurb*, 125, 66 eat, drink, nin-gu-tu šu-kun (KB ii 252); 134, 46 (KB ii 256—7) it-ti (amêl) LUB^MEŠ (= zammerê) e-peš nin-gu-ti (*cf* 132, 21; 312, 74). K 2711 *R* 20 see nabnîtu *c*). Asb x 95 ina e-le-li nin-gu(-u)-ti with playing of music (but Boissier, PSBA xx 164 § 2: qu'ils passèrent le reste de leur vie *à gémir et à soupirer*); V 33 v 40 ni-ga-ti-šu-nu ra-ba-a-ti lu-u e-pu-uš their (the gods') great festivals I arranged. K 2852 + K 9662 (margin) 1 (end) e-biš ni-gu-tu.

nâdu *1, 2.* see na'adu & nâ'idu.

nâdu *3.* (נאד) skin, leatherbag, -bottle {Fell, Lederschlauch} with or without determinative SU = mašak. T^M 124. Sn iii

---

na-gir-tum see na-kir(-piš?)-tum. ∼ nag(k)-ru-tum *cf* naqrûṭum (V 21 *a-b* 63). ∼ NI-GIŠ (*or* IÇ?) see šamnu elû ‖ Oel.

80 mē (mašak) na-a-di ka-çu-ti (*q.v.*) ašti (BA ii 256 *fol*). IV² 56 iii 54 lu-u na-ša-a-ti na-a-du ša çu-um-me-e-ki; 40 *b* 31 ki-ma mē nādi (written SU-A-EDIN-LAL) ina ti-ki liq-tu-u, like as the water of a leatherbottle may they perish by being poured out. NE 17, 45 (10, 40) mē na-da-a-ti (*var* -te) water from leatherbottles (J^W 96 & *rm* 6; ZA ii 437); 43, 38 (mašak) na-a-da mu-na-.... na-ši-ša. Neb 211, 4—5 a-na (mašak) nu-u-ṭu *pl* u na-a-da. AJP xix 386 nādu originally: inflated, swollen.

nādu *4.* Rm 339 *O* 5 (= dupl. of II 40 *no* 3) na]-du-u = na-a-du ša ṭi-ṭi for na-du-u, 3 = na-du ša IM (II 40 *c-d* 45).

nadū *1.* see kulūlu, 2.

nadū *2.* *pl* (mē) na-da-a-ti see nādu, 3.

nadū *3.* pr iddi; ps inadi (& i-nam-di NE 63, 28 + 31); ip idi; pm nadi; pc li-du-u (let them throw, § 22; lu-ud-di Cuthean-*Creat.*-legend ii 16). AV 5916; ZDMG 27, 515 *rm* 5; ZK ii 15 *ad* ideogr. RU (IV 38 *b* 39; 23 *b* 34—5; 10 *b* 37—8) § 9, 78; Br 1434. — *a*) throw, throw down, -away {um-, hin-, wegwerfen} NE 48, 180 ana pāni-ša id-di (*var* is(z, ç)-max); perh 54, 1 na-di-ma Eabani (55, 21); XII vi 11 ša ina su-qi na-da-a ik-kal & 6 the man ša ša-lam-ta-šu ina çēri na-da-at (whose corpse is thrown away upon the field) (KB vi, 1, 265); *del* 231, 238 (= 256, 265) *cf* mašku; 235 (262) a-a id-di-ma. Creat.-*frg* IV 112 see kamāriš; TP viii 20 a-na e-pi-ši a-xi la-a ad-du-u; III 15 ii 9 na-di-e a-xi ul ir-ši; V 64 *a* 38 a-xi la ad-da I did not lay down (expressing great activity); *cf* S^c 1 *b* 12 ... ni-di a-xi (Br 1848; AV 6197; ZA i 391; D^Pr 140); TP viii 65 whosoever my documents a-na mē i-na-du-u; Esh *Sendsch.* *R* 55—6 ina mē i-nam-du-u (see BA ii 140 for further examples), Mer.-Bal.-stone (Berl.) v 28 (end) ana mē RU (= inamdu)-u; IV² 39 *b* 18 (see mīšu), 19 a-na mē i-na-du-u; I 70 *c* 1 ana mē i-nam-du-u; III 4 *no* 7, 6 my mother id-dan (*var* -an)-ni (or נדן?) a-na nāri; V 25 *b* 7 a-na na-a-ru i-na-ad-du-šu (ideogr. SE, Br 4417; S^c 85): into the river they shall throw her (§§ 66; 140; HOMMEL, *Sum. Les.*, 111); Bu 88, 5—12, 21 a-na nāri i-na-du-ši-na-ti (JRAS '97, 610—11); T^M iv, 44 (tad-da-a); Asb iv 51; IV² 50 *b* 42, see miqtu. Bu 91—5—9, 407, 11—12 iš-tu di-im-tim i-na-da-ni-iš-ši (he may throw her, JRAS '99, 106—7; or נדן?); T^M iii 91 ana išāti lu-ud-di (1 *sg*); 101 see miqtu. Sarg *Khors* 38 id-du-u they throw down (the corpse); Bu 88—5—12, 75 + 76 ii 16 ... id-du-ma; H 87, 6 ša ina i-ku na-du-u; 10 (see katamu, ג); 13 (see namū, 2); perh II 16 *f* 12—13 u a-na çi-rum ta-nam-da; 80—7—19, 19 *O* 3 ana mi-tu-tu a-na-ad-di-ka I will put thee to death; IV² 3 *a* 21—22 see xamaṭu, 2 ג^t; K 2361 + S 389 i 41 (ZA iv 237) see gibšu; ši-ka-ra i-na na-di *cf* šikaru; IV² 10 *b* 37—8 see ru-šum-tu, also for IV² 16 *b* 21—22 (Br 8992), same ideogr. = na-a-du II 25 *g-h* 73. — *b*) pull down, destroy {niederreissen, zerstören} Sarg *Ann* 288 Dūr-Ladinna na-da-a (pm) is lying in ruins; IV² 31 *b* 23 la ta-na-da-aš-ši do not pull it (the gate) down! (KB vi, 1, 81); I 27 *no* 2, 28 my palace la i-na-di (he may not destroy); KB iii (2) 62 *no* 10, i 27 the temple ša u-ul-la-nu-u-a na-du-u (had gone to ruins); IV² 1 *a* 10—11 see karru, 1 (& Br 5580); 83, 1—18, 1331 iv 5 na-du-u ša kar-rum. — *c*) with uš-še, *etc.* lay foundation {Grund, Fundament legen}. V 65 *a* 40 ad-da-a uš-šu-ša, *cf* 64 *b* 5 + 27 (innamdū, § 53, accent); *c* 32; Sarg *Bull* 56 upon such & such uš-še-e-šu ad-di-ma; TP vii 83 *fol* ina muxxišu uš-še bīti ša pu(-u)-li ad-di; Sarg *Cyl* 61 uš-še-e-šu ad-di(-ma); V 66 *a* 12 a-na na-di-e uš-šu ša Esagila; *a* 16 ad-di-e uš-ši-šu; V 60 *c* 1 na-di-e parakkē ‖ šu-šub ma-xa-zi; *del* 286 (324) u uš-ši-šu la id-du-u. — With libittu, 1 (libnāti, *q. v.*) Asb x 82; Bu 88—5—12, 75 + 76 iv 15; III 8, 89; 82, 5—22, 1048, 3 li-bit-ti ul na-da-at; V 63 *a* 33 ad-da-a libnatsu; ZA iii 314, 68 li-e (*i. e.* bit)-su ul id-da-a (*Bell* 30 i-da-a). — Sarg *Khors* 160 du-nu-šin (*i. e.* of the ēkallāte) ad-di-ma. — With šubtu = locate, settle {Wohnstätte gründen; ansiedeln, wohnen} ‖ ramū (BA ii 282). K 2527 + K 1547 *O* 19 šu-]ub-ta id-di (= ip; also see *l* 33); Sn iv 25—6 id-du-u | šu-bat-sun; Asb ix 116 Ušû ša ina a-xi tam-tim na(*var* id)-da-ta(*var* -at) šu-bat-su (whose habitation was located at); KB ii 254—5 (SMITH, *Asurb*, 131), 17 ša kirib mê na-da-at šu-bat-su (BA i 417); K 2675 *R* 6 na-da-ta šu-bat-su; V 35, 31 cities which ištu ap-na-ma na-du-u šu-bat-su-un. — KNUDTZON, 72 *O* 3 ša (mât) Il-li-pi na-du(-ma); *R* 3 na-da-tu; TP ii 37 *U* ša i-na (šad) Pa-na-ri na-du-u; V 70, 1 lu-u ad-di (I founded); III 9 *no* 1, 8 kussû-u-a ad-di (ROST, 16); K 10 *R* 22—23 a-na tar-çi a-xa-meš na-du-u they are encamped opposite each other (Hr^{L} 280). — *d*) with qâtu: put hand on (= ana) something {Hand anlegen}. III 38 *no* 1 *O* 14 who a-na eš-ri-e-ti (mât) Akkadi qât-su id-du-u (= SMITH, *Asurb*, 251); KAT^2 570, comp. Deut 19:5. KNUDTZON, 108 *R* 11—12 qa-su-un ša limut-tim [i-na lib-bi-šu] | na-du-u; *del* 72 (76) qa-ti ad-di I put my hand to ... (but KB vi, 1, 235: ich legte meine Hand hin). — *e*) with double *acc*: put, place something (*e. g.* fetters, *etc.*) on (or around) one {etwas jemandem auflegen} *etc.*; § 139. Sn ii 70; III 12, 23. II 67, 20 see bîr(i)tu, 2 *a* (ad-di-šu-nu-ti); Asb ix 22; also see šum-ma-nu & çirrîtu (Sarg *Cyl* 9); H 122 *O* 7 *cf* ingâu. Perh K 2971 (IV^2 56 *add* 11) 4 a-šu-uš-tum ta-nam-di-i AN-GIŠ-BAR. V 47 *a* 57 (iç) il-lu-ur-tum ši-ri-ja na-da-a i-da-a-a (Z^B 54: *terminus technicus* for: putting a man in fetters); 82—3—23, 4344 + 4373 + 4593 the bird catcher še-e-tam id-di-ma; Cyr 281, 3 si-me-ri-e parzilli id-du-uš-šu; also Nabd 559, 8 na-du-u. NE 54, 16 see xargullu (where 3 more instances are given); KB vi 220, here also NE 69, (47) 48; *del* 243 (278) (iç) elippu gi-il-la (*q. v.*) id-du-ma: threw the ship upon the waves. — *f*) do, place (in general) {tun, legen (im allgemeinen)} I 28 *b* 23 mê a-na qir-bi-ša ad-di. T^{M} viii 79 ana libbi karpati .... ŠUB (*i. e.* i)-di-ma; IV^2 26 *b* 35—6 (37—8; 46—7) ana (& a-na) libbi i-di(-ma) put into it (the vessel); T^{M} 149; H^{V} 53. TP viii 86 famine *etc.* ana mâtišu lid-di ‖ IV^2 39 *b* 42 lu-ka-ja-an; I 27 *no* 2, 96 li-du-u; also KB i 4, 11 (see xušaxxu) = ZA ii 313 *no* 8. *del* 61 (65) see xišixtu *b*); 57 (60) see lânu, 2. — *g*) break forth in ..., pronounce {ausbrechen in ..., aussprechen}. H 122 *O* 18 see zarbiš. šiptu nadû, pronounce an incantation, spell *etc.*, usually the work of the âšipu. IV^2 21 *no* 1 B, *R* 1—2 i-di-šu-ma (= NAM-ŠUB[or RU]-BA-AN-SE, Br 4417) šip-tu pronounce the incantation over him (T^{M} 119—20). i-di (& MU) šipta T^{M} (often); IV^2 6 *b* 44 šip-tum elli-tum ina na-di-e-a. H 12, 122 ŠUB (or RU) = na-du-u. IV^2 22, 1 *R* 13 ana mê-šu-nu-ti ši-pat-ka elli-ti i-di-ma (also, 20); 3 ii 16 mê šip-ti e-li-šu i-di-ma. Creat.-*frg* III 101 (+43) ad-di ta-a-ka; T^{M} vii 27 ad-di šipta a-na ra-ma-ni-ja; 38 ad-di-ka šipat (il) Ê-a bêl Eridû (BA iv 161). — *h*) with ru'tu (*q. v.*) = spit, vomit {spucken, speien} H 87 i 60 see limniš & Br 537; II 35 *c-d* 42 UX-(KA + inserted LI) = ni-id ru-'u-ti Z^B 78; Br 780; 43 same id + KIM = ki-ma na-di ru-'u-ti (Br 8305); JENSEN in LEHMANN, ii 112: auswerfen von Gift; KB iii (1) 127 *rm***. — *i*) place, throw {legen, werfen}. T^{M} vii 70 eli (iç) dalti u (iç) sikkuri na-du-u (pm) xar-gul-lu (also i 54 i-di-i = ip), 11 na-da-at (i 56 i-di-i) ši-pat-su-nu; the kaššaptu *etc.* (*q. v.*) ša ina sûqâ-ta na-da-tu še-is-sa (her net). K 2148 iii 22 ana šu šal-li-šu RU (= nadât) ZA ix 116; *ibid* 419 na-da-at (K 8337, 15); IV^2 23 *no* 3, 13—14 ina aš-ri elli ad-di-ka (= RU); 15* *R* i 17 see na'alu נאל. — K 870 *O* 7 (astron. report) i-na-an-du (ps); K 787 *O* 9 (il) Adad pî-šu i-na-du-u-ni (*cf* K 747 *R* 4 (il) Adad pî-šu it-ti-di = it thundered (THOMPSON, *Reports*, vols i & ii). — K 890 *O* 4 a-ki-e la na-da-ku-u (BA ii 634); 1 a-na me-e-ni ki-i elippi-e ina qabal nâri-e na-da-ki. See also ja-ru-ra-ti. — T. A. (Lo.) 8, 12—13 la-a ti-id-di (BEZOLD, -du) mi-ma i-na lib-bi-qa do not take it to heart (BEZOLD, *Diplomacy*, 69 √ידי). — 83—1—18, 1846 *R* ii 2 (12) tad-da-a (PSBA xviii 256—7); V 47 *a* 60 id-da-an-ni (or nadanu?). — *Zû*-legend (K 3454 + K 3935) ii 21 he assumed na-du-u par-çi; K 4810 i (= IV^2 21 *a*) 46 their eight sisters an-na-RU-di T^{M} 145 "I will add" (but see ^{il} Na-ru-di). On nadû libittu *e. g.* K 3399 iv 6 i-na be-ru-šu-nu i-ta-di libittu; iv 15 i-na bît a-li-te xa-riš-ti: VII ûmê li-na-di libittu (KB vi, 1, 286—7; ZIMMERN, ZA xiv 292) see Exod 1:16 & SPIEGELBERG, ZA xiv 269—76.

H 51, 38 IN-TAG = id-di; S^{b} 297 ta-ag | TAG | na-du-u (Br 3800); S^{b} 1 *O* iii 3 ku-u | KU | na-du-u (H 33, 796; Br 10542); perh also S^{c} 85 (Br 4417; see nadanu); H 109 iii 20 = V 12, 18 = D 120, 117; V 14 *e-f* 56 ša ina tap-kir-ti na-du-u (Br 5261); 13 *a-b* 5 KAK-NI-LAL = na-du-u sikkati (close the door; Br 5289; 5366—7); V 24 *c-d* 13 see maqatu Q (end); II 48 *c-d* 23 $^{(e\check{s})}$ BI = na-du-u (ZA ii 88—9) = II 15, 197; Br 2565. — On kalakku nadû (= ana *k n*) see kalakku (*p* 385) where read ZA ix 270—2 (not 370) & add Nabd 620, 9 ŠE-BAR ina ka-lak-ku ša kissat *etc.* na-da-a-tum . . kalakku nadû Nabd 558, 8 = pm of nadû (>< BA i 531).

NOTE. — *Johns Hopk. Circulars*, 69, 17 on *del* 8 reads ša 18 na]-da-ta what is placed no longer. — KB vi 230 u i-n]a a-xi na-da-at(-ta) and yet thou liest on thy side ‖ und doch liegst du auf der Seite; JASTROW: sir-ḫa-am (*q. v.*). — *del* 33 (30) man?]-dîma (JENSEN, 370; 403 *fol*); ZIMMERN, ZA ix 105 id-]di-ma (so HAUPT, NE 135, 39); but KB vi, 1, 232 e]n-di-ma: nachdem (mich) Bel verflucht hat.

Q^{t} = Q. — *a*) throw {werfen} Asb iv 85 the bones at-ta(-ad)-di a-na na-ka-ma-a-ti (I threw into heaps), *var* a-na ka-ma-a-ti. T^{M} iii 23 at-ta-di la [. . . . xer-tum], at-ta-di i-ša-tum (BA iv 157); ZA iv 238, 40 ta-at-ta-di; NE 8, 34 the goddess Arûru ṭîṭa iq-ta-ri-iç it-ta-di ina çêri; also K 3399 + K 3934 iv 4—5 (ZA xiv 286—7; KB vi (1) 286—7); KB vi (1) 130 *col* v 35 *b*; 132, 43; & *col* vi 26 (NE) a-na-ku] at-ta-di-šu ina šap-li-ki. — *b*) throw down, destroy {niederwerfen, zerstören} ‖ abatu; *cf* K 2619 ii 4 against the will of Šamaš dûr-šu ta-bu-ut-ma ta-ta-di tarbaç[su?]; S^{P} 158 + S^{P} II 962 *O* 8 it-ta-di. — *c*) place, found, lay foundation, *etc.* {legen, Grundlegen, *etc.*}. I 44, 64 at-ta-di its foundation; IV^{2} 8 iii 52 at-ta-di pi-šir-tu; Asb viii 103 there & there at-ta(-ad)-di uš-man-ni, I encamped. *cf* SMITH, *Sen*, 93, 74; K 2619 i 7 ta-ta-di (2 *sg*) šu-bat-su. — *d*) K 10 *R* 8—9 qât-su-nu a-na lib[-bi . . . . .]-ti-šu-nu | it-ta-du-u, they put their hands upon . . . . — *e*) D 99 *R* 14 it-ta-di çir-ri-e-ti i-di-šu-[nu], he placed their hands in fetters; Asb ix 107 see laxû, 1. — *f*) TP vi 83—4 ni-sig-ge^{pl}-ja | lu-u at-ta-ad-di; K 2148 ii 18 . . . . šu a-na lil-šu un-qa-a-ti i-ta-ad-da-a (ZA ix 118—9); *del* 54 (= 57) at]-ta-di b(p)u-na-šu (see bûnu; JENSEN, 372 & KB vi, 1, 232—33 >< ZA iii 417); *del* 206 (227) ši-ba it-ta-di see KB vi (1) 247; H 120 *R* 14 see lîtu, 1 (II^{OV} 33), translated by BOISSIER, *Rev. Sém.*, viii 151 *rm* 1: la pêcheresse s'est couchée près du bord (à la base? ina li-id dûri) du mur; IV^{2} 8 ii 51 (end) e-li-šu it-ta-du (= BA-AN-RU); IV^{2} 13 *b* 27 it-ti aš-ṭu-te la at-ta-da [. . . .] Br 10100. — *g*) *del* 273 (= 306) it-ta-di qu-lul-tum (*cf* KB vi, 1, 4, 14); NE 48, 175 it-ta-di a-ru-ru-ta broke out into a curse {"warf" einen Fluch "hin"}; perh K 890, 13 . . . . . u-ni it-ti-di-i ri-ga-an-šu, & Nabd-Cyr *Chronicle* (= Nabd *Annals*) 16 . . . . du-um-mu it-ta-du-u. — T. A. (Ber.) 6 *O* 18 it]-ta-du-u (? or √'adû?).

Q^{tn} Creat.-*frg* IV 91 (= D 98, 8) it-ta-nam-di ta-a[-ša] breaks out {stösst ihre Bannformel aus} §§ 52; 53 *a*; KB vi (1) 20—7; K^{M} 21, 73 e-nu-ma $^{(il)}$ Adad ina ki-rib šame-e pû-šu it-ta-na-an-du-u (*ibid*, *l* 25 id) = thundered {donnerte}.

J^{t} II 16 *b* 52 utadda see nâku; perhaps V 31 *no* 3, 13 *cf* mûšu (end).

Š KB iii (1) 162—3 v 45 whosoever this boundarystone a-na me-e u-ša-ad-du-u (causes to be thrown into the water); KB iv 41 *c* 18 *fol* a-na mê a-na išâti u-šad-du-u. IV^{2} 56 *no* iii 45—6 li-šad-di-ki (Anu, thy father, Antum, thy mother) may throw it down for thee; AV 5916 quotes also II 9, 37 ina pi-i a-ri-bi u-šad-di.

N *a*) be thrown {geworfen werden} Asb ii 116 pa-an $^{(amêl)}$ nakiri-šu pa-gar-šu li(-in)-na-di-ma (118: in-na-di-ma). IV^{2} 13 *a* 42—3 na-an-di (= ip

NUN-KI-RU-DA) Br 2648; § 110; ana išāti RU (= innadu)-u Z^Š v/vi 60, 73, 83 *etc.* K 2333 *R* 9 (= Z^Š iv 59) ana mê RU (= linnada)-a; BA ii 412. — *b*) be overthrown, ruined {gestürzt, zerstört werden} SCHEIL, *Nabd*, x 13 (the temple) ša in-na-du-u 54 šanāti; V 35, 10 see dadmu. — *c*) TP vii 60 *fol* uš-šu-šu ul i(n)-na-du-u (for 60 years the temple's foundation was not laid); KB iii (2) 90—1 ii 36 without thee ul in-na-an-da šu-ub-ti no dwelling is founded; ABEL & WINCKLER, *Texte*, 60 *fol* (= HOMMEL, *Sum. Les.*, 123—4) *R* 13 (end) ana lu-li-e na-an-di.

𝔔^t IV² 60* C *R* 7 meširūtūa sup-puxā it-ta-ad-da(?-na, IV R)-a a-xi-tum (§ 110).

NOTE. — On nadū = nadānu, see nadānu, NOTE 2.

Derr. perhaps (bît) ma-an-du (*q. v.*) & these 6 (?):

nadū *4. adj f* nadītu. — *a*) deposited {niedergelegt} see nadītu (below); & Nadītu (*i. e.* šubtu) in P. N. of towns *e. g.* Sn iv 59 ^(al) Na-di-tu; Asb v 77 (residence in Elam). — *b*) ruined, destroyed {eingerissen, zerstört} *etc.* Sarg *Cyl* 34 ana šūšub na-me-e na-du-te to make inhabitable the desolate ruins; *bull-inscr.* 37 (na-du-ti); TP III *Ann* 19 dadmê na-du-u-ti; T^M iv 22 a-na ekimmi xar-bi (*q. v.*) na-du-ti tap-qi-da-in-ni; IV² 30* *b* 31—2 šu-bat-ka bītu na-du-u (= ŠUB-BA) [xur]-bu the ruined house (*Rev. Sém.*, vi 150); II 16 *a-b* 60 ana bīti na-di-i (= E-ŠUB-KU); see above, *p* 204, *col* 2; § 80. — *c*) spit, vomited {ausgeworfen, ausgespuckt} IV² 16 *b* 55—56 ru-'u-tum na-di-tum pi-i be poured out like water (Br 537); 57—8 *cf* kišpu. — Nadâ P. N., Cyr 183, 6 (+ 10) ^(sal) Na-da-a.

nadūtu (?) ZA x 211, 15 .... GA { kan-nu (*q. v.*) na-du-tu (AV 4127).

nadītu treasure {Schatz} AV 5915; Br 1637. V 13 *a-b* 21 EN-NU-UN NA-DI-TUM (evidently = na-di-tum) = ma-çar na-di-ti; preceded by EN-NU-UN NA-KAN-TUM (*i. e.* na-kan-tum) = ma-çar na-ka-an-ti.

ni(î?)dū(u?) *c. st.* nid in ni-id ru'ti see nadū (Q *h*); T^M 119, below; AV 6375.

NOTE. — nidū (= parhelion) nadi in astronomical reports = casting a shadow or image, or reflection. See THOMPSON, *Reports of the Magicians and Astrologers of Nineveh and Babylon*, vol ii pref. xxvii. 81—2—4, 79, 9 ina imitti Šamši (gloss: i-mit-ti ^(il) Ša-maš) ni-du na-di; also K 799 *R* 3, K 119, 1 + 3 + 5 + *R* 1; K 188 *O* 3; S 86 *R* 4 ina ni-du (with a parhelion); also K 774 *O* 7, *etc.*

nudu (?) Br 10196 *ad* 80, 11—12, 9 *O*, *col* 1  = nu-du.

nidūtu — *a*) delapidation, destruction, desolateness {Zerstörung, Verfallenheit}. Sarg *Khors* 139 these people ki-rib-šu u-šar-me-ma u-še-ši-ba ni-du-us-su (KB ii 72—3); also *Ann* 367; I 49 *b* 12—13 see minūtu; also MEISSNER, 119—20. — *b*) desert {Wüste}. IV² 15* *b* 27—28 the evil spirits ina ni-du-ti er-[çi]-ti it-te-ni-en-bu-u (√נבא, Br 9788); 41—42 see xalalu 𝔔^{tn}; Z^B 54; II 31, 726 ka-an-kal | KI-KAL | ni-du-tum (= H 68, 26); 68, 22 KI^(ki-iz-lax) UD = ni-du-tum (Br 9759, 9788), maš-ka-nu (21), te-rik-tum (23) & tur(AV 9033 ṭu)-ba-lu-u (24) = II 52 *g-h* 68 *foll*; ZA i 185. AV 6201.

na-a-du 5. (?). II 25 *g-h* 73 = id of na'alu (Br 8991) with pronunciation na-a (?) Br 8992.

ni-id libbi see perhaps nītu.

nadbu Sarg *Khors* 158 la-mid pi-ri-š'-ti an-du-šun na-ad-bu-ti (*Ann* 419).

nidbu freewill offering {freiwilliges Opfer} ✕ sattukku (*q. v.*). SCHEIL, *Nabd*, iv 33 u-kin ni-id-ba-šu; also PSBA xi 208, 23; KB iii (2) 50 *col* 3, 24 ba-aṭ-lu ni-id-ba-a-šu (+ 51); ZA ii 135 *foll.* *pl* Neb *Grot* i 4 ni-id-ba-a-šu e-ol-lu-u-tim (*cf* duššū).

NOTE. — NE 40, 46 ana nid-bi-šu-nu it-taš-bu-ni: liessen sich nach Belieben nieder; but KB vi, 1, 124 ud-bi-šu-nu: setzten sich auf ihren Sitzplatz.

nidabū & nindabū (> niddabū, intensive-form., BA i 180 *rm* 2) offering {Opfer} id = dues to a goddess (JENSEN, *Diss*, 34 *rm* 1; LATRILLE, ZA i 37; K^M 18 *R* 13); D^II 20; BA i 3 (bel.); 176; 279; J^{I-N} 47 (= נְדָבָה); POGNON, *Wadi-Brissa*, 84, 85; LOTZ, *Quaest. Sabbath*, 50 (*ad* IV 32 *a* 33); Z^B 24. id see V 11 *d-f* 1 AM-PAT-AN- | PAT-AN-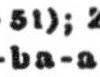 | = nin-da-bu-u (H 108 ii 1; 110 + 113, 47) ‖ takli-mu (2); qi-iš-tu (3); Br 4778; 9982. Šalm, *Balaw*, vi 6 nindabû el-lu. T^{M} ii 126 na-din nin-da-bi-e ana ilâni (il) Igegê. DT 71 *R* 4 ni-da-bu-u pa-ri-is-ma WINCKLER, *Forsch*, i 541: den Opfergaben mache ein Ende. V 60 iii 6 iD + ^{pl}; 64 *c* 37 sat-tuk-ku u nin-da-bi-e eli ša maxri u-ša-te-ir-ma. IV^{2} 9 *a* 32—33 Nannar mu-kin nin-da-bi-e; ZA v 59 *R* 11 see kitrubu, 1 (*p* 460); x 201 *R* 10 qat-ta-ri ša nin-da-bi. iD, *e. g.* SCHEIL, *Rec. Trav.*, xvii 178, 16 GIŠ-RU-BA nindabê tar-rin-ni ana ilâni šu-nu-ti u-kin da-riš; Anp i 23 xa-nin nindabê a-na ilEni rabûte; also IV^{2} 55 *no* 3 *O* 12 (beg); 35 *no* 6, *a* 14; ZA iii 97, 5 *no* 2.

NOTE. — HOMMEL, *Sum. Les.*, 59 (bel): nindabû > nin-dab(g), as also nidaba (nisaba). dab(g) contained also in sag(dag) whence šangû; √dag perhaps also in 𒋗 (but see above, *p* 241). — JENSEN in HASTINGS, *Dict. of the Bible*, i 216: freewill offering: nindabu; originally consisting of a gift of corn (Sumerian Nidab) to the goddess Ištar.

Nidaba see Nisaba.

nadbaku (√dabaku, *p* 230) mountain-wall, -slope; incline, precipice {Gebirgswand, Abhang, *etc.*}. Anp ii 114—5 pagrê-šunu xur-ru (*q. v.*) na-ad(*var* da-)ba-ku (ZA i 355 *rm* 3; 376) ša šade-e u-ma(l)-li; i 53 (ii 18, 37) the others xur-ru na-ad-ba-ku šade-e(-i) (lû) êkul (devoured {verschlang}); Anp *Mon*, *R* 33 X na-ad-ba-ku šade-e u-mal-li. Samš iv 3 between such & such places | attabalkat na-ad-bak šade-e (KB i 184—5); TP III *Ann* 64 xur-ri na-ad-bak šadi-i u-mal-li [pagrê-šu-nu]; Sn iv 77 na-ax-le na-ad-bak šad-di-i a-du-ra I feared the torrents coming down the (Elamitic) mountain slopes; *cf* I 43, 43 na-xal-lum na-ad-bak ša-di-i; Sn iii 75 see xurru (end). K 3456 *O* 15 xur-ru na-ad-ba-ku u-šat-ba-lum šadû U-a-i (& *l* 29). Perhaps S^{c} 5 *b* 2 na-ad(t)-ba[-ku?] Br 2976. 83, 1—18, 1330 *O* ii 15 nagû ‖ nadbaku. AV 5918.

NOTE. — 1. According to MEISSNER & ROST, 105, 9 ša-an-da-bak-ku (*q. v.*) perhaps a compound of ša + nadbaku.

2. See DELITZSCH, *Zeitschr. f. kirchl. Wiss.*, vol iii, '82, 342 *rm* 2; D^{Pr} 105, 180; ZDMG 40, 723; ZA ii 111 *fol*; BA i 8; 15 *rm* 2 (on connection between nadbaku & tabaku); 42 *no* 37; 175—6. § 65, 31 *a*.

nidugallu chief watchman {Oberwächter} K^{M} 53, 20 ana (il) Nedu ni-du-gal ša erçitim lupaqid; (il) Nidu ni-du-gal ša erçitim maççartašu lidannin. To *N.*, the chief watchman of the netherworld may he deliver him {dem Gotte *N*, dem Oberwächter der Unterwelt, möge er ihn übergeben}; also IV^{2} 1 ii 50 niš (il) Ne-du ni-du-gal erçitim lû ta-ma-tu.

ni-du-du ZA x 205 *R* 8 NI-KIL: ni-du-du: šam-ni nu-u-nu fishfat {Fischfett}?

nadilu (?) Br M. 84, 2—11, 136, 6 (PEISER, *Babyl. Vertr.*, ci) III-ta ka-a-su siparri, ba-ṭu-u siparri, na-di-li siparri; some instrument of siparru. Dar 302, 9: I na-di-il-lu siparri.

nadanu pr id(d)in (ni-id-din, 1 *pl*, § 101; id-di-in, Camb 193, 8; id-din, 215, 9; 1 *sg* addin & a-din, § 22); *ps* inamdin (§ 52; PSBA xix 138, 5 ina-an-din, he shall give; a-na-da-an NE 93, 12; a-nam-da-aš-šu Cyr 280, 9); & id(d)an (in later inscriptions); ip id-ni (*ndin: (i)din: idin, ZA xiv 373—4) NE 69, 34; pm na-din, give {geben} Br 4202, 4418; AV 5909; iD SE § 9, 66; SE-nu(-na) either iddi-nu(-na) or nadnû(-na); H^{F} 43, 53; § 100; ZDMG 10, 280; 23, 355. — *a*) give, grant {geben, verleihen} TP i 2 (il) Ašur .... na-din xaṭṭi (*q. v.*, & *cf* IV^{2} 9 *a* 35, see nabû Q *a*); i 32 ša ..... xaṭṭu elli-tu na-ad-na-ta-šum-ma (= pm) ZK i 160 *rm*; ZA v 15 people ša na-ad-na-ta ana jEši which thou hast given unto me; *Khors* 175 aššu ša-ṭa-pu na-piš-ti *etc.* na-da-nim-ma, *Ann* 435; KB iii (1) 122 (Xammurabi) *g* i 13 id-di-nu-nim (*pl*); 124, 17 ša (il) Marduk id-di-nam; Marduk na-di-in xêgalli *Rec. Trav.*, ii 78, 3. Asb vii 105 whom to govern Ašur & Ištar id-din-u-ni (§ 56 *b*). Beh 4 (+ 10) Auramazda šarrû-tu anâ-ku id-dan-nu; NB 21

Nudimmud *cf* Nugimmud. ~ nidmirtu see nitmirtu.

anā-ku id-dan[-na]-nā-ši-ni-ti (§§56*b*; 135). KB vi (1) 76 *R* i 4 a-na-an-di-na-ak-ku, I will give thee; K 2852 + K 9662 iii 25 ana na-da-ni to give {zu geben}; K 2401 iii 18 la a-di-nak-kan-ni (+ 20: a-di-nak-ka-a), 24 ta-di-na, thou hast given. KB iii (1) 130—1 when Bēl to Marduk the rule over the world (7) i-ti-nu-šum; 17 ri-ja-im i-din-nam; Beh 96 in-da-na-aš-šu-nu-tu he gave them; K 512 (V 53 *no* 4) 22 the mistress of life, who .... ta-da-nu-u-ni (has granted, ZA i 6; BA ii 196—7). K 13 *R* 22 id-dan-nak-ku-nu-šu he used to give you (Hr[L] 281), 25: ta-nam-di-na-na-a-šu ye shall give unto us; K 519, 10 ni-din-u-ni we gave (Hr[L] 108); K 528, 32 ni-id-din we will give (Hr[L] 269); K 528, 31—2 (IV² 47 *no* 2) ma-a-ti nu-tir-ra-am-ma a-na šarri bēli-ja | ni-id-din; K 562, 6—7 (IV² 47 *no* 1) a-na šar mātāti be-ili-ja lid-di(n)-nu. — II 53, 51 ni-id-dan (see maxaru & leqū); 16 *b* 55 *cf* mannu; H 128 *R* 3 a-nam-din (21, ul) Br 4202; also IV² 12 *a* 25—6. — *b*) bring sacrifice, offering {Opfer, Gaben darbringen}. T[M] i 47 ana ilāni ša šame-e mē a-nam-din; iv 126 anā[-ku] mē a-dan-ma; na-dan(-din) zību (see 278 *col* 1); also kitrubu, 1 (K 7592 + K 8717 + DT 363, 11); V 33 v 46 ki-ša-at-šu-nu (קשׁת) lu-ad-din; vi 9—10 lu-ad-din (ki-ša-a-ti of silver & gold), + 13; ii 31 lu-u-ad-di-nu-ma; K 183 *R* 18 when a peace offering a-da-na-aš-šu-nu-ni (Hr[L] 2). — *c*) pay tribute {Tribut zahlen} Cyr 64, 11 man-da-at-ta-šu (*q. v.*) i-nam-din (also 12); Sn ii 63 na-dan bilti; iii 27 (& *var* -da-an), 40 (see mandattu); III 12, 30 + 32; Asb ix 118 the inhabitants ... la i-nam-di-nu *etc.* (see *p* 561 *col* 2) BA i 585; § 152; K 2675 *R* 18 ēpiš ar-dūti u na-din man-da-at-ti; ZA iii 312, 53 a-na na-dan mandatti. — *d*) pledge oneself with an oath {Eid leisten} II 65 *O* 1, 4 see above, *p* 554. — *e*) nadanu qātā lay one's hands on; K 469 *R* 7—8 a-da-an | a-na-ku qa-ta-a-a ina kib-sa-ti I shall lay hands on the rascals (Johnston, JAOS xviii 152). — *f*) pānu nadanu show oneself, be seen {sich zeigen, gesehen werden}. V 60 i 15 the picture of the sungod pa-ni-šu la id-din-šu; IV² 60* B *O* 4 ili al-si-ma ul id-di-na pa-ni-šu I cried unto my god, but he did not show himself. See also pānu. On nadanu pānu ana = dagalu ana in T. A., an Aramaism, see ZA ix 275 *fol.* — *g*) give in marriage. Nabd 243, 5 thy daughter id-din (= give!) to my son (+ 8, id-din, he gave); see also 990, 4; Cyr 311, 6—7 (i-din); Bu 91—5—9, 407, 5—6 see mutūtu. — *h*) deliver, give up {übergeben, preisgeben}. Asb vii 45 his corpse a-a ad-din a-na ki-bi-ri, I did not commit to burial (§ 144; BA i 460 *rm* 2); Smith, *Asurb*, 117, 3 those fugitives ul a-din-šu (BA ii 248); Šalm, *Obel*, 153 id-dan-nu-ni, they gave up to me. K 819, 6 + 7 idda-an(-ni), he will give; ZK ii 324 (326), 7 id-dan-nu (3 *pl*); K 405, 16: 10 ma-na kaspi i-dan (he shall pay); T[M] iv 9 see kamū & kasū; 82, 9—18, 3737, 14 ni-id-din-ka šar-ru-tum; II 53 *no* 2 *O* 51 ni(or çal?)-la-ki ni-id-dan. BO iv 131, 22 see xišixtu (end); Cyr 26, 11 lu-ad[-din]. K 824 (Hr[L] 290) 11—12 a-na dāki id-din-u-ka they have given thee over to destruction. — *i*) restore, grant, deliver, return {erstatten, verleihen, abliefern, zurückgeben} (ZA ix 270). Esh iii 7 aš-šu na-dan ilāni-šu. the return of the statue; *del* 246 (276) minā ta-ad-dan-na-ma i-ta-ar ana māti-šu; 251 (281) ad-dan-nak-kum-ma (KB vi. 1, 250—1); IV² 61 *c* 22 long days *etc.* a-na Ašuraxiddina a-da-an-na (57 a-da-nak-ka, § 56*b*; AJSL xiv *no* 4), *a* 20—21 na-ka-ru-te-ka u-ka-a-ça | a-da-na-ka; 33 a-da-na, I will deliver; V 67 *no* 3 *O* 10 ta-nam-din (ZA iii 21); ZA iv 9, 8. Neb 4, 14 (end) id-din-šu (has given him); Dar 37, 16; ZA iii 220, 24: IV šiqlu kaspu ki-i at-ru id-di-in-šu; Neb 268, 7 ad-dak-ka; Nabd 346, 4 i-nam-di-in (see maš-šartu); Camb 42, 7 + 8 i-nam-din (3 *sg*); 46, 8; VATh 378, 8; III 47 *no* 5 (K 350) 5 (end) id-da(n)-an (he will deliver). 6 šum-ma la-a id-di-ni; Cyr 64, 8—9 mu-çip-tum .... ta-nam-din (3 *sg*), 11 i-nam-din; 22, 3 barley ša .... SE (= nad)-na-at (3 *sg*); 12 SE-na (= *pl*); also Camb 281, 12; 62, 24; Nabd 177, 7 ana SE-nu; 659 [16], 22 + 26 ša SE-n'a;

VATh 78 (KB iv 308) 14 they will deliver unto (= i-nam-din-nu-'-; + 17 + 29); also Camb 400, 5; KB iv 314—15, 17 (amêl) na-din-na-' (the sellers) . . . 19 i-nam-din-'u (§ 53c); 316—17, 8 Bêl-eṭir i-nam-din + 9 la id-dan-nu + 10 i-nam-din + 16 i-nam-di-nu; 206—7, *no* xi 12. Strassm., *Stockholm*, 3, 4 ina ki-it arax *X* . . . i-nam-din; ki-i la id-dan-nu (he will give, but if he should not give); 4, 9 id-da-aš-šu-nu-tu; Rm 157 iii 5 kaspu na-din the money was delivered; Cyr 227, 6 i-na-ad-din; 205, 7 i-din (give!). Neb 14, 4 *fol*; but Camb 298, 5 read na-*ši*; Peiser, *Babyl. Vertr.*, xxvii 10 ta-ad-da-aš-ši, has delivered unto her. K 180, 10 a-na *M* . . ni-dan; K 363, 11 i-da(n)-an; ZA iii 138, 16 in-nam-din-nu; 82—3—23, 607, 12 in-na-aš-šu > idnaššu > idinnaššu, give him! (*Rec. Trav.*, xix 105—6). Ana maççarti nadanu, deposit (see maççartu). — *k*) present, give {schenken} (il) Nin-ib na-di-in ax-xi-e (*Rec. Trav.*, xix, *no* xxv, Repr. *p* 15 *no* 12); V 33 viii 6 lid-di-iš; Cyr 337, 11 lu-ud-dak-kam-ma I will give unto thee; nadanu ša šarri *etc.*, see ṭâbu, 1 ג; V 61 vi 6 na-dan šarri; K 589 (Hr[L] 187) Bêl . . . . ṭûb libbi . . . ana . . . (12) lid-din-nu. Merod.-Balad.-stone iii 10—11 a-na na-dan | eqli a-na çâbû ki-din-nu. III 43 vi 6 whosoever claims eqlu ul na-dan (KB iv 70 = nadin) BA ii 137—8; KB iv 58—9 *col* 3, 1. I 70 ii 17 (see mulugu). T^M iii 50 id-di-nu-ki AN-GIŠ-BAR qu-ra-di. P. N. Nabû-id-din-nu Dar 362, 16; 17 Nâdin-aplu; VATh 378, 13 Bêl-id-dan-nu; VATh 78 the wife of Nabû-axê-id-dan-nu; also Bêl-axû-iddin; KB iv 318—9, 20 Nabû-na-din-šum; Kaššû-nâdin-axê *etc.* (KB iv 82, i, 13). — *l*) sell {verkaufen} >< maxaru (*q. v.*) ZA ix 275 *fol.* VATh 575, 8 ana kaspi na-da-nim to sell (the slave) for money; 11—14 a-na mi-nim la ta-ad-di-in-šu-ma ar-xi-iš i-di-iš-šu-ma; V 25, 28 u ma-na kaspi i-nam-din-šu, and sells him for money; III 46 *no* 7, 2 ta-da-a-ni; Camb 145, 5—6 money to the amount of 17 šekel ša na-da-nu u ma-xar-ri i-nam-din, see *p* 527 for other instances; V 68 *no* 2, 37 bîtu šu-a-ti ul na-din-ma kaspu ul ma-xi-ir (& KB iv 300, 23 *fol*; Dar 37, 25; 134, 1 *foll*); Dar 67, 2; Ner 68, 8 i-nam-din; KB iv 88 *col* 4, 19 na-da-na ul i-ši-ma; ZK i 48, 25 id-di-iš-šu-nu-ti has sold them. — ag nâdinu seller {Verkäufer} Neb 4, 6—7 na-din bîti >< maxirânu (*q. v.*) bîti; Peiser, KAS 115; AV 5911; 5913. na-di-nu Nabd 116, 5; 18 na-din (eqli or šêm), 260, 14; 203, 51 (amêl) UŠ-BAR na-di-in eqli; 293, 46; KB iv 306—7 *col* 6, 8; (amêl) na-din še-im cornmerchant {Getreide-händler} Cyr 254; 15; also P. N. mâr Na-din(-)še-im Nabd 346, 15 (AV 5914); 504, 3 Na-din(-)še-e. ZK i 49, 45 na-di-ni-e eqli; Nabd 178, 48 + 55; 1113, 27 (amêl) na-di-na nudunnû; P. N. Na-di-ni II 67, 26; ša (amêl) Na-di-nu u (amêl) Tab-ni-i (AV 5912); Cyr 233, 18 na-di-na-at bîti; II 56 *c*(-*d*) 19 (il) na-din me-e ga(?)-ti (AV 5248; Br 1639). — *m*) permit, let {zugeben, zulassen} IV 31 *R* 46 šum-ma nap-ṭi-ri-ša la ta-ad-di-nak-kam-ma (KB vi, 1, 90); NE 8 iv 12 ul] i-nam-din-an-ni; KB vi, 1, 154, 47 a-na šu-ru-bi ul i-nam-din; *del* 135 (142) Mount Niçir took hold of the vessel and a-na na-a-ši ul id-din did not permit it to get away (lit[y]: to shake). — *n*) show, indicate, announce {zeigen, angeben, kundtun}. IV² 60* O *R* 13 u a-dan-na si-li-'-ti-ja bârû ul id-din; 15 ii 47—8 ša lim-nu-ti si-bit-ti-šu-nu . . . . . ur-ta-šu-nu lid-din-ka; T^M ii 75 at-ta-m]a na-din ur-ti u ṭe-e-me. K 2527 + K 1547 *O* 3 ad-dan ṭe-mu, I will report (BA ii 392—3). NE 67, 17 (*cf* 69, 34) minû it-ta-ša jâši id-ni id-nim-ma it-ta-ša jâši (*cf* 18) what is its direction, show unto me (o Sabitu), show unto me its direction! K 10, 24—5 pi-i-šu-nu id-dan-nu-nu, they sent a message. T^M ii 73 to the great gods purussa-a ta-nam-din, thou announcest decision; viii 90—1 ta-nam-din šiptu ‖ 59 šipta mu-nu-ma (see manû, 1). — *o*) in later time also: make, create {machen, schaffen} = banû Bezold, *Achaemeniden*, inscr. xii (*passim*); *p* 51 ša du-un-qu a-na nišê id-din-nu.

II 45—6, 15—16 (ana itti-šu) IN-NA-AB-SU-MU = i-na-din-šu (also

128 *R* 3—4 = i-nam-din; 128, 22, see D[K] 72 *rm* 2 on *l* 21); 17 IN-SE = id-di-in (69, 14 id-din); 18 IN-SU-MU-UŠ (H[OV] 31 *rm* 20) = id-di-nu; 19 IN-SU-MU = i-na-ad-din (H[F] 54 *fol*); 55, 47; 46, 20 IN-SU-MU-NE = i-na-ad-di-nu; 21 id-din-šu (69, 15); 22 id-di-nu-šu; 23 i-na-ad-din[-šu] (II 15 *d* 55 i-na-din); 24 i-na-ad-din (= di-nu)-šu; 25 id-din-šu-nu-šim; 26 id-di-nu-šu-nu-šim; 27 i-na-din-šu-nu-ši; 28 i-na-di-nu-šu-nu-ši; also 65, 37 *foll* id-din (II 8 *f* 58), i-nam-din (V 40 *a-b* 57), i-nam-di-nu, ul i-nam-din. — ina-an-din he shall give PSBA xix 137 *no* 8, 3; ina-ad-din ZA iii 218, 9 (end); iv 69 *rm* 3.

S[b] 2, 7; S[c] 86 si-i | SE | na-da-nu; S[b] 348; H 18, 302; II 40 *c* 76; perh also H 109, 21; V 12, 19; D 129, 18; = MU (§ 9, 52) in P. N. (Br 1228); RU(M) in P. N. *e. g.* Anp ii 23 eponymate of Ašur-i-d(t)in, *var* ⟶; III 17, 53 SE (= id-din)-na; Asb i 8 Ašur-ax-SE (= iddin; *var* ⟶)-na; P. N. Bēl-id-dan-nu, RU also in II 9 *c-d* 13 NI-RU = id-din; *c-d* 16 MI-NI-RU = id-din-šu.

NOTE. — 1. For various forms in *c. t.* see T[C] 160—162 (a rich collection); PEISER, *Babyl. Vertr.*, 330—1; KB v 22*. — *pr* id-din (Nabd 17, 16), id-di-in (257, 7), i-din (56, 4), i-di-in (157, 3); SE-na (22, 14); id-di-id-ma (687, 7), id-din-su (116, 29), id-di-in-su (263, 26); ta-ad-din (533, 6; ta-ad-di-in, Neb 198, 5); ta-ad-di-na-an-ni (1113, 22, ta-ad-da-aš-šu VATh 66, 15 + 22 ta-nam-din); *pl* id-din-nu-' (685, 7), id-di-nu-'- (336, 7), id-di-nu (18, 6), id-din-nu (718, 4) *etc.*; ni-id-din-ka (720, 9), ni-id-di-din-ma (356, 9); *pm* nadin, nadnu; na-ad-na-ta (576, 9); *ip* id-din (343, 5), i-din (709, 5), i-de (din)-in Cyr 296, 8; *ac* na-da-nu (Nabd 356, 5; 687, 3); *ps* i-na-ad-di-in (299, 8), ina-ad-din (282, 7), i-na-ad-da-aš-šu (1031, 12), ta-ad-da-aš-šu (Neb 101, 6), ad-dak-ka (Neb 266, 7). —

For T. A. forms see *e. g.* BEZOLD, *Diplomacy*, xxxi *fol*; 100 *fol*. Lo. 21, 4 bēlu-ka ti-di-nu; 6, 49 id-di-nu (1 *sg*); i-din-an-ni (6, 26); *pc* 1 *sg* lu-u-din (35, 55); li-id-din-an-na-ši-ma (Ber. 248, 29); *ip* id(t)-na-ni Ber. 77, 42; 41, 40; Lo. 62, 18; *pm* 3 *sg* na-da-an (Lo. 50, 26), na-di-en (14, 13) lu na-din (24, 46); 1 *sg* na-ad-na-ti (Lo. 16, 38; *cf* Ber. 67 *R* 17), 3 *pl* ša na-at-na-ta (Rost. 3, 31); ZA vi 262; *ps* u-ul i-na-an-di-nu-na-ši (Lo. 1, 66); la i-na-an-di-na-a (Ber. 24 *R* 48), 1 *sg* a-na-an-din-šu-nu (Lo. 1, 76; *cf* 78; Ber. 22 *O* 31); 3 *pl* i-na-an-din-nu-ni m (Lo. 31, 13).

2. On nadū & nadanu see TALLQVIST, *Babyl. Schenkungsbriefe*, 9; and again, MEISSNER, 149 *ad* 89, 10; JENSEN, ZA vi 352.

3. V 30 *e-f* 26 SUB-SUB = bu-ul-ṭu SE (= nada)-nu, *cf* bulṭu (Br 858; ZK ii 18 *rm* 1).

4. On names of officials Nadan, *var* Nadannu, Nādinu, Nadin + compounds, see BEZOLD, *Catalogue*, 2131.

5. On Phoenician נתן, Hebr נתן, Assyr nadanu, Syr *netal*, Arm *netán* see WINCKLER, *Forsch*, i 70.

6. šumu nadanu = give a name, *i. e.* transmit a name, see šumu.

7. On nadanu construed with double accus. see BELSER, BA ii 149; HAGEN, *ibid*, 239.

8. See also natanu, nāptu, *etc.*

Q[t] give, deliver, entrust; sell {geben, abliefern, übergeben; verkaufen}. T[C] 4 *ad* § 48; BA iii 468. T[M] iv 55 see kamū & kasū, Q[t]. *del* 91 (95—6) a-na *P*(amēl) malaxi ēkallu at-ta-din a-di bu-še-e-šu; IV[2] 26 *b* 22—3 (24—5, 28—9) u-ri-ça ana na-piš-ti-šu (for his life) it-ta-din; Sm 1064 *R* 12 (RP[2] ii 180—1) pi-i-šu it-ti-din he has given command (Hr[L] 392); III 43 iv (edge) 6 i-ta-ad-di-nu he has given; K 112 *R* 2 (AJSL xiv 9) *S* ana *N* ardi-šu it-ti-din (Hr[L] 223); BrM. 8 475, 5 u-sa-lim (> uš-talim?) it-ti-din has given him completely (KB iv 120—1); K 363, 12 i-ti-din. PEISER, *Babyl. Vertr.*, xl 13 it-ta-nu; *f* tat-ta-din (cxiii, 18). NE 51, 22 at-ta-din qātā-a[-a]; AH 1090, 83, 1—18, 5 it-ta-din. K 2401 iii 5 ta-at-ta-an-na-šu-nu she gave unto them (BA ii 628 *fol*); Cyr 247, 4 Ba-zu-zu ana bīt karē it-ta-din; Cyr 1, 4. Camb 71, 4 it-ta-din-nu (§ 53*c*), has delivered; 363, 4 it-ta-din, has given; KB iv 314—15, 11 it-ta-din-'u has sold; Nabd 222, 4 it-ta-din; 10, 8; 21, 3, *etc.*; 343, 7 ta-ad-di-nu-ma; 310, 9; 70, 2 at-ta-din; *pl* it-ta-dan-nu-' 756, 12; 1113, 20 ta-at-ta-an-na-an-ni (3 *f sg* + suff. 1 *sg*); Neb 70, 4 (*var*) it-nam-din; Cyr 64, 3 ta-ad-di-in (3 *f sg*); III 4 *no* 2, 4 this seal ... ša-ri-iq ta-din. An expression often used in deeds of sale and barter is kas-pu ga(m)-mur ta-din = the money has all been paid Rm 167, 9 (also III 46 *no* 5, 10 *fol* & 9, 11; 48 *no* 2, 10; *no* 3, 17; *no* 5, 6; 49 *no* 3, 15; *no* 5 *O* 7; 50 *no* 4, 11). K 405,

10—11 *k. g.* ta-din-ni; KB iv 122—3 *no* xi 15; III 46 *no* 6, 11—12 (ta-ad-din; also III 40 *no* 1, 10; K 306, 14; 317, 16); III 46 *no* 1, 13 *k* gam-mur ta-a-din; III 46 *no* 10, 11 ta-SE-ni; see, above, 224 *col* 1; & Feuchtwang, ZA v 25. — Scheil, *Rec. Trav.*, xvii, 177, 4 mu-ta-din (?) kur-me-ti (*q. v.*); K 4332 (II 55) ii 5—6 mut-ta-ad-di-na-at ar-da-a-ti (Br 11167, said of the goddess). — H 55, 49 (D 92, 31) AB-BA-SE = it-ta-din.

T. A. Lo. 1, 89 it-ta-di-in; Ber. 3, 9 ta-ad-ta-di-in; Ber. 188 *R* 11 te-te-en-da-ni.

ℑ T. A. tu-da-nu-na šu-te-ra a-ya-tu but the return of an answer has not been granted (Lo. 14, 23; KB v 180); nu-da-nam we will give (Lo. 12, 34; KB v 409 *ad p* 128—9: and if he establish-ed (inf. absol.) the princes in their coun-tries); Ber. 71, 6 u la-a (?) tu-da-nu, but they have not given (?); 58, 44 u-ul tu-da-nu (but they gave me not) troops.

ℑ' mu]-uš-ta-ad-di-nu KB iii (2) 4 *col* 2, 34; see ZA iv 160, 79; 82—5—22, 48, 4 + 5 ilu ikkal ... xunni *pl* eli mäti uš-ta-ad-du-nu | uš-ta-ad-da-nu šu-ta-du-nu mit-lu-uk (= will be given) Thompson, ii *no* 195.

ℑ PSBA xix 135 *no* 2, 5 one plot of garden ground (?, see kašbaqqu) which in-na-ad-nu (has been added); T. A. (Ber. 3, 7) ul in-na-ad-di-in, has not been given; Ner 9, 3—4 ša a-na | ēkalli ana kaspi in-na-ad-nu; perh Cyr 302, 10 (in-na-am-din, or Q?); ZA iv 281, 7 id-dan-na-'-?

ℑ' K 1285, 11 for I will bestow upon thee (at-ta-na-ad-da-nak-ka) godly speech, S. A. Strong, *IX. Or. Congr.*, ii 207; perh K 619, 10 ja-a-ši it-ta-an-na-a-dan (the king) has given to me (Elip, or Q^tn?, JAOS xx 251—2).

Derr. ma(n)dattu (*p* 561), taddanu (tadānu), tidintu (AJSL, xiv *p* 13) & these 7:

nadnu *adj* given {gegeben} P. N. Na-ad(t)-nu Sarg *Ann* 281, & Na-din (often); Cyr 144, 9 mār-šu ša Nad-na-a (KB iv 296—7, *no* ii 12).

nidnu, in Asb ix 50 šu-tam-mu ina ni-id-ni .... imdanaxarū gammalē u amēlūtu (received camels & slaves), Jensen, ZA vii 178 = נדנה. P. N. Ni-id[-nu]-um (mār) Šu-ba-ri-im.

nidintu, nidittu, *f* gift, present {Gabe, Geschenk} ‖ tidintu; *c. st.* nidit (?) whence Ezech נדן (BA ii 122; Tallqvist, *Schenkungsbr.*, 9). V 61 vi 35 ni-din-ti šarri. III 43 iv (edge) 2 whosoever says: eqla annā ul ni-di-it šar Bābili (that this field is not a present of the king of *B.*); 41 ii 7 eqlê ul ni-di-it-ti šarri (KB iv 74, 76); perh II 39 *c-f* 32 GAR-SE(?)-MU = ni-[-din-tu?] Br 12051. Neb 247, 15 ni-din-ti; Nabd 297, 2 bīt ni-din-it šarri; 455, 8 ni-din-tum (šarri), *etc.* Often in P. N. Camb 1, 2 (+ 6) Ni-din-tum Bēl (= present of Bēl); III 39, 31 *etc.*; Cyr 144, 11 Ni-din-tu mār ša E-til-pi; Ni-din-ti-Bēl, *e. g.* KB iv 306—7 *col* 6, 14; 308—9 *col* 8, 9 + 10; 310—11, 15; KB iv 314, 15 + 21 Ni-din-tum (ilu) Anim mār ša Ta-nit-tum (ilu) Anu; also simply Ni-din-tum (BO i 76, 2); Camb 347, 2 Ni-di(n)-it-tum; also Ni-id-na-tum & Ni-id-na-at (*c. l.*). AV 6199, 6200.

nindanu (> niddanu) gift, tax, tribute {Gabe, Abgabe, Tribut} BA i 163; ZDMG 43, 199; Sarg *Khors* 158 such & such a priest šu-par (?) it-xu-xu nin-da-an-šu-un (of the gods); *Ann* 418. II 7 *e-f* 27—8: (....ig) ZU & (...da-na) NA = nin-da-nu. Br 13869.

nudnu *m* dowry {Mitgift, Aussteuer} of a girl about to be married. Anp ii 124 *fol* axat-su ištu (‖ III R 6 a-di) nu-ud-ni-ša (III R 6 nu-du-ni-ša) ZUN (= ma'adi, III R ma-'-di) binâti ra-būtišu ištu nu-ud-ni (III R ni-tu-ni)-ši-na ma-a-di amxur. A ‖ is:

nudun(n)ū & nu-du-nu; *pl* nudunânê (§ 65, 38; *cf* 1 Kings 9, 16; BA iii 470; Talm נְדוּנְיָא). Šalm, *Mon*, *R* 26 (28) his daughter, *etc.* it-ti nu-du-ni(-ša) I re-ceived from him; *R* 23 it-ti nu-du-ni-ša ZUN (= ma'adi); *O* 41; Asb ii (65) 78 his own daughter it-ti nu-dun-ni-e ma-'-di; II 65 *O* ii 35 iš-tu nu-du-ni-ša ma-'-di (KB i 198—9); KB iv 82 (1) 15—16 see mulūgu; 322—3 iii 36 nu-dun-na-a-šu ana bīt abišu i-ta-a-ri[-ma]; also *l* 23, 28, 32; iv 8, 13 nu-dun-nu-u ma-la nu-dun-nu-u | i-nam-din-šu; 18 nu-dun-ni-i-šu; 20. Nabd 356, 4 (3 1/2 minas of money) nu-dun-na-a-a he took; 6 kasap nu-dun-ni-e-a (*cf* 22); 31 ku-um nu-dun-ni-e-šu; 38 kaspi nu-dun-na-šu (Nabd 243, 17). Neb 403, 5 nu-du-un-ni-e; 161, 4—5 ina ri-ix-tum (9—10 ri-xi-tu) nu-dun-nu-u; *cf* KB iv 322 *col* 3, 28; Nabd 348, 7 ri-ix-ti nu-dun-ni-e. Cyr 143, 5 (8); 6 a-na nu-du-nu-u; 183, 25—6 a-na nu-dun-nu-u .... id-din; Nabd 348, 14; Neb 198, 5, 6 (ta-ad-din), 283, 8; Strassm., *Stockholm* (*VIII.*) *Or. Congr.*, 32, 6 nu-dun-nu-u ša aššatu A-dir-tum; 27, 1 + 17; Cyr 130, 1; 332, 3 + 7; Nabd 243, 10—11 (+ 13: 1 ma-na ša nu-dun-ni-e); 82—3—23, 3368, 4—5 nu-du-nu-u-a | ša abu-u-a id-di-nu (*Rec. Trav.*, xix 107—8); D 125 *no* 3, 7 a-na nu-dun-ni-e (Camb 193, 6; 215, 7; 214, 3) ki-i ad-dak-ka (Neb 265, 7; 368, 6 id-da-aš-šu) + *R* 1 nu-dun-nu-u; *O* 10 ku-um nu-dun-e-šu; also see Peiser, KAS 115 *col* 1 & kalabuttu. Dar 379, 64 nu-dun-na-ni-e ša aššati-šunu ilteqû. II 9 *c-d* 5 *foll* nu-du-nu-u; nu-du-nu-šu; *n* ip-qi-su (פקד); *n* i-pu-uš, Br 4418, 7152. Br M. 84, 2—11, 61 Amti-Bêlit nu-dun-na-ni-e ana Ṭab-tum u Tabanni mar-ti-šu ul-tu nu-dun-ni-šu ta-nam-din.

Also = gift, present }Geschenk{ Etana-*frg* (BA iii 366—7; KB vi (1) 108—9) *R* 17 (*l* 31) kîma e-ri-ši nu-dun-na-a lut-lim-ka, according to thy pleasure I will bestow upon thee a gift. A ‖ is

nudinnû, *e. g.* Neb 91, 1 ri-xi-it nu-din-nu-u (the remainder of the dowry), + 20—1: IV manê ri-xi-it nu-din-nu-šu ta-šal-lim; Nabd 44, 2 bît nu-u-di-ni-e.

nadinânu seller }Verkäufer{, form like paqirânu. K 11571 viii 22 na-di-na-an-šu the seller (of the slave), BA iv 80; KB iv 86 *col* 3, 2 na-din-an; 314, 17 (end) (amêl) na-din-na-' (+ 21); 320—1, *col* 2, 18 na-di-na-nu (× ma-xi-ra-nu) ...., 21 i-nam-din; Nabd 518, 17 na-di-na-nu.

nadaqu (??). 𝔔 IV² 44 *b* 11 ta-ad-di-qan-ni (but??) = *del* 210 (232), but rather √takû (*q. v.*); KB vi (1) 246—7: tu-ad-di-kan-ni at-ta: stiessest du mich. — 𝔑 kak-ke-šu-nu in-na-ad-qu (BA ii 428 *ad* K 2619 *O* 14) M[8] 63; KB vi (1) 61: ihre Waffen wurden losgemacht. See dikû 𝔑 (above, *p* 246 *col* 1).

nadaru be fierce, rage }grimmig sein, wüten{ ‖ galatu, § 84. KB vi (1) 4, 28 [lab-biš] i-na-dir. IV² 1* iv 25—6 a-na nišê na-ad-ru, against the people they (the seven evil spirits) rage (= ZI-GA-A-MEŠ, *var* ŠU-ZI-GA-MEŠ, Br 2318, 7124), see on this text Halévy, *Rev. Sém.*, iv 150, 245, 344. Johnston, JAOS, xix 72. 𝔔 = to lavish, thus K 13 (Hr[L] 281) *R* 14 a-na bêl ṭâbâtešu (written EN-MUN-XI-A-MEŠ-šu) id-dur he used to lavish upon his partisans. — 𝔑 be made fierce, be put into a rage, rage, act fiercely }wütend gemacht werden, wüten, ergrimmen{. ac na-an-du-ru, *c. st.* na-an-dur (BA i 181; §§ 11; 52; 101). Sn v 54; III 15 i 2; Sarg *Khors* 40 see labbiš. K 2867, 27, the lions, devouring (ukulti) cattle, sheep (?) *etc.*, in-na-ad-ru; K 793 *R* 4 nakṭûti *pl* in-na-da-ru(-nu), brigands will be rampant; K 712 *R* 2 xab-ba-a-tum in-na-an-da-ru; S 375, 7; K 1378 + 83—1—18, 780 *R* 1 in-nam-da-ru; III 60, 115 UR-MAX[MEŠ] in-nam-da-ru (62 *a* 27 + 30); 62, 29 ÇIR-MEŠ in-nam[-da-ru]; also 64 *a* 34; 61 *b* 10; 62 *b* 6; 60, 35 kakku in-nam-da-ru; 54 *c* 40 in-na-an-da-ru. IV² 24 *no* 1, 33—4 na-an-'u-rat (= ŠU-BA-AN-ZI, Br 2318) = pm; Scheil, *Rec. Trav.*, xx 201 *no* 39 kakku (il) Ša-aš-ši bar(?)-ku na-an-du-ru xi-u (or, *adj*?); K 706, (III 54 *no* 10) 2 na-an-du-ur nešê u axê; also K 793 *O* 2 (-dur); III 58 *b* 58 *foll.* II 38 *g-h* 2 TIK-DA-RI = na-an-du-ru (or √adaru) Br 3283. — NE XII *col* 3, 29 in-ni-id(?)-ru-ma(?) BA i 70 (KB vi, 1, 262—3 leaves reading & translation undetermined). — 𝔑tn II 28 *a* 11 i-ta-nam-dar; III 60, 64 lions it]-ta-na-da-ru; VI² 95 *no* 2 *a* 21 eb-ri u tap-pi-e (?) it-ta-nam-da-ru-in-ni, nišê alija it-ta-nam-da-ra-nin-ni (they are angered at me, § 101). Derr. these 3:

nadru *1. adj* fierce, raging }grimmig, wütend{ AV 5953. ZA iv 238, 9 nir-ka na-ad-ri, thy fierce yoke. Esh *Sendsch*, *O* 24 (end) kalbu na-ad-ru; *R* 14 zi-bu na-ad-ru. Asb vi 60 u-na-as-si-xa rimē (il) na-ad-ru-u-ti (or rimā-an?) ZK ii 316. I 7 *no* ix E 3 see labbu, 1 & read na-ad-ru-ti. IV^2 5 *a* 21—22 the fifth (xa-aš-ša) of the seven evil spirits is ab(p)b(p)u na-ad-ru. Creat.-*frg* III 27 (85) GAL-GIR-MEŠ (= ušumgallē, KB vi, 1, 309—10) na-ad-ru(-u)-ti. II 6 (*a*-)*b* 34 na-dir-tum (said of the kalbatum); 8—9 UR-ŠU]-ZI-GA (Br 11298) & UR-KA]-GAB-A (Br 11269) = na-ad-ru (see kattillu), D^M 34; also II 24 *e-f* 2; S^c 3, 8 na-ad-ru (Br 2318).

nadriš *adv* T^M ii 138 a-ra-ab-bi-eš na-ad-ri-eš.

nanduru *2.* Scheil, *Nabd*, xi 12: II kakkē na-an-du-ru-ti two terrible weapons {zwei furchtbare Waffen}.

nad(t)ru *2.* V 27 *c-d* 46 in a list of birds IT-UŠ (= [cuneiform]) -XU = na-ad(t)-ru, AV 5953; Br 6590.

nādušum fresh, green herbage {frisches, grünes Kraut; Spross} √edešu. AV 5917. II 23 *c* 4 na-du-šum ‖ pi-ir-xu (*q. v.*). BA i 160; 176; ZDMG 43, 198 perhaps √*n-d-š*.

(mē)nadāti see nādu, 3 (*p* 645 *col b*).

nadītu, nidūtu see *p* 649 *col a. b.*

nidittu see nidintu (*p* 654 *col b*).

naụaddu favorite {Liebling} TP iv 35 the temple of Bēltis xi-ir-te rabīte na-ụad-di (il) A-šur; vii 56 šarri ṭa-pi-ni na-ụad (il) A-šur; Anp i 33 na-ụad (il) Adad. So *e. g.* Scheil, *Šamši-Ramman IV*, 33 *fol* (*ad* I 32, 18, where, however, KB i 174—5 reads bēlit ši-na-at: der Herrin der Satzungen); Jensen, 444 √ودّ = nadadu, 3; ZDMG 43, 200 *no* 9.

Against reading namaddu & derivation from √madadu see Hommel, PSBA xix 314, where he says: naụaddu & šadadu were borrowed from the Arabic in the time of the Arabic dynasty of Hammurabi. — ZA ii 116 *rm* 1 našaddu (√šadadu, love); ii 111: a Nifal-formation. See also L^{TP} 142 + 175; D^{Pr} 97.

NU-ZU = ul īdī I know not (often) *e. g.* II 39, 49 *fol*; 8 iii 60; 37, 7; V 31 *f* 47 (ZK ii 88 & 86; 299, 13; ZA i 393 *rm* 1).

nazū Bu 91—5—9, 419, 8—9 certain persons iz-zu-u-ma (recognized); Pinches, JRAS '99, 112 √nazū, connected with nazazu in its meaning of "to witness"; *ibid*, he says: "some forms now considered irregular under nazazu belong to this verb", *e. g.* K 657, 6—7 it-tal-ka ina pa-ni-ia | i-ti-ti-zi ma-a (Hr^L 102); K 539, 7—8 ina pa-an ...... | i-ti-ti-zu (Hr^L 206); C. A. Thompson, *Reports of the Magicians, etc.*, 96, 3 Jupiter stood (it-ti-it-zi) within the halo of the moon; also 106, 7, where it is preceded by iz-za-az and izziz; *ibid*, 180, 8; 228, 8 it-ti-ti-zi; 235, 8 ki-ma it-te-mid (or ziz?) it-ti-ti-iz šu-u-tu, when it stands and waits; 236 G *R* 1; 251, 1.

niz(ç)ū excrements, dung {Excremente, Mist} see mašaru, 3. Sn vi 20—1; I 44, 54; III 14 (*Bav*) 39 written u-maš-še-ru ni-ša-a-šu-un. Perh √נצה, Brown-Gesenius, 633.

nizū 83, 1—18, 1330 iv 7 te-e | TE | ni-zu-u, M^S 63.

nēzu see nēçu.

nūzu Strassm., *Stockholm (VIII.) Or. Congr.*, *no* 22, 1—2: II GUR 102 QA suluppu ša nu-u-zu, ša bīt Ba-zu-zu.

naz(ç)b(p)ūtu Delitzsch, *Kappad. Keilschrifttaf.*, *no* 15, 12—13 a-na na-az-bu-tim | i-za-az.

nazabu *cf* naçabu; **nuzābu** see nuçābu.

nazazu, pr iz(z)iz (H^F 53; Knudtzon, *no* 115 *O* 5; *R* 10 i-zi-zu & i-nam-zi[-zu], *ibid*, 143 *O* 4; pc lu-zi-iz I will take my stand (§ 83, 1 *b*); ip iziz (ZA iv 15, 16 i-ziz), izzi-za-am-ma, Knudtzon, *p* 47—8; ps iz(z)az (analogy to פ"א verbs); §§ 90*a*; 100. D^{II} 49; H^F 52; Hebr. ii 6 *rm* 1; AV 4893, 4939, 5930. stand, step, tread {stehen, sich stellen, treten}. — *a*) stand (literally) {stehen}. NE 44, 50 the allallu-bird iz-za-az (*var* a-šib) ina ki-šu-tim (*var* id), now stands (sits) in the forest. D 99 *R* 21 (end) eli-ša iz-za (*var* zi)-za stood up upon it; 97, 16 iz-ziz-zi-ma he stood firm upon it (Jensen; but Barton, iç-mad-zi(m)-ma he harnessed it; Hebr. ix 19). NE 60, 12 iz-ziz (Haupt: iç-bat) | ṭe-en-šu-ma

(KB vi 204), 61, 4 ša iz-zi-zu-ma ina puxur ilāni; *del* 7 ki-i ša ta-az-ziz ina puxur ilāni (*Johns Hopk. Circ.*, 69, 17; BA i 116); 181 (201) iz-za-az ina bi-ri-in-ni. KB vi 266, 5 ta-az-za-az thou standest; IV^2 19 *a* 52 ki-ma at-ta ta-az-ziz-zu; 14 *no* 1, 30 iz-za-zu ‖ uš-ša-bu (31; 3 *sg*). T^M ii 87 ma-xar-ka (*q. v.*) lu-uz-ziz (1 *sg*); ii 22 (end) a]z-za-zu-ma; i 94 iz-za-az-zu (3 *pl*); iii 6 DU(= izza)-az ina sūqi (3 *sg*) also *l* 93; BA iv 162 *ad* T^M vii *col* 4 (beg) 4 [ša bābi]-ja iz-za-zi (il) Nergal; 5 [ša] ic iršija iz-za-zi il Lugal-edin-na. Anp i 105 where the statues ..i-za-zu(-u)-ni, there ṣa-lam šarrū-ti-a ..... u-še-zi-iz; KB iv 30—1 (*no* iii) 15 see kutallu; perh K^M 11, 27 (end) da-riš lu-ziz-ku; K 183 *R* 14—15 ša ina libbi ēkalli i-za-zu-u-ni (Hr^L 2). I 7 F 20 memorial slabs(?) ... ša a-xi ul-li-e ina mi-xir-ti-šu i-za-zu; K 155 *O* 21; Neb ii 69—70; 83, 4—19, 13 *O* 71 see kamasu; 82—7—4, 82 *R* 8—9 iz-zi-iz-zu ka[-am-su]; K^M 1, 21 kan-sa-ku az-za-az a-še-'-ka ka...; 21, 11 ana ma-]xar-ka az-ziz a-še-'-ka (22, 57); II 19 b 28 a-na tab-ra-a-ti iz-za-zu. — *b*) stand, make a halt, establish oneself {stehen, Halt machen, bleiben}. IV 31 *a* 23 i-zi-zi be-el-ti la ta-na-da-aš-ši halt, my lady! (H^F 53; § 101); K 664 (Hr^L 175) *R* 1—3 la-a ina ma-ṣar-te | ša (al) Ni-nu-a i-za-zu; NE 24, 1 iz-zi-zu-ma (*cf* 27, 44; KB vi 158) i-nap-pa-at-tu kištu they stood there admiring the forest. K 515 (Hr^L 89) 10 (elippu ... ina Bāb-bitqi) ta-za-az-za the ship is (*i. e.* has halted) at *B.* — *c*) *n* ina muxxi (or eli) or ana = rely upon someone(-thing), have confidence in, depend on somebody(-thing) {sich auf jemanden (etwas) verlassen, Vertrauen haben} IV^2 61 *a* 16—18 a-a-u-te di-ib-bi-ja | ša aq-qa-ba-kan-ni | ina mux-xi la ta-zi-zu-u-ni, upon which of my words that I have spoken to thee couldst thou not place confidence? (AJSL xiv 270); *ibid*, vi 49—50 da-ba-bu pa-ni-u | ša a-qa-ba-kan-ni | ina mux-xi la ta-zi-zi (*ibid*, 276); 50—2 u-ma-a | ina eli ur-ki-i | ta-za-az-ma. Salm. *Obel* 89: 12 kings of the Xatti-land ana idān a-xa-miš iz-zi-zu (trusted upon their combined forces). — *d*) stand as witness, assist, be witness at something {assistieren, als Zeuge dienen}. Such & such persons were present as witnesses (iz-za-az-zu) I 66 *b* 16; V 61 vi 26; KB iv 88—9 *col* 4, 10 iz-za-az-zu; Merod.-Bal. stone v 14—5 iz-za-zi (3 *pl*). GUB(= DU)-BA = ina nazazi (‖ ina ašābi) in presence of {im Beisein von} *coram*; Belser, BA ii 136 × T^C 103: ina manzazi; III 43 ii 1; K 433, 25 ina naza-zu; Camb 135, 5; Nabd 866, 7; 174, 8 i-na naza-zu NN. nadi-in. — *e*) stand up, arise {aufstehen, sich erheben} *etc.*, thus ‖ tebû (KB vi, 1, 306); K 2333 *R* 16 li-iz-ziz (il) Ninib bēl kakkē li-ni-is-si pušqa; *R* 27 li-iz-ziz (il) Papsukal bēl (iç) xaṭṭi bi-ri-iq mur-ṣu; I 70 ii 9 whosoever to seize this field iz-za-az-zu-ma (arises, ‖ il-lam-ma, 7); KB vi 130, 31 Uruk ma-a-tum iz-za-az eli[-šu]; Creat.-*frg* III 11 al-ka (il) Ga]-ga qud-me-šu-nu i-ziz-ma (before them stand up!)]; 79, 7—8, 178, 6 see muttiš; K 8571 *O* 13 i-ziz stand! Sm 949 *O* DU(= iziz)-za-am-ma, *aye!* (D 16 *rm* 2); also i-ziz-za-am-ma up! (§ 101); K 256 *O* 43—44 (= IV Rawl 17) (il) Šamaš i-ziz-ma; T^M ii 117 ina di-ni-ja i-ziz-za-am-ma (+ 132); iii 82; i 13 i-zi-za-nim-ma (2 *pl*); V 61 vi 34 mannu arkū .... iz-za-az-zu-ma (shall sit in this palace as king in later days). Sm 1371, 5 ta-az-za-az ina orçi-tim, *etc.* Smith, *Asurb*, 119 (= III 32) 27 a(*var* az)-zi[-iz?]-ma (KB ii 250 × Hehr. ix 160—1). *Adapa*-legend *R* 2 (see bābu, Note 4); IV^2 59 *a* 6 ina ik-ri]-bi u te-is(ç)-li-ti iz-za-az-ku (= ka); 7 ilišu li-iz-ziz; 8 .... šu li-iz-zi-iz-ma; 17 *a* 18 ana nu-ux lib-bi-ka .... iz-za-az-ku (*cf* 30; Br 7056); *R* 22 ilāni rabūti?] ša šame-e u orçi-tim eli-ša iz-za-az-zu-ka (Br 7057; *cf* 43—44) also 16 el-çiš iz-za-az-zu-ka; 49 *a* 13 i-zi-za-nim-ma ilāni ra-būti. V 31 *no* 3, 13 kal mu-ši ul iz-za-zi does not rise the whole night (but, ZA i 234; Jensen, 146 nazazu in astronomical texts = disappear {verschwinden} see babalu 1, biblu 2; and, again, compare Thompson, *Reports*, Vol. ii (*passim*). — *f*) make a stand, step, stand on one's side, locate {Stellung, Stand nehmen; treten, sich stellen} TP iii 50 (54) on the mountain lu iz-zi-zu-nim-ma; they made a stand (*cf* v 86). V 64 *a* 19 Marduk u Sin .... iz-zi-zu ki-lal-la-an (*q. v.*), stood at either side (of me). V 50 *a* 10 ilāni rabūti [ina] pa-ni[-ka] iz-za-az-zu-ka (sit before thee); 12 .... ana pa-ra-si iz-za-az-zu-ka; IV[2] 61 ii 25—6 the 60 great gods round about thee i-za-zu. H 75 *R* 2 see dînu; 89, 41 (97, 8 + 17) ina re-ši-šu li-iz-zis (= XE-EN-GUB-BA); 99, 49. Asb x 1—3 A-a-mu .... it-ti *A.* i-zi-zu-ma. NE 28, 38 ur-ri]-ix i-ziz-za-aš-šu (KB vi, 1, 160—1); K 112 *R* 10 ina pa-an (amēl) ikkari lu-u la i-za-az (AJSL xiv 9; Hr[L] 223); T. A. (Ber.) 152, 24 u li-iz-az-ma | i-na pa-ni šarri bēli-ja and if he comes before the king, my lord. Sm 954 *O* 23—4 to 31—2 a-na šu-ta-bu-ul te-ri-e-ti az-za-az git-ma-liš (*q. v.*) az-za-az; NE 4, 16 az-za-zi a-na-ku. — K 183 *R* 9 ina pa-ni-ja li-iz-zi-zu, let them enter my service (Hr[L] 2); ina pān šarri nazazu = become the king's body servant = ina pān šarri erebu. K 183 *R* 11 may also Gula my son ... ina pa-an šarri bēli-ja li-zi-iz. K 469 *R* 23 (Hr[L] 138) ina pānija i-za-zu, they are (stand) with me (*R* 16 li-zi-zu, let them stand); perh Asb iv 34 (Tammarîtu) ina max-ri-ja i-zi-zu-u-ma (ZA x 80); H 120 *R* 12 ina pa-ni-a .... iz-ziz-zi. K 2701 *a* Nusku ina pān iz-za-az Winckler, *Forsch.*, i 92 (med); T. A. Lo. 18, 10—11 for a long time Abd-aširta pa-na-nu iz-zi-iz (has been besieging me); izzaz pāni, see manzazu. II 51 *no* 1 *R* 11 ma-xa-ri ilāni rabūti li-zi-zu-ma (*ibid*, 13 DU-zu-ma; ZK ii 323); IV[2] 30 *R* 4 (= II 125, 14) ilāni ša šame-e ta-šur (?) a-na ta-xa-zi iz-za-az-zu-ka (Br 9402); V 50 iii 32 ilāni ša-qu-tu ša šamê u erçi-tim ša-a-šu iz-za-az-zu-šu (*cf* 34). KB iv 40 *no* iii 16—18 a-na ba-ag-ri-šu ki-ma çi-im-da-at šarri | iz-za-az; 44—47 *no* iv 17—18 a-na ba-ag-ri-šun ki-ma çi-im-da-at-tum | iz-za-a-az-zu. K[M] 6, 122 ilu ša la šālimu li-iz]-ziz ina imni-MU (= ja); 9, 16 + 17; 10, 21; 22, 17 + 18; 53, 22 li-iz-ziz (il) šigaru nam-ç(z)a-ki-šu-nu; 2, 30—31 ittika li-iz[-zi]-zu (*var* li-ziz-zu) ilāni šu-par (il) Bēl (& Ē-KUR); 6, 72 al-si-ki bēlti-MU (= ja) i-ziz-zi[-im-ma ši-me]-i ja-a-ti (7, 10; 37, 8) = 4, 27 (i-ziz-zi-ma). IV[2] 8 iii 44—5 the evil charm ina a-xa-a-ti li-iz-ziz (H 138); 7 i 12—13; K 246 (H 93) iii 10 the evil demon ina a-xa(-a)-ti li-iz-ziz (+ iv 48) = to step aside, withdraw. — Sn vi 72 may Ašur nak-riš li-zi-is-su, stand against him as an enemy; I 70 iii 16—7 ina pa-rik-ti li-iz-ziz-su; also KB iv 72 (iv) 11 (= III Rawl 43); IV[2] 5 *a* 50—51 in the wide heavens lim-niš iz-za-zu (= GUB/GUN-GA); K 111 *R* i 28 (il) Gibil ana ra-bi-çu-ti-šu li-iz-ziz (= IV[2] 15 *fol* iii); III 15 *a* 23 (ilat) Ištar i-da-a-a ta-zi-iz stood at my side (§ 101); Sn v 24 i-da-a-ni i-zi-iz (= ip); III 41 ii 1 whosoever a-na i-di li-mut-ti iz-za-az-zu-ma. — *g*) take possession of; settle {Besitz ergreifen} *etc.* IV[2] 30* *R* 19—20 ina bîti lu-uz-ziz (GA-BA-GUB), also 22 + 24 (I will not rest in the house); H 61, 41—2 when he has brought the money | [ina] eq-li-šu iz-za-az he may take possession of the field (= BA-AB-GUB-BA); 55, 31 çibtu ki-ma maxîri iz-za-az (= GUB-BA); 56, 18 mil-qi-ti-šu-nu iz-zi-iz-zu (also 19); 57, 20 iz-za-az-zu; 21—22 iz-zi-zu.

Cyr 302, 9 ni-iz-zi-iz; Neb 135, 3 iz-zi-iz-zu; K[M] 7, 41 i-zi-za-ma; 42 li-iz-zi-zu; also pr = izuz; 82—5—22, 63, 6 (il) Marduk ina mûši i-zu-uz; K 87—1 *R* 8 .... ul az-zi-iz; 10 u-zu-za-ku-ma; *O* 2 u-zu-us-su (Thompson, *Reports*, 247 A.). — H 52, 70 IN-GUB = iz-zi-iz (120, 12; 125, 2). 20, 351 gu-up DU na-za-zu. II 20 *a-b* 29 AD-GUB = na-za-zu; 30 see xepû (330 *col* 1).

On ina bāb (*etc.*) nazazu see *p* 142 NOTE 4, where read lu-uš-ziz *ad* H 118 *R* 12; also see KB vi *p* xviii on K 8743, 17 + 18.

T. A. izziz & izzaz (often); Lo. 30, 23 i-zi-iz-mi; 12, 61 'i-zi-iz. 1 *sg* pm iz-zi-iz-ti (Lo. 57, 28, *cf* Bezold, *Diplomacy*, xxxii & *rm* 4); KB v 337 *rm* **; ip i-zi-iz ana (occupy! Lo. 23, 15). Ber. 41, 33 u la-a ti-zi-za | (il) Çu-mu-ra *S* cannot hold her own; Bor. 77, 14 (al) Çu-mu-ra i-zi-za-ti.

Q^{t}. — *a*) stand, stand still, be unable to move {stehen, stehen bleiben; sich nicht von der Stelle bewegen können}; NE 7, 13 (= 11, 27) his knees could not move (see birku); *del* 185 (142) a-na šad Niçir (II 51 *a* 21) i-te-ziz (KB vi 238 -mid) elippu; BA iii 366—7 (*Etana*-frg) *R* 10 u-ri-dam-ma it-ta-ziz ina eli ri-mi (& stood upon the wild ox). — *b*) take place, place oneself, step {Stellung nehmen, treten} IV^2 7 *a* 12—13 his goddess ina a-xa-a-ti it-ta-ziz (= BA-DA-GUB).

NOTE. — Br 8995 reads II 119 *O* 17 it-ta-sis, others -lil (see natalu); Br 9599 reads IV^2 3 *a* 18 (end) li-zis-ka, but read li-⊢<-la.

Q^{tn} *ittananzaz = ittanamzaz = ittandzaz (§§ 52; 101). IV^2 2 v 16—17 (55—6) su-la-a a-na (*var* ana) da-la-xi ina sūqi (*var* su-ki) it-ta-nam-za-az-zu šu-nu (& it-ta-na-za-zu šu-nu) § 53*c* (auf die Strasse treten sie) H 175 *no* 7; IV^2 30* *no* 3 *R* 15—16, 17—18 ina eš-rit ili bīti (*Rev. Sém.* vi 149 (il) Bīt) & ina tub-qat bīti la ta-at-ta-nam-za-az la ta-as-sa-na-ax-xar(xur), do not advance; ZA iii 344 it-ta-nam-za-az.

ℑ II 60 *c* 8—9 ui-šu kun-zu-ba e-li-'i | a-na-ku nu-ux-xu(?)-za a-li-'i; II 11, 39 u-za-as-su (36 i-zu-us-su) AV 5930, 6408.

Š ušazix (Cyr 364, 9 u-ša-zi-zi) > ušazzix > ušanziz (§ 52 *rm*; Hilprecht, *Assyriaca*, 46 *rm* 1); ušēzix (§ 100); uš-zix (contracted on the analogy of verbs מ״ד; Cyr 382, 19 uš-zi-zi) § 37 (end), but *cf* Hilprecht, *Assyr.*, 45 *rm* 2; Haupt, Hebr. ii 5—6; ZK ii 272; Z^B 22; u-uš-zix (§ 10, I put up); ušzizzū (*c. t.*) § 53*c*; ulzix (§ 51; BA i 164; often in TP III *Ann* 44, 76 *etc.*); Sarg *Ann* 69. — *a*) place, set up, erect; also spread out {setzen, stellen, aufrichten; aus-, verbreiten} D 94 (K 3567) 2 (end) uš-zi-ix + 4 (end), KB vi, 1, 30; *Creat.-frg* IV 19 uš-zi-zu-ma ina bi-ri-šu-nu lu-ba-šu iš-te-en; ZA v 59, 9 (il) Marduk uš-ziz-ma xar-ra-nu. Xammurabi (KB iii, 1, 115 *col* 4, 1; 113 *col* 2) li[-it-ka?]šu-zi-ix. V 33 iv 2—4 i-na eli šub-tim-šu šu-bat (iç) erini lu-uš-zi-zu-ši(-ma). *Rec. Trav.*, xiv 109. H 118 *R* 12 lu-uš-zix see bābu NOTE 4, & gallū. IV^2 11 *b* 44 ina çi-e-ni tuš-ziz; Asb x 38—9 see danānu; & Smith, *Asurb*, 216, h; Asb v 26 + 127 see gārū; Esh iv 40—1 (see lītu) u-ša-zi-zu-ni (3 *pl*); Anp i 98 u-ša-zi-iz ça-lam šarrūti-ja (I had erected a statue of my royalty), + Šalm, *Mon*, *R* 56; u-še-zi-iz, Anp i 69, 105; ii 7, 91; u-še-ziz Šalm, *Obel*, 31, 72, also 156 (× KB ii 146); *Mon*, *O* 27, 51; *R* 44, 63; ul-ziz Šalm, *Obel*, 93; I 67 *a* 24 la uš-zi-zu šarru ma-ax-ri; Sn ii 7 a narū .... ul-ziz; *Bell* 26; Neb *Grotef* (I 65) i 44—5 rīmē ērī e-iq-du-tim u çir(or muš?)-ruš-šu še-zu-zu-u-ti uš-zi-iz; on ana tabrāt ušāzix, *etc.* see G § 68; Latrille, ZK ii 336. II 67, 80 a-na tab-ra-a-te u-ša-az-zi-iz; Esh *Sendsch*, *R* 53—4 ana tab-rat .... ul-ziz (see tabrītu). Sarg *Cyl* 42 šu-zu-zi (= pm) were put up; also 36 šu-zu-zi-im-ma. Neb *Bors*, ii 11; V 62 *a-b* 56 see miqittu & Bezold, *Diss*, 24 *rm* 1. Sm 954 *O* 29—30 ja-a-ši a-bi (il) Na-an-na-ru ul-zi-iz-za-an-ni (= MU-UN-NA-GUB-BA, EME-SAL); 88—5—12, 75 + 76 ix 12 çīriš nakiri lišzizanni (ZA ix 270—2) above my enemies may she place me. — Knudtzon, 115 *O* 4 Ašur-ax-iddi-na šar (māt) Aššur (ki) i-na pa-ni-e-šu lu-ša-zi-is[-su]; & *R* 9 u-ša-zi-is[-su]; 46 *O* 7 amēlu šu-a-tu l]i-bu-kam-ma ina pāni-šu [l]u-ša-az-zi-iz. Nabd 13, 6 da'ānē maxaršunu uš-ziz-zu; 356, 35 ina duppāni-šunu uš-ziz-zu (*cf* 936, 10 ša .... šu-uz-zu-zu = pm); II 61 *a-b* 22 ana manzazāni uš-zi-iz (= II 8 *c-d* 56); 70 *a-b* 46 ana qātāte uš-zi-iz (Z^B 16 on *a*) — settle, make to dwell {ansiedeln, wohnen lassen} Asb iv 40—1, I let *T.* and his family live in my palace (ki-rib ēkalli-ja ul-ziz-su-nu-ti), ii 94; iii 91; Sn ii 7. NE 42, 10 lu-še-iz-ziz-ka (Z^B 104). — *b*) make, or cause to rise, thus also: take away {aufstehen machen; wegnehmen} V 35, 25 ap-ša-a-ni la si-ma-ti-šu-nu šu-zix(?)-su-nu, BA ii 232 (× KB iii, 2, 124—5); see, however, Prince, *Diss*, 82 & AJP xiv 115, who translates V 50 *a* 51—2 ša ra-bi]-çu lim-nu ša-rat (ZK ii 27 *rm* 2) zu-um-ri-šu uš-zi-zu by: on the hair of whose body the evil rābiçu has caused to stand up (*i. e.*, in fear; not "take away"); *l* 60 (end) šar-ra e-li-šu šu-ziz-ma, let the king step upon it, Br 2327. H 82—3, 6 (pm) see zumru (§ 88; Br 2327). — *c*) put up, *i. e.*, collect {aufstellen, *i. e.* zusammenbringen}. Dar 384, 5: II gur suluppi *N* itti *P* . . . u-ša-az-xu-ma ana *M* inaddinu, 2 *gur* of dates shall *N* & *P* collect and deliver to *M*. ZA iv 66 *rm* 1, uš-xi-iz. — deposit {deponieren} VATh 459, 6 u-ša-az-za-az-ma (Peiser, *Babyl. Vertr.*, *no* 137).

Zimmern, *Beitr. zur babyl. Rel.*, 122 *no* 26 i 34 (end) er]ši šarri tu-ša-za-ax. T. A. Lo. 1, 45 nu-še-zi-ix; Ber. 8 *R* 15 i-na ri-ši ki-i ul-zi-xu-šu (ZA v 148) = 3 *sg.*

Š^t Beh (25) 26 anāku u-qu ina aš-ri-šu ul-ta-az-zi-ix (Bezold, *Achaemeniden*) I settled the people again in their (old) place. Knudtzon, 308 on 46 *O* 8 [ṭa-ab kīma ina p]āni-šu ul-t[a-az-x]i-xu-uš; T^M vi, 124 ul-te-ix-xix, ich werde Platz nehmen lassen (die Götter).

𝔑 K^M 9, 15 ti-i-ru (*var* ti-ru) u na-an-za-zu liq-bu[-u damiqtim], also see *ibid*, *p* 47; *Rec. Trav.*, xx 205 *foll*; *col* v 7. Sn *Kui* 4, 11 cedars which . . . . . . na-an-zu-zu (stood = pm, § 80); also l 67, 22 ša . . . . . na-an-xu-xu ka-a-a-nam.

𝔑^t it(t)ašix (but ZA xiv 374—5 = 𝔔^t of נשׁג). V 55 *a* 42 and king Nebukadr. it-ta-ši-ix i-na li-ti; K 10 *R* 19—20 it-ti-šu it-ta-ši-ix-xu they placed themselves on his side (= Hr^L 280; Pinches, *Texts*, *p* 6; § 100); K 19, 7—8 ana (kak-kab) aqrabi ina tarbaç Sin it-ta-ši-ix when Scorpio stands within the moon's halo. K 84, 31—2 (Hr^L 301) aš-ša it-ti bēl da-ba-bi-ja ta-ta-ši-iz-xa (= IV^2 45 *no* 1; RP^2 ii 185—9; JAOS xv 314 *fol*); K 18, 30—1 (Hr^L 281) ina eli amāt-ja ta-at-ta-ši-ix-xa-'a. (Johnston = 𝔔^t; š due to dissimilation). V 55 *a* 20 ni-ši-qu ša rabūti sisū it-ta-ši-ix-xu u ša et-li qar-di qit(or pu?)-ri-da-šu it-tu-ra (KB iii, 1, 104—5).

Derr. muzzix (see *p* 517; ZDMG 43, 203), manzazu, man(x)zaltu, manzazānu (see *p* 561—2), šūzuzu; uzuz(zu) & ušuzzu (see Appendix).

naxazu 2., nizzatu see nasasu, nissatu.

nuziztu so ZDMG 43, 197, perh for nubattu (*q. v.*).

naxaku 1. T. A., see nasaku.

naxaku 2. 𝔑^t Bu 89—4—26, 11 *R* 5 u enna a-na libitti it-ta-ax-ki-in-ni, and now to brick work he has set me (C. R. Thompson, *Reports*).

naxamu 1. weep, lament? {weinen, wehklagen?} ℑ IV^2 51 *b* 20 ina šur-ki šum ili-šu i-me-šu u-qad-di-šu u-na-az-zi-mu ik-lu-u. — ℑ^t perh ZA v 156, 22: ut-te-ix-zi-im (see *ibid*, 157 *rm* 9); KB vi (1) 282 *col* iv 28(+25) [ ] bēl ut-ta-x(ç)a-ma ta-ni-še-ti.

Der. izimtu (?) V 49 vii 22.

naxamu 2. Š Hilprecht, *OBI*, I pl 32—33 *col* 3, 36—7 a-na ta-ab-ri (*var* ra)-a-tim lu u-ša-ax-zi-im-šu, McGee, *Diss*, 17: admirabiliter illud adornavi (√asamu?).

naxaqu 1. = Arm נזק, Barth, *Etym. Stud.*, 51—2 comp. نقص, with which Fränkel, BA iii 81 agrees conditionally. K 196 (Pinches, *Texts*, 11—15) iii 25 the lord of that house ina-an-ziq will suffer harm (damage); II 47 *b* 2—3 mātu ina-an-ziq (or 𝔑?); K 588, 4 ana šarri bēli-ja i-na-ax-za-qa. Perh P. N. Nabū-u-xu-uk, II 64, 20, AV 5753. 6108. — Š harm, bring harm upon, injure {schädigen, Schaden zufügen, *etc.*} III 61 *a* 52 gir-ret nakri māta u-ša-ax-za-qa, hostile invasions will harm the country (§ 101); V 45 vi 46 tu-ša-an-zaq. Rm^2 139, 13 . . . . ma u-še-ziq (when a man harms his wife), 14 zikaru xīrtašu i-še-ir-ma u-še-ziq; 28 . . . . a-ni u-še-ziq : ul-tab-bar; 30 . . . . amēlu u-še-ziq lu-(?)-qa i-ma-al-li; Z^Š 57 refers to this Š also Šurpu iv 67 ar-nu ma-mit ša a-na su(for šu)-us-suq amēlūti iš-šaknin. — 𝔑 K 8713 *R* 6 (end) mātu ina-an-ziq (see also under 𝔔).

Derr. these 2:

naxāqu *2.* harm, injury {Schaden, Schädigung} III 65 *a* 15 (32) na-za-qu iš-šakan-šu, harm will come to him. Z^Š 4 : 64 na-xaq-šu; Craig, *Rel. Texts*, 74, 8 na-za-qu; K 7674, 17 na-zaq lā çalali; K 779 *R* 4 na-zaq māti, harm to the land (K 124 *R* 2; K 813 *O* 6; 82—5—22, 61 *O* 4). Thompson, *Reports*. A ‖ is:

niziqtu. K 196 i 1 *b* ni-ziq-tum sadrat-su (+21, end); T[M] vii 126 qu-lu k[u-ru ni-is]-sa-tu ni-ziq-tu imṭu-u ta-ni-xu. V 31 *g-h* 29 ni-ziq (written sik)-tu = ni-ziq-ti. V 48 vi 13 on the 13th (day?) ni-zi-iq-tum; 49 vii 19 on the 16th ni-ziq-tum; K 1395, 6 ni-ziq-tum ub-ba-lu; 81—2—4, 79, 6 ni-ziq-tu ub-ba-la.

NOTE. — Does it-ta-zu-uk-šu, T. A. Ber. 92, 3 belong to this stem?

nazaqu 3. whence epithet of door na-zi-iq-tum (AV 5932) II 23 *e-f* 65 = da-al-tum, *i. e.* something that moves (on hinges); AV 6108 (na-ça-qu), JENSEN, 339; *cf* II 30 *e-f* 42 BAR (?) = na-za-qu (Br 1776), preceded by kamû.

NOTE. — 1. According to some, here also Creat.-*frg* IV 101 iz-zuq mulmullu, the spear quivered; JENSEN, 339, but see KB vi, 1, 28—9 & נזק.

2. u-ša-za-ku-ni (HILPRECHT, *OBI*) = ušazakûni, *Zohâb*-stele i 12 = ušazzakûni > ušanzakûni (§ 79β) = move, remove something.

DERR. munziqqu & namzaqu.

nazaru pr izzur; *ps* inanzar curse {verwünschen, verfluchen} ‖ araru & ezeru. SCHWALLY, ZDMG 52, 511 comp. Arb. نزر: ungestüm fordern; perh im-ma az(s, ç)-ru-nim-ma (so KB vi, 1, 4 instead of im-ma-aç-ru-nim-ma, √maçaru, see above, *p* 573 *col* 1); V 50 *a* 67—8 ša pu-u lim-nu ix-zu-ru-šu (= NAM-TAR-RU-DA, Br 2111) ‖ 69—70 ša li-ša-nu li-mu-tum i-ru-ru-šu. Perh NE 16, 5 [lu]-uz-zur-ki ix-ra raba-a; 15, 20 (sal) u-xat ta-na-an-za-ar (or √נצר?) KB vi 138. K 2022 i 63 AŠ-BAL[-E?] = ir-ri-tu ša na-za-ri (II 29 *no* 1, add) BA ii 570; V 30 *a-b* 66 AŠ-BAL-E = na-za-rum (between ar-ra-tum & arrat). Perh IV² 60* C *O* 9 (end) na-za-ri. — Q[tn] NE 45, 84 Gilgamesh it-ta[-na]-az-za-ra-an-ni curses me; but see also zêru, 1. Der.

nizirtu curse {Verfluchung} M[S] 64 *ad Esh Sendsch*, *R* 39 ša Tarqû šar (mât) Muçur u (mât) Kûsi ni-zir-ti ilûtišunu rabîti, the object of the curse of their great deity.

naz(s, ç)ru some kind of peg, pole, *etc.* {eine Art Pflock} V 26 *c-d* 24 GIŠ-KAK-SAL-LA = na-az-ru (= II 44 *c-d* 43). Perh. rather naçru, √naçaru.

nazzaru, sword {Schwert} see namçaru.

nazarbubu, *cf* KB vi (1) 307; zarbabu & S[c] 5 *b* 6 (Br 2070); also kutlalu.

nazrabtu V 39 (*a*-)*b* 66 na-az-rab-tum = 65 na-aš-rap-tum; Z[B] 70 (end) √zarabu; but better naçraptum (Br 3769).

nazititum (?) AV 5934 quotes Sp 117, 2; 3 na-ti-ti-tum (?).

nâxu 1. pr inûx, *ps* inuxxu (in rel. cl.); ip nûx, rest, become rested, quiet down {ruhen, ruhig werden, sich beruhigen} ‖ pašaxu; AV 5941; Br 6387, 10540, 10607; § 138; D[H] 5; see libbu for IV 31 *R* 16; I 49 ii 15; Sm 954 *R* 9/10—15/16 (K[M] 12, 88); K 4623 + 79—7—8, 24, 19 (= H 122 *O* 15; + *R* 8). T[M] iii 83 ki-ma] šadi-i ina kibri (il) nâri i-nu-ux-xu; IV² 21* *no* 2 *O* 8—9 be-lum ša libba-šu e-liš la i-nu-xa-am (10—11 šap-liš); 12—13 e-liš u šap-liš la i-nu-xa-am; 26—27 libbušu ina pu-uš-šu-xi li-nu-xa-am; 32—33 lib-bu nu-ux, nu-ux. Bu 88, 5—12, 103, 24 (libbi bêli) i-nu-ux; K 2852 + K 9662 i 35 ag-gu lib-bi ul i-nu-ux; 24, ag-gu lib-ba-ka li-nu-xa-am-ma. NE 15, 44. Creat.-*frg* IV 135 i-nu-ux-ma be-lum ša-lam-tu-uš i-bar-ri (= *R* 52) KB vi 30—1. SCHEIL, *Nabd*, i 28 i-nu-ux-ma uz-za-šu; vii 38; *del* 125 (132) the abûbu i-nu-ux (rested, ceased). S. A. SMITH, *Asurb*, ii pl. 1 (K 2867) 18 lib-bi ilâni ul i-nu-ux ul ip-šax ša e-xu-zu ka-bit-ti bêlûti-šu-nu. K[M] 6, 80 li-nu-xa ša i-gu-gu; *cf* 7, 27; 21, 68; 27, 20; 28, 12; 46, 5. IV² 57 *b* 19 li-nu-ux lib-ba-ka (il) Marduk; KB ii 246—7, 66 libbi (il) Ašur ag-gu ul i-nu-ux-šu-nu-ti; Cyr 174, 7 P. N. Li-nu-ux libba be-ili. IV² 8 iv 13—16 (šiptu) nu-ux AN-GIŠ-BAR qu-ra-du | it-ti-ka li-nu-xu šadê nârâte | it-ti-ka li-nu-xa nâr Diqlat u nâr Purâtu | it-ti-ka li-nu-ux A-AB-BA ta-ma-tum rapaš-tim; 18 *no* 2 *O* 9/10—13/14 ER-ka (Ba-bi-lu; (il) A-nim) ..... nu-ux liq-bi-ka (ZK i 208); *R* 9—10 ilâni ša šamê u erçitim be-el nu-ux liq-bu-ka; *cf* 1/2—5/6 nu-ux = KU-MA´, EME-SAL; *O* 5/6 = A (which = pašaxu, Br 11349); K 3600 *R* 17 nu-xi mârat (il) Sin. P. N. Nu-xi-ja KB iv 14, 7. — pm (in passive meaning). K 181 *O* 28 ma-a u-ma-a mât-su ni-xa-at (Hr^{L} 197; *cf* JAOS xx 250—1; JOHNS, PSBA xviii 227); *Adapa*-legend, *R* 20 (li-ib-ba-šu ez-za) nîxa-at (BA ii 419); but KB vi 98: iç-ça-*ba*-at. V 31 *b* 56 ša-pa-su ne-e-ix (his) anger was quieted. On K 4832, 19 (above, 442 *col* 1, *l* 3) see KB vi 10 *l* 21.

83, 1—18, 1330 iii 38 si-id |  | na-a-xu (‖ pa-ša-xu, 39) PSBA xi; ZA ix 157; V 40 *c-d* 12 TE = na-a-xu (‖ pa-ša-xu, 13) Br 7698; V 21 *c-d* 39 TI = *n* (Br 1702); *g-h* 46 NE = na-a-xu (Br 4591); II 48 *a-b* (= K 4386 iv) 5 ku-uš | KUŠ | na-a-xu (Br 6387); H 24, 478; H^{F} 40, together with manâxtu & la a-ni-xu; see also Z^{B} 31 (med) on II 48 *e-f* 60.

Q^{t} KB vi 98, 20 it-tu-ux li-ib-ba-šu then his heart quieted down (*Adapa*-legend), but?.

ב *a*) to calm, make quiet {beruhigen} Asb iv 88—9 ilânišunu .... u-ni-ix (1 *sg*); K 1282 (*Dibbara*-legend) *R* 4 ^{il} I-šum ma-lik-šu u-ni-xu-šu-ma (quieted him). ZA iii 344 li-ni-ix-ki; IV^{2} 21* *O* 24—5 libba-šu el-lum lu-ni-ix; 24 *no* 3, 24—5 ša-mu-u li-ni-ix-xu (= KU-MA'-EME-SAL), also D 57 *O* (JENSEN, 424 *rm* 1); Sm 954 *R* 11—12 lib-ba-ki li-ni-ix (= XE-EN-KU-E) ‖ ka-bit-ta-ki li-paš-ši-ix (14). Sp III 286 + R III, 1, 14 lib-ba-ka ne-ix-tum li-ni-ix (HOMMEL, *Sumerische Lesestücke*, 120 *fol*). K 8214, 17 ... a-tum $^{(il)}$ Nin-kar-ra-ak u-na-ax-xu (KB vi 100); SMITH, *Asurb*, 121, 38 (ana) nu-ux-xi ka-bit-ti $^{(il)}$ Marduk; 122, 41 *b* a-na nu-ux libbi (of such & such gods); K 4648, 9 (H 178, 78); I 49 iii 6 ana nu-ux-xi lib-bi ilu-ti-ka rabîti; 81—6—7, 209, 12 a-na nu-ux-xu libbi ilûti-šunu (HEBR. viii 114; BA iii 260); IV^{2} 4 iii 15 $^{(ilat)}$ Iš-tar ša ina nu-ux-xi (Br 6264) ul-çi ul-la-nu-uš-šu; V 52 iv 20 ša a-na nu-ux lib-bi ilâni rabûti šu-lu-ku; 3, man-nu u-na-ax-xa-an-ni who shall pacify me? Sm 690 *O* 5—6 ilu mu-ni-ix lib-bi abê-šu (Z^{B} 114); K 2852 + K 9662 iv 19 lil-bur mu-ni-ix-libbi-Ašur. — II 32 *a-b* 16 ûm nu-ux libbi ‖ ša-p(b)at-tum (*q. v.*); ZA iv 274—5; also 83, 1—18, 1330 i 25 see xarmaṭu; ZA iv 232, 10 Ê-sag-gil ša ta-ram-mu nu-u-xu. — *b*) over-power, bring to order; extinguish, *etc.* {bezwingen, zur Ruhe (Ordnung) bringen; auslöschen, *etc.*} T^{M} v 125 ina mê ša mûti libbakunu u-ni-ix (I overpower your heart). TP i 67 *fol* ša .... šarru ja-um-ma i-na tam-xa-ru ira(t)-su-nu | la u-ni-xu (I Rawl. -ti, or perh. 'u?); L^{T} 98; ZK i 120; TP iv 47—8 mu-ni-xu | i-na qabli ša-ni-na i-na ta-xâzi la i-šu-u, AV 5497. Sarg *Khors* 13 ina epêš qabli u taxâzi ul êmura mu-ni(-ix)-xu; see *Cyl* 8; *Ann* 4; Samš iv 23 e-peš taxâzi-ja dan-ni ša mu-ni-xa la išu-u; iii 29 (mu-ni-ix-xa), § 11; Sarg *Nimr* 4. T^{M} v 158 šadû li-ni-ix-ku-nu-ši (iv 122); Creat.-*frg* III 109 ip-šu pi(-i)-ku-nu $^{(il)}$ girru li-ni-ix-xa (*etc.*), KB vi 8 *etc.* IV^{2} 8 iv 2 kinûna ap-pu-xu (see napaxu) u-na-ax; 5, u-na-ax-xu; also II 51 *b* 19 u-ni-ix (& 22 -xu); K 2852 + K 9662 ii 6 lišân GIŠ-BAR (= li'bi?) mu-na-ax-xi; K 4832, 16 iššâtu li-ni-ix-xa; + *R* 35 libbu]-uk li-ni-ix-xa. Neb 329, 7 tu-ni-xi; V 45 ii 40 tu-na-a-xa; see 55 (& ZA i 96 *rm* 1); 56 tu-na-a-xa-an-ni, 57 tu-na-xa-šu-nu.

Š^{1} K^{M} 33, 3 muš?]-te-ni-ix uz-zi ili u [iṣ̌tarti?] who appeaseth the anger of god and [goddess?].

NOTE. — 1. Nûx-napištim see napištu, NOTE 1.

2. uštanix, SMITH, *Asurb*. 118, 7—8; JENSEN, KB ii 248—9 √nâxu rest (said of sun & moon, *Kosmologie*, 106 *foll*); K 1406 *O* 1 uš-ta-ni-ix (of an eclipse) see anaxu.

Derr. manâxu, manâxtu, 1 &:

nîxu *f* nixtu, *adj.* quieted, quiet, calm, peaceful {beruhigt, ruhig, friedlich} esp. in connection with šubtu. III 6, 46 šub-tu ni-ix-tu a quiet (peaceful) house; LEHMANN, L^{4} ii 28; TP vii 34 šu-ub (*var* šub)-ta ni-ix-ta u-ša (*var* še)-ši-ib-šu-nu-ti; V 35, 36 šu-ub-ti ni-ix-tim u-še-šib. šu-bat ne-ix-tim ZA ii 119 *b* 8; 360 ii 9 (KB iii, 1, 122—4); Br. M. 12215 ii 10; *Khors* 190 (ni-ix-ti); *Ann* 413 (ne-ix-tu). II 43 *a-b* 14 šubtu ne-ix-tum = e-bi-tum; 83—1—18, 215 *R* 12 (end) .... ne-ix-tu u-še-šib; 83—1—18, 242 *O* 7 šubtu ne-ix-tum. K 2711 *R* 39 šubat ne-ix-tu; 80—7—19, 63 *O* 8 šu-ub-tum ne-ix-tum (a peaceful home will be to the land); K 2801 + K 221 + 2669, 43 ša . . . . u-še-ši-bu šu-bat ne-ix-ti. IV^{2} 3 *b* 17—8 see manzaltu (Br 8424, 8458); 20 *no* 1, 17—8 i-ru-um-ma ir-ta-me šu-bat-su ni-ix-ta (= IM-DUB-DUB, Br 7028), he entered & inhabited his peaceful home. AV 6209.

***nâxu* 2.** be fat {fett sein}. II 27 *c-d* 38 NI-ŠAX = na-a-xu ša šaxē (*cf* šaxū), Jensen, ZA i 310 (× Z^{B} 31); also see III 56, *no* 2, 4; 62 *b* 29 NI of the šaxū. **Der.:**

nūxu. fat, oil {Fett, Oel} used for oiling SU (*i. e.*, leather). II 44 *c-f* 69 SU-LU-UB (= lu-ub-bu, 64) NI-IÇ = nu-u-xu; 70, = a-a-çu; 65 SU-LU-UB-MAR-TU-KI = ku-ša-nu.

nixū? II 37 *no* 7 *R* . . . LI = ni (or xal, çal)-xu-u, AV 6210; Br 13911.

naxbū, naxbâtu quiver {Köcher} properly: hiding place of the arrows √xabū, 1, *p* 290. D^{Pr} 175, 1; § 65, 31 *a*; BA i 176. K 4200, 10 . . . LAL = na-ax-bu-u (AV 7031, Br 14377); perh T. A., Ber. 28 ii 43: I na-ax-bu-u ša kaspi; iii 63: III na-ax-bu-u ša abni. Bm 2, 27, 13 NA-AX-BA-TUM = ŠU *i. e.* naxbâtum, M^{S} 36.

naxbalu snare, net, trap {Schlinge, Fallstrick} as a means of ruining, √xabalu, 1. Z^{B} 93 *rm* 1; RÉJ xiv (27) 157; AV 3291, 5942. II 22 *a-c* 20 GIŠ-EŠ-SA-DU = na-ax-ba-lu ‖ (qū?) na-ax-ba-lim; Br 10007 *fol*; K 2022 i 50 see xaštu, 1. IV^{2} 22 *a* 14—5 . . . na]-ax-ba-lu (= GIŠ-EŠ-SA-AD) še-ip-šu lul-lu (or nar-tib?)-b(p)u-um-ma. ‖ is:

naxbaltu II 60 *c* 11 ri-da-a i-šu ki-i na-ax-bal-ti.

nuxxuṭu V 20 *e-f* 32 nu-ux-xu-tum (ṭu?) ‖ kunnû (*q. v.*), Br 9076, Jensen, 440: desire. ZA iv 274—5 has nu-ux-xu-ṭu (i 23) ‖ supp(bb)ū, sullū = prayer; PSBA '88 (Dec.) (*i. e.*, 83, 1—18, 1330 i 21 *foll* = zu-ur); V 45 ii 45 tu-na-ax-xaṭ-ṭa; perh II 47 *a-b* 9—10 nu-ux-xu-ti (for ṭi)-šu i-dal-la-xu (Br 4277, 6580 *ad* nuxxu).

***naxalu* 1.** ℶ dig, bore a hole, deepen {aushöhlen, vertiefen} *etc.* V 36 *d-f* 42 bu-ru ¦ ⟨ nu-ux-xu-lum (Br 8721; Z^{B} 98 *rm* 1: oppression); D^{H} 48—9, but see RÉJ x 301; D^{Pr} 151 & again RÉJ xiv (27) 158. Knudtzon, 308 *ad* 33 *R* 11 šumma mār-tu na-ax-lat (? šat, qur?). — **Derr.** these 3:

naxlu *1.* — *a*) narrow ravine, narrows, shaft {enge Schlucht, Schacht} Z^{B} 55 *rm* 1. II 32 *g-h* 18 SI-DUG-GA (Br 3420) = na-ax-lum ‖ šu-ut-ta-tum (17); also ‖ šu-xarruru & xa-aš-tum. K 328, 4 kim-matu na-xal (KB iv 146—7). Z^{S} viii 23, 37 kup-pu na-ax-lu; also iii 62. — *b*) valley, ravine; brook {Thalschlucht; Bach} § 27. III 35 *no* 4 *O* 12 na-xal (mât) Mu-çur ašar nāru lā išū; Sarg *Cyl* 13 na-xal (mât) Mu-uç-ri; Esh i 56; Winckler, *Forsch*, i 26; D^{Pa} 310; Sn iv 77—8 see nadbaku. P. N. Na-xal-šu. The same two meanings has:

naxallu — *a*) K 4341 i 26 (II 36 *no* 3; *e-f* 61) MAX-DI = na-xal-lum (‖ šu-ut-ta-tum, 60 & xa-aš-tum, 62) AV 5936; Br 1057. II 35 *c-d* 41 UX-ŠIT-TA = na-xal-lu (Br 8310); VATh 244 iii 18 UD-RI-IG = na-xal-lum. — *b*) Sn iii 75 see nadbaku; K 420, 10 + 21.

nixlu excavation, deepening {Aushöhlung, Vertiefung}? V 36 *d-f* 41 bu-ru ¦ ⟨ ni-ix-lu (Br 8720); IV^{2} 19 *b* 22 šiptu : ni-'-mil ni-ix-lu (*var* li), gu-ux-xu, xa-ax-xu, ru-['-tu] = Z^{S} vii 97 (viii 1): Bangigkeit; thus read *s. v.* guxxu; M^{S} 37. See, however, KB vi (1) 451.

***naxalu* 2.** II 39 *g-h* 24 na-xa-lum ša še-im (*cf* xabašu) AV 5935; S 896, 5; D^{S} 79; 120. **Der.:**

naxlu *2.* K^{M} 12, 4 še-am na-ax-la taš-pak (= date-palm?); *cf* Cyr 355, 6 na-xa-lu-u-tu.

naxlu *3.* some kind of garment {ein gewisses Kleidungsstück} AV 5944. V 15 *e-f* 51 KU-TUR-[cuneiform] = na-a[x-lu?], 52 KU-EB-LAL = ni[-i-ru?], 53 KU-GAR-EB-LAL = xu[-ul-la-nu]; V 28 *c-d* 71—2 . . . [cuneiform] (= u?) d(t)up-lum = na-ax-lum & sa-an-qu (a tight garment or bandage?); but see naxtu, 3.

naxaltum ? Nabd 78, 13 (çubât) na-xal-tum SEG; *var* (çubât) na-xal-ap-tum na-ba-su (78, 7) BA i 494, bel. K 1151 (Hr^{L} 95) *O* 11 a-dan-niš na-xal-a-te.

naxlapu cover, garment {Decke, Kleid} √xalapu. V 28 *c-d* 85 na-[ax]-la-pu

= lu-lu-un-tum u-ri-e (Pinches, ZK ii 332, 5; Z^B 95). ‖ is

naxlaptu. § 65, 31 *a*; AV 5943; also see nabāsu; IV^2 30* *b* 1—2 na-ax-lap-ta (= KU-TIK-UD-DU) sa-an-ta (Br 3293; see *Rev. Sém.*, '98, 148—51 on this text) = $Z^Š$ viii 45. K 2674 i 17 KU-TIK-UD-DU-šu iš-ru-ṭu (Smith, *Asurb*, 142). NE 43, 31 see xalapu 𝔍ᵗ. V 28 *c-d* 68 *foll* na-ax-lap-tu (*d*) = e-pa-ar-tu (68 *c*); 69 naxlaptu bur-um-tu = ka-šu-ri-tum; 70 = e-kal(?lap, rib)-tum, 71 a-ta-bi ki-ša-di; 72 *c* na-ax-lu-up-tum = naxlaptu su(or SU?)-xu-um-bi (ZK ii 332); 73 *c* .... it-tum = *n s* & 74 *c* .... ri-it-tum; 75 ... a-çu ....; 78 e-kil (rim?)-tum = *n* ça-lim-tum; 79 sa-am-tum = *n* çi-ri. V 15 *e-f* 51 KU-TIK-UD-DU = na-ax-lap-tum; id also Cyr 241, 6. II 25 *g-h* 40. ‖ are:

naxluptu & **naxallaptum** (T^C 73, 1). Nabd 78, 17 (+ 21) KU na-xal-ap-tum (see lines 6, 7, 10) BA i 494.

naxamu P. N. mār ša Mu-na-xi-im-mu, Strassmaier, *VIII. Or. Congr.* (*Stockholm*), 20, 2.

naxmaçu (√xamaçu, *q. v.*) Neb 108, 7 du-u-du ina muxxi na-ax-ma-çu maškānu; Neb 199, 5 du-u-du u na-ax-ma-çu (?) maškānu.

naxnaxtu ala of nostril (Johnston) & **naxnaxūtu** breathing {Atmen} K 510 *R* 9—12 (Hr^L 108) i-na maxri u ina eli ¦ na-ax-na-xi-e-te ša ap-pi ¦ u-mu-du (√עמד); na-ax-na-xu-tu ¦ u-ṭa-u-bu, they interfere with the breathing; *cf* OLZ '99, 158.

ni-xe-nun-na-ku, Jensen, ZDMG 50, 261 "Ein Lehn- oder Kunstwort" *ad* IV^2 54 *a* 52, not zāzāku (*q. v.*), as others read.

nixesu. pr ixxis, ps inaxxis, inamxis; ip ixis (AV 5087) cedo, recede, go away {weichen, weggehen}, ZA v 99; BA i 201 × § 110; *Rev. Crit.* '90 (482) aller rapidement. K 79 *O* 14—5 (Hr^L 26 = IV^2 46 *no* 3) ar-ka-niš a-na (mât) Elamti ki-i ix-xi-su, later on when they had fled to Elam; *Il* 14 a-na (mât) Elamti ¦ ul ax(or ix?)-xi-is. K 145, 18 ki-i ix-xi-su-nu a-na Bābili e-tir-bu-nu; 22 la i-na-ax-xi-is(-ma). K 831 *R* 3 (Hr^L 214) la i-nam-ax-xi-is-ma (*cf* K 1250, 2); *del* 280 (316) ana-ku lu-ux-xi-is; IV^2 58 *d* 27 the daughter of Anu like smoke ... la i-na-ax-xi-is. K 81, 26 (Hr^L 274 *R* 3—4) it-ti-ia a-na Uruk ¦ ta-nam-xi-is-ma (§ 52). NE 68, 31 šum-ma la na-ṭu-ma i-xi-is arki-k[a?] (then return!); VATh 73, 48 i-ni-xi-is-'u (Jensen, 427—8); Nabd 715, 11 ittišunu i-na-xi-su (*cf* 18); Neb 51, 6 i-ni-xi-is (+ Cyr 128, 25); Cyr 376, 18 ana ku-tal-la i-ni-xi-si; Camb 378, 7 ina libbi i-na-ax-xi-is. V 31 *e-f* 14 aš-šu a-la-ku u ni-xi-e-šu ša kakkab GUD[-UD?]; *cf* ZA v 128 & nikimātum. — *b*) of buildings *etc.* = anaxu. IV^2 39 *b* 3 the gate e-na-ax-ma ¦ ix-xi-is u i-nu-uš. — T. A. detain {aufhalten} Lo. 58, 8 lū la i-na-ax-xi-is-su, do not detain him; Ber. 234 (238) *frg*, 11 la i-na-ax-xi-is e-ib-ši-it-šu-nu (Ber. 24 *R* 56, 58, 61).

𝔔ᵗ = 𝔔 *del* 108 (115) in the heavens the gods were afraid of the stormflood, it-te-ix-su (*var* it-tax-su; *cf* K 350, 13 it-tax-çu-u!) i-te-lu-u ana šamē ša (il) A-nim, they receded to the heaven of Anu (§ 110); IV^2 27 *a* 39 i-bak-ki it-xu-su (= uç) ul i-kal-la; K 114 *O* 19 see kutallu. Nabd 119, 3—4: I mana X šiqlu ṭu-ux-xu-u it-te-ix-si (Cyr 368, 8); Camb 85, 16 ni-ix-te-ix-su (amêl) mu-kin-nu; Dar 260, 21.

𝔍 V 45 *col* ii 43 tu-na-ax-xa-as, 46 tu-na-ax-xa-sa; V 36 *d-f* 44 bu-ru ⟨ ¦ mu-ux-xu-su (Br 8728); Nabd 234, 11 mu-ni-xi-is.

Š V 45 vi 38 tu-ša-an-xa-as (but Knudtzon, 237 derives this from axazu). Perh K 359, 8 us-su-an-xi-i[s-su?] or Šᵗ; 21 u-ša-an-xu-çu (S. A. Smith, ii, √נחץ). Cyr 1, 7 u-ša-xi-su. Der.

nixsu. V 36 *d-f* 43 bu-ru ¦ ⟨ ¦ ni-ix-su (Br 8722); K 7, 7 ni-ix-su xurāçi ZA i 247 (see, above, *p* 353 *col* 1, note to ṭibū).

naxasu demand {verlangen} Peiser, *Babyl. Vertr.*, *no* cviii 10 (mim-ma ma-la ul-tu kaspu *K* itti *S* ta-na-xi-is (Br. M. 84, 2—11, 150) as much money as *K* asks of *S*; also see Nabd 715, 11 + 18.

---

nixappū read niqilpū (נקלפ) *q. v.* ∼ naxaçu, innixaç *cf* nakadu.

naxaçu. K 8204, 4—5 u-na-xa-aç çur-ri çir-xi-iš šu-um-u (PSBA xvii 137, *rm* † comp. نخص *mucio confectus fuit*; BA i 201: נחץ = antreiben, drängen). V 45 ii 43 (*cf* naxasu); 42 tu-na-ax-xaç. KNUDTZON, 115 *O* 9 u-ša-da]-b[a-a-b]a u-ša-an-xa-aç-ça; *cf* 116 *O* 10; 118 *O* 7; *R* 12 u]-ša-an-xa-çu u-ša-da-ba-bu, all of which KNUDTZON derives from √axazu.

naxaru 1. Q pm perh KNUDTZON, 152 *O* 18 e-zib ša ("heed not that", R. F. HARPER) .... ma na-ax-r[u]. — ℑ V 45 ii 41 tu-na-ax-xar. — Š V 45 vi 41 tu-ša-an-xar (or √maxaru?). See also P. N. Na-xa-ra-a-u III 4 *no* 4 (K 416) 14.

naxru, T. A. Ber. 21, 33: I na-ax-ra ma-aš-ši (so perh against above, *p* 337 *col* 2 s.v. xaramu); 81—7—27, 56 *O* 1—2 GIŠ-ŠA'-AB-LAX = iç-çu na-ax[-ru], GIŠ-ŠINIG-UD-DA-TAR-DA = bi-nu na-ax[-ru], a plant? M^S 64.

naxaru 2. T^M vi 100 u [šam] NU-LUX-XA-ma u-na-xa-ra kal kiš-pi-ki; destroy, cut off {vernichten, abschneiden} T^M 140; ℑ' T^M v 38 ki-ma šam NU-LUX-XA SAR lit-tax-xi-ra šaptā-ša may her lips be pierced through.

naxiru 1. a bird {ein Vogel} 81, 7—27, 56 *O* 5—7 TE(?)-US-XU; .... ZI(?)-XU; ..... XU = na-xi-rum (XU) M^S 64.

naxiru 2. some large sea animal {ein grosses Meertier}. AV 5940; KGF 20; FOX TALBOT, PSBA v 351 = dolphin √naxaru breathe, snort {schnaufen}. Anp iii 88 KA-MEŠ (= šinnē) na-xi-ri bi-nu-ut tamdi (among the tribute of the people living on the Mediterranean coast) KB i 108—9; L^T 161 *ad* I 28 *a* 3 na-xi-ra ina tāmti rabīti i-du-uk; *b* 16: II na-xi-ri-MEŠ and other animals, of (aban) AD-BAR served as ornaments of the portals. Lay. 43, 12. HOMMEL, *Gesch.*, 532 *rm* 4: Der durch die Nase schnaubende; ist etwa eine Hippopotamusart gemeint? (doch sein Merkmal sind wertvolle Zähne; dazu passt diese Erklärung nicht); IDEM in HASTINGS, *Bible Dict.*, i 182: a sea monster, properly: snorting.

naxīru nostril {Nasenloch} III 65 *a* 15 na-xi-ir imitti-šu his right nostril; 16 na-xi-ra-šu both his nostrils = נְחִירַיִם. K 519 *R* 14—15 pi-i na-xi-ri liš-ku-nu ša-a-ru i-ka-si-ir (Hr^L 108) RP^2 ii 182 *rm* 4. K 3445 + R 396 *O* 37—8 ip-te-e-ma na .... | na-xi-ri-ša ub.... M^S 64.

nuxar II 26 *c-d* 85 Ê-ŠI + Ê-NIR = nu-xar = ziqquratum (*q. v.*). *cf* V 41 *e-f* 22 nu-xa-ar = ziq]-qur-ra-tu. BA iv 378.

nuxaru, V 17 *c-d* 3 (II 26 *no* 1, *a-b* 6) šam A (or ZA?, ZK i 344)-A-[sign]-GUŠ-KIN = nu-xa-ri (or IŠ xa-ri[-iç?]). Br 9809 reads šam (a-a-ar) GUŠKIN; also Br 11698. MEISSNER & ROST, 26—7: vielleicht, Schmuckgegenstand.

nuxuru. II 44 *no* 1 (add) AV 6411 .... KAL = nu-xu-rum, Br 81.

nuxurtu a plant {eine Pflanze} 81, 7—27, 56, 3 *fol* KA-LAX(LUX)-XA-SAR, NU-LAX-XA-SAR = nu-xur-tum. See T^M v 38 & *p* 140; and naxaru, 2.

naxarmuṭu & **naxarmumu** see xar-maṭu & xarmamu (*p* 338 *col* 1).

naxa(u)rtu = namxa(u)rtu (√maxaru) receipt, income {Einkommen} K 660, 12 (Hr^L 86) na-xar(mur?)-tu ša ardi-ka.

naxšum (na-ax-šum) AV 5945 see xā'iru.

naxašu 1. superabound, exist in abundance {strotzen, in Überfluss vorhanden sein}. AV 5939; D^{Pa} 148; P^{Pr} 72; 200; BAER-DEL., *Ezech*, pref. xiv; see, however, ZK ii 350—1; RÉJ xiv 158; ZDMG 40, 730. Q S^c 78 ša-ar | ŠAR | na-xa-šu ša nu-ux-ši (Br 8227); K 806 *O* 6 (māt) Akkadu[ki] i-na-xi-iš; šar Akkadi[ki] i-dan[-nin]; also 83—1—18, 310 *O* 7; perh KNUDTZON, *no* 33 *R* 11 (see naxalu, 1). — ℑ V 45 ii 42 tu-na-ax-xaš; II 67, 78 dalātē erini (iç) šur-man (= šurmēni) tu-'a-ma-te mu-na-ax-xi-ša e-ri-bi-ši-na (AV 5486; KB ii 24—5); Esh (Berl. Mus.) *O* 7 Adad bēl ra-aš-bu mu-na-xi-iš umūnātē-ja (ROST, *p* 117); K 3600 *R* 12 (end) see labnu (said of goddess Ninā); P. N. Mu-na-ax-xiš(s?) Marduk (AV 5487, Mu-na-ax-xi-iš Marduk) PEISER, *Babyl. Vertr.*, xxii 5; also lxi 12; Camb 375, 2 *fol.* Derr.:

naxāšu 2. abundance {Überfluss} K^M 8, 3 rīmi-nin-ni-ma (ilat) Iš-tar ki-bi-i na-xa-ši command abundance.

nuxšu abundance, luxury {Überfluss, Üppigkeit} Br 4051; AV 2134; 5573; 6413; G § 2; Z^B 97 *rm* 2. TP viii 28—9 see mašrū & § 92*b*; I 27 *no* 2, 52—3 see duxdu; Xammurabi (KB iii, 1, 122) *col* ii 7; I 66 *c* 16 see xegallu; KB iii (1) 122 i 17 nu-xu-uš ni-ši (+ ii 23); ZA ii 360. Neb iv 57—8 see zananu, 1 Š; & also for *del* 36 (43). Ner ii 10—11 mi-e nu-ux-šu la na-pa-ar-ku-ti ukîn ana mâti (AJP xi 501); KB iii (2) 8—9 *col* ii 7 me-e nu-ux-ši dam (or perh nik?)-lu-tim *i. e.* artistic waterbasins (AJP xi 498). TP III *Ann* 12 nu-ux-še mê. II 51 *b* 25 Tigris is called ba-bi-lat nu-ux-ši (D^H 67 *rm* 1); 50 tu-bil nu-ux-ša, she brought a (great) abundance of water, name of a canal. IV^2 18 *no* 1 *O* 12—3 šu-bat nu-ux-ši (= XE-NUN-NA) u-še-šib (Sn *Bav* 31); Asb i 51; Sarg *Ann* 454 nu-xuš; *Cyl* 37 mê nu-ux-še (Lyon, *Sargon*, 67); nu-xuš ma-a-ti the abundance of the world (JRAS '91, 402, 9); *cf* V 63 ii 47 nu-xu-uš ta-ma-a-ti; 83—1—18, 219 *O* 6 nu-xu-uš nišê; 83—1—18, 35 (Hr^L 427) *O* 6 (il) Adad nu-ux-še ina libbi am-ba-si (= -te) il-lak (AJSL xiv 5); nagab nuxše see nagbu. V 40 *c-d* 30 XE-NUN = nu-ux[-šu]; S^c 76 ša-ar | ŠAR | nu-ux-šu; II 28, 608; Br 8228.

naxâšu *3.* (?). Sp II 265 *a* v 8 (ZA x 5) ....ti (?) bêl pa-an (M^S parçi) ša uç-çu-pu-šu na-xa-šu (M^S 64 √ nâxu).

Nuxâšu P. N. V 67 *c* 51 (S + 326 *R* 4) mâr Nu-xa-šu; Nabd 153, 7 (amêl) Nu-xa-a-šu.

nuxuštum T. A. Lo. 73, 22 u (?) nu-xu-uš-tum ša-'-(?).

naxatu. Only in ℑ nuxxutu, always preceded by ša ina šiqil pit-qa *i. e.* by the one shekel-piece coined, Pinches, RP² iv 105. Camb 315, 1—2: I ²/₃ manê kaspi ša ina I šiqil pit-qa nu-ux-xu-tu ša la ginû (BA iii 454 in Einzelsekelstücken), see also ZA iii 216; Nabd 368, 1; 750, 1; 1084, 1; 786, 2; Cyr 275, 1—2; Dar 156, 2—3; 131, 2; 349, 1 (6) kaspu piçû nu-ux-xu-tu (so for -ru, see M^S 64); BOR ii 57 (*no* 97) 2; Br. Mu. 84, 2—11 (middle) see Kohler & Peiser, ii 70; KB iv 310—11 (below) 3 + 7; Peiser, KAS 32 (vi) 15; 34 (vii) 11: ana ¹/₂ mana kaspi pi-çu-u nu-ux-xu-tu id-din coined {gemünzt} (but see BA i 517 *rm*); Peiser, *Babyl. Vertr.*, 321 *col* 1: coined, struck; *cf* PSBA '84, 105; ZK i 120 (med) *Rev. d'Assyr.*, i ('84) 9; Halévy, JA viii ('88, Dec.) *vol* 12, 514 = نحت, cut, scratch, so also Lehmann, ZA xiv 362 *foll*: but with the technical meaning: *radendo aptavit*; kaspu piçû nuxxutu, Lehmann says: Schekel weisses Silber, das in einzelne Schekel abgeteilt ist (jeder einzelne Schekel) geglättet (resp. justiert [reads bat-qu]) *i. e.* vollwichtig. ša la ginû: die nicht normalwichtig sind. BA iii 454 √ נחת be small (>< D^{Pr} 33; 118) ℑ = make small; nuxxutu perh = coined, struck. See also BOR iv 5 (engrave); ZA x 49 (monnayée). V 45 ii 44 tu-na-ax-xat; 47 tu-na-ax-xa-ta. III 61 *no* 2, 23 nu-ux-xu-ut u-di-e; V 46 *a* 55.

nuxxîtu Ner 15, 9 pu-ut nu-ux-xi-tum | šil-bir-tum ša ¹/₂ šiqil pit-qa ša ina maxar *M* & *N* i-na-ši (?); *cf l* 24 nu-ux-xi-tum ša ši-bir-[tum]; ZA vii 273; M^S 64.

naxtu *1.* name of the young of the paspasu-bird {das Junge des paspasu-vogels} D^S 106; D^{Pr} 120 *rm* 1; AV 5946. II 37 *d-f* 11 TUR(?)-UZ]-TUR-XU = na-ax-tu ni-ip-çu ‖ mâr iç-çur ra-bi-i; II 40 *no* 1, *R* (*e-f*) 27 na-ax-tum = ni-ip[-çu?]; BA iii 454: a small fowl, chicken; Br 14055, *cf* 14056.

naxtu *2.* despondency {Niedergeschlagenheit} III 4 *no* 4, 48—9 xar-ba-šu ta-xa-zi-ja im-qu-su-ma | ir-ša-a na-ax-tu.

naxtu *3.* in a list of garments is mentioned KU-EB (or TUM)-EŠ & KU-EB-LAL = na-ax-tum V 14 *e-f* 51—2 (Br 4928, 4964); id of 52 also = ni-bit-tum (53) AV 5946. See naxlu, 3.

nixatbutum (?) V 33 *e-f* 56 bu-ru | ⟨ | ni-xat (or pa?)-bu-tum, Br 8719.

nuxatimmu baker {Bäcker} Zimmern, ZDMG 53, 115—8, on *Rec. Trav.*, xx 127 & *Compt. Rend*, '98, 221 *fol*, *ll* 10—12 it-ti nu-xa-tim-me nu-xa-tim-mu-ta ip-pu-uš it-ti nu-xa-tim-me ša Eridi nuxatimmûta ippuš | a-ka-la u me-e ša Eridi û-mi-šam-ma ip-pu-uš (see KB vi, 1, 92—3) = נַחְתּוֹמָא, Etymology: Sumerian NU (= amêlu) + xatimmu (?) form like nukaribbu (also title of an official); so also Hommel, *Expository Times*, Jl. '99, 460 *col* 2; Sep. '99, 567 *col* 1; Jensen, *ibid*, Aug. '99. Halévy, *Rev. Sém*, viii ('99) 278 *fol* agrees with Zimmern as to the meaning, but rejects the etymology; the form a Nifal of נחת "sceller, imprimer un nom, marquer". — II 31 *a-b* 29 ŠU-QA-GAR = šaqû cup-bearer foll. by rab (*i. e.* SAG)-MU = chief of the bakers = rab nuxatimmu; *cf* K 8669 where the rab MU and rab SAG are mentioned together. rab-MU (81—2—4, 161) also name of an eponym. II 31 *b* 90 (amêl) MU bît-[ili] = temple-baker. 82—8—16, 1 i 23—4 (S. A. SMITH, *Misc. Texts*, pl. xxv *fol*) EN-ME-GI (en-gi-ma) & EN-ME-NU (en-di-ib) = šu & nu-xa-t[um?]; Rm 338 *R* 16 MU-KIT(?)-UZU = nu-xa-tim bît na-aç-ri, foll. by ša mut-ta[-ti], ṭa-bi[-xu] & preceded by Asû (physician) & munâ'išu (veterinary surgeon); see ZA ix 274.

nûṭu some vessel, receptacle of leather {ein aus Leder gefertigtes Behältnis}. نَوْط, T[C] 103; BA i 635 basket (made of the bast of the date-palm). Neb 211, 4 see nâdu, 3; 402, 13 (mašak) nu-u-ṭu; 173, 1; Nabd 31, 3.

nûṭânu (*pl?*) Nabd 824, 11; Neb 383, 2 (mašak) nu-ṭa-nu.

naṭû *ps* **inaṭṭû** AV 5950. be feasible, passable, acceptable {passend, geeignet sein} *etc.* K 638 (Hr[L] 328) *R* 15 ša bêl E-KI (= Babylon) u-çab-bit i-na-aṭ-ṭu; II 62 *no* 3, *a-b* 64 (= K 64 i 6) e-li-tu (u) ša-pil-tu i-na-aṭ-ṭu (= AN-AG-A) Br 459; 2788; also II 62 *no* 3 (K 49 ii 19—20); II 30 *c(-d)* 4. *pm* naṭû TP ii 73—4 eqil pa-aš-qi ša a-na me-tiq narkabâti-ja | la-a na-ṭu-u, (Mount Aruma) a rough territory, impassable for the moving of my chariots; iii 20 (24) see kibsu; also iii 45 (49) la-a na-ṭu-u. IV² 3 *a* 52—3 muruç qaqqadi kîma šadi-e ana nu-uš-šu (√נוש) la na-ṭu-u (= NU-UB-ZU-A), the *m q* like a mountain cannot be shaken. NE 67, 18—19 šum-ma na-ṭu-ma .... šum-ma la na-ṭu-ma; ‖ 69, 35 where once written na-tu(!)-ma; 68, 31 (see naxasu). — **Der.**

naṭû, *adj* suitable, right {passend, recht} Anp ii 10 maxâzi-šu-nu bîtâti-šu-nu na-ṭu-te u-ša-aç-bi-su-nu their cities & houses as far as feasable, I let them occupy; also III 6, 46 na-aṭ-ṭu (KB i 92—3). II 35 *a-b* 8 la na-ṭa-a-tum = la a-ma-ra-a-tu (AV 5117). H 82—3 i 18 la na-ṭa-a-tu (ŠA-NU-SUR-RA, Br 2977, 12027) la ki-na-a-tu (see *l* 27). IV² 51 *b* 8 la na-ṭa-ti (*var* na-ṭa-a-tu, Z[Š] ii 65) šu-xu[-zu], interrog. sent.

nuṭû V 30 *e-f* 11 TA-KAB-BE-BAR = nu-ṭu-u (Br 3962).

naṭbaxu ‖ maqâçu (*p* 577 *col* 2) AV 5951; ZDMG 40, 729; BA i 176.

NOTE. — nabbaxu (§ 65, 31 *a*; D[H] 29; D[Pr] 75) does not exist (RÉJ ix 149—9; x 296).

naṭalu *pr* iṭṭul, *ps* inaṭ(ṭ)al look {schauen} AV 5947; D[H] 40; D[Pr] 33 + 98; Z[B] 105, 55. — *a*) look, look up {schauen, hin-, aufschauen} *intr.* K 3399 ii 20—1 i-na-ṭal (3 *sg f*, ZA xiv 284); NE 70, 12 Pêr-napištim ana ru-ki i-na-aṭ-ṭa-la[-am-ma?], 18, 19, 20 a-na-aṭ-ṭa-lam-ma I look {ich schaue}; 65, 10 ina-aṭ-ṭ[a-la-am-ma]. Creat.-*frg* IV 67 i-na-aṭ-ṭal-ma eši malakšu (D 97, 32); IV² 10 *b* 3—4 see katamu Q *b*) & read a-na-ṭa-al (= NAM-MU-UN-GAR, EME-SAL, Br 4485); 56 *b* 36 ênâ-ki na-ṭi-la-a-ti thy seeing eyes (T[M] ii 31; iii 95); Esh v 53—4 ša a-xi-en-na-a pa-na u ar[-ka] | i-na-aṭ-ṭa-[la] (compare with this KB vi, 1, 106, 45 + 46). K 2652, 31 um-ma ta-na-aṭ-ṭa-la a-na opiš; KB ii 250—1, 59 um-ma ta-na-ṭa-la a-na e-piš ša-aš-ši. — *b*) behold, look upon, inspect {anschauen, anblicken, besehen}. Anp *Balaw*, *R* 16—7 (V Rawl. 70) the gods ina ni-ši enâ-šu-nu kinêš(-eš) li-ṭu-lu-šu. Sarg *Ann* 238 Marduk ep-šet (amêl) Kal-di limnûti i-ṭul-ma; Asb iii 120 šabrû i-na-aṭ-ṭa-al šuttu; KB ii 250—1, 50 ištên (amêl) šab-ru-u u-tu-ul-ma i-na(-aṭ)-ṭal šuttu. SCHEIL, *Nabd.* vi 21—22 šuttu | ši-i ša iṭ-ṭu-lu; 23 ša ta-aṭ-ṭu-lu (2 *sg*) which thou sawest; x 47—8 see na'alu. Creat.-*frg* IV 63 (twice) the gods i-ṭul-lu-šu; + 64 (= D 97, 28—9), ZIMMERN *apud* GUNKEL, 412; but KB vi, 1, 24—25 i-[dul]-lu-šu: sie laufen um ihn herum. K 3454 + K 3935 ii 5 (*Zû*-legend) ep-šet Bêl-u-ta i-na-aṭ-ṭa-la i-na-šu (his eyes beheld, BA ii 409; KB vi, 1, 46—7). NE 6, 43 i-na-aṭ-ṭa-la šu-na-te-ka (13, 24 -lu); 13, 15 u-ṭul pa-ni-šu (KB vi, 1, 130); 14, 14 šu-na-ta aṭ-ṭul mu-ši-ti-ja (6, 45);

49, 209 šu-na-ta i-na-aṭ-ṭal (he saw a dream); 50, 29 *fol*; 55, 20 ū-um šutta iṭ-ṭu-lu; 12, 31 i-na-aṭ-ṭa-la (?) pa-ni-ša; 66, 31 pa-nu-ša i-na-aṭ-ṭa-lu pa-an (il) Šamši. *del* 2 a-na-aṭ-ṭa-la-kum-ma. K 3474 i + K 8232 i (ZA iv 7 *fol*) 36 i-na-aṭ-ṭa-lu nu-ur-ka; *l* 48 na-aṭ-la-a-ta = pm; Sp II 265*a* xxv 7 ri-ši-MU (= ja) ul ul-lu qaq-qa-ri a-na-aṭ-ṭ[al]; ii 7 na-aṭ(?)-la-ta-ma nišē mit-xa-riš a-pa-a-tu[m]. ZIMMERN, *Beitr. z. Kenntn. d. babyl. Rel.*, 116 *foll*, *no* 24, 7 šamnē ina mē na-ṭa-lu (*cf* II 58 31), Öl auf Wasser beschauen (also 118, 13); K^{M} 6, 116 šuttu aṭ-ṭu-la ana damēqtim (šuk-na); 10, 18; 12, 113 (end) luṭ-ṭul (*var* šutta damēq-ta lu-mur); 18, 2 . . . i-na-ṭa-lu pa-nu-uk-[ka]; 18, 7 (*var*) šīrē^{pl}-šu-nu ta-na-[ṭal] *var* to ta-bar-ri. IV^{2} 19 *a* 43—44 all the Anunnaki i-na-aṭ-ṭa-lu; 55—6 i-na-aṭ-ṭa-la-ka-ma (Br 4485, 5360), *a* 47—8 see Br 9392; 59 *no* 2 *b* 21—22 šup-ra-an-ni-ma šuttu damēq-tu luṭ-ṭul ‖ šuttu a-na-ṭa-lu lu-u damqa-at, šuttu a-na-ṭa-lu lu-u GI (= kīn)-na-at (also *l* 23); see IV^{2} 57 *b* 44. S^{P} 158 + S^{P} II 962, 10 (end) i-na-aṭ-ṭal É-KUR. II 36 *a-b* 20 ŠI-LAL = a-ma-rum ša (= *i. e.*) na-ṭa-li (EDGAR P. ALLEN, '86); K 7331 ii ŠI-GAB na-ṭa-lum ‖ çu-ub-bu-u & a-tu-u.

NOTE. — BA i 270—1 reads V 60 *a* 12 la na-ṭil ma-na-ma nobody found it; but HAUPT: la na-aš ma-na-ma, not holding anything, *i. e.* it was robbed of everything.

Q^{t} *a*) look {schauen} K 3456 *O* 25 at-ta-aṭ-ṭa-lam-ma (PSBA xxi 38); perh NE 69, 40 on the 3^{d} day it-ta-ṭal (or -ri?) KB vi 220. — *b*) behold {sehen, anblicken} PINCHES, *Texts*, 15 *no* 4 (DT 83) 8 ar-ba-'i kib-ra-a-ti (*q. v.*) lit-ta-aṭ-ṭa-la zi-me-šu. T^{M} vii 122 ša at-ta-ṭa-l[u] ū-me-šam what I behold daily. Perh *del* 87 (92) ša ū-mi at-ta-ṭal (or -ri? √tararu) b(p)u-na-šu, KB vi (1) 236—7. *Zū*-legend (see above) 10 (il) Zu-u it-ta-aṭ-ṭal-ma a-bi ilāni; also 17 ša it-ta-aṭ-ṭa-lu. — *c*) find {finden} K 3456 *O* 26 see mirītu. — *d*) H 61 iv 30—4 bīta, eqla, kīrā, amta, arda a-na kaspi it-ta-ṭa-lu (ŠI-NE-NE-GAB, Br 4485, 9328) ZK ii 272: the house *etc.* was open for inspection; also *l* 38 (= ŠI-NE-NE-GAB).

Q^{tn} *Zū*-legend (see above) 7 dupšimāti ilūtišu (il) Za-a it-ta-na(?)-ṭal-ma, + 8 it-ta-na-ṭal-ma.

𝔑 KB iii (2) 88 i 39 la in-na-aṭ-ṭa-la u-çu-ra-ti-ša not were seen *etc.* (also ii 19; *cf* I 69 *a* 48). Derr.:

nāṭilu, *adj* Merod.-Balad. stone (Berl.) v 26 sak-lu la še-ma-a la na-ṭil ša-lim-ša (KB iii, 1, 192—3); but BA ii 265 (273) ša pāni-ša, a short sighted {einen Kurzsichtigen}. Perh II 28 *a* 18 . . . . za na-ṭi-lu.

niṭlu *c. st.*, niṭil *m* look {Blick}. ZA iv 241, 26 ni-ṭil-šun; perh K 3182, 42 (ZA iv 11) ma-la kap-pa ni-ṭi (or ki?)-il enā^{II}-šu. IV^{2} 30* *no* 3 *O* 14 see mūšu. K 2270, 8 ina enā-ka lu-u na-mir ni-iṭ-lu, T^{M} 147 may the look in thine eyes be bright. Creat.-*frg* IV 70 ni-ṭil-šu-un i-ši their look became confused (K 3437; D 98, 35).

naṭāšu leave, neglect {verlassen, vernachlässigen} 𝔑 80—7—19, 58 *O* 7 rub šar-ru-ti i-na-ṭi-iš, the prince of the kingdom has been neglected. (THOMPSON, *Reports of the Magicians & Astrologers*, ii, *p* lxx).

nuk *adv* ‖ muk (*q. v.*), especially in letters. K 582, 23 (beg. = Hr^{L} 167); K 678 *R* 15 (= V 54 *b* 49); K 943, 20 a-ša-'-al nu-uk; K 554 *O* 5 & K 104 *O* 5 (= Hr^{L} 100; 144). K 3456 *O* 36 nu-uk ki-ir(-?)ra-ma nu-uk i-si-ki . . . ? (PSBA xxi 38 *foll*). JENSEN, 424 perhaps = ša or aššu.

nāku. II 16 *b* 51—2 na-a-ku šu-nu-qa ‖ u-da-at-da (Br 3911; 8993); *l* 4 ina la na-ki(-)mi e-rat-me; BA ii 278 = haurire (*cf* nāk mē drawer of water {Wasserschöpfer}; but see ni(a)qū, BRÜNNOW, ZA viii 127) and then: concipere; *ibid*, 280 JÄGER reads II 16 *b* 56 ina burti ša lā mē ināk: der schöpft aus einem Brunnen, in welchem kein Wasser ist. AV 5916, 5968; Br 3911, 6120, 8993; ‖ dalū. BOISSIER, *Rev. Sém.*, 1900, 95: nāku = concipere, although primitive meaning possibly: coucher avec; avoir commerce avec

naṭaru, AV 5948 see eṭ(d)eru; naṭru, naṭirtum, AV 5949, 5863 see nadru.

une femme; he translates: "concevoir et allaiter—elle a été établie", *i. e.* la femme a pour mission de concevoir et d'allaiter". See also HOMMEL, *Sum. Les.*, 28, 331 & 38, 425. K 126, 9—10 u ina zi-e | ni-ià na-ak zi-ka-ru-ta xu-uà-šu-ux-šu i-na bi(= pi?)-ki limni, said of the zikaru.

nakû = נכה cut off {abschneiden}? T. A. (Lo.) 61, 18 ta-an-na-ku (KB v 442).

nakû, *noun*? T. A. (Ber.) 28 ii 8 u na-ku-u ša abni.

naki'atu? K 126, 8 pu-tu u arkati na-ki-a-as-su (*Rev. Sém.*, i 160).

***nakadu** 1.* pr ikkud(?), *ps* innikud. KB vi (1) 198 *rm* 1: perhaps originally; palpitate, said of the heart {vielleicht ursprüngl. "klopfen", vom Herzen}. AV 5958; JENSEN, 513; HEBR. ix 22 *rm* 33. II 25 *no* 6, 8 (*g-h* 73) ... BU(?)-A-NA' = na-a-du & na-ka-du; V 16 *c-d* 77. KB vi (1) 198 (*ad* NE 74) 18 ul i-nak-ku[ud ....]. MESSERSCHMIDT, *Stele Nabuna'ids*, 64, 22 see mâšu Q pr. *Rec. Trav.*, xx 205 *foll* iv 17 ša ...lip-lax lik-kud-ma at-riš. Creat.-*frg* IV 100 in-ni-kud (?) libbaša-ma pa-a-ša uš-p(b)al-ki, KB vi (1) 26. Asb vii 31 he heard of the approach of my messenger & ik-ku-ud lib-ba-šu ir-ša-a na-kut-tu his heart was afraid and fright overtook him (KB ii 212—13), *cf* SMITH, *Asurb*, 293 *a-e* Nadnu ip-lax-ma ir-ša-a na-kut-tu (& 229, 53). V 64 *b* 52—3 ak-ku-ud aš-xu-ut na-kut-ti ar-še-e-ma; *a* 36 ap-la-ax ak-ku-ud na-kut-ti ar-še-e-ma; also KB iii (2) 90, 26—7 ap-la[-ax] ak-ku-ud ar-ša-a ni-ki-i[t-ti], I became afraid and fear seized me. — Š perh V 45 vi 45 tu-ša-an-qat (= kad?).

Derr. nakdu 1, nakuttu & nikittu.

nakadu *2.* IV^2 86 ii 20 ū-mi ša na-ka-da (Br 8994); 21, 23 ar-xi ša ši-ṭa-ru-da | ša-at-ti-šam | la na-par-ka-a (KB iv 62—3).

nakdu *1. adj a)* timid {ängstlich}. Sp II 265 *a* ii 11 na-ak-di pa-li-ix làtar (or √נקד?); Z^B ii 4 mar-çu nak-du na-as-su šu-ud-lu-bu. —. *b)* frighful, terrible {furchtbar} JENSEN, 470 *ad* K 128, 5 mur-çu nakdu.

nikdu. a plant {Pflanze} ZA vi 291 iv 5 ni-ik-du.

naklabu, *cf* naglabu; T. A. (Ber.) 28 i 66—7 na-ak-la-bu ša xurâçi; iii 4, 5 na-ak[-la-bu?] ... ša siparri.

nakalu. pr ikkil be smart, artful, crafty, cunning; skilful {verschlagen, arglistig, klug sein}. P^{Pr} 33, 155; LYON, *Sargon*, 70; ZK ii 345; ROST, 108 on kazabu & nakalu. K 2675 *O* 43 (= SMITH, *Asurb*, 43) ik-ki-lu nik-lat-sun they perceived their cunning (plans); perh Bu 88—5—12, 77 vi 12 i-ki-lu ši-ki-in-šu-un (BA iii 248—9 *rm* *††); K^M 6, 29 ak[-kil]. pm Sn vi 44—45 the palace ša eli maxrīti ma'diš šu-tu-rat ra-ba-ta u nak-lat. IV^2 30* *no* 3 *O* 24 a-ši-pu (*var* šip) Èridu ša ši-pat-su nak-lat a-na-ku (= is admirable, *Rev. Sém.*, vi 148—51).

NOTE. — JASTROW, *Religion of Babylonia*, derives ik-kal *del* 146 (153) from nakalu = cautiously (he waded in the mud), but rather √akalu, eat.

Q^t perhaps here it-ku-lum, i-tak-ku-lum (= ℑ^t) as suggested on *p* 129. V 30 *g-h* 21 (= H 215) DI-TIK = it-ku-lu (Br 9545; AV 3954); followed by DI-GAR-RA = ša di-ni-ti; Nabd 964, 14—15 nik-lu ana eli at-ti-ik-lu; see also niklu.

ℑ *a)* devise or execute cunningly {arglistige Pläne planen oder ausführen} 80, 7—19, 19 *R* 5—6 ka-a-a-ma-nu ni-ik-la-a-tum | u-nak-ka-la, but he has always acted craftily (Hr^L 416). — *b)* prepare skillfully, tastily, artistically {kunstreich, kunstvoll ausarbeiten}. Sn vi 32 la nu-ku-lat epištaš his workmanship was not artistic (KB ii 112; HEBR. vii 70; § 92); Sn *Bav* 18 la u-nak(?)-ki-lu nik-la[-as]-su they had not enhanced its (Nineveh's) artistic character; Sn *Kui* 4, 22. ZA iii 315, 72 u-nak-ki-lu šipiràa; *cf* Sn *Bell* (Lay. 64) 46 *fol* (J^W 51—2); V 64 *b* 8 u-nak-ki-lu ši-bi-ir-šu, BA i 413. Bu 88—5—12, 75 + 76 iv 16 u-nak-ki-la ni-kil-tuš, BA iii 244 *fol*: sein kunstvolles Werk verschönerte ich; MEISSNER & ROST, 100 *R* 3 mu-nak-kil nik-la-te-šu-nu. II 67, 79 whose forms ma-'-diš nu-uk-ku-lu (KB ii 24—5; AV

nakadu, 3. *cf* naqadu. ~ nikidu see nâqidu.

6420); IV^2 12, 25 ep-še-tu ša nu-uk-ku-la. K 3449 *a*, *R* 2 (end) ki-i nu-uk-ku-lat [ep-šet-sa] KB vi (1) 32. — ‎נכל(?) K^M 22, 12 nam-kil-lu-ni-ma.

Derr. these 4:

naklu, *adj* fine, artistic {fein, kunstvoll}; AV 5972; G § 117; see kammu. aš-ru nak-lu a well-built, fine place, ZA iii 373, 63. Asb i 24 see markasu *c*); Neb i 31 *cf* na'adu Q^{tn}. S^b 362 li-il | LIL | nak-lu, Br 4706; V 20 *a-b* 4 .... KUD = na-ak-li(!) AV 5975; Z^B 92 reads -su. Merodach-Balad. stone ii 48 bar-su-u nak-lu the wise decider (BA ii 261, 267 >< KB iii (1) 186); 81, 11—13, 465 *O* 1 na-ak-lu; ZA iv 230, 7 naklu mun-tal-ku (*q. v.*; Q^t of malaku). II 44 *c-f* 46 (karpat) ša (amēl) nak-lu | mu-çar(?)-riš-tum. K 252 (III R 66) i 20 daltu na-kil-tu çalmāni *pl*. Sarg *Khors* 157 suk-ke nak-lu-ti (*Ann* 417); Rm 97, 5 te-re-tu-šu nak-la-a-tum ša la uš-te-pi-el-lu, AV 8956; Br 4706.

nakliš, *adv* artistically {kunstvoll}, AV 5971. Sarg *Ann* 425 great bull-colossusses nak-liš aptiq (BA iii 192 *rm* ** ippatqu-ma); *Bull*-inscr. 76; II 67, 70 see kazabu ג. Esh v 51 a palace nak-liš u-še-piš; I 7 F 16—17. SMITH, *Senn*, 91, 50 large ships ibnū nak-liš (*Kui* 2, 13); I 52 *no* 3 (ii) 21 na-ak-li-iš (see maççartu); also *cf* Neb vi 7, 53.

nikiltu, *c. st.* niklat; AV 6215 = ‎נְכָל; *pl* niklāti, § 32*aa rm* craft, cunning {Kunstgriff, Arglist}. Asb iii 85 ina ši-pir ni-kil-ti by treason; also SMITH, *Asurb*, 153, 18; KB ii 240—1, 25 ina šat(t) mu-ši ši-pir ni-kil-ti; LEHMANN, ii 10, 27 ina ši-pir ni-kil-tu maliciously {in boshafter Absicht} often. KNUDTZON, 1 *O* 10 u i-na mimma ši-pir-ti ni-k[il-ti], or by any work of diplomacy; also *cf* 12 *O* 11; 150 *R* 11; 17 *O* 7. Merod.-Balad. stone v 24 whosoever with this tablet i-bau-nu-u ni-kil-tu ma-am-man (BA ii 265); V 62 *a* 26 (ša) ina ši-pir ni-kil-ti i-pa-aš-ši-ṭu; *cf* V 61 vi 42; 81—6—7, 200, 40 (BA iii 260 *foll*); KB iv 98—99 *no* iv 15 i-na ši-pir ni-kil-tu u-xal-la-qu. — *b*) smartness, intelligence {Klugheit, Verstand}; niklāti smart, wise thoughts, ideas. Sn vi 41 ina nik-lat lib-bi-ja, in the wisdom of my heart (KB ii 112—13); Sargon *Silv* 26 nik-lat. Merod.-Balad. stone iii 3—4 u-zu-un ni-kil-tu ša (il) Ēa, the wise intellect of Ea; II 67, 67 see xasīsu. Šamš i 22 see karšu 1, *b*; + K 3258 *O* 17 (KB vi 320). I 35 *no* 2, 3 (Nabū) abkal nik-la-a-ti. Sarg *Cyl* 47 ma-lu-u nik-la-a-ti; Šalm, *Mon*, *O* 2 Ēa šar apsī ba-u (? SCHEIL: ba[-nu]-u) nik-[la-]ti, KB i 150—1. AV 5971 quotes nak-liš ina nik-lat .... u-še-piš. — *c*) skilfulness, artistic work {Feinheit, kunstvolle Arbeit}. ZA iii 313, 63 ši-pir ni-kil-ti works of skill; Senn *Bell* 36; Bu 88—5—12, 75 + 76 vi 10—11 ina ši-pir ni-kil[-ti] | n]ak-liš u-še-p[iš] BA iii 246—7. Creat.-*frg* IV 136 (= *R* 53) i-ban-na-a nik-la-a-ti and creates artistic works (KB vi (1) 307; JENSEN, 343; JAOS xv 314 *fol*).

niklu. IV^2 45 *a* 11 (K 84) nik-lu šu-u it-ti-kil; Nabd 1118, 5 nik-li-šu (speaking of Bēl-rimanni); also see nakalu Q^t. *adj* niklu, *pl* niklūtim *cf* nuxšu *ad* KB iii (2) 6—8 *col* 2, 7. Ni-ki-il enā-šu *cf* niṭlu.

nukiltu. IV^2 31 *O* 27 nu-kil-tu ša kip-pe-e (see kippū).

Nik(kal) = šarratu, > NIN-GAL (see NINGAL), consort of Sin the moongod. JENSEN, *Theol. Litztg.*, Feb. 1, '96 *cols* 66—7; also HOFFMANN, *ibid*, *no* 11 *col* 258; JENSEN, ZA xi 293 *foll*; LEHMANN, i 51; written ‎נכל on the stele of *Nērab*. AV 6264 *fol*; V 30 *a-b* 38 AN-NIŠ (= šarru)-GAL = (ilat) Nin-gal (and see *ll* 39—46). V 64 ii 38 (ilat) NIN-GAL is called ummu ilāni rabūti (*l* 18); Sarg *Cyl* 62 Ēa, Sin, Nin-gal, Adad, *etc.* K 655, 4; 625, 4; 620, 4; 647, 3 (= Hr^L 132, 131, 91, 210).

nakamu 1. *pr* ikki(u?)m, *ps* inákim heap, heap up {anhäufen}; Z^B 5 *rm* 1; ZA ii 206 comp. ‎كَوَّمَ (?); AV 5959. K 40 iii 7 na-ka-mu, Br 762. I 44, 90 ša ak-qi-mu a-na na-kam-ti ša ēkalli šātu. TP viii 68 whosoever my tablets .... pi-ši-riš i-na-ki-mu. T^M vii 6 u-sap-pax kiš-pi-ki ša tak-ki-mi mu-ša u ur-

nukalabb(pp)u see nukaribbu. ~ nikilmû (Br 7556, 9310, 9358) *cf* ‎נכלמא.

ra, which thou heapest up day and night (or √akamu?, T^{M} *p* 145). Sarg *Ann* 197 ak-ku-ma (??). — ℶ Neb vii 20—1 bu-ša-šu-num i-na ki-ir-bi | u-na-ak-ki-mu ‖ 22 u-ga-ri-nu makkuršun; viii 17—18 ni-çir-ti šar-ru-ti | u-na-ak-ki-im lib-bu-uš-šu. T^{M} vii 2 [^{amêl}] kaššapu u-nak-ka-ma; Pognon, *Wadi-Brissa*, 33 u-na-kam. פִּעֵל nuk-kumu see nakamtu (§ 89).

NOTE. — ZDMG 43, 197 reads nu-uk-kum instead of nu-ug-gat (see nuggatu); *ibid* 203 also ikkimu is derived from nakamu & see KB vi (1) 435. Derr.:

nakmu *1.* *f* nakam(n)tu *adj* heaped up {an-, aufgehäuft} § 65, 6 *rm*; AV 5960, 5978. K 40 iii 8—10 na-ak-mu (see Br 2416, 12093, 12094). Esh i 10 nak-mu makkuršu his heaped-up possessions, = niçirti ēkallišu. K 2619 *O* 22 na-kam bu-še-e Bâbili ta-šal-lal at-ta (KB vi (1) 60); ZA v 67, 31 ud-du-uš ilâni^{pl} na-ak-mu-ti to renovate the (statues of the) gods which were thrown into a heap. Sn *Bell* 46 $^{(iç)}$ ki-max-xe-šu-un nak-mu-ti their heaped up coffins.

nakamtu, nakantu, treasure {Schatz} § 49a. Anp ii 64 ni-çir-ti(-te) ēkalli-šu na-kan-te-šu (*var* bît na-kan-ma-te-šu) KB i 80—1. Smith, *Asurb*, 132, 22 na-kan-ti ēkalli-šu (KB ii 254). K 493, 7—8 XXV u-ra-a-te ' ša na-kan-te ša III pi-ir-ra-a-ni (Hr^{L} 440). Xam-murabi (Br. Mus. 13936) 6 *fol* še-am a-na na-kam-tim ša bît $^{(il)}$ Šamaš. V 18 *a-b* 20 see nadîtu, Br 1607. — **bît na-kanti** treasury {Schatzhaus, Schatzkam-mer} § 49*a*; *cf* 2 Kings 20: 13 (Isa 39: 2). D^{Pr} 141; ZDMG 40, 731; ZA ii 266 Hebrew borrowed from the Assyrian; also Brown-Gesenius, *Lexicon*, 649; Haupt in Cheyne, *Isaiah* (SBOT) 119; Meinhold, *Jesaja-erzählungen*, 15—17. Winckler, *Sargon*, 172 (Lay 34) 21 ina bît na-kam-te šu-a-ti; I 27 *no* 2, 35 bît na-kan-te-šu; K 646, 18 ina bît nak-kan-du (AV 348); Asb v 132—4 ap-te-e-ma bît nak (*var* na)-kam-a-ti-šu-nu | ša çarpu ^{pl} $^{(var\ carat)}$ xurâçu ^{pl} $^{(var\ carat)}$ ŠA-ŠU-MEŠ namkûru | nu-uk-ku-mu ki-rib-šu-un (KB ii 202—3; § 73); also without bît, III 8, 81 na-kan-te lu ap-ti ni-çir-tu-šu la a-mur (KB ii 170).

NOTE. — Asb iv 85 *var* at-ta-di a-na na-ka-ma-a-ti (to ka-ma-a-ti) would be from nakamtu heap ‖ Haufe; G § 44; Tiele, *Geschichte*, 382.

nakamu 2. K 40 iii 6—7 (D 82) GE & KA-NIK-DUG-GA = na-ka-mu (Br 6318).

nakmu, *f* nakimtu (AV 5694). IV^{2} 28* *no* 3, *a* 11 thy servant (o Ištar) li-še-çi (may drive out) nak-ma u na-kim-ti ša zumrija. ZA iv 237 ii 13 ki-i na-ak-mi šu-çu-u (K 2861 + S 389 ii); *cf* V 47 *b* 21 kîma na-kim-tum šu-çi-i; perh. IV^{2} 2 *b* 25 u-tuk-ku lim-nu n[a]k-mu-šu. K 40 iii 8—10 AMÊL-GIŠ-GI-KA-SAR; ŠA AMÊL-UR; ŠA-AMÊL-UR-SUD-UD = na-ak-mu; 11 ID-QU (or it-qu) = na-ki-im-tum (Br 6587).

nikimêtu. V 31 *e-f* 14 ni-ki-mi-e-tum (AV 6214) aš-šu a-la-ku u ni-xi-e-su (*q. v.*) ša $^{(kakkab)}$ GUD(-UD), ZA v 128; Jensen, 427 & *rm*: Schleife (des Planeten-laufes)? √*k-m-'*.

nakmaru, net, rope {Netzgeflecht, Seil-werk} BA i 521; 635; T^{C} 82 compares מַכְמָר. Nabd 104, 6 na-ak-ma-ru (545, 2 -ri); 146, 5 nak-ma-ru (845, 9); 680, 1: ište-en $^{(iç)}$ xu-ul-la-nu itti $^{(qân)}$ nak-ma-ru; 252, 6 na-ka-ma-ru.

niknakku, the vessel used for smoke offer-ings {das zum Rauchopfer verwandte Ge-rät} so Zimmern, GGA '98, 826; *Beitr. z. Kenntn. der babyl. Relig.*, 94—5; 102, 81 (end) niknakka tu-nam-mar sollst das Rauchbecken anzünden; *cf ll* 84; 87; *p* 106 *l* 165 *etc.*; 102, 92 niknakka u-nak-kar-ma thou shalt remove the *n.* IV^{2} 30*, 3 *O* 33—4 nik-nak-ki (*var* ‖ i. e. ŠA-NA) si-bit-ti šu-nu; IV^{2} 57 *a* 4 ŠA-NA burâši (which very often in K^{M}); *R* 17; IV^{2} 5 *c* 65. K^{M} 178: a vessel for incense, censer. 82—5—22, 1048 *R* 6 (JRAS '91, 407) ŠA-NA = nik-na-ki el-lu. Also perh T. A. (Ber.) 26 iv 29: 1 nik-na-ak-gu siparri. — Delitzsch; M^{X} 96; Boissier, *Rev. Sém.*, vi ('98) 148 *fol* read šanakku.

nakasu. pr ik(k)is, ps inakkis cut off,

nakmû, AV 5974; Br 5773 see naqmû.

hew down {abschneiden, abhauen}; § 9, 106; AV 5961. ak-ki-za POGNON, *Wadi-Brissa*, 170; ZA i 357 *fol*; kirāte-šu ak-kis III 5 *no* 6, 55; D 133, 16; Sarg *Ann* 347 (gišimmarē); V 50 *b* 77; a-kis Šalm, *Balaw*, III 4 (IV 5 akšiṭ); II 67, 24; TP iv 68 trees lu ak-ki-is; Anp iii 89 lu-u ak-kis; iii 91 a-ki-si; Šalm, *Ob* 30 a-kis (+ 97 + 100 + 140; Anp iii 109); TP III *Ann* 204 çip-pa-a-te .... ak-kis. T^M vii 64 bal-ta-ki a-k[is?] BA iv 162. SMITH, *Asurb*, 99, 13 ikkisū-ni(mma) §§ 53*d*; 150; II 66 *no* 2, 4—5 ina qit-ru-ub ta-xa-zi ik-ki-su | qaqqadu Teumman; Cyr 331, 8 ik-ki-is-su. V 56, 60 (end) kirē u $^{(iç)}$ gi-šimmarē la na-ka-si; KB vi (1) 68 (= K 1282 *O*) 9 a-na na-ka-si ul u-ma-ak(g, q); Z^B viii 45 ban through naxlapti na-ka-su: tearing of garments. KB vi (1) 162 *col* ii (iii) 41 (*end*) ni[-nak-kis qaq-qad-su]; 78 ii 13 (end) ga-ga-as-sa a-na na-ka-si (= T. A. Lo. 82, 31); Esh i 18 + 46 ak-ki-sa qaq-qa-su. VATh 354, 9 a-na-ku ul ak-ki-is (PEISER, *Verträge*, 65). V 56, 57 lik-ki-sa na-ap-šat[-su]. S^P III 2 *O* 13 ..... u TUR (= māru) ik-ki-is. Asb iii 36 ak-kis qaqqad Teumman (*cf* KB ii 254, 101); vii 47 qaqqad-su ak-kis; iv 15—16 ša ik-ki-su | (3 *sg*) a-xu-ur-ru-u ummānāti-ja | um-ma i-nak-ki-su-u (3 *pl*) qaqqadu šar ^{māt} Elamti (on *ll* 12—18 see WINCKLER, *Forsch.*, i 247 & ZA x 79 *fol*); SMITH, *Asurb*, 144, 1—2; 145, 3 ana na-kas qaqqad ramānišu; *cf* T^M vi 47 a-na na-kas $^{(iç)}$ bīni; K^M 50, 23 ša ana na-kas napišti-ja illika, which may come to cut off my life. III 61 *no* 2, 13 (end) xabbatu SAG-DU (= qaqqadu) KUD (= inak)-is. Anp ii 76 šadū marçu .... ina kalabāti (*q. v.*) parzilli a-kis (*var* ki-si). II 31 *b* 89 $^{(amēl)}$ na-ki[-su] BA i 289; AV 5965; Br 1688. V 39 *e-f* 61 KUD = na-ka-su (II 9 + 204. 22); 42 *a-b* 45—6 ... KUD = na-ka-su followed by nakasu ša ši-i-ri (*q. v.*) Br 14308.

Q[t] KB vi (1) 78 ii 8 xu-d[u]-ma-a-ša i-na ta-ar-ba-ç[i] it-ta-ki-is he cut off (= T. A. Lo. 82, 26).

ℶ cut off, hew down (in larger quantities) {abschneiden, abhauen}. TP i 81 qaqqadē-šu-nu lu-na-ki-sa; vi 6 qaqqadē-šu-nu ki-ma zi-ir-qi u-ni-ki-is, & see iii 99 (§ 33). Anp iii 106 u-na-kis; ii 18—19 qaqqadē muq-tab-le-šu-nu KUD-is (*var* u-ni-kis) — Šalm, *Mon*, ii 73 u-na-kis. T. A. Ber. 8 *R* 12 (ZA v 148) šēpā-šu ki u-na-ak-ki-su after he had cut off his feet (KB v 26—7). KB vi (1) 108, 56 (*Etana*-legend) u-nak-ki-is kap-pi-šu (*q. v.*) I cut off its wings; 106, 27 nu-uk-kis kap-pi-šu (= K 1547 + K 2527; BA ii 393—4; BA iii 363 *foll*; see nubal(l)u, 3), Sn v 85 sapsapāte u-na-kis. The Suteans ... az-li-iš u-nak-kis-ma; Sarg *Khors* 131; Sn vi 76 kišādātešunu u-nak-kis az-liš; vi 2 u-na-ak-kis; Sp II 265 *a* xiii 4 bi-e-ra lu-na-ak-kis.

niksu *c. st.* nikis. — *a*) cutting off of a head, decapitation {Enthauptung} nikis qaqqadu; also = the cut off head; Asb iv 13 eli ni-kis SAG-DU = qaq-qadi, the cut off head of Teumman; also KB ii 256, 53 + 55 + 60. KB vi 58 (K 8571) *O* 17 (end) ni-ip-la-xu ni-ki-su. — *b*) slaughter, killing {Gemetzel, Tötung} Asb iv 59 who la-pa-an ni-kis paṭri parzilli ... i-še-tu-u-ni (see ZA x 80 *fol* on *ll* 59 *foll*). — *c*) cutting through a wall, *etc.*; breach, opening {Durchschneidung einer Mauer, Wand, etc.; Bresche, Öffnung} JENSEN, *Lit. Centralbl.*, '94 *col* 54. Sn iii 16 cities were taken with the help of pil-ši nik-si u kal-ban-na-te (*var* -ti), HEHN. vii 61; KNUDTZON 1 *O* 7 lu-u i-na ni-ik]-si lu-u i-na bēl (= pil)-ši $^{(iç)}$ i-pal u ki-pal; 17 *O* 6 lu-u ina si-'-u-tu lu]-u i-na da-na-na lu-u i-na ni-ik]-si lu-u *etc.* KNUDTZON, *p* 76: axe, hatchet {Hacke, Beil}; see also na-balkattu, *c.* K 186 *O* 5 (Hr^L 222) ma-a ina lib-bi ni-ik-sa-u-ni; 12—14 ina eli bīti .... nik-su ina lib-bi ni-ki-si (§ 97 = פּוּ) çābē ina lib-bi nu-še-rab; *R* 6 a-ni-ni çābē ina lib-bi nik-sa-a-ni nu-si-ri-ib. — IV^2 31 *a* 20 ki-ma ni-kis $^{(iç)}$ bi-[n]i KB vi 82. — Is II 28 *a* 26 a ‖ of paššūru perhaps to be read ni-ik-si li-qu (√לקח), or ni-ik (√niqū) si-li-qu? On niksu see also BOISSIER, PSBA xxii 108—9.

$^{(amēl)}$ **ni-ki-si** $^{(meš)}$ — butchers {Metzger} KB iv 180, 31.

nukkusu, *adj* cut off {abgehanen} Asb iv 74 širē-šu-nu nu-uk-ku-su-u-ti, § 65, 24.

nukasātu (?) Br. Mus. 84, 2—11, 164, 7 šēr nu-ka-sa-a-ta (Peiser, *Bab. Vertr.*, cvii); ZA vi 443 compares מִכְסָא, Schlachtvieh.

nakis(š)tum (?) II 22 *e-f* 41 ME-ME-A = na-kis(š)-tum, AV 5967; Br 10453.

nikasu, properly, possessions, treasure {Habe, Vermögen, Schatz} Meissner, 145 (*no* 79). H 108, 4 (111, 50) AM-ŠIT(LAG) = ŠA-ŠIT = ni-ka-su (*cf* 22, 489) = V 11 *e-g* 4; D 127, 52, ‖ kirbānu (S^b 241) AV 6212. IV² 32 ii 23 epeš ŠA-ŠIT (= nikasi) = ἱερὰ ῥέζειν; D 86 i 17, Br 5975 reads .... ŠIT = iç-çi nik-kas-s[i]. 81, 11—3, 111 *O* 7 calls Marduk = Na-bi-um ša nikasi; 80—7—19, 19 *O* 5+8 ŠA-ŠIT-ja. Occurs mostly in *c. t.* Neb 403, 2; 334, 18 ŠA-ŠIT. ŠA-ŠIT ittišunu epšu often in Nabd: 948, 13 e-piš ŠA-ŠIT; *cf* Neb 388, 41 epeš nikasi ša arxi. Nabd 810, 5 ŠA-ŠIT-ka-su ul e-puš; 575, 15 epeš ŠA-ŠIT-šunu; Neb 125 (ša la) ni-ka-su; 283, 18 when *S* is dead ni-ka-si-šu pa-ni *G* da-gal, the property is at the disposal of *G*; 376, 6 ni-k]a-su ina ittišu ul epši; Cyr 118, 16 nikasu ep-šu. II 31 *b* 84 (amēl) GAL-ŠA-ŠIT = rab nikasi, who is mentioned also in Nabd 387, 16; 780, 2; Neb 98, 3. Perhaps also Strassm., *Stockh. Or. Congr.*, *no* 5, 1: VIII nik-kas qanāte eqlu ki-ru-bu-u; & 11: nap-xar VIII nik-kas. — See Lotz, *Quaestiones*, 52; D^Pr 33, 186 (× Fränkel, *Lehnwörter*, 98); *Johns Hopk. Circ.*, *no* 59; Hebr. iii 107—110; BA ii 42. Schwally, *Idiotikon*, 120: Spende; vielleicht sogar term. techn. für ein bestimmtes Opfer, ursprüngl.: Schlachtopfer (bloody sacrifice) = נְסָכִים; T^C 104—105; Zehnpfund, BA i 535: Übergabe; 'Ablieferung' einer bestimmten Waare; ferner, Verpflichtung zu einer zeitlich bestimmten Ablieferung; davon, "Verpflichtung". See also Peiser, ZA iii 370; *Babyl. Vertr.*, 236; 253—4; 350; KAS 103: Lieferung, Leistung; Hommel, *Sum. Les.*, 58: Wohlstand, eigentl. "Getreide".

nakapu 1. break lose, storm, rush on, overcome {losbrechen, stürmen, anstürmen, stossen} ‖ šēru (שור) = נגף; Br 9144. ZA vi 236, 35 murçu ik-ki-ip ina (mât) MAX; IV² 1* iv 14—15 gal-lu-u al-pu na-ki-pu (= UL-UL) a storming bull (H 29, 664); H 52 iv 1 IN-SU-UL = ik[-kip]. *Rec. Trav.* xix 46—7 *R* 12 ma]-an-ma i-na-ki-ip Marduk bē-lija; K 769, 8 šarru itti mātišu u nišē zi(=çi)-ni i-na-kap(kip), the king with his land & people will repel the enemy (Thompson, ii 21). — Q^t = Q IV² 3 *a* 1—2 muruç qaqqadi ina çi-e-ri it-tak-kip; *b* 31—32 ki-ma a-gi-e it-tak-kip; 44—45 ki-ma ki-is lib-bi it-tak-kip; K 7906 ū-mu lim-nu ša ina çi-rim i-tak-ki-pu (T^M 124; Bezold, *Catalogue*, 1579; M^S 65 *col* 2); IV² 22, 1 *O* 46 bu-ul çi-ri im-qut(or -xaç)-ma ki-ma ki-ri-e ša xa-ru-u na-as-xu ištē-niš it-ta-kip (= UL-UL); IV² 5 *a* 1—2 ūmē mut-tak-pu-tum ilāni lim-nu-tum šu-nu; III 9 *no* 3, 27 it-tak-ki-pu-ni (?), KB ii 27; Rost, 118 (= TP III *Ann*, 127). — ℑ Asb ix 78 Bēltis u-na-kip nakirē-ja ina qarnāte-ša gašrāte (knocked down, overthrew); IV² 20* 4 B ii 13 enā-šu u-na-kap (& Bezold, *Catalogue*, 1710; M^S 65); K 12388 + 13101 *O* 5 šarru māt nakirišu u-nak[-kap]; & u-na-kap (K 172, 3 = Pinches, *Texts*, 3 *no* 6); V 64 *b* 14 ri-i-mu zaxalē ebbi mu-nak-kip ga-re-ja; 80—7—19, 63, 6 šarru a-šar u-sa-na-qu u-nak-kap; 83—1—18, 242, 4 a[-šar?] u-sa-na-qu u-na-kap: and, wherever he presses on he will overcome.

See Hommel, *Säugethiere*, 429; Lotz, *Quaestiones*, 37; G § 111; Z^B 56 *rm* 1; *Chald. Genesis*, 99; RP² v 163 *foll.* On Barth, *Nominalbildung*, 34, see Fränkel, BA iii 77.

nakapu 2. K 2034 ii 18 ZAG-UD-DU = na-ka-pu ša dūri (Br 6510 iššūti, but adding??; = ⊕ 253 *d* 13; *cf* II 48 *e-f* 60) ‖ zamū ša dūri (*p* 282 *col* 2).

nakapu 3. K 2034 & 80, 7—19, 308 (= ⊕ 253 *d*; M^S *pl* 4) 1/2, SAG-TA-DUG-GA; SAG-SIG-GA = na-ka-pu ša ...., Br 3569, 3601; 3/4, UL = *n* ša alpi (?); 5, SI-XUB = *n* ša ...., Br 3468; 6, KUR-KU = *n* ša a-mi-e (Br 7417; 3897; AV 5957);

nakasu. V 20 *a-b* 4 read naklu.

7, RU-TIG = *n* ša ubāni; 8/9, SI-GA = *n* ša çu-ba-ti & *n* ša ku-si-t[im], Br 3398; Sch. 2 in ZA ix 219 *no* 2.

nakkapu & nakkaptu. K 2034 ii 11, 12 KI-NAM-A-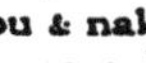-RA = nak-ka-[pu], SAG-KI = nak-kap[-tum?], Br 3645, 9660; AV 5957; also see GGA '98, 821 against M[S] 65 *col* 2.

nikiptu some spice {eine Spezerei}, T. A. Ber 18 *R* 15: II ⁽ⁱˢ⁾ ni-kib(p)-tum ra-n-bu-tim ul-te-bil-ak-ku. Also see M[S] 65 *col* 2. ⊕ 253 *d* 10 RIG-AN-NIN-IB = ni-kip[-tum] Br 5168, AV 5957.

nakaru 1. pr ikkir (for orig. ikkar, BA ii 386 *rm* 1); ps inákir(kar) be or become different, strange, change; desert from some one, rebel against {anders sein oder werden; anfeinden, feindlich auftreten; von jem. abfallen, sich wider jem. empören} (itti, ina qāt or pron. suff., § 38); D[Pr] 195 *rm*; §§ 100, 101; SCHEIL, *Šamš*, 36; AV 5962; Br 1143. Asb iv 100 those, who ik-ki-ru it-ti-ja (KB ii 194—5); Šamš i 50/*fol*: the 27 cities which itti Šulmānu-ašarid ik-ki-ru-u-ni (KB i 176—7); Rm 194 *R* 4 axu axi KUR (= inak)-ir; K 727 *O* 4 ⁽amēl⁾ nakru i-na-kar. K 528, 12—13 ša i-na qāt šarri bēli-ja | ik-ki-ru he revolted from the king my lord (Hr[L] 269); K[M] 59, 9 kam]-sa-ku a-na-kar ir .... KB iv 12, 27 ša a-pi (= ma)-at dup-a-ni-im i(?)-na-ka-ru; S[P] II 987 *O* 14 (beg). i-nak-kar (he changeth) + 12. K 4316 (= II 33 *no* 2) *d-e* 2 IN-KUR-E-MEŠ = ik-ki-ru (K 211), & *l* 1 ik-ki-ir, Br 1143. Beh 40 annūtu mātāte ša ik-ki-ra-'-in-ni, which had revolted against me; 68 ik-ki-ra-an-ni (§ 56). KNUDTZON, 2 *O* 6—7 i-n]a-ki-i-ri ilu-ut-ka rabīti na-ka-a]-ra ša ⁽mât⁾ Ma-mit-ar[-šu]; *R* 5 itti Ašur-ax-iddi-na ... i-na-k[i-ru]. — Creat.-*frg* III 127 mi-na-a nak-ra KB vi (1) 21: was hat sich geändert? SCHEIL, *Nabd*, ii 21—22 ša it-ti šar .... na-ak-ru-ma (3 *pl*). K 2756 *b* (NE 2, 1 *b*) i-nak-kir-šu bu-ul-šu (NE 10, 44; 11, 14), KB vi (1) 126, 14 (so dass) ihn sein Vieh *nicht* mehr *kennen* wird. V 31 *c-d* 18 BA-AN-KUR = i-nak-kir. KB iii (2) 78, 35 qibītika kēttim ša la na-ka-ri; *cf* I 67 *b* 33; Neb *Bab* ii 27 i-na pi-i-ka el-lu ša la na-ka-ri; IV² 55 *no* 2 *R* 5 ša la na-kar ‖ ša la šanan (K[M] 13, 11); ZA i 342, 27 ša la na-ki-ri-im; Z[Š] iii 38 ma-mit ina ū-me e-di iku ša-'-a-lu u na-ka-ru *etc.*; *cf* 39; 55 ma-mit ç(z)a-ma-ni še-me-e u na-ka-ru; viii 41, 42 na-ça-ru(m) | u na-ka-ru (*cf* 51, 55). V 30 *e-f* 4 BAL (Br 272) = na-ka[-ru] betw. nu-kur[-tum] & da-ba-bu; II 22 *no* 2 (*add*) = K 4248, 11 KUR = na-ka-ru (AV 5962).

T. A. (Lo.) 50, 23 my youngest brother na-ka-ar iš-tu ja-ši; 35, 37 the kings of *N* na-ak-ru it-ti-ja (64, 22); Ber. 63, 46—7 a-na alāni ša na-ak-ru iš[-tu .... (BA iv 121); 34 *a* 27 na]-ak-ru-nim it-ti-ja (are hostile to me); 177, 22 i-na-ki-ir; 24, 74 a-na-ag-gi-e-ir; 8 *R* 10 u amēlišu i-na-ak-ki-ru-ka (and its inhabitants will become hostile to you); 128, 5 for all the lands na-ak-ra-at to Azīru (& 10).

Q[t] = Q ittakir. K 2852 + K 9662 ii 35 by their command which not?] it-tak-ka-ru; IV² 11 *a* 1—2 .... ru it-ta-kir; 16 *b* 22 it-te-kir (H 219); KB iii (2) 4, 36—7 i-na qi-be-ti-ka çi-ir-tim | ša la it-ta-ak-ka-ra; K 84 *R* 3—4 aš-ša-a ni-it-te-ki-ru-uš (Hr[L] 301) because we have rebelled against him (§ 148); *cf* Beh 16 + 30 (it-te-ik-ru-' la-pa-ni-ja); Rm 277 i 19 it-ta-ki(?)-ir changes (his view); KB vi (1) 154 (NE IV) ii 49 ina sūqi it-te-ik(g, q)-ru; *cf ibid* 276 i 27 ni-šu .... it-tak(q, g)-ru wurden feind; 278 ii 40 (followed, 41, by ik(g, q)-ru-ni. Z[Š] ii 10 (end) it(?)-te(?)ik-ru, but see AJSL xiii 147.

Q[tn] T. A. (Lo.) 2, 26 šum-ma it-ti ..... ta-at-ta(-na)-ak-ra(-ma) KB v 16—17; ZA v 152—3: wenn du dich verfeindest. Bu 88—5—12, 75 + 76 ii (= K 192 *O*) 12 see mitxariš.

Ʒ una(k)kir change, alter {ändern} Br 1164, ‖ ušanni (HINCKS, ZDMG 10, 517; OPPERT, *ibid*, 808), D[H] 42; § 33 u-na(k)-ki-ir & unīkir; § 37*c*: unak-karu & u-na-ak-ru. IV² 12 *R* 25—26 u-nak-ka-ru-ma, Br 3449; Anp ii 3 the

---

nakapu 4. see naqapu. ~ nakparu & nakpartu (§ 65, 12*a*) see naktamu, naktamtu.

old wall of the city u-na-kir (I changed), *cf* ii 132; the city's former name I changed: u-nak-kir Sn ii 25; *Bell* 32; *Kui* 1, 16. Neb *Bors* ii 7 a-šar-ša la e-ni-ma la u-na-ak-ki-ir te-me-en-ša; 81—6—7, 209, 40 (ša) lu-u a-šar-šu (of the inscription) u-nak-ka-ru (BA iii 260 *foll*); KB iii (1) 162 *col* v 48 whosoever this boundarystone u-na-ak-ka-ru = IV 62 iii 17 u-na-aq-qa-ru; *cf* iv 58 *col* 3, 3 abnu šuatum i-na aš-ri-šu u-nak-ka-ru (Esh *Sendsch*, *R* 54 u-nak-kar-u-ma, Merodach-Balad. stone v 28 u-na-ka-ru; V 64 *b* 44—45 I found the inscription of Ašurbanipal and la u-nak-kir (1 *sg*), *c* 45—6 may inspect the inscription, but la u-nak-ka-ar; KB i 4 (*no* 5) 7 who mu-ša-ri-ja u-na-ka-rum. Scheil, *Nabd*, iv 20 Anunit whose dwelling place a former king had changed (u-na-ak-ki-ru-ma); see also Lehmann, S^1 29; S^3 86; S^3 68; P^1 32. Merodach-Balad. stone iii 21—22 kudurrêšina | nu-uk-ku-ru (BA ii 262); II 16 *d* 12 ana nu-uk-ku-ri-ka (ZK i 120); Sn vi 71 mu-nak-kir šiṭ-ri-ja u šu-me-ja "refers probably to the custom of the kings, simply to turn old inscriptions against the wall and write on the back" (Haupt). I 6 *no* vi 6 mu-ni-kir; Bu 88, 5—12, 108 vi 6 mu-nak-kir ši-ṭir šumi-ja; also Bu 88, 5—12, 80. Lay 17, 3 mu-na-ki-ir mal-ki-šu-nu deposing, removing their kings (KB ii 4—5); Sarg *Cyl* 28 mu-nak-kir šu-bat (al) Pâpa (by transplanting its inhabitants), AV 5488; *cf Ann* 459. NE 13, 2 ši-ma-tu u-nak-kar (KB vi (1) 128), + 20 nu-uk-ki-ra še-rit-ka (change thine anger, KB vi, 1, 130—1); 6, 39. K^M 12, 60 muruç šak-na nu-uk-kir nu-us-si di-xu ša zumri-ja = IV^2 57 *a* 60. S 1708 *O* 12 u-nak-ki-ir (= BA-AN-KUR) = IV^2 *R* 18* *no* 6; H 51—2, 58 IN-KUR = u-na-ki-ir; 60, IN-KUR-EŠ = u-na-ki-ru; 62, IN-KUR-RE = u-na-ak-kar; 64, IN-KUR-RE-NE = u-na-ka-ru; $Z^{Š}$ iv 74 li-na-kir di-xu, drive away the disease! I 27 *no* 2, 91 ep-še-ti-šu lu-na[k-ki-]ir, KB i 122—3 may destroy his works; Sarg *Cyl* 76; K 2852 + K 9662 iv 7 šumi-šu-nu maxrê u-nak-kir (he changed); I 28 *b* 9 see maxrû; Zimmern, *Beitr. z. Kenntn. d. babyl. Religion*, 102, 92 see niknakku. P. N. Mu-ni-kir name of an official III 48 *c* 53.

$\mathfrak{J}^t$ utákkar be changed, altered {geändert werden} § 53*a*. Anp i 5 Ninib ša la-a ut-tak-ka-ru si-qir šap-ti-šu, the word of whose mouth cannot be changed. V 65 *b* 30 ina qibîtika çîrti ša la ut-tak-ka-ri; *l* 31 uš-te-pi-lu. ZK ii 340; Hilprecht, *OBI*, i *pl* 33 *col* 3, 40—1 ša la ut (*var* it)-ta-ak-ka-ra; *cf* T^M i 120 BAL (= uttakar)-ra; IV^2 20 *no* 3 *O* 18—19 ki-bit-ka ki-ma ša-me-e ul ut-tak-kar (= NU-KUR-RU-DA, H 138; ZK ii 340) | in-nin-nu-u (Asb x 9); IV^2 18 *a* 5—6 u-çu-rat šamê u erçitim ša la ut-tak-ka-ru; H 80, 32 (il) Ninib ki-bit-ka ul ut-tak-kar (shall not be violated); K^M 60, 7 dânu çîru ša ki-bit-su la ut-tak-ka-ru & id + ru 12, 19; 19, 31; 33, 36; 53, 23; 59, 11; + rum 1, 50; + ar 12, 96. *Rec. Trav.*, xx 205 *foll* i 14 ša çi-it pi-šu la ut-tak-ka-ru; K 3477 *O* 28 *fol* see mašalu, $\mathfrak{J}^t$. Creat.-*frg* II 9 la ut-tak-kar mim-mu-u a-ban-nu-u [a-na-ku] = III 68 + 121; KB vi (1) 12—13. Hilprecht, *Assyriaca*, 14—15 *R* 2 ku-dur-ra-ša ul ut-ta[k-k]ar shall not be removed; 5, ut-tak-kir; *cf* KB iv 64 *R*; perh II 16 *f* 10 tu-kak-ga-r[um].

$\mathfrak{J}^{tn}$ K 782, 4 ana (kakkab) Dil-bat ..... ça ut-tu-nak-kar (Thompson, *Reports*).

$\mathfrak{S}$ ušamkir seduce, or induce to rebellion {verleiten, zum Abfall bewegen} §§ 49*b*; 101. ZK ii 409. Asb iii 105 all of them it-ti-ja u-šam-kir he induced to revolt against me; vii 102, the inhabitants of Arabia it-ti-šu u-šam-kir (KB ii 184; 216); vii 50 *Š* .... ša it-ti-šu a-na šum-ku-ri (mât) Elamti il-li-ku, to cause a rebellion in Elam; K 5407, 6 ana šu-uk-ku-ru ša mâti; Sarg *Ann* 54; 234 u-ša-an (*var* šam)-kir(-šunûti); Šams i 43, see magaru $\mathfrak{S}$. V 45 vi 40 tu-ša-an-kar.

$\mathfrak{N}^{tn}$ (or $\mathfrak{Q}^{tn}$?) Lehmann, ii 26 (L^4) iii 18 pa-nu-uš-šu it-ta-nak-ka-ru their (subservient) conduct toward him was changed.

Derr. these 7:

na(â?)kiru, *noun* foe, enemy {Gegner,

Feind} *pl* nakirē. AV 5966; § 65 *no* 9, 7. iD (amēl) KUR often (KNUDTZON, *etc.*), *pl* KUR-MEŠ, TP vi 53 kibis KUR-MEŠ also see viii 40; 82 ina pa-an KUR-MEŠ-šu; iii 96 ina ašaridūtija-ma ša KUR-MEŠ-ja *etc.* T. A. (Lo.) 74, 9 iš-tu KUR-MEŠ da-nu(?)-ti, BEZOLD, *Dipl*, but KB v 338 da-na(?)[-at]; 9, 32 (amēl) KUR-MEŠ. — K 82, 5 (Hr^L 275) ul-tu i-na māt na-ki-ru a-na-ku; K 11, 14 ina māt na-ki-ri (Hr^L 186); Creat.-*frg* IV 125 e-li na-ki-ru; K 2748 ii 6—7 ki-šit-ti na-ki-ri (BA iii 208); NE 51, 17 (amēl) KUR-šu; Asb ii 116, 118 *etc.* K 2619 i 16 ki-i šal-lat na-ki-ri; *pl* na-ki-ri *e. g.* ZA iii 314, 70; Esh iv 55; vi 49; III 16 v 4; KB iii (2) 66, 42; Neb x 15; *Bors* ii 21; *Bab* ii 31; V 66 *a* 27 irnintija | eli na-ki-ri; Sarg *Cyl* 7; Bu 88—5—12, 75 + 70, ix 12; KUR-MEŠ-ja TP iii 92, vi 53; Asb x 39, 69. V 34 *c* 48 na-ki-re-ja; V 65 *b* 41 šil-lat (ZK ii 351 *rm* 1) na-ki-ri-ja; Esh iv 40. D 95, 14 u-ša-as-si-ku eli ilāni na-ki-ri-šu, JENSEN, 206. L^4 ii 16 kakkē na-ki-ri ti-bu-te the weapons of the approaching enemies. Esh *Sendsch*, *O* 10 sa-pi-nu na-ki-ri-ja, *R* 34 a-na ra-sa-ap na-ki-ri, + 53 (end); also 24 šu-qiš da-ad-me na-ki-ri-e-šu; kul-lat na-ki-ri, see kullatu (*p* 391), Anp i 35 (>< ZA i 365); K 2852 + K 9662 ii 26; 81—6—7, 209, 35; Esh iv 42 na-ki-re šad-lu-u-ti, Sn v 61 *n* lim-nu-ti; Sarg *Khors* 14 mātāte na-ki-re ka-li-šun. ZA i 342, 31 ka-ak na-ki-ri-im (= KB iii, 2, 64); Neb iv 50 ka-ak-ku na-ki-ri-ja. IV^2 12 *R* 44—45 see malū 3 (*p* 542 *col* 2), Br 1143; 46—7 ana māt na-ki-ri-šu liš-lu-lu (?), Br 272. *Rec. Trav*, xix 60, *no* 2, 6: qa-mu-u na-ki-ri-ka; see Creat.-*frg* IV 16 (end); K 647 (Hr^L 210) *R* 2 (amēl) KUR-ka. V 41 (*a*-)*b* 50 sanaqu ša (amēl) KUR, see sanaqu.

nakru, *f* nakirtu. *adj* hostile {feind, feindlich} *pl* nakrūti (§ 53 *a*), *f* nakrāte; also used as a *noun*. §§ 9, 110; 65, 7 *rm*; Br 1144, 11263, 11278; AV 5966, 5976. axi nak-ri Asb iv 50, 54; vii 100; iD vii 49: see also KB vi (1) 62—3 *col* ii 16 + 19 (beg); NE 51, 17 + 17 (-šu); T. A. (Lo.) 13, 24 iš-tu qa-at na-ak-ri-ja; 55, 22. IV^2 39 *b* 25 li-ša-na na-ki-ir-ta (*var* -kir-) AJSL xii 152. V 64 *b* 37 (amēlāti) na-ak-ru-te-ja; TP i 52 maxāzi u malkē nakru-ut (il) Ašur; *cf* v 47; vi 85; vii 39; I 7 F 7 a-na ra-sa-ap nak-ru-ti (māt) Aššur; T. A. (Lo.) 48, 36 amēlūti na-ak-ru-tu; III 3, 16 la pa-du-u na-ki-ru-ut (il) Ašur (KB i 12, 5). Esh vi 11 mātāte nak-ra-a-te (iD TP viii 43); K 233 *R* 2 amēlāti nak-ra-a-tu foreign women. — TP i 9 kib-rāt KUR-MEŠ; iv 41; vi 49. — used as a *noun*: IV^2 19 *b* 45—6 nak-ru dan-nu (Br 1038); 33—4 nak-ru gab-šu, *cf* H 181 *no* xii *O* 21—22; KB vi (1) 300, 17 (amēl) nakru da-an-na; Esh ii 22 (māt) Par-na-ki nak-ru aq-çu; KB vi (1) 72, 20 ina nak-ri i-kab-bit (>< BA ii 432, ina nak-ri-i kab-bit-t[i-šu], where, however, JENSEN's reading is suggested on *p* 436). K 41 *a* 8 nak-ri (the enemy) + 12 nak-ri šu-u, + 18; iD, 6 + 8. II 16 *c-d* 15 + 17 (amēl) KUR-RA (H 40, 186) = nak-ri(-ru); IV^2 61 *b* 34 a-a kan-šu-u na-ak-ru (but see AJSL xiv 272); I 27 *no* 2, 68 who na-ak-ra a-xa-a, *etc.* shall send; IV^2 48 *a* 12; Asb vi 66. V 40 *e-f* 8 (H 39, 175) U-A = šu-bat nak-ri (BA ii 296 perh = an other) Br 6094; V 52 *a* 63 na-ak-ru (S^b 1 ii 20; Br 1388) = IS ki-e-nu, Asb iv 6; V 55, 46 i-na nakru-u-ti u mun-dax-çu-ti (& 48).

H 12 & 219, 107 ku-ur | KUR | nak-ru; H 198 *no* 4 (= V 16 *a-b*) 36 = nak-rum (II 49 *c-d* 33) ‖ axū & bi-e-šum (Br 6404); H 186, 18 = V 38 *no* 2, *R* 49 na-ak-ru. II 29 *g-h* 52 UR = nak-ru (= K 2022 ii 53). D 83 (K 40) iii 48 KUR = na-ak[-ru], 54, 55 KUR, UR = na-ak[-ru]; 49—51 .....-GUR (Br 3364), ... GE (Br 6319), ... BAL = na-ak[-ru] ša a-ma-ti (= II 26 *e-f* 30 *foll*).

nakriš, *adv* hostile {feindlich} Sn ii 72 nak-riš; vi 72 (ZK ii 336).

nakaru 2. (*i. e.* nakkaru, § 65, 24) hostile, enemy {feindlich, Feind} *pl* nakarūti, § 65, 6. 80—7—19, 130, 6 alpu na-ka-ri; I 70 *b* 22 whosoever sends na-ka-ra a-xa-a; Creat.-*frg* III 66 (end) na-kar-ku-nu dan-nu; IV^2 21 *no* 1, 51—2 (Nergal) qar-ra-du a-a-ab Ê-KUR na-kar Ṭ(D)UR-AN-KI; 61 *a* 9 na-ka-ru-te (*var* -ti)-ka thy enemies (+ 14

+20). II 49 *no* 3, 36 the planet Mars has the name na-kar (*cf* II 51 *a-b* 70). AV 5962; III 57 *a* 62 UL na-ka-ru; JENSEN, 120; ‖ is:

nikru (nekru), *pl* nikrūtu rebel {Rebell, Aufrührer} §§ 57 *d*; 65, 9 *rm*. AV 6216. Beh 51 ni-ik-ru-u-tu, 87 ana u-qu ša Bābilu ni-ik-ru-tu; *cf* 50, 54, 55 ni-ik-ru-tu a-ga-šu-nu; 46, 52; 65 u-qu ni-ik-ru-tu, 48; perh NR 21 (?) ni-ik-ra(-ma), people living in enmity.

nukurtu, *f* hostility, enmity {Feindschaft} usually in māt nukurti, the enemy's country. § 65, *5*; AV 6418; Br 2126, 10930. TP i 43 māt nu-kur-te (*var* -ti); Esh *Sendsch*, *R* 23 mušamqit māt nu-kur-ti (Anp i 34; ZA i 365); 83—1—18, 180, 2 nu-kur-tu ina māt ibaš-ši. K 257 *O* 33—4 (H 127) māt nu-kur-tum (= KI-BAL-A-NI), *cf* IV^2 18 *no* 3, *b* 1/2; 22/3; IV^2 13 *b* 1/2 see nabū Q *a*. ina māt nu-kur-ti (Br 272) NE 48, 40; DT 71 *R* 14; K 257 *R* 16 (H 129); IV^2 18 *no* 3 *O* 35—6; ana māt nu-kur-tim K 133, 12 (H 81) = KI-BAL-A-KU; II 19 *a* 46—7 (Br 4386); *b* 9—10 xa-tu-u bīt māt nu-kur-tim (Br 2647, 2697); 67—8. IV^2 30 *no* 1, *O* 9; 26 *a* 1—2 (*cf* 8—9) Nergal sa-pi-in māt nu-kur-ti (KI-BAL-A) JENSEN, 221; JEREMIAS in ROSCHER's *Ausführl. Lexikon*, iii *col* 256 (≍ J^{26} 65). K 4995 (H 124) 3 ana bīt māt nu-kur-ti (+11 -tim), *cf* 4, 6, 7, 12, 16, 20. D 83 iii 52—3 BAL = nu-kur-t[um]; KI-BAL = māt nu-kur-ti (Br 272); = II 26 *e-f* 34—5; *cf* V 30 *e-f* 3. II 50 vi/v 1 KUR-KI [.... BA]L = māt nu-kur-tim (ZDMG 53, 657 *foll*, on this text). II 38 *g-h* 17 (= V 20 *e-f* 47) KI-BAL = māt nu-kur-ti ‖ māt pa-li-e (16) & māt nabalkatti (18).

T. A. (Ber.) 189, 14 nu-kur-ta mux-xi-ja u ç[a-ab]-tu-mi (KB v *no* 134; BA iv 121); 104, 25 ça-ba-ta-ni nu-kur-tu ana ja-a-ši; BEZOLD, *Dipl*, xvii *rm* 2, *ad* (Lo.) 23, 17 nu-kur-tum 𒀸►►►, but KB v 176 reads nakrūtu. nu-kur-tum (Lo.) 12, 14+40; 23, 20; 28, 74; 30, 14+61+63; 48, 37; 44, 1; 50, 29; 73, 16; 61, 9 nu-kur-te; 73, 8 nu-kur-ti-MEŠ; 43, 15 nu-kur-ta; often ID.

nukkurrūtu. ZK ii 83, 20 nu-uk-kur-ru-tu (Br 1143); perh II 26 *e-f* 38 (= D 83 iii 56) KUR-RA-AN-DI = nu-kur-ru[-tu?] Br 7410.

ni(?)k-ku-ri (?) V 33 iv 44, but see JENSEN, KB iii (1) 144 *rm* 7.

nakkuru, see namkur(r)u.

na-kir(piš?)-tum ‖ kulūlu, 2 *b* (*q. v.*).

nakrū trouble {Weh}. √כרה, BA ii 432—3 *ad* K 1282 *R* 20 i-še-ti ina nak-ri-i kab-bit-t[i-šu], but see nakru, & BA ii 436.

nakrītum, BA ii 208—9 *ad* V 35, 6 ana na-ak-ri-tim evil intention {böswillige Absicht} √נכר, or sorrow {Betrübnis} √כרה, BA ii 230; perh read ma-ag-ri-tim (see *l* 24) & magrū (*p* 512).

nukaribbu (pp?). V 40 *e-f* 3; 16 *g-h* 72 (= II 38 *no* 3, 71) U-A = nu-kar-rib-bu, Br 6091; AV 6417; ZDMG 40, 197. K 4560, 12 nu-ka-r[ib-bu] between ma-xi-çu & ša-an-da-bak[-ku].

NU-KAR-KI, see JENSEN, 223—4 & šu'ēlu.

nakrimānu, something made of leather {etwas aus Leder verfertigtes}, *cf* kirūmu (*p* 438 *col* 1). Nabd 386, 1 (mašak) na-ak-ri-ma-nu a-na ki-re-mu ša šikar ŠE-BAR; also *ll* 4, 6, 9, 10, 11. ZA vi 205 *rm* 2: Lederschlauch.

nakašu. II 22 *no* 2, *add* na-ka-šu, AV 5963.

nukušū, (> NU-KUŠ-ŠA, *i. e.* lā šuni-xu?) a part of the door; gate; usually in *pl* showing that there was more than one found on each door; doorhinge {Thürangel} AV 6419; Br 2001. H 38, 64+65 NU-KUŠ-ŠA = nu-ku-šu-u, la a-ni-xu. K 246 (H 95) iii 54, 55 ina nu-ku-ši-e e-li-i; šap-li-i (= GIŠ-NU-KUŠ-U [*i. e.* = ŠA]-AN-TA; KI-TA). IV^2 16 *a* 58—9 ša ina (iç) ka-nak-ki nu-ku-še-e (H 220, below, = GIŠ-NU-KUŠ-ŠA) i-çar-ru-ur, preceded by (57) ša ina as-kup-pa-ti u çir-ri, *etc.* II 23 *c-d* 40, 41 nu-ku-šu-u ‖ ni-ir dalti & mu-kil dalti. Neb viii 7 as-ku-up-pi u nu-ku-še-e (also vi 13; ix 14); KB iii (2) 30 *col* 3, 26; FLEMMING, *Neb*, 50. V 64 *c* 2; V 65 *b* 6 written NU-ŠAK (TELONI);

---

nakrūtu, see naqruṭum. ∼ nakratu, WINCKLER, *Sargon*, 120, (*Khors*) 128 a-šar nak-ra[-ti], but read naq-ra-bi (KB ii 70). ∼ nakištum see nakistum.

see also KB iii (2) 112 *rm* 8. K 2061 *b* 9; *etc.*

NOTE. — Sa v 32 see nakalu, 3; read la nu-ku-še by ABEL & WINCKLER, *Keilschrift-texte*, Glossary.

nakuttu, see nakadu. terror, fright {Angst, Furcht}. K 625 *R* 9 na-kut-tu ra-aš-ši (Hr[L] 131) WINCKLER, *Forsch.*, ii 21, 304—5. A ‖ is:

nikittu, see nakadu Q; V 65 *a* 23 ma-'-diš ap-lax-ma ni-kid-ti ar-ši (ZK ii 340—1); AV* 49 *col* 2: ni-bit-ti √נבא. Perhaps LEHMANN, ii 12 (L[4] 28) i-raš-šu-u ni-kit-tu (*cf* nibittu, 4).

naktamu (?). V 28 *g-h* 46 na-ak-tam (or par?) pi-i ‖ iš-pa-ar. AV 5978; cover, lid {Deckel, Verschluss}. T. A. (Ber.) 26 iv 17: I na-ar-ma-ak-tum (iç) DU (ZA v 163 *rm* 9: qa-du) na-ak-ta-mi-šu ša siparri (ZA v: ein Spendegefäss nebst seinem Deckel); also (Ber.) 25 iii 18: XXV šu gab-ša imēri qa-du na-ak-ta[-mi-šu]; see Ber. 28 ii 40; 25 i 71, ii 1; iii 20, 32. Tim אנתכא, FRÄNKEL-BARTH, ZA iv 378.

naktamtu (?) perh cover, lid {Deckel, Verschluss}. II 44 *no* 8, 53 nak-tam(par?)-tu ‖ kal-kal-lu-u.

(šad) **Na-al**, ROST, 46, 28 (Lay 18, 29): ša (mât) Ur-ar-ṭi ša ku-tal (šad) Na-al; 52, 41 (mât) Ul-lu-ba (mât) Kil-xu ša šepā (šad) Na-la.

nallu. II 23 *e-f* 55 na-al-lu ‖ kištu; read qa-al-lu, AV 398; GGA '98, 821.

nîlu *1*. √נאל? K 126, 1 if a man approaches his wife ig-lud-ma ni-il-šu bul-lul (*Rev. Sém.*, i 68; 169) & loses his *semen* {Samenerguss}; *cf l* 26.

nîlu *2*. V 22 *b-d* 38 A-DAN = ni-i-lu, preceded by mi-lu, high tide {Hochwasser}; perh = nîlu, 1.

NOTE. — M[S] 104 reads ni-il-šu (K 126) as NI (= šamna) il[-la] *etc.*

nalbabu, fury {Wut}; ZA iv 288 iii 5, 7 see lababu II, end; perh also S[c] 3, 12, Br 2319; KB vi (1) 305—6.

nalbubu, fierce {wütend} *cf* lababu II. K 2061 *R* 50 muš-ruš-šu na-al-bu-bu, eine sich züngelnde Schlange (BA iii 297). V 47 *a* 26 ‖ ši-gu-u.

nalbanu, *m* I 44, 62: 200 ti-ip-ki i-na na-al-ban-ia rabi-i ana elāni ušaqqi rēšu. BA i 176: brickbuilding {Ziegelbau}. MEISSNER & ROST, 57—8: Ziegelform. √labanu, 2, whence also:

nalbantu. 82, 5—22, 1048 *O* 8 libitti ul nadât na-al-ban-ti (= GIŠ-U-RU) ul ba-na-at, a foundation was not yet laid; brickwork not yet constructed (JRAS '91). KB vi (1) 38: Ziegelform; *ibid* 36 (*p* 40) na-]al-ban-ti ib-ta-ni. KB iii (1) 209: nalbantu = "das Geräth zum Ziegelformen". CRAIG, *Rel. Texts*, i 78, 20 še-'-i-tu na-al-ba-na-a-te (M[S] 52 *col* 2). V 31 (*a*-)*b* 5 (xi-bi-eš-šu) RU-NA-GIM (perh = nad-na kîma) na-al-ban(?)-ti (amēlu) ba-nu-u, Br 13933. Also KB vi (1) 360.

nalbanattu. K 196 iii 20 bîtu na-al-ba-na-at-ta RU (= na)-di, PINCHES, *Texts*, 14.

nalbašu, garment, dress {Gewand, Kleid}. √labašu, = מַלְבּוּשׁ; § 65, 31 *a*; AV 5984; Z[B] 95, bel. V 28 *c-d* 52—3 (= II 25 *g-h* 24—5) na-al-ba-ši ‖ ku-max-um & ša-ta-ru; V 23 *a-d* 54 .... A | ME | ša KU-ME: na-al-ba-šu, S[c] 4, 9; Br 10377; II 39 (*c*-)*d* 53 na-al-ba-šu preceded by lu-bu-uš-tum, Br 10567. II 47 *e-f* 34—5 AN-TIK (Br 3219, *p* 31, *note* 2) & AN-MA (Br 489, 6778) = na-al-ba-aš šamê; *cf* Eponym of 798 (KB i 206) Bêl-tarçi-AN-MA (JENSEN, 21—22); also KB i 210 *ad* 782 AN-MA-li' (III 1 *c* 35); KB i 204 *ad* 881/80 reads ša nalbaš-šamê (AN-MA)-dam-qa; Anp ii 86; III 6 *O* 28; II 63 *col* 8, 17 Nalbaš-šamê-çur-tu. II 51 *a* 55 the canal nalbaš-šamê-mi-šar-rat. — Sn *Kui* 4, 20 see kâru, 6. K 3454 + K 3935, 6 na-al-ba-aš ilû-ti-šu (*i. e. Zû*-legend) his divine garment. T. A. (Ber.) 57 *R* 16: I ta-bal na-al-ba-ši na-ad-na-ti aq-ru-tu: I gave one pair (?) of garments as a present (for the Xabiri).

ne-lu-du-u, see biḷludû.

nalaku (?) T. A. (Ber.) 28 iii 59: XXI šêdu ša abnu na-la-ku.

---

nâlu, 1. lowland ‖ Niederung, see na'âlu, 2. ∾ nâlu, 2. roe ‖ Hindin, § 18 see na'alu, 4. ∾ ni-lu ša šamê see çal-lu, 1; (šam) ni-lu erišti *cf* çallu, 2; ni-lu-ti in lu-bar ni-lu-ti see çallitu. ∾ na-la-b(p)u V 28 *e* 86, AV 5980, read naxlapu, *q. v.*

ni(çal?)lummu II 49 *R* iv 16; 18—21 see mešxu, 2.

nalpatu, knife {Messer}. T^C 89; M^S 54. K 4378 (D 87) iii 44—5 [GIŠ-LIŠ] TUR (which also = tannu), & [GIŠ-LIŠ]-NI (which also = napšaštu) = na-al-pa-tum(-tu). Perh Neb 92, 6 na-al-pa-a-ta. T. A. (Ber.) 28 iii 6 *fol*: 41 na-al-bad-du ša (amēl) gallabi ša siparri; 5 na-al-bad-du ša siparri qatušunu ša (iç) ušu; ii 9: 4 na-al-bad-du çupru ša xurāçi; & *ll* 52, 54; 26 iv 6: 35 GIŠ-LIŠ.

nalšu & nalašu, rain, cold {Regen, Kälte}. AV 5981, 5987. IV^2 58 *a* 18 kīma na-al-ši ša kakkabāni; V 22 *a-b-d* 32, 38 na-al-šu & na-la-šu, together with zu-un-nu : za-na-nu (31), šur-p(b)u & šar-p(b)u, as equivalents of še-ig | A-AN. ZA i 248; Br 11394—5. K 4219 *R* 3 na-la-šu between u-pu-u & šu-ri-pu (M^S plate x). II 57 *a-b* 37 goddess (ilat) Ša-la is called thus as the goddess ša nišē u na-al-ši (or -lim?, Sayce, ZA ii 96: ghost??!), but probably read *qa*-al-lim (see qallu servant, slave, just as in II 23 *e-f* 55).

nūltum, corpse {Leichnam} ‖ mittu (*q. v.*) & nabultu, AV 6422.

nallūtu. V 15 *d* 48—50 na-al-lu-tum prec. by ma-a[k-ça-ru], kannu *etc.*, & foll. by kannu & qū. AV 5986. Z^B 66; ZK ii 43 (√אלל, bind); ZDMG 48, 199 *no* 8: rope? same √ as ni'lū (*q. v.*). BA i 182.

nullatu, *pl* nullātu. so perhaps for ul-latu, 2 (*q. v.*), see naṭū; AV 6421; K 246 i 27 see murçu & maruštu; IV^2 17 *b* 20 nu-ul-la[-tu] *cf* kišpu. II 35 *no* 3, *g-h* 41—8 see migirtum, magrū. Sp II 265 *a* xxiv 9 šar-ku-uš (*var* -šu) nu-ul-la-tum. √נול.

namū 1. go to ruin, decay {verfallen} Z^B 84; ZK ii 43 *rm* 2; ZA ii 273—4 ‖ anaxu, rixū, xarabu. — Q *pm* KB iii (2) 50 *col* 3, 18 (ša) na-ma-a-tu iç-ra-at[-sa] Jensen, 352: walls settling in the sense of subsiding; ZA ii 184 *a* 3; PSBA xi 216 (giš-ra-at-sa). T^M v 91 na-mu-u (= *ag*). — 𝔍 ruin, destroy {ruiniren, zerstören} Sarg *Cyl* 22 see dadmu, *a* (AV 5491); Scheil, *Nabd*, i 8—9 *cf* xarabu Š. S^P 158 + S^P ii 962 *R* 15 u-na-a-ma man-za-as-su, + 23 u-na-am-ma-am-ma (laid in ruins); K 3600 i 18 mu-na-am-mi bīt .... — 𝔑 be ruined, destroyed {zur Ruine gemacht werden}. Neb *Bors* i 31 (= I 52 *no* 4 *a* 14—5) the temple tower ultu ūm ri-e-ku-tim(-tu) in-na-mu-u; *cf* KB iii (2) 88 *col* 1, 35 ‖ e-mu-u kar-mi-iš. V 34 *c* 10 the temple ša ul-tu pa-nim in-na-mu(-ma); IV^2 48 *a* 1 māt-su in-nam-mi (= *ps*) Boissier, *Diss*, 7; ZA ii 134 *a* 24.

Derr. these 4:

namū *2.* *m*; *pl* namē ruin {Ruine} ‖ karmu = נְוֶה KB vi (1) pref. *p* xi; Lehmann, i 137; AV 5996. id A-RI-A. IV^2 30* *no* 3 *R* 27—8 (K 3152) let the evil alū go ana na-me-e (Br 11457) ‖ ana ni-sa-a-ti (nišrāti, 26), *l* 32 see nadū, 4; *O* 27—8 a-šib na-me-e ana na-me-ka tūr o thou that dwellest in ruins, to thy ruin return; *Rev. Sém.* vi 149—50. K 758 *R* 2 na-mu-u šumqutu *pl* fallen ruins; K 727 *R* 6 (amēl) nakru na-me-e-a i-kam-mi'š' (Thompson, *Reports*). II 16 *a-b* 58 a-na na-me-e i-lu-šu-nu itūru, into the desert {in die Wüste} BA ii 281, but see ZA viii 129; Br 11456; II 61 *a* 31 xa-rab na-me-e, Br 11456. H 87 ii 12—13 a royal prince ša ina çi-e-ri u na-me-e [n]a-du-u, Br 6254. Sarg *Cyl* 34; *bull*-inscr. 37, see nadū 4. *Rec. Trav.* xvi 178, 11 see madbaru (& KB iv 102); xix 42, 8 šum-ma i-na na-me-e-im ša Larsam (BA iv 94). Smith, *Asurb*, 81 (K 2675 *R*) 9 see xarabu Š & translate: devastated so that it became ruins; Šalm, *Mon*, *R* 99 šal(?)[-ma-te-]-šu-nu | pa-an na-me-e u-šam-li (KB i 172; AJSL xiv 4); IV^2 48 *b* 8 see kamaru 𝔑. S^P III *R* 7 .... mar(?)-ru ana na-me-e. T^M iv 23 a-na çēri qe-di u na-me-e tap-qidainni. III 52 *a* 30 ina ali u na-me-e-šu (*cf* 41, 39 eli); K 2619 ii 21 (al) Dūr-ili (ki) a-na na-me-e? [ ] KB vi (1) 64—5, *D* zur Wüste [ward gemacht]. 83, 1—18, 1335 iii 46 *foll* (81, 11—18, 465) AL-TAR = al-ta-ru, pu-us-su-u, na-mu-ti, ra-ka-nu (M^S 103 *col* 2). See also KB vi (1) 379.

namūeš, *adv* like ruins {ruinengleich} § 80 *b*. IV^2 20 *no* 1, 3—4 city, plain and heights u-ša-li-ka na-mu-iš (Z^B 84 *ad* H 182, 14) he ruined ‖ tilāniš imni.

namūtu condition of ruins, decay, ruin {Zustand des Verfallenseins, Verfall, Ruine} AV 6004. Šalm, *Mon*, *O* 38 *fol* (*R* 52) his cities na-mu-ta(-tu) u-ša-lik (1 *sg*); Bu 88, 5—12, 103, 10 na-mu-ta il-li-ku-ma (‖ e-mu-u ki-ru-bi-eš); Sn *Bav* 6 ša .... na-mu-ta šu-lu-ka(-ma) KB ii 116; perh 53, eli ša a-bu-bu na-mu-ut-ta-šu u-ša-tir. II 35 *a-b* 37 UB(= AR)-RI = na-mu-tum, Br 5791 ‖ xittu, *q. v.* 83, 1—18, 1335 iii 46 *foll.*

nummu *1.* K 948 (margin) 3 nu-um-ma-ša ni-pa-aš its destruction we shall accomplish (?).

nammu *1.* ZA x 208 *O* 17 pi-it-tum : nam-mu : sag[-ba-nu].

nammu *2.* K 4603, 9 TE-A-AN = nam-mu | = mi?, Z[B] 72; Br 7735; AV 6029.

nammû. K 2020 *R* 16 nam-mu-u | mi .....

nummu *2.* 82, 5—22, 915 nu-um-ma (XU) = zi-i-bi or עֹרֵב? see zību, 2 & II 6 *c-d* 1. ZA vi 340 *rm* 1.

nīmu. II 23 *e-f* 36 ni-i-mu = el-pi-e-tum, between aššgu & pu-uq-da-tum, ‖ pu-qu-ud-tum (37), AV 6280.

[il]**Ni(or çal?)-mu** III 66 *O* 2 *b* & [il]**Ni(çal?)-mu-du**, *ibid* 24 *a*.

namba'u, fountain, spring, well {Quell, Quelle} √נבע. ZA ii 113 compares מַבּוּעַ; Lyon, *Sargon*, 70; § 65, 31 *a*; BA i 8; AV 6005. Asb ix 31 see kuppu. Sarg *bull-inscr.* 30 I built *D-Š* i-na eli nam-ba-'e ša šēp Muṣri šadê elênu Ninâ; *Cyl* 44 (KB ii 46—7). K 3445 + Rm 396 *O* 39—40 iš-pu-uk ..... nam-ba-'e.

nambūbtu (> nabbûbtu, √נבב) a bird {ein Vogel}. II 37 *e-f* 14 nam-bu-ub-tum = a-dam-mu-mu. same stem as imbūbu. D[8] 37; 66; 107; Br 13965; AV 6007; §§ 63; 65, 28; BA i 182.

nambaṭu, hilarity, joy {Heiterkeit, Freude} √נבט. II 43 *a-b* 26 nam-ba-ṭu ‖ ul-lu-uç lib-bi, AV 6006.

NAM-BUL-BI incantation, charm, ban {Beschwörung, Zauber, Bann} so with GGA '98, 821 against M[S] 65—66 nam-bulbu; also *cf* Zimmern, *Beitr. z. Kenntn. d. Babyl. Rel.*, 113 *rm*: NAM-BUL-BI = tapširtu perhaps, but by no means nambulbu; see pašaru ℑ *ad* IV² 17 *R* 15; K 2277 *O* 8 *foll*, *R* 1, 4. K 168, 17 pa-aš ša NAM-BUL-BI ma-'-du-te, Lehmann, ii 77. *ibid* line 29 ina qâtê a-sa-kan-ka NAM-BUL-BI an-nu-ti; IV² 60 *R* 35 speaks of the series NAM-BUL-BI-MEŠ. K[M] 62, 12; *p* 129: a somewhat general term for evil. K 769 *R* 7 see Thompson, *Reports of the Astrologers, etc.*, vol. ii *pp* xlvii *fol.* K 712, 10 me-i-nu xi-iṭ-ṭu NAM-BUL-BI-šu lu e-pi-iš. 82—5—22, 52 NAM-BUL-BI li-pu-u-šu; 82—5—22, 48 *R* 8 NAM-BUL-BI šarru be-ili li-pu-uš, let the king, my lord, make a *n.*-ceremony to avert the evil; K 772 *R* 4, I send to the king, my lord, and they shall make a NAM-BUL-BI-ceremony for the eclipse.

namgaru, see naggaru & nangaru. AV 6010, 6057; Br 11165; S[a] iv 4; BA i 283.

nīmedu, room, dwelling {Zimmer, Raum, Wohnung} √עמד₄. Neb viii 19 ni-me-du šar-ru-ti-ja; Z[B] viii 31 ib-ra-tum u ni-mi-di-ša Wohnung & Gemächer; *cf* T[M] v 41. III 66 *col* 9, 39 ni-me-du parakki, PSBA xxi 127; 81, 4—28, 327. II 23 *e* 4; D 86 ii 2; Sn iii 36, iv 8 *etc.* see kussû (*p* 414 *col* 1) = royal seat in the palace, Br 11519; ZA iii 327; AV 6221; Haupt (XI, 7, '88); II 33 *a-b* 70 (*cf* 28 *a* 47) KI-UŠ-SA = ni-me-du, together with šub-tu & ib-ra-tu; UŠ-SA = pa-rak-ku, 67; II 35 *c-d* 56 BAR-KI-KU-GAR-RA = ni-me-du (Br 6909), 57 BAR-KA-SI-GA = ni-me-du e-li-ti (Br 6883). § 65, 31 *a*; D[Pr] 75, 2. BA i 6; 176; AV 6221. See also below, after nimittu.

nĕmdu (?) II 24 *no* 1 *R* 20 U-GAL = iš-kip-pu = ma-aç-çar ne-im-di some worm {ein Wurm}?

namzû some house-utensil {ein Hausgerät} √mazû; Nabd 761, 6 nam-zu-u par-zilli. From same √:

namzītu, *f* a vessel {ein Gefäss}, *pl* nam-ziâte, namzâtu, *etc.*, ‖ xarû, 3 (*q. v.*); Z[B] 43 *rm* 4; ZK ii 216; ZA i 187; BA i 176; Peiser, *Babyl. Vertr.*, Mischkrug; AV 6016; 6018; AV *46 *col* 2. K 4220, 4 nam-zi-ti, M[S] plate x. Camb 330, 5 ištēn-it nam-zi-tum (BA iii 463); 331, 13: II nam-zi-a-tu, *cf* 14; also Nabd 600, 4 + 14.

---

ni-mu see çalmu. ∼ numbû lamentation, *etc.* see nubû. ∼ namaddu, 1. see naqaddu. ∼ namaddu, 2. *cf* namandu. ∼ namduru (√עדר, *q. v.*) see na'duru, nanduru.

Neb 441, 7. Cyr 183, 28; 355, 6—7 naxalûtu ša (karpat) nam-zi-tum (Nabd 278, 14; 787, 13); Nabd 258, 12: šani-it nam-za-tum, + 15—16: II gangannu (*q. v.*) ša nam-zi-tum. VATh 387, 11 II[ta] nam-za-ti (Peiser, *Vertr.*, *no* 148); *Cuneif. Texts in Metropl. Mus.* (N. Y.) i *no* 14, 2: II[ta] nam-za-a-ta u II[ta] nam-za-ra-tu. Anp ii 67 na(m)-zi-a-te siparri (BA i 473); §§ 38; 49 *a*; 69. ZA vi 75—5: goblets. IV² 14 *no* 1 *a* 28 *cf* lamsītu, KB vi (1) 57: ihr Mischkrug ist (aus) blankem Lazurstein. V 32 *c* 37 + 42 *c* 31 nam]-zi-tum; perh V 46 *c-d* 28 to be supplemented. S[b] 168 see kakkullu (& Br 8857; Jensen, 411 *rm* 2; Hommel, *Sum. Lesest.*, 26, 314; 76). — II 20 *b* 44 nam-za-tum .... RA (Br 14203, AV 6063, BA i 622); also *cf* nisannu, 2. T. A. (Ber.) 28 ii 35 we read: III na-an-zi-du.

namzaqu, key {Schlüssel} AV 6034. II 23 *d* 50 nam-za-qu ‖ mušelû (*q. v.*). V 13 *c-d* 9—10 AMÊL-UD-DU (Br 7887) & AMÊL-ŠA-KAK-TI (Br 12072) = ša nam-za-qi (BA i 384) porter {Pförtner}; IV² 17 *a* 5—6 ina ši-gar šame-e el-lûti sik-kat nam-za-ki (ŠA-KAK-TI); D 87 ii 69 littu (*q. v.*) nam-za-qi & add Winckler, *Forsch*, ii, 2, 307—8 × Br 10852, 10854. 81, 2—4, 219 *R* i a nam-za-aq ilâni rabûti, *Rev. Sém.*, vi 359: le chef des grand dieux, in the meaning of = order, decree. K[M] 53, 22 li-iz-ziz (is) šigaru nam-za-ki-šu-nu. IV² 33* *a* 25 par-ka nam-za-q[u]; II 23 *e-f* 66 nam-za-qu (not ik-ni-tum) ‖ daltum (GGA '98, 821 + 814); √ nazaqu, 2.

namxaçu, some wooden instrument {ein Instrument aus Holz} AV 6019; K 4378 (= II 45 *b* 16) vi 62 GIŠ--tum = nam-xa-çu, Br 5211; KB vi (1) 392; √ maxaçu, 1.

namxaru, a sacrificial dish {ein Opfergefäss} √ maxaru. TP ii 50 nir-ma-ak [siparri *pl*] u nam-xar siparri *pl* rabûti; ii 58: I nam-xar siparri I nir-ma-ak siparri I dedicated to god Ašur. L[T] 125; AV 6020. Nabd 258, 13 ištên-it nam-xar-ri *pl*; Cyr 183, 23 ištên nam-xa-ru; Nabd 600, 14; 787, 18 see namzītu; Camb 331, 13 ište-en nam-xa-ri. Rm 358 *O* 2 nam-xar sa-bi-i (*q. v.*). ZA v 158, 37 nam-xa-ra (xurâçi rabûti) = T. A. (Lo.) 8; Ber. 25 iv 58 nam-xar *pl* as-pi; ZK ii 216 nam-xar ši-ka[-ri]. II 33 *c-d* 10 DUK-BIR-SI-DI (*cf* birsidu) = nam-xa-ru in one group with nar-ma-ku (8) & nar-ma-ak-tu (9), Br 8509; see also II 24 *no* 1 (add) & namâçu. A ‖ is:

namxartu. Peiser, *Vertr.*, *no* 148, 14: II[ta] nam-xa-ra-ti, AV 6020.

namxurtu present, offering {Geschenk, Opfer} *i. e.*, what is received, BA i 180 *fol*; K 46 ii (II 57) 28 nam-xur-tu ‖ man-da-tu (29) & tam-gur-tu (30) Br 7169; AV 6022; see nanxurtu.

namxarû; thus AV 6021 reads II 43 *b* 69 (šam) nam-xa-ru-u DIR (?).

namkû, AV 6024 *ad* II 26 *no* 2 (*add*).

NIM-MA-KI = (mât) Elamtu, Elam. IV² 38 *a* 19; Sn iii 62; Asb iii 27; Beh 48; II 6 *a-b* 15. D[S] 39; D[Par] 320 *foll*; AV 6430. 2223.

nimakku. T. A. (Lo.) 82, 15 ni(?)-ma-ak(?)-ki ut-ta(?)-xa-az (*cf* BA iv 130—1 on this text); KB vi (1) 78 reads i-ba-ak-ki ut-ta-xa-as she weeps (and) mourns.

namkur(r)u & **nakkuru** = makkûru (*q. v.*) goods, effects, property {Eigentum, Habe, Besitz} § 65, 31 *b*; BA i 4; 160; 176. L[T] 117; § 88 *rm*: something earned, earnings; AV 6025. TP i 83 (93) šal-la-su-nu bu-ša(-a)-šu-nu (u) nam-kur-šu-nu; ii 80 *fol*; iii 9—10, 27—8, 62—3, 81—2; v 1. bu-ša-šu-nu nam-kur-šu-nu iii 102; iv 23—4; vi 9; du-muq nam-kur-ri-šu-nu ii 52 (Anp ii 133); a-di nam-kur-ri-šu-nu iii 8. S[P] ii 987 *O* 5 nam-kur šu-par Bâbili, the property of B. — *del* 21 (26) n]a-ak-ku-ra zirma, Jensen, 396 (following Halévy) × BA i 124 (*Johns Hopk. Circ.*, 69, 18 *col* 1) na-aq-ku-ra zirma: leave what is doomed to destruction. J[I-N] 33. Barth, ZA ii 384 reads ina-ak-ku-ra (√ naqaru). II 47 *c-d* 49 NAM-KU-TU (BA i 176: a ℨ-formation; AV 6026) = na-am-ku-rum (Br 2218; § 53 *rm*). id *e.g.* Cuthean-legend

namz(ç)abu = nanç̣abu, (*q. v.*).

iv 20 namkurra-ka (ZA xii 321 *foll*, KB vi, 1, 298); JENSEN, KB vi (1) 254 *ad* DT 42, 7 (end), usually read kusumnat-ka; perh also Asb iv 65.

namkūru. V 28 *a-b* 92 nam-kur i-ni ‖ nāmaru mirror {Spiegel} *q. v.*

nimlū. 82—8—16, 1 *R* 11 me-il | KI-NE | i-za-ak-ku : nim-lu-u, betw. ximṭētu, & qilūtu, Br 9709; HOMMEL, *Sum. Lesest.*, 98; √malū. See KB vi (1) 447—8.

namalu, reeds {Rohrstand} KB vi (1) 40—41 (82, 5—22, 1048) 32 . . . n]a a-pa na-ma-la iš-ku-un, ... Schilf und machte einen Rohrstand.

namallu. II 23 *c* 63 na-ma-al-lum ‖ of ir-šu, bed, couch {Bett, Lager} in the language of the Suteans; AV 5989; D^{Par} 230; HAUPT, *And. Rev.*, '84 Jl., *p* 93 *rm* 1; HOMMEL, *Gesch.*, 275; WZKM, ii 157; ZA iv 384; vi 60.

namullum. K 4172, 1—2 GIŠ-NA-MU-UL-LUM = ŠU-lum, & lu-'-tum, some wooden instrument, furniture {ein Gegenstand aus Holz} M^{S} 52 *col* 2; 66. BEZOLD, *Catalogue*, 1893. GIŠ-NA-MUL = na-mul-lu.

nīmelu, nēmalu, produce, gain; possession; welfare, strength {Gewinn; Vermögen; Kraft} √עמל. Z^{B} 17; 91; 100 ‖ emūqu; AV 6222; § 65, 31 *a*; BA i 228—30 (but *cf Rev. crit.* 23 Je '90, 482); 326 properly: result of labor. K 601 *R* 7—9 ni-me-el māt $^{(il)}$ Ašur $^{(ki)}$ | ni-me-el māt Akka-d[i-i] | ni-me-el mātāte kāli-šina, BA i 625 (Hr^{L} 7); IV² 60 B *O* 26 ū-mu ri-du-ti $^{(ilat)}$ Iš-tar ni-me-la (*var* -li) ta-at-tur-ru (& C *O* 6) the time spent in the service of Ištar was gain and riches. K 2024 *R* 5 ūma ni-me-el pa-la-ax ili ta-ta-mar, when thou beholdest the gain of the fear of god, MEISSNER, 108. KB vi (1) 186 *col* 3, 1 (= NE 18, 1) ni-mil(?)-šu xul-liq, destroy his riches! Sp II 265 *a* vii 8 il-ku ša la ni-me-li a-šu-aṭ ap-ša-nu; IV² 54 *b* 11 me-nu-u ni-me-il-šu. K 618, 8—11 ilāni rabūti ša šarru be-ili | šum-šu-nu is-sik-u-ni ni-ma-al-šu | a-na šarri be-ili-ja | lu-kal-li-mu, BA i 224—5; Hr^{L} 9. K 666 *O* 11 (Hr^{L} 12; V 53 *col* 2) ni-e-ma-al-šu ana, *etc.* (BA i 626—7); K 167 (Hr^{L} 1) *R* 1 ni-me-el ina ri-šu-uš-šu | az-zi-zu-u-ni (BA ii 24); K 565 (Hr^{L} 77) *O* 15, *R* 1 ni-me-il-šu šarru be-ili li-mur (perh: favorable result); K 1197, 10 (Hr^{L} 15) ni-me-il xa-ri-pa-a-ni (HEBR. x 110). K 245 ii 4 [AZAG?]-ID-TUK = ... ni-me-li (H 69, 4), *ibid* 2 ta-at-tu-ru; *ll* 37—41 (H 70) ni?]-me-lu, nīmelu ma-la ba-šu-u mit-xa-riš i-zu-zu, the gain, as much as there was, they divided in equal parts (MEISSNER, 16 *rm* 2); also see ZA iv 10, 48 (& *p* 28) & kaçapu Š^{t}; 15, 11 ni-me-la. V 40 *c-d* 29 [ID?]-TUK = ni-me-lu (Br 6639), between še-bu-u & e-mu-qu; & see II 27 *no* 1 (K 2008) iii 8. P. N. Bu 91—5—9, 366, 8 ana . . . . mar Ne-me-lum. T. A. (Ber.) 9 *R* 22 a-na šarri ni-me-lu i-ba-aš-ši, to the king belongs the property, + 24. To the same stem belongs probably:

namlu, power, strength {Macht, Kraft} T. A. (Lo.) 61, 16 ša-ni-tu ki-i na-am-lu tu-um-xa-su (= zu = çu).

namandu > namaddu, √madadu, extension, width, measure {Ausdehnung, Maass} KGF 520 *rm* 1. AV 5990; Br 4659, S^{b} 196 gu-ur (HOMMEL = כר) | [cuneiform] | na-man-du; ZA i 403—4; AJP ix 421 *rm* 5; § 63. ‖ ittū, nindanaku. T. A. (Ber.) 28 ii 41: III na-ma-an-du. Br 2579 *ad* II 22 *d-f* 13 (DUK)-RI (TAL) | tal-lu | na-man[-du?]; *cf* V 42 *c-d* 10 DUK [cuneiform] = na[-man-du].

namsū & nam-si-u (BA i 474) place of cleansing, purification {Waschungs-, Reinigungsort} √misū, 1. Z^{B} 97; 103; J^{w} 90; JENSEN, ZA ii 249—51; §§ 38; 65, 31 *a*. *del* 229 (254) take him and ana nam-si-e (§ 66, note) bil-šu, and bring him to the place of cleansing (236 [263]). T^{M} viii 56 (+ 60, 65, 80) kaššaptu ša qēmu ina libbi erī nam-si-e [te-iç-çir].

nimsū K 11890, 5 . . . . PAR-RA = nim-su-u ša $^{(amēl)}$ ašlaki, M^{S} 58 *col* 2.

nimsētu. K 11890, 4 . . . . LAX-XA = nim-si-e-tum; IV² 14 *no* 1 *O* 29 nim-si-is-sa me-su kas-pa u [xurāça], KB vi (1) 57: her washtub of pure silver & (gold); IV² *R* reads *lam* instead of *nim*, see lamsītu.

namsuxu. I 28 *a* 29 nam-su-xa, one of the presents sent with other sea-animals (umāmi tāmdi) to the king of Assyria by the king of Egypt. L^T 198; KB i 126; BA i 180 *rm* 1. OPPERT, from Egypt. *emsuḥ* = crocodile; HOMMEL, *Gesch.*, reads tum-su-xa = crocodile, also *Sum. Lesest.*, 57.

Nampagāti (*pl* of *nampagtu). name of a town. (al)Nam-pa-ga-a-te Sn *Bav* 10; D^{Par} 188; POGNON, *Bavian*, 116; BA i 176.

namāçu, some kind of vessel for milk {ein Milchgefäss} II 24 *no* 1 (K 152) i 67 (*add*) + V 32 *c* 38 DUK-BIR-SI-DI = ŠU-u | na-ma-çu ša šiz-bi.

namūçu, K 4172, 4 GIŠ-NA-MU-ÇU = ŠU (MEISSNER, 105; M^S 66).

(iç) nim-pi (*i. e.* [illegible] ?)-çi-tu, II 28 *f* 14.

namçaru, *pl* namçarē sword {Schwert} √maçaru, 1. L^T 146; AV 6035. IV^2 21 (K 3197) 1 B *R* 18—19 (il Gibil) nam-ça-ru (= GER-GAL, Br 318) mu-sax-xi-ip nam-ta-ri; K 1279 (BEZOLD, *Catal.*, 257) il BIL-GI called GER-GAL (= namçaru) MAX (*i. e.* rabū) = il Gibil miš-lax çīru. Sn vi 4; Sm *Asurb* 124, 55 see zaqtu; Sn *Kui* 4, 12, Sarg *Ann* 133 see karru, 2. K 3600 *R* 2 na]mçaru pe-tu-u | ulmū zaqtu (GGA '98, 823). $Z^Š$ v/vi 198 u mu-šal-li-ma-ta-ma at-ta na-az-za-rak-ka, and an avenger with the sword art thou; II 19 *b* 2 see kiššādu & Br 318 (GIR-GAL). NE 75, 5 nam-çar šip-pi-ja the sword on my belt, KB vi (1) 136—7. S^b 210 u-gur | UGUR | nam-ça-ru, H 29, 637; 37, 18; Br 8859; Br 1191 quotes AV 7067, 6 KUR-E-A-KA-GA = nam-ça-rum pi-qi-tu.

namçarūtu ? T. A. (Tel-Hesy) 14: u III nam-ça-ru-ta three swords {drei Schwerter} BA iv 153—4; OLZ ii *nos* 1 & 2 *ad* KB v *no* 129, *p* 340.

namçarratum T. A. (Lo.) 41, 24 nam-çar-ra-tum ik-šu-ud-šu-nu, BEZOLD, *Diplom.*, distress? KB v *p* 102 reads nam-xar-ra-tum & translates: have captured them by force.

namçartum K 152 i 77 + V 32 *d* 47 = ša (*i. e.* karpat ša) nam-çar-tum.

namqu. H 106 *c* 18 QI-IB = XI (or DUG) = nam-qu; id = ṭābu. Br 4212, 8229; AV 6064.

nīmequ & **nēmiqu**, wisdom {Weisheit} √עמק; §§ 30; 65, 31*a*; I 65 *a* 4; Neb i 7. AV 6223; BA i 5; 165; 176. id ZU = nīmequ 'depth'; ZU also = be wise, wisdom; hence nīmequ = wisdom, JENSEN, 244; also Br 2209. apsū (*i. e.*) bīt ni-me-ki IV^2 52 *b* 34 ($Z^Š$ ii 150) where original meaning still evident; K^M 21, 57 apsū ni-me-ki; I 27 *no* 1, 4 Êa bēl ni-me-qi; II 48 *a-b* 32 (K 2081 *R* 10, 12 *etc.*; Br 12226) bel ni-me-ki; *cf* I 44, 77; Lay 43, 3 see xasīsu. II 58 *a-c* 56 Êa is called AN-NIN-ŠI-AZAG as ša ni-me-ki (LE GAC, ZA vii 140); Sarg *Cyl* 47; Merod.-Balad. stone iii 2 ina ni-me-ki, + 8 (il) Bēl-nīmeqi (wr. AN-NIN-ŠI-AZAG); Sarg *Cyl* 38 see milku, *b*. V 61 *d* 41 ina ni-me-qi ša (il) Êa. IV^2 52 *a* 2 Ištar ni-me-ki, of the goddess (ilat) Ši-du-ri = $Z^Š$ ii 172. Asb i 31 I learned (a-xu-uz) ni-me-ki (*var* -qi) Nabū kullat dupšarrūti; Neb i 7: Nebuchadnezzar muštālum (*q. v.*) a-xi-iz ni-me-ki, BA i 165 *rm* 1; *cf var* after Asb iii 123 axiz ni-me-qi-ja. L^4 i 11 ix-zi ni-me-qi-šu the acquisition of wisdom. KB iii (4) 78, 4 Marduk ba-an ni-me-qi; Rm III 105, 5 (Nabū) bēl ni-me-ki u ši-tul-ti; Sp II 265 *a* vi 2 gi-mil (?) na-qab ne-me-ki il-lu uk-taš[-šad], ZA x 5 *fol*; PSBA xvii 141 *foll.* IV^2 14 *no* 3, *a* 3—4 NAM-AZAG-ZU (Br 9894) = ana ni-me-ki (of Nabū). V 33 viii 15—18 il Êa | bēl naqbi | ni-me-qam | li-šak-lil-šu. ni-me-qi(-ki, -iq) Nabū often in colophons, *e. g.* II 21 *a* 31 (-ki); D 49, 37; II 23 *a* 55; T^M i 151 (-iq); II 33, 73; K 2867, 8 (S. A. SMITH, *Asurb*, ii 1); T^M ii 21 (-qi); II 39 coloph. 19 ni-me-ki-šu-nu pal-ku; K 155 *R* 23. SCHEIL, *Rec. Trav.*, xix 46, 9 ina ne-me-ki çi-ri; 14 aš-xi ap[-pa]-at ne-me-ki. IV^2 38 *b* 7 see melultu (end). KB vi (1) 78 ii 17—18 lu-uš-ku-un tu-up-pu | ša ni-mi-e-qi a-na ga-ti-ka, I will place into thy hand the tablet of wisdom = T. A. (Lo.) 82. — V 30 *a-b* 48 ZU = ni-me-qu (Br 136); H 37, 3; *cf* II 57 *a-b* 35. II 16 *b* 64—5 the prudent, the wise | ša ni-me-iq-šu ēn-šu | la xa-as-su, of whose wisdom

---

namçītu see namsītu.

his lord is not mindful, BA ii 280; also see V 31 *c* 15; K[M] 13, 16; 41, 3.

nāmaru *1.* mirror }Spiegel{. V 28 *a-b* 86—93 na-ma-rum is a ‖ of ab(p)-rum (86), a-ka-rum (87), a-du-rum (88), a-ma-rum (89), mu-ša-lum (90), muš-šulum (91), nam-kur i-ni (92), si-mat pa-ni (93). II 25 *e-f* 58—61; Fränkel, ZA iii 51 (√نمر). T. A. (Ber.) 25 ii 56 (+58): I na-ma-ru ša kaspi; 28 ii 74 *foll* na-ma-ar.

nāmaru *2.* (?) something made of leather }ein Gegenstand aus Leder{. V 32 *b-c* 51 SU-NA-MA-RU = ŠU (*i. e.* nâmaru) ‖ ka-ri-im-pi-du.

(māt) **Nam-ri**, P. N. of country }Landesname{ D[K] 30—1 *rm* 5; D[Par] 186—7; 205; Bezold, *Catalogue*, 2132: district in Babylonia. V 55, 47 *foll* māt Na-mar.

Winckler, *Forsch.*, i 292 changes זמרי, Jer 25: 25 into נמרי, see, however, Cornill, *Jeremiah* (SBOT); Marquart, *Philol. Suppl.* VI, 648 *rm*; Rost, *Untersuchungen*, *p* 103 *rm*.

nāmuru (prop. 𒐏 ac of amaru, see) appearance, apparition }Erscheinen, Erscheinung{. Sin ina] na-mu-ri-šu (agā a-pir) when the moon (god) at its rising has a crown, III 58 *a* 30, usually written ŠI-LAL-šu; III R plates 51, 54, 58, 60 *passim*; also AV 6002; 83—1—18, 317, 6; perh also T. A. (Ber.) 150, 15; BA i 187, & again § 88, note (end).

namaru 1., seldom ***nameru***, pr immir, pc li(m)mir (§ 22); pm namir; ps inammar, Pinches, *Inscr. Babyl. Tablets*, *no* 12, 9 U-AN-TIM šu-ma-a-tim ta-na-am-ma-ar this contract is shown (*i. e.*, appears, shines), but? ZA i 234; Z[B] 43; Halévy, *Rech. Crit.*, 95 = נהר; AV 5992. — *a*) be or become light, bright; shine }licht sein oder werden; scheinen{ H 78—9 (K 44) *O* 19 le-lil le-bi-ib li-im-mir; *R* 28 ki-ma ki-rib šame-e lim-mir (Br 7930); IV² 57 *a* 69 like alabaster nu-ri lim-mir, may my light shine; Z[B] vii 88 a-me-lu mār ili-šu li-lil li-bi-ib li-im-mir. V 55, 26 (36) bit (? pit?) i-mit-ti | šarri bêlišu la im-mir-šu-ma. 82—3—23, 4344 + 4478 + 4593 (end) ū-mu-ka nam-mar, thy day make bright (PSBA xviii 257—8); K[M] 1, 5 nam-rat urru (Jensen, 105 *rm*: çît)-ka ina šame-e; II 54 *no* 1, 28 Sin is called AN-UD-SAR?]-RA as ša çi-su (>çit-šu) nam-rat; also II 52 *a* 1 (end) & K 710 *O* 1 (end); K 788 *O* 3, 4 ÇAB (= inam)-ir. K 2279 *R* 8 see niṭlu; Lehmann, ii 26 *col* 3, 10 (end). K 2401 ii 7 a-ki çi-it (il) Ša-maš na-mir, like the rising sun he shines; perh K 257 *R* 25 (end) na-mir. Sp II 265 *a* ii 4 na-am-ra-tum zi-mu-ka; 9, na-am-ra-a be-lu meš-ri-e; 81—2—4, 88 *O* 6 irat-ça nam-rat zib-bat-ça e-ṭu-at. TP vii 101 u-šar-rix na-me-ri-šu I made great its brilliancy (§ 32 *aγ*; ZA v 98; AV 5999). K 806 *O* 8 e-šu-a-ti i-nam-mi-ra ‖ dal-xa-a-ti i-zak-ka-a (9), troubles will be cleared up and complications unravelled. ZA iv 240, 12 (hymn to Nebo) a-šar ek-lit nam-rat še-zu-zu; used especially of the beginning of day, daybreak; Anp ii 53—4 mu-šu a(d)-di na-ma-ri ar-te-di, I marched (all) night until daybreak. V 31 *c-d* 19 UD-ZAL-LI = na-ma-ru (Br 7908; II 62 *c-d* 7; *cf* uddazallū); *del* 92, *etc.*; NE 75, 45 see mimmū (*p* 565 *col* 1); P. N. IV 31 *b* 12, 13, 23 Uddu-šu-na-mir (bright is his light), KB vi (1) 86 reads Açū-šu-na-mir; *Rec. Trav.*, xx 62—3 *no* xxxiii frag. Uddu-šu-nam-ir pa-te-si itti Ri ...., *etc.* T. A. (Lo.) 57, 14 + 16 u la-a na-mi-ir, but there is no light; 1, 35 a-na na-ma-ra bīti-ši (= amaru); see also xamū, note.

V 12 *no* 5, 38—9 ZI = na-ma-a-ru (Br 2320) & na-pa-a-xu (Br 2321) ZA ii 196 *rm* 3; V 24 *c-d* 3 še]-e-ri = na-ma-ru (V 28 *a-b* 38). K 40 iv 1—2 PA (zu-ud), & PA (ku-sa) = na-pi(= ma)-a-ru (Br 5582; AV 8895; H 21, 396; ZK ii 18; ZA ii 206—7; 297; Z[B] 86 *rm* 1); iii 82—3 SU-LU-UG & ŠU-ZU-UZ-LU-UG-LUL = na-ma-a-ru (Br 288; ZA i 63; ii 49; Br 7080, 7209); iv 5—6 UD (ba-bar) & UD-DU = na-ma-a-ru ša ū-mi (Br 7785, 4890, 7881; *cf* Hommel, *Sum. Lesest.*, 24, 286; II 27, 586; ZA i 194 = çi-it šam-ši); On V 21 *g-h* 67 ŠI = na[-ma-ru] see ZA i 238; Br 9277; S[c] 267 see Br 10548. V 30 *g-h* 19 BAR = na-ma-ru (20, = ša-am-šu) Br 1775; H 215; 18, 146; AV 5992; V 38 *a-b* 42 ši-ir | BU | = na-ma-ru (ZA ii 196; 282; Br 7525), also V 36 *a-b* 33; II 47 *e-f* 58 ZAL = na-ma-ru (59 = mašû), *cf* 48 *a-b* 42, Br 5319; K 4225 *dupl.*, 8 AR = na-ma-ru, Br 9425.

b) be or become joyful, brighten up *etc.*, orig. of face, then also of disposition {fröhlich, heiter sein oder werden} D^{Pr} 153. IV^2 60* C *R* 19 im-me-ru pa-nu-šu his face brightened, ‖ kabittašu ipperdû; V 35, 18 im-mi-ru pa-nu-uš-šu-un (BA ii 210); V 65 *a* 39 im-me-ri pa-nu-u-a; I 69 *b* 7 im-mi-ru zi[-mu-u-a]; I 69 *c* 18 (KB iii (2) 82 + 86; 92 ii 51); V 61 *d* 39 see zîmu (end); K^M 8, 10 lim-mi-ru zi-mu-u-a; IV^2 20 *no* 1, 20 im-me-ra ma-li ri-ša-a-ti, was bright, & full of joy; *Khors* 194 na-mar ka-bit-ti (*q. v.*) = *Ann* 452; II 36 *c* 24; IV^2 12 *R* 12 (see appendix to IV^2 *R*); ZA iv 241, 34 see nuparu. II 117 (K 4931) *O* 23—4 ka-bit-ti ul im-mi-ir, ZA i 34; Br 8145; on *l* 23 *cf* II 27, 581 la-ax = na-ma-ru; K 40 iv (= D 85; II 8 *a-b*) 3—4 KA-KA-XAB-RA & EB-DAM = na-ma-ru ša amêli (Z^B 57; Br 594, 4979).

Q^2 shine, be brilliant {glanzen, erglänzen} II 40 *no* 2, 12 a stone is called, ŠA (*i. e.* ši + lu)-LA = ^{aban} a-la-di = ^{aban} it-ta-mir = λίθος ἵππωτις, ZA xiv 357—8. IV^2 57 *b* 14 like heaven lu-lil (1 *sg*), like earth lu-bi-ib, kîma ki-rib šamê-e lu-ut-ta-mir (may shine, § 101); at-ta-am-ma-ru in *c. t.*

𝔍 — *a*) make light, bright, brilliant, *etc.* {hell, licht, glänzend machen} § 36; u-nam-mir, Lehmann, S^2 29; S^3 15; L^3 4; L^3 R 4; P^2 15. K 44 (H 78) 13—14 mê u-nam-me-ru (3 *pl*); Esh iv 48 the temple .... u-nam-me-ra (*var* -mir) ki-ma û-me; I 65 *a* 38 bîtu ki-ma û-um lu u-na-am-mi-er (§ 66); V 84 *a* 52 the chambers u-na-am-mi-er ki-ma û-um; Neb vii 8 the temples û-mi-iš u-na-am-mi-ir ‖ kîma šarûru šamšu uššbi (= uššûpi); KB iii (2) 92, 18; V 63 *b* 39; II 67, 80 u-nam-me-ru (1 *sg*) mu-çu-u. Scheil, *Nabd*, viii 50 u-na-am-mir û-mi-iš. V 64 *b* 25 ki-ma çi-it arxi u-nam-mi-ir ša-ru-ru-šu; 65 *b* 8 ki-ma šu-u û-mi u-nam-mir-šu; ZA iii 318, 89; ZA v 67, 39 u-nam-mir-ši kîma ša-rûri (11) šamši a[-çi-i], I made it brilliant like the splendor of the rising sun. — Sarg *Ann* 201 mu-nam-mir; Merod.-Balad. stone ii 5 mu-nam-mir gi-mir e-kur-ri. IV^2 26 *a* 39—40 mu-nam-mir (= LAX-GA-AB) ek-li-ti, said of the fire-god (ZA iii 349); IV^2 19 *a* 37—8 be-lum mu-nam-mir (= ŠI-BE-BIR, Br 9294) ek-li-ti; IV^2 21, 1 B *R* 20 end (Br 9369, 9440); K^M 58, 17 mu-na-mir uk-li; 1, 2 Sin id-diš-šu-u mu-nam-mir. Ištar mu-na(m)-mi-rat mu-ši IV^2 1* iii 35—6; IV^2 50 iv 13 el-lit (= 3 *sg* pm) Ištar mu-nam-me-rat šim-ti (T^M iii 180; Jensen, 118). 81—11—3, 111 *O* 8 Marduk is called Sin mu-nam-mir mu-ši. — K 3927 *R* 3 (H 75) ina ek-li-ti-ja nu-um-mir; *cf* IV^2 54 *a* 44 nu-um-mir [pa-ni-šu]; perh IV^2 59 *no* 2 *R* 17 nu-mir-an-ni-ma; K^M 11, 20 e]-ša-ti-ja nu-um-me-ir (*var* mir) said to Marduk; pm Sn *Kui* 4, 28 ša nu-um-mu-ru (3 *pl*; BA iii 193 *rm* **). — adorn, *e. g.* NE 44, 65—66 the gardener of thy father ša ka-a-a-nam-ma šu-gu-ra-a na-šak-ki | û-mi-šam-ma u-nam-ma-ru pa-aš-šur-ki (KB vi, 1, 170—1). — *b*) light a fire, kindle, fan {anzünden, anfachen} IV^2 49 *b* 37 I have taken a torch u-nam-mir ka-a-ša (or to *a*) as T^M 39?); Zimmern, *Beitr. z. Babyl. Rel.*, 102, 81 (end) niknakka tu-nam-mar (*cf* lines 84, 87; 106, 165 *etc.*), K^M 40, 11. II 44 *c-d* 6 NE (or ṬE) = nu-mu-rum (or -ri?) followed by ṭipârum; Br 4593; AV 6420. — *c*) make joyful, gladden {freudig, heiter machen} Esh vi 43 ina ..... nu-um-mur ka-bit-ti; K 601 *R* 12 (BA i 625; Hr^L 7; AV 6433); Bu 88—5—12, 75 + 76 viii 31 xu-ud lib-bi nu-um-mur pa-an | u ṭu-ub ka-bit-ti. V 51 *c* 25 + 57 (end) li-nam-mir-ka may gladden thee (see bûnu, *b*) *p* 178 *col* 1); *ac* Scheil, *Nabd*, viii 5 nu-um-mu-ru zi-mu-šu, to cause his face to shine. H 50, 16 IN-LAX = u-nam-me-ir, ZK ii 270. V 38 *a-b* 34 ši-ir | BU | nu-um-mu-rum, Br 7526; also see AV 6432.

Š V 45 vi 49 tu-ša-an-mar.

Š^t (§ 85) I 7 D 6 the temple of Nergal kîma û-me uš-nam-mir I made to shine {liess ich erglänzen}. IV^2 57 *a* 35 at-ta-ma (Marduk) kîma šamši ek-lit-si[-na] tuš-nam-mar (= K^M 12, 35); T^M ii 71 ek-li-e-ti tu-uš-nam-mar;

ii 21, 22 tuš-nam-mar bīt [ek-li-e-ti] & gi[-pa-ri]. Sn *Kui* 4, 8 ū-me-iš uš-nam-mir; K 11152 (hymn to Ištar) 5 ga-bu-tum ša ša-ru-ru-ša uš-nam-ma-ra(-ru) ik-li-ti; V 65 *b* 20 liš-nam-mir; IV 61 *c* 35 nu-ur ša il-me-ši ina pān Ašuraxiddina u-ša-na-ma-ra, I will cause to shine, Z^B 104. K 3312 iv 18 Šamaš muš-na-mir uk-li (*cf* ZA iv 12), KB iii (2) 108, 30; K 3474 + K 8282 i 15 muš-na-mir pi-tu-u [. . . .]; K 8030, 10 (K^M 39) muš-na-me-rat. See also kinūnu.

IV T. A. (Lo.) 27, 10 en-nam-mu-ru (BEZOLD, *Dipl*, KB v 243: my eyes shone brilliantly, *i. e.* Q); Ber 90, 16 en-nam-ru ēnā-ja. 81—2—4, 88, 7 qarnāt ^{pl} ça nin-mu-ra its horns are brilliant. when at the moon's appearance xar-bi-iš na-an-mur (it appears high) K 1395, 5; 81—2—4, 79, 5 (THOMPSON, *Reports*).

NOTE. — MEISSNER & ROST, 118: namaru developed from √ נהר (na'aru) & from this was borrowed נָהָר = نَهر; see, however, SCHWALLY, *Idiotikon*, 121; HAUPT, BA iii 280 *rm* *: nūru perhaps a softening of numru.

Derr. nanmurtu (?) & these 16 (?):

namru *1.* *f* namirtu, *adj* light, bright, brilliant }hell, licht, glänzend} *pl* namrūti, *f* namrâti. AV 6042, 6000, 6043; K 2396, 16; § 65, 7. T^M ii 111 (end) ilu nam-ru; *ibid* 102 (107) mim]-ma nam-ru, was turned into darkness. IV^2 17 *b* 12 nūr-ka nam-ru kàl nišē i-bar-ri; T^M ii 26 a-na nūri-ka nam-ri; viii 17 (il) Nūru ellu nam-ru; Esh *Sendsch*, *O* 5 Sin nannaru nam-ru. V 42 *a-b* 52 MUL-ŠU-PA = kakkab na-am-ru, Br 202. *Rec. Trav.*, xvi, 177, 7 (ilat) Ištar kak-kabū na-mir-tum šamē. IV^2 1* v 21 —22 Sin bēl (*var* be-el) nam-ra çi-it, the lord glorious in his rising (= ša çēšu namrat, § 73); Sm 949 *O* 8 Šamaš lit-tu çir-tu ša bēl nam-ra çi-it, Br 58, 2818. ZA iv 230, 13 see birbirru, where other references. K 695, 5 šarru nam-ru, also II 55, 67. — I 65 *a* 30 (*b* 20) xurāçu na-am-ra-am (KB iii, 2, 33); Neb *Bors* i 18 xurāçu na-am-ri; Neb iii 6 xurāçi nam-ri, + 47 kaspi nam-ri (+ 29); Sarg *Ann* 199 siparru namru; *Khors* 116 erē nam-ri; *Ann* 422; Asb x 101 erī nam-ru; see also Sn vi 49; Asb vi 29. OPPERT in GGA '84, 331: namru & ruššū with metals = pure & mixed metals. — Sarg *Khors* 156 eš-re-ti nam-ra-a-ti; ZA ii 134 *a* 23 Ē-bar-ra ki-iç-çi na-am-ri. — ū-mu nam-rum II 32 (*a*-)*b* 11 (JENSEN, 130, the bright day, a name of Marduk); T^M ii 4, beg.; IV^2 5 *a* 35—6 ina ū-me nam-ri, Br 8146. V 30 *e-f* 24 see na'duru & Br 7936. ZA iv 12, 7 na-mir-ta urrika. II 36 *e-f* 23 bu-un-ni-šu nam-ru-ti (see namrū-tu?), V 61 *d* 43; AV 1396; KB iii (1) 132 iv 6 written na-[cuneiform sign]-ru-tim, see būnu, *p* 178 *col* 1; KB iv 92 *R* 4; SCHEIL, *Nabd*, vii 20. II 66 *no* 1, 2 see zīmu; V 65 *b* 11; 64 *b* 40 Šamaš & Ištar çi-it libbi-šu na-am-ra (*i. e.* of Sin); on II 19 *a* 38—9 see Br 9187. II 24 *a-b* 48 (33 *a-b* 28) UD-KA-BAR = nam-ru (together with ellu & ebbu, 46, 47). Br 1775, 7817 (V 23 *f-h* 17), 7806 (V 23, 35); H 27, 584; ZA i 3 *rm*. II 27, 597 la-ax | LAX | nam-ru ‖ nu-u-ru (598) Br 7931. — DT 83, 4 (PINCHES, *Texts*, 15) na-am(? PINCHES pa-xi)-ru nu-ur ša-ma-mi (PSBA xvii, 138 on this text); T^M vii 31 šamnu ellu, š ib-bu, š nam-ru. — In connection with ardu it means also: light of skin, white }hell von Hautfarbe; weiss} >< nišē çal-mat qaqqadi, MEISSNER, 101. VATh 1176, 8—9 ardu nam-ra-am (PEISER, *Vertr.*); KB iv 38 *no* ii 11 (ardāni) nam-ru-tim. — ēnu (ēnā) na-mir-tu(m) *etc.* = a clear, bright eye, often in colophons: II 21 *a* 28; 23 *a* 45; 33 *e-f* 65; 38, 67; 51, 65; D 49, 31; V 30, 40; T^M i 149 *etc.*; written ŠI II LAX-tum, II 51 *no* 2 *R*, colophon 2, *etc.* K 2801 + K 221 + K 2669 *O* 26 ēnā-ša nam-ra-a-te (*var* -ti); 82—8—16, 12 nam-ri ‖ te-lil-tum. — P. N. *e. g.* Nam-ra-am-ša-ru-ur *Rec. Trav.*, xvii 35 (*no* xvi); KB iv 2, 9 Na-[cuneiform sign] (= mà)-ru-um-ili; 196 (*no* xxviii) 3 ana (amēltu) Na-mir-tu(m) = Neb 334.

NOTE. — On namraçīt = askaru = new-moon, see JENSEN, 104 *fol.* *Ibid* also against HOMMEL, PSBA '85—6, 119 *foll* on Nimrod = namraçīt; repeated by HOMMEL, PSBA xv ('93) 291—300; prop. Narūdu (V 21 *b* 30 AN Na-ru-du; III 66 *col* 4, 14 (il) Na-ru-du (ilat) Ištar) = Namra-uddu: a star-god; also xvi ('93) 13—15; see, however, JENSEN, ZA ii 76; 191 *foll.* GESENIUS[12] *s. v.*; BROWN-GESENIUS, 650 under נִמְרֹד. HALÉVY, ZA ii 397 Namra-ud(d)u = Namra-çît = light of the East = נִמְרֹד. On Nimrod compare also BA ii 538 *no* 117; LAGARDE, *Mittheilungen*, i 198. On Nimrod and Nasimaraddash (V 44 *a-b* 26: client of Ninib) see BROWN-GESENIUS, *loc. cit.* KB i 196, 24+26; D^{K} 27; BA i 183—4; *Johns Hopk. Circ.*, XII (My, '93) *no* 96; HOMMEL, *Gesch.*, 164, 175, 417; SAYCE, *Crit. & the Monuments*, 101; HILPRECHT, *Assyriaca* & WINCKLER, *Forschungen*, *passim*.

nâmiru, *nomn?* KB i 12, 10 i-ru-bu na-mi-[ri-šu]-nu; perh also TP vii 101.

namriš, *adv* brightly {glänzend} AV 6041; Neb iv 65 the temple na-am-ri-iš e-pu-uš (1 *sg*); also KB iii (2) 30 *col* 1, 43; Neb iii 60—1 & POGNON, *Wadi-Brissa*, 54 nam-ri-iš; K^{M} 9, 23 ma-xar-ka nam-riš a-dal-lu-ka.

nam'â'ru *2.* IV^{2} 15* i 21 where mu-ši .... u na-ma-ri are used side by side, Br 7905. ZA iii 315, 71 bît na-ma-ri, observatory (S 1894).

namru (?) *2.* II 42 *a-b* 42—43 U-XA-XI-A & U-XA = $^{(šam)}$nam(?)-rum, Br 11825, 11848.

nimēru. II 28 (*e*-)*f* 56 n]i-me-rum, ZA viii 383 (AV 2030 u-me-rum).

namrir(r)u, splendor {Glanz} of the rising stars, *etc.* G §§ 61, 63, 113; GGA '81, 901 (*ad* L^{T} 83); JENSEN, ZK ii 33; BA i 150 all √נמר; DELITZSCH in L^{T} √namaru. AV 6040. KB iv 102—3, 6 $^{(il)}$ Sin il na-ma-ri ... ša lit-bu-šu nam-ri-ri (*cf* K^{M} 46, 15) who is clothed with light. In a hymn to Šamaš (K 3474 i + K 8232 i) 18 nam-ri-ru-ka im-lu-u, ZA iv 8. K 155 *O* 7 ma-lu-u nam-ri-ru-ka. SOMMEL, ZA x 292, 11 ma-lim nam-ri-ir-ru-uš-ša; I 27 *no* 1, 5 nam-ri-ri $^{(il)}$ Marduk. DT 83, 16 çu-bat nam-ri-ir[-ri?] = PINCHES, *Texts*, 15 *no* 4; ZA iv 229, 13. IV^{2} 30* *b* 3—4 çu-bat nam-ri-ir-ri (= IM-GAL-LA, *cf* H 40, 231); Asb i 84 nam-ri-re $^{(il)}$ Ašur u $^{(ilat)}$ Ištar is-xu-pu-šu; vii 75. Šams i 13 who like the sungod nam-ri-ri šit-pu-ru, sends out splendor; Šalm, *Ob*, 6 Sin šar a-gi-e ša-qu-u nam-ri-ri; *cf* TP i 6; Sarg *Khors* 163 ma-lu-u nam-ri-ri; *Ann* 425 (on which see BA iii 192—3 *rm* **); *bull*-inscr. 72: *del* 100 (105) the Anunnaki ina nam-ri-ir-ri-šu-nu uxammaṭu mâtum. Neb ii 53 u-še-piš nam-ri-ri šam-ši. K 133 (H 80) 16 nam-ri-ir-ri ina na-še-e-šu, and when he displays his magnificent power, Br 8455. IV^{2} 18 *no* 3 *O* i 29—30 kak-ku ša nam-ri-ir-ri (= IM-GAL-A); K^{M} 8, 10 eš-te-'-u nam[-ri]-ir-ri-ki, I have sought thy light.

numru *1.* joyfulness, gladness {Freude} AV 6433; II 43 *a-b* 21 nu-um-ru ‖ xu-ud lib-bi; WINCKLER, *Sargon*, 178, 2 nu-mur pâni.

numru *2.* ZA iv 362, 7 nu-mur Ba-bi-li, the interior of B; *cf* II 26, 35 (add, *no* 1) BIT-[cuneiform] = nu-mur (AV 2932; 6427; Br 6266), followed by zig-gur-ra-tum.

namarîtum. IV^{2} 49 *a* 3, see bararîtu, T^{M} i 3.

namrûtu (?) V 65 *b* 21 i-na bu-ni-ka nam-ru-tu, xi-du-tu pa-ni-ka.

NOTE. — KB iii (2) 4, 50 samtu bi-ir na-[cuneiform]-ru-tim (× ZA iv 110, 95) = the *sandu*-stone shining with brilliancy. na-[cuneiform]-ru-tu > namrûtu; *cf* birû (189 *col* 2).

namirtu, (properly *f* of namru, § 65, 7). light, brightness {Licht, Helligkeit} AV 5998. K 155 *O* 3 Sin ša-ki-in na-mir-ti a-na niše; H 75 *O* 11 ša-kin na-mir[-ti]; T^{M} ii 127 (K 2455 *R* 15) ša-kin na-mir-ti a-na $^{(il)}$ A-nun-na-ki. NE IX *col* v 46 (KB vi, 1, 208) na-mir-tu šak-na-at, es entsteht Helligkeit. II 8 *a-b* 7 (K 40 iv) UD-ZAL-LA = na-mi[-ir]-tum, followed by nu-u-ru. Z^{B} 81 reads na-mi-ra-tum, dawn of morning (Br 7906); ZK ii 285 *rm* 2; ZA iii 98—99.

namartu *1.* joyfulness, hilarity {Fröhlichkeit, Heiterkeit}; *pl* II 49 *no* 4, 56 MUL-TAG-GAR-ŠI-A-GUR = na-ma-ra-a-tum ina mâti ibašša; L^{T} 152, AV 5991; ZA v 373.

namurtu *1.* splendor, brightness {Glanz, Helligkeit}. II 54 *no* 1, 18+19 Sin is called ša na-mur-te & ša na-ma-ri.

namurtu *2.* jewels {Schmuck, Geschmeide} K 1221 (1101) *R* 5 ša a-nu-ut bît na(?)-mu-ra-a-te ša šarri (HEBR. x 198); K 660 *O* 13 na-mur (or xar? *q. v.*)-tu ša ^{arax} Ṭebetu kar-ma-tu-u-ni (Hr^{L} 86); K 5464 *R* 19 ... na-mur-tu ina mux-xi-ja na-ça (but *cf* 24).

namru *3.* T. A. (Lo.) 12, 42 ki-na-na ti-eš-ku-nu nam-ru a-na be-ri-šu-nu,

mu-šu-nim; Ber 63, 12 u la-a ji-na-mu-šu, and I will not revolt from thee; Ber 61, 42 i-na-mi-šu (3 *pl*), *cf* 189, 63; 154, 52 u la-a ji-nam-mu-šu but they do not cease (summoning); 52, 7 u la-a aa-na-mu-šu, but I have not departed [from the cause]; 156, 19 u ti-na-ma-šu (and though a brick) be moved; + 22 —3 u a-na-ku la-a i-na-ma-šu (*cf* Lo 57, 17 + 20; Rostow 13 + 15); 58, 40 u ti-na-mu-šu eli-ja and they will desert from me (*cf* Lo 57, 17). DT 363, 1 (is) e]-ri-ni ša na-miš (ZA iv 231).

Q¹ break up, start {aufbrechen} pr ittamuš, usually ittumuš, ittumša, § 101 (BA ii 298 √ שמא). Often in Anp & Šalm in the meaning of moving from (TA or iš-tu), leaving a city or country. Anp iii 14 (twice) at-ta-muš, *var* to at-tu-muš, for which see Anp i 70, 113; ii 31, 33, 34, 39, 51, 60 (*var* a-), 62, 65, 87, 88, 92, 94, 98 (*var* a-tu); iii 5; Šalm, *Ob*, 45, 119, 120, 135, 163; *Mon*, *O* 19, 23, 26 *etc*. at-tum-šu *var* at-tu-muš Anp iii 3 (see 2); a-tu-muš Anp ii 103; iii 8; ii 76, *var* a-tum-ša; it-tu-muš (3 *sg*). Šalm, *Ob*, 164, 168; at-tum-muš Anp iii 5, 9, 15, 28; at-tum (*var* a-tu)-muš Anp i 58; at-tum-ša Anp ii 2, 12; iii 101, 109; Asb viii 100; ix 12 ul-tu (*var* TA) ali at-tu-muš.

ℑ V 45 *col* v 48 tu-nam-maš; K 11148 *R* 14—15 i-da-tu-u-a ma-a-dak-tu u-nam-ma-aš (Hr[L] 242).

ℑ¹ K 774 *R* (kakkab) muštabarrū-mūtānu ut-ta-me-eš (will go); 81—2 —4, 79 *R* 3 (kakkab) *m-m* is-su-ux-ur | ut-ta-me-iš (= ina pa-na-tu-uš-šu .... il-lak) Thompson, *Reports* (√ amašu).

See § 101 note; BA i 408 (>< ZA i 369), 412, Kraetzschmar; and Philippi, *ibid*, ii 381.

Derr. these 2:

nammaštu, every living thing; creature, reptile, beast {Jedes lebende Wesen, Kreatur; Getier} K[M] 32, 10 šik-nat na]?-piš-ti na-maš-ti qaq-qa-ri ta-bar-ri-i; DT 41, 6 b(p)u-ul çêri pu-n]x-ri nam-maš-ti gi-mir nab-ni-ti & *l* 10; see KB vi (1) 42—3, & 360; perh 82 —5—22, 65, 2 gab-šu nam-maš[-tu?] Thompson. II[1] 52 *a* 2 kîma nam-maš-ti aqrabi (also *a* 11) G § 76; Jensen, 156 *fol*. IV² 19 *b* 4 be-el nam-maš-ti (= A-ZA-LU-LU, Br 11702) Z[B] 20; 103; id usually = tênišêti (H 116, 7—8) & amêlûtu, = Z[S] vii 77; also *cf* ZA ix 159 *fol* a-za-lu-lu explained by nam-maš-tum zêr-mandu (zêr-ma-an-tum) & tenišêtum; Lehmann, ii 34; K 2836, 12 (ZK ii 214 *rm* 1).

nammaššû, bustle of animals, animals small and large {Gewimmel von Tieren, Getier, klein und gross}. DT 41, 4 b(p)u-ul çêri [u-ma-am] çêri u nam-maš-še-e [ali ib-nu-u] KB vi (1) 42—3, & see *l* 6. K 120 A *O* 6 when a halo surrounds the moon and Jupiter stands within it šumqu-tim bûli na-maš-še-e ša çêri, there will be a slaughter of cattle & beasts of the field, Thompson, *Reports*; also 83—1—18, 290, 3 šumqu]-tim bu-lum u nam-maš[-še-e]; 82—7—4, 82 *R* 5 he made bu-u-lum ša-ak-ka-an u nam-maš-šu-u (PSBA xx 152 *foll*); IV² 48, 2 (Adad) nam-maš-še-e çêri-šu *etc*., destroys through famine. K[M] 32, 10 .... ru-ki na-maš-šu-u; 27, 10 bu-ul (il) Nergal nam-maš[-še-e qa-tuk-ka ip-qid]. IV² 59 *no* 2 *b* 16 lim-xur-an-ni nam-maš-šu-u ša çêri; 56 *b* 51 a-na pa-an nam-maš-še-e ša çêri (*cf* III 54 *b* 33) pa-ni-ki šuk-ni (J[I-N] 60 *rm* on *ll* 39—52). NE 12, 35 am-me-ni it-ti nam-maš-še-e ta-rap-pu-ud (*var* -da) çêra, why, o Eabani, doest thou chase over the field with the bustlings animals? 11, 1 + 5 nam-maš-še-e mê (9, 41) the reptiles of the waters (?). J[I-N] 47 *rm* 23. K 263 (II 49 *no* 3) *O* 48 MUL-NU-MUŠ-DA = na-maš-šu-u = ilu Adad; V 46 *a-b* 44 = (il) ša-gi-mu, the roarer; Br 2008; Jensen, 140, 148. V 31 *g-h* 24 IT-DAM = na-maš-šu-u : bu-lum, Br 4555, 6635.

V 41 *R* 6 *g-h* û(?)-mu-u = nam-maš-šu-u, ‖ a-lum, Z[B] 103; 82, 5—22, 1048, 5 nam-maš-šu-u ul ša-kin, KB vi (1) 38—9: Gewimmel war noch nicht (in die Stadt) hineingesetzt (& see *l* 38); Zimmern-Gunkel, 419: keine Wohnung war bereitet; Jastrow, *Religion*, 444: conglomeration; Ball, *Light from the East*, 21: no animal crept about.

namašu perhaps cognate of רמש, Gen 44

1, 21 *foll.* Z^B 13; 103; L^T 167 *rm* 1; AV 5993; Pognon, *Wadi-Brissa*, 171; also see Haupt, KAT² 70, 448; ZA iii 37; 57.

namšu (?) III 67 *O* 53 ša nam-še, Z^B 48; IV² 58 iii 36 ra-bu-u kakkē-šu nam-ši-šu bu-a-ni ....

namša. T. A. (Ber.) 28 ii 49—50 na-am-ša šum-šu, called namša; iii 37, 67. W. Max Müller, OLZ ii *no* 4 = Egypt. *nmst*: a bulky vase {eine dicke Vase}; also see BA iv 105—6.

n'ă'm'ă'šu (?). T. A. (Ber.) 28 ii 64 (65) I na-ma-ši (468).

nēmašu. II 23 *e-f* 10 ne-ma-šu ‖ i-çu wood or wooden instrument {ein Holz oder Werkzeug aus Holz} AV 6220 (or qum-ma-šu?).

nam-iš-tum *1.* see kamāru, 3.

nam-iš-tum *2.* V 39 *c-f* 66 nam-iš-tum ša nam-ça-bi.

nimšištu. ZA ix 109 reads V 28 *c-f* 10 nim-ši-iš-tum ‖ abbūnu > ana būna & piqāma; or num-ši-iš-tum; see ki-šištum; AV 6225; Br 7971; see GGA '98, 813—14.

nammušu. in Asb ii 21 illik nam-mu-ši-šu (Winckler, *Forsch.*, i 246); read NAM (= šīmat) mu-ši-šu, see mūšu; Jäger, BA ii 298 says: nammūšu halte ich für ein infinitives Nomen vom Nifal, mit der Bedeutung: "Weggang, Tod"; whence the *adj* nammušišu; V 41 *no* 3 *R* 49 ..... XI = na-mu-ši-šu (50, ... DUN [ZK i 124 *rm* 2]; 51, ... BAD) preceded by na-mu-ši-ša-tu. Jensen, KB ii 167: perhaps "Blut, Ader".

nimittu, literally: foundation {Gründung} √עמד. D^{Par} 215; Flemming, *Neb*, 47; Tiele, *Gesch.*, 447; BA i 176; ZA iv 309—10; AV 6226—29. Ni-mi-it-ti-Bēl name of the outer wall (šalxū) of Babylon; Neb iv 67 *foll.* Pognon, *Wadi-Brissa*, 142, 171. II 50 viii/vii *a* 26 BAD (= dūr) ni-mit AN-EN-LIL = šal-xu-u-šu; 29 [BAD] ni-mit AN-ZUR-UD (*i. e.* Marduk) šal-xu-u (ZDMG 58, 659—60). II 52 *a* 57 ni-mit-ti-šarri^ki; 53 *a* 31 ER (= ālu) ni-mit ^(ilat) Ištar; I 49 *d* 20 ni-mit-Bēl šal-xu-šu (*i. e.* of Babylon).

ni(or çal?)mādu, nimēdu, *f* **nimattu** (or çalmattu, KAT² 216 *rm* ††; Flemming, *etc.*), with prefix ^(iç) = something belonging to the furniture of the king's palace. Streck, ZA xiii 72 ni-mat-tu, Bettgestell; BA i 176 armchair or litter {Sessel oder Sänfte} AV 7175. Šamš iv 31 eršu šarrūti-šu ni-mat šarrūti-šu ni-çir-ti ēkallišu, KB i 187 the royal litter. Scheil, *Šamš* reads çal-lat, √çalalu, s'étendre, repose; a sort of canopy. Sarg *Ann* 339 ^(iç) ni-mit-du xurāçi; 291 *no* 22 ^(iç) ni-ma-at-tu, *no* 33 ^(iç) ni-mid kaspi (see Winckler, *Sargon*); *Khors* 131: Merodach-Baladan left behind among the royal furniture the ^(iç) ni-mat-ti xurāçi. Anp ii 123 paššūru *etc.* ^(iç) ni-mat-tu šinni ^pl xurāçi (ux-xu-zu-ti) which, together with other things formed the ni-çir-ti ēkallišu; iii 68 ^(iç) ni-mat-ti ^pl (+ 74). III 6 (Anp *Mo*, *R*) 40 ^(iç) ni-ma-ta-a-te. I 35 *no* 1, 20 ^(iç) ni-mat-ti šinni ein Bett aus Elfenbein, KB i 190—1; III 66 *col* 11, 18 + 19.

nu-ma-at bīt abišunu: das Inventar des väterlichen Hauses, Meissner, 79—80; 100, 11—12; 108. by-form of nūptu, *q. v.*

namtāru, fate {Geschick} id NAM-TAR *e. g.* $Z^Š$ iv 79; AV 6045; Br 2110; ZA i 193. According to many a compound of NAM + TAR = fate decider. K 246 (H 84—5) i 50—3 nam-ta-ru mar-çu, namtaru dan-nu | *n* ša amēla la u-maš-ša-ru | *n* la a-çu-u | *n* la te-bu-u, *n* lim-nu, always = NAM-TAR, ‖ as(š)akku; Hommel, *Sum. Lesest.*, 215. IV² 1* iii 39—40 nam-ta-ru (= NAM-TAR) a-šak-ku ša māta i-na-as-sa-šu (*var* ina-q[a-ru?]); *ibid* 7—8 the evil "seven" are mārē šipri ša nam-ta-ru (*var* -ri) šu-nu, Br 5943; 16 *a* 21—22 nam-ta-ru lim-nu; 27 *no* 6 *R* 9—10 nam-ta-ru a-šak-ku kab-tum (see *l* 1); 29 *no* 1 *b* 21—22 nam-ta-ru ašakku sa-m[a-nu], *cf* 31—32; *no* 2 *a* 3—4 nam-ta-ru lim-nu ša a-na na-piš[-ti amēli .....]. II 42 *no* 5, *O* 34—5 mentions three plants NAM-TAR ardi & išdu NAM-TAR ardi, ZK ii 215. K 4152 i 5—6; K 165, 39; H 14, 169; K^M 12, 42; K 161, 1 ^(iç)

---

nu-um-tu. Camb 117, 8 to be corrected to nu-up-tu (*q. v.*) WZKM iv 127. ∼ numitiu, J^{u} 63 *rm* 4, see nubattu.

nam-tar, ZK ii 4. V 50 *a* 37—38 ša nam-ta-ru iç-ba-tu-šu.

[il] Namtar is the sukkallu of Allatu, IV 31 *O* 65—66; *R* 30, 31, 35; J^{W} 71, 72; J^{L-N} 41: die Pest = [il] Nam-tar. For [il] Nam-tar see also $Z^{\check{S}}$ iv 81, *etc.*; NE XII *passim*; JEREMIAS, *Hölle und Paradies bei den Babyloniern*, 17: der Pestgott. K^{M} 1, 49. IV^{2} 21 *no* 1 B, *R* 18—19 see namçaru; 1 ii 52 al-ti nam-ta-ri; i 5—7 nam-ta-ru ma-ru na-ram (il) Bêl. KB vi (1) 74 *no* 1, 7 Nam-ta-a-ra šu-uk-k[a-l]a-[š]a of Erìškigal (= Allatu); also *ll* 8, 10; *no* 2, 6 Nam-taru (+ 10), + 12 Nam-ta-a-ru; *R* i 33 iq-ta-bi a-na Nam-ta-ri; 78 ii 9 (il) Nam-ta-ra ça-a-bi-šu.

NOTE. — 1. HALÉVY, *Rev. Sém.*, iv 344 √נתר = נזר, Eth *matára* cut, cut off.

2. KB vi (1) 280—1 *col* iii 10 + 14 (end) namtâru = Seuche; *ibid* 12 + 16 a-sa-ku occurs; 282 *rm* says: Vielleicht ist murçu jede Krankheit, namtâru dagegen eine tötliche.

3. *P* 487 *col* 2 lines 16—17 read šimta-šu li-lam-min & see ZIMMERN, GGA '98, 821.

4. On namtar = μοῖρα, & namtar = νόσος see ZA i 188.

(ilat) **Nanâ**, a goddess {eine Göttin} written Na-na-a-a, Na-na-a & Na-na, § 13; AV 6049; Br 1594; 3049—51. Na-na-a, KNUDTZON, 102 *O* 3 (+ 6), *R* (3 +)5; 103 *O* 3 + 4; $Z^{\check{S}}$ ii 156; T^{M} v 59. L^{4} iii 12 bêltu ša A-ga-de Na-na-a. KB iii (1) 130—1, *no* vii 3 Ana (?) (ilat) Ninna, ša (ilat) Na-na-a-a; JASTROW, *Religion of Babylonia and Assyria*, 81, 82; *Rev. d'Assyr*, ii 12. On Nanâ of the Gudean cylinders see PRICE, AJSL xvii 51; LEHMANN, i 140—41 on pronunciation (Νάναια); D^{Par} 222, 247; ZK ii 309—10; HOMMEL, VK 262; 386. Mentioned as consort of Nebo, with Tašmêtu; K 523, 6 (Hr^{L} 334) [il] Nabû u (ilat) Na-na-a; also K 476, 6 (Hr^{L} 54) (ilat) Na-na-a u (ilat) Tašme-tum; K 1239, 4 (Hr^{L} 219); K 81, 4 *etc.* BA i 191. Asb vi 107 (ilat) Na-an-na-a who 1635 years ago had been taken away I brought back to her temple at Erech, D^{K} 68; LEHMANN, i 71—2; JASTROW, *Religion*, 202 on Nanâ, the Ishtar of Erech, meaning: "lady" par excellence. II 59 *R* 2, (ilat) Na-na-u (*cf* also Br 10829); I 43, 21. V 56, 48 (ilat) Na-na-a with other gods mentioned as gods ša (mât) Na-mar. TP III, *Platt.-Nimr.* (1) 15—16 Na-na-a be-lit Bâbili, LEHMANN, i 95, 98. Nabd 243, 12 P. N. (sal, ilat) Na-na-a-ki-ši-rat, Neb 265, 12; Cyr 252, 6 (ilat) Na-na-a-ki-li-li-uçrî; 254 (beg.) ina muxxi Ri-mut (ilat) Na-na-a, BA iii 394; KB iv 176 *col* 3, 10 (ilat) Na-na-a-karabi. Na-na-a-bêl-uçur PEISER, *Babyl. Vertr.*, *nos* 11; 12; 18. *Rec. Trav.*, xx 205 *col* i, 1 (ilat) Na-na-a bêltu çir-ti; 6, called ta-lim-mat (il) Šam-ši; iii 1 + 3. IV^{2} 46 *c* 5 (= K 79; Hr^{L} 266) ilat Na-na-a; K 528 *O* 6 (Hr^{L} 269); K 81 *O* 4 (Hr^{L} 274). I 65 *b* 34 parakku Na-bi-um u Na-na-a bêlê-e-a (*cf* 28); III 66 *col* 11, 26 (il) Çir-gal (ilat) Na-na-a; *cf col* 8, 32; 9, 14; K 3600 *R* 13 da-lil šar-ra-ti (ilat) Na-na-a; KNUDTZON, 102 *O* 3 (6); *R* (3) 5; 103 *O* 3, 4; 101 *O* 3. V 46 *a-b* 10 MUL-BAL-UR-A = (ilat) Na-na-a, Br 295. same id in 45 = kakkab bal-tum. KB iv 314 *foll*, 5 (ilat) Na-na-a (+ 32); 16 + 21 mâr ša (ilat) Na-na-a-iddin (P. N., masc.); on compounds with Nanâ see AV 6051—54.

(ilat) **bêlit Ni-na-a.** III 66 *col* 11, 15; II 39 *a* 63—4; KB iii (1) 20 *rm* 4; SAYCE, *Hibbert Lectures*, 116 *rm* 1; 266. On (ilat) Ninâ see also LE GAC, ZA vii 142, who with Sayce, maintains that Ninâ = Nanâ, both being dialectic forms derived from NIN = bêltu, lady. AV 6238. K 3600, a hymn to Ninâ she is called xirat [il] Mu-'u-a-ti. K^{M} 61, 21. JASTROW, *Religion*, 86—88 on KB iii (1) 107, 109. On Ninâ of the Gudean Cylinders see PRICE, AJSL xvii 50—1.

(al) **Ni-nu(na)-a** = Nineveh. II 53 *no* 2 *O* 2, capital of the Assyrian Empire. H 19, 332; § 9, 237. I 7 F 13 (al) Ni-na-a maxaz be-lu-ti-ja. id ER-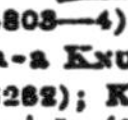-KI V 23 *a-c* 6 (AV 6238; Br 4803—4); Anp i 101 (Br 4802). (âl) Ni-na-a KNUDTZON, 69 *O* 11; *cf* II 63, 12 (AV 6282); K 614 *R* 1—2 la-a ina ma-çar-te | ša (al) Ni-nu-a (Hr^{L} 175; WINCKLER, *Forsch.*, ii 310—11); S 747 *O* 7 Ni-na-a[ki]. T. A. (Lo.) 10, 13 (Tušratta's letter to Amenophis III) speaks of the moving of the statue (çalam) of Ištar ša (al) Ni-i-na-a bêlit mâtâte to Egypt; also see III 17, 62; Asb x 51; K

4629 *R* 8 (Br 4805, 5865, 7350). AV 6261; D^{Par} 260; BA iii 87 *foll*; 107 *foll*; 107 *rm* * against TIELE, *Gesch.*, 84; 90. LEHMANN, i 137 *foll*, 140, 141; ii 112 (on Ni-nu-u-a), 137: "ich halte die alte Herleitung vom Stamme נוה: Stätte, Niederung für die richtige"; JENSEN, ZA viii 240: Ninua perhaps Hypokoristikon of Nina = Ištar (so HILPRECHT); but see JEREMIAS, BA iii 107 *rm* * (end): "vielleicht, fruchtbarer Weideplatz". On etymology see also HEBR. ix 150 *rm* 1.

NIN — *a*) in NIN-šum-šu, NIN-šip-ru, *etc.* read mimma (*q. v.*) AV 6236. — *b*) = bêl or bêltu (AV 6236, 6287) KB iii (1) 25 *rm* †† in expressions like NIN-A-ZU NE XII *col* i, 29; ii, 20 (KB vi, 1, 258—9: mother of Ninazu, AV 6239); iii 1, 8, 16. Br 10087 AN-NIN = bêltu; IV^2 19 *b* 7—8 = bi-el-tum; 1 *b* 27—8 (see bêltu). IV^2 15 *b* 36; Allat (or Bêlit) consort of Nergal (*q. v.*) or Ninazu (Br 11100; WZKM xii 64 *rm* 1; J^w 66; PINCHES, RP^2 ii 133 *rm* 1); NIN-SUN NE XII *col* ii 27, a female deity. See also Ninib(p), Ningal, Ningirsu, *etc.*

NI-NI. V 34 *b* 52 = ilâni; see NI = ilu S^a i 20; IV^2 26 *b* 62—3; 59 *no* 2 *b* 5, 9; *Rec. Trav.*, ii 4 ana NI-NI; also KB i 12, 5.

nannû (nanniu). Sarg *Cyl* 56 na-an-nu (*var* -ni)-uš-šu-un la muš-pi-e-lu at-ta-ki-il-ma; AV 6063; KB ii 48—9 their word, as LYON, *Sargon*, 72; Z^B 23; 66 ‖ annu √חנן grace, favor {Gnade}; ZDMG 48, 199 : 4.

nûnu *1*. fish {Fisch} id XA; *pl* XA-XI-A *del* 117 (124); § 9, 33: used as a determinative after names of fish. D^B 5; ZK i 161 § 10; ZDMG 27, 706 *fol*; §§ 31 & 64. H 36, 879 XA-A = nu-u-nu; II 7 *g-h* 25; V 39 *g-h* 29 XA = nu-nu, Br 11821; S^b 200 a-rum ša nûni see âru, 2 (*p* 90 *col* 2) Br 4677; Sarg *Cyl* 21 ki-ma nu-u-ni. IV^2 26 *a* 25 ina?] i-ta-an-ni ša nu-nu (= XA) ul uç-çu-u; id also II 62 *c-d* 45 (Br 11841); IV^2 59 *no* 2 *b* 15. I 65 *a* 9; 66 *c* 13 nu-u-nim mentioned together with iç-çu-ru, *etc.* See also bu'aru (*p* 139); V 50 *b* 41 (40) see bašalu, note; also *cf* nidudu. II 40 *no* 2, 18 TAG-XA = aban nu-u-ni, Br 11822; 2644, *i. e.* os sepiae, ZA xiv 356. *Adapa*-legend (KB vi 94) 3 a-na bi-i-t[u nu-ni]-e; *cf* 96 *R* 17 a-na bi-it nu-ni (15 nu-ni a-ba-ar), see maçalu, *p* 572. Creat.-*frg* IV 137 see mašdû, and add: BALL, *Light from the East* says: mašdû from Sum. MAŠ + DU = çabîtu (gazelle); NU-NU = šîru (flesh), thus translates: he rent (her) like the body of a gazelle in twain; but see JENSEN, KB vi (1) 343. isix nûni ZA vii 192; *cf* II 27 *c-d* 49; i 65 *b* 29 i-si-ix nu-u-nim. II 51 *a-b* 40 nâr nu[-nu] name of a canal; (= XA in *a*) followed by nâr iç-ç[ur]; V 51 *b* 75—6 a sacrificial gift: nu-na iç-çu-ra si-mat ap-pa[-ri]. — As the twelfth sign of the Zodiac nunu is written  *i. e.*  , JENSEN, 81 *foll*, 314.

NOTE. — 1. BALL, PSBA xx 10—11 explains nûnu (נוּן, fish,) from √נון strictly = teeming or multiplying [see MUSS-ARNOLT, *Babylonian Months*, 9]; from this same root he derives also Ninâ^{ki} Sarg *Cyl* 54 *etc.* = Hebr נִין, offspring, Gen 21 : 23; D^H 20.

2. P. N. Nu-nu-a, son of Nadin-aplu; PEISER, *Babyl. Vertr.*, lxxxvi, 11.

nûnu *2*. II 19 *b* 65—66 nu-na (= NUN, Br 2627, 2631; AV 6435, 6609) ša si-ha ab-ra-šu, JENSEN, 343: must be a kind of spear (?) the common weapon of Ninib. V 30 *g-h* 30 NUN = nu-nu (II 7 *g-h* 26; AV 6435, Br 2627); 31, NUN-UD-KA-BAR = nu-un-nu (written $\frac{nu}{nu}$) Br 1971, AV 6442. II 57 *c-d* 34 AN-NUN-NIR = $^{(il)}$ Ninib ša qab-li, AV 6441.

nunu. II 28 *a* 16 nu-un-u ‖ pa-aš-šu-ru (*q. v.*) AV 6436.

nunnu, chapel? {Kapelle?} S^P II 987 *O* 15 the king of Elam (is there) who has built Ɪ nun-nu (the chapel) of Ê-sag-gil u . . . (*Jour. of Trans. of Victor. Institute*, 29, 53).

ninnu. II 49 *no* 5, 68 . . . . NA = DUP ni-in-nu, AV 6278.

nînu, nîni (> anînu, *etc.* §§ 39; 32 *a* β) we, us {wir, uns} §§ 40; 55. K 115 (IV^2 46 *a*) *R* 15 ni-i-ni; K 515, 15 ni-i[-ni]; H 119 *O* 24—5 ni-nu (= ME-EN-NE-EME-SAL) ina âli-šu i ni-il-lik-šu, as for us, let us go to his city, ZA viii 121; ix 121 *foll*; Br 10409. *Etana*-legend (K 2527 + K 1547) *O* 38 (end) i ni-ku-la ni-nu, let us eat (BA ii 393—4; KB vi 106

—7); K 3473 + 79, 7—8, 296 + Rm 615 *R* (*i. e.* Creat.-*frg* III) 128 la ni-i-di ni-i-ni, KB vi 20—21; 4, 15 urruxiš ni-i-nu . . . . i ni-il-lik; 98, 25 ni-nu minā nippussū (BA ii 421; 438). P. N. Ištu-Adad-a-ni-nu & Ištu-Adad-ni-ni, Eponym of 679, KB i 207. — T. A. (Lo.) 41, 12 + 27 ni-i-nu; 46, 3 ni-e-nu; 3, 11 *etc.* ni-nu; 82, 4 ni-i-nu-u; 41, 29 + 83 ni-i-nu-ma; Ber. 54, 33 ni-nu-um.

ninum, ni-nu-um, ni-nu-mi-šu, ni-nu-šu, when, at the day (, time) when {als; am Tage, zur Zeit, als}. Ni-nu KB iii, 1, 130 *col* 1, 1, followed by ni-nu-šu (13) = when . . . ., at that time. Neb i 40 ni-nu-um; I 65 *a* 8; V 34 *a* 11; KB iii (2) 46, 22; I 51 *no* 1 *a* 10; & *no* 2 *a* 7 (followed by i-na ū-mi-šu-ma, 11); KB iii (2) 56 *col* 1, 15. I 66 *c* 27 ni-nu-šu at that time {damals}; V 34 *c* 5 ni-nu-mi-šu; KB iii (2) 50 *col* 3, 13; I 51 *no* 1 *a* 27; ZK ii 24 *rm* 1; ZA ii 183. ni-nu KB iii (2) 62 *col* 1, 17 (when); *l* 25 ni-nu-mi-šu = then, at that time. ni-nu-mi-šu-um KB iii (2) 6 *no* 2 *col* 1, 10; Scheil, *Rec. Trav.*, xvi 185, 6 + 13 ni-nu-um, followed by ni-nu-mi-šu. AV 6260. √ ēnu time {Zeit}, ZK ii 24; Flemming, *Neb*, 30 √ ענה; see also ZA ii 64; Amiaud, *Jour. Asiat.*, '79, *p* 241 (from ūmu); ZK i 81.

ninū = נִינְיָא, a gardenplant {Gartengewächs} D^{Pr} 84 *rm* 2; V 39 *g-h* 28 (= II 7 *g-h* 24) U-KUR-RA (šim-bi-ri-da) SAR (u-ku-ra ni-sig-ga-a) = ni-nu-u, Br 6057; id also T^M v 30 (see *ibid p* 140). ZA iv 293 i 19 ni-nu-u SAR.

nēnu. V 28 *g-h* 56 ne-nu (55, qar-nu) = u-lap lu-ub-bu-tim.

Ninib, name of a god {Name eines Gottes}, god of the city of Nippur, son of the old Bēl of Nippur, K 133, 5 *foll* (il) Nin-ib šarru mâru (il) Bēl. According to Jeremias, = Lord of Ib; formerly read Adar (AV 147), or Nindar. Br 11096; AV 6241. Occurs first in the inscr. of Ašur-rēš-iši (KB i 12, 6 i-na siq-ri AN-NIN-IB) 1150 B. C.; the mighty one among the gods; Jastrow, *Religion*, 213 *foll*. According to Jensen, 457—75 he is: die Ost-, Frühsonne. ZA vi 112. Ninib and Ningirsu are closely related to Nergal in early Babylonian times (Jeremias); according to Hommel they are idential, KB iii (1) 20 *rm* 4. Ninib is also identified with Anu, Jensen, 130 *fol*; 191 *fol*; III 69 *a* 5; II 54, 4. — (il) Nin-ib KB iii (1) 110—111, 11 (Xammurabi); I 29, 1—25 (incl.) is a hymn to Ninib (KB i 174—79; Jensen, 466—71; RP^2 i 9—10; ZA ii 317); K^M 2, 25 a-ša-rid ilāni qu-ra-du; K 2333 *R* 16 called bēl kakkē; on kakku in connection with Ninib see PSBA xxi, 135 § 46. — Asb i 17 (KB ii 154 *rm* 6); V 56, 39 calls him šar šamê u erçitim; *Rec. Trav.*, xix 57 *no* 174 = (il) Nin-ib ra-xi-im gi-ri-im. A hymn to Ninib is published in Abel & Winckler, *Texte*, 60 *fol*; H 79 *fol* (= K 133; Hommel, VK 404; PSBA xvi 227 *fol*) called often qar-ra-du; šar-ru ma-ru ša (il) Bēl. TP i 11 speaks of him as qar-du ša-giš lim-ni u a-a-bi (also see vi, 58, 61, 76; vii 6 (*var* AN-BAR, so also Anp i 1, 10; Asb ix 84), 37; Sarg *Cyl* 61 (il) Nin-ib mu-kin te-me-en a-du(-uš)-ši. *Del* 15 (17) gu-zalû-šu-nu (of the gods) (il) Nin-ib; 98 (103) il-lak (il) Nin-ib; 164 (176) (il) Nin-ib pāšu ēpušma iqabbi. Written (il) BAR $Z^{\check{S}}$ iv 43, 75; K^M 50, 29; 55, 2; III 66 *O a* 20, *d* 26, *e* 27 (Br 1778); T^M vi 2 (il) IB; IV^2 23, 1 *R* iii 11—12 AN-IB-A-KID = be-lum (il) Nin-ib, Br 10492. V 37 *a-c* 18 nin-nu-u = 50 = (il) Nin-ib (17 = (il) Bēl); KB iii (1) 23 *rm* *† on Ur-Bau iii 6. — On Ninib = (il) maš-maš see mašmašu. S^c 1, 1 (H 13, 194) [ma-aš] | MAŠ | ma-a-šu | (il) Nin-ib, ZA i 390; ii 203—4; Br 1778. II 57 *c-d* 17—76 contains idd & readings for Ninib: 17, (il) Nin-ib = (il) Nin-ib ša pi (Br 1096, III 67 *c-d* 63)-riš-ti; 18, = AN-AG; 19 + 20, see nāb(p)ū, Br 11098 *fol*; 21, AN-EN-KUR-KUR = (il) Nin-ib (Br 2892); 22, = be-lum še-ix-ši-u (?); 23, AN-EN-TUR-DA = (il) Nin-ib ça-bit EŠ-BAR ilāni; 24, AN-XAL-XAL-LA = (il) Nin-ib; 26, AN-ME-MAX = (il) N. (Br 10390); 28, AN-KA-LUM-MA = (il) N.; 29, a-ni-ku = a-ni-xu; 30, AN-ID-KAL-MAX = (il) N. bēl e-mu-qi, Br 6597; 1033; 31, AN(u-ra-aš)IB = (il) N. ša ud-da-zal-e (*cf* II 59 *a-c* 10), Br 10479; 32, AN(u-rum) APIN = (il) N. ša al-li (Pinches: of planting, fertility; *cf* III 67 *c-d* 64 AN-

IB = (il) N. ša al-li, Br 10479); 33, AN-ŠAR-ŠAR (*i. e.* 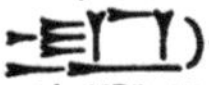 [cuneiform sign])-RI = (il) N. ša na-aš-b(p)an-ti (III 67 *c-d* 65 AN-ŠAR-ŠAR (*i. e.* [cuneiform sign])-RA = (il) N. ša na-aš-pa-ti, Br 8274); 34, AN-NUN-NIR = (il) N. ša qab-li (III 67 *c-d* 66 AN-NU-NIR = il N. ša me-ix-ri; JENSEN, 343—4 & nûnu, weapon; K^{M} 27, 1 & *var*); 35, AN (ti-iš-bak) ŠUX = il N. ša ram (III 67 *c-d* 67 ra-am)-ku-ti, god of libation, Br 3022, KB vi (1) 44 : 20; 365 (& 441—2) Gott des sich Waschens; 36, AN-ŠU (šu-ša-na-bi) [cuneiform sign] = (il) N. ša qar-ra-di, Br 7230; 37, AN-AŠ-TU-[cuneiform sign]-PI-NU = AN-ZA-[cuneiform sign]-[cuneiform sign]-AN-MAB-TAB-[cuneiform sign], Br 11761; 38, AN-LU-LU = the same; 39, AN-KU-KU = AN-NIN-[cuneiform sign]-TIN-AN-BAR, Br 11103; 40, AN-SAG-KUD = il Nin-ib (II 37, 31; JENSEN, 136; 191; which id also = Anu, III 69 *a-b* 5, Br 11097); 41, AN zi-za-nu, 42, AN-ra-bi (iç)gu-za (Br 6376), and 43, AN-LA-LAL(?)-ra-bi = il Ninib ina SU; 47, AN-A-DA-E-NE; 48, AN-ŠU-ŠI-NA-AK, 49, AN-DA-AK-BA-AK, all three = il N. ina Elamti, Br 11555, 7225, 6665; 50, see Br 3874, same id as ûmu eb-bu-u (V 16 *e-f* 47) & (il) Šam-ši in IV^{2} 19 *a* 47—8, Br 7828; 54, AN z(ç)i-ir-ku (AV 2995, Br 2369); 55, AN šad-da-ri (Br 7413); 57, Br 1211 & V 44 *c-d* 36 il Nin-ib a-ša-rid-su-nu = III 67 *e* 24 & II 60 *a-b* 13; 61, AN a-bu-ub la-ap (?) Br 11577; 63, Br 14430; 65, Br 11007 & III 68 *g* 21; 66, AN lil-lu (Br 6700); 68, Br 4614, same id = Nabû e-muq li-i-ti; 70, AN-ZA-[cuneiform sign] [cuneiform sign], Br 11761; 74, AN-NIN-GIR-SU (Br 10994; II 59 *d-f* 26); 76, Br 12238—9, Z^{B} 15, JENSEN, 461—2 on AN-UT-GAL-LU = Sturmsonne. — III 67 *c-d* 68 il Nin-ib ša qu-ul-ti (√qâlu?), same id in II 57 *c-d* 64; Br 3007, 3045; *cf* II 60 *a-b* 10; III 67 *a-b* 54 AN-AMÊL = il Nin-ib, Br 12904. — III 68 *g-h* 17; 25—30 where Ninib's daughter, consort, sister, messenger & servant seem to be mentioned. — II 59 *a-c* 7 AN-[cuneiform sign]-LU-A & 8, AN-[cuneiform sign]-KAL-A = il Nin-ib = il MAŠ, Br 8832; 8820; 11096; *cf* IV^{2} 21* *no* 2 *R* 8—9.

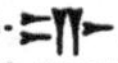

Ninib was one of the names of Saturn, JENSEN, 136 *foll.* — II 57 *a-b* 50—55 we have in *b* il Ninib and in *a*, 50, MUL-LU-BAT (Br 10709, same id = bibbu), 51, MUL-NIN-A-ZU, Br 11101; 52, MUL-KAK-SI-DI tar-ta-xu Br 5279; 53, MUL-ID-XU-ZA-[cuneiform sign] [cuneiform sign] (Br 6565); 54, AN-NIN-GIR-SU-AN-KA-DI, Br 10996; 55, see Br 4002. — IV^{2} 33 *col* iv (end) 4 month Tammûz = ša qu-ra-du il Ninib (WINCKLER, *Forsch.*, ii 267—8 on this text). — zikir (il) Ninib peasant {Bauersmann} = kiçir (il) Ninib, J^{I-M} 46 *rm* 16 on NE 8, 35; 9, 4; but KB vi, 1, 121: eine Heerschaar Ninibs. On Ninib as Ningirsu = god of agriculture see T^{M} viii 78; JENSEN, 199 *rm* 1; 239. — On compounds with Ninib see AV 6242—59; BEZOLD, *Catalogue*, 2185—6.

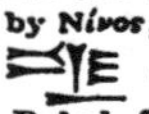

On reading and etymology see HOMMEL, *Expos. Times*, April '98, 330 *col* 1 *rm* 1 (there is no Assyro-Babyl. Adar); PSBA xix 134 § 42 pronunciation Ninib proved by *Nίνος*; 312 *fol*: once written AN-NIN-[cuneiform sign] (*i. e.* TUM = IB) PINCHES, *Inscr. Babyl. Tablets*, 61 *no* 18, 1; + 66. Also Bu 88—5—12, 210 AN-NIN-IB (= TUM) a-bi, MEISSNER, *no* 95 who however reads Bel-tum a-bi = Bêltis is my father. HOMMEL, PSBA xxi 168—9 discusses a cylinderseal which reads AN-NIN-IN = *Nίνος*, which may be = Ninib; but PINCHES, *ibid*, believes NIN to be the name, & IN only a phonetic complement. On the other hand, the reading Adar is defended by C. H. W. J(OHNS), PSBA xix, 79. Of special importance is JEREMIAS' article in ROSCHER's *Ausführliches Lexikon der .... Mythologie*, iii 364—9. Also see PINCHES, *Jour. of Trans. of Victoria Institute*, 28, 17—18. — For the pronunciation of the name in Ašurbanipal's time see perhaps Asb i 105 Pu-kur-ni-ni-ip, BA i 353 *no* 15. — On (al) Bît-Nin-ib in T. A. (Ber) 106, 13—5 = And now, indeed, the city of the land whose name is Jerusalem, *Bît Ninib*, see HAUPT, *Independent*, (New York) 12 Ja. '99 = temple of the Israelitish god of war and thundershowers; see also T. A. (Lo) 12, 31—2, "where, however, it must be a sanctuary further north" (HAUPT) — the Assyrian scribe substituted the name of the Assyrian deity Ninib for the Canaanitish Jahweh. On this text see also ZIMMERN, ZA vi 262—3; PINCHES, PSBA xvi ('94) 225—29. T. A. (Ber) 73, 39 Abd-Nin-ib. See also MUSS-ARNOLT, *Expositor*, Dec. 1900, *pp* 422, 423.

nannabu, shoot, offspring, sprout, progeny {Spross, Leibesfrucht, Nachkommenschaft} ZDMG 28, 135; D^H 65; D^{Pr} 75 *rm* 2; 83 *rm* 2; 114; § 65, 81*a*; BA i 176. III 43 iii 30 may the gods take away na-an-nab-šu; IV^2 12 *R* 33—4 his name, his seed, his offspring | ki-im-ta-šu na-an-nab-šu (= LI-LI-A) . . . lixalliq. KB iii (2) 68—9 *no* 13 *col* ii 12—3 *etc.* see zêru (*p* 295 *col* 1); II 44 *a-b* 70 TI = na-an-n[a-bu??] Br 1703. LEHMANN, S^1 22 šum-šu zē]r-šu pi-ir-i-šu na-an-na-bu-šu may Nebo destroy; *cf* III 41 ii 38 š. z. pi-ri-'i-šu na-an-nab-šu; also KB iv 86 *col* ii 17; PINCHES, *Texts*, 16 *no* 4 *R* 5 see ma'adu, 1 Š (*p* 505 *col* 1). Sm 2052 *O* (dupl. of K 2040 = II 29 *no* 3) 17 *foll* ni-ip-rum, a-ru, tu-ça-tum, pa-a-ar, na-an-na-bu, *etc.* as ‖ of zi[-ru].

ninnabaku (wr. ša-na-ba-ku) > nin-na-bi (wr. ša-na-bi) forty {vierzig} semiticized šinipu (*q. v.*) HOMMEL, PSBA xxi 115.

nangugu (= nâgugu = na'gugu) see nagagu 27. II 36 *g-h* 32 ŠA (= LIB)-IB-BA = na-an-gu-gu; II 20 *c-d* 39; AV 6058; Br 8034; BA i 181.

nangigu (?) perh II 20 *d* 31 na]-an-gi-gu followed by nu]-ug libbi; see nagagu.

(ilat) **NIN-GAL** (AV 6264) = Nikkal (*q. v.*) = bêltu rabîtu, consort of Sin. K^M 1, 31 (Ištar is called the firstborn of Sin, the offspring of Nin-gal), JENSEN, 14 *rm* 3.

Ningirsu, *i. e.* lord of Girsu, the political & religious metropolis of the Patesi of Lagash; called the mighty warrior & son of god EN-LIL-LA = Bêl, DE SARZEC, pl. viii of the Ur-bau inscr. (KB iii, 1, 18—9); see also JENSEN, KB iii, 1, 11—12 *rm* 7 & *passim*. Patron deity of the royal house of the period of Gudea & husband of Bau. PRICE, AJSL xvii 49; AV 6268; Br 10994. Later, he was identified with Ninib, the warrior, II 57 *c* 74; peasants were called servants of Ningirsu (see "Ninib") JENSEN, 199 *rm* 1; 239. III 66 ii 21 (il) Nin-gir-su; vii 2 (+ 12), PSBA xxi, 118 *fol.* V 16 *c-f* 39; II 56, 46; II 66, 44; 61, 64; $Z^{\check{S}}$ iv 43 + 80; viii 18.

nindû, if {wenn}. VATh 244 i 13 i-gi-in-zu = ni-in-du-u, ZA ix 159; ZIMMERN, *ibid*, 110 > nimdû √medû (see *p* 514 *col* 1); amplified to **nindêma** = min-dêma, OLZ ii *no* 5 *col* 157. K 13 *R* 3 nin-di-e-ma šarru bêlija i-qab-bi; 8—9 nin-di-e-ma .... ip-pu-šu-ma (if they will bestir themselves, JOHNSTON).

NOTE. — On mindêma *etc.* see BOISSIER, PSBA xxi 107 § 2 against ZIMMERN; & *cf* piqâ-ma

nindabû = nidabû (*q. v.*).

nandi, see 27 of nadû & HOMMEL, *Sum. Lesest.*, 123—4 (= ABEL & WINCKLER, *Texte*, 60) *R* 13 (end) ana lu-li-e na-an-di. The same verb perhaps also in *Rec. Trav.*, xx 202 *no* xl 12—13 ib-bi an-nu-u-te u ni-en-di, 'il a dit ces choses et nous étions présents' (or √medû?).

nindanu. Such & such classes of priests šu-par it-xu-zu nin-da-an-šu-un (*i. e.* of the gods) la-mid pi-ri'š'-ti *etc.* ma-xaršun (ukîn) Sarg *Khors* 158; AV 6270; √nadanu (??). II 7 *e-f* 27—8 . . . (...ig) ZU & . . . (...da-na?) NA = nin-da-nu; BA i 163 *no* 4; 176; ZDMG 43, 199.

nindanâqu, with prefix GI *i. e.* qanû measuring-rod {Messrohr}; HILPRECHT, *OBI*, i 33 *col* ii 25 i-na (qan) ninda-na-qu umandida mindiâtu (so read KB iii, 2, 4). IV^2 14 *no* 3, 7—8 Nebo mut-ta-bel (qan) nin-da-na-ki (= GI-NIN-DA-GAN, Br 4660; ZA i 408); S^b 197 Nin-da | ib | it-tu-u (measure). ZDMG 43, 199 *rm* 5; PSBA xxi, 115. V 32 *d-f* 43; M^S 66 *col* 2.

nênzu (?) TP III *Ann* 53 D Gun ne-en-zu siparru; & *l* 99. ROST, 117, perh: a metal {ein Metall}.

nanzazu. *Rec. Trav.*, xx 208 *col* v 7 ilâni mala ina eli narûa annî | šur-šu-du

---

nimbûtu & ningûtu, see nabatu 2. & nigûtu; AV 6263; Br 6677; BA i 176. ∼ nangaru see naggaru, & add: JENSEN, 293 *rm* 2; AV 6057; Br 11165. ∼ nindag(g)aru Asb i 125 see magaru Ω ∼ Nindar see Ninib. ∼ nanduru 1. √אדר see na'duru; Br 11292. ∼ nanduru 2. √נדר (*q. v.*). *Rec. Trav.*, xix 81: *no* 2, 13 Tabnit Sirpurlaki na-an-du-ru. ∼ nanzabu see nançabu.

na-an-zu-zu. pm II of nazazu, *q. v.* & M[S] 64 *col* 1.

nanaxu, a gardenplant {Gartengewächs} D[Pr] 84 *rm* 2; BA i 182; ZA vi 291 *col* 1, 10 na-na-xu SAR.

nanxurtu see namxurtu; III 52 *b* 52 bi-ib-li na-an-xur-ti. III 32, 16 (= SMITH, *Asurb*, 119) in the month of Ab, arax na-an-xur-ti MUL-BAN. ZA i 234; 238 reads nanmurtu; so also KB ii 248—9; JENSEN, 108; RP vii 67.

(ilat) **Nin-ki-gal**, AV 6271; K 432, 8; IV[2] 31 *a* 24 *etc.* read Ereškigal & see KB vi, 1, 80 = Allatu, consort of Nergal; goddess of the netherworld; Z[B] viii 19; JEREMIAS, ROSCHER, *Ausf. Lexikon der .... Mythologie*, iii *cols* 268—70.

nankul, nankullat, *e. g.* IV[2] 54 *a* 18 kabtassu na-an-kul-lat; ZA iv 239, 39 na-an-kul libbi II pm & *ac* of נכל (*q. v.*).

nançabu; naçabu. AV 6033, 6107; D[Par] 142; J[w] 30. — *a*) some vessel or jar {ein Gefäss, Behälter} K 4150 (ZA vi 74; 156 *no* 2) 14 *foll* [pi]-sa-an-nu = na-an-ça-bu ša içi; [am, or ku?]-ru-um-mu *etc.* = *n* ša xaçbi (or epinnū); [e]-lal-lu-u = *n* ša qanē. II 33 *c-d* 4—6 (pi-sa-an) ŠIT = na-ça-bu ša içi (Br 5976; H 22, 442; ZA vi 73); ŠIT (pisan) NA = ša LA (AV 6107; Br 5983: epinni); (a-lal) 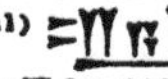 = *n* ša qanē (Br 6007, 6014; H 23, 446); these in one group with ç(z)ir-ki ki-it-ti. — *b*) V 29 *g-h* 21 TAG]-NUM = nam-ça-bu followed by am-ru-um-mu (see above), JENSEN, 440, Br 14343 part of a door, perhaps stone-threshold {Teil einer Thür, vielleicht Steinschwelle}; K 11409, 6. K 2866, 6 (= Z[B] viii 59) mâmit urû na-an-ça-bu (M[S] 68: Ständer) sip-pu šigāru, daltu, sikkūru, u par-kan-nu. V 39 *e-f* 66 see namištum. — *c*) some gardenplant (stalk?) {ein Gartengewächs (Stengel?)} ZA vi 295 *col* 3, 4 na-an-ça-bu SAR.

ninçabu support {Stütze} Dar 129, 10 nin-ça-bi (iç) gušurē ša (il) Zamama-iddin jānu. M[S] 68.

nunçabâti (*pl* of *nunçabtu). NE 51, 14 the še-e-du ša Uruk su-pu-ri | it-tu-ru a-na š(s)ik(q)-k(q)e-em-ma it-ta-çu-u ina nu-un-z(ç)a-ba-a-ti; BA i 176; § 65, 31*b* perhaps hole {Loch}? ZDMG 48, 197 > nuzzabâti √ na-zabu.

nannaru, nan(n)iru. perhaps: light, lightbearer, enlightener, luminary {Licht, Leuchte, *etc.*} AV 6062. V 64 *a* 18 (34) (il) Sin na-an-na-ri šamē u erçitim; I 70 *c* 18 (il) Sin na-an-na-ru a-šib šamū ellūtim. SMITH, *Asurb*, 126, 78 + 79 (= KB ii 252) arax Sin na-an-nir šamē u erçitim. Šalm, *Mon*, *O* 2 (il) Na-nir šamē erçitim, KB i 150—1. Creat.-*frg* V 12 (il) ŠEŠ-KI-ru; *cf* IV[2] 5 *a* 74 ina ma-xar (il) ŠEŠ-KI (= nanna)-ri il Sin, *etc.* (H 77, 42; 37, 40), *c* 40—1 [kîma] il Na-an-na-ri id-di-ši-i. T[M] ii 20 (il) ŠEŠ-KI-ra. H 77, 30 mār ru-bi-e na-an-na-ri (il) Sin (V 52 *a* 24); IV[2] 9 *a* 3/4—17/18 a-bu (il) Na-an-nar (= AN-ŠEŠ-KI; § 9, 60); also V 38 viii 3. Esh *Sendsch*, *O* 5 (il) Sin nannaru namru. V 23 *R* 32 I-IT = AN-ŠEŠ-KI = na-an-na-ru ‖ çi-? Br 7572, 7860; AV 6060. S 954 *O* 30 ja-a-ši a-bi (il) Na-an-na-ru; Sarg *Khors* 110 a-di-i (il) Nannari (WINCKLER, *Forsch.*, ii, 2, 372); K[M] 1 *O* 1 (il) Sin (il) Nanna-ru šu-pu-u (*cf* 16), GGA '98, 825; *Rec. Trav.*, xvi 177, 6. S[P] II 265 *R* 13 (corrected by K 3452) šar katmi na-an-na-ru ba-nu-u a-pa-a-ti. PINCHES, *Texts*, 15 *no* 4 *O* 3 na-an-na-ri. See further K 4870, 29 (+41); II 49 *a-b* 54. Local deity of Ur.

BA i 7 (> nanmaru, with progressive assimilation), 166, 176, 179, but see 461 *rm.* JENSEN, 102; & ZA ii 82 & ZDMG 48, 199, LYON, *Manual*, 121 √ נהר; ZDMG 43, 499 *no* 7; § 49*b*. HOMMEL, *Sum. Lesest.*, 21 (*no* 247) √ *nar-nar*. Also see HALÉVY, *Rev. d'hist. Relig.*, xvii 171 (× SAYCE, *Hibbert Lectures*, 155—6): same √ as *nār*, *nēr*, *nūr* light, fire. JASTROW, *Religion*, 75—9; MUSS-ARNOLT, *Babylonian Months*, 12; KB vi (1) 348.

(amêl) nin-ku an official, see ša-ku. ∼ nanmurtu, BA i 176 *etc.*; see nan(m)xurtu. ∼ nu-un-nu-nu (?), written nu-un-$\frac{nu}{nu}$ see nûnu, 2.

ninšubu. K 4349, 14 LAM-LAM = nin-šu-bu, AV 4891; Br 9047; M^{S} 104.

nanšû. 83, 1—18, 1330 iii 14 DAX$^{(DU)}$ = na-an-šu-u.

nanšuxu. T^{C} 7; Nabd 558, 11 na-an-šu-xu some vessel {ein Gefäss} √נשׁח.

(ilat) **Ni-ni-tum** (or Çalçaltum) ša Suti III 66 *col* 7, 27; Br 12696.

nâsu, na'asu see for the present nâçu, 2.

nisû, pr issi, ps inissi = נסע; D^{Pr} 47; ZDMG 40, 721 + 723, 12; ZA v 89. — *a*) trans.: remove, put away {entfernen, wegtun} IV^2 48 *b* 17 the gods i-ni-is-su-u ad-ma-an-šu-un, will remove their shrines (see kiççu, *pp* 425—6); pm kings ša ni-is-sa-at šu-bat-su-un, *Khors* 146 whose dwelling is afar off (§ 110); *Ann* 384 *var* šu-bat-su-un ni-sa-at; ZA iv 239 (K 2361 iii) 14 see xu-šaxxu (*p* 345 *col* 1) & ni'u Q pr (*p* 626); Z^{S} viii 63 mi-ix-ru la ṭa-a-bu li-is-su-u (3 *pl*). Perh Sp II 265 *a* vi 3 (end) ma-lik ni-si (*var* -su) mi-lik, ZA x 5; PSBA xvii 142. — *b*) intr.: move, withdraw, leave, move away, give way; set out, depart {sich entfernen, weichen, weggehen} ‖ açû. Sp II 265 *a* xxii 3 see libbu *b*). IV^2 2 *a* 28 ana pa-ni-šu i-si ana ar-ki-šu i-si; T^{M} v 166 i-sa-a i-sa-a depart! depart! (+ 170). Z^{S} vii 20 a-me-lu ša ili-šu it-ti-šu is-su-u (*cf* DT 150, 6) einen Menschen, von dem sein Gott gewichen. IV^2 15 ii 5—6 (end) a-na (*var* ana) šame-e šu la (a-)a-ri is-su-u. Z^{S} iv 66 lis-si, lit-ta-kiš, li-dip-pir ar-nu; iv 51 qil-la-ti li-is-su-u, 60 qil-la-tu-šu lis-su-a. IV^2 1* iii 47—48 ina SU (*var* zu-um-ri)-šu li-is-su-u (‖ ina zumrišu li-iç-çu-u) Br 7882; Z^{S} iv 84, 86. — KB iii (2) 6 *no* 2, 14—17 (nâr) Purattu is-si-šu ma | a-na ku-ud-duš (קדשׁ, so rather than -dul, as *p* 372 *col* 2) bêlûtišunu | me-e i-ri-e-qu a-na sa-a-p(b)u (ZA ii 73, 144; AJP xi 501), the waters receded and diminished so as to disappear entirely. Ner ii 2 during the reign of a former king mu-u šu-a-tu .... is-su-u i-ri-e-qu a-na sa-a-p(b)u. K 492, 15—16 mâr šarri | li-is-si, Hr^{L} 3; BA i 628 *foll*; AV 6071 let the son of the king set out; perh K 638 (Hr^{L} 328) 15 ul i-nis-si, + K 644 (Hr^{L} 336) 11. II 20 *a-b* 34—37 BAD (Br 1525; H 12, 124), SUD-UD (Br 7625), RI (Br 2567), SAR (with enclosed A-LAL) = ni-su-u, AV 6283; II 30 *no* 4 *R* 19 (= *l* 47) BAR (Br 1779) = ni-su-u, followed by BAR = nu-uz-zu-u (for nussû? AV 6407; Br 1780); *cf* 35: BAR = ri-qa-a-tu (‖ nisâtu, PSBA xii 308); V 40 *c-d* 5 TE = ni-su-u (Br 7699; ZA iv 275); see also Br 5823 & ZK ii 20; perh Sp II 265 *a* xxii 6 lillidu nis-su (or > niš-šu?, but see nissu), 3 ni-si-ma.

Q^{t} move, go away, depart {sich entfernen, weichen} NE 11, 25 bu-ul çêri it-te (*var* ti)-si ina zumrišu; IV^2 7 *a* 11 his god ina zumri-šu it-te-si (= BAD-DU) has left him (Z^{b} v/vi 12 it-te-is-si); Babyl. Chron. (84—2—11, 356) i 7 ana tarçi Nabû-naçir Bar-sip^{ki} itti Bâbili it-te-si, had separated from Babylon.

ℑ = intensive of Q remove forcibly, tear away, carry off {mit Gewalt entfernen, wegreissen, wegnehmen} I 51 *no* 1 *b* 2 zunnum u ra-a-du u-na-as-su-u (tore away) libittašu. IV^2 54 *a* 15—16 ab(p)uxxu anûnu xattum pi-rit-tum have silenced him and u-na-as-su-u ni-is-sat-su and have even carried away his lamentation; 57 *b* 4 kîma pi-sâni (GIŠ-RIT) lu-ni-is-su-u (may they tear away) my disease (XUL^{MEŠ}-ja); *a* 60 see nakaru ℑ. K 2333 *R* 26 li-ni-is-si pušqa may remove the distress (Z^{S} iv 75 purîdu); Sarg *Cyl* 23 mu-ni-is-si who led away, AV 5409. K^{M} 12, 73 kîma (iç) kunukku lu-ni-is-su-u (*var* li-is-su-u) limnêtija; 60 nu-us-si (= ip) see nakaru ℑ. KB vi (1) 132, 42 ul-te-le]-'-a nu-us-su (= NE 6, 49) but thou canst not shake him off; PINCHES, RP^2 ii 183 (11) Ninip linissi muttaliki. Sarg *Ann* 322 (*Khors* 127) dûrišu rabi-i u-ni-is-si-ma (?).

Š cause to, make one recede, depart, remove {zum Weichen bringen; entfernen} IV^2 54 *a* 40 see ṭi'û (348 *col* 2), also K 1438 *O* 19, T^{M} 148. T^{M} iii 147 ekimmu (*var* utukku) ri-da-a-ti .... u-ša-as[-si?] BA iv 159. IV^2 50 *a* 16 u-ša-as-si (= 3 *sg f*) ilija u ištarija ina zumrija (wr. SU-MU), she (the witch) caused my god and my goddess to leave me; *cf* 49 *a* 6 u-šes-su-u eli-ja. Neb ii 28—9 ra-ag-ga u çi-e-nim | i-na ni-ši u-še-is-si (= deport); ix 40—41 ga-an ta-xa-zi-šu u-ša-as-si (ich hielt fern); K 3600 *R* 23 šu-us-si-i zu-um-ru-šu.

Š¹ K 4832 *R* 36—37 liš-te-is-si | qi]-bit šap-tuk.

Š3 K 8204 iv 12 dunqi tašarraq tuš-na-as-si xi-du thou removest sin, Bezold, *Catalogue*, 905. M^{S} 66—7; see nassu.

N be or become removed {entfernt werden}. K 155 *R* 10 + 13 li-in-ni-is-si *etc.* (= K^{M} 1, 45 + 48; see *ibid*, *p* 14); Hebr. xi 102—3; also K^{M} 33, 28 + 32; 30, 12 written BAD-si. IV^{2} 30* *no* 3 *R* 12 u-tuk[-ku lim-nu] na-an-si-' a-lu-u lim-nu te-bi (*Rev. Sém.*, vi 149 *fol*) = ip. See perh K 8204 iv 11 na-as-si (PSBA xvii 139; Bezold, *Catalogue*, 905; or Q?).

Derr. mesû, mesûtu (*p* 567 *col* 1) and these 3:

nisû *2. adj* far, removed {fern, entfernt} § 65, 7; *f sg* ni-su-tum Rm 131 *R* 15. TP i 39 pu-lu-ge ni-su-te far-off districts; iv 49 mâtâti šarrâ-ni ni-su-te; vi 41 xur-ša-a-ni ni-su-ti (*var* -te). ZA iv 8, 41 šid-di .... ni-su-ti far-off regions (& 11, 23); Neb ii 13—14 mâtâte ru-ga-a-ti ša-de-im ni-su-u-ti. Neb 320, 17 see nagû. IV^{2} 30* *b* 25—6 u-tuk-ku lim-nu çi-i ana ni-sa-a-ti (*i. e.* ašrâti?) = KI-BAD; *Rev. Sém.*, vi 150, ‖ ana namê.

nisiš *adv.* II 19 *a* 55; Neb vi 27 *etc.* see ṭaxû (354 *col* 1, *ll* 9—12); ZK i 7 *foll*; ii 415; KAT^{2} 380; AV 6282.

Nisannu (> nisânu) *1.* = Nisan, the first month of the Assyr.-Babyl. year. ⊕ 116 i 11 (H 44 + 64, 1; II 43, 3; V 29 *a-b* 1) ^{arax} BAR-AZAG-GAR = ni-sa-an-nu, AV 6687; Jensen, ZA ii 209—11. Sarg *Ann* 309 ^{arax} Nisannu, arax a-çi-e $^{(il)}$ Bêl ilâni; id also Knudtzon, *passim*. V 43 *b* 1 *fol*; Br 10837; 1781; 6877; 6903; AV 6274, 6687; § 46; Muss-Arnolt, *Assyro-Babyl. Months*, 5, 6.

nassu, sad {betrübt} Z^{B} ii 4; see nakdu. Perh K 8204 iv 12 du-un-qi ta-šar(ṭi?)-rak-ku na-as-si xi-du (but see Š3 of nisû). √nasasu, whence also:

nissu. Sp II 265 *a* xxii 6 see lillidu (481 *col* 2); ZA iv 15, 16 ta-qab-bi nis-su.

na-sa-'-is. Sarg *Ann* 258 ušabṭila na-sa-'-is.

nassab(p)u, a vessel {ein Gefäss}. II 22 *d-f* 14 DUK-RI-A = na-as-sa-bu ‖ na-man .... preceded by tal-lu. K 4220, 7 ... diqar ša me-e | gan-gan-nu ša na-as-sa-bu; Br 2610, AV 6074; ZA ii 266; BA i 182; M^{S} 67 *col* 1.

Nisaba. — id AN-ŠE-ELTEG = Nidaba (82, 8—16 i 28 = nidabu); III 66 vii 7 (PSBA xxi 124), Br 7454; § 9, 60; *Johns Hopk. Circ.*, 69, 18 *col* 1; ZK ii 55 *fol*, 421 & *rm* 3; Jensen, 93, 109, 236 *rm* 1, 498; Zimmern, ZA xiv 278, 283. — *a*) a deity {eine Gottheit}. IV^{2} 16 *a* 27—8; 29—30 the demon ša a-na ku-š'ur-ri-e ša $^{(il)}$ Ni-sa-ba i-çar-ru-ru sa-pa-ru ana $^{(il)}$ Ni-sa-ba lik-su-šu (Z^{B} v/vi 178, 181; viii 19). See Pinches in S. A. Smith, *Asurb*, i 108. 82, 8—16, 1 *col* i 28 ME-AN-NIDABA $^{(mat-ku)}$ = i-šip-pu ša $^{(il)}$ Nisaba, S. A. Smith, *Miscell. Texts*, *p* 25. Babylonian god prior to Xammu-rabi, Jastrow, *Religion*, 101, 102; Price, AJSL xvii 52. — *b*) some field fruit: grain, barley? {eine Feldfrucht: Getreide, Gerste?} Lyon, *Sargon*, 69 *ad* 41. Asb i 48 ešêr ebûru na-pa-aš nisaba (KB ii 156 = piširtu?) see lines 46, 47; ZA ii 228; ZA x 242—44 × Meissner, *ibid*, 76. Smith, *Asurb*, 100, 19 nisaba ba-laṭ napištim nišê; IV^{2} 17 *b* 19 ina $^{(il)}$ Nisaba elli-ti çalmê-šu-nu ab-ni; 8 *a* 4 (+ 7) see Jensen, *Diss*, 85, 86. IV^{2} 28 *a* 14 e-ri-iš nisaba, o planter of grain, BA ii 417; Br 9158; *cf* III 69 *c-d* 42; NE 8, 37 pi?]-ti-iq(k) pi-ir-ti-šu ux-tan-na-ba ki-ma $^{(il)}$ Nisaba, KB vi (1) 120—1: die?] .... seines Haupthaares reckt sich wie Weizen; J^{I-N} 47 *rm* 2. — Hommel, *Sum. Les.*, 49, 59: Nidaba & nisaba > nin-dab > nin-dag = grain-gods {Korngötter}; on grain-gods see Hoffmann, ZA xi 262; Ball, *Genesis* (SBOT) *p* 100 *ad* 42: 1 is corrected, *ibid*, by Haupt.

nissabu, cereals {Getreide} 82—1—18, 181, 2 na-pa-aš ni-is-sa-bu, an increase of

---

nasbu see naçbu. — nasbû (AV 6076) *cf* naçbû.

cereals; *cf* 81—2—4, 132 *R* 2 na-pa-aš (il) Nisaba; 83—1—18, 178; THOMPSON, *Reports*, ii *nos* 220—222.

nisibtu (p?), a vessel {ein Gefäss}. K 152 i 76 DUK-ŠA-GUL = ni-si-ib-tum ‖ kur ....; id = akk(qq)ullu. AV 6276; Br 12136.

nisiggu. TP vi 88 būl çēri gimirta u iççur šamē mut-tap-ri-ša e-im ni-sig-gi ^{pl}-ia lu-u attaddi. L^T 168; BA i 182: trophy {Trophäe}? AV 6277. Perh √nasaqu?

***nasaxu* 1.** pr is(s)ux, ps inassax, ip usux; id ZI. AV 6064. ZA ix 107 = نسخ. — *a*) tear out, pluck out, draw, pull, remove, drag away; transplant {aus-, herausreissen, ziehen, entfernen, mit Gewalt fortführen; wegführen} *etc.* pr as-su-ux P^{w} 120; Šalm, *Balaw*, III 4 ebūr-šu a-su-xu (‖ a-kis); IV 5 ebūr ^{pl}-šu a-su-ux; TP vi 88 is-su-xa, they carried away; Sarg *Ann* 359 temēnšu as-su-ux; 22 as-su-xa-am-ma; 295 is-su-xa-am-ma; Šalm, *Ob*, 126 a-su-xa; Anp ii 31, 33; iii 43. Lay 17, 13 Puqudu *etc.* ul-tu aš-ri-šu-nu as-su-xa-šu-nu-ti (KB ii 6—7; BA ii 306 *foll*); Esh *Sendsch*, *R* 47 ul-tu (mât) Mu-çur as-sux; *cf* SMITH, *Asurb*, 94, 77 (KB ii 242); Asb ii 42 ul-tu man-za-al-ti-šu-nu as-sux(-ma). Creation-*frg* VII 20 ša .... is-su-xu who tore out (KB vi, 1, 36—7); S^P 158 + S^P 962 *O* 8 is-sux-ma it-ta-di; IV² 34 *a* 9 is-su-xu. K 824, 8 libbašu ZI (= issux)-xa, took away his understanding (JOHNSTON); V 63 *a* 30 e-pi-ri kir-bi-šu as-su-ux(-ma); I 69 *c* 32 as-sux; I 51 *no* 2 *a* 21 is-su-ux(-ma); 81—6, 7, 209 (dupl. K 6346) 32 its ruins as-sux (I removed) PAOS, May '91, *p* cxxxii; HEBR. viii 114; BA iii 260—3. IV² 27 *b* 51—3 u-ri-ça ša libba-šu ta-as-su-xu. II 9 *c-d* 16 a-na aplūtišu is-su-ux-šu; *cf* 8, 53 *fol* qa-as-su-nu is-su-xu. H 51, 52—3 IN-ZI & IN(si-id)BU = is-su-ux; II 39 *c-d* 38 is-sux, Br 5821. — *pc* TP viii 78—9 the gods išdi kussē šarrūti-šu li-su-xu (may uproot); I 70 *c* 12 (III 43 *c* 27) the gods išid (& e-ši-is)-su li-is-su-xu; *d* 4 li-is-su-ux (may tear out); IV² 38 *c* 35—6; IV² 14 *no* 2, 28 (il) Šamaš ina a-çi-šu da'ummatsu li-is-sux (= ZI; H 78, 29) may *Š* in his rising remove the darkness in which he is; ZA i 406, 23 li-su-xa; IV² 15 i 30 (× Br 2324) see ṭaradu; also *l* 40 ina zumrišu li-is-sux-ma. T^M vii 29—30 kiš-pi ša zumrija li-is-su-xu (3 *pl*) ilāni rabūti; *ibid* 15 li-is-sux-šu-nu-ti. — ip KB vi (1) 266, 15 = NE 93 u-sux tear out! {reiss heraus!}; *Etana*-legend (BA ii 394—5; KB vi, 1, 108) 16 b(p)il-ti u-sux-ma; IV² 3 *a* 40 ina man-za-zi u-sux-šu-ma (*cf* ZA iv 233, 3); IV² 26 *b* 42—3 u-sux (= ⟨-ME-NI-BU); 26 *b* 47 us-xi sikkāte-ki; 27 *b* 46—7 the heart of the uriçu u-sux-ma. T^M ii 64 u-sux-šu-nu-ti ina zumrija. SCHEIL, *Rec. Trav.*, xix 43 (last line) u-su-ux-šu-nu-ti. — *ps* *del* 97 (102) tar-kul-li. il I(U)ra(-ra)-g(k)al i-na-as-si(a)x, JENSEN, 423; KB vi (1) 236—7; *cf* K 3500 i 12 li-is-su-xu, WINCKLER, *Forsch.*, ii *pp* 10 + 16. KB vi (1) 198, 24 i-na-sa(i)x; IV² 1* iii 39—40 (ZI-ZI) see namtāru (they destroy); IV² 4 *b* 20 man-nu i-na-as-sax (= ZI-ZI) man-nu u-šat-ba, speaking of the muruç qaqqadi. ZIM., *Rit.* *no* 68, 8 ila tu-šat-ba ku-ul ta-na-sax. KNUDTZON, *no* 55 *R* 9 i-na-as-s[u-xu šu-u *etc.* — *ag* Sarg *Nimr* 8: *Sargon* na-si-ix (mât) Xa-am-ma-te who transplanted by force the inhabitants of Hamât, + 11; Pp IV 35; *Cyl* 18 (+ 25 = tearing out). K 2107 *O* 20 ..... (il) SUX(?)-KIL = mu-bal-lu-u nap-xar a-a-bi na-si-ix rag-gi; 18 (il) ZI (šad) SI = na-si-ix ša-bu-ti, AV 5411; 6068; Br 14392; see Creat.-*frg* VII *O* 28, 29; KB vi (1) 36—7; & *cf* the article "Marduk". T^M viii 125 ilāni ša ma-çar-te na-si-ix lib-bi. — *pm* IV² 3 *a* 19—20 he that is stricken by the muruç qaqqadi ki-ma ša lib-ba-šu na-as-xu it-ta-nab-lak-kat; Sarg *Ann* 40 milik limutti ša na-six *etc.*; IV² 22 *a* 45 see nakapu Q^t. — *ac* I 70 *b* 8 ana na-sax kudurri annī to pull up this boundary stone; Asb x 24 ana na-sax(?) niqē (e-lu-u) KB ii 230 *rm* 3; I 27, 92 marulta ša na-sax (KB i 122) iš-di šarrū-ti-šu; IV² 30* *no* 3 *O* 26 I am come a-lu-u lim-nu ana na-sa-xi-ka; IV² 56 *a* 21 la-az-za u labartu nasa(= ZI)-xi; *b* 5 see ṭaradu; $Z^{Š}$ iii 25 šammē ina çēri na-sa-xu; + 40

(= KB iv 212 *foll*) u ni-is-xu a-na eli ul i-na-sa-xu; while KOHLER-PEISER, ii 23 *rm* 1: nisxu perh draft, bill of exchange {Wechsel}. Nabd 65, 19 ni-is-xi ana muxxi ul ta-na-as-sa-xi; 118, 9—10 ni-is-xu a-na mux-xi ..... ul i-na-as-sa-xi; 356, 9 a-na nis-xu niš-ša-am-ma. Abstr. noun:

nisxûtu. Neb 402, 4 ni-is-xu-tum.

nasixû. V 42 *c-d* 56 .... TA-SAR-RA = na-si-xu-u in one group with a-la-nu-u & mun-nar-bu, perh: fugitive {Ausreisser}.

nusâxu, deduction, reduction {Abzug}? K 2729 *O* 31 ŠE] nu-sa-xi-ši-na la in-na-su-xu BA ii 566 *fol*; KB iv 144—5; *Rec. Trav.*, xvi 176, 10) of corn they shall make no reduction {vom Getreide soll man keinen Abzug machen}. K 4289 *R* 8—9 ŠE nu-sa-xi-ši-na la in-na-sa-xu (BA ii 572); KB iv 104, 19 ŠE nu-sa-xi-šu la in-na-su-xu; 154 (K 330) 25 of the corn a-na la ši-ib-še la nu-sa-xi, ist weder Steuer noch Abgabe (zu leisten); BA ii 569 = nisxu, in neo-babylonian contracts.

nisixtum. K 2024 *c* 10 ittika luçlal ilu ša ni-six-ti (= ZI-GA) šûkil. K 4152 *O* 10 *b*; AV 6278 (ni-si-ix-tum).

***nasaxu* 2.** determine {bestimmen, abfassen}? THOMPSON, *Reports*. Q K 870 *R* 4 u-il-tu ša-ni-tu a-na-as-sa-xa a second report I have determined; 81—2—4, 380, 6 ... i-na-sa-xa. — Q[t] K 712, 9 ik-šu-ud at-ta-as-xa, so I determine; 83—1—18, 287, 110 at-ta-as[-xa]; K 1049 *R* 9; S 1368 *O* 12 (Hr[L] *nos* 38, 857); — Ꝛ 83—1—18, 197 *R* 4 a-ki an-ni-e in-na-sa(?)-xa u-ma-a; K 760 *R* 3 aš-šu la in-na-sa-[xu?]. But this verb should better be combined with nasaxu, 1.

nasxapu, some object made, or composeds of reed {ein Gegenstand aus Rohr} √sa-xapu; M[S] 71 *col* 1. Rm 2, 27, 12 GI-MAL-na-as-xa-pu = ŠU. Neb 402, 14 na-as-xa-pu; Camb 355, 3 + 7: VII šeqel kaspi šuqultu kip-pa-tum (√קפף?) na-as-xa-pi.

nisxiptu. Camb 265, 3—4: ana pu(?)-di-e nis-xi-ip-tum ša xa-ša-du ša (il) Ea.

nasaku. pr issuk, ps inas(s)uk, ip usuk place, put, lay; appoint; do, perform {setzen, legen; einsetzen; tun} AV 6065; D[H] 20; D[Pr] 47; § 99; ZDMG 40, 719; G § 56; HEHR. vii 89 *rm* 17. Nabd 966, 11 i-na-as-su-uk ana xarrâni. NE XII i 18 (KB vi, 1, 256—7) pit(?)-pa-na a-na erçi-tim la ta-na-suk; J[I-N] 41; *Etana*-legend (KB vi, 1, 114, 28 + 30 + 32) is-su-k[a-am-ma] he fell down {er fiel hinab}; Creat.-*frg* IV 101 is(z)-s(z)uk(q) mul-mul-la (KB vi, 1, 339); *del* 282 (298) šannûtum is-su-k(q)aš-šu a-na pir-ri-šu, KB vi (1) 250. T[M] viii 65 ana libbi erî nam-si-e ta-na-suk ii 167 ki-ma šu-]šu-rat igâri a-na-as-suk-šu-nu-ti (*cf* 156 ana na-sa-ki-ja), GGA '98, 821; 82—3—23, 845, 4 ta-na-as-su-uk (*Rec. Trav.* xix 106—7): Sm 526, 33—4. Rm 282 (KB vi, 1, 46) *R* 4 us-kam-ma fahr hinab! 7; is-su-kam-ma; IV[2] 3 *b* 66—7 u-suk (= ŠUB)-ma, Br 1436. — V 55, 11 Nebuchadrezzar na-sik šarrâni, who appoints kings, or *c. st.* of nasiku? 56, 36 who this document (memorial slab) a-na nâri i-na-su-ku; III 41 ii 41 a-na bûr i-na-as-su-ku (BA ii 140); also see KB iv 90 *col* v 2. — II 39 (⊕ 59 ii) *g-h* 12 RI = na-sa-ku ša A....; 13 RI-RI = ra-xa-çu ša .... Br 2568. — T. A. Ber 92 *O* 31 a-na lib-bi i-ša-ti a-na na-xa-ki u-ba-u-ka.

Q[t] T. A. Ber 92 *O* 3 ša a-xu-šu i-na ba-a-bi it-ta-xu-uk-šu (*cf* 11).

Q[tn] M[S] 67 *col* 1, quotes BOISSIER, *Doc*, 27, 9 šumma kip-pa-a kisalîti it-ta-na-suk (+ 10).

Š K 8522 *R* 14 (D 95) u-ša-as-si-ku eli ilâni na-ki-ri-šu (JENSEN, 296, 362, see našaku, 2). BA iii 280 derives also K 2801 *R* 20 li-šam-si-ku (möge fördern) from nasaku, but see masaku.

Derr. — perh massaku (567 *col* 2) & these:

nasîku, prince {Fürst} *pl* nasîkâni & na-sîkâti, § 70 *b*. AV 6070; D[Pr] 111; = נסיך, WEINEL, ZA '98, 17. Anp ii 24 Nûr-Adad (amêl) na-si-ku ša (mât) Dagara (iii 45); K 10 *O* 14 (Hr[L] 280); *ibid* 19 (amêl) na-si(?)-ka-a-ti of Lachiru & the tribe (?) Nu-gu-u-'u. See also Sarg *Ann* 255 na-si-ka(-a)-te (*var* -ti) = authorities,

na-si-ix-tum AV 6060 see nasištum. ~ nasxuru AV 6073 (& našxuru) *cf* saxaru 27 &, BA i 181.

rulers; *Ann* 267 na-sik-ku; *Cyl* 18 *T* ša (amēl) na-sik-šu-nu, K 4207 na-si-ku; on iḏ see Br 3820. 83—1—18, 47 *R* 8—9 (amēl) na-si-ku (māt) Ia-di' (amēl) [na]-si-ku u (amēl) na-si-ka-tu. Sn vi 15 the king of Elam & the king of Babylon (amēl) na-sik-ka-ni ša (māt) Kal-di. KB vi (1) 417: Ausgiesser, Opferer.

nasikūtu. III 6 *R* 42 (end) Artešnu his brother ana (amēl) na-si-ku-te aš-kun (KB i 92).

nasīkatu *1.* *f* of nasīku, see above; Neb 109, 3 (amēltu) na-si-ka-tum.

nasikatu *2.* II 39 *c-d* 76 .... DA = na-si-ka-tu (so against 181 *col* 1 ba-si-ka-tu) in one group with pi-xa-tu (73) & bi-ir-tu (75), Br 14214. K 2361 + S 389 ii 12 na-si-ka-tuš lu-ub-ba-bil (or -ne?), ZA iv 237.

nasku, fallen {gefallen}. IV^2 40 *a* 29 (il) Bēl mātāti a-šib E-LAX ([cuneiform])-UL ça-bit qātā na-as-ku. Craig, *Relig. Texts*, i 1, 22 e-ṭe-rat ka-mi-i ça-bi-tat na-as-qu (= ku, AJSL xiv 173—4); *cf* K^M 9, 36 ça-bi-ta-at qātā na[-aš?-ki].

nis(š?)akku. *a*) a (high) priestclass, or -order {eine bestimmte Priesterklasse} iḏ NU-AB. AV 6362, also: priest. Sarg *Cyl* 1: Sargon NU-AB; I 6 *no* vii 2; § 9, 59. Zimmern, *Beitr. z. Kenntn. d. babyl. Relig.*, 116 *foll*, *no* 24, 27 ri-xu-ut (amēl) ni-sakki: aus priesterlichem Geblüt. 81—7—27, 130, 9 [li]-ša-an ni-sak-ki Priestersprache(?), see Weissbach, *Die Sumerische Frage*, 155; ZA iv 434 *foll*. H 13, 153 ...... eš | NU-AB | ni-sak-ku = II 32 *e-f* 7 (Br 1979) followed by ra-am-ku & a-ši-pu. Rm 8, 105 i 10 *b*: (amēl) ni-sak-ki (amēl) TU-bīti (il) Nabū; JRAS '92, 350 *foll*; S^P 158 + S^P II 962 *O* 25 ni-sak-ka-šu a-mat i-qab-bi-šu, 37 (end) ni-sak-ku (also, 7). Pinches, *Victoria Institute Trans.*, xxix 59 = prince, chief. — *b*) offering {Opfer} S^b 89 ni-sag | iḏ | ni-qu-u & *var* ni-sak-ku (Br 6710; H 24, 508; S^b F 1, 10); perh also 82, 9—18, 4159 iv 32 *fol* ni-sag | NI-SAG | ni-sag-gu & ni-sag riš-tu-u.

See L^T 176, where also Pognon & Guyard are cited; Lyon, *Sargon*, 58 *rm* 1. McCurdy, vol i 115; Sayce, *Hibbert Lectures*, 60 *rm* 1 (√na'š'aku sacrifice); also *cf* Le Gac, ZA vii 138—9, on G § 32.

Nusku. — iḏ AN-PA-KU, a Babylonio-Assyrian god, perhaps originally local deity of Nippur, in whose pantheon he is the scribe, as Nebo in that of Babylon. Mentioned very early (ZA xi 268 *fol*); occurs in Babylonian as well as in Assyrian cult (Tiglath-pileser's grandfather: Mutakkil-Nusku). In Šalm. II *Ob* 11 he is called na-ši xaṭṭi elli-ti, perhaps in explanation of PA-KU (= stylus); 12 he is named ilu mul-ta-lu (see *p* 614 *col* 2); Asurb x 83, 118 (KB ii 268, 106) as belonging to the 12 great Assyrian gods. II 59 he is mentioned in a list of deities after Ninib: *a-c* 13 .... ÇI-IB | AN-EN-[cuneiform]-XI (= DUB) Br 2896; 14, ... U-A | AN-EN-[cuneiform]-PA; 15, AN-ŠE (Br 2867 MU; 8799)-DU-RU = AN-EN-PA & all = AN-PA-KU (see III 66 *O* 10 *a*; 25 *d*; 36 *c*, *R* 9 *a*, *etc.*); K 1024, 6.

He was a solar deity (while Nabū a water-deity), Jeremias; Jastrow, *Religion*, 220 *fol* god of the midday sun and thus = fire-god; IV^2 26 *no* 3; T^M *no* ii.

iḏ AN-PA-KU (§ 9, 60; Br 5682; 5683), *e. g.* V 64 *b* 18; 42, called suk(k)allu çi-i-ri (as messenger of the gods; by no means a subordinate position); IV^2 23 *a* 4 (Jensen, 91; Br 6241); V 44 *c-d* 16 (Br 6456 = AN-ŠEŠ-KAK); II 19, 56—7; H 76, 6—8 *etc.*; T^M i 122, 144; ii 1, 8; iii 139; v 22, 99; viii 1. Hommel, *Sum. Lesest.*, 47, 14. IV^2 49 *b* 35 *foll* (T^M i 122 *foll*) he is called šur-bu-u i-lit-ti il A-nim, tam-šil abi bu-kur (il) Bēl (whose favorite & lofty messenger he is); tar-bit ZU-AB (= apsî), bi-nu-ut (il) E-a (T^M ii 111; K^M 6, 24); also see T^M ii 1 *foll*, 17; KB vi (1) 319—20. T^M 26 *foll*; Jastrow, *Religion*, 276 *foll*: a special feature (Erscheinungsform) of Gibil (fire), as Jensen, 137; Jeremias, on the contrary, maintains that he is near related to the firegod, but not to be identified with *Gibil*.

IV^2 26 *no* 3; 54 *no* 2; 49 *b* 56 he is called ma-lik ilāni rabūti.

In Harran, whither his cult was transplanted from Nippur, Nusku is the sukallu of god Sin; & is called נשכ on the stele of Nerab (ZA xi 233; 293*foll*); also Nušku occurs *e. g.* Nu-uš-ku-Malik (Johns, *Deeds and Documents*, 20, 113) see Hoffmann, ZA xi 267 § 16.

In later Babylonia his cult was, again, revived by Nabonidus.

S^b 212 nu-uz(s)-ku | PA-KU | nu-uz-ku, followed by ri-'-u; D^K 52 *rm* 2; H 21, 404. His wife is Sa-dar-nun-na, II 57 *a* 17; 59 *c* 16; V 52 *a* 17; 64 *b* 18; AV 6237. In *c. t.* we have P. N. I-bi (amêl) Nu-us-ku, etc. AV 6444.

NOTE. — 1. See especially Jeremias in Roscher, *Lexikon*, iii 482—87; Hoffmann, ZA xi 260*foll*; Jensen, *ibid*, 293*foll*. — Z^B 25; 32; 36. *Proc. Am. Or. Soc.*, Oct. '87, *p* xxxiii *rm* 1; Pinches, *Jour. Trans. Vict. Institute*, xxviii 19.

2. On Nusku & *Nisroch.* (נסרך) see Halévy, JA viii ('79) 387 = *Mélanges de critique* ('83), 177: נסך whence נסכך, & then, נסרך; √ נסך, anoint. See also *Rev. d'hist. Relig.*, xvii, 187 against Sayce, *Hibbert Lectures*, 113—119; Meinhold, *Jesaja-erzählungen* ('98) 73. On the other hand, Kittel, *Bücher der Könige*, (1900) 280 & others: who believe in an intentional change of the name Nusku into *Nisroch*; or, rejecting connection with Nusku, explain it as from נסרך (Winckler, *etc*). — See, in general, commentaries on 2 kings 19; 37 = Isa. 37, 38. Haupt in Cheyne *Isaiah* (SBOT) *p* 178.

nismatu, will, desire {Willen, Wunsch} or the like; Jensen, 341; 515. Esh *Sendsch*, *O* 30—1 ik-šu-da | ni-is-mat-su. I 49 *c* 5 tušakšidu ni-is-ma-ti, BA iii 220 —1, dessen Herzenswunsch du erreichen liessest; also 81—6—7, 209, 11 ni-is-mat-su ušakšiduš, BA iii 260*foll*. Creat.-*frg* IV 126 after ni-is(ç, z)-mat (ilu) Nu-g(d)im-mud ik-šu-du (ilu) Marduk qar-du, KB vi, 1, 28; Winckler, *Unters.*, 143 (= KB iii, 1, 132) 14—15 of Šamsi-iluna ni-is-ma-at libbija kima ili kašadam. Winckler, *Sargon*, 192 B 8 epištuš šullima lik-šu-da ni-is-ma(t)-su, that he may obtain his desire. KB iii (2) 8 *no* 3 i 14 u-ša-ak-ši-du ni-is-ma-su. Perh Pinches, *Texts*, 16 *no* 4 *R* 6 (end) li-ik-šu-da ni-is-mat (or -sat)-su; PSBA xvii 136 derives from √ נשם, thirst; then: desire, aspiration.

nisannu *1.* see, above, *p* 698, *col* 1.

nisannu *2.* K 4220, 4 [karpat] ša ni-sa-an-ni = gan-gan-nu ša nam-zi-ti.

***nasasu** 1.* prs inassus wail, mourn, lament {jammern, wehklagen} Z^B 93; D^{Pr} 63—4; ZDMG 40, 729. K 891 *R* 12; L^3 *R* 10 see kûru, 1. II 20 *a-b* 29—30 AD-DU = na-za-zu; BAR-SI-EL = *n* ša xi-pi-e, Br 1889. IV^2 11 *O* 23—4 ina?] ni-is-sa-ti (AD-DU) ina-(as?-)su-[us?] = AD-DU-MU.

Derr. — nassu, nissu &:

nissatu, lament(ation), grief, weeping, *etc.* {Wehklage, Kummer, Weinen} ‖ kûru, 1 (431—2) which see for IV^2 59 *no* 1 *b* 15; Sm 949 *O* 19; NE 72, 29 + 37; Sp II 265 *a* iii 8. id SAG-PA-RIM, BA ii 282. T^M 148; AV 6285; Z^B 23; 92; 97; J^W 86 *rm* 2. K 196 i 14 nissatu u la ṭûb šîri (Pinches, *Texts*, 11); Z^Š iv 63, 64 ni-is-sa-su (> nissat-šu). T^M vii 40 u-šat-bi qu-lu ku-ru ni-is-sa-tu ša pag-ri-ka, BA iv 161; K 185 *R* 7 ina ku-u-ri u ni-is-sa-te ittanallak (Hr^L 74); *var* to *del* 119 (126) reads ina nu-ru-ub(p) ni-is-sa-ti. NE 59, 4 ni-is-sa-a-tum i-te-ru-ub ina kar-ši-ja sadness has entered my heart (§ 141); ibašši SAG-PA-RIM NE 65, 8; 73, 4 + 11; 77, 17 (ni-is-sa-tum), 9, 49; 62, 33 ina ni-is[-sa-ti] *cf* line 35. Sp II 265 *a* xxv 1 ri-me (*var* mi)-na-a-tu eb-ri ni-is-sa-tum še-te-'-me; xiii 5 be-ir-ta lu-ul-lik ni-sa[-at]-ti lu-xu-uz; i 7 . . . ri-id-ma ni-is-sa-tum lu-u-ta-me-šu. KB vi (1) 4, 10 qu-lu liš-ša-kin-ma ni-is-s[a-tu libbi]. III 38 *no* 2 *R* 66 see ma'âlu (507 *col* 2, 7—9); IV^2 30 *a* 27 —8 *cf* Br 3996 & maqatu Q *b* (*p* 578 *col* 1); IV^2 54 *a* 12 ni-is-sa-ta; 16 see nisû 3. IV^2 19 *a* 13—14 ed(t)li u ar-data ukassû ni-is-sa-ta (*var* -at; = AD-DU) umallû (Z^B vii 14; Br 4177). V 49 ix 30 ni-is-sa-tum, BA ii 288. ZA iv 237 ii 16 (K 2361 + S 389) be-lum pal-ku-u id-da-a a-šu-uš-tum ni-is-sa-t[um]. V 22 *e-h* 14 i-si-iš | A-ŠI | ni-is-sa-tum; *cf* 52 (Br 11714; 11613). II 20 *a-b* 31—33 (i-si-iš) A-ŠI (Br 11614); SAG-PA-RIM (Br 3602); KU-KI-SAG (Br 10630) = ni-is-sa-tum, AV 6205. — (šam) ša-mi ni-is-sa-ti = azallû K 4418, 8 (II 41 *a-b* 47). — 81—6—7, 209, 11 see nismatu.

***nasasu** 2.* 3 II 20 *a-b* 41—43 SUD-SUD = nu-us-su-su ša zibbati, AV 6445; Br 7617); DUB-DUB-BU = *n* ša pir (? çabt?)-tim (Br 7038); SI-SI-IN = *n* ša tur-ru-ki (תרך, Br 3486). Perh NE

14, 4 l]i-na-as-si-sa k(q)im-mat-su, KB vi (1) 140—1 (+436): möge schütteln sein Haar; ‖ limxaç (3); T^M vi 81 ša tu-na-sis-a-ni kim-mat-ku-nu ja-a-ši (against, above, *p* 400 *col* 2).

nisip(p)u, a measure of capacity {ein bestimmtes Hohlmass}. BA i 633 perh √ספא, properly: Sammelkrug. Nabd 108, 1: 30 ni-si-pu (245, 6 -pi?) ša šamni; 185, 1: 8 ni-sip-pi ša šam-ni (798, 1—2); 322, 1: so & so many ni-sip ša šam-ni (or ša NI-IÇ, 329, 7); Cyr 290, 1: 11 ni-sip-pi ša šam-ni. T^C 105 נסף.

naspanu. K 4378 (D 87) i 63, 64 GIŠ-DA(-ŠU)-QI-GA = na-as-pa-nu (Br 6693, 6685; AV 6075) = II 46 *a-b* 48—9; BA i 176; preceded by pitnu, *q. v.*

naspantu. Sm 1366 (= H 118) *R* 1 gal-lu-u bi-el na-as-pan-ti, the demon, lord of destruction {Herr der Niederwerfung} Br 3400; ZK ii 281; Hommel, *Semiten* (VK), 244.

na-as-pa-ra-an-na Cyr 84, 3.

naspātu see salū, 1.

nasaqu. *pr* issuq, *ps* inasaq glorify, praise {verherrlichen, rühmen, preisen}. Hebr. vii 89—90 *rm* 17; D^H 55—6; § 99; BA i 228; G § 56; Br 3019. KB vi (1) 186 (+460) = NE 53, 41 for twenty kaspu as-su-qa i-ça[-ki ṭa-a-ba] I have admired thy beautiful wood. K 4815, 2—3 a-xi ra-man-ka la ta-na-sa-qa (= NU-SUX-E-EN). K 4225 (+dupl.) 20—21 SI | SUX | lu-us-su-uk-ka & na-sa-qu, preceded by lu-'-ud-ka (√na'adu) H 185; Br 3387; AV 6066. ג decorate, ornate splendidly {verzieren, herrlich einrichten, schmücken}. TP vii 95 a house which by the skill of the builder ma-'-a-diš nu-su-qu (pm). I 7 E 3—4 ša kīma še-im ça(-ax)-xa-ri ši-kin(*var* šikin)-šu nu(-us)-su-qu; *cf* I 44, 72 the *ašnan*-stone ša kīma zēr qiš-še-e šikinšu nu-su-qu. Sn *Kuj* 4, 16 (see Meissner & Rost, 12, 15+16; 58).

nasqu *adj.* magnificent, precious {kostbar. auserlesen} *etc.* V 56, 2 Nebuchadrezzar rubū nādu (*q. v.*) | na-as-qu; 22 šarru na-as-qu; Sn iii 72 it-ti $^{(amēl)}$ mutīr pu-ti šēpi-ja na-as-qu-ti (Hebr. i 184); V 33 ii 42 abna namra *etc.* ša šum(??)-šu na-as-qu; L^4 i 19 it-ti il-li na-as-ki. Sargon, *Ann* 203 na-as-qu; 329 mundaxçēja na-as-qu-ti. K 2801 (+K 221+2669) *R* 30 abnē na-as-qu-ti, kostbare Steine, BA iii 260. Rm 2, 66 (Šalmaneser I) na-as-qu-ti ummān Qu-ti-i. V 14 *b* 26 na-as-qa-a-tum (*scil.* šipāte) of woollen stuff, AV 6077.

nisqu, *c. st.* nisiq splendor, grandeur, preciousness *etc.* {Pracht, Herrlichkeit, Kostbarkeit u. dgl.}. V 55, 20 ni-is-qu ša rabūte sisē the splendor of the large horses; murnisqi, see mūru, *p* 584 *col* 1. Neb ix 7 $^{(iç)}$ šu-ur-mi-ni ni-is-ki bērūtim, Flemming, *Nebuchadn.*, 58; 61. nisiq abnu precious stones, jewels *etc.*, properly: preciousness of stones, Neb iii 31 ni-si-iq abnu (viii 10); ii 30 ni-si-iq abnu šu-ku-ru-ti, Flemming, *ibid*, 32. — **ni-siq dup-šar-ru-ti** the best of the art of penmanship; often in colophons, AV 2092; 6279. II 21 *a* 28; 51 *no* 2 *R*; IV^2 4 *a* 39; 6 *a* 45; 19 *b* 26 *etc.*; V 15 *a* 42; 51 *a* 49; T^M often in colophons; ni-siq dup-šar-u-ti, II 23 *a* 40; ni-siq dup-šar-ru-u-ti V 30 *e* 42; II 33, 67; ni-siq NAM-DUB-SAR V 16 *c* 64. — Pognon, *Wadi-Brissa*, 173—4 *rm* 1, reads ni-šim & translates "les hommes d'écriture", *i. e.* les hommes des sciences; for 𒈨 = šim see Latrille, ZK ii 241; also 82—7—14 i 9 (ZA ii 169); ZA ii 136; iii 308.

nisiqtu ‖ nisqu. Sn iii 34, 35 see guxlu, *p* 215 *col* 2; 47 xurāçu abnē ni-siq-ti = jewels; literally stones of splendor, precious stones. AV 6280; aban nisiqti ‖ aban aqartu D^H 55; ZK ii 343. I 65 *b* 21 gold, silver TAG-TAG (= abnē) ne-se-iq-tim; V 63 *b* 38 in aban ni-siq-tim šuk-lu-lu; 64 *b* 1 aban ni-siq-ti šu-qu-ru-tu; IV^2 18 *no* 3 *R* iv 6—9 aban ni-siq-ti (= TAG-ZA-ŠUX) el-me-šu, Br 11744; T^M viii 74; Z^B 104; H 39, 124. usually **nisiqti abnu** (nē), splendor of stones, *i. e.* precious stones, jewels. Asb ii 39 kaspu xurāçu ni-siq-ti abnē (*cf* vi 12); ZA iii 311, 56; II 67, 26+83; I 49 *a* 17; L^2 13 (Lehmann, ii 18, while P^2 14 ni-siq-tu abni). I 51 *no* 1 *a* 20 ni-se-iq-tim ab-nam (*var* -nim); Neb iii 40 ni-se-iq-ti abnu; I 52 *no* 3 *a* 24 i-na kaspi xurāçi ni-se-iq-tim abnē šu-ku-ru-u-tim; V 34 *b* 1; KB iii (2) 48 *col* 1, 38 ne-se-iq-tim abnē. II 67, 28 ni-siq-ti abnē bi-nu-ut tam-dim. V 31 *g-h* 29 ni-siq(ziq?)-tu : ni-ziq-ti.

nussuqu *adj.* precious, splendid, select {kostbar, herrlich, erlesen}. V 62 *a* 51—2 par-çi-šu-nu šu-qu-ru-tu bil-lu-du-šu-nu | nu-us-su-qu-tu (KB iii, 1, 150—1; LEHMANN, ii 58); Sp ii 265 *a* vii 2 il-lu nu-us-su-qu; also xxiii 2 u-çur nu-us-su-qa se-kar at-mi-e [. . . .

nussuru. II 29 *g-h* 54 (supplemented by K 13608) bi-e-šum, nu-us-su]-ru, zu-um-šum; perh Rm² 139, 25 ilišu is-su-ur (*i. e.* Ⓠ pr) aran ili-šu na-ši.

na-sa-ru-ru (√סרר). 83, 1—18, 1335 iii 26 = KUD (ku-ud); M⁸ 74 *col* 2.

nasištu. V 28 *c-d* 86 na-si-iš-tum ‖ lu-luntum u-ri-e, ZK ii 332.

nāpu, in the phrase nu-up-tum i-na-a-pu (‖ inamdin?) FEUCHTWANG, ZA vi 442—3: (der Miether) übernimmt zur Reparatur (KOHLER); also see WZKM iv 127, 128 *rem* 1; PSBA ix 308 il en déclarera la déclaration. PEISER, *Vertr.*, 44, 7—8 nu-up-ta i-na-a-pi; 135, 8—9: in the months of Nisan, Ab (?) & Kislev nu-up-tum i-na-a-pu (Dar 256, 10; 25, 8); also 134, 8. Br. M. 84, 2—11, 102 (toward the end): in Nisan, Āru and Kislev [nu]-up-tum i-nu-up-pu-u-' (*cf* Dar 163, 14) sie werden *n* leisten (KOHLER & PEISER, ii 58). STRASSM., *Stockholm* (VIII.) *Or. Congr.*, *no* 32, 9 ša ina mu-kin-nu šarri nu-pu-'-u.

nūptu(m) a tax {Abgabe} PINCHES, *Inscr. Babyl. Tablets*, 71 *l* 11 nu-up-tum ša ešten šiqli kaspi i-nam-din, a tax of 1 shekel of silver he shall pay. PEISER, *Vertr.*, 41, 7 nu-up-tum i-nam-di-nu-'; Nabd 9, 9 nu-up-tu; ZA iii 140 *no* 16, 8; Cyr 158, 12. Written nu-um-tum, MEISSNER, 108; Camb 117, 8 nu-um-tum i-na-pu-'. WZKM iv 127.

PINCHES, *loc. cit.* from √נוב = nābu, sprout, germinate, increase = profit, earnings, capital, amount; thus P. N. Nu-ub-ta-a, Nabd 356, 21 (AV 6448) *etc.* not = "my bee". but "my treasure".

nāpu, na'apu. II 16 *c-d* 23 pu-uq(k)-li na-'-pi; D⁸ 79; BA ii 296: Kraft des Wurmes; AV 5926; see nābu, 1.

nuppu perh in IV² 45 *b* 45 (K 13) a-na pa-ra-su ša (amēli) ša-ar (= up) nu-up-pu i-nam-di-nu; also lines 48, 51; M⁸ 98 šarnuppu, ein Beamter.

napagu. II 39 *c-d* 64 [cuneiform]-RI-A = na-pa-gu, together with ša-lu-u (62) & ti-bu-u (63), AV 6078; Br 4827.

Der. nampagtu (*q. v.*).

napadu ? 83, 1—18, 1335 ii 22 ku-ud KUD | na-pa-du.

napdū ? K 10053, 2+3 we have a-gi-it-tum, nap-du(?)-[u?] followed by ša-lal . . . & maksū (*q. v.*).

napaxu, pr ippux, ps inappax. — *a*) trans: kindle, fan, inflame {anzünden, anblasen, entflammen}. IV² 8 *a* 2+5 see kinūnu (*p* 408); II 51 *R* 9 ina ṭi-pa-ri tap-pu-xu (ZK ii 322); perh nap-xat pit-pa-nu (or נבה, see nībxu, NOTE 1). — *b*) intr.: flare up (of fire), rise, rise brilliantly (of sun and stars); dawn, ZDMG 30, 312 {aufleuchten, aufgehen (von Sonne und Sternen)}. IV² 20 *no* 2, 1—2 o Šamaš ina išid šamē tap-pu-xa-am-ma (= XI-I-NI-BU) § 150; T^M vii 152; viii 73 a-di tap-pu-xa (2 *sg*), o Šamaš. Anp ii 106 see lām. TP iii 104—5 I conquered the city a-di šuššān-ti ū-me ša (il) Šamaš na-pa-xi; L^T 139. D 94, 15 see lilātu, *p* 483: but KB vi (1) 32—33 reads na-pa-xi i-[na ma-]ti. ZIMMERN, *Beitr. z. Kenntn.*, = *Ritualtafeln*, *etc.* 112 *foll* 3: ina še-rim la-am (il) Šamaš na-pa-xi; Z^Š iii 43 (il) Šamaš ina ZI (= napaxi)-šu. I 35 *no* 1, 11 (*cf* 6) the great sea ša na-pax (il) Šamši; *no* 3, 6 the great sea ša KUR-xa (*var* na-pax) (il) Šam-ši = east, >< J. OPPERT, GGA '82, 817: south; II 67, 3 to the mountain Bikni ša KUR(?) (il) Šam-ši (KB ii 10) >< šul-mi šam-ši. K 2401 ii 4 ištu bīti i-nap-pa-xa-an-ni (where he brightly arises), BA ii 627 *foll.* IV² 56 *col* 1, *add* 4 ri-bu-u . . . i-nap-pa-xu. III 57 *b* 61 MUL DIL-BAT ina šabāṭi KUR

---

nasru, Br 5296 see nasru. ~ ni-sur *cf* NI-ŠUR. ~ nasrap(t)u see naçrap(t)u. ~ nisiītu *cf* nisūtu. ~ nāpi' *cf* nabū, 3. ~ ni-pi-'i (AV 6288; Br 2028) see nib'u. ~ napšidiš see nabāṭiš. ~ nipsu read either nibxu or nipçu, 1 (*q. v.*).

(= ippux)-xa ina šo-ri-e-ti, ZA i 253. S 954 *O* 2 nu-ur šamo-e ša ki-ma i-ša-tim i-na ma-a-tim nap-xat (>< Hilprecht, *Assyriaca*, 45 *rm* 8: nap-pa ℑ of פחו) at-ti-ma; *R* 2 ša ina šu-puk šame-e nap-xat (*var* -xa-tum, Reisner, *Hymns, no* 53) Br 4327. Knudtzon, 44 (+ 295) ZI-MEŠ-xa = napxā, 3 *f pl* of pm ZI-ix, *ibid* 108 *R* 18; 72 *R* 8 = napi-ix (*cf p* 52). V 29 *e-f* 60 GI-NE(=BIL)-LAL = n[a-pa-xu] followed perh by NE-GAR(=ŠA) = nu[-up-pu-xu] Br 2478 *fol.* H 19, 323 . . . . bi | NE | na-pa-xu (II 39 *g-h* 28, Br 4592, ‖ ša-xa-nu, 29); 26, 555 KUR = na-pa-xu (§ 9, 176; Br 7395); 558 bu | BU | na-pa-xu; H 51 (= II 11 *c-d*) 56 IN [(bu)] BU = ip-pu-ux, Br 7528; V 12 *no* 5, 39 see namaru, ZA ii 196 *rm* 3; Br 2321. AV 6079; BA ii 551 *no* 283, where literature is cited; Thompson, *Reports*, agrees with Oppert's rendering: be high, culminate.

Q[t] = Q trans.: IV² 8 *b* 51, 52 at-ta-pux i-ša-ta | kinūna at-ta-pax; *cf* II 51 *R* 14 *foll*, ZK ii 320; T[M] iii 22 (BA iv 157); viii 76 it-tap-xa [(il)] Šamaš (Š leuchtet auf); Zimmern, *Ritualtafeln*, *no* 26, 35.

ℑ intens. of Q. L⁴ iii 10 ab-re nu-up-pu-xu ‖ ṭi-pa-ri ki-e-du (קיד), wood-piles were put on fire {Holzstösse wurden angefacht}. IV² 38 ii 16 u-mi-iš (??) nu-up-pu-xi, or nu-ub-bu-ṭi, KB iv 62 (see nabaṭu. ℑ). V 29 *c-f* 61 see Q.

Š perh V 45 vi 45 tu-ša-an-pax.

N become inflamed, kindled; glare, flare up (of fire *etc.*) {entflammt, angezündet werden; aufflammen (von Feuer, *etc.*)} NE 58, 17 (= Sm 1040) in-na-pi-ix i-ša-a-tum; V 55, 30 i-na bi-ri-šu-nu in-na-pi-ix i-ša-tu. Sm *Asurb*, 126, 73 pa-nu-uš-ša iššātu in-na-pi-ix ez-zi-iš, KB ii 252—3: eine Flamme wird auflodern.

N[t] II 28 *a* 5 libbu it-tan-pax the heart became enraged ‖ libbu ēgug. V 42 *c-d* 47 KAR [(kar-kar)] KAR = i-tan-pu-xu (Br 3188), ‖ itanbuṭu (*q. v.*) Z[B] 102; § 49 *b*.

Derr. tanpaxu & these 4:

napxu *adj* napixtu *f*, kindled {entflammt} IV² 51 *b* 53 ina kinūni nap-xi = Z[B] ii 110. H 129 (K 257 *R*) 11—12, 13—14 i-ša-tum na-pi-ix-tum šit-pu-qu anšku; i-ša-tum na-pi-ix-tum ša ina kirib šadī u-šar-ra-pu anšku, ZA i 451; Br 4327.

nipxu, *c. st.* nipix the brilliant rising of sun or stars (>< Oppert, Thompson, culmination of the sun; zenith) {der glänzende, flammende Aufgang der Sonne und Sterne} AV 6294. I 28 *a* 14 ina ūm (or tam?)-at ni-pi-ix kakkab mešrī (*q. v.*) KB i 124—5; L[T] 170; ZA ii 96—7; BA ii 544 *no* 188; 545 *nos* 196, 196 *a*; 548 *no* 261; 549 *no* 261; 551 *nos* 282—87; also see *nos* 292, 296. Rm 201 *O* 7 ina ni-pi-ix [(il)] Šamši (Pinches, *Texts*, 2 *no* 4; ZA i 436—7); K 871 it is said of Jupiter in line 6: ni-pi-ix-šu ki-ma ni-pi-ix [(il)] Šamši ga-mir (Thompson). Sarg *Khors*, 144 ina qabal tam-tim ni-pi-ix šam-ši (also 69). V 64 *b* 34 i-na ni-ip-xi u ri-ba KB iii (2) 103: beim Aufleuchten und Verschwinden (>< ZA i 286; *cf* I 69 *b* 19). II 35 *e-f* 9 ni-ip-xu ‖ ša-ru-ru, followed by im-mu ‖ xa-ar-xu & šuxnu (11); K 252 (III *R* 66) ii 18 [(il)] Ni-ip-xu çalmu (*cf* נִבְחוֹן, PSBA xxi 118 *fol*; Br 12702); vii 9 + 23 [(ilat)] Ištar ni-ip-xu ša Suti. ZA v 58—9, 42 (hymn to Marduk) (ilu) reš-tu-u a-ša-rid . . . . | ša ina ni-ip-xi-šu u-kal-la-mu ça-ad-du ki[-rib?]. K 126, 41 zikaru ina ni-pi-ix kakkab nīri ana aššatišu iṭxi (*Rev. Sém.* i 170 *foll*). According to some also V 60 *a* 18 = the splendor of the face of Šamaš, BA i 270, but see nīb(i)xu.

[(amēl)] **nappaxu** smith {Schmied} AV 6096. S[b] 93 (*cf* S[b] F 1, 13) si-i (*var* si-mu-ug) : 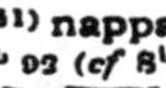 | nap-pa-xu, Br 6720; Berl. Vok i 17; AV 6096; ZA i 256; Jensen, 293 *rm* 2; Peiser, ZA ii 448; ZA v 103; > nappaxu bellows {Blasebalg}, BA i 16 *no* 16; 176. Often in *c. t.* [(amēl)] nappaxu parzilli, Neb 92, 3; blacksmith; [(amēl)] nappaxu siparri, Nabd 220, 3 = coppersmith; *cf* III 47 *no* 10, 13 + 14; 46 *no* 2, 7. [(amēl)] nap-pa-xu Nabd 666, 13; 86, 2 [(amēl)] nap-pa-xu siparri; id in Nabd 89, 3 + 8 *etc.*; 118, 5; 119, 6; 673, 2 (+ MEŠ); Camb 126, 6 according to BA iii 491: der bei den Räucheropfern die Kohlenbecken anzündet. II 58 *no* 5, 8 NIN-ID-GAL | AN + iḍ | .[ii] Ê-a ša nap-pa-xi (Br 6723; TIELE, *Gesch*, 520 *rm* 4; ZA i 256; ZA ii 448; and again, ZA vii 140); see also ZK i 122; ii 324 *foll*; PEISER, KAS 115; HOFFMANN, ZA xi 267.

nappaxtu. smelter {Schmelzofen} III 61 *a* 27 nap-pax-tum in-nap-pax; IV² 51 *b* 55 ina nap-pa-xa-ti (= $Z^Š$ ii 112; T^M iv 26; $Z^Š$ iii 15 = K 2390 *O* 14); $Z^Š$ viii 58 kinûni KI-UB-DA u nap-pa-xà-tu.

nu-pax-ti T. A. Lo. 29, 56.

nupuxâtu see nubuxâtu.

napxaru. totality {Gesammtheit} AV 6091; § 65, 31 *a*. WINCKLER, *Forsch*, 2te Reihe, ii 255 *foll* ('99) compares מבחר, Isa 22, 7. ZA iv 64 *no* 22. *c. st.* nap-xar (alâni-šunu) TP ii 82; iii 8; iv 5 (*var* nap-xar, caret); šarrâni-šunu v 8 + 81; mâtâti-šunu v 84; a-a-bi, K 2107 *O* 20; Br 14392; AV 5411; šarrâni V 35, 28 (end); rag-gi D 95, 31; KB vi (1) 36; kiššat nišê Esh *Sendsch*, *R* 26; mâti-ja Asb ix 44; ki-du-die, ZA iii 313, 61; kiš-ša-ti ZA iv 8, 44. zi-qi-qu ša nap-xar ni-ši V 50 *a* 26; also V 35, 12 (BA ii 210—11); K^M 6, 40. KB iii (2) 66, 39 na-ap-xa-ar ma-da a-a-bi; *Khors* 17 nap-xa-ar Gu-ti-um; a-na nap-xar um-ma-ni-ja V 35, 27 (end), da-ad-mi, 10. a-di nap-xar dad-me-šu I 43, 17; ina nap-xar ZA iv 15, 7; ina nap-xar çal-mat qaqqadi, Merod.-Bal.-stone i 22; mâtâti K 8474 i 47 (ZA iv 8—9); 81—6—7, 209, 41. mâtâte nap-xar-ši-na all countries Šalm, *Ob*, 18; *Mon*, *O* 11; K 1282 *R* 27; *O* 5 qu-la-ma (listen!) nap-xar-ku-nu (KB vi, 1, 68); Creat.-*frg* III 126 Igegê nap-xar-šu-nu; K 2610 iv 18 (‖ na-gab-šu-nu); ilâni nap-xar mâti-šu-nu SMITH, *Senn*, 88, 26; *cf* mašlu 1. BANKS, *Diss*, 18 *foll*, *no* 2 (8—10) 35 û-mu nap-xa-ri; also 10 *no* 1 (4) *O* 37 (-ra). II 54 *a-b* 7—8 [il] ?? bêl ša nap-xa-ri Z^B 85; Br 6191; 3221 *ad* 9); IV² 23 *b* 13—14 be-el nap-xar (= TIK) ma-a-ti (also 15—16); K 44 (H 78) *O* 26—7; IV² 1 *a* 1—3 nap-xar (= NIGIN-NA, Br 10335; 7238—9); K 5267, 5 (H 180 *no* viii); IV² 25 iii 44—5 ina nap-xar mâtâti (Br 8257); 9 *a* 26—7 nap-xar ma-a-ti (Br 8220; *cf* K^M 52, 5). S^c 3, 13 [ŠI?] = i-lu ša nap-xa-ri, ZK ii 23 *rm* 1; Br 9271. V 31 *e-f* 5 up-pi ‖ nap-xa-ru, Br 5802; *cf* 10, Br 9435. S^b 1 *O* iii 2 ni-gi-in | NIGIN | nap-xa-ru (ZA i 183 § 6; Br 10335); S^c 155 ta-ab | TAB | nap-xa[-ru] Br 3705; H 109, 40 (= V 11 *d-f* 40; D 128, 88) TIK (or GU)-MAR = GU-GAR = nap-xa-ru (Br 3279, 3320). K 738 GUD = nap-xa-ru, BOR ii 39. Br 3309 . . . SI = nag-bu ša nap-xa-ri, see also nagbu. II 31 *no* 2, 7 . . . . nap-xa-rum. Br 5897 *ad* D 86 i 27. √פחר, *q. v.* In *c. t.* often in the meaning of sum total, written PAP (TP iv 83; vi 39) & NIGIN, Cyr 188, 15; by some read napxariâ, Br 1145. Neb 403, 2 nap-xar nikasišu. BA i 209.

napaṭu II 47 *c-d* 31 see nabaṭu, 1. Br 5769, AV 6080.

nap(d)ṭarum. II 39 *g-h* 51 ŠA (= GAR) GIŠ-KU-UR = nap-ṭa-rum (AV 6093; Br 12080) √פטר, whence also these 2:

napṭi(î?)ru. IV² 31 *R* 46 šum-ma nap-ṭi-ri-ša la ta-ad-di-nak-kum-ma, if she does not grant thee liberty {wenn sie dir ihre Loslassung nicht gewährt}.

napṭartu. peg to open a door; key {Pflock zum Öffnen der Thür, Schlüssel} ‖ nap-têtum; AV 6105; BA i 170—77. I 27 *no* 2, 41 ša ki-i êkalli-ja la e-ri-bi nap-ṭar-tu, KB i 118—9 *rm* ††. II 22 *a-b* 3—4 GIŠ-KAK-ŠA-GAB = nap-ṭar-tum, nap-te-tum (II 44 *a-b* 44—5) Br 4488, 5303. Also K 12848 *R*, followed by nap-te-e-tum.

napkapu. Neb 92, 7 na-ap-ka-pu.

nappillu, so perhaps better instead of nabbillu. See GGA '98, 821.

napilu some siege instrument, catapult {Belagerungsmaschine, Mauerbrecher} or the like. Anp iii 53 I besieged the city ina pil-še na-pi-le ça(-a)-bi-ti(-te); *cf* 111 ina pil-ši [(iç)] ça-pi-te u ni-pi-še maxâzu akšu-ud.

niplu. M^S 68 reads V 23 *g-h* 26 GIŠ-ŠE-

---

napâṭiš *cf* nabâṭiš. ∾ naplu, AV 6094 see nablu. ∾ napâliš *cf* nabališ. ∾ napalu, 1 (AV 6081) see nabalu, 1. ∾ napalṭû (AV 6082, Br 5531) *cf* nabalṭû. ∾ napalkutum (AV 6083) see nabalkutu (√balkatu); napalqa(t)tu *cf* nabalkattu, *c.* ∾ napša(à)u. AV 6086 see nabasu.

RU = ni-ip[-lu] >< [-ru, D^{Pr} 83 *etc.*] ZA ii 340; Br 7459; see also AV 6295 *ad* K 90, 31 <<< ni-ip-lu ša û-mi.

napalû an official {ein Beamter} ZK ii 302 *ad* K 2012, 5 MULU]-PAL = na-pa-lu-u, apparently ‖ tur-gu-man-nu, Br 274.

naplaxu. √פלח. ZA v 68, 10 kurunnu ša nap-la-xi wine for the temple service. See banû, 1 Q^{t} (end) *p* 175 *col* 1.

naplis & **naplusu** (ac) see palasu, whence also:

naplusu. V 21 *a-b* 64 nap-lu-su = re-e-mu favor, grace {Gnade, Erbarmen} AV 6095.

nipilsû. K 5418 iii 3—4 ša-lum-mat ni-ši mu-ši mu-u-tu namtâru a-ru-ur-tu (or -šu?) n]a-mur-ra-tu xar-ba-šu ni-pil (KB vi 296: bi-is, or b(p)il)-su-u ni-ib-ri-tu, ZA xii 321 *fol.* √פלסא.

naplasatu. D 85 *R* 30 ŠI-TAB-IMÊRU = nap-la-sa-tu, ZA v 378, Br 9317. √פלס.

napalsuxu, *adj?* V 16 *e-f* 44 (= II 49 *a-b* 26) KI-LAL = na-pal-su-xu (√פלסח), AV 6084; Br 9812; BA i 508. Also V 11 *a-c* 21—22 UR-ÇI-ÇI = UR-DUN-DUN = na-pal-su-xu (H 107 + 112; D 127) Br 4841; 4844; also S^{c} 270 (Br 10544); II 26 *a-b* 19, Br 10581.

napalsuxtu (*sc.* kussû) low chair, footrest niedriger Sessel, Schemel} II 23 *a-b* 8 na-pal-su-ux-tum (& šu-šu-ub-tum) ‖ ku-us-su-u ša-pil-tum. AV 6085.

naplaštu. D 84 *R* 31 AB-LAL (Br 3842 *ad* ZA iv 31) = nap-la-aš-tu in a group with derivatives of פלס. Lehmann, ii 43 *rm* 2: scales {Wange} >< Z^{B} 18. BA i 176.

napaltum. S^{P} 158 + S^{P} II 962 *O* 34 .... ša-na kat-te-e u-ša-an-na-a na-pa-al-tum. Pinches, *Vict. Inst. Journ.*, xxix: the *k* repeated the matter (?).

nipêsu? III 15 *a* 13 aš-šu e-peš šarrû-ti bît abi-ja ni-pi-sa šangûti-ja (I prayed to the gods). Harper, *Diss*, 32, bel.; Pinches; KB ii 140 ni-pi-ir.

napsamu. bridle; rein and bit of a horse {Zaum und Gebiss}. § 65, 31*a*; BA i 177. V 47 *b* 40—41 ina pi-i gir-ra ēkili-ja id-di nap-sa-mu (il) Marduk, into the mouth of the lion that threatened to devour me, Marduk put a bit. nap-sa-mu = ma-aq-ça-ru (*q. v.*) ša pî sisê; ‖ kulûlum. AV 5895; ZK ii 333 *col* 3, 5.

napsanu. 83, 1—18, 1847 *R*, *col* 5, 2 (mât) bi-it na-ap-sa-nu, PSBA xviii 256.

ni-pa(or **xat?**)**-pu-tum** (?) V 36 *d-f* 56; form like nirarûtum?

napaçu. *pr* ippuç, *ps* inappaç break to pieces, shatter, smash, overwhelm, kill, slay {zerbrechen, zerschmettern, töten, erschlagen} AV 6087; Br 7029; RÉJ xiv 149 >< D^{Pr} 39 *rm.* I 70 *d* 25 may the gods (a-di û-um ça-a-ti) lip-pu-çu zêr-šu, may destroy his race. IV^{2} 16 *b* 10 (end) ar-da-tum i-nap-pa-çu (= MU-UN-DUB-DUB-BU-NE) ‖ edlu išab-biṭu. Strassm., *Stockh. Or. Congr.*, 6, 2 ša na-pa-çu u e-pi-šu erçi-tim. Scheil, ZA x 202, 5 arki] in-bi i-nap-pa-aç. S^{b} 155 du-ub | DUB | na-pa-çu, H 25, 534; II 48 *c-d* 42 (= K 4386); S^{c} 296 ta-ag | TAG | na-ba-çu, Br 3799.

Q^{t} H 25, 536 du-ub | DUB-DUB | it-pu-çu (= II 48 *c-d* 43) Br 7037; Z^{B} 102; § 49*b*.

Q^{tn} K 161 *b* 24 itanapaç kîma nûni, ZK ii 10, 11.

ℑ kill, slay in great numbers {töten, erschlagen} § 33. Asp ii (83) 114 their soldiers u-nap-pi-iç; ii 36 u-na-pi-iç; iii 53 u-ni-pi-iç; Šalm, *Balaw*, III 1 muqtablêšu u-nap-pi-çi. III 38 *no* 2 *R* 9 qu-ra-]di-ja u-nap-pi-iç. Sarg *Ann* 332 ki-ma az(s)-li ..... u-nap (*var* tap)-pi-ça qurâdêšu I cut down {mordete ich}. NE 43, 35 êkallu mu-nap-p[i-ça-at] qar-ra-de(-di) KB vi (1) 168—9: a palace which will smash this mighty one.

$ℑ^{t}$ u-tap-pi-ça see ℑ. i-tap-pu-çu ac K 4386 iii (II 48 *c-d*) 44 = ŠU-DUB-DUB, Br 7206; §§ 49b; 88; 101.

Derr. these 3:

nipçu *1.* a broken-off piece of metal, or the like {ein abgebrochenes Stück Metall}? AV 6296. II 30 *b* 39 ni-pi-iç erê; same id = ep-ri erê (40 *b*). H 82—3, 21 ni-pi-iç bu-a-ni = SA-ŠA-DUB, Br 12103.

nuppuçu *adj* broken, smashed {zerschlagen, zerschmettert}. II 30 *b-c* 74 GUL-DUB-DUB-BU = nu-up-pu-çu-ti (said of narṭabê, *q. v.*) AV 6446; Br 7029, 8969.

nappaçu (> nanpaçu). V 26 *a-b* 21 GIŠ (e-si) KAL = nap-pa-çu (‖ ešû, martû) Br 6203; *cf* II 40 *a-b* 20; 44 *a-b* 39—40; AV 6097. BA i 177.

nipçu *2.* ‖ naxtu, 1. *q. v.* Br 14055.

napaqu. Perh = Aram פקנ herausgehen, أفق überragen. V 42 *c-d* 59—60 . . . . . XU = na-pa-qu, followed by nu-up-pu-qu. K 49 (II 62) *c-d* 30—31 XAR-DA = pu-uq-qu (פוק) & nu-up-pu[-qu] Br 8577 (>< AV 6394). II 24 *no* 4 *R* (K 4188 iii) 54, 55 = nu-up-pu-qu, AV 6447. V 47 *b* 11 see lagabbiš (*p* 476 *col* 2). V 30 *g-h* 29 (= H 215) ÇUR = nu-pu-qu, Br 9072.

nappaqu. ZA iv 237, 49 (252, 25) kīma li-e ša ina nap-pa-qu p(b)al-qu.

naprû. a weapon {eine Waffe}. K 8076 iii 26 URUDU-ŠUN-ID-LAL = nap-ru-u, ZA viii 77.

(bir) na-pi-ru-ti see note to namrûtu; P. N. Na-pi-ru(-rum) ili KB iv 2, 9.

nipru. sprout, offspring, child, or the like {Spross, Sprössling, Kind} D[S] 142 see nannabu. II 30 *c-d* 40 ni-ip-ru ‖ ma-ar; 36 *c-d* 49 = ma-a-ru & *a-b* 58 ni]-ip-ru = lil-li[-du] AV 6190. II 22 *b-c* 61 BU-BU-I = ni-ip-ru, followed by šu-uk-qu-u, Br 7580.

T. A. Lo. 41, 9 **na-ap-ri-il-la-an** = emûtu, a word belonging to the Dunip-language; Sayce, PSBA xxii 172 would connect this with nipru and translate „priests".

nīpiru. a fortified position, cover {befestigte, gedeckte Stellung, Deckung} Anp iii 39 Azilu relied upon his forces and in the city of *K.* ni-pi-ri lu iç-bat (KB i 100; Hebr. i 178 *rm* 5; vii 100 *rm* 31; AV 6289).

napparu. Delitzsch, *Weltschöpfungsepos*, 58 *ad* S 747 *O*: çu-çu-u : nap-pa-ru; but Jensen, KB vi (1) 303: ap-pa-ru.

nup'ā'ru. perh disposition, feelings {vielleicht Gemüt, Gefühl} Esh vi 38 all my subjects . . . u-ša-li-ça nu-pa-ar-šu-un (Hebr. vii 99). Sarg *Khors* 168, I offered rich presents to the gods and u-ša-li-ça nu-pa-ar-šu-un (= *Ann* 432); Pp IV 130 (3 *sg*); ZA iv 241, 34 lim-mir nu-par[-šu].

Hommel, PSBA xix 78 § 21: as lubāru 'dress' from lubāšu, so perhaps nupāru "wind" from nupāšu, √נפש.

Nippur(u) city of Nippur (Niffer) iδ EN-EN-KIT[KI] *i. e.* Bel's city, Br 2877; AV 6293. Bezold, *Catalogue*, 2136. II 50 *a-b* 28 (Br 8409) DUR-EN-KIT; H 38, 79 Ni-pu-ru; 50, 14 ina ka-ri Ni-pu-ru. II 53 *a-b* 4, Br 2877. K 83 *R* 3 ki-i i-xu(bak)-ku-an-ni ina Nipûri (Hr[L] 202); II 19 *a* 55 a-na Ni-ip-pu-ri nisiš la ṭexê; V 44 *c-d* 39; 82—8—22, 1048, 6 Ni-ip-pu-ru ul êpuš, was not yet built. ZA iv 430 (80—7—19, 126) ina Ni-ip-pu-ru pa-rak-ki çi-ri-ša. Nippura'a, 81—2—4, 125. Local deities were Bêl & Bêltis. On the names Nippur-Niffer-Nuffar see Nöldeke, in Hilprecht, *Assyriaca*, 86 *rm* 1; also *cf* Friedrich, *Kabiren*, 14 *foll.*

Nipur(i), a mountain to the East of the Tigris. Anp i 70—3 (šadû) Ni-pur; Sn iii 69, 71. AV 6292. Lehmann, i 77, 78, 80, 98.

niperdû, sometimes napirdû, *adj* brilliant, bright, shining, light {glänzend, scheinend, hell} √פרד. TP i 40 Tigl. Pil. calls himself û-mu ni-per-du-u whose splendor overthrows the world (R. F. Harper, AJSL xiv 2). V 16 *a-b* 34 + Rm 2. III *col* 1, 18 (H 108 *no* 4, 35) UD-BAR-LAX-GA = û-mu ni-per-du-u (*cf* Sn *Kui* 4, 16; Z[B] 69; Br 1934, 7835; L[T] 106). 82, 9—18, 4159 ii 5 UD (ba-ab-bar) ni-pir-du[-u]. IV² 20 *no* 1, 15—16 they all looked at e-til-la na-per-da-a šu-lu-la, Br 10006. — used as a noun in KB vi (1) 46 *no* iii 4 ni(>< BA ii 467 *fol* sa)-pir-du-u ellûti mê, the brightness of the clear water.

na-pa-ra-ax-tum, Nabd 558, 13.

napraxatum see maškanu, 3.

naparkû. ceasing {aufhörend}. Ner ii 10 mi-e nu-ux-šu la na-pa-ar-ku-ti unceasing flow of water, AV 6088, AJP xi 501.

napraku. bolt, cross-bar {Riegel}. V 47 *a* 21 nap-ra-ku explained by pi-ir-ku ‖ me-di-lu. AV 5260, 6095; § 65, 31 *a*; BA i 177. ⊕ 287 vi (*R*) 5—6 GIŠ-ŠU-GI & GIŠ-GIL = nap-ra-ku, Br 7128, 1392; Z[B] 39.

---

napurru *cf* naburru.

naprušu. II 30 *e-f* 38 RAB = nap-ru-šu (Br 1787; AV 6099) see parašu.

naprašu (?) ZA iv 240, 1 pu-ṭur ku-un nap-ra-šu (= naprasu?).

nēpišu (nībišu). √epešu. — *a*) action, procedure; treatment, method {Treiben, Handeln; Handlungsweise, Verfahren}. IV² 23 *no* 1, iv 26 ni-pi-šu NAM-UŠ-KU (= kalûti, *cf p* 382, kalû, 6) = astrology. V 47 *a* 39 ni-pi-ši explains ag-ag-ṭu-u, see also ki(t)-kit-ṭu; Jensen, KB iii (1) 204 *rm* 9. K 626, 7 ina eli nipi-še (Hr^L 24); K 1026, 6 (Hr^L 118). See also makaltu (end) *p* 536 *col* 2, where read with Zimmern, *Ritualtafeln*, 89 *rm* 4: ni-pi-šu ša ba-ru[-ti]; "makaltu wol: Schale oder Becher zum Wahrsagen". çubāt ni-pi-še(-ši) Kultusgewand, Zim., *Rituall.*, *no* 26, 35; 55, 7. — *b*) witchcraft, charming {Zauberei} K 168, 18 ni-pi-e-še ša ašipūtu; 22 ... ma-a pa-na-at ni-pi-eš an-nu-ti, Lehmann, ii 76—77. perh ni-pi-šu ^il Sin, Craig, *Relig. Texts*, 65, 3. Zimmern, *Ritualtafeln*, 116 *foll.*, *no* 24 *R* 8: das (Wahrsage)gerät des Sin. — *c*) with or without prefix ^(iç), a siege machine {Belagerungsapparat} BA i 177; 326. Anp iii 111 see napilu. II 67, 21 i-na bi-ru-ti (*p* 197 *col* 1) u ^(iç) ni-pi-ši. II 65 ii 3 Nebuchadrezzar ni-bi-še-šu iš-ša-a; 6, aš-šu ni-bi-še la a-bu a-ge-šu ina išîti iš-ru-up, KB i 198. AV 6184, 6200. Pognon, *Wadi-Brissa*, 85, 86.

nipištu *1.* structure, work, production {Bauart, Werk, Machwerk} § 65, 31a. Sn vi 42 a palace ni-piš-ti ^(mât) Xa-at-ti, ‖ êpištu. ZA v 291; BA iv 244. — product {Erzeugnis} Sarg *Khors* 148 Ušu- & Urkarînu-wood ni-piš-ti mâti-šu-un (= *Ann* 388).

napašu 1. pr ippuš; ps inappuš (& -paš?) be or become broad, extended, widen, expand, breathe {weit sein, sich weiten, ausdehnen, atmen}. AV 6080. Brown-Gesenius, 659 *col* 1: orig., breathe, blow ‖ rapašu (Gesenius[12]), then: to extend, expand. Z^B 99. *del* 190, 198 (210, 213) šit-tu ki-ma im-ba-ri i-nap-pu-uš eli-šu sleep fell (literally: expanded) upon him like a storm; but KB vi 244—5: bläst Schlaf wie ein Wetter über ihn hin. KB vi (1) 10, Tafel ii *b*, *R* 5 ... kab-ta-taš lib-bu-uš li(u)p(b)-p(b)u-uš, {dass .... aufatme}, *p* 317. IV² 54 *b* 4 loosen his fetters lip-pu-uš sur-riš, so that he breathe freely at once. II 60, 7 a-na-ku na-pa-a-ša a-li-' (AV 6089). — spread out, expand, thrive, increase {sich ausbreiten, ausgedehnt, zahlreich werden, sich mehren} II 37 *g-h* 1 name of a bird: kap-pa ip-pu-uš. Asb i 48 ŠI-DI (= ešer) ebûri na-pa-aš ^(il) Nisaba; also 83—1—18, 178, 3; 81—2—4, 182 *R* 2; 83—1—18, 181 *O* 2; Bu 88—5—12, 75 + 76 *col* ix 15 (Thompson, *Reports*); H 68, 14—15 (= K 4170 + K 4322 *R*) ebu-ru ip-pu-uš, ebûru ul ippuš, *cf* Bu 89—4—26, 18, 2 ebûru ina-pu-uš; 83—1—18, 222 *R* 5; 83—1—18, 176 *R* 5. — Of maxîru (KI-LAM) price {Kaufpreis} it is used often, *e. g.* III 54 *c* 3 maxîru ina-pu-uš; 60, 73 maxîru LAL (= maṭu)-u ina-pu-uš; II 43 (*d*)-*e* 15 na-pa-aš maxîru. — T. A. Ber 48, 9 *foll* ia-nu še'i a-na a-ka-li a-na ia-ši-nu mi-na a-na-pu-šu, KB v 410 *ad* 148—9: what shall I nourish my peasants with? — S^c 125 pi-eš | PEŠ | na-pa-šu ša .... (Br 6935) same id, 21 rapašu.

ℑ allow to, let breathe {aufatmen lassen}. IV² 60* C *R* 5 the whole day my pursuer pursued me, during the night ul u-nap-pa-ša-an-ni sur-riš, he does not allow me a moment's breath. K 578, 10 ša a-na e-pa-ša | DUG-GA u-ni-ip-ša (Hr^L 273; AV 6089). 81—6—7, 209, 12 Esh (ana) nu-up-pu-uš kabit-ti-šu-nu (of the gods) ‖ ana nuxxu libbi ilûtišunu (BA iii 260) see KB vi (1) 317. V 21 *c-d* 18 nu-pu-šu preceded by bu-'-u & a-tu-u (AV 6898, Br 7207). P. N. Mu-ni-piš-ilu III 48 *no* 6, 20.

ℑ^t be extended, enlarged {ausgedehnt, erweitert werden}. II 47 *a-b* 18 mâtu ut-ta-pa-aš expl. by mâtu DAGAL-iš (= irapiš), it will be enlarged (§ 101).

Derr. These 6:

napšu *adj* widening, increasing {sich weitend, steigernd}. II 43 *b* 28 KI-LAM

napramu see nabramu. ~ naprar'ū' (BA i 177) read nabrarû & niprêtu see nibrêtu. ~ naparšudu *cf* פרשד 23.

(= maxīru) nap-šu; III 54 *c* 1—2 maxīru nap-ša ibašši (?).

napšu abundance {Überfluss}. K 86 *R* 2 mātu-ša nap-ša ik-kal, the land will eat abundance (THOMPSON, *Reports*); also K 815, 5—6.

nipšu. flavor, odor {Duft} JENSEN, KB vi (1) 252 on *del* (272) 304: çīru i-te-çi-in ni-piš šam-mu, a serpent smelled the flavor of the herb.

napištu, *c. st.* napšat, *pl* napšāte; id ZI, Br 2322 (H 15, 191 = na-piš-tu) § 9, 28; *pl* ZI-MEŠ *del* 20 (25); also ŠI (Br 9279). — *a*) breath, life {Atem, Leben} AV 6090; § 65, 7. — Asb ix 33 mē balāṭ napištim-šu-nu (K 81, 5 a-na TI-ZI-MEŠ) ak-la (WINCKLER, T. A., KB v: balāṭ napšāti provisions); iv 95 ba-laṭ napišti-šu-nu (*var* na-piš-ti-šu-nu); K 523, 7—8 a-na ba-la-ṭa nap-ša-a-ti for the preservation of life (Hr^{L} 324; BA i 189 *fol*). Asb ii 8; ix 112; *del* 21 (26) see bulluṭu (*p* 162), K 620 *R* 11—13 (Hr^{L} 65) *cf* bulṭu (*p* 164); D 99, 26 (Creat.-*frg* IV 100) see eṭeru; K 2852 + K 9662 ii 23 aš-šu .... eṭir na-piš-ti-šu they came out before him. TP ii 54; v 12; Neb iv 38 (also KB iii, 2, 48 *col* 2, 42 + 49); IV^2 54 *b* 7; 21 *a* 59—60 (Br 6812) *etc.* see gamalu (*p* 221); Creat.-*frg* IV 17 na-piš-ta-šu gi-mil. K 7674, 14 ur-ru-uk nap-ša-ti. Destroy one's life, kill some one {jemandes Leben vernichten, töten} see bullû (*p* 159 *col* 2), xulluqu (*pp* 318—9), quttû; V 61 vi 58; Asb iii 125 *etc.*; Creat.-*frg* IV 18 tu-bu-uk nap-šat-su. — Sn v 60 (iç) tar-ta-xu pa-ri-' nap-ša-te; v 77 aq-ra-te nap-ša-te-šu-nu u-par-ri-' gu-'-iš; *cf* Creat.-*frg* IV 31 nap-ša-tu-uš pu-ru-'-ma; IV^2 3 *b* 11 na-piš-ta-šu rukusma; IV^2 9 *no* 2, 4: In these passages perhaps = part of the body: throat {Kehle} GGA '98, 822. — Also see sāqu, usīq. — Esh ii 34 18 ušēxibu nap-šat-su; III 5 *no* 6, 13 a-na šu-zu-ub napšāti-šu; TP ii 40 a-na šu-zu-ub | nap-ša-a-te-šu-nu. — SCHEIL, *Nabd*, viii 10—11 (ilat) Taš-me-tum na-çi-rat na-piš-ti-ja; V 34 *c* 7 the goddess Ninkarrak na-çi-ra-at na-bi-iš-ti-ja; 46 šu-ul-li-im na-bi-iš-ti; *cf* KNUDTZON, 144 *O* 6 ša-lam ZI-MEŠ-šu, dass sein Leben erhalten wird. KB iv 198 (*no* xxix) 7 nap-ša-ti ša (amēl) gal-li-ka u-šal-lam-ka. I 44, 94 the bull-god na-çir nap-ša-a-ti, protecting life. TP v 28 a-na na-piš-ti umaššeršu, I let him go; Sn vi 23 ša a-na nap-ša-a-ti u-çu-u, who had escaped with their lives; K 2852 + K 9662 i 17 a-na nap-ša-a-ti muš-šir-an-ni. Neb ix 52 na-ap-ša-ti a-ga-ar-ti a-ra-mu. Sarg *Ann* 435 see šaṭapu. Asb iv 56 ša .... nap-šat-su-un pa-nu-uš-šu-un te-qir-u-ma, to whom (their) life was too dear (*cf* vii 32); iv 95 ba-laṭ na-piš-ti-šu-nu aq-bi; na-piš-ta H 75 *R* 7. — šakanu napištu give up the ghost, die {den Geist aufgeben, sterben} Asb iii 135; iv 80; ix 35; K 3474 i + K 8232 i 23 šu-par na-piš-ti šak-na (ZA iv 8). KB ii 244—5, 55 see kalû 2. Q^t. nap-ša-ti-šu TP III *Ann* 92; nap-šat-su S^{P} II 987 *R* 3. IV^2 3 *a* 25—6 the poor man it-ti na-piš-ti-šu. nap-šat niše *pl* ZA iv 14 *col* 3, 21. *del* 22 (27) šu(?)-li-ma zēr nap-ša-a-ti ka-la-ma (+ 84). KB vi (1) 46 *R* 3 ku-nu-uk-ku na-piš-ti-ka dein Lebenssiegel (+ 6 -šu); II 51 *b* 26 lip-šur na-piš-ti ma-a-ti (*i. e.* the Euphrates). I 65 *b* 15 a-na ša-ṭa na-bi-iš-ti ni-šim Ba-bi-lam^{ki} (KB iii, 2, 34). P. N. Sin-na-bi-iš-tim IV^2 34 *a* 17; PSBA xxi 136—7; § 49. — ši-kin na-piš-ti, I 27, 70 = living being, creature; IV^2 29** *no* 5 *O* 2 (= H 115) šik-na-at na-piš-ti (Br 2322); IV^2 28 *no* 1 *b* 7—8 (Br 12018); 29 *no* 1 *a* 43—44; 19 *b* 38; II 19 *a* 22; II 51 *b* 31 mu-ti-la-at šik-nat na-piš-ti, epithet of a canal. 82—7—4, 82 *R* 4 ši-ik-na-tum na-pi-iš-tum (PSBA xx 152 *foll*); II 43, 54; IV^2 9 *a* 49—51 (end) ŠI-MA-AL = šik-na-at na-piš-tim; also *a* 24 (-ti); *b* 4 (Br 9364). — soul {Seele} K 2852 + K 9662 i 31 ši(?)-i-gi na-piš-ti-ja la tap-la-xu the anger(?) of my soul thou didst not fear. — *b*) living being, creature, person, people {lebendes Wesen, Kreatur, Person}. IV^2 5 *c* 30 (šar-ru) na-piš-ti (= ZI, 37) māti u-kal-la, controls the people of the country;

napšû AV 6191 *ad* V 21 *a b* 53 nap-šu-u ‖ ri-e-mu; but see napšuru.

IV^2 34 *R* 3. *del* 163 (174) a-u-um-ma u-çi na-piš-ti, "ist (da) irgend ein Lebewesen entkommen?". Sn *Bell* 18 (Lay 63, 9) na-piš-tu ul ezib ‖ Sn i 57 e-du ul ēzib (AV 6090).

NOTE. — 1. V 33 iii 43 a xulālu-stone ina na-piš[-ti-šu] I laid, KB iii (2) 143 "auf seine Kiemen (??)" & see *ibid*, *rm* *.

2. K 4030 ina nap-šat ēkalli is contrasted to ina rēš ēkalli & ina qabal ēkalli. BOISSIER, PSBA xviii ('96) 237—9.

3. The name of the famous ancestor of Gilgameš: 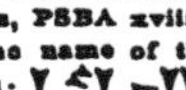 is read variously: HOMMEL, PSBA xv ('92—3) 243 nūx-napištim (= נֹחַ), so also BALL, *Light from the East*, = rest of the soul, whence Hebr נוּחַ, rest. — JENSEN, KB vi (2) reads ŪT-napištim (or Ūm-napištim, *p* 310); as against *Kosmologie der Babylonier* ('90) 213 *fol*, 227, 384 *fol*: Çit-napištim = "he that has escaped", from destruction. — ZIMMERN, *Cheyne-Black*, i *col* 1056 favors Par-napištim = sprout, or offspring of life; see also JASTROW, *New York Independent*, 10 & 17 Febr. '98; ZA xii 288—301. — HAUPT, KAT^2 ('83) Šamaš-napištim (Z^B 26 *rm* 1) = "the sun of life"; he now reads: Pīr-napištim.

nappašu (> nanpašu). — *a*) airhole, loophole, window {Luftloch, Luke, Fenster} § 65, 31 *a*. *del* 129 (136) ap-ti nap-pa-ša-am-ma urra im-ta-qut eli dūr ap-pi-ja. H 93, 29 ina bi]-ti nap-pa-ši ša ērubšu. ZA iv 240, 15 ta-sa-niq arad-ka nap-pa-šu. — *b*) airhole for a stove {Ofenloch}. V 39 *a-b* 62—64 (*cf* 42 *a-b* 33—35) KA-KAK (Br 659) = nap-pa-šu (see pi-ka-lu-lu ‖ ka-par ti-nu-ru, lines 61, 60); KA-BAL (Br 556), ŠA-TAB (Br 3766, 12087) = *n*; this last in 65 also = na-aš-rap-tum & na-aç-rap-tum, Br 3769 (Z^B 70, V 42 *a-b* 47). 82, 8—16, 1 iv 16 (di-ni-ig) | KI-NE | nap-pa-šu (15 = ku-u-ru, Br 9707) HOMMEL, *Sum. Les.*, 98: bellow {Blasebalg}. ZK i 122 *fol*; ii 52; ZA i 64, 1; BA i 1 & 177.

nipištu *2.* some sort of ulcer {ein Geschwür}? II 28 *b-c* 17 SA-BU-I = ni-pi-iš-tu (AV 6291, Br 3141).

napašu 2. card, pick wool {zupfen, zerrupfen, von Wolle} *etc.* 83, 1—18, 1330 i 14 pi-uš | SU-KAD | na-pa-šu, ni-ip-šu, nu-up-pu-šu. Ⓠ perh K 883, 15 giçu ašabirma axartinnu ana ni-ip-ši a-nap-pa-aš, BA ii 633—4. ℑ IV^2 7 *b* 28 kīma SEG-ŠIT (idqi) an-ni-i in-nap-pa-šu-ma; *b* 35 kīma idqi annī li-in-na-pi-iš (§ 101); lines 38, 45, *var* li-in-na-piš, said of çirpu (dyed wool); also see *b* 48 + 55. HOMMEL, PSBA xix 78 § 22 √ of napasu, naba'š'u.

nipšu *2.* see napašu 2. woolflakes {Wollflocken} ZIMMERN, *Ritualt.*, 60, 20 ina ni-ip-šu ina nabāsi qātē-šu tarakkas; & 67 *O* 4.

nipšu *3.* NE 46, 140 ina ša[-ni](-i) [n]i-[i]p-š[i]; 143 i-na šal-ši ni-ip(b)-ši, KB vi (1) 174.

napišu (?) NE 11, 10 + 17 li-ki-e (& il-ti-ki) na-pis-su (> napiš-šu?). KB vi (1) 156 *ad* NE IV *col* v 3 (end) ri-um-ma na-p(b)is-su: und Wind sein Atem, thus *masc* of napištu. J^{I-N} 48 *rm* 34 translates NE 11, 10: betöre seine Seele; if there is a masc. form napišu: life, soul, then *del* 265 (296) belongs here, see nibittu, 2.

napšuru. grace, favor {Gnade, Gunst} √pašaru. V 21 *a-b* 53 ri-e-mu = nap-šu-ru; 65 nap-šu-ru = ri-e-mu, BA i 181. ZA iv 236, 2 nap-šur-ka. K 3500 + K 4444 + K 10235 i 9 see WINCKLER, *Forsch*, ii 10, 16. III 66 *col* 10, 9 nap-šur pi-ti-tim. perh in ar-rat la nap-šu-ri, a curse without escape, K 2619 i 31; III 41 ii 15; 43 iii 25; i 70 iv 23. KB iii (1) 192—3, 37 (= Merod.-Bal.-stone v la nap-šu-ru) ‖ la pa-ša-ri IV^2 38 *c* 33—4. AV 6102. Fem is:

napšurtu. II 34 *g-h* 72 UL$^{(ša)}$DU = nap-šur-tum, AV 6103, Br 9152.

nipšaru, salvation, relief {Errettung, Erlösung} D^K 26; BA i 177; Camb 298, 4 P.N. Nabū-ni-ip-ša-ri. *cf* P.N. Nabū-ni-ip-ša-ri Neb 103, 1 *foll.*

napšaštu, napšaltu, AV 6100; BA i 177. — *a*) ointment, anointing {Salbe, Salbung, Einreibung}. IV^2 57 *b* 7 see nabšaltum, which T^M 123, 124; K^M 57 refer here; 49 *b* 20 nap-šal-ti šam-me lim-nu-ti ip-šu-šu-in-ni, with ointments of bad herbs they have rubbed me (= T^M i 106). IV^2 55 *a* 32 (end). 83—1—18, 2 *R* 18 (Hr^L 391) lik-ru-ur nap-šal-tu (R. F.

---

napašu see nabas(s)u, nabašu. ∼ napištum see nakirtum ‖ kulīlum. ∼ napšaltu see napšaštu.

Harper, AJSL xv, 141). — *b*) means or instrument, vessel for anointing, brush? {Mittel oder Werkzeug, Gefäss zum Salben, Einreiben; Bürste, Pinsel?} II 46 *f-g* 38 GIŠ-LIS-NI 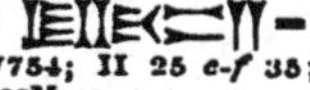 = nap-ša-aš-tum, Br 7754; II 25 *e-f* 35; D 87 iii 46; id also in K[M] 12, 8 + 15 + 116 (*cf* IV² 57 *a* *O* 8 *etc*).

nupuštum, so Br 14001 *ad* V 16 *g-h* 4 . . . EN = nu-pu-uš-tum, AV 6293.

napatu. NE 24, 1 iz-zi-zu-ma i-nap-pa-at-tu (iç) kištu, KB vi 159 (443 > inabbâṭṭu = innabâṭu √נבט), still standen sie und betrachteten den Wald, thus = examine, observe; also 27, 45 on which see KB vi (1) 152 *rm* 5. perh II 28, 49 (*add* 4) nu-up-pu-tum, instead of nubbutum.

naptû. Rm 353 *O* 2 has sik-kat nap-te-e (Br 4494; 5283); II 22 *a-b* 5, perh = נִפְתָּ.

niptû key {Schlüssel}. II 23 *c-d* 49 ni-ip-tu-u ‖ mu-še-lu-u, BA i 163 *rm* 2; 177; § 65, 31*a*, *rm*; AV 6297.

naptētu. H 39, 142 = II 44 *a-b* 45 (K 4399 *O* 14) GIŠ-KAK-ŠA-GAB = nap-te-tum, see napṭartu; Br 5304. Also K 8676 iv 12 [URUDU?]-TUR-TUR = nap-te-e-tu, M[S] 79; AV 6106; Hommel, VK 73; §§ 32*aγ*; 65, 31*a*.

naptanu. meal, feast {Mahl, Schmaus} √patanu. AV 6104; ZK ii 18; ZA i 53; BA i 177; Barth, ZA iii 57—8 compares Syr מתותא × BA i 161 *rm* 1. Hommel = Hebr מִפְתָּן. Šalm, *Ob*, 70 nap-tan xu-du-tu aškun a feast of joy I made {ein Freudenmahl machte ich} KB i 134. Sarg *Cyl* 42 šurrux nap-ta-ni ši-mat paš-šûri ili u šarri. Peiser, KAS 46, 11 kur-ru-bu nap-ta-nu ša (il) IB. *Bab. Vertr.*, xxiii 19 nap-tan. Nabd 247, 12. IV² 7 ii 1 a-na nap-tan ili u šarri la illakû (BA i 390). ZA iv 13, 28 (+16) nap-tan kib-ra-a-ti u zi-bi (= sacrifice), *cf* ZA iv 226; ZA v 68, 9 nap-tan a-pa-ta-nu ul i-ṭe-xa-a, to the feast, I had prepared, he did not come. K 2711 *R* 31 . . . . lu (ŠE) sil-lat an-nu-u a-na nap-tan ilû-ti[-šu rabî-ti] BA iii 264 *fol.* K 2852 + K 9662 iii 30 cattle, sheep ana niqê bêli-ja u nap-tan šarrû-ti-ja (my royal table). Sp III 586 + R III 1, 16 nap-ta-an i-lu-ti-ka liš-ša-kin-ku (*var* -ka). T[M] ii 9 ina ba-li-ka ul iš-šak-kan nap-ta-na ina É-kur; = vi 95 (nap-tan); Lehmann, *Šamš*: L⁴ iii 9 mimma šum-šu nap-tan; Z[B] vi 66. KB vi (1) 276, 35 il-tak-nu ana nap-ta[-ni mârtu] *cf* 280 ii 48; Banks, *Diss*, 24—26, 2 *nos* 8—10, 68 nap-tan(-nu) ša-qu (*var* ku)-u. Zimmern, *Rituall.*, 60 *R* 28 nap-tan qa-ti; 78, 71 nap-ta-an pu-ux-ri ša ilâni rabûti.

nâçu 1. K 4341 i 23 (II 36 *e-f* 58) ŠI-TUR = na-a-çu (AV 6117; Br 9320) in one group with ša-a-ṭu (= ŠI-TUR-TUR), despise {verachten}? ‖ qullulu; Hebr נאץ. Delitzsch in Baer-Del., *Ezek*, pref. xvi (bel.); Jensen, 361. Haupt in Toy, *Ezekiel* (SBOT) 80—1 says: it does not occur in any connected text; but *cf* K 655 (Hr[L] 132) *R* 6 an-nu-çu a-ça-ba-[s]u, I despise him and put him in fetters, Winckler, *Forsch*, ii, 2, 302; Sp ii 265*a* viii 2 u-çur-ti ili ta-na-çu (ZA x 6; PSBA xvii 148). — Ʒ V 45 ii 20 tu-na-'-aç. KB v 410 *ad p* 154—55: T. A. (Ber) 71, 14 ti-na-i-zu despise me?; 23 u ja-an-aç-ni, despises me.

Rec. Trav. xx *no* xxxv, 9 a-na-aç; but KB vi (1) 300 a-na-xi; also see ZA xii 330.

nâçu 2. *c.st.* na-aç. Rm 2. 454 + 79, 7—8, 180 *O* 18 see kappu, 1 (420 *col* 1); KB vi (1) 113 translates: gegen die Stümpfe meiner Flügel leg' [deine Hände]; see line 21. Perh. = Hebr נוֹצָה: plumage, BA ii 395—6; Brown-Gesenius, 663. See also K 3651 *O* 14, 16.

nâç(z, s?)u 3. Zimmern, *Ritualtafeln*, *no* 11 *R* 6 (iç) erina ina pI-šu u-na-['-aç], *var* Rm 145 & K 2364 i-na-'-iç: Cedernsaft mit seinem Munde soll er schlürfen; see also *no* 75—78, 16.

nâçu *4.* 82—2—4, 144 *R* 8 i-na]-ap-ra na-aç u pa-ni-tu, Thompson, *Reports*, ii 31.

naçû *1.* in karân na-ça-' çi-e some species of wine; II 44 *g* 11, together with *k* me-zu, AV 5920; Br 12639.

naçû 2. perh hasten to, or from; come quickly; flee, run away {viell.: herbeieilen oder enteilen; entfliehen, fliehen, flüchten} AV 6118. Mostly in pIII K 5464 *R* 19 na-mur(xar?)-tu ina mux-xi-ja na-ça

(Hr^{L} 198); K 350, 5 see nībirtu, *b*; *l* 10 a-na Elamti na-aç-çu-u (S. A. Smith, ii 51). K 513 *R* 4: 380 napšāte na-aç-ça (Hr^{L} 245); K 686, 7 $^{(amēl)}$ rab-kiçir . . . na-ça (3 *sg*; Hr^{L} 173); K 504, 9 (*ibid*, 90): 138 cedar-trees na-çu-ni = have arrived; K 1461, 15 (*ibid* 120); K 286, 9 which *M* . . . na-ça-an-ni (KB iv 148—9: herausgebracht hat); also K 417, 14 + 17 (*ibid*). K 125 (Hr^{L} 196) 9 it-tal-ku-ni ma-da-tu na-çu-ni (11 + 19: na-çu-u-ni) have come; tribute they brought, PSBA xvii 236—7; K 525 *R* 1 na-çu-u-ni ana šarri bēlija (Hr^{L} 252); K 683, 4; K 582 (Hr^{L} 167), 8 na-çu-ni-ni (3 *pl*); K 186 *O* 3—4 a-ni-ni | $^{(al)}$ Darāte na-ça-ni (Hr^{L} 222; V 53 *no* 1; BA ii 61) we have left; K 181 *R* 20—8 u-gir-tu . . . . $^{(amēl)}$ rab biti ša $^{(sal)}$ axat-abi-šu ištu $^{(māt)}$ Ta-bal na-çu-u-ni (Hr^{L} 197). Rm 2, 97 *R* (*ad* 709: . . . tu ša $^{(al)}$ Dūr-Ia-kin na-ça. T. A. (Ber) 71, 76 na-çu-ni ja-nu a-na ša-šu, they did not take out (= pay the tribute?) to him. P. N. Strassm., *Warka*, 66, 1 Ilu-na-zi. — Q^{t} perh IV^{2} 61 *b* 32 çi-xi-ri-ka a-ta-ça-ak-ka, in thy youth did I come to thee (?). — Š V 45 vi 28 tu-ša-an-ça; perh K 122, 8 la i-din-u-ni la u-ša-an-çi, Hr^{L} 122.

nēçu. Sm 2052 *R* 20 *c-d* ga-ab-rum, ne-e-çu, i-ru = ga-aš[-rum] M^{S}, texts, 20. K 4260 *O* 2 ne-e-xu = ra[bū?]; M^{S}, texts, 11; II 29 *e* 36 [ne?]-e-xu; GGA '98, 820.

nīçu (?) Berl. Orient. Congr. ii 1, 361 *a*: šar-ri-ṭu u ni-iç ša e-kal-lum.

niçū. I 44, 53 see nizū.

***naçabu* 1.** whence nançabu (naççabu) & ninçabu (*q. v.*).

***naçabu* 2.** T. A. (Lo) 29, 11 ša it-ta-ça-ab all the lands; KB v 271 *rm* * נצב or אסף (who collects?); Lo 30, 42 i-na maxri nabali (?) ni-ta-ça-ab, we are shut in from the land. Ber 107, 18 u lu-u ni-zi-ba elišunu, and we will besiege them. Bezold, *Diplomacy*, √ ezebu.

naç(z, s)bu V 28 *c-d* 89 na-aç-bu ‖ b(p)it(d) a-xi. AV 6119; ZK ii 338.

nuç(z)ab(p)u. $^{(šam)}$ A-A [sign] KU-BABBAR = nu-ça-bu ☉ 84 iv 5 (= II 26 *a-b*) followed by nuxaru (*q. v.*). V 17 *c-d* 2 (ZK i 345). Br 9018, AV 6449. perh = silver ear-ring.

naçbū (√ נצב ,ח?) — *a*) K 242 iv 4 (= II 22 *d-f* 4) GI-GUR-A-GE-A = na-aç-bu-u, AV 6120, Br 2457; *cf* K 152 i 50. — *b*) K 242 iv 11 (*cf* K 152 i 51) DUK-LA-XA-AN-GID-DA = na-aç-bu-u = ka-ni(z[ç]al?)[-lu?]. Br 1012. — *c*) K 4200, 11 . . . . LAL = na-aç-bu-u (AV 6076, 7031, Br 14376) preceded by naxbū.

Naçibīna (& *var* Naçibna) City of Nisibis. II 52 *a* 25 + 38; *c* 7 + 17 + 36 + 44; 53 *a* 43; *d* 9. Na-çib-i-na & Na-çi-bi-na, KB i 208—11. Rost, *Tiglath Pileser*, prf. xiii *rm* 3; Bezold, *Catalogue*, 2133; AV 6110.

naçbaru. some instrument, *etc.* √ çabaru, M^{S} 80. Nabd 432, 2: 5 na-aç-ba-ru; Cyr 84, 3—4: 2 na-aç-ba-ra-an-nu, 3 un-qu^{pl} (BA iii 437); perh also Nabd 1046, 2: 2 na-ça-ba-ru^{pl}.

naçabtu (?). I 27 *no* 2, 32 see nasaxu ℶ *a*.

naçbatu. Nabd 555, 2 na-aç-bat ša dalti.

naçalu (?) T. A. (Ber) 91, 17 Gebal alone iz-zi-la-at šar-ri, is saved for the king, KB v 412. 83, 1—18, 1332 i 15 [XAL] = na-ça-lum. Š, M^{S} 68, ušamçil, see maçalu.

naçmadu a span (of horses) with the harness? {Gespann, mit Geschirr} ‖ çin(m)du, çimittu, √ צמד, *q. v.* Sn vi 58 na-aç-ma-di sisē parē . . . . šuk-nuše ana nīri to break in (literally: to make submissive to the yoke) the spans of horses & mules. G § 66; BA i 177. Creat.-*frg* IV 51 iç-mid sim (Zimmern: iz-ziz-zim-ma) er-bit na-aç-ma-di idušša ilūl, KB vi (1) 24—5: er spannte ihn (den Wagen) an, das Viergespann schirrte er an ihn; § 128. Perh V 32 *a-b* 37.

naçaru, *pr* iççur (& iççar?); *ps* inaç(ç)ar, inamçar; *ip* uçur, guard, keep watch over, observe, protect, keep {wachen, bewachen, beschützen, bewahren, beobachten}. AV 6109; § 9, 110; ZDMG 28, 368. id URU, § 9, 165; Br 6443. S^{b} 280 u-ru | URU | na-ça-ru (II 48 *c-d* 39); Haupt

---

naçbūtu see nazbūtu. ~ nuçxu, Br 1229 compare nusxu. ~ naçaqu (AV 6108, Br 1776) see nazaqu.

xe, *Isaiah* (SBOT), 99—100: identical with uru, Sumerian — pr Smith, *Asurb*, 284, 94 ṭa- ı iç-çur-ma; *cf* Asb vii 86 ı-pu-šu-uš la iç-çur-u-ma; a-di-ja la iç-çu-ru, 72 aššu ıi-iç-çu-ru because we did not ii 51 + 113 ša a-mat .... la ı (3 *sg*). I 60 *c* 32 (iç) parak- aç-çur (*cf* K^M 8, 9). NE III ı r-šu iç-çur protected his friend; *surb*, 106, 17 who la iç-çu-ru . DT 71, 20 aç-çu-ra ma- Dar 128, 14—5 from the 20th to has Bēlit ma-aç-çar-tum ta- u; 88—1—18, 174 *R* 2—4 ina ti qablīti .... iç-çar-ru. Bu 2, 212, 10 iš-tu šu-mi iç-zu- ckler, *Forsch*, ii ('98) 92. II 30 olophon) Ašurb. ša .... iç-çu- u-us-su, whose kingdom Nebo rotect. D 86 i 13—15 GIŠ-UX, -ŠEŠ, GIŠ-IM-ID-LAL = ia-a-ri (but?). — pc V 65 *b* 26 i-iç-çu-ur (*var* to li-iç-çi-ru); the gods ana ana-ku li-iç- '-]in-ni, § 135 (end); K 669, 27 r; 629, 40 nap-ša-a-te ša šarri li-iç-çu-ru. — ip K 82, 22 tu uç-ra-a-ma (Hr^L 275; BA i 84 *c* 47 u-çu-ur še-e-ri-ja, , 44—5 protect my family; ZA i çur. K 10, 8 (Pinches, *Texts*, 6) . KB vi (1) 208, 23 pagrika] ZA xii 323). — ps K 590, 26 u .... ta-na-çar-u-ni. NE 60, a-aç-ça-ru (3 *pl*; also *l* 3); 5, 29 -na-an-ça-ar. IV^2 8 *a* 24 (end) -aç-ça-rak-ka (see Jensen, : 2401 iii 13 ta-na-ça-ra a-di-e ti (BA ii 628 *foll*); ZA iv 15 (K 11 ta-na-çar (2 *sg*); II 14 (= H zēr-šu i-na-ça-ar (Br 2838; n, 12 *rm* 3; Idem, ZA ix 276 *fol*; , *Sum. Les.*, 108). Rm 277 viii 19 herd shall watch the field (i-na- ır-ma), BA iii 504; iv 82. 81—2 *R* 7 maççarti ša šarri bēlija çar. Knudtzon, 29 *O* 9; 130 *O* 9 -ça-a-ra; Camb 42, 10 see xa- K 478 *R* 5—7 (Hr^L 254) see ırtu. K 678, 16 ni-na-çar (= V Perh K 883, 23 an-çar-ka (BA ii 633 *foll*), 24 ša kal la-ma-ri un-na-ni-ka u-çur, u-çur up-pa-aš-ka. DT 42, 10 i-na-aç-ça-ru bāb-ka, they will guard thy door (KB vi (1) 254—55). — pm V 63 *a* 9 lib-bu-uš pa-al-xu-ma a-mat ilāni na-aç-ru. IV^2 15* *R* i 48—49 (il) I-šum na-çir na-bu-u; ina mu-ši lu-u na-çir-šu, Br 2850. — ag Scheil, *Nabd*, x 50 Ēsaggil is called bīt na-çi-ir na-piš-ti ilāni rabūti; viii 10—11 (ilat) Taš-me-tum na-çi-rat na-piš-ti-ja; ix 27 (the great gods) na-çir na-piš-ti-ja. V 55, 5 Nebuch. calls himself na-çir ku-dur-re-ti. Sarg *Khors* 30 Ambaris of Tabal la na-çir ket-ti; Sn i 4, *Bell* 2. I 44, 94 šēdu na-çir nap-ša-a-ti; *cf* Sarg *Ann* 440; *Khors* 189 šēdu lamassu na-çi-ru, *Cyl* 71; Esh v 44.

Asb viii 67 la na-çir māmit ilāni rabūti. K 2720 *O* 9 a-na pa-li-xi na-çir a-mat šarrūti-šu, BA ii 566. VA 208 iv 20 na-çir-šu, but he that keeps it (KB iv 98). IV^2 21, 1 B *R* 16 na-çir pi-ri'š'-ti ša (il) Bēl. V 65, 33 na-çir pi-ri'š'-ti ilāni rabūti (*cf* Zimmern, *Ritualtafeln*, 117) (K 2486) 10 (amēl) um-mānu mu-du-u na-çir piri'š'ti ilāni rabūti, also Rm 601 *O* 5; V 65 *a* 12 na-çir na-piš-ti-ja; Šamaš na-çir V 44 *b* 11. II 23 *e-f* 67 na-çi-ir-tum ‖ daltum, *q. v.* KB iii (2) 50 *col* 3, 46 Ninkarrak na-çi-ra-at nabištija; V 34 *c* 7; K^M 9, 38 na-çi-rat napišti; 22, 6 (end) Nabū na-çi-ru na-piš-ti. III 66 *col* 8, 17 na-çir tarbaçi, PSBA xxi, 126. (amēl) na-çi-ru often in Knudtzon (*p* 381), also K 89, 4 (Hr^L 281), II 67, 6. AV 6111—2. V 28 *c* 72 na-çi-ru = ik[-kil-lum?]. ac. Asb i 20 a-na na-çir mār šar-rūtija, (KB ii 154 & *rm* 7; Lehmann, i 34 *rm* 6; ZA v 9 *rm* 1; §§ 32*e*; 65, 11; BA i 585). Sarg *Cyl* 50 a-na na-çar kētti u mīšari. Z^B viii 41 na-ça-ru u na-ka-ru (*cf* 51, 55; 42 -rum). K 319, 6 šum-ma la na-ça-ru iddi-ni, KB iv 186—7. K 2852 + K 9662 iii 27 aš-šu a-di-e na-ça-rim-me, to protect, observe the laws. V 30 *a-b* 66, Br 6760 see naxaru.

On naçaru, naçir in P. N. see Bezold, *Catalogue*. v 2133; AV 6113—15.

Q^t see maç(ç)artu (*p* 574); K 481 *R* 1—2 ma-çar-tu ni-ta-çar, K 83, 14 ittišu ni-it-ta-çar (Hr^{L} 141, 202); K 585, 23 ta-at-ta-çar; K 669, 22 i-ta-çar; K 233, 16 it-taç-ru. I 8 *no* 2, 18 at-ta-çar a-na-ku (KB ii 262—3); T^{M} v 15 la i-ta-aç-ça-ru. VATh 348 *R* 18 š]a [a]t-ta-ça-ar, KNUDTZON, but KB vi, 1, 96 [. . . *š*]*a* [l]a ta-a-ar. Perh IV^{2} 61 *b* 22—3: 60 ilāni rabūti is-si-ja | it-ti balāṭ-su it-ta-çar-u-ka, but *cf* HILPRECHT, *Assyriaca*, 47.

Š ušançir, let guard {liess bewachen}. Asb viii 13 u-ša-an-çir-šu, I made him guard the gate of Nineveh; 29 (ix 111) u-ša-an-çir-šu (ilç) ši-ga(r)-ru; ix 32 see maççarū (*p* 578); perh K 8468 *col* 2 ki-du-di-e ilāni la šum-çu-ri = Sp II 265 *a* viii 3 kidudē ili ana la šu-uç-çu-ru, the sanctuaries not to guard, was thy heart's intention, ZA x 6; PSBA xvii 148. V 45 vi 39 tu-ša-an-çar.

NOTE. — T. A. has these forms: iz-zu-ru (1 *sg*) Lo 71, 12; i-çur 31, 6; Ber 21, 32 may my gods & those of my brother li-iç-çu-ru-šu-nu; Ber 39, 14 in order that we may defend (li-na-aç-çur) the lands of the king (BA i 426 *no* 2); Ber 57, 9 u-çur mi lu-u na-çar-ta, defend yourself & then you will be protected; Lo 71, 9 u-çur; 11, 27 u-zu-ur-šu; i-na-zi-ra, Lo 30, 27 (BEZOLD, *Diplom.*, xxxii *rm* 2); i-na-zi-ru-na, 3, 27; 30, 32; Ber 44, 15; ti-na-ça-ru (3 *f. sg.* agreeing with noun in *pl*) Lo 16, 20; 24, 8; a-na-ça-ru Lo 57, 81; a-na-az-zu-ur, Ber 33, 10; a-na-ça-ar 71, 53; 76, 82; i-na-ça-ru (1 *sg*) Lo 70, 26; *cf* 77, 14; i-na-ça-ru-na, 19, 12; ni-na-ça-ru, 42, 9+30; a-na-an-çur, 30, 16; 29, 61; na-aç-ra-ku, Lo 27, 11; 47, 5 na-aç-ra-ti; ki-ma ša na-aç-ra-at Ber 144, 25; ROSTOW, 4, 10 lu-u na-aç-ra-ku, I am guarding; Ber 161, 7; Lo 71, 21 na-ça-ri; 18, 33+40, 20 na-ça-ar. — Q^{t} it-ta-ça-ar-ka, Lo 11, 22. — 3 Lo 21, 12 uz-zu-ru; 61, 8 uç-çur-ru-ma; 61, 28 u-çur-ru-ma; 61, 31 u-çur-ru-šu-nu. See also KB V^{*} 24.

DERR. — maç(ç)aru, maçarūtu, maç(ç)artu, maççaštu (*pp* 575—5) &:

niçirtu. AV 6299; § 64, 4. — *a*) guard, watch, safety {Bewachung, Bewahrung, Sicherheit}. Neb *Bab* ii 12 ni-çi-ir-tim Ēsagila u Bābili aš-te-'e-ma (*cf* 22; ZK ii 293); Neb viii 34 In Babylon, al ni-çi-ir-ti-šu (of Marduk) *cf* vi 56; Sn ii 10 maxāzē dan-nu-ti bīt ni-çir-ti-šu; I 43, 37 (§ 124); V 52 iv 28 (end) ni-çir-ti ap(?)-kal-lum. — *b*) treasure {Schatz} ‖ nakamtu, *q. v.* Sn iii 37 ni-çir-tu ka-bit-tu; *Bass* 7 ni-çir-ti ka-bit-tu; *Bell* 8 (-tu); ni-çir-ti ēkallišu *Kui* 1, 32; Anp ii 64, 124; iii 56; Sarg *Khors* 80; Esh i 22; TP III *Ann* 155 ni-çir-ti šarru-u-ti ‖ mimma aq-ru. niçirtu katimtu, see katmu (*p* 459 *col* 1); Sn *Bav* 47 ŠA-GA perh = niçirtu. bīt niçirti = treasury {Schatzhaus, Schatzkammer}. aptēma bīt ni-çir-ti-šu, Sn i 27; *Kui* 1, 6; = ŠA-GA; Sn v 19, also often in *c. t.*; Camb 212, 4 *etc.*, T. A. Ber 73, 15 a-šar ni-çi[-ir-ti], treasure house. — *c*) secret {Geheimnis} ni-çir-ti (il) A-nim [(il) Bēl u (il) Ea], ZIMMERN, *Rituall.*, *pp* 117, 7+17; 118, 13 & *p* 89; *cf* piriš̆tu. a-mat ni-çir-ti *del* 9, 252 (282), BA i 122; *Hopk. Circ.*, 69, 17; HAUPT in CHEYNE, *Isaiah* (SBOT), 143; KB vi (1) 281. V 36 *a-c* šu-u | < | ni-çir-tum, Br 8724. — BA iii 234 (K 2801 *O* + K 221 + K 2669) 4 (end) a-šar ni-çir-ti, Punkt seiner Sichtbarkeit (*i. e.* of Jupiter); also 244, 4 & see *ibid* 278, below; but JENSEN, *Theol. Litztg.*, '99 *no* 2 says: ašar niçirti of a planet: ist die Gegend, in der er hinter (oder vor?) der Sonne unsichtbar wird. — *d*) = napištu. K 8522 *R* 9 see karū, 2. (430 *col* 2); KB vi (1) 36—7 *rm* 13 (>< G § 101); JENSEN, 363. — II 48 *c-d* 38—9 PAP-XAL = ni-çir-tum (Br 1155, 1146); ŠA-ŠES (Br 12006) = *ša* na-ça-ri.

naçirtum ‖ daltum (AV 6166) see naçaru Q *ag* & daltum.

naççaru see namçaru.

naçru *1.* T. A. Lo 58, 8 na-aç-ri-iš safely, in safety; or speedily? Lo 5, 40; Ber 12, 11+15; 14 *R* 7. Perh also Ber 144, 25.

naçru *2.* see nuxātu & nazru, Br 5295, AV 6122; K 654, 26 dib-bi-ja na-aç-ru-ti.

Niç(s)ir name of a mountain in *del* 134—8 (141—3) a-na šad Ni-çir (KB vi 238—41; D^{Par} 105; HAUPT, *Sintfl.*, 26 *rm* 19; HOMMEL in HASTINGS, *Dict.*, i 221 = rescue; so also JASTROW, *Religion*, 503; BOISSIER, *Rev. Sém.*, vi 52—3, § 25; see, however, BA i 135. — Anp ii 34—6 mentions (šad) Ni-çir as mountain(s) of Tokma & Pir-Omar-Gudrun, BEZOLD, *Catalogue*, 2138; situated between Tigris & Lower Zab

---

naçaru 2. see nazaru. ∼ naçrabtu (Br 3769) *cf* nasrabtu.

(ZIMMERN-CHEYNE, *Encycl. Bibl.*, i 1056); II 51 *a* 21 (šad) Ni-çir (lip-šur) = šadû Gu-ti-i.

naçrab(p)u ? PEISER, *Vertr.*, cvii 7 šer na-aç-rab[-tum?], ZA vi 448; √çarabu burn {brennen}?

naçraptu retort, crucible {Schmelztiegel} II 34 *a-b* 64—5 AL-BAD-BAR-TÚR; ŠI-BIR (kur) AG-A = na-aç-rap-tum (Br 5754, 9453; ZK i 123; Z^B 70; AV 6121); V 39 *a-b* 66 (Br 12038) preceded by naš-raptum, BA i 177. √çarapu, 1 (ZK ii 190; ZA vii 80: purification {Läuterung}).

nâqu 1. *pr* inûq howl, lament {heulen, wehklagen} Z^B 22. II 45 *c-f* 34—7 (K 4314) na-a-qu, id ending in U (*i. e.* ŠI-LU, Br 14355), A (Br 11348), & I. S^c 127, Br 3981; S^a vi 25 i?]-it | A | na-a-qu. II 29 *g-h* 37 GAR = na-a-qu (Br 11967) betw. un-ni-nu & ni-e-šu. Creat.-*frg* III 126 see marçiš (end) *p* 591 *col* 1. Perh K 3456 *R* 17 b(p?)al-ça-a-ma i-na-qa, says the ox to the horse. K 8063 + K 8066, 13 (end) aššat-su na-a-a-qat (?) his wife laments; *l* 14 (end) aš-šatu na-id ta-na-a-a-ku (?), BEZOLD, *Catalogue*, 892.

nâqu 2. see Sn *Bav* 53, nabalkattu; and against MEISSNER-ROST compare M^S 62.

naqû (& ***niqû***). *pr* iq(q)i, *ps* inaqqi, *ip* iqi = נקה. — *a*) pour out, make a libation for sacrificial purposes {ausgiessen, zu rituellen Zwecken, libieren} AV 6120; id BAL, PUL, §§ 9, 102; 25; 108; Br 271; H 37, 12 ‖ ta-ba-ku (13); ZK i 300; ZA iii 336; Z^B 76; KNUDTZON, *pp* 82—4. I 7 *no* ix A 3 (= D 121 *no* 10) karâna aq-qa-a e-li-šu-un. ZIM., *Ritualt.*, 81, 8 a-nak-ki-ku-nu-ši (+ 11) mê (šad) Xa-ma-ni; 9 ta-na[-ak-ki] + 86, 9; IV² 59 *no* 1 *a* 33 (end) ta-nak-ki; 55 *no* 2, 10 šikara u karâna tanaq-ki (+ 10); ZA iv 12, 46 i-naq-qa-nik-ka, they pour (wine) out for thee. — *b*) make offering, sacrifice in general; then especially of the sacrificial lamb {opfern im allgemeinen; dann speciell vom Opferlamm}. Sarg *Khors* 178 ma-xar-šu-un aq-qi; KB ii 38, 20; V 61 *d* 32 iq-qi-ma. TP III *Ann* 47 ana ilâni] | rabûti bêlê-ja aq-ki; Sarg *Cyl* 50 (60) (immêr) niqâ (= a sacrificial lamb) ak-ki s(z)ir-qu as(z)-ru-uq; Sn *Bav* 38 (immêr) niqâ eb-bi-ti lu aq-qi. Asb x 106—7 (immêr) niqâ taš-ri-ix-ti | aq-qa-a to the gods my lords; Esh (A) vi 29—30 (immêr) niqê taš-ri-ix-te eb-bu-ti | ma-xar-šu-un aq-ki; V 65 *b* 45; also 81—6—7, 209, 38 (BA iii 262—3) liq-qi; Esh *Sendsch*, *R* 59—60 niqû liq-qi let him make an offering; Sarg *Ann* 457 ni-qa-a liq-qi; TP viii 48—9 aq-qi; 57 liq-qi; ZA iii 319, 94; Sn vi 60; I 67, 12 niqê ellûti .... aq-qi (+ 37); *cf* Lay 17, 16 (KB ii 6). ZIM., *Ritualt.*, *p* 100, 73 niqê ta-naq-ki-ma (106, 154), darauf sollst du ein Opfer darbringen; I 27 *no* 2, 10 rêšê-te (of fruit & wine) ana (il) Ašur ... a-qi (Anp. iii 135 BAL). POGNON, *Wadi-Brissa*, 125 na-qa na-qa-a MEŠ, he who sacrifices; V 65 *a* 26 ana ša-at-ti ni-qa-a ak-ki-šum-ma. IV² 23 *no* 1 *a* 14—15 qa-ta-u-a ellêti iq-qa-a ma-xar-ka (BA ii 417); IV² 32 *a* 32, *b* 17 *etc.* ni-qu-u ul BAL-ki. Perh K 168, 15 kal ep-šat qa-ab-ru na-ki-i-u. T. A. Lo 6, 12 ti-na-ku ni-qa-am, you were celebrating a sacrificial feast.

Q¹ = Q *b*. NE 17, 45 (19, 40) see kaçû, 2. TP vii 15, 16 pu-xa-di-e *etc.* it-ti (immêr) niqê-ja ellu-te a-na (il) Ašur bêli-ja at-ta-qi; viii 9, 10 lu at-ta(-aq)-qi, KB i 40—42; § 53 *a*; *del* 147 (156) at-ta-qi ni-qa-a.

3 pour out {ausgiessen}. IV² 8 *a* 4 + 7 see kabatu, 3 (369 *col* 2); II 51 *b* 24 u-naq-qu-u, + *b* 10 (ZK ii 320); K^M 22, 79 aš(or ina?)(-)li-i-te nu-uk-ka(?) gam-ra-a-ti.

3¹ KB vi (1) 162, 48 (= NE 57) u]b(p)-nat-su ut-te-qa-a schüttete sein u-mehl [in die Grube]. V 29 *g-h* 8 (II 25 *no* 4 *add*) u-taq-qu-u, better √aqû, Br 5327.

27 be poured out {ausgegossen werden}. IV² 19 *b* 37—8 ina .... bît pi-ri'-ti-ki da-mi ki-ma me-e in-naq-qu-u, Br 3801; § 110. V 52 *a* 64—5 ša ka-ra-na im-lu-u (or: in-na-ku-u) ta-ni-xu it-ta-an-ki, Z^B 75: where wine is wont to be poured out, there he now pours forth sighs, Br 6709.

NOTE. — 1. Here belongs especially the expression nâq mê water-pourer ‖ Wasserausgiesser, a priestclass. *Lit. Centralbl.*, Mr 16, '89; J^W 42; 53 *rm* 4 (but see HAUPT, BA i 316); BRÜNNOW, ZA viii 127 >< JÄGER, BA ii 278. Also BELSER, BA ii 147; JEREMIAS, *Hölle & Paradies bei den*

Babyloniern, 11. IV² 12 *R* 33—4 where, in a curse, it is said Bêl zêrašu lilqutma (amêl) naaq mê (= AMÊL-A-BAL-A, II 31 *a-b* 80, Br 271) a-a ir-ši, may destroy his seed, not may he have a *n. m.* (Br 11381). The Assyrians & Babylonians believed that the dead needed water; the greatest shame for a man was not to have a *n m* after his death. KB iv 86 ii 19 naaq mê; Asb vi 75—6, K 891 *R* 1—2 (KB ii 262—3), see kispu; also L⁴ *R* 1; L³ *R* 1. III 4 *no* 7, 7 + 8 Ak-ki (amêl) nâq mê.

2. Jensen, ZA vii 174 *rm* 1 šangû, priest, = ša naqî, the man performing (or presiding at) the sacrifice; bêl niqê only a secondary development; see also Jastrow, *Religion*: he who sacrifices, *i. e.* the priest as one who presides over the sacrifices. Winckler, *Forsch.*, ii 2, 314. Haupt, *Jour. Bibl. Lit.*, xix 80 *rm* 42: šangû 'sacrificer' (BA i 169 *rm* 2; 178 *rm* 3) is a *shaf'el*-form & may be connected with נקי 'to sacrifice'.

Derr. — tamqîtu (?) & these 2:

niqû libation, offering; then, especially, lamb of offering, sacrificial lamb {Libation, Trankopfer; Opfer, Opferlamm} § 65, 9 *m. c. st.* niq (ni-iq Sarg *Ann* 434; *Khors* 172). ideogr. *c. g.* S^b 158 si-giš-še ¦ ideogr. | ni-qu-u, H 29, 656, § 9, 260, Knudtzon, 32—34; 101 *O* 4 (?). AV 6302. II 45 *e-f* 38, ÇUR + inserted še & 39, DÊ (Br 6727; II 25, 509) = ni-qu-u; 40, ÇUR-KA-GA (Br 9093) = niqû na-qu-u; 41, DÊ = niqû ša ši-ka-ri (BA i 280; ZA vii 150); 42, ... RA = ši-kar ni-ki-i (Br 14344, wine used for libations). V 47 *a* 43 te'š-li-tum ta-ši-ma-tum, ni-qu-u is my command. V 28 *d* 20 çu-ba-tu ni-ki-i, sacrificial garment (also AJSL xv 79; AV 6213). IV² 18* *no* 6 *R* 1—2 mu-ur ni-ki ši-iz-bi (GA-NAG, Br 4988); D 29, 246. K 246 (H 98—99) iv 53 ina ni-iq (= 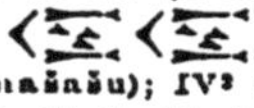) re-e-me šul-me (see mašnašu); IV² 20 *no* 1 *R* 3—4 = ni-ki-e. 82, 9—18, 4159 iv 34 ni-sag | NISAG | ni-qu-u; S^b 89; Br 6709. Šalm, *Bal*, vi, 1 u-šam-xi-ra (3 *sg*) ni-qa-a-šu el-la; *Obel* 82 niqû ..... êpu-uš; Asb iii 112 e-piš (immêr) niqê-ia. K 2745 iii 10 (immêr) niqû (*i. e.* ÇUR + še inserted) taš-r[i-ix-ti] eb-bu-u[-ti], BA iii 285; Asb x 24, end. V 65 *b* 51 ana ni-k(q)i-i ma-as-xa-ti; 81, 7—1, 9 *R* 31 ni-ki-e (§ 29). AV 8500 on II 63 *c* 30 a P. N. Šumma-ni-iq-ilâni. Zim., *Ritualt.*, *p* 112, 10 ni-qa-a u-ka-an, soll Opfer veranstalten, 12 ni-qa-a i-paṭ-ṭar, das Opfer soll er "auflösen". IV² 17 *a* 56 ni-ga-a-šu mu-xur. K 3364 *R* 12 ni-qu-u ki-bit pi-i si-mat qu]t-rin-ni. Perh *del* 65 (69): except one *sar* of oil ša e-ku-lu ni-iq-qu; 152 (162) bêl niqê, the sacrificer (BA i 287; Zimmern, *Ritualtafeln*, *p* 95: der Opfernde, nur ja nicht der Priester!; *cf* Phön בעל הזבח).

NOTE. — Here belongs perhaps II 23 *a* 26 ni-ik si-li-qu a ‖ of pa-aš-šu-ru.

naqû *2.* see naqû 1. Q.

niqqu. II 49 *no* 3, *add*, BUL-BUL | tu-ma-gu | niq-qu ša ba-nu-u, AV 6304, Br 14399; IV² 29* *b* 12 ša tittu ni-iq-qa-ša.

naqabu, pierce, bore through; break through from under the earth's surface {durchbrechen, aus der Tiefe hervorbrechen}. K 3456 *O* 27 it-taq-bu-šu mê naq-bi (= Q^t) and there welled forth from it the waters of the deep, PSBA xxi 38 *foll.* Sarg *Cyl* 11 e-te-ib-bi-ru (*Khors* 15 e-tib-bi-ra) na-qab be (*var* bi)-ra-a-ti; *Ann* 6. V 36 *d-f* 37 < | bu-ru | na-qa-bu, Br 8718, AV 6128.

Derr. these 2:

naqabbiš, like a torrent. S^p 158 + S^p II 962 *R* 12 (end) u-ri-du-ma na-qab-bi-iš.

naqbu — *a*) piercing through; deep, depth, hole {Durchbruch; Tiefe, Abgrund, Vertiefung}. ZDMG 28, 132 *rm* 5; Jensen, 7; 243; 259 *etc.*; JA '97, Ja-F., 112 *foll* on apsû, tâmtu, naqbu. esp. in phrase mê naqbi waters of the deep {Grundwasser}. ideogr. BE § 9, 10, Br 1520. Sarg *Khors* 128: 21 cubits he dug until ik-šu-da mê naq-bi, he reached the waters of the deep, *Ann* 323. I 28 *b* 26 iš-tu eli mê naq-bi-ša. IV² 2 v 32—33 ina na-qab (= BE, *var* naq-bi) ap-si-i; also 36—7 (Jensen, 247); 30 *no* 1 *a* 12—13 mi-na-a ina na-aq-bi (= BE-MA), what should be in the deep (‖ tâmtum). ZA iv 11, 9 mê naq-bi da-ri-i, the waters of a perennial spring. — *b*) well, fountain {Quelle, Quell} naqbê ‖ bûrâti. 81—11—3, 111 Marduk is called, *O* 2, ša naq-bi (*Jour. Vict. Inst.*, 28, 8 *foll*); IV² 57 *a* 28 Marduk bêl BE^pl (*i. e.* naqbê) ša-di-i u tâmâte. V 33 *col* 8, 20 (Marduk) be-il na-aq-bi, Herr der Quellhöhlung (Jensen, 246); *ibid* 15—16 (il)

Ê-a bēl naqbi (Jensen, 251); II 55 *c-d* 48 AN (na-aq-bu) BE = (il) Ea (AV 5069, Br 1482); Sn *Bav* 28 see kuppu (420 *col* 2). Asb i 45 (il) Ê-a u-paṭ-ṭi-ra naqbē-šu. Sarg *Harem*-B 4, O Êa naq-bi-ka šu-up-ta-a open thy wells! *Cyl* 70 (il) Ê-a mu-uš-te-šir naq-bi-šu, name of the city-gate of Sargon's city. — Anp i 3 (il) Ninib pi-tu-u naq-be; 6 (il) Ninib bēl naq-be u tāmāti. — V 56, 41 (il) Adad ašaridu (= GU-GAL) šamū u erci-ti bēl naq-bi u zu-un-ni. V 59 *a* 4 iš-tu šadi-i ra-bi-i ša-ad naq-bi ina a-çi-ka (of the sun). K 3445 + Rm 396 *O* 36 naq-bu up-te-it[-ta-a?], 37 ip-te-e-ma na[-qab?]. K 4386 i 28 (II 48 *e-f* 18—20) BE = naq-bu, followed by SI = *n* ša nap-xa-ri (thus = nag-bu) & GU-LA = *n* ša GIŠ-U-GER (*i. e.* ašagi, thus = naqpu) AV 6128. KB vi (1) 288 *col* 2, 15 ina n]a-aq-bi, ZA xiv 278; ZA iv 228, 7 ina na-aq-bi ni-me-qi; 83—1—18, 197 *R* 1 (il) Ê-a naq-bi-šu .... i-nam-din. Perh II 51 *a* 51 (canal) .... na-qab (or gab?) nu-ux-šu (AV 5897, Br 2618); Sp II 265 *a* vi 2 (+ K 9280 + K 8452) na-qab ne-me-ki el-lu. K 3399 + K 3934 ii 45 + 55 ja (ul) iš-ša-a me (*var* mi)-lu i-na na-aq-bi (also ii 30). KB vi (1) 284—5, see ZA xiv 277—92. S^{c} 6, 6 BE = naq-bu, Hommel, *Lesest.*, = canal.

naqbaru. funeral; grave {Begräbnis, Grab} √קבר, BA i 177; § 65, 31 *a*. V 30 *g-h* 38 Ê-KUR-BAD (Br 6262) = na-aq-ba-ru together with ir-çi-tu, bît mu-ti; see also mîtum (V 16 *e-f* 40). H 23, 466; 215, 37. AV 6127. ZA ii 113, 2; J^{W} 62 *rm* 4; 63 *rm* 10; D^{Par} 121; Jensen, 222; 510 (Raum = Unterwelt). A ‖ is:

naqbiru. K 2729 *R* 27 ša ul-tu naq-bi-ri bît ça-al-lu i-di (*var* -ik)-ku-šu, BA ii 566; KB iv 144, 60, whosoever disturbs him in the grave, the house wherein he rests.

naqadu. Zim., *Ritualtf.*, *p* 104, 112 eine Leber, *etc.* lu-u naq-da-at, werde punktiert, be punctured.

nâqidu herdsman, shepherd {Hirte}. D^{H} 20; D^{Pr} 47; ZA iii 199, 2—3; ZDMG 40, 728. K 8522 *R* 25 ša (amêl) re'ê u na-ki-di (*var* -kid), *cf* S. A. Smith, *Asurb*, ii 2 (K 2867) 30 (amêl) rê'ê (amêl) na-qi-di. ⊕ 51 iv 8 ... na-ki-du = re-id alpi; ZA iv 8, 81 na-qi-du = ri-'-u. Perh II 31 *b* 89 officer na-ki[-du]. K 2801 + K 221 + K 2669 *O* 34 ... ri-e-u tak-lum na-qid çalmat qaqqadi. K 3474 i + K 8232, 24 (hymn to Šamaš) at-ta-ma na-qid-si-na ša eliš u šapliš, thou art the shepherd of those. Name of Elamtic city (al) ša na-qi-da-a-ti Sn iv 62; Asb vii 66. IV^{2} 35 *no* 5, 4 read na-gid = nâqidu, shepherd of Ur; also in Gudea *F* iv 12 (KB iii, 1, 58—9), Jensen-Zimmern, ZA iii 208 *foll*; KB iii (1) 4.

niq'û'du. ZA vi 244, 50 iç-çur ap-pa-ri = ni-qu-du. On P. N. Niqûdu see D^{Pr} 212; Peiser, *Vertr.*, 342 *col* 1.

naqmû, (√qamû) cremation, burning, fire {Verbrennung, Brand} BA i 177. II 34 *a-b* 69—70 AL-GAR-NE-PA-GA, & NE-PA-GA = naq-mu-u, AV 5974, Br 5773.

naqmûtu: Sn iv 68 qu-ṭur na-aq-mu-ti-šu-nu the smoke of their (the elamitic flames') fire. ZDMG 27, 513 *rm* 2; Z^{B} 94; 97.

naqapu mutilate {verstümmeln}. ZDMG 35, 763 (or נגף?, Zimmern, *Ritualtafeln*, 223). Q pm ša ubân-šu naq-pat whose finger is mutilated, Zim., *ibid*, *p* 97, 5. ⊕ 253 *d* 7 na-ka-pu ša ubâni, AV 5957. Br 1461. — **Der.**:

naqpu. II 107, 10—11 (D 126, 10—11) naq-pu. naq-pi ubâni, Zim., *Ritualtafeln*, *no* 24 *O* 32; K 161 iii naq-pu[-šu], ZK ii 11. See also nagpu. On the term lišânu naqpu (H 133) see Haupt, *Sintfluther.*, 22, 3; ZK ii 268; AJP v 68—84; Prätorius, ZDMG 35, 763; Z^{B} 84 *rm* & 119; PSBA xi, 16 *fol*; Weissbach, *Die Sumer. Frage*.

naqaru. pr iq(q)ur, ps inaqar (& iqqar) see Barth, ZA ii 384 *ad* § 90 I *a*, ip uqur. tear down, destroy {niederreissen, zerstören} of buildings *etc.* AV 6124. II 15 (K 56 iv) *a-b* 32 i-na ra-ma-ni-šu ik-gur (= IN-KAL, Br 6202) i-pu-uš, on his own responsibility he can pull down & rebuild. u-qur ZA iii 315, 75; Beh 68; uq-qur Asb x 75. K 85, 4 i-naq-qar. Mostly in connection with nabalu (*q. v.*)

---

niqilpu see נקלפ. ∾ nu-uq-qum read nu-ug-gat & see nuggatu.

cf Esh *Sendsch.*, *R* 43—44 ab-bul aq-qur ina išāti aq-mu; TP III *Ann* 51, 110, 160, 162, 164, 180, 188, 189. Asb vii 14 ab-bu-lu aq-qu-ru aš-lu-lu šal-lat-su. KB ii 266, 97 thy cities a-na-qar; I 7 F 24 whosoever this old house i-na-aq-qa-ru (& builds anew), PEISER, KAS ix *rm* 2. I 69 *c* 31 i-ga-ri-šu-nu aq-qu-ur. IV² 28* 4 *R* 34 *b* ālum ša naq-rum, the city that is destroyed, 36 Nippur ša naq-ru. ZA iii 132 *no* 4, 16 ta-na-qa-ri. III 58 *r* 56 the enemy ina-qar (will destroy) the sanctuary; *c* 43 i-na-qar the city gates. *del* 20 (24) u-qur bīta see nagaru; 21 (26) see nam-kur(r)u. JASTROW, *Papers of the Philadelphia Oriental Club*, i ('94) 127 *foll*: bītu šuātu ša naq(a)ru u ep(e)šu: a property: to lie idle or to be made productive; espec. in Babyl. documents (see *p* 204 *col* 1, *h*). KB iv 162 *col* 3, 17 bītūti ab-tūti ša na-qa-ru u e-pi-šu. II 26 *add*, 6 na-qa-ru ša biti (AV 6124, Br 13865). II 9 *c-d* 54 ik-ka-ar, Br 278. — *b*) devastate, a field *etc.* {verwüsten, ein Feld, *etc.*} IV² 38 *c* 16—17 who that field u-ša-aq-qa-ru | i-na-aq-qa-ru, commands to devastate, or himself devastates. — *c*) of other objects: destroy, break {von sonstigen Gegenständen: zerstören, brechen}. V 56, 35 who (aban) narā an-na-a i-na abni i-naq-qa-ru. IV² 22 *a* 32 çi-la-ni kīma e-lip-pi la-bir-ti i-na[-qa-ru? Br 5536]. — *d*) perhaps IV² 61 *a* 15 ina pān šūpē-ka ak-kar-ru-u-ni. — K 46 (II 60) iv 14 i-na pa-ni-šu iq-qur (or ig-gur?) = II 18, 14. AV 5809; 108, 22 (114, 10 = V 11 *d-f* 22) A-KA(= DUG)-GA | MA(?GIŠ?)-DU = na-qa-r[u]; *cf* V 12, 7. Br 6808, 11405. II 24 (= V 19 *c-d* 12—13) *no* 3 *O* 36—37 NUM = na-qa-ru ša TAG-XAR (Br 273, 9015); RU-TIK = *n* ša TAG (Br 1462) cut (a stone) like cut glass. II 26 *no* 1 (*add*) *c-f* 4 (su-un) BE = na-qa-ru (Br 1521, AV 6124); 5 A-GE-A = na-qaru ša maxāzi (Br 11543); 7 BAL = *n* ša narkabti (Br 14146); 8 DAG-GA = *n* ša elippi (Br 5536); 9 RU-TIK = *n* ša abni (JENSEN, 439); 10 KI-ŠU-DUG-GA = *n* ša qaq-qa-ri (Br 7086, 9778). 80, 11—12, 9 *O*, *col* 1 = na-qa-ru (Br 10194).

Q = Q¹ Their cities at-ta-bal at-ta-qar, see nabalu.

3 V 47 *a* 25 na-al-bu-bu tap-pi-e u-nam-ga-ra-an-ni; perh also K 2361 iii 16 b(p)it-ri-e u-nam-ga-ru kar-ra (ZA iv 236). V 45 ii 58 [tu-na-aq?]-kar; followed by tu-na-aq-qa?]-rum.

Š cause, command to destroy {zerstören lassen}. KB iii (1) 162 v 43 whosoever this tablet la mu-da-a u-ša-aq-qa-ru. III 60, 84 šu-uq-qur dūrāni-šu iq-bu-um; perh K 5467, 6 ana šu-uk-ku-ru ša māti (or √nakaru?). See also Q *c*.

ℑ be destroyed, laid waste {zerstört werden} III 61 *a* 9 (+ 14) dūrāni in-na-ga-ru the walls will be destroyed. K 3500 + K 4444 + K 10235 ii 26 in-na-ga-ru-u-ni (3 *pl*) WINCKLER, *Forsch*, ii 12. K 196 iii 18 (end) that same house in-na-qar (PINCHES, *Texts*, 14); K 815 *R* 7 in-na-qa-ru.

nuqāru. V 14 *c-d* 27 SEG-MUG-XUL = nu-qa-ru, literally a bad muqqu; perh: torn, shabby, AV 6450, Br 99.

niqru some wood {ein Holz}?. V 26 *a-b* 29 [mi-iš-su-un] BE = ni-ik(q)-ru, between bu-lu-u & i-çu la-bi-ru, AV 6212, Br 1522.

naqrabu fight, battle {Kampf, Schlacht} √qarabu, 1. Sarg *Khors* 128 u-'ša'al-lum maxāzi a-šar naq-ra-bi-šu mā umalli (KB ii 70—1), ‖ text reads a-šar mit-xu-çi, *Ann* 325.

naqruṭum grace, favor, compassion {Gnade, Erbarmen} V 21 *a-b* 63 naq-ru-ṭum ‖ ri-e-mu, GGA '98, 825 (not nagrūtu, nor nakrūtu, BA i 181) AV 5977. ZA iv 234, 6 naq-ru-ṭu ana ardika; 241, 30 naq-ru-uṭ riši-šu (*i. e.* of aradka) ti-ru-nu (*cf* V 21 *a* 62); Sp II 265 *a* iv 11 naq-ru-ṭu li-gi[-me?].

naru 1., neru 1. pr inār (inīr, inēr), *ps* inār (inarru) strike, kill, destroy {schlagen, töten, vernichten} *etc.* AV 6137; D^{H} 58; D^{Pr} 98—99; J^{W} 30 = √נגר; §§ 93 *rm*, 114, 115. IV² 5 *a* 44—7 ni-ir-tu ana na-a-ri (= SAG-GIŠ-RA-RA, Br 3610) to bring about destruction, ina

naqrimānu, see nakrimānu.

maxri illakūni *i. e.* the evil seven; *a* 8—11 nir-tu ana na-a-ri (>< Z^B 88 *rm* 1). KB iii (2) 66 *no* 12, 44 a-na na-a-ri a-a-bi-ja may they come to my assistance. IV^2 18 *b* 9—10 qar-ra-du ša ta-na-ru (Br 4391); 30 *b* 11—12 ta-na-ar u tuš-mit; 27 *b* 25 (Br 3609). II 19 *a* 23—4 qar-du ša ša-di-i ša ta-na-ru (iD BAD, Br 4391) = kill; *b* 14 nir-ta i-nar[-ru?] Br 3610. V 50 *a* 47—8 ša gal-lu-u rabu-u i-na-ru-uš (= SAG-GIŠ-BA-NI-IN-SI) H 187, Br 3604. KB iii (2) 2, 29 ib-ba-ru-um a-na-ru (ZA ii 146 *b* 1). Asb i 38 the gods i-na(-ni)-ru ga-ri-ja (KB ii 156—7 *rm* ^{oo}). Smith, *Asurb*, 144, 5 a-nar-šu-nu-ti, I killed them; 181, 113 i-na-ru-uš (3 *pl*) ina $^{(iç)}$ kakki (KB ii 268—9). III 15 ii 19 i-na-ru-šu (3 *pl*) ina kakki; iii 18 a-na-ar ina kakki. I 43, 18 the inhabitants of Cilicia a-nar ina kakki. Esh ii 31 who the troops of Išpakā i-na-ru ina kakki; Sarg *Ann* 308. S^P 158 + S^P II 962 *R* 34 rubūti . . . i-na-ri ina kak-ki. Asb iv 49; KB ii 268—9, 107; III 15 i 9; Sarg *Harem* A 8 see gārū (*p* 280) § 142. III 38 *no* 1 *O* 4 Nergal who i-na-ar-ru ga-ro-e-e-šu. I 49 *c* 4 za-ma-n]i-ja ta-na-ru (2 *sg*; BA iii 220); K 4832, 24. Neb ii 24 la ma-gi-ri a-na-ar ‖ ak-mi za'irē; Sarg *Ann* XIV 9; Anp i 20 who i-ni-ru all his adversaries, Lyon, *Man*, 7, 18. IV^2 39 *a* 24—5 who . . . . . i-na-ru (3 *sg*); Salm, *Ob*, 20; *Mon*, *O* 12. IV^2 34 *no* 1 *O* 6 Sargon ša i-ni-ru. 2 (ša) . . . i-na-ru; I 35 *no* 3, 13. Asb ix 122 the inhabitants of Acco nišē la kan-šu-ti a-nir, I struck down }schlug ich nieder{. NE 48, 170 iš-tu a-la-a i-na-ru, after he had killed the heavenbull; 71, 9 alā ni-na-ru; KB vi (1) 148, 17 (24) end i-na(r)-ru, 3 *pl*; 198 v/vi 8 tu-na-ra (2 *sg*) + 6. Creat.-*frg* IV 105 ul-tu Ti-āmat i-na-ru (Jensen, 379). Bu 88—5—12, 75 + 76 ix 8—9 li-na-a-ru a-a-bi-ja; V 65 *b* 41 lu-nar za-'-ri-ja (ZA iii 309); Hilprecht, *OBI* i *no* 84 *col* 1, 27 Su-ba-ru-um a-na-ru. T^M v 162 šadū li-nir-ku-nu-ši; ip perh ii 110 nir-šu-nu-ti; ac vi 83 šēpa-a-a na-a-ru; T^M 169 >< 89. Scheil, Notes, xxxiv 6 (*Rec. Trav.* xx) iš-tu 6 šu-ši li-mi um-ma-ni i-ni-ru (KB vi, 1, 298—9) 3 *sg*. KB vi (1) 292 *col* 1, 8 ša . . . . i-na-ru (3 *sg*). K 2619 (*Dibbara*-legend) iv 16 li-na-ru a-xa-meš they shall kill one another. K 3454 (*Zū*-legend) ii 29 $^{(il)}$ Za-a li-nar-ma (36 ni-ir] ^{il} Zā i-na kakkika; also 57 + 80) see KB vi (1) 48—52. P. N. *e. g.* K 2852 + K 9662 iv 17 li-nir-a-a-im-di; 21 (end) Ašur-i-nar-ga-ru-u-a (Winckler, *Forsch*, ii 40). — V 18 *a-b* 17—18 SAG-GIŠ-RA = ni-e-rum; & nir-tum ni-e-rum (Br 3606, 3607, 3610) ‖ bi-e-çu (9) ri-e-su (15) Z^B 17; ra-sa-pu (25). V 28 *e-f* 1 sa-a-du = na-a-ru, Jensen, 341. II 32 *e-f* 26 . . . . nab? = na-a-ru, Br 14036. S^c 48 ga-al | GAL | na-a-rum between ka-a-nu & ba-šu-u, Br 2244.

ℑ Anp i 35 (iii 131) mu-ni-ir a-a-bi-šu, AV 5500.

Derr. — These 2:

nīru *1.* destroyer }Vernichter{? AV 6805. Esh *Sendsch*, *R* 25 ni-ir a-a-bi-e-šu. IV^2 39 *a* 2—3 Adad-nirāri ni-ir ṭap-nu-ti ‖ mu-xi-ip (5); P. N. Nabū-ni-ir-da-bi-bi, Merodach-Balad.-stone v 14. To this Boissier, PSBA xxii 109 refers also S 31, 52 *O* 3 (ZA x 202) kis$^{(iç)}$ ku-^{tu}kut = ni-'-[ru]. kiskuttu (*q. v.*) = 'coup violent'. — 83—1—18, 187 *O* 2 šar Akkadi^{ki} ni-ir-šu iš-šir-ma (Thompson: the rule of the king of *A* will prosper).

nīrtu *1.* perh murder, slaughter }vielleicht Mord, Totschlag{ AV 6350, see ℚ of nêru; also perh Sarg *Khors* 122 zi-ir ni-ir-ti. Asb iii 81 šap-la-nu libba-šu ni-ir-tu (KB ii 184—5; § 152). Sp II 265 *a* xxiv 9.

nāru *2.* = נהר river, stream; canal }Fluss, Strom; Kanal{. iD A  (Sarg *Ann* 266) = i-id, K 4322 iii 46. II 50 vi/v 5 . . . ID = na-a-rum; 6, ID-MAX = çi-ir-tum *i. e.* high (deep?) river, ZDMG 53, 657—8. AV 6135—6; ZDMG 40, 699; Lagarde, *Übersicht*, 140. It is used as a determinative before names of rivers & canals, *e. g.* II 51 *col* 1; § 9, 1; Br 11647. H 36, 873 = V 27 *a-b* 11 = na-a-ri (Br 8407). *del* 11 $^{(nār)}$ Pu-rat-ti, *etc.* *pl* nārāti (§ 70 *a*). Often in Z^B. II 50 *c-d* 16 nār el-li-tu; 14, nār ez-zi-tum. Esh *Negoub* 8 nāru ša-a-tu (*Rec. Trav.* xvii 81—2) + 11; BA iii 206—7. I 65 *a* 26 ki-ma me-e na-a-ri (§ 72 *b*) la ni-bi-im (*q. v.*); Šamš iv 29 ki-ma mē nāri; KB iii (2) 6 *col* 2, 10; H 89 ii 26 see kibru. IV^2 59 *no* 2 *b* 17 mē nāri ālikūti (written A-MEŠ A-[sign] DU-MEŠ), id also 15 (end). Su *Kui* 3, 2 [nār] U-la-a na-a-ru ša kib-ru-šu ṭābu. I 28 *b* 20—1 nāru (the canal which *A* had dug), ri-eš nāri ša-a-ti (+ 22). Sp II 265 *a* ii 6 na-a-ri xu-bur teb-bi-ri; *cf* K 2001 iv 3, & xubur, where add Jensen, ZA x 94—5. KB iii (1) 172, 33 kal-li na-ri kal-li ta-ba-li (see kallū, 383). V 25 *a-b* 8 (= D 131) a-na na-a-ru (= A-ID-DA) i-na-ad-du-šu (§ 66); II 16 *e-f* 19 ina na-ri tab-ba-ši-ma; 48 *e-f* 37 ši-kin na-a-ri, Br 11639. NE 75 (+ 88) 44 zik-ru ša na-a-ri, KB vi (1) 143 (*cf* vi (2) 402) a likeness of the river {ein Bild des Flusses}. V 50 *b* 28 see mīlu (544 *col* 2). IV^2 1 ii 30 na-a-ru la ib-bi-ru; 11 *R* 24 it?]-ti na-a-ra uš-ta-bel (Br 6736); 22 *b* 10—11 ina pi-i na-ra-a-ti (= A-[sign]) ki-lal-li-e (*q. v.*), at the mouth of the two rivers, *i. e.* Tigris & Euphrates; *del* 184, 185 (204, 205) ina pi-i nārāti; ZA vii 111: wol im persischen Meerbusen. KB i 212—3 *ad* 745 B. C. a-na be-rit nāri it-tal-lak; Rost, *Tiglath Pileser III*, pref. xi *rm* 1 = Arm: בית נהרין. Asb v 81 bērit nāri (Winckler, *Forsch*, i 240 × KB ii 201). IV^2 29* *no* 4 C *R* 11 ba-a-çu ša na-a-ri, mud from the river; 54 *a* 42 see didru, Zimmern, GGA '98, 822, however, reads ina na-ri-ṭi (*q. v.*) eṭ-ra-aš-šu. id + *pl* we find often, III 66 *col* 9, 42 nārē kib-rat erbit-tim. atān nāri, ka-kiš nāri, mi-xir nāru, kullē nāri see those words; bāb nāri see bābu, 1 (141 *col* 2 § 4) and add M^8 21; also *cf* xarū & petū. V 16 *f* 23 perh na-ar-rum. — Names of canals are given in Bezold, *Catalogue*, 2183 *fol*. In astronomical texts, according to Thompson, *Reports*, nāru is probably the *corona*, *e. g.* 83—1—18, 47 *O* 8: when a 'river' surrounds the moon, there will be great inundations & rain. — On Na-ri-ma in T. A. see ZA vi 258 *rm* 3 = Euphratland = *Naharīna*, *Naharaiim*; Brown-Gesenius, 626 *col* 1; Winckler, *Forsch*, i 149; 384.

(ilu) **Nāru** P. N. of god?. T^M ii 63 ina kibri (ilu) Nāri elli-ti: am Ufer der glänzenden Flussgöttin, but see Jastrow, *Religion*, 282 *rm* 1. II 62 *e-f* 40; K 44 *O* 22—3 (= IV^2 14); II 56 *c-d* 26 AN (I-ID) A-[sign]; 27, AN-A-[sign] ÇI-GAL; 28, AN-A-[sign]-SI-LI-MA-DI; 29, AN-A-[sign]-AMĒL-RU-TIK all = [ilu] Nāru; T^M 132—33 suggests identification with Nergal who in II 59 *d* 39 is called šar ID-DA.

(māt) **Na-ar-ti.** Knudtzon, 85 *O* 2.

nāru *3*. II 25 *a-b* 79 . . . . . [sign] = na-a-ru = II 32 *e-f* 26, in a list of officials. §§ 9, 174; 25. ZA iii 328; D^{Pr} 47, = נגר. Pinches, PSBA xviii, 254—5 quotes na-a-ru among officials (83—1—18, 1866 *R* i) together with a-ši-pu. id Esh i 52 it-ti AMĒL (*var* TUR) NAR-MEŠ (read zammērē), perh also TP viii 90. *masc.* of:

nārtu. female singer, songstress, musician {Sängerin, Musikantin} II 32 *no* 5 *add* (ZK ii 300, 12; 413) SAL[na-ar]LUB = na-ar[-tu] Br 7274, 10950; AV 6034, 6151; preceded by zammārtu. Hommel, *Sum Lesest.*, 23 *no* 269: von nāru vielleicht Lautwert *nar* für *LUB*.

nūru, *m* light {Licht} id BER (or ÇAB?) Br 8147; Z^B 72 *col* 1; AV 6456; § 65, 3. V 31 *e-f* 33 BER-ri (or bir-ri?) = nu-u-ri Br 5859, 8152; *cf* IV^2 57 *a* 69 (nu-ri īni). NE 63, 36 ša-pat ek-l[i-tum-ma ul i-]ba-aš-ši nu-ru, KB vi (1) 206—8. K 44 (H 79) *R* 12—13 with thy bright fire ina bīt ek-li-ti nu-ra (= BER) ta-šuk-kan. IV^2 31 *O* 9 nu-u-ru ul im-ma-ru(-ra) light they see not (§ 66) *i. e.* they live not; 7 (& NE 17, 37; 19, 32) see zamū 3. IV^2 51 *a* 32 see כלם (388 *col* 1). S^P II 987 *O* 22 before him the gods il-la-biš nu-u-ri, were clothed with light (+ 26), *Jour. Vict. Inst.*, 29, 52. V 52 iv 20 who has established nu-ri ana nišē e-ša-a-ti. T^M vii 151 šiptu: bīt nu-ru (& *ibid*, *p* 148); K 61, 5; IV^2 60 *O* 30; K 54 (end) idī šipta bīt nu-ri, *etc.* Bīt nūru, ZA iii 36—7, name of a temple.

IV^2 61 *c* 33 nu-ur ša il-me-ši; ZA iv 8, 32 nu-ur kiš-ša-ti, 38 nu-ur-ka, 50 ana nu-ri-ka; PSBA xviii 158, 1:

nu-ur kiš-šat nišē. IV² 57 *a* 69 see namaru Ⓠ *a*. 8 iv 23 (end) nu-rak-ka; III 66 *col* 10, 32—4 u ki-ri-ru (קרר) ṭābu | a-na nu-ri-šu-nu | lib-ši. IV² 17 *b* 12 nūr-ka nam-ru kal nišē i-bar-ri, thy shining light beholds all mankind; 13 *b* 20—1 edlu na'idu ša ni-iš nu-ur (= GIŠ-ŠER) i-ni-šu (niš inišu = ŠI) ana axāti šaknu, BA i 404. II 19 *b* 20 ša ki-ma ū-me nu-ri šu-pu-u. In colophons: nu-ur šarri ilāni (il) Ašur (T^M i 154, *etc.*). *Šamaš* is called nu-ur ilāni rabūte, IV² 17 *b* 22; Šamš i 11; Asb iii 113; V 64 *c* 11 (§ 125); *Marduk*: nu-ur ilāni, Nerigl. ii 32, KB iii (2) 78, 29; *Ninib*: nu-ur šamē u erçi-tim, Anp i 8. IV² 19 *no* 2, 52 at-ta-ma nu-ur-šu-nu, 42 a-na nu-ri-ka u-paq-qu ilāni rabūti, Br 4638. DT 83, 4 nu-ur ša-ma-mi, Pinches, *Texts*, 15 *no* 4; PSBA '95, 181 *foll.* Banks, *Diss*, 18 *foll* *no* 2, 66 nu-ri (*var* ur) . . . . ša ša-me-e; S 954, 2 nu-ur šame-e . . . . . at-ti-ma, Br 7631. D 80 iii 1 TAG (iç) nu-ur in a gloss *bi-ir*; 82 iv 8—12 GAR (ga-ar), Br 11971; ŠER (Br 1650); GIŠ-ŠER (Br 1650; V 11 *a-c* 37; H 113, 33 = D 127, 35); BU (or ŠER; ZA ii 196); UD-UD (Br 7932) = nu-u-ru; V 38 *a-c* 32 see Br 7530, 1648; 33 = na-ma-rum; 42 = na-ma-ru ša . . . . . (ZA ii 282); K 4195 *R* 9 SI = nu-u-ru, AV 6614; V 29 *g-h* 61 nu[-u-ru] Br 4638. — In P. N. nūru occurs quite often, II 63 *c* 37 Nu-ur-un-ni-ilu = our light is god, AV 6452; nu-ur-a-ni-Nabū III 16 *no* 3, 39. Nu-ur (il) Nin-gir-su; Nu-ur-i-li-šu, Bu 91—5—9, 704, 12; Nūr-il, II 63, i 19: Nu-ur-ili, AV 6455; ii 22 Nūr-AN-UT (= il Šamaš, AV 6461); Cyr 332, 8 + 9; III 66 *col* 7, 11 il Nu-ru çal-mu; V 67 *c* 41 nūr (il) Sin, AV 6460; Cyr 64, 3 Nūr-Sin-at-kal-a-na Marduk; also Lu-ušēçi-nu-ur. Bezold, *Catalogue*, 2138.

Bīt nūri = candlestick {Leuchter} Peiser, *Vertr.*, *no* 121, 10 + 11: bīt nu-u-ru; ib 101, 5 (iç) bīt nūri.

Derivative tinūru, BA ii 295, connected perh with Syr *nūrā*, fire, & نار. nūru perh a softening of numru (II 43, 21; Z^B 17; ZA ii 282) Haupt, BA iii 580, *rm* †.

nīru 2. *m.* — *a*) yoke {Joch} for animal & slave, § 64; AV 6318. ib šu-du-un |  = ni-i-ru, S^b 45; § 9, 31; H 34, 828; Br 10275 *foll.* On the dialectic form see Br 7229. It is usually prefixed by (iç) and read nīru; § 121. TP ii 54—55 ni-ir bēlūtija kab-ta, the heavy yoke of my rule (ii 93; iii 85). Sarg *Ann* 20 ni-ir (il) Ašur ēmidsunūti, *Bull-inscr.* 10; *Cyl* 33 ni-ri (il) A-šur. TP III *Ann* 18 n]i-ir-ri il Ašur; Esh ii 21 kab-tu ni-ir be-lu-ti-ja (BA i 386 *rm* 1); iv 15 mighty lords who la kit-nu-šu a-na ni-i-ri; III 16 iv 7. Asb iii 16 he submitted ana (iç) nīri-ja (*var* ni-ri-ja), v 42; iv 103 (iç) nīr (il) Ašur (AV 6309) ša is-lu-u e-mid-su-nu-ti; Sm *Asurb* 284, 94 is-la-a (iç) nīr bēlu-u-ti-ja = Asb vii 87 (§ 152; Sm *Asurb* 97, iv, 2). Asb v 92 *U* ša la ik-nu-šu ana (iç) nīri-ja; x 29 (iç) nīr (iç) ša ša-da-di u-ša-aç-bit-su-nu-ti, 37 the unsub-missive u-šak-ni-šu (3 *pl*) a-na (iç) nīri-ja. V 65 *b* 45 lišdudu ni-i-ri. ZA iii 314, 69 a-na ni-ir-ja la ik-nu-šu; see also kānu ℶ *e* (402 *col* 2). III 66 *R* vii 22 (ilat) PAT (= Ištar?) ni-ru ša Sūti, Br 13464; PSBA xxi 124; also *col* v 33, Br 12638. Sp II 265 *a* xx 9 ša-di-id ni-ir ili; ZA iv 236, 9 nīr-ka na-ad-ri. ☉ 237, 5 ni-i-ru; P. N. of cities, K 2852 + K 9662 iv 22 Aš(š)ur-ni-ir-šu-u-rap-piš, Aš(š)ur-ni-ir-ka-rap-piš. T. A. Lo 57 + 38 (iç) ni-ri | xu-ul-lu (= על) of my lord, the king, is upon my neck; Ber 26 iv 39: X ni-i-ru, followed by (40): X çi-mi-it-tum. — I 44, 66 in order to break the chargers ana ni-i-ri; NE 48, 21 parū-ka] ina ni-i-ri ša-ni-na a-a ir-ši, KB vi (1) 168—9. H 124 (K 4995) 13 lu-u ša ina ni-ri ça-an-du, AV 7180; Rm 283, 9 (end) çi-mit-ti ni[-i-ri] Winckler, *Forsch*, ii 19; TP iii 8 çi-mit-ti ni-ri-šu-nu; vii 28 narkabāti-ja çi-im-da-at ni-i-ri; K 3600 *R* 22 mūrnisqē çi-in-da-at ni-ri-[-šu]; Šamš ii 2 sisē çimda-at ni-ri; ib Šalm i 18, 22, 48 (çimda-at); ii 3, 58, 62 (çimda-at); II 67, 63; Sarg *Ann* 330 çimitti ni-ri; see also mašaddu (*p* 600 *col* 1). Asb v 42 pa-an (iç) nīri-ja u-tir a-na Aššur, turned my span of horses toward Assyria; see çimittu. 82—5—22, 99 *R* 5—6 sisē ša ni-i-ri (Hr^{L} 373; AJSL xiv 16); 81—2—4, 57, 9/10 (16/17, 21/22) sisē ša ni-i-ri, BA i 207 Zugpferde. See also Sn ii 7, 8; iii 49; iv 2, 78.

b) part of the door {Teil der Türe} ‖ nukušū, *q. v.* II 23 *c-d* 40; AV 6305.

c) some ornament, jewelry worn around (on?) the neck, necklace, collar {ein Schmuckgegenstand, um den (an dem) Hals getragen, Halskette, -binde} Z^{B} 6 *rm* 1; J^{v} 30; BA i 494, 498. II 37 *g-h* 57 TAG [illegible]-TIK (Br 8182) = ni-i-ru; id = crimmatu ša kišādi, *cf* IV^{2} 31 *a* 49, *b* 43. V 15 *e-f* 26—28 KU-NIR-LAL-LAL, Br 6304; KU-NIR-TIK-LAL. Br 6296; KU-TIK-NIR-RA, Br 3281 = ni-i-ru, *cf* V 15 *e-f* 52. Bezold, *Catal.*, 1721 = [ ] 4 ša eli ni-ri kaspi.

d) V 18 *a-b* 24 ...... BU-SAR-DA = ni-ru ša šame-e, literally: yoke of heaven; PSBA xviii 25. Halévy, *Rev. d'hist. des Rel.*, xxii 190 perh connected with Mod. Hebr ניר, see Brown-Gesenius, 644, II ניר.

V 46 *a-b* 47 MUL-MU-ŠIR-ŠAR-DA = ^{il} ni-ru rak-su, Jensen, 18, 441: Anu als Nordpol der Ekliptik, Br 12089, while same id in II 47 *e-f* 16 = ^{il} A-num rabu-u ša šame-e (= V 46 *a-b* 12).

nīrtu *2.* T. A. Ber 25 i 70 ni-ir-ti, perh *f* of nīru, necklace.

nīru *3.* in Omens. ina ni-ri Ne-ša(?) ša-ki-i[n], Knudtzon, 6 *R* 4; ina qaqqad ni-ri KAN-tum RU(= nadn?)-at 72 *R* 6.

nīru *4.* V 18 *a-b* 20, 21 SAG-UŠ-SA; UŠ-SI-IL-LA = ni-rum ša eqli (Br 3586, 5066); 22 NIR = ni-rum ša aš(or til?)-li (Br 6285) AV 6305. Perh = ניר, the tillable, untilled, fallow ground.

nīru *5.* compassion, pity {Mitleiden, Erbarmen}. V 21 *a-b* 60 ni-i-ru ‖ unni-nu. Or, rather: wailing, crying, √na'aru, howl (Jensen).

nēru *2.* S^{b} 2, 11 pi-ri-ik | NER | ni-e-rum Br 9189; H 30, 670 (pi-rik, √paraku?).

nēru *3.* II 23 *e-f* 8 ne-e-ru ‖ i-çu.

nēru *4.* = numeral 600 {Zahl 600} = ὁ νῆρος. §§ 29; 75. Br 8717. Schrader, ZDMG 26, 241; 27, 405 *rm* 3; Delitzsch, *Aeg. Zeitschr.*, '78, 56—70; BA ii 543 *no* 169; ZK ii 279; AJP viii 271; Lehmann, i 130. H 110, 41 (= V 12, 39) ne-e-r[u] following 1, 2, 3, 4 šu-ši. V 18 *a-b* 23 [illegible] = ni-e-ir, H 32, 750, Br 10148. Sarg *Ann* 423.

narū. memorial tablet, slab of stone with inscription thereon {Gedenkstein, Steintafel mit Urkunde} ✕ temē(n)nu, *q. v.* AV 6138; usually written (aban) NA-RU(= KAK)-A Sn ii 4; § 9, 151; ZK i 170; Esh *Sendsch*, *R* 51 (aban) narē ši-ṭir šumi-ja; 54 (aban) narē šu-a-tam; 58—9; KB ii 202 iv 24 nara-a an-ni-i; Beh 98, 106; V 34 *b* 47, 50 i-na (aban) narē aš-ṭu-ur; *Rec. Trav.* xvi 178—9, 15 + 23; Merod.-Balad.-stone v 22 (šu-a-tu); I 70 *a* 22. K 5418 *a* i 4; iv 8, 11 (aban) narē an-na-a (+ 12) KB iv 295—7. See also *Rec. Trav.*, xx 208 iv 18 TAG-RU-A; v 6. T. A. Lo 17, 36 if my lord does not send me word quickly a-na dup-bi u na-ri-šu. III 43 *a* 32 na-ra-a an-na-a u-ša-aš-šu-u, and has this tablet carried away; *c* 23 i-na mux-xi na-ri-e an-ni-i; IV^{2} 39 *b* 12 na-ri-ja (*cf* 8) šu-me šaṭ-ra (+ 16); KB iv 164—5 v 5 (aban) na-ra-a ka-nik; 13, i-na ka-nak duppi šu-a-tu; (aban) na-ra-a Peiser, KAS 16 v 5. TP viii 48 I wrote all i-na narē-ja u tem-me-ni-ja (+ 57 + 63 + 71). D 87 i 53 na-ri-e. Rm 339 *O* 6 na]-ru-u a-su-mit-tum, K 240 *R* 11—13 (= II 40 *no* 3) NA-RU-A = ši-ṭir šu[-mi] Br 1631; šu-mu zak-r[um] Br 1632; na-ru-u (Br 1636, Pognon, *Bav*, 95); 14, na-ru-u = a-su-mit[-tu] Br 1592. See also Bezold, *Catalogue*, vol. v pref. xxix.

Knudtzon has the following forms: 106 *R* 4 ki-i amēlu ša šum-šu i-na libbi ni-'-a-ra an-na-a šaṭ-ru; also 125 *O* 2; 126 *O* 2, *R* 6. 120 *R* 7 ni-ja-'-ri. 116 *O* 2, *R* 9 ni-ja-a-ri. 116 *R* 12 ni-ja-a-ri-im-ma. 116 *O* 4 ni-ja-ri-im-ma (*cf* 117 *R* 9); ni-a-ri 95 *O* 2; 97 *O* 2, *R* 7; 107 *O* 3; 119 *R* 4. ni-a-ra 107 *R* 9 *etc.* na-a-a-ru 94 *R* 3.

See Jensen, 4—5; 489 *fol*; KB iii (1) 36 *rm* 1; 37 *rm* *. Le Gac, ZA ix 337; Leh-

70—71: simply 'document'; t, *Sargon*, 188 *rm*: the front of HALÉVY, *Rev. d'hist. des Relig.*, : narū tablet not NA + RU ngraved in relief' (>< JENSEN), d. Hebr *neyâr*, usually translated nt, or paper'.

3 iii, 2, 8; AV 6358) see (il) Gir-*col* 2).

some weapon, a club? {eine 65, 31 *a*, *rm*. I 28 *a* 12 lions ina 'a-am-te u-šam-qit; L^T 196; *rm* 1; 177: spear.

48 *e-f* 32 (di-ig) NI = na-ra-labaku, 469 *col* 2, which also u) Br 5320, AV 6129; H 21, 388. p i 4 Ninib is called mu-nir-bu *. Anp*, 26; AV 5501). — Il^t perh —12 çi-ta ir-ta-ši | a-na su-n-ru-ub; but might be Q^t of > itérub).

— 1. munnar(i)bu. IV^2 30* *b* 9—10 na-zi ki-ma i-me-ri mun-nar-AR-RA), *Rev. Sém.* vi, 149: comme onagre lorsqu'on lui lance le lasso. Sn a-na-rib-šu-nu ša a-na nap-u-çu-u. V 42 *c-d* 58 KAR?]-RA nar-bu, same group with na-si-a-la-nu-u, more probably √ נרב; see also M^S 15 = BA ii 400.

AS, *AJSL*, xvi 251, narabu cognate, a stem from which we get אֲרָבִים

ab?)-bu. ZA iii 313, 65 (Sn *Bass* 38) Nineveh where my royal an-nnually e-rib la nar-ba-a-ti, sing income, the tribute *etc.* re-ee *ibid*, *p* 328). Sarg *Ann* 312 see *p* 468); 418 sat-tuk-ke la nar-is-qu-uš-šu-un u-kin-na, 157; KB ii 77: unaufhörliche en. WINCKLER: unceasing {be-ohne Aufhören}; MEISSNER & ROST, 434 tam (or per?)-qe-ti la nar-= *Khors* 173.

769 reads S^b 149 LAL-U (perh = nar-ba-a-tum (see libbā-d; *p* 476 *col* 1).

c. st. nurub perhaps: a piece of ell. ein Stück Fleisch} K 2527 *R* u-ub širi iš-te-ni-'i-i, BA ii vi (1) 106; 415: wird des Fleisches erforschen; thus √erebu, from lso the following 3:

nēribu entrance, pass {Eingang, Pass} §§ 32*aγ*; 45; 70*b*; AV 6318; KGF 147; L^T 143—44; AJP viii 275; BA i 4; 175; 177. *pl* nēribē, nēribâ, nēribēti. — *a*) entrance to a house, gate {Eingang eines Hauses, Tores} NE 24, 3 they saw of the forest ni-rib-šu, its entrance. Asb viii 14 ni-rib masnaqti adnāti (*q. v.*); ix 110. Sn iv 59 a-di maxāzāni ša ni-ri-bi, as well as the cities at the entrance toward ... V 65 *b* 7 like ni-ri-bi qin-ni-e (the entrance to a nest) I strengthened it; also 13, 16, 32. Sarg *Ann* 112 bîrtu ša ina ni-rib māti; *Khors* 161 u-rat-ta-a ni-rib-šin, and put them up in their entrances (BA iv 253) = *Ann* 422. BANKS, *Diss*, 24—6, 2 (*nos* 8—10) 82 ina ni-ri-bi tar-çu-tum (-ti) be-el-tum. II 67, 80 lion- & bull-colossusses ni-ri-bi ušaçbit. Neb v 63 iš-ta-ap-pi-la ni-ri-ba-ši-in, their entrances had become too low, FLEMMING, *Neb*, 30; BA i 393; § 67, 4. T^M v 135 abulli u ne-ri-bi la ter-ru-ba-ni, durch Tor & Eingang sollt ihr nicht eintreten. Z^S iii 63 ma-mit ni-ri-bi. KB vi 110—111 (below) 3 + 5 ni-rib ša bābi: at the entrance of the gate. KNUDTZON, 11 *b*, *O* 5 ni-ri-bi ša al S. li-še-rib; 35 *O* 6, *R* 10; 31 *O* 2. WINCKLER, *Sargon*, 166, 23 i-na ni-ri-bi(-ti)-ši-na, in their (the doors') entrances; perh II 48 *e-f* 9 ni-rib erçi-tim, JENSEN, 197 *rm* 1; 219. — *b*) entrance to mountains, pass, cleft, ravine {Eingang zu Gebirgen, Engpass, Schlucht}. Mighty mountains ša ni-rib-šu-nu aš-ṭu, whose entrance is steep, Sarg *Ann* 5; *Khors* 14; *Cyl* 10. POGNON, *Wadi-Brissa*, 173 ni-ir-bi-e-ti. T^P iv 53 ṭūdā (*q. v.*) marçūte u ni-ri-bi-te | šup-šu-qa-a-te .... ušētiq (57, end); Anp ii 40—1 ina ni-rib ša bi-rit (šad) *L* (šad) *B* ... ēru-ub; ii 33 a-na ni-ri-bi (*var* ni-rib) ša (al) Ba-bi-te ēru-ub; 19 *fol* ina (šad) ni-ri-bi (*var* -rib) ša *B* etera-ab; Šalm, *Ob*, 24, 25; 42; *Mon* i 15; Anp i 59. Šalm, *Mon*, ii 65—66 ina ni-ri-be ša šade-e ēru-ub ina ni-ri-be ša (māt) Kir-ru-ri | ina rēš Arba-il u-çi-a (1 *ag*). Sn iv 10 i-na ne-ri-bi-šu-nu qi-qu-ti šūnu-xiš e-ru-um-ma into their (the mountains') ravines I entered with difficulty.

I 43, 38 a-di ne-ri-bi ša (šad) Bīt-Bu-na-ki. NE 59, 8 when I arrived at night a-na ni-ri-bi-e-ti ša šadī, to the clefts of the mountain. A ‖ is:

nīrubu. Anp ii 24 (šad) ni-ru-bu ša Ba-bi-te (*cf* 20).

nīribūtu II 9 *a-b* 17—19 ni-ri-bu-tu, ni-ri-bu-su, „ iš-kun; ið NAM]-GA-BAR-TU-RA, Br 1072, 14186; AV 6314.

niribu (?) K 2867 *O* 25 la i-šu-u ni-ri-bu, said of the kiššti, çuçē, S. A. Smith, ii, 2.

narbū, nirbū. greatness, might, glory of the gods }Grösse, Macht, Herrlichkeit{ √rabū. Z^B 97; § 65. 31 *a* & *rm.* K^M 6, 16 nir-bi ilū[-ti-šu?]; 21, 7 nir-bi ana nap.... ZA iv 231, 24 nir-bu-ša rabū, ZA v 58. K^M 2, 41 nar-bi-ka lu-ša-pi (6, 69); ‖ da-li-li-ka lud-lul; 5, 8 lu-ša-pi nar-bi-ka; 7, 2; 12, 93; 18, 17 la-ta-am nar-bi-ka ana nišē rapšāti (§ 93, 1 *b*); 21, 23 + 71; 23, 5; 50, 27; 27, 24 nir-bi-ka lu-uq-bi; 6, 94 nar-bi-ki lu-ša-pi; 2, 8; 7, 32; 30, 15 + 17 nir-bi-ki lu-ša-pi (& -pu-u). IV^2 54 (= IV 61) *a* 46 nar-bi-ka ‖ qur-di-ka (28, end), ZA iv 241, 36. H 121 *R* 1—2; IV^2 59 *no* 2 *b* 27 *etc.* see dalalu. IV^2 29 *no* 1 *b* 13—4 nar-bi-ka (IV^2 17 *b* 4) O Marduk aq-bi, Br 1046, 1612, 2123. KB iii (1) 115 *col* 4, 2 na-ar-be du-ni-šu, the greatness of his power. Perh NE 61, 10: 12 kuspu nar-ba[...]; or lib-ba, KB vi (1) 206—7.

narbūtu. Šalm, *Mon*, *O* 49 see dalalu Q (*p* 250 *col* 1; Craig, *Diss*, 27). 81—2—4, 219 *O* ii 9 lip-pu-du nar-bu-u-tu. *Rev. Sém.* vi *no* 4.

Nirbu name of a country. Anp i 112; ii 9 + 15 (māt) Ni-ir-bu (Streck, ZA xiii 82); ii 129 (māt) Ni-ri-be; iii 122 (?) māt Ni-rib ša bi-ta-ni; L^T 176; Belck, ZDMG 51, 561 *rm* 3, on the location of Nirbu (= das Land der Pässe); see also Hommel, *Gesch*, 563—4.

Nirba, Br 7454, see Nisaba.

narbaçu. camp, dwellingplace }Lagerplatz, Lager, Wohnort{ § 65, 31 *a* = מַרְבֵּץ. Sarg *Khors* 144 Uperi who here & there like a fish šit-ku-nu nar-ba-çu (= *Ann* 370); Pp IV 57 nar-ba-a-çu, BA i 326. DT 57 *O* 11 get up ki-ma iççur xurri ina nar-ba-çi-ki, from thy hiding place. K 2606 *O.* 5 ... lu-u qin-nu nar-ba-as[-su] BA ii 399. K 4174 + K 4583 iv 39 KI[-KU] = šub-tum, mu-ša-bu, ru-ub-çu, nar-ba-çu, M^S 88.

naragū, an official? }ein Beamter?{ K 194, 3 ina eli na-ra-gi-e (Hr^L 144) Bezold, *Catalogue*, 2133.

Nergal. P. N. of the city-god of Cutha (2 Ki 17: 30), the modern Tel-Ibrahîm, some ten miles east of Babylon = נֵרְגַל, Νηριγλι(σαρος) § 29. Belongs to the Babylonian pantheon prior to Xammurabi, Jastrow, *Religion*, 65—8; *ibid*, 218—9 on his occurrence in later times. AV 6321.

ið AN 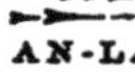-RA, § 9, 60; II 54 *no* 5, 67 *foll*; AN-LAM (?) IV^2 24 *O* 6 *foll*; D 28, 233; II 61 *b* 18, 17, 53 *etc.*; LAM according to S^b 210 = u-gur (Br 8858, 8860); AN-GIR (or NE?)-URU (Br 9202)-GAL; IV^2 24 *O* 1, 5 *foll*; II 60 *a-b* 12; III 68 *a* 75; V 65 *b* 49; AN-ŠI-DU, *i.e.* ilu ālik maxri, Br 9330.

Originally the god of the burning heat of the sun; then also war god & lion-god. God of the hunt, chase, I 7 *no* ix D, 3 (AN-LAM); lord of weapons & bow, III 43 iv 21 il Nergal (= AN-LAM) bēl be-li-e u qa-ša-ti. As god of war, he is the god of destruction, who overthrows the enemy's army & land; see (māt) nukurti; he is called git-ma-lu ša tam-xa-ri (the wise god), Šalm, *Ob*, 11; III 38 *no* 1 *O* 1 il Nergal (= AN-LAM) qar-ra-du git-ma-lum; IV^2 24, 1 *O* 48—9 git-ma-lu ša dan-nu-us-su šu-tu-qat; IV^2 2 *a* 19 qar-ra-du dan-nu ša (il) Bēl. NE XII *col* iii 21, 22, 26 qar-ra-du eṭ(d,t)-lu il Nergal; *cf* V 46 *c-d* 17 AN-UL gu-ud gu-ud UL = il qar-ra-du = the warrior-god. T. A. Lo 5, 13 + 37 ið = god of iron; here he seems to be a hostile, evil god. Anp ii 25—6 with the help of .... Nergal, who went before me with the mighty weapons that Ašur has given unto me; 27 with the lofty help of Nergal, who walked before me (Šalm, *Mon*, i 44; ii 70); thus no doubt because of his ið AN-ŠI-DU (81—7—27, 152, 4 + 6, end; BA iv 162) which also = Ninib. TP vi 58; II 67, 12. Scheil, *Nabd*, ix 23—5 mentions Bēl, Nabū & Nergal (AN-GIR-URU-GAL) as ilāni rabûti; also I 35 *no* 1, 24. K[M] 27, 4 (ilu) Nergal (AN-LAM) kaš-kaš ilâni. Sn v 50; Esh & Asb (i 48 *etc.*) reckon him among the twelve great gods.

Consort of Eriškigal (= Allatu, on which see WZKM xii 64 *rm* 1; IV² 15* *b* 36) the mistress of the netherworld with whom he shares the rule of this kingdom, KB vi (1) 78, 15 *foll*; J[w] 66; JEREMIAS, *Hölle & Paradies bei den Babyloniern*, 16; his name Urra-gal = hell-god. Also mentioned as consort of La-az, (*p* 477 *col* 2). II 59 *d-f* 37 AN-‹ (= bêl)-[cuneiform] = AN-GIR-URU-GAL *i. e.* king of Aralû, kingdom of the dead; J[w] 62 *no* 4; IV² 26 *a* 3—4. His temple in Cutha: E-ŠIT-LAM, KB iii (1) 80 *no* 5; thus he is called AN-ŠIT-LAM-TA-UD-DU-A *i. e.* coming out of ŠITLAM, IV² 35 *no* 2; ZA ii 292. NE XII *col* ii 25 (iii 3, 10, 18) ra-bi-iç (ilu) Nergal la pa-du-u, perh one of the monsters, supposed to be in his retinue. KB vi (1) 527: lisum.

Ninib, as well as Ningirsu, are closely allied (or identical?, HOMMEL) with Nergal in early Babylonian literature. I 28 *a* 1 *etc.* mentions Ninib & Nergal (written AN-ŠI-DU). Sometimes identified with Nusku (*q. v.*) the god of the all-destroying midday-sun; and with Gibil, the fire-god, IV² 24 *a* 54. As god of the glowing sun he appears also in lion's shape (see, however, JENSEN, 489). V 46 *c-d* 22 AN šar-ra-pu (*i. e.* burner {Verbrenner} = *Seraph*, DELITZSCH) = AN-LUGAL-GIR-RA-MAR-KI = Nergal in the Westland (Canaan, JENSEN, 484 *foll*).

II 59 *d-f* 36—40 (J[w] 66—7); 36, AN-‹ (= bêl) ŠE-ZI-DA = AN-NIN-GIŠ-ZI-DA = ŠU (J[w] 66 *rm* 3); 37 (see above); 38 AN-‹-A-AB-BA = AN-LUGAL-A-AB-BA; 39 AN ‹-ID-DA (= the river of the dead); 40 AN-‹-AB-A (*i. e.* the water-house).

III 67 *c-d* 69 AN-GIR-URU-GAL = AN-LAM ša qa-ab (AV -ba)-ri; 70, AN-‹-[cuneiform] = AN-LAM ša xa-a-a-ṭe, Br 8860; 71 AN-XUŠ-KI-A = AN-LAM ša ši-ib-ṭe, Br 8607, AV 6321.

K 170 *R* 15; III 66 *O* 21 *a*; *R* 14 *e* see Br 9190.

V 44 *c-d* 55 *cf* Br 8978. — V 46 *c-d* 18 (ilu) s(ç)ar-bu-u = il bêl s(ç)ar-be; 19, see JENSEN, 478.

Planet Saturn (later Mars) was sacred to Nergal (HOMMEL, *Ausland*, '91, 382 *foll*, JEREMIAS-ROSCHER, iii 266—7; ZA vi 221; >< JENSEN, 181 *fol*, 313 *rm* 1, 504). — Mars originally sacred to Ninib (*q. v.*); also the *Gemini* (tušmu) are connected with Nergal, JENSEN, 64—5. IV² 33 iv (end) 9 Kislev ša UR-SAG-GAL-AN-LAM, WINCKLER, *Forsch*, ii, 3, 368.

V 21 *c-d* 25 AN-NIN-GIR (*i. e.* bêl emûqi) = al-mu; 26, AN-NIN-GIR-[cuneiform] = a-la-mu (JENSEN, 64); 27 AN-NIN-GIR-BAN-DA (*i. e.* lord of youthful vigor) = bi-ib-bu shows that Nergal as a planetary god retains the character as warrior-hero; compare with these lines, V 46 *c-d* 20—21 AN-al-mu = AN-LUGAL-GIR-RA (22 + 24; ZA i 56 *fol*; J[w] 69 *rm* 3; also II 59 *d-e* 46; S[b] 2, 14; S[c] 1 *b* 8; III 66 *O* 21 *d*, Br 1846); 21, AN-al-la-mu = AN-ŠIT-LAM-TA-UD-DU-A (23 + 25; S[c] 1 *b* 9; Br 1847). See also K 4810 (IV² 21 *O* 42 *foll*); T[M] 143. On S[c] 1 *b* 22, 23 see Br 1906, 1907.

NOTE. — 1. See, above all, JEREMIAS' article in ROSCHER'S *Lexikon der griech. u. röm. Mythologie*, III 250—71; & *Hölle u. Paradies bei den Babyloniern*, 16—19; JENSEN, 476—90: Ner(i)gal-Ur(r)gal. PINCHES, *Jour. Trans. Vict. Inst.*, 28, 16. WINCKLER, *Forsch*, i 218 *fol*; MUSS-ARNOLT, *Assyro-Babyl. Months*, 32—33; HEBR. ix 8 *rm* 8.

2. Etymology: Ne-uru-gal is a popular etymology; = lord of the wide land: bêl ša erçitim rapaštim, *i. e.* of the netherworld. }— HOFFMANN, ZA xi 287: Dass Nergal = dem "Geiergott" [Hebrew] ist, ist nicht so unmöglich, sofern [Hebrew] als Wortbildungsendg. vorkommt. (§ 65 *rm* 30: JA VII *vol* 12, *p* 440; ZA v 61, 30. -ak bildet im Mahri adjectiva & Partizipien.

3. (ilu) EN-NU-GI, *del* 18, perh for (ilu) EN-KUR-NU-GI = Nergal; the occurrence of the name, in Z³ iv 83, at the side of Nergal (79) may be due to later differentiation.

4. On Nergal + compounds see BEZOLD, *Catalogue*, 2137—8; AV 6323—46.

nergallu lioncolossus {Löwenkoloss} Br 11270. Sn *Kui* 4, 27 large pillars çi-ir ner-gal-li-e ul-ziz (Lay 41, 33). Sarg *Ann* 423 *var* to nêšê, but see JENSEN, 495—6: reads gir (or ur)-gal-li-e; see *ibid* 489—90: nergallu: Löwe, existiert nicht; also see JEREMIAS-ROSCHER, iii *col* 254; reads urgallu. MEISSNER & ROST, 36: liegender Löwenkoloss.

nargîtu large bandage {grosser Verband} AV 61448, 6945. V 28 *g-h* 12 na-ar-gi-tum ‖ pa-as(z)-ka-rum foll. by xa-zi-qa-tum (*p* 308 *col* 2) & patinnu as ‖ of paršîgu. II 29 *no* 5, *d* 76 nar-gi[-tu]. K 8827, 9 na-ar-gi-tum. AV 2999 *ad* V 15 *e-f* 56 nar[-gi-tum], followed by zi-ir-[qu-tum] & xa-zi[-qa-tum].

(ilat) **Na-ru-du** III 66 *col* 6, 2 (il) VII-bi, (ilat) Na-ru-du (= 39); & *col* 2, 13; PSBA xxi 118 *foll*; Br 1591; 1593 *ad* IV² 2, 1 B *O* 23 (*a* 46 >< T^M 143; *cf* 25 *b*) = sister of the "seven". ZIM., *Ritualtaf.*, *no* 45 iii 1 çalam (ilat) Na-ru-da (47 ii 13; 54, 25 & 42 ii 14 -di) AV 6130.

nar(nir)damu. road, way {Weg}. II 46 *no* 4 *b* 68 nar-da-mu; Br 14235; V 21 *a-b* 30, Br 11116; D 89 vi 57, Br 5507; § 61, 31 *a*, *rm*; AV 6144. II 38 *d* 31 nir-da-mu, prec. by da-rag-gu, ki-ib-su, AV 6348. BA i 162—3: the *i*-vowel is the original; the *a*-due to the influence of the following *r*; see also BA i 461 *rm* *; JENSEN, 42 compares رَدْم 'dam'.

nurzu (?). Merod.-Balad.-stone iv 31 nu-ur-zu kišâd nâr šarri, BA ii 263 *n* at the bank of the king's canal; KB iii (1) 190: nu-'-zu.

nurîxu. T. A. Ber 28 ii 46: 1 nu-ri-xi šanîtu ša kaspi.

naraṭu. Q ul i-nir-ru-ṭa (= inéruṭa, BA i 461 *rm* *) šêpâka SMITH, *Asurb*, 125, 69; S. A. SMITH, *Asurb*, iii 12 (K 2652, 36). KB ii 252—3: thy feet shall not become weary, give away {deine Füsse sollen nicht widerstreben} §§ 98; 101. II 127, 50 a-šib pa-rak-ki i-ru-bu-u-ni (רחב) i-xe-šu-u-ni (√xâšu) i-nar-ru-du-nim[-ma] = MU-UN-DA-AL-PA-PA-GI . . . Br 5583. BANKS, *Diss*, 16, 1 *no* 4, 154 (end) er-çi-te i-nar-raṭ ‖ i-ru-ub-bu, 152. KB vi (1) 355; 512—13: regungslos, unbeweglich sein.

ℑ SMITH, *Asurb*, 136, 71 (KB ii 256) u šu-nu | u-nir-ri-ṭa e-piš šarrû-ti-ia and who had resisted the exercise of my royal rule. Asb iii 58 mu-nir-ri-ṭu epêš šarrûtija, who opposed {die sich widersetzten}; vi 72 mu-nar(*var* -nir)-ri-ṭu šarrâni abêja (KB ii 207; >< J^W 54—55; HOMMEL, VK 490 *rm*). II 66 *no* 1, 5 Ištar dâlixat tâmâte mu-na-ri-ṭa-at xuršâni, AV 5493. BANKS, *Diss*, 1 *foll*, *no* 1, 15 a-mat-tum ša šap-liš erçi-tim u-nar-ṭu (23, u-nar-raṭ); 18 *foll*, *no* 2, 21 šamê u-ra-bi erçi[-tim] u-nar-raṭ. S 954 *O* 43, 44 šamê u-ra-ab er-çi-tim u-nar-raṭ (*var* ra-aṭ, REISNER, *Hymnen*, *no* 53) ta-na-da-tu-u-a (D 135; G § 99; Br 5583); 45, 46 mu-rib-bat šamê mu-nar-ri-ṭa-at erçi-tim ta-na-da-tu-u-a. V 45 v 52 tu-nar-raṭ. Šalm. *Throne*-inscr. iii 7 Mu-nir-ri-te kib-ra-a-te, name of the rampart of city of Ašur.

Derr. perh these 3:

nariṭṭu. ZA iv 237, 44 (46, 48) ittaziz ina na-ri-iṭ-ṭu ka-li ina ru-šum-du he descended into a *n*, is kept back in a *r*. ZIM., GGA '98, 822 reads IV² 54 *a* 42 ina na-ri-ṭi eṭ-ra-aš-šu. KB vi (1) 504; 513: Sumpf, Morast.

nurruṭu. Šamaš. L⁴ i 22 as-ma-ra-ni-e nu-ur-ru-ṭu-u-ti heavy lances (lit^y hard to handle, obstreperous) {Schwere Lanzen}.

nirṭu (or nirîṭu). K 2729, 59 (KB iv 144) ni-ri-iṭ bêl ṭâbti bêl damiqti ša šarri bêlišu šûtuni, BA ii 566 *foll*; M^S 69 *col* 1. KB iv: grave {Grab}. *del* 209 (231) an ni-riṭ šit-tum ir-xu-u e-li-ia, KB vi (1) 248—9: Einen Zustand der Erstarrung und Schlaf ergossen sie über mich. J^{I-N} 38 reads an-ni-riṭ (נרט) ich war hingesunken.

narṭabu *1.* irrigation-machine, waterpail; watering, irrigation {Bewässerungsmaschine, Wassereimer; Bewässerung} § 9, 220; Br 1025, 8950; AV 6145. ið T^M vii 20 kîma GIŠ [cuneiform] erçi-tim ir-xu-u, as the ground loves watering; also IV² 52 *b* 1 ina axi narṭabi ša-'-il, Z^S 117. IV² 31 *b* 34 akalê GIŠ-APIN (= narṭabi) ali lu a-kal-ka (KB vi, 1, 402); V 32 *b* 56 kurussu ša narṭabi; Z^S iii 41 ma-mit narṭabu ça-ba-tu; also Cyr 173, 5. II 30 *b-c* 68 [cuneiform] (*i. e.* SUN) = nar-ṭa-bu; S^b 339 su-un | SUN | nar-ṭa-bu. V 29 *g-h* 64 GIŠ (a-pi-in) [cuneiform] = nar-ṭa-bu, prec. by it-tu-u. II 26 *no* 1 *add* = ⊕ 84 i 6 . . . . . . (Jur) [cuneiform] = ap-pat ša GIŠ ; BA i 167 & *rm* **. √ra-ṭabu.

NOTE. — arṭabu Cyr 316, 1 + 6 has nothing to do with narṭabu (JENSEN, ZA xiii 335 >< HILPRECHT), but is Persian (= ἀρτάβη). GIŠ-APIN = Bewässerungswerk = ناعورة; *cf* nāru = mirišu, Gerät zum Bewässern. Eines der beiden GIŠ-APIN entsprechenden Wörter: epinnu & narṭabu, wol auch = Bewässerungseimer.

narṭabu *2.* IV^2 56 *b* 56 see laxamu (478 *col* 1).

narṭibbu IV^2 22 *a* 15 (end) nar-ṭib-bu (= GIŠ-BAB-MAX) Br 4245, or lub-lubu, *q. v.*

narkabu. PEISER, *Babyl. Vertr.*, 218 *no* 148, 15 ištēn-it (aban) xarri u (aban) nar-ka-bu.

narkabtu. *f, pl* narkabāte, wagon, chariot, war chariot {Wagen, Streitwagen} > mar-kabtu = מֶרְכָּבָה; id GIŠ (= MAR), § 9, 31; Br 10225; BA i 177; §§ 58*a*; 120; AV 6146. NE 42, 10; 43, 20; H 39, 155; 209, 15—16 = nar-kab-ti (Br 6208); $Z^{\check{s}}$ iii 27, 57; viii 60. T. A. (*passim*). IV^2 12 *R* 25—6 whosoever nar-kab-tum šu-a-tum, Br 614. TP iv 66 ina narkabti-ja (often in TP). II 19 *a* 2 (beg) nar-kab-tu-ka; II 16 *c* 36 nar-kab-ta ça-[am-da-ni] BA ii 285—6, Br 12106); Anp iii 68 narkabtu eb-bi-tu(-te); Sn i 67 (iç) narkabat šēpi-ja; Sarg *Ann* 222; *Khors* 85, 114; TP III *Ann* 69; Creat.-*frg* IV 50. *pl* Anp ii 120 narkabāte ra-ki-su xallupti (i 86; iii 57 + 59; KB i 92—3); iii 48 narkabāte-šu ra-ki-su; 45 narkabāte-šu LAL-su. II 65 *b* 12 (KB i 198). BA iii 169 *rm*: *u. r.* ganz mit glänzendem Blech beschlagene (bepanzerte), stets aber mit blanken Metallschienen versehene Streitwagen. — Asb iv 64 narkabāte (iç) ša ša-da-di *etc.* .... u-bil-u-ni a-di max-ri-ja. II 65 *b* 5 narkabātešu; *ll* 8, 10 (& see zūku, 289 *col* 1); Anp iii 58, 60, 63; III 5 *no* 6, 11: 1121 narkabāte-šu KB i 140 *rm* 1. TP ii 9—10 xu-(u-)la (see AJP xix 386) for the advance narkabāte-ja & my troops; also 42; 65: with 30 narkabāti-ja going at my side. Sn v 82 narkabāte taxāzi-ja. (amēl) bēl narkab(ā)ti(e) charioteer, Lay 72, 3; also see III 12, 25; TP III *Ann* 97. II 27 *a-b* 23 *foll* TI = ṭa-pa-nu ša narkabti (Br 1698); GA = ça-ma-du ša *n*; DUL-DU = e-lu(?)-u ša *n*; *g-h* 43 GIŠ--ŠU-GI = ma-xa-rum ša *n*, Br 10225. GIŠ-MAR = nar-kab-tum, D 89 vi 75; H 39, 144 (Br 5815); KB iii (1) 172, 37 narkabti la ra-ka-si. A ‖ is:

nirkabtu. IV^2 12 *R* 21—22 nar(*var* nir)-kab-ti šu-a-ti; id same as in *ll* 25—26 (see above).

narāmu *1.* √רמם-rāmu. KAT^2 414; ZK i 14, 15; AV 6180; § 65, 31*a*. — *a*) love {Liebe} V 64 *a* 14 Bēl ... i-na na-ra-am šarru-u-ti-ja, aus Liebe zu meiner Königsherrschaft; KB iii, 2, 98—99 *rm* *; on the other hand see Neb i 34; TIELE, *Gesch*, 482. H 123 *R* 3—5 Šamaš xa-'-i-ri na-ra-me-ki = KI-AG-ZU; *cf* 31, 715—16 KI-AG (or RAM) = na-ra-mu & da-du (Br 9717) K 4386 (= II 48) iii 16, 17. IV^2 15 ii 13, 14 eb-ri na-ram-šu, to his beloved friend; 24 *a* 24—5 na-ram Ē-KUR. 82—7—4, 82 *R* 15—16 and he renewed Babylon al na-ra[-am-šu]. KB iii (2) 6, 12 Sippara .. na-ra-am of Šamaš & A-a; 88 i 33 Larsa a-lu na-ar-mi-šu; iii (1) 120 *f.* ii 8 of Babylon al na-ar-me-šu (see, 121 *rm* **; § 37*c*); 126 b ii 14, 15 where Borsippa is called al na-ra-mi-šu (*i. e.* of Marduk) Neb iii 36; Sarg *Khors* 34 *Q.* al na-ram-i-šu, his favorite city; SMITH, *Asurb*, 119, 19. Asb x 51, 52 Nineveh al çi-i-ru na-ram Bēlit (*var* Iš-tar); viii 91, 92. II 58, 33 (iç) orinu na-ram ilāni rabūti. — *b*) object of one's love, favorite, darling {Gegenstand der Liebe, Liebling} K^M 6, 19 Nusku called na-ram (ilu) Bēl; 22, 5 Nabû, na-ram (ilu) Ea; also see 27, 4; 60, 6 (of Šamaš). I 49 i 6 *var* na-ram (ilu) Marduk; I 51 *no* 1 *R* 17 (*O* 3); Xam-murabi na-ra-am (ilu) Marduk anāku, KB iii (1) 119 *col* 2, 15—6. Kurigalzu calls himself na-ram (ilu) Bēlit, HILPRECHT, OBI, i *no* 41, 3; TP i 18 na-ra-me bi-bil lib-bi-ku-un. KB iii (2) 6 *col* 3, 1 Nebuchadrezzar na-ra-am li-ib-bi-ja. Sp III 586 + R III 1 (hymn to the setting sun) (ilu) Mi-ša-rum .... na-ra-am-ka; *cf* TSBA viii 167 *foll*; HOMMEL, *Sum. Lesest.*, 120 *fol.* IV^2 1 *a* 5—7 na-ram (ilu) Bēl; 24 *a* 15, 16 na-ram lib-bi (ilu) Bēl. ZA v 67, 17 Açurnaçirpal na-ram-ki (in a hymn); Neb i 6 Neb. na-ra-am Na-bi-um (i 34); v 22 I, na-ra-am libbi-šu; V 60 *b* 21 Nabupaliddin na-ram (il) A-nim u (il) Ēa (*cf* II 58, 26; Anp i 10); V 64 *b* 39 ina maxar Sin na-ra-mi-šu. Rm III 105, 4—5 na-ram (il) Bēl (of Nabû), 8 na-ram (il) Marduk. V 55, 11 na-ra-am (il) Marduk; I 35 *no* 2, 5. Esh *Sendsch*, *R* 22 na-ra-am šar-ra-ti ‖ migir (il) Anim. — P. N. Naram-Sin, AV 6131; V 63 *a* 31 Na-ra-am-Sin; KB iii (1) 98, 99; Na-ra-am-ba(?)-ni *Rec. Trav.*, xvii 36 *no* xvi, 2; Bezold, *Catalogue*, 2133.

narāmtu, *f* object of one's love, favorite {Gegenstand der Liebe, Liebling}. *Rec. Trav.* xx 205 *foll* i 6 Nanâ is called na-ram-ti il A-sa-ri. Asb x 27 Bêlit, the mother of the great gods xi-ir-tu na-ram-ti (il) Ašur (?); *cf* Smith, *Asurb*, 302, 11; ZA i 69; K^M 6, 126; 10. 23 (but?); written na-ra-am-tum, Berlin. Congress, ii, 1, 349*b*; KB iv 16 *no* ii 1 + 5. K 5157 *R* 15 (H 181 XII) xi-ir-tum na-ram-ta-ka um-mu rabi-tum. Scheil, *Nabd*, viii 39 Çarpanitum is called na-ra-am-ti (il) Marduk. Zim., *Ritualtaf.*, *p* 102, 104 (+ 107) ilat A-a xi-ir-ti na-ram-ti-šu; KB iii (2) 88, 51 A-a kal-la-tim na-ram-ti-šu (of Šamaš); I 69 *a* 60 kal-lat na-ram-ti-šu; Sp III 580 + R III 12 il A-a xi-ir-tum na-ra-am-ta-ka.

ṇarāmu 2. V 15 *c-d* 19 in a list of garments we have KU-UN-IL = na-ra-mu, AV 6130, Br 5916.

nurmû, a tree or wood? or fruit? {Baum, Holz? Frucht?}. V 26 *g-h* 21, 22 GIŠ-NU-UR-MA = ŠU-u *i. e.* nurmû; GIŠ 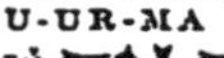-RA = nu-ur-mu-u (Br 1988, 3341); followed by 23, GIŠ-NU-UR-MA-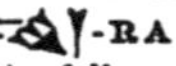 = ku-dup-pa-nu, 24 GIŠ-NU-UR-AL-XAB-RA = lap-pa-a-nu. K 40 iii 1 aban GIŠ-NU-UR-MA, following upon aban su-luppi, Br 731. AV 6458, 6459. Zim., *Ritualtaf.*, *no* 67, 10 (iç) nu-ur-ma *pl* (& 66 *O* 12); also a piece of jewelry {Schmuckgegenstand}. T. A. Ber 25 ii 4: 5 nu-ur-ma-a aban ....; 38: 7 nu-ur-ma çixrûti xurâçi.

nirmu (> nirmû, √ramû, 1). foundation {Grund, Fundament} § 65, 31*a*, *rm*; D^H 58; D^Pr 46; Z^B 91, 97; ZA ii 274, 1; AV 6354. II 35 *e-f* 44 ni-ir-mu ‖ iš-du; du(?, šu?)-ub(p)-lu (43), du-ru-uš-šu. Meissner-Rost, 104 *rm* 4 (irmu = nirmu); Barth, ZA iii 374 *rm*.

NOTE. — KB i 4 ma-xa-zu ni-ir-mu(?)-ti, IV² 39 *a* 3, is to be read ni-ir dap-nu-ti um-ma-a-ni; *cf* Meissner & Rost, 104 *rm* 2.

ni(a)rmaku. jar, pitcher {Krug, Topf} § 65, 31*a*, *rm*. AV 6147, 6358; BA i 162, 163. ši-i-mi nar-ma-ku ša siparri Camb 153, 1—2 (BA iii 402—3: Spendekrug); H 93, 35 [ina] ... ša-ti nar-ma-ki; II 33 *c-d* 8—10 DUK-XI-UŠ-SA = nar-ma-ku, Br 8258; nar-ma-ak-tu, Br 5537; & namxaru. TP ii 30: 5 nir-ma-ak siparri, mentioned among spoils (§ 128); see also namxaru TP ii 49, 58 *etc.*; L^T 124, 125; Lotz, *Quaestiones Sabb.*, 50. A ‖ is

ni(a)rmaktu. Sarg *Ann* 292 nir-ma-ak-tu; Anp iii 86 nir-ma-ka-te siparri among the tributes brought to Anp. T. A. Ber 26 iv 17 see naktamu.

nurupu. *var* after *del* 119 (126) reads ina nu-ru-up(b) ni-is-su-ti (NE 139 *rm* 25); KB vi 238 *rm* 5; 415: nurup perh √'-r-p: be sad {düster, traurig sein}.

NER-PAD-DU. id for bone(s) {Gebein, Knochen} so first Halévy; § 9, 261; D^Pr 155 *rm* 2; G § 26; J^W 54; AV 6357. KB ii 176 *rm* 5: perh = tuk-te-e (Smith, *Asurb*, 172, 17 = KB ii 264: tor-ra tuk-te-e abi ba-ni-ka; but see Winckler, *Forsch*, 246; 252). Asb ii 117 liš-šu-u-ni NER-PAD-DU (*var* DA)-šu let them carry away his bones, + 118; iii 64 NER-PAD-DU (*var* DA)-MEŠ abi ba-ni-šu-nu; iv 83 NER-PAD-DU-MEŠ-šu-nu-ti; vi 74. S^P ii 987, 13 kalbu ka-si-is NER-PAD-DA; IV² 56 *b* 40 (44) NER-PAD-DU ‖ šîru. II 28 *d-e* 66 KUD-DA = pa-ra-su ša NER-PAD-DU. II 22 *a-b* 9; Br 6303.

NOTE. — Tiele, *Gesch*, 296 *rm* 1. √rapadu, stretch out; but see BA i 163; Hommel, *Sum. Lesest.*, 35 *rm* * on 403. √KIR = man + BAD = dead; thus dead man's bones.

narpuxu. K 9949, 7 nar-pu-xu(-)šu LU-NITA. M^S 89 & Tafel 15, foll. by la-ax-ru & çi-e-nu.

narpasu an agricultural implement: threshing roller or sledge {Dreschwagen, -schlitten} √rapasu, crush to pieces, thresh. AV 6148; § 65. 31*a*. V 17 *c-d* 32 GIŠ-MAR (= narkabtu)-ŠE-RA-AX = na-ar-pa-su, Br 5830. id also in Sn *Bav* 30 bâb nâri u narpasu a-na ra-ma-ni-šu ip-pi-ti-ma Pognon, *Bavian*, 67; Winckler, *Forsch*, i 280: ein Bestandteil der Schleuse.

narpusu, properly *ac* or *pm* of 𝔑 of rapasu. *adj*. V 17 *c-d* 33, 34 SAG-A-NA´-A = na-ar-pu-su ša ma-na-ax-ti, AV 6149; BA i 181. KB vi (1) 392: Zerschlagenheit, Ermüdung.

naru(q)qu. something made of leather {ein aus Leder gefertigter Gegenstand} AV 6140. H 87, 61 na-ru-qu (= SU-A-SA, *var* GA´-LAL) up-ša-še-e ša lim-niš rak-sat, Br 242, 244. K 3172 *R* 3 na-ruq-qu ra-kis-ti, ZK ii 275.

nararu help, aid, assist {helfen, Beistand leisten}. II 39 *c-f* 3 id ID-DAX = na-ra-rum ‖ xa-ta-nu (*q. v.*) Br 4536; AV 6132. DT 83, 2 na-ra-ru, Pinches, *Texts*, 15 *no* 4. Sch 2, 7 na-ri-ru(m), ZA ix 219 *no* 2. T. A. Lo 24, 20 na-ri-ri. IV^2 30 *a* 35—6 see nâgiru. — 𝔑 KB v 415 *ad* Ber 222, 3 in-ni-ri[-ir?]; Lo 64, 21 en-ni-ri-ir, Bezold, *Diplom.*, xxxiii.

Derr. these 3:

nararu, neraru. *m*, helper, help {Helfer} §§ 9, 182; 34 *d*; 63; 65, 11. Sarg *Khors* 113 eli Argišti ne-ra-ri la mu-šo-zi-bi-šu it-ta-kil-ma. P. N. Ašur-na-ra-ra; Bêl nirari, IV^2 39 ii 65; *cf* II 47 *e-f* 68. Belck & Lehmann, GGN '99, 83 *fol*, *etc*. P. N. Ašur-ni-ra-ri-ni; A-da-di-ni-ra-ri-e-xi (= son of Adadnirari) in chaldic inscriptions. *AJSL* xii 150.

narâru. help, assistance {Hilfe, Beistand} T. A. Ber 240, 13 il-si-i' na-ra-ru' he cried: help! (KB vi, 1, 94—5; BA iv 128 *foll*; ii 418 *fol*)) *R* 4 il-su-u (3 *pl*) na-ra-ru. Rostow. 4, 15 [a?]-di na-ra-ru-qa until thy assistance.

ni(a)rarûtu. help, assistance {Hilfe, Beistand} BA i 461 *rm*. ID-DAX & ZAB-DAX, § 9, 25; ZDMG 28, 89; AV 6133, 6307. Asb i 75 a-na na-ra-ru-u-ti ša ilâni; Smith, *Asurb*, 38, 12 see xa-mâṭu; 103, 45 a-na na-ra-ru-ti (il) Bêl u (il) Nabû I called in my troops. TP ii 18 ša a-na šu-zu-ub u ni-ra-ru(-ut)-te ša (mât) Qummuxi il-li-ku(-u)-ni; iv 98 ša a-na ni-ra-ru-ti-šu-nu il-li-ku-ni; v 74 a-na na-ra-ru-ut (*var* ri-çu-ut) (mât) Muçri (Winckler, *Tigl. Pil.*, I, 1893, *p* 15). Sarg *Khors* 71 a-na ni-ra-ru-ti-šu al-lik, I came to his assistance. II 65 ii 10 nar-kabâti (u) zu-ki a-na ni-ra-ru-te iš-pu-ur; iii 31 a-na ni(II Rawl. na)-ra-ru-ti ša M. . . . il-lik (32). H 27, 600 ZAB-DAX = na-ra-ru-ut çâbê (V 21 *c-d* 19 + 20, D 26 *rm* 3; Br 4536, 8161, 8162; 624, 2566); H 38, 112 (= V 30 *g-h* 32)

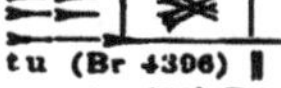

(um-ba-ra) = ni-ra-ru-tu (Br 4396) ‖ ki-di-nu (30) ri(ta?)-mu-tu (31) BA i 497.

naršundu, naršunnatu. an epithet of the witch {eine Eigenschaft der Hexe} √רשׁם. T^M iii 41 e-li-ni-tum (*var* -ti) [nar-šun]-da-tum (vi 22); iv 105 kaššapat nar-šun-na-at I am released; vii 94 nar-šun-du-u *pl* li-pu-šu-ki.

na-ru-tum, AV 6141 see našubtum. ni-ri-ti AV 6316 *ad* II 24 *a-b* 15 read qa-an ir-ri-ti & see V 32 *e* 47.

nurîtum. ZA vi 243, 35 nu-ri-e-tum ša (arax) Du'uzu (?) ana (il) Lugal-ku-azagga.

nirûtu (?) T. A. Ber 71, 14 u ti-na-i-s(z)u ni-ru-tu; 90, 44 let the king have a care of these (amêl) nir ni-ru-ti šu-nu-tu.

nirtanîtu. T^M viii 16 (*cf* iii 40) kaššaptu nir-ta-ni-tum; but iii 85 read e-li]-ni-ti-ja, BA iv 158.

nâši. we {wir} properly us {uns} Jensen, KB vi (1) 244—5 *ad del* 183 (203) end: na-ši-ma.

naššu? T. A. Ber 28 i 33 na-da-ni rab na-aš-ši.

nâšu. *pr* inûš, *ps* inâš & inaššu = נוש, Ps 69, 21 sway, quake, tremble, shake {schwanken, erbeben, zittern} Z^B 118; D^{Pr} 64 *rm* 3; ZDMG 40, 724. Thompson, *Reports*, vol. ii *pp* lxxxi: especially used for heaven & earth quaking at the approach of a god. S^P 158 + S^P 962 *R* 17 e-šar-ra i-nu-uš ki-gal-la; *O* 23 i-nu-uš aš-ru-ti, he shook the holy places, Pinches, *Jour. Vict. Instit.*, 20 pt. 1. KB vi (1) 154 (= NE IV *col* ii) 50 i-ga-ra i-na-uš, the wall is swaying. V 65 *b*

44 ana zikir sumija kabtu kul-lat na-ki-ri lit-tar-ri (תרר) li-nu-šu. IV² 39 *b* 3 see nixêsu. III 3, 21 i-nu-šu-ma e-nu-xu. IV² 28 *no* 2 *a* 11—12 ⁽¹¹⁾ Adad ina e-zi-zi-šu er-çi-tum i-na-as-su (trembles) ‖ i-ta-na-ar-ra-ru-šu (quakes before him). II 19 *a* 3—4 ina a-la-ki-ka šamu-u u erçi-tim i(n)-nu-uš-šu, Br 10288. IV² 31 *R* 32 ⁽ᵃᵇᵃⁿ⁾ askuppāti ça-'i i-na-ša ⁽ᵃᵇᵃⁿ⁾ PA-MEŠ; 36 u-ça-' i-na-ša (but see KB vi 1, 88—9). *Del* 135 (142) Mount Niçir took hold of the ship a-na na-a-ši ul id-din, and dit not let it slip away (lit: sway), BA i 18 *rm* 23; 135. V 36 *a-c* 58 šu-u | ⟨ | na-a-šu, Br 8715. Perh T^M iii 141 am-me-ni na-aš (BA iv 158).

ℑ causative of 𝔔; see naṭû, 1 & Br 10288. V 16 *c-d* 47 SAG-BU-BU = nu-uš qaq-qa-di, AV 6464; Br 3518, 3633, 7571. Br 11828 compares S 1708 (= IV² 18 *no* 6) *O* 6—7 un-ni-iš; ið almost same as that of nušū.

ℑ¹ 1 65 *a* 50 the great wall ša ki-ma sa-tu-um la ut-ta-aš-šu, which like a mountain could not be shaken (K 8258 *O* 23; ZA i 340); also JAOS xvi 74, 22.

NOTE. — 1. ℑ^{I-N} 55 *rm* 1c8 reads K 2774 iii 23 (= NE XII) lu-niš tak-ka-ap erçi-tim (+ 27); also K 3475 vi 2; but see KB vi (1) 262—3.

2. BA ii 208 *rm* * explains IV² 7 *a* 14—15 i-ta-na-ša-aš-šu as 𝔔^{tn} of נשׁ: er rüttelt ihn; Jensen, *Diss*: et perturbavit (?) eum.

našu (> naša'u § 38); *pr* iššî, 3 *pl* iššû (§ 49*b*); *pc* la-aš-ši for luašši BA ii 632—33; K 2401 iii 34; *ps* inaš(š)i; *ip* iši; *pm* n'a'ši (§ 32*β*), na-šu-u, ZK i 88, 6; *ag* našû § 42, nāši *c. st.* nāš, § 89. lift, carry, take {heben, tragen, nehmen}. ZDMG 32, 21 *foll*; ZA iv 66, 67; BA i 37; D^{Pr} 29; AV 6157, 6158. ið mostly GA-ṬU = EL(I), Br 6148.

Trans. — *a*) lift, lift up {heben, aufheben}. aš-ši-am-ma, I lifted up Pognon, *Wadi-Brissa*, 9. KB iii (2) 62 *no* 10 *col* 1, 19—20 ana bēlūt māti iš-ša-an-ni-ma (3 *sg*); KB vi (1) 112, 16 al-ka lu-uš-ši-ka-ma ana šamê. II 65 *O* i 12 such & such a-na šarru-u-te a-na eli-šu-nu iš-šu-u, they raised up to the kingship over them, KB i 194. Šalm, *Ob*, 148 (KB i 146). NE 21 *a* 9 i-di-šu iš-ši; 58, 49 lu-u aš-ši pa-a-šu (KB vi 187: hatte ich die Axt erhoben); 69, 40 i-ši Gilgameš xaçina (= *ip*); 44 iš-ši xaçina; XII vi 4 abu-šu u ummu-šu res-su na-šu-u, lift up his head; i 20 šab-bi-ṭu a-na qāti-k[a] la ta-na-aš-ši, KB vi (1) 256—7; *del* 154 (164) iš-ši she lifted up; 247 (277) u šu-u iš-ši pa-ri-sa (3 *m*, *sg*). Creat.-*frg* IV 37 iš-ši-ma, he lifted up (+ 49). T^M i 135 aš (= GA-ṬU)-ši ṭi-pa-ru, I lift up the torch (= IV² 49 *b* 47; l. 37 aš-ši). IV² 20 *no* 2, 8 ⁽¹¹⁾ Šamaš a-na ma-a-ti ri-ši-ka taš-ša-a (2 *sg*) *cf* III 57 *a* 10 ina māti na-ši, ZA ii 202. NR 27 ša kussū attūa na-šu-u (3 *pl*). Abel & Winckler, *Texte*, 60 *O* 29 (end) ina na-še-e šu-ma[-šu]. On našū erina, lifting up the cedar-staff on the part of the bārû, see Zimmern, *Ritualtafeln*, 89. — *b*) in many phrases used literally & figuratively: — *a.* raise, lift up the hand, *i. e.* pray, offer prayer {die Hand aufheben zum Gebet, beten}. KB iii (2) 64 *col* 2, 12 aš-ši ga-ti | u-sa-ap-pa ša-aš-ši; 90, 34. III 15 i 6 qa-a-ti aš-ši, I lifted up my hand. I 66 *c* 43 aš-ši ga-ta; ZA ii 132, 86 e-ma ga-ta-a na-šu-ka. Neb ix 46 ga-ti aš-ši; *cf* 80—7—19 *R* 4—5 qātā² . . . ul-te-li (Hr^L 416). Perh Abel-Winckler, *Texte*, 60, 10 qa-at-ka iš-te-niš (?) la taš-ša-a. — *β.* lift up one's head {sein Haupt erheben} ‖ kullu (כלא) ša rēši; šaqû ša rēši, II 30, 1. IV² 24 *a* 24—5 be-lum na-ša-a (= SAG-EL, *ag*) ri-e-ši çi-ru. Perh IV² 28 *no* 1 *a* 13—14 Šamaš mi-ša-ru re-is-su i-na-aš-ši-ik (= ši-ka?, Br 2560; GGA '98, 822). H 127, 32 ri-is-šu ul in-na-aš[-ši]; 128, 78 e-na (?) a-na-aš-ši[. . .]-ra a-na-aš-ši. II 26 *c-d* 57 —9 TIK-UŠ (Br 3269, 5040); TIK-ZI (Br 3242 = ša-qu-u ša ri-ši, II 30 *a-b* 4); SAG-EL (Br 3612) = *n* ša ri-e-ši. T. A. Ber 6 *R* 24 u ši-i ri-e-ši la iš-ša-a, and she did not lift up my head (when I was in sorrows); 7, 14 when my health was not good and my brother ri-e-ši [ul iš-ši] did not comfort me, + 17 am-mi-ni ri-e-ši la iš[-ša-a], why does he not comfort me? P. N. Ašur-reš-i-ši KB i 12; L^T 192, 193; I 6 v 2; Nabû-reš-i-ši *etc.* — K 660 *R* 5 ri-[ša-ni?] ni-iš-ši we will hold up our heads *i. e.* we shall be relieved of embarrassment, JOHNSTON, JAOS xviii 169. — γ. lift up one's eyes on high {seine Augen aufheben} našû îni (înâ) ana, D^{Pr} 48 & *rm*: to show favor to one, love and cherish. II 26 *c-d* 60, 61 ŠI-GAL, ŠI-EL, ŠI-LAL, ŠI-GAB = na-šu-u ša i-ni ‖ ša-qu-u ša i-ni II 30 *b* 7 (Br 2245, 9307; 9352; 4484, 9391, 10101; 9327, 9399); II 26 *c-d* 21 see Br 11152. Sn *Bav* 2 the great gods who in all lands to rule the people e-nu i-na-aš-šu-u i-nam-bu-u malku Sinaxerba; perh KB iii (1) 194—5, 6 n]a-šu-u e-ni na-šu-u zik-ri ma-al-ku (LEHMANN, ii 12—13) = L^{4} 6. See ni-šit înâ & ni-iš înâ. — *c*) bear, carry {bringen, tragen}. II 65 i 13 iš-ša-a (3 *sg*); TP ii 58. I 49 *d* 10 aš-ši(-ma) ‖ ušazbil; also Bu 88—5—12, 72 vi ku-dur-ru ina qaqqadi-ja aš-ši-ma (BA iii 245 *rm* *††). NR 10 i-na-aš-šu-nu they bring (§§ 90 *c*; 135). Asb iii 24 his tribute iš-šu-u-ni a-di max-ri-ja. Sn ii 57 before me iš-šu-nim-ma (3 *pl*) iš-ši-qu šepê-ja. SMITH, *Asurb*, 55 *R* 5; 97, 100; Esh iv 27—8; NR 10 mandattu anâku i-na-aš-šu-nu. K 890 *O* 5 ina û-me in-bu aš-šu-u-ni (1 *sg*); Lay 43—44, 16 lu(-u)-aš-ša-a, I brought. V 64 *a* 21 i-ši (= ip) libnâti; Sarg *Khors* 90 (153) na-še-e & la-na-še-e bil-ti; TP i 65, 66 kings na(-a)-aš bilti u madatti ša (ilu) Ašur; Sargon, *Asdod*, 30. IV^{2} 18 *no* 3 i 14—15, 16—17, 18—19 na-aš bil-ti said of mountain, field & acre, orchard, Br 3334. ZA iv 414 *ad* WINCKLER, *Sargon*, 64, 283 ar-du-ti u ana na-ši-e bil-ti (*Ann* 42 na-še-e), *Ann* 385 iš-šu-u-ma mandattu kabittu. lu-uš-ši-ka I will carry thee, KB vi (1) 112, 16; 114, 10. II 67, 84 palaces . . . na-ša-a xegalli. Babyl. Chr. iv 7—8 ana Aššur na-ši. III 58 *c* 42 a mighty enemy kakkê-šu ana mâti i-na-aš-ša-a, *b* 55 ina mâti GA-ṬU-ša. ZA x 292, 15 kib-ra-a-tum mit-xa-riš na-ša-šu xi-iç-ba. IV^{2} 56 *b* 54 lu-u na-ša-a-ti (2 *sg f*, pm; § 93, 2). NE 43, 17 lu-u na-šu-nik-ka (*var* lu-u-na-šu-ša-ka, § 93, 2) bil-tu (KB vi 166—7); 43, 37 + 38 na-ši-ša he that carries it {seinen Träger}; 44, 65 who . . . . . šu-gu-ra-a na-šak-ki; 63, 48 na-ša-at i-ni-ib-ša, bears as fruit, 51 in-ba na-še-ma fruit it bears (*cf* 50); 65, 7 i-ši šêr ilâni ina zumrišu er hat Fleisch der Götter an seinem Leibe (*var* išû; KB vi (1) 210) 66, 29 as long as the river iš-ša-a milim, carries the waves to the sea. III 4 (*no* 7) 7 iš-ša-an-ni nâru the river carried me along. IV^{2} 23 *a* 19 a-na par-çi ki-du-di-e na-šu-ka (they bring to thee); 32 *b* 9 Sin agâ taš-rix-ti ana mâti na-šu-u (*var* GA-ṬU-ši, or to *a*?), *cf* line 2; 25 *b* 46—7 ša-lum-ma-tu na-ši e-til-lu-tu (Br 467 na-ši-e be-lu-tu, same ID as V 21 *a* 24; see 5 *c* 40—41); 15* i 21 ina qa-ti-šu lu-u na-ši, Br 2245; H 89, 35 ša bu-bu-tu i[-na-a]š-šu-u. Creat.-*frg* III 21, 79 na-šu-u tam-xa-ri they take up the fight (KB vi, 1, 36—7); IV 114 še-rit-su na-šu-u, they bore his wrath. PEISER, *Vertr.*, *no* 145, 6 a-na-aš-šam-ma, I will bring (KB iv 200 *col* 1, 5); 95, 10 i-na-ša-aš-šu (Neb 246, 8 i-na-aš-ša-am-ma); 93, 11 i-na-aš-ši (Camb 42, 11; KB iv 262—3). Neb iii 19 a-na e-bi-šu Êsagila na-ša-an-ni (‖ abalu) li-ib-bi; *cf* niš libbi; perh V 55, 20 il-lik (lak) šarru na-as-qu ilâni na-šu-šu (KB iii, 1, 164—5; § 56 *b*). T. A. Lo 8, 35 li-iš-ša-am-ma, let him bring; 19, the 20 minas of gold ša na-ša-a, which he brought; Ber 7 *R* 25 xuraçu ša na-šu-ni, the gold which they brought (ZA v 14; 144). Perh II 46 *c-d* 48—50 DA = našû ša amêli (Br 6651); DA-RI = *n* ša amêli TUR (= çaxri? Br 6664) & = *n* ša al-mat-ti (Br 6663). — *d*) take, take away {nehmen, wegnehmen}. TP ii 32 aš-ša-a (iii 81; vi 9; Anp ii 62; Šalm, *Ob*, 141); iš-šu-u ii 40 (3 *pl*); viii 14 stones i-na šadê-ni . . . lu(-u)-aš-ša-a, I fetched {holte ich}. II 16 *c-d* 14—18 tal-lik taš-ša-a (ZK i 242; BA i 10) e-qi-el nak-ri | il-lik iš-ša-a e-ki-el-ka nak-ru (BA ii 296; JENSEN, ZA x 244). *dcl* 272 (305) šam-ma iš-ši; 278 (314) e-du-u i-na-aš šam-ma (Z^{B} 77; PSBA Nov. '84, 35). I 27 *no* 2, 30 la i-na-ši let him not take away; I 66 (*no* 2) *a* 8 la na-še-šu-nu (KB iv 67); PINCHES, *Inscr. Babyl. Tablets*, 42 *O* 5 i-na-aš-ša-am-ma. K 831 *R* 7 ši-pir-ti liš-ša-'u, let him take the letter. KNUDTZON, 150 *R* 9 fortresses which the Manneans iš-šu-u-ni, had taken; *ibid*, 100 *O* 12 (*pm*) EL (= našu)-u-ni. Neb 430, 4 iš]-tu pi i-rib-bi iš-šu-u-'-ma. A-na na-ši (na-aš) = in accordance with (kanikišu = this tablet, contract), KB iv 34 i 10 a-na na-aš-ši ka-ni-ki-ši (transl. by Peiser: dem Überbringer einer Siegelurkunde), ii 9; 38 ii 16; see Meissner, 102. pu-ut . . . naši, nāši, našāta, našū in contract tablets see pūtu & T^C 107—8. — *e*) carry on one's person, *etc.* a garment, sceptre, armature *etc.* }tragen, von Kleidern, Scepter, Waffen, *etc.*}. IV^2 56 iii 54 lu-u na-ša-a-ti thou shalt carry (on thy person); IV^2 14 (*no* 3) 5—6; Šalm, *Ob*, 11 (na-ši); Šamš i 27—8 see xaṭṭu (311 *col* 2) & ZA xi 295. na-aš pi-laq-qi II 25 *a-b* 76 AMÊL GIŠ-BAL-SU-UL = na-aš pi-laq-qi a temple-servant, charged with the slaughtering of scrificial animals. II 32 *e-f* 23 (Br 7220, 9145); Rm 338 iv 9; K 691, 11 (Hr^L 45) (iç) pi-laq-qu šu-u-tu a-na (il) Dil-bat a-na-aš-ši. (amēl) na-aš paṭ-ri (id GIR-GAL II 31 *a* 36) II 31 *c-d* 9; H 109, 48; 113, 41; D 129, 94 (= ME-RI (*var* IR)-LAL) Br 309, 10101, 10425; id also Neb 72, 2; 156, 2; K 2619 ii 11 na-aš paṭ-ri na-aš nag-la-bi qup-pi-e u çur-[ti]; see (nāš) paṭrū-tu. V 60 *b* 25 na-aš pit-pa-ni ez-zi-tim; V 35, 8 (§ 58). na-aš (iç) ka-ba-bi Sarg *Khors* 117 = *Ann* 400. TP III *Ann* 199 (*cf* 198). Creat.-*frg* III 34, 92 na-aš (iç) kakkē la pa-di-i (*cf* I *c* 26, KB vi 6—7; II *a* 6; III 40), III 98. Knudtzon, 100 *O* 12 ša be-li (weapon) našu-u-ni. na-aš ṭi-pa-ri(-ru) IV^2 26 *a* 39—40; aš-ši ṭipāru (see *p* 358 *col* 1); V 64 *c* 22 the mistress of the battle na-ša-ta (iç) qašti u iš-pa-ti. Creat.-*frg* IV 53 šin-na-šu-nu na-ša-a im-ta, their fangs carry poison. ZA iv 11, 27 na-aš kīsi; *del* 64 (68) çūbē na-aš (iç) su-us-su-ul-ša (KB vi 234—5: seine "Korbträger"). Neb iv 61—62 Sin na-aš ça-ad-du damiqtija who holds the çaddu of my safety; V 46 *a-b* 39 (kakkab) SAG-ME-GAR explained as na-aš ça-ad-du a-na da-da-mu. KB iv 102—3, 4 na-ši duppi ši-mat ilāni. II 19 *b* 54, 56, 58, 60 in my right, left *etc.* a weapon na-ša-ku (Br 2245; § 110*a*); also see *ibid* 2 (end), 5, 7 *etc.* Asb ix 80 Ištar . . . . me-lam-me na-ša-a-ta (*var* ša-at) was clad in splendor (§ 58*c*) *cf* IV^2 27 *a* 49 ša pu-lux-tu me-lam-mi na-šu-u (*pm*). K 3456 *R* 13 a-ri-ri na-ša-a-ta (2 *sg*). K 2148 ii 6 ina šumēli-ša še-ir-ra na-šat-ma (ZA ix 118; 417) iii 8 (end) a-ka-la na-šat-ma. K 164, 19—20 zi-iq-tu ša qanē ṭābi ta-na-aš-ši (BA ii 635—6). V 21 *a-b* 24 AN-TA-MU = i-ša-an-ni raise me!, followed by i-la-an-ni, Br 461; ZA iv 230, 3.

H 23, 451; 186, 8 i-li | GA-ṬU | na-šu-u (II 26 *c-d* 43; V 38 *c-d* 39, *e-f* 66, see ZK ii 62 *foll*); ZA iii 408; II 44 *no* 9 *g-h* 68; Br 14174; S^b 1 *O* ii 10. H 23, 452 gu-ru (*var* -ur) | GA-ṬU | na-šu-u = II 26 *c-d* 45; H 23, 453 ga-a | same id na-šu-u (II 26 *c-d* 44; G § 43; ZK ii 323). S^a ii 53 na-šu-u; II 44 *c-d* 46 (a-ga-na-te-nu-u) GA-ṬU = na-šu-u, Br 3180; H 48, 37 IN-EL = iš-ši. II 26 *c-d* 65, 66, 67 *add* see Br 14380, 14388, 14153; AV 6158. Br 13917 on II 26 *c-d* 33. S^c 3 i 11 ZI = na-šu-u, Br 2325; II 46 *c-d* 47 AN-KU- (= GAN?) = našū ša mimma; 48 GAL = n ša ka-la-ma (Br 10608, 2246); II 27 *a-b* 18 GAL = na-šu-u, between da-ku-u & e-mi-du, Br 2245. Br 14264 quotes II 26 *c-d* 69 . . . . = na-šu-u ša še-im; & 68 našū ša mas(bar)-si-e Br 14101.

Intrans. — rise, be high }sich emporheben, -steigen, hoch, erhaben sein} *cf* نشا. T^M viii 89 to the right & to the left iši-ma, rise up! Sn *Bell* 47 see gegunū (*p* 213); *Bass* 73. KB vi (1) 278 ii 30 ul iš-ša-a mi-lu ina na-uq-bi (*cf* iii 45, 55); Creat.-*frg* IV 77 at-ti . . . . e-liš na-ša-a-ti[-ma], KB vi 26—7: die du hoch emporgehoben bist. H 80, 16 (end) ina na-še-e-šu (= GA-ṬU-BU-NA) ‖ ina a-ša-bi-šu. — II 26 *c-d* 52 (zu-us) KU = našū ša e-ni (H 34, 801; Br 10545); 53, 54 A (& UŠ)-ZI-GA; 55, ŠA (= LIB)-ZI-GA, 56 ŠA-TIK-BI-GE-A = n ša mi-lim (Br 2325, 5059, 8270).

Q^t — *a*) lift one's hand in prayer }seine Hand zum Gebet erheben} Sarg *Cyl* 54 at-ta-ši qa(-a)-ti(-te), 60 at-ta-ši ŠU-EL(-LAL)-KAN (= niš qāti, KB ii 48; Winckler, *Forsch*, ii, 1900, 310—2). — *b*) lift up the eye }das Auge erheben auf}

NE 42, 6 a-na du-un-qi ša (ilu) Gilgameš i-na it-ta-ši ru-bu-tu (ilat) Ištar; 44, 67 i-na ta-at-ta-ši-šum-ma, thine eyes thou didst lift up to him (§ 110). — *c*) carry, bring {tragen, bringen}. K 378, 4 ina pu-u-xi it-ti-ši wird es gegen Quittung bringen; K 381, 5 (ina pu-u-xi it-ta-çu); K 1429, 8; Neb 246, 10 if, however, in the month of Ab *Š* kaspa la it-ta-ša-am-ma, does not bring the money; ZA iv 66 *rm* 2 = kī lā išallimu; ZA iv 116 (*no* 7) kaspu-šu-nu la it-ta-šu-u; Br. M. 84, 2—11, 844 (toward the end) ki-i kas-pi ana pān (amēl) dā[ini] la it-ta-šu-ni, if they have not brought; K 81, 24 (amēl) rab-kiçir a-na mux-xi-ka it-ta-ša-'a (Hr^L 274; BA i 199). T. A. Lo 8, 25 Gilia, my messenger, my brother's message a-na ja-ši it-ta-ši. Peiser, *Vertr.*, iii 10 on the day when *N* bīta it-ta-ša-am-ma & gives the money to *B*. — *d*) take, carry away {nehmen, wegnehmen} K 646, 40 that & that ul-tu lib-bi it-ta-ša-a. KB iv 318 (*no* xii) 8 ša .... it-ta-šu-u-nu (3 *pl*); K 552, 13 at-ta-ša-a, I have carried away (Hr^L 255). K 8718 *R* 14 TIN-TIR-KI ix-te-pu-u u bu-še-e ša TIN-TIR-KI it-ta-šu-u; 80—7—19, 19, 5 (amēl) Çil-la-a nikasi-ja it-ta-ši, has carried away my property (& see *R* 4) Hr^L 416. V 25 *col* 3, 8 ina su-ki-im it-ta-ši. — *e*) nourish, support {unterstützen} Bu 91—5—9, 2, 474, 6 *A*, her mother, it-ta-aš-šu-ši-i-ma, has nourished her. — *f*) assume {annehmen} Bm 191 *R* 3 Mars šarūra it-tan-ši, has assumed a brilliance, Thompson, *no* 146. K 1101 + K 1221 (Hr^L 152) 13 + *R* 1: in-ta-aš-'i.

Qtn lift, support, assist {heben, stützen, helfen}. K 3459, 14 ta-at-ta-na-aš-ši la li-am-ma, thou, o Marduk, raisest up the weak (ZA iv 15; § 110); H 81, 22 (Ninib ša) ina bi-ri-šu-nu ki-ma ri-i-me ra-bi-e qar-na-a-šu it-ta-na-aš-ši (Br 6148). Bu 91—5—9, 407, 18, 14 as long as *J* lives, *A* i-ta-na-ši-ši, shall support her (JRAS '99, 106, 107). K 583, 8 (end) a-ta-na-aš-ši; perh III 59 *no* 8, *b* 40 gloss: it-ta-na-aš-i (Br 11970). Nabd 854, 7 it-ta-na-aš-šu (or √ natanu?).

Š ušašši (§ 49*b*) make one carry, command, cause to carry {tragen lassen}. ZA iii 314, 69 u-ša-aš-ši-šu-nu-ti-ma, I made them carry. V 65 *b* 11 and zi-i-me nam-ru-tu u-ša-aš-ši-ma, KB iii, 2, 112—13. I 44, 81 I let the female (?) lamassi carry (u-ša-aš-ši-ši-na-ti) thresholds. Sn i 68 narkabāte šepija i-na ti-ik-ka-a-ti (*var* -te) u-ša-aš-ši, I made (them) carry by means of ropes; *Bell* 21; see also dupšikku (*p* 264) & Sargon *Stele* 43; *Ann* 294 .... NE 15, 141 u ana-ku(-u) ar-ki-ka u-ša-aš-ša-a ma-la-a pa-gar-š[a]; Sarg *Cyl* 35 u-xu-um-mi zaq-ru-ti bil-tu šu-uš-še-e çur-ru-uš uš-ta-bil. I 70 *c* 14 Marduk agalatillā ..... li-šiš-ši-ša, BA ii 142 (*ad* III 43 *c* 31). — let take {nehmen lassen} III 41 *b* 10 whosoever (abaa) narā an-na-a u-ša-aš-šu-ma (KB iv 76—77); *cf* III 43 *a* 32 (u-ša-aš-šu-u); I 70 *b* 24. Esh *Sendsch*, *R* 34 a-na ra-sa-ap na-ki-ri u-ša-aš-ša-a i-da-a-a (he held, supported). Perh V 45 vi 36 tu-ša-an-ša. II 45 *e-f* 31 .... LAL = šu-uš-šu-u (Br 14383), followed by .... TUK = i-šu-u. H 128 *R* 2 see karātu (443 *col* 1).

Št let carry, endow with something {tragen lassen, beladen, ausstatten}. Creat.-*frg* III 28 (68) with Jensen, KB vi (1) 14—15 read me-lam-mi uš-taš-ša-a, belud sie mit schrecklichem Gleissen (≍ *p* 269, dašū); see also KB vi (1) 6, 14 & *p* 309. K 8743, 12 ....] ma-la-a ul-taš-ši-šu let him carry. KB vi (1) 94, 15 (= Adapa, VATh 348) .... l[a]-a[u]š-te-eš-ši-šu; *cf* IV^2 31 *R* 2 ma-le-e na[-ši?].

N be brought {gebracht werden}. Scheil, *Nabd*, v 9—10 ana be-lu-ti māti an-na-ši-ma (I was proclaimed). K 8204 (PSBA xvii 138—9) 1 ša la-ka-a-ta ina ilāni ul in-na-ši [ri-ša?] or Q? Nabd 50, 14 ri-eš qanē in-na-aš-šu-u (or Q?) KB iv 210. Berl. Congr. ii 1, 350 *a* in-na-ši-im-ma (*var* in-na-ši-i-ma). II 16 *b* 71 in-na-ši ri-is-su; 47 *c-d* 52 A-UN-KU-MAL = mīlu ana māti in-niš-ša-a.

Nt(?) IV^2 32 *no* 2 (K 13; Hr^L 281) *R* 17 (end) it-tan-na-aš-šu, they levy, collect (Johnston).

NOTE. — 1. (amêl) ša šikaru na-ši-šu Nabd 116, 42; 373; 854. (amêl) šikara ša na-ši-šu Nabd 238; 239, 2; (amêl) ša na-ši-šu Nabd 43; 79; 246; 275; 916. PINCHES, *Inscr. Tablets*, 42 *R* 10 (end) mar ša (amêl) ša BI (= šikaru) na-ši-šu. Nabd 920, 3 read (amêl) ši-riq ša na-ši-šu *Š* the cupbearer ‖ *Š* der Mundschenk, BA i 635.

2. V 60 *a* 12 la na-aš ma-na-ma, see naṭalu.

3. Z^{Š} iii 126, 127 ma-mit na-ši-e Bann durch einen Hohen, ma-mit la-ki-e, Bann durch einen niedrigen.

4. For *c. t.* forms see T^{C} 107—109.

5. 83—1—18, 172 (THOMPSON, *Reports*, 243 B) *R* 2 Mars ina na-šu (kakkab) Dil-bat izziz, stands in the *n* of Venus.

Derr. muššu (?) & these 2:

***nîšu** (niššu, niš'u) *c. st.* **niš** lifting up }Erhebung{ § 138; AV 6360: Br 6149. — *a*) niš qâti handraising, lifting up of hands in prayer, prayer }Erhebung der Hand zum Gebet, Gebet{ ‖ ikrêbu, supû, *etc.* G § 59; ZA ii 99 *no* 18; iii 78 *rm* 3. Asb ii 121 ša ina ni-iš qâtê-ja ilâni tik-li-ja .... u-šap-ri-ku; IV^2 20 *a* 10 ek-ri-bi-ja šu-un-xu-ti ni-iš qa-ti-ja u la-ban ap-pi-ja; 83—1—18, 296 *R* 3, 7 (it-ti) ni-iš qa-ti. T.A. Lo 37, 64 + 65 niš qa-ti-šu K 257 (H 127) 58 ni-iš qa-ti-ja (= EL-LA-MU) šame-e e-mid. K^{M} 12, 88 a-na niš qâti-ja; TP viii 25 ni-iš qa-ti-ja li-ra-mu. IV^2 17 *a* 53—4 ana ni-iš qa-ti-ja, Br 12087; III 32 *a* 43, 44 a-na ni-iš ŠU^{II} (= qâtâ)-ka ša taš-ša-a ênê-ka im-la-a di-im-tu (= SMITH, *Asurb*, 123, 48). Neb ix 60 see magaru Q ip (*p* 510 *col* 2) & KB iii (2) 62—3 *no* 9 i 17. II 19 *a* 5—6 a-na ni-iš i-di-ka; IV^2 21, 1 B *O* 2 ana ni-iš i-di-šu-nu çu-ba-tu sa-a-mu at-ru-uç, ZIMMERN: upon their raised hands I spread a dark garment. P. N. KB iv 82 *no* 1, 3 (šar) Niš-ga-ti-rim-ma. K^{M} *p* 13 on colophon line: INIM-INIM-MA-ŠU-IL-LA^{il} Sin *etc.*, quite often in his texts, except *no* 35, 14 where ni-iš qa-a-ti ša (ilat) Bêlit. id also IV^2 58 iii 43, iv 20; 55 *no* 2 *R* 6; K^{M} 40, 10 + 13. — *b*) ZA iv 12, 44 ina ûm niš-ši ri-ša-ta, in the days of raising shouts. — *c*) niš îni. — *α*. lifting up of the eye, look, glance }Erhebung des Auges, Blick{ K 257 (H 128) 68 ina ni-iš i-ni-ja man-nu uç-çu; perh K 901 *R* 12 ni-iš ŠI (= ênê)-ja Hr^{L} 117. IV^2 13 *b* 20—21 see nûru. P. N. Ni-ši-i-ni-šu, *c. t.* — *β*. loving look, favor, grace }liebevoller Blick, Gnade{ V 64 *b* 33—4 Sin šar ilâni ša šamê u erçitim i-na ni-iš înâ (*var* i-ni)-šu damqâti xa-di-iš lip-pal-sa-an-ni-ma. V 70, 16 the gods ina ni-ši ŠI^{II} (= înâ)-šu-nu ke-niš-eš (= kêniš) li-ṭu-lu-šu (√נטל) may cast their eyes upon him, lifting up their countenance upon him, *i. e.* blessing him. BP^2 iv 80 *foll.* — *γ*. favorite, darling }Günstling, Liebling{ Lay 17, 2 TP ni-iš ini (il) Bêl. Neb vii 34, 35 ina Bâbili âli ni-iš ŠI^{II}-ja ša a-ra-am-ma; 16, i-na âli ni-iš i-ni-šu-nu. — *d*) niš libbi, impulse of the heart, will, desire. IV^2 49 *b* 13 the conjurer and the witch who ni-iš lib-bi-MU (= ja) iç-ba-tu. — *intrans.*: V 22 *b-d* 40 A-KAL (or DAN) = ni-šu.

nišit (*c. st.* of nišîtu) in nišit îni favorite, darling }Günstling, Liebling{ DELITZSCH, 1882. AV 6364; KAT^2 160; 618; LYON, *Sargon*, 58; see kiribtu (435 *col* 1). Šalm, *Mon*, *O* 6 Šalm. ni-šit e-ni (il) Bêl, KB i 152—3. Sarg *Cyl* 1: Sargon ni-šit ŠI^{II} (il) A-nim u (il) Da-gan (Lay 33, 1; KB ii 34—5); Anp, *Stand*, 1. Anp i 10 Ašurnaçirpal ni-šit (il) Bêl u (il) Ninib ‖ na-ra-am (il) A-nim u (il) Da-gan. Esh *Sendsch*, *R* 21—22 ni-šit (il) Ašur (il) Nabû u (il) Marduk (‖ ni-bit, mi-gir, *ibid*). ZA xiv 289 *rm* 4 on KB vi (1) 280 *col* 3, 8 + 284, 41 (see 280 *col* 3, 3) reads: la i-ça-ba-tu ni-ši-tu, ergreifen sie nicht "Erhebung", *i. e.* Erhebung des Auges der Götter, = Gnade. But see nišîtum (*p* 742 *col* 1).

NOTE. — On the origin of Hebr נשיא see HAUPT in TOY, *Ezekiel* (SBOT), *p* 82 & JBL xix 63 *rm* 40.

niš(u) a word of very indefinite meaning }ein Wort sehr unbestimmter Bedeutung{ AV 6360. IV^2 7 *b* 2, 12, 22, 32, 42, 52 ni-šu ‖ ma-mit; 8 *b* 3. Z^{Š} viii 27 ni-iš-ka curse (?) upon thee }Fluch über dich{ K 2866. IV^2 57 *a* 52 (K^{M} *no* 12) murçu lâ ṭâbu ni-šu ma-mit. — IV^2 1 *b* 26 (28, 30 *etc.*) niš be-el .... lu-u ta-ma-a-ta; 2 v 22 ni-iš (*var* ZI = niš) (il) Sin ... lu-ta-ma-tu, 24 (Br 2326). Br. M. 84, 2—11, 172 ni-iš Šamaš u-ša-az-ki-ru-šu, Anrufung des *Š.* liessen sie ihn sprechen. ● 116 ii 42—3 (H 67, 1—5;

72, 47 = II 40 *no* 4, 23—26) ša ni-iš ili-šu-nu it-mu[-u], ša ni-iš šarri-šu-nu iz(s)-ku-ru, Br 56. Asb viii 50 ni-iš ilâni rabûti la ip-lax-ma. III 38 *no* 1 *O* 12 (end) ša ni-iš ilâni rabûti la [ip-lax-ma?]. I 70 *a* 20 a-na paq-ri la ra-še-e ni-iš ilâni rabûti ...... iz-kur. Asb i 21 a-di-e MU (= šum) ilâni = viii 45 a-di-e ni-iš ilâni rabûti u-ša-az-kir-šu-ma (Esh i 42 šum ilâni rabûti, § 138), I made them swear (obedience to) the laws by the name (?) of the great gods. H 83 *foll* 7, 10, 17, 22, 29, 34, 44, 49 (ta-ma-mat), 54, 59, 71; ii 5, 15, 21, 36, 44 *etc.* niš (= ZI) šame-e lu-u ta-mat niš erçi-ti lu-u ta-mat, o spirit of heaven conjure, o spirit of earth enchant; Br 2326; § 138; G § 50; J[w] 70 *rm* 2; Jensen, ZK i 321; ii 20 (Aram-Syr ܡܘܬܐ); ZA ii 319; JA vii ('86) 556 *rm* 1; Hommel, VK 489; Babelon, *Rev. crit.*, 15 Ap. '83, 144. K[M] 164. H 78 *R* 4 ma-mit niš šame-e lu-u ta-ma-a-ti, niš erçi-tim lu-u ta-ma-a-ti; H 15, 192 ZI = ni-iš-šu. — Meissner, 155 *no* 100, 9 ana niš ili, gemäss der Entscheidung eines Gottes. V 21 *a-b* 41 see lû 1 (462 *col* 2, end).

nišû *f* people, nation, mostly used in *pl* nišê people, subjects {Volk, Nation, meist als *pl* gebraucht} AV 6366; L[T] 110; ZDMG 28, 354; 29, 211; G § 32; D[Pr] 168; Lyon, *Sargon*, 59. ið S[b] 246 u-ku | UN | ni-šu (*cf* ûqu in Beh) Br 5915; § 9, 83. Xammurabi *Louvre* i 11—12, 20—21, 28—9; ii 1—2 UN (= niš) šu-me-er-im u ak-ka-di-im; ii 3 ni-ši-šu-nu sa (ZA ii 451)-ap-xa-tim lu-u-pa-ax-xi-ir, KB iii (1) 122—4; ZA ii 360; KB iii (1) 113 *col* 2, 9 ni-šu ra-ap-ša-tum. V 55, 4 (end) ni-ši-šu ‖ mâti-šu; Neb *Senk* i 9; Ner i 16; Neb ii 27; Asb x 88 UN-MEŠ mâtija, my subjects {meine Untertanen}; K 2745 ii 5 nišê mâtâti; IV² 20 *no* 1, 16 ni-ši ma-a-ti. Sn *Bav* 7 nišê-šu (of Nineveh); K 1288, 8 ana ša-qa-aš ni-ši; IV² 19 *a* 9—10 ni-iš (= UN-LU-A) da-ad-me ušamraçu (*q. v.*), Br 10745; & Banks, *Diss*, 12, 73 a-mat-su ni-ši u-šam-ra-aç, ni-ši un-na-aš. V 65 *b* 9 a-na tab-ra(t)-a-ti ni-ši (& often); *a* 5 rê'û ni-šim (char. šig, sig, Jensen, 194 *rm* 1) rapšâti; 12 UN-MEŠ; II 16 *c* 24 ina ni-ši-ja among my people; IV² 39 *b* 36 xa-la-aq ni-ši-šu destruction of his subjects. Winckler-Abel (T. A.) 240 *R* 32 la ba-al-ṭa-ta a-a ni-iš da-a[-la-t]i [(11)] Êa be-li, BA iv 128 *foll*. V 50 *a* 26 nap-xar ni-ši, Br 6409. IV² 24 *no* 3, 13 ... pu-lux-ta-ka ga-lit-tum ma-a-ta u ni-ši (= MU-LU) tar-me; 30 *no* 2 *a* 30—1 ni-ši (MU-LU) ‖ a-me-lu-ti (*cf* gamaru Q *ag*, *p* 223). nuxuš ni-ši, epithet of a canal, ZA ii 360 *col* 1, 18 = KB iii (1) 122—3. Samsuiluna ii 1 ni-ši-im ra-ap-ša-tim (KB iii, 1, 130) the numerous subjects; Sn *Bav* 7 ni-šim ra-ap-ša-a-ti. I 65 *a* 10; 66 *c* 18 ni-šim ra-ap-ša-a-ti (ið, K[M] 18, 17), die ausgedehnten Menschen(schaaren), 28 ni-šim ra-be-a-tim; *b* 15 ni-šim Ba-bi-lam[ki]; *c* 24 ku-ul-la-at ni-šim. Merod.-Bal.-stone i 20—21 kul-la-tan nišê (written UN-ME). KB iv 58 ii 13 a-na ni-ši ax-ra-a-ti. IV² 32 *a* 2 rê'u nišê ra-ba-a-ti (*var* GAL-MEŠ), 29, 40; *b* 14, 40; 19 *a* 55—6 nišê rap-ša-a-ti. KB iv 58 iii 11 [(11)] Ê-a pa-ti-iq ni-iš, creator of mankind; H 121 *R* 2 ni-šu lid-lu-la. KB vi (1) 276, 27 ni-šu = mankind {die Menschen}; 278, 39, where read with Zimmern, ZA xiv 277 *foll*: ni-šu i-na šu-par-ki-e [napišti bal-ṭa-at]; 284, 42 + 52 a-na ni-še. Scheil, *Rec. Trav.*, xx 57 *fol col* 2, 13 u-ub-ba-al ga-ti a-na ni[-ši] KB vi (1) 290—1. *del* 116 (123) a-na-ku-um-ma ul-la-da ni-šu-u-a-a-ma (KB vi, 1, 238—9), 160 (170) u nîši (writt. UN-MEŠ)-ia; 172—3 (188, 190); 175 (194) with *var* mâtu (KUR). V 35, 3 UN-MEŠ çal-mat qaqqadi, KB iii (2) 128 refers to people in general; also see BA ii 210—11; Winckler, *Unters.*, 132 & ✕ BA ii 231; Br 5920. IV² 29, 1, 42 a-me-lu-tum ni-ši çal-mat qaqqadu.

Construed as *masc.* in the meaning of people {Leute}. Asb iv (70) 73; vii 73 nišê ša-a-tu-nu; Smith, *Asurb*, 243, 90; 117, 92. K 4249 *R* 10 u nišê ša-a-tu-nu (BA ii 572); K 383, 11 nišê šu-a-tu, these people. individual: III 49 *no* 4, 3 napxar 3 niše-e; sons of *A*; Amiaud, *Rev. d'Assyr.*, ii 13 on III 46 *no* 2, 2. V 21 *a-b* 40 ni-šu ‖ û(lax, AV 4691)-mu; perh also V 22 *d* 40. On reading ni-šim for ni-sig see nisqu. Connected with nišu is:

nišūtu (nisūtu in *c. t.*). family; servants, including relatives, usually in connection with sa(l)-la-tu {Familie, Diener, und Verwandte} AV 6284. D[Pr] 163 *rm* 4 & 5. BELSER, BA ii 137 nišūtu & salātu ‖ of kimtu, perh male & female relatives. Asb i 29, 30 the bît ridûti where Esarh kim-tu u-rap-pi-šu ik-çu-ru ni-šu-tu u sa-la-tu (KB ii 154, 155). Sarg *Khors* 31; K 2390; V 68 *no* 1 *R* 37; *no* 2 *R* 35, 36; KB iv 300 *no* ii 21; ZA iii 220, 31; VA 208, 44 see kimtu (390). I 70 *b* 2, 3 whenever in later days one of the brethren, sons, relatives ni-šu-ti u sa-la-ti ar-di-en u ki-na-a-ti of Bît-Xabban. III 43 iii 3 see KB iv 70, 71. V 51 iii 19 ni-šu-ut šar-ru-ti. II 9 *c-d* 52 šumma matēma ni-šu-su e-te-lam-šu (Br 190). K[M] 11, 23 kim]-ti-ja ni-su(*var* šu)-ti-ja u sa-la-ti-ja. Nabd 203, 33 *fol* ki-im-tum ni-su-tu u sa-la-tim ša (ZK i 48); 178, 37; 110, 35 i-na axē mārē kim-ti ni-su-tu u sa-la-at ša X; 687, 29, 30 ki-im-ta ni-su-tu u sa-la-ti ša X; Neb 135, 26, 27 kimti ni-su-ti sa-lat; Dar 26, 26 kim-tum ni-su-tu u sa-lat. Br. M. 84, 2—11, 103, 23—4 ma-ti-ma i-na axē mārē kim-tum ni-su-tum u sa-la-tum; PEISER, *Vertr.*, *nos* 94; 117, 27—8. See also T[C] 106.

nēšu *1.* AV 6364, *m* lion {Löwe}; **nēštu**, AV 6373, *f* lioness {Löwin} nouns to ni-e-šu (*p* 680). id UR-MAX, § 9, 82. NE 72, 31 ni-ša nim-ri *etc.* lion, panther; 74 *b* 21 kima neš-ti (KB vi 226; 198) S 954, 14 ni-e-šu ša ina qir-be-ti it-tanallakū atti (D 135; Br 11271); H 41, 275 UR(= LIK)-MAX = ni-e-šu (II 49, 40; 29, 38) *cf* NE 44, 51. II 5 *b* 7—8 zu-um-bi (*q. v.*) ni-e-ši & ni-eš-ti; 6 *b* 31 ni-eš-tum after kalbatum. V 21 *a-b* 39 see labbu; some also refer to lines 40, 41 (but, ??). On nēši gal(-at)-ti K 943, 14 see BA iv 255. id in *del* 172 (188) see nadaru; also compare nābar-tum, šigaru. UR-MAX-MEŠ ša ad-du-ku I 7 *no* ix A 2; *ibid* B 1—2 UR-MAX ez-zu (ZK ii 321) ša çēri-šu (C 1; D 2) BA ii 281. II 67, 79; TP vi 77; Sarg *Ann* 423 (& BA iii 192—3 *rm* **). UR-MAX ša qaq-qa-ri *del* 277 (312). J[W] 93 *rm* 5. K 4378 i 21 UR-MAX qaq-qa-ri ‖ xu-la-[lu-u?]. id also K 2148 iii 25 paq-ru nēši, a lion's body. K 3500 + K 4444 + K 10235, 7 ... ina qātē nēši a-ki-li. HALÉVY, BROCKELMANN, ZA xv 394 & others compare לַיִשׁ, Arm לֵיתָא. BA i 161; BARTH, ZA iii 60.

nēšum *2.* V 28 *g-h* 59, 60 ba-la-tu (see *p* 168 *col* 1) = ša-ṭa-pu & ne-e-šum, AV 6365, end.

nušū perh = נְשָׁיָא = نَسًّا. Br 11704; AV 6465, 8794. IV[2] 18 *no* 6 *O* 6—7 tar-ba-ça ki-ma nu-še-e (= A-XA-AN) un-ni-iš, T[M] 126—7; II 33 *a-b* 74 A-X]A-AN = nu-šu-u ‖ qū & ga'ū (*p* 208).

nišū *1.* Sn *Bar* 39 ni-ša-a-šu-un, see nīxū.

nišū *2.* 83—1—18, 1330 iv 7 te-e | TE | ni-šu-u.

našabu blow {blasen}. ℑ be blown away {weggeblasen werden} T[M] v 57 li-in-na-aš-bu kiš-pu-ša ki-ma pū liq-qal-pu ki-ma šūmi; vi 31 li-in]-ni-eš-bu.

nišbū satisfaction, becoming sated {Sättigung, Sattwerden} √šebū, § 65, 31 *a*. Asb viii 119 lu iš-tu-u mē niš-bi-e; Sarg *Cyl* 39 ti-'u-u-tu niš-bi-e. Sp II 265 *a* iii 9 a-na niš-bi-e. LYON, *Sargon*, 68; Z[B] 97; ZK ii 114; BA i 3, 159, 177, 180. A ‖ is:

nišbūtu. IV[2] 56 *b* 39 iš(43, ta)-ta-na-at-ti da-mi niš-bu-ti ša a-me-lu-ti, J[I-N] 60 *rm*.

našbu, našbūtum (*pl*) II 30 *e-f* 68—9 na-aš-b(p)u-tum. AV 6161; Br 6889, 6886 for col *e*; 12237. Br 5206 reads II 30 *b* 67 na-aš-bu (AV 6160); & Br 1207 has II 30 *no* 5 *R* 77(—78) na-šub-tum, with id similar to našbūtum (≍ AV 6141).

našabbu. Dar 84, 2: $^1/_2$ mana $5^1/_2$ šiqlu kaspi ana epešu ša ki-it-tum ša na-ša-ab-bu.

našbaṭu. V 26 *e-f* 47 GIŠ-PA-KUD-DA-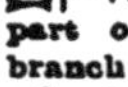 = na-aš-ba-ṭu ‖ u-ru-u, part of the gišimmaru, staff, twig, branch (?); AV 6159; Br 5598; D[Pr] 38 √שׁבט; BA i 177.

našxu 81, 2—4, 219 *O* ii 8 lu-ça-a eli na-aš-xu xu-ux-xa-xu, Boissier, *Rev. Sém.*, vi *no* 4.

našxu, našux, name of a god; in P. N. (as first part) coming from the neighbor-hood of Harran; *cf* Johns, *PSBA*, xxi 285: naš-xu a-a-li; *n*-id-ri; n-sa-ma-'a-ni; *n*-sa-kap.

našxiptum. some instrument {ein Werkzeug} AV 6162; T^{C} 7; Peiser, *Vertr.*, 305. Nabd 571, 15: ištēn-it na-aš-xi-ip-tum (926, 4); 784, 2: ištēn-it parzillu na-aš-xi-ip-tum; Camb 18, 5—6; BA iii 479; *Cuneiform texts from New York Museum*, 1 *no* 14, 12 mar-ri parzilli na-aš-xi-ip-ti.

našxuru I 35 *no* 2, 7, & našxira, Br 6340; see saxaru II.

našaku 1., **iššuk** bite {beissen} § 49 *b*; ZDMG 43, 188; Hebr. vii 90 *rm* 17 *c*. IV^2 5 *b* 54, 55 when Êa heard this ša-pat-su iš-šuk (*var* šu-uk, = KA-NE-IN-TAR) he bit his lip, H 76, 24; Z^B 32; 74; Br 562). IV^2 31 *R* 21 taš-šu-ka u-ba-an-ša she bit her finger (in anger) {biss sich in den Finger (aus Zorn)} § 92. Perh K 5464 *R* 9 iš-šu-ka, Hr^L 108; PSBA xvii 231.

Q^t = Q Creat.-*frg* II (K 4832) *O* 19 ša-p]at-su it-taš-ka, he bit.

3 = intens. of Q. NE 44, 63 and his hounds u-na-aš-ša-ku 'šap(b)-ri-šu tore to pieces his skin (Fell?) KB vi (1) 170—1. K 3886, 8 šumma sīsū iš-še-gu-ma lu tap-pa-a-šu lu amēlūti u-na-šak, Bez., *Catal.*, 574. II 6 *b* 33 mu-na-šik-tum (*i. e.* kalbatum) AV 5492. TSBA v 59 mu-na-ši-ku ga-re-šu, name of a dog.

II perh Abel-Winckler, *Texte*, 60; (Hommel, *Sum. Lesest.*, 128) *R* 17 ki-ma ba-ša-mi na-aš-ri it-ba(-ma?) a-mi-lu li-in-niš-ka. — **Der.**:

nišku *c. st.* nišik bite {Biss}. KB ii 244, 58 Bēl-iqīša ina ni-šik xumçiri (or piāzi?) iš-ta-kan nu-piš-tu.

našaku 2. *pr* iššik put, lay down {stellen, niederlegen} S^P 758 + S^P II 962 *O* 8 da-lat Ištar iš-šik (threw down) ‖ is-sux-ma it-ta-di.

Q^t K 3449 *a R* 5 qašta it-ta-šik, KB vi (1) 32.

Š usually with dupšikku, *q. v.* Sarg *Cyl* 5 mu-ša-aš-ši-ik dup-šik-ku Dūrilu mu-šap-ši-xu niši-šu-un; *Bull*-inscr. 6; Pp IV 6; *Bronce* 11; AV 5598. *Khors* 8—10 u-ša-aš-šik dup-šik-ki Dūrilu *etc.* . . . u-šap-ši-xa niši-šu-un, *Stele* i 13 u-ša-aš-ši-ik dup-šik-ki; to these expressions corresponds in Sarg XIV 4 *fol* (Winckler, *p* 80): of these cities ān du-ra[-ar]-šu-un (*q. v.*) aš-kun-ma; see also Pp V 6 *foll*; thus perh = made them lay down. freed them from the dupšikku. K 8522 (D 95) 14 ap-ša-na en-du u-ša-as-si-ku eli ilāni na-ki-re-šu, who took away from the gods his enemies the yoke he had put upon them.

naškapu a stone {ein Stein}. Camb 223, 2: IV TA xaçbattu (aban) erū (aban) na-aš-ka-pu.

na-šal-lu-lu, Br 2980, AV 6154; S^c 5 *a* 4 see šalalu, II.

na-še-mi-u T. A. Ber 28 *a* 55; *cf* OLZ ii *no* 4; BA iv 105—6.

našmū, nišmū. hearing {Gehör} √šemū. Z^B 97; § 65, 31 *a*; BA i 177. V 47 *b* 10 he took away their (the ears') deafness & ip-te-te niš-ma-a-a.

ni]-iš-ma-k(q)e-ja ni(?)-ši-ma šu-un . . . . . KB vi (1) 158, 35.

našpux. IV^2 39 *b* 36 na-aš-pu-ux mā-tišu = naspux, see sapaxu.

našpaku *1.* some large vessel {ein grosses Gefäss} II 22 *c-d* 19 DUK-SAB-GAL = na-aš-pa-ku (*cf* ga(i)rrānu) AV 6163; Br 5680; also K 4204, 60 (II 24 *no* 1 *add*). √šapaku. BA i 177 compares שפך; BA i 636: Schütte; Jensen: Gefäss zum Ausgiessen.

našpaku *2.*, našpakūtu *1.* storing {Aufspeicherung} KB iv 34 *col* 2, 3 a-na na-aš-pa-ku-tim, auf Grund der Aufspeicherung, but Meissner, 18: grain was borrowed ana na-aš-pa-ku-tum, for sowing purposes; *cf* se-am a-na na-aš-pa-ak.

našaddu, na-šad (AV 6152) see naçaddu. ～ nišxu see nisxu. ～ našaxu: ša-na-aš-xu, AV 6153, Br 7539 *cf* nasaxu II. ～ niš-ṭi-nu, Br 1374 see mandinu. ～ našku. K^M 9, 56 see nasku. ～ nišakku, AV 6363 *cf* nisakku.

našpakūtu *2.* flood, inundation?? {Flut, Überschwemmung?} *Rec. Trav.*, xx 55 *f*, *no* xxx *col* 2, 14 li-ša-az-ni-in na-aš [-pa-ku-tu?] qu'il fasse pleuvoir l'inundation; but see KB vi (1) 288.

našpantu, našpa(t)tu, overthrow {Überwältigung} for naspantu √sapanu. ZA ii 212—13; JENSEN, 430. Ninib is called AN-ŠAR-ŠAR-RI as the god ša na-aš-pan-ti (Br 8274) II 57 *c-d* 33; in ‖ passage (III 67 *c-d* 65) AN-ŠAR-ŠAR-RA as god ša na-aš-pa-te (BA i 162 *rm* 1; ii 297—8); II 49 *no* 4, 41 it is said na-aš-pan-ti shall prevail in the country, Br 11277, same id = axū. H 118 *O* 7 be-el na-aš-pa[n-ti], *R* 2 be-el na-as-pan-ti.

našparu, našpartu, AV 6164. mission, message, command, order; messenger, delegate {Sendung, Botschaft, Befehl; Bote} § 65, 31 *a*; T^C 108 reads našūtu; BA i 177, √šaparu. Bu 88—5—12, 333, 14 ^(amēl) na-aš-pa-ru ša il-li-kam, the messenger who came. SCHEIL, *Nabd*, v 17 na-aš-pa-ar-šu-nu dan-nu a-na-ku their powerful messenger am I. V 65 *a* 8 na-aš-pa-ri xa-an-ṭu ša ilāni rabūti (*cf* מַלְאָךְ). Asb v 7 Teumman whom I had beheaded ina na-aš-par-ti ^(il) Ašur (KB ii 196—7). K 2852 + K 9662 i 1 šu-u na-aš-par-ti šar-rūti-ja. K 1066 *R* 4 i-na na-aš-pa-ar-ti ša Bēl-ibni, Hr^L 277. V 48 iv 7 the 6th day of Tammūz na-aš-par-ti ^(il) Šamaš, a message from *Š.* K 528, 22 na-aš-par[-tu ša šarri], the king's behest, Hr^L 269. III 41 ii 22 ilat ba-ri-ri-ta na-aš-par-ta-ša ša uz-zi, KB iv 79. T^M v 88 u na-aš-pa-rat .... ša tal-tap-pa-ri ja-a-ši (vii 7); vii 74 na-aš-pa-ra-ti-ki ša lim-mut-ti thy baneful intention (vii 110). KB iv 320—1 *no* 2 ii 6 na-aš-par-tum (ana eli . . .) la ir-ku-su. Cyr 311, 2; 218, 1; Camb 135, 4 ina na-aš-par-tum (-ti) ša X; 127, 5 na-aš-pa-par-tum. Nabd 85, 5 i-na na-aš-par-ti ša ^(il) Bin-ad-du-na-ta-nu; 653 (end); KOHLER-PEISER, ii 58. Dar 362, 7 ina na-aš-par-ti ša *M.* PEISER, *Vertr.*, 14, 8 ina na-aš-par-tum ša Çi-ra-a. DELITZSCH, *Kappadoc. Keilschrifttafeln*, 20, 9 na-aš-bar-tum (*cf* 9); 15, 8 na-aš-be-ir-ta-ga; 15, 16 na-aš-be-ir-ti-ga; 21, 15 na-aš-be-ir-tam. A ‖ is

našpaštu. Camb 338, 19 ina na-aš-pa-aš-tum ša X. ZA vii 181.

nišpatu. judgment, justice {Gericht, Recht} ZA ii 280; § 65, 31 *a*; BA ii 297—8. P.N. Ni-iš-pa-ti-^(il)Bēl = Bel is (my) judgment, C^a 95. BA i 162 *rm* * & 177 compares מִשְׁפָּט.

našaqu, pr iššiq, ps inašiq kiss {küssen} AV 6155, Br 204; = נשׁק = نشق (smell), LAGARDE, *Novi Psalt. Spec.*, 24; BARTH, *Etym. Stud.*, 46; FRÄNKEL, BA iii 79. NE XII (K 2774) i 24, 26 thy wife (thy son) ša ta-ram-mu la ta-na-šiq. K 3869 i 8 qaq-qa-ru i-na-šiq (ZDMG 53, 117). Creat.-*frg* III 69 uš-ken-ma iš-šiq qaq-qa-ra ša-pal-šu-un, KB vi (1) 16—17; ZIMMERN, *Ritualtafeln*, 67 *R* 2 . . . i-ša-qi-ši šapta-ša i-na-šiq. Mostly in connection with šēpē (id NER^II) feet, as sign of submission, subjection. Sn ii 57 iš-ši-qu šepē-ja they kissed my feet. H 119 (DT 67) *O* 20—1 na-ša-gam il-ta-mad she learns kissing. K 164, 6 šāpā ta-na-šiq, BA ii 635—6; also line 21. II 47 *c-f* 38 KA-TA-SU-UB = na-ša-qu (32, = ka-ra-bu) Br 638; H 37, 6 + 57.

ℑ = Q u-na-šiq qaq-qa-ru (dū-rāni) ZA iv 413; *cf* Sarg *Ann* 55 *foll.* SMITH, *Asurb*, 194, 5 u-na-aš-ši-qa qaq-qa-ru, they kissed the ground *i. e.*, fell to the ground in subjection. IV² 9 *a* 59—60 the Anunnake qaq-qa-ru u-na-ša-qu (= MU-UN-SU-UB-SU-UB, EME-SAL) ‖ Igigē appa ilabbinū (see labanu, 1). NE 15, 38 (end) ma-al-ka ša qaq-qa-ri u-na-aš-ša-qu šēpē-ka, KB vi (1) 138—9; NE 6, 34 u-na-ša-qu šēpē-šu, KB vi 180—1; 43, 15 li-na-aš-ši-qu šēpē-ka. Sarg *Khors* 149 (*Ann* 270) u-na-aš-ši-qu (3 *pl*) šēpē-ja. II 67, 27 ša ..... la il-li-kam-ma la u-na-aš-ši-qa šēpē-šu-un, now they came before me and u-na-aš-ši-qu šēpē-ja. Asb ii 67; iii 19 u-na-aš-ši-qa (*var* -šiq, + ii 72, 80) šēpē-ja. WINCKLER, *Sargon*, 184, 44 u-na-ši-qu. Esh ii 39 u-na-aš-ši-iq šēpē-ja; iii 6, 45 (*var* šiq); iv 28 u-na-aš-ši-qu šēpē-ja (Asb ii 87; TP III *Ann* 5, 255); III 15 ii 26 each year he comes to Nineveh &

u-na-aš-ša-qa šêpē-ja (and kisses my feet). V 35, 18 u-na-aš-ši-qu še-pu-uš-šu; (30 še-pu-u-a). T. A. Lo 82, 38 u-na-aš-ša-aq-ši, he kisses her, KB vi (1) 78, 20; BA iv 130, 131.

Š (?) SCHEIL, *Nabd*, v 5 u-ša-aš-ši-qu še-pa-a-a.

𝔑 Perh Creat.-*frg* III 132 in-niš-qu a-xu(-)u a-xi, they kissed each other {küssten einer den andern} KB vi (1) 220; ZIMMERN-GUNKEL, 410 *rm* 1.

našru. eagle {Adler} AV 6166. D[8] 105; BROWN-GESENIUS, *Lexicon*, 676. id ID-XU, *Etana*-legend; KB vi (1) 100. 3, 6; 102, 10, 14; 104, 22; 106, 35, 37, 39, 45; 108, 50, 52; 110, 8, 9, 11; 112, 14, 24, 29, 31, 36; 114, 8, 29, 31, 33, 35, 36; AV 3639; § 9, 25. Asb iv 76. See also našaku, 1 𝔑. Sn iii 68 kīma qin-ni ID-XU (= našri) a-ša-rid iççurâti; Šamš ii 52 kīma našri; II 37 *d-f* 9 ID]-Xu = e-ru-u & na-aš-ru Br 6564 (>< POGNON, *Bav*, 82) 13970. II 57 *a-b* 53 (kakkab) ID-XU (il) Za-ma-ma | (il) Nin-ib. II 49 *R* v 16; III 57 *a* 55 (kakkab) ID-XU. T. A. Lo 5, 26 one (amêl) ša-i-li našri (wr. ID-XU-MEŠ).

nišru *1.* Nabd 321, 4 (aban) di-gil niš-rum, name of a stone.

našaru, pr iššur, ps inašar. reduce, shorten, take away {vermindern, verkürzen, wegnehmen} Arm נתר; نسر. JENSEN, *Diss*, 76. AV 6156, Br 108. KB vi (1) 278 ii 31 i[š-š]ur eqlu es verringerte das Feld seinen .... (iii 46, li-šur, 56); ZA xiv 278—9 *ad* SCHEIL's deluge text i 17 (KB vi, 1, 288, 18) li-iš-š]ur eqlu iš-bi-ke-šu. IV² 16 *b* 53—4 ma-ru-uš-tu ša e-mu-ke i-na-aš-ša-ru (= BA-BA). ZA iv 13, 7 na-ši-ir a-kal ....; 236, 10 ta-na-aš-šar xi-iç-bu thou takest away the super-abundance. K 4225, 8 na-ša-ru (H[T] 185; *Sintflutber.* 26 *rm* 16); H 46 i 31 IN-BA = iš-šu-ur; 34 IN-BA-EŠ = i-šu-ru; 37 IN-NA-AN-BA = iš-šur-šu (D 91 i 15, 18, 21). 80, 11—12, 9 *O* i: na-ša-rum ina .... (Br 10195).

𝔔[2] Br 168 *ad* K 257 *O* 58 (H 127) end im-da[-aš-šar?].

𝔍 = 𝔔 H 46 i 40 IN-NA-AN-BA-E = u-na-šar-šu. IV² 8 *b* 30—31, 36—37 (Z[8] v/vi 153, 159) qa-a çi-ra qa-a raba-a qa-a bit-ru-ma qa-a mu-na-aš-šir ma-mit, H 190. IV² 1 *a* 3 šu-ru-ub-bu-u xar-ba-šu mu-na-aš-šir nap-xar, *Rev. Sém.*, iv 155. IV² 1* iv 8, 10 mu-na-aš-šir šamê u erçitim še-e-du mu-na-aš-šir ma-a-ti.

𝔑 KB iii (2) 88, 93 in-na-ši-ir-ma, they were removed. IV² 13 *b* 3—4 ina šul-me-ka e ta-an-na-šir, shall not be reduced, shortened (= NAM-BA-DA-AB-E, Br 5848). — Derr. these 3:

niširtu. diminution, reduction {Verminderung, Abzug} BA ii 138—9; BOISSIER, *Diss*, 32. III 43 *c* 21 whosoever ni-ši-ir-ta ki-iç-ça-ta ina libbi eqli annī i-ša-ak-ka-nu (KB iv 70), diminution (or parcelling?) of this field undertakes. III 41 *b* 6 whosoever ki-iç-ça-ta ni-šir-ta i-šak-ka-nu (KB iv 76); I 70 *b* 15 whosoever ni-šir-ta ki-iç-ça-ta i-na lib-bi i-šak-ka-nu (KB iv 80). WINCKLER, *Forsch*, i 500 *R* 35 whosoever ni-ši-ir-ti gi-iç-ça-tu ud-da-a (?) .... ina libbi i-šak-ka-nu. A ‖ is:

nuššurū. (§ 65, 38) V 61 vi 39 who ina libbi akâlē nu-šur-ra-a išakka-nu-ma (BA i 277, 292; HILPRECHT, *Assyr*, 38; 42), makes a deduction from the eatables. Nabd 265, 8 the creditors of thy father nu-šur-ru-u ina lib-bi i-šak-ka-nu. ⊕ 84 iv 31 BA(bi-bi)BA = nu-šur[-ru-u] >< Br 116, AV 1099. K 3600 *R* 23 nar-tu nu-šur-ru-u šussi. PEISER, *KAS*, 70, 5 compares משורה, *munus*, *donum*, 1 Sam 9, 7; Isa 57, 9; ZA iv 343. Another ‖ is:

nišru *2.*, nišir. HILPRECHT, *Assyr*, 12—13, 14 (see *ibid p* 35) ni-š]i-er še'ū zūri ig-zu-uz-ma, schnitt einen Teil des Kulturlandes ab. K 196 iv 1 enuma ina bîti amēli ni-iš-ru ibaš-ši. Nabd 118, 2 niš-ri, 356, 9; 276, 5 niš-rum.

nuširtu (?) KB iv 86 *col* 3 12 nu]-šir-ti-šu-nu; 20 .... nu-šir-ti.

nišru *3.* sum, amount?? *Cuneif. Texts fr. Metrop. Museum, N.Y., no* 14, 8 u niš-ru gab-bu-tu and the entire amount: T[C] 108. Probably identical with nišru, 2.

ni-šur : NI-ŠUR, *e. g.* kannu ša NI-ŠUR, see kannu, 1 (406 *col* 1, bel.), AV 6367. Often in the phrase (amêl) NI-

ŠUR-GI-NA., *Cuneif. Texts from the Metropol. Mus. of N. Y.*, I *no* 28, 18; belongs, no doubt, to the large class of temple-officials. V 20, 40—42. (amêl) NI-ŠUR Nabd 792, 2; 1060, 15; — gi-ni-e Nabd 346, 4; 390, 5; AV 6368; — GI-NA Nabd 755, 14; 802, 4; — sat-tuk, Cyr 349, 2. See T^C 105 where many other passages are cited. PINCHES, *Inscr. Tablets*, *p* 43 *no* 12 *O* 4 (+ 18) mâr (amêl) NI-ŠUR-gi-ni-e; see *ibid*, *p* 45: temple-treasurer. *Pal. Expl.-Fund Quart. Stat.*, July 1900, 265, 4: overseer of the dues.

nišurûtu (?). Camb 182, 2 (amêl) NI-ŠUR-u-tu; Nabd 424, 2 + 8; 712, 2; Neb 349, 4.

našramu (√šaramu S^b 219) AV 6165; BA i 177; § 65, 31 *a*, a sharp-edged tool {ein scharfes Werkzeug}. D 87 i 40 (= II 45 *b* 64) GIŠ-BA-ŠAB = na-aš-ra-mu, Br 111.

našraptu. V 39 *a-b* 65 .... TAB = na-aš-rap-tum ‖ naçrabtu (*q. v.*), Br 12039; ZK i 122; ZA i 64, a weapon {eine Waffe} BA i 177; M^S 98 *col* 2. K 8670 iii 28 URUDU-ŠUN-ŠIK = na-aš-rap-tu; *cf* K 4362 *O* 3 *a* (ZA iv 161).

nišîtum. V 31 *g-h* 30 ni-ši-tim ‖ maš-ši-tim oblivion, forgetfulness {Vergessenheit} perh √ = נָשָׁה (BROWN-GESENIUS, 674 *col* 2) AV 6364. KB vi (1) 280 iii (iv) 3 & 8; 541.

na-tu(-ma) NE 69, 35 see naṭû.

natû. strike, crush; split {schlagen, zerschlagen; spalten} AV 6174, 6940. ZK i 346. V 17 *c-d* 47 PA-TU du UZU = na-tu-u, followed by natû ša pa-ni (48, 49) Br 5620, 5603, 9351. IV^2 56 *add*, 3 šal-šu paṭ-ru [ša qaq]qadu i-nat-tu-u. Perh K 8466, 4 see muxxu (518—19).

ℑ crush, smash {zerschlagen, zerschmettern}. I 7 *no* ix D 4; Creat.-*frg* IV 130 see muxxu (518—19); IV^2 26 *a* 27—8 mu-nat-ti šadi-i zaq-ru-u-ti. KB vi (1) 342. Der. perh.:

nîtu, in ni-it libbi, oppression, misery {Bedrängnis, Unglück}. LEHMANN, i 139 = nîtu surrounding {Umschliessung}. AV 6375 on II 37, 75 *add*; II 37 *c-f* 53—55; perh II 39 *a-b* 75 ni-it xi[??].

nîtu detention, surrounding {Zurückhaltung, Hemmung}. AV 6383. LYON, *Manual*, 122; LEHMANN, 138 √נוי; § 114 √נאי; HEBR. ix 10. JENSEN, KB vi (1) 309: Umschliessung; see *Kosmologie*, 250; 288. Creat.-*frg* IV 110; SCHEIL, *Rec. Trav.* xvii, 83 *no* 28, 6; V 19 *c-d* 20—1 (Br 8181); II 24 *c-d* 45, see lamû (*p* 484 *col* 2); H 38, 87. Sn v 13 a-na-ku ni-tum al-me-šu (§ 139; *Andov. Rev.* v 545); *Bav* 44 (end) the city ni-i-ti al-me, KB ii 116—7. III 15 *b* 4 the governor of Ur ni-i-tu il-me-šu-ma içbatu mûçâšu. Sarg *Ann* 127 ni-i-tu almê, 308 ni-i-ta ilmûšunûti. K 2674, 41 ni-i-tum il-mu-u. V 41 *e-f* 61 see Br 1577. SMITH, *Senn*, 94, 75 ni-ti-iš il-ma-a. Asb v 76 *etc.* read çal-ti-ia.

nittum *1.* K 7331 *O* 8 *a-b* ni-it-tum, together with ra-bi-çu & šar-ra-qu, M^S 70.

nittum *2.* ⊕ 252 *R* 9 ..... ⟨⟨ = ni-it-tum, AV 8073; Br 14325.

nîtu. V 17 *d* 51—2 ni]-i-tu; *n* ša Êa, JENSEN, 251, 511.

nitû. V 16 *g-h* 33 ZI = ni-tu-u, AV 6380; Br 2328.

natbu Sarg *Khors* 158 see nadbu.

nutabu. V 26 *a-b* 27 GIŠ?]-BAD = nu-ta-bu some wooden instrument, article {ein hölzerner Gegenstand} AV 6466; Br 1526. SCHEIL, *Šamš*, 39 compares נְתִיב. See sunnu.

natbak(q)u (G §§ 4; 25) see nadbaku.

natbalu. V 16 *g-h* 77 LIBIT-TAB-BA = na-at-ba-lu, followed by u-ru-ba-a-tum (see urbatu, 2). AV 5952, Br 11200, BA i 177. √tabalu.

nataxu *1.* WINCKLER & ABEL, T. A. (Ber) 240 *R* 20 it-tu-u(x) li-ib-ba-šu; BA ii 418; iv 128 *foll*; KB vi (1) 98—99: da beruhigte sich sein Herz (see nâxu Q^t). ZIMMERN, *Ritualtafeln*, *no* 58, 9 k]i-ma riksu it-tu-xu; IV^2 57 *b* 27 (beg).

nataxu *2.* AV 6168 lintuxu, intatax *etc.* see mataxu.

nataku. pour forth, be poured out {sich ergiessen, zerfliessen}. IV^2 20, 3 *O* 14—16 u-šum-gal-lu ša iš-tu pi-šu im-tu la i-na-at-tu-ku, *var* da-mu la i-çar-ru-ru (Br 5212); BA ii 292 & *rm* *.

Catchline of K 13663 . . . A?-DE = na-ta-ku, BEZOLD, *Catalogue*, 1329.

ℨ perh V 45 ii 60 tu-na-at]-tak.

Š¹ šumma ištu murçi šapti-šu uš-ta-nat-tak, BOISSIER, *Doc*, 23, 7; M³ 70.

ℨ¹ T^M ii 134, 135; i 32, 140 see xâlu.

Der.:

natiktum. vessel used for magic purposes {ein zu magischen Zwecken bestimmtes Gefäss} AV 6173. II 22 *e-f* 33—35 + V 32 *c* 43—5 e-gu-ub-bu-u = karpat te-lil-te (*var* -ti) & karpat na-ti-ik-tum (Br 2113), ša-ti-ik-tum which = DUK-NAM-TAR.

nituktum (?) perh V 42 *c-d* 20 ni-tu[-uk-tum], same ideogr as maškalum (21) *q. v.*

NU-TUK(G)-A = ša . . . . lā išû, see išû did not have {hatte nicht}; ZIMMERN, *Ritualtafeln*, *no* 54, 22 *etc.*

NI-TUK-KI. (AV 6381) see Dilmun & Dilmunû (*p* 251 *col* 1) & *cf* BEZOLD, *Catalogue*, 2006, 2046.

natkil see takalu, 1. ℨ.

natkiltu. T. A. Ber 26 i 21: II na-at-ki-la-a-tum ša maški. √נכל, 2.

natalu. pr ittil, *ps* ittal (?) lie, lay down, go to sleep {liegen, sich legen, sich schlafen legen} Z^B 117; G § 53. *del* 201 (221) u ûmi ša it-ti-lu (3 *sg*) ina i-ga-ri elippi; *cf* 203 (223); 188 (208) ga-na e ta-at-til well! do not go to sleep! Asb vi 20 ša ina mux-xi u-ši-bu it-ti-lu whereon they had sat & lain down, BA i 426. IV² 31 *a* 79 it-til ed(t)-lu i-na kum-mi-šu it-til ar-da-tum ina a-xi . . . . . ša; see *R* 9—10 (KB vi, 1, 86 —7). Rm 197, 2 mâr šarri li-it-til (+4+6) THOMPSON, *Reports*, 274 Q. NE 14, 12 it-ta-lu e-da-nu-uš-šu, KB vi (1) 140. K 3186, 5 la na-at-la (= pm ZA iv 234).

Q¹ = Q H 119, 17 (= DT 67 *O*) ina er-ši el-li-tim it-ta-til (× Br 8995). On a sumptuous couch she slept ‖ ina kussî ellitim ûšib. Z^B ii 101 ina erši ta-mi-i it-ta-til.

nitmirtu. 82—8—16, 1 iv 17 ku-ni-lu-ug | KI-NE | = ni-it-mir-tu, followed by tumru. Br 9708. HOMMEL, *Sum. Les.*, 98 chimney {Rauchfang}.

natanu (AV 6170) = nadanu, AJP xvi 119; ZK ii 326; 168 & *rm* 2; 379 *fol* pr ittan. Anp i 83 all rebels u-ça-bi-tu-ni i-ta-nu-ni (3 *pl*; see above, *p* 131 *col* 2 under itânu) & perh Šalm. *Ob*, 153. Samsu-iluna 7 i-ti-nu-šum, has given him, KB iii (1) 130 *col* 1; ZA ii 140 *a* 13 i-ti-nam. K 625, 15 u-sa-xi-ir a-ta-na-aš-šu-nu; K 662 *R* 14 a-na šarri bêli-ja it-ta-nu; K 609 *R* 5 it-ta-an-u-ni; K 619, 20 it-ta-an-na; K 573 *R* 5 it-ta-nu-ni; K 513, 8 i-ta-an-na (Hr^L 131; 211; 126; 174; 180; 245). K 2401 ii 3 kip-pat erbit-tim ⁽ⁱˡ⁾ Ašur it-ta-na-šu; iii 5 ta-at-ta-an-na-šu-nu (BA ii 627 *foll*). Nabd 497, 4 P. N. Il-tam-meš-na-ta-nu. PINCHES, *Jour. Trans. Vict. Inst.*, 28, 19—20; 38 *ad* K 961, 15. P. N. Tam-meš-na-ta-nu. Nabd 85, 5 ina našparti ša ⁽ⁱˡ⁾ Bin-ad-du-na-ta-nu (356, 2 na-tan; KB iv 234); Nabd 854, 7 šaṭâri kî iš-ṭur-ru it-ta-na-aš-šu, he returned to him (or √našû?). PINCHES, PSBA viii ('86) 242 on Babylonian forms it-ta-nu, it-ti-nu. Bu 91—5—9, 296, 12 i-na-an-ti-in, he will place (& -nu, 16) JRAS '97, 590. T. A. Lo 11, 40 i-na-an-ti-nu (*ps*). pr would be ittin = יִתֵּן. Lo 8, 69 (end) lu-ut-ti-in, I will give, ZA v 162—3; KB v 38—9. DELITZSCH, *Kappad. Keilschrifttafeln*, 26—7: Golenischeff 11, 4: i-ti-nu they gave; a-ti-in, I gave.

P. N. Na-ta-nu-ja-a-ma, AV 6169; PSBA xv 13—15; JASTROW, ZA x 230.

nitunu ‖ nudnu (*q.v.*) KB i 92—3; perh also T. A. Ber 21, 38 nu-te-en-ni-šu-nu, as presents for them.

na-at-na-ta-šum(-ma) TP i 32 *etc.*, see nadanu Q *a*; AV 6175.

nataru. II 30 *no* 4 *O* 13 BAR] = na-ta-ru. Br 1777; 83, 1—18, 1335 iii 21 ta-ar | TAR | na-ta-rum; perh S^c 5 *b* 1 na-ta[-ru?] AV 6172, Br 2981.

natru, Br 6590 see nadru.

nu-tuš, K 678 *R* 15 (V 54 *b* 49) read nu-ku & see nuk.

ס

SU (AV 6763) = mašku skin {Haut} II 16, 57 *etc.* Thus correct AV 6766 su-a-šu-a-ti into (mašak) a-šu-a-ti = aškti (see 123, *col* 2).

Su, abbreviation for Suri (not Sutî); WINCKLER, *Forsch*, ii, 2, 255; ZA xiv 174.

sâ'u. V 41 *c-d* 51—55 sa-a-u; id ending in TUR, LUB, KA (+li inserted).

sa'û. V 26 *g-h* 1 GIŠ-MA-NU (= eru)-MIR-A = sa-'-u. AV 6491; Br 6799, 6923.

si'û. pr isi'i, throw down, overthrow, overcome, storm {nieder-, überwerfen, stürmen} סעה. V 17 *c-d* 8 ŠU-UŠ-SA = si-'u-u followed by sa-ka-pu (9); II 34 *a-b* 16; AV 6634; Br 7165, 14106. III 58 *c* 32 nakru dannu mâta i-si-'i (THOMPSON, ii 119, 6); 61 *no* 2, 11 (end). T^M v 27 like a lion li-sa-a eli-ša. V 16 *g-h* 32 .... GAR (= ŠA) = si-'u-u, Br 14476. K 595, 12 *foll* i-sa-u adanniš u ilâni rabûti ša šamê erçitim mala šumu nabû inišunu is-su-u (= Q^1) Hr^L 6.

NOTE. — Instead of xu-si-i (xusû, 328 *col* 1) we may perhaps read XU (= iççur) si-i. — Der.:

si'ûtu. storm, storming {Sturm, Ansturm} KNUDTZON, 309; *no* 1, 6 lû ina si-'-u-tu lu-u ina da-na-na (17 *O* 6; 12 *R* 8), JENSEN, *Lit. Centralbl.*, '94, 54.

su-u ‖ daltu. II 23 *c-d* 18. but here we read ik-zu [cuneiform] su-u, which perhaps means rather that ik-zu as well as ik-su-u can be read.

(aban) **su-u.** Br 216 *ad* V 30 *g* 62; AV 6763; K 133 *R* 23—4 (H 81) Br 231.

sa-i-di. II 52 *d* 61 dun-nu sa-i-di(ki?).

suadu. a spice {Spezerei}. Rm 367 + 83, 1—18, 461 *a* iii 6 GIŠ-SIM-DU = su-a-du (II 42 *a* 13). AV 6765; M^S 70.

suâlu. Z^B vii 30 g]u-ux-xu su-a-lu i-rat-su u-tan-niš, through asthma and cough his breast was weakened (*p* 60 comp. سُعَال); K 141 (BEZOLD, *Catalogue*, 50) šumma amêlu su-a-lam mariç.

si-el-lu see sellu.

סאס. ג V 45 v 41 tu-sa-'-as.

sa'aru xurâçi. Anp iii 62 sa-'a-ru(-ri) xurâçi ša tam-li-te (65), perh = שהרנים; Syr סהרניא, necklace; they were made often of gold, ZA i 357. KB i 105, 107: Silberner (goldener) Korb. AV 6492.

si'eru II 29 *c-d* 36 ŠU-UŠ-SA = si-'e-ru, preceded by te-šu-u.

si-e-ru *1.* V 28 *e-f* 2 *cf* mêsi (565 *col* 2) Br 10432.

si-e-ru 2. K 2009, 8 ŠU [cuneiform] = si-e-ru (?) AV 6751, followed by pa-ša-ṭu; same id = sanaqu ša dalti.

si-e-rum *3.* S^c 267, according to Br 10548.

su-eš-šu, *cf* daqqu (365 *col* 2); also II 36 *a* 37; or SU = (mašak) eš-šu (AV 6757 si-eš-šu) AV 2408.

si-e-tum. K 4195 *R* 7 SI = si-e-tum. Br 3392; AV 6614. Perh II 35, 31 (AV 6619) = si-[cuneiform]-tum; 32 *g-h* 11 = si-i-tum (Br 3404, 3444).

siba, sibi, *f* **sibittu,** sibit seven {sieben}, Br 12206—12209. §§ 65 *no* 6; *rm*; 75. Z^B 73. II 19 *b* 14 ša ..... si-ba (VII-NA, 13; Br 12206) qaq-qa-da-šu, its heads are seven (§ 67, 4; AV 6620; Br 3518); *b* 66 nu-na ša si-ba ab(p)-ra-šu. Written id *del* 149 (158); KB vi (1) 78, 4; § 129, seven incense-vessels each. NE IX *col* vi 29. K 2801 + K 221 + K 2669, 12 ^{il} VII ilâni qar-du-ti; III 66 iv 12 ilâni VII-bi (*cf* vi 2) + 19 ilâni ša bît ilâni VII-bi. Esh *Sendsch*, *O* 10 (^{il}) VII-bi ilâni qar-du-u-ti (JENSEN: sibitti-šu-nu qar-du-u-ti). K 3500 + K 4444 + K 10235 i 5 ^{il} si-bit-te ilâni qar-du-te the seven-gods, the strong gods. Sn *Bav* 1 ^{il} VII-bi ilâni rabûti. IV^2 33 *col* iv 12 Addar ša VII-bi ilâni rabûti. K 2606 *O* 17 ^{il} si-bit-tum the seven-gods; 9 si-bu-tum ^{il} A-nun-na-ki. H 78, 11 mâre ap-si-i si-bit-ti-šu-nu (= IV^2 14 *no* 2) Br 12209. H 76, 33—4, 37—8 si-bit-ti-šu-nu ilâni lim-nu-tum, seven they are, the evil gods; IV^2 5 *a* 66—7, 70—1; IV^2 15* *R* i 30 lim-nu-ti si-bit-ti-šu; *cf* IV^2 30* *no* 3 *O* 34. IV^2 1* iii 13—14, 19—20 si-bit (= VII-A-AN, Br 12208) ilâni lim-nu-tum; 21—22 si-bit la-bar-tum lim-nu-tum, 23—4 si-bit la-ba-çi .... lim-nu-tum; 21, 1 B *R* 21—22 ilâni si-bit mu-xal-liq lim-nu-ti, BA ii 436; IV^2 2 v 30—1 to 34—5 si-bit-ti (= VII-NA, AV 6619) šu-nu seven they are {sieben sind *sie*}, 58—9 si-bit-ti-šu-nu si-bit-ti-šu-nu si-bit a-di ši-na šu-nu, seven they are, seven they are, twice seven they are. 5 *a* 27—8 si-bit-ti-šu-nu mār šip-ri ša (il) A-nim; 3 *b* 6—7 ki-çir si-bit a-di ši-na ku-çur. KB vi (1) 58, 6 (il) sibitti-šu-nu; 66, 22; 72, 24. IV^2 1* iii 25—6 ina šamē si-bit ina erçitim si-bit-ma (= VII-A-AN); 59 *no* 2 *b* 13 si-bit šārē, the seven winds (§ 128); D 97, 12 šārē ša ib-nu-u si-bit-ti(-)šu-nu = Creat.-*frg* IV 47. K 4810 i 45 šar-ri si-bit-ti seven kings = IV^2 21, 1 A 45. P. N. Si-bi-it-ti-bi-'-li (III 9, 51; KAT^2 185) & — bi-'-el (II 67, 57) AV 6618.

NOTE. — 1. JASTROW, *Religion*, 264 *foll*: a sacred number among Semitic nations.

2. On siba and samānu (> š) see HALÉVY, *Mém. de la soc. de linguist. de Paris*, xi 77; JENSEN, ZA xiv 182—5.

3. Has si-ba, the pronunciation of PA + LU (S^b 213, V 13 *a* 55, Br 5684) any connection with siba, seven?

sibū (sebū) seventh {siebenter} § 37; *f* **sibūtum** (§ 36); § 32 *aβ*; LOTZ, *Quaestiones*, 24 *fol*. IV^2 5 *a* 25—6 si-bu-u (= VII-KAN-MA, Br 12212); H 41, 300; IV^2 56 *add*, *col* 1, 7. T. A. Lo 82, 4 i-n]a si-e-bi-i (il) I-lu(dib?)-tu KB vi 78; BA iv 130. Asb vi 10 a-di sibē-šu (§ 129); IV^2 26 *b* 48—9 a-di si-bi-šu, Br 12207, up to the seventh time (*cf* NE 55, 24); IV^2 31 *a* 60 sebu-u bāba he let her enter. NE VII *col* vi 8 si-ba-a (*i. e.* ū-ma); XII *col* iv 5 siba-a (pa-ri-sa?) KB vi 222; Creat.-*frg* V 17 ina ūm sibī (id). SCHEIL, *Rec. Trav.*, xix 61—2 (Repr., 25) *no* 3, 9 sib-ti ūmi between seš-šit-ti & sa-man-ti (see also HILPRECHT, *Assyriaca*, 89). *del* 123 (130) si-bu-u ū-mu i-na ka-ša-a-di; 139 (146) siba-a ū-ma i-na ka-ša-a-di (BA i 133, 134). Perhaps, arax si-bu-ti Sn *Bell* (Layard 63, 1) AV 6622; see MEISSNER, WZKM v 180, who quotes arax si-bu-tim (see *p* 275 *col* 1) & compare za-bi-in for sāpin; JA '89, xiii 297.

sibitān. T. A. often. VII-šu VII-da-an (& ta-am) am-qut, Ber 100, 8; 154, 3; VII-šu u VII da-am, Ber 138, 9; VII u VII ta-am Lo 71, 5; VII-šu u VII-ta-an, Lo 70, 4 (BA iv 126 *foll*); also VII-it u VII-it uštanaxixen Lo 82, 8—9; Ber 132, 7—8 VII-šu a-na pa-ni VII-ta-an-ni am-qut. VII u VII mi-la-an-na, Ber 101, 5 (Lo 67, 4; 68, 4); VII u ši-ib-i-ta-an, seven & seven times = שבעתים, Ber 140, 4; Lo 60, 6 (see JENSEN, ZA x 324 *rm* 1 on this Assyrian form); also simply 7 u 7, Ber 98, 3; 99, 3; VII-ta-am u VII ta-am, Ber 102, 4; VII-šu u VII-it-ta-am, Ber 88, 6—7; a-na šibi-šu u] ši-bi-ta-am am-qut, Ber 159, 2—3; see also BEZ., *Dipl*, § 32 on *š* for *s* in T. A.

sibūtum. in the seventh place {siebentens, an siebenter Stelle} *del* 207 (220) si-bu-tum (§§ 77; 129); also see DELITZSCH, *Kappadoc. Keilschrifttaf.*, *no* 14, 25.

(KI) **Sa-ab-'-a-a** II 67, 53; III 10 *no* 2, 38 (end) lit^y of the Sabaeans, Br 6478; perh V 12 *e-f* 49, 50 sa-a-bu (KI), D^{Par} 106. But ZA xv 247 A]-a-bu.

(šad) **Sa-bu(-a)** Anp ii 68 name of a mountain. KB vi 54 (*Zû*-legend; IV^2 14 *a* 3—4) 4 ina šadī Sa-a-bi (Br 3165); II 51 *a*(*-b*) 1. D^{Par} 105.

(aban) **sāb(p?)u** a stone {ein Stein}. II 44 *c-d* 37 a-ban?] sa-a-bu = (aban) a-bi ab-ni, which latter also = e-pi-ir-ru (38) & e-rim-ma-tu (39); mentioned also in I 44, 83 (aban) AN-ŠE-TIR (= aš-nan) (aban) DUR-MI-NA-TUR-DA u (aban) sa-a-bu, as material used for the building of the ēkallu. ZDMG 55, 234.

sabū sesame-wine {Sesamwein} *cf* kurunnu (V 19 *a-b* 28, Br 3655) = סְבָה, سباء. ZA iv 12, 45 ši-kar si-bi-'-i (ka-a-ri), the noble drink; 46 ši-kar sa-bi-'u (see *ibid*, 241) AJSL xvii 142. AV 6471, 6474. Rm 388, 2 see namxaru; & ZK ii 216. Perh. (amēl) sa-bi-e, BEZOLD, *Catalogue*, 1393. N 3554 *O* 5 maxar-ki bīt sa-bi-i na-ra[-am]; 11 (end) ina bīt (amēl) sa-bi-i maš-šad; 13 karan (?) sa-bi-i (PSBA xxiii, 120).

PSBA xii 407; ZA ix 197, 8; Br 12811 *ad* 45 *no* 4 (*add*) *R* 1 GIŠ sa-bu, AV 6473. FRÄNKEL, *Aram. Lehnwörter*, 157—8.

sābu (?, **sabū?**) perh K 3351, 22 ša tam-tim gal-la-ti i-sa-am-bu-' qu-ub-bu-ša. K 118 libbū mē i-sa-am-bu-'.

sab(b)i'u, sabbi'itu. II 32 *g-h* 14 I(çi)ZI = sa-bi-'-u ‖ igaru & amartu; H 38,

102, 103 (AV 6472, Br 3990). II 28 *b-c* 64 SA-UŠ-BI (Br 3125) = sa-ab-bi-'-u; 65, NU-SA-UŠ-BI (Br 1977, 3125) = sa-ab-bi-'i-tu, AV 6477. *cf* NU-SA = dāmu, blood.

subbu. T. A. Ber. 26 i 58: I ša su-ub-bi su-u-li-i xurāçu; ii 43: I ša (?) zu-ub-bi gu-uš-šu-ti.

sibixûti. a garment {ein Kleidungsstück} Camb 295, 10 (çubât) si-bi-xu-tum.

sa-ba-ku, Cyr 373, 16; P. N. Sa-ba-ki-ilu (*c. st.*, Neb) AV 6470.

s(š)ab(p)-ku NE II iv *a* 8 (KB vi 140).

si-ib-ka-ru-u. Nabd 801, 2.

sibultu Delitzsch, *Kappad. Keilschrift-tafeln*, 18, 21 nu-ur ki-li si-bu-ul-tam.

(amêl) **sab(p)sinûtu.** Nabd 172, 3 (7) where the acquirement of the (amêl) sa-ab-si-nu-tu qa-ti-tim is mentioned.

sibû a garment {ein Kleidungsstück}. II 26 *e-f* 18 (Br 7012); V 28 *c-d* 64 si-bu-u ‖ kar-rum, AV 6621. *Cf* Rm 2, 555, 5 si-bu-u ša SEG (= šârti?). 83, 1—18, 1331 iii 17 si-bu-u.

su-bi-si II 30 *b* 30. KB vi (1) 511.

sabasu, isbus be angry {zürnen} see šabasu.

sabbaru. K 4152 *R* 32 sa-ab-ba-ru ‖ ša ..... M^S texts, *p* 7.

Subartu (*sc.* mâtu) highland {Hochland} *cf* êlamtu; then name of country. D[S] 119; D[Par] 234 *foll*; ZK i 71; ZA i 196; Winckler, *Forsch*, i 153; 224; ii 47. K 2619 iv 10 Su-bar-ta su-bar-tu shall not spare (KB vi (1) 381). TP iii 1 (3) maxâzâni ša Su-bar-te (& Šu-bar-te, 3); ii 89 Šu-ba-ri-i šib-çu-ti. II 50 *c-d* 48—51 SU-EDIN-KI (Jensen, 481 *rm* 1; V 14 *c* 15; V 28 *b* 28), SU-NER-KI, SA-NER-KI (Br 3148), XU-BU-UR-KI (Br 2081, 198, 234) AV 8384) = su-bar-tum; *ibid*, 60 (šad) Su-bar-ti; ZDMG 53, 656; 662—4:

Subari = Šubari; Subartum = Šubarte. (Š)Subari the original name of the tribe; š(s)ubartum name of the country inhabited by them. (Subari = Suri of T. A.). T. A. Ber 52 *R* 7 i-na (mât) Su-ba-ri i-na lu-qi; 42, 17 a-na (mât) Su-ri (but *cf* Knudtzon, BA iv *no* 3; KB vi (1) 381) i-na lu-qi. Bezold, *Catalogue*, 2192: part of the district of Su (?). See also V 16 *a-b* 17—19 (Br 234, 3147, 2080); ib of 17, 18 also = e-lam-tum, 14, 15. KB vi (1) 307—8. The Inhabitants perhaps are the

Subarî, mentioned in Hilprecht, OBI, i 84 *col* 1, 27 Su-ba-ru-um a-na-ru; see Messerschmidt, 7, 8. Also IV² 39 *a* 5 (+ 33) Šu-ba-ri-i, 33, (mât) Šu-ba-ri-i ra-pal-ti; Šalm I: Rm 2, 606. T. A. Ber 101 *R* 7 Su-ba-ri. Hommel, *Gesch*, 500; Winckler, *Forsch*, i 390.

sibirtu (?). Nabd 10, 4 (çubât?) si-bi-ri-it; Cyr 158, 2 si-bi-ir-t[um?].

sabašu, isbuš be angry {zürnen} see šabasu.

sabîtu *1.* originally epithet of the (ilat) Si-du-ri & then used as ‖ of Siduri; also = Aram סָבִיתָא (*pl*) barmaids. NE 65 (X *col* 1), 1 (ilat) Si-du-ri sa-bi-tum (ZA iv 113); + 10; 67 ii 20 sa-bit said unto Gilgameš; 72, 30 ana bi]-it sa-bit ul ak-šu-dam-ma. According to Hommel, *Altisraelitische Überlieferung*, 35 perh = the one from *Sabu*: a district in Arabia; Jastrow, *Religion*, 491 perh = Saba in South-Arabia; J[W] 86. KB vi (1) 470.

sabîtum *2.* K 11020 sect. ii 5 *foll*: šumma sa-bi-tum elippi (kirru, nûnu, šaxû) ibaš-ši. Bezold, *Catalogue*, 1131.

sa-ga see sanqu.

sagû. Creat.-*frg* IV 12 plentifulness a-šar sa-ge-šu-nu lu-u ku-un aš-ru-uk-ku (KB vi, 1, 22), while they are in want, shall be given to thy sanctuary, BA ii 155 (bedürftig sein); Boissier, *Rev. Sém.*, vii 51. K 2020 *R* 5 sa-gu-u, preceded by xa-an-ça-tu & ši-ib-bu, ‖ gab .... M[S] texts, *p* 4. To the same stem belongs:

sugû need, want {Not, Mangel} I 70 iv 17 Nabû su-ga-a u ni-ib-ri-ta liš-ku-na-aš-šum-ma; III 41 *b* 34—5 Nabû û-um su-gi-e u ar-ra-ti a-na ši-ma-ti-šu li-šim-šu (KB iv 79).

sagîtu. K 546, 6—7 sa(?)-ga-a-te (mašak) ma-ga-' (Hr[L] 75) AV 6488.

sagabu (שגב) Winckler, KB V *ad* T. A. (Lo) 29, 53 and the wall of bronze ša is-ku-bu (which protects him).

sig(k, q?)-du an insect {Insekt}? V 27

sagbanu. *cf* šakbanu.

g-h 4 XU-BER-DI-A = si-ig-du; II 5 *c-d* 14 ‖ a-du-dil-lum, Br 9567; AV 6658, 6665.

si-gi-iz-zu Cyr 163, 6.

su-gil-lu. AV 6780 *ad* III 70, 101 (with S + *R*). Or SU(= mašak)gil-lu?

sagilatu a plant {Pflanze} K 4565 (šam) sa-gi-la-tu.

sugullātu (*pl f*) herds {Herden} AV 6781. TP v 5 su-gul-lat sisē xapšāti large droves of horses (Sarg *Ann* 341); vi 105 su-gul-lat sisē alpē imērē *etc.* ... ak-çur; vii 4—5 u su-gul-la-at (*var* lat) na-a-li ajalē *etc.* ..... u-tam-mi-xu; 10, su-gul-la-te-šu-nu ak-çur. I 28 *a* 7 young wild-oxen he captured alive, su-gul-la-a-te-šu-nu ik-çur (*cf* 21, 27). The *sgl* sugullu perh H 74 *col* 3, 1 ša su-gul-li, of the flock, herd; also S^{P} II 987 *O* 10 su-gul-lum u kalbē bît xab-ba-a-tam, the herd and the dogs of the house of X (he favors?), Pinches, *Jour. Trans. Vict. Inst.*, 29, 52. Perhaps also K 161 *R* iii 7 sug(k)ullu mentioned with supūru, tarbaçu, šigaru. — GGA '79, 807; D^{ii} 20; D^{Pr} 34; § 65, 22; Barth, *Etym. Stud.*, 64, 65; Hebr. iii, 107—110; ZA v 93 √סגל = collect, heap up.

sigmu (?) VATh 793, 14—15 si-ig-mi-šu-nu | mu-xu-ur-ma their *s* accept, BA ii 563—4.

sag-pa-rim *i. e.* SAG-PA-RIM = nis-satu (*q. v.*).

(amēlūti) **SA-GAS** *pl* often in T. A.; also merely (amēlūti) GAS; Lo 74, 11—12 (amēlūti) SA-GA-AS | (amēlūti) xa-ba-ti; 49, 26 (amēlūti) SA-GAS *pl*; Ber 96, 27 u qa-du (amēlūti) SA-GAS *pl*-ja. AV 6480. KB V = the *Xabīru*, but Haupt in SBOT (*Joshua*) 53 *rm* *: SA-GAZ only id for xabbatu, spoiler (*i. e.* raiding nomads).

sigru see sikru, 1.

***sâdu** 1.* pr isād destroy, kill {niedermachen, vernichten, töten}. Creat.-*frg* IV 123 see kamū, 1. Q. V 28 *e-f* 1 sa-a-du ‖ na-a-ru (AV 6588); perh K 194, 10 çābē dal-xu-te ša i-si-šu-nu i-sa-du-u-ni a-di (amēl) šaqē ... di-e-ku (Hr^{L} 144).

sādu *2.* pasture {Weide?) Johnston, JAOS xviii 138 *ad* K 524 *R* 13 ina sa-a-du li-ku-lu; 21, a-na sa-a-du ša (māt) Ēlamti ip-te-ir-ku (Hr^{L} 282).

Su-u-du. so read T. A, with KB v & Prášek, *Expository Times*, Aug. 1900, 508 instead of Ia-u-du (*q. v.*). — On the other hand, ZDMG 53, 655 *foll* reads II 50 i/ii 1—5 Eri(not Su)-du.

sadab(p?)u. V 45 v 37 tu-sa-da(ṭa)-ab(p).

suddû'. √sadû, Peiser, KAS 97 = manû count {zählen} properly count by the sexagesimal system; T^{C} 109; ZK i 7 *rm* 1. Neb 76, 6 kaspu ša ina 1 ṬU su-ud-du-', he shall pay. 68, 5 written VI-' (*i. e.* suddu-'); 65, 6: I šiqlu VI-' mā (wr. LAL)-ṭi kaspi. Nabd 880, 6: VII ṬU VI-' xurāçi; Neb 112, 1: 24 ṬU su-ud-du-' LAL-ṭi (?) kaspu BA i 517 *rm* 1.

***sadadu** 1.* ב Beh 112, these men lu ma-a-du su-ud-di-id (= ip). KB iv 214, 5—6 a-na pa-ni-ka su-ud-di-di-in-ni, zu dir nimm mich und befreunde mich. Nabd 697, 10 ta-ab-kiš-šu ta-du-ur-šu u tu-sa-ad-di[-id-ma], KB iv 244—5; Cyr 377, 21 su-di-da-aš be-friend him. Dar 257, 9 (348, 9) pūt su-ud-du-du re'ītum u maçartum alpi bu-uš-tim Ubar naši. AV 6487; befriend {befreunden}.

***sadadu** 2.* = šadadu (?). II 11 *g-h* 54 BU = is-du-ud (Br 7535).

sadidu old {alt} M^{S} 70; texts, *p* 24. Rm 2, 200 A 4—6 qu-ud-mu, ul-lu-u, sa-di-du = max[-ru-u].

'Sad-nu, PSBA xxii 110 *ad* S^{b} 187, × Br 3077 kurnu.

sudinnu(ṭ, t?) *1.* garment, dress {Kleid}. V 14 *c-d* 50 KU-ŠA-NE(or LAM)-UŠ = su(or perh çit)-din-nu; KU-ŠA-LAM = lamxuššû. *Cf* T. A. Ber 26 i 44: II sa-ti-in-nu bi-ir-mu, in a dowry list. Schwally, *Idiotikon*, 121—22 combines it with σινδων, Targ סְדִין.

---

saggilimut see šaggil(i)mut. ~ si-gar *i. e.* Sarg *Bull* 77, see šigaru (AV 6626). ~ si-gir (AV 6627) TP i 28 *cf* siqir (siqru). ~ sigrāti see zikrāti, zikirtu; Haupt in SBOT: *Ezra-Nehemiah*, 66 reads šigrāti. ~ si-gur-ra-a-tu, AV 6630, TP viii 53 (vii 87, 102) *cf* ziqur(r)atu. ~ sadilātim in um-ma-nim sa-ad-li-a-tim, *cf* šadlu. ~ sa-da-ni-iš = šadāniš (*q. v.*).

sudinnu *2.* a bird living in clefts {ein in Spalten nistender Vogel} D^{S} 110; AV 1610. Sn i 17 *fol* see nigiççu. Sarg *Khors* 125—6; *Ann* 290 see mûšiš. II 37 *c-f* 23 *cf* gilgidânu, AV 6783, Br 13962. K 41 *c* 4 ki-ma su-din-nu XU (= SU-DIN-MUŠEN, 3) Pinches, PSBA xvii 65 *foll.*

(mâr) **Su-da-nim**, KB iv 8 (*no* ii) 20.

suddinnu (?) ⊕ 287, 7 GIŠ-SU-UD] TIN-[illegible] = su-ud-din-nu, AV 6787, Br 14368, between sik-kat ni-i-ri & çi-mid-tum.

sadaru, isdir (§ 36), isaddir arrange, put in order; range in order for battle {reihen, ordnen; in Schlachtordnung stellen}. Barth, *ESt*, 56 = سَرَدَ; see, however, Fränkel, BA iii 85. K 2674 *O* 12—13 si-id-ru (battle-array) ša Ašur-ban-aplu ... it-ti (against) Te-um-man is-di-ru. K 788 *R* 9 is-dir-u-ni. ip K^{M} 21, 88 [ana] ia-a-ši aradka ana ṭu-ub-ba-ti si-di-ir-ma. 83—1—18, 41 Edge, 14—16 & *R* 1 a-sa-dir mi-i-nu ša šarru be-ili i-qab-bu-u-ni (*cf* R. F. Harper, *AJSL*, xiv, 11). DT 81 vi 11—12 der Lehrling soll das Geld i-sa-ad-dir-ma (aufzählen) BA iii 501—3, iv 83. Knudtzon, 309 *ad* 85, 3 mât Ašš]ur^{ki} i-sa-da[-ra]; K 493, 14 la-as-di-e-ri I will put to order (BA i 212; § 93, 1 *b*). K 1113, 26 a-sa-di-ir, I will put to order (Hr^{L} 71 *R* 11; BA ii 45); III 16 *no* 2, 3 a-ta-a dup(?)-pi-ki la ta-sad-di-ri (Hr^{L} 308); *cf* Hommel, *Gesch*, 694 *rm* 4; Tiele, *Gesch*, 406, 413; Johnston, *Hopk. Circ.*, 126, 91 *foll* & JAOS xx 244 *foll*; Scheil, ZA xi 49; Winckler, *Forsch*, ii 58—9, √שטר. V 65 *b* 51—2 before Bêl, Nebo & Nergal .... lu-u sa-ad-ra-ak tal-lak-ti ana darâti. pm also perh Strassm., *Stockh. Or. Congr.*, 18. 7: 2 GUR aš-a-an sat-tuk ša bîtu sad-ra-tu. K 126, 31 zi-karu ina sûqi erbitti xarimta sa-dir; 43, zikaru çaltu sad-rat-su ûmê-šu KIL-DA-MEŠ (BA i 170 *foll*). Rm^{2} 139, 20 limnu-šu sa-dir. KB ii 238—9 (= K 2675) *O* 16 is-di-ra mi-ix-rit ummânâteja. V 44 a-b 20 perh an-nu-tum šarri-e ša arka a-bu-bi a-na sa-dir a-xa-meš la šaṭ(or sad?)-ru these are the kings after the deluge, but they are not placed according to order, Hommel, *Gesch*, 175; ZA ii 310. Pognon, JA '88 (XI) 544 *foll*; D^{K} 20; Halévy, RÉJ xvii 6 reads šaṭ-ru for sad-ru. In omens, K 196 i 1 (end) & 21 (end) see niziqtu; *ibid* i 4 bîtu šuâtu BAD (= nisû) sa-dir-šu (*cf* ii 28) Pinches, *Texts*, *p* 11; *ibid col* ii 17 ti-bu sa-dir-šu (26 = ZI-GA for ti-bu). Thompson, *Reports*, ii 126 *col* 2: prevail, *e. g.* 83—1—18, 222 *R* 2 ... imbaru sa-dir pa-li-e mâti; 4, imbaru ûmê u-sa-dir; K 1412 + 1508 *R* 6 (sa-dir); Bu 89—4—26, 181, 3; K 760, 4; 83—1—18, 176, 2 (+ 4 u-sa-dir); K 1826, 1; K 1880, 4 ana sa-dir-ma i-nu-uš; = u-sa-dir, 83—1—18, 287, 3 (+ 9, *R* 6); 81—2—4, 344, 3—4 ana u-sad-dir-ma i-[nu-uš]; K 763, when a northwind prevails (sad-rat)-ma il-lak (Thompson, *loc. cit.*, lvi). Babyl. Chron. iii 37 si-xi ina (mât) Aššur sa-dir, a rebellion was organized in Assyria; S 760, 14 ul-lu-a-te sa-ad-ra (Hr^{L} 424) + 22, AV 6490. ag Sp ii 265 *a* xx 9 ša-di-id ni-ir ili lu-u-ba-xi(ṭi) sa-di-ir a-[illegible]-šu.

ג See above. Pognon, *Wadi-Brissa*, 120 u-sa-ad-di-ru. V 45 v 35 tu-sa-ad-dar (?). K 891 *R* 7 su-ud-du-ru-u-ni (3 *pl*) ka-a-a-an (Pinches, *Texts*, 18); L^{3} *R* 5; perh III 38 *no* 1 *O* 22 su-ud-du-ra. ZA v 58, 28 su-ud-du-ru gug-ga-ni-e tar-ri-ni (are placed in order), perhaps also 22 thou hast given righteous judgment su-ud-ra-su (> sud-rat-šu?). Craig, *Rel. Texts*, 54, 16 bêlu urpîti su-ud-di-ra-ši-ma. Derr.:

sidru. *a*) row; arrangement {Reihe; Anordnung} K 2674 i 8 ina sid-ri šapli-i. Nabd 768, 4 (end) a-na si-id-ri. — *b*) battle-array {Schlachtordnung} Sn ii 77 before Altaqû el-la-mu-u-a si-id-ru šit-ku-nu, they had placed their battle-array against mine. (= מַלְחָמָה, ZDMG 40, 74). Sn *Kui* 3, 3.

sidirtu. battle-array {Schlachtordnung} AV 6648; § 65, 4. II 65 *O* ii 15, 16 for the second time si-dir-tu ša narkabâte ... iš-kun; iii 3 at the foot of Inlman si-dir-tu lu iš-kun, KB i 198, 200. Šamš iv 41 si-dir-ta ša ummanâte-šu iškun-un (KB i 186). Sn v 48 ellamûa šit-ku-nu si-dir-ta. Sn *Bav* 36 against

Ummanmenanu .... aš-ta-kan si-dir-ta. Šalm, *Mon*, ii 72 si-dir(*var* dar)-tu lu iš-kun. TP iii *Ann* 136 ina mux]-xi-šu-nu iš-ku-na si-dir-tu. Haupt, Hebr. i 175—6 comp. שְׂדֵרֹת 1 Kin 8 : 15; 2 Chr 23 : 14.

sadirtu *pl* perh I 28 *a* 20 ina sa-di-ra-a-te u-te-im-me-ix (*cf* diritum, 269 *col* 1), KB i 124—5.

sadarū. M^{S} 71, quotes Boissier, *Doc*, 3, 19 bēl bīti šuáti ul-tab-bar sa-da-ru-u illaku.

sudūru. In a list of jewelry, II 37 *g-h* 55 TAG-ŠA-TAG(=ŠUM)-GA = su-du-ru, between ti-iq-nu (54), e-rim-ma-tu (56) & ni-i-ru (57) AV 6785, Br 12041.

siduru in $^{(ilat)}$ Si-du-ri; see sabītum; perhaps compare also ši-du-ri, II 32 *c-d* 27 ši-du-ri ‖ ar-[da-tum]. KB vi (1) 578—9.

sadru. Thompson, *Reports*: copious ‖ dax-du. K 750, 13 [zunnē] dax-du-tu mē-lē ^{pl} sad-ru-ti. A ‖ is

sidru. K 871, 8 zunnē dax-du-ti mēlē si-id-ru-ti; K 742, 6.

sazargu. T. A. Ber 26 iii 39 ša sa-za-ar-gu (?).

sadāta. KB vi 106—107, 24 (end) sa-d(ṭ)a-a-ti it-ta-na-al-lak; 47 sa-d(ṭ)a-a-ta [it]-ta-na-al-lak, BA iii 366 >< BA ii 393—4, 54: ir-ṭa-a-ti.

sazzaru *cf* seseru, sisseru.

saxu *1.* V 41 *c-d* 56 ... TAG-GI = sa-a-a-xu.

***saxu** 2.* desire (?). King, *Xammurabi*, *no* 75, 5 ša be-li i-si-xa-am, which my lord has desired; also *no* 87, 7 i-si-x[u...].

sīxu a perfume {ein Parfüm} made of the cypress. R 367 (= V 26 *no* 2) + 83, 1—18, 1461 *a* 2, 15 GIŠ[-ŠIM]-LI-LAX (or TU?) = si-i-xu, between bu-ra-šu (14, 16); 31 GIŠ[-ŠIM]-ZA-LUM = sīxu. II 45 *g-h* 50, same id = di-šu (V 27 *g-h* 28) AV 6642, Br 1135.

sixu a plant {eine Pflanze}. II 42 *a* 11 $^{(šam)}$ si-xu, AV 6643, Br 12342, D^{Par} 107; *cf* perh T. A. Ber 25 iv 41 $^{(iṣ)}$ si-ix-xu.

sixū pm si-xi. — *a*) desert, rebel; refuse {abtrünnig werden, abfallen; verweigern}. K 13, 22 (beg) si-xu-šu-nu-tu (Hr^{L} 281; Johnston, JAOS XVIII: are in a state of revolt); Scheil, *Rec. Trav.*, xix 48 (Konst. 1109) 6 the people ša ..... is-xu-ni-iq-qu = King, *Xammurabi*, *no* 77. BA iv 91 *fol*: ungehorsam, widerspenstig sein. Rm^{2} 139, 4 ar-ka-ti-ša iš-te-ni-'i i-si-xi il-bi iššakan-šu. — *b*) swoon away, lose one's senses {schwinden, Besinnung verlieren} Creat.-*frg* IV 68 sa-pi-ix ṭe-ma-šu-ma si-xa-ti ep-šit-su (KB vi 26—7; 335; Jensen, 335). — Q^{t} Sn v 5 in the 8th campaign arki Šu-zu-bi is-si-xu-ma (ZA v 303 √נסח), had revolted. Asb v 15, 16 ul-tu $^{(māt)}$ Elamtu ta-si-xu-u (KB ii 196—7; ZA x 80). — Q^{tn} (?) ZK ii 88, 5 it-te-ni-is-xi = id-dal-lax.

Derr. these 2:

sixu (si-xu *i. e.* sixū) desertion, rebellion {Abfall, Empörung, Aufstand} AV 6643. Sn v 12 *etc.* see bašū כ (109 *col* 2, end). KB iii (2) 144 si-xu *ad* 827—822; also KB i 210—12 *ad* 762—59 (si-xu, & -xi), 746. K 10 *R* 17 si-xu a-na eli *U* i-te-pu-uš. Especially in si-xu bar-tu ‖ saxmaštū (*q. v.*). Šamš i 40 si-xu-bar-tu (ZA ii 97—8 >< KB i 178) a-mat limut-ti u-šab-ši, *cf* Smith, *Asurb*, 335. Knudtzon, 224—6 reads sixu maštu (usually written XI-GAR) but *cf* Meissner, *Theol. Litztg.*, '94 *no* 10. Knudtzon, 110 + 127 *O* 5 si-xi bar-ti; 115 *O* 6, si-x]u maš(bar?)-tu 1,15 *R* 11; si-xu(-xi)-XI-GAR, often. Rm III 105, 15—16 es entstanden in Borsippa e-ša-a-ti dal-xa-a-ti si-xi u sax-ma-ša-a-ti. Babyl. Chron. iii 34—5 Senacherib aplu-šu ina si-xi idūku[-šu]; *ibid*, 14 Kudur, king of Elam ina si-xi ça-bit-ma dīku; i 16 Šamaššumukīn bēl si-xi (KB ii 276 *foll*). See also sadaru Q pm.

saxū *2.* IV^{2} 51 *b* 7 maš-ru pa-ar-šu pi-i-šu, maš-da sa-xa-a šap-t[a-a-šu?], $Z^{Š}$ ii 64 šap-ta-šu: sind trügerisch, widerspenstig seine Lippen. KB vi (2) 335. KB ii 248 v 3 (= Smith, *Asurb*, 117) qi-bit pi-i-šu sa-xu-u ul amgur.

***saxū** 3.* ב destroy, ruin {zerstören, vertilgen}. Sarg *Cyl* 76 see būnānu, *b* (179 *col* 2). V 60 i 7 the temple of Šamaš which the Suteans u-sax-xu-u (had destroyed, BA i 278); *cf* V 65 *a* 18 the temple of *Š* ša ... su-ux-xa-a uçurá-tušu; ZA ii 151, 14; ZA iii 178, Sn *Bav* 58 whosoever (the work that I have accomplished) u-sax-xu-u. KB iv 66, 23 e tu-sax-xi mi-iq[-ra]. Scheil, *Nabd*, i 10 u-sa-ax-xi u-çu-ra-a-ti. IV^2 51 *b* 23 paššûru kun-na (*p* 405 *col* 1) u-sax-xu-u (Z^Š ℶ of saxû 1). S^P 158 + S^P 962 *R* 16 ina?] nibxi Ê-an-na u-sax-xi (& *O* 19) uçurta-šu; *O* 14 sux-xa-' u-çur-ta-šu. Perh V 45 v 38 tu-sa-ax-um (?). ℶ^t KB iv 64 *no* ii *R* 1 mi-çir-ša ul us-sax-x[a] (5, -xi pr) ‖ ut-tak-kar Hilprecht, *Assyr*, 14—15; 54.

sixû, with or without determinative $^{(amêlu)}$ usually in connexion with paqir(r)ânu (*q. v.*); pût sixû *etc.* see pûtu. AV 6644.

suxxu. T. A. Ber 25 iii 55 su-ux-xi xu-râçi; something of gold.

suxû. 83, 1—18, 1331 i 29 mu-u MU su-xu-u.

saxxu. V 55, 19 not could be had mê sax-xu u p(b)u-ut-tu-qu maš-qu-u. Haupt in Toy, *Ezekiel*, (SBOT) 68: pit, well (= בּוֹר), *cf* שׁוּחָה. *s* for *š* as in xursaniš, *etc.*; also *cf* mê šaxâtu H 114, 14 where šaxâtu is perh *pl* of שַׁחַת. The ח of the verbal stem of secondary development.

sixb(p)u part of the narkabtu. T. A. Ber 26 i 2: 1 narkabtu ...... si-ix-bi-šu gap-pa (√חפף?).

saxaxu. ZA iii 314, 69 as-xu-xa-am-ma *var* as-su-xa-a-am-ma. Nabd *Ann* i 5 is-xu-xu-ma ul iš-ši (or -lim?, er fand kein Gelingen, KB iii, 2, 128). Perh V 40 *c-d* 11 TE = sa-xa-xum (or -lum?), but see ZA iv 276.

saxalu 1. pr isxul, ps isaxal. pierce, transfix {durchbohren} I 7 *no* ix B 3 with the javelin in my hand as-xul zu-mur-šu (*i. e.* of the lion); T^M v 32 kîma sixlu (wr. U-ZAG-XI-LI-ŠAR, see *ibid*, *p* 140) li-is-xu-lu-ši. Sarg *Ann* 139 libba-šu is-xu-ul, he committed suicide. Sm *Asurb* 135, 56 ina paṭri parzilli šib-bi-šu is-xu-la ka-ra-as-su (KB ii 256—7). K 577, 9—10 si-ix-lu šu-u ištu bi-it i-sa-xal-an-ni-ni since that thorn had pierced me (Hr^L 203).

ℶ ‖ Q IV^2 60* C *R* 8 pa-ru-uš-šu u-sax-xi-il-an-ni (a staff has pierced me) zi-qa-ta dan-nat; V 47 *b* 1 $^{(iç)}$ pa-ru-uš-šu u-sax-xi-la-an-ni zi-qa-tum dan-nat. V 45 vii 10 tu-sax-xal. ℵ^2 K 577, 12 is-sa-ax-lu (Hr^L 203).

— **Der.**:

sixlu point; thorn {Spitze; Stachel, Dorn} or the like. *del* 255 (285) šam-mu ša ...... si-xi-il-šu kîma a-xa(u)r-t(ṭ, d)in-nim-ma u-sa(i)[x-xa-al qât-k]a, KB vi (1) 250—1, sein Dorn wird wie (der) einer 'Dornrebe' deine Hand durchbohren; *cf* 260 (291) šu-u il-qi šam-ma-ma is-x[u-ul qa-ta-šu]. K 4905 *R col* 3, 2 (IV^2 15*) $^{(šam)}$ ZAG-XI-LI-ŠAR = six-lu; see also ZA x 81 *ad* Asb vi 79. Perh K 8727, 4—5 .. SAR = six-lu (?), & = zêr six[-lu?], M^S texts, *p* 14. BA iv 159 read si-xi-il, T^M iii 153, beg.

$^{(šam)}$ **sixlû**. K 4152 *O* 10 $^{(šam)}$ six-lu-u (M^S texts, *p* 6); *cf* IV^2 55 *a* 36; 58 *a* 33; GGA '98, 822.

sixîlu (?) AV 6639. V 22 *h* 5 si-xi-lu; but very doubtful, preceded by bu-ub[-bu-lum?].

suxalziqu (or SU (= mašak) xal-zi-qu, *p* 313 *col* 2; so KB vi, 1, 88—9: Der *Xal-ziqu*-Schlauch). IV^2 31 *R* 18—19. J^W 39 grotto {Loch, Quelle}, but *cf* Jensen, 233 *fol*; Kennedy, JRAS, 1900 Ap., 348 and Jastrow, *Religion*, 572, follow J^W.

suxumu. Rm 2, 24, 10 su-xu-mu, preceded by du-ru-u (8), du-ku-u (6) M^S 71.

suxummu (?) II 29 *c-d* 14 U (*i. e.* ŠI + IB) = su-xu-um-mu, Br 14357; *cf* perh Sarg *Ann* XIV 50 sux-xi-ma-ti. AV 6797.

suxumbi (?) V 28 *c-d* 72 (naxlaptu) su (or SU?)-xu-um-bi = na-ax-lu-up-tum, some kind of dress {eine Art Kleid} AV 6796.

saxmaštu, *pl* saxmašâtu, uprising, rebellion {Aufstand, Empörung} AV 4453, Br 2615 (kitbartu), ZA ii 98; 358. Asb x 11 his country rebelled against him and la-pa-an six-maš-ti ardâni-šu .... ip-par-šid-ma; III 25, 120. IV^2 39 *b* 40 a-bu-bu | imxullu sa-ax-ma-aš-tu te-šu-u | a-šam-šu-tu su-un(*var* um)-qu *etc.* ... lu ka-a-a-an. III 69 *no*, 53 (sax-maš-tu); 56 *no* 3, 34 sax-ma-ša-tum, revolts. II 47 *c-d* 15 sax-maš-tum ‖ šan bar-tum (& see III 66, 95; 62 *a* 7). Rm III 105, 16 see sîxu. Xammurabi-Biling iv 11 mu-še-ib-bi sa-ax-ma-ša-tim (KB iii, 1, 115; Br 11211).

sixûnu (?) Neb 305, 2 TU K si-xu-nu.

saxxanu. Nabd 1067, 5 sa-ax-xa-na.

suxindu. rate {Rate}? AV 6792. T^{C} 4 *d* for *t*, fem. ending. Nabd 228, 4 ina su-xi-in-di; 678, 15; 1047, 6 (-du; WZKM iv 120); 1048, 1 (+11). Camb 34, 3 *foll*: istēn su-xi-in-du 5 mana xurāçi 2 su-xi-in-du $1^{5}/_{6}$ mana 6 šiqlu xurāçi. PSBA ix 272, 290 Babyl. for šuxindu.

saxapu. pr is(š)xup (§ 46), *ps* isaxxap. throw down, overthrow {niederwerfen, über den Haufen rennen}. ZDMG 32, 21*foll*, D^{H} 55; 62; D^{Pr} 21; 180. AV 6495; Br 10839 id I. The land(s) *etc.* ki-ma til abūbe aš-xu-up, TP ii 78, iii 76, v 100. Asb iv 61—2 sa-par ilāni rabūti .... is-xu-up-šu-nu-ti; II 67, 13 the Puqudi kīma sa-pa-ri as-xu-up (TP III *Ann* 37); Sams ii 6 (Nairi) kīma sa-pa-ri as-xu-up. Sarg *Ann* 279 kīma] ti-ib me-xi-e as-xup; Sn ii 11 ki-ma imbāri as-xu-up. *Bav* 44 ki-ma im-ba-ri as-xu-up-šu. IV^{2} 50 *col* 3, 47—8; T^{M} ii 150, 161; ZA iv 10, 38; II 67, 15 + 32; Sarg *Ann* 60, 411 see xuxaru, xuxariš (309 *col* 1). TP ii 39 lu iš-xu-up (*var* is-xup)-šu-nu-ti (iii 70 + 74); Šalm, *Mon*, *O* 22; Sarg *Ann* XIV 14; Z^{B} vii 8 (= IV^{2} 19 *a*); NE 60 8; II 67, 27 see melammu (*p* 550); III 15 i 20 pu-lux-ti ilāni rabūti is-xup-šu-nu-ti; also Sn iii 30. K 2675 *R* 24 see xattu (*p* 347 *col* 1); Smith, *Asurb*, 103, 48. Sn ii 43 ra-šub-bat kakkē (il) Ašur is-xu-pu-šu-nu-ti (see also namrir(r)u, Asb i 84; vii 75 *etc.*). Sn *Bav* 38—9) xar-ba-šu taxāzija (wr. AG-ZAB) dan-ni is-xup-šu-nu-ti. I 44, 53; Sn vi 16—7 is-xu-up. TP III *Ann* 4 na-mur-rat (il) Ašur bēli-ja is-xup-šu-nu-ti. V 50 *b* 55 amēlu šu-a-tum ina bīt ram-ni-šu te-šu-u (*cf* IV^{2} 5 *a* 41) is-sa-xap-šu (H 187—88) a *tešū* throws down this man in his own house; *b* 28 (end) is-xu-up[-šu]. H 80, 8 qar-ra-du ša šu-uš-kal-la-šu a-a-bu i-sax-xa-pu; IV^{2} 17 *b* 13 sa-xi-ip (= pm) šu-uš-kal-la-ka pu-xur mātāte (see further, šuškallu). ZA iv 8, 38 çalūla-ka sa-xi-ip mātāte; 46 sax-pat (= pm) *cf* namurratu; II 67, 40. tasaxxapanini Bez., *Catal.*, 1045. S^{c} 2, 8 šu-u | ŠU | sa-xa-pu; H 34, 824. V 36 *a-c* 49 (Br 8737), *d-f* 7 šu-uš | ⟨ | & 16 u-mun = sa-xa-pu.

3 Šalm, *Mon*, ii 72 u-sax-xi-ip he crushed {er zertrat}. TP i 41 see melammu; iii 4 *b* me-lam qar-du-ti-ja u-si-xi-ip-šu-nu-ti. IV^{2} 21 *no* 1 B *R* 18—19 see namçaru. II 22, 18 see musaxxiptum (567 *col* 1, >< Br 8091). IV^{2} 28 *a* 13—14 the mighty mountains su-ux-xu-pu-šu (break to pieces) before Adad's wrath. Br 8000. IV^{2} 30* *no* 3 *O* 12 Elu lim-nu ša amēlu ki-ma al-lu-xap-pi u-sa(IV *R* -ra)-xa-pu at-ta, *Rev. Sém.*, vi 148 *fol.* V 45 vii 11 tu-sax-xap.

Derr. isxappu (??), nasxapu, nisxiptu & these 2:

sixpu *1.* prostration; dejection {Niedergeschlagenheit} V 19 *a-b* 50 ..... DA = six-pu, between ki-im-ru & kib-su. AV 6495 (saxpu). Smith, *Asurb*, 285, 7 si-xi-ip māti. L^{4} ii 20, but doubtful.

sixpu *2.* ZA iv 11, 41 kal si-xi-ip dadmē all the overthrowers of habitations (?). But see K 3182 i 20.

NOTE. — V 22 *h* 51 we have perh si-xi-ip[-tum?] preceded by bu-ub[-bu-lum], both same id.

sixpu *3.* II 45 *e-f* 56 GIŠ-BAR-XUR = si-ix-pi a wood {ein Holz}? AV 6645; Br 1935. *Cf* kiškanū (450 *col* 1).

sixipū. V 36 *f* 39 si-xi-pu-u; § 65; 38 *rm.*

saxaru, pr isxur, *ps* isaxxar; pm sa-xi-ir (Pognon, *Wadi-Brissa*, 86; 108) § 101; AV 6194, 6497. — *a*) turn, turn around {wenden, sich wenden}. KB iv 82, 18 kirū is-xu-ur(-ma). II 65 *O* ii 7 ina ki-rib-šu im-xaç is-xur-ma [ana mātišu itūr], turned and went back to his own country. Sarg *Khors* 123 the Elamite king šu-u a-na ri-çu-ti is-xur-ma (he came to his assistance); 130, ša i-da-a-šu is-xu-ru il-li-ku ri-çu-us-su. Sn iv 40 šar (māt) Elamti ša idā-šu is-xu-ru-ma (BA i 402). Creat.-*frg* III 17 (75) is-xu-ru-šim-ma ilāni gi-mir-šu-nu. II 57 *c*(-*d*) 61 name of Ninib in Elam: il a-bu-ub la KIL-KIL (= NIGIN), Jensen, 462 (sāxiri). V 35, 10 sa-ax-ra a-na napxar dadmē (had gone about?). K 625, 14 (Hr^{L} 131) sa-xi-ir di-na-aš-šu-nu; 15, u-sa-xi-ir a-ta-na-aš-šu-nu; *R* 5 when the king i-sa-xu-ru-ni (returns), Winckler, *Forschungen*, ii (2) 304—5. KB ii 248 v 12 enā-šu is-xur (*var* xi-ir?) his eyes were rolling {seine Augen verdrehten sich} WINCKLER, *Forsch*, i 252. H 75 *R* 1 a-na-ku .... as-xur-ka eš-e-k[a], I turned to thee, I beseeched thee (Z^B 14; 22). IV^2 60 *O* 34 ... šar šame-e u erçi-tim eš-'e-ka as-xur-ka; *R* 19 as-x]ur-ku-nu-ši a-še-'e-ku-nu-ši (Z^B 105). — *b*) turn to in mercy, assist (‖ tāru, salamu) {sich in Gnaden, hilfreich zuwenden} V 21 *a-b* 58 sa-xa-ru ‖ i-te-'e-lu-u, be merciful. Rm^2 139, 12 $^{(il)}$ Ninib sa-xi-ir-šu. III 66 *c* 17 ilat sa-xi-ir-tu (Br 12314). On LIB NIGIN = libbu saxir, suxxuru see KNUDTZON, 51. — *c*) surround {umschliessen}. Neb ix 34, 35 me-lam-me šar-ru-ti | i-ta-ti-šu sa-ax-ra-a-ma (= pm). KB vi (1) 100, 18 li]t-bi-ma si-im-mu mur-çu lis-xur. IV^2 49 *b* 6 ... u-ni is-xu-ru-ni u-ša-as-xi-ru-ni. V 64 a 25 Ummanmanda sa-xi-ir-šum-ma (surrounds it). Sn i 6 Senn. sa-xi-ru dam-qa-a-ti (*Bell*, 2), G § 112, end; HEBR. vii 57, AV 6500. II 41 *c-d* 9 U-KI = ri-tu sa-xa-rum preceded by ri-tu šu-te-'u-u, Br 6084. — *d*) Nabd 668, 18—19 aš-šu ma-ti-ma la sa-xa-ri-im-ma a-na eli amēlūtu šu-a-tu (annul {umwenden, rückgängig machen}).

Q^t issaxur (> istaxxur) turn {sich wenden}, issaxrā, issaxrūni, is(s)ux-ra. *Etana* (KB vi, 1, 108) 54 še-rit-ka i-si(a)x-xu-ra a-na mux-xi-ja they would turn against me (>< BA iii 366—7). — *a*) return, come back {um-, zurückkehren} Rm 2, 197 *ad* 709 šarru ultu Bābili is-su-ux-ra returned from Babylon. DT 59 *O* 12 e tas-sax-ri a-na çib-ti-ki. Anp iii 31 (45) ina gi(r)-ri-ja-ma a-su-ux-ra, I returned. *del* 141, 143, 146 (149, 152, 155) the dove, the swallow is-sax-ra (returned), the raven ul is-sax-ra (§ 152). IV^2 5 *c* 77—8 the evil demons .... a-a is-sax-ru-u-ni shall not turn (Br 10339). 83—1—18, 236 *R* 2 i-da-a-ti ina $^{(arax)}$ Simāni i-sa-xu-ur; 81—2—4, 79 *R* 2 Mars is-su-ux-ur, has turned (THOMPSON, *Reports*). K 5464 (Hr^L 198) 27 i-su-ux-ra, *R* 21 is-su-xar. K 113, 11 i-sa-xu-ru-ni (Hr^L 183). PSBA xvii 230 *foll*; JAOS xx 280—1. — *b*) surround; befall {umschliessen, befallen}. KNUDTZON, *no* 147, 2—3 muruç ..... is-sax-raš-šum-ma (+ 9; & *p* 265). KB i 214—15 *ad* II 69 *frg*, 4 is-su-ux-ra ēkallāti u ..... TA (Ber) 9, 16 a(?)-sa-ax-xu-ur. — *c*) turn to in mercy, be merciful, gracious {sich in Gnaden zuwenden, gnädig sein}. TP viii 24 Anu & Adad kēniš li-sax-ru-ni-ma, BA i 440—1.

Q^{tn} turn hither & thither, to and fro, roam about {sich hin u. her wenden, sich umhertreiben}. IV^2 16 *a* 45 the demon ša ina a-xa-a-ti is-sa-na-ax-xu-ru (= NIGIN-E, § 98 *ps*) Br 10339. IV^2 30* *b* 15—16, 17—18 see nazazu, Q^{tn}; T^M iii 5; RS vi 140 *fol*. KB vi 48, 26 [i]-la-a-ti is-sa-na[-ax-xa-]ru a-na ṭe[-me-šu] the goddesses turn at thy command. SCHEIL, ZA x 292, 19 ra-bu-tum $^{(il)}$ Igigi is-sa-na-xu-ru. — T^M ii 190 a-na la ṭa-ab-ti ta-as-sa-na-ax[-xar-in-ni], zum Unheil hast du mich betört. In astronomical texts we have: when ^{kakkab} LU-BAD is-sa-na-ax-xur, III 54 *c* 30.

ℨ turn {wenden} V 47 *b* 42 (end) u-sax-xar. *a*) turn away {sich abwenden} H 115 *R* 7—8 a-di ma-ti be-el-ti su-ux-xu-ru (NIGIN-NA, Br 10339, *pm*) pa-nu-ki, how long o lady will thy face be turned away? (= IV^2 29** *no* 5). IV^2 51 *a* 21 u-sax-xi-ru, preceded by u?]-da-a-çu. Creat.-*frg* IV 108 the gods u-sax-xi-ru(-ra) ar(*var* al-)kat-su-un, turned to flight (KB vi, 1, 28—9). K 8466, 10 (end) sux-xu-rat ar-kat-su. K 613 *R* 8—9 ištu pa-an me-xi-ri-šu | la u-sa-ax-ra (Hr^L 85); *cf* K 567, 10 (u-sa-xi-ra-an-ni); K 582, 22 (u-sa-xi-ir); K 662, 9; K 629, 24 u u-sa-ax-xar (Hr^L 248; 167; 211; 67). IV^2 48 *a* 27 (Marduk) māt-su a-na nakiri-šu u-sax-xar; he will deliver .... over. — *b*) turn to in favor {sich in Gnaden zuwenden} IV 20 *no* 1 *O* 11 sa-li-ma?] ir-ši-ma ki-šad-su u-sax(six?)-xi-ra (Br 10339). TP viii 24 ke-niš li-sax-ru-ni (3 *pl*). V 60 *c* 18 Šamaš sa-li-ma ir-ši-ma | u-sax-xi-ra pa-ni-šu. SCHEIL, *Nabd*, vii 17 *foll* a-na su-ux-xu-ru pa-ni-šu; pa-ni-šu tu-sax-xi-ram-ma. K 143 *O* 16 to my sighing and to my raising of hands (= prayer) sux-xi-ra-ni pa-ni-ku-nu (*cf* L^4 ii 30); perh Šamš i 32 (beg) su]-xur lib-ba-šu (= pm). K 4623 *O* 19 ki-šad-ki su-xi-ir-šum-ma (H 128; Br 3366); and so also supply H 115 *O* 16. 81—2—4, 188, 15 look upon me ki-i su-ux-xu-ra-ki libbi (that through thy turning toward me the heart of thy servant may be strong) § 94; ZA v 66 *fol*; King, *First Steps*, 251. Perhaps V 35, 11 u-sa-ax-xi-ir; ZA iv 236, 6 u-sa-xir; Sarg *Silr* 29 u-sax-xir. 81—7—29, 199, 12 be-ili lu-sa-xi-ra-ni (Hr^L 382; R. F. Harper, AJSL xiv 6—7). K 2852 + K 9662 ii 6 a-na $^{(al)}$ Ub-bu-nu u-sa-xir-ma. — let go: VATh 793, 18 su-xa-ri-e-šu-nu let them go; Bu 88—5—12, 65 *R* + *foll* a-na a-ma-tim u su-xa-ri-e la ta-gi(?)-a (or *noun* here?).

ℑ^{t} perh K 762, 4 at-ta-na-šu us-sa-xi-ir us-si-ri-ba.

Š u-ša-as-xi-ir, Pognon, *Wadi-Brissa*, 119. Neb v 37 two great walls dūr Bābili u-ša-as-xi-ir (1 *sg*), *cf* vi 29, I let surround, enclose Babylon. V 34 *b* 16, 25; I 65 *b* 6; I 52 *no* 3, *b* 7. ZA iii 316, 80 u-ša-as-xi-ra. Neb ix 21 with a great wall šadāniš u-ša-as-xi-ir-šu (I enclosed the palace mountain high); I 66 *c* 40. Esh vi 7 si-el(*var* il)-lu(m) .... u-ša-as-xi-ra (1 *sg*) gi-mir bā-bā-ni. II 67, 81 (end) u-ša-as-xir (ZA v 302 *ad* KB ii 24—5). Lay 39, 19 (u-ša-as-xi-ra), ZA iii 316, 80; K 2711 *R* 18; KB iii (2) 68—9 (*no* 13) i 14—17 see kisū (412, 413). KB iii (2) 78, 27 u-ša-xi-ir probably a mistake for u-ša[-as]-xi-ir (*cf* JAOS xvi 73, 15). Sarg *Khors* 165; *Ann* 428; *Bull*-inscr. 79 u-ša-as-xi-ra (1 *sg*). K 3426, 10 ana] [È]-sagila ša ta-ram-mu šu-us-xi-ra pa-ni-ka (*Rev. Sém.* ii 76). T^M i 92 is-xu-ru-ni u-ša-as-xi-ru-ni.

Š^{t} = Š uš-ta-as-xi-ir, BOR ii 229, 19. § 84, caused to surround, & ultesxir (§ 84*a*). Neb vi 52 ka-a-re a-gu-ur-ri uš-ta-as-xi-ir-šu-nu-tim (*i. e.* the waters of the artificial lake). V 55, 41 ul-te-is-xi-ir limutti, he turned away the evil. I 66 *b* 14 ap-pa-ri-am lu-uš-ta-aš-xi-ir-šu (ZA ii 169 *a* 16); Br. Mus. *no* 12215 (Xammurabi) i 19. K 2606, 19 maxaz $^{(il)}$ Igigi šu-tas-xu-ru (BA iii 399); L^4 iii 11 šu-tas-xu-ru (3 *pl*, pm). IV^2 25 *b* 48—49 mi-lam-me šu-ta-as-xur (= NIGIN, Br 10339) he (the moon-god) is surrounded with splendor (§ 89); 18 *no* 3, *O* i 33—34 the lofty weapon me-lam-me ez-zu-ti šu-tas-xur (= NI-GIN-NA, Br 7020).

𝔑 be turned, turn; of god's wrath: become merciful, have mercy {gewendet werden; von dem Zorne des Gottes: sich wenden, barmherzig werden}. H 115 *O* 11—12 rim-ni-tum ša na-as-xur-ša ṭa-a-bu, merciful one, to whom to turn is good (or, who turnest in favor) = IV^2 29^{**} *no* 5, 12. I 35 *no* 2, 7 ri-me-nu-u ta-a-a-a-ru ša na-aš-xur-šu ṭābu (Br 3366; ZK ii 260), Z^B 22; 102; BA i 181. *Rec. Trav.* xx 205 *fol*, 16 ša-da(?)-at ri-mi-ni-i na-as-xur-šu ṭābu. IV^2 21^* *no* 2 *O* 30—31 lib-bu na-aš-xi-ra (ip) našxira (written 𒐖) liq-qa-bi-sum (Br 6324, 6340) = GE-U-EME-SAL twice in *l* 30 ‖ libbu nu-ux nu-ux. II 21 *d* 30 na-as-xu-ru ša libbi ‖ rēmu, inclination, favor.

𝔑^{t} perhaps T. A. (Ber) 29, 10 and when a-na mux-xi-ka | it-ta-as-xa-ru (they returned to you).

𝔑^{tn} turn to {sich an (zu) jem. wenden}. IV^2 10 *b* 5—6 ana ili-ja rem-ni-i at-ta-na-as-xar (I turn, = NIGIN-NA-AN-ŠI-EB, EMESAL, Br 10339) un-ni-ni a-qab-bi. III 15 i 26 ida-a-a it-ta-na-as-xa-ru, they declared themselves on my side (KB ii 142—3; § 98). Scheil, ZA x 292, 12 (end) u-da-'a-as-si-ma (√da'açu?) it-ta-na-as-xar-ši. NE 74, 22 it-ta-n[a]-as-xar a-na pa-ni (ib-ri-šu) KB vi (1) 198—99: er wendet sich seinem Freunde zu.

Note. — *Rev. Ét. Juives*, xiv 150; ZK i 183 § 6; Z^B 23.

Derr. as-xar[-ru?] *q. v.*, tasxiru & these 13 (?):

saxru, *c. st.* saxar. II 32 *a-b* 18 sa-xar ū-me ‖ lil-la-a-tum evening: the wane of the day {Tageswende}.

saxiru (ā?, ī?). II 21 *c-d* 10 GIŠ-UD-SIR-GAL = sa-xi-rum (Br 7861, AV 6500); KB vi (1) 186 (NE VII) 45 šu-ku (dur)-ki sa-x(s)ir-ki u ša-gam-ma-ki (see *ibid*, 460: wohl ein Bogen), *f* saxirtum (?). K 4574 *O* 7 [s]a-xir-tum (of a bent, or drawn, bow) = qa[-aš-tu] ma-li-tum. Nabd 884, 1. II TAK (= aban) sa-xir-ra-a[-ta?]. II 21 *c-d* 19 UZU-ŠA (= LIB)-NIGIN (or DAN?) = ir-rum sa-xi-ru-ti, Br 14071; BOISSIER, PSBA xxii, 110; KB vi (1) 456.

sâxiru *1.* H 108 ii 16 (D 128, 64) sa-xi-ru, *var* sa-ki-rum; see mi(e)xru, 1 end (*p* 532 *col* 2) Br 6338.

sâxiru *2.* 89—10—14, 224 *O* 1 ištēn-it alpu sa-xir-tum (one young heifer); 8 alpu sa-xir-tum xa-si-il-ti, the heifer weaned (*Rec. Trav.*, xix, 110—111). *Cf* Z^{8} iii 82 mâmit ekimmē sax-xi-ru-ti, Bann durch behende Aufpasser.

sâxiru *3.* *f* saxirtu magician; witch }Zauberer, Zauberin{. T^{M} i 77 (ii 39) sa-xir]-MU (= ja) [u sa]-xir-ti-ja. iii 132 aš-bu ina libbiša sa-xi-ru u sa-xir-tu. Perhaps here also:

saxxiru, ZK ii 302 sax-xi-ru between a-kil (? = [sign]) li-mi and um-ma-nu. M^{8} 71 *col* 2: six-xi-rum (K 12027, 8).

suxarû, *noun*? Bu 88—5—12, 65 *R* 4 *foll* a-na a-ma-tim u su-xa-ri-e la ta-gi-a.

sixru. *c. st.* sixir some jewel, ornament }ein Schmuck{ AV 6646; D^{II} 8 *rm* 2; 36. II 21 *c-d* 9 TAG-ID-ZA-SUX = si-ix[-rum] Br 6641; *cf* šubû. IV^{2} 50 *b* 43 o witch ki-ma si-xir (aban) kunukki an-ni-e | li-çu-du (*cf* çâdu & BA ii 297 *rm* 1) li-ri-qu pa-nu-u-ki. Perhaps also V 44 *c-d* 34 AN (?) ..... A-EDIN (*cf* II 56 *c* 59) = si-xir (?) ilat Çar-pa-ni-tum (ZA i 265).

sixru turn, turning }Wendung{ L^{4} i 23 ki-ma as-sa-ri u-ša-as-xar si-xi-ir ma-gar (or ša?)-ri. LEHMANN, ii 22.

sixirtu, *c. st.* sixrat (§§ 37 *a*; 65, 4 & 6 *rm*). — *a*) surrounding wall, enceinte of a city or palace *etc.* }Umfassungsmauer, Ringmauer einer Stadt oder eines Palastes{, but see JENSEN, ZA xiv 183. TP vi 12 their 3 great brick walls and si-xir-ti âli-šu I destroyed. Sn iii 3 (i 50) di-mâte si-xir-ti âli; Sn *Kui* 4, 32. AV 6638 *ad* Anp i 94; AV 6640. Esh vi 3 si-xir (*var* xi-ir)-ti êkalli šâtu. V 65 *b* 30 ilâni-ja u ilâni si-xi-ir-ti bîti, perh. belong to: — *b*) surrounding territory, circuit, extent, totality }Umgebung, Umfang, Ausdehnung, Gesammtheit{ TP i 92 the country a-na si-xir-ti-ša (in its totality), ii 56, iv 22, v 70, vi 37 (*var* a-na paṭ gim-ri-ša, see also Asb ix 45); ZA iii 315, 75; K 2852 + K 9662 iii 16; 83 —1—18, 215 *R* 5; Asb iii 35; v 40; x 75 Sarg *Ann* 188, *Khors* 17, 82; II 67, 15 + 22 (-šu); Esh ii 40 a-na si-xi-ir-ti-ša. Sarg *Ann* 7 + 340 si-xi-ir-ti mâti. TP III *Ann* 128 alâni ša si-xir-ti-šu (+ 129): and its neighboring towns. II 67, 25 the countries a-na si-xir-ti-šu-nu; Sn vi 34 that palace a-na si-xir-ti-ša I tore down; I 44, 59; III 16 v 9; Esh v 5 (xi-ir). I 28 *b* 12 the great city-wall a-na si-xir-ti-šu I rebuilt. KB iii (2) 48 *col* 2, 53 i-ga-ar si-xi-ir-ti E-ŠIT-LAM. III 29 *no* 2, 12 the country ina si-xir-ti-ša i-be-el. IV^{2} 34 *O* 1 Sin ana sixir-ti-šu çi-lil. Sn i 31 si-xir-ti um-ma-a-ni mala bašû. A | is perhaps:

sixxirtu, *c. st.* sixxirat. II 21 *c-d* 16—18 six-xi-rat (= NIGIN) du-ri (Br 4386, 10341), âli (Br 917), u-ga-ri (Br 4393), extent }Umfang{.

suxxurtu repulse, overthrow, flight }Zurückwerfung des Feindes, Flucht{. Sn v 66, sux-xur-ta-šu-nu aš-kun I brought about their overthrow (§ 88, note; HEBR. vii 68).

su-xur. S^{b} 359 su-xur = kim-ma-tu (properly: enclosure) perh. √סחר.

suxûru name of a constellation: goatfish, *i. e.* capricorn of the zodiac }Ziegenfisch; Steinbock{ JENSEN, 73 *foll*, 83, 277, 313 *fol.* KB iii (1) 62 *rm* °, 144—5 *ad* V 33 v 1; but see, on the other hand, DELITZSCH, *Weltschöpfungsepos*, 127 *rm* 1; also *cf* ZIMMERN, *Ritualtafeln*, *no* 50 ii 8 (end) & *rm* *b*.

suxru, suxur. K 4152 *R* 3 su(?)-xu-ur a-ga-lim (M^{8} 71 *col* 1), but better ti-ri-ku a-ga-lim (DELITZSCH).

suxarru (?) III 56 *a* 20 KI-GAR su-xar (mur, xur?)-ri niššē ibašši; 27, su-xar-ri niššē ibašši KI-GAR.

s(ç)i(a)xxar(r)u. a vessel }ein Gefäss{. AV 6501. II 21 *c-d* 11 (karpat) BUR-ZI-ṬU-NA = sax-xa-ru [...] (Br 6977); II 44 *e-f* 52 (karpat) BUR [...] Z]I-TUR = sax-xar-ru | kal-kal-l[...]-u. Neb 457, 14: 2 (karpat) sax-xa-rû [...] ZIMMERN, Ri-

tuallafeln, 26 vi 28 s]ix-xar-ri; 66 *O* 21 (karpat) si-xa-ru ša dišpi; 68 *O* 24 (25) (karpat) six-xa-ru.

sixarrû (?). II 6 *c-d* 34 ŠAX si-x(m)a(u)r-ra = ŠU-u (*i. e.* sixarrû) some wild animal {ein wildes Tier} AV 6657, 6696; Br 3456. ZA xv 236. Perhaps connected with:

suxîru *m* the young of an animal {das Junge eines Tieres}. Asb ix 65 ba-ak-ru su-xi-ru b(p)ûru kirru (JENSEN, KB ii 227: Eselsfüllen); Sm 276, 40. P. N. Su-xi-ru III 48 *a* 29 (KB iv 100); K 326, 26.

su-xur-du-u II 37, 64 see surdû.

saxašu. II 29 ii 35 ŠU-XA-LU (= DIB)-BA = sa-xa-šum between ba-a-ru & e-še(?)-šum, AV 6498, Br 7245.

sixšu. II 28 *b-c* 49 (Br 8387); 33 *c-d* 74 IM-NU-GAL-LA = si-ix-šu (AV 6647), followed by si-xi-tu (50; 75) & çir-ri-tu.

suxuššu II 23 *a-b* 28 pa-aš-šur tak-ni-e ‖ paššur su-xuš(ruš?)-ši. ZA xii 410.

(elip) **s(š)ax-xi-tum** D 88 v 10 (II 48 *c-d* 10) = GIŠ-MA'-ŠA (= LIB)-XA.

sixîtu see sixšu. √sixû, 1, & KB vi (1) 335.

suxatu (?) K 4159, 8 su-xa-tum, preceded by i-si. T. A. (Ber) 26 i 9: 2 ša su-u-xa-ta-a-tí xurâçi kaspu uxxuzu.

saṭâdi see sa-da-a-ti.

sâku (סוך) anoint {salben} ZIMMERN, *Ritualtafeln*, 26 i 24 (ii 7) i-su-ak.

saku. K 8515 (BEZOLD, *Catal*, 933) za-nin sa-ki-šu ri-ē-a-um ma-ti-šu. M^8 71: who adorns his *s*, the shepherd of his land; *cf* III 66 *R* 20*e*; III 68 *col* 10, 20 (sa-ka) see PSBA xxi 129—30.

sakku *1. adj*, properly: stopped, closed; deaf {eigentlich verstopft: dann taub}; in connection with sak-la *etc.* also used of mental depravity. (√סכך). occurs mostly in deprecations, curses. I 70 ii 21 or who orders ..... sak-la sak-ka sa-ma-a, a fool, a deaf or a blind and has this memorial stone removed; thus also: III 41 *b* 9 sak-la sak-ka nu-'-a; III 43 i 31 sak-la sak-ka sa-ma-a; KB iv 58—60 iii 6 lu sak-lam lu suk-ku-ka lu sa-ma-a. V 56, 34 lu sak-la lu sak-ka lu sa-ma-a. IV² 38 *iii 11* lu sak-la lu [sak-ka?] lu la ši[*mû*]. Merod.-Balad. stone v 25—6 whosoever sends sak-ku sak-lu la še-ma-a, *etc.* KB iii (1) 162 *col* v 41 (amêl) sa-ak-la sa-ak-ka la mu-da-a. Perh. ZA iii 316, 77 sak-ki (or pint?). S^c 6, 4 BE | e-dim-mu | sak-lu, sak-ku, suk-ku-ku, BA ii 139.

sakku *2.* L^4 i 18 ka-ak-ku sa-ak-ku b(p)al-lu. II 23 *a* 29 KA (iç) sa-ak-ku (?).

sakû in P. N. (amêl) Sa-ka-a-ilu, III 47 *c* 11. Lay 98 *no* 3 a-lap (nâr) Sa-ki-e-ja, HOMMEL, *Gesch*, 602; SCHEIL, *Šulm*, 91: hippopotamus, ZA viii 212—3.

sakkû enclosure {Einschliessung, Umfassung} S^P 158 + S^P II 962 *O* 14 šup-ri-sa-a (√parasu) sak-ki-e-šu, cause its enclosure to be cut through ‖ suxxâ' uçurtašu; *R* 29 (end) šu-xur-ru-ur sak-ki-e-šu.

sak-ki-u & **sak-ki-lum** ‖ ku-ub-šu, see ט.

sik-ku NE 51, 14 (KB vi 1, 272—3) see šikku.

sikû (?) ZA v 68, 15 a-di ma-ti bêltu murçu la na-par-ku-u xal-qu si-ki-ja (is destroying my members??).

sukku, *pl* sukkê. — *a*) dam, river-bank {Damm, Uferwand} properly: defense {Abwehr}. D^{Pr} 195; § 25; AV 6808. I 52 *no* 4 *R* 4 of asphalt & brick ab-na-a su-uk-ki-ša, I constructed its (the canal's) dams, ZA ii 128 *a* 27. Ner ii 7—9 the East-canal, which a former king had built, but la ib-na-a su-uk-ki-šu, this I dug out again i-na ku-up-ri u a-gur-ri ab-na-a su-uk-ki-šu. — *b*) an enclosed, separated room within a temple; a shrine, dwelling of a god {ein abgeschlossener Raum innerhalb eines Tempels, Göttergemach, Stätte einer Gottheit}. HOMMEL, HASTINGS, *Dictionary*, i 216 *col* 2. Sarg *Khors* 157 ešš-re-ti nam-ra-a-ti suk-ke nak-lu-ti (= *Ann* 417); *Cyl* 54 i-na suk DIM-GAL-KALAM-MA (KB ii 46—7), in the sanctuary of. Z^3 iii 69 ma-mit suk-ku u p[a-an-p]a-a-nu. III 66 *col* 9, 38 su-uk-ku, followed by ni-me-du, parakku, *etc.* (PSBA xxi 126—7; BA i 282). S^c 80 du-u (S^b 1, 9*a*) | DUL su-uk-ku ‖ šub-tu, du-u (ZK i 17 *rm* 5; JENSEN, 234); thus perhaps V 65 *a* 37, 39 DUL-MEŠ = sukkê; Br 9587. Perh. also S^c 5 *b* 8 su-uk[-ku] Br 2985. II 33 *a-b* 64, + 28 *a* 41 SUG = suk-ku (see dū, *p* 235; Br 10306); II 35 *a-b* 14, 15 suk-ku & pa-an-pa-an = pa-rak-ku.

sikdum (AV 6658) see sigdum & sīqtum (sīqu).

(sam) **suk-ki-di,** Br 13488 *ad* II 43 *e* 61 (but??).

sakaku in *ac* sa-kak uz-na deafness {Taubheit} Merodach-Balad.-stone v 38 (KB iii, 1, 192—3). PSBA x 291 compares سَكَّ close, stop; fasten a door. ℑ pm IV^2 10 *b* 29—30 amēlūtu su-ku-ka-at (= U-XUB-A-AN).

Derr. sakku, 1, sakkū, sukku, sikkatu & these 4:

sukkuku; *cf* sakku & II 39 *e-f* 22 *foll* GIŠ-KU-ŠI = xa-as-su; GIŠ(?)[-KU?]-PI-LAL = ṭu-um-mu-mu; .... ŠU = a-mi-ru; ..... A = pi-xu[-u?]; [U?]-NER = suk-ku-ku. BA ii 139. V 40 *e-f* 9—10 U-X[UB?] u U-NER (Br 14167, 6073) = su-uk-ku-ku (11, = pi-xu-u ša mār abkalli); Rm 79, 7—8 gal-lu-u suk-ku-ku (= GIŠ-KU-PI-LAL) i-b[ak]-ki. V 47 *a* 23, *b* 9 xa-šik-ku = suk-ku-ku. Rm 3, 105 ii 2 zamanū limnūti su-ku-ku-u-ti la šēmi'a, the evil, deaf spirits that do not listen to me.

sukkukūtu deafness; stupidity {Taubheit; Stumpfsinn} V 23 *b-d* 24 suk-ku-ku-tum one of the equivalents of TUR-TUR (Br 4111; AV 3017).

sakikē, *pl* mud, properly closing up {Schlamm, eigtl. Verstopfung}. V 56, 42; III 42 iv 4 see malū ℑ, *p* 541 *col* 2. I 52 *no* 4 *O* 18 the eastcanal of *B*, which had gone to ruin for many days and ši-ix-xa-at epirē is-sa(-an)-nu-u-ma im-lu-u sa-ki-ki.

sakikku. IV^2 60* C *R* 10 sa-kik-ke-ja iš-xu-ṭu (amēl) mašmašu ‖ u te-ri-ti-ja (amēl) bārū u-taš-ši. 83—1—18, 2 (Hr^L 391) 12 sa-kik-ki-e-šu la u-ša-ax-ki-me (HARPER: AJSL xv 139 perh.: = murçu, constipation?). See also KB vi (1) 389 √SA-GIG.

sakalu. K 40 (D 81) ii 63, 64 SA-GE-A (Br 3135) = sa-ka-lu; ŠU-KAT = *s* ša zi-bi (Br 7099), be foolish {töricht sein} or: a fool? {Tor?} AV 6508. WINCKLER, *Sargon* (text, *p* 26 *no* 55, 14) is-ki-lu madattu they refused (?) tribute. ℑ V 16 *c-d* 50 SAG-NAM-NU-SI = suk-ku-lu; AV 3018, Br 3550. Derr.:

saklu perhaps: stupid; fool {vielleicht: töricht; Tor} often in connection with sakku (*q. v.*). III 61 *b* 20 liššānu sa-kil-ti mātu ibēl (GGA '98, 822); IV 33 *a* 39 nišē sak-la-a-ti foolish people {dumme Leute} KB iii (1) 137. ZA iv 12, 55 sak-la-a-ti ša li-ša-na da-bi-bu (foolish things). S^c 6, 4 BE = sak-lu; K 168, 40 (amēl) sa-ak-lu. S. A. SMITH, ZA iii 100; BROWN-GESENIUS, 698; BA ii 139.

sakiltu foolish actions {Torheiten} *pl* sak-la-tu-u-a ‖ limnētūja (6) CRAIG, *Rel. Texts*, 7, 7. ZIM., *Ritualtafeln*, 26 iii 7.

sikiltu. K 40 (D 81) ii 70—72 BAR-ŠU-GAL; ŠU-BAR-ŠU-GAL; .... ŠU-GAL = si-ki-il-tum (ZA iii 100; AV 6650; Br 1927, 7112; BOR i 125. V 44 *c-d* 47 (amēl) BAR-ŠU-GAL-AN-UD-KA-DE = si-kil-ti-Adad, name of an ancient Babylonian ruler. PINCHES, PSBA xvi 226: servant.

(GIŠ)-SAK(G)-K(G)UL see sikkūru.

suklum (or zuqlum?) *f* some measure of length {ein Längenmass} perh. id SUK-LUM. AV 6809. Bu 88—5—12, 75 + 76 vi 37 ina (iç) suk-lum rabī-ti mišix-tašu amšux. Sn *Kui* 4, 1 *fol*; *Bell* 50 *fol*; *Rass* 77 ina suk-lum rabīti sak-ki (ZA iii 316). D 86 (K 4378) i 1 GIŠ-SUK-LUM = ŠU-lum (II 45, 5, Br 10315). On suklum rabīti see JOHNS, *Expositor*, 1901, March, *pp* 216—7.

sak-kul-lu (?). II 45 *no* 4, 51 GIŠ-ŠA(= LIB)-DAN = sak-kul-lu (II 18, 52; AV 6515) a wood? {ein Holz?}.

III si-kal-li-tum, Nabd 258, 35 an instrument, implement {Gerät}. TALLQVIST, *Schenkungsbriefe*, 11, 12.

s(š)uk(k)allu, *m* ambassador, messenger, supervisor {Bevollmächtigter, Botschafter, Aufseher}. id LUX, S^b 77 šu-uk-kal | LUX | suk-kal-lum, *var* lu-ux | LUX | su-kal-lu, § 9, 161; see also S^a III 13—14 (same id = pāšišu, he that anoints); H 23, 455, 456. Used mostly of gods. *Nebo* su-uk-ka-al-lam çi-i-ri, Neb *Bors* ii 16 (KB iii, 2, 46, 11); FLEMMING, *Neb*, 45 *ad* Neb iv 18; I 70 iv 16 su-kal-lu çi-i-ri; III 41 *b* 34 sukkallu çi-ru; 43 *d* 1 su-kal-lu çi-ru (BA ii 143). IV^2 14 *no* 3 *a* 1—2 to Nebo suk-kal-li çi-i-ri (= LUX-MAX). *Bunčne*: V 65 *b* 82 su(?)-kal-la-ku (*var* ka) MAX (*var* çi-i-ri) who stands before thee. K 5201 *O* 17—18 LUX-MAX-A-AN = suk-kal-lum çi-ru (H 182, XIII). Asb ix 86 Nusku sukkallu na'idu; II 19 *a* 56—7 Nusku suk-kal-lu. IV[2] 5 *b* 36—7 be-lum ana suk-kal-li-šu (LUX-A-NI) (il) Nusku i-šes-si (H 76, 5—6) + 38—39; see also II 31 *d* 36—7. ZK ii 301 we have ša suk-kal-li preceded by ša pa-an [man-zaz] & followed by ša ar-kat ..... Sp III 586 + R III, 1, 8: [il] Mi-ša-rum su-uk-kal-lum, Hommel, *Sum. Les.*, 120 *fol.* *Cf* also Creat.-*frg* III 2, 3. T. A. (Ber) 240 *O* 8 (KB vi 94) Anu [a-na š]u-uk-ka-li-šu (il) I-la-ab-ra-at i-ša-a[s]-si; 10 šu-uk-ka-la-šu; (Lo) 82, 7 nam-ta-a-ra šu-uk-k[a-l]a-[š]a (KB vi, 1, 74 *no* 1); (Lo) 9, 46 [amēl] LUX (= sukkal)-li. The sukkallu *par excellence* was Papsukal: AN-PAP-LUX, III 68 *c* 64 gloss pa-ap-su-kal to AN-PAP-LUX-LUX. He was su-kal-li ilāni rabûti III 43 *d* 25, the messenger of the great gods. IV[2] 31 *R* 1 (*cf l* 30 of Namtāru); 33 *col* iv (end) 10. month Ṭebet ša [il] Pap-sukal sukallu [il] A-nim u [ilat] Ištar. III 66 *col* 8, 30 (il) Pap-su-kal ša al Bīt (il) NIN, *col* 7, 32 (ilat) Ištar pap-su-kal ša Sûti (PSBA xxi, 124—7); also *cf* II 59 *R* 23; JRAS '91, 401, 3; *Trans. of Vict. Inst.* xxviii 19. V 61 vi 20—1, Ibasilu is called (amēl) sukallu, BA i 291. KB iv 256, 7 + 25 (amēl) sukallu, ZA xi 260 *foll*, § 12 perhaps: Gerichtspräsident. The Babylonian surgeon (asû) calls himself the sukkallu (il) zuqaqīpu, the superintendent of the divine scarifying scorpion (BA iv 220 *foll*; AJP xxi 105). II 34 *no* 3 *g-h* 31 mu-šar-bi-du ‖ su-kal-lu. K 4567, 11 LA-BAR = suk-kal-lum (KB vi, 1, 462) 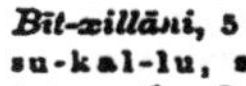 Br 993; 12 see Br 10307; 13 .....BI-IR (AV 8438, Br 14298); see also M[S] 71 *col* 2. Against Meissner & Rost, *Bīt-xillāni*, 5 *rm* ** on Ḳ 1014 *O* 1—2 bīt su-kal-lu, see these authors in BA iii 212 *rm* *. Cyr 128, 15 (amēl) suk-kal-tum. — Jensen, ZA xi 293 *foll*; Halévy, *Rech. crit.*, 33; 253; D[Pr] 111; Muss-Arnolt, *Assyrio-Babyl. Months*, 34, 35. AV 6803; Br 6158 *foll*, 6170.

sakanu care for, help (with ana) {für jemanden sorgen, helfen} T. A. Zimmern, ZA vi 248 *rm* 9, Hebr סכן. T. A. Ber 102, 34 u li-i]s-ki-en šarru a-na māti-šu; 38, u li-is-kin; 103, 13—17; 87, 8 danniš a-di ti-is-k[i-in?]; Lo 28, 52 u ja-nu a-ja-ka-mi ni-is-kan mītu.

(amēl) **sukīnu**. Knudtzon, 48 left edge 2: (amēl) su-ki-nu. *Cf* T. A. (Lo) 64, 9 pa-ni (amēl) ra-bi-çi ‖ zu-ki-ni šarri bēlišu (= סֹכֵן) before the officer his lord the king.

sik-ka-nu. D 89 vi 66 (Br 2357, AV 6659) see sikkatu.

siknat AV 6662 *cf* šikittu, šiknat.

si-ki-nu-nu Neb 299, 2,

sakapu (rarely šakapu) pr is-kip (Pognon, *Wadi-Brissa*, 175), ps isakip. AV 6507; KB vi (1) 306 = Hebr-Arm שׂכב. — *a*) *trans*: cast down, overthrow, upset {stürzen, umstürzen}. V 33 viii 44 (may Ašur & Bēlit) ezziš | [li]s-ki-pu-šu-ma overthrow him by force. Sn vi 73 Ašur lis-ki-pa palā-šu; *Bav* 60 (-pu); DT 71 *R* 9 pala-a-šu tas-kip his rule overthrow! (Winckler, *Forsch*, i 541); KB ii 246—7, 69 pale-e šarrū-ti-šu iš-ki-pu (see also Rost, 119). K 2867, 10 šarru-us-su iš-ki-pu ‖ palāšu ēkimū (S. A. Smith, *Asurb*, ii 1 *fol*); TP viii 77 šarrū-su lis-ki-pu, may they overthrow his kingdom. ZA ii 318, 9 = KB i 4 *no* 5 šarru-su li-is-ki-ip. Sarg *Ann* 459 lis-kip šumu-šu. IV[2] 10 *b* 35—6 o mistress arda-ka la ta-sa-kip (Z[B] 73; Br 3365). Often in colophons: IV[2] 20 *no* 2 *R* 28 (57 *b* 68) the gods ag-giš iz-zi-iš lis-ki-pu-šu-ma; also 58 *c* 44; 19 *b* 32 lis-kip-u-šu-ma (49 *b* 66; 50 *c* 38; V 51 *d* 70); IV[2] 6 *a* 55 lis-ki-pu-šu-u-ma (56 *a* 54) § 53 *d*. *cf* T[M] i 156; iv 143 *etc*. IV[2] 57 *a* 68 arrat limut-tim ana a-xi-ti li-is-kip. P. N. Našxu-sa-kap, PSBA xxi 285. Of enemies: defeat {besiegen}. I 69 *a* 14 a-na ..... sa-ka-pu (amēl) nakirē-ja (*b* 17, *c* 48 sa-kap *etc.*); III 15 *a* 16 sa-kap za-'-i-re-ja (*cf* R. F. Harper, *Diss*); KB iii (1) 196, 24 a-na .... sa-kap (amēl) nakirē. II 43 *a-b* 4 sa-kap KUR (= nakri) ‖ šu-šur-tum; II 64, 25 P. N. Nabû-sa-kip, AV 5837;

V 54, 48 (K 613 *O* 11); II 10 *b* 18 sa-kip (Br 6537) ta-xa-zi ez-zi; V 60 ii 26 sa-kip (amêl) nakiru lim-nu. Neb v 46—7 name of a gate in Babylon: Nanâ-sa-ki-pa-at-te-e-bi-ša; also *cf* P. N. Ištar-sa-ki-pat-te-e-bi-šu, Pognon, *Wadi-Brissa*, 77 *fol* (= Istar throws down his aggressors). — *b*) *intr* lie down, rest {sich niederlegen, ruhen} V 17 *c-d* 9—10 ZAG-SAG = sa-ka-pu (8, si-'-u) Br 6501; [KU]$^{ku-ku}$KU = sakapu ša ça-la-li, *i. e.*, *s* in the meaning of çalalu (Br 10646) AV 6507. *Etana*-legend (KB vi, 1, 110 *no* III *a* 7) a[-xi]-ir (*var* -xir) a-sa-kip. BA ii 395—6 refers this to *a*). Creat.-*frg* III 20 (78) ez-zu (they are full of wrath), kap-du la sa-ki-pu, they plan without resting (night and day). ℑ = 𝔔 *a*). Perh IV² 18* *no* 6, 21—22 su-kip-ma. Derr. the following:

sikpu, *c. st.* sikip. K 4525 *R* 8 (amêl) ax-la-mu-u ša si-kip-šu-nu ..... (Winckler, *Forsch*, ii 574).

sikiptu overthrow, defeat {Niederwerfung, Niederlage} § 65, 4; Hommel. i 175; AV 6651. Anp i 30 who si-kip-te la ma-gi-re-šu il-ta (*var* tak)-ka-nu, KB i 56—7. Sn *Bav* 36 *fol* si-kip-ti ummânâte-šu-nu aš-kun. K 84 *R* 17—18 (Hr^L 301) si-kip-ti (il) Marduk a-ga-a that smitten one by Marduk. K 1550, 31 si-kip-ti arrat ilâni Nabû-bêl-šumâti; K 1250, 14 si-kip-ti (il) Bêl arrat ilâni *N.*, smitten of Bêl, accursed of the gods (Hr^L 400). K 13, 39 (IV² 45 *b*). II 38 *g-h* 4 'ši'k-pi-e-tu (AV 6663, Br 3321).

sakkapu bolt {Riegel} sa-ak-ka-pu ‖ mi-di-lu (*q. v.*, *p* 516 *col* 1) AV 6513.

sakaru, **se-ki(a)r** see zakaru, zikru and saqaru, seqi(a)r.

sikeru (ZA v 99; §§ 32 γ; 34 β); pr iskir; ps isakir shut up, stop, lock up, dam up, dam (a river or canal) {schliessen, sperren, dämmen, abdämmen} AV 6653; ZK i 113; Nabd-Cyr Chron. ii 9 Babylon is-kir-ma (BA ii 224—5 >< KB iii, 2, 136 is-si-ma). Šalm, *Bal*, iv 5 nâra-šu as-ki-ir (KB i 134—5); Sarg *Ann* XIV 68 askir. IV² 22 *a* 26 i-sik-kir. *Rec. Trav.* xxii (Scheil *no* LIV, 3) te-sik-kir. Neb viii 39 pa-la-ga-šu la e-es-ki-ir his (Marduk's) canals I did not dam up; *cf* Z^Š iii 52 ma-mit palgi tap-pi-e si-ki-ru. Smith, *Asurb*, 128, 97 ina (amêl) pagrê-šu-nu (nâr) U-la-a-a as-ki-ir (KB ii 252—3). II 23 *c-d* 43 si-ke-ru ‖ e-di-lu, sa-na-qu; II 7 [*c*-]*d* 15 si-ki-ru, preceded by zi-ka-r[um]. K 4560, 8 .... A-[sign]-DA = si-ki-ru, AV 8415, a list containing names of workmen & officials; Meissner, 115 *rm*; sa-ki-rum *var* of sa-xi-ru *q.v.*, AV 6509. — ℑ in mu-sa-kir-a-te (*cf* 568 *col* 1). — ℑ^t be stopped, shut up: of ears {gesperrt, verschlossen sein, von Ohren} *etc.* V 47 *b* 9 see xašikku, *p* 345 *col* 2. — 𝔑 KB vi (1) 278 ii (v) 30 is-sa-kir šap-l[iš] below (rain) was shut off *i. e.* a drought came about; 284, 45 li-i]s-sa-kir šapliš; 51, is-sa-[kir] šap-liš.

Derr. these 4:

sakru *1. noun* prison, imprisonment {Gefängniss, Einschliessung}. IV² 31 *R* 28 sak-ru u za-mu-u limxaçu lîtka; but KB vi (1) 403 reads šakru u çamû: der Trunkene u. der Durstige.

sakru *2. adj.* bolted, locked up; in connection with "gold" probably = זָהָב סָגוּר *i. e.* gold shut up and thus rare, fine (Brown-Gesenius, 689 *col* 1); Cheyne, PSBA xxi 246 massive, or solid gold. K 538, 18 + 19: 3 talents of xurâçu sak-ru, 4 talents la-a sak-ru. (Hr^L 114; RP² ii 184). III 46 *no* 5, 23—4: 10 minas kaspu LAX(-u), 1 manê xurâçu sak-ru (48 *no* 5, 17). Sarg *Ann* XIV 42 + 47; *Ann* 47.

sik(k)ûru — *a*) stop, dam, lock {Sperrung, Versperrung} AV 6655. ZA ii 108; ZDMG 29, 80; § 65, 29. V 39 *a-b* 9 KA-GIG (Br 1394) = si-kur pi-i (lock jaw?); also *cf* names of plants II 41 *no* 10 (K 4418) *a-b* 54, 55 (šam) si-kur-rat eqli, (šam) si-kur eq-li ‖ (šam) pu-qut-tu (63) >< Br 12353. — *b*) lock, bolt of a door {Türverschluss, Riegel} H 94—5, 50 ina sik-kur bîti (= GIŠ-SAG(K)-G(K)UL, § 9, 31), H 30 138. ⊕ 287 *R* 7 GIŠ-KAN-NA = sik-ku-ru; id usually GIŠ-SAG(K)-G(K)UL (Br 3545) T^M vii 10; IV² 31 *O* 11 eli dalti u GIŠ-SAG(K)-G(K)UL ša-pu-ux ep-ru; 17 sik-ku-ru a-šab-bir = amaxxaç daltum. II 15 *a-b* 1—3 da-al-tu | u si-ku-ru (= GIŠ-SAG(K)-G(K)UL) | ku-un-nu; Z^Š iii 66; viii 59. II 23 *c-d* 32, 33 sik-ku-rum ‖ ši-ga-ru & mu-kil šu-ul-bi-i ‖ mêdilu. IV² 16 *a* 52—3, 54—

li-il | KIT | ki-i-tu : si-li [. . . .], translating it by: end, extremity.

sellu, sillu *1.* *m* (√סלל?) breastworks {Schutzwehr, Brustwehr} or the like, AV 6681; ZA ix 107, 17; Brown-Gesenius (699 *col* 2) for references to Semitic equivalents. Sn *Kui* 4, 9 of bricks (aban) KA *etc.* us-sima si-el-lum ni-bi-xi u gi-mir pa-as-as-ki-su. Esh vi 3 *foll* sixirti ēkalli šâtu ni-bi-xu (*q. v.*) pa-aš-qu ša (aban) KA *etc.* . . . ušēpišma . . . si-el-lu (*var* il-lum) mat-gi-gu ki-ma AN-TIR-AN-NA (Jensen, *Theol. Litztg.*, '90 *no* 2: Milchstrasse) ušasxira gimir bā-bāni. K 4574 (M^S texts, *pl* 12) *R* 12 kap-pu (GGA '98, 811), & 13 ŠU-u = si-el-lu; 14 sa-as-sa-an-nu = si-el-[lum?] (here perh = sellu, 2 basket, Br 14265); 11 (*cf* II 22 *no* 1 *add*) qa-an sil-li = sil-l[i?]. AV 6680—1, 6577. Meissner & Rost, 4; 29 Architrav, KB ii 138; again Meissner & Rost, BA iii 193, 214: Mauerbogen (falsches Gewölbe); Archivolte.

sellu, sillu *2.* Jensen, ZA xiv 184 *fol* = סַל (Hebr); סילתא (Arm); WZKM iv 127 *rm* 2 basket {Korb}. St. Nabd 239, 16 Nisannu, Dûzu, Kislimu 3 GI (*i. e.* qan) si-el-lu ša ta-bi-lu inamdinū (BA iii 423—4); Neb 318, 5 (qan) sil-li (see also, *no* 1); Camb 147, 10. Sp iii 6 *O* ii, 1 [su]-us-su-lu; 3—4 sa-al-tum; 6 sil-lu (PSBA xvi 308—9).

sillu *3.* (?) K 64 ii 5—6 (II 62 *no* 3) GIŠ-PA [ ] = sil-lu ša; GIŠ-PA-(tu[ ] & PU-BA [ ] = sillu ša, followed by ⟨ . . . . = s ša ta-kal-ti.

sul(l)ū *1.* *m*, *pl* sul(l)ē originally: a portion of the street (sūqu), sidewalk (?), then street {urspr. Teil der Strasse, Fussweg?, dann Strasse} AV 6818. IV^2 2 v 16—17 (55—56) su-la-a (= E-SIR-RA) a-na (& ana) da-la-xi ina SIL-A (= sūqi, *var* su-ki) ittana(m)zazzū šunu (H 175 *no* 7; Br 5881); 15* i 20—21 mu-ši su-u-qu su-la-a u na-ma-ri ina qa-ti-šu lu-u na-ši; 26 *b* 5 su-u-qa su-la-a ina a-la-ki-šu; 27 *b* 33—34 ina su-li er-çi-ti, Br 5883. V 65 *b* 36 ina (*var* i-na) su-u-qu u su-la-' (BA i 590) li-da-am-me-qu e-gir-ra-u-a; *b* 47 ina su-li-e-šu a-tal-lu-ku; ZA iv 11, 32 [ina] su-li-e çēri mut-tag-gi-šu (*cf* nagašu); K 2866 *O* 35 SIL (= sūqu) su-lu-u (*cf* $Z^Š$ viii 31) street and path (S. A. Smith, *Miscell. Texts*, *pl* xvii *foll*). Asb iv 87 ul-li-la su-ul-li-e-šu-nu lu-'-u-ti (BA i 10 = סְלָיָה), Smith, *Asurb*, 167, 22. K 1451 (Meissner-Rost, 108) be-lit te-lil-ti bēltu a-li-kat su-li-e (also Pognon, *Wadi-Brissa*, 79). T^M v 40 sūqu u su-lu-u; 88, 1—18, 1835 iv 20 *fol* TAR = su-lu-u ša sūqi, su-lu-u ša barbari. Neb v 38—9 A-a-bu-ur ša-bu-um su-le-e Bābili, name of a street the mašdaxu of Marduk (*cf* v 61). S 954 *O* 8 ka-a-ši su-li-e (= SIL, Br 353, 380) ket-ti i-kar-rab-ki. Sp II 265 *a* xiii 9 bi-ri-iš lu-ut-ṭe-'(-)lu-šib (or me?) su-li-e lu-ça-a (ZA x 8; PSBA xvii 149). I 67 *col* 2, 6 suli-e šamši açē (+ 8), KB iii (2) 74 & *rm* 1.

sulū *2.* V 36 *a-c* 27 u | ⟨ | su-lu-u, Br 8742.

***salū* 2.** — *a*) perhaps throw {werfen} IV^2 28* *no* 4 *b* 35—6 Nippur ša nak-ru u ana me-e sa-lu-u (= סלה); GGA '98, 822: das überschwemmt ist. — *b*) throw off, shake off {abwerfen, abschütteln} *i. e.* the yoke (nīru, *q. v.*) § 150; Smith, *Asurb*, 284, 94; Asb vii 87; iv 103; also ii 115. Sarg *Khors* 28 X who ni-ir (il) Ašur is-lu-u-ma (*cf* 55) & *Ann* 163; III 35 *no* 4 *O* 8 (the people) ša ni-ir (il) Ašur is-lu-ma. KB ii 244, 57 is-lu-u (ic) nir bēlūtija; K 653, 10 (Hr^L 154) ša ana šarri bēlija is-lu-ni; see also sil-latu, 2. — Der.

sullū *2.* in Sarg *Khors* 38 a-mat su-ul-li-e (*i. e.* nir) u s(ç)ar-ra-a-ti id-bu-ub-šu-nu-ti words of derision {Hohnworte}.

***salū* 3.** Q perh trust in or upon {vertrauen ir, oder auf} K 1450, 28 ana eli šarri bēlišu sa-lu-u; also K 155, 14, 14 the great gods i-sal-lu-ka-ma (= K^M *no* 1). — ב with *acc.* pray to somebody, invoke some one's help, favor or mercy {zu jemandem beten; jemandes Hilfe, Gnade, Erbarmen erflehen} AV 6528. IV^2 60* B *O* 5 u-sal-li (ilat) Iš-tar-ri ul i-šaq-qa-a ri-ši-ša (Z^B 41). Scheil, *Nabd*, vi 3 u-sal-li-šu-nu-ti, I emplored them; vii 10 u-sa-al-li-šu-nu-ti, + 18 u-sa-al-li-šu-ma; I 66 *c* 43—44 I raised (my) hand u-sa-al-la-a bēl bēlē, ana Marduk . . . . illikū su-pu-u-a (KB iii, 2,

38); Neb iii 34 ud-da-kam u-sa-al-la-a (I prayed daily); V 63 *a* 10, 13 Nabd who aš-šum i-na pa-ra-aç ilāni la ša-la-ṭi u-sal-lu-u (AJP xi 502 >< KB iii, 2, 114) ilāni rabūti. L^{4} ii 28 ša a-lak ilū-ti-šu bāni-a u-sa-al-la u-sa-ap-pa rabū-ut (*var* rabī-tu) ilū(t)-su, followed by a prayer. K 824, 13 (to my Lord Ašur) u-sal-an-ni-i-ma (I prayed, Hr^{L} 290); S 1028, 9 (end) to Marduk & Çar-pa-ni-tum u-sal-la; K 523 *R* 2 u-sal-la; K 478 *R* 1 (u-sal-lu 1 *sg*); K 81, 5; K 528, 7 (= Hr^{L} 418, 324, 254, 274, 269). P. N. Nabū-u-sal-lu, ZA i 200, 13; iv 11, 22 um-mi sal-la (GGA '98, 814). JENSEN, KB vi (1) 238—9 reads *del* 135 ki-ma u-ri mit-xu-rat u-s(ṡ)al-lu, as soon as daylight appeared, I prayed, but see *ibid* 498—9. Derr.: te(a)slītu &:

sullū *3.* prayer {Gebet}. V 21 *a-b* 52 su-ul-lu-u ‖ xas-si-tum (51, te-is-li-tum) AV 6821; JENSEN, 503. II 35 *h* 33 PI = su-ul-lu-u perh ‖ la-ban ap-pi, *q. v.* (Br 14300) sec 31. 83, 1—18, 1330 i 23, 24 ZUR = su-up-pu-u, su-ul-lu-u (PSBA Dec. '88; ZA iv 274—5). K 3312 *col* 3, 18 see karābu, 2. Br 13905 *ad* II 49, *add* (AV 6821) ..... LA-KA-GA = su-ul-lu-u.

salū 4. K 512, 11—13 a-na me-i-ni ta-sa-al-li (to which is answered): a-na šarri bēli-ja a-sa-al-li (V 53 *no* 4; Hr^{L} 204), or to salū, 3?

silū in P. N. K 518, 11 (amēl) Bur-si-la-a. (Hr^{L} 140; see R. F. HARPER, AJSL xiv 11, 12). AV 6677; K 4248 (II 22, 74 *add*) si-lu-u followed by ul-lu-xu, ud-du-du, Br 4229.

salaxu, *pr* islux, *ps* isallax sprinkle, besprinkle {besprengen, bespritzen} with double acc. (§ 139) ‖ saxalu, 2; ZA iv 276. AV 6519; *cf* Hebr סלח. According to ZA v 42 = נסך. id ŠUD, so mostly in ZIMMERN, *Ritualtafeln*. IV^{2} 31 *R* 34 (ilat) Ištar mē balāṭi su-lux-ši-ma li-qa-aš-ši ana max-ri-ia; 38 is-lux-ši-ma *etc.* K^{M} 62, 29 ta-]sal-lax. IV^{2} 59 *no* 1 *b* 9 that man mē i-sa-la-ax, he shall sprinkle with water; 22 *b* 14—15 amēlu mār ilišu su-lu-ux-ma (= <-ME-NI-ŠUD, Br 7604; H 26, 564); 16 *b* 37 with that water amēlu šu-lux-ma (U-MU-E-NI-SE); ZA iii 347 (bel) su-lux. Sarg *Cyl* 29 Sargon who kullat nakirē is-lu-xu i-mat mu-u-ti(-te); *Khors* 131 i-mat mu-u-ti as-lu-xa si-it-ta-at nišē mul-tax-ṭu; *Ann* 338 i-mat mu-ti as-lu-xa nišēšu. IV^{2} 6 *a* 19—21 the talk (rigmu) of an evil man im-tu amēlu i-sal-lax. T^{M} v 115—16 a-sal-lax lib-ba-ku-nu; a-sal-lax la-'-me-ku-nu; see also šuluxxū. 83, 1—18, 1330 iv 10 te-e | TE | sa-la-xu.
Derr. these 2 (?):

salāxu T. A. (Ber) 26 iv 26: 5 ša sa-la-xi siparri = 5 sprinklers of bronze.

salixu Z^{Š} iii 60 ma-mit sa-li-xu u na-rāti *pl*. *Rev. bibl.*, July '01, 398 *rm* 3 cp. שלח = *šiloax* = canal.

salxu. K 1769 + DT 3 i 17 sa-al-xu, apparently = šalxū, *q. v.* MEISSNER & ROST, 80 *no* 2.

sulxū K 8204, 3 see šulxū.

si-lak-ku V 41 *g-h* 8 si-lak-ku ‖ of a-lum; Sm 949 *O* 34 (+ Sm 787) ana çēri kak-ki u si-lak-ki lū at-ma. Z^{Š} iii 7 ma-mit (il) si-lak[-ki ..... r]i-tu-u. See perh III 69 *a* 71 AN (?) si-lak-ku, Br 12343. JENSEN, *Diss*, 80.

sililītu. V 43 *c-d* 5 (arax) si-li-li-ti a name for the month shebat; AV 6671. Also 83—1—18, 187, 1 + 4 ina (arax) si-li-li-ti (arax Šabiṭu, 4).

salamu, *pr* islim (PHILIPPI, BA ii 387 *rm* †††); *ps* isi(a?)lim; *ip* silim; *pm* salmu, turn to lovingly, graciously; assist, help {sich liebevoll, gnädig zuwenden; helfen, beistehen} with itti of person, whom to assist. id DI (or SILIM). K^{M} 8, 12 (twice) lu tas-lim, propitious be (13, 10). V 64 *a* 15 (Bēl) a-na maxāxi u bīti ša-a-šu is-li-mu ir-šu-u ta-a-a-ri; KB iv 30 iii 5 P. N. a-na A-xa-am-ni-si-lim (+ 16). Bu 88—5—12, 21, 8 sa-la-a-mi-ša i-sa-li-im (she) shall care for her welfare; Bu 91—5—9, 2176 A 23 sa-la-mi-ša i-sa-lim (JRAS Jl. '97, 607—8). K 168, 30 i-sa-al-mu. perh II 51 *b* 13 (end) ina ū-me an-ni-i lis-li-mu it-ti-šu. Z^{Š} iv 55 li-is-li-mu (3 *pl*). V 46 *a-b* 32 (il) muš-te-šir si-lim (on *a* see ZA i 259 *rm* 1). P. N. (Bu-ni-tum) si-il-mi (&-mu) BOR i 137—8; Camb 379, 4 Nabū-si-lim (+ 15); Nabd 693, 3 (ilat) Na-na si-lim, O Nana have mercy! K 143 *O* 4 O my god si-lim, have mercy ‖ o my goddess nap-ši-ri. II 123 (*no* 19) *O* 21—22 (K 4623) ana ardiki ša ta-gu-gi si-il-me (= SILIM-MA-AB-EME-SAL) it-ti-šu (*cf* H 188 *no* 101), turn in mercy to thy servant, against whom thou wert angry. IV^2 57 *b* 2 DI (= sil)-mu itti-MU (= ja) turn to me in mercy; 55 *no* 2 *a* 10 ilu, šarru *etc.* itti-šu a-na salâ-mu (+ 12, 22). Asb ii 117 see šalamu. K 183, 12, 13 ilâni sa-al-mu, the gods are propitious (Hr^L 2; BA i 617; PSBA 23, 351), AV 6527.

ג K 1282 *etc.* (KB vi, 1, 70) 32 the gods of the country, who had been angered tu-sal-la-am ana ru?[. . . .], thou shalt reconcile. K 669, 16 u-sa-li-im-šu-nu (Hr^L 246), Delattre, PSBA 23, 51 *fol*: je les ai rétablies. Perb. V 45 vii 21 tu-s̀al-lam. P. N. Bêl-u-sal-li-im (BOR i 137, 7); K^M 2, 24 tu-sal-lam ar-xiš thou art quick to favor (the man); 21, 87. IV^2 61 b 31 a-na-ku . . . . $^{(il)}$ Ašur is-si-ka u-sa-lim, I have made Ašur propitious to thee (or ג'?). *cf* K 168, 21 u-sa-li-mu. Z^{Š} iv 84 $^{(il)}$ Gibil mu-sal-lim ili zi-ni-i u ištar zi-ni-tu.

Z^B 57: šalamu = common Semitic שלם; salamu = saxaru (only found in Assyrian); see also Haupt, *Beitr. z. Assyr. Lautlehre*, § 9. Hommel, *Sum. Les.*, 30, 359 derives salamu from silim (S^b 185).

Derr. these 9:

salâmu welfare {Wolfahrt} see above; & KB iv 310—11 *no* ix 23 mâr Sa-la-mu.

salîmu *m*, literally: turning to, attention {Zuwendung, Zuneigung}. AV 6527; § 65, 14. — *a*) kindness, grace, favor, goodwill {Güte, Gnade, Wolwollen} V 33 i 2 Agum] ka-ak-ri-me . . . . šar taš-me-e u sa-li-me (KB iii, 1, 136). K 874 *R* 3—4 taš-mu-u | u sa-li-mu ina mâti ibašši. III 59 *b* 47 sa-lim kiš-ša-ti; 54 *a* 9 sa-li-im kiš-ša-ti; 64 *b* 23 DI (= sali)-im kiš-ša-ti. Knudtzon; *no* 1 *O* 9 *etc.* lu-u i-na pî ṭâbi u sa-lim tu(= ṭu)-ub-ba-a-ti (15 *R* 10; *ibid, O* 5 si-lim); 12 *O* 10 (Knudtzon, *p* 77); also 19 *O* 6—7. — *b*) alliance, treaty {Bündniss, Bund}. Asb i 128 to Tarkû they sent a-na ša-kan a-di-e u sa-li-me (*cf* sulummû); Smith, *Asurb*, 42, 38. Sn iii 61 bêl sa-li-me-šu, his ally, the king of Elam (KB ii 98—99); T. A. (Ber) 6 *R* 19 ax-xu-tum ṭa-bu-tum sa-li-mu u a-ma-tum. — *c*) of gods: compassion; merciful & loving kindness; grace, forgiveness {Erbarmen, Liebe, Gnade, Vergebung}. V 60 iii 17 Šamaš sa-li-ma ir-ši-ma, took pity (BA i 282). Merodach-Bal.-Stone i 19 of Marduk = ir-ša-a sa-li-me. ZA v 60, 21 ša is-bu-us-su li-ir-ša-a sa-lim-mu, let him who has offended obtain forgiveness. KB iii (2) 52, 32 Marduk ir-ta-ši sa-li-mi. 81—6—7, 209, 18 Marduk a-na Bâbili$^{(ki)}$ sa-li-mu ir-šu-u (BA iii 262). Perb. IV^2 20 *no* 1, 11 sa-li-ma] ir-ši-ma. V 49 *col* x 28: on the 25th of Tebeṭ sa-li-mu; K 3515 *O* 14 tu-šar-ši-i sa-li-mu. II 60 *no* 2, 40 AN SILIM-MU-UN-ZAL = $^{(il)}$ Nabû $^{(il)}$ mu-uš-ta-bar-ru-u sa-li-mi (Br 9543); and thus read H 121 *R* 34 (DT 67) sa-li-ma] uš-ta-bar-ra-ši. V 43 *c-d* 30. Neb *Senk*, i 19 Marduk ana bîti šuâti (i)-ir-ta-šu sa-li-mu (§ 134, end); K 143 *O* 19 sa-li-ma šuk-na-ni (*ip*, *pl*). V 21 *a-b* 59 a-ni-mu-u ‖ sa-li-mu, preceded by sa-xa-ru *etc.*, in a list of words meaning: mercy, favor, compassion. P. N. Nabû-sa-lim.

Note. — On $^{(âlu, or mât)}$ U-ru-sa-lim T. A. (Ber) 106, 14 see Sayce, *London Academy*, '91 Febr. 7, 138; *Higher Criticism*, 176; against him, Zimmern, ZA vi 252, 254, 262 *rm* 7; Haupt, *Independent* (N. Y.), 12 Ja. '99. translates: the land Urusalim, whose name is Bît-Nin-ib; Jastrow, *JBLit*, xi 106 sides with Sayce = Uru (city) + Salim (name of a deity). See also Ursalimmu, D^{Par} 288. Sn iii 8 (20, 32) Ur-sa-lim-mu (III 12, 27 + 29).

salimiš, *adv*. full of grace, mercy {huldvoll, gnädig} V 35, 22 e-nu-ma a-na . . . . . Bâbili e-ru-bu sa-li-mi-iš (or perhaps confusion with šalamiš; thus, apparently KB iii, 2, 125).

Salim(a)tu, *pl* salimêti. P. N. of Babyl. port Bâb-sa-li-me-ti, Asb iii 99; Bu 91—5—9, 366 (wedding contract) 3 Sa-li-ma-tum (JRAS '97, 605); III 49 *b* 32 ŠI (= pân) Sa-lim-du (an official).

silmu, grace, favor {Zuwendung, Entgegenkommen}; *c. st.* si-lim, Knudtzon, *no* 150 *O* 5; AV 6672. K 4623 *O* 2 DI-MA-AP = si-il-me. II 40 *no* 2, 14 TAG-GUG (= $^{(aban)}$ sându) si-lim ‖ aban ra-a-me, Oefele, ZA xiv 358 = λίθος σεληνίτης. Dar 82, 12 P. N. Si-lim-Bêl, *etc.* (AV 6674—6), Si-lim-Ašur, K 400, 2 (III 50 *no* 2), Si-lim-Adad, Si-lim-ilu, Bezold, *Catalogue*, 2186.

silimtu (?) Perh. II 62 (*c*-)*d* 14 si-li[-imtu?] BA ii 290.

sullumu reconciliation }Versöhnung} Scheil, *Nabd*, x 8 su-ul-lu-mu ilâni zunu-tu or ג ac of salamu?

sulummû *m* § 65, 38; AV 6819. *a*) affection, favor, sympathy }Zuneigung, Gunst, Mitleid}. II 65 *O* ii 27 ṭu-ub-ta su-lu-um-ma-a ga[-am(-ma?)-ra] it-ti axa-meš iš-ku-[nu; *cf* iii 18 + 24 (KB i 198—99) they treated one another in friendly spirit & complete harmony; Asb v 41 ina ta-a-a-ar-ti-ja ša sul-lumme-e (but see Winckler, *Forsch.*, 249); Sarg *Khors* 35 su-lum-mu-u u-ša-aškin I brought about friendly relations; Knudtzon, 87 *R* 3 su-lum[-mi-i?]. T. A. (Ber) 24, 6 your father wrote to me el zu-lu-um-me-e (of friendship); *cf* (Ber) 16, 1. — *b*) treaty }Bündnis} Hehn. i 170 *rm* 4; BA i 320. Asb i 124—5 su-lum-mu-u ina bi-ri-in-ni liš-ša-kin(-ma) = Smith, *Asurb*, 42, 30; *ibid* 290, 53 a-na ša-kan a-di-e su-lum-me-e.

Salamânu. P. N. K 1518, 8 u Sa-la-ma-nu (Hr^L 140); see AJSL xiv 11—12.

salmu. Sarg *Khors* 99—100 it-ti (amêlu) qu-ra-di-ja ša a-šar sa-al-me (KB ii 65 whither I lead) idâ-a-a la ip-par-ku-u I went to Asdod; 85 it-ti nar-kabât šepê-ja u (imêr) bit-xal-li(*rar* lim)-ja ša a-šar sa-al-me i-da-a-a la ip-par-ku-u (+ 114); *Ann* 223.

sal(*i. e.* SAL)-mi-e Asb v 26 read mim-me-e (& see mimmû, *p* 565 *col* 1) also SAL-mu (& ma) = mimmû, Knudtzon, 305.

silammu a plant }eine Pflanze}. II 42 *c-d* 17—18 (K 4345) (šam) šu-ul-tu = (šam) si-lam-mu, Br 12355, AV 6669.

silammaxu state-garment, royal robe }Prachtgewand, Herrschergewand} AV 6668; D^S 112. V 28 *g-h* 38—9 al-lu-rum & zu(= çu)-bat bẹ-lu-tim (which in 40 = çu-bat šar-ri) = si-lam-ma-xu.

sulumxû (AV 6818) see zuluxxû, zulumxû (*p* 282 *col* 1) & M^S 33, 34.

ʼSill'â'n see under çît'â'n.

salsalu. Knudtzon (*p* 128) 30 *R* 7 ša sa-al-sa-lu ina libbi kalumi an-ni-e izzi-za-am-ma.

suluppu *m* date }Dattel} iď KA-LUM-MA, § 9, 39; Br 764; T^C 111; AV 4062; 6820; H 37, 56; S^b 319 = su-lu-up-pu, Br 5966; & KA-LUM, Rm 277 vii 17; II 52 *g-h* 67. II 15 *c-d* 42 i-na šu-ru-ub-ti su-lu-pi (= KA-LUM-MA) (H 68, 20), 44 ši-ni-pat KA-LUM-MEŠ (+ 47), 49 su-lu-up gišimmari, spring date, Br 7284 (>< AV 6816 su-lu-ku). II 16 *e-f* 23—4 su-lu-up-pa-ka (= KA-LUM-ZU) mar-tum. IV² 7 *a* 47 kîma su-lu-up-pi (KA-LUM-GIM) liš-ša-xi-iṭ (let it—the curse—be plucked away), *b* 8 kîma KA-LUM-MA an-ni-i iš-šax-xa-ṭu (& 15, liš-ša-xi-iṭ), Jensen, *Diss*, 40. II 5 *c-d* 33 UX-KA-LUM-MA = kalmat su-lu-up-pi (see *p* 389 *col* 2); II 31 *g* 82; V 27 *h* 21 (Br 8303). V 19 *a-b* 55 TAG-KA-LUM-MA = a-ban su[-lu-up-pi] Br 765, 14192; AV 4062. H 21, 381—2; 38, 120; D 81 ii 82. V 19 *a-b* 56 see Br 3186. suluppu imittu dates paid by the tenant to the proprietor as rent. Often in *c. t.* Neb 564, 1: 3 gur suluppi i-mit-tum ša N ina eli N; Nabd 353, 1; Neb 347, 1: 34 gur suluppi i-mit-ti ša eli gišimmarê; iď ZAG-LU, Nabd 623, 1 *etc.*; 309, 10 suluppu ri-ix-ti i-mit-tum ša šatti VIII; 47, 1: 3 gur suluppi ri-ix-tum imittum ša M ina eli N. BA iii 385 *foll* √emedu impose }auferlegen}, thus: Auferlegung, Auflage. See also D^H 51; D^{Pr} 137 *rm* 2; Z^B 97; BA i 523; 634—5; ii 299; ZA iii 45. ZA xiv 183 (below).

s(š)allapânu. K 4354 i 5 (šam) sal-la-pa-nu ‖ šam s(š)eš-a-nu, a plant }eine Pflanze}.

salaçû. S^r 295 sa-la-çu = ba-a-rum. Br 3802, AV 6523.

salaqu. II 62 *c-d* 26 sa-la-qu ša šêri ‖ ša-ra-qu, AV 6524, Br 7059.

Derr. silqu, 2, salqu, siliqu?

silqu *1.* a plant }eine Pflanze}. 81—7—6, 688 S. H. iii 1 si-il-qa SAR = סִלְקָא: Mangold (Gemüse) ZA vi 295. *pl* Nabd 386, 12: 4 nakrimânu ana kirêmu si-il-qa-a-tu u šikar ŠE-BAR. T^C 111.

siliqqu (?) AV 8221, Br 6958 *ad* II 44 *e-f* 83 si-liq-qu.

silqu *2.* in šêr sil-qu boiled meat; see for the present šilqu & HAUPT, JBL xix 60 & note 105, *p* 78. ZIMMERN, *Ritualtafeln*, 1—20 *ll* 52 + 109; ‖

salqu, *ibid* 61 *no* ii 13 [šir] xinçâ(?) sa-al-qa NI (or -ni?).

siliqu perhaps in ni-ik-si-li-qu II 23 *a* 26 *a* ‖ of paššûru.

sulaqu. V 28 *a-b* 17 su-la-qu ‖ lu-ba-šu, AV 6812.

silaru. ZA x 202, 9 bi-bi-en-du : si-la-ru ^ bi-bi-en-du : pu(a)l-lu-uk-ku.

salatu *1.* II 20 *a-b* 73, + 27 *b* 6 DAR (da-ar) sa-la-tum in a group with litû (*p* 501 *col* 2) & xuppû; Br 3492, 6975; AV 6525. H 16, 237; S^c 118. To this belongs also:

saltum. Sp III 6 *O* ii 4 [DA?]-RA = sa-al-tum followed by xi-pu-u & li-tu-u; PSBA xvi 308—9.

sal(l)atu (salâtu?) relatives {Verwandtschaft} usually in connection with kimtu & nisûtu (*q. v.*). PSBA xiv 169; D^{Pr} 163 & *rm* 4; ZA ii 99; 227—8; JENSEN, 113 *fol*; *Rev. Sém.* v 57 *rm* 2: membres féminines de la famille. Asb i 30 sa-la-tu (*var* sal-la-tum). On Cyr 277, 6 see TALLQVIST, *Schenkungsbriefe*, 17, 18; often in *c. t.* Nabd 193, 23 sa-lat. V 67 *no* 2, 42 two persons are called sa-la-ta-ni-šu. Also P. N. Sa-la-tum. On lišân sa-lâti, see WEISSBACH, *Sumerische Frage*, 155. Xammurabi, Br. M. 12837, 6: *X* sends *S* officials [a-na] za(= sa)-la-tim ša li-li-ka, to form members of his court.

salatu *2.* cut up {zerschneiden} ik-rib (iç) erina sa-la-ti-ma, ZIMMERN, *Ritualtafeln*, 75—8, 62: Gebet beim Cedernholz zerschneiden (= šalat(ṭ)u?), *cf* 76.

siltu *1.* ZIM., *Ritualt.*, 75—8, 57 ki-iç-ra sil-ta heaps of chips {Haufen von Holzschnitzeln} *cf no* 100, 40.

salītu. K 8466, 13 u-çi ina sa-li-ti (WINCKLER, *Forsch.*, ii 28—9).

sûlatu (?) HILPRECHT, *OBI*, i *no* 2, 7—8 su-u-la-ti il Bêl: the dominions of Bêl (*cf* סללה, Jer 33, 4?).

siltum *2.* Camb 258, 4: 7 mašixi ša si-il-tum, perh. ‖

sillatu *1.* = סלת some kind of grain {eine Kornart, Getreideart}. K 274, 24: 24 (imêr) ŠE sil-la-a-tu, = 24 Homer of *s*-grain; *ibid R* 31: lu (ŠE) sil-lat a-nu-u a-na nap-tan ilûtišu rabîti (BA iii 264—9; 361), also K 1989 *R* 6. To this TALLQVIST (*p* 145) refers also T^M vi 62 si-lit riqqu gam-gam. ZIM., *Ritualtafeln*, *no* 66 *O* 8: 7 QA akalê ša (ŠE) sil-lat (& *rm* 9); *ibid* 9 si-il-ti (& *rm* 18).

s(š)illatu *2. f* impudence, rebellion {Vermessenheit, Empörung}; thus for sil'atu √סלה (salû 2), (M^S 72). Asb iv 66, 67 (amêl) çâbê ša-a-tu-nu sil-la-tu pi-i-šu-nu ša ina eli (il) Ašur ilija sil-la-tu iqbû (KB ii 192—3; BA i 441); also KB ii 256—7 (= SMITH, *Asurb*, 137) 76 *M.* who against my goddess iq-bu-u sil-la-tu rabî-tu. K 3364 *O* 5 sil-la-tu. Bu 91—5—9, 183 *R* 2—4 (Hr^L 340) ma-a mârâni Bâbili ina (mât) Ba-ni iç-çi-e-u-ni si-il-a-te-ši-na (R. F. HARPER, AJSL xiv 211—12); perh. K 660 *O* 15 (Hr^L 86) u çi-il-la-a-te (JAOS xviii 167—9). $Z^Š$ iii 131 ma-mit šar-ri u si-la-a-ti. II 36 *g-h* 4, 5 (+ ⊕ 276) PA(lu-ga)GA = sil-la-tum; GA-GA = sillatum ša KA (= pî). V 21 *a-b* 21 K]A?-Ê-GAL = 'šil-la-tu, followed by tu-uš-šu & bar-tum (Z^B 73: curse). V 47 *a* 60, 61 see zillûtum (*p* 282 *col* 2) & תפה.

sili'tu, silêtû defect, frailty, weakness, sickness {Gebrechen, Krankheit}. D^{Pr} 136. IV^2 60* C *R* 13 a-dan-na si-li-'i-ti-ja (‖ mur-çi-ja) (amêl) bârû ul id-din, an end of my frailty no priest could set. V 47 *a* 54, 55 ap-pu-na-ma e-te-rik si-li-e-tum. si-li-e-tum = GIG (*i. e.* murçu). K 747 *R* 2 šu-mu an-ni-u si-li-a-te šu-u . . . . (THOMPSON, *Reports*). Also see M^S 71—2 *ad* BEZOLD, *Catalogue*, 1437.

silītu favor, mercy, compassion {Gnade, Erbarmen} Z^B 20; but very doubtful. S^b 1 *R* (V 38 *c-f*) v 17  = si-li-tum, together with i-b(p)u & ri-i-mu Br 5520; Br 5932 reads S^c 211 si-li[-tu]. K^M 30, 14 šur-qim-ma šumu u zîru lu rêmu si-li-ti : lu-ša-pa zi-kir-ki, grant me name & posterity, mercy & compassion, and I will praise thy name.

sil-lu-tu, AV 6682, Br 8964—5 *ad* II 30 *a-b* 75—76 *cf* xašlu (*p* 346, where read xaš-lu-*tu*).

sâmu 1. be dark {dunkel sein}. K 763 *R* 4 the sky i-si-mu was dark, THOMPSON, *Reports*, ii *p* lvi & 36; Br 9298 li-sa-ma; V 62 *a* 62.

Der.: sâmtu, 1 & 2, &:

sâmu 2. *f* sâmtu. iṡ DIR dark colored {dunkelfarbig}. BA i 507 *rm*: reddish-brown; ZA xiv 182; KB vi (1) 570 = fuscus, perh. = سهم. AV 6541. II 6 *a* 22 kalbu] DIR (= sâmu), *c* 41. II 45 *e-f* 55 see kiškanû (450 *col* 1) Br 8554; see also V 28 *c-d* 79; IV² 30* *b* 1—2 (*cf* naxlaptu), 3—4 çu-ba-ta sa-a-ma (= DIR & *cf* namrirru); 21 *no* 1 B 1—2 çu-ba-tu sa-a-mu (= DIR) at-ru-uç. V 28 *c-d* 34—40 see ubâru (*p* 473 *col* 2). Anp ii 54 see mitxâru (at daybreak?) *p* 622 *col* 1. V 14 *b* 22 perh. šipâti sa-ma-a-tum; also T. A. (Ber) 26 i 36. Nabd 489, 4 (+8) xurâçu sa-a-mu; Camb 1, 1 imêru samânu-u sa-a-mu ša ši-in-du ina mux-xi-šu ja-a-nu, an 8 year old dark colored donkey, without a spot (KB iv 282—3, BA iii 478: kein Mal). II 26 *e-f* 44 *foll* DIR = sa-a-mu; GUG = sa-am-tum (& 46, Br 2448), sa-ma-nu (47); 39 *b* 47 SI a-a-mu Br 3403; 47 *c-d* 33 AL-DAR-DAR-NU (= bur-rumu) = sa-a-mu, Br 5759. S^b 179 sa-a | DIR | sa-a-mu ‖ ad-ru (178); H 16, 242, Br 8745; K 40 (D 83) iii 62 DIR = sa-a-mu; *cf* III 59 *no* 8, 1 si-a-mu gloss to DIR, AV 6615. Br 2601 la sâmu *cf* lasamu. sâmtu see below (*p* 767 *col* 2).

(11) **Sa-a-mu.** III 66 *col* 3, 31; Br 12316; PSBA xxi 120—1.

sâmu 3. of a bird {von einem Vogel gesagt} II 37 *c-d* 29 iççurf] sa-a-mu, with ur bal-lum and xa-xar; Br 11846.

samû? 1. be or become sick; esp. of blindness {krank sein oder werden; namentl. in Bezug auf Blindheit}. Q¹ šêpâka la is-sa-nam-ma-a (lâ i-nar-ru-ṭa qâtâka) K 2652, 35, 36 let thy feet not become sick (lame?). — ℑ V 45 v 40 tu-sa-am-ma; T^M v 33 li-sa-am-mu-ši kiš-pu-ša, may her charm blind her.

Derr.: samânu & these 2:

samû 2. sick; then, blind (physically and intellectually) {krank; blind (physisch und geistig)} see sakku, & saklu.

simmu. sickness; blindness {Krankheit; Blindheit}. AV 5565, 6698; Br 744. K 6057 si-im-mu ma-'-du šu-mi-šu-nu ul i-di (BEZOLD, *Catal.*, 759). I 70 *d* 6 si-im-mu(-ma); III 41 *b* 30; 43 *d* 16; K 3500 + K 4444 + K 10235 i 4 sim-ma, (KB iv 86 ii 20—21) see lazzu. Perh. K 3456 *R* 5 e-la ja-a-ti tur la si-me PSBA xxi 40 *foll*: upon me bring no sickness. K 2061 ii 19 (H 203) GIG (= marçu) = si-im-mu, Br 9238. IV² 29* *no* 4 C *a* 10—11 ina ša-me-e ša-a-ru i-zi-qam-ma ina i-in amêli si-im-me iš-ta-kan; 14 ana i-ni mar-ça-a-ti si-im-me (*var* -ma; iṡ GIG-GA) iš-ta-kan (see *Hopkins Circ.* 114 *p* 118 on this text). KB vi 100, 18 see saxaru (& KB vi (1) 413—4). ^amêl GIG = ^(amêl) simmu in *c t.*, Nabd 161, 8; Neb 190, 4 *etc.*

NOTE. — BA ii 287 (*ad* II 16 *c-d* 44: si-im-me) √סמם be dark (connected with sâmu), be sad, lament be sick, whence also ummatu (*cf* Hebr אִימָה) according to JÄGER, BA ii 288 this verb also in su mu ug ga H 76, *foll* (= adaru *cf* Br 181 and HOMMEL, *Sum. Les.*, 11 *no* 129) the ug ga um ma mimmation on the other hand HAUPT, BA 168, umug-ga a modification of sunqu *c. st.* sunuq (see, however, BRÜNNOW, ZA viii 127). BA ii 146—7 simmu = poison ‖ gift, Aram סַמָּא. so *Lit. Centralbl.* '77 *col* 346.

sammu in P. N Sa-am-mu-ra-mat I 35 *no* 2, 9. HAUPT, ADLER, *Hopkins Circ.*, 55 (Ja. '87) 51; BA i 163 *rm* ††: Die Taubenliebende: lover of doves (≍ HOMMEL, *Geschichte*, 632 *rm* 1); also BA i 323 *fol* ≍ HOFFMANN *Phönis. Inschriften*, 51. DELITZSCH-MÜRDTER, 278 Liebhaberin von Wolgerüchen. See also BA ii 287—8, *rm* *; 598 *rm* ***. LEHMANN, *Berl. Philol. Wochenschr.*, '04 *no* 8 (*p* 239) ≍ WINCKLER, *Gesch. Babyl. u. Assyriens*; J^I-N 68 *foll.*

samû 3. II 62 *no* 1 *R g-h* 7 DI-GA = sa-mu-u, AV 6542; Br 9554.

summu (√סמם?). II 32 *a-b* 17 su-um-mu = si-ma-nu, appointed time AV 6831; D^S 116.

sammû sweet odor, incense {Wolgeruch} Z^B 37. Hebr סַמִּים; DT 363 *O* 85 ^(iç) i-ni (^(iç)) sa-am-me-e, ZA iv 247; but *cf* M^S 72.

sama'anu (?) in P. N. Našxu sa-ma-'-a-ni PSBA xxi, 285.

samēdu, in iç-çur sa-me-di see diqdiqqu (*p* 265 *col* 2); AV 6537 quotes a U (= šam?) sa-me-du. Br 8157, 13898.

summuzzū. T. A. (Ber) 28 iii 26 summu-uz-zi-e (+ 29).

samaxu add {hinzutun}. ZIMMERN, *Ritualtafeln*, *nos* 1—20, 47 tu-sa-max-ma (2*sg*); *cf* IV^2 59 *b* 22.

samaxxu. V 26 *c-d* 65 GIŠ-SA-MAX = ŠU (*i. e.* samax)-xu, AV 6531, 8002; Br 3088.

samxaçu. AV 6544 *ad* II 45 *no* 4 (*add*) 2 (iç) sa-am-xa-çu, preceded by (iç) sa-b(p)u.

'šamxatu see uxātu & šamxatu.

samaku. ‏ג‏ T^M v 44 ki-ma kib-si kirri li-sa-am-me-ku-ši-na li-ti-qu-ši.

simāku. Some kind of shrine, sanctuary, abode of the gods {eine Art Heiligtum, Götterschrein}. MEISSNER & ROST, 18; KB vi (1) 379. Aram סְמִכָא, סְמִיכָא. PSBA xxi 74. ‖ ganūnu. SCHEIL, *Nabd*, iii 27—9 (il) Lamassu la si-mat E-an-na | u-še-ši-bu | i-na si-ma-ak-ki-šu they let dwell in their shrine (also viii 28). Merod.-Balad. ii 12 see kūmu (*p* 393); Sarg *Cyl* 43 see banū, 1. ‏ש‏ (175 *col* 2, below). K 3445 + K 390 *R* 11 ina si-ma-ak-ki-šu. ZA iv 240, 24 li-pu-uš si-ma-ak-šu. Also *cf* AV 6684 si-ma-ak (il) Šamaš.

sumāku. V 29 *g-h* 70 ID-TU-A = su-ma-ak TAR (= sûqi) AV 6827, Br 6560; ZA i 411—12; 191 *rm* 1 in a list denoting "offspring" (ilitti bīti, tarbū, lillidu), J^{P} 34 *cf* II 46 *d* 48 li-du-tum šu-ma-ki. JÄGER, BA i 483 says: suwâq (sûqi) secondary development from su'âq (فُعَال).

simkurru. some wild animal {ein wildes Tier} I 28 *a* 25: wild asses and gazelles barbarē si-im-kur-re meš u-šam-qit (he killed); Lay 44, 19 si-en-ku-re meš (KB i 124—5). ZA i 307.

samullu. a tree or plant {ein Baum oder ein Gewächs} AV 6548. II 45 *c-d* 49 GIŠ-ŠIR (usually = nūru, light) = sa-mul-lum (H 39, 134; Br 1651). SCHEIL, ZA v 399 *foll* reads V 63 *b* 36 (end) ina sa-mulli for in (aban) giš-šir-gal; so also PINCHES, PSBA xvi 228 *ad* H 81 *R* 26 (Ninib) qar-ra-du (aban) GIŠ-ŠIR-GAL, the warrior of white limestone (?, II 19 *b* 47; 38 *b* 42). It is not = סֶמֶל.

samēnu. some plant {eine Pflanze} 79, 7—8, 19 *col* 2, 22 [(šam?)] sa-me-nu. M^S texts, pl 25.

simānu *1*. Sn v 78 *fol* see munnu (559 *col* 1); translated by HAUPT, *Jour. Bib. Lit.*, xix 80 *rm* 120: I scattered their entrails and bowels over the vast field.

simanū. Asb vi 17—18 (iç) be-li qa-ra-bi si-ma-nu-u | mim-ma e-piš taxāzi si-mat qātā-šu (KB ii 204—5). Dar 4: 8 .... šiqlīu kaspi ana si-ma-nu-u .... še-e-nu ša (amēl) çābē qašti.

samnu eighth {achter} K 146, 10 sam-na mu-šu the eighth night; especially in a-ra-ax(-rax)-sam (*var* sa-am)-na H 44 (64) 8 *etc.* see arxu, 4. D^{Par} 132; § 129. *f* sa-man-ti (ū-mu) HILPRECHT, *Assyr*, 90 *fol.* SCHEIL, *Rec. Trav.*, xix 62—3 *no* 3, 10; Sm 1064. Br 1030. a ‖ is:

samānū, § 75. See sibū & ZA xiv 182—3. KB vi 76 ii 4 i-na sa-ma-ni-i, eighthly {zum achten} BA iv 130; T. A. (Lo) 82. NE 54, 8 sa-ma-na-a (KB vi 192); 55, 24 see sibū; written VIII-a NE 70, 6; & also see Sn v 5 ina samāni-e gir-ri-ja; Asb v 63. K 4810 i (= IV^2 21 *a*) 46 sa-ma-nu-tu a-xat-su-nu (il) Na-ru-di. Camb 1, 1 imēru samānu-u, BA iii 478.

samānu. some sickness {eine Krankheit}, also a demon specially feared {auch: ein besonders gefürchteter Dämon}. II 26 *e-f* 47 = D 83 iii 65 SA-MA-NA′ = sa-ma-nu, (V 21 *a-b* 3) AV 6534, Br 3136; *cf* K 246 i 20 (H 82—3) see maškadu. IV^2 29 *no* 1 *b* 21—22 (see namtāru) has the same id. BOISSIER, PSBA xxii 110; CRAIG, *Relig. Texts*, 18, 20 asakku sa-ma-nu murçu. See also KB vi (1) 160, 10; 574.

sīmānu. appointed, due time {festbestimmte, übliche Zeit} usually in the phrase = ina lā sīmānišu out of season {zur Unzeit} AV 6686; V 31 *e-f* 46 ša ina la si-ma-ni-šu kun-nu u-tu-lu. III 64 *a* 28 Sin ina lā si-ma-ni-šu ŠI; *a* 29 (30) (uxxi-ram-ma ŠI & la ŠI); 54 *b* 1, 2; *c* 29 (unexpectedly). ZA iv 169 māru ālid ina si-man-ni-šu (a son born under her

—the moon's—sign). BANKS, *Diss*, 1 *no* 21, 160 e-bu-ri ina si-ma-ni-šu u-ṭa-ab-bi (zur Reifezeit). Perhaps also Sn vi 1—2: I cut off their hands ki-ma bi-ni kiš-še-e si-ma-ni (= ina simânišu). √סמן (KB vi, 1, 370—1).

Sīmānu (= siṷânu) = Sivan, name of the third Babylonian month. AV 6087; = סִיוָן. ideogr. (araz) LIBIT-GA; MUSS-ARNOLT, *Jour. Bib. Lit.*, '92, 82 *foll*. V 43 *a-b* 9—14 (Br 4200, 4852, 9349, 10602, 11197, 11207, 11584. II 44 *a-b* 71, Br 5125. §§ 44; 46.

simānu ***2.*** Nabd *Ann* 3, 17—18 be-la (*p* 159 *col* 1) ša mimma ina Ê-sag-gil u êkurâtê | ul iš-ša-kin u si-ma-nu ul itêti-iq, BA ii 222—3, 247, 256: nobody's weapon entered *Esaggil*, nor did a flag come in {niemandes Speer kam nach *E* hinein, auch kein Feldzeichen rückte ein}.

simēnu (?). 82—5—22, 78 *R* 1 si-me-in dul-li šu-u. THOMPSON, *Reports*.

simānu ***3.*** among list of plants, II 41 *no* 9, 40 ..... si-ma-nu, preceded by .... ru si-ma-ti.

simūnu. K 1197, 8—9 ma-a mi-i-nu si-mu-nu | lu-te-ru-ba (Hr[L] 15).

summunu. Camb 438, 8 (16) .... QA šamaššammi ša ištēn su-um-mu-nu.

Samsu in P. N. Sa-am-su-i-lu-na KB iv 36 *no* 4, 22; 34 *no* 1 *foll*; KB ii 286 *col* 1, 7 BA iv 375 *foll*; name of canal Samsu-iluna na-ga-ab nu-ux-ši, BA iv 376, 408. On samsu, šamsu, šamšu see § 46 *rm*.

sumassuxu. K 2020 *O* 5 su-mas-su-xu. M[S] texts, pl. 4.

sumqu *cf* sunqu.

simurrū, AV 6696 see sixarrū; **sumurru** (?) *cf* suxarru.

su-mur-du-u *cf* surdū.

simēr'ū'. Cyr 281, 3 si-me-ri-e parzilli iron fetters {eiserne Fesseln}, BA iii 433; Targ. סְמַר. Br. M. 81, 6—25, 45, 9 *M.* gives to *A-B* his wife a piece of land *etc.* instead of ..... 5 manê kaspu qu-lu u si-me-ri (and a ring) BOR ii 3; ZK ii 84, 20 XAR ..... = si-me-ru.

(al) **Sa-me-ri-na** (§ 46). II 53 *no* 4, 55, followed by (al) Di-maš-qa, among tribute-paying cities of Syria. AV 6539; also III 34 *b* 95; 35 *no* 4 *O* 11 (TP III *Ann* 228).

samašurū. AV 6536 quotes sa-ma-šu-ru-u; from a late Babylonian text.

Sumaštu see Subartu.

samētu wall {Mauer}? KB vi 116—17 (& 424) *ad* NE i (1) 12 sa-me-ta-šu ša la u-maš-ša-ru. K[M] 21, 26 (*cf* 16) sa-me-it dūri (ZA xi 101); T[M] iv 24 (v 134) ana dūri u sa-me-ti tap-qi-da-in-ni. Perh. CRAIG, *Relig. Texts*, 81, 11 xur-ri nadbaku u sa-ma-a-ti ša šadī. √סמה?

sāmtu ***1.*** ZIMMERN, *Ritualtafeln*, 1—20, 101 as soon as the horizon of heaven sa-am-ta im-tax-ṣu (is covered with darkness).

sāmtu ***2.*** *f* of sāmu, 2, & sându some gem, precious stone {ein Edelstein} usually with prefix TAG = aban. AV 6546; Br 11862—3. K 40 (I) 83) iii 63, 64 GUG & GI-RI-IM (ZA x 371—2) = sa-am-tum. II 19 *R* 47, 48 ša-ad (aban) GIŠ-ŠIR-GAL sa-an-ti (= TAG-GUG) uk-ni-i qa-ti-ia u-ma-al[-li]. ABEL & WINCKLER, *Texte*, 60 *fol*, *O* 22 ana xu[-la-li sa]-an-di uk-ni. IV² 18 *no* 3 *R* iv (5+)8 xu-lat i-ni muš(ṣir?)-gar-ru xu-la-lu sa-an-du (= TAG-GUG, which occurs also IV² 31 *R* 56, see KB vi, 1, 405; II 40 *no* 2, 14) uk-nu-u, a list of precious stones. H 39, 125; 209, 16—17; NE 75, 47.

NOTE. — See H[P] 43, 2; D[Par] 131 bel; MEISSNER & ROST, 25: pearls ‖ Perlen, properly the gray gem; connecting therewith sandaniš (*q. v.*); etymology accepted by HAUPT; see, however, JENSEN, ZA x 368 *foll* perh Malachite ‖ Malachit, found especially in Meluxxa (II 51 *b* 17; V 30 *g-h* 63); KB vi (1) 570: vielleicht Porphyr; on KB iii (2) 4, 50 see JENSEN, ZA ix 127.

sammatu. NE 42, 13 [a]-na bīti-ni i-na sa-am-ma-ti (*var* -mat) (iṣ) erini er-ba KB vi (1) 166—7 (& 574) into our house enter, into the sweet odor of cedarwoods.

summatu *f* dove {Taube} *pl* summâti, Br 1078, 1084. ideogr. TU-XU, § 9, 98; *del* 140, 141 (147, 148); Sn vi 19 (see kaš-šudu, 449 *col* 1); *pl* TU-XU[-MEŠ]. See damamu (*p* 253) for IV² 26 *b* 56—7, 27 *no* 3 *a* 30—1 (BA i 163 *rm* ††, on *p* 164), H 115—16 *R* 9—10 (= IV² 20* *no* 5; Br 7718); NE 51, 10 (J[I-X] 15). S[b] 2, 3 tu-u | TU | su-um-ma-tum; II 12 & 219, 105. IV² 27 *b* 14—15 su-um-ma-ti (= TU-XU) ina a-pa-ti-ši-na i-bar-rum, they fetch the doves from their houses; *cf* 3 *b* 69 mu-ru-uṣ qaq-qa-di [ki-ma su]-um-ma-ti ana ap-ti. K 41 *c* 2 ki-ma su-um-ma-tum u(or šam?)-ri-it-ti i-na gu-šu-ri a-bit, PINCHES, PSBA xvii 65 *foll.* II 37 *a-c* 42 su-um-mu (or SU-UM-MU?) XU = su-um[-ma-tum]; D^{S} 116, AV 6881, Br 194. — Z^{B} 30; D^{Pr} 157; G §§ 41 *rm* 2; 56. HOMMEL, BA ii 354 *rm* *: *smn* (Egypt) = goose = سُمانى, quail; summatu < sumnatu.

sīmtu *f*, *c. st.* si-mat (& se-mat) √סמן. AV 6688, 6698; id ME-TE, § 9, 116; Br 10440—1; *pl* simāti; what is fitting, pertinent, suitable; fitness, propriety {Gehörige; Gehörigkeit} also = spolia; further: ornament, decoration {Schmuck, Zierde}; also of food and drink {auch von: Speise und Trank. Sarg *Ann* 198 see misū, *p* 566 *col* 2; si-mat bēlu-u-ti insignia of lordship L^4 i 26; si-mat qa-ra-du-ti, L^4 i 21; si-mat ilu-u-ti or šarru-u-ti NE 43, 27—8; 15, 30—1 *etc.* V 33 ii 52—3 a-gi-e be-lu-ti si-mat i-lu-ti; V 65 *a* 16 *Ebabbara* .... si-mat ilu(-u)-ti-šu, + 21 a-na si-ma-at i-lu-u-ti-šu, & *b* 2 the temple ša .... šu-lu-ku a-na si-mat ilu-u-ti-šu, + 25. SCHEIL, *Nabd*, iii 32 the 7 lions si-mat i-lu-ti-šu; Asb ii 11 a golden chain si-mat šarrū-ti-šu (*cf* vi 12 + 16 + 18, see simanū); TP III *Ann* :25 (-ia); 23 si-mat līti u dannūni. Bu 88—5—12, 80 *col* viii mu-sa-ru-u si-ma-ti-ia ‖ ši-ṭir šumi-ia in Bu 88—5—12, 103 vi 7 (BA iii 226). Neb viii 14 (24) see makkūru. TP vii 88 *fol* two great ziqqurāte which a-na si-mat ilū-ti-šu-nu rabī-te šu-lu-ka; *cf* IV^2 18 *no* 1 *O* 8—9 a-na si-mat (= ME-TE) ilū-ti-šu šu-lu-ku. I 49 *d* 27 si-mat da-ra-a-ti, an ornament for ever. Asb vi 61 wild oxen .... si-mat bābā-ni. V 60 *c* 21 šikin-šu u si-ma-ti-šu; 81—6—7, 209, 25 the wise ruler who si-ma-a-ti iš-tak-ka-nu, added decorations, improvements; 32—33 ki-ma si-ma-ti-šu la-bi-ra-a-ti, in harmony with his former decorations, BA iii 262—3. LEHMANN, S^2 19 ištak-ka-nu si-ma(-a)-ti; S^2 27; L^2 6; si-ma-a-te L^2 7. Bu 88—5—12, 75 + 76 v 15 si-mat É]-sag-ila (BA iii 246—7); Merod.-Balad. stone ii 46—7 who for the great gods iš-tak-ka-nu si-ma-tu (BA ii 261, 267 Prunkgeräte niederlegte >< KB iii, 1, 186—7); Asb iii 117 aš-tak-ka-nu si-ma-a-te (*cf* WINCKLER, *Forsch.*, i 247 >< KB ii 186). ABEL & WINCKLER, *Texte*, 60, 17 (end) ana si-ma-a-ti na-aš-kin. SCHEIL, *Nabd*, iii 37 ⁽ⁱˡ⁾ lamassu la si-mat E-AN-NA; + 34 ⁽ⁱˡᵃᵗ⁾ Ištar la si-ma-a-tu (die nicht hingehörte), viii 52—3 ki-ma si-ma-a-ti-ši-na ri-eš-ta-tum, in harmony with its original decorations. ZA v 68, 11 see zamū ℶ *pm* (*p* 283 *col* 1); I 65 *b* 50 se-ma-a-ti ri-eš-ta-a-ti; KB iii (2) 92, 57 u-ça-ab-bu-u si-ma-a-tim; Sarg *Khors* 166 aš-tak-ka-na si-ma-a-ti (*Ann* 430; II 67 *R* 28). K 3364 *R* 12 (end) si-mat [qu]t-rin-ni DELITZSCH, *Weltschöpf.*, 54, but see KB vi (1) pref. xviii *fol.* — I 65 *a* 19 ⁽ˢᵃᵐ⁾ šu-um-mu pi-la-a si-ma-at (*c* 14 se-ma-at, *b* 30) ap-pa-ri-im, a name of rushes {Rohrnamen}. V 51 *b* 75—6 nu-na iç-çu-ra si-mat ap-pa[-ri] = ME-TE-ZUG-RA; IV^2 4 *b* 27 si-im-ti a-bi (GGA '98, 813). IV^2 14 *no* 1, 24—5, 26—7 um-mu ša ana si-ma-a-ti (= ME-TE) šit-kuna-at (KB vi 54), 15—16 a-na iç-çu-ri (& ⁱˡ Zi-i) si-ma-a[-tu lu-pu-uš] = NAM-ME-TE; also IV^2 18* *no* 3 *R* iv 11—12; 27 *no* 2 *a* 25—6 (end) si-mat (= ME-TE) bīt gi-gu-ni-e. V 51 iii 17 enbu eššu?] ba-nu-u si-mat (= ME-TE, 16) be-lu-tim; II 55 *c* 55 Damkīna is called ME-TE ZU-AB = simat apsī. — **Lā simātē** (= lā bānātē), desecration, indignities, violation, unworthiness {Verunzierung, Schändung, Unwürdigkeit} KB vi (1) 370—1. a-šar la si-ma-te-ka at a place not befitting thee = unworthily of thee, L^4 ii 31; *cf* Asb vi 109 a-šar la si-ma-te-e (*var* ti)-ša (§ 74, 2); Sn v 17 speaks of a hated rival as having been a-na la si-ma-te-šu "improperly" put on the throne of Babylon. IV^2 39 *a* 1 Adadnirāri rubū ellu si-mat ili (AJSL xii 167: used by Adadnirari to emphasize his worthiness to occupy the throne of Assyria); V 35, 25 (end) ap-ša-a-ni la si-ma-ti-šu-nu, the yoke which dishonored them (BA ii 212—3); 6 (beg) pa-ra-aç la si-ma-a-ti-šu-nu (BA ii 208—9; 250 >< KB iii, 2, 120—1). — V 28 *a-b* 93 si-mat pa-ni (Br 601)

— na-ma-rum (see nāmarum), JENSEN, 349 *rm*: picture {Bild}. V 39 *a-b* 9, Br 1894 si-kur (mat?) pi-i. V 40 *c-d* 2, 3 ME-TE & TE (H 40, 211) — si-im-tum (ZA iv 275; Br 10440, 7705); V 29 *e-f* 67 ME; ME TE — si-im-tum : si-ma-a-tum (H 33, 788); V 16 *c-d* 7 PAT^(kur) DIR — si-im-tum, Br 9935.

^(kakkab) **si-mu-tu.** Br 12348 *ad* K 4915 *c* 8 (AV 6697).

simētu. AV 6693 *ad* K 8665 *a-b* 3 .... e-tu | si-me-tu. M^S texts, *pl* 14.

^(il) **Sin** name of the moon-god {Name des Mondgottes} § 46; usually written ►►+<<< (§ 9, 60; TP i 5; Br 9988. 9995) *i. e.* god of the thirty; IV² 31 *R* 2; Asb iii 121; K 2701, 4 + 12 + 16; AV 6700. iD AN-EN-ZU (pronounced ZU-EN, SCHEIL, ZA vii 192 *rm*; Br 2819; K 4870, 29; IV² 1 *b* 53—4 — AN-<<<); AN-ŠEŠ-KI (Br 6455; II 61, 48; IV² 1 *b* 29—30; 5 *a* 60—1; V 52 *a* 25 *etc.*). H 77, 41—2 EN-ZU — ^il Sin, mentioned together with Šamaš and Adad; H 18, 289 du-mu-gu | TUR-KU | ^il Sin. Written Si-in in IV² 61 *b* 9 P. N. ^(sal) Si-in-qi-ša-a-mur (or Sinqu?). JENSEN, ZA vii 177 *rm* 1 reads Šin (as before him, OPPERT, GGA '78, 1032) and believes that šattu & Šin are of the same root. BALL, PSBA xii 408 √Akkadian. See also JASTROW, *Religion*, 219—20; JENSEN, 101 *foll*; MUSS-ARNOLT, *Babyl. Months*, 11—18; PINCHES, *Jour. of Trans. of Victoria Institute*, 28, 15—16. — Sin was the local deity of *UR*, H 37, 30. Simān is the month ša ^(il) Sin mār reš-ti-i ša ^il Bēl, IV² 33 *col* iv (coloph.) 3. See now KAT³ 361—7.

On Sin bēl agē, see HOFFMANN, ZA xi 241 (bel). Sarg *Cyl* 58 says qar-rad ilāni ^il Sin. Sin ša a-gi-e ša-qu-u nam-ri-ri, I 27, 4; TP i 5—6; IV² v 21—22 called bēl nam-ra-çi-it (*q. v.*) Br 2821.

On Aku — ^il Sin see JENSEN, 100 *foll*; HOMMEL, *Überlieferung*, ('97) 161 *fol*; ZIMMERN, *Theol. Rundschau*, '98, 321; MEINHOLD, *Jesajaerzählungen*, 72—3 — "אריוך, Gen 14: 1, 6; Dan 2: 14, doch wol — Eri-Aku — Arad-Sin"; but WINCKLER reads Rim-Sin, II 48 *a-b* 48 AN-A-KU — AN <<<; V 44 *c* 52—3; Br 11680.

On compound names see BEZOLD, *Catal.*, 2187 *foll*, AV 6701—6719. Sin-axe-erba — Sennacherib (often); ^(il) Sin-i-din-nam (Xammurabi, KING, vol i pref xxxv *fol*); ^(il) Sin-karābi-iš-me, Neb 161, 6; KB iv 4, 31 ^(il) Sin-i-ki-ša-am (14, 1 -šam); 6 ii 17 ^(il) Ri-im ^(il) Sin; Camb 386, 8 ^(amēl) Sin-ša-du-nu; & Sin-ta-qiš-bul-liṭ; Cyr 64, 3 Nūr-Sin-ut-kal-a-na-Marduk; Sin-tal-lak, eponym ruler of 740—39 B. C. Against P. N. Si-ni-ja, JENSEN, ZA vii 177 *rm* 1 see TALLQVIST, *ibid* 284 *rm* 1.

On Bur-Sin and other names with Bur-, see DELITZSCH, BA ii 622 *foll*; also LEHMANN, ZA x 84 *foll*. Sin-uballiṭ, § 46. Sin-gamil & Ga(i)mil-Sin see *p* 221 note 2; also *cf* Ig-mil ^(il) Sin, KB iv 29, 60; ZA x 91 *foll*.

II 48 *a-b* 33 ^(du-mu-gu) TUR-KU — ^(il) Sin, Br 4159; 48 AN-A-KU — ^il Sin; *c-d* 30 an-ta-lu — a-da-ru ša ^il Sin, Br 474. II 49, 50 *add* MUL-AN-NA — ^il Sin, AV 6700; (Br 450), *cf* K 257 *O* 29 E-AN-NA — bīt a-a-ak; II 56 *c-d* 44 *cf* Br 6458, 9665; AV 6700. II 57 *a-b* 56 (Br 4616), 57 (Br 10571), 58 (Br 10637), 59 (Br 2876), 60 (Br 8281), 61—2 (Br 7801, same iD as ūmu lā padū; II 19 *b* 59—60), 63 (Br 7479; II 19 *b* 19—20), 64 (Br 681), 65 EN-ZU-MU-ŠA (— GAR) — ^(il) sa-pi-in a-a-bi (Br 3142), 66 (Br 5986), 67 (Br 7825; II 19 *b* 57—8), 77 (Br 7922), 78 (Br 6134), 79 ^il Nam-tar-ru. II 58 *a-b* 18 see Br 10004; 47 *e-f* 66 ^(lam-ga) AN  — ^il Sin (Br 11166). On V 37 *d-f* 42 *cf* ZA i 228; ii 81 *rm* 3. III 66 *O* 11 *e*, 24 *d* AN-EN-<< (Br 2910).

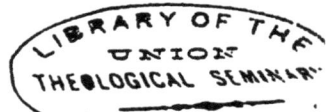

In Observatory reports the name is written also without prefix ►►+ (K 172, 1 *etc.*). II 44 *no* 1 *add* (AV 6700, Br 7545, 9872, 10349). V 36 *a-c* 6 u | < | AN-EN-ZU, Br 8740.

-sun — -šunu, written ►—◄, ZA i 182 *rm* 2; BOISSIER, *Diss*, 19; IV² 48 *b* 5, 9 pron. suffix. 3 *pl m.*

-sin — šina, *e. g.* kul-lat-si-in V 35, 8 their totality; pron. suffix. 3 *pl f.*

sānu. II 48 *a-b* 51 ^(šam) sa-a-nu, Br 12317; AV 6556.

(bīt) sa-a-ni (?) T. A. (Ber) 199, 7 ma-k(q)u-ut i-na bīt-sa-a-ni i-ba-aš-ši.

Sannu. name of a fisher's net made of reed {ein Netz aus Binsen oder Schilf}. K 242 i (II 22 *a-b*) 24 GIŠ-SA-GIŠ-GI = sa-an-nu & še-e-tum ša (amēlu) ŠU-XA (*i. e.* bā'iri) AV 6505, Br 3128.

sūnu *1.* loins (between hipbone and false rib) {Hüftenbein} HAUPT, *Jour. Bib. Lit.*, xix 76 *rm* 93 against KB iii (1) 181, 10 šīr sūni, II 44 *g-h* 16; ZA i 247 *rm* 2. Also see BA i 287. T^C 111—112; AV 6834. III 65 *a* 30 sūn (written UR) imitti. H 118 *R* 6 su-ni (5, UR) ip-te-ma. IV² 61 *b* 57 ina su-ni-ki ta-šak-ni. II 35 *g-h* 68—71 (id UR), see mutu (620 *col* 1), & çubātu; also *l* 68. II 19, 346 UR = su-nu (= S^b 276 su-u-nu, Br 4887) between iš-du and ut-lu; id also IV² 31 *O* 35 lubkī ana ardāti ša ina sūn (amēli) xa-i-re-ši-na (*R* 21). V 28 *e-f* 19 su-nu ‖ ut-lum. K 5418 iv 16 at-ta ina su-un sinništi-ka šipir lu KAK (= tēpu)-uš, mayest thou perform thy work in the lap of thy wife {mögest du im "Schoose" deines Weibes dein Geschäft verrichten, KB vi (1) 298—9, and 316 *ad* 10, 20; ZA xii 321 *foll.* *Rec. Trav.* xxii (SCHEIL, *no* liv, 7) ina su-un ardati (etli) tu-še-li-i.

sūnu *2.* sloop, tie, band {Schleife, Binde, Band} or the like ‖ mu(i)gru (*p* 512 *col* 2), AV 6884 *fol.* V 15 *c-d* 20 KU-TU = su-u-nu (Br 11912), *c-d* 48 u-la-pu su-u-ni, Br 7077, 12166, AV 5463. T^C 111 *ad* Nabd 320, 11 (826, 12) su-u-nu ša (il) *N-N*, combines *nos* 1 & 2: a garment for the lower portion of the gods (statues); 320, 9 su-un-ni-e ša (il) Šamaš u (ilat) A-A; 694, 26 su-ni-e. ZA i 182 *rm* 2 reads V 28 *a* 7 te-di-iq sun-ni (instead of be-ni).

NOTE. — V 25 *c-d* 1—3 u-zu-bu-šu i-zi-iţ(d)-ma \| i-na su-ni-ša ir-ku-uš \| ina biti uš-ç-iš (BOISSIER, *Diss*, 4) Br 4835. Not sure whether to *no* 1 or 2.

sunnu. Perhaps V 26 *a-b* 25 GIŠ-BAD = su-un-nu in same group with nu-ta-bu (27) Br 1531.

sunnu V 27 *e-f* 33 see šinnu.

sinnu? Nabd 973, 7 si-in-nu; 799, 11 sin-nu.

sinū. BROWN-GESENIUS, 702 compares סְנֶה thorny bush {Dornbusch}. 81—7—6, 688 S. H. i 12 si-ni-e SAR (ZA vi 293).

sanabu. II 34 *a-b* 13 BU = sa-na-bu (Br 7535, AV 6547) followed by ZI = si-in-bu.

sanābu. II 42 *c*, *R* 66 (šam) a-a-ar sa-na-bu = صناب (*σίναπυ*) STUCKEN, *Astralmythen*, i 5 *rm* *.

sinbu *1.* see sanabu.

sinbu *2.* in a list of clothing {ein Kleidungsstück} V 15 *c-d* 45 KU-ŠA-IB (= ulāpu)-AN-RA = si-in-bu. AV 6722, Br 3331, 12164; but *cf* ZK ii 266.

sangu (AV 6560) = šangū, *q. v.*

singu something of fur or woolen stuff {etwas aus Tierpelzen oder Wollstoffen gemachtes}. V 14 *c-d* 28—9 SEG-ŠU-KAT, SEG-SAG-DIM-GA = si-in-gu, AV 6723; Br 7100, 3560.

sungiru. K 4334 i (II R 60) 8 su-un-gi-ra (K 9287 ii 4) i-na lap-ti, *Rev. Sém.* ix 187 *rm* 2, "plante de marais".

sandu = sāmdu = sāmtu, 2. *q. v.*

su-na-a-di Sn iii 80 *i. e.* SU (= mašak) na-a-di (see nādu, 4).

sindu. Nabd 644, 2 (end) si-in-du; P. N. Pa-ar-si-in-du, Anp ii 69, *var* Par-sin-du.

sindū. a tree whose wood was used for building purposes {ein Baum dessen Holz für Bauzwecke verwandt ist}. Sn *Kui* 4, 3 (iç) si-in-da-a (BA iii 193 *rm* **: Pistazienholz (?); MEISSNER-ROST, 14 + 25 = buţnu).

sandaniš *adv.* Sarg *Cyl* 21 Sargon who ina qabal tāmdim the Ionian sa-an-da-niš kīma nūni ibārūma, HAUPT, *Proc. Am. Or. Soc.*, Mr. '94, *p* civ *rm* †: like a pearldiver. (plural of *sāndu) AV 6502. See Note to samtu, 2.

sanxu. a stone {Steinart} Nabd 490, 3 + 4 sa-an-xu.

senkurru *cf* simkurru.

sunkirtu. V 47 *a* 52 u-lil (? çip?) explained by su-un-kir-tum.

sin-na-nu *cf* šinnānu; **su-un-nu-nu,** Sarg *Cyl* 39 (end) AV 6840, read zunnunu (*q. v.*).

sinuntu (& d, § 48; BA ii 295) swallow {Schwalbe} §§ 63; 65, 18; id NAM-XU, § 9, 116; *del* 142 (150, 151). AV 6721, 7237; IV² 27 *b* 18—19 si-nun-tu (= NAM-XU) ina qin-ni-ša u-šap-ra-šu, the swallow they make to fly out of her nest. Br 2101, 2137. II 37 *a-c* 30 KIB-ŠU-XU

— ŠU (*i. e.* kib(p)šu) — çi-nun-du, 40 see kîsu, 2 (412 *col* 1); II 40 *c-f* 37 si-nun-tum; II 45 *b* 63 su-pi-in si-nun-ti (D 87, 89) Br 2101. II 51 *a-b* 59 (Br 10666) a star of the Euphrates is explained by si-nun-tum. TALLQVIST, ZA vii 285 *rm* quotes P. N. (sal) Sinūnu, Neb 138, 22 written (sal, il) Sin-u-nu.

sanasu. ℑ V 45 v 39 tu-sa-na-as.

sanaqu *pr* isniq, *ps* isaniq. press {drängen} AV 6549. *a*) trans.: 1) harass, oppress, afflict {bedrängen, drangsalieren}. 81, 2—4, 219 *O* ii 3 ri-eš sa-na-ki, at the beginning of the oppression. II 65, 3 a-na za-an-ki bir-ti ša māt [Aššur]. TP iv 87—88 i-na šu-mur kakkē-ja ez-zu-te as-ni-qa-šu-nu-ti. HILPRECHT, *OBI*, i 32—33 *col* i 4 ([il] Bêl) za-a-ni-ik (il) A-nun-na-ki. K 2361 *R* iv 15 ta-sa-niq arad-ka (ZA iv 240). Šalm. *Throne-inscr.* iii 9 *foll* name of a gate (10) sa-ni-qa-at mal-ke. K[M] 46, 12 (Ner-gal) sa-ni-qu, who harasses. V 41 *a-b* 47—50 SAG-BU (Br 7536) = sa-na-qu ša ŠEŠ (= axi, or limnit?), GI-NA = *s* ša (amêl) IM (the man of the tablet) Br 2899; SAG-BU & KU-NU (Br 10588 = qirêbu) = *s* ša (amêl) KUR (= na-kiri) Br 8630, 10589. — 2) push, press together, connect something with another thing (itti) {zusammenfügen, etwas mit etwas anderem fest verbinden}. Neb v 51 it-ti ša a-bi i-pu-šu e-is-ni-iq (KB iii, 2, 20—21) & *l* 31; V 34 *a* 30 ik-zu-ru e-se-ni-iq (+ *b* 19). ZA ii 128 (Br. M. 79, 2—1, 1) *a* 25 nār mu-çi mi-e-šu as-ni-iq-šu. espec. in colophons: iš-ṭur is-niq ibrēma, II 36, 26; 21 *a* 32; IV² 34 *no* 1 *b* 85. V 41 *a-b* 46 ..... KAK = sa-na-qu ša dup-šar-ru-ti (*q. v.*) perh. = condense, Br 5266. — 3) grasp, hold fast {festpacken, festhalten}. V 66 *b* 19 man-da-at-ti-šu-nu lu-us-ni-qi (*var* -ik). II 48 *c-d* 26; V 41 *a-b* 43—5 sa-na-qu ša ŠU (*i.e.* qâti?); V 29 *e-f* 70—71 DIB-BA = sa-na-qu ša ça-ba-ti (Br 10692; H 34, 805; II 27 *a-b* 38); ŠU-GID-DA (Br 7536) = *s* ša amēli. V 41 *a-b* 61 da-ab DIB | sa-na-qu ša (amêl) DIB; 58 KI-LAL = *s* ša šu-qul-ti (Br 10110). — 4) provide {besorgen} PEISER, *Vertr.*, xxii 11—12 PAT-XI-A i-sa-an-ni-iq-ma. — 5) of animals: force into the yoke, tie, harness {ans Joch festbinden, ins Joch zwingen}. Sn v 80 horses and mules is-ni-qa çi-in-de-šu (§ 139). V 41 *a-b* 60—61 see Br 9019; 56 SAG-DU = sa-na-qu ša ri-ši mu-tu(m), Br 3576. V 29 *e-f* 72 GIŠ-GIŠ-LAL = sa-na-qu ša iš-ka-ri (fetter) Br 10104. — 6) lock, lock up, shut up {schliessen, verschliessen}. I 44, 56 e-kal ku-tal-li (see *p* 457) ša ana sa-na-a-qi mimma šum-šu; Sn vi 29 (the palace built by my royal fore-fathers) ana šukšur karāši pa-qa-a-di sisê sa-na-ki mimma šum-šu (BA i 374 *no* 56). II 23 *c-d* 42 sa-na-qu ‖ e-de-lu; *c-d* 1 sa-niq-tum ‖ da-al-tum, AV 6553. K 8364 *R* 10 ina sa-naq at-me-e-ka. L[5] 2 (= KB iii, 1, 194); K 128 *O* 1 see mitxurtu, 2. V 41 *a-b* 51, 52 TIK-GI (Br 3246, 6390), TIK-GIG (Br 3235, 7536) = sa-na-qu ša bîti; 53—55 TIK-BU (Br 3288, Z[B] 88), TIK-GIG (Br 3234), ŠU-GU-ŠUR = sa-na-qu ša dalti (Br 7171, 7211); 62, 63 KA-GI-NA = sa-na-qu ša pi-i or a-ma (*char.* pi)-tim (& *cf* 57; Br 10693, 619, 9813); perhaps also 64, 65 DUG-GA-ZI = sa-na-qu ša ki-bi-tim (AV 684; Br 12332); 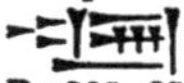-ZI = *s* ša šap-di (*i. e.* šapti, Br 805, 2899).

b) intrans.: 1) push, press against something, intrude {gegen etw. drängen, an-drängen}. JAOS xvi 73 *foll* 9: a-na Ba-bi-lam[ki] la sa-na-qi. TP iii 58 (62—3) a-na ālāni ..... šam-riš lu as-niq (*var* ni-iq). S[P] 158 + S[P] ii 962 *O* 7 is-ni-qa ana bābi çîri (pressed on to the supreme door; + 15), 21 see limniš. IV² 2 v 26 (end) la DIM-DIM = tasaniq (Br 6320 la tunakkir); H 12, 110 di-im | KUR-KUR | sa-na-qu = V 29 *e-f* 69. IV² 15 ii 57—8 a-bi, the firegod a-na çi-it (il) Šam-ši is-niq (Br 1666); 56 *b* 19 šum-ma a-na pulāni mār pulāni ta-tur-riš-šu (√târu) ta-sa-ni-ki-šum-ma, & *cf* K 2971 (IV² 56 *add*, 11) 6 a-na zumri pulāni mār pulāni la KUR-KUR (= sana)-ki; IV² 57 *b* 5 a-a TE (= iṭxa)-a a-a DIM-DIM (or KUR-KUR)-qa; H 75 *R* 11. — 2) approach, arrive at {nahe kommen, an-kommen} Neb *Grot* ii 8 in order that an enemy a-na Ba-bi-lam[ki] la sa-na-ga-am (& ZA i 339, 9; see also *no* 1). KB vi (1) 298, 24 e ta-as-niq-šu, do not approach him (ZA xii 323). KING, *Xammurabi*, i pref. xxxv *foll*; Br. M. 17298 *R* 2—3 a-na Bâbili^ki zi-in-ga-am (arrive at *B*); 23152, 8 a-na Bâbili^ki za-na-ki-im; 12837, 9 *foll* ina ^(arax) Araxsamna ûm XII^kan i-sa-an-ni-ku-ni-ik-qu | i-nu-ma iz-za-an-ku-ni-ik-qu (when they reach thee; BA iv 89—90 reads -ma- instead of -ku). — In legal documents: summon before a judge ‖ ṭaradu: Br. M. 23337, 12—13 within 2 days | li-is-ni-ku-nim (let them arrive, be summoned); Br. M. 23148, 19, 20 a-na Bâbili^ki li-is-ni-ku-nim; Br. M. 23139, 11 ar-xi-iš li-is-ni-ga-am: MEISSNER, 125, 127. — In astronomical forecasts: 83—1—18, 198 *R* 1—2 when Mercury is-niq (approaches) Mars; followed by la is-niq. — II 35 *e-f* 23 sa[-na]-qu ‖ qa-ra-bu; V 40 *c-d* 7 TE = sa-na-qu (8, = ṭe-xu-um) ZA i 456; iv 275. V 29 *e-f* 69 [cuneiform] [cuneiform] (with gloss di-im) = sa-na-qu (= II 27 *a-b* 37) ZK ii 54; Z^B 50. — 3) press, throng, crowd together, *i. e.* be submissive, obedient {zusammendrängen, sich ducken (in Gehorsam, Unterwürfigkeit)}. Asb ix 117 *foll* the inhabitants who a-na pâxâtišunu la sa-an-qu (did not obey) § 152; viii 63, 64 ina pu-lux-ti ^(iç) kakkê ^(il) Ašur ka-ši-du-ti | is-sa-an-qa-am-ma, KB ii 221: he approached {er kam heran} see also WINCKLER, *Gesch.*, 288; *Forsch.*, i 251. V 41 *a-b* 67 . . . . ZA = sa-na-qu ša i-[cuneiform] (lim?) Br 14464; 68 . . . . KI = *s* ša U (or u?)-si (Br 14360). K 4143 *O* 6 s]a-na-qu (M^S texts, *pl* 5). II 48 *c-d* 7 LAL = sa-na-qu; V 41 *a-b* 59 KI-LAL = sa-na-qu ša çarpi, 58 = KILAL ša šu-q(g)ul-ti (Br 9814, 9815). H 50, 1, 3 IN ^(di-im) [cuneiform] [cuneiform] = is-ni-iq; IN-[cuneiform] [cuneiform]-EŠ = is-ni-qu. V 40 *c-d* 7 TE = sa-na-qu (?) Br 7704.

ʒ T. A. (Ber) 8 *R* 2 su-ni-iq[-šu-um-ma] ZA v 17 press him hard; K 1101, 8—11 ^(amêl) rêb qa-qul-la-te | ša la šarri | ša la mâr šarri | i-çab-ta u-sa-ni-qa-a-ni = the *r q* has . . . . put me into prison (Hr^L 152); K 194, 9 u-sa-ni-iq-šu-nu, and has put them into prison (*ibid*, 144). 83—1—18, 242 *R* 4 & 80—7—19, 63, 6 see nakapu, 1.

ʒ^t K 527 *R* 5, 6 e-ta-am-ru iç-çab-tu-ni-šu | us-sa-an-ni-qu-u (or -šu) Hr^L 32.

Š IV² 57 *a* 67 the plant may not let approach (a-a u-šes-ni-qa) to my throat anything evil (JENSEN); K^M 12, 67; *ibid* 109 tu-ša-as-ni-qa ja-a-ši. T^M vi 6 la u-ša-as-na-qa ru-xi-e a-na zu-um-r[i].

Derr. masnaqtu & these 2 (3?):

sanqu, *adj.* *a*) narrow {enge}. V 28 *c-d* 62 sa-an-qu ‖ u(?) d(ṭ,t)ub(p)-lum; *cf* naxlum. AV 6566. — *b*) submissive, obedient {unterwürfig, gehorsam}. Esh ii 28 the inhabitants of the country Manna'a qu-tu-u la sa-an-qu. Z^Š ii 40 la a-mir-ti i[q-ta-bi l]a sa-niq-t[i]. Neb *Winckler* i 9 Neb. 'ašru sa-ga *etc.*, but KB iii (2) 46 reads '-aš-ru sa-[an-]qa, for the usual ašru šaxtu. II 48 *a-b* 45 NU-DIM-DIM-MA = la sa-an-qu, Br 1168; preceded by la šemû (44) & la mâgirum (43) in one group. Also II 27 *a-b* 41 (Br 13448); V 36 *d-f* 20 u-mun | [cuneiform] | sa-an-qu, Br 8738.

sunqu. need, famine {Not, Hungersnot} often with bubûtu, xušaxxu, *etc.*, *q. v.*, & Asb viii 36 ina su-un-ki xu-šax-xi. AV 6841. III 65 *a* 33, 38 the land su-un-gam im-mar (shall see famine); *a* 37 su-un-qu u dannatu mâtu içabat; Asb ix 58 su-un-qu ina bi-ri-šu-nu iš-ša-kin (broke out among them); SMITH, *Asurb*, 100, 18 see nibrêtu. II 29 *c-d* 37 U-GUG = su-un-qu, same id = ki-ib-bat išâti, xu-šax-xu, ub-bu-ṭu, *etc.* (Br 6096, 6099). K 1066 *R* 12 u su-un-qu i-na ^(mât) Elamti ša-kin-ma, *etc.* (Hr^L 277). I 27 *no* 2, 94 (*cf* POGNON, *Bavian*, 94, 162; BA i 168; ZA x 43). Also si-in-qi, Bu 91—5—9, 110 (Hr^L 756).

NOTE. — H 76, 1 su-mu-ug-ga perh. √ sanaqu, explains nanduru; also H 181; BA i 168, 11. See Note to simmu.

sinqu (?) II 23 *c-d* 70 sin (or eš)-ki e-ri-im. See also above Sin, § 1.

^šam **sunuš**. II 42 *a-b* 38 ^(šam) su-nu-uš = ^(šam) pi-pi. AV 6836; Br 186.

sanašu. ʒ T^M iii 20 u-sa-an-niš ina ka-lâtiki e-ra [qa-ma-ki?] (BA iv 157—8);

ibid viii 14 era ina kalâtiša tu-sa-na-aš (& T^{M} *p* 149), Br 6790. IV^2 55 *b* 35 paṭru ina libbi tu-sa-an-niš ‖ 56 *b* 24 tu-ša-an-niš. K 2496 *O* 4 . . . ga ina lib-bi tu-sa-an-na-aš.

sinništu, sineštu, sometimes **sinniš**, female, woman {weiblich, Weib}, *pl* sinnišâti (>< man), AV 6725; Br 7294, 10920, 10928; § 65, 24 *rm*. id SAL *e. g.* K 126, 3; II 28 *f* 40; IV^2 26 *b* 11—12 = sin-niš-tum; H 60, 13 ana SAL-šu; *pl* Sn ii 29 sinnišâti (written SAL-UN-MEŠ). libbi êkallišu, PSBA '81 Nov. 8 *p* 12; Bu 91—5—9, 2463, 18—19 iš-tu zi-ka-ri-im | a-di si-ni-iš-tum, from male to female. PINCHES in S. A. SMITH, *Asurb*, iii 98 si-in-niš; Asb ii 40 nišê zik-ru u sin-niš. II 35 *no* 4, *g-h* 61—62 ardatu ša ki-ma sin-niš-ti—ardu la-a i-ki-pu-ši (*cf* kipû & AV 4270, 7571; Br 3970, 11392). T^{M} 128—9 *ad* S 1981 + K 4355. S 752, 5 SAL-A-AN ša kîma sin-niš-ti. NE 8, 36 Êabani [nu-?]up-pu-uš (√napašu) pi-re-tu kîma sin-niš-ti, KB vi 120—1; NE 11, 13 + 19 ši-pir sin-niš-ti. IV^2 8 *col* 3, 27 sin-niš-tu (= SAL, 26). IV^2 2 v 39—40 ul zi-ka-ru (*var* zikru) šûnu ul sin-niš-a-ti (-tum) šûnu (§ 143). See zikru for other instances. III 53 *b* 30—1 (ilat) Dil-bat (= star Venus) sin-ni-ša-at (id SAL) & zi-ka-rat (*cf* 281 *col* 2). sin-niš-tu (= SAL) it-peš-tu IV^2 14 *no* 1 *a* 24—25, 26—27 (Br 11243), the wise woman (KB vi, 1, 154—55); IV^2 3 *b* 4—5 sin-niš-tu (= SAL, Br 2082) pa-ris-tu. K 4949 (= IV^2 26) 15 sin-niš-tu ša ru-xi-e qât-su ilta-pat, T^{M} 117 (also IV^2 26 *b* 12). BOR i 145 *R* 3 idnî-ma si-niš-ta-ki-ma an-nu-u lu muti-ki give me thy womanhood and he shall be thy husband; šupîlu (√שפל) ša sinništi, pudenda mulieris, see šupîlu. I 35 *no* 2, 9 SAL êkalli; II 58 *no* 2 *b* 5; II 32 *c-d* 19—21 iš-šu = si-n[i-iš-tu], as well as zi-ni-iš[-tum] & aš-bu-tum; 36 *d* 76 [zi]-ni-eš-tu. H 35, 833 SAL (?) = sin-niš-tu. II 27 *a-b* 45 (e?-rum) [illegible] = sin-niš-tum, preceded by zikaru, Br 3676); H 130 *R* 49—50, 53—54 NU-[illegible] = sin-niš-tu ana zi[-ka]-ri Z^{B} 15; Br 2013; same id = bêltu; 51—52 ša zi-ka-ri ana sin-niš-tum; 47—48 zi-ka-ri [ana] sin-niš-tum, Br 2013. — BARTH, *Etym. Studien*, 60—61 reads çinniš & *cf* Eth ፀንስት፡ pregnant {schwanger}; BA ii 298 √ perh. zinnu (= sunnu); LEVIAS, AJSL xvi 250 > šiçintu, *cf* Aram. אִנְתְּתָא. — Dupl. of K 38396 reads [Ti]-amat ša si-in-ni-ša-at T. who is a woman.

sinnišaniš *adv.* Esh *Sendsch*, *R* 57 zik-ru-šu sin-niš-a-niš lu-ša-lik-šu may degrade his manliness to womanishness. So perh. also K 2619 (*Dibbara*-legend) ii 10, see KB vi (1) 62—3.

sântu > sâmtu, *q. v.*

su-na-tum KB iv 4 (VATh 815) edge bîti u su-na-tum ša Sin-i-ki-ša-am, the house & *s* belongs to *S.*

sunnatu. II 37 *a* 38 su-un-nat ša-nu-xu (or XU?) = ku-pi-tu (*q. v.*, *p* 425 *col* 1) AV 6838.

santakku see below after sattûku.

sasû. K 890, 17 (al) Aššur tal-lak ta-si-si-i nu-bu-u, BA ii 634.

sa-as-su (-si) *1.* V 65 *b* 33 *etc.*, see šaššu.

sâsu *a*) moth {Motte} = סָס. §§ 27; 62, 2; AV 6574. S^{c} 13 [u-xu?] | UX | sa-a-su ‖ ub-lu (H 28, 612; Br 8298); II 5 *c-d* 41 UX-SEG = sa-a-su preceded by a-ša-šu (Br 8331); II 49 *no* 4, 64 when a star ana sa-a-si itûr (65, ana kal-ma-ti) Br 12318; see nâbu, 1. — *b*) precious stone {ein Edelstein} V 30 *e-f* 62 (aban) ZA-TU-BE = sa-a-su, Br 11805; KB vi (1) 210 *ad* NE 64, 26.

sassu *2.* 79, 7—8, 170, 10 sa-as-su, M^{B} texts, *pl* 26.

sisû *m* horse {Pferd, Ross} § 65, 38 *rm*; id usually (imêr) KUR-RA (§ 9, 244); *pl* (imêr) KUR-RA-MEŠ (Beh 59, 75 *etc.*) = sisû *pl* sisê; often in TP III *Ann*, *etc.* AV 6727. BA i 206; ii 46. Cyr 252, 4 (amêl) rê'û sisê (Nabd 932, 11); 320, 18 (amêl) rê'û si-si-i (AV *51 *col* 2); also Nabd 474, 11 (601, 12); Neb 4, 29 (KB iv 300—1); ZA iii 396, 12: V çimitta ša si-si-i, ZA v 142. IV^2 2 v 10—11 si-su-u (= (imêr) KUR-RA) ša ina šadî irbû šûnu (+ 49—50) Br 4994. IV^2 18* *no* 6 *O* 8—9 a[sak]ku ina u-re-e si-si-i uš-ni-il-ma, BA i 211. *pl*: KUR-RA-MEŠ, K 1252 *a* 13 (Hr^{L} 520); K 1113 + K 1229 *R* 8 imêr KUR-RA-MEŠ rak-ka-su-te (Hr^{L} 71); 80—7—19, 20, 12 *etc.*; TP v 5; also Šamš iii 16 (-šu-nu); Šalm, *Ob*, 49 (-šu); Asb ii 40, 73, 132 (rabûte); Sarg *Ann* 375 sisê taxâzi-šunu; *Khors* 183 (= *Ann* 440) sisê $^{(mât)}$ Mu-çu-ri çi-mit-ti ni-i-ri rabûte; Esh iv 16 sisû ru-ku-bi-šu-nu; Sarg *Ann* 126 rukub sisê. 80—7—19, 26, 10: altogether 16 KUR-MEŠ ša ni-i-ri; also KUR-MEŠ K 549, 12 (Hr^{L} 63); 83—1—18, 42, 9 *foll* (Hr^{L} 376). BOR ii 3 *R* 9 P. N. Mâr si-si-i = mâr rê'i sisê son of the master of the horse. See also Br 4986 *ad* S 1708, 9, and *cf* parû, çumbu, çimittu. — T. A. (Ber) 169, 24 u sisê ‖ su-u-[su], and horses (ZA vi 156 *no* 7); Lo 6, 22 $^{(imêr)}$ KUR-RA (76, 9 *etc.*); *pl* $^{(imêr)}$ KUR-RA-MEŠ Lo 1, 85 *etc.*; 26, 25 $^{(imêr)}$ KUR-RA-ja-ZUN; 3, 6 a-na si-si-ka, with thy horses; 72, 9 $^{(sal\ imêr)}$ KUR-RA-ja; Ber 7 *R* 12 u V çi-mi-it-ta ša si-si-i, and 5 span of horses. JENSEN, 91, 93 sisû (in Astronomy) = Pegasus am Himmel. — D^{Pr} 128 & *rm* 2; *cf* ZDMG 40, 719; ZA i 461. HOMMEL, *Gesch.*, 195; BALL, PSBA xiii 94 *rm* 2; BROWN-GESENIUS, 692; JENSEN, ZA xv 230 *rm* 1. A ‖ is

sûsu *1.* see, above, T. A. (Ber) 169, 24.

sûsu *2.* KB i 150 *ad* Šalm, *Ob*, (relief-inscr., *no* 3) su-u-su mentioned among the tribute of Muçri with pi-ra-a-ti (,) ba-zi-a-ti, *etc.* HOMMEL, *Gesch.*, 602; SCHEIL, *Šalm*, 91: a species of Antelope {Antilopen-art}; TIELE, *Gesch.*, 57 *rm*; AV 6844; ZA viii 210 √ Egypt *šôšu*: Kuhantilope.

sûsab(p)înu an official {ein Beamter} K 2012 *R* 12 LI-BI-IR = su-sa-p(b)i-nu (ZK ii 299; 302; 402; ZA i 398); *ad* LI-BIR = nâgiru, see this and Z^{B} 60, 61. Br 6967, 1134. ZA ii 460, 2 comp. Aram שׁוּשְׁבִינָא; also see (JENSEN) KB iii (1) 47 *rm* °; ZA xiv 183.

sussuku. Z^{B} iv 67 ar-nu ma-mit ša a-na su-us-suk (for evil {zum Unheil}) amêlûti iššak-nu; but *ibid*, *p* 57 šum-suk (√masaku) or šunzuq (√nazaqu).

sissiktu, *pl* sissikâtu dress, robe {Kleid, Kleidung}? (§ 61, 16; Z^{B} 105). KB iii (2) 50 *col* 3, 25 si-is-si-ik-ti $^{(il)}$ Marduk ça-ab-ta-ku-u (WINCKLER, ZA ii 175, 7—8; BOR iv 59; PSBA xi 208; but see KB iii 2, 114—115). V 63 *a* 8 Nabonidus who ça-ab-tu si-is-si-ik-[t]i ilâni, takes hold of the garment of the gods. AV 6720. K 6082 ii 8 si-si-ki-ti-šu (ZA v 151; & 150 *rm* 7). id KU-SEG *e. g.* KB vi (1) 44—5, 16 Sin ina sissikti-šu; *ibid*, *p* 364—5: "Schnur, oder ähnliches, aber nicht Kleid". id also L^{4} ii 27. V 15 *c-d* 24 KU-SEG = sis-sik-tum (Br 10783); V 28 *g-h* 57 si-sik-tum = e-ṭa-pa-tum. V 31 *a-b* 51 KU-SEG-ZUN = sis-si-ki-e-tum (Z^{B} 104; AV 6784; Br 10659).

si-si-el-tum ‖ arurtu (*q. v.*) trembling, earthquake {Erschütterung, Erdbeben} Z^{B} 118; ZA i 245 *rm* 1.

sussulu basket; amphora, jug {Korb; Krug} *del* 64 (68) 3 SAR çâbê na-aš $^{(iç)}$ su-us-su-ul-ša i-zab-bi-lu šamna, KB vi (1) 234—5 & 489: 3 Saren trugen die Leute, seine "Korbträger" (von) Öl herbei. So against ZA iii 419; see also JENSEN, 410; 516. Br 10201 *ad* 80, 11—12, 9 *R* iii 7, 8 bu-gin = su-us-su-lu; & ‖ bu-gin-nu ša me ....; see also *l* 9; K 4188, 5; Ner 28, 24. Sp III 6 (PSBA '94 Dec.) su]-us-su-lu followed by saltu, sillu.

sissimu. 81, 4—28, 327 *R* 14, 15 si-is-si-mu & si-is-si-ru = i-'š'it-tum, M^{S} texts, *pl* 26.

sassannu. K 4574 *R* 14 sa-as-sa-an-nu = si-el-lu (*q. v.*) AV 6577; Br 14261.

sasinu. name or title of some workman or official {eine Berufs- oder Arbeiterklasse} S^{b} 163 za-di-im | [illegible] | sa-si-nu (Br 101; AV 6573). V 61 iv 17 ^{il} NIN-ZADIM transl. in BA i 283: god (or lord) of the sculptors or stonecutters {Herr der Steinbildner}. Also IV^{2} 25 *a* 41. II 58 *no* 5, 14 (*c-d* 64) ^{il} Êa ša $^{(amêl)}$ [illegible]. According to HOMMEL, *Sum. Les.*, i 4 from Sumerian.

sisânu *1.* a grasshopper species {Heuschreckenart}. K 4373, 12 (+ K 10028) XU-BIR-MAL-AN-NU-GIG = $^{(arab)}$ si-sa-nu, evidently = zizânu (*q. v.*). M^{S} 73 *col* 2.

si-sa-nu *2.* *cf* šešânu.

sisinnu some winged bird {ein Vogel}. III 15 i 15 ki-ma iççur si-si-en-ni mup-parši ana sakap zâ'irêja aptâ idâa. See R. F. HARPER, HEBR. iv 148, vi 154;

x 200; also vii 100. BA i 19 *no* 25; 167 *rm* 3; 324 = Hebr סוס, Jer 8: 7. On II 49, 11 see BA i 167 *rm* 3.

sissinnu. part of the date-palm {ein Teil der Dattelpalme}. § 61, 1 *b*; *cf* סַנְסִנִּים. II 29 *a-b* 72 (+ K 2008 i 5; II 27 *a-b* 6) AN = sis-sin-nu (Br 435; H 10 + 205, 31) & šubultu (HALÉVY, *Rev. Sém.*, vi 277—8). V 26 *g-h* 45 GIŠ AN-NA-[illegible] = sis-sin-ni, part of the gišimmaru (*q. v.*) Br 456. Cyr 128, 17 sis-sin-nu (BA iii 404—5: Dattelzweige) e-li nâri u šu-pa-lu nâri. Camb 58, 17 ši(but character is not clear)-sin-nu ul e-ṭir-ru-'u (written mostly sis-sin-nu in *c. t.*, Camb 55, 8; 108, 11 *etc.*). IV² 7 *b* 20 like this date which a-na sis-sin-ni qa-at-pu lâ itûru, JENSEN, *Diss*, 55—6 (ZA i 55); T^{C} 112; Z^{Š} v/vi 75: Datteltraube. STRASSM, *Liverpool*, 12, 12 sis-sin-nu (amêl) zikar kirî (?) ul e-ṭir (AV *63 *col* 1); *Stockholm*, 26, 14 sis-sin-nu u (amêl) gu-gal .... | e-ṭir (*cf* Nab 347, 18). PEISER, *Vertr.*, xlvi 10 sis-sin-nu u[l e-ṭir]; xx 20 sis-sin-na-šu ul e-ṭir (Nabd 623, 9). Also see Camb 42, 11 sis-sin-ni i-na-aš-ši (KB iv 262—3). See also ZA iv 128 *no* 8. For discussion see BA i 634, 635 (& *cf* kabbaru); PEISER, KAS, 102, 105; *Vertr.* 240: Anteil des Pächters; but ZA vi 445: Blätter der Dattelpalme.

sasqû. II 49 *no* 3, *add* (AV 6578, Br 14288) .... TIR | sa-as-qu-u = man-di aš-a-an.

sa-su-ru (AV 6575) *cf* šassûru, 1.

sasiru (?) perh NE 58, 45 (KB vi, 1, 186) šu-ku(or dur)-ki sa-x(s)ir-ki u ša-gam-ma-ki.

seseru, sisseru *1.* child, youth {Kind, Jugend}. se-se-rum ‖ ma-ar (*cf* mâru, 581 *col* 1) AV 6733; & si-is-si-ru II 36 *a* 49 (AV 6785) & sa-az-xa-ru (AV 6586 = sassaru?; צער be small, ZA i 395 *rm* 3; i 47 √צער) *a* 46; also sa-az-xa-ar-tum (*a* 48; AV 6576 *xa* instead of *za*) ‖ çi-ix-xe-ru-tu. Perh. *cf* P. N. סִיסְרָא, D^{Pr} 199 *rm* 3.

sisseru *2.* *cf* sissinnu.

sissêrinûtu. 81, 4—28, 327 *R* 11 si-is-si-ri-in-nu-tu. M^{S} texts, *pl* 26.

sa-sa(i)r (*i. e.* [illegible])-**tum.** K 4558 *O* 7 an epithet of pit-pa-nu.

?sassatum? K 4174 + 4583 *col* 2 *c-d* 21 .... sa-as-sa-tum. M^{S} texts, *pl* 8—9.

sisâtum. Bu 89, 4—26, 112, 9 (šam) si-sa-tum, M^{S} texts, *pl* 32.

sisîtum. S^{b} 91 (dupl.) di-im | [illegible] | si-si-tum *var* to ši-ki-tum; also S^{b} F 1, 12; H 25, 511; Br 6728. KB vi (1) 364 ‖ ikkillu: Geschrei oder Geheul. K 2148 iii 29 a description of an idol (Göttertype) si-si-it rit-ti ša (ZA ix 119; *cf* 124).

sâpu *cf* nisû Q & Hebr סוף; also perh. II 47 *c-d* 61 sa-a-pu. Rm 341, 3—5 sa(?)-pu, sa-a-pu, si-i-pu. D^{Par} 105, 106; AJP v 76.

sappu *1.* 82, 9—18, 4159 iv 9 UD-KA-BAR = sa-ap-pu, hence also V 23 *c-f* 13 sap-pu.

sappu *2.* sappatu, see šappu, šappatu.

sa(i)pû Q pray {beten}? perh. Anp i 9 Ninib ilu rem[-nu]-u ša si-pu-šu ṭâbu; II 66 *no* 1, 9 Ištar il-tim rem-ni-ti ša si-pu-ša ṭâbu. AV 6620, Z^{B} 22. 3 usappû, pray to some one {zu jemandem beten, ihn anflehen} AJP xi 502; see salû, 3. KB vi 282, 31 tu-sa-pa-a pray {betet}. V 63 *a* 6 a-na ilâni u ištarâti gi-na-a u-sa-ap-pu-u; K^{M} 50, 20 (end) u-sa-pi[-ka], I besought thee. ZA v 67, 23 be-lut-ki ul u-sap-pa-a ka-a-a-an, and to thy ladyship (o Ištar) I (Asurnaçirpal) did not pray without ceasing; perh NE 77, 18 lu-sap-pa-a; Asb iv 9 ina su-up-pi-e ša Ašur u Ištar u-sap-pu-u, KB ii 188, 189 in answer to the prayers I prayed to *A* & *I.* KB iii (2) 64 *col* 2, 12—13 aššî ga-ti, u-sa-ap-pa ša-aš-ši, I prayed to the sun; 18 iš-ma-a su-pi-e-a. ZA v 68, 17—18 mu-sa-pu-u be-lut-ki, who prays to thy ladyship. L^{4} iv 3 ça-lam šarrû-ti-ja mu-sa-ap-pu-u ilu-ti-šu-un maxaršun ulziz. II 39 (*c-*)*d* 65 su-up-pu[-u] together with teçbîtu, teslîtu & šutêmuqu (H 87, 52; AV 6774; Br 719). See also IV² 29* *b* 1 li-sa-pa-a-ni mê tâmti; IV² 29* 4 B, *b* 21 (*add*)

---

su-sir-ru (stable) read su-pu-ru (*q. v.*).

li-is-sa-pa-ni-im-ma. — GUYARD, ZK i 113; HOMMEL in HASTINGS, *Dict. of the Bible*, i 216 suppû 'pray' from sippu, threshold; also the same in TRUMBULL, *Threshold Covenant*, 314, 1 *foll.* **Der.:**

sup(p)û originally ac of ג petition, prayer {Flehen, Gebet} ‖ sullû (*q. v.*). AV 6851; ZK i 113; HEBR. i 206; AJP viii 290; ZA iv 274—5; 11, 18 = su-la-a = ka-ra-bi. K 155 *R* 8 lil-ma-da su-pi-ja. V 63 *a* 12 a-na su-pi-e u te-me-qi ar-ki ilâni ri-du-u; V 65 *a* 36 ina te-me-qu (il) Šamaš bêli-ja ina su-pi-e-šu ša ilâni rabûti. SCHEIL, *Nabd*, vii 43 aç-bat-ma su-pi-e-ja I implored him {ich flehte zu ihm}. *Rec. Trav.* xx 205 *foll* i 4 (ilat) Nanâ še-ma-ti su-pi-e. KB iv 102—3 (*Rec. Trav.* xvi 177), 7 (ilat) Ištar ma-xi-rat su-pi-e. Neb ii 5 (il) Marduk im-xu-ru su-pu-u-a. NE 59, 11 to Ištar .... illakû su-pu-u-a, go my prayers (KB vi 1, 202—3); I 66 *c* 44. K^{M} 8. 1 .... ṭa-a-bu su-up-pu-u-ki. K 2852 + K 9662 i 33 (end) ul am-xu-ra su-up-pi-šu (see also Br 7212, 8053); Šalm, *Balaw*, vi 5 (the great gods) iš-mu-u si-pi-šu (of Šalmaneser); III 66 *col* 8, 9 liš-me-u su-pi-e (PSBA xxi 126); K 3456 *O* 6 (*ibid* 37, 38). ZA iv 232, 14 il-tum rêmi-ni-tum ša su-up-pi-e ta-ram-mu. KB iii (1) 122 *col* 4 šemû su-pi-e-šu; Sp II 265 *a* iv 6 su-up-pi-e. K 3364 *R* 15 see sullû & laban appi. Neb i 52 Marduk ut-ni-en su-pi-e-šu aç-ba-at, I besought, addressed to him prayers. SMITH, *Asurb*, 74, 18 lil-li-ku-uš su-up-pu-ka (§ 119). Sn *Bav* 30 su-up-pe-ja iš-mu-ma. V 52 *no* 1 iv 26 a-na .... še-mi-i su-up-pi-šu to listen to his prayers (= IV² 53 *R* iv 43). Neb ix 61 ši-ma-a su-pu-u-a. Sn v 53 su-pi-e-a urruxiš iš-mu-u. V 64 *b* 42 su-pi-e-a li-iš-me-e-ma; *c* 48 su-pu-u-šu li-iš-mu-u. Sarg *Khors* 120 i-na su-pi-e u te-me-qi u-s(ç)al-la-an-ni; *Ann* 315. 83—1—18, 1350 *O* 31 suppû (or çuppû?) see kutennû, kanû, 1.

supû *2.* K 490, 17 si-i-ru su-pi[-e?] Hr^{L} 119; part of a building?

supû *3.* Antioch. Inscr. (ZA iii 138) 15 u in-nam-din-nu su-pu-u (?).

suppu. KB iv 160 *col* 2, 30 the property, a house on the northside, a garden to the south, u II ina su-up-pu erçi-tim gi-šimmar šadî.

sîpu. K 1285 *R* 9 thy sins like si-pi ina pa-an me-e i-šu-'-u (CRAIG, *Relig. Texts*, i *p* 6 -*la*- instead of -*šu*-); M^{S} 73 reads pi-i si-pi ina pa-an šamê ilâ' (thy adversaries) will become weak as *s* on the firmament (>< STRONG, *IX. Or. Congr.*, ii 203). On the other hand ZIM., *Ritualtafeln* (*p* 162 *rm* 12) reads ki si-pi ina pân mê išu', and explains sêpu as a grain-sort {eine Getreideart}. See *ibid no* 66 *O* 8: VII akal si-e-pi; 67 *O* 8; 68 *O* 4. K 164, 35 where read akal si-pi (BA ii 636); & *cf* K 2619 (*Dibbara*) ii 16 kî šeim ina pân mê imaššû'.

sipp(bb)u, *pl* sippê threshold {Schwelle} § 63; סף Exod 12: 22. D^{Pr} 34. ZA vii 21; MEISSNER, 9 *rm* 3; POGNON, *Wadi-Brissa*, 142; AV 6741. KB vi (1) 305: "könnte Lehnwort aus dem Sumerischen sein". IV² 31 *O* 18 a-max-xa-aç (*q. v.*) si-ip-pu. K 2401 iii 19 ma-a ša si-ip-pi ša (mât) Aššur (BA ii 629); V 65 *b* 13 sip-pu ši-ga-ri me-di-lu u dalâti (+ 25). I 65 *a* 36; Neb iii 49—50 see kanakku (407 *col* 1); vi 18 si-ip-pe-ši-na, their (the gates') threshold. Ner (I 67) i 22 ti(-?)ri-i-mu kaspi ša se-ip-pi-e (+ 31; KB iii (2) 72); ii 19 u-ra-ak-ki-su se-ip-pu-šu; KB iii (2) 78 *col* 2, 10 si-ip-pu-šu la ku-un-nu-um; + 24 si-ip-pu-šu u-ki-in-ma. M^{S} 74 quotes K 8665 *a-b* 9/10 ti?]-ip-qu = si-ip-pu, & = ri-kis sip-pi. K 4256 *O* 4 where si-ip-pu is mentioned between tu-ša-ru & za-mu-u. 81—2—4, 188 *O* 27 ana sip-pi nešê *pl* tab-bi-in-ni (ZA v 67). IV² 54 *a* 52 sip-pe-ka (end) ‖ ši-ga-re-ka (51, beg); 21 *no* 1 B *O* 32—35 ina sip-bi (= ZAG-GAB) bâbi; thus also I 65 *a* 44, compared with V 34 *a* 19 a-na se-ip-pi (= *pl*) abullâti-šu. K 2061 ii 11 (H 203) ZAG(du)GAB = si-ip-pu, II 48 *e-f* 58, Br 6504. Compare also Z^{B} viii 59; Šalm, *Obel*, 131 si-pe-ša ak-çur (KB i 144); ZIMMERN, *Ritualtafeln*, *no* 26 iii 21 sib-bi-e imni u šumêli: Pfosten rechts und links.

NOTE. — Some passages me-sir (*cf* mê-siru) *p* 568 *col* 2 might be read sip-pu, thus *e. g.* K 483, 2 bîtu ep-šu sip-pu rak-su.

sipû. V 28 *d* 64 si-p(b)u-u, a garment {ein Kleid} = kar-rum (3). PSBA xxiii 353 combines with this (KU) sip-pi, usually read ku-z(ç)ip-pi (*q. v.*) & V 28 *c-d* 56.

sapadu mourn {trauern} Q^1(?) perh. K 2867, 31 i-sa-ap-pi-du da-ad-me ur-ru u mu-šu, S. A. SMITH, *Asurb*, ii 9.

Derr. sipittu and these 2:

sapādu mourning {Trauer}. K 3426, 6 a-xu-laṷ i-na mâti-ia ša ba-ki u sa-pa-a-du; *l* 7 nu-um-bi-e u ba-ki-e. 83, 1—18, 1331 iv 11 DIR | su-u | sa-pa-du. D^H 20; D^{Pr} 34; *Lit. Or. Phil.*, i 198; ZDMG 35, 762; *Rev. Sém.*, ii 76. A ‖ is:

sipdu. IV^2 49 *a* 12 (e-li-li nu-bu-u) xi-du-ti si-ip-di, my joy has been turned into mourning, MEISSNER, *ZA* ix 274—5. Perh. Camb 277, 10 lubar sip-du (?).

sapaxu, *pr* ispux, *ps* isappax scatter, loosen; break to pieces, destroy {zerstreuen; auflösen; zerstören} LEHMANN, ii 42—43; BAER-DELITZSCH, *Ezechiel*, pref. xiii. ‖ pararu. IV^2 50 *c* 6 li-is-pu-ux (id BIR)-ku-nu-ši [ilu] GIŠ-BAR ez-zu (*cf* T^M iii 169, 173). Bu 88—5—12, 75 + 76 *col* ii 8 ... a-na sa-pax (*var* pan) mâti u nišê (= K 192 *O*). TP III *Ann* 42 ana la sa-pa-ax na-gi-i-šu; SMITH, *Asurb*, 292 X: sa-pa-ax mâti-šu; also KB ii 208 *rm*, *l* 17. K 12388 + 13101 *R* 2 BIR-ax mâtâti (THOMPSON); K 1383, 2 only BIR. K 2852 + K 9662 i 34 (end) it-ta-ça-a sa-pa-ax mâti-ka. BANKS, *Diss*, 12, 1 *no* 4, 77 a-mat-su šap-liš ina a-la-ki-ša ma-a-tu i-sa-ap-pa-ax; *ibid*, *l* 63 (end) ma-a-ta i-sap[-pax?] ‖ bîtâta u-xat-tu & u-ab-bat (61). 83, 1—18, 1335 iii 18 ta-ar | TAB | sa-pa-xu. *pm* sapxu. *Etana*-legend (KB vi (1) 104 *l* 7) sa-ap-xu ad(ṭ,t)-mu-u-a (BA ii 392; iii 364 *foll*); *Creation-frg* IV 68 see sixû; perh. K^M 32, 11 the nations sa-pi-ix-ti (= 2 *f*); 5, 7 (end) su-pu-ux (= *ip*) ta-ni[-xi?]; 6, 53 ša sa-ap-xi. II 39 (*e-*)*f* 44 sa-pi-ix, AV 6583; Br 5681.

ᗡ $Z^{\breve{S}}$ ii 53 kin-na pu-xur-ta u-sap-pi-xu; IV^2 51 *b* 15—16 ina puxri šu u-sap-pi-xu (= $Z^{\breve{S}}$ ii 78), ina el-la-ti ka-çir-ti šu u-par-ri-ru (both, questions). V 64 *a* 31 u-sap-pi-ix ‖ upar-rir, I scattered. Sn *Bav* 37 pu-xur-šu-nu u-sap-pi-ix-ma u-par-ri-ir el-lat-su-un, their army I destroyed and ruined their power. Sn iv 42 ellâte-šu u-sap-pi-ix-ma u-par-ri-ir pu-xur-šu MESSERSCHMIDT, *Stele Nabuna'ids*, 64, 24 u-sap-pax el-lat ..... (WINCKLER, *Forsch.*, i 492—3); T^M vii 5 u]-sa-ap-pax urpîta-ki ‖ u-xal-laq ûma-ki; 6, u-sap-pax kiš-pi-ki; v 5 u-sap-pa-ax kiš-pi-ki (also v 86, 87). K^M 11, 37 su-up-pi-ix-ma adi VII-šu pu-ṭur. IV^2 39 *a* 32 mu-si-pi-ix el-la-at (mât) Šu-ba-ri-i rapalti (AJSL xii 168). Esh ii 27 mu-sap-pi-ix nišê (mât) Man-na-a-a. KB vi (1) 36, 30 mu[-sap]-pi-ix a-di-šu-nu, AV 5590. IV^2 60* C *R* 7 meš-re-tu-u-a su-up-pu-xa ‖ i-ta-ad-da(?)-a a-xi-tum.

ᗡ¹ IV^2 16 *b* 27—8 bi-na-ti-šu us-sap-pi-xu (= BA-BIR-BIR-RI-EŠ).

נ Creat.-*frg* IV 106 ki-iç-ri-ša up-tar-ri-ra pu-xur-ša is-sap-xa, her host was broken up, her throng was scattered; LEHMANN, ii 42. DT 59 *O* 13 na-as-pi-xi (*ip f*) kîma im-ba-ri. IV^2 30 *b* 36 see šapaxu. **Derr.:**

sapxu *adj* scattered {aufgelöst, zerstreut} Sarg *Cyl* 31: Sargon mu-pa-xir (mât) Ma-an-na-a-a sa-ap-xi mu-ta-ki-in (mât) El-li-b(p)i dal-xi, LYON, *Sargon*, 64. Perhaps also the šapxu (*q. v.*) of Xammurabi. II 62 *no* 2, 9 a-na pu-ux-xur nišê sap-xa-a-ti, *etc.* (ZK ii 352). Perhaps also Sargon, *Ann* XIV 12; POGNON, *Wadi-Brissa*, 120, 121 sa-ap-xa-a-ti. id in Merodach-Balad. stone i 33. A ‖ is:

suppuxu *adj* Nabd 293, 1 gišimmarê su-up-pu-xu-tu (PEISER, KAS 85, below); AV *52 *col* 1.

sapku *cf* šapku.

sa-pi-ku. P. N. V 53 *no* 1 *O* 1.

saplu. bowl, plate {Schüssel, Schale} AV 6584; KAT^2 208; FRÄNKEL, *Lehnwörter*, 67 *fol.* Anp i 122: 3000 kappê siparri (sa-ap-li siparri a-ga-na-a-te si-parri); ii 64 (67) sa-ap-li (siparri). KB i 80, 82, 92; also Anp ii 92; KB i 150 *no* 2 sap-lu xurâçi. K 164, 3 sa-ap-lu šamni *pl* ṭâbi, BA ii 635; see also si-qîtu.

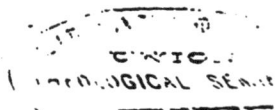

sup'ă'lu. V 26 *e-f* 30 GIŠ-ŠE-RU (= KAK)-A = su-pa-lu preceded by šu-u-šum, AV 6847, Br 7464. ZIM., *Ritualtaf.*, 75—78, 7 (iç) su-pa-li. GGA '98, 811 *ad* M^{S} texts, *pl* 8 (K 4174+4588) iv 24 su-pa-lu, & see M^{S} 54 *sub* lardu. II 23 *e-f* 22 su-pa-lum (& ti-ja-rum) = GIŠ erinu (H 34, 821; Br 10805). Sm 8+1297, 10 U-KI-AN-ŠEŠ-KI = su-pa-lu followed by a-çu-çi-im-tu, Br 6075. LÖW, *Pflanzennamen*, 279 compares Aram סְפָל; see also HOMMEL, PSBA xxi 136: Syr סַפְלוֹלָא, *Aristolochia.* SCHEIL, Notes LX, 5 (*Rec. Trav.*, xxiii) (šam) su-pa-lam.

sapalginu. a plant {eine Pflanze} K 4398; AV 6579; Br 6054, 13091. See kurkanū.

sapanu (& very rarely **šapanu**) *pr* is(š)-pun, *ps* isap(p)an, *ip* supun. ‖ katamu. AV 6580; Br 4420, 7605. H^{W} 52; 74; *Proc. Am. Or. Soc.*, xiii 52. ZA iii 60; iv 155; v 40. cover; overpower, and then, destroy {bedecken; überwältigen, zerstören} *etc.* Sn *Bav* 52 ir-çi-is-su i-na mē as-pu-un, I covered (the city's) ground with water. — Creat.-*frg* IV 54 sa-pa-na lam-du, they know how to destroy; *R* 2 (med) ana sa-pan mātāti. IV² 18, 3 *O* i 36 see maqatu Š (579 *col* 1, 1—3). V 34 *c* 49 (command) sa-pa-nim māt a-a-bi-ja! I 49 *a* 20 .... a-na sa-pan māti xul-lu-qu nišē (he planned); also see JASTROW, *Dibbarafragm.*, *p* 5. Bu 88—5—12, 75+76 iii 8 see sapaxu; 83—1—18, 215, 4 .... (māt) Aššur sa-pan māt nakirēšu (WINCKLER, *Forsch.*, ii 8, 4). SCHEIL, *Rec. Trav.*, xx *no* xxxv (= KB vi, 1, 300) 20 .... Ak-ka-di-i sa-pa-nu. — Sp ii 265 *a* ii 5 na[. . . .]-nu-ma is-pu-nu il-la-ku urux mūti. Asb iv 71, whom Sennacherib .... is-pu-un (had killed; ii 120) ... 73, nišē ša-a-tu-nu ..... as-pu-nu (MEISSNER, ZA x 81; LEHMANN, ZA xiv 376). II 67, 22 a-bu-biš as-pu-un-ma ‖ u-šax-ri-ba da-ad-me-šu (Sarg *Ann* 272); *ibid*, 2 a-bu-biš is-pu-nu. I 35 *no* 3, 13 is-pu-nu a-bu-ba-niš (KB i 188—9). I 49 *c* 3 a-bu]-biš tas-pu-nu; DT 71, 19 a-bu-ba-niš tas-pu-un, 21 tas-pu-na ti-la-niš te-še[-me]; Šalm, *Obel*, 21 iš-pu-nu (§ 46) = *Mon*, *O* 12 is-pu-nu; *Ob* 158 aš-pu-un (I 43, 7); *cf* III 10, 28; V 64 *b* 38 (il Sin) li-is-pu-un ga-ri-ja. — KB iii (2) 66 *no* 12, 40 su-pu-un kullatsum ‖ xulliq napxar māti a'ābi. — K 1282 *etc.*, *O* 7 (end) nišē a-sap-pan (KB vi (1) 68—9); *del* 122 (129) me-xu-u i-sap-pan mātu (BA i 133; NE 140, 129; KB vi 238—9); S 954 *R* 5—6 ša-di-i il-te-niš a-sap-pan (= NE-IB-SE-SE-GI-EME-SAL). TP viii 64 whosoever my tablet and foundation-document i-xap-pu-u i-sa-pa-nu. — Esh i 11 calls himself sa-pi-nu gi-mir da-ad-me-šu (of Sidon); TP ii 87 *TP* sa-pi-nu gimir alṭūti (*cf* iii 33); Anp i 7 Ninib sa-pin māt nākirē. S^{P} II 987 *O* 24 sa-pi-in-nu māti kāli[šu?]; Sarg *Cyl* 29 sa-pi-in (māt) An-di-a. V 44 *b* 14 P. N. of a king: Sa-pi-in māt nukurti. Zürich-inscr. of TP III, 2 (end) etlu gar-du sa[-pi-in] PSBA xviii 158—9. IV² 21 *no* 1 B *R* 17 the firegod sa-pi-in (= SE-SE-A-AN) a-a-bi; 26 *a* 1—3 Nergal .... sa-pi-in māt nukurti; also *cf* IV² 24 *no* 1, 57—8 (H^{CV} xxxviii). V 64 *b* 16 two laxmu of ešmarū-stone ša-pi-in a-a-bi-ja; *c* 35 (Anunītum) sa-pi-na-at (amēl) na-ak-ru. Sn v 57 the mighty warchariot is called sa-pi-na-at za-'-i-ri; v 82 sa-pi-na-at rag-gi u çe-ni. Written sa-bi-in in Xammurabi-biling., 8 & often. — S^{c} 92 si-i | SE | sa-pa[-nu]; perh. S^{c} 156 ta-ab | TAB | sa-pa[-nu] Br 3768; V 42 *c-d* 54 GUŠUR-GUŠUR = sa-pa-nu in one group with ba-'-u & etequ (Br 5506).

Derr. naspanu, našpa(n)tu &:

sapannu, *c. st.* sa-pan, obscurity, darkness {Verborgenheit, Dunkel, Tiefe} ‖ katimtu (*q. v.*). Sn *Kui* 4, 12 ša parūti .....i-na sa-pan (šad) Am-ma-na-na ušaptūni pānišu; Sarg *Bull* 33 *fol*, who the corpses of his warriors i-na sa-pan tam-tim ugarrinu gurūniš. K 509, 8 the Birtaeans a-na sa-pan-ni ap-pa-ru ša Bābili ki-i aš-pu-ru (Hr^{L} 259) into the darkness of the swamp. Neb 131, 11 ŠE-BAR grows ina sa-pan ap-pa-ri. See also Sn *Rass* 76; BA i 241; ii 400; MEISSNER & ROST, 30.

sapnu. K 10244 šumma GIŠ-BU sa-ap-ni nēši šakin. Bezold, *Catalogue*, 1075.

sup(p)innu. K 4378 i 35 GIŠ-BA = su(-up)-pi-in-nu; 36 GIŠ-BA-ŠU = *s* qa-ti; 37 GIŠ-BA-KA = *s* çur-ri (followed by mu-maš-ši-xu); 39 GIŠ-BA-NAM = su-(up)-pi-in si-nun-ti (AV 6850); 49 GIŠ-BA-BAL = su-pi-in(-nu) pi-laq-qi; 50 GIŠ-BA-BAL-BAL = *s* pi-laq-qa-ati (*var* -te). D 86—7; Br 111; Hommel, *Sum. Lesest.*, i 5 wahrsch. cover {Umhüllung, Decke}. IV² 18 *no* 3 ii 3—4 ina su-pi-in[-ni-ka elli] followed by ina pa-šul-ti (6); ina bu-'u-di (8; II 45 *b* 67, 70); K 4138, 19 su-up-pi-in-nu preceded by b(p)u-kan-nu, M^S texts, *pl* 5.

supanū (?). K 5464 *R* 13 su-pa-ni-ja lu-pa(-xat?, *p* 346)-ti (Hr^L 198; PSBA xviii 230 *foll*).

sappandu. Rm 367 + 83, 1—18, 401 *a* iii 7 GIŠ-ŠIM-EŠ-XA-RA = 's'ap-pan-du. M^S 74 *col* 1.

sapsapāte, *pl* some part of the body {ein Körperteil}. Sn v 85 sa-ap-sa-pa-te u-na-kis; Lhotzky, *Diss*, 28: ear-lap {Ohrläppchen}. Haupt-Pinches: testicles; Lyon: extremities, limbs. *Cf* Bezold, *Catalogue*, 1516 šumma GIŠ-BU lišān-šu ina sa-ap-sa-pi. (!)

sapsuptu *f* BOR iii 30 *ad* IV² 61 *c* 23 sa-ap-su-up-ta-ka ra-bi-tu anaku (*i. e.* Ištar). Banks, AJSL xiv 273: thy great supporter (?) am I.

saparu 1. surround {umgeben} ZA v 15 reads T. A. (Ber) 26 i 46 ša . . . . su-up-pu-ru, which is surrounded (ℑ pm); L⁴ i 24 iš-ta-na-as-bar (?) is also refered to this verb by Lehmann, ii 68; but *cf* ZA x 82 *rm* 2 (√šaparu).

saparu *2.* net {Netz}. id (GIŠ)-SA-PAR, Br 3126; AV 6581. Hommel, VK 418; D^H 29; D^Pr 21 *rm*. V 50 *b* 48 ana šamē sa-par-šu uš-pa-ri-ir-ma (KB vi, 1, 338); IV² 16 *a* 13—14 sa-pa-ru (= SA-PAR, H 38, 85) la a-çi-e ša ana lim-ni tar-çu; *a* 29—30 see kasū, (412 *col* 1); 15* iii 16—17 see na'alu, 1 Š³ *no b* (end) *p* 629 *col* 1; also see saxapu (TP III *Ann* 37; II 67, 18). Creat.-*'ry* IV 41 e-pu-uš-ma sa-pa-ra šul-mu-u kir-biš Ti-āmat; 44, i-du-uš sa-pa-ra uš-taq-ri-ba; 95 (end) sa-pa-ra-šu u-šal-mi-ši; 112 sa-pa-riš (= ina sa-pari) na-du-ma (KB vi, 1, 338). K 3449 *a*, *R* 1 sa-pa-ra ša i-te-ep-pu-šu; Asb iv 61 sa-par ilāni rabūti . . . ša la na-par-šu-di (ZA x 80 on *ll* 59 *foll*); Zimmern, *Ritualtaf.*, 75—78, 34 sa-pa-ru a-na ^(il) Šamaš u ^(il) Adad. ZA v 59, 3 ar-mu ina sa-pa-ri-ka. IV² 26 *a* 22—23 SA-PAR (22), iu 23 še-e-tu šu-par-ru-ur-tu & sa-pa-ru ša ana tam-tim tar-çu. II 22 (K 242) i 13 GIŠ-SA-PAR = sa-pa-ru ‖ še-e-tum. Perh. H 128 *R* 8 be-li-ku sa-par-ra (??) çi-i-ri ina za-ki-ki šur-b(p)u-ça-at anāku.

sapparru. K 4152 *R* 32 sa-ap-par-ru between z(ç)a-'-i-ri-in-nu & la-a-tum, AV 6585.

supūru *m* enclosure, wall {Umschliessung, Mauer} AV 6778; Br 5558. — *a*) of a city {einer Stadt} esp. in the phrase: Uruk su-pu-ri, Erech the well-walled, fortified {das festummauerte Erech} often in NE 1, 9; 51, 12; 12, 36; 13, 6; 48, 174; *del* 266 (297); 282 (320); Z^B ii 167. J^(I-N) 7; Z^B 73; Jensen, 171; KB vi (1) 424. P. N. Neb vi 57 ṭa-a-bi su-pu-ur-šu name of the wall of Borsippa (*cf* V 34 *b* 22); also II 50 (*a*-)*b* 27; 59; ZDMG 53, 657 *foll.* — *b*) resting place of cattle, sheep, *etc.*; fold {Pferch, Hürde} ‖ tarbaçu (šuparruru, III 64, 13). JRAS vol 23 ('91) 400, 30: im-mir su-pu-ri the sheep of the fold; Banks, *Diss*, *p* 14, 1 *no* 4, 103—4 ču-u ū-mu . . . . su-pu-ri i-na-as-sax. S^b 248 a-ma-aš (*cf* amašu ‖ abaru, surround) | id | su-pu-ru; IV² 4 *b* 30—31 milk brought iš-tu su-pu-ri el-lu (‖ ištu tarbaçi elli, 29); 18* *no* 6 *R* 3—4 ina su-pu-ri-ši-na (of the she-asses) i-dir-tu iš[-ta-kan]; 9 *b* 3—4 *cf* marū, 1 Š (584 *col* 2). — id in V 43 *a* 16, Month Tammuz is the month of the feast of the god šarri supūri. supūru & tarbaçu in astronomy: of halo of the moon & the sun, *cf* Thompson, *Reports*, vol ii pref. xxiv, and, again, KB vi (1) 338.

^(amēl) **sipiru,** an official {Beamter}. Nabd 245, 9 ina naza-zu ša X ^(amēl) si-pi-ri; see also ZA iii 135, 137, 8. Meissner, *Diss*, 21; AV 6737; T^C 112. Cyr 177, 2 *G* ^(amēl) si[-pi]-ri ša mār [šarri], KB iv 272—3; Cyr 44, 4 ^(amēl) si-pi-ri ša šarri; AV* 52 *col* 1. Strassm., *Stockholm*, *no* 3, 7 one of the witnesses mentioned is Qu-qu-u (amēl) si-pi-ri. S + 329, 76—11, 17, 5 (amēl) si-pi-ri (amēl) qal-la (BOR ii 15; 48).

sip(b)ru Neb 201, 8 si-ip-ru ša ina a-me-lu-tum ib-ba-aš-šu-u (KB iv 192, 193).

siparru *m* a metall: bronce, or copper {ein Metall: Bronze oder Kupfer?} id UD-KA-BAR AV 6739. S^b 113 za-bar UD-KA-BAR | si-par-ru (H 27, 583; § 9, 26; Br 7819). V 23 *g-h* 11 *fol* UD-KA-BAR = si-par-ru, also = qu-u, 'š'ab-bu, *etc.*; AV 2786; ZA viii 76 *no* 2. Sarg *Ann* 207 ma-xi-ri kaspi ki-ma si-par-ri ina kirib Aššur i-šim-mu. Sarg *Cyl* 51 kaspi u siparri^{pl}: in silver and copper (KB ii 46). Esh vi 8 siparri namri, *cf* Sarg *Ann* 190. Br. M. 79, 2—1, 1 *l* 23 si-pa-ar-ri (ZA ii 128). H 129, 24 (end) a-na-ak si-par-ri (= UD-KA-BAR-DA) + 30. id often, *e. g.* TP ii 30, 50, 58, 59; vi 15, 20; + MEŠ ii 50 *etc.* V 33 *d* 43 ina a-ša-at siparri. Many things are made of siparru *e. g.* gullātu, narmaku (Camb 153, 2). In T. A. id often, Lo 20, 53; 30, 47; Berl 27 *b* 40 (ZA v 15) *etc.* — § 65, 21 (sipirru); Hommel, VK 244; ZDMG 45, 340 √za-bar = bronce; ZA i 2 *rm* 3; Pognon, *Wadi-Brissa*, 144; Halévy, ZK i 182 § 4; reading çipa(i)rru; Winckler, *Forsch.*, i 160—63, *etc.*; ii 165: bonds, fetters {Fessel} K 653, 6 si-par-ri parzilli = fetters of iron (Hr^L 154); K 655 *R* 7 (Hr^L 132). Idem, *Forsch.*, ii 303: siparru: Babyl.: bronce; Assyr.: copper; while eru = Babyl. copper, and Assyr. bronce. Johnston, JAOS xxii 15 same √ as sapâru "net" & supūru "enclosure".

Sippar(-ra) Babylonian city {Babylonische Stadt}. § 46; AV 6736. Br 7902, 7940. II 59, 16 i-na ka-ri Si-par (= UD-KIB-NUN-KI); id also KB iii (2) 6 *no* 2 *col* i 11; ii 5. S 1028 (Hr^L 418) 18; Asb iv 84, 92. II 50 *cols* viii/vii 33 BAD]-UD-UL-KAK-A = dûr UD-KIB-NUN-KI = Stadtmauer von Sippar (Latrille, ZA i 26; Lehmann, ii 53; KB iii (1) 201 *rm* ††; ZDMG 53, 650 *fol*). V 62 *a-b* 54 du-u-ru Si-ip-par. Merodach-Balad. stone ii 8 Sip-par(ki). — Bezold, *Catalogue*, 2190 = ספרוים; but see J. Halévy, ZA ii 401—2; *Rech. critiques*, 259; Brown-Gesenius, 709; Friedrich, *Kabiren*, 9—14. On the location of Sippara, see W. Hayes Ward, *Proc. Am. Or. Soc.*, Oct. '85.

sippirū. V 26 *e-f* 26, 27 GIŠ[ ]Ï-UD (Br 7792); GIŠ[ ]Ï-UD-KIB-NUN-KI (*i. e.* of Sippar) = sip-pi-ru-u, something made at Sippar (?). AV 6736, 6740.

s(š)ipp(bb)ūru. K 2148 ii 4 sip-pu-u-ra rak-sa-at, followed by irat-sa pi-ta-a-at, in a description of an idol (Göttertype; ZA ix 118, 417); also 8, ištu qaq-qadi-ša ana 'š'ip-pu-ri-ša (vom Kopf bis zur Mitte des Körpers?? Nabels??); 10, ištu sip-pu-ri-ša ana ka-an-tap-pi-ša. Or mēb(p)uru?

sipittu mourning {Trauer} √sapadu. § 65, 14; ZA i 262. Asb vii 15 e-ru-ub u-šib-ma ina si-pit-ti *etc.* (KB ii 210, 211); also Sarg *Khors* 78 nišē a-ši-ib lib-bi-ša e-me-da si-pit-tu u çir-xa; *Ann* 136; *Stele* i 45. II 35 *e-f* 31 perh. si-pit (or e?)-tum?

saççaru see sesseru.

sâqu. *intr.*: be narrow, thin {eng, schmal sein} G § 106. V 21 *g-h* 68 KIL = sa[-a-qu] ‖ karû. Perhaps also press, distress {drücken, bedrängen} 81—2—4, 188 *O* 11 Ištar mimma ša bul-lu-lu i-si-iq-ša (distresses her). ZA v 67; King, *First Steps*, 249 *fol.* — ℑ shorten {verkürzen} K 8522 *R* 9 (KB vi, 1, 36; 353) see ni-çirtu, *d* (*p* 480) & karû, 2, where also Asb ii 54; KB ii 242, 49; Sn v 13 nap-ša-tuš u-si-qa (1 *sg* pr). ZA iii 302; V 45 v 42 tu-sa-a-qa. Perhaps also V 65 *b* 6 u-si-qa-ma, see KB iii (2) 112 & *rm* 11; BA iii 214.

Derr. these 3:

sīqu. narrow, short, slim {eng, kurz, schmal} = ضيق, Hebr. i 231; AJP viii 267. S^c 6, 8 BE = si-ku : pu-u (§ 25). K 4378 (D 88) vi 8 GIŠ-MA'-SIG-GA = (elip-pu) si-iq-tum, a short; narrow vessel, preceded by (elippu) a-rik-tum (II 62 *no* 2, 37) Br 11875; Haupt, *Sintflutbericht*, 30.

sūqu (& sūgu) *m* street {Strasse} *pl* sū-qāni & sūqāti (§§ 64; 70 *b*) AV 6857; Br 379, 5878—80. id SIL (NE 22, 49;

IV^2 31 *R* 8; *O* 78; S^b 304) & E-SIR(-RA) which = sulû, mašdaxu. H 9 & 202, 20 si-la SIL | su-u-qu (II 33 *c-d* 11); Cyr 361, 7—8. See also § 9, 106; HOMMEL, *Zwei Jagdinschriften*, 61; J^w 34; BA i 102 *rm* *. IV^2 2 *col* v 23—4 ni-iš (ilu) I-šum(-taq) na-gir su-qi (H 175 *no* 7; see nāgiru); *ibid*, 55—6; IV^2 15 i 20—21; 26 *b* 5 see sulû; IV^2 26 *b* 1—2/3 su-ga-am (= E-SIR-RA) ina a-la-ki-šu, as he walked in the street; 28* *no* 4 *R* 70 su-u-qu (= E-SIR) ša la-la-a la aš-bu-u. V 25 *c-d* 8 ina su-ki-im (= SIL) it-ta-ši. II 9 *d* 33 ina su-ki šu-ru-ub; *b* 12 a-na su-qi it-tin-ru-ub. NE 49, 196 su-qa ša Uruk rak-bu-u[-ni] (KB vi (1) 176—77); XII (vi) 12 ša ina su-qi na-da-a (see also Sp II 265 *a* xxi 7; iv 4 su-qa). Neb viii 37 su-uq-šu (*i. e.* of Marduk) la e-nim. I 7 F 14 uš(??)-rab-bi su-qi-šu. V 65 *b* 36 see sulû. K 2852 + K 9662, margin, 1: ... ina (?) su-ki-e-šu xa-du-u, on its street(s) rejoyced. Often in *c. t.* (T^C 109—110). PEISER, KAS 22, 15. *Vertr.* 132, 2; 31, 12 ra-šu-tu ša Gi-mil-lu ša ina su-u-qa (*ibid*, *p* 249); also perh. Nabd 838, 3 money which *N* ultu sûqi iššû; 498, 6 suluppu ša ina su-u-qu-'-. On Nabd 781, 15 see KOHLER-PEISER, i 2; ii 28. — K 2061 ii 5 E-SIR = su-u[-qu]; 6, E-SIR-SIG = su-qa[-qu-u?] *i. e.* a small street, a lane; 7, E-SIR-DUG-TAB-MA = su-qi ir-bit-ti; thus read II 38 *c-d* 11 SIL = su-u-qu; 12 SIL-DAMAL-LA = sûqu rap-šu (‖ rêbitu; Br 405, also K 126, 31 in *Rev. Sém.* i 171—2), 14 su-qa-qu-u, 16 su-ki ir]-bit-ti. IV^2 13 *b* 51 a-na su-uq ir-bit-ti (id also IV^2 59 *b* 24, end) § 128*b*. — ZIMMERN, ZA x 18 reads Sp ii 265 *a* xxv 8 (end) ina sûqi Sli id-d[a ...; but STRONG, PSBA xvii 151 ina puxur it..... Sumak sûqi see sumāku. *pl* Sn *Bell* 61 birûti u su-qa-a-ni; ZA iii 318, 89 bi-ri-e-ti u su-qa-a-ni uš-per(?)-di-ma; BA iii 100; IV^2 56 *a* 2 su-qa-a-ti (MEISSNER & ROST, 70 *C* 8); Asb iv 82 SIL-MEŠ ‖ re-ba-a-ti. P. N. Su-qa-a-a (often).

suqāqu (later šuqāqu), alley, lane {Enge Strasse, Gasse} Arm שְׁקָקָא. Br 5882; see sûqu, & III 48 *no* 3, 10 su-qa-qi; thus also III 48 *no* 2, 2 (K 316) mu-çu-u a-di su-qa-qi (against *p* 571 *col* 2). JENSEN, ZA xiv 183; BA iii 582; SBOT, *Ezechiel*, *p* 64.

saqqu *cf* šaqqu 1, 2.

suqû Camb 318, 6 ŠE-BAR su-qu-u in distinction from ŠE-BAR ša irbi ša bābi, BA i 633.

siqdum see sigdum.

saqalu. K 4309 *R* (30) 4 sa-qa-lum followed by pa-a-du, pādu ša mimma.

saqapu, isqup, see zaqapu, izqup.

suqārum. V 28 *no* 4 *e* 80 su-qa-a-rum = ri-e .... AV 6855.

saqaru, isqur & išqur (DELITZSCH, ROST & others) for zakaru (*pp* 279—80), *ad* TP i 38: *TP* whose name, as ruler over the four quarters (of the world), he (Ašur) proclaimed (iš-qu-ru) forever; 27, ye have called (taš-qu-ra). Sarg *Cyl* 49 day & night ak-pu-ud az-□-ma epessu aqbi. H 50 iii 19, 22; Ⓢ 116 ii 44 (= H 67 iii 1—4); Esh i 42; I 70 *a* 22; Ṡ Asb viii 45; i 22; SMITH, *Asurb*, 283, 91. — 𒀀ᵗ V 35, 35 lit-taš(s, z)-ka-ru a-ma-a-ta; I 27 *no* 2, 93; V 65 *b* 28; Sargon, *Khors* 188. See however zakaru; HAUPT, BA i 76 note **; *Jour. Bibl. Lit.*, xix 68 *rm* 40.

siqir (AV 6627), **seqar** *m* speech, word, command, order {Rede, Wort, Geheiss}. II 66 *no* 1, 2 (si-qir-ša kabtu); Anp i 5; Creat.-*frg* II 138 se-qar šap-ti-ja (III 64, 122); IV 9 se-qar-ka = çi-it pi-i-ka; TP i 31 i-na si-qir (ilu) Šamaš (III 5 *no* 1, 5); 44 i-na si-qir Bêl; vi 61, 76 i-na si-qir (ilu) Ninib, see zikru, 1 (*pp* 280, 281). KING, *Magic*, 22, 10 ina se-ik-ri-ka kabti; II 66 *no* 1, 2. BARTH, *Etym. Studien*, 64 *cf* סכר; JENSEN, KB vi (1) 320 sikru, sikir.

sa-qa-tum *cf* çirku, 1.

sâru 1. *pr* isâr *rage* {toben}. V 55, 32 a-šam-ša-tu iç-ça-nun-da i-sa-ar me-xu-u (*q. v.*). Perh. II 42 *no* 3 *O* 10 sa-a-a-ru & II 29 *c-d* 56 (AV 6599, Br 7137).

sâru 2. ZIMMERN, *Ritualtafeln*, *nos* 1—20, 99 su-ur-ta tu-sa-ar; 39, 4 .... su-ur-ta ta-sa-ar-ma; *ibid*, *p* 103 *rm* 8: surta surru a technical term of the barû-service not yet explained; Sm 747 *R* 8 *fol*: su-ur-tum ša bārûti, explaining u-sar-rum (?). See surtu, 2.

NOTE. — On surta surru consult MEISSNER, ZA xv 415—16. sāru 1 & 2 perhaps the same with general meaning of make noise ‖ ausgelassen sein, VATh 4105 iii 9 Sabītu says to Gilgameš: ur-ri u mu-ši su-ur u me-li-il (sei ausgelassen und vergnügt).

sāru *3.* ring {Ring}? ZIMMERN, *loc. cit.*, *no* 61 ii 8 sa-a-ri tu-še-taq, the rings thou shalt remove; see *no* 62 *R* 6; & *ibid*, *pp* 178, 179 *rm* 14; refers to K 8669 ii 29, iii 19 where (iç) sa-a-ri, *pl* sa-ra-a-ni are carried in one's hands; *ibid*, iii 25 (iç) sa-a-ri us-si-tu-qu.

sāru *4.* an animal {ein Tier}. BEZOLD, *Catalogue*, 1247 *ad* K 12504 šumma sa-a-ri, mentioned together with turāxu, çabītu, and nēšu.

sāru *5.* K 55 *R* 11 IM  -A = sa-a-ri, preceded by di-i-ru & di-ru-tu; M^{S} texts, *pl* 1.

saru (?) in name of star kakkab rēš sa-ri III 57 *a* 42.

sa-rum, II 47 *e-f* 54 *cf* dāmu (251 *col* 2, below); H 28, 630; AV 6600, 8739; Br 8672. KB vi (1) 575.

sarru *1.* *adj* obstinate, rebellious; also as *n* rebel {aufrührerisch; Empörer} Z^{B} 6 *rm* 2, (√sararu); *pl f* sarrāte (amāte) = rebellious, seditious words; rebellion, *etc.* AV 6610; Br 7275; KB vi (1) 324. H 127, 55—6 sa-ar-tum (ZA i 400; Br 1346); Z^{S} iii 131 ma-mit sar-ri u si-la-a-ti (*q. v.*). II 49 *no* 3 *e-f* 33 star (kakkab) LUL-LA (THOMPSON, *Reports*, ii, pref. xxxv *rm* 1) = sa-ar-rum (JENSEN, 120: the refractory; KB vi, 1, 324); 36, nakar; 37, ša-nu-um-ma; 38, a-xu-u; also see H 26, 546; II 51 *no* 2 *O* 33. V 16 *c-d* 48 SAG-BAL-E = sa-ar-ru, Br 3538. Perhaps IV^{2} 51 *a* 34 ul i-di sar-ti ili (or šertu?, K^{M} 12). *pl* Creat.-*frg* IV 72 u-kal sar-ra-a-ti (KB vi, 1, 26—7: sich von jemandem lossagen; HEHN. ix 20); also KB vi, 1, 36 line 26 ša sa-ar-ti u[-šat-mi-ix?] and *ibid*, 354; Z^{K} iii 12; Sm 2022 (WINCKLER, *Sargon* "Asdod", 188) 32 da-bab(bib?) sa-ar-ra-a-ti (KB ii 64 *rm* **); Sarg *Ann* XIV 48; *Khors* 38; *Ann* 75 (*cf* dababu). Sp ii 265 *a* xxiv 5 sar-ra-a-tum u lā kēnātu išruqušu sa-an-tak-ku. T. A. (Ber) 40, 22 A-mu-ri amēlūti sa-ru-du; 24 *a* 32 a-na amēlūti sa-ar-ru-ti; Lo 35, 7.

sarru *2.* II 32 *c-d* 28 sa-ar-rum, together with šu-gu-u & pur-šu-mu a ‖ of ši[-i-bu??] old, old man {alt, Greis} AV 6610. KB vi (1) 569.

sarru(m) *3.* KB iv 12 (*l* 4) 26—7: ʾšar-ru-um | MI ʾšar-ra-am.

sīru. hedge, wall {Umfassung, Wand} = סִיר; but GESENIUS-BROWN, 690 compares √שור. AV 6751. V 42 *g-h* 25, 26 IM-BE, IM-ŠA(=LIB)-RA-AK = si-i-ru followed by šal-la-ru (Br 8336, 8471). V 32 *a-c* 21 IM-ZI = šal-la-ru & si-i-ru (Br 8388); *d-f* 49 GI-KAK-A = si-i-ru ‖ maçallu (*q. v.*) ša rē'i (Br 2481) resting place of the shepherd, which also = dūru (48) & tarbaçu (50). II 28 *b-c* 52 we have MU-SA-DUL-LA = si-i-ru (33 *c-d* 77) Br 1263, 14235. See also supū, 2.

sūru rebel {Rebell} T. A. (Ber) 171, 6 (amēl) su-u-ru. KAT^{3} 28 *rm* 1.

Sūri in T. A. see Subartu (Subarī); Ber 42, 17 a-na (māt) Su-ri, BA iv 181 *foll*; AV 6861, 6868.

surru *1.* moment {Augenblick} KB vi (1) 324 √sararu; thus properly: motion, change {Bewegung, Veränderung}. ⊕ 116 ii 5 (H 65) ŠU-GAR-TUR-LAL = sur-ru, followed by ŠU-GAR-TUR-LAL-BI = šum-ma. Sp II 265 *a* iii 4 ku[ ]-ma a-na sur-ri; xx 11 (end) ta-rab a-na sur-ri. — mostly found as **issurri** (= ina surri), issuri, isurri, properly: at the moment when, as soon as, when {im Augenblick als, sobald als, wann}. K 525, 6 is-su-ur-ri (10, i-su-ur-ri) šarru bēli iqabbi ma-a, as soon as my lord, the king inquires, Hr^{L} 252. K 691, 9 is-su-ri *etc.* (Hr^{L} 45); K 1234 *R* 1 Sin i-su-ri (as soon as Sin has entered his temple) Hr^{L} 134. BA i 248. *adv* of surru is:

surriš. at once, suddenly, hastily {augenblicklich, plötzlich, eilends} ‖ zamar (Z^{B} 99; IV^{2} 54 *b* 2). IV^{2} 54 *b* 4 ru-um-me ma-ak-si-šu lip-pu-uš sur-riš, see napašu; & also for IV^{2} 60* C *R* 5; *O* 20 (beg) sur-riš uš-ta-d\[i\]r za-mar ux-ta-maç; I 49 *b* 15 sur-riš lib-ba-šu i-nu-ux; perh. also ⊕ 13 (BA iii 218)-KB vi (1) 280—1 *col* 3 (4) 10 sur-r]iš li-çi ri-gim-ši-na namtāru (+ 14, *sar*-ri-iš). K 8364 *R* 9 sur-riš ta-ta-mu-u.

surru 2. see mutamētu (624 *col* 1).

surrū 1. magician, priest {Magier, Priester} *cf* kalū; JENSEN, ZA vii 174. S^b 287 sur-ru | ið | sur-ru-u (288, ka-lu-u); see surmaxxu.

surrū 2. *cf* šurrū.

sarbu 1. mourning, lamentation {Gram, Trauer, Wehklage}. V 35, 26 nu-xu-ut-su-nu u-pa-aš-ši-xa u-ša-ap-ţi-ir sa-ar-ba-šu-nu their sighing I stilled, their mourning I made cease (BA ii 253). NE 62, 33—35 ina ni-is-sa-ti ina sar-bi . . . . 35, ina ta-ni-xi.

s(š)arbu 2. KB vi (1) 164 *col* 3, 3 ētiq š(s)a(i)r-bi, there passed by a cold wind {es zog vorüber ein kalter Wind}, KB vi (1) 447.

's'arbillu. S^d 95 = II 109, 47 ME-IR-SIG = MIR-SIG = sar-bil-lu; perh. NE 58, 3 sar-bi-il[-la?].

s'arganu. strong, mighty {stark, mächtig}. II 31 *no* 3, 27 sar-ga-nu ‖ dan-nu (ZK i 271; L^{TP} 89).

saradu. hitch, bind {anspannen, binden}. AV 6593. II 24 *a-b* 55 (*cf* 33 *a-b* 35) LAL = sa-ra-du ša imēri, with makkaru ša imēri (*p* 540 *col* 1) in one group; Br 10105; ZK ii 260 *rm* 2: to hitch said of an ass, bind to a yoke ‖ çamadu, rakasu. 𐎚 V 45 ii 5 tu-sar-rad. **Derr.**:

sirdū (*pl* sirdē?). reins {Zügel} *etc.* JA '81 *col* xviii *p* 240—42: si-ir-da-a. HAUPT in CHEYNE, *Isaiah* (SBOT), 137 = שׂרד. II 23 *a-b* 5 ku-us-su-u si-ir-di-e = ša-di-it-tum (*a*) √šadadu, AV 6755. I 65 *a* 12 a-na ša-a-ţam si-ir-di-e-šu, to drag his (god Marduk's) yoke (I bent my neck). V 63 *a* 14 a-na ša-a-ţi si-ir-di-e-šu-nu ku-un-nu-šu ki-šad-su. AJP xi 498; ZK ii 261 *rm*; ZA v 407. Neb ii 9 a-na ša-da-da se-ir-di-e-šu ušatkanni libba.

sirdu 1. command {Gebot}. K 4370 *O* 5 (*R* 21) palaxu axāzu si-ir-du [ilāni?) šitē'u.

sirdu 2. a tree and a wood {ein Baum und eine Holzart}, MEISSNER & ROST, 16. Sn *Kui* 4, 37 in the parks vine *etc.* $^{(iç)}$si-ir-du u riqqē MA-GAL (= rabiš) iš-mu-xu + 41 (end) kisal $^{(iç)}$ sir-di u xi-bi-iš-ti.

surdū. a bird; perh. falcon (PINCHES) {ein Vogel, vielleicht Falke} AV 6865. II 37 *a-c* 15; *b-c* 64 see kasūsu, *b* (416 *col* 2), Br 6393. ið *e. g.* Asb x 15 ki-ma SUR (= SAG)-DU(= KAK)-XU a-bar-šu; also V 27 *c* 15. IV^2 30* *no* 3 *O* 38 surda-a iç-çu-ra. K 626, 15. — See PINCHES, PSBA vi ('84) 57 *fol*; HOMMEL, PSBA '10, 314 § 33 compares Georgian *Shavardem* (?), falcon; also see JRAS '97, 117—8 (PINCHES); BOISSIER, *Rev. Sém.*, vii 130 § 27; MEISSNER, BA iv 418—22.

$^{(šam)}$ **'s'ur-du-nu-u.** K 5424, 4 (AV 8579; Br 14358), of the parallel column there is preserved only . . . . di; also Br 13984; 14013 (K 5424, 5 + 6).

siriddatum. Dar 301, 4 ištēnit si-rid-da-tum ša šikari ţābi.

sirxu, sirix in P. N. Nabū-a-na-ka(?)-tum-si-ri-ix, Nabd 1054, 3.

siriam (sariam), coat of mail, cuirass {Panzer} Z^B 54 *rm* 1. Sn v 55 see labašu 𐎚^t (*p* 474 *col* 2); also see ZA iii 312, 57 si-ri-ja-am. V 32 (*b*)-*c* 54, 55 sir-ja-am (✕ AV 1365); in *col b* read SU (*i. e.* mašak) ul-lu-lu (K 4547; Z^B 59). Neb 408, 23 Axat-ābišu is to receive annually a $^{(çubāt)}$'š'ir-a-am. Ner 28, 25 išten-it $^{(çubāt)}$sir-a-am ša $^{(iç)}$ a-mil-tum. K 419, 17 we read si-i-ru su-pi, which has been connected with siriam (Hr^L 119). T. A. (Ber) 26 iii 37 (+ 38): I SU sa-ri-am (+ 39 sa-ri-am). KB i 150 *no* iv perh. sir (not bu)-u-ja.

NOTE. — JASTROW, *Religion*, on *del* 6 reads sir-ja?]-am thou hast placed upon thee; but HAUPT k]i-a-am; JENSEN, KB vi (1) 230 u i-n]a a-xi na-da-at[-ta], und doch liegst du auf der Seite; ZA iii 417 ša la-a] na-da-at-ta (see also *Hopkins Circulars* 69, 7).

saramu. 𐎚 *ag* mu-sa-ri-mu ummāni, leader of troops {Leiter, Führer der Truppen}? MESSERSCHMIDT, *Stele Nab*, *p* 70.

sarme. II 23 *e-f* 57 sa-ar-me = ki-iš-tum, Br 12315; AV 6603.

saramū K 943 *R* 10 $^{(iç)}$sa-ra-me-e la

si-ru-bu-tu; K 82, 14 (Hr^L 176) so AV 6753, but read mutir-ru pu-tu (& see BA i 240—6). ∼ sarbatu *cf* çarbatu.

ga-mu-ru, Hr^L 452; MEISSNER & ROST, *Bīt-xillāni*, 10—11.

'šarmaxxu *n* reading of GIŠ-SAR-MAX = kirû çîru; § 73 *n* a large, grand garden, park {grosser Garten, Park}; Esh vi 14 (iç) sar-max; Asb x 104 (KB ii 234); Sn *Kui* 4, 32 (iç) sar-max-xu.

'surmaxxu. Sarg *Khors* 157; *Ann* 418 (amêl) sur-max-xi, mentioned together with (amêl) ram-ki *etc.*; compound of surrû + MAX (?), see maxxu. § 73 *rm.* highpriest {Oberpriester}?

si-er-in-ni II 49, 11 see sisinnu (& BA i 18; 167).

sarsarru. IV^2 9 *b* 14 sar-sar-ri ša .....

sarsarāni (*pl*) K 2401 (oracle to Esarhaddon) ii 10 an-nu-šim (amêl) sar-sar-a-ni an-nu-ti. BA ii 631 √סרר; so also PRINCE, AJP xv 114.

sirsiratu. chain {Kette}. T. A. (Ber) 24 *R* 83 as I put them i-na sir-sir-ri-ti (in chains).

sirapu, sirpu, *pl* sirapē some implement; shears {Schere} used for the gizzu (see *p* 214 *col* 2). Nabd 258, 15: II (parzillu) si-ra-pu (TALLQVIST, *Schenkungsbriefe*, 11—12); 874, 2 (-pi); Camb 331, 9—11: ištēn-it (iç) šid-da-tum, išten in-gu-ri-nu, šelalti si-ra-pu; 330, 4 *foll* there is mentioned as part of the dowry of Xunnatu 1 in-gu-ri-nu, 3 si-ir-pu (BA iii 463—65); Nabd 960, 3. PEISER, *Babyl. Vertr.*, 287 *rm* 10; BA i 530 *fol.*

saraqu, pr isruq, pour out, offer a libation {aufschütten, ausgiessen}. Aram סְרַק. K^M 18, 13 na-ša-ku nindabû a-sa-raq ....; 1, 20 as-ruk-ka si-riq (& see K^M *p* 12); 30, 3 as-ruk-ki si-riq; 57, 9. ZIM., *Ritualtafeln*, 52, 11 (end) ta-sar-[raq]; 75—78, 62 (end) sa-raq-qi; *l* 75 sa-ra-ki, *l* 76 these prayers ša sa-raq niknakki. Sarg *Cyl* 60 niqu aq-qi sir-qu as-ru-uq-ma, a libation I poured out (so perhaps against *p* 297, za-raqu). Nabd 16, 9 a woman *R* offers a sacrifice (ta-sar-ra-qu), *l* 1 ta-sa-ra-qu. BA ii 218—19 (239) reads Nabd-Cyr Chron. ii 8 is-ruq-ma. S^c 37 du-ub | DUB sa-ra-qu (Br 3929) ‖ šapaku, 35; tabaku, 36; AV 6595. H 17, 274; 48, 47 IN-DUB = is-ru-uq. K 2361 *O* ii 45 sa-ra-qu, ZA iv 238. — ℑ H 49, 51 IN-DUB-DUB = u-sa-ar-ri-iq; L^4 iii 8 az-li ṭu-ub-bu-xu li-e bu-ul-lu ki ar-man-ni sur-ru-qu (LEHMANN, ii 27: ward Weihrauch gestreut). Derr.:

sirqu. drinkoffering, libation {Trankopfer} see, above, and ZIMMERN, *Ritualtafeln*, 120 *no* 24 *R* 9: II sir-qu rabûti, two large libations. K 3650 *R* 48 sir (*var* si-ir)-ki-ši-na (ZA iv 12). T^M iv 59 (end) ...si-ir-ki-ku-nu. A ‖ is probably:

surqînu, which read perhaps for zurqînu (*p* 297 *col* 2). § 65, 35; JENSEN, KB vi (1) 416—17 (& 501); *del* 148 (156/7) at-ta-qi ni-qa-a | aš-kun sur-qi-nu (KB vi 241: machte ein Schüttopfer); see also *del* 157 (167/8). V 60 *a* 26/8 sattukku šu-a-tum ip-pa-ri-is-ma ba-ṭil sur-qi-nu (BA i 280).

sarraqu, one that pours out libations. K 8233 ii 31 [mu-tax-li]-lu sar-ra-qu, ZA iv 11.

sarqûtu. L^4 ii 22 sar-qu-tu da-me bloodshed. {Blutvergiessen}.

sararu. change; be refractory, rebellious; rebel {sich verändern; aufrührerisch sein} D^M 20. H 127 *O* 53—54 ša sar-rat-mi i-qab-bu-ni (Br 5369; Z^B 6 *rm* 2), who is it, that is obstreporous (or unsteady?) answered in 56: bêliku sa-ar-tum ana bîti u-še-ir-ri-ib, I am the lady, strife I let enter the house. pm Creat.-*frg* IV 9 la sa-ra-ar se-qar-ka (KB vi, 1, 324). — Q^t BANKS, *Diss*, *p* 10 *no* 4, 53 (end) ba-ru-u šu-u is-sa-ra-ar; followed by ša-i-lu šu-u is-sa-ra-ar. — ℑ K 1304 *R* 12 u-sa-ri-ir; V 63 *b* 32 mu-'š'ar-ri-ir ummâni nakri. — ℑ 83, 1—18, 1335 iii 26 ku-ud | KUD | na-sa-ru-ru.

Derr. sarru, 1 & 2, [surru, surriš] & these 2 (or 3?):

surtu. misdeed, evil deed, rebellion {Missetat, Empörung} *pl* surrâte. KB iii (1) 162 *col* v 40 whosoever causes the destruction of this boundary stone ina su-ur-ti ma-la ba-šu-u, by some evil deed. Asb i 120 êmuru ep-šit sur-ra-a-te (*var* ti)-šu-un, they saw their rebellious actions (see WINCKLER, *Forsch.*, i 251). K 2675 *O* 44. Asb vii 91—2 as Elam da-bab sur-ra-a-te Akkadê iš-me-e-ma; viii 68 da-bab sur-ra-a-te it-ti-ja id-bu-ub-ma (SMITH, *Asurb*, 243). K 2852 + K 9662 i 20 ru-bi-e ma-li-ki-ia sur-ra-a-ti la šal-ma-a-ti id-bu-bu it-ti-ia.

sarrūtu. enmity {Feindschaft} T. A. (Ber) 92, 14 u-ul ti-i-ti za-ar-ru-ut-da ša amēli, as if you did not know the hatred of the people; + *l* 37 a-ụa-ti *pl* za-ar-ru-ut-ti, thoughts of hatred (in your heart). See, however, ZA vi 246 *rm* 5; & šarūtu.

sarūru. K 618, 21 but the great gods . . . 24 a-na balāt napšāti ša šarri bēlija 27 a-na sa-ru-ri (V 53 *b*; Hr^L 9; AV 6602). Prince, AJP xv 114: protection {Schutz} a derivative of good sense of סרר originally: press together, be firm.

surāru. D 90 *frg l* 7 (end) ki-i su-ra-ri u-ma-çi; K 1268, 27 su-ra-a-ri ša šar-ri bēlija.

surtu 2. see sāru, 2; and Zimmern, *Ritualtafeln*, *nos* 75—78, 11 ana maxar su-ur-ti ana qāt ili nadanu (+ 22, 23, 24, 48, 49, 51, 54 etc.), see *ibid*, *p* 223 *col* 2. Perhaps S 747 *R* 7—8 su-ur-tum ša (amēl) bārūti.

sērāš (šireš). some beverage, drink, must {ein Getränk, Most}. I 66 *c* 15 ti-bi-ik si-ra-aš la ne-bi ma-mi-iš ka-ra-nam (Pognon, *Neb*, C vii 29: si-e-ra-aš; A vii 17 si-ra-aš); 65 *b* 31 da-aš-pa-am se-ra-aš. Creat.-*frg* III 135 ši-re-sa mat-qu; with sweet drink (KB vi (1) 20—1; 322). KB vi (1) 234—5 reads *del* 69 (73) si-ri[-šu ku-ru-]-un-nu, *cf Biblical World*, Febr. 1894. NE 137, 73 & *rm* 15. Ball, PSBA xx 18 spiced wine; Pognon, *Wadi-Brissa*, 18, 10—11; 117. On the original form sirasu *cf* Haupt in Ball, *Genesis* (SBOT), *p* 81; Jensen, 279, *rm* 2. On (il) Siris *cf* KB vi (1) 371. OLZ '02 Apr., *cols* 141, 142 says: ši-ri-sa Creat.-*frg* III 135 points to √שרש thus: Wurzeltrank, Kräuterwein.

sirašū, sirēšū. one who has to do with the sērāš {einer der mit sērāš zu tun hat} AV 6747, 6750. V 16 *e-f* 41 ZIR(or KUL?)-LUM = si-ra-šu-u (II 49 *a-b* 23) Br 1688. V 19 *b* 27 (+ II 34 *c-d* 15) ZIR-LUM = si-re-šu-u, Br 1689, in one group with sa-bu-u & ça-xi-it ka-ra-ni (28, 29). V 13 *c* 44 the same ideogram is = ba-ru-u (*cf* Zimmern, *Ritualtafeln*, *pp* 86—7). — Knudtzon, mentions 43 *O* 5 (māt) Si-ri-iš & 43 *O* 11 (māt) Si-ri-iš-a-a. Jensen, 279 *rm* 2; 411—12; ZA xv 254 & *rm* 1.

sartu. K 321, 22 sa-ar-tu a[-na kal ša-nāti]. ZA xiii 258, 268: this is the obligation for all years {dieses ist die Obliegenheit für alle Jahre}, *ad* KB iv 132—33: die Eingangsportel. Johns, PSBA xxi 79: sartu (= שער, Talm) = measure, taxation, *etc.*, sartennu = the judge who imposes the sartu. In Assyrian contracts = a fine imposed as a penalty for wrong done = damages'; çibtu bennu ana mē ūmē sarta ana kāl šanāti (*cf* Johns, *Deeds*, *no* 94) = the profit and service of a 100 days shall be the compensation for every year, *i. e.*, a slave, in place of full service, shall compound for the year's work by one 100 days' service; but against Johns, see Peiser, *OLZ*, ii *no* 4, *col* 181. Johns, √סאר.

sartennu. (T^C šartennu). IV² 40 *R* 27 (amēl) sa-ar-te-nu. III 49 *no* 4 (K 416) 22 (amēl) sar-tin-nu. Johns, *Deeds*, 164 has (amēl) sar-tin-nu. Also *Doomsday book* 5 ii 6 'š'ar-tin, chief justice. V 29 *e-f* 8 . . . . BA = sar-tin-nu, Br 13850; Nabd 1128, 6 (10) lawsuits are carried before the (amēl) sar-te-nu u (amēl) da'ānū (written DI-TAR-MEŠ); 64, 3 (amēl) sar-te-nu (& 4—11 (amēl) DI-TAR); 55, 9. Cyr 128, 15 (amēl) sar-te-en-na (amēl) suk-kal-tum u (amēl) da'ānē. Some kind of judge {eine Richterklasse}.

sešŝu (> sedšu) sixth {sechster} § 76. IV² 5 *a* 23—27 seš[-šu] = VI KAN-MA; NE 55, 24 see sibū. 82, 7—14, 864 *col* 3 *a-b* 14 siš-šit (Meissner, ZA vii 28 & *Diss*, *p* 6: VI GIN GUŠKIN NI-LAL-E = siš-šit šiq-lu kaspu i-šaq-qal, 6 šeqel of silver he shall pay. Also *cf* Hilprecht, *Assyriaca*, 69, 71; on the other hand KB vi (1) 78, 3 has še-iš-ši.

seš-a-nu *cf* šeššānu.

sātum. V 41 *c* 27 sa-a-tum.

sa-tu-um (-im) = šadū mountain (*q. v.*).

sūtum. a vessel of small size {ein kleineres Gefäss}. V 42 *c-d* 16 DUK ^ba-an-da^ BAR = su-u-tum; same ideogram = kupputtum (*q. v.*) & adagur(r)u. BA ii 632; PSBA xii 397; AV 6875; Br 1827; Haupt, *Sintflutbericht*, 27 *rm* 20; Del., *Chald. Gen.*, 320; KB vi (1) 501—2. V 36 *a-c* 28 u

| ⟨ | su-u-tum (Br 8741); 37 *d-f* 49 ba-a | ⟨⟨⟨ | su-u-tum (Br 9989).

sutū. V 14 *a-b* 14 SEG-ŠID-MA = si-pat su-ti-i, Br 5999, 10788; undoubtedly connected with the name of the Suteans: Sutī, IV^2 39 *a* 20 the axlamū u Su-ti-i (WINCKLER, *Forsch.*, i 146—7); Sutī (*varr* Sutium, Sutū) part of the district of Sū? (BEZOLD, *Catalogue*, 2196); IV^2 36 *no* 1 *O* 23 *a*; IV^2 50 *b* 19; V 60 *a* 6, *b* 27. III 66 *col* 8, 2 ilāni ša (māt) Su-tu (PSBA xxi 124—5) see *col* 7, 17 *foll.* K 2619 ii 8 Su-ti-e Su-ta-a-tu, KB vi (1) 63 Beduinen und Beduinenfrauen; iv 12 Su-ta-a Su-tu-u did not spare (KB vi, 1, 67; 376). AV 6874; also ZDMG 48, 489. — Mentioned in T. A. (Ber) 96, 27 (amêlûti) Šu-te-ja; (Lo) 74, 12 *fol* (amêlûti) xa-ba-ti u (amêlûti) Šu-ti-i (ZA x 330—1). See KB v Registers 40* *col* 2.

sittu, sītu, *adj* the other {der andere}, *pl* sitūti, *f* sit(t)āti the others, the remaining ones {die andern, die übrigen} D^{II} 44. Esh ii 19 si-tu-te-šu-nu (III 15 iii 11 si-it-tu-ti-šu-nu); Sarg *Khors* 115 that city a-di LXII maxāzē dan-nu-ti si-tu-ti-šu al-me. TP III *Ann* 170 si-tu]-u-ti-šu-nu ša .... ipparšidu. Asb vii 6 si-it-tu-ti (*cf* viii 35); iii 133 si-it-tu-u-ti; ix 36; si-it-tu-te-šu-nu, the balance of them, Sn iii 5 (*Kui* 1, 26); Asb ix 125 si-it-tu-ti-šu-nu; Sarg *Khors* 24 si-it-tu-ti i-nu-šu-nu u-ša-xi-iz (KB ii 54, 55); V 35, 5 si-it-ta-a-tim ma-xa--za, the other cities (§ 67, 4).

sittu, *noun.* rest, remainder {der Rest, der übrige Teil} *pl* sit(t)āti, sitēti. Asb iii 61 si-it-ti mārē, the remainder of the children of... (*cf* iv 92); thus perhaps also KB ii 258, 81 (= SMITH, *Asurb*, 137); ii 1 u si-it-ti maxāzē (*cf* vi 97); Sarg *Cyl* 20 Sargon who defeated such & such people ša si-it-ta-šu-nu he drove away; Sn vi 6 si-it-ti (amêl) rabûte-šu. I 43, 40 si-it-ti nišē mātišu; Sn iii 58 (also Asb iv 70; LEHMANN, ZA xiv 376). ZA iii 312, 60 si-it-ti šal-la-ti (*gen* for *c. st.*). Anp i 53 si-ta-ti-šu-nu (*cf* iii 113; AV 6758); ii 18 si-ta-te-šu-nu (ii 37; iii 36); i 64 si(*var* sit)-ta-te-šu-nu; ii 108 si-ta-ti (*var* te)-šu-nu; Sarg *Ann* 31 si-it-ta-ti-šu-nu (ZA iv 142); 96 (-te-); 271; Botta 75, 5; AV 6762. Sarg *Khors* 131 si-it-ta-at nišē multax-ṭu (+ 133). TP III *Ann* 38 si-ta-at mundaxçēšunu. I 28 *a* 31 si-te-it u-ma-a-me ma-'-di; AV 6759. TP i 85 si-te-it ummānātešu(nu); iii 16—17; iv 27; v 54; Šalm, *Mon*, *O* 21. K 2660 (III 38, 2) *R* 7 [ina?] si-ta-at nišē. Anp iii 41 si-ta-at ummānātešu (42; ii 9). TP ii 1 si-te-it (mât) Qummuxi.

sītu. II 32 *g-h* 11 SI-BAD = si-i-tum; same id = ēlat šamē, AV 6760. KB vi (1) 349: spitzer Vorsprung, Zinne? *Ibidem* 542 on Br 3404.

sataku. V 45 vi 37 tu-sat-tak. From this verb probably the following 4:

satāku. I 69 *c* 35 sa-ta-ku eli ša pa-ni u-ša-tir, the tribute I increased beyond the former.

sattakka, sattakam, *adv* continuously, constantly, always {beständig, immerwährend} § 80 *a*. Ner ii 12 ana Êsagila u Êzida la ba-aṭ-la-ak (*q. v.*), sa-at-ta-kam (KB iii, 2, 74). V 34 *c* 52 qi-be-i sa-at-ta-ak-ka (>< KB iii (2) 45 *rm* **).

sattūku, sattukku, *m* originally perhaps: the established, regular standard of value {der feststehende Gehalt} intensive formation from סתק; then, a fixed, perpetual sacrifice ‖ ginū (*q. v.*). id DI-KA *i. e.* SA-DUG, probably from sattukku (WZKM iv 116 *rm* 5); V 60 *a* 20 + 26 sattukku šu-a-tum (BA i 279); I 49 *d* 27—8 sattukkē-šu-nu ba-aṭ-lu-ti. Bu 88—5—12, 75 + 76, vi 18. Sarg *Ann* 364 sat-tuk-ki-šu-nu baṭlūti, *Khors* 137; *Ann* 418 sat-tuk-ki la nar-ba-a-ti, *Khors* 157. KB iii (1) 196, 17 (Šamaššumukīn) sat-tuk-ki Ê-sag-il, die Tempelabgaben von *E* (KB ii 258, 11). Esh *Sendsch*, *R* 49 sat-tuk-ki gi-nu-u ... u-kin; also Asurb iv 106/7 (WINCKLER, *Forsch.*, i 248 >< KB ii 195); iv 90/1 sat-tuk-ke-šu-un ša i-me-çu .... ina šalmē utīrma u-kin (KB ii 192). IV^2 53 *c* 38 Asurb. zānin ešrēt ilāni rabûtim mu-kin sat-tuk-ke-šun. V 35, 7 sat-tuk-ku u-šab-ṭi-li. V 62 *no* 1, 10 sat-tuk-ke Êsagila ... u-kin (+ 7, sat-tuk-ki-ši-na baṭ-lu-tu); V 65 *a* 4 Nabd. ... mu-dax-xi-id sat-tuk-ku; 64 *c* 37 sat-tuk-ku u nin-da-bi-e .... uššštir. V 52 iv 22 (end) mu-kin sat-tu-ki-šun; *cf* 81—6—7, 209, 17 (BA iii 260—3); K 2801 *O* + K 221 + 2669, 39 *fol*. A. H. 82, 7—14 ii 5 sa-at-tu-uk-ku. K 3600 *R* 26 pa-ri-su sat-tuk-ki ša ili u (ilat) Iš-ta-ri. KB iii (2) 50 *col* 3, 22 bi-it-ru-su sa-at-tu-ku (& 78, 19); I 65 *a* 18 sa-at-tu-ku-šu du-uš-šu-u-tim, *etc.*: his fat (rich) offerings (I encreased); *b* 38 sa-at-tu-uk ilâni rabûti. Often in *c.t.* written sat-tuk (BA i 279; ZA iv 72 & *rm* 1). Nabd 672, 1 ina sat-tuk ša Addari (33, 3); 683, 3 a-na sat-tuk ša ....; 350, 2 ‖ guqqanû; 49, 8 such & such, sat-tuk ša Addari ša ilu Adad. Camb 314, 1—2 see maššartu (612 *col* 2); 62, 1 *foll*; 200, 1 *fol*; 112, 2—3; 12, 1 *foll*; Cyr 50, 1—2; 66, 1 *foll*, see makkasu, 2 (538 *col* 2); also Cyr 118, 11 AŠ-A-AN sat-tuk ša (arax) Dûzu. STRASSM., *Stockholm*, 16, 8; 5 + 7. Neb 1, 1—2 see mašixu (where also other passages). mašixu ša sat-tuk, a technical term. Dar 90, 1 *foll*, + 5 *fol*; Nabd 912, 1 + 5; ZA iv 125 *no* 3. On the sat-tuk ša arxi see T^C 113. — The superintendence of the sattukku was given to the (amêl) rê'û sattukki (Nabd 298, 3 *etc.*).

NOTE. — 1. On Sadugga in name Ammi-sadugga see צדק

2. mastaku see maštaku.

3. See § 65, 39 *rm a*; PEISER, *Babyl. Vertr.*, 286; 290; LATRILLE, ZA i 36; JENSEN, ZDMG 5 · 261; ZA ii 219 *foll*; JASTROW, *Religion*, 667. BA iii 287 *foll*: nicht nur festgesetztes Opfer, sondern auch festgesetzter, regelmässiger Gehalt. ZA iv 72 & *rm* 1. POGNON, JA viii (*vol* xi) 1888, *p* 546; HOMMEL in HASTINGS, *Dictionary of the Bible*, i 206 *col* 2 (√sa-dug: probably a word originally borrowed from the Arabic).

santakku ‖ ka'amânu. AV 6567. Sp II 265 *a* xxiv 5 (end) sa-an(*var*-at)-tak-ku (*var* omits); Rm III 105 i *b* 12 (end) pu-tuq-qu sa-an-tak (WIN., *Forsch.*, i 254—55; JRAS '92, 350 *foll*). K 4587 *R* 8 *foll* s]a-an-tak *foll* by ka-a-a-ma-nu. ZA iv 239 (iii) 11 ku-nu-uk-ka sa-an-tak(-)ki-na-a-ti; 83—1—18, 483 + 1272 *R* 5 sa-an-tak-ku = ka-a-a-ni. V 13 *c-d* 37 ZAB𒁹 = çâbê sa-an-tak-ki. tikip santakki often in colophons: nimêq(i) Nabû ti-kip sa-an-tak-ki ma-la ba-aš-mu I wrote on the tablets (AV 6567); II 42, 55; 21 *a* 31; 23 *a* 59; D 49, 37; often in IV² Rawl. V 51 *a* 55 (sa-tak-ki); 16 *c* 72; 30 *e* 48; K 155 *R* 23. Also the colophons in $Z^Š$ & T^M. Th word, according to HALÉVY, ZA iii 346 is a ‖ of sattukku. D^{L4} = Schriftzeichen.

'šattakku. K 49 (II 62 *no* 1) *col* 3, 11 AŠ (= DIL) III-TE = sat-tak-ku.

sutukku. K 55 *R* 17, 18 IM-DAG-GA & IM-AN-NA = su-tuk-ku, M^S texts, *pl* 3. su-tuk-ku Nabd *Ann* iii 16 read SU (= mašak) tuk-ku (≍ KB iii (2) 134). K 4174 + 4583 iv 24, perhaps rather su-pa-lu (GGA '98, 811).

sut(t)innu, *cf* sud(d)innu, where also satinnu.

sitmatum. II 22 *e-f* 42 ME-ME-A = si-it-ma-tum, AV 6761; Br 10454.

sataru. perh. mu-us-ta-ru, AV 5519 (*q. v.*).

su-ta-ri KB iii (2) 126 *ad* V 35, 29 read kuš-ta-ri.

פ

pû *1. m* mouth {Mund} § 62, 2. gen. pî (bî); acc. pâ. Z^B 97; AV 7099; Br 538, 817, 836; id KA § 9, 39; H 86—7, 62 KA = ina pi-i; IV² 30* *no* 3 *O* 32 ana pi-ja = KA-MU; IV² 22 *no* 2, 20—21 ina pi-i (= KA) ka-ra-ši; II 8 *b* 29, 31 pi-ja = KA-MU; H 76, 23—4 with woe pi-i-šu (= KA-BI) was filled; 10 + 207, 40 (where many passages are given). IV² 25 iv *R* 53 ana pi-ka (= KA-ZU) + 55. V 39 *a-b* 1; 31 *e-f* 62 KA = pu-u(-um); 50 *a* 67; S^b 1 iv 26 ka-a | KA | pu-u followed by ap-pu (27). — V 47 *b* 40 i-na pi-i gir-ra; 41 (end) KA = pî (sisê); i-na pi-i kal-bi (*q. v.*) e-ki-im-šu, i-na pi-i a-ri-bi u-nad-di K 245 (II 9 *c-d*) iii 34, 36 (≍ BA i 636). of donkeys: IV² 18* *no* 6 *O* 11 pi-i-šu-nu; naktam pî and makçaru ša pî see these. abau pî ça-bi-ti, Esh iii 28 (ZK ii 9 but *cf* KB ii 131 *rm* **). — usually of the mouth of persons or gods: Creat.-*frg* IV 100 (end) pa-a-ša (*i. e.*, Tiâmat) uš-p(b)al-ki, opened wide her mouth. S 28, 36 pi-i-šu i-pi-ti, see also pît pî. KB vi (1) 34, 17—18 let not the(se) words be forgotten ina pi-i çal-mat qaqqadi; 19, pa-ši-na lit-tab(p)-b(p)al, bring forth their mouth (KB vi, 1, 353—4); K[M] 22, 8 ina pî niše; 9 ina pî-ka ket-ti; 9, 13 šuškin kettu ina pi-ia; Esh ii 24 i-na pi-i niše it was called thus; KB iii (1) 50, 23 Eulla's income i-na bi-i ip-pa-ar-ku-u (was not ordered?). ZA ix 118, 16 description of an idol: ina pi-šu mu-u šu-gal-lu-lu-ni. BA ii 418; KB vi (1) 94, 5 (end) ki-ma i-na bi-i-šu iq-bu. K 3182 iii 20 a-na xar-ri pi-i-šu. IV² 18* *no* 6 (S 1708) 11 ša .... pi-i-šu-nu u-mal-li-ma; V 50 *a* 67—8 ša pu-u lim-nu (= KA-XUL-GAL-E) iz-zu-ru-šu (see nazaru); H 84—5 i 32 pu-u lim-nu (= KA-XUL-GAL); iḋ IV² 1* iii 46. V 33 *a* 48 the great gods i-na pi-i-šu-nu el-lim ..... iq-bu-u; K 2701 *a* (beg.): ina pi-i-šu el-li la muš-pi-li; Antioch. Cyl 46 ina pi-i-ka el-li (I 52 *no* 3 *col* 2; 27; L⁴ ii 33); H 78, 9 pu-u el-lu = purifying word. — K 2401 iii 34 mû ina pi-ia la-aš-kun (BA ii 627 *foll*). ina pi-i-ka I 51 *no* 1 *R* 31; KB vi (1) 108 *c* 18 (li-ça-am-ma); Asb ix 34 food and drink u-ša-qir a-na pi-i-šu-nu. Bu 88—5—12, 75 + 76 ii 9 (see maršu 2, end). IV² 39 *R* 37 i-na pi(*var* KA)-šu-nu kabti. — çît pî (literally: that which issues from the mouth; utterance, word) = qibîtu. V 39 (= II 30) *a-b* 12 KA-TA-UD-DU = çi-it pi-i; I 29, 20 çi-it pi-i-šu dan-dan-nu; Creat.-*frg* II (KB vi, 1, 8) 14 (+ 22) li-kun çi-it pi-i-ka; III 48; IV 9; Banks, *Diss*, *p* 14, 1 *no* 4, 101; *Rec. Trav.* xx 205 i 14 (pi-šu); I 66 *c*-46 ši-mi çi-it bi-ia, hear the word of my mouth; ZA iv 11, 14 çi-it pi-i-šu-nu; Anp i 4 ki-bit pî-šu; K 3364, 12 qi-bit pi-i; KB ii 248 v 8 qi-bit pi-i-šu ša-xu-u, the request of his haughty mouth; also simply pû without preceding çît: K 10, 24 (Hr[L] 280) pi-i-šu-nu | id-dan-nu-nu, they sent a message; S 1064 (Hr[L] 392) *R* 12 pi-i-šu it-ti-din, he has given his command. ZA v 67, 31 ina pi-i-ki u-ça-a, from thy mouth came forth (the command).

IV² 15 ii 50 see magaru (511 *col* 1, 1—2); Asb iv 66 sil-la-tu pi-i-šu-nu. II 27 *e-f* 7 pu-u pur-ru-šu (Br 3497: same iḋ = xuppû); parû ša pi-i see parû 2; la-ak pi-i (Br 11441); si-kur pi-i (II 39 *a-b* 9) see lâku, 2 (479 *col* 2) & si-k(k)ûru; miqit pî see miqtu (579 *col* 2). — Knudtzon has the forms: pi-a-šu 2 *R* 4 (+ 3); pi-ia 150 *R* 6; otherwise iḋ KA. — Pâ epešu, open one's mouth (= to speak) {seinen Mund (zum Reden) auftun} § 152; KB vi, 1, 315, 318. GGN '80, 516 *rm* 1; see zakaru. Creat.-*frg* III 1 Anšar pa-a-šu i-pu-šum-ma. K 2527 + K 1547 *O* 15 Šamaš KA (= pî)-šu i-pu-ša-am-ma .... izakkar (KB vi, 1, 104—5); also KB vi (1) 106, 37 našru pa-a-šu i-pu-ša-ma i-zak-ka-ra ana ... 108, 50 + 52; *c* 17 (11) Šamaš pi-i-šu i-pu-šam-ma; IV² 31 *O* 21 + 66; *R* 29; Rm 282 *R* 1 ... pa-a-šu i-pu-uš-ma (KB vi, 1, 46). S[P] 158 + S[P] II 962, 11 pî-šu êpuš-am-ma. Merod.-Balad.-stone iii 14 pi-šu ib(p)-ši-ma. Creat.-*frg* I i *c* 36 ep-ša pi-i-ku-nu; II ii *c* 8 ep-šu pi-ia (KB vi, 1, 8 + 12); IV 23 ep-ša pi-i-ka (= speak!); III 51 + 109 ep-šu pi-i-ku-nu; 62 + 120 ep-šu pi-ia; 57 + 115 ep-šu pi-i-šu; II 39 *a-b* 8 e-peš pi-i. Smith, *Asurb*, 146, 2 i-na e-peš pi-ia. — Also = tongue {Zunge} Asb iv 69 pi-i (*var* lišâni, Br 836) aš-lu-uk, their tongues I tore out. — ša pi-i in oracles: from the mouth of *e. g.* IV² 61 *no* 1, 29; 2, 9 *etc.* — word {Rede} often in: pâ šakanu itti: to ally oneself with. Asb iii 106 (it-ti-šu) iš-ku-nu pi-i-šu-nu; vii 101 iš-ta-kan pi-i-šu (see 109); viii 48, 49 u šu-u it-ti *N* pi-i-šu iš-kun-ma, 69; KB ii 6—7, 21 iš-ku-na pi-i-šu ... it-ti. K 6332, 6—7 it-ti-šu-nu ..... pa-a e-diš iš-[kun]; Sarg *Khors* 34 pa-a e-da u-ša-aš-kin-ma; Winckler, *Sargon*, *p* 221. — iš-tu pi-e adi xurâçi, from start to finish; lit[y] from the word to the gold, Pinches, *Inscr. Tablets*, 60, 18 (& *p* 63); KB iv 12, 22—23 iš-tu bi-e a-na xurâçi (*ibid* *rm* ** >< Meissner, 145). — pû ṭâbi = friendly speech, Knudtzon, *etc.*; pû ilû-ti-ka rabî-ti (*ibid* 23, 47, 299); IV² 45 *no* 3 *R* 9 pi-i (amêl) zi-'i-ra-ni. K 174, 15 šarru ša pi-i-ni lišmi, let the king listen to our word (Hr^{L} 55); K 562, 12 *foll* šarru ša pi-i-šu liš-mi (Hr^{L} 260); III 43 i 10 ki-i pi šarri (BA ii 116 *foll*; KB iv 68, 69); 22 ki-i pi-i *M.*; a-mat-tu ša pi-i-šu I 27, 86 (80, ša pi-i-šu). — Also = contents, K 2729 *R* 32, 35 (see dannītu 2, *p* 262 *col* 2). — Babyl. Chron. iii 21 pū-šu ça-bit-ma at-ma-a la li-'-. — To make people of one mind (or, of one tongue), TP vi 46 pa-a ište-en u-še-eš-kin-šu-nu-ti (1 *sg*); TP III *Ann* 18 pa-a ištēn u-ša-aš-kin-šu-nu-ti; Sarg *Cyl* 73 ba'ūlāt arba'i .... pa-a ište-en u-ša-aš-kin-ma (*Bull-inscr.* 95); Asb iv 99 the inhabitants of Akkad, whom *Š* a-na ište-en pi-i u-ter-ru. — mouth of a river, or canal {Mündung eines Flusses, oder Kanals}. *del* 184, 185 ina pi-i nārāte; ina KA (*var* pi-i) nārāte; IV^{2} 22 *no* 1 *R* 11 see kilallā (386—7); Sn *Kui* 2, 31 raq-qa-at pi-i nāri, the swamps around the river's mouth; *Bav* 54 i-na pi-i nāri; KB iv 66—67 *no* iii (1) *col* 2, 2 ša pi-i (nār) Çal-ma-ni. Anp iii 31 I turned away ištu pi-a-te $^{(nār)}$ Xa-bur (KB i 100; ZA i 369 *pl* of *pītu; Hoffmann, ZA xi 211—12).

On PN ša-pī-Bēl (Nabd 6, 16; Asb iii 54 + 68; Strassm., *Stockholm*, 7, 10); ša-pī-Marduk Dar 26, 6 + 14; ša-pī-$^{(il)}$IB Peiser, KAS 81, 28 see BA i 385.

V 20 *c-d* 56 pu-u (= KA) ba-ba-nu-tu (Br 617); T. A. (Ber) 75, 11—12 a-na pī | bi-i = in accordance with the demand of *A.* (Lo) 22, 24 iš-tu bi abulli, from the gate; K 519 *R* 14 (Hr^{L} 108) pi-i na-xi-ri within (properly: in the mouth of) the nostrils.

V 39 (= II 39) *a-b* 1—3 KA; $^{(u-nu)}$TE-UNU (S^{c} 94; Br 7728); $^{(mu-ru-ub)}$SAL <ϒ ϒ (*p* 585 *col* 2; Br 10963) = pu-u-um; 4 pū pitū; 6—7 pīt pi-i see pitū; 5 pū uš-šu-ru (*cf* ašaru, 3; Br 610); 8 e-peš pi-i. sanaqu ša pi-i see sanaqu.

pī (*i. e.* gen. of pū) is also used as a preposition {auch als Präposition gebraucht}: In accordance, in agreement with; according to; in harmony with, corresponding to {in Gemässheit von; gemäss; entsprechend}, as kī (368 *col* 2); BA i 385 *rm* *; § 81*c*. Asurb x 46 ki-i pi-i an-ni-ma; V 61 *e* 18 kīma pi-i an-nim-ma; colophon to S^{c} (327) ki-i pi-i duppāni, *etc.* Sarg *Cyl* (41) 52 ki-i pi-i dup-pa-a-ti *etc.*; K 5268, 38 (see duppu); Rm 277 ii 13; V 52, 30; Esh v 42 ša ki-i pi-i šik-ni-šu-nu, BA i 278; often in *c. t.*, Nabd 566, 9; 668, 16; 715, 13; KB iv 320—1 (*no* 2) ii 10 ki-i pi-i u-il-tim. Beh 101 kī pī ša; also kīma pī, ZA iv 341—2. 82, 9—18, 3737 *R* (end) ki-i pi-i GIŠ-LI-XU-SI-UM ša a-na pi-i ša-ṭa-ri qu-ul-lu-pu; VATh 352, 1 ki-i pi-i ū-mu ša arxi, in accordance with the days of the month; without kī *e. g.* I 27 *no* 2, 45—46 (*p* 569 *col* 1, musarū 2, where read pi instead of pī); 54 ki-i pi-i; also see *ibid* 78—80. ša la pi-i ku-nu-uk-ki-šu Peiser, *Jurisprud. Babyl.*, 38—9; ana pi-i ni-is-xi (*q. v.*) like the original, ZA iv 262, 43; ki-i pi-i at-ri Neb 135, 20; KB iv 158, 15 (Hilprecht, als Bachschisch).

pū *2.* chaff, straw, stubbles {Spreu, Stroh, Stoppeln} M^{S} 74 *fol*; KB vi (1) 453—4: pas. NE vi 104 i-ba-aš-ša-a] 7 šanāti p[e-e]; *cf* 11: 7] šanāti pe-e. S 21 *R* 4 IN-BUL-BUL = pu-u, ZA viii 108; V 42 *g-h* 23 IN-BUL-BUL = (ṭi-iṭ) pi-e (Br 4242, 8420). T^{M} v 11 mannu IN-BUL-BUL (= pā) ib-bat ŠE-BAR u-qaç-çir; v 15, 57; vi 31; viii 74 + 79; IV^{2} 55 *O* 12 (id). Connected with this is probably Strassm., *Stockholm*, 31, 3: zirē zaq-pi u pi-i šul-pu (Camb 407, 11; 257, 6); VATh 208, 7: 4 GUR zēru pi-i šu-ul-pi, KB iv 95 .... a-di kirē zaq-pi; also *l* 36 (KB iv 96). Perhaps also Zim., *Ritualtafeln*, 60, 4 ina eli karpat pi-'- inaqqi.

pū *3.* = Egypt. *pw* (??) T. A. (Ber) 60, 52—54 read a-na $^{(al)}$ I-[n]am-ta al-ka u pu-u en-ni-ip-ša a-na $^{(amēlūt)}$ GAZ-MEŠ (= xabbūti?): but it (the city) had fallen into the hands (power) of the robbers, BA iv 105.

PI. a Babylonian measure. 1 GUR = 180 QA; 1 PI = 36 QA; thus 5 PI = 1 GUR; Oppert, ZA i 87 *foll*; Peiser, *Babyl. Vertr.*, 316; Zimmern, BA iii 489; Pinches, *Inscribed Tablets*, *p* 15. Camb 56, 7: ina ma-ši-xi ša I PI (BA iii 461) *etc.*

pa'ū (?) a bird {ein Vogel}. II 37 *e-f* 20 pa-

'u-u ‖ qa-qa-nu, Br 13969, AV 6887; D[S] 109.

p(b)iāzu. some fourfooted animal {ein vierfüssiges Tier} AV 7038; *cf* xumçiru. D[S] 61: Gepard; JENSEN, ZA i 311 & KB vi (1) 538: hog. II 6 *d-e* 47 pi-a-zu; S[b] 1 *O* iii 15 [sign]-TIN (ki-iš) = pi-a-zu; V 38 *no* 2 *R* 44; Br 11937; id also III 56 *no* 2, 11; K 626, 12 (Hr[L] 24). PINCHES, PSBA '96, 251 on id. II 49 *no* 4 *a* 45 when a star ana bi-a-zi itūr; 49, ana xumçiri.

pijāmu written pi-ja-a-mu ‖ qar-radu, *etc.* (*q. v.*) AV 7034. II 31 *no* 3, 60 a-li-lu = pi-ja-a-m[u] ZA ix 274 *rm* 1; and thus correct V 41 *a-b* 24 *var* reading. 81, 4—28, 327 *R* 10 ga-a-ga-mu = pi-ja-a-mu, S 2052 (+S 1051) ‖ of qarradu is pi-[ja]-a-mu, BA iii 276—77.

pi-e-çu. S[c] 67 da-ar | DAR | pi-e-çu, (preceded by šu-ut-tu-ru) Br 3489; 83, 1—18, 1332 *col* iv 4 pi-e-çu; ip. IV[2] 26 *b* 44—45 ṭa-ab-tu el-li-tu u(?)-xu-lu el-lu pu-uç(z, s?)-ma; see also bi-e-çu (139 *col* 1). — [sign] V 45 vi 15 tu-pa-'-aç. AV 7063.

pa'aru. K 125 (Hr[L] 196), 21: 7 biltu ištu libbi ni-ip-ti-ar. M[S] 75: select {auswählen}; JOHNS, PSBA xvii 234—5: pay {zahlen}.

pijāru. K 21, 8 (Hr[L] 51) ma-a a-na pi-ja-a-ri e-pu-uš ū-mu la DUG-GA (= ṭābi).

pa'itū? T. A. (Ber) 92 *R* 29 (amēl) Pa-ma-xa-a ša Xa-an-ni pa-i-te-e-i-u, KB v 25* *col* 2: perh: secretary (?).

pābu. T. A. (Ber) 26 i 27 pa-a-ab a-ça-am pa-an-ša.

pagu 1. JOHNSTON, JAOS xx 251—2: take away {wegnehmen}, to which he refers II 65 i 27 karassu (il) urigallešu i-pu-ga-šu. K 619, 14 your cities pi-e-gu (are taken away) Hr[L] 174; AV 7035. 83—1—18, 6 (Hr[L] 421) *R* 5 u-ma-a eqla pi-ga-ku, now I am deprived of my land.

pagu 2. see for the present pāqu (paqū?).

pūgu (?) so ZA ix 222 *ad* S 31—52 *R* 19 GIŠ-SA-TUR = pu-u-gu, between mešeštum & te-šu-u; V 26 *d* 68 pu-u[-gu?] Br 3103.

paggu T. A. see pakku.

pagū; usually **pagītu, pagūtu.** AV 6880. I 28 *a* 29 pa-gu-ta rabī-ta nam-su-xa (*q. v.*) (imēr) nāri u-ma-a-mi ša tāmdi rabī-te, sent by the king of Muṣrū to Aššur (BA i 180 *rm* 1); Anp iii 87 mentions among the tribute of the kings of the Mediterranean Coast pa-gu-tu rabī-tu pa-gu-tu çixir-tu, also *l* 76. Lay 43, 12 Anp brought to Kelach pa-ga-a-te rabīte pa-ga-a-te çixrūti (KB i 108 *rm*); 44, 18 pa-gi-e pa-ga-a-te (ZA i 307 *rm* 1); K 2675 *R* 3 .. [ba?]-za-a-ti pa-gi-e u(-)qu-pe tar-b t šad-d -šu-un (KAT[2] 450). ZA iv 362 (82—7—14, 509) *O* 7 .... pa-gi-tum turāxu *etc.* S 2037, 11 pagīti. T. A. (Ber) 28 ii 47: 1 pa-ku-du u mārti-šu. W MAX MÜLLER ZA viii 211 *rm* 2: "wenn pagū, *f* pagūtu eine Affenart bezeichnen würde (HOMMEL, *Gesch.*, 582, aber nicht wahrscheinlich), so wäre es kaum ein ägyptisches Wort", vielleicht: afrikanische Meerkatze.

pagadu see paqadu.

pagdarū *cf* pakdarū.

pagūgu. V 30 *g-h* 38 GI-GI = pa-gu-gu, followed by BAR-ŠU-IK = pu-ṭu-ru, AV 7100; H 215, 38, 39 (reads GI-IK?); Br 2438.

pagalu. 80, 11—12, 9 *O col* 1 [sign] = pa-ga-lum, Br 10197.

pagalu, pagilu & pagulu names of vessels {Gefässbezeichnungen}. ZIMMERN, *Ritualtafeln*, 61 *no* i 2—6 (karpat) pa-ga-al; 69 *R* 4. pa-gu-lu, *no* 61, iii 4; 62 *O* 10; pa-gul, 64, 10 *etc.*; pa-gi-li 66 *O* 6; 68 *O* 8.

paglu TP ii 9 see xūlu, 2 (313 *col* 1) and *cf* CHR. JOHNSTON, AJP xix 386 = xarrānu, road.

puglu, perhaps radish {Rettig} = פֻּגְלָא; D[Pr] 84 *rm* 2. — ZA vi 295 iii 3 pu-ug-lu SAR = laptu (*q. v.*); ZDMG 39, 294, 2. Also see II 44 *a-b* 29 GIŠ (dab(?)-im(?)-[sign]) ŠAR = pu-ug(k, q)-lu; V 26 *a-b* 10, Br 10176; M[S] 75 & puqlu.

pa-gal-tu, Nabd 327, 7.

pagūmu (AV 6879) see daššu, 2 (269 *col* 2).

pāgumu. T. A. (Ber) 26 i 48: 1 (mašak) pa-a-gu-mu.

puginnu see buginnu (*p* 147 *cols* 1, 2) & KB vi (1) 420—1; 489—90.

pagru, *c. st.* pagar, *m.* D^{Pr} 34 פֶּגֶר; G § 36; AV 6878. — *a*) body {Leib}. Cuthean Creat.-*legend* iv 22 (iii 23) pa-gar-ka u-çur pu-ut-ka šul-lim, ZA xii 323 thy body protect, thy breast preserve intact (KB vi, 1, 298); *ibid* i 4 (end), 9 pag-ri u p(b)u-u-ti & iii 2 (KB vi, 1, 292, 294; ZA xii 319 *foll*). KB vi (1) 118 *col* 2, 2 ça-lam pag-ri-šu; 126/7 (NE 11), 26 ul-lu-la pa-gar-šu; *del* 227 (252) see malū 2 (end; 544 *col* 1, where add: Jensen, KB vi (1) 400—401: malū = karru: Trauertuch). K 2148 iii 37; ii 9; Rm 279 *O* 9 see merīnu (589 *col* 1). K 2148 ii 20 pag-ru (iii 9 pa-gar-ša) pir(?)-xa kakkabāni ma-li; iii 25 pag-ru nēši; T^M vii 40 (end) pag-ri-ka ‖ zumri-ka (39), BA iv 161. KB vi (1) 298 i 15 pa-ag-ri u um-ma-ni lu-še-çi (see KB vi (1) 506); IV^2 19 *a* 28 see zarabu ℑ (295 *col* 2). V 46 *a-b* 28 pa-gar asakki (Br 1527); S. A. Smith, *Asurb*, 87, 67. II 30 *no* 4 *O* 19 (46) BAR?] = pag-ru followed by zu-um-ru, Br 1753. — *b*) corpse {Leichnam} id (amēl) BAD (§ 9, 10). Asb iii 9 see mašaru, 2. Q^t; Smith, *Asurb*, 95, 85; Asb ii 116 (118) before his enemy li-na-di (& innadi) pa-gar-šu; v 45 (amēl) pagri-šu a-a ad-din a-na qi-bi-ri (KB ii 212—3; § 144; BA i 460 *rm* 2) his corpse I did not commit to burial; see also K 2729 *R* 31 (BA ii 566 *foll*); TP ii 21 pa-gar muq-tab-li-šu-nu; Asb iv 79 (amēl) pagrē nišē; ix 123 (amēl) pagrē-šu-nu; Sn i 58 (amēl) pag-ri-šu-un; iii 3; v 84 pag-re qu-ra-de-šu-nu. Sn vi 18 over the pag-ri of their troops they ran; v 68 gim-ri (amēl) BAD-MEŠ-šu-nu; Anp ii 55 pag-ri-šu-nu I filled the streets (+ 88 pag-ri-šu-nu at-bu-uk + ii 41 id; 114 & *var* id + MEŠ, Br 1527); i 29 pag-ri (*var* pa-gar) gi-ri-šu; 109 id + MEŠ (*var* pag-ri)-šu-nu. TP i 79; ii 15 BAD-MEŠ-šu-nu; *cf* iii 15, 55; v 95; vi 7; viii 86; Anp i 53; Rm 191 *R* 5; 83—1—18, 244, 5.

NOTE. — 1. Bezold, *Diplomacy* (xxv *rm* 2) reads T. A. (Lo) 9, 8 (amēl) pag-ra-ti-ka, but KB v *no* 16 reads xu-ra-ti-ka; also see *ibid*, *nos* 1, 83; 83, 9.

2. I 28 *b* 4 bît ša pag(q?)-ri, KB i 126—7.

3. Nabd 304, 1 see xūrū & BA i 633.

pagru 2. see paqru (paqaru).

pugurrū *cf* puqurrū.

pādu, pr ipīd. Sarg *Cyl* 18 Sargon ša-lil (māt) Tu-'a-mu-na ša (amēl) na-sik-šu-nu i-pi-du-ma (Scheil *ad* Šamš iv 34: i-ue-du) Lyon, *Sargon*, 61: put in fetters; KB ii 92, deposed. *Cf* P. N. Sin-pi-di-ma (or √padū?); K 4300 *R* 5, 6 pa-a-du; *p* ša mimma, preceded by sa-qa-lum, AV 6883.

pādu 2. *cf* pāṭu.

pa-du see xaramu (*p* 337 *col* 2).

padū. loosen, scatter, defeat; also, cease; usually set free, spare {lösen, auflösen, zerstören; aufhören; gewöhnlich: losgeben, freigeben} Z^B 97; AV 6884. K 8522, 15 a-na pa-di-šu-nu to release them (KB vi, 1, 34; 315; but Zimmern-Gunkel: in their stead, *cf* pāṭu). IV^2 22 *a* 38 al-pa ul ip-di (Br 6150); 15 *b* 1—2, 3—4 ul ip-du-u (Br 7874; id as II 26 *c-d* 37). ag padū used as *adj.* — pm T^M vi 82 pa-da-at-ti thou art my savior {du bist meine Erlöserin} + viii 35; but?? — ℑ Knudtzon, 21 *O* 8 . . . ip-p]a-di-i; *R* 6 . . . . ip]-pa-du-u.

Derr. napdū, tapdū, ipdū (?) & these 2:

padū. usually with lā: giving no quarter, no pardon; without mercy, relentless {kein Pardon gebend; schonungslos} Esh *Sendsch* *O* 20 (+ 23) la pa-du-u (+ *R* 23), the merciless. Anp i 7 (+ 20) Ninib (& Anp) tizqaru la pa-du-u (*var* ez-zu). T^M ii 96 (il) Gibil ez]-zu la pa-du[-u]; iii 53 la pa-di-tum ša sinnišāti, said of the kaššaptu (§§ 41; 68); Anp i 34; iii 127 kakku la(-a) pa-du-u, the relentless weapon (Lay 38, 6); i 41 kakka-šu la(-a) pa-da-a (iii 118, 130); Creat.-*frg* III 34 kakkē (92, *var* kak-ku) la pa-di-i; III 25 la pa-du-u at-ta-['-i?] + 83; IV 130 see miṭṭu (& KB vi, 1, 328—9). I 43, 5 ši-bir-ru la pa-du-u; K^M 20, 15 + 17; 46, 18; 5, 9 ud]-da-kam la pa-da-a; ZA iv 236, 12 la pa-du-uk gir-ri. Sarg *Ann* XIV 6 xuršāni la pa-du-ti; III 3, 16 la pa-du-u na-ki-ru. Anp *Stand* 14 šarrāni eqdūte la(-a) pa-du-te (Anp iii 131). IV^2 60 *a* 44 la pa-da-a-ti. IV^2 5 *a* 3—4 še-e-du la pa-du-tum (= UŠ-NU-KU); K 247 iii 3(—5) *i. e.* II 26 *c-d* 37—9 ū-mu la pa-du-u (Br 7898, 5057; 6150, 7800; 7956, 10846)

ZA iv 231—35. NE XII *col* 3, 18 ra-bi-iç AN-LAM (= Nergal) la pa-du[-u] KB vi (1) 262; also *ll* 3 + 10; *col* 2, 25 *etc*. V 16 *g-h* 76 (H 38, 117) UŠ-KU (*i. e.* KA + inserted ša): pa-du-u Br 5057 (75, = ba-ṭa-lum).

pidū. ransom-money {Lösegeld} Z^B 99. IV^2 54 *a* 47 muxur kat-ra-šu li-ki pi-di-e-šu (or šidū?); perh. K 168, 12 a-na pi-di-šu-nu, LEHMANN ii 76; T. A. (Ber) 7 *R* 35 pi-di]-e-šu li-te-ir-ru-ni-i[š-šu] that they may refund his ransom, ZA v 144 (but?).

padd(ṭṭ)ū. NE 72, 35 [ ]a-ši pa-ad-di-'-i, KB vi (1) 226—7.

pi-du-u ša pi-i = DAX, 83, 1—18, 1330 iii 20.

pi-du-u V 12, 31 *etc.* (AV 7036) read a-du-u.

pi-id see pittu.

p(b)u-da(du) *etc.* read giṭṭu (*p* 315 *col* 2).

p(b)ūdu. side, especially of a human being {Seite, namentlich des Menschen} *pl* (or *dual*?) pūdā. AV 1352; Z^B 6 *rm* 2. NE XII *col* 1, 30 (2, 21) pu-da(-a)-ša el-li-e-tum (*var* -ti) KB vi 259 & 525—6 whose shining shoulders; KB vi (1) 100, 21 .... lal pu-u-du (see *ibid*, 414); NE VI 45 ša pu-di-im-ma (KB vi (1) 168; 480). IV^2 22 *a* 30 the muruç qaqqadi pu-u-da (= LIBIT) kîma kib-ri 'i-ab-bat, Br 11196; II 30 *no* 4 *O* 21 BAR(?) = pu-u-du (AV 7100; Br 1792); 26 *c-d* 35, 36 (K 247 iii 1—2) BAR & LIBIT (mur-gu) = pu-du-um ša amēli (AV 7111; 7101; 1358; 5560; Br 433, 11195); V 29 *a-b* 55 ZAG = pu-u-du, Br 6487 (56: pu-u-tum); II 32 *c-d* 82 (AV 7140, Br 6517); see also būdu (*pp* 147—8); and KB vi (1) 506 on *del* 181 (201).

pudū. Camb 265, 4 *cf* nisxiptum.

puddulu. SCHEIL, *Notes d'épigr.*, *no* lv (Etana-*frg*) *col* 1, 10 si-bi te-ba pu-ud-du-lu e-lu da-ap-nim (or buṭṭulu?, *Rec. Trav.*, xxiii).

pudilxu read by SCHEIL & others pu-aš-xu (*q. v.*), also parumxu.

Pudīlu. P. N. *e. g.* K 6303, 4 (end) Pu-di-il a-bi ša-ak-ni Bēl; IV^2 39 *a* 14 Pu-di-il ša-ak-ni Bēl. ZK ii 108, 7; 79—7—8, 303; I 6 *no* 3 A 2; B *no* 1, 2; C 2 (name of Assyrian king); also see Pu-di-ba-al, ZK ii 303; SMITH, *Asurb*, 62, 118; Asb ii 83 (+ 91).

padānu, *m* road, way, path {Weg, Pfad} AV 6882; D^{Par} 135. Asb i 74 those kings ..... ur-xu pa-da-nu ušaçbitsunūti, I made them find road and way. Neb ii 18 ur-xu-um aš-tu-tim pa-da-num pi-xu-ti I traversed; ZA iv 238, 14 ur-xu pa-da-nu; Sp III 586 + *R* III 1, 20 a-lik pa-dan-ka li-šir (TSBA viii 167 *fol*). K 155, 24 ur-xi lid-me-iq pa-da-ni li[-šir], ZA xi 100 (>< K^M 1, 24); K 3456 *R* 6 (end) ul i-ba-'-u pa-da-na (PSBA xxi 40 *foll*). II 38 *c-d* 28 NER = pa-da-nu followed by ki-ib-su & da-rag-gu, Br 9191; H 40, 244; S^c 8 gi-ru-u | GER | pa-da-nu (V 16 *a-b* 24 = tal-lak-tu), see also H 204, 26. II 62 (K 49) *a-b* 33—35 (ga-a-gu-nu-u) GAN (Br 3182), XI-EN-DU-DU (Br 8251); XI-EN-GI-SAR (Br 8250) = pa-da-nu. V 16 *c-d* 51 [SAG]-AŠ (or DIL?)-BAR = pa-da-nu, Br 3531.

pidnu see pitnu.

puddutum (?) II 28 *e-f* 25 pu-ud-du-tum = pu-ṭu-ut-tu.

pidātu in çābē pi-da-ti. T. A. (Letters of Abdi Xeba); W. MAX MÜLLER. ZA vi 64 (& *Asien u. Europa*, 13) compares Egypt. pedit?, *pl* -ati, -ate, mercenaries {Söldner, Soldaten} literally: one belonging to the bow. See also ERMAN, ZA vi 250—1 *rm* 7; JASTROW, *Jour. Bibl. Lit.*, xi 108—9, *rm* 30; BOISSIER, ZA vii 349 √פדה.

pazadu. 83, 1—18, 1330 i 13 pi-eš | SU-KAD | pa-za-du (‖ na-pa-šu, ka-za-rum) see also ZA xv 400—1.

pazazu, crush {zerdrücken}. IV^2 29* 4 C *a* 7 ina pi-i-ka te-xi-pi ina qātika te-pe-ziz. JOHNSTON, *Johns Hopk. Circ.*, 114 *p* 118.

pāz(s, ç)nuqu, piznaqu *adj* weak, weakling {schwach, Schwächling}; **piznuqiš** *adv.* Sp II 265 *a* xxiii 8 u-šal-qa (*var* -qu) iš-šik-ki (*var* ku) ša pi-iz-nu-qu ti (*var* te)-'- u[t-tu]; xiii 10 bi-is-nu-qiš ana kir-bi lu-tir (ZA x 8 + 11);

---

pasadu. T. A. read un-du, M^S 10 *b*. ∼ paskaru see paskaru. ∼ puzzulum *cf* buççulum (baçalu).

NE IV *col* vi 30 my friend pi-iz-nu-qiš (like a weakling) KB vi (1) 156—7. K 2361 + S 389 iv 6 pi-is-nu-qiš lal-la-riš (Z^B 94; ZA iv 240); K 3459 *R* 13 pi-iz-nu-qa tu-rap[-pa-aš] ZA iv 15. S^c 6, 10 BE = pi-iz-na-qu, between ulālum & la li'ū, with same id).

pazaru, hide, be hidden, safe {verbergen, verborgen sein} § 84. ℑ *del* 66 (70): il SAR šamni u-pa-az-zi-ru (amēl) ma-lāxu (Jensen, 411; KB vi (1) 490); V 45 vi 14 tu-pa-az-zar; $Z^Š$ iv 6 a-na [ ] pu-uz-zu-ru it-ti-ka-ma, to hide thou art able. — Š II 23 *e-f* 69 mu-šap-zi-ir-tum one of the many ‖ of da-al-tum.

Derr. tapzirtu and these 2:

pazru, *adj* concealed, hidden (away), secret {verborgen, geheim}. Sn *Rass* 73 ki-max-xe-šu-un pa-az-ru-ti (ZA iii 315; 325); Sn *Bell* 48 (*var*). Asb vi 65 kiššātē-šu-nu pa-az-ra-a-ti, their secluded forests (into which no stranger enters).

puzru, *c. st.* puzur. D^{Par} 208: concealment, secrecy {Verborgenheit, Heimlichkeit}. Creat.-*frg* IV 32 ša-a-ru da-mi-ša a-na pu-uz-ra-tum lu-bil-lu-ni, the winds may carry her blood to secret places {die Winde mögen ihr Blut ins Verborgene tragen}; 131—2 u-par-ri-'-ma uš-la-at da-mi-ša ša-a-ru il-ta-nu a-na pu-uz-rat uš-ta-bil. K 3182 i 9 pu-uz-ru sat-tak-ku šu-xu-zu. Strassm., *Stockholm*, 6, 45 ina pu-uz-ru iš-ša-mu. III 4 *no* 7, 4 (57) ina pu-uz-ri u-lid-an-ni, in secret she bore me (KB iii, 1, 100; AV 1409). Sn *Kui* 4, 11 cedars which on mount Sirara ina pu-uz-ri na-an-zu-zu (stood in concealment); $Z^Š$ iv 79 pu-uz-ra-a-ti, the most secret places. Sarg *Khors* 41 he fled from his city and ina pu-uz-rat šadī marçi a-di-riš ūšib (see Haupt in Cheyne, *Isaiah* [SBOT] 168 on Hebr. equivalent); Asb vi 31 God Susinak ša aš-bu ina pu-uz-ra-a-ti (who lives in concealment). *Rec. Trav.* xx 205 *foll*, *col* v 1 whosoever this tablet lu pu-uz-ru u-šax-xa-zu. — *b*) secret, mystery {Geheimnis, Mysterium}. IV^2 32 *a* 33 a-šar pu-uz-ri (amēl) bārū amāta ul išaka-an. K 3597 (Bezold, *Catalogue*, 547) šarru ..... a-šar pu-uz-ri a-ma-tam ul i-ša-kan (Zimmern, *Beitr. z. babyl. Relig.*, 88 & *rm* 1); also IV^2 18 *b* 44; 33 *b* 6 + 40; 15* ii 57, 58 my father (Ea) the firegod ana çīt šamši isniqma pu-uz-rat-si-na (= KA-BI, Br 523) it-ṭi-xa-a. Asb vi 69 my warriors ... e-mu-ru pu-uz-ra-sin (of forests) iq-mu-u ina išāti (and burned them down). — *c*) safety, security {Geborgenheit} *del* 90 (95) Pu-zu-ur(-) (il) KUR-GAL (amēl) ma-lāxu (Jensen, 420 *fol*; KB vi, 1. 236—7 & 493: he who is hidden in the great mountain, the latter a symbol of safety; ZA iv 54 *foll*; J^{I-N} 53 *rm* 88). — II 58 *c* 40 AN (pu-zu-ur) ⟨⟨, the equivalent broken off (AV 1360; Br 9953 = il Bēl?); also V 37 *d-f* 26 bu-zur | ⟨⟨ | pu-uz-rum, Br 9954); *ibid*, 16, 17, Br 8668; II 42 *no* 3, *O* 13 *b*; II 18, 45. V 48 ii 31: 26th of Aru: pu-zu-ra-tum; vi 19: 18th of Elul: pu-zu-ra-tu; 49 viii 26: 22d of Marxešvān: pu-zu-ra-tum; x 24: 21st of Ṭebet pu-zu-ra-a-tum.

pa-xu K 422; V 28 *c-d* 90 see pit a-xi.

pāxu ‖ šupīlu see pēlu. ℑ puxxu exchange {tauschen} in early Babylonian law, Meissner, 130; originally: change {verändern}. II 28 *e-f* 40 (K 247 ii 14) BAL = pu-ux-xu ša sinništi (Br 277; J^W 31; AV 7104); 43 = šu-pi-lu ša sinništi. Meissner, 100, 13 u-ba-ax-xu-ši (3 *pl*); V 45 vi 12 tu-pa-a-xa. ZA vi, 236, 41 nišē mārē-ši-na ana kaspi ubixxu.

Derr. puxātu, pixātu, 1, puxītu, puxtu, Puxātum & these 2:

pūxu. exchange, barter {Tausch} Meissner, 10. II 28 *c-f* 42 ŠA(= GAR)-SAG-EL-LA = pu-u-xu (Br 12035) same id = zuqqurūtu (Br 12036; *p* 291 *col* 2) AV 7103. IV^2 13 *b* 52—3 pu-ux-šu (= ŠA-SAG-EL-LA-NI, Br 12035) ana [sign]-pi ša ma-a-ti iz-ba-am[-ma]. V 16 *c-d* 12 SAG = pu-xu (Br 3521; 11 qar-nu; 13 di-na-nu); *cf* S 747 + S 949 *O* 3 pu-xu-u-a ša u-kin-nu (il) Ē-a, followed by di-na-nu-a ša ib-ba-nu-u (il) Marduk Martin, *Textes Assyriens-Babyloniens*, 20/21 + 24 both = corps: body (= le personne); K 4228 iii 31—2 pu-ux-šu i-ta-ra-ad. in his stead he will send down (munāgiršu). BA iii 495 *fol*; *ibid* 30 u lū (amēl) munāgiru igūr pu-ux-šu, or rents a hireling in his place (see *ibid*, *p* 407); perhaps K 930 *a* 5 ina eli çalam pu-u-xi ša šarri bēli ana (amēl) ardišu išpurani (Hr^L 46); K 2085 *R* 11 (il) Bēl u (il) Nabū ma-ta-a-ti gab-bi a-na pu-ux šarri bēli-ja lid-din-nu (Thompson, ii *pp* lxxxv + 98: may *B* & *N* give all lands to the king, my lord); K 703 *R* 6 liš-pur-ma a-na pu-xi šarri A-MAX-MEŠ *etc*. Jensen, 420. 80—7—19, 20 (Hr^L 359) 7—8 ina muxxi šarri pu-u-xi (or -ṭe) ša šarru be-ili iš-pur-an-ni. K 112 (Hr^L 223) 13 šar pu-u-xi (or -ṭe) ša (mât) Akkadū[ki] ittīti uš-tax-ra-an-ni; 16, ina libbi .... šar pu-u-xi (-ṭe) tu-še-ši-ba. (R. F. Harper, AJSL xiv, 8—9). II 15 *a-b* 40 Ê-KI-BI-ŠA (= GAR)-RA = bīt pu-xi; Ê-KI-BI-ŠA-RA-BI-KU = bīt a-na pu-xi-šu, Br 9786, same id = ina ta-kul-ti. Perh T. A. (Ber) 18 *R* 13 pu-u-xi ku (?) 3 ma-na šuqultu-šu. — Also: receipt {Quittung}. K 1429, 3 a-na pu-u-xi it-ti-ši (KB iv 121: gegen Quittung wird er bringen; but Oppert, ZA xiii 246 loan {Darlehen}); K 381, 5 ina pu-u-xi it-ta-çu, they will give away upon a receipt; K 287, 7 ina pu-u-xi i-ta-çu (III 47 *no* 10) see also našū ($\mathfrak{Q}^t$ *c*); KB iv 121 *rm* †† suggests connection with pūxatu, occurring in old Babylonian contracts. A ‖ perhaps:

pīxu. PSBA xix 289, 12—13 ga-du-um ša i-na pi-ix-šu a-ta-di-na (√nadanu) or = "enclosure"? (*ibid*, 291).

pixū 1. pr ipxi, ps ipaxi, ip pixi close, lock {schliessen, verschliessen} § 100; D^H 13. Babyl. Chron. ii 33 Ištarxundu took his brother prisoner and bābu ina pāni-šu ip-xi (and threw him into prison, literally: shut the door into his face); iii 7—8 bābu ina pa-ni-šu ip-xu-u (= *pl*), KB ii 278, 280 (ZA ii 154, 156). K 41 *R* 13 .... ina bīti pi-xu-u (= pm) PSBA xvii 65 *foll*. *del* 84 (89) pi-xi bāb-ka. D 100 frg, 4 e pi-xi elippi[-ka], but see KB vi (1) 254, 255 &, again, 520; BA i 314. I 27 *no* 2, 34 bābša (of the palace) la i-pa-xi, he shall not lock. T^M iv 33 çal-māni-ja ina igāri tap-xa-a (ye have locked up), also 35. III 4 *no* 7, 5 ina iddū bi-ja ip-xi (*i. e.* my mother). S 702 *R* see AV 7039. Perhaps KB iii (1) 162 *col* 6, 4 išid-su lip-xu (?). V 42 *c-d* 51 SAG-GI = pi-xu-u (Br 3556) between up-pu-qu & ka-ta-mu; perh also V 36 *a-c* 45, Br 8731. — $\mathfrak{Q}^t$ *del* 89 (94) end ap-te(*var* -ti)-xi ba-a-bi. — $\mathfrak{J}^t$ K 517 (Hr^L 327) 19 nu-up-tax-xi a-na pit-xi, we close tightly; K 638, 42 up-ti-ix-xa-ni (AV 6895). — $\mathfrak{N}$ šumma rīmu ina maxar abulli irbiç nakru abul-la ali içabatma abullu šuatu ip-pi-ix-xi (Bezold, *Catalogue*, 1710).

Derr. pitxu &:

pixū 2. *adj* closed, shut, locked {verschlossen, geschlossen}. IV² 16 *a* 43—44 a-na bi-ti pi-xi-e (= SAG-GA-NA) li-še-ri-bu-šu. II 33 *d* 15 su-u]-qu (*q. v.*) pi-xu-u; Neb ii 18 see padānu. AV 7039; also in meaning of: deaf, a ‖ of sukkuku; S^c 6, 7 [BE] = pi-xu-u preceded by sakku & sukkuku (*q. v.*); V 40 *e-f* 11 U-NER = pi-xu-u ša mār abkalli (written NUN-ME) Br 6072.

puxxu. II 41 *c-d* 10 U-LAL-LAL = pu(l)-ux-xu (AV 7104; Br 6080), something connected with plants {etwas mit Pflanzen zusammenhängendes}.

pixū 3: control, command, direct {controllieren, dirigieren, lenken}, Jensen, 420. *del* 90 (95) a-na pi-xi-i (e) ša elippi (ZA iv 54; KB vi, 1, 236—7 & 492—3; J$^{I\text{-}N}$ 34; see also KB vi, 1, 408). 88, 1—18, 1330 iii 6 du-u | DAX | pi-xu-u ša elippi; here perhaps S^e 6, 7. H 51, 45 IN-GAB = ip-xi (or ṭe?) ZK ii 270; Br 4486.

Derr. paxātu, pixātu &:

(amēl) **pixū.** Nabd 180, 1: ½ šeqel of silver a-na (amēl) bi-xi-e ša elippi; 2 QA of oil a-na ke-pi (to the captain).

puxadū, lamb, kid {Lamm, Zicklein} *f* pu-xadtu. AV 7102; Br 5489; Jensen-Schulthess, *Homonyme*, 90: eigentl.: Schüchterling. TP vii 13 pu-xa-di-e kirrē (or as[x?]li?) nab-ni-it lib-bi-šu-nu. 81—11—3, 478, 6 pu-xa-du followed by pu-xa-du ši-zib, Pinches, PSBA '96, 252 suckling lamb; Amiaud, ZA iii 45: le bélier. ZA iv 116 *no* 8 mentions: 6 pu-xa-di-e. Nabd 490, 3 pu-xa-du MEŠ; id Neb 247, 10. V 38 *c-e* 19 pu-xa-du = S^b 1 *R* v 19. — IV² 5 *c* 34 ša-rat pu-xat-ti la pi-te-te ṭi-me-ma. S 954 *O* 11 (D 135) see bar-

baru (190 *col* 1), where read li-*ki*-e and see leqû, 1 *a* (494 *col* 2). *c. st.* pu-xa-at Berl. *Congr.* (= STRASSM., *Warka*, 68, 7 + 69, 7) II, 1, 329; *ibid* ana pu-xa-ti-šu. S 2148: 3 pu-xat-tu (ZK ii 8). See also laxru. ZIMMERN, *Ritualtafeln*, *p* 216, 36 *foll*: aslu = alter Wildwidder; puxâdu = junger Wildwidder.

paxazu. WINCKLER *ad* Sarg *Ann* 293 reads ip-xaç(z) urxašu, he obstructed his way {er hemmte seinen Weg}. ℑ V 45 v 51 tu-pax-xaz. 𝔑t II 28 *a* 15 i-tap-xu-zu. (= ac). D^Pr 155.

paxaxu. II 30 *no* 4 *O* 8 (*l* 35) [BAR] = pa-xa-xu, AV 6890.

puxâlu 2. Ner 28, 22 a furniture is called (iç) pa-ni pu-xa-lu.

puxmax(xu). II 21 *no* 2 (*add*) AN-TUK-TUK = pu-ux-ma-ax, AV 7106; Br 14440.

paxanu. II 29 *e-f* 41 pa-xa-nu = ru-bu-nim (or NIM?).

paxasēmunu. Dar 388, 2: X TA bilti ša šammu pa-xa-si-e-mu-nu ša Nabû-nadin-šum.

puxpuxu, a plant {ein Gewächs} II 42 *a* 17 (K 274) (šam) pu-ux-pu-xu, AV 7107, Br 13125.

puxpux(x)û, roar, noise; strife {Geräusch, Schnauben; Hader}? AV 7107. Z^B 86; LEHMANN, ii 63. II 62 *a-b* 34 IM-BA-RA-AX = pu-ux-pu-xu-u ‖ çârixu; II 42 *c-d* 17, Br 8377. III 65 *b* 27 AMĒL-NE (= çaltu) u pu-ux-pu-xu-u iššaka-nu-šu. K 891 *R* 6 ina mâti çalta ina bîti pu-ux-pu-ux-xu-u la ip-par-ra-su it-[ti-ja] (*cf* L³ *R* 4), or id [-a-a-a?]; 82, 9—18, 4159 i 18; M^S 75 *col* 2. *Rec. Trav.*, xxiv 104.

paxaru, *pr* ipxur; *ps* ipax(x)ar, collect, assemble, gather {sich sammeln, sich versammeln} AV 6891. Sn v 11 fugitive *etc.* . . . çi-ru-uš-šu ip-xu-ru-ma, assemble around him; STRASSM., *Berl. Congr.*, ii, 1, 328 a-lum ip-xu-ur-ma. Beh 54—55 the rebels ip-xu-ru-nim-ma gathered together, and. K 3474 (+ K 3182) i 45 (47) çi-tuk-ka ip-xu-ru ilani *pl* ma-a-ti; at thy rising assemble the gods of the countries. K 528, 29 (Hr^L 269) a messenger of the king my lord may come and (mât) Akkadû gab-bi ni-ip-xur-ma, and we, all Akkad, will assemble, and it-ti-šu ni-il-lik-mu. T. A. (Lo) 28, 61 ip-xu-ru-nim (3 *pl*) elippê-šu-nu; 30, 66 ip-xu-ur (3 *sg*) elippê çâbê. See also SCHEIL, *Notes d'epigr.*, *no* 45 in *Rec. Trav.* xxii. P. N. Rm 187, 6 eponymate of Lip-xur-ilu, *etc.* (KB iv 106). — pm NE VI 197 pax-ru etlê ša Uruk, there assemble the men of Uruk; perh H 125 *R* 17 pa[-ax-ru-ka] *cf* IV² 30 *b* 7, Br 3222. II 51 *b* 10 pa-xir; V 54 *c* 57 pa-xi-ir (= K 620, 24; Hr^L 91). — NE XII (i) 17 [i or ip? = 𝔑]-pax-xu-ru-ka they gather around thee; K 7906 ina çirim i-pax[-xa-ru?] T^M 124. II 34 *e-f* 65 (bu-ur) BUR = pa-xa-ru ša . . .; perh II 29 *g-h* 11, Br 343; on II 34 *e-f* 66—68 see Br 9472—74; H 39, 165; II 26 *e-f* 12, 13 (Br 7203), 14 (Br 12222); H 32, 757 (= II 34 *e-f* 64) ni-gi-in | [illegible] | pa-xa-ru ša a-la-ki (Br 10337; ZK i 121).

Q^t = Q *del* 152 (162) ilâni kîma zumbê eli bēl niqê ip-tax-ru, the gods gathered like flies around the sacrificer (§ 37 *b*). Babyl. Chron. (KB ii 282—3) iv 4 the palace-prefect bi-xir-tum ip-te-xir, convened an assembly (ZA ii 159).

ℑ *a*) gather, collect {sammeln, versammeln} u-pa-ax-xi-ir(-ma), I gathered together, V 65 *a* 32; 63 *a* 48; u-pax-xi-ir, Sarg *Ann* 24; *Khors* 98 my whole army ul u-pax-xir, I did not call out; Esh i 27 u-pa-xir-ma (the kings of the land of Xatti). Asb i 18 u-pa(x)-xir (3 *sg*) the inhabitants of Assyria; ii 23 u-pax-xi-ra (3 *sg*) el-lat-su (& ZA ii 360 ii 4); vi 3 treasures which the former kings u-pax-xi-ru iš-ku-nu. TP III *Ann* 168 nišê-šu] u-pax-xir(-ma); 161. Bu 88—5—12, 101 ii 13 u-pa-xi-ir. KB vi 172, 105 (= NE VI) t]u-pa-xi-i[r še-um]; *l* 112 [še-um up-ta]x-xi-ir (1 *sg*). T. A. (Ber) 72, 28 in order that he may not bring together (ụe-pa-xi-ra) all the Xabiri and capture Šigata (+ 48, 77); 62, 14 and now, before they bring together (ụi-pa-xi-ru). — IV² 52 *no* 2, 44 u-pax-

puxâlu 1. see buxâlu & add Neb 20, 1: XXII kirru bu-xal; Camb 194, 1. ~ puxlalû *cf* buxlalû.

xa-ru-ma, they collect. — KB vi 152 *ad* NE IV *col* ii 39 (NE 22) ma-a-tu pu-ux-xu-rat; T. A. (Lo) 18, 20 pu-xi-ir, has assembled. — Sn v 23 pu-ux-xir um-man-ka, gather thy army (‖ dikâ karaška); K 7599, 5 .... pu-ux-xi-ra-šu-nu-ti-ma, let them be assembled. T. A. (Ber) 74, 17 and now pu-xi-ir all the Xabiri against Šigata (*cf* 86 *R* 19; 56, 23). — T. A. (Lo) 1, 27 a-na .... pu-xu-rum, to collect; 70, 6 and I am seeking pu-xi-ir xarranâti i-na qa-at axi-ja; (Ber) 112, 23—4 and have commanded pu-xi-ri alu-mi, to levy [the people of] the city. — *b*) gather together; collect something or somebody scattered about; strengthen, fortify {etwas aufgelöstes, zerstreutes sammeln, zusammenbringen; Halt verleihen, stärken}. IV^{2} 39 *b* 4 aš-ra ša-a-tu u-pe-xi-ir, those (ruined) places I strengthened again; also see AJSL xii 160—70. I 49 *d* 29 + 32 mârê Bâbili .... u-pa-xi-ir(ma), 1 *sg*; V 35, 32 u-pa-ax-xi-ra-am-ma (all the cities' inhabitants); Merodach-Balad.-stone ii 20 nišê da-ad-me sapxâti u-pax-xi-ru (1 *sg*); *ibid* i 33 mu-pa-ax-xi-ru sapxûti (KB iii, 1, 184—5), of Marduk. Sarg *Cyl* 31; V 62 *no* 2, 9 (Br 9161; 11373) see sapxu; Neb *Grot* iii 24 (I 66 *c*) u-pa-ax-xi-ir (1 *sg*); KB iii (1) 122—4 ii 4 lu-u-pa-ax-xi-ir. Bu 88, 5—12, 75 + 76 iv 14 (amêl) dim-gal-li li-'-u-ti mu-kin-nu (iç) xar-ri ištê-niš u-pax-xi-ir-ma (BA iii 244—7); viii 23 lu-pax-xir. H 80, 11—12 um-man-šu u-pax-xir (-xar). *del* 186 (206) ana kâša man-nu ilâni u-pax-xa-rak-kum-ma (see, however, KB vi, 1, 245 & 507). — V 45 v 49 tu-p(b)ax-xar, ZA i 98 (but V 45 iii 8 tu-ba-ax-xar); II 39 *e-f* 49—50 pu-ux-xu-rum : KIL | pu-ux-xu-rum, AV 7105; Br 10109, 10336. P. N. V 44 *c-d* 50 Šamaš-u-pax-xar (= DUL-DUL, as H 80, 11) Br 9585, Šamaš gives strength; K 133 *O* 11 (ZK ii 273); K 4350 iv 2 u[-pa-ax-xar]; 361 *rm* 1; H 52 iv 2 1N-DUL-DUL; Eponym-list (KB i 204—5) ii for 875 Ša-maš-u-pa-xir; AV 5520 mu-pa-xir.

ℑ' — ℑ *a*) TP i 71 (iii 41) my chariots and my troops lup-te-xir, I collected (§ 33). Sp II 265 *a* xii 9 up-te-ix-xir libbu ..... (K 9290 ii 6). K 669, 14 (amêl) mutir pu-te up-ta-xe-ir (Hr^{L} 246; PSBA xxiii 51 *foll*); K 679, 6 annu-šim gabbišunu nu-up-ta-xir, now we have all assembled (Hr^{L} 212). Smith, *Asurb*, 186 C up-tax-xa-ru-u (S *pl*). NE 49, 184 up-tax-xi-ir Ištar her hierodules (KB vi, 1, 176); T. A. (Ber) 22 *R* 9 up-te-ix-xir I have collected; perh 24 *R* 81 (KB v 64); also see Rm 2, 1 *R* 28 up-ta-at-xu-ru (Hr^{L} 408).

Derr. sapxaru and these 7:

(amêl) **paxîru**, an official {ein Beamter}? K 505, 8 Niq-ili (amêl) pa-xi-ru (Hr^{L} 166).

puxuru *1. adj* assembled, collected {versammelt}. Z$^{\check{S}}$ ii 53 kin-na pu-xur-ta (*var* -tum) u-sap-pi-xu.

puxuru *2. noun* totality {Gesamtheit} Neb 104, 14 pu-xu-ru; Nabd 958, 3 pu-xur-ru.

puxru. *c. st.* puxur. ib § 9, 225; § 65, 3; AV 7108. — assemblage; then, totality, the whole, *i. e.* all the assembled {Versammlung; dann, alle versammelten, Gesamtheit}. S^{b} 266 (Br 902). K 1285 *R* 5 ina pu-xur en-sa-as-si-ja, in the multitude of my sins, Strong, *IX. Or. Congr.* (London), ii 208. KB ii 4, 11 pu-xur nišê-šu; see also III 10, 27 (KB ii 32). In a more specific meaning the word means: — *a*) army, the assembled hosts {Heeresmacht} ‖ ellatu, *etc.* Sn iv 42 u-par-ri-ir pu-xur-šu (see sapaxu, ℑ); v 42 pu-xur-šu-nu in-nin-du (עמד); ib Anp i 51. III 15 i 25 ina puxri-šu-nu iq-bu-u um-ma an-nu-u šar-a-ni, in their whole army the cry was heard: "this is our king". ZK ii 301 rab pu-ux-ri, an officer, ZA iv 279 *rm* 1. — Creat.-*frg* IV 106 see sapaxu ℨℨ; DT 41, 7 + 10 pu-u]x-ri nam-maš-ti (*q. v.*). The following belong here or to *b*): Creat.-*frg* III 60 (+ 118) šuk-na(-a)-ma pu-ux-ru, assemble then together (K 292 *R* 6 -ra); II 134; III 74 (Tiâmat) pu-ux-ru šit-ku-na-at (KB vi, 1: schaart zusammen; Delitzsch: nimmt ihre ganze Kraft zusammen; but see KB vi, 1, 305; 561), also III 16; 37 i[š]-kun-ši [pu-ux-ra], + 95 (-ri) ušašqi (il) Kingu; 97 mu-ir-ru-ut puxri (+ 39). — *b*) assembly, especially of the gods to take counsel {Versammlung, Ratsversammlung, speziell von Göttern} ina puxur ilāni u-šar-bi-ka, Creat.-*frg* III 43, 101; Anp i 8; *del* 112 (120) ina pu-xur *var* to ma-xar ilāni; iδ also Creat.-*frg* III 132; I 49 *b* 22 (axē-ja); K 3351, 12 be-lum ra-aš-bu ša ina pu-xur ilâni rabûti, *etc.*; *cf* K 3454, 37; 82—7—4, 42 *R* 8 pu-ux-ru ilāni šu-par šamē erçitim. IV² 48, 30 ina pu-ux-ri-šu-nu. Creat.-*frg* IV 15 ti-šam-ma i-na pu-xur (lu-u ša-ga-ta a-mat-ka); DT 41, 1 ina pu-ux-ri-šu-nu. NE 56, 20 ina pu-xur kul-la-ti. Merodach-Bal. i 42 ina pu-xur šu-par ma-al-ku. — II 11 + 216, 84; S^b 266; Sp II 265 *a* xvi 1; xxiii 9; V 21 *g-h* 63 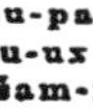 = pu-ux-rum (Br 7991; II 39, 49); II 35 (*no* 1) 10 (K 4320) pu-ux-ru ‖ ši-pa-ri. V 30 *g-h* 16 GA'-GA' = pu-ux[-ru] between emūtu & kiš-ša-tu (H 215, Br 5433); V 47 *a* 29 i-na xa-aš pu-ux-ri. See also Br 9844.

NOTE. — 1. Against puxru = [illegible] (so originally HOMMEL & ZIMMERN) see GUNKEL, *Schöpfung & Chaos*, 310 *rm* 3; JENSEN, ZA x 339—40 (note), and *cf* pūru.

2. BA iv 168—4; 326 reads KB v *no* 219, 7 (Tel-Hesy) pu-ux-ri-iš = together ‖ zusammen, *cf no* 163, 24; PEISER, OLZ ii *cols* 5/6 (Jan. '99) reads pu-xa-ri, da hatte Z. die Stadt aufgeboten; so also WINCKLER, *ibid*, *col* 64 (Feb. '99).

paxāru 2. assemblage, assembly {Versammlung} SCHEIL, *Nabd*, x 30—1: Marduk the king of the gods iq-ta-bi pa-xar-šu-nu, commanded their assemblage.

(amēl) **pixīru** governor {Statthalter}. Nabd 438, 17 Bēl-ušallim mār (amēl) bi-xi-ru (or = paxxaru?).

pixirtum. gathering, assemblage {Versammlung}, see paxaru, ℚ¹. II 51 *b* 15 pi-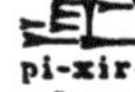-ta; V 47 *b* 37 qat(d)-ru ina pi-xir-ti a-ba-'. IV² 34, 1 ana pixir-tišu çirip zaqīqi, (the moon) at her setting with the color of a dust-cloud.

puxrēti. BA i 132—33; KB vi (1) 238 *ad del* 120 (127) pu-ux-ri-e-ti, form like karummēti; see, however, also KB *loc. cit.*, *rm* 8.

pax(x)aru potter {Töpfer}. iδ usually (amēl) DUK-QA-BUR V 32 *e-f* 18 (KB vi, 1, 544); *d* 19, Br 5898: amēl) DUK-QA-BUR & (amēl) ŠU-GAL-AN-ZU = pa-xa[-ru]; ⊕ 84 i 19, 20 (II 26 *e-f* 12, 13) same iδδ = pa-xa-rum & p. mu-di-e ka-la (Br 5894; JENSEN, 293 *fol*, 514; LEHMANN, BA ii 600 & *rm* *†); K 55 *O* 19 DUK?]-QA-BUR = zi-e pa-xa-ri potter's clay? DT 67 *R* 19—20 pa-xa-ru (= DUK-QA-BUR) ina z(ç)ar-ba-bi-šu (H 120); II 58 *no* 2, 7 (*c-d* 57) NUN-UR-RA | (il) DUK-QA-BUR = (il) Ē-a ša pa-xa-ri (Br 5896); iδ often in *c. t.* Nabd 854, 14; 1025, 3 *etc.*; T^C 114; PEISER, *Vertr.*, xxx 8 (end) & *p* 248; also see PINCHES, PSBA xxiii, 204, 9—10.

(amēltu) **paxxirtu.** PEISER, *Vertr.*, xcvii, 1 (amēl) pax-xir-tu.

pūxatu. KB iv 26, 5 pu-xa-ti-šu, the object of barter for it (is) {das Tauschobject dafür (ist)}.

puxtu. K 530 *R* 18 (Hr^L 158) pu-ux-tu.

Puxūtum, P. N. Pu-xu-tum mārat Sin-pu-uṭ-ra-am. PEISER, *OLZ*, Dec. 1900, *col* 477 on SCHEIL, *Notes d'Épigraphie*, *no* li.

pīxatu. exchange, barter {Tausch} MEISSNER, 130. II 28 *no* 4, 41 BAL = pi-xa-tum, AV 7031, Br 9734. II 13 *c-d* 56 KI-BI-GAR (=ŠA) = pi-xa-tum, (H 60, 46; Br 9785), 57, KI-BI-GAR-RA-BI = pi-xa[-ti-šu] (but see H 60, 47; II 39 *c-d* 73—74 KI-BI-IN-GAR-RA = pi-xa-tum [Br 6237, same iδ as lānu, igaru, ugaru] & ša-niš pi-xa-tum, Br 9733; ZK ii 307); 58, KI-BI-GAR-RA-BI-KU = a-na pi[-xa-ti-šu]; II 40 *g-h* 53 TAK-ŠIT-LA (?, or KI?)-BI-GAR-RA = kunuk pi-xa-ti. N 3554 *O* 10 pi-xa-ti an-ni-ti na-ša-ti at-ti (PSBA xxiii 120).

paxātu. *a*) prefecture {Präfektur}, Hebr פֶּחָה GUTHE, *Ezra-Nehemiah* (SBOT), *p* 41. bēl paxâti = prefect {Statthalter} written (amēl) EN-NAM, Babyl. Chron. i 16 (KB ii 276); Sarg *Khors* 32; Sn v 9; K 518, 7 & *R* 1 + 6 (Hr^L 140; AJSL xiv 11); KNUDTZON, 30 *R* 4; 33 *O* 2; *pl* (amēl) EN-NAM-MEŠ, Esh iv 32; K 678, 11 (Hr^L 506) Esh *Sendsch*, *R* 48; III 43 ii 4 + 28; iii 9; KNUDTZON, 31 *R* 5. Sarg *Khors* 22 bēl pa-xa-a-ti, *Ann* 437 (amēl) bēl pa-xa-ti. V 69, 20 the wide countries of Naïri ana pa-xa-at gim-ri-ša ‖ Anp ii 131 ana pāṭ gimriša, AV 6892 (*ad* III 4, 6 + 14), KB i 94, 95. On KB ii 8, 36 see Tiele, ZA v 301 *fol.* — *b*) governor {Statthalter}. Cyr 257, 2 Šamaš-axē-iddin (amēl) pa-xa-tu. id (amēl) NAM, Knudtzon, 310; Esh i 34; *pl* (amēl) NAM-MEŠ Asb ix 117; i 110; V 54 *no* 1, 15; K 678, 12; Knudtzon, 406; 109 *O* 3. Sarg *Khors* 178 (amēl) pa-xa-ti mātija the prefect of my country. KB iv 88—9, *no* 1, 11 before *I-M* pa-xat (the prefect). A ‖ to *a*) perh.:

puxātu. BA iv 122 on T. A. (Ber) 189, 59 pu-xa-at i-ça-ba-tu (KB v *no* 134).

pixātu. *a*) office or district of viceroy, province, district {Satrapie, Verwaltungsbezirk, Provinz}. AV 7038; Oppert, ZK i 55; G § 108; § 65, 12; ZA viii 84—5. Sarg *Khors* 58, the cities I added eli pi-xa-at (māt) Paršuaš; 60 (64) eli pi-xa-ti-šu (see *Ann* 67, 70); NAM = pi-xa-tu, H 14, 164; S^c 59, Br 2099; Esh i 34; V 40 (*c*-)*d* 46 pi-xa-tu-šu-nu. — *b*) territory in general {Bezirk, Gebiet überhaupt} Merod.-Bal.-stone v 14 itti pi-xat šarri (royal territory). BA ii 263. Pinches, *Inscribed Tablets*, *no* 4, 1 (end) pi-xa-tum. Babyl. Chron. i 34 ina NAM (= pixât) Dûr-ilu(ki); iii 8 ina pi-xat Nippur. Peiser, KAS 66 (xx) 1 + 5 pi-xa-at Dilbat. pi-xat Bābili Cyr 174, 1—2 (KB iv 270—1: im Verwaltungsbezirk von B.); 188, 4 pi-xa-at Bāb-ili^{ki} (BA iii 427; ZA iii 210); 26, 4 pi-xa-at Sippar. TP III *Ann* 208 ina pi-xa]-at ālišu. See also Peiser, *Vertr.*, xcii 8; xciv 2.

pāṭu. *a*) boundary, border, limit, surroundings {Grenzlinie, Grenze, Umgebung} D^{Pr} 34; Rost, 120; Lehmann, ii 51, 52. Sarg *Khors* 18 far Media ša pa-aṭ (šad) Bi-ik-ni; Pp i 12 Ellipi & Ras ša pa-aṭ Elamti (= i-te-e iii 9 + 12); *Ann* XIV 11—12 he fled before Sargon ana itê (māt) Mu-çu-ri ša pa-aṭ (māt) Me-lux-xa. Esh iv 10 ša pa-a-ṭi (šad) Bi-ik-ni (= III 16 iv 4); 33 my governors ša pa-a-ṭi māti-šu-un; Sn iv 18: 33 places ša pa-a-ṭi na-ge-šu. K 4337 ii 21 (II 50 *c-d* 63) KUR-ZAG-GU-TI-UM-KI = [(māt?)] pa-aṭ Gu-ti[-i] Br 6484. IV^2 26 *a* 20—1 ça-ad-du ina pa-aṭ (= ZAG) kiš-ti (see *p* 452 *col* 1) ri-tu-u. ZA v 14 *rm* ša pa-a-ṭa la išû (T. A.) see pâtu. II 38 *c-d* 8—11 [ZA]G = pa-a-ṭu (Br 6485; 6524; AV 6898); *p.* ki-re-e; *p.* eq-li; *p.* ma-a-ti (ZA iv 67). — *b*) territory, district {Gebiet, Bezirk}. IV^2 39 *a* 19 pa-aṭ Qu-ti-i ra-pal-ti; 12 *no* 1, 3—4 see gimru. Sarg *Khors* 60: 6 alāni pa-ṭi-šu; 63: 6 na-gi-i pa-ṭi-šu; 70: 5 na-gi-i ša pa-ṭi-šu; also *Ann* 193 (pa-a-ṭi); 162. Samsu-iluna iv 1—4 pu-lux-ti me-lam šar-ru-ti-ja pa-aṭ šamê u erçitim lu ik-tum (KB iii, 1, 132); Sn *Bav* 11 ul-tu pa-a-ṭi (al) Ki-si-ri adi [libbi] Ninua (KB ii 116); ZA iii 318, 87. S 31—52 *R* 7 pa-ṭi(di?) xu-xa-rum; 14 pa-a[-ṭu?]. K 8522, 15 see paddū, 1. — Note especially: (a-na) pāṭ gimri(šu) the whole territory, totality {Gesammtgebiet, Gesammtheit}. Sarg *Khors* 78 the land of Urarṭi a-na pāṭ gim-ri-ša (+ 88); Šamš ii 5; TP iii (30) 34 a-na pāṭ gim-ri-ša (‖ ana si-xirtiša, i 92); see also II 67, 12 + 32 (-šu-nu); Asb ix 45; Sarg *Ann* 182, 412 (pa-aṭ). IV^2 39 *a* 17—18; Asb iv 102, vi 100 see gimru. Anp i 19 kāšid alāni (u) xuršāni pāṭ gim-ri-šu(-nu) & see *l* 27; ii 131 & V 69, 20 see paxātu. II 38 (*c*-)*d* 8 read pa-a-ṭu (not aš-a-ṭu).

paṭṭu'u (?) NE 72, 35 [ ] a-ši pa-aṭ-ṭi-'-i(-) u-mu, KB vi 226. See paddū.

pūṭ, ina pūṭ see pūtu.

paṭaru (& *paṭaru*, BA ii 142; § 143), *pr* ipṭur, *ps* ipaṭṭar, *ip* puṭur. AV 6896; Br 4488, 7158. split, tear asunder, break through, in proper as well as in transferred, figurative meaning: loosen, set free, pardon {spalten, zerreissen, durchbrechen, in natürlichem und übertragenem Sinne: lösen, freimachen, vergeben}. III 15 i 24 ta-xa-za-šu-nu ra-ak-su tap-ṭu-ur (KB ii 142), Ištar broke through their close battlearray. L^4 ii 16 rak-su ip-ṭu-ru, she loosens (the fetters) of the bound. II 35 *g-h* 70—3 (S 1981 + K 4355) ardatu ša et-lu dam-qu šil-la-ša la ip-ṭu-ru, a girl whose virginity a noble husband has not yet destroyed (T^M 128; AJP xv 112). — K 3182 iii 17 ša šuk-çu-ra ta-paṭ-ṭar, those that are bound thou loosest; iii 51 el-lit-si-na ta-paṭ-ṭar, wilt loosen their bands. Sarg *Ann* 335 his finger ap-ṭur, I cut off. Scheil, *Nabd*, iii 22 ip-ṭu-ru (3 *pl*) çi-mi-it-tuš; K 653 (Hr^L 154) *O* 8 li-ip-ṭu-ru (Johnston, JAOS xxii 25). K 3500 + K 4444 +

K 10235 i 11 see markasu (588, 1—2). K 8235 + K 8234 ii 6 ta-paṭ-ṭ[ar], ZA iv 229. H 85, 41 see kirimmu, & II 33 *a-b* 3 ŠU-KAL-GAB = pa-ṭa-rum ša kirimmu (II 25 *g-h* 76; Br 7196). IV^2 16 *a* 54—55 (daltu u sikkūru) markas la pa-ṭa-ri (SA-NU-GAB-U-DA) lik-lu-šu, a bolt that cannot be broken, may bar him out; Bu 88—5—12, 75 + 76 v 4 markas ilāni la pa-ṭa-ri (& Bu 88—5—12, 77 vi 1 *foll*) BA iii 246—7. III 43 *c* 32 ri-ik-su la pa-ṭe-ra; I 70 *c* 14 ri-ki-is-su la pa-ṭe-ra (§ 32 *a γ*), BA ii 141. — On riksa paṭaru, to put away a sacrificial meal (>< rakasu) see ZIMMERN, *Ritualtaf.*, 94—5. — pa-ṭi-ir-tum ∥ daltum II 23 *c-d* 10 (AV 6897); Neb 10, 2 ma-xa-ri xi-in-du pa-ṭir-tu. IV^2 54 *a* 48 see maksū (538 *col* 2). Perh. ZA iv 240, 11 pu-ṭur ku-un nab-ra-šu ∥ xipū il-lu-ur-ta. H 87 i 74 šu-pa-tu ša ina zumri amēli paṭ-rat. PINCHES, *Insc. Tablets*, *p* 67 *no* 15, 5 qat-su ina lib-bi paṭ-rat. — KB iii (1) 158, 29 eqlu šu-a-tu ip-tu (for ṭu)-ur, he redeemed this field. IV^2 49 *a* 40 e-ga-a pa-ṭi-ra pa-šir ul ibaš-ši (T^M i 41); 59 *no* 1 *a* 20 e-il-ta-šu pu-ṭur (ip); 26 *no b* 18—19 'e-il-ta-šu pu-ṭur-ma; 19 *b* 12—18; 17 *b* 29 pu]-ṭur e-il-ti. H 75 *R* 7 i-il-ti pu-ṭur na-piš-ta (Z^B 103). K 2487 + K 8122, 23 whosoever has sins ta-paṭ-ṭar ar-nu. K^M 11, 39 an-ni pu-ṭur; IV^2 54 *a* 39 (end) pu-ṭur a-ra-an-šu. IV^2 7 *a* 35—36 ma-mit-su pu-šur-ma ma-mit-su pu-ṭur-ma (= <-ME-NI-GAB); 8 iv 12 sin and anger lu pa-as-sa-šu lu pa-aṭ-ra-aš-šu (= *pm*). K 2852 + K 9662 i 24 (end) pu-ṭur en-nit-ti, free me from my guilt; K 2866, 64 ina ū-mi an-ni-e lu-u pa-aṭ-ra-nik-ka lu-u pa-aš-ra-nik-ka lu-u pa-as-sa-nik-ka. Also note the frequent use of lip-ṭur (*i. e.* such and such a temple, or god) IV 52 *b* 28—37, 41—3, 53—6, *a* 1—2; *pl* lip-ṭu-ru, 26—7; ip pu-ṭur, *b* 15, 19, 20 *etc.*; *pl* pu-uṭ-ra *b* 23—25. TP v 14 ap-ṭu-ur, I loosened; ZA iii 318, 17 i-paṭ-ṭar, he delivers; II 39, 20 lu-u tap-paṭ-tar (or צר?). NB 70, 9 u šu-u ip-ṭur qabal-šu, KB vi (1) 222—3; 474. K 164, 49—50 ma-a iç-xa-at pa-aṭ-ra-at | ma-a me-i-nu iç-xa-at pa-aṭ-ra-at, BA ii 636; see also *l* 44. IV^2 60* B *O* 9 $^{(amēl)}$ MAŠ-MAŠ ina ki-kit-ṭi-e ki-mil-ti ul ip-ṭur. P. N. Sin-pu-uṭ-ra-am; Sin-pa-te-ir (= pāṭer?) KB iv 12, 13; 26, 23. PEISER, OLZ, Dec. 1900, *col* 477. — ZIMMERN, *Ritualtafeln*, *p* 112, 12 ni-qa-a (*q. v.*) i-paṭ-ṭar, soll er "auflösen". V 50 *b* 75 perh. pa-ṭir-ka, it is opened to thee. H 51, 44 IN-GAB = ip-ṭu-ru (II 11 *g-h* 44); 61, 53 ul i-paṭ]-ṭar. S^b 345 [ga-ab | GAB] = pa-ṭa-rum, § 9, 143; H 18, 308; V 16 *a-b* 26 (Br 5817). In *c. t.* paṭ-rat = it is dissolved (of business relations) KOHLER-PEISER, ii 59 & *rm* 5; Neb 116, 1. 83—1—18, 175, 6 pa-ṭar $^{(al)}$ bi-ra-a-ti, there will be an overthrowing of fortresses; ∥ a-rad ma-aç-ça-ra-ti, & a downfall of garrisons (THOMPSON, ii *p* 13); also K 878 *R* 1 (*ibid*, 38). Rm IV 97, 2 paṭ-rat, departed was (her might) PSBA 23, 198. paṭaru ša šarri in T. A.: to desert the king, commit high treason {Verrat am König üben, ZA vi 246 *rm* 7. Ber 40, 35 la a-pa-aṭ-ta-ar a-di ta-ri-iš (I will never depart), & (-ṭar) 38, 17; 31, 18; 36, 8; Lo 36, 6 la a-paṭ-ṭar (+ 28, i-paṭ-ṭar-ru); 13, 22 pa-ta-ra-ma tu-ba-u-na, they are intending to desert. Ber 102, 8 pa-ṭa-ar-mi (= *pm*; *A* has revolted from, — ina pāni, his lord); *l* 35 pa-ṭa-ra-at alāni, the cities . . have fallen away; 103, 50 [lu-u] pa-aṭ-ra-an-ni, has revolted from me; 105, 5 *M.* la-a i-pa-aṭ[-ṭa-ar], has not revolted, + 11 mâtu gab-bi māt šar-ri pa-ṭa-r[a-at] (BA iv 127). — 199, 16 u lu-u ni-ip-tu-ur $^{(al)}$ U-ru-sa-lim^{ki}; Lo 14, 28 pa-aṭ-ra (3 *sg*), + 47 + 50 pa-aṭ-ra-ti, I am gone with (qa-du) the people *etc.*; Ber 159 *R* 12 pa]-aṭ-ru they have left; Lo 19, 28; 25, 14 (3 *pl*); 36 *R* 15 lip-ṭir(?)-šu-nu let (my lord) redeem; Ber 76, 47 i-pa-ta-ra-ni; Lo 43, 19 i-pa-ṭar a-na-ku, and I withdraw; Ber 95, 20 u [i-ip-tu-ra a-na mu-xi-ia, and he fled to me; 54, 26—28 (so that I may not have to give the city up) u i-pa-ta-ra a-na mu-xi-ka al-lu pa-ta-ri (= *pm*); 63, 18 that man pa-ta-ri (has departed); 31, 29 iz-za-az a-di pa-ta-ri-šu, until his departure; 162, 11 iš-tu pa-ta-ri çābē bītāti (since . . . abandoning me); 38, 24 li-ip-tu-ur = לִפְטֹר to free (themselves from the king of Xatti); 38, 41. — In astronomical texts, *e. g.* K 178 *R* 2 of the halo of the moon la ip-ṭu-ru, is uninterrupted.

𝔔^t split, open; loosen, free, deliver {spalten, öffnen; lösen, befreien}. Sn 1064, *R* 2—3 ši-ir-ṭu ša ina libbi ça-bit-u-ni ap-ta-ṭar, I undid the bandage JAOS xix *no* 2, *p* 75; Hr^L 392; RP^2 ii 181. K 183, 24 those that have been imprisoned for many years tap-ṭa-tar (2 *sg*) BA i 618; Hr^L 2; IV^2 57 *R* 14 lup(lip)-ta-aṭ-ṭi-ru ki-çir limnūtija; Nabd 697, 10 ta-ap-ta-ta-ṭu-ur-šu (see § 83 on form); Peiser, *Jurispr. Babyl.*, 38—9 ta-ap-te-ṭir. T. A. (Ber) 56, 18 ip-ta-tu-ur iš-tu mu-xi-ja, then he will depart from me.

ℑ = 𝔔 TP III *Ann* 200 taxâzi-šu-nu | u-paṭ]-ṭir (§ 39); V 54 *c* 48 u-pa-ṭar i-ra-še (rašû?). IV^2 60* C *R* 6 ina i-tab-lak-ku-ti pu-uṭ-ṭu-ru rik-su-u-a, by tearing asunder my bonds are loosened; 49 *a* 34 kiçrūša pu-uṭ-ṭu-ru (= pin) epšētuša xul-lu-qa; 48 *b* 10 rik-si-šu-un u-paṭ-ṭar-u-ma, he will loosen; *b* 13 Nebo rik-sat mâti-šu u-paṭ-ṭar-ma a-xi-ta i-šam; 52 *b* 52 li-paṭ-ṭi-ru ma-mit-sun (§ 93, 1*a*), may they release. Scheil, *Nabd*, v 33—4 u-pa-aṭ-ṭi-ru | a]-ma-a-ti-šu-nu they broke their commands; Asb i 45 Êa u-paṭ-ṭi-ra naqbēšu, opened his wells (§ 92). K 2660 (III 38 *no* 2) *R* 17 . . . . . la tu-paṭ-ṭa-ra mi(m)-dil bābi. V 45 i 4 tu-paṭ-ṭar; 5 tu-paṭ[-ṭar]-šu-nu (ZA i 95). VATh 793, 20 pu-ut-te-ir-šu-nu-ti, free them! Smith, *Asurb*, 122, 45 O Ištar . . . pu-uṭ-ṭi-ri-šu, set loose (*cf* KB ii 250—1). K 232 *O* 30 [ça-bi]-ta-at mu-paṭ-ṭi-rat (see Martin, *Textes Assyriens-Babyloniens*, *p* 110). — On putter for puṭṭer see BA ii 557—8. T. A. (Ber) 142 *R* 18 u-pa-ṭar, I will drive out (the Xabiri).

ℑ^t I 51 *no* 1 *b* 8 a-gu-ur(*var* gur)-ri ta-ax-lu-up-ti-ša up-ta-aṭ-ṭi-ir, burst asunder {brach entzwei}; Sm 1034, 10 bītu up-ta-ṭi-ir (BA i 614; Hr^L 389). I 67 *b* 22 the palace i-qu-up-ma up-ta-aṭ-ṭi-ri çi-in-du-šu; K 501, 35 up-ta-ṭar; K^M 12, 83 kīma ki-rib šamê lu-ut-ta-mir lip-ta-aṭ-ṭi-ru ki-çir limnēti-*pl*-ja; 30, 13 lip-ta-ṭi-ru, may he loosen (the grief of my heart).

Š loosen, set free {lösen, freimachen}. V 35, 26 see sarbu. Sp II 265 *a* v 7 . . . . ki-mil-ti AN-ŠAG šup-ṭu-ri ZA x 5 (× Strong, PSBA xvii 142 *foll*: ki-iš-ti-il ti-i-ru ṭu-ri).

Šℑ perhaps K 8235 + K 8234 ii 7 tuš-paṭ-ṭar, ZA iv 229.

𝔑 be torn asunder, be loosened *etc.* {zerreissen, gelöst werden} *Adapa-legend* i 14 (KB vi, 1, 92—3) u ba-lu-uš-šu pa-aš-šu-ra ul ip-paṭ-ṭar, see Zimmern, *Ritualtafeln*, *p* 94. III 41 *b* 26 agalatillā ša ri-ki-is-su la ip-paṭ-ṭa-ru; IV^2 8 *a* 9 ki-çir ik-çu-ra lip-pa-ṭir, 10 lip-paṭ-raš-šu; 17 *a* 57—8 ina ki-bi-ti-ka en-ni-is-su lip-pa-ṭi-ir; 59 *no* 2 *R* 12 'e-il (written AN)-ti lip-pa-ṭir, + 11 lip-paṭ-ru ar-nu-u-a; 16 *b* 60—1 ri-kis-si-na lip-pa-ṭir (= XE-EN-GAB-A); Z^Š vi 183 (ZA x 401); iv 56 lip-paṭ-ra-aš (v/vi 184 -raš)-šu. Sarg *Cyl* 15 li-pit-su ip-pa-ṭir-ma; II 51 *R* 21 ip-paṭ-ra (ZK ii 322); K 3456 *O* 19 ša xa-ru-ub-ti erçi-tim ip-pa-ṭir ki-rib-ša PSBA xxi 37—8. KB iv 318—19, 12 lip-paṭ-ṭar, werden gelöst werden. 83—1—18, 2 *R* 2—3 ultu pa-an šarri be-ili-ja ip-pa-ṭar (Hr^L 391).

Derr.: ipṭīru, napṭarum, napṭartu, napṭiru & these:

paṭru *m* sword {Schwert} *pl* paṭrāti. See KB vi (1) 374 and passage quoted under natû, 𝔔. id GIR (Br 309) & ME-RI, § 9, 103. S^b 165 gi-ir | GIR | paṭ-ru; S^c 7 [gi]-ri | GIR | pa-aṭ-ru; H 9 + 202, 24; AV 1639; 6900. K 4378 i 33 = V 27 *c-d* 7 see Br 309. KB vi (1) 140 (iv *b*) 44 paṭ-ri-ka, thy dagger; 60, 24 (end) za-qip paṭ-ru; see also zaqapu (289 *col* 2). V 56, 54 (ul-tu) paṭ-ru ina kisādi-šu | u qup-pu-u ina i-ni-šu. paṭ-ri zaq-tum H 116, 4 (K 4931; L^T 160); pa-ṭar qāti, Br 7160. Anp i 49; ii 51 kīma zi-qip paṭri parzilli (see ziqpu, *b*), KB ii 256—7, 56. DT 67 (H 120) *R* 22 . . . . ru-u ina paṭ-ri (= ME-RI, 21) u pa(Br 10395 di)-ṭar-ri. II 19 *b* 1—2 nam-ça-ru paṭ-ru. K 306, 3 bīt pa-aṭ-ru ina max (KB iv 134—5: das

Dolchhaus??). ZA x 208 *O* 16 see mašla'tum (*p* 606 *col* 2). — (amêl) nâš paṭri swordbearer {Schwertträger} see našû, Q *no* 5; ZA vi 352; Br 309, 10101, 10395, 10425; BA i 289. *pl* napalsuxu šeššu paṭ-ra-tum, ZK ii 324, 2 (*cf* K 4931 *O* 4), the weight of six swords.

paṭrûtu, in nâš paṭrûtu written (amêl) GIR-LAL & (amêl) GIR-LAL-u-tu, K 4395 i 11 & v 29, the association of swordbearers, a military and a priestly office, belonging to the temple service. T^C 114; Neb 247, 2; 416, 2; V 61 v 25 (BA i 289); see also šelûtu & tukâltu.

paṭru *adj* L³ *O* 10 a-mat abi bânija ul paṭ-ru inviolable {unverbrüchlich} Lehmann, ii 63.

puṭûru *adj* AV 7109. Nabd 1113, 1 (19) X arad pu-ṭu-ru kaspi ša (amêltu) Ga-ga-a, ZA iii 87—9: a slave, redeemed with money, *i. e.* a slave redeemed by his original owner from the man who had caught the slave as a fugitive; Meissner, *Diss*, 42 says: a slave having bought his freedom with his own money. See also WZKM iv 117. V 30 *g-h* 40 BAR-ŠU-GAL (or IK) = pu-ṭu-ru, Br 1926 (together with pa-gu-gu); H 215, 39; id = gallabu (gullubu) Br 1925.

puṭûru, *noun* in puṭur îni, name of a bird {Name eines Vogels}. II 37 *e-f* 2 pu-ṭu-ur i-ni ‖ ri(ar?) . . . . zu; *b-c* 69 pu-ṭur i-ni ‖ . . . . . zu; see also KB vi (1) 491.

pa(or xaṭ?)-ṭu-ti II 30 *e-f* 65 = AL-BUR-RA, AV 6899, Br 6887; *ibid* 64 = pi-tu-ti.

piṭru, a plant {eine Pflanze} T^M 118. 82—8—16, 1 *R* 1 xi-ri-im | KI (= KAN)-KAL | ki-i gu-ru-ša-ku | pi-iṭ-ru (or pitru?).

pakû. V 35, 19 be-lu ša . . . . . ina pu-taqu u pa-ki-e ig-mi-lu kul-la-ta-an (see gamalu, Q pr). L^M 124 fear {fürchten}.

pakkû (?) Hilprecht, OBI, I 32 *col* ii 20—21 (ina libbim šundulu ša ilu bânija ašaršanni [KB iv 4: ša ta-ar-sa-an-ni]) i-na pa-ak-ki-ja ra-be-im | u-ša-ta-ad-di-im-ma. (On the other hand see KB iii, 2, 4 *col* ii 21—22).

pakku. T. A. (Lo) 53, 14 + 16 read lu pa[-a]k-ku & lu pa-ak-[k]u, perh. ax-lu pakku, so BA iv 324—5, against lu-pakku (OLZ ii '99, *cols* 39—41); *ibid* reads T. A. (Ber) 153, 19 [ax?]-li pa-ak-ku, & (Ber) 200, 17 ax-li ba-a[k-k]u; (Ber) 26 iv 28 x]u-lu-up pa-a-ag-gu; (Ber) 28 i 11 perh. aban ax-l]i pa-ak-ki, BA iv 416.

pukku (?) KB vi (1) 260—1 *ad* NE XII *col* 2, 29 ûma p(b)u-uk-ku a-na erçitim im-xaç-an-ni-ma (+ *col* 3, 13); see also *ibid*, *pp* 521 net {Fangnetz}?, for the usual reading tammabukku; 83, 1—18, 1332 i 10 [XAL] = pu-uk-ku, M^S 105.

p'û'ku. Scheil, ZA x 292, 19 ud-du-u is-ki-šu-un ma-xa-ru p(b)u-ki-šu-un.

pakdâru. II 28 *b-c* 48 PA-AG-DA-RU = pa-ak--da-ru-u, forming a group with da-ru-u and šur-ru-u. II 33 *c-d* 73; AV 6905; Br 5608.

pikal(l)ul(l)u. V 42 *a-b* 30—32 < IM-ŠU-RIN-NA (Br 8825); KA-KAK-IM-ŠU-RIN-NA (Br 664); KA-KAK (Br 660)-pi-kal-lul-lum; V 39 *a-b* 59—61 = pi-ka-lu-lu (see nappašu). ZK i 123 some vessel, pan; perh. chimney {Ofenloch}? it denotes a hole for a tinûru (*q. v.*).

pa-ki-tu, *var* to bi-ki-tu (*q. v.*) Sarg *Ann* 295, perh. der. of pakû, *q. v.*

pâl. T. A. (Ber) 115, 33 i-na pa-al; KB v 25* *col* 2: at once? surely? perhaps also (Ber) 25 iv 35 pa(?)-lum.

pêlu change, exchange {ändern, tauschen, vertauschen} Rost, 120—1; ‖ enû, ZA vii 187; § 106; G § 52. Peiser, *Vertr.*, xlii 7 lu-pi-el-lu, (3*sg*). Haupt in Toy, *Ezekiel* (SBOT), *p* 87 √פעל = בעל = subdue; the *p* in ušpêlu due to partial assimilation of the ב to the preceding causative š; see also BA ii 259. It occurs as Š³ and Š³ᵗ. — Š³ pr ušpêl, *ps* ušapêla, *ac* šupêlu, *ag* mušpêlu. III 38 *no* 1 *R* 10 ina çi-it pi-i-šu-nu ša la uš-pi-e-lu; Scheil, *Nabd*, iii 20 uš-pi-el-lu (3*pl*), have changed. Lay 17, 3 Tigl. Pil. mušpil nišê mâti eliš u šapliš (KB ii 4—5). IV² 16 *a* 6—8 u-çu-rat šame-e u

pakadu see paqadu. ∼ pa-ku-du T. A. *cf* pagâtu. ∼ puk(q)ânu 1, 2 see buk(q)ânu 162 *col* 2. ∼ pâkurtu see pitiltu.

erçi-tim ša la ut-tak-ka-ru ilu iš-ta-a-nu la muš-pi-lu (= BAL, Br 281), no god is able to change. K 2971, 3 see zīmu (*p* 283 *col* 2). K 2701 *a* ina pi-i-šu el-li la muš-pi-li (Winckler, *Forsch.*, i 92). I 52 *no* 3 *b* 30 at thy lofty command ša la šu-bi-e-lu, which cannot be overruled. ZA iv 14 *col* 3, 2 a-ra-an-ši-na uš-pi-lu. AV 5620 muš-pi-e-lu. Sarg *Cyl* 56 see nannū; 61, in the month of Ab, arax a-rad (il) GIBIL mu-uš-pil (*var* bi-il) am-ba-te ra-ṭu-ub-te (KB ii 48 *rm*); TP III Pl. i 3. Knudtzon (*pp* 39; 42 *etc.*) has the forms uš-pi-lu (& lum), uš-pil (& pi-el)-lu. K 247 ii 17—19 (II 28 *no* 4, 43 *foll*) BAL; [ ]-BAL = šu-pe-lu ša sinništi (Haupt: pudenda mulieris) Br 281; [ ]-BAL = šu-pel-tum (see puxxu). V 45 vi 52 tu-ša-pa-a-la.

Š^{t} V 65 *b* 30—31 see nakaru J^{t} (& § 106). Merod.-Balad.-stone i 14—15 çīt pīšu ša la uš-te-pil-lu ‖ la in-nu-nu-u (BA ii 259; 267; KB iii, 1, 184, 185); Banks, *Diss*, 14, 1) *no* 4, 101 (-lum); KB vi (1) 38—9, 29 çi-it pi-i-šu la uš-te-pil (& pi-el)-lu a-a-um-ma (*p* 359; G § 52); Rm 97, 5 see naklu (end).

NOTE. — 1. pēlu Q *etc.* see bēlu, 1 (*p* 155, 156).

2. Peiser, KAS, 90; T^{C} xi; 113: šupēltu, exchange ‖ Austausch.

pālu (?) be dark {dunkel sein} Thompson, *Reports*, Q pm K 729, 2 its (the moon's horns) ud-du-da-ma pi-il, are pointed and dark; *ibid*, 4 pi-lu, explained by sa-a-mu.

palū, *m* (§ 25) iD BAL. — *a*) a weapon or ornament of the king, insignia of royalty {eine Waffe oder Schmuck; Abzeichen des Königs}. D^{S} 133; § 129; ZDMG 27, 518; 28, 135; AV 6907, 6915; Jensen, 331 *fol.* Boissier, *Rev. Sém.*, viii, 150: meaning not definitely known, perh.: bâton, bâton de commandement, puis plus tard: poteau, pieu, c'est à-dire le latin palus; a compound is xut-palū (*q. v.*). H 9 + 204, 23 (§ 9, 102) BAL = pa-lu-u, between na-ka-su and paṭ-ru. II 28 *f-g* 61 BAL = pa-lu-u in one group with uš-pa-ru (59), xa-aṭ-ṭu (60) and ši-bir-ru (62) Br 275. Boissier, PSBA xxiv, 228 = *clavus annalis*. Thus also Creat.-*frg* IV 29 u-uç-çi-pu-šu (iç) xaṭṭa (iç) kussâ u pa-la-a (KB vi 23; 326—9; 563); K 48, S. AH. 82, 7—14, 631 iii 10 *fol* lištēlipu palūa, compare with ZA ii 129 ii 5 *foll.* BA iii 558. II 38 *g-h* 15, 16 KI-PAL = ŠU-u (ki-palu-u, or √קבל, *Rev. Sém.*, viii 150; Br 9650, 9653), & māt pa-li-e, Br 276 (V 20 *e* 46), followed by māt nu-kur-ti, māt na-bal-kat-tu. — *b*) rule, reign (of the king) {Regierungszeit, Regierung (des Königs)} §§ 30; 66. V 35, 22 Bēl and Nabū ir-a-mu pa-la-a-šu. Neb *Bors* ii 21 la-ba-ri pa-li-e, length of reign (see labaru, *p* 471 *col* 2). Scheil, *Nabd*, vii 25 (Nabū) mu-ša-rik pa-li-e-a; ix 26 ra-'-im pal-e-a (*cf* V 33 ii 14; viii 19). K 601 *R* 14 šul-bur pa-li-e (Hr^{L} 7) *etc.* DT 71 *R* 9; KB ii 246—7, 69; Sn *Bav* 60; Sn vi 73; K 2867, 19 see sa-kapu, Q. K 183, 9 pa-lu-u damqu ūmē | ki-nu-u-ti šanāti ša me-ša-ri (Hr^{L} 2). K 2801 *O* + K 221 + 2669 *R* 8 kutunni palē-ja; see Sarg *Khors* 174; II 36, 26. 81—6—7, 209, 18 ina ū-me BAL-šu (& 36). V 62 *no* 1, 8 ina BAL-e-a, during my government; V 66 i 28 šarrūtu mīšari pa-le-e bu-a-ri (*Mél. Renier*, 130); KB vi (1) 294—5, 31 (& *p* 554) a-na pa-le-e mi-na-a e-zib. — Used at times to designate the single, individual year of reign, Bu 88—5—12, 75 + 76 viii 29; Šalm, *Ob*, 26 i-na ište-en palē-ja; 32, ina II palē-ja *etc.*; see *ll* 52, 54; 35, ina III BAL-MEŠ-ja; also *ll* 67, 78 *etc.* The ištēn palē-ja is usually preceded by rēš (or šur-rat) šarrūti-ja; *cf* II 67, 5; Sarg *Cyl* 71. TP vi 45 adi V palē-ja. — On palū & šattu see ZA ii 303; Winckler, *Sargon*, pref. xxxvii *rm*; & *p* 224 *col* 2. On Winckler, KB i 131 *fol*, *ad* BAL-MEŠ see Hilprecht, *Assyriaca*, 55 *rm* 1. Streck, ZA xiii, 57: palū = offizielles Regierungsjahr.

(aban) **pīlu (pēlu)** & (aban) **pūlu.** dressed stone {Quader} ? § 64 *rm*. AV 7045, 7110. K 1247, 13 tikpi ša (aban) pu-u-li. NE VI 39 pi-i-lu m[u . . .] dūr abni (KB vi, 1, 449 compares Armenian *bur*: Kalk; so also Belck). I 44, 82 a temple of (aban) pi-i-li. Sarg *Khors* 165 as-kup-pi aban pi-i-li rabūtā (= pi-li, *Ann* 427); *bull*-inscr. 56 pi-el-šu uštriqa; *Bronce*, 39 pe-e-le. TP vii 84 the foundation of the temple I made of pu(-u)-li. IV² 39 *R* 6 aŝru ŝštu u-pe-xi-ir dannasu akŝud. it-ti pu(*var* pi)-li u epri ŝa (ŝi) U-ba-si-e (*cf* II 53, 33) ēpuš JASTROW, AJSL xii 152, 32; *ibid*, 150, 28 ŝa i-na pa-na it-ti pi-li u ṭi-ṭi ēpušu; *ibid*, 168; see also ZA x 44, 45. Esh v 9 i-na (aban) pi-i-li aban ŝadi-i dan-ni tamlā ušmalli. Bu 88—5—12, 75 + 76 ix 22—5 mentions (aban) çalamdu; (aban) a-lal-lum; (aban) pi-i-lu pi-çu-u, this latter usually translated: white alabaster {weisser Alabaster}. a palace of (aban) pi-i-li u (iç) ērini is mentioned in Sn vi 42; I 44, 64; Esh v 48; Sn vi 51, 52 i-na (aban) pi-i-li pi-çi-i ŝa ina erçit (al) Baladā innamru I had bull-colossusses made; also I 44, 74 (it-ti); Sn *Kui* 4, 17 *fol* (aban) pi-i-li pi-çi-e (*cf* 26); ZA iii 316, 81; 318, 90 (aban) pi-i-li pi-çi-e; Anp ii 5 a statue of myself ŝa (aban) pi-li piçi-e ēpuš. II 66 *no* 2, 13 ina pi-i-li iš-ki (with mighty, massive, dressed stones) ŝi-kit-tašu u-rab-bi, KB ii 266—7. Rm 339 *O* 7 pi-i-lu = abnu pi-zu-u. agurru pīli piçī = white marble tile (ZA vii 123 *rm*). — See D. H. MÜLLER, *Die Keil-Inschrift von Aschrut-Darga*, Wien '86, *p* 18; pūlu or pēlu stone from Vannic to Assyrian, BA i 175 *rm*; 325; ZA ii 225; see, however, ZA ii 107—8; vii 261 *rm* 1. ROST, 121 declares II 67, 71 (aban) pi-lu-u dannu (KB ii 23) a mistake of the scribe. MEISSNER & ROST, 23: Alabaster; see, however, JENSEN, ZA ix 128; &, again, MEISSNER & ROST, BA iii 210; iv 243—44; 275; AJP xvii 121; pīlu: Alabaster, später ganz allgemein: Gebirgsstein; pūlu = pīlu. Also see ZA viii 377; LEHMANN, ii 114. MEISSNER, WZKM xvi ('02) *part* 200: Kalkstein. — On pīlu = canal; or, perhaps, the embankment of a canal, see LEHMANN, WZKM 1900, pt 4. — Pu-la-ni an-nu-te ZA viii 376 *pl* of pūlu.

pelū, pilū. I 65 *a* 19 (šam) šu-um-mu pe-la-a; *b* 30 bi-la-a; 66 *c* 13 bi-e-la-a. Neb *Pogn.* C vii 21 (šam) šu-um-mi [cuneiform]-a = pela-a; POGNON, *Wadi-Brissa*, 62: rouge. K 247 iii 7—8 SI-IS & [cuneiform] = pe-lu-u (II 26 *c-d* 41, 42; Br 8452). K 40 (D 83) iii 66, 67 si | TAB | = pe-lu-u (Br 8490, H 16, 234) & pe-lu-tum (Br 2329; II 26 *e-f* 48); ZI & [cuneiform] = pe-lu-u. V 19 *a-b* 19—21 (Br 8491, 8181) + II 34 *c-d* 6—9 .... XI = pe-lu-u; .... (gab) KA = *p* ša karšni; .... [cuneiform] = *p* ša XU (= iççūri); .... [cuneiform]-SA = *p* ša BI (= šikari); S^b 297 nu-nu-us | [cuneiform] | = pe-l[u-u], followed by pi-ir-'-u, Br 8178; HOMMEL, *Sum. Lesest.*, 24. OPPERT, ZA ii 107 (bel): blue, or bluish-gray. AV 7047.

pillu, piltu? S^b 2, 5 + 6 in | IN | pi-il-lum, pi-il-tum, AV 7048, 7051; Br 4227—8. HOMMEL, *Sum. Lesest.*, 74: Herr, Herrin (?). II 27 *e-f* 44—46 IN = pil-tum; IN-TAG = *p* xa-tu-u (Br 4233); IN-DUB-DUB-BU = *p* ub-bu-lim (Br 4238 reads up-pu-ši; KB iii (1) 47 *rm* reads: ub-bu-ši √יבש).

p(b)illu, a plant {eine Pflanze}. II 45 *e-f* 60 GIŠ-GEŠTIN-BIL = p(b,d,t)il-lum; see billum, *p* 160 *col* 1.

pīlu. elephant {Elefant} PINCHES, JRAS n. s. ('87) xix 319 quotes pi-i-ru followed by pi-i-lu. So first HINCKS, *Dubl. Univ. Mag.*, Oct. '53.

palgu. canal {Kanal}. II 29 *a-b* 20 A(e-ni-gi-in) [cuneiform] = pa[-al-gu], Br 11670 (⨯ AV 2285); H 36, 871; *cf* II 38 *a-b* 15 = a-mi-ra-nu (Br 1183); AV 6916 = פֶּלֶג, GGA '82, 814; D^Par 142 *no* 30. BA ii 142—3: Stromteiler. IV² 14 (*no* 3) 11—12 ilu ša ina ba-li-šu i-ku u pal-gu la (?) .... Br 796, 1183; also see K 48 *R* 5. I 69 *b* 6 + 8 id KUR (= BAB)-E (= palgi); H 38, 58; JENSEN, ZK ii 17 *ad* IV² 7 *a* 54; Neb 247, 12 *etc.* I 52 *no* 4 *O* 12 pa-al-ga; *R* 9 ti-tu-ur pa-al-ga, a bridge over the canal; Neb viii 39 pa-la-ga-šu (= *pl*; FLEMMING, *Neb*, 48) la e-iz-ki-ir, AV 6909; § 65 *no* 6, *rm*. See also zaqpu (*p* 290). A denominative is perhaps:

palagu, spread, flow off {sich verteilen, verfliessen} Sn *Kui* 4, 31 naššu ūmiŝamma

---

puilū see bulū. ~ pallum (AV 6922) *cf* ballum (*p* 154 *col* 2). ~ pu-ul-lu-u (AV 7115) *i. e.* bullū (*q. v.*).

mē dilûti max-xum ip-li-gu. *Cf* MEISSNER & ROST, 37 *no* 80.

pulug(g)u, pulungu, *m pl* pulu(n)gē. district, territory, country {Bezirk, Gebiet, Gau}. AV 7111, 1382; BA ii 142—3. TP i 39 Tigl. Pil. ça-bit pu-lu-ge ni-su-te ša itāte eliš u šapliš, the conqueror of distant lands, which form the boundaries on North and South. Sarg *Cyl* 24 Sargon ... mu-rap-pi-šu pu-lu-un-gi-šu-un(*var*-gi-e-šu). Perh. connected with pulukku, pulūku, *q. v.*

pilgu see pilku.

(iç) **pal-lag-du** see dudittu, explained as ‖ of pilakku, *q. v.* JENSEN, *Diss*, 73—4. ZA iii 341 (end) reads pal-laq-tum. Z^B 114 = talm. פילכא. ZA xvi 162 reads IV^2 56, 50 (iç) BAL (= pilakku, pilaqqu?) šid-du.

palaou. II 22 *no* 2, *add* (K 4243, Br 1147) ḲUR = pa-la-du (but M^S 76 *col* 2 -mu?); Š Camb 404, 9: X šiqlu kaspi .... šup-lu-du; or √*b-l-d* whence billudû?

palaxu, *pr* iplax, *ps* ipal(l)ax; *ip* pilax (T^M 116) fear, be afraid {sich fürchten, erschrecken} construed with ištu pān(a), ultu pān, lapān, ina pān, ana, or absolutely. AV 6910, 6914. — D^{Pr} 176 separates Syr פלח = فلح from palaxu; see, however, SCHWALLY, *Idiotikon*, 124; also KB vi (1) 352; RÉJ xiv 155; 158. — Cappadocian balaxu (see DELITZSCH, *Kapp. Keilinschr.*, 43, 44), thus PNN. Be(i)-la-ax-A-šur & Be-la-ax-Ištar; Sin-bi-la-ax, MEISSNER, 82, 10; 108, 25. — *pr* Anp iii 103 the whole country ip-lax; K 41 *b* 14 (end) šu-u ul ip-lax-an-ni, PSBA xvii 65 *foll.* NE 59, 7 mu-ta ap-lax-ma; Asb x 79 la-pa-an ešrēti ilāni rabûti ap-lax (but better: I worshipped .... before the shrines of); *del* 107 (114) ilāni ip-la (*var* -tal)-xu a-bu-ba-am-ma; J^W 60 *rm* 1. Creat.-*frg* IV 108 (the host of Tiamat) it-tar-ru ip-la-xu (= 3*pl*). KB vi (1) 288 ii 19 u-ul ip-la-xu (3*pl*); 58, 17 ni-ip-la-[x]u ni-ki-su; TP iii 14 (18) ša i-na pa-an kakkēja ezzûti ip-la-xu; Asb iv 57; II 67, 20; SMITH, *Asurb*, 164, 113; III 8 (= Šalm. *Mon* ii) 79; TP III *Ann* 163; Šalm. *Ob* 36 ištu pa-an kakkēja dannûte ip-lax (*cf* 152). V 70, 16 + 31 ištu pa-an ..... ip-la-xu; Šalm. *Mon*, *O* 21; Šamš iii 28—30; ii 44—5 iš-tu pa-na .... ip-la-xu (3*pl*); iv 22—3 ul-tu pa-an .... ip-la-xu (see namurratu). V 65 *a* 23 ma-'-diš ap-lax-ma; Sn ii 72 ip-lax lib-ba-šu-un; III 12, 23; V 64 *a* 36 ana qibītišunu çirti ap-la-ax. K 2852 + K 9662 i 31 see napištu (end); Nabd 697, 10 ta-ap-lax-šu (3*sg f*) ta-du-ur-šu. V 34 *c* 15 ak-ku-ud ap-la-ax-ma (KB vi (1) 465). Asb v 96 ip-la-xu ana nībarte, they were afraid to cross over; iv 56 ša mi-tu-tu ip-la-xu. Sn vi 7—8 ša la-pa-an ta-xa-zi-ja ip-la-xu (*pl*); Bu 89—4—26, 161 *R* 5 ina a-xi-ja la-ap-lax (Hr^L 435; AJSL xiii 210), K 991 *O* 4 ni-ip-lax-u-ni (Hr^L 117). — *ps* KB iv 58 iii 5 šum ar-ra-a-ti a-na-a-ti i-pal-la-xu-ma, or if he is afraid of these curses; IV^2 54 *b* 12 (end) i-pal-lax; 61 *a* 6 + 25; *b* 16, 33, 61; *c* 38 (a-la-ka) la ta-pal-lax, be not afraid, see KB vi (1) 464; KB vi (1) 298, 14 la ta-pal-lax la ta-tar-ru-ur (K 5418); K 883, 20 la ta-pal-lax (*bis*) BA ii 633—5; & line 25; III 32, 42 (KB ii 250—1, 47); KB v *no* 75, 90 xu-ub-ši-ja a[-pa-l]a-ax, BA iv 308; T. A., Rost. 26 ul ta-pa-la[-ax] *cf* KB v 409 (bel) *ad* 134—5. Rm 177, 6 *B* ta-pal-lax-šu (will serve: wird dienen) KB iv 146—7; vi (1) 352 (*med*). Nabd 697, 17 i-pa-al-lax; Rm 77, 28 i-pa-lu-xu (Hr^L 414). — *pm* KB vi (1) 76 *R no* 1, 3 la-a pa-al[-xa-a-ta]; H 75 *R* 8 pal-xa-ku, I fear; NE 9 iii 8 pal-xa-ku-ma. 83—1—18, 205 *R* 8 pa-al-xa-ku. T. A. (Lo) 1, 87 for, because pal-xu-ni-ik-ku, they fear you; (Ber) 38, 28 pal-xa-ku, I fear (31, 22; 33, 40; Lo 23, 28); (Lo) 12, 43 pa-al-xa-ti danniš, I am very greatly afraid, Lo 24, 23; Ber 58, 121 pal-xa-tu; 49, 11 behold: (al) Çur-ri (= Tyre) la na-pal-xa-ti (has acted rebelliously). — *ag* K 175 *R* 4 thy servant pa-lix ištu pa-an bēli-ja (= V 53 *b* 51; Hr^L 221); K 2729 *O* 29 pa-li-ix šarrū-ti-ja. — especially in the meaning of: fearing the gods, *etc.*: be reverent, show reverence to; revere. K 3364 *R* 19 pa-la-xu da-ma-qa ul-la-ad; IV^2 60* C *O* 5 û-mu pa-la-ax ili ṭu-ub lib-bi-ja. HILPRECHT, OBI i

pal-lu-da, AV 6623 *ad* II 37 *e* 48, see balludu, *p* 160 *col* 2. ~ pil-lu-du, Br 5646 read billudū.

32—33 *a* 16—17 ša pa-la-ax ili u ištar li-it-mu-du (KB iii (2) 2); ZA iv 107, 17; perh. Esh *Sendsch*, *O* 35 ša pa-lax ili u iš-ta-ri [lit-mu-du?]. V 35, 7 (end) pa-la-xa (il) Marduk *etc.* (BA ii 208—9); 23, ûmišam a-še-'-a pa-la-ax-šu, (BA ii 210—11 ✕ PEISER, KB iii (2) 124 *rm*); K 183, 13 pa-lax ili ma-'i-da the fear of god is prevailing (Hr^{L} 2; BA i 617—8); K 2024 *R* 5 pa-la-ax ili (MEISSNER, 108); L^3 *R* 11 ana la pa-li-xi; 81—7—27, 19, 12 pa-lax ilâni (pl). — KB iv 66 (*no* ii) 14 zi-kir (il) GUR u (ilat) NinÊ i-pal-la-xu (= 3 *sg*), HILPRECHT, *Assyr*, 16—17 reads: i-pal-la-a-ax. IV^2 16 *a* 36 ša ilâni rabûti la i-pal-la-xu (= IM-BA-RA-NU-TUK-A, Br 8495). *Rec. Trav.* xx 205 *fol col* iv ša .... (17) lip-lax; 55 *fol*, *no* xxx *col* ii 19 [the gods] u-ul ip-la-xu (= KB vi, 1, 288). K 3459 *R* 6 ki-i .... si-qar-ka pal-xu, ZA iv 15. — V 63 *a* 9 lib-bu-uš pa-al-xu-ma (8, a-na pa-lax ilâni ba-ša-a uz-nâ-šu). K 164, 50 ilâni ša pal-xu; K 3182 iii 52 pal-xa-ka, those who fear thee. S 6 + S 2 *O* 13 pal-xa-ku-ma ad-ra-ku u šu-ta-du-ra-ku (*Rev. Sém.* '98, 142 *foll*). — esp. in *ag* L^3 *R* 13 ki-i la pa-li-ix ili u ilti ip-ša[-ku] LEHMANN, ii 85 *col* 2. V 62 *no* 2, 12 aš-ri pa-lix-ku-nu, Br 8365, Merodach-Balad.-stone i 28 pa-lix ilûtišu (§ 131); v 27 la pa-lix ilâni rabûti (KB iii, 1, 192; BA ii 265; *cf* II 36 *coloph.* 14). Anp i 18 + 38: *Anp* pa-lix ilâni rabûti. Rm III 105 i 10 (end) pa-lix ilu-u-ti-šu. Sarg *Asdod* 37 I, Sargon, pa-li-ix (ZA ii 73 *b* 8) ma-mit Nabû, Marduk (WINCKLER, *Sargon*, 188); V 35, 27 to me, Cyrus the king, pa-li-ix-šu (*i. e.* Marduk), 36 šarru pa-li-xi-ka, 17 Nabuna'id la pa-li-ix-šu. K 2852 + K 9662 ii 27 (end) la pa-li-xu-ti lip-la-xu be-lut-ka. I 49 *a* 5—6, Esarh pa-lix Nabû u Marduk & *var* pa-lix ilû-ti-šu-nu rabî-ti (BA iii 218 *rm* *); Esh ii 45 la pa-li-xu zik-ri bêl bêlâni, who did not heed the command of the lord of lords (Sarg *Khors* 122); K 2729 *O* 9 a-na pa-li-xi (BA ii 566); ZA v 67, 17, I, Anp. pa-lix ilû-ti-ki; 68, 16 pa-lix-ki; ZA iv 14 (ii) 2 pa-li-ix kit-mu-su. Sp II 265 *a* ii 11 pa-li-ix (ilat) Ištar; IV^2 3 *a* 6 la pa-li-ix ilišu (= IM-NU-TE-NA-DINGIR-RA, Br 8464); II 66 *no* 2, 2 pa-lax (or lix?)-ša (KB ii 265 her worshipper), *ibid* 16 pa-lax (or -lix) ilu-ti-ki rabîti; Asb ii 125 me, thy servant, pa-lix-ka; iv 68 u ia-a-ti rubû pa-lix-šu; vi 71 their kings la pa-li-xu-u-ti Ašur u Ištar bêlê-ia. — K 4386 i 59, 60 (= 48 *e-f* 49, 50) ÇI-NU-TUK = la pa-l[i-xu], irreverent (V 16 *c-d* 76, AV 6918); ME-ÇI-TUK-ZU = ardu pa[-li-xu?] Br 10415. — II 35 *c-d* 9 LUX = pa-la-xu, Br 6168; H 26, 570 TE = pa-la-xu (569, a-da-ru); ZA x 207 (ii *O*) 7 (end) a-da-ri : pa-la-xu. According to some V 28 *e-f* 85 ba-ra-ru = pa-la-xu (not -mu!), Br 7700.

NOTE. — II 37 *e* 49 read is-xu not pa[-la]-xu, ZA vii 192 ✕ Br 6526.

Q^t = Q K 610 *R* 13 ip-ta-al-xu (Hr^{L} 310; AJSL xiv 179). K 168, 32 ip-tal-xu (3 *pl*) & see *l* 34. NE 59, 9 ap-ta-lax a-na-ku; *del* 107 (114) see Q. Asb ii 105 the Gimirraeans who la ip-tal-la-xu (§§ 53 *a*; 37 *b*) abêia; K 8466, 12 .... la-a ap-tal-la-xu, I fear not (WINCKLER, *Forsch*, ii 28—9); SMITH, *Asurb*, 143, 46 Bêl u Nabû ša ap-tal-la-xu ilu-us-su-un; K 479, 18 ap-ta-la-ax. V 56, 32 šarru u ilâni-ša la ip-tal-xu-ma, also see Beh 20. Neb i 10 Nebuch. .... bi-it-lu-xu (AV 1332) bi-e-lu-ut-su-un (BA i 2; § 151); i 39 pi-it-lu-xa-ak bêlûtsun (ii 11); i 50 (ZA vi 419 *rm* 1); AV 7095; also POGNON, *Wadi-Brissa*, 27. DT 71, 14 E-la-mu]-u ša la pit-lu-xu rabî-tu ilu-us-su; K 2675 *R* 6—7 ša ..... tak-lu-ma la pit-lu-xu bêlût Ašur. — ip SMITH, *Asurb*, 74, 17 šarru-su pit-lax (§§ 88 *b*; 94). — Q^{tn} = Q Asb vi 37 the gods ša šarrâni Elamti ip-tal (*var* ta-na)-la-xu ilu-us-su-un. — Ʒ K^{M} 53, 6 (il) Šamaš ekimmu mu-pal-li-xi, o Šamas, thy spectre which striketh fear. — $Ʒ^{tn}$ K^{M} 53, 8 ina kâl mûši up-ta-na-lax-an-ni, has striken me with terror; *cf* ZIM., *Ritualtafeln*, 41—42 i 54 up-t]a-na-al-la-xa-an-ni; *ibid* ii 9 & *no* 45 *col* i 15. — Š Bu 88—5—12, 72 *col* vi šup-lu-xu be-lut-su, BA iii 245 *rm* *††; K 2619 ii 10 (*Dibbara*-legend) ša a-na šup-lu-ux niši, KB vi, 1, 62—3 to teach fear unto mankind. Bu 88, 5—12, 193 ii 11 (BA ii 224).

Derr.: naplaxu, pitluxu & these 4:

palxu, *adj* reverent, god-fearing {ehrfürchtig, Gottesfürchtig} § 73; AV 6918. V 63 *a* 4 lib-ba pa-al-xu; KB iii (1) 120 (Br. Mus. 81, 8—30, 9) 9 pal-xu še-mu-u (il) Šamaš; 13, aš-ru pal-xu; V 63 *a* 47 libbu pa-li-ix the pious heart. K 3459 *R* 3 .... pal-xu-u-ti a-di-ra (ZA iv 15). K 4386 i 58 (= II 48 *e-f* 48) ÇI-TUK = pal-xu, Br 4217.

palxiš, *adv* reverently {ehrfürchtig} AV 6917. V 34 *c* 3 pa-al-xi-iš. Neb ii 61 pa-al-xi-iš u-ta-ak-ku-šu (√aqū); *cf* I 65 *a* 11; V 34 *a* 15; KB iii (2) 46, 26; V 64 *a* 23. Asb x 49 see kanšiš. KB iii (2) 78 *col* 2, 7 pa-al-xi-iš at-ta-'-id-ma; 82—7—4, 42 *R* 10 (PSBA xx 152*fol*); V 65 *a* 15 pal-xi-iš uš-te-mi-iq. Šalm. *Bal* vi 3 pal-xiš; K 2801 (+ K 221 + 2669) *R* 20 *b*.

pulxu, *c. st.* pulux *m* fear, terror {Furcht, Schrecken} §§ 37*b*; 65, 5; AV 7114. TP ii 38; Šalm, *Mon*, *O* 22 (Sarg *Khors* 111); *Ob* 158—9; II 67, 27; Sn ii 35; iii 30; III 12, 30 (*ibid* 18 pu-lux-ti) see melammu (*p* 550); also see saxapu (I 45 *no* 3, 17). V 61 *e* 42 is-ku (= tukultu?) pu-ul-xu = service. worship (BA i 290).

puluxtu, *c. st.* pulxat (§§ 37*b*; 65, 5), *pl* pulxāti (§ 69). AV 7012, 7113; Br 8366, 8465. — *a*) fear {Furcht}. Anp iii 23 pul-xa-at bēlū-ti-ja, the fear of my lordship. III 8 (= Šalm, *Mon* ii) 79 pul-xa-at bēlūti-ja; Asb viii 63 ina pu-lux-ti (iç) kakkē (il) Ašur ka-ši-du-ti; ZA iv 11, 26; K 41 *b* 12 ina pu-lux-ti. Sn *Kui* 1, 18 pu-lux-ti mēlammē. KB vi (1) 96, 8 pu-lux-ta-šu i-mur; II 67, 81 pu-lux-ta u-šar-ši (ZA v 302—3 on KB ii 24—5). K 3182 iv 3 the god Luxmu [.....] ša ma-lu-u pu-lux-ta, who is filled with terror. Sarg *Cyl* 27 ina pu-lux-ti-šu rabī-ti, in great fear of him. *del* 88 (93) ūmu a-na i-tap-lu-si pu-lux-ta i-ši, KB vi 236—7. IV² 30* *no* 3 *R* 2 ša pu-lux-ti im-xa-aç, which inspires fear (*Rev. Sém.* vi 149). — *b*) grandeur, terribleness {Furchtbarkeit} K 2675 *R* 24 see xattu (*p* 347 *col* 1). NE 60, 7 the scorpion-men ša ra-aš-bat pu-ul-xat-su-nu-ma imratsunu mūtu, *l* 10 pu-lux-ta. Šamš i 14 Ninib who ma-lu-u pul-xa-a-ti; Rm III 105, 13 ša pul-xa-a-ti ma-lu-u; Asb iv 120 see saxapu; NE 22 *no* 9 *R* 2 ana pul-xa-a-ti ša UN-MEŠ (+ 5). Samsu-iluna iv 2; IV² 27 *a* 48—50; II 19 *a* 40—41; *b* 23—6, 43—44 see melammu (*p* 550 *col* 2). IV² 18 *no* 1 *O* 8—9 pu-lux-ta (= IM) ša-lum-ma-ta; & see IV² 24 *no* 1, 18—19. Creat.-*frg* III 27 (85) ušum-galle na-ad-ru-u-ti pul-xa-a-ti (*var* pul-xa-ta) u-šal-biš-ma, the fierce monster-vipers she (Tišmat) clothed with terror. K 5209, 2 be-lum pu-lux-ta-ka gal-ta-at (?); H 183 XVI, perh. also IV² 24 *no* 3, 25; 12—13 (see galtu, *p* 220 *col* 1). H 80, 10 Ninib pu-lux-ti çil-li-ka a-na ma-a-ti tar-ça-at, *N*, the majesty of thy protection is spread over the country. K 2487 + K 8122 *O* 13 ša pu-lux-tu lit-bu-šu (of Ninib). — *c*) reverence, worship {Ehrfurcht, Verehrung}. Neb i 38 a-ra-mu pu-lux-ti i-lu-ti-šu-nu (§ 151); 69—70 šu-ri-'-im-am-ma pu-lu-ux-ti i-lu-ti-ka (ii 7; viii 31); ix 58 pu-lu-ux-ti ilūtišu (Marduk gave into my heart); V 63 *a* 5 Nabd. ašru kanšu ša ra-šu-u pu-lu-ux-tim; Esh ii 48 pu-lux-ti Bēl u Nabū; III 15, 20 pu-lux-ti ilāni rabūti; I 69 *b* 47 ina pu-lux-ti ša Ištar, in reverence of; *a* 21 pu-lux-ti (il) Sin, the worship of Sin. See also saxapu. — S^c 285 ni-i | IM | pu-lux-tu; H 28, 617; S^b 41; V 28 *h* 66. K 3182 iii 26 i-ti-qu (= αg) pu-lux-ti. — K 13, 16 + 18; K 1250, 10, 11 (Hr^L 281; 480) read pu-lux-ti (Johnston, JAOS xviii 141; xix 44 against M^S 77 pu-pit-ti).

NOTE. — V 41 *h* 65 pu-ul-xi-ti read bu-ul-ṭi-ti & see *p* 166 *col* 1.

palaṭu. T.A. (Ber) 1719, 51 i-pa-al[-l]i-iṭ, then I shall live (BA iv 284); (Ber) 189 (= KB v *no* 184) 25 pa-li-iṭ-mi (+ 33; BA iv 121) = balaṭu (*q. v.*).

palaku divide, separate {teilen, abgrenzen}. Meissner & Rost, 39 & *rm* 85. Q KB iv 64 *no* 2, 3 ša [ana; Hilprecht, *Assyr*, 10—11: ki-i] pil-ki ip-lu(?)-uk-ma, which (the king) has separated off as a district; see also Jensen, ZA viii 221 *rm* 2; Hilprecht, *ibid*, 366; Oppert, x 60; against whom see Jensen, 152, 162 (= enclose, surround). K 4080 enuma ina rêš êkalli ŠU-SI uçurta pala (written [sign])-kat, BOISSIER, PSBA xviii, '96, 237—9. 83—1—18, 1335 i 9 (du-ub) DUB = pa-la-ku ša pil-ki (PSBA vii *pl* 12); II 30 *no* 4 *O* 9 [BAR?] = pa-la-ku, AV 6911; Br 1784. — T. A. (Lo) 36, 17 all the lands i-pal-la-ka (KB v: will subject themselves, & *l* 27); 57, 23 pa-nu-ka i-pal-la-ak (and subjects himself to you). Rm iv 90 *O* 6 .... [ip]-pal-gam-ma tup-ki, *etc.* — ג divide off, separate, constitute into a district, or territory {abgrenzen, zu einem District, Bezirk machen} Sn *Bell* 58 eqil tamirti elēn âli .... a-na mârê Ninâ pil-ku u-pal-lik-ma u-šadgila panuššun (*Rass* 86; ZA iii 318); Sarg *Cyl* 18 mu-pal-li-ku (AV 5521) gu-un-ni-šu see gunnu (226 *col* 1) & balaqu (167). — On V 53 *no* 4, 50 see balaṭu ג¹ (163 *col* 1).

pilku *c. st.* pilik, district, territory {Gebiet, Bezirk}, see palaku; KB iv 66 *no* 2 *R* 10 eqlu šu-a-tum a-na pil-[ki]-šu u-tir-ru, that field they incorporated into their territory (see, however, HILPRECHT, *Assyr*, 14—15); III 41 *b* 28 Ninib ..... pi-lik-šu le-ni, may min his territory. BA ii 142—3 reads pilgu & compares פְּלַגּוֹת, Jud 5, 15 *fol.* K 620 *R* 4 (amêl) rab pil(char. bil)-ka-ni, Hr^L 91; perh. V 28 *h* 86.

pal(l)ukku *1.* perh. = pulukku (*q. v.*) 83, 1—18, 1335 *O* 12 (me-en-bulug) DUB = pal-lu-uk-ku (PSBA, Dec. '88); & S^b 170 (me-bu-lu-ug) id = pa-lu-uk-ku (ZA v 105—6).

pallukku *2.* Camb 126, 2: I mana (rik) pal-lu-uk-ku, 1 Mina of *p*-wood; *ibid* 3—4 AŠ buršâu a-na ki-nu-nu; BA iii 491; see also K 4346 ii 9 *fol* (II 45 *g-h* 56, 57) with id GIŠ-ŠIM-MU[G?] & GIŠ-ŠIM-BA[L?], probably a fragrant, sweetsmelling species of wood (AV 1000; Br 5166—7; see silaru). According to BOR i 78 perhaps name for the cypress. Rm 145 *O* 8 has qa-ni-e pal-lu-uk-ku. See also ZA xv 421 *ad* ZIMMERN, *Ritualt.*, 190, 7. There may be some connection with:

puluk (?) in V 55, 56 pu-lu-uk u imêr ŠIM-LI (= buršâi) la na-da-ni. ZA x 202, 9 has bi-i-en-du : si-la-ru { bi-bi-en-du : pul(or rather pal)-lu-uk-ku; 6, še-ru-'u (JENSEN, 311: thorn) { ša ir-ri aš-ta-pi-ru pal-lu-[uk-ku] SCHEIL: une plante grimpante; a creeper. √palaku, enclose.

pulukku, circle, district {Kreis, Bezirk} ZA vii 139; JENSEN, 162; 505—6; *Theol. Litztg.*, '90 *col* 174; POGNON, *Wadi-Brissa*, 82 (following OPPERT) compares فَلَك, orbis coelestis. AV 6924, 7111. Neb *Bors* ii 23—4 i-na li-'i-ka ki-i-nim mu-ki-in pu-lu-uk ša-mi-e u er-çi-tim, KB iii (2) 55; OPPERT, *Rev. d'Assyr*, i 104; V 66 *b* 15 OPPERT, *Mélanges Renier*, 228, & JENSEN, ZK ii 352, read i-na xaṭ-ṭa-ka çi-i-ri mu-kin pal-lu-uk-ku šamê u erçi-tim (>< HOMMEL, *Gesch.*, 793 bel). Merodach-Bal.-stone iii 20 pu-lu-uk-ku la šit-ku-nu, BA ii 261; KB iii (1) 186—7. WINCKLER, *Forsch.*, i 498 *R* 4 during the disturbances and revolutions in Akkad pu-lu-uk-ka-šu-nu iš-ni-ma, their boundaries were changed. S^b 169 bu-lu-ug | [sign] | pu-lu-uk-ku, AV 1379, Br 2769. II 52 *a-c* 53 is thus to be read BULUG-KI = pu-lu-uk-ku = bît xa-ri-e, AV 1380, Br 2771; also as gloss in II 48 *e-f* 16 pu-lu-uk = qa-ra-šu (*q. v.*) ša içi, AV 1376. — pulukku in astronomical texts; according to ZA viii 224 die Krippe; ZA v 285 = crab {Krebs}, so also JENSEN, 311; on the other hand, see London *Academy*, Dec. 6, 1890, *no* 970, *p* 532.

palku. T. A. (Ber) 165, 13 (19) pal-ku (?).

pilakku spindle {Spindel}. IV² 8 *b* 28—9 šipâte piçâte šipâte çalmâte qa-a eç-pa ina pi-lak-ki (= GIŠ-BAL, Br 278; § 25) iṭ-me, = Z^Š v/vi 151; § 65 *no* 23; JENSEN, *Diss*, 73—4 (*cf* ZA i 59) = Talm פילכא; id same as pilaqqu, *q. v.* Z^B 114; LEHMANN, i 127. GESENIUS¹² 626 פֶּלֶךְ.

פלכה (זב) be wide, be wide open {weit sein, weit geöffnet sein} § 117. — Q pm (?) Sm 1719 pal-kat uz-ni, said of goddess Ištar — Š make wide, open wide {weit auftun} Creat.-*frg* IV 100 Tiâmat pa-a-ša uš-pal-ki, *T.* opened wide her mouth. V 65 *b* 15 bîtu ana erêbi Šamši bêlija šu-pal-ka-a (= pl) bābānišu, the gates of the house are opened wide for the entrance of Šamaš my lord. K 3182 iv 14 read muš-pal-ku-u da-lat da-ad-me (Gray, AJSL xvii 142) instead of Brünnow (ZA iv 14) çir-ti ku-u-da ⟨ šamē.

palkū *adj* wide, ample {weit, geräumig} AV 6920. — *a*) wide open, all-embracing {weit geöffnet, allumfassend} Jensen, 318; Lehmann, ii 64. ZA iv 287 i 33 be-lum pal-ku-u (286, 241); Sp II 265 *a* xxii 1 li-'-u pal-ku-u; xxv 3 ri-e-šu pal-ku-u; K 112 *R* 6 i-sa-al ma-a i-na muxxi ša p(b)al-ku-te ša ma-a-ti -du-bu-ub (Hr^L 223; AJSL xiv 9). Mérod.-Balad.-stone iii 6, 7 xa-si-sa pal ka-a u šat-li-mu-šu, KB iii, 1, 186—7; uznā palkū, an intelligent, receptive mind, *e. g.* Sarg *Cyl* 48 *etc.* see xissatu; Winckler, *Sargon*, 166, 14 (pal-ka-a-ti); II 67, 67; Lay 38, 4; Sargon *Harem B*, 6 *etc.* see xasisu (*pp* 328—9); also L⁴ 20 xa-si-su pal-ku-u. Sarg *Cyl* 47 see mērišu, 1 (*p* 593); 59 on a festal day of the son of Bēl ŠI (= ige)-gal-l pal-ki-e (Lyon, *Sargon*, 73). II 36 *coloph*, 19 ni-me-qi-šu-nu pal-ku .... V 37 *d-f* 2 bu-ru |⟨| pal-ku-u, preceded by rap-ša uz-nu & pi-ta uz nu (36 *d-f* 6). — *b*) perh. numerous, or fat {zahlreich oder fett, feist}. III 9 *no* 3, 55 LU-BAD-MEŠ (= kirrē) pal-ku-ti (KB ii 31 = TP III *Ann* 155) § 117. K 2711 *R* 28 xa-ṭa(da)-a-a pal-ki-e, BA iii 268—9. V 62 *no* 1, 25 niqē pal-ki; see also V 15 *e-f* 1 pal-ku (Br 9345). II 32 *g-h* 75 *cf* mērišu, 2 (593 *col* 2).

paliāmu. some garment {ein Kleidungs-stück} § 65, 36. V 28 *a-b* 7 pa-li-ja-a-a-mu = te-di-iq sun (ZA i 182 *rm* 2)-ni, AV 6913.

pillumgu (?) **pilingu** (?) K 4206, 5 pi-il-lum-gu-XU = pi[-li-in-gu?]; II 37 *a-c* 58 pi(?)-il-lum-gu(?)-XU = ši (or rather pi)-li-in-gu = pu-ri-du, *q. v.* AV 7049.

palamu. 82, 1—18, 4154 + 4155 i 6 (ku-ur) KUR = pa-la-mu.

pulānu see pulpul.

palānu. T. A. (Ber) 184, 30 ki-ma pa-la-nu-ka (?) i-ti-lu. KB v 258 *rm* * suggests a mistake for la-pa-nu-ka = before thee (?).

פלס. Iı *pr* ippalis, *ps* ippalas; *ac* naplusu (BA i 181; IV² 40 *a* 24 nap-lu-su); *ip* naplis (na-ap-li-is, ZA i 40, 26; ii 128, 20), see, look {sehen, ansehen} AV 6012; § 84; H^F 53; G § 100; ZK i 75; Z^B 17, 18; Fränkel, ZA iii 55 *no* 8 compares Jew-Aram בלש = examine. — *a*) see, look, look at, in a general sense {sehen, schauen, anschauen, in allgemeiner Bedeutung}. V 65 *a* 23 ap-pa-lis-su-ma ma'diš ap-laxma. Banks, *Diss*, 10, 1) *no* 4, 39 (end) i-nu ul ip-pal-la[-as]; 40 šu-ut-ta-tum ša la nap-lu-si; 18, *no* 2 (8—10) 37 (end) i-ni ul ip-pal-la-as. IV² 24 *b* 5—6 ana gegunī (*q. v.*) a-šar la nap-lu-si ip-pal-su (Br 4010, 9295, 9297). IV² 5 *a* 11—12 ip-pa-lis-ma; *del* 126 (133) ap pa-al (*var* pal)-sa-am-ma; 132 (139) ap-pa-li-is. IV² 9 *a* 22—3 ši-xa kat-ta ša ana nap-lu-si (Br 4010) as-mu, a plant fine to behold; *b* 23—4 nap-lis (21—22; Br 9359). V 55, 34 ed-lu bēl narkabti ul ip-pal-la-sa ša-na-a ša it-ti-šu, KB iii (1) 166—7. DT 67 (H 120) *R* 7—8 ip-pa-li-is-ma nap-lu-us mu-tim-ma (Br 4006, 4010; Z^B 26; ZK i 219). KB vi (1) 98 *no* iii 2 šu-u ip(b)-p(b)[a-la-as], + 8 ip]-pa-lis-ma. *Adapa*-legend *R* (= T. A. (Ber) 240) 9 *D* & *Z* a-xa-mi-iš ip-pa-al-su-ma (+ 25 ip-pa-la-su-ma). Rm 2, 454 *R* 17 (20, 24) eb-ri nap-li-is (‖ du-gul) BA ii 396—8; 25 ap-pal- am-ma, S 1708, 27 ip-pa-lis-ma (AV 8794 Br 9324); S 752 *R* 4; IV² 7 *a* 16 (il) Marduk ip-pa-lis-su-ma (+ 22 *a* 48); 18* *no* 6 *R* 11—12 (Br 9359). V 65 *a* 25 pa-pa-xu (il) Šamaš ... na-pa-li-sa-ma (2 *pl* ip), 37 ip-pal-su-ma pa-pa-xi u kummē i-xi-ṭu-ma; 38 (+ 28) ap-pa-lis (ZA i 340, 19 -li-is). IV² 17 *a* 25—6 tap-pa-al-la-aš, id same as Zür. Vok. iv 25 (ZK ii 400; Br 9297); see also K 4207, 16. — *b*) select, choose, inspect {ersehen, auserseheh} Halévy, JA '79 *vol* xiii 518; Lehmann, ii 41 (× ZK ii 352). KB iii (2)

---

* palkatu, AV 6919 *cf* balkatu (*pp* 165, 166). ~ pa..lu, BA ii 260 read balalu & see above, *pp* 166, 167.

38, 47—8 temēna *B* ša ki-ri-ib-ša ip-pa-al-sa; V 63 *a* 32 (ap-pa-li-is-ma); 62 *a-b* 41 (11) to do thus & thus the great gods xa-diš lu-u ip-pal-su-in-ni-ma (Br 4010), have selected me; I 43, 4 among all the other princes ke-niš ŠI-BAR (= ippalsa)-ni-ma. — *c*) look upon with favor, graciously, with compassion, love {mit Wolgefallen, Teilnahme, Mitleid, Liebe jemanden ansehen}. ZA v 68, 18 nap-li-si-ni-ma, look upon me (with compassion); IV² 59 *no* 2 *b* (K 254) 10 my goddess nap-li-si-in-ni-ma. KB iv 66 (*no* ii) 16 may Gur and Nina ..... ke-niš lip-pal-sa-su-ma *etc.*, see kēniš (*p* 404); 81—6—7, 209, 4 (end) ke-niš ip-pal-la-su; also see xadiš (*p* 307); ZA ii 131 *a* 11—12 na-ap-li-is-ma; V 63 *b* 42; KB iii (2) 4, 34—5; 68, 6—7. 81—6—7, 209, 34 xa-diš lip-pa-lis-ma; V 35, 14 (end) xa-di-iš ip-pa-li-is; V 64 *b* 34 xa-di-iš lip-pal-sa-an-ni-ma (3 *sg*). H 115 (K 101) *O* 7—8 a-me-lim tap-pa-la-si (Br 4010) amēlu šū iballuṭ (ZA iii 99); *R* 3—4 ke-niš nap-lis-in-ni-ma = IV² 29 ** *no* 5; also simply ip-pa-li-is-ma, III 43 *a* 7; Samsuiluna iv 7 the gods .... lu [ip]-pa-al-su-nim (KB iii, 2, 182); see also V 61 *d* 46 ip-pa-lis-su-ma (3 *sg*). Scheil, *Nabd*, vi 35 (damqiš) ap-pa-lis-šu-nu-ti. K^{M} 2, 37 mu]-up-pal-sa-ta (*var* mu-up]-pal-sa-at) ki-niš nap-lis-an-ni, thou art pitiful, truly pity me; 27, 17; 4, 26 [nap?]-lu-us-sa taš-mu-u, whose regard is prosperity; 8, 2. S^{c} 3, 22 [ŠI] = nap-lu-su (preceded by a-ma-ru) Br 9280, AV 6095; H 41, 255. D 84 (= Zür. Vok.) iv 25 ŠI-BAR (Br 9297); 26 ŠI-TAB (Br 9316); 27 ŠI-SE (Br 9324, same id = amaru, 9323; H 41, 255); 28 ŠI-GAB (Br 9326); 29 ŠI-GAB-BAR-RA (Br 9330) all = nap-lu-su; 32 ŠI-BAR-BAR = mu-pal-su (Br 9299). K 4587 *R* 8—10 *c-d* a-tu-u = a-ma[-ru], da-ga[-lu], nap-lu[-su].

Ꝋ¹ see, look {sehen, schauen}. IV² 26 *b* 13—14 la mi-sa-a it-tap-la-as (Br 9324); NE 51, 23 (KB vi, 1, 272) ... i-tap-la-si Barsip-^{ki}. *del* 88 (93) see puluxtu, *a*; § 49*b*.

Ꝋ¹ⁿ = Ꝋ¹ K 126, 16 when a man looks upon (it-ta-nap-la-as) upon a woman, that is not his wife; + 18 (end); *Rev. Sém.* i 170; L⁴ i 29, beg. II 28 *a* 16 it]-ta-nap-la-as followed by [i]-ta-na-mar. NE 24, 2—3 ša (1?) erini it-ta-nap-la-su (3 *pl*) mi-la-šu; ša (1?) kišti it-ta-nap-la-su ni-rib-šu (KB vi, 1, 160—1).

NOTE. — 1. VATh (Ber) 991 *col* iii šum-ma ... a-na amēli ša-ni-tim up-ta-al-li-is-ma, Peiser, *Jurispr. Babyl. reliqu.*, 35: si aliam mulierem respicit.

2. V 21 *h* 37 ša-a | RU | pa-la-su (ZK ii 418; Br 1437); D 85 *R* 33—4 ŠI-TAB-GA-GA & IMĒR-ŠI-TAB-TIK-SE-KI (?) = pu-lu-su ša imēri (Br 9316); 35 IM-A-ŠI-BAR-ŠE-GA-GA = pu-tal-lu-su (Br 8499); *ibid* 30 ŠI-TAB-IMĒR = nap-la-sa-tu, *q. v.* (Br 9317). S 19 *c-d* 5 mu-pal-su (ZA iv 32; viii 196; 382; Br 9299); 6 pu]-tal-lu-su (ZA iv 35; viii 383). — See also balašu, 163 *col* 1.

Der.: naplusu.

palsū a weapon of the gods {eine Götterwaffe} pul-su-u II 43 *d* 28.

פלסא see nipilsū.

פלסח. Ꝋ pr ippalsix; ac napalsuxu (*q. v.*) Br 4841, 4844, 9812, 10544, 10581. throw oneself down, sink down {sich niederwerfen, hinsinken} Sarg *Ann* 294 Merodachbaladan qaq-qa-riš ip-pal-si-ix, threw himself on the ground (as an expression of mourning) Winckler, *Sargon*, 50. Bit edlu ip-pa-la-sa-xu | bīt šubat (11) Marduk, Bez., *Catal.*, 1776.

Ꝋ¹ = Ꝋ NE XII (K 2774) iv 11, 12 [ina e-pi]-ri it-ta-pal-si-ix, KB vi, 1, 265 & 530: hat sich im Staube niedergekauert; also DT 67 *R* 5—6 (H 120); so Boissier, *Rev. Sém.*, viii 151 § 1 (end) not it-ta-bal-kit; J^{I-N} 42.

Š bīt šu-pal-su-xi edlūti, Bezold, *Catal.*, 1776; M^{S} 76.

Derr.: napalsuxu (Br 4841, 4844), napalsuxtu.

palīpu. Neb 402, 14 BAR-ṬU çarpi ša a-na pa-li-pi na-aç(z, s)-xa-pu.

PULPUL (?), read by Z^{B} 28; K^{M} *p* 167 and others pulānu (= פְּלוֹנִי) see, however, BA i 114 *rm* (bel) & 319. K 3377 + K 7078, 6; Asb viii 46 (*var*); II 51 *R* 3 + 12 (ZK ii 320); H 75 *R* 1; Br 10347—8; id + tum (= *f*) often, Z^{B} ii 3 *etc.*

pilpilānu. Zim., *Ritualtafeln*, 24 *O* 33 pi-il-pi-la-nu; *ibid*, *rm* h: certainly a name for a bodily defect {jedenfalls Bezeichnung für einen Körperfehler}. See also MEISSNER, ZA xv 417.

palaçu in P. N. I-li-ip-pa-al-ça-am ra-bi(-a)-nu-um, KB iv 32, 25; perh. K 3456 *R* 17 pal-ça-a-ma i-na-ka (PSBA xxi 41; *ibid* 45 √balaçu).

palaqu, perhaps = balaqu destroy, kill, ravage {zerstören, töten, verwüsten} *p* 167. IV² 22 *a* 37 ..... ra-ba-a kîma al-pi i-pal-liq. piḷḷ see nappaqu. 83, 1—18, 1330 ii 34 ṬU (tu-un) pa-la-qu. — ℶ = Ⓠ I 34 iv 43 see balaqu. L⁴ iii 8 az(s,ç)-le ṭu-ub-bu-xu li-e pu-ul-lu-ku, thus read perhaps *p* 463 *col* 1 (lû, 3). Also see V 64 *c* 35.

pilaqqu, *pl* pilaqqâte (§ 70*a*) axe, hatchet {Axt, Beil} § 65, 23. id GIŠ-BAL (§ 25) Br 278; II 39, 132; H^V 55 *rm* 5; ZK ii 44; AV 7044. See paraçu & sup(p)innu. III 65 *a* 41 pi-la-ka-at mâti TAR-as. nâšpilaqqi see našû (*p* 734 *col* 1); II 25 *a-b* 76, BA ii 32. On bird's name pi-laq-qi (ilat) Ištar see xanzizîtu (*p* 326).

NOTE. — On pilaqqu & πέλεκυς see LAGARDE, *Gesammelte Abhandlungen,* 49, 10; PRÄTORIUS, *Lit. Or. Phil.*, i 195; HAUPT, BA i 171 *rm* 1.

pilurtu. Rm 2, 1 *R* 6 ina libbi (iç) pi-lu-ur-te ka-ri-ru-u-ni mar-di-tu, Hr^L 408.

palašu 1. bore, dig through {bohren, durchbohren}. V 36 *d-f* 23 bu-ru | ⟨ | pa-la-šu, Br 8726. HEBR. vii 61 *rm* 13. Asb ix 106 see laxû, 1 (*p* 478). KB v (T. A.) *no* 119 (Ber 91) 19 pa-la-ša, has destroyed (see *ibid*, 412), Lo 45, 17. V 63 *b* 31 see kaskasu (*p* 415 *col* 1); II 61 *a* 41 u uznâ-šu pal-šat, and his ears are bored through. Perh. K 4207, 19—20 bi-ru-u-um bît agurri i-pal-la-aš (Br 12248) not -rum, as on *p* 188 *col* 2.

ℶ Sn v 68 all their corpses u-pal-li-ša (1 *sg*). III 53 *a* 19 the star  ana DIR-MEŠ pu-ul-lu-ši. Der.

pilšu excavation {Aushöhlung}. V 36 *f-d* 24 bu-ru | ⟨ | pi-il-šu (Br 8727; ZA vi 11).

special meanings are: *a*) hole {Loch} Šalm, *Bal,* v 1 ki-ma še-li-bi ina pil-še (*var* ši) u-çi like a fox he escaped out of the hole (KB i 136). — *b*) breach, fissure {Bresche, Loch} JENSEN, *Lit. Centralbl.*, '94 *col* 54; & mine {Mine}. See nabalkattu, *c*; niksu, *c*); nêpilu; nipišu, *c*.

pulluštu. a furniture, house implement {ein Hausgerät}. T. A. (Ber) 26 iv 27: 1 p(b)u-ul-lu-uš-tum siparri.

palašu 2. weigh {wägen} LEHMANN, ii 43 *rm* 2, whence naplaštu (*q. v.*). See, however KB vi (1) 528—9: hole {Loch}.

palašu 3. IV² 20 *no* 1, 10 a-pal-lu-uš, see balašu.

paltu *1.* a weapon {eine Waffe} > paštu (*q. v.*) ZA viii 77 *col* 4, 30; 78. ZK ii 299, 13, 14 pa-al-tu (see *ibid*, *p* 412; AV 6930).

paltigu. II 28 *a-b* 6 pa-al-ti-gu ‖ ku-us-su-u xar-ra-ni, literally: a traveling chair {ein Reisestuhl} § 61, 3; AV 6929.

palatu PEISER, KB iii (2) 124 *rm*, *ad* V 35, 23 (end): and daily I visited his pa-la-tu, but BA ii 220—11 reads pa-la-ax (-šu): worship {Verehrung}.

paltu *2.* in xi-il pal-ti see xilbalti (*p* 312 *col* 2).

pûmu (?) MEISSNER, 57 *no* 65, 1 šub-tum pu-um garret, storehouse {Speicher, Vorratshaus}.

(amêl) **pamaxû** some official (?) T. A. (Ber) 92 *R* 29 (amêl) pa-ma-xa-a ša Xa-an-ni; see also Ber 7 *R* 30.

pinnu see gungupinnu, *p* 227 *col* 2.

pânu *c. st.* pân *m*; id ŠI § 9, 86; Br 9281; S^c 3, 15 [ŠI] = pa-a-nu; H 7, 191; 16, 225; 30, 679; AV 6940. D^H 20; ZDMG 40, 723; HAUPT: properly an old plural of pû. *pl* pânû, pânê. — *a*) countenance, face {Antlitz, Gesicht}. K 2148 iii 23 pa-nu amêli; NE 72, 28 (end) pa-nu-u-a, my countenance, KB vi (1) 226—7; pa-ni-ka V 65 *b* 21; H 115 *R* 8; K 3426, 10 (end) see saxaru Š. pa-nu-uk-ka, K^M 14, 10 (-ku V 65 *b* 17); 18, 2 followed by pa-nu-ka; DT 67 *O* 13 (H 119) pa-nu-ša

pal-lu-çi-tum, AV 6952 see balluçîtum (*p* 167 *col* 2). ~ pa-laq-tum (see ZA iii 166; 341) read pa-rit-tum. ~ pallurtu (AV 6926) see ballurtu. ~ (šam) paltu (AV 6930; Br 7915) see baltu, 1. ~ pa(u)ltu see baltu, 2. ~ paltû, Creat.-*frg* IV 16 see *b-l-ṭ* (*pp* 164, 165.) ~ pu-ma-lu see gitmâlu.

dim-tu dul-lu-xu, Br 11332. IV² 31 *O* 64 pa-ni-ša ir-'-ub; pa-na-ka ZA iv 8, 39. K 991, 15 ul-tu pa-ni-e-šu. H 85, 31 pa-an (= ŠI) lim-nu-ti, evil countenance, Br 3644; IV² 30* *no* 3 *O* 38 ina pa-ni-ka lim-nu-ti; II 16 *b-c* 28 pa-an al-pi (= ŠI-UL) a-li-ki; V 60 *a* 18 ni-ib(p)-xa ša pa-an (or PA-AN? *i. e.* parçi) ⁽ⁱˡ⁾ Šamaš u-šat-ri-ça-am-ma, the splendor of the face of the sun; *see*, however, King, *First Steps*, 30: an enclosure (?) before Šamaš he erected. IV² 19 *a* 43—44 all the Anunnaki inaṭ-ṭalū pa-ni-ka (= SAG-ZU), o Šamaš; also *a* 38, Br 3520. NE 13, 15; 12, 31; 66, 31 see naṭalu. NE 9, 50 see mašalu (*p* 604 *col* 2 bel); KB vi (1) 198, 11; NE 14, 17 uk-ku-lu pa-nu-šu; NE 60, 11 i-te-kil pa-ni-šu; Sm 1702, 2 a-kal pa-nu (shew-bread; *cf* Haupt in Paterson, *Numbers* [SBOT], 50 line 50; and in Guthe, *Ezra-Nehemiah* [SBOT], 70; also *Jour. Bib. Lit.* xix (1) 59 & *rm* 82: literally: advance bread); il-lu-ur pa-nu V 27 *b* 4, Br 14815; KB vi (1) 198 *col* v (vi) 7 qud-du-du pa-nu-ka (+ 200, 14; 216, 2), see also 198, 11. *del* 34 (41) end: ul a-šak-kan pāni-ja-a-ma (NE 136, 41 & *rm* 2; KB vi, 1, 233; BA i 233: I turned to); IV² 31 *R* 13 i-na ..... šu-kun pa-ni-ka; Asb iii 53 eli ...... aš-ku-nu pa-ni-ja; I 42, 41 ana ..... iš-ta-kan pa-ni-šu, he betook himself. IV² 56 *b* 51 see nam-maššū; K 13, 18 pa-ni-šu-nu ana ⁽ⁿˡ⁾ Š šaknu, their faces turned toward (*i. e.* going in the direction of) Š. H 99, 41 (Allatu) pa-ni-ša ana aš-ri ša-nim-ma liš-kun (J^W 72; H^F 57); V 33 i 52 pa-ni-šu iš-ku-na (*cf* ii 4). Smith, *Asurb*, 126, 76 panuššu taškun (Sag *f* § 147, 1 *b*). Creat.-*frg* IV 60 to Tiāmat's place pa-nu-uš-šu iš-kun; see also K 2619 iv 21 (KB vi (1) 383). Smith, *Asurb*, 290, 56 pa-ni-ja damqûte eli-šu aš-kun. pa-nu-uš-šu-un, their countenance, § 74, 2. namaru pânu see namaru ℚ *b* & ℷ *c*. KB vi (1) 4, 21 (end) i m-me-ru pa-n[u-u-šu]; V 61 iv 9 pa-nu-šu ir-ti-šu, his face rejoiced (BA i 278). K 890 *O* 7 see xilū (*p* 312 *col* 2). KB ii 253 (III 32, 66) 69 pa-nu-u-ka ul ur-raq, thy face shall not blanch; IV² 50 *b* 44 li-çu-du li-ri-qu pa-nu-u-ki (T^M iii 103); V 64 *a* 36—7. Anp iii 26 see xuribtu (*p* 336 *col* 2); Šalm, *Mon*, ii 99 *cf* namū (desert) >< KAT² 195. dagalu, dāgil pān(u) see dagalu (*p* 240 *col* 1, *b*); Lehmann, ii 82 *b*; Nabd 356, 12—14 a-na ū-mu ça-a-tu pa-ni-ja u-šad-gil-ma, and (this house) belongs to me forever; + 23, 25 pa-ni-ja šu-ud-gu-lu; 380, 12; 668, 15; 697, 14; 1098, 6; ina pa-ni tu-šad-gil, 65, 13. pāna nadanu (*q. v.*) ana, in T. A. (ZA ix 275 *fol*), V 60 i 15 the likeness of the sun-god pa-ni-šu ul id-din-šu, did not show itself to him (the seeker); IV² 60* B *O* 4 ul id-di-na pa-ni-šu, = show oneself to {sich zeigen, sehen lassen}. L⁴ iii 18 pa-nu-uš-šu (§ 11) it-ta-nak-ka-ru, they changed their attitude toward him. Asb iv 57, 58 see napištu (& translate: because their life was dear in their own eyes). Sp II 265 *a* vii 10 il-an-nu kuççudu pa-na-an-ni lil-li (ZA x 6); VATh 348 *O* 27 pa-ni ba-nu-ti, a beautiful face (KB vi, 1, 96); *cf* K 2619 i 13 la ba-ne pa-ni; not light (*i. e.* angry) was his face; also K 3182 iv 16 (AJSL '01, Apr.). V 28 *a-b* 93 si-mat (*q. v.*) pa-ni ‖ nāmaru; — Sn iv 69 the smoke of their fire pa-an šame-e rap-šu-ti u-šak-tim. See also pitū. — *b*) front {Vorderseite} = maxru; id ŠI, *del* 57 (60) see lānu, 2. — *a.* of space: front, head {Front, Spitze}. III 15 i 10 pa-an ummānātē-ja ul ad-gul; TP ii 75 pa-an qu-ra-di-ja aç-bat, I placed myself at the head of my warriors. The land Xarusa which lies pa-an Mu-us-ri (*i. e.* on the eastside of) TP v 91. Sn v 49 see mašku, *d* (*p* 608 *col* 1); Asb v 42 see nīru; manzaz pāni *cf* manzazu (*p* 562; Br 6368, 9201); II 36 *c-d* 8 ID-TUK = be-el pa-ni, Br 6637, together with ālik maxri & bēl ēmūqi, Sp II 265 *a* xxiii 11. II 62 *no* 2 *R* 74 GIŠ-ŠI-MA' = pa-an e-lip-pi, Br 9314. — With prepositions: used as a prepositional expression, ina, ana pān(i), or pān alone = *coram*; at the head of (§§ 9, 86; 81 *b*), before. ina pān (of the king) 83—1—18, 41 *R* 5 (Hr^L 378; AJSL xiv 11); K 233, 18 (i-na); 83—1—18, 3 *R* 10 (Hr^L 301; AJSL xv 141); K 504, 10 (Hr^L 157); K 528, 26 (Hr^L 269); K 5291, 6; K 542, 12 (Hr^L 192; AJSL xiv 13). I-na (*var* ina) pa-an (il) Sin (or Êa) IV[2] 31 *R* 4/5; 1: pa-nu [il Šamaš]; 14, 15 (end) i-na (& ina) pa-ni-ka li-ix-du (may welcome thee, KB vi, 1, 87); K 3351, 30. K 94, 24 i-na pa-ni-ja in my presence (Hr[L] 287); DT 67 *R* 11—12 (H 120) ina pa-ni-a (Br 3644; 3654; ZA ii 64, 9), written DIŠ ŠI-MU, H 75 *R* 6; see also Q[t] of naxazu. K 257 *O* 65—66 (H 128) ina pa-ni-ja, Br 4007. K 3351, 30 (before). Creat.-*frg* IV 39 ina pa-ni-šu, before him. T. A. (W-A 236 + 239 *a* + 234 + 237) 37 pa-a[-nu-u-te il-l]i-ku-ma, [i-na pa-ni]-ja la it-bu-u (BA iv 131—2). Ina pa-ni .... qibî, say in the presence of, K 1274 *R* 5. ina pân(i) paqadu (*q. v.*). Asb ii 122 ša .... ina pa-an abi bâni-šu u-šap-ri-ku, what he had done against his own father. ina pa-ni-ka K 468, 8 + *R* 10 i-na pa-ni-ja (Hr[L] 121); K 592, 6 (Hr[L] 305); Rm 282 *R* 3 (end) i-na pa-ni-ka; 6 (end) ina pa-ni-šu (KB vi, 1, 46—7). H 60, 14 ina pa-ni-šu at his disposal; K 10, 17 qaqqar ina pa-ni-šu-nu ru-u-qu, a long stretch of ground lay before them (Hr[L] 280). II 10 *b* 17 ina pa-ni-šu — ana pân. T. A. (Tel Hesy) 23 a-n]a pa-ni-ja, to me (OLZ ii *cols* 15, 16); *Adapa*-legend (T. A. Ber 240) *R* 10 a-na pa-ni (il) A-ni šar-ri. NE VI 171 a-na pâni (il) Šamaš; 172 ana pa-an (il) Šamaš. K 615, 12 a-na pa-ni-ni (Hr[L] 258; PSBA xxiii *no* 2); K 831, 6—7 a-na pa-ni-ja ul il-lik-ku (Hr[L] 214), they did not come to me. K 13, 38 ana pa-ni-šu-nu a-šap-par, I will send to them; + 39 kî .... ana pa-ni-šu-nu it-tal-ka (Hr[L] 281). IV[2] 45 *no* 3, 13—14 man-ma ma-la a-na pa-ni-ku-nu i-ma-aq-qu-ta, (= K 647; Hr[L] 210). — ina pân (KB iv 110 *no* iii 6 *etc.*) according to Oppert, ZA xiii 249 = claim of *Z* against *A* {Forderung des *Z* an *A*}. — lapân before {vor} § 81 *b*; D[H] 21; D[Pr] 132 *rm* 1; ZDMG 40, 739; Asb x 11 see siximnaštu; vii 70 ša la-pa-an (iç) kakkê (il) Ašur u (ilat) Ištar ... in-nab-tu; see also iv 25; Esh i 15. Asb iv 59 see niksu, *b*. Sarg *Ann* 300; I 43, 22. Sn v 14 see xattu (*p* 347 *col* 1); III 15 iv 26 la-pa-an (iç) kakkê-ja (ipparšidu) = ša ul-tu la-pa-an (iç) kakkê-ja ip-par-ši-du. K 890 *O* 11 (+ 3) see kalû 5, where read tuk-tal-li. Knudtzon 130, 7 + *R* 11: la-pa-an. ZA iii 366, 5 la-pa-ni. KB ii 246, 82 la-pa-an da-a-ki Te-um-man; *cf* K 528, 14, 15 (= for the purpose of) see dâku, *p* 244 *col* 1, bel. la-pa-ni Beh 9, 16 *etc.*, in Achaemenian inscriptions (Bezold, *Diss*, 26 *rm* 2) with naçaru = protect against; see also nakaru (Q[t]), rebel against. Bu 88—5—12, 343, 8 la-pa-an *M*, before *M*. (ZA iii 228; KB iv 168). Nabd 245, 2: 11 minas of silver ša la-pân X .... na-ša-a; usually written la-ŠI (= pân) in *c. t.* (T[O] 89, 90); la-pa-ni, Nabd 312, 4; 702, 4; 708, 7; KB iv 316, 11; Nabd 411, 5 ša la-p(b)an-na-ni; in *c. t.* ina pân = ina qâti. T. A. (Ber) 229 *R* 7 la-pa-na = "antea". — ištu pân kakkêa dannûti e-li Anp iii 45 (ii 78); 18 ištu pa-an; ii 7; K 890, 22 ištu pa-an xa-bi-ri-ja. Also pân, alone; see especially KB iv 108 *foll* = *coram*, mostly interchanging with ina pân. Asb ii 116 pa-an (*var* DA) amêl nakri-šu his body shall be thrown. K 2619, 17 ... pa-an um-ma-ni, *etc.* (KB vi, 1, 60—1; & *rm* 3 × BA ii 427—8). K 519 *R* 18 šumma pa-an šarri maxir, if it be acceptable to the king (Hr[L] 108); K 18, 32. K 552, 10 [ša] pa-ni *A* šarri (Hr[L] 255); K 4931 *R* 7—8 ub-lim pa-ni-ja (H 117); Smith, *Asurb*, 126, 73 see napaxu, 27 (before her); II 66 *no* 2, 15 (end) may this kisallu lim-ma-xir pânu-uk-ki, be pleasing unto thee. K 4574 *R* 16 pa-an ar-ki; IV[2] 20 *no* 1 *O* 3—4 pa-ni u ar-ku; V 65 *a* 31 im-nu u šu-me-lu pa-ni u ar-ku; Esh *Sendsch*, *R* 14 a wild wolf pa-nu-uš-šu er-um-ma. K 2660 (III 38 *no* 2) *R* 14 pa-nu-uš-šu at-ta-çi. Sn iii 74 pa-nu-uš-šu-un (= ana pâni-šun) aç-bat, I marched against them. KB ii 256, 52 u-qa-'-u pa-an ši-kin ṭe(-e)-me-ja; P. N. Nabû-a-lik-pâni-ja, AV 5709. — Tigl. Pil. I uses eli ša pa-an, *e. g.* TP vi 35; vii 29; Anp has ša ina pa-an ii 133 *etc.* See also naparšudu (*p-r-š-d*), palaxu, and paraku. — *β.* of time {zeitlich} *n.* beginning {Anfang} in the phrase pân šatti = spring, springtime {Frühjahr, Frühling} Haupt. (Hebr. vii 67; Muss-Arnolt, *Babyl. Months*, 2). Sn v 43 ki-ma ti-bu-ut a-ri-bi ma-'-di ša pa-an šat-ti; III 13 *no* 3,

26. Perh. ina pa-an çal-tim-ma K 3364 *O* 13. — 2. former time, former(ly) {Vorzeit, frühere Zeit}. ZA iii 317, 83 eli ša ū-mu pa-ni above that of former days. I 35 *no* 3, 24 šar pa-ni, a former king {ein früherer König} KB i 188; ZA ii 388. V 55, 48 ina šarri pa-na. TP vi 35 tax and tribute eli ša pa-na uttir, I increased more than before; I 69 *c* 35 (pa-ni). Scheil, *Notes d'épigr.*, *no* xxxv 5 e-li ša pa-na u-ya-at-te-ir (*Rec.Trav.*, xx). I 65 *b* 35 eli ša pa-nim udaxxid (*q. v.*) pāni also = ūm, ū-me pa-ni, more than before, Winckler, *Sargon*, Texts ii *no* 55; Sn i 78; Asb i 115 (pa-ni); ki pa-na, T. A. (Ber) 71, 83 = *sicut antea.* ul-tu ū-me pa-ni (or -na), of old {von Alters her} NE 47, 43; 19, 35; Esh ii 14; III 15 *c* 7; K 891 *O* 10 ul-tu ū-um pa-ni. II 32 *a-b* 5 ūmu pa-ni; I 34, 47; K 576 *R* 5 ul-tu pa-an zi-i-qi (Hr^L 110; AJSL xv 141); ul-tu pa-ni Nabd i 89; ii 29 (KB iii, 2, 84—5); ul-tum pa-na T. A. (Ber) 3, 6; 7, 37; also ina pa-na (& -an) formerly (§ 78). IV^2 39 *b* 2 (the temple) ... ša i-na pa-nu .... ep-šu, which had been built long ago. *del* 182 (202) i-na pa-na (formerly: P.-N. was a human being) 183 (203) e-nin-na-ma, but now! Anp ii 133 çalam Ninib šu-a-tum ša ina pa-an la-a bašu-u .... ab-ni; see also pa-na[-ma] KB ii 116 (Sn *Bav*) 13. Neb vii 9 pa-na-ma ul-tu ū-mu ul-lu-ti (AV 6982) .... a-di, formerly, many days ago .... until.

Notice especially ālik pāni predecessors (= ālik maxri) used *a*) locally {dem Orte nach}. Creat.-*frg* III 39 a-li-kut (97: ku-ut) max-ri pa-an um-ma-ni; IV 105 Tiāmat a-lik pa-ni; Anp *Mo*, *O* 4 the great gods a-li-ku-ut pān ummānātē-ja; II 65 *b* 13 a-lik pa-an ummānātē-šu; Anp iii 20. KB ii 38, 33 (Lay 33) the ēkallu ša Ašurnaçirpal rubū a-lik pa-ni-ja ina pa-nu e-pu-šu; Anp ii 26 + 50; 27, 28; a-lik pāni-ja, Šalm, *Mon*, *O* 44; *R* 70. V 30 *e-f* 8 KAL-GA-VII = a-lik pa-na, Br 6210, preceded by muq-tab-lu. II 30 *h* 72 a-lik pa-ni, id ŠI-DU, II 31 *c* 52, Br 4928. — *b*) of rank: headship, leader(ship) {Führer, Leiter} § 73. ālik pānūtu. Sarg *Ann* 297 a-li-kut pa-ni mu-'i-ru-ut māti. K 312 (S. A. Smith, *Asurb*, ii 49) 11, a-na a-lik pa-nu-ti (Hr^L 289). — *c*) of time {der Zeit nach} Sarg *Ann* 303 šarrāni a-li-kut pa-ni-ja; *Khors* 152 šarrāni a-lik pa-ni-ja (*Ann* 374). Anp i 102 Šalmaneser, the great, a-lik pāni-ja (*var* pa-ni-a); iii 132 a-lik pa-ni-a. Šalm, *Mon*, *R* 37 Tiglathpileser abu rubu-u ālik pāni-ja. — II (+ V) 39 *a-b* 11 KA-KA = pa-a-tum: nu, Br 577; II 44 *a-b* 14 GUL = pa-a-nu(?) Br 8960. V 18 *c-d* 14—16 see xarašu (& Br 2454—6); II 47 *c-d* 50, 51 gi-gur-pa-nu; pa-nu-qu-b(p)u, names of plants, Br 7548. 80, 11—12, 9 *R* iii 13 u-mu-un | UMUN | pa-a-nu, Br 10281. — II 58 *b* 42 (!!) ra-ab(p)(-)pa-an ku-ux-bi (*col a* lost) Br 12895.

pānātu, properly *pl f* of pānu. AV 6936 front {Vorderseite} *a*) of space: front, head {Front, Spitze}. Anp iii 70; IV^2 61 *a* 23—4 see kalū, 5 *p* 382 & KB vi (1) 464. NE 67, 25 and deep are the waters of death ša pa-na-as-sa par-ku, which are placed in front of it (the crossing), KB vi (1) 216—7; *del* 227 (251) amēlu ša tal-li-ka pa-na-as-su, the man, in front of whom thou walkedst. Camb 187, 1 bītāte ša pa-na-at abulli ereb Šamši, houses located in front of the west-gate (ZA iv 128 *no* 9; Nabd 845, 6); KB iv 298—99 *no* iv 2. Šalm, *Ob*, 142 (160) I sent off the tur-ta-nu ... ina pa-na-at ummāni-ja (§ 120); 149, ina pa-na-at um-ma-ni-ja karāši-ja; 176 ina (!) pa-na-at ummāni-ja (Hilprecht, *Assyr.*, 27 *rm* × KB i 148). K 622 *O* 5 ina pa-na-at (amēl) xubtē xannūti (Hr^L 306). Merod.-Balad.-stone iv 33 (44) tap-tu-u (*var* -te-e) ša pa-na-at GIŠ-SAR (= kirrē). — *b*) of time: former time, formerly {Vorzeit, frühere Zeit, ehemals} Beh 3: eight of my ancestors ina pa-na-tu-u-a (before me) have ruled as kings. K 469, 20 Šupri'ā šubtu ina pa-na-tu (beforehand) uš-šešibu (Hr^L 138). — Peiser, *Vertr.*, 279: das was über seinem Einkommen ist: Überschuss, *ad* 91, 12 pa-na-at GIŠ-ŠUB-BA. — K 168, 22 ... ma-a pa-na-at ni-pi-eš an-nu-ti, Lehmann, ii 76—7; Strassm., *Stockh.* (VIII.) *Or. Congr.*, 23, 3 (end) zīrē ša ina pa-na-a-ta.

NOTE. — SI-ŠI-šu-nu maxaçu = šilimšunu maxaçu, see maxaçu, 1 & šilmu.

pānīu (> pānāiu) *f* pānitu, *adj* former, earlier {erster(er), früher} ⨯ arkīu, arkū. KB iii (1) 172, 34 (amēlu) pa-nu-u (ZA i 261); K 4609, 6 ir-tum pa-ni-tum ša amēlu ik-ka-lu (AV 6939, Br 9281). K 181 *O* 23 ma pa-ni-u ša aš-pur-an-ni (JAOS xx 250—1; PSBA '95, 222—3). Bu 89—4—26, 161, 2—3 e-gir-ti pa-ni-it-ti, of my former letter (Hr^{L} 485; AJSL xiii 209); III 51 (*no* 8) 3—6 an-nu-ti (of stars) pa-ni-u-ti ša ina pa-ni-ti in-namerūni. K 146, 4 sisē pa-ni-a-te ⨯ sisē arkiāte, (Hr^{L} 102) BA i 205. KB iv 22 (ii) 25 ši-bu-tum pa-nu-tum, the former elders. Sp II 265 *a* xxii 9 li-il-lu ma-ru pa-na-a i-al-lad. K 525 *R* 2 (end) (amēl) çābē pa-ni-te (Hr^{L} 252; BA ii 56). ša ina pa-ni-ti (viz. ētti) formerly III 51 (*no* 9) 15, 32; K 168, 39.

pānānu, formerly, earlier {ehemals, früher} T. A. (Ber) 11 *R* 2 ina ba-na-ni, in former times; 24, 64 ki-i ša pa-na-a-nu; 22, 32 el ša pa-na-a-nu; 24, 72 iš-tu pa-na-a-nu-um-ma; 45, 21 ša-ni-tu pa[-na-nu?] ša-ap-ra-ti; 71, 75 pa-na-nu; 87 *R* 22; 60, 24; Lo 18, 10 (BA iv 300); 19, 14; 10, 20 i-na pa-na-a-nu-um-ma; 41, 6 i-na pa-na-nu-um-ma (Ber 36, 9).

panū 1. turn, turn to? {zuwenden, sich zuwenden?} KNUDTZON, 2 *O* 4 pa-ni-šu i-pa[n-ni-e].

panū 2. (פנה) be first {erster sein}; but T^{C} 115 = panû 1. Nabd 356, 37 i-pi-en-ni i-šal-lim, er hat vorweg erhalten; Neb 193, 13 (end); KB iv 236—7 & *rm* † see bânu (*pp* 172, 173).

panītu, *pl* panāti = banītu (banû, 8) see *p* 177 *ad* T. A. (Lo) 8, 20; 9, 17.

pūnu (Br 3042) face, form, see būnu.

pingu. IV^{2} 18* *no* 3 *R* iv (7—)10 abnu ša pi-in-gu-šu xu-ra-ça ux-xu-zu, MEISSNER & ROST, 36, 73 Einfassung ‖ ix-zītu. Neb 451, 6 BAR ma-na çarpi ša pi-in-gu. See also MARTIN, *Textes Assyriens-Babyloniens*, *p* 7 *rm* 1 on CRAIG ii 1, 22 kīma ū-me u-nam-me-ra pi-in-gi-šu; *p*: an ornament.

panagu. ZA v 15 *ad* T. A. (Ber) 25 iii 61 (+ 57) p(b)u-un-nu-gu is enchased {ist eingefasst}.

pungulu = pugGulu see פגל.

pindū, *pl* pindē. III 65 *b* 9 when a new-born child pi-in-di-e ma-li, is covered with *p*.

panxa (?) K 4344 v 6 ni-šu pa-an-xa e-li-'- (*Rev. Sém.*, ix 148).

pinnanaru, pinnaru. II 29 (K 2022 iii) *c-d* 82—84 BIR-ṬAR (Br 8510); BIR-ṬAR-ṬAR (Br 8511) = pi-in-na-ru; DIM-ŠU-DUB-UR = *p* ru-si-e (Br 4256); II 35 *c-d* 36 XAR-ṬAR-ṬAR-NU (Br 8552) & K 240 *O* 25 EN-GI-ŠAX, both = pi-in-na-na-rum (*cf* xipindū), AV 7052—3.

panpanu. a chamber set apart for a god (or gods) in a temple, sanctuary {ein für eine Gottheit abgeschlossener Raum in einem Tempel, Götterkammer} § 61, 1*a*; AV 6941; BA i 282. II 33 *a-b* 65 .... U(*i. e.* ŠI+LU)-NA = pa-an[-pa-nu] in one group with suk[-ku] 64, du-u 66, & pa-rak-ku 67; Br 14356. II 35 *a-b* 15 pa-an-pa-an, between suk-ku & di-'-u, ‖ of pa-rak-ku; also see II 28 *a* 42; Z^{B} iii 69. — According to HOMMEL in HASTINGS, *Dictionary of the Bible*, i 216 *col* 2: one of the special divisions of the holy of holies.

panaqu. *pr* ipnuq. IV^{2} 30 *a* 12—14 mi-na-a ina na-aq-bi mi-na-a ša la ip-nu-qu (= NU-MU-DA-DI, Br 6690, 9523, which also = la tak-šu-da), perh. = panagu. BOISSIER, PSBA xxi 43: who does not rejoice; *ibid* 37—8 quotes as ג. K 3456 *O* 12 (end) bi-i-šu u-pa-na-aq. V 45 vi 15 tu-pa-an-naq.

pantū. T. A. (Ber) 93, 10 i-na pa-an-te-e ⟨ ba-aṭ-nu (-ma) *q. v.* (*p* 151 *col* 2) & KB v 284—5. KB vi (1) 562 = pāntū: das Vordere. HALÉVY, *Rev. Sém.*, vi 274 *foll*, note 3: ban-da in V 28 *a-b* 38 = bandū = child √בנד, which also occurs in T. A. (*loc. cit.*): panṭu an incorrect spelling for bandū & ‖ Phoenician *baṭnu* (= בטן) "ventre", bandū = "issu du ventre, enfant". ZA vi 156 translates: ich falle nieder mit Bauch und Rücken.

pēntu. coal {Kohle} > pēmtu √פחם. PINCHES, PSBA xiii 29 *rm*: fire; LOTZ, *Quaestiones*, 51; Z^{B} 76 *rm*; ZA i 65; HAUPT,

AJP viii 288. II 28 (*d*-)*e* 54 pi-]en-tum followed by la]-'a-bu, ni-me-rum, ṭi-ta-al-lum. II 51 *R* 17 (end) pi-en-ta (ZK ii 323); 82—8—16, 1 *R* 22 i-si pi-en-tum (Br 9710; HOMMEL, *Sum. Lesest.*, 98); IV² 32 *a* 30 (+*b* 15; 33 *c* 3 + 35) see bašalu (*p* 201 *col* 1). PEISER, *Vertr.*, xxiii 9 (is) kan-kan-na pi-en-tum; ZIMMERN, *Ritualtafeln*, 75—78, 27—8 nik-nakka p]i-en-ta tumalli-ma, the censer thou shalt fill with coals; pi-en-ta mullī-ma; *cf ibid*, 89—90, 18; 95, 22 + 25; 96, 9 pi-en-ti.

passu. PINCHES, JRAS '98, 444 name of a plant {Pflanzenname}.

pussū, *adj* 83, 1—18, 1335 iii 47 AL-TAR = pu-us-su-u, together with al-tar-ru, na-mu-ti & ra-ka-nu (*cf* 81, 11—13, 465) M^S 103 *col* 2.

pīsu. V 18 *a-b* 12 GIŠ(?)-KIL (= RIM)-MAR = pi-i-su, Br 14394; AV 7055. 82—5—22, 946, 17 GIŠ-LAGAB-MAR = pi-i-su *var* pi-i-zu mar-ri "enclosure", or body of the vehicle, PSBA 23, 202.

pissu *1.* V 26 *e-f* 21 [GIŠ . . .] 𒁹-AN-ZA = pi-is-su, Br 496; 29 *g-h* 73 . . . . .] AN-ZA = pi-is-su, Br 14465; AV 7058. √pasasu?

pissu *2.* JASTROW, HEBR. v 294 on Šalm, *Ob*, 121 a-na pi-is-si (māt) A-ma-da-a-a . . . attarad; KB i 142 te-is-si; D^K 30; SCHEIL, *Šalm*, 62—3 a-na me-is-si; see also STRECK, ZA xv 298 *rm* 1. ROST, *Untersuchungen*, 74: US-SI = usu, Grenzmark.

pisū. V 18 *a-b* 13, 14 . . . . 𒁹 PI-IR; . . . . 𒁹 PI-EL-LAL = pi-su-u, Br 14301—2; AV 7056; II 39 *c-d* 61 . . . . RU(? Br 14193 KAL)-KAL-LA = pi-su-u. — ℑ K 2020 *R* 11 pu-us-su-u = tak-(šum) . . . .

pusikku see pušikku.

pas(z, ç)k(q)ītu *cf* sellu.

pas(z, ç)karu some kind of bandage, band {eine gewisse Art Binde}. V 28 *g-h* 12, 13 see nargītu & xaziqātu. AV 6945. T. A. (Ber) 26 ii 12: I pa-as-ka-a-ru xurāçi.

pasallu. MEISSNER & ROST, 36 *no* 74 ixxit pa-sal-li u kaspi: Überzug aus ciseliertem Erz und Silber. Sp II 265 *a* xxiii 7 (ZA x 18) umallū pa-sal-lu (*var* la) ša xabbilu (*q. v.*). M & R refer to this also V 20 (*a*-)*b* 9—11 pu-us-su-lum (AV 7116; Br 6623, 6561, 6630), see buç-çulum.

pasil(l)u. *m* some sacrificial animal {ein bestimmtes Opfertier} I 65 *b* 27 see bitrū (*p* 207 *col* 2); POGNON, *Neb*, C vii 18 pa-si-lum & see zuluxxū; also *cf* bazillu, *p* 149 *col* 2.

p(b)is(š)lu, picture {Bildniss} šiptu pis]li pis-li qe-di-e qe-di-e. T^M iii 192; iv 1 (& *ibid* 138: פֶּסֶל).

pasamu. ℑ T. A. (Ber) 240 (*Adapa*-legend, KB vi, 1, 94) 14 an-n[i]-ka-a (il) Ê-a ša ša-me-e i-di-il pu-us[-su]-m[a li-i]l-[g]u-ni-šu, BA iv 128; 418.

Derr. napsamu, pasuttu & these 3:

pusmu. V 28 *c-d* 72 pu-us-mu = b(p)it a-xi, AV 1398; ZK ii 338 (iii) 4.

pusumtum. Sm 1702, 4 pu-su-um-tum.

pasuntu. IV² 15 *a* 61 (*add*) pa-su-un-ti išxuṭu (= pasuttu?).

pasanu. Beh 102 kī dib-bi an-nu-tu ta-pi-is-si-nu ana u-ki, but if thou doest conceal these words from the people, § 34 *a*; see napsanu.

pisannu (pisānu) *pl* pisannāti. §§ 25; 65, 12; AV 7054. a receptacle of clay, earthen or wooden jar, used for storing (valuable) things; reservoir; granary {Behältnis aus Thon; irdenes oder hölzernes Gefäss; Reservoir, *etc.*} D^{Par} 77 & 142; PSBA 5 Nov. '89, 39—40. V 42 *g-h* 34 IM (te-e) ŠIT = pi-sa-nu (Br 8439; IM = ṭīṭu, clay); *ibid* 18 *a-b* DUK (pi-sa-an) ŠIT = pi-sa-an[-nu] preceded by alallum; V 26 *a-b* 61 GIŠ (pi-sa-an) 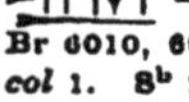 = pi-sa-an[-nu]. H 22, 443. Br 6010, 6015; see also M^S 10 *col* 2; 77 *col* 1. S^b 242 pi-sa-an | ŠIT | pi-sa-an-nu (Br 5978); *cf* S^c 145; S^a 3, 3—6, here perhaps receptacle for writing materials; ZA iii 22 amēl pisanni: scribe; see also nançabu. Also: cave, cavity {Höhlung} in general. JENSEN, KB iii (1) 57 *rm* & reference to AMIAUD, ZK i 247 *fol.* — V 47 *b* 14 šam-ma-xu ša ina unçi it-tar-ru-u ki-ma pi-sa-an-ni ir(?)-rak-su, perh. water pipe {Wasserröhre}. 81—11, 3, 11 *O* 13 (il) Šu-qa-mu-nu = Marduk ša pi-sa-an-nu (reservoir). S 31—52 *R* 10 pi-sa-an-nu, preceded by a-lal-lum. K 5418 iv 19 pi-sa-an-na-ti-ka še-im-ka kaspaka ...... šu-rib (KB vi, 1, 298—99; 556—7; LYON, *Sargon*, 68).

pisnuqiš see piznuqiš.

pasasu, pr ipsus smash, break, destroy; also remove, forgive (of sins) {brechen, austilgen; auch entfernen, vergeben (von Sünden)}. Br 614; D^{Pr} 54. SCHWALLY, ZDMG 53, 198 compares Hebr (cease). Asb iv 38 see kaçaru, 2, *p* 428 *col* 1 where read pa-si-su instead of *mu*-pa-si-su. 88—5—12, 86 viii pa-si-su e-piš-ti. IV^{2} 57 *b* 7 the herbs *etc*. lip-su-su lumnu-u-a (K^{M} 12, 76; $Z^{Š}$ iv 50; T^{M} *pp* 123, 124). IV^{2} 8 *a* 12 še-rit-su ...... lupa-as-sa-šu (see paṭaru), JENSEN, *Diss*, 88; $Z^{Š}$ v/vi 186; *ibid* iv 57 lu pa-sa-aššu (= 3 *pl* pm). K 2866, 64 ina ū-mi an-ni-e ..... lu-u pa-as-sa-nik-ka, T^{M} 124; $Z^{Š}$ viii 30, 32, 38, 6[5]. II 129, 18 ša ed-lu muttallum pa-si-sat pi-šu ana-ku, Br 10838. V 42 *a-b* 56 BAR pa-sa-su (& xa-sa-su) Br 1770.

ℑ = ℚ IV^{2} 12 *R* 21—22 whosoever bu-un-na(-an)-ni-e narkabti šu-a-ti u-pa-as-sa-su-ma (= KI-EB-ZI-IR-RI-E-A, Br 614); 52 *a* 20 the gods li-pa-as-si-su li[-paṭ-ṭi?]-ru li-šat-bu-u ma-mit-su (= $Z^{Š}$ ii 190). Nabd 697, 13 (+ 499; PEISER, KAS 88) duppi mārbānūtu ša ju-pa-as-si-is (he broke, smashed). Cyr 368, 6 tu-pa-as-si-si. H 51, 42 u-pa-si-is together with uš-xal-çi, AV 6942. KB iv 308—9 *no* viii 6 ri-ik-sa-a-ti-šu-nu u-pa-si-su (PEISER, *Vertr.*, *no* 83), they have broken their contracts. K^{M} 50, 22 pu-šur kiš-pi-ja pu-si-si xi-ṭa-ti[-ja]; 62, 10 mu-pa-si-su.

ℑ¹ K 6074 ii 15 up-ta-sis, ZA vii 30 broke {zerbrach}; $Z^{Š}$ iv 60 xi-ṭa-tu-šu lip-tas-si-sa, his sins may be blotted out.

pasusātu (?). IV^{2} 56 *col* i (*add*) = K 3377 + K 7087, 3 pa-su-sa-tum i-qab-bu-ši, GGA '98, 823.

paspasu. a bird {ein Vogel} AV 6946. II 37 *d-f* 10 [UZ?]-TUR-XU = pa-as-pa-su ‖ iç-çur rabi-i, Br 14056, see naxtu 1, nipçu. id also Sargon *Nimrud* 19 (end) KB ii 38—9. — D^{S} 105; AMIAUD, ZA iii 47 peacock, or pheasant; POGNON, *Wadi-Brissa*, 59, 60 compares Mish; also see WINCKLER, *Sargon*, *p* 222; BA ii 234; T^{C} 47 & *ibid* under UZ-TUR-XU, JENSEN, ZA vi 349 duck {Ente}.

pasaqu. K 8383, 3—5 dūru ša ēkalli ša im-qu-ta-a-ni nu-up-ta-si-iq, the wall of the palace which had caved in, we have repaired. BEZOLD, *Catal.*, 922; M^{S} 77 *col* 1.

pasqu, *var* to pašqu *q. v.*

pasaru, pussuru (AV 7117) see basaru & § 65, 24.

pusirrum, AV 7118; II 30 *no* 3, 37 pu (*i. e.*)-šir (bu, pu)-rum = ma-ar (māru).

pa-as-ru BE, ZIMMERN, *Ritualtafeln* 66 *O* 22, perh. for bašru = bišru (?).

pasuttu (> pasuntu > pasumtu?) II 22 *a-b* 22 GIŠ-SA-LAL = pa-su-ut-tum, Br 2751, 8159; AV 6944 ‖ še-e-tum. D 89 vi 51.

pappū see babbū (*p* 142 *col* 1).

(šam) **pi-pi.** II 42 *a-b* 38 see (šam) sunuš. Br 186, 13194; AV 7059; Br 5170 on II 42 *a-b* 37. See also 37 *d* 37—8 (šam)  -pi-pi, Br 13700; followed by U ŠA-MI-XA-XI-MEŠ = (šam) pi-pi ina māt Akkadī (Br 12134); Rm^{2} 139, 7 ina (šam) pi-pi u-ça-bit-si. Br 13193 reads II 43 *a* 50 (šam) pi-pi-nu-nu, AV 7059; *cf* II 41 *a* 69; 70 (šam) pi-pi-pi-šum (or -tak) Br 13196.

pipī. 82—3—23, 845, 11 a-na pi-pi-i ša amēlti. PINCHES, *Rec. Trav.*, xix, 107 (& JRAS '98, 444) perh. reduplication of pī (pū) thus: according to the chattering of a woman.

papāxu (§ 61, 1 *b*) *pl* papāxāni (& -āti § 70 *a*), AV 6949 shrine, sanctuary {Kammer, Gemach, speziell: Götterkammer, Tempelgemach} ‖ massaku (*p* 567 *col* 2). KB iii (2) 92, 13 pa-pa-xi šu-ba-at ilūti-šunu. I 65 *a* 29 pa-pa-xa šu-ba-at be-lu-ti-šu (ZA ii 183); *a* 35 Ēzida pa-pa-xa (il) Nabū ša kirib Ēsagila. Neb ii 43 Ē-KU-A pa-pa-xa Bēl ilāni Marduk; iii 25 pa-pa-xa bēlu-u-ti-šu (KB iii, 2, 46, 31); iii 48 dalāti bāb pa-pa-xa; 54, ta-al-la-ak-ti pa-pa-xa. Neb *Bors* i 17 pa-pa-xa bi-e-lu-ti-šu. V 65 *a* 25 pa-pa-xu u kummē (or ašrāti) a-na si-mat ilūtišu (+ 31, + 37 -xi, + *b* 10) 35 pa-pa-xu (il) Šamaš (+ 38 -xi; 39; *b* 7 + 20); IV^2 20 *no* 1, 19—20 bâb SU-ŠI (= šalummati) pa-pax be-lu-ti-šu. KB vi (1) 298—99, 10 i-na pa-pax (il) Nerigal. STRASSM., *Stockholm*, *no* 4, 3 bît pa-pa-xi (il) Šamaš; KB iv 206—7 *no* ii 4 i-na pa-pa-xi ili bêl mâxâzi-ja (= PEISER, *Vertr.*, *no* 38); 214—5, 9 pa-pa-xu (il) IB (= PEISER, KAS 18). KNUDTZON, 106 *R* 5 bît pa-pax (il) Marduk (*cf* *O* 5). V 33 iv 40—41; v 10—11 i-na pa-pa-xa-at (il) Marduk u (ilat) Çarpanîtum; vii 30—31 Agum ša pa-pa-xa-at (il) Marduk (*cf* v 38) e-pu-šu (AV 6949); *cf* vi 43 pa-pax (il) Marduk. Neb iii 44 pa-pa-xa-a-ti (il) Nabû within the temple of Êzida at Borsippa (ZA ii 186: a collective plural like "aedes"; see also 182—3; PEISER, KAS 116 *col* 1). Sn *Kui* 4, 6 i-na ba-rak-ki ša ki-rib bîti pa-pax meš-ni ap-ti. BA 265 papaxâni: kleine Gemächer. Pa-pa-xu-um in *c. t.* chamber, room in a house. Nabd 283, 8—10 šu-bat *pl* ša pa-pa-xu *pl* ša ilâni Sippar. — See MEISSNER & ROST, 26. HALÉVY, *Rech. crit.*, 177 √paxpaxu; KNUDTZON √פחה, whence also pixâtu.

(šam) **pa-pa-xat** (or -pa?) a plant {eine Pflanze}. II 41 *no* 3 *e* 15; Br 12748; equivalent broken off; according to AV 6952: (šam) a-rá-ru.

papallu(m) sprout, shoot; germ; twig {Spross, Sprössling; Keim; junges Reis} see nipxu; ‖ pirxu. AV 6950, 7522; MEISSNER & ROST, 41. Sn *Kui* 4, 38 nap-xar içê išîxûma u-çar-ri-šu pa-pa-al-lum, Lay 42, 46. Bu 88—5—12, 75 + 76 viii 25 lu-çar-ri-šu pa-pal-lu (BA iii 254). SCHEIL, *Rec. Trav.*, xvii 190 *no* 9 quotes fragm. S 4 (Constantinop.) 8 lirap-pišu papallum & explains (iç) papal karâni as "rejeton de vigne" > palpallum (JENSEN, 331) perh. √palû. II 44 *h* 79 pa(?)-pal-lum (*cf* libû, 2 *p* 469 *col* 2); 45 *d-e* 72 (iç) pa-pa-al karâni = pa[-pa-al-lum] Br 5632; 83, 1—18, 1332 ii 35 (mu-lu) MUL = pa-pal-lum.

pappaltu (?) II 40 *no* 2, 8 TAG-MU-ZU = ša libbi u-ru-la-ti-šu = pap (or kur?)-bal-tu ša bir-ki amêli. K 240 *O* 23 (II 40 *a-b* 58) [TAG]-BUR u-ru-la-ti-šu = pap-pal-tum ša UŠ (= ridi?) amêlûti.

papallatum (?) Nabd 258, 34: III pa-pal-la-tum 3 si-kal-li-tum *etc.*, an instrument.

puppulu see bubbulu.

papânu *1.* a plant {eine Pflanze} Br 11852, 12749; AV 6951, see xadilu (*p* 307 *col* 2).

papânu *2.* beating {Pochen}? K 2148 ii 12 (description of an idol) pa-pa-an libbi-ša a-gi-i i-ta-ad-du, ZA ix 118 (417) das Pochen (?) ihres Herzens bewegt die Meeresflut.

puppânu part of the body {ein Körperteil} K 9387 (BEZOLD, *Catalogue*, 1020) šumma amêlu ina (burki aššati) pu-up-pa-ni-šu ça-lil (M^8 77).

puppâniš. V 47 *a* 51 ki-i u-lil-tum an-na-bi-ik pu-up-pa-niš an-na-di; also see ZIMMERN, *Ritualtaf.*, 72—82 ii 7 ma-kalta ina pu-up-p[a-ni?].

pappasu. payment, remuneration, compensation for work done (BA i 494 > pas-pasu); provisions (PEISER, KAS 89—90); support (PEISER, *Vertr.*, 362, 28 & KB iv), mostly used in *c. t.* {Bezahlung, Entschädigung, Gehalt, Lohn für getane Arbeit; Unterhalt} perh. also ‖ sattukku, BA iii 486. II 60 *a* 47 (K 4334) such & such ina pap-pa-si ta-pat-tan. Dar 5, 8 pap-pa-su (amêl) MU-u-tu (see *p* 620 *col* 2). Camb 162, 1: 1 šiqil kaspi ina pap-pa-su (amêl) NI-ŠUR-u-tu; 281, 12: I ma-ši-xi ina pap-pa-su ša bît (ilat) Gu-la. See also T^C 116; K 61, 3 half an ophah of pa-pa-si (ZK ii 12—13); P. N. Pap-pa-su Nabd 842, 5.

(il) **Papsuk(k)al.** appears to be a general title for gods in a serving capacity. HOMMEL, VK 480, 494; JENSEN, 313 *rm* 2; AV 6953. III 68, 64 AN-PAP (pa-ap-su-kal) [cuneiform] (= LUX) | [cuneiform] | right column wanting; also II 65 *no* 1 *R* 27; II 50, 23. III 67 *c-d* 54; 55 AN-LUX = AN-PAP-LUX ša an-ti, Br 6171; 60 AN-GA-AN-GU (Br 6119; 6117 -DU) = (il) Papsukal ša še-ir-ti (*cf* K 4349; Br 13855), + 61 called (il) suk-kallu ša la-ma-ti (Br 6192); III 66 *col* 7, 32 il Papsukal ša Su-ti. V 44 *cf* 23 see Br 6225 & lamassu (*p* 489). IV^2 33, 45 Pap-suk-kal mâr šipri Ani u Ištar, JENSEN, 77: Nabû; also see JASTROW, *Religion*, 130; but also used of other gods. IV^2 31 *R* 1 see J^{w} 34, 35; KB vi (1) 86. D^{Pr} 111 *fol*. Šamš iv 24 Dūr-Pap-su-kal, name of a city.

p-p-r (?) T. A. (Lo) 44, 7—8 ia-nu šip(b)-ru pu-pu-rat (*cf* šibru) BA iv 305 & again, 413, 414. T^{M} v 101 has pa-pa-ru kiš-pu.

pu-pu-rum *cf* pusirrum.

pu-pa-tu read puxadtu & *cf* puxadū.

papatu (?) I 27 *a* 71 i-pa-pi-tu, perhaps mistake for i-pa-ši-tu?

papātum. K 4373 iii 13 pa-pa-a-tum preceded by iz-zi-bu-u & mu-çu-u, *q. v.*

pupittu see puluxtu (end).

pāçu. II 36 *h* 19 pa-a-çu ...... TAG, AV 6058.

pīçu. V 18 *a-b* 12 ....] KIL-MAR = pi-i-çu. V 47 *a* 47 see lu'ūtu, *p* 466 *cols* 1—2 (perh. √[illegible]?). — ℑ V 45 vi 13 tu-pa-a-ça.

pēçu see pi-e-çu.

peçu be white, clear {weiss, klar sein} Z^{B} 20 *rm* 1; 38; ZA ii 194, 195. KB vi (1) 284, 47 mūšāti lip-çu-u ugāri (at) night may the fields be white; 57, mūšāti ip-çu-u ugāri. — Camb 415, 1—3: III ma-ši-xi la-bi-ri XV $^{(i\varsigma)}$ kib-su la-bi-ri a-na pi-çu-u u ça-bat bat-qa ana B nadna, (ZA iv 157 *no* 4, 1: to polish). — Q^{t} *del* 205, 216 (226, 238) see kamanu (*p* 396 *col* 2, J^{I-X} 38); Jensen, KB vi (1) 247; 511: ist weiss geworden dein Röstbrod. — ℑ D 83 iii 77—81 ŠA(= LIB)-SUD-UD (Br 8056); ŠA-GIŠ-BA-AB-GUR (Br 8030), UM (or DUB, Br 3900); $^{(ba-bar)}$ UD (Br 7780; II 27, 580); UD-AG-A (Br 7849) = II 26 *e-f* 50 *foll* = pu-uç-çu-u ša GI-DUB-BA (*i. e.* qān duppi) AV 7120. Nabd 115, 1—3 mu-pa-çu-u (*cf* WZKM iv 125 *rm* 2).

piçū *f* piçītu, *adj* white {weiss} >< çalmu black {schwarz}; seldom paçū. AV 7084; Br 7788. A. H. 83, 1—18, 1162 (KB iv 272, 3) 1: X KU-DA pi-çu-u ša lu-bu-uš-tum; 81, 11—28, 33, 8 + 11 id = çubāt piçā (AJSL xv 75; also IV² 55 *a* 7 (end) šaxi 𒆳 (= piçi)-e; see also II 6 *c-d* 30. II 124, 23 (K 4095) a-ri-ib-šu pi-çu-um-ma his raven is white (Br 1660) >< ça-al-mu-um-ma, *ib.* II 45 *e-f* 53 see kiškanū (*p* 450 *col* 1). Šamš iii 31 ana šadi-e pi-çi e-lu-u (KB i 180—1), the white mountain (ZA xv 371; Hommel, *Gesch*, 625: der Elvend bei Hamadān; der 8 Monate im Jahre mit Schnee bedeckt ist). V 14 *a-b* 20 SEG-UD = pi-ça-a-tum (sc. šipātum) Br 7780; perhaps also *c-d* 8 (but?). IV² 8 iii 29 ši-pa-a-te pi-ça-a-te (H 90—1 ii 55, -ti; Z^{S} v/vi 151) id K^{M} 40, 6. T. A. (Ber) 9, 10: II sisē pi-xu-ti; Dar 387, 1 ŠE-BAR pi-çi-tum; II 39 *e-f* 14 $^{(ba-ab-bar)}$ UD = pi (or pa?)-çu-u. See also pīlu, for other instances. K 4239 *R* 1 DI-UD = (šikaru) pi-çu-u; *cf* Nabd 811, 4: III Qa šikaru pa-çu-u, also Cyr 384, 1. II 49 *no* 3, 29 MUL-UD = pi-çu[-u] name of a star, = II 51 *a-b* 68 (Jensen, 125 = Jupiter). II 26 *e-f* 48 $^{(si)}$ DAR = pi-çu-u, pi-lu-tum; 56 UD = pi-çu-u (H 27, 579; D 83 iii 74); 57 GUŠKIN-XI-ID = xu-rāçu pi-çu-u (Br 8267; D 83 iii 75); 58 UD$^{(ud-su)}$ID-KI = pi-çi(-)it-ki (Br 7942, 7945; AV 7060; ZK ii 416; D 83 iii 76). — Note especially xurāçu piçū, which, according to Peiser, *Vertr.*, pref. xix § 5; 258, 259 is >< ginū, 2 (see *p* 227 *col* 1). kaspu (*q. v.*) pi-çu-u ZA iii 216, 1 *etc.*; KB iv 294—5; Nabd 193, 13; T^{C} 116; Cyr 3, 14 ši-pir-tum pi-çi-tum; Nabd 726, 1: dul-lu piçu-u ša X išparu id-din(u); 826, 1.

NOTE. — 1. On paçū, piçū *cf* Boissier, RS vii 51—3: there are three meanings to the verb paçū (1) separate, deliver, free; (2) purify; (3) "blanchir", make white, bleach. With no (1) compare Syr [illegible] (Hebr [illegible]) & *cf* puça'ītu = l'affranchie; a freed slave and also II 29 *g* 74 pu-uç-çu[-tum] in a list of words denoting "fiancée" (kallātu), so also M^{S} 77; not = a woman in white (>< Jensen, WZKM vi 210), but rather = la jeune fille pure, la vierge; so also xurāçu piçū not shining, white gold, but pure gold.

2. Hommel, PSBA xix 79 § 23 piçū 'white', literally: egg-colored from biçu ([illegible]).

puça'ītu. Nabd 340, 5: X k(q?)al-lat-su pu-ça-'i-i-tum; see preceding note, 1.

$^{(amēl)}$ **puçāa** fuller {Tanner} BA i 512; Nabd 281, 5 $^{(amēl)}$ pu-ça-a-a; also Nabd 117, 5; 237, 15 $^{(amēl)}$ pu-uç-a-a; garments are sent "to be fulled" ana puçū, Nabd 115, 10 eçu a-na pu-çu-u; 492, 8 ia a-na pu-uç-çi; qaqqaru puçē fuller's earth or fuller's field also in *c. l.*, but K 2745 ii 15 qaq-qa-ru bu-çi-i (BA iii 208—9) = der Schlammboden. še'u paçī fuller's meal (CHEYNE, PSBA xxi 254—55). Neb 51, 7 b(p)ūd(t) pu-çi-i.

pūçu see bûçu (*p* 181 *col* 2) & read there: V 47 *b* 25 bu-çi[-iš]; also see II 60 *c* 19 mi-na-a-ti diš-pi e-ri pa-ni ana (?) bu-çi maš-la-ka (KB vi (1) 476). NE 72 (X) 31 .... ka-a-sa b(p)u-çu, KB vi (1) 427; 550: Höhlenvögel. BA i 512 reads puçū & translates dove {Taube}; BA iv 421 falcon {Falke} as D^{8} 113.

p(b)u-çi Rass 609 *R* b(p)u-çi (?) ZA vii 18; BA iii 215; Camb 290, 5 u pu-çu i-na i-ni-šu (?).

paçadu (?) Sp II 265 *a* xii 8 up-te-çi-id nišē (K 9290 ii) or up-te çi-it nišē?

paçillu *cf* pasillu.

puçammūtu (?) Cyr 318, 6 (amēl) pu-ça-am-mu-u-tu qa-tu-u ulammadsu, the complete *p*-art he shall teach him. Perh. (amēl) MU-u-tu (*p* 620 *col* 2) = pu-çammūtu.

puçinnu *cf* buçinnu (*p* 182 *col* 1); perhaps a der. of piçū, puççū.

puçununu (?) K 2852 + K 9662 iv Margin 3 .... ina (?) eš-šu-u-ti še-la-bu u pu-çu(?)-nu-nu, or pu-çu nu-nu (??).

paqu כ look, care for, heed, pay attention to, wait for something {schauen, blicken, genau acht haben auf, harren auf etwas} ܐܩܫ, BARTH, *Etym. Stud.*, 2; FRÄNKEL, BA iii 64. Z^{B} 60 *rm* 1; Fl^{N} 39; OPPERT, ZA iii 21. Sm *Asurb* 9, 6 (& 187 *f*) u-pa-qu zi-kir šaptija (KB ii 237); *cf* L^{4} ii 8 (3 *pl*); S. A. SMITH, *Asurb*, iii 77, 24 ša ana šārika ṭābi u-paq-qu-u. IV^{2} 17 *a* 19—20 ša kiš-šat ma-a-ti ra-biš u-paq-qu-ka, all the countries look intently upon thee, o Šamaš, Br 1869, 7278 (= LUB-BAR-AG); *cf* V 50 *a* 14 (end) u-paq-qa-ka (they behold thee, Br 8578); IV^{2} 19 *a* 41—42 a-na nu-ri-ka u-paq-qu (= DUG-GA-AG, Br 685) ilāni ra-būti ‖ inaṭṭalū (*q. v.*) pānika; see also ZA iii 349 bel. NE 8, 22 (KB vi, 1, 118; 571) ina pu-uk-ki (*var* -ku, 9; or aš-bu-uk-ki?) šu-ut-bu-u. Bu 89—4—26, 161 *R* 13—14 gab-bu um-ma-a-ni | u-pa-qu-ka (Hr^{L} 435; AJSL xiii 210). V 65 *a* 1 Nabonidus ša a-na (ana) (ṭe-me) ilāni pu-u-qu (pm), who heeds the (command of the) gods (LATRILLE, ZA i 28 + 32, wrong). II 62 *c-d* 30 see napaqu (Br 8576); II 25 *no* 4 (*add*) .... AK-A pu-uq-qu (AV 1410; Br 14221 ..... DA; 13999 ... AK-A); & u-taq-qu-u (√פקו?) Br 13998; K 4188 *c* 56—7.

כ¹ = כ Perhaps Sp II 265 *a* xii 10 up-te-iq ilu ..... (= K 9290 ii; ZA x 7); SCHEIL, *Nabd*, viii 25—7 šarru ša ..... ga-ga-da pu-tuk-ku-ma. V 63 *a* 4 Nabonidus ša a-na a[-mat?] ili u ištari ra-bi-iš pu-tuq-ku (ZA v 406 × KB iii 2, 114). IV^{2} 20 *no* 1, 5—6 ša ana ta-mar-ti-šu gag-da-a pu-tuq-qu (= AB-TA-BU-BU-LU which usually = šitē'u, Br 3581, 8571, 7584), who was always looking at the aim before him; 15—16 kul-lat-si-na pu-tuq-qa-šu (= XAR-RA-AG-A) ‖ ib-tar-ra-a, were all mindful of, Br 8571. Variant to I 49 i 6 reads šarru šax-tu ša ultu ū-me çi-ix-ri-šu be-lat-su-nu pu-tuq-qu, BA iii 218 *foll.* Neb iii 20 ga-ga-da-a bi-tu-ga-ak, I am always thinking of (AV 1320; see, above, *p* 205, footnote, end); thus a bye-form of putuq(q)ák (?); SMITH, *Asurb*, 187 *y*; see R. F. HARPER, AJSL xiv 5—6.

Another irregular formation is perhaps also V 35, 19 pu-ta-qu (Q^{t}? BA ii 232; 252—3; Z^{B} 60 *rm* 1, × KB iii, 2, pu-uš-qu), see pakū.

pāqu 2. V 23 *b-d* 28 pa-a-qu, one of the equivalents of TUR-TUR (Br 4105), preceded by enšu, dallu, *etc.*; AV 6962. Here perhaps K 890 *O* 2 šap-pu-ru paq-qi ki-i ba-tu-qu aš-li-ki, BA ii 634; K 2401 iii 7 ta-qab-bi-a ina libbi-ku-nu : ma-a Ištar pa-aq-tu ši-i (BA ii 628 *foll*: is powerless).

piqū, *adj* Sn iv 10 see nēribu, *b* (*p* 725 *col* 2, below) & HEBR. vii 63.

piqā, piqāma, *adv* K 8848, 3 pi-qa-ma; Bu 88—4—26, 165, 5 (M^{8} *pl* 15 + 32). II 16 *e-f* 42—44 (GA-NAM-GA) see balaṭu & mūtu, 2 Q *ps*, Br 6122. V 28 *e-f* 10 pi-qa-ma ‖ ki (or nim, GGA '98, 813—4)-ši-iš-tum, ZA ix 109. AV 7065. HOMMEL, VK 478: since, because, indeed; D^{Pr} 137 *rm* 2; JÄGER, BA ii 305 perh

---

pi-çu AV 7061 *ad* Anp I 92 read pi-rik. ∼ pi-çu-u AV 7062 *ad* TP viii 84 li-ip-çu read li-ib-riq. ∼ piçnuqiš see pixnuqiš. ∼ puçru, puçur see puzru.

√ב₂פק (pa'-qu-u), related to פקד (so also WINCKLER, *Forsch.*, i 392; HAGEN, BA ii 282); thus piqû, confidence, trusting, looking up to {zuversichtlicher Blick, Vertrauen}. REISNER, ZA ix 161, 19 ID-IS = a-kiç = pa-gu-u = pa-qu-u; paqû, whence piqâ, evidently {ersichtlich}; also *cf* BOISSIER, PSBA xxii 109, 110.

paqadu, pr ipqid (lapqid, BA ii 30), *ps* ipaqid (K[M] 58, 3 ta-pa-qid); *ip* piqid. AV 6959, Br 1122; T[C] 116. — 1) look after, take care of {in Obhut nehmen} in the sense of: *a*) keep, preserve {bewahren, aufbewahren} ‖ sanaqu, KB vi (1) 409, 410. Sn vi 29 see sanaqu Q *no* 5 (& § 65, 11); I 44, 56 (pa-qa-ad), + 66 ana ni-i-ri u pa-qa-du. Esh vi 25, 26 see kalâmu (*p* 388 *col* 2). K 3182 i 23 nišê *pl* mâtâte kul-lat-si-na ta-paq-qid (thou protectest), + 31; 24 (end) paq-da-ta, thou art a protector (GRAY, AJSL xvii 134). Cyr 247, 5 (immêr) lax-ra-tum a-na pa-ga-ad (ša?) ina pân Zêrûtu man-na-ta, BA iii 434 ist überwiesen worden. — *b*) oversee, inspect; rule, direct {überwachen, Acht haben auf, die Aufsicht führen über; regieren, leiten}. Neb iv 20 a righteous scepter a-na pa-ga-dam ka-al da-ad-mi; i 60 xa-ra-na i-šar-tu ta-pa-qid-su, the straight road thou leadest him. S[P] 158 + S[P] II 962 *O* 20 paqid (?) AT-GI-GI; especially in *ag.* guardian, ruling {Wächter, Leiter} *etc.* § 27; Br 1122; AV 6902 *ad* ⊕ 252 *R* 7. V 51 iii 27 (il) Marduk pa-qi-du rabu-u (Br 5977); K 4872 *R* iii 18. KB iv 102, 103 i 2 Marduk ... pa-qid eš-rit ilâni kališina; *Rec. Trav.* xx 205 *foll* i 18 (il) Êa ša pa-ki-du eš-ri-e-ti; V 43 *c-d* 27 (il) Nabû pa-qid kiš-šat (*q. v.*) šamê u erçitim; I 35 *no* 2, 3; 51 *no* 1 *a* 13; V 52 iv 18; KB iv 58 iii 14 (il) Nabû pa-qid šûpû .... V 44 *c-d* 37 P. N. Ninib-pa-ki-da-at (= SAG-LI-TAR-ZA-E-ME-EN; ZA ii 198 *rm* 3; v 2 *rm* 1). — *c*) look, after, take care of {Acht haben auf etwas}. NE XII vi 9 ša e-kim-ma-šu pa-qi-da la i-šu-u whose *e* has none that looks after it. (KB vi, 1, 264—5; BA i 70; J[W] 56; J[I-N] 43); NE 20 *a* 18—19 [ni......]-in-ni-ma ni-ip-qi-dak-ka šarru; [ta......m]a ta-pa-qid-da-na-ši šarru (KB vi, 1, 144—5); IV² 3 *a* 9—10 ša (ilat) Iš-tar pa-qi-da la i-šu-u (= LI-TAR-NU-TUK-A) ‖ la pâlix (*q. v.*) ilišu, § 131 *rm*, whosoever does not respect the goddess Ištar. T[M] iv 21 a-na êkimmu murtap-pi-du ša pa-qi-da la i-šu-u. T. A. (Lo) 43, 35 u li(m)-pa-qa-ad mâti-šu šarru, and let the king therefore take care of his country. Also perhaps V 63 *b* 21 (end) ap-qid (SCHEIL >< POGNON, *Wadi-Brissa*, 104; KB iii, 2, 118) & *b* 5 (beg). — *d*) muster, inspect {mustern, inspicieren}. KB vi (1) 106 (*Etana*-legend) 45 našru ip-qid šîra, the eagle inspected the meat, + 46 iš-ni-' ip-kid šîra. Esh vi 51 gimir ummânâti, *etc.* ... lu-up-qi-da ki-rib-ša (= III 16 vi 10). K[M] 40, 13 mamlu, gitmâlu, pa-ki-du gimir, *etc.*; perhaps 42, 12 ša paq-du (= פקד) pi .... — 2) give into custody, commit, intrust {in Obhut geben}. — *a*) intrust, commit something to the care of someone (ana), place one in charge of something or someone {jemandem (ana) etwas zur Bewahrung, Bewachung anvertrauen; anbefehlen}. Merod.-Bal.-stone i 35—6 who .... ši-bir-ru mu-šal-lim nišê ip-qid qa-tuš-šu (= ana qâti-šu) KB iii (1) 184, 185; BA ii 259, 267. Creat.-*frg* III 42 + 100 ip-qid-ma qa-tuš-šu, and she intrusted to him; Anp i 6 Ninib ... ša kip-pat šame-e erçitim qa-tuš-šu paq-du. Sm 1371 *O* 8 Šamaš šib-ṭa u purussâ qa-tuk-ka ip-qid (KB vi, 1, 266—7); K 3158 *O* 44 (IV² 54 *no* 1) pi-qid-su i-liš ba-ni-šu, commend him to his god, his begetter! IV² 4 *O* 44—45, 47—49 (Br 6322, 4419) a-na Šamaš ..... pi-qid-su (§ 98); Šamaš .... šalmûšu ana qâtâ damqâti ša ilišu lip-qid-su; *cf* IV² 19 *b* 18—19 pi-qid-su-ma. IV² 59 *no* 2 *b* (K 254) 26 a-na Marduk (êkal ilâni bît balâṭi) a-na damiq-tim a-na qâtâ (*var* qa-at) damqâti piq-dan-ni, ZK ii 315; see also K[M] 11, 29 (ti-pi-iq-da-ni). K 125, 12 bîd(t) ana mât Ku-mu-xa-a-a pa-aq-du (Hr[L] 196; PSBA xvii 236, 237); Sm 1034, 7 bît .... ša šarru bêli ip-qi-da-ni-ni, concerning the order of my lord regarding the house (BA i 614); V 33 vi 15—16 ṭa-a-bu u dam-qa | ap-ki-id; K 501, 14 šul-mi ba-la-ṭi itti šarri bēli-ja lip-qi-du (Hr^{L} 113); 83—1—18, 35 *O* 13—15 (Hr^{L} 427); 83—1—18, 223 *R* 8 (amēl) SAG lip-qi-du; SCHEIL, *Nabd*, v 19—20 their people ga-tu-u-a paq-da, are intrusted to my care; see also K^{M} 27, 10. T. A. (Ber) 97, 31 ji-ip-ki-id-ni i-na qāt P, and he has placed me under P. (Lo) 28, 9 the king my lord ip-ki-id-ni, has commissioned me; (Ber) 99, 21; 155, 31 for the king ip-ki-da-ni, appointed me; (Lo) 30, 7 I guard the king's city ša ip-ki-id i-na qa-ti-ja, which he intrusted to my hand; (Ber) 99, 28 let the king give his attention to his servant u li-ip-ki-id a-na (amēl) rābiçu-šu, and command his officer. V 65 *b* 51 ana ni-ki-i ma-as-xa-ti pa-qa-du; 81—7—1, 9 *R* 31; K 168, 41 pa-qi-di ina pa-an, *etc.* K 825, 8 (as for the *G*) ša ina pa-ni-ja paq-da-tu, whom thou hast intrusted to me. Camb 212, 4 such & such ... ina pān N ša bit niçirti pa-qa-da-tum (3 *f* pm); KB iv 298—99 (Neb 3) 3—4: II Minas of silver pu-qu-ud-du-u (= a deposite) ša ... ina pa-ni *N*. .... pa-qid; also ZA iii 137 *no* 13, 2. KB iv 316—17, 2 + 9 (end) in accordance with the decision of the king ša ana mux-xi paq-du šaṭ-ri (+ 11 + 13); STRASSM., *Stockholm* (VIII.) *Orient. Congr.*, *no* 24, 10 paq-du ša Ar-'-en-nu. WZKM iv 120; 307 on paqadu = deposite {deponiren}, & PSBA ix 292 *fol.* KB iv 318 *no* xii 12 pi-qid, are deposited. Neb 334, 13 the dates ša a-na X ma-na kaspi ki-sip u a-na paq-du ma-na-a-an, KB iv 196—7. II 27 *c-d* 62—64 ŠI-BIR (ku-rum) = pa-qa-du (H 30, 683; Br 9450); SAG-LI-TAR = *p* ša pi-qit-ti (Br 3542); ŠIT-KAK = *p* ša mi-nu-ti (Br 5268, 5977, 5988). — *b*) deliver, in general {übergeben, im allgemeinen}. Camb 347, 10—11 ša a-na Bēl-šu-nu ni-ip-ki(?)-du, which we have delivered to *B*. III 35 *a* 56 (= SMITH, *Asurb*, 285, 4) išāti ušaxxizma ip-ki-du ana AN-GIŠ-BAR (on which see JENSEN, *Diss*, 54, 55). T^{M} 4, 27 çalmāni-ja a-na pagri tap-qi-da (2*pl*) + 32 + 46; 19 (+ 20 + 22—25) tap-qi-da-in-ni, ye have delivered me. K 2867 *O* 17 uxalliqū napšatsu ip-ki-du-šu a-na erçit lā tārat; 29 ki-i tap-di-e Dibbar-ra tap-qid ša-lam-tu (amēl) mītūtē. Perh. *Rec. Trav.* xx 204, 8 nap-xar an-ni-u ip(?)-qid. II 9 *b* 35, 36 bīt u u-na-ti-šu ip-qi-is-su, he intrusts to his hands. — 3) Appoint somebody to or over (ana) something {jemanden zu (ana) etwas bestellen, einsetzen}. Asb i 118 those kings ma-la ap-qi-du, as many as I had appointed (+ 113 ap-qid-su-nu-ti); + ii 16 ašur abū bānīa .... a-na šarru-u-ti ip-qid (*var* ki)-du-uš (*var* -šu) § 58 *c*; + 18 a-na (ilu) X ap-qid; LEHMANN, *Šamaš*, P^{I} 15 Šamaššumukīn a-na šarru-u-tu Bābili ap-ki-id; *cf* V 62, 12 (ap-kid) & often in LEHMANN, *Šamaš*. Esh *Sendsch*, *R* 49. TP III *Ann* 226, Idibi'ilu ana (amēl) qipu-u-ti eli (mât) Mu-uç-ri ap-qid. ZA v 108 (bel) rabšaqqu lip-qi-du; K 168, 52 lip-qi-di; K 501, 14 lip-qi-du (3 *pl*); K 10 *R* 3 ša ...... ap-ki-du, whom I had appointed (Hr^{L} 280); K 547 *R* 10 šul-mu is-si-ka lip-qi-du, may they ordain prosperity with thee (Hr^{L} 62). II 9 *c-d* 7 (nu-du-nu-šu) ip-qi-su (he appointed him; or, delivered to him?) Br 4419. Perh. S^{c} 80 si-i | su-un-nu | pa[-qa-du] Br 4419; *cf* S^{b} 347. KNUDTZON, *no* 116, 5 li-ip-ki-su kīma ip-taq-du-uš; 43, 9 ik-[tap-d]u *ps* 116 *R* 12 i-pa-qi-du-šu. KNUDTZON, 240—1.

Q^{t} — *a*) give heed to {Acht haben auf etwas} § 89. ZA v 67, 17 anāku (*i. e.* Anp) ... pit-qu-du na-ram-ki, in a prayer to Ištar. Anp i 24 Anp who .... pit-qu-du (looks after). — *b*) appoint someone to something (ana) {jemanden zu etwas bestellen} Nabd Cyr. Chron. *R* 20 Gu-ba-ru pi-xu-šu (amēl) pixāti ina Ē-KI ip-te-qid (KB iii (2) 134—5; BA ii 222—3). KNUDTZON, 116 *O* 5 ip-taq-du-uš; 126 *R* 8 ip-te-iq-du-uš (*ps*). K 1066 *R* 5—6 a-na pa-ni šarri bēli-ja .... ip-te-qid-su (Hr^{L} 277; PSBA xxii 290—2); NR 22 (Ahuramazda) anāku (= me) ina muxxišina ana šarru-u-tu ip-te-qid[-an-ni] § 34 *a*. K 616 *R* 7 ap-ti-qid-su-nu (Hr^{L} 127).

ℑ appoint, order, *etc.* {einsetzen, beauftragen, *etc.*}. Asb i 58 šarrāni (amēl) qi-e-pa-a-ni ša .... u-pa-ki-du (3 *sg*) abū bānūa (+ 111). K 167 *R* 8 (amēl) MAŠ-MAŠ-MEŠ u-pa-ga-da (1 *sg*) dul-la-šu-nu e-pu-šu (Hr^L 1); K 3182 iii 16 everyone pu-uq-qu-du qa-tuk-ka, is subject to thy hand, AJSL xvii 140; K^M 53, 20 (end) lu-pa-qid. — deliver {übergeben} T^M ii 40 ša ana pagri pu-qu-du-in-ni (pm). — Šalm, *Bal*, vi 1 u-paq-qid (3 pr) bîta, SCHEIL, *Šalm*: he visited, frequented.

ℑ^t Beh 27 anā-ku up-te-ki-id, I ruled {ich regierte}.

ℑ2 be intrusted, commended to {anvertraut, (an)befohlen werden}. IV² 4 *O* 3—4 a-na qât damqâti ša ili-šu lip-pa-qid (= XE-EN-ŠI-IN-GE-GE, Br 6322); 8 *b* 48—9 ana qa-at dam-qa-a-ti ša ili-šu lip-pa-qid. IV² 28 *a* 23 lip-pa-qid-ma.

Š Perhaps V 33 v 44 lu-u-ša-ab(p)-qid(lil?) KB iii (1) 144.

Derr. piqittu, piqittûtu, pitqudu & these:

(amêl) **paqûdu.** Cyr 328, 2(+7) (amêl) pa-qu-du ša (al) Šax-ri-in, KB iv 282—3 the mayor {der Amtmann} AV 6963.

puqdatu *1.* II 35 *h* 35—36 pu-uq-da-tu; the synonym is deleted. Here perhaps 82—3—23, 607, 11—12 p(b)u-gu-da-ti in-na-aš-šu, *Rec. Trav.* xix 105—6 (Late Babylonian) or √בגד? Also Dar 439, 1 (+7+11).

piqdu. III 45 *no* 2, 7 pi-iq-da ša Bît-A-da a-na âli-šu u-na la pa-qa-di, administration {Verwaltung}.

puquddû, perh. deposit {Depositum}. KB iv 298 *no* i, 1: II ma-na kaspi pu-qu-ud-du-u ša *I-M* ... ina pa-ni *N* pa-qid. Also Neb 3, 1—4; 5, 2 *foll*; 8, 1: II ma-na kaspi pu-uq-du-u. III 69 *no* 2, 41 AN-ŠE-ELTEG-NI- .... ša pu-qud-di-e.

puqdatu *2.* see puquttu.

puqûdu (?) = puquttu? II 27 *c-d* 65 (H 38, 90) SI-LAL = pu-qud-du[-u?] Br 3467 (pu-qu-du) & *cf* KB vi (1) 577.

paqalu ℑ make strong, mighty, great {stark, gewaltig, gross machen}. V 64 *a* 25 pu-ug-gu-lu (pm) e-mu-ga-a-šu, powerful are his forces (§ 67, 4); Sm 2052 iii 14 du-un-nu-num = pu-uk-ku-lum (LATRILLE, ZK ii 339). BANKS, *Diss*, 24—26, 2 *nos* 8—10, 96 ša âli-ka (of thy city) e-mu-kan pu-ug-la-tu (*var.* pu-ug-gu-la-at) u-šal-pi-it. Perhaps S^c 1 *b* 29.

puqlu. strength {Stärke} II 16 *d* 23 pu-uq-li na-'-pi (see nâpu) AV 5926.

paqlu, *adj* strong, mighty {stark, mächtig}; used: of (sacrificial) animals {von (Opfer)-tieren} Neb, *Grot*, iii 9 GUD-IL-E-IL-E (= alpê ellûti) pa-aq-lu-ti; V 61 iv 30 gumaxxê paq-lu-ti; POGNON, Neb. C vii 16 gumaxxê pa-aq-lu-tim, POGNON, *Wadi-Brissa*, 32, 108. — *b*) of human beings: Sarg *Cyl* 24 the kings of Urarṭu and Musku i-da-an paq-la-a-te. — *c*) of trees {von Bäumen}. Neb ix 5 (iç) a-šu-xu pa-aq-lu-ti; *cf* V 63 *a* 39 (& ašuxê); ZA iii 297; V 65 *b* 8 (iç) erinu pa-aq-lu-tu; 81—7—1, 9 *l* 22 (KB iii, 2, 108—9). II 31 *no* 3, 29 (*cf* V 41 *a-b* 31) pa-aq-lum ‖ eš-qu (L^T 89). AV 6906. A ‖ is:

pungulu (= puggulu = puqqulu) IV² 57 *a* 22 Marduk gaš-ru pu-un-gu-lu; K^M 143, below.

p(b?)uq(g,k)lu. — *a*) some kind of irrigation-instrument {eine Bewässerungsmaschine} II 80 *e-f* 70 = pu-uq-lu, preceded by našpûtum (68), Br 1203. — *b*) IV² 22 *a* 27 .... pa-a-xi kîma pu-uq-li i-xaš-šal (*cf* 345 *col* 2, where also another passage), *l* 26 kîma it-ti-e, which is a ‖ of narṭabu. — *c*) V 26 *a-b* 10 GIŠ-KIL = pu-uq-lu in one group with mekkû (see *pp* 535—6) Br 10176; II 44 *a-b* 29.

puqulu (?) Nabd 558, 15: V ma-na pu-qu-lu.

paqamu see baqamu.

piqannu. II 38 *g-h* 28 .....]'U' = pi-qa-an-nu, in one group with ru-ub-çu (26), ka(=qa)-bu-u (27, fold, enclosure). Br 10249; AV 7066.

paqaru (Babylonian also ***bagaru***); pr ip-kur(kir?); ps ipaqqar (ibagar) & ipakir, dispute, claim, lay claim to another man's property {beanstanden, reklamieren, gerichtlich (zurück)fordern} AV 6960; PEISER, *Vertr.*, often; BA ii 152. STRASSM., *Warka*, (*Berl. Congr.* ii, 1) 57, 17 ip-ku-ur-ma; 78, 11 ip-ku-ru-u-ma. ZIMMERN, *Ritualtafeln*, 1—20, 51 (end) ta-pa-ki-ir (2*sg*). KB iv 22 ii 1—4 aššum (concerning) the garden of *S* which *A* has bought but which Ilu-ba-ni a-na çi-im-da-at-tu-uš ip-ku-ru-ur-ma (= ipqurû, Meissner, 128), *I* ..... claims again; 17 kirû *I* ip-ku-ur-ma; 30—1 *S* shall not come and lai-ba-ga-ru-ma, shall not claim. KB iv 13—14 (above) 14 *S* zit-tu-šu u-ul i-ba-ga-ar-ar-ma, shall not dispute his share. KB iii, 1, 156 *col* 3, 4 ša a-na Bêla-ni na-ad-nu šarru ip-qir-ma, he took back again. III 41 i 36 whosoever ..... i-pak-ki-ru u-šap-qa-ru (claims himself or has someone else claim for him) i-tab-ba-lu u-šat-ba-lu. K 196 i 33 that house pa-ki-ru (a claimant) iraš-ši, Pinches, *Texts*, 11.

ℑ K 433, 22 in-nu-u u-paq-qa-ru; see also KB iv 158 *col* 2, 1. V 61 iv 37 whosoever the gift of the king u-paq-qa-ru-ma | ana ša-nim-ma i-šar-ra-ku (BA i 291—2; Peiser, KAS 8 ii 1); 84, 2—11, 72 (end) tu-paq-qir-an-ni she demanded of me, Kohler-Peiser, ii 73—4. Neb 100, 6 mu(?)-paq-qir-ra-nu ‖ (amêl) paqirânu; KB iii (2) 46 *col* 1, 18 gu-gal-lum ga-ar-dam (קרד) mu-ba-ak-ki-ir ga-ar-ba-a-tim; also perh. 42, 8.

Š̀ see Q.

NOTE. — According to Feuchtwang, ZA vi 439 paqaru = sich eines Gutes entäussern, sich aus einem Privat = in ein Gemeingut verwandeln; paqirânu = officieller Gerichtsvollzieher = sixû.

paqâru, *n* KB iv 314—15, 14 û-mu pa-qa-ri ana mux-xi ši-iš-šu ša û-mu, am Tage der Zugrechtsklage betreffs des "Sechtels" der Tage. Peiser, *Vertr*, lxi 8 u la pa-qa-a-ru .... na-ši. Nabd 405, 12 pa-qa-ri e-li X u-šab-šu-u; 356, 27; Cyr 332, 15. T. A. (Ber) 12, 18 (amêl) pa-ga-ri-ka ul ja-ga-ar-ri-ib it-ti-šu-un, let not your customs officer come too near them; also 14 *R* 5. A ‖ is:

Paqru, *n* reclamation {Reklamation}. Meissner, 97: Weigerung. V 61 vi 14 all this the king has granted (i-rim) to his servant u ana paq-ri la rašo-e (as irrevocable property) iq-nu-uq-ma ana û-um ça-a-ti iddinna; also Merod.-Balad.-stone iv 52—53 (KB iii, 1, 190). DT 81 r 6 a-na ba(?)-ag-ri la i-šu, darf keine Ungültigkeitsklage entstehen. KB iv 88 *col* ii 34 aš-šu paq-ri la ra-šo-e, not to permit a reclamation; 40 iii 16 a-na ba-ag-ri-šu, if he puts in a reclamation. I 70 *a* 20 the bride-groom of the girl, presented with this property, a-na paq-ri la ra-še-e niš ilâni rabûti .... iskur. K 11571, 21 when somebody a slave i-ša-am-ma ba-ag-ri ir-ta-ši na-di-na-an-šu ba-ag-ri-šu i-ip-pa-il (the seller must make good the loss). Perhaps I 28 *b* 3 bît ša paq-ri (KB i 126 pag-).

paqir(r)ânu, claimant, plaintiff {Reklamant, Kläger} ✕ nabalkattânu, *q. v.* AV 6903; T^C 117; often in Peiser, *Vertr*. V 68 *no* 1, 39 (*no* 2, 36) pa-ki-ir-a-ni (pa-kir-a-nu; Lay 53, 27 -an) kaspa im-xuru a-di XII ta-a-an itanabbal; also KB iv 172 *no* 2, 22 (amêl) pa-qir-ra-nu; Neb 135, 31—2. Oppert, JA '80 xv 540 *rm* 8; ZK i 53 & 62; ZA i 303; iii 118, 17; Peiser, *ibid* 91; Peiser, KAS 116 *a*. Ball, PSBA xvi 168: the bargain-breaker. Pût (amêl) sixî (u) (amêl) pa-ki(r)-ra-nu, *etc.* see pûtu.

puqurrû, *n* claim {Reklamation} ZK i 53; Jensen, ZA i 67; § 65, 38. II 67 (K 4317) 5—6 KA-GAL(= IK)-LA = pu-gur-ru-u & ru-gu-um-mu-u, Br 611; followed by 7—9 puqurrû (& rugummû) ir-ta-ši; 10 *p* ip-pal; 11—12 KA-GAL-LA-BI = pu-qur-ru-šu & ru-gu-um-mu-šu.

paqâtum, *n* an instrument {ein Werkzeug}. II 22 *a-b* 19 GIŠ-SA-PAR-KAK = pa-qa-tum (Br 3092) ‖ mu-sax-xi-ip-tum (*p* 567 *col* 1), AV 6961; both adjectives belonging to še-e-tum net {Netz, Fallstrick}. *cf* BAR-KAK = çabîtu, gazelle. II 22 *e-f* 9 GI-MA-AN-SE (or SIM)-GAM-MA = pa-qa-tum (KB vi, 1, 521) = mu-sa[x-xi-ip-tum], and also 10, GI-MA-AN-SE-ŠU-IK = mi-ik-ku-u ‖ musaxxiptum. Br 2503, 2501 *ad* II 24 *a-b* 29.

puquttu (*i. e.* puqudtu) & **puqdatu,** 2; with or without determinative (šam) = thorns, thornbush {Dorngenist, Dorngestrüpp} AV 7122—3. II 41 *a-b* 54 *foll* mentions (šam) pu-qut-tu in *col b* as synonym of 54, (šam) si-kur-rat eqli; 55, (šam) si-kur eqli; 56, (šam) um-mat eqli (Br 3904); 57, (šam) um-mat (Br 3903); 58, (šam) xa-xe-in (Br 11845); 59, (šam) GIR-xa-ax (Br 322); 60, (šam) alap xa-ax (Br 9163); 61, (šam) pu-uq-da-tum (Br 13120); 62, (šam) GIŠ-KIL (Br 5720) which = pu-uq-lu in V 26 *a-b* 10; 63, (šam) pu-qut-tu = (šam) ša-mi çu-rat (?); also II 42 *a* 9 (šam) pu-qut-tu equivalent broken off (Br 13117); 35 *h* 35—6 p]u-uq-da-tu (AV 7123); 23 *e-f* 37, 38 pu-uq-da-tum (& ga-ab(p)-ga-b(p)u) ‖ pu-qu-ut-tum, in a list of words for thorns (= baltu, ašagu, *etc.*) ZA v 373. V 40 *e* 26 [(iç)] pu-qut-tu, Br 13118. III 43 iv 5 Adad ta-mi-ra-ti-šu li-mi-la-a pu-qut-ta, may fill his fields with thorns (BA ii 189); I 70 iv 13 pu-qut-tu li-iš-mu-ux, thorns may grow up luxuriously (JENSEN, ZA i 409 *foll* ✕ G § 70); III 41 ii 33 ki-mu Nisaba pu-qut-tu li-ix-nu-bi (KB iv 78—9); ZA iii 237 (above); ZK ii 31; AV 7122. Esh iii 28: 140 miles bāçū pu-qut-tu u (aban) pī ça-bi-ti, swamps filled with *p* & *p ç*; III 15 iv 12 pu-qut-tu; III 69, 81 pu-qut[-tum] mentioned as a weapon of gods.

piqqūti, a gardenplant (wild cucumbers?) {ein Gartengewächs} D^{H} 24; D^{Pr} 84 *rm* 2; ZK ii 424, bel.; ZA vi 207 *col* iv 8 pi-iq-qu-ti.

piqītu (?) 81—2—4, 263, 2 KUR-E-𒐉 (= ditto) = pi-qi-tu (AV 7067; Br 1188); *ibid* 7 same id as namçaru, Br 1192; *l* 1 same id as atabbu, in II 38 *a-b* 17, Br 1196; also same id as mūkaltu, rā-ṭu, *etc.*

piqitu (?) 81—7—27, 199, 11 ina muxxi pi-qi-te-ja bū-ili lu-sa-xi-ra-ni. Hr^{L} 382.

piqittu. appointment, command, post {Anstellung, Posten} AV 7068. Asb i 112 (these kings who at the approach of Tarqū) pi-qit-ta-šu-un u-maš-še-ru, had left their posts .... I brought them back, = u-tir-ma a-šar pi-qit-ti-šu-un ...... ap-qid-su-nu-ti. K 618, 6 (= V 53 *no* 3; Hr^{L} 9; BA i 224 *foll*) pi-qit-ti ša bīt ku-tal-li, the stable watch. K 666, 6 a-na (amēl) pi-qit-ti ša (ilat) Bēlit parçi (written PA-AN) Hr^{L} 12. With (amēl) K 583, 10 (Hr^{L} 5); K 482, 8 (Hr^{L} 178) a-na pi-qit-te ša (ilat) Bē-lit par-çi (+ *R* 1) BA i 621; *cf* K 601, 4 (-ti; = Hr^{L} 7; BA i 625). 83, 1—18, 1335 iv 26 su-lu | TAR | pi-qit-ti. Nabd 245, 2 (end) bēl pi-qit-tum; 558, 7 bēl pi-qi-it ša Ésagila (+ 19); 7, 6 bēl pi-qit-ti.

piqittūtu, the office of the (amēl) piqittu. KNUDTZON, 116, 4 ana pi-qit-tu-u-ti lipqisu; 126, 4 (amēl) bēl pi-qit-tu-tu (& 122 *O* 8 -ti) official {Beamter}.

pa-ru *1.* Asb i 24 read aš-ru (ZEHNPFUND ✕ KB ii 154, 155).

pa-ru *2.* V 28 *c-d* 91 (K 169) pa-ru = p(b)it(d)?a-xi, ZK ii 383. ZEHNPFUND, *Trans. VIII OC.*, Sem. Sec. B., 270—1 believes that V 28 *c-d* 90, 91 aš-xu (K 422 pa-xu) & aš-ru (K 422 pa-ru) are correct.

pāru 1. pr ipār seek {suchen}. Sn *Bell* 10 five days i-pa-ru-nim-ma ul innamir ašuršu, they sought but could not find its place. SMITH, *Senn*, 26, 7; ZA iii 59 & *rm* 1 comp. Arab فَارَ. ‖ of bu'u (*p* 186 *col* 1, bel); II 36 *no* 3 *O* 46 (Br 10751); Rm 343 *R* we find pa-a-ru in one group with par(?)-ru & bu-'-u; see also AV 6983. Against BARTH, *Etym. Stud.*, 22 see FRÄNKEL, BA iii 72.

pāru *2.* Sarg *Cyl* 33 Sarg. mu-ab-bit (māt) Kar-al-la ša pa-a-ri A-šur-li-' (amēl) bēl alāni-šu-nu il-lu-ri-iš u-si-mu (AV 6983); *Khors* 56 has: ma-šak Ašur-li' a-ku-uç-ma. KB ii 45 skin {Haut}? L^{S} 64 (bel), connected with פרא?, thus for par'u: the flayed skin? II 30 *e-f* 43 [BAR?] = pa-a-rum, prec. by naxaqu (Br 1782).

pāru *3.* ‖ ze-rum offspring, product {Frucht, Erzeugnis}. Sm 2052 ii 20 pa-a-ar = ze-rum; K 2020 *R* 23 pa-ar nu-ub-tu = dišpu.

parru *1.* (Br 691 bar-ru) in: ša ina a-ša-gi par-ru *etc.*, see mašaru, 1. & mašru.

parru *2.* see pāru, 1.

parū 1. cut, cut off, cut in, cut through {ab-, ein-, zerschneiden} § 108 note. Z^{B} 93; 104; LYON, *Sargon*, 64; K 2861 + S 389 i 43 a-na pa-ra-'-a li-e-mu, ZA iv 237. IV^{2} 22 *a* 29 .... ki-ma ki-e me-xi-e i-par-ra[-'], ‖ i-šal-laṭ (31) Br 373, 395. Asb iv 135 their heads I cut off šaptē-šu-nu ap-ru-', their tongues I cut out, KB ii 196—7; SMITH, *Asurb*, 247 K. K 41 *b* 18 nak-ri šu-u uk-ni-i ip-ru-'-ma

(= DA-AN-KUD) PINCHES, PSBA xvii 65 *foll*: this enemy has cut off my jewelry (& given it to his daughter). Sn v 60 (iç) tar-ta-xu pa-ri-' nap-ša-te; Sp II 265 *a* xxi 6 (end) pa-ra-a i-šid dīni (STRONG, PSBA xvii 141 *foll*: i-rid-di); perh. KB iii (2) 2, 28 ib-ba-ru-um, broke. IV² 22 *b* 19 ina ši-me-tan pu-ru-'u-ma = Creat.-*frg* IV 31. — ℑ = Q (intens) Creat.-*frg* IV 131 u-par-ri-'-ma uš-la-at da-mi-ša; Sn v 77 aq-ra-te nap-ša-te-šu-nu u-par-ri-' gu-'-iš (see also qû; IV² 8 iii 41); vi 4 see xuçannu, *p* 333 *col* 1. Asb ix 85 Ninib with his sharp arrow u-par-ri-'i napištim nakirēja. Sarg *Cyl* 22 mu-par-ri-' ar-ma-xi, *cf* AV 5522. ZA iv 8, 42 tu-par-ri xatta, thou spreadest terror (?). Z$^{\check{S}}$ v/vi 163 Marduk son of Eridu ru-bu-u ina qâtō-šu ellēti u-par-ri-' (= IV² 8 *b* 40).

Der. perhaps:

par'u *adj* cut through, burst, broken {zerschnitten, geborsten} H 87 i 64 (K 246) šênu labirtum me-si-ru (*q. v.*) pa-ar-'u (= EB-BA-GAB-A, Br 4487).

parû 2. II 27 *e-f* 5—6 .... ŠI-IL = pa-ru-u (Br 14350); .... UD-DU-NE = *p* ša pi-i (Br 7895, 14297); 7 KA-DAR-DAR = pu-u pur-ru-šu (or -u?) Br 3497; AV 6984, 7133. V 41 *d* 50 pa-ru-u between i-ta-ak-tu-mu & i-te-ik-lip-pu-u.

parû *3. m, pl* parē, mule {Maultier} ROST, 122. Chief id (IMÊR) [cuneiform] (§ 9, 244); *pl* same id + MEŠ, Sn i 24; v 30; *Kui* 1, 5; *Bell* 7; AV 6984. K 9287 ii 12 pa-ra-a a-qaç-ma tibnu u-ma-al-la. II 16 *b-c* 35 a-ga-la-ku[-ma] ana pa-re-e (id in *b*, Br 4091) ça-an-d[u-ku], heifer that I am, to the mule I am yoked, BA ii 285 *fol.* TP v 6 sisē pa-re-e a-ga-le *pl*; Šalm, *Mon*, *R* 51 sisē-šu (imēr) pa-re-šu a-ga-le; 63, 64 alpē-šu-nu | çi-ni-šu-nu sisē (imēr) pa-ri-e a-ga-li; Sarg *Khors* 29 sisē (imēr) pa-ri-e, *cf Ann* 45 *etc.* V 65 *b* 34 pa-ri-e qar-du-tu; TP III *Ann* 30 sisē-šu pa-ri-e-šu alpē-šu, *etc.*, for which II 67, 63 (KB ii 20—1) has IMÊR-NÊR-NUN-NA-MEŠ (KB ii 16 *rm* 3), called the çim-da-at (iç) ni[-ri]; id also II 44 *e* 8 preceded by (imēr) KU-DIN *pl* see kudinu (374 *col* 1). IV² 55 *a* 11 (14, 16, 18, 20, 22) 4 pa-ri-e. ZA xvi 184 & *rm* 7: evidently a precious stone. — HAUPT, *And. Rev.*, Jl. '84, 97—8; *ad* D^{H} 65; D^{Pr} 114, 119, see BA i 114 *rm*; 319 bel. ZDMG 40, 734; PINCHES, JRAS *n. s.* xix 320; JENSEN, 109, 239.

parû 4. a plant {eine Pflanze} II 42 *a-b* 44 (šam) pa-ri-e = U-NA = (šam) ša(i)m-rum ša šadi-i.

parru 3. see laxru, *f* laxratu, *p* 479 *col* 1. PINCHES, again, in *Pal. Explor. Fund*, *Quart. Statement*, 1900, 265, 1 + 5 has (immēr) par-ra-tum *pl* = ewelambs; for the reading parratu is quoted Neb 326, 1 .... pa-ar-ra-a-ti; 5—6 pu-ut e-ṭe-ru pa-ra-a-ti na-ši, AV 6996. T^{C} 117.

(iç) **par-ru** (Br 5532), see for the present giš-parru (*p* 233 *col* 2); others read isparru, √sparu = net, a form like ismaru.

(aban) **parru** a precious stone {ein Edelstein} Nabd 245, 12 (aban) par([cuneiform])-rum; see 321, 6; 719, 1; Neb 280, 1; Br 7799, 11810 *ad* V 30 *e-f* 69 TAG-ZA-ṬU par-rum = par-rum-u (?) AV 2829, 6997.

pûru 1. NE XII ii 1 i-rat-sa ki-i pu-ri šap-pa-ti [ul šad-da-at?]; ii 22 irat-sa ki pu-ur šik-ka-ti ul šad(?)-da-at(?), KB vi (1) 259 (526) whose breast is not like the bowl (Schale?) of a box; i 16 ša-man p(b)u-u-ri ṭa-a-ba la tap-pa-ši-i[ā] (= 27) KB vi (1) 523 (or from pûru wild young ox {Wildkalb?}) *cf* bûru 2, *p* 187 *col* 1; see also the id in ZIMMERN, *Ritualtafeln*, 41—48 i 18 (IV² 58 *c* 27) and *ibid* 147 *rm* k: Topf: wol eigentlich "Steintopf", wird dasselbe Wort sein wie pûru 'Stein' (REISNER, *Hymnen*, 31 *O* 11 *fol*; see JENSEN, *Lit. Centr. Bl.*, '96 *no* 50 *col* 1803) & wie pûru 'Loos' (BA iv 65; JENSEN in WILDEBOER, *Esther* ["Kurzer Hand-Commentar z. A. T."], *pp* 173, 174 = פּוּר of Esther 3, 7. See also JENSEN, ZA x 339—40 *rm*; KB iv 106—7 (Rm 2, 19) 26 (amēlu) ša-kin (al) Kal-xi ina šani-e pu-ri-šu, where in *rm* ** PEISER quotes Šalm, *Ob*, 174 pu-u[-ru] ag(k)-ru-ru; WINCKLER, *Forsch*, ii 3, 334 *fol*: "ich warf das Los" [but *cf* KAT³ 518]. JOHNS, *Expositor*, August, 1896, 152—4, translates: "in his second term of office". Bēldānan was eponym in B. C. 744, and, again, in B. C. 734. Nabd 787, 7 ašar pu-u-ru, nach dem

Lose. — II 29 *no* 4, *c-d* 63 (pu-rum) (KB vi, 1, 363); IV² 10, 1 *R* 17 kīma pu-ur xi-me-ti liš-tak-lil; & see Z^Š vii 90/92 ki-ma pu-ri (*var* -ur) šik-ka-ti lim-te-is-si; ki-ma pu-ri xi-me-ti liš-taq-qir. II 28 *a-b* 27 pu-u-rum a ‖ of pa-aš-šu-ru (KB vi (1) 408); S^c 119 bu-ur BUR ' ab-nu : p[u-u-ru].

pūru *2.* So JENSEN, KB vi (1) 363 and others for būru = young wild ox {Wildkalb} on account of pīru = p(b)ûru. See būru, 3 (*p* 187) where in NOTE, add: "On Pūr-sin see also LEHMANN, ZA x 84 *foll*". *Cf* II 29 *no* 4, *c-d* 62 (A-MAR); KB vi (1) 40, 28. 81—11—3, 478, 8 LU maš(s)-gal-lum = pu-u-ru, PSBA '96, 252. *f* pūrtu see būrtu, 2 (*p* 195 *col* 2). AV* 54 *col* 1 quotes: 4 alpu pu-ra-tum šu-li-e-tum. Also see JENSEN, ZA x 248—9.

purru. *adv* purriš. DT 363 *O* 89 (hymn to Bēl-Marduk) ana dariš šur-qa pur-riš gu-u da-pa-a [. . . .

pu-ru *3.* mentioned in WZKM iv 127 *rm* 2 with gi-dil & pītu (*q. v.*) is no doubt to be read gid-dil (see giddu).

purrū *adj* II 35 *c-d* 54 BAR-SI-EL-LAL (Br 3448): PA-AN (*i. e.* parakku) pur-ru-u; same id = nakaru (IV² 12, 32); preceded by parakku malū.

pir'u, shoot, offspring, progeny {Spross, Sprössling, Nachkommenschaft} AV 7071. id , S^b 298 = pi-ir-'u (297 = pilū) Br 8179; 81—6—7, 209, 29 (beg). id + ka, Z^Š viii 28. Lay 63 (Sn *Bell*) 13 Bēlibni pi-ir-'i Bābili, born in *B.* TP viii 79 pir-'i bēlūtišu lu(li)-bal-lu-u. I 70 *c* 12 li-xal-li-qu pir'i-šu, BA ii 141; III 41 *b* 38 his name, his seed, pi-ri-'i (KB iv 78: -ix)-šu na-an-nab-šu . . . . li-xal-li-qu; III 43 *c* 29; see also xēru & nan-nabu; LEHMANN, S¹ 32; KB iv 86 *col* 2, 16 id + šu; LEHMANN, L⁸ 23. V 34 *c* 47 ki-in-ni bi-ir-'i-ja ‖ uçur še-.-.-ri-ja, strengthen my family; *c* 8, the go.ldess X nāçirat nabištija (*q. v.*) mušallimat bi-er-'i-ja. KB iii (2) 50 *col* 3, 47 mu-ša-al-li-ma-at pi-ir-'i-ja, ZA ii 135 *O* 22; perh. KB iii (2) 4, 50 šāmtu bi-ir na-'-ru-tim (but *cf* JENSEN, ZA ix 127). IV² 30* *b* 7—8 (*no* 3 *R*) pi-ri-'i (= GIŠ-GUL-SAR, which also = ziqpu, *q. v.*) bal-ti (*cf p* 168 *col* 1) et-ti ina sikka-tim a-lul (-nar, *Rev. Sém.* vi 149 *fol*). IV² 12 *R* 32 (last two signs) pir'i-šu; 57 *b* 6 ina pāni-ka šu-mi u pi-ir-i (*var* pi-ir-'i, K^M 12, 75) li-šir, my name & my progeny. V 47 *b* 14 ki-ma pi-ir an-ni-ni (or ¹¹ NI-NI?) rak-su. — NÖLDEKE, ZDMG 40, 734 *ad* D^Pr 114; 129, √פרא jump, leap; JENSEN, in SCHULTHESS, 90 √פרע. BROWN-GESENIUS has pir'u, posterity (√פרה), *p* 826; & pir'u, sprout, progeny (√פרע), *p* 828.

NOTE. — 1. On Pir-napištim see napištu, NOTE 3; and add, JASTROW, *Religion*, *pp* 488; 507 *rm* 1. SCHEIL's fragment (KB vi, 1, 290) vii 21 reads ta-ar-ku-ul-li Pi-ir[-napištim]; see, however, JASTROW, *Independent* (New York), 17 Febr. '98, *p* 7 *col* 3. Also KAT³ 545 (Ut-napištim).

2 On the Ancient Babylonian name (ilu) Pi-ir-Ištar mār Pi-ir a-bu-um (MEISSNER, 17, 13) see LEHMANN, ZA x 278.

pīru *m* elephant {Elefant}; *pl* pīrāti (§ 70 *a*) & pīrāni; § 64 *rm* √פור be strong, power-ful (thus same stem as pūru, young wild ox); Aram *pīlā*; Arab فيل, SCHRADER, *Proc. Berl. Akad.*, '87, 502 *rm* 2; PINCHES, JRAS, *n. s.* xix 319 (*cf* bīru, 2). id usually AM-SI (§ 9, 53), TP III *Ann* 89; 154. So first HINCKS (1857), *cf* BA ii 546 *no* 207. D 88 iv 4 KA-AM-SI = šin-ni pi-ri, ivory {Elfenbein} see šinnu; II 46 *e-f* 4; Esh i 20, 21; Sn iii 36, 37 mašak pīri, šinni pīri; see KB iii (2) 4 *col* i 43 i-na šinni pīri; I 49 iv 12; Br 650. See also OPPERT, *Lit. Or. Phil.*, iii 85, 86; L^T 160 *foll*; *Lit. Centr. Bl*, '89, *col* 1586. xa-lam-ši šini biruxe, a picture, statue of ivory, in Mitanni-language borrowed from the Assyrian, ZA v 188 *fol.* T. A. Lo 4 + B 17, 20 (iç) usū šin bi-ri; B 13, 7: V erū II ši-in[-ni ša b]i-ri; also B 14, 8; B 6 *R* 7 içi šu ši-in-ni li-il-pu-tum, let wood be inlaid with ivory; B 218 *R* 11; 14 *O* 4; B 24 *R* 90 perh. mašak (?) bi-ru. — TP vi 72 AM-SI^pl bal-ṭu-te (*var* ti), 74; I 28 *a* 8 (KB i 124, 125), also *ibid* 7 AM-SI-^pl. NE VI 36 pi-i-ru (KB vi, 1, 168); WINCKLER, *Sargon*, Texts II *no* 55 mašak pīri. *pl* Šalm, *Ob*, iii (Lay 98) pi-ra-a-ti^pl men-tioned among the tribute of Muṣri (KB i 150, 151); HOMMEL, *Gesch*, 603 *rm* 1. TP vi 70: X AM-SI^pl b(p)u-xa-le dan-nu-te. D 81 (K 40) ii 56 TU-XAL-LA

= xa-an-dil(-)pi-ru, AV 7074. Perh. in STRASSM., *Stockholm* (VIII. O. C.), *no* 29, 3 + 10 (al) ka-par (? [cuneiform]) ša(-?)pi-ri.

parab, fivesixths {fünf-sechstel} AV 6972; ZDMG 27, 698; L^T 180; § 77. S^b 54 kin-gu-si-li [cuneiform], pa-rab, II 35, 847. See V 37 *a-c* 19, where <<< << *i. e.* 50 has the gloss gi-gu-sil-la; also line 20, where we have in *c* pa-ra-as : rab (parab?), perh. = paras (√parasu) Br 10043. HOMMEL, *Sum. Lesest.*, 31, 373; K 519, 10 (Hr^L 108).

purbāni. K 146 *R* 3—6 i-si-niš sisē | ga-mu-zu | lip-šu-xu pur-ba-a-ni (Hr^L 192); see burbāni; BA i 204, 207.

pargāniš *adv* (of pargānu?) THOMPSON: securely {in Sicherheit; gewiss}. Merod.-Balad.-stone iii 18 the old fields of the Babylonians which the countries' enemies had taken possession of, and which they ..... par-ga-niš bašo-e (KB iii 188: ik-kal), BA ii 268; 269 × MEISSNER & ROST, 106, *rm*. Asb vi 106 umām çēri māla bašū par-ga-niš u-šar-bi-ça ki-rib-šu-nu (RP^2 i 83 *rm* 2: in safety). III 58 *b* 29 būl (māt) Akkadē par-ga-niš ina çēri NA' (= irbi)-iç; *cf* PINCHES, *Texts*, *no* 1 (III 58 *no* 11) 13 *fol*: bu-lim (māt) Akkadū par-ga-niš i-na çēri i-rab-bi-çu. III 61 *b* 2, 16 pa-ar-ga-niš; see also K 92, 8 (= III 58 *no* 5; DT 148, 6; K 773, 6 (THOMPSON, *Reports*, *nos* 124, 129, 136 *O*). Sarg *Ann* 277 nagū šuátu eli ša maxri par-ga-niš u-šar-bi-iç (& I placed over it the governor of Gambul). POGNON, *Wadi-Brissa*, 179: pa-ar-ga-niš; 125, par-ga-niš.

paragu be bright, shine {hell sein, scheinen, leuchten} THOMPSON, *Reports* on Rm 194, 4 e-du-u ina pa-an (il) Šamaš pa-ri-iq (alone before the sun she [the moon] was brilliant).

paradu be impetuous, strong {ungestüm, stark sein} D^H 45 *rm* 1; AV 6966 perhaps also: be anxious. S^c 57 mu]-ud | MUD | pa-ra-du (Br 2279); *cf* 83—1—18, 1332 iii 36, followed by pirittu, *q. v.* 88—5—12, 101 i 4 his gods and his goddesses ip-ri-du-ma, BA iii 273; 88—5—12, 108 i 13 (BA iii 224). — $\mathfrak{Q}^t$ see $\mathfrak{I}^t$. — $\mathfrak{I}$ V 45 iv 1 tu-par-rad, followed by tu-par-rad-da (√פרדא?). D^{Pr} 94 *rm* 2: hasten {eilen}. K 41 *b* 10 qa-ti-šu ub-lam-ma u-par-ri-da-an-ni (PINCHES, PSBA xvii 65 *foll*: drove me forth). — $\mathfrak{I}^t$ KNUDTZON, 42, 7: up(*var* ip)-tar-ri-du, (a word from my mouth) is quickly gone forth {hat sich übereilt}; also 1 *R* 6: a word may have been passed over in haste. — $\dot{\mathfrak{S}}^t$ KB vi (1) 130—1, 30 ul-tap(b)-r(š)id(ṭ, t)k(q)i-is-su-š[u]ma.

Der. pirittu.

purīdu *1.* (AV 1415—16); V 31 *a-b* 43 bi-rit pi-ri-du = git-pu-ul (AV 7070) *noun.* S^a 203 [pa]-ap-xa-al PAP-XAL | pu-ri-du, Br 1156 (& pu-uš-qu), II 12, 118. V 16 *g-h* 79 ZA-XA-AŠ = pu-ri-du (80, = pu-uš-qu) = II 38 *h* 78 + *g* 79; II 41, 286 & 287; Br 11800. H 128 *O* 68 + 70 ina ni-iš i-ni-ja man-nu uç-çu ina pi-it pu-ri-di-ja man-nu ip-pa-raš-šid; *cf* IV^2 26 *a* 42 ina pi[-it?] pu-ri-di-ka man-nu ip-pa-ra-aš-šid. IV^2 60* C *O* 22 ina çi-bit ap-pi izammur elēla ina pi-it pu-ri-di uzarrab lallarēš (*q. v.*). IV^2 5 *b* 46—7 Nusku to Ea in the ap-si-i pu-ri-du (= PAP-XAL) il-lak (II 76, 16). Sp II 265 *a* xx 5 ša am-mi-e pu-ri-di-šu za-mar i-xal-liq. D^{Pr} 94 *fol* = פָּרִיד eilig, Eilbote; HOMMEL, *Säugethiere*, 113. *Del* 209 ki-ma aš-bu-ma ina bi-rit pu-ri-di-šu, sowie er auf seinem Hintern sitzt, KB vi, 1, 244—5; *ibid* 428 "Beine", & 508 reads also V 55, 21 u ša et-li qar-di pu(or qit?, ZK ii 411)-ri-da-šu it-tu-ra. SCHEIL, *Rec. Trav.*, xxii, note LIV 10 ki-ma ši-na-a-ti ina bi-ri-it pu [-ri]-di çi-i. II 37 *e-f* 47 bi-rit pu-ri-di (Br 3455) ‖ [git?]-pu-lu, in a group with kalītu (kidney), išku (testicle), biç-çuru (genitals), KB vi (1) 508: Schamgegend, Schamteile, oder penis? *i. e.* die Gegend zwischen den Beinen. To the same stem belongs:

purīdu *2.* a bird {ein Vogel}. II 37 *b-d* 8 .... BI-XU (*a-c* 58 .... IL-LUM-BI-XU) = ši(or pi?)-li-in-gu = pu-ri-du, Br 7932; AV 1416, 7049, 8222: PI-EL-LUM-GU-XU. On BARTH, *Etym. Studien*, see FRÄNKEL, BA iii 64.

פרדא. $\check{\mathfrak{S}}$ lighten up, make light, bright, shining {hell machen, erhellen}. K 2801 + K 221 + K 2669 *O* 6 (il) Šamaš muš-par-du-u; 8 (il) Marduk ..... ša šu-par-du-u u šu-šu-pu ba-šu-u it-ti-šu. I 35 *no* 2, 5 Nebo ša šu-par-du-u u šu-šu-pu bašû ittišu. Sn *Bell* 61, *Rass* 89 birêti u sûqâni (*q. v.*) uš-per-di ‖ unammir kîma ûmê. Anp i 8 Ninib, the light of heaven & earth, muš-par-du kirib apsê (who makes bright even the depths of the sea) AV 5625. Lhotzky, *Anp* 28; L^T 106. K 3182 iv 8 muš-par-du-u e-ṭu-tum muš-na-mir uk-li, thou who makest the darkness shine, who makest bright the deep darkness (AJSL XVII 143; ZA iv 12; BA iii 228, 6). — 2T be bright, shine; be merry, joyful {hell, heiter, fröhlich sein oder werden}. KB iii (2) 92, 50 ka-ba[-at]-ta ip-pa-ar-da. IV^2 60* C *R* 20 kabittašu ip-per-du (Z^B 44 *rm* 1); IV^2 31 *R* 10 ul-tu lib-ba-ša i-nu-ux-xu kab-[ta-]as-sa ip-pe-rid-du-u. TP ii 67 my warriors ša mit-xu-uç tap-di-e li-per-du I took along (§ 145, end). Perhaps NE VI 204 man-nu-ma ni-pi]-ir?-du[-u?]. III 61 *b* 10 ûmê ip-pi-rid-du-ma (62 *b* 5). — 2T' V 47 *b* 29 du-u-tum (V 40 *c-d* 34) um-mul-tum it-ta-per-di.

NOTE. — 3 perhaps K 2862 + K 9662, 10 mu-per-du-u qab-li .... ta-xa ši. V 45 iv 2 see 3 of paradu, above.

Derr. šiperdû, naperdû.

pardîsu preserve, park {Garten, Park} see Brown-Gesenius, 825 *col* 2. Cyr 212, 3 we have an (amêl) u-ra'-šá ša par-di-su, from Persian *pairideça*, ZA vi 290 *rm* 3. Lagarde, *Armen. Stud.*, 1878; ZDMG 32, 761; 36, 182.

purzigallu see burzigallu, *p* 190 *col* 2, & add: Halévy, *Rev. Sém.*, iii 91 comp. ברזא 'courroie'.

פרזח Š I 65 *b* 38 sattuk ilâni rabûti uš-pa-ar-zi-ix (Winckler: I increased; *cf* 39, u-ša-ti-ir). Perh comp. Arb *façaxa* 'appear in full glory'; *façuxa* 'be pure'?

parzillu. Iron {Eisen}. id AN-BAR; Br 1780; AV 1050, 6987; §§ 9, 60; 27; 61, 3. Sarg *Ann* 200 (mât) E-li-pu du-ri-ni ib-ba-ni par-zil-lu; *Khors* 180 gold, silver, *etc.* erû par-zil-lum (*Ann* 430); 142 par-zil-la; *Nimr* ii 8 (-li); ZA ii 128 *b* 5 in pa-ar-zi-il-lum e-lum-tim, in shining iron. See also birtu, 2; birîtu, 2 (*pp* 196, 197), nappaxu, *etc.* — id often in *c. t.*, Camb 18, 3 *foll* (see marru 1, *p* 584). TP vi 67 šu-ku-ut parzilli (Winckler, *Forsch*, ii 163). V 30 *a-b* 51, 52 BAR(?)-GAL (Br 1924) & UD (Br 7787) = bar-zi-lu in a group with ni-me-qu (48), kaspu (49), xurâçu (50), çar-pu (53), a-na[-ku] (54). — par-zal-li, AV 6986 *ad* II 62, 7 see ud-zal-li. — BA i 2 on Hebr form; also *Johns Hopk. Circ.*, 114 *p* 111 *b rm*. Hommel, ZDMG 45, 340 on etymology.

purzîtum. T. A. (Ber) 26 iii 13—14: I pur-zi-tum xurâçu X šiqlu i-na šuqulti-šu; 14 purzîtum kaspu *etc.* Keb 457, 15: III pur-si-tum.

paraxu germinate {keimen} 3 V 45 iv 3 ta-p(b)ar-rax. *Proc. Berl. Acad.* '88, 1353 quotes u-pa-ra-xa-an-ni. 82—9—18, 3454 + 4155 iv 11 p(b)ur-ru-xu ša ši-kari, GGA '98, 816.

Derr. Perh. naparaxtum, napraxatum (*q. v.*); & these 2:

pirxu, *c. st.* pirix. sprout, offspring, shoot {Spross, Sprössling, junger Keim}. See mâru (581 *col* 1, *med*). AV 7076, 3906. *Cf* Hebr פִּרְחָח, Gen 4 : 5 (Ball, *Gen*, *p* 50, SBOT); D^S 143; D^H 34 & *rm* 2. II 23 *O* 15—27 (*add*, K 4375) mentions pi-ir-xu as ‖ of pa-pa-al-lum (15), is-pu (16), ni-ip-rum (17), na-an-na-bu (18), [li?]-gi-mu-u (19), na(?li?)-gi-mu (20), ši-it-lum (21), šik-ka-tum (22), (qân) am-ma-lu (23), ši-ix-tum (24), a-lu-u (25), ba-aq-lum (26), e-lu-u & e-di-šum (Delitzsch). II 23 *e-f* 1—6 pi-ir-xu (in *f*) = la-a-xu (1), ba-ku-xu-u (2), eš-šum (3), na-du-šum (4), il-lu-rum (5), pi-ir-xu (6), Br 7531. Rm 76, 13 pir-xi lil-li-du (Hr^L 358); perh. K 2610 iv 3 la i-šam-mu-xa pi-ri[-ix]-šu, BA ii 428—9; KB vi (1) 66, 67. K 2148 ii 20 pag-ru pir(?)-xa kak-kabâni (meš) ma-li (ZA ix 118—9). III 43 *c* 29 see pir-'u. On Barth, *Etym. Stud.*, 22 see Fränkel, BA iii 12. — See also marru, 2.

piraxu (?). ZA x 208 *O* 20 GIR = pi-ra-xu.

purxu *1.*, **purxiš** see burxu *p* 191 *col* 1, where read I 28 *a* 26 and add: *b* 16; T. A. (Ber) 24 *R* 88 pu-ur-xi-iš.

purxu *2.* T. A. (Ber) 26 i 7: II ša pu-ur-xi xurâçu uxxuzu VI šiqlu xurâçu.

paraku 1. *pr* iprik, *ps* ipar(r)ik, *ip* pirik, separate, bar, bolt, shut off, lock {verriegeln, versperren, abschliessen} AV 6968; RÉJ x 304. IV² 18 *b* 55—56 ke-im aš-na-an elli-ti bâba ka-ma-a pirik[-ma]. Sm 1017 *O* ⁽ⁱˢ⁾ ka-na-ki bîti la ta-pa-ar-ri-ik, thou shalt not bolt. NE 67 (X, ii) 25 u bi-ra-a mê muti ša pa-na-as-sa par-ku, KB vi (1) 216—7. Asb iv 125 the city of *B-I* ša ki-ma dûri rabi-e pa-an Elamti par-ku, which like a great wall barred the way in front of Elam (KB ii 194/5).

𝔔^{1} Peiser, *Jurisp. Babyl. reliqu.*, 38 ta-ap-te-rik. K 524 *R* 21—22 (kî ..... ištên immêru) a-na sa-a-du ša ⁽ᵐâᵗ⁾ Elamti ip-te-ir-ku, if a single sheep (is separated from your flocks and) gets over to the Elamite pasture (?) Hr^{L} 282; Johnston, JAOS xix (2) 77. Perhaps KB vi (1) 154 *ad* NE IV *col* 2, 46 (end) ip-te-rik ki[-ib-su].

𝔍 III 43 *d* 27 Papsukal ba-ab-šu li-par-ri-ki, may bolt his doors. Asb iv 82 the corpses ša sûqâni pur-ru-ku (which blocked up the streets) malû rêbêti (KB ii 192), BA i 18 *no* 28. See also Winckler, ***Forsch***, i 473 *rm*. V 45 iv 6 tu-par-rak.

𝔑 perh. T^{M} vii *col* 4, 6 a-a ip]-pa-rak-kim-ma ša bâbi-ja ⁽ⁱˡ⁾ Nergal (BA iv 162); III 64 *a* 3 ip-pi-ri-ik; V 50 *a* 62—3 ip-par-ku-šu; K 3927 *R* 6 ip-par-ri-ku id same as in napraku, Br 1392.

Derr. napraku (possibly: parkannu, piriktu) and these 3:

parku *1.* *n* part of a lock, or bolt {Teil eines Türverschlusses, Riegel} ‖ markasu, *b* (*p* 588 *col* 2) & šulbû. AV 6988. Creat.-*frg* IV 139 iš-du-ud p(b)ar-ku, KB vi (1) 30/1; 344; 564/5: schob einen Riegel (davor). Perh. also K 655 *R* 4 ma-a par-ku ina eli abi-a | ak-ta-ra-ra (Hr^{L} 132), einen Hinterhalt gegen meinen Vater habe ich gelegt; & IV² 33* *a* 25 par-ka.

parku *2.* *adj f* pariktu barred, bolted, locked {verriegelt, versperrt}. III 43 *d* 30/31 the great gods xar(?)-ra-an-na pa-ri-ik-ta li-še-iç-bi-su, may cause him to take a barred road. Dar 267, 2 pa-ri-ik-tum (or *n*?) ûlênîtu.

pirku. *n.* — *a*) bolt {Riegel}. V 47 *a* 21 nap-ra-ku is explained by pi-ir-ku. — *b*) a stretch of land partitioned off; territory {ein abgeschlossenes Gebiet, Bereich}. II 67, 24 gišimmarê-šu ša pi-rik mâti-šu (Rost, 123; KB ii 14—15); TP III *Ann* 19; AV 7073. Anp i 91 ma'a-dûti ina pi-rik mâti-ja a-ku-çu maškêšunu (Peiser, ZA ii 448; KB i 66—7: im Gebiete (?) meines Landes). perh. S^{b} 2, 11 pi-ri-ik = ni-e-r[u]. See also AV 7077.

paraku 2. *pr* iprik, *ps* iparrik use force, display violence, compel, either with *acc* of object or ina pân = against; tyrannize {Gewalt verüben, zwingen} Jastrow, ZA ii 354 *foll* (✕ Lehmann, *ibid* 214 *foll*); Belser, BA ii 148. 83—1—18, 2 (Hr^{L} 391) *R* 12 pa-ri-ik-tu lip-ri-ku (see R. F. Harper, AJSL xv 189 *foll*; Martin, *Rec. Trav.*, xxiv 107, 108). I 27 *no* 2, 64—66 who ina pa-an | musarê⁽ᵖˡ⁾-ja man-ma ki-i la a-ma-ri u la ša-si-e i-pa-ar-i-ku (whosoever .... damages). IV² 16 *b* 3—4 še-id-du lim-nu ka-a-a-na ip-rik-ma (= SAG-BA-AN-GIG-BA). Br 4000 *ad* IV² 18 *b* 13—14. Perh. Zimmern, ***Rituall.***, 66 *O* 17 ⁽ᵏᵃʳᵖᵃᵗ⁾ kal-lu ša qi-ir-ši qâtâ [ ] ta-pa-ri-ik.

𝔖 = 𝔔 usually with ana pân, ina pân. T^{M} ii 8 ⁽ⁱˡ⁾ Nusku a-ri-ru mu-šap-rik za-a-a-ri (conqueror of the enemies); also see Sn i 7. Asb ii 121—122 ep-šit ⁽ˢᵃˡ⁾ limut-tim ša .... | ina pa-an abi bâni-šu u-šap-ri-ku (KB ii 176—77; BA i 14 *no* 8 פרך); KB ii 268—9, 101 [ep]-šit ina pân Te-um-man u-šap-ri-ku (I inflicted; = Sm *Asb* 179). TP viii 72—3 but whosoever plans something evil and a-na pa-an ⁽ᵃᵇᵃⁿ⁾ narê-ja u-šap-ra-ku, thus injures this my memorial slab. I 27 *no* 2, 44—5 pa-an kiššu-ti-ja šu-bat šarrû-ti-a la u-ša-pa-ra-ak. See also 82—7—4, 42 *O* 6 (PSBA xx 155 *foll*). Perhaps K 666 (Hr^{L} 12) *R* 15 ma-a šu-up-ru-ku (?) BA i 627.

𝔖𝔍 Perh. KB vi (1) 62—3, 3 a-bu-bu la uš-pa-[-rak?].

𝔑 H 75 *R* 5/6 u mimma ep-šit a-mo-lu-ti | ša ana pâni-ja ip-par-ri-ku šu-zi-ba-an-ni-ma, J^{K} 158 *rm* 1.

L⁴ ii 22 ul ip-pa-rik pa-rik[-tu] violence was not done.

ZT[in] K 2866, 33 thy sin .... the charm .... the evil upšašū of men, who a-na kūša a-na bīti-ka .... it-ta-nap-ri-ku (S. A. SMITH, *Miscellaneous Texts*, XVII, *p* 18, 3); also see ZS viii 29. III 61 *b* 16 antalū rixçu murçu mûtum .... maxar Sin it-ta-nap-ri-ku; 62 *b* 12. AV 5992. — Der.:

pariktu. violence, outrage, violent act {Gewalt, Vergewaltigung, Gewalttat}. Esh ii 47 whosoever the countries ina pa-ri-ik-te it-ba-lu-ma. III 15 *c* 23 ina pa-rik-ti. I 70 *c* 16—17 may Šamaš ina pa-rik-ti li-ix-xi-su, proceed against him with violence. Here belongs perh. also:

parku 2. SCHEIL, *Rec. Trav.*, xx 201 *no* 30 kakku (il) Ša-naš-ši-p(b)ar-ku.

(iç) **parakku** T. A. (Ber) 28 ii 20: V (iç) pa-ra-ak-ku xurāçu uxxuzu; also *ll* 21 + 63; (Ber) 25 ii 36. Probably of same stem as:

parakku (Sn: barakku), *pl* parakkē (& āni) § 65, 20; H 25, 520 ba-ra |  pa-rak-ku, S[b] 354; § 9, 255; Br 6878; AV 6969. — *a*) in general: dwelling place, room, chamber {im allgemeinen: Wohnraum, Gemach, Kammer}. Creat.-*frg* IV 1 id-du-šum-ma pa-rak ru-bu-tim, thereupon they (the gods his fathers) placed him (Marduk) into a royal chamber. K vi (1) 584, 17 la ba-nu-u iš-ti-ni-iš pa-ra-ak-ku (for the king). gi-mir pa-rak-ki (*i. e.* parakkē) ZA iv 13, 14. Sn *Kui* 4, 6 i-na ba-rak-ki ša ki-rib bīt pa-pax (pl)-ni ap-ti bi-ir-re u-pat-ta-a; 8: çu-lul ta-ra-a-ni ša ki-rib ba-rak-ka-ni eṭūšun ušaxlā. Lay 39, 28 ba-rak-ka-a-ni (see MEISSNER & ROST, 4; 26; § 73). 80—7—19, 126 see Nippur(u), BA iv 205. AV 3399 pa-ra-ki read gi-pa-ra-ki (PSBA xxiii 120 *foll*). II 35 *c-d* 53—55 BAR-A-GI-SI = (parakku) ma-lu-u; BAR-SI-EL-LAL = *p* pur-ru-u, BAR-SAG-GAR(= ŠA)-RA = *p* a-ši-ir-tum. — *b*) specifically: dwelling place of the gods, sanctuary, shrine (because of its being a separated room) {Göttergemach, Allerheiligstes}. PINCHES, *Texts*, 16 *O* 10 mu-ud-di-šu pa-rak-ki ‖ ba-ši-mu eš-ri-e-ti. V 62 *no* 2, 19 ša ilāni ra-būti a-ši-ib pa-ra-ak-ka (LEHMANN, ii 9). ZA v 59, 7 ina gi-mir ilāni *pl* a-šib pa-rak-ki. NE 24, 6 mu-šab ilāni pa-rak (il) Ir-ni-ni. *Rec. Trav.* xvii, *p* 33 pa-rak (XI-A = *pl*) ša Bēl Bēl apli. V 60 *c* 1 na-di-e parakkē. Asb iv 86 ina ši-pir i-šip-pu-ti BAR-MEŠ (= parakkē)-šu-nu (*i. e.* of the cities) ub-bi-ib (KB ii 192—3); vi 124 (the great goddess) u-šar-me-ši parak da-ra-a-ti; see I 49 *d* 26 parakkē-šu-nu u-šar-ma-a (the great gods); III 27 *b* 84; S 1089, 6 .... mu-ša]r-mu-u pa-rak da-ra-a-t[i], WINCKLER, *Forsch*, ii 515 *fol*; 81—6—7, 209, 21 u-še-ši-bu pa-rak-ka da-ra-a-ti, BA iii 260—3. I 69 *c* 32 (end); Neb v 14 DU-AZAG pa-ra-ak ši-ma-a-ti; *cf* I 67 *a* 33 (JENSEN, 86); Neb ii 55; iii 1 *fol*; iii 57 du-u BAR-BAR (= parakkē) & viii 37. IV² 54 *a* 49 xegalli xi-iç-ba pa-rak-ka-ka li-ša-ax-nin, Z[B] 90; ZA v 67, 19. V 51 *c* 34 ina pa-rak-ki rabūti ša šamē u erçitim ša-a-šu ix-xa-ax-xu-šu; 36 u-çu-ra-tu-ši-na (referring to parakku, thus = *f*). K 2606 *O* 24 Bēl i-xa-aṭ pa-rak-ki šame-e, BA ii 309 *fol*. II 33 *a-b* 67 (+ 28 *a* 44) UŠ-SA = pa-rak-ku, Br 14107; preceded by du[-u], pa-an[-pa-nu], suk[-ku]; II 35 *a-b* 14 see sukku; 15, 16 pa-an-pa-nu & di-'u = pa-rak-ku, Br 5650, 9559. — Also: dwelling place, royal chamber of a king {Königsgemach}. V 35, 28 nap-xar šarre a-ši-ib BAR *pl* (= parakkē) ša kališ kibrāte, the throne-occupants of all the lands (BA ii 212—3). I 7 *F* 10 gi-mir mal-ke a-šib pa-rak-ki. Sn i 12 eli gi-mir a-šib pa-rak-ki u-šar-ba-a (iç) kakkēa, and gave me victory over all the (priest?) kings. II 35 *c-d* 51, 52. BAR-KU-GAR-RA (Br 6910) & BAR-BAR-KIT-E-NE (Br 6906) = a-šib pa-rak-ki. — *c*) also = king (abbreviated from āšib parakki). II 31 *no* 3, 4 pa-rak-ku ‖ šar[-ru]; V 41 *a-b* 4; V 30 *a-b* 27 BAR-GAL-AN-NA = šarru.

NOTE. — BA i 282: √ perhaps paraku), thus = enclosed room; see also PRINCE, *Diss*, 82; HALÉVY, *Mélanges*, 187; *Journal of Phil.*, 13, 283; ROST, 123. ZA ii 182—4; D[H] 127; TIELE, ZA vii 80 *fol*. HOMMEL, PSBA xxi 115 √BARA (Sumerian); so also LEHMANN, i 121 *foll*; ii 47, 115; *Berl. Phil. W'sch.*, '91 no 25, *cols* 789 (and ✕ HAGEN, BA ii 233).

p(b)urk(q)u? *n* III 50 *no* 4, 21 (so & so many minas of silver and gold) ana pur-ki (ilat) Ištar a-ši-bat Ninâ[ki] išaka-an (KB iv 129: wird in die Casse der Ištar .... niedergelegen); also III 46 *no* 5, 24; 48 *no* 5, 18; KB iv 132 (K 321) *no* 1, 16: X ma-na kaspi I ma-na xu[râçi] ina pur-ki Ninib(p) a-šib (al) [Kal-xi] | išaka-an (see ZA xiii 268—9 on this text: Schatz des Gottes Ninib). K 482, 17 (Hr[L] 178 *R* 5) šarru .... ina pur-ki-e-šu li-in-tu-xu. IV² 61 *a* 60, thy son, thy grandson šarrû-tu ina pur-ki ša (il) Ninib u-pa-aš. 83—1—18, 14 (Hr[L] 406) *R* 14 šarru be-ili ina pur-ki-šu | li-in-tu-ux, AJSL xiii 211 (R. F. HARPER), on M[S] 25 *col* 2: reading burku & stating: Sicher ist es ein Körperteil. BA ii 21 (√ paraku: scheiden, trennen, wahren; thus: Verwahrung). V 27 *g-h* 64—66 U-GUG = el-pi-tum; U-GUG-A-BUR-RA, & U-A-GUG = el-pîtum me-e pur-ki (AV 1426; Br 1385, 6981, 11428). M[S] 25 quotes twice ina (& ana) bur-ki aššati. T. A. (Ber) 26 iii 27: I ša bur-ki.

parukâti (?). Nabd 776, 1 (end) pa-ru-ka-a-ti.

פרכ. § 117; AV 6968; Br 3035—7, 5441. — 𝔖 (causative of 𝔑) make cease, stop {aufhören machen}. TP v 41: I imêr kur-ba-a-ni ša a-ba-ri ma-da-at-ta, every year, a-na la šu-par-ki-e elišunu u-kin. Perhaps a mistake for *na-*. ZIMMERN, ZA xiv 277 *foll* reads KB vi (1) 278 i 39 ni-šu i-na šu-par-ki-e napišti bal-ṭa-at.

𝔑 *pr* ipparku, *ps* ipparakkû, *ag* mup(p)arkû, *ac* naparkû (AV 6088). — *a*) give way, recede, yield {weichen, zugeben}. Sarg *Khors* 85 in the anger of my heart I marched with my war chariots and the horse ša a-šar sa-al-me i-da-a-a la ip-par-ku-u (+ 90/100; 114); *Ann* 223, 447. K 246 iv 51 (= H 90) a-a ip-par-ku, of *Išum*, Br 3194; ii 43 (H 80) a-a ip-par]-ku-u (= *pl*); iv 9 + 19 (H 97) id (= nagnâu; 1. 𝔍'); see also H 15, 219. IV² 5 *a* 66—8 day and night to stand (u-zu-uz-zu) la na-par-ka-šu-nu-ti (uma'iršunûti). Esh vi 57 the bull-colossuses a-a ip-par-ku-u i-da-a-šu may not be removed from its (the palace's) side; *cf* I 44, 99; *Kui* 4. 43. *Khors* 190 a-a ip-par-ku-u i-da-šu-un. K[M] 6, 124 a-a ip[-par-ki] râbiçu šul[-mu]; 10, 22 a-a ip-par-ki, *etc.* I 35 *no* 1, 3 *R-N* la mu-par-ku-u (or to *b*?). H 107 (= V 11) 14 (& 112, 13) SUX-GA = SUX-GA (*var* DU) = na-par-ku-u (marû), Br 3035; 15, SUX-NAM-BA-AN-GA-GA = SUX-NAM-BA-AN-NAM (*var* DU)-MA = a-a ip-par-ku (marû) Br 3026; also H 38, 84. — *b*) cease, desist {aufhören, ablassen}; lit[y]: be held back. TP viii 19 ak-pu-du-ma la a-bar-ku-ma (*var* -u) ana epêši axi la addû. V 63 *a* 20 a-na xi-in-na-a-ti Ê-sag-il u Ê-zi-da | ul ap-pa-ra-ak-ka-a ka-a-a-na (ZA i 37 *rm* 1 = baṭalu with ana). I 65 *a* 5 Nebuch. na-a-dam la mu-up-pa-ar-ku-u. IV² 12 *O* 9—10 na-'i-du la mu-up-par-ku-u (= GA-LA-NU-DAG-E-DA); 1* iv 35—6 a-kil da-mi la mu-par-ku-ti (= SUX-NU-DU-MU-MEŠ, *cf* BA ii 290) šu-nu; ZA v 67 (Anp) 18 la mu-par-ku-u. — la na-pa-ar(*var* par)-ka-a. *adv*, unceasingly {unaufhörlich} *e. g.* Neb *Senk*, ii 25; *Bab* i 22 ud-da-ak-ku la na-pa-ar-ka-a. I 69 *a* 16 ûmi-šam-ma la na-par-ka-'a; *b* 18. IV² 12 *O* 17—18 û-mi-šam-ma la na-par-ka-a (= GAL-LA-NU-DAG-E-DA); 20 *no* 1, 7—8 (= SUX-NU-DU-MA). Creat.-*frg* V 14 ar-xi-šam la na-par-ka-a, every month without exception. III 15 ii 25 šat-ti-šam (-ma) la na-par-ka-a; ZA iii 313, 65; Esh vi 50; III 16 vi 10. IV² 38 *b* 23 (KB iv 62/3). Asb iv 109; K 2852 + K 9662 i 14; Esh *Sendsch*, *R* 50—1. — KB iii (2) 50 *col* 3, 22—3 bi-it-ru-su sa-at-tu-ku | i-na bi-i ip-pa-ar-ku-u.

𝔑¹ = 𝔑 V 25 *a-b* 18 when a slave .... it-ta-ba-ta it-ta-pa-ar-ka, flees or otherwise ceases to work, WZ iv 303; Br 3194.

Der.: naparkû *adj* which see *p* 709 *col* 2, bel., where add perhaps: SCHEIL, *Nabd*, viii 28—9 u-mi-ša-am la na-par-ku-u a-na-ku; ZA v 64, 15 murçu la na-par-ku-u.

pa(u)rkullu, see ba(u)rgullu, *p* 190 where

read: II 34 *no* 3 *g-h* 36 ça-dim-mu ‖ b(p)ar-g(k)ul-lum. ⊕ 51 iv 32 (amêl) ALAM-GU-U = pur-kul-lu, see naggaru (644 *col* 1). K 4815 ina pur-kulli (= BUR-GUL) ìuṭur. — Der.

purkullūtu, with determinative (amêl) = stonemason, sculptor {Steinmetz, Steinarbeiter}. II 67, 77 abnū ši-pir (amêl) pur-kul-lu-ti ab-ni ina us-si-ma bāba (KB ii 22—3); BA iii 246—7 on K 192 *R* 19. Cyr 325, 4 a-na (amêl) purgul-u-tu ‖ a-na Qud-da-a-a (amêl) pur-kul .... id-din.

parkannu. bolt {Riegel}? Z[Š] vii! 59 itti ma-mit daltu sikkūru u par-kan-nu. perhaps KB vi (1) 60 (iii) 29 [ ] park(g)an-ni tu[š-ta .....]. Beh 105 (??; KAT³ 214 *rm* 2).

pirik(q?)tu. II 30 *b-c* 78 ša pi-rik-ti, in a list, with determinative of narṭabu.

parīmu (?). KB iii (2) 48 *col* 2, 20 la na[-aš-ku]-nu pa-ri-im, that no harm may be done to it. Dupl. reads la na-aš-ku-un na-ba-lum, PSBA xi 197; KB *loc. cit.*, *rm* 3. AV 6970; ZA iv 238 (K 2361) iii 1 .... pa-ri-im (but??).

purīmu, *m* wild ass {Wildesel} id IMÊR-EDIN-NA (§ 9, 244) = the ass of the desert. D 17, 134; § 65, 36. HAUPT, *Andov. Rev.*, Jl. '84, 97 *rm* 5. Sn iv 22 before my powerful weapons kīma pu-ri-me ig-ru-ru, they ran away like wild asses. IV² 3 *a* 23—24 ki-ma pu-ri-me (id, Br 4992) ìa xa-am-ra êna-šu u-pi-e ma-la-a; 56 *col* iii (*b*) 48 ki-ma pu-rim çêri, (swift) as a wild ass šu-da-ki ru-uk-bi (§ 72*a*, note). III 41 *b* 18 ki-ma pu-rīmi i-na ka-mat ali-šu li-ir-tap-pu-ud; I 70 *c* 20—1; II 60 *a* 52; Asb viii 69 IMÊR-EDIN-NA-MEŠ (= purīmê) ça-bâti *etc.*; also vi 104; I 28 *a* 24, 25.

NOTE. — JOHNS, *Expositor*, X '99, 393—4: pu-rīmê = "wild asses", added to sum of minas of bronze = a name for a mina of bronze; it is highly improbable that a mina of bronze should bear an animal name, save from a coin device.

parammaxu & barmaxxu (> BAR + MAX = parakku çīru) holy sanctuary, shrine, temple-chamber {erhabenes Heiligtum, Tempelgemach}, § 73 note; SMITH, *Sn* 119. H 80, 15, 16 ina ku-us-si-e pa-ram (Br 6884 ra)-ma-xi (= BAR-MAX) ina a-ša-bi-šu, ZK ii 273. Sarg *Bull* 47 a-na zuqqur BAR-MAX-xe admān ilāni rabûti *etc.*; *Cyl* 49 (see LYON, *Sargon*, 71).

parumxu, purumxu see for the present paîxu, puaîxu.

parmusatu (?) Rm IV 97 (33, 541) 8 A-ga-de(ki)-i-tum tab-ku ša pa-ar-mu-sa-as-su di-ku bêl la-li-e-šu, transl. by PINCHES, PSBA 23, 198: the Agaditess wept, that her elder was slain, the lord of her well-being.

pirrāni. K 493, 7—9 (Hr[L] 440) 25 u-ra-a-te ša na-kan-te ša 3 pir-ir(*i. e.* pirra-a-ni | ša (al) Kal-xi | ša (al) Ni-nu-a | ša (al) Dûr-šarru-kin (BA i 210), *pl* of pirru or pirrānu (?).

(iç) **p(b)uranū.** Nabd 1033, 5—6 a-na (iç) pu-ra-ni-e nàd-na; also Lab. 1, 6; 9, 8 something made of reed {etwas aus Rohr gefertigtes}.

parasu, pr iprus, ps iparras. — *α*) part, divide, separate, hinder {scheiden, trennen} AV 6971; ZA i 418; ii 47; idd § 9, 106 & 114; Br 374, 375. — *a*. scatter {zerstreuen} K 3182 iii 40 a-na šārê erbā ar-kat-si-na ta-par-ra-as, to the four winds thou wilt scatter their hinder parts (AJSL xvii 142, 143). — *β*. part, estrange, alienate {trennen, abwendig machen}. IV² 51 *a* 22(—30) itti māri aba ip-ru-su *etc.*; 50 *b* 55—6 tap-ru-si (o witch) itti-ja ili-MU (= ja) u Ištar-MU (= ja) tap-ru-si itti-ja še-'a še-'i-tu axa axāta (= T[M] iii 114, 115). Asb iii 108 Šamaš-šumukīn .... ip-ru-sa axu-u-tu (KB ii 185: verwehrte mir die Bruderschaft); iii 83 ardāni da-gil pa-ni-ja ip-ru-us-ma (KB ii 182 *rm* **; WINCKLER, *Forschungen*, i 247 on *ll* 82—86; or pa-raçu, 1.?). SCHEIL, ZA x 205, 13 (end) nis-xu (*q. v.*) pa-ra-su (*cf* 14). — *γ*. hem, restrain, hinder {hemmen, zurückhalten}. KB ii 254—55, 37 ri-gim a-me-lu-ti ap-ru-sa çêru-uš-šu, the cry of mankind I restrained. III 4 *no* 4, 38, 39 violent & continuous storm i-na bir-tu-uš-šu-nu a-la-ku la i-par-ra-as (did not prevent); SMITH, *Asurb*, 59, 88 on sea & on land .... a-lak-ta-šu ap-ru-us, I cut off his way. T[M] ii 14, 15 (= IV² 50 *a*) i-na im-ti-ša (with her saliva) ip-ta-ra-as (*i. e.* the pursuing witch) a-lak-tu; ina ru-xi-ša (with her charm) iš-di-xi ip-ru-us, she stopped my foot. T^{M} i 143 lip-ru-us (+ v 155); IV^{2} 49 *a* 10 u-pu-un-ti pī-MU (= ja) ip-ru-su (= T^{M} i 10). Sp II 265 *a* xxi 2 i-lu a-na šar-ra-bi ul pa-ri-is a-lak-ta. Sarg *Ann* 272 (*var*) ana šēpā Kaldī pa-ra-si-im-ma, to stop. TP vi 54 šēp nakirē i-na māti-ja lu(-u)-ap-ru-us, the foot of the enemies I restrained in my country (*i. e.* I always prevented an inroad of my enemies into my country). Asb vii 89 ana ša-'-al šul-me-ja šēpešu ip-ru-us-ma (*cf* SMITH, *Asurb*, 284, 95). Sn vi 13, 14 until the fourth hour of the night it continued (then finally) da-ak-šu-nu ap-ru-us (I stopped the slaughter). K 3600, 26 pa-ri-su (= ag) sat-tuk-ki ša ili, *etc.*; DT 71 *R* 4 see nidabū (630 *col* 1). K 312, 5—9 ak-ka-a-'i ina libbi ša ēna-a-a ina eli-ku-nu | u la-pa-an xi-iṭ ša Nabū-bel-šumāte ..... (9) ap-ru-su-ku-nu-ši; IV^{2} 49 *b* 55 = T^{M} i 143 see xâtu (*p* 346 *col* 2). K 2852 + K 9662 (iv) Margin 2: ap-ru-us, I detained. IV^{2} 11 *a* 17—8 ... ša bi-el-šu ar-kat-su la ip-ru-us. *Cf* IV^{2} 60* B *O* 6. Pa-ri-is-tum, the restraining one, an epithet of the door (da-al-tum), II 23, 9 (AV 6982). T. A. Lo. 11 + Murch, 24 the embassies .... la ip-r[u-su], they have not restrained; 29, la ta-pa-ar-ra-as, do not restrain! — *b*) decide {entscheiden} especially with purussū (*q. v.*). K 2711, 14 ap-ru-us, I decided, BA iii 264. V 50 *a* 11—12 [ana purussē?] ana pa-ra-si they sit before thee, Br 10005. K 3182 ii 22 ta-par-ra-as, thou decidest, AJSL xvii 138. 83—1—18, 227, 2 written TAR with gloss ip-ru[-us]; 80—7—19, 58 *R* 3 ū-mu ri-ša-a liš-ši-ma lu-up-ru-us-ma, (may the lord—of kings when his face is favorable) lift up my head, that I may decide; K 1393 *R* 3 a-mat pa-ri-is-tum, a sure report; K 8391, 7 a-mat (?) la pa-ri-is-tum (THOMPSON, *Reports*, 179; 210; 52; 272 C). HILPRECHT, *OBI*, i 32—33 *col* ii 35 the gods *A* & *M* ap-ru-us-ma (I consulted); *ibid* 39 ilāni rabūti ina pa-ra-si (but KB iii (2) 4, 36 reads di-pa-ra-am. ZA iii 221 = KB iv 168, *no* ii 6—7 di-in-šu-nu u-par-su-ma xur-ša-an ina mux-xi-šu-nu | ip-ru-su; also Nabd 13, 11; Neb 116, 7 ip-ru-us-su. STRASSM., *Stockholm*, 4, 11 bītu (il) Za-ma-ma ina eli Šum-iddina ip-ru-su. KING, *Xammurabi*, 56, 23 *foll* bārūti ta-ma-'-ri-a[m-ma] pi (= ṷa)-ar-ka-tu li-ip-ru-s[u-ma], order the bārūti, so that they may reveal the future; IV^{2} 60* B *O* 6; see also KB iii (2) 64 *col* 2, 20—22 pi-ši-ri ka-la Šamaš Adad u Marduk ap-ru-us. K 62, 6 ... ta-par-ra-sa ši pat-ku-nu balāṭu. IV^{2} 45 *b* 45 (= Hr^{L} 281; K 13) see nuppu; *ibid* 48 pa-ra-su ša šar-nuppi. See also piristu, purussū. V 24 *a-b* 36, 37: ma-am-man arkat-su ul ip-ru-us (= NU-UN-SAR, Br 4328); kab-tum arkat-su ul ip-ru-us (NU-UN-KUD). IV^{2} 3 *b* 4—5 sinništu pa-ris-tu (= SAL-MUD-DA-GE-A, Br 2082). HAUPT, *ASKT*, 201 reads IV^{2} 22 *b* 19 ina ši-me-tan pu-ru-us-ma (instead of pu-ru-'-ma). K 883, 11 ... ina bir ....ni lip-ru-us, BA ii 633. — *c*) break to pieces {zerbrechen}? ZA v 68, 7 par-sa-ku-ma, I am broken to pieces (Aram פְּרַס).

H 9 + 201, 17 KUD = pa-ra-su; V 31 *g-h* 64. II 28 *d-e* 65 BAR = pa-ra-su (H 13, 141; Br 1785; AV 6971; II 30, 37 = parašu); 66, KUD-DA = *p* ša NER-PAD-DU; 67, PA-KAB-DU = *p* ša si-ri, Br 5653; 68, UBUR (šu-ub) ŠUB = *p* ša tu-li-e, Br 1438, 5556; 69, RI = *p* ša ri-xu-ti, Br 2570; 70, ... GE-A = *p* ša SAL (or rak?) Br 14200; 71, [KUD?]-DA = *p* ša pi-[ris-t]i,? Br 14214; 72, ... ME = *p* ša up (or ar?)-ti, Br 14400. 83, 1—18, 1335 ii 6 (*cf* 81, 11—13, 465) ku-ud | KUD | xa-ra-mu ša pa-ra-su. — ZA iii 307 barašu = parasu.

Q^{t} *a*) hem, restrain {hindern, hemmen, abhalten} IV^{2} 50 *a* 7 ina re-bi-ti ip-ta-ra-as (*i. e.* the witch) a-lak-tu (= T^{M} iii 7), see also Q. KB iii (2) 50 *col* 3, 22 bi-it-ru-su sa-at-tu-ku (*q. v.*). K 890, 22 ištu pa-an xa-bi-ri-ja ip-tar-sa-an-ni a-a-ši. NE 22, 37 ip-ta-ra-as a-lak-ta, KB vi, 1, 152; K 3057 i 15 a-lak-ta ip-tar-sa. — *b*) divide, partition off {abteilen} *del* 58, 50 (62, 63) ap-ta-ra-as (KB vi, 1, 488; H^{NE} 136; see also ZA iii 419).

3 K 613 (V 54 *a* 39; Hr^{L} 85) 7 ardāni

ša bīt bēlija ša šarru bēli û-mu an-ni-u u-par-ri-su-u-ni, PSBA 23, 61 *fol*, has set apart. S. A. SMITH, *Asurb*, iii 3, 61 see mešrû, *p* 611 *col* 1, med. Asb ix 46 camels, like small cattle u-par-ri-is, I divided (and parcelled out) among the inhabitants of Assyria, D^{Pr} 154 *rm* 2. V 45 iv 5 tu-par-ra-as(ç?). H 37 ii 17 pur-ru-su la ....

Š stop, hinder {hemmen, hindern} Sarg *Ann* 368 a-na šup-ru-us šēpâ (wr. NER^{II}) amēlu Elamû (*Khors* 139), to stop the advance of the (hostile) Elamite. Neb ii 19, 20 a-ša-ar kib-si šu-up-ru-su | še-e-pi la i-ba-aš-šu-u (KB iii, 2, 12, 13; AV 8543). S^P 158 + S^P ii 962 *O* 14 see sakkû (755 *col* 2) & *Jour. Trans. Vict. Inst.* 29, 58.

Š^3 BANKS, *Diss*, 16, 1 *no* 4, 164 mannu tuš-par-ra-as.

𝔑 *a*) be separated, withheld {geschieden, getrennt, verwehrt worden} K 891 *R* 6 see puxpuxxû. KB vi (1) 284, 285, 42 li[p(b)-par]-sa-ma, es mögen abgesperrt werden den Menschen die ....; 52 ip-p[a]r-su a-na nišē e-ti-ta; & 282 *O* 28. T. A. (Ber) 8 *R* 9 i-na bi-ri-ni mār ši-ip-ri ip-pa-ar-ra-as, and the messengers [*i. e.* trade] between us will be cut off (*cf* ZA v 148). IV^2 20 *no* 1 *O* 7—8 ina zu-um-ri-ja la ip-par-su-u-ma (= NU-KUD-DA, H 200 *no* 11); *cf* T^M v 165 (+ 184) ina zumri-MU lu-u tap-par-ra-sa-ma. IV^2 28* *no* 4 *b* 43, 44 a-lum ša še-um ip-par-su-šu (= KUD-DA), a city from which supplies are withheld. V 60 *a* 27 this sattukku ip-pa-ri-is-ma ‖ ba-ṭil. L^3 *R* 4 la ip-pa-ra-su, they do not cease. BANKS, *Diss*, 14, 115 see mākalû (536 *col* 2). SCHEIL, ZA x 205 *R* 6 a-ru-u lip-pa-ri-is. — *b*) be decided {entschieden werden}. Perhaps i 27, 103 ip-par-ra-su. See also purussû. — V 31 *c-d* 47 ul KUD = ul ip-par-ra-as. — Derr.:

puru(i)ssû decision, decree {Entscheidung, Urteil} D^H 40; AV 7129; Br 48; § 65, 38; id EŠ-BAR (§ 9, 93). II 57 *c-d* 28 (Br 2659); H 37, 1 AŠ-BAR = pu-ru-us-su-u; 41, 250 EŠ-BAR (II 28 *e-f* 73, Br 1008). often in KNUDTZON, 312. id Merod.-Balad.-stone i 38 purussû kiš-šat nišē. V 38 *c-d* 33 ga-ra-aš | id | pu-ru-us-su-u (S^a 2, 16) = ka-[su-]u (ZA i 188; ii 298; ZK ii 62 *foll*); S^b I *O* ii 4 (BA ii 284; Br 6132); H 186, 2; III 32, 10 EŠ-BAR-šu ša la in-ni-nu-u; also V 63 *b* 5; Šalm, *Balaw*, VI 2 a-na bīt purussē-šu ki-ni uš-kin-ma. KB iii (2) 64, 34 Šamaš eṭlu ka-ab-tu bēli muštēšir pu-ru-us-si-e ki-it-ti; usually in connection with parasu. KB iv 84—5, *col* 2, 2—3 Šamaš ... di-in-šu u purussī-šu | a-a ip-ru-us; *cf* Esh *Sendsch*, *O* 6 Šamaš ... pa-ri-su purussī-ja. On pāris purussē see T^M 29—30, *rm* 6. 31—2—4, 188 (Prayer to Ištar of Nineveh), 7: a-na pa-ri-sa-at purussē, to her who determines decrees. V 65 *a* 11 Šamaš ... pa-ri-is pu-ri(-is)-si-e (ZA i 59 *rm* 1); 26 purussī-a ap-ru-us-su (KB iii, 2, 111). V 50 *a* 12 purussē]-a (*cf* 11 EŠ-BAR) ana pa-ra-si iz-za-az-zu-ka. T^M ii 74 ša ka-a-ta ilu ma-am-man purussâ ul i-par-ra-as. KB vi (1) 266, 10 (= Sm 1371 + Sm 1877) pu-russâ-šu-nu ta-par-ra-as (also K 256 *O* 24); 13 purussa-a a-na pa-ra-s[i]; 14 [purussa-a a] pur[us]; also *l* 8. T^M v 21 (end) pari-is pu-ru-us-si-e-ni (BA iv 160). IV^2 59 *a* 5 pu-ru-us-si-e-šu pa-ra-a-si. Sp III 586 + R III, 1 (hymn to the setting sun) 24, 25 dA'En ša pu-ru-us-si-e-ša muštēširša at-ta; TSBA viii 167 *fol*: judge of its decisions; HOMMEL, *Sum. Lesest.*, 120 *fol*. IV^2 17 *a* 43, 44 (K 256) a-ma-as-su li-mad pu-ru-us-sa-šu pu-ru-us (Br 1785); *a* 23, 24 pu-ru-us-sa-a ta-par-ra-as-su-nu-ti (Br 9801); & *cf* IV^2 8 iv 25 EŠ-BAR-a KUD-us; K^M 12, 59. K 2085, 8 pu-ru-us-su a-na Uru^{ki} na-din (a decision to Ur is given, THOMPSON, *Reports*, 268); id K 750, 7; K 702, 3 (*ibid* 271; 272 *B*). III 67 *c-d* 56 Papsuk(k)al is the god ša pu-ru-si-e. II 35 *e-f* 5 pu-ru-us-su-u = da-a-nu; 52 *c-d* 64, *cf* Br 552; 54 *a-b* 5 AN-DI-TAR = ilu Bēl ša purussē, AV 1933, Br 9544.

pirsu perh. division, partition {Scheidung. Lostrennung}. II 38 *g-h* 12, 13 (Br 3278); V 20 *e-f* 42, 43 (Br 3562, 3048) SAG-KI (*var* TIK)-GIŠ-SAR (Br 4329), TIK-GIŠ-SAR = pir(*var* pi-ir)-su, AV 7078; the latter id also = na-bal-kat-tum (44); JENSEN, 221 (Grenzland).

pirsānu (?) IV^2 29* *b* 8 dāma ina pir-sa-a-nu u-qa-an-na-an.

piristu decision, especially = divine decision; oracle {Entscheidung, Orakel} § 65, 4; AV 7072. Asb v 129 Šušan mūšab ilāni-šun a-šar pi-ris-ti-šu-un ak-šu-ud; vi 30 (il) Šušinak il pi-ris-ti-šu-nu. K^M i (K 155) 17 pi-ris-ti ilāni^{pl} rabūti^{pl}; *cf* IV^2 21, 1 B *R* 16 (Br 4169). *del* 10 u pi-ris-ta ša ilāni ka-a-ša lu-uq-bi-ka (KB vi, 1, 230); 176, 177 (195, 196) pi-ris-ti ilāni rabūti. ZA v 68, 44 pi-ris-ti ket-tu, the just decree; Sarg *Khors* 158 la-mid pi-ris-ti. K 2801 (+K 221+K 2669) *R* 22 šu-ru-ub pi-ris-ti, to render the decision; 29, mār um-ma-a-ni li-'-u-ti mu-di-e pi-ris-ti; II 57 *c-d* 17 perhaps: (il) Nin-ib (*q. v.*) ša pi-ris-ti (III 67 *c-d* 68); II 58, 32 (coloph) ta-kal-tu ša pi-ris-ti (*Jour. Bibl. Lit.*, xix, 59 *rm* 62, 63). Zɪᴍ., *Ritualtafeln*, (*p* 116 *foll*) 24, 10 (amēl) um-mānu mudū na-çir piristi ilāni ra-būti. V 48 *c-d* 32 (= II 60 *no* 2, 33) Nebō as ba-nu-u pi-ris-ti is written AN-GI-XAL (ZA iv 279); V 29 *e-f* 68 NAM : SAG-►— (= AŠ?) = ši-im-tum : pi-ris-tum (Br 2100, 3528); *a-b* 73 ZAG (Br 6486) = pi-ris-tum; V 36 *a-c* 51 šu-u | ⟨ | pi-ris-tum, preceded by ni-çirtu (Br 8732). IV^2 30, 1 *O* 11 kab-tum ša ina pu-šu-uq : pi-ris-tum .... la uç-ça-a, Br 2012; ZA iii 363, 63 šu-bat pi-ris-ti. IV^2 19 *b* 37, 38 ina E-UL-BAR bīt pi-ris-ti-ki (= BAR-RA-ZU, Br 1788) dāmē kīma mē in-naqqū; V 52 *a* 62, 63 bīt bi-ri-iš-ti (= BAR-RA, ZA iii 307; *cf* II 30, 37); Sᴄʜᴇɪʟ, *Nabd*, viii 32 bīt pi-ris-ti (il) Marduk u (ilat) Çar-pa-ni-tum.

Hᴀᴜᴘᴛ in JBL xix 74 *rm* 63 reads pi-rištu; also in Pᴀᴛᴇʀsᴏɴ, *Numbers* (SBOT) 51; see also Jᴇɴsᴇɴ, KB vi (1) 230 (secret: Geheimnis), 481, 506.

Zɪᴍᴍᴇʀɴ, *Beitr. z. babyl. Religion*, 86, 89 pirištu (not piristu) = mysterium; (amēl) XAL = the man of the mysterium; | niçirtu, *Theol. Litztg.*, '00 *no* 2, *col* 33 against BA iii 236, 22+29; 234, 4; 244, 4.

parsu, *adj* IV^2 30* *no* 3 *R* 30 man]-za-az-ka aš-ru par-su (= KUD-DA); *cf* *Rev. Sém.*, '98, 148—51; KB vi (1) 488: ein abgesperrter Ort.

par(pir?)su. part, portion {Teil} in colophons *etc.*: IV^2 58 *c* 30; ZA ii 161, 39 par-su reš-tu-u (KB ii 284: pars prima); K^M 48, 18: VII-u par-su. See pirsu, 834 *col* 2.

parsū, see massû, *pp* 565, 566; Br 14101 on II 26 *c-d* 68; mentioned in one group with im-qi mu-di-e par-si-e, *Rec. Trav.* xix, 16 (note xxvii *no* 356). BA ii 261 ii 48 b(p)ar-su-u nak-lu: the wise decider.

parsāti (?) Zɪᴍᴍᴇʀɴ, *Ritualt.*, 66 *O* 15: VIII (karpat) par(pir?, tam?)-sa-a-ti ša dišpē, name of a vessel.

(māt) **Parsua.** I 35 *no* 1, 8 (māt) Pa-ar-su-a; (māt) Par-su, 83—1—18, 589; also (māt) Pa-ar-su *etc.*, AV 6092; see Sᴛʀᴇᴄᴋ, ZA xv 308 *foll*; Bᴇᴢᴏʟᴅ, *Catalogue*, vol v *s. v.*; AV 6093.

pa(ā)ri(ī)su. guide, oar, rudder, pole {Ruder, Ruderstange}. Jᴇɴsᴇɴ, 145; 410; ZK ii 283; J^{v} 88 *rm* 1 (√פרס, split); *del* 61 (65) a-mur pa-ri-su, I found me a rudder, pole (Hᴀᴜᴘᴛ: mast); 247 (277) u šu-u iš-ši pa-ri-sa, KB vi (1) 250—51: hat er (Gilgameš) doch die (Schiffs)stange erhoben; Hᴀᴜᴘᴛ, JAOS xxii, 10: he unstepped the mast. NE 60, 41 e rid ana kišti-ma pa-ri-si ša xamilti GAR ta-an ku-pur-ma šu-kun tu(tam?)-lu-a, KB vi (1) 220, 221; & *l* 45; 70, 2 (+4 +5+6+7) li-qi pa-ri[-su, or sa?]; 8, ug-dam-me-ra pa-r[i-si]; D 89 vi 59 (60) GIŠ-GI-MUŠ = gimuš-šu (*q. v.*, AV 1549) & pa-ri-su (Br 2514); çir-rit pa-ri-su (Br 13987); II 45 *a-b* 13, 14.

p(b)ars(š)igu, *pl* parsigē bandage {Binde, Verband} AV 7000; 5090; J^{w} 90 *fol*; BA ii 561. *del* 232 (258) lu-u ud-du-uš par-si-gu ša qaq-qa-di-šu; 239 (267) u-te-id [-diš par-si-gu ša] qaqqadi-šu. II 34 (*no* 3) *g-h* 42 a-gi-it-tu-u = KU-BAR-SIG (*i. e.* parsigu) & çi-in-du ša A-ZU (= asī), bandage used by physicians. V 15 *e-f* 54 may be read par-[si-gu] as against *p* 601 *col* 2, bel (maš [-xu]); see BA i 515; II 62, 66; IV^2 25 *b* 21. V 14 (*a*-)*b* 36 woollen clothing, stuff ša par-si-gi (to be used for bandages); II 62 *a-b* 67, 68 KU-BAR-SI-ŠA (= LIB)-GA, & KU-BAR-SUN (see sūnu)-ŠA-GA = par-si-ig ša-pil-tu (Br 6982; ZA i 194); 66, KU-ŠA(= LIB)-GA = ša-pil-tu. V 28 *g-h* 14 pa-tin-nu pa-ar-ši-gu = na-ar-gi-tum (*q. v.*) & Nabd 726, 1; MEISSNER, 105: ein Kleid. iḋ KU-BAR-SI Cyr 4, 6; 232, 26; 253, 7 (ša (ilat) Gu-la); 259, 5; 241, 17 (end): II (çubāt) parsīgu. Neb 87, 4 (çubāt) par-si-gu, see also nabāsu; BA i 512 (*cf* 514, 15) reads Nabd 284, 20 (end) par-šu-ga, a byform to paršigu.

pursaggu & pirsidu see bursaggu & bir-sidu, *p* 193 *col* 1.

paraçu 1. pr ipruç tell lies, lie {lügen} AV 6073; D^{Pr} 154 *rm* 2 (see kazabu). K 617, 16, 17 This *M-B*, bēl xi-i-ṭu šu-u (amēlu?) par-ri-çu šu-u, is a liar (JAOS xx 251 (>< Br 1980, 6562); *cf* Rm 2, 1 *R* 25  pa-ri-çu-u-te. Asb iii 83 see pa-rasu. BEZOLD, *Achaem*, 53 on Beh I—IX; this is *NN* ša ip-ru-çu-um-ma, who lied thus. On K 480, 15—17 (III 51 *no* 9) read by JENSEN, 30/1 ša ina pa-ni-ti a-na šarri bēlija aš-pur-an-ni par-çiš (wr. NU-UG) see BA ii 35 *rm*. V 19 *c-d* 17 (II 62 *g-h* 14, 15) NU-UG = pa-ra-çu ša amēli, to lie; & pa-ri-iç (or is?) ilasum (Br 1980, 1981, 6562).

ℷ = Q Beh. 97 amēlu ša u-par-ra-çi (+ 105 u-par-ra-çu).

ℷ' = ℷ Beh. 90 (91, 92) up-tar-ri-iç (§§ 84; 98) i-qab-bi um-ma, he lied, speaking thus (§ 152). — **Der.**:

pi(a?)riçtu, *pl* pirçātu. lie {Lüge} § 70 *a, n*. Beh. 100 pir(par?)-ça-a-tum ši-na (§ 140), they are lies; KNUDTZON, 108 *O* 22 lu-u ina pir-ça-te lu-u i-na pa-ni xar-du-u-ti. K 2889, 11 gabbi pi-ir-ça-a-ta, nothing but lies. KB ii 266—7, 80 whom *N* ina pi-ir-ça-a-ti u-çab-bi-tu, has caught by means of fraud. *Cf* Cyr 307, 4 when *T* is seen (ta-ta-nam-mar) with *K* u ina pi-ir-ça-tum | i-tab-ka-ši(-ma), and he has seized her by unfair means, (BA iv 10 *fol*); see also KB iv 282—3, *rm* 3.

paraçu 2. pr ipruç perh. break, break through {brechen, durchbrechen} BARTH, *Etym. Stud.*, 7; BA iii 66. V 19 *c-d* 14—16 KA (ki-ir) AG-A = pa-ra-çu (Br 627); KA (kir-xu-ur) XUR = paraçu ša pilaqqi (of a hatchet) II 11 + 212, 63 zerhacken (??) vom Beile, Br 740; TIK-NER-TAR = *p* ša dūri (of a wall) Br 376, 3298. SMITH, *Asurb*, 42, 84 ip-ru-çu ma-mit-sun (*cf* 854 *col* 2, above).

parçu 1. sepulchre, grave {Grab}. S^b 191 AB + infixed 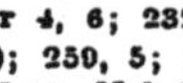 *i. e.* dark dwelling (u-nu-gi) = par-çu; H 19, 383 (‖ qabru, 384); V 23 *a-d* 9 (Br 4785, 4787) *cf* S^b 190 unu = šubtu; S^b 130 GI = mūšu, šklitu (V 18 *a-b* 11, + 16; H 109, 27). JENSEN, 220. J^w 63: 5 read xiç-çu.

paraçu 3. decide {entscheiden}. pm KB iv 162 (iv) 5 (end) pa-ri-çi, it was decided; ℷℷ L^4 iii 29 ip-par-çu. — **Der.**:

parçu 2. *c. st.* paraç *m* command, order, law; edict, especially of a god or king {Gebot, Befehl, Gesetz} *etc.* *pl* parçē(ū). iḋḋ PA-AN (Br 5644, 5647—8); ME; AV 6994; MEISSNER, 125. V 19 *c-d* 32—34 (K 2008 iii 34—36) ME (Br 10374) = parçu (II 27, 15); (ku-uš) PA-AN = *p* ša ili (H 21, 401); (gar-za) PA-AN = *p* ša šarri (V 37 *a-c* 20); S^b 214 ga-ar-za PA-AN | par-çu ‖ tērtu, H 21, 400. V 28 *a-d* 52 ME-ME | mi-mu-u | par-çu & *cf* S^b 188 me-e | ME | par-çu; H 109, 38 (113, 31) MAR-ZA = PA-AN = par-çu, Br 5836; = V 11 *e-f* 38. V 62 (*no* 2) 12 ana šul-lum par-çi (Br 11851), zur Wiederherstellung der Gebote (LEHMANN, ii 44); 21 par-çi-šu-nu šu-qu-ru-tu. K 2711 *R* 21 .... u-šal-la-mu par-çi-e-ša. KB iii (1) 194, 3 Nabū ... [xa-mi-im] par-çi (= *pl*); also see xa-mīmu & KB vi (1) 367. PINCHES, *Texts*, 16 *no* 4 *R* 9 (end) li-šal-lim par-çi-šu. Merodach-Balad.-stone ii 10 *M-B* calls himself mu-šal-lim par-çe-šu-nu (BA ii 260; 267 >< KB iii (1) 181). V 60 *a* 9 par-çu-šu im-ma-šu-ma, so that his commands were forgotten (BA i 270), *ibid* 18. Nerigl. (I 69) *a* 20 pa-ar-çu ri-eš-tu-tu, the laws of old (§ 67, 5; JBL xix 67 *rm* 38); V 63 *a* 10 aššum i-na pa-ra-aç ilāni la-ša *etc.* (? = la išū?), but PEISER la ša-la-ṭi. Anp i 24 PA-AN-MEŠ (*var* par-çe) škurrē mūtišu (KB i 56—7); see also IV^2 31 *a* 44, 47, 50, 53, 56, 59, 60 (ki-a-am PA-AN-MEŠ-ša); 38 ki-ma parçē la-bi-ru-ti; on *R* 54 see KB vi, 1, 90—1, *rm* 4 & 405; perh. Asb iv 100 ana pa-ra-aç (*var* -raç) ra-ma-ni-šu-nu (WINCKLER, *Forsch.* i 248: auf eigene Faust) ik-ki-ru it-ti-ja; x 62 Ištar ša Arba-ilu[ki] ilat šarrat (BA i 227) parçē (PSBA Je. '86, 244; KB ii 232—33); I 27 *a* 10—13 Ištar reš-ti šame-e erçi-ti ša paraç qar-du-te šuk-lu-lat (KB i 130, 131); V 35, 6 pa-ra-aç la si-ma-a-ti-šu-nu (BA ii 250 × KB iii, 2, 121). H 116 *O* 2 šuk-lu?]-lat par-çi Bēl; 6, muš-tak-li-la-at par-çi (& V 51 *b* 51); 14, be-el-tum šur-bu-tum ša par-çu-ša šu-tu-ra, great lady whose command is overpowering. *Rec. Trav.*, xx 127 *foll* 9, eb-bu el-lim qa-ti pa-ši-šu muš-te-'-u par-çi, KB vi (1) 92, 9. K 3454 (*Zû*-legend) 48 (end) na-du-u par-çe (KB vi, 1, 50—1: das "Hinwerfen" der Gebote, & *cf l* 92; 48, 21); also see KB vi (1) 48, 14 lu-be-li par-çi. Creat.-*frg* IV 82 a-na pa-ra-aç [il] Anu(-nu)-ti, against the divine command, & see KB vi (1) 336. *Dibbara-legend* (K 2619) ii 14 par-çe-ši-na i-te[-ik-ru?] KB vi (1) 62. IV[2] 30* *no* 3 *O* 18 šangammaxu mu-ul-lil par-çi (*Rev. Sém.* vi 149: sanctuaries) ša Eridu a-na-ku (on id see KB vi, 1, 552); 34 (end) ša par-çi el-lu-ti ana qa-ti-ja u-ma-al[-li]. 81—6—7, 209 (dupl. K 6346) 2 (ana) Ištar of Uruk ru-ba-a-ti çir-ti li-qa-a-ti pa-ra-aç [(il)] A-num-u-tu (BA iii 263 *foll*). K 629 *R* 10 pa-ar-çi ša ilāni, the commands of the gods (Hr[L] 65; × AV 6991); II 19 *a* 38, 39 nam-ru ina ap-si-i par-çi ez-zu-ti li-qu-u. S[P] 158 + S[P] II 962 *O* 18 it-bal par-çi-šu, took away its ordinances. 81—2—4, 188 (a prayer to Ištar of Nineveh) 4 a-na šar-rat ilani[pl] ša par[-çi ilāni ra-bûti[pl] šu-ut]-lu-mu qa-tuš-ša, ZA v 66. KB vi (1) 288, 32 read par-çi-šu, his command; K 3351, 18 ina Ê-kur bīt taq-na-a-ti ša-qu-u par-çu-u-šu. Rm III 105 i 12 ša ana pa-ra-aç Nabû bêl mātāti i-ši (or -lim?) bu-tuq-qu, *etc.* (WINCKLER, *Forsch*, i 254 *foll*). I 35 *no* 1, 4 read mu-kil PA-AN (= parçē) Ê-kur; *cf* Šamš i 31 (KB i 176, 177). 83—1—18, 14 *O* 9 PA-AN il-ki (Hr[L] 406; AJSL xiii 211). V 16 *a-b* 8 A-QAR(?)-BI (= KAŠ)-NU-ŠUR = par-çu, Br 11552; MEISSNER 125: ein Stück Land. IV[2] 23 *a* 19 a-na par-çi ki-du-di-e na-šu-ka; 22, mu]-ši-im par-çi ša šamē u erçitim. On paraç kiškanê see BA i 302, 9 & *rm* *; and JENSEN, 249. T. A. (Lo) 15, 39 ti-i-di pa-ar-ça-ja. Whether KB iv 66 (*no* ii) *R* 8 par-si e i-ta-ni e i-ša-lu-ma, belongs here is doubtful.

NOTE. — 1. KB iii (1) 200—1; JENSEN, 220; MEISSNER & ROST, 18 maintain for parçu meanings: (1) command, (2) chamber, abode (but see BA ii 258 *foll*). In support of *no* (2) see V 33 *b* 18, 19 i-na biti ša [(il)] Šamaš i-na pa-ra-aç arki I placed it; Neb *Grot*, iii 41 pa-ra-aç šar-ru-ti šu-lu-ux be-lu-tim ina libbišu ušāpam (KB iii (2) 38, 39); TP vii 105 e-lal-la-a pa-ra-aç of their great godhead, therein I established. Rm 88. 5—12, 75 + 76 *col* vi 12, 13 par-çi Ê-sag-ila qa-aš-du-te ana ašrišunu utir (BA iii 246—7: Heiligtümer).

2. II 62, 37 [(il)] Nabû xa-mi-mu par-çi (Br 1042?); 67, 27 [(il)] Ninib xa-mi-im PA-AN-MEŠ MAX-MEŠ (*i. e.* parçê çirûti), AV 3165.

paraqu. 83, 1—18, 1335 ii 22 (ku-ud) [KUD] = pa-ra-qu.

pirqêti, Sarg *Khors* 173 (*Ann* 434) *cf* narbû (narbâti); or tamqêti √naqû?

parqu. KB iv 308—10 *no* ix, 17 it-ti 1 GUR tu-xal-la .... par-qu.

pararu, pr iprur, break, kill {zerbrechen, töten} AV 6974. Br 1849 reads II 62 (*c-*)*d* 17 i-par (or tak, dag?)-ru-ur-rum.

ב break, smash {zerbrechen, zerschmettern} § 22. Sarg *Ann* XIV 7 u-par-ri-ir ellat; III 14, 37. IV[2] 16 *a* 62, 63 ki-ma xa-aç-bi (*q. v.*) li-par-ri-ru-šu (= XE-EN-ŠU-UŠ-RI-E-NE, 3 *pl*); DT 71 *O* 17 tu-par-ri-ir el-lat-su; *R* 15 (el-çi-iš) tu-par-ri-ir (WINCKLER, *Forsch*, i 541); NE 59, 18 im-xa-aç .... u-par-ri-ir. Z[B] ii 73 ina il-la-ti ka-çir-ti ša u-par-ri-ru; iv 48 li-par-ri-ru (3 *sg*). K 2852 + K 9662 ii 77 u .... ma u-par-ri-ru ka-çir el-lat-su. TP v 90 lu-pi-ri-ir (1 *sg*; § 33); V 45 iv 4 tu-par-ra-ar. 83, 1—18, 1335 iii 25 (ta-ar) TAR = pur-ru-ru. III 3, 17 mu-par-ri-ir el-la-te-šu-nu (KB i 12, 6); Sn iii 53 (*cf* III 29, 9) u-par-ri-ru (1 *sg*); v 42 u-par-ri-ir pu-xur-šu; mu-par-ri-ru, AV 5523; Anp iii 116 mu-pa-ri-ru ki-iç-ri mul-tar-xi.

ב[t] be broken {zerbrochen werden} Creat.-*frg* IV 106 ultu Tiâmat inâru ki-iç-ri-ša up-tar-ri-ra.

NOTE. — ZA iv 156, 11 pur-ru-ru, read by ZA v 43 šurruru (?).

Der. — perh. naprarû (?), but see nabrarû.

piruru (?) K 9287 iii 8 šum-ma pi-ru-ru-ti; 12 a-di pi-ru-ru-ti *Rev. Sém.* ix 153: si des jeunes moutons.

purrurtu. Rm 131 *R* 11 pur-ru-ur-tum.

parašu 1. 𝔔 II 30 *no* 4 *O* 10—11 (37, 38) pa-ra-šu (Br 1786); 𝔑 nap-ru-šu (Br 1787). AV 6076.

𝔓 (?) BA iv 119 *fol* on T. A. Ber 63, 18 u-[u-]pa-ra-aš be-ri-ku-[n]i; 61, 34 u tu-pa-ri-šu-nu be-ri-ku-ni, haben unter einander Worte gegen mich genommen.

𝔖𝔓 Anp iii 26: *Anp* whose face is directed toward the desert a-na ši-tap-ru-šu (Z^B 14; § 98) xu-te-ni-šu i-ça-xa libbu-šu (G § 48; JENSEN, 113; AV 3467 × KB i 98, 99).

𝔑 see 𝔔.

parašu 2. H^F 57; D^Pr 95; NÖLDEKE, ZDMG 40, 736; ZA i 417. — 𝔖, causative of 𝔑 make, cause to fly {fliegen machen}. IV² 27 *b* 18/19 (BA-AN-RA-AN-RI-RI-E-NE) see sinuntu, Br 2571, 2592. Sarg *Khors* 129 my warriors eli nârâtišu a-ra-niš u-šap-riš(-ma), I caused to fly like eagles (*Ann*, 330). L⁴ i 21 u-çu u-ša-ap-ra-aš si-mat qar-ra-du-ti, let fly the arrow, the indication of my heroic valor.

𝔖^t ag muš-tap-ri-šu, see muttaprišu (624 *col* 2).

𝔑 fly; then also hasten {fliegen} § 84. POGNON, *Wadi-Brissa*, 180 ip-pa-ar-ša-a (3 *pl*, *f*). TP ii 42 (iii 69) ki-ma iççuri (lu) ip-par-šu, they flew. Sn i 18 e-diš ip-par-šu (3 *sg*); iii 57 iç-çu-riš ip-pa-riš, he fled {er floh}; Sn *Kui* 3. 9 a-ri-biš ip-par-šu (3 *pl*); *Zû*-legend (K 3454 + K 8935 ii) 22 ⁽ⁱˡ⁾ Zu-u ip-pa-riš(-ma) KB vi (1) 48. KB vi (1) 300 ii 6 ip-par-šu-in-ni (escaped me); NE 78 (K 8582). T. A. Rost. 2, 23 (u-ul iç-çu-ru-u) ip-par-ra-šu-u-ma i-il-la-ku, but they should hasten & come. ag D 97, 17 ra-xi-çu mu-up-par-ša; Šamš ii 49 iç-çur mu-par-šu, a winged bird (§ 122); III 15 i 15 *cf* sisinnu (?). Also *cf* su-dinnu & mupparšu.

𝔑^t = 𝔑 IV² 4 *b* 1, 2 ki-ma iç-çu-ri ana aširi rapši lit-tap-ra-aš (= XA-BA-NI-EB-RI, Br 2571), let him escape (§§ 93, 1 *a*; 97). ag muttaprišu see *p* 624 *col* 2; S^P 987, 11 a-ri-bi mut-tap-ri-šu i-ra-mu, the raven who has wings, he loves (*Jour. Trans. Vict. Inst.*, 29, 52).

𝔑^tn it-ta-nap-raš, it flies (§ 97); it-ta-nap-ra-šu BEZOLD, *Catalogue*, 1472.

purrušu in pu-u pur-ru-šu (AV 6984, 7133; Br 632, 3497) see parû 2.

pi(a?)ršu *1.* fecal matter, contents of the intestines, filth {Mist, Excremente} = פֶּרֶשׁ. Sn v 83 da-mu u pir-šu ri-it-mu-ku ma-ša(or gar?)-ru-uš, blood and filth ran (dripped) down its wheel; Asb ix 37 for their thirst they drank dâmê u mê pir-šu (*i. e.* the water gathered in the stomach of a camel) HAUPT, Hebr, iii 120; BA i 175, and in MOORE, *Judges* (SBOT) 80; also see ZA x 83. Perhaps II 31 *b* 83 officer pir-šu.

paršu *2.* perhaps in II 43 *a-b* 62 U ka-ni-nu par-šu | U xa-lu-ku(?); *ibid a(-b)* 60 U a-xu-lap par(pir)-šu.

paršu *3.* Z^Š ii 63 maš-ru pa-ar-šu pi-i-šu, ist lose, unflätig sein Mund; see also II 35 (*no* 1) *a-b* 7 par(?)-šu, to which the scribe adds a-mat la i-du-u (Z^Š *p* 54).

parašu, Xammurabi-letters = parasu *b*; BA iv 481.

paršû see mašâšu, 596 *col* 1; Br 14370 on K 4200, 12; AV 7081.

parišû (?) Nabd 78, 16 III KU pa-ri-ši-i, BA i 534, 8: bandages {Binden}?

paruššu *m* staff {Stab}. IV² 60* C *R* 8; V 47 *b* 1 see saxalu (𝔓) *p* 750 *col* 1.

pu(a)ršu'û flea {Floh} Hebr פַּרְעֹשׁ, § 61, 3. AV 7002, 7135. II 5 *c-d* 25 ⁽ᵘ⁻ˣᵘ⁾ UX = pur-šu-'-u; H 28, 611; S^c 12; V 29, 62; ZDMG 34, 758; Br 8295—6.

parašû, in ka-lab pa-ra-ši-i, II 6 *a-b* 10, between kalab Êlamti & kalab mâ. TSBA v 53 a swift dog (√פרש) AV 6975; *cf* JENSEN, ZA xv 280 identifies Parašî with marxaši = die Susiana; *cf* II 50 iii/iv 23; ZDMG 53, 656 *foll.*

paršigu (AV 7000) see parsigu.

פרשד. 𝔑 *pr* ipparšid, *ps* ipparaššid, ac naparšudu, flee, flee away {fliehen, entfliehen} Br 1439; AV 6998; often with pa-ni, ina pân, ištu pân, lapân. or without preposition. ip-par-ši-id (& -šid) TP III *Ann* 45, 178, 200; 170, the rest who ip-par-ši-du lapân kakkê ⁽ⁱˡ⁾ Ašur dannûti. Sn i 82 who la-pa-an kakkēja ip-par-šid-du; Sarg *Khors* 133. Sams iv 18, 19 nišē ša pa-ni kakkē [-ia] ezzûte ip-par-ši-du. TP i 85 who i-na pa-an kakkēja ip-par-ši-du, ii 2, 3; v 55, 56 who i-na pa-an kakkē ša (il) Ašur ip-par-ši-du; see also Anp i 68 (ip-par-ši-du-ni), ii 9; i 72; ii 82 + 90. Asb vii 119 ip-par-šid-ma in-na-bit ana ru-qi-e-ti; x 12 e-diš-ši-šu ip-par-šid and took to the mountains (Smith, *Asurb*, 55, 72); iv 62 e-du ul ip-par-šid (no one escaped; ix 40); I 44, 54 e-diš ip-par-šid-du-ma ma-tu-uš-šu-un, and escaped alone to their country; *cf* Sn i 23; *Kui* 1, 5; *Bell* 6; I 43, 8 a-na mât tam-tim e-diš ip-par-šid. Esh iii 41 who ul-tu la-pa-an kakkūja ip-par-ši-du; Asb ix 56 ša la-pa-an kakkē (il) Ašur bēli-ja ip-par-ši-du; Sarg *Ann* 31. II 19 *b* 3—4 ša šadû ina qa-ti-šu la ip-par-šid-du (= KUR-ŠU-NA-NU-SUB-BU, Br 1439); V 60 *a* 11 his (Šamaš') picture and its adornment i-na qāti ip-par-šid-ma, had disappeared, BA i 270. Bu 88—5—12, 75 + 76 vii 33, 34 ina qātē ip-par-ši-du (3 *sg*); also see ZA vi 236. H 128 (K 257) *O* 69—70; IV² 26 *a* 42 see purîdu, 1. Sarg *Ann* 127 iççuriš ip-par-šid-ma. Written iD + šid Knudtzon, 56 *R* 6; *ac* R[U-š]id-di, 57, 8. Creat.-*frg* IV 110 na-par-šu-diš (*cf* nîtu & lumû); Asb iv 62 sa-par ilâni ša la na-par-šu-di isxupšunûti. Smith, *Asurb* 59, 88 *b* ina me-si-ri dan-ni ša la na-par-šu-di, a blockade which could not be run (§ 143). — 𐎼ᵗ Peiser, *Jurisprud. Babyl.*, 38, 39 it-ta-par-šid & it-ta-par-ši-id. — 𐎼ᵗⁿ Ultu šade-e bit mar-ki-ti-šu a-šar it-ta-nap-raš-ši-du (whither they had fled), Asb x 14.

parašd(t)innu. K 2061 i 5 (H 202) . . . KIRRUD (= xurru)-DA = pa-ra-aš-din-nu (Br 14368, AV 6977).

פרשׁם. ℑ K 597 *R* 6—7 may my lord, the king ana mâr-mârâni lu-par-ši-im, attain old age (extending) to (the times of) our grandchildren (Hr^L 283; AJP xvii 490). K 595 *R* 7 (Hr^L 6) see R. F. Harper, AJSL x 197; xiii 210, 211; Rm 76 *R* 14 (Hr^L 358). — ℑᵗ K 501 *R* 15, 16 mârē-šu-nu mâr-mârē-šu-nu | up-ta-tar-šu-mu, their sons and their grand sons shall attain old age. — 𐎼 Rm 76 *R* 8, 9 (Hr^L 358) ina libbi da-ru-te | ša šarri be-ili-ja šarru be-ili ip-par-ši-man-ni (BA iv 509 *foll*).

paršamu, pa(u)ršumu, *f* **paršumtu,** old, aged, venerable; old man, old woman; elder, sheikh {alt; Alter, Greis, Greisin; Scheich} BA i 230; = פַּרְתְּמִים, Haupt in AJP xvii 490 *rm* 3; S. A. Smith, ZA iii 101; § 61, 3, AV 7003, 7036. K 492, 18 (*R* 3) anâku (amêl) par-šu-mu (I am an old man) ša ṭi-en-šu la-aš-šu-u-ni (Hr^L 3; BA i 631): K 618, 15 (= V 53 *no* 3; Hr^L 9) a-na kalbi-šu ana ardi-šu u par-šu-me (BA i 224 *foll*); K 183, 16 (amêl) pur-ša-mu-te i-ra-qu-du (amêl) çixrûte i-za-mu-ru (Hr^L 2; BA i 617); K 482 *R* 6, 7 li-in-tu-xu par-šu-mu-a-te ina zi-ik-ni-šu-nu li-mur (BA ii 20). S 526, 17—18 pur-šum-tu (= UMMA, EME-SAL) ‖ ši-i-bu (31, 32); K 3500 + K 4444 + K 10235 ii 6 (end) (amêl) par-šu-mu-te ša mâti-ka (Winckler, *Forschungen*, ii 12 *foll*). V 29 *g-h* 62 UKKEN (me-is) MIS = pur-šu [-mu], ZA i 403, 405 *rm*; Br 905. II 32 *c-d* 30 pur-šu-mu (& sa-ar-rum, šu-gu-u) ‖ ši-i[-bu], ZA i 405, 408; *c-d* 66, 67 (= K 2051 iv 24, 25) UM-MA(+GAL) = pur-šu-um-tum (AV 1439; Br 3901, 3902; ZK ii 412); also see *ll* 68, 69 (Br 14422, 14455). V 42 *e-f* 66, 67 pur-šu-un-tum & BAR-BIL-GI = ši-[ib-tum]. III 68 *c* 10 (il) pur-šu-me (Br 13024).

Jensen, ZA vii 217 > paššumu]/ *p-š-m* = Hebr פשׂם, the bearded {der bärtige}.

pirtu 1. hair of the head {Haupthaar} = פֶּרַע, Jensen, 325; Jensen-Schulthess, *Homonyme*, 90. *pl* pirêtu. NE 8, 36 read perhaps: (Êabâni) [nu?]-up-pu-uš pi-ri-tu kîma sin-niš-ti; 37, pi]-ti-iq pi-ir-ti-šu ux(ix?)-tan-na-ba (KB vi, 1, 120—21; 425 refers to V 19 *a-b* 7 xanabu ša pir-tim); KB vi (1) 154 (iv) 6 uš-šur-tum pi-ri-tu. II 20 *a-b* 42 nussusu (see nasasu, 2) ša pir-tim. See also muttatu; ziqnu (beard) & šartu hair (of the body).

pirtu 2. see kannu 1. (*p* 406 *col* 1, beg.), AV 7079.

pirtu *3.* K 122 *R* 24—6 māru-šu ištu pi-ir-ti-šu i-za-az (Hr^{L} 43). BA iv 514, 515.

paritum. II 35 *g-h* 42 pa-ri-tum, apparently a ‖ of nullatum (*q. v.*) & mi-gir-tum, AV 6988.

parittum (paridtum, pašittum?) *adj* or *n*?. IV² 22 *a* 5 (K 2869) la-bar-tum pa-rit-tum does not permit me to sleep (Br 727). Rm 131 *O* 13 pa-rit-tum between ka-bi-is-tum & xa-liq-tum; M^{S} plate 20.

pa(i)r-ri-tu. K 2148 ii 19 .... par(?)-ri-tu ina li-ti-šu (see *p* 500 *col* 2) ša-kin.

parūtu. Rost, *Diss*, 55, Thesis *no* 4; *Tigl. Pil. III*, *pp* 122—3 & BA iii 210 limestone {Kalkstein}; so also Hommel, ZDMG 55, 528; also Meissner-Rost, 23; AJP xvii 121. On the other hand, Jensen, ZA ix 128: ein wertvoller Stein; also KB vi (1) 449—50; Haupt, *Johns Hopk. Circ.*, 114, 111 *col* 2: alabaster (agreeing with Jensen); also Abel, ZA vii 123 *rm* 1. Winckler, *Forsch*, i 271, 272: marble. — AV 6985. ideogram most likely (aban) GIŠ-ŠIR-GAL (Esh v 19; II 38 *b* 42; Br 1057; § 9, 151) & (aban) GIŠ-NU-GAL. Sarg *Khors* 159, 160 speaks of tablets of xurāçi, kaspi, uknê, (aban) aš-pi-e (aban) pa-ru-tim; *Ann* 421; written (aban) GIŠ-ŠIR-GAL Sarg *gold*-inscr. 34; *silver* 42; *Magnesite* 20 (see Winckler, *Sargon*, index). II 67, 80 askuppāte ..... (aban) pa-ru-ti aç-li (KB ii 24, 25 × -kup); Anp *Stand.* 20 beasts of mountain and sea ša (aban) pi-i-li pi-çi-e u (aban) pa-ru-te ūpu-uš. See also V 33 *e* 4; H 81, 25. V 30 *no* 5 (*h* 59) 1 (aban) pa-ru-tu foll. by (8) (aban) aš-pu-u (Br 12745); II 19 *b* 47, 48 speaks of ša-ad (aban) GIŠ-ŠIR-GAL (sa-an-ti, uk-ni-i *etc.*) & see Asb vi 49 where *-NU-* occurs as *var* of *-ŠIR-*. T. A. (Ber) 26 iv 7: I ŠU te-la-a-an-nu ša (aban) GIŠ-ŠIR-GAL, preceded by (aban) ja-aš-pu; also see *ibid* 10.

pārūtu, perh. = bārūtu in T. A. (Ber) 22 *R* 32, that my brother a-na pa-ni (amulu) pa-ru-ti-ja .... may greatly favor me, KB v 44, 45.

Purā(t)tu, name of the river Euphrates {Name des Euphratflusses}. § 27; AV 7120; D^{Par} 169; KAT² 39. ideogram (nār) UD-KIB-NUN-KI (Br 11665) = pu-rat-tum, II 50 *c-d* 8 & often; I 67 *b* 21 (end); the same ideogram in II 48 *a-b* 47 = u-ru-ut-tum (*q. v.*); called in II 51 *a-b* 26 na-piš-ti ma-a-ti. §§ 9, 1; 26; ZDMG 53, 657 *fol.* Bezold, *Catalogue*, v 2159. Sm 1366 (H 118) *R* 3—4 ina gi-ir-si-e (*cf p* 232 *col* 2) ša a-ax Pu-rat[-ti] Br 10423. Often in Šalm, *Obel*, 27, 33 *etc.*; also ideogram (nār) A-RAD (Br 11444; D 113, 1 = III 5 *no* 6; thus also II 67, 9). Neb v 8 a-bar-ti Pu-ra-at-ti. TP vi 42 a-di e-bir-ta-an (nār) Pu-rat-ta (*var* te); also iv 71 (-te); v 56 (-ta). Anp iii 48 ina šidi am-ma-ti ša (nār) Pu-rat-te (& 49). *del* 11 (12) Šurippak [i-na kišā]di (nār) Pu-rat-ti šak-nu, situate on the bank of the Euphrates river. NE 49, 194 ina (nār) Pu-rat-ti im-su-u qa-ti-šu-nu. Neb 251, 4 nār ki-la-a-tum ša (nār) Pu-rat-tum; Sarg *Khors* 128 ul-tu ki-rib (nār) Pu-rat-ti. V 60 *c* 22, 28 ina e-bir-ti (nār) Pu-rat-ti. H 75, 4, 5 mê Pu-rat-ti (= (nār) UD-KIB-NUN-KI). H 36, 875 BU-RA-NU-NU | ideogram | [pu-rat-tum]. II 35 *c-d* 6 (nār) SA-XA-AN = pu-rat-tu, Br 3168.

Halévy, *Rech. crit.*, 259 *fol*, compares: קרת = פרת, √פאר, thus originally: branch, twig: a branch river.

pirit(šit?)tu. fright, terror, fear, oppression {Angst, Drangsal}. IV² 54 *a* 15 (= IV 61) see xattu (847 *col* 1). NE 77, 13 pi-rit-tum (Z^{B} 93). V 28 *a-b* 33 see xaštu, 1. and read thus AV 5367 instead of me-šit-tu. 83, 1—18, 1332 iii 35 + 37 MUD = gi-lit-tum & pi-rit-tum. ZA x 208 *O* 21 pi-rit-tum. T^{M} v 76 (78) pi-rit-ti a-dir-ti ja-a-ši taš-ku-nu-ni; vii 128 gi-lit-tum pi-rit-tum a-dir-tum. Knudtzon, 41—42 bi-rit-ti ŠI (= āmu)-ru, oppression I have experienced; also written pi-; for ideogram MUD *cf* S^{c} 57 = pa-ra-du; thus also IV² 21* *no* 2 *O* 18, 19 ina zum(çu?)-ri-ja bi-rit-tu iš-ku-na ‖ 17, ina qa-ti-ja a-ru-ur-ti iš-ku-na (Br 8463).

paratitinašu (?). T. A. (Ber) 26 i 4: I ma-il-dax-xu-ku rak-bi ša GIŠ (= epri) xurāçu uxxuçu pa-ra-ti-ti-na-šu.

pāšu 1. increase, add {vermehren, erweitern} ℑ IV² 61 *a* 70 see purku, & AJSL xiv 277. Perh. K 4225 dupl. 15 lu-up-pa-ši-ka (Br 9278).

pāšu 2. Q¹ K 1335 + 80—7—19, 335 *R* 3

(e-ta-am-ru) ip-tu-šu, Thompson, *Reports*, vol ii, they have passed off.

pāšu *3. m.* axe {Axt}? Zimmern, *Ritualtafeln*, 141 *rm* 5. AV 7012. Neb 92, 4 ište-en (?) pa-a-šu, preceded by (3) V xa-çi-na-a-ta, made by a smith. NE 53, 49 (+ 37, end) lu-u aš-ši pa-a-šu, KB vi (1) 187; 459—60. IV² 18* *no* 3 iii 9—10 pa-aš (= GIŠ-ṬU) il-pu-tu, preceded by pit-pa-nu; additions (Rm 2, 133) 10/11 pa-a-šu il-pu-tu-ka pa-a-šu. S^b 1 *O* ii 12 tu-un | ṬU | pa-a-šu (Br 11910; PSBA xv 297: torah), followed by qu-du & ta-kal-tum. V 38 *c-d* 41—43; H 36, 883, 884; 186, 10—12. II 44 *no* 6 *e-f* 35 GIŠ-ṬU = pa-a-šu (Br 11911) & 36, qud-du; *ibid* 30 GIŠ-MIR = a-gu-u, 31, GIŠ-MIR-ṬU = agû a-pa-ši (evidently mistake for pa-a-ši); see S (Scheil) 31, 52, 13*fol* where we have a-gu[-u], agû pa-a-[ši]; II 20 *c-d* 45—47 where a-gu-u pa-a-ši = GIŠ-MIR-ṬU, A-MI-A; ŠE-KU (Br 11594, 7493). *f* see pāštu.

pašu *1. e.g. del* 143 (149) i-pa-aš-šum-ma, see bašû & KB vi (1) 500; S^a ii 54*fol*; AV 7013; Br 2238; also D 134 *c* 19, ip-pa-aš-ši.

pašû *2.* Nabd 1128, 22 (end) sûqu pa-šu'-u (name of a street).

pûšu (?) a plant {eine Pflanze}. II 41 *g-h* 50 xammu ša bērâti = ^(šam) p(b)u-u-(?) ša . . .

piššu *1.* a plant {eine Pflanze} ZA vi 294 ii 15 piš-šu SAR. Can פשת be compared?

piššu *2.* ointment {Salbe}? √pašašu; see mašqu, end (*p* 608 *col* 2).

pašaxu. *pr* ipšax, *ps* ipaššax, *pm* pašxu, become soothed, appeased, set at rest, calm, reconciled {sich besänftigen, beruhigen; versöhnt werden}; of a sick person: recover {von einem Kranken: wieder besser werden, genesen}. AV 7004; Br 3062, 3067. H^F 31; § 138; RÉJ XIV 158; Jensen, ZA i 188; iv 268; vii 219; xv 182, 183; KB vi (1) 512, 513 = פשח = فسح, Barth, *Etym. Stud.*, 9. — Sm 949 *O* 15 see dullu, 2 (*p* 248 *col* 1). K 2619 iii 19 an-na-a ēpuš-ma a-pa-aš-ša-xu (and I am now satisfied) KB vi (1) 64, 65. IV² 7 *a* 22, 23 ina mi-ni(-i) i-pa-aš-šax, Jensen, *Diss*, 33, how can he (the sick) recover? (IV² 22 *a* 54, 55, Br 6323). IV² 21 *b* 11 whose heart . . . šap-liš la i-pa-ši-xa-am (but H 200, 201: i-pa[-aš-ša]-xa-am), 13 la i-nu-xa-am; if IV² is correct, then = נח > ippašix. K 11, 41 ni-ip-šax, BA ii 26; Hr^L 186. K 2852 + K 9662 i 34 (end) ul i-pax-šu ez-zi-tu ka-bat-ti (‖ ul i-nu-ux); K 61, 8 i-pa-šax (ZK ii 12); Rm iv 90 *O* 20 thy sickness lip-šax-ma (may it ease). H 128 *R* 10 (end) ka-bit-ta-ki lip-šax (*cf* nâxu); 115 (K 101) *R* 5—6 (end) lip-ša-xa (= TE-EN-TE-EN-EME-SAL, Br 7718) = IV² 29** *no* 5. ZA iv 227 (K 3216) 2. Sm 954 *R* 9, 10 (*cf* 17, 19 *etc.*). Perh. IV² 59 *no* 2 *R* 9 ana mu-u-tum pa-aš-xi (Z^B 100); on V 65 *b* 17 (beg) see ZA iii 304. — T. A. (Lo) 51, 20—21 pa-ši-ix lib-bi-ja danniš, my heart is perfectly at rest. (Ber) 61, 31 pa-aš-xa-ti, I will live in peace; (Ber) 184, 40 pa]-aš-xa-at, is peaceful; *3 pl* (Lo) 12, 37 pa-aš-xu; (Lo) 25 *R* 7; (Ber) 63, 10 (they have rest); (Lo) 12, 27 u pa-aš-xa-tu-nu, and you will then have rest. — 88, 1—18, 1330 iii 39 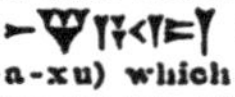 (si-id) = pa-ša-xu (& na-a-xu) which also in II 26 *c-d* 16 (Br 3062); 17, 18, 19 see Br 7883, 8457, 7718. ID with gloss še-e in S^c 242; S^c 44 ga-al | GAL | pa-ša-xu (H 14, 175) Br 2247. H 185 (K 4225) 6 ^(e) A = pa-ša-xu, followed by a-ša-bu; A = nâxu, *cf* 661 *col* 2 (bel), Br 11350. See also Br 5584 *ad* K 4225 dup. *O* 10, 11.

NOTE. — 1. K 146, 21 (Hr^L 192) lip-šu-xu. 2. Bu 88, 5—12, i 24 ip-šul, perhaps mistake for ip-šax (BA iii 274).

Q^t K 3216, 2 + 4 i-tap-šax kab-ta-tuk (ZA iv 227).

ᴣ appease, calm, quieten, reconcile; heal (?) {besänftigen, beruhigen, versöhnen; heilen (?)} M^S 78 *col* 2. pušuxu, appeasement of the wrath of god, Zimmern, *Ritualtafeln*, 92 *rm* 9; *Jour. Bibl. Lit.*, xix 73 *rm* 60. Sm 954 *R* 14 *cf* nâxu ᴣ (*p* 662) where read li-pa-aš-ši-ix. Also see IV² 24 *no* 3, 26, 27; IV² 21* *no* 2, *O* 26—27 (28, 29) libbu-šu (libbi bēlûtišu) ina pu-uš-šu-xi (Br 7883) linûxam; 36, 37 ana pu-uš-šu-ux libbi-šu. V 35, 26 an-xu-ut-su-un u-pa-aš-ši-xa, their sighing I quieted;

others, their delapidation I repaired. T^M vii, 41 u-pa-aš-ši-ix bu-a(?)-ni(?) mi-na-ti-ka NU ṭābāte ^{pl} (BA iv 161; Sarg *Cyl* 41: šamnu ^{pl} mu-pa-ši-ix bu-a-ni; Lyon, *Sargon*, 59; AV 5524); vii, 33 šamnu mu-pa-aš-ši-ix (šēr) bu-a-na ša a-me-lu-ti; 49 [ ] ⋿-šu-ut Eri-du li-pa-aš-ši-xu SU-KI(?). IV^2 22 *no* 2, 15 (end) ul u-pa-aš-ša-ax-šu (Br 7718); *a* 39 ul u-pa-aš-šax. ZA iii 48 (bel) arallū called bît xarrāni mu-pa-šix-tu, rest, restingplace. IV^2 30 *no* 2, 31 ana xar-ra-ni .... mu-pa-ši-xat (Br 1528) a-me-lu-ti; thus is called the road to arallū (ZA iv 43, 44; J^w 49); Nabd 1133, 13 (end) mu-pa-ši-xi.

ℑ^1 Banks, *Diss*, 16, 163 u-ta-tap-šax kīma ša ūmi ul-lu-ti.

Š Asb v 120 I smashed their idols u-šap-ši-ix (il) (or ān, *c. st.* of ānu? *var* caret) ka-bit-ti bēl bēlē (Jensen, ZA xiii 334 = an(a) = Arm ל, nota accusativi). I 49 *c* 7 (ana) šup-šu-ux ka-bit-ti-ka (BA iii 220, 221); Sn *Kui* 4, 36. K 4648, 11 ina šup-šu-ux ka-bit-ti-šu (II 178, 78). IV^2 19 *b* 7, o the goddess Gula ina me-šid qa-ti-ša el-li-te li-šap-šix-šu. V 65 *b* 18 li-šap-ši-xu kab-ta-at-ka. IV^2 54 *O* 34 (end) li-šap-šax lib-bu-uk-ka. T^M v 144 (il) Marduk li-šap-šix-ku-nu-ši, *M* may calm you; L^4 ii 17 u-šap-ši-xu pitpānē-šu-un ma-l[a-ti?], und setzten zu Ruhe ihre (mit Pfeilen) gefüllten Bogen. T. A. (Ber) 57 *R* 11 ju-ša-ap-ši-xu, and gives peace (to his lands). ZA iii 344 li-[šap-ši-ix]. ZA v 67, 35 mā'al mu-šap-ši-ix ilū-ti-ki. Sarg *Cyl* 5 Sargon ..... mu-šap-ši-xu nišē-šu-un, who brought rest and peace to their inhabitants (AV 5590; *cf* Rp 6); 21, Sargon who .... u-šap-ši-xu(-xa, *Khors* 9) (māt) Qu-e u (al) Çur-ri, brought peace to Q. & Tyre. BA iv 284 on T. A. (Lo) 18 *R* 32 (KB v *no* 94) šu-up-ši-ix. Zimmern, *Ritualtafeln*, 79—82 iii 9 qāt nu-ri u-šap-ša-ax šamnu šaman piš-ša-te ša rubū(-e). K 232 *R* 25 i-nam-din te-e ša šup-šu-xi ši-pat balāṭi (Craig, *Relig. Texts*, ii 17; Martin, *Textes religieuses*, 107, 108.)

Š^t IV^2 54 *no* 1 *R* 3 liš-tap-ši-ix šer-ta-ka ka-bit-ta, Z^B 90.

Š3 K 8286 ii 9 uš-pa(-aš)-šax; K 9459, 6 (ZA iv 14; 227).

ℜ see ℚ and perhaps 79, 7—8, 178 *R* 3 .....]-ni at-me-šim-mu ši-i lip-pa-aš-xa (KB vi (1) 10, 11).

Derr. šupšuxu, tapšaxu, tapšuxtu & these 2:

pašāxu *n* (?) T. A. (Lo) 29, 11—12 (he who puts to sleep all the lands) i-na pa-ša-xi (in peace), KB v 271 compares נחבש. ZA v 68, 22 lim-qu-ta pa-ša-xi (my peace); also K^M 8, 7 (end) pa-ša-xa šuk (-ni?), do thou give consolation.

pušxu (?) IV 61 *b* 43—5 ka-kiš-a-ti pu-uš-xa-a-ti ša i-da-ba-bu-u-ni.

pašxu (or **pašaxtu?**). T^M vii 46 ina] qātē (II) pa-aš-xa-ati ša (il) Nin....ga (BA iv 161); *ibid* 36 [ša (il) Ē-a id-di-nu] a-na pa-aš-xa-a-ti.

pašxu. So perh. (with KB i 124) instead of parumxu, and thus also puašxu (*cf* na'adu and nu-a-du), *pl* pašxāti, a weapon {eine Waffe} KB i 125 on I 28 *a* 11: 120 lions .... ina (iç) pa-aš-xi i-duk (spear {Speer}); Lay 44, 24: 370 lions ina (iç) pu-aš-xi a-duk (*ibid. rm* 8, below). Šalm, *Obel*, relief inscr. II (end) (iç) pu-aš-xa-ti (Scheil, *Šalm*, 72—73; KB i 150—1); *ibid* IV (iç) pu-aš-xa-a-ti.

NOTE. — KAT^2 208: burāxu; others b(p)u-dilxu. REJ x 4; Hommel, *Gesch*, 613 *rm* 1; Hastings, *Dictionary of the Bible*, i 184 *col* 2; & pa(u)rumxu.

pašaṭu, *pr* ipšiṭ, *ps* ipaššiṭ; *ip* pišiṭ expunge, destroy, blot out, obliterate, efface, especially some writing, so as to write something else on top of it; literally: smear, cover writing with clay = mašadu & katamu {vernichten, tilgen, auslöschen, namentlich etwas geschriebenes}, AV 7005. V 62 *no* 1, 26 *fol* ša šu-me šaṭ-ru u šum ta-lim-ja ina šipir nikilti i-pa-aš-ši-ṭu (*cf* 61 vi 42), whosoever destroys maliciously my signature and the name of my twin (?) brother. P^1 29, 30; S^1 28; L^5 31; S^2 64; S^3 83; L^1 21; L^2 26; P^3 26 (Lehmann, *Šamaššumukin*); S^c 332, 333 ša šu-me šaṭ-ru i[-pa-aš]-ši[-ṭu] šum-šu i-šaṭ-ṭa-ru | (il) Nabū DUP-SAR gim-ri MU-šu lip-pi (*var* ši)-it(ṭ); Le Gac, ZA ix 386, 4 šum-šu lip-ši-du (= ṭu). Esh *Sendsch*, *R* 54, 55 whosoever šu-me šaṭ-ru i-pa-ši-ṭu-ma šum-šu i-šaṭ-ṭa-ru; SCHEIL, *Rec. Trav.* xvi, 178, 179 MU-SAR la ta-pa-šiṭ (2 *sg*) = KB iv 102, 26; see also *ibid* xx 208 *col* 5, 2—3 (i-pa-ši-ṭu); TP viii 69; IV^2 39 *R* 14, 15 (ZA v 41); see also KB i 4, *no* 5, 5—6 (i-pa-aš-ši-ṭu); K 5201 colophon (last but one line) ša šu-me šaṭ-ru i-pa-aš-ša-ṭu (H 184). I 27 *no* 2, 71 perhaps: ša .... i-pa-ši(l)-tu (for ṭu)? K 4335 iii 7 pa-ša-ṭu; K 2009, 9 see si-e-ru (Br 7175; ZA iv 155; v 40).

𝔓 = 𝔔 AV 7525, 7005 mu-pa-šiṭ-ṭu si-ma-te-ja, *etc.* Sarg *Cyl* 66; *Silv* 51; *Cyl* 76 who si-ma-te-ja u-pa(-aš)-ša-ṭu-ma, *bull*-inscr. 104; see also *Cyl* 41. I 70 *c* 5 whosoever this inscription u-pa-aš-ša-ṭu-ma ša-nam-ma i-šaṭ-ṭa-ru. AV* 53 *col* 2 has li'ū duppūnišunu pu-uš-šu-ṭu.

𝔓^t V 56, 33 if some one šu-um ili u šarri ša šaṭ-ru up-taš-ši-ṭu-ma ša-nam il-ta-aṭ-ru (KB iii, 1, 170, 171).

𝔖̌^{3} ZA iv 229, 11 tuš-pa-aš-šaṭ (K 8235 + K 8234 ii).

Der. — šipšīṭu.

pašku. Camb 102, 5—6: pa-aš-ku *pl* i-na-aš-ši.

pušku. Nabd 492, 6—7: UR pu-uš-ku; 696, 32; 1090, 5—6: 3 kib-su .... 3 šal-xi, 1 UR pu-uš-ku. UR = šūnu, na-palsuxu, kibsu, Br 4835 *etc.*

p(b)uš(s)ikku, some special kind of fur or woollen material {Eine besondere Art Fell oder Wollstoff}. V 14 *a-b* 15—18 SEG-GA-ÇU-AG-A (Br 6128; ZK ii 43 *rm* 3); SEG-GIŠ-NI (Br 5715); SEG-LAB-BA-DU (Br 6212); SEG-DU (Br 5250) = pu-šik-ku. PSBA xiv 158 translates: particoloured, speckled.

pašalu 1. AV 7006. V 19 *c-d* 35—37 (K 2008 iii 37—39) U-SAR-KI-TAG-GA = pa-ša-lum (Br 6050; V 42 *a-b* 62); KU-KU-RU = pi-še-lum (AJP viii 280, 25; AV 7081; Br 10651, same id = ka-lu-u ša me-e, Br 10650; raxaçu ša ašabi, II 24 *a-b* 45, *etc.*); U-TAG-TAG = pi-taš-šu-lum (§ 98; Br 6048), in a group with i-taš-lu-lum. Z^B 50; 73—75: beseech, Syr פתל turn to (?); ZIMMERN, *Ritualtafeln*, *p* 148 *rm* *e*. T. A. (Ber) 28 iv 9: 19 (iç) ga-çu ša šin-piri pa-aš-lu (& 26 ii 61).

𝔔^t K 4623 (H 123) *R* 1, 2 be-el-tum qa-ta-a-a ka-sa-ma ap-ta-šil-ki, Br 6076: U-RI-A-RA-AB-TAG-TAG; Z^B 71: o lady my hands are bound, yet I beseech thee (??).

𝔔^{tn} perhaps IV^2 10 *b* 7 ap-ta]-na-ši-il.

𝔓^t see 𝔔.

𝔖̌ see MEISSNER & ROST, 100 *R* 3: adi 1 šiqlu šup-šu-lim-ma; K 9873 *O* 7 ina iddē ša tu-šap-ši-lu (?).

Der. pišālu see pašalu, 𝔔.

pašalum 2. ZA x 208 *O* 13 xa-ba-tum ša a-la-ku: pa-ša-lum (Z^B 58) ina dup (pu) ul ša[-ši-tum].

pašallu see pasallu, & KB vi (1) 278/9 *rm* 8.

paš(s)ultu, some instrument, implement {ein Gerät, Werkzeug} AV 7014. D 87 (K 4378) i 43—45 GIŠ-BA-SU (Br 111), GIŠ-BA-KA, GIŠ-BA-SEG (which, 46, = pu-u-dum, *var* pu-'u-du) = pa-šul-tum. See also supinnu.

pišannu. BA i 498; 632 √*p-š-š*, whence piššatu, cover {Decke}, AV 3822. Nabd 186, 5: 5 minas a-na pi-ša-an-ni; 213, 2: 5 1/2 šiqlu ... a-na pi-ša-an-na for the temple of the 'queen of Sippar'; 1029, 7 ta-bar-ri a-na dul-lu ša pi-ša-an-ni; see also Cyr 190, 6; Camb 24. 1—2: 5 ma-na kaspi a-na di(or ṭi)-mi-i-tum (√ṭamū?) ša pi-ša-an-na; Camb 158, 6; KB iv 284—5 *rm* †† compares Hebr קשׂת. 82—5—22, 940 *R* 7 GI-MA-MA = pi-ša-an-nu su .... (PSBA xxiii 200—1).

NOTE. — HOMMEL, PSBA xix 315, § 37 ('97 Dec.) = epišannu: a third variant epišānu occurs in Camb 61, 4; 66, 7; 121, 6. But PEISER, *Or. Lit. Ztg*, i *col* 61: "besser zu streichen".

pašaqu. be high, difficult; painful, full of trouble {hoch, schwierig; schmerzvoll, beschwerlich sein}. 𝔔 NE 67, 24 pa-aš-qat ni-bir-tum šup-šu-qat u-ru-ux-ša; 60, 21 ša e-bir-ši-na pa-aš-qu (KB vi, 1, 204).

𝔓^t K 651, 12 up-ta-ši-iq (Hr^L 338).

𝔖̌ L^3 *R* 9 death encompasses me u-šap-ša-aq (and causes me trouble). K

---

pašalu 3. see bašalu (*p* 201); pišlātum see bišlātu (*ibid*).

3182 ii 9 šup-šu-qat u-ru[-ux-šu], whose way is steep, AJSL xvii 137; & see Q. Su *Kui* 3, 29 the bull-colossusses ina da-na-ni u šup-šu-ki (qi, Lay 38, 12), they had brought with great trouble and difficulties; K 41 *c* 6 ina bīti-ja ki-ma iç[-çu-]ri u-šap-šaq-an-ni, PINCHES, PSBA xvii 65 *foll*: he putteth me in anguish. Sp II 265 *a* xxii 4 see lūtu, 2 (*p* 501 *col* 1, above). *del* 74 (78) šup-šu-qu-ma, was difficult }war schwierig{. Perhaps K^{M} 9, 14 šup-ši-ka (= qa); *cf* 13 šu-uš-kin; also 22, 14—15; 42, 16 mu-šap-šiq (or piq?).

Š̆^tn Šalm, *Mon*, *O* 8, *Šalm*. ša ana tib taxāzišu danni kibrāti ul-ta-nap-ša-qa (§ 83, quake) ixilū mātāti .... išdašina. HAUPT, BAL 104, 13; HEBR. iii 124; KB i 152, 153; POGNON, *Bavian*, 153; also K 1349, 5 šamū erçitim ul-ta-nap-ša-qu.

Derr. — šapšaqu, šupšuqu & these 3:

pašqu, *adj* AV 7015. — *a*) strong }stark{ ‖ kapkapu (*q. v.*, 422 *col* 1). — *b*) steep, difficult, troublesome }steil, beschwerlich, mühevoll{ ‖ marçu, šupšuqu; H^{F} 68. TP ii 73 on mount Aruma eqil pa-aš-qi; iii 46 šadē pa-aš-qu-te; ii 77 gi-sal-lat šadi-i (ii 8 gir-re-te-šu-nu) pa-aš-qa-a-te. Asp i 43 ar-xi (45, gi-ri) pa-aš-qu-te; SMITH, *Asurb*, 55, 73 ur-xi pa-aš-ku-u-ti (KB 168, below). Sarg *Cyl* 11; *Khors* 15; Su iv 4 see ṭūdu (*p* 353 *col* 2).

pašqiš, *adv* with difficulty }beschwerlich, mühselig{. III 15 i 17 the road to Nineveh pa-aš-qi-iš ur-ru-ux-iš ur-di-ma. K 2675, 13 see namraçu, 1; K 2852 + K 9062 i 39 see marçiš, 1.

pušqu. *m* distress, sorrow, pain, trouble }Drangsal, Not, Beschwerde{ AV 1447, 7137. K 8522 *O* 9 (D 95) i-na pu-uš-ki u dan-ni ni-çi-nu šāršu ṭābu. V 44 *c-d* 58, 59 ... ina pu-uš-ki u dan-na-ti qa-ti ça-bat (Z^{B} 25; Br 1002), a Proper name (JENSEN, 361: help me in my distress and trouble); V 16 *g-h* 80 ZA-XA-AŠ = pu-uš-qu (H 41, 286, 287; ZK ii 410; Br 11801); followed by pu-ri-du. id also K^{M} 9, 35; 31, 6 (PAP-XAL, Br 1155); T^{M} ii 12. IV^{2} 30 *no* 1 *O* 11 kab-tum ša ina pu-šu-uq (= PAP-XAL, = strength?) pi-ris-tam (*q. v.*) la uç-ça-a. H 12, 112 PAP-XAL = pu-uš-qu; S^{c} 302, Br 1157; id also IV^{2} 59 *no* 2, 24 (see kimru, 1, *p* 398 *col* 1), and thus also *l* 22; K 2333 *R* 16 (end), T^{M} 130. Xammurabi mu-bi-it-ti pu-uš-qi šadē a-aš-tu-tim, KB iii (1) 117: der da öffnet die Unwegsamkeit unzugänglicher Berge. KB v 409 on (Lo) 12, 52 (end) pu-uš[-qam], and has seen his distress; (Ber) 80, 25 pu-uš-kan is explained by ma-na-rum.

NOTE. — On V 35, 19 (KB iii, 2, 124) see pāqu & pakū, BA ii 232—3.

paš(s)qū, an architectural technical term: copings }Stufenabsätze, Zinnen{. Esh vi 4 see nīb(i)xu, *p* 635, where add: "KB vi (1) 430 & sellu". II 67, 75 ul-tu šu-pul mē a-di pa-aš-qi (MEISSNER & ROST, 4; 27; 30 *rm* 44; BA iii 213); here perhaps also K 4378 (D 87) i 48 GIŠ-BA-BAL = pa-as (*var* aš, Br 111)-qu-u, same id = supin(nu) ša pilaqqi (*q. v.*).

pašaru, *pr* ipšur, *ps* ipaššar; *ip* pušur. id BUR (Br 327; AV 1411) H 9 + 204, 27; S^{b} 172 (Br 344); HEBR. ii 144; K^{M} 22, 12 BUR-RU-DA = pāšir; AV 7007; 7016; FRÄNKEL, *Aram. Fremdwörter*, 286. — *a*) loosen, free }lösen, befreien{ ‖ paṭaru. SCHEIL, *Nabd*, i 20 ul ip-šu-ur ki-mil-ta-šu. IV^{2} 49 *a* 22, 24, that & that lip-šur-an-ni; 16 *a* 9, 10 ilu u amēlu la ip-pa-aš-ša-ru; 8 iv 8 goddess Siris is called pa-šir ili u amēli; Rm 113 *O* 10 (BA ii 416, 417); see also II 51 *R* 10, 20, 25. IV^{2} 49 *a* 40; 7 *a* 35, 36; K 2860, 64, K^{M} 11, 10; 2, 38 see paṭaru. V 20 *e-f* 11 (Br 344, 2181) see mamītu (554 *col* 1; H 205, above); H 92—3, 18 (Br 3534); IV^{2} 57 *a* 9 lip-šu-ru-ni-šu ma-mit. T^{M} i 41 pa-ṭi-ra pa-šir (= *pm*); iv 97—110 pa-ši-ra-ak; i 20 lu pa-aš-ru, may be freed; i 60 kirru i-pa-aš-šar; iv 90, 91 ša mūši ip-pu-ša-nim-ma | ša kal ū-mu a-pa-aš-šar-ši-na-ti (& *cf* 92, 93). IV^{2} 54 *a* 32 i-pa-aš-šar-kum-ma, will he free thee? (Z^{B} 89). — lipšur, often. II 51 *a* 1 *foll*, *b* 25 *foll*; K^{M} 12, 78 lip-šu-ru, + 84 lip-šur-an-ni. V 48 ii 20: XVIII day of Aru: za-qu-tu pu-šu-ur (T^{M} 2, 65 pu-šur); K^{M} 50, 22 see pa-sasu, J. IV^{2} 38 *c* 33 ar-rat la pa-šu-ri (& often); H^{F} 14; Z^{B} 90; ZA i 220. Sarg *Ann* 340 ušaçbita pa-ši-ru. III

66 *O* 19*c* $^{(ilat)}$ pa-še-ir-tu (Br 12751); K 655, 2 ardu-ka Nabû-pa-šir; K 625, 2; K 1234, 2 (Hr^{L} 182, 131, 134). — *b*) interpret a dream {einen Traum deuten} BA i 181 *rm* **; JBL xix 69 *rm* 42; ZA iii 233 (end). V 30 *e-f* 13 ME-GAL-ZU = šu-ut-tu pa-ša-ru (KB vi, 1, 552—3; Br 10439); K^{M} 6, 5 & 6 pa-šir û-mi, 7 *p* šunâti (?). NE 6, 44 šu-na-ta BUR-ar, izzak-ra a-na ummišu; 50, 210 it-bi-e-ma Êa-bani šu-na-ta i-pa-aš(*var caret*)-šar; KB vi (1) 431; ZA iv 26, 38. K 3182 i 54 ..... iš-me ša-i-li pa-ši-ri (*var* -še-ru) šunâte *pl* (AJSL xvii 136 & *rm* 29); iii 14 çi-it pi-i-šu-nu ta-pa-aš-šar at-ta, the words of their mouths thou wilt interpret. T. A. (Ber) 22 *R* 20 u la lu-u pa-aš-ra im-ma-ti-ma, & may that never happen (KB v 45). Here perhaps also II 24 *a-b* 4; V 32 *no* 4, 36 NAM-NE-RU = qa-au pa-ša-ri (Br 2179, 2431), instead of *ma* (or *li*, or *tu*)-ša-ri; see esp. Br 2181 where NAM-NE-RU-BUR-RA = mamîtu pašaru. — *c*) spend, give away money *etc.*; waste money; also sell {sich Geldes *etc.* entäussern, weggeben; verschleudern; verkaufen}. I 49 *a* 17, 18 since the Babylonians gold and gems a-na $^{(mât)}$ Elamti ip-šu-ru ma-xi-riš, wasted money on Elam as purchase price (BA iii 218 *fol*). Bu 88—5—12, 75 + 76 ii 6 (= K 192 *O*). Asb vi 15 gold, silver *etc.* which they a-na kit-ri-šu-nu (*p* 460 *col* 2) ip-šu-ru a-na $^{(mât)}$ Elamti (BA ii 204). DT 81 vi 8 u mi-im-ma bi-ša-am a-na pa-ša-ri-am id-di-in, BA iii 501 *foll*; also Rm 277 i 18 i-na pa? [-ša?]-ri-am, *ibid* 503, 504. V 22 *d* 25 pa-ša-ri, Z^{B} 116; Br 11757. Peiser, *Vertr.*, 250, 251: einlösen; *no* cxxx 20 such & such to Iddin-Nabû a-na pa-ši-ri aš-ku-nu; *ibid*, 10/11 P. N. Ta(p)-pa-šir. Also Peiser, *Jurisprudentiae Babyl. reliqu.*, 33 (VATh 1036, 6).

𝔓 loosen, free, set free {lösen, freimachen}. IV^{2} 40 *b* 48 the mighty firegod šipat-su-nu li-pa-aš-šir; 17 *b* 14, 15 O Šamaš thou art mu-di-e rik-si-šu-nu ‖ mu-xal-liq rag-gi mu-pa-aš-šir (= NAM-BUL[R]-BI-E, see *p* 680); 59 *a* 9 pu-uš-šu-ru u-pi-šu (+ 4) KB vi (1) 470. II 65 *a* 53 çi-lip-t[a-ša] | li-pa-še-ra ana ka-liš kib-ra-[a-te] KB i 203: verbreiten; T^{M} iv 50; v 123 anâku ana pu-uš-šur kiš-pi-ja u ru-xi-e-a. II 34 *g-h* 70, 71 ŠA(= LIB)-TA-KI(N)-GA (Br 8020); ŠA-AB$^{(bu-ru)}$-BUR-NUM (Br 8018) = pu-uš-šu-ru(m) Br 344; AV 7138; followed by nap-šur-tu[m]. V 13 *c-d* 53 mu-pa-šir [-šunâti?] preceded by mu-še-lu-u & ša-i-lu, *etc.*

𝔓^{t} Z^{8} iv 81 (3 *pl*) see mamîtu; IV^{2} 22 *b* 22 di-'-u ša qaqqadi-šu lip-ta-ši [-ir].

𝔑 *a*) be freed, released, loosened {gelöst, befreit werden}. T^{M} 1, 70 a-ma-ti la ip-pa-aš-šar. IV^{2} 7 *a* 48 mâmit .... kîma pi-til-ti lip-pa-šir (= XE-EN-BUR-RI), § 93 note; *b* 18—25; K 155, 47 may the poisons that are upon him lip-pa-aš-ru, be loosened (K^{M} *no* 1); also T^{M} v 58; K^{M} 6, 13; 11, 2 [nap]-šur-šu a-bu ri-mi-nu-u. arrat la nap-šu-ri (KB iv 82 i 30; 214, 30 [-ru]; IV^{2} 12, 8 *foll*; ZA iii 72. 73) see napšuru. — *b*) be freed from anger; calm down; become reconciled {beschwichtigt, wieder gut werden}. ZA v 67 (81—2—4, 188) 14 ana zik-ri-a šum-ru-çi ka-bit-ta-ki lip-pa-šir (let thy mind be opened). IV^{2} 54 *b* 2 za-mar nap-šir-šu. K 8204, 4 nap-ši-ra ja-a-ša (= ip) PSBA xvii 138. — *c*) be explained. K 734, 3 ul ip-pa-aš-šir, it has not been explained (Thompson, *Reports*, ii *no* 83). Perh. P. N. $^{(amêl)}$ NINI ip-pa-aš-ra-am (*c. t.*).

𝔑^{t} 82—5—22, 63 *R* 1 ina še-e-ri it-tap-šar, Thompson, ii *no* 170: in the morning it shall be explained.

Derr. — napšuru, napšurtu, nipšaru, tapširtu (?) & these 4:

pašru *adj* II 32 *g-h* 67 [ŠE]-BUR-RA = pa-aš-ru (*sc.* še-um) AV 7016; Br 344.

piš(î?)ru, perh. interpretation {Deutung, Erklärung} 83—1—18, 37 (Hr^{L} 355) *O* 6 lik-ru-bu ina eli pi-iš-ri; 12/13 iš-šak-ku-nu pi-iš-ru-a-te ša šu-me ša arxê (AV 7082) + *R* 1 pi-iš-ra-te-šu-nu (Harper, AJSL xiii 212). III 51 *no* 9, 23 (29, 30) pi-šir-šu (& K 1304 *R* 9; Jensen, 30—2); KB iii (2) 64 *col* 2, 20 (ana ebêš bîti šuâti) pi-ši-ri ka-la Šamšu, Adad u Marduk aprus (K 3600). 83—1—18, 222, 2 [izziz] an-ni-u pi-še-ir-šu; K 8393, 3 an-nu-u pi-ši-ir-šu, THOMPSON, ii *nos* 111, 144 D; BEZOLD, *Catalogue*, 1759.

pišîriš *adv* AV 7083. TP viii 68 whosoever my memorial slab and my foundation stone ..... heaps up as rubbish (pi-ši-riš inakimu) in some dark place where they cannot be seen (but very doubtful); AJP viii 280, 25: as objects of interpretation, BA i 6 = ina pišêri (& 14 *no* 8).

piširtu *1.* IV² 8 *b* 52 kinûnu at-ta-pax, at-ta-di pi-šir(?)-tu. (AV 7084; ZK ii 31 *rm* 3); G § 113 (end), perhaps some implement to extinguish fire; a cover placed on the fire.

piširtu *2.* T^M iii 129 ina bi-rit qarnâti-ša na-šat pi-šir-tum. II 34 *g-h* 69 IN-DUB = pi-ši-ir-ti (Br 4237, AV 7084).

paširâti (?) JOHNSTON, JAOS xix (2) 45 + 76 guarantee, credentials (properly: explanation). K 13 *R* 2 a-na-ku pa-ši-rat-ti a-na Ummanaxaldâšu lu-še-bil-šu, I will send it (the royal signet) as a guarantee (*i.e.* to give force to my request); *ibid R* 4 ši-pir-ta-a pa-ši-rat-ti .... ašappar (Hr^L 281); *OLZ* ii *no* 5, *col* 157 explains it as: secret; secretly {Geheimnis; insgeheim} M^S 79 *col* 1.

(iç) **paširâte** (?) ZIMMERN, *Ritualtafeln*, 67 *O* 10 (iç) pa-šir-a-te + 68 *O* 15 where III (iç) pa-šir-a-te ša ŠE-PAD-ŠE-SA-A are mentioned.

paširu (?) II 32 *g-h* 15 (ni-gi-in) NIGIN = pa-ši-ru, H 32, 768; Br 10338; AV 7010.

paššûru table {Tisch}, or anything, whereon eating is placed (>< § 65, 28) AV 7017; ZA iii 53. main id GIŠ 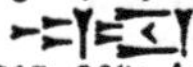 (H 11 & 217, 86; § 9, 31), Br 907, 908; Anp ii 67 where id & *var* GIŠ pa-šur (ZA i 365—6) xuraçi; Neb 312, 23 *etc.* Sarg *Cyl* 42; I 65 *b* 34. JENSEN, ZA vii 216 *rm* 3 = ; *cf* BA i 323. Esh vi 36 ina paššur tašilâti = Asb iii 90 ina paššur tak-ni-e | ul-ziz-su-nu-ti, BA ii 184; i 161 *rm* *; SMITH, *Asurb*, 153, 22. Nabd 258, 34: III (iç) pa-aš-šu-ru *pl*; id 990, 13. IV² 13 *a* 55, 56 ina pa-aš-šu-ri elli a-ka-lu ellu a-kul. V 24 *c-d* 48 *foll* tir-xa-as-su [ina?] pa-aš-šu-ri iš-ku[-nu]. NE 44, 66 û-mi-šam-ma u-nam-me-ru pa-aš-šur-ki. *Rec. Trav.* xx 127—8, 13 ina] ga-ti-šu el-li-ti pa-aš-šu-ra i-rak-kas; 14 u] ba-lu-uš-šu pa-aš-šu-ra ul ip-paṭ-ṭar see ZIMMERN, *Ritualtafeln*, *p* 94: Opfertisch oder Altar (properly: bowl: Schüssel), *p* rakasu >< *p* paṭaru; see also KB vi (1) 92—3; 407—8; 571. K 4378 (D 87) iii 53—55 (= II 46 *c-f* 33 *foll*) GIŠ-ŠU-KAT, (Br 7098); GIŠ-BI-BUR (S^b 64), Br 5215; GIŠ 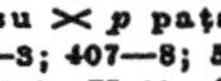 (S^b 269) = pa-aš-šu-ru; followed by *p* ra-bu-u (56), çi-ix-ru (57), ša qaq-qa-di (58); pa-aš-šur ili (59), *p* šar-ri (60); *p* ma-ak-ka-nu-u (61), *p* me-lux-xu-u (62), *p* u-ru-u (63), *p* ak-ka-du-u (64); *p* šak-ki (65), *p* a-šir-ti (66); it-gur-ti pa[-aš-šu-ri] Br 7751, AV 8620 (67); çu-pur paššûri (70); id in all instances = *l* 55. — II 23 *a-b* 13—27 has pa-aš-šu-ru ‖ of ..... li-u (13), gu-du-ut-tu-u (14), ... (xi-bi) (15), nu-un-u (16), e-ri-qa-u (17), mi-eš(-?)gag-gu-du-u (18), mi-eš te-gur-ru-u (19), mi-eš te-gu-du-u (20), mi-eš qa-lal-lu-u (21), tiš-ku-u (22), ka-ap-rum (23), gu-ub(p)-rum (24), (xi-bi) (25), ni-ik(-)si(-)li-qu (26), b(p)u-u-rum (27); 28, pa-aš-šur tak-ni-e = *p* su-xuš-ši. A ‖ is perhaps:

pašru. T. A. (Ber) 26 *c* 11: I pa-aš-ru kaspi uxxuzu I šu-ši šiqlu kaspi i-na libbi-šu na-di.

paššaru (??). KB iv 32—33 (*no* III) 16 and Idin-Sin pa-aš-ša-ar (*var* BANŠUR siparri) (11) Rab-KI-SUR-NA in-na-ši-im-ma, was brought to the copper altar of god *R.* (?).

pašašu (K^M 58, 8 pa-ša-šu), *pr* ipšuš, *ip* pušuš, *ps* ipaššaš, *ag* pâšišu, anoint, rub {reiben, einreiben, salben} with double *accus.* § 139. Z^B 28 *rm* 2; AV 7008. TP viii 48 the memorial slab of *Š*, my predecessor NI *pl* (*i. e.* šamnê) ap-šu-uš; 57 may he cleanse (li-ip [*var* lip]-šu-uš) with oil my memorial slab and the foundation cylinder. T^M vii 37 ap-šu-uš-ka šaman balâṭi (BA iv 161); i 106 see napšaštu. V 62 *no* 1, 25 my narû NI-IÇ (mostly written 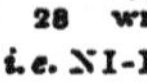, almost = kisallu, thus Z^B 28 wrong; more correctly  *i.e.* NI-IÇ, Sn *Bell* 63; *Bass* 94: lip-šu-uš, ZA iii 389) lip-šu-uš. Esh *Sendsch*, *R* 59 šamna lip-šu-uš (*i. e.* the ^aban narû); also see Sn vi 69; V 64 *c* 49; Sarg *Ann* 437; 81—6—7, 209 (Esarh. text) 38 (BA iii 260—8); Asb x 112. V 64 *b* 44; *c* 9 (ap-šu-uš). Esh vi 68 šamna pu-šu-uš (BA i 440); III 16 vi 20; IV² 26 *b* 48, 49 (Br 10814) with magic ointment seven times zu-mur amēli šu-a-tu pu-šu-uš-ma. K 3500 + K 4444 + K10235 i 17 šamni ina pa-ša-ši-ku-nu lu-xal-li-qu (Winckler, *Forsch*, ii 12 *foll*). IV² 56 *b* 52 (K 2971 *c* 18) see mixru, 1 (532 *col* 2, 1—3), § 98 & ZA xvi 108. II 25 *e-f* 26 MA(?)-NI-LU-AG-A = pa-ša-šu ša KU (Br 6309). Sᵇ 1 *col* iii 18 ŠE-EŠ  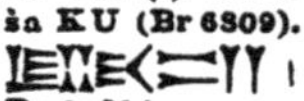 | pa-ša-a-šu, H 34, 819; Br 10814.

$\mathfrak{Q}^t$ = $\mathfrak{Q}$ *Adapa*-legend (T. A. Ber 240) *O* 22 ša-am-na u-ka-lu-ni-ku-ma bi-iš-ša-aš, KB vi (1) 96—7; BA ii 418 *foll*, 423); IV² 56 *col* 1 *add*, 2 (K 3377 + K 7087) 2 (end) ip-ta-ša-aš; *ibid* iii 34 ip-ta-ša[-aš], Zimmern.

$\mathfrak{J}$ K 4359 iv 8—9 BU ⁽šu-uš⁾ AG-A = pu-uš-šu-šu; ŠU-QI-A = *p* ša IN-NU, Br 7243, 7547; AV 7139. 83—1—18, 2 (Hr[L] 391) *R* 21 šarru li-pi-ši-iš (AJSL xv 141).

$\mathfrak{N}$ be anointed {gesalbt werden}, or rather reflexive: anoint oneself. Asb vi 21 ša ... ina libbi e-ku-lu iš-tu-u ir-mu-ku ip-pa-aš-šu (were anointed, > ippašišu, § 97; BA i 426: woraus man salbte; Winckler, *Forsch*, i 249 × KB ii 204, 205). Perh. K 576 *R* 4 šarru lip-pi-ši-iš (Hr[L] 110; AJSL xv 141; Martin, *Rec. Trav.* xxiv 105, 106); NE XII *col* i 16 see pūru, 1 (do not anoint thyself).

$\mathfrak{N}^t$ = $\mathfrak{N}$ *Adapa*-legend, *R* 29 [il]-gu-ni-šu-um-ma it-ta-ap-ši-iš (KB vi (1) 98, 99; BA ii 418 *foll*).

Derr. napšaštu (napšaltu) and these 3:

pāšišu (properly ag). an official, title of a priest {ein Beamter. Priester}, or a class of priests, magicians, charged with the anointing or preparing anointment. AV 7011; Haupt in Cheyne, *Isaiah* (SBOT) 82. H 32, 777. Bu 88—5—12, 75 + 76 vi 20 ra-am-ki pa-ši-ši (BA iii 246, 247). IV² 11 *a* 33, 34 pa-ši-is-su (= UX-ME-BI, EMESAL, Br 8327) ina ku-uz-bi it-ta-çi (also 29, 30). Scheil, *Rec. Trav.*, xvii 83 (*no* xxiii) ¹/₃ [šarru] dan-nu ...... pa-šiš ilu. *Adapa*-legend (KB vi (1) 92) 9 (end) pa-ši-šu muš-te-'-u par-çi (see *ibid* 368: Gewaschener, aber mit Öl; also *pp* 462—3). II 25 *c-f* 30—32 pa-ši-šu = UX-ME (*cf* NE 17, 49 + 19, 44, in Hades there live pāšiš apsī, written UX-ME-ZU-AB-MEŠ, ša ilāni rabûti; KB vi (1) 188—9; 559—60; 575; Meissner, WZKM xvi, '02, 201); LAX (LUX Br 6169; same id as sukkallu; see also T[M] 6, 102, 110 LAX-XA-ti-MU = ja); MAR-MAX (Br 5824). V 23 *a-b-d* 51 ME ⁽me⁾ = pa-ši-šu = S[c] 4, 6 (Br 10375); V 52 *b* 57 (Br 10810) = pa-ši-šu (58). Or pašlišu, Jensen, Zimmern, (KAT³ 590).

pāšišūtu. office, class of anointer, or preparing ointments {Stand, Klasse der Ölsalber}. D 134 *C* 19 qarçi akāli a-šar pa-ši-šu-ti (= NAM-LAX; Br 2191) ip-pa-aš-ši, Meissner, 147 *rm*; Hommel, *Sum. Lesest.*, 119.

piššatu. *a*) salve, ointment, oil {Salböl, Salbe, Öl} Meissner, *Diss*, 42; Z[B] 28 *rm* 2; J[w] 97 *rm* 3; AV 1263, 7085. II 9 *c-d* 47—50 see lubuštu (475 *col* 1) to which II 39 *c-d* 51 NI(?)BA = piš-ša-tum is evidently a glossary. Nabd 697, 7 + 11; Cyr 339, 5; KB iv 214—15, 7. II 25 *e-f* 27—29 NI-BA = piš-ša-tum (Br 5336); NI-BA 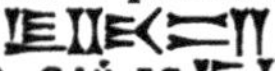 = piššatum (Br 5337); GIŠ-IG 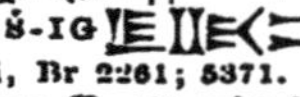 = da-lat piš-ša-ti, Br 2261; 5371. I 27 *no* 2, 58 see katamu $\mathfrak{Q}$, 457 *col* 2, bel. & KB i 120—121. *del* 72 (76) ap(b)-t[e šik-kat] piš-ša-ti, KB vi (1) 235 opened a salve box. NE 49 (VI) 191—2 six *gur* of oil ..... | ana piš-ša-ti eli-šu ⁽ⁱˡ⁾ Lugal-banda i-qiš (KB vi, 1, 176, 177). — *b*) salve box {Salbenbüchse} T. A. (Ber) 25 *b* 43: I bi-iš-ša-tum.

p'ā'štu *f* Jensen, KB vi (1) 460 a two-edged sword {eine zweischneidige Axt} Syr פוסתא; Pinches, PSBA xxiii, 195. IV² 6 *b* 40 qa-an pa-aš-ti ša ša-l(q)um-ma-tu ra-mu-u, Br 258. Rm iv 90 *R* 6 da-mu ina pa-aš-tum (with a two-edged sword) li-im-xa-aç, PSBA xxiii 205; V 17 *a-b* 42 SAG-GI-PA (= SIG)-GI = maxaçu ša pa-aš-ti, Br 3558, preceded by (40) *m* ša u-çi (arrow). K 537 *O* 11 (end) ⁽māt⁾ pa-aš-ša-te (Hr[L] 208). K 8676, 29 pa-al-tu, same iδ as IV^2 6 *b* 39, 40; ZA viii 76 *foll.*

pa-šu-ut li-ši-i ka-çir-tu, 83—1—18, 33 *ll* 11—12. BA iv 513 der feste Lappen (pašûtu) der Leber (lišû).

pu-uš-tum, II 88 *h* 78; Br 11801; see pušqu.

pišâti. NE 45, 73 + 86 see bi'šu (end) *p* 140 *col* 2; KB vi (1) 170, 171; 172, 173 leaves pi-ša-a-ti & er-ri-e-ti untranslated; also see *ibid*, *p* 451; the meaning of the word is certainly very doubtful; some compare Phoen ב־שׁתמא: malitia.

pâtu corner, side, boundary, limit {Ecke, Seite, Grenze} ‖ pâṭu (*q. v.*). D^{Pr} 34: פָּאתָא; *cf* פֵּאָה (ZDMG 40, 615 & 725; ZK ii 282 *rm* 2; Brown-Gesenius, 802). II 50 *c-d* 63 KUR-ZAG-GU-TI-UM-KI = (šad) pa-at Gu-ti[-um?] ZDMG 53, 656 *foll*: Grenzgebirge von *G*; Br 6524; AV 7019; also V 35, 31 (BA ii 212, 213; Prince, *Diss*, 83); same iδ in V 29 *a-b* 56 = pu-u-tum (Br 6484). S^b 364; AV 6898; Br 6484; Sarg *Khors* 69 (mât) Ma-da-a-a ša pa-ti (amêl) A-ri-bi; perhaps also II 67, 14 (al) Pi-il-lu-tu ša pat-ti (mât) E-lam-ti (KB ii 12, 13); II 39 (= V 39) *a-b* 11 KA-KA = pa-a-tum: nu (Br 577); *cf* KA = pu-u (1) AV 7030 (or to pû?); V 41 *c* 26 pa-a-tum = ??. Sm 1034, 11—12 pit uš-še pa-te | uš-še .... kar-mat BA i 614, 616; perh. *del* 132 (139) appalis kib-ra-a-ti pa-tu tâmti (KB vi, 1, 238—9, + 499: an der Grenze). — iδ ZAG also T. A. (Ber) 24, 24 ZAG la i-šu, has no limit; written pa-ta la i-šu *ibid* 43. — See Haupt, *Johns Hopk. Circ.*, 114, *p* 109 *fol.*

pàti. V 43 *c* 16 gloss pa-a-ti see mu-'u-a-ti, AV 7022; & again, Lehmann, i 143, 144.

pûtu. so instead of bûtu (*p* 147, 148) *f* front, entrance, border {Front, Frontseite} AV 7140; BA i 203, 205; ii 134, 135 (>< Rost, 120 *f* to pû). iδ SAG; SAG-KI, both also = pânu (§ 9, 166). V 20 *g-h* 48 pu-u-tum (preceded by šid-du & followed by šuplum, mîlû, rupšu) Br 3511; K 4558, 3 SAG (= RIŠ) = šid-du u pu-u-ti. V 29 *a-b* 56 SAG(ZAG) = pu-u-tum, Br 6488. *del* 181 (201) see lapatu, 493 *col* 1; § 74; and, again, KB vi (1) 506; *ibid* 298, 23 (end) p(b)u-ut(d)-ka šul-lim; 292, 9 where pag-ri u pu-u-ti (294, 2 [Zimmern, ZA xii 321, 322: in eigener Person]; 300, 15, reads pa-ag-ri u um-ma-ni); 555: Leib. H 91, 57—8 (Br 9482) see amartu (*pp* 61, 62) Br 2307. K 2107, 18 na-si-ix ša pu-ti. D 87 ii 59—61 GIŠ-SAG-GU-ZA = pu-u-tum (*var* -tu) Br 111; 8062. Sn v 63 a-na šid-di u pu-te ..... ana nakri a-zi-iq (288 *col* 2); II 38 *d* 4 šid-du pu-u-tum, which are often found together; written iδ UŠ (šiddu) u SAG (KI) = pûtu; Bu 88—5—12, 75 + 76 vi 30, 31 (BA iii 246, 247) & KB iv *passim*; K 433, 10, BA ii 134 *fol*; Peiser, KAS i 17, 19. K 4558, 3 šid-du u pu-u-ti. Nabd 760, 9 SAG (= pûtu) ki-i SAG-KI (= pûti), BA iv 22; Knudtzon, 38—40 has pu-ut, & usually SAG-KI (often); K 126, 8 pu-tu u arkati, RS i 169. Neb 134, 4 ma-xi-iç (523 *col* 1) pu-ti-šu (24, 3—4 pu-tu-šu); Cyr 128, 12 aš-tar-tum ša VIII ŠU-SI pu-ut-su. III 66 *col* 4, 9 ilâni ša pu-tu, the gods mentioned afore? (PSBA xxi 120). — Note especially **mutir pûti**, satellite, body guard, "properly: he who stood at the entrance and turned back the approaching" (C. Johnston); Delattre, PSBA xxiii 57 *foll*: un commissaire royal. KB iv 166 *no* II, 9 + 11 (amêl) GUR-ru (*i. e.* mutîru) pu-u-tu; II 31 *a-b* 66 (pu-u-ti) Br 12345. K 79 *R* 25 (amêl) GUR-ru pu-tu. K 4395 *R* v 7 (amêl) GUR-ZAG with gloss (amêl) GUR pu-u-te; see III 46 *no* 3, 34. Sn iii 72 it-ti (amêl) GUR pu-ti (>< AV 1745) šêpêja nas-qûti. K 526, 9 (amêl) mutîr pu-tu; K 82, 14 + 18 (amêl) mutîr-ru pu-tu; K 609, 14 (amêl) mutîr pu-te; K 497, 6—11 (represents the king); K 664 *O* 12, 13; K 582 *O* 20; K 622 *O* 3; K 618 *R* 2 (Hr^L 226, 275, 246, 165, 336, 167, 306, 85; BA i 203; 242; 530; PSBA xxiii 53 *foll*). 83, 1—18, 10 *R* 11 mutîr pûtu tak-lu, a trusty satellite. — **pût, ina pût** (§ 81 *b*), Zimmern, BA iii 449; T^C 54, 55. — *a*) opposite, in front of, before, at the entrance (of a town, *etc.*) {gegenüber, am Eingange von}. NE 9, 43 see mašqû (608 *col* 2). V 60 (title in right upper corner, *l* 1 end) ina pu-ut ap-si, at the entrance to the ocean, BA i 269; Anp i 89; ii 109; iii 108 + 84 *etc.*; Šamš iv 41; also written ina

SAG, Anp ii 19; Šalm, *Mon*, *R* 66. Šamš ii 9 *K* ša pu-ut (al) Gar-ga-mis; Anp i 62 a mountain peak ša pu-ut (al) *N*. III 5 *no* 6, 46 (8) see 147 *col* 2; 61: mount *B* ša SAG (*i. e.* pût) tam-di. Bu 91—5—9, 296, 19—20 an-nu-u a-na an-ni-im ma-xi-iç pu-ti, one for the other strikes the responsibility, PINCHES, JRAS '97, 590—591. K 520, 10 ina pu-tu-u-a ta-az-zaz; K 678, 13, 15 ina pu-tu-ni (in front of us); maççartu ina pu-tu-šu-nu ni-na-çar (Hr^L 80; 506). Nabd 1128, 16—17 mu-çu-u ša ina pu-ti-šu, *cf* Neb 105, 1 ina .... pu-ut-tu? V 67 *no* 3, 42—44 *B* pu-ut še-e-pi | ša *N* muti-šu | .... na-ša-a-ta. K 786 *R* 2 ina pu-ut (il) Šamši na-pa-xi he shall pray; K 8713 *R* 13 so that I may raise myself pu-u-tu šarri bēlija (THOMPSON, *Reports*, ii 254, 272). Cyr 311, 1 pu-ut (amēl) mu-kin-nu-u-tu .... na-ši; Nabd 348, 2. — *b*) instead of, for (*ἀντί*) {anstatt, für} especially in these combinations: *a.* in the case of debtors assuming an obligation for payment (ZA iv 402); see MEISSNER, *Diss*, 45, & above, *p* 148 *cols* 1, 2. ište-en pu-ut ša-ni-i na-šu-u ša kir-bi | kaspi i-nam-din, Neb 138, 7—9. STRASSM., *Stockholm O. C.*, 27, 16 ana eli na-še-e pu-u-tu, to assume the obligation. KB iv 174 *no* II 6—7 ište-en pu-ut ša-ni-i na-šu-u (3*sg*); also 176 *no* iii 7—8. Camb 315, 14—15 ište-en pu-ut šani-i na-šu-u ša kirbi kaspi .... eṭṭir; 145, 10 *B* pu-ut e-ṭir na-aš-ši, assumes the obligation for the payment; 1, 6—7; 81, 13—14 ište-en pu-ut | šani-i na-šu-u. Neb 51, 7 pu-ut b(p)u-çi-i na-ši; 283, 7 pu-ut ṭu-ub-bu ša šikari na-ši, he guaranties for the quality of the date wine; KB iv 308—9 *no* IX 15 ištēn pu-ut ša-ni-i a-na e-ṭe-ir na-šu-u. pu-ut e-ṭir (e-ṭe-ru) ša kaspi *N* na-ši, *N* guaranties the refunding of the money, Nabd 68, 1 *foll*; Cyr 177, 13 *fol*; BA iii 398. Neb 346, 8—9 pu-ut xi-li-qu u mi-tu-tu ša *N*, in case of flight or death of *N*; KB iv 318—9, 12 pu-ut xar-ru u xa-laqi ... na-ši. Nabd 990, 8 pu-ut zitti ša *Z* = gemäss dem Mitbesitz der .... Neb 284, 4 SAG-KI-XA-LA-šu = pût(?) zitti-šu. — *β.* In the case of a slave the seller assumes guaranty of ownership to the buyer of the slave. AV^w 50 *col* 2; BA iii 449—50; iv 44. KB iv 166—7 *no* II 5 pu-ut si-xi-i u pa-qir-ra-nu .... na-ši. Nabd 336, 8 pu-ut (amēl) si-xi-i (amēl) pa-qir-ra-nu (amēl) arad-šarru-u-tu u (amēl) mār-bān-nu-tu; Neb 346, 6 *foll*; Nabd 1044, 6 *foll*; 693, 11—12; 257, 7; Camb 334, 11 *foll*. Neb 386, 8 pu-ut si-xi-i pa-ki-ra-nu u (amēl) bān-u-tu; 70, 5 *foll*; 201, 6—10 pu-ut si-xu-u | u (amēl) pa-qir-ra-nu u (amēl) mār-bānu-u-tu (ZA i 89) u si-ip-ru ša ina a-me-lu-tum ib-ba-aš-šu-u *G* ina qāti *N* | na-ša-tum (KB iv 102—3); Nabd 274, 6 *foll*; 300, 5 *foll*, 126, 6 *foll*. Camb 309, 6 *foll* pu-u-tu | (amēl) si-xu-u (amēl) pa-qi-ra-a-ni u mār-bānu-u-tu ša *X* .... na-šu-u; also Camb 15, 6—8 (BA iii 472—3); 307, 7 (pu-ut si-xi-i pa-qir-ra-ni); Cyr 146, 5 *foll* (BA iii 417—8); V 67 *no* 2, 45 pu-ut si-xu-u u pa-qi-ra-nu ša ina eli *N* ... na-ši.

pitū, petū, seldom ***patū*** (Sn *Bav* 27; perh. V 37 *b* 13; Br 8730); *pr* ipti (§ 18); *ps* ipatti & ipeti, *ip* piti; *ag* petū (§ 32 *aβ*) K 3474 i + K 8182 i 17 pi-tu-u, ZA iv 7; *pm* pi(pe)ti, ZA ii 200—202; D^{II} 62; AV 7091; §§ 32γ; 34/3; 38. — *a*) open {öffnen} K 3445 + R 396 *O* 37 ip-te-e-ma (§ 32 *aγ*); KB vi (1) 262 *col* 3, 23 + 27 (end). V 47 *b* 13 (end) ip-ti; *del* 257 (288). IV^2 31 *O* 39 ip-ta-aš-ši (§ 56 *b*) ba-ab-[šu], he opened for her the (his) gate; 37, pi-ta-aš-ši ba-ab-[ka]; 14, 15 pi-ta-a (§ 94) ba-ab-ka, pi-ta-a ba-ab-ka-ma; 16, šum-ma la ta-pat-ta-a ba-a-bu (I will smash it). Asb iii 17 up-na-a-šu ip-ta-a, he opened (imploring) his hands (Z^3 *p* 59); SMITH, *Asurb*, 96, 92. IV^2 25 *a* 55 pi-ka ina i-š'ip-pu-ti ip-ti (Br 2258). K 2527 + K 1547 *O* 32 ip-te-e-ma lib-ba-šu ka-ra-as-su iš-ṭu-uṭ. KB vi (1) 286 iv 7 (end) tap-te-ši (& *p* 544). IV^2 20 *no* 2, 3—4 O Šamaš ši-gar šamē tap-ti, Br 2248; 5, 6 da-lat šamē tap-ta-a (Br 2258; ZA ii 190 *foll*; § 150); ap-te-e-ma bīt niçirtu (*q. v.*) Sn i 27; *Kui* 1, 5; Sn v 19; Sarg *Ann* 47 ap-ti (*var* te)-e. Asb v 132; III 8, 81 see nakamtu (671 *cols* 1, 2); Sn *Kui* 4, 6 see papāxu.

Etana-legend (KB vi, 1, 110—11) III *a* 6 ki-çir-ta ap-ti; *del* 129 (130) ap-te (*var* -ti) nap-pa-ša-am-ma; 279 (318) ra-a-ṭa ki-i ap-tu-u. SCHEIL, *Notes d'Epigr.*, xxiv 7—8 bûr mê [ka]-çu-ti | ina lib-bi-šu ap-tu-u (*Rec. Trav*, xix 46). Sp II 265 *a* xiii 6 bi-e-ra lu-up-ti. KB vi (1) 276—277, 32 the mother ul i-pa-ti bâbi-ša to the daughter (see *ibid* 539); K 3500 + K 4444 + K 10235 ii 13 (end) ta-pat-ti (*i. e.* the letter thou shalt open); 83—1—18, 223 *R* 8 that, whosoever opens the document (= ša un-qu i-pat-tu-ni). K 2852 + K 9662 i 6 pe-ta-a up-na-a-šu (WINCKLER, *Forsch*, ii 28), his hands were opened. Rm 67, 8 (Hr^{L} 348) u ma-a ênâ-ja la a-pat-ti (AJSL xv 140, 141). K 890 *O* 6 pa-ta-ni (*i. e.* patâ-ni) up-na-ja-a a-na (ilat) Be-lit šamê u-çal-la, BA ii 634; GGA '98, 828. III 66 *col* 10, 9—10 nap-šur pi-ti-tim ana (al) Aššur pi-ta-a. K 1066 *R* 11 (Hr^{L} 277) uznâ .... i-bat-tu-u (PSBA xxii 290—2). S 954 *O* 42 (ilat) Ištar pi-ta-at (Br 2593) ši-gar šame-e el-lu-ti; IV^{2} 14 *no* 3 *O* 10 pi-tu-u be-ra-a-ti (Br 2258, 8062, 9305); Anp i 3 pi-tu-u naq-bi; K^{M} 12, 29 (= IV^{2} 57) pitu-u kup-pi u be-ra-a-ti. II 23 *e-f* 70 pe-ti-tum, epithet of da-al-tum (AV 7090). K 1282 *R* 22 u-zu-un-šu a-pi-it-ti (KB vi, 1, 72—3); KB vi (1) 280—1 (& 541) ii 34 uzun-šu pi-ta-at. IV^{2} 17 *a* 10 dal-tu ra-bi-tu ša šamê ellûti ina pi-te-e [-ka?]; II 140—1; Br 2258. V 43 *a-b* 10 the month pi-te bâbi, epithet of Tammûz. V 13 *a-b* 13 AMÊL ŠI (= IGE)-BAR-BAR-RA (V 30, 4) = ša pi-ti i-nim (Br 1850; 9300). IV^{2} 60* C *R* 16 pi-ti (= pm) KI-MAX. V 39 *a-b* 4 KA-BAR-RA = pu-u pi-tu-u; Creat.-*frg* V 97 ip-te-ma pi-i-ša Ti-âmat. K 3158 *O* (IV^{2} 54 *no* 1) 43 [pi-te] il-lu-ur-ta-šu. (amêl) KA ša bâbi, Nabd 116, 15; (amêl) BAD ša bâbi, Nabd 841, 17 *i. e.* iD of "door keeper" = (amêl) NI-GAB (AV 6192) IV^{2} 31 *O* 13, 14, 21, 25, 37, 39, 43 *etc.*; see also II 49 *c-d* 21; K 180, 4 *etc.* V 13 *a-b* 6 KAK-NI-GAB = pe-tu-u (= ag) sikkati, Br 5352; & see sikkatu. — *b*) open, *i. e.* lay bare, unveil }öffnen, *i. e.* entblössen, blosslegen{. NE 11, 9—16 ur-ki pi-te-ma (= ip); ur-ša ip-te-e-ma, KB vi, 1, 428. Neb vii 59, 60 te-me-en-ša ap-te-e-ma šu-pu-ul me-e ak-šu-ud, KB iii, 2, 24/5. II 118 *R* 6 su-ni ip-te-ma, + 5, bir-ki-ja ip-te-ma; I 69 *c* 31 uš-še-šu-nu e-ip-ti, I laid bare, § 34*a*. Perh. K 2148 ii 5 iratsa pi-ta-a-at, BEZOLD, ZA ix 118: is open, *i. e.* filled with milk; PUCHSTEIN, *ibid* 417: is nacked. K 2619 i 28 (2 *sg*) see munnu (*p* 559 *col* 1); HAUPT. JBL xix 80 *rm* 120; KB vi (1) 374. — *c*) reveal, announce }eröffnen, kundtun{. *del* 9 lu-up-te-ka (§ 32*aγ*) a-mat ni-çir-ti (*q. v.*); 252 (282) lu-u-up-te (§ 93, 1 *b*); 170 (195) a-na-ku ul ap-ta-a, I have not revealed. V 47 *a* 44 see katamu Q *a* (457 *col* 2). KB v *no* 71, 33 ip-ti, I confessed (my sin unto the gods) BA iv 315. ZIMMERN, *Ritualtafeln*, 24, 39 ta-mit pi-ris-ti ul i-pat-tu-šu. ZA iv 12, 9 (K 3182 iv) pi-tu-u ek-li-ti (i 17), who uncoverest the gloom (AJSL xvii 142). Perhaps IV^{2} 19 *a* 37, 38 o Lord (Šamaš) munammir ekliti pi-tu-u pa-nu (Br 8921); 18, 1 *O* 14. 15 a-na lib-bi-šu ip-tu-u, ZA ii 200; Br 1416. — *d*) open *i. e.* dedicate }eröffnen: einweihen{ so perh. Sn *Bav* 27 a-na pa-te-e nâri šu-a-tu I commanded the magicians. — *e*) open a way, road; dig a course for a river by means of a canal }einen Weg öffnen, bahnen{ Sarg *Cyl* 10 mighty mountains with steep passes ... ip-tu-ma; III 14, 42. V 42 *a-b* 65 (du-un) DUN = pi-tu-u ša nâri (Br 9870): iD = xirû & xararu (*q. v.*). Perh. T^{M} iv 37, 38 bûri tap-ta-a, a well (which) you have dug (see *ibid*, *p* 138). Sarg *Cyl* 66 mi-ix-rit VIII šârê VIII abullê ap-te-e-ma (KB ii 50, 51); Creat.-*frg* V 9 ip-te-ma abullê ina çi-li ki-lal-la-an (KB vi, 1, 80—1); Sarg *Nimr*, 17 (end) ap-ti (KB ii 38, 39). — *f*) cultivate a field }ein Feld urbar machen{ Sarg *Cyl* 34 a-na .... pi-te-e ki-ru-bi-e za-qap çip-pa-a-te iš-ku-un u-xu-un-šu. KB 44, 45. — *g*) loosen (from a ban, curse, charm) }lösen, befreien{ IV^{2} 22 *no* 2, 10. 11 see ma(u)ššakku (603 *col* 1) § 39; Br 1529. — *h*) leave an interval, THOMPSON, *Reports*, ii 127 *etc.*; K 712 *R* 10 ultu libbi an-ni-e i-pat-ti il-lak; *O* 9 pa-a-te (= pm) la iṭ-xi; 83—1—18, 107 *R* 8 la i-ṭa-ax-xi i-pa-at-ti. — K 4143, 4 81 = pi-tu-u (5, ur-ru-u; 6, še-lu-u) Br 8402. H 38, 73 GAL-[sign] = pi-tu-u (on ID see IV^2 14 *no* 3, 9—10; 20 *no* 2, 3—4; 17 *a* 9—10; 25 *a* 54—55 *etc.*); II 36 *no* 2 (*add*) pa-te-e qab-ri, Br 3428, AV 7029. S^b 222 ba-ad | BAD | pi-tu-u; H 12, 123; V 42 *a-b* 51; Br 1520; S^c 46 ga-al | GAL | pi-tu-u; H 14, 177; Br 2248. V 42 *a-b* 52—54 UD-DU = pitû ša bābi, Br 7884; (ga-al) GAL = *p* ša me-e, Br 2240; (tu-ux) GAB = pitû ša pi-i, Br 4480. II 39 (V 39) *a-b* 6, 7 KA-BAD-DU & KA-BA (8, = e-peš pi-i) = pi-it (*c. st.* of ac) pi-i, Br 558, 606, 1558, 555, 110. IV^2 25 iii *R* 65 an-nu-u ina la pi-it pi-i, Br 4490. V 16 *e-f* 50 GE-GE = pi-tu-u ša pa-ni (II 40, 50) Br 6337; H 23, 475. II 35 *no* 3 *g-h* 10 ... SU(?)-U = pi-tu-u.

$\mathfrak{Q}^1$ open }öffnen{. K 1285 *R* 1 ip-te-te Ašurbanipal up-ni-šu (CRAIG, *Relig. Texts*, i *no* 6). K 1304 *R* 11 up-te-te; 83—1—18, 197 *R* 12 pa-ni-šu ip-ti-e-ti, THOMPSON, *Reports*, ii 89 & 112); V 47 *b* 10 ip-te-te niš-ma-a-a. K 2401 ii 12, 13 (oracle to Esarh) at-ta pi-i-ka tap-ti-ti-a ma-a a-ni-na, BA ii 628 thou openest thy mouth.

$\mathfrak{P}$ *a*) open }öffnen{ Sn *Kui* 4, 6 bi-ir-ri u-pat-ta-a, BA iv 265. K^M 6, 107 šame-e tu-pat-ti; T^M vii 143 *c* .... še-e-ru pu-ut-ta-a, BA iv 162—3; II 37 *e-f* 67 ši-i-ru pu-ut-tu-u. T. A. (Lo) 82, 27 ba-ba-a-tu lu pu-ut-ta-a, the gates shall be opened }die Tore sollen geöffnet werden{ KB vi (1) 78 *no* II 9—10; BA iv 130, 131. T. A. (Ber) 154, 46 u ju-pa-at-ti. ZA iv 13 *B* 6 Marduk mu-pattû bu-ur kup-pi. Perh. K 5464 (Hr^L 198) *R* 13 su-pa-ni-ja lu-pa-ti (but see xatû, *p* 436 *col* 2). — mupattitu, key }Schlüssel{ see *p* 570 *col* 1; Br 4490, 5271. ZIMMERN, *Ritualtafeln*, *no* 49, 7 ṣalme an-nu-ti = 7 Ellen von der Vorderseite der Opfer-Zurüstung tu-pat-ta-šu-nu-ti (sollst du abstehen lassen). — Especially note **uznâ puttû**, open one's ears, *i. e.* communicate with, inform some one, BA i 235. IV^2 60* B *O* 8 (end) ul u-pat-ti uz-ni. K 95, 12 *foll* ša im-ma-ru u ša i-šim-mu-u; *R* 1—2 uznâ ša bēli-šu u-pat-ta (Hr^L 288), whatsoever he will see or hear, he will communicate to his lord; *R* 2 *foll* en-na (behold!) ba-ni ša taš-pu-ra PI$^{2\,pl}$ (= uznā)-ja tu-pat-tu-u. BA i 232 *foll*: K 8258 *R* 12 la naparkâ li-pat-ti uz-nu, without ceasing let him make known. — *b*) in meaning of $\mathfrak{Q}$ *c*. u-pat-ta ZA ii 60, 15 (& 61): 17 tu-pat-tu-u. TP ii 86 (§ 72 *a*) see durgu (268 *col* 1); K 11152, 8 še-e-ru ša ur-xa-ti u-pat-tu-u. Bu 88—5—12, 75 + 76 vii 38 girra-šu-nu u-pat-ti. IV^2 9 *a* 39 mu-pat-tu-u [urux?] ilâni at-xi-šu, Br 4461. Šalm, *Mon*, *O* 8: Šalm. mu-pat-tu-u ṭûdâti (*q. v.*) § 131; ZA iv 13, 6; Sarg *Khors* 15 mountains, without number, u-pat-ti-ma šumura du-ru-ug-šu-un. POGNON, *Wadi-Brissa*, 156 u-pa-at-ta-a. See also pušqu. — *c*) in the meaning of $\mathfrak{Q}$ *f* Camb 102, 5 tap-tu-u u-pat-ta. V 45 i 1—3 tu-pat-ta, tu-pat-tan-ni, tu-pat-ta-šu-nu. See also K 2085 *R* 2 (end) lu-pi-it-tu-šu; THOMPSON, *Reports*, ii *no* 268.

$\mathfrak{P}^1$ Perhaps K 3445 + Rm 396 *O* 36 naqbu up-te-it[-ta-a?].

$\mathfrak{P}^{tn}$ K 1285, 1 up-ta-na-at-ta-ka, I confess to thee, o Nebo (CRAIG, *Relig. Texts*, i *p* 5; HEBR. x 76, 77; but see M^S 79 *col* 1; & ZIMMERN, GGA '98, 823 reading addanab]ub ta-na-at-ta-ka.

$\mathfrak{S}$ *a*) cause to open; open }öffnen lassen; öffnen{ § 94. Sarg *Harem*, B 4 see naqbu (*p* 719 *col* 1, *ll* 5, 6). — *b*) cause to see, reveal, disclose }sehen lassen, eröffnen{ *etc.* Sn *Kui* 4, 12 u-šap-tu-ni pa-ni-šu (see šapannu, *p* 778 *col* 2).

$\mathfrak{SP}$ K 3182 iii 41 kal si-xi-ip da-ad-me uz-ni-ši-na tuš-pat-ti.

$\mathfrak{N}$ be opened }geöffnet werden{. IV^2 31 *R* 14: VII bâbē erṣit la târi lip-pi-t[u-u] i-na pa-ni-ka (KB vi (1) 86, 87). K 8522 *R* 25 (D 96 *R*) ša rē'i u na-ki-di li-pat-ta-a uz-na (*var* uznâ)-šu-un, let it be known, communicated to }sei es mitgeteilt, kundgegeben{. KB vi (1) 359.

DERR. — naptû, niptû, naptētu (see *p* 713 *col* 1), taptû, teptītu & these:

pitû, *c. st.* pet, pit, *f* pitī(ē)tu, §§ 34 *δ*; 65, 7. *a*) opened, open }geöffnet, offen{. II (V) 39 *a-b* 4 KA-BAR-RA = pu-u pi-tu-u, Br 609, 1791. Sn *Kui* 4, 21 see urmaxxu (102 *col* 2) § 67, 3. [82—5—22, 174, 10 read: mar-ça-at a-dan-niš la ku-sa-pi ta-kal >< M[S] 79 *col* 2.] — *b*) open, clear }offen, klar{ of the weather. 83—1—18, 48 *R* 7 ûmu pi-tu-u, THOMPSON, *Reports*, ii *no* 155; perhaps also Nabd 954, 10 û-mu XX [kam] û-mu pa-tu-u. — *c*) opened, made open, of roads *etc.*; espec. in 1Š pitû unbeaten }ungebahnt{. TP iv 57 see durgu (268 *col* 1); Sn iv 4 see ṭûdu (353 *col* 2). — *d*) unsheathed, drawn, of weapons }gezückt (von Waffen){. K 3600 *O* 12 na]mçaru pe-tu-u, GGA '98, 823. K 2852 + K 9662 i 26 ša maxar kakkê pi-tu-ti (vor den drohenden Waffen). — *e*) in sexual meaning it is used in IV² 5 *c* 34, 35 ša-rat u-ni-ki la pi-ti-ti, ša-rat pu-xat-ti la pi-te-te (= UŠ-NU-ZU); also *cf* IV² 3 *a* 42—3; *b* 3 (Br 5050). — II 30 *e-f* 64 AL-BUR-RA (Br 6887) = pi-tu-ti (*pl*, *m*) the line giving the noun to which the adj. belongs is erased. AV 7094. II 30 (*c*-)*d* + e-li-tu pi(?)-tu(m) Br 3252.

Especially note: **pit uzni**, of an open mind }empfänglichen Sinnes{ § 73. V 36 *d-f* 61 pi-ta uz-nu (BA ii 602—3); II 60 *no* 2, 44 AK = pi-it uz-ni & AK = rap-ša uz-ni, epithet of Nebo; V 43 *c-d* 43, Br 2789. Lay 43, 8 pi-it uz-ni ni-me-qi. open for (words of) wisdom. pit xasisi see xasîsu (328, 329). — **pit pāni**, clear, perspicuous }offen von Gesicht, *i. e.* klar, erkennbar{ L⁴ i 16 e-it-gu-ru-ti ša la i-šu-u pi-it pa-ni, dreams which are not clear; LEHMANN, ii 65, which had not yet been interpreted.

pitû? *noun?* H 130, 56 (58) bêl (la) pi-ti-i, Br 6816 reads bît (?) instead of bêl.

pitûtu (?) perh. Nabd 456, 2 (658, 2) (amêl) NI-GAB-u-tu ša .... K 883 (oracle of Beltis to Ašurbanipal) 7 (çubât) pi-tu-tu i-rak-kas (BA ii 633).

pittu *1.* *noun* (> pit'u, פֶּתַע) moment, twinkling }Augenblick{ BA i 238; D[H] 19 (פִּתְאֹם); HAUPT in PATERSON, *Numbers* (SBOT) 45. On BARTH, *Etym. Stud.* (بَغْتَة) see FRÄNKEL, BA iii 71—2. K 657 *R* 7—8 pi-ti dul-la .... 9) .. e-pa-šu-ni (Hr[L] 102), immediately the work shall be done. — usually in adverbial phrase: ina pitti, ina pittimma, ina pi-te-ma, suddenly, at once, immediately }sofort, augenblicklich{ § 78. Asb ix 61 all the curses put down in their laws the gods ina pit-ti i-ši-mu-šu-nu-ti, destined for them at once. *del* 207 (229) si-bu-tum ina pi-it-tim-ma; 218 (241), KB vi, 1, 247. K 504 *R* 6 ina pi-it-ti (Hr[L] 157); perh. also K 685, 11 (AV 7098). K 915, 8 ina pi-it-ti linnipiš, let it be done at once; K 540 *R* 14 ina pi-it-ti ni-pu-uš (Hr[L] 149); K 486, 10 + *R* 1 a-na-ku ina pi-te-ma aq-ṭi-bi, I have given orders at once (Hr[L] 308; § 78). III 53 *no* 3, 11 (*b* 60) ina pi-it-ti-i. PSBA xxiii 347—8; 350. ina pitti(m) ‖ of appitti(mma) in meaning of: avec raison; avec à propos. Bu 91—5—9, 210 (Hr[L] 403) 4 + 13. Xammurabi-letters 34, 8; 81, 8 ki-ma bi-tim, BA iv 463, 495.

pitītu, *f* to pittu, 1. V 31 *c-d* 2 ina bi-ti-ti = ina pi-ti-tim; AV 7090, Br 54. Perh. III 66 *col* 10, 9 nap-šur pi-ti-tim, PSBA xxi 129.

pittu *2.* in appitti = an(a) pitti. K 84 (Hr[L] 301) 19 ap-pit-tim-ma la; K 95 (Hr[L] 288) 9 ap-pit-ti amêlu *etc.* PSBA xxiii 347.

pittu *3.* V 31 *a-b* 40 up(b)-p(b)u = pi-it (*ṭ*, *d*).

pittu *4.* see nammu, 1 (680 *col* 1); ZA x 208: un genre des poignards ou glaives.

pittu *5.* Rm 2, 1, 159 *O* 13 a-na ma-mit il-qu(-)in-ni-ma p(b)it-tum in-ni na-da(?)-ku; see also MARTIN, *Textes religieux*, 54.

pittu *6.* in pit a-xi. V 28 *c-d* 87—92 = mu-kil ši-ip-ri; e-du-tum; na-az(s, ç)-b(p)u; naš(or pa, ZK ii 338)-xu; aš(or pa?)-ru, pu-us-mu; Z[B] 39 *rm* 1: *c. st.* of pittu > pid-tu = אטד. See also bittu (*pp* 204, 205); JASTROW, AJSL xv 79 reads V 14 *a-b* 19 e-ṭum (dark) instead of b(p)it-tum (>< Br 9006).

pītu *1.* II 52 *no* 2 *c* 61 name of city ša k(q)ub(p)-b(p)u-tu ina a-xi pi (?, thus with JOHNS)-tum, *i. e.*, situate at the mouth of a canal; ZA xv, 243, 244; origin-

---

pit in pit maškānu see bîd (*pp* 148, 149) & maškānu, 1 (*pp* 603, 604) where bîd is read mal.

ally perhaps: front, as in V 55, 26 (+ 36) pit i-mit-ti šarri bēlišu = in front of the right hand of the king (see *p* 148 *col* 2, NOTE, & 205 footnote). Here perhaps also Sm 1034, 11 pit uš-še; K 538, 20 (Hr[L] 389; 104) BA i 616.

pītu *2.* BA i 511; 633 row, furrow, line }Reihe, Furche{ esp. onions bound in rows }Zwiebeln in Reihen gezogen{ >< WZKM iv 127 *rm* 4: a part of the garlic; see gidlu (*p* 214 *col* 1). Nabd 663, 5: 2000 pi-tum ša šūmi bab-ba-nu-u (also 933, 1); 160, 1: 26 pi-i-ti ša šūmi 600 gid-dil ša šûmi (17, 7 + 10, 11 *etc.*, pi-i-tu); *c. st.* pi-it 122, 2; 169, 8 pi-i-ti u gid-dil ša šūmi; 184, 1 (180, 1): 865 (1300) pi-i-ti ša šūmi. Perhaps also Merodach-Balad.-stone iii 51 (see xāzu, ב, end, *p* 276 *col* 2).

patū *1.* goal }Ziel{ T. A. (Lo) 8, 76—77 may these words ina pa-ti-i-šu-nu li-ik-šu-du, reach their goal; ZA v 163; KB v 40, 41 = pātu.

patū *2.* Sarg *Khors* 33 (112) *NN* amēlu pa-tu-u lim-nu, AV 7029. D[S] 55; 85: frivolous, fickle }leichtfertig, leichtsinnig{ D[Pr] 103 & *rm* 1: *i. e.* open to evil influences. GESENIUS[12] 647 *col* 1 (פחז); ZDMG 40, 735; WINCKLER, *Forsch*, i 548; ii 132 reads xattū.

patū *3.* In P. N. Šarru-pa-ti-i-Bēl, Eponym of 832 B C. (KB i 206—7; AV 8086).

pattu *1.* (so probably instead of šuq-tu), *pl* pattāti. aqueduct, canal }Wasserleitung, Kanal{. G § 57; ZA iii 318. Anp iii 135 (nār) Pa-ti-XE-GAL šumša (*i. e.* of the canal) abbi; *cf* I 27 *no* 2, 6 (nār) ba-be-lat-XE-GAL. TP III (Lay 52 *no* 1, 4): (nār) Pa-at-ti [-xegalli ša] ultu ūmē rūqūti nadāt-ma .... axrāma, ROST, *Tigl. Pil. III*, *pp* 2—3. Esh vi 20 see xababu, 2 ש (300 *col* 1). Sn *Bav* 12 Pat-ti-Sin-axē-erba, name of an aqueduct; 19 mē pat-ta-a-ti ša ušaxrū, the waters of the canals which I had dug. Bu 88—5—12, 75 + 76 vii 30 xi-ri-e pat-ta-a-ti ‖ za-qa-ap çip-pa-a-ti. Perh. also Neb 301, 10. *Adv* to this is:

pattiš. Sn *Kui* 4, 35 see xababu, 2. ש. ZA iii 318 (322) 88: I caused it to irrigate thoroughly.

pattu *2.* T. A. (Ber) 26 *b* 54: II BAN(?) *pl* ša pa-at-ti apsī ki-za-al-li-šu-nu; & 63: tam-lu-u abnu uknū banū ša pa-as-zu (> pat-šu?) xurāçu uxxuzu, whose margin is enchased with gold (KB v* 47 *col* 1).

pat(t)u(ū?) *pl* pat(t)ūte, AV 7031. TP vi 81 see maqatu, ש; I 28 *a* 10 with a stout heart *etc.* ina narkabtišu pa-at-tu-te, ina šepā-šu ina (iç) pa-aš-xi idûk nēšē; Lay 44, 23: 257 wild oxen, big ones, ina narkabtija pa-tu-te ina qi-it-ru-ub bēlūtija u-šam-qit, KB ii 124—5: "mit Pfeilen", perh. K 4200, 3 ... AN-GAB (DAN) = pat-tu-u; *ibid* 1 na-ax-bu-u.

pattū, see buninnu, 180 *col* 1 & Br 10305; AV 7031. V 39 *a-b* 15—17 GI-PA (Br 2519. 13929); GI-ŠU-A (Br 2536, also = šutukku & kupū, 421 *col* 1); GI-ŠU-BIL-LAL (Br 2505) = pat-tu-u (Z[B] 17 *rm* 2: šuk-tu-u). II 22 (K 242) iv 6 GI-PAD = ŠU = pat[-tu-u] reed thicket, jungle }Rohr-, Schilfdickicht{; KB vi (1) 330.

pataxu, *pr* iptix, dig a hole, dig out, dig, bore through }ein Loch graben, bohren, durchbohren{. D[H] 32; D[Pr] 182. V 34 *c* 15 this appalisma akšud ap-te-ix-ma (changed by some to ap-la-ax). V 36 *d-f* 50 bu-ru | < | pa-ta-xu; Dar 358. 8 ina pa-ta-xu ša.

ב V 45 i 6, 7 tu-pat-tax, tu-pat-tax-šu-nu; ZA ii 381. K 1550, 28 al-pēšunu 500, 600 kī u-pat-ti-xu it-tassū.

ב[t] transfix oneself, kill oneself }sich durchbohren{. Asb vii 37 he and his attendant with an iron girdle-dagger up-ta(-at)-te (*var* ti)-xu a-xa-meš (killed one another) KB ii 212. — Der.

pitxu *1.* hole }Loch{. V 36 *d-f* 49 bu-ru < pit-xu, preceded by xurrum.

patixu, *f* patixatu. II 44 *e-f* 67, 68 SU-LU-KU (*i. e.* UB)-PA-TI-XU = pa-ti-xu; SU-LU-KU PA-TI-XA-TUM = pa-ti-ti (mistake for xa)-tu[m]. AV 7023; Br 239; SU-LU-UB = lu-ub-bu (64). IV[2] 56 *b* 55 pa-ti-xa-tu limalliki (>< M[S] 37*a* pa-ti-xa lix-dir-ki), GGA '98, 818; *cf* IV[2] 55 *b* 25 where iD SU-BIR *pl* = patixātu.

pitxu *2.* K 517, 19 (Hr^{L} 327) see pi-xû, 1 ℶ^{t}.

patalu. III 65 *b* 57 when is-pu libbi^{pl}-šu pat-lu. KB vi (1) 154 iv 8 ip(b)-te-la ina bâbi-ma. See also pitiltu.

ℶ V 45 i 8 tu-pat-tal.

pitiltu (so perhaps instead of pikurtu). Z^{8} *p* 58 = פתיל cord, loop {Schnur, Schlinge} KB vi (1) 451. IV^{2} 7 *a* 48 kîma pi-til-ti (= ŠU-SAR, Br 7150) lip-pa-šir; *ibid b* 18 *foll*; 25 id an-ni-i, indicating the existence of also a masculine form of the same noun. IV^{2} 4 iv 25 *fol* pi-til-ti šu-uš-lu[-uš-ti] (= ŠU-SAR-𒐈) KB vi (1) 480. T^{M} ii 153 ki-ma pi-til-ti ana pa-ta-li-ia; 164 kîma pitilti a-pat-til-šu-nu-ti; Hebr. xi 109 *rm.*

pitluxu (AV 7095) see palaxu, Q^{t}.

patanu 1. פתן ipattan. AV 7020 eat {essen}, or the like. ZK ii 18, 19 *rm* 1; ZA i 53, 54. II 36 *g-h* 61 U-SUD-SUD = pa-ta-nu (Br 6058); 62, [sign]-AG-A = *p* ša a-ka-li; 63, DUN (du-un) DUN = *p* ša amêli, Br 9880. V 16 *g-h* 74 KA-AG-A = pa-ta-nu, Br 628; = II 38 *g-h* 73; H 31, 730. II 60 *a* 44, 47 (K 4334, 8 + 6) that & that ta-pat-tan; ina pap-pa-si ta-pat-tan; + 50, 53, 57, 60; *c* 15 a-pat-tan. ZK ii 4, 3 [sign] (= lâ) pa-tan; 5, 10 ba-lu pa-tan, without tasting it. ZA v 68, 9 nap-tan a-pa-ta-nu, I have prepared.

Derr. — naptanu & iptennu.

patanu 2. K 3600 *R* 23 lip-tu-nu šur-ru-u (hymn to Goddess Ninâ).

ℶ perh. V 47 *b* 18 u-pat-tin qi-ni-e a-ma-liš iz-qu-up (subject: Bêl); qi-nu-u explained by [sign] (qin?)-u.

pattanu in P. N. (amêl) Êa-pat-ta-nu Neb 81, 6; KB iv 204—5, *no* 1, 25 Bêl pat-ta-nu; Êa-pa-at-ta-an-ni, also occurs.

pitnu *2.*, **pitin** in P. N. Bêl-e-di-pi-ti-in; Bel-e-di-pit-nu, *etc.*

pit([sign] *?*)**-ta-nu.** T. A. (Ber) 26 iii 26 (end).

pitinûtu (?) Nabd 441, 6 a-ma-lu-tum pi-ti-nu-tum.

pitnu *1.* (or pidnu?) AV 7037, Peiser, *Vertr.*, 302 *rm*: stand {Ständer} K 4378 (D 86) i 58 GIŠ-DA = pi-it-nu (Br 6652; Anp ii 123; II 26 *c-d* 25); 59, 60 GIŠ-DA-GAL = *p* ra-bu-u; GIŠ-DA-TUR = *p* ça-ax-ru; 61, GIŠ-DA-ŠU = pi-it-nu qa-ti (Br 6683); 62, GIŠ-DA-ŠU-1 = *p* gal-la-bi (Br 6684). id of 58 also in *c. t.*, Nabd 95, 5; 219, 2; Cyr 31, 3; 140, 7; KB iv 316—17, 26 transl.: table {Tisch}. S^{b} 61 na-a | ŠA | pi-it-nu, H 25, 538; Br 7048; same id also in inscr., BA iv 221: ŠA-GUB = pitna-mukîn, translated by Zehnpfund (225, 226): Pflasterstreicher. II 26 *c-d* 26—28 .... GUD-UD = pitna ša šame-e (Br 14147; J. Oppert, JA xvi ['90] 319 = horizon × Lotz, *Quaestiones*, 80, 31: the furrow of heaven *i. e.* ecliptic, near to Jupiter; see, however, Jensen, 132. 310; KB iii (1) 25, 26); ...... A = *p* ša ZAG-ŠAL (or RAG) Br 14458; ... AD-GI-GAZ-ZA = *p* ša AD-KIT. Also written pi-da-nu (Nabd 394, 2 a-na pi-da-nu; 431, 6 a-na pi-da-nu aš-ši. + 12) which would point to reading pidnu, rather than pitnu.

patinnu some kind of dress, or cover {ein Bekleidungsgegenstand} AV 7025. III 41 *a* 26 (çubât) pa-tin-nu. Nabd 78, 4 (+ 9) (çubât) pa-ti-in-nu (+ 19); V 19 *a-b* 17 (+ II 34 *c* 5) NAB-NAB = (çubât) pa-tin-nu, Br 3852; perh. V 12 *c-d* 47, Br 7673. V 32 *c* 43, 44 pa-tin-nu, among articles made of leather, Br 14287. V 28 *g-h* 14 pa-tin-nu ‖ pa-ar-ši-gu, BA i 534. Cyr 157, 5 ši-pa-tum pa-tin[-nu] BA i 534; 636; ii 152. — (il) Pa-tin XI-DU (?) III 68 *e* 22, Br 12757.

putuntu. Scheil, Constant. *no* 583 *R* 9 [sign] ZAG-XI-LI-ŠAR pu-tu-un-tu (*Rec. Trav.*, xxiii, notes d'épigr., *no* lx).

Patesi. TP vii 62, 63 *Š-A* pa-te-si Ašur, son of Išme-Dagan likewise pa-te-si of Ašur. KB i *pp* 2 *foll* *NN* pa-te-si il A-šur, & see note 1 *ibid.* II 53 *a* 13 Pa-še-ki (AV 7009) pa-te-si^{ki} (Br 12753; ZK ii 179 *foll*; ZA ii 314; 389 *fol*; iii 348 & iv 292). *Rec. Trav.*, xx 62—3, *no* xxxiii mentions Uddušu-namir pa-te-si. AV 7026—7. pa-te-is-si PAOS '85 *p* xii. Lehmann, *VIII. Or. Congr.*, Sem. Sec. *B* 173; 178; princely priest {fürstlicher Prie-

pitxallu (§ 67, 5) see bitxallu (*p* 205). ~ pat-xa-riš see mitxariš. ~ pa-ta-ku, V 65 *b* 10 read maštaku (& see *p* 614 *col* 1).

ster} = der Fürst mit teilweise priesterlichen Functionen. See also LEHMANN, BA ii 614; *Šamaššumukin*, i 95, 98; JENSEN, KB iii (1) 6: a high official of the king; IDEM, ZDMG 50, 254: Patesi = Stellvertreter >< LEHMANN, *ibid*, 49, 302—3; HOMMEL, *Gesch*, 294; 334: Priesterkönig (title of Gudea of Sirpurla) >< OPPERT: governor }Statthalter}; AMIAUD: 'lieutenant' before the name of a land; 'vicaire' before the name of a god. LE GAC, ZA vii 138: il est surtout pontifical; JASTROW, *Religion of Babylonia, etc.*, 198: religious chief. See also LYON, *Sargon*, 12 *fol*. — On a possible etymology of the word see WINCKLER, *Forsch*, ii, 2, 313 ('99). BA iv 488 = iššakku (114, 115).

pit(?)pānu (§ 61, 16). *f* (§ 71), seldom *m* (K 2652 *R* 47 pit-pa-nu šu-a-tu, III 16 *no* 4, 51); *pl* pitpānāte (§ 70*a*), AV 5207. IV^2 22 *a* 47 ki-ma pit-pa-a-nu (id GIŠ-PAN Br 9101) ba-aš-me (Br 334) mimma šumšu i-zak-kir. IV^2 18* *no* 3. iii 7—8 pit-pa-nu (GIŠ-RU, Br 1431) a-rik-tu, a long bow; see also in additions to this plate. V 60 *b* 25 Nabû-baliddin na-aš pit-pa-ni ez-zi-tim (BA i 271, 25; 357). I 7 *no* IX A 2 (iç) pit-pa-a-nu ez-zi-tu ša (ilat) Ištar. II 19 *b* 10 (end) pit-pa-na u ka-ba-b[a], Br 210. K 2801 + K 221 + K 2669 *O* 12 (il) sibi ilāni qar-du-ti ta-me-xu pit-pa-nu u uç-çi. Sn vi 57 išpāte pit-pa-na-te u uç-çi, quivers, bows, and arrows. NE XII (1) 18 see nasaku (701 *col* 2); 19, see maxaçu Q *b* (523 *col* 1, *med*); K 2619, 24 see nibxu, note 1 (685 *col* 1). T. A. (Ber) 26 *a* 42: 1 pit-pa-nu ša ça-mi-ri a-na V(?)-šu xurāçu uxxuzu. II 22 *no* 1, *add* (⊕ 51) 2 pit-pa-nu = qa-aš[-tu]; 3, = a-rik(lik?)-tum; K 4574 *O* 3 *foll*; K 4558 *O* 3 *foll*. 82, 5—22, 574, 7 MU]-RU & GIŠ-BAR = pit-pa-a-nu. — ZA iv 212 > papanu > panpanu √panann, be brilliant, shine; ZDMG 43, 205 reads baṭpānu; see also LEHMANN, ii 83 *b*.

pataqu & pitequ; *pr* iptiq; *ps* ipattiq, form, make, prepare }machen, bereiten} AV 7021. — *a*) make, build, form }machen, bauen, bilden} see JENSEN, *Theol. Litztg*, '95 *no* 20. K 2711 *O* 37 .... ina pi-ti-iq (il) NIN-A-GAL ap-ti-iq-ma; BA iii 264 *foll*. Sarg *Cyl* 54 bit xilanni .... mixrit bābānišin ap-tiq (= u-še-pi-ša, *Khors* 162); Rp 21 (31) ap-ti-iq (*cf* BA iv 250 *rm* **); *bull*-insc. 54 in the month of Āb when (ša) all the çal-mat qaqqadi ana rimūtišina i-pat-ti-qa çu-lu-lu; 76, nak-liš (*q. v.*) ap-tiq. Neb iii 5 the parakku ša šarru maxri i-na kas-pi ip-ti-ku bi-ti-iq-šu; iv 24 i-na kupri u agurri e-ep-ti-iq (§ 34*a*) pi-ti-iq-šu (I built its structure); viii 53 between the ramparts bi-ti-iq a-gur-ri e-ep-ti-iq (§§ 10; 34*a*) = ab-ni (POGNON, *Wadi-Brissa*, 39 *rm* 1); I 44, 78 (end) ap-ti-qu, I was going to build. Asb x 77 pi-tiq-tu ap-tiq. Creat.-*frg* III 9 (end) lip-ti-qu ku-ru-na (+ 134), wine they prepare (KB vi, 1, 319). II 38 *a-b* 22, 23 pit-qu; [ ] pa-ta-qu. V 21 *no* 3, 57 pa-ta-qu (56, ba-nu-u) both = KAK (ru); II 21, 385; Br 5264. — *b*) make, create }machen, erschaffen} ag = creator }Schöpfer}. S^P 158 + S^P II 962 *R* 14 A-num pa-ti-ik-šu-nu, their creator. K 2801 + K 221 + K 2669 *O* 4 (end) Ea ..... pa-ti-iq kul-lat. Sarg *Harem*, B 1 Ea bēl nimēqi pa-ti-qu kal gimri; KB ii 236, 1; KB iv 58 iii 11 (il) Ea pa-ti-iq ni-ši. Creat.-*frg* III 81 um-mu xu-b(p)ur pa-ti(*var* te)-qat ka-la-ma; IV^2 56 *b* 10: 82—7—4, 82 *R* 4 (end) see nabnitu (*p* 638); V 66 *a* 21 šar-rat pa-ti-qat nab-ni-ti (§ 131). Sp II 265 *a* xxiv 3 šar-ra-tum pa-ti-iq-ta-ši-na. K 8522 *R* 12 (D 96) ip-ti-qa (*var* tiq) dan-ni-na. — *c*) of money: coin }vom Gelde: prägen} BA iii 454; T^C 119. K 245 (II 69) ii 6 [AZAG?]-IM-BA-AG-A = [pa?]-ta-qu, Br 9917. Nabd 598, 2, 4: 55 minas and 22 shekel of silver ša a-na pi-te-qu iddi-na; of which 1/2 mina 5 shekel silver ina pi-te-qu LAL (= maṭû?); 88, 4—6 & 119, 8 see maṭû, 534 *col* 2. Nabd 860, 2: 42 1/2 shekel silver a-na pi-te-qu šu-bul.

Q^t K 245 ii 7 [AZAG?]-IM-BA-BA-AN-AG-A = ip-ta-ta-aq, Br 9917.

Š or Š^t HILPRECHT, *OBI*, i 32—33 ii 3 u-ša(*var* ša)-ap-ti-iq agurra; thus also KB iii (2) 4 *col* 2, 7.

N be made, created }gemacht, geschaffen werden}. K 2801 *R* 51 ša .... ina ši-pir um-ma-nu-ti la ip-pa-ti-iq-ma. Sarg *Bull*, 71: VIII UR-MAX ru'āmū . . . . ša (i-na) ši-pir (11) NIN-GAL ip-pat-qu(-u)ma; *Khors* 163; *Ann* 426; *Ann* XIV 74; BA iii 102—3 *rm* **.

Derr. these 5:

pitqu *1.* (& **bitqu**); *c. st.* pitiq. AV 1265, 7088; T^C 119. KB vi (1) 384 on original meaning. — *a*) work, workmanship, building, structure {Machwerk, Bau} BA i 510 *rm* 2; Z^B 44. Asb ii 41: 11 (12) tim-me çīrūti pi-tiq (*var* ti-iq) x(ç)a-xa-li-e eb-be; vi 29 qarnē (*var* qar-ni, § 70)-ša ša pi-tiq (BA i 402) erū nam-ri; 49 (XXXII çalmē šarrūni) pi-tiq kaspi xurāçi *etc.*; see also Ⓠ *a* of pataqu. pi-ti-iq e-ri, Pognon, *Wadi-Brissa*, 38 and often. V 42 *g-h* 80 IM-KAK-A pit-qu, Br 8426; see also Br 8431. K 1282 *O* 8 (end) u-šel-li ina pit-qi, KB vi (1) 68. Sn *Kui* iv 3 pi-ti-iq GU-AN-NA, BA iii 103 *rm* **, preceded by pi-ti-iq u-ru-di-e. Nabd 467, 4 a-na pit-qa tu-un-ša-nu (BA i 525; T^C xviii); Neb 414, 1—2: VIII šiqli xurāçi a-na pit-qu ša šu-kut-tum (zur Anfertigung). Perh. NE 8, 37 pi]-ti-iq pi-ir-ti-šu, see pirtu, 1. — *b*) of money: coining, forming (engraving) {Anfertigung, Prägung von Geld}; so for bitqu, 1 (*q. v.*) *p* 207. T^C 119; BA i 516—17; 633; BOR ii 57; ZA x 49 *fol*; ZA iv 124 šiqlu pit-qa. Br. Mus. 84—2—11; Neb 388, 17: V TU pit-qa kaspu. Nabd 84, 13 . . . . a-tu-nu u pi-it-qu. — *c*) child {Kind} in language of *Su*, II 30 *c-d* 48 pi-it-qu, AV 7090 ‖ ma-ar: see pitēqu.

pitiqtu = pitqu *a*). ZK i 173; T^C 119. II 15 *c-d* 39 pi-ti-iq-ti (= IM-AG-A, Br 8427) i-ta-ti-šu i-lam-mi (Z^B 44); 29, pi-ti-iq-ti i-[ga-ri-šu i-lam-mu]. IV² 29* (*add*) 4 C *b* 18; 25. T^M ii 154 ki-ma pi-ti-iq-ti a-na na-bal-ku-ti-ja, & 165. — Against T^C 119 *ad* Neb 158, 2 pit-qat see BA i 634; ZA vii 272 = bīt qāti, see qātu, 2. — Also *cf* pataqu Ⓠ *a*.

pitēqu (> *putāqu?) child {Kind}. AJP viii 280 & *rm* 3; ZA iv 384; § 65, 12; AV 7089; Haupt, *Andover Rev.*, Jl. '84, 93 *rm* 1; II 30 *c-d* 51 pi-te-e-qu = ma-a-ru (*q. v.*).

putuqqū. perh. coining, coinage of money {vielleicht: Prägung des Geldes}. K 245 (H 69) ii 5 [AZAG?]-IM-BA = [pu?]-tuq-qu-u, Br 9916. V 16 *g-h* 39: . . . . A]K-ZA = pu-tuq-qu-u, AV 1454; Br 14091.

pitqu *2.* Camb 374, 5—6: III gur AŠ ki-me šaṭ-ru | I gur 𒐊 PA ki-me pit-qa; Cyr 316, 2. See also Neb 201, 3: for 4 1/2 minas of money ša ina ištēn šiqli pit-qa; 454, 2—3 (KB iv 200, 201); & compare nuxxutu (*p* 666).

pitqudu (√paqadu) *adj* heedful, mindful {achtsam, aufmerksam} AV 7097; § 65, 40. Anp i 24 *Anp* ša a-na šu-te-šur *etc.* pit(*var* piš)-qu-du, KB i 56, 57. Šalm, *Mon*, *O* 6 *Šalm.* šakkanakku Aššur pit-qu-du, KB i 152. Lay 33, 10 Sargon mal-ku pit-qu-du, KB ii 38, 39; Sn v 70 Xumbanundaša et-lum pit-qu-du, KB ii 108, 109; Beh 80; Sarg *Ann* 386. KB vi (1) 158, 159, 40 pit-qu-du a-me-lu.

pataru *1.* *Rec. Trav.*, xx *p* 57 (Scheil) vii 18 li-ip-te-ru šu-u, KB vi (1) 290—1. Scheil: que celui-là fabrique. P. N. Sin-pa-te-ir.

pataru *2.* KB iii (1) 158 iii 29 ip-tu-ur = ipṭur; √פטר, *q. v.* BA iv 454 *no* 23, 8 ip-tu-ru[-nim-ma], sie sollten sich auf den Weg machen (& 492).

patarru (?) H 120 *R* 22 ina paṭ-ri (see paṭru) u pa-tar-ri (or פטר?); 21, BA-DA-RA-NA.

pattaru. K 8676 iii 31 pat-ta-ru ‖ xu-ut-pa-lu-u (both = URUDU-ŠUN-TAB-UD-KA-BAR-XUŠ-A), preceded by pa-al-tu; see xutpalū and Boissier, *Rev. Sém.*, viii 150 § 1.

patiru. some kind of fat, lard {eine Art Fett}. II 44 *c-f* 66 SU-LU-KU(= UB)-SEG- = pa-ti-ru (‖ lubbu) AV 7028; Br 289.

putru (??) II 38 *g-h* 31 p(b)u-ut(𒀀)-ru, AV 1364. preceded by qabūt imēri.

pitru. *del* 287 (325) read by KB vi (1) 254 [p]i-t[i-i]r bīt (ilat) Ištar, of the (sacred) precinct of the house of Ištar (see *ibid*, *pp* 504—5; 519—20); *del* 288 (326)

putuqtum (AV 7141) & putiqtum see butuq(tiq)tum, *p* 207.

III sar u pit-ru (*var* pi-t[i-i]r) Uruk; 82, 8—16, 1 *R* 1 KI-LAL (xi-ri-im) = pi-it-ru, Br 9760; see also piṭru.

pitrū. II 6 *c-d* 35 pit-ru-u (?) or bitrū (?, AV 1335); Br 2152. See KB vi (1) 345—6; ZK ii 49 *rm* 1; ZA i 308; 390 = nâšū-ridu. This would also include V 20 *g-h* 39, Br 2154.

pi-tar-ti bîti-a-ma, Meissner, 118, 110 = a-tar-ti (יתר); here also belong such forms as suluppē pi-at-ru-tim, Rm 277 ii 15 (ZA vii 17) kaspu pi-at-ra-am *etc.*

pi-tu-šu. II 35 *f* 24; equivalent in *col e* broken off; AV 7093.

pita(ā?)tum. ZA x 207 ii *O* 9 (xi-bi eš-šu) aš-šum pi-ta-tum ša dup-pi. V 47 *a* 30 a-na qa-ab damqāti-ja pi-ta-as-su (> pitat-šu) xaš-tum; Sp II 265 *a* vi 7 gi(= qi)-il-lat UR-MAX (= nêši) i-pu-šu pi-ta-as-su xaš(*var* xa-aš)-tum.

צ

çi (§ 39) = ip açū, *q. v.*

ça'u *1.* pr açî devastate, ruin, destroy }zerstören, verheeren, vernichten}. D^{Pr} 160 *rm* 2: צאי; KB vi (1) 542 perh. always: zur Ruhe, Untätigkeit bringen, zwingen. Anp iii 40 his warriors I killed, his chariots a-çi-'i; 36, a-iç(mistake for çi?)-'i (KB i 100 & *rm*). Šalm, *Co*, 102 a-çi-'i (KAT² 208; Scheil, *Šalm*, 104).

NOTE. — IV² 31 *R* 32 usually read (aban) askuppāte ça-'i; 38, u-ça-'i (3 *sg*) followed in both cases by inšâš (√ שׁשׁ) (aban) PA *pl*; but KB vi (1) 88 & 403 reads za-'-i-na (& u-za-'i-na) & translates: klopf' an die Steinplatten, *etc.*; referring to zu'unu, mentioned above, *pp* 271, 272. — Derr. çîtu (çâtu) &:

çî'u destruction }Untergang{ V 30 *e-f* 21 UD-TU = çi-i šam-ši, followed by ereb šam-ši Br 1077, 1865, 2521; II 75. lit^{y}: destruction (*i. e.* setting) of the sun. AV 7190.

ça'u *2.* KB vi (1) 280 *col* iii (iv) 10 (abnē) sur-r]iš li-çi ri-gim-ši-na namtāru, may silence at once }alsbald möge zum Schweigen bringen}. KB vi (1) 282, 14 i-çi; & *ibid* 542, where also V 30 *e-f* 21 is referred to this ça'u, 2.

ça'u 3. see za'u (zi'u) *p* 271 *col* 1.

ç(z)a-'i-i-i. 83—1—18, 1846 *R col* 1, 3 in a list of officers, followed by da'ânu, PSBA xviii 256, 257.

ça'irinnu. K 4152 + K 4188 *R* 31 ç(z)a-'-i-ri-in-nu = ši-pa[-tum?], AV 7152.

çi-a-tim *etc.* see çîtu, *pl* çâtu.

çi-e-tu (?) K 4195 = 81; preceded by qarnu, šu-xar-ru-ru, a-ra-mu.

çâbu (> çabbu > çab'u) man, soldier, warrior }Mann; Krieger{ AV 7144, 7148. mostly used in *pl* & written id (amêl) ZAB *pl* = men }Leute{ Br 8170; K 114 *O* 15 (IV² 46 *no* 1). § 9, 182; II 6, 162; ZDMG 34, 757; 40, 726. Pognon, *Wadi-Brissa*, 78; 708; *Bavian*, 120; on çâbu & ummânu see also KB vi (1) 549. S^{b} 296 e-rim | ZAB | ça[-a-bu] (Br 8148); H 27, 599; S^{c} 2, 8+9 ça-ab & e-ri-im | ZAB | ça-a-bu, id same as ummânu, 2; thus ZAB + ni = ummâni (BA ii 254 *rm* **) × çâbâni (Schrader). *Dibbara-legend* (K 2619) i 16 (end) ça-ba-šu, his army. Perh. K 7673, 20 ..... max-xu (amêl) rak-bu u ça[-bu]. id + *pl* in II 65 *a* 10; TP ii 101; Anp i 48, 62; II 43 *a* 23; often in Knudtzon, (*p* 314) with or without prefix (amêl). See also the second word in çâbē mundaxçē (Anp i 64, *etc.*) *pp* 523—4; çâbē muqtablē, TP ii 13, 79; iv 18 (קבל Q^{t}); çâbē kidinnu (373 *col* 1); çâbē šâlûti; çâbē tidûkišu; çâbē maç(ç)arti; çâbē bîtâte, ç. šarrûti; Strassm., *Stockholm Or. Congr.*, *no* 13, 6 (amêl) ça-ab šarri; Nabd 103, 15. id V 13 (*c*-)*d* 30—41 (Br 8154—57; 8162—64); 39+40 mu-ir çabi; ri-'u ça-bi, captain of the soldiers,

---

ça'anu 1. fill, see çânu & compare eçenu 1, *pp* 86, 87. ~ ça'anu 2. decorate, see za'anu, *p* 272 *col* 1. ~ ça'aru, see za'aru, *p* 272 *col* 2 & zâru, *pp* 293, 294. ~ çaiâru, ça'irânu see zaiâru & za'irânu, *p* 294 *col* 1.

Br 8158; 43, Br 8151. V 21 *c-d* 19, Br 8162. ça-ab xub-ši, *Khors* 33; the Sutī are called ça-ab çēri, *Khors* 19: see also 123, 136; & ça-ab qaš̀ti *Khors* 82 (*var* çāb). Beh 38 (amēl) çābē i-çu-tu, a few people; Sn *Bar* 24, 25 (amēl) çābē an-nu-ti (e-çu-ti); 33 (šu-nu-ti). SCHEIL, *Nabd*, ix 38 a-na ça-ba ku-um-ma-ku (MESSERSCHMIDT, 36 & 55). KB vi (1) 431 refers here also 83—1—18, 1332 *O* ii 25*foll* MULU = kakkabu, ç(z)abbu (*q. v.*), šiṭru, used of stars and constellations. V 32 *f* 5 ça-ba = mu-nu, 6 ça-ba MUL = mu-nu, see mūnu (550 *col* 1). T. A. (Lo) 3, 5 it is well a-na ça-bi-ka, with thy soldiers; 82, 9 an (= ana) Nam-ta-ra ça-a-bi-šu ṭēma iškakkan (KAT³ 583 ≻; KB vi (1) 78, 79).

çābu 2. see zābu, 272 *col* 2.

(šam) **ça-ba.** BA i 528 *no* 22 reads Nabd 514, 2 a-na (çubāt) šam ça-ba; but T^C 35 (çubāt) u-za(ça)-ba, √צבא₄.

çabbu see zabbu, 272—3; K 2001 *O* 24 (II 52 *e-f* 20, Br 8379); II 25 *a-b* 78 AMĒL-IM-ZU-UB = ça-ab(p)-b(p)u preceded by max-xu-u, AV 2793; see, above, *p* 518 *col* 2; see also çābu, 1 (end).

çabu, çibu 1. want, wish, desire; also: behold, inspect {wollen, wünschen; schauen, beschauen} Arm צְבָא, ZDMG 27, 517; LYON, *Sargon*, 66: צבה; G § 98; D^Pr 42 *rm* 1; 159 *rm* 1; RÉJ xiv 147; ZK i 120; AV 7197, 7281; § 110. prm çibi, 1*sg* çebāku. Sarg *Cyl* 52 ša ka-sap eqli la çi-bu-u, who did not want money for the field; see also ZA iii 151, 10; Cyr 168, 10 XA-LA-šu a-šar çi-bu-u i-çab-bit (≻ PEISER, KAS 99); *ibid* 12 ku-um XA-LA a-ki çi-bu-u i-çab-bit. KB iv 314—15, 25 mim-mu ma-la . . . . . çi-bu-u, all that he . . . desires: 316, 10; 318, 15 ina ū-mu . . . ša *B* çi-bu-u. IV² 46 *no* 3 (K 79) *R* 14, 15 ki-i šarru . . . . | . . . çi-bu-u (Hr^L 266), if the king desires. (JAOS xviii 146—8). NR 24 whatever I command them they do lib-bu-u ša ana-ku çi-ba-a-ka (because I want it) BA i 442; § see (in accordance with my will); STRASSM., *Liverpool*, *p* 8, 13—14 a-šar çi-ba-a-tu ta-al-la-ak, she can go wherever she pleases; ZA iii 182 (çi-ba-ta). Neb 409, 5—6 a-šar ça-ba-ta. Nabd 608, 6 iq-bi-ma lu i-çi-ib-bu-ma. — Perhaps here also *del* 231 (257) ça-pu (*var* zu-pu. perh. = 𝔔 pm) & iç-ça-pi (pa, pu) = 𝔑; 288 (266) see above, *p* 351 *col* 1 § 2; KB vi (1) 515 (& *ibid* 394 on *zu* for *çu*); also K 678 (Hr^L 506) *O* 13 ina pu-tu-ni . . . . . a-çap-pi. V 65 *a* 37 ça-pi, he was seen. Sarg *Cyl* 6 (7) Sargon who ki-i ça-ab (il) A-num u (il) Da-gan išṭuru zakūt-su (see *pp* 278, 279), pledged, according to the will of *A* & *D*, the freedom of Haran, OPPERT; LYON: G § 98; ≻ WINCKLER, *Sargon*, 164; 223 *col* 2; KB ii 40, 41; KB vi (1) 431 transl.: as soldier of *A* & *D*; a ‖ of zik-ru ša (il) A-nim, KB vi (1) 120, 33; & ki-çir (il) Nin-ib (*ibid* 35); see also Sarg Pp IV 12; *bull*-inscr. 10; *Bronce*. 14.

𝔔 desire, be on the lookout for; inspect, see, behold {wünschen, begehren; besichtigen; schauen (auf etwas)} Z^B 18: 104 (med); çu-ub-bu (AV 7269). T^M vii 58; 65 (end) see nabnītu, *b* (638 *col* 2); Lay 38, 8 in my mother's womb kēniš ŠI-BAR (= ippalsa)-an-ni-ma u-çab-ba-a nab-ni-ti. L⁴ i 7 (end) u-çab(p)-b(p)u-u (3*sg*). V 65 *a* 39 pa-pa-xi bēlūtišu u sukkē (or kummē?) u-ça-ab-bi-ma (I inspected); KB iii (2) 92, 57 u-ça-ab-bu-u (3 *pl*) si-ma-a-ti. *del* 285 (323) te-me-en-na xi-i-ṭi-ma libitta çu-ub-bi, KB vi (1) 254—55; BA ii 402, and inspect the brickwork. VATh 4105 iii 12 zu-ub-bi çi-ix-ra-am ça-bi-tu ga-ti-ka, look upon the little one, catching hold of your hand. Rm 2, 454 + 79, 7—8, 180 *O* 26 (KB vi, 1, 112—3) çu-ub-bi (= du-gul, 25) tam-tum i-da-te ša Ē[-kur?]; II 35 *e-f* 28 çu-ub-bu-u = da-ga-lu, AV 7281. ZA v 67, 38 u-lil-ši ana çu-ub-bi-e; 13, ul u-çab-ba-a, I cannot see (*cf ibid p* 74 bel)-K 7831 ii see naṭalu 𝔔, end (668 *col* 1). D 85 iv 20—22 ŠI-SUD-UD-AG-A, ŠI-SUD-UD-BAR-RA, ŠI-ŠA (= LIB)-BAR-RA = çu-ub-bu-u, Br 9366—68; Z^B 104; 108; D^Pr 153. 83, 1—18, 1330 i 21 *foll* see kunnū (*p* 405 *col* 2).

𝔔¹ (?) KB iii (2) 88 i 38 la uç-ça-ab-bu-u ki-su-ur-šu ‖ la in-na-aṭ-ṭa-la u-çu-ra-ti-ša (39).

𝔑 perh. be asked, requested. Nabd 113, 8 (end) N (who made the donation of her own will) ul iç-çi-bi-e-ma (had not been requested to do so); TALLQVIST, *Schenkungsbriefe*, 19, 20 (= Q^t).

NOTE. — çibû in legal language also: dispose of ¦ verfügen, OPPERT; FEUCHTWANG, ZA vi 438; vii 83 *rm* 2.

Derr. çibûtu, 2, teçbîtu.

çibu 2. surround, catch }fest umgeben, fangen{ S^c 40 du-ub | DUB | çi-bu-u (39, = lamû. *q. v.*) H 17, 275; Br 3930. D^{Pr} 171 *fol*. — ℑ V 30 *c-d* 65 see labû, 2 (467 *col* 1). Perh. also SCHEIL, *Nabd*, x 35—7 ça-lam (11) Sin ana zi-ki-ir šu-mi-šu u-ça-ab-bu-u-ma, MESSERSCHMIDT, *p* 58.

Der. tiçbû.

çibû ***3.*** *adj.* dyed, tinctured (?) }gefärbt{ D^{Pr} 171. 172 צ₂צבע. II 30 *e-f* 71 A-DI-A (= puqlû) = çi-bu-tum (*m. pl*); 62 A-SUD-A (Br 6893) = çi-bu-tum. A-DI-A = çarapu, çirpu (*q. v.*).

NOTE. — According to PRINCE, *Daniel* (*p* 221)] çebû also çubbu (?) finger, fingertip, Finger, Fingerspitze; § 46. See çubbân.

Derr. naçbu (*q. v.*) & çibutum, 1

çubb(pp)u name of an animal (lamb?) }Tiername (Lamm?){ K 152 iv 19 çu-ub(p)-b(p)u ‖ pasillu (*q. v.*).

çababu see zababu (*p* 275 *col* 2) Br 11748; and III 52 *a* 82 kappi iççûri imitti u šumêli ça-bi-ib.

Q^t K 3880, 12 šumma sîsû iç-ça-bi-ib-ma maškâšu ikkal, BEZOLD, *Catalogue*, 574.

ℑ V 45 ii 33 tu-ça-am-bab (?). III 35 (*no* 4) *c* 7 birds ša çu-ub-bu-bu a-gap-pi (WINCKLER, *Untersuchungen*, 98).

çubabû, part of a tree }Teil eines Baumes{ Rm² 67 + 83, 1—18, 461 *a* ii 8 GIŠ-BIR-GAM-MA-U-KU = çu-ba-bu-u.

(Iç) **çi-bi-il-ti,** AV 7195; AV^b 54 *col* 2, a tree }ein Baum{, or iç-çi bi-il-ti (?)

çubbân a measure of length }ein Längenmass{. BA iii 246 (K 192 *R*) 20 .... aš-lu çu-ub]-ban šiddi aš-la X çu-ub-ban pûti kîma maxrimma êpuš (see *ibid*, 358—9), a measure, smaller than ašlu; Bu 88—5—12, 75 + 76 vi 30, 31 aš-lu çu-ban šiddi | aš-lu çu-ban pûti; ZA iv 362, last line: mi-lu-šu 1 UŠ (ta-a-an) çu-ub-ban.

çabaru 1. *pr* içbur (& içbar), *ps* içabbar perh. to get into one's power, get hold of, seize, snatch }in seinen Besitz, seine Gewalt bekommen. wegraffen{. V 50 *a* 49—50 [ša] ilu lim-nu meš-re-ti-šu iç-bu-ru, Br 2574 = he whose muscles an evil god has taken hold of; iÐ same as çibratu, *q. v.* LEGAC, ZA ix 386, 5—6 ku-dur-ra-šu li-iç-ba-ri. Perh. also KB vi (1) 582—3 *b* 16 and a scepter of lapislazuli la ç(z)a-ab(p)-ra-at, had not been taken possession of. II 20 (*a*-)*b* 45—47 ç(z)a-ba-rum (Br 2251, 13871, 14117; 50. çabaru ša GIŠ-BAL (*i. e.* pilaqqi; perh. to çaparu, 2); 51, ça-baru ša meš-re-ti.

Q^{tn} II 20 *b* 52 i]ç-ça-nam-bur (?).

ℑ = Q intensive. II 20 *c-d* 1—10 we have 1, A-ŠA (= LIB)-DIB-DIB & 2. E-KAL-KAL-GA = çu-ub-bu-ru ša i-ki. PSBA xiii 95 bank up a canal, a ditch. Br 10696, 11588; 5876, 6224. 3, DU-DU-GA-NU = ç ša a-la-ki, Br 4921, 5428; 4—7 AN-TA-ŠUR-RA. (Br 471); 5, ŠA (= LIB)-DIB-BA (Br 1074, 8070. 10696; II 40, 221 = zi-nu-u, ša-ba-su); 6, ŠA-NI-NI-BI-IR (Br 8068, 8273); 7, ŠA-SAR-DA (Br 4334, 8025) = ç ša lib-bi; 8—10 ŠA (= LIB)-SUR-RA (Br 2938, 8015); ŠA-ŠU-DIB-DIB-BA (Br 8054, 10698); 10, È-LIBIT-NUL (Br 6276) = ç ša ir-ri. Br 5435, 3995 reads II 34 *g-h* 10, 11 GA-GA & I-RI = çu-ub[-bu-ru] (ša ...).

Š Z^B ii 60 u-kan-nu u-bar(*var* ba)-ru u-ša-aç-ba-ru.

NOTE. — LEGAC, *loc. cit.*, quotes L⁴ i 24 iš-ta-na-as-bar (but?; unless we assume mistake of uš instead of iš): ZA x 280. BA iv 491 assumes value *uš* for the sign *iš* (in Xammurabi, and T. A.).

Derr. naç(*z*)baru & these:

çaburtu. oppression; injustice? }Vergewaltigung; Ungerechtigkeit{ Z^B 54. IV² 60* A *O* 3 (B *O* 3) ça-bur-tum (*var* -ti) u-ta(-aç)-ça-pa; V 47 *a* 34, 35 ça-bur-tum explained by ru-ub-tum. ZEHNPFUND, *Theol. Litbl.*, '91 *col* 606 comp. Hebr צרבת. T. A. (Berl.) 40, 23 ça-bu-ur-ta itti-ja (+ 30). See also çaparu, 2.

çabburîtu *f* epithet of the witch (ax-xu-di-tum). IV² 50 *a* 54 çab-bu-ri-tu. T^M 15 *rm* 1: 'Zischerin', thus √ça-paru, 1.

çab-ra-ti III 61 *a* 17.

çabaru 2. understand, hear }verstehen, hören{ ZIMMERN. KB vi (1) 44, 4 a-na rim-ma-ti-ši-na ul i-ç(z)ab-[bar], do not listen to their howling.

$\mathfrak{Q}^1$ Creat.-*frg* III 5 .... ti-iç-bu-ru te-le-'u, KB vi (1) 318, with ZIMMERN: [den Befehl meines Herzens] sollst du willig hören.

$\check{S}$ Creat.-*frg* III 14 Anšar has sent me te-rit libbišu u-ša-aç-bi-ra-an-ni ja-a-ti-um-ma (72, u-ša-aç-bir-an-ni) ZIMMERN-JENSEN, narrate }erzählen{.

$\mathfrak{A}^1$ II 20 *c-d* 23 TIK-KI-IZ-KI-IZ = i-ta-aç-bu-ru ša amēli (§ 98; Br 3300; 9742); or çaparu, ?.

çabāru. Nabd 1040, 2, so & so much a-na ça-ba-ru-MEŠ.

çib(p)ru 1. some precious stone, lapislazuli; then, also, necklace of lapislazuli, and necklace in general }ein Edelstein, Lapislazuli, Lasurstein; auch Geschmeide aus solchem Stein; dann Geschmeide im Allgemeinen{. V 29 *g-h* 45 uk-nu[-u] ‖ çib(p)-ru; II 40 *a* 48, 49 (aban) çi-ib-rum ‖ (aban) ZAGIN [ ] Br 12497 & (aban) ku-nu[-ku?] AV 7243; Br 14412. II 20 *c-d* 11—15 çib(p)-rum has the id (aban) ZAGIN-SIG(ŠIK) Br 11787; AV 2052; aZ-AŠ (*i.e.* ⟶) Br 27; 11777; aZ-AŠ-AŠ. Br 11778; aZ-TIK, Br 11779; aZ-NI-A. Br 11781; 16, 17, aZ-NI-A-GUŠKIN & (aban) A-TIK-ZAG-GA (Br 11782, 5862) = ç xurāçi. Perh. also *del* 155 (165) lu-u (aban) ZAGIN-TIK-ja = lū çibri-ia, KB vi (1) 240—1; 503; JENSEN, 441. Connected with this is probably:

çibrēti. II 37 *g-h* 58 (aban) NUNUS (= pilū, Br 8184)-TUR-TUR (KB vi, 1, 503) = çib-ri-e[-ti, or tum?]; according to *l* 57 a small erimmatu, *i.e.* necklace.

çibru 2. III 52, 55 kakkabu ša ina pāni-šu ç(z)ib(p)-ra ina arki-šu zibbu (a tail) ŠA(= šak)-nu; also *a* 59, 60; thus read II 49 (K 250) iv *e-f* 13 UL ša ina pāni-šu çib(p)-ru ina arki-šu zibbu ŠA (= šaknu); KB vi (1) 503 *ad* JENSEN, 154, 157. 159, 505. Perhaps better = çipru.

çibāru (?). See dakū, *p* 246 *col* 2; Br 6026, AV 7192. K 61, 26 (šam) çi-ba-ru; 35, (šam) çi-bu-ru, ZK ii 208; 83, 1—18, 1335 *R* iii 15 (PSBA xi 54 *foll*); also šumma šarat qaqqadišu kīma çi-ba-ri zaq-pat. See OEFELE, ZA xiv 359 on […] U çibāru (MEISSNER, ZA ix 276—7: etwas pflanzenartiges, eine Pflanzenart); the sign […] means probably: inimical, enemy to the plant }Pflanzenfeind{; thus the meaning probably: Nachtschnecke; not as HOMMEL-MEISSNER: Unkraut; or BERTIN: menuro.

çabatu, *pr* içbat, *pl* içbatu (§ 27), so after içabat (*ps*), PHILIPPI, BA ii 387 *rm* †, for original içbut (see Anp; Šalm; K 683, 19 aç-bu-ut; K 3182 ii 6 [11] Šamaš ša di-na-ti iç-bu-tu); *ip* çabat; *ps* iça(b)bat; Beh 17; 82, & içabbit. AV 7144; catch, grasp, take }fassen, nehmen{ chief-id LU (= DIB) § 9, 44; Br 10894. Sᵇ 1 iii 13 di-ib | LU | ça-ba-tum; V 38, 42. K 5157 *O* 1 ça-bat, H 181 XII; Br 2397.

a) catch, grasp, take hold of }fassen{ in general. K 3600 (hymn to Ninā) 18 bless Sargon ça-bit qa-ni-ki; also ZA v 68, 17 *Anp* ça-bit qa-ni ilū-ti-ki, who takes hold of the staff of thy divinity; KB iv 102—3, 3 Nabū ça-bit qān duppi elli (see also V 52 iv 19); 100—101 i 30 pān (amēl) a-ba ça-bit dup-pi. K 3182 ii 51 (& 54) ça-bit (iç) zi-ba-ni-ti, he who holds the scales (+ 56); KB iv 120 *no* IX (Rm 107) 25 (amēl) a-ba ça-bit e-gir-tu, & see dannitu, 2. IV² 7 *a* 55 like this onion šur-šu-šu qaq-qa-ru la i-çab-ba-tu, whose root does not ground in the earth (+ IV² 8 *b* 11); *del* 199 iç-bat qa-ti-ja-ma, he took me by the hand; perh. Creat.-*frg* IV 98 im-xul-lu ça-bit ar-ka-ti, KB vi. 1, 26—7; 338. S 1064 *R* 2—3 ši-ir-ṭu ša ina libbi | ça-bit-u-ni, the bandage which held it on. — Especially note these combinations: *a.* šēpē(ā) (id NĒR) çabatu, take hold of one's feet, *i.e.* to express submission to some one. NĒR *pl*-ju (lu) iç-ba-tu (3 *pl*), TP i 86, 87; iii 71; iv 27, 28; v 87; 78, 79; (lu) iç-bat ii 46; vi 26. iç-bu-tu (3 *sg*) NĒR²-ja, SMITH, *Asurb*, 140, 1; 120, 105; Anp i 66—7 (ii 10 + 78) NĒR 2 *pl*-a DIB (*var* iç-bu)-tu; 81, NĒR *pl*

çab(p)ru. AV 7150, Br 11759—60, see zabru (275 *col* 1). ∼ çab(p)ru *del* 262 (203) end, see pir-ru, BA i 142, 143.

(*var* ?)-(j)a DIB (*var* iç-bu)-tu; i 115 NÊR$^{2\,pl}$-ja la-a iç-bu-tu; iii 52 (NÊR-a, *var* -ja); iii 88 (ZA iii 419); Asb v 21 iç-ba-ta NÊR-ja. Šalm, *Mon*, *R* 86 NÊR^{2}-ja iç-bu-tu; *R* 74 NÊR$^{2\,pl}$-ja iç-bu-u-tu; *Ob* 184 (154 iç-bat). Asurb ii 98 NÊR^{2} Ašurbanaplu ça-bat (ip); K 2675 *R* 17 NÊR$^{2\,pl}$ ru-bu-ti-šu ça-bat. — *β*. qât(ā), usually written ŠU^{2} (or ŠU^{II}) çabatu, literally: grasp one's hand *i. e.* help, assist, support, take under one's protection {die Hand jemandes fassen, *i. e.* ihm helfen, beistehen, *etc.*} G § 119; Z^{B} 25; 28; D^{Pr} 155 *rm.* Smith, *Asurb*, 100, 20 corn I gave him and aç-bat qât-su, KB ii 244. K 2487 + K 8122 *O* 21 ta-çab-bat qât en-ši. K 512, *R* 10, 11 (Hr^{L} 204; V 53 *d* 58) the mistress of life ši-i qāt-su ta-ça-bat. III 43 *d* 24 God *Zamāma* šar ta-xa-zi i-na ta-xa-zi qât (*i. e.* ŠU)-su la i-ça-bat, may not help him in battle. IV^{2} 10 *a* 59 aš-ta-ni-'-e-ma man-ma-an ga-ti ul i-ça-bat; *b* 37—8 qa-as-su ça-bat (help him!) Br 7583; K 5157 *O* 1—2 qa-ti ça-bat, H 181 *no* XII. See also V 64 *b* 18—20; V 44 *c-d* 59 ina pu-uš-qi u dan-na-ti qa-ti ça-bat (come to my succour, Z^{B} 25). P. N. Nabû-ça-bit-qâtâ, AV 5842; see Nabû-qat(?)-an-ni, AV 5845; II 64, 21; Nabû-ŠU^{2}-ça-bat, AV 5846, II 64 *d* 9; Asb vii 47; K 101 (H 115) *O* 15—16 kišadki sux-xir]-šum-ma ta-ça-ba-ti ŠU (qât)-su. KB ii 180 below, *no* ii 3 *T* qat-su iç-ba-tu-ma, *T* came to the assistance of his (wounded) father. S^{P} 158 + S^{P} II 962 *O* 29 ti-iç-bat qat-su (ip like tîšab?) *Jour. Vict. Inst.* xxix 79, seize his hand! ZA iii 369 māru ça-bit qâtâ-i-ni, our adopted son. — çabatu qâtâ ša ^{il} Bêl, *etc.* on zagmuku-festival *etc.*, see Jensen, KB iii (1) 139 *rm* **; Rost, *pref.* x. Winckler, *Diss*, Thesis 4: ZA ii 301 *foll*; *Sargon*, *pref.* xxxvi: leitet den rechtmässigen Regierungsantritt eines babylonischen Herrschers ein; es muss diese Ceremonie an jedem Neujahrstage von neuem vorgenommen werden. L^{4} iii 29 Šamaššu-mukîn .... qâta ilû-ti-šu rabî-ti ça-bit (pm); *cf* Asurb vi 119 qâti ilû-ti-ša rabî-ti at-mu-ux. V 33 ii 10—12 ŠU $^{(il)}$ Marduk u $^{(ilat)}$ Çar-pa-ni-tum lu iç-ba-tu-nim-ma. — *γ*. abûtu ça-batu = go surety for one; & rêmu (*q.v.*) çabatu, intercede for one. ZA v 68, 25 çab-ti a-bu-us-su, intercede for him (o Ištar!). K 4623 (H 123) *R* 5 (end) a-bu-ti (id see S^{b} 360) çab-ti-ma, Z^{B} 25; 60; 118; Pognon, *Wadi-Brissa*, 182 *fol*). L^{4} ii 9 as for the king my father çab-tak ab-bu-su-nu, I intercede for them; Sm *Asurb*, 9, 7 (KB ii 236—7; see also *ibid* 178); K 183 *R* 19 (Hr^{L} 2) ab-bu-ut-ti i-çab-bat-u-ni, BA i 624. V 64 *b* 43 Nusku .... li-iç-ba-at a-bu-tu. K 3182 ii 43 who does not accept a bribe ça-bi-tu a-bu-ti en-še, but has regard for the weak, AJSL xvii 138, ZA iv 10; K 3474 ii 27. DT 109 *O* 19 ça-bi-tat a-bu-tu (also Boissier, *Rev. Sém.*, viii 152 § 4); 22 ça-bi-tat (na-as-qu?) & *cf* 83—1—18, 1847 ii 7—10 (AJSL xiv 173—4); K 2801 *R* 43, 44 ça-bi-ta-at ab-bu-ut-ti. On abûtu çabatu see also KAT^{3} 410 *rm* 6. — *δ*. grasp, seize {packen, festhalten}. I 7 ix *B*) 1/2 a mighty lion of the desert ša uznâ-šu aç-bat; *C* 2. V 47 *a* 18—19 a-tam-max; [ta]-ma-xu: ça-ba-tum. KB ii 252, 85 iç-bat-su xat-tu, fright seized him (§§ 51; 53*a*). NE VI 123 .... iç]-bat-su-ma (grasped him), & 146; KB vi (1) 162, 41 [ni]-çab-bat $^{(il)}$ Xum-ba-ba; 154 *ad* NE IV *col* iv 2 çab-[t]a dan-nu, they seize the giant; 196 ii (iii) ni-iç-ba-tu, we grasped (the heaven-bull); 198, 15 ša iç-ba-tu[-ka ka-a-ši]; 204 ii 22 (= ZA xii 320 *foll* ii 16) end, ja-a-ti lu-uç-bat. *Etana*-legend (K 2527 + K 1547) *O* 26 (end) at-ta ça-bat-su ina kap-pi-šu, grasp him by his wing; 48 (end) çiru iç-ça-bat-su, *etc.* *del* 135 (142) Mount Niçir elippa iç-bat-ma and let it not go again (see nâšu). IV^{2} 8 *b* 14 (ruxû?) a-a iç-ba-tu i-çi-en çi-ru. Perh. K 150 i 38 a-na ça-ab-ti ça-bat-su(-ma) .... iq-bu-u (IV^{2} 51 *col* 1). Smith, *Asurb*, 192, 13 the ship of Tammaritu ša ši-ik-nu di-ru-u ru-šum-tu iç-ba-tu. — *ε*. mend a rent, a tear in the wall, *etc.* see batqu; 207 *col* 1; BA iii 309, & Cyr 228, 7—8 ur-ru i-ša-an-ni u bat-qa ša a-su-ru-u i-çab-bat (177, 16); Camb 182, 5 (end); 415, 3 (ana) ça-bat bat-qa; 306 *R* 2 bat-qa ša a-sur-ru-u ta-çab-bat;

KB iv 202—3, 9 u-ri i-ša-an-na bat-qa ša a-sur-ri-e i-çab-bat; see also T^C 120; PEISER, *Babyl. Vertr.*, 47, 11 (a-ça-ba-ta); 58, 19 (a-çab-bi-ta). — ζ. grasp, in a mental, intellectual way; understand, apprehend }fassen, in geistigem, intellektuellen Sinne; begreifen, verstehen{. kul-lum ša ça-ba-ti, Br 11797, see *p* 380 *col* 1. § 2. *Adapa*-legend (KB vi, 1, 96; BA ii 419 *foll*) 34 what I have told thee lu ça-ab-ta-ta, hold fast in thy memory; *cf* IV² 19 *b* 47—8 ṭême ul çab-ta-ku (= NU-MU-UN-DIB) ra-ma-ni ul xa-sa-ku; perh. ZA x 205 *R* 15 ku-šur lib-bi liç-bat (& 10—19); Anp iii 76 treasures whose weight la-a çab-ta-at (iii 66, 67), cannot be apprehended; Šalm, *Mon*, ii 75 (KB i 170—1: ist unberechenbar).

b) take, receive, accept }nehmen, empfangen{. IV² 39 *a* 5 ça-bi-it ki-šat ni-ši, who receives the gifts of the people (MEISSNER, 112 *rm* 2; KB i 4, 5). IV² 1 *a* 47 ša ilušu ana (*var* ina) ku-ru-um-ma-ti iç-ba-tu-šu. Šalm, *Ob*, 184 li-ṭi-šu aç-bat, see liṭu. Cyr 270, 8—9 ša . . . . maš-ka-nu (see *pp* 603—4 & BA iv 427) çab-ta-ta (pm with passive meaning), who was taken as a guarantee, a pledge; 154, 8—9; Nabd 390, 8; 391, 6. Cyr 321, 8—9 çab(*var* ça-ab)-ta-tu (+ 10, end: ça-ab-ta-at, BA iii 395); Nabd 239. 5 house of X ša Y maš-kan . . . . çab-tu. K 517, 39—40 (the inhabitants of Nippur) ša nira ša ^(māt) Ašur ^(ki) iç-bat-u, have accepted the yoke of *A.* (Hr^L 327; PSBA xx 67). 82—3—23, 845, 3 ta-aç-bat-ma ina rim-ki-it ta-na-as-su-uq, *Rec. Trav.* xix 106—7; 5—6 ul man-ma-am-ma-' i-aç-ça-bat-šu-ma. no one at all shall take him. See also TP III *Ann* 173. 174. — Especially note: *a*. take a person or thing for something. see liṭûtu. 479 *col* 2. Sn ii 25 the city a-na (âl šarrûti u) dannat naçê šuâtu aç-bat; also see birtûtu, *p* 197 *col* 2. — *β*. with urxu & xarrânu = take the road = go toward, travel " uštêšera xarrânu; also "arrive at", *e. g.* a mountain. TP III *Ann* 134 aç-ba-ta ur-xa; NE 59, 7 ur-xu çab-ta-ku-ma. Sn v 20 u-ru-ux ^(māt) Akkadî iç-ba-tu-nim-ma (3 *pl*); I 43, 44 *etc.* see xarrânu, *a* (338 *col* 2). Asb vi 120, 121 xar-ra-nu (*var* -an) i-šir-tu . . . . ta-aç-ba-ta (3 *f sg*) ana Ê-AN-NA. KB ii 244, 47 aç-ba-ta xar-ra-nu; 49 arka-šu aç-bat. Anp iii 70 (28) ina bi-rit such & such a mountain . . . . a-ça-bat. TP III *Ann* 163 who feared and šadu-u iç-ba-tu, and took to the mountains; Asb v 112; x 12 iç-ba-ta (3 *sg*) šadû; v 20 like fish iç-bat šu-pul mê ru-qu-u-ti. SCHEIL, *Nabd*, iv 36 iç-ba-tu (3 *sg*) u-ru-ux ši-im-ti. — *γ*. take in hand, take charge of }etwas übernehmen{, see sis(s)iktu, ‖ dulla çabatu (248 *col* 1), perform a duty, a task. K 5464 *O* 16 ina qatâ-ku-nu ça-ab-ta-ma, take into your hands (Hr^L 198). — *δ*. offer a sacrifice to a god }einer Gottheit Opfer darbringen{ Šalm, *Ob*, 29 (70) ^(immer) niqê a-na ilânija aç-bat; offer prayer, Neb i 52, see supû. — *ε*. take in, collect taxes }Steuern einziehen{ BA ii 569 on K 2729. 34 [çi]-bit (BA ii 566 [ina] biti?) alpê-šu-nu çênê-šu-nu la i-çab-bat; KB iv 104. 21.

c) take possession of }Besitz nehmen von einer Sache{ § 69 i. in general: T. A. (Ber) 189, 59 pu-xa-a[t] [i]-ça-ba-tu ilâni *etc.* (BA iv 121, 3 *pl*); 48, 12—13 ça-bat-ši la i-li-u, but to take it, they were not able. TP i 69—70 Kum-mu-xi iç-ba-tu (3 *pl*); iii 2. Anp i 103 my royal city a-na aç(= ça)-ba-ti il-li(m)-ku, to capture they came (ZA i 376); iii 76 (see above, *a* end). K 186, 9 (V 53 *a*) ma-a al da-ra-a-ti ni-çab-bat. S^c 4 ça-bi-tu = possessor. *Babyl. Chron.* iv 3 ^(al) Çi-du-nu ça-bit (+ 20 + 26; iii 22) KB ii 282—3. NE 56, 19 lu-çab-ta bit xi-im [. . .]. Asb ix 89 me-ix-rit um-mânâtija iç-bat-ma. took the lead of my army. Perh. K 112 *R* 8, 9 bît dûrâni ina bat-ta-ta-a-a çab-bi-ta (Hr^L 223); K 13, 33 a-na muxxi ça-ba-ta, with reference to the capture (Hr^L 281). Cyr 168, 10 XA-LA-šu . . . . . i-çab-bit, took possession of. KNUDTZON has the following forms: ac ça-ba-a-ta 1, 14 *etc.*; ça-bat 17, 9; DIB-bat 15 *R* 8; DIB 1, 10. — *ps* i-çab-bat-u-ma 149 *R* 8; *pr* iç-ba-tu-uš 72 *R* 3. — *pc* li-iç-bat-ma 69, 3. — Note especially *a*. rebuild. take possession again of a ruined city. KB iv 102, 11 *K* . . . . aç-bat, I rebuilt (*Rec.*

Trav. xvi 178). TP vi 17 that city a-na la(-a) ça-ba-ti I commanded. See also ROST, *Annal. Tigl. Pil. III*, pref. xii *rm* 4; xxii. C^h *R* 81 [a1] Birtu çab-ta-at (KB i 212—3 *ad* 787 = II 52 *a-b* 35). Ana eš-šūti çabatu, see eššūtu (124 *col* 1); Sarg *Ann* 188. — *β*. in a military sense: take up a position }Stellung nehmen{ Anp iii 39 see nipiru; TP iii 17 see gab'u (208 *col* 2). Sn *Kui* 3, 4 me-li-e (see 545 *col* 1, *b*) ummāni-ja çab-tu (3 *pl*). Sn v 49 pa-an maš-ki-ja çab-tu (3 *pl*). — *γ*. capture, put into prison }jemanden gefangen nehmen{. IV^2 51 *a* 31 çab-ta la u-maš-ši-ru; 33 (see above *a*, *δ*). Beh 95 iç-ba-tu-', they caught. K 2675 *O* 45 such & such iç-bat-u-nim-na, they took prisoner. V 56, 5 in city and country ça-bat amēlu la ša-ka-nu. K 181 *R* 2 (*N*, the *turtān*) ça-bi-it, is taken prisoner; K 183, 23—4 who many years ça-bit-u-ni (had been in prison) tap-ta-ṭar (Hr^L 2; BA i 617). K 5464 *O* 18 the prefects ina qâtā ça-bi-ta, were captured (Hr^L 198; PSBA xvii 230 *foll*). TP III *Ann* 163 Bur-da-da ina qa-ti aç-bat; *Khors* 26, 58. SMITH, *Asurb*, 97, 5 ša-a-tu-nu bal-ṭu-su-nu ina qâtā aç-bat. Asurb viii 24—26 ša-a-šu bal-ṭu-us-su iç-ba-tu-nim-ma. Sn iv 39 balṭuan (see balṭūtu) ina qâtē aç-bat-su (§ 136). K 655 *R* 6 a-ça-ba-[s]u, Hr^L 132; *Babyl. Chron.* ii 2; iii 23 *M* ça-bit. K 94, 8 ba-ni ša taç-ba-ta-šu-nu-ti, it is well that thou hast taken them (Hr^L 287; PSBA xxiii 61 *foll*). — *δ*. snatch away, grasp }wegraffen, packen{ ‖ šalalu, tabalu. Asurb iv 43 ni-ib-ri-e-tu iç-bat-su-nu-ti. NE XII *col* i 28 ta(-az)-zi-im-ti erçi-tim i-[ç]ab-bat-ka (KB vi (1) 258—9; *ibid* 525: Eindruck machen, ergreifen); ii 19 ta-z[i-im-]ti erçi-tim iç-ça-bat [-su] = Ꝗ^t; ii 24 [il] Namtāru (*q.v.*) ul iç]-bat-su a-sak-ku ul iç-bat-su erçi-tim iç-bat-su; iii 2, 3, 4, 9, 10, 11, 17, 18, 19. V 50 *a* 38. II 60 iv 13 see *p* 318 *col* 1, 1—3; Br 160. — *ε*. çabatu ṭēmu, become distracted, distraught, insane, see ṭēmu, 355 *col* 2. NE 60, 12 (BA i 118); KB ii 256, 58 ša-ni-e ṭe-e-mi iç-bat-su-nu-ti. — *Babyl. Chron.* iii 21 pā-šu ça-bit, see KB ii 281. — pān ça-batu, take the lead *etc.*, see pānu.

II 34 *a-b* 11 DIB-BA = ka-lu-u ša ça-ba-ti, Br 14415. II 26 *no* 5 *add* ZA-ZA = kul-lum ša ça-ba-ti (see above); H 34, 805 di-ib | LU | sa-na-qu ša ça-ba-ti; V 29 *e-f* 70, Br 10692. H 40, 210 BU-DA = ça-ba-tu; 52, 72 IN-DIB = iç-ba-at; V 31 *c-d* 44 DIB-DIB-ta-ma = ti-iç-bu-ta-ma = Ꝗ^t; V 21 *g-h* 33 RA = ça-ba-tu, Br 6363.

NOTE. — 1. Kappadocian inscr. 21. 5 iz-ba-at (3 *sg*); *ibid* 8 i-za-ba-at (see DELITZSCH, *Kappad. Keilschrifttafeln*).

2. T. A. has these forms: Ber 73, 36 iç-bat (al) Gub-la; *ac* ça-ba-ta šlu (Lo) 17, 22 & ça-ba-at (al) B. (Ber) 55. 20; *ps* (Ber) 22 *R* 19 my brother ina libbišu i-ça-ab-ba-tu-an-ni, has imagined: ÷ 41 ša i-na çili-šu i-ça-ab-pa-tum; *pm* Lo 13, 8 ça-bat (+ 17, he has seized) ÷ ça-ab-bat (11) & ça-ab-tu (*pl*: 37). dullu (*q. v.*) ša ça-ab-ta-ku-u, (Ber) 3 *R* 14: (Lo) 2, 15—16 (ZA v 150): (Ber) 104, 25 ça-ba-ta-ni nakrūtu ana ja-a-ši.

Ꝗ^t *a*) take hold of, seize }fassen{ — with šēpē = Ꝗ *a a*. Anp iii 69 NĒR^2-a iç-çab-tu; Šalm, *Ob*, 138 NĒR$^{2\,pl}$-ja iç-çab-tu. — with qâtā. KB i 214 *ad* 720/8 šarru qât(â) [il] Bēl DIB(= içça)-bat. — mend }ausbessern{ batqa ša a-sur-ri-e iç-ça-bat, AV^* 7 *col* 1. — KB vi (1) 62 i 30 libbašu iç-ça-bat, sein Herz wurde "gepackt"; 48 (*Zū*-legend. I) 11 uk(q.g)-su [il] Bēl-u-ti iç-ça-bat i-na lib-bi-šu (see 468 *col* 2). — *b*) grasp }packen{. NE VI 134 iç-ça[-bat-ma]. Br. M. 84, 2—11, 72 aç-ça-bat (§ 48), I grasped; KOHLER-PEISER. ii 73—4. Cyr 328, 7 (KB iv 282). V 50 *b* 47 tu-ra-xa ina qaq-qa-di-šu u qar-ni-šu iç-ça-bat, the *I* by its head and horns he grasps. — *c*) offer, sacrifice }opfern{ TP III *Ann* 16 aç-çab-ba-ta CCXL kirrē qat-ri-e a-na Ašur bēli-ja. — *d*) take, capture, conquer. KNUDTZON, 48 *R* 7 iç-ça-ba-tu-nim-ma. — *e*) take, with arxu, urxu, xarrānu (*q. v.*). Anp iii 57 (a-na) Karchemish a-ça-bat (§ 22) ar-xu. *Khors* 114 aç-ça-bat u-ru-ux-šu (I marched against him); Sn ii 8 a-na (māt) Ellipi aç-ça-bat xar-ra-nu (BA i 591 *rm* 3); *Kui* 1, 13; Sn iii 50; iv 74, 79, 8 çi-ir (against). — Anp iii 28 xu-ri-ib-tu a-çab-ta I took (the road through) the desert. NE VI 195 iç-çab-tu-nim-ma il-la-ku-ni; see also KB vi (1) 154

& 484 *ad* NE IV ii 48. IV^2 18* *no* 4, 9. — *f*) Šalm, *Ob*, 136 šadû marçu iç-çab-tu, they took (position on a) steep mountain. Anp i 77. ši-di (nâr) Xa-bur a(ç)-ça-bat, KB i 65; § 22. — Creat.-*frg* I (KB vi, 1, 6) 26 na-aš (iç) kakkê ti-iç-bu-tu, das Erheben der Waffen zu beginnen; see *ibid* 318—4; Creat.-*frg* III 40 + 98. K 8522 *R* 22 li-iç-çab-tu-ma, sie mögen festgehalten werden (KB vi (1) 39).

(Q^{in} Scheil. Notes d'Epigr. LX (*Rec. Trav.* xxiii) Constant. *no* 583 (a medical text) 23, 24 ta-tur-rak in A-KISAL-SAR ta-la-a-aš ta-aç-ça-na-bat-su-ma.

Ƶ *a*) grasp, seize {fassen, packen}. IV^2 50 *b* 49 at-ti-e (o witch) ša tu-çab-bi-ti-in-ni. II 84—5 i 30 ša bu-un-na-ni-e amêli u-çab-bi-tu (= DIB-DIB-BI), whatsoever affects the constitution of a man, be it an evil countenance, or an evil eye. IV^2 49 *b* 51 mimma lim-nu mu-çab-bi-tu (*var* -bit, see T^M i 139) a-me-lu-ti. T^M vii *col* 4 supplied by 81—7—27, 152 *R* 9 kišpi-ki ru-xi-ki u-ça-ab-ba-tu-ki ka-a-ši KA + LI šiptu (BA iv 167); see also T^M vi 97 (end) çu-ub-bu-tu-in-ni (pm). K 3377 + K 7078 (IV^2 56 *add*), 1: meš-ri-ti tu-çab-bi-ti ¦ tu-ab-bi-ti bi-na-a-ti. K 3456 *R* 11, 12 i-na SU (or su?)-me-ja çu-ub-bu-tu | i-na buânê-ja çu-ub-bu-tu, PSBA xxi 40 *foll*: rigor? thus a *noun*). V 33 iv 46—9 ša-gam-mi-ši-na ina (?) ku-ru-us-si ša eri mi-si-i lu-u-çab-bit (1 *sg*); see also iii 40 (KB iii, 1, 142—3). — *b*) take possession of something; carry off {in Besitz nehmen; wegschleppen}. Asb ii 53 on water and on land gir-ri(-e)-ti-šu u-çab-bit, I cut off his way; iii 132 see muçû (571 *col* 2). — *c*) capture, take prisoner, man or beast {fangen, gefangen nehmen (Menschen oder Tiere)}. TP vi 73: IV pîrâni bal-ṭu-te (*var* ti) lu(-u)-ça-bi-ta. I 28 *a* 8, pîrâni bal-ṭu-te u-ça-ab-bi-ta (3 *sg*). Anp i 83 see natanu; ii 72: XX çâbê TI-LA-MEŠ (= balṭûte) ina ŠU (= qâti) DIB-ta, *var* u-çab-bi-ta, 1 *sg*; iii 83; ii 108 (*var* u-ça-bi-ta) + 36; iii 20 (end) ina qâti u-çab-bi-ta; III ina qâti u-ça-bi-it. Sarg *Khors* 43: CCL zêr šarrûtišu i-na qa-ti (*var* ŠU^2) u-çab-bit; *Ann* 108. TP III *Ann* 66 .... [ina] qâtâ-ja u-çab-bit (1 *sg*). Asb iii 39 ina ŠU^2 (= qâtê) balṭûti (*var* bal-ṭu-sun ina qa-ti) u-çab-bit (1 *sg*) mun-dax-çi-e-šu; ix 21 (the son of Ti'ri) ina qabal tam-xa-ri bal-ṭu-us-su-un u-çab-bit ŠU^2 (*var* ina qa-ti); x 90 u-çab-bi-tu. KB ii 266, 9: whom *N* .... u-çab-bi-tu. K 82, 22 be on your guard çu-ub-bi-ta-niš-šu-nu-tu (& capture them; § 94) = Hr^L 275 *R* 5 (BA i 242 *foll*; PSBA xxiii 53 *foll*). — V 45 iii 63 tu-çab-ba-ta; perh. 60 tu-çab-bat (or -sap-pad?).

Ƶ^t capture, take prisoner {gefangen nehmen} § 84. Šalm, *Ob*, 153 mâr Su-ur-ri a-di çâbê bêl xi-i-ṭi uç-çab-bi-tu it-tan-nu-ni. Beh 51 bal-ṭu-tu uç-çab-bi-tu-nu (3 *pl*; § 51); Beh 87; 90: IX šarrânišunu uç-çab-bit; also 67 + 70. K 82, 26 (*R* 6) ki-i it-bu-u uç-çab-bit-su-nu-tu. *del* 221 (245) [ša ...]-e-ja uç-çab-bi-tum ik(q)-k(q)i-mu; KB vi (1) 247; 513—4. Perh. K 1203, 24 uç-ça-bi-tu; + 28 uç-ça-bi-su-nu-tu.

Š *a*) cause to seize, grasp {fassen, packen lassen}. T^M v 64 utukku limnu tu-ša-aç-bi-ta-an-ni *u. l.* li-iç-bat-ku-nu-ši, the evil demon, whom you made take hold of me, may grasp you; iii 29 the firegod li-ša-aç-bit-ki xa-bol-ki. K 525 *R* 6 ina libbi mâti-šu u-ša-aç-bat-su ....nu (Hr^L 252). — *b*) cause to take, let take {nehmen lassen} TP III *Ann* 133 (âl) ku ..... u-ša-aç-bit; K 82, 9 the cities ša ..... u-ša-aç-bi-tu (1 *sg*; Hr^L 275) 82—5—22, 90 *R* 12 (sisê) lu-ša-aç-bi-tu (Hr^L 378; AJSL xiv 16); KB iii (2) 6 *col* iii 12, 13 allu narkabtu lu-u-ša-aç-bi-it, liess (meinen Sprössling) Strang u. Wagen ergreifen. V 33 *d* 5—8 a-di aš-ra-ti | i-lu-ti-šu-nu ra-bi-ti | u-ša-aç-bi-tu-ma (1 *sg*): KB iii (1) 143 *rm* ***. S^P II 987, 27 ra-bûti (??) ina šul-lat u-še-iç-bi[-it?] 3 *sg*. K 528, 8—9 (amêl) xi-'a-la-a-nu tu-ša-aç-bat-ma (*i. e.* xarrânu), Hr^L 269, troops thou shalt put upon the march; § 134. Sn iv 32 u-ša-aç-bi-ta (1 *sg*) xar-ra-an (mâti) Aššur. V 35, 15 u-ša-aç-bi-it-su-ma xarrân Bâbili. III 43 *d* 30, 31 see **xarrānu** (338 *col* 2; & BA ii 148). T. A. (Ber) 240 *R* 1 xar-r]a-an ša-me-e u-še-iç-bi-is-su-ma. — *c*) take possession of, esp., as residence; thus = settle, station, post, place {von etwas Besitz nehmen lassen; bewohnen lassen} *etc.* T. A. (Lo) 82, 34—5 lu-še-iç-bi-it-ka (1 *sg*) | šar-ru-ta i-na er-çi-e-ti ra-pa-aš-ti (KB vi, 1, 78 *ll* 16—17; BA iv 180, 181). Anp i 103 the Assyrians *etc.* whom Šalm. Xal-zi-lu-xa u-ša-aç-bi-tu-šu-nu-ni, had settled in X (I let them dwell in), KB i 69; ZA i 361. Anp ii 90 alānišunu u-ša-aç-bi-su-nu (1 *sg*); ii 10, their cities, their houses .... u-ša-aç-bi-su-nu; ii 8 in the city of *Tušxa* u-ša-aç-bi (*var* bit)-su-nu, I made them settle; iii 54 (134, end) ina (al) Kāl-xi (& ina libbi) u-ša-aç-bit; see also Merodach-Balad. stone iii 28 (KB iii, 1, 188). Sarg *Khors* 82 in the land of Kammana I made the captured archers of the Sûti live (u-ša-aç-bit); *Ann* 189; 267. KB vi (1) 60 on K 2619, 27 damē ... tu-ša-aç-bi-tam ri-bit āli. ZA iv 111, 130 u-ša-aç-bi-it; II 67, 15 ina ki-rib (māt) Aššur u-ša-aç-bit. K 2675 *R* 12 nišē maxāzi ša-tu-nu ki-šit-ti qātē-ja as-sux-ma ki-rib (māt) Mu-çur u-ša-aç-bit (KB ii 174 *rm*); Smith, *Asurb*, 80, 15; 83, 8. Creat.-*frg* IV 139, 140 see maççaru, 573 *col* 2. K 662, 23 nu-ša-aç-bat-u-ni (Hr^{L} 211). — *d*) place, erect {aufstellen}. Great lamassu ... a-na er-bit-ti ša-a-ri u-ša-aç-bi-ta (*Ann* 340) SI-GAR (= šigar)-šin (*var* ši-in) as-mu, I placed toward the 4 directions at their (the palaces') beautiful gates, Sarg *Khors* 164; *Ann* 427 *etc.* without as-mu; *bull*-inscr. 76 *fol*; *Ann* XIV 76; Pp IV 119 *fol.* Sn vi 53 the lofty lamassu im-na u šu-me-la u-ša-aç-bi-ta šigar-šin. Esh v 46, 47 lamassu & šēdu of stone .... imna u šumēla u-ša-aç-bi-ta šigar-ši-in; also K 2711 *R* 7. — *e*) send for {holen lassen} V 60 *a* 23 (amēl) XAL u-ša-aç-bit (1 *sg*). V 45 *g* 43 tu-ša-aç-bat. K 7599, 6 .... E-KUR šu-uç-bit-su-nu-ti (= ip).

Š^{t} cause to take, let take {nehmen lassen}. Creat.-*frg* IV 34 u-ru-ux šu-ul-mu u taš-me-e uš-ta-aç-bi-tu-uš xar-ra-nu, Jensen. 280, they made him take the road to. — *b*) cause or order to take up a position, post, place. Creat.-*frg* IV 42 the four regions uš-te-iç-bi-ta (he placed). K 80, 8—9 tak-pi-ir-tu da-at-tu u-sa-aç-bit; K 582 *O* 12 çilla (?) (written GIŠ-MI) u-sa-aç-bit K 991 *O* 9 a-ni-in-nu gab-bu nu-us-sa-aç-bit (Hr^{L} 52. 167, 117). K 683 *O* 9 xu-ub-tu u-sa-aç-bi-it.

Š^{tn} K 126, 29 zikaru UŠ (= ridû?)-šu sinništa uš-ta-na-aç-bat, *Rev. Sém.* i 170 *foll.*

IV Perh. VATh 793, 8 ša ix-li-ku-ma iç-ça-ab-tu, who had gone astray and were caught again, BA ii 563—4. NE IV *col* 4. 12 iç-çab-tu-ma mit-xa-riš, KB vi (1) 155: wurden gepackt zusammen. 83—1—18, 47 *edge* 2 iç-çab-tan-ni (Thompson, *Reports*).

Derr. naçbatu; çabtu, çibtu 2; çibittu, çubātu (?), çabitānu.

çabtu prisoner {Gefangener}. Z^{B} iv 53 ka-su-u li-šir çab-tu li-i[r?]-pu(or, mu?), the bound be free, the captive be delivered; ii 29 çab-tu la u-maš-ši-ru ka-sa-a la u-ram-mu-u ‖ 30 ša bīt çi-bit-ti; 31 a-na ça-ab (*var* çab)-ti ça-bat-su-ma.

çibtu *2. c. st.* çibit. AV 7193, 7200. — *a*) content, lit^{y}: the carrying power {Fassung, Gehalt} NE 49, 191 see 386—7. — *b*) possession, property {Besitz, Eigentum} Asurb ix 105 see xutnū, *p* 348 *col* 1, & Boissier, PSBA xx 163, § 1. KB iv 104—5, 21 çi-bit alpē u çēni la i-çab-bat (he shall not take); *Rec. Trav.* xvi 178. Bu 91—5—9, 418, 14: X *gan*, a field, çi-bi-it = the property of. II 35 *c-d* 44 UX-KA-DIB = çi-bit ap-pi (Br 8302, 10695). D^{S} 79 an insect; lit^{y}: what attacks the face; IV^{2} 60* C *O* 21 ina çi-bit ap-pi izammur elēla. To this noun may also belong çib(p)tu ‖ bennu (2 & 3; see *p* 179 *col* 1) a ‖ of qāt-ili (KB vi. 1, 389) an illness accompanied with fever; properly: Gepacktheit, or: Fallen, Neigung zum Fallen, ‖ miqtu. KB iv 132—33 translates K 321, 21—22 çib-tu ben-nu [ana 100 ūmē] sa-ar-tu a-n[a kāl šatti], die Kopfsteuer ist bezahlt für 100 Tage, die Eingangsportel für alle Jahre; on the other hand, Oppert, ZA xiii 268 has: Willensfreiheit u. Ruhe für 100

Tage, das ist die Obliegenheit für alle Jahre. Johns, *Assyrian Deeds and Documents*, iii §§ 648—51. — çibit pî muteness }Stummheit{ properly: seizure of the mouth; perh. here also II 27 *a-b* 64, 65 . . . . . . çib-tum; ç ša GIG (= murçi) AV 2925 (zibtum).

çibittu *a*) imprisonment }Gefangenschaft{ AV 7196; G § 74. II 9 *c-d* 9 EN-NU-UN = çi-bit-tu; 10 EN-NU-UN-KU = a-na çi-bit-ti, Br 2830, 9661; *ibid* 1 = ma-çar-ta; 10 EN-NU-UN-[illegible]-TA = iš-tu çi-bit-ti, followed by ištu ç u-še-çi. Creat.-*frg* IV 127 over the gods that were captive çi-bit-ta-šu u-dannin-ma, he strengthened his hold. K 246 (H 88—89) ii 22, 23 ša ina bu-bu-ti (çume-e) u çi-bit-ti (EN-NU-UN-TA) i-mu-tu(or, -ut). Sarg, *Khors* 135 çi-bit-ta-šu-nu a-bu-ut-ma, their imprisonment I ended (*Ann* 360). IV² 48 *a* 41 çi-bit-ti lu . . . . i-çab-ba-tu. — **bît çibitti** prison }Gefängnis{ IV² 48 *a* 20 & 22 a-na bît çi-bit-tim šu-ru-bu; 34 i-na çi-bit-ti a-a-bi ir-rid-du-u; thus ša bît çibitti perh. = the prisoner; IV² 51 *a* 32 ša bît çi-bit-ti la u-kal-li-mu nu-u-ru (3 *pl*; a question) BA i 385—6. See also K^{M} 10, 29 (bît) çi-bit-ti-ka. J 27 *no* 2, 37 men & women ša ša bît çi-bit-te, who are prisoners (he shall not lock up therein) KB i 118 *rm.* — V 13 *a-b* 15 ma-çar çi-bit-ti = jailer, see maççaru, 573 *col* 2. — *b*) possession, property }Besitz, Eigentum{ Sarg *Cyl* 74 mârê (mât) Aššur mu-du-te i-ni ka-la-ma a-na šu-xu-uz çi-bit-te (*var* ti) pa-lax ili u šarri (amêl) ak-li (amêl) ša-pi-ri u-ma-'-ir-šu-nu-ti, KB ii 51: dass sie Wache halten sollten über die Verehrung Gottes u. des Königs (after Lyon, *Sargon*); *bull*-inscr. 96; *bronze*, 53; *Ann* XIV 69 (Winckler, *Sargon*, 90). — ZA iii 216, 5 has ku-um çib-te-e-ti, *cf* çibtu, 1.

çubâtu, also zubâtu (§ 19) *m.* id KU § 9.41; Br 10551; AV 7267; GGN '80, 528 *rm* 3; Z^{B} 71. BA i 519: gefärbtes; buntes Kleid (צבע׳); erst in zweiter Linie: Kleid, schlechthin. — *a*) garment, dress }Gewand, Kleid{; id used also as a determinative before words indicating garments and materials of which garments or other articles of wear are made. S^{b} 1 *O* iii 4 tu-u | KU | çu-ba-tum. V 14 *c-d* 32—36 KU with glosses tu-u, te-ug, te-e, mu-u (H 33, 793—5) & MAŠ-LU (*cf* KB vi, 1, 394; Br 1941: mašlû, 606 *col* 1) = çu-ba-a-tum, see kusîtu. IV² 30* *no* 3 *R* 3—4 çu-ba-ta (= KU) sa-a-ma çu-bat (= KU) nam-ri-ir-ri, *cf* naxlaptu; Zimmern, *Ritualtafeln*, 84, 2 = IV² 21 *no* 1 B = ein dunkles Tuch. IV² 10 *b* 43—44 my many evil deeds ki-ma zu-ba-ti (= KU) šuxuṭ. IV² 7 *b* 50 mâr (amêl) ušpari a-na çu-ba-ti la u-ba-ra[-mu]; *a* 15 qu-lu ku-u-ru kîma çu-ba-ti ik-tum-šu. NE XII i 30 whose shining white shoulder-çu-ba-a[-t]a (*var* tu) ul kut-tu-ma; ii 21 çu-ba-ta (KB vi, 1, 525—6: cover. spread }Tuch{); i 14 çu-ba-ta za-ka-a. clean garments; thus also çu-bat kap[-pi] IV² 31 *O* 10 (*cf* NE 19, 84), & 60—1 çu-bat bul-ti (KB vi, 1, 397—8) ša zu-um-ri-ša (ia); *R* 30 (KB vi, 1, 526 *ad* 394); see also use of KU in V 14 *c-d* 36 *foll.* On çubat qaqqadi see BA i 519 turban. headgear }Kopftuch{, IV² 3 *a* 35 ki-ma (il) Ša-maš a-na bi-ti-šu e-ri-bi çu-ba-ta qaq-qad-ka kut-tim-ma, ZA iii 191. II 35 *no* 4, 67—70 a maiden who ina su-un (*q. v.*) mu-ti-ša çu-bat-su la iš-xu-ṭu; Prince, AJP xv 112, perh. = šillû = 'hymen'? Camb 66, 1—2: so much a-na KU-tu sun ša (il) Šamaš u (il) Bu-ne-ne; 3—4 a-na KU-tu (sun) *etc.*; evidently *pl* is meant; K 41 *a* 16 çu-ba-a-ti iš-xu-uṭ-ṭa-an-ni-ma, he tore from me my garments (and clothed therewith his wife). NE VI 25 [KU?] pag(?)-ri u çu(?)-ba-a-ti. — V 28 (*c-*)*d* 6—12 çu-ba-tu; 13 ç ba-nu-u (a bright garment, Z^{B} 37); 14—15 ç damqu; 16 ç ili; 17—19 ç ku-lu-li; 20 ç ni-ki-i (a sacrificial garment); 21 ç be-lu-ti; 22 ç 'a('i?)-li. *g-h* 38 al-lu-rum & 39, zu-bat be-lu-tim = si-lam-ma-xu; 40. = çu-bat šar-ri (§ 72*a*, *n*; AV 8009); III 4 *no* 4. 45—6 KU çu-ba-tu be-lu-ti-šu u-šar-riṭ (3 pr) = his royal robe. çu-bat a-riš-ti II 7 *c-f* 42—44 = KU-MU-SIG (mu-ud-ra) BU (Br 1298); KU-BAR-RA-SI-IL-LA & KU-ŠA (?ŠUR?)-MUX-GAM-MA (Br 1920. 10585; 10591); the last two also = çu-bat e-li-tum (= II 30 *g-h* 22, 23; Br 1921; 21, KU-BAR-RA = çu-bat e-lu-ti Br 10584, 10586, 10665). See also V 15 *e-f* 47—49. çu-bat a-dir-tu V 28 *a-b* 10 = kar-ru (*q. v.*); *d* 28 çu-bat a-dir-ti; çubat muqqu (Br 7733) see muqqu, 576—77. K 2852 + K 9662, 3 ba-ša-mu çu-bat bēl ar-ni. II 5 *c-d* 39 UX-KU-BA = kal-mat çu-ba-ti (Br 8328; see *p* 389 *col* 2). V 14 *c-d* 31 ŠA(= LIB)-SIG-ŠUR-RA = it-tu(, 1, *q. v.*) ša çu-ba-ti, Br 8078. — *b*) part of the date palm, the gišimmaru. V 26 *g-h* 44 çu-ba-tum; id Br 9606; perh. bark }Rinde{.

NOTE. — II 51 *b* 41 mentions a city çu-bat xa-ma-a-tu(m), among cities of Central & Southern Syria; see also *ibid* 37.

çabitānu, *m* bailiff }Häscher{. V 56, 55 a-na ça-bi-ta-ni-šu ap-pa-šu lil-bi-im-ma; 56, but he did not listen to my beseeching.

çab(p)-tim see nasasu, 2 (703 *col* 2, below).

Cabtāni P. N. V 60, 16 ça-ab-ta-ni.

ça-bit-tum (?) II 48 *a*(-*b*) 12 see ça-mit-tum.

çubūtu in name of City, II 53 *no* 3, 60 (+ 72) [al] Çu-bu-tu, a tribute paying city in Syria.

çib(p?)-tu *1. c. st.* çi-bat. id 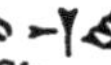 (ZA ii 303, 304; HALÉVY, *Rev. Sém.*, vi 275 *no* 2) Br 2029; § 9. 230; AV 7200. II 13, 154 = çi-ib-tu (Br 1816). in general: increase, addition to property }Zuwachs, Mehrung des Besitzes{. id also = lalū & id + IMĒR = būlu, *q. v.* — *a*) increase in cattle }Zuwachs an Vieh{. V 55, 55 çibat alpē u çēni, Z[B] 29; PINCHES; BA ii 53. 30, 7—10, 26, 16: IV çi-ib-tu ša KUR [pl] (māt) Ku-sa-a-a, four additional animals, horses from the Kuseans; *ibid* 8: III KUR [pl] çi-ib-to ša (māt) Ku-a-a-a. Nabd 1054, 7 pa-ni (amēl) rab çib-tum, KB iv 254, 255. STRASSM., *Stockh. VIII. O. C.*, *no* 27, 1 kaspu u-du-u ku-mu çib-tum. Perh. II 47 *d* 57 çib(?)-ti bu-lim. S[c] 1 *a* 11; S[c] 1 *b* 13 ma-aš | MAŠ | çib-tum, following tu'āmu. — *b*) interest in money, grain. *etc.* }Zinsen, in Geld, Korn, Getreide *etc.*{ ‖ xubullu; thus AV 2025 quotes ma-na-ma ša ul-tu ūm an-na-a kas-pi a-na çib-tum še-im a-na xubulli ana Š i-nam-di-nu; AV* 54 *b*; MEISSNER, 109, 110 (later on = tithe *i. e.* ešrū). *c. st.* çi-bat kas-pi-šu II 13, 27; KB iv 28—9 *no* V = MEISSNER, *no* 12, 2. DEL., *Kapp. Keilschriftafeln*, *p* 46 on 5, 8 if he pays not a $^1/_2$ mina of silver i-ša-tim zi-ib-tam uzāb (KB iv 52 *no* IV 8); also 6, 11 (KB iv 52 *no* V); 7, 18; 3, 9 (KB iv 50 *no* II 9 *foll*); *ibid* 8, 8 kaspu u zi-ba-te-šu; 16, 24 a-na kaspi u zi-ba-te-šu.

NOTE. — On Sargon *Stele* II 32, 33 & *Khors* 110 see WINCKLER, *Forsch*, ii (3) 373 & *rm* 3. V 40 (= H 62 *no* 3) *a-b* 47, 48 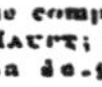 = çib-tu; id + BI = çi-bat-su; 49, id + BI-KU = a-na çib-ti-šu; 50 a-na  iš-kun; 51 çi-bat (il) Ša-maš; 52 çi-bat Ša-maš DU (which in *col a* = GI-NA, thus = kūnu: V 46, 52; ZK ii 272) *i. e.* the fixed tax, or interest for *Šamaš*; 53 çibtu ki-i-ni (shows that the word is masculine noun; MEISSNER, 8: „der gewöhnliche Zinsfuss“); 54 *ç k* u-ç-çap(b), followed by *ditto* i-šak-kan: 56 *ç k* uç-çap(b); 57 *ç k* i-nam-din; 58 *ç k* u-ru-u; 59 ša la çib-tum (= free of taxes). 60 çib-tum i-ši; 61 çib-tum ul i-ši; 65 id + id = çi-bat çib-ti (compound interests); 66 çi-bat çib-ti i-ši. With these compare H 54 (K 46) 1 *foll* as reconstructed by HAUPT; 55, 28 MAŠ-ŠE-GIM = çi-ib-tu kima še-im, (interest like (in) corn); *etc.*: 33/4 çi-ib-tu ki-ma āli çibtu it-ta-bal-kit, he refuses to pay interest as paid in the city; 35 çi-bat ša-na-at, yearly interests; 36 çi-bat a-ra-ax, monthly interests; *etc.* 69. 1 çi-bit-su i-ma-da-du, he measures what is due him.

çibtu *3.* Nabd 320, 8: II manē šuqultu lubūšum u (çubat) çib-tum ša (ilat) Bēlit, BA i 519: ein Kleid. welches man umnimmt, festhält{ (√צבת) see, however, JASTROW. AJSL xv 77. To this root also muçib(p)tum. BA i 634. T[C] 120, 121. 81, 11—28, 33 (AJSL xv 75) 3: II (is) šal-xu IV (çubat) çib-ti (four cloaks); Cyr 325, 9 (end) di-mu çib-tum. A ‖ is:

çibbatu. Nabd 320, 4: XX manē šuqultu (çubat) çib-ba-tum ša [il] [ ]; BA i 519; a tight fitting dress; T[C] 120, 121. Camb 414, 4 KU (*i. e.* çubat) çib-ba-tum.

çabītu (§ 65, 6 *rm*) gazelle }Gazelle{. id MAŠ(or BAR)-KAK, Br 1908; T[M] v 50; vii 28. II 6 *c-d* 14, 15 MAŠ (Br 1797), MAŠ-KAK = ça-bi-t[um] (>< AV 7145); on *c-d* 17 see ZK ii 418, below. H 13, 148; *cf* 168, 3; S[c] 4; S[c] 1 *a* 3 ça-bi-tum: bu(pu)-lum; AV 7147. H 71, 13 ça-bi-ta u-kaš-ša-ad, he chases away the gazelle; D 92, 4. KB vi (1) 196, 11 (NE VIII) .... ça-bi-ti. ZA iv 362, 5 ça-bi-tum ab-su-su-u nim-ru ki-sa .... see daššu, 1, the *m* of çabītu. ìD + *pl*, Asb vi 104. — (aban) pî çabīti, written KA-MAŠ-KAK, III 15 iv 12 a stone: gazellemouth }Gazellenmaulstein{, Esh iii 28 see puquttu. Delitzsch, ZK ii 93 *rm* 2; Br 608. — Haupt, GGN '83, 92 & *rm* 5; D^{H} 19.

ç(z)āb(p)itu, some machine, engine, instrument for beleaguering a city }Belagerungswerkzeug{ see nâpilu, nîpišu, pilàu. Pognon, *Wadi-Brissa*, 85, 86. See perh. T. A. (Ber) 25 ii 2 ça-bi-ti (context broken off).

çibûtum *1. tinctio, immersio*, AV 7199. — *a*) V 15 *e-f* 13 KU-A-GE-A = çi-bu-tum, *id quod tinctum est* (15 = çirpu) Br 11544; 1208 on II 30 *e-f* 71 & 62. — *b*) *abstr. noun.* IV² 7 *b* 41 as this hide of a kid a-na ši-pir çi-bu-ti la illaku (+ 21) = Z^{B} v/vi 86 & 106: wie sie zur Ausschmückung nicht mehr taugt (but see Meissner, ZA x, 400, who also maintains that the meaning: tinctio etc. is wrong; it is the same as the following çibûtu, 2; ana šipir·çibûti = for the purpose for which it was intended.

çibûtu *2.* will, desire. wish }Verlangen, Wunsch{ AV 7199; Jensen, ZK ii 26, 27. Rost, 124; Feuchtwang, ZA vi 438—9. V 21 *c-d* 11 ID-AŠ = çi-bu-tu, together with ereštu, 1; xišixtu, *etc.* K 114 *R* 15 (IV² 46 *col* 1) šarru çi-bu-us-su i-kaš-šad. 81—2—4, 105, 5—6 a-na çi-bu-ti ša šarri. Neb 406, 8 ki-i gid-dil a-na çi-bu-ut; see also Nabd 619, 9 (-tu); 375, 10 a-na çi-bu-ut-tu; perh. KB iii (2) 4 *col* II 35 çi-bu-ut mi-in-di-a-tim. VATh 575, 6 çi-bu-ti u-ul te-pu-šu-am, und du hättest meinen Wunsch nicht erfüllt (BA ii 561, 562; iv 89, 90). K 13, 60 (IV² 45 *no* 2) ki-i a-mat ša a-na çi-bu-ut bēl šarrāni (Hr^{L} 281 *R* 27); BA ii 559, 13 a-na çi-bu-tum, nach Wunsch. S^{b} 341 AŠ = çi-bu-tu (340 = ar-ra-tu); S^{c} 225 aš AŠ = çi-bu[-tu] Br 6751. On çibûta damiq(tu) itēpša see ZA vi 433; vii 330 *rm* 2 (on *p* 331).

According to Jensen, ZK ii 26—7 here also II 67, 68 çi-bu-ta-at mâti-šu-nu (ni-çir-ti šarrûti); *pl* formation (like isitâti. Anp i 109 from isittu *etc.*); so also Rost, 124; KB ii 21.

çâdu (צוד) *1.* hunt {jagen} *pr* içûd; *ps* içâd; *ag* çâ'idu (§§ 13; 64); AV 2810, 7151, 7159. II 24 *e-f* 5 (= K 152 iv 42) UR (ni-gi-in) NIGIN = ça-a-a-i-du (∥ *col* broken off) Br 10342, 11295; H 32, 762; Le Gac, ZA vi 200, 206; ìD indicates: dogs hunting in a pack. II 6 *a-b* 28 UR(NI?)-NIGIN = ça-i-du, followed by ka-lab il-la-ti, AV 7159. II 24 *a-b* 50 (see lamû, 484 *col* 2 & Br 10343); 51, LAL-E = ça-a-du ša is-qi-ti (ZK ii 81 *rm* 2); *cf* II 33 *a-b* 30, 31; H 32, 761; Br 13853. NE 46, 122 [.....] i-çu-dam-ma (ilu) EN-KI[-ba-ni ....]-šu alû (KB vi, 1, 174; 454). IV² 27 *b* 22—23 ûmû rabûtum utukkû limnûtum ça-i-du (NIGIN-NA) šu-nu, they are hunting, Br 10342. Z^{B} iii 81 ma-mit utukkû [ça-a]-du-ti. II 34 *k* 73—5 ça-a-du; ç ša .... (AV 7151). II 48 *c* 19 (al) dun-nu ça-i-du, Br 13444. Sp II 265 *a* xxi 7 i-na su-ki zi-lip(or -lul[-šu, but M^{S} 80 -tum], see Strong, PSBA xvii 150) [-ta?] i-ça-a-a-ad ab(p)-lum. (ZA x 10) Banks, *Diss*, 12, 67 ki-ma ka-tim-ti kat(?)-mat-ma ina kir-bi-e-ti i-ça-ad.

Q^{t2} hunt, chase; storm {jagen, einherjagen; einherstürmen}. IV² 1* iii 11, 12 a-bu-bu ša ina mâti iç-ça-nun-du (= NIGIN-NA, see *ibid*, *rm* 7) šu-nu (§§ 11; 52), a whirlwind sweeping over the country, they are (ZK i 29); 5 *a* 31, 32 a-šam-šu-tum ša ina šame-e ez-zi-iš iç-ça-nun-du (= NIGIN-NA) šu-nu; 48 *a* 14 see zilulliš, where read IV 55 (= IV² 48) and perhaps šu-*par* (instead of *ud*). V 55, 32 see *p* 520 *col* 2 (bel).

Derr. these 4(?):

çâ'idu, ça'adu (çaiadu), **çâdu.** hunter, trapper {Jäger, Fänger} BA i 462: in NE used of the "hunter" of Gilgameš, see 2, *no* 1 *b* (last but one line) ça-a-a-du i-tal-lak; *no* 1 *c* 3 + 5; 9, ii 42 (ça-a-a-du xa-bi-lu amēli, J^{I-N} 45 *rm* 25: Menschenfänger) + 45; iii 1; 10, 48. ça-a-a-di (*gen*) NE 9 iii 13; 10, 39; (*voc*) 10, 40; 10, 45 ça-a-di (a mistake according to BA i 462). K 3182 iii 29 ça-a-a-du (*var* da) ma-xi-çu mu-tir-ru būli; ii 11 xar-ra-na-a-ti ša la am-ra ça-'-i-da, paths that have not seen a hunter, AJSL xvii 136/7. On ça'adu (çā'idu) in NE see JASTROW, *Religion*, 475; AJSL xv 200 *foll.*

çidānu *1.* hunter's net }Jagdnetz} §§ 64; 65, 35, AV 7203. M[S] = hunting }Jagen}. STRASSM., *Stockholm*, 15, 5 ri-ik-su .... a-na çi-da-nu.

çidītu (if √צור) or çidētu (if √צרה), provisions, stores }Reisekost, Proviant}. PEISER, *Babyl. Vertr.*, 242; BROWN-GESENIUS, 845 √צור (but??); perh. *cf* צֵידָה. III 15 *a* 13 çi-di-it gir-ri-ja ul aš-pu-uk, provisions for my expeditions I did not collect. SMITH, *Senn*, 92, 68 çi-di-tu ad(ṭ, t)-qa, I collected; *Kui* 2, 22. Nabd 824, 1 çi-di-tum ša a-na (Cyr 280, 4); 1054, 2 a-na çi-di-i-tum a-na Bēl-šu-nu ... nadi-in. II 30 *d* 67 ma(??, ke??)-im çi-di-ti. AV 7204 quotes Sel 68, 5 ša çi-di-it ilāni, + 7 + 12 + 20.

çidinnu, hunter's shirt, garment }Jagdhemd, Jagdanzug?} ZK ii 265 *ad* V 14 *d* 50 çi-din-num, in a list of garments.

çādu 2. pr içūd, ps içād (& içûdu, in relative clauses) shine, be fiery, brilliant, yellow }leuchten; feurig, glänzend, gelb sein}. ZA i 255 *foll*; HAUPT, GGN '83, 93: 9 & *rm* 6; ZK i 360. LE GAC, ZA vii 141 comp. Hebr צהב. IV² 50 *b* 43, 44 see sixru (754 *col* 1) & transl.: may shine and grow pale thy face (T[M] iii 120, 121); BA ii 297 *rm* 1: wie die Rückseite einer Tafel soll fahl und bleich werden dein Antlitz (çâdu ‖ araqu), >< JENSEN, ZA i 256. I 28 *a* 15 see (kakkab) mešrī (611 *col* 2). III 61 *b* 19; 62 *b* 13 i-ça-ad, said of the sun. II 24 *a-b* 49 (33 *a-b* 29; H 25, 512) di-e | | ça-a-du ša erū, ZA i 256; V 27 *a-b* 16 *foll.* K 12026, 6—7 (M[S] *pl* 17) .... = ça-a-du (1); 8 (= II 24 *a-b* 49) = ç ša erē; 9 ..... A = çi-da-nu. T[M] i 91 çu-ud?] pa-ni ša-ni-e ṭe(-e)-mu (& *ibid p* 123); iv 15. K 3714 (see BEZOLD, *Catalogue*, 557) colophon irpu piçū ina pānišu i-ça-ad. — ℑ[t] T. A. (Ber) 1, 17 (this gold) uç-çi-id-du, hat geglüht, oder ist geschmolzen; *cf* T. A. (Ber) 7 *R* 25.

DERV. maçādu (872 *col* 1) &

çīdānu *2.* fever, fever's heat }Fieberglut} JENSEN. KB vi (1) 76, 7 mentions the following evil demons (il) Bi-e-e[n-na (il) Çi-i-da-a-na (il) Mi-qi-it (il) Bi-e-el-ub(p)-ri]; see *ibid* 78 ii 4, 5, 6 & *pp* 390; 569 where it is explained as name of a disease; iδ same as çādu 'hunt', an Assyrian 'rebus'. IV² 19, 15—16 (= Z[S] vii) SAG-NIGIN (Br 3656, 10342) = çi-da-nu i-š[ak-ka-nu]; IV² 14 *b* 37 lib-bi çi-da-nu. Z[S] *p* 60. V 21 *a-b* 6 SA-AD-NIGIN (BOISSIER, DAN. Br 3113) = çi-da-nu; šag(k)-ba-nu (4) & ra-pa-du (5); BOISSIER, PSBA xxii 110, perhaps a disease of the breast (cancer?); 82—9—18, 4159 *R* 27 çi-da-nu (M[S] *pl* 31), preceded by (26) çi-id (il) Šamši (= U-UT-KID), for çīd √çādu (JENSEN, ZA xv 212 *rm* 2). K 610 *R* 15 çi-e-da-nu a-sa-kan-šu-nu (Hr[L] 310; AJSL xiv 179).

çīdu? II 43 *e-f* 55 U (= šam) çi-i-du tam()-šil (or xaz,) = U iš-hab(q, kur)-tum; the latter is 56 = (šam) ša-mi çūri, AV 7205.

ç(z?)addu *1.* net, snare, trap }Netz, Schlinge, Falle}, or the like. AV 2812. √צדד. D[M] 29 *no* 2; ZK i 350; RÉJ x 298; D[Pr] 75 *rm* 4, & 76; RÉJ xiv 149; ZDMG 40, 730; also see ZK i 81. IV² 26 *a* 20, 21 (iδ XUL-SAR) see pāṭu, ‖ saparru (*q.v.*) ša ana tāmtim tarçu, Br 9510. Sarg *Cyl* 57 see kalamu (388 *col* 2) KB ii 48. K 2801 + K 221 + K 2669, 5 (BA iii 228, 274, where JENSEN's (127 *rm* 1) çaddu = idāti is accepted provisionally). ZA v 59, 42 ša ina ni-ip-xi-šu u-kal-la-mu ça-ad-du ki[rib?] who (*i. e.* Šamaš) by his rising brings to light the snare in .... K 576 (Hr[L] 110) 8 ina eli (iç) ça-di, *R* 12, 13 ba-si (iç) ça-di i-xa-li-qu; but, MARTIN, *Rec. Trav.*, xxiv 105, 106 reads iç-ça-di & transl.: au sujet de la courbature (*i. e.* stiffness, lameness); OEFELE: écorchure de la peau.

ç(z?)addu *2.* perh. side, *e. g.* back of a chair }Seite, Lehne eines Stuhles}, Neb iv 61 Sin na-aš ça-ad-du da-mi-iq-ti-ja (Z[B] 105 above; KB iii, 2, 19: welcher trägt den *çaddu* meiner Gnade). V 46 *a-b* 39 see našū, 1 Q, trans. (*e*).

çadū (?) ℑ give to eat, feed }zu essen geben, füttern} IV² 58 i 27 (end) tu-ça-ad-di-

ši; iii 48 li-çad-di-ki, es gebe dir zu essen; 55 *b* 30 çu-di-e an-nu-ti tu-ça-ad-di-šu-nu-ti. — Q[t] IV² 56 iii 41 tal-tam-di-i (> taçtaddī) mārat [(il)] Anim a-kal dim-ma-te, ZIMMERN, GGA '98, 824 >< J[I-N] 60 *rm*.

Derr. çudū, see above, & perh. çiddētu (ZIMMERN).

çadu (?) ℑ destroy, devastate }zerstören, verheeren{ III 9 *no* 1, 8 in his palace kuššā u-ça-ad-di (1 *sg*); but ZIMMERN, GGA '98, 824; ROST, *Tigl. Pil. III*, 16 read kussu-u-a ad-di!

ç(z)adidu. V 32 *b-c* 28 ça-di-du ‖ of [a-ma]-mu-u & gu-ux-lu (*q. v.*) = II 30 *a-b* 36 [ ] ŠA (= GAR)-ZA-DIM (Br 14486) = ça-di-du, preceded by a-ma-mu-u (32), gu-ux-lu (33—35) & followed by lu-lu-u (37). Br 13922; AV 2808; ZA viii 75, 76; M[S] 27, 28. GGA '98, 816 (below); see also šību.

çadimmu sculptor, jeweller }Steinschneider, Juwelier{? JENSEN, 352 *rm* 1. ⊕ 51 iv 31 [(amēl)] TAG-ÇA-DIM-MA = ça-dim[-mu?], see naggaru (644 *col* 1). II 34 *no* 3 *g-h* 36 see parkullu (*pp* 831, 832). V 63 *b* 38 mentions [(il)] NIN-ZA-DIM; V 61 iv 17, on which see JENSEN, 353, *rm*.

[(al)] **Çidu(n)nu(i)** = Sidon. Babyl. Chron. iv 3 [(al)] Çi-du-nu ça-bit. I 35 *no* 1, 12 *etc.*; Sn ii 35 Lulī šar [(al)] Çi-du-un-ni (38); III 15 *b* 27, 30. AV 7206; § 11 (Çi-du-un-nu); T. A. [(al)] Çi(& Zi)-du-na; Zi-tu-na, often.

[(amēl)] **Çidunā'a**, inhabitants of Sidon. Anp iii 86 [(mât)] Çi-du-na-a-a (§ 41); K 614, 6 (WINCKLER, *Forsch*, ii, 2, 310, 311). Sn ii 48; III 12 *b* 14; 5 *no* 6, 25; [(amēl)] Çi-du-un-na-a, KNUDTZON, *pp* 109, 111. § 13 (Çi-du-un-na-a-a). See also Çurru, Çurrā.

çu-da-nu II 7 *c-f* 27, 28 (Br 13940) see nindanu (*p* 695).

çidinnu see sudinnu, 1 (*p* 747 *col* 2).

צדק, be just }gerecht sein{ Q pm T. A. (Ber) 103, 32 behold, the king my lord ça-du-uq a-na ja-a-ši, is just to me (ZA vi 252: hat mir Weisung zugehen lassen?); to the same √ also:

Çi-id-qi-ilu (P. N.) Eponym of B. C. 764 (AV 7207). KB i 204—5 *col* vi = my justice is god. KAT³ 473, 474.

NOTE. — See also za-dug-ga, *p* 275 *col* 2 bel. POGNON, JA (Je. '88) xi, 544 za-du(g)-ga = çaduqa = صادق, צדוק; JENSEN, ZA x 343 *rm* (Ammi) saduga (zaduga) hardly √צדק: perh. = saduga, whose later Assyro-Babyl. equivalent is satukku (*q. v.*) = ginū (√gina, which also = kettum); thus Ammi-zaduga; not of foreign (*i. e.* Arabic, so HOMMEL) origin. The same, ZA xiii 325—6 reads Am-mi-DI-ta-na & Samsu-DI-ta-na = Ammi-satāna *etc.* = Ammi-šadāna, *A* is our mountain. HOMMEL, *New ki. Zeitschr.*, '98, 633 *rm* 3: '*Ammī-šaddai* = Ammi-sa-ta-na (KB iv 34—39; KB ii 286 *col* 1). See also WINCKLER, *Alter. Forsch.*, i 146: ii 390.

çudūru. V 28 *c-d* 67 [(çubat)] çu-du-rum ‖ el-lu-ku, AV 7270; KB vi (1) 397; II 25 *h* 37, 39; K 12022 *R* 1.

çidarū see zidarū (276 *col* 1); K 2801 *R* 39 šubat of [(iç)] mis-ma-ka-na [(iç)] çi-da-ri-e (or: iç-çi da-ri-e?, ZA iii 299 *rm* 1); K 1794 x 25, 35 mentioned with [(iç)] mus(s)uk(k)annu (S. A. SMITH, *Asurb*, ii 19); BA iii 281.

çâxu 1. (צחה, צוח) stare at, be astonished; desire, find pleasure in, rejoice at }anstaunen; begehren; sich freuen an{? JENSEN, KB vi (1) 440. Q pm NE 63, 51 (KB vi, 1, 208 & 469) in-ba na-ši-ma a-na a-ma-ri ça-a-a-ax (BA i 462); Anp iii 26 Anp ša .... ana ši-tap-ru-šu xutēnišu (see *p* 347 *col* 2) i-ça-xa (KB i 98, 99: desired). — *Adapa*-legend, KB vi (1) 98, 99 *l* 30 Anu looked at him and iç-çi-ix i-na mu-xi-šu; *ibid col* 3, 4 i-çi-ix-ma.

Q[tn] *Adapa*-legend (KB vi, 1, 96—7) 26, the two will look at each other and iç-çi-ni-ix-xu, will be astounded; *ibid R* 10.

ℑ *del* 154 (164) Ištar iš-ši NIM-MEŠ rabûti ša [(il)] Anim ēpušu ki-i çu-xi-šu, which Anu had made according to her desire (suff. -šu also in preceding line, referring to fem. subject).

çâxu 2. *adj.* ça-ax = [(il)] Šamaš (Cossaean) ZA iv 209 = clear, bright. — name of two birds, *a*) II 37 *a-c* 44 NER-GI-LUM-XU = ça-a-a-xu ‖ a-ra-bu[-u?], AV 7155; Br 9109. — *b*) see laxantu (this *no b*, perh. √צוח cry, § 114 *rm*) RÉJ xiv 158; D[S] 96, 116 (hawk }Habicht{); Br 712.

çuxxu (çûxu) desire }Begehr{ ‖ sullū (*q. v.*). K 2022 i 3 çu-ux-xu followed by qu-lu-lu & kup-pu-du; 83, 1—18, 1330 i 23 zu-ur | ZUR | çu-ux-xu, ZA iv

274—5: desire. V 29 *e-f* 31 çur-ra = çu-u-xu followed by nu-ux-xu[-tum], see kanû, 1 (405 *col* 2, end). KB vi (1) 150, 151 on NE III *col* 3 *b* 45 Enbani çu-xi (my desire), JENSEN, 440, 441. Z[S] viii 56 itti ma-mit xi-du-ti çu-u-xi qa-bu-u (promise) and then to refuse it. 82, 9—18, 4159 ii 15 bi-ir | UD | çu-u-xu (M[S] *pl* 30).

çixtu, *pl* çixâti perh. astonishment, wondering }Erstaunen, Verwunderung{. IV² 27 *a* 22, 23 qar-na-a-šu ki-ma ša-ru-ur (ilu) Šam-ši it-ta-na-an-bi-ṭu, ki-ma kak-kab šame-e na-bu-u ma-lu-u çi-xa-a-ti, id I-SI-IŠ, (Br 3097), same as in V 22 *e-h* 51 I-SI-IŠ | 𒀸𒌋𒀸𒁇 çi-ix-tum (Br 11717); *ibid* 13 A-SI-IŠ (Br 11616) | A-ŠI | çi-ix[-tum] (Z[B] 33; 92) between ba-ku-u & ni-is-sa-tum, perh. originally: cry of astonishment; then cry in general; also lamentation, moaning. AV 7214. K 41 iii 17 çi-xi (= ix?)-ta-šu (= I-SI-IŠ) u-ša-na-aš-an-ni, PSBA xvii ('95) 64 *foll*: for its lamentation will make me sad.

çâxu 3. V 34 *c* 13: III libnâti ça-xi apsî. BALL, PSBA, may '88, 366—7: reads za-xi-er-tim, translating: 3 brick cylinders.

çixamiru II 60 *c* 22 ki-ma çi-xa-mi-ri, AV 7208; or ki-ma çi-xa mi-ri-i??

***çexeru* (*çaxeru*)** = צחר AV 7153; pr içaxir; pm çixir (çixra) be small, young }klein, jung sein{ §§ 32 γ; 34 β; 65, 11; 84. ZMDG 29, 18; 34, 758. BROWN-GESENIUS, 858 *col* 2 = צער. pr perh. *Berl. Congr.* ii 1, 356 *a* (below) kîrû iç-xu-ur-ma. II 34 *g-h* 34 kar(?)-bil(?)-lu-u : ça-xa-rum, AV 2828. ps III 61 *a* 25, 26 še-gu-um TUR & TUR (= içaxi)-ir. *del* 267 (298) ši-i-bu iç-ça-xir amêlu, already an old man, he will yet become young again (name of a magic plant) or 2?? J[W] 93; BA i 143; KB vi (1) 517. pm *del* 268 (299) a-na-ku lu-kul-ma lu-tur a-na ša (BA i 385) çi-ix-ri-ia-a-ma (*var* çu-ux-ri-a-ma, in which case = a noun: of my youth), KB vi (1) 517: I will return to the vigor of my youth. H 117 *O* 17—18 (K 4931) ul-tu û-um çi-ix-ri-ku (Br 4083), since the days when I was a child. KB iii (1) 160, 27 ul-tu anaku çi-ix-ri-ku (§ 91); T. A. (Lo) 9, 12 ultu çi-ix-ri-ku, when I was young (or little?). K 2867, 11 ul-tu çi-xi-ri-ja ilâni rabûti šimâti išimûinni; 14 ul-tu çi-xi-ri-ia a-di ra-bi-ia (also K[M] 11, 30). IV² 61 *b* 32 çi-xi-ra-ka a-ta-za-ak-ka, when thou wert young. S 787 + S 949 *O* 20 çi-ix-ra-ku-ma, when I was young. I 49 *a* 5—6 (*var*) ultu û-me çi-ix-ri-šu, since the days when he was young; 81—6—7, 209 (Esh-text) *Esh.* ša ultu çi-xi-ri-šu, BA iii 260, 261. T. A. (Lo) 5, 12 çi-xi-ir, it was little. It is very probable, that in many of the above instances we have a *noun* or *adj* instead of the pm. ag Neb 125, 1 il-ta (= ištu) ça-xi-ir a-di ši-bu-tu, from youth to old age.

ᑐ *a*) make small, little; diminish, reduce; belittle }verringern, verkleinern{. Sn ii 18 u-ça-xir (*var* xi-ir) mât (*var* ma-a)-su, I reduced his country (in size); iii 26 u-ça-ax-xir (*var* u-ça-xi-ir) mât-su (see *Kui* 1, 30). KB ii 242, 67 u-çax-xi-ir nap-xar mâti-šu. Sn *Rass* (ZA iii 313) 66 the palace in Nineveh kummu ri-mit bêlûti ša zu-ux-xu-ru šu-bat-su, whose area had become too small (*Bell* 39: çu-ux-xur, ZA iii 329). Sn vi 31 šu-bat-sa çu-ux-xu-rat; I 44, 57 çu-ux-xu-rat šu-bat-sa. I 7 F 19 gir-ri šarri ana la çu-ux-xu-ri, that it may not be made smaller. KB iii (2) 90 *col* 1, 53 [çu]-ux-xu-ru ši-pi-ir-šu. IV² 13 *b* 6 rab-bu-ut-ka el çu-ux-xu-ri (against calumny) lim-ra-aç, Br 4114; or *adj*? (= the miserable). Perh. *del* 172, 173 (188, 190) would that a lion had come and niši li-ça-ax-xi-ir (had reduced mankind, BA i 138). tibût eribê ibûr mâti uçax-xar, an army of grasshoppers will reduce the country's crops (often in III Rawl. pl. 51—65). — *b*) deprive some one of something; withdraw, withhold; expel }jem. etwas verkürzen; entziehen, verwehren{. V 25 *c-d* 32 a-la-am u-ça-ax-xa-ru-šu (id see Br 10340), they expel him from

---

çuxdu, çaxalû, çaxannu see suxlu, saxalû, saxannu (277 *col* 2). ⁓ çaxmaštu, Br 11211 cf saxmaštu.

town, do not permit him to live in town (MEISSNER, 15; 152 × GGN '80, 524 *fol* & II^F 2; see also BA i 15 *no* 14). II 25 *b* 20, 21 i-na lib-bi ki-çir bîti u-ça-xa-ar; (id same as H 53 iv 60 TUR-RI = u-ça[-ax-xar], 61 un-na[-aš]; 62 un-na-aš-[ši]). V 45 ii 38 tu-ça-ax-xar (vii 12 tu-sax(çax?)-xar); perh. IV² 13 *b* 57 lim-nu pa-ni-šu la u-ç(s?)ax-xa-ru.

צר KB iv 52 *no* v 17 kaspa i-ça-xi-ir, the money is made less; see *ibid note* ***, & ?.

NOTE. — T A. (Lo) 10, 16 lu-ul-lik-ku-me lu-uç-ça-xi-ir; 20, 21 u i-ça-xar še-xu-šu (KB v its sound passes away?), 23 la-a i-ça-xar še-xu, + 44; 9—10 ša i-ba-li-iṭ i-na še-xi-šu ṭâbu u i-ça-xir; 16, 25 (furthermore when) ji-xa-xi-ra-am a-na ja-ši[-ia]. they turned against me. (Ber) 77, 50 and the people in the city will flee (xi-ix-ra). — 23 Lo 4 + Ber 7, 17 and when your messenger iç-ça-xar (returns?); also Ber. 23 *R* 37 iç-ça-ax-xa-ru. KB v (Index) all to a çaxaru, 1 = saxaru, to which also V 25 *c-d* 32.

Derr. — meçxirûtu (*q. v.*) & add: S 787 + S 949 *O* 19 meç-xi-ru-ti, MARTIN, *Textes religieux*, *pp* 14 & 17; & these 4:

çaxru (AV 7157) *f* çaxirtu; & **çix(çex)ru** (Br 4085; AV 7213), *f* çixirtu, çi-ix-ri-tu (AV 7211); *c. st.* çixir & çixrut, § 37 *b*; ZA i 179 *rm* 2; ii 307; v 69; §§ 34 *d*; 65, 4 *rm*, 7 & 8 *rm*. small, young {klein, jung}; id TUR § 9, 139; TP iv 1; H 18, 285. Perh. Hebr צָעִיר, Arab صغير. Sn *Bell* 13 see mirânu (584 *col* 1). SCHEIL, *Nabd*, iv 38 Labaši-Marduk mâr-šu ça-ax-ri. V 64 *a* 29 arad-su ça-ax-ru. *Etana*-legend (KB vi, 1, 104 *a* 10; 106 *b* 39) ad(ṭ,t)-mu çi-ix-ru. Nabd 693, 4—5 (sal) q(g)al-lat-su-nu ça-xir-tum ša VI šanâte-šu; 106, 3; Neb 100, 3 mârta-šu ça-xir-tum mar-tum III šanâte. H 91, 52 ina u-ba-ni-šu çi-xir-ti; S 1064. 23 ubâni çi-xi-ir-te, the little finger (Hr^1. 392 *R* 8). IV² 28* *no* 4 *R* 47, 48 ša mu-ux-ça çi-ix-ru (Br 4121, 10024 see muççû, 571 *col* 2); 58, 59 çi-ix-ru u ra-bu-u (§ 127); 54, 55 mar-tum çi-xir-tum (= TUR-DA) a-bi-mi. Of similar meaning as ša muç-ça çixru, is probably e-mu çix(çi-ix)-rum, V 39 *a-b* 44 (= II 32 *no* 5, 70) SAL (mu-us-sa) UŠ-DA; ZK i 71; ii 209; ZA i 394; Br 10937, 10939; V 42 *e-f* 52; Z^B 48; 84; AV 5623. According to FRIEDRICH, *Kabiren*, 10, 11 = *membrum genitale* (also id for zikaru); while êmu rabû = *pudenda muliebra* (V 39 *a-b* 43 *etc.*). *Dibbara*-legend (K 2619) i 20 çi-ix-ru u ra-ba-a kill together (BA ii 427—8; KB vi, 1, 60. 61). IV² 19 *a* 11, 12 çi-xir ra-bi (= EL-ŠI-GA), great & small; V 56, 29 çi-xir ra-bi malû bašû (*i. e.* of the cities): Sarg *Ann* 94. S^P II 987 *O* 5 (end) ça-xi(a)r u ra[-ba-a?]. Asb ii 130 maxâ-zânišu dan-nu-ti a-di çixrûti (= TUR-MEŠ) ša ni-i-ba la i-šu-u; also v 105; Sn i 74; ii 13; Esh ii 16; KB ii 240—1, 37 (çi-ix-ru-ti). Esh v 4 êkalla TUR-ra (or RA?) šu-a-tu; III 16 v 9. Z^B ii 37 ina çi-xir-ti it-ta-din ina ra-bi-ti im-t[e-eš], im Kleinen hat er gegeben, im Grossen verweigert (see, however, AJSL xiii 147). II 36 *a-b* 57 [çi]-ix-ri-tum | çi-xi-ir-tum; Br 14062 .... SAR(XIR) = çi-xi-ir-tu, AV 7241. K 4386 (II 48) iv 20, 21 (tu-ur) TUR (Br 4084) & GI (EMESAL, Br 2398) = ça-ax-rum, in one group with ra-bu-u. II 13 *c-d* 28, 29 maxîru rabu-u & çi-ix-ru (= TUR-RA), H 59, 18, 19. K 4378 (D 86 *foll*) i 59, 60 pitnu (*q. v.*) ra-bu-u, ça-ax-ru (Br 4084, 6669); iii 56, 57 paššûru (*q. v.*) ra-bu-u, çi-ix-ru; iv 7, 8 kutû (*q. v.*) ra-bu-u, ça-ax-ru (Br 8113); id always GAL & TUR. V 23 *b-d* 33 TUR-DA = çi-ix-ru, Br 4133. V 42 *c-f* 20, 30 DUK-GAL & DUK-TUR = [mašqalillu?] ra-bi-tum & *m* çi-xir-tum, Br 4086. S 31—52 *R* 16, 17 GIŠ-SA-GAL = ra-bi-tu; GIŠ-SA-TUR = çi-xir-tu, ZA ix 221—222. II 37 *e-f* 62 qu-ta-at-tu : ra-pal-tu çi-xir-tu. V 38 *a-b* 16 see Br 4158. Sm 1538 (+ Sm 1290 + Sm 1409) ii: ši-pat Šu-[me]-ri ša çi-ix-ri ba-'-ki-at (or -tu, ta?) nu-ux. II 65 *a* 16, 18 Ku-ur[-ri]-gal-zu çi-ix-ru (KB i 196—7), see WINCKLER, ZA ii 308; LEHMANN, ZA v 413 *rm* 2; WINCKLER, again, ZA vi 454; *Forsch* i 137. — T. A. (Lo) 72, 40 axê-ja zi-ix-ru-tu, my younger brothers; perh. (Ber) 28 i 35, 52, 53, 56: u I zi-ix-ru; ii 45 (end) = a small jug (?). II 37 *g-h* 50 TAG-ŠA-TUR-TUR = (aban) çi-ix-xir[-tu?], Br 12045 = a very small weight. 51, TAG-½ ṬU =

(aban) çi-ix-ri[-tu?] = weight of 1/3 sekel, Br 11223. A ‖ is:

çi-xa-ru, *adj* ‖ la-ku-u II 36 *a* 38 (AV 7209). Another ‖ is:

çixxiru. § 65, 29 *rm.* IV² 3 *b* 38, 39 a-gi-i çi-ix-xi-ru-ti (= TUR-TUR-LAL) >< a-gu-u rab-bu-ti (= floods) Br 4113; 30 *no* 2 *b* 10, 11 çi-ix-xi-ru-tu-šu (= TUR-TUR-BI) >< rab-bu-tu-šu; 16 *b* 11, 12 çi-ix-xi-ru-ti (= TUR-TUR-RA, Br 4107) perh. T. A. (Ber) 26 iv 2 .... çi-ix-xi-ru-u-tum.

cix(x)irūtu smallness; young of man or animal }Kleinheit; Kleines, Junges von Mensch oder Tier{. AV 7210, 7212. V 23 *b-d* 21 TUR-TUR = çi-ix-xi-ru-tum, Br 4107. II 36 *b* 46 *foll* çi-ix-xi-ru-tu ‖ of sa-az-xa-ru (46). ax-ru-u-tu (47), sa-as-sa (AV 6576 -xa)-ar-tum (48), si-is-se-ru (49), da-qa-ki-ta (50), du-qa-qu-u (51), çi-xe-ru-tu(m, 52); zu-xa-ru-u (53). T. A. (Ber.) 44 *R* 17 .... z]i-xi-ru-ta.

çixrūti youth }Jugend{ IV² 31 *b* 47 Tammûz xa-mer çi-ix-ru[-ti-šu]; a ‖ is:

çuxru *noun* see çaxaru ① pm.

çaxxaru (??) small }klein{? I 7 *E* 3 kīma še-im ça(-ax)-xa-ri, small like a grain of corn; V 32 *c* 2 xaç-bu (*q. v.*) ça-ax-xa-ru; AV 7157; see also Zimmern, *Ritualtafeln*, 67 *rm* 14. T. A. (Ber.) 28 ii 1: XIII ça-ax-xa-ru ša xurāçi, 12 small golden bottles; 53, XI small silver bottles; iii 70: one ça-ax-xa-ru ša abni piçī, called zi-la-ax-da.

ça(i)xxarru. II 44 *e-f* 52 (pursigallu) TUR = çax-xar-ru (Br 4085) *etc.* see saxxarru (754, 755).

çuxrētu (?) youth }Jugend{. KB vi (1) 168, 169 on NE VI 46 to Tammûz xa-mi-ri ç[u-ux]-re-ti-ki.

çixirtu. II 47 *e-f* 26 EBŪR-ŠA-TU-BA (Br 981) çi-xir-tu, perh.: the cutting down of grain (?); preceded by xa-ar-p(b)u (Br 980). V 26 *c-d* 67 çi-xir-tu, Br 3104.

çuxxūru miserable }elend{? H 210, 6—7 on IV² 13 *b* 6 (see çaxaru ℑ, *a*); perh. also IV² 18 *a* 42 ina çu-ux-xu-ri nag-mir, Br 4083, 4108.

çuxēru IV² 34 *no* 1, 1 (med) a-na çu-xi-e-ri ša šarrāni ša li-mi-ti-ka il-tak-nu-ka-ma, a laughing stock for the neighboring kings thou hast been made.

çux'ā'r''ū' KB vi 394, see zuxarû, 277 *col* 2. & çix(x)irūtu. Bu 91—5—9, 418, 8 zu-xa-ar-šu its (the plantation's) smaller part. T. A. (Lo.) 9. 37: I (amêl) zu-xa-ru I (amêltu) zu-xa-ar-tum I have sent; 1, 80 u-ul ba-na-at zu-xa-ar-ti. the maiden is not beautiful (& 97); (Ber.) 180 *R* 2: II māru zu-x[a-ru?]. Delitzsch, *Kappad. Keilschrifttafeln*, 20, 18 zu-xa-ru-um, + 22 zu-xa-ra-am; 17, 4 zu-xa-ru-a, = my little one.

çuxarūtu. 83—1—18, 198, 8 when Nergal in its disappearing ina zu-xar-u-tu šakin (-in), grows smaller (Thompson, *Reports*).

çax(u)rū Zehnpfund, BA i 526—7; T^C 46 enzaxurû. — Occurs in *c. t.* Nabd 538, 2 IX (= lubšu, *i. e.* material for garments) ça-xu-ri-tum; 428, 8 lubšu ça-ax-ri-tum; 794, 1 *l* ça-xu-ri-e-ti. Cyr 190, 8 ... lubšu ça(?)-xu (written *ri*, a mistake)-ri-tum; 253, 4—5 lubšu ça-xu-xu (here a mistake for *-ri-*) du(?) ša çi-pi. Neb 180, 2: IX ṬU lubšu ça-xu-ri-e-[tum?]. Camb 11, 2: II ma-na IX ça-xur-e-ti. BA i *l. c.* perh. = צְחֹר white }weiss{, *ibid* 635 suggests also šaxurû (*cf* Nabd 538, 6 = çaxurû, the former, however, only a mistake of the copyist); Zehnpfund, *Theol. Litbl.*, 1901 *col* 606 *ad* Ezek 27 : 18: çaxur-Wolle im neubabylonischen Reiche war hochgeschätzt.

çixiš. IV² 20 *no* 1 *R* 35 ša-ma-]me u qaq-qa-ri çi-xi-iš [it-ta]-ṭa-lu (ilu) Marduk qar-du; see Martin, *Rec. Trav.*, xxiv 96—99: dans sa splendeur (√צחה?).

çaxat(d,ṭ)u; ag çāxit. V 10 *a-b* 20 (II 34 *c-d* 17) (amêl) GEŠTIN-SUR-RA = ça-xi-it ka-ra-ni (Br 5011, AV 2827, 7154), perh. vintager, vinedresser }Winzer{ ið see mazû, 2 (517 *col* 1).

ℑ V 45 ii 39 tu-ça-ax-xat; vii 12 tu-çax(ça)-xat. V 31 *c* 69 ēne-šu uz-za-xa-ta, AV 2825.

çaxittu (?) P. N. La ça-xi-it-tum. Br.M. 84, 2—11, 214.

çuxxurtu see suxxurtu. ∼ ça-xar(xur)-tu see çamurtu. ∼ ça-ki-qu, AV 7160 see zaqiqu (290, 291).

çalû 1. locate; pm çal'i & çali, be located, situated {legen; pm gelegen sein, liegen}. ROST, 124—5; KGF 142 *rm*; L^{TP} 137. ‖ šakanu & nadû, AV 7167, 7170. Hebr צלע. II 67, 80 askuppâte IM-BAB-BAR (= gaççi, *p* 220) parûti ina šap-lišunu (*i. e.* of the lion, *etc.*, colossusses) aç-li (× KB ii 24 + 30 -kup). TP iii 62 the cities, situate (ša .... ça-al-'u-ni) at the foot of the mountains (§ 100, *cf* ظَلَعَ); *cf* ii 37 ša .... na-du-u. Anp iii 12 the city .... ina šûp am-ma-te ša (nâr) Pu-rat-te ça-li (+ 15); 16, ina qabal (nâr) Pu-rat-te ça-li, KB i 96, 97. — Š = Q IV² 54 *a* 53 li-ša-aç-li-ka za-'-i e-ri-ni *etc.*, let him put down for you (sacrificial gifts).

çêlu (> çal'u > çal'u = צלע), *pl* çêlê, çêlâni. — *a*) rib {Rippe} HAUPT, Hebr. i 180. S^b 106 ti[-i] | TI | = çi-lu; H 13, 139; Br 1704. II 44 *g* 16 (šêr) TI = a part of a sacrificial animal; PEISER, *Vertr.*, CVII, 6 (šêr) ga-an çi-li (see gannu, 1). — Of the rib, skeleton of a ship. D 88 vi 28 GIŠ-TI-MA' = çi-il (*var* -el, & -li) elippi (Br 1713), followed by GIŠ-TI-TI-MA' = i-ga-ra-a-te elippi. II 45 *no* 3 *a-b* 37; 62 *no* 2 *R* 62, 63; AV 7216. IV² 22 *a* 32—33 (TI-TI) see nagašu, 1. — *b*) side (in general) {Seite (im allgemeinen)} AV 7222. Sarg *Cyl* 66 (56) in front and behind i-na çi-le ki-lal-la-an, at both sides; *Ann* XIV 78; *bull*-inscr. 82; Creat.-*frg* (D 94) 9 see kilallân (386 *col* 2). II 40 (*a*-)*b* 24 we read sik-kat çi-li.

çalû 2. פ pr uçallâ, ac çullû (§ 65, 32*d*) pray, implore {jemanden anflehen}. On original meaning see HAUPT, *Jour. Bib. Lit.*, xix 78 *rm* 106. AV 7170; construed with ana & aššu = for. Z^B 41. TP III *Ann* 238 u-ça-la-ni. Asurb iii 17 to save his life up-na-a-šu ip-ta-a u-çal-la-a bêlu-u-ti; + 10: they approached me on account of these matters and u-çal-lu-u be-lu(-u)-ti. Esh iv 30 be-lu(-u)-ti u-çal-lu-ma erišuinni kitru (*cf* III 15 *col* 2, 28; Sarg *Khors* 120 u-çal-la-an-ni = 3 *sg*, e-riš-an-ni kitru; *Ann* 408); iii 7 aššu nadân ilâ-nišu (the return of his gods) u-çal-la-a-ni (§ 56 *b*); SMITH, *Asurb*, 283, 90 aš-šu ilâni-šu imxuranni-ma u-çal-la-a šarru-u-ti. K 2675 *R* 25 u-çal-la-a (3 *pl*) be-lu-u-ti (ZA iv 231, 4); *R* 17 çu-ul-la-a (= ip) be-lut-su (= SMITH, *Asurb*, 74; KB ii 170—1); see also K 2852 + K 9662 i 6 (end). K 890 *O* 9 (end) u-çal-la; K 595 *R* 5 (end) nu-ça-al.... la; K 79 *O* 7 Ištar ... & Nanâ | a-na ba-lâṭ napšâte ša šarri bêli-ja-ma u-çal-li; K 476, 8 (end) & 15 u-çal-lu-u; K 647, 7 nu-çal-li (= 1 *pl*); K 528, 7 (or Dt) = Hr^L 6; 266; 54; 210; Asb iv 83 (see KB ii 190—1); i 65 aš-ši qâtâ-ja u-çal-li, and I implored Ašur & Ištar; ii 116; L⁴ i 32. V 45 ii 1 tu-çal-la; Beh 22. P. N. KB iv 178 *no* ii, 11 (ilu) Šadû-rabû-u-çal-lum. K 112 *R* 11 (Hr^L 228) (amêl) Nabû-u-çal-li; II 64, 2; AV 5754. K 2852 + K 9662 i 5 ina te-me-ki çu-ul-li-e la-ban ap-pi, *etc.* פ^{tn} SMITH, *Asurb*, 290, 54 ana šakan adû sulummê (*q. v.*) epêš ardûtija u-ça-na-al-la-a be-lu-u-ti (he besought. § 83). K 890 *O* 12 at-ti-i a-na me-ni tu-ça-na-li-ni, BA ii 634.

Derr. Çallâ, çulû, çalûtu; & teçlitu, which, however, perh. better teslitu (| salâ).

(amêl) **Çal-la-a-a.** P. N. K 112 *R* 1 (Hr^L 223; AJSL xiv 9).

çalû 3. be at enmity, hostile {feindselig, feindlich sein}. SMITH, *Asurb*, 247, i (K 3062, 9): who ana Aššur ikpudu limut-tu [eli] Sinaxêrba [e-pu]-šu çi-lu-u. — פ ag muçallû (*p* 572 *col* 2); K 3312 = K 3182 (AJSL xvii 140, 141).

NOTE. — KB v* 27 *col* 1 says: √çilu & compares T. A. (Ber.) 92, 25: why do you make peace with a prince with whom another prince iz-zi-il, is at enmity. (Lo.) 1, 66 az-zi-el eli (*I am angry at*) your messengers.

Derr. — çultu, çillê 2, çiltu, çulštu, çe-lûtu, & perhaps:

çal(zal, ni?)lu *1.* IV² 49 *a* 31, 32 pû-ša (of the witch) lu-u çal-lu liššânša lu-u MUN (= ṭabtu), ša iqbû pû limut-tim-MU (= ja) ki-ma (*var* kîma) çal-lu lit-ta(-at)-tuk.

çallu *2.* perh. an apron {ein Schurz} T^C 71; BA i 534 *no* 45 | צלל cover, hide {decken, bedecken}. Nabd 1034, 1 (mašak) çal-lu; 836, 5 (mašak) çal-la-nu; Cyr 214, 3 (mašak) ça-al-la, by the side of (mašak) ab-še-e (leather strap); 148, 5 (mašak) çal-la *pl* ip-pu-uš-šu. Does here belong

Camb 40, 2: ša [cuneiform] sal (*i. e.* [cuneiform])-la ša SIG-ZUN (= šipātum). K 2022 *R* 7 na-bar çal-lu.

çallum *3.* V 19 *c-d* 29 A = çal-lum ša ri-xi-e; 22 (*a*-)*d* 47 A-A | a | a-a-u | çal(or ni?)-lum ša ra-xi-e (see also nīlu, 2, *p* 678 *col* 1); II 27 *g* 12 cal-lum ša ..... AV 2851; Br 11350. √çalalu, 1.

callu *4.* a plant {eine Pflanze}. K 4345 *R* (*col* iii) = II 42, 14—16 ^(šam)^ çal-lu e-riš-ti = ^(šam)^ aš-šu-ul-tu; ^(šam)^ ša-lam-bi TUR-RA (= çixru) = ^(šam)^ a-ra-ru-u, ^(šam)^ aš-šu-ul-tu.

çallu *5.* see çalalu, 1 (pm). Banks, *Diss*, 16, 122 ki-ma qa-ni e-di çal-lu kab-tu.

çillu *1.* *m* shade, protection {Schatten, Schirm, Schutz} *etc.* id GIŠ-MI (K 582 *O* 12 = Hr^L^ 167); §§ 9, 81; 27; 63; AV 7224; Br 8925—29. — *a*) shade {Schatten} II 109 iii 27—29 (= V 12, 25 *foll*; D 129, 124—6) [ ] | GIŠ-MI | çi-il-lu (H 39, 152); ..... SI-IB | GIŠ-MI-XI (= DUG)-GA = çillu ṭa-a-bu; [... DA]-MA-AL = GIŠ-MI-DAGAL = çillu rap-šu. H 94—5, 48 ina çil-li [bīti]; IV² 12 *a* 12, 13 pa]-nu-šu çil-li (= GIŠ-MI) kiš-te xa-aç-bu; 15* *col* 1, 62 ana bīt el-lu ša ki-ma kiš-ti çil-la-šu tar-çu, which like a forest spreads its shade (H 219); 31 *b* 26 GIŠ-MI (= çilli) dūri; Anp ii 6 a-na ni-iš i-di-ka çil-lu ta-ri-iç. Asurb iv 64 narkabāti ^(iç)^ ša ša-da-di ^(iç)^ ša çil-li (= baldachin); Sarg *Khors* 132; *Ann* 338 narkabāt kaspu ^(iç)^ ša çil-li xurāçi. NE 24, 8 ṭa-a-bu çil-la-šu, beautiful was its shade. V 16 *e-f* 45 çil-li (= GIŠ-MI) tam-xi-e = twilight, Br 7910, 7998; V 47 *a* 17 (end) ta-ra-nu, expl. by çil-lu. — *b*) protection {Schirm, Schutz}. 81—6—7, 209, 12 çillu-šu-nu da-ru-u | it-ru-çu eli-šu, BA iii 260, 261. K 2729 *O* 24 (id) see kanū, 1 Q (405 *col* 1); Beh 4, 7, 9 *etc.* II 80, 10 see puluxtu, *b.* II 18 *d* 45 ina çil-li pu-zur amēli (see *c*); P. N. Ṭa-ab-çi-la-šu, often. Eponym list, KB i 204 iv (716) Ṭab-çil-Ē-šar-ra; 206 ii (807) Çil-Bēl; also name of a king of Xazīti (Sn iii 25); III 49 *b* 30 Çil-Bēl-tal-li, an official. Cappadocian Zi-li-Ištar. *etc.* Çil-Ištar. KB i 206 iii (788); Çi-li-Ištar, KB iv 24 *no* 3, 8: Çi-li ^(il)^ Šamaš; 26, 27 Ṭa-ab-çi-la-šu; see also KB iv 6 *col* 2, 7 + 19. Çil-Aššur, III 49 *a* 43; K 1393 Ṭāb-çil-Marduk, name of royal astronomer. Çil-Nabū, Çil-Ninib *etc.* often (see Bezold, *Catalogue*, vol v). Neb, *Grot*, iii 23 a-na çi-il-li-šu da-ri-i (under its, *i. e.* Babylon's eternal protection) I gathered all the nations amicably. — Camb 386, 7—8 P. N. ^(amēl)^ Çil-la-a mār Na-ba-a-a. — *c*) part of a ship {Teil eines Schiffes} D 88 vi 34 GIŠ-GIŠ-MI-MA′ = çil-lum elippi. II 62 *no* 2 *R* 70; BA iv 242 *rm* *: Schiffsrippe (nicht Kammer), evidently combining it with çi-el (çi-li) elippi, Br 8929. II 85 *g-h* 72—75 see paṭaru & šillu.

NOTE. — an çilli see zillu, 2 (292 *col* 1) & GGA '98, 815.

çillu *2.* a plant {eine Pflanze}. K 4174 + K 4588 i 30 U-GI-IŠ-GI-IG-GA-KU = çi-il-lu, preceded by ku-ša-ru; GGA '98, 811 *ad* M^S^ *pl* 31.

çilū *1.* 83, 1—18, 1330 iii 13 ^(du)^ DAX = çi-lu-u ša qut-rin(?)-nu; M^S^ 81 compares צלה broil, fry {braten}.

çillū. II 44 *e-f* 38 GIŠ-ŠI-KAK(DU); 62 *c-d* 78 GIŠ-ŠI-KAK-TUR; V 26 *e-f* 48 GIŠ-ŠI-KAK-TIR = çil-lu-u (Br 9344, 9348) a tree {ein Baum}? same id as II 44 *e-f* 38 we find in II 35 *g-h* 72 ŠI-KAK = çil (or šil?)-la-ša.

çilū *2.* K 3062, 9 e-pu-šu çi-lu-u, see çalū, 3 & çilūtu.

çulū prayer {Gebet, Flehen} Rm 196 *R* 4 ^(il)^ Marduk u ^(ilat)^ Çar-pa-ni-tum çu-li-e of your people (they) will hear, Thompson, *Reports.* Perh. V 42 *g-h* 13 (Br 8442); K 2852 + K 9662 i 34 çu]-ul-li-e-šu ul aš-me.

çalabu see çalapu.

çalbānu. Peiser, *Babyl. Vertr.*, XLII 5 (VATh 129) ša gi-meš ša çal-ba-nu ša it-ti ..... lu-pi-el-lu, & also 10; *ibid* 12 duppu ša ça-al-ba-nu La-a-ba-ši.

çil(li)bāni. 83—1—18, 2 (Hr^L^ 391) *R* 9—10 i-na šar-ki-ma (Martin, *Rec. Trav.* xxiv 107: i-na-šar ki-ma; but see, again, BA iv 520, 521) çi-il-ba-ni ina pa-an šarri u-še-rab-u-ni (AJSL xv 139). Zimmern, *Ritualt.*, 67, 5 še-i]x-tu ^(iç)^ ga-ça-a-ti ^(iç)^ ç(z)il-li-ba-ni; K 494,

5—6 ina eli ka-ra-ni | ša çil-li-ba-a-ni (Hr^{L} 19). BA iv 520: Süssholz (?).

ça-lu-bu (??) T. A. (Ber) 28 iv 6.

çalaxu (?) K 10507 ça-la-ax ça-la[-ax], Bezold, *Catalogue*, 1093.

zi(-il)-la-ax-da. T. A. (Ber) 28 ii 1, 54; iii 70: = מַפְתֵּחַ key {Schlüssel} BA iv 105, 106.

çalaku (*z*?) PSBA xvii ('95) 233 *ad* K 5464, 18 ina mux-xi-ja i-ça-al-ka-a-ni, transl.: against me they advanced. K 582 *R* 2 i-ça-al-ka bi-la (??) Hr^{L} 167.

çalalu 1. pr içlal, ps iça(l)lal, pm ça-lil (§ 97) sink down, sink to rest. AV 2845, 7162. — *a*) lie down, to rest as well as to sleep {sich hinlegen, um zu ruhen oder zu schlafen} || utûlu. id KU, Br 10550. IV^{2} 3 *a* 64, 65 DA-KU-KU = i-çal-lal. K 7674, 17 na-zaq la ça-la-li. IV^{2} 49 *a* 8 em-de[-ku] la ça-la-lu mûša u urra (here) I stand without lying down night or day (T^{M} i); Sm 949 *O* 16; H 88—89 ii 18 ša û-ma ..... lu-uç-lal. IV^{2} 13 *b* 39 (end) a-di u-bal-li-ṭu-ka la aç-la-lu-ma, I shall not cease. Asurb vi 75 e-kim-me-šu-nu la ça-la-lu e-me-id, I did not allow their shades to rest, *i. e.* I left their corpses unburied. J^{W} 54. NE XII *col* vi 8 e-kim-ma-šu i-na erçi-tim ul ça-lil, KB vi (1) 264, 265. K 2729 *R* 23, 24 i-ça-al-la-lu e-ma bi-bil libbi-šu (so that he may rest, where his heart desires), a-šar ça-al-lu la ta-dak-ki-šu (& where he rests, he shall not be disturbed; 27, ša ul-tu naq-bi-ri bît ça-al-lu, BA ii 566 *fol*, KB iv 144, 145 (*ll* 56, 57. 60). IV^{2} 27 *b* 38 ul i-çal-lal (= KU-KU); *cf* Z^{B} iv 64 ûm la ça-lal-šu, restless days. T^{M} vi 13 lu-u çal-la-a-ta la te-tib-ba[-a], thou mayest lie down. NE 21, 10 why to my son Gilgameš libbi(-bi) la ça-li-la te-mid-su (KB vi (1) 140 *col* 2 *a* 18); 50, 208—9 u-tu-lu-ma (*var* çal [or ni?]-li) etlê ina ma-a-a-al (507 *col* 2) mu-ši çal-lu; u-tu-ul-ma (*var* ·a-lil) Êabani šunata(-tu) inaṭṭal, the heroes slept, stretched out upon their couches & Êabani slept, & saw a vision in his sleep; see also KB vi (1) 192 on NE VII *col* vi 6 (28) end: the third and fourth day ç[a-li-il] & NE XII *col* vi 1 + 29 (ii 20 *etc.*) ša çal(or ni?)-lat ša çal-lat um-mu (il) Nin-a-zu ša çal-lat, KB vi (1) 258—9 (+ 525) die da ruht, die da ruht, die Mutter des *Ninazu*, die da ruht (or çalalu, 2 ?). K 2619 iii 20 on the day when fate snatched me away a-çal-lal ina .... (KB vi, 1, 64—65; BA ii 429). Rm 2, III 150 *R* 10 lu ça-al-la-ta ça-li-lu (& *ibid* 8 *O*); T. A. (Ber) 73, 14 i-ça-lu-ul (he encamps). IV^{2} 23 *no* 1 i 24—31 .... çal-lu be-lum ša çal-lum a-di ma-ti ça-lil, *etc.* (§ 97) id NA'-A (Br 8987, 8999); 29 šadû rabû a-bu Bêl ša çal-lum a-di mât, *etc.* KB vi (1) 228 (*cf* 477—8) reads NE 66, 33 çal-lu u mi-tum, the resting & the dead. Scheil, "Notes d'Epigr." xxx coloph. dup-pu 2 kam-ma i-nu-ma çal-lu a-mi-lum, *Rec. Trav.* xx ('97) 55, 56. K 413; (omens concerning accidents that may happen to a man) it is said: ina ça-la-li-šu; K 6759 [šumma] sinništu ina erši i-çal-lu-ma; K 9517 ça-lil, Bezold, *Catalogue*, 597; 808; 1020. See also sakapu (V 17 *c-d* 10). — Sometimes perh. in the meaning of sexual intercourse (with prep. eli) *e. g.* NE 11, 12 eli-ki li-iç-lal, 18, eli-ša iç-lal, J^{L-N} 48 *rm* 34. — See also çallum, 3. — *b*) sink, decay, go to ruin {hinsinken, verfallen}. I 27 *no* 2. 3 the city e-na-ax-ma iç-lal (or perh. √zalalu, *p* 282 *col* 2, where also V 24 *a-b* 35: BA-DIB = zu-ul-lu-ul, Br 10700); Anp iii 133 (KB i 116, 118). T^{M} vii 8 ça-lil (iç) nibiru ça-lil ka-a-ru; 9 (end) ka-li-šu-nu çal-lu.

ב *del* 31 Gilgameš is told when the ship is completed e?]-ma apsî ša-a-ši çu-ul-lil-ši, KB vi (1) 230—1 (& 485): beim Weltmeer 'leg' es hin; Haupt, H^{CV} xlii; BA i 127; PAOS Oct. '87 *p* lii & in Ball, *Gen* (SBOT), 52, 53: cause it to be immersed = launch. K 196 i 24 of the foundation of a house it is said la u-ça-lil (Pinches, *Texts*, 12). Here according to KB vi (1) 343 also Creat.-*frg* IV 138 mišluašša iškunamma ša-ma-ma u-ça-al-lil; if so, then also, Sarg *Silver inscr.* 31: beams of cedar & cypress wood elišina u-çal-lil (I placed over them); see also K 2675, 20 u-ça-lil (S. A. Smith, *Asurb*, vol ii); ll 67, 77 (with beams of cedar wood *etc.*) u-ça-lil-ši-na[-ma], lit^{y}: caused to be immersed. 82—7—4, 42

R 1—2 [burûmu] el-lu-u-tu | ša u-ça-al-li-lu | ri-it-tu-uš[-šu] PSBA xx 153*foll.*

ڪ let sleep {schlafen lassen} IV² 22 *a* 6—7 la-bar-tum pa-rit-tum ul u-ša-aç-lal (KU-KU Br 10550), does not let (him) sleep; in view of this id IV² 3 *a* 65 (*cf* 64) perh. i-çal-lal; IV² 21 *no* 2 *O* 3—4 mu-ša-aç-lil (id KU-KU).

NOTE. — SCHEIL, *Šamš* reads Šamš iv 31 çal-lat šarrûti-šu but see nimattu (690 *col* 2).

DERR. çallu, 5; maçallu (872 *col* 2), muçlalu, taçlîltu, & çallûtu, 1.

***çalalu* 2.** perh. a denominative of çillu (*q.v.*) id ŠUR, which is id for çalmu, dark, black & adaru, be darkened. According to some to this çalalu belongs NE XII *col* 1 *foll.* KB iii (2) 64 *col* 2, 17—19 i-na kakkê ez-zu-ti | te-bu-ti ta-xa-za lu-zu-lu-ul um-ma-ni-ja (protect my army!). See perh. KB iv 102, 5 (end) ✕ *Rec. Trav.* xvi 177.

ℶ çullulu. LEHMANN, ii 66 & 115 (& i 90) make dark, then also: shield, protect, L⁴ i 17 aš-ta-si kam-mu nak-lu ša Šumêri çu-ul-lu-lu (M^S 87 — *adj.* dark; see also OPPERT, ZA vi 451); K 7592 — K 8717 + DT 363 *R* 14 li-ça-li-lu en-ta-at-ka, may they protect thy might (ZA v 59). K^M 21, 78 mu-çal-lil ū-mi. Here belong perh. T. A. Ber 43, 38 Jan-xama mu-ça-li-il šarri be-li-ja i-ši-mi (KB v *no* 85); Rm 283, 10 (end) u-çal-lu-lu bêlû[-ti-ja].

DERR. — perh. muçallu (872 *col* 2); çallu çalûlu, çulûlu, çulultu, çallûtu 2, çililitu (?).

çalîlu (?). K 3554 *O* 10 it-ti-ki li-ru-ba ça-lil-ki ṭa-a-bu, PSBA xxiii 120*foll*; AV 2380.

çalûlu — *a*) protection {Schirm, Schutz}. Anp i 44 ina max-ri-i (*var* e) palê-a ša Ša-maš dân kibrâti ça-lul(*var* AN-ŠUR, Br 6385; § 9, 60)-šu eli-a iš-ku-un, in the beginning of my reign, when Šamaš . . . placed me under his gracious protection (AV 7171). — *b*) protector {Schirmherr, Schutzherr}. Anp *Stand* 13: Anp. rê'û ça-lu-lu (*varr* -ul; & AN-ŠUR) kibrâte.

NOTE. — OPPERT, ZA vi 448; PSBA xx 27, & ZA xi 315 *rm* 2 çalullu = σκιάσμός, a solar eclipse ✕ mânâxtu √anaxu, ἔκλειψις.

çulûlu *m* §§ 63; 65, 19; AV 3024. — *a*) shade {Schatten} Asurb viii 83 they entered ki-šâte ša çu-lul-ši-na rap-šu, forests whose shade was dense (literally: wide). — *b*) shady place, protecting place {schattenspendendes Obdach} Sarg *bull*-inscr. 54 see pataqu & translate: in the month of Ab when all the blackheads build a shady place for their habitation. — *c*) roof {Bedachung} POGNON, *Wadi-Brissa*, 181. KB iii (2) 48 *a* 41 a-na zu-lu-ul E-MAX-TI-LA *etc.* u-ša-at-ri-iç; V 34 *b* 4 (çu-); Neb *Grot.* ii 19 e-ri-num çu-lu-li-šu, its roof of cedars; Neb iii 30 erinu zu-lu-lu (+ 43 + 46); ix 8 cedars *etc.* a-na zu-lu-li-ša (Neb *Grot,* iii 37; V 64 *c* 1); iii 24 (28) a-na zu-lu-lu E-KU-A. Sn *Kui,* 4, 8 see parakku, 1. I 44, 84—5, u-šat-ri-ça çu-lul-šu, I adjusted its roof. — *d*) protection {Schirm, Schutz}. K 1794 x 27—8 eli Marduk bêli rabi çululšu aprus(ma), S. A. SMITH, *Asurb,* ii 19. — id Sarg *Cyl* 6 çulû-la-šu it-ru-çu-ma; *bull*-inscr. 9(?) + 54; *bronce* 13 (✕ OPPERT, ZA vi 114*fol*). On ukin çu-lûlu (S³ 18 *etc.*) see LEHMANN, ii 115, 116, where of Asurbanipal it is said: he unfolds his protection. Asb x 64—5 çu-lul-šu-nu ṭâbu çalû-la-šu-nu ša ša-la-me it-ru-çu eli-ja (KB ii 233 ✕ ZA vi 448). P. N. V 44 *c-d* 7 (amêl) Marduk-çu-lu-lu (= AN-ŠUR-MU, Br 6392), *i. e. M* is (my) protection; IV² 21* *no* 1 *C R* iii 6 Marduk zu(*var* çu)-lul ma-a-ti. Merodach-Bal.-stone iii 33 iš-ta-kan çu-lu-li (BA ii 262; KB iii (1) 186, 187).

çulultu roof {Bedachung} V 65 *b* 5 cypress trees *etc.* (iç) çu-lul-tum bîti u-šat-ix (*var* mi-ix)-ma, KB iii (2) 112, 113, for the roof of the house.

çililîtu a bird {ein Vogel}. II 37 *b-c* 19 (+ 68) çi-li-li-tum(-tu) ‖ of aš-ki-ki-tu & ab-ki-ni-ni-tum(-tu), Br 14393, AV 7219; on id see BA ii 234 *rm.*

çalamu, be or become dark, black {düster, schwarz sein oder werden}. V 48 v 11 (49 vii 30; ix 4, 14; xi 7) I-NE (= pânu?) ça-lim (✕ immêru pânu, see namaru). NE XII i 29 *etc.* is read by some ša çal-mat, which is dark {die da finster ist} but see çalalu, 1; III 59, 31 (*no* 13) see JENSEN, 66.

ℶ V 45 ii 2 tu-çal-lam.

DERR. these 4:

çalmu *1. f* çalimtu *adj* dark, black {finster, schwarz} AV 7175, 7168; >< piçû, *q. v.* iD usually MI; H 29, 640; § 9, 50; Br 8922—24. II 45 *no* 4, 57 GIŠ-MI = iç-çi çal-mi. H 92—3, 32 ina çal-mi followed by ina ek-li-ti (a-a e-ru-ub-šu). kiš-kanû çal-mu (see kiškanû, Br 8568). V 15 (*c*-)*d* 12 ša çal-me (Br. 11155; or to çalmu, 2?). V 28 *c-d* 78 na-ax-lap-tu ça-lim-tum ‖ çubat e-kil-tum, AV 7168. *del* 93 (98) end: there rose up ur-pa-tum ça-lim-tum. 83—1—18, 483 *R* 4 Me-lu-xi-e MI *pl* = Meluxxê çal-mûti, black *M* (JENSEN in WINCKLER, *Forsch.*, ii 578). V 14 *b* 22 (šipâti) çal(?)-ma-a-tum (PINCHES), *i. e.* dark woolen materials. H 90—91, 58 ši-pa-a-ti çal-ma-ti (= MI); see also IV² 8 *col* 3, 29; $Z^{\check{S}}$ v/vi 151. — Note especially the phrase (nišê or šiknâte) **çalmât qaqqadi** (Babylonian: çalmât gaga-dam), the blackheaded, *i. e.* the human race. DEL., *Chald-Gen*, 301; ZA i 320; Br 3637; § 70*a*, note: perh. a *plur tantum*. On SAYCE, *Hibbert Lectures*. 101 see HALÉVY. *Rev. d'hist. des Relig.*, xvii 186: les peuples de la surface noire = terre, en face des corps célestes qui sont lumineux. PINCHES, *Jour. Trav. Vict. Inst.*, 28, 5 *rm*: perh. the dark race in contradistinction to the fair sons of Japhet; see also MEISSNER, 101. — Sn i 13—15 ul-tu tâmti e-le-ni-ti ša ša-lam šam-ši a-di tam-tim šap-li-ti ša çi-it šam-ši gim-ri çal-mat qaqqadu u-šak-niš še-pu-u-a, from the upper West Sea to the lower East Sea (KB ii 82—3); vi 54 a-na šu-te-šur çal-mat qaqqadi ‖ pa-qa-di mur-ni-is-ki. ZA iii 352, bel. 82—7—4, 42 *R* 13 (middle) ça-al-ma-tum qa-qa-du. See also K 8571 *O* 10 (KB vi, 1, 58 & 83 of mâtu, die); iD in K 2801 + K 221 + K 2669 *O* 34 na-qid *ç. q.* K 11152, 10 çal-mat qaqqadi. Neb x 19 my successors may rule forever ça-al-ma-at ga-ga-da. Neb *Grot*, iii 59 çal-ma-at ga-ga-dam; Ner ii 42 ça-al-ma-at ga-ga-dam; i 9 rê'ûti ça-al-ma-at ga-ga-dam; V 12 *a-b* 37 SEB-SAG-MI-GA = re-'u çal-mat qaq-qa-di, Br 5690; H 38, 94; Merodach-Bal.-stone ii 54—55 a-na ri'u-ut çal-mat qaqqadi. I 52 (*no* 6) 8 ça-al(l)-ma-at ga-ga-dam li-bi-e-lu. V 35, 13 nišê çal-mat qaqqadi KB iii (2) 128; WINCKLER, *Untersuchungen*. 132: the Babylonians especially; but see BA ii 281. IV² 17 *a* 45, 46 O Šamaš thou rulest çal-mat qaq-qa-di (= SAG-MI-GA); 29 *no* 1 *a* 41, 42 a-me-lu-tum ni-ši çal-mat qaqqadi, Br 5920; 54 *b* 27 Gula is um-mu a-li-da-at çal-mat qaqqadi, the mother giving birth to mankind.

NOTE. — 1. On [il] Çalmu & צלם as part of P. N.; Çalmu, as name of star, see Br 6283, HOFFMANN, ZA xi 246 § 2; LEHMANN, i 10 & *rm* 1; JENSEN, 115.

2. Çal-mat-tu, AV 7175 see zimattu (C9) *col* 2).

ça-lam-ma^{MEŠ} (?) PEISER. *Babyl. Vertr.*, *no* 107, 5 ûmu AB-AB-MEŠ ba-a-a-ta-nu ça-lam-ma-^{MEŠ}.

çalamtu — *a*) some kind of snake {eine best. Schlange}. II 24 *c-f* 12, 13 ÇIR-MI-A = çi-ir mu-ši = çir çal[-mi]: ÇIR-MI = ça-lam-tum = çir çalmi AV 7165, Br 7652. — *b*) a bird {ein Vogel}. II 37 *b-c* 30 (40 *no* 1 *R* 28) (iççur) çu-la-mu & iç-çur mu-ši = ça(l)-lam-du, AV 7164, Br 14191.

çulâmu, AV 7273 see çalamtu, *b*.

çulmu, çulum. K 3452 *R* 10 šar-xu (?) z(ç)u-lum; V 26 (*e*-)*f* 33 . . . . . çu-lum. AV 7274; Br 5987; *cf* V 42 *g-h* 18 same iD = çu-lu[-mu?].

çalmu *2. c. st.* çalam, *pl* çalmânu, picture. statue {Bildniss, Denkmal} AV 7165, 7175. 7163; iD usually ALAM; but S^b 378 ça(?)-la-am | 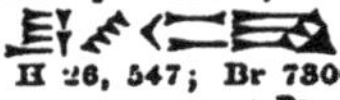 | ça-al-mu. § 9, 237; H 26, 547; Br 7800; ZDMG 23, 343 *rm* 4; 40, 738, >< D^{Pr} 141; HOMMEL PSBA '98, 291 *foll.* ça-lam šarru-u-ti-ja V 65 *b* 9, 22; ç šarrû-ti-ja II 67, 27; D 114, 22; Šalm, *Ob*, 31 (u-še-ziz), 92, 93 (ul-ziz), 124 (ašqup); 71 ç-š šur-ba-a e-pu-uš, a great statue of my majesty I erected (72, ina qir-bi-ša aš-ţur, BA ii 231); 156 (êpu-uš); *Mon*, *R* 44, 55, 65; TP III *Ann* 23, 175 *etc.* Anp i 104, 105 (97, 98) a-šar ça-lam ša Tukulti-pal-ešarra u Tukulti-Ninib . . . . i-za-zu(-u)-ni ça-lam šarrû-ti-a ab-ni. I 49 *d* 25 ça-lam ilâni rabûti ud-diš (a statue!); on çalam ilâni rabûti, Lay. *pl* 19 *etc.* see TIELE, ZA vii 78, IDEM, ZA v 302, 303 on II 67, 81 as in KB ii 27 & 29.

Also STRONG, RP^2 v 128 *rm* 1. V 60 (inscr. on left corner of picture), 1 ça-lam (il) Šamaš bêli rabî (ZK i 270 *fol*; PAOS '87, Oct.; BA i 268, 269; KB iii (1) 175); V 60 iii 31 çal-mi šu-a-tum; 21, 22 u-ṣur-ti çal-mi-šu. ZIMMERN, *Ritualtafeln*, *no* 54, 18 *foll*; SCHEIL, *Nabd*, x 35 ça-lam (il) Sin; V 61 iv 12—13 ana e-peš çal-mi šu-a-tum | u-zu-un-šu ib-ši-ma, his mind was bent upon; KB iii (1) 116, 117, 1) Xammurabi iv 14: ki-ma ça-lam ṭi-ṭi-im. See also bûnûnu (179 *col* 1). IV^2 21 *no* 1 B *O* 16/18, 20/21, 36/38 (A-LAM) = ça-lam; V 50 *b* 57, 58 ça-lam an du-na-ni-šu (Br 3618), ša tal-pi-in-ni ina qaq-qa-ri (Rm 110 *b* 25—6); K 1284, 33; Anp i 68, 97, 104; ii 5, 91; iii 24 ça-lam bu-na-ni-a; KB vi (1) 118, 119 ça-lam pag-ri-šu; 228, 229 (478) *ad* NE X vi 34 (NE 66) of death ul iç-çi-ru ça-la[m-šu]. *pl* Beh 106 çal-ma-a-nu a-gan-nu-tu, these pictures (§§ 57; 67, 2). Asurb vi 48: XXXII çalmâni (written ALAM-MEŠ) of Elamite kings (pi-tiq, *i. e.* made of, kaspu, xurâçu, erû, pa-rûtu, *etc.*); see 53—55 (used of 'idols'). V 15 *c-d* 12 see çalmu, 1. K 2801 *R* 38 ça-al-me .... u-šag(k,q)-li-du ušan-biṭu kîma (il) Šamši. P. N. 81—11—3, 11 *R* 4, 5 (amêl) mu-bar-ru-u ça-lam Da'âni; (amêl) za-zak-ku ça-lam Pa-pil-sag *Jour. Trans. Vict. Inst.*, 28, 8 *foll*. iD also NU (Br 1963) *e. g.* Anp ii 135 NU (il) E-a (§ 9, 59); especially in incantations (T^M often; IV^2 49 *a* 15, 43; *b* 10, 47). — V 27 *g-h* 43, 44 mu-ša-lum = šû, but scarcely = mušâlum (*q. v.*) & çal-mu (Br 1296—7).

NOTE. — 1. PRINCE, *Daniel*, 208: çalmu used of 'idol', Asurb vi 53, *i. e.* picture (originally) & çalmu 'black' from the same stem; possibly owing to the dark color of the material of which the Assyrian images were generally made.

2 K 2401 ii 26 an-nu-u šul-mu ša ina pân ça-al-me, STRONG, BA ii 628 compares god (il) Çalmu (III 66 ii 26; see also ii 18; vii 9, 11) perhaps identical with the god (il) A-lam (*ibid* 69 *f* 67) and may be the same name as the sungod (II 48 *a-b* 49); a god Ça-lam, Ça-al-me, also III 69 *f* 66; II 49 *no* 3, 42. See, however, PRINCE, AJP xv 114: "this (referring to the benefits just described) is the blessing which is in the presence of the image", *i. e.* the image of the shrine where the oracle was given. See also KAT³ 475—6.

(il) **Çalmûdu**, *cf* Nimûdu (680 *col* 1).

çalamtu *2.* a tree }ein Baum{ V 26 *e-f* 55, 56 ça-lam-tum ‖ i-ka-du, Br 8040, 8057; *cf* K 192 *R* 23 . . . (aban) ça-lam-ti, a statue }ein Standbild{ BA iii 248—9 *rm* ††† & 359; Palmyr. צלמתא, female picture, NÖLDEKE, ZDMG 24, 100; also Bu 88—5—12, 75 + 76 ix 23 (aban) ça-lam-du *etc.*, BA iii 254: unbekannte Steinart; vielleicht = (aban) KA (= Basalt); *cf* V 30, 63 (aban) KA-tu.

Çillannîtum, P. N.? KB iv 34 (i) 5 a-na ga-bi-e Çil-la-an-ni-tum, at the instruction of *Ç*.

çalapu. II 32 *no* 4 *O* 2 ça(za)-la-pu(bu?), AV 7166 offend, sin against; II 30 *e-f* 29, Br 1798. — ℑ V 45 ii 4 tu-çal-la-pa, preceded by tu-çal-lap(b); Colophon to Creat.-*frg* iv see (ki)pî (789 *col* 2).

Derr. these 4:

çalpu *1.* injust }ungerecht{ K 3474 *b* 25 da-a-a-na çal-pa; K 3182 ii 41 & 5 tu-tar-ra çal-pa ša la mu-u[...] AJSL xvii, Apr. '01. T^M ii 129 (il) Gibil al-la-lu-u mu-ab-bit aklê u z(ç)al-pi *pl*, der du die Listigen und Frevler zu Grunde richtest. K 3183, 11 z(ç)al-pa, ZA iv 250.

çalpu *2.* *n* unrighteousness }Ungerechtigkeit{ Rm 201, 1 ça-lap mâti, THOMPSON, *Reports*, *no* 181.

çaliptu, *c. st.* çalpat intrigue, plot; meanness }Intrigue; Bosheit{ AV 7160. Sarg *bull-inscr.* 19 the princes lâ âdir zikri ilâni da-bi-bu ça-lip-ti; *Khors* 95 the Hittites da-bi-ib ça-lip-ti (*Ann* 219); 113 Muttallum ka-pi-du lim-ni-e-ti da[-bi-bu ça-lip-ti]; *Cyl* 26 Pisiri da-bi-ib ça-lip-te. TP i 8 (il) Šamaš xa-a-iṭ ça-al-pat a-a-bi. Perh. TP III *Ann* (III 9, 31) ša ina xi-iṭ-ṭi-šun ça-lip-te a-na *A* e-ki-i-mu (KB ii 26—7; LOTZ, TP 85); ROST: ša ina xi-iṭ-ṭi u qul-lul-ti; so also HOMMEL, *Gesch*, 660.

çiliptu — *a*) Synchr. Hist. iv 28, 29 ša (mât) Šu-me-ri. (mât) Ak-ka-di-e çi-lip-t[a-ša] li-pa-še-ra a-na ku-liš kib-ra[-a-te], KB i 202, 203 the wickedness of *Š* & *A*. — *b*) H 72, 28 çi-lip-ta (iD ≻+-NUN = xi-il-çu, Br 1867—8) ana çi-lip-te u-še-çi, GGN '80, 528 *rm* 4; ZA i 409 *foll*; one çiliptu after another he brings out, AV 7221.

çaltu enmity, hostility, fight {Feindseligkeit, Kampf} √çalû, 3. D^{Par} 216; Lotz, *Sabbath*, 52; AV 2855, 7176. Asurb i 88 in my stead etappalū bēl çal-ti-ja i-na (*var* ni)-ru ga-re-ja; also v 76 (& kaçaru, , 427 *col* 1); bēl çal-ti III 38 *no* 2 *O* 15; K 1285 *R* 5 bēl za-as-si-ja = bēl çaltija (*lt* = *ss*, ZA viii 380 *rm* 2; xi 94). K 3364 *O* 9 a-šar çal-tim-ma (where there is enmity); 10 ina çal-tim-ma [. . .]; 13 ina pa-an çal-tim-ma; 14 lu-u çal-ta-ka-ma . . . .; 15 çal-tu-um-ma šu-ut [. . . .] še-di-tum; 18 it-ti bēl çal-ti-ka (= thy enemy) . . . . šu-ut(-)me-in, followed by ēpiš limuttika, rag-gi-ka, çir-ri-ka. Nabd-Cyr Chron *R* 14 Sippar ba-la çal-tum ça-bit, was taken without fighting; 15, 16 (KB iii, 2, 134, 135; BA ii 222, 223, & 247. Xammurabi letters 15, 6 a-n]a ça-la-tim (= *pl*) ša li-ti-ka (+ 23), BA iv 449. Especially çaltum epešu = fight {kämpfen}. Bab. Chron. i 7—8 çal-tum ša Nabû-nâçir | a-na libbi Bar-sip$^{(ki)}$ i-pu-šu (KB ii 274—5; ZA ii 150); also i 34, 37; ii 2; iii 4. Nabd-Cyr. Chron. iii 12 in the month Tammûz Cyrus çal-tum . . . . ēpu-šu. Beh 49 ça-al-tum itti-šu-nu i-te-pu-uš. — D 134 *C* 16—17 AMĒL-NE-DA, Br 6416 = ça-al-tu, see kinKtûtu, 411 *col* 1. H 82—3, 16 UD-UR-DUG-GA = ça-al-tu; II 36 *a-b* 7 same id = çal-tum (Br 7059), in one group with tu-qu-un-tum (6, = AMĒL-NE); S^b 329 du-u | AMĒL-NE | çal-tu (Br 6414; ZA i 14, 15; id also III 68 *b* 45; 65 *b* 27 see puxpuxxû). II 35 (K 4320) *a-b* 9 da-ça-a-tum çal-ti.

NOTE. — V 37 i 22 MAŠ-GI (Br 12246) | (ZA i 181 = four times <) with glosses ni-si-gu-u ša(= gar)-bi i-gi-gub-bu-u [*cf* V 19 *a* 57—60] = ni (perh. better than çal)-tum ša$^{(amêl)}$XAL, Br 12247.

çiltu ‖ of çaltu. Sn v 55 see xulimm (314 *col* 1); ZA v 99; another ‖ is:

çulātu, *pl* Creat.-*frg* III 22 (+ 80) puxru šit-ku-nu-ma i-ban-nu-u çu-la-a-[ti], & started the revolt (KB vi, 1, 307). II 23 *a-b* 30 zu-la-ta ‖ ta-xa-zu (see *p* 282 footnote), AV 3022, 3044; also perh. V 28 *no* 4, 83 zu-la(!)-at = ta-xa[-zu], Zimmern. Rm III 105 i *b* 20, and with the people of Borsippa ip-pu-šu çu-la-a-ti, they waged war (& *ibid*, ii 5) Winckler, *Forsch*, i 254, 255.

çēlûtu enmity, hatred {Feindseligkeit, Hass} abstr. noun of *ag* çēlû. Asurb iii 123 ik-pu-du limuttu ip-pu-šu çi-e (*var*: caret)-lu(-u)-tu (K 3062, 9), whosoever plans evil against Ashurbanipal and begins hostilities. II 35 *e-f* 41.

çallîtu. T. A. (Ber) 26 i 39: one ça-a-al-li-e-tu siparri.

çillātu, *pl* K 660 *O* 15 u çi-il-la-a-te laššu (Hr^L 86); JAOS xviii 167—9; xix 77; perhaps 'shelter' (for the storage of wine); see also sillatu, 2. √çalalu, 2.

çallûtu *2.* abstr. noun of *adj* *çallu shade, darkness {Schatten, Finsternis}. V 28 *c-d* 41 ¹¹ -ŠUR-lil (*i. e.* çâlil) = god of pestilence ‖ lu-bar çal-lu-ti, = garment of darkness (so perhaps instead of Peiser, KAS 82: a prayer gown), AV 2854.

çallûtu *1.* K 3756 (omens) beginning: šumma amēlu in ça-al-lu-ti-šu, at his lying down; Bezold, *Catalogue*, 561.

çalûtu (?) K 3456, 28 ir-ši-ma ul-ça lib-ba-šu-nu ip-pu-ša ça-lu-u-ta. PSBA xxi, 38—40 ‖ ulçu. √çalû, 2. (?)

***çamu** 1.* (KB iv 144, 62 *etc.*) see zamû (282, 283).

***çamû** 2.* thirst {dürsten}. Bezold, *Achaem.* 54. Here perh. II 62 *a-b* 49 GIŠ-ZU-A-AN-TUK = ça-a-am i-šu, he is thirsty. AV 2856; V 47 *a* 45 im-mu ça-ma im-ma, *etc.*; Br 140; also IV^2 31 *R* 28 instead of xamû (282 *col* 2), so KB vi (1) 403.

Derr. çûmu, çummû, çumāmu, çumāmītu, çumāmētu.

çamû *3.* D 85 iv 24, see also xamû, 1. Meissner & Rost, 20: west {Westen}, but Jensen, ZA ix 127; KB vi (1) 403: rather an architectural term. K 4256 *O* 4 ça-mu-u, preceded by si-ip-pu & tu-ša-ru (II 48 *e-f* 56 *foll*); AV 7178.

çûmu (> çummu, > çum'u) *m* thirst {Durst} AV 7277; § 65, 3. H 11 + 214, 71 im-ma (§ 25) | | çu-u-mu, V 31 *e-f* 37; Br 827; H 87 ii 3 çu-mu limnu, an evil thirst. K 31 *R* 19—20 see mâtu, 2 (618 *col* 1). IV^2 19 *b* 35, 36 ina šli-ki reš-ti-i U-ru-uk çu-mu (Br 734) it-taš-kan, water famine has broken out. BROWN-GESENIUS, 854 *col* 2.

çummû (& çumû, properly צמא) thirst, famine {Durst, Wassernot} AV 7278. K 31 *O* 20 bu-bu-tu (*q. v.*) u çu-um-mu-u (IV² 46 *no* 2). K 517, 26 ja-a-nu ina çu-um-me-e la ni-ma-ta; 35 ina çu-um-me-e la qât šarri la ni-il-li; 40 iç-bat-u ina çu-um-me-e (Hr^L 327); IV² 56 iii (*b*) 54 see nâdu, 3 (645—6): carry thy waterbag for thy thirst. H 88—9, 23 (Br 828), see bubûtu & çibittu. K 2517 + K 1547 B *O* 20 (*R* 24) see bubûtu, *a* (end), & BA iii 366; KB vi (1) 104, 105. Anp iii 37 ina çu-me-e. Sn iii 80 mê (mašak) na-a-di ka-çu-ti (*p* 425 *col* 1) a-na çu-(um-)me-ja lu aš-ti; *Kui* 1, 41 çu-me-ja. Asurb viii 87 (122—3) a-šar çu-um-me qal-qal-ti (Esh iii 26); 106 qaq-qar çu-um-me a-šar qal-qal-ti; ix 35 ina çu-um-me qal-qal-ti iš-ku-nu na-piš-te, through thirst and famine they lost their lives; 37 a-na çu-um-me-šu-nu (ištattû dâmê, *q. v.*, u mê pi(a)ršu), to quench their thirst.

çumbu (> çubbu, as zumbu > zubbu), *pl* çumbē(-âti) § 70*f*; wagon, covered wagon, freightwagon {Lastwagen, Karren} × narkabtu (*q. v.*). D^H 20; D^Pr 84; § 52. AV 7279; Br 5831. Also çûbu, § 52 *rm*. Sarg *Ann* 280 çu-um-bi *pl*. Sn i 24 narkabâti sisê (iç) çu-um-bi parē (KB ii 82—3); *Kui* 1, 5; *Bell* 7; Asurb vi 61; Sn v 29; i 48, 49 narkabâti (iç) çu-um-ba-a-ti; 44, 88 (iç) çu-um-ba-te narkabâti; Asurb vi 22 narkabâti (iç) ša ša-da-di (iç) çu-um-bi (KB ii 205); x 85 speaks of (iç) çu-um-bi *pl* (mât) Elamti. D 85, 9—10 [GIŠ-ŠI-DUB]-BIN-MAR-GID-DA = i-nu (center, lit. eye, of the wheel, nave; see înu, 5) ša çu(m)-bi, Z^B 81; S^c 290 dub-bi-in | id | çu-um-bu, preceded by maššarum, *q. v.*, Br 2717.

çamadu, pr içmid, pm çamid, çandu. properly: bind, tie, join; then, fasten (cattle) to the yoke; yoke. harness {festbinden, zusammenfügen; dann speziell: anspannen, anschirren}. id LAL = ça-ma-du. § 25; H 32, 745; ZK i 296 — of animals & men. SCHEIL, *Nabd*, iii 14, 15 the lofty princess ša ça-an-da-ti 7 la-ab-bu, who harnesses 7 lions; 33 iç-mi-id-zu (*i. e.* the lion); S. A. SMITH, *Asurb*, ii *pl* III (Lo. *no* 64) 10—11: the Elamite kings ina (iç) ša ša-da-di rukûb šarrûtija LAL (*var* aç-mid)-su-nu-ti, KB ii 264—5; II 66 *no* 2. NE VI 12 lu-u ça-an(*var* am)-da-ta (2 *m sg*) ûm-(m)iš ku-da-nu rabûti, KB vi (1) 166, 167. V 63 *b* 28 (beg) bit-xal-lu ça-mi-id (& *ibid* 11 + 14); V 65 *b* 34 ça-mi-id pa-ri-e qar-du-tu. II 16 *c-d* 35 see parû. K 4905, 13 (H 124) see nîru, 2 (AV 7180, Br 998, 6817) — of wagons. Creat.-*frg* IV 51 iç-mid-sim-ma *etc.*, *cf* naçmadu (714 *col* 2: where read iç-mid-sim *etc.*); T. A. (Ber) 9, 11 one chariot la ça-mu-ut-ta, without a span of horses; *l* 9 a king's chariot zu(?)-mut(?)-ta, KB v 30—1; K 2008 (II 27 *no* 1 *a-b* 24) i 23 + II 29 *no* 4 (*add*) SI-GA = ça-ma-du ša narkabti (Br 3405, AV 6624, 7177), in one group with ṭa-pa-nu ša *n* (see 357 *col* 2). — Here some also Asurb i 34, but better ça-bat. — figuratively: IV² 19 *no* 3 *b* 41, 42 O my lady ma'adiš šal-pu-ti ça-an-da-ku (= LAL), greatly I am fettered to misfortune, Br 10107. K 4931 (H 116, 117) *O* 17—18 ça-am-da-ku (see H 179; Br 4775). — put on weapons: V 35, 16 his numberless troops kakkē-šu-nu ça-an-du-ma i-ša-ad-di-xa i-da-a-šu, KB iii (2) 122, 123; BA ii 210 *foll*; § 152. — Creat.-*frg* IV 85 lu-ç]a-an-da-at um-mat-ki, then may thy host be tied (lu rit-ku-su šu-nu (iç) kakkē-ki = then may thy weapons be bound).

Š NE VI 10 lu-še-iç-mid (or bat?)-ka (iç) narkabtu, KB vi (1) 166—7; GGA '98, 824.

NOTE. — According to KAT³ 339, 340 çamadu also = weigh, pay {abwägen, bezahlen. שקל ša-qalu, *q. v.* See also WINCKLER, *Forschungen*, ii 90 (+ 83) *ad Isa* 5, 10. Bu 91—5—9, 2185, 10—12: I littu (written LID) bu-ur-ta-am be-ili at-ta šu-bi-lam-ma V mana kaspi lu-uç-mi-id-ma, I shall pay 5 minas silver; 20: V mana kaspi' . . . a-ça-am-mi-dam-ma; 41: V mana kaspi a-ça-am-mi-da-am-ma. WINCKLER reads Kappod. Keilschr. Golenisch. 5, 9; 6, 12: VI ma-na u-ça-mad(mid) not u-za-ab (as DELITZSCH).

DERR. naçmadu, çimdu (çindu) & çimittu, all three of which refer always to chariots, never to horsemen, HAUPT, in CHEYNE, *Isaiah* (SBOT) 129.

çimdu, çindu, *m* § 65, 4. — *a*) coupling strap, leash, rope to fetter or bind together prisoners {Koppel, Seil, zum festbinden oder aneinanderbinden von Gefangenen}, H[F] 72. IV² 22 *no* 2, 12—13 see maruštu (id KU-AK-LAL-A, Br 4776); ZK i 308 translates: to his great distress he has no relief of his fetter (*i. e.* it is not taken off). I 49 *b* 9, 10; *d* 31 a-na çi-in-di u bir-te zu-'u-u-zu, see birtu, 2 (196 *col* 1); also Bu 88—5—12, 101 i 11, 12. KB iv 48 (*no* 2) 16 zi(= çi)-im-da-an šarri. — *b*) bandage of a physician {Verband des Arztes}. II 34 *no* 3, 43 a-gi-it-tu-u ‖ KU-BAR-SIG *i. e.* parsigu (*q. v.*) & çi-in-du ša asî. — *c*) firm structure {festes Gefüge} used of buildings Ner (I 67 *b*) ii 22 see paṭaru ג¹; II 29 *g-h* 50 BAL = çi-in-du followed by BAR-BAR-RI = bi-ir-tu & preceded by kun-nu, Br 1799; AV 7238: MEISSNER & ROST, 19. — *d*) of stars, bound together into a constellation. Sn *Bell* 35 (*Rass* 62) Nineveh whose picture is formed and šu-pu-u çi-in-du-šu (whose constellation shines from of old on the heavenly expanse). — *e*) Neb 283, 2: a-na XXIII (?) çi-in-du-u šikari ṭâbi, KB iv 192, 193: zu 23 Gefässen guten Dattelweins; also Neb 188, 2 çindû ša ximētu. — *f*) harness, yoke with which animals are yoked to the wagon; then also (as çimittu & naçmadu) a couple, pair, a span (of horses *etc.*) = צֶמֶד. Sn v 30 see sanaqu, Q 5; *Khors* 124 uš-te-ṣe-ra çi-in-de-ja (*Ann* 283, 317) akçura ušmânî, I collected my teams and gathered the camp together. WINCKLER, *Sargon*, 191 (bel) šul-li-ma çi-in-di-šu, keep in order the teams. Perh. V 42 *e-f* 14 (Br 4586); III 38 *no* 2 *R* 10 (end) i-bir çi-in-di-ja.

çimdêtu. IV² 29* *no* 4 B *O col* ii 9 çi-im-di-ti li-qir-ri-bu.

çumuxu. T. A. (Ber) 28 i 15 abni çu-mu-xu, *etc*, + 10 + 38; iv 4 + 6 (where: 44 lux-ni çu-mu-xu, are mentioned).

çumlalû a spice {Spezerei}. Rm 367 + 83, 1—18, 461 *a* ii 30 GIŠ-ŠIM-GAM-MA = çu-um-la-lu-u, M[S] *pl* 23.

çumâmu, thirst {Durst}. § 65, 36; a-šar çu-ma-me, III 10 *no* 2, 34, the desert {die Wüste}; 15 iv 11 (*cf* Esh iii 26), Neb ii 22 u-ru-ux zu-ma-mi, AV 3027. Esh *Sendsch*, *R* 38 a-šar çu-ma-a-me .... šal-miš lu at-tal-lak.

***çumâmâ'u,** *f* çumâmâitu, *adj* thirsty {durstig} BEZOLD, *Achaem*, 54 & 88 *ad* H 11, 12, 19. 20 qaq-qar çu-ma-ma-i-tum, a thirsty, dry ground, desert (§ 65, 37); BA i 477.

çumâmêtu, desert {Wüste}. K 4354 ii 11 šam çu-ma-me-tu, plant growing in the desert {Wüstenpflanze} = II 43 *no* 2 *R* 57; AV 7276; K 267 iv 18 kiš-šu-u (p) ša çu-ma-me-ti.

çamânu see zamânu (284 *col* 1).

çamuçiru see zamuçiru (284 *col* 1).

çamaru think, plan {im Sinne tragen, planen} FLEMMING, *Neb*, 26; GGA '84, 338—9; G § 112; POGNON, *Bavian*, 85. — Q perhaps K 644, 6 i-da-bu-bu um-ma : ni-il-mir (> niçmir) followed by sisê ni-max-xa-ra, we will buy the horses. Hr[L] 336; PSBA xxiii 338 *foll.*

Q[t] pm tiçmur (> çitmur) § 83 *n*. Neb i 14 (*Bab* i 18) *Neb* who a-na zin-nâti Esagila u Ezida û-mi-ša-am ti-iç-mu-ru(-u)-ma; KB iii (2) 62, 10 libba ti-iç-mu-ur, the heart (*i. e.* I) was thinking of. KNUDTZON, 43, 6; 47, 4 *etc.* ti-iç-mu-ru-ma.

ג = Q[t] IV² 21* *no* 1 C *R* iii 9 e-ma u-ça-am-ma-ru lukšud; perh. also SCHEIL, *Nabd*, v 11 (see *p* 284 *col* 1). Sn *Bav* 43 Babylon ša a-na ka-ša-di u-ça-am-me-ru-šu, which I had planned to take (KB ii 116, 117). V 45 ii 34 tu-ça-am-mar. T[M] vii *col* 4, 13 .... u-ça-am-ma-ru çu-um-mi-ra-ti-ja lu-uk-šu-ud, BA iv 167. pm K 8182 i 52 O Šamaš upon thy light çu(-um)-mu-rat mit-xar-tum(-ti); AJSL xvii 136, 137, they think in harmony. K 2907, 10 ša çu-um-mu-ru. V 16 *c-d* 44 SAG-DUB = çu-um-mu-ru followed by itekîimmû (see כלמא, 389 *col* 2). Br 3626. AV 7280. Rm 345 *R* 13 ..... GA = çu-um-mu-ru. — **Der.:**

çum(m)êrtu, desire, wish (of one's heart), the hidden thoughts of the heart {Wunsch. verborgener Herzensgedanke} § 65, 29 *rm*, *a*. SMITH, *Asurb*, 199, 3 *Asurb* who ik-šu-du çu-um-me-rat libbi(-bi)-šu; 245, 2; 125, 68 a-di (until) u-šak-šu-du (I *sg*) çu(-um)-me-rat libbi(-bi)-ka, the wish of thy heart has come to pass (III 32, 65;

BA ii 253; HEBR. ix 162. K 3182 iii 50 çu-um-mi-rat ik-pu-du tu-šak-šad at-ta, ZA iv 12, the plans which they have in mind thou wilt prosper. K 4001 *O* 37 zu-mi-ra-ti-šu ikašša-ad. See also çamaru, ב.

çimru multitude, fulness {Menge, Fülle, Reichtum, *etc.*} √*çamaru, complete, fill up. AV 7233. K 8522 *O* 7 see kubuttû (*p* 371 *col* 2), & see, again, JENSEN, KB vi (1) 351. HOMMEL, *Jour. Trans. Vict. Inst.*, 28, 34 transl. "creator of leaves! & vegetables", but this is out of question. V 21 *g-h* 21 (Br 9892) = çi-im-ru, preceded by ba-šu-u & followed by ku-bu-ut-te-e; *ibid* 12, = el-lum, 13, te-lil-tum; this passage evidently a commentary on K 8522. ZA x 293, 35 (37) çi(zi)-im-ru-šu duššupu rabû tiqnu.

çimērtu II 28 *b-c* 7 ŠA (= LIB)-TA-XA-AR-GIG = çi-me-ir-tu, followed by ki-çir-tu, AV 7232, Br 8021.

ça(çu?)murtu. JOHNS, *Doomsday Book*, 81: the first son is called ça-mur-tu; a child is called çu-mur-tu. JOHNS: completion, fulfillment; but perh. rather connected with çum(m)ērtu, wish, desire (of one's heart). Here also K 481 *O* 9 çu-um-rat libbi (Hr^{L} 141).

ç(z)amru, a plant {eine Pflanze}, whose exact nature is not known, written ça-am-ri, JOHNS, *Doomsday Book*. 3 i 6; 8 ii 5 + iii 8; perh. Hebr צֶמֶר.

çāmiru (??) T. A. (Ber) 26 i 42: one pit-pa-nu ša ça-mi-ri.

Çimirra, *var* Çimirri = city of Simyra (τὰ Σίμυρα = צְמָרִי) II 53 *no* 3, 57 Çi-mir-ri (73; *no* 4, 60 -ra); III 9, 46. K 598, 21 (end) ana (al) Çi-mir-ri (Hr^{L} 190). Perhaps Nabd 1005. 7. AV 7221. See BROWN-GESENIUS, 856 *col* 1, where large literature is given.

ça-mit-tum. II 43 *a-c* 12 same id as e-pi-iq-tum, perh. with JENSEN in SCHULTHESS, *Homonyme*, 23 = צמיתא.

çimittu (> çimidtu. § 65, 4). *c. st.* çim-dat (rarely used, instead of the more frequent çimitti, *gen.*) *pl* çimdāti (§ 32*a*, *rm*) = span, team {Gespann} id LAL (§ 9, 125) or GIŠ-LAL, Br 10108. AV 7230; always used concretely of the team, harnessed to wagon or chariot. On the syntactical use, see § 124. TP iii 4 (8) narkabāti çi-mit-ti ni-ri-šu-nu, vii 28 (*pl*); K 3600 *R* 22; Rm 283, 9 (end); Šamš ii 2 *etc.* see nīru, 2. *Khors* 183, 184 (imêr) KUR-RA *pl* (= sisê) (mât) Mu-çu-ri çi-mit-ti [ni-i-ri ra-bu-]ti, KB ii 78, 79: large Egyptian wagon horses; see also *Ann* 333, 440; III 15 i 11 sisê çi-mit-ti niri, KB ii 142—3; PAOS '87, *p* xxxv. ZA iii 396, 12: V çi-mi-it-ta ša si-si-i, 5 span of horses (also ZA v 142, 12); Z$^{\check{S}}$ iii 109 (end) u çi-mit-ti. II 67, 63 LAL (= çinda)-at ni[-ri]. Anp i 86 sisê (iç) LAL (= çindat)(-at) ni-ri-šu (*cf* Šalm, *Ob*, 170, 171; 182, 183 written sisê LAL-at (iç) ni-ri, *Mon.* *O* 18 + 22; *R* 58 + 61—2 sisê LAL-at GIŠ-GIŠ). Anp ii 121: 460 sisê LAL-at (iç) ni-ri-šu; iii 22 narkabāti(-šu) sisê LAL-at (iç) ni-ri-šu, his chariot & his chariot horses; also iii 45 (çimdat-su). Sm *Asurb*, 130, 4 the chariots & wagons, horses & mules çi-mit-ti ni-i-ri, which were used for draught animals. K 3600 (hymn to Ninâ) *R* 22 šul-li-me mur-ni-is-qi çi-in-da-at ni-ri[-šu], CRAIG, *Religious Texts*, vol 1. Sn v 80 the horses çi-mit-ti ru-ku-pi-ja; IV² 48 *a* 38 çi-in-da-at alpê. Camb 322, 15 ša muxxi çi-in-da-a-ta. — T. A. (Lo) 8, 84: X çi-mi-it-tum sisê, also 10: wooden chariots, with all their appurtenances. (Ber) 7 *R* 12: V çi-mi-it-ta ša si-si-i: (Lo) 9, 40 (-tum); (Ber) 26 iv 39; 41; 26 iv 40 see nīru, 2. — *b*) in meaning of çindu *c*). SCHEIL, *Nabd*, iii 22 ip-ṭu-ru çi-mi-it-tuš, preceded by ad-ma-an-šu id-ku-ma. — *c*) KB iv 22 (ii) 3 (ša) Ilubani a-na çi-im-da-at-tu-uš (= auf Grund seiner Leistung als Gespannfrohnde) zurückverlangt hat; here perh. also PINCHES, PSBA xix 132 *no* 1, 10 (= KB iv 38 *no* 1) ki-ma çi-im-da-at šar-ri, translated: like a decree of the king it shall be. Bu 88—5—12, 234, 17—18 (MEISSNER, *no* 3; KB iv 40—1 *no* 3). MEISSNER, 97 & PEISER, KB iv 38, 39: yoke {Joch}. ⊕ 287 i 9 GIŠ-LAL?] | | çi-mit-tum. Xammurabi-letters 19, 12—13 di-nam ki-ma çi-im-da-tim šu-xi-ix-xu-nu-ti, BA iv 452 (480) lass sie Strafe empfangen gemäss den Rechtssatzungen.

çēnu *1. adj* good, docile {gut, recht, lenkbar} >< raggu. AV 7235/6; DELITZSCH in L^{TP} 87; D^{H} 47; D^{Pr} 87—88; *cf* RÉJ xiv 150; ZDMG 40, 736. TP i 8 Šamaš .... mu-še-ib-ru çe-ni. Sn v 82 my chariot overthrowing rag-gi u çe-ni, good and bad (without exception) >< HEBR. vii 69; see also T^{M} iv 2, where with TALLQVIST (*p* 170) read rag-gu u çi-e-nu. Neb ii 28 ra-ag-gu u çe-e-num i-na ni-ši u-še-is-si (I threw down, √nisû); AJSL xiv 5—6. Perh. K 1208, 32. K 2061 i 15 (H 202) ŠA (= GAR)-ID-ZI = çi-e-nu, AV 7236, Br 12101, preceded by rag-gu & a-a-bu, H 41, 297. S^{P} 158 + S^{P} II 962 *R* 33 çi-e-nu Elam(ki)-u perhaps = the good Elamite, in an ironical meaning; id NIG-A-ZI[-DA] = good, he who is right (>< PINCHES, *Jour. Trans. Vict. Inst.*, xxix 79); also *O* 33 Elamû çi-e-nu.

çēnu *2. n* small cattle, usually of sheep and goats in one flock {Kleinvieh, Schafe und Ziegen} BROWN-GESENIUS, 838 *col* 1. §§ 29; 32 *a* γ written çi-e-ni(-nu), çe-ni, (immer) çe-ni; & id 'U-LU-ZUN(pl) *etc.*, mostly in connection with alpē (= cattle); § 9, 44 + 271, id LU; H 34, 812 = çi-e-nu followed by lu-li-mu; Asb ii 133 & Br 10697; G § 71; *pl* LU-MEŠ, perh. V 58 *b* 52 (K 175 *R* 5); TP ii 51 *fol* alpē (immer) çi(-e)-ni. Sn ii 17 alpē u çi-e-ni (*var* 'U-LU-ZUN; *cf* Z^{B} viii 40; T^{M} vii 25; Br 10230); iii 18 *fol.* AV 7235—6; V 58, 55 çibit alpē u çi-e-ni ša šarri (see also KB iii, 1, 172, 37, id); Asb vi 93 alpē u 'U-LU-ZUN *pl* (Br 10253, *var* çi-e-ni); vii 8 the others .... ki-ma çi-e-ni u-za-'-iz (*cf* K 2852 + K 9662 iii 18). Anp i 88 alpē-šu (immer) çe-ni-šu (Šalm, *Ob*, 167); i 52 like a mar-šit (LU) çe-ni, + 56 (id); II 67, 38 alpē-šu-nu çi-e-ni-šu-nu (*cf* TP III *Ann* 39, 138, 207); + 39 ud(par?)-ra-a-ti(pl) u çi-e-ni; 41 alpē u çi-e-ni (*cf* TP III *Ann* 46, 156; Asb vi 101); K 2867 *O* 27. Esh *Sendsch.*, *R* 46 çi-e-ni-šu (of Tarqû) without number; ZA iii 312, 60 ki-ma çi-e-ni; TP III *Ann* 96; Asb ix 5 gam-malē u çi-e-ni (*cf ibid* 46); KB vi (1) 68 *O* (K 1282) 8 ki-i a-gir çi-e-ni, like a hired herdsman. D 96 *c* 8 kīma çi-e-ni li-ir-ta-a ilāni gimrašun. IV^{2} 11 *b* 43—44 ina çi-e-ni, Br 4207, 5863. Nabd 785, 15 XIV-ta (immer) çi-e-nu; KB iv 178 *no* III 5: VI ma-na ša-lal-ti ša (= for) çi-e-nu ša Axušunu; see also Nabd 278, 8; 754, 2 (where çi-e-nu instead of e-çi-nu); 952, 12; 1050, 2. T. A. (Ber. 169, 11 çēni | zu(?)-u-nu : za-zi-lu (*q.v.*), ZA v 156. Simply LU *pl* in Anp i 95; ii 23; iii 4; Šalm, *Ob*, 185, 182. See also gizzu (*p* 214 *col* 2); V 21 *no* 4, 58—9 R I = çi-e-nu & ri-'-u, Br 2575. — LAGARDE, *Übersicht*, 136 çēnu a derivative from açû. 1 (*q. v.*).

çânu, ça'anu (צאן?), *pr* içān, içēn, 1 *sg* eçēn; *ps* içān fill, load {füllen, laden} construed with double *acc.* = fill something with ....; ZIM., *Ritualtaf.*, √צאן; D^{Pr} 176; BA ii 142; HAUPT in TOY, *Ezekiel* (SBOT) 77. ZIMMERN, *Ritualtaf.*, 1—20, 62 (+ 130) te-çi-en (IV^{2} 55 *no* 2 *a* 16: 2 *sg*); 60, 27 (K 8380) i-çi-en (3 *sg*). Creat.-*frg* IV 99 ez-zu-ti (*var* -tum) šārē kar-ša-ša i-ça-nu-ma, the terrible winds filled her stomach; 115 the eleven creatures šu-par pul-xa-ti i-ça-nu. III 41 *b* 25 Marduk a-ga-lā (wr. NU)-til-la-a .... li-ça-an ka-ra-as-su, may fill his belly with dropsy. *del* 77—79 (81—84) mimma išû e-çe-en-ši, with all that I had I loaded it (the ship) *etc.*, BA i 97 *rm* 2. Also I 67 *a* 27 & IV^{2} 26 *a* 14, 15 belong here rather than to zananu, 2 (*p* 287 *col* 2); & perh. Bu 91—5—9, 2176 A 21, 22 (çe)-ni Ta-ra-am-Sag-ila Il-ta-ni i-çi-ni; Bu 88—5—12, 21 (MEISSNER *no* 89) 7 zi-ni-ša i-zi-in, JRAS July '97, 613 (see, above, *p* 272 *col* 1, za'anu). *pm* perh. K 3600 *R* 23, 24 zu-um-ru-šu çi-in-nu (in a curse!). **qutrinna çēnu** = fill up *i. e.* place down incense (smoke) offering = sacrifice. IV^{2} 20 *no* 1. 26, 27 zi-i-bu šur-ru-xu çe-e-n (= *pm*; NE-IN-SI-SI, id = malû, 1) qut-ren-na; 25 *b* 64, 65 qut-ri-in-na la çe-e-nu (= *pm*; XAR, id of eçenu, smell); K 1282 *R* 14 a-a i-çi-in-na

çanazu (Br 180) see zanazu (286 *col* 1). ~ ç(z)anaq(k)u V 45 *b* 37 see zanaqu. ~ çançaliqu *cf* zanzaliqu.

qut-rin-na, not shall he heap up a smoke offering (KB vi, 1, 72, 73), also *O* 15 çi-nu qut-rin-na. Bu 91—5—9, 183 *R* 2—4 see sillatu, 2 (764 *col* 2).

NOTE. — 1. V 33 *b* 49; *c* 12 see za'anu. — As ℑ of ça'anu JENSEN, KB vi (1) 430 explains also *ibid* 128—9 (NE I) v 11 + 17 (*p* 130, 131) zu-'-na [ku-u]z-ba.

2. V 42 *e-f* 14 DUK ba-a-<<< PA = çi-in[-nu??].

çinnu insect }Insekt{ K 3600 *R* iv 24 çi-in-nu e-ri-bu mu-xal-liq aš-na-an. MARTIN, *Textes Relig.* ('03) 201: 'funeste', 'bruyant' (?).

cinnabu (?) 82, 9—18, 4159 ii 30 la-ax UD | çi-in-na-bu, M^{S} *pl* 30.

çinundu(-tum). II 40, 37; 37, 39; AV 7237; Br 5220 see sinnuntu.

cançirat(u) Sp 131, 47 iççur GIŠ-SAR (= kirī) & ça-an-çi(wr. zi)-rat, ZA vi 244.

çinnatu. K 2001 *O* 2 çi-in-na-tu (ilat) Ištar ša ša-bu-u (?) . . .; CRAIG, *Relig. Texts.* MARTIN, 66 'good'; √צנן?

çinnitu. K 3600 *O* i 15 (8) ša malīli çi-in-ni-ti; MARTIN, 200: a musical instrument. K 6335, 18, 19 sik-ka-tum çi-en-nit-tum, BEZOLD, *Catal.*, 781.

çinnitan. V 26 *a-b* 24 + Vok. Const. GIŠ (u-ri) URI-KI = çi-in-ni-tan ‖ ap-pa-tan (22) & çir-ra-tan (23) Br 7310—12; AV 7239; D^{Par} 197; HOMMEL, VK 255 = palmtree; also, HALÉVY, RHR xxii 190; M^{S} 14*a*, following JENSEN, ZA vii 219: reins }Zügel{, a dual. Amos iv 2 (?).

çappu *1.* IV^{2} 55 *R* 7 çap-pi (immer) bak-kar-ri-i çap-pi šaxī piçi-e; perh. also K 4609 *O* 23 ana pān ubāni^{pl}-ja ina bi-rit çap-pi u-bal-lu (MARTIN, *Textes religieux*, 64: perhaps some part of the body). ZA xvi 176 *rm* 14; IV^{2} 58 *b* 54—6.

çappu *2.* K 3558, 3 (kakkab) ça-ap-pi; 5 (il) ça-ap-pi.

çuppu K 4780 *R* 7, 8 ina eli (iç) paššūri çu-up-pi ukulāti, Hr^{L} 26.

çu-up-pu (?) ZA iv 155 (K 2009), 6; v 41: hide, cover; AV 7269.

çi-pa. TP vi 14 abnu^{pl} çi-pa (or -xat?) ina muxxišu az-ru (III 5, 25) see zarū, 294 *col* 1. AV 7240, Br 12494; L^{T} 154.

K 3456 *O* 28 çu-çu-u . . . . . lu-lu çi-pa (??; see çuçū!) il-tak-nu.

çīpu. BA i 635 perh. matting }Geflecht{ for which the leaves of the datepalm were used: comp. צִיף; Talm. צִיפָא. Nabd 1072, 2: XXIV ma-na of wool [a-na] çi-e-pu (are given to the weaver); 214, 6 a-na çi-pu ša A'āri; Cyr 253, 5 see çax(u)rū. *Cf* T^{C} 121.

çaplu. T. A. (Ber) 26 iv 31: X ça-ap-lu siparri, perh. = saplu, *q. v.*

çapanu. set (of the sun) }sinken (von der Sonne){ T. A. (Lo) 20, 10 i-na ça-pa-ni-šu, when he sets.

çapūnu in P. N. (il) Ba-al-ça-pu-nu, K 3500 + K 4444 + K 10235, 10 (end) = בעל צפון; also *cf* šadū Ba-'-il(& li)-ça-pu-na, Sarg *Ann* 204; III 9, 27 (= TP III *Ann* 127); ZA x 360 = mount Hermon. T. A. (Ber) 138, 16 city Ça-pu-na = Saphôn. KAT^{3} 479.

çaparu *1.* *ps* içappur, speak, cry, howl }sprechen, rufen, schreien{ HALÉVY >< ZK ii 310; KB i 83 *rm*; JENSEN, 337; KB vi (1) 500—1 twitter }zwitschern{. IV^{2} 1 *a* 14, 15 e-liš i-šag-gu-mu šap-liš i-çap-pu-ru (KA-BAL-BAL-A, Br 557). Anp ii 76 the tribute of the country Sipirmena who kīma SAL^{pl}-te (= sinnišāte) çap-ru-ni. Perhaps also II 20 (*a*-)*b* 48, 49 ça-ba-rum ša iççuri (Br 2787, 14373); DT 57 *R* 1, 2 ina še-rim la-am iç-çu-ri ça-ba-ri, AV 2787; JENSEN, 505 *ad* 150. ZA v 98. ℑ *ag f* muçap(p)irtu, Br 10597, 10945, 10968; >< ZA v 98). K 2051 ii (ZA ii 300 & 413) SAL(ga-]ga)-GA'-GA' (Br 10945) = mu-tar-ri-tu; [SAL . . .] . . . GA'-GA' & [SAL]-KU(?)-GUB-BA = mu-ça-pir-tu, Br 14097; AV 5527; followed by zammērtu, *q. v.* IV^{2} 16 *b* 60, 61 šap-tan mu-uç-çap-ra-tum (Br 796, 803) ša li-ta-ma-a ri-kis-si-na lip-pa-ţir, speaking lips, which talk, whose charm is broken. Z^{S} ii 9 mu-uç-çap-ru, speaking low }flüsternd{ ZIMMERN. V 45 *c* 61 tu-çap-par. Perh. as Š we have Z^{S} vii 12 in city and in country u-šad-ma-mu çi-xir ra-bi u-ša-aç-pa[-ru]. — ℑ^{1} see çabaru. *Cf* çabburitu.

çapū, çuppū see çabū, çubbū; çibū, 1. ~ ç(a)šp(b)u see muçippu, muçiptum, 872 *col* 1. ~ çappu, 3 see zabbu.

çaparu 2. scratch, destroy }kratzen, zerstören{ Q ps I 27 *no* 2, 71 or, who sends some one else and my picture and inscription i-pa-ši-tu (√פשט) i-ça-ap-pi-ru (blots out and destroys) Delitzsch >< KB i 121. See çabaru, 1 & çaburtu.

צ V 47 *b* 21 kīma na-kim-tum šu-çi-i u-çap-pi-ra çu-pur-a-a. T^M v 31 like ..... li-çap-pi-ru-ši kiš-pu-ša, may her charm destroy her; perh. a denominative of

çupru (& **çuppāru**) *c. st.* çu-pur, ZA i 221, 44; fingernail, claw }Fingernagel, Klaue{ § 46; D^{Pr} 43; AV 7284. H 87, 63 li-qit (see *pp* 497/8) çu-up-ri, Br 2726. Zim., *Rit.*, 100, 13 of a gazelle imnu (see *ibid*, *rm* 18) xu-up-pa-ar-šu (whose right foot). NE 14, 19 çu-pur a-ri-e çu-pur-a-šu, lion's claws are his nails. K 1547 + K 2527 B *O* 27 (end) cut off abri-šu u [çu-up]-ra-šu, while *R* 22 nubal-li-šu (his talons); K 1220 *O* 7 ina muxxi çu-pur a-gap-pi, & *R* 6 (Hr^L 271; AJSL xiv 178). K 2148 ii 21 (end) the nails (?) of his feet xu-up-ra ši-na, are claws, ZA ix 118, 119. Rm 279, 7 šēpu ša imittišu xu-pur iççuri-ma (ZA ix 407); Rm 2, 19 *l* 1: ka-um kunūki-šu-nu çu-pur-šu-nu iš-kun-nu, followed by çu-pur *NN*, *etc.* (KB iv 104; also *ibid*, *pp* 100 ii 1 *foll*; 108 *foll*); III 48 *nos* 1—4. S^c 289 & S^b 1 *R* 4 dub-bi-in | DUBBIN | çu-up-ru(m), Br 2718; see also Br 2722, 2723, 2728. D 89 vi 69; 87 ii 55 & iii 40 (II 46 *no* 4 *c-d* 39); 87 iii 70 çu-pur paššūri (= II 46 *no* 4, 57). çu-pur alone also used = *loco sigilli* Strassm., *Stockholm* (*VIII.*) *O. C.*, 5 : 24, *etc.*, see Hoffmann, ZA xi, 235—6: Anhang zu 215, who explains: çupur as: Griffelspitze, Unterschrift. — A derivative of çaparu, 2 perh.:

çapru, *adj* (?) T^M v 121 taš-te-ni-'-a ru-xi-e çap-ru-ti, wicked charms.

çaparu 3. perh. 83—1—18, 205, 8 [e-di]-du ça-pa-ru ša [qarni]; Bu 89—4—26, 159 *R* 1 e-di-du : ça-pa-ru ša qar-ni, be sharp, pointed }scharf, spitz sein{ Thompson, *Reports*; a derivative of this may be çupru.

çaparu 4. T. A. (Ber) 26 i 46: 1 ŠU bat-ti-in ka-ak ša TUL-TUL xi-me-ta xu-up-pu-ru; ii 12, 13: one pa-az-ka-a-ru xurāçu ša ki-i šipir xa-aç-xi xu-up-pu-ru 14 shekels in weight (or value). Connected with this is perhaps:

çupru *2.* T. A. (Ber) 28 ii 13: IV na-al-bat-du xu-up-ri ša xurāçi.

çipru (*ad* çaparu, 3) in ki-ma çip-ri tar-ta-xi the point of a spear }Lanzenspitze{ Winckler, *Untersuchungen*, 98; Jensen, 505 (*ad* 159).

çip(b)rātu, *pl.* II 20 *c-d* 18—22 çi-ip-ra-a-tum (*d*) = [cuneiform]-DA-RI; [cuneiform] (du-ku-uš) KA-KA; [cuneiform]-ŠID (pa-pa) ŠID. [cuneiform]-TUR-DI-TUR-DI; SA-EN-KI-EN-DU (Br 5521, 3053, 3055, 3054, 3098); AV 7242; ZA v 103 *rm* 1; ZK i 306; ii 310; Jensen, 130 *rm* 1. Perh. to çaparu, 1.

çipparātu (?). K 649, 9—10 ina çip-par-ra-a-te ri-ix-te, Hr^L 56.

çipirētu. Camb 235, 2 çi-pi-ri-e-tum ša çu-up-pa-a-tum; Camb 44, 18.

çapitu (*1.*) Cyr 236, 1 has ..... bil-tum ša ça-pi-tum a-na eli EDIN-NA; see also Peiser, *Verträge*, xxv 15.

çāpitu (*2.*) see çābitu (Anp iii 111; KB i 112/3).

çapītum (*3.*) see zapītum; AV 7182. II 37 *a-c* 50 & read x(ç)a-pi-tu(m) XU = x(ç)a[not ša?]-pi-tu(m) = aš-ki-ki-tum.

çuppūtu. Dar 382, 22: 1 GUR çu-up(b)-p(b)u-u-tu.

çuppātu. Nabd 781, 1/2 so & so many mana of [cuneiform] ..... a-na çu-up-pa-a-ta. Camb 235, 2 see çipirētu. Neb 286, 3.

ç(z?)ippatu *1.* a reed }ein Rohr{. V 32 *d-f* 64, 65 see kīsu, 2 (412 *col* 1) & Br 2430; AV 7241; perh. K 9287 ii 13 çip-pa-ta a-rak-kas(-ma), *Rev. Sém.*, ix 149. M^S 82 *col* 1.

çippatu *2.* *pl* çippāti. orchards }Obstpflanzungen{ and perh. also more general: trees *etc.* AV 7241, çip-pa-tum GIŠ-SAR followed by çi-xi-ir-tu, dab(p)-ru-u. Sarg *Cyl* 34 za-qap çip-pa-a-te; *bull.* 38; *Ann* XIV 67 za-qip çip-pa-ti; Lyon, *Sargon*, 65. Bu 88—5—12, 75 + 76, vii 30 za-qa-ap çip-pa-a-ti, plant orchards, BA iii 246, 247. Also Sn *Bell* 46. 58; *Bass* 67, 86 see xaqapu. K 1282 *etc.*, *O* 9 ki-i la za-qip çip-pa-tu. ZA iii 318, 88 ki-rib çip-pa-ti ša-ti-na; Asb i 50 çip-pa-a-ti šu-um-mu-xa inbu (KB ii 156, 157 & *rm* **). TP III *Ann* 204 çip-pa-a-te ša ni-i-ba la i-šu-u ak-kis, ROST, 125. L⁴ iii 10 çip-pat mu-šarê. KB iii (2) 128 A 11 (iç) çip-pa-a-tum inbu (Sᵇ 45) ma-la ba-šu-u, BA ii 216, 217. V 33 vii 24*foll* çi-pat iç[u kiri] (BA ii 216 reading: çi-pat-t[um]) a-na da-riš (?) in-ba ṭa-a[-ba] li-te-il-li (KB iii, 1, 150, 151 & *rm* *). K 3600 *R* 25 mu-ub-bil çip-pa-a-ti; perh. II 60 *a* 50 (= K 4334 *R* i 9) u çip-pa-ta ina qêmi lâ misi ta-pat-tan; II 35 *c-d* 2, AV 833. MEISSNER & ROST, 39 *rm* 84 perh. Tlm. [illegible] sallow }Weide{.

çaçâku, çaçâti see zazâku. zazâti, 277 *col* 1 & also ni-xe-nun-na-ku, 664 *col* 1.

çâçu. K 2852 + K 9662 iii 28 after these people aš-al u-çi-iç a-xi-iṭ, I inquired, I asked, *etc.*; *cf* צִיץ or צוּץ, Cant. ii 9 (WINCKLER, *Forschungen*, ii 36 *foll*).

çuçû, *m* marsh, marshy land, fernland; or, also, an artificial island in the midst of a lake (Sn *Kui* 4, 36) }Marsch, Marschland; auch eine künstliche Insel inmitten eines Teiches{. id ZUG Z³ iii 26; Br 10310; H 33, 771 = çu-çu-u, see buniunu, 180 *col* 1. K 246 (H 88, 89) ii 28 ša ina çe-rim u çu-çi-e (= ZUG) i-mu-tu, who died in the desert or on the marsh. K 2867 *O* 25 qanâti çu-çi-e uš-te-li-b(p)u (see S. A. SMITH, *Asurb*, vol ii; ZA ii 132); S 747 *f* 3 çu-çu-u nap (so DELITZSCH, *Weltschöpf.*, 58; but KB vi (1) 303: ap)-pa[-ru]. Creat.-*frg* I 6 (D 93) see gipâru (229 *col* 1) and add: see KB vi (1) 304; Babyl. dupl. [82—7—14, 402] reads çu-ça-'a. IV² 19 *b* 49, 50; 26 *a* 47, 48 see damamu, *p* 253; Br 10309; these passages as KB vi (1) 304 says show rather a meaning like: das im Marschlande oder Sumpfe wachsende Rohrdickicht; see also JENSEN, 326 *fol.* K 3456 *O* 18 çu-çu[-u?] .... la qar-ba-a-tum, no fields; 28 çu-çu-u .... ÇI-PA (= çippâti?) il-tak-nu, PSBA xxi 37, 38. ZA iv 241, 33 [ki]-in-gi u çu-çi-e liš-te-šir ad-man-šu. — Sn *Kui* 4, 36 (nâr) a-gam-mu ušabšîma çu-çu-u ki-rib-ša as-ti-il. — Dᴾᵃʳ 241; Dᴾʳ 64 *rm* 2; G § 49. On [illegible] & çuçû see NÖLDEKE, ZDMG 40 ('86), 725; BROWN-GESENIUS, 425. On Ezek. 24, 7—8 see HAUPT in TOY, *Ezekiel* (SBOT) 79.

çâçu moth }Motte{. K 3726 i sect. 3, 1 šumma ça-a-çu ina bît amêli ibši & destroys the clothing, *etc.*; BEZOLD, *Catalogue*, 553.

çiççu, with or without derminative (iç) = fetter, iron clasp }Fessel, Kette, Klammer{, *cf* ציצת; WINCKLER, *Forsch.*, i 495 *rm* 2; DELITZSCH in BAER-DEL., *Ezech*, pf. xxxvi *ad* Ezek 8, 3. Asb iii 59, 60 ina (iç) çi-iç-çi iš-qa-ti parzilli, *etc.* u-tam-me-xa (KB ii 183); ii 109. Sarg *Khors* 112 ina çi-iç-çi [is-qa-ti] bi-ri-tu parzilli id-di-šum-ma (KB ii 66, 67); *Ann* 411 i-na çi-iç-çi u is-qa-ti. Perhaps Sp II 265 *a* iii 3 ku-u-ri (see *p* 364 *col* 2) eb-ri çi-iç-ka il(?)-mad. V 17 *a-b* 48 .... XA ∣ çi-iç-çi ma-xi-iç, Br 14468; AV 7244.

çaçallû. T. A. (Ber) 26 iii 36: X ça-ça-al-li-e, *cf* ZA v 13 *rm*.

çaçumtu, çaçuntu, a plant }eine Pflanze{ AV 7184. K 274 = II 42 *a* 10 (šam) ça-çu-um-tu, Br 13889. K 4566, 8 (šam) ça-çu-un-tu ∥ (šam) a-ši-i. K 4345 ii 3 (šam) ça-çu-'u-tu (*i. e.* II 42 *no* 2 *R* 2).

çâçiru some destructive insect, like grasshopper; locust? }ein heuschreckenartiges zerstörendes Insekt{ AV 7183; BALL, PSBA xii 413 a cricket. II 5 *c-d* 8, 9 XU-BER .... PA(?)-AG = ça-çi-ru, Br 5425; XU-BER ¶¶ TIR-RA = ç kiš-ti (of the forest), Br 5426; *ibid* 20 *c-d* we have ça-çi-ru with id of kisimmu (see 416 *col* 1) & gloss (ša-ri-in); H 22, 423; Sᵇ 251. D⁸ 77; Br 5549. K 6429 + K 6619 šumma ça-çi-ru ina êli (?), BEZOLD, *Catalogue*, 786. K 4152 *R* 10 ça-çi[-ru]; *cf* K 4376 *c* 6 (M⁸ *pl* 7; 12) GGA '98, 824.

çiçîtu (?) NE 76, 18 ina çi-çi-ti ma-lu-u eqla (?); 20 iç-ru-ux-ma çi-is-su ki-i i-ša-ti. II 41 *no* 7 *g-h* 24 ... çi-zu-ti, among names of plants.

(iç) **çaq-qal.** DT 83 *R* 11 šu-uš-qu-us-su ina (iç) çaq-qal; PSBA xvii 138*foll*; here, perhaps, a musical instrument made of the çaqqal woods; *cf* II 40 *a* 54.

(aban) **çi-q(k)ir-tum** Nabd 321, 6.

çâru *1.* (?) ZA vi 241, 9 BAR = ça-a-ri.

çâru 2. KB vi (1) 349 on Creat.-*frg* V 14 (end) ina a-ge[-e] u-çir. suggests √çurru = make great }gross machen{ and refers to

KB iii (1) 132 *col* 3, 21 (Samsu-iluna says:) Bābilu erçi-tim-šu lu-u-çi-ir, translated there by WINCKLER: I enlarged, increased; and connected with çīru great. — pm of Ⓠ perhaps T^M ii 4 ū-mu namru ša qi-bit-su çi-rat, whose command is lofty; also KM 60, 11. See çīru, 2 *a*.

çarru *1.* (√çararu, 1.) *adj* IV² 16 *a* 23, 24 the demon who a-na me-e çar-ru-ti (= SUR-RA, Br 2987) ša Ea 'i-ir-ru, BA ii 292: the flowing water {das fliessende Wasser}; JENSEN & others: the bright, shining water. Perhaps also 80, 11—12, 9 *R col* 3, 40 ça-ar | id | ça-ar-r[u]; same id = (il) Šamaš.

çarru *2.* (√çararu, 2.) foe, enemy, oppressor {Feind, Gegner, Dränger}. III 57 *a* 63 UL çar-ru, mentioned together with UL na-ka-ru, UL lim-nu, *etc.*, as one of the seven names of the star muštabarrū mūtānu, *i. e.* planet Mars. A ‖ is

çirru *1.* (= çerru, çarru) see çaltu. D^Pr 164 *rm* 1 ‖ raggu. K 3364 *R* 21 a-na çir-ri-ka preceded by a-na e-piš limut-ti & a-na rag-gi-ka.

çirru *2.* oppression, vexation {Drängung, Peinigung}. IV² 49 *a* 78 EN (= bēl) çir-ri-MU (= ja) u bēlit çir-ri-MU (= ja); = T^M i 80; *cf* ii 42.

çēru, çīru *1.* צאר *n* § 65, 1; AV 7250. — *a*) back {Rücken}. T. A. (Ber) 93, 11 çi-ru(-ma) is explained by zu-ux-ru (KB v 234/5); see *Rev. Sém.* vi ('98) 274 *foll*; ZA vi 156 *nos* 4/5. Also (Ber) 94, 15; 95, 9. Šalm, *Ob*, relief-inscr. i: III gammalē (udrāte?) ša šu-na-a-a çe-ri-ši-na = dromedaries? (KB i 150/1). III 4 *no* 4, 49, 50 ul-tu çi-ir sisē qaq-qa-riš im-qu-ut, from the horse's back he fell upon the ground. Here according to KB vi (1) 166/7 also NE VI 2 (end) e-li çi-ri-šu = upon his back; & *ibid* 230/1 on *del* 6 (end) e-li çi-ri-ka; see, however, HAUPT, *Johns Hopk. Circ.*, *no* 69, 17; BA i 320; also ZA iii 417. II 37 *e-f* 61 çe-e-ru ‖ e-çi-en (*q. v.*) çi-ru = spine. IV² 8 *col* 3, 14 (end) = Z^B v/vi 136. II 62 *g-h* 64 e-çi-en çir (*var* çi-ri) elippi, Br 3313. Br 3312 on II 48 *c-d* 52. — *b*) upper part (in general) {Oberteil}, whence the prepos. çir (see like process with elū, muxxu) = upon, over, over against (in hostile meaning) § 81 *b*; mostly written id EDIN, which properly = çēru, 2, field, desert; see H 185, 186; § 9, 240. Also id GAB, KNUDTZON, 313. — *α*. upon, on {auf}. Sn vi 41 çi-ir tam(?)-li-e ša-a-tu; iii 69 çi-ir zuq-ti (šad) Ni-pur, on the top of Mount Nipur (§ 72 *a*); ii 6 such & such çi-ru-uš-šu (= ana çīrišu) u-ša-aš-ṭir (1 *sg*; *cf* L⁴ iv 5); Esh *Sendsch*, *R* 53 çir-uš-šu u-ša-aš-ṭir; *Bell* 26; *Bav* 56 çi-ru-uš-šu-un (*i. e.* on the statues) ušašṭir. I 7 F 26 çi-ir bītišu, upon his house; Asb ii 74 more than . . . . . u-kin EDIN-uš-šu; iv 107 sattukkē *etc.* u-kin (see kānu) EDIN-uš-šu-un. Sn ii 46; iii 11 *etc.* tribute *etc.* u-kin çi-ru-uš-šu; iii 29 çi-ru-uš-šu(-un); Sarg *Cyl* 64 u-kin çi-ru-uš-šin. AV 7248. V 35, 4 u-ša-aš-ki-na (3 *sg*) çi-ru-šu-un. K 2852 + K 9662 i 14 (end) ki-in (= ip) çi-ru-uš-šu-un. I 44, 61 çi-ru-uš-šu, upon it (I reared a structure). Sn *Kui* 4, 3 çi-ru-uš-šin ul-ziz-ma (BA iii 103 *rm* **; see further *sub* nazazu, 3). ZA iii 317, 82 çi-ir max-ri-e, above the former. NE 11, 15 + 20 EDIN-ka (& -ša), see dādu *b*) *p* 241 *col* 2, & KB vi (1) 428. Asb v 30 they placed me çi-ir (v 127; x 39 id) ga-ri-ja. K 2801 *R* 50 çir-ruš-šu na-al-bu-bu çi-ir (aban) a-lal-lum . . . . u-šar-bi-ça. Sargon *RP* 22 çi-e-ru-uš-šu, WINCKLER, *Sargon*, 166. — *β*. around {um}. Sn v 11 see paxaru Ⓠ. — *γ*. over against, against {gegen, wider}; Sarg *Ann* 304 I sent çi-ru-uš-šu, *Cyl* 54. Sn v 15 ki-i ri-kil-ti . . . . çi-ru-uš-šu baši; iv 2 çi-ir Ma-ni-ja-e . . . . . aç-çabat xarrānu. Asb iii 129 EDIN NN uštešēera xarrānu: viii 83; *cf* iv 112. v 64 (*var* çi-ir, Br 4581; also iii 21); viii 77, the verb mostly ad-ki = I gathered (my troops). T. A. (Lo) 17, 17 and he will march [a-na] çi-ri-ja (against me) + 15; (Ber) 184, 31 a-na zi-ri-ja.

NOTE. — i-zir & i-zi-ir = ina çir, KB iv 60 (i) 4; (ii) 20; *cf* 84 (viii) 20 i-na zi-ir a-bi-ja u i-na zi-ri-ja, & *ibid rm* *.

çiriš *1.* a by-form of çīr. Creat.-*frg* IV 128 Marduk çi-ri-iš Ti-āmat . . . i-tu-ra ar-ki-iš. 88—5—12, 75 + 76 ix 12 *foll*: çi-riš na-ki-ri liš-zi-za-an-ni, may place me over mine enemies, BA iii 256—7;

ZA ix 270—2. ZA iv 237 (i) 38 çi-riš it-tab-šu-u; K 2807 *R* 52 çi-riš tāmtim; *cf* eliš = (ina) eli, II 65 *O* ii 17.

çu'ru, T. A. back {Rücken} see zu'ru, *p* 272 *col* 2.

çîru 2. *adj* high, lofty {hoch, erhaben} *f* çîrtu, *c. st.* çîrat; *pl* çîrûti, *f* çîrâti, AV 7249; § 65, 9 *rm*. Neo-Babyl. zîru, § 19. id MAX, § 9, 109; H 12 & 208, 11; S^b 336 ma-ax | MAX | çi-i-rum, Br 1047 ‖ rabū, maxxu. D^Pr 1; Nöldeke, ZDMG 40, 718. II 31 *no* 2 *c-d* 22 MAX = çi-i-ri, which also = tizqāru. K 40 iii 25, 26 (= D 82) MAX; [. . . .]-AL = çi-i-rum (Br 5749; II 8 *c-d* 25, 26); see T. A. (Lo) 51, 13 ki-ma ri-ki (like a weed) AL: zi-ri; K 5337 iii 6 A-AK(?)-MAX = çi-ir-tum. — It is used in connection with *a*) gods: Šamaš, V 63 *a* 41 called DI-KUD (= dajānu) çi-rim of heaven and earth; Neb iv 19 da-a-a-nim çi-i-ri; IV² 28 *no* 1 *a* 19, 20 da-a-a-nu çi-ru (*b* 5, 6); & see dānu, 2. (288, 289); also V 65 *a* 11; *b* 32 (*var* to MAX). — Šamaš & A-a, V 65 *b* 13, 14 ana ni-ri-bi ilu-u-ti-šu-nu çi-ir-ti. — Anu & Adad, TP vii 111 i-na šub-ti-šu-nu çi-ir (*var* çir)-te. — Sin, IV² 9 *a* 54 (56) ina šame-e (erçi-tim) man-nu çi-i-ru at-ta e-diš-ši-ka çi-rat (§ 91: thou art exalted); id MAX. — Nebo, V 66 *a* 16 Nabū mâr çi-i-ri; Neb i 35 a-lak-ti i-lu-ti-šu çir-ti. — Marduk, Neb i 69 be-lu-ut-ka çir-ti; *cf* ii 6; 12 ina tu-ku-ul-ti-šu çir-ti; KB iii (2) 78, 28 e-te-el-lu çi-i-ri; 6, 36 i-na ki-be-ti-ka (*q. v.*) çi-ir-tim. See also I 52 *no* 3, ii 30 (KB iii (2) 56, 57); V 65 *b* 30; 66 *a* 24; T^M i 120 ina qi-bi-ti-ka çir-ti; Sarg *Cyl* 58 i-na ki-bi-ti-šu-nu çir-ti (*var* -te). I 67 *b* 33, 34. Hilprecht, OBI, i 32—33 *col* 3, 42. Messerschmidt, *Nabd*, 68, 18 = Winckler, *Forsch*, i 492, 493. — Nergal, Šalm, *Mon* 44 ina idât çi-ra-a-ti. — Ea is called mas(par?)-si-e çi-ri of heaven, IV² 5 *a* 58. — IV² 15* (i) 34 ^(il) Gibil e-mu-qan çi-i(?)-ir-ti, *etc.* K 5201 (beg.) ina er-çi-ti at-ta çi-ra-ta, H 184; see also ZA iv 230, 7; K 3182 ii 26. 82—7—4, 42 *O* 6 (of a god) la-u-ti-šu çi-ir-tim, his exalted might, PSBA xx 155 *foll.* Asb x 9 ina qibit ilū-ti-šu-nu çir-tu; V 35, 28 i-lu-ti-šu] çir-ti, BA ii 212, 213; also DT 71, 15 ana ilū-ti-šu çir-tum. See also sukkallu, *pp* 756, 757. P. N. V 44 *c-d* 22 Çi-rat (id MAX)-ki-bit-^(il) Marduk. — Ištar of Uruk ru-ba-a-ti çir-ti, 81—6—7, 209, dupl. K 6346, 2. Henn. viii 113 *foll*; BA iii 260 *foll.* L¹ 14 Ištar is called bēltu çir-tu. S 6 + S 2, 21 ina a-mat ru-bi-ti-ki çir-ti. *Rev. Sém.*, '98, 142 *foll.* Pinches, *Texts*, 16 *no* 4 *R* 4 Zi-ir-pa-ni-tum ru-ba-tum çir-tum. KB iii (2) 48 *col* 2, 44 a-na Gu-la ru-ba-a-ti çi-ir-ti; *Rec. Trav*, xx 205 *foll*, *no* i ^(ilat) Na-na-a bêlit çir-ti. Also *cf* dalīlu, 250 *col* 2, end. — *b*) demons, *etc.*: H 98/99, 47/8 of lšum: na-gi-ru rabu-u ra-bi-çu çi-ru (= MAX), the lofty demon; 123 *R* 15 [gallū]-ki çi-i-ru. IV² 17 *O* 12 [??] çi-ru-ti ša šame-e (*cf* *l* 10). K 7906 ū-mu çi-ru ša ina çi-rim [DU-A]; ū-mu ez-zu ša ina çi-rim i-ziq, T^M 124. NE 8, 35 Aruru created Ea-bani i-lit-ti çir-ti (*cf* KB vi, 1, 120, 121; 425). — *c*) kings: III 8 (*no* 6) 15 ir-šu çi-i-ru qar-rad tam(ū? 𒀸)-tal(ri?) [-ku?] Nebuk. iššakku çi-i-ri, Neb *Bors* *a* 3; *Bab* *a* 6; I 66 *c* 1 (zi-i-ri). Neb i 5 Neb. pa-te-si çi-i-ri; see also V 65 *a* 3. Anp i 32 çîra (*var* giš-ra)-ku. KB iii (1) 130 Samsuiluna to whom Bêl šu-ma-am çi-ra-am i-be-u-šu. — *d*) other human beings: III 15 i 18, 19 gi-mir qu-ra-di-šu-nu çi-ru-ti, all their powerful troops; TP iii 39 i-na e-mu-qi çi-ra-a-ti, with the mighty forces; iv 7 (*var*); 43 (çi-ra-te); also I 7 (ix) A 1 (end); KB ii 36, 6 to whom Ea gave e-mu-qa-an çi-ra-a-te; Asb v 110 mundaxçêšu MAX-MEŠ (*var* çi-ru-ti); i 60 ad-ki-e ^(amêl) e-mu-qi-ja çi-ra-a-te. — *e*) cities, temples, *etc.* Asb x 52 Nineveh maxāzu çi-i-ru na-ram ^(ilat) Bêlit; Sn *Bav* 17; Nabopol. (Winckler) A i 12 = KB iii (2) 6 *no* 2: Sippar ma-xa-zi zi-i-ri. ZA iii 313, 61 ma-xa-zi çi-i-ru. TP viii 17 ad-ma-na çi-i-ra; *cf* V 65 *a* 6 ad-ma-nu çi-i-ri; ZA iv 430 (80—7—19, 126) see Nippuru, 719 *col* 2; ZA ii 361 *b* 18 dūra çi-ra-am. Pinches, *Texts*. 15 *no* 4, 5 (end) Esagila çi-i-ri; 15 Babylon ma-xa-za çi-i-ru; Sn vi 43 êkallu çi-ir-tu; II

23, 69 mu-šab zi-ir-tum, AV 8006; III 38 *no* 2 (K 2660) 8 ma-xa]-zi çi-ru-ti. — *f*) other nouns: IV^2 15* i 18 ina šip-ti çir-ti (šipat Eridu ša têlilti); Neb iv 7 the sacrificial house a-ki-ti çi-ir-ti, BA ii 238. K 2801 *R* 10 uz-nu çir-tu, BA iii 285. IV^2 14 *no* 3 *O* 6 na-aš xaṭ-ṭi çir-ti; ZA i 40, 11. IV^2 8 *c* 31 qa-a çi-ra (= MAX) qa-a raba-a ($Z^{\check{S}}$ v/vi 153); H 128 *R* 8 sa-par-ra çi-i-ri ina çi-e-ri, *etc.*; V 33 ii 50, 51 a-gi-e ga-ar-ni çi-ra-a-ti (*cf* KB iii, 1, 140—1 & *rm* °; LEHMANN, BA ii 590, 591). TP i 21 a-ga-a çi-(i-)ra, the lofty crown; vi 59 qa-a(t)-su-nu çi-ir (çir)-ta; II 50 *col* iv/v 6 ID-MAX = (nâru) çi-ir-tum, ZDMG 53, 657 *fol.* *Rec. Trav*, xvii 81, 82, 12 giš(?)-max-xi-ša çi-ru-ti; Asb ii 41 (iç) dim-me MAX-MEŠ (*cf* dimmu); I 69 *b* 12 (iç) erini çi-ru-tum; V 64 *c* 2 dalâtê erini çi-ra-a-ti; ZA ii 128 *a* 22 da-la-a-ti çi-ra-a-ti: SMITH, *Sen* 91, 58 (= *Kui* 2, 12) elippê çi-ra-a-ti noble vessels.

Derr. these 3:

çîriš ***2.*** KB vi (1) 40, 16 çi-riš im-bu-u, they called it (*i. e.*, Babylon) by a lofty name.

çîrtu ***1.*** K 2852 + K 9662 ii 4 ina zir(=çir)-ti mu-ši, in the height of the night, WINCKLER, *Forsch.* ii 34 *fol.*

çîrûtu, greatness, loftiness {Hoheit, Erhabenheit}. TP i 23/4 Tigl. Pil. ša .... a-ša-ri-du-ta çi-ru-ta qar-du-ta ta-qi-ša-šu, to whom you have given supremacy, majesty, and valor. Sp III 586 + R III 1, 10 a-na E-babbar-ra bît Šamši šu-bat be-lu-ti-ka çi-ru-ut-ka šu-u-pi, Br 1047; PINCHES, TSBA viii 167 *foll.* S^3 58, 59 gušûrê | er-nu u šur-man çi-ru-ut tar-bi-ti, LEHMANN, ii 16, 17.

çêru 2. throw down, overthrow {umwerfen, niederwerfen} (??). IV^2 8 *a* 18—20 pu-lux-ta-šu ça-'-i-rat (= KA-DÚ-A); also perh. D 82 (K 40) iii 23, 24 (*cf p* 293 *col* 2, below); IV^2 22 *a* 23, 24 i-ça-ar (*cf p* 293 *cols* 1, 2); ‖ u-kan-na-an (*p* 408 *col* 1, above). K 164, 29 mârtu še-sa-a ta-ça-ar-ru (karpat) qa-b(p)u-tu, BA ii 636. D 82 iii 17—19 çi-e-rum (Br 3272, 3240, 3239); 20, ç ša kiššdi, Br 3273, 5268 (= II 8, 17—20).

çêru, çîru ***3.*** *m* plain, prairie, desert {Niederung, Ebene, Steppe, Wüste}. Main id EDIN, § 9, 240; Br 4529—30; AV 7250. §§ 29; 32*aγ*; H 185, 186; D^{Par} 144 *rm* 41; H^F 5 *rm* 3; GGA '82, 814. S^b 1 *O* ii *r* e-di-in (*var* -din) | EDIN | çe-e-ru (8, = e-di-nu), H 18, 313; 186, 7; V 38 *c-d* 38 & *ibid*, 65. D 82 (K 40) iii 27—32 EDIN; AN[-NA?]-EDIN; BE (Br 1530); ZUG (zu[ug]?) (Br 10308); KIB (u[l]); ZAG (Br 6492) = çi-e-rum; V 29 *a-b* 61. V 50, 29—30 ina çi-ri (= EDIN-NA); IV^2 8 iii 48 ana çi-rim; K 257 *R* 9—10 ina çi-rim; IV^3 3 *a* 2 ina çi-e-ri (Br 454, 4142), + 22 (Br 477, 4530). K 7906 see nakapu, 1 (673 *col* 2). IV^2 11 *b* 27—8 [muruç] qaq-qa-di ina çi-e-ri (= EDIN-NA) Br 6820; also 25—6; $Z^{\check{S}}$ v/vi 165. IV^2 18 *no* 3 *O* 33—4 çi-e-ru eq-lu na-aš bil-ti; 18* (S 1708) *O* 8 (end) alû limnu ina çi-rim tar-ba-ça ib-ta-'-u; 20 *no* 1, 3—4 çi-i-ru ba-ma-a-ti (*cf* V 29 *a-b* 60, 61 & bamâtu [*p* 172 *col* 2] for IV^2 19 *b* 1/2; II 32 *g-h* 12; Br 10308, 10312); 27 *a* 7 kim-mat-su ina çi-e-ri arta la ibnû; 16 *b* 2 utukku limnu ina çi-ri ir-bi-i[ç] Br 1937; K 1283, 6 e-kim-mu lim-nu ina çi-rim i-ku-uš; see also H 128 *R* 8 in çi-e-ri; 10 ina çi-rim. NE 10, 44 bu-ul-šu ša ir-bu-u ina çêri-šu, & 11, 14 (KB vi, 1, 124). *Rec. Trav.*, xx notes d'epigraphie, xxxv 3 (end) u-ma-al-li çi-ra. H 83 i 2 u-tuk çi-e-ri, the demon of the desert; 87 ii 12 see namû, 2 (670 *col* 2); i 70 ša-ar çi-rim, the blast of the desert (wind); 89 ii 28 see çuçû; 29 ša ina çi-rim (il) Adad ir-xi-çu-šu. — TP vi 57 mu-'-ur çe-ri (508 *col* 2); I 28 *a* 1 (+ 32) bu'ur çêri. K 517 *R* 21 see çummû. id Sn v 85 ta-xa-az çêri = field battle. II 16 *g* 12, 13 u a-na çi-rum (?) ta-nam-da. II 62 *a-b* 40 a-çi-tu ša çi-e-ri (& 41) Br 3959. 3961, 3966. Camb 81, 10 mim-mu-šu-nu ša âli u çêri ma-la ba-šu-u, their property in city and country. bu-ul çêri see bûlu, *pp* 154, 155; Br 2033; also IV^2 22 *a* 45, 46. V 50 *b* 51 ri-ma ša çi-rim u-šak-niš, the wildox of the desert he lays down. umâm çêri see umâmu, 2. I 7 *no* ix B 2, C 1, D 2 nêšu (*q. v.*) ezzu ša EDIN-šu (BA ii 281; ZA ii 321); NE 71, 6 nimru ša çêri; purim çêri see purîmu; nam(m)aššû (-še) ša çêri see nammaššû. bît çêri, see *p* 204 *col* 2, & kultâru, 891 *col* 2. On Bêlit çêri, NE VII 47 (KB vi, 1, 190—1) see KB vi (1) 463; KAT³ 637; also Z^{Š} viii 7. naxlaptu çe-ri see naxlaptu (664 *col* 1); lubâr çêri see murxu, 587 *col* 2. — V 21 *a-b* 45 tu-ša-ru = çi-e-ru. Also see rapadu, NE 59, 2 + 5; 67, 10. T. A. (Ber) 6 *R* 8 ša-am-mi ša çi-e-ri, ZA v 14 *bel*; (Ber) 60, 48 i-na zi-ri, by land (?).

çâru (?), **çarru** *3.* V 21 *a-b* 36 ça(za)-ar-u = çi[-ru?] snake, serpent, followed by names for scorpion, *etc.* With this is perhaps connected II 5, 31 u-z(ç)ab(p)i-ça-ar, name of an insect or reptile (see za-ar, 208 *col* 1).

çir(r)u *3.* *m* snake }Schlange{, AV 7245; iδ ÇIR & MUŠ, § 9, 178; H 26, 562; *del* 270 (292) çiru i-te-çi-in, KB vi (1) 252—3. Z^{B} 73 *rm* 4. Esh iii 29 ÇIR u GIR-TAB, snakes & scorpions. KB vi (1) 582, 8 .... çi-ru çi-ru serpent, serpent! IV² 1 *a* 32, 33 ina dal-ti ki-ma çi-ri it-ta-nâ-la-lu(!) BA ii 292 *rm*; Br 7639. çi-ir mu-ši ‖ çir çal-mu (*q. v.*); also KB vi (1) 102, 7; Br 7653. K 282 *O* 5—6 man-nu-um-ma çiru; tam-tu-um-ma çiru Ti-âmat. ka-nanu ša çi-ri, see qanannu, Br 7644—5. K 242 (= II 22 *c-d*) iv 29 DUK-ÇIR = kar-pat çi-(ir)-ri, AV 7256, a ‖ of karpat ṭâbâti (see ṭâbtu, 2), ZA vi 75; Br 5901, 7639. (šam) ki-sa-at çi-ri see kisat (419 *col* 1); II 51 *b* 45 nâr çi[-ri], name of a canal. — Boissier, PSBA xxii 107 çiru designe tout animal rampant, les ophidiens et les sauriens. Connected with this çiru are perhaps the following 6:

(il) **Çir.** V 52 *a* 20 Çir (but see ZA iii 169) ra-bi-iç Ê-šar-ra; II 59 *a-b* 21; Br 7641.

(il) **Çir-gal.** III 66 *R* 26 *b* (Br 13136); PSBA xxi 129 *foll*; H 79 (K 133) 4 e-muq la-bi çir-gal-li; see PSBA xvi 227 *foll*, on this text.

(kakkab) **Çir.** II 49 *c* 4 + 12; V 46 *a-b* 29 = il NIN-KI-GAL (= Allatu); D^{S} 87; Br 13134. KAT³ 501 & *rm* 1.

çirgarru. See for the present, mušgarru (*p* 599).

çirmaxxu, great serpent }grosse Schlange{ = çir + maxxu (*p* 518). II 19 *b* 14 ša ki-ma çir-max-xi si-ba qaq-qa-da-šu, Br 7643. KB vi (1) 6, 10 it-ta-lad çir-max-xi-e; & Creat.-*frg* III 24 (end) + 82 (end). KAT³ 504 (mušmaxxu). A ‖ is:

çirruššû, some kind of large serpent = çir + ruššû, *q. v.* apparently a ‖ of xul-mittu, 315 *col* 1. D^{Par} 146 *no* 43; Jensen, 277. K 3473 + 79, 7—8, 296 + Rm 6, 15 *O* 31 çir-ruš-šu (+ 89). ÇIR-RUŠ-MEŠ, KB vi (1) 6, 17 *etc.*; see *ibid*, 310; 364; S^{P} II 987 *O* 14 (*Jour. Trans. Vict. Instit.*, vol 29 pt 1). K 2801 *R* 50 see çîr(u), upon. II 19 *b* 17 speaks of the ÇIR-RUŠ tam-tim; Neb vi 5 + 17; I 67 *a* 26: VIII ÇIR-RUŠ e-ri-e (of bronze) še-zu-zu-u-ti; Scheil, *Nabd*, viii 56 ÇIR-RUŠ e-ri-i (*cf* Neb, *Bab*, ii 9); I 65 *a* 45 ÇIR-RUŠ-RUŠ še-zu-zu-u-ti uš-zi-iz; iδ also V 33 *c* 13 (KB iii, 1, 148 dragon: properly: fierce serpent). KAT³ 503 muš-ruššu.

çirru *4.* *m* some part of the door, different from nukuššû (*q. v.*, 677 *col* 2); = ציר. Brown-Gesenius, 852 *col* 1: pivot (of a door); hinge }Türangel{; like nukuššû there was an upper & a lower çirru. H 94, 95 *ll* 56, 57 ina çir[-ri] e-li-i, & šap-li-i [a-a e-ru-ub-šu]; H 89, 160 = GIŠ-ZA-RA-AN-TA (& -KI-TA). IV² 1 *a* 35 ina çir-ri ki-ma ša-a-ri i-ziq-qu; 16 *a* 56, 57 (= GIŠ-ZA-RA) see nukuššû (Br 11770); 27 *no* 5 *col* ii ina çir (= GIŠ-ZA-RA) ki-ma ....; 6 *c* 44 GIŠ-ZA-RA : çir-r[um?]; 24 *a* 48, 49 (end) ina çir-ri (iδ ZA-RA); Meissner & Rost, 45 *no* 3 √çararu, go to & fro }hin- u. hergehen{.

NOTE. — Some read çir(-)la-lu(la) instead of muçlalu, see *p* 572 *col* 2.

çurru *m* heart }Herz{ properly: pericardium; also thoughts }Gedanken{. AV 7290; K 7674, 15 rit-pu-uš çur-ri; Šamš i 22 (Scheil, *Šamš*, 35); Merodach-Balad.-stone ii 49—50 see karšu, 1 *b* (441 *col* 2); Esh vi 39; Sn *Kui* 4, 42 see mukaru (539 *col* 1). IV² 20 *no* 1, 7—8 ûmi-šam la na-par-ku-a çur-ri qid-da-a-ti ina zumrija lû ipparsûma, not a single day did thoughts of despair (?, distress) forsake me; see also Martin, *Rec. Trav.*, xxiv 96—7; Br 169. Sp II 265 *a* xxii 2 li-id(t)-mu(-)um-ma çur-ra-ka ilu ta-da-a-a-aç (ZA x 10, 11; PSBA xvii 150). LYON, *Sargon*, 65, 66 *ad Cyl* 35 çur-ru-uš uš-ta-bil(-ma), AV 7293. II 36 *e-f* 52 çur-rum ‖ libbu, Br 8898; *cf* S^b 255, where same id = lib-bu; perhaps also K 40 iii 47 (Br 13992); K 8204, 5 see naxaçu (665 *col* 1); K 4378 i 37 see sup(p)innu & Br 5437. — *Lit. Centralbl.*, '81, *col* 735; ZDMG 32, 185 √צרר = enclose.

NOTE. — 1. See zumru (end) *p* 295 *col* 1 and JENSEN, KB vi (1) 322—323 on Creat.-*frg* III 135, who denies the existence of çurru, reading zurru = belly, stomach; not heart.

2. ina çu-ri-in IV² 21* *no* 2 *O* 19 (Br 8463) = zumrija, see zumru

(mât) or (al) **Çurru** = city & district of Tyre. II 67, 66 (al) Çur-ri; & *ibid* Metenna (al) Çur-ra-a-a (*i. e.* the Tyrians; § 65, 37); III 12 *no* 2, 18; Asp iii 86 the tribute of the king of (mât) Çur-ra-a-a (mât) Çi-du-na-a-a; III 5, 63; Sarg *Cyl* 21 (mât) Qu-e u Çur-ri. I 35 *no* 1, 12 mentions (mât) Çur-ru Çi-du-nu; Ash ii 49 Ba-'-li šar (mât) Çur-ri. T. A. (al) Çur-ri, often. BEZOLD, *Catalogue*, 2196; BROWN-GESENIUS, 862—3.

çurû (?). Nabd 271, 2—3 man-ga-ga (la) çu-ru-u; 385, 2—3 & 7—8.

çarabu. burn, scorch {brennen}. II 28 *d-e* 60 (K 4361 i 7) PA(*i. e.* SIG)-GA = ça-ra-bu in one group with kababu, kubbubu. Camb 88, 1—2 a-na ça-ra-bu ša a-gur-ri, to burn bricks. — ℶ II 34 *a-b* 59, 60 (K 4324, 13. 14) ÇI-ÇI & BAR-TAB-GER (which = xamaṭu, burn) = çur-ru-bu, Br 4201, 1830; AV 7292; S^c 159 ta-ab | TAB | çur-ru-[bu], Br 3769. Here according to Br. also IV² 10 *a* 54, 55; 19 *a* 27, 28; II 16 *e-f* 17, which see under xarabu, *p* 295 *col* 2.

Derr. naçrabu & these 2:

çarbu. V 46 *c-d* 18 (il) Çar-bu-u explained by (il) Bêl çar-be, a name of god Nergal; Br 10241 *ad* II 54 *c-d* 72 (il) Çar-bu-u = (il) EN (= bêl) çar-bi; POGNON, *Wadi-Brissa*, 46 *rm* 1 reads šarbu. JASTROW, *Religion*, 243 *rm* 1, connects with š(s)arap(b)u = burn: *i. e.* fiery lord. See also I 65 *b* 48; III 66 *col* 9, 22 (il) NIN-çar-be; Br 10241.

çiribtu fire; fire's heat; fever heat, fever {Brand; Brandhitze, Fieber}. AV 7247. II 34 *a-b* 52—55 (K 4324, 6—9) BAR-TAB-GER (Br 1829); BU (si-ir) (Br 7537); GIG (uš) BAD (Br 9248); GIG-TAB (Br 3769; 9245) = çi-rib-tum ša (xi-bi-eš); see also V 42 *a-b* 47 & ziqittum.

çarbatu *1.* BANKS, *Diss*, 16, 130 kima çar-ba-ti e-di ina kib-ri u-ša-man-ni.

çarbatu *2.* a tree {ein Baum}. V 26 *g-h* 19 (K 4346 iii 3) GIŠ-TIR-GIŠ-A-TU-GAB-LIŠ = kiš-tu(-ti) çar-ba-ti; AV 914, 2904, 4446; Br 7671, 11415. id also Z^B iii 133, & see *ibid* 56 + 80. GIŠ-A-TU-GAB-LIŠ = luluppu (*q. v.*), Br 11414.

çurbu. a plant {eine Pflanze, Gewächs} ZA vi 201 (iv) 5 çu-ur-bi, *ibid* 296 = σεσέλι, ferula asa foetida.

çaraxu, *pr* içrux, *ps* içarrax cry, roar; be excited, rage, be in passion {schreien, toben; aufgeregt sein; in Aufregung geraten} H^V 23; ZDMG 40, 728; ZA i 238 (>< G §§ 40; 48; *Rev. Sém.*, vi 363). K 1282 *R* 18 (amêl) xaumméru ša i-çar-ra-xu ul i-ma-ti ina šib-ṭi (KB vi, 1, 72—3; 387); KB vi (1) 208, 209 (& 468, 469) *ad* NE IX *col* v 35 (end) i-çar-ra-ax, he cries aloud; NE 76, 20 (K 8560): iç-ru-ux-ma. K 494, 7—8 ça-ri-ix a-dan-niš lu ça-ri-ix, Hr^L 19. KB vi (1) 128 *ad* NE I *col* v 1 lu-uç]-ri-ix, I will cry out (in the midst of Erech); preceded by iv 47 da-nu[-niš] lu-qab[-bi-ma]. II 20 *a-b* 14—18 we have ça-ra-xu (*b*) = SAR (14) Br 4333; SAR-SAG (15) Br 4358; SUR (16) Br 2986; H 178, 54; SAR (17); TUK (18) Br 11230. On id in 16 & 17 see H 134. AV 2892. *Ibid* 19 NE = çaraxu [ša lib-]bi, Br 4597; 22—27 (AV 2899) KA-RA-AX (22) Br 690; I+LU-DUB-DI (23) Br 4026; I+LU (du) KA (24) Br 4024; H 38, 104; I+LU-DI (25) Br 4028; I+LU-KA-KA (26) Br 4025; I+LU-DI-DI (27) Br 4029 = ça-ri-xu = crier, herald, *etc.*; 28 ma-aç-ra-xu (*q. v.*, 576 *col* 2). II 34 *g-h* 33 a-ša-ru = ça-ra-xu.

çarbabu see zarbabu. ∾ çirdu see kullu, *p* 383 *col* 1 & M^R 35 *col* 2 (zirdu) ∾ çir-ri-du see puridu.

$\mathfrak{Q}^{t} = \mathfrak{Q}$ IV² 11 *b* 29—30 . . . . iç-çar-ra-ax-šu (= SAR-MU-NA-AN-RA, EME-SAL) qu-bi-e i-qab-bi-šu.

$\mathfrak{P}$ II 67, 77 a-na çur-ru-ux si-ma-a-ti; ROST, 125 (glänzend zu machen × KB ii 23); Br 4024—26.

$\check{\mathfrak{S}}$ roar, cry out (in going to battle) {in Geschrei ausbrechen}. K 8204, 4 u-ta-çal ($\mathfrak{P}^{t}$ of אצל) ra-ma-ni lib-bi u-ša-aç-ra-xa . . . PSBA xvii 137. Sarg *Khors* 127 u-ša-aç-ri-xa taxāza (? KB ii 70, 71; he sounded the battle cry); *Ann* 295: Merodachbaladan . . . . tore his garment . . . . . . and u-ša-aç-ri-xa bi-ki-tu. III 15 i 1.

$\mathfrak{N}$ properly: become alarmed, excited; then to rage, rave {in Unruhe versetzt, aufgebracht werden; toben; *pr* iççarix & iççarux (§ 97). III 15 ii 13 libbi i-gug-ma iç-ça-ri-ix ka-bit-ti; see also i 2. Asurb i 64 eli epšēti annāti libbi e-gug (*var* i-gu-ug)-ma iç-ça-ru-ux (*var*-ri-ix) ka-bit-ti; SMITH, *Asurb*, 38, 10. Bu 88—5—12, 75 + 76 ii (= K 192 *O*) 7 . . . ka-bit-tuš (of Bēl) iç-ça-ri-ix.

$\mathfrak{N}^{tn}$ K 196 iii 28 the owner of the self same house it-ta-na-aç-ra-ax (PINCHES, *Texts*, 11 *fol*).

Derr. maçraxu (?) & these 6:

çirxu cry, howling, lamentation {Schrei, Geschrei, Wehgeschrei}. Sarg *Khors* 78 see sipittu. IV² 11 *b* 33, 34 çir-xa (= SAR-KU, EME-SAL, Br 4333) i-qab-bi; K 4648, 6—7 çi-ir-xa lu-uq-bi-šu. Sm 1366 *O* 14 ša çir-xe (= SAR-RA) gal-lu-u (H 118). T^M v 127 çi-ri-ix libbi-ku-nu u-še-çi; IV² 21* *no* 2 *R* 6 see zamaru $\check{\mathfrak{S}}$, *p* 284 *col* 1 & Br 4333, 6824. I 27, 103 çir-xa ina māti-šu [ukin?-]nu. II 20 *a-b* 20, 21 DUB-DI (Br 7042; see also kandu, 406 *col* 2) & KA-DUB (Br 710 = nagagu) = çir[-ri?]-xu, AV 2994. A ‖ is perhaps:

çurxû. K 494, 11 çu-ur-xi-e, Hr^L 19; &

çarāxu. Bu 88, 5—12, 103, 7—8 ina ug-gat libbi-šu u ça-ra-ax ka-bit-ti-šu, BA iii 224. Also:

çirixtu. Asurb v 37 ina çi-ri-ix-ti libbi-ia, in the anger of my heart, BA i 436; KB ii 199. K 8760 çi-ri-ix-ti libbi, a disease (?; BEZOLD, *Catalogue*, 959).

çirxu, çirixtu, *adj* (?). S^P II 987 *O* 12 a-ri-bi çir-xu tab-bi-ik mar-tum (*Jour. Trans. Vict. Inst.*, xxix, pt 1). IV² 29* 4 C *R* i 3 lis-la-ni-im-ma li-ki-iç-ça-ça (קצץ; IV *R* reads -*a* for -*ça*; see kaçû, 425 *col* 1) iššātu çi-ri-ix-tu ša libbi enā-šu. JOHNSTON, *Johns Hopk. Circ.*, 114 *p* 118: may they (the goddesses) drive away and cut out the raging fire within his eye (or to a çaraxu, 2? see KB vi, 1, 468. 469: sparkle, flicker {funkeln} id. same as zārixu); see above, 296 *col* 2; also KB *loc. cit.* 448. 449 (× JENSEN, 158).

çirxiš *adv* see naxaçu, 665 *col* 1.

çarxu see zarxu, & perhaps K 3183, 14 ça-ri-ix-šu, ZA iv 284.

çurxu arm {Arm}? T. A. (Ber) 104, 14 ç(z)u-ru-ux šar-ri dannu, the strong arm of the king.

çirku *1.* name of a bird {Vogelname}. II 37 *a-c* 45, 46 NER-GID-DA-XU = sa-qa-tum (AV 6588; D^S 116; PSBA xii 181, 182); še-ip a-rik = çir (or, muš?)-ku, which in 47 is also = gam-gam-mu, *q. v.*

çirku *2.* perhaps II 33 *c-d* 7 GAN-GID-DA = çir-ki ki-it-ti, AV 7252; Br 3196. AV 2995 reads II 57 *c-d* 54 AN zi(= çi?)-ir-ku (ilu) Nin-ib.

çarmu. BA iv 289 *fol* reads T. A. (Ber) 58, 29 Abd-aš-ra-ti u a-na [ça-a]r-mi alu(-ki).

çaramu (Br 8743) see zaramu & KNUDTZON, 1 *O* 6 i-çar-ri-mu-u i-kap-pu-du[-u]; they will succeed with their plans; 12 *O* 8; 70 *O* 4; 75, 6; 35, 6; 48, 5 i-çar-ri-i-me; 48, 7 li-iç-rim lik-pid; 38, 2; 43, 13; KNUDTZON, *pp* 139, 140; 314, 315, succeed, accomplish.

çarramu, audacious, THOMPSON, *Reports*; 83—1—18, 198, 12 mātu çar-ra-mu ikašad, an audacious land they will overcome.

çirmalaxxu see NOTE to malaxu, 546 *col* 1; Br 7647.

çarapu *1.* *pr* içrup; *ps* içarrap (?); *pm* çarip. color, dye {färben}, construed with double accus. or ina & ana, § 139. AV 7185. TP iv 20, 21; Anp i 58; ii 17, 18; Asurb iii 43; Šalm, *Mon*, i 47; ii 78; IV² 23 *no* 2 *R* 4, 5 (= TAR-XAR) see

çirmu, çirmû see zirmu (ū) *pp* 296, 297. ∼ ça-ri-mu *cf* za-ri-mu, 297 *col* 1.

nabasu, nabassu, 638, 639. Sarg *Khors* 130; Šalm, *Mon.* ii 50 see nabasiš; Sarg *Cyl* 35 *cf* xamma'u, 320 *col* 2. Anp ii 55, 56 BE^{pl} (= dāmē)-šu-nu | bītāte-šu-nu aç-ru-up (KB i 80, 81); ii 114 dāmē-šu-nu šadu-u aç-ru-up, with their blood I colored red the mountain; Šalm, *Mon.* ii 73 dāmē mun-dax-çe-šu šadu-u aç-ru-up. Pinches, *Inscribed Babyl. Tablets*, *no* 11, 6 (the brick work) i-lab-bi-in-nu u i-çar-rab-bi, they shall build and color it (or √çarabu, burn?). III 9 *no* 3, 55—56 fat sheep ša šipātu-šu-nu ar-ga-man-nu çar-pat (dyed with crimson; AV 7188), winged birds of heaven ša a-gap-pi-šu-nu a-na ta-kil-te çar-pu (= TP III *Ann* 155, 156; KB ii 30, 31). T. A. (Ber) 6 *R* 7 let the wood li-iç-ru[-pu-u], be colored; + 7 (ZA iv 84; v 12 *rm*). — ℑ KB ii 110 *ad* Sn vi 20. see zarabu, 295 *col* 2. — Derr:

çirpu *1. m a)* dyed wool }gefärbte Wolle{. IV² 7 *b* 48 (*cf* 55) šiptu : kīma šipat çir-pi an-ni-i (see napašu, 2, *p* 712) = Z$^{\check{S}}$ v/vi 113 & 120. AV 7254; Hommel, PSBA xix 78 § 22. — *b)* a dyed, colored piece of cloth: garment }gefärbter, farbiger Kleiderstoff{ V 15 *e-f* 15, 16 KU-A-DI-A (Br 11635) & KU-ŠU . . . . RA (Br 7201) = çi-ir-pu; preceded by çibūtum (13) & ši-ni-tum (14): Jensen, ZK ii 26; 28.

NOTE. — On V 15 *e-f* 18, 19, 20, 21, 22, 23 see Br 12064, 12063, 12052, 12049, 12002, 12137.

çurpu. T. A. (Ber) 181, *s* (karpat) rik-ku xu-ur-pi, a vessel with çurpu-spices; perh. rouge? }Schminke?{. Thus √ça-rapu, 1 (?).

çarapu 2. smelt, refine, test }läutern{; Z^B 70; AV 7185 see çurrupu.

Derr. naçraptu and these 4:

çarpu *1.* silver }Silber{ iD KUBABBAR (= kaspu; originally, every kind of precious metal); H 32, 736; 79 *R* 18, 19 see damaqu, ℑ, *p* 254 *col* 1. II 58 *d* 66, 67 see xurāçu. AV 7188; Br 9914—15; 9919. iD + *pl*, Asb v 133. Sarg *Ann* 431 çar-pi ebbi " *Khors* 168 kaspi eb-bi. V 30 *a-b* 53 UD (= BABBAR) = çar[-pu] Br 7793; between par-zi-lu (51—2) & a-na-ku (54. 55); *a-b* 49 see Br 138; also *cf* V 29 *g-h* 47 (Br 13913); KB iii (1) 140 on V 33 *b* 24. — In T. A. (Lo) 5, 19 + 20 (iD); 7, 18 (kaspu) ça-ar-pa usually = money, in general; except 35, 44 xurāça u çar-pa. ZA x 261 *rm* 1.

çurrupu *adj* refined, unmixed, pure }geläutert, lauter{ Z^B 73. IV² 4 *b* 40, 41 ki-ma çar-pi (KUBABBAR) çur-ru-pi, like pure silver; Br 9451. H 41, 259. A | is

çarpu *2. adj f* Z$^{\check{S}}$ iii 21 ma-mit ina kasi (?) la ça-rip-tum me ša-tu-u, a charm caused: by drinking water from an impure cup he solves.

(ilat) **Çarpānītu** (*f* of form *fa'alānū* of çarapu, be pure, shine) properly: the "silverybright one" }eigtl. "die Silberhell-glänzende"{ Jastrow. AV 2910. BA i 195; *Journal of Bibl. Lit.*, xi ('92) 167. Consort of Marduk (see 586, 587); usually called bēlit mātāti, ZA v 57 *foll.* III 66 *col* 11, 28 (ilat) Çar-pa-ni-tum, Br 10240; see also IV² 18 i *O* 10, 11. II 48 *a-b* 37 (ga-ša-run) iD (Br 12223—4) = ilat *Ç*; Bu 91, 5—9, 284 ii 24; BA iv 346 (a Sumerian list); also 380 *no* 4; 403. Z$^{\check{S}}$ ii 153 (= the queen of Esagila); iii 144. Pinches, *Texts*, 16 *no* 4 *R* 4 Zi-ir-pa-ni-tum ru-ba-tum çir-tum lik-tar-ra-ba *etc.* (a late Neo-Babylonian text; the scribe being, no doubt, under the influence of the current etymology).

Rm 76, 4 (il) Marduk u (ilat) Çar-pa-ni-tum; (il) Nabū u (ilat) Taš-me-tum; K 538 *O* 4 (il) Ašur (il) Šamaš (il) Bēl (ilat) Çar-pa-ni-tum. K 646, 3 (il) Marduk u (ilat) Çar-pa-ni-tum (+ 13, end); K 476 *O* 4—5 daily to (il) Bēl (*i. e.*, Marduk) (ilat) Çar-pa-ni-tum I pray; 9 (ilat) *Ç* bēltu çir-ti; Sm 1028, 6—7 a-du-u ū-mu-us-su (il) Marduk u (ilat) Çar-pa-ni-tum . . . . (9. end) u-çal-la [see Winckler, *Forsch*, ii 2, 308; PSBA xxiii 335 on this text] (Hr^{L} 358; 114; 478; 54; 418). Neb 368, 7 in-nu-u (il) Marduk u (ilat) Çar-pa-ni-tum (283, 19—20). Scheil, *Nabd*, viii 33, 34 bīt pi-ris(š)-ti (il) Marduk u (ilat) Çar-pa-ni-tum; 39, 40 (ilat) *Ç* na-ra-am-ti (il) *M.* Agumkakrimē (about 1700 B. C.) often mentions (il) *M* u (ilat) Çar-pa-ni-tum, V 33 ii 10—11, 13, 30. 34, 43—44; iv 40. 41; v 11, 12; vi 30, 31; vii 8, 9. Bu 88—5—12, 75 + 76 vii 41, 42 *M* & *Ç* are called ilāni ti-ik-li-ja; *ibid* v 31 we read šubat (= ri-mit, 19) (il) *M* (u) (ilat) Zēr-bāni-tu (= the begetter of posterity), this the later etymology, on the analogy of zēr-ma-ši-tum; or as Kar-ba-ni-ti, a popular etymology, Asurb i 77; BA i 595 *no* 26; thus also II 67. 12 ana Bēl (*i. e.*, Marduk) (ilat) Zēr-bāni-ti; Ba-ni-tum (Camb 193 *passim*, *etc.*) occurs also as P. N. and may have helped along. JENSEN, ZA iv 352 makes (מִבְנָה) מְנָה = banîtu, an epithet of Ištar.

I 65 *a* 27, 28 ina parakki (il) Marduk u (ilat) Zar-pa-ni-tum bēlē-e-a; 32, 33 bītu a-na Zar-pa-ni-tum be-el-ti-ia ku-uz-ba-am u-za-'-in.

II 59 (*a*-)*c* 50, 51 (ilat) Çar-pa-ni-tum DAM-BI-SAL (*i. e.* consort of Marduk, mentioned in 46—49); see also *l* 55; HOMMEL, *Lesestücke*, 51.

V 46 *c-d* 35—38 we read AN-KUR-NUN-NA-AN-KI (*i. e.* lofty offspring of heaven & earth) Br 1177; AN-NIN-Ê-NA-MA, Br 11050 (II 54 *g-h* 55); AN-NIN-ŠE-NA-UD-DU, Br 11061 (II 54 *g-h* 56); AN-ME-ZU-AB; Br 10386 (II 54 *g-h* 57) = (ilat) Çar-pa-ni-tum. *ibid* 39—45 (39) AN-LA-NA-MUN (Br 1014) = (ilat) Ç NI-TUK-KI (ZA i 265 *rm* 3); (40) AN-E-RU-U-A (V 62 *b* 38; Br 5856; II 54 *e-f* 59) = (ilat) Ç NI-TUK-KI [ZA iv 263; see also V 66 *a* 19, 20 where Nebo is called mâr reš-tu-u ša (il) Marduk i-lit-ti (ilat) Eru-u-a šar-rat pa-ti-qat nab-ni-ti, *i. e.* who causes birth. The popular etymology Zēr-bāni-tum led to the epithet (ilat) E-ru-u-a (הרה); see LEHMANN, ii 36—38 who reads Neb i 23: since bēl (il) Ir-u-a (il) Marduk created me; see also ZA vii 80; on the other hand KB iii (2) 10, 11]; (41) AN-E....RU, Br 5855 (II 54 *c-f* 60; ZA i 265 *rm* 3); (42) AN-NIN-[sign]-GI-[sign], Br 11056, 8804 (II 54 *g-h* 61; 59 *a-c* 50); (43) AN-NIN-TAB-<<. Br 11066 (II 54 *g-h* 62 reading AN-NIN-[sign] [*i. e.* LID]-NIŠ); (44) AN-NIN-ZU-AB, Br 4278, 10993, 7339 (II 54 *g-h* 59 + 63; 59 *a-b* 52); (45) AN-NIN-TE-LA-AM, Br 7712 (II 54 *g-h* 64). II 54 *g-h* 65 AN-E-LA-GU = Çarpānitum NIM-MA-ki (= Êlamti, Br 5852).

V 44 *c-d* 34 AN (?) .... A-EDIN (ZK i 71; Z^B 84 A-RI; ZA i 265 *rm* 3, reading A-RU) = Si-xir (ilat) Çar-pa-ni-tum, Br 11484; also 46 *a* 46; II 56 *c-d* 59. Col. *c* of V 44 is evidently compiled as a sort of cryptogram for (ilat) Çarpānitum, indicating the etymology, current in the days of the Babylonian scribe, *viz* AN = ilat; A = ba-nu-u (*e. g.* H 35, 854); EDIN = çi-e-ru (H 18, 313). — On V 18 *c-d* 27, 28 see xiršu, *p* 341 *col* 2; (ilat) Çar-pa-ni-tum in Sumerian line, 27.

Etymology. — *Berliner Philol. Wochenschr.*, '91 *col* 794 √ çarapu be bright, pure; LEHMANN, ii 37. JENSEN, KB iii (1) 22 *rm*; 200 *rm* 1 & ** (>< ZDMG 49, 3-6) = the goddess of daybreak; also ZA vi 153 & ZDMG 50, 25-, believes in a possible connection of šêru 'morning' and 'morning dawn' and Šerûa = Çarpānitu, >< LEHMANN, who combines Šerûa with Erûa (הרה). — HALÉVY, *Mélanges de critique*, 162; *Rev. crit.*, 23. Je. '90 (*no* 25) *p* 482 would connect with צרפת, the tutelary goddess of Ashkelon in Philistia.

On Çarpānitu & סכות בנות (II Kings 17, 30) see MUSS-ARNOLT, *Jour. Bibl Lit.*, xi ('92) 167. — בנות no doubt, equivalent of Ba-ni-tum: סכות, the Hebr. author may have considered Çar (*i. e.* Zar) as a masculine formation of the Assyrian zarâtu, tent, hut. (*see p* 298 *col* 1).

The name occurs in the pantheon of Xammurabi, JASTROW, *Religion of Babylonia*, 121 *foll*; 449 on Çarpānitum & Zērbānitum: Assyrian Pantheon, *ibid*, 224.

See especially Jeremias' excellent article in ROSCHER's *Lexikon*, II 2370 *foll*: personification of the morning dawn, BA ii 623 *rm*.

G. FOSSEY, *Rev. d'hist. des Religions*, 1900, Mr-Apr., 163 65 believes that A-ru-ru (NE 8, 30 + 33 + 34) is an id A = mâr, aplu; RU (= ŠUB) = nadû; māru & nadû ‖ of zēru & banû; thus A-ŠUB-ŠUB = zēr amēlûti ittišu ibtanû (*cf* Creat.-*frg*, second account, *ll* 20, 21); he suggests as the Assyrio-Babylonian equivalent the name of Çarpānitu. See also BA iii 283.

***çarapu* 3.** perh. II 34 *a-b* 61, 62 çur-ru-pu(bu?) ša abni (Br 5191, 5234, 5235, 7013; AV 6121); 63 uç-çar-rap (IM-IŠ(DA?, Br 5420)-RA-GA'-GA'; perh. ZT in ZK ii 82, 32 GIŠ-GA' = in-na-aç-rip(b)-ma. — **Der.**:

çarpūtu. Bu 88—5—12, 75 + 76 *col* ix 26 mu-šar-e IM çar-pu-ut; BA iii 256—7.

***çarapu* 4.** acquire by purchase, buy }erwerben, käuflich erwerben, kaufen}? often in *c. t.* usually in connection with leqû, 1 Q *b* (see 495 *col* 1); and III 46 *no* 1, 10 the female slave up-pu-šat çar-pat laq-qi-at, was bought, acquired and received; *no* 9, 12 bitu šu-a-ti ça-rip laq-qi; 48. *no* 3, 18; *no* 2, 11 (KB iv 114); 50 *no* 5, 7 bîtâte šu-a-te ça-ar-pu laq-qi-u. Rm 167. 10 nišê šu-a-te çar-pu laq-qi-u (KB iv 120, 121); III 50 *no* 4, 12 eqlu ça-rip la-qi; Rm 2, 19, 10 (KB iv 106, 107); Rm 157, 6 (the money was handed over) *A* ça-rip (was paid) KB iv 124, 125. III 4 *no* 1, 16 ça-ar-pat la-qi[-at], KB iv 100, 101. In Cappadocian inscriptions (KB iv 50 *foll*), DEL., *Kappad. Keilschrifttafeln*, *p* 46, *no* ii 1—3 so & so many shekels za(*i. e.* ça)-ru-ba-am i-çi-ir (= ina çir) Da-ši-ja; *cf no* iii 1—3; *pp* 54—55 *no* viii 6; also *Rec. Trav.*, xviii 74, 1—2: VII 1/2 ma-na kaspi za-ru-ba-am i-zi-ir A-xa-na-ar-si (but KB vi, 1, 371: reines Silber).

Q[1] III 46 *no* 3, 11: *N* has the slave ina libbi (for) . . . ištu pân (from) . . . i-zi (= çi)-rip it-ti-ši (acquired for himself & takes her away); III 49 *no* 2, 10 iç-zi-rip is-si-ik-ki (??).

çarapu *5.* ב IV^2 38 ii 1 *N* as whose grandfather Rimêni-[il]Marduk li-çir-ri-pu-u (is mentioned ??) KB iv 60, 61.

çirpu *2.* V 60 iii 20 see xaçbu, 3 (*p* 332 *col* 1) & perh. zirbu (*p* 296 *col* 1). Br 8491.

çirpu *3.* T. A. (Ber) 188 *R* 3 my messenger brings çi-ir-pa to your city and to your house.

Çariptu, P. N. of town = צרפת: see literature in BROWN-GESENIUS, 868 *col* 2. Sn ii 39 [al] Ça-ri-ip-tu.

çirpêtu, *pl f* (?). II 34 *a-b* 56—58 çir-pi-e-tum = NI-ŠE-RI-A (Br 3363); GA-ŠE-RI-A (Br 6126); GAN-ŠA-LA-LA-RI (Br 4066); AV 7247, 7253.

çurçubbu (?) 82—5—22, 946 *R* 14 DUK KISIM-IMINA-BI = çur-çu-ub[-bu] PSBA xxiii 200; *ibid*, 204 quotes from an unnumbered fragment (1) ur-ru-ub [-bu], (2) ur-çu-ub-bu, (3) çur-çu-ub-bu.

çarçaru *1.* perh. cricket, locust {Grille}? = صَرْصَر. II 5 *c-d* 17 XU-BER-DUB-KA-NA = çar-ça-ru (Br 7033); § 61, 1*a*. See BARTH, *Etymolog. Stud.*, 41 & FRÄNKEL, BA iii 78.

çarçaru *2.* see zarzaru (*p* 296 *cols* 1, 2): AV 2907. Z^{N} 3, 58; MARTIN, *Textes relig.*, 92, 4; 96 √çararu, 2 (?).

çar-çar-tum II 23 *e-f* 58 ‖ ki-iš-tum (*q. v.*), AV 2908.

çararu *1.* *pr* içrur, *ps* içarrur light up, shine brilliantly {aufleuchten, strahlen}. JENSEN, 154 *foll*; *Jour. Asiat.*, '80, *p* 59; 519; ZK i 302; ZA ii 82, 83. BA ii 292 flow, slide along {fliessen, dahingleiten}. See also JENSEN, *Theol. Literaturztg.*, '95 *no* 13: "von gleitendem Wasser, von gleitenden Sternen gesagt, auch vom Huschen auf einen Menschen" (Add. to IV^2 35 *no* 4) id SUR; AV 7186. III 52 *a* 49 [il] Šamaš iš-qam-ma kakkabu iç-ru-ur-ma, lights up, begins to shine; III 52 *a* 1, 2 (*i. e.* K 710) kakkabu SUR (= içrur)-ma çi-ri-ir-šu kîma UD-DA (= urri) na-mir, ina ça-ra-ri-šu kima nam-maš-ti GIR-TAB (= zuqaqîpi) zib-bu ŠA (= iššak)-in (if so, it is a favorable omen); 80—7—19, 59 *R* 2 SUR-ma. K 1304 *R* 6 [il] LU-BAD iç-ru-ur (-ma); see THOMPSON, *Reports*. II 49 *e-f* 19 ça-ra-ar kakkabi (AV 2894) = ni (or çal, zal)-lum-mu-u, *q. v.* JENSEN, 157: a meteor. IV^2 3 *a* 11, 12 the muru qaqqadi ki-ma kak-kab ša-ma-me i-çar-ru-ur (SUR-SUR-RA, Br 2987) = like the heaven's star it flares up. ‖ kîma mê mûši illak. IV^2 20 *no* 3, *O* 15—17 (= BI-IZ-BI-IZ-E-NE, Br 5212) see nataku & dâmu; id BI-IZ-BI-IZ = i-ta-aš[-lu-lu] II 39 *g-h* 36. V 31 *e-f* 12 see mišxu (end) 602 *col* 1, & read muš-xi *aš*-šu ça-ra-ru, Br 7049. ag perh. Sp II 265 *a* v 9 . . . . dir ça-ri-ri i-xi-ṭa a-na šamê(-ma)-mi. On kakkab çâriru see JENSEN, 158, 159.

ℨ 81—2—4, 105, 3—4 (a great star from the north) a-na [šar] šûti | iç-ça-ru-ur, shone to the south, THOMPSON, *Reports*, *no* 201.

Derr. çarru, 1. and possibly maçarru (*q. v.*): çariru, çarûru & çurâru, and these 3:

çirîru see çararu, Q.

çarrûtu. V 31 *no* 3 *e-f* 9 çar-ru-ti (= çari-rûti??) explained by ša bi-ir-çu šak-nu aš-šu kakkab ME-NI-BU (JENSEN, 494); PINCHES, *Texts*, 18, 6.

çirçirru see zirzirru, *p* 296 *col* 2. ~ çirq(k)inu see muškinu. ~ çarartu *cf* çaliptu.

v 31 we read šubat (= ri-mit, 19) (ilu) *M* (u) (ilat) Zēr-bāni-tu (= the begetter of posterity), this the later etymology, on the analogy of zēr-ma-ši-tum; or as Kar-ba-ni-ti, a popular etymology, Asurb i 77; BA i 595 *no* 26; thus also II 67. 12 ana Bēl (*i. e.*, Marduk) (ilat) Zēr-bāni-ti; Ba-ni-tum (Camb 193 *passim*, *etc.*) occurs also as P. N. and may have helped along. Jensen, ZA iv 352 makes (מַבְּנָה) מְנָה = banītu, an epithet of Ištar.

I 65 *a* 27, 28 ina parakki (ilu) Marduk u (ilat) Zar-pa-ni-tum bēlē-e-a; 32, 33 bītu a-na Zar-pa-ni-tum be-el-ti-ja ku-uz-ba-am u-za-'-in.

II 59 (*a-*)*c* 50, 51 (ilat) Çar-pa-ni-tum DAM-BI-SAL (*i. e.* consort of Marduk, mentioned in 46—49); see also *l* 55; Hommel, *Lesestücke*, 51.

V 46 *c-d* 35—38 we read AN-KUR-NUN-NA-AN-KI (*i. e.* lofty offspring of heaven & earth) Br 1177; AN-NIN-Ê-XA-MA, Br 11050 (II 54 *g-h* 55); AN-NIN-ŠE-XA-UD-DU, Br 11061 (II 54 *g-h* 56); AN-ME-ZU-AB: Br 10386 (II 54 *g-h* 57) = (ilat) Çar-pa-ni-tum. *ibid* 39—45 (39) AN-LA-XA-MUN (Br 1014) = (ilat) Ç NI-TUK-KI (ZA i 265 *rm* 3); (40) AN-E-RU-U-A (V 62 *b* 38; Br 5856; II 54 *e-f* 59) = (ilat) Ç NI-TUK-KI [ZA iv 263; see also V 66 *a* 19, 20 where Nebo is called mār reš-tu-u ša (ilu) Marduk i-lit-ti (ilat) Eru-u-a šar-rat pa-ti-qat nab-ni-ti, *i. e.* who causes birth. The popular etymology Zēr-bānitum led to the epithet (ilat) E-ru-u-a (ערוה); see Lehmann, ii 36—38 who reads Neb i 23: since bēl (ilu) Ir-u-a (ilu) Marduk created me; see also ZA vii 80; on the other hand KB iii (2) 10, 11]; (41) AN-E....RU, Br 5855 (II 54 *c-f* 60; ZA i 265 *rm* 3); (42) AN-NIN-[cuneiform]-GI-[cuneiform], Br 11056, 8804 (II 54 *g-h* 61; 59 *a-c* 50); (43) AN-NIN-TAB-[cuneiform]. Br 11066 (II 54 *g-h* 62 reading AN-NIN-[cuneiform] [*i. e.* LID]-NIŠ); (44) AN-NIN-ZU-AB, Br 4278, 10993, 7339 (II 54 *g-h* 59 + 63; 59 *a-b* 52); (45) AN-NIN-TE-LA-AM, Br 7712 (II 54 *g-h* 64). II 54 *g-h* 65 AN-E-LA-GU = Çarpānitum NIM-MA-ki (= Elamti, Br 5852).

V 44 *c-d* 34 AN (?).... A-EDIN (ZK i 71; Z^B 84 A-RI; ZA i 265 *rm* 3, reading A-RU) = Si-xir (ilat) Çar-pa-ni-tum, Br 11484; also 46 *a* 46; II 56 *c-d* 59. Col. *c* of V 44 is evidently compiled as a sort of cryptogram for (ilat) Çarpānitum, indicating the etymology, current in the days of the Babylonian scribe, *viz* AN = ilat; A = ba-nu-u (*e. g.* H 35, 854); EDIN = çi-e-ru (H 18, 313). — On V 18 *c-d* 27, 28 see xiršu, *p* 341 *col* 2; (ilat) Çar-pa-ni-tum in Sumerian line, 27.

Etymology. — *Berliner Philol. Wochenschr.*, '91 *col* 794 √çarapu be bright, pure; Lehmann, ii 37. Jensen, KB iii (1) 22 *rm*; 200 *rm* 1 & ** (>< ZDMG 49, 300) = the goddess of daybreak; also ZA vi 153 & ZDMG 50, 25-, believes in a possible connection of šēru 'morning' and 'morning dawn' and Šerūa = Çarpānitu, >< Lehmann, who combines Šerūa with Erūa (ערוה). — Halévy, *Mélanges de critique*, 162; *Rev. crit.*, 23. Je. '90 (*no* 25) *p* 482 would connect with אטרגתיס, the tutelary goddess of Ashkelon in Philistia.

On Çarpānitu & סכות בנות (II Kings 17, 30) see Muss-Arnolt, *Jour. Bibl Lit.*, xi ('92) 167. — בנות no doubt, equivalent of Ba-ni-tum; סכות, the Hebr. author may have considered Çar (*i. e.* Zar) as a masculine formation of the Assyrian zarātu, tent, hut. (see *p* 298 *col* 1).

The name occurs in the pantheon of Xammurabi, Jastrow, *Religion of Babylonia*, 121 *foll*; 449 on Çarpānitum & Zērbānitum; Assyrian Pantheon, *ibid*, 224

See especially Jeremias' excellent article in Roscher's *Lexikon*, II 2370 *foll*: personification of the morning dawn, BA ii 613 *rm*.

G. Fossey, *Rev. d'hist. des Religions*, 1900, Mr-Apr., 163—65 believes that A-ru-ru (NE 8, 30 + 33 + 34) is an id A = mār, aplu; RU (= ŠUB) = nadū; māru & nadū ‖ of zēru & banū; thus A-ŠUB-ŠUB = zēr amēlūti ittišu ibtanū (*cf* Creat.-*frg*, second account, *ll* 20, 21); he suggests as the Assyrio-Babylonian equivalent the name of Çarpānitu. See also BA iii 283.

çarapu 3. perh. II 34 *a-b* 61, 62 çur-ru-pu(bu?) ša abni (Br 5191, 5234, 5235, 7013; AV 6121); 63 uç-çar-rap (IM-IŠ(DA?, Br 5420)-RA-GA'-GA'; perh. 27 in ZK ii 82, 32 GIŠ-GA' = in-na-aç-rip(b)-ma. — **Der.**:

çarpūtu. Bu 88—5—12, 75 + 76 *col* ix 26 mu-sar-u IM çar-pu-ut; BA iii 256—7.

çarapu 4. acquire by purchase, buy {erwerben, käuflich erwerben, kaufen}? often in *c. t.* usually in connection with leqū, 1 Q *b* (see 495 *col* 1); and III 46 *no* 1, 10 the female slave up-pu-šat çar-pat laq-qi-at, was bought, acquired and received; *no* 9, 12 bītu šu-a-ti ça-rip *çarašu.* 3 see zarašu (297, 298) & papallu. MEISSNER & ROST, 41 *no* 92. Bu 88—5—12, 75 + 76 *col* vii 25 lu-çar-ri-šu pa-pal-lu, BA iii 254, 255: may let sprout the twig }möge ich den Spross gedeihen lassen{; perhaps Aeth. ሠረጸ, Hebr. שׂרין (ROST). ag mu çarrištu (*q. v.*, *p* 576) some instrument; also II 44 *e-f* 46, where it occurs as name of a vessel, Br 879.

Der. — Perhaps çuršu, see zuršu, *p* 298.

çirratu, çirritu 2. rope, reins, or the like }Seil; Zügel, oder dergleichen{ JENSEN, 56, 166 *rm* 3, 340; KB vi (1) 341. AV 8627, 7257. II 44 *a-b* 49, 50 GIŠ-[cuneiform] (Br 8848) = çir-ri-tum (= šibirru, II 28, 60; II 120 *R* 16); GIŠ-TI-BA-KUR-RA = ç i-me-ru = donkey's reins (others: donkey's goad) Br 1706. Here perhaps Asb ix 107 see laxû (478 *col* 1) and nadû, *e* (647 *col* 1). K 2745 ii 2—4 šurrâni ša kibrât arba'i id-du-u çir-ri-e-tu, BA iii 208, 209. Sarg *Cyl* 9; *Khors* 14; *bronze*-inscr. 22; Rp 11 (see xammamu ... KB ii 40, 41). Creat.-*frg* IV 117 = K 3437 *R* 34 see nadû Q¹ *e* (648 *col* 2). D 89 vi 60 see pârisu. Xammurabi-*Louvre* i 14 when Anu & Bêl çi-ir-ra-zi-na ana gâtija umallû, their (the nations') scepter (lit^y: reins) put into my hands (*Rec. Trav.*, ii '79, *pp* 9—11; KB iii, 1, 122); see also KB iii (1) 120 *col* ii 4—5; ZA ii 360. I 69 *c* 26 when Šamaš & Anunit çi-ri-ti ka-la nišû qa-tu-u-a uš-ma-al-lu-u (*cf* V 64 *c* 20, 21) BA i 160 *rm* 2. IV² 18 *no* 2 *R* 13, 14 çir-rit ni-ši li-kil (*cf* kâlu, 379 *cols* 1, 2); also Esh *Sendsch.*, *O* 24 mu-kil çir-rit ma-li-ki. K 13733, 7 t]a-me-ix çir-ri[-ti?], who holds the reins. WINCKLER, *Forsch*, ii 19, 20; 23. — See also LOTZ, *Tigl. Pil. I.*, 183; D^K 75, 58; HAUPT, *Andover Rev.*, July '84. 97.

çurtu 1. knife }Messer{. K 2619 ii 11 (KB vi, 1, 378); Sarg *Ann* 136, see naglabu. √צרר, be sharp (?); & compare צר (E. T. HARPER).

çurtu 2. *c. st.* çurat perh. in Br 13842 (šam) ša-mi(-)çu-rat; 13338 (šam) çur-tu(m; [cuneiform]) AV 2688, 7122.

çirratan, AV 8000, 7255; see çinnitan.

çîtu, çêtu 1. (çi-e-tu) √ça'u. — *a*) devastation, destruction }Verheerung, Vernichtung{ (Sm 787 +) Sm 949 *O* 12, 13 see xulqu (319 *col* 1); KB vi 542 explains it as "wol ein körperliches Leiden". ZIMMERN, *Ritualtafeln*, 45, 12 lu xi-bil-tu lu çi-tu; also perh. çi-ta-a-te in connection with sa-rab-a-te, K 1292. — *b*) some animal, vermin destroying field fruit *etc.* }ein Felder verwüstendes Tier{ ‖ urbatum (see 97 *col* 1; JENSEN in SCHULTHESS, *Homonyme*, 47); AV 7262; Br 14006; D^{Pr} 160 *rm* 2

çîtu or çêtu 2. (> çi'tu) √açû, 1 *q. v.* § 65, 4. AV 7260. — *a*) literally: exit, departure, marching out }Ausgang; Ausrücken{. KNUDTZON, 52 *a* 5 (see *ibid p* 29) UD͡DU (= çî)-ti, of the marching out of the army. II 9 (*a*-)*b* 11 çi-ta ir-ši, he granted exit (?). Perh. NE 76, 20 çi-is-su ki-ma i-ša-ti (?? see çiçîtu). V 27 *a-b* 21 çi-it xur-ri (Br 5084; >< AV 7263) ‖ mu-su-u, *q. v.* & see V 28 *e-f* 11: xu-ur-ri = ana çi-a-tim, Br 2085. II 26 *h* 7 UD͡DU-BA-RA = çi-it. T. A. (WINCKLER) 236 + 229 *a* + 234 + 237, 40 (end) çi-i-it-ta-ka (BA iv 182 = KB vi, 1, 76 *R* 20); Rm 982 (end) çi-ta-šu. Perh. T. A. (Ber) 9 *R* 18 why should not the messengers remain i-na çi-ti (on the march, journey?), also *ll* 21, 23, 26, 29. KB iv 92 *no* ii *R* 3 ana çi-i-ti la uç-çi(?). — *b*) what proceeds from the mouth: word, speech, edict, in çît pî, see pû mouth (788 *col* 1) Br 640, 7886. — *c*) product, offspring, sprout }Produkt, Sprössling{ *etc.* see libbu, 468 *col* 2, below. Br 2252 (*ad* II 9 *c-d* 22), 8005. Also IV² 61 *b* 58 (end)—60 ja-u, çi-it libbi-ja çêra tu-šar-pi-di. KB iii (2) 6 *col* 3, 9; MESSERSCHMIDT, *Nabd*, 64, 25 (-šu). Neb ix 4 (iç) erini dannûti çi-i-ti ša-di-i e-lu-ti, grown on the lofty mountains. Sn *Kui* 4, 12 the gods granted me to see çi-i-su-un. their (the cedars') growth. V 35, 27 Kambuzija mâr çi-it libbi[-ia] says Cyrus; Nabd 380, 6 + 8. II 29 *e-f* 67 çi(!)-i-tu = i-li-it-tum (PINCHES in S. A. SMITH, *Asurb*, ii 68). —

çurîtu see zurîtu, *p* 298 *col* 2. — çarbtu read xarîtu: ça-ri-tum see za-ri-tum, *p* 298 *col* 1. — çir-ri-tum see mušṭal-tum (*cf* mušṭalu √ שׁאל).

d) the going or coming out, in the meaning of beginning of the moon, month *etc.* }Aufgang des Mondes; Beginn des Monats} *etc.* S^b 87 i-tu | iǒ | ar-xu, *var* çi-it arxu; H 12 (Br 971) + 217, 93. On the epithet of Sin = bēl nam-ra-çi-it *etc.* see Sin (769 *col* 1) & namru (686 *cols* 1, 2). — *e*) It is used especially of the coming out, rising of the sun; sunrise }vom Sonnenaufgang} ≍ erēb šamši. $Z^{\check{S}}$ ii 121 ina çi-it (ilu) Šamši(-ši) u ereb (ilu) Šamši(-ši) ša-'-il (IV² 52 *b* 5); IV² 3 *b* 34 iš-tu çi-it (= UD͡DU, Br 7886) (ilu) Šam-ši ana e-reb (ilu) Šam-ši; V 60 *b* 17, 18 (e-re-eb). Anp iii 131, 132; Sarg *Ann* 228; *Khors* 153 (tam-tim ša çi-it (ilu) Šam-ši); *Nimr* 5; ZA iv 414 bel. K 2675 *O* 1 šarrāni çi-it (ilu) Šam-ši u erēb (ilu) Šam-ši; Lay 17, 2 ul-tu çi-it (ilu) Šam-ši a-di e-reb (ilu) Šam-ši; Esh i 7; Sn *Bav*, 18, 19 (ultu *etc.*); KB i 50, 51 *no* 2, 8—9. T^M i 44, 45 where ana çīt (ilu) Šamši is followed by ana çi-it (ilu) Šam-ši. T. A. (Ber) 92 *R* 35, 36 [ištu?] çi-it Šama-aš [a-di] e-ri-bi Šam-ši. K 8474 (K 8182) i 45 (47) see paxaru, Ⓠ; IV² 15 ii 38, 58 (Br 7934), 2?—4 si-bit-ti šu-nu ina šanat(?,d?) çi-it (ilu) Šam-ši ir-bu-u. H 27, 516 ba[-ab]-bar | UD | çi-it šam-ši (Br 7794; ⊕ 59 i 17); V 42 *c-d* 41 AN-UD-UD͡DU = çi-it (ilu) Šam-ši (Br 7934), followed by erēb šamši. — Cyr 281, 5 ina la zi-tu bīt Šamaš (??), BA iii 434. On bīt çīt Šamaš = E-BAB-BAR-RA, II 30 *e-f* 17, see BA i 277; Pognon, *Wadi-Brissa*, 19; Latrille, ZK ii 358, 359. — *f*) Also of the rising of the stars }vom Aufgang der Sterne}. TP vii 100 its walls ki-ma ša-ru-ur çi-it kakkabāni u-si-im, I made brilliant like the (splendor of the) rising stars.

Note. — 1. Jensen, KB vi (1) 343, & ZA xv 243 suggests reading çīd (> çād) šamši = U-UT-KID, 82—9—18, 4159 *R*. √çādu, 2. See çīdānu, 2.

2. For Çēt-napištim see napištu, Note 3 (712 *col* 1).

Derr. the following three:

Çātu *1.*, **çāti** (*pl* of çītu > çiātu, Haupt) ≍ ullu; properly: beginnings, the remote past; then usually: eternity; also the remote future }Anfang; ferne Vergangenheit; später: ferne Zukunft} § 70 *a*, *n* = תאצ. G § 50; ZK i 194; AV 7189; KB vi (1) 398. KB iii (2) 8 *col* ii 20 ana çi-a-tim. used either alone: çāti, or with ūmu : ūm çāti, çāti ūmē; ū-mu ça-a-ti, eternity. 81—6—7, 209, 21 (end) ki-šit-ti ça-a-ti, BA iii 262—3. III 43 i 13 a-na ça-ti i-ri-en-šu, BA ii 116 *foll*, KB iv 68, 69. Sn *Bell* 35, Nineveh tim-me-en-nu da-ru-u du-ru-uš ça-a-ti (*Rass* 62). ZA iv 439 *rm* 2 a-di ça-a-ti-šu, to its (the series' = KU-GAR) end. K 5464 *R* 21 ça-tu, forever (Hr^L 198; PSBA xvii 230 *foll*); K 84 *R* 1 u ša ça-tam (Hr^L 301; PSBA xxiii 344). II 32 *a-b* 25 iš-tu ça-a-ti ‖ [iš-tu] ul-la-nu; ZA v 67, 34 & 28. D 96, 11 lībil ana ça-a-ti. Winckler, *Sargon*, 182, 57 ça-ti-iš = forever (see also M^S 3 *col* 2 *sub* egirtu). KB iv 314, 10 ana ū-mu ça-a-tu (25, -tum); Cyr 277, 12—13. Merodach-Baladanstone iv 55 a-na ūm ça-a-tu (KB iii, 1, 190); also TP v 15, 16 ana arkât ūmē a-na ū-um ça-a-te (viii 50, followed by: a-na ma-te-ma); KB i 12—13, 11 (-ti); V 61 *f* 16. Peiser, KAS 18, 19 a-na ū-mu ça-a-tu; *Vertr*. 96, 7 a-na ūm ça-a-ti; NE 67, 22 ul-tu ū-um ça-at. Nabd 356, 14 ūm ça-a-tu; 564, 6; Neb 115, 13; Nabd 1098, 8 (-tum); Neb 247, 13; 416, 5 (-ti); ZA iv 261, 16. I 34 *c* 66, 67 a-na ū-mi ça-ti; I 35 *no* 1, 22—23. TP iii 74 (78) iš-tu ū-um ça-a-te (*cf* ZA ii 176, 16); V 56. 9 a-na ū-um ça-ti; ZA ii 119 *b* 13 iš-tu ū-mu çi-a-tim; H 40, 218 a-na ū-me ça-a-ti; V 65 *b* 45; IV² 13 *a* 24, 25 (iǒ see Br 7939, 9154); K 22, 24; K 638, 8 (Hr^L 334 *R* 12; 328). K 4874 *O* 1—2 ana ū-mi ça-a-ti. Esh *Sendsch*. *R* 54 ana ça-at ū-mi; TP ii 55 (-me); viii 16 (+ 46 ūmē).

S^c 1 *b* 35 BAR ¦ ba-a-ru ça-a[-tu?]; II 30 *no* 4 *R* 36. Br 1765. V 20 *g-h* 9 UL = ça-a[-tum] Br 9154.

çītan (çītān) & **çītaš** ‖ of çītu, *d-e*). AV 7259. Sarg *Cyl* 57 i-na arax çi-i-tan (taš) arax bi-in (ilu) DARA-GAL (KB ii 48, 49; Winckler, *Forsch*, ii 370—2). See also V 43 *a-b* 9 = Simānu (ZA v 131); Jensen, KB vi (1) 348; ZK ii 312. — Usually found together with (rather in contrast to) ši(l)lān. § 80*c*: from beginning to end; from top to bottom. K^M 9, 41 o Lady çi-ta-aš u ši-la-an, the mistress of Bēl. I 7 F 9 ul-tu çi-tan a-di šil-la-an = ul-tu ri-eš a-di q(k)i-it, from beginning to end, Br. M. 49934 *R* 5. Sarg *Silber-inscr.* 4—5 Sargon a king who ul-tu çi-ta-an a-di šil-la-an has taken possession of the four regions; *gold*-inscr. 5 *fol* (çi-tan); *Khors* 165, 166 dadmē mātitān ša ul-tu çi-tan a-di šil-la-an .... ak-šud-du-ma; *Ann* 428. Rm III 105, 10 i-na çi-tan u šil-la-an. V 42 *c-d* 43—44 GIŠ-NUM (Br 5718) = çi-tan (usually = eliš); GIŠ-SIG = ši-la-an (usually = šapliš); ZA i 184 *rm* 1; 393 *rm* 1. (zenith & >< horizon).

çītan. Meissner & Rost, 68, 9: Culminationspunkt; Jensen, ZA ix 130 = East (>< *Kosmologie*, 13 *fol*); see also ZA v 131; vi 170 *rm*; xv 248 *rm* 1: Ostgegend, Gegend des Aufganges. Hommel, *Expository Times*, July 1897: šīlān & çītān were with the Babylonians the two culminating points: šīlānu, the southern one under the earth; çītān, the northern one over one's head = Zenith.

çātum *2.* V 31 *a* 11 ça-a-tum ša duppi XVIII: extracts of the XVIII tablet (?) AV 7189. *Cf ibid a* 37 ça-a-tum u šu-… pi-i ša duppi XXVII. ZK ii 74.

çutammu. some official {ein Beamter} Asb ix 50 see nidnu, 654 *cols* 1, 2 where read *çu*-, not *šu*-.

P.

QA, a measure {ein Maass} K[M] 22, 31 (a QA of qēmu); 62, 25; K 13, 56 (IIr[L] 281); K 629 *R* 8 (IIr[L] 65); K 871, 11; K 742, 8; K 750, 14. AV 7206. Lehmann in Meissner, 98 *foll.* Thureau-Dangin, ZA xvii 94.

-qu = -ku in Old-Babylonian. 2 *sq.* Meissner, 106; BA ii 559.

qū (gū) *1.* *m* cord {Garn, Faden, Schnur} Z[B] 103; *gen* qē; *acc* qā; *pl* qē; id GU, Br 11139; § 114 *rm.* IV² 6 *a* 15, 16 amēlu šū ina ni-ši qa-a e-ša-a ana šēti tar-çu, has spread a destructive cord as a net; KB vi (1) 335: eine kreuz und quer gelegte Schnur; 8 *b* 30—1, 36—7, 40—1 qa-a çi-ra qa-a raba (*var* ra-ba)-a qa-a bit-ru-ma qa-a munaššir, *etc.*; Jensen, *Diss*, 72—3; *b* 42—3 ma-mit qa-a-ša ana çe-rim aš-ri el-li li-še-çi; 28—9 qa-a eç-pa (& 5 iii 31); 17 *b* 17 Šamaš mu-šal-li-tum ki-e lum-ni, who cuts off the rope of the evil. K[M] 62, 11; Z[S] v/vi 151, 153, 159, 165. T[M] vii 106 liššānki ša limuttim ina qi-e lik[-ka-çir] + 113. Inscr. of TP III (Zürich) 8 it-gu-ru-ti ki-ma ki-e u-šal-li-tu-ma, PSBA xviii 158—9. H 89, 45 ki-e na-b[a-si] el-lu-ti, pure cords made of *u* (*q. v.*) Br 11150. IV² 22 *a* 29 ....ta ki-ma ki-e me-xi-e i-par-ra[-'-?]. K 7592 + K 8717 + DT 363 *R* 6 šu-uš-ru-xu qi-e, strong are the cords. Perh. K 3474 i 37 (= K 3182 i 39) .... ki-ma ki-e ka-sa-ta (but??). K 3456 *O* 33 (amēl) naggaru mu-du-u it-ta-rak(q) qi-e .... PSBA xxi 38—9. V 15 *c-d* 53 qu-u preceded by kan-nu & nallūtu (*q. v.*); here perh. = זק, fetter. Also *cf* ZA x 211, 14. A ‖ is perh. qītu (*q. v.*). *adv*:

qūiš Sn v 77 (gu-'-iš) see parū, 1 ב. § 80 *b*; BA i 451, 456 *rm.* another *adv.*

qieš see qidēš.

qū, gū *2.* see gū, 2 (208 *col* 1) id GU. Jensen, 497; Halévy, *Rech. crit.*, 232. Ball, PSBA xvi, 196 *fol*: comfrey, *ad* IV² 27 *a* 12, 13 qu-u ša ina mu-sa-re-e (see musarū, 1) mē lā ištū, Br 1138. Sn *Bav* 7 ša-ta-a ki(or ṭi)-e (-) it-tu-ti, the plants drank ittūtu (but??; see ṭīṭu, *b*, 355 *col* 1). V 21 *e-f* 8 SAR = qu-u (7 = še-im; 10 = ar-qu) AV 7393, Br 4321. K[M] 12, 30 xa-a-a-aṭ (11) aš-na-an u (11) la-xar ba-nu-u še-am u ki-e mu-diš-šu-u šam urqītu; K[M] =

çi-tu Meissner, 104 *rm* see zittu, 1 (296 *col* 2). ~ çu-u-tum AV 7206, Br 9077 *ad* V 29 *e-f* 31 read çu-u-xu, (*q. v.*). ~ çatrū *cf* satrū, 299 *col* 2, & Br 8460.

barley. Rm 201 *R* 3 u qu-u la išširu *pl*, THOMPSON, *Reports*, ii *no* 181: vegetables?

qû *3.* II 33 *a-b* 73 GU = qu-u together with nu-šu-u (*q. v.*) & ga-'a-u. Br 1139, 14471. D^{Par} 142, 13; AV 7393.

qû *4.* IV^2 49 *a* 9 qu-u im-ta-na-al-lu-u pi-ia. T^M = qû, 1.

qû *5.* bronce {Bronze}? ideogram UD-KA-BAR which = siparru, Br 7814/5. read thus V 23 *g-h* 12 qu[-u] ZA viii 75—6. usually as ki-e maš-ši see maššu, 1 (597 *col* 1) & mašašu (612, 613). Probably = qû 1. perh. here also NE I 11 ša ki-ma qi-e ni[-]-?-s[u] KB vi (1) 116—7; 424.

qa'u 1. (קוה) ℶ pr uqî (ukkî); ps uqâ wait, await {warten, erwarten} AV 7814; Z^B 16; BA i 451. BROWN-GES., 875 *col* 2. TP i 72 arka-a ul u-qi, I did not hesitate. III 15 i 10 one day (or much less) two days ul uq-ki, I waited not, § 127; thus SMITH, *Asurb*, 246 *b* ul u-qi. K 706, 1 when the moon la u-qi-ma, does not wait for the sun. IV^2 34 *no* 2, 2 (end) ina (al) Zaq-qa-lu-n tu-ki-i-an-ni; 6 (*med*) u-ki-ia-an-na-ši. SMITH, *Asurb*, 134, 52 the two magnates ša ina maxri-ia ak-lu-u (√kalû) u-qa-'u-u pa-an ši-kin ṭe(-e)-me-ia, KB ii 256—7; BA i 485; § 13; ZA vi 207. V 63 *a* 28 to rebuild this temple Marduk the great lord u-ga-a-an-ni (awaited me); V 65 *a* 27 Šamaš the lofty lord .... ia-a-ši u-qa-ma-an-ni, ZK ii 239; ZA ii 260; 278; iii 14 *rm* 1; 298; §§ 49*a*; 115. KB iii (2) 90, 9 u-qa-a-ma-an-ni, he commanded me. SCHEIL, *Nabd*, x 5 my lord Marduk u-ga-'-an-ni-ma. Perh. K^M 8, 8 u-ki-' qaqqada-ki; K 8204, 3 u-qa-a-u ka-a-šu (§ 18), I wait for thee. NE 52 (*no* 24) 48 u-qa-a-a. KB vi (1) 48, 17 ni-rib q(k)i-iç-çi .... u-qa-a-a. K 2660 (III 38, 2) *R*? u-ki-šu, I awaited him. KB iii (1) 111, 14—15 at-ta ma-an-nam tu-ga-a. IV^2 23 *no* 2 *O* 8 u-qa-a-kâ (3 *sg*), Br 9005. K 3456 *O* 34 i-da-ki ku(qu?)-bu-ru-ni-ma u-qa-a-u, PSBA xxi 38—40; L^4 iii 13 u-qa-'-u. Rm III 105 i *b* 13 šip-ri ša-a-ši u-qa-a-a-an-ni-ni ušadgil pânija, WINCKLER, *Forsch*, i 254—55; JRAS '92, 350 *foll.* KB iii (2) 64, 11 u-ga-a-am ša-aš-ši, I waited for the sun; perh. KB iii (1) 206, 11 my brother li-iq-qa, may be patient {möge sich geduldeu}. T^M vii 152 u-qa-a-ka. T. A. (Lo) 16, 38 u-qa-mu, I am expecting (BEZOLD, *Diplomacy*, xxxvii). V 45 vii 39 tu-qa-a-'a. VATh 244 i 8 u-qa-a (ZA ix 156 × *ibid* 110). — Where belongs II 19 *a* 43 (il) A-nun-na-ki ilâni rabûti qa-'u ir-ru-šu.

qâ'u 2. (קיא?) spit {speien}. Z^Š iii 59 ma-mit nâru ša-a-nu u nâru ka-a-a, Bann durch: in einen Fluss pissen oder in einen Fluss speien.

qi-a-šu *1.* surname {Beiname} §§ 12 & 64; קיש, Br 1243. V 27 *g-h* 48 MU-AŠ-AŠ = ki-a-šu, preceded by MU (= šûmu) a-xu-u. AV 4558. BEZOLD, *Catalogue*, 518.

qi-a-šu 2. K 4219 *O* 8 qi-a-šu = ša-ra [-qu?) M^S texts, pl. 10. See qâšu, 1.

qaâtum. Cyr 80, 9: III GUR a-na qa-a-a-tum ..... ša bît Bêlit Sippar.

qâbu. small water ditch; reservoir {kleiner Wassergraben; Reservoir}? S^b 244 (H 22, 429) e | E | qa-a-bu, Br 5842. same ideogram = ik(q)u; AV 7302; JENSEN, ZK ii 17 (= *Diss* 47); D^{Par} 142—3 *no* 39; D^{Pr} 113 *rm* 2. A ‖ is:

qabû *1.* S^b 245 (water)reservoir {(Wasser)-behältnis} Z^Š iii 39 ma-mit: qa-bi-e ša-'-a-lu u na-ka-ru; Nabd 558, 12 u 𒐀 ša qa-bu-e.

qabû 2. (קבא) ℶ V 45 iii 29 tu-qam-ba-'.

qabû *3.* stable, fold, pen {Stall, Hürde} *etc.* AV 3903. 80, 11—12. 9 iv 15 (ba-ru-un) 'U = qa-bu-u ‖ ki-sil-lum, Br 10248. II 38 *g-h* 27 see piqannu, Br 10247. Camb 194, 2 ina UZ-TUR-XU qa-bi-e (im Gänsekoben) + 10 nikûsu ša qa-bi-e. does this perhaps explain II 60 *no* 1 (K 4334) *R* 14 .... UZ qa-bi-e ša ina ba-çi šu-nu-lu? — Connected with qabû is:

qabûtu *1.* II 38 *g-h* 29—30 ['U?]-GUD = ka-bu-ut al-pi; ['U-IMÊ]R = *k* i-me-ri, Br 14145. Cyr 206, 9 (Camb 239, 2) ina maxar (amêl) rê'ê ša qa-bu-tu ina bît karê. Nabd 296, 6 the lambs are given to *NN* a-na qa-bu-ut-tum; 312, 7 a-na qa-bu-ut; 1043, 2. ZA iv 119 *no* 15, a list of cattle is summarized as the qa-bu-ut Ia-a-bi-bi.

qabûtum *2.* Br.M. 84, 2—11, 342, 12: II-ta ka-a-su A (= mê) ša qa-bu-tum mu-ki-in-ni = PEISER, *Babyl. Vertr.*, *no* 121. *pl* perh. qabuâte cups, goblets {Becher} Šalm *Ob* relief inscr. II: qa-bu-a-te (iç) xurâçi; KB i 150; KAT^2 208; Scheil, *Šalm*, 72—3; 90; Hommel, *Gesch*, 612, 613. Barth, *Etym. Stud.*. 8. ZA ix 185 *no* 12; K 164, 29 (end) ^{karpat} qa-bu-tu (BA ii 636).

qabbu (?) KB vi (1) 372 *ad* 58, 5 siba(-a) q(g)ab-ba(-)ma(-)me, *cf* Hebr קַב; *pl* perh. Nabd 973, 13: li-ta qa-ab-ba-a-tum. On Nabd 606, 10 see Peiser, *Vertr.*, 206.

NOTE. — 1. On the qâbu (qabbu?) ša šarri in Nineveh see Oppert, ZA xiii 256—7.

Has ki-be siparri, Anp iii 66 (KB i 108 & *rm* 1), preceded by nirmakâti siparri. some connection with the preceding words? It belongs to the u-nu-ut škalli.

qebû 1., qabû 4. (§ 34β; K^M 27, 14 qa-bu-u); AV 7803. *pr* iqbi (iq-bi, I 49 *c* 19; § 34*a*; 2*sg m* ša taq-bu-u), *ps* iqabbi (Babyl. i-ga-ab-bi, § 48); *ip* qibî; *pm* qi-bi, qa-ba (T. A.). *idd* KA, Br 531; BI (= KAŠ) Br 5124; DI, Br 9528. — *a*) speak, say, announce {sprechen, sagen, verkünden} § 84. H 120 *R* 4 ana a-ma (*char.* pi)-at ^{ilat} ištar iq-bu-u (Z^B 87); 123 *R* 10 iq-bi-ki (3*sg f*). K 2619 *v* 7 the words which Išum iq-bu-šu, spoke to him; followed by (8) u ki-a-am iq-ta-bi, and thus spoke. IV^2 22 *a* 53 a-di-ši-na iq-bi-šum-ma, Br 6648. Asb iii 7 ki-i (ša) ..q-bu-u (as I said) I shall do; iv 14 the king of Elam me-ri-ix-tu (*q. v.*) iq-bu-šu (+ 18, iq-bi); v 99 ki-a-am iq-bi-šu-nu-ti um-ma. K 41 *c* 15 aq-bi-ma, I said. VATh 575, 5 never aq-bi-qu-ma + 9 (BA ii 561, 562); 574, 16 lu-uq-bi-ma, I will speak (*ibid* 560, 561). K 13, 27 aq-bak-ku-nu-šu um-ma (§ 56*b*); K 625 *R* 12 ..... di-ib-bi iq-ba-na-ši-ni, was said unto us; (Hr^L 281, 131). Neb i 54 ššâšu aq-bi-iš (Schmidt, *Nabd*, vi 30). Smith, *Asurb*, 123, 47 la tapallax iq-ba-a, fear not, she said. Sp II 265 *a* ii 1 na-a-a-du eb-ri ša taq-bu-u i-dir-tum. 3 *pl*: iq-bu-u, KB ii 256—7, 76; III 15 *a* 25; V 65 *a* 37 ja-a-ti iq-bu-nu, they said unto me. — *pc* ZA v 146, 24 li-iq-ba-ak[-ku], he may confirm it to thee (T. A.); IV^2 49 *a* 55 liq-ba-nik-kim-ma, let them say to thee (but thou shalt not listen to them). Sp III 5866 + R III, 1, 3/4 šul-mu liq-bu-qu, may give thee greeting (ZA iii 40 on qabû šulmu or šulum, often in Asurb). V 35, 35 li-iq-bu-u, may they say; liq-bi-ku IV^2 59 *a* 7 + 8 (§ 56*b*); liqbika (often) see nâxu, 1 (661 *col* 2). Sp II 265 *a* i 1 (end) lu]-uq-bi-ka, *cf del* 10 (end), §§ 93, 1*b*; 135. II 51 *b* 12 liq-bu-u; K 82, 4 (Hr^L 275). H 116 *O* 16 teslîtim lu-uq-bi. — *ps* I 27 *no* 2, 63 whosoever: "a-na-ku la i-di" i-qa-ab-bu-u. I 70 *b* 18 (i-gab-bu-u); III 41 *b* 7; 43 *c* 6, 7, 17 (§ 142). IV^2 30* *b* 19, 20—23, 24 ina bîtu luzziz ... la ta-qab-bi (= NAM-BA-AB-BI-EN); *del* 32 (33) at-ta ki-a-am ta-gab-ba-aš-šu-nu-ti. ZA iv 15, 16 ta-qab-bi: nis-su. Smith, *Asurb*, 124 (III R 32) 61 at-ta ta-qab-bi-ši um-ma, thou sayest to her, KB ii 252, 253. — Bu 88—5—12, 21, 17—18 thou art not my husband i-ga-bi-i-ma (JRAS '97, 610, 611; Meissner, *no* 89); IV^2 11 *a* 31, 32 (29, 30) thus ul i-qab-bi (NU-MU-NI-EB-KI, EME-SAL); 10 *b* 5, 6 un-ni-ni a-qab-bi (= NE-RA-AB-BI, EME-SAL); 61 *a* 17 a-a-u-te di-ib-bi-ja ša aq-qa-ba-kan-ni, which I speak to thee (*a* 48 a-qa-ba-kan-ni). S^P 158 + S^P II 962 *O* 25 a-mat i-qab-bi-šu, a command he gives unto him. KB iv 88 *col* 3, 1 whosoever ... i-qab-bu-u, says. K 883, 8 (end) i-qab-bu-u-ni. III 16 *no* 2 (K 1619, 13; Hr^L 308) 5 u-la-a i-qab-bi-u (people might say); *ibid* 4 im-bu-ki la ta-qab-bi-i. JAOS xx 244—249. Beh 1, 2, 3, 4 *etc.* Darius the king ki-a-am i-qab-bi, spake thus; also 90, 91, 92, see paraçu, 1 ℑ^t. K 5291 *O* 10 whatever I hear, to the king a-qab-bi, I will tell, Hr^L 317; III 43 *c* 7 who i-qa-bu-u, 3 *sg* (+ 16 + 17); *Adapa*-legend (*no* II) *O* 27 a-na $^{(il)}$ A-ni i-ga-ab-bu-u (3 *pl*); see *R* 20; *O* 33, 34 a-ma-ta ša aq-ba-ku; K 2527 + K 1547 *O* 42 a]-ma-tum i-qab-bi. K 257 *O* 53, 54 ša sar-rat(-)mi i-qab-bu-ni (H 127). K 125, 18 ni-qa-bu-u-ni, we have told (Hr^L 196; PSBA xvii 236, 287); 20, the merchants iq-ţi-bu-u-ni, have said. K 539 *R* 8 ina pa-an šarri ni-qa-bi (Hr^L 206). i-qa-bu-niš-šu-un-ni, Knudtzon, *no* 48, 4; probably suffix of 3 *sg* as šu-ni in Anp ii 34 + 77; Šalm, *Mo*, ii 36 (Knudtzon, *p* 152). — pa-a-šu e-pu-uš-ma i-qab-bi, often (§ 152); IV^2 31 *O* 31; *R* 29 & see zakaru. — pm Nabd-Cyr. Chron. *R* (iii) 19, 20 Cyrus šu-lum ana ... qi-bi, BA ii 222, 228. — ip NE XII *col* iv 1 ki-ba-a ib-ri ki-ba-a ib-ri; 8, ul a-qab-ba-ku eb-ri ul a-qab-ba-ku; 21 (end) a-qab-bi-ka (KB vi. 1, 263—5). K 4623 + 79—7—8, 24 (H 122) 15 qi-bi-šu (also, 13), say unto him (thy heart be at rest); II 115 *R* 6 = IV^2 29^{**} *no* 5, ki-bi(-ma). Schen., *Nabd*, vi 28 qi-ba-a | ia-a-ši; K 112 *O* 18 ana pān ikkari qi-i-bi (or pm?) Hr^L 223. BA ii 559 on ki-be-ma um-ma in Old-Babylonian letters, written ki-bi-ma (K 2641 = III 4 *no* 5). — ac IV^2 27 *no* 3 *a* 41, 42 e-piš-ti ul ša qa-bi-e. Perh. Sp II 265 *a* ii 6 (end) qa-bu-u ul-tu ul-la (ZA x 3, 4). — *b*) speak aloud, cry {lautsprechen, schreien}. III 15 *a* 25 ina puxrišunu iq-bu-u um-ma (he is our king!); IV^2 11 *b* 33, 34; K 4648, 6—7 see çirxu. — *c*) ina libbi (*q. v.*) qubū = to converse with one's heart, *i. e.* think, consider (BA i 188); K 2401 iii 6 ma-a ta-qab-bi-a ina libbi-ku-nu, BA ii 628 *foll.* Asurb v 25 ki-a-am [iq]-bi [it-ti] lib-bi-šu um-ma. thus he thought within himself (= אָמַר בְּלִבּוֹ). — *d*) call, name {nennen}. II 67, 10 til xam-ri ša [(al)] Xu-mut(d) i-qab-bu-šu-u-ni, which they call X. — *e*) order, command {befehlen} TP ii 100 to increase his territory iq-ba-a, he commanded; i 49 thus iq-bi-u-ni (*var* iq-bu-ni) *i. e.* the gods [§ 38]; vi 28 see nabalu, 1 Q (636 *col* 2); vii 75 iq-bu-u-ni (3 *pl*). I 27 *no* 2. 79 when any one .... i-qa-ab-ba-aš-šu, orders him; I 28 *a* 13 iq-bi-u-ni-šu, they commanded him. V 33 *a* 50 Marduk [ta]-ar-šu iq-bu-u, commanded his return to Babylon. Esh *Sendsch*, *R* 36, 37 since Ašur .... iq-bu-u-ni (3 *sg*). *del* 28 (33) u-mu-u]r be-li ša taq-ba-a at-ta (KB vi, 1, 232); D 101 *frg* 17. V 64 *a* 24 ša taq-bu-u epešu, which thou commandedst to build. K 883, 14 ..... šu-ni-tu laq-bak-ka ma-a (BA ii 633). NR 24 what X a-qab-ba-aš-ši-na-a-tu (§ 56*b*). *Rec. Trav.*, xx 57 *foll*, *col* vii 14 a-bu-bu ša ta-ga-ab-b[u-u] 2 *sg*; KB vi (1) 290—1. 83—1—18, 41 *R* 1, whatsoever the king i-qab-bu-u-ni (Hr^L 375; AJSL xiv 11); Bu 91—5—9, 210 (Hr^L 403) 10 man-di-e-ma ta-qab-ba-a. Knudtzon, 48 *O* 4 & 8 i-qa-bu-niš-šu-un-ni; *ibid p* 23 qa-bi-i (= pm). V 61 iv 5, 6 ša epi-eš çal-mi šu-a-tum | qa-bu-šum-ma. KB iv 34 i 5 a-na ga-bi-e, at the order of ..... Nabd 1000, 1 ina qi-bi ša. *del* 113 (120) when .... aq-bu-u limuttu; 114 (121) ki-i aq-bi; 115 (122) qab-la aq-bi, I ordered the storm. Creat.-*frg* IV 22 (+ 24) qi-bi (= command!); 25 (26) iq-bi. V 34 *c* 51 ki-be-i, command!—especially in connection with alaku, to march. Šalm, *Balaw*, IV 2; TP iii 39, 40 a-na a-la-ki iq-ba-a (*i. e.* Ašur); V 35. 15 to Babylon a-la-ak-šu iq-bi. — Neb *Bab*, ii 29 qi-be li-it-tu-u-ti (‖ i-be, √קבא). — *f*) promise {versprechen}. Nabd 760, 18 ša taq-bu-u, who had promised. K 245 ii 58—61 (= II R 8) qa-ba-šu (= DUG-DUG-GA-NI, Br 576) id-din | it-ta-din | iš-kun; literally: he did (made) his word (*i. e.* he did as he had said). III 66 *O* 28*c* [(il)] qi-bi du-um-qi (+ *R* 29*f*) Br 13544. I 51 *no* 1 *b* 28 ki-bi (*var* -be) du-um-ku-u-a, *etc.* (& see dumqu, 255—6) V 47 *a* 30 a-na qa-ab(p?) dam-qātija; *cf* IV^2 54 *no* 2 *O* 45 [(il)] Guzalū qa-ab damqāti (also *l* 21), who commands good things; see also damiqtu. II 58 *a* 12 [(il)] iq-bi da-mi-iq. V 64 *b* 41 li-iq-bu-u (3 *pl*) damiq-tim. — K 4335 iii 3 ....] KA = qa-bu-u. II 39 *no* 2 *O* (= ⊕ 59 i) 7—8 MU-UN-NI-KA = ki-bi-šu; U-MU-UN-NI-KA = ki-bi-šum-ma. S^c 321 (H 11 & 208, 47) KA = qi-bu-u. V 39 *a-b* 32 KA-KA-GA = (amātum) qa-bu-u (Br 580; Z^B 84; 87); 33, KA-DI-KI (Br 748) = the same. Also see *ll* 34 (Br 580) & 35 (Br 656). In P. N. often iq-bi & qi-bi. AV 5719. Nabū-balasu (> balaṭ-su) iq-bi, V 44 *c-d* 8, Br 7906.

Q^t *a*) speak, say {sprechen, sagen, reden} K 619, 9 iq-ṭe-bi ma-a; K 666 *R* 9; K 983 *R* 5; K 82. 16 iq-ta-bu-nu-um-ma (BA i 242; § 90*c*); K 539 *R* 10 nī-iq-ṭi-bi ma-a; K 524, 20 iq-ta-bu-niš-šu um-ma; K 621, 9 i-qi-ṭi-bu-ni-šu ma-a; K 5464 *R* 20 iq-ṭi-bi-a (he has said); K 1227 *R* 7 aq-ṭe-ba-šu-nu-ni (I said to them) = Hr^L 174; 12; 35; 275; 206; 284; 515; 198; 314. K^M 11, 25 iq-ta-ba-an-ni-ma. IV^2 61 *c* 39 la ta-pal-lax šarru aq-ṭi-ba-ak .(§ 56 *b*). K 883, 12 (ilat) Bēl]-tu taq-ti-bi; ZA iii 395, 26 aq-ta-ba-aš-šu (*ibid* 28). ZA v 59, 13 (K 7592 + K 8717 + DT 363 *R*) qaq-da-a ṭa-biš liq-tab-ba. III 51 *no* 9, 21 iq-ṭi-bi-u-ni-ma-a = I said, and. When so & so says (iq-ta-bi) thus, V 25 iii 25, 30, 37, 43; iv 5, 11 (§ 142). — *b*) command, order {befehlen} K 486 *R* 1 a-na-ku aq-ṭi-bi, I have ordered it at once (Hr[L] 303). Šalm, *Balawat*, V 4 a-na Bābili iq(-ta)-bi a-la-ku. SCHEIL, *Nabd*, x 30 (Marduk) iq-ta-bi. — c) promise {versprechen} K 3364 *R* 26 šum-ma taq-ta-bi-ma (2 *sg*) i-din.

𝔔[tn] K 2852 + K 9662 i 7 (end) iq-ta-nab-ba-a a-xu-lap. K 126, 7 (end) zi-karu ana aššatišu .... ki-bi (*var* bit)-su iq-ta-nab-bi.

𝔍 scream, lament, cry {schreien, wehklagen, rufen} V 45 viii 52 tu-qab-ba. *ac* qub(b)ū, used as a noun, *q. v.*

Š speak {sprechen, sagen} K 6172, 8 sibitti šanītu ana pān (il) Šamši tu-šaq-ba-šu, FOSSEY, JA '02, Mr., 864—5: sept fois ... tu lui ferns dire (ces paroles). AV 7303 (end) u-ša-aq-bu-šu a-na *etc.* — let command {befehlen lassen} KNUDTZON, *no* 122 *O* 6 u-ša-qa-ba-a.

𝔑 *a*) be spoken, be said {gesprochen, gesagt werden} IV[2] 21* *no* 2 *O* 30, 31 (32) heart, be quiet again .... liq-qa-bi-šum (let it be said to him) Br 11238; IV[2] 15* i 45, 46 (end) liq-qa-bi (Br 9413); IV[2] 13 *b* 42, 43 ba-la]-ṭu iq-qab-bi (Br 2213; 9528) ši-i lu-u ki-a-am. — *b*) be commanded, ordered {befohlen werden}. K 2852 + K 9662 ii 35 iq-qa-bi ša-lal niše-ka (§ 110). NR 10 ša la-pāni-ja at-tu-u-a iq-qab-ba-aš-šu-nu, whatsoever has been commanded them by me. — *c*) proclaim {ausrufen, proklamieren} S 954 *R* 4 šar-rat šame-e e-liš u šap-liš liq-qa-ba-a ta-na-da-tu-u-a (D 136).

NOTE. — T. A. has these forms: 𝔔 *pr* 3 *sg f* ti-iq-bu-na (Lo 45, 29); te-iq-bu-na (Lo 16, 10; 43, 16); 2 *m* ti-iq-bi (Lo 14, 45). tiq-bu (Lo 15, 7); 1 *sg* iq-bi (Lo 20, 57); iq-bu (Lo 43, 25). — *ps* 2 *sg m* ti-qa-bu (Lo 61, 28); ta-qa-ah (Lo 1, 35) & the regular taqábi, often. 3 *pl m* i-qa-ab-bu-u; i-ga-ab-ba-aš-šu, ZA v 40, 22. 1 *sg* a-qab-bi-i (Lo 8, 49). — *pc* (Lo) 82, 32 a-ma-ta lu-uq-ba-a-ku (BA iv 130, 131); *pm* ana *NN* qi-be-ma (ZA v 150); 2 *sg m* qa(b)-ba, qa-bi(be)-me *etc.* — 𝔔[t] a-ka-an-na aq-ta-bi (& I said thus); aq-ta-ba-aš-šu (ZA v 156, 157 *rm* 2); iq-ta-ba-a, ZA v 140, 19; iq-ta-pi (Ber) 22, 14; i[q-t]a-bi (Ber) 236 + 1617 + WA 289 β, 13 (BA iv 123); ta-aq-ta-bi, thou hast said; ni-iq-ta-bi Ber 8, 10 (ZA v 146).

DERR. — qabū 5, qibū 2 (?), qubbū 1, qubbūtum, qibītu.

qabū 5. *noun.* speech, word {Rede, Wort} NE VI 178 iš-me-ma (il) Ea-bani an-na-a qa-bi-e (ilat) Ištar, when *E* heard this word of Ištar (§ 57 *b*); NE I *col* iv 40 (KB vi, 1, 138—9) ma-gir qa-ba-šu (*var* qa-ba-a-a). I 44, 72 (abanu) qa-bi-e ma-ga-ri *etc.* (an amulet?); K[M] 9, 19 see magaru 𝔔 (end) *p* 511 *col* 1 (below). II 35 *g-h* 44 (see magrū, 512 *col* 1, bel). Perh. II 47 *e-f* 23 UD-DU = ki-i qa-bu-u, Br 7878. II 8 *e-f* 57 *foll* qa-ba-šu, his command (AV 7297; Br 531, 576). K 1206 *R* 5 li-qi un-ni-ni-ja ši-mi qa-ba-a-a (IV[2] 57 *a* 59; hear my cry; CRAIG, *Relig. Texts*, i 12); also IV[2] 5 *a* 59. II 25 *a-b* 58 GAL-GAL-DI = qa-ab libbi, Br 6863. See also gabū, gabbū (209 *col* 2).

qubbū 1. (form like nubbū, *q. v.*). wailing, lamentation {Wehklagen} G § 89. id I-LU, Br 4020; H 180 *no* IV (K 4926, 11). IV[2] 10 *b* 1—2 qu-bi-e a-qab-bi, I cry aloud (but no one listens to me); 11 *b* 29—30 qu-bi-e i-qab-bi-šu. H 122, 10—11 see xalalu, 314 *col* 1. IV[2] 26 *b* 52—53 ina qu-ub-bi-e (Br 4738) mar-çu-ti; 54 *a* 21 see zarabu Š (295 *col* 2). H 17, 284 I-LU = qu-ub-bu-u. See also Sarg *Ann* 137.

qibū 2. command, order {Befehl} in *c. t.* ina qi-bi Nabd 33, 2; 86, 6; 570, 2 ‖ ina il-ki, 741, 1. Here perhaps also V 30 *e-f* 14 ME-GAL-ZU = ki-bu ša-ka-nu = give command (?), Br 10438; same id (13) = šu-ut-tu pa-ša-ru (Br 10437). See also KB iv 182 *col* 3, 18 + 22; 108 *no* 1, 3 ki(b)-bu šik-nu.

qababu. Sarg *Ann* 251 iq-bu-bu (3 *pl*) li-me-is-su, they covered, surrounded her (the city's) enceinte. T[M] i 98 eçēnçiri-ja iq-bu-bu, sie haben mein Rückgrat krumm gemacht. — 𝔍 V 45 viii 34 tu-qab-bab.

qabābu *n* shield {Schild}. Sarg *Khors* 117 na-aš (iç) ka-ba-bi, shieldbearer, squire; *Ann* 400; *Nimr* i 58. Sn *Rass* 56 narkabâte ga-ba-bi as-ma-re-e (ZA iii 312; 320; 328, 57). Lay 72 *no* 2, 5 ka-ba-bi as-ma-re-e (KAT[2] 261); *cf* TP III *Ann* 199; L[4] i 24 q(k)iškittē kîma [(iç)] a-ra-a-te [(iç)] qa-ba-ba-te, LEHMANN, ii 68. II 19 *a* 9, 10 see pitpānu (Br 210); perh. II 34 *c-d* 62 (Br 201). V 32 *b-c* 46 ka-ba-bu ‖ tuk-ku & a(?)-ri-tum (see xa-ri-tum, 298 *col* 1); II 32 *g-h* 35. ZA x 82 *rm*: qabābu not only: shield, but also a kind of bow.

qubbū *2.* (?). T. A. (Ber) 26 iii 27, 28: I šu-zu-ub ša kitî ša (?) kub-bu-u I lu-buštu šu-zu-ub ša kitî ku-ub-bu-u; *cf* Neb 457, 12 [(karpat)] qub(p)-b(p)u-u & see kubbū.

qabduqqū see kapduqqū.

qabalu oppose, fight {einem gegenübertreten, feindlich begegnen} see also kabalu. K 2001 *O* 8 a-ku-ku-tum ša qab-la qab-lat, CRAIG, *Relig. Texts*, i 15. Sp II 265 *a* vii 11 a-na abi liq-bil (ZA x 6); STRONG, PSBA xvii 148 reads at-taš-pil. K 719, 6 itti nakri ummāni i-qab-ba-al, THOMPSON, *Reports*, *no* 174. KAT[3] 195 suggests √קבל for ti-ka-bi-lu, T. A. (Lo) 61, 17: und sie haben nicht angenommen.

Q[t] ag **muqtablu** warrior, soldier {Streiter, Krieger} *pl* muqtablē; AV 5543. Anp ii 18, 36, 83; iii 36, 53: muq-tab-li-šu-nu (TP ii 21; iii 79); Anp *Mon*, *R* 32 [(amēl)] çābē muq-tab[-le]-šu-nu; Anp ii 114 çābē muq-tab-li([pl]-ni)-šu-nu (see KB i 90, 91 & *rm* 19; ZA i 367); see also TP i 74; ii 13; iv 18; vi 4 (without [(amēl)]); [(amēl)] muq-tab-le-šu Šalm, *Bal*, III, 1; *Mon*, ii 73 the heads of muq-tab-li-šu; Asb x 21 pa-gar muq-tab-li-šu-nu. V 30 *e-f* 7 KAL-GA-VI! = muq-tab-lu (Br 6220), = 8 a-lik pa-na.

ℑ Perhaps V 45 iii 30 tu-q(k)am-bal (> tuqabbal).

NOTE. — Instead of bu-bu-lu read perhaps q(g)it-b(p)u-lu (see mu'aru, 508 *col* 2). KB ii 36 *rm* **. On קָרָב = fight (Esther ix 23 + 27) see OLZ '02, *no* 10.

DERR. — these 3 (4?):

qablu, *c. st.* qabal midst {Mitte}; also: fight, contest {Kampf} AV 1474, 7304. ideogr. see S[b] 88 mu-ru-ub | | qab-lum (*var* qa-ab-lu); H 24, 507; § 9, 254. V 26 *c-d* 9, 10, see Br 4478, 8160; 7279 8166. — *a*) midst {Mitte} KNUDTZON, 315, 316. Mostly used as an *adv* ina qabal, properly: in the midst; then (like ina qirib) simply: in; ultu qabal, out of, from; also simply qabal; § 81 *b*. SMITH, *Asurb*, 76, 27 rapašti qabal tāmtim, in the wide ocean (§ 121, end); V 65 *b* 34 qa-bal-šu (ça-mi-id parē); *del* 64 ina qabli-ša. K 3182 iv 12 (end) qab-lu, ū-me, in the midst of day. Asb i 69: 22 kings ša a-xi tam-tim qabal tam-tim u na-ba-li; Sarg *Khors* 16 (146 i-na qabal); Sn iii 57 the city *N* ša qa-bal tam-tim; Esh i 9 ina qabal tam-tim, + 16; Asb ii 85 the sons of *I* a-šib qa-bal tam-tim; 86 ul-tu qabal tam-tim they went. — Sn i 22 ina qabal tam-xa-ri, in the fight; vi 9; Asb ix 21; SMITH, *Asurb*, 122, 45 ina qa-bal (*var* qabal) tam-xa-ri. I 43, 35 abul qa-bal ali ša Ninâ, a gate into Nineveh. NE VI (*p* 44) 77 ina qa-bal manāxti; Creat.-*frg* IV 65 qab-lu-uš Ti-a-ma-ti i-bar-ri, KB vi (1) 25 & 335. H 127, 42 ina qab-lu ašassi; 44 ina ga-bal ša-di-i ašassi (ideogr. ŠAB-ŠAB-BA; ŠAB, Br 5670, 5678); as a ‖ of libbu see giš-rinnu, Br 7280. III 64 *a* 14, 16 qabal šame-e, the midst of heaven, meridian (54, 36); on IV[2] 61 *c* 32 ina qabal šamē, see JENSEN, 16. — *b*) encounter, battle, fight {feindliche Begegnung; Kampf, Schlacht}. TP iii 38 sa-pi-nu qa-bal tar-gi-gi; SMITH, *Asurb*, 121, 35 Ištar i-lat qab-li be-lit ta-xa-zi; ZA ii 128 *b* 23 e-ma ga-ab-li u ta-xa-zi; ideogr. K 2852 + K 9662 i 32; *ibid* 27 .... la iš-nu-u qa-bal-šu šarru man-ma-an; *ibid* 10 muperdū qab-li. III 41 *a* 24 (çubât) ša qab-lu. Asurb ii 25 to defeat my warriors id-ka-a qa-bal-šu (KB ii 166—167; BA i 11), he gathered his host. K 3454 ii 35 a-a i-ni-'i qa-bal-ka (+ iii 79). K 2487 + K 8122 *O* 14 [(il)] UT-GAL-LU [ša la im-]max-xa-ru qa-bal-šu. *del* 105 (111) ki-ma qab-li eli nišē u-ba-'-u [....] (KB vi (1) 236, 237; see, however, NE 108 *rm* 3), like an onslaught in battle it rushed in on the people; *del* 123 (130) a-bu-bu qab-la; *del* 122. NE VI 53 a horse na-'-id qab-li, terrible in its attack; see also K 3456

R 5 (PSBA xxi 40 *foll*). Often with epešu. Anp i 38 (ii 25; iii 35) a-na e-peš qabli u taxāzi, Šalm, *Ob*, 62; 145 a-na epi-eš qabli taxāzi; TP iv 80 a-na e-peš qabli u ta-xa-zi (*var* taxāzi); in all these instances written KA + inserted çab; so also in K 2675 *R* 25 ba-lu e-peš qabli, without fight; *O* 16 + 60; K 2867, 13; Asb i 79 *fol*; V 35, 17 ba-lu qab-li u ta-xa-zi; IV² 12 *R* 39, 40 a-šar qab-li u ta-xa-zi. II 36 *a-b* 21 ŠUN-ŠUN-SAG-GE-A = qab-lu la max-ri, Br 253, 255 (II 37, 7); see also IV² 24 *a* 54, 55 ša qa-bal-šu. II 57 *c-d* 34 Ninib (*q. v.*) is called (1) NUN-NIR as god ša qab-li (see mēxru, 532 *col* 2) Br 2637. 81—11—3, 111 *O* (name for Marduk) 5: NE-URU-GAL = Marduk ša qab-lu, *Jour. Trans. Vict. Inst.*, 28, 8 *foll*. Perhaps S^b 159 ib | TUM | qab-lum followed by xar-da-tum (II 20, 364) Br 4958; see also S^b 289 (Br 3716).

NOTE. — 1. In the meaning of waist ; Lendenmitte, (BEZOLD) qablu (*id* = S^b 159) occurs in IV² 15* *no* 4, 3; 29 *no* 2, 16. IV² 31 *O* 54 (*R* 41) aban aladi ša qablate-ša, KB vi (1) 84, 85; NE 70, 9 u šu-u (Ēa-bani) ip-ţur qabli-šu also *cf* Sn vi 6; KNUDTZON, 51 *etc*

2. JOHNS, *Doomsday-Book*: qablu also some sort of garden, or enclosure.

qablū, *f* qablītu *adj* middle ⸤Mittlerer⸥ AV 1473. II 39 *e-f* 12 EN-NUN-[…]-BA = qab-li-tum, between barārītum & šad-dur-rum(-u), all adjectives to maççartu (*q. v.*) Br 2855; ZK ii 285. K 8583 ii 5 ina ba-ra-ar-ti qab-li-ti šad-ur-ri, BEZOLD, *Catalogue*, 942. NE 58, 8 [ina] qab-li-ti šit-ta-šu u-qat-ti.

qabaltu. — *a*) midst ⸤Mitte⸥. TP III *Ann* 97 ina qabal-ti ēkalli; Asurb ix 48 ina qa-bal-ti māti-ja, in my country = SMITH, *Asurb*, 275, 32; 286, 11: qa-bal-ti māti-ja. See also PEISER, KAS 2, 12; ZA iii 315, 73; Sarg *Ann* 289. I 27 *no* 2, 40 ina qabal-ti ali; Sn *Bell* 47. VATh 208, 12 ina qa-bal-ti maxāzi (KB iv 94); VATh 4105 ii 11 I ran around . . . . ga-ba-al-tu çi-ri, in the desert. *Adapa-legend* *R* 14 a-na bi-it be-ili-ja i-na ga-a-ab-la-at ta-am-ti nu-ni a-ba-ar (KB vi, 1, 96, 97). § 9, 254. — *b*) bosom ⸤Busen⸥ NE 11, 7 dannu (etlu) š(s)ag-ga-ša-a ša ga-bal-ti çēri KB vi, 1, 126, 127. — *c*) fight ⸤Kampf⸥ TP i 14 mu-šarrixat qablā^{pl}-te; perh. KNUDTZON, 112 *R* 4 [qab]-la-ti.

qabbaltu. II 29 *c-d* 31 XU-NER = qab-bal-tu, preceded by kab-bar-tu.

qibaltu see kibaltu, *p* 365 *col* 2.

qabasāte. 83—1—18, 38 *R* 2—5 ina eli bit libitti | ša a-bu-sa-a-te | qa-ba-sa-a-te | it-ta-mar (Hr^L 367).

q(k)absu. K 614 *R* 3 qab-si alu I-du-kin (Hr^L 175); Bu 89—4—26, 160 *R* 3 ina qa-ab-si ēkalli; perh. (māt) Bīt-kab-si, 83—1—18, 215, 12. WINCKLER, *Forschungen*, ii, 2, 310, 311 district ⸤Bezirk⸥. *Cf* qapsu.

qabaçu. K 4201 *R* 11 ka-ba-çu in a group with xanašu, eçepu, kuppuru, xabaçu.

qiberu, *pr* iqbir, *ps* iqab(b)ir, iqebbir bury, hide ⸤begraben, vergraben⸥ AV 4660. I 27 *no* 2, 59 whosoever this picture ina e-pi-ri i-qa-bi-ru-šu. IV² 38 *c* 20 whosoever this memorial slab i-na erçiti i-qab-bi-ru (BA ii 140; KB iv 60 *foll*); IV² 56 *b* 26 ina tub(p)qat dūri te-qeb-bir-ši (§§ 34 *a*,3; 97); K 2729 *R* (22) 31 his corpse ina la ki-bi-ri, without being buried. T^M iv 31 çalmāni-ja ina QI-MAX pagri taq-bi-ra (+ 36, 37, 38). Ina ēkal Šargina ki-bir, he was buried. Babyl. Chron. 3 (KB ii 272, 273); *ibid* 5. K 4362 (*R* of II 34 *no* 6) 15 ga (*i. e.* qa)-ba-ra-ki.

3 Šalm, *Mon*. *R* 100 see nabrarū (639 *col* 2); V 45 viii 35 tu-qab-bar; perh. IV² 56 *col* 3 *b* 47 qu-ub-bi-ri ki-e-ki (ZA xvi 168: schneid ab deine Stricke; KB vi (1) 384).

Derr. — naqbaru, naqbiru (719 *col* 1) & these 3:

qabru grave ⸤Grab⸥ AV 7305. S^b 192 u-ru-gal | id | qab-ru (Br 4781); id literally = large city; also = arallū; H 19, 334. K 168 *O* 15 qa-ab-ru (Hr^L 487). K 4982 (H 204 *no* 25) ki-rib qab-rim (Br 8948); K 4362 iv 12, 13 id AP + insert gal; & KI = qa-ab-ru. *Cf* H 17, 266 eš | AP | bītu. T^M i 108 see na'alu […] *a* (629 *col* 1); H 82, 83, 3 u-tuk qab-ri; 92, 93, 40 ina ni-gi-iç-çi qab-ri; also *l* 28. II 34 *no* 6 (add) u-ru-gal = qab-ru (AV 2667), see also Br 4784, 4788. Nergal (*q. v.*), III 67 *c-d* 69 *i. e.* AN-NER-URU-GAL as god ša qa-ab-ri. II 38 *a-b* 1 SI-GI-URU-GAL = [pa; Br 3428]-te-e qab-ri. V 36 *a-c* 31 u ⟨ qab-rum. On kašid qabru see kabru (387 *col* 1). *Pl* Anp ii 89 maxaz or (al) qab-ra-ni-šu (KB i 86, 87), but see kapru, 1 (423 *col* 2). K[M] 30, 11 read puṭ(not qab)-ri ka-si-ti (M[S] 12).

qibīru. funeral, grave }Begräbnis, Grab{ § 65, 21. V 61 vi 55 ki-bi-ra a-a ir-ši, a grave shall not be granted to him; see also KB iv 86—7 *col* 2, 25. Asurb vii 45 his corpse a-a id-din a-na ki-bi-ri, I did not grant a burial, ZA v 98; § 144; BA i 460 *rm* 2. NE X *col* 2, 6 a-di . . . qi-bi-ri ul addin-šu, see *Mittheilungen der Vorderasiatischen Gesellschaft*, 1902. *no* 1, *p* 5 on KB vi (1) 214, 215; VATh 4105 ii 6 u-ul ad-di-iš-šu a-na ki-bi-ri-im. V 16 *c-f* 43 KI-DU = ki-bi-ru, preceded by mītum; see also K 4364 iv 7 (Br 9723). V 31 *g-h* 25 ki-bi-ru ‖ (māt) bi-ru-di, PINCHES, ZK ii 81.

qubūru. II 35 (*a*-)*b* 21 qu-bu-ri, preceded by šuttatum, AV 7397.

NOTE. — Connected with qabru is perhaps the name of the town (al) Qa-ab-ri-na, Asurb v 56 = קברין, form like Niçibina. See also above.

qibirru in ki-is(ç)-ki-bir-ru see NOTE 2 to kisū (413 *col* 1). Br 10870 on V 26 *a-b* 16; AV 4267.

qi(n)burru. birdnest }Vogelnest{. II 27 *a-b* 60; H 33, 773 ki-bur | [sign]-ALAL qi-bur-rum ša iççuri, preceded by qinnu ša iççuri, Br 10819. HOMMEL, *Sum. Lesest.*, 30, 363 hole }Loch{; see also JENSEN, ZA v 132 *fol*; KB vi (1) 528. id in V 52 *b* 46 = a-ta-bu-ru, which M[S] 20, 21 proposes to emend into qiburru.

qubāte (?). K 1231 *R* u-tar-qu-šu-nu qu-ba-te-šu-nu il-la-ku-u-ni.

qubēti. stables }Ställe{? PSBA xxi 124, 125 *ad* III 66 *col* 7, 15 ilāni ša qu-be-ti.

qubbatum. T. A. lamentation }Wehklage{ (Ber) 6, 5 (+11) qu-ub-ba(-a)-tum. √qebū.

qibītu *f* (√qebū) § 65, 11; AV 4268/9; Br 582. — *a*) speech, word }Rede{. K 3364 *R* 12 ki-bit pi-i, the word of my mouth; KB ii 248 *col* v 3; Sp II 265 *a* viii 6 ki-bit pi-i ili il-ti, *etc.* K 155 *R* 8 ina qi-bit pi-ki = K[M] 1, 43. — *b*) order, command }Geheiss, Befehl, Auftrag{. V 35, 33 (end) i-na ki-bi-ti (il) Marduk, *etc.* V 44 *c-d* 22 P. N. Çi-rat ki-bit (il) Marduk. IV[2] 48 *b* 6 ina qi-bit (il) Êa. Esh iii 35 ina (& i-na) ki(qi)-bit (il) Ašur + 56; vi 41; Ash v 63; vi 126; ix 87; Sn iv 80; v 63; Sarg *Khors* 124. V 64 *c* 34 Anūnit who executes ki-bit (il) Bēl (23, ki-bi-it); see also III 55 *b* 32, 37. D 121 *no* 10, 3. ZA iv 238, 12 qi-bi-tuk-ka lu-u šu-mu[-u?]. Neb x 1 ki-bi-tu-uk-ka, at thy command (§ 80*e*); see also I 52 *no* 6, 8; Sargon *Khors* 191 ki-bi-tuš, at his order; SCHEIL, *Nabd*, ii 6 ki-bi-tu-uš-šu (= ina qibītišu); K 3600. 28 i-na qi-bi-ti-ki; ZA i 342, 20 (& often) ina ki-bi-ti-ka ki-it-ti; V 60 ii 10. id K[M] 54, 5 DUG(= KA)-GA (= qibīti)-ka kit-ti. — ina (*var* i-na) ki-bi(& be)-ti-ka çi-ir-tim, I 52 *no* 3 ii 30; KB iii (2) 4, 36; V 66 i 23 (-ti); V 65 *b* 30; ina ki-bi-ti-ša çir-ti III 15 i 26; Sarg *Cyl* 53 i-na ki-bi-ti-šu-nu çir-ti (*var* -te); Ash x 9 ina qi-bit ilūtišunu çir-tu (*var* -ti). Asurb. Nebo inscr. 8 ina ki-bi-ti-šu rabī-ti; II 66 *no* 2, 2 (-ša). IV[2] 17 *a* 57, 58 i-na ki-bi-ti-ka (= DUG-GA-ZU-TA); IV[2] 21* *no* 1 C *R* iii 8 ina DUG-GA-ka ka-bit-ti lubluṭ. Merodach-Baladan stone i 16 la in-nin-nu-u ki-bit-su. T[M] iii 182 ina ki-bit iq-bu-u (il) GIŠ-BAR-RA ru-bu. I 35 *no* 2, 2 Nebo ša ki-bit-su max-rat (is supreme); SCHEIL, *Rec. Trav.*, xx 205 *foll.* i 8 ša ki-bit-su ma-ag-rat. II 127 (K 257 *O*) 34 a-mat qi-bi-ti-ja çir-tum māt nu-kur(?)-tum qa-tum u-ab-bat. Asb vi 116 *fol* a-mat ki-bit ilūtišu(nu) ša . . . . iq-bu-u, their divine command which they gave. IV[2] 20 *no* 3 *O* 18, 19 ki-bit-ka (= DUG-GA-ZU) kima šamē ul ut-takkar; II 80, ~~25~~—6. II 28 *d* 50 . . . . IÇ šu-pil-tum ša ki-bi-ti, AV 8535, Br 14142. H 10 + 207, 44 KA (*i. e.* DUG) = ki-bi-tum. V 41 *a-b* 65 sanaqu (*q. v.*) ša ki-bi-tim. *pl* Nabopol (Hilprecht) i 21 i-na ki-be-a-tim (il) Nabū u (il) Marduk (= HILPRECHT, OBI, i 32/33). V 51 *b* 50 ina ki-ba-a-ti (= KA-DU-DUG-GA) ša (il) Šamaš. See also Br 654 on K 4872 *R* 80.

qigallu see kigallu, 371, 372.

qādu *1.* with {mit} T. A. see gūdu (213 *col* 2) *e. g.* (Lo) 12, 22 (BA iv 300); 47, 50; (Ber) 96, 27 *fol* (ZA x 330, 331).

qadu ***2.*** fire, burn {an- brennen} קדח. II 35 *e-f* 14—16 qa-a-du = ša-ra-pu; qa-mu-u = šarapu; qamū = qa-lu-u. IV² 27 *no* 6 (*add*) 35 UD-DU = ta-qad-ma; IV² 27 *b* 55. K 9287 ii 13 i-ša-ta-a-qad-ma, *Rev. Sém.*, ix 149. K 66 (IV² 55 *no* 2) *O* 17 GI-BIL-LAL (= gibillu) ina išāti kibir nāri ta-qad-ma (thou shalt kindle) ab-ra tuš-ta-xaz. ip qi-di-e see pišlu; perh. T^M iv 23 a-na çēri qe-di u na-me-e tap-qi-da-in-ni. pm L⁴ iii 10 see napaxu ℑ (706 *col* 1). — See also ki-e-du & ṭipāru (end).

NOTE. — Scheil, *Rec. Trav.*, xx 68 *fol* (no xxxv) 9 reads a-ka-ad (קדר), but Zimmern, ZA xii 330 & KB vi (1) 300 suggest a-ka-la, became dark.

Der.: Perh. maqaddu (577 *col* 1) &:

qidēš. T^M ii 137 šiptu : qi-e-eš (like a cord) li-bi-iš qi-di-eš; viii 7 šiptu : qi-eš libbūš qi-di-eš.

qadū *1.* a bird {ein Vogel}. II 37 *a-c* 14 (Br 14444) .... IB-A-NU = qa-du-u & ak-ku-u; *ibid* 63 ‖ a-ku-u. AV 7311; *cf* Targ קַדְיָא = כוס; Z^S iii 64 ma-mit a-tu-du qa-du-u, AJSL xiii 146 or [na]-du-u, *cf* K^M *p* 146; GGA '98, 824. Hommel, Hastings, *Dictionary*, i 214 *col* 2: horn-owl.

qadu ***2.*** K 7673, 18 in(?)-ni]-si ina rēbit ali i-qa-ad-di qa-du-u, = to cry like the *qadū*-bird. See qadū, 4.

NOTE. — *del* 245 (273); 250 (280) see šāṭu (שקט) & KB vi (1) 516. M^S 83 *col* 2 reads i(ta)-qad-du (√קדד).

qadū ***3.*** an official {ein Beamter}. K 1347, 10 ana ^(amēl) qa-di-e ... aš-pura; M^S 84 *col* 1.

qadū ***4.*** (?) ℑ IV² 54 *a* 16 xattum pirit-tum, qud-du-šum-ma, have silenced him (?); see nisū ℑ, 697 *col* 2 & qadū, 2; Z^B 94 > quddudu; see also §§ 89 ii 1, & 97 (end).

qadū ***5.*** — **Der.** maqdū (577 *col* 1).

qadū ***6.*** & **qadūtu** (qaduttu) some earthen vessel, jug {ein Thongefäss, Krug} *etc.* V 27 *a-b* 7—11 IM-TIK = qa-du-ut-tum (Br 8401); IM-TIK-TIN-NA = *q* ši-ka-ri (Br 8405); IM-TIK-EN-NA = *q* ši-ka-ni (Br 8403); IM-TIK-A-AB-BA = *q* tam-ti (Br 8406); IM-TIK-A -DA = *q* na-a-ri (Br 8407). — V 27 *e-f* 16—18 IM-TIK = qa-du-ut-tum; IM-TIK-EN-NA = *q* ši-ka-ni; IM-TIK-BI-TIN-NA = *q* ši-ka-ri (Br 8404). AV 7312, 7313. V 32 (II 32) *a-c* 24—26 IM-TIK-EN-NA = qa-du-u ši-ka-ni = šik-nu ša nāri (AV 7311, Br 8402); IM-TIK-TIN-NA = qa-du-ut ši-ka-ri = šur-šum-mu ša BI-SAG (Jensen, ZA i 309; Br 8405; KB vi (1) 487: Schlamm des Flusses); & = qa-du-tum = d(ṭ)i-du (ZA viii 75 *rm* 1; Br 8401). K 257 (H 127) *O* 35, 36 ina bur-ti ša-di-i qa-du-tam (= IM-TIK) am-xu-ux (ZK i 242).

quddu, qudu, AV 4486. K 4408 (II 44 *no* 6) *g-h* 36 GIŠ-TU (see Br 10189, 11909) = qud-du (& pāšu); V 26 *a-b* 14 GIŠ (gi-iš-ku-ur) KIL = qud-du. S^b 1 *O* ii 13 ṭu-un | ṬU | qu-du, Br 11908, between pa-a-šu & tu-kal(?)-tum; V 38 *c-d* 42; H 36, 883; 186 (Sm 23) 11; AV 7309. K 4200 *R* 15 ..... -DA = qud-du (Br 14026, AV 8415). Hommel, Hastings, *Dictionary*, i 219 "cup".

qiddu. Ner 28, 9: II ši-pi ša ki-id-di (in a dowry-list).

qadadu, pr iqdud. bow down, bow, incline, humble oneself {sich beugen, neigen, senken} AV 7306; ZDMG 28, 137; ZA v 36. V 65 *a* 22 ina la a-dan-ni-šu ša bīti šu-a-ti ri-ša-a-šu iq-du-du ut-tab-bi-ka (*var* ku) mi-la(-a)-šu, KB iii, 2, 110, 111. III 6 A 11 a-na-'-du qa-di-id. T. A. (Lo) 35, 4 i-na ga-ta-ti-ia, I am prostrating myself; Reisner, *Hymnen*, 26 (VATh 298 *R*), 22 ki-šad-ka ina qa-da-da. K 40 (D 80) ii 7 GAM = qa-da-du (Br 7317); 8 TIK-GAM (21 = kanašu ša amēli, Br 3286); 9 TIK-GAR (Br 3318, 11963); 10 TIK-GA'-GA' (Br 3276); 11 TIK-KU-ŠE-GAR (Br 3310, 10627); 12 TIK-KI-KA-GA'-GA' (Br 3301, 9825); 13 TIK-KI-LU-LAL (Br 3302, 9827); 14 TIK-AKA-GA'-GA' (Br 3268); 15 IM-KI-KU-LAL (Br 8485) all (8—15) = qa-da-du ša amēli. See also AV 4010.

Q^t Rm IV 90 *O* 10 (end) ki-šad-su (of a man) iq-ta-du-ud (he bent down).

Q^{in} V 31 *g-h* 26 GAM-GAM-UD (or -ud?) = iq-ta-na-ad-du-ud, he bowed down (§ 98).

ℶ — *a*) make bow down, bend, humiliate {niederbeugen, biegen; erniedrigen}. T. A. (Lo) 82, 30 i-na ša-ar-ti-ša u-ki-id-di-da-aš-ši-im-ma (BA iv 130, 131; KB vi, 1, 78, 79). IV² 21* *no* 2 *O* 14, 15 the lord who u-qa-ad (*var* qad)-di-da-an-ni (= IM-MU-UN-GAM-MA, *var* IM-MA-AN-GAM-E-EN, EME-SAL) u-qa-at-ti-an-ni (IM-MU-UN-TIL-LA), has laid me low & has ruined me, BA i 417. KB vi 198 *ad* NE VIII *col* v/vi 7 qud-du-du pa-nu-ka (also see 200, 14; 216, 2). V 21 *a-b* 27 GAM-MA-MU = qu-di-da-an-ni (§ 98, incline me), preceded by šup-pil-an-ni (26). H 26, 547 ga-am | GAM | [qu-ud-du-du]; *cf* II 27 *no* 4, 27 (*add*). — *b*) sink, lower {senken, niederschlagen} IV² 31 *R* 1 Papsukkal gu-ud-du-ud ap-pa-šu pa-nu-šu [ur-pu] KB vi (1) 86—7.

ℶ^t = ℶ K^M 11, 6 [kîma] ši-bi (*var* ki-ma ši-bi-im) uq-ta-ad-di-da-an-ni (*var* uq-ṭa-ad-di-da-ni), he has bowed me down like an old man.

NOTE. — According to Boissier, *Rev. Sém.*, vii 134, 135 § 84 from qadadu also quddu, whence gu-ud-du (S^b 151, where read gu-ud-du = kab-tum).

Der. — maqdadu (?), 577 *col* 1, qiddu (?)! and these 6 (?):

qadādāniš, *adv* bent; bowed down {gebeugt, gebeugten Hauptes}. IV² 24 *no* 2, 11, 12 iš-tu É-KUR kab-tum qa-da-da-niš (= GAM-GAM-MA-NI, EME-SAL, Br 7317, 5333) i[-tal-lak?].

qududū (?) K 183, 19 qu-du-da-a-te i-šak-ku-nu (Hr^L 2) see BOR i 125; BA i 618, 619; PSBA xxiii 351 *foll.*

qudādu, *adj* bent, bowed down; frail, delapidated {gebeugt, hinfällig}. ⊕ 51 iv 14 .... DIM = gu-da-du ‖ la-'u-u & la-ku-u, *q. v.* K 2061 i 20 (H 202) NE-EN-ÇI-IR = ku-da-du, Br 4053.

qiddatu *1.* *pl* qiddāti. — *a*) V 36 *d-f* 35 bu-ru | ⟨ | qi-id-da-tum, perh. = sinking, lowering (?); Z^B 82; Br 8701. 82, 9—18, 4156 i 13 (*fol*) [NAR] = qid-da-tum; & qid-da-tum ū-mu; ii 16 [NAR] = ki-id-da-tum. — *b*) depression {Niedergeschlagenheit}. IV² 20 *no* 1, 7—8 see çurru (Br 7318); IV² 21* *no* 2 *O* 22 see kidūtu (375 *col* 2). — V 31 *g-h* 56 [qi?]-da-ta = ki-id-da-tum.

qiddatu *2.* (?) Smith, *Sen*, 91, 62 (Sn *Kui* 2, 15) I ordered the Phenician sailors qi-rib Diqlat itti šināti (*i. e.* with the vessels) a-na qid-da-ti a-di ^(al) U-pi-a u-še-qil-pu-u na(?)-ba-liš. (ZA viii 82 & *rm* 4 reads šid-da-ti & translates: to the coasts {nach den Küsten}). *Cf* also קלפא.

qadmu ‖ ilu. K 2100 iv 8 qa-ad-mu = i[-lu] PSBA ix 377; ZA iii 193; KAT³ 477.

qudmu — *a*) locally: front {Vorderseite, Front} II^F 73. II 36 *c-d* 64 DUB-SAG = qud-mu (Br 3937, AV 7401) *cf* muttu (*p* 620); *pl* DUB-SAG-MEŠ, Nabd 687, 3. Rm 2, 200 A 4 qu-ud-mu = max-[ru-u]. Creat.-*frg* III 11 al-ka ^(il) Ga-]ga qud-me-šu-nu i-ziz-ma (before them stand!); perh. also KB vi (1) 283, 33 ana qud-me-ša. — *b*) temporally: aforetime, ancient time {Vorzeit}. I 35 *no* 3, 25 Bēl-kap-ka-pi šarru pa-ni | a-lik max-ri qu-ud-mu šarrūti ša Su-li-li (KB i 188, 189; ✕ Amiaud, ZA ii 206 *rm*). NE i 4 read qu-dum ni-me-qi, the primeval knowledge of everything Haupt, JAOS xxii *p* 11 (✕ KB vi, 1, 116).

qudmiš, *adv.* KB vi (1) 584, 12 ku-ud-mi-iš A-ni-im i-na ša-ma-i ša-ak-nu, lay before Anu in heaven (Scheil, *Rec. Trav.*, xxiii).

qudmū, *adj* of olden time, of old; ancient, belonging to the past {aus der Vorzeit, vorzeitlich, uralt}. I 65 *b* 51 sūmāti reš-tāti bil-lu-di-e ku-ud-mu-u-tim ša ^(ilat) Ištar-Uruk .... utēr ašruššun.

qudūmu (?). K 761 *R* 2 a-na qu-du-mi-šu lil-lik.

qadašu. Q 82—9—18, 4159 *O* 56 UD = qa-da-šu, followed by na-ma-rum, ni]-per-du-u, *etc.*; 54 = qud]-du-šu M^S texts *pl* 30. KAT³ 602, 603.

ℶ cleanse, dedicate {reinigen, weihen}, see Q. IV² 51 *b* 20 ina šur-ki šum ili-šu i-me-šu u-qad-di-šu unazzimū iklū (Z^Š ii 76, 77). Br. M. 81, 7—1, 9 *col* i i 32 u-qa-ad-diš, I dedicated, KB iii (2)

qadnu see qatnu.

qigallu see kigallu, 371, 372.

qādu *1.* with {mit} T. A. see gādu (213 *col* 2) *e.g.* (Lo) 12, 22 (BA iv 300); 47, 50; (Ber) 96, 27 *fol* (ZA x 330, 331).

qadu 2. fire, burn {an- brennen} קאד. II 35 *e-f* 14—16 qa-a-du = ša-ra-pu; qa-mu-u = šarapu; qamū = qa-lu-u. IV^2 27 *no* 6 (*add*) 35 UD-DU = ta-qad-ma; IV^2 27 *b* 55. K 9287 ii 13 i-ša-ta a-qad-ma, *Rev. Sém.*, ix 149. K 66 (IV^2 55 *no* 2) *O* 17 GI-BIL-LAL (= gibillu) ina išāti kibir nāri ta-qad-ma (thou shalt kindle) ab-ru tuš-ta-xaz. ip qi-di-e see pislu; perh. T^M iv 23 a-na çēri qu-di u na-me-e tap-qi-da-in-ni. pm L^4 iii 10 see napaxu ℑ (706 *col* 1). — See also ki-e-du & ṭipāru (end).

NOTE. — SCHEIL, *Rec. Trav.*, xx 65 *fol* (no xxxv) 9 reads a-ka-ad (קדר), but ZIMMERN, ZA xii 330 & KB vi (1) 300 suggest a-ka-la, became dark.

Der.: Perh. maqaddu (577 *col* 1) &:

qidēš. T^M ii 137 šiptu: qi-e-eš (like a cord) li-bi-iš qi-di-eš; viii 7 šiptu: qi-eš libbūš qi-di-eš.

qadū *1.* a bird {ein Vogel}. II 37 *a-c* 14 (Br 14444) .... IB-A-XU = qa-du-u & ak-ku-u; *ibid* 68 ‖ a-ku-u. AV 7311; *cf* Targ קַדְיָא = כוס; Z^S iii 64 ma-mit a-tu-du qa-du-u, AJSL xiii 146 or [aa]-du-u, *cf* K^M *p* 146; GGA '98, 824. HOMMEL, HASTINGS, *Dictionary*, i 214 *col* 2: horn-owl.

qadu 2. K 7673, 18 in(?)-ni]-si ina rēbit ali i-qa-ad-di qa-du-u, = to cry like the *qadū*-bird. See qadū, 4.

NOTE. — *del* 245 (273); 250 (280) see šāḳu (שׂחט) & KB vi (1) 516. M^S 43 *col* 2 reads i(ta)-qad-du (√קדד).

qadū *3.* an official {ein Beamter}. K 1347, 10 ana $^{(amēl)}$ qa-di-e ... ašpura; M^S 84 *col* 1.

qadū 4. (?) ℑ IV^2 54 *a* 16 xattum pirit-tum, qud-du-šum-ma, have silenced him (?); see nišū ℑ, 697 *col* 2 & qadū, 2; Z^B 94 > quddudu; see also §§ 89 ii 1, & 97 (end).

qadū *5.* — Der. maqdū (577 *col* 1).

qadū *6.* & **qadūtu** (qaduttu) some earthen vessel, jug {ein Thongefäss, Krug} *etc.* V 27 *a-b* 7—11 IM-TIK = qa-du-ut-tum (Br 8401); IM-TIK-TIN-NA = *q* ši-ka-ri (Br 8405); IM-TIK-EN-NA = *q* ši-ka-ni (Br 8403); IM-TIK-A-AB-BA = *q* tam-ti (Br 8406); IM-TIK-A [sign] -DA = *q* na-a-ri (Br 8407). — V 27 *e-f* 16—18 IM-TIK = qa-du-ut-tum; IM-TIK-EN-NA = *q* ši-ka-ni; IM-TIK-BI-TIN-NA = *q* ši-ka-ri (Br 8404). AV 7312, 7313. V 32 (II 32) *a-c* 24—26 IM-TIK-EN-NA = qa-du-u ši-ka-ni = šik-nu ša nāri (AV 7311, Br 8402); IM-TIK-TIN-NA = qa-du-ut ši-ka-ri = šur-šum-mu ša BI-SAG (JENSEN, ZA i 309; Br 8405; KB vi (1) 487: Schlamm des Flusses); & = qa-du-tum = d(ṭ)i-du (ZA viii 75 *rm* 1; Br 8401). K 257 (H 127) *O* 35, 36 ina bur-ti ša-di-i qa-du-tam (= IM-TIK) am-xu-ux (ZK i 242).

quddu, qudu, AV 4486. K 4408 (II 44 *no* 6) *g-h* 36 GIŠ-TU (see Br 10189, 11909) = qud-du (& pāšu); V 26 *a-b* 14 GIŠ (gi-iš-ku-ur) KIL = qud-du. S^b 1 *O* ii 13 ṭu-un | ṬU | qu-du, Br 11908, between pa-a-šu & tu-kal(?)-tum; V 38 *c-d* 42; H 36, 883; 186 (Sm 23) 11; AV 7309. K 4200 *R* 15 ..... [sign]-DA = qud-du (Br 14026, AV 8415). HOMMEL, HASTINGS, *Dictionary*, i 219 "cup".

qiddu. Ner 28, 9: II ši-pi ša ki-id-di (in a dowry-list).

qadadu, pr iqdud. bow down, bow, incline, humble oneself {sich beugen, neigen, senken} AV 7306; ZDMG 28, 137; ZA v 36. V 65 *a* 22 ina la a-dan-ni-šu ša bīti šu-a-ti ri-ša-a-šu iq-du-du ut-tab-bi-ka (*var* ku) mi-la(-a)-šu, KB iii, 2, 110, 111. III 6 A 11 a-na-'-du qa-di-id. T. A. (Lo) 35, 4 i-na ga-ta-ti-ja, I am prostrating myself; REISNER, *Hymnen*, 26 (VATh 298 *R*), 22 ki-šad-ka ina qa-da-da. K 40 (D 80) ii 7 GAM = qa-da-du (Br 7317); 8 TIK-GAM (21 = kanašu ša amēli, Br 3286); 9 TIK-GAR (Br 3318, 11963); 10 TIK-GA'-GA' (Br 3276); 11 TIK-KU-ŠE-GAR (Br 3310, 10627); 12 TIK-KI-KA-GA'-GA' (Br 3301, 9825); 13 TIK-KI-LU-LAL (Br 3302, 9827); 14 TIK-AKA-GA'-GA' (Br 3268); 15 IM-KI-KU-LAL (Br 8485) all (8—15) = qa-da-du ša amēli. See also AV 4010.

Q^t Rm IV 90 *O* 10 (end) ki-šad-su (of a man) iq-ta-du-ud (he bent down).

Q[tn] V 31 *g-h* 26 GAM-GAM-UD (or -ud?) = iq-ta-na-ad-du-ud, he bowed down (§ 98).

ℑ — *a*) make bow down, bend, humiliate {niederbeugen, biegen; erniedrigen}. T. A. (Lo) 82, 30 i-na ša-ar-ti-ša u-ki-id-di-da-aš-ši-im-ma (BA iv 130, 131; KB vi, 1, 78, 79). IV² 21* *no* 2 *O* 14, 15 the lord who u-qa-ad (*var* qad)-di-da-an-ni (= IM-MU-UN-GAM-MA, *var* IM-MA-AN-GAM-E-EN, EME-SAL) u-qa-at-ti-an-ni (IM-MU-UN-TIL-LA), has laid me low & has ruined me, BA i 417. KB vi 198 *ad* NE VIII *col* v/vi 7 qud-du-du pa-nu-ka (also see 200, 14; 216, 2). V 21 *a-b* 27 GAM-MA-MU = qu-di-da-an-ni (§ 98, incline me), preceded by šup-pil-an-ni (26). H 26, 547 ga-am | GAM | [qu-ud-du-du]; *cf* II 27 *no* 4, 27 (*add*). — *b*) sink, lower {senken, niederschlagen} IV² 31 *R* 1 Papsukkal gu-ud-du-ud ap-pa-šu pa-nu-šu [ur-pu] KB vi (1) 86—7.

ℑ[t] = ℑ K[M] 11, 6 [kîma] ši-bi (*var* ki-ma ši-bi-im) uq-ta-ad-di-da-an-ni (*var* uq-ṭa-ad-di-da-ni), he has bowed me down like an old man.

NOTE. — According to HOMMEL, *Rev. Sém.*, vii 134, 135 § 84 from qadadu also quddu, whence gu-ud-du (S[b] 151, where read gu-ud-du = kab-tum).

Der. — maqdadu (?), 677 *col* 1, qiddu (?)‡ and these 6 (?):

qadādāniš, *adv* bent; bowed down {gebeugt, gebeugten Hauptes}. IV² 24 *no* 2, 11, 12 iš-tu E-KUR kab-tum qa-da-da-niš (= GAM-GAM-MA-NI, EME-SAL, Br 7317, 5333) i[-tal-lak?].

qudūdū (?) K 183, 19 qu-du-da-a-te i-šak-ku-nu (Hr[L] 2) see BOR i 125; BA i 618, 619; PSBA xxiii 351 *foll.*

qudādu, *adj* bent, bowed down; frail, dilapidated {gebeugt, hinfällig}. ⊕ 51 iv 14 .... DIM = gu-da-du ‖ la-'u-u & la-ku-u, *q. v.* K 2061 i 20 (H 202) NE-EN-ÇI-IR = ku-da-du, Br 4053.

qiddatu *1.* *pl* qiddāti. — *a*) V 36 *d-f* 35 bu-ru | ⟨ | qi-id-da-tum, perh. = sinking, lowering (?); Z[B] 82; Br 8701. 82, 9—18, 4156 i 13 (*fol*) [NAR] = qid-da-tum; & qid-da-tum ū-mu; ii 10 [NAR] = ki-id-da-tum. — *b*) depression {Niedergeschlagenheit}. IV² 20 *no* 1, 7—8 see çurru (Br 7318); IV² 21* *no* 2 *O* 22 see kidūtu (375 *col* 2). — V 31 *g-h* 56 [qi?]-da-ta = ki-id-da-tum.

qiddatu *2.* (?) SMITH, *Sen*, 91, 62 (Sn *Kui* 2, 15) I ordered the Phenician sailors qi-rib Diqlat itti šināti (*i. e.* with the vessels) a-na qid-da-ti a-di [(al)] U-pi-a u-še-qil-pu-u na(?)-ba-liš. (ZA viii 82 & *rm* 4 reads šid-da-ti & translates: to the coasts {nach den Küsten}). *Cf* also קלפא.

qadmu ‖ ilu. K 2100 iv 8 qa-ad-mu = i[-lu] PSBA ix 377; ZA iii 193; KAT³ 477.

qudmu — *a*) locally: front {Vorderseite, Front} II[F] 73. II 36 *c-d* 64 DUB-SAG = qud-mu (Br 3937, AV 7401) *cf* muttu (*p* 620); *pl* DUB-SAG-MEŠ, Nabd 687, 3. Rm 2, 200 A 4 qu-ud-mu = max-[ru-u]. Creat.-*frg* III 11 al-ka [(il)] Ga-]ga qud-me-šu-nu i-ziz-ma (before them stand!); perh. also KB vi (1) 283, 33 ana qud-me-ša. — *b*) temporally: aforetime, ancient time {Vorzeit}. I 35 *no* 3, 25 Bēl-kap-ka-pi šarru pa-ni | a-lik max-ri qu-ud-mu šarrūti ša Su-li-li (KB i 188, 189; ✕ AMIAUD, ZA ii 206 *rm*). NE i 4 read qu-dum ni-me-qi, the primeval knowledge of everything HAUPT, JAOS xxii *p* 11 (✕ KB vi, 1, 116).

qudmiš, *adv.* KB vi (1) 584, 12 ku-ud-mi-iš A-ni-im i-na ša-ma-i ša-ak-nu, lay before Anu in heaven (SCHEIL, *Rec. Trav.*, xxiii).

qudmū, *adj* of olden time, of old; ancient, belonging to the past {aus der Vorzeit, vorzeitlich. uralt}. I 65 *b* 51 sūmūti reštāti bil-lu-di-e ku-ud-mu-u-tim ša [(ilat)] Ištar-Uruk .... utēr ašruššun.

qudūmu (?). K 761 *R* 2 a-na qu-du-mi-šu lil-lik.

qadašu. Q 82—9—18, 4159 *O* 56 UD = qa-da-šu, followed by na-ma-rum, ni]-per-du-u, *etc.*; 54 = qud]-du-šu M[S] texts *pl* 30. KAT³ 602, 603.

ℑ cleanse, dedicate {reinigen, weihen}, see Q. IV² 51 *b* 20 ina šur-ki šum ili-šu i-me-šu u-qad-di-šu unazzimū iklū (Z[B] ii 76, 77). Br. M. 81, 7—1, 9 *col* i i 32 u-qa-ad-diš, I dedicated, KB iii (2)

qadnu see qatnu.

108, 109. ZIMMERN, *Ritualtafeln*, 46—47 i 3 tu-qad-daš, thou shalt cleanse; *no* 52, 2. K 126, 3 zikaru ana sinništi la ku-ur-u gi-na-a ku-ud-du-uš amēlu šuātu i-la-an, *Rev. Sém.*, i 169. Perhaps KB iii (2) 6 *no* 2 *col* 1, 15 a-na ku-ud-duš be-lu-ti-šu-nu (R.F. HARPER).

ℶ[t] ZIMMERN, *Ritualtafeln*, 1—20, 29 tu-u]q-ta-ad-da-aš, thou shalt dedicate, sanctify thyself }du sollst dich heiligen{; *cf ibid*, *no* 58, 2; Sm 1513, 3. K^{M} 30, 20 ina ūmi magūri liq-te-diš (so ZIMMERN, *loc. cit.*, 172 *rm* 2).

NOTE. — KB vi (1) 439 qašādu (*q. v.*) > qadāšu, √ קדש.

Derr. — these 3:

quddušu *adj* brilliant, shining, clear }glänzend, rein{. AV 4487; ZA v 5; HAUPT in PATERSON, *Numbers* (SBOT) 44. V 24 *c-d* 8 qud-du-šu ∦ el-lum. NE 12, 44 a-na bit el-lim qud-du-ši mu-šab (il) A-nim (ilat) Iš-tar (KB vi (1) 128, 129); 1, 10 ša E-a]n-na qud-du-ši šu-tum-mi el-lim. T^{M} viii 17 šiptu: (il) Nāru ellu nam-ru qud-du-šu (BA iv 158); vi 36 šadê ellūti qud-du-šu-ti. K 2001, 22 aṭ-bu-xa-ak-ki niqē ellā qu[d-du-ša. ZIMMERN, *Ritualtafeln*, 45 ii 10 (end) bīnu qud-du-ši, a dedicated, sacred tamarisk; *ibid* 98—99, 7 (immer) puxāda ella qud-du-ša.

qadišu, *f* **qadištu** a temple-prostitute }Hierodule{ *cf* קְדֵשָׁה; AV 1490, 7309. D^{H} 12 *rm* 1; J^{I-N} 60: jede Buhlerin hiess qadištu (die Geweihte) *i. e.* der Göttin Ištar; JOHNS, AJSL xix 101 *fol*. KAT^{3} 423, 603. iṣ NU-GIG, lit^{s}: not sick; SAL-NU-GIG, Z^{N} viii 52. V 25 *c-d* 7 ar-ka-nu ga-di-iš-tum (= NU-GIG-A-NA, Br 2017) ina su-ki-im it-ta-ši; 11 ga-di-iš-ta. II 32, 83, 11—12 qa-diš-tu ša lib-ba mar-ça; iš-ta-rit (iṣ NU-GIG, as in 11) (il) A-nim la [a-ni-xu ??]. II 32 *no* 2, 3 *fol* q]a-diš-tum, followed by zēr-ma-ši-tum, *q. v.* IV^{2} 30 *a* 44 the witch is called .. SAL-NU-GIG (ZA viii 81—2); 58 *c* 37 qa-diš-tu mārat (il) A-nim. T^{M} iii 44 (dupl.) qa-diš-tum ti-giš (or iš. ix, iç?)-tum (perhaps the phonetic spelling for SAL-ME, BA iv 157, 158).

qadiltūtu (> qadištūtu) *abstr. n.* of qadištu, Br 2017, 2135. V 25 *c-d* 10 ina rāmešu ga-dil-du-us-su (= NAM-NU-GIG-A-NI) i-xu-us-su, although she was a temple-prostitute he yet married her (?) J^{I-N} 60. ZIMMERN (KB vi, 1, 439 bel) reads ga-aš(!)-du-us-su = Eigenschaft einer qadištu.

qadišu (??). T. A. (Ber) 71, 32 qa-di-šu u mar-xu-u danniš (death or the like?).

qaṭalu (??) Š SCHEIL, *Rec. Trav.*, xx 55 *fol*, i 11 ni(?)šu (il) Adad li-ša-aq-ṭil; ii 11 li-ša-aq[-ṭil, li]-ga-ax[-ziz] (קצץ). JENSEN, KB vi (1) 288, 289.

qâlu 1. *pr* iqūl, *ps* iqāl speak, call, howl, lament }sprechen, rufen, heulen, klagen{ Z^{B} 99. T^{M} i 68 a-qu-la. IV^{2} 61 *b* 36 a-na-ku qa-la-ku-u-ni, I speak. NE 9, 47 [innadir] uš-xa-ri-ir i-qu-ul-ma; 67, 11 ki-ki-i lu-qu-u[-lu]; 71, 20 (lu-qul). KB vi (1) 200, 35; + 466 reads ki(-)ki-i lu-us-kut (סכת) ki(-)ki-i lu-qul-ma, how, how can I be silent, how, how shall I cry? K 5464 *R* 14 at-tu-nu qa-la-ku-nu, I call on you (Hr^{b} 198); T. A. (KB v) 134, 67 iš-tu ša-[š]u la-a i-qa-al (BA iv 121, 122); (Lo) 12, 48 why will you neglect (? ta-qa-al) your land; *ibid* 13 u-ul ta-qa-al; 14, 15 qa-la-ta (*pm*, 2 *m sg*); 41, 29 ga-a-la-nu (1 *pl*); *cf* BEZOLD, *Diplomacy*, xxxvii (√ קלל?). ZIMMERN, ZA vi 157 translates T. A. (Ber) 104, 45 šumma qa-al šarru (when the king laments) & *ibid* 46 la-a ja-ku-ul. K 144 *R* 5 liqi unninija šimi qa-la-a-a (my lamenting). S^{b} 187 me-e | ME | qa-a-lu (H 33, 775; Br 10360); II 42 *no* 3 *O b* 6 qa-lum. *pm* (?) 81—7—27, 199, 4 a-ta-a be-ili qa-la ana-ku, *etc.* *ag* K 8204, 13 al-ta-na-si ilānima qa-liš qa-a-a-al (PSBA xvii 139), I call to the gods, crying aloud. AV 7319 quotes (il) Ēa qa-a-lu i-šim-me; also Sp 31 (margin).

Q[t] call aloud, howl. V 47 *a* 32, 33 ūmu šutānuxu mūšu girrūni arxu qi-ta-a-a-u-lu (= ac) i-dir-tu šattu; qi-ta-a-a-u-lu qu-u-lu. Z^{B} 14 *rm* 2:

qasaru see qaçaru. ⁓ qizulī'ū' *cf* kizullu, 577 *col* 1. ⁓ qaṭnu see qatnu. ⁓ qaṭ(a)pu read qat(a)pu. ⁓ quṭru, quṭrennu see qutru, qutrinnu.

moaning, lamentation; see also *ibid* 23; 100; 108; BA i 296, 4.

3 IV² 34 *no* 1 *b* 9 [ri?]-qi-šu ellātešu u-qa-i-la ana A-ga-ne-ki u-še-ri-bu (KB iii, 1, 106—7; *Rev. Sém.*, x, Apr. '02, 275 *fol*); perhaps Creat.-*frg* IV 72 (or √ kālu, 1).

Derr. — qa'ālu, qultu, the following two:

qūlu, *m* speech, call, cry {Rede, Ruf, Geschrei} AV 7404. IV² 7 *a* 5, 6 qu-lu (= GAR-ME-GAR, Br 12159) la ṭa-a-bu, the disastrous speech (meaning a curse); *a* 14, 15 qu-lu ku-u-ru (= GAR-ME-GAR-RA), & *cf* 3—4 (Br 7271); IV² 1 *a* 42, 43 qu-lu ku-ru (= U-DI-GAR-ME-GAR); T^M vii 40 (BA iv 161). II 121 *O* 8, 9 qu-lu šu-kun (Br 10430); *cf del* 126 (133 end); ša-kin qu-lu (BA i 134 *rm* 2 ša-qi); see also KB vi (1) 48, 28 (end); Creat.-*frg* I *b* 10 (I 44) [q]u-lu liš-ša-kin-ma, KB vi (1) 4 & 305 qūlu šakanu = cry, call. K^M 12, 36. S^b 136 me-e ME | qu-lu (II 33, 776; Br 10370); II 42 *no* 3 *O* 5 *b* qu-lum. V 36 *a-c* 29 u | < qu-lum, Br 8707.

qāliš *adv* loud {laut} M^S 83 *col* 1 *ad* K 8204, 13 see qūlu. S. A. Smith, *Asurb*, iii 80, 24.

qalu 2. pr iqūl inspect, look upon, pay attention to {anschauen, auf etwas schauen, Acht nehmen}. IV² 48 *a* 1—5 šarru a-na di-ni la i-qul *etc.*; 2, a-na di-in māti-šu la i-qul; 4, a-na abkalli-šu la i-qul, when the king does not pay attention to the law; the law of his country, *etc.* (misfortune will arise); 6, when a-na is-xap-pi i-qul; 7, but when a-na ši-pir ilu Ê-a i-qul the great gods will bless him; *a* 16 (when the king has listened to the complaint of the Babylonians, but a-na qa-li tur-ru (but can be turned to partiality). IV² 17 *a* 53, 54 O Šamaš a-na ni-iš qa-ti-ja qu-lam-ma, hear my prayer (Z^B 69; Br 9390); 54 *b* 6, 8 qu-ul ši-ta-al-šu. K 1282 *O* 5 qu-la-ma nap-xar-ku-nu, pay ye all heed (KB vi, 1, 68 *foll*).

3¹ perh. K 519 *O* 12 uq-ti-il i-da-te. Martin, *Rec. Trav.*, 23, 160 *fol*: il a tenu compte des présages.

qa'ālu. II 47 *a-b* 12 qa-a-a-lu = šar-ru ek-ki-mu, AV 7318, Br 4272. BA ii 280 Schreier, Prahlhans.

qallu. *m* servant, slave; in *c. t.* also: assistant (Camb 43; 62, 20; 161; 257; 391) {Knecht, Sklave, Diener; in *c. t.* auch Gehülfe}; *f* qallatu. ZA v 276, 2; Z^B 61; 28 *rm* 2. iD usually (amēl) GAL-LA, K 79 *R* 7 + 16 (Hr^L 266); Peiser, *Vertr.*, 27, 1; 40, 1; also perh. 73, 3; 74, 6; 90, 3 (amēl) GAL-LA-šu; see also Peiser, ZA iii 82; KAS iii *b*. Nabd 1008, 4; 244, 1; 194, 1; ZA iv 120 *no* 17 (amēl) gal-la ša šul-lum (AV 1504); KB iv 200 *no* i 8; BA iii 458, 459. K 479, 21 bīti-a u (amēl) qa-al-la-a (BA i 245; ZA iv 70 & *rm* 1 √ קלל). Beh 44 & 53 such & such (amēl) gal-la-a (māt) Par-sa-a-a. NE 66, 35 (amēl) qal-lu(-)u (amēl) e-dil(?)-u, KB vi (1) 228, 229; see *ibid* 478 where it is identified with kallū, *q. v.* K 1606 *R* 9 (amēl) qa-al-lu, Thompson, *Reports*: magician. Perh. II 57 *a-b* 37 see nalšu, 679 *col* 1. Peiser, *Vertr.*, v 3 *N* qal-la-šu, his slave *N*; lxxiii 11 (amēl) qal-li-šu; Nabd 751, 5; 789, 11; 518, 21 (-šu-nu); 13, 4 qal-la-a; 386, 4 (amēl) GAL-LA interchanges with (amēl) MU. BA i 200; iv 484. KB iv 198 *no* xxix 7: nap-ša-ti ša (amēl) qal-li-ka u-šal-lum-ka. See also BA i 244, 245; ii 43; 124; 526 & kallū (383). — **qallatu,** AV 1505. Nabd 679, 1 gal-la-tum ša *N*; 682, 1 (amēl) gal-la-ta; 1008, 2 (-tum); 243, 12 gal-lat ša *N* (KB iv 228, 229); 196, 8; (sal) gal-lat-su ça-xir-tum mārat erbit-ta šanāte; 693, 4 (see çaxru); 253, 8; 143, 4 (sal) gal-lat. Peiser, *Vertr.*, xxiv (VATh 107) 4; xxxiv 4; lvi 3. Camb 334, 3 (sal) gal-lat-su (KB iv 292, 293); Neb 386, 3 (end).

NOTE. — WZ iv 307, 4: name for slave in neo-babylonian contracts = qallu: in syllabaries & older contracts we find ardu.

qallu *2.* lowly {gering, niedrig} AV 7323; II 36 *a* 40 qa-al-lu; 34, la-ku-u. — Neb 12, 1 kaspu qal-la (= gering, verringert) la ša gi-in[-nu]; or qal-la-la? √ קלל. *adv*:

qalliš. frivolously {leichtfertig} IV² 60* B *O* 22 niš ilišu kabti qal-liš izkur.

qallu *3.* forest {Wald} for nallu (see 678 *col* 1), AV 7323.

qullu. Br. M. 84, 2—11, 88, 6—7 kaspu ra-šu-tum ša ina eli xurāçi qu-ul-lu, Peiser, *Vertr.*, xciii; see *ibid p* 280, would combine with qalū (ZA iii 214 *no* 1, 1)

= Camb 45; *ibid* 10, 11 qu-ul-lu u xarrê i-na-aš-ši.

qalû 1. *pr* iqlû, *ps* iqallu. burn {brennen, verbrennen} G § 33; AV 7320; § 19. T^M v 130 aq-lu. K 3341 (IV^2 49) *R* 57 aššî ṭ(d)i-pa-ru çalmâni-šu-nu a-qal-lu (= T^M i 135; *ibid*, *p* 126; § 110). T^M ii 68 at the shore of the shining river-goddess a-qal-li-šu-nu-ti a-šar-rap[-šu-nu]-ti. TP viii 60 whosoever this memorial slab *etc.* i-na NE^{pl} (= iššâti) i-qal-lu-u; KB iv 90 *col* v 1. Sp 93, 24—5 ša šani-i i-qa-la-a-'a. IV^2 39 *R* 19 (i-qa-lu-u); III 43 *c* 34; 41 *b* 11 i-qa-al-lu-u; I 70 *c* 4 has instead of these i-šar-ra-pu; K 689 (Hr^L 312) *R* 16 i-ka-al-la, 8 ka-lu-te. Zimmern, *Ritualtafeln*, 60, 30 (end) a-na ma-aq-lu-te i-qa-lu. ip T^M ii 98 o firegod qu-li; 100 qu-li-šu-nu-ti; 185 qu-li, + 203 (BA iv 157 -me?); iv 116; 118 qu-li-ši-na-a-ti; ag to the firegod qa-mi-e qa-li-e ka-si-i (T^M iv 10, 56, 73—4; 94—5). pm perh. T. A. (Ber) 92, 31 a-na lib-bi i-ša-ti a-na na-za-ki u-ba-u-ka u ga-lu. H 19, 320 bi-il NE | qa-lu-u; II 35 *e-f* 16 qa-lu-u ‖ qa-mu-u; perh. II 24 *e-f* 57, Br 4587.

𝔔t 81—2—4. 58 *R* 7 ma-qa-la-tu aq-ṭu-lu, Hr^L 301.

𝔇 K 185 *R* 4, 5 lu-u i-ša-ti me-im-ma u-qa-al-li (Hr^L 74).

𝔖 V 56, 36 whosoever this stone ... iššâti u-šaq-lu-u; also i-ša-ta u-ša-aq-[lu-u] BA ii 140.

𝔑 Rm 2, 139, 6 iq-qal-li.

Derr. — maqlû, maqlûtu (see *p* 577); qilû; qalûtu, qilûtu. KB vi (1) 380 also taqlîmu = Hebr קלי cake ‖ Backwerk, but see taklîmu.

qalû *2.* K 55 *R* 1 GAR-SA-SA; *O* 10 GAN-ŠE-SA-A = qa-lu-u (the latter id in *O* 11 = la-ap-tum); K 8676 iv 10; M^S texts, *pl* 3. See also Br 3163 on II 24 *e-f* 58.

qalû *3.* & **qûlu** (?) in connection with kaspu. KB iv 316—17, 1: ²/₃ ma-na kaspi qa-lu-u šul-šu (Antiochus-text) ZA iii 137; also *ibid* 214, 1: 1 ma-na kaspa qa-lu-u. Neb 38, 2; Dar 84, 1; 393, 1. Br. M. 81, 6—25, 45 *ll* 7—9 (BOR ii 3). *M* gives to *A-B*, his wife, a piece of land *etc.* instead of 80 mana kaspi piçû 2 mana xurâçu 5 mana kaspu qu-lu u si-me-ri; Pinches, *ibid*: refined silver. T^M combines with qalû, burn, also qu-lu ku-ru (see above) = burning, fever {Brand, Entzündung}. Hrozný, BA iv 546, wol etwa: gebrannt, geläutert.

qilû. Rm 76 *R* 12 (Hr^L 358) ki-li-a, my funeral pyre {mein Scheiterhaufen} BA iv 511.

qullû (?) K 8669 ii 28 qu-ul-li-i me-me-e-ni, ZDMG 53, 117—8.

q(k,g)alad(ṭ)u 𝔇 Bu 91—5—9, 290, 10 *foll* at-ta tu-ka-al-li-da-an-ni šu-bi-lam-ma, if thou art favorable to me = קלט = magaru, Winckler, *Forsch*, ii ('98) 133. — 𝔖 K 2801 *R* 38 ça-al-me .... u-šaq-li-du u-ša-an-bi-ṭu kima (il) Šam-ši.

qalalu, be light, small, insignificant {leicht, gering, geringfügig sein} AV 7316. II 48 *g-h* 31 PIL (= NE) (pi) LAL = qa-la-lum, Br 4635.

𝔇 make light of, hold in contempt, slander, slight {gering achten, verachten, verleumden, schlecht handeln} D^{Pr} 140. K 3177 *R* 2 ar-ni ša u-qal-li-lu, Craig, *Religious Texts*, i *pl* 14. ZA v 67, 41 ina mi-ni-e u-qal-lil-ki-ma, in what have I hold thee in contempt? Esh *Sendsch*, *R* 35 ana (il) Ašur ix-ṭu-u u-qal-li-lu i-ši-ṭu (ZA viii 115); K^M 11, 10 mannu lâ i-ši-iṭ ja-u la u-qal-lil (so instead of ukallil). IV^2 10 *b* 33, 34 lu-u u-qal-lil (Br 4741, 9500) lu-u u-dam-me-iq mimma ul idî (Z^B 21, 72; Zimmern, ZA xi 89 >< dummuqu). Perh. K 41 *c* 19 (end) ra-man-ki ki-i tu-g(q)al-li-li (Pinches, PSBA xvii, '95, 64); V 45 iv 25 tu-q(k)al-lal. Bu 11—5—9, 354, 35 ga-ga-di-ka tu-ga-la-al; also *cf* T. A. (Lo) 72, 38—9 i-nu-ma ŠIK-ja | ji-ki-il-li-mi u KAB | ji-ka-bi-id | a-xi-ja xi-ix-ru-tu, KB v 322—23: so that he looks upon me with contempt and honors my younger brothers. II 48 *g-h* 32 XUL = qu-ul-lu-lu (H 16, 247; AV 7406); 33 XUL-MU-UN-ŠI-EB = u-qal-li-la-an-ni (Br 9500). K 2022 i 4 qu-lu-lu between çu-ux-xu & kup-pu-du. perhaps also H 107, 13 = V 11 *a-c* 13; D 126, 13 (Br 3578—9, 3594—5), but not certain; see H 112, 11 = qul-lu-u.

𝔇t see mâšu 𝔔t, 595 *col* 2.

ꝗ (?) Bu 11—5—9, 2185, 2 *l* 26 among my brethren ka-ag-ga-di la i-ga-al-li-il, let my head (= myself) not be held in contempt.

ꝗ¹ Perhaps K 2401 ii 16 at-ta-qa-al-la-al-la, I am distressed; STRONG, BA ii 628; but see MARTIN, *Textes relig.*, ('03) 196.

DERr. qallu 1 & 2 (?), qalliš; perh. killu, 2 (see above, 883 *col* 2), qalqaltu, and the following 6 (?):

qullultu, & **q(g)ulultu** *1.* — *a*) some misdeed, nefarious act, sin {Schmach, Schandtat, Sünde}. Sn iii 6 (see xiṭṭu); Esh ii 19—20 (not 61); TP III *Ann* 131, see xiṭṭu (*pp* 310, 311). IV² 60* C *O* 14 ša damqat ra-ma-nu-uš a-na ili qul-lul-tum, what appears to one pleasing (good), is evil in the sight of god. Sm 949 *O* 20 gu-lul-tu KAK (= êpu)-šu anū-ku ul i-di, I know not that I have committed an evil deed. — *b*) curse {Verwünschung}. *del* 273 (306) it-ta-di qu-lul-tum (see nadū Q¹ *g*; 648 *col* 2).

q(g?)ulq(g?)ullatu contempt {Verachtung}? T^M iv 32 çalmāni-ja a-na qul-qul-la-ti tap-qi-da.

qallatu dishonor, disgrace {Schmach, Entehrung}. Z^S iii 13 charm by: ka-bit-ti (= honor) ul qal-la-ti he loosens; but M^S: through something heavy or light. See also kullatu, 1. — A ‖ is:

qullatu. T^M iii 17 the intellect of the witch ina qul-la-ti ag-da-ri.

qillatu so G § 50 (*p* 44, *med*); ZIMMERN, ZA xi 89; Z^S *pp* 68; 80; KB vi (1) 242 on *del* 170 (185) be-el qil-la-ti e-mid qil-lat-su; instead of xablatu (see *p* 301); K^M 12, 78; 2, 39 *etc.*; Rm 601, 5 [...] xi-iṭ-ṭa-šu gi-il-la-tu-šu; 10 [....] ar-ni xi-ṭi u gi-il-la-ti itti Marduk i-za-ak-ku-u; *Rev. Sém.*, vi *no* 4; K 2333 *R* 9.

qallalu *1.* *n* K 55 *O* 23 [GAR(= ŠA)-SA]-SA = qal-la-lum; but K 8676 iv 8 reads the same id = qal-qal-lum, see M^S 84 *col* 2.

qallalu *2.* *adj* Ner 28, 21: II ⁽ⁱˢ⁾ maššānu *pl* rabûti II ⁽ⁱˢ⁾ maššānu *pl* qal-la-lu-tu; Cyr 370, 6 iš-pu-ru kaspu qa-al-la-al (>< kaspu kab-d(t)u, 8).

qulālu (?) K 638 *R* 17 ki-i ad-bu-bu qu-la-li-ja (Hr^L 328) √*q-l-l* (?).

qa-lal-lu-u, II 23 *a-b* 18 see paššūru.

qulultu *2.* Sp iii 6 *R* 9 (+ II 32 *no* 7, 62) GI-BAR(?, ME?)-GI = qu-lul(p?)-tum, in a list of trees, bushes *etc.*, PSBA xvi 308—9.

qullultu *2.* K 4166 *O* 4 BU-SU-UD = qul-lul-tu.

qalmu. II 36 *a* 41 qa-al-mu one of the 17 synonyms for small, weak (çixru?), AV 7325 ‖ qallu; D^Pr 90 & *rm* 3, >< HALÉVY, RÉJ x 302.

qalisu, √קלס (?). K 666 *R* 11, 12 ma-a ⁽ˢᵃˡ⁾ Çu-ux-ru | qa-li-su bi-la-a-ni a-na êkalli lu-še-e-li (Hr^L 12; BA i 626); AV 7317 reads qa-li su-bi-la-a-ni (?).

qalapu, peal *e. g.* an onion (?) {abschälen, eine Zwiebel, *etc.*}. H 38, 79 NUN = qa-la-pu. Babyl. Chron. iv 10 after UD-DU : ⁽ᵐᵃᵗ⁾ Aššur ana ⁽ᵐᵃᵗ⁾ Mi-çir DU (= illiku) qi-lip (perh. = xip(b)i: was destroyed, blotted out), KNUDTZON, >< WINCKLER, KB ii 282.

ꝗ IV² 7 *a* 51 ki-ma šûmi an-ni-i i-qal-la-pu (§ 22), like this onion which is pealed off; *a* 46 kīma šu-mi liq-qa-lip (§ 93*n*); *b* 5 kīma šûmi an-ni-i liq-qa-lip-ma, Br 2626; JENSEN, ZK ii 15; BA i 441; T^M v 57 liq-qal-pu kīma šûmi. — **Der.**:

qalp(b?)u. Neb 13, 2 ša mar-ri u qa-al-pu.

קלפא. Š see qiddatu, 2; also SMITH, *Sen*, 92, 64 (§ 117).

Š³ (?) K 2096 *O* 18 u muš-qa-al-pi-ti ilāni *pl* ša qid-da-a-ti (les dieux des abîmes, MARTIN), CRAIG, *Religious Texts*, i 56.

ꝗ *pr* iqilpū; *ac* niqilpū; *ag* mu(q)qalpū (ZA viii 80—82). — *a*) go, walk along, pass along, take the road to {gehen, dahingehen, den Weg nehmen} *etc.* *Adapa*-legend i 20 (end) ⁽ⁱˢ⁾ elippi-šu iq-qi-lip-pu, KB vi (1) 93: and his ship passed along (see *ibid*, 410, 411); III 58 *no* 7, *b* 40 when the moon through (ina) the clouds DIR-pu (*var* i-qi-lip-pu) mīlu illak; with gloss, 42, ni-iq-il-pu-u : a-la-ku (K 736 *R* 1; THOMPSON, *Reports*, ii *no* 130). BANKS, *Diss*, 12, 75 a-mat-su e-liš ina ni-qil-pi-ša ma-a-tu u-šam-ra-aç; IV² 9 *a* 61, 62 kâtu amâtka e-liš ki-ma ša-a-ri ina ni-qil-pi-[e] (= DIRI-GA) when thy command passes along on high like a stormwind. IV^2 50 *a* 49 the witch (kaššaptu) mu-la-'-i-tum ša šame-e mu-kal-pit-tum ša erçi-tim. See also ZA viii 81 on IV^2 3 *a* 55 (*add*: kima erpiti muq-qal-pi-ti) + IV^2 *add* 9 *a* 62 (Br 3741). Craig, ***Religious Texts***, ii 20: 91—5—9, 294, 7 elippu mexirtu u mu-ki-el-bi-tu. — *b*) with *acc.*: cross, cross over {überschreiten; über etwas setzen}. Smith, *Sen*, 92, 69 with the horses qu-ra-du-u-a i-na elippê i-qil-pu-u (nâr) Pu-rat-tu, my warriors crossed the Euphrates (ZA viii 82 *rm* 4). Smith, ***Asurb***, 193, 2 who ina ki-rib mar-ra-ti i-ki-il-pa-a ēmuru maruštu. D 88 (K 4378) vi 10 GIŠ-MA'-DIRI-GA-BA-BAD = mu(q)-qal-pi-tum (*i.e.* elippu) AV 5541, 8575; Br 3754, 6922 = a ferry boat, preceded by ni-bi-ru, *q. v.* II 62 *c-d* 48—51, DIR; ŠU = ni-qil-pu-u (Meissner, ZA viii 80; Scheil, ix 219 *nos* 2, 3; AV 6207; Br 10836); IR-TA-SUD-SUD = *„* ša zu-'-tu (? or -pi?) Br 5405, 7616; LU(lu-lu)LU = *„* sa mur-çi (H 25, 519; Br 6922), perh. be smitten by sickness.

3 ac V 41 *d* 57, 60 i-te-iq-lip-pu-u (followed by itaktumu, √כתם), same id as II 62 *c-d* 51, see 3.

qalaçu. Perh. 82, 9—18, 4159 ii 12 (bi-ir) UD = ka-la-çu, M^8 29; 47. — ב V 45 viii 1 tu-qal-la-aç.

qulqullu (?). K 8466, 4 .... du-u qul-qul-li; *cf* K 2852 + K 9662 ii 10 qul-qul-li-šu-nu ir-çi-pu di-ma-ti-iš, their *q* they built like pillars. Winckler, ***Forsch***, ii 28, 29. Neb 426, 2 q(g)ul-q(g)ul-lu ball {Kugel}? if so √גלל.

qulqullânu. a plant {eine Pflanze}. II 48 *a-b* 63 (šam) qul-qul-la-nu (Br 8971, 13319) = (šam) inbu ka-si çiri; 64 (šam) zēr qul-qul-la-nu (Br 1674) = (šam) ki-sa-at çiri: 66 (šam) qul-qu-la-a(?)-nu = (šam) ki-sa-at çiri (Br 1680); perhaps also 68 (šam) q(g)ul-lu-a(?)-nu (Br 1684) = (šam) zēr ki-sa-at çiri (Br 1686). Also II 42 *a-b* 45 (šam) qul-qul]-la-a-nu-um (?) = (šam) U (or šam?)(-)ra-nu; Br 13320; AV 1723. 79, 7—8, 19, 4 (šam) qul-qul-a-nu = (šam) ki-sat [çiri] AJSL xiii 220.

qalqaltu, hunger, famine {Hunger, Hungersnot, Verschmachtung}, form like panpanu, § 61, 1*a*; Z^B 15. Asb viii 87, 123, 106; ix 35; Esh iii 26 see çummû; Sarg *Ann* 266. K 2022 iv 17 (+ II 31 *c-d* 2—5) [ŠA = GAR]-GAR-GAR = qal-qal[-tu], in a group with bu-bu[-tum], um[-çu?], ni-ib[-ri-tu?]; V 11 *e-f* 43; D 128, 91; H 109, 43; ZK ii 270 *rm* 1; Br 8048, 8090; preceded by xu-ša-xu. See also xarxarru, *b* (387 *col* 1). √קלל.

qalatu. V 45 vii 44 tu-qa-al-lat(d, ṭ).

qil(î)tu. a plant {eine Pflanze}. K 4565 (šam) qi-il-tum, followed by (šam) qil-tum qar-ni. II 41 *no* 9, *g* 56 (šam) qi-li-tu, apparently a ‖ of (šam) e-pi-ta-a-tu; see also kilîtu, 2 (391 *col* 1). IV^2 61 *c* 52 Esh ka-a-su ša ma-lu-u qi-il-te.

qultu. III 67 *c-d* 68 god Ninib is called AN-ŠUR- 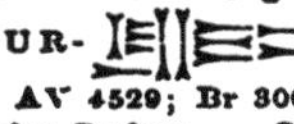 as god ša qu-ul-ti, AV 4529; Br 3007; KB vi (1) 573: Ninib des Rufens. — See also Rm IV 97 (83, 541) 20 (end) a-me-tum gu-ul-tum, translated by Pinches, PSBA xxiii 197: abundance of affliction (קלף?); IV^2 28 *no* 4 (K 4811) 4 (end) qu-ul-tum; same id as qûlu (Br 12160).

qalûtu. K 1133, qa-lu-tu ina eli ka-nu-ni lu-bi-la (Bezold, *Catal.*, 231; M^8 105 *col* 2). K 689 *R* 8 (the soldiers) qa-lu-te i-si-ja u-si-çi (AV 7322; Hr^L 312); √qalû, burn.

qilûtu. burning {Verbrennung} § 65, 9. S^b 42 gi-bi-il |  | ki-lu-tum (also = maqaddu) § 9, 272; Br 10867, 10871; H 34, 826; GGN '80, 541; ZK ii 15. K 4174 + K 4583 iii 8 gi-gi-bil | GI-GI-BIL gi-maš-tin-eš-še-ku | gi-bil-lu | ki-lu[-tum]; 82—8—16, 1 *R* 12 see Br 9702; Hommel, *Sum. Lesest.*, 98; Br 10978 on II 24 *e-f* 59. K 3476 *O* 29 qi-la-te] jarurâte.

qaluâte (?) K 1304 *R* 10 ina ili (iç) qa-lu-a-te bi-it šarri, *etc.*

קלתא. Perhaps 3 *del* 207 (220) si-bu-tum ina pi-it-tim-ma il-pu-us-su-ma iq(*var* i-te?)-qil-ta-a amēlu; 218 (242) te-et[-te]-qil-ta-a at-ta, KB vi (1) 246—47 and the man arose frightened {und der Mensch schrak auf} &, then didst thou arise frightened {da schrakest du auf}.

Also KB vi (1) 202, 203 on NE IX i 13 at night he laid down to sleep i[q-]qil-tu-ma šu-ut-tum; & 110—11 on *Etana*-legend, part iii 13 uq-qal-tam-ma at-ta-ru-r[u]; see *ibid* 419. — 27ᵗ see above, & *del* 195 (215) li-iq-qil-ta-a amēlu.

qāmu. T. A. see qā'u, 1 (ℑ *pr*) end.

qamū *1.* crush, said of grain, grind {zermalmen, zermahlen}, *cf* קמח, Jensen, ZK ii 31; 56 *rm* 2; 235; 238. Peiser, KAS 103, *med.* V 19 *c-d* 47 (+ K 2008 iii 49) KA (+ inserted ku) + KA (+ inserted ku) with gloss (mu-u mu-u) between the two signs, preceded by KA (+ inserted ku) with gloss (mu-u) = te-e-nu ša KU-DA (= qēmi) Br 810, 859. IV² 1* iv 21, 22 ma-a-tu(-tum) ki-ma ke-me (*var* mi; id ZID-GIM) i-qam-mu-u. — Der.:

kēmu = qēmu. grain, flour {Korn, Mehl} or the like. Br 10431; G § 70; BA i 280; KB iii (1) 27 *rm* **. III 65 *b* 43 mātu ke-im-ša i-ta-kal. Peiser, *Vertr.*, xxiii 13 ki-me i-nam-din. Camb 112, 2—3; 156 [mašīxi] ke-me ma-ak-ka-su ina sattuk ša Ābi. Cyr 187, 3—4: I AŠ ke-me ana (amēl) çab ša nāru (?) [i]-xi-ru-u i-din; 209, 6: I PI ke-me. In *c. t.* GAR-ZUN either: akālu or qēmu (see Ball, PSBA xii 57; BA i 280 on V 61 iv 54 & v 21); also *var* ki(qi)-me *i. e.* qēmē (= *pl*) found interchangeably. Nabd 24, 1; 113, 2; 21, 1; 29, 1; 62, 1; 86, 1 *etc*; 420, 1 510, 4 + 7; Tᶜ 123 below. ZK ii 31; ZA iii 237; KB iv 210, 211. — Also KU-DA, *e. g.* Neb 104, 3; 209, 1; 387, 2; 427, 1—4; 433, 1. GGA '98, 817 & 824 quotes IV² 3 *a* 37 (end) ki-ma (= KU) e-çir-ma; 13 *b* 55, 56 ke-im (= KU, Br 7484, 10531) aš-na-an elli-ti bāba ka-ma-a pi-rik-ma. K 166, 12 ke-im (= KU) qip-ti; see ZA i 13; KB vi (1) 374; Br 10432. Sᵇ 1 *O* iii 5 zi-i | KU | ki-e-mu, Br 10430. II 5 *c-d* 38 UX-KU-DA = kal-mat ke-mi, meal-worm (Br 8329, 10531); also IV² 2 *c* 20, 21. V 42 *a-b* 15 DUK-KU-DA = kar-pat ke[-mi], Br 10620, see karpatu, 440 *col* 1.

qamū *2.* *pr* iqmū, *pc* liqmū, *ip* qumu, *ps* iqammi(-mu); burn, burn up {brennen, verbrennen} § 19; Hᶠ 47, 8; AV 6094, 7326. Tᴹ v 79 aq-mu-ku-nu-ši; TP ii 82 all their cities i-na NE *pl* aq-mu. Sp II 265 *a* vi 9 gi-riš ina ū-um la ši-ma-ti i-qa-am-me-šu (*var* i-qam-meš) ma-al-ku. ina išāti aq-mu, often: TP III *Ann* 85, 175 *etc.* (interchanging with ina išāti ašru-up, 41 *etc.*); I 43, 39; Esh *Sendsch*, *R* 43. 44; Asb ii 131; v 57; vii 122 (iq-mu-u); KB ii 240, 39 ab-bul aq-qur ina išāti aq-mu. *Rec. Trav.*, xx 205 *foll col* 4, 20 ina išāti i-qam-mu-u; xix *pp* 62, 63 *no* 2, 6 qa-mu-u na-ki-ri-ka. 81, 2—4, 219 *R* i 13 i-qam-mu-u i-lam-mu-u, they burn, they besiege (*Rev. Sém.*, vi 359—61). IV² 7 *a* 52 like this onion (date, *etc.*) . . . ana išāti innadū | (il) NE-GI qa-mu-u i-qam-mu-u, which the burning god (the god of fire) burns up (+ *b* 9, 19, 29, 39, 49); *b* 6, 16, 26, 36, 46, 56; 8 *b* 20 (il) GIŠ-BAR qa-mu-u liq-mi; IV² 50 *a* 28 (il) NE-GI liq-mi-ki, may burn thee (Tᴹ iii 28; *cf* 85 + 165). *ip* qu-mu, Tᴹ i 115; ii 97; qu-mi, ii 15 *etc.*; qu-mu-šu-nu-ti (& -ši-na-a-ti) ii 99; iv 117. *ag* qa-mu-u, Tᴹ i 110; ii 130; iv 12, 58; see also qalū, *ag*; qa-mi-ku-nu, v 183. *ac* II 34 *a-b* 70 NE-PA-GA = ka-mu-u (preceded by naq-mu-u) Br 4626. II 35 *e-f* 14—16 see qādu, 2. V 19 *c-d* 48 (K 2008 iii 50) NI (za-al) NI = qa-mu-u ša nab-li, Br 5359; also see *l* 47; & K 2852 + K 9662 i 1 (end) ša ki-ma nab-li i-qam-mu-u a-a-bi i-ku-la.

ℑ NE VIII v (vi) 11 heat q]u-um-mu-u (or perh. -lum?) pa-nu-ka, has scorched thy face, KB vi (1) 216—17; 200, 18. V 28 *e-f* 87 ku-u-u (AV 4459) = qu(m)-mu-u ša i-ša-tum (AV 7410), the former only a late pronunciation of the latter, see Jensen, KB vi (1) pref. xi. See also Zᴮ 16; ZA ii 280; BA i 453 *rm* 2; Lehmann, i 15.

Š KB iii (1) 162 *col* v 44, whosoever this boundary stone i-ša-ta u-ša-ak-ka-mu.

27 IV² 8 *b* 8 ki-ma ZI (= qēm?) zēr upunti an-ni-i ina išāti i[q-qa-mu-u].

Derr. — naqmū, naqmātu (719 *col* 2); perh. also dikmēnu (> tiqmēnu), see 247 *col* 1.

qamū 3. (?). 82—7—4, 42 *R* 9 u-qa-mu-u ri-es-su. PSBA xx 252 bend {beugen}.

qimaxxu (mostly written with initial *g* & *k*), *m pl* qimaxxē, perh. coffin, urn {Sarg,

Urne}. id KI-MAX, ZIMMERN, *Ritualtafeln*, 48, 10; 44, 1; T^{M} iv 81; K 3454; K 14223 (BEZOLD, *Catalogue*, 543, 1369). K 168 *O* 13 bît KI-MAX ni-ta-pa-aš-šu (Hr^{L} 437; epešu). Sn *Bell* 46 the river T .... uabbitu $^{(iç)}$ ki-max-xe-šu-un nak-mu-ti u-kal-li-mu $^{(il)}$ Šam-šu; ZA iii 315 (325) 73 ki-max-xe-šu-un pa-az-ru-ti; I 48, 8 ul-tu ki-rib KI-MAX ix-pi-ir-ma; id also *Rec. Trav.*, xxii (SCHEIL) Notes d'épigraphie li, 5—7 KI-MAX a-ni-a-am a-na aš-ri-šu li-te-ir; 11 KI-MAX mûši a-ni-am, *etc.* Asb vi 70—3 ki-max-xe šar-râni-šu-nu .... abbul aqqur u-kal-lim $^{(il)}$ Šam-ši. IV^{2} 60* C *R* 16 pi-ti KI-MAX. V 40 *c-f* 56 KI-MAX = iç-çu-u gi(& ki, Sm 1701 *R*)-ma-xi; ZA i 400 *rm* 1.

NOTE. — See § 73*n*; MEISSNER & ROST, 22; M^{S} 84 *col* 2. JENSEN, *apud* BROCKELMANN, *Lexicon Syriacum*, & ZA ix 268; x 83; *Theolog. Literatur-ztg.*, '95 *no* 10; HOFFMANN, ZA ix 337. BROCKELMANN, ZA xiii 327 *fol*; J^{W} 64, 65; O § 73. S. A. COOK, PSBA xxi ('99) 74; HALÉVY, *Rev Sém.*, iii 87.

qamxurû, part of the palmtree {Teil des Palmbaumes}. V 26 *e-f* 43 qa-am-xu-ru-u, same id in 42 = u(or U = $^{(šam)}$?)(-)qu-ru (Arm קורא). Br 8058; JENSEN, ZK ii 26; AMIAUD, ZA iii 45; AV 7327. See perh. II 43 *c-f* 58 $^{(šam)}$ qa(?)-am-xu-ra = $^{(šam)}$ a-[sign]-ar-tum (?).

qamaku (?) T^{M} iii 20 (end) e-ra qa-ma-ki (+ 21, beg.; BA iv 157).

qummalu = some animal (like bûlu) {ein Tier}. V 31 *c-d* 48, 49 qu-um-ma-lam (lu) = bu-lum, AV 7412.

qummulum. NE VIII v/vi 11 see qamû, 2 ℑ.

qumullu, see 808 *col* 1.

qamaçu, bend the knee, kneel down {das Knie beugen, knien} see also kamaçu (397 *col* 2). Dupl. to Creat.-*frg* III 70 iq-miç (or ik-mis, *var* i-šir) KB vi (1) 16, 17. K 1285 *O* 19 ka-me-iç ina ki-in-çi-e-šu, CRAIG, *Religious Texts*, i *p* 5 (see kinçu, 408 *col* 2).

ℑ V 45 vii 43 tu-qa-am-maç (a, š).

Š K 3464 *O* 15, 16 tu-še-li-ma ina kin-çi-šu tu-šaq-mas-su, CRAIG, *Religious Texts*, *pl* 66. — Der.:

qim(& n)çu. KB vi (1) 164 *ad* NE V *col* 4, 6 $^{(il)}$ Gilgameš ina qin-çe q[a-miç]; see *ibid*, *p* 321. BOISSIER, *Documents*, 32, 1 šumma aqrabu kim-çi imnašu, *etc.* T^{M} vi 8 qin-ça-a-a ‖ šêpâ'a; also K 2148 iii 16 (ZA ix 120).

qumqummu. T^{M} vi 19 kaššaptu qu-um-qu-um-ma-tum, a name for the witch.

qumaru. K 2148 iii 28 qu-ma-ar-šu ša imitti-ša, in the description of an idol, ZA ix 117—19.

qummarû (?) II 35 *g-h* 39 qu-um-ma(?)-ru-u = e-ri-eš-ša-nu, a plant {eine Pflanze}; AV 7413 read *-qa-* instead of *-ma-*.

qummašu see nêmašu, 690 *col* 1.

qumtu so HAUPT, *Jour. Bib. Lit.*, xix 64 *rm* 28: stature, figure; for kumtu, see 399 *col* 2. ZIMMERN, *Ritualtafeln*, 221 *col* 1 reads gattu *ad* 24, 28 + 30; see also kittu, Sn *Kuj* 4, 22; ZA xv 417.

qanû 1. perh. acquire, produce {erwerben, vollbringen} Deut. 32, 6; Prov. 8, 22. See kanû, 1 (405); K 1101, 16 what my father ..... iq-nu-u-ni, has acquired, Hr^{L} 152 (he has taken away).

ℑ V 45 vii 40 tu-qa-an-na.

qanû 2. AJSL xi 102 reads K 155, 21 a-qan-'a-ka (√קנא?) against K^{M} *no* 1, a-ša-'-ka.

qanû 3. be angry {zürnen} קנא T. A. (Lo) 61, 64 qa-nu-u (3 *pl*). ZA vi 158.

qanû *4.* *m* (§§ 27; 65, 6). — *a*) reed {Rohr} *pl* qanâti (§ 70*a*); id GI (§ 9, 16); H 2 + 178, 48; 15, 193. AV 7328; D^{H} 34; ZA iii 420. KB vi (1) 38 *no* 2, 2 qa-nu-u ul a-çi. IV^{2} 8 *a* 5, 6 (id GI) *cf* xaçaçu, ℑt (333 *col* 1); 19 *b* 45, 46 nak-ru dan-nu ki-ma qa-ni-e (= GI) i-di u-'š'ip-pa-ni. BANKS, *Dirs*, 16, 122 ki-ma qa-ni e-di çal-lu kab-tu; ki-ma qa-ni-e e-di çal-lu, *etc.* K 4395 v 18 $^{(amêl)}$ ša eli qa-na-a-te (= II 31 *a-b* 77) Br 13841, AV 7330. Neb 421, 4 $^{(amêl)}$ rab qa-na-a-tu. *Rec. Trav.*, xix 62, 63 (SCHEIL, Notes, 2) 11 Tabnît A-ga-ne^{ki} qa-na-a-ti. Sp III 6 *O* ii 10—11 GI-BIL (& -LA) = qa-nu-u šu-ru-up-tum, "cane of burning", torch (?) *cf* 18 id = ṭi-pa-ri; 12 = SU (*i. e.* gibillu)-u; *R* ii 3 GI-AŠ-DU-A = qa-nu-u š(s)in-na-nu; 6 GI-UR-GI = iš-di qa-ni-e; 7 GI-ŠA-GI = lib-bi qa-ni-e, followed (8) by ar-tum qanie & qu-lul-tum qanie. Note qânu appari or apparâte reed {Binsen} *e. g.* KB vi (1) 40, 25 ap-pa-ri qa-na-a. — qa-an ir-ri-ti = bīt šaxē, V 32 *e-f* 47 (Br 2488). — qa-ni-e a-pi WINCKLER, *Sargon*, I (*no* 31, 8) 202; ZA iv 412; see also Esh *Sendsch*, *O* 32; Anp i 23. — qa-an u-ru-ul-lu II 24 *a-b* 14; V 32 *c-d* 46 (Br 2445). — qa-an be(or til?)-la-ti (Br 2462); & qa-an ma-lal-li-e (Br 2463, see 169 *col* 2); also see mamītu, 554 *col* 1 (*med*). — qa-an taxāzi (*q. v.*) Neb vi 22; viii 42; ix 40 = spear {Speer} Br 2446. — qa-an pāštu (*q. v.*). — qa-an d(t)uppi & qa-an dup-ba-an (*var* -ni) AV 2048, see duppu 262, 263. ZIMMERN, *Ritualtafeln*, 1—20, 14 *etc.* qa-an tup-pi; Br 2468—9, 3943, *cf* KB vi (1) 268 *no* I *b* 5 qan-t(d)up-pā(pa)-ti (+ 11): Schreibtafelrohre. — qān kunināti see kuninu, 1 (408 *col* 2). — qa-an tap-šir(?)-ti, *q. v.* Br 2506. — qa-an ša-la-lu (Br 2522) *q. v.* — qa-an mi-ix-ri *etc.*, see mexru, 2 & qa-an ma-ša-ri (*q. v.*). — rikis qanē (Br 2444) see riksu. — xuppū ša GI (= qanē) II 27 *g-h* 57 see xipū. — lubšu ša qanāte *cf* lubšu. — na(n)çabu ša GI see na(n)-çabu. — qān tēlilti (Br 2540) *cf* tēliltu. On qanū ṭābu see KAT³ 600 *rm* 5. — *b*) staff {Stab} ZA v 68, 17 ça-bit qa-ni ilū-ti-ki, who takes hold of the staff of thy divinity. K 3600 *O* 18 Šargina ça-bit qa-ni-ki, CRAIG, *Religious Texts*, vol i. — *c*) a measure of length, longitude {ein Längenmass}; *cf* our "rod"; also an acre {ein Acker} T^{C} 124. — 1 GAR = 12 U; 3 qanē = 1 1/2 GAR; 1 qanū = 6 U. GGA '78, 1061 *foll.* HAUPT, *Proc. Am. Or. Soc.*, Oct. '88; lxxxix; AJP ix 421 = double-rod. On qanāte, Cyr 128; 168 *etc.* in description of property see BA iv 65; often in STRASSMAIER, *Stockholm* (*VIII. Or. Congr.* Cyr 308, 13: 2 qa-nu-u ugāri; Nabd 360, 3 qa-ni-e *etc.* — Etymology: see DELITZSCH, *Lit. Centralbl.*, '85, 354; H^{F} 49; H 178, 48; D^{Par} 60.

qannu *1.* qa-an-nu a-a-lu SAR name of a plant {Gewächsname} 81—7—6, 688 iii (ZA vi 291). K 1118, 9 a-na qa-an-ni la u-çu-u (*cf ibid* 19). See also JOHNS, *Doomsdaybook*, texts 3 i 8: 300 qan-ni za-am-ri; see *ibid p* 44: "byeform of qanū", used to denote: 'stalks or shorts'.

qannu *2.* district, boundary {Gebiet, Grenze}. K 1026 *R* 10 qa-an-ni a-xi-ia ni-za-ax (V 54 *no* 1; Hr^{L} 118). K^{M} 18, 9—10 çab-ta-ku-ma ki-i ti-i-ri ina qa-an-ni-ka. K 2701 *a*, 11 ina qa-an-ni (al) Xarran. See KNUDTZON, 109, 7 (amēl) qēpāni ša qa-an-ni; 108, 8 [amēl qē]pāni ša qa-a-ni. K 525, 8 (BA ii 55). See KNUDTZON, 228 (× BA ii 60). — T. A. (Ber) 24 *R* 84 a-na āli-ia ša qa-an-ni māt-ti, to my city on the border of the land; (Lo) 2, 20. JOHNS, *Deeds*, *nos* 331, 6; 472, 10.

qannu *3.* KB vi (1) 210, 211 on NE X *col* 1, 3 ip(b)-šu-ši q(k)an-nu, she is protected with a covering {sie ist mit einer Hülle umhüllt}; *ibid*, 578—9 connects with kannu, 2 (406 *col* 2).

qannu *4.* = qinnu 1. Perhaps also qa-ni (al) Til-abni, JOHNS, *Doomsdaybook*, 29 *no* I 1, 24 *etc.*: in the district of T. M^{S} 85 *col* 1, see qanuu, 2. √qananu.

qinnu *1.* AV 7383; D^{Pr} 34; Z^{B} 88. — *a*) birdnest {Vogelnest} see qananu, Q. *pl* qi-ni & qi-in-ni (§ 19). *Etana*-legend (KB vi (1) 104) *no a* 18 .... qin-na[-šu]; *b* 5 eu-ni-na qin-ni[-ia] + 6. K 2686 *O* 5 ..... lu-u qin-nu nar-ba-as[-su]. Asb viii 110 a desert where iççur šame-e la i-šak-ka-nu qin-nu; Anp i 49 kīma ki-in (*var* qin)-ni u-di-ni; 51 (figuratively) see xepū Q 329 *col* 2. Sn iii 68 see naššru, 741 *col* 1. V 65 *b* 7 ki-ma ni-ri-bi qin-ni-e u-dan-nin, like the entrance to a nest I fortified it (but see M^{S} 85 *col* 1). II 33 *a-b* 5 U-KI-SE-GA = qin-nu (D 80 ii 1 qin-nu : qa-an[-nu] Br 6077) 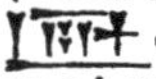 = tak-ka-pu (KB vi, 1, 528). II 27 *a-b* 59 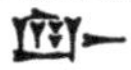 A-LAL (ab-lal = suspended house) = qin-nu ša iççūri (Br 10318; see qiburru); H 33, 772. — V 42 *a-b* 62, 63 U(gu-ud)KI-SE-GA = qin-nu (see also V 52 *a* 60, 61 & kisikku, 414 *col* 2); (ab-lal)  (usually = xammu, Br 10278 *foll*) = qinnu ša XU. V 32 *e-f* 56—59 qin-nu ša iççūri ‖ ašā-šu, xišu, uššštum, adattum; see also HAUPT in CHEYNE, *Isaiah* (SBOT) 133. H 109 iii 26 = D 129, 123 = V 12 *e-f* 23 ŠA-UR = qin-nu, Br 12178. K 4174 + K 4583 *col* 2 *c-d* 26. IV² 14, 1 *R* 6 ul-tu qi-ni (= U-KI-SE-GA) (il) Zi-i it-be-ma; same id also: 27 *no* 5, 19—20 see sinuntu. — *b*) family {Familie} *pl* qinnāte. Asb iii 10 his brothers qin-nu-šu zēr bīt ābišu they killed with their weapons; iv 23; vi 82 the daughters and the sisters of the kings a-di qi-in-ni max-ri-ti u arkī-ti ša šarrāni Elamti; ix 4 his mother, his sisters, his wife, qin-nu-šu. IV² 45 no 2 (K 13) 8 his wife, his sons and (amēl) qin-na-aš-šu gab-bi (Hr^L 281) §§ 53 rm; 74, 1 note. Sargon *Ann* 47, 64, *Khors* 56: *NN* a-di qin-ni-šu, and his family. TP vi 31: 300 qi-in-na-a-te^pl (bēl) xi-i-ṭe^(pl) = 300 families implicated in the rebellion. K 6, 4 (9, 15, 20, 25) *NN* qin-ni ša bīt (amēl) Ga-xal, ZA i 424. K 615, 8 (amēl) qin-na-a-ta (Hr^L 258; PSBA xxiii *pt* 2). K 114 *R* 7—8 a-di (amēl) qin-ni-šu u (amēl) A-ra-mi-šu. Rm 76 *R* 47 (48) a-du qin-ni-šu (Hr^L 358; PSBA xxiii 357). √qananu.

qi-in-nu-u (id QI, QIN) see JAOS xxii 218.

qi-nu (?) ZA xii 410—11, 14 GIŠ-GIŠIM-MAR] ... TUR-TUR = qi-nu, preceded by ‖ ta-a-lu; *cf Rev. Sém.*, x 248 *fol* on Sp II 111, 1—2: tālu ša qin-nu (Halévy, קִנְ׳ן), le très jeune palmier.

qinū. V 47 *b* 18, see patanu, 2 ב.

qunnu (?) V 42 (*e-*)*f* 57 qu-un-nu[-nu??] AV 7414, Br 6207; II 26 *no* 2 *add.*

qunnab(p)ru. V 41 *c*(-*d*) 13 qu-un-nab(p)-ru, *col d* broken off.

qunduxu. V 41 *g-h* 8, 9 a-ša-šu & si-lak-ku = qu-un-du-xu : a-lum.

qin(n)ā'zu. perhaps: whip, or the like {Peitsche, oder etwas Ähnliches} KB vi (1) 450. Br 227, 8189—90. V 47 *a* 60, 61 qi-na-zu id-da-an-ni; qi-na-zu = (iç) tax-ri. IV² 60* C *R* 2 qi-na-zi id-da-an-ni; see also taraku & IV² 30* *no* 3 *R* 10 ina qi-na-zi (= SU + id of S^b 209; Br 227) ki-ma i-me-ri mun-nar-bi zu-mur-ka u-tar-rak, *Rev. Sém.* vi 149; IV² 28 *no* 1, 16 (il) Šamaš rag-gu ki-ma qi-na-zi it-tar-rak-ka; 24 *a* 44, 45 qar-ra-du ša qi-na-as-su, *etc.* S^b 299 qi-na-zu (Br 8189, 8190; Hommel, *Sum. Lesest.*, 24, 291: Schlauch); H 27, 601. T. A. (Lo) 30, 48 (iç) gi-na-zu. — *b*) name of a bird {Name eines Vogels} tu-bal-la-aç ki-na-sa see 167 *col* 2.

qananu, pr iqnun. build a nest, nest {ein Nest bauen, nisten}. Sn *Kui* 4, 38 in the orchards iççur šame-e .... qin-nu iq-nun. V 42 *a-b* 64, 65 UŠ = qa-na-nu ša qi[n-ni?] Br 5035; ÇIR-TIK-GIG = *q* ša çi[-ri] Br 3233; *cf* II 33 *a-b* 7 (Br 7644; AV 7329). D 80 i 6, 7 GIR-TIK-GIG-DUG-GA (Br 7645); ÇIR-DI-XUŠ (Br 7655, 9559) = ka-na-nu ša çiri.

ב V 45 vii 41 tu-qa-an-na-an. D 80 ii 3, 4 ŠA(=LIB)-SIG (Br 8083); ŠA (si-ir)PU (Br 8055) = qu-un-nu-nu, §§ 63; 88. IV² 6 *a* 13, 14 ina ša-sur ni-ši çīra u-qan-ni-nu (= TIG-GIG-DUG-GA, Br 3236). See also piršānu.

qanap(b)u. V 45 vii 42 tu-qa-an-nap(b).

(riqqu) **qu-nu-pu.** Bu 80—4—26, 5 (Hr^L 368) 12: hemp {Hanf}.

kanaku, *i. e.* psp. pr iqnuq, ps ikanak (iqanaq), ip kunuk, ag kāniku. seal {siegeln} perh. originally: press, imprint. T^C 82. V 61 vi 15 all this he has given to him u ana paqri la rašē ik-nu-uk (ma), he has sealed; Peiser, *Vertr.*, xxxi 9 + 13; xxvi 6 (ik-nu-ku-ma)-; ZA iii 221, 11; Nabd 356, 18; Cyr 277, 5; K 4289 *R* 7. BOR ii 3, 7 ik-nu-uk-ku(ma); Neb 334, 3 ik-nu-ku-u-ma. KB iv 82 (I) 15 ik-nu-u-kam-ma, + 24 a-kan-nak(-ma); 21 ik-nu-ku-ma; 26 eqlē ik-nu-kam-ma (+ 34, 36). K 1274 *R* 8 (amēl) rāšu ik-nu-ku-u-ni, the officer who executed the contract (Hr^L 220; JAOS xviii 178 *foll*). Creat.-*frg* IV 122 see ki-šibbu (446 *col* 1). Neb 283, 3 tak-nu-ku-ma (3 *f sg*); see also Peiser, *Vertr.*, xxvii 3 + 10; xxvi 9 tak-nu-uk-ma tu-šad-gil .... pa-ni *etc.* (& see *ibid*, *p* 245); also T^C xiii on similar expressions. Cyr 368, 3 tak-ka-nu-uk-ma. 1 *sg*: K 7856 i 7 *fol* ak-nu-uk(ma); K 2729 *O* 27 i-na un-ki šarrū-ti-ja ak-nu-uk. Perh. Cyr 277, 9 + 11 i-uk-nu-ma (T^C 18). — pc li-ik-nu-uk, ZA v 144, 22. T. A. (Ber) 7, 22 (+ 24). — ip ZA iii 366 (Nabd 380) 10 ku-nu-uk; Cyr 311, 5 (KB iv 282); Br. M. 84, 2—11, 72; also KB iv 158 —9, 14 duppa-šu ku-nu-uk-ma bi-in-ni. — pm Nabd 356, 24—5 mimma ša kan-gu-ma pa-ni-ja šu-ud-gu-lu whatsoever has been sealed and legally given me; 1113, 24 a-na kaspi ka-na-ak ardu a-na-ku. KB iv 68—9 *col* 1, 23 according to the order of N. ... ka-ni-ki (3 *pl*); 70—1 *col* 3, 7, and says: kunukku ul ka-nik-ma; see also III 43 *col* 3, 17 u kunukku ul ka-ni-ki; KB iv 164—5 *col* 5, 5 (aban) na-ra-a ka-nik. — *ps* NE 65, 26 as long as ni-kan-na [-ak duppa?], we seal tablets (*i. e.* make treaties?) KB vi (1) 228—9; Br. M. 84, 2—11, 72: a-di la duppi ik-ka-na-ka (Kohler-Peiser, ii 73, 74); Nabd 50, 15 ik-ka-na-ak-ma (or נכך?). — ac Merod.-Balad.-Stone iv 56 ina ka-nak duppi šuāte .... iz-za-zi (KB iii (1) 190); v 15; (BA ii 264—5; 271 ✕ ZA vii 190); I 66 *b* 5; T^C 83; Strassm., *Stockholm. Orient. Congr.*, 2, 20. = to ratify. *Rec. Trav.* xx 205 *col* 3, 5; ZK i 49, 38; & 52. V 61 vi 17; Nabd 990, 21. Cyr 277, 20 ina ka-nak-kam duppi šuatim (BA iii 428—9). KB iv 66—7 *no* iii (1) *col* 2, 5; 94, 18; 90—1 *col* vi 14 i-na ka-nak kam-gi ša-a-tu. Dar 37, 30 i-na ka-na-ku duppi šu-a-tim; 32: III šiqli kaspi ki(= qi)-iš-tum ka-na-ki (for the sealing); *cf* Cyr 188, 35. P. N. ka-nak bābi, Nabd 993, 31. II 28 *f-g* (*i. e.* K 4361 ii 1—3) 55 TAG-ŠID-RA-RA = ka-na-ku (Br 5996, 6371); 56, TAG-ŠID-GUR = *k* ša kunukki (Br 3362; II 39 *g-h* 11; Br 3926); 57, TAG-ŠID(du)GAB = *k* ša ša-bi-e (*cf* šabū; Br 4470). II 39 *g-h* 10 KA-KAK = ka-na-ku, Br 658. On kanaku & ina kunukki baramu, see WZKM iv 307.

Q¹ K 666 *R* 5: III dup-pa-a-ni ak-ta-nak (BA i 627); K 664 *R* 5; K 578, 12; K 538 *R* 2 (end) ik-ta-nak, he sealed it up; K 5464 *R* 23 a-ta-xar ak-ta-na-ak (PSBA xvii 229 *fol*); 83—1—18, 2 *ll* 13, 14 e-gir-tu | ak-ta-nak us-si-bi-la (AJSL xv 141; Martin, *Rec. Trav.*, xxiv 106, 107) = Hr^L 12; 179; 180; 114; 198; 391. Also 81—11—3, 478 iii 7 ik-ta-[n]a-ak, PSBA xviii 258.

ℑ Perhaps: oppress, bend down {vielleicht: niederdrücken, zu Boden drücken}. IV² 50 *b* 50 at-ti-e (o witch) ša tu-kanni-ki-in-ni; V 45 viii 45 tu-kan-nak.

Š KB iv 318, 319 *ll* 15—16 (amēl) muše-du[-u?] u-šak-kan-nak-ku (ZA iii 138).

NOTE. — 1. See also ZK i 112; ZA iii 88.
2. Against kanaku = qanaqu see Brünnow, *Indices*, pref. vi, vii.

Derr. kāniku, kanniku, kanīku (?), kānku, kunuk(k)u, kingu, and according to some also šakan(n)akku (*q. v.*).

kāniku (orig. qāniqu) & **qāngu**, name of an official, notary (?), who is charged with the sealing of tablets, documents, contracts *etc.*, thus rendering them legal {Bezeichnung für einen Beamten, vielleicht Notar?}. V 42 *g-h* 14 IM-ŠID-ŠUB-ŠUB-BA = ka-ni-ku (Br 8446). V 32 *a-c* 18, 19 IM-Ê-ŠA-DUB-BA = ša-an-da-ba-ku ‖ kan-gu ša ša-kas-si; IM-ŠID-DUB-BA = ka-ni-ku ‖ kan-gu ša bābi. Cyr 37, 33 Šu-zu-bu mār ka-nik bābi.

kanniku, an official {ein Beamter}. V 13 *a-b* 12 (amēl) ŠID-PAR-PAR-RA = kan-ni-ku, Br 6002.

kān(i)ku, tablet, document {Tafel, Urkunde} see kanaku, Q; & Pinches, JRAS, July '01, 601. KB iv 34 *no* I 10 a-na na-aš-ši ka-ni-ki-šu (see *no* II 9; 38 II 16); Meissner, 102. VATh 1176, 10 *fol* ka-ni-ik-šu i-xi-ib-bi-e (Meissner, 6—7), he will destroy his (the former owner's) tablet (when he buys the slave). H 72, 38 u pi-i ka-ni-ki-šu, and according to his contract, Meissner, 101, 102; ZA vii 28. Strassmaier, *Stockholm*, 6, 43 kīma kan-gi-šu. DT 81 vi 14 ka-ni-ik kaspi, a receipt for the money. — On Armenian *kniχ*, see Lagarde, *Armen. Studien*, 1167; *Mittheilungen*, i 288. Hübschmann, ZDMG 46, 241 *fol*; Jensen, *ibid* 48, 463; TSBA viii 288; Meissner, 101 *fol*.

kanīku, *adj* (?). VATh 809, 17 kaspa ka-ni-ik-tu šu-bi-lam, BA ii 559, 560, sende mir geprägtes Geld, *i. e.* mit einem Siegel versehenes. Bu 88—5—12, 172, 18 on kaspa kanku; and on use of *f* for *m* see kaspa gamirtu & *k* gamru.

kunuk(k)u, the act of sealing; seal {Siegelung; Siegel}. chief id. TAG-ŠID § 9, 151; Br 5971; H 89, 122; KB iv 104 (Rm 2, 19) 1. — H^{OV} xxxv; § 65, 28 *rm*; ZA vii 30; Meissner, 117. — Nabd 85, 12 ku-nu-uk maxiri: Kaufbrief. II 40 *g-h* 42 TAG-ŠID (Br 5971) = ku-nu-uk-ku; 43, ku-nu-ka-šu; 44, ku-nu-ka-šu-nu; 45, TAG-ŠID-EB-RA = bi-ri-im TAG-ŠID; 46, TAG-ŠID-EB-RA-BI = ku-nu-uk-ku ku-nu-ku-šu (Br 4970); TAG-ŠID-EB-RA-NE-NE = *k* ku-nu-ki-šu-nu; 48, TAG-ŠID-NU EB-RA = ul bi-ri-im TAG-ŠID; 49, TAG-ŠID-KUR-TUK = kunukku xu-bu-ul-li; 51 kunuk zi-it-ti (KB iv 24 *col* 3, 2—3: ku-nu-uk zi-it-ti-šu, die Urkunde seines Besitzers). II 9 *c-d* 42—44 i-na ku-nu-uk ši-bu[-u]-ti ib-ru-um; on *c* see Br 5971, ZA i 407. Rm 282 *R* 3 ku-nu-uk-ku na-piš-ti-ka (+ 6, -šu) KB vi (1) 46, 47. Golenischeff 20, 4: III šiqil kaspu ku-nu-ki-ni; see also Bu 91—5—9, 2176 A 24 (JRAS '97, 607—8). Bu 91—5—9, 387, 11 ku-nu-kam ša la ra-ga-mi, a document that could not be quashed (JRAS '97, 601—3). ZA iv 239 *col* 3, 11 see santakku. V 42 *g-h* 10, 11 IM-ŠID-ŠUB = ŠU(?)-qu (?) Br 8441 & ku-nu-uk[-ku]; the same id in 12 = ši-mat . . . . . KB iv 8—9 *col* 2, 15, 16 e-zi-ib pl (written KA) ku-nu-ki-š[u]-nu. Peiser, *Jurispr. Babyl.*, 38, 39 ša la pi-i ku-nu-uk-ki-šu. V 27 *g-h* 41 MU-SAR-RA = ku-nu-uk šu-mi (Br 1270, 4322); 83, 1—18, 1335 i 22 (ki-ši-ib) DUB = ku-nu-uk-ku (PSBA '84, Dec.). II 40 *b-c* 49 see Br 14412 & çibru, 1. KB iv 22 *no* II 12 ku-nu-uk-ki la ix-te-pu(-ma), the document (concerning it) he has not destroyed. T. A. (Ber) 25 ii 29: 1 kûxazzu çixru ša gu-un-nu-ki xuräçu.

kingu *1.* (*i. e.* qinqu). II 28 *g-h* 58 GI-ŠEŠ-KA-NA-GUB-BA = ki-in-gu ša bâbi, Br 2497. See perh. also Nabd 880, 13 ina ki-in-gi-šu, & kangu.

Kingu *2.* (= Qinqu?) P. N. of husband of Tiâmat in the Creation account. Jastrow, *Religion of Babylonia & Assyria*, 440. Bezold, *Catalogue*, 1600 on Rm 275. BA ii 434 *rm*: the god of fire {der Feuergott}.

NOTE. — Delitzsch, *Weltschöpfungsepos*, 129: kingu vielleicht von √קנק, wenn Semitisch (dies das wahrscheinlichere) oder KINGI Land (II 39 *c-d* 9) wenn Sumerisch; daher Hommel = ursprünglich Personifikation der Erde.

Kingu *3.* 81—11—6—478 ii 2, 3 Ki-en-gi: Šu-me-ri, & ma-a-tum. IV² 36, 3 Karaindaš šarru dannu šar Bâbili, šar Ki-en-gi Urţu šar Kaššû šar Karduniaš.

NOTE. — Weissbach, *Sum. Frage*, 176, 177: ki-in (or en)-gi bedeutet schlechthin "Land", nicht nur Land Sumer — doch "Land" κατ' ἐξοχήν nur so genannt von seinen Bewohnern. Bewohner von *kingi* = Sumer, waren die Sumerer. See also Winckler, *Forsch.*, i 206—7: Tiefland; *Mitth. d. Berl. Akad.*, '87, 12; Rost, xxvi (*ibid* xxv on names with kingi-; Tiele, *Geschichte*, 231); Halévy, *Rev. Hist. Rel.*, '88, 30 *rm*.

qinattu, qinâtu see kinattu, kinâtu (410, 411).

qintaru, see kintaru, 411 *col* 2, & Zimmern, GGA '98, 816 *foll*, reading kap-ta-ru.

qanqannu, qanqânu see gangannu (227 *col* 2) & Camb 330, 5; 331, 13; Neb 441, 4; also kamkammatu (395); & kankannu (407 *col* 2) & KB vi (1) 536, 537; Zehnpfund, *Theol. Litbl.*, vol 49, *col* 582, comparing Heb מכנות, 1 Kings vii 27 *foll*.

Qîsu. P. N. Qi-i-su, in the Eponym-list, KB i 204, 205 *col* 6 (755 B. C.) AV 7384.

qêsu (?) K 8380 qâtâ bêl niqê i-ça-bat qi-e-su KA-GA (= išasi?) i-pa-ţar-šu, let him say *qêsu* & free him, M⁸ 83 *col* 1; Bezold, *Catal.*, 921.

qâpu 1. = קוף. pr iqûp decay, tumble down, go to ruins {verfallen, einfallen, einstürzen}. Sn vi 33 i-qu-pa re-ša-a-ša (*i. e.*, of the palace), its top had tumbled down. V 63 *a* 27 bîtu šu-a-ti i-qu-up. Rm III 105 i *b* 7 i-qu-pu-u (3 *pl*) Winckler, *Forsch.*, i 254, 255. I 67 *b* 22 (the palace) i-qu-up, had gone to ruins. V 64 *b* 52 ša bîtu šu-a-tim i-qu-pu i-ga-ru-šu. V 62 *a* 17 the temple of Šamaš which had become old and i-qu-pu in-nab-tu (אבת), had tumbled down and become a ruin; *b* 55 i-ni-šu (אנש) i-qu-pu; also Šamaš-šumukîn, L³ 17; P³ 17. 81—6—7, 209, 31 i-qu-pu igarâtišu (BA 260—3); see also Peiser, *Jurispr. Babyl.*, 38, 39. III 52 *a* 36 ina libbi êli igarâte i-qub-ba (= *pl*). II 15 *a-b* 10 bît la-be-ra igâru-ša i-qu-up-pu (= GIŠ-ZI-DIRIG-GA, Br 3735), the old house, whose walls have tumbled down; *ibid* 24, 25 i-ga-ru ša i-qu-up-pu eli-šu [im]-ta-qu-ut, AV 3833. II 26 (⊕ 84 iii) 23 DIRIG-GA = qa[-a-pu] ša i-ga-ri, Br 3734.

Š Hilprecht, OBI, i 32, 33 *col* i 33 (Zikkurât Bâbili ša ullanûa) un-nu-ša-tu šu-ku-pa-at išidsa (ZA iv 108; KB iii (2) 4, 35).

Derr. these 2 (3?):

quppu *adj* tumbled down {eingestürzt} I 67 *b* 28 i-ga-ru-ša (of the palace) qu-up-pu-tu ad-ki-e-ma.

qaāpu *adj* tumbling down, delapidated {einstürzend, baufällig}. V 63 *a* 29 i-ga-ru-šu qa-a-a-pu-tim ad-ki, ZK ii 344; KB iii, 2, 114.

qūpu (?). Creat.-*frg* IV 136 šār ku-pu, see KB vi (1) 30, 31; 342, 343; M[R] 44 & 105 connects with ku-u-p(b)u, see, above, 421 *col* 1.

***qapu* 2.** = קיפ, pr iqīp; ps iqāp(?). — *a*) deliver, entrust something to somebody {jemandem etwas übergeben, anvertrauen}. Neb i 42 since Marduk the rule over the whole nation i-ki-pa-an-nim, had entrusted to me (§ 56 *b*; see also V 63 *a* 17; Scheil, *Nabd*, ix 22); ix 51 (i 65) the royal dominion over the whole nation ta-ki-pa-an-ni, hast thou entrusted to me. Flemming, *Neb*, 30. V 64 *a* 44, 45 which Sin, Šamaš *etc.* ja-ti i-ki-pu-nu; Knudtzon, 64, 5 i-qi-pu-u-ni. Nabd (Winckler) i 37 i-qi-pu-u. — *b*) give over, deliver unto {überliefern, übergeben} K 183, 21—22 (Hr[L] 2) see muātu (509 *col* 1). — *c*) with qiptu: K 46 i (II 56) 65—67 a-na qip-ti; qa-a-pu, a-na qa-a-bi (id ŠI-DUB-TI....., Br 9433; AV 7302, same id = tukultu); preceded by (63) ul a-na xubulli a-na ki-ip-ti. II 26 (Ⓒ 84) iii 21, 22 [....am] UD = qa[-a-pu], [ ]-DUB-TI = ša a[.....]. — *d*) trust somebody, believe in {jemandem trauen, glauben}. K 84, 6 ša-a-ru la ta-qi-pa-šu, lies! do not believe them! (Hr[L] 301; IV[2] 45 *col* 1; PSBA xxiii 344); K 79 *R* 16 šarru .... la i-qap-šu (Hr[L] 266; IV[2] 46 *col* 3), let not the king trust him; K 824, 34 u a-na-ku a-qip-pu-u (Hr[L] 290 *R* 13; JAOS xviii 148; PSBA xxiii 63), I believe (§ 115). See also Sn *Bav* 24 ina qa-a-pi.

Q[t] deliver, entrust. Creat.-*frg* V 12 (11) Nannaru uš-te-pa-a mu-ša iq-ti-pa.

ℑ K 469 *R* 13 ša u-ka-ip[-u]-ni (Hr[L] 138), who have appointed, put in charge (JAOS xviii 151). Perh. VATh 244 i 29 AN-NA-AŠ AL-TI-TI = am-me-ni tu-qip-an-ni.

Derr. These 5:

qēpu, qīpu, *pl* qē(ī)pāni, usually with determinative (amēl); literally: one entrusted with something, ambassador, governor {einer dem etwas anvertraut ist, Bevollmächtigter, Militairgouverneur} AV 7386. II 31 *no* 5 (K 4395) iii 1 (amēl) qi-e-pu (Br 13545 *ad* II 31 *c* 26); 2, (amēl) TIL-LA-GID-DA (II 26 *c-d* 44; Br 5752; AV 4380); thus probably id for qēpu; *cf* BA i 528 & IV[2] 33 i & K 114 *O* 8 (amēl) TIL-LA-GID-DA-MEŠ (= qēpāni) ša (al) Bīt Dakuri; + 17 (amēl) ke-pa-nu; thus also Asb iv 104 & Smith, *Asurb*, 108, 109 (K 374). II 26 (Ⓒ 84 iii) *c-d* 24 = ki-i-pu (Br 5752); V 16 (*g*-)*h* 40. K 3500 + K 4444 + K 10235 ii 12 (amēl) qi-e-bi; Merod.-Balad.-Stone v 19 lu-u šarru lu-u mār šarri lu-u (amēl) ki-i-pu; Asb v 1 *J* (amēl) qi-e-pu ša *B.* (& see *var. ibid*; Br 6861: amēl rāb-GIŠ-BAN); Sn i 53 *NN* (amēl) ke-pi (al) Xa-ra-a-ti (*Bell* 17; *Kui* 1, 8). III 10 *no* 2, 37 (amēl) qi-e-pu ina mux-xi-ša aš-kun, I placed over her an overseer. Nabd 662, 15 (end) (amēl) ki-i-pi; also Cyr 2, 3; 292, 2—3 ša ina a-mir-tum ša (amēl) ki-i-pi la a-mar. Nabd 22, 6—7 (amēl) qi-pi; 906, 3 (amēl) qi-e-pi. KB iv 188 *no* xii 16 *N* (amēl) ki-i-pi ša māt tam-tim (+ 22), followed by (18) (amēl) šanu-u, *i. e.* second in command. Nabd 180, 1—3 see (amēl) pixū; also *cf* T[C] 122, 123. — K 168, 34 ke-pa-a-ni ša Akkadī. Esh. *Sendsch*, *R* 48 (end) (amēl) qe-pa-a-ni. Asb vi 84 (amēl) ke-pa-a-ni (amēl) xa-za-na-a-ti; i 58 šarrāni (amēl) ke(*var* qi-e)-pa-a-ni which my father had appointed in Egypt (ZA ii 100); also i 75; ii 32. Perhaps K 543, 14 (amēl) qi-ba-a-ni, Hr[L] 442; AV 7375. Nabd 170, 3 (amēl) qi-pa-nu.

NOTE. — IV[2] 31 *O* 13, 14 *etc.* read pit mû & see pitū — A ǵ of qēpu is probably:

qēpānu (?). T. A. (Ber) 7 *R* 21 ana pān ga-a-a-pa-ni ma-am-ma la u-ma-ša-ar, (+ 24). ZA v 142.

qēpūtu. *abstr. noun.* governorship {Stellung eines Bevollmächtigten, Militairgouverneurs}, or the like. V 56, 28—29 or some one else ša a-na ša-kin-u-ti ša (māt) Na-mar iš-šak-ki-nu lu-u ki-pu-ut (māt) Na-mar, KB iii (1) 168—9; AV 4260. TP III *Ann* 226 a-na (amēl) ki[-pu-u]-ti eli (māt) Muçri ap-qid (Winckler, *Untersuchungen*, 91 *rm* 1). III 43 *c* 14 lu-u ak-lu lu-u ki-pu-tu ša Bīt-A-da (BA ii 120, 121). See also paqadu, Q *no* 3.

qīpānu Johns, *Doomsdaybook*: a district, county: ruled over by a qēpu: *no* 1 i 40 ina ki-pa-a-ni (+ 50); ii 7 + 45 (see *ibid*, *p* 35); *no* 9 iii 8 ina kip-a-ni, *etc.* & *p* 68: here occurs in the context the iδ NI-GAB (Br 5353) which, Johns says, supports the explanation of NI-GAB = qēpu. See also Knudtzon, 108, 18; T^C 123; Anp iii 93; AV 7385.

qīp(b)tu. loan {Darlehen} see xubullu & qēpu ℚ *c*; also qēmu. AV 4277. Meissner, 117: capital ‖ xubuttatu & qaqqadu. Rassam 609 *R* 3 še-im qip-tum, preceded by še-im xu-bul-lum, še-im xu-bu-ut-ta-tum, & followed by še-im šu-pil-tum (BA iii 215). K 245 i (II 8 *b*) 50 ki-ip(b)-tu; 51, 52 *q* (ul) i-ba-aš-ši; 54 [ki]-ib-ta-šu, Br 13902.

qupp(bb)u *1.* — *a*) box {Kasten} AV 7415. III 4 *no* 7, 5 iš-kun-an-ni i-na qup-pi ša šu-ri i-na iddû bi-ja ip-xi (KB iii (1) 100, 101); also see 81—11—8, 154 *R* *col* 3, 14 ina qu-up-pi (PSBA xviii 257—8). — especially: moneybox, cashbox, safe {namentlich: Geldkasten} T^C 122; BA i 536; 636. Nabd 84, 11 kasap qu-up-pu; 9 ina qup-pu (?); 347, 4; 1058, 2 (*cf* 6) BAR ma-na çarpi ir-bi | ša bābi ul-tu qu-up-pi (nadin); 10 *N* ša it-ti qu-up-pu ana Bābili illiku; 574, 9 ša qu-up-pu i-na-ça-ri (?); 551, 8 ša ina eli qup-pu; 1101, 1 kasap ša ultu qu-up[-pu?]; 746, 20 ina?] qu-pu iddin-nu; 1099, 19. Neb 265, 5: 3 ma-na çarpi ša ina qu-up-pu. Cyr 267, 12 maççar qu-up; 271, 14 amēl ša eli qu-up-pu ša Ē-BABBAR-RA. See also ZA iii 132 (*no* 5) 2. — *b*) (bird)-cage {Käfig (eines Vogels)}. Sn iii 20 ša-a-šu kīma iççūri qu(-up)-pi ki-rib (âl) Ur-sa-lim-mu ..... e-sir-šu. TP III *Ann* 203 ina pi-xa]-at ēli-šu ak-çur-ma kīma iççur qu-up-pi e-sir-šu. — S^b 132 sa-b(p)u-ra | [cuneiform] | = qu-up XU-MEŠ (= iççurāte, Br 1408. 1412).

quppu *2.* Peiser, *Vertr.*, ic 3: VIII minas of money nu-ux-xu-tu a-di I ma-na kaspi qu-up-pu, which is coined in one shekel pieces; see also *ibid* ci 2; x 8 ša ul-tu qu-up-pu ša Kaš-ša-a iš-šu-u Ba-la-ṭu; Peiser, *ibid* 231 + 286: Privatvermögen der Frau, in addition to her dowry; ZA iii 76 *rm* 3.

quppū *1.* (& qubū) some sharp instrument {ein scharfes Instrument} BA ii 485. V 56, 54 see paṭru (dagger); K 2619 ii 11 & Sarg *Ann* 186 see naglabu, 643 *col* 1; & KB vi (1) 62, 63.

quppū *2.* see qubbū.

qūpu. K 2675 *R* 3 see pagū. Winckler, *Untersuchungen*, 105, 106 compares קוף 2 Kings 10: 22; but Jensen, ZA x 360: perhaps Egyptian *kupi* = κῦφι: Räucherwerk; so also Brown-Gesenius, 880 *col* 2.

(iç) **kipal(u)** Knudtzon, 1 *O* 7 see niksu, 672 *col* 2. Knudtzon, 73 compares קבל. Boissier, *Rev. Sém.*, viii 150 § 10. See KI(?)palē; & kipalū, 422 *col* 2.

qapsu. K 497 *R* 4, 5 (mât) Man-na-a-a | ina qa-ap-si māti-šu ik-ta-la; K 614 *R* 4 qap-si āli i-du-qi; K 662 *R* 9 ša ina qap-si (âl) Kal-xa aš-mu-u-ni (Hr^L 165, 175, 211); Winckler, *Forsch.*, ii (2) 310—11. See also qabsu.

qapašu (?) ℶ V 45 viii 33 tu-qap-pa-aš. — ℶ¹ Rm 194 *R* 7 when the stars of Sibzianna are brilliant, kab-tu uq-da-ap-pa-ša-am-ma, heaviness will weigh down (Thompson, *Reports* ii, *p* xlviii) & 23.

qappatu (Br 12040), see gabbatu, 229 *col* 1, where read ZA vi 291 and add: AV* (Liverpool) 23*a*, 55*a*: IV-ta qa-ap-pa-tum; also Nabd 271, 4 + 9 + 13.

qupputu. II 52 *no* 2, 61 see kapatu, 424 *col* 1 & add: ZA xv 243, 244 reads (a-xi) pi-tim instead of tam-tim.

qaçu, pr iqūç flay {schinden, die Haut abziehen} with or without mašku. Anp i 68 *B* ina Arba-il a-ku-uç (§ 55*b*) maška-šu dūra u-xal-lip (KB i 62—3); 110 a-ku-uç (*var* çu) *etc.*; 90, the magnates ..... a-ku-çu, + 92 + 93 a-ku-su (> a-kuç-šu). III 6, 42 *B* bēl xi-iṭ-ṭi a-ku-su, KB i 92. Sarg *Khors* 35 ša-a-šu ma-šak-šu a-ku-uç, KB ii 56—7. *Ann* 47; *Ann* XIV, 52; Winckler, *Sargon*, 191, 5.

ℶ IV^2 61 *a* 20 I, Ištar of Arbēla na-ka-ru-ti-ka u-ka-a-ça a-da-na-ka

---

qapadu, iqpudu see kapadu, 421, 422.

(AJSL xiv 270), I will flay thine enemies (and) give (them) over to thee.

Der. maqāçu, 577 *col* 2).

qîçu. summer {Sommer}? KB v *ad* T. A. (Lo) 24, 11 ūmē gi-e-zi, during summer.

qaçapu. break to pieces {zerbrechen}. T^M vi 117 ^(ilat) Nisaba šar-ra-tu mu-qa-aç-ça-ap-ma qarnāti-ki.

qaçaçu, gaçaçu (ZK ii 16) see gazazu (igzuz, igazzaz) 214 *col* 2. § 25; AV 1547; also kasasu, 416. Hilprecht, *Assyriaca*, 12/13, 14 see nišru, 2 (741 *col* 2); K 2867, 26 lions thrived therein and without number ig-çu[-çu the herds?]. IV² 58 *col* 3, 31 qaç-ça-at mārat ^(il) Anim; 56 *b* 33 (ZA xvi 160—1: ist zornig); 6 *a* 23—25 lib-ba-šu i-gaç-ça-aç) id same as S^b 265: ka-sa-mu); 1 *col* 1, 9—11 e-liš ig-çu-çu-ma šapliš karra iddû, Br 933, 7514. ⊕ 84 (= II 26 *add*; AV 8282) iii 37—41 KA-GAZ = ga-ça-çu (also II 45 *e-f* 5; Br 653, 1747); KA^(zu-su-ud-rat) RAT = *g* ša šin-ni (Br 613, 2298, 8283; ZK ii 6 *rm* 1; ZA viii 78 *rm* 1); BU ^(bu-u) = ba-qa-mu, Br 7513; ŠAB-BA = ga-ça-çu (Br 5673; AV 1547); ID-SER-RA = *g* ša kap-pi (Br 1597, 6607, 7514).

ג cut off {abhauen}. IV² 16 *a* 65, 66 who kap-pi-šu (*i. e.* of the evil one) li-gaz-zi[-zu-šu], id TAR; 29* 4 C *R* i 3 li-ki-iç-ça-ça (Johnston, see kaçû, 425 *col* 1), may they cut out the raging fire within his eye. Scheil, *Rec. Trav.*, xx 55 *col* 2, 11 li-]ga-az[-ziz]. V 45 vi 7 tu-qaç-ça-az. Perhaps K 257 (H 129) *R* 19, 20 (Br 9842) see kasasu, 416 *col* 2.

ג^t IV² 49 *b* 32 ki-ma ti-rik abnē ubānē-šu-nu lig-ta-az-zi-zu, may their fingers be cut off.

Derr. — maqaççu (577 *col* 2); perhaps qiççu in qiç libbi (Z^B 24; 56), see kisu, 411 *col* 2 and xuççu 2 on IV² 59 *no* 1 *b* 16 where qaç perhaps = GAZ *i. e.* qiç (libbi) or = xip (√xepû) libbi; but it could be a *c. st.* of qaççu; & these 2:

qaçāçu cutting apart, down {Zerschneidung} T^M ii 141 ka-ça-a-çu i-za-an-nun.

qiççatu cutting up, diminution (BA ii 138—9) see niširtu, 741 *col* 2.

qiççu dwelling, residence, shrine; & T. A. (Ber) 26 ii 20; 25 ii 37 see kiççu, 425—6.

qaçaru (§ 9, 111), 1 see kaçaru 1 (426—7; & *Jour. Bib. Lit.*, xix 73 *rm* 60).

qaçru, qiçru, 1 see 427 *col* 2.

qiççuru 1 & 2 see 428 *col* 1.

kaçiru. T. A. (Ber) 115, 13 u la-a-mi ni-li-u ka-zi-ra = קצר, harvest (= and we are not able to harvest); perh. also T. A. (Ber) 25 iii 68, 69 KAR-KAR *pl* ša ka-zi-ri *pl*.

qaçaru *2.* see kaçaru, 2 (428 *col* 1); where dele (Asb v 38) *mu* before pa-si-su, reading ik-ki-mu pa-si-su. On id ŠU-KAD (83—1—18, 1330 *O* i 16) see ZA xv 41.

qiçru *2.*, qiçirru, qiçirtu see 428.

qaqû, a bird {ein Vogel} Br 13964. II 37 *e-f* 19 qa-qu-u ‖ tar-ma-zi-lu, AV 7886; D^S 100.

quqqu, qūqu (= קוק). *del* 39 (46), 83, 84 (88 + 91) mu-ir ku-uk-ki, KB vi (1) 234—7; 485—6: die Gebieter der Finsterniss. Perh. V 23 *a* 16 ku-uk-ki (Br 8348, 8989) = *d* 16 e-ṭu[-tu]; 17, ek-li[-tu]; 18, ta-ra[-nu] Br 8946; 19, da-'-[mu] Br 8941; 20, du-'-u-mu. S^b 1 iii 7 gu-ug | GUG | ku-uk-ku ‖ da-la-xu (8) = V 38 *col* 3, 36; Br 6916; see also NE 72, 43.

Der. qūqānu.

quqqû & quqqanû see guqqû & guqqanû (229 *col* 2); T^C 80; KB iv 314—15, 6 gu-uq-qa-ni-e ūmu AB-AB-MEŠ. Bu 88—5—12, 75 + 76 vi 16 guq-qa-ni-šu-nu ellūti (BA iii 246, 247); Peiser, *Vertr.*, cxl 1 (VATh 388). Also see sattukku.

qaqadā (& **gagadā,** Babylonian), **qaqdā,** *adv.* firm, constant *etc.* {fest, beständig}. Neb iii 20; IV² 20 *no* 1, 5—6 (= SAG-UŠ = kajânu & kâmānu, Br 7584); Scheil, *Nabd*, viii 25—28 see pāqu, ג^t. I 66 *c* 4 see kajānu, 1 (404 *col* 2). Sp II 265 *a* iv 9 m]i-ša-ri qaq-da-a; K 4587 *O* 12 qaq-da-u = ka-a-a-ma-n[u], *q. v.* ZA v 59, 13 qaq-da-a ṭa-biš liq-tab-ba.

qaqqadu (AV 7339; § 61, 1 *b*); Babylonian

---

qapaçu see kapaçu, 422—23. ～ qaçû see kaçû 1 & 2 (425 *col* 1). ～ ququbānu (§ 61, 1 *b*), ququbātu, see kukubānu, kukubātu, 378 *col* 2.

gagadu (AV 1483; § 43) — קָדְקֹד D^{H} 20; KB vi (1) 396. — *a*) head {Kopf, Haupt} id SAG-DU (§ 9, 131; Br 3513), IV^{2} 31 *O* 42 (-ša), 43 (-ja); H 16, 246, preceded by ri-e-šu. S^{b} 1 *R* iv 18 . . . . . du | SAG-DU | qaq-qa-du, Br 3575. id T. A. (Lo) 70, 18 qaqqadu-nu | ru-šu-nu — our head. Bu 11—5—9, 2185, 2, 3: ka-aq-ga-di ku-ub-bi-id (o Lord, now) honor my head; Bu 11—5—9, 354, 35 ga-ga-di-ka tu-ga-la-al (T. A. Ber 196, 38—9). IV^{2} 2 vi 12 qaq-qa-su im-xaç-ma ana qaq-qa-di-šu iš-kun; 3 *a* 34, 35 (SAG-ZU) see katamu, 3 (458 *col* 2); 4 *a* 31, 32; 3 *a* 44, 45 & *b* 8, 9 (SAG) see marçu, 2 (591 *col* 1). II 19 *b* 13, 14 si-ba qaq-qa-da-šu (— SAG), its heads are seven (§ 67, 4) Br 3513; V 16 *e-f* 47 nu-uš qaq-qa-di (see 732 *col* 1). V 50 *b* 46, 47 (SAG-GA-NA) see çabatu, Q^{t}; also IV^{2} 22 *no* 1 *R* 17 . . . . li qaq-qa-su ru-ku-us-ma. parsigu ša qaqqadišu see parsigu. H 86—7, 11 ša qaq-qad-su (= SAG-BI) e-pi-ri la kat-mu; 90—1, 66—7 qaq-qa-su-nu ana qaq-qa-di-šu (a-a iš-ku-nu, a-a iṭ-xu-u); 127, 38 ina bur-ti ša-di-i Dil-mun qaq-qa-du (— SAG-GA) am-si. Hilprecht, OBI i 82, 83 *col* 3, 3 ṭi-iṭ-ṭam i-na ga-ga-di-ja lu(-u) ax-bi-il (— KB iii (2) 4 *col* 2, 65, 66) & see xabalu; T. A. (Lo) 182 (BA iv 130, 131; 418*foll*; KB vi. 1. 78*foll*) *R* 13 a-na ga-a-ag-g[a-r]i ga-ga-as-sa a-na na-ka-si; see also nakasu & niksu for further instances. VATh 4105 iii 11 ga-ga-ad-ka lu me-si. NE 51, 17 ul i-šak-kan qaqqad-sa: Ištar could not make head against its (Uruk's) enemy (Haupt, *Philadelphia Oriental Club*, i 271 *rm* 20 & in *Ezra-Nehemiah* (SBOT) 70, 8 — נתן ראש; on the other hand see KB vi (1) 272—3.

qaqqad ubāni — tip of the finger, S 1064, 22. — qaqqad pilaqqi see pilaqqu. — çalmat qaqqadi see çalmu, 1. — muruç qaqqadi *cf* murçu (591, 592). — paššur ša qaq-qa-di (D 87 iii 58) brain-pan {Hirnschale} see paššūru. — Johns, *Deeds*, *no* 53 *O* 3; 57 *O* 5; 105 *O* 5 ina qaqqadi (ilu) iddišē ša arxi — exactly at the beginning of the month (KB vi, 1, 396). P. N. Ummu-qaqqadi — blockhead {Dickkopf} BA iv 223. II 24 *d-f* 25 [ ] ⟨ A-ZA-AT(D) | bi-bi-nu | qaq-qa-du, Br 14463. — *b*) sum, total; capital {Summe, Gesammtbetrag; Capital} Meissner, 117; ZA iv 72 so often in *c. t.* KB iv 54 viii 19—20 kaspu ina ga-ga-ad J . . . . ra-ki-is. Cyr 37, 5—6 kaspu ina qaqqadišu — the capital, without interests {das Geld in seiner Hauptsumme, *i. e.* ohne Zinsen}; Nabd 44, 6; 888, 1; BA iii 406; Nabd 18, 6; 446, 4*foll* ina qaqqadišu gamirtum; Neb 205, 3; 345, 10; Camb 195, 5; 409, 5 kaspa a-an XII šiqlu ina qaqqadi-šu i-nam-din-nu-'u (here — complete(ly) {vollständig}. KB iv 48, 49 *no* ii 18 *Š* ga-ga-a-tu-šu, ist ihr Garant (lit: hält seinen Kopf), perhaps shortened from mukīl qaqqadišu; see *ibid* 48—9 iii 9—11 *Š* mu-ki-il ga-ag-ga-di-šu (Meissner, *no* 61) — sein Beschützer, Rechtsvertreter (see also Meissner, *no* 40).

Derr. these 2:

qaqqadū, headgear, cover for the head {Kopfbedeckung} ‖ kubšu (*q. v.*, 369 *col* 1). K 13600, 5*fol* irrit qaq-qa-di-e, M^{8} *pl* 17.

qaqqadānu. — *a*) some species of grasshopper {eine Heuschreckenart}. K 4373 i 9 XU-BIR-SA-AD-NUM — êribu (or êribu?) qaq-qa-da-nu; see šaššaṭu. — *b*) commander in chief {Oberbefehlshaber}. K 1111 (Bezold, *Catalogue*, 227) (amēl) qaq-qa-da-a-ni; 81—2—4, 60 (see *ibid*, 1757). IV^{2} 47 (K 181) *no* 3, 30 P. N. SAG-DU (— qaqqada)-a-nu.

qaqūlu, qaqullu *1.* Neb 131, 19—20 (amēl) ir-ri-še-e | ša (çubat) qa-qu-lu; Dar 47, 1 (çubāt) qa-qu-ul-l[u].

qaqullu *2.* a bird {ein Vogel} see kulukuku (385 *col* 2) & II 37 *c* 70; AV 7337.

qaqullu *3.* a plant, vegetable {ein Gartengewächs} D^{Pr} 84 *rm* 2; qa-qu-ul-lu SAR, ZA vi 291 ii 5 — קָקוּלָא — cardamom. K 4174 *O* qa-qu-lu & ša-me-ṭu with same id as man-gu (M. I. Hussey, JAOS xxii 212); also K 4588 i 7. ZA xvii 94 (šam) GAM-GAM — qaqqultu.

qaqqullum *1.* ‖ nam-xi-tum; see kakkullum, 378 *col* 2; KB vi (1) 371; JAOS xxii 208.

qaqqullu *2.* Reisner, *Hymnen*, 8, 66 amātsu qaq-qul-lu (— GAKKUL) katimtu qiribšu mannu ilammad, M^S 85 *col* 2. ‖ ?:

qaqqultu. IV^2 16 (*add*) *b* 13, 14 qaq-qul-ti (= GAKKUL) la pa-te-e li-ik-tum; KB vi (1) 371: Mischkrug. See also Reisner, *Hymnen*, 2, 61; 4, 23.

qaqqultu ŠI. K 11185, 7 qaq-qul-ti ŠI (M^S *pl* 16 *k*; KB vi, 1, 371).

qaqultu. III 69 *no* 3, 76 mentions a weapon of Marduk as qa-qu-ul-tu. K 1101, 8 (amêl) rab qa-qu-la-te (Hr^L 152); some officer.

qiqallu see kigallu, 371—2; S^P 158 + S^P II 962 *R* 17 [ina?] Ê-ŠAR-RA i-nu-uš ki-gal-la; Pinches, *Jour. Trans. Vict. Inst.*, 29, 61: in (?) the temple shook the platform.

qaqq(kk)ulânu (*varr* kakkullâni, ka-kulânu, *etc.*) name of an official. K 567, 7 ka-ku-la-nu (amêl) mutîr pu-te (Hr^L 248); III 46 *a* 61; *b* 11 + 23 + 66; III 50 *no* 3, 13 + 16; Bezold, *Catalogue*, 2067.

qaqânu a bird {ein Vogel}. II 37 *c-f* 20 qa-qa-nu ‖ pa-'-u. D^S 109; AV 6887, 7335; Br 13969.

qûqânu, gûqânu. — *a*) a disease of the eye: blindness? {eine Augenkrankheit: Blindheit?} ZK ii 47; AV 3769; 7416. K 246 ii 51 (H 90—1) a charm against (ana) qu-qa-ni ša i-ni-šu (= ŠI-GU-LAL-E-ŠI, Br 9398); lit: darkness of the eye; the same id in II 36 *g-h* 60 (Br 9397). — *b*) some animal of lower order {ein Tier niederer Ordnung}. II 36 *g-h* 59 NIM-MAŠ-XUŠ (Br 9022) = gu-qa-nu. V 40 *no* 5 *R* 44 qu-qa-nu qaq(AV 7416: ni?)-qa-ri. *Theol. Litblatt*, 1900, *no* 5: Krebs, der auf dem Fussboden sich bewegt (*i. e.* Fresser; qûqânu auch: Frass *i. e.* Krebs am Auge); on the other hand, see Benzinger, *Prot. Real Encycl.*^{3}, viii 30; GGA '98, 825. — See also kukkânîtum, 378 *col* 2; & ja-quqânu, 361 *col* 1.

qaqsallû. V 26 *c-d* 23; II 41 *no* 4, 42 GIŠ-KAK-SAL-LA = ŠU-u *i.e.* qaqsallû(?) followed by ‖ nazru (661 *col* 1).

qaqaru. ג blot out, root out, destroy {austilgen, zerstören} § 61, 1*b*. III 4 (*no* 2) 2, 11 mu-[qaq-]qir šiṭri-ja šumija. KAT^2 459 *rm* 2, but KB i 10, 11 mu[-nal]-kir. Q^t perhaps K 8204, 6 al-ta-pil (שפל) ina çâbê aq-ta-qur na-a-a-al (PSBA xvii 138, 139 reading ak-ta-kam).

qa-qa-rat (?). IV^2 34 (K 2130) 12 . . . ina šumêli ÇI i-lat qa-qa-rat. *Rev. Sém.* x 275 (April '02).

qaqqaru, AV 7341; § 61, 1*b*. Babylonian **ga-]ga-ru,** AV 1811; § 43; Bezold, *Achaemeniden-inschr.*, pref. xi; H^{OV} xxxix. — *a*) ground, earth, floor; country, land {Boden, Erdboden; Land}. I 49 *c* 13 ina ša-ma-me qaq-qa-ri (KB ii 122 -riš) i-ši]-ra is-kim-mu-uš, BA iii 220, 221. III 38 *no* 1 *O* 19 ina ša-ma-mi u qaq-qa[-ri]. V 64 *c* 18 i-na ša-ma-mi u ga-ga-ri. ‖ erçitum; IV^2 31 *O* 1 ana erçit la târi qaq-qa-ri . . . . NE 58, 15 il-su-u šamû qaq-qa-ru i-ram-mu-um. K 3182 ii 40 ka-pi-du e-ni qaq-qar-šu, who plans to oppress his land; K 3188 *O* (IV^2 54 *no* 1) 48 ina qaq-qar šul-me, in the land of peace. Sarg *Nimr* 14 of the foundation of this building e-li du-un-ni qaq-qa-ri ki-çir šadi ul šur-šu-da iš-da-a-šu (KB ii 38, 39). V 55, 47; 56, 8 qaq-qar (mât) Na-mar, the land belonging to Namar. Achaemenian-inscr. *O* 2 Auramazda who has created qaq-qa-ru a-ga-a; 17, Darius šarru ša qaq-qa-ru agâta, ‖ mâtu. On qaqqaru rapaštu in the Achaemenian-inscr. = ארץ רבה, see Haupt in Toy, *Ezekiel* (SBOT) *p* 99. — Asb iv 29 see ziqnu, 289 *col* 2. IV^2 7 *a* 55 like this onion whose šur-šu(-šu) qaq-qa-ru la i-çab-ba-tu, root does not take hold of the ground (8 *c* 11); ZA v 68, 14 a-na e-li-ni pa-an qaq-qa-ri, on the face of the earth. Sp II 265 *a* xxv 7 ri-ši-MU (= ja) ul ul-lu qaq-qa-ri a-na-aṭ-ṭ[al]. K 2745 ii 15 qaq-qa-ru bu(?)-çi-i, BA iii 208, 209: Schlammboden. V 50 *b* 57, 58 ça-lam an(-)du-na-ni-šu ša tab-pi-in-ni ina qaq-qa-ri (of clay?) e-ç(s)ir-ma, (id KI, Br 7436, 9634, where other instances are given). D 101 frg, 14 + 10. KB vi (1) 292, 14 ina qaq-qar ib-uu-u ilâni a-lu-šu (ZA xii 319 *fol*). V 63 *a* 30: 18 (ammât?) qaq-qar u-ša-ap-pil, 18 (cubit? of) earth I dug out, KB iii (2) 114, 115. Neb vi 25: 4000 ammât ga-ga-ri; viii 45: 490 am-ma-at ga-ga-ri; ZA iii 395, 20 ga-ag-ga-ru. Rm 2, 454 *R* 35 ana qaq-qa-ri, to the ground (KB vi, 1, 114). *del* 33 (41) [ana] qaq-qar (ilu) Bêl ul a-šak-kan pāni-ja-a-ma, KB vi (1) 232, 233; NE 136, 41 & *rm* 2, perh. H 87, 72 see maksūtu, 538, 539. — T. A. (Lo) 82, 31 see qaqqadu; (Ber) 51, 11 iš-tu qa-qa-ri, by land; 7, 20 ul ga-ag-ga-ru ki-ir-bu-um-ma the road is not short. — TP vii 76 qaq-qar-šu u-me-si, I cleared its ground (*i. e.* the whole place from the rubbish that was covering it). — On qaqqaru našaqu see našaqu, 740, 741. K 8669 i 5 qaq-qu-ru; 8 qaq-qu-ru i-na-šiq; 11 qaq-qa-ri, ZDMG 53, 117—18. — šax(xu) qaq-qa-ri, see xallūlā(i)a, 314 *col* 2. — nēšu ša qaq-qa-ri see nēšu, 738 & KB vi (1) 518. — II 26 *no* 1 (*add*) *e-f* 10 see naqaru (Br 9778) Q (end) 720; and nigiççu, 644 *col* 1 *ll* 2—3; V 21 *a-b* 12 ni-gi-iç-çu qaq-qa-ri, Br 9683. K 4378 vi 25 (D 88) GIŠ-KI-MA' = qaq-qar elippi, bottom of the ship (?) Br 9669; II 45 *no* 3, *a-b* 34; II 62 *no* 2. — KAS(GAL)-GID (BU; see kasbu, 414) qaq-qa-ri, see JENSEN, *Kosmologie*, *s. v.* & KB ii 202 *rm*; KUGLER, ZA xv 383 *foll.*

b) a piece of land; place, property {ein Stück Grund und Boden; Eigentum} K 2619 iv 26 im-ta-ni qaq-qar-šu, KB vi (1) 68, 69: rechnete (den Berg *S*) als seinen Boden *i. e.*, property. K 3456 *R* 29 imru-ka t(d)ax-xu qaq-qa-ri. Esh v 6 qaq-qa-ru ma-'a-du, a large piece of land. III 16 v 10 (amēl) Pu-qu-du ina qaq-qa-ri-šu-nu aš-bu; K 82, 30 = Hr^{L} 275 *R* 10; + 33 u a-ni-ni xi-ṭu ša qaq-qa-ru ni-quṭ-ṭu, BA i 246; PSBA xxiii 53 *foll.* qaq-qar çu-um-me & çu-ma-ma-i-tum, see these. K 890, 16 .... da-a qaq-qar xi-bi-la-te, BA ii 634; qaq-qar ṭābti Esh iii 26 see ṭābtu, 3 (352). KB iv 158, 159, 5 qaq-qa-ru šu-u I received from *I-N*; 7, qaq-qa-ru i-ba-aš-ši; 12, u qaq-qar which I have bought from *I-N.* V 36 *a-c* 30 u ⟨ | qaq-qa-rum, Br 8695. qaq-qar ket-ti ZIMMERN, *Ritualtafeln*, 1—20, 2; 75—78, 19: Rechtsstätte; Sm 788, 7 + Rm 145 *O* (end) ana qaq-qar ket-te ša Šamaš u Adad isaniqma.

c) In astronomical texts, qaq-qar = moon's orbit {Mondbahn} ZA xv 119.

qaqqariš, *adv* on, to the ground {auf den Erdboden, gleich dem Erdboden} AV 7340. III 4 *no* 4, 49 from his horse qaq-qa-riš im-qu-ut, he fell to the ground (578 *col* 1). Sarg *Ann* 294 see פלס, 2T. II 67, 21 the city qaq-qa-riš am-nu (§ 80*b*) see manū, 1 Q (556 *col* 2).

qaqqūru ‖ qaqqaru see above, & K 124 *R* 14 qaq-qu-ru bi-it ni-ik .... K 97, 9; also K 472, 13; K 1049 *R* 7; K 689, 9; K 554 *R* 8 (ka-ku-ru); 79—7—8, 138 *R* 5 (Hr^{L} 177; 88; 312; 100; 438). Another ‖ perhaps:

qaqqiru. BA ii 635, 10 karānē ... ana qaq-ki-ri itabuku. T. A. (Ber) 103, 37 ga-ag-gi[-ru] gloss to u-ri-e. field. ZA vi 253 *no* 15.

qāru. an officer, official? {Beamter?} see kalū 6 (382 *col* 2).

qarū (?) JENSEN, KB vi (1) 474 on 222 (NE X *col* iv) 11 ina kap-pi-šu ka-ra-a u-š(s)aq(k)[-ki-ma], and erected the mast with his own hands {und brachte mit seinen Händen den Mastbaum in die Höhe}. See also remarks under karū 3*b* (431 *col* 1, below) & see qaritum.

(šam) **qu-ru** see qamxurū & ZA x 202, 10 GIŠ-SAG (= LIB) gišimmar = (šam) qu-ru : šad-li-i : da-lu; ZK ii 26; ZA iii 45: Palmenmark; ZA viii 198, 10; M^{S} 83 *col* 1. Br 8060; id also IV^{2} 57 *R* 15 (end).

q(k, g)ur-ru-u. V 27 *no* 6, 45 in one group with çalmu, 2 (*q. v.*).

qīru. *del* 62 (66) see kīru, 1 (432 *col* 2) & KB vi (1) 489; also HAUPT in KAT^{2} 516; PRINCE, *Daniel*, 227: I poured out for caulking.

qirrū. STRONG in PSBA xvii 137 on PINCHES, *Texts*, 16 *R* 7 (DT 83) qir-ri-e dum-qi u taš-me-e, with exclamations of good will & submission (*cf* Prov 20, 6); but probably = kirū 3 (433 *col* 2).

qarabu* & *qirebu (AV 7344; § 19) pr iqrib & iqrub (83—1—18, 194, 6 ul iq-ru-ub); ps iqarib & iqarrub. approach {sich nähern} Z^{B} 114, 115; ZA ii 348. K^{M} 7, 57 a-a iq-ru-bu-ni, shall not approach. Sn v 41; I 43, 46 (*med*) ana šar Bābila a-na a-xa-meš iq-ri-bu-ma, they joined forces to wage war. II 51 *b* 2 iq-ri[-ib] ZK ii 320. IV^{2} 29* *no* 4 C *R* 11 am-me-ni iq-rib-ki-na-ši, why does he offer you (mud from the river). Sn iii 1 against (a-na) Ekron aqrib, I marched; *Kui* 1, 25. K 181 (Hr^{L} 197) 44 see madaktu & JAOS xx 250, 251, his camp no vulture can approach. Perh. K 146 *R* 2 i-qar-bu-u-ni-ni (Hr^{L} 192; BA i 204). *del* 155 some read iq-rib i-ša-ax-xi (BALL, *Genesis* [SBOT], 54), came near wading; but KB vi (1) 240 reads ik-kal (אכל); see also K 2148 ii 6 (end). K 164, 45 mê šamnê i-qar-ri-bu (karpat) ma-si-tum ša àikari. T^{M} vii 151 i-qar-ri-ba(-bu, vi 63; vii 149); 3 *pl* la i-qar-ri-bu-ni ja-a-ši vi 65; also la i-qar-ru-bu, shall not approach; T^{M} v 18 (+ 20, -ba). IV^{2} 40 *c* 25 i-qar-ru-ub-šu-nu-tu. — pm 83—1—18, 198 *R* 2 la is-niq ina mux-xi la qur-bu; perh. K 88, 7 ul qir-bi-ka (Hr^{L} 202); PSBA xxiii 331 *fol.* — qârib bar(mas)-xâti, AV 7346, see 190 *col* 2; BA iv 121 reads T. A. (Ber) 189, 33 (KB v *no* 134) u b[i]t [ešti]-en ga-ri[b]. II 35 *e-f* 23 qa-ra-bu ‖ sa[-na]-qu, *q. v.*; II 48 *c-d* 28 KU-NU = ki-re-bu, in one group with ṭaxû, sanaqu, emedu (25—27); ZA i 456 *rm* 1; Br 10588, same id = sanaqu ša nakri (V 41 *a-b* 50). See also II 35 *e-f* 25 (AV 7348). *Adapa*-legend ii *R* 11 (Adapa) ina qi-re-bi-šu, when he approached (KB vi, 1, 96—7). — T. A. (Ber) 12, 19 (your customs officer) ul ja-ga-ar-ri-ib, came not too near (them); 14 *R* 6 ul i-gi-ri-ib eli-šu-nu. 3, 16 ki-i a-na a-xa-mi-iš ki-ri-bi-ni (+ 18), that we may be nearer related to one another; (Lo) 24, 17 qa-ar-bu, they have drawn nigh.

𝔔^{t} advance against, approach to (ana). Anp i 74, 79, 107 *etc.* to the cities aq-ṭe-rib; iii 51 (§§ 18, 34*a*; 53*a*); Šalm, *Ob*, 32, 55, 86; 169, 171, 177 (a-na *etc.*) iq-te-rib; see also 163, 165; 161 ina libbi alâni iq-te-rib. On Anp ii 52 (aq-ṭe-rib) see KB i 78 & *rm* 4. KB vi (1) 292, 298 i 10 ina mâti (✕ ZA xii 319 *foll*: šatta) ul u-še-ṣi-ma ul aq-ta-rab-šu. K 146, 8 iq-ta-ra-bu-u-ni (Hr^{L} 192), they will arrive. 83—1—18, 107 *R* 5 u-di-na ina libbi la i-qar-rib ki-ma iq-ṭi-ri-ib; also 81—2—4, 80 *R* 3 (beg); K 870 *R* 3. — ip perh. KB vi (1) 282, 35 qit-ra-ba-ma (ZIMMERN). — pm Creat.-*frg* IV 94 ša-aš-meš it(d)-teb(lu?)-b(p)u qit-ru-bu ta-xa-zi-iš (KB vi, 1, 26, 27); KB vi (1) 208, 48 qit-ru-ub, he approaches. — *ac* **qitrubu**, marching out, approach, attack, battle, war = taxâzu and sometimes = offering, gift, § 65, 40*b*; AV 7891. IV^{2} 20 *no* 1 *R* 23—4 (beg) qit-ru-ba-aš-šu, Br 9091. Sn i 25 the chariots which i-na (ina) qit-ru-ub taxa-zi had been left; iii 15 ina šukbus arammê u qit(*var* qur-, on 80, 7—19, 1)-ru-ub šu-pi-i, with battering of rams and the assault of engines; vi 10 ina qit-ru-ub ta-xa-zi dan-ni. I 28 *a* 10; TP vi 78 see metlûtu, 623 *col* 1. II 66 *no* 2, 4 ina qit-ru-ub; BA ii 264, 265: im Ansturm der Schlacht.

𝔓 bring nigh; cause to approach {heranbringen, vor sich kommen lassen}. MEISSNER, 107 u-qi-ir-ri-bu-niš-šu-nu-ti (*c. l.*), man brachte (vor den Richter). K 1396, 10 ina pânikunu lu-qar-ri-bu (Hr^{L} 185); K 871, 3 (arax) Simânu u-qar-rib-ma (approach); also K 742, 1. KNUDTZON, 114 *R* 9 u-qar-ra-ba-šum-ma; K 8380, 24 (end) u-qar-rab; 28 (end) tu-qar-rab. KB iii (1) 160 *col* 4, 26 ul qu-ur-ru-ub, had not come; *ibid* 42 a-na ax-xu-u-ti la qir-bu(!). IV^{2} 57 *b* 8 a-a u-qar-ri-bu-ni uz-zu nu-ug-gat ili. V 45 v 55 tu-qar-rib (= rab?). *c. l.* u-qar-ru-bu-ni, T^{C} 8. Sm 1371 + Sm 1877, 22 u-qar-rib-ka, I have brought thee; tu-qar-rab, ZIMMERN, *Ritualtafeln*, 60, 12 + 17 + 24 *etc.*; 101, 1 (end) u-qar-rab-ku-nu-ši, I bring before you. Nabd 862, 3 elippê ša ŠE-BAR ana Âl-(il)Šamaš u-qar-ru-bu-ni. Sacrifice: K 168 *R* 16 ina parakki gi-nu-u lu-qar-rib (Hr^{L} 437). — pm ZA iii 133 (*no* 5) 12 qur-ru-ub; see also 𝔔^{t}; & perh. K 1044 *R* 10 qur-ru-bu (Hr^{L} 241); AV 7430.

Š̆ V 64 *c* 43 šu-uq-ri-ba (ip) damiq-tim; ZA i 237 šuq-ri-ba.

Š^{t} bring near to {an etwas heranbringen}. Creat.-*frg* IV 44 see sapâru, 2. Creat.-*frg* V 24 šu-taq-ri-ba-ma di-na di-nu (KB vi, 1, 33: nähere dich und richte das Gericht!); 21 (end) šu-taq-rib-ma.

𝔑^{t} T. A. (Lo) 1, 20 there is none among them [ša it]-ta-ka-ri-ib, who stood near.

Derr. naqrabu (720 *col* 2), taqrubtu, & these 10 (?):

qarābu. (properly αc), war, battle, fight {Krieg, Schlacht, Kampf} § 65, 11. (iç) elippē qa-ra-bi (ma-la it-ti-šu .... u-çab-bi-tu ina qātē) = men of war; III 28 (K 2675 *O*) 23 (Smith, *Asurb*, 40); KB ii 238—9. Asb vi 17 (iç) be-le qa-ra-bi. K 610, 14 (end) if qa-ra-bu (war) you desire to make (Hr^L 174; JAOS xx 252); written qa-ra-a-bu, 83—1—18, 40 (Hr^L 407) 6; AJSL xiv 179, 180.

q(k)irbu (§ 19 on *k* for *q*) *c.st.* kirib (§ 65, 2; H 169, 170; D^H 20, 13) interior, midst {Inneres, Mitte}. It refers *a*) to the viscera of the thoracic cavity (heart, lungs, *etc.*) while karšu denotes the viscera in the abdominal cavity (stomach, liver, *etc.*) Haupt, *Journ. Bibl. Lit.*, xix 70 *rm* 99. Creat.-*frg* IV 102 ixtēpi karassa (of Tiāmat) | kir-bi-ša u-bat-ti-qa u-šal-liț libba. V 61 *c* 13 mi-šil (šēr) kirbi. — *b*) to the interior of places, localities *etc.* II 79 (K 44) *R* 28 ki-ma ki-rib šame-e (= ŠA[= LIB]-AN, Br 7087, 8044) lim-mir; IV^2 57 *b* 14 kima ki-rib šamē lu-ut-ta-mir; see namaru Q^t, 685 *col* 1. — K 4386 (II 48) iii 56 AN-ŠA(LIB)-GA = ki-rib šame-e (& II 47 *c-d* 18); II 27, 593; 37, 43; preceded by e-lat šamū. Sp II 205 *a* viii 5 ki-i ki-rib šame-e ‖ libbi šamē TP vii 98. — qir-bi suluppi, Nabd 375, 7; 619, 6. KB iii (2) 68, 69 *col* 2, 2 ki-er-ba-šu, its interior.

As a prepositional phrase we find kirib, ina kirib (or kirbi); ana, ištu & ultu kirib (§ 80*b*). — **kirib & kirbi** = in. V 35, 30 (end) heavy tribute they brought ki-ir-ba Bābili. Banks, *Diss*, 12, 66 ki-rib-šu; Sarg *Cyl* 73. Pinches, *Texts*, 16 *no* 4 (DT 83) *R* 9, 10 kir-bi Ê-KUR (& Ba-bi-lim); 8 (end) ana ki-rib Bā-bili. V 63 *a* 30 e-pi-ri kir-bi-šu (of the temple); Sarg *Cyl* 75 kir-bi(-e)-šu; I 49 *b* 8 nišē a-šib qir-bi-šu. *del* 15 qir]-ba-šu, therein, KB vi (1) 230, 231. V 63 *a* 40 kir-ba-šu (u-še-ri-ib); 38, ki-rib-šu. I 66 *c* 22 ki-er-ba-šu = in (Babylon); *c* 48 ki-er-bi-šu. Hilprecht, OBI i 32, 33, iii 54, 55 when Marduk i-ra-am-mu-u ki-ri-ib-ka = KB iii, 2, 6, 56. ZA iv 113, 171. KB iii (2) 8 *no* 3 *col* 2, 15 ta-ra-am-mi-im ki-ri-ib-ša; I 68 *c* 53 lumxur ki-ri-ib-ša; Sn *Bav* 12 ki-rib-ša; I 27 *no* 2, 30; Neb vii 50; K 3456, 19 (end). K 2867 *O* 26 qi-rib-ši-in; KB iii (2) 48 *col* 1, 52—3 the great gods a-ši-ib ki-ri-ib-ši-na u-ša-ar-ma-a ki-ri-ib-bi-ši-in. Neb vi 48 bu-tuqti ki-ir-ba-šu-un | la šu-ub-ši-i. With šațaru often: *e. g.* Bu 88—5—12, 75 + 76 ix 33, 34 ki-rib-šu-un aš-țur. — Asb v 40 (māt) Elamti I entered victoriously; Sarg *Cyl* 20. V 35, 17 ki-rib Bābili; 81—6—7, 209, 7. D 49, 43; Neb 329, 17 ki-rib tam-dim, in mid-ocean; I 44, 52 ki-rib tam-xa-ri. — **ina kirib (kirbi)** = in. KB vi (1) 292—3, 17 ina ki-rib šadē (ZA xii 319 *foll*); TP ii 13 (xuršāni); 27 (tam-xa-ri). TP III *Ann* 12 i-na kir-bi-e-ša; 90, ina ki-rib um-ma-ni-ja (= among); Sarg *Cyl* 35 ina kir-bi-šu-nu (& -ši-na, *bull*-inscr. 98). I 66 *c* 56, 57 li-bu-u-a i-na ki-er-bi-ša; KB iii (2) 68 *a* 7/8 i-na ki-ri-bi-ša. V 65 *b* 24 ina ki-ri-bi-šu; 63 *a* 23 i-na ki-ir-bi-šu-un (*i. e.* Esagil & Ezida). H 129, 14 ina ki-rib šadi-i. used adverbially: Neb vii 20 their treasures i-na ki-ir-bi | u-na-ak-ki-mu. Instead of ina kirbišu, *etc.* we find **kirbuššu** (§ 80*e*) in it, into it. K 3445, 11 kir-bu-uš-šu ma-xa-za-šu; Sarg *Cyl* 43, 54, 62. *del* 12 (13) the gods kir-bu-šu (*var* uš), in it (the city of Šurippak). I 51 *no* 2 (KB iii, 2, 58) 15 ki-ir(*var* kir)-bu-uš-šu, its interior, PSBA x 290 *foll.* KB iii 66 *no* 12 (iii) 29 u-ki-in ki-er-bu-uš-šu. Neb x 12 ki-ir-bu-uš-ša, in it (the palace); Sarg *Cyl* 62 kir-bu-uš-šu, in it (the city). — **ana kirib (kirbi)** in, into, to {in, nach}. a-na ki-rib (māt) Aššur, to Assyria, often; ‖ passages, where only ana is used. Smith, *Sen*, 95, 80 a-na ki-rib tam-tim I threw. Nerigl. i 36 a-na ki-ri-ib Bābili = Neb vii 25 (ki-ir-bi). V 35, 33 (med) a-na ki-rib Bābili; 34 (end) a-na ki-ir-bi maxāzēšunu. — **ištu, ultu kirib (kirbi)** from, out of {aus, ... von weg} Šamš iv 13 iš-tu ki-rib ali šu-a-tu (iv 34; ii 57); Anp i 65. I 48, 9 ul-tu ki-rib kimaxxi. Sarg *Khors* 125 ul-tu ki-rib Bābili. Esh i 45 ul-tu ki-rib šadi-i; 17, ul-tu ki-rib tam-tim. Sn iii 19 (iv 16, 19) ul-tu kir-bi-šu(-un, *i. e.* the city, cities) I led them away. V 64 *b* 54 ul-tu ki-ir-bi-šu (the temple); IV^2 17 *a* 1/2, 3/4 iš-tu ki-rib šamê [ellûte]; 20 *no* 1, 18 iš-tu ki-rib limni-ti E-lam-ti (H^{OV} xxxi below); Asb vi 113; V 62 *a* 44 (Br 8896); IV^2 19 *a* 1/2, 3/4 ul-tu ki-rib ap-si-i (šame-e) Br 7987. — V 21 *g-h* 42 (+51) $^{(ir)}$ XU = kir(?)-bu, Br 8535; H 28, 623. — **Der.**:

qirbiš = ana (ina) kirib, in the phrase kirbiš-tišmat. D^{Par} 147 *no* 44; Halévy, *Rev. Sém.*, iv 192. Creat.-*frg* IV 41 ēpušma sapāra (*q. v.*) šul-mu-u kir-bi-iš ti-āmat; 48, kir-biš ti-āmat šu-ud-lu-xu tibû arkišu. K 8522 *R* 5 ša kir-biš ti-āmat i-tib-bi-[ru]; perh. K 4832 *R* 34.

Note. — Delitzsch, *Weltschöpfungsepos*, 132—134; Jastrow, *Religion*, 426 life (to destroy) the of *T*. — Jensen, KB vi (1) 329, 331 = kirib tiāmat = Tiāmat (>< Jensen, *Kosmologie*). — Hommel, *Neue kirchl. Zeitschrift*, 1890 *nos* 2 & 3; & *Jour. Trans. Vict. Inst.*, 28, 34 *fol* = in the midst; Pinches, *Jour. Trans. Vict. Inst.*, 28, 37: the central ocean, *i. e.* the waters under the earth, as distinguished from tiāmat in general. See also Meissner, ZA ix 270—2.

qirbîtu *1.* ‖ qirbu, 1. KB vi (1) 104, 16; & 415 *ad Etana*-legend: ina qir-bit ûme, in der Mitte des Tages. Perh. also *del* 59 (63) qir-bi-is-su I divided into 9 parts, KB vi (1) 234; 488 (>< ZA iii 419). Banks, *Diss*, 12, 67 ina kir-bi-e-ti i-ça-ad (& 66). KB iii (2) 68, 14—16 ina ki-er-bi-it pi-ri-'-ja ša-al-mi-iš šu-te-ši-ri ta-li-it-ti. Meissner, 48 *no* 48, 2 ina ki-ir-bi-it Pa-al-çu, in the limits of P.

qirbu *2.* *f* **qirubtu**. T. A. (Ber) 7, 20 ul ga-ag-ga-ru ki-ir-bu-um-ma, the road is not short; 27, ma-tum ru-uq-tu-u i-ba-aš-ši u ki-ru-ub-tum i-ba-aš-ši, be the land remote or near (?) ZA v 140.

qurbu (?) K 61, 7: Ɣ QA qu-ur-bi, one ephah of the flesh of the entrails (??).

qarbâti, a *pl f* meadows, fields {Fluren, Gefilde}. KB iii (2) 46, 18 Nabd mu-ba-ak-ki-ir ga-ar-ba-a-tim ik-ka-ri Ba-bi-i-lu. Rm 3, 105 *col* 1, 15 (JRAS '92, 305 *foll*). K 3459 *O* i 10 .... pi-e i-lu qar-ba-a-ti (*ibid* 226); *cf* gar-ba-a-tim A. H. 82, 7—14, 1042 (PSBA ix 125; x 369). K 3456 *O* 13 çu-çu .... la-qar-ba-a-tum; 30, bamâtum ub-ba-lu ir-xu-ça qar-ba-a-tum, PSBA xxi 37—9. Perh. Merod.-Balad.-stone iii 21 qar-ba-ti kudurri-ši-na, BA ii 262: ihre Gebietsumfriedigungen.

qirbîtu *2.* *pl* qirbâti & qirbêti, meadows surrounding a city {Flur einer Stadt} § 136; AV 4408, 8536. TP v 17 great herds of animals u mar-šit kir-be (>< Streck, ZA xiii 58 -bat)-te-šu-nu without number. II 67, 24 umallâ kir-ba-a-ti. K 1282 *O* 35 kir-bi-e-tum ša uš-tax-ri-ba, KB vi (1) 70—1. Pinches, *Inscr. Tablets*, *p* 60, 6 ki-ir-bi-tum, the aqueduct (or footpath). S 954 *O* 13, 14 nēšu ša ina kir-bi(*var* -e, Reisner, *Hymnen*, *no* 53)-ti (= ŠA [= LIB]-DU-EME-SAL, Br 8032) ittanallaku atti (D 135), a lion, walking about the fields thou art, J^{I-N} 62. IV^2 23 *no* 1 i 10, 11 the great bull ib-ta-'a kir-bi-ti. S^b 1 *R* iv 10 qir-bi-tum, preceded by eq-lum. Perh. II 60 *a-b* 32 $^{(il)}$ ki-iš-šat ša kir-bi-ti$^{(ki)}$; also II 55 *c-d* 11 um-mu ša ina kir-bi-ti šu-pat (?) Br 5463, 8032.

qirubû, *pl* qirubê. *m* meadow, field, piece of land or ground; parcel {Gefilde, Stück Land, Grundstück} Delitzsch in Del.-Baer, *Ezech*, xiii; § 65, 38 *rm*. Oppert, ZA x 52; Jensen, 517; Meissner & Rost, 57 (>< BA ii 130: Baumpflanzung); Lyon, *Sargon*, 65. Sarg *Cyl* 34 pi-te-e ki-ru-bi-e, to open up fields; *bull*-inscr. 38 (qi-ru-bi-e); Meissner, 122. Strassmaier, *Stockholm VIII. O. C.*, 5, 1: eqlu ki-ru-bu-u; also 8, 1; KB iv 172—3 *no* ii 1. V 68 *no* 1, 2—3 mi-ri-šu u ki-ru-bu-u šap-la-nu. I 44, 60 ki-ru-bu-u ma-a-du, a large piece of land; Sn vi 35 (ma-'a-du) ‖ qaqqaru ma'adu, Esh v 6; also KB ii 134 & 148. I 44, 61 i-na ki-rib (= upon) ki-ru-bi-e. IV^2 33* *c* 17 ki-ru-ba-a. Cyr 188, 2—3 ki-ru-bu-u | e-la-a-ni nâr ša .... (BA iii 427); *ibid* 19; Nabd 116 ki-ru-bu-u; Neb 95, 3 ki-ru-ba-a. ZA iii 219, 220. VATh 130, 6 gi-ru-bu-u ma-lu xitti-šu, Peiser, *Vertr.*, *no* 43. *Adv.*:

---

qurbanû (T^C 124) see babbanû (§ 65, 36 & *rm*). ~ qurubtum *cf* gurubtum, 231—2 ~ q(g)urb(p)u-u-te, AV 1745; Sn iii 72 read mutir pu-u-te, *q. v.*

qirubēš ‖ karmeš (437 *col* 2). Bu 88, 5—12, 103, 12 e-mu-u ki-ru-bi-eš, BA iii 224.

קרד. be strong, valiant {gewaltig, stark, mächtig sein}. — ג V 45 v 54 tu-qar-rad. H 2061, 1 (H 202) q(g)ur-ru-du. Perh. Rm 76, 21 (end) a-na-ku ax-xu-ur ik-ki u-qar-ad(t), Hr^{L} 358.

גt K 1316, 25 (amēl) šangû uq-ṭa-ri-da-aš-šu, M^{S} 86 *col* 1.

NOTE. — *Del* 85; NE 10, 47; 67, 27 see ka-šadu Q¹ 448 *col* 1.

Derr. — qitrudu, taqridu & these 6:

qardu (AV 7350; § 53*a*), Babylonian **gardu** (AV 1559; § 48), *f* q(g)arittu (AV 1519, 4230, 7347) *adj* strong, mighty, valiant {stark, mächtig, tapfer}. iδ UR-SAG (§ 9, 82); H 35, 852 qar-(*var* -ra)-du; Knudtzon, 30 *R* 6: GU-UD. — It is used of gods & goddesses. Ninib: TP i 11 (qar-du); Anp i 1 UR-SAG (Br 11281; *var* qar-du); I 27 *no* 1, 6. — Marduk: Creat.-*frg* IV 126; IV² 20 *no* 1 *R* 35 (end) (il) Marduk (il) qar-du, Br 5742. — H 77, 44 (= IV² 5 *b* 75) (il) Adad qar-du, Br 11281. IV² 49 *b* 46 the fire-god qar-du; see also T^{M} iii 183 (end); Asb ix 57 (+82) Dibbar (Gir, U)-ra qar-du. II 19 *a* 24 qar-du (= UR-SAG, 23) ša-di-i ša ta-na-ru. — Of Ištar: K 257 *O* 18, 19 (H 126) Ištar mar-tum qa-rit-tum (UR-SAG) il Bēl; K 155 *O* 29 qa-rit-tu(m) (ilat) Ištar. V 33 i 8, 9 Ištar ga-rit-ti i-la-a-ti; Asb ix 76; *ibid* 10 called mārat (il) Sin qa-rit-tu; 87 bēlit qa-rit-tu. Sm 122, 44 at-ti qa-rit-ti ilāni (BA iii 263*foll*). K 3464 *O* 22 (end) qa-rit-tum Ištar (Craig, *Religious Texts*, 66); N 3554 *O* 16 Ištar mātāti qa-rit-tum i-la-tum. — *Rec. Trav.*, xx 205*foll col* 1, 1/2 (ilat) Nanâ .... qa-rit-ti | i-lat i-la-a-ti (17, il A-e qar-du). Esh *Sendsch*, *O* 10 the seven gods qar-du-u-ti; K 3500 + K 4444 + K 10235 i 5 (il) Si-bit-te ilāni qar-du-te; also K 2801 + K 221 + K 2669 *O* 12 (il) sibi ilāni qar-du-ti. — Of kings, rulers & others. I 35 *no* 3, 14, Anp. zi-karu qar-du. Sn i 7 Sen. zi-ka-ru qar-du (*Kui* 1, 1; *Bell* 3). V 55, 7 zi-ik-ru qar-du (& 3). Sarg *Cyl* 17 Sargon ed(t)-lu qar-du; *Nimr* 4; Pp iv 13; TP ii 85; TP III (Zür. Inscr.; PSBA xviii 158, 159) 2. V 55 (58) *a* 21 see purīdu, 1. Sp II 265 *a* xxii 10 li-'-u qar(*var* -ra)-du. See also gugallu (212 *col* 2) & qar-bāti. V 37 *a-c* 31 qa-rit-tum (Br 6992) with be-el-tum & šar-ra-tum (iδ, with gloss ga-ša-an). II 43 *a-b* 1—3 a-rik-tum, a-lik-tum, qa-rit(šit?)-tum; also II 22 (K 242) *a-b* 21; Br 3122, AV 364. — IV² 5 *a* 41 (end) qar-du-te šu-nu (Br 741); V 65 *b* 34 pa-ri-e qar-du (*var* ru)-tu. — 43 *c* 12 arax qar-da-a-ti = arax ŠE-KIN-KUD.

qardūtu. power, strength, might {Kraft. Stärke, Macht} AV 7351, Br 2244. TP i 23 see qīrūtu. Šalm, *Mo*, *O* 9 *cf* metlu, 623 *col* 1. Neb 329, 9 (end) qar-du-ti-šu. I 27 *no* 1, 10 Ištar ša paraç qar-du-ti šuk-lu-lat; Šalm, *Ob*, 13 (-te). V 20 *e-f* 24 [NAM]-UR-SAG = qar-du-tum, Br 11281; H^{F} 29.

qarradu (§ 65, 24) ‖ qardu. iδ UR-SAG (§ 9, 82; Br 11282); AV 7357. — Asb ix 84 AN-BAR (= NIN-IB) tar-ta-xu qar-ra-du rabu-u; also K 133 (H 80) *O* 7—8 *R* 3—4, 13—14 *etc.*) Ninib qar-ra-du (= UR-SAG); *ibid R* 25—26 qar-rad-su-nu (25, QAR-RA-DU-UM-BI, Br 6539; ZK i 99 § 5). II 19 *a* 23/24, 52/53, 62/63; Abel & Winckler, *Keilschrifttexte*, 60, 1/2 (Ninib) qar-ra-du; also 18/19. K 3351, 29 qar-rad ilāni ni-bit-su. — II 57 *c-d* 36 Adar ša qar-ra-di (Br 7230). — III 38 *no* 1 *O* 1 Nergal qar-ra-du gitmālum dandannu ilāni; Smith, *Asurb*, 217, k, qar-rad ilāni. Banks, *Diss*, 18, 37 qar-rad (il) Nergal (+39). IV² 26 *a* 1, 2 (*cf a* 3) qar-ra-du (= UR-SAG) abûbu ezzu; IV² 2 v 18, 19 ina ma-xar (il) Nergal qar-ra-du dan-nu. NE XII *col* 3, 21—22 a-na qar-ra-di e[d-li il Nergal i-qab-bi] | qar-ra-du ed-lu il [Nergal] +26. Banks, *Diss*, 24—26, 36 (Adad) qar-rad ša la im-max-xar. — IV² 17 *a* 3, 4 qar-ra-du ed-lum il Šamaš; H 123, 5 ana qar-ra-di ed-lum (il) Ša-maš; also V 62 *no* 2, 30. Sp III 586 + R III 1, 18 qar-ra-du ed-lum (il) Šamaš. — V 62 *no* 2, 16 be-lum ra-bu-u qar-ra-du (il) Marduk; Šalm, *Balaw*, V 4 (Marduk) qar-rad ilāni. — H 126, 17 anaku qar-ra[-du]; IV² 50 iii 47 kīma še-e-ti u-kat-ti-mu qar-ra-du. K 2619 iv 22 (il) sibitti-šunu qar-rad la ša-na-an (KB vi, 1, 66—7). KB vi (1) 58—9, 7 (il) Dibbar (Gir, U)-ru(-ra) qar-rad ilāni. II 57 *d* (end) 7 qar-rad ša i-ša-riš aš-bu, Br 4544. — Anp i 33 qar-ra-da (*var* UR-SAG)-ku. III 3 (*no* 6) 15 see çīru, 2. V 33 *a* 16 qar-ra-du [eq-du]; also 26. Esh *Sendsch*, *O* 22 (end) calls himself qar-ra-du git-ma-lu. NE 43, 35 ēkallu munappiçat qar-ra-di. IV^2 30 *a* 5 qar-ra-du (= UR-SAG) ra-bu-u ša ki-ma erçi-tim ri-tu-u (& *l* 9). Sm 2052 (+ Sm 1051) iii/iv 28—43 has qar-ra-du as a ‖ of: (28) ša-nu-du, (29) ur-ša-nu, (30) ur(or ruz, s, ç)-zu-nu, (31) qar-du, (32) qar-ra-du, (33) qu-ra-a-du, (34) pi-ja-a-mu, (35) d(ṭ)a-ap-nu, (36) da-at(d)-nu, (37) al-ru, (38) it-bu-šum, (39) bi-i-ru, (40) ka-as-su-su, (41) mu-tu, (42) a-ru-um, (43) ka-šu[-šu], ZDMG 43, 193; BA iii 276, 277. V 41 *a-b* 21—26 (+ II 31 *no* 3, 20—24) qar-ra-du ‖ of (21) [ǎ]a-nun-du, (22) ur-ša-nu, (23) ka-šu-šu, (24) a-li-lu & pi-ja-a-mu[u], (25) al-lal-lu & ma-am-lu, (26) e-tel-lum & ša-ga-pi-ru. — S^b 1 *R* iv 21 gu-ṭu | id | qar-ra-du, Br 3679; same id in II 36 *a-b* 2 = (ma-a-a-al) qu-ra-di, Br 3680. V 36 *d-f* 21 u-mun | ⟨ | qar-ra-du, Br 8699. V 46 *c-d* 17 AN-GUD-(gu-ud-ga-ud)GUD = (il) qar-ra-du, Br 5741. II 52, 67 [.... UR-SAG-E]-NE(-KI) = ka-pi qar-ra-di = ki-šu, ZA xv 246.

qarradūtu ‖ qardūtu. AV 7358, Br 2245. K 2852 + K 9662 i 7 qur-di (il) Ašur bēli-ja u ta-nit-ti qar-ra-du-ti-ja; also SMITH, *Asurb*, 318, *m*; KB vi (1) 72, 16 (K 1282 *R*). II 67, 74 see metlu. Esh *Sendsch*, *R* 51 (end) ta-nit-ti qar-ra-du-ti (il) Ašur bēli-ja. II 19 *a* 15/16, 17/18; *b* 51/52 (ZK i 306 *rm* 1): a-na i-di qar-ra-du-ti-ka (& -ja); also IV^2 18 *a* 20, 21 of Ninib (Br 11282); L^4 i 21, 29.

qurdu (AV 7425), Babylonian **gurdu**. — *a*) = qarradūtu. IV^2 40 i 26, 27 man-nu ša ka-a-šu la i-dib-bu-bu qur-di-ku, who should not proclaim thy power? (§ 119). K 1282, 27 li-na-du qur-di-ja (KB vi, 1, 72). TP viii 39 li-ta-at qur-di-ja. Anp iii 89 a-su-me-tu ša qur-di. K 2852 + K 9662 i 17 (end) [lu]-šad-lu-la qur-di-ka; also see qarradūtu. K 3158 *O* (= IV^2 54 *O*, *no* 1) 45 (end) lit-ta]-'i-id qur-di-ka; IV^2 59 *no* 2 *b* (K 254) 28 (end); IV^2 20 *R* 37 (end) qur-di. Šalm, *Mon*, i 49 qur-di-šu-nu u-ša-pa. ZA v 60, 18 lu-šar-ri-ix qur-di-ki, I will magnify thy might. III 20, 97 qur-di ilāni-ja dan-nu-ti; Asb iv 35. II 67, 39 qur-di ta-nit-ti ša (il) Ašur (KB ii 18, 19). K^M 5, 9 .... ud]-da-kam la pa-da-a qu-ru-ud-ka lud-lul. K 2801 + K 221 + K 2669 *O* 33 qur-us-su-nu (§ 17), their power. DT 71, 8 .... qu-ru-us-su lud-lul. Also P. N. Qur-di-Ašur; Qur-di-Adad *etc.*, AV 7426, 7427. — *b*) multitude, mass, massiveness {Fülle, Masse, Massenhaftigkeit}. Neb viii 16 gu-ur-du ta-aš-ri-ix-tum ‖ ni-çir-ti šar-ru-ti (17) I heaped therein, AV 1750.

qurādu ‖ qarradu (§ 65, 13; AV 7418). KB vi (1) 68 *no* iii 17 a-na qu[-ra-di (il) Dibbar (U)-ra] + 18 qu-ra-du (il) Dibbar-ra; 64 *R* 23; 66, 19 (beg) + 24 (end); 60, 10. *del* 14 (16) ma-lik-šu-nu qu-ra-du (il) Bēl; *del* 164, 167, 168 (177, 181) ana qu-ra-di (il) Bēl; atta ab(p)-kalli ilāni qu-ra-du. K 2487 + K 8122 *O* 26 qu-ra-du at-ta (of Ninib). NE 8, 28 ma-rat qu-ra-di, + 35 ib-ta-ni qu-ra-du. IV^2 33 iv (end) Tammūz: ša qu-ra-du (il) Nin-ib; Tišrīt ša (il) Šamaš qu-ra-du (see *ibid* iv 11). T^M iii 60 (il) GIŠ-BAR qu-ra-du (BA iv 158); IV^2 8 iv 13. VATh 4105 i 9 Gilgameš said a-na ku-ra-di-šu (il) Šam-ši (*Mittheilgn. der Vorderasiat. Gesellschaft*, '02, *no* 1). *Cuthean*-legend ii 10 (end) (il) Šamaš qu-ra-du (KB vi, 1, 294; ZA xii 320 *foll*); also see KB vi (1) 216, 23 (= NE 67) & 472; *Etana*-legend (K 2527 + K 1547) *O* 30; TP iv 45 (-di). II 36 *a-b* 2 *etc.* see qarradu (end) Br 9801.

It is mostly used in the *pl*: qurādē = warriors {Krieger}, lit^y: braves. qu-ra-de-ja$^{(pl)}$, my soldiers TP i 71 (*var* to ummānātēja); ii 6, 75; vi 23 (qu-ra-(a)-de-ja); v 45; ii 66. Sarg *Khors* 99 (amēl) qu-ra-de-ja; Sn *Kui* 3, 6 qu-ra-du-u-a. — S^P 158 + S^P II 962 *O* 12 ana kal-la qu-ra-di-e-šu. Asb v 109 qu-ra-di-e-šu (§§ 20; 74, 2) ‖ mund(t)ax-çi-e-šu (110). TP III *Ann* 195 (amêl) qu[-ra-di]-šu, + 185; also Sarg *Khors* 81, 130. Šalm, *Mon*, i 39 ši-lim qu-ra-de-šu; Synchr. Hist. (KB i 200, 201) last line. TP i 77 qu-ra-de-šu-nu; iii 24, 53, 55; iv 20, 91; v 71, 93; qu-ra-a-de-šu-nu, ii 23. Sn v 84 pagrê qu-ra-de-šu-nu, III 16 iv 24 pa-gar gu-ra-de-šu-un; 15 i 18 gi-mir qu-ra-di-šu-nu | çi-ru-ti.

q(k, g)ardamu. K 2061 i 16 (amêl) GIL-GIL = qar-da-mu (H 202; AV 7349; Br 1397) followed by aš-ṭu. Perh. also IV² 12 *R* 6 la a-ni-xa bir-ka-šu-nu, u-šab-ba-ru qar(?)-da-mi la [muštêširûti], their knees weary not, they break (= destroy) the *q*, if they give not a right decision. Hommel, *Expos. Times*, Febr. 1900, 234, comparing חַרְטֻמִּים.

קרט, whence naqrûṭu, 720 *col* 2.

qirṭunu (?) V 42 *g-h* 33 IM(la-ak)ŠIT = qir(biš, piš?)-ṭu-nu, a vessel {ein Gefäss} Br 8437.

קרם. ℑ V 45 vi 1 tu-qar-ram.

qirmu. cover {Überzug}? Nabd 258, 10 qi-ir-mu u bi-ir-ri qâtê; 386, 1 + 11 ki-ri-mu (see however kirêmu, 438 *col* 1 & nakrimânu 677 *col* 2). Peiser, *Vertr.*, 287 *rm* 3.

qaranu, *pr* iqrun heap up {aufhäufen}; originally: bring together, strengthen, bind, Samš iv 30 šal-ma-ta qurâdêšunu a-na gu-ru-ni-it lu-u aq-ru-un (see also Sarg *Ann* 208), I heaped up; Sarg *Ann* 455 the presents *etc*. la-aq-ru-na ki-rib-ša, I will heap up therein.

ℑ = ℚ *int*. (§ 43) heap up high. AV 1551. Sp II 265 *a* vi 8 gi-ix-bar-ri-e (Strong, PSBA xvii 148: gi-iç maš-ri-e) bêl pa-ni (*var* -nu) ša gur-ru-nu (*var* gu-ru-un) ma-ak-ku-ru. Neb vii 22 u-ga-ri-nu (3 *pl*) makkûršun; viii 15 bûšâ *etc*. u-ga-ri-in (1 *sg*) kiribšu. TP ii 21 *fol*, the corpses of their warriors a-na gu-ru-na-te ina gisallât šadê lu-ki-ri-in (1 *sg*); iii 54 (57) ina bamât šadî a-na gu-ru-na-a-te lu(-u)-ki-ri-in (H 169); iv 19 çâbê muqtablêšunu ina gisallât šadê a-na gu-ru-na(-a)-te lu-ki-ri-in. Sarg *bull*-inscr. 34, the corpses of their warriors .... u-gar-ri-nu gu-ru-un-niš.

Derr. these 3:

qarnu 1. bond, tie {Band, das Verbundensein} or the like. V 28 *g-h* 55 qar-nu | u-lap lu-ub-bu-tim.

gurunniš, *adv* in heaps {haufenweise} see qaranu, ℑ.

gurunâte & gurunêti (*pl*; § 70*a*) heaps {Haufen}. ZA v 92 comp. גֹּרֶן. See qaranu, ℚ & ℑ.

qarnu 2. *f* horn {Horn}; *pl* qarnê & qarnâte, D⁸ 107. ℑ SI; § 9, 65; Br 3388; AV 7354. Sb 177 si-i | SI | qar-nu; H 8 + 178, 61; 16, 231; 24, 502. *pl* SI-MEŠ-šu-nu; TP vi 68. — *a*) horn {Horn} in its proper sense. — IV² 9 *a* 19—20 b(p)u-ru ek-du ša qar-ni (= SI) *etc*. kabba-ru (*q. v.*); 27 *a* 21, 22 ki-ma re-mu ek-du ... qar-na-a-šu (= SI) kîma šarûr Šamši ittananbiṭu (see נבט), Br 7470; 22 *a* 40, 41 qar-ni-šu (= SI-BI) his horn(s). Asb ix 78 Bêltis u-nakip nakîrêja ina SI*pl*-ša gaš-ra-a-te. H 81, 22 ina bi-ri-šu-nu ki-ma ri-i-me ra-bi-e qar-na-a-šu (Br 6553; II 24 *c-d* 50) it-ta-na-aš-ši. NE VI 185 ina qar-ni-šu (of the heaven-bull); 169, ina bi-rit ti-ik-ki qar-ni (see KB vi, 1, 176, 177); 188, ku-bur qar-ni-šu, the dimensions of his horn. V 50 *b* 47 tu-ra-xa ina qaq-qa-di-šu u qar-ni-šu iç-ça-bat. K 3182 ii 39 as for him who protects wickedness qar-na-šu tu-bal-la, his horn thou wilt destroy, AJSL xvii 138, 139. Scheil, *Rec. Trav.*, xxii (notes liv 5) ina qar-ni-ki tu-šar-di-i. — *b*) in a figurative sense: *α*. of the "horns" of the moon {von den "Hörnern" des Mondes} K 172 *O* 1—2 Sin ina tamartišu | SI-MEŠ-šu ud-du-da, Pinches, *Texts*, 8. Creat.-*frg* V 16 qar-ni na-ba-a-ta, that the horns shine. III 58 *a* 35 qar-nu imitti-šu, its right horn. IV² 28 *no* 2 *O* 15, 16 qar-ni ba-nu-u (= SI-SAR-SAR). — *β*. of the "horns" *i. e.* the projecting corners of a tower {von den "Hörnern", *i. e.* vorspringenden Ecken eines Turmes}. *pl* qarnê. Asb vi 29 u-kap-pi-ra qarnê (*var* qar-ni, § 70)-ša ša pitiq erê namri (KB ii 204, 205). — *γ*. V 33 *b* 50 a-gi-e ga-ar-ni çi-ra-a-ti, KB iii (1) 140, 141: grossartige Hörnermützen; Lehmann, BA ii 590, 591, headgear with horn-shape projections. — *δ*. part of a ship {Teil eines Schiffes}.

pl qarnâti; Gr. *κέρας*; perhaps the yard of a ship, D[8] 137; ZA i 43 *rm* 1. K 4378 (D 88) vi 26, 27 GIŠ-SI-MA′ = qar-ni (-nu) elippi; GIŠ-SI-SI-MA′ = qar-na-a-ti (-te) elippi, Br 3438, 3435. II 45 *a-b* 35, 36; 62 *g-h* 61. — *e.* part of a wagon or chariot {Teil eines Wagens} NE VI 11 ša ma-ša(gar?)-ru-ša xurâça-am-ma el-me(*var* mi)-šu qar-na-a-ša, KB vi (1) 166, 167; § 74, 2. — V 16 *c-d* 11 SAG = qar-nu, Br 3515; same id = di-na(or ta?)-nu & pu-xu. ku-ut qar-ni (= SI) see kutû, 456 *col* 2.

qarnû, *adj* horned {gehörnt}. Banks, *Diss*, 24—26, 84 ri-i-mu qar-nu-u a-bi Adad.

qarnu *3.* a herb, plant {Kraut, Gewächs} see qiltum.

qarnânu, *adj* IV² 26 *b* 35, 36 epithet of u(or U?)-xu-lu (id = SI), *p* 313 *col* 1; AV 7352. II 30 *e-f* 73, 74 ‖ puqlu (= SI-UD-DU & SI-SAR-A, Br 1204, 1205).

qirsu. K 511, 9—10 nu-še-ri-ba-a ina qir-si; K 568, 7 a-na ki-ir-s[i?]; K 89, 9 ina lib-bi qi-ir-si | i-ba-aš-ši; K 113, 6 ki-ma a-na ki-ir-si it-tal-ku; 81—2—4, 58 *R* 3 (Hr[L] 21; 4; 181; 183; 361).

qursînu, *dual* qursînâ, *pl* qursînâti; so Haupt, *Journ. Bib. Lit.*, xix 77 *rm* 100, instead of kursinnu, 440 *col* 1.

qursêtu. K 623 *R* 2 šulmu .... | a-na g(q)ur-si-e-te | a-na êkalli | ana dûri | ana bitâti ša ali gab-bi, Hr[L] 191.

qurpîsu. AJPh xix 386 *ad* Anp ii 92/3 (96) gur-pi-si (siparri) buckets or baskets (סכס = קבץ) of copper; instead of gur-pîsu, 232 *col* 2; see also Streck, ZA xiii 77 on III 6 *R* 52 *foll.*

qaraçu. G § 26; D[Pr] 155. — *a*) pinch off, clip off {abkneifen} see Q[t] & qirçu. KB vi (1) 286 iv 5—6 [XIV gi-ir]-çi taq-ri-iç; VII gi-ir-çi ana imni taš-ku-un | [VII gi]-ir-çi ana šumêli taš-ku-un. Sp II 265 *a* xxiv 2 šar-xu [(il)] Zu-lum-ma-nu ka-ri-iç (*var* -çu) ṭi-iṭ-ṭa-ši-na; T[M] ii 171 ina bi]-rit êli iq-ri-çu-u-ni di-i-[ṭa-]ki; GGA '98, 825. — *b*) gnaw, gnaw off {nagen, benagen}. IV² 56 *b* 40, 41 .... amêlûti šîr(-)ša la a-ka-li NER-PAD-DU(-)ša la ka-ra-a-çi. — *c*) in figurative sense = gnaw at one's reputation, slander {verleumden} see k(q)arçu.

Q[t] NE 8, 34 Arûru ṭi-ṭa iq-ta-ri-iç, pinched off a piece of clay; T[M] iii (= IV² 50 *a*) 17 ša kaššapti ina kul-lati aq-ta-ri-iç ṭîṭa-šu. K 651 *O* 13 aq-ṭi-bi mu-uq-ta-ri-iç (Hr[L] 383).

Derr. — these two:

qarçu. slander {Verleumdung}. V 21 *a-b* 19 EME-ŠIG(K) = qar-çu ‖ taš-gi-ir-tu (שקר), ZK ii 279 (bel); Br 14473. found mostly in the phrase kar-çi akalu = calumniate, slander {verleumden}; properly: eat to pieces (§ 132). Sm 61, 14 (D 131) kar-çi a-ka-li (= EME-ŠIG-KU-KU) Br 854 & *cf* pâšišu. On *q. a.* compare ikkiba akalu = eat guilt, *i. e.* take guilt upon oneself, *i. e.* do wrong, IV² 51 *b* 13 (ZA vi 246); K 122 *R* 9 qar-çi-šu e-ta-kal; K 824, 9—10 since Ummanigas kar-çi-ka ina pâni-ia i-kul-u, has slandered thee in my presence (Hr[L] 43, 290; JAOS xviii 148; PSBA xxiii 63). K 2729 *R* 15 ina] eli pi-i ša a-kil qar-çi za-'-ra-ni la tal-lak, BA ii 566 *fol.* K 3364 *R* 5 ša a-kil kar-çi. DT 109, 19 a-ki-lat kar-çu (AJSL xiv 173, 174; Boissier, *Rev. Sém.*, viii 152 § 4). Also in T. A. (ZA vi 246 *rm* 4; ‖ xa-ba-lu harm, hurt {schädigen}, Jastrow, *Jour. Bib. Lit.*, xi 116 *rm* 40). (Ber) 102, 6 i-ka-lu ka-ar-zi-ia, with gloss u-ša-a-ru (= שור; *ibid* 21, 24); 34 *a* 33 ša i-kal-lu-u-nim kar-çi-ia, who slander me; 112, 16 a-nu-ma a-ka-lu ka-ar-zi-ia xa-ba-lu-ma, that is a slander against me (and) a shame. (Lo) 35, 8 ša i-ka-lu-u-ni kar-çi-ia; 61, 14 u i-li qa-bi qa-ar-zi-ia ši-ir-ti before my lord, the king. K 2051 i 30 EME[(ku-ku)]KU-KU = a-kil kar-ç[i] followed by emetukû (*i. e.* II 32 *a-b* 58, 59; Br 840). V 12 *a-b* 41 EME-ŠIG-KU-KU = a-kil [kar-çi] Br 854; V 31 *a-b* 67, 68 EME-ŠIG-KU-ME-E = kar-çe in-nak-ka-lu, Br 841; AV 7355; ZK ii 72 *foll*; V 48 ii 32 âkil qar-çi, see also vi 18; H 216, 80.

qirçu, a piece of clay {ein Stück Ton}. V 42 *g-h* 15 IM[(ki-id)] [illegible] = ki-ir-çu, Br 8285; see also qaraçu Q.

qirçappu, see 440 *col* 2 & BA iii 281, 282.

qararu. K 4256 *R* 7 ka-ra-r[um?]. ZA iv

15 (K 3459) 18 qa-ri-ra (or noun?) te-ip-ti.

ℶ V 45 vi 3 tu-q(k)ar-ra-ar. Perh. K 161, 13 (end) tu-qar-ra-ar.

ℸ V 45 iii 52 tu-šaq(k)-ra-ar.

The verb perhaps means: dry, be singed, burn {vielleicht vertrocknen, versengt werden, brennen}.

Derr. — these 5:

qarūru. drying {Abtrocknung}. *del* 145 (153) il-lik a-ri-bi-ma qa-ru-ra ša mê i-mur-ma, KB vi (1) 241 & 500: Schwinden des Wassers; Haupt: decrease of the water. Ball in *Genesis* (SBOT) 54: saw the *bottom* of the water (*cf* قرار, bottom of the sea); perhaps V 30, 13 (AV 4196) ka-ru-ru.

qarurtu. famine {Hungersnot}. II 44 *a-b* (*no* 7) 68 ka-ru-ur-tum = bu-bu[-tum]; II 29 *c-d* 40 U-GUL-TA = ka-ru-ur-tu, AV 4197, together with sunqu, ubbuṭu, xušaxxu, Br 6071.

kararū fire, heat {Feuer, Hitze}. Sm 9, 10 ka-ra-ru-u ‖ i-ša-tu; II 28 *no* 5 (*add*) AN]-NE = ka-ra-ru[-u?] AV 4183; Br 14070. IV² 15* *R* i 18, 19 ina ka-ra-re-e (= AN-NE) mu-ši u ur-ra ina ri-ši-šu lu-u ka-a-a-an, Br 4588, *cf* NE = la'bu.

qirīru lamp {Lampe}? III 66 *col* 10, 32—33 u ki-ri-ru ṭābu | a-na nu-ri-šu-nu lib-ši, PSBA xxi 129: and a good lamp, or fire?

qurāru. IV² 58 iii 41 (end) ina gu-ra-ri, in the fire (?) ZA xvi 176, 177.

garašu. cut {zerschneiden}, AV 7345; *ps* iqarraš, igaraš. D⁸ 53 *rm.* II 48 *e-f* 15 (ki-it)  = qa-ra-šu (AV 1376; Br 1413); 16 (bu-lu-ug) 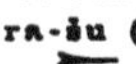 = *q* ša içi (Br 340); 17 .... ŠUK (or PAD) = qu-ra-aš-tum (AV 7420; Br 11931). K 4373 *O d* 2+4 qa-ri-šu, M⁸ *pl* 12. 83, 1—18, 1335 ii 18 (ku-ud) KUD = ga-ra-šu. — Perh. Neb 247, 9 ul i-ga-ra-aš; 416, 3 (i-qar-ra-aš).

ℶ V 45 vi 2 tu-qar-raš.

NOTE. — Winckler, *Forsch.*, ii, 2, 400 *ad* KB iii (1) 36 *col* vi 39 kir-sa-nim, compares קרש = board ‖ Brett.

Derr. — Perhaps these 3:

quraštu see qarašu.

qiršu. Zimmern, *Ritualtafeln*, 66 *O* 17 (karpat) kal-lu ša qi-ir-ši.

quršu. V 17 *a-b* 43 maxaçu ša qur-ši.

qarratu. K 10624 (beginning of a section of incantations) qar-ra-ti-ja qar-ra-ti-ja; Bezold, *Catalogue*, 1102; M⁸ 86 *col* 2; see perhaps karattu, 442—3.

qarītum. some kind of beam, wood {eine Art Balken, Holz}. 81—7—27, 200 *col* 3, 23 *foll* u-rum = gu-šu-rum (both ID GUŠUR), qa-ri-tum, followed by giš-rum. Perh. = قَرِيع. ZA ix 268 *no* 5; also 81, 4—28, 327 *R* 12 a-ru-u explained by qa-ri-tu[m]; 83—1—18, 14 *O* 6—8 ina muxxi e-pa-še ša qa-ri-e-ti ša šarru be-li iš-pur-an-ni; 12 *foll* ṭa-ba qa-ri-tu | ana e-pa-še .... li-pu-šu (Hr^L 406; see R. F. Harper in AJSL xiii 211). K 2401 iii 25 .... li ša qa-ri-ti, BA ii 628, 629.

qartuppāti (?) KB vi (1) 268, 269 (Rm 908) 4 l]i-' qar-tup-pa-a-ti ri-kis qabli-šu-nu, mächtig der Schreibtafel ....–e der Binde ihrer Hüften (see *ibid* 585: ein „Tafelgriff", womit man die angebrannte Tafel aus Ton beim Schreiben oder sonst anfasst); *cf* karru, 2 (431 *col* 2 *med*).

qâšu, *pr* iqīš, *ps* iqâš, *ag* qâiš(u), qâeš(u). give, present, donate {geben, schenken} ID BA (§ 9, 8; Br 107); GAB (= ŠA)-BA (§ 9, 84). G § 5 ‖ šaraqu. AV 7359. TP ii 60 (iv 6) such & such ana Ašur (& Adad) a-qiš; vii 8 the gods who love me .... i-qi-šu-ni, have given me; i 24 see qîrūtu. K 2711 *O* 38 ... a-na Bêl bêlija a-qiš a-na qiš-ti (& *R* 1); KB iv 46 *no* 1, 4 i-ki-i-iš, he has presented. NE VI 192 see piššatu. L⁴ i 12 i-qi-ša-an-ni a-na qiš-ti. Asb ii 14 chariots, horses, mules a-na ru-kub bêlū-ti-šu a-qis-su; ix 128 my numerous army which Ašur i-ki-ša; K 2675 *O* 59. Merod.-Balad.-stone iii 6 i-ki-šu-šu; iii 34 qi-ša-a-tu i-qis-su-nu-ti-ma. aqi-eš = aqiš, I 8 *no* 3, 7 (§ 30); I 69 *a* 15 lū a-qi-iš (ZK ii 260); ZA v 67, 30 ta-qi-ši-ma (2 *sg f*) ki-nu-ti (thou hast granted). Šalm. *Obel* 83 ŠA-BA-MEŠ

qirtu, qirâte see kirū, 1 (433). ∼ qartabbu *cf* kirçappu (440 *col* 2) & see qirçappu.

(= qîšâte) a-na ilâni rabûti aq-qiš (KB i 138, 139); Nabd 854, 4 a-qiš-šu. Cyr 337, 15 i-ki-iš. ana ba-la-ṭi-šu i-ki-iš often on seal-rings *etc.* = i-ki-iš. — *pc* II 19 *a* 16 + 18 (end) qiš-ta li-qiš-ka; K 10, 5 li-qiš-šu (Hr^{L} 280). — *ps* ZIMMERN, *Ritualtafeln*, *no* 52, 14 + 17 qi-šâti (& qîšta) ta-qa-su-nu-ti. — *ip* Cyr 337, 11 qîštu ki-ša-an-ni-ma, a present give unto me! IV^{2} 59 *no* 1 *a* 29 napiš-ti qi-šam, grant life! NE VI 8 in-bi-ka ja-a-ši qa-a-šu qi-šam-ma (KB vi, 1, 167; § 133: give, I pray thee!); II 66 *no* 2, 18 (ja-a-ti) qi-šim-ma. — *ag* Anp i 9 Ninib qa-iš balâṭi; KB iv 102, 103, 4 Nabû .... qa-iš balâṭi. K^{M} 22, 5 (il) Êa qa-i-šu balâṭi. II 66 *no* 1, 9 Ištar qa-i-šat balâṭi, who grants life, J^{W} 100. K 2001, 3 (ilat) Gu-še-e-a qa-i-šat gu-ša-a-ti (ZA viii 351); K^{M} 4, 25. II 60 *no* 2, 32 qa-eš-še, giving (§ 30). — *ac* K 4225, 20 (H 125) SI = ka-a-šu; K 4350 i 29 & 32 (= II *R* 11; H 46; D 91, 13 & 16) IN-BA, *pl* IN-BA-EŠ = i-ki-iš, i-ki-šu; 35 IN-NA-AN-BA = i-ki-is-su. ZK i 70 (bel). — Note especially the use in proper names: V 43 *c-d* 31 AN-AB-BA = (il)Nabû qa-eš-še ab-bu-ti; V 44 *c-d* 18 (ilat) Ba-u ta-ki-ša bul-liṭ, o Bau thou hast granted that he may live; Br 107; Camb 336, 14 (il) Sin-ta-qiš-bul-liṭ. V 44 *c-d* 53 (il) Sin ta-ki-ša lubluṭ. Camb 315, 24 Iqîša; 62, 5 Ta-qiš (ilat) Gu-la. Esh iii 53 Bêl-BA (= iqî)-ša. KB iv 4, 31; 14 (*no* 1) 8 (+ 15, 16, 21) ana Sin-i-ki-ša-am (& -šam). Marduk-qišanni, see ZA vii 281, 282. On AN-BA-NI-NI = (il) Taqîš-ili see KB vi (1) 552; MEISSNER, *no* 8, 11 (110, 26) Qi-iš-i-li.

ג give plentifully. K 7856 i 8 *foll* qi-ša-a-ti a-na ..... [u]-qa-a-a-iš. Šalm. *Balaw*, v 5 (immer) niqâ-šu ušamxira u-qa-i-ša (3 *pr*) qîšâ (wr. ŠA-BA-MEŠ)-te; vi 4, 5 qîšâte u-qa-i-su (= iš-šu)-nu-ti. Sarg *Khors* 144 all this to the gods Bêl *etc.* u-qa-i-ša ki-ša-a-ti, I gave as presents (see also WINCKLER, *Sargon*, 180, 22); Sn *Bav* 29 all this a-na (il) Êa u-qa-a-a-iš ki-ša-a-ti. K 4350 i 38 (H 46; D 91, 32) IN-NA-AN-BA-E = u-qa-as-su. K^{M} 39, 14 qu-ši-ma (= *pm*?).

ג^{t} IV^{2} 23 *no* 1 *a* 24 ... a-na (il) Bêl liq-ṭa-'i-iš (23 ‖ lip-pa-qid).

Derr. these 2:

qîšu & qîštu (§ 64); *pl* qîšâte, present, gift {Geschenk, Gabe} id ŠA-BA (often in *c. t.*, T^{C} 123; Br 11988); HEBR. i 179, see qâšu. Creat.-*frg* IV 44 he drew to his side the net qi-iš-ti abi-šu (il) A-nim. Dar 87, 32: III šiqil ki-iš-tum ka-na-ki; IV^{2} 39 i 8 (?? MEISSNER, 112 *rm* 2). V 33 v 46 ki-ša-at-šu-nu lu ad-din (§ 51); vi 10—13 ki-ša-a-ti ša kaspi u xurâçi ana ilâni Êsagila lu addin; vii 4 ki-ša-a-tim mârê um-ma-ni. S 747 *R* 6 [u?]-še-ri-bu k(q)at-ra-šu-un ki-ša-a-tu. H 108, 3; 111, 49 (D 127, 5; V 11 *d-f* 3) AM-BA = ŠA-BA = ki-iš-tu(m) *var* qiš-tu; Br 4752. Perhaps Bm 609 *R* še-im qiš-tum (BA iii 215); T. A. (Ber) 24, 83 ki-i-ša-a-ti *pl* which my brother sends. — SCHEIL, *Rec. Trav.*, xvii 84 (*no* xxiii *col* 2 bel) the king of Anšan it-ti ir-bi u ki-ša; Merod.-Balad.-stone ii 17 ir-ba u ki-ša-a-ti; BA ii 260; ZA vii 187: Zoll und Geschenke. Perh. here also kîšu, 2 (446 *col* 1). A ‖ is:

qûštu, *pl* qûšâti (BA iii 274) see qâšu ק *ag*.

qašû oppress {unterdrücken}? ק^{t} 81—11—3, 478 iii 5, 6 iq-ta-ši, iq-ta-ša, PSBA xviii 253.

qiššû. probably cucumber, pickle {Gurke} ZK ii 424; ZA vi 296, 297; *cf* קִשֻּׁאִים. I 44, 72 the ašnân-stone is compared to zêr kiš-še-e. Sn vi 1 see simânu, 766, 767, ZA i 53. Perh. also 83—1—18, 483 *R* 2 (WINCKLER, *Forsch*, ii 8). S^{b} 46 u-ku-uš | 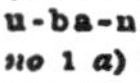 | kiš-šu-u (Br 10887; ZA i 52; KB iii, 1, 64 *rm* 4). II 44 *g-h* 4 id + SAR (Br 4320, 10898) = kiš-šu-u, followed by u-ba-nu & ti-gi-lu-u. K 267 iv 5 (= II 41 *no* 1 *a*) kiš-šu-u, followed by (6) u-ba-nu; (7 & 8) ša-ru-ru; (9) zêr kiš-še-e; (13) ... kiš-šu[-u ša] çu-ma-me-ti (*q v.*). — See also kiššû, 446 *col* 1.

q(k, g?)iššu. II 48 *e-f* 24 qiš-šu followed by qiššu ša SAR-MEŠ & qiššu ša mu-sa-ri-e, Br 1839.

qašdu *1. adj* splendid, lofty, sublime {herrlich, erhaben} ‖ ellu (KB vi, 1, 439, where connection with קדש, quddušu is suggested). IV^{2} 58 *a* 4 Ê(?)-UL-BAR qa-aš-du; Bu 88—5—12, 75 + 76 vi 12 see parçu, 2. NOTE 1. NE 28, 37 NIN-DINGIR-RA-MEŠ (= ilāti; but KB vi, 1, 150: enēti) qa-aš-da-a-ti; see KB vi, 1, 489; 573. T^{M} vi 27 mārē .... š]a qa-aš-da-a-ti (+ 38). Fragment of a hymn to Ištar (K 11152) 13 qaš-da-a-ti ša muš-ba(?)-i-ki. Perh. V 11 *a-c* 16 NU-GA = NU-UG-UD = ul qal-du Br 1993, 6110. III 66 *col* 9, 21 (ilat) qa-al-da-i-tu. To the same stem belong the following 3:

qašdu *2.* *n.* V 28 *e-f* 4 qa-aš-du ‖ al-lum, AV 7360.

qūšudu (> quššudu) *adj* ‖ qašdu, 1. TP vii 90 a splendid mansion ad-ma-na qu-šu-da, AV 7431.

qašdūtu. V 25, 10. See for the present qadiltūtu.

qašaṭu see kašaṭu, 449, 450.

qašalum (??) V 40 *a-b* 1 ŠA (= GAR) = qa-ša-lum.

qašp(b)u. II 30 *c-d* 67 qa-aš-pu, apparently ‖ of raṭ-bu, *q. v.* But *cf* našbu, 738 *col* 2.

qišqittū see kiški(a)ttū, 450 *col* 2 & KB vi (1) 456—7.

qašaru see gašaru, 233, 234; also K 2711 *R* 6 (end) ma-aq-tu ag(q)-šir.

qušaru; qiširu (?) 82—5—22, 946 *R* 1—2 qu-ša-ru; 3—5 ki(qi?)-ši-ru, PSBA xxiii 200, 201.

quššutu. T. A. (Ber) 25 *c* 52: I ŠA-BAN (= qaštu) gu-uš-šu-ti xurāçu uxxu-zu; 26 *b* 43: I ŠA (?) zu-ub-bi gu-uš-šu-ti ŠIT-LAL-šu.

qaštu, (§ 62, 1) AV 7361. *pl* qašāti *f* bow {Bogen} § 69 note; D^{S} 128, 129; Hebr. i 175. id GIŠ-BAN, § 9, 31; IV^{2} 45 *no* 3 *R* 3 (Hr^{L} 210); II 39 *c-f* 31; Creat.-*frg* IV 38. TP vi 56 id + su-nu. Barth, *Nominallehre*, 7 perh. √קשׁי be curved {krumm sein}. K 13, 42 (Hr^{L} 281) ina qašti ra-mi-ti, GGA '98, 825 × JAOS xix 78. K 4574 *R* 3; K 4558 *O* 3 *foll* see pitpānu. Smith, *Asurb*, 143 *no* I: šu-li-e (iç) qašti. Esh *Sendsch*, *R* 29 (iç) qaštu dan-na-tu u tar-ta-xu giš-ru. III 48 *d* 21 see bēlu, 3 (159 *col* 1). K 3351, 19 i-na pa-an qaš-ti-šu ez-zi-ti. II 47 *d* 59 see malū, 1 (Š^{3t}, 543 *col* 1) & D^{Pr} 155 *rm.* id also Esh i 32; v 1 (qašti-ia) see xubtu, 304 *col* 2. Camb 334, 4 (end) ina xu-bu-ut qašti-šu. Perh. II 19 *b* 8 qa-aš[-tu (Br 9100) a-bu-ba-niš na-ša-ku]; also see ZA ii 333 *no* 16. — (amēl) çāb(ē) qašti = archers, bowmen {Bogenschützen}. id Asb vi 88; Nabd 23, 9 (amēl) çābē ša GIŠ-BAN; 987, 13 (iç) qaš-tum; Sarg *Khors* 82 (amēl) Su-te-e ça-ab (*var* çābē) qašti. Nabd 215, 3; 228, 13; 1058, 4 (amēl) rab (iç) qašti. Asb vi 86 (amēl) rab qašti^{pl}, commander of the archers. On BA iii 106 *ad* II 31 *b* 53 see Jensen, *Theol. Litztg.*, '95 *no* 20. qaqqab qašti = bow star = Syrius. Hommel in Hastings, *Dictionary*, i 218. See IV^{2} 54 *a* 11; V 46 *a*(-*b*) 23; ZA i 258, 259 *no* 4. Dar 307, 2 (430, 4) ša ina bīt (iç) qašti, name for a locality. See Kotolla, BA iv 553 & 560—1 on bīt qaštu = Bogenland; & bīt ešrū = Zehntland.

qištu. forest {Wald} Jensen, KB vi (1) 362/3; 445 for kištu (452).

qatu *1.* (קתי) present, give away, lend {weggeben, verleihen}. § 116. V 34 *c* 44 ba-la-ṭam qu-ti (*ip f*) ana kalie littū-tija.

qātu *2.* AV 7368; Babylonian gātu, AV 1578; § 43. *f* hand {Hand} id ŠU (= 𒋗) Br 7071, with or without dual sign (𒈫); *pl* or *dual* qātē, qātā; id ŠU ^{pl}, ŠU 𒈫 (or ŠU^{II}; ŠU^{2}). § 9, 89; H 25, 539; Br 8670 on V 36 *a-c* 29. T. A. (Ber) 28 ii 17 ga-du; in Cappadocian inscriptions ga-tim (-ti) *etc.* *pl* also qa-tu-a-te (a-xi-in-na-a u-ki-in-ma) K 2801 *R* 22; BA iii 236, 237. ni-iš qa-a-ti, K^{M} 35, 14, *etc.* see nīšu, niš, 736. epšit qātija see epištu & Sarg *Cyl* 76 (+ 68) ep-šit qa-ti-ja; TP vii 51 ep-šit qa-ti-šu, his handiwork; Anp i 24 (*var* ŠU-šu); šip-ru qa-ti-ja I 44, 79, the work of my hand; see also liptu, lipittu, 493, 494. ŠU 𒈫-u-a, Nabd *Scheil*, x 8; ga-tu-u-a, my hands (§ 41) & in my hand (§ 80*e*) I 51 *no* 1 *a* 14; I 69 *c* 26 (qa); qa-ti-ja, II 19 *a* 48; Asb iv 63 ina ŠU 𒈫-ja im-nu-u ŠU 𒈫 (*var* qa-ta)-u-a; ŠU 𒈫-a-a Sn i 25; ŠU 𒈫-a, Beh 96. qa-ta-a-šu, his hands, KB vi (1) 34, 18; V 35, 18 (end) ša u-ša-ak-ši-du qa-ta-a-šu. IV^{2} 23 *a* 15 qa-ta-a-a (= ŠU-MU) ellēti iq-qa-a ma-xar-ka. V 66 *a* 10 ina ŠU 𒈫-ja el-le-ti; IV^{2} 25 *a* 43/44, 49 ŠU 𒈫 (& ŠU)-šu (=

qâtêšu) ellêti; ina ga-ti-šu el-le-ti, KB vi (1) 192—3, 13. Creat.-*frg* IV 8 to exalt and to humble ši-i lu-u ga-at-ka (of Marduk), KB vi (1) 324 & 563 qâtu = work {Werk}? NE 69, 37 qa-ta-a-ka. ŠU-su V 47 *b* 4; H 115 *O* 16; ZK i 346; Anp iii 117; qa-su his hand IV² 39 *O* 26; qa-a-su, Sarg *Cyl* 15 + 21; qa-as-su, *bull*-inscr. 22; qa-as-su-nu II 8, 50. Sn vi 2 unakkis qa-ti-šu-un, I cut off their hands; qa-tuk-ka, K^M 2, 18; ZA iv 11 (K 3182 iii) 16; qat-ta-ka, K^M 25, 59; *del* 256 (286) qa-ta-a-k[a], thy hands. DT 81 v 8, 9 mi-im-ma ša ga-ti-šu i-ba-aš-šu-u (BA iii 501—3). H 88—9, 46 ina qa-at (= ŠU) el-li-tim; 90—1, 68 qa-ti-šu-nu ana qa-ti-šu, their hands to his hands. — qa-tuš-šu (& -ša) & qa-tuk-ka(ki) *etc.* = ina qâtišu, *etc.*, often. NE VI 194 ina (nâr) Pu-rat-ti im-su-u qa-ti-šu-un, see misû, 566, for further passages. — On qât(a) damqâti (IV² 8 *b* 48/9 ŠU = qa-at) see paqadu (820—22), & damqu, 254, 255. — binût qâti(ki) *etc.* see binûtu, 180 *col* 2; šikin qâti *cf* šiknu; littum qa-ti, littu, 501 *col* 2; gisallum qa-ti, gisallum, 228 *col* 1; tiriç ga(qa)-at see tirçu; nap-tan qa-ti, Zimmern, *Ritualtafeln*, 60, 28. u-ba-'-u qa-tuš-šu (> ina qâta-šu), see ba'u, 136. — qâtu abalu, put one's hand to {seine Hand legen an} K 41 *a* 8—12 nakri šu-u qâtâ-šu la me-si-a-ti ja-ši ub-la qa-ti-šu ub-lam-ma.... nak-ri šu-u qât-su u-ub-lam-ma. I 49 *a* 15 qât-su-nu u-bi-lu-ma; IV² 32 *a* 34; Asb vi 5. K 150 (IV² 51) ii 11, 12 a-na kišpi u ru-xi-e ŠU-su u-bi-lu. KB vi (1) 290 vii 13 u-ub-ba-al ga-ti a-na ni[-ši?]; *Rec. Trav.* xx 57 *foll.* — qâtu nadû, see nadû, 3 (647 *col* 1 *d*; 648 *col* 2 *d*); manû ina qâtâ, deliver, see manû, 556, 557; qâtu lapatu, *cf* lapatu, 493 *col* 1 *b*. qâtu malû, mullû see malû, 1 (540—543); it-ti qa-ti ma-li-ti (*var* ma-da-ti) I returned to Nineveh, Asb ii 47. maxaru ina qât *N*, *etc.* see maxaru, 525—529. nakaru ina qâtâ (written ŠU ᴵᴵ), revolt, see nakaru, & also balkatu. — qâtu našû see našû Q *b a*; Q¹ *etc.* (732 *foll*); H 128 *O* 60 bê-liku it-ti qa-ti-ja qa-tu ša iš-ša-na-nu (שנן) ul i-ba-aš-ši. niš qâti, see above. qâtu çabatu; ina ŠU, ŠU-te, qa-ti, ŠU ᴵᴵ, ŠU^{pl} *etc.* çabatu, çubbutu *cf* צבת; also balṭu, balṭûtu; kašadu, kišittu. VATh 4105 iii 5 *foll*, the gods, after they had created mankind, ba-la-tam ina ga-ti-šu-nu iç-ça-ab-tu, retained life in their own hands. IV² 54 *a* 30 a-xu-uz ŠU ᴵᴵ-su = help him! qâtu (ina qâti) *etc.* paqadu, entrust, see paqadu; qâtu talamu & *q.* tamaxu see these; ina qât(â) *X* šaparu, Asb ii 122 *etc.*, see šaparu, = ביד; thus in T. A. ina qât(i) & ana qât(i) = through {durch}. KB vi (1) 78, 17—18 lu-uš-ku-un tu-up-pa ša ni-mi-e-qi a-na ga-ti-ka. qa-tum ša dup-pi V 32 *a-c* 8; 11—17 (see Br 13953, 8383/4, 8392, 8394, 8480, 8497, 8500); V 47 *a* 58 (??); Aram קתא, handle; qa-tum musarû, *q. v.* V 32 *a-c* 9, 10 (Br 14317). See also T. A. (Ber) 28 iii 7. pitnu qa-ti II 26 *c-d* 46 see pitnu. še-im qa-ti in *c. t.* qâtâ (= ŠU ᴵᴵ) u šêpâ (NER ᴵᴵ); or qâtê u šêpê, Asb v 4; ix 22; iii 60; i 131; Smith, *Asurb*, 289, 42; 44, 45 usually with: I put into fetters. II 27 (*c-*)*d* 43 ŠU ᴵᴵ u NER uz-zu-la-ti, see eçelu, 1. IV² 8 iii 39 ša amêlu šu-a-tu qaq-qa-di-šu qa-ti-šu še-pi-šu u-rak-kis. — ⁽ᴵᴵ⁾ Qa-at-ra-bu-tu, III 66 *col* 9, 23 (PSBA xxi 126, 127; § 73). Qât-ili; qât-Ištar *etc.* Zimmern, *Ritualtafeln*, 45 i 5 *etc.* on qât-ili, a disease, see KB vi (1) 557. P. N. ⁽ⁿᵃʳ⁾ Niš-ga-ti-rim-ma, KB iv 82 (i) 3; Asb vii 47 Nabû-qâtê-ça-bat; II 64 *d* 9.

Ša ga-ti(-ja) *etc.* in Xammurabi: indicates the relation of an official to his master, or of a body of troops to the officer in command or control. King, *Hammurabi*, I pref. xlvi *foll.*

Qâtu also used of animals. K 3500 + K 4444 + K 10235 i 7 ina qâtâ nêši, in the claws of a lion.

qa-at KB ii 284 iv 41 = for {für}. ZA v 140, 37 ina ga(qa)-at šar-ra-ni. among the kings. — NE VI 69 u qâti-ka šu(?)-te-ça-am-ma (KB vi, 1, 170—1), according to ZA ix 297/8; J^{I-N} 24; 51 note 61: a euphemism for *membrum virile.*

On Qât-Sin & Ga-ti-Marduk see Delitzsch, BA ii 625 *rm* 2; Hilprecht,

Assyriaca, 105 *rm*; LEHMANN, ZA x 84 *foll*; 268 *foll*.

qātu *3. pl* qātātu. mostly in the phrase bit (= bīt) qāt (written ŠU II) & qa-ti, Br 7157; PEISER, *Vertr.*, 241; ZEHNPFUND, BA i 634 money-drawer {Kasse}; TALLQVIST, ZA vii 272 × T^C 119; KOHLER-PEISER, iii 17: Vorratshaus. Nabd 782, 2 ultu bīt qa-ti (*cf* 292, 6/7 ul-tu ir-bi ša bābi); bīt qāti ša bābi: Torkasse. Nabd 337, 6 he has given the money ultu kaspi ša ina bīt qāti. K 538, 20 ina bīt qāti (Hr^L 114). Nabd 407, 3 ša bīt qāti, an official; see also K 2801 *R* 26, & BA iii 280/1, cashier. Neb 345, 8 (*cf* 1) I mana 1/3 šiqli 2 ŠU II-ta-a-tum kaspi, *etc.* (T^C 123). K 245 ii 42—58 (= II 8 *e-f* 40 *foll*; H 70, 71, AV 7366): qa-ta-tu; a-na qa-ta-te iddin, id-din-šu, uš-zi-iz (as *q* he fixed); qa-as-su il-qi, i-laq-qi, il-qu-u, i-laq-qu-u; qa-as-su-nu il-qu-u, il-laq-qu-u, is-su-xu, in-na-aš-xu; a-na qa-ta-te-šu-nu uš-zi-iz.

qatū *1.* be at, or, come to, an end, cease {zu Ende sein oder gehen; ein Ende nehmen} AV 7369; Z^B 7 *rm* 1; HEBR. vii 89 *rm* 15. *pr* iqtī, *ps* iqattū(?), *pm* qatā *etc.* NE 72, 30 lu-bu-uš-ti iq-ti, my garment had gone to ruin, KB vi (1) 227; KB vi (1) 186 *col* 3, 7 (4) ..... KUR la i-qat-tu-u ana [d]u-[u]r da-a-ar. K 82, 29 (my lord the king knows) ki-i bīt A-muq-a-ni iq-tu-ma (Hr^L 275); BA i 242 *foll*; PSBA xxiii 58 *foll*: that the house of *A*. has come to an end. SMITH, *Asurb*, 145, 2 Urtaku (although severely wounded) la iq-tu-u napšāti (wr. ZI-MEŠ), did not loose his life; K 2674 ii 4 iq-tu-u; KB ii 244—5, 53. *e. t.* epēš nikasi qa-tu-u (pm) see T^C 125. IV^2 23 *no* 2 *O* 11—12 ša ku-zu-ub-šu la qa-tu-u (= NU-TIL-LA, Br 1512); 49 *b* 31 see nādu, 3 (645, 646). — V 61 vi 52, 53 ina un-ṣi u bubūti na-piš-tuš liq-ti, in oppression and famine may his life end. K 2455 (T^M ii 83) see ma'adu, 1 Q (505 *col* 1); IV^2 38 iii 38, 39 i-na li-mu-ut-ti u la ṭu-ub šīri liq-ti-ma, KB iv 62 *fol.* KB iii (1) 192 (Merodach-Baladan-stone) v 44 ina ši-xaṭ šīri liq-ta-a mašak-šu (BA ii 271: zumuršu), his body may perish. — *pm* xi-iṣ-ba la qa-ta-a (?) K 3459 *R* 8 (ZA iv 15); dib-bi .... qa-tu-u; die Klage ist beendet, Br 84—2—11, 138; KOHLER-PEISER, ii 26; ZA iii 217, 18—19; KB iv 200 *no* 1, 8. *Proc. Berl. Akad.* '89, 825 di-in-šu ul qa(?)-ti, his lawsuit is not completed. KB vi (1) 198 (v/vi) 8 qa-t]u-u zi-mu-ka (+ 200, 15; 216, 3). Cappadocian inscr.: ga-ta-tum iš-du. K 824, 19 qa-ta-a-ta (thou wouldst have perished) Hr^L 290. Sp II 265 *a* xxi 8 (end) a-na ka-ti-i ti-u(= šam)-ta. S^c 214 ti-il | TIL | = qa-tu-u (Br 1512; H 13, 125).

Q^t Neb 307, 8 the debtor has sworn by God Sin ki-i arax Nisān [ul] iq-ta-tu-u | a-di kubšu a-na *X* | e-it-ti-ra, that the month *N* should not come to an end, before he had returned the *kubšu* to *X*. Nabd 849, 14 iq-ta-tu.

ג *trans* of Q. — *a*) complete, finish {vollenden, zu Ende führen}. Sn *Kui* 4, 40 ul-tu šip-ri ēkallija u-qat-tu-u. Sarg *bull*-inscr. 98 ul-tu ši-bir (*var* ip-ri) āli u ēkallate-šu u qat-tu-u, after I had completed the building of. Nabd 553, 13 u-qa-at-tu-u; 373, 8; Neb 379, 4 u-qa-at-ta. LEHMANN, S^3 51 ša za-ru-u-a la u-qa-at-tu-u, what my ancestor had not finished (KB ii 258, 259, 16); L^1 8; P^1 17. — IV^2 20 *no* 1, 7—8 on a fine couch la u-qat-ta-a (= NU-TIL-LA-E-DA-NI, Br 1512) šit-ti, I did not finish my sleep, *Rec. Trav.* xxiv *no* 1/2. K 3657 i 11 ina ma-a-a-li u-ul u-qat-ta ši-it-ta (3 *sgl*) + ii 11; NE 58, 8 šit-ta-šu u-qat-ti. IV^2 59, 1 *R* 16 a-na xu-uṣ-ṣi u kis (qiṣ) libbi li-qat-ta-a šanātē-ša. II 35 *c-d* 63 TIL-TIL = qut-tu-u (Br 1551), 64 = lu-uq-qu-tum. AV^* 55 *col* 2: ni-si-xu e-li-šu-nu gab-bi-šu-nu qut-ti-'. — *b*) finish some one; kill {den Garaus machen, töten}. quttū & šuqtū napištu = murder, kill; while šakanu napištu = lose life, through famine, *etc.* Sarg *Cyl* 27 ina kakki ra-ma-ni-šu u-qa(t)-ta-a na-piš-tuš, KB ii 42, 43. Sp II 265 *a* iii 8 ku-u-ri u ni-is-sa-tum u-qat-ti-ki. Sarg *Khors* 77 with his own hand .... na-piš-ta-šu u-qat-ti, he put an end to his life; *Ann* 189 (§ 55*c*, *a*). Asb iii 126 u-qat-ta-a nap-šat-su-un, I shall kill them (with dagger, fire, hunger & pest). IV^2 61 *c* 50 with my hand nakīrē-ka u-qa-at-ta (1 *sg*). IV^2 52 *b* 45 kīma bi-tum ma-ru-uš-ti u-qat-tu-šu, he has destroyed him; IV^2 21* *no* 2 *O* 14, 15 (Br 1512) see qadadu, ℑ; IV^2 50 *b* 41 Sin .... li-qat-ta-a pa-gar-ki. T^M iii 100; v 72 ina ni-ši u ma-mit tu-qat-ta-in-ni (2 *pl* + 1 *sg* suff).

ℑ^t — *a*) finish, complete {vollenden}. Zimmern, *Ritualtafeln*, 26 i 19 kīma tak-pi-ra-a-ti tuq-te-tu-u, when thou hast finished the expiatory rites; ii 8 tuq-te-it-tu-u. — *b*) make an end, finish, destroy {ein Ende machen, vernichten}. *del* 228 (253) see mašku *c*) 603 *col* 1; KB vi (1) 248/9; 515; J^W 90; ZA ii 249. K 82, 7 since the tribe of Puqud bīt Amuqāni .... uq-te-it-tu-u. IV^2 4 iii 8 ša ed(t)-li be-el e-mu-ki e-mu-ki-šu uq-ta-at-ti (= MU-UN-DA-TIL) Br 1523. — *c*) *pass.* be finished, completely routed, ruined, destroyed {geendet, aufgerieben, vernichtet werden}. Sm 949 *O* 17 ina çabāt libbi u lā ṭūb šīri ra-ma-ni uq-ṭa-at-ti, I am completely ruined. IV^2 25 *b* 16 kīma tu-]uq-ta-at-tu-u (Zimmern).

Š exterminate, kill, finish {ausrotten, töten, beenden} TP vi 67 four wild oxen .... na-piš-ta-šu-nu u-šeq-ti, L^T 160.

Š^t uš-taq-tu-u, K 3554 ii 3: as he had finished; BA ii 409; KB vi, 1, 46/7.

Derr. taqtītu & these two:

qatū *2. adj* complete, ended, finished {vollkommen, beendet, fertig}. V 62 *no* 1, 2 ši-pir Êsagila la qa-ta-a (also L^2 12) u-šak-lil, the incomplete work on Esagil I finished. In *c. t.* especially in the meaning: complete, completely {ganz und gar; gründlich} T^C 28. Cyr 325, 8 $^{(amêl)}$ pur-kul-lu-tu qa-ti-ti (Nabd 172, 7 -tim) ulammadsu; 248, 5/6; see also puçammūtu, Cyr 318, 6. Tallqvist, *Schenkungsbriefe*, 28. II 23 *c-d* 22 ar-ka-bi-in-nu = daltum la qa-ti-tum. V 47 *a* 61 see zillātum, 282 *col* 2 &, again, KB vi (1) 374.

qutū *1.* Esh ii 28 calls the inhabitants of Mannâ qu-tu-u la sa-an-qu; *cf* III 15 iii 16 (KB ii 129; 147). Perhaps connected with

Qutū *2.* IV^2 39 *a* 4 ummān kaš-ši-i qu-ti-i lu-lu-me-i u šu-ba-ri-i (+20); K 2619 iv 13 qu-ta-a qu-tu-u. K 4386 iii (= II 48 *c-d*) 14 [cuneiform]-ŠU-AN-NA (Br 943) = qu-tu-u, a-mur-ru-u, ur-ṭu-u. T^M iv 100 kaššapāt qu-ta-a-ti, between *k* e-la-ma-a-ti & su-ta-a-ti. V 35, 31 a-di pa-at $^{(māt)}$ Qu-ti-i; *cf* II 50 *col* 2, 21; D^{Par} 233.

NOTE. — Winckler, *Forsch*, i 486 (*ad* Esh ii 27, 8) combines both: Kutäer = qutū: d. h. einer von den unbotmässigen Nordvölkern, ein Barbar. — See also *ibid* ii 255 *foll* (Sarg *Ann* 337, 361; *Khors* 130, 136); & against Gesenius^{13} 665 (קֹוַע = qutū, abbr. to qū) he says not = קוע, which is a mistake for קיר (= *Qir*), a people, living near the Sutī. See also Bezold, *Catalogue*, 2034.

qītu *1.* T^M ii 160 (149) ki-ma ki-i-ti a-kab-bil-šu-nu-ti. ‖ of qū, 1.

qītu *2.* end {Ende}, see kītu, 455.

qitū see kitū, 455—6; & *cf* KB vi (1) 394; Syr ܩܛܘ.

qi-ta-a-a-u-lu, see qālu, 1 ℑ^t.

qit-b(p)u-lu (Br 3274) see gapalu, ℚ^t, 228 *col* 2.

qatanu. pr perh. II 59 *a* 37 iq-tu-un. pm K 8860 + K 8950 *col* ii 63, 64 šumma šārat qaqqadi qa-at-ta-an, is short {ist kurz} ✕ kabbar. Winckler, ZA vi 454. Bezold, *Catalogue*, 571; & ZA viii 142 *rm* 1.

Derr. these 3:

qatnu. *adj* short, small, thin {kurz, dünn} KB vi (1) 456 (465 refers here also qut-tēnu). IV^2 22 *a* 34—35 ša(= LIB)-max-xu kīma ir-ri qat-ni i-çab-[bat], said of the muruç qaqqadi. V 28 *a-b* 13 (*c-d* 31) qa-at-nu ‖ (?) çu-bat ra-bu-u (BA iii 551, ein feines, dünnes Tuch). V 14 *b* 32 qa-at-na-a-tum (*sc.* šipāti) *f pl.* AV 7370. — name of a street: Cyr 361, 7 sūqu qat-nu; 8 sūqu qa-at-nu; also Peiser, *Vertr.*, cxvii 7 sūq qa-at-nu (& la) a-çu-u; KAS 116 *b*; Tallqvist, *Schenkungsbriefe*, 12, 13; Dar 275, 2. — II 25 *no* 1 *R* 3 qa-at-nu (the equivalent is broken off). K 1312 *R* 6; 82—5—22, 56, 6; 83—1—18, 210, 1—2: qa-at-nu. — Anp iii 5 ina $^{(ṣi)}$ qa-at-ni asakan mit-tak, AV 7371. K 335, 6 xarrān qa-at-

---

qat-bal-la-tum see kat-pal-la-tum, 460 *col* 1. ∼ qut-ta-xu *cf* tar-ta-xu. ∼ qaṭalu AV 7264 see kalū, 1 ℚ^t. ∼ qitqittum *cf* kitkittu, 457 *col* 1.

ni, KB iv 110 *no* iv. II 60 *a* 30 (ilu) qa-at-nu, & *b* 29 (AV 7365).

qattinu. Scheil., *Textes élam Sem.*, I 102, 35. KB vi (1) 536 on NE 51, 6 qat]-tin-nu.

(amēl) **qatinnu.** Johns, *Doomsdaybook*, 64, perh. storekeeper, √qātu 3, store {Vorratshaus}. K 185, 11 (amēl) qa-tin-nu šarri (Hr^L 74); II 31 *no* 5 *col* iii 38 (amēl) qa-tin, AV 7308.

qutānu (?) Nabd 351, 15 *foll* (end); 644, 6 *foll* (end); 1111, 11 ina qu-ta-nu.

qatapu. pluck off, fell {abpflücken, fällen} Z^B 93. NE 67, 29 ina libbi kišti i-qa-tap ur-na, he broke off (fell) a urnu (KB vi (1) 216). II 29 *c-d* 27 qa-ta-pu, AV 7362, Br 7520; followed by ša-ma-ṭu. Nabd 606, 6 a-na qa-ta-pu.

Derr. — these 2 (?):

qatpu. *adj* plucked, broken off {abgepflückt, abgebrochen}. IV^2 7 *b* 10 (Z^B v/vi 75) see sissinnu.

qitpu (?) Nabd 708, 9 qi-it-p(b)u.

qataru 1. burst, strike {bersten, brechen, schlagen}? 83—1—18, 188, 1 imbāru iq-tur; Bu 89—4—26, 18, 5 *etc.* K 1242 *R* 4 (Hr^L 50). K 8669 *R* iii 8 qa-tu-a-ri. Where does K 3456 *R* 8 at-ta ma-a e duk-ku taq-ṭi-ra (PSBA xxi 40 *foll*) belong to?

Q^t perh. Nabd Cyr. Chron. iv 3 DAN-MEŠ iq-ta-tur.

ℑ IV^2 19 *b* 43, 44 o my lady tu-qat-tir-in-ni-ma (= SIR-SIR-RA, Br 7570) marçiš (591 *col* 1) tuššēminni, thou hast stricken me & made me sick, Z^B 77; H 179. Nabd 761, 5 mu-qa-at-ti-ir-tum siparri kal-lu ša dan-nu-tu. K 2385 qu-ta-ri ša šiptu (ilu) Bēl qaqqadi-MU (= ia) ma-la a-na KA-ŠAR-MEŠ (= riksāti) šaṭ-ru Ⲧ<< bullil(?)-ma tu-qat-tar-šu šiptu (ilu) Bēl qaqqadi-MU mu-nu, T^M 143.

ℑ^t Rm^2 139 *O* 16 when a man marries another woman, uq-ta-at-tar. K 7988, 5.

Š K 3445 + Rm 396 *O* 33 šu-uk-tur im-[ ].

Derr. — these two:

q(k)atru. *adj* something like: defeated, vanquished {besiegt, geschlagen}. I 66 *c* 30 see kanašu ℑ^t (409 *col* 2); III 60 *O* 28 *a* see *ibid* Q ip.

qutāru see qaturu, 1 & Zimmern, *Ritualtafeln*, *no* 26 i 8 q]u-ta-ri eb-bu-te; 27, 6; also IV^2 55 *b* 14 ina eli 3 qu-ta-ri mu-nu-ma; *a* 37 annū qu-ta-ri, M^S 87.

qataru 2. Q K 13663 *R* 3 .... TU-RI = qa-ta-ru; T^M vi 44 .... ina bīti-ki i-qat-tur qut-ru. — ℑ Zimmern, *Ritualtafeln*, *no* 75—78, 56 u-qat-tar-ku-nu-ši, ich räuchere euch (reines Cedernholz) + 58 + 77. K 3821 (Omen) šumma iššātu ina kinūni šarri içē ab-lu-ti u-qat-tar, M^S 66, 87. H 78 *R* 5 kibir (ilu) Nāri tu-qat-tar-šu.

ℑ^t Zimmern, *Ritualtafeln*, *no* 11 *etc.* *R* 9 (end) ina iššāti uq-ta-at-tar, soll er räuchern.

qutru *1. c. st.* qutur smoke {Rauch} Z^B 44 *rm* 2; Hebr. i 176; GGA '84, 1018. IV^2 61 *c* 69, 70 at thy right qut-ru u-qa-at-t[ar], I will cause smoke to ascend. ‖ 71, 72 at thy left (iššātu u-ša[-kal]) I will cause fire to consume, AJSL xiv 274. Sn iv 68 qu-tur na-aq-mu-ti-šu-nu, the smoke of the fire (destroying the Elamite cities) kīma zē kabti pān šamē rapšūti ušaktim. T^M iii 170 qut-ri AN-GIŠ-BAR li-ri-ma pa-ni-ku-nu. IV^2 3 *b* 17/18 (= I-NE) see manzaltu, 562 *col* 2 (>< Br 4008 tar-ru); 18 *a* 6/7 ki-ma qut-ri; 49 *b* 53 qu-tur-ku-nu li-tel-li šame-e (T^M v 153; i 141; v 80; v 50 qu-tur-ša li-ib-li). DT 57 *O* 14 ki-ma qut-ri etelli ana šamē ša Anim, Jensen, 11/12; see also T^M v 169. II 51 *no* 1 *R* 4 kīma qut-ri, ZK ii 322. 81—2—4, 63 *O* 9 *foll* ūmu zi-mu-šu ki-ma qu-ut-ri ina pān ša-at-ti Adad raxi-iç.

qutru *2.* a plant {eine Pflanze}. K 4174 *O* + 4583 i 9 qu-ut-ra | U-KI-AN-IM u-ki-i-iš-ku-rak-ku | qu-ut-ru (Hussey, JAOS xxii 213).

qutrinnu, qutrēnu. *m* incense, incense-, smoke-offering {Räucherwerk, Räucheropfer} Jensen, 418. Zimmern, *Ritualtafeln*, 75—78, 44 qut-rin-na ina niknakki nadē-ma (+ 48; 95 *R* 27; 100, 28). Sarg *Khors* 172 qut-rin-ni šur-ru-xi, preceded by zi-i-bi el-lu-ti maxaršunu akki (√niqū); *Ann* 434. ZA v 58, 28 see *p* 748 *col* 2 קטר ℑ, where read qut-ri-ni. IV^2 20 *no* 1, 26 zi-i-bu šur-ru-xu çi-e-ni qut-rin-na; see çēnu, 2. T^M ii 10 without thee the great gods ul iç-çi-nu qut-rin-nu; vi 96. K 3364 *R* 12 see niqū, 718 *col* 2. NE 21 *a* 8 (before) Šamaš qut-rin-na iš-kun, he offered an incense offering; 23, 32 see kabatu, כ (369 *col* 2). IV² 31 *R* 58 nitūte (*q. v.*) li-lu-nim-ma qut-ri-in li-iç-çi-nu, KB vi (1) 90/1; Boissier, ZA xii 395—6. V 13 *c-d* 47 ŠA-NA-RI(?) ... ŠI-BAR-RA = ba-ru-u ša qut-rin-ni, Br 12000. A ‖ is perhaps:

qatrinnu. Scheil, Notes d'épigraphie, LX (*Rec. Trav.*, xxiii) on Const. *no* 583 *O* 21 ina A būri ka-la ū-mi ina IM qatrin-ni te-sik-kir (+ *R* 17); & *ibid* notes *no* LIV (*Rec. Trav.*, xxii): or šurin-nu?

qatrū see katrū, 460 *col* 1; & on IV² 48 *a* 11 *cf* ZA xv 41. S 747 *R* 6 [u?]-šeri-bu k(q)at-ra-šu-un; 7, kat-ru-u da-'-a-tu; also Zimmern, *Ritualtafeln*, *no* 75—78, 59.

qatriš *adv* see katriš, and add: V 64 *b* 15.

qi-ta-ru (Br 1469; AV 7389) see qintaru.

qitrubu see qarabu, Q^t.

qitrudu, *adj* strong, brave, valiant {stark, tapfer} √qaradu. AV 7391. II 31 *no* 3, 25, 26 (V 41 *a-b* 27, 28) qit-ru-du ‖ taq-ri-du & ša-ka-du. Sm 2052 iii 32 ki-it-ru-du ‖ git[-ma-lum]; V 65 *a* 9 šakkanakku qit-ru-du, ZK ii 261. Sarg *Cyl* 25 qit-ru-du la a-dir tuqma-te.

qit-ri-du, Br 11800, 11892. See purīdu, & Hommel, *Sum. Les.*, 90.

qatattu. some part of the body {ein Körperteil} AV 7367. II 37 *e-f* 62 qa-ta-at-tu ‖ ra-pal-tu çi-xir-tu.

ר

ra'u, VATh 244 ii 23 ID-GIŠ-AK-A = ra-'-u; ZA ix 157.

ru'a, rūa; *f* ruttu (> ru'tu) neighbor, friend, companion {Nachbar, Freund, Genosse}. Z^B 32; H^{OV} xxxiv (רֵעַשְׁלְ). ZDMG 54, 154 *cf* רֵעַ; BA iii 368. K 2390 ru-'u-a u it-ba-ru, preceded by eb-ri u tappi-e, d(t)ar-ka-ti u te-ni-ki(qe), kim-ti u ni-su-tu, T^M 138. K 2061 i 18 + Rm 345 *R* 13 XI ^(du) UŠ-SA = ru-u-a ‖ ta-li-mu, H 202, AV 7625, Br 8257. T^M iv 89: VI riksi-ši-na, VII-bit ru-u-a. K 150 (IV² 51) i 30 itti ru-'u-a ru-'u-a-šu ip-ru-su (BA i 456 *rm*), preceded by abu, māru, ebru, *etc.* III 16 *no* 3, 9 na-bu-u ki-i ru-'u-a. 81, 2—4, 219 *O* ii 15 id-du-ku (√dāku) šu ni-bi-ri ru-u-a (*Rev. Sém.* vi *no* 4). Sm 1051, 11 ru-ut-tum, followed by ši-i-it-tum (*cf* še'ū) & eb-ru. K 2061 i 21. — P. N. Ru-'u-a amēlu Sarg *Ann* 282, *etc*; *Khors* 19 (Ru-'u-u-a) AV 7686. K 94 (Hr^L 287) 7 ^(amēl) Ru-u-a-a (PSBA xxiii 61). See also ru-xi T. A. (Ber) 104, 11. — Der.:

ru''ūtu *1.* friendship {Freundschaft} K 3456 *O* 21 ox and horse ip-pu-šu ru-'-u-tu, PSBA xxi 37—8.

ru-u (?) V 22 (*a*-)*d* 51, Br 11356.

re'u, *pr* ire'i. pasture, feed; lead, govern, rule {weiden, füttern; leiten, regieren}. V 34 *a* 12 ni-šim ri-e-a-am (= *ac*) .... uma'iranni. K 3459, 14 te-re-'i ulāla, thou leadest the weak (ZA iv 15; 226; 271). K 11152 (frg. of hymn to Ištar) 10 çal-mat qaqqadi te-re-'-i kīma i-la-a-ti. Xammurabi-Louvre I *col* ii 8 lu-e-ri-ši-na-ti, I governed them, KB iii (1) 122, 123 & *rm* **†. K 3182 (+K 3474) i 25 (end) ta(te)-ri-'i, thou shepherdest, ZA iv 81; AJSL xvii 134. Nabd 915, 11 alpē ša ina çēri ir-ru-u. KB iii (1) 130 *col* 1, 19 the countries a-na ri-ia-im i-din-nam.

Q^t *intr.* pasture {weiden}. Asb viii 90 a desert in which purīmē çabāti la ir-te-'-u ina libbi, BA i 244. — *trans.* pasture; lead, govern, rule {weiden; leiten, regieren}. TP vii 59 Ninib-pal-Ē-KUR ša .... ummānāt Aššur kēniš ir-te-'u-u (AV 7565). Sarg *Cyl* 72 ba'ūlāt arba'i māl(a) ir-te-'u-u (= *ps*) nūr ilāni bēl gimri (AV 7464); *bull*-inscr. 98; *bronze*-inscr. 50; *Ann* XIV 87; *Rp* 25. K 8522 *R* 8 kīma çi-e-ni li-ir-ta-a ilāni gimrašun, like sheep may he pasture the gods, them all. Bu 88—5—12, 75 + 76 viii 14, 15 ina ket-te u mi-ša-ri lu-ur-te-'-a, BA iii 254 (1 *sg*). Anp i 45 xaṭṭa | mur-te-'-at nišē, AV 5569; KB i 60, 61.

Q^{tn} KB iii (2) 78, 3 ni-ši-ja ra-ap-ša-a-tim i-na šu-ul-mi ar-ta-ni-'-e, my great nations I govern in peace.

Derr.: miritu, mirûtu (?) 585 *col* 1; rûtu 2 (?); ritu 1 & the following 4:

rē'ū (originally: ag; §§ 32*aβ*; 42) *m* shepherd; leader, ruler {Hirte; Leiter, Regent} AV 7564. רֹעֶה, راع (ZDMG 43, 324 *no* 6); G §§ 47, 103; BA i 485, 486. id SEB. S^b 213 si-ba | SEB | re-'e-u; § 9, 156; H 21, 405; V 13 *a-b* 55; Br 5638. S^c 308 . . . . . u | 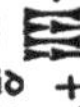 | re-e-um; IV^2 27 *a* 1—2 same id + BA = re-E-um (Br 4940) be-lim (ilu) Du'ūzu (+ 3); DT 67 (H 120) *R* 15, 16 = re-Ē-u ina šibirrišu li-dūkši. — IV^2 1 *a* 45 AN-GAL (MULU) ri-'-um (*var* u, = SEB) muš-te-'-ú ri-ta ana amēli; 23 *a* 30, 31 ri-'-u mu-ši-im ši-ma-a-ti. K 8522 *R* 25 (= SEB) see nâqidu (*p* 719), where also other instances. K 3182 i 33 ri-'-u šap-la-a-ti (of Šamaš) ‖ na-qi-du e-la-a-ti, AJSL xvii, 134. Pinches, *Texts*, 15 *no* 4, 9 ar-re-'i-i za-ni-ni-šu, *etc.* (to the king) § 49*b*. K 3600 + DT 75 (hymn to Ninā) 19 ri-'-u (mât) Aššur(-ki) a-lik ar-ki-e-ki, Craig, *Relig. Texts*, i 54. V 12 *a-b* 37 SEB-SAG-MI-GA = ri-'u çal-mat (*q. v.*) qaq-qa-di (Neb x 19), followed by rē'ū u-tul(-?)la[-a-ti?] Br 8874; and, rē'ū ku-ça(za)-la-a[-ti?], Br 5690, 5694 *fol.* V 13 *c-d* 40 ri-'u ça-bi (Br 3624, 8156); rē'ū nišē see nišu (737, 738). II 31 *no* 3, 44 perh. ri]-'-u = be[-lum?], followed by e]-nu = be[-lum] (V 41 *a-b* 6, 7); *ibid* 47, 48 perh. ri]-e-tum & en]-tum = be-el[-tum] (V 41 *a-b* 9 reading šu instead of ri, but adding?), AV 1208. — V 12 *a-b* 35 SEB = re-Ē (character *bit* = ē)-a-um; V 33 *a* 24 ri-ē-u (+ 22); 27 ri-ē-a-um. I 48, 2 ri-ē-um (§ 66) ba-xu-la-a-ti (H 38, 11 6); Sn i 3 *Sn* ri-ē-um it-pe-šu (= *Rassam* mutnennû); *Kni* 1, 1. *Neb* ri-ē(-a)-um ki-i-num (*q. v.*), Neb *Bors* i 2; *Bab* i 3; V 34 *a* 12; TP i 34 SEB-ja ki-i-nu (*var* -ni); i 19 (BA i 296; § 12); I 65 *a* 2; *var* to I 49 *a* 5 (BA iii 218 *rm* *). IV^2 18 *no* 3 i 20, 22 ša šarri re-ē (= SEB) mâti-šu. — II 52 *no* 2, 66 [X S]EB-E-NE(-KI) = ka-pi (*not* -par) re-'-i = XARSAG-KALAMA, Fels des Hirten, ZA xv 246. II 31 *c* 50 (amēl) rab rē'ē (written SEB-MEŠ) D^8 135; Br 12997. (amēl) SEB sisē see sisû. — On the (amēl) rē'û sattukki see sattukku (end). It interchanges with (amēl) rē'û gi-ni-e (Neb 20, 7 *etc.*). maçallu ša (amēl) SEB see maçallu, 572 *col* 2. NE VI 58 ta-ra-mi-ma (amēl) SAB (= rē'û?) ta-b(p)u-la. — On BA iii 500 (Sm 26 i (?) 14—16) see BA iv 84: rē'û pān (not ši) i-ši. V 44 *a-b* 23 Ku-ur-gal-zu = ri-'i-i bi-ši-i (AV 4589) see Jensen, ZDMG 48, 433 (>< Lehmann, ZA ix 88) reading kaš-ši-i instead of bi-ši-i. Hilprecht, *OBI*, I *nos* 41 & 46, 3 ku-[r]i-gal-zu ri-ja-um [na-ram ilat Bēlit], & KB iii (1) 120 (81, 8—30, 9) ii 8 ri-'i-u. — V 27 *c-d* 41 SEB-XU = ri-'u-u ‖ allallu, name of a bird (II 31 *c-d* 69; Br 5689).

TP i 30; Anp i 21 LIT-KU, a title of the king (or rim-ku?, *q. v.*). III 68, 21 LIT-KU-GAL = a great litku; epithet of two gods, *i. e.*, the great shepherds of Anu (KB vi (1) 574, 575). V 12 *a-b* 40 LIT-KU = u-tul[-lu?], perh. a ‖ of rē'û (37—39). II 32 *a-b* 51 (u-nu) LIT-KU (Br . . . . LU) = ri-'i]-i; 52 = *r* u-tul [-lu]; 53 (u-tu-ul) LIT-KU = u-tul[-lu]. V 21 *g-h* 59 RI = ri-'-u.

rē'ûtu. rule, government, lordship {Hirtenschaft, Regentenschaft} AV 7566. Šalm, *Mon*, *O* 13 re-'u('e?)-ut (mât) Aššûr. ZA iii 319, 93 ri-e-u-tu; KB iii (2) 64, 12 ri-e-u-ti ṭa-ab-ti. Sn vi 65 ri-ē-um-ut (= rē'ût) mâti u nišē; Lay 64, 63. V 60 *c* 9 ana ri-'u-ut nišē e-pe-ši. I 67 (Ner.) *a* 19 a-na re-ē-u-ti çalmat ga-gadam e-bi-e-šu. IV^2 12 *O* 21, 22 re-ē-us-su (= NAM-SEB-DA-BI) Br 5688; 15* *b* 57 ša (ilu) Ē-a ri-um-ta-šu (= rule) . . . . (63) tar-çu (Br 4919, 4944). TP vii 47 a-na SEB-ut (mât) Aššûr kēniš ib-bu-šu; Asb vii 105 SEB-si-na e-pe-ši, to exercise my sway over them (§ 132); I 49 *c* 8. KB iii (1) 132 *col* iv 11 ri-ja-u[t ki-ib]-ra-at ar[-ba]-im.

rē'ītum, *f* to rē'û, *q. v.*

re'ītu *f* herd {Herde}. II 32 *a-b* 54 (u-tu-ul)
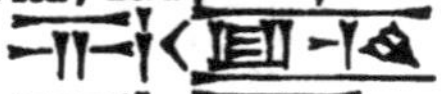 & 55 (u-tu-ul)
 = ri-'i-i[-tum?] & *r* i[....

ra'abu (rābu?), *1.* pr ir'ub, *ps* irab. be angry, try to get at one, attack violently {zornig sein, auf Jemanden einstürmen, Jemandem heftig anfahren}, רעב. IV² 31 *O* 64 Allatu beheld her (the goddess Ištar) and ina pa-ni-ša ir-'u-ub (§ 20), flew in her face (KB vi, 1, 84/5; 396/7: zürnen, betrübt sein) quoting K 2764 ra'bāku between uššušāku & zenāku (I am angry). T. A. (Ber) 92, 41 a-na (mātu) Ki-na-ax-xi gab-pa-ša ki-i i-ra-u-ub. Nabd *Ann* ii 16 Cyrus šap-la-an (al) Ar-ba-'-il (nār) Diqlat i-rab-ma (strove toward the Tigris). K 126, 39 zikaru šuātu lā ellil ana arkāt ūmi qāt-su i-ra-'-ub, *Rev. Sém.* i 170*foll.* K 979 *R* 3—6 šarru be-li la i-ra-u-bu, let the king, my lord, not be angry against me (Hr^L 47; BA iv 503). See also M^S 87 *col* 1. 82—5—22, 63 *R* 4 ki-i tar-'-u-bu ru-'-ub-ti, when thou art angry. II 35 *e-f* 33—36 ra-'-a-bu (AV 7461) ‖ [ug]-ga-tum, um-mu-lum, ma-am-lum & ṭ(d)a-ax-rum, AV 1807. —

Derr.:

ru'ubtu anger {Zorn} see above; & perh.:

ra-'i-bu violent {heftig}. Knudtzon, 71 *O* 6 (see *ibid*, *p* 29) between šabsu (angry) & uššušu (sad); KB vi (1) 399: traurig, finster. S 28, 8 ṭ(d)i-'-u šur-bu-u ra-'-i-bu, AV 7463; Br 8416. Perhaps also H 83, 25 SEG-DUB-SEG-DUB-BA = ra-ib-tu ra-ti-tu (Br 10790), same iḋ in *l* 63 = ub-lu ma-lu-u.

ra-'a(?)-zu. K 4309 ii 25 GAR (ga) in one group with ra-ma-çu (24) = XAR-RA & uxxuzu, ZA iv 158, AV 7466, Br 11072. — ℑ perh. V 45 v 16 tu-ra-'-az(ç, s?).

ri-e-zu see kammaru (398 *col* 2), AV 7567, Br 4241.

ri-um-ma, wind {Wind} perh. = ריח, KB vi (1) 442; see napišu (712 *col* 2).

רים, whence nir'amtu, 725 *col* 1.

Ra-'-su-nu. K 655 (Hr^L 132) 8 (+14), a P. N. (?).

riā(a?)šu. mealworm {Getreidewurm} §§ 20; 47; 65, 12 = רקב. II 5 *c-d* 34 UX-ŠE-KU-E = ri-a-šu. V 27 *g-h-i* 22 ri-'-a-šu = kal-mat [še-im]; *cf* H 40, 223; II 31 *e-g* 83; 24 *f-g* 22, Br 8323.

ru'utu *2.*, **rūtu** *1.* (§§ 64, 65, 3) *f* saliva, spittle {Speichel, Spucke}. Syr רותא, Jensen, *Diss*, 62. AV 7637. iḋ  in IV² 16 *b* 55, 56 see nadū, 4 (649 *col* 1); 57, 58 see kišpu (450 *col* 2, below). IV² 19 *a* 32 see rupuštu, 2 (= Z^S vii 32; *ibid* 97). K 246 (H 86—7) i 60 see nadū, 3 Ⓠ *h* (647 *col* 2, *med*) & limnis (488 *col* 2, below); i 69 ru-'-tu li-mut-tu ša e-pi-ri la kat-mu. T^M vii 93 u-ma-al-la ru-'-a-ta ēn[ā-ki]. S^b 85 u-xu 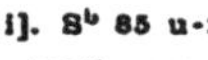 ru-'-tu (Br 8132), *var* ru-u-tum (Br 8133) ZA i 66; H 81, 27—28 same iḋ = ku-ši-i (see *p* 445 *col* 2). H 11 + 208, 68; 27, 596; also see AV 7602. V 23 *h* 4 ru-'-tu ‖ rupuštu, imtu, *etc.* (ZK ii 11 *rm* 2; Z^S 60). II 35 *c-d* 42, 43 see nadū 3, Ⓠ *h* (647 *col* 2) & Br 792, 8297, 8304, 8305.

rabū *1.* pr irbi, *ps* irabbi. AV 7442. Arm רְבָה, Dan iv 8, 17. — *a*) be or become tall, large, great; grow up {gross sein oder werden; aufwachsen}. Sarg *Cyl* 38 the king who ... i-na mil-ki ni-me-qi ir-bu(-ma). Sn *Bell* (Lay 63) 13 Bēl-ibni who kīma mirāni (584 *col* 1) çaxri in my palace ir-bu-u, AV 7157. Asb i 27—8 where Esarhaddon .... ('i-) al-du | ir-bu-u; x 59 aš-šu ki-rib bīt ridu-u-te šu-a-tu ar-ba-a. K 2729 *O* 19 ki-rib ēkalli-ja ina šumi dam-ki ir-bu[-u-ma], grew up, BA ii 566, 569; Lehmann, i 11. NE 10, 44 bu-ul-šu ša ir-bu-u eli çēri-šu; 11, 14. K 5419 E (Creat-*frg* I) 11 (end) a-di ir-bu-u ‖ 82, 7—14, 402 a-di(-)i ir-bu[-u], KB vi (1) 2—3; 305. K 3454 (*Zū*-legend) ii 37 šu-mi-ka li]-ir-bi, *cf* 81 (KB vi (1) 48 + 52). K 2401 ii 5 bītu i-rab-bu-u-ni. K 164, 5: III-šu ištu irši ta-rib-bi-a (10, ta-rib-bi), 28, III-šu i-rib-bi-u (BA ii 635). IV² 15* i 53 ir-bi (Br 5845); ii 23—4 the seven .... ir-bu-u (= BA--A-MEŠ, Br 1665) ‖ 'ialdu; iii 3—4; ii 19—20 ēkāma al-du ēkāma ir-bu-u, where were they born, where did they grow up? IV² 2 v 11 si-su-u ša ina šadi-i ir-bu-u (Br 7885) šu-nu (+38). KB vi (1) 288/9 i 8 i-ra-ab-bu, wird gross werden. *pm* ZA iv 282, 11 be-lat šar-xat ra-bat ša-qa-at ba-na-at. II 60 v 14 see ṭapašu (358) & bubūtu (147 *col* 1). Sn vi 45 ra-ba-ta ‖ šu-tu-rat (3 *f sg*). V 44 *c-d* 57. IV² 10 *a* 36—7 ra-ba-a (= MAX-A-AN, EME-SAL, Br 1045) xi-ṭa-tu-u-a, great are my sins (*cf* 38/41). *Auramazda* ra-bi, is great; ša ra-bu-u ina muxxi ilāni gabbi, H 1 (§§ 41; 89 i). Creat.-*frg* IV 77 at-ti ša ra]-ba-a-ti, KB vi (1) 27 du, die du gross geworden (ZIMMERN-GUNKEL, 412 šap-liš rab]-ba-a-ti, drunten gewaltig warst du). — *b*) grow, increase of interests, increasing the capital (with ina (& ana) muxxi, ina (& ana) eli = added to) {anwachsen, vom Zins} AV 7442; AV* 55, 56. T^C 126. PEISER, *Vertr.*, 323 *col* 2. Often in Neo-Babylonian *c. t.* ZK i 88 *no* 2, 5; ZA i 199, 6; 430; iv 117 *no* 11; v 277, 14. ZA iii 289 (81, 2—4, 147) *O* 7 tar(r)abbi. K 291, 5 ir-rab-bi ZA iii 240, 241, 4; Camb 219, 4—5 ina mux-xi-šu i-rab-bi, wächst ihn belastend hinzu. (Neb 45, 9; 65, 6—7 [KB iv 184 *no* VIII]); 341, 5 i-rab; 16, 3 i-rab-ba-'. Cyr 254, 6 (BA iii 394); 227, 5 (KB iv 276, 277); 94—6—11, 36, 5 (ZA x 398; KB iv 176 *no* III). Nabd 585, 5 kaspu ina muxxišu i-rab-bi (he will pay interest thereon); see also 187, 5—6; 282, 4 *foll*; 552, 4—5. — In Assyrian *c. t.* we have: III 47 *no* 5 (K 350) 7—8, the 2 talents a-na III-su-šu-nu i-rab-bi-u, werden um ihr Drittel anwachsen (*i. e.* yield 33 $^1/_3$ percent), KB iv 126—7. III 46 *no* 8 (K 381) 6, kaspu a-na IV-ti-šu (= ribūtišu?) GAL (*var* i-rab)-bi, Br 6846, the money increases by one fourth (*i. e.* pays 25 %). III 47 *no* 6, 11 (7, 4) a-na IV-tu-šu GAL (*var* i-rab)-bi; 47 *no* 3, 6 the money ina IV-tu-šu irab-bi (i-rab-bi, *no* 2, 7); 9, 5: V šiqlē kaspi ša arxi irab-bi, 5 silvershekel are added each month (to the four minas owed); *no* 10, 8 the money a-na III-su-šu i-rab-bi. K 381, 6 kaspu a-na ribu-ut-ti-šu irab-bi; K 378, 6 ta-rab-bi (3 *sg*?) KB iv 148—51. See BARTH. *Etym. Stud.*, 29 & FRÄNKEL, BA iii 74. — S^c 71 ša-ar | ŠAR | ra-bu-u, Br 8231.

See also maçū, 2 (570 *col* 2). V 38 *b-c* 27—29 (on *col a* see ZA iii 348/9) ⟩ = ra-b(p?)u-u (Br 7431), ru-ub(p)-b(p)u-u (Br 7432; *cf* V 40 *c-d* 16, Br 7702), tar-b(p)u-tu (AV 7632) followed by li-qu-u, li-qu-tu.

NOTE. — KB iii (2) 50 *col* 3, 27 Marduk be-ili ja-ti i-ra-ba-an-ni, translates: stärkte Marduk, der Herr, mich.

𝔔^t = 𝔔 *a*. K 5418 (+ K 5640) i 11 (= 17) ina ki-rib šadē ir(-ti)-bu-ma i-te-it-lu-ma, KB vi (1) 292, 293; ZA xii 319 *foll.* IV² 28 *no* 2 *O* 25, 26 Nannar (the moon god) ina e-lat šamē ir-ta-bi, Br 4820. *Etana*-legend (Rm 2, 454) 23 u-dan-nin-ma ir-ta-bi bi-lat-su, and great became his burden, KB vi (1) 112, 113.

𝔍 — *a*) make great, raise, lift up {grossmachen, erhöhen, erheben}. Esh vi 17 kisallaša MA-GAL (= danniš) u-rab-bi (1 *pr*); Bu 88—5—12, 75+76 v 25. II 66 *no* 2, 13 (I strengthened its site) see (aban) pīlu. Sarg *Khors* 96 Yaman u-rab-bu-u elišun; *Ann* 221; 141 elišunu u-rab-bu-u; *Khors* 36 *etc.*; ZA iv 412; II 51, 28. K 7673, 19 ..... (ilat) Iš-tar ina ru-ub-bi-e-ša (§ 98). H 50 *b* 5—7 u-ra-ab-bu-u, u-ra-ab-ba (?), u-ra-ab-bu-u (*col* 1 broken off); 72, 34 zēr-šu u-rab-ba. — *b*) bring up, raise, educate {aufziehen} III 57 *no* 4, 45 šu .... ki-ma ābi ummi u-rab-bu-u-šu. III 4 *no* 7, 9 (62) see mārūtu, 582 *col* 2. K 6065, 5 .... u-r]ab-ba-an-ni-ma (KB iv 156—7: hat mich aufgezogen). K 883, 25 do not fear mu-u-ri (see 583/4) | ša ana-ku u-rab-bu-u-ni; BA ii 633—5. Camb 273, 6—7 mārē-e-a | çix(?)-ru-tu-u (my small children) u-rab-bi, I shall bring up, BA iii 427. See also 𝔔 *ac.* — *c*) of interest {von Zinsen} K 363, 9—10 kaspu a-na $^1/_2$ šiqli-šu u-ra-ba, KB iv 132, 133, er wird das Geld um seinen halben Seqel anwachsen lassen.

𝔍^t = 𝔍 Creat.-*frg* III 46 (104) li-ir-tab-bu-u zik-ru-ka, great be made thy name. *Dibbara*-legend *R* iii 15 [.....] ur-tab-bi-ma, KB vi (1) 64, 65 I shall make great.

𝔖 make great, enlarge, increase {grossmachen, vergrössern}. KB vi (1) 72, 15

(*Dibbara*-legend) ša . . .] šu(?)-me u-šar-bu-u (3 *sg*); 28 (end) li-šar-ba-a šu-me. Sn i 12 Ašur eli gi-mir a-šib pa-rak-ki u-šar-ba-a kakkē-ja, KB ii 82—3; Sarg *Ann* 244; Sn *Kui* 1, 2; *Bell* 4; I 69 *a* 62 u-šar-bi, ZA iii 317, 84; iv 228, 8; I 44, 85 the former palace MA-GAL u-šar-bi u-šaq-qi-ši u-šar-ri-ix-ši; I 49 *d* 23, 24 Êsagila *etc.* I had rebuilt u-šar-bi | u-šaq-ki u-šar-ri-ix. See also II 67 *R* 25 (u-šar[-bu-u?]). Esh *Sendsch*, *R* 33 šarru-u-ti u-šar-ri-ix-ma u-šar-ba-a zik-ri šumi-ja. 82—7—4, 42 *O* 8 . . . Anunnaki . . . . u-šar-bu-u [šarrussu], PSBA xx 155 *fol.* ZA iv 280, 12 (Bēl) u-šar-bu-ka. K 3454 (*Zū*-legend) ii 30 (end) who . . . . li-šar-bi (3 *sg*) šumi-šu (will make great his name); ZA v 68, 27 lu-šar-ba-a (1 *sg*). Neb 329, 8 tu-šar-ba. — pm V 60 *b* 27, 28 ša šur-bu-u xi-ṭu-šu-un, whose sin is great. K 3600 iv 14 (hymn to Ninâ) šur-ri-xa ba-ni-i-tu šur-ba-a ru-çu-un-tu; Craig, *Relig. Texts*, i 54. K 3258 *R* 14 šu-uš-ru-ux zi-kir (il) Ašur šur-ba-a-ta ilu-us-su; *ibid*, *pl* 34. IV^2 55 *b* 10 šur-bat mārat (il) Anim. Creat.-*frg* III 45 lu-u š[ur-ba-ta-ma]. ag III 38 *no* 2 (K 2660) 3 . . . eli abi-šu ar-na šu-tu-ru šur-bu-u xi-ṭu-šu kab-tu. Messerschmidt, *Nabuna'id*, 64, 23 a-na šur-bi-i be-lu-ti-ka. — ag AV 5595. TP i 17 the great gods mu-šar-bu-u šar-ru-ut Tukulti-pal-ēšara; i 46; Anp i 77 (ZA i 360); Šalm, *Ob*, 14. I 27 *no* 1, 11 ilāni mu-šar-bu-u šarrūti (§ 131). Anp i 17 Ašur mu-šar-bu-u šarrū-ti-a; 41; iii 118; *Mon*, *O* 26; also I 27 *no* 2, 48, 49 (lu-šar-bu-u, 3 *pl*); KB iii (2) 46, 10 (-šu); 48, 45 ((ilat) Gula) mu-ša-ar-ba-ṭi zi-ki-ir šar-ru-ti-ja. Pognon, *Wadi-Brissa*, 183, mu-šar-ba-ti. Asb ix 86 read mu-ša[-ar]-bu-u bēlu-u-ti, Winckler, *Forsch.*, i 251, 252.

Š3 enlarge, increase {grossmachen, vergrössern}. I 7 F 14 (*cf* Peiser, KAS ix, 2); ZA iii 318, 89 uš-rab-bi ri-ba-ti-šu (§ 85). Sn *Bav* 5 ša Ninâ šubatsu MA-GAL uš-rab-bi (1 *sg*); Sn vi 60; I 44, 66—7 *cf* kanū, 2 (405 *col* 2). Creat.-*frg* III 38 (end) ša-a-šu (?) u]š-rab[-bi], +96 ša-a-šu uš-rab-bi-iš (KB vi, 1, 14 + 18). NE VI 106 [u ana b(p)u-u-li tu-]-uš(?)-rab-bi šammē, KB vi (1) 172, 173.

Note. — T. A. — Q^t (Ber) 1, 8 amēlu ir-ta-bi, is grown up. — 3 (Lo) 11, 27 Nap-xur-r[i-ja] ru-ub-bi u u-zu-ur-šu, magnify *N* & shield him! (Ber) 16, 17 am-mi-nim du-ra-ab-bi.

Derr.: narbū, nirbū, narbūtu (726 *col* 1), šurbū, šurbūtu, tarbū, tarbatu, tarbītu, tarbittum, tarbūtu, & these 8:

rabū 2., rabiu (orig. form), *c. st.* rab (§ 39; but ZA vi 307), *f* rabītu ᐅ rabī-atu, §§ 37*a*; 41; IV^2 21* 2 *O* 34 ra-bi-ti); *pl* rabūti (§ 69), *f* rabāti, *adj* great {gross} § 65, 7. AV 7441, § 38 on case-endings. main id GAL (Br 6845); also GULA (Br 11143). — *a*) great, large of measure, number, *etc.* {gross, an Mass, Zahl, *etc.*}. Perh V 33 i 19 A-gu-um ra-bi-i. I 65 *a* 42 see dūru (268 *col* 1, *ll* 3/5); S 954 *R* 7/8. KB iii (2) 4, 21 see kirū, 1. (433 *col* 1). V 33 iv 52 UD-GAL-LA = ūmu rabū (KB iii, 1, 144/5 & *rm* *†; Jastrow, ZA iv 158). karru rabū (GAL-u) see kargulū (436 *col* 1); kutū rabū (456 *col* 2); paššūru rabū & pitnu rabū, see these. NE 15, 32 lu-ub-ši ra-ba-a. V 35, 24 zēru GAL; ZA i 341, 17 lu-la ra-bi-a. T. A. (Ber) 28 *b* 37/38: I kar-patu ra-bu-u, *c* 62. Camb 197, 6 bābu rabi-i, Hauptkasse, BA iii 488; ša bābi rabi-i, Hauptkassirer. KB iv 82 i 12 māri-šu ra-bu-u, his eldest son; see also *ibid* 88 iv 32. *pl* id I 49 *b* 22. Sp II 265 *a* xxi 5 ra-bi a-xi; IV^2 7 *a* 41 axi-šu rabi-i. çixru rabū *etc.* see çixru. — iççur rabi see naxtu, 1 (666 *col* 2, & paspasu). Scheil, *Notes d'Épigr.*, xxxv 7 ta-ap-da-a ra-bi-a (*Rec. Trav.*, vol. xx). KB iii (1) 116/17 (Xammurabi) i 14 ki-ma sa-tu-im (= šadīm) ra-bi-im; 124, 10 in e-bi-ri ra-bu-tim (ZA ii 360 ii 10; I 65 *b* 10). II 47, 15 (ra-bi-ta) id ma-ta-a-ti, AV 7440. kitkittu ra-bi-tum, see 457 *col* 1; maššartu rabītu (612 *col* 2, below); V 33 vi 7/8 tarimte . . . ra-bi-ti. On ammatu rabītu see ZA iv 265, 26; suklu rabītu see *p* 756 *col* 2. dal-tu ra-bi-tu (= GAL) IV^2 17 *a* 9/10; *pl* GIŠ-IK-MEŠ GAL-MEŠ V 33 iv 36; ii 32 lu-bu-uš-ta ra-bi-ta V 42 *no* 2 *O* 29 DUK-GAL = (maš-qalillu) ra-bi-tum, a vessel; see *ibid* 38.

S 31, 52 *R* 16 (GIŠ) SA-GAL = ra-bi-tum, ZA ix 222; & see V 26 *c-d* 66 (Br 3187; *cf* samaxxu, 766 *col* 1). V 69, 7—8 a-ab-ba (*var* tam-di) GAL-te (= rabī-te); *cf* tâmtu. KB ii 246, 63 še-er-ta-šu rabī-tu. Perhaps Sarg *Cyl* 15 rabī-tum qa-a-su; Anp i 39 (§ 121) his great (strong) hand. — I 65 *b* 12; Neb vi 41 mê ra-be-u-tim, see kaššu, 1 (444 *col* 1). V 50 *b* 38, 39 (Br 11143). TP vi 11 dûrānišunu GAL-MEŠ. V 52 *b* 46, 47 a-ta-bu-ru (?) ra-bu-tim (= GAL-GAL-LA). IV^{2} 28 *no* 2 *O* 14 ša-du-u ra-bu-tu (= GAL-GAL-E). — Sn vi 59 e-mu-ki ra-ba-a-te; V 35 v 40, 41 ni-ga-ti-šu-nu ra-ba-a-ti. IV^{2} 32 *a* 2 (end) + 29 nišê ra-ba-a-ti (*var* GAL-MEŠ). — *b*) great in value, position, rank, *etc.* {gross an Wert, Stellung, Rang, *etc.*}. V 65 *a* 14 bêlu MAX (*var* ra-bu-u); I 69 *b* 16 (il) Šamaš bêlu rabu-u. Neb *Senk* i 7 Marduk bêlu ra-bu-u; KB iii (1) 124 *h* 1/2 ana (il) Marduk be-li-im ra-bi-im; V 34 *b* 55 bêlu ra-be-u (il) Marduk; ZA i 341, 17 (ra-bi-a); I 65 *a* 8 bêlu ra-be-u; I 52 *no* 2 ii 23; V 34 *a* 11; *Bors* i 10; ii 5; *Bab* i 15; ii 23. Šamaš-ra-bi (a P.N. or pm?) KB iv 16 *b* 1; ra-bi-ilu (or -an?) II 67 *a* 5. S 954 *R* 14 be-lum ša-du-u rabu-u. V 44 *c-d* 57 (il) Sin ra-bi (*c*, GU-LA); TP iv 35 Bêlit xi-ir-te rabī-te; KB iii (2) 48 *b* 48 a-na Gu-la be-el-ti ra-be-ti. KB iii (1) 113 *b* 12/13 ta-na-da-ti-ka ra-bi-a-tim; Sarg *Khors* 156 (il) Ninib u xi-ra-ti-šu-nu ra-ba-a-ti; *Ann* 416. — ilu rabu-u, ra-bu-u; ilâni rabûti (GAL-MEŠ, with or without complement -ti, -te) *etc.*, often = the great god(s). Creat.-*frg* IV 3, 5 ina ilâni ra-bu-tum. ilûtu ra-bītu, often; I 49 *c* 6—7 ilû-ti-ka rabī-ti; V 33 ii 47, 48 i-lu-ti-šu-nu ra-bi-tim; iv 6, 7 (-ti). — V 30 *a* 48 gallû GAL (= rabu)-u. IV^{2} 31 *O* 22 ana rabī-ti (ilat) Ištar; 42, 43 MIR (= agû) raba-a, the lofty crown; *R* 45 a-gu-u ra-ba-a. 81—6—7, 209, 41 (ilat) Ištar bêltu rabī-ti (34, šur-bu-ti). See also nâgiru (644 *col* 2). II 31 *c* 46 (amêl) rab-u-te, AV 7443, Br 13002. (amêl) GAL-MEŠ-šu K 181 *O* 28 (Hr^{L} 197); NE 42, 12; *cf* III 66 *col* 8, 1 Anunnaki GAL-MEŠ (= rabûti); and, again, KB vi (1) 582/3 *b* 1 ra-bu-tum (il) Anunnaki.

Rab (written GAL) forms the first part of a great many titles of officials, for which, in most cases, see the noun, mentioned as second component part (II 31, 28 *foll*) AV 7443; (amêl) rab-A-BA Rm 203 *R* 5; 82—2—4, 144 *R* 9; K 779 *R* 5 (III 51 *no* v); K 693, 5 (III 51 *no* ii), Thompson: chief astrologer; (amêl) rab-a-ši-pa, K 2085, 18; (amêl) rab-asû, K 693 *R* 1, chief physician; K 4395 iii 21 (amêl) rab ešre-te, II 31 *c* 46; Cyr 2, 4 (-tim), he who is placed over ten; thus also (amêl) rab xanšâ, II 31 *c* 45 (Br 13005); (amêl) rab alâni-šu, K 525, 8 (Hr^{L} 252); K 678, 27 (Hr^{L} 506 = V 54 *no* 2); rab a-la-di-nim ša rab am-tim, KB iv 55/55 *no* vii 7 (but, Delitzsch, *Kappad. Keilschrifttafeln*, *no* 11 reads: ša rab zi-ki-tim); (amêl) rab bîti = *major domo*; written (amêl) GAL-Ê, K 13 *R* 19 (Hr^{L} 287); (amêl) rab bu-lu, Pinches, *Inscr. Tablets*, 8, 15 + 19, chief of the cattle (herders); (amêl) rab be-li, II 31 *c* 51; (amêl) rab-bâni, written (amêl) GAL-KAK, Camb 2, 7; 43, 4; 284, 14; 313, 10 *etc.*, see bânû (176); (amêl) rab-dup-šar-ri, K 715 *R* 1 (amêl) rab-DUP-SAR; 80—7—19, 56 *R* 1 (see dupšarru); (amêl) rab BI-LUB(L), AV 7445, chief cupbearer {Obermundschenk} (?), III 49 *a* 52; II 53 *a* 20; 31 *a-b* 28 *foll.* Zim., *Ritualt.*, 45 vi (*p* 156/7) Ober-*Bierschenk*. (amêl) rab LUB = rab zammaru (?) 83—1—38, 358 *R* 6 rab za-am-ma-ri, ZDMG 53, 117—8. (amêl) rab da-ni-be (see 259 *col* 2); (amêl) rab p(b)il-ka-ni see pilku. (amêl) rab dan-dan, II 31 *c* 41; ra-bi (& rab) zi-ka-tim, see 293 *col* 1; (amêl) rab kar-ma-ni, see 438 *col* 1 & K 122 (Hr^{L} 43) 18 (amêl) rab kar-man, the chief overseer of the vineyards (ZA xvii 92 × BA iv 514: Ruinenmeister). (amêl) rab karani (K 14 = Hr^{L} 42, 11) = Kellermeister; (amêl) rab bir-te, *cf* bîrtu 2 (196 *cols* 1, 2) and add II 31 *c* 29 = rab xalçi; (amêl) rab mašmašu (607 *col* 2); (amêl) NU kirî = (amêl) rab kirî, vine-dresser, husbandman, Johns, *Doomsdaybook*, *pp* 20, 31; (amêl) rab ša-kil (? [illegible]) Br 13006,

II 31 *b* 34; rab pu-ux-ri, ZK ii 301; (amēl) rab mu-gi, see 509 *col* 2; KAT^3 590 *rm* 5; 651. JOHNS, *Doomsdaybook* 5, ii 22 (& *p* 54) = master of the horse; (amēl) rab malāxi (*q. v.*) III 48 *b* 31; (amēl) rab MU see nuxatimmu, 666—7, & again, DELITZSCH, BA iv 484, more probably = rab qalla (see qallu); (amēl) rab kiçir (427 *col* 2); & kāçir; (amēl) rab qašti; (amēl) rab nikasi; rab ka-a-ri & kar-ri, see kāru, 2 (429 *col* 2); (amēl) rab-šaq (?) II 31 *a* 34, Br 12991; 83—1—18, 47 *R* 10; AV 7446; (amēl) rab-ŠAQ-MEŠ C^b *O* 19, *R* 20 (Br 12992; KAT^3 278, 651) & see šāqû, 5; (amēl) rab ša-(?)riš see ša-(?)-riš & also rēšu; ra-ab šik-ka-tu, see šikkatu, 1; (amēl) rab ši-iš-ku; (amēl) rab šim (riq?)-ki; II 58 *b* 42 (il) ra-ab(p?) pa-an ku-uz-bi, Br 12895.

K 4378 i 59 GIŠ-DA-GAL = ra-bu-u, Br 6682. H 12 (+218) 102 ma-ax | MAX | ra-bu-u (‖ maxxu, çīru); S^b 337; § 9, 109; Br 1045. H 15, 211 nu-un | NUN | ra-bu-u, S^b 129, Br 2628; S^b 124; H 25, 516 ga-al | GAL | ra-bu-u, § 9, 169. H 28, 607 ša-ar | XI | ra-bu-u; 38, 60 ZIR-GA. II 48 *a-b* 18 GIŠ = ra-bu-u, 19 MU EME-SAL = rabû, Br 1280, 5704; II 29 *f* 45—47 ra-bu-u (‖ *col* destroyed); II 31 *no* 3, 14, 15 (52, 53); V 41 *a-b* 14, 15 ra-bu-u ‖ ba-qa-šu, šu-pu-u; II 43 *a-b* 10 see maçû, 2 (570 *col* 2); II 44 *c-d* 2, 3 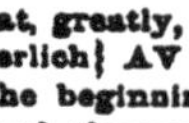 (= šar? [ru?], 1) & KIL = ra-bu[-u] Br 1165, 10200.

T. A. (Ber) 6 *R* 10 *X* ra-ba-a-ka, thy officer (+12).

rabiš, rabeš, *adv* great, greatly, solemnly {gross, grossartig, feierlich} AV 7439; Br 6845. Anp i 44 at the beginning of my reign, as on the royal throne rabi-iš ūšibu (1 *sg*); Šalm, *Ob*, 23; *Mon*, *O* 15. TP i 22 whom ye, o gods, to the dominion over the country of Bēl rabi-eš tukinnāšu, ye have solemnly appointed. V 34 *a* 14 since Marduk ... ra-bi-iš uma'i-ranni, = KB iii (2) 46, 25 (see 508 *col* 2); ZA ii 119 *O* 16; I 52 *no* 3 i 18; KB iii (1) 130 *col* 2, 4. V 63 *a* 37 ra-bi-iš e-pu-uš, I constructed on a grand scale; *BOR* ii 230, 22—3. III 66 *col* 3, 19 ur-rik (written çu) ra-biš, PSBA xxi 126. II 19, 2 *O* 27 ra-biš šu-lu-ku; IV^2 16 *b* 35. BANKS, *Diss*, 12, 63 a-mat-su ra-bi-eš ina alaki bītāte. IV^2 9 *a* 15, 16 Nannar ša šarrûtu ra-biš (= GAL-LI-EŠ, EME-SAL) šuk-lu-lum; V 51 *c* 45 (ZK ii 342); see also MA-GAL (510 *col* 1) Br 6884.

rabiānu. president, presiding officer {Präsident, Vorsitzender}? STRASSM., *Warka*, (Berl. Congr. II, 1, 357) 30, 34 maxar Sin-im-gur-an-ni ra-bi-a-nu, KB iv 24, 25; *Warka*, 48, 14 ra-bi-a-nu-um ša āli, the presidents of the district, KB iv 30, 31; *ibid* 25 *I* ra-bi(-a)-nu-um. Xammurabi-letters 19, 4 ra-bi-a-an (al) *M* (+7); ‖ sartēnu, *q. v.* On ditargallu, rabiānu, & rab(i) zikāti see ZA vii 27; MEISSNER, 5.

rabûtu. in P. N. Ra-bu-ut-Sin, KB iv 16 *b* 18. arax ra-bu-tim, early Babylonian name for Nisān (MEISSNER, 135; WZKM v 180); axu rabû-tu, I 8 *no* 2 *O* 18, KB ii 262—3; ZA vi 455 (Mündigkeit; Mündigkeitserklärung).

rubû *1.* (§ 41; AV 7629), *f* rubâtu (AV 7628) & rubītu (S 6+S 2, 21 ina a-mat ru-bi-ti-ki çir-ti, or *noun*?, *Rev. Sém.*, '98, 142 *foll*); *adj* great, lofty, sublime {gross, erhaben, hehr, herrlich} § 65, 13. id NUN, § 9, 119; Anp i 24 NUN-u (*var* ru-bu-u), & KU (Br 10547). Esh *Sendsch*, *R* 58 ru-bu-u ar-ku-u, some later ruler (81—6—7, 209, 36; TP viii 51); *R* 36 ru-ub-bu-ti u-šam-mal-lu amēlu-ut-u-a (SCHRADER; but WINCKLER, *Forsch.*, ru-up-pu-ši u-mal-lu qa-tu-u-a). Nabopolassar (KB iii (2) 2—3) 13 calls himself ru-ba-a-am na-'i-dam (see nā'idu, nādu, 2, *p* 628); I 68 *no* 3, 6 Nabd. ru-bu-u e-im-ga, the wise prince (ZA iv 107; V 34 *a* 2); I 68 *no* 4, 3 ru-bu-u git-ma-lu. K 2801 = K 221+K 2669 *O* 24 [(il) Taš-me-tum] rubu-u mun-dal-ku (+32). T^M iii 182 (il) GIŠ-BAR-RA ru-bu, BA iv 159, 160. IV^2 12 *no* 1, 9—10 E-kur ru-bu-u, Br 2629; 8 iii 40, 41; K 4567, 5, 6 TUR-NUN-NA = mār ru-bi-e. PINCHES, *Texts*, 15 *no* 4, 6 ar-ru-bi-e (il) Marduk (see karabu, Q^t, 434 *col* 2). IV^2 27 *no* 2, 27 see Br 10967; IV^2 5 *col* 2, 48—49 ana ru-bi-e (= NUN); H 76, 18. —

Scheil, *Nabonidus*, ix 21 NUN (il) Marduk (*cf* IV^2 48 *a* 26); iii 11, 12 Ištar of Nineveh ru-ba-a-ti çir-ti. ZA x 292, 26 il-tum kun-nu-tum ru-ba-tum. DT 83 *R* 4 Zi-ir-pa-ni-tum ru-ba-tum, Pinches, *Texts*, 16 *no* 4; KB iv 54 *no* vii 3 ru-ba-um u ru-ba-tum (see *ibid* 55); L^4 i 32 ru-bat i-la-a-ti. K 5157, 11 ru-ba-tum rabî-tum be-el-tum *etc.* (H 181 xii) Br 10966. 81—6—7, 209 (dupl. K 6846) 2 (ilat) Ištar of Uruk ru-ba-a-ti. KB iii (2) 48 *col* 2, 44 a-na Gu-la ru-ba-a-ti çi-ir-ti (ZA i 40, 10). K 257 (H 126) 9 ru-ba-tum. IV^2 59 *no* 1 *b* 20 at the command ru-ba-ti bêlit ilâni. Rm III 105, 7 ru-bat ilâni (ilat) Še-ru-'-u-a (Winckler, *Forsch.*, i 254 *foll*). K 11152, 4 (Ištar) ru-ba-tum ša it-ti (il) Bêl šit-lu-ṭa-at. K 4629 *R* 8 ru-ba-tum kit-tum NIN 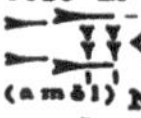-ki (AV 6238, Br 7350). — *pl* (amêl) NUN-MEŠ, Sn ii 69; iii 2; NUN-MEŠ *Khors* 178; NE VI 16 (end); KB vi (1) 72, 19 eli šarri u rubê; Smith, *Asurb*, 9, 6. Sarg *Ann* 331 ru-bu-ti šarrûtišu. V 35, 18 ru-bi-e (§ 67, 4) u šak-kan-nak-ka (BA ii 210). K 2852 + K 9662 i 20 ru-bi-e ma-li-ki-ia. K 2085 *R* 8 (end) ru-bi-e. — V 44 *c-d* 20 (ilat) Ba-u ru-bi-ma (= NUN) du-me lu-mur (Br 4078, 6849). V 52 *a* 24 mar ru-bi-e (= NUN, 23) rabu-u na-an-na-ru (il) Sin (H 77, 30). K 13 (Hr^L 281) *R* 20 (amêl) GAL-MEŠ-šu, his nobles. — V 13 *a-b* 43—45 NUN (= II 29 *e-f* 42; Br 2629) & KU (Br 10547; K 4870, 29) = ru-bu-u (H 34, 802); (sal) KU = ru-ba-tu (Br 10990; H 41, 272; ZK ii 269). V 39 *c-d* 66 (sal) KU (*i. e.* NIN) = ru-ba-a-tu (65, be-el-tum; 64, a-xat-tum); V 36 *d-f* 17 u-mun | < | ru-bu-u (Br 8736); II 31 *no* 2, 18 MAX = ru-bu-u (Br 1046; V 16 *a-b* 55); II 31 *no* 3, 13 (Br 2629); V 41 *a-b* 13 ru-bu[-u] ‖ ka-ru-bu. II 29 *e-f* 40 perh. ru(?!)-bu-u = ru-bu-tu, 41 pa-xa-nu = ru-bu NIM, *i. e.* in the language of Elam (?) or ru-bu-nim (?); 43, 44. II 47 *a-b* 17 (Br 9769, 10547). — II 67, 5 (amêl *sar* mât) Ru-bu-'u (AV 7630) followed by (amêl) Ru-ub-bu (AV 7632).

rubû 2. interest {Zins}. K 411, 6—7: II ma-na kaspi a-di ru-bi-e-šu, KB iv 156, 157 Zwei Minen Geld sammt seinem Angewachsenen (*i. e.* Zins). Dar 427, 8 pût ru-bu-u u maxrûtum. Perh. *Rec. Trav.*, xx *p* 203: ŠE-BAR-um (= še'um) ru-bi-e-ša.

rubûtu. greatness, splendor, loftiness, majesty {Grösse, Erhabenheit, Herrlichkeit} AV 7631. Creat.-*frg* IV 1 pa-rak ru-bu-tum; L^4 iii 14 šu-bat ru-bu-ti-šu. K 2852 + K 9662 i 26 (end) a-mat ru-bu-ti-šu, his princely word {sein Fürstenwort}. NE VI 43 (& *cf* 68) a-na ru-bu-ut(-ti) (ilat) Ištar; perh. NE 34, 10 ru-bu-sa (> t-ša?). ZA v 60, 18 see qurdu. ZA x 293, 29 binti (ilat) Nannar is called te-li-ia-a-tum ru-bu-tum. Smith, *Asurb*, 74, 17 šêpê ru-bu-ti-šu (of Ašurbanipal) çabat (= ip). IV^2 9 *a* 17, 18 ša ina ti-di-iq ru-bu-ut (NA-AM-KU-NA, EME-SAL, Br 1627, 10547) i-šad-di-xu. T. A. (Ber) 106, 10 mât (al) ru-bu-te, the land of the city of holiness (Haupt, *Independent*, New York, Jan. 12 '99). V 20 *e-f* 20, 21 NAM-NUN-NA (Br 2629) & NAM (e-gi, ZK i 366) KU-RA (Br 10547) = ru-bu-tum (H 42, 20); II 33 *a-b* 68 . . . GUL = ru-bu-tu, Br 14337.

rubîtu see rubû, 1.

rubuttum. 83—1—18, 1846 *R col* iv 7 P.N. (sal) ru-bu-ut-tum, followed by (sal) NUN (= rubu)-ut-tum.

râbu 1. = רוב, *pr* irûb sink, settle (of the foundation of buildings *etc.*), quake (of the earth) {sinken (von Gebäuden, *etc.*); beben (von der Erde). 83—1—18, 287, 8 i-ru-ub (of the earth) Thompson, *Reports*, ii, pref. lxxxi *fol*; & *no* 264 (& *passim*). H 127, 50; Banks, *Diss*, 16, 152—4 see naraṭu Q (728 *col* 1 where read רוב *not* רחב); Banks, 12 *fol*, 88 ina a-ma-ti-šu e-liš šame-e ina ra-ma-ni-šu-nu i-ru-ub-bu. III 61 *a* 27 (31, 35, 39, 43, 47, 51, 55, 60; *b* 3, 7, 11) when in such & such a month from the first to the 30th day attalû ittabši or . . . . ri-i-bu i-ru-ub, then such & such will happen; 62 *b* 7. III 51 *no* v, 7 when in Ṭebet ri-i-bu ŠU (= iru)-ub (K 779, 7) the king shall live in the city of his enemy; 11 when ina mûši KI (= erçitu) i-ru-ub (= the earth quakes). K 124 *O* 12 ri-i-bu i-ru-ub; also *R* 11 (+ K 813, 1) + *O* 14 erçitu i-ru-ub (& K 779 *R* 8) apparently ‖ *R* 1 i-nu-uš. Also ŠU alone, 83—1—18, 287 *R* 1; *ibid* *O* 8 i-ru-ub, + *R* 6 i-ru-ub-u-ni (= *pl*). K 2852 + K 9662 iv 19 P. N. Ša-ni-ni a-a ir-r[u-ub] — pm rūb. K 8391, 5 (end) ru-ub, *R* 2 + 3 (in all cases preceded by KI = erçitu).

Q¹ III 51 *no* v, 6 (= K 779) mūša an-ni-u (this night) ri-i-bi ir-tu-bu.

ℑ *a*) put out; extinguish (a fire *etc.*), blot out {auslöschen} *trans.* IV² 8 *a* 3 (+ 6) = Z³ v/vi 177 (+ 180) iššātu aš-ru-pu u-ra-a-ba (u-rab-bu-u; II 51 *no* 1 *R* 23), the fire, I started, I am (now) putting out, ‖ unāx; JENSEN, *Diss*, 84. ið TE = ru-ub[-bu?] V 40 *c-d* 16. II 51 *no* 1 *R* 19 (*b*) iššātu aš-ru-pu u-rab-bi, ZK ii 321. ZIMMERN, *Ritualtafeln*, 46, 47 *l* 13 (end) šu-lux-xi (*var* -xa) tu-rab-ba, die Besprengungen sollst du auswischen. — *b*) blot out, destroy, kill {austilgen, vernichten, töten}. K 2148 iii 8 ina ki-la-te-ša a-ka-la na-šat-ma a-na pi-ša u-rib. Lay 38, 14 the river Tebil(nā)ti, which with its immense flood u-ri-ib-bu tam-me-en-ša, has destroyed its (the palace's) foundation; Sn *Kui* 3, 31 u-rib-bu; *Bell* 47 u-ri-ib-bu; *Rass* 74 u-ri-bu. Sm 954 (D 135) *O* 43, 44; 45, 46 (= AL-DUB; AL-DUB-DUB, EME-SAL, Br 7031); BANKS, *Diss*, 18 *foll*, *no* 2, 21 see naraṭu ℑ (728); 1, 13 a-mat-tum ša e-liš šamē u-rab-bu (+ 23). V 45 v 14 tu-ra-a-ba. Sarg *Cyl* 19 mu-ri-ib ^(mât) Bît-Xu-um-ri-a rap-ši (KB ii 42, 43). Anp mu-ri-ib (& -rib, AV 5552) a-nun(-un)-te (šar kal malkē) who destroys all resistance, Anp i 20; iii 27 mu-rib a-nun-te; Sarg Pp IV 22 Sargon mu-rib malkē ^(mât) Amatti, *etc.* — **Der.**:

rību *1.* earthquake {Erdbeben} THOMPSON, *Reports*. See rābu Q & Q¹. 83—1—18, 287, 1 ina eli ri-i-bi ša šarri [be-ili] iš-pur-an-ni an-ni-u [pi-šir-šu]; K 12281, 1; K 813 *R* 1.

ra(i)bū *3.* Q disappear, be or become invisible {verschwinden, unsichtbar sein oder werden}? THOMPSON, *Reports*. K 706, 1 Ana Sin Šamšu ina u-qi-ma ir-bi; K 782 *R* 1; *pl* K 725, 4 ir-bu-u; Bu 91 —5—9, 14 *R* 3 ša ir-bu-u-ni; ið BUL, 81—7—27, 23 *O* 6. *ps* K 712, 3 ūm XV^(kam) i-rab-bi(-ma). *ac* IV² 55 *no* 1 *R* 31 in the evening i]a-am ^(il) Šamaš ra-bi-e, before the sun has disappeared (ZA xvi 194/5; KAT³ 548 *rm* 3). Q¹ IV² 28 *no* 2 *a* 24, 26 Šamaš ina išid šamē i-te-ru-ub, ZA i 453 (× i 236; or √erebu?); ^(il) Nannar ina elat šamē ir-ta-bi; ZA ii 197 *rm* 1. IV² 30 *no* 2 *O* 25 ^(il) Šamaš ir-ta-bi-šu ana erçitim mītūti, JENSEN, 226: Let *Šamaš* make him disappear unto the land of death. Bu 91, 5—9, 14 *O* 7—8 la ni-e-mur | ir-te-bi; K 725 *O* 1 ^(MUL) DIL-BAT ina çît Šamši ir-ti-bi. ℑ perh. 82—2—4, 144, 3 ^(ilat) DIL-BAT u ^(il) GUD-UD a-na ru-u-bi il-lu-ku; or *noun*? — **Der.**:

rību *2.* K 8713 *R* 5 ana ri-bi-šu il-lak, of a star. × nipxu, *q. v.* V 64 *c* 18, *b* 34; I 69 *b* 19; ZA xvii 200 *rm* 2.

ribannu (?) III 53 *a* 71 kakkabu erītu (??) ša ina ri-ba-an-na (kakkab) ši-bi u (kakkab) ^(il) A-nim izza-zu. WINCKLER, *Forsch.*, iii 208: im Bereich (?).

rābu *2.* (רוב?). K 2852 + K 9662 i 16 concerning the Assyrian who has run away C-a ri-bi-šu lu-ri-ib, I will give a hundred. — Perhaps also H 46, 44 i-ri-ib, 46 + 48 i-ri-bu; 50, i-ri-ib-bu (or √erebu, 1; see 95 *col* 2).

NOTE. — With ר־־, HOMMEL, *Dict. of Bible* (Hastings) i 190 *col* 1 *rm* * connected I-ri-ba tuk-te-e (SCHEIL, *Nabonidus*, ii 13 ‖ u-tir gi-mil-li, 11; see MESSERSCHMIDT, *p* 43) = vengeance took (the king of the Manda) = Arbak, Arbaces (LEHMANN), ‖ turru tuktē & šakanu gimilli (MESSERSCHMIDT, 68, 17). M³ 15 √ריב.

ribbu, in Creat.-*frg* see labbu 1, NOTE (466 *col* 2, below; KB vi (1) 44/5 *rm* 5; & KAT³ 498 *rm* 2).

ri-ib, in P. N. Ri-ib Addi T. A. (*passim*) = servant of Adda {Diener des A} ZA xi 248 § 5.

rību *3.* II 22 *c-e* 18 DUK-ŠA(= GAR)-DAGAL = ri-i-bu, preceded by ru-up-šu & rap-šu; same ið; H 24, 494. AV 7555; Br 5456, 12077. Perh. √רחב.

rību *4.* II 35 *e-f* 37 ri-i-bu = AN-NUN-GAL, AV 7555; Br 2641. The AN-NUN-GAL-MEŠ = Igigi.

rababu *1.* = rabū 1 (but see KB vi (1) 315—316). Q perh. 82—7—4, 42 *R* 7 ri-it-tu-uš-šu rab-ba-a-ta, PSBA xx 152 *fol.*

Š³ Creat.-*frg* III 52 (K 4832 *O* 17) see magšaru; 512 *col* 2 (= let his power increase) & KB vi (1) 315. — Derr. these 5:

rabbu *1.* great, mighty, powerful {gross, mächtig}. II 19, 19 šar-ru rab-bu (il) A-nim a-ša-rid ilāni. IV² 3 *b* 38—9 a-gu-u rab-bu-ti >< a-gi-i çi-ix-xi-ru-ti. Banks, *Diss*, 10, 38 a-mat-su mi-si ra-ab-bu-ti (= GIŠ-MIŠ-GAL-GAL-LA), & see mēsu, 565 *col* 2. Sm 1871 *O* 2 O Gilgameš rab-bu ša nišē. Sn i 8 *Senn*. rab-bu; *Kui* 1, 2; *Bell* 3. Nabd 357, 3: XVI alpē ra-ab-bu-tu. T. A. (Lo) 3, 5 ana ra-ab-bu-ti-ka, to thy magnates (ZA v 138, 7); (Ber) 7, 5 + 7; also içē rab-bu-te, *etc.* Ūmu rab-bu-tum (= GAL) great storms, IV² 1 *a* 18, 19 (Br 6848; § 67, 5; KB vi (1) 316). V 14 *b* 35 (šipātum) rab-ba-a-tum; Esh v 29 ēkallāte rab-ba-a-ti; *cf* DT 83 (Pinches, *Texts*, 15/16 *no* 4) *O* 12 Ē-KUR-MEŠ-šu rab-ba-a-ti.

rabbiš. *adv.* Banks, *Diss*, 12, 61 a-mat-su rab-bi-iš ina a-la-ki-ša ma-a-ta u-ab-bat (= Reisner, *Hymnen*, 8) ‖ rabiš.

rabbūtu. greatness, might, majesty {Grösse, Macht, Hoheit}. IV² 13 *b* 5, 6 rab-bu-ut-ka (= KIL-RA-ZU) el çuxxuri limraç, Br 1021.

rubbu (?) torrent, flood? {Flut *etc.*}? I 34 iv 25 ina ru-ub-bi mē, KB i 186—7: in der Hochflut des Wassers. Perh. also K 3351, 22 (= Craig, *Rel. Texts*, i 43 *l* 16) ša tam-tim gal-la-ti i-sa-am-bu-' ru-ub-bu-ša (Martin: ruppuša √רפש).

rubbū = rubū (?). Nabd 758, 21 a-na ru-ub-bi-e-ša.

rababu 2. Š TP v 65 mu-šur-bi-bu (see 612 *col* 1) ka-liš mul-tar-xe ‖ mušim-qit lā magirē; AV 7434, who makes submissive, oppresses {der willfährig macht, unterdrückt}. V 45 v 21 tu-šar-bab.

Note. — With this may perhaps be connected KB iii (1) 113 *col* 1, 21 Šamaš & Adad ra-bi-ba-ku (sind dir zu Willen?). T^M vii 45 ina ri-kiš ra-ba-bu ša (il) ..... la, BA iv 161. Lehmann ii 69 *ad* L⁴ ii 18 ir-bu-bu akçūti, kraftlos (?) waren die gewaltigen; M³: be humble, submissive ‖ demütig sein. — Der.:

rabbu *2.* submissive, oppressed {willfährig, unterdrückt}? S^b 334 ra-ba | RAB rab-bu, AV 7449, Br 4244. V 28 *b-c* 27 rab(p)-b(p)u one of the 9 equivalents of TUR-TUR ‖ dal-lu, Br 4106.

rabb(pp?)u *3.* H 122 *O* 8—9 ina qāti]-šu ša ina rab-pi šu-nu-xat.

rabbū (?) Peiser, *Vertr.*, lxx 1: arxa 4 rab-bu-u ša tak-ka-su-u (monthly 4 *r* for *t*); 7 mār (amēl) pa-še(-ki) rab-bu-u ša PAT-XI-A (= kurummati).

rabū *4.*, **ribū**, **rebū** (§ 32*aβ*) fourth {vierter}. √רבע whence arba'u, irbā (four), erbā (forty) § 76. Reisner, *Hymnen*, 109, 64 ra-bu-u (= IV-U-KAM-MA-MU) iššātu napixtum. IV² 5 *a* 19, 20 IV-KAN-MA = re-bu-u (AV 7556, Br 12043; H 41, 295). T. A. (Lo) 82, 2 (end) i-na ri-e-bi[-i], KB vi (1) 78—9; BA iv 130—1. IV² 56 *add*, *col* i 4: ri-bu-u; Nabd 228, 12. NE 70 (X, iv) 4 ... šana-a šal-ša u ri-ba-a (KB vi, 1, 222); KB vi (1) 192, 6: šal-ša ūma u ri-ba-a ūmu. NE 55, 23 šal-ša ū-ma u ri-ba-a ū-ma. *del* 137 (144) šal-ša ūmu ri-ba-a ūmu. — 205 (226), 216 (238) ribū-tum, fourthly {viertens}. *pl f* ribātu, V 40 *c-d* 53 ŠI-IV-GAL-LA = re-ba-a-tum, fourths {Vierttteile}. K 56 (*cf* H 68 *R* 5) iii 25—27 (H 78) ri-ba-a]-tu, [a-na ri-ba-a]-ti, a-na ri-ba-a-ti u [-še-çi], AV 7558. Perh. ZK i 48, 23: III ri-ba-a-ta. K 3364 *R* 6 ina ri-ba-a-ti (Delitzsch, *Weltschöpfungsepos*, 54); H 74, 5 miksu (toll) ša ri-ba-a-ti, § 77; Br 9406. Xammurabi-letters 21, 5 re-ib-ba-a-tim ša çēni, die vierten Teile des Kleinviehs, BA iv 452, 453. Note also **rebūtu** & **rebītu** *c. st.* rebāt, rebīt (?) = fourth of a shekel. AV* 57 *b*. Cyr 156, 4: V ma-na XV šiqli III re-bat (bit?); IV-ut, often in *c. t.* Nabd 190, 1: III re-but, *etc.*

rebūtu. *noun.* K 381, 6 kaspu (a)-na ribu-ut-ti-šu i-rab-bi. See rabū, 1. Q *b*. Strassm., *Stockholm* (VIII.) *Or. Congr.*, 16, 10 𒁹 ri-ba-a-ta kaspi. Nabd 131, 1: III ri-ba-a-ta kaspi; 178, 25 & often.

rubānu (??) Nabd 1074, 12 ... ru-ba-nu kaspi. Probably from same stem as ribū.

rabušēni. K 527, 17 ina šal-še-ni ina ra-bu-še-ni (Hr^L 252; BA ii 55).

rabadu. III 65 *a* 22 the weapon of the king i-rab-bi-di, the land will be conquered.

— Š II 34 *no* 3, 31 mu-šar-bi-du ‖ su-kal-lu, AV 5594.

rabaṭu, Br 4463, 7572 *ad* muttaširabiṭu see שרבט.

(šam) ribxu (?) II 28 *e-f* 21 (šam) ri-ib(p)-xu = (šam) , followed by su-pa-lum, *q. v.* AV 7604; Br 2607, 5218. ið also Nabd 486, 2.

rabaçu, pr irbiç (ZDMG 43, 187), ps ira(b)biç, lie down, rest, encamp {sich legen, liegen, lagern}. D^H 5; D^{Pr} 52 *rm* 1. IV^2 16 *R* (*b*) 2 (end) ir-bi-i[ç]; K 8063 + K 8066, 18 (Bezold, *Catalogue*, 892). III 58 *b* 29; K 700 (Pinches, *Texts*, *no* 1) 13—14 see pargāniš; K 92, 8 NA′-is = irabbi-iç; DT 148, 6 i-rab-bi-iç. I 27 *no* 2, 42 (end) ina libbi la i-ra-ba-çu, may not rest in it. *Etana*-legend (K 2527 + 1547) *O* 40 suppose now that in this wildox çiru ra-bi-iç (a serpent should hide) KB vi (1) 106—7. II 50 iii/iv 29 KUR-MIN-NAD-A = māt a-bur-ri rab-çu, ZDZG 53, 656 *foll.* II 42 *no* 3 *R* 23 U-SAL-LA-NA′-A = aburriš ra-ba-çu, Br 8997; BA ii 282; V 22 *e-h* 54 (or ra-ba-bu?). IV^2 27 *a* 19, 20 ina šadē kima ri-mi eq-du rab-çu (= NA′-A) H 138. *del* 109 (116) ilāni .... rab-çu (= 3 *pl*). Z^B 31 (med) supplies II 48 *e-f* 61 ra-ba-çu; *cf* H 29, 649. II 36 *a-b* 24, 25 ŠAR & NA′ = ra[-ba-çu] together with ru-ub-çu (23).

Q^t V 52 *R* 43 ina bi-ki-tum ir-ta-bi-iç (Br 10546) to which V 22 *h* 54 ra-ba-çu is probably a commentary, Br 11715. L^4 ii 16 kakkē na-ki-ri ti-bu-te ir-tab-çu (came to a halt, rested); VATh 244 ii 25 r(š)it-b(p)u-çu, ZA ix 157.

Š let rest, encamp, live, dwell {lagern lassen, wohnen lassen}. K 2801 *R* 51 u-šar-bi-ça. Sarg *Ann* 277; Asb vi 106 see pargāniš. IV^2 12 *O* 19/20 (end) māt-su a-bur-riš šur-bu-çi, to make his land live in peace. KB iii (1) 130—1 (Samsuiluna) i 20 ar(?)-ba a-bur-ri š]u-ur-bu-ça-am, to make inhabited the 4 aburri. — H 128 *R* 8 (end) be-ili-ku sa-par-ra çi-i-ri ina çi-e-ri za-ki-ki šur-bu-ça-ṭt (?? Br 7102) ana-ku. — ip T^M ii 108 (end) šur-bi-iç. V 45 v 22 tu-šar-ba-aç.

Derr. — narbaçu (726), tarbaçu, tarbiçu, &:

rubçu. AV 7633. — *a*) resting place, stable, fold {Lagerstätte, Stall, Hürde}. IV^2 18* *no* 6 *O* 10, 11 the evil demon has filled the mouth of the donkeys with dust and ru-bu-us-su-nu (= KI-KU-BI, usually = šubtišu) unakkir; IV^2 58 *b* 61 ru-bu-u[s-sa]. K 4609, 41 (il) Ê-a ina ru-ub-çi-šu um-me-du-šu, Br 8998. II 38 *g-h* 26 see piqannu (also II 38 *g-h* 28, Br 10250); & see rabaçu (ið ʼÚ). Constant. 583 *O* 19 (end) ru-ub-çi ši-ip-ra-ti (a medical text, perh. to *b*) Scheil, *Rec. Trav.*, xxiii notes lx. See also narbaçu. H 33, 765. ZA iii 202. — *b*) womb {Mutterleib} II 37 *e-f* 56 ri-e-mu = ru-ub-çu; 40 *a-c* 6 .... GAR-RA = ri-e-mu = ru-ub-çu, Br 14481.

rabiçu *m.* *a*) name for a demon {ein gewisser Dämon}. ið MAŠKIM, written 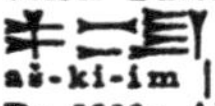 or 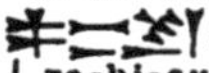; S^b 216 ma-aš-ki-im | ið | ra-bi-çu, H 21, 402, Br 5659; AV 7438; KAT^3 460. K 7331 *O* 12, 13 ra-bi-çu followed by š(s)ar-ra-qu, M^S *pl* 13. See also Br 13906 on Ⓢ 252, 10; AV 8073. K 246 ii 61 (H 90/1; D 133); IV^2 16 *a* 15, 16; 29 *no* 1 *b* 24—26 ra-bi-çu lim-nu (= MAŠKIM-XUL) together with gallū limnu & ilu limnu. See also V 50 *a* 51, 52 (*b* 59, 60). KB vi (1) 292—3 *col* 2, 5 ra-bi-çu lim-nu-te; IV^2 15* i 31, 32, Br 1822. K 3197 i B *R* 13 (= IV^2 21) mu-šam-qit (579 *col* 1) ra-bi-çi lim-ni. NE XII ii 25 ra-bi-iç (il) Nergal; iii 3, 10, 18 (KB vi, 1, 258 *foll*; 527; 553). — *b*) guardian, watchman, *etc.* {Aufseher, Wächter}. K 246 iv 47 (H 98, 99) Išum is called ra-bi-çu çi-ru ša ilāni J^W 69, 70. See also IV^2 15* *col* 2, 47—8. K 2619 (*Dibbara*-legend) i 6 il Dibbar]-ra (or, Ira, Jensen, Zimmern) ra-bi-çu abulli-šu, KB vi (1) 60, 61. III 66 *col* 3, 30 (il) ra-bi-çu biti, the guardian of the house, PSBA xxi 120, 121; Br 12897. T^M i 135 (see *ibid*, *p* 127) ra-bi-çu between še-e-du & e-kim-mu. V 52 *a* 20 see (il) Çir (*p* 891 *col* 1), Br 11318; KAT^3 504. KB vi (1) 76, 77 *R* 6 (il) Ra-a-bi-i-ça; 78, 79, 3; 389. — (amēl) ra-bi-zi T. A. (Lo) 64, 9 (explained by zu-ki-ni) Jastrow: Diener, Gesandter; Müller, *Asien & Europa*, 274 *rm* 3: Laurer, Aufpasser. (Ber) 80, 19 i-na (amēl) ra-bi-çu šarri (ZIMMERN, ZA vi 247 *rm* 13). id often in T. A. as (amêl) rābiçu šarri (Ber) 102, 17; 119, 16 (amêl) rabiçu rabi-iç ša šarri bēlija. See also BA iv 415 *ad* 311. KAT³ 192, 195. Abstract noun is:

rabiçūtu. IV² 15* (K 111) *R* i 28 AN-GIŠ-BAR (= il Gibil) ana ra-bi-çu-ti-šu li-iz-ziz, T^M 127 protection {Schutz}.

ri-ib-šu (?) K 3364 *O* 19 (end). DELITZSCH, *Weltschöpfungsepos*, 54.

ri-bi-iš, KB iii (1) 186 *ad* Merodach-Balad.-Stone ii 39, see talbišu.

rūbatu hunger {Hunger}. √רעב?. V 27 *g-h* 62, 63 U-GUG (Br 1377, 6100) = ru-ba-tum (II 29 *c-d* 38, 39; Br 6096) §§ 47; 65, 3. K 4174 *O, c-d* 13 ru-pa-tum same id as ku-na(GGA '98, 811; or uš(?), JAOS xxii 212)-tum (11), ur-ba-tum (12) & el-pi-tum (14). K 4583 *O* 29 ur-ba-tum followed by ru-pa-tum, el-pi-tum (id U-GUG); also REISNER, *Hymnen*, 10, 128; but M^S 88: a tree {ein Baum} not = hunger.

rubtu (?) V 47 *a* 35 see çaburtu.

rēbitu, *f* √רבא₃, § 35; AV 7554; H^F 16; BAL 94 *rm* 2; JOHNS, *Doomsdaybook*, 50. — *a*) surroundings of a city, town; open space, unfenced land; precincts {Weichbild, Umgebung einer Stadt; offenes Land} Sarg *Khors* 23 ina re-bit Dūr-ilu (ki) aškuna taxtâšu, *Ann* 20; *Cyl* 17; Lay 33, 7 (‖ pixâtu, *b*; in Babylonian Chronicle). Esh i 53, 54 ina re-bit Ninâ etettiq, I marched into the suburbs of *N*. Magganubba, a suburb of *N*, lay ina eli namba'ē u re-bit (al) Nina-a, Sarg *Cyl* 44. D^Par 260, 261; JEREMIAS-BILLERBECK, BA iii 100 & *rm* **. P. N. Ri-bi-it-Sippar, KB iv 14, 12. — *b*) Broad street, place, square {Breite Strasse, Platz, Marktplatz} id SIL-DAMAL-LA = re-bi-tu = sūqu (*q. v.*) rapšu (H 37, 8—9); § 9, 106. IV² 16 *b* 52 pour out the waters ana re-bi-ti (Br 404); 53, 54 maruštu ..... re-bi-tu lit-bal; 22 *b* 22 ina re-bi-ti i-di-ma; 26 *no* 5, 4 re-bi-tu(-tam) ina ba-'a-i-šu (§ 138), when he walks on the street; 58 *a* 49 (*cf* ZA 16, 172/3). Sams. iv 29 dāmē-šu-nu ki-ma mē nāri (DELITZSCH × KB i 186 a-ax) re-bit āli-šu-nu lu-u-šar-di. K 2619 i 27 see rādu, 1. Sn *Bell* 61 ša (al) Ninâ ... re-ba-ti-šu u-ša-an-dil (שׁרל); *Rass* 89 (ZA iii 318) ušrabbi ri-ba-ti-šu (314, 67 ri-ba-a-ti); *Bav* 45, 46 with their corpses ri-bit(-mit?) āli-šu u-mal-li. NE 51, 12 (KB vi, 1, 272—3; HAUPT, JAOS xxii pt. 1) the gods i-xab(p)-b(p)u-b(p)u ina ri-ba-a-ti. IV² 50 *a* 4 the witch da-a-a-li-tum ša bi-re-e-ti xa-a-a-ṭi-tum ša re-ba-a-ti; 7 ina re-bi-ti ip-ta-ra-as a-lak-tu (*cf* parasu Q¹). III 41 *b* 24 i-na ri-bi-it āli-šu (KB iv 78, 79). Sp II 265 *a* xxv 5 ri-bit āli-ja u-ba-'-u ir(?)-xi-iš. Asb iv 82 see sūqu (end) & BA i 15, 23.

ragabu (?). K 433, 2 (end) bītu ŠIN rag-bu (but PEISER, *Jurispr. Babyl.*, 38—9, bīti i-qu-pu). — Q¹ 82—7—14, 864 iii 25 rit-gu (= ku?)-bu, ZA vii 21; 28, said of a house in good condition; ZA xiv 419, JENSEN, perh. = רכב cover {bedachen}. — ℑ¹ *del* 58 (61) ur-tag-gi-ib(p)-ši a-na VI-šu (KB vi, 1, 232; 488: von der Bedachung des Schiffes ist die Rede; √רכב).

ri-ga-b(p)u. II 37 *h* = ir-ka-bu (*g*), in a list of birds; Eth. *regêbe*, pigeon? AV 3861, 7557; Br 13968.

ragagu. perh. be bad, wicked {schlecht, böse sein} L^TP 86. *del* 199 (219) rag-ga-at a-me-lut-tu i-rag-gi-ig-ki, KB vi (1) 244, 245: ist dir das Schlimme des Menschen schlimm (??; see *ibid* 509). — ℑ ZA iv 11 (K 3182 iii) 15 ša rug-gu-gu (as for him who has done evil) tu-mas-si dīnšu.

DERR.: targigu & these 2:

raggu *adj* or *noun*. evil, the evil, wicked {böse, schlecht} AV 7453. — wickedness {Böses, Schlechtigkeit}. D^M 15. KB vi (1) 380 = Hebr רע. × çēnu (but ZA xviii 47 *rm* 4 *cf* ضغن, hate) & kēnu, *q. v.*, for Sn v 82; Neb ii 28; T^M iv 2. IV² 17 *b* 15 Šamaš muxalliq rag-gi. K 710 *O* 5 rag-gu ixaliq, THOMPSON, *Reports*: violence. V 64 *c* 24 Anunītum sāpinat (*q. v.*) (amêl) nakru muxalliqat ra-ag-gu (*c* 35 rag-gu); IV² 49 *b* 24 (= T^M i 111); Neb ix 36 ra-ag-gu la i-ša-ra. K 3182 i 56 kit-mu-su rag-gu u ki-na, AJSL xvii 136. IV² 51 ii 10 i-te-e rag-gi i-ti-qu. Sp II 265 *a* xxiii 5 u-ka-an (*var* kan)-nu rag-ga (*var* gu) ša an zil-la-šu, ZA x 11. K 2061 i 13 (H 202) ŠA-NE-RU (*cf* NE-RU = a-a-bu) = rag-gu, followed by a-a-bu; çi-e-nu. Br 4607; H 41, 291. Same id in IV^2 1* iv 33, 34 gal-lu-u ša rag-gu ma-lu-u šûnu; 28 *no* 1, 11—12 O Šamaš ke-na ti-di rag-ga ti-di; 15, 16 rag-gu ki-ma qi-na-zi it-tar-rak-ka; V 50 *a* 27, 28; II 16 *a-b* 62. K 3364 *O* 20 a-na rag-gi-ka. K 2107, 20 na-si-ix (*q. v.*) rag-gi ‖ muballû napxar a-a-bi, Br 14392; AV 5411. *f* raggatu see ragagu. Perh. IV^2 50 iii 2 a-tab-bak ana qaqqad rag-ga-ti šim-ti-ki. See also KB vi (1) 64, 28.

riggatu. wickedness, injustice {Schlechtigkeit, Ungerechtigkeit} Sarg *Cyl* 52 aš-šu ri(-ig)-ga(-a)-te la šub-ši-i, not to do injustice, KB ii 46, 47; AV 7558.

ragamu, *pr* irgum (ZA iii 87); *ps* iraggum & iragam. AV 7452. Lagarde, *Mittheilungen*, ii 177. Eth. *ragâma*, Arb رجم. — *a*) cry, shout, call {schreien, rufen}. D^H 50; AJP iv 349. S^c 320 gu-u |KA| ra-ga-mu; H 10 + 208, 50; Br 540 & see rigmu. — *b*) object, make objection; claim (in court), sue {einwenden; Einspruch und Anspruch erheben, reklamieren, klagen (vor Gericht)} chiefly in *c. t.* (T^C 126, 127; Peiser, *Vertr.*, 323). AV* 56 *a* quotes ni-ir-gu-mu; tar-gu-mu (3 *f sg*). Pinches, *Inscribed Tablets*, 54—55, 4 and Y. ir-gu-mu-ma, laid claim; 23, a-xu-um a-na a-xi u-ul i-ra-ga-mu. Nabd 668, 19 a-na eli amêlut-tu šu-a-tu la ra-ga-mu, and that there be no suit concerning this slave-woman; 356, 12 a-ar-gum-ma (1 *sg*); 477, 29 i-ra-ag-gu-mu. V 29 *c-d* 46 ana la-a ra-ga-mi (ZA vii 22; H 69, 41 -me; BA i 292), preceded by ana la-a e-ni-e. Bu 91—5—9, 511, 8 ir-gu-mu-ši-im-mu, they made claim against her; *ibid* 16 u-ul i-ra-ga-mu; 387, 11 ša la ra-ga-mi (JRAS July '97, 601; *ibid* 597 *foll*: Bu 91—5—9, 367, 15 u la i-ra-ga-am, he shall not make claim); KB iv 160 (below) i/ii 2; Neb 135, 25. KB iv 158, 30 ana a-xa-meš ul i-rag-gu-mu (ZA iii 220, 32 i-ra-ag-gu-mu). V 68 *no* 1, 38 ša i-rag-gu-mu um-ma, who will put in the following claim. V 25 *c-d* 6 u-ul i-ra-ag-gu-um-ši, he shall not claim her (Meissner, 103; Br 676). KB iv 46 *no* i 6 u-ul i-ra-ag-ga-mu-ši-im; 14, 8 i-ra-ga-mu-ma (= 3 *pl*) construed with a-na (against). Perh. II 9 *b* 55 [i-rag]-gu-mu. Bu 91—5—9, 704 (dedication of a temple) 13, 14 a-na ša-gu-ti-im u-la i-ra-gu-um, against the priesthood he will not bring action; 17 ša i-ra-ga-mu, but he who brings action (JRAS '99, 105); Bu 91—5—9, 419, 25 a-na ri-šu-tim la ra-ga-mi, JRAS '99, 106, 107.

Q^t K 168, 23 tar-tu-gu-mu, (3 *f*).

Š KB iii (1) 160, 34—5 i-da-ab-bu-bu i-rag-gu-mu | u-šar-ga-mu u-ma-'-a-ru.

Derr.: targumânu, turgumannu & these 5:

ragâmu *nom. n.* Peiser, *Vertr.*, cxiii 20 mimma dînu u ra-ga-mu, any suit or claim.

rugummû. reclamation, complaint {Anspruchserhebung, Klage} AV 7635; § 65, 38. ‖ puqurrû, *q. v.* rugummû apalu perh.: refute a complaint. V 68 *no* 2, 31—2 a-pil (= *ac*) ru-gum-ma-a (ZK i 161) ul i-ši ul i-tur-ru-ma; a-xa-meš ul i-rag-gu-mu (& *ibid* 1, 35—6). See also Neb 135, 24—25; KB iv 158 i 28, 29; 160 (below), 1; 88 iv 34, 35; Br. M. 84—2—11, 138. Bu 91—5—9, 2468, 11 ru-gu-mi-šu-nu i-zu-xu, they rejected their claim. V 67 *no* 1, 31—2 ap-lu ru-gu-um-ma-a; Peiser, *Vertr.*, 96, 12; 97, 25. II 48 *g-h* 28 (K 4317 *O* 6) KA-GAL-LA = ru-gu-um-mu-u, Br 540; 612 (K 4317 *O* 12).

rigmu, *m. c. st.* rigim, AV 7559. — *a*) cry, shout, lamentation {Ruf, Schrei, Wehgeschrei}. S 747 *R* 10 (end) rig-mu ša im-bu-u. Asb vi 101 ri-gim a-me-lu-ti (*var* amêlûti) *etc.* .... uzammâ ugârêšu (KB ii 208—9; Winckler, *Forsch.*, i 252); KB ii 254, 37 ri-gim a-me-lu-ti ap-ru-sa çêru-uš-šu. K 774, 4 ri-gim nakri ibašši. VAT 4105 ii 7—8 a god saw and answered a-na ri-ig-mi-ja, *Mitth. der Vorderasiat. Gesellsch.*, '02, *no* 1. Sp II 265 *a* xxv 6 ri-ig-mu ul iš-ša-bu iš-ša-pil at-mu-u-a. KB vi (1) 280, 281 *col* 3, 10 sur-r]iš li-çi ri-gim-ši-na namtâru (+ 282, 14; also 280 iii 2; 284 iii 40); 288, 289 *col* 2, 18 ri-ig-ma u-še-lu; *col* 1, 5 ri-g[i-i]m-ši-in. IV^2 6 *col* vi 20 ça-'-i-rat ri-gim-šu, Br 700. V 48 vi 29;

49 xi 5 ri-gim ki-di; K 44 (H 78) 25 ri-gim ša kîma a-li-e. *del* 111 (118) the mistress of the gods is called ṭa-bat rig-ma (KB vi, 1, 239, die schönstimmige; H^F 56; BA i 131, 132; $J^{I\text{-}N}$ 34, die freundlich redende). IV² 1* *col* iv 2 niš (il) IM be-ili ša ri-gim-šu ṭa-a-bu. K 4623 (H 122) *O* 12, 13 O Lady, ina zurub libbi rig-me zar-biš ad-di-ki (see zarbiš, 295 *col* 2); V 21 *c-d* 20 (Br 624); K 890, 13 it-ti-di-i ri-ga-an-šu, thus rigamu perh. = rigmu, BA ii 634. NE IV (v) 3 (il) Xum-ba-ba rig-ma-šu (‖ ikkillu) a-bu-bu; V 40 *g-h* 8 (ta-al) AŠ = ri[-ig-mu], followed by ši-s[i-tum], ta-nu[-qa-tum], ik-ki[l-lu]; see also Jeremias, *Diss*, 41 on K 4119 *O*. — *b*) noise {Geräusch}. NE XII (i) 23 ri-ig-ma (of the feet) a-na erçitim la ta-šak-kan (KB vi, 1, 258—9); K 712, 6 ša-ni-iš ri-ig-mu išúkan. IV² 24 *a* 40 ša ana ri-gim še-pi-šu; II 19 *a* 2 see ramamu (Br 700). Sn iii 53 ri-gim kakkēja dannūti (he feared); *Kui* 1, 35; Sarg *Khors* 26. ri-gim (= KA) ta-xa-zi ez-zi, IV² 13 *b*, on edge of the tablet; *ibid* 22, 23 rig-ma (= KA) ez-za. T. A. (Lo.) 29, 15 iš-tu ri-ig-mi-šu; 13, he who id-din ri-ig-ma-šu (= thunders) in the heavens. KAT³ 450 *rm* 9. — *c*) noise, made by flies {Gesumme von Fliegen} *etc.* V 40 *e-f* 47 see zumbu, 283 *col* 2. — S^c 317 gu-u | KA | ri-ig-mu (H 10+209, 51) Br 541. V 16 *a-b* 23 AD-SAR-A = ri-ig-mu zar[-bu?] Br 4174. Z^B 55 also S^b 1 *R* iv 2; V 38 *g-h* 2 rig(or šim?)-mu. K 4166 *O* 6 GIŠ = rig-mu, M^S 104 × 81 *col* 2. See also ZA xvii 268 *ad* 81, 2—4, 206 *O* 22.

ragimu, *f* ragintu. Epithet of Adad. KAT³ 446. ZA iv 215 ra-gi-mu. K 168 (Hr^L 437) 23 (sal) ra-gi-in-ti (26, -tu) Lehmann, ii 76: Ruferin. K 883, 1 (oracle of Beltis) (ilat) Bēltu kab-ta-at (sal) ra-gi-in-tu, BA ii 633, 634. K 540 *O* 6—7 ra-gi-in-tu ša ki-zip-pi ša šarri (Hr^L 149).

raggimu, some title. Bezold, *Catalogue*, 1739 mentions Quqî (amēl) rag-gi-mu.

rigimtu (?). K 9287 iii 3 a-na ri-gim-tu. Xammurabi-*letters* 27, 10: I ri-gi-im-tu (something that was to be taken along on an expedition) BA iv 457.

ragā(n)nu (?). Xammurabi-letters 6, 15 (+6) ra-ga-a-nu-um; BA iv 442 der Schurke; but see *ibid*, 488.

רגן & רגץ see margannu, margunu, marguçu.

rādu *1.* thunderstorm, torrent, rain {Gewittersturm, Regen} §§ 27; 32 *aγ*; 47; 65, 1. G § 9 (רעד); AV 7459; Jensen, ZA i 245 *rm* 1: > radju √radū, flow. III 34 *b* 52 see gabšu, 211 *col* 2. Neb *Bors* ii 1 *etc.* see zunnu, 285 *col* 2. Sarg *Nimr* 15 i-na ra-a-di ti-ik šame-e. *var* to *del* 122 (129) shows ra-a-du almost ‖ a-bu-bu. KB vi (1) 238, 239; H^{NB} 140 *rm* 3: *Dibbara-legend* (K 2619) i 27 ūšmā-šu-nu ki-ma mê ra-a-di tu-ša-aç-bi-tam ri-bit Eli, KB vi (1) 60, 61. 83—1—18, 47 *O* 8 ri-ix-çu u ra-a-du rabûti *pl* ibaššû *pl*.

rādu (?) ***2.*** pursue {verfolgen}? Q $Z^Š$ ii 56 ki-nu-u i-ru-ud (*var* car)-du i-rat-tu-tum, pursues (and) oppresses the just (3 *sg pr*).

rūdu (?). Dar 11, 5: V šiqlu kaspi ša irbi ana muxxi ru-u-du; Camb 295, 13.

radū, ridū 1. *pr* irdi (§ 108); *ps* iré(d)di, *ip* rid(it?); *ag* redū, *c. st.* red (rid). KB vi (1) 317 original meaning: tread, whence (1) follow after, pursue, (2) subdue, *subigere*, (3) cohabit. *id* mostly UŠ. AV 7460. thus — *a*) tread, walk {einen Schritt tun, gehen} Zimmern, *Ritualtafeln*, 1—20 *ll* 75, 82 *etc.* mir-di-tu ... ta(& te)-red-di. H 127 (K 257) 52 a-šib pa-rak-ki kib-sa iš-ten i-ri-id-du-ni (§ 110). Asb i 77 ur-ru-xi-iš ar-di-e-ma, ‖ al-lik; viii 81 ir-du-u (+105) ur-xi ru-qu-u-ti (= 3 *pl*) ‖ il-li-ku (& KB ii 236—237, 14); V 55, 23 i-red-di (3 *sg*) ‖ il-lak (22). Asb ix 14 the whole night ar-di-e-ma (‖ al-lik a-di, *etc.*); v 90. Sarg *Ann* 143. — *b*) follow {folgen, nachgehen} TP III *Ann* 33 ar-ki-šu-nu (161—2 ar-ki-e-šu) ar-di-e-ma. V 63 *a* 12 seu suppū. *ip* perh. S^P II 967, 7 rid-di (*Jour. Trans. Vict. Inst.*, xxix 52: descend, √aradu?). Scheil, *Rec. Trav.*, xx 57 *foll*, *col* vii 23 li-ir[-di ... Sp II 265 *a* xxiii 11 u ja-a-ši id(t)-nu-šu bêl pa-ni ri-dan-n[i?], ZA x 11. — *c*) fetch {holen} Xammurabi-*letters* 34, 7 a-na ..... ri-di-e-im. — *d*) flow {fliessen} see Š & perh. V 22 *h* 50 ra-ma-at ra-di i-ni, preceded by ši-gu-u, Br 11615; Z^B 28; 93. Also P. N. of river Radānu. — *e*) pursue {verfolgen} (ZA iii 200). TP iv 100 lu ar-di-šu-nu-ti, I pursued them. Anp iii 42 ar-di-šu. Sn iii 81 ina ubānāt xuršāni ar-di-šu-nu-ti, up to the mountain peaks I pursued them. IV² 60* C *R* 4 kal ūmu re-du-u i-ri-id-da[n-ni], continually the pursuer pursues me. IV² 49 *a* 79 bēl ri-de-MU (= ja) u bēlit ri-de-MU (*cf* H 128, 70—71); IV² 48 *a* 34 i-na çi-bit-ti a-a-bi ir-rid-du-u (or ℵ?). K 4289 *R* 11 di-ku-ut māti ir-ri-du[-u] BA ii 572; K 2729 *R* 2 (35) di-ku-tu la ir-ri-du-u, BA ii 566: Aushebung soll man nicht veranstalten. pm TP III small-inscr. i 24 xu-ša-xu ra-da-at nišē, famine pursued the people. — T. A. (Ber) 9 *R* 15 (amēlu) Su-ti-i ra-di-e il-qu-u-ni. — *f*) drive {treiben}. II 24 *a-b* 57 (33 *a-b* 37) UŠ = ri-du-u (preceded by makkaru ša imēri, 540 *col* 1); 60, (II 33 *a-b* 40) GUD-UD-DA-UŠ = redū ša alpi (Br 5748: raise cattle); thus ⊕ 51 iv 9 re-id alpi, *cf* nāqidu, (719); ZA ii 200 *no* 2. K 4386 (II 48) i 21 KI-KU(ku)-AMĒL = re-id alpē (Br 9826) together with ikkaru. K 4395 (II 31 *no* 5) iii 29, 30 (amēl) UŠ (imēr) A-AB-BA *pl* = rid udrātē, & (amēl) UŠ (imēr) gam-mal *pl* = rid gammalē, camel driver; iv 3 (amēl) UŠ (imēr) ABAD = rid imēri, donkey driver. Lo 101 iii 13 Marduk .... i-na limut-ti li-ir-di-šu, BA ii 146. *Rec. Trav.*, xix 43 *ll* 2—3 (from the top) a-na KA-AN-RA-KI li-ir-di-a-aš-šu-nu-ti (BA iv 89/90: bring them). VATh 4105 i 4 (never) me-e i-ri-id-di ša-ri, does the wind drive the waters, *Mitth. Vorderas. Gesellsch.*, '02 *no* 1. — *g*) lead, govern, rule {leiten, regieren}. Asb i 29 whence Esarhaddon gimir malkē ir-du-u. IV² 48 *a* 8 the gods .... UŠ^me-šu = iredū-šu. Perh. II 67, 7 (amēl) Ra-di-e; AV 7457. II 24 *a-b* 58 (II 33 *a-b* 38) MIR (u-ku-uš) UŠ = ri-du-u ša çābē, Br 5041, 6960; BA iv 485 = ag Militärbehörde; see also ZK ii 302; BA iv 85—7 (K 4228 iii 28 *fol*). JOHNS, AJSL, XIX 171, a "ganger" (on his civil side), or a "field-cornet" (on his military side). Br 12222 reads II 26 *e-f* 14 (pa-xa-rum) ri-du-u ša en-še-e. II 16 *b-c* 33 ip-pi-ra ri-dan-ni, Br 5041; BA ii 285; and see ZA xvi 204, 5 (end), 220, 31 ebūru ired-di, ZA xvi 238. — II 24 *a-b* 57, 59 (II 33 *a-b* 37, 39) UŠ = ri-du-u (S^b 228; Br 5041); DUL = ridū ša ri-du-ti (Br 9586), JENSEN, KB vi (1) 317 succession {Nachfolge} against DELITZSCH, HWB, 614 *col* 1: IV רדה. V 15 (*c*-)*d* 11 ša ri-di-i (preceded by kut-tin-nu, *q. v.*); AMIAUD, ZA iii 44; Br 14434.

Q^t *a*) tread, march {gehen, marschieren} Anp ii 54 the (whole) night ar-te-di (104); *Mon*, *R* 22 (§ 34*a*). Neb ii 23 u-ru-ux zu-ma-mi e-ir-te-id-di-e-ma, I traversed; K 3182 iv 5 mi-xir-ti nāri ša ir-te-du-u, who travels along the river, AJSL xvii 142—3. — *b*) follow {folgen, nachgehen} 81—7—27, 152 *R* 12 xu-u]d libbi ṭu-ub šīri li-ir-te-da-an-ni, may follow me; BA iv 167. 'with arki = after one = pursue {verfolgen}. Anp iii 41 arki-šu ar-te-di (III 5 *no* 6, 14); ii 114 arkē(?)-šu-nu ar-te (*var* ti)-di; *Mon*, *R* 32; Šalm, *Ob*, 80, 167; *Mon*, *R* 69; III 4 *no* 1, 40—41; Šamš ii 50 (-te-); iii 31/2 (-ti-). — *c*) drive, lead {treiben, führen}. III 41 *b* 37 the gods ana limut-ti u la ṭāb-ti li-ir-te-id-du-šu (§ 110), may drive him to evil and misfortune. III 43 iv 14 (li-ir-te-di-šu); I 70 *c* 24 (li-ir-te-id-di-šu). Lo 103 vi 14 (UŠ-UŠ-šu). — I 27 *no* 2, 51 the gods ina le-te .... li-ir-ta-du-šu. IV² 2 vi 3/4, 5/6 the evil demon ... ir-te-di-šu (i⊃ UŠ), is leading him. — *d*) rule, govern {regieren, lenken} Šamš i 28 *NN*. mur-te-du-u ka-liš mātāte; Šalm. *Ob*, 16; *Mon*, *O* 6; Br 5069. H 75 *O* 9 mur-te-id-du-u (or ℑ^t?).

Q^tn Neb i 29 a-la-ak-ti ili er-te-ni-id-di, I walk god's way.

ℑ uraddi add {hinzufügen} with eli; ZK i 314; ZA iii 48. TP i 60 to Assyria land, to its inhabitants people lu-rad-di (I added); vii 32 lu-ri-id-di (*var* lu-rad-di). Sarg *Khors* 60 (64) 6 cities (districts) eli pixātišu u-rad-di (1 *sg*); 36: 200 chariots, 600 horses from the inhabitants of Hamath eli ki-çir šarrū-ti-ja u-rad-di. Lay 18, 36 ina eli pixāt biti (amēl) tur-ta-ni u (māt) Na-'-ri u-ra-ad-di (KB ii 8/9; ZA v

301); TP III *Ann* 180. Sn ii 23 these cities eli miçir (māt) Aššur u-rad-di; *Bell* 31; *Kuj* 1, 15 (u-re-di); Sn iii 28 mandattu .... u-rad-di-ma; III 12, 30; ZA iii 312, 59; 317, 84; Asb iii 26 (see mandattu); vii 5; 79—81; ix 126—128 see kaçaru, 2; kiçru, 2 (428). Neb viii 58 the structure it-ti ēkalli abi u-ra-ad-di-ma (1 *sg*); K 81 *O* 18 am-mar-ma u-rad-di-e-ma (Hr^L 274; BA i 198—200). IV^2 53 *c* 31 ma]-'a-du-tum ul am-ni ina libbi la ru-ud-du-u (= pm), has not been added; 7 *a* 28/29 mi-na-a lu-rad-di-ka (= RA-AB-DAX-E, Br 4538), what shall I add; 22 *b* 5/6 ‖ lu-uç-çip-ka. H 18, 314 da-ax | DAX | ru-ud-du-u; 51 (K 4350) iii 51 IN-TAB = u-rad-di (Br 3707), preceded by uš-te-ni & e-çi-ip; 53, 64 IN-SU-SU = u-ra-da (Br 174); 55 (K 46 i) 46 AB-BA-DAX = u-rad-di (Br 4538) preceded by NE-IN-DAX = uç-çi-ip, he added; also 54, 9. K 46 iv 15 MI-NI-IN-ZU = u-ra-ad-di, Br 137. V 45 iv 40 tu-rad-da.

Š let go, cause to go {gehen lassen} (§ 84). Smith, *Sn*, 93, 70 (*Kuj* 2, 24) to Bāb-salimēti u-šar-da-a ur-xi, I caused myself to go. Creat.-*frg* III 67 il-lik (il) Ga-za ur-xa-šu u-šar-di-ma; IV 59 uš-te-šir ma[-lak-šu u]r-xa-šu u-šar-di-ma. — *b*) let flow, make to flow {fliessen lassen}. TP i 79/80 dāmē-šu-nu xur-ri | u ba-ma-a-te ša šadi-i lu-šar-di; iii 29/31; 59/60; v 95/96; *cf* ii 15/16. Šalm, *Mon*, *R* 99 (u-šar-di); Asb iii 42 dāmē-šu-nu (nār) U-la-a-a u-šar-di; Šams iv 29. Sn *Bav* 12 mē šu-nu-ti u-šar-da-a (1 *sg*) ki-rib-ša (*i. e.* the canal), KB ii 116/117; *Kuj* 4, 35 ma-a-me dārūti a-šar-ša (in it, the canal) u-šar-da-a; Sarg *Khors* 128 u-šar-da-a ta-mir-tuš, he caused the Euphrates to overflow the (city's) pasture land (KB ii 70/71); *Ann* 324. Sn v 79 u-šar-da-a see munnu (559 *col* 1), simānu, 1 (766 *col* 2) & KB vi (1) 374. *del* 98 (108) see mexru, 1 *c* (582 *col* 2; & KB vi, 1, 236—7); H^{NE} 78 (beg). u-šar-da-a gul(zir?)-mu. IV^2 26 *a* 18, 19 bu-tuq-tum (a flood) which by night šur-da-at (breaks loose) = UD-DU-A (§ 89). II 34 *a-b* 18 [....] UŠ = šur-du-u ša A (= mē) Br 5041; in one group with bu-tuq-tum (17) & a-çi(?)-tum ša kib-ri (19). — *c*) pursue {verfolgen}? K 2852 + K 9662 i 2 (end) i-tar-ru-ra šur-da-a-šu (*cf* tararu). Scheil, *Notes d'Epigr.*, liv 5 ina qar-ni-ki tu-šar-di-i (*Rec. Trav.*, xxii).

Š^t 79, 7—8, 178 *R* 5 (KB vi, 1, 10) .... xar-r]a-an-ša-ma u-ru-ux-ša uš-tar-di, pursued its way. — Xammurabi-letters 4 *R* 4/5 mu-u a-na ši-ib-ri-im ga-am-ri-im | la uš-ta-ar-du-u, the water was not lead into the whole structure {das Wasser hat man in den Gesammtbau nicht hineinfliessen lassen} BA iv 440 *fol.*

Š3 cause to, let add {hinzufügen lassen}. Esh v 8 qaqqaru ma'adu .... e-li-ša uš-rad-di (1 *sg*; § 85); III 16 v 11 (-šu) KB ii 148; I 44, 61. Creat.-*frg* III 24 uš-rad-di (3 *sg*) ka-ak-ki (*var* -ka) la max-ri.

Derr.: mardītu, mirdītu (587), šurdūtu, terdū, terdeanu & these 3 (?):

rid(d)u(ū) 2., **ra-du.** son, child; servant {Sprössling, Sohn, Kind; Knecht}. II 30 *c* 30 (31) ‖ māru (581 *col* 1 § 2). Perh. KB vi (1) 92, 6 Ēa ki-ma rid-di ina a-me-lu-ti ib-ni-šu (KB vi, 1, 406; Scheil: pour gouverner l'humanité); Scheil, *Nabd*, iv 39 Labaši-Marduk .... la a-xi-iz ri-id-di (Messerschmidt: der nicht zu regieren verstand; thus properly ac of Q.) Rm III 105 i *b* 11 ri-du-u mut-nin-nu-u, Winckler, *Forsch*, i 254, 255; JRAS '92, 305 *foll.*

ridūtu. succession {Nachfolge}. So perh. with Jensen, KB vi (1) 317. AV 7562. Esh ii 41 māt tam-dim ... ri-du-ut axišu u-šad-gil pa-nu-uš-šu; III 15 ii 24. IV^2 38 i 14, 15 bīt Tu-na-mi-is-sa-ax | ša ri-du-ti (KB iv 60, 61). Asb iii 18 Erisinni mār ri-du (*var* UŠ)-ti-šu, Br 5041. K^M 53, 9 ri-du-su ušzīzu. K 2729 *O* 14 ša ultu ri-du-ti a-di e-peš šaru-u-ti, BA ii 566; KB iv 142, 143. IV^2 60* C *O* 6 ū-mu ri-du-ti (ilat) Iš-tar ni-me-la ta-at-tu-ru, BA i 229. IV^2 60* B *O* 11 a-mur-ma ar-kat ri-da-ti ip-pi-ru. BA iv 158 (below) reads T^M iii 147 ekimmu (*var* utukku) ri-da-a-ti xarrāni-ki u-ša-as-[si]; but whether these belong to this ridūtu, is not quite clear. — Note especially the phrase **bīt ridūti**. Asb i 2 Ašurbanipal mār-šarri rabū ša bīt-ridu (*var* UŠ)-u-ti (I 48 *no* 5, 8); x 51 bīt UŠ-u-ti, explained as te-ni-e ēkalli; 55, bīt UŠ-u-ti (i 23) šu-a-tu, + 103 (BA iv 276), + 110; 59, ki-rib bīt UŠ-u-te šu-a-tu; 91, ana epeš bīt ri-du (*var* UŠ)-u-ti šu-a-tu (*cf* 87) Br 5041. See Knudtzon, 68/9, 206, 219 *fol*, 222 *foll*. Meissner, ZA x 75: Regierungspalast (but see Asb x 51) nicht Harem, >< KB ii 152; see Jensen, ZA x 243. II 65, 27 *add* (AV 1822); Nabd 780, 3 bīt ri-du-tu. K 1619 *B* (III 16 *no* 2; Hr[L] 308; Hommel, *Gesch*, 694 *rm* 4; Amiaud, BOR ii 197 *foll*; Scheil, ZA xi 49; Winckler, *Forsch*, ii 58—59; JAOS xx 244—49) *R* 2 mārtu rabī-tu ša bīt UŠ-MEŠ-te; 6, mār-šarri rabū ša bīt-UŠ-MEŠ-te. V 21 *c-d* 18 DUL-LAL = ri-du-tu followed by Ē-DUL-LAL = e-du-lu-u, Br 9610. Bīt-ri-dūti = I-ridūti = Ἰριδώτις (Arrian, *Indica*) see Sachau, ZA xii 60.

ruddū. increased, enlarged, greater {vermehrt, vergrössert, grösser} V 61 v 28, 29 ina gi-ni-e i-çi u ru-ud-di-i, BA i 275.

radānu, name of a river. D[Par] 186; AV 7455; Anp ii 52 (nār) ra-da-a-nu.

radiānu, an officer (?). K 657, 9 ra-di-a-ni la-aš-šu, Hr[L] 102.

ridanū, offspring {Sprössling} Zimmern, *Ritualtafeln*, 61, 5 + 10 (ilu) Anunnaki ri-da-ni-e be-li-e rabu(-u)-ti; 62, 7.

ridū *3. phallus, penis*, Z[B] 67; but *cf* KB vi (1) 317. S[b] 228 uš | UŠ | ri-du-u (H 20, 371), AV 7561; Br 5041; II 24 *a-b* 57; ZK ii 302, 3. K 126, 18 zikaru itti sinništi ina šu-ta-ti-šu UŠ-šu it-ta-nap-la-as. II 16 *c* 11 see naxbaltu (663 *col* 1).

ridū *4*. V 28 *a-b* 22, 23 ri-du-u & rit(šit, kal, lak)-tum & kab(p)-b(p)u ‖ šit (rit)-tu-ku, AV 7561.

ri-du (?) S[c] 5 *b* 7, AV 7560; Br 2983.

r-d-m, see na(i)r-damu, 728 *col* 1.

radub(p)u. 82—8—16, 1 *O* NU-UN-ME = ra-du-b(p)u, preceded by taq-qa-ku.

radadu pursue {verfolgen} AV 7454. Sarg *Ann* 70 (140) ir-du-du. TP v 92 ab-ku-su-nu lu ar-du-ud, defeated I pursued them. NE 78 (K 8582) arki-šu-nu ar-du-ud ax-muṭ ur-ri-ix. Sn vi 21 a-na ra-da-di-šu-nu (*i.e.* the enemies). K 2924 *R* 9 SAR = ra-da-du : A-RI-A = xa-ra-bu, Br 4330. KB vi (1) 300 *col* ii 7 ar-du-ud; ZA vi 242, 15 ana aššakku i-rad-da-ad. — ir-du-ud IV[2] 15* ii 10 see šadadu. ג V 45 iv 38 tu-rad-da-ad. ש P. N. Al-Ušardid (in Nippur), an early king.

riznu, ruzzunu see risnu, ruççunu.

ra-ax im-tu, II 28 *c-e* 4 = A-GAL-LA-TIL-LA, which in *l* 3 = ma-li-a me-e (see malū, 3 *p* 544 *col* 1); AV 7468; Br 11569.

ra-ax ki-di see ki-di (372 *col* 1).

(amēl) **ru-xi** T. A. (Ber) 104, 11 a-na-ku (amēl) ru-xi šar-ri, Jensen, ZA vi 256 compares רֵעֶה. KB v 309: officer; KAT[3] 650: Freund (?) oder Hirt (?) des Königs, see *ibid*, *rm* 1.

rēxu (?). K 747, 4 il-lak u-çu-um-me (√ açū) ri-e-xi a-na; Thompson, *Reports*: breeze.

rexū 1. *a*) pour, water, inundate {(be-, er-) giessen, überfluten}? *del* 219 (231) .... šit-tum ir-xu-u e-li-ja, KB vi (1) 243: Schlaf ergossen sie über mich; (*cf* 210). K 3182 ii 4 i-ri-ix-xi-šu-ma šit-ta ... N 3554 *R* 11 kīma šamu-u ir-xu-u er-çi-ti im-i-du šam-mu, AV 7577; but PSBA xxiii 120 *foll* reads er-çi-ti-im i-du-u-mu. Reisner, *Hymnen*, *p* 130, 25 bēlu Bēl ri-xu-ut ma-a-tum ana šadi-i tar-xi, 27, ri-xu-ut šadi-i ana māti tar-xa-a. Sp II 265 *a* iii 9 ku-ru-ra ir-xi-e (?) a-na niš-bi-e. T[M] vii 23 a-ra-xi-ka ra-ma-ni; 26, nar-ṭabu erçitim ir-xu-u; 28, li-ir-xi; see also vi 26? Perh. H 86—7, 68 mu-u ša ina ša-te-e ri-e-xu (NIR-A, Br 1417; BA i 475). — *b*) especially *a*. in sexual sense: cohabit. NE 11, 21 six days & seven nights Ēabani te-bi-ma Uxāt (ta) ir-xi (*var* i-ri-xi). DT 67 (H 119) 18, 19 i-ša-ri ri-xa-a il-ta-mad = MU-BA-AB-DUG-GA, EMESAL; to love aright she learned, Br 1249. H 108, 19 (II 48 *a-b* 25) MU-DUG-GA, EME-SAL = ra-xu-u (AV 7473) followed by ra-a-mu, = 114, 7; D 128, 67; V 11 *d-f* 19. S[c] 34 [g]i-iš | UŠ | ri-xu-u, Br 5042; S[c] 24 [du-ug] | XI | ri-xu-u, Br 8232. *β*. beget {schwängern, zeugen}. IV[2] 1* v 1/2—3 it is said of the evil utukku ša ri-xu-su-nu (= A-RI-A) iš-ta-at(?, Br 11459 -nu) ina ri-xu-ut (= A-RI-A) (il) A-nim | ib-ba-nu-u šu-nu; 1 i 22/23 ša ri-xu-ut (= A) (il) A-nim ri-xu-u (A-RI-A, Br 11358, 11458); 2/4. IV^{2} 21* *no* 2 *R* 1/2 (il) ANUNNA ša ri-xu-ut (il) A-nu ra-xu-u = pm (= AN-NA-A-RI-A). Rm 117, 24 ri-xu-ut ru-bi-e (?) ra-xu-u. T^{M} i 78; ii 40 ra-xi-MU (= ja) u ra-xi-ti-MU (= ja), see *ibid* 15 *rm* 1. V 31 *e-f* 6 ra-xu-u ‖ ba-nu-u aš-šu e-pe-ši. V 22 *a-d* 47 (raxû); 19 *c-d* 29 (rixû) see çallum, & Br 11359.

𝔔^{t} = 𝔔 *a*) IV^{2} 54 *a* 14 murçu *etc.* eli-šu ir-te-ix-xu-u im-ṭu-u ta-ni-xu (AJP xxii 462 √rēxu, remain).

ℑ IV^{2} 50 iii 36, 37, 38 AN-u (= šamû) a-na-ku] ul tu-lap-pa-tin-ni KI (= erçi)-tum ul] tu-ra-xi-in-ni zi-qit GIR-TAB ul tu]-kab-ba-si-in-ni, = T^{M} iii 151 *foll*; BA iv 159. T^{M} vi 54 .... u-ri-ix-xa-an-ni, hat mich vernichtet (?).

𝔑 II 47 *a-b* 27, 28 nišē māti adi ulla i-ri-xa-a (> irrixâ) explained by nišē ig-gam-ma-ra.

Derr. marxîtu (588 *col* 1), tirxâtu (?) and:

rixûtu. *a*) liquid {Flüssigkeit} KB vi (1) 44, 23 (Rm 282) taš-pu-ra-an-ni be-el ri-xu-ut nāri [....], das Nass des Flusses. Perh. IV^{2} 3 *b* 20 ki-ma [ri]-e-xu[-ut me-e?] tab-ku-ti ana erçitim li-rid, BA i 475 *rm* *. V 22 *a-d* 44 a-a | A | ri-xu-tum, properly: pouring out; then: what is poured out; also of the *semen virile*, but not exclusively, Jensen, KB vi (1) 365, 366. AV 7578; Br 11353. — *b*) *semen virile*; cohabitation, *etc.*; see rixû, 1. V 22 *a-d* 59 (UŠ-DUG-GA; same id = (la-a) ri-xa-tu, S 752, 5). K 4886 iv 24 (II 48, 24) XI-NIR = ri-xu-tum (Br 8232, 8264) together with ra-xu-u (25; Br 5053), zaraqu & zirqu. II 28 *d-e* 69 see parasu. V 46 *a-b* 46 (kakkab) A-EDIN (or RI) = ba-na-at ri-xu-tum. Reisner, *Hymnen*, *no* 71 *R* 23/4 Ê-DUG-GA = [bît] ri-xu-ti. Zimmern, *Ritualtafeln*, *no* 24 *O* 27 ri-xu-ut (amêl) nisakki, aus priesterlichem Geblüt; also 100, 36. Rost, 128: Geschöpf, Erzeugnis ≍ Z^{B} 83 *fol.*

To rixû as a derivative, Jensen refers also:

ruxû ‖ kišpu & ru'tu, spittle, saliva {Speichel, Geifer} id [illegible]-ZU; T^{M} 175 *col* 1. AV 7638. K 246 (H 90/1) ii 64 kiš-pu (*q. v.*) ru-xu-u (Br 795, 800) ru-su-u (Br 797); also K 2866, 63. IV^{2} 51 (K 150) ii 11/12 a-na kiš-pi u ru-xi-e qât-su u-bi-lu (3 *ag*). IV^{2} 26 *b* 15 sin-niš-tu ša ru-xi-e qât-su iltapat, a witch has touched his hand; 50 *a* 15 ina ru-xi-ša the witch has halted my walk ‖ ina imti-ša; 8 *b* 7 kiš-pu ru-xu-u ru-su-u; 49 *a* 20 [kiš]-pu-ša ru-xu-ša ru-su-u-ša lu pa-aš-ru; 57 *b* 12/13 like heaven may I become pure ina ru-xi-e ša ep-šu-u-ni; like earth may I become clean ina ru-si-e lâ ṭâbûti; *b* 37 e(-?)tammur (xur?) kiš-pe ru-xi-e zi-ru-ti; 17 *R* 23 ina mu-ux-xi bêl ru-xi-e-a lu-ta-lal a-na .... T^{M} vii *col* 4, 9 (supplemented by 81—7—27, 152 *R*) ... kiš-pi-ki ru-xi-ki, *etc.*, BA iv 167.

rêxu 1. leave over, as a rest {übrig lassen, als einen Rest} BA i 510 *fol.* T^{C} 127. Br. M. 84, 2—11 (*med*) ri-e-xi 15$^{1}/_{2}$ ṬU (šiqlu) kaspi, there remain 15$^{1}/_{2}$ *š* (Kohler-Peiser, ii 61), Peiser, KAS, 24—5; 90. KB iv 322—3 *col* 3, 27—8 a-ki ni-kâsi-šu | ša ri-e-xi (das geblieben ist). K 282 *R* 19 ri-xa u-çu-ra-a-te, Craig, *Relig. Texts*, ii *pl* 17. Scheil, *Rec. Trav.*, xx 202 (*no* XL) *col* 1, 10 ša ri-xu-u-ni. Perh. K 518 *R* 7 ri-e-xu e-gir-tu ina mux-xi-šu liš-pur-u-ni, Hr^{L} 245. Nabd 224, 6—7 ri-ix-tu i-di bîti ša *R* | ina pân *Ç* ri-e-xi, the balance of the house rent of *R* was placed at the disposal of *Ç* (for later payment).

𝔔^{t} T. A. (Ber) 86, 18 Beruna ir-ti-xa-at, is left over; 56, 21 Gebal alone ir-ti-xa-at (to me); 62, 10; 53, 8 (ir-ti[-xat?]); 89, 9—10 only *G* & *B* ir-ti-xa (*pl* or *dual?*) a-na ia-ši; 77, 54 and there is no city ša-a ti-ir-ti-xu, that would remain yours. (Lo) 12, 22 ir-ti-xu (= *pl*); (Ber) 74, 9; 75, 27; 77, 12 & 49; 84, 11. IV^{2} 54 *a* 14; BA iv 295; AJP xxii 462 (it remained).

ℑ IV^{2} 51 *b* 21 im-i-ru u-ri-ix-xu i-ku-lu (questions) = Z^{Š} ii 78 (3 *ag*). V 45 v 17 tu-ra-a-xa. — Derr. these 5:

rēxu *2. noun.* the rest of, remainder {der Rest von}. KB iv 92 *col* 2, 1 ri-xi eqli. ZA iii 132, 19 ri-xi $^{2}/_{3}$ ma-na 8 šiqlu 1 ba-ra (?) kaspi; Cyr 147, 15—16 su-luppe ri-xi ša, the dates are the rest of (the claim of); Camb 129, 1 ri-xi ŠUK-ZUN (PAT-XI-A = kurummati?); 144, 1—2: $^{1}/_{2}$ mana 7 šiqlu kaspi ri-ix-xi šīmi, the remainder of the price for. PINCHES, *Inscr. Tablets*, 3, 13 ina ri-xi, of the tax.

rēxu *3. adj* remaining, left over {rückständig, übrig}. Nabd 262, 4: $^{1}/_{2}$ mana 7 šiqlu kaspi re-xi. K 504 *R* 5 (Hr^{L} 157) end: ri-xu-ti (*i. e.* inscriptions). T. A. (Ber) 24 *R* 20 ardāni-ja ri-e-xu-tum; (Lo) 8, 6 a-na a-xa-ti-ja u a-na ri-e-xi-ti (or *noun*?) aššāti-ka (ZA v 154, 6); (Ber) 23, 41 ri-ix-ta u-nu-ta.

ruxxu (?) Neb 132, 19 alpē ru-ux-xu-ti.

rexānu, rest, remainder {Rest}. Nabd 273, 8 ku-mu ri-xa-ni ša çi-e-ni ša Bēl. Neb 249, 6 (18, 21) ri-xa-an ša šatti. PEISER, *Vertr.*, cliii 5 (+ 10, end) ri-xa-nu ša bīti (amēl) mār-šarri; cxxvii 5; P. N. see AV 7570 on K 679, 18 (amēl) Ri-xa-a-ni, Hr^{L} 212. a form like pa-qirānu.

rēxtu *1.*, **rēxi(ī?)tu, rixūtu** (?); *c. st.* rīxit (> rēxit?), *pl* rixēti, rixāti (?) rest, remainder {Rest, das Übriggelassene} T^{C} 127; ZA iv 69 *rm* 1. AV 7576, 7580. Anp iii 41 ri-ix-ta-šu-nu šadū Purātu ēkul, what remained of them, was destroyed (lit^{y} eaten) by the mountain (and) the river Euphrates. Esh *Sendsch*, *R* 45 (and often) ri-ix-ti mārē-šu, his other sons. Asb iv 81 the corpses of their inhabitants, ri-xi-it u-kul-ti kalbē šaxē, (as much as) remained of them after dogs and swine had eaten thereof (WINCKLER, *Forsch.*, i 473 *rm*), K 1252 *a*, *O* 12/13 mu-muq ri-ix-ti | sisē(-) ka(-)a-li-i, Hr^{L} 529. Bu 89—4—26, 161, 1 an-ni-u ri-ix-ti | da-ba-a-bi ša (Hr^{L} 435; AJSL xiii 210). K 2701 *a* 15 ri-ix-ti ma-ta-a-ti (HEBR. ix 1—3). III 58 *b* 37 ri-ix-ti di-ib-bi (55 *c* 44). Z^{B} iii 120 (ma-mit) ri-xi-e-te (*var* -ti) ta-me-i ša-tu-u; *cf* iii 22; 124 ri-xi-it bēl ar-ni. — Nabd 299, 7 a-xi (a part of) kaspi ina mišil šatti u ri-ix-ti kaspi ina kīt šatti inaddin; Cyr 228, 5—7 a-xi kaspi ina ri-eš šatti u ri-ix-tum kaspi ina mi-šil šatti i-nam-din; Camb 97, 7; Cyr 130, 13 ri-ix-ti kaspi. BA i 510. Camb 12, 3—4 ri-xi-ti sat-tuk ša Ṭebēti; 128, 1—2 V ṬU (šiqlu) kaspi ri-xi-tu ša pap-pa-si; 231, 1 ri-xi-it šīmi, the remainder of the price. Cyr 320, 1 ri-ix-ti šīmi of the field of . . . (also ZA iii 214, 1). Neb 91, 1: IV ma-na kaspi ri-xi-it nu-din-nu-u, the balance of the dowry of . . .; also 9/10; 350, 1: XX šiqlu kaspi ri-ix-tum i-di, the balance of the rent; 165, 1: II ma-na kaspi ina ri-ix-tum nu-dun-nu-u (& 9: ri-xi-tu). Sp 38, 1: III mana IV šiqlu kaspi ri-xi-e-ti. Cyr 248, 3/4 Ri-xi-e-ti gallu, a P. N. (AV 7575); Nabû-ri-ix-tu-uçur. On rixtum with imittum, see suluppu. T. A. Rostow. 2, 9 aššatika a-na ri-xu-ti aššātika.

raxaxu (?) V 29 *g-h* 14 SUD-SUD = ra-xa-xu, followed by zi-ir-qa-tum, Br 7618. II 35 *e-f* 46 ra-xa-xu ‖ ta-xa(?; AV 7468 ma)-xu.

רחל = whence marxallu (587 *col* 2).

raxultu. T. A. (Lo) 1, 61 ki-i ta-na-an-din mārātika a-na ra-xul-ta (in trust?) √raxaçu, 1.

raxamu (?). be piteous; *cf* P. N. Raximū; Ra-xi-ma-a (JOHNS, *Doomsday-Book*, 1 ii 27; & *ibid*, *p* 37; also *no* 3 iii, end); Ra-xi-im-ilu; HILPRECHT, *Babylon. Expedition of the Univ. of Pennsylv.*, A, IX *p* 69 *col* 1. — Also SCHEIL, *Notes d'Epigr.*, xxvii *no* 174 (il) Nin-ib ra-xi-im gi-ri-im, *Rec. Trav.*, xix: *N* aime la guerre. In T. A. we have (Lo) 2, 34 šum-ma ta-ra-ax-ma-an-ni (ZA v 152, 153); 37, 41 a-ra-ax-am, I love; (Ber) 43, 40 i-ra-xa-mu(-ma). Either a loan-word or a by-form of rāmu, PSBA xxi 254.

raxapu. IV^{2} 30* *no* 3 *O* 12 i-ra-xa-pu, but read *sa*, instead of ra & *cf* סחף.

raxaçu 1. *pr* irxuç & irxiç. *ps* iraxxuç. await, trust, have confidence in, with eli, ana eli {warten, harren, vertrauen} AV 7470. D^{Pr} 42 & *rm* 1; NÖLDEKE, ZDMG 40, 726. Asb v 102 e-li šutti an-ni-ti ummāni-ja ir-xu-çu, upon this dream my army trusted. K 3456 *O* 30 ir-xu-ça qar-ba-a-tum; 32, aš-rat la mi-riš-ti ir-ri-ša ra-ax-çu, PSBA xxi 38, 40.

Bu 88—5—12, 101 ii 6—7 lib-bi ar-xu-uç-ma. K 17 *R* 19 li-ir-xu-uç; + 18 ru-xu-uç ša ardē'a. IV² 47 *c* 33 šarru bēlija lu-u ra-xu-uç (perh. K 2085 *R* 5). K 175 (Hr^L 221) *R* 5—6 (and who in due reverence to my lord) ina eli LU-MEŠ | be-ili li-ir-xi-ça-aš-šu (trusts); K 524 *R* 14 a-na mux-xi-ni ta-ra-ax-xu-uç, (in order that) you may have confidence in us (Hr^L 282; Johnston, JAOS xviii 134—8). K 646 *R* 2 a-na eli šarri be-ili-ja ra-ax-ça-ku (Hr^L 498). P. N. KB iv 164 *col* iv 35 a-na Ra-xaç u mārē-šu.

Q^t K 2801 + K 221 + K 2669 *R* 27 (end) at-ṭa-kil-ma ar-ta-xu-uç, BA iii 236.

Š inspire with confidence, trust {Vertrauen einflössen}. Bu 88—5—12, 75 + 76, vii 30—1 zaqap çippāti . . . u-šar-xi-is-su-nu-ti, BA iii 246—7. Sarg *Ann* 250 u-šar-xi-su-nu-ti. Esh iv 2 grace I granted him and u-šar-xi-is-su lib-bu, and made (his) heart confident. V 45 v 23 tu-šar-xa-aç. Smith, *Asurb*, 123, 47 (III 32, 42) fear not, she said, u-šar-xi-ça-an-ni lib-bu (and made my heart confident, § 90*c*).

Derr.: marxaçu, 1 (587 *col* 2); raxultu; &:

rixçu, confidence {Vertrauen} I 44, 72—3 aban qa-bi-e ma-ga-ri (511 *col* 1) u ri-ix-çu; but M^S 88 *col* 2, below, to rixçu, 2.

raxaçu 2. *pr* irxiç & irxuç; *ps* iraxxaç. inundate, flood {überschwemmen}; to bathe, wash, sprinkle {baden, waschen}; also used figuratively. Nöldeke, ZDMG 40, 727; Halévy, RÉJ xiv 158. AV 7470. H 88—9 ii 29 ša ina çi-rim ⁽¹¹⁾ Adad ir-xi-çu-šu, Br 6361. V 50 *b* 44, 45 the birds of heaven ki-ma ⁽¹¹⁾ Adad ir-xi-iç (= IM-MI-IN-RA-AX, Br 6373; H 187). TP III *Ann* 172 kīma ri-xi-iç it-ti (but Rost, *TP. III Ann*, corrects to ri-xi-iç-ti) ⁽¹¹⁾ Adad ar-xi-iç-su [-nu-ti-ma]. K 175 *R* 6 ina eli kirrē bēli li-ir-xi-ça-aš-šu, (Hr^L 221). I 70 iv 11 ⁽¹¹⁾ Adad ugāršu li-ir-xi-iç & *cf* III 41 ii 32 (IV² 39 *R* 38/39) ⁽¹¹⁾ Adad i-na ri-xi-iç li-mu-ti li-ir-xi-su. V 65 *b* 40 lu-ur-xi-iç mât a-a-bi-ja. K 19 *R* 2 ⁽¹¹⁾ Adad i-ra-xi-iç. Constant. 583 *O* 22 (a medical text) ina . . . . (karpat) nam-xar ta-tab-bak i-ra-ax-xa-aç (+ 24, end: et il se lotionnera). — *pm* K 1460, 2 umma] ra-ax-ça-tu-nu-u (a question); 3, ... ra-ax-ça-a-ni. 81—2—4, 63 *O* 9 *foll* ⁽¹¹⁾ Adad RA (= raxi)-iç & *cf* K 1399 *O* 1 iraxi-iç. 82—5—22, 49 *O* 7 (end) RA = raxiç. — *ag* TP i 9 ⁽¹¹⁾ Adad ra-xi-iç kib-rat nākirē mātāte; i 78 the corpses of their warriors I slaughtered ki-ma ra-xi-çi; iii 25/29. Anp iii 120 kīma ⁽¹¹⁾ Adad ra-xi-çi eli-šu-nu aš-gu-um; Creat.-*frg* IV 52 (= D 97, 17) nišē] la pa-du-u ra-xi-çu mu-up-par-ša. Rm 290 *O* 5 ra-xi-iç kul-lat la ma-gi-re ‖ mušaknišu. — H 114, 12—13 A-MAR-RA (Br 11521) = A-GAR-RA (Br 11707) = mê ra-xa-çu (*var* -zu) Br 5434, 5818, 6831 (14, = mê ša-xa-tu); A-MA-MA (Br 11567) = A-GA-GA (Br 11510) = *m r.* S^c 180 ra-a | RA | ra-xa-çu, Br 6361; § 9, 76; H 23, 475. II 39 *no* 2, *O* 13 *g-h* RI-RI (Br 2591) = ra-xa-çu ša . . . preceded by na-sa-ku (*q. v.*) ša A[-MEŠ?] = mê. V 22 *a-d* 76 me-e A | a-a-u | ra-xa-çu [mu-u??] Br 11351. II 24 *a-b* 42—45; 33 *a-b* 22—25 GAR = ra-xa-çu ša . . . (Br 11973); NER-ŠU-GE-GE = raxaçu ša amēli; NER-GA-GA = *r* ša šēpi (Br 9215); KU-KU-RU (Br 10652) = *r* ša a-ša-bi.

Q^t K 8905 vii 25 ⁽¹¹⁾ Adad ir-ta-xi-i[ç].

N Esh (Negoub-tunnel) 13 . . . bi . . . ir-ra-xi-iç-ma, was flooded, BA iii 206, 207; Scheil, *Rec. Trav.*, xvii 81, 82.

N^tn III 61 *a* 11 that ⁽¹¹⁾ Adad i-ta-na-ar-xi-iç, will inundate, BA ii 387.

Derr.: marxaçu, 2; marxuçu (587 *col* 2) and these 3:

rixçu 2. inundation, flood {Überschwemmung, Flut} § 65, 4. See raxaçu 2, and, TP i 42, 43 nab-lu šur-ru-xu ša ki-ma ti-iq ri-ix-çi a-na māt nu-kur-te šud-nu-nu. Anp *Mon*, *R* 24 kīma ⁽¹¹⁾ Adad ša ri-ix-çi eli-šu-nu aš-gu-um; and, thus, with KB i 88 read Anp ii 106 kīma ⁽¹¹⁾ Adad ša NER-BAL (= rixçi) eli-šu-nu aš-gu-um. 83—1—18, 197 *R* 11 . . . ri-ix-çi la iq-ri-ib; Z^B 8, 18 ⁽¹¹⁾ Ram-ma-nu ri-ix-çu. See also rādu & rixçu 1. II 43 *d-e* 20 me-iṭ-ru = ri-ix-çu (*ibid* 16*d*); & ‖ di-xu, 23; 24, ri-ix-çu dan-nu ‖

di-xu MI. AV 7579. V 31 *a-b* 60 SAL (?, or ŠI?)-RA = pa-an ri-ix-çu(m).

rixiç(l)tu, inundating rain, torrent, cloud-burst, *etc.* {überschwemmender Regen, Platzregen, Wolkenbruch} D^{Pr} 177; RÉJ x 305; xiv 156. AV 7573—4. TP iv 89—91 ša-qal-ti um-ma-na-te-šu-nu rapšāti ki-ma ri-xi-il-ti [il] Adad lu aš-ku-un. Šalm, *Mon*, *O* 46; *R* 98 like Adad eli-šu-nu ri-xi-il-ta u-ša-az-nin; *R* 50 ina eli-šu-nu ri[-xi-il]-tu u-ša-az-nin (KB i 166—7; KGF 134). II 32 *b* 15 ū-um ri-xi-iç-ti [il] Adad; Br 4963, 7896. II 27 *a-b* 51 . . . NE-RA-RA = RA (= rixil)-ti [il] IM (= Adad) Br 7864; IV^{2} 5 *a* 40, 41 ri-xi-iç-ti (= UD-NE-RA-RA) [il] Adad te-šu-u qar-du-te šu-nu.

raxxiçu. IV^{2} 58 *d* 32 ra-ax-xi-ça-at mut-tab-bi-lat mārat [il] Anim, ZA xvi 181 overthrowing, destroying, is the daughter of Anu (said of the Labartu).

raxaçu 3. T. A. (Lo) 26, 31 u lu-u ti-ra-xa-aç çābē bi-ta-at ša šarri bēli-ja, and may the troops of my lord . . . dash to pieces. (Ber) 184, 32 u an-nu-u ri-xi-iç mi amēlūti-ja, and behold! he has beaten my people. Rather to raxaçu, 2. in a figurative meaning. KB v רחץ √; KAT^{3} 653; but see HAUPT, AJSL xx 161.

raxāçu (?) V 30 *e-f* 20 USAN⊕DU = ra-xa-aç ū-me (Br 6349), H 24, 490; preceded by same id = ši-me-ta (H 24, 480 -tan); ZK i 315 *rm* 2 = evening.

רחש, *cf* marxašu (587 *col* 2; and add: JENSEN, ZA xv 229 *fol*).

ra-ax-ta. T. A. (Ber) 28 i 36 an Egyptian word.

raxatu (?) K 609 *R* 2 am-mar ša . . . . ri-xa-tu-u-ni, Hr^{L} 126.

rixtu 2. *c. st.* rixat, *pl* rixēti, AV 7571. — *a*) destiny, fate {Bestimmung, Geschick}. K 186, 29 (Hr^{L} 222 *R* 12) see mūšu (598 *col* 1, below). — *b*) offering (?) {Opfer, Darbringung} ROST, 127, 128 Abgabe. I 35 *no* 1, 24 Babylon, Borsippa and Cutha ri-xat Bēl, Nabū, Nergal lu-u iš-šu-ni. Sarg *Ann* 297 the inhabitants of Babylon and Borsippa . . . . ri-xa-at Bēl Çarpanīti Nabū Tašmētu . . . adi maxrija ublūnim(ma). K 589 *R* 1—4 ri-xa-a-te | ša [(il)] Nabū | a-na mār-šarri bēli-ja | u-si-bi-la (Hr^{L} 187; AJSL xiv 14 desires, orders or decisions; JOHNSTON, the greetings from Nabū). TP III *Ann* 7 ri-xat [il] Bēl, Nabū, Nergal a-di max-ri-ja [u-bi-lu-ni], see ROST, pref. xv & *rm* 1. NE 58, 7 . . . ri-xat niše eli-šu im-qut (??). Sm 193, 3 + 4 I, Ašurbanipal ri-xi-e-ti šarrū-ti-ja u-še-bil-šu ri-xi-e-ti ša-a-ti-na im-xur.

rāṭu *1.* (Hebr רַהַט?) ‖ pišannu (*q. v.*) receptacle, perh. in Sarg *Cyl* 39 (si-mat šarrū-ti zu-un-nu-nu) ra-ṭi-šu-un. then also: gutter, trough {Wasserrinne, Wasserbehältnis}. D^{Par} 142; D^{Pr} 1; 2 *rm*; ZDMG 40, 742. JENSEN-SCHULTHESS, 90: nur: Wasserlauf. IV^{2} 27 *no* 1, 9 il-daq-qu ša ina ra-ṭi-šu la i-ri-šu, PSBA xvi 197. 82, 5—22, 1048 *O* 11 i-na ša ki-rib tam-tim ra-ṭu-um-ma, KB vi (1) 40—41; 360; 519; 566: nur Brunnen, Wassergrube, Wasserlauf, >< JASTROW, *Religion*, 436. *del* 279 (315) ra-a-ṭa (*var* ṭu) ki-i ap-tu-u[-ma], + 302 (BA i 142, 145). II 38 *a-b* 18 BAB(, PAP?, KUR?)-E-RAD = ra-a-ṭu (19, me-kal-tum); BAB-E = palgu, *q. v.* JENSEN, KB vi (1) 566 compares also id A-RAT for purattu = Euphrates. Sp II 111 *no* 2, 8 ra-a-ṭu followed by me-ṭir-tum (9); 81, 2—4, 268, 5—6 (Br 1184) BAB-E-RAD = ra-a-ṭu, mi-iṭ-ru, *etc.* S^{b} 282 ši-ta | RAD | ra-a-ṭu, Br 2295. V 42 *g-h* 31 IM-DU(= KAK)-A = ra-a-ṭu, Br 8428; *l* 30 = pitqu. V 22 *h* 50 see ra(e)dū.

rāṭu *2.* K 55 *O* 22 U = ra-a-ṭu (a vessel?). K 8676 *R* 7 *a-b* U(?)-U = ra-a-ṭu.

rūṭu, spelled ru-u-ṭu, ru-ṭu, ru-ṭi; after numbers, perh. = our 'foot' in 3-foot *etc.* JOHNS, *Doomsday-Book*, 80 below.

raṭabu. be moist {feucht sein} *del* 205, 215 (225, 237) šanūtum muš-šu-k(q)at šalultum raṭ-bat. J^{I-N} 38; KB vi (1) 246—7; 511. AV 7544 reads V 22 *h-k* 55 ra-ṭa[-bu??]. ℑ moisten, wet, irrigate {befeuchten, bewässern}. K 10483 i (?) 8

---

ri-xi AV 7572 on Sarg *Cyl* 31 see dalxu (249 *col* 2); so also AV 7578 on K 194, 9; AV 7571 on K 3027, 3 nu-um-mir ri-xa-ti-ja, see dalixtu.

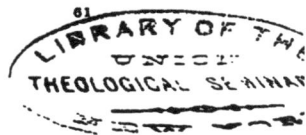

.... pa-šu u-ra-aṭ-ṭa-ab. V 45 iv 38 tu-raṭ-ṭa-ab.

Derr.: narṭabu, 1 (728—9) & these 5:

ruṭṭubu, *adj* II 30 *b-c* 69 SUN-A-SUR-RA = ru-uṭ-ṭu-bu, followed by ri-si-it-tum, AV 7640, Br 8973.

raṭbu *1. noun.* ditch {Graben}? Peiser, *Vertr.*, xxv 12 raṭ-bu ul u-ma-ru; lii 14 raṭ-bu u i-da-ak; see *ibid*, *p* 244.

raṭbu *2. adj. f* raṭubtu irrigated, moist, fresh {bewässert, saftig, frisch}. V 40 *e-f* 2 U-A = iç-çu raṭ-bu (Br 6088), a verdant, green tree. Sarg *Cyl* 61 am-ba-te ra-ṭu-ub-te, AV 7475; AJSL xiv 5. II 30 *b-c* 65  = raṭ-bu. *Cf* šapulu, 2.

riṭbatum. III 61 *a* 45 ri-ṭ-ba-tum will not prosper; perh. plantations, fields (?).

ruṭbu. moisture, irrigation {Feuchtigkeit, Befeuchtung} *etc.* § 25; AV 7544, 7639. V 22 *a-d* 61 (73) A (a-a) & (me-e) = ru-uṭ-bu, Br 11358.

rāku (?). II 36 *e-f* 72 XI (= SAR) = ra-a(??)-ku ša (Br 8230).

raku. T. A. (Lo) 35, 32 iš-tu-mi pa-ni Xa-an-ni ti-ir-ta-ki-i, from X ye have withdrawn (KB v 123 & *rm* *); from same stem as markītu (588 *col* 2).

rakabu, *pr* irkab, *ps* irakab (Barth, ZA ii 383/4; Knudtzon, *ibid* vi 417); *pm* rak-pa-ak (1 *sg*; L⁴ i 20; Lehmann, ii 67); *ip* rukub. AV 7478. — *a*) embark, enter (a vessel) {(ein Schiff) besteigen}. *del* 242 (272) $^{(11)}$ Gilgameš u Ur-ninim ir-ka-bu $^{(12)}$ elippu; NE X *col* iii 47 (= 11^{NE} 67) KB vi (1) 220, 221. NE 70, 16 ra-kib $^{(12)}$ elippi. I 28 *a* 2/3 ina elippē .... ir-kab. Smith, *Asurb*, 39, 21 ki-rib elippi ir-kab, KB ii 238. K 41 *b* 4 elippi ar-ka-bu, PSBA xvii 65 *foll.* — *b*) mount, a chariot, wagon {in einem Wagen fahren}. Creat.-*frg* IV 50 nar-kabta .... ir-kab. Sn vi 9/11 nar-kabāte .... ša ra-ki-bu-ši-in di-ku-ma, the chariots whose riders were slain, = רְכַב, BA iv 586 & *rm* *. 83—1—18, 187 *O* 1 when Sin in the month si-li-li-ti $^{(12)}$ narkabta ra-kib; also K 815, 3 (Thompson, *Reports*). V 65 *b* 33 ra-kib (*var* ki-ib) narkabta, said of Bunene (*cf* Ps 18, 11). id XU-SI in IV² 32 *O* 32; *R* 17 + 43; 33 *R* 5 + 38 šarru narkabtu ul XU-SI (= irakab); see also V 48 iii 23; 49 ix 26 elippa (& narkabta) NA-AN-XU-SI. — *c*) ride on horseback {zu Pferde reiten} Sarg *Ann* 109. Sn i 67 i-na sisē ar-kab; *Kui* 1, 10; *Bell* 21; L⁴ i 20 ši-tax-xu-ṭa-ku mur-ni-is-ki rak-pa-ak xi-iš-ša-tiš. — NE 49, 196 içça-btunimma illakūni su-qu ša Uruk rak-bu-u[-ni], they rode through the streets of Erech. III 56 *a* 17 Ummanmanda shall come and ana māti i-ra-ka-ba (‖ māta i-šal-lal); shall forage in the country. NE III (ii *a*) 14 (H^{NE} 20 + 80) gi-ir-ru ša la i-du-u i-rak-kab. — Of a mountain, that is to be ascended. IV² 56 *b* 48 ki-ma pu-rim çēri ša-da-ki ru-uk-bi, like a wild ass of the desert ascend thy mountain; also IV² 11 *a* 41, 42 ša-da-a ir-kab, Br 11352. T. A. (Lo) 72, 17 ir-ka-ab (= 1 *sg*). — Used figuratively Šamš i 10 Ninib ra-kib a-bu-bi, riding upon the whirlwind (§ 131). — To rakabu belong perhaps also II 33 *a-b* 11—14 XI-NIR = r]a-ka-bu (Br 8263) [which = rixūtu, & may perhaps have the same sexual meaning as rexū ("besteigen"; Syr רכב = cohabit); here perhaps also K 126, 12 zikaru ir-kab-šu rak-bi mitxariš ilikki; 14 (when a man approaches the bed) zi-ka-ru-ta ēpu-uš (, & sleeps with his wife)]; GUŠUR (Br 5498, = ka-tamu) = *r* ša ka-lal-lum; E-NE-SUD-UD-DA = *r* ša u-ma-ši (Br 7634; 5872 -mi); AN-TA-NA = *r* ša .... (Br 3967).

Q¹ *del* 243 (273) $^{(12)}$ elippu [gi-il-la id]-d[u]-u šu-nu ir-tak-bu; NE X iii 48; KB vi (1) 220/1; 248/9; J^{I-N} 54 *rm* 99. Sn v 56—58 i-na narkabat taxāzi-ja çir-ti ar-ta-kab xanṭiš. IV² 11 *a* 43, 44 ša-da-a ir-ta-kab.

Š embark people on a ship {ein Schiff besteigen lassen}. Sn iii 56 ilāni .... ki-rib elippē u-šar-kib, the idols .... he embarked; iv 31 ki-rib elippē u-šar-kib (1 *sg*). Smith, *Sen*, 92, 67 (Sn *Ku* 2, 21) i-na ki-rib elippē u-šar-kib-šu-nu-ti. Xammurabi-letters 34, 10 at once (ki-ma bi-tim = kīma pittim) the goddess in a ship šu-ur-ki-ba-am-ma, embark (also 19).

Št Creat.-*frg* IV 36 mul-mul-lum (550, 551) uš-tar-ki-ba, he burdened himself with (*i. e.* seized) the *m.* — H 81 (K 133) *R* 17, 18 šada-a uš-tar-kib (Br 8022), he rode up the mountain. — BOR i 48, 8 u-sa-ar-ki-pi, 1 *sg.* K 527, 20—21 ina eli sisē u-sa-ar-kib-šu (Hr^L 32 *R* 3, 4).

Derr.: narkabtu, nirkabtu (*p* 729), & these 5:

rakbu *1. c. st.* rakab (whence iD RA-GAB = mâr šipri, AV 7451); *pl* rakbē. § 65,16 *rm.* properly rider; then, messenger, envoy, ambassador {Reiter; Bote, Gesandter}. Sarg *Ann* 279 (*var*) rak-bu; 391; *Khors* 111 rak-bu-šu-un la išpu-ru. Sn iii 41 iš-pu-ra (he sent) rakbu-šu; ZA iii 312, 58. Asb ii 100 (amēl) rak-bu-šu iš-pu-ru (3 *pl*); Smith, *Asurb*, 72, 92; also Sarg *Ann* XIV 48; Šalm, *Balaw*, IV 2 u-ma-'i-ra rak-ba-šu. Bu 91—5—9, 418, 28 ra-kab-ja a-na be-li-ja lu-ub-lam; K 7673, 20 .... max-xu (amēl rak-bu u ça[-bu?]. Asb i 124 umâ'erū (amēl) rak-bi-e-šu-nu; + 129. Perh. also T. A. (Ber) 52 *O* 27. II 39 *g-h* 47 RA-GAB = mâr šipri; K 2675 *R* 19 *etc.* A ‖:

rakūbu (?) T. A. (Ber) 52 *R* 3 ra-ku-ba.

rakbu *2.* (?) T. A. (Ber) 26 i 4: I ma-il-dax-xu-ku rak-bi ša GIŠ xurāçu uxxuzu.

rakkabu. II 22 *a-b* 10 GIŠ-NIR-TUK (?) = rak-ka-bu, AV 7483; Br 6299, some object made of wood; perh. same as III 41 *a* 16 (+ 18): VI (+ II) rak-kab sisē (+ imēr) KB iv 74, 75; BA ii 151, saddle, harness?

rukūbu. — *a*) riding, driving {Reiten, Fahren} § 65, 19; BA i 177. Asurb i 34 where I had learnt ... ru-kub sisē narkabti (Sarg *Ann* 126 ina ru-kub sisē), to ride and to drive; ii 14 wagons, horses, mules I presented him a-na ru-kub bēlū-ti-šu. III 37 *a* 62; Nabd i 20 i-na sisē ru-ku-bi-ka. — *b*) wagon, chariot, cart {Wagen, Gefährt}. Esh iv 16 themselves, with their army, sisē ru-ku-bi-šu-nu. Sn v 80 see lasmu (492 *col* 1). II 66 *no* 2, 9—10 ina (iç) ša-da-di ru-kub šarrū-ti-ja açmidsunūti, KB ii 264, 265. I 7 *no* ix E 4 narkabta ru-kub šarrūtija. Neb 2, 4—5 a-na (iç) ru-ku-bu ša (ilat) Ištar; iii 72 ru-ku-bu ru-bu-ti-šu. K 8239, 10 GIŠ-MA'-XU-SI = ru-ku-bu; K 4560, 5 .... MA'-XU-SI | (malaxu?) ša ru-ku-pi (§ 19; Br 14041; M^S *pl* 12). T. A. (Ber) 28 ii 17 ru-ku-bu zi-xi-ru-ti (which are drawn by hand).

rukbu. — *a*) V 28 *a-b* 21 ši-pat ruk-bi ‖ a-ru in a list of clothings. does IV² 56 iii 48 (end) ru-uk-bi, belong here? — *b*) Zimmern, *Ritualtafeln*, 41—42 i 20 tarbaça ūra ruk-bi-e-ti (*var* -tu) apâti tultappat, den Hof, das Dach, die Balken (= the beams), die Fenster sollst du berühren. K 9873 *O* 6. ZA xv 119: perhaps connected with ritgubu, an architectural expression (ZA vii 20) & urtaggibši. See also M^S 89 *col* 1. — VATh 244 ii 28 ša ruk(q?)-bi ši-iq-bi, he of the riding on šiqbi (ZA ix 158: a kind of upright saddle).

rikbu 83, 1—18, 1332 iii 26. M^S 89.

rik(g, q?)ib(p)tu. AV 7581. V 22 *a-d* 45 a-a | A | ri-kib-tum (Br 11354) same iD = rixūtum; perh. the act of רכב in a sexual meaning.

rakūbu (q, p)? II 36 *a* 36 ra-ku-bu, one of the many synonyms for small, little (la-ku-u), AV 7482.

rukbūtu see ruqbūtu.

rakaku. M^S 89, 1/2 quotes Reisner, *Hymnen*, 110, 27 ina šubē u ukni ra-ak-ka-at. T. A. (Ber) 25 ii 28: X xarrē qāti ša parzilli ra-ak-ka-tum.

rikiltu, see rikistu, *d.*

ra-ki-mu. II 48 (*c*-)*d* 17 = ER-KI-RAM-ME-ME; (Br 9721, AV 7480) preceded by **rak-na-na** = ER-KI-RAM-AN-NANA (*i. e.* ⊢ΨY) Br 9719, in one group with (15) da-tu-nu. II 50 *a-b* 68 [RA-AK]-AN-ME-ME-KI = ra-ki-ma (Br 9655, 13883, 14408, preceded by RA-AK(?)-NANA-KI = ra-ak-na-na, AV 7484. ZDMG 53, 655 *foll* says: ME-ME = (ilat) Gu-la (Br 10449); Gu-la = rabū (Br 11143); rabū = MU (Br 1230); thus AN-ME-ME = mu; RA-AK-AN-ME-ME-KI = Ra-ak-mu(-ki).

rakanu. M^S 103 *col* 2. 83, 1—18, 1335 iii 46 *foll* (+ 81, 11—13, 465) AL-TAR, explained by al-ta-ru, pu-us-su-u, namu-ti, ra-ka-nu.

rakasu, *pr* irkus (ZA iii 366, 15 ir-ku-us); *ps* irakku(a)s (ZK ii 8 i-rak-kus-su; ZA iii 45; iv 431); *ip* rukus (KB vi, 1, 298, 22 ru-ku-us); AV 7479. — *a*) bind {binden}. D^H^ 28 *rm* 1. I 43, 36 at the central gate of Nineveh ar-ku-su (> ar-kus-šu) da-bu-u-eš, I tied him like a pig; Asb viii 12 itti ásì kalbi ar-ku-us-šu. K 2711 *R* 9 ar-kus ur-max-xi ⁽ⁱˡ⁾ Zi-i, *etc.*; *O* 19 ar-ku-us (= I dedicated); 20, ar-kus; 22, ar-ku-su. NE VI 4 (end) ra-ki-is a-gu(-ux)-xa, und bindet das Wams (?) fest (*cf* NE 29, 4; 30, 4; 37, 4). V 25 *c-d* 2 i-na su-ni-šu ir-ku-us (= NAM-NE-IN-SAR). IV² 22 *no* 1 *R* 17 .... li qaq-qa-su ru-ku-us-ma (= ⟨-ME-NI-SAR). T^M^ iv 88 i-rak-ka-sa-a-ni rik-si, they tie with bands. iD TAR IV² 25 *b* 21; *b* 18. H 88—89, 48 ina im-ni-šu ru-ku-uz-su-ma; 90—91, 59; *l* 57 ru-kus-ma. IV² 3 *b* 9—11 qaqqad; kišād marçi, napištašu ru-kus-ma (= ⟨-ME-NI-SAR); also *a* 44/45, 46 ru-ku-us-ma, ZK i 303. IV² 3 *a* 26 (end) it-ti mu-u-ti ra-kis; 4 *b* 6 ṭi-'i-u ina šamē ra-kis. imērašu la ra-ka-si, narkabta la ra-ka-si, ZA iv 202, 36/7; KB iii (1) 172 = not to take. — *b*) tie, join, unite firmly {fügen, zusammenfügen} III 15 i 24 (see raksu); Sn *Bav* 58 (see rikistu, *a*). Sarg *Ann* xalçē ir-ku-su. — K 9287 ii 11 BIR xul-dub-bi-e a-rak-kas; 13 çippa-ta a-rak-kas. — I 8 *no* 2 *R* 2 offerings *etc.* which had been omitted ar-ku-us (I enjoined, KB ii 262, 263). *Rec. Trav.*, xx 127—8; KB vi (1) 92, 13 *etc.* see paššūru; also K 164, 44. TP III *Ann* 16 (+51+73) kat-ri-e ana ⁽ⁱˡ⁾ Ašur bēli-ja ar-ku-us, als Angebinde darbringen (see Rost). — I 66 *a* 9 a-na la ra-ka-si-im-ma, nicht zur Frohnde nehmen. V 56, 44 an enemy day and night lu-u ra-ki-is it-ti-šu, shall pursue him. KB iii (1) 170 (× BA i 462 nakis). — Peiser, KAS 87, 19: make a contract, *e.g.* Nabd 380, 4; 13, 8 *etc.* — In Cappadocian texts, KB iv 54 *no* vii, 22 (end) the money ra-ki-is (is placed safely); viii 10 ra-ak-su-ni; *pm* also V 47 *b* 14 (end) rak-su; IV² 1 *a* 48 (end) rak-su(-)šu-nu (*var* K 4846 it-ta-na-al-la-ku šu-nu) Br 4918, 5068. Knudtzon, 21 *R* 10 ra-kis, usually written XIR-is & XIR (see Knudtzon, *s. v.* qabaltu). H 87, 61 see naru(q)qu (781 *col* 1); *ibid* also K 3172 *R* 8. K 2148 ii 4 šip(me?)-p(b)u-u-ra rak-sa-at, ZA ix 118; 417. K 433, 2 bītu ep-šu 'š'ip-pu (or me-sir?) rak-su. K 164, 30 xašxuraku *pl* i-ra-ku-su ištu gu(!)ga-am-li, BA ii 636. 82—5—22, 1048, 17 ⁽ⁱˡ⁾ Marduk a-ma-am ina pa-an me-e ir-ku-us, KB vi (1) 40, 41. K 883, 7 see pitūtu. V 30 *e-f* 12 ŠU-PA-PA = ra-ki-su, Br 7180. K 4256 *R* 10 ra-ka-su, M^S^ *pl* 11. K 4850 (H 48) ii 38 IN-SAR = [ir-ku]-us; H 18, 295 sa-ar | SAR | ra-ka-su. II 48 *g-h* 29 ⁽ᵏᵘʳ⁾ KIL | ra-ka-su (Br 10202); H 32, 758; *ibid* 744 = la-al | LAL |. S^b^ 349 ki-eš-da = [ra-ka-su] ZA i 69 *foll*; Jensen, 171; Br 4331; BA i 501 *rm*.

Q^t^ *a*) tie, combine {fügen, binden} Creat.-*frg* IV 85 see çamadu Q. IV² 61 *b* 26 qabal tuqmāti ir-tak-su (3 *pl*). II 48 *g-h* 30 MU-UN-NA-AB-KIL (*i.e.* KUR)-RA = ir-tak-sa-an-ni, he has bound me. K 891 *R* 4 see xuluqqū (319 *col* 1). Perhaps L³ *R* 3 why is the evil sickness tied to me (rit-ku-sa (?) itti-ja). — *b*) saddle a horse, mule, *etc.* {satteln, einschirren}. Rm 2, 1 *R* 10: II mules ... ar-ta-kas (I have saddled, + 25); 12 (end) ir-ta-kas (Hr^L^ 408).

ℑ *a*) bind, tie, wind something around somebody, surround {binden, festbinden, umwinden, umschliessen}. IV² 8 *b* 36—39 qa-a mu-na-aš-šir ma-mit | .... this man's head, hands and feet u-rak-kis (he has tied) = SAR-SAR; 3 *b* 12 meš-re-ti-šu ruk-kis-ma (= ip ⟨-ME-NI-SAR-SAR). Esh v 39; Sarg *Khors* 161, *Ann* 422; I 28 *b* 11; I 27 *no* 2, 17—8 (16); V 70, 7; I 44, 71; II 67, 79; Sn vi 49, 50; Asb x 100 see mēsiru (568 *col* 2); Asb ii 11—12; 52; 93—4; iii 92 (u-rak-kis); I 44, 52; Sn v 73 (ruk-ku-sa) see laqtu (end) 497 *col* 2. *del* 258 (289) u-rak-ki-is abnē kab-tu-t[i ana šēpišu], tied heavy stones to his feet. Bu 88—5—12, 75+76 v 36 (BA iii 246, 247). Sarg *Ann* 120 ru-uk-ku-sa (*pm pl*). — *b*) tie, join {festfügen, zusammenfügen} TP III *Ann* 117 tuklātišu u-ra-kis (3 *sg*? KB ii 26. 27) a-na *etc.* — *c*) build {bauen} Neb v 9 u-ra-ak-ki-su; V 34 *a* 39 u-ra-ak-ki-is (he had built); Neb vi 36 (1*sg*). TP vii 104 tax-lu-bi-šu (*cf* taxlūbu) i-na a-gur-ri u-re-ki-is. Sn iii 21, 22 xal-çāni elišu u-rak-kis-ma. — *d*) II 65 *a* 2, 3 Karaindas & Ašurbêlnišišu rik-sa-a[-ti] ina bi-rit-šu-nu a-na a-xa-meš u-ra-ki-su, entered into a mutual agreement. — *e*) Asb i 115, 116 u-rak-ki-sa rik-sa-a-te(-ti), I made stricter the commands (orders). — K 4350 ii 35 (H 48) IN-SAR-SAR = [u-rak-ki]-is. V 45 vii 29 tu-rak-kas.

ℑ[t] S 1064, 12—14 ta-al-i-tu ina eli | ur-ta-ki-is (ina ap-pi-šu | ir-tu-mu) I applied (bound on) a dressing (Hr[L] 392).

Š *a*) erect, build, construct; or order such to be done {errichten, bauen lassen} *etc*. Sarg *Khors* 139 at the boundary toward Elam u-šar-kis (al) bir-tu, I had a fortress built; *Ann* 366, 368. TP vi 102 narṭabê (?) i-na nap-xar (mât) A-šur gab-be lu-šar-ki-is (set to work; Johns, *Doomsday-Book*, 19). Perh. KB vi (1) 186—7 on NE VII ii 50 a-ma lu(-)u-šar-ki-i[s-ma], hatte einen Baldachin zusammenfügen lassen. — *b*) prepare, order, arrange, or have done so {einrichten, ordnen, vorkehren lassen} *etc*. TP vii 80 narkabâti-ia ..... eli ša pa-na | u-tir u-šar-ki-is (1*sg*; I harnessed?). ag see mušarkisu (612, where in *col* 2 *l* 4 change the; to follow after K 596, 4). Also see 83—1—18, 28 (Hr[L] 344) *O* 3 (amêl) mu-šar-ki-si *pl* (+8); BA ii 27 on K 11, 12 (Hr[L] 186).

Derr.: markasu (*p* 568; KB vi (1) 494); murâkisu & these 7:

raksu & rakasu 2. *a*) *adj* bound {gebunden} AV 7485. L[4] ii 16 (end) rak-su ip-ṭu-ru (Lehmann, ii 69). III 15 i 24 ta-xa-za-šu-nu ra-ak-su tap-ṭu-ur, their compact battle array she broke up. V 46 *a-b* 47 (il) Ni-ru (?) rak-su (= SAR-DA) Br 12689; PSBA xviii 25. — *b*) used as a *noun* (?). Anp ii 102—3 ina rak(*var* ra-ka)-su-te Diqlat e-te-bir. TP III *Ann* 1 .... (nâru) .... [i]-na rak-su-ti e-bir, BA ii 51. — (amêl) rak-su II 31 *b* 92 (Br 13556); *pl* (amêl) rak-su-ti = general, BA ii 50; K 658, 14; K 550, 9; 583, 9 (amêl) rak-su-ti (Hr[L] 154, 64, 304). Rm 77 *O* 6 (amêl) rab rak-si (Hr[L] 414).

rakīsu, see narkabtu (729 *col* 1); ZA vi 8; AV 7481.

rakkasu. K 1113, 26 *foll* sisê rak-ka-su-te me-sa-a-a ša .... u-rak-ka-su-ni (Hr[L] 71). Pinches, TSBA vii 114; BA ii 46, 47; perh. ‖ sisê ša ni-i-ri, draught horses.

riksu, *c. st.* rikis *m.* AV 7582. — *a*) bandage {Binde}. V 28 *g-h* 6 ri-ik-su a ‖ of sûnu (*q. v.*). V 28 *g-h* 19 ‖ agû, bânu *etc.*, of a turban. KB vi (1) 268—9 (& 535) *no* I *b*, *O* 4; 5 ri-kis qabli-šu-nu (&-ša), die Binde ihrer Hüften. K 8827, 7 ri-kis qaq-qa-di & mar-kas. — *b*) alliance, bond {Bund}. V 28 *g-h* 50 ri-ik-su ‖ u-la-pu (*q. v.*). ℑ T. A. (Lo) 29, 12 explained by xa-ab-ši. — *c*) ban, charm {Bann}. IV[2] 16 *R* 60, 61 (end) ri-kis-si-na lip-pa-ṭir; 17 *b* (*R*) 14 O Šamaš thou art mu-di-e rik-si-šu-nu. Perh. K 232 *O* 14 (Craig, *Religious Texts*, ii 16); T[M] vii 45 ina ri-kis (BA iv 161). III 43 *c* 32; I 70 *c* 14; IV[2] 48 *b* 10; 58 *d* 49 (ZA xvi 180, 181) see paṭaru 𝔔 & ℑ. On riksa paṭaru & rakasu see Zimmern, *Ritualtafeln*, 94 *no* 1: riksu, Zurüstung eines Opfermahles. Perh. here also K 3182 i 53 (end) a-na ri-kis (iṣ) erini, at the preparation of the cedar (AJSL xvii 137), followed, 55, by ša rik-sa-a-ti. — *d*) bond that holds together {Band, das zusammenhält}. Perh. T[M] iii 60 (il) GIŠ-BAR .... ri-kis-ki li .... (BA iv 158). K 8665, 10 ri-kis si-ip-pi M[S] *pl* 14. IV[2] 21, 1 B *O* 21 (end) ina ri-kis bîti ul-ziz, Br 4332; Zimmern, *Ritualt.*, *p* 168: Verschluss. Creat.-*frg* V 6 ana ud-du-u rik-si-šu-un (um ihre Schranken kenntlich zu machen). — *e*) joint, wrist (in a human body); sinew, tendon {Gelenk, Sehne} see buânu. IV[2] 60* C *R* 6 (see paṭaru ℑ & translate: "members of my body", rather than "bonds"). K 4386 ii 38 (= II R 48 *g-h* 28) SA (usually = buânu) = rik-su, Br 3082. — *f*) foundation {Fundament}. V 65 *b* 7 u-dannin ri-kis (*var* ki-is) bît pa-pa-xi be-lu-ti-šu. rikis samê (*q. v.*) = foundations of heaven; Lay 33 (Sarg *Nimr*) 15 ir-mu-u rik-su-šu, its foundation was giving away (KB ii 38). V 43 *c-d* 30 Nabû called (ilu) A-A-UR as the ri-kis ka-la-ma. — *g*) sum total {Summa} ‖ napxaru. K 8522 *R* 18 ri-kis parçêja kâlišunu *etc.* (KB vi, 1, 38, 39). 81—6—7, 209, 3 ša ri-kis te-ri-e-ti xa-am-mat, BA iii 260—1; Hebr. viii 114 who makes fast the bond of laws. — *h*) tax {Abgabe, Frohnde} Camb 276, 3 ri-ki-is qabli, the *q* tax; Nabd 103, 15 kaspu ša a-na ri-kis-si qabli. H 71, 22 (end) ri-ki-is bilti. — *i*) contract, document {Vertrag} Peiser, KAS 87; ZA iii 82. Nabd 85, 12 ri-ik-su ša bîti šu-a-tim, a contract concerning this house; Nabd 945, 10. Cyr 332, 21 ri-ik-sa-a ša ištu šatti VI Nabuna'id, the contracts from the 6th year of Nabonidus. KB iv 320, 321 *no* ii 6—8 ri-ik-su ša na-aš-pir-tum a-na eli la ir-ku-su. — II 51 *no* 1 *R* 21 + 25 ri-ki-is-su; see also Cyr 293, 10; Nabd 103, 15. — S^b 164 di-im | DIM | rik-su, perh. = rope {Seil} Br 2741. S^b 235 (H 15, 215) ši-ta | <⊏YYY | rik-su, ‖ šuk-lu-lu, Br 9166. V 21 *a-b* 29 GIŠ-SAR-DA = rik-su (Br 4332, 4376) together with eššepû. V 29 *a-b* 65 ZAG = ri-ik-su, Br 6491. II 29 *a-b* 60—62 .... SAR = ri-ik-su (Br 4332); .... DIM = ri-kis qa-ni-e (Br 2444, 2471; V 32 *no* 4, 53 see kišibu, 446 *col* 1). .... DIM-KUR-KUR-RA = *r* ma-ta-a-ti, Br 2762.

rikistu, *c. st.* riksat; *pl* riksâti. — *a*) foundation (?) {Fundament}. Sn *Bav* 58 whosoever .... rik-sa-a-te ar-ku-su i-paṭ-ta-ru, breaks up the foundations (of the canal which) I have made. KB iii (2) 78, 15 ri-ik-sa-ti-ša (of the front of a temple) la du-un-nu-nim ‖ sippušu la kunnunum iššakkan. — *b*) laws and regulations of the country {Gesetze und Ordnungen des Landes}. IV² 48 *b* 13 see paṭaru, ℑ & translate: may Nebo destroy the organic union of his land. Asb i 115, 116 see rakasu, ℑ. — *c*) preparation {Zurüstung}, see riksu, *c*). — *d*) agreement, contract {Vereinbarung, Vertrag}. Nabd 356, 29 the judge listened to dup-pa-nu u rik-sa-a-tu (+ 39). KB iv 308, 309 *no* viii 6 see pasasu, ℑ. II 65 *a* 2, 3 see rakasu, ℑ. D^K 7; RP² iv 24 *foll.* Strassm., *Stockholm* (VIII.) *Or. Congr.*, *no* 27, 1 kaspu u-du-u ku-mu çib-tum ri-kis-tum nu-dun-nu-u. — *e*) agreement against one; conspiracy {Vereinbarungen gegen jemanden; Verschwörung}. Sn v 15 ki-i ri-kil-ti (but ZA v 304 = רכיל; so also BA iii 284) u qil(ZA ix 89)-la-ti çiruššu bašî. Bu 88—5—12, 75 + 76 i (= K 192 *O*) 4 .... šu u-šab-ṭa-lu u-šab-šu-u ri-kil-tu.

rakistu. K 3172 *R* 3 GAR(= ŠA)-SAR-DA = ra-kis-ti, Br 12050, 4332. Z^B iv 47 ra-kis-t[a lip-ru-s]u bonds {Bande}.

rikâsu. contract {Vertrag} Br. M. 84—2—11, 72 (Kohler-Peiser, ii 73, 74) toward the end: ri-ka-si ki-i u-ti[r-ru]. Nabd 1113, 8 (end) ri-ka-su ša ar-du-tu.

rakapu (?) T. A. (Lo) 29, 14 tar-ku-up(b) gab-bi mâti, (so that) the whole land shakes at his noise, Bezold, *Diplomacy*, xxviii.

ra-ka-šu. V 41 *c* 29.

rukšu (?). ZA iv 237, i 42 kib-ri ru-uk-šu.

rukûšu. property, possessions {Besitz}. § 65, 19; D^{Pr} 47. Asb ix 36 gammalê ru-ku-ši-šu-nu u-šal-li-qu; *cf* רְכֻשׁ. Haupt, Hebr. iii 110 compares in addition, רכש. KAT³ 647: Kanaan. Lehnwort im Assyr.?

râmu 1. = רחם (§ 47); *pr* irâm & irêm (§ 106); *ps* irâm (i-ra-mu, they love, § 17) & in relat. connection irammu; *ip* rîm (ZA vii 61 *ad* § 107); *ag* râ'imu (§§ 32β; 42). H^{OV} 36; H^F 52, 5; BA i 21; Z^B 20; 22; 58. AV 7462, 7511; ib RAM, Z^B 6 *rm* 2; § 9, 147; Br 4745. — *a*) have pity on some one; pardon some one {sich jemandes erbarmen; ihn begnadigen}. TP iv 28 (v 37) a-ri-im-šu-nu-ti, I pardoned them; IV² 60* C *R* 15 ul i-ri-man-ni (ilat) Iš-ta-ri (3 *m* for 3 *f*; § 90 *c*); III 4 *no* 7, 11 ... Iš-tar lu-u i-ra-man-ni. K^M 8, 3 ri-NIN(= min)-ni-ma (ilat) Ištar, BA iv 531. Perh. IV² 15 ii 14 ib-ri na-ram-šu it-ti-šu 'i-ram-ma, Br 4894. — *b*) turn in love to some one; love {sich in Liebe jem. zuwenden; lieben}. TP viii 25 ni-iš qa-ti-ja li-ra-mu (may they love). Neb i 38 ina gimir libbija kênim a-ra-mu (I love) puluxti ilûtišunu (§ 92, ix 52; vii 35 in Babylon .... ša a-ra-am-ma, the city, I love; ix 57 ki-ma ša a-ra-am-ma puluxti ilûtika; i 56 a-na šarri ša ta-ra-am-mu-ma (2 m). Asb vi 123 the temple ša ta-ram-mu (3 f, ps). L⁴ i 30 i-ra-man-ni. V 44 *c-d* 38 ⁽ⁱˡ⁾ Ninib ša kun-na-a i-ra-mu (ZA ii 91); V 35, 22 Cyrus ša Bêl u Nabû ir-a-mu pa-la-a-šu (& Anp i 25). NE VI 48 (51, 53, 58, 64) ta-ra-mi-ma, thou didst love; 79, u ia-a-ši ta-ram-man-ni-ma, and now thou also lovest me. IX *col* 3 (NE 69, 30; 67, 12; 71, 21) eb-ri ša a-ram-mu (V 65 *b* 48); XII i 24 (26) aš-šat-ka (ma-ra-ka) ša ta-ram-ma; ii 15 (17) aš-šat-su (ma-ra-šu) ša i-ram-mu. ZA iv 232, 10 É-sag-gil ša ta-ram-mu nu-u-xu (662 *col* 1/2). Scheil, *Rec. Trav.*, xvii 18 (notes xix) 2 ina qâtu ša a-ra-am-mu. S^P II 987 *O* 11 i-ra-mu, he loves. ZA v 67 (81—2—4, 188) 20 the desire of thy heart ša ta-ra-me (which thou lovest); 14 (+ 10) ana il(?)-tim rem-ni-ti ša me-ša-ra i-ra-am-mu. VATh 4105 ii 2 Êa-ṭâbu ša a-ra-am-mu-ma (*Mitth. Vorderasiat. Gesellsch.*, '02, *no* 1). K 95, 11 (ša) i-ra-'-a-mu (ZA ii 60; who loves); K 183, 42 (= *R* 18) la i-ra-'-mu-un-ni, they do not love me; K 824 *R* 12 ardu ša bît bêli-šu i-ram-mu (Hr^L 288; 2; 290). IV² 18 *a* 4 bi-i-tu ša i-ra-am-mu; 19 *b* 10/11 Marduk .... ša mi-ti bul-lu-ṭa i-ram-mu; 29 *no* 1 *a* 23, 24 (see mîtu & balaṭu, ב); KAT³ 378 *rm* 4 says: im Sinne von Totkranke gesund machen. ag ra-i-mu (§§ 20; 47; AV 7477). V 28 *e-f* 20 ra-i-mu ‖ šu-da-du. K 2729 *O* 6 I Ašurbanipal .... ra-im ket-ti; Sn i 4: *Sen* ra-'-im mi-ša-ri (*q. v.*) ‖ na-çir ket-ti; V 65 *a* 5; *b* 31. Sn *Kui* 4, 10 Ašur u Ištar ra-'i-mu šangûtija. TP vi 76 at the command of Ninib ra-'i-mi-ja; vii 73 the great gods RAM (= râ'i)-mu šangû-ti-ja; id + ja also TP ii 62; iv 6; vi 61; Esh *Sendsch*, *R* 28 Iš-tar be-el-tum ra-'-i-mat šangû-ti-ja; III 15 *a* 22 Ištar ra-'-i-mat ša-an-gu-ti-ja. V 34 *c* 6 (the goddess) be-el-ti ra-'i-im-ti-ja; KB iii (2) 50, 45; Neb iv 45. II 66 *no* 1, 6 ra-i-mat ki-na-te. K 13 *R* 29 (end) ra-'-i-mu; K 595, 8 ra-'i-mu ša niše (Hr^L 281; 6). Scheil, *Nabd*, ix 26 the great gods ra-'-im palê-e-a.

V 33 ii 13, 14 *M* & *Ç* ra-im palê-e-a; 4 *M* ra-im palê-e-a; viii 19. K 501, 7—8 ilâni an-nu-u-te rabûti ra-i-mu-te šar-ru-ti-ka (Hr^L 113); perh. ZA x 293, 30 ra-ma-a-tum ul-la-a-ti i-lat u be-li-ti. ip (either to *a* or *b*) KB vi (1) 108, 109 *l* 51 rim(?)-an-ni-ma, have mercy upon me (see *ibid*, *no* 2). P. N. Marduk-ri-man-ni (AV 5160); Nabû-ri-man-ni (AV 5706; II 64 *a* 25; Z^B 68); Êa-ri-man-ni, V 61 vi 21. ⁱˡ Ri-im ⁽ⁱˡ⁾ Sin, in *c. t.*; KB iv 6 ii 17. See also BA iv 383 *foll* (IV² 35 *no* 8 Ri-im A-nu-um); 385 *nos* 13 & 14. Çi-ni Ištar son of Sin-ri-me-ni (Strassm., *Berl. Congr.*, 17 *l* 23). — *c*) favor one with something; present, grant {jemanden mit etwas begnaden, *i. e.* beschenken} constr. with double *acc*. — See tarîmtu. V 60 ii 10 such & such .... i-rim (61 iv 13); iv 53 i-ri-mu (BA i 281; ZA iv 327 note 2); Merod.-Balad-Stone iv 52. III 43 i 13 a-na ça-ti i-ri-en-šu (§ 49 *a*); iv (margin) 6 a-na ûmê ça-ti i-ri-in-šu (BA ii 116 *foll*; KB iv 68 *foll*). See also KB vi (1) 58, 7. Scheil, *Rec. Trav.*, xx 202 (notes xl,) 10 i-ri-mu-u-ni. IV² 38 ii 29 a-mur-ti-iš i-rim-šu (KB iv 62, 63); see KB iv 58 i 15 a-mur-ti-iš i-ri-mu. Nabd 65, 18—19 a-na ri-e-mu-u-tu ul(-?) ta-a-ri-me. — KB iv 92 *no* 2 *R* 2 šarru li-ri-man-ni-ma the rest of the field of my father's house; 94, 17 i-ri-mu. — *d*) follow {jemandem anhangen}. T. A. (Lo) 14, 51 the people ša i-ra-a-mu-ni, who have followed me. — Sp II 265 *a* iv 8 .... i-ri-im-mu a-na ....; Knudtzon, 130, 6 i-ra-'-a-m[a]; *R* 20 i-ra-'-a-mu (*ps*). V 25 *c-d* 9 ina ra-me-šu (Br 4745, 8069). — P. N. Bu 91—5—9, 2176 A 18 ši-bi Ta-ram-Sag-ila (JRAS '07, 607). — H 47 i 77—8 IN-AG-E(-NE) = i-ra-am(-mu); 79, IN-NA-AN-AG-E = i-ra-am-šu, Br 4745. II 40 *no* 2, 14/15 TAG-KI-AG-GA = aban ra-a-me (Br 9720; 11865), ‖ TAG-GUG (= sându?)-si-lim (ZA xiv 357—8: λίθος σεληνίτης); TAG-NU-KI-AG-GA = aban la ra-a-me (Br 2021) ‖ TAG-XUL-GIG (= stone of hatred, זיר). S^b 204 a-ka | RAM | ra-a-mu; H 19, 340. H 108, 20 (112, 12; 114, 8; D 128, 68; V 11 *d-f* 20) KI-EN-

GA-AD = [KI?]-AG = ra-a-mu (Br 9664); see also raxamu.

Q^t love {lieben}. Neb vii 17 my royal ancestors ina alâni ni-iš i-ni-šu-nu a-ša-ar iš-ta-a-mu (= irtâmu) êkallâti iteppušû (PSBA xi 160; KB iii 2, 24).

ℶ conciliate, make one favorably inclined toward {versöhnen, barmherzig machen}. IV² 54 a 35, 36 te-mi-qu-šu e-liš li-rim-ka | in-xu u ri-e-ma a-xu-lap liq-ba-ka, H^CV xxxvii: his sighing prayer make you, above, incline favorably, *etc.* KNUDTZON, 151 *O* 5 u-ra-am-mu-u (?). V 45 v 15 tu-ra-'-am. 81—7—27, 19 *O* 11 tu-ra-ma šarru be-ili, do thou grant, o king my lord. Perh. II 22 no 2 (*add*) . . . . . SAL | tu-ra-am-an-ni (Br 14426; AV 8151).

Š V 45 v 30 tu-šar-'-a[m?].

Šℶ show mercy {Mitleid zeigen}. Neb i 69 be-lu-ut-ka çir-ti šu-ri-'-im-am-ma (§ 106); also SCHEIL, *Nabd*, vii 22 taš-ri-im-mi (> tušrimmi?) ra-am-mu, she showed mercy unto me.

NOTE. — T A tablets have the forms: pr (3 *sg m*, 2 *sg* & 1 *sg*) Lo 20, 23 if the king i-ra-am his faithful servant; 10, 2 + 3 ša a-ra-'-a-mu (+ 15) u ša i-ra-'-a-ma-an-ni, + 5 ša i-ra-'-a-mu-ka (who loves thee); 8, 4 (-mu-u-ka), + 8 to thy wives ša ta-ra-'-a-mu; 8, 2 ša i-ra-'-am-an-ni u ša a-ra-am[-mu-uš]; 9, 15 ša i-ra-'-ma-an-ni-ni ja-bu-u-ta, + 24 i-ra-'-am-ka, + 26 ta-ra-'-am-šu. — 53, 22 ti-ra-am; 9, 27 [ta]-ra-a-mi. Ber 102, 18 ta-ra-ju-mu, (2 *pl*) you are favorable to. pm Ber 58, 72 ra-im, is attached to; ac Ber 24 *O* 35 i-na ra-'-a-mi (+ 40); ag Ber 24 *O* 67 aššat ra-'-im-ta. — Q^t Lo 8, 14 ša ni-ir-ta-'-a-mu an-ni-ta, + 29 lu ni-ir-ta-'-am, we would continue friendly. pm Ber 23, 10 ri-ta-'-[mu-ku?]. — Q^{t-t} Lo 8, 10 ir-ta-ta-'-a-mu, they were on friendly terms; 11, ta-ar-ta-ta-'-a-am (ZA v 11; 154 *rm* 7). — Q^{tn} Lo 8, 12 (28, 31, 78, 70) ni-ir-ta-na-'-a-mu, ZA v 156; 11 + Murch 10 (22) it-ti-ja ir-ta-na-'-am-mi(-me), was friendly with me.

Derr. narâmu 1, narâmtu, šerîmtu (?), tarîmtu & these 9 (8?):

râmu 2., ra'mu grace, favor {Gunst, Gnade} §§ 29; 32 *a γ*. AV 7588. K 183 *R* 5—7 šarru be-ili ra-a-mu . . . . uk-tal-lim (Hr^L 2), BA i 617; PSBA xxiii 351 *foll.* 82—5—22, 55, 1—3 mi-i-nu ra-'-a-mu an-ni-u ša ^(ilat) Ištar ana šarri bêlija ta-ra-'-a-mu-u-ni. A ‖

rammu, see rêmu, 1 Šℶ.

ra(â)i(î)mu (?). Bu 91—5—9, 210 (Hr^L 403). *R* 1 Ardâni-ja u ra-im-a-ni-ja (& my friends) PSBA xxiii 348 *foll.* K 890, 19 is-si-šu aš-ba-ku-u ša ra-i-ma-ni-ja; K 84, 13 ra-i-ma-ni-šu it-ti-ja lu-ba-iš (Hr^L 301) PSBA xxiii 344—48. M^S 87 *col* 1: merciful {barmherzig}: ra'i-mânu a *pha'ilânu* form. — T. A. (Ber) 71, 47 amêlûti ra-i-mu-ja.

rêmu. — *a*) compassion, mercy, grace, favor {Erbarmen, Gunst, Gnade} § 65, 1. H 99, 58 amêlu muttalliku ina ni-iq ri-e-me (Br 5522); see *p* 718 *col* 1. Rm² 139, 15 re-mi ket-ti be-en-ni ibašši. K 183 *R* 20 ri-e-mu ina eli ardašu li-iç-bat-su. K 3515 *O* 14 ta-šak-ka-ni ri-e-mu. K 824 *R* 5—6 ri-mu aš-kun-ak-ka (Hr^L 290; PSBA xxiii 63), I have shown favor unto thee. IV² 57 *b* 1 li-šak-na ri-e-mu, may grace prevail. — especially with rašû, take compassion on one, show favor to {Erbarmen zu jem. fassen; Gnade erweisen}. K 2729 *R* 28 (end) a-a ir-ši-šu ri-e-mu. TP v 25, 26 ri-e-ma ar-ša-šu (+ 11); K 2852 + K 9662 i 24 ri-e-ma ri-ša-an-ni(-ma) + 35 ri-e-mu ul ar-ši-šu; ii 23 aš-šu ra-še-e ri-e-ma . . . . K 4623 + 79—7—8, 24 *l* 20 (H 122, 17) ana ardiki . . . . ri-e-mu ri-ši-šu. Sp II 265 *a* xxv 10 ri-ma li-ir-ša-a ^(ilat) Ištar ša . . . . Asb iii 20 ri-e-mu ar-ši-šu-u-ma (§ 53*d*); ii 8 + 62; iv 94 (-šu-nu-ti); ix 114; SMITH, *Asurb*, 48, 58; 123, 49 ar-ta-ši [cuneiform sign] (*var* re-e-mu); Sarg *Ann* 62, *etc.* IV² 54 *a* 38 ri-ši-šu ri-e-mu, o god! (§ 110). H 24, 500, ‖ napšuru (712 *col* 2); V 21 *a-b* 61—68 ri-e-mu ‖ un-ni-nu (61), ti-ra-nu (62), naq-ru-ṭum (63), nap-lu-su (64), nap-šu-ru (65), ti-ni-nu (66), ti-ni]n-tum, ? (67). V 29 *a-b* 71 ZAG = ri-e-mu (Br 6489). — *b*) womb {Mutterleib}. IV² 9 *a* 24, 25 ri-i-mu (= [cuneiform sign] EME-SAL) a-lid nap-xa-ri; Br 5455; ‖ rubçu (*q. v.*); sili-tum (764 *col* 2); Br 5518, 5519. III 32 *col* v 44. — Perhaps √ramû, 2.

NOTE. — With rîmu according to some also P. N. Agum-ka-ak-ri-me V 33 *passim*. D^K 56 & *rm* 3; but see JENSEN, KB iii (1) 134.

rîmûtu. pardon; grace {Vergebung; Gnade} usually with šakanu = show mercy, have compassion upon {jemandem Gnade erweisen, Gnade gewähren}. AV 7590 *foll.*. Anp iii 56 ri-mu-tu aš-ku-na(-aš)-šu-nu; iii 76, 77 a-na šu-a-šu ri-mu-tu aš-ku-na-šu, § 56 *b*: I showed mercy to him. Šalm. *Ob*, 170 ri-mu-tu aš-ku-na-šu; *Mon*, *R* 58. V 30 *g-h* 31 see kidin(n)u, *b* (373 *cols* 1/2). Often as P.N. Nabd 697, 1—2 a slave Ri-man-ni-Bêl-Ri-mut, Ri-mut-Bêl, Strassm., *Stockholm Or. Congr.*, 13, 12; Ri-mut (ilêt) Na-na-a, Cyr 254, 3; *cf* 292, 11. V 67 *b* 13 (amêl) Ri-mut-bêl-ilâni, (AV 7591 *foll*); KB iii (1) 122—3 coloph. 2, Ri-mut (ilat) Gu-la; 83—1—18, 245 *R* 9 (amêl) Ri-mu-tu; 82—5—22, 68 *R* 8. — *b*) present, fief {Geschenk, Lehen, Schenkung}. D^K 58 *rm* 2. Merodach-Balad.-stone v 33—35 ri-mut ..... i-ri-mu, the present which ..... (he) has made, BA ii 271; KB iii (1) 192. KB iv 214—15, 25 ri-mu-tu ul i-ri-me. Nabd 65, 18 a-na ri-e-mu-u-tu | ul(-)ta-a-ri-me.

ra'mûtu, friendship {Freundschaft}. T. A. (Ber) 23, 11 it-ti-ja ra-a-mu-u-ta xaš-xu; 22 *R* 31 my brother ra-'-mu-ti u-kal-lam; Lo 11 & Murch, 30 ra-'-mu-u-ta; 28, ra-'-mu-ut-ta-šu; 26, ra-'-mu-ut-ka. A ‖ is:

ri'mûtu. T. A. (Lo) 8, 55 ri-'-mu-u-ta li-še-im-'-id-an-ni.

ramâtu (?). Sarg *Ann* 72 Bît-ra-ma-tu-a.

rêmênû (§ 32 *a a*), **rîmînû** & **rimnû** (§ 37 *c*) *f* rîm(i)nîtu (§ 65, 37 *rm*) gracious, merciful {barmherzig, erbarmungsreich}; mostly of gods. AV 7586. *Marduk*: (il) Marduk ri-mi-nu-u, K 2493 *O* 7 (*Rec. Trav.*, xxiv 103, 104); I 49 *b* 14 ri-mi-nu-ú (il) Marduk; Neb x 2; I 66 *c* 44 a-na (il) Marduk ri-mi(me)-ni-i; IV^2 59 *no* 2 *b* 26; 29 *no* 1 *a* 21, 22 ri-mi-nu-u ina ilâni (*b* 9, 10; also *a* 23, 24; *b* 11); S^P III 2 *R* 8 (end) rim-nu-u (*Jour. Trans. Vict. Inst.*, xxix 48); *cf* IV^2 19 *b* 10, 11. K 8522 *O* 16 re(= ri)-me-nu-u. IV^2 88 *a* 34 P.N. Ri-me-ni (il) Marduk. — V 46 *c-d* 34 (il) Ni-bi-ru = ri-mi-nu-u (ZA i 265 *rm* 3). — *Šamaš*: IV^2 19 *a* 39, 40 ilu ri-mi-nu-u (Br 3574); 28 *no* 1 *b* 7, 8 ri-me-nu-ú ša ma-ta-a-ti. — *Sin*: IV^2 9 *a* 26, 27 (il) Sin .... rim-nu-u (= ŠA [= LIB, Br 8070]-LAL-SUD) ta-a-a-ru (ZK i 104 § 14); 59 *no* 2 *b* 8 be-ili ta-a-a-ru ri-mi-nu-u, o gracious, merciful lord; 26 *b* 58, 59 ana ili-šu ri-mi(me)-ni-i; 27 *a* 32—34 (Br 5523); *c. t.* P. N. Sin-re-me-ni. — *Nebo*: I 35 *no* 2, 4 (il) Nabû re-me-nu-u; 7, re-me-nu-u ta-ja-a-ru. — IV^2 10 *R* 6 ana ili-ja rim-ni-i I address all my sighing. — DT 363 *R* 14 iltum rêm-ni-tum ša su-up-pi-e ta-ram-mu (ZA iv 232). II 66 *no* 1, 9 to *Ištar* il-tim rem-ni-ti; S 6 + S 2 *O* 5 ..... i-li bêlit ša-qu-ti ummu rem-ni-ti (of Ištar), *Rev. Sém.*, '98, 142 *fol.* KB iii (2) 68—9 *no* 13 *col* 2, 5 (ilat) Nin-max ummu ri-mi-ni-ti. 81—2—4, 188 (ZA v 66) 10 see râmu Q. IV^2 29** *no* 5 *O* 12 (H 115) rim-ni-tum to whom it is well to turn (Br 8070); ZA i 40, 24 ri-mi-ni-ti. Sp II 265 *a* xxv 1 ri-me (K 3452: mi)-na-a-tu eb-ri nissatum ši-te-'-me, ZA x 13.

NOTE. — Anp i 9 perh. ilu rim[-nu?]-u; *cf* II 66, 9.

***rîmu** *1.* *f* rîmtu, the beloved (?). Asb ix 75 see ma'u 3 (504, 505); § 65, 14. Perh. P. N. in Neb 386, 1 (sal) Ri-mat, AV 7585. Reisner, *Hymnen*, 107, 16 + 18 ri-im-tum šakûti. or √רחם?

rîmu *2.* *m* wildox, buffalo {Wildochs} = רְאֵם. AV 7587. TSBA v ('77) 336 *foll.* § 65, 2. *pl* rîmê & rîmâni. H 186 *no* 90; Hebr. i 180. D^S 32; D^H 67; D^{Pr} 15—17; 23. ZDMG 40, 742. Hommel, VK 497 *rm* 246. *Florence Orient. Congr.*, i 224, 225. Haupt in *Proverbs*, SBOT 34; *Isaiah*, SBOT 88; *E-vowel*, *p* 10; Margolis, AJSL 1903, 162—3. S^b 97; H 18, 316 [a]-ma | AM | ri-i-mu; § 9, 53; ZK ii 68, 5. Br 4531, 4545. Neb iii 48 ri-i-mu; 59, id. IV^2 27 *a* 19, 20 ša ... i-na šadê *pl* ki-ma ri-mi (= AM) ek-du rab-çu. *Etana*-frg (KB vi 106, 107) 44 it-ta-ziz ina eli ri-me, BA iii 366, 367; *ibid.*, KB vi 104, 105 *b* 17 ri[-ma mi-i-tu]; 106, 107, 31 çi-ir [ri-e]-mi; 35 (+ 40) šir rîmi an-ni-e. Šalm. *Mon*, *R* 52 his lands I trampled down kîma (alap) AM; Sn iii 74 kîma AM ek-di (*Kui* 1, 39 alap AM). V 50 *b* 50, 51 AM-GUL (Br 4553) = ri-ma (*var* ri-im) ša çe-rim ušaknîš (3 pr) H 187. *cf* I 28 *a* 4 AM-MEŠ-GUL-MEŠ šu-tu-ru-te; TP vi 62: IV pu-xal AM-MEŠ dan-nu-te šu-tu-ru-te. H 81, 22 see qarnu; also qarnū. T. A. (Lo) 3, 26 ša ri-mi. — *pl* AM-MEŠ also I 28 *a* 6; Asurb vi 60 unassixa (1 *sg* pr) AM-MEŠ-an (= ri-mān?) na-ad-ru-u-ti (see nadru, 655—656; ZK ii 316); Lay 43—44, 17 end; Anp iii 48: fifty (alap) AM-MEŠ-ni dannūti ..... eight (alap) AM-MEŠ balṭūti. *f* perh.:

rīmtu (?). K 2001 *O* 7 ri-im-tum mu(?)-nak-ki-pat kib-ra-a-ti, CRAIG, *Relig. Texts*, i *pl* 15.

rīmāniš, *adv* Sn i 69 (*Kui* 1, 10; *Bell* 21) see nagašu Q[t] and read at-tag-giš.

rāmu 2. (רעם) whence murta'imu (595 *col* 1) & perh. S^b 204 a-ka  ra-a-mu, *var* ra-ma-mu. Der?:

rīmu *3.* thunder {Donner}. III 67 *c-d* 46 Adad (or Rammān? see KAT[3] 445) is called the god ša ri-mi, followed by ilu ša bir-qi. K 9290 + K 3452 (PSBA xvii 141 *foll*) *var* to Sp II 265 *a* vi 4 ri-mu šam-ṭu.

rāmu 3. be high {hoch sein}. Eponymlist *col* v (677) Abi-ra-mu. See also HOMMEL, PSBA, May '94; PRAŠEK, *Expos. Times*, F '00, 252. — ℑ perh. II 28 *c* 5 e-ri-a mu-ri-im, Br 8052. — But mu-rim, Sarg *Cyl* 67 *etc.* is read mu-kil, see kâlu (379 *col* 2). — ℑ[t] K^M 61, 13 (end) ana nap-šat ili u šarri qa-ti at-ta-ra[-am] — or Q[t]? — Derr. perhaps tarāmu &:

rūmu, *f* rūmtu. honored, respected {angesehen, geehrt} § 65, 8. Perh. II 67, 6 (amēl) Ru-um(-mu-lu-tu), AV 7643. II 31 *no* 3, 16, V 41 *a-b* 16 ru-um (sign: dub)-tum ‖ ka-bit-tum, AV 7644. 81—6—7, 209, 4 (of ištar) ru-um-ti ti-iz-qar-ti BA iii 263 *foll.* SCHEIL, ZA x 292—3, 28 ru-um-tum (il) E-a bēl xa-si-si. Perhaps also II 62 *g* 62 ru-um[-tum] followed by ru-ma[-tum?].

ramu 1. = רָמָה. §§ 108 *foll.* ZA vii 78. pr irmi, ps iram(m)i(u). AV 7512; Z^B 91; 7 *rm* 1. — *a*) throw, throw down, prostrate {werfen, niederwerfen}. V 50 *a* 45, 46 ša e-kim-mu lim-nu ina mu-ši ir-mu-šu (= BA-AN-DA RI-A), whom the evil spirit prostrates during nighttime; *a* 55, 56 (Br 2573). K 255 *O* i 16 ša ina taxāzi-šu la i-ram-mu-u qab-li, CRAIG, *Relig. Texts*, II *pl* 14 (M^8 89 √ramû, 2). — *b*) in connection with šubtu, *etc.* = settle, dwell. V 62 *no* 1, 9 šu-bat-su ir-me; *no* 2, 18 šu-bat-su el-li-ti ṭa-biš lu-u ir-mi. V 35, 23 since the time when in the palace of the princes ar-ma-a šu-bat be-lu-tim. Neb vii 19 there ir-mu-u (3 *pl*) šu-ba-at-su-un. 81—6—7, 209, 19 ina E-sag-ila .... ir-mu-u šu-bat-su, BA iii 260. L^4 ii 31 ra-ma-ta šub-tu, thou hast established the dwelling place. V 64 *a* 10 šu-ba-at ṭu-ub lib-bi-š[u ra]-mu-u ki-ri-ib-šu. IV[2] 5 *a* 78, 79 the goddess Ištar it-ti (il) A-nim šar-ri šub-tu elli-tim ir-me. V 61 iv 28 ir-ma-a šu-bat-su, he founded his house. IV[2] 9 *a* 24, 25 Nannar who with (it-ti) the living creatures šub-tu elli-tim ra-mu-u. K 3600 iv 17 (il) Sin ri-me-i šub-tuk-ki, CRAIG, *Relig. Texts*, i 54. — Without šubtu. Esh vi 44 ki-rib-ša da-riš lu-ur-me; KB iii (2) 78, 9 ša ra-am-ku-tim ki-ni-iš-ti E-sag-il ra-mu-u ki-ri-ib-ša (see *ibid* *p* 79 & HOMMEL, *Gesch.*, 776). TP III *Ann* 10 tuklat Ašur bēli-ja i-na lib-bi ar-me (+ 180). Sp II 265 *a* xxi 4 i-na ki-rib (iç) dun-ni ra-mi bu-kur-šu. PEISER, *Vertr.*, x 11 a-šar ša ta-ra-am-u, an dem Orte wo sie wohnt. Sarg *Khors*, 157 ir-mu-u (3 *pl*); *Ann* 417. IV[2] 13 *b* 11, 12 (end) ki-gal-la lu-u ra-ma-a-ta. Neb vii 50 the palace ša Nabū-bal-uçur i-ir-mu-u ki-ri-ib-ša, in which *N* had dwelt. III 4 *no* 7, 2 the brother of my father i-ra-mi ša-da-a, lived in the mountains. KB iii (2) 6 *col* 3, 54—56 when Marduk i-na ri-si(= šì?)-e-tim i-ra-am-mu-u qiribka; 8 *no* 3 *col* 2, 15 ta-ra-am-mi-im kiribša, thou enterest it. P. N. Ina-Êsagila-ra-mat. — With parakku (*q. v.*). V 64 *c* 14 parakka da-ru-u i-na ra-mi-e-ka (§ 66 *rm*). — With double *acc.* = to put, place something on some one, endow. K 2001, 5 bēltu ša ša-lum-ma-tu ra-ma-at ra-šub-ba-tu lab-šat. IV[2] 27 *a* 49, 51 to the god .... ša puluxtu melammê na-šu-u ûmu ṭapinu ša ra-šub-ba-tu (= IM-XUŠ) ra-mu-u (= RI-A); *a* 53, 54 namtāru rabū ša ra-šub-ba-tu ra-mu-u, the great *n* who is clothed with terror; 25 *b* 48, 49 bu-un-na-an-ni-e ra-šub-ba-tu ra-mi (Br 2573, 7135), his person is endowed with majesty; 26 *a* 35, 36 the god of fire ša ša-lum-mat (= SU-ZI) ra-mu-u (= ME-IN-RI); 6 *b* 41, 42 qa-an pa-aš-ti ša ša-lum-ma-tu ra-mu-u (= RI-A); 18 *no* 1 *O* 8, 9 [ša] .... pu-lux-ta ša-lum-ma-tu ra-mu-u (= RI-A); 18 *no* 3 *O* i 29, 30 kak-ku ša nam-ri-ir-ri ra-mu-u (= RI-A) Br 11460. — II 31 *no* 2, 25—26 RA = ra-mu-u & a-ša-bu (Br 6362); II 26 *a-b* 18, 19 (Br 2573); H 15, 198. P. N. of god Ta-ra-mu-u-a, III 66 *col* 7, 6.

Q¹ = Q Scheil, *Nabd*, i 15 ir-ta-me šu-bat-su, took up his abode. IV² 20 *no* 1, 17, 18 i-ru-um-ma ir-ta-me šu-bat-su ni-ix-ta. *Rec. Trav.*, xxiv *nos* 1/2.

ℑ ip K 469 *R* 5, 6 šubat çābē ra-am-me, establish a military post (Hr^L 138).

Š with šubtu or parakku = settle some one, let some one dwell. ZA ii 134 *a* 32 u-ša-ar-ma-a. V 64 *a* 22 i-na ki-ir-bi-šu šu-ur-ma-a šu-ba-at-su; Scheil, *Nabd*, x 9 šu-ur-ma-a šu-bat-su-un. K 2711 *R* 41 (end) u-šar-ma-a šu-ba-a-te (BA iii 268, 269). V 35, 32 the gods I returned to their place and u-šar-ma-a šu-bat dūra-a-ta (BA ii 212, 213). Asb vi 124 ina Ê.... u-šar-me-ši parak da-ra-a-ti. I 49 *d* 26 parakkē-šu-nu u-šar-ma-a. IV² 9 *a* 32, 33 mu-šar-mu-u šub-tum. — Without šubtu: Sn ii 2 the fugitives (in such and such cities) u-šar-me, I settled. Sarg *Cyl* 20 ša ..... u-šar-mu-u (3 *sg*) ki-rib ^(māt) Bit-Xu-um-ri-a; *Khors* 139 (these people) ki-rib-šu (*i. e.* in Bit-Yakin) u-šar-me-ma; *Ann* 367; *Ann* XIV 88 (u-šar-ma-a); *Cyl* 73; KB iii (2) 88 i 49 (u-šar-mi, 3 *sg*); 90 ii 31 u-ša-ar-mi kiribšu; 48, 53 u-ša-ar-ma-a (1 *sg*) ki-ri-ib-bi-ši-in.

Šℑ Creat.-*frg* IV 146 Anu, Bēl and Ea ma-xa-zi-šu-un uš-ram-ma (3 *sg* *pr*) KB vi (1) 30, 31.

Š¹ II 19 *b* 50 ^(il) A-nun-na-ki ki-ma xu-um-çi-ri ina ni-gi-iç-ça-te uš-tar-mu[-u], Br 4950. — **Derr.** nirmu(ū) &

rimī(ē)tu *1.* dwelling, habitation {Wohnung, Haus}. Sn *Rass* 66 (ZA iii 318, 329); *Bell* 30; *Kui* 4, 29 see kummu, *b* (393 *col* 2); *Kui* 3, 23 the palace which former kings a-na ri-mit be-lu-ti-šu-un ušēpišu; Sn *Rass* 72; *Bell* 45, 46 (ri-me-ti); Sn vi 26 (& I 44, 82) a-na ri-mit šarrūtija. Sarg *Bull* 54 (ana) ri-me-ti-ši-na; *Ann* XIV 70 (× Oppert, ZA vi 450 *rm* 1: tab-re-ti-ši-na). K 806, 7—8 ri-me-t[u] a-na gi-mir-ri-ša, KB iv 136—7. Bu 88—5—12, 75 + 76 v 19 ri-mit (= šu-bat, 31) ^(il) Marduk *etc.* (BA iii 246—7). Z^Š iii 166 + iv 1 (end) u ri-me-ti. — T. A. (Lo) 26, 44 ri-mi-tu, Canaanite rendering of dūra-ši, its castle.

ramū *2.* *adj* IV² 45 *b* 42 ina qašti ra-mi-ti (Hr^L 281 *R* 9) = durch einen Bogenschuss (Zimmern, GGA '98, 825 × Johnston, JAOS xix 44: with bow relaxed, unstrung; also BA iv 531).

ramū 3. pr irmū. relax, become loose, give way, decay {sich lockern, locker werden, nachgeben, nachlassen, zu Grunde gehen}. IV² 59 *no* 2 *b* 12 see kusītu (419). Sn vi 33 iš-da-ša ir-ma-a, its (the palace's) foundation had given way. Lay 33, 15 see riksu, *f.* V 47 *b* 16 ki-ša-di-ša ir-mu-u. Perh. V 22 *h* 50 ra-ma-at ra-di i-ni (AV 7509) see radū & Z^B 93. — ac see under ℑ.

ℑ loosen, uncover (?) {lockern, lösen, entblössen} Z^B 91, 92. IV² 51 *a* 31 see kasū, 2 (412 *col* 2). IV² 17 *a* 7—8 midil šamē ellūti [i-na] ru-um-mi-ka (= SI-IL ....). K 89 *R* 4—5 me-me-ni | la u-ram-ma-na-ši (Hr^L 181); K 11 *R* 2 tu-ra-am-me (Hr^L 186). KB vi (1) 76 *R* *no* i 11 ub-bi ru-um-mi(-ma), mach das Tau (?) los, BA iv 131, 132. Z^Š iv 40 (pc) see kasītu. V 47 *a* 49 la-ba-ni i-ti-ku u-ram-mu-u ka-ša-du, with the explanation i-ti-ki : ra-mu-u : še-bi-ru — of the mother's womb (?): H 85 (K 46) i 42 (= TU-LU) see kirimmu (438 *col* 1; Br 1096; AV 7642); *ibid* (438) also for II 33 *a-b* 4 (= ŠU-KAL-TU-LU, Br 7194). — NE 11, 8 ru-um-mi-i, + 16 ur-tam-mi ^(sal) U-xat di-da-ša (KB vi (1) 427—8; 540: bosom {Busen}). *del* 171 (186) ru-um-me a-a ib-ba-ti-iq, KB vi (1) 243: (aber) mach (ihn) los, (dass) er nicht "abgeschnitten" werde; KAT[3] 550.

ℑ[t] see ℑ & Z^{B} vii 34. — **Derr.**: rimētu, 2, rimûtu.

NOTE. HAUPT, ZA ii 274 & AJSL xx 167 (30): ramû, dwell & ramû relax, are identical; the common meaning being: settle.

rimētu 2. KB i 12, 9 the temple of .... which since the time of Šalmaneser .... i-na ri-mit i-nu-xu, had remained (lain) in ruins.

rimûtu (?) K 8396 *R* 10 kal pag-ri-ia i-ta-xaz ri-mu-tu.

rimgiddû, a vessel. Thus Br 12060 reads V 42 *e-f* 18.

rimxu. V 22 *a-b* 75 me-e | A | = ri-im-xu, AV 7596; Br 11355. Perh. = rimku, *q. v.*

ri(tal?)-max-xu. II 22 *d-f* 15 a vessel = DUK RI-MAX.

ramaku, pr irmuk, ps irammu(a)k. AV 7486. H^{F} 30. Usually = pour, pour out {ausgiessen, vergiessen}; but JENSEN-ZIMMERN: wash {sich waschen}; and, again, WZKM xvi 190: pour out, (and) wash. Asb vi 21 ša .... ina libbi e-ku-lu iš-tu-u ir-mu-ku ip-pa-aš-šu. I 70 *d* 7—8 da-ma u šar-ka ki-i A-MEŠ (= mû) li-ir-muk; III 43 *d* 17—18 šar-ka u da-ma ki-i-ma mê li-ir(-mu)-muk (§ 23 *rm*). *del* 271 (303) he went into the well mê i-ra-muk (KB vi (1) 253 und wäscht sich mit Wasser). *Zû*-legend, K 3454 + K 9335, 18 e-nu-ma (ilu) Bêl i-ra-mu-ku mê ellûti, wie Bêl sich mit reinem Wasser wäscht; KB vi (1) 48—9; 367—8. IV[2] 54 *b* 33 (at that time) A (me) i-ram-muk. K 2852 + K 9662 ii 29 (end) arki niqê-ka ta-ra-muk mê, WINCKLER, *Forsch.*, ii 34—37. VAT 4105 iii 11—12 me-e lu ra-am-ka-ta, wash thyself in water (*Mittheil. Vorderas. Gesellsch.*, '02, *no* 1). K 11 *R* 14 ša i-ra-ma ka-a ni (Hr^{L} 186). ZIMMERN, *Ritualtafeln*, *no* 11 *R* 3 (*p* 112) ina še-rim la-am (ilu) Šamaš na-pa-xi (amêl) bârû egubbâ i-ra-muk (*var* mu-uk). T. A. (Ber) 28 *a* 37 šaš] ra-ma-ki; *b* 85 karpâti?? zi]-xi-ru-ti ša ra-ma-ki ša siparri. II 48 *e-f* 33 ŠU-[illegible] = ra-ma-ku, followed by ri-is-nu (34) Br 7155. H 48, 48 IN-DUB = ir-mu-uk, Br 3928.

Q^{t} = Q III 41 *b* 31 šarka u dâma ki-ma mê li-ir-tam-muk. Sn v 83 see pi(a)ršu, (838 *col* 2).

ℑ H 49, 52 IN-DUB-DUB = u-ra-am-me-ik (Br 3928, 3940); IV[2] 31 *R* 48 mê el-lu-ti ra-am-me-ik (= ip; §§ 30; 98 > rummêk). T^{M} i 105 ina [..... lu?]-'u-ti u-ra-me-ku-in-ni; K 72, 16 *a*: u-ra-me-ku-šu.

ℑ[t] pr ur-tam-mi-ik um-te-is-si, see misû ℑ[t] (566 *col* 2).

ℑ[tn] K 10255 i 6 tu-ur-ta-na-ma-ak-šu-ma iballu-uṭ, ZA x 122 *rm*; BEZOLD, *Catalogue*, 1075.

Š, with double *acc.* = causative of Q. IV[2] 54 *a* 51 šam-na (with oil) ši-ga-re-ka kîma mê li-šar-me-ik.

Derr.: ni(a)rmaku, ni(a)rmaktu (730 *col* 2) & these 4:

ramku, *pl* ramkê. JENSEN (KB vi (1) 367—368): one that has been cleansed {ein (einmal) Reingewaschener}; so also KAT[3] 590 & *rm* 4; × the usual (LOTZ, *Quaestiones*, 50, *etc.*) priest, as the one who pours out the libations; BA iii 246—7 *etc.* With or without prefix (amêl). Bu 88—5—12, 75 + 76 vi 20 ra-am-ki pa-ši-ši. Sarg *Khors* 157 (= *Ann* 418) see 'š'ur-maxxu (784 *col* 1). IV[2] 8 iv 1 ra-am-ku ellu ša (ilu) Ê-a .... a-na-ku = Z^{B} v/vi 175. II 51 *b* 16 ram-ku ellu eb-bu ša (ilu) Ê-a. II 32 *e-f* 8 'Š'UX-BU (Br 3038) = ra-am-ku between ni-'š'ak-ku (702 *col* 1) & šangamaxxu. 83, 1—18, 1330 iii 38 (su-us-bu) SUX = ra-am-ku. H 33, 782—3 me-e | ME | = ra-am-ku, & i-ši-ib | ME | = ramku; S^{b} 139, Br 10376; see išippu. V 23 *a-b-d* 49 me | ME ra-am-ku, together with išippu, šî pu ellu *etc.* V 24 *c-d* 5 ra-am-ku is explained by el-lum.

NOTE. Here perhaps râmku (rim-ku) TP i 30 *TP.* ar ka ma k bš bêlê rim-ku, *etc.*; Asp i 21; AV 4793 lid(t)-ku.

ramkûtu. *abstr. n.* the act of washing oneself {das sich Waschen} AV 7514. II 57 *c-d* 35; III 67 *c-d* 67 see *p* 694 *col* 1, 8—12; KB vi (1) 365. Also see ramû, 1 Q.

rimku. *m* washing; or, sprinkling, pouring out? {Waschen; oder, Ausgiessung}. IV[2] 7 *a* 33, 34 aš-šu bit] rim-ki el-li li-ki-šu-ma, AV 7597. IV[2] 26 *no* 5, 6—7 ri-im-ka ṭâb-ka, Br 7156. V 51 *b* 20, 21 ana bît rim-ki ina e-ri-bi-ka; also *b* 48—9, 54—55, 68—9 (Br 7158; iD also 4447); Hebr. xi 107 (ûm) rim-ki. K 979 *O* 7—8 ina ši-a-ri ša-ba-a-ṭi (KAT[3] 594 *rm* 2) ri-in-ku ina (al) Tar-bi-çi. K 168, 18 bît rim-ki ša-la-me-e, name of a temple (Lehmann, *Šamaššumukîn*); Zimmern, *Ritualtafeln* = Waschhaus; see *ibid*, *no* 26 iii 22.

rimkîtu. 82—3—23, 845 (late Babyl. text) 3—4 ta-aç-bat-ma ina rim-ki-it ta-na-as-su-uq, *Rec. Trav.*, xix 106, 107.

ram-kuš (?) V 27 *a-b* 39 (Br 1114).

ramamu (ramemu), ṗr irmum, *ps* iramum. AV 7487. cry, howl, bellow; roar, thunder {schreien, heulen, brüllen; donnern}. Z^B 18 & 87; PSBA '83, 73; ZK ii 166. IV^2 3 *b* 35—6 the muruç qaqqadi (see 591—2) i-ra-mu-um i-ša-as-si; 28 *no* 2 *a* 17—8 a-na ra-mi-mi-šu (= XAR-DU-BI, EMESAL), at the roaring of Adad, ‖ a-na ša-ga-mi-šu (§ 32*γ*; ZA iv 215). II 19 *a* 2 nar-kab-ta-ka ana ri-gim ra-me-me-ša (= XAR-DU-BI, 1), with its thundering sound, AV 6146. K 6071 šumma çiru ana ši-na in-na-dir-ma i-ram-mu-um (hisses {zischt}). NE 58, 15 il-su-u šamu-u qaq-qa-ru i-ram-mu-um; K 3764 *b* 15 (il) Adad ir-mu-um. II 49 *no* 5 *g-h* 52, 53 [ ]-DU; [ ]LA (Br 14482 NIN)-MA = ra-ma-mu; 54, 55 XAR & XAR-DU = ra-mi-mu, AV 7510; 56 XAR-DU = ri-im-mu. II 22 *e-f* 57 SAR-SAR = ra-ma-a[-mu?]; K 2043, 31 XAR-DU = ra-ma-mu; 32 TUM-DAM-MA = ra-ma-mu, Br 4980; 33, 34 XAR & XAR-DU = ra-mi-mu (Br 8539, 8557). S^b 204 *var* (Br 4746) see râmu, 2.

Ǫ[t] *del* 94 (99) (il) Adad ina libbi-ša ir-tam-ma-am-ma (§ 97).

Derr. these 3:

ramîmu see Ǫ (above). P. N. in K 83, 9 ša Ašur-ra-mi-im-šarri (Hr^L 202).

rimmu. howling, bellowing {Geschrei, Gebrüll}. K 2043, 28 BAD(zu-ša)DU (Br 1557); 29, A-AN .... (Br 14466, AV 7598) = ri-im-mu; also 27 (Br 8546); 35 (Br 8558); 30, SU(za-al)NI = ri-im-mu ša amêli. See also rimu.

rimmatu. howling, lamentation. Rm 282 *O* 4 a-na rim-ma-ti-ši-na ul i-z(ç)ab[-bar?], ‖ 3, a-na ik-kil-li-ši-na ul ... KB vi (1) 44, 45. II 22 *e-f* 55, 56 SAR-SAR (or KA-KA?) = ri-im[-ma-tum] & ri-im-ma[-tum].

ramânu, ramênu, r'âmnu (§§ 32*aγ*; 37*c* [and, again, Hilprecht, *Assyriaca*, 45 *rm* 2]; 55*c*; 63, 35) AV 7488; Z^B 22; perh. originally: highness √רום; then with pronominal-suffix = self {mit Pronominalsuffix = selbst}. KB iii (1) 132 *col* 2, 11 in e-mu-qan ra-ma-ni-a I built such & such; *col* 3, 12 in ram[a]-ni-šu-nu. NE 72, 29 [e-te]-te-z(ç)iq(k,g) ra-ma-ni (= myself) KB vi (1) 226—7. *del* 277 (312) ul aš-ku-un dum-qa a-na ram-ni-ja. K 41 *b* 22 .... ra-ma-ni-ja aš-ra-a-ti eš-te-ni-'-e (I will seek); *c* 19 thou hast destroyed it ra-man-ki (thyself), PSBA xvii 65 *foll.* I 49 *d* 11 ra-ma-ni, myself; K 8204, 4 (PSBA xvii 137). Banks, *Diss*, 14, 93 (16, 122) ina ra-ma-ni-ja u-ši-ib-ba-an-ni. Anp iii 104 (amêl) šaknu ša ra-ma-ni-a, my own governor (i 89 ša ra-ma(*var*-me)-ni-ja). V 47 *a* 59 maš-kan ram-ni-ja. K 2729 *O* 21 i-n]a bi-bil libbi-ja mi-lik ra-ma-ni[-ja]; 25 e-pu-šu bîd (bît?) ra-me(*var* ma, Rm 308)-ni-šu (KB iv 142—143), BA ii 566, 567. Šalm *Bal* IV 4 ra-ma-ni-šu, himself. S^P 158 + S^P II 962 *O* 24 (end) .... uk-kiš ra-man-šu, he hid himself. Sarg *Khors* 125 xat-tu ram-ni-šu im-qut-su, terror seized him; *Khors* 136 the lands which the Suteans .... ra-ma-nu-uš-šu-un u-tir-ru (+ *Ann* 361); see Smith, *Asurb*, 92, 54 a-na (i-di) ra-ma-ni-šu-nu. Šalm. *Mon*, *R* 79 ina kakkê ra-ma-ni-šu-nu they slew *G*, their lord. Esh iii 57 ki-i ṭe-im ra-ma-ni-šu, of his own free will. Sn iv 37 who the dominion over Šumer and Akkad ra-ma-nu-uš u-tir-ru; vi 12 the chariots .... ra-ma-nu-uš-šin ittanal-lakâ. Asb ii 113 a-na e-muq ra-man-i-šu it-ta-kil-ma (i 57 ra-ma-ni-šu), he relied upon his own strength; iv 31 ra-man-šu im-nu-ma; 100, ana pa-ra-aç ra-ma-ni (*var* man-i)-šu-nu (see parçu, 2; 837 *col* 1); vii 34 ana (amêl) ki-zi-e ra-ma-ni-šu iq-bi;

viii 3 (Uāte) ša ra-man-šu had made king of Arabia. K 2675 *O* 5 the cities u-tir ra-ma-nu-šu. Asb i 121 im-li-ku ra-man-šu-un; *cf* Merodach-Baladstone ii 51 ma-li-ku ram-ni-šu (= who takes his own counsel); KB iv 308—9 *no* viii 5 i-na ra-ma-ni-šu-nu. NE X *col* iv 14 it-ti ra-ma-ni-šu he counselled (KB vi (1) 222—3). III 15 *c* 23 *NN.* who the lands u-tir-ru ra-ma-nu-uš, diverted to his own use. I 7 E 6 (end) ra-ma-nu-uš. 80—7—19, 130, 7—8 alpu ra-ma-ni-šu, one's own ox; Beh 17 Cambyses mi-tu-tu ra-man-ni-šu mi-i-ti, committed suicide. Bu 91—5—9, 210, 9 ra-man-ku-nu a-na (amēl) *B* tu-ut-te-ra (PSBA xxiii 348 *foll*); K 84 *O* 23 u ra-man-ku-nu (*cf* 38) ina pān ili la tu-xaṭ-ṭa-a; 34, ina eli ra-mi-ni-ku-nu u-xaṭ-ṭu-u (*ibid*, 344—48); K 125, 14 ra-me-ni-šu-nu (Hr^{L} 403; 301; 196). NE VI 62 ka-par-ru ša ram-ni-šu, his own *k.* V 61 vi 41 whosoever lu-u ina ram-ni-šu utarru (takes it for his own use); *cf* Rm III 105 i *b* 22 (Winckler, *Forsch.*, i 254, 255); Winckler, *Sargon*, *p* 176, 49 ina qātē ram-ni-šu; ZA iii 20 *rm* 1. Camb 320, 11 (end) ul-tu ram-ni-šu, of his own accord; ultu ra-ma(n)-ni-šu Nabd 601, 19; Neb 182, 8. Banks, *Diss*, 12, 88 the heavens ina ra-ma-ni-šu-nu i-ru-ub-bu (rābu, 1). IV^2 21* *b* 34 (end) ša di-e-ni ra-ma-ni-šu i-din-nu; 19 *b* 47 ra-ma-ni ul xa-sa-ku; 9 *a* 22 en-bu ša ina ra-ma-ni-šu ib-ba-nu-u (also H 80 *O* 5—6; Br 8466). V 50 *b* 54, 55 amēlu šu-a-tum ina bīt ram-ni-šu (= IM-TE-A-NI; H 187—88) te-šu-u is-sa-xap-šu, in his own house; *cf* V 51 *b* 38, 39. K 56 iii 46 (= II R 15 *c-d*) ina za-bal ra-ma-ni-šu (= IM-TE-NA, Br 3615; IV^2 14 *no* 1 *a* 13, 14); & *cf* iv 31 i-na ra-ma-ni-šu (Br 8468) iq-qur i-pu-uš. S^{c} 286 ni-i | IM | ra-ma-nu ‖ emûqu; H 28, 614 *foll.* On itti ra-ma-ni-šu in *c. t.* see Meissner, 125 *no* 55.

NOTE. — K 619 (Hr^{L} 174) 16 ra-am-me-ja ma-a a-na-ku, Johnston, JAOS xx 251—2: I for myself.

(il) **Ramān(u)** P. N. of a Syrian-Aramean god = Hebr רִמּוֹן. But KAT^3 445: schon im babyl. Semitisch zu Hause; √ramamu. From Babylonian the word passed into the other dialects. $Z^{\check{S}}$ viii (K 2866) 19 (il) Ram-ma-nu ri-ix-çu. K 349, 7 (il) Ra-man-nu. KB i 206—7 (Eponym-list) *col* 1, 848 P(B)ur (il) Ra-ma-na (*var* -man); see Lehmann, ZA x 88 >< Oppert, ZA ix 313. K 429, 22 Ra-ma-nu-u, as P. N. ZA vi 161 where god Ra-ma-a-nu-um is mentioned with the goddess Aš-ra-tum (*Ištar*); & KAT^3 433; 442—51.

NOTE. — For AN-IM, usually read (il) Ram(m)ān, see (il) Adad; Johns, *Deeds and Documents*; § 9, 5; and "Addenda".

ramapu, AV 7508; Br 8563, see ra'azu.

rimtū (??). D 87 ii 58; iii 69 GIŠ-RI-GU-ZA = rim(xab, gil?)-tu-u. Br 2586, 2608; AV 3078.

rimētu *3.* T. A. (Ber) 25 *b* 4 lu-u ri-me-ti abnu šāmtu.

runē. Pinches, JRAS, '98, 444 name of a gardenplant.

rannūnu (?) a medical term. Constant. *no* 583 *O* 2 (end). U(=šam?)ra-an-nu-un (or šam-ra-an-nu-un?) + 5 + 16; *R* 5. Scheil, *Notes d'Epigr.*, ix (*Rec. Trav.* xxiii).

rininu. KB iv 60 *no* iv 13 li-rik ri-nin-šu(-ma), his whining shall last long {sein Gewinsel dauere lange}. P. N. Gu-la-ri-nin-ni, name of a female, AV 1719.

ren-nin-ti (?) Su *Bell* 29 ugārešun ren-nin-ti (?) D^{Pr} 155 *rm*; § 65, 29 *rm b.* or xab-çu-ti? see šaxarratum.

rēsu 1. smash, break, *etc.* {zerschlagen, brechen, *etc.*} = רסס. V 18 *a-b* 15 SAG-GIŠ-RA = re-e-su : šu, AV 7601; Br 3608; same id = nēru, nāru (721 *col* 2, above), rasab(p)u, *etc.* perh. V 41 *c* 21, 22 ra-a-su, ra-sa-bu; ZA iv 158 ‖ axazu. JAOS xv 6 + 16 compares רעש (Judges v 4) & Arab رَعَسَ, tremble. See šapasu.

ג Creat.-*frg* IV 16, thy weapon may not succumb, li-ra-i-su na-ki-re-ka, let it crush thine enemy. V 45 v 16 tu-ra-'a-as(z, ç?). — Der.:

rēsu *2.* V 18 *a-b* 16 SU-KU (*i. e.* KA + inserted ša = gar)-A = ri-e-su, Br 179. Same id in II 7 *g-h* 5; V 39 *g-h* 7 = xu-šax-xu, Br 178.

ri-e-su *3.* & **ri-si-a-tim**, late Babylonian for rēšu, 1 & rīštu, *q. v.*

rusū, *pl* rusē. *m* witchery, hoax {Hexerei, Spuk}?? ‖ kišpu & ruxū, *q. v.* AV 7645; Jensen, *Diss*, 63 (Gift, Vergiftung). id -RI-A; = ruxū. T^{M} iii 156 ru-su-u[-ki up-ša-šu]-ki; K 12916 reads instead: ru-su-ki, *etc.*, BA iv 159. See also pinnaru (814 *col* 2) & Br 4256.

rasab(p)u. *ps* irasib strike, smash, pierce, kill {schlagen, zerschlagen; durchbohren, töten} ZA iv 280; AV 7516. I 27 *no* 2, 42 nap-ṭar-tu la i-ra-si-pi, the key he shall not smash. Perh. *del* 171 (186) end: šu-du-ud a-n i[r-ra-si-ib?], BA i 138; KB vi (1) 242—3. I 7 F 7 ana ra-sa-ap nak-ru-ti; *cf* Esh *Sendsch*, *R* 34. V 18 *a-b* 25 (V 41 *c* 22) see rēsu, 1. & Br 14195. ra-si-pu, crushing, Sarg *Ann* 209 *etc.*

ב slay, kill {erschlagen, töten} GGN '83, 105. usually with ina kakki(ē). K 2675 *O* 18 (çābē) tuk-la-ti-šu u-ra-as-si-bu ina kakki (KB ii 238—9). Sarg *Khors* 84 *NN.* whom his son i-na kakki u-ra(-as)-si-bu-šu. Esh ii 9 *Teušpa* and his whole army u-ra(-as)-si-ba ina kakki; III 15 *c* 2. Sn vi 24 whosoever among them had escaped, u-ra-sa-bu (3 *pl ps*) i-na kakki. Asb iv 2 him and his family u-ra(s)-sib (3 *pr*) ina kakkē; v 110 ina kakkē u-ras (*var* ra-as)-sib (1 *pr*) mundaxçēšu; vii 35 ra-si-ban-ni (= ip) ina kakkē (H^{F} 60) § 98; vii 42 his swordbearer who u-ra(-as)-si-bu-šu ina kakkē (see ZA x 83 on *ll* 39—43); vii 118 the Arabians u-ra(-as)-sib (= 1 *pr*) ina kakkē. Scheil, *Nabd*, i 40, 41 (the son) i-na kakki | u-ra-as-si-ib-šu (*i. e.* the king of Assyria). — Without ina kakki; Asb ix 88 [il] Dibbar (Gir, Ur, Ir?)-ra u-ra(-as)-si-pa (*var* -ba) ga-re-ja. Sarg *Khors* 16 the great gods who u-ra-as-si-ba na-gab ga-re-ja; Pp IV 62 u-ra-si-bu (*var* ba); XIV 21. Smith, *Asurb*, 285, 2 u-ra-si-bu (3 *pl*); Rm III 105 i *b* 19 axamēš u-ra-sa-a-bu (Winckler, *Forsch*, i 254, 255). — **Derr.**:

rasbu (?) K 596, 6. So M^{S} 89 *col* 2; but see raçpu.

risbu (AV 7603); *f* **risbatu** (AV 7601). V 18 *a-b* 26, 27 .... KU (*i. e.* KA + inserted ša = gar) = ri-is-bu (Br 13920; 13897 & see rēsu, 2); .... MU = ri-is-ba-tum, preceded by rasabu. II 39 *g-h* 50 ri-is-ba-tu = di-ik-tu (Br 2608).

risbītu (?). KB ii 192—3 on Asurb iv 98 ša ina šib(p)-ṭi ris-bi-ti u ni-ib-ri-e-ti i-še-tu-u-ni. slaughter {Gemetzel}. See šaqqaštu.

risibtu ruin, destruction {Zerstörung}? K 2608 + 2638 + 3101 *b* + 3435 *O* 22 si-kip-tu ri-si-ib-tu u xi-im-ça-a-ti ša ummān nakiri šuátu. Martin, *Textes Relig.* ('03) 304/5.

ri-si-xi (?). Neb 132, 9 (end).

רסן whence perh. Šalm. *Throne-inscr.* iii 15 ra-si-nat (✕ Craig, *Diss*, Appendix: mat). — Q^{t} mur-ta-as-nu, an epithet of Adad, ZA iv 215 (see *p* 595 *col* 1). Perh. = pour out {ausgiessen, ausschütten}. — **Derr.**:

risnu (*z*, *ç*?). II 48 (K 4386 i 44) *e-f* 34 A-ŠU- -A = ri-is-nu (AV 7568, Br 11571), preceded by ra-ma-ku. Perh. Sp II 265 *a* xxv 11 ri-is(or iç?)-ni (il) Šamši (ZA x 13, but *cf* PSBA xvii 151 *fol*).

risittu (?). II 30 *e-f* 72 A-BUR-RA = ri-si-it-tum, Br 1209; see *ibid* 70 *b-c* & Br 8972. AV 7600.

rapū ? *pc* li-ir-pu. Z^{B} iv 53 (see *ibid*, *p* 56) perh. mistake for li-ir-mu (ramū 3, *q. v.*).

rappu V 23 *c-d* 27 see rabbu, 2; H 122 *O* 9 see rabbu, 3.

ruppu. D 89 vi 63 (iç) ru-up-pi, AV 7647; perh. better: giš-ru up-pi KB vi (1) 392—3.

rapadu 1. AV 7518. *pr* irpud; *ps* irappud. Jensen, KB vi (1) 429; 471 run (away) {(davon)laufen, rennen} against Z^{B} 18; G § 103 *note* 2 & others: be stretched out, stretch out, lie down, encamp. NE 12, 35 why Êabani itti nammaššē ta-rap-pu-ud (*var* -da) çēra (also see KB vi, 1, 192, 12)? 11, 24 imurāšuma Êabani i-rap-pu-da çabāti (also 15, 42); 59, 2 Gilgameš weeps bitterly for Êabani his friend i-rap-pu-ud çēra (67, 10; KB vi (1) 202); 59, 5 (71, 5) mūta aplaxma (*q. v.*) a-rap-pu-ud çēra; 67, 19 if it be possible çēra lu-ur-pu-ud (KB vi

(1) 214). Sarg *Ann* 346 ir-pu-du kîma šaxê. Bu 89, 4—26, 209 *O* 19 (il) Sin bêlu rabu-u tax-sil[-ti]-šu lu-šag-lid(t)-su ma (il) šêdu balâṭi li-ir-pu-ud MARTIN, *Textes Religieuses*, '00 *p* 12 on CRAIG, *Relig. Texts*, ii *pl* 2. id + *pl* = irpudûni Nabd *Ann* iii 19 *cf* xarinê & PSBA xxiv 224. K 2867 *O* 32 (S. A. SMITH, *Texts*, ii 1 *fol*) i-ir-ap-pi-du da-ad-me ur-ru u mu-šu. VATh 244 ii 22 rap-ta(= da)-at, he encamped (?, ZA ix 157; pm). II 29 *c-d* 45 ŠU-DAG = ra-pa-du (AV 7458, Br 7179: ra-di-du), preceded by ŠU-DAG = šur(?; II R)-pu-du, Br 7178. H 22, 413 da-ak DAG | ra-pa-du = II 27 *a-b* 47; together with lasamu & nabalṭû, Br 5533. II 35 *e-f* 57 ra-pa-du ‖ a-la(?)-a-ku.

𝔔t run away }davon laufen} Sarg *Ann* 163/4 šadû u madbaru, *q. v.*, ir-tap-pu-du šar-ra-qiš (like a thief). III 41 ii 18; I 70 iii 20; KB iv 164 v 12 see kamâtu, *p* 399 *col* 1; BA ii 144; ZA vii 181. K 4470 ii 8 ir-tap-pu-ud imêru (+ 3 + 9); KB iii (1) 100 *rm* 5. perh. Sp II 265 *a* xiii 7 (end).

𝔍t mur-tap-pi-du (see ZA iv 31, 33). K[M] 53, 15 ekimmu mur(!)-tap-pi-du (× MEISSNER, ZDMG 50, 750 *fol*); T[M] iv 21 a-na ekimmi mur-tap-pi-du ša pa-qi-da la i-šu-u, KB vi (1) 429: ein ruhelos dahinfahrender Totengeist; also see KAT[3] 460.

𝔖 IV[2] 61 *b* 60 (= v 20) ja-u çi-it lib-bi-ja çêra tu-šar-pi-di. See also above, 𝔔.

Derr. these 2?:

rapâdu *2.* some disease }eine Krankheit}. H 82—3 i 20 (SA-NUM-MA-LAL) see maškadu, 603 *col* 2; Br 3145. II 28 *c-d* 25—28 SA-AD-GAL (Br 3108); SA-PAT (Br 3153); SA-PAT-BA-AG-A (Br 3154); SA-XI-RA-RA (Br 3148) = ra-pa-du. V 21 *a-b* 5 see çidânu, 2 & Br 3156.

ripittu. VATh 244 iii 28 A-ZA-LU-LU = ri-pi-it-tum (ZA ix 163).

רפח, see narpuxu, 730 *col* 2; & perh. (šam) ripxu, see ribxu.

rapasu. beat, crush to pieces, thresh }schlagen, zerschlagen, dreschen}. AV 7521. V 17 *c-d* 27—29 [SAG-GIŠ]-RA = ra-pa-su ša še[-im?]; SAG-GIŠ-RA-RA = *r* ša da-a-ki (= in the meaning of: kill); ŠI-PA-PA = *r* ša pa-ni (Br 6372, 5521, 9350). See nâru, nêru, 1. Perh. II 16 *b-c* 28, 29 pa-an al-pi a-li-ki ina up-pi ta-rap-pi-is (Br 6372). 81—2—4, 294, 7 ki(-)a(-)da (or ki?) a-ṭa su-xa-ti ir-pi-is(ç?). — See on etymology also FRÄNKEL, BA iii 76 *ad* BARTH, *Etym. Stud.*, 33.

𝔑 see narpusu, 731 *col* 1.

Derr. — narpasu (731 *col* 1) &:

ripsu. V 17 *c-d* 30, 31 ŠA-XAR-RA-TUR-TUR (Br 12128) = ri-ip-su; ŠA-RA-AX (Br 6374, 7480) = *r* ša še-im, AV 7605. III 51 *no* 9 (K 480) 20 ina ri-ip-si la ix-xi-kim.

rapaqu. H 72 ii 4 eqla ina ix(ax)-zi u-rap-pi-iq (= BA-AB-AG-TA, Br 2791), perh. = the field he protects by a fence, AV 7519. Arab رَفَقَ. II 38 *e-f* 7 (amêl) AL-AG-A = ra-pi-qu, Br 5758; AV 7526; *cf* II 65, 5.

NOTE. — IV[2] 39 *a* 7 (mât) Ra-pi-qu, Sarg *Ann* 7; II 60 *b* 8 šar ša Ra-pi-qa (ki), Br 12800. On the cities Rapiqu, Rabiqu, see ZA xv 217, 219; WINCKLER, *Forsch.*, i 156 *rm* 1; AV 7525.

rapašu. pr irpiš, ps irappiš. be or become wide, extend }weit sein oder werden} § 84. Hebr רחב, Arm רפס. id DAGAL, § 9, 247; often in Astronomical texts. AV 7522. K 479, 33 bît-ka i-ra-ap-pi-iš, thy house will increase (*i. e.*, prosper); 35, under the protection of the king, my lord, li-ir-pi-iš. III 66 *R* 20 *e* ur-çu ra-piš (perh. = pm); Asb viii 83 forest ša çu-lul-ši-na rap-šu. II 47 *a-b* 18 see napašu 𝔍t (710 *col* 2, below). V 20 *e-f* 73 see muççu (571 *col* 2); Br 10918. V 36 *a-c* 59 šu-u | 𒀀 | ra-pa-šu, Br 8734. S[c] 121 pi-eš | PEŠ | ra-pa[-šu] & see *ibid.*, *rm*; H 35, 832. S[c] 1 *b* 30 (Br 1882).

𝔔t K 7674, 14—15 ur-ru-uk nap-ša-ti | rit-pu-uš çur-ri.

𝔍 make wide, widen, broaden, increase }erweitern, mehren} § 33; Beh 107. TP i 61 the dominion of my land u-re-piš, I enlarged. Asb x 97 eli ša max-ri šu-bat-su u-rap-piš (1 *sg*), ‖ u-šar-ri-xa ep-še-te-e-šu (KB ii 234—5). K 2852 + K 9662 iv 22 names of cities: Aš(š)ur-ni-ir-šu-u-rap-piš; Aš(š)ur-ni-ir-ka-rap-piš (= ip?), WINCKLER, *Forsch.*, ii 40—8. Sarg *Khors* 82; *Ann* XIV 12, 13 see kisurru (418 *col* 2). Esh vi 18 tal-lak-ta-ša ma-'-diš u-rap-piš. Sn ii 29 u-rap-piš (1 *sg*) ma-a-ti. I 35 *no* 3, 17—18 Adadnirāri .... ša (ilāni) .... ri-çu-šu | i-li-ku-ma u-ra-pi-šu māt-su. pc Bu 88—5—12, 75 + 76 viii 22 kimti lu-rap-piš (1 *sg*), BA iii 254; *cf* SCHEIL, *Rec. Trav.*, xvii *p* 190, *no* IX (S 4, Constant.). Rm 76 *O* 14 li-rap-pi-šu (= *pl*) [pa-pal]-li (Hr^{L} 358) BA iv 508; DT 83 *R* 5 zi-ru-šu li-rap-piš-ma ‖ li-šam-'-i-du na-an-nab-šu (PINCHES, *Texts*, 16 *no* 4). — ps K 3182 iii 8 u[-rap]-pa-aš kim-ta; *cf* 81—6—7, 209, 89 (BA iii 260—8). ZA iv 15 (K 3459 *R*) 13 pi-is-nu-qa (?) tu-rap-pa-aš; IV^{2} 9 *b* 4 (end) u-ra-pa-aš (= MU-UN-DA-MA-AL-LA). — ip K^{M} 5, 4 ru-up-piš li-im-id lil-li-ki. ru-ub-bi-ši (= *f*) ze-ri-im (see zēru, *c*; 295 *col* 1), § 66. ac TP i 49 miçir mātišunu ru-up-pu-ša (extend § 98) iqbiūni; ii 99 a-na ru(-up)-pu-ši. Esh *Sendsch*, *R* 35, 36 mi-çir (mât) Aššur ru-up-pu-ši. Asb x 75 aš-šu ru-up-pu-uš (*var* -šu) tal-lak-ti-šu. K 601, 14, 15 ru-up[-pu-uš] zēri (Hr^{L} 7), BA i 625. ag Lay 33 (Sarg *Nimr*) 9 Sargon mu-rap-piš mi-çir (mât) Aššur; Sarg *Cyl* 24 mu-rap-pi-šu pulungišun (*q. v.*). I 35 *no* 3, 15 Ašurnaçirpal mu-ra(p)-piš da-ad-mi. I 43, 5 xaṭṭu i-šar-tu mu-rap-pi-šat mi-iç-ri. Sarg *Cyl* 70 bēlit ilāni mu-rap-pi-šat ta-lit-ti-šu (*cf* *Ann* XIV 83; Sn *Kui* 4, 39 urappišu talittu). KB iii (2) 76, 29 xaṭṭu mu-ra-ap-pi-ša-at ma-a-tu; *cf* 82—7—4, 42 *R* 19. S 1708, 9 a-ta-nu mu-rap-pi-iš-tu ša-as-su-ru (Br 5451, 8010). 76, 11—17, 56 (*cf* S^{c} 121 *rm* 1) E-PIŠ-PIŠ = bitu mu-rap-piš. AV 5546. — With uznu. K 698, 2 šar māti uz-nu u-rap-[pa-aš]; NE 6, 41; 13, 22 *etc.* u-ra-pi-šu uzunšu = made him intelligent.

ℑ¹ = ℑ H 81 (K 133) *R* 17, 18 (Ninib) ze-ra ur-tap-pi-iš (= BA-PI-PI, Br 7968).

Šℑ I 7 F 18 see xarīçu, 1 (340 *col* 1), I caused to be made wide, § 85.

Derr. ritpāšu, tarpašū and these 8 (?):

rapšu, *f* rapaštu (BA i 375) & rapaltu (§ 51) wide, large, broad {weit, gross, breit} §§ 37*b*; 65, 6. AV 7529. id DA-GAL, H 24, 492. § 9, 247; Br 5452. H 110, 29 .... DA]-MA-AL | GIŠ-MI-DA-GAL | çillu rap-šu (= D 129, 126) Br 6681. II 37 *e-f* 62 qa-ta-at-tu (*q. v.*) ra-pal-tum (AV 7520): çi-xir-tu. — *a*) wide, extensive; distant {weit, zahlreich; entfernt}. V 33 i 34 šar māt Bābili ra-pa-aš-tim. TP ii 56 Qum-mu-xi rapaš-ta; IV^{2} 39 *a* 19 Qu-ti-i ra-pal-ti. TP III (Lay 17) 24 (end) (mât) Ur-ar-ṭi rap-ši (ii 39 ra-ap-ši). I 48, 5 rap-šu na-gu-u; III 8, 100 na b(p)-ra-ru-u rap-šu. Šalm, *Mon*, *O* 39 çēru rap-šu. KB vi (1) 92, 22 ina tam-ti ra-pa-aš-ti (*Adapa*-legend). K 3474 i + K 8132 i 33 ta-ma-tum ra-paš-tum. Merodach-Balad.-stone ii 15, 16 xi-çib tam-tim rapaš-tim. V 47 *a* 50 kum (kat?)-ti rap-ša-tu (see 399 *col* 2; & qumtu). V 52 *b* 49 see mērištu, 1 (593 *col* 2); also see mērišu, 1 (*ibid*). K 3182 iv 1 erçi-tim ra-pa-aš-ti (+ 11, tum); 9, erçi-tim rapaš-tim; KB vi (1) 44, 18 ma-a-tum ra-pa-aš-tum; K 3238 i 13 (Br 6679; § 68 *rm* 1); IV^{2} 1* iii 15—16 (-ti). H 5 ina qaq-qar a-ga-a rap-ša-a-tum, on this wide earth; on qaq-qaru rapaštu in Achaemenian inscrr. = ארץ רבה, see HAUPT in TOY, *Ezekiel*, *p* 79. V 69, 19—20 rapšāti (*i. e.* DA-GAL-MEŠ) mātāti Na-i-ri (§ 121); see also SMITH, *Asurb*, 76, 27. I 66 *c* 33 in i-ra-at er-zi-tim ra-pa-aš-tim. KB vi (1) 78 *R* ii 17 ina er-çi-e-ti ra-pa-aš-ti. IV^{2} 1 *a* 25 u-ri rap-šu-ti. sūqu rapšu see sūqu. šamē rap-šu-ti Sn iv 69; v 46; IV^{2} 1* *col* 3, 14 si-bit ilāni šame-e rap-šu-ti (= DAGAL-LA-MEŠ); followed by (16) ma-a-ti ra-pa-aš-ti; see also IV^{2} 5 *a* 50.

libbu rapšu (§ 73) *e. g.* Asb iv 37 lib-bu rap-šu, magnanimous, *etc.* K 283, 7 ilāni uzna rapaš-tu u lib-bi rap-šu il-tak-nu-ku-nu-ši.

rapšu uzni, of a far-reaching, open, mind. II 21 *a* 27 uznā rapal-tu (in colophon); II 23 *a* 41 *etc.* ZA v 68 (below). IV^{2} 3 *b* 41 rap-ša uz-ni (Br 6979); 15 *b* 63 (Br 6978); II 60, 44 (*i. e.* Marduk); on id see LEHMANN, BA ii 599 *fol.* D 49,

29 uznu (*var* uz-nu) ra-pa-aš-tum (*var* to rapaš-tu; *cf* T^{M} iii 196; i 148; L^{4} i 10, -tu); V 37 i 1 rap-ša uz-nu. V 43 *c-d* 43 epithet of Nabû: pi-it uz-ni rap-ša uz-ni (Br 2790); also K 2361 + S 389 i 34 (ZA iv 237). Merodach-Balad.-stone ii 48 *M-B* calls himself rap-ša uzni. — *b*) numerous }zahlreich{. TP iii 52 um-mānāte-šu-nu rapšāti; III 8, 99. V 35, 16 um-ma-ni-šu (24, -ja) rap-ša-a-tim. nišē rapšāti, see nišu, people (737 *cols* 1, 2) & KB iii (2) 78, 3 ni-ši-ja ra-ap-ša-a-tim; KB iii (1) 112, 113 *col* 2, 9 (ra-ap-ša-tum). V 33 i 17 i-na zēr (?) rap(?)-šu (*cf* KB iii, 1, 136). kimtu rapaštu, see kimtu.

rapšiš, *adv* AV 7528. Neb viii 40 see kummu, *b* (393 *col* 2). Haupt, ZK ii 274 supplies rap-šeš (as AV 7528) to H 80, 18 after xa-diš (17, DAGAL-LA).

rapaštu *1.* greatness. power, *amplitudo* }Grösse, Macht{ AV 7523. II 43 *a-b* 9 ra-pa-aš-tum ‖ me-til-lu-tum.

rapaštu *2.* some part of the body. K 4609 *O* 11 ina eli ra-pa-aš-ti iš-di-xu um-mid-ma, Craig, *Relig. Texts*. ii *pl* 11.

rupšu *c. st.* rupuš. width, breadth }Weite, Breite{ AV 7648. *dcl* 25 (30) lu-u mit-xur ru-pu-us-sa u mu-šal(rak, g?)-ša, KB vi (1) 230—1: einander entsprechend sollen sein seine Breite und seine Länge. I 7 *F* 23 see mašaxu, 1 Q. (600 *col* 2). NE 53 (*no* 26) 44 (end): II GAR ru-pu-uš-ki, KB vi (1) 186—7. H 24, 493 DAGAL = ru-up-šu (= V 20 *g-h* 51), preceded by šiddu, pūtum, šuplum, milū, Br 5453; V 29 *e-f* 75; see rapašu. S 1708 *O* (= IV² R 18* *no* 6) 11—12 ru-pu-us-su-nu u-nak-ki-ir.

rappašu (?) maxme, 522 *col* 1, below.

ripšu (?) H 70, 36 ri-ip-šu.

rupuštu *1.* K 3445 + Rm 396 *O* 29 ru-pu-uš-tu ša ti-[. . . .

rup(b?)uštu *2.* AV 7648. saliva, foam. spittle? }Speichel, Geifer, Schaum{ or the like. IV² 19 *a* 31, 32 ru-'-tu ru-pu-uš-tu (. . . . . DIB-BA) pišu imtalli, Jensen, *Diss*, 91 & *rm* 2 (= Z^{B} vii 32). Jensen-Schulthess, 90: Hebr-Talm. רְפַשׁ, Isa 57:20 = رفش. V 23 *h* 5 ru-pu-uš-tu (Br 8134) preceded by ru-'-tu, and followed by el-la-tu, im-tu, *etc*.

ru-pa-tum, see rûbatu, hunger.

ripûtu (?) T. A. (Lo) 63, 17 riqqu ÇAR *pl* | mu-ur-ru ana ri-pu-u-ti; for medicinal purposes, KB v 299 *rm* *; KAT³ 653 compare רְפוּאָה.

ripītu. Zimmern, *Ritualtafeln*, *no* 66 *O* 8 akal ri-pi-tu; 67 *O* 7. Zimmern: eine Getreideart, *cf* רִיפוֹת. Also perhaps Johns. *Doomsday-Book*, 15, 1 bīt ri-pi-tu (*p* 69) = granary (?); and *no* 7, left hand edge ii 3: 1 ri-bit.

rêçu. help, be helpful, assist }helfen, hilfreich sein{. AV 7607. Delitzsch in L^{T} 153. IV² 60* C *R* 14 ul i-ru-ça ili qātī ul içbat. K 3464 *O* 18 e-li-šu ru-çi, + 24 a-na ja-a-ši ru-çi, come to his assistance! Craig, *Religious Texts*, i *pl* 66; PSBA xxiii 115 *foll*. K^{M} 53, 4 (ilu) Ê-a u (ilu) Šamaš u (ilu) Marduk ja-a-ši ru-ça-nim-ma; *cf* T^{M} vii 139. T. A. (Ber) 50 *R* 17 a-na ri-zi-ja, to help me.

ג ZA ii 128 *b* 24 lu-ri-çi. V 51 iv 25 a-šar ta-xa-zi lu-ri-çu-ka (Br 6579; 4537: ID-DAX-ZU-XE-A), they have, indeed, helped thee (or: lu re-çu-ka, *noun*?). T. A. (Lo) 73, 17 ja-nu-ma amēl-lum ša ij-ri-zu-ni, there is no one to rescue me (KB v 379 *rm* * √riç û).

Derr. these 4 (5?):

rêçu. helper, comrade }Helfer, Beistand{. ib § 9, 25. Sn i 20 a-di ummān Êlam ti re-çi-šu; *Kui* 1, 4. Asurb viii 34 re-çi-e-šu a-duk, his comrades I killed. Šalm, *Mon*, *O* 29 with the assistance of the gods re-çe-šu, his helpers. Sarg *Ann* 326 adi ri-çi-šu (& see Winckler, *Sargon*, 57 *rm* 2: foreign auxiliary troops of Merodach-Baladan); *Khors* 120, 121 Ni-bi-i a-di um-ma-an e-la-mi-i ri-çi-i-šu; *Ann* 249 ri-çi-e-šu. IV² 34 (K 2130) *R* 9 ri?]-çi-šu u ellāte-šu u-qa-i-la, Boissier, *Rer. Sém.*, x 275 *foll*. KB iv 102—3, 8 (end) the gods . . . . ri-çi-šu, his helpers. Scheil, *Nabd*, ii 2—3 ri-çu id-din-šum-ma ‖ tap-pa-a u-šar-ši-iš (√rašû). Samsu-iluna (KB iii, 1, 132) ii 17 (*etc.*) Adad ri-çi-ja, my helper. V 44 (*c*-)*d* 61 (ilu) Ša-maš ri-çu-u-a. T^{M} ii 89 at-ta-ma da-a-a-ni at-ta-ma ri-çu-u-a. In P. N. Nergal-ri-çu-u-a, AV 6343; KB iv 300—1, *no* ii 9 Bêl-ri-çu-u-a; II 64 *c* 50, 51 Nabû-ID-DAX-u-a; Nabû-re-çu-u-a (§ 74, 1 *rm*), Nebo is my helper. Ašur-ri-çu-u-a, Rm 2, 3

(Hr^L 380) *O* 2; K 181 *R* 4 (end; Hr^L 197); 81—7—27, 199 (Hr^L 382) *O* 2 ardu-ka Ašur-ri-çi-u-a (R. F. Harper, AJSL xiv 6/7). K 620, 24 (Hr^L 91 *R* 5) ri-çu-a i-ma-gur. Creat.-*frg* IV 107 u ilāni ri-çu-u-ša, and also the gods, her helpers. Perhaps Sp II 265 *a* xxv 2 ri-ça-an (PSBA xvii 151, -am-ma); 4, ri-ça u šik-la-tum za-mar ul a-mur; 9, ri-ça liš-ku-nu [il] Ninib ša id[....]; ZA x 13. II 39 *e-f* 5 SAG-TAB = ri-çu, followed by a-lik ṭap-pu-ti (H 38, 91); K 49 (II 62 *no* 1) ii 27 SAG-TAB = re-e-çu, Br 3567. A ‖ is:

rūçu *1.* in P. N. Camb 135, 3 Nergal-ru-çu-u-a (BA iii 467).

rēçtu, *c. st.* rēçat, *f* to rēçu. II 19 *b* 5—6 re-ça-at (= ID-DAX) ed-li a-rik-ta (AV 7606; Br 6579), the bow, the helper of the noble; H^{OV} xxxiii.

rēçūtu, help, assistance {Hülfe, Beistand} usually in phrase: alaku (ana) rēçūtu, come to the assistance of. AV 7608. ZA ii 152, 36 ri-çu-tum. TP v 83 who a-na re-çu-ut (mât) Mu-uç-ri iš-ša-ak-nu. Anp i 76 ina ri-çu-ti ša ilāni, with the help of the gods; iii 119 ina ri-çu-te ša Ša-maš u Adad ilāni tik-li-a. Šalm, *Mon*, 48 ana ri-çu-ut a-xa-meš i-tak-lu-ma. Sarg *Khors* 123 (*Ann* 231) + 130 see šaxaru Q (751 *col* 2); 119 il-li-ka ri-çu-us-su, he came to his assistance; *Ann* 407; 36. Sn ii 75—6 who il-li-ku re-çu-us-su-un; iv 40, 41 the king of Elam who idā-šu is-xu-ru-ma il-li-ku ri-çu-us-su; v 53—4 the gods il-li-ku ri-çu-ti (to my assistance). I 43, 36 the king of Elam ša ri-çu-ut (amêl) Bābili (ki) il-li-ku. Asurb iv 32 aš-šu .... a-lak re-çu-ti-šu, to come to his help; iv 36 the gods which il-li-ku re-çu(-u)-ti; ix 92 (re-çu-ti); see also KB ii 276, 277 *l* 36 ša a-na ri-çu-tum .... il-li-ku; Asurb vii 99, 100 a-na ri-çu-tu Šamaššumukīn .... iš-pur-am-ma; *cf* iv 6—7; viii 32—33 (ri-çu-u-ti). V 65 *b* 38 i-na ši-ip-ri-ka šu-qu-ru lil-lik-ki ri-çu-u-tu. III 4 *b* 52 (*no* 6, 1) ina ri-çu-te ša (il) Ašur. Scheil, *Nabd*, ii 7 u-ša-lik ri-çu-ut-zu; *cf* 23, 24. ZA iv 240, 4 še-e-ru ri-çu-ti-ja. T. A. (Ber) 76, 44 çābē ri-zu-ti; (Ber) 36, 31 ... ri-iç-çu-ti-ja. 81, 2—4, 219 *O* ii 19 so and so many kings it-ti-šu-nu ana ri-çu-ti-šu-nu.

Note. — Neb (*Jour. Am. Or. Soc.*, xvi 74) ii 24 reads lu(-)ri-çi-tu kul[lat balāṭi]ja.

rūçu *2.* Perhaps II 6 *b* 35, 36 ru(m, *i. e.* ▸—)-çu, name of an animal: runner {Läufer}?

raççu. Nabd 82, 1 one hundred ra-aç-çi.

רצן. ℑ S^c 11 (41) ga-al | GAL | ru-uç-çu-nu (Br 2050); S^c i 41. AV 7649. *Etana-legend* (KB vi, 1, 110—111 *no* III) 9 [....] ru-uç-çu-na-at? [....], sie war [.....] herrlich (+ 419). **Der.:**

ruççunu, *adj* ‖ kabtu (*q. v.*; see *p* 370 *col* 2). V 41, 20; Sm 2052 iii/iv 30 ‖ qar-ra-du (BA iii 276—277). hoary, dignified? Prince, AJP xvi 175, 176 reads ruzzunu √רזן. K 4587 *O* (M^S *pl* 13) 5—9 ru-uç-çu-nu ‖ ba-nu-u (beautiful) & mu-us-su-u (washed, cleansed). *f* perhaps K 3600 iv 14 Ninâ is called ru-çu-un-tu (Craig, *Relig. Texts*, i 54). Perhaps also these 4:

riç(s?)nēti. a *pl.* V 31 *c-d* 16, 17 ri-iç-ni-e-ti ša dalti ‖ a[-ša?]-a-ti and (mašak) a-šu-a-ti, AV 7568, Br 245, 11696.

Raçunnu (?) P. N. of a prefect of Damaskus, written ra-çun(*i. e.* NI-A)-nu, III 9, 50.

riçinnētum. Nabd 413, 3 a-na ri-çi-in-ni-tum ša arxi Aru; probably *pl* of:

riçittu. Camb 155, 4 ana ri-çi-it-tum ša ûm 11 KAN ša (arax) Aru.

raçapu. pr irçip, ps iraçip. join, fit together, erect, build {fügen, zusammenfügen, aufbauen} *etc.* AV 7530. Anp ii 25 dūra ir-çi-pu (3 *pl*). TP vi 20 bīta ša a-gur-ri ar-çip, a house of brick I built; viii 7 the house i-na a-gur-ri ar-çi-ip (*var* çip); thus also vi 11, 12 its 3 great walls ša i-na a-gur-ri ra-aš (= aç)-pu (= pm); vi 18 the walls of the city ana la-a ra-ça-pi I ordered. Sn vi 61, 62 see naburru (639 *col* 1). Asurb x 96 ultu uššī-šu a-di tax-lu-bi-šu ar-çip; Sarg *Nimr* 17; K 891, 3 ar-çip; + 7; Šalm, *Mon*, 16; *throne*-inscr. ii 14. I 28 *b* 13 (ana eššu-ut-te ar-çip). I 27 *no* 2, 11; III 3 *no* 11, 52. 81—4—7, 209. 33 (BA iii 260—3). K 617 (Hr^L 208) *R* 12—13 ana eli eqli li-ir-çip lu-ši-ib, let (each man) cultivate a farm (and) live (on it), Johnston. K 1227 (Hr^L 314) *R* 8 bît-su li-ir-çi-bi, let (each man) put up his house. K 620, 15 (Hr^L 91) i-ra-çip; K 609 (Hr^L 126) 12 bīt dan-nu a-ra-çi-pi; K 1027 (Hr^L 247) *R* 4 bi-tāte-šu-nu i-ra-çi-pu (AJSL xiv 179). See also dimtu, 2 (256 *col* 2); K 2852 ii 10 *cf* qulqullu. K 12021 *R* 3 ra-ça-pu between li-ku-u (1/2) & ka-pa-ru (4). T. A. (Rostow) 1, 29 ra-aç-pa-ti (= pm), I have fortified (the city of M.).

Q^t dūru an-ni-u ar-ti-çi-ip, Jensen, ZA viii 376, 377. — **Derr.:**

raçpu (?) K 596 (Hr^L 190) *O* 6 bītāte ra-aç-pa-a-ti ši-na (+ 13); PSBA xxiii 342—44.

riçiptum. Lay 78*β* ri-çip-tum ziqqu-rāti ša $^{(al)}$ Kal-xi. *Rec. Trav.* xxvi 26 le bâtiment.

raçaçu (?). K 1304 edge 2 . . . i-ri-çi-çi mār Šatti, Thompson, *Reports*, *no* 89.

requ 1. pr irēq, = pm. — *a*) be or become distant, removed; recede, remove {fern sein; sich entfernen. II 35 *c-d* 61 BE (= TILA)-DU = ri-e-qu, AV 7610; Br 1556; KB vi (1) 355. ip T^M v 166, 167 where ri-e-qa, ri-e-qa is followed by bi-e-ša (also = ip). See also ZA ii 73, 144 (= KB iii (2) 6); Ner ii 2 *cf* nisû (697 *col* 1, below). IV^2 9 *a* 36, 37 see libbu, 1 *a*. VATh 4105, 14 ri-ke-e-it ik-li-tum, distant remain darkness. (*Mitth. der Vorderasiat. Gesellschaft*, '02 *no* 1). pm NE 60, 19 ru-qa-tu ur-xa. K 3182 iii 23 ša ru-qat kim-ta-šu ni-su-u alu-u-šu; TP III *Ann* 221 ša a-šar-šu-un ru-u-qu. T. A. (Ber) 7, 22 ma-tum ru-ga-at, the land is far away; + 29, ki mātum ru-ga-tu-ma, + 32, ki-i gi-ir-ru ru-ga-a-tum, that the way was really far (ZA iii 396; v 16; 140). Esh ii 7 a nation ša a-šar-šu ru-u-qu (§ 89 i); I 35 *no* 1, 9 (ru-qu); Esh iii 25 nagû ša *etc.*; III 15 iv 10; Sarg *Nimr* 8; Asurb viii 57; Smith, *Asurb*, 289, 46, *etc.* Esh iv 22 $^{(mât)}$ Ma-da-a-a ša a-šar-šu-nu ru-u-qu. — *b*) be wide, numerous, extensive {weit, zahlreich, ausgedehnt sein}. K 3258 *O* 19 Ašur ša ki-bit-su ru-qa-at (= pm) § 89 i.

ℑ K 824 (Hr^L 290) 13 $^{(il)}$ Ašur . . . . u-raq-an-ni-i-ma, Ašur keeps me away from; K 2333 *R* 27 (= $Z^Š$ iv 76) li-ri-iq mur-çu, let (Papsukal) remove the sickness; preceded by li-ni-is-si; $Z^Š$ viii 63 li-is-su-u li-ri-qu. 83—1—18, 9 *R* 3—5 (Hr^L 386) lil-li-ku dul-la-šu-nu | li-e-pu-šu | li-ri-qu-u-ni, let them come, perform their duty, and depart.

Derr. these 5:

rūqu ***1.*** *adj* (§§ 31; 47) *f* rūqtu; *pl* rūqūti, *f* rūq(g)āti, rūqēti (§ 32 *aγ*). AV 7650. ideogr. § 9, 177; H 5, 152; 26, 561 su-ud SUD | ru-u-qu; Br 7608. — *a*) far {fern} *a.* locally {örtlich}. *del* 184 (204) ina ru-u-qi, afar off, + 205 (ru-qi). Sn ii 36 a-na ru-uk-ki he fled (§ 11); V 51 *b* 67, 68. T. A. (Ber) 24, 56 ru-uq-ki. IV^2 14 *no* 1 *O* 2 ana šadi-i a-šar ru-u-qi (= SUD-UD-DA) § 122: a distant place. VATh 4105 iv 6 I am Sursunabu who is known ru-u-ki-im (as the "far off", "distant"), 14 ri-ga-am!, 11 ur-xa-am ri-ki-e-tu, distant ways. Asb ii 96 Lydia aš-ru ru-u-qu, a far-off country; K 2676 *R* 13. K 10 (Hr^L 280) 17, 18 qaq-qar ina pa-ni-šu-nu ru-u-qu, they had a long stretch of ground before them. NE X *col* v 24 (NE 70) Pīr-napištim ru-qa, *P*, the far-off; *del* 1 a-na *P* ru-u-qi; 194 (214) ru-qi; 244 (274); NE X iv 12 (NE 70) *P* ana ru-ki i-na-aṭ-ṭa-la[-am-ma]. — V 33 ii 9 ana māti ruq-ti; 82—5—22, 53 *R* 2 māti ru-uq-ti; K 809 *R* 3 (ideogr. + ti); 83—1—18, 184 *O* 5. ZA iii 395, 22 ma-tum ru-ga-at; ZA iv 140, 22; Sarg *Ann* 278 šubat ru-uq-ti. T. A. (Ber) 7, 27 ma-tum ru-uq-tu-u i-ba-aš-ši; 9 *R* 10 ma-ta-tum ru-qa-tum. NE I *col* i 7 ur-xa ru-uq-ta il-li-kam-ma. Asb v 20 šu-pul mē ru-qu-u-ti; Botta 75, 4 $^{(mât)}$ Ar-ba-a-a ru-u-qu-ti (KAT^2 277); Sn ii 30 $^{(mât)}$ Ma-da-a-a ru-qu-ti, the far-off Medes; *Kui* 1, 17; *Bell* 33; Sarg *Nimr* 12 (ru-qu-u-te); *Khors* 17 (-ti); see also *Ann* 100; 452. Neb ii 13 mātāte ru-ga-a-ti (‖ ša-di-im ni-su-u-ti), § 69: distant lands; IV^2 39 *a* 31 a-na ru-qa-ti, to the far-off distance (or temporal?). Asb vii 120 in-na-bit ana ru-q(k)i-e-ti; Sn ii 10; iv 14; *Kui* 1, 13; *Bell* 27. H 80 *O* 13, 14 ana ru-ki-e-tim (= SUD-UD-BI-KU). Sarg *Ann* 162 na-gi-i ru-qu-ti; 286 (šadē). Asb viii 81 irdū ur-xi ru-qu-u-ti; NE X *col* iii 5 (+ 12) [ana] a-lik ur-xe ru-qa-ti (+ i 9 *etc.*) pa[-nu-ka maš-lu], + 27 u[r-xa ru]-qa-tu (NE 73) KB vi (1) 218, 219. NE X *col* iii 28 xar-r]a-nu ru-q[e-tu]; also v 18 + 19 (see KB vi, 1, 224). — *β*. of time }zeitlich}, especially in the phrase ûmê rûqûti (§ 67 *b*) = far-off days or times (of past as well as of future). Sarg *Khors* 146 ul-tu û-me (*var* ûmê, *Khors* 110) ru-qu-ti; *Ann* 100 (ru-qu-u-ti); 92 (ru-u-qu-te); TP III *Ann* 11; K 1024 *R* 3 (Hr[L] 28). Asb i 3 ul-tu ûmê SUD-MEŠ (= rûqûti) + vi 107. Neb *Senk* i 13 iš-tu û-mu (*var* -mi; ûmu-um) ru-qu-u-ti; ii 18 balâṭ ûmê (*var* û-mi) ru-qu-u-ti. K 4623 (H 123) *R* 5—6 ba-laṭ û-me ru-qu-ti (= UD-SUD-SUD-EME-SAL); V 65 *a* 27 ul-tu û-me ru-qu-tu; see also Scheil, *Nabd*, vii 32. K 601 *R* 13 la-bar ûmê ru-qu-ti (Hr[L] 7; BA i 605); Sarg *Ann* XIV 86. ZA iii 366, 13 a-na û-mu ru-qu-tu, forever. — lîpu ru-qu (Br 8105) see lîpu (492). *b*) wide, extended, extensive }weit, zahlreich, ausgedehnt}. IV² 29* *col* ii 13 iš-tu šame-e ru-qu-ti; V 37 *d-f* 4 ša-mu-u ru-qu-u-tum. IV² 19 *no* 2, 52 kip-pat šame-e ru-qu-u-tum, the uttermost ends of heaven, Br 3544. — especially in the Achuemenian inscriptions (*cf* Bezold, *Achäm. Inschr.*) O 18 Darius ša qaqqaru agâta ra-bi-tum ru-uq-tum; D 8 Xerxes ša qaqqaru agâta rabî-ti ru-uq-ti; E 12 ru-uq-qu-ti, ‖ passage F 18 ra-bi-tum ra-pa-aš-tum. — libbu rûqu (§ 78) see libbu 1 *a* (467 *col* 2); Banks, *Diss*, 14, 97 lib-bu ru-u-qu ša a-mat-su ki-na-at; KB vi (1) 38/9, 32; 359; 566. Adv. of rûqu, 1 is:

rûqiš. distant, far-off }fern, in der Ferne} § 80 *b*. Sarg *Khors* 102 the approach of my expedition ru-qiš iš-me(-ma), + 148; 111 a-na ru-qiš [iš-me-ma].

rûqu *2.* distance }Ferne}. L⁴ ii 21 xar-ra-nu ru-qi-e = ein Weg der Ferne = eine weite Reise.

rêqu *2.* = rûqu, 1. *q. v.*

rêqûtu distance }Ferne}. — *a*) of the (far) past. I 51 *no* 1 *a* 31 ul-tu û-um re-e-ku-tim = of old; 52 *no* 4 *a* 14 (-tu); Rm 673 (KB iii, 2, 66—7) iii 22 iš-tu û-um ri-e-qu-u-tim. — *b*) of the future. KB iii (2) 6 *col* 3, 48 a-na û-mu ri-e-ku-tim (ZA iv 113, 163; Hilprecht, *OBI*, i pl 32/33 iii 50 ri-e-qu-te [*var* -tim]); 8 *no* 3, *col* 2, 22 a-na û-mi-im ri-e-ku-tim; Rm 673 iii 33 ba-la-aṭ û-um ri-e-qu-u-tim. Perhaps II 30 *no* 4 *R* 7 BAR = re-qa-a-tu (AV 7609; Br 1793) in a group with ax-ra-tu, ar-ka-tu, ça-a-tu.

rêqu *3.* = ריק. be empty }leer sein}. III 61 *b* 12 see karû, 3 (430 *col* 2, below). Nabd 787, 12 (end) dan-nu ri-qu (or *adj*?); perhaps S + 448, 2: u 20 dan-nu ri-i-qu (+ 6). — **Der.**: rêqu, 4 (râqu?):

NOTE. — K 645 *R* 6 (Hr[L] 444) we read i-si-nu-te (= ištenûte = the ones; see *l* 8 i-si-nu-te-ma = the others) i-ri-ku-ni.

rêqu *4.*, **râqu** (?). *adj* empty }leer}. See dannu, 2 (258 *col* 1), & *Cuneiform Texts from Metropol. Mus. of New York*, I *no* 14, 1: 40 (karpat) dan-nu-tu ri-qu-tu; Neb 825, 1; KB iv 196, 197 translating: eleven censers }elf Weihrauchgefässe}, see riqqu); Nabd 204, 1: 10 dan-nu-tu ri-qu-tu. K 121 *R* 8 iš-šik-ki (??, AV 7610) ri-qu-te i-ma-al-lu. T. A. (Ber) 28 *c* 72, u-nu-te *pl* ri-ku-du ša abni; (Ber) 71, 21 a-zi (amêl) mâr šip-ri-ia ri-qa, my messengers have gone forth (from Egypt) empty-handed; *ibid* 10 ri-ku-tu; (Lo) 22, 17 uç-ça-am ri-ku-dam; 2, 35 ri-qu-ti-šu-nu ku-uš-ši-da-šu-nu-ti, let them depart empty-handed (ZA v 17 *rm* 2; 152, 11). Xammurabi-letters 14, 4 as the year has KI (= ašru) ri-ga-am (a gap, break: eine Lücke), BA iv 490; 37, 11 ina MÁ-NI-UM ri-ki-im çi-nam-ma, verlade es (das Getreide) auf ein leeres Frachtschiff, BA iv 466. — ra-qu, perhaps = idle, unemployed; Johns, *Assyrian Doomsday Book*, *no* 6 VIII 1 *Š* ra-qu = Š idle (without allottment); *ibid* 3 VIII 11: 6 amêle ra-qu-ti; Neb 62, 6 alpu (written UL?) ra-a-qu. See also Nabd 159, 2 KI-LAL (= šuqultu) ra-qa-tum ša ki-suk(?)-ku(?); 916, 16 ra-qu-ti-šu-nu.

rêqu (?) *5.* KB vi (1) 170—1 *ad* NE VI 67 i-na ta-at-ta-ši-šum-ma ta-ri (or tal?)-q(k)iš-šu; + 172 i-ri(tal?)-qu-nim-ma a-na pa-an (il) Šamaš.

raqû = רקח. polish, anoint }polieren, glätten, salben} ZK ii 355, 356; ZA i 55; BA ii 280. ⅃ Sn *Kui* 4, 41—2 kisal (ic) sir-di (*cf* sirdu, 2) u xi-bi-iš-ti u-raq-qa a-na ru-uš-ti (*var* te); Lay 42, 50. Perhaps Peiser, *Vertr.*, 97, 3: qaqqad-su ru-uq-ka; II 48 *a-b* 41, 42 A-LI = ruq-qu-u (AV 7651); N I[(11)] = *r* ša kisalli (H 21, 389), Br 5309, 5324. II 16 *a-b* 57 ma-ša-ak la ruq[-qi?], BA ii 280: Haut ohne Salbung (a *noun*?). V 45 vii 27 tu-raq(-šal?)-qa. Connected with this verb are perhaps the following 4:

riqqu (*kk*?) *m*; id ŠIM-MEŠ (Br 5163); ŠIM-ZUN (§ 9, 149) *i. e.* ŠIM + *pl* indication. *sg* occurs in Rm 367 + 83, 1—18, 461 iii 10 GIŠ-ŠIM = riq-qu; also M[S] *pl* 23. Sarg *Khors* 143 (urkarinu, cedar and cypresswood) ka-la ri-ik-ki biblat (šad) Xamāni ša ērisunu ṭābu. id + [pl] in Sarg *Ann* XIV 66; *Khors* 160; ŠIM-ZUN V 64 *b* 2. id also KB vi (1) 160, 10 (+ 444). Esh vi 15 a great park .... ša ka-la ŠIM-ZUN u GIŠ-ZUN (*var* GIŠ-MEŠ, *i. e.* iççē) xurrušu. Sn iv 37 see sirdu, 2. — von Oefele (ZA xv 109) = Kräuter (*herbae*) in medical language; Hebr רקח (Jensen, ZA vi 350), not: Wohlgerüche. Fr. Küchler: ein immergrüner Baum oder Strauch; then, Z[B] 37 ירק would be correct. Rost, *Tigl. Pil.*, 128: ein harziges Gewächs. — Nabd 317, 7 + 10 has an (amēl) rab rik-ke; 496, 6 *etc.*; 1010, 15 (amēl) riq-qi; Camb 126, 7 (*cf* BA iii 491); Cyr 332, 16 (*med*). BA iv 32—34. T. A. (Lo) 51, 13 ki-ma ri-ki (AL) zi-ri; (Ber) 181, 8 (karpat) rik-ku xu-ur-pi (*cf* KB v 330—1, 388—9; see çurpu).

riqqiūtu. Cyr 332, 19 (end) (amēl) riq-qi-u-tu; see also BA iv 78—9.

riqītu. III 66 *col* 10, 30 MUN (= ṭābtu) GAR(= ŠA)-BA (= gift) ri-ki-ti. PSBA xxi 130: of fragrant plants. See also Neb 183, 5 ri-qi; 247, 8 šīr ri-qi-ti; Peiser, *Vertr.*, cvii 7 šīr ri-qi-tum, *ibid* 289, 15: ein Bestandteil des Schafes.

ruqqu, *pl* ruqqē. TP ii 30: (3 Soss) ruq-qe erē [pl]: unguentaries of bronze; see *ibid* 49 + 61; iii 103: 1 (*var* 2) šu-ši ruq-qi urē [pl] (mentioned as objects of tribute).

raqqu. *m* to raqqatu, 2 in name of Nagite-ra-aq-qi Sn iii 56 (see *p* 645).

raqbūtu (?) putridity, rottenness {Fäulniss}?? T[M] vii 100 u ak-ka-a-ši ru-uq-bu-ta u-ša[-kil-ki?], und dir selbst gebe ich Fäulniss zum Essen.

raqadu, pr irqud; ps iráqud. hop, jump {hüpfen, springen}; *cf* רקד, dance. Isa 13: 21; Eccl. 3: 4 (S. A. Smith, ZA iii 102). AV 7532. K 183, 6 see paršamu (839 *col* 2) & translate: the aged hopped (and) the young sang; *R* 12 (end) ni-ir-qud (Hr[L] 2; BA i 618; PSBA xxiii 354).

3 83—1—18, 1846 *R col* 1: words indicating offices held by men, *l* 8: ru-qu-ud-du = (amēl) TU-IGI-GUGU, PSBA xviii 256, 257.

Š V 45 v 24 tu-šar-qad.

raqundu (perhaps > raquddu) Neb 419, 7 (end) ra-qu-un-du parzilli (T[C] 4 *ad* § 48).

raqqidu Br. M. 93080 *R* 14 ANŠU]-UD-GUD-UD = rak-ki-du, ZA xvii 240 *rm* 10: ein tänzelnder Esel, resp. Kamel.

raqunqu (?) Neb 419, 5 ra-qu-un-qu, but not certain, one sign preceding *ra-* being effaced.

raqraq(q)u. stork {Storch} see laqlaqa (497 *col* 1; Br 13977). Z[B] 37 = ירקרק; Barth. *Nominalformation*, § 148; Pognon, *Wadi-Brissa*, 129; AV 7534. for the id see D 83 (K 40) iii 69, 70 (Br 2069, 11550); II 26 *R* 51, 52.

raqqatu *1.* some garment {ein Gewand}. V 14 *c-d* 38 KU-BAR-LU-SAL-LA = raq-qa-tum, Br 1949, 10925; AV 7533. V 28 *c-d* 51 ra-aq-qa-tum ‖ lu-bu-uš-tu. Perh. Nabd 831, 3 raq-qa-ta; also Dar 301, 12. T. A. (Ber) 25 ii 28: X xarrē qâti ša parzilli ra-ak-ka-tum xu-rāçi uxxuzu.

raqqatu *2.* swamp {Sumpf} *pl* raqqāti. KB ii 272—3: Babyl. Chronicle, A (or Smith) v 5, *E* ina raq(?)-qa-ti ša bīt Xaš-mar ki-bir (was buried). Smith, *Sen*, 94, 77 (= *Kuj* 2, 31) the vessels of my warriors a-na raq-qa-at pi-i nāri ik-šu-da, arrived at the swamps of the river's mouth. Cyr 59, 1—2: ŠE-BAR ir-bi ša ir-ri-še-e'ša 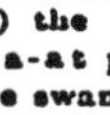 raq-qat (written ŠU[II]) [il] Šamaš: Gerste, eingeliefert von den Bauern, von der .... des Šamašsumpfes, BA iii 436. Nabd 178, 16 (198, 4) raq-qa-tum; 203, 17 ra-aq-qa-tum ša kišād Diqlat. AV* 56 *col* 2. See also ZK i 47, 5; 58.

raqqāti (?). KB iv 170—1, I 2: II ša-an-ša-nu pa-an raq-qa-a-ti ša (il) Malik; perhaps connected with raqqatu, 1.

raqutū (?) K 5464 *O* 26 iš-lim-a ma-a ra-qu-te-e (?) Hr^L 198; PSBA xvii ('95) 230 *foll.*

rāšu, be abundant {reichlich sein} Q pr 3*sg* e-lam-ma di-i-šum i-ra-aš dux-du eš-še-ba zēr (diš-šu būli), K 2519 *O* 17. MARTIN, *Textes Relig.*, ('03), 222; ZIMMERN, *Ritualtafeln*, 100, 17 (zēr šip-kat būli). Perhaps K 12849, 5 ra-a-šum, XI-LI = ra-a-šum ... LI, M^S 87; Br 1113.

rēšu *1.* & **rāšu** *2.* (§ 32 *a* γ) head, top, beginning, *etc.* {Haupt, Spitze, Anfang} § 65, 1; ZDMG 29, 7 & 425; AV 7516. id usually SAG, § 9, 131; Br 3522.

a) head {Haupt} in its literal meaning. ‖ qaqqadu. Sn v 56 with a helmet ... a-pi-ra ra-šu-u-a (HEBR. i 178); *cf* Creat.-*frg* IV 58 (KB vi, 1, 24—5). IV^2 19 *a* 48, 49 di-ka-a (*cf* ZA xvii 246) ri-ša-ši-na (*cf* 246 *col* 1 & Br 2308). IV^2 60* B *O* 5 u-sal-li (ilat) iš-tar-ri ul i-šaq-qa-a ri-ši-ša (& see šaqū, 1). IV^2 59 *no* 2 *R* 24 ina SAG-MU (= rišija) lu DU (= kā)-an. IV^2 15* *b* 18 ṭi-'u *etc.* ina ri-ši-šu (id SAG) lu-u ka-a-a-an (Br 4588), also *ll* 25 & 40, end. *del* 200 + 202 (220 + 222) ši-tak-ka-ni (= ip), & iš-tak-ka-an (= pr) ina ri-ši-šu, lege sie zu seinen Häupten. IV^2 14 *no* 1 *R* 4 ... ku-ba-ra ina ri-ši-šu iš-kun. On šakanu ša rēši, *del* 41 = resist, see HAUPT, *Proc. Am. Or. Soc.*, '94, vol xvi, *p* cviii & *cf* NE 51, 17 ul išakan qaq-qadsa (she, the goddess Ištar, could no longer resist its [Erech's] enemies), not ‖ našū ša rēši, as MEISSNER, 138. See also HAUPT in GUTHE, *Ezra-Nehemiah*, (SBOT) 70. BANKS, *Diss*, 18 *foll*, 68 be-lum [ ] ša re(*i.e.* ri)-e-šu (§ 29) ša-qa-a-tu (*var* -qa-at). — rēšu ullū (علی) = הֵרִים ראשׁ see D^{Pr} 155 *rm.* I 67 *a* 15 Marduk ri-e-ši-ja u-ul-lu-u. Sp II 265 *a* xxv 7 ri-ši-MU (= ja) ul ul-lu. SMITH, *Sen*, 98, 71 i-na ul-lu-u re-ši-ja, when I lifted up my head. — kālu ša rēši see *p* 379 & BA ii 566 *foll.* KB vi (1) 64 (below) 28 raggu u mu-kil re-eš šarri. mu-kil re-eš limuttim (& damiqtim) see KAT^3 461. — rēšu našū, see našū Q *b* β (732 *col* 2) & Br 3242, 3243, 3269, 3280, 3612 (‖ šaqū ša rēši). IV^2 20 *no* 2 *O* 7/8 (end) re-ši-ka (= SAG-GA-NA-KU) taš-ša-a. ZA iv 228, 12 na-ša-a ri-ša-a-ka ina bīt ta-ši-la-a-ti. P. N. Ašur-rēš-i-ši, III 3 *no* 6, 1; TP vii 42 *etc.* 82—7—4, 42 *R* 9 see qamū. — H 89, 41 ina re-ši-šu li-iz-ziz (see 658 *col* 1); T. A. (Ber) 11 *R* 15 ina ri-ši ki-i ul-zi-zu-šu (ZA v 148; KB v 27). gurruru ša re-ši *cf* גרר, 2 (233 *col* 1). KB iii (1) 132 *col* iv 16—19 daily in ri-ši-in e-li-ja-tim | in [ri?]-ša-a-tim | u xu-ud li-ib-bi-im | a-ta-al-lu-kam, WINCKLER, *Untersuch.*, 143, JENSEN, 502 on *p* 113.

b) head of something; officer, leader, chief, commander {Jemandes Haupt, Leiter, Befehlshaber} *etc.* T. A. (Lo) 19, 35 ri-šu-šu-nu, their sheiks. Sp II 265 *a* xxv 3 ri-e-šu pal-ku-u; *cf* I 49 (*var*) i 5—6 ri-e-šu mut-nin-nu-u, das betende Oberhaupt. Bu 91—5—9, 183 *R* 5 ri-eš narkabāte-šu-nu, der Hauptmann der Streitwagen (Hr^L 340). Sm 61, 17 u-bar-ru ina ali ša-nim-ma re-e-šu (= SAG-GA), a servant in another city becomes a lord, KING, *First Steps*, 293. rab ša ri-e-šu, chief of the heads or princes? = רַב־סָרִים, Dan 1, 3. WINCKLER, *Untersuchungen*, 138; PINCHES, *Academy*, June 25, 1892, *p* 618 *col* 2; JENSEN, ZA vii 174; KAT^3 649; see also šariš. (amēl) rūšē (written SAG *pl*) in lists of military offices, Asb vi 89 *etc.* *pl* perhaps S 1028, 20 (Hr^L 418 *R* 6) (amēl) ra-ša-ni ša (māt) Kal-du, die Häuptlinge (PSBA xxiii 337, 338; *cf* II 35, 31—4, AV 3066 compares muraššū ‖ xabbatum √רשׁה; rašānu, *pl* of rašū, *i. e.* ceux qui ont été pillés par les Chaldéens; see rašū, 2). Also *cf* TP III *Ann* 3; Pl i 15 ((amēl) ra-'-sa-a-ni ša (māt) Kal-di); ii 17. KAT^3 214 *rm* 2.

c) top of something, *e. g.*, a mountain, tower, house {Spitze eines Berges, Turmes, Hauses} *etc.* I 44, 59 iṭ(t)-ru-ra (*cf* טרר, 359 *col* 2) ri-ša-a-ša (of the ēkal ku-talli), *var* -ša-a, + 30; 63, u-šaq-qi ri-e-su (> rūš-šu). V 63 *a* 27 it-ru-ra ri-e-ša-a-šu. I 51 *no* 1 *a* 26 u-ul-

rarubatu, see rašubbatu. ∼ ri-ru-uš-šum, so AV 7612 on II 42 *cf* 20, 21; Br 4431, 4434.

la-a ri-e-ši-ša, *b* 15; see also I 52 *no* 3
b 20. K 618, 7 (= V 53 *no* 3) see mataxu Q^{t} (621 *col* 2). V 62 *no* 1, 18 kīma
šadī ri-e-ši-i-šu (§ 29) ul-li; ZA iv 239,
112, 141—2. V 63 *a* 43 parak xurāçi
šimat ilūtišu ša ab(p)-ru ra-šu-uš-
šu *etc*. ZA v 399 *foll* >< KB iii (2) 116.
IV^2 27 *a* 17 ri-ša-a-šu, Br 3223. KB iii
(2) 6 *col* 3, 24, 25 ri-e-ši-šu lu-u-ul-
lu-im; also *ibid* 4 *col* 1, 38—9 ri-e-ši-ja
ša-ma-mi a-na si(= ši?)-it-nu-ni he
commanded, ZA iv 108. 81—6—7, 209
(Esh text) 33 (end) high as a mountain
ri-e-ši-šu ul-li, BA iii 260—3. KB iii
(1) 132 *col* 3, 17—18 ri-ši-šu-nu ki-ma
sa-tu-im u-ul-li; (2) 78 *col* 2, 12 la ul-
lu-u (= pm) ri-e-ši-ša. II 67, 72 u-
šaq-qi ri-is-si-in. Z^{Š} iii 62 ma-mit
ri-e-ši u na-ax-li; viii 22 šadū elūti
ri-ša-an e-la-a-ti. V 65 *a* 22 see qadadu Q. Neb ix 18 *cf* lamū Š &
kilīlu, 1.

d) the best, choice {das Beste}. V 63
a 21 ri-eš mimmā (?) dam-ga ušērib
kiribšun.

e) front {Vorderseite}. Sarg *Cyl* 66
i-na ri-e-še u ar-ka-a-te ina çilū
kilallān (886 *col* 2); *Ann* XIV 78 ina
ri-e-še u arkāti. KB vi (1) 566 on
ibid 36 *R* 4. IV^2 55 *R* (*b*) 15 ina ri-eš
erši (of a bed) u še-pi-ti erši (zu Füssen
des Bettes). In *c. t.* = Flanke eines Feldes,
Grundstücks, see T^{O} 126 (id SAG).

f) beginning, origin, source, *etc*. {An-
fang, Ursprung, Quelle}. id SAG, see
super-inscription of TP *col* 1. a city called
ri-eš e-ni, *cf* V 69, 10; Anp ii 128; iii 122
(D^{Par} 25) ištu rēš (nār) e-ni. On rēš
ēni & mūçū see Haupt in Cheyne, *Isaiah*
(SBOT) 156, 157. rēš nāri = ראש הנהר,
KAT^2 29, see nāru, 2 (722 *col* 1). rēš
tāmti III 5 (*no* 6) 61 see tāmtu. K 122
R 4 (Hr^{L} 43) ultu ri-e-ši, from the beginning. 81, 2—4, 219 *O* ii 3 see sanaqu
(771 *col* 1) Q *a* 1. K 3454 + K 3935 ii 17
(end) u-qa-a-a re-ši ū-mi, awaited the
beginning of day (KB vi, 1, 48—9). TP vi 44
iš-tu rēš (*var* ri-iš) bēlū (*var* šarrū)-
ti-ja ... adi v palēja, from the beginning of my government. KAT^3 325:
Regierungsantritt, Zeit vom Antritt bis
zum Jahresabschluss. See also BA iii 277,
278: erstes Jahr nach der Thronbesteigung.

Asb iii 5 ultu ri-e-ši. IV^2 18 *no* 1, *O* 22,
23 re-eš šat-ti (= [ZA]G-MUG) = ראש
השנה, the beginning of the year, celebrated
by a festival, see zagmuku; KAT^3 514;
370—1: babyl. Neujahr; Brockelmann, ZA
xvi 391 *fol*; Meissner, ZDMG 50, 297; also
ZDMG 55, 390; Winckler, *Forsch.*, iii (2/3)
52. Neb ii 56 re-eš ša-at-ti (§ 73 note);
vii 23—25; Lehmann, ii 111. Cyr 228, 5—6
ina ri-eš šatti (>< ina mišil šatti);
& often. Camb 97, 6—7; Br. Mus. 84. 2—
11, 102 (Kohler-Peiser, ii 52—3); BA iii
422—3; Nabd 48, 12 (ri-eš šatti); 996,
10 ri-e-šu šatti; 1030, 15 (>< ki-it
šatti); also K 3456 *O* 26 ina ri-eš šatti
u ki-it šatti. Br. Mus. 49934, 5 ul-tu
ri-eš a-di ki-it, from beginning to end.
III 53 *a* 3 ri-eš me-riš-te šur-ri, see
mērištu, 2 (594 *col* 1). II 22 *a* 53 ri-eš
šur-ri-e (see šurrū, begin, open); & *cf*
(ina) rūš šarrūtija = ina šurri šar-
rūtija.

H 16, 245 sa-ag | SAG | ri-e-šu,
followed by qaq-qa-du. II 7 *e-f* 36; 27
g-h 25; 36 *e-f* 63 SAG = ri-šu, followed
by qud-mu, mu-ut-tum, max-ru.

V 29 *a-b* 70 ZAG = re-e-šu, Br 6490;
19 *e-f* 32 see Br 12048; V 21 *g-h* 34 ri-
e-šu ar-kat (Br 2041); 35 AN = ri-e-
šu (Br 434). II 30 *g-h* 14—17 SAG-IL
(Br 3693), SAG-UŠ (Br 3584), TIK-AN-
NA-UŠ (Br 3230), TIK-AN-BA-KU-
ZI (Br 3231) = re-ša-an e-la-a-tum,
KB vi (1) 402; Jensen, 118; 502 *fol.* also
88, 1—18, 1330 i 40. M^{S} 87. ZA v 105;
PSBA '88, Dec. — perh. = *dual*? In names
of places, *e. g.* KB iv 314, 5 Bēlit ša Bīt-
ri-eš.

Derr. — rāšiš 1, reštu, reštū &:

rūšu (-nu) *1.* T. A. (Lo) 70, 18 our head,
translation of qaqqadu-nu; KAT^3 652.

rāšu 3. pr irāš, pc lirūš, pm rēši. = רוש,
jubilate, shout, hail {jauchzen, jubilieren},
ZK ii 343; Z^{B} 44. ZA v 58 (DT 363) 21
li-riš-ka Bābilu^{ki}, let *B* shout joyfully unto thee; 29, i-ra-a-ša Bābili^{ki},
B shouts. Lehmann, ii 69 *ad* L^4 ii 7 ēkal
ina e-ri-bi-ja i(?)-ra(?)-aš. V 65 *b* 17
li-re-šu-ku (*var* ka). IV^2 31 *a* 40 (end)
Kutū $^{(ki)}$ li-riš[-ki] ‖ ēkal erçit lā
tāri li-ix-du ina pa-ni-ki. IV^2 17 *b* 11
re-šu-nik-ka (§ 141) mātāti, the countries may shout joyfully to thee (& see

xabaçu, *p* 302 *col* 1; KB vi (1) 323); IV^2 21* *no* 1 C *R* iii 19 Bēl lix-du-ka (o Marduk), Ēa li-reš-ka; IV^2 28* *no* 3 *a* 19 O Ištar šamu-u u apsû li-re-šu-nik-ka.

Q^1 = Q V 61 iv 9 pa-nu-šu ir-ti-šu i-te-li-iç kabtassu (§ 92).

ℑ ag perh. K^M 9, 3 (58, 18) mu-riš, who causes *E* to rejoice.

ℨ^1 perh. K 2519 *O* 19 (*med*) i-ta-ra-ša ri-'-u ina çēri, Martin, *Textes relig.*, ('03) 222, 223: et il se plait à paître dans les champs. Zimmern, *Ritualt.*, 216, 217 leaves word untranslated.

Derr. — rīšātu &:

rīšu. joy, shouting, jubilation {Freude, Jauchzen} *etc.* N 3554 *O* 17 xu-di-e u ri-ši al-ki (PSBA xxiii 120 *foll*); IV^2 19 *a* 50 xa-du-u u ri-i-šu (but AJSL xix 221 = 3 *pl* pr); H 41; 271.

rēšu *2.* slave, chattel {Sklave, Eigentum} perh. ultimately same as rēšu, 1. *cf* ἀνδράποδον & κτῆμα. PSBA x 298; xi 211. V 47 *a* 24 a-tur a-na ri-e-ši, I have become a slave; re-e-šu, explained by (amēl) ardu; also V 19 *c-d* 42. K 2008 iii 44 *foll*, SAG = re-e-šu, in one group with abdu & ar-du. Sm 305; Meissner, 92. Here, according to some, also KB vi (1) 64 *col* 3, 28 mu-kil re-eš šarri tuš[-ta-mat], he that holds back the slave of the king (see rēšu, 1, *a*). Perh. V 52 iv 34 (middle) ri-e-šu (but??). — *adv* rēšiš, 2 & *abstr. n.* rēšūtu, see below.

ru-šum *2.* V 11 *c-d* 49, H 109, 49; 111, 40; D 129, 97 iꝺ ME-ÇI[-IR] & MU-BU (which latter = mašaddu, 600 *col* 1, & nīru, yoke), *var* ur-ru-šum (see *p* 106 *col* 1) AV 7658; Br 10412—14; H^{CV} xxx; ZA i 311 *rm* 1, a weapon. According to Jensen, 17 & Hommel, *Sum. Les.*, 61 *rm* (ur-)ru-šum means: diadem, crown. Br 1800, where reference is also made to IV^2 4 *O* 40—1 (same iꝺ MU-BU-BI), see nabaṭu ℨ (635 *col* 1), the word here being considered as = ruššû (splendor, brilliancy?). Where does V 47 *b* 27 ru(šub?)-šu-uš u-zak-ki, followed by ru(šub?)-ši-iš ib-bi(?), 28, belong? *Cf* AV 7656.

rašû. pr irši, ps iraš(š)u; ip riši, pm raši, AV 7540. — *a*) take, show, turn to {fassen, erweisen, zuwenden} in connection with rēmu, *q. v.*, = take compassion on one, have mercy upon, show favor to. Peiser, *Vertr.*, xxvii 5—6 ri-e-mu ana mārišu ta-ar-še-e-ma (3 *f*), had shown favor to. P. N. T. A. (Lo) 48, 3 Abd-tir-ši. Asb vii 55 ir-ša-a xi(ṭi?)-ip(ib?) libbi. K 3456 *O* 23 see çalūtu. — *b*) take, acquire {nehmen, erwerben, sich aneignen}. KB vi (1) 134 (NE I) 39 a friend a-na-ku lu-ur-ši, may I gain. I 69 *a* 23 a-a ir-ša(-)a-an xi-ṭi-ti. I 68 *b* 29, 30 a-a ir-ša-a xi-ṭe-ti, not may he commit sin. V 63 *a* 7 ana la ra-še-e xi-ṭi-tim, not to commit sin. IV^2 57 *a* 69 (end) i-dir-tu a-a ar-ši, sadness may not overcome me. In *c. t.*: which *NN.* ... i-ra-aš-šu-u, is yet to acquire. K 2801 (= K 221 + K 2669) *R* 26 a-xi la ta-raš-ši, be not indolent; III 15 *b* 9 la na-di-e a-xi ul ir-ši. a-na paq-ri la ra-še-e ‖ la i-šu ‖ TUK-e, see paqru (*p* 823). ZA v 60, 21; V 60 *c* 17; Merodach-Balad.-stone i 19; 81, 6—7, 209, 18; IV^2 20 *no* 1, 11 see salīmu, 762 *col* 2. III 59 *b* 56 TUK-ši with gloss i-ra-aš-ši. K 625 *R* 9 na-kut-tu ra-aš-ši (Hr^L 131), see *p* 678 *col* 1, and add: Asb vii 81; Smith, *Asurb*, 293 *a-e*; 229, 53; V 64 *b* 52—3; KB iii (2) 90, 26—7, which see *p* 669 *col* 1 (nakadu). V 65 *a* 23; L^5 28 see nikittu (678 *col* 1); also *cf* naxtu. — *c*) possess, own, have {besitzen, eignen, haben} ‖ išû, iꝺ TUK; written often TUK-ši in Thompson, *Reports*. K^M 11, 12 wickedness la a-ra-(aš-)ši, I have not. V 63 *a* 5 ašru kanšu ša ra-šu-u pu-lu-ux-tim, who has piety. K 3182 iii 3 i-raš(*var* ra-aš)-ši bil-ta (+ 8, end). Sarg *Cyl* 40 (end) the joy of thy heart .... ba-ṭil-ta la ra-še-e; Sn iii 38 ir-šu-u (3 *pl*) baṭ (not *be*; so against above, *p* 172 *col* 2, bēltu, 3) -la-ti; *cf* Neb *Bab* ii 31 mu-ga-al-li-tu a-a ar-še-e (Hincks in Norris, *Dict.*, 8); Neb x 16 ‖ a-a i-ši nakiri. Sams i 21 Ninib ra-aš (= ag) e-mu-qi (§ 110). K 1282 (*Dibbara*-legend; KB vi, 1, 68 *foll*) 17 (ša) ma-xi-ra a-a ir-ši; NE VI 21 ni-i-ri ša-ni-na a-a ir-ši. II 16 *b-c* 32 la ra-aš ta-šim-ti (BA ii 285 *foll*; Br 11239); en-qu-ti ra-aš ṭe-mi, V 63 *b* 1, *etc.* see ṭēmu; Sn v 3 *U* la ra-aš ṭēmi u milki. Nabd 356, 3 *N* a-na aš-šu-tu ir-ša-an-ni-ma (KB iv 234, 235); see also Neb 359, 6 (ar-šu-ka); 359, 7 abla u mārta itti [axâmeš?] ul ni-ir-šu. Neo-Babylonian rašū = early Babylonian axazu, = Assyrian liqū, in the phrase: take a wife. T. A. (Lo) 1, 58 i-ra-aš-šu-u (= axazu) your daughters. — *d*) induce }bewegen{. V 63 *a* 47 to do so & so ... libbu pa-li-ix ra-ša-ku. — *e*) grant }zulassen, gewähren{ V 61 vi 55 *cf* qibīru; Sarg *Ann* 42 ana lā naši bilti ir-ša-a. V 37 i 9 ra-šu-u ša uz-nu, grant a hearing (Br 8735). Sp II 265 *a* viii 1 ki-na ra-aš uz-ni (or to *c* = have?). — *f*) become }geraten, werden{. 81—6—7, 209, 37 when .... ši-pir šu-a-tu in-na-xu-ma ma-qit-ti i-raš-šu-u (& the thing is broken down, has become a ruin).

NOTE. — 1. V 54 *c* 48 (K 620, 15) reads i-ra-še, but Hr[L] 91 -çip.

2. P. N. Ra-ši-ilu (or an?) PEISER, *Vertr.*, lxx 15, lxxiv 10 *etc.*

3. On rašū in legal texts see also OPPERT, ZA vi 281.

Q[t] *a*) take }fassen{. Neb *Senk* (I 51 *no* 2) i 19; KB iii (2) 52, 32 see salīmu (762 *col* 2). S[P] 158 + S[P] II 962, 14 Anu ... ir-ta-ši ki-mil-tum (*q. v.*). SCHEIL, *Nabd*, i 5—6 ta]-a-a-ru ul [ir-ta-ši], has no compassion. V 35, 11 ir-ta-ši ta-a-a-ra (BA ii 230, 231; 251); *cf* V 64 *a* 15 ir-šu-u ta-a-a-ri; K 8522 *O* 13. — *b*) acquire }erwerben, sich aneignen{. K 5418 *a* i (11—12) ir-ta-šu-u mi-na-ti (ZA xii 319 *foll*; KB vi (1) 292, 293 *l* 18) = increased (see minūtu, 558 *col* 1). paqru, puqurrū & rugummū ir-ta-ši, see these words, & II 67, 7—9; 69, 24 (= BA-AN-AG). On Neb 101, 11 iš-ta-aš-šu-u, see KB iv 186 *rm* 7; M[S] 88 *col* 1. Sp II 265 *a* xv 9 ir-ta-ši. — *c*) grant }gewähren{. II 9 *b* 11 çi-ta ir-ta-ši, he granted an exit, Br 2792; II 40 *g-h* 29.

Ʒ[t] (?) MEISSNER, WZ xvi 198 suggests here uštaššā (KB vi, 1, 6, 14). See, however, našu Š[t] (735 *col* 2).

Š grant, *etc.* }gewähren{ K 3515 *O* 14 see salīmu (762 *col* 2); also 82—7—4, 42 *O* 5 u-ša-ar-ši ri[-e-mu] PSBA xx 152 *foll*. Asb ii 112 (see *p* 151 *col* 2); KB ii 174, 175. Nabd 356, 34 the judges .... la u-šar-šu-u, did not grant to ...., KB iv 236, 237. See also PEISER, *Vertr.*, ix 6 Balaṭu hatte auf das Einkommen keine Hypothek genommen (la u-šar-šu-u). SCHEIL, *Nabd*, ii 2—3 see rēçu, helper. KB vi (1) 138 (= NE 11 *col* 3 *b*) 33 and Gilgameš tap-pa-a u-šar-šu-ka ka-a-ša. II 67, 81 pu-lux-tu u-šar-ši (1 *sg*) KB ii 24; ZA v 302, 303. V 45 v 18 tu-šar-ša. HILPRECHT, *OBI*, i pl. 32/33 ii 19 u-ša-ar-sa-an-ni = donavit mihi. *ip* K[M] 13, 28 šur-ši di-ni.

Š[t] see tiqnu.

On (amêl) Mu-ra-šu-u as P. N. see especially HILPRECHT, *OBI*, ix, *passim*; BA iv 555 *foll*.

DERR. — maršītu (583 *col* 1), raššītu, raššūtānu, rišūtu, 1 (?), &:

rašū *2.* creditor }Gläubiger{ properly: owner, ZA i 431, 10; ii 328 (bel.). Often in *c. t.* (amêl) ra-šu-u ša-nam-ma, another creditor, PEISER, *Vertr.*, xxviii 10. Cyr 177, 8 (amêl) rašu (= TUK)-u ša-nam-ma ina mux-xi i-šal-laṭ (adi *NN* kaspašu išallim) KB iv 272—3; BA iii 397; T[C] 129; Nabd 103, 9—10; 304, 9—10. BA iv 559 *foll* on HILPRECHT, inscr. *A*, ix, 19, 11—12. Nabd 817, 7. KB iv 88—9 (IV) 33 *K* ra-šu-u; 90, 39 ra-ša-a ul zak-ki, has not been satisfied. id (amêl) TUK-u, Camb 81, 10, *etc.* — *f* ra-ši-tum, PEISER, *Vertr.*, lvi 11.

rašū *3.* break }brechen{?? Ʒ see mu-raš(š)ū, 598 *col* 1. K 2051 i 32 EME-(e-me-tu-ku) TUK = mu-ra-šu-u ‖ emetukū, literally: tongue-lasher. VATh 244 i 23 TE-TE = ru-uš-šu-u; 26, 27 XI-TE-TE & XA-TE-TE = lu-ra-aš-ši-ka; 29, A-NA-AŠ-AL-TE-TE = am-mi-ni tu-raš-ša(?)-an-ni. — Ʒ[t] *ibid* i 24 MA-TE-TE = tur-taš-ša-an-ni; 25, GAB-TE-TE = mur-taš-šu-u (*cf* 595 *cols* 1/2); 28, AMÊL-TE-TE = mu-ur-taš-šu-u.

ruššū (> ruššiju) § 69; ‖ xuššū (*p* 344) & sāmu, 2 (765 *col* 1). D[Pr] 194 *rm* 1; AV 7660; KB vi (1) 570; G § 83; Br 8608, 8612—14. LYON, *Manual*, 131 √ = genuine; OPPERT, GGA '84, 334 (with metals) mixed; WINCKLER, *Sargon*: rötlich funkelnd (wie die Sonne). id XUŠ-A (see xuššū); H 40, 288 = ez-zu (Br 8608, 8613, 8600); perh. = shining, brilliant (of gold, metal *e. g.* çarīru, *q. v.*, and other mining products). IV² 12 *R* 21, 22; Neb ii 47; iii 69, 70 see xurāçu (340 *col* 2); V 61 iv 18 ina xurāçi ru-uš-ši-i; Sn v 73; *Khors* 141 *a* ruš-šu-u, followed by kaspu eb-bu. K 2711 *R* 3 mar-ri xurāçi ru-uš-še-e, BA iii 266 *fol*. Neb ii 33 silver, gold *etc.* xēgallu ru-uš-ša-a, a shining treasure; K 2801 *R* 30 see çarīru. in-bi ru-uš-šu-tim (šumux çippāti) Pognon, *Neb Bav*, C vii 23, rotglänzende Früchte; A vii 12 in-ba ru-šu-tu; A iv 48 aš-na-an ru-uš-ša-a; C vii 27 bi(?)-du ru-uš-ša-a; also ru-ša-a, Pognon, *Wadi-Brissa*, 36; 185. — V 61 vi 44 see zīmu (283 *col* 2); KB vi *loc. cit.*, rotglänzende Gesichtszüge; some connect this with rāšu, rāšu, shout, jubilate, and translate, his joyful face; BA i 277: mit seinen vollen Gesichtszügen. — Of garments: V 14 *c-d* 41, 42; *e-f* 40, 41; *c-d* 22, 23 see xuššû; AV 7659. — Of serpent, *etc.* see çirruššû (& KB iii, 1, 142—3); also *cf* xuššû, *c* (*p* 344 *col* 2). A Derivative ruteššû, see below, and compare, also, mullilu (549 *col* 2).

rašabu, be mighty, powerful, terrible {gewaltig, furchtbar, schrecklich sein} KB vi (1) 570. pm Sarg *Cyl* 54, that goddess ra-ši-bat Ninua, is the mighty one of Nineveh. NE 60, 7 see puluxtu (806 *cols* 1/2) ‖ gal-tu (8).

NOTE. — TP vi 11, 12 see raçapu Q. — Derr.:

rašbu, *adj* mighty, powerful, awe-inspiring, terrible {gewaltig, schrecklich, ehrfurchtsgebietend} AV 7543. K 3351, 11 be-lum ra-aš-bu ša ina pu-xur ilāni rabūti šin-na-as-su la ib-ba-šu[-u], Craig, *Relig. Texts*, i *pl* 43. V 34 *a* 46 kiççi (425 *col* 2) ra-aš-ba-an(-bu, KB iii, 2, 46, 27; 90 ii 14, -ba). Sarg *bull* 57 parak-ki ra-aš-bu-ti ‖ *Cyl* 62 ra-aš-du(-u)-ti(te). II 31 *no* 3, 31 see mitru (625 *col* 2); II 35 *e-f* 18 see kummusu, 397 *col* 2. BA ii 261 reads Merodach-Balad.-stone ii 37 TE (= temēnu) raš-p(b)u, *etc.* — A ‖ is:

rašubbu. IV² 50 iv 15 AN-GIŠ-BAR (= Girru?, KB iii, 2, *p* 2 *l* 27 [il] Gir-ra ra-šu-ub-bu) ra-šub-bu, KAT² 478 on רשף; Pietschmann, *Phönizier*, 150; Ed. Meyer, ZDMG 31, 719. II 35 *e-f* 17 ra-šub-bu ‖ šar-xu. K^M 14, 16 + 21 + 93; 49, 25; T^M ii 109; iii 182. — ZA v 67, 25 at-ti-ma [ilat] Ištar u-šum-gal-lat ilāni ^pl^ ra-šub-ti, but thou, o Ištar, mighty princess of the gods.

rašubbatu. awe, awefulness, terror, terribleness {Furchtbarkeit, Schrecklichkeit} ZA ii 88. H 40, 233 IM-XUŠ (id for rušššû) = ra-šub-ba-tu. Esh iv 25 pu-lux-tu ra-šub-bat [il] Ašur bēlija isxupšunūti; also Asb ii 20, 21; Sn ii 42, 43 see saxapu, Q (751 *col* 1). III 6 *R* 51 (end) ra-šu-ba-at bēlū-ti-ja ‖ na-mu-ra-a-at kakkēja. NE 60, 10—11 pu-lux-ta u ra-šub-ba-tu i-te-kil pa-ni-šu. K 2001, 5; IV² 25 *b* 48, 49 (Br 8474; Winckler, *Forsch.*, i 250 *rm* 1 ✕ ZA ii 88); IV² 27 *a* 49, 51; 53, 54 see ramû, 1 Q.

ruššubu. K 2044, 4 . . . GAN = ru-uš-šu-bu (AV 7661); 1 = si-xi-ip ma-a-ti, 3 = ka-šu-u.

rašibu (?) destroyer {Vernichter}? L⁵ 10 ra-ši-bu the great lord, my lord.

ru-šub(?)-tum. V 41 *c* 25.

rašadu, S establish, lay foundation {gründen, fest gründen} AV 7538, 8590. Anp i 12 ša tu-šar-ši-da (2 pr) palššu. ZA v 67, 40 u-šar-ši-si (> id-ši) ina Ēbabbar šu-bat la-li-ši. Creat.-*frg* V 6 u-šar-šid (3 *sg*; Marduk) man-za-az [il] Ni-bi-ri ana ud-du-u rik-si-šu-nu, KB vi (1) 30, 31; Winckler, *Forsch.*, iii 202. I 35 *no* 1, 3 u-šar-ši-du (= 3 *pl*) kussûšu. Sarg *Cyl* 65 on lofty stones (?) . . . u-šar-ši-da (1 pr) te-me-en-šu; *bull* 81 (*var* še-). KB iii (2) 6 *col* 3, 47 thus šu-ur-ši-id (= ip) the foundation of my throne forever. Neb vii 61, 62 mixrat mē i-ši-id-sa u-ša-ar-ši-id (1 *sg*); viii 60, 61 (ZA iii 318, 88 u-šar-ši-da-a); vi 1—3 (u-šar-ši-id), I 66 *a* 35; TP viii 8; ZA i 340, 30; see also I 52 *no* 3 *col* 2, 18—19. 1 *sg*: KB iii (2) 48 *col* 2, 28 (u-ša-ar-šid); u-šar-ši-id Pognon, *Wadi-Brissa*, 75; Sarg *Ann* XIV 78; KB iv 102, 13 u-šar-šid (1 *sg*). — pc KB iii (2) 8 *no* 2 *col* ii 10—12 ki-bi-ir nāri šu-a-ti i-na kupri u a-gur-ri lu-u-ša-ar-ši-id; I 67 *b* 25, 26. TP viii 38 šangūti . . . kīma šadē kūniš lu-šar-ši-du (3 *pl*); Lehmann: S² 44; S³ 99 li-šar-šid. — pm Lay 33 (Sarg *Nimr*) 14 on firm rock ul šur-šu-da iš-da-a-šu

(§ 89: had not been laid), KB ii 38. IV² 27 *R* 16—18 lofty mountain whose peak vies with heaven ap-su-u el-lim šur-šu-du (Br 5068) uš-šu-šu, while its foundation is grounded in the shining ocean. V 63 *a* 45 šu-ur (KB iii (2) 116 un)-šu-du ‖ tu-uq-gu-nu. Sarg *Cyl* 62 (-du); *Ann* XIV 71 ul šur-šu-da. — ip IV² 18 *no* 2 *R* 13, 14 iš-di kussē šarrū-ti-šu ṭābiš šur-ši-di (Br 1278) & see IV² 12 *O* 20 (= MU-UN-ŠU-UŠ-EME-SAL); ZA iv 113, 162 šu-ur-ši-di. — ac II 36 *c* 22 šur-šu-du kussē šarrūti-šu. V 65 *a* 24 ana šu-ur-šu-du(-dam, ZA iv 108, 37). te-me-en *etc.*; *ibid* 7 mu-šar-šid. — Hilprecht, *OBI*, i 32/33 *col* 1, 35 a-na šu-ur-šu-dam (KB iii, 2, 4, 37). — ag Šalm, *Throne inscr.*, iii 12 mu-šar-ši-da-at a-rat-te-e (Scheil, *Šalm*, 77). Scheil, *Nabd*, viii 40; IV² 9 *a* 30, 31 mu-šar-ši-du eš-ri-e-ti (Br 1440).

rašdu, *adj* Sarg *Cyl* 62 see rašbu & gennu (227 *col* 1); also *Rp* 17.

rašamu (?). K 3600, 16 (hymn to Ninā) ba-a-lum ur-pi-tu erib (= SU) tam-di ra-ši-ma.

rušumtu, mud, mire, slime, marsh {Schlamm, Morast}. Same root as šuršummu; ‖ na-riṭ(t)u (728 *col* 2); Z^B 73, 118; ZA i 309 *rm* 1; see also naršundu, naršunnatu (731 *col* 2). V 42 *g-h* 16, 17 IM-TA-KIL (= ṭiṭṭu & duxxudu); IM-RI-A (= רזם, 2) = ru-šum-du. IV² 10 *b* 37, 38 ina me-e ru-šum-ti (= IM-RI-A, Br 8398) na-di qāsu ççabat, he (thy servant) lies in the mud, help him out; 16 *b* 21, 22 ina ru-šum-ti (= SU-BUR-RA, Br 177) na-di, lies in the mud. IV² 50 *c* 9, get away kīma šaxē ina ru-šum-ti-ja (= T^M iii 176; ZA i 309 *rm* 1); T^M vi 75 ina ru-šum-di-MU (= ja). Sm *Asurb*, 192, 13 the ship of Tammaritu ša ši-ik-nu di-ru-u ru-šum-tu içbatu.

ru-šim-tu, II 26 *no* 1 *a-b* 11 read ta-šim-tu.

ra-aš-pu, TP vi 12 see raçapu.

ri-ša-qu. 83, 1—18, 1330 iii 21 DAX ^(tu-ux) = ri-ša-qu ša amēli; *cf* M^N 90 *col* 1 *ad* Boissier, *Doc.*, 37: 2 ru-uš-šu-qat.

rišqu (AV 7620) ‖ ba-ša-mu, u-du-u see šaqqu.

ru-šu-qu read šup-šu-qu (*q. v.*).

ri-ša-šim (riq?) V 21 *e-f* 1 = ... BAR; Br 1794, 13952; AV 7613.

ruštu (?) see raqū. Meissner & Rost, 41 *no* 96: Menge, Fülle, Masse; same √ as ruššū. See Nabd 424, 9 a-na ru-uš-tum.

REŠ-TAN see a-ša-ri-du, S^c 278; Br 6204, *etc.*

rēšiš *1. adv* of rēšu, 1. V 65 *b* 2 ri-ši-eš *var* to eš-ši-eš (u-še-piš), ZA iii 297.

rēštu, *pl* rēšēti & rēšāti § 65, 1. — *a*) top, peak, summit of something (tower, mountain, building *etc.*) {Spitze, Gipfel, oberster Teil}. V 56 ii 47 Šumalia, the mistress of snowcapped (el-lu-ti) mountains, a-ši-bat re-še-e-ti. Šalm, *Mon*, *O* 7 *Šalm.* mukabbis re-še-ti-e ša šade-e kāliš xuršāni (KB ii 152, 153; §§ 30, 32*aa*). Boissier. *Doc.*, 23, 13 šumma ultu ri-še-ti ana še-pi-ti ultu še-pi-ti ana ri-še-ti, (from head to foot *etc.*). — *b*) the highest, most exalted (person), princess {die Höchste, Erhabenste; Fürstin}. I 27 *a* 10 Ištar reš-ti šame-e erçi-ti; Šalm, *Ob*, 18; II 66 (*no* A) 1. TP i 13 Iš-tar reš-ti ilāni, the foremost among the gods. — *c*) best, choicest, highest {das Beste, Höchste}. Sarg *Cyl* 3, Sargon .... whom Ašur & Marduk have called zi-kir šu-mi-šu u-še-iç-çu-u a-na ri-še-e-ti, proclaiming his name as best; *bull* 5; *Nimr* 2 (KB ii 36—7); *Khors* 5; AV 7615. V 34 *b* 43 the renewal of Babylon which .... aš-ku-num a-na re-e-eš-e-tim (*var* re-še-e-tim), which I had made best. šaman reš-ti, choicest oil, Pinches, *Texts*, 16 *R* 12; Esh vi 40 written NI-SAG, & explained as šaman gu-la-a. Sn i 61 suluppu re-še-te-šu; *Bell* 19; *Kui* 1, 9 (re-še-ti-šu). Sarg *Khors* 170 re-še-it mātāte (conquered by me); *Cyl* 40 re-še-e-te. Asb vi 125, vii 1 niši u šal-lat ^(māt) Êlamti ša ... ax-bu-ta ri-še-e-ti (the best of) a-na ilāni-ja aš-ruq. Neb iii 21 bi-tu-ga-ak re-e-ša-a-ti ^(iç) erini-ja, KB iii (2) 15: die besten Cedernstämme (BA i 474; AV 7614). K 2852 + K 9662 iv 11 li-ša-a-nu ri-še-e-ti ana pul-pul (Winckler, *Forsch.*, ii 40—43). — *d*) beginning {Anfang}: of the month Tammūz i-na ri-iš-ti-šu, at its beginning, *Rec. Trav.*, xvii *p* 36 (*no* xvi). —

V 38 *no* 2 *O* 16 ZAG = ri-iš-tum (AV 7622); but read mut-ta-tum.

reštû, *adj f* reštitu. — properly: situated at the top (rêštu) = first in order, or in time; hence "in the beginning" (§ 76). id SAG § 9, 131, Br 3522; AV 7621. — *a*) highest, first (of rank), chiefest {oberster, erster (an Rang), vornehmster} ‖ ašaridu. — Esh *Sendsch*, *O* 2 A-nu giš-ru reš-tu-u; V 33 *a* 18, 19 mâr (aplu; TUR-UŠ) reš-tu-u ša A-gu-um ra-bi-i. Anp i 12 Ninib aplu reš-tu-u. Asb iv 111, in the month of Sin .... mar reš-tu-u a-ša-ri-du ša (il) Bêl; viii 97; also IV² 33 iv (end) Sin mar reš-ti-i ša (il) Bêl. IV² 8 *b* 25, 26 Marduk mâr (& mar) reš-tu-u (TUR-SAG) ša ap-si-i; 22 *b* 29, 30; H 99, 57; 97, 5 (ša (il) Ê-a); IV² 30* *no* 3 *O* 22 mar reš-ti-i ša (il) Ea. K 7592 + K 8717 + DT 363 *O* 32 (Marduk) bu-kur (il) Ea reš-tu-u; + *O* 41 (end) (il) reš-tu-u a-ša-rid. V 66 *b* 5 Nabû bu-kur (il) Marduk reš-tu-u; see ZA v 58, 32 & bukru. V 34 *a* 41 I (Nebuchad.) a-bi-il-šu (of Nabopolassar) re-e-eš-ta-a-am. Neb v 21 ia-ti apil-šu re-eš-ta-a. KB iii (2) 4/5 *col* 2, 70 (Neb) bu-uk-ru ri-eš-tu-u; I 68 *b* 25 Bêlšazar mar reš-tu-u (çit libbija); Sn iii 63 *Esarh.* mar reš-tu-u | tar-bit bir-ki-ia; *cf* V 66 *a* 19. *Rec. Trav.*, xx 205 *foll*, *no* xli *col* 1, 7 Ištar is called bu-kur-ti (il) A-nu reš-ti-ti. ZA ii 161, 39 see parsu (835 *col* 2). On aplu ašaridu, reštû, & talimu *cf* WINCKLER, *Forsch.*, i 517; II 193 *foll*. — *b*) original, primeval, ancient, of old {anfänglich, ursprünglich, uralt}. I 65 *b* 50 (‖ billudê qudmûtim); SCHEIL, *Nabd*, viii 52, 53 see *p* 768 *col* 2, *ll* 9—13. I 67 *a* 30 ki-ma se-ma-a-ti-šu re-eš-ta-a-ti; 20 pa-ar-çu re-eš-tu-tu; Asb iv 106 sattukkê gi-ni-e SAG-MEŠ (= reštûti), KB ii 195 ✕ WINCKLER, *Forsch.*, i 248 (rišêti). *Creat.-frg* I (S 747) 3 apsû-ma reš-tu-u (zârûšun), the primeval ocean. IV² 19 *b* 35, 36 ina âli-ki reš-ti-i U-ru-uk. III 35 *no* 4 *O* 5 ina (arax) Nisanni arax reš-tu-u, in Nisan the month of the beginning. I 66 *c* 32; KB iii (2) 4 *col* ii 43, 44; I 52 *no* 6, 4 see kigallu, *b* (372 *col* 1). V 64 *b* 23 E-XUL-XUL ri-eš-tum, the old temple *E*; ZK ii 347 *fol*. — II 31 *no* 3, 33 (71) mar-ma-ru ‖ reš-tu(m); V 41 *a-b* 35. II 7 *e-f* 40, 41 KU-SAG (V 14 *e-f* 42) & KU-SAG-ZA-SAG = reš-tu-u; Br 3524, 11154, 12057; see also V 14 *c-d* 49.

rêšiš 2. *adv* K 2852 + K 9662 i 4 ri-e-šiš e-me, made himself like unto a slave.

rêšûtu. slavery, servitude, service {Sklaverei, Knechtschaft} BA iii 271 √רוש, be poor, miserable; also BA ii 280. I 49 *b* 11 the inhabitants of Babylon il-li-ku re-e-šu-tu; *d* 30 who a-na re-e-šu-ti šu-lu-ku (✕ KB ii 123); also Bu 88—5—12, 80 ii 23 il-li-ku ri-e-šu-tu; Bu 88—5—12, 101 *col* i 13, 14 (-ta). V 34 *a* 7 *Neb* ša ana Nabû u Marduk kitnušuma ip-pu-šu ri-e-šu-su-un, who is subject to *N* & *M* and does service to them. KB iii (2) 46 *col* 1, 18 (ri-[šu-su]-un). Bu 91—5—9, 419, 25 a-na ri-šu-tim la ra-ga-mi, to slavery (he was) not to be claimed.

NOTE. — II 16 b 71 in-na-ši ri-es-su. JÄGER, BA ii 280, 281, 286, (sein Mangel tritt ein, nicht) erhebt sich wieder sein Haupt; supplying *ul* before innaši. PRINCE, AJP xiv 117, his poverty is increased, referring to V 18 *a-b* 15 (see rêšu). BRÜNNOW, ZA viii 130 (dessen Begehr wird erfüllt und) es erhebt sich sein Haupt (*cf* našû ša rêši; & H 127, 32 a-li aš-tal-lum ri-es-šu ul in-na-aš[-ši], the town, I destroy, will never recover). HAUPT, *Papers of Philadelphia Orient. Club*, i 250, 269 *rm* 23; 271 *rm* 29: (their want set in and their?) suffering was heightened.

rîšâtu, rêšâtu, *pl tantum* (?, § 70 *a*, note; see below); §§ 64; 65, 11 *rm*: *rêštu (= *sg*); AV 7614; Z^B 47. IV² 18 *no* 1 *O* 6; I 65 *a* 40; *b* 23; I 51 *no* 2 *b* 14; Neb iv 9; Rm 198 *R* 4; KB iii (2) 50 *col* 2, 69 see xidûtu (307). Asb i 23 ina xidâti ri-ša-a-te (& *cf* KB ii 258—9, 10); V 65 *a* 40. K 126, 14 (when a man approaches the bed) zi-ka-ru-ta êpu-uš that man enjoys life (u ri-ša-a-tum iššakana-šu). I 69 *c* 38 (*b*) li-id-di-šu balaṭ ri-ša-a-ti (KB iii (2) 86—7). V 35, 28 i-na ul-çi u ri-ša-a-tim; Bu 88—5—12, 75 + 76 viii 30 (-ti); L⁴ iii 15; BA iii 254. IV² 20 *O* 12, 13 xar-ra-an šu-lu-lu u-ru-ux ri-ša-a-ti (triumphant return), Br 4400; same id as S^b 352 a-si-la-al | id | ri-ša-a-tum (ZA i 191, 192); 19, 20 (im-me-ra) ma-li ri-ša-a-ti (Br 9151; 10391) + *R* 31 (see also NE 24, 8; V 65 *b* 15), war voll Jubels; *Rec. Trav.*, xxiv *nos* 1/2 on this text; KB iii (2) 6 *col* 3, 54 (when Marduk) i-na ri-si-e-tim i-ra-am-mu-u ki-ri-ib-ka (*ibid*, 20, 21 i-na ul-çi-im | u ri-si-a-tim = HILPRECHT, *OBI*, i 32/33 *col* 3, 29/30; ZA iv 112, 137); KB iii (1) 132 *col* iv 17 see rêšu, 1 *a*). — *sg* see ZIM., *Ritualtaf.*, 31—37 i 31 Êa, thy father .... reš-ta lim-la, be filled with joy; perh. also K 306, 2 bît ri-ši-tu (or = rašûtu?) KB iv 184, 185; see Anp iii 90 bît xi-da-te. — Sm 954 (D 135) *O* 33/34 (*bis*); 35/36 (*cf* ZA i 191) EL-LU-EME-SAL = i-na ri-ša-a-ti (Br 11182, 11633) same iD as lallartu (483 *col* 1). V 47 *a* 40 a-mur-ma ar-ka-t[um] ri-ša-a-tum ip-pe-e-ši. IV² 54 *a* 54 ar-man-ni re-ša-a-ti (= precious odor) ṭu-pu-uš aš-na-an, (see 358 *col* 2). K 3182 *col* III 44 i-na ûm niš-še ri-ša-ta il-la-ta u xi-da-a-ti, *AJSL*, xvii April, '01. — II 7 *e-f* 47, 48 ZAG-AŠ (Br 6497) & GAR-ME-GAR (Br 12161, which also = qûlu, *q. v.*) = ri-ša-a-tu (ZK i 298). V 16 *c-d* 6 KI-LI = ri-ša-a-tum (Br 9658); see also LEHMANN, Š¹ 16; P² 10 (-te); L⁵ 16 (-tu); S² 26 (-ti), *etc.*

rašûtu *f* literally: creditorship, then: claim }Guthaben, Forderung{ AV 7542. Nabd 669, 1 ra-šu-tu ša X ša ina muxxi Y, (and often). Ner 36, 1: $1^2/_3$ mana kaspi ra-šu-tu ša *B*; Cyr 245, 1 ina ra-šu-ti-šu ša ... (kraft seiner Schuldforderung) BA iii 409, 410. Dar 128, 6 ra-šu-ut-ta-a ina mux-xi-šu ku-um ra-šu-tu, Cyr 337, 2, Ersatz für eine Schuldforderung (BA iii 428, 429). PEISER, *Vertr.*, xvi 21 ra-šu-tu ma-la ba-šu-u; cl 3 ra-šu-ta-a ina mux-xi. Often: e-lat ra-šu-tu (max-ri-tum), unbeschadet der (früheren) Schuld, Camb 164, 9—10. HILPRECHT, *OBI*, ix 91, 9 ra-šu-u i-šal-lim (= innițțer); 104, 9; 103, 10 ra-šu-us-su in-niț-te-ru; 95, 10 a-di .... (amêl) rašû-su in-ni-țe-ir (BA iv 559 *foll*).

NOTE. — According to OPPERT (ZA iv 400 *foll*; vi 281 *foll*) U-AN-TIM an iD for rašûtu & rikeu (BA ii 534 *no* 337); also ZA iii 170 *rm* 2 >< PEISER, *KAS* 95; *cf* Aram [illegible], ZA iv 68, 69; vi 444; PSBA ix 180.

rašûtânu, creditor }Gläubiger{. PSBA ix 250 *foll*; 296 *foll*. AV 7541. STRASSM., *Liverpool* (AV* 56 *a*) 132, 4 + 7; 134, 7 ra-šu-ta-nu.

rišûtu *1.* ‖ of rašûtu HILPRECHT, *loc. cit.*, 19, 11—12 (amêl) rašu-u ša-nam-ma a-na mux-xi ul i-šal-laț a-di-i Bêl-nadin-šum ri-šu-ut-su in-ni-țe-ru. BA iv 559 *fol.* PINCHES, PSBA xix 137 *no* 3, 6 ri-šu-u[-tu?]; Nabd 17, 16; Neb 141, 5.

rišûtu *2.* (= SA-DUBBIN-AG-AG) *cf* xarasu (339 *col* 2). Br 2726, 3095 read tal-qat-tum.

ri-ša-ti, III 67 *c-d* 73 Nergal is written [AN ...]-DUN-GA as god ša ri-ša-ti.

rîtu, *f* pasture; feed }Weide; Futter{ √rê'u (*q. v.*). § 25; G *p* 105 *rm* 1; Z^B 32; iD Ú (Br 6025). K 2852 + K 9662 iii 30 (end) ri-i-tu ța-ab-tu (treffliche Speise) 31, u-ša-az-nun (besorgte ich) WINCKLER, *Forsch.*, ii 36 *foll.* V 50 *b* 52, 53 bu-ul çêri ina ri-i-ti uš-tam-qit (3 pr; Br 6025); H 187; AV 7623. IV² 23 *no* 1 i 8, 9 see kabasu a) 365 *col* 2; BA ii 417. IV² 1 *a* 45 see rê'û; 9 *a* 61, 62 kêtu amatka eliš kîma šâri ina niqilpû [ri]-i-tu u maš-ki-tum u-da-aš-ša. H 39. 170 U-QI = ri-tu šu-te-'u-u (Br 6083/4), followed by *r* sa-xa-ru (see 752 *col* 1); II 41 *no* 2 *c-d* 8—9; 37 *b-c* 28 in a list of birds we have (*b*) še-u ri-ta ina (or AŠ?). V 40 *e-f* 5 (Br 6089); H 39, 174; Sn i 41, 42 (a-šar *etc.*) see mašqîtu, 608 *col* 2. Dar 257, 10 pût suddudu (see 747 *col* 2) ri-'-i-tum u maçartum alpi buštim ubar naši. Artax 3, 6 zêru pî šul-pu, explained by bît re-e-ti = pastureland.

rittu *1.* seal, sign, *etc.* }Siegel, Zeichen, *etc.*{ AV 7563. PEISER, *Vertr.*, 243 document, tablet }Urkunde{. S^b 121 ki-ši-ib (*cf* kiššibbu, 446 *col* 1) | ŠIT | ri-it-tum, Br 5979 (according to HOMMEL, *Sum. Les.*, 76 = finger, arm, see rittu, 2 & laqtu). 82—7—4, 42 *O* 1/2 see çalalu, 1 ג (end); 6, ta-mi-ix ri-it-tu-uš-šu; + 18 [u-šat]-mi-ix ri-it-tu-uš-šu (which passages would perhaps determine the reading rittu in stead of laqtu in some of the instances quoted on *p* 497 *col* 2). Xammurabi-letters 8 *R* 5, 6 a-ụa-tum ša ta-aš-pur-am .... ki-ma ri-it-tim-ma ša-nu-um(-ma?) BA iv 489 *foll.* KB iv 88, 89 *col* iii 26; iv 24 alpi ša rit-ti (or = rêtu?); KB iv 298, 299 *no* iv 9 ina eli ištēni-it rit-tu = at one time {auf ein Mal} >< T^C reading minûtu; 308, 309 *no* ix 13; Ner 31, 6 ina ištēnit ri-it-tum. Nabd 59, 5 (KB iv 212, 213 & *rm* *) rit-ta-šu ana šu-mi-šu (ištur), und dessen Handzeichen *N* auf seinen Namen geschrieben hat.

rittu *2.* — *a*) finger, fist {Finger, Faust} see laqtu. ZA ix 119; 417. Rm 279 B (Rm 422) 11 ri-it-ta-šu, his fist (ZA ix 407); thus also K 2148 iii 29, 30 si-si-it rit-ti ša; & ri-it-ta-šu ša ...; ii 8 .... šakna-at rit-ta ša amēli (or šit-ta??). ZA xvi 180, 181 reads rit-ta-a-ša in IV² 58 *col* 3 (& *add*) *d* 30 instead of laq-ta. Perh. K 12846, 14 (M^S *pl* 17) r]i?-it-ta-an, a dual? (GGA '98, 825). — *b*) handle {Henkel}. T. A. (Ber) 25 ii 43: 1 bi-iš-ša-tum (= piššatu) ri-it-ta-šu of a certain stone; + 45 + 47 + 49 + 51 *etc.*; iii 42: III ŠU tam-lu-u ri-it-ta-šu of a certain stone; + 45 + 46 *etc.*, ri-e-it-ta-šu-nu.

NOTE. — NE 60, 10 read šit-ta(-šu) & *cf* KB vi (1) 214, 216.

rit-ti-ja TP vii 73 *etc.* read šangû-ti-ja & *cf* šangûtu.

retû, erect, fortify, strengthen, make firm {errichten, befestigen, festmachen} AV 7547; D^Pr 41 *rm*; Flemming, *Neb*, 20; ZA iii 302: רתה. V 34 *c* 37 the temple .... ša-da-ni-iš e-er-ti, I erected mountainhigh; Neb iv 13 (e-ir-te); KB iii (2) 78 (iii) 25 e-ir-ta-a ^(ic) dalâti, § 34*a*. *pm* KB iii (2) 92, 14 ša .... ri-tu-u te-me-en-šu; IV² 30 *no* 1 *a* 4, 5 qar-radu rabû ša ki-ma erçitim ri-tu-u (Br 5585); 16 *a* 11, 12 gišparru la e-ti-qu ša ana lim-ni ri-tu-u (= KAK-A); 26 *a* 21, 22 see pâṭu, *a* (798 *col* 1) Br 378. S^c 202 du-u | KAK | ri-tu[-u], Br 5265. — *ps* II 15 *a-b* 37 (K 56 iv) in its wall a peg ul i-ret-ti, Meissner, 12 *rm* 2. NE VI 15 (a-rat-tu-u) see KB vi (1) 449.

Q^t Neb vi 14, 15 (11, dalâti erini) e-ma bâbâni (written KA-KA)-ša e-ir-te-it-ti (KB iii, 2, 22—23); viii 9; ix 16 ir-te-it-ta-ma; vi 38 e-ir-te-it-ti-ši-na-ti (I placed firmly into the gates).

Q^tn K 1285 *O* 1 ... ar-ta-na-at-ta-ka ^(il) Nabû, I address myself to thee (Martin, *Textes relig.*, '03, 26: a prayer to Nabû.

ℶ = Q place, put in or at (with or without *prep.* ina, e-ma). II 67, 79 doorwings e-ma bâbâ^pl-ni u-rat-ti (KB ii 24, 25). V 64 *b* 12 (dalâti) u-ra-at-ta-a i-na bâbâni-šu, ZA ii 128 *a* 24; I 69 *a* 12 e-ma bâbâni-šu u-ra-at-ta. Anp *Stand* 21 ina bâba^pl-ša u-ri-ti; V 70, 8; I 27 *no* 2, 18 (ina bâbi-ša) u-ra-ti; Anp ii 4 (u-ri-te); Sn vi 50 u-rat-ta-a bâbâ^pl-ši-in; I 44, 71 (-šin); Sarg *Khors* 161 u-rat-ta-a ni-rib-šin (= *Ann* 422) = at their (the palaces) entrances. *Silv.* 24 (u-rat-ti); *bull* 68 (u-rat-ta-a); Asb x 100; Scheil, *Nabd*, viii 54; Bu 88—5—12, 75 + 76 v 37. H 73 (K 56) 12 du-la-a-ti (251 *col* 2) u-rat-ta (= AB-KAK...E, Br 6624), I fixed, placed; D 92, 10; Meissner, 12 *rm* 3; Johns, *Doomsday Book*, 19. V 45 iv 37 tu-rat-ta; see also gašišu (234, 235).

ratû *f* ratîtu, AV 7546 see rê'ibu.

ra-ti ^(il) Adad, AV 7445; see râdu.

rûtu (?) S 1708, 11 KI-KU-BI-KU = ru-us-su-nu, AV 5962; Br 9823 (KI-KU = šubtu & rîtu, Br 9826).

rûtum. AV 7662 U-XU | id | ru-u-tum, *cf* ru'utu, 2.

ruttu *1.* V 27 *a-b* 13 ru-ut-ti ^(il) Nâri, apparently the same as 12, kib-ri ^(il) Nâri. KB vi (1) 487 = Schaum des Flusses; then perh. = ru'utu, 2.

ruttum *2.* AV 7663 on K 2061 (H 202) 20 MA-LI = ru-ut-tum, followed by ba-a-a-šu (see *p* 141 *col* 1), Br 6785.

rit(šit)-tum & **rit(šit)-tu-ku** see ridû, 4.

רתת ℶ tu-rat-tax V 45 iv 39. **Der.** perh. tar-ta-xu.

NOTE — Q perh. V 22 *g-h* 56 ra-ta[-xu?].

ratamu, *pr* irtumu, bind, wrap {binden, umwinden} S 1064, 13—14 ina ap-pi-šu ir-tu-mu, (which) covered (enveloped) his face (nose), Hr^L 392; Johnston, JAOS xviii, 101—3. M^S √רתם Q^t.

ritpâšu. *adj* wide, open; receptive {weit, offen; empfänglich} § 65, 40*a*; ZA iv 52. V 35, 23 lib-bi ri-it-pa-šu (§ 73) ša mârê Bâbili, BA ii 210, 211. Lay 38, 4 see karšu, 1 (441 *col* 2). √rapašu.

ruteššû ‖ ruššû, *q. v.* V 23 *d-f* 30—42 TUR-DIŠ = ru-uš-šu-u (39), ru-te-eš-šu-u (40), uk-ku-du (41), mul-li-lu (42). V 38 *a-c* 9, preceded by ru-uš-šu[-u], 8 (Br 4151, 4152).

ratatu, oppress {unterdrücken} see rādu, 2.
rattitu (?). T. A. (Ber) 25 iii 53 PA rat-ti-ti (??) abnu XI-LI-PA.

ש

ša (> šā?), properly *acc* of šū, he (§ 58; Haupt, *J. H. Circ.*, 114 *p* 111); Hommel, ZDMG 32, 711 *foll*; Kraetzschmar, BA i 379—442; Knudtzon, 26. In Xamm.-*code* ša is used for nom., gen. & accus. — 1. Demonstr. pron. (original meaning): he, she, it; this; that {der, die, das} BA i 384—6 = annû, which later on ousts ša entirely. Used *a*) of persons, indicating rank, profession, with following *gen.* (amēl) ša (= ذو) eli qa-na-a-te, see qanû, 1. K 524 (Hr^L 282) 18 + *R* 1 (amēl) Pu-qu-du | ša i-na (al) *T.* K 469 *R* 22 (Hr^L 138) (amēl) ša bit-xal-la-ti, the cavalry. ša bābi rabī, head cashier, BA iii 488. ša ṭe-mi, the councilor. ša bīt šikari, butler {Kellermeister} BA i 536, 630. (amēl) ša šikari na-ši-šu, wine merchant; (amēl) ša ṭa-ab-ti-šu Nabd 1048; (amēl) ša MUN-ti-šu Nabd 148 *etc.*; ZA ii 322 (on -šu). ša a-bu-sa-tu, AV 7694. ša bīt çi-bit-ti, the prisoner, lit^y, the man of the prison; *cf* V 13 *b* 8—10; I 27 *no* 2, 37 men & women ša ša bit çibitti, who are prisoners. V 18 *a-b* 13 ša pi-ti i-nim, Br 1850. Xamm.-*code* xxxvi 76 ša ma-xi-ir-tim freightagent {Spediteur}; 77, ša mu-uk-ki-el-bi-tim = ferryman. ša with following ꞉ *e.g.* ša dāki, ša xa-bati, ša šalali, see these verbs. Also P.N. ša ilu-ma damiq; ša Ištar gub-bu, ša Ištar-šu-u. AV 7795—97. ša Nabû-šu-u, AV 7963. ša na-ši-šu, Nabd 855, 3, AV 7969; ša pi-i Bēl K 618 (AV 8007), name of a fortress, Esh iv 3; Asb iii 54, 68; ša pi-i kal-bi AV 8008; ša ri-di-i V 15, 11 (AV 8047). On compounds of ša *e.g.* šabrû, ša(k)kanakku, šangû see Jensen, ZA vii 174 *rm* 1 & these words. — *b*) of things with following *gen.* {von Sachen} iš GAR, Bezold, *Diss*, 30, 31. frequently in phrases like eli ša pāna(i); & maxri (*cf* kānu, ℑ & mandattu). (iç) ša šadadi; (iç) ša çilli *etc.* see these words. ša me-e = Wasserbecher (?, Peiser, *Verträge*, 287). S 1064 (Hr^L 392) 11—12 ša ku-ri Inā-šu, Johnston, *Diss*, *no* 14. ša pi-i-šu = his word, command, report. ebrûtum ša ûmākal kînātûtu ša dārāti Sm 61, 9 + 11. ša û-um a day, for a day, Neb *Grot*, i 16; ii 26, 36. H 87—89, 16—19 ša û-ma, but Prince, AJSL xix 215 reads ša-tam-ma. Nabd 67, 3 ša arxi, by the month; ša šatti, Nabd 796, 4. ša ba-la-ṭi-ja, during my lifetime, Neb ii 1.

2. Genitive-particle. BA i 386—95; Anp i 117 ša (BA i 398) çābē mādûti ēnā šunu. Beh 1 *foll*. *del* 87 (92) ša ûmi at-ta-ṭal (or ri?) b(p)u-na-a-šu, ZA iii 421; also in local meaning, Anp ii 110 = from (a further development, Johnston), K 629, 16 ša libbi ad-ri ēkalli, from the palace enclosure (he will go) Hr^L 65. K 519 *R* 2 ša damē ša ap-pi-šu il-lak-u-ni, blood came from his nose, Martin, *Rec. Trav.*, xxiii 160.

3. Relative pron. Beh. 7 *foll*; BA i 399 *fol*; TP i 85, who, which; for all genders, numbers, and cases. In T. A. often ša-a, Bezold, *Diplomacy*, xxii § 15, *a*. Rm 76 (Hr^L 358) 15 ša = as regards the matter of, BA iv 508 *foll*. Br 11974.

4. Conjunctive particle: that {dass}. K 524, 17 (mār šipri) ibaš-ši ša (Hr^L 282), a messenger has come to him (with the news) that; K 95 (Hr^L 288) *R* 3 ba-ni ša, it is well that; K 94 (Hr^L 287) 7. In *c. t.* especially after kunnu & mukinnûtu, *cf* T^C 130 (above). — ša la = except, Neb 72, 4; 283, 15; T^C 87; *del* 165 (178). — ša = arki ša, TP iii 92 (96). — ša = kī ša, as soon as, Asb ii 30; K 528 (Hr^L 269) *R* 14 ki-i ša; = how (K 79 *R* 15); *cf* K 79 *R* 16/17. — a-di ša = until K 79 *R* 8 (Hr^L 266). — ina libbi ša = because, K 824 (Hr^L 290) 17 + *R* 4. K 81, 12 ša mi-i-tum a-na-ku, because I was dead (= aššu), §§ 82; 148, 1;

BA i 200; 441 *fol*; Asb ii 49 *foll* (51, *var* aš-šu); i 132 *fol*; iv 66 *foll*. *del* 112 (120) aš-šu & *var* ša. when, as {wenn, als} BA i 403 *fol*.

On the syntax of ša in Xamm.-*code* see Ungnad, ZA xviii 41 *foll*.

II 31 *no* 2 *f-g* 14 AMÊL = ša-a (+ 29) Br 6406; 1340 (MU-LU = ša). V 21 *g-h* 40, 52 RA = ša-a, Br 6364; V 22 *d* 30 ma-a : ša-a : ki-i (Br 11398; AV 7665; GGA '80, 528); *cf* S^c 278, Br 9637. V 27 *a-b* LI = ša-a, Br 1116. V 22 *a-b* 67, Br 11362.

Note. — 1. Preposition ša does not exist, BA i 583 ≍ BA i 295—98.

2. ša also a variant of šu, BA ii 231; 252; 279.

3. On construction of ša see T^C 23—27.

šu, relative pron = ša. Xamm.-*code* iv 1, 9, 29; ZA xviii, 41, 42.

šū *1.*, he; *f* **šī**, she; *pl* **šūnu, šun** (Br 10471); *f* **šīna**, they; §§ 21, 27; AV 8360—7. Ges.^{12} 185 (הוּא); Brockelmann, ZA xvi 402. K 8522 *R* 17 šu-u ki-ma ṭa-a-ti-ma; Rm 67, 11 (Hr^L 348), AJSL xv 140. *del* 260 (291) šu-u. KB vi (1) 98 *no* III 2; 290, 15 (ma-an-nu šu-u, whosoever he may be), + 18. Asb iv 73 šu-u, he himself. u šu-u, NE X *col* iv 9; I *col* iv 2 + 29 (KB vi (1) 427; 429) = KB vi (1) 124, 2; 126, 29; *del* 228 (247) šu-u mu-tum-ma, that means death; 247 (277); Asb iv 127, v 60 (but he); vii 119; viii 15. TP III *Ann* 45 šu-u = he; Sn iii 51; III 29, 47 + 51; Banks, *Diss*, 14, 103 šu-u ū-mu, it, the storm. Sarg *Khors* 30. K 112 *R* 12 šu-u gab-bu (Hr^L 223; BA i 212; ii 28); K 498, 6 (Hr^L 522) šu-u, the said {der bewusste}; K 617, 16 (Hr^L 208) this mār Bêl-iddina bēl xi-i-ṭu šu-u, is a rascal; + 17 par-ri-çu šu-u, is a liar, JAOS xx 251; 83, 1—18, 2 *R* 8 li-pu-uš šu-u (Hr^L 391; AJSL xv 141). — KB vi (1) 100, 14 ši-i lu-u ki-a-am (*ibid* 411; 568; IV^2 13 *b* 43; 23 *no* 2 *R* 5, be it thus); K 3449 *a R* 5; ZA ix 159. 79, 7—8, 178 *R* 7 (KB vi, 1, 10—11): K 2401 iii 7 see pâqu, 2. IV^2 60* C *O* 7 ik-ri-bi šarri ši-i xi-du-ti, to bless the king that was my joy, BA i 229. Asb vi 110 u ina ūme-šu-ma ši-i u ilāni abē-ša; Beh 18. Neb 101, 4 lu-u aššati ši-i, she shall be my wife, KB iv 186/7. Nabd 356, 33 ši-i u mu-ti-šu, she & her husband. Creat.-*frg* IV 8 ši-i lu-u ga-at-ka, that be in thy hand. K 595 *R* 13 an-ni-tu ma-a ši-i ṭa-ab-tu a-ta-mar, BA iv 505, that I consider a benefit; K 512 *R* 10; K 828 *R* 1 ma-la ša ši-i di-ki-e-ma; K 84 *R* 5 ul bil-tu ši-i (Hr^L 6; 204; 291; 301); also šim-me, ZA v 156, 18 & *rm* 3. — *pl* šu-nu liq-tūma (*cf* qatū) anaku lum'id, let them perish but let me increase (§ 150). K 512 *R* 3 šu-nu, they; Asb iv 121. KB vi (1) 58, 11 + 12 šu-nu, they! šu-nu (= E-NE-NE-NE) often in IV Rawl., IV^2 1 *fol* i 12/13, 28/30 *etc.*: = MEŠ, IV^2 1 *fol* i 12/13—22/23 *etc.*; Br 5870. K 1249 *R* 11 šu-u-nu (Hr^L 326). Beh 100 par-ça-a-tum ši-na, lies they are! Sn vi 11. K 3182 iii 53 ši-na, as for those, *etc.* (AJSL xvii 142—3); Bu 88—5—12, 21 (Meissner, *no* 89) 37 u ši-na = and they. — V 20 *a-b* 59 ŠE = šu-u (Br 7435; ZK i 315); V 21 *c-d* 53 NI = šu-u (Br 5329); V 27 *a-b* 36 LA = šu-u (Br 987), followed by LI = šu-a-tu; *c-f* 60 BI = šu[-u?] Br 5132; K 101 *O* 7/8; IV^2 4 *b* 36/37; V 27 *e-f* 63 *foll* for equivalents of šū & šūnu, Br 5869. V 36 *a-b* 48 (Br 8785); V 37 *e-g* 56 (Br 9995). *Cf* also P. N. Nabū-šu-u, AV 5670.

Here belongs perhaps also the šu-u (šu) in bilingual vocabularies, indicating that the word in the right column is the same as that in the left column, + ending -u. II 32 *a-b* 59 *etc.* — šu-ma = *ditto* (§§ 55; 79). šu-ma IV^2 27 *a* 59; K 991 *O* 11 ina ūme šu-ma; Br 9993 on V 37 *a-c* 4. On šu-ma. ši-ma after ummā introducing direct discourse (= *hic*, *haec*) see Meissner, 124.

On šu-u in *del* 123 (129 *var*) see BA i 133 *fol* (≍ Jensen, 431) = a kind of article to abūbu; or = *ditto*, Lotz, *Tigl. Pil.*, 107; § 55 *rm*. Jensen, KB vi (1) 239 *rm* 11: šu-u belongs to šûtu = Südwind, a synonym of mexū; or = he (the hurricane).

T. A. forms see Bezold, *Diplomacy*, xxi § 14 (*a*).

šū *2.* demonstr. pronoun; § 21, used as a postpositive adj. he, that, the same (= šuātu); *f* **šī** (AV 8125); *pl* **šūnu**, usually **šu'nūti**; *f* **šinâti** & **šinâtina**, they, them. JA xvi ('90) 533 *foll*; § 57 *a*. — *del* 12 âlu šu-u, that same city; I 27 *no* 2, 2; H 115, 8 amēlu šu-u, and that man; *cf* ina ūmi(-)šu-ma, at that time (H^{CV} xxxvi); KNUDTZON, *pp* 139, 140; TP i 89 *etc.* aš-ru šu-u IV^{2} 39 *b* 10; pa-rakku šu-u, Neb iii 1; K 112 *R* 9 (Hr^{L} 223); K 41 *b* 18 nak-ri šu-u. V 69, 21; Anp iii 133 (= *acc*). *del* 254 (284) šam-mu šu-u (= *nom*; 264 (295) šam-mu an-nu-u); 256 (286) šum-ma šam-mu ša-a-šu (= *acc*); IV^{2} 22 *a* 8 (Br 5866). — ēkallum ši-i, Anp ii 5; 134; III 32, 53 (+60). Camb 42, 12 a-ki-i u-il(or an?)-tim ši-i. K 562, 12 (Hr^{L} 260) a-lak-ti ši-i; IV^{2} 26 *a* 45/46 tam-tum ši-i gal-ta-at, Br 9284. — S 1708 *O* 11 (= IV^{2} R 18*) ša i-me-ri-e šu-nu-ti *etc.* Asb iii 90 mārē Bābili šu-nu-ti; çābē šu-nu-ti, Šalm, *Ob* 154; ilāni šu-nu-ti, *Khors* 35. — KB vi (1) 92, 5 ina ša-na-a-ti ši-na-a-ti, in those same years. abullāte ši-na-a-ti, Neb v 64; vi 19; (bābāni) Ner i 30; (êqlū) Nabd 687, 17 + 18; 31 (-ta); Esh ii 40 (= ša-ti-na, III 15 iii 25; § 57 *a*); ši-na-ti, III 41 ii 2. IV^{2} 39 *b* 23 (see irritu, 1, *p* 109 *col* 1, & *cf* I 27 *no* 2, 67). TP iv 33 ša mātāte ši-na-ti-na. I 49 *b* 20 ep-še-e-ti ši-na-ti.

On šu = šūtu (Esh iv 20) see BA ii 60; Hr^{L} 252 *R* 8 *b*.

šū 3. name of stone }Steinname{ ‖ šū, 2 & ušū. K 240, 1 (Brit. Mus., Texts XIV 5) + K 4232, 1 (*ibid* 17) TAK-DAN-GA = (abnu) šu-u; K 240 *b* 8 = (abnu) šu-u.

ša'u pr išū', ps išā' fly }fliegen{ = שׁוא, § 116. PSBA vi (Jan. '84) 58 surdū (see 783 *col* 2) its prey ina pīšu iprurma ana pān šarri i-šu-'-u. K 4470 ii 11 i-ša-'-u. Asb viii 85 (a desert) ša iççur šame-e la i-ša-'-u ki-rib-šu, to which no bird of heaven flies (= 110 la i-šak-ka-nu qin-nu).

ša'ū (?). II 28 *b-c* 44; 35 *c-d* 69 LUB-KIL = ša-'u-u in one group with šu-ta-mu-u & u-tal-lu-u (] 'alū' curse?); Br 7282, AV 7770. G § 109 compares شكا, speak.

šē'u 1. pr eš'i (1 *sg*); ps iše'i; pm še'ī. AV 8176. D^{Pr} 39, 40 = שׁעה; G §§ 49; 77; 112. — *a*) see, look, behold }sehen, schauen, erblicken{. Creat.-*frg* I 6 çū'çā la še-'i, see gipāru (229 *col* 1) & çuçū; IV 66 (] ibarri); II 75 (see mekū, 585 *col* 2; KB vi (1) 317). K^{M} 1, 21 kan-sa-ku az-za-az a-še-'-ku; *cf* Rm 76 (Hr^{L} 358) *R* 12 ša-a-u i-ni-šu-u-ni a-na a-a-ši (PSBA xxiii 357: are turned toward). — *b*) look for someone or something, inquire, seek }nach jemandem (etwas) suchen{ NE 1 *col* iv 41 mudū libbašu i-še-'a eb-ra. KB vi (1) 584 *c* 21 u šarru i-ši-'i[-na ma-a-ti], + 28. H 75 *R* 1; IV^{2} 60 *O* 34; *R* 39 see saxaru Q *a* (end), 752 *col* 1 (*ll* 3—8). *del* 20 še-'-i napšāti, seek life (*i. e.* save) J^{I-N} 83; *del* 7 ina pu-xur ilāni ba-la-ṭa (see 163 *col* 2 *b*; & again, KB vi (1) 231) taš-'-u (*var* um); 187 (207) balaṭa ša tu-ba-'-u. Here then also II 35 *e-f* 27. V 35, 23 (end) ū-mi-šam a-še-a (KB iii, 2, 124 *rm* 2). II 37 *b-c* 28 še-u (?) ri-ta, name of a bird? Sp II 265 *a* vii 7 il (= ina?) la-ba-an ap-pi u te-mi-ki e-še-' (ilat) iš[-tar-ti]. K^{M} 27, 8 ta(*var* ti)-ši-'.

Q^{1} — *a*) seek }suchen{ V 35, 12 (Marduk) iš-te-'-e-ma (§ 53 *d*) malki išaru (BA ii 210); 38 (med) aš-te-'-e-ma. Neb i 53 a-ma-at libbi iš-te-'-u. V 65 *a* 34 te-me-en la-bi-ri ši (*var* šu)-te-'-ma (= ip); Sp II 265 *a* vi 11; xx 10 (end); xxv 1; V 65 *a* 15 aš-te-'-e-ma; I 65 *a* 4 *Neb* mu-uš-te-'u-um ba-la-ṭam. IV^{2} 1 *a* 45 see rē'ū; & *cf* ZA iv 107, 21. K 4341 i 12 (II 36 *e-f* 46—48) QI-QI = ši-te-'u-u with pa-a-rum & bu-'u-u, AV 8348, Br 10754. H 34, 815 (*var* šu- = Ʒ^{1}). — *b*) be careful, pay attention to, be mindful of }Sorge für etwas tragen, auf etwas bedacht sein{ Neb iii 25—6 ana xulūlu Ē-KU-A aš-te-'-e-ma (viii 41) i-ta-am libbu. 81—6—7, 209, 32 aš-te-'-i-ma; 37, liš-te-'-e-mu (BA iii 280—3); I 52 *no* 4, 19—20. V 63 *b* 6—7 the aš-ra-a-ti of Šamaš and Adad aš-te-'e-ma (+3); Ner ii 3. V 62 *no* 1, 17. V 85, 25 aš-te-'-e mārē Bābili (I took care of). KNUDTZON, 143. 11 liš-te-'. IV^{2} 15 ii 60—61 aš-ra-ti-šu-nu ši-te-'-a (= ac) xi-šam-ma, IV^{2} 12 *a* 12 ši-te-'-a (Br 7588) mu-du-u. KB iii (2) 8 *no* 3 I 16 mu-uš-te-'-e-im; V 63 *a* 2 rubū nādu mu-uš-te-'-u aš[-ra]-a-ti ilāni rabūti; KB vi (1) 92, 9 muš-te-'-u par-çi. Sp II 265 *a* vii 4. — *c*) plan, think out }planen, sinnen{. I 27 *b* 88 (ša) . . . . li-im-ni-ti il-te-'-u. — *d*) Xammurabi-*code* xl 18 aš-ri šu-ul-mi-im eš-te-i-ši-na-šim, ZA xviii 31, ich suchte ihnen aus.

Q^{1n} — *a*) look around, seek, search for }umblicken, suchen{. KB vi (1) 106, 45—46 iš-te-ni-'-i ša pa-ni-šu u ar-ki-šu. — *b*) be mindful of, take care of, pay attention to, *etc*. Neb i 8—9 ša a-lak-ti i-lu-ti-šu-nu iš-te-ni-'-u (+ 17; K 3182 i 11; § 151), + 28 aš-ra-a-ti ili aš-te-ni-e. Ner i 20 aš-te-ni-'a-a; ii 14; Neb i 48; K 2606 *O* 25 (BA ii 399); K 41 *b* 22. Smith, *Asurb*, 121, 33 a-na-ku aš-re-e-ki aš-te-ni-'a-a, KB ii 250/1. V 63 *a* 8 (ša) iš-te-ni-'-u ba-la-ṭi (+ 11); V 35, 14 i-na ki-it-tim u mi-šu-ru iš-te-ni-'-e-ši-na-a-tim (BA ii 210; § 56 *b*). IV^2 10 *a* 38—9 aš-ta-ni-'-e-ma (= MU-UN-GI-GI-E-AN, Br 10754). — *c*) plan, think of }planen, auf etwas sinnen{ Asb i 128 iš-te-ni-'-u (3 *pl*) a-mat limut-tim; *cf* iii 79 iš-te-ni-'a-a limutti; v 24; Sm 118, 5. T^M v 121 tuš-te-ni-'-a (= 2 *pl*) ru-xi-e; ii 189. IV^2 5 *b* 28, 29 li-mut-tu iš-te-ni-'u-u šu-nu (= pš; Br 10754); see also limuttu, 480 *col* 1, *ll* 21—4.

ℑ perh Sp II 265 *a* xvii 2 ma-an-nu i-na šu-'-u ta[. . . .].

ℑ^t IV^2 19 *no* 3 *O* 9—10 (ul-te-'u); V 52 *a* 60—61 (Br 1014), *see* 414 *col* 2. II 179, 7—8 (Br 7977); pm 81—7—27, 19 *O* 12 ša pa-lax ilāni šu-tu-u-ni, (grant) . . . that they pursue the worship of the gods. Thompson, *Reports*, 257. II 41 *no* 2 *c-d* 8; H 39, 170 (AV 8624, Br 10755) see rītu.

NOTE. — K^M 175 derives from this verb šūtu, moment, time (??).

šēu, *pr* **išē**, come hastily, haste }eilends kommen, eilen{. Anp ii 86 *Anp* arki-šu-nu kīma (*var* ki-ma) iççurāte i-še-'i; i 63 i-še-'u (3 *pl*); iii 105 (× G § 49); ii 107 see zū, 3 (271). Šamš ii 52: in one day kīma našri eli-šu-nu a-še-'e. Creat.-*frg* V 23 (D 94, 23) ši-um (or -ta?) ba-'i-i u-ru-ux-šu (KB vi (1) 32/33). II 35 *c-f* 27 see bā'u, 2 (136).

Q^t (?) Sarg *Ann.* 210 i-na ši-te u-na tur-ri gi-mil-li-šu.

ℨ perhaps K 83, 10 un-qu (?) | ša šarri bēli-ia | ša X | a-na mux-xi-ja lišša-', the order . . . . was brought to me quickly; K 831 *R* 7 ši-pir-ti liš-ša-', let him take the letter (Hr^L 202; 214). — Or √našū (?).

With this šēu may perhaps be connected these 2:

še[-'u?] V 22 *d* 54 in the same group with mū (water), perh. = rapidly flowing water; &

še'itu. K 2491 iii 20/22 še-'-i-tu na-al-ba-na-a-te (& šap-li-tu), Craig. *Relig. Texts.* i 78. Martin, *Textes relig.*, ('03): la rigole (gutter }Rinne{), ou bassin, puisqu'on faisait couler de l'eau dessus.

ša-u-a (??) V 40 *e-f* 4 = U-A$^{(E)}$ Br 6098; ZA iii 334.

šu-u-u, AV 8368 = šummū, *cf* šamū (שמה).

šu-u. V 65 *b* 3 ki-ma šu-u ūmi u-nam-mir-šu; ZA iii 297.

šu'u *m* sheep, lamb }Schaf, Lamm{ Hebr שֶׂה, id LU-ARAD, Z^S 55, 35; Haupt, JBL xix 79 *rm* 109. Sarg *Khors* 168 see gu-maxxu (220 *col* 2); *cf Ann* 311 + 432; *Nimr* 19. L^4 iii 23 šu-'-e ma-ru-ti. Z^S iv 25 šu-'u. Brown-Gesenius, 961, 962.

šu'u. *f* **šu-e-tum**, master, mistress? Sp II 265 *a* xx 11 li-'-u pal-ku-u šu-e ta-šim-ti (ZA x 10/11; PSBA xvii 150); xxiii 3 šu-e-tum of the universe; xxiv 3 see šarratu. K 7592 + K 8717 + DT 363, 27 mit-lu-uk mil-ki ši-it[-al] (√שאל) šu-'i-i-ti ši-tul-tu (ZA iv 281; v 58: he who would be well counselled and make wise decisions). KB iii (2) 48 *col* 2, 41 a-na Gu-la šu-'-e-ti ba-la-ṭam (+ 48). V 41 *a-b* 8/9 šu (or ri?)-i (*var* e)-tum & en-tum = be-el-tum; II 36 *a-b* 64, Zimmern, GGA '98, 825.

še'ū, *f* **še'ītu, ši'ittu.** IV^2 50 *b* 56 see parasu (832 *col* 2, *med*) mentioned together with ebru, tap-pu-u, ki-na-at-tu, following god & goddess. Jensen, 327 suggests: father & mother; Sm 1051 (M^S *pl* 19) 12 š]i-i-it-tum between ru-ut-tum (11) and eb-ru (15). V 39 *d* 59 še-'-a-tu (Bezold-Pinches, ZA ii 460 *rm* 1; T^M 137).

še-i *1.* Sn *Bar* 33 alpi še-i (?) immēre du-uš-šu-ti . . . . aq-qi.

še-i *2.* K 1374, 18 ina qātāšunu kī ip-laxu ana še-i ixteliq. Perhaps connected with še'ū.

ši-ja-u = dan-nu-tum Sm 2052 *R* 9. M^b *pl* 20.

šu'û. V 21 *a-b* 9 = SA-SAR-SAR (AV 8408, Br 3120), see maškadu (603 *col* 2). Z^B 16 = ᒍ ac; BOISSIER, PSBA xxii, 110, some disease. Same id in V 30 *c-d* 65, 66 = çu-ub(p)-b(p)u-u & lu-ub-bu[-u?].

ši-u. Sm 2052 i 6 between šul(dun)-u & ba....bu; a ‖ of ça]-ax-rum, M^B *pl* 19.

šeu, written še-um (AV 8177), še-im (AV 8236, = *gen*), še-am (= *acc*; V 25 *b* 21) grain, corn {Getreide}. id ŠE, BA ii 284; § 9, 87; Br 7433. *pl* še-im-MEŠ TP vi 103 (MEŠ indicating quantity). HALÉVY, ZA iv 58 √שעע; KAT³ 340; 651 = סְאָה. kima še-im ça(-ax)-xa-ri see çaxxaru. KB iv 42 *no* 1, 1 a-na mit-xur še-e, to buy grain. II 16 *f* 34, 38; II 39, 73. V 20 *a-b* 43 (Br 11985); S^b 258 (Br 6892). See the second word in še-im karê (431 *col* 1, *a* end); še-im xamadiri (320—1); *š* liqtâti (495 *col* 1); *š* kišpi (450 *col* 2); and Rm 609 *R* (*add* to II 32 *O* 2), ZA vii 18; BA iii 215; and the first in: šaq-qu ša še-im; kal-mat še-im (389 *col* 2); kannum ša *š* (406 *cols* 1, 2); šubultum ša ŠE (= ear of corn); šapilti ša še-im; me-riš še-im, K 3182 i 18 (see mêrišu, 2); na-din še-im, cornmerchant, Cyr 254, 15 (& nadanu, Q *l* ag, 652 *col* 2); kur(ur)-ri-e še-im, I 66 *c* 25. — Also the verbs in xašalu ša še-im (345 *col* 1); naxalu ša *š* (⊕ 59 ii 24; 663 *col* 2); šapaku šeim; maxaçu ša *š* (522 *col* 2); rapasu (ripsu) ša šeim; še-im xu-un-nu[-bu], 325 *col* 2; paxaru še-um.

With šeum is used madadu (see *pp* 514. 515); šaqalu with kaspa. V 17 *a-b* 35 (Br 7483); 20 *a-b* 46 (Br 7095); 21 *e-f* 7 SAR = še-im (Br 4357).

NOTE. — 1. On šu[-u] .. šeu, KB vi (1) 278 n (v) 34; 540.

2. Sum ZIG, ZID, whence (HOMMEL, in HASTINGS, *Bible Dict.*, I 211 *col* 1, bel.) זֵרַע & šeu, wheat.

3. al še .. a farm: âlu often only .. section, with only one family. Out of the original âlu grows the maxâzu, JOHNS, *Doomsday-Book*, 8; see *ibid*, *pp* 33 & 35.

4. še-im-nu .. ŠE-IN-NU tibnu, *q. v.* — ŠE-IN-NU-XA .. enninu, eine Getreideart.

5. ŠE-BAR-um, BA i 515; AV 8219; T^C 130 *Rec. Trav.*, xx 203. Camb 314 (beg.) see mašartu. EISENLOHR, ZA xii 234 *foll*: ŠE-BAR = ... grain ; Korn, PEISER, KAS vi 1; vii 1; a harvest ; Ernte, MEISSNER, *no* 77, *p* 143. PEISER, KAS xiv 19 ŠE-BAR ebûri = Frucht der Ernte; Cyr 59, 1 ŠE-BAR ir-bi (BA iii 436: Gerste). ZA xii 237 *ad* Cyr 226 *etc.*: maš-ku = Haut, Hülse (?) des Korns. — ŠE-ZIR (šêzir) = field, acre ; Feld, *i. e.* Flächeninhalt des Feldes (EISENLOHR). See also BA ii 130, 171; ZK i 64 (see, above, *pp* 294. 295, & JOHNS, *Doomsday-Book*, 19. — II 44 *a-b* 66 ŠE-BAR .. še-a-tum (AV 8127) JENSEN, 372 on D 101 *frg*, 7. Nabd 189, 2; 18. 5; 36, 5; 367, 12 (ŠE-BAR-su); Dar 3-7, 1 ŠE-BAR pi-çi-tum; indicate that the noun is a *fem* (BA iii 38-). — ŠE-GUR (= כֹּר, KAT³ 340) .. gur (*c. st.* of gurru) še'im, bushel of wheat; wheat to the amount of a bushel.

šu-i-ib-da. T. A. (Ber) 26 ii 61. MÜLLER, OLZ ii *no* 4, perhaps Egypt. loan-word from the Semitic.

ša'alu (שאל, § 46); pr iš'al (§ 47; iš-'-a-lu, § 20 *rm*); ps iša'al; ip ša'al ask, inquire, consult {fragen, befragen} AV 7767; Z^B 99. ZA v 140, 31 ki a-ša-lu(-ma), I asked (= T. A. Ber 7); Lo 1, 83 why ašša-a-li-šu, should I have asked him? KB vi (1) 294, 12 a-šal-ma; 296, 22; V 33 ii 8; Nabd 720, 14 i-ša-lu-ma iqbû; Cyr 312, 10. In the prayers published by KNUDTZON, the phrase often occurs: (11) Šamaš bêlu rabu-u ša a-šal-lu-ka an-na kêna a-pal-an-ni, O Sungod, great lord, whom I ask, answer me faithfully (see *ibid* 43 *foll*). ZIMMERN, *Ritualtafeln*, 88 on ša'alu in connection with oracles. judicially: Sm 1371 + Sm 1877, 7 ta-šal (KB vi, 1, 287). JOHNS, *Doomsday-Book*, *no* 3 viii 16 i-ša-'u-lu ina mux-xi, shall inquire concerning. K 155 *O* 14 the great gods i-šal-lu-ka-ma, consult thee + 16 (K^M *p* 3 i-çal-lu). T. A.: call to account. Lo 79, 6 let not the king, my lord, ... a-šal-ni (hold me responsible?); Ber 105, 10 (BA iv 126 *foll*); 90, 29 a-na ša-al alâni. ta-ša-'-al-ma (T. A.) ZA iv 83; v 12 *rm*; 138, 11 & *rm* 4; iii 395, 11. Ber 7, 28 mâr ši-ip-ri-ka ša-a-al, ask thy messenger; + 31 ki-i ..... a-ša-lu; Lo 12, 51 verily ... ša-al-šu (ask him!) 14, 35—6 amêlešu ti-ša-la(?)-na, his people reproach me, KB v 410. S^c 296 ta-ag | TAG | ša-a-lum, Br 3803. — K 498, 13 my lord, the king, liš-al-šu; 83—1—18, 28

R 10; K 655 *R* 14; K 537 *R* 5 (= V 54 *col* 3) liš-al; K 11 *R* 5 (BA ii 20); K 82 *R* 8 my lord, the king, liš-'-al-šu-nu (BA i 242*foll*; PSBA xxiii 58*foll*); K 615, 4; Rm 69 *R* 2 (end) liš-a-lu-šu (+7), let him inquire; K 112 *R* 12 liš-a-lu; K 825, 5 (end) liš-'-a-lu, I pray. K 483 *R* 8 a-na man-ni la-aš-al, +5 la-aš-al-šu (§ 93, 1 *b*; BA i 212; ii 20); K 595 *R* 8 *N* ša-al-šu (= ip BA iv 505), +10 la aš-al-šu, I could not ask him; K 483, 9 attama ša-'-al (§ 20; ZA v 140, 26 ša-a-al; BA i 220) = Hr^L 522, 344, 132, 205, 186, 275, 258, 429, 223, 263, 55, 6. pm IV² 51 *b* 48 ša-'-il ša-'-il; 49 ina irši ša-'-il; —59; 52 *b* 1—13, perh. = he searches. Jastrow, JBL xix 98, 99: one should seek an oracle on the couch, on the throne *etc.* — šulmu ša'alu see šulmu.

Q^t ask {fragen} BA i 197. K 507, 9 a-sa-'-al-šu; K 943 *R* 2; Rm 77 *R* 12; K 512, 11 ana me-i-ni ta-sa-al-li, +13; K 686, 9 a-sa-al-šu; K 194, 18 an-ni-e i-sa-al-šu-nu; K 518 *O* 10 ma-a : ša-al ni-is-sa-al (AJSL xiv 11); K 112 *R* 6 i-sa-al (= Hr^L 88, 452, 414, 204, 178, 144, 140, 223). Asb ix 89 the inhabitants of Arabia iš-ta(-na)-'-a-lum a-xa-meš, asked one another. K 1523 + K 1436, 25 ši-tal = pronounce (the oracle concerning = eli; +26) PSBA xxiii 220*foll.* V 60 *a* 14 ši-kin-šu iš-ta-al. decide {entscheiden} IV² 54 *b* 6+8 qu-ul ši-ta-al-šu. 83—1—18, 1335 iii 32 ta-ar | TAR | ši-tu-lum; K 4600, 6 (ZA iv 162). T. A. (Ber) 24 *O* 9 (end) ši-ta-a-al(-šu-nu-ti) = ip +46 (-ši) ZA v 146, 23. ag muštālu, multālu, see 614 *col* 2; & add "see KB vi (1) 531: der nur nach vorherigem Ausfragen sein darum gerechtes Urteil fällt: also = vorsichtig. klug (*cf* ŠA-KUŠA); aber nicht Entscheider." — Jastrow, JBL xix 99 "muštālum, addressed to Šamaš, *etc.* = he who gives the answer to an inquiry & hence 'decides fates'."

Q^tn see Q^t; ZA v 12 (*rm*) il-ta-na-'-al-šu. K 194 *R* 1 a-sa-na-al (+6, i-sa-na-al) me-me-ni, Hr^L 144. KB vi (1) 94, 21 il-t[a-n]a-a-[l]u-ka, they will ask thee.

ℑ in connection with kakkū 'weapons' = make the weapons decide, appeal to. Sn ii 77—8 they placed their battle array against mine u-ša-'a-lu kakkē-šu-nu, appealing to their weapons (Haupt, *Andov. Rev.*, July '86); +v 49 (ZA v 306 √šalū, draw); III 15 *a* 19 (u-šal-lu). Smith, *Asurb*, 122, 43 Teumman ..... u-ša-'-a-la kakkēšu (KB ii 251); Creat.-*frg* IV 92 u ilāni ša taxāzi u-ša-'a-(a-)lu-šu-nu kakkē-šu[-nu]. KB vi (1) 26—7. KB vi (1) 337—8; 564 & 568: combines with TP i 36, 37 kakkē-šu u-ša-xi-lu.

Š Rm 76 (Hr^L 358) 22 lib-bi u-ša-aš-al. PSBA xxiii 355*foll*; BA iv 508*foll.*

Derr. — šālūtu (government?), šitultu, tašiltu; perh. maš'altu (593 *col* 1) &:

ša'ilu, *f* ša'iltu. — *a*) name of a class of priests, enchanters. Haupt, JBL xix 63 *rm* 21: interpreter of dreams, as Zimmern, *Ritualt.*, 89*foll*, whose specialty the pašēru šunāte. See also Zimmern, ZA iii 98 & 233; Z^D 14 *rm* 4 (√ša'alu); Haupt in Paterson, *Numbers* (SBOT) 61. He is mentioned with the bārū (185). āšipu (177 *col* 1) & mašmašu (607). V 13 *cd* 48—51 (AV 7795) has EN-ME-]LI = ša-i-lu; EN-ME-LI (Br 2022). XA]R-RA-AŠ (see Br 14232), AMEL-MA (Br 6780) = ša-il-tu. See KB vi (1) 417 on the ideogr. IV² 22 *no* 2, 10—11 ša-i-lu (as EN-ME-LI) with bārū (8/9); *cf* maššak(k)u (603 *col* 1) V 47 *a* 36 (& Zehnpfund, *Theol. Litbl.*, 1900 *no* 5). Banks, *Diss.*, 18, 17 ba-ra-a ul i-ši ša-i-li (*var* lu) ul i-ši (+1, 19); 10, 58 a-mat-su ana ša-i-li ib-ba-bal-ma ša-i-lu šu-u is-sa-ru-ar. KB vi (1) 294, 20 a-a-u LIK-BAR [....] ša-il-tu; see also V 28 *b* 2/3 (*cd* 22). KB vi (1) 418. ZA iv 8 (K 3182 i 54 ....] iš-me ša-i-li (*var* .... mu-ši-ni ša-AN-MEŠ) *etc.*, which would thus be = man of god; but may be a popular etymology. See ZA iv 26; v 88; GOA '98, 825; ZK ii 301—2; 413—14; 423 (ša-'i-li). T. A. (Lo) 5 *O* 26 (amêl) ša-i-li našri uš-še-ra-an-ni, send me an eagle-inquirer!

Del § 65 √ša + ilu (god); *HWB* ša + 'ilu (ban, charm): Jeremias, *Hölle u. Paradies bei den Babyloniern*, 20: der Totenbeträger (& *cf* ZA iii 233). Jastrow, JBL xix 96*fol* (& *Religion*, 360) would separate šā'ilu from šā'iltu (?- ša + 'iltu), and derive *b* from *a*); but *cf* KB vi (1) 418; *ibid*, 417—18: der Träger des 'ilu or ''iltu.

b) an insect of the genus grasshopper. II 5 *c-d* 10 XU-BER(= â(ô)ribu, grasshopper)-EN-ME-LI (Br 2022) = ša-'-ilum; 11 EN-ME-LI-A-ŠA-GA (Br 2924) = š eqli, AV 7769; KB vi (1) 518. שׁאל also K 4373 (M[S] *pl* 12) i 10, 11; *ibid* 18. 19 ša-'-il ir-bi-i; ša-'-il eqli = TUR-SAL..., & mar-...

šu'âlu (??). D 80 ii 33 ka-ni-iš(-ki) = ŠU-ER(= âl?)-ki; 83 iii 57 nu-kar-ki = ŠU-ER-ki. See kanšu, NOTE (410 *col* 1). Br 673.

Muss-Arnolt, *Assyro-Babylonian Months*, 33 & *rm* 91, where add: Zimmern-Gunkel, 154 *rm* 5, doubting connection with Hebr שְׁאוֹל, and denying it in KAT[3] 636; see also Schwally, *Leben nach d. Tode*, 59 *rm* 2; 194. D[Pr] 145 *rm* 2; § 46 *rm*; Halévy, RHR, xvii 340. Connection with שְׁאוֹל is maintained by Jastrow, *Religion*, 550: place of inquiry (of the nature of a religious oracle), & AJSL xiv 165—70. J[W] 62: place of deciding, judgment. Jensen, ZA xv 243 *rm* 1 on šî (l) lan & שְׁאוֹל; Hommel, *Expos. Times*, July, '97.

ša'irru. K 3351 *O* 11 a-na te-bi-šu ez-zi ša-'-ir-ru ul ib-ši. Martin, *Textes relig.*, '03 220—1, il n'est pas personne qui résiste (√שׁאר: résister not ša '-ir-ru √אמר, as *ibid*, 162).

šu'uru. II 32 *e-f* 5 ŠI-KIN-BAR-RA = šu-'-u-ru, AV 8409, Br 9395.

ši'âru, šiâru, see after šêru, morning.

šuâšu, usually contracted to **šâšu** (ša-a-šu. AV 8095; BA i 20. 28 > šâšu = š-âtu = âtu-š); *f* **šâša** (after the analogy of -šu & -ša); *pl m* **šâšun(u)**, *f* **šâšina**. = *gen* & *acc* of pron. pers. of 3 pers.: (to) him, her *etc.* §§ 55 *b*; 57 *a*. NE i *col* 2, 43 ša-a-šu uštamxiršu; 3, 8 + 23 a-na ša-a-ši(šu), 40 & often. a-na ša-šu-ma izzakaru *del* 1. 8 *etc.*; ana ša-ši-ma 191, 198 (211, 218); 26 (31) ša-a-ši (*i. e.* the ship) çullilši. + 57 (60). NE x *col* 3, 31; 5, 22 ki-i ša-šu-ma-a, like himself. IV[2] 31 *b* 46 a-na ša-ša-ma tûr; *a* 75 ana ša-a-ša gab-bi-ša-ma. Neb i 54 ša-a-šu (= *dat*) aq-bi-iš, to him I said; *Khors* 35. *acc* in Sn iii 20, ii 59; Asb iii 131; iv 2; KB ii 238/9, 19; V 56, 37. Rm III 105 i *b* 13 šip-ri ša-a-ši. Anp iii 76 a-na šu-a-šu re-mu-tu aš-ku-na-šu, to himself I showed mercy. V 27 *b* 38 ana šu-a-šu, preceded by LI = šu-a-tum, Br 1118/19. Sm *Asurb*, 291 *O* ša-a-ša bal-ṭu-us-sa; Asb viii 24 ša-a-šu. K 3600 i 10 e-la ša-a-ša mannu mi-na-a ip-pu-uš. BI = ša-a-šu, Br 5188; V 51 *b* 31/2, 33/4 see Br 5865. T. A. has ša-a-šu (-ši, -še), ša-šu *etc.* Bezold, *Diplom.*, xxi § 14 *a*. — *pl* Creat.-*frg* III 12 šu-un-na-a ana ša-a-šu-un. Neb i 47 ša-a-šu-nu, them (*i. e.* the gods). K 525 *O* 20 (Hr[L] 252) a-na šu-na-šu-nu. *Khors* 96 ki-ma ša-a-šu-nu, like unto them. — *f* Knudtzon, 150, 8 ša-a-ši-na; *R* 11 ša-ši-na; V 47 *b* 29 ša-šin (??).

NOTE. — V 64 *a* 11 e-li šli u bîti ša-a-šu libbuš izûzma, explained as mistake for ša-a-tu; but see *ibid* 15 & *c* 33; while *a* 12 bîtu šu-a-tim. Also KB iii (2) 90, 12; I 7 F 23/4 nišû ašibût maxaz ša-a-šu. ZA v 148, 16 amûlûti ša-šu-nu. Sarg *Cyl* 43 âlu ša-a-šu, *cf* 40, 51 & 75. Knudtzon, 150, 8 bi-ra-a-ti ša-a-ši-na — these fortresses. Thus showing that šâšu *etc.* is also used as a demonstrative pronoun.

šuâtu(m) §§ 21; 57; AV 8370; šuâti(m): **šâtu** (§ 38 *a*); *f* **šiâti**; *pl m* **šuâtunu, šâtunu**; *f* **š(u)âtina**, that, the same: those; *adj* used postpositively. § 57 *a*: only adjectively, but *cf* KB vi (1) 92, 4 a-na šu-a-tu, to the self same. KB iii (1) 132 *col* iv 5 a-na šu-a-ti, therefore, for that reason. Jäger, BA i 480; Hommel, BA ii 359 *rm* **. amêlu šu-a-tum IV[2] 7 *a* 10. + 23 (-tu); 22 *a* 55 (-tu); V 50, 55; II 93, 14; 99, 55. V 20 *a-b* 60 ŠI = šu-a-tum (Br 9284); V 27 *a-b* 37 = LI. שׁ BA (Br 113); BI (Br 5184). šip-ri šu-a-tu, ZA iii 314, 68; D 49, 35. âla šu-a-tu (= *acc*) TP ii 34; v 38; vi 8 + 17. âla ša(*var* šu)-a-tu TP iv 8 (BA i 383 *rm* 3); bîta (& nâra) ša-a-tu vii 68 + 79. bîtu šu-a-ti (= *nom*) V 63 *a* 27; + 28 (= *acc*): ana bîti šu-a-ti, Neb *Senk*, i 18; bîta ša-a-ti Neb ix 29; šu-a-tim Nabd 85, 7. In *c. l.* bîtu u Ê-NUN ša-a-ti (= the same). êkalla çixra šu-a-tu Esh v 4, that small palace; êkalla ša-a-tu, Sn vi 34 (KB ii 110); 61 + 66; I 44, 57. eqlu šu-a-tum KB iv 58 *no* 1, 21. Asb iii 2 nagû šu-a-tu (*var* -šu) ak-šu-ud, this *n*; K 2852 + K 9662 ii 1 ina kirib na-gi-e šu-a-tu. Sn vi 41 çi-ir tam-li-e ša-a-tu. see tamlû. II 66 *no* 2, 15 ki-sallu šu-a-tu. TP v 33 ina ta-lu-uk gir-ri-ma šu-a-tu, in the course of that same campaign. I 70 *a* 22 ina narû šu-a-tum; Beh 106 (-tu). Ina ka-nak dup-pi šu-a-ti, often. Anp ii 133 ça-lam Ninib šu-a-tum; Beh 66 u-qu šu-a-tim; še-am šu-a-ti (= *acc*) Ḫammurabi-*Letters* 56, 27. — JOHNS, *Deeds & Documents*: šuatu also written ḪAR-tu, 241, 12; 612 B. E. 2; ḪAR-MEŠ = *pl* 175, 8. ki-ma šu-a-tu(-ma) KB ii 248, 7 & see KB vi (1) 313 on 6, 22 kîm(a) šu-a-ti. The *masc* form is apparently also used with *fem* nouns & plurals: nišū šu-a-tu III 49 *no* 1, 11 (KB iv 112, 113), these people. K 321, 8—9 amēltu šu-a-tu (KB iv 132): & šu-a-ti (see gašîšu). IV^2 12 *R* 21/22, 25/26 narkabti šu-a-ti (Br 113). K 2729 *R* 32 + 35 dan-ni-te šu-a-tu, this document (KB iv 146); + KB iv 100 *no* 1, 9/10. Nabd 668, 19 a-na eli amēlut-tu šu-a-tu; *cf* III 46 *no* 5, 11 amēlāti šu-a-tu, these slaves, KB iv 140, 141. I 68 *a* 14, 19, 25 ziq-qur-rat šu-a-ti. Asb v 57 ālāni šu-a (*var* nu)-ti.

In later incriptions written šumāti. PINCHES, *Inscr. Tablets*. *p* 43 *O* 8/9 u-an (ilī)-tim šu-ma-a-tim, this contract. STRASSM., *Stockholm Orient. Congr.*, *no* 6, 18 mi-šix-ti bîti šu-ma-a-ti. Neb 135, 30 eqlu MU-MEŠ (= šumāti) + 28 (end) ina eli eqli šu-a-ti: Merod.-Balad.-stone iv 56 (KB iii, 1, 190). & often in *c. t.* (T^C 132; 137 *ad* Neb 433, 8). SCHEIL, *Rec. Trav.*, xvii 31/2 (below) 3 GIŠ-BAR šu-ma-a-ta; 33: 5 AŠ-GAN eqli ši-ma-tim. Perh. also K 679, 7 a-na šu-ma-a-ti (Hr^L 212); PEISER, KAS 28, 26; ZA vii 189 *fol.* — *f* ina šatti-ma ši-a-ti, in that same year, Šalm, *Obel*, 50 (KB i 132, 133); *Mon*, ii 75; ZA ii 150, 3; AV 8126.

pl m KB ii 248/9 v 4 mun-nab-ti šu-a-tu-nu; na-gi-i šu(*var* ša)-a-tu-nu Sarg *Khors* 71 + 107; *Ann* 261, 289; *Khors* 58 ālāni šu-a-tu-nu; TP III *Ann* 8; 179. K 2852 + K 9662 iv 2 (+ 4, šu-tu-nu): Asb vii 73 nišê ša-a-tu-nu; K 4289 *R* 10. Asb ii 132 ālāni ša-a-tu-nu; iii 109; vi 85; iv 66 (amêl) çābē ša-a-tu-nu. a-na šarrāni ša-tu-nu TP v 10; vii 20 içū ša-tu-nu; see also Asb i 72; iv 66 (ša-a-tu-nu). Sn *Bav* 12 gu-bu-uš mē ša-tu-nu. Note: TP vi 20 biriq siparri ša-a-tu-nu.

f Rm III 105 i *b* 8 ša aš-ruk-ka-ti šu-a-ti[-na]. WINCKLER, *Forsch*, i 254, 255. II 67, 23 mātāte šu-a-ti-na; also ZA iii 312, 59 (ša-ti-na); 318, 88 (ša-a-ti-na). TP iv 33 mātāte ši-na-ti-na; viii 53, 54 sigurātu ša-ti-na. Sarg *Khors* 40 ana kašād mātāte ša-ti-na; 166 ēkallāti ša-ti-na; see also *Ann* 429; 59 ša-a-ti-ši-na, 71 ša-a-ti-na; III 15 *c* 25 see šū, 2 (*pl f*). K 4289 *R* 8 ša eqlê kirê šu-a-ti-na; K 2729 *O* 30 ša eqlê kirê ša-a-ti-na; + 34 eqlē kirē šu-a-tu-nu, KB iv 142, 144.

NOTE. — Against HAUPT's etymology of šuatu (H^V 12 *rm* 4; JAOS xiii *p* lii) see KRAETZSCHMAR, BA i 391 *rm* 3 (reading šāatu); but scarcely correct; see also HILPRECHT, *Assyriaca*, 56, 57.

ši'atim? KB vi (1) 582 *b* 15 (7) i-na ši-'a-tim, at that time {damals}, meaning only suggested as a possibility; 586/7. ši-'a-tim would be = šiati *f* of šuātu. i-na = time {Zeit}.

šāb(p)u *1.* K 12021 *R* 9 (M^8 *pl* 17) ša-a-b(p)u. between ša-a-xu and ma-al-ma-al-lu.

šābu ***2.*** be or become gray, old {grau sein oder werden; alt, greis sein}. Sm 1806 ḪAL (Br 82) & ŠU-GI (Br 7129) = ša[-a-bu?] D 4 *rm* 1; ZA ii 117; BA i 218; pm KB v *no* 71 (Ber 71) 29 ši-ba-ti, I am an old man, BA iv 315/6. — Q^t K 2370 ii 10 šum-ma ina ûmê rûqûti i-sa-ab(-)ni, MARTIN, *Textes rélig.*, '03, 23.

Derr. šābu, šîbu 1; šābtu, šîbtu; šū(l)bûtu, 1.

šābu ***3.*** T. A. (Tel Hesy) 22 ša-a-bu (= שָׁבוּ) u uš-ši-ir-šu, (KB v *no* 219); OLZ ii *no* 2 (Feb. '99) >< PEISER, *ibid*, *no* 1: t]a-a-bu. See also BA iv 153, 154; 326.

šabbu *1.* shining, brilliant {scheinend, glänzend}. 76—4—13 M. *O* + V 23 *g-h* 13 šab-bu, one of the equivalents of UD-KA-BAR; ZA viii 75, 76 (>< Br 7820): perh. *cf* שַׁבְּבָא, armlet, bracelet.

šabbu ***2.*** S^b 218 ša-ab | ŠAB | šab-bu, Br 5671 (but see BA i 635—6) & see šappu.

šabbu ***3.*** Ner 14, 10 pût ša-ab-bi u murçu našû, M^8 91.

šabū 1., šebu 1. press. oppress, attack, overpower {drücken, bedrücken, angreifen, überwältigen}? SCHEIL, *Salm*, 88 سبي, but see KB vi (1) 355. II 28 *f-g* 57 see פּכּפּ (i. e. qanaqu in the meaning of šabû) Br 4479; the same id = dakû, dikû (on which see MEISSNER, ZA xvii 244—47) & labanu (see *p* 470); AV 7685. 83, 1—18, 1330 iii 6 (du) GAB = ša-bi-e ša qāti (PSBA Dec. '88). Perh. IV² 12 *no* 1, 18 (end) a-pi(= me?)-lu-ka(ki) še-bi-e (= SI-SI-E, Br 8015); M^S 91 *col* 1 to šebû, שׂבע.

Q¹ overpower, conquer; usually with aktašad. Šalm. *Mon*, *O* 16, 24, 34; *R* 2, 19, 64 a-si-bi (> aštabi); Šamš iv 20; Anp i 82, 107, 115; ii 17, 55; Šalm, *Balaw*, iii 5 the mountain peak e-si-bi, I stormed. MARTIN, *Textes relig.*, '03, 324 *col* 1 adds also K 3351, 16 ša tam-tim gal-la-ti i-sa-am-bu-' ru-up-pu-ša, de la mer immense il domine l'immensité; see sabû, 745 *col* 2, below. Perhaps also K 2401 i 12 il-ti-bu-ka, they lead thee away captive, BA ii 628 (or √la'abu?, see 465 *col* 2) & il-te-bu (II 56, 25) >< JENSEN, 131.

ב BANKS, *Diss*, 14, 93 kab-tu ki-ma ša-a-ri ina ra-ma-ni-ja u-ši-ib-ba-an-ni; 16, 122 ina ra-mu-ni-ja u-ši-ba-an-ni (= REISNER, *Hymnen*, 9, 93 + 122) = has ruined me. IV² 15 i 67 (*add*) u-šib-bu (= SIG-GI), ZIMMERN, GGA '98, 825. M^S 91 suggests reading u-šib-ba-an-ni, IV² 19 *b* 46 (end) instead of u-šib-pa-ni (see NOTE to šēpu, foot). Xammurabi *Biling.* iv 11 mu-še-ib-bi za-ax-ma-ša-tim (see 750 *col* 2, below). Xamm.-*Code* xlii 59, 60 te-ši (a revolt) ša šu-ub-bi-im ga-zu, which his hand cannot control. — **Der.:**

šabû 2. oppressor (?). Neb vii 46 name of street of Babylon: A-a i-bur ša-bu-u (§ 39); v 15 a-a i-bu-ur ša-bu-um su-li-e Bābili; v 35 (ZA vi 228) + 45; ZA iii 4—6; not may an oppressor become victorious. I 51 *no* 1 *a* 22. Perhaps also K 2107 *O* 18. See "Marduk", 586 *col* 2, below. P. N. (il) Marduk-ša-ba-an-ni, Camb 330, 9.

šabû 3. see mez(ç)ax, 517 *col* 2.

šibbu 1. Senn., ZA x 208 *O* 10 xa-ţ-ma-ţu = ši-ib-bu.

šibbu 2. Dar 254, 2 suluppu imitti ... ša ši-ib-bu.

šibbu 3., *pl* šibbē. girdle, belt }Gürtel{ KB vi (1): Hüftentuch. J^w 31. II 34 *c-d* 65, 66 (K 4362 iii 13, 14) A-GE (Br 11542) & MIR = šib-bu; see also H 186, 15 = V 38 *c-d* 46. AV 8144 refers here also to II 19 *no* 2 *O* 8 ši-ib-ba (= MIR, 7) ša a-na a-me-li i-ţi-ix-xu-u. IV² 31 *O* 54, 55; *R* 41 šib-bu (aban) TU (KB vi (1) 84 = alādi) ša qabli-ša, KB vi (1) 397: der Gebärsteingürtel ihrer Hüften. NE IX *col* 1, 16 *etc.* iš-lu-up [nam-ça-ar] šib-bi-šu (KB vi (1) 202). NE 75, 5 nam-çar šip-pi-ja. Sn v 72 paţar šib-bi xurāçi, a golden belt-dagger (vi 5); Asb ii 12; vii 36; KB ii 256, 56; Sargon *Khors* 79. KB iii (2) 128 A 12 ši-ib-bi-ši-na (whose girdles). H 25, 523; S^c 10 MIR = šib(*var* ši-ib)-bu (Br 6954); S^b 1 *O* ii 17; JAOS xxii 220. V 28 *c-d* 31 qa-at-nu: (çubāt? šib-bu.

šibbu 4. TP ii 76 ki-ma šib-be(*var* bi) er-xi-ku(-ma), I wormed myself through like a lizard (HAUPT). JENSEN, KB vi (1) 505 (*ad* 345) refers to ZIMMERN, *Ritualtafeln*, 126 (*no* 26) 21 LU-MAŠ *pl* u 'š'ib-bi-e which ZIMMERN (*loc. cit.*) combined with sippu (see 776 *col* 2, below); but JENSEN suggests: shepherd }Hirte{, which ZIMMERN, KAT³ 599 *rm* 1 accepts, referring also ZA v 67, 27 (KAT³ 382) >< sippu (see 776 *col* 2); BA ii 629, 10.

šibbu 5. K 3216, 5—7 Marduk ša a-ma-ru-uk šib-bu ga-pa-aš [....] ZA iv 227.

šūbu. TP ii 20 + 80; v 94; vi 5 the enemy's troops ki-ma šu(-u)-be(bi) (lu) uš-na-il (& u-me-çi); ZA v 92 ich goss aus wie Wasser, comparing شَوْب. AV 8379. JENSEN, 418, šūbu, often in connection with A-AN = zunnu = Regenguss; III 57 *a* 7; 64 *a* 13; 65 *b* 20; II 49 *no* 4 (*a-b*) 43, 45, 61, 63.

šub(p)û 1. war-engine. BA iii 101 & *rm* *: Sturmmaschine. KNUDTZON (*p* 77 √š-p-'; see also ROST, 93) 1 *O* 8 (iç) šu-bi-i; 17 *O* 7; 12 *O* 10. II 67, 16 (*cf* 21) the city of *S* ina ši-pi-ik epirē [u (iç) š]u-pi-i ak-šud, KB ii 12, 13. Sn iii 15 ina šuk-bus arammē (366 *col* 1) u qit-ru-ub šu-pi-i.

šubû 2. a precious stone }ein Edelstein{ = שְׁבוֹ. D^H 36; D^Pr 84/5; ZA i 461; KAT³ 649. Sm 954 *O* 19, 20 (ilat) Ištar ša šu-kut-ti (= TE-UNU-LAL) šu-bi-[e] (= ZA-SUX *i. e.* ŠUB) šak-na-at

(= LAL) Br 7730. IV² 18* *no* 3 *R* iv 15, 16 ab-nu] rabûti .... (aban) šu-bu-u GAL *pl* (rabûti). II 26 *no* 1 *a-b* 1 TAG]-ZA-SUX = šu(× Z^B 27)-bu-u, followed by a-a-ni-bu & ki-bal-tum; on id see V 22 *a-d* 17, where in *a* the gloss šu-ba, Br 11745.

šēbu *1.*; **šību** *1.* (Hebr שׂיב) AV 8139. — *a*) gray, grayhaired {grau, grauhaarig} III 65 *b* 7 when (of a newborn child) its head is full of gray hair (qaqqad-su ši-ba-a-ti ma-li). — *b*) old man, grandfather; elder {Alter, Grossvater; Ältester} Z^B 45, ZA i 405. Arm שָׂב, Ezr v: 5. IV² 56 *a* (*add*) 34 iz-xiz ši-i-ba, she approaches the old man. *del* 267 (298) ši-i-bu(bi) iç-ça-xir amēlu (see ça-xeru, Q & KAT³ 578). NE 75 *no* 39, 1 ši-ma-in-ni ši-bu, hear me, old man! (KB vi (1) 136 & 482). K 883, 9 (BA ii 633). KB vi (1) 58, 14 ki-i ši-i-bi ir-ki, wie ein schwacher (?) Greis. *pl* Nabd 300, 8 (amēl) ši-i-bi. *del* 80 (35) ālu um-ma-nu u ši-bu-tum, to the town, the people and the elders. KB iv 22 *no* II 19—20 a-na a-na-a-ši u ši-bu-tim; 25, ši-bu-tum pa-nu-tum; 30, 15 pān ši-bu-ut a-lim iš-pu-ru-nim-ma (*var* to iz-zi-zu-ma). V 65 *a* 32 ši-bu-tu āli, the elders of the town; *cf* T. A. (Lo) 42, 4. Bu 91—5—9, 418, 24; Cyr 319, 4. IV² 34 (K 2130) 37 ši-bu-ti māt kā-lāmi (KB iii (1) 106—7; Boissier, *Rev. Sém.* x 275 *foll*: les habitants). Bu 91—5—9, 2176 A. 18 ši-bi *T* i-mi-zi-i, the parents of *T* shall recognize (JRAS '97, 607—8). *f* šibtu, šēbtu; & abstr. noun šībûtu, 1.

II 32 *d* 61 AB-BA = še[-e-bu]; *c-d* 62 ŠU-GI = še-e[-bu]; *cf* V 42 *c* 68; Br 7130; ZA i 404; § 9. 89. S 526, 31 & 32 (Br 3821) see paršumu (839). II 32 *c-d* 28—30 see sarru, 2 (782 *col* 2). S^c 96 ab AB ši[-i-bu] Br 3821. V 39 *e-f* 68.

NOTE. — 1. KB vi (1) 248, 249 (see also ZA ... 219; xiv 182 3) explains also *del* 235 (262) to-... š-qu ši-pa a-a id-di-ma e-de-šu li-diš, ... : soll das Gewand nicht "graues Haar abwer-... m", sondern neu (neu) verbleiben: connecting it ... 5th *del* 298 (227) xumul-tum ši-ba [it-ta]-... š ; 217 (239); see KB vi (1) 511, 512; but M^S 90 ... plains this ši-b(p)a as: a condiment {Gewürz, ... and then adds: dieselbe Bedeutung hat šību ... ru.

2. ši-i-bu ‖ naxlaptu urâ "stable garment" (*i. e.* an old garment), may also belong here.

3. II 16 *e-f* 25—29 aš-šar-šu-ma šu-u ša al-ti-šu-ma; a-ma-aš-ša-as-su[-ma šu-u li-bit-tum-ma, I honor him, and he is also (honored) by his family; I polish it, and it is a brick (BA ii 302, 304; answer: šêbu, 1 old man *etc*; & šêbu, 4 = brick); BA ii 303: both from same √[illegible].

šību *2.* (√שׂהד?) witness {Zeuge vor Gericht}; in the case of documents: expert {Sachverständiger} Meissner, 5. II 9 *c-d* 88 ŠI-AMĒL-KA[-KA-MA?] = i-n]a ma-xar ši-bi, in the presence of a witness; *cf ibid* 43. Xammurabi-*letters* 2, 12 (amel) ši-i-bi; 11, 11 ši-bu. Perh. 88—1—18, 1846 *R* i (bel) ši-i-bu (twice) in a list of officials, PSBA xviii 256/7. Often in Xammurabi-*code* (R. F. Harper, edited) *p* 184. II 32 *c-d* 64 (amel) KA-KA-MA = še[-e-bu] Br 591; id same as āšipu, šiptu. & šibûtu, 2. T^C 7; Peiser, *Vertr.*, 283. Abstr. noun: šibûtu. 2.

šību *3.* enclosure, border {Einfassung, Leiste, Borde}, AV 8139; § 25 *rm* 2. V 32 *a-c* 30 + K 4602 IM-ŠIM-GUŠKIN = ši-i-bu & šin-di xuraçi; 27 *e-f* 7 ŠIM-GUŠKIN (Br 5200) = ši-i-bu, between šin-du xu-ra-çu & lēru, līru (*q. v.*). II 30 *a-b* 43, 45, 47 ŠIM-GUŠKIN, IM-GUŠKIN, ŠIM-BI-GUŠKIN (Br 9900, 8487, 5188) = ši-i-bu, which, KB vi (1) 510 = Goldlehm, Goldpaste; 44, 46 ŠIM-BI [cuneiform] [cuneiform]. ŠIM-IŠ (Br 5186, 5177) = ši-i-bu „ lēru (as also, 47; see *p* 498). M^S 90 separates šību = lēru = condiment {Gewürz} from the other passages, where it is an architectural term. Neb iii 30 ši-i-bi šap-la-nu (iç) erini zulûlu I decorated with gold and precious stones. Meissner & Rost, *Bit.cilkani*, 9 = šūpu (perh.: die untere Schichte der Decke). I 67 *b* 29, 30 (iç) erini dan-nu-tim a-na ši-i-bi-ša .... u-ša-at-ri-iç. V 65 *b* 4 (ZA iii 299—300 & Fl.^N 40: šīpu = ספּ); KB iii (2) 108 *rm* 1 = šību: Fertigung. K 4152 *R* 21—23 (M^S *pl* 7); V 39 *e-f* 69 ši-bu = a-ma-rum. Where belongs H 121 *O* 4/5 ši-b(p)u-šu kima ṭi-ṭi e-me? (= šūpu, foot? *cf* ši-bi, feet, Bu 91—5—9, 2176 A, 17).

šību *4.* brick {Backstein} II 32 *c-d* 63 APIN (u-ru) KI-GAR-RA = še[-e-bu], Br 1031.

šebû 2. (§ 34 β; ZA vi 306; Heb שָׂבַע); pr išbi; pc lišbi, lušbi (§ 92); ps išebbi, be or become sated, filled, satisfied; satisfy one's self }satt sein oder werden, sich sättigen{, with *acc.* AV 7692, 8140; G § 103; Pognon, *Bavian*, 99 *rm* 2. NE 11, 22 *etc.*; K 195 *O* 3 (the owner of the house shall enjoy its magnificence) see lalû 480 *col* 2 (end). NE X *col* 5, 28 (H^{NE} 72) ul išbu-u pa-nu-u-a, nicht sättigte sich mein Antlitz. K 8204, (9) 18 du-un-namu-u ša tak-lu-ka i-šeb-bi duxdu, PSBA xvii 138, 139. IV² 28 *no* 4 *R* 70 (see sûqu; 781 *col* 1, *ll* 11—13); 69: NU-GE-GE, EME-SAL. IV² 21* *no* 1 C *R* iii 18 (= K^{M} 9, 23) ma-xar-ka nam-riš a-d(t)al-lu-ka lu-uš-bi; 60* C *O* 25 i-šeb-ba-a-ma i-ša-an-na-na ila-šin, if they (the apâti) are satisfied, they become like unto their god; & KB vi (1) 114, 26. — ip Zimmern, *Ritualtafeln*, 75—78, 58 (end) ša-ba-a (also 87, 10) (iç) erina, sättigt euch am Cedern(duft)! — pc *ibid* 59 (iç) erina liš-bu-ma; lišbi; lu-uš-ba-a, lu-uš-bi-im, lu-uš-bu; & *cf* šebû in connection with lalû see 480 *cols* 1/2; bu'âru. 140 *col* 1; & littûtu, 500 *cols* 1/2. Rm 76, 11 ši-bi-e li-tu-ti (Hr^{L} 358; BA iv 506 *foll*); *Creat.-frg* III 8 (end) ina ki-ri-e-ti liš-bu(??). II 24 *a-b* 54 (ša-ša u) ⧗ | še-bu-u (Br 10841) preceded by li-e-mu (52) & baru-u (53). V 40 (*c-*)*d* 28 (?).

Q^{t} K 183 (Hr^{L} 2) *R* 1 ba-ri-u-ti is-sab-bu, they hungry have been satisfied, BA i 618, 622. ZA iv 241, 38 dadmu liš-te-ba-a nar-bi-ka. NE 58, 18 iš-tab-bu-u ! iz-za-nun (were filled). K 382, 9—10 whom .... tu-šab-šu-u-ni (√bašû) taš-tab-bi-'-u (3*f sg*) KB iv 154, 155. P. N. Ta-aš-te-bi, AV 8832.

Q^{tn} = Q^{t} V 31 *f* 26 ba-la-ṭu iš-te-ni-ib-bi, with life he was sated, ZK ii 81; or √šabû 1, see Br 8015.

ב satisfy }sättigen{. Asb ix 67 see karšu, 1 (441 *cols* 1/2; § 138). K 538, 12—13 see littûtu; K 501, 7—12 ilâni ..... lu-šab-bi-u; K 627, 13 (Hr^{L} 114, 113. 115).

ש IV² 9 *a* 22, 23 in eš-še-bu-u (= NU-GE-GE. EME-SAL, Br 6325) see lalû, 480 *col* 2. above. Perhaps also Sp II 265 *a* xxv 6 see rigmu (or √šabû 1?); Martin, *Textes relig.*, '03 ש of šapû, être proféré.

Derr. nišbû, nišbûtu, but see ZA xvi 162 & *rm* 7; našbûtu? & šabû, 2.

šabû 2.; *pl* T^{M} i 103, 104 .... ša-bu-ti u-ša-ki-lu-in-ni (√akalu); .... ša-bu-ti iš-qu-in-ni (they made me drink); ZA xvi 162, 163.

šababu. burn }brennen{ ‖ xamaṭu, 2 (321) & kababu (364 *col* 2, bel). G § 113. V 19 *a-b* 26 + II 34 *c-d* 14 (*cf l* 64) ŠU-XU-UZ (Br 7105, 7116) = ša-mu-u ša ša-ba-bi. Ball, PSBA xii 413. *del* 120 (127) *var* š(s)ab-ba (to kat-ma) šap-ta-šu-nu, KB vi (1) 238 *rm* 6: glow }glühen{?: PAOS Apr. '93, xi; BA i 120.

Derr. šabbu 1, šibbu 1, šibbatu & these 2.

šibûbu. splendor, brilliance }Glanz{. II 35 *e-f* 8 ši-bu-bu ‖ ša-ru-ru, AV 8141: § 63. *Theol. Litztg.*, '95 *no* 20; BA iii 84 = שְׁבִיבָא, Dan iii 22.

šubâbu. Kar = šu-ba-bu JAOS xxii 215.

šibâga. Nabd 707, 3: II ši-ba-a-ga parzilli.

šabaṭu pr išbiṭ; ps išabbiṭ beat, strike; kill }schlagen; erschlagen{ K 3219 *O* 5—6; Craig, *Relig. Texts*, i *p* 17, 17 see KAT³ 603 *rm* 6. K 979 (Hr^{L} 47) 7 ina ši-a-ri ša-ba-a-ṭi, KAT³ 594 *rm* 2, 603: vielleicht vom kultischen Schlagen (an die Brust). IV² 16 *b* 9 ed-lu i-šab-bi-ṭu (= MU-UN-GE-GE-NE, Br 6327), the master they kill, ‖ ardatum inappaçu (708 *col* 2), said of evil demons. IV² 27 *b* (*no* 5) 20/21 al-pi i-šab-bi-ṭu im-me-ra i-šab-bi-ṭu (= iD IN-GE-GE-E-NE, EME-SAL) D^{H} 46; D^{Pr} 38; RÉJ x 301; xiv 149; ZDMG 40, 736. BA i 138—9 suggests *del* 174 (192) end: mâtu lišbiṭ, may strike the country; see also KB vi (1) 242.

Q^{t} perhaps V 16 *a-b* 33 + Rm 2 III *col* 1, 33 (H 198 *no* 4) IM-AN-DA-RU-RU : ša(-a)-ru iš-ta-biṭ-su, Br 1441; or šabatu? see šibṭu.

Derr. našbaṭu & these 4 (?):

šibṭu *1.* § 65, 2. AV 8149; ZA iv 278 *foll* (. . D^{Pr} 38 & *rm* 3) & KB vi (1) 387. — *a*) staff }Stab{ with which to strike. Haupt in Cheyne, *Isaiah* (SBOT) 82 compares שֵׁבֶט. rod. IV² 24 *no* 1, 27/8 šib-ṭu (= GI, Br 2413) u pu-ru-us-su-u, scepter & rule.

Xamm.-*code* xlii 87, 88 a-šar ši-ib(p)-ṭi-im u pu-ru-zi-im, in the place of judgment & decisions (HARPER, 104, 105), ZA xviii 25. Sm 1371 *O* 8 see paqadu Q 2 (820 *col* 2); see also BA iv 2 *R* 8. II 66 *no* 1, 5/6 (Ištar) ša la-iu-ša ina E-ŠAR-RA šib-ṭu ul i-ma-ga-ru-ma (JENSEN, 197; 256 and KB vi (1) 387; as well as ZA iv 278 *foll* read šip-ṭu throughout √šapaṭu judge, decide; also see KAT³ 647, 650). In the meaning of Strafgericht it is mentioned in ZŠ iv 79; IV² 21 *a* 44; III 67 *c-d* 71. — *b*) slaughter }Gemetzel, Blutbad{. Asb ix 120 among the insubmissive inhabitants šib-ṭu aš-kun; Asb iv 93; Anp ii 107 see rišbītu. K 662 *R* 17 (šarru bēli) a-na ši-ib-ṭi liš-kun-an-ni; K 679 *R* 7 a-na-ku ultu pān šib-ṭu ša šarri bēli iš-pur-an-ni; K 145 *R* 2 (end) = H^L 211, 212, 436. — *c*) epidemy, pestilence }Seuche, Pest{ K 1282 *R* 18 see çaraxu & KB vi (1) 387; + 25 paṭar šib-ṭi ul i-ṭe-xi-šu. K 87—1 *O* 8 . . . . . tum u ši-ib-ṭu (THOMPSON, *Reports*, 247 A).

NOTE. — See also šab(p)attu.

šābiṭu. K 2012 *O* 15 ša-bi-ṭu some official ZA iv 279 (שֹׁפֵט); M^S 91; & *pl* 4.

šabbiṭu = שַׁרְבִיט, sceptre }Scepter{ properly stick, staff. KB vi (1) 524. NE XII *col* 1, 20 šab-bi-ṭu a-na qāti-ka la ta-na-aš-ši, den (Herrscher)stab erheb' nicht "zu" deiner Hand. V 26 *g-h* 7—8 GIŠ-MA-NU-KAL-GA & GIŠ-MA-NU-ŠU-KAL = šab-bi-ṭu, Br 6206, 6798; 7191, 6801; AV 7696: between giš-kal-lu & xaṭ-ṭu.

šab(p)ṭ(d)ātu, *sc.* šipātu, *pl f* of *adj.* said of cloth, woollen stuffs. AV 7699. V 14 *b* 29 šab-ṭa-a-tum. Perhaps some connection with:

šibṭu 2. (?) Camb 66, 3—4 ana çubā-tu^(pl) šib-ṭu çubā-tu^(pl) ku-lu-lu; PEISER, *Vertr.*, 143, 2 has še-ib-ṭu-tu-ša ²/₃ U rap-šu (ṣ which were ²/₃ cubits long).

Šabāṭu = *Šebāṭ*, name of the 11th Assyrio-Babylonian month. § 46. ZA iv 272 *fol.* KAT³ 603 *rm* 2 (on etymology); MUSS-ARNOLT, *Assyrio-Babylonian Months*, 35. 36. ⊕ 116 i 11 ša-ba-ṭu; iD (arax) AŠ (-A-AN; Br 6767), on which see KAT³ 556, below (= eine bestimmte Getreideart). V 43 *c-d* 1—6 (Br 4378, 11641, 10009, 10490, 3428, 7538). III 15 i 14 (KB ii 142); Cyr 22, 3 + 12; Br 4354 on II 60 *no* 2 (*add*) 2; Br 6752 on Sp 129. AV 7671.

šubṭulu see baṭalu Š (151 *col* 1).

šabikū. V 28 *g* 29 ša-bi-ku-u ‖ kubšu (369 *col* 1), AV 7686. BOISSIER, *Rev. Sém.*, vii 51 compares شَبَكَة, *retum reticulatum*; BROWN-GESENIUS, 959 *col* 1 שְׂבָכָה, hair-net.

šabakilu. V 32 *d-f* 46 GI-DIM-DIM] : qa-an u-ru-ul-li(lu) ‖ ša(-)ba-ki-lu. AV 7672; Br 2445. BOISSIER, *Rev. Sém.*, xii 51. 52 = סְבִיכָא, *rameau entrelacé.*

šubakilu. ZIM., *Ritualt.*, 24 *O* 33 šu-ba-ki-lu pi-il-pi-la-nu.

šab(p)ulu, šab(p)ultu, see, for the present, šapulu, 1 & 2.

šubēlu see pēlu (801, 802).

šubalū, AV 8372, *cf* šupalū.

šu-bu-lu = Š pm of a₅balu, 2 (*q. v.*).

šēbulu. Asb vii 25 šu-par še-bul Nabū-bēl-šumāte (see *ibid* 43, 44) concerning the delivery of *N.* KB ii 248—9, 91 a-na še-bu-li nišū ša-a-tu-nu; 93, še-bul-šu-nu ul aq-bi-šu. prop^y ac of Š of a₅balu, § 113. Of the same verb are derived the following three nouns:

šūbiltu, present }Geschenk{. T. A. (Ber) 29, 12—13 šul-ma-na aš-pur u šu-bi-el-ta [a-na] mux-xi-ka ul-te-bil, + *R* 6. *pl* in (Ber) 13, 14 šu-bi-la-a-te-e ša u-šo-bi-la.

šūbultu *1.* desire, wish }Wunsch{. K 2370 i 2, 3 mimma šu-bul-ta libbi-šu ub-la, CRAIG, *Relig. Texts, p* 4. *cf* T. A. (Ber) 9. 13 ša šarri rab-bi šu-bu-ul-tu ka-an-na-a; (Ber) 16, 18.

šībultu. If a man gives silver, gold *etc.* a-na ši-bu-ul-tim, with a commission for transportation, Xammurabi-*code* xviii 57; 64 be-el ši-bu-ul-tim, the owner of the transported gods; 73. √abalu.

šu-bal-ku-tu, II 32 *g* 75, AV 8378 see balkatu (165 *col* 1. below).

šubultu *2.* (§ 37 *a*) ear (of corn, *etc.*) }Ähre{ D^II 34 *rm* 2; § 65, 19; AV 8383. II 36 *a-b* 43 šu-bu-ul-ti in-bi ‖ çixru, *etc.*;

šibkū, Br 11301. See mekū, 535 *col* 2. — šib-lu-uk-ku, Br 6805 *ad* gb 170, read pa-lu-uk-ku (807 *col* 1).

thus indicating something small, light, easy to sway or bend by wind & weather. II 29 *a-b* 70, 71 (a-nu) AN (Br 440) = šu-bu-ul-tum; (ci-šu) AN = AN (*i. e.* šubul)-tum ša še-im (Br 422, 441); H 10 & 206, 33 & 34. HALÉVY, *Rev. Sém.*, vi 277 *nos* 2 & 5. BALL, PSBA xii 40 reads an-tum ša še-im. Asb i 47 see KB ii 156—7. K 5414 *a*: ina šu-un-bu-ul-te ši-qi (= kin?) ubānu VII-tum, M^S 91 mit der Ähre ist er 7 Zoll hoch. šu-bu-ul-ta-šu often in *c. t.* Neb 72, 1: 31 Gur ŠE-BAR šu-bu-ul-tum (T^C 113 = šu-piltum, exchange) ša suluppi. SCHEIL, ZA x 211 *col* 2 *R* 6 šu-bu-ul-tum : ši-it-ri (perh. = ŠE-TIR?),

šabnu. II 22 *c-d* 2 (*add*; AV 5051, 7701) GI-MAL-KIL-DA = ša-ab-nu (as well as = ša-ru) = nu-us-xu (700 *col* 2) Br 2484.

šubnū *e. g.* Sarg *Cyl* 43 see banū, 1 Š (175 *col* 2, below).

(amêl) **ša-bi-na-a-ši-šu** OPPERT, ZA iii 110, 177; EVETTS; T^C 130; AV 7689. *ad* Nabd 116, 42. read (amel) ša BI (= ši-kari) na -a)-ši-šu; *cf* šikaru.

šabasu, sabasu & šabasu, pr i'šbus, ps' i'šabas be angry }zürnen{ Z^B 24 originally: turn away, still discernable in šabasu kišadsu, *etc.* IV² 10 *a* 52—3 Ištar e-li-ja is-bu-us (= ŠA [= LIB]-DIB-BA, Br 8075 = zinū); IV² 60 *a* 43 is(?)-bu-sa eli-MU ‖ ix-nu-u itti-MU. Merod.-Balad.-stone i 18 see ki-miltu (425 *col* 2), Asb vi 108 the goddess Nanā who 1635 years ta-as-bu-šu (*var* -su); Sm *Asurb*, 249 *h.* ZA v 60, 21 ša is-bu-us-su liršu salimmu. K 8522 *R* 31 ina sa-ba-si-šu (when he is angry) uz-za-šu ul imaxxaršu ilu mammam. V 31 *e-f* 65 i-ša-ba-as-ma : i-sa-ba-as-ma, AV 7678. K 2619 *R* 15 (ilat) Iš-tar i-gu-ug-ma is-sa-bu-us eli Uruk; ZA iv 237 i 67 ta-as-sa-bu-us eli ar-dika. V 60 *c* 14 Šamaš who for a long time had been angry at Akkad (and) is-bu-su ki-šad-su, had turned his neck away. I 69 *a* 46 the god kišādi]-šu is-bu-su-ma; ‖ pānu or kišādu saxaru. S 6 + S 2 *O* 18 ana ilu āli-ja ša šab-su-ma (17, ana ilija zi-ni-i). II 29 *c-d* 10 TIK-ŠUB-BA = ša-ba-su (Br 3237), preceded by zi-nu-u. Perh. also KB vi (1) 286 *col* iv 17 šab-su, see, *ibid.* *p* 548.

NOTE. — See HAUPT in CHEYNE, *Isaiah*, 116 & BALL, *Genesis*, 61 (SBOT) on the original form sabasu. — Derr. these 3 (?):

šabsu, *adj* angry, provoked }erzürnt{ III 65 *a* 11 ilāni šab-su-tum ana māti GUR-MEŠ (= itūru)-nim-ma, ‖ zi-nu-tum II 61 *a* 75. IV² 59 *no* 2 *b* 5 NI-NI-MU (= ili-ja) šab-su, o my angry god, ‖ o my goddess ša te-zi-zi. Asb iv 68 ilāni-šu-nu zi-nu-u-ti ištarāte-šu-nu šab-sa-a-te(ti) unīx (= 1 *ps*); *cf* K 3182 ii 25 (AJSL xvii 138, 139).

šapāsu, *noun.* anger, wrath }Zorn, Unmut{ V 31 *a-b* 56 si-qi(n)-tu = ša-pa-su ne-e-ix, the anger was calmed, appeased, 57 ra-su = ša-pa-su dan-nu. See also KNUDTZON, *no* 71, 6 (*p* 29). A ‖ is:

šibistu. M^S 91. ZIMMERN, *Ritualt.* (b) 11, 10 ša šib-sa-at ili eli-šu baša· he upon whom the wrath of god is laid. K^M 27, 12 šib-sat (!) ili u ištar; IV² 57 *a* 57 (beg.)

šabsū & šabšū V 32 *d-f* 21, 22 see bašu Š (199 *col* 2) & bašamu (201 *col* 2, NOTE) AV 7702. K 4152 + 4183 *R* 41 e-piš ba-ša-me = su-[ab-su-u?] perhaps indicates sab(p)sū as best reading. (M^S *pl* 7).

šabaçu. V 28 *e-f* 13 ša-ba-çu = ux-xu-ru, AV 7676. — Der.:

šabçu. V 28 *e-f* 12 ša-ba-çu : ša-ab-çu, AV 7703.

šabaru 1., šebiru 1., pr išbir, ps išabir break, smash }zerbrechen{. še-bi-ru Z^S viii 39, 43, 45; 83, 1—18, 1335 ii 42. III 15 i 23 (Ištar) qašat-su-nu taš-bir. *Adapa*-legend *O* 36 ka-ap-pa-ša iš-bi-ir; *R* 13 *k* te-e-eš-bi-ir. KB vi (1) 100—1, 13 iš-bi-ru. IV² 12 *R* 41, 42 Ninib ..... kak-ka-šu liš-bir (iš-TAR). K 883, 25 e(?)-ta-al-la gi-çu a-šab-bir-ma. IV² 31 *O* 17 sik-ku-ru a-šab-bir ‖ amaxxaç daltum. P. N. AV 8824 *ad* II 63 *b* 32 taš(or la?)-bi-rum.

Q¹ *Adapa*-legend (KB vi (1) 94—5) *O* 12 ša šu-u-ti ka-ap-pa-ša iš-te-bi-ir. NE VI 49 kap-pa-šu (of the

šibsū. Br 3262 see m..šū (764—7)

eagle) tal-te-bir (2 *sg*). Perhaps WINCKLER, *Sargon*, 184, 74 māt-su liš-tab-bar.

ℑ *Adapa*-legend ii *O* 5 ka-a[-ap-pa]-ki lu-u-še-bi-ir. TP III *Ann* 197 kakkē-šu-nu u-šab-bir-ma. III 48 *d* 22 Nergal ..... ka-ak-ke-šu li-še-bir (see *p* 377). TP viii 80 kakkē-šu lu-šab-bi-ru (8 *pl*); AV 7679; § 93, 1 *a*. V 34 *b* 26 mu-ša-ab-bi-ir (kakkē na-kirēja), AV 5572. KB iii (2) 60, 38 šu-ub-bi-ir kakkēšun; D 98 *R* 28. V 70, 20/1 Ištar kakkēšu lu-u tu-ša-bir (§ 93, 1 *b*), will break to pieces his weapons. Asb v 119 u-šab-bir (1 *sg*) ilāni-šu-un; Sn *Bav* 48 u-šab-bi-ru-ma. K 7673, 7 .... in-niš ik-sir-ma u-ša-ab-bi-ri (+ 11 [end] u-šab-bi-ra). I 27 *no* 2, 32 gušūrēša la u-ša-bar, KB i 118, 119. IV² 12 *R* 6 see qardamu.

ℑℑ¹ *Adapa*-legend ii *O* 6 ša [šu-u]-ti ka-ap-pa-ša it-te-eš-bi-ir, was broken.

Derr. the following 3:

sabru, šabartu. AV 7681. TP iv 1: 30 biltu eri ša-b(p)ar-ta bu-še ta-tur 30 loads of copper broken in pieces (fragments) RP² i 108 *rm* 4; *cf* K 1990 i 15. But ZA v 98 reads ša-par-ta = Talm שַׁפִּיר, schön und gut; schönes, kleines Gerät.

šebiru *2.* *adj* Xammurabi-*code* xxxv 1 (NER-PAD-DU) še-bi-ir-tam, broken (limb); ZA xviii 46.

šibirtu *1.* REISNER, *Hymnen*, 37, 15 LAGAB-ZA-GIN-NA = ši-bir-ti uk-ni-ja. Br. M. 38128 *O* i 8 [cuneiform sign] = ši-bir-tum, fragment, morsel.

šabaru 2., šebiru 3. *ps* išebbir; used in connection with certain work on the field at harvest time (ina ūmi ebūri): reap, gather?? H 71—2 (K 56) i 19 (37) eqlu i-še-ib-bir (bi-ir). AV 7679; Br 6326 = GIŠ-AB-GE-GE (which = šabaṭu), preceded by eqla išakkak. BERTIN, RP² III 94: he rakes the field. II 36 *g-h* 28 GIŠ-]TAR & NAŠ = še-bi-rum ša içi, Br 383; 29 [cuneiform sign]-PAD(=DU) = *š* ša ši-bir-ti, Br 14372. V 47 *a* 49 (end) i-ti-ki : ra-mu-u : še-bi-ru, see ramū, 2. Or √= שׁבר examine, inspect?

šebiru *4.* some instrument, or vessel }ein Werkzeug oder Gerät{. V 26 *a-b* 36 GIŠ-(za-aš) TAR (Br 383) = içu (*var* iç-çu) še-bi-rum (ZA i 184 *rm* 2, on *p* 185: some sharp, cutting instrument. II 46 *no* 6 (*add*) *g-h* 65 same id = (iç) še-ib(p)-ru, Br 384; AV 8134. Perh. also V 20 *a-b* 2/3 ši-ib(p)-rum; AV 8154. K 4995 *O* 14, 15 (H 124) GIŠ-APIN-NAŠ-BI = še-bi-ir e-pi-in-ni-šu, Br 382, 1022.

šibru *1.*, **šibirtu** *2.* II 36 *g-h* 27 AZAG-PAD?]-DU = ši-ib-ru (AV 8154; Br 4900); 30, = ši-b(p)ir-tum, Br 9918; for 28. 29 see šebiru. K 46 (H 61/2) iv 24—26 AZAG-PAD-DU = ši-bir-tu (MEISSNER, 10: die Nebenkosten beim Kaufe); AZAG-PAD-DU-A-NI = ši-bi-ir-ta-šu; AZAG-PAD-DU-NI-IN-SE = šibirtašu id-din; 35—38 ši-bir-ta-šu la-a ša-ki-il-ta (שׁקל) D^{Pr} 149 & *rm* 4: unbezahltes Sendschreiben; ša a-na šib-ru-ti i-zi-bu u kaspa it-ta-ṭa-lu; 50—53 ši-bir-ta-šu la-a ša-qil-ta; ..... ti [ul ip-pa]-ṭar (AV 8136); also II 69 (K 245) 11—15 ši-bi-ir-tum, *etc.* Cyr 188, 25 napxar 1⅔ mana kaspi ši-bi-ir-ti ina qāt N. ma-xir, ZA iii 220. See also PEISER, *Vertr.*, cxvii 22; xciv 17 id AZAG-PAD-DU; KAS 92 (bel); 99 (above), & 117: agreeing with FEUCHTWANG, ZA vi 437. in the explanation of: price }Kaufgeld; Abschlagszahlung{: شُبْرٌ, Erbrecht; √שׁבר buy; שֶׁבֶר Teilzahlung; not √שׁבר break. Or to šipru, šipirtu?

šibru *2.* grain, corn }Getreide{ BA iv 305 (>< *ibid* 413, 414). T. A. (Lo) 44, 7 = שֶׁבֶר. see *p-p-r*, 818 *col* 1, above.

šebirru (?) Nabd 48, 11 gušur še-bir-ri u-xal-lap, als vom Mieter vorzunehmende Reparatur. Perh. = šipru structure, edifice }Bau{.

šebirtu. IV² 58 *b* 40 (iç) ga-çu še-bir-tum. ZA xvi 173 *foll*: some precious stone.

šibirru. staff, stick (as a weapon, *etc.*) }Stecken, Stab{ § 65, 21; AV 8135; PAOS '87, clxx *rm* 7; SCHRADER, ZDMG 28, 135 Streitaxt; POGNON, *Wadi-Brissa*, 28—9. Sarg *Cyl* 73 see metlu (623 *col* 1). Merod.-Balad.-stone i 35—6 ši-bir-ru mu-šal-lim nišē (= völkerbeglückend) ip-qid

šibçu, Asp ii 106, 107 see šipçu, 2. ∼ šibru 3. & šebiru *cf* šipru & šāpiru (*i. e.*, Marduk) qa-tuš-šu (of *M.-B.*) BA ii 259; 267. Esh *Sendsch* 33 (end) ši-bir-ru ez-zu ... u-ša-aš-ša-a i-da-a-a. I 43, 5—6 ši-bir-ru (*var* GIŠ-KU, *i. e.* kakku, SMITH, *Sen*, 8) la pa-du-u ana šumqut zā'irē u-šat-me-ix laq-tu-u-a. V 64 *c* 20 xaṭṭi u ši-bir-ri ki-i-nim ..... lu-bi-il for ever; KB iii (2) 64 *col* 3, 13/14 (ši-bi-ir-ri). H 120, 15—16 rē'ū ina ši-bir-ri-šu (Br 8849) li-duk-ši, the shepherd shall kill her with his staff (*Andov. Rev.*, July '84, 97). KB vi (1) 584/5, 19 (11) xa-ad-du-um me-a-nu-um ku-ub-šum u ši-bi-ir-ru. II 28 *f-g* 62 (ši-bir) = ši-bir-ru, together with uš-pa-ru (59), xa-aṭ-ṭu (60), pa-lu-u (61). H 12 & 218, 95. K 4378 (D 89) vi 74 GIŠ = ši-bir-ru, (*cf* urinnu, çirritu) (D^{Pr} 196); GIŠ-KAK = sik-kat šibir-ri, Br 5293.

šibrū. 80, 11—12, 9 *O* i KIL = šib-ru-u; same = barū, Br 10203, 10175; S 60, 5 (ša-am) šib-ru-u = (šam) .....

šabrū, *f* šabrātu. seer, interpreter, magician }Seher, Magier{. SMITH, *Asurb*, 123, 50 during that night ište-en (amēl) šab-ru-u u-tu-ul-ma inaṭṭal šutta igilti. K 2652, 25 iš-tin šab-ru-u. S^b 217 (ša-ab-ra) PA-AL = šab-ru-u. Br 5663, 6205; AV 7705; II 51 *c-d* 35. V 16 *a* 6. S^P 158 + S^P II 962 *R* 10 i-nu-um ša-bu-ru-u iš-ta-nu lim-nam-šu-un, JTVI xxix, 61: if the magicians repeat their evil.

G § 60; Pl.^{Nab} 43: POGNON, *Wâron-Nâdar*, 104, ZK ii 348, 10. BA i 16, *rm* 2; ZA v 155 *rm* 11; vii 174 *rm* 1 > ša bari: der Mann des Sehens; ZIMMERN, *Ritualtafeln*, p 86: in dessen Bereich das "Traumedeuten" gehört; HOMMEL, *Expos. Times*, '01, Febr. 230. But, again, see JBL xix 69 *rm* 42.

šubarū *1.* prop^y ac of ש 3 of barū, 4 (185 *col* 2). AV 8378. K 2801 *O* 41 ša-kin šu-ba-ri-e Nippur$^{(ki)}$, BA iii 232/33, 275/6; Sarg *Cyl* 4; *bull*-inscr. 5. *bronze* i 7 šakanu šubarū(ē) ‖ zāninūtu epešu (*q. v.*). WINCKLER, *Forsch.* i 95. Bu 88—5—12, 75 + 76 vii 14 çābē ki-din šu-ba-ri-e, BA iii 253: Schützlinge, Schutzbefohlene; *cf* Šalm, *Bal*, vi 4 (KB ii 136/7). IV^2 48 *a* 30 çābē šu-nu-tim ilāni ..... šu-ba-ra-šu-nu u-kin-nu, these people the gods will richly take care of. IV^2 40 *a* 32 (šu-bar-ru-šu-nu); KB vi (1) 100, 10 (& 413) Ēa šu-ba-ra-šu iš-kun. *cf* P. N. Ni-id[-nu]-um mār Šu-ba-ri-im.

Šubarū *2.* name of a people. See Subari & Subarū (746); Šubarte (AV 8374, 8375, 8377). VATh 575, 7 (amēl) Šu-ba-ri-i, the *Š* (slave); BA ii 561/2.

šēburu (§ 104) see eberu Š ac (10 *col* 2).

šibburu (or me-sir-ru?). some wooden object }ein hölzerner Gegenstand{. V 26 *a-b* 49 (Br 3261) see mesū (566, 567); V 32 *a-b* 40 *cf* mezax (517 *col* 2), AV 8147.

šabašu. K 2729 *O* 32 ŠE-]IN-NU-ši-na la i-šab-ba-aš (*i. e.* ▶—, or rum? SCHEIL, *Rec. Trav.*, xvi 178/9), between la in-na-su-xu (31) & la i-çab-bat (33); KB iv 145: soll nicht geheischt werden; BA ii 566 *fol.* K 4280 *R* 9 la iš-šab-ba-aš (BA ii 572); both texts are charters, grants; KB iv 104, 19. V 16 *g-h* 28 ŠU-NU = ša-ba-šu, AV 7682, Br 7115. "Šabašu expresses the levy of grain or fodder which royal officials could take from a field. usually in phrase tibnušu (eqli) lā iššabaš": JOHNS; i-ša-ba-aš, *Deeds and Documents* 625 *R* 7; iššab-ba-aš, 627, left edge 2; i-šab-bu-šu, 622, 1.

ℑ IV^2 58 iii 45 (end) mārat (il) Anim ša u-šab-ba-ša la-'-[u-ti], ZA xvi 180/1: die die kleinen quält. — Der.:

šibšu. levy of grain or fodder (JOHNS). *var* to tibnu in phrases quoted above from *Deeds and Documents*; & ŠE šib-še-šu, 622 R. E. 1; ši-ib-še, 81 *R* 4; 1/10 še nusaxi (another levy) 1/4 šibšu, 623 *R* 15; eqlu zakūtu la šibšu la nusaxi. 621 *R* 10. PEISER, *Vertr.*, cxliii 3 says of 2 gušūrē (*l* 1) in *l* 3: ši-ib-šu gab-zu-u ša 5 1/2 U (= ammāt) ar-ki. K 330, 25 eqlu za-ku-u ŠE ana la ši-ib-še la nu-sa-xi KB iv 154. K 13 *R* 10 (end) ŠE-BAR šib-ši (Hr^L 281) + 15 ŠE-BAR a-ga-a ša šib-ši, this tax-corn, JOHNSTON, JAOS xix 81. Nabd 167, 2: ši-ib-šu eqli, + 758, 9. KB iv 52 *no* 5, 17 i-na-ma-ru šib-ši-šu (see *ibid.*,

---

šibbūru see 'š'ippūru & mesirru. ∾ šubarkū *cf* רכש (831 *col* 1, end).

note [**]). Cyr 26, 12 ši-ib-šu eqli, *etc.* (KB iv 264), + 20.

šabšu. ZA xii 319 *foll* reads K 5418 *a* + K 5640 i 8 (= KB vi, 1, 292, 7) ša ši-ik-la-šu šab-šu, but KB reads ša igi-gal-la-šu rê'û-šu.

šubšî (AV 8385) & **šubšû**, $\stackrel{*}{=}$ ip & *ac* of bašû (199 *col* 2).

šub(ru?)-šu-uš? V 47 *b* 27; 28 šub-ši-iš.

šubašuku. T. A. (Ber) 28 ii 14: 11 narkabâti ša [(iç)] šu-ba-šu-ki xurâçu ux-xuzu (+ 15). part of a wagon {Teil eines Wagens}.

šabatu. V 28 *e-f* 14 ša-ba-tu ‖ ga-ma-ru, ZA iv 272; 277; AV 7683; D[Pr] 38; 88; ZDMG 40, 736. — K 4359 *O* 19—27 we have: 19, SA]G-SAG-GAR-RA = ša-ba-tu ša ka[-ap-ti??] Br 8566; 20/22 ..... GUŠUR (Br 14135) = š ša [ûri, ZIMMERN]; 24 = š ša a-bu-bi (Br 14134; JENSEN, KB vi, 1, 553 "vor sich herwehen, treiben"; KAT^3 556: wol identisch mit šabaṭu); 23 ... [cuneiform] = š ša pit-nim (Br 935); 25 ..... GAR-RA = š ša kib-ri, 26 .... ŠA-AG-A = š ša še-im (Br 14000); 27 LU(?)-BA = š ša karpati (Br 14416); 28 (Br 14351). ZIM., *Ritualt.*, 1—20, 55 u-ri ta-šab-bit, du sollst eine Opferzurüstung veranstalten = ûru rakasu = riksu rakasu. prop^3: (rein)fegen. Also qaqqaru šabatu, den Boden (das flache Dach) abwischen. See JENSEN *apud* ZIMMERN, *loc. cit.*, 196, 197 *rm β. ibid, no* 79—82 i 8 qaqqaru [t]a-ša-bit; often written KI-SAR in ZIMMERN, *Ritualt.* Also see K[M] 26, 5. 83, 1—18, 1330 i 25—27 (ša-bat-tim) see xarmatu 2) (338 *col* 1). For שׁ[t] see šabaṭu.

Derr. perhaps these 3:

šubtu *1.* 83, 1—18, 1330 iv 25 TU = šub-tum = abûbu = der verheerende, zu Boden werfende Sturm; JENSEN, 388, 389 & KB vi (1) 583.

šibtu. II 27 *a-b* 58 IM-RI-A (*cf* RI-A = zâqu, blow) = ši-bit (?) IM (= šâri) Br 14887. See šabaṭu, שׁ[t].

šabtum. 83, 1—18, 1330 ii 30 [(tu-um)] TU = ša-ab-tum; or šaptu? *q. v.*

šab(p)attu. some special day. II 32 *a-b* 16 ša-pat-tum ‖ ûm nu-ux lib-bi, AV 7684, 8004. 82, 9—18, 4159 i 24 u | UD ša-bat(⊢—⊣)-tum. Also *Cuneif. Texts*, XII 6, 24; 10, 25 *etc.* ZA iv 274; KAT^3 592—4 √šabatu, ablassen, aufhören; or > šabaṭtu, *i. e.*, Tag des Schlagens (in kultischer Bedeutung). GUNKEL, *Schöpfung & Chaos*, 155 & *rm* 3: šabattu & שבת, identical; LYON, *New World*, 1900, 181: = day of rest of the heart = day for appeasing the anger of a deity. That such a day fill on the 7th, 14th, 21th & 28th of the month lacks proof; that on the four days no work was permitted, is disproved by the evidence of commercial records. See also PINCHES, PSBA xxvi 51—6: Day & word for it of non-Semitic origin; the -bat- in ša-bat-tu of same origin & meaning as the -bat- in nu-bat-tu & bat-tu(ti) in K 6012 + K 10684, 11 + 16; *l* 13 ša-pat(= šuk)-ti, fifteenth day. Also UD | [cuneiform] | ša-bat(⊢—⊣)-tum, *Cuneiform Texts from Babyl. Tablets.* XII *pl* 6, 24 = the day *par excellence.* PINCHES, *ibid*, 55 also suggests to read Creat.-*frg* V 18 ša]-pat-tu shalt thou then encounter. ≻, KB vi (1) 32] XIV-tu. But ZIMMERN, ZDMG 58, 199—202: PINCHES' reading bat-ti is wrong; read til-ti = ninth day; his suggestions concerning šabattu & nubattu are not acceptable. Whether šabattu or šapattu is the original, cannot be determined at present. The 15th day -šapattu- perh. = full-moon-day ≺ the 1st day, the newmoon-day. On šapatu, cease, discontinue and its connection with šapattu, see KÜCHLER, *Beiträge zur assyr.-babyl. Medizin*, 90 *fol.* — šapattu, statt "ablassen, aufhören des göttlichen Zornes" könnte auch "Abnehmen des Mondes" bedeuten (ZDMG 58, 202 *rm* 3). — *Ibidem*, 458 ZIMMERN, "Nochmals Sabbat" ≻ DELITZSCH in *Zeitgeist*, April 18, '04, who reads now ša pat-ti = the (day) of pattu, *i. e.* the incision, division, of the month. thus, also, Creat.-*frg* V 18; while in the vocabularies he still reads šap(b)attum = שַׁבָּת. — HOMMEL in NIELSEN, *Die Altarabische Mondreligion und die Mosaische Überlieferung* (Strassburg. '04) *pp* 69; 87. 88: šabattum (whence Hebr שבת) a variant of šubtu = (moon)-station {Mondstation} √ישב; thus the Assyrian from the Early Arabic.

ši-be(bat)-tum, ZA vi 291 *i* 18 = שביתא = dill = *anethum graveolens*; see also JOHNS, *Doomsday Book*, 21.

šebītu, a musical instrument {musikalisches Instrument}. K 3600 + DT 75 i 7 šu-par GIŠ-ZAG-SAL (*cf* PINCHES, *Texts*, 16 *R* 11) še-bi-ti u ka-an-za-bi, MARTIN, *Relig. Texts*, perh. Hebr. (בְּ)שבח = play.

ši-ib-i-ta-an, seven times, T. A. (Ber) 140, 4. See sibitān (745).

šubtu *2. c. st.* šubat; AV 8878; §§ 39; 65, 5. √ašābu, 1 (111, 112); ideogr. KI-KU, § 9, 40. — *a*) dwelling, habitation, settlement {Wohnung, Wohnsitz}. TP vi 94 ēkallāte šu-pat (*var* bat) šarrūti. Sn iii 70 the cities ša .... šu-bat-sun šit-ku-na-at; — nadū šubtu, ramū (šurmū) šubtu & šakanu šubtu, see these verbs. — Esh i 11 dūr-šu u šu-bat-su assux. V 35, 23 I entered the ēkal ma-al-ki šu-bat be-lu-tim (32, šu-bat dūrū-a-ta; *cf* V 65 *b* 11); 34 (end) šu-ba-at ṭu-ub lib-bi of the gods is the name given to the maštaku; 36 (end) šu-ub-ti ni-ix-tim ušūšib (see 662/3 for more instances). K 3182 ii 46 ēkalla šu-bat rūbē*pl*. I 66 *a* 29 calls the ēkallu the šu-ba-at ri-ša-a-ti u xi-da-a-tim. IV² 31 *a* 4 mu-šab (*var* šu-bat) (ilu) Ir-kalla. V 62 *a-b* 47 see Br 6881. Nineveh is called šu-bat šarrūtija, Sn *Bav* 17; and, Uruk is designated šu-bat (ilu) A-nim u (ilat) Iš-tar, K 2619, 5 (KB vi, 1, 62/3). Z^{Š} ii 155 šu-bat ilāni rabūti; is written KI-KU, iii 23; viii 44. Creat.-*frg* IV 142 apsū is called šu-bat (ilu) Nu-gim-mud. IV² 18 *no* 1 *O* 12/13 see nuxšu (666 *col* 1). IV² 30* *no* 3 *R* 32 šu-bat-ka (= [KI]-KU-A-ZU) bīt na-du-u [xur]-bu. On KI-KU (Br 9824) see also Neb 247, 12; 416, 4; H 31, 721. K 469 *R* 5 KU = šubat ṣābē, a military post; Br 10553. IV² 40 *a* 16 šub-ta-ka. *pl* K 2711 *R* 41 .... u-šar-ma-a šu-ba-a-te, BA iii 266—9. Xammurabi-*code* iv 14, 15 mu-šar-ši-du šu-ba-ti-ši-in. Nabd 283, 8 + 11 šu-bat-MEŠ. — *b*) seat {Sitz} ‖ kussū (*q. v.*); also KB vi (1) 138/9, 37 & 435. — *c*) ambush {Hinterhalt} Anp ii 71 cavalry & (amēl) kal-la-pu a-na (ana) šub(*var* šu-ub)-te u-ši-šib (*var* ši-ib), I placed into ambush. K 469 (Hr^{L} 188) 19/21 (Šu-pri'E) šu-ub-tu ina pa-na-t[u] u-še-ši-bu, the Š had laid an ambush beforehand (AJSL xiv, 8). V 40 *e-f* 8 U-A = šu-bat nak-ri (H 39, 175) Br 6094.

S^{c} 25 [du-ul | DU]L | šub-tu, H 31, 704; Br 9588; S^{b} F 1, 1. S^{b} 190 u-nu ideogr. šub-tum (Br 4792, 6712); Nabd 553, 8; 103, 15; H 19, 330. S^{b} 80 *cf* Br 4467/8; S^{c} 272, Br 9639. II 34 *a-b* 8 TIR = šub-tum, Br 7662, preceded by ad-ma-nu in one group with pa-pa-xu & ma-as-sa-ku. I 65 *a* 29 pa-pa-xa šu-ba-at be-lu-ti-šu, ZA ii 183. II 33 *a-b* 68 (28 *a* 45) .... GUL = šub-tu, with ni-me-du, *etc.* ideogr. TIN (= balaṭu)-TIR (= šubtu)-KI = šu-bat ba-la-ṭi = Babylon (145 *col* 1 *c*); KAT³ 529 *rm* 1); V 62 *a* 44/46 šu-bat ba-la-ṭu; Šalm, *Balaw*, v 5.

NOTE. — 1. AJSL xiii 212 reads 82—5—22, 174 *O* 10 *b* la šubat-sa pi-ta-tan & translates: her bowels (?) are out of order (Hr^{L} 341).

2. On AN-TIR-AN-NA = šubat šamê = the milky way, *cf* JENSEN, *Theol. Litztg.*, '99 no 2. See also, KAT³ 628 *rm* 5.

3. PSBA xxiii 202 explains marru, 1 as chariot, cart in general; this would fit Nabd 753, 22: a-na šu-ba-tum ša mar-ri.

šubtu *3.* a garment, dress {Kleid}? T. A. (Ber) 25 iv 3 lubuštu (?) šu-ub-tum ša ta-kil-ti.

šībtu, šēbtu, *f* to šību, 1. old woman, grandmother {Greisin, Alte, Grossmutter} Z^{B} 6 *rm* 2; AV 8156. II 32 *c-d* 65 DAMAL-SEG (Br 5469, 10780): ši-ib-tu = UM-MA: [ši-ib-tu?]; 66, UM-MA = pur-šu[-um-tu]; 67, UM-MA-GAL = ummu rabītu. V 42 *e-f* 66, 67 see puršumtu (839 *col* 2 & ZA i 408).

šē(ī)būtu *1.* old age {Greisenalter} *e.g.* ši-būtu lukšud *etc.* see kašadu Q (447 *col* 1, *med*); & Šx (449 *col* 1, above); & littūtu (501). AV 8142. TP vii 54 see labirūtu (478 *col* 1). Sarg *Khors* 191 ši-bu-ta lil-lik; Pp IV 142; *Ann* 448 (-tu); šibūta alaku = reach old age (§ 138). K 512 (Hr^{L} 204) *R* 7 ši-bu-tu, lit-tu-tu-tu; K 1146, 14 ši-bu-tu u ṣi-xi-ru-tu. Neb 125, 1—2 il-ta (= ištu) ṣa-xi-ir a-di ši-bu-tu, from youth to old age. II 33 *e-f* 10 NAM-AB-BA-A-NI-KU = ana ši-bu-ti-šu, Br 2165, 3821; preceded by ana ab(p)lūtišu, axxūšišu, *etc.* T. A. (Ber) 71, 29 perh. ši-ba-ti u mur-zu, old age & distress.

šībūtu *2. abstr. noun* of šību, 2. T^C 7 & 69; PEISER, *Vertr.*, 233. K 83 (Hr^L 202) *R* 15 (amēl) ši-bu-ti. Nabd 194, 7—8 *NN.* a-na (amēl) ši-bu-u-tu ina u-il (an?)-tim ša *Y* a-ši-ib, *NN.* guaranties as a witness the debt of *Y.* 903, 8 the mother of the seller a-na ši-bu-tu ina libbi aš-ba-at (‖ amēl mu-kin-nu-tu, 538 *col* 2); Neb 104, 14. II 40 *g-h* 40 (amēl) KA-KA-MA = ši-bu(pu?)-tu followed by ar-xu ū-mu u šat-tu (41). — Perh. T. A. (Ber) 24 *O* 45 ma-am-ma ši-i-bu-u-ta u-ul a-qab-bi, no one has spoken in his capacity of a witness. Xammurabi-*code* v 59; 68 a-na ši-bu-ut .... u-zi-a-am-ma = bear witness, ZA xviii 18, 14; 14 *rm* 1 on šību & mukinnu.

šibbatu. K 4361 i 9 (= II 28 *no* 5, 62) NE-TAR-TAR-RI = ši-bat išāti; AV 8143 reads II 22 *a* 47 ši-ib-bat pi-i (but??); √šababu.

šub-taq-tu, see rušumtu.

ša-ga, *i. e.* ŠA-GA = makkūru (539 *col* 2) or niçirtu (716 *col* 2); AV 7708; ZK ii 303 *nos* 6/7.

šagum & **šagūtu** see šangū & šangūtum.

šugū (AV 8395) & **šegū** *1.* old, old man }alt; Alter, Greis} ‖ šību, see sarru, 2 (782 *col* 2); also ID for šību, 1. III 61 *a* 26 še-gu-um TUR(= içax)-ir, the old man will become young (again); *cf* III 53 *a* 73 (kakkab) šu-gi; & *b* 71 (kakkab) ši-bi u (kakkab) il A-nim (WINCKLER, however, *Forsch*, iii 208*foll* explains it as: die Pleiaden, das Gestirn des Gottes *Sibi*, die bösen Sieben); III 59 *c* 14, & *no* 10, 1; JENSEN, 48; AV 8392. P. N. Ši-gu-u-a in *c. t.*, AV 8163. Perh. compare Hebr שֵׂיבָה.

šegū 2. (= שגע), ***šigū 1.,*** be violently excited. — *a*) rage }toben, wüten}. V 47 *a* 26 na-al-bu-bu (469 *col* 2) explained by ši-gu-u. 83, 1—18, 1331 iii 12 [DIR] = še-gu-u. — *b*) lament, howl }wehklagen, heulen}. V 22 *e-h* 10; *g-h* 49 (e-ir) A-ŠI = ši-gu-u, Br 11617. — ℑ V 45 vii 8 tu-uš-šag]-ga, ZA i 95*foll.* — ℑℑ become mad. K 3886, 8*foll* šumma sisū iš-še-gu-ma lu tap-pa-a-šu lu amēlūti u-na-šak. — ℑℑ^n K 4038 (catchline) šumma kalbu it-te-niš-gu-u.

Derr. these 2.

šegū *3.*, **šigū** *2.* (prop^y ac) raving, raving prayer, penitential prayer; lament }Rasen; heftige Klage, Bussgebet; Wehklagen}. AV 4808; H^F 59; PSBA xii 216 (error); BA i 105 *rm* 1 (√שגא; see Z^B 1 *rm* 2). IV² 54 *b* 32: 3 days, morning and evening, ši-gu-u KA(= iša)-si; *b* 39 ina ūm ŠE-GA ši-gu-u ana (il) Ea iša-si. K 2581 ši-gu-u (BEZOLD, *Catalogue*, 456). V 16 *c-d* 2 (38 *c-d* 63) NAM-TAG (which = annu, arnu, šērtu = sin; Br 2161) = še-gu-u, followed by ik-kil-lum & id-ra-nu; H 38, 67; 108, 10. AV 8162. Perh. K 2852 + K 9662 i 31 ši(?)-i-gi na-piš-ti-ja la tap-la-xu, the anger of my soul thou didst not fear.

šegū *4.* fierce, savage, mad }tobend, wütend}. AV 8162; D^Pr 89. II 6 *a-b* 26 [UR]-BE (V 33 iv 53; JENSEN, 277; KB iii, 1, 144—5) = kal-bu še-gu-u, a savage dog, preceded by ŠU-mu, which perh. = idimmu; see V 30 *g* 44 i-di-im, gloss to BE = aš[-ga-gu?]. S^c 6, 12 [BE] = še-lu-u : še-gu-u.

šagbānu *1.* V 21 *a-b* 4 SAG-BA-NA′ = šag(k)-ba-nu, with ra-pa-du & çi-da-nu, 2. K 152 i 3. Br 3537; BOISSIER, PSBA xxii 110.

šagbānu *2.* ZA x 208 *O* 17 see nam-mu, 1 (680 *col* 1), followed by 18, šag-ba-nu = ma-mit (Br 3533); šag : ma-mit.

šagubbu. Br 8033 *ad* V 42 *e-f* 16 (LUD) ŠA (= LIB)-DU (= GUB) = ŠU (= šagub)-bu.

ša-gi-gu. Br. M. 93080 *R* 13 (ANŠU) GU (= KA)-DE = ša-gi-gu (12, = na-gi-gu) = a braying donkey, or, camel; ZA xvii 242; *ibid rm* 9 suggests: mistake for ša-gi-mu.

šagiggu. Br 8066 *ad* V 42 *e-f* 15 ŠA-GIG = ŠU-gu.

šu-gi-du (??); ‖ (*i. e.* šu-da-du) V 28 *e* 21 = (*f*) šu-nun (mistake for gid?)-du : a-pi(= me?)-lu; AV 8393.

šagalu (?) K 97 *R* 4 šumma anšku u-ša-ga-lu ka-nu-ui. Connected with this are perhaps these 3:

šagalūtu. *Ibid* 4 *O*: ultu pān ša-ga-lu-ti ša (māt) Aššur.

šagilatu. K 4565 (šam) ša-gi-la-tu together with qiltu (*q. v.*).

ša-gal-la-tum. ZK ii 324: Il-ta unqâtum ša dalâte Il-ta ša-gal-la-tum.

šigallu see šiklu.

šuglu(d)du (§ 88*b*, *n*) see גלד (218, 219).

šaggil(i)mut. some kind of stone {eine Steinart}. Esh iii 31 the country of Xazû šad-di (aban) šag-gil-mut; III 15 iv 14. V 30 *h* 65: 1 (aban) šag-gil-mut. II 40 *a-b* 56 (aban) tar-ma-nu = (aban) šag-gi-li-m[ut] Br 409; *cf* 40 *d-e* 16; 37 *g-h* 67. 81, 7—27, 147, 7 šag-gil-li-mut ‖ mu-çi-il-tum.

ša-gal-ti, AV 7710 see √שקש.

šaga(i)mu, pr išgum; ps išaggum (BA ii 386). howl, roar, cry, shout {brüllen, heulen}. AV 7711; Z^{B} 6 *rm* 2; 56 *rm* 2. Anp iii 120 see raxaçu. 2 & Šalm, *Bal*, III 3; Anp *Mon*, *R* 24; Anp ii 106 (§ 152). Sn v 62 çi-ir gimir ummânâti nakirê zarbiš (295/6) ûmêš al-sa-a kîma Adad aš-gu-um. Sams iii 69 kîma Adad ša-gi-mi (§ 32γ) elišunu aš-gum (KB i 182/3). Scheil, *Rec. Trav.*, xix 47/8 notes xxv 3 iš-gu-um Dibbarra. IV² 1 *a* 14/15 (= KA-DE-DE-A-MEŠ) see çaparu, 1; 20/21 eš-še-pu ša ina âli i-šag-gu-mu šûnu; 11 *a* 41/42 be-el-šu (43/44 be-lit-su) iš-gu-um-ma, Br 1532; 28 *no* 2 *a* 17/18 a-na ša-gi-mi-šu (Br 817) ‖ a-na ra-mi-mi-šu; 24 *no* 3, 3 ina (?) ša-ga-mi-ka (H 208—9). K 2924 *R* 7 KA-DE = ša-ga-mu, Br 701. II 21 *a-b* 19—23 ša-ga-mu; on *a* see Br 814—818; 13888/89. II 36 (*e*-)*f* 40—43 ša-ga-mu, š ša Adad, š ša nêši, š (il) ; *e* broken off. S^{c} 318 gu-u | KA | ša-ga-mu; H 10 & 208, 49; Br 544.

Š Br 817 reads IV² 22 *a* 21/22 u-ša-aš-[ga-am]: but??

Derr. these 3 (4?):

šagîmu. loud cry, shout {lautes Rufen}. K 4832 *O* 22 (*Anšar*) ša-gi-mu-šu uš-tax-xa-ax (KB vi (1) 10—11).

šâgimu. V 46 *a-b* 44 MUL-NU-UZ (or MUŠ, Jensen, 140)-DA = il ša-gi-mu.

šigmu noise {Geräusch} IV² 12 *R* 4 a-na ši-gim še-pi-šu-nu.

šigimmu. K 96, 9 ši-gim-ma ina libbi âli (Hr^{L} 302).

šagammu. V 33 iv 46 ša-gam-mi-ši-na (of the door) i-na ku-ru-us-si .... lu-u-çab-bit (KB iii, 1, 144, 145). KB vi (1) 186/7, 45 šu-dur(ku)-ki sa-x(s)ir-ki u ša-gam-ma-ki .... (NE 53 *no* 26). 83, 1—18, 1332 iii 23 ša-gam-mu ša.

šugammumu = šagamu of the storm, *etc.* II 21 *a-b* 18 .... ŠUR = šu-gam-mu-mu ša û-me, AV 8391. Or *š-q-m-m*?

šagapû(î)ru, *f* **šagapûrtu.** mighty, strong; leader, master {mächtig, stark; Leiter, Meister, Machthaber} AV 7709; ZK i 309; ii 417—18. Nerigl. i 13 (il) Dibbar-ra ša-ga-pu-ru; KB iii (2) 46, 6; 72 i 13 *D. š.* ilâni. Rm III 105, 2 (ilat) Nin-sag-ga called ša-ga-pu-ur-ti rap-ša gim-ri (Winckler, *Forsch*, iii 254 *foll*: die Fürstin des weiten All). S^{b} 268 ši-li-ig | id | ša-ga-pu-ru (Br 920); II 11 & 217 *no* 87; see also IV² 15 ii 45, K 4219 *O* 5 (M^{S} *pl* 10). Sams i 2 to god Nînib ša-ga-pi-ri šur-bi-i; ‖ qarradu, *q. v.* II 31 *e-f* 62 e-til-lum : ša-ga-pi-ru[m]; L^{TP} 89 = V 41 *a-b* 26 (see qarradu); II 57 *c* 14 ša-ga-pu-rat Igegê.

ša-gu-un-nu & ša-gu-uç-çi (AV 7718 *fol*) see gunnu, NOTE 2 (226 *col* 2).

šagaçu. Sm 1637, 3 ša-ga-çu = שקץ?

ša-gar šaptê K 883, 4 (BA ii 633).

šiga(â?)ru. AV 8160. id GIŠ-SI-GAR, Br 3465. *pl* šigarê. Used as *m* & *f.* § 9, 65. Hebr סוּגַר (*i. e.* סִיגַר) borrowed from (Assyrian-)Babylonian; ZK i 113; ZA ii 198; iii 61 & 114; BA i 372; Hebr. i 226; Haupt in Toy, *Ezekiel* (SBOT) 71. — *a*) bolt, lock {Türriegel, Türschluss} Creat.-*frg* V 10 ši-ga-ru ud-dan-ni-na šu-me-la u im-na (KB vi, 1, 30/31). KB vi (1) 92/3, 18 (& 409) ûmi-šam-ma ši-ga-ar Eridi iš-ša-ar. IV² 17 *a* 5/6 when thou, o Šamaš, ina ši-gar šamê ellûti puttest in the bolt; 20 *no* 2 *O* 3/4 ši-gar šamê ellûti tapti (o Šamaš); D 135 *O* 42 see petû 1 Q *a* (AJSL xix 218: thou hast opened the bolt of the shining heavens). Sp III 586 + Rm III 1, 4 ši-gar ša-me-e el-lu-tum šul-mu liq-bu-qu ‖ 6, da-la-at ša-me-e lik-ru-ba-a-ku. II 23 *c-d* 32/33 see si(k)-kûru, 758/9. Neb *Grot*, i 36 si-ip-pu-šu ši-ga-ru-šu u (iç) ka-na-ku-šu (of the shrine of the gods). V 65 *b* 13 + 25; Neb iii 49, 50; IV² 54 *a* 51/2 see sippu

(776 *col* 2). D 136 *R* 7/8 ši-gar-šu-nu rabu-u ana-ku, I am their great bolt (Br 3453; AJSL xix 207). — Perhaps also: entrance {Eingang}. K 2711 *R* 7 (*O* 11) SI-GAR bâbêša; Sarg *Khors* 164 (ušaç-bita; *cf* נצב Š) SI-GAR-šin (Esh v 47; I 44, 75); *Ann* 427; *bull* 77. H 95, 51 ina ši-gar bîti lâ êrubu. KB vi (1) 535: also vault, arch {Gewölbe}. Rm 908 (NE 89) 8 .... be-lit šamê GIŠ-SI-GAR uknî. — warehouse {Speicher} KB iii (1) 186/7 & *rm* *: Merod.-Balad.-stone ii 4 *M-B*. mu-dax-xi-id ši-gar-šu-nu, but BA ii 260; 267: der ihren Schrein triefen lässt; see also M[S] 92. BA i 273 on V 61 iv 34: Türschlösser. — BA iv 253 *ad* Esh v 45—47: der durch die Säulenstellung (wie Stäbe eines Käfigs) markierte Königsweg (tallakti šarri); 266: "Das Säulengehege, welches sich von einem Tore zum andern hinzieht; .... auch das Torgewände der Portale einer Halle." — *b*) animal cage {Tierkäfig} Asb viii 29 see naçaru Š (716 *col* 1); + 11 (iç) ši-ga-ru aš-kun-šu-ma, I made a cage for him, and let him guard the city-gate; ix 111 I put on him a dog-chain and at the Eastgate u-ša-an-çir-šu (iç) ši-ga-ru (Sm *Asurb* 281 GIŠ-SI-GAR-ru). — V 26 *a-b* 39 see nâbaru (639 *col* 1); 43, 44 GIŠ-MA-NU (H 37, 147) & GIŠ-ŠA-SI-DI (Br 12033) = ši-ga-[ru], ZK i 193; Br 6789—92. H 43, 40 GIŠ-SI-MAR = GIŠ-SI-GAR = ši-ga-ru, Br 3453. II 39 *c-f* 19—21 GIŠ-MA-NU = ši-ga-rum (Br 6792), GIŠ-AZ-LAL = *š* kalbi (Br 3875), GIŠ-TIK-XA-ZA = *š* nêši (Br 3317). II 29 *no* 1 *O* 48 (*add*) ši-ga-ru ša ki-šâ-di (Br 3873) followed by e-ri-in-nu. Also *cf* Br 3469, 9680, 9816, 11891.

šigrîtu. *pl* šigrêti = ladies of the Harem = שֵׁגָל, Ps 45, 10. Haupt in Guthe, *Ezra-Nehemiah* (SBOT) 66, 46; 67, 11; "connected with šigaru "lock, cage", which passed into Hebrew as סוגר, miswritten שגל". So for zikrûti, *pl* of zikirtu (281/2). ZA xv 396. Sm *Asurb* 200, 5 (sal) šig-re-te-šu *etc*. I took away as captives.

šagurrû. V 21 *a-b* 55 ša-gur-ru-u ‖ ta-a-ru, compassion, mercy {Mitleiden, Erbarmen}, AV 7720; Z[B] 102; § 73*n*: ŠA (= LIB), heart + GUR (= turn).

šugurû. NE VI 65 (Išullanu) ša ka-a-a-nam-ma šu-gu-ra-a na-šak-ki, KB vi (1) 171 (451), der dir beständig Blumensträusse zuträgt; King: costly gifts. Connected with šûquru.

še-gi-ru ? II 16 *a* 32 še-gi-ru mi-lam uš-ziz; + 35.

šugarû. A product of the datepalm {Produkt der Dattelpalme}. Nabd 973, 10 man-ga-ga šu-ga-ru-u, preceded by tu-xal-la (9). Cyr 316, 8—9 tu-xal-la gi-p(b)u-u man-ga-ga šu-ga-ru-u bil-tum ša xu-ça-bi; *cf* 377, 17 (a-na eli) šu-gar-ru-u ib-ša-'; 123, 9—10 itti 1 GUR tu-xal-la gi-pu-u man-ga-ga bil-tum ša xu-ça-bi ište-en (karpat) da-ri-ki šu(?)-gar-ru-u i-nam-din. K 9891, 7 šu-ga-ru-u, between xuççu & im-bu-bu.

šugu(r)ruru. Neb 360, 9—10 imêru šu-gu-ru-ru ša ina eli ap-pi-šu ši-in-du.

šagašu *cf* šaqašu.

šigušu. V 26 *e-f* 22 [GIŠ ....]-ŠEŠ = ši-gu-šu, some instrument, weapon *etc*.; AV 8164. Br 4194, 14210. Perh. √שׁגשׁ.

šugêtu. concubine. Xammurabi-*code* xxiv 31 if a man set his face to take a concubine (sal šu-ge-tim); 36 (-tam); 40 (-tum); *etc*. Harper, *The Code of Hammurabi* (1904).

šiggatu. some sickness ?? K 10625 § 3 šumma amêlu ši-ig-ga-tu mariç; or a part of the body? M[S] 92.

šad mûši, **šad** urri see šat.

šadû *1*. be high {hoch sein} D[Pr] 95 *foll*, see however, ZK ii 405. existence of verb quite uncertain, KB vi (1) 386. If it exists, the following forms may belong to it. — Q 83—1—18, 218, 4 i-šid-di (Thompson, *Reports*, 194 A); NE XII ii 1 + 22 whose breast .... ul šad-da-at (or שׁדד?), does not rise; but is quiet like a pûr šap-pa-ti, *etc*. *Rec. Trav.*, xx 206. 16 ša-da-at (of Nanâ) ri-mi-ni-i. — Q[t] III 16 iv 24 (R. F. Harper, *Diss*, *p* 34) ki-ma aš-ta-di pa-gar gu-ra-di-šu-nu. — 3 83—1—18, 300, 5 u-šad-da-ma (Thompson, 208 A).

Derr. these 2:

šad(d)û *2*. East {Osten} § 46. id KUR (which = napaxu) & IM-KUR-RA (properly: Eastwind) Br 8462; II 29 *g-h* 3; H 40, 232; § 9, 54; K 196 *b* 26. II 29 *g-h* 1 IM-ER-LU = šu-u-tum; 2, IM-SI-DI = il-ta-nu; 4, IM-MAR-TU = a-xur-ru.

šad(d)ū *3.* *m* mount, mountain {Berg, Gebirge} § 65, 6 *rm*; *gen* šadī & šaddē (§§ 30; 66). *pl* šad(d)ē (āni) AV 7754. id KUR (Br 7396), mostly + phonetic complement *u*, *a*, *i*) §§ 9, 176; 23; *pl* KUR-MEŠ (Br 8553)-e (TP i 51); KUR-KUR-MEŠ, TP ii 76 (§ 29), + -ni (ii 86); ša-di-e, šad-di-i; IV² 28 *no* 2 *a* 13/14 XAR-SAG-GAL-GAL-E = ša-du-u ra-bu-tu.

V 62 *a-b* 58 re-ši-šu kima ša-di-i .... ul-li (= XAR-SAG, EME-SAL); II 98/99, 36—7 ša-du-u (= XAR-SAG); 127, 36 + 38 ina bur-ti ša-di-i (= BUR-KUR-RA-GID, Br 10268), 44 ina qabal ša-di-i; + 46 + 48; IV² 26 *b* 46/7 ištu šadi-i (= KUR); 30 *b* 14 ina ša-di-i (= KUR-RA). + 12; V 50 *a* 2 (+ 4 + 6) ^(il)^ Šamaš ul-tu ša-di-i ra-bi-i (= KUR-GAL-TA) ina a-çi-ka, Jensen, 201—12 (on šad ereb Šamši ≺ šad çīt Šamši). — KB vi (1) 106, 30 the serpent went, i-ti-iq ša-da-a (crossed the mountain), + 104. 16; 108, 18 (preceded by a-lik ur-xa) + 110, 18; KB vi (1) 415 suggests: Gefilde (this being the original meaning); see *ibid* 70, 30: ša-[d]a-šu ta-šak-kan, where. perhaps = Hebr שׂרה & Syr ܪܒܪܐ, "Trift"; 50, 45; 52, 89 a-na ša-ad la '-a-ri; 50, 49 (52, 72 + 93) ša-du-us-su ik-su (?); 54, 23 ul-tu ša-di-i i-ta-ra-a. NE 1 *col* v 23 la-am tal-li-ka ul-tu ša-di(-im)-ma; iv 2 u šu-u ^(il)^ Ēa-bani i-lit-ta-šu ša-du-um-ma; IX *col* ii 1 ša ša-di-i še-mu-šu Ma-šu[-um-ma]; + 2. *del* 96 (101) šadu-u u ma-a-tum. over mountain and land. IV² 56 *b* 47 ša-da-ki ru-uk-bi. Rm 76 *R* 12 (Hr^{b} 358) ina libbi ša ša-da-i. u-kan-ni-šu-u-ni, BA iv 511 (refers to the funeral. burying, of a person). I 7 *no* E. 6 i-na šēp ^(šad)^ Ni-pur šadi-i (*var* šad-di-e); Esh iii 31; iv 10; III 16 iv 14. Sarg *Khors* 164; *Ann* 426.

IV² 30 *a* 18 gimir ma-al-ku šadi-i u xur-ša-ni. — TP viii 12 ^(abnu)^ KA-GI-NA (= šadānu) i-na šadē-ni ša māt(āte) Na-i-ri (KB i 44, 45). Sn *Kuj* 4, 33 the trees bib-lat šad-di-i; Sn iv 73 kirib šad-di-i rūqūte; iv 78; I 43. 41. Neb ix 4 çi-i-ti ša-di-i e-lu-ti; ii 14 ša-di-im (§ 67, 1) nisūti. Smith, *Asurb*, 69, 93 xarrāni šaib ša-di-e ša-qu-u-ti (*cf* TP ii 41). III 4 *no* 7, 16 ša-di-i šap-lu-ti; 15 ša-di-i e-li-u-ti (+ 23); II 19 *b* 46 ša-di-e zaq-ru-te; TP iii 46 (pašqūti); ZA iv 7, 17 = K 8182 i 19 (gaš-ru-ti). — D 138 *R* 6 + 8 ša-di-i (= KUR-KUR-RA, 5 + 7). III 29 (K 2675) *R* 3 pa-gi-e (u-)qu-pi tarbit šad-di-šu-un (ZA x 360). — KUR-MEŠ-e u tā-māte, Šalm, *Mon*, *O* 10. IV² 57 *a* 28 ša-di-i u tāmāte.

šadū marçu see marçu, 1 (590 *col* 1). — Also *cf* kāpu, 1 (420), kiçru (428) & nadbaku (650).

V 28 *h* 83 ša-du-u between ša-ku-u & ga-ab(p)-lum. D 129, 100 me[-li]-e (see mēlū) šadi-i, Br 7409, 7412. S^{a} v 13 ša-ad = ku-u-ru (Syr ܟܘܪܐ); S^{b} 303 ku-ur | KUR | ša-du-u; H 26, 553. S^{b} 122 i-ši | IŠ | ša-du-u (same id in IV² 14 *no* 1 *a* 3/4); H 20, 376. V 16 *a-b* 12 ga-bi-ri (or GA-BI-RI?) = ša-du-u; see gabīri (211 *col* 1). II 50 *c-d* 53—56 KUR, X(U)AR-SAG (AV 3258; Br 8553), E (Br 5846), GA-BI-RI (Br 6124) = ša-du-u, ZDMG liii 656 *foll.* V 17 *a-b* 15 see AV 7751. II 29 *no* 1 (*add*) .... šu-ul ša-du-u (AV 7754, Br 14263).

In Babylonian texts we find these spellings: ki-ma sa-tu-um (ZA i 340, 22; 344; 346—7); I 65 *a* 50; *a* 21; *b* 32 (ši-ka-ar sa-tu-um); ZA iv 110, 93 (134. 139) abni sa-tu-i u ti-'-a-am-ta. I 66 *c* 21 bi-ši-it sa-tu-um; *cf* Neb ii 34 bi-ši-ti ša-di-im (§ 72*a*). — KB iii (1) 117 *col* 1, 14—15 ki-ma sa-tu-im ra-bi-im; also 124, 21; BOR ii 220, 14 *fol.* Br. Mus. 12215 i 14—15 (King = šadī + *mimmation*); Hommel, *Anc. Hebr. Trad.*, 109; PSBA xxi 115—117. — *Rec. d'Assyr* iv 73. Thus in Gudea-inscr. sa-tu-im = šadū. AV 6613.

P.N. Ša-ad-da-šu; V 44 *d* 60 Ē-sag-gil-šad-du-u-ni (is our rock).

T. A. (Lo) 12, 17 eqli-ja | ša-ta = שָׂדֶה (≺ KB v 128); (Ber) 103, 56 u-ga-ri | ša-te-e, ZA vi 157 *no* 9; KAT³ 652.

NOTE. — On the etymology see also D^{Par} 102; J. P. Peters, *Jour. Bib. Lit.*, xii ('93) 54 *fol*; Barth

Etym. Stud., 65, 66; WINCKLER, *Forsch*, ii ('94) 192 (= שַׂדַּי); JÄGER, BA ii 292; but SCHWALLY, *Idiotikon*, 119 (*cf* [illegible]).

Connected with šadû 3. are šadânîš & perhaps the following 2:

šadû 4. in such phrases as: ⁽ⁱˡ⁾ Ašur šadu (*var* ša-du)-u rabu-u, Sn i 10; Asb viii 5; ⁽ⁱˡ⁾ Bêl šadû rabû (*p* 158 *col* 1); KAT³ 357—8 perhaps = שַׂדַּי; compare Çûr as P. N. of a god & Hebr צוּר. KB iv 178 *no* ii 10, 11; S 954 (D 136) *R* 14 belum ša-du-u rabu-u ⁽ⁱˡ⁾ Bêl; IV² 27 *a* 15—17 ša-du-u rabu-u (= KUR-GAL) ⁱˡ EN-LIL-LA; 23 *no* 1 *a* 28, 29; 18 *no* 2 *O* 15.

See on the connection with שַׂדַּי also Dᴴ 48 *rm*; Dᴾʳ 96 & ZK ii 286 *rm* 1 (>: HALÉVY, ZK ii 405—7; RÉJ x 301; xiv 150; JENSEN, ZA i 251; NÖLDEKE, ZDMG 40, 735—6: verb šadû not in existence). — Against NÖLDEKE, ZDMG 42, 481 on שַׂדַּי see LAGARDE, *Nominalübersicht*, 138 *rm* *. VOLLERS, ZA xvii 310 combines שַׂדַּי & שֵׁדִים (instead of שַׂדַּי); *šaddai* shows: Anlehnung an √שדד. See also the views of G. HOFFMANN, *Phön. Inschr.*, 53 *fol*; BARTH, *Nominalbildung*, § 231 *y*; SCHWALLY, ZDMG 52, 136.

šêdu 1. summit, top of a mountain }Gipfel eines Berges{. Anp i 49 šadu-u kîma zi-qip paṭri parzilli še(-e)-su (>šêd-šu, ZK ii 289; 292; ZA i 206 *rm* 2 √שרה × ZA i 251) na-a-di; *cf* ii 41 (KB i 60, 61; AJSL xiv 8). — highness, majesty }Hoheit, Majestät{ III 55 *a* 23 palû-šu BE (= ilâbar) še-su innad-di.

šad-da. NE 10, 50; 11, 1, but read with KB vi (1) 124 ikašada(-da).

šu-ud(t) in šu-ud šaqê *etc.* see šu(p)-par.

šid(d)u 1. (√šadadu) *m*; properly: extent, direction — then: *a*) region, district; shore, bank of river }Landstrich, Bereich, Bezirk; Uferstrecke{ AV 8174; Dᴾᵃʳ 194. K 3182 i 48 i]-na šid-di ša la i-di nisu-ti (in regions unknown and distant, AJSL xvii 136, 137); ii 40 e-peš šid-di (the fixer of boundaries); 47; 49 a-na šid-di rûqûti. TP vi 41 ši-di (at the side) of far-off mountains; vi 96 (in the big cities) ša ši(-id)-di mât-ti-ia (gabbe); + 71 in Harran u ši-di ⁽ⁿâʳ⁾ Xabur (Anp i 77; iii 96); Anp ii 96 in the cities ša ši(iii 102 šid)-di xu-li-(i)a (= along my route); see xûlu (*p* 313), and C. JOHNSTON, AJP xix 386 (xûlu = xarrânu, road); also MARTIN, "Mélanges Assyriologiques" viii (*Rec. Trav.*, xxv *pp* 225, 226). 83—1—18, 14 *R* 16, 17 ina ši-id-di TAG (gloss xu-u-li) lu id-ku (Hrᴸ 406; AJSL xiii 211); 81—2—4, 55 *O* 6 i-na-gi-e (= ina nagê) ša šid-di tiâmat (which is a region of the sea) Hrᴸ 381; AJSL xiii 212. Sn vi 38 see mašdu (599 *col* 2. below); ⁽ᵃᵐᵉˡ⁾ A-ru-mu ša šid-di ⁽ⁿâʳ⁾ ....., TP III *Ann* 135; see also 146, Siannu ša šid-di tam-tim. *c. st.* šid. Sarg *Cyl* 69 the gate .... ša ši-id iltâni. šid-di šadê = mountain-slopes, 83—1—18, 215 *R* 8. — *b*) side, longside, length (iš UŠ, BA ii 134; MEISSNER & ROST, 20) }Seite, Flanke. Langseite{, with pûtu (*p* 848). Neb 13, 6 a-na šume-la šid-da ša ....; Br 4896/7, AV 7743. V 20 *g-h* 46. 47 UŠ (*not* DU) = šid-du, & ša-da-du. followed by pu-u-tum. K 4558 (II 38 *c-d*) 3 šid-du u pu-u-ti(-tum); 4 šid-du u šup-li; 5 šid-du ar-ki; 6 šid-du ku-ru-u (AV 7140, Br 14217/8, 14824). V 23 *d* 36 TUR-DA = šid-du, Br 4135. K 4378 vi 24 (D 88) GIŠ-AD-UŠ-MA' = šid-di ša e-lip-pi, Br 4178, 4181.. Another vocabulary mentions šid-du ša ud-di (*i. e.* elippi) THUREAU-DANGIN, ZA xvii 193 šiddu & uddu = le bord.

šiddu 2. some piece (or part) of furniture }ein Hausgerät, oder Teil eines solchen{? Tᶜ 131 compares Mod. Hebr שִׁדָּה, سُدَّة, chest }Kiste{. Neb 278. 3: 4 (?) ⁽ⁱᶜ⁾ šiddu *pl* (Camb 36, 2); Nabd 502. 2 (+ 4): 2 ⁽ⁱᶜ⁾ ši-da-nu; *cf* 590, 2; 163, 2: 4 (UŠ) šid-da-nu. Here perhaps also IV² 23 *no* 1 iv 1, 2 (end) šid-du ša-da-di; šid-du BU (= GID *i. e.* šandda)-ad; 24 (end) šid-di tu-na-ax. On šiddu šadadu see ZIMMERN, *Ritualtafeln*, *no* 56 *rm* *a* & 9: ein seiner genauen Bedeutung nach noch dunkler, bestimmter Ritus. See šiddatu, 1.

NOTE. — ZA xvi 162, 163 reads IV² 56, 50 GIŠ-BAL šid-du instead of ⁽ⁱᶜ⁾ pa-lag-du.

šiddu 3. see šittu, 3.

šidê (= *pl*) written ši-di-e, Sarg *Ann* 431, 454; *Khors* 153, 168; Sn ii 55, 56; read with ZIMMERN-JENSEN (KB vi, 1. 564) ŠI-DI (= igise)-e & *cf* II 39 *c-d* 58. Perhaps also IV² 54 *a* 47 ŠI-DI = igisê.

šêdu. *m* bullcolossus }Stierkoloss{; *i. e.* the god or demon represented by such figure. BA iv 266. Dᴾᵃʳ 153 *foll*; ZDMG 32, 183;

Hommel, ZDMG 46, 529 √שער = سعد; Haupt, AJP viii 279; ZA vi 124; KAT^3 460 *rm* 4: "Stiergestaltig und wol auch als Sturmdämon gedacht"; 461/2: whence Hebr שֵׁדִים. AV 8171. iD AN [illegible] (= ALAD) K 4337 (II 50 *c-d*) iii 11; S^b 175 a-la-ad | AN-KAL (or DAN) | = še-e-du (Br 486, 6253); § 9, 60; II 10 & 206, 36; Both iDD often in K^M & Z^Š. S^P 158 + S^P II 962 *O* 18 (+ *R* 3, 7, 25) .... ur-rid še-du-uš-šu, JTVI 29, 58: there came down his winged bulls. T^M vii 124 še-id rag-gu ‖ u-tuk-ku lim-nu. — we find the word used for — *a*) a destructive god. KAT^3 459, 460. IV^2 1* iv 9 + 11 še-e-du (= ALAD) munaššir māti še-e-du munaššir māti ša emūqāšu ša-qa-u. IV^2 5 *a* 3/4 see padū, 791 *col* 2, below; § 67, 5. IV^2 40 *b* 48 u-tuk-ku še-e-du rābiçu ēkimmu. IV^2 16 *b* 3/4 see paraku, 2 Q (829 *col* 2). H 82/3, 4 še-e-du lim-nu a-lu-u, *etc.* (Br 11308, 11314). — *b*) a protecting deity (šēdu dumqi × utukku limnu) usually mentioned together with lamassu (*p* 489). Sarg *Khors* 189; I 44, 94; see also KAT^3 455. NE 51, 12 še-e-du ša Uruk supūri ‖ 11, ilāni ša Uruk supūri, KB vi (1) 232/33; Haupt, JAOS xxii *pl* 1; BA iii 99 *fol.* Perhaps also K 523 *R* 5 mar šip-ri ša du-un-qu of Bēl and Nabū may walk by the side of the king (Hr^L 324; KAT^3 456 *rm* 4). — On V 52 *a* 15, 16 see Jensen, 196. Perh. name of town, Šalm, *Ob*, 115 Bît-ši-e-di.

Note. — On the šid(d)ēti of alabaster and ivory, see BA iv 265; ZA vi 130 *rm* 7.

šud(d)ū *1.* KB iii (2) 50 *col* 3, 19 whose kisurū la šu-du[-u] Š pm of idū, could not be recognized (ZA iii 366, 15); see also KB vi (1) 198, 21 kīma neš-ti šu-ud-da-at me(? šip?)-ra[-nu?-šu?].

šuddū *2.* I 35 *no* 2, 5 Nabū ša šu-ud-du-u šu-šu-pu ba-šu-u it-ti-šu, BA i 404: to whom belongs wisdom (√idū) & conjuring (oracle). See 117 *col* 1.

šaddabakku see šandabakku.

šaddaggu, šaddaggiš, *f* **šaddagṭu, šaddagtiš,** Harper, AJSL xiv 13: adverb of time; ZA xvii 391 *no* 6: before, formerly, earlier {früher, vorher}? K 525 *O* 17 nišē māti ša šad-dag-ṭiš ina šal-še-ni ina ra-bu-še-ni ..... (19) ixliqūni; K 582 *R* 31 ina šad-dag-ṭiš; K 154 *O* 15 šad-da-giš; K 1107 *O* 11 ul-tu šad-da-giš; K 117 *O* 4 lik-ru-bu ša-dag-ṭiš; K 639 *O* 9 šad-da-giš ultu; K 615 *O* 14 (= Hr^L 252, 167, 238, 84, 328, 258). S 152. 10 (Hr^L 778) ina ša-dag-ṭiš; S 984, 7 (Hr^L 481) ina ša-dag-ṭi-iš.

šudgulu. See Š of dagalu (240, 241).

šadadu pr išdud, il(r)dud, ps išaddad. Hebr שׂרד. draw, drag, pull {ziehen} iD GID (§ 9, 11). AV 7743. — *a*) *del* 259 (290) the stones il-du-du-šum-ma, dragged him down (into the ocean). V 65 *b* 45 ana ūm çâti liš-du-du ni-i-ri. V 59, 59 as long as he lives maruštu li-iš-du-ud, ZK ii 218. Sp II 265 *a* xxi 3 i-šad-da-ad i-na be(mit)-ra-ta za-ru-u elippa; xx 9 ša-di-id ni-ir ili; *cf* Sarg *Khors* 36 + 70 & see nīru, 2. IV^2 15 ii 9/10 rubū ašaridu çīri(u) ana šamē ir-du-du (*var* iš-du-ud; § 51, 3) = IM-MA-AN-GID(= BU)-I-EŠ (*cf* 6), BA i 168; 182 *rm*; Lehmann, i 159 & *rm*; Jensen, ZA vii 179. šadadu serdē (see sirdū, 783 *col* 1); KB vi (1) 92—3, 17 ina ma-a-a-li ina ša-da-di. — $^{(iç)}$ ša šadadi = the royal carriage {der Galawagen} ‖ šadittu & thus = $^{(iç)}$ kussū ša šadadi. T. A. (Lo) 64. 10—11 see çamada Q; TP III *Ann* 69 $^{(iç)}$ ša ša-da-di. Asb iv 64 narkabāte $^{(iç)}$ ša ša-da-di $^{(iç)}$ ša çil-li, the chariots, the royal carriage, (and) the canopy; x 29 see nīru, 2 (723 *col* 2); 30, to the temple gate iš-du-du ina šapliia; vi 22; II 66 *no* 2, 9 (KB ii 264—5). — KB iv 58 *col* 1, 17 ša-di-id eqli, perhaps = cultivator; farmer; M^S 92: a legal term. Xammurabi-*letters* 34, 20 people ša-di-id aš-li-im, who pulled the rope (in propelling the ship) šu-ku-un-ma (= order!). Creat.-*frg* IV 139 iš-du-ud par-ku. — *b*) I 43, 27 the king of Elam a-na Bābili il-du-du-nim-ma, they made come to B. *del* 171 (186) šu-du-ud a-a i[r....], KB vi (1) 242 (& 505) zieh ihn heran zu dir.

K 615, 15—16 a-na mux-xi-ni il-du-du-ni, have made them come to us; K 528, 13 since Bēl-iqīša ik-ki-ru $^{(mât)}$ Êlamtu il-du-da-am-ma (& took along Elam, *i. e.* brought Elam over to his side against us); K 824 *R*

8/10 nakru u bu-bu-u-ti . . . . ul taš-du-ud (Hr[L] 258, 269, 290). Meissner, no 74, 23—4 i-ša-ad-da-du-u-ma. perhaps: zurückgeben, "vom Felde", am Endtermin der Mietezeit. — II 62 *a-b* 44 (= K 64 iv 5) see madadu (✕ Br 1800, 7084, 7938, 9135). — *c*) consider {in Betracht ziehen} IV[2] 5 *a* 53—55 Bēl a-ma-ta ana lib-bi-šu iš-du-ud (Br 7557 = BA-AN-BU-I), considered carefully. — H 51 iii 54 IN-BU (= GID) = is (mistake for iš)-du-ud.

Q[t] 85—5—22, 63 *R* 5 ni-il-ta-da-ad, we draw near.

ℑ Perhaps V 45 vii 30 & 36 tu-šad-da-ad (??).

ℑ[t] V 42 *c-d* 48 GID[(si-id)] GID | ši-ta-du-du (= ac; § 98), together with muççuru (573 *col* 1) Br 7539, 7575. Nabd 697, 10 see sadadu, 1 (747 *col* 2).

Š cause to pull, let or make to carry, drag {ziehen, schleppen lassen}. I 7 E 8 [(iṣt)] zazāti u-šal-di-da (*var* -id, 1 *sg*) ki-rib Ninā (ZA iii 314, 70); Sn *Kui* 4, 17; Esh v 26 building-material of wood and stone mar-çi-iš pa-aš-qi-iš a-na Ninā u-šal-di-du-u-ni; also K 2675, 13. Winckler, *Sargon*, 176, 36 u-šal-di-da nīr Ašur.

Derr. — mašaddu (600 *col* 1), šiddu, 1 & 2; šadittu & šiddatu.

šu-da-du. V 28 *e-f* 20 | ra-i-mu. ZK i 361; ZA ii 111; Jensen, 443; AV 8399.

šidādu (?) in P.N. [(sal)] ši-da-da-lu-mur, Neb 147, 3 *fol*.

šudxu, šudri, see laxxu (478 *col* 1) & laxru (479 *col* 1).

šadaxu, pr išdix; ps išaddix, BA ii 210, 211. proceed, advance, walk, especially in solemn procession, march {vorrücken, einhergehen, besonders feierlich, gemessen einherschreiten. K 7940, 14 ēnuma ina arax . . . . LU-ZU iš-di-xa [cuneiform sign]. K[M] 8, 5 iš-di-xu. Rm III 105 i *b* 3 i-šad-di-xi u-ru-ux, Winckler, *Forsch*, i 254, 255: schreitet er den Pfad. V 35, 16 (marched at his side) see çamadu Q end (§ 152); + 24 my troops ina kirib Bābili i-ša-ad-di-xa šu-ul-ma-niš. Pognon, *Wadi-Brissa*, IX *col* i 1 *foll* [i-ša]-di-xa-ma iramū kiribšu; VIII *col* vii 29 *fol*. L[4] iii 6. V 65 *b* 35 god Bunēnē ša i-ša-ad-di-xu a-na max-ri-ka, who marches before thee. IV[2] 9 *a* 17, 18 Nannar ša ina ti-di-iq ru-bu-ut(-tu) i-šad-di-xu (= SUD-SUD-EME-SAL, Br 7619). Asb viii 98 on the 25th of Sivān ša-da-xu ša Be-lit Bābili; *cf* IV[2] 33 *col* 3, 22 (KB ii 220, 221); K 734, 1 [(il)] Sin ina ša-ta-xi-šu. II 35 *g-h* 3 ša-da-xu | alaku; BA ii 39; AV 7744.

Q[t] pr ištamdix (> ištādix); ps ištamdax); = Q; § 98. Šalm, *Mon*, O 10 *Šalm* who . . . . iš-tam-da-xu (§ 53) šadē u tāmāte (*var* ta-ma-a-te). Sn III 76 (nadbak šadē, *etc.*) ina [(iç)] kussē aš-tam-di-ix, KB ii 98, 99. *Kui* 1, 39 aš-ta-am-di-ix (§ 52). I 43, 31 to Nineveh iš-tam-di-xu.

ℑ *Rec. Trav.*, xx 205 *foll* i 11 it is said of Nanā: ma-li-kat igēgē mu-šad-di-xat xur-ša-nu.

ℑ[t] Smith, *Sen*. 104, 31 šúnu ana Uruk uš-tam-di-xu. Esh iv 58, 59 [ana] šit-mur sisē ši-tam-du-ux (§ 52) nar-kabāti nāru šuátu imiçannima (§ 98). III 16 *col* v 6.

Š Pognon, *Wadi-Brissa*, IX *col* iii 12 *fol* u-ša-aš-di-ix-ma (see *ibid pp* 74 & 96).

Derr. išdix(x)u (114 *col* 1) & mašdaxu (600).

šid-du-xu-[u?] II 33 (*a*-)*b* 15, Br 1418.

šadalu. be wide, large {weit, gross sein} see perhaps ZA x 202, 10 *b* šad-li-i : da-lu. D[H] 50; RÉJ x 301; D[Pr] 101 *fol*; RÉJ xiv 151, 152; ZDMG 40. 735; ZA iii 61 *rm* 1. — ℑ ušandil (> ušaddil); ac šum(u)-dulu. — *a*) make wide, large, ample {weit, ausgedehnt, geräumig machen}. Sn *Bell* 55 (*Bass* 83; ZA iii 317) u-ša-an-di-la ši-kit-taš, I widened its (the terrace's) structure. Sn *Bell* 61 (*Bass* 89; ZA iii 318) see rēbitu; *ibid* 40: šum-dul (to make wide) rēbāti (of the city). Neb viii 35 a-na šu-un-du-lam šubat šar-ru-ti-ia, to enlarge my residence; ZA ii 133 *a* 7. I 52 *no* 4 *R* 10, 11 titūr palga (803 *col* 2) ak-zu-ur-ma u-ša-an-di-il ta-al-la-ak-ti, KB iii (2) 60, 61. I 44, 58 a-na šu-uš-mur sisē (for the sheltering of horses) ul šum-du-la (was not roomy enough) ka-nu-u (405 *col* 2) ki-sal-lu. I 35 *no* 3, 22 Šalmaneser mu-šam (*var* šan)-di-il Ē-XA(U)R-SAG-KUR-KUR-RA (explained as) [bīt?] ša-ad ma-ta-a-ti. Xammurabi-*code* xliii 58 li-ša-ad-di-il-šu; iii 18 mu-ša-ad-di-il (HARPER). — *b*) increase, enlarge {zahlreich machen, vermehren}. V 64 *b* 36 my days li-ša-rik (may he lengthen, √ארך) šanāteja li-ša-an-di-il; ZK ii 352—3. Bu 88—5—12, 75 + 76 viii 24 pir'u lu-šam-dil, BA iii 254. ip šu-um-di-li, see zēru *c*) *p* 295 *col* 1.

Derr. these 2:

šadlu, *f* šadiltu, *adj*; HEBR. i 226. — *a*) wide, extensive, large {weit, ausgedehnt}. K 3182 i 35 te-te-ni-bir tam-tim rap-ša-ti ša-dil-ta (*var* K 3474: ta-ma-tum rapaš-tum ša-di-il-ta), AJSL xvii 136/7: the wide, broad sea. Sn v 79 çi-ir er-çi-ti ša-di-il-te, on the broad plain. Neb vi 35 abullānišu ša-ad-la-a-ti, their (the walls') wide gates; ZA ii 127, 20. — *b*) numerous {zahlreich} ‖ rap-šu. Esh iv 42 ki-šit-ti na-ki-re šad-lu-u-ti, the spoil of the numerous enemies. ŠI-DI (= igise)-e šad-lu-ti, Sarg *Ann* 431; *Khors* 168; Sn ii 55—6. KB iii (2) 4/5 *col* 2, 2 um-ma-nim sa-ad-li-a-tim, numerous artisans; ZA iv 109 *rm* 1. SCHEIL, *Nabd*, ix 20 bu-še-e ša-ad-lu-ti.

šundulu (> šuddulu), AV 6061, 8521. — *a*) large, extensive {weit, weitumfassend} ZA i 41, 32. Sams (I 29) i 22; Merod.-Balad.-stone ii 49—50 see karšu, 441 *col* 2, *b*. — *b*) splendid, precious, gorgeous {herrlich, prachtvoll}. Sams i 24 (*Kelax*) ki-iç-çi el-li aš-ri šum(šun)-du-li. Neb *Bab* i 26 mi-im-ma šu-um-šu šu-ku-ru šu-un-du-lam (KB iii, 2, 56—7); Neb viii 12. — AV 8510 reads S^r 70 šum-du-ul, instead of šum-du-'-u, Br 8236.

šadlū. S 80, 10 kippat šad-li-e (ZA x 202); also K 4903 *O* ii (see V R 26) 4/5 kippat šad-li-e; ZA xvii 199, 200.

šudlupu see dalapu Š (248 *col* 2).

šidimmu, AV 8169 see idimmu (20 *col* 2) and add: = (kalbu) šegû (*q. v.*) & KB vi (1) 6 *rm* 4.

šudmaši, see šutmaši.

šadānu, a precious stone {eine wertvolle Steinart} ZA xiii 58 *foll* iš TAG-KA-GI-NA (*cf* IV² 18 *b* 22/23; II 38 *e-f* 13 & katū, 455 *col* 1). K 183 *R* 23/24 (= II 81) = ša-da-nu (AV 7746, Br 620). TP viii 12 (aban) KA (aban) XAL-TA (or xal-ta?) u (aban) KA-GI-NA i-na šadā-ni ša māt(āte) Nairi lū aššā.

šu-ud-du-nu(-ma), Xammurabi-*letters*, 22 *R* 5 = Š of nadanu, *q. v.*

šudnunu, AV 8407 see dananu Š (260 *col* 2). KB vi (1) 568 reads TP i 48 šuznunu.

šadāniš, (§ 67, 2) *adv* of *šadānu = šadū, 3; mountainlike, mountainhigh {berggleich, berghoch} AV 7745; ZA i 340 *R* 1; POGNON, *Wadi-Brissa*, 187 (below). Neb *Bab* ii 6 kārē xirītišu .... ša-da-ni-iš ab-ni-ma; see also Neb vi 34; iv 13; viii 51; ix 21; I 52 *no* 3 *b* 20; V 34 *c* 37.

šidintu (?) PEISER, *Vertr.*, cxxvii 7, ši-din-tu ra(?)-tu(?)-qu.

šadappu (?) Cyr 84, 5: I-it ša-da-ap-pu. BA iii 437 suggests a-da-ap-pu & comp. Esh v 15 *foll* (iç) a-dap-pe.

šadaru 1. ‖ qibū, nabū; command, order {gebieten, befehlen}. DELITZSCH in BAER-DEL., *Ezechiel*, xii; D^Pr 102—3 = Talm סדר. Neb *Bab* ii 29 & *Bors* ii 25; I 49 *b* 12/13 (see 558 *col* 1, above); but JENSEN, 162, & others šuṭur, √šaṭaru.

Derr. Perhaps:

šidru. command, order {Befehl, Gebot} Z^B 96 (end); IV² 54 *a* 34 ši-id-ru ša (il) Ea lišapšax libbukka. But rather √šaṭaru.

šadurru see šat urri.

šu-dur-ki. KB vi (1) 186, 45. So perhaps for šu-ku-ki. √aduru, be wide, *etc.*

šūduru. Nabd-Cyr *Chron* 14: III ū-mu šu-du-ru, mourned for 3 days. √aduru, be afraid; lament; Š. Or, from:

šadaru 2. (?) ZIMMERN, *Ritualtafeln*, 101, 8 l]ibbi pal-xu-u-ni ša-du-ru-n[i], my heart fears and is oppressed {mein Herz ist furchtsam und bedrängt. K 4174 + 4583 *c-d* 17 ša-da-ru (GGA' 98, 811). — ℑ ZA ii 83, 12 šu-ud-du-ru.

Derr. — Perhaps these 3 (?):

šudru, *c. st.* šudur. IV² 30 *b* 31 the Igege and Anunnaki i-na šu-dur-šu-nu (of the great gods) ezziš likelmūšu.

šaddaru (?). II 57 *c-d* 55 (il) šad(ṭ)-d(ṭ)a-ri = (il) Nin-ib, AV 7766.

šiduri. girl, wench, *etc.* {Mädchen, Dirne, *etc.*} AV 8173. II 32 *c-d* 27 ši-du-ri (me-me-tum & mērtum, see 583 *col* 2) ‖ ar-da-tum, Br 13364; KAT³ 574 *rm* 3. Z^N ii 172 (ilat) ši-du-ri lip-ṭur. See sidūru (749 *col* 1) & KB vi (1) 470, 578/9. Perhaps originally = timid {furchtsam, bezagt}.

šadûtu. K 476 *R* 1/2 (Hr^L 54) Bēl & Nebo pa-an | ša-du-ti ša šarri bēli-ja .... (5) liš-ku-nu, BA i 195/6: Huld, Gnade; ein freundlich Antlitz. — MEISSNER, 106—7 also has ša(n)dûtu, name of a month (arax šan-du-tim) WZKM v 180 *fol.* KB iv 48 *no* IV 10.

šadittu (▷ šadid-tu) properly *adj f*, kussû to be supplied; a royal throne-chair pulled by ropes. See sirdû. AV 7749. ZA xvii 242: ein transportabler Sessel von einem Esel gezogen.

šiddatum *1.* an implement, furniture {ein Hausgerät} *etc.* Cyr 183, 16: III kussē; I-it šid-da-tum; Camb 331, 11: I-it (12) šid-da-tum; 330, 6. Nabd 258, 16 (end) I-en gan-ga-nu ši-da-tum. Neb 42, 2: šid(?)-da-a-ti-šu-nu (ša alpē). See also POGNON, *Wadi-Brisa*, 84. Perhaps V 23 *a-d* 15, Br 3352. See šiddu, 2.

šiddatum *2.* SCHEIL, *Rec. Trav.*, xvii 35 ši-id-da-tum u-ul i-šu-u-ma, il n'y a pas de réintégration à faire. šiddatum: action de šadadu. MEISSNER, 141.

šizbu *m* (KAT^3 442 *rm* 2), *c. st.* šizib, milk {Milch} id GA, Br 6114; AV 8161. — *a*) of animals. Asb ix 67 see karšu, 1 (441). IV^2 4 iii 31 (& 39) ši-iz-bu (= GA) brought from a clean stable; 18* *no* 6 *R* 1/2 mu-ur ni-ki ši-iz-bi ši-iz-ba ul ....; 28* *no* 3 *b* 6/7, 8/9 ši-iz-bi en-zi, goat-milk, Br 7036. Nabd 1119, 6 ši-iz-bi ša ....; I 65 *a* 20 + 33 *cf* ximētu. ši-zib la-a-ti el-li-ti see littu, 1 (500 *col* 2). 81, 11—3, 478, 7 puxâdu ši-zib, a suckling lamb, PSBA '96, 252; ZK ii 216. II 46 *e-f* 14; V 42 *a-b* 9 DUG-GA = karpat ši-iz-bi, AJP v 72 *rm* 1; H 23, 450. ku-ut ši-iz-bi see kutû; mamâçu ša šiz-bi, see namâçu (683 *col* 1). H 81, 6 e-muq ši-iz-bi (= GIR-GA-NI?). K 2001 (CRAIG, *Rel. Texts*, i 15) 20, 21 šizbu, elli-tu, milk (&) cake, KAT^3 442 & *rm* 2. — *b*) of woman. II 35 *g-h* 74, 75 see çirtu, NOTE, *p* 897 *col* 2. Camb 365, 3 marat-su-nu ša ši-zib | ša eli ti-lu-u, a suckling child. *Rec. Trav.*, xxii Notes d'Epigr. LIV 8 .... šimma-tum ki-ma ši-iz-bi ina tu-li-e. K 2619, 21 [la] a-niq ši-zib še-ir-ru la te-zi-ba a-a-am-ma, KB vi (1) 60—1. BALL, PSBA x 300 rends šiçbu & compares שצף, outpouring, overflow.

šûzib & šēzib — ip *Š* of ezebu, 25 *col* 2; *cf* P. N. Šamaš-še-zib, AV 7938.

šûzub(u) *1.* AV 8419. *ac Š* of ezebu. Arm שיזב, D^{Pr} 140. V 16 *g-h* 17 ŠU-TA-KAR-TAX = šu-zu-bu, Br 7147. Also used as P. N. Dar 37, 33 Šu-zu-bu (mâr) ka-nik bâbi. Sn iv 35 *etc.* abbreviated for Nergalušēzib; Sn iii 45; v 8 + 41 for Mušēzib Marduk (BEZOLD, *Catalogue*, v 2196; WINCKLER, *Altor. Forsch*, i 204).

šûzubu *2.* T. A. (Ber) 26 iii 27, 28: I šu-zu-ub ša qîti ša kub-bu-u I lubuštu šu-zu-ub ša qîti ku-ub-bu-u.

šûzuzu. *adj* TP v 43 *Tigl. Pil.* šu-zu-zu a-bu-ub tam-xa-ri; AV 8413. √ezezu.

šēzuzu *1.* ZA iv 240, 12 (hymn to Nebo) a-šur uk-lit nam-rat še-zu-zu; perh. also K 3216 (ZA iv 227) bēlum šēzuzu linûx. provoked, angry {erzürnt, zornig} √ezezu.

šēzuzu *2.* see çirruššû, and Neb vi 17 çirruššû še-zu-zu-ti; V 34 *a* 21; KB iii (2) 72 *a* 26. AV 8180. upright, erect {aufrecht, aufrechtstehend} √nazazu. FLEMMING, *Neb*, 51.

šuzuzzu H 88, 6 = *pm Š* of nazazu (*q. v.*); also see zumru.

šuzmuru *cf* zamaru *Š* (284 *col* 1).

šazanu. LYON, *Manual*, 131 on Asb iv 21, see 48, footnote; also BARTH, *Etym. Stud.*, 52 & FRÄNKEL, BA iii 82.

šu-zu-ta (?) T. A. (Ber) 28 i 28 .... qat-ti xurâçu tam-lu-u šu-zu-ta.

ša-xu. T. A. (Ber) 48, 9 explained by še'i-ja = grain. Perhaps also T. A. (Lo) 31, 9 a-na na-da-ni še-xu.

šaxû, šixû 1. *ps* išaxxi. wallow in the mud {im Schlamme waten oder wühlen}; but see KB vi (1) 500. *del* 146 (155) the raven ik-kal (√אכל; or iq-rib?) i-ša-ax-xi. S^c 2, 7 šu-u | ŠU | ši-xu-u Br 10842; = a-ša-rum (6). sa-xa-pu (8). & ka-ra-mu (9). ℑ Perhaps K 483 *R* 6 amēlu lu-šax-xa-ni (Hr^L 55); BA i 222.

Derr. šaxû, 2 & 3 (?), & šaxîtum.

šaxû *2.* swine, pig, hog {Schwein} JENSEN, ZA i 170 *rm* 2; 306—11; KB iii (1) 130, 1. properly: the animal wallowing in the mud; and thus ŠAX (§§ 9. 118; 25; AV 7771) is used as part of id of such animals; Br 11114. II 6 *c-d* 21, 22 ÇI-IX

(KB vi, 1, 500) & ŠAX = ša-xu-u; AV 7783; Br 4208, 974. IV^2 13 *a* 41 at-ta-ma e-pi-ši-ka ki-ma ša-xi-e lu-u çal-lat, KB vi (1) 538. id also IV^2 50 *c* 9; Sarg *Ann* 139; Esh iii 4. I 28 *a* 23 ŠAX GIŠ-GI-MEŠ = šaxê abi. Rm 2, 588 *O* 43 GI-IR-PIŠ = ša-xu-u, M^S *pl* 25. II 29 *no* 1 *add* (K 2022) *a* 61, IR-DAM = ir-ri-tu ša šaxê, Br 3161; and V 32 *d-f* 47. kukubānu ša šaxê, see 378 *col* 2; nāxu ša ŠAX (= šaxî) see nāxu, 2 (663 *col* 1; Br 5342, 5409). šax(ū) qaq-qa-ri ‖ xallūla(j)a see 314 *col* 2 § *b*. *Cf* also JAOS xxii 214.

šaxū *3.* Neb 312, 1 $^{(iç)}$ ša-xu-u ša a-na Su-la-a $^{(amēl)}$ ašlaku nadnu.

šūxu (?). K 678 *R* 1 šu-ux ŠE-IN-NU (= tibni) Hr^L 506; also *ibid* 9/10 šu-ux $^{(amēl)}$ i-tu-'-e ša šarri bēli iš-pur-an-ni. K 653, 4 šu-ux *M* (concerning *M* of whom the king has written to me); K 1235, 4 (Hr^L 154, 155)

šuxū *f* šuxītu. T. A. (Lo) 6, 20 + 21 ište-en $^{(iç)}$ ir-šu $^{(iç)}$ ušū xurāçu šu[-xa?]-a u narkab-tum šu-xi-tu i-na xurāçi; KB v 87 a bed of ušū-wood, gilded; also a gilded chariot.

šīxu 1. pr iši(ē)x; Hebr. שיח. grow, grow up, become tall, high }wachsen, hochwachsen{. G § 49; D^H 62; D^{Pr} 34; 180; ZDMG 40, 725. Sn *Kui* 4, 11 see kabaru (366 *col* 2); *ibid* 38 cypresses nap-xar içē i-ši-xu; Sarg *Cyl* 38, *Sargon* who i-na mil-ki ni-me-qi ir-bu-ma i-na ta-šim-ti i-še-e-xu (KB ii 45; 293. Lyon, *Sargon*, 67). K 3456 *O* 18 i-na ki-ši (in the forest) .... i-ši-xu šam-ni, PSBA xxi 37—8; K^M 53, 8 i-šix(-šu). IV^2 18 *no* 3 i 42/43 kiš-ti elli-ti ša i-çu-ša ši-i-xu (= pm; § 116, GID-DA .... UD-DU, *i. e.* id of açū, S^b 84; Br 7564, 7880).

ℑ V 45 vi 34 tu-ša-a-xa. ag V 31 *c-d* 33 mārtu mu-ši-xat & mu-us-si-xa-at (= ℑ^1) paššūrē (or √masaxu? 567 *col* 1) AV 5518.

Derr. mušixxu (692 *col* 1); šīxtu; šutaxu (šutamxu) &:

šīxu *2.*; **šēxu.** *adj* grown tall, tall, lofty }hochgewachsen, hoch{. V 65 *b* 8 a-šu-xu ši-xu-ti (*var* ši-xu-u-tu). II 67, 76 gušūrē erini še-xu-u-ti; ZA ii 133 *a* 20. See also karū, 3 (end; 431 *col* 1). IV^2 22 *a* 36 see na'alu, 1 Š^3 *b* (629 *col* 1) and translate: (the muruç qaqqadi) cuts down the tall like a willow (?); see V 47 *a* 50 kum(qum, gat)-ti rap-ša-tu urbatiš ušnillum. IV^2 9 *a* 22/3 en-bu ša ina ramānišu ibbanū ši-xa gat(kum?)-ta.

šīxu *3.* some animal of lower order, destructive to plants and vegetation }ein den Pflanzenwuchs zerstörendes Tier niederer Ordnung{. II 5 *c-d* 18 see kisimmu (416 *col* 1) Br 5550; AV 8184.

šīxu *4.* some weapon or instrument. K 8676 iii 27 URUDU-ŠUN-XAŠ-LUM = ši-i-xu (ZA viii 77).

šexxu (?). II 41 *c-d* 10 .... LAL = še-ix-xu.

šaxxū. a cloth }ein Tuch{. KB vi (1) 92, 19 $^{(iç)}$ šaxxītum ir-kab-ma, bestieg er das Segelschiff (see *ibid* 410); id see II 46 *c-d* 10; D 88 v 10 GIŠ-MA-ŠA(G) [= LIB]-XA = (elip) šax-xi(*var* xu)-tum, AV 7785; Br 8082. — V 15 *e-f* 44 KU ŠA(G)-XA = šax[-xi-tum] or šax[-xu-u] followed by kar[-ru] & u-ra[-šu] & ‖ bašamu, KAT^3 603: Büssergewand. id also IV^2 25 *b* 16 (a šaxxū kussū for a god); 29* 4 C *R* ii 7; 56 *no* 2 *a* 16; Zimmern, *Ritualtafeln*, 48, 12 & *rm* 11. See also IV^2 58 *a* 44 e-pu-šak-ki (make unto thee) makurru šax-xu-tu u-še-el-li-ki ina libbi.

šuxdū see Š of xadū (307 *col* 1); Hr^L 290, 14.

šūxuz(u) *ac* Š of axazu; Sarg *Cyl* 74 ana šu-xu-uz çi-bit-te, KB ii 50, 51. AV 8419.

šuxzuzu. VATh 244 iii 29 A-ZA-LU-LU = šu-ux-zu-zu.

šaxaxu, pr išxux, *ps* išaxxux & išaxxax AV 7773. K 8454 ii 52; iii 75 ....]-šu ilāni i-šax-xu-xu BA ii 410; 413: ihm haben sich die Götter zu beugen; thus = bend, bow down; but KB vi (1) 53 leaves passage untranslated. V 49 viii 14 (end) i-šax-xax. T^M vi 33 like a .... wall liš-xu-xu kiš-pu-ša. K 4309, 20 ZI-ZI = ša-xa-xu ša .... (Br 2348; ZA iv 158); *cf* K 2009, 15 UŠ-ZU-A-RI-A = ša-xa-xu, ZA iv 155 & v 44; Br 5051.

ℑ oppress, press (ZK i 190). IV^2 22 *a* 19/20 zu-mur u-šax-xa[-ax?]. IV^2

3 *a* 10 (end) UZU-MEŠ (= šêrē)-šu u-šax[-xa-ax] or šaxaṭu, 2?

$\mathfrak{J}^t$ K 4832, 22 (21) see šagimu.

Here also belong the T. A. forms, (Ber) 93,9 uš-xi-xi-in i-na pa-an-te-a \ ba-aṭ-nu-me, (ZA vi 150); (Ber) 94, 13; 114, 8; 186, 7 = I throw myself, I prostrate myself. — $\mathfrak{Q}^t$ (Lo) 50, 12 lu-u iš-ta (Ber 123, 11 -ti)-xa-xi-in; 53, 7; 52, 8 lu-u iš-tu-xu-xi-in.

Derr. šaxxû & šixxatu.

šaxaṭu 1. *pr* išxiṭ, *ps* išaxxiṭ, go up, mount, ascend {steigen, aufsteigen, besteigen} ZIMMERN, *Ritualtafeln*, 217 *rm* 17. NE VI 145 iš-xi-ṭam-ma Êa-bani; + 175 iš-xi-iṭ xup-pa (KB vi (1) 176—77). K 2519 *R* 11 (ZIMMERN, *Ritualtafeln*, 100, 36) puxatta] šatti ištênit (-kan) ša na-lu la iš-xi-iṭ-ṭu (= MARTIN, *Textes rélig.*, '03, 324/5). IV² 31 *R* 7 a-na bur-ti alpu ul iš-šax-xi-iṭ (see *O* 77; KB vi (1) 399. K 8486, 7 .... m]a-ša-ru i-šax-xi-iṭ. *pm* KB vi (1) 48 (= K 8459 ii) 19 šax-du-ma i-na (iç) kussê a-gu-šu šak-nu.

$\mathfrak{Q}^t$ — Creat.-*frg* III 30 (88) it is said of the ušumgallu : zu-mur-šu-nu liš-tax-xi-ṭam-ma, (ZIMMERN-GUNKEL: ihr Leib schwelle an) la i-ni-'-u i-rat-su-un; see KB vi (1) 309. — *b*) mount {ersteigen} *etc.* Sn iii 76—77 a-šar a-na (iç) kussê šup-šu-qu i-na šêpê-ja aš-tax-xi-iṭ (I went up afoot); *Kui* 1, 40. IV² 18* *b* 8 ina axâti iš-ta-xi-iṭ; perh. 83—1—18, 40 (Hr^L 407) 8—9 atalû ultu šadê is-sa-ax-aṭ (or šaxaṭu, 2?) AJSL xiv 179.

$\mathfrak{J}^t$ L⁴ i 20 ši-tax-xu-ṭa-ku murni-is-ke, I mounted the charger, LEHMANN, ii 67. — ZIMMERN, *Ritualtafeln*, 26 (K 3245) iii 4 the king upon .... uš-ta-xaṭ-ma (ascends).

$\check{\mathfrak{S}}$ Rm 282 *R* 5 u-ša-aš-xi-iṭ ur-pa mi-xa[-a?]; *ibid* 2 šu-uš-xi-iṭ ur-pa mi-xa-a, let a cloud rise up, let the storm .... (KB vi, 1, 46—7).

Der. perhaps:

šixṭu. V 55, 15 ši-ix-ṭa iš-ta-ka-an a-na 30 kas-bu, he advanad about 30 *k*. Also see KB iii (1) 172, 7—8.

šaxaṭu 2. *pr* išxuṭ, *ps* išaxaṭ & išaxuṭ, tear, tear off, flay, peel {zerreissen, abreissen, schinden, schälen} AV 7774; H^W 46; HAUPT in PATERSON, *Numbers*, *p* 50. IV² 60* C *R* 10 see sakikku (756 *col* 1); 60 *b* 25 çubat-su i-ša-xaṭ-ma; *cf* ZIMMERN, *Ritualtafeln*, 40, 3; 54, 4; 60, 21: the singer idâ-šu i-šax-xu-uṭ (soll seine Arme entblössen). K 2852 + K 9662 i 3 lu-bul-ti šarrû-ti-šu iš-xu-uṭ. II 35 *g-h* 67—70 ardatu ša ina su-un mu-ti-ša çubat-sa la iš-xu-ṭu, Br 3406; see çubâtu & *cf* 81—7—1, 98 i 19, 20 et-lu ša ina su-un aš-ša-ti-šu çu-ba-ta la iš-xu-ṭu; *Jour. Trans. Vict. Inst.*, xxvi 153. IV² 10 *b* 43, 44 my many sins ki-ma zu-ba-ti šu-xu-uṭ (= MU-UN-PA-PA (= SIG-SIG)-GA, EME-SAL) Br 5623; 59 *no* 2 *b* (K 254) 14 lu-uš-xu-uṭ lum-ni (the bird carry it up to heaven). K 41 *b* 16 çu-ba-a-ti iš-xu-uṭ-ṭa-an-ni-ma, he tore away from me, PSBA xvii 65 *foll.* NE V *col* i (?) 41 ... xa-lip-ma 6 sa-xi-iṭ šu-nu .... (KB vi, 1, 162—3). K 490 *R* 15 li-iš-xu-ṭu šarru bêli (Hr^L 119); Rm 216, 13 igarâte (?) i-ša-xu-ṭu. NE I *col* iii 42 ši-i liš-xu-uṭ lu-bu-ši-ša (& 22), KB vi (1) 124—5. Asb x 5 mašak-šu aš-xu-uṭ; ii 4 iš-xu-ṭu; SMITH, *Asurb*, 137, 77—8 (148, 3) lišân-šu-un (*var* -nu) aš-lu-up aš-xu-uṭ(ṭa) SU (= mašak)-šu-un (KB ii 256—7).

$\mathfrak{Q}^t$ K 2083, 8 il-ta-xa-aṭ (draw off, away).

$\mathfrak{J}$ IV² 12 *R* 22/24 mala bašû | u-ša-ax-xa-ṭu. Here perhaps IV² 3 *a* 9/10 the muruç qaqqadi šêrê-šu u-šax-xa[-aṭ, ZK ii 302] = PA-PA-GA (see also zurbu, šaqummatu; Br 5587 & IV² R read [-ax]).

$\mathfrak{J}^t$ K 4309 *R* ši-tax-xu-ṭu (AV 8841; § 48), together with sa-a-ru, me-lu-lu & mêlultu; ZA xv 415, 416. Rm 345 *O* 2 ši-tax-xu-ṭu between bir-qu & qu-'-u.

$\check{\mathfrak{S}}$ K 3245 iii 15 (ZIMMERN, *Ritualtafeln*, 26) he said thus: lu(-)šu-uš-xu-ṭa lim-ni-tu-u-a, may my evil deeds be extirpated.

Derr. these 2:

šixṭu. II 39 *c-d* 57 ŠA-XAR-GUD = ši-ix-ṭu, decrease?, preceded by XAR-GUD = im-ru-u (56). AV 8187; Br 12122. — ZIMMERN, *Ritualtafeln*, 61 ii 9 še]-ix-ṭi-šu i-ša-xaṭ; literally: his tearing off he shall tear off; *i. e.* he shall deliver him completely; also *no* 62 *R* 6. Here perhaps Merod.-Balad.-stone v 44 i-na ši-xaṭ šîri liq-ta-a mašak (or zumur?)-šu (>< BA ii 205; 271).

šaxxūṭîtu, literally: one who tears to pieces }Zerreisserin{ an epithet and, then, name of the witch. T^{M} III 54 ša-ax-xu-ṭi-tum.

šaxṭu humble, see šaxtu.

ši-xaṭ so ZEHNPFUND in J^{I-N} 54 *rm* 98 on *del* 235 (262): das Gewand soll keine Falten werfen; but see ši-pa, above; *s. v.* šîbu, 1 NOTE 1.

šaxalu 1. call, announce }rufen, verkünden{ D^{H} 20; RÉJ xiv 158; ZDMG 40, 725. AV 7775. V 19 *c-d* 30 (83, 1—18, 1333 i 14); K 2008 iii 41 (II 27 *g-h* 22; H 14, 166) si-im | SIM | ša-xa-lum, in one group with nabû, šûçû; Br 2102. See LYON, *Sargon*, 12 on *Cyl* 3; L^{TP} 105; ZK i 98, § 2. Perhaps KNUDTZON, 144, 10 iš-xal eli.

ℑ TP i 86—7 ša-tam-mu çi-i-ru ša A-šur kakkê-šu u-ša-xi-lu, which according to KB vi (1) 337/38; 564, & 568 = uša'ilu. V 45 viii 20 tu-šax-xal.

šixlu. some officer }ein Beamter{. K 658 *R* 8 (amêlu) ši-ix-lu | ja-a-ši lid-din-u-ni, Hr^{L} 154.

šaxalu 2. whence mašxalu (602 *col* 1).

šaxalu *3.* K 7940, 10 ênuma ina arax Adaru .... ša-xal šîri; 11 .... LU-ZU ša-xa-al šîri.

šaxalu 4. KB vi (1) 294, 8 (& 553) aš-xul = asxul (ZA xiv 182).

šaxalam ? K 4740, 18 .... lu TIN-TIR-KI (*i. e.* Babylon) ša-xa-lam.

šaxîlu. some vessel, furniture, or the like?? PEISER, *Vertr.*, ci 7: II ša-xi-li siparri; Dar 301, 9 ištên ša-xi-il-lu siparri.

ša(u)xluqtu (√xalaqu). ruin, destruction }Vertilgung. Vernichtung, Verderben, Zerstörung{ AV 7786. IV^{2} 39 *b* 17 see manû, 1 (557 *col* 1 *ll* 1/4). § 65, 33 *b*. BANKS, *Diss*, 1 *no* 4, 17 .... (il) A-nun-na-ki in-ne-eš-ri-šu { ša ša-ax-lu-uq-ti; 119 ul i-šu-ka (= not is to thee) šux-lu-uq-ta; *no* 2, 15. III 61 *a* 21 ša-ax-lu-uq-ti bîti. — V 11 *d-f* 13 (= II 108, 13; 114, 2. D 128, 61) NA-AM-GIL = NAM-GIL = ša-ax-lu-uq-tum. IV^{2} 30 *no* 1 *a* 22—23 NA-AM-GIL-LI-AM-MA, EME-SAL = ša-ax-lu-uq-ti; also 11 *b* 21—22 (H 220, 14—16) Br 1891, 1627, 2129; IV^{2} 30 *no* 2 *O* 39; *no* 1 *O* 24 (= H 125 *R* 11, 12) ilâni ina ša-ax-lu-uq-ti tal(*var* ta)-lu-tu(ut?); see also H 191. From the ideogram was formed a new word, šaxalamma, which *e. g.* in III 60, 71 (middle) ša-xa-lam-ma ina mâti ibašši (§ 49*a*, *rm*); also *ll* 83 (*med*) + 88; III 65 *b* 3 + 22; id also K 712 *R* 4; K 1834, 7 šax-lu-uq-ti, THOMPSON, ii *nos* 88, 114.

ša-xul-la-tum SAR. ZA vi 291 (i) 17 a plant }ein Gartengewächs{.

šaxamu. Perhaps ℑ V 45 viii 16 tu-ša]x-am.

šuxmu ‖ šuxnu, flame, heat }Flamme, Hitze{. II 35 *e-f* 12 šu-ux-mu (some read here la-'-mu) & ṭi-ṭi-lu ‖ di-iq-me-en-nu. Perhaps II 26 *a-b* 14 šux-me = xi-i-mu. See also ušxamu (114 *col* 1).

šuxummu (?). Sp II 265 *a* xxiv 10 + K 9290 + K 3452 šar-ri-iš ka-la mi-nu šu-xu[-um-me] aš-šu la i-šu-u i-ri(?)-tu.

šaxanu. flare up, become hot, burn, glow }aufflammen, lodern, glühen{ ZA i 451. 452. *Cf* שָׁחַן. ⊕ 51 iv 36 (= II 39 *g-h* 29) NE (bi-bi) NE = ša-xa-nu [ša iššiti], preceded by na-pa-xu, Br 4617; AV 7777. See JENSEN 424 *rm* 1 on DT 57: iššitum-ma šaxinat.

ℚ¹ K 3182 iv 7 a-a-ta kib-ra-a-tum ša la iš-tax-xa-nu na-mir-ta urrika. ZA iv 12; AJSL xvii 143, what regions have not sparkled with the brilliancy of thy light?

ℑ T. A. (Lo) 29, 66: and wood a-na šu-xu-ni-ja (to keep me warm).

Derr mušaxxinu (602) &

šuxnu ‖ zarxu (see 296 *col* 2).

ša-xa-an, V 28 *a-b* 25 = ša-ka-nu = שׁכן, AV 7776; Br 12181; LEHMANN, i 15 *rm* 5.

šuxindu see suxindu. 751 *col* 1.

šaxsasutu. K 122 (Hr^{L} 48) *R* 17 ina la šax-sa-su-te (√חסס) la ṣa(written pi)-lu-up, without monition he has not grown up }ohne Mahnung ist er nicht aufgewachsen{.

šaxapu 1. whence našxiptu, 739 *col* 1. AV 7778.

šaxapu 2. TP ii 38 išxup (*var* to isxup); ii 78 aš-xu-up, see saxapu (751).

šux(u)pu. Nabd 1012, 4: 1V (or ša?) šu-xu-up ša (iç) at-ta-ri.

šuxubbattum, something made of leather. T. A. (Ber) 25 ii 41: X ŠU (mašak) šu-xu-ub-bat-tum; perh. *cf* Nabd 1012, 4.

šuxuppatu. S^h 44 šu-xu-ub | 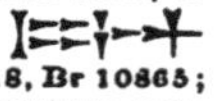 šu-xu-up-pa-tum, AV 8418, Br 10865; see parû 3 (825). HOMMEL, ZDMG 32, 178; HAUPT, *Andover Rev.*, '84, *p* 97 = mule; § 9, 244.

NOTE. — There is probably a connection between šux(u)pu & šuxupbattum; and perhaps of both with šuxuppatu; the hide of the mule being used for leather.

šaxaru, whence ušašxir, uštašxir (Xammurabi-*code* ii 60 mu-uš-ta-aš-xi-ir), našxuru, see saxaru (751—3).

ša-ax-ri gate }Tor{. T. A. (Ber) 115, 16 gloss to a-bu-ul-li. ZA vi 156; Hebr. שער.

šaxrû, šaxurû see çax(u)rû & Nabd 214, 1 lubšu ša-xu-ri-e; 2, lubšu ša-xur-ri-e; BA i 498—99; 635. Nabd 637, 5 (end) ša-ax-ri-e-tum.

šaxûru. BA i 499 quotes Rm-*frg* ša-xu-ru ‖ ibšu, aburru; fence }Umfriedigung{. probably ‖ סחר.

še-xi-ri ‖ šêri, morning, see šêru; KB vi (1) 337/8; AV 8183.

šexru. V 22 *a-d* 36 A-DAN = il-mi : ši-ix-ru (or -tu?), AV 8188, Br 11539.

šaxarrabû (?). IV^2 34, 2 u amêni dibbu-kunu a-na ša-xar-ra-bi-e maš-lu; see 604 *col* 2, *med.*

(ki-gal-lum) **šu-ux-ru-ub-tu,** Sarg *Cyl* 36, a desert waste, AV 8422.

šu(?)xarrum. II 21 *c-d* 26 $SA^{(xi-ir)}SAR$ [šu?]-xar-rum, Br 3115; II 21 *c-d* 22 see Br 4340.

šuxarruru *1.* = שחרר, § 117, 2; G §§ 51; 86; Z^B 5; 55. be or become narrow; be or become in trouble, afraid, in need }enge, beengt, bange sein oder werden{. KB vi (1) 354: still, ruhig sein oder werden; erstarren, starr, regungslos werden. *pr* ušxarir. *del* 125 (132) uš-xa-ri-ir-ma im-xul-lu KB vi (1) 239: der Unheilsturm ward still; ‖ inûx; iklû. NE I ii 47 (= H^{NE} 9) uš-xa-ri-ir i-qu-ul-ma; NE 58 (KB vi, 1, 164) 16 û-mu uš-xa-ri-ir u-ça-a ek-li-tum. ZA iv 238, 48 uš-xa-ri-ir i-lak-šu. II 21 *c-d* 20 ZI-IN[ ] = šu-xar-ru-rum, Br 2358. S^P 158 + S^P II 962 *R* 29 šu-xur-ru-ur sak-ki-e-šu, PINCHES, *Jour. Trans. Vict. Inst.*, xxxix 80 (√חרר). — $Ʒ^t$ NE i *col* ii 45 uš-tax-ri-ru pa-nu-šu, KB vi (1) 121, ward sein Antlitz starr.

NOTE. — Against HAUPT's view (BA i 178 *rm* 3 √—ר) see SCHULTHESS, *Homonyme*, 78 & *rm* 2: Syriac & Mandaic have the root —ר, be afraid; originally, no doubt, be narrow.

Derr. these 6:

šuxarruru *2.* *adj* V 19 *a-b* 11 SI-DUG-GA (see naxlu, 1; 663 *col* 2) = šu-xar-ru-ru, Br 3422. *Cf* Rm IV 97 (33, 541) 11 (end) mu-çi-e šu-xu(a)r-ru-ru-tu, PSBA xxiii 105.

šaxrartu straits, oppression, need }Enge, Bangigkeit, Not{. Sn *Kui* 3, 17 eli Êlamtim rapaštim it-bu-ku (3 *pl pr*) ša-ax-ra-ar-tu = SMITH, *Senn*, 98, 102; §§ 65, 29 *rm* 6; 117, 2.

šuxarriš, *adv* III 38 *no* 2 *R* 24 [e-ru-um?]-ma a-na (al) X at-ta-šab šu-xar(mur?)-riš.

šaxarratu; ‖ of šaxrartu. JENSEN, KB vi (1) 236 *rm* 9: quiet, stiffness, torpidity }Stille, Erstarrung{. Sn *Bell* 29 eli ugârêšun xab-çu-ti (KB vi, 1, 323; or rin-nin-ti?) ša-xar-ra-tum at-bu-uk, ‖ šaqummatu, Asb iii 3. KB vi (1) 354 Ruinen, Trümmerstaub; or: Öde, Schweigen. See also Sarg *Ann* 382. K 3454 + K 8935 ii 23 it-ta-at-bak ša-xar-ra-tum, KB vi (1) 48—9: ergoss sich Stille. II 38 *g-h* 23 [PA]-PA (= SIG-SIG) = ša-xar-ra-tu; 24 = ša-qu-um-ma-tu, Br 5588, 5624. II 21 *c-d* 21 SI-SI-G[A = ša]-xar-ra-tum (Br 3437); also perhaps V 20 *c-f* 54. S^c 306.

šuxarratu. KB vi (1) 36—7, 28 mu-uk-kiš šu-x(m)a(u)r-ra-tu, der die Stille vertreibt; see *ibid* 354/55.

šu(a)xarratu. some vessel }ein Gefäss{, lit^y: *f adj*: narrow. IV^2 22 *a* 21/22 kîma kar]-pa-ti ša-xar-ra-ti u-ša-aš[-ga-am??]; 26 *b* 33/34 me-e bu-u-ri .... kar-pa-tu šu-xar-ra-tu (= DUK-SAR-RA) mul-li, T^M 149. II 21 *c-d* 25 $DUK^{(sa-xar)}SAR$ = šu-xar-ra-tum (Br 4341); V 42 *e-f* 31 $DUK^{(sa-kar)}SAR$ = ša-xar-ra-tum, Br 4339. — JOHNS, *Deeds & Documents*, has the following forms: 1007, 4 šax-xa-rat, & often; 1030 i 1 ša-xa-rat; 1095, 4 ša-xar-ra (MEŠ =) te.

šaxatu *1.* be or become afraid, timid }furchtsam, bange, zaghaft sein oder werden}. J^{I-N} 48 *rm* 34. V 64 *b* 52/53 see nakadu. III 10 *no* 2, 36 (= TP III *Ann* 214, 215) the queen of Arabia taš-xu-tam (or -ut?)-ma before my mighty weapons. NE I *col* iv 10 e(-)taš-xu-ti li-qe-e na-pis-su, KB vi (1) 127 scheue dich nicht; + 17 ul iš-xu-ut. Here also Mer.-Bal.-stone ii 21 iš-xu-ṭu (for -tu). Where does IV^2 29* *no* 4 B *R* 16 (ta-aš-xu-tu) belong?

ג Perhaps V 45 *col* 8, 17 tu-šax-xa-at.

גᵗ NE I *col* iv 26 ul-tax-xi-it Ea-bani ul-lu-la pa-gar-šu; KB vi (1) 126—7. — Der.:

šaxt(ṭ)u. *adj* humble {demütig}. Anp i 11 *Anp* šax-tu narâm libbika, ZA ii 206. I 52 *no* 4 *O* 3 *Neb* aš-ru ša-ax-ti pâlix ilâni rabûti. Ner i 11 *I* (*Nerigl.*) aš-ru ša-ax-ṭu; also ZA ii 73 *b* 2; 124, 2 a-aš-ru ša-ax-tim, ZA ii 74, 75. K 3258 *O* 18 mut-lil-lu-u ša zi-kir-šu šax-tu. KB iii (2) 72, 25; 2 (i) 16; see also *var* to I 40 *a* 5/6 (šarru šax-tu); ZA v 67, 16.

šaxatu 2. be angry, rage {zürnen, wüten}. V 48 *col* iv 5 (on the 4th of Tammuz) šu-xat UR-MAX u ša-xat ÇIR (= çiri, serpent); v 8 (on the 7th of Ab) ša-xat UR-MAX. — Der.:

šuxtu, *c. st.* šuxut. anger, wrath {Zorn, Wut, Grimm}. Sarg *Khors* 34 (97) i-na šu-xu-ut libbi-ja, in the anger of my heart; *Ann* 59. KAT^3 398.

šaxatu 3. K 40 ii 11 (II 108, 26; 114, 14; V 11 *d-f* 26) A-MAR-RA = A-GAR-RA = mê ša-xa-tu (Br 5819, 11520, 11708, 11977); D^{Pr} 119 = maqatu; AV 7779; same id = mê ra-xa-çu & thus perhaps = sprinkle, besprinkle {giessen, begiessen}; see saxxu, 750 *col* 1. — K 3464 *R* 6 bâb bîti ta-ša-xat, Craig, *Relig. Texts*, 66; PSBA xxiii 115 *foll.* Scheil, *Notes*, liv 9 ki-ma zu-'-ti ina ša-xa-ti.

šuxtu 2. KB vi (1) 556; *Deu. Lit:ty.*, '00, *no* 47 compares Syr שוחתא = verdigrise {Grünspan}. 82—9—18, 4159 *R* 14 UD-KA-BAR = šu-ux-tum; 83—1—18, 1335 i 10 same id = šinnu; K 8676 iv 16 = šu-ux-tu. V 23 *h* 18. Perhaps ‖ êrû copper.

šuxtu 3. V 47 *b* 28 explains mammû, 2 (552 *col* 1).

šax'ā'tu (?) ***4.*** perhaps: side {Seite} see gulibat (216 *col* 1); AV 7779; Br 6666. id DA (= idu, side; itti, with; lit: at the side of); which also in IV^2 1* iv 37/38 the demons ana tub-ki u ša-xa-ti a-a i-tu-ru-ni, Jensen, 165: they shall not return to the inside nor to the outside. Br 6653, 6666. II 30 *no.* 4 *O* 7 (*l* 34) [BAR?] = ša-xa-tu, Br 1801. Rm 283, 3 kîma našri ina ša-xat šadi-e šit-ku-nat [šubat-su], Winckler, *Forschungen*, ii 9 *fol.*

šaxatu 5. destroy, ruin {verderben} Hebr. שחת? Zimmern, ZA vi 158; fall {fallen} KB v 30* *col* 1 (*cf* Gen 38 : 9); surround {einschliessen} BA iv 305. T. A. (Ber) 31. 25—6 for if Dunip iš-xi-it, falls; 33, 40 and I am afraid iš-tu ša-xa-ti-šu la i-li-'-e; 43, 10 u a-nu-ma i-na-an-na ši-ix-ta-at; 12, ša-xa-at-ši i-li-u u ça-bat-ši la i-li-u, BA iv 305: und siehe; jetzt ist *S* bis zu seinem Tore ein-geschlossen; es einzuschliessen vermochten sie; es zu besetzen vermochten sie aber nicht}; (Ber) 99, 39 iš-xa-ta mât šarri; 150, 21 the city i-nu-ma ša-ax-ta-at. (Lo) 61, 20 ki-i a-na-ku i-ša-xa-tu.

Qᵗ (Lo) 19, 19—20 u an-nu-u i-na-na iš-ta-xu-at-ni (3 *sg*) A-zi-ru.

šextu. Zimmern, *Ritualtafeln*, 60, 13 še-ix-tu tašakkan; 64, 11 še-ix-tu tu-šar-ra; see also 66 *O* 5, 6, 7; 67 *O* 5, 6, 7.

šîxtu, sprout, shoot, germ {Spross, Keim} or the like. (√šîxu) ‖ pirxu (828 *col* 2); AV 8189; D^{Pr} 83 *rm* 2; §§ 64; 65 *no* 2.

šaxîtum. perh. *f* of šaxû, 2. II 6 *c-d* 44—46 ša-xi-tum; on id see Br 7540, 13945. S^b 71 ša-xi-tum; also perhaps K 749, 7 (sal) ŠAX (= šaxîta)-a, Thompson, *Reports*, *no* 277. AV 7782.

šixxatu. I 52 *no* 4 *a* 16 see sakikê (756 *col* 1); perh. = subsidence of earth. (√šaxaxu?); or √šaxaṭu = torn down masses of earth; if so, then a *pl* of šixṭu.

šuxattu. K 4606, 8 šu-xa-at-tum; ZA iv 162.

šâṭu 1. — Hebr. שוט or שאט slight, neglect, despise {verachten} *pr* išîṭ. Baer-Del., *Ezech*, pref. xvi; Jensen, 361; Haupt in Toy, *Ezekiel* (SBOT) 80, 81. AV 7792; Br 9322. ‖ na-a-çu. 1 (713 *col* 1); qul-lulu (*q. v.*). Esh *Sendsch*, *R* 35; K^M 11, 10;

K 769 *R* 7 šarru la i-ša-ṭu, Thompson, *Reports*, 82.

Derr. perhaps these 2:

šîṭu. K 1250 *O* 7 u ši-i-ṭu mātāti gabbi, Hr^L 460.

šēṭūtu. Sarg *Khors* 55 (*Ann* 47; *Ann* XIV 41) the people ša ni-ir (11) Ašur is-lu-u il-qu-u še-ṭu-ti, KB ii 60/61; Winckler, *Forsch*, i 107. See leqū, *a* (494 *col* 2). K 1349, 29.

še-ṭu, see šindu, 1 & šīmtu, 2.

šâṭu 2. pr išūṭ, *ps* išāṭ draw, pull; carry, bear {ziehen, schleppen; tragen} ‖ šadadu. AV 7792. See Teloni, ZA ii 100; Lehmann, *ibid*, 214—18; Jastrow, *ibid*, 353—56. šāṭu si(e)rdē see sirdû (788 *col* 1). šāṭu ab(p)šānu see abšānu (11 *cols* 1/2) & Asb vii 88 i-šu-ṭu ap-ša-a-ni; ii 77 + 125 (la-šu-ṭa > lūšūṭa, § 93, 1 & 2*b*; BA i 15 + 314; Lehmann & Bezold & Pinches in S. A. Smith, *Asurbanipal*, II 93, 89, 98 & 99; Bezold, ZA i 376; iv 289. Sn ii 64; Sarg *Ann* 228; *Khors* 70 & 109 (§ 152). K 2852 + K 9662 i 13 (end) li-šu-ṭu (3 *pl*). Sp II 265 *a* vii 8 il-ku ša la ni-me-li a-ša-aṭ ap-ša-nu. I 44, 70 great cedarbeams ana Ninā i-šu-ṭu-nim-ma (3 *pl*). T. A. (Ber) 28 ii 17: VI ru-ku-bu zi-xi-ru-ti ša i-ša-aṭ ga-du. *del* 245 (275), 250 (280) i(& ta)-na-xa i(& ta)-šu-ṭa; Haupt, JAOS xxii 10 *rm* 5 = proceed laboriously, move with effort; KB vi (1) 515.

šuṭubbu, Br 2206; see ṭâbu ŠJ (350 *col* 2).

šaṭaṭu. K 2527 + K 1547 *O* 32, the serpent ip-te-e-ma libbašu (of the wildox) ka-ra-as-su iš-ṭu-uṭ, KB vi (1) 107 suggests: penetrated into its stomach {drang in seinen Bauch hinein}; see *ibid* 104, 18 [šu-ṭu-uṭ].

šaṭ(d)ap(b)u. Sarg *Ann* 435 (*Khors* 173) I sacrificed to the gods ..... aš-šu ša-ṭa-pu na-piš-ti. V 28 *g-h* 59; *e-f* 59 ša-ṭa-pu & ne-e-šum ‖ bu-la-tu, AV 7742. — K 2608 + K 2633 + 3101 *b* + 3435, 12 (end) Marduk ša-ṭe(or xi?)-ip ga-ri-šu. K 232, 29 sa(for ša)-ṭi-pat. See Hebr. שׁטף & šatapu.

šaṭaru 1. pr iš(l)ṭur, 1 *sg* ašṭur, § 27 & alṭur, § 51; ip šuṭur; *ps* išaṭar; *pm* šaṭir & šaṭra BA i 420 *rm* 1. id SAR, § 9, 141. Br 4336; AV 7791. write {schreiben}. ZDMG 32, 367; ZK i 268/9 *no* 14; WZKM 1, 29. S^P II 987 *O* 17 e-gir?]-e-tum ša taš-ṭu-ru-um-ma, the letter which thou hast written, JTVI 29, 53. duppu šaṭaru, see duppu (263); also simply aš-ṭur, KB iv 142—3 *no* IX 26. duppi marūtišu niš-ṭur-ma, often in *c. t.*; ni-iš-ṭu-ur(-ru), Neb 359. 8; 84—2—11, 165 (end). duppi ap(b)-lu-ti-šu iš-ṭur-šu II 9 *a-b* 32; Meissner, 15 *rm* 4. dup-pa-a-nu iš-ṭu-ru-ma, they wrote documents, Br. M. 84—2—11, 79. KB iii (1) 160 *col* iv 39 duppē (?) a-na xur-ša-an il-tu (for ṭu)-ra-aš-šu-nu-tim-ma, + V 14/16. KB iv 174 II 31 ša-ṭir duppi, writer of the document; 124 I 15 ša-ṭir u-il (or an?)-ti; *cf* Hebr. שׁטר, KAT^3 649. V 56, 25 tup-sar ša-ṭi-ir nari an-ni-i (§ 131). K 5418 *a* iv 8 narā aš-ṭur-ka (KB vi, 1, 296/7). II 65 iv 24 lil-ṭu-ur-ma; 27, whosoever finds it liš-me ma-la ša-ṭi-ir. iš-ṭu-ru zu-kut-sun see zakūtu, 278/9; also *cf* mitgurtu, 621 *col* 2. III 16 *no* 2, 3; V 44 *a-b* 20/21 see sadaru (748). I 28 *a* 37 the record of these events la ša-ṭi-ir, had not been written down. KB iii (2) 50, 40 [çi-e-ri] kalbu xa-aç-ba ša-ṭi-ir-ma; ZA ii 150, 8 (KB ii 274 & **) ul ša-ṭir, it was not recorded. — Such & such ana (amêl) mu-kin-nu-tu šu-ṭur (see 538 *col* 2) = number among, add to; assign. See Xammurabi-*letters* 43, 4 ša a-na BARA-UŠ *pl* ta-aš-tu-ru-šu, die du den Truppenführern zugeschrieben hattest; *ibid* 7 aš-tu-ur-šu-nu-ti; BA iv 471 *foll*. *pm* 3 *f* šaṭ-ra-tum, is written, Peiser, *Vertr.*, lxxiii 4 (Nabd 693, 7); *ibid* cxix 8—10 ša-ṭa-ri ša ..... taš-ṭu-ru (3 *f sg*). Also see šadaru. — Notice in particular:

a) eli (ina eli), ina kirbi, ina libbi, ina .... šaṭaru = write on, upon. Sarg *Khors* 53 eli-šu aš-ṭur; Esh iii 48. i-na mux-xi al-ṭu-ur TP vi 18/19; Asb ii 13 (aš-ṭur). Šalm, *Obel*, 72 ina kir-bi-ša aš-ṭur; Bu 88—5—12, 75 + 76 ix 33, 34 see q(k)irbu (928 *col* 2, beg.). K 522 *O* 9—11 ma-a i-zir-tu-u me-me-ni ina libbi ša-aṭ-rat (Hr^L 31; BA i 215). Such & such ina libbi aš-ṭu-ur (*var* al-ṭur) Anp i 98; *cf* 69; iii 25; i 99 ina libbi SAR (*var* al-ṭur); ii 6 (SAR); ii 91 al-ṭur (*var* SAR). Anp *Mon*, *R* 3 al-ṭur-ru. TP viii 44 such & such i-na .... al-ṭu-ur; V 34 *b* 47 i-na narê aš-tu-ur, + 50 (see narû, 724, 725). Asb ix 60 ina ar-ra-a-ti ma-la ina a-di-e-šu-nu šaṭ-ru; iii 121 ša-ṭir (*var* ṭi-ir) see kigallu (372 *col* 1).

b) Often in colophons to tablets: nisiq dupšar(r)ûti ..... nîmêq(i) Nabû tikip santakki mala bašmu(e) ina DUB-MEŠ aš-ṭur as-niq ab-re-e-ma, II 21 *a* 32; 23 *a* 63; IV^2 50 *coloph.* 37; IV^2 56 iv *coloph.* 50; D 49, 39; K 161 *col* viii (ZK ii 2) *etc.* H 184 *frg* 5201 coloph aš-ṭur as-niq. II 36, 26 iš-ṭur; D 90, 6; IV^2 34 *no* 1 *b* 35.

c) Often also in colophons: kîma BE (= labiri)-šu ša (= LIB)-ṭir ma ba-a-ri, said either of the gabrû (copy), or of the duppu (tablet); IV^2 16 *b* 67 (§ 53*c*); 9 *b* 42 kim-ma BE-šu ša-ṭir ma ŠI-GAN; V 25 *a-b* 29. IV^2 21* *no* 2 *R* 27 ki-ma la-bi-ri-šu SAR-ma ba-[a-ri]; 10 *b* 54 kîma labiri-šu ša-ṭar-ma ba (written ⟨⟨⟨)-rim; 11 *b* 51; H 181/2 *no* XIV (K 24) 3. K 5268, 38 ki-i pi-i duppi gab-ri Kûti ša-ṭar-ma ba-ri; ZA iv 363 kîma la-bi-ri-i-šu ša-ṭi-ir-ma ba-ri; V 32 *no* 4 coloph. (ZA i 401); 46, 61; 36 *a-b* 42 (Br 8756). Bezold, *Catalogue*, vol v *pref* xxix šaṭir-ma bâri = copied. and also revised.

d) šum-šu it-ti šumi-ja lil-ṭu-ur, let him write his name next to mine, TP viii 59; but who (69) šum (written MU) šaṭ-ra (BA i 420 *rm* 1) i-pa-ši-ṭu-ma (70) šuma-šu i-ša-ṭa-ru. I 70 iii 6 who ša-nam-ma (something else) i-šaṭ-ṭa-ru; Esh *Sendsch*, *R* 54, 55 who šu-me šaṭ-ru i-pa-ši-ṭu-ma šuma-šu i-šaṭ-ṭa-ru. S^c 332, 333 ša šu-me šaṭ-ru i[-pa-aš]-ši-[ṭu] šum-šu i-šaṭ-ṭa-ru, *etc.* V 70, 14/5 MU-ka itti MU-ja šu-ṭur ana aśri-šu te-ir (restore it). IV^2 56 *coloph.* 50 man-nu ..... šum-šu itti šumi-ja i-šaṭ-ṭa-ru; II 42 *no* 5 *R* 5 (BA i 428). *Rec. Trav.* xx 205 *col* 5, 2—4. See also pašaṭu, 842—8. — H 18, 294; S^b 2, 8 sa-ar | SAR | ša-ṭa-ru. V 27 *g-h* 40 MU-SAR-RA = ša-ṭar šu-mi, Br 1271; V 36 *a-c* 42. H 50—51, 31 IN-SAR = iš-ṭu-ru; 33 IN-SAR-EŠ = iš-ṭu-ru (= *pl*); 35 IN-SAR-RE = i-ša-ṭa-ar; 37 IN-SAR-RE-NE = i-ša-ṭa-ru.

Knudtzon has these forms: pr iš-t(ṭ)u-ru 46, 8; 98 *R* 7; ps i]-ša-aṭ-ṭa-ru[-u-ma] 133, 2; pm *sg* ša-aṭ-ru-u-ma, 114 *R* 8; šaṭ-ru, often; ša-aṭ-rat-tu, 116, 5; *pl* šaṭ-ru-u-ma.

𝔔^t V 56, 38 see pašaṭu 𝔍^t 843 *col* 1. K 991 *O* 10 u dup-pa-a-ni is-si-ni-ni-is-sa-ṭar (> ništaṭar); K 525, 2. —22 ina lib-bi e-gir-te-MEŠ i-sa-ṭa-ru (BA ii 55 *foll*); K 112, 8 a-sa-ṭa: (Hr^L 117, 252, 223).

𝔍 Sn *Bass* 92 such & such ki-rib-šu (*i. e.* on the musarû) u-šaṭ-ṭir, ZA iii 319. IV^2 38 iii 25 u-ša-ṭa-ra-ma (KB iv 62—3).

Š cause, order to write {schreiben lassen}. Sarg *Ann* 35 çiruššu u-ša-aš-ṭir ina qirbišu ul-ziz (ZA iv 412); also *cf* Sn ii 6; *Bav* 56; *Bell* 26. Esh *Sendsch*, *R* 53 da-nu-an ep-še-te-ja ..... çir-uš-šu u-ša-aš-ṭir (Esh iii 11). I 49 iii 23 ud-du-uš É-sag-ila u-ša-aš-ṭi-ra ana mu-xiš (BA i 448 reads: ana MU (= ja)-tum, to me). Bu 88—5—12, 75 + 76 iii 10 see BA iii 244. Meissner, 1.5 *no* 100, 13 u-ša-aš-ṭi-ru-ši-ma, sie haben aufschreiben lassen. In the sense of *conscribere*: Xammurabi-*letters* 1, 10 i-na bi-i ka-an-ki-šu u-ša-aš-ṭi-ra-an-ni, BA iv 487.

𝔑 Xammurabi-*letters* 14, 6 li-iš-ša-te-ir, es werde geschrieben.

Note. — Xammurabi-*code*: write, assign, deed. For forms of 𝔔 & 𝔔^t see Harper's edition, '04, *p* 185.

Derr. maš(l)taru & these 4:

šaṭru *adj* in the phrase šum(u)šaṭru, id MU-SAR, a written name, signature; also = inscription with the name of the author {geschrieben; Namensschreibung. und Inschrift mit dem Namen ihres Urhebers}. BA i 480. ‖ šiṭir šume & šaṭar šu-mi V 27, 40; AV 7789, Br 127.. See šaṭaru 𝔔 *d*. IV^2 39 *R* 12 + 14; V 62 *no* 1, 26 *fol*. Esh *Sendsch*, *R* 54/5; K 5201 coloph. *etc.* see pašaṭu, 842 .. IV^2 12 *R* 27—8 who šu-ma šaṭ-ra (= MU-MU-DU-A-NA-KIT) pi-ši-ir-ma (= pm). ZA vii 330 *rm* 7. narâ an-na-a šaṭ-ri ša abni, copy of a tablet. See also Xammurabi-*code* xli 10; xlii 53 (ša-aṭ-ra-am).

šaṭāru 2., šaṭarānu. writing, copy, document {Schrift, Schriftstück, Dokument} AV 7791. ZA iv 66—7 note {Schuldschein}; PEISER, KAS 97, below. Colophon to Creat.-*frg* IV see 789 *col* 2 (ki-i pi-i). il-qu-u & il-te-qu-u in connection with 1-en (ta-a-an) ša-ṭa-ru, often. BA iii 466 *no* 15; 477 *no* 27. Nabd 760, 25 ištēn (ta-an) ša-ṭa-ri il-qu-u; 243, 17—18; Cyr 338, 10—11; 337, 18—19; 242, 10; also see 245, 9 where we have simply ište-en (a-an) il-qu-u. Camb 257, 12—13 ište-en (a-ta-a-an) ša-ṭa-ri il-qu-u; 388, 14. Also written ša-ta-ri, PEISER, *Vertr.*, 324 *col* 2. Neb 334, 19 ištēn (ta-a-an) ša-ṭa-ra-nu il-qu-u, AV 7790, they each took one copy (document).

šiṭru *c. st.* šiṭir. — *a*) writing {Schrift}. Sn vi 71 munakkir šiṭ-ri-ja u šu-me-ja; Mer.-Bal.-stone iv 53, 54; V 65 *b* 9 ši-ṭir šu-mi-ja (§ 73 note); ZA iii 316, 81; I 51 *no* 1 *b* 12 (ši-ṭi-ir); I 27 *no* 2, 46/7 (who) ta-me-tu šiṭ-ri-a la uš-te-nu-u (+ 56), the wording of my document; *cf* 62, 63. I 69 *c* 22 ši-ṭir šumi-šu ša-ṭi-ir (= pm); KB iii (2) 92, 30 it-ti ši-ṭi-ir šu-mi-ja; II 40 *c-d* 46 (Br 1631). 81—6—7, 209, 38 + 40; 88—5—12, 103 vi 7; III 16 vi 17 *foll*; Esh vi 64 *fol*; Asb x 111—16 see musarū, 2 (569); also *cf* V 64 *b* 43—5. II 60 *d-e* 34 AN-KIM-SAR = (il) Nabū ba-nu-u ši-iṭ-ri DUB-SAR-ru-ti. See also narū, 724 *col* 2.

b) šiṭir šamē, *cf* KAT[3] 634 *rm* 2. IV[2] 38 *b* 26—27 a-na du-um-mu-ki ki-ma ši-ṭi-ir šame-e. šiṭir burūmi *cf* burūmu (191); Sn *Rass* 62 (ši-ṭir). KB vi (1) 431.

šiṭirtu, said of the firmament: the starry sky. KB iii (2) 48 *col* I 30 Ēzida ..... I made shine ki-ma ši-ṭi(*var* ṭe)-ir-ti ša-ma-mi; *cf* V 34 *b* 2; Neb *Bab* ii 2; ZA ii 141 *a* 23. 83—1—18, 1332 ii 27—8 MUL = šiṭru & šiṭirtum; 48 banū ša šiṭirtum, to shine said of the *š* (PSBA Dec. '88).

šiṭāruda. IV[2] 38 ii 21 ar-xi ša ši-ṭa-ru-da (Q[t] of ṭaradu?) KB iv 63, Monde die sich drängen (?).

ša-ku (or šaqū, 3?) mayor {Bürgermeister} or the like; espec. in *c. t.*, AV 7813, 7818. BA ii 262, 36; 269. Merod.-Bal.-stone iii 36—7; iv 51; v 10, 11. Rm III 105 i *b* 8 + 10 (amēl) ša-ku together with (amēl) ki-pi. KB iv 94, 23 ša-ku māti. Nabd 170, 2; 962, 6. Neb 109, 19. S 1028, 3 (amēl) ša-ku ša Bābili; Bu 91—5—9, 183 *R* + (amēl) ša-ku MEŠ, + *O* 23; K 517 *R* 11; *pl* K 1107, 9 (amēl) ša-ku-u-ti (but?) (Hr[L] 418, 340, 327, 238). See also K 114 *O* 12 (IV[2] 46*a*). √šakaku, 1 (??).

šakū 1. Sarg *Cyl* 53 a-na (il) *D* u (il) *Š* da-i-nu-te te-ni-še-te ta-li-ma-ni ina te-me-qi u-šak-ki-ma. V 28 *h* 82 ša-ku-u (ZA i 251).

šakū 2. = šakanu, in *c. t.* i-ša-ka-šu-u-ma *etc.* Here perh. also *p* 235 *col* 1 *ll* 6—8 (see gašīšu).

šak-ki-u. V 28 *g-h* 28 ‖ kubšu (369 *col* 1); AV 7828.

šakku in paššur šak-ki (= GIŠ-BAN-SUR-ZAG-GU-LA, Br 6523) see paššūru (846 *col* 2 *l* 15). √šakaku, 1. From the same verb we have:

šakkū ‖ parçu. command, control {Gebot, Befehl, Gewalt} or the like. IV[2] 60* C *O* 4 te(a)s(š)-li-ti ta-ši-ma-ti (√שׂים) ni-qu-u šak-ku-u-a, sacrifice was my command. V 47 *a* 48 te(a)s(š)-li-tum ta-ši-ma-tum ni-qu-u šak-ku-u-a; šak-ku-u, explained by par-çi.

šikku *1.* some animal; perh. a mouse {ein Tier; vielleicht Maus}. J[I-N] 46, 8. Sarg *Ann* 336 see xallalāniš (314 *col* 2); NE 51 (K 3200) 14 see nunçabāti (692 *col* 2) & KB vi (1) 273 *rm* 8; 518; 537—8: pig {Schwein}?

šikku *2.* some vessel, pot {Gefäss} or the like. V 42 *a-b* 13 DUK-AL-UŠ-SA = kar-pat ši-ik-ki; II 8 *c-d* 22; D 82 (K 40) iii 22 [....] (su-ur) [cuneiform] = eçennū ša karpat ši-ik-ki, Br 3295, 5763; II 22 *e-f* 32 (šik-ki); see karpu (440 *cols* 1, 2). Perhaps K 55 *R* 17 IM-DAN-GA : SU (= mašak?) šik-ku, M[S] *pl* 3. AV 8201. BOISSIER, *Doc.*, 2, 12 šumma eribē ina karpat ši-ik-ki innamru. See šikkatu, 3.

šikbu. VATh 244 ii 29 MULU-LUM-LUM-AK-A = e-pi-iš ši-ik(g,q)-bi; preceded by (28) ša ruk-bi ši-iq-bi (see rukbu); ZA ix 158.

šikbū (?). PEISER, *Vertr.*, cxliii 4: 1 (iç) gu-šur š(s)ik-bi-i ša 5 1/2 U (= ammāti) arku.

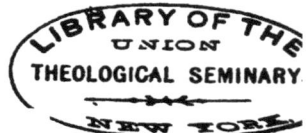

ši-ka-b(p)u. V 41 *d* 34.

šakbānu *1.* & *2.* see šagbānu, 1 & 2.

šu-uk-bu-tu, said of the size of dogs. See kabatu, NOTE (369 *col* 2).

ša-ka-du (AV 7799) ‖ qitrudu, *q. v.*

šukūdu. spear {Speer}. JENSEN: Pfeil; ‖ tartaxu. TP vi 66 see mulmullu (550, 551) & KB vi (1) 327—8. V 28 *e-f* 79 u-çu (85 *col* 2) = šu-ku[-du]. II 49 *no* 3, 48 MUL-KAK-SI-DI (which = tar-ta-xu K 263 *O* 46) = šu-ku-du; AV 8431, 8815; Br 5294, 7240 & 10714; ZA i 257; iii 251. JENSEN, 150 on K 128, 8: Ninib is called šukūdu lā nīxu.

šakadu, whence maškadu (603 *col* 2) &:

šikdu. ZA iv 281 *R* 7: VII ši-ik-di; Rm 2, 588 *R, c-d* 22 EŠ (?) = ši-ik-du. See also mān'ā'xtum, 2 (503 *col* 1).

šakdū ‖ agū & kubšu. V 28 *g-h* 26 šak-du-u; or: ŠAG-DU-u, *i.e.* qaqqadu-u? AV 7820.

šakxuku. K 10452, 3 ša-ak-xu (or bak?)-ku, some vessel. M^S *pl* 16.

šakaku. 1. (Arb شَكَّ, *etc.*, pierce, transfix) meaning not certain. V 19 *a-b* 30 (II 34 *c-d* 18) UD-DU (= açū) = ša-ka-ku (Br 7888); 32 TIK-UDDU-PA (= SIG)-GA = š ša šik-ka-tim (Br 3294, 7888); AV 7800. the id points to a meaning like: loom up, come out, project. — ℑ^t perhaps K 87—1 *R* 3 lu uš-tik-kak(-ma), THOMPSON, *Reports*, 247 A. ZIMMERN, *Ritualtafeln*, 112, 113, 8 UD-DU (= iššak-kak) = er soll aufreihen; thus also IV^2 55, 14 *foll*, espec. 21; IV^2 57 *a* 13.

Derr. Perhaps šakku, šakkū, & šikkatu, 1.

šakaku 2. H 71 (72), 17—18 (35—36) ina ūmi e-bu-ri eqlu i-ša(-ak)-ka-ak (= GIŠ-AB-GUŠUR-RA, Br 5499), followed by eqla išebbir (see šabaru, 2) & i-šal-la-aš (= GIŠ-GA-AN-PEŠ-A), JENSEN, 409. Xammurabi-*code* xiii 14, the field which he has neglected, he shall break up with hoes, he shall harrow (i-ša-ak-ka-ak-ma) & he shall return to the owner of the field; xiii 29 (HARPER, *The Code of Hammurabi*, 25, 27). Here probably also V 19 *a-b* 31 ZA-A = ša-kaku ša TAG (= abni) Br 11795. Based on the use of id GUŠUR this verb is usually explained as meaning to "fence in". *Cf* Hebr. שׂכך; מְשׂוּכָה. — ℑ see šik-katu, 2; & V 45 iii 53 tu-šak-kak. If the meaning given is correct, then belong here also T. A. (Ber) 25 i 72 (iii 53, 54) ša abni (& xurāçi) šu-uk-ku-ku (see kuxaššu, 376, 377); 27 ii 17 šu-ug-gu-gu; 26 i 5 one abnu xulālu banū i-na lib-bi-šu šuk-ku-uk (53, šuk-ku-ku); 28 i 8 šu-uk-ku-ga-at; enchased, set {eingefasst}. ZIMMERN, *Ritualtafeln*, 113, connects T. A. passages with šakaku, 1.

Der. — šikkatu, 2.

šakalu 1. ℑ V 45 iii 47 tu-šak-kal. — See also aškallum, 115 *col* 1; & šuškallu.

šakalu 2., whence maštakal? (614 *col* 2).

šakalu 3. see mušākil (603 *col* 2); BA iii 279—80; Nabd 306, 3.

NOTE. — If this stem *š-k-l*, 3. is correct, there could belong to it also S 760, 18 20 sisē-ka ša-ki-il (= ℑ ip > šakkil) a-di mār šipri a-'š'ap-par-kan-ni, feed thy horse until I have sent to thee a messenger (Hr^L 424).

Der. would be:

(amēl) **šākilu** *1.* Nabd 714 *R* 6 (amēl) ša-ki-il iç-çur[-re], ZA iii 130.

šākilu *2.* K 5464 *O* 20 ma-a ki-ma a-si-me (√šemū) ša-ki-il ina eli *etc.* (Hr^L 198); see PSBA xvii ('95) 230 *foll* on this letter.

šakkilu. AV 7830 šak-ki-lum ‖ kubšu (369 *col* 1).

šakkullu, some tree. II 45 *e-f* 51 GIŠ-ŠA (= LIB)-DAN = šak-kul-lum, Br 8046. Perhaps here also 79, 7—8, 179 *O* ii 25 ēnuma birqu šak(g)-k(g)ul-li (or ŠAG-GUL = šaqi-li?) ana šārā erbitti ibriq, CRAIG, *Astron. Texts*, 63.

šiklu, clever {klug}. From √šakalu = שׂכל, شكل. ZIMMERN, ZA xii 319 *foll* reads KB vi (1) 292, 7 ša ši-ik-la-šu šab-šu, as against JENSEN's ša ige-gal-la-šu rē'ū-šu. Here belong, also, Hymn to Adar (ABEL & WINCKLER, 60 *foll*) 15 ša (ilu) A-nun-na-ki ilāni rabūti lu-u ši-ik-la-šu-nu at-ta; Sarg *Cyl* 59 i-na ūm AB-AB ša mār Bēl ši-ik-li pal-ki-e Nabū. V 66 i 17 Nabū ši-ik-la ilāni; I 35 *no* 2, 1 (??). IV^2 49 *a* 18. Usually read either ši-gal-lu or ŠI (*i. e.* igu)-gal-lu. AV 8204. Perh. II 30 *e-f* 60; Sm 2052 *R* 29 ši-ik-lu | e.... See also šiqlu, 2.

Derr. — probably these 2:

šiklūtu cleverness {Klugheit}. K 2801 (= K 221 + 2669) *R* 12 ina ši-ik-lu-ti ša (ilu)

Ašur .... ip-tu-u xa-si-si, BA iii 234—5.

šiklatum. Sp II 265 *a* xxv 4 ri-ça u šik-la-tum za-mar ul a-mur.

šukkallu, AV 8438, see sukkallu, 756—7.

šuklu *1.* see suklu, 756 *col* 2.

šuklu *2.* Banks, *Diss*, 1 *no* 4 (= Reisner, *Hymnen*, 7) 27 ša be-lum a-mat-su ap-pa-ra ina šu-uk-li-šu (= AN-PUL) uš-ma-a-at; 18*foll*, *no* 2, 25 [ina] šuk-li-šu (= MAŠ-PU). See also Sp II 265 *a* i 3 (end).

šuklulu. completed, complete, perfect {vollendet, vollkommen, fehlerfrei} §§ 63 & 88. √kalalu, 385—6. AV 8441. Esh iii 59 gumaxxê šuk-lul šam-na (see 220 *col* 2; Budge, *Esarh*, 93). Neb 140, 1 ište-en alpu šuk-lu-lu; Nabd 54, 8 (+ 11); 127, 3—4; Zimmern, *Ritualtafeln*, 24, 28 + 31; 79—82, 3. T^C 81. S^b 236 ši-ta | id | šuk-lu-lu; Br 9167 & 9142; § 9, 89. *pl* šu-uk-lu-lu-u-tim, Pognon, *Wadi-Brissa*, 25, 100*fol.* id also I 65 *a* 16 (end), *b* 26, *c* 10 (= *pl*).

šuklultum. completion, perfection {Vollendung, Vollkommenheit}. AV 8200. IV² 57 *a* 58 šuk-lul-ti pag-ri-ja. V 47 *b* 26 šuk-lul-tum pag[-ri]-ja; šuk-lul-tum explained here by la-a-nu (1; see 491 *col* 1). II 67, 82 a-na šuk-lul-ti-ši-in, KB ii 25, zu ihrer Vollendung.

šûkultu *1.* √akalu, 1. NE XII *col* vi 11 šu-ku-la-at d(ṭ)i-qa-ri ku-si-pat a-ka-li, KB vi (1) 264—5 & 531: Essen gelassenes (im) Topfe, die Reste vom Essen (die auf die Strasse geworfen wurden) ik-kal (isst er). See diqaru (266 *cols* 1, 2) & kusīptu (417 *col* 2). From same √:

šûkultu *2.* Cyr 57, 1 immĕr šu-kul-tum, BA iii 484, Mastschaf.

šukāmu. KB vi (1) 367 intelligence {Klugheit} or the like. I 35 *no* 2, 4 Nabû ta-me-ix qân dup-pi a-xi-zu šu-ka-mi (*var* me). K 2361 + S 389 i 34, 36 Nabû rap-ša uz-ni a-ši-ši šu-ka-a-mu, ZA iv 237; 252, 10 + 12. KAT³ 401 *rm* 4 reads qât ka-mi, Schreibschaft; see also kâmu, 392 *col* 1.

šakanu. put, place; do, make {setzen, legen, in eine Lage bringen; tun, machen} AV 7802; T^C 134. idd ŠA (= GAR) §§ 23; 9, 84; Br 11978; GA(*i.e.* [cuneiform sign])-GAL, Br 5421, *etc.* III 4, 39 ina ša-ka-a-ni; *dcl* 13 (14) a-na ša-kan a-bu-bi; *pr* iškun; (-ma) Anp iii 100 (§ 53*c*); iš-kunnû II 65 *O* i 23 (pause, § 53); iš-ka-nu-ni, Anp ii 83; iš-ka-nu-u-ni, K 14 *R* 3 (Hr^L 42); *pc* liškun; lu-uš-kun (ku-un) K 61, 7 (ZK ii 12); II 16 *b* 53, *f* 45; ZA v 142, 19; liš-ku-nu (3 *pl*) II 51 *b* 17; *ip* šukun, IV² 31 *b* 13 šu-kun; ZA v 142 šu-ku-un; Camb 428, 13 P. N. Nabû-rēmu-šuk-nu; Nabd 356, 28 šuk-na (2 *pl m*); *f* šuk-ni T^M 5, 25; H 117 *R* 6; *pm* ša-kin, often (AV 7808) K 2148 ii 17, 19; šaknu (§ 89 i; Asb ii 1). *f* šak-nat; 2 *sg* šak-na-a-ti (§§ 91, 93, 2); *pl* ša-ak-nu-u-ni, Anp iii 93; ša-ak-nu, TP iii 57 (61); *ps* išakkan (§ 17 i-ša-ka-an-u-šu, they made it); K 183, 19 (Hr^L 2) i-šak-ku-nu. Haupt, JBL xix 78 *rm* 107: perhaps a Š of كان.

a) lay on, upon {auferlegen} with ina muxxi (or eli). thus tribute (ma(n)-dattu), hostages, *etc.* i-na mux-xi (& eli)-šu(-nu, -un) aš(iš)-kun (= u-kin), TP v 20, 31 (aš-ku-un, *var* u-kin), *etc.* Anp ii 79 e-li-šu-nu aš-kun (*var* GAR-un); K 84 *R* 1 ša-kan bil-te, imposition of taxes (Hr^L 301).

b) place, put down, deposit {hinterlegen, deponiren} espec. in *c. t.* ‖ paqadu, T^C 134; Meissner, 117, 118. *Rec. Trav.* xvi 178—9, 24 ina aš-ri ša-num-ma la ta-ša-kan. TP viii 16 the (precious) stones .... i-na bît xam-ri ... aš-ku-un (*var* u-kin); viii 46. III 4 *no* 7, 5 iš-kun-an-ni (3 *m* for 3 *f*) i-na kup-pi ša šu-ri, KB iii (1) 100. I 27 *no* 2, 24 gold *etc.* ina lib-bi (*i. e.* the palace) aš-kun. Asb vi 3 iš-ku-nu (3 *pl*). Cyr 332, 10 as a pledge ina pân *A* iš-ku-nu-ni-šu (gave him to); see maškânu, 1 (603—4). KB iv 318 *no* XII, 11—12 ša-kin ‖ pi-qid; 24 *no* III 5 ša-ak-nu; KB vi (1) 78 *R* ii 17 lu-uš-ku-nu .... a-na ga-ti-ka. I 70 *d* 7 si-im-ma .... i-na zumrišu liš-kun-ma; III 43 *d* 17 (§§ 48; 49 *b*). — See also napišta šakanu = die (711 *col* 2, *med*).

šu-ku(-ki) see šu-dur(-ki). ~ šakbītu, Hommel, *Sem*, 500 *rm* 260 read šaqqaštu. ~ ša-ku-du, AV 7815 *ad* Anp iii 90 read ša-da-du.

c) erect, establish, build; in connection with madaktu (515, 516); qinnu of a bird; Anp ii 83 such & such [al] dannūtišunu iš-ka-nu-ni (ZA i 368/9; KB i 84/5); TP ii 6; Šamš ii 50 & dannūtu (262). — *pm* be situate {gelegen sein}. *del* 11 (12) *etc.* see Purātu (840 *col* 2); TP iii 60, 61 (see gisallu, end, 228 *col* 1). Anp iii 98; i 50.

d) place, put, appoint {anstellen} Sn ii 63; Anp i 76; IV^2 27 *b* 48, 49 (šu-kun, ip); K 2852+K 9662 i 13; KB vi (1) 582 *b* 14. Xammurabi-*letters* 25, 14 ša-ak-na-an-ni-a-ši-im, sie sind für uns bestellt.

e) K 183 *R* 13, 14 my eyes itti šarri bēlija šak-na (are directed toward the king) Hr^L 2; BA i 623.

f) put on. IV^2 56 iii 53; K 41 *b* 6 see šēnu, 2.

g) do, make, perform, accomplish, create {tun, machen, herstellen, veranstalten, schaffen} *etc.* Bu 91—5—9, 210 *O* 11, 12 ša at-tu-nu .... te-tip-pu-šа a-na eli ardēja šak-na-tu-nu (Hr^L 403). — adanna [(1)] Šamaš iš-ku-nam-ma (appointed; ZIMMERN, *Ritualtafeln*, 88; but see KB vi, 1, 480). — *del* 164 (183) a-bu-ba taš-kun; 172—5 (187, 189, 191, 193) taš-ku-nu (2 *sg m*). — çalūlšu šakanu, see çalūlu. — u-bur-ta iš-ku-nu-šu-nu-ti, IV^2 34 (K 2130) 3. — su-un-qu iš-ku-nu ‖ ibbašū nibrētu, SMITH, *Asurb*, 100, 18; also I 70 *d* 17, 18. — amāta šakanu, make an utterance, speak (of a priest, *etc.*) IV^2 *pll* 32, 33 & 33*; ZIMMERN, *Ritualtafeln*, *p* 88. — uzna šakanu see uznu (26, 27); BA ii 283 *rm*; KB vi (1) *pref* xiv; IV^2 31 *R* 18 (end) uz-na šu-kun, *etc.* — pānu šakanu (& Q^1) eli, ana, ana pān, ina see 811 *col* 1. — lišānu šakanu see lišānu, 499 & KB vi (1) 318, 319. — qūlu šakanu see qūlu. — puxra šakanu (& Q^1) see puxru (796 *col* 2). — šakanu ša rēši = resist see rēšu & HAUPT, *Papers Philad. Or. Club*, i ('94) 271 *rm* 29; *Proc. Am. Or. Soc.*, Mar-Ap., '94, cviii; GUTHE, *Ezra-Nehemiah* (SBOT) 70. — dumqu šakanu ‖ epešu (Q^1) see dumqu (255 *col* 2). — a-bi-ik-ta-šu-nu lu aš-kun, TP i 76, 77; iii 28 (27); viii 81 a-bi-ik-ti um-ma-ni-šu liš-ku-nu (3 *pl*) = defeat = šilmu šakanu, Sn i 21 aš-ta-kan ši-lim-šu; Šalm, *Ob*, 64 ši-lim-šu-nu aš-kun (+89); Asb i 55; iv 69; vii 116. — taxtā (Q & Q^1); tapdā; šaqalti; sikiptu (Q & Q^1; 758 *col* 1); kamāru (398 *col* 1) šakanu, see these nouns. — lītu (u danānu) šakanu see *pp* 260, 261 & 500. — šikkatu šakanu see šikkatu, 1. — sidirtu šakanu (& Q^1) see 748, 749. — ina zaqīpi šakanu (& Q^1) see 290 *col* 2. — ta-am-tu lu aš-ku-nu (or -nam)-ma V 33 iii 33, 34 (KB iii, 1, 143). — šu-ma šuk-na-an-ni, KB vi (1) 108 *c* 16, create me a child. — ša-kin namirti, H 75 *O* 11; also KB vi (1) 208, 46. — isinnu šakanu, H 80, 18 ina i-sin-ni šak-nu-uš. — H 79 (K 44) *R* 12, 13 nūra ta-šak-kan (= AB-GA-GA) see nūru (722 *col* 2) & KB vi (1) 329. — nigūtu šakanu (& Q^1 & Ꝟ) see 648 *col* 2. — šubarū šakanu see šubarū. — ṭēmu šakanu (& Q^1) see 356 *col* 1; K 81 *R* 5 ṭe-e-mu i-šak-kan-ga, Hr^L 274; BA i 201, 202 ✕ HALÉVY, *Rec. crit.*, '90 *no* 25; MEISSNER, 133. KB vi (1) 96, 33. — tapšuxtu *š cf* this noun. — gimillu šakanu (& Q^1) see gimillu (222) & MESSERSCHMIDT, 63, 17; Br 7260; WINCKLER, *Forsch.*, i 492, 493. — rēmūtu šakanu see rēmūtu & K 3515 *O* 14 ta-šak-ka-ni ri-e-mu ‖ tušarši salīmu.

h) with double *acc*: ul-li kalbi aš-kun-šu, Asb viii 28; +11, [(ic)] ši-ga-ru (*q. v.*) aš-kun-šu. V 56, 43 see § 53*d* & KB iii (1) 170, 171. V 25 *c-d* 27 abbuttum (see 12 *col* 1) i-ša-ak-kan-šu, Br 5269; H 60, 4; Z^B 59; 117. Xammurabi-*Louvre* ii 5, 6 mirītu u mašqītu lu aš-ku-un-ši-na-ši-im (§ 56*b*; KB iii, 1, 122); Br. M. 23154, 31 a watch šu-uk-na-aš-šu-nu-ši-im-ma, place over them.

i) it-ti a-xa-meš niš-ša-kin, we will band, work, together, KNUDTZON, 2, 3 (*cf* PEISER, KAS, 104: ša-kin); 115, 3 ša-ak-nu; 103, 2 šak-na-tu. — e-peš ardūti-ja it-ti-šu aš-kun, SMITH, *Asurb*, 287, 26; *cf* Asb ii 9; K 572 *R* 3 a-di-e liš-ku-nu; Asb i 123 a-na šu-kan a-di-e u sa-li-me; SMITH, *Asurb*. 42, 38; 290, 53; II 65 *O* ii 27 see sulummu (763 *col* 1). — pā šakanu itti see 75‥ *col* 2. Xammurabi-*letters* 22, 7—8 itti amēlē ta-ak-lu-tim šu-ku-un-ma.

BA iv 453; 492: šakanu itti, sich mit jem. ins Vernehmen setzen.

intr. — perhaps IV² 9 *b* 2 ina er-çi-ti ina ša-ka-ni (be, exist) Br 6818.

S^b 281 ma-ra | MAR | ša-ka-nu (H 22, 428) Br 5820. S^c 45 ga-al | GAL (H 14, 172) Br 2258; S^c 148 ga-a | MAL (H 21, 391) Br 54?1, 6818. H 100, 33 (112, 26) MA-MA | G[A]-GA | ša-ka-nu ma-ru-u (II 26 *a-b* 37) Br 5487, 6832, 6833. — 109, 34 (112, 27) MA?]-AL | GAL š xa-am-ṭu (II 26 *a-b* 35) Br 5442, 6125. — 109, 35 (112, 28) MAR | GAR | š (II 26 *a-b* 36) Br 2253, 5820, 6810. H 47—8 (= D 91—2) 10 (+ 12) IN-GAR(-RE-EŠ) = iš-ku-un (& nu); 14 (+ 16) IN-GAR-RE(-NE) = i-ša-ka-an (& nu); 18 (+ 20) IN-NA-AN-GAR(-RE-EŠ) = iš-ku-un (& nu)-šu; 22 (+ 24) IN-NA-AN-GAR-RE(-NE) = i-šak-ka-an(-u)-šu; & GA-GA in 26, 28, 30, 32; *cf* II 15 *a-b* 19. V 11 *d* 31 see Br 8744, 11624, 11626, 11628 & bikîtum. II 39 *g-h* 56 UX-MU-MA šur-ru-u & ša-ka-nu, Br 8308, 8309. — V 28 *a-b* 25 see ša-xa-an.

Q¹ iš(t)ta(k)kan; 1 *sg* aš-tak-ka-na (§ 92); il-ta-kan, Peiser, *Vertr.*, cxxx 9; Sp II 265 *a no* vii 9; § 53 *a*; *pl* ni-il-ta-kan, 81—2—4, 104, 7 (Thompson, *Reports*, 240); isakan (§ 51); 1 *sg* asikin (§ 35, *add*); pm šitkun (> šitakunu, additions to § 37 *d*; §§ 88 *b* & 94).

a) place, put {legen} w. double *acc.* K 655 *R* 7 ina si-par-ri a-sa-kan-šu, Hr^L 132. Sn *Kui* 2, 36 (ana) šit-kun šêpi amêli, for the landing of troops. — K 2619 iv 21 (KB vi, 1, 66—7). *del* 200 (220) well! bake ku-ru-um-ma-ti-šu ši-tak-ka-ni (= ip) ina re-ši-šu; 202 (222) iš-tak-ka-an (*m* for *f*) ina re-ši-šu.

b) deposit {niederlegen}. Neb viii 25 the royal treasures ul aš-ta-ak-ka-an kirbi mâtitân; *cf* ZA i 341, 12; ii 128 *b* 14. KB iii (2) 4, 57—8 my royal picture i-na te-me-en-na lu aš-ta-ak-ka-an; Mer.-Balad.-stone ii 46—7; Asb iii 117 see simtu (768); also 81—6—7, 209, 25 (BA iii 260).

c) encamp, erect, establish, build {lagern, errichten, bauen} *etc.* see mit-tak (622 *col* 2); Knudtzon, 320 (madaktu) il-ta-kan. Esh iii 55 who like a fish šit-ku-nu šub-tu (had taken up abode) in the water. KB vi (1) 48, 40 (*Zû*-legend) ina kib-rat er-bit-ti ši-tak-ka-na (= ip) ma-xa-zi-ka. See also AV 8354. — be situate {gelegen sein} Sn iii 69, 70; I 48, 21 (ša .... šit-ku-na-at).

d) direct, turn {lenken}. H 179, 78 kib-si iš-ta-kan (see additions to IV² 19). iš-ta-kan pa-ni-šu I 43, 41.

e) place, put, appoint; determine {einsetzen, anstellen}. Asb iii 104 the kings whom iš-tak-ka-na qâtâ-a-a (Smith, *Asurb*, 154, 36); iv 105 governors aš-tak-ka-nu e-li-šu-un. Sarg *Cyl* 16 (3 *sg*); V 56, 32 whosoever .... il-ka il-tak-nu. Merod.-Balad.-stone iii 20 see pulukku (807 *col* 2). NE 66, 38 iš-tak-nu mu-ta u ba-la-ṭa (determine), but *cf* KB vi (1) 480.

f) make {machen} in various shades of meanings. Neb *Bors* i 18 xurâça namri (& namram, I 65 *a* 30) ša-al-la-re-iš (lu) aš-tak (*var* ta-ak)-ka-an. See also abiktu, šilmu, lîtu, sidru, sidirtu. NE 17, 44—5; 19, 39—40 to the priest of Anu & Bêl iš-tak-ka-nu šu-me-e ši-i-ri (*var* še-e-ri) e-pa-a iš-tak-ka-nu ka-çu (*var* -ça-a)-ti it(*var* iš)-taq-qu-u (√šaqû) mê na-da-a-te; KB vi (1) 188—9. — Creat.-*frg* III 74 puxru šit-ku-na-at-ma (80, šit-ku-nu-ma). — V 66 *a* 18, 19 Nebo ... ša a-na ta-na-da-a-ti šit-ku-nu (is made); — *b* 16 i-na pi-i-ka el-li liš-tak-ka-nu du-un-ki-ja. Pinches, *Texts*, 16 *no* 4 *R* 10 (end) liš-tak-ka-na xi-du-tu; NE VI 207; K 610 *R* 9—10 nišê pi-i paṭar parzilli i-sa-ak-nu (Hr^L 310); K 525, 24 (Hr^L 252); AJSL xiv 179. — K 233, 7 the gods uzna rapaš-ti u lib-bi rap-šu il-tak-nu-ku-nu-ši, Winckler, *Forsch.*, i 469. H 54, 6 çib-tu (*q. v.*) iš-ṭu (= ta)-ka-an.

g) Sn v 72 their nobles ša paṭar šibbi xurâçi šit-ku-nu (which were girded with; I 44, 51; see paṭru).

h) bring to one's side i(s)si; often in Anp. isi'a a-si-kin, ii 53, 72, 103; iii 58, 60.

Q^tn IV² 26 *b* 60, 61 tânîxa marçam iš-ta-na-ka-an (= BA-DA-RA-AB-GA-GA), the sickly plaint is made to him, AJSL xix 225 (but see § 98). Knudtzon,

75, 6 il-ta-nak-kan-u(a)n (*ps* or *pr*); GAR-MEŠ-un, 30 *R* 6; see also 612 *col* 1, NOTE 1. — L^4 i 27 ṭe-e-mu aš-ta-nak-kan a-na rabûti.

𝔍 see KB i 202, 203 on II 65 iv 23 u-ša-ka-nu-šu-ma (= *pl*); *ip* IV^2 31 *R* 18 šu-kin rēšēka, HROZNY, WZKM xvii 324 ≍ KB vi (1) 88, 89.

𝔍^t K 5481 ii 2 kilu uš-tak-kan-ma.

Š — *a*) causative of šakanu *trans.* Sarg *Khors* 35 su-lum-mu-u u-ša-aš-kin (1 *sg*); K 3182 ii 14 tu-ša-aš-kan kap-pa. — establish. Sn iii 71 at the foot of the mountain ka-ra-ši u-ša-aš-kin-ma; 82—7—4, 42 *O* 10 gu-gal-lum šamē erçitim mu-ša-aš-ki-in xi-gal-la; Neb iv 35; AV 5597. — direct. K 2675 *O* 13 the way to Egypt u-ša-aš-ki-na šēpā-šu-un; Asb ix 8. SCHEIL, *Nabd*, x 6 the renewal of the abodes of the gods u-ša-aš-kin qātu-u-a. — order, determine. KB iii (2) 92, 47 u-ša-aš-ki-ni (3 *pr*) i-na ter-ti-ja; 64, 25—27; V 63 *b* 9 (+ 5, end, iš-šak-na; ZA v 409). — combine, unite. TP vi 46 (§ 84) & see pū, 1 (789 *col* 1, above). — place (?). V 35, 4 u-ša-aš-ki-na çīru-šu-un. KB iii (2) 62 *col* i 8 into the mouth of the people mu-ša-aš-ki-in the fear of the great gods. See also I 69 *a* 22 šu-uš-ki-na-a-ma; *c* 55; I 68 *b* 28 (BA i 398 on *ll* 24—28); K^M 9, 13. — bring to one's side Šamaš i 43 the Assyrians it-ti-šu u-še-š-kin.

b) causative of šakanu *intrans.* settle, cause to dwell, let be {wohnen lassen, bleiben lassen} V 33 v 8 lu-u-ša-aš-ki-in-ma (1 *sg*), see KB iii (1) 144—5 (subject: Marduk). Neb ii 8 the reverence for his godhead u-ša-aš-ki-in ina libbi-ja ‖ ušabši (iii 1); I 68 *no* 1 *col* ii 15 + 28 (šu-uš-kin).

Š^t V 33 i 40 šarru muš-ta-aš-kin (or -qi?) kib-rat ar-ba-'i, KB iii (1) 138—9. K 168 *R* 7 nu-sa-aš-kin-šu-nu, Hr^L 437. *Cf* KB vi (1) 204 *col* 3, 2 ki lu-uš-tak(q)-k(q)an-ma, + 300 *col* 1, 14 (= but what shall I do?).

𝔑 iššakin (§ 49*b*). — *a*) be placed, appointed, made, found {gelegt, bestellt, gemacht, gefunden werden}. III 43 *c* 15 future officials ša iš-ša-ki-nu-ma. Neb *Bors* ii 31 *Neb* lū šarru zāninan li-iš-ša-ki-in i-na pi-i-ka (may be found in thy mouth); *cf* KB iii (2) 55; 86—7 on I 69 *c* 52; KB vi (1) 62—3, 31. KB iii (2) 56 *col* 2, 26 see damiqtu (*pl*), 255; & V 66 *col* 2, 28—9. Asb i 125 *cf* sulummū, *b* (763 *col* 1). I 49 *c* 21 ina ma-kal-ti (on which see ZIMMERN, *Beiträge zur Babyl. Religion*, 89 *foll*; KB vi (1) 572) bārūti šīrē tukulti iš-šak-nu-nim-ma, KB ii 292 *ad* 122. I 35 *no* 2, 6 Nebo without whom in heaven la iš-ša-ka-nu mil-ku. ABEL & WINCKLER, 60—61, 17 $^{(aban)}$ GIŠ-ŠIR-GAL ina bīt ilāni rabûti ana si-ma-a-ti na-aš-kin (*pm*), + *R* 19 gurgurru ka-a-ta liš-ša-kin-ka. — be built, erected. Sp III 586 + Rm III 1. 16; T^M ii 9 *etc.* see naptanu, 713 *col* 2. Also V 31 *a* 11; *d* 21 *etc.* (or šaki-in?). — be changed into. KB vi (1) 60—1, 13 zi-im lab(?rib?)-bi taš-ša-kin-ma. — befall, happen to {befallen} *etc.*; § 84. IV^2 3 *b* 27—8, 29—30 the muruç qaqqadi a-na amēli iš-ša-kin (= MU-UN-GA-GA); also *a* 13—14. IV^2 57 *b* 1 li-šak-na re-e-mu, grace befall him; *cf* ZA i 40, 28; & see parimu, 832 *col* 1. — lie down {sich legen} KNUDTZON, 320: iš-ša-kan-aš-ši.

b) come to pass, happen, occur {geschehen, werden, eintreten}. TP v 88 see rēçūtu; also Sarg *Ann* 35. Asb ix 58 see sunqu, 772 *col* 2 (& SMITH, *Asurb*, 286, 18). *del* 174 (192) see xušaxxu (345 *col* 1). — Asb iv 42 the people ša it-ti Šamaš-šumukin iš-šak-nu, who had been brought over to Š.

𝔑^t ittaška(i)n, §§ 49*b*; 97. be placed, happen, befall {gelegt, getan werden, befallen, eintreten}. IV^2 7 *a* 1—2, 19—20 ar-rat limut-tim kīma gal-li-e ana amēli it-taš-kan (= BA-NI-IN-GAR); *a* 3—4, 5—6 qūlu kūru (& la ṭābu) e-li-šu it-taš-kan. IV^2 19 *b* 36 see çūmu; Br 5820. K 13, 19 u et-ti su-un-qu ina māti-šu-nu it-taš-kin. Hr^L 281: when need came upon their country. ZA iv 233 & v 74 (below) e-taš-kan; Br 5269.

𝔑^{tn} K^M 6, 83 (*var*) it-ta-na-aš-ka-nam-ma, + 7, 19; also gloss to GAR-GAR-NU K 748, 4 (it-ta-na-aš-kan). THOMPSON, *Reports*, 248.

NOTE. — T. A. has such forms: Q (Lo) 5, 12 i-na lib-bi-ka la-a i-ša-ki-in (+35 ša-ki-in, ip?), thou doest not know, ZA v 20; DELATTRE, PSBA xiii 544, & again, BEZOLD, *Diplomacy*, xxx. (Ber) 11 *R* 4 la-a ta-ša-ga-an i-na lib-bi-ka. (Lo) 2, 23 it[ti-]ka i ni-ša-ki-in, we will make an alliance with thee, ZA v 152, 153. 3 *f sg* ti-eš-ku-nu. ip šu-ku-un, appoint (Lo) 44, 27; 1, 64, establish, bring about! *pm* 3 *sg m* ša-ka-an (Lo) 13, 5; *f* ša-ak-na-ti, (Ber) 104, 32 (ZA vi 258 *rm* 1); 2 *m* šumma ša-ak-na-ta-ni (Lo) 28, 47, since thou hast appointed me. ša-ki-in (Ber) 78, 3 *rm* is; 198 *R* 13 i-ša-ak-ni. — Q[t] (Lo) 19, 31 ji-iš-ta-ka-nu. — 3 *pm* ki-i it-ti-ja na-aš-ku-nu (Lo) 2, 29; ZA v 17. *ac* it-ti-ja a-na na-aš-ku-u-ni (Lo) 2, 25; ZA v 152. — 3[t] (Lo) 2, 27 šumma ta-at-ta-aš-ka-na, ZA v 152—3.

DERr. — maškanu, 3 (604 *col* 1), šikittu, šukuttu, & the following 8:

šaknu *1. f* šakintu, *adj* made, prepared, ready {gemacht, hergerichtet, bereit, fertig} *etc.* IV² 23 *no* 1 *col* ii 25—6, 27—8 see makkūru, 539 *col* 2 end of first §.

šaknu *2. c. st.* šakan & šakin (× AV 7839 ša-laṭ) § 65, 1; AV 7835; ZK i 10 *rm* 1; BA ii 47, 48; literally: the appointed; thus: deputy, prefect, governor {Stellvertreter, Statthalter}. D[H] 13; BROWN-GESENIUS, 688 סגן borrowed in Hebr. from Babylonian, KAT³ 649. STRECK, ZA xv 306: Landesgouverneur, dem die innere Verwaltung oblag; nāgiru = Militärpräfekt den Heerbann kommandierend. id GAR (§ 9, 84) + nu (complement), Br 11979; *pl* šaknūti. — IV² 39 *a* 2 Adadnirari ša-ka-an erçit ilāni; 14 Pu-di-il ša-ak-ni (il) Bēl (§ 72*a*); K 6303, 4, the deputy representative of Bēl; I 6 *no* vii 1; Sarg *Nimr* 1; *Cyl* 1; Esh i 34. V 60 ii 5 kurmat (amēl) šak-ni ša Ēsaggil. Merod.-Balad.-stone v 20 lu (amēl) šak-nu lu (amēl) ša-tam lu (amēl) xa-za-an-nu, KB iii (1) 192—3. V 55, 52; 56, 17 + 18 + 22 + 23 ša-kin; (amēl) ša-kin, KB iv 94, 20; Rm 187, 6—7 (KB iv 106 *no* 4); Nabd-Cyr, *Chron*, ii 22 (BA ii 220—1). WINCKLER, *Forsch*, i 498 *R* 4 (amēl) ša-kan u (amēl) ša-pi-ru. III 9, 37 ša-ki-ni-ja, my prefect. Rm 157, 9 (amēl) ša-kin-ni-šu (KB iv 124). K 94 (Hr[L] 287) *R* 8 (amēl) šak-ni-ku-nu šu-u. Anp i 89 (amēl) šak-nu ša ra-me(*var* ma)-ni-a, my own deputy (§ 55*c*). Asb iv 104 (amēl) ša-kin *pl* (amēl) qēpūni ši-kin qātā-ja aš-tak-ka-na (§ 92) e-li-šu-un. Sarg *Cyl* 16 Sargon who (amēl) šu-par-šāqē-šu (amēl) šak-nu-ti eli-šu-nu iš-tak-ka-nu, had placed his generals as prefects over them; Rp 11; *Ann* XIV 10 (ša-ak-nu-ti); *bronze* 23 (amēl) GAR-nu-ti; *bull* 20 a-na (amēl) NAM-u-ti (see below); LYON, *Sargon*, 79. GAR-MEŠ, KNUDTZON, 69, 4 *etc.* (see *ibid* 229).

NOTE. — See also aškandu (115 *col* 1) and add: JENSEN, ZA vii 174 ašgandu > šagannu (ZA vi 351); Nabd 314, 16 (see below) as compared with 665, 2 aš-kan-du.

šakintu. *f* to šaknu, 2. KB iv 122 *no* XI, (= 82—5—22, 34) 12 + 19 (sal) ša-kin-te; III 47 *no* 8, 4 (sal) ša-ki-in-te, the deputy's wife? see also *ibid* 132—33 I (K 321) 5 & *rm* † (ZA xiii 267—69 on this text): Händlerin (?).

šak(i)nūtu, prefecture, governorship {Statthalterschaft}. SMITH, *Asurb*, 35, 13 his servants a-na šarrū-ti (amēl) NAM-u-ti (*var* GAR-nu-u-ti, ZK ii 313 *no* 5) eli šunūti u-pa-qi-da (3 pr). V 56, 28 whosoever a-na ša-kin-u-ti ša (māt) Namar iššakkinu. Sarg, *bull* 20 a-na (amēl) (EN)-NAM-u-ti; *stele* i 35; Rp i 21. III 43 *a* 15 eqlu bīt ša-ak-nu-ti.

(amēl) **ša-kan-na** prefect, governor {Statthalter} Nabd 314, 16.

šiknu *c. st.* šikin; properly: laying, placing, putting in position; then:

a) what is placed, put, made = object {Gegenstand}. — *α.* structure, edifice {Bauwerk, Gebäude}. Neb *Grot*, (I 65) ii 23 with gold, silver *etc.* uza'in ši-ki-in-šu (*i. e.* of Ezida); *cf* KB iii (2) 92 *col* 3, 7; ZA i 340, 21; narkabta (*q. v.*) ši-kin la maxri, Creat.-*frg* IV 50. — *β.* heap {Haufe} Esh, *Negub* Cylinder 10 ina ši-kin eprāti, BA iii 206, 207. — *γ.* picture, statue {Bildniss, Denkmal}. V 60 i 10 (of the sun-god) ši-kin-šu u simātišu (had been lost); written GAR-šu, i 14; iii 21; *cf* i 16 ça-lam-šu u simātišu, BA i 278. Perh. Bu 88—5—12, 77 vi 12 i-ki-lu ši-ki-in-šu-un (of the gods and goddesses) BA iii 248, 249 *rm* ***. — *δ.* creature, created being {Kreatur, Geschöpf}. I 27 *no* 2, 70 lū amēlūta ši-kin napišti *etc.* Asb iii 136 *U.* ši-kin qātā-ja, a creature of my hands; iv 104: but KB vi (1) 333 = he who has been appointed by my hand = my šaknu.

b) nature, kind, condition {Natur, Wesen, Art} 83—1—18, 2 (Hr[L] 391) 9 ši-ki-in murçi-ja an-ni-ja-u, the nature of this my sickness. See AJSL xv 141; MARTIN, *Rec. Trav.*, xxiv 106, 107; also *cf* IV² 60* C *R* 12. Esh v 42 šēdē u lamassē ša abni ša ki-i pi-i šik-ni-šu-nu (BA i 278) ir-ti lim-ni u-tar-ru (according to their position?). I 7 *E* 3 (*var*) end: ŠA (= GAR, *i. e.*, šikin)-šu; MEISSNER & ROST, 58 (der gesetzt war wie ein Gurkenkörper); see also I 44, 72; but rather ša-šu, *cf* šāšu, 1.

c) execution {Ausführung} ši-kin ṭe(-e)-me-ja, of my order(s) see 356 *col* 1 (*med*).

d) sediment of a river, mud {Satz des Flusses, Schlamm} JENSEN. AV 8206. K 4386 i 47 A-LAL-A-[illegible]-DA = ši-kin na-a-ri, preceded by ušultum ša IM (115 *col* 2). II 48 *e-f* 37 (Br 11639). V 27 *a-b* 14. SMITH, *Asurb*, 192, 13 see rušumtu; V 32 *a-c* 24, 25 see qadû, 6. Sn *Kui* 2, 35—7 the shore of the ocean ša a-na ši-ik-nu a-na e-li-e sisē u šitkun šēpi amēli la na-ṭu, which owing to mud (sediment) was not fit for the disembarking of horses and the landing of troops.

e) name of a street. sûqi šik-nu, KB iv 172 ii 3.

f) šikin adanni, see ZIMMERN, *Ritualtafeln*, *p* 88.

NOTE. — Should Creat.-*frg* IV 4+6 be read ši-kin-ka instead of ši-mat-ka?

šikânu. AV 8193 = šik-nu ša nāri, sediment of the river {Satz des Flusses} KB vi (1) 476. See qadû 6, qadûtu (908 *cols* 1/2) Br 2817.

šukānu. IV² 60* C *R* 16 pe-ti qimaxxu (opened is the *q*) ir-šu-u šu-ka-nu-u-a. I 27 *no* 2, 30 see KB i 118, 119 (das Niedergelegte), MEISSNER & ROST, 28. ZIMMERN, *Ritualt.*, 68, 12 a-du šu-ka-ni-ša.

šukunnû. Z[B] viii 64 šu-kun-ni-e ili u ištar (Machenschaften).

šakkanu *1.* 82—7—4, 42 *R* 5 bu-u-lum ša-ak-ka-an u nammaššû, PSBA xx 152 *foll.* *Cf* V 40 *a-b* 50 UR(?)-TAB-MA = (bu-lum) šak-kan & see V 50 *a* 15, 16 UR-TAB-MA = ša er-ba še-pa-šu; thus perhaps = quadruped {Vierfüssler} AV 7822.

šakkanu *2.* V 32 *no* 4 *c-d* 45 GI-NER-LAL = šak-ka-nu = qa-an .... (AV 7824); *cf* II 24 *a-b* 18 (Br 251[P]); II 34 *c* 33. Also perh. IV² 6 *b* 43, 44 GIŠ-ŠA(= LIB)-KA-NA-TA = šakannu (?) AJSL xix 206 & *ibid rm* 18: probably = reeds.

šikkanu *cf* sikkanu (757 *col* 2).

šukunnû (Br 12185). See kanû, 1 Š (405 *col* 2); H 74, 17 GAR[-GAR]-GIŠ-SAR = šu-kun-ni GIŠ-SAR (= kirî); *ibid* 18. AV 8433. M[S] 94 from √šakanu.

šukinnu, šukînu (properly: *ac* Š³ √kânu, 1; 400 *col* 2) homage, prostration, worship {Huldigung, Verehrung, Anbetung}; ZIMMERN, *Ritualtafeln*, 95. K 3812 (8812) iii 19 see kamasu Q¹ (397 *col* 1, above); AJSL xvii 140, 141. KB vi (1) 321. II 35 (*g-*)*h* 29, 30 šu]-kin-nu, with ikribu, labân appi, *etc.*; the ‖ were ending in -çu & -nu; ZA iv 271; AV 8429. V 30 *e-f* 25 id (Br 860) with gloss (su-ub) = šu-kin-nu (H 11 & 214, 74; AV 8550); 26, = bu-ul-ṭu SE (= nada)-nu; see *p* 164 *col* 2, above; for the id see perhaps II 62 *a-b* 70 = ša šap-la-ti i-ta-mu-u, one who speaks lowly, humbly.

šakkanak(k)u. AV 7823. id NER-ARAD (§ 9, 261: Machthaber). I 48 *no* 5, 2 (6, 2) NER-ARAD Bâbili, JENSEN, 477. V 62 *no* 1, 4 *etc.* Neb *Bors* i 6 *Neb* ša-ak-ka-na-ku la a-ne-xa; & V 34 *a* 4, as compared with Neb i 71 NER-ARAD la a-ne-xa; ix 64 Nebukadrezzar ša-ak-ka-na-ak-ku it-bi-šu. V 35, 18 ru-bi-e u šak-kan-nak-ka (§ 67, 4). K 2012 *R* 7 NER]-ARAD = šak-ka-nak-ku (OPPERT, ZA ii 302; Br 9195). IV² 1 *b* 42, 43 GIŠ-BEL šak-ka-nak-ka (*var* ki) (= SAG .... LA) erçi-tim; JENSEN, ZA x 248. For id see also V 30 *c-d* 20—22; II 30 coloph. 14; V 65 *a* 9 (ZK ii 261). K 2619 ii 13 šakkanakku eq(k,g)-su, KB vi (1) 68: einen gewaltsamen Statthalter. On Asb iii 63 (amêl) TIG-EN-NA & Rm 338 *O* 13 (ZA iv 437) see ZA ix 274 *no* 3; x 78; M[S] *pl* 21. — id NER = e-mu-qu (S[b] 2, 14); ARAD = zi-ka-ru, ar-du. — ZA iii 138, 16 u šak-kan-nak-ku i-gam-mar.

HINCKS: ruler, vice-regent (*cf* GGA '77, 1483). — G § 32 > šakan (= שכן) + akku. — LYON, *Sargon*, 79 NOTE 2 (on *Bull* 2) √šaq (*c. st.* of šaqû, high) + kanâku (gate) — BALL, RP² iii 194 & *rm* 1: a priestly rather than a secular personage; perhaps: highpriest. IDEM, *Light from the East*, 216: the grand gate-warden. — Sargon called šakkanak Bābili: SCHRADER· Hohepriester von Babylon; LEHMANN, *Šamaššumukīn*: Oberpriester (?), priesterlicher Statthalter; following WINCKLER, *Sargon*, *pref.* xxxvi *rm* 6; WINCKLER, *Forsch.*, i 258 *rm* 2 (on Nebukadrezzar, KB iii, 1, 165): Sargon called himself šakkanak Bābili, instead of šar Bābili, after the conquest of Babylon; also see KAT^3 73 JENSEN, ZA i 403; vii 174 *rm* 1; x 248: ša kanak(k)i, he that is in charge of locking the city's gate. WINCKLER, *Forsch.*, ii (2) 314 ('99): der Mann des Siegelns (כנך). BA iv 456 *ad* Xammurabi-letter 24, 7 governor (as KING) BROCKELMANN, ZA xvi 391 on the question why the kings of Assyria preferred to call themselves *š* of Babylon rather than kings of Babylon.

šuk-nu-še, Anp i 42 *etc.* see kannšu Š (409—10) & Br 7333.

šakassi, AV 7712, Br 8448 see šandabakku.

šakapu (AV 7803) iš-ki-pu, see sakapu (757 *col* 2).

šakapu whence naškapu, *q. v.* (739 *col* 2).

ša-kap-pi, AV 7804 see kappu, 1 (420 *col* 1).

šik-pi-e-tum see sikiptu, (758 *col* 1).

ša-kaç-çi, Br 8470 *ad* IV^2 21, 1 B *O* 30, 31 ša-kaç-çi read ša gaç-çi & see gaççu (220).

šakaru. be or become drunk }trunken sein oder werden} AV 7805. *pr* iš-ku-ru MEISSNER & ROST, 33 *rm* 58; K 613 (Hr^L 85) *R* 5—6 these 3 men ša-ak-ra-nu-tu šu-nu, (are drunkards) ki-ma i-šak-ki-ru (as soon as they drink) PSBA xxiii 61. Perh. K 164, 33 i-ša-ki-ru, BA ii 636. II 27 *a-b* 20 SE = ša-ka-ru, S^b 346; Br 4423.

ℑ perhaps V 45 iii 48 tu-šak-kar.

Derr. — these 4:

šikaru. intoxicating drink, date-wine }Rauschtrank, Dattelwein} AV 8194; § 65, 9 = *σίκερα*; & שֵׁכָר; HAUPT, AJPh v 72. ZK ii 205; ZA iv 337; vii 150; BA i 280; KAT^3 600. ið BI (or K(G)AŠ) Br 5126; H 20, 378; ið in *c. t.*, but also spelled out, Nabd 80, 1 ši-ka-ri; T. A. ið (Ber) 92, 23; (Lo) 35, 22 *etc.*; (Ber) 71, 10 ši-ka-ra ul išti, ZA v 138. I 65 *a* 21 see dašpu (270 *cols* 1/2) & *b* 32. K 2801 *R* 46 see kurūnu, 439 *col* 2, *med*; & Bu 88—5—12, 75 + 76 iv 12; also šadū, 3 (end). K 3182 iii 45 (end) ku-ru-un(-ši-na) explained as ši-kar ši-bi-'-i ka-a-ri (+ 46). IV^2 14 *no* 1, 30, 31 ina ši-kar iz-za-zu (& uš-ša-bu) ta-ši-la-ti (& ri-ša-a-ti) KB vi (1) 56, 57. K^M 2, 29 ši-kar aš-na-an. D 85, 16 ši-ka-ra (also ZA iii 395, 10; x 83—4) i-na na-di (>< Br 5155). ši-ka-ru ma-zu-u see mazū, 2 (517 *col* 1); V 52 *b* 52—3 see mazū, 1 (517 *col* 1); niqū ša šikari, ši-kar niqū see niqū (718 *col* 1, *med*); pelū ša šikari (803 *cols* 1/2); kannu ša *š* (406 *col* 1); kūt *š* (456 *col* 2); šuršummu *š* (*q. v.*). ZA iv 157 *no* 4, 2 ši-kar ti-gi-i; ZA vi 85, perhaps: circular bowl or dish; or a certain drink; *cf* the German: Bowle. i-ši-id bīti ši-ka-ri-im, MEISSNER, 122 *no* 35: Grundgeschoss des Bierhauses. V 27 *e-f* 18 IM-TIK-BI-TIN(?)-NA = qa-du[-ut?] ši-ka-ri, & see *a-b* 8, Br 9856. V 32 *a-b* 25 karpat šikari (§ 23). ZK ii 216, 2 nam-xar ši-ka-ri (681 *cols* 1/2). (amêl) ša BI na(-a)-ši-šu (>< AV 7689) *etc.* = wine-seller }Weinschenk} often in *c. t.*, Nabd 116, 42; ša bīt šikari = butler }Kellermeister} BA i 536, 636. II 61 *c-d* 19 É-TIN-NA = bīt ša [šikari?]. V 60 *b* 4 BI-SAG = finest, choice šikaru = kurunnu. On the ingredients of šikaru see BA i 524.

šikru *1.* perhaps intoxication, drunkenness, the condition of being drunk }Rausch, Berauschtheit}. Creat.-*frg* III 136 ši-ik-ru ina ša-te-e xa-ba-çu zu-um-r[i], KB vi (1) 20—1; 323. AV 8209. V 30 *g-h* 25, 26 NAG (im-me-li) = ši-ik-ru (H 11 & 216, 76; 215, 25); NAG = *š* ša-tu-u (H 11 & 216, 77; 215, 26) Br 874, 875.

šakkūru. *adj* drunken, intoxicated }trunken, berauscht} § 65, 28. AV 7805, 7833. II 27 *a-b* 21, 22 BI-SE-SE-KI = šak-ku-ru-um, Br 5144; BI-NAG-NAG = *š* ša ši-ka-ri, Br 878; 5142.

šakrānu drunkard }Trunkenbold} see šakaru, Q.

šakru, AV 7836 see sakru, 2 (758 *col* 2), *ad* IV^2 31 *R* 28 šak-ru u ça-mu-u, the drunken & the thirsty }der Trunkene und der Durstige}; so also HROZNY, WZKM xvii (03) 328: a combination like raggu u çēnu = bad & good; or çixir rabī, small (&) great, a circumlocation for: every body. šakru u çamū in IV^2 31 used with special reference to context.

šaki(r)ru. a vessel }ein Gefäss{. H 11 & 216, 81 = II 22 *d-e* 28 ša-ki-ir ša-ki-ir-ru. id also H 120 *R* 19 DUK-SAKIR-RA & *cf* REISNER, *Hymnen*, 130, 13. Br 885, 886. AV 7810, 7811.

šakiru. a plant }eine Pflanze{ K 4174 *O* *a-b* 37 ša-ki-ra = U (or ŠAM) (= GUR?); followed by ša-ki-ra = U-KI-AN-UD. *cf* ZA xvii 180 *rm* 3 perhaps ‖ iṭṭittu.

šakirū. HOMMEL, *Sum. Lesest.*, 96 *ad* 82—8—16 *O* 1/2 ša-ki-ru-u bolt }Riegel{; perhaps also gloss in II 33 *a* 9.

šak-ka-ru-u. V 26 *f* 51 some part or kind of the gišimmaru; AV 7825.

šu-kur(?)-ru = d(ṭ)a-i-mu. V 28 *e-f* 15; AV 1809, 8435. K 883, 22 (iṣ) šu-kur-ra ina bi-rit tulê^{pl}-ia a-šak-kan-ka (BA ii 633; 645). ZŠ iii 28 mamit paṭri siparri u (iṣ) šu-kur-ri upaššar; & *var* GIŠ-ŠI-KAK; also viii 60; ZŠ *p* 55: spear }Speer{.

šik(g,q)ru *2.* S^{b} 375 ga-am | | ši-ik-ru, AV 8200, Br 1216. Same id in S^{b} 374 with gloss zu-bu = gam-lum (221 *col* 1). HOMMEL: a weapon }eine Waffe{. 83—1—18, 1330 ii 20 id with gloss ga-am = ši-ik-rum ša GIR (= paṭri). See also V 46 *a-b* 3 where MUL (*i. e.* kakkab) + id (S^{b} 375) = kakku ša qāt (il) Marduk.

šikru *3.* K 6012 + K 10684, *col* iii NU-GIG = šik(g,q)-ru. Perhaps part of the body, or an organism. See K 159, 11 šumma SA-TI (= bamātu, swelling, ulcer) eli kubši NU-SI u šikru išidṣa BAR, PSBA xxv 23 *rm* 2. Perhaps also II 43 *f* 19 ši-ik-ru[m?].

ši-ki-ru, Br 13996, AV 8415 on K 4560, 8 .... AK-DA = ši-ki-ru; but M^{S} *pl* 12 reads si-ki-ru.

šikirtu (?). ZA iii 136, 11 (SU?) ši-kir-tu gam-ru; 13/14 ittadin kaspa ½ ma-na lib-bu-u (SU) ši-kir-ti-šu gab-bi.

'š'ukkutu. 83, 1—18, 1332 iv 18 DAR = 'š'uk-ku-tum.

šīktum (?). ši-ik-tum = la-ga-u (see 476) M^{S} 94 *col* 1 quotes Camb 4, 2 ana (ṣubāt) šik-tum ša (ilat) Bēlit Sippar, & explains the word as = garment; see also ZA iv 109, 60 ana ši-ik-tu ša (il) Marduk.

V 15 *c-d* 23 among a list of garments we have 'š'ik-ka-tum = KU-ṬU-SAR-DA, *i. e.* a tied KU-ṬU; ṬU = takāltu, repository }Behälter{ thus šikkatum a purse which can be tied, or tied around one }ein zu- oder umbindbarer Geldbeutel{, or bag, in general (KB vi, 1, 491). KU-ṬU = sūnu (770 *col* 1). See šikkatu, 3.

šikkatu *1.* AV 8200. — *a*) point, peak, mountaintop }Spitze, Bergspitze{ TP iii 18 see xuršu (341 *col* 2, below) & HAUPT, BA iii 580 *rm* * = שִׂכָּה barbed iron, Job, 40, 31. — *b*) germ, sprout }Keim, Spross{ or the like; ‖ pirxu (828 *col* 2) & im-bu-'-u (55 *col* 2). — *c*) ‖ li-ki-e li-ti (500 *col* 2, *ll* 1, 2) control, triumph, victory. rab šikkati = commander, victor }Befehlshaber, Sieger{. Rm 338 *O* 5, 6 ... GE-GE = ma-li[-ku]; Š]IK-AT(? AD?)-GE-GE = ra-ab šik-k[a-ti] M^{S} *pl* 21; also perhaps Nabd 1099, 2 officer rab šik-kat.

šikkatūtu. *abstr. n.* Craig-*frg* 1 *col* i *c* 27 (šik-ka-tu-tu); III 41 (& 99) šu-par tam-xa-ri ra-ab šik[-ka-tu-(u)-ti], KB vi (1) 314 perhaps: Heeresspitze; but rather: chief, supreme in authority.

šikkatu *2.* fence? }Zaun?{. H 73, 5—6 gan-na-ti šik-kat mu-sa-ri-e u-ša-ak-ka-ak.

šikkatu *3.* NE XII *col* ii 1 (+22) see pūru, 1 (825 *col* 2) & KB vi (1) 259: whose breast is not .... like the bowl of a box; *ibid* 491 ‖ šappatu bag }Beutel{; *ad del* 72 (76) quoting 83, 1—18, 1330 i 5 (ša-ka-an) = šik-ka-tum; 6 (ša-man, or niš?), same id = šap-pa-tum. K 10040, 3—5 (M^{S} *pl* 16) Br 10813. According to ZŠ *p* 60: Alum }Alaun{. See also IV² 55 i *R* 23 & 28 (of a wood) GIŠ + id (used for NI-GIŠ or IZ = oil or fat). IV² 19, 1 *R* 16 kīma p(b)u-ur [šik]-ka-ti (id ŠAGAN); 20 *no* 2 *R* 3; ZŠ vii 90. With this KB vi (1) combines šikkatu in II 34 *no* 3, 41 (see ṭappanu, 357—8), called an a-šu-u aq-rum. *Cf* ešû V 28, 5—7 ‖ rikṣu & sūnu. V 15 *c-d* 23 see šiktum.

šikittu, *f. c. st.* šiknat (AV 6662, 8205); *pl* šiknāti. — *a*) work, structure }Machwerk, Bau{ *etc.* Asb x 80 ši-kit-ta-šu (of the tamlū) ul u-šaq-ki ma-'-diš; *ibid* 76 maš-kan ši-kit-ti-šu. II 66 *no* 2, 13 see 803 *col* 1 (*med*) & KB vi (1) 333; *ibid* 582—3 *b* 11 (3) ša-ki-nu ši-ki-it-tim (& 586). Sn *Bell* 55 *etc.* see šadalu, ℑ. Rost, 131 on II 67, 75. — *b*) condition {Lebenslage}. Sarg *Khors* 13 the gods u-ša-te-ru ši-kit-ti (as compared with others). — *c*) creature, living being {Lebewesen; Geschöpf} šiknat napišti, see napištu, 711 *col* 2 (*med*), Br 6819, 8004, 9364, 12018. Scheil, ZA x 292, 26 ši-ik-nat nab-nit (il) Da-gan; Zimmern, *Ritualtafeln*, 84—85, 2 ana (?) te-ir-te ši-ik-na-a[t, zum Vorzeichen der Geschöpfe. — *d*) in legal phraseology (*c. t.*). Ev. Mer. 12, 8 ina qaqqadišu inamdin ina ši-kit-ti-šu išalim; Ner 43, 8 kaspu qaqqadušu ina ši-kit-ti-šu-nu mala bašû išallimu ši-kit-ta-šu-nu maškanu ša *I-M.* Nabd 130, 2; 145, 6; 169, 9. — Br 9845—6; 11980 on II 26, 40, 41 & 44 (*add*, AV 4279).

(iç) **šikittu** a wood {eine Holzart}. Zimmern, *Rituall.*, 75—78, 7 (iç) ši-kit-ti, *etc.*

šukuttu, *f* (AV 8436; § 49*b*); *c. st.* šuknat, Jensen (ZA viii 293 *A*; KB ii 204—5 *rm* °°; iii (1) 29 *rm* *; vi (1) 404—5) >< Rost, 133: Gerät, Machwerk. L[TP] 159; Z[B] 11; D[Pr] 85. V 33 iii 45, 46 šu-kut-ti [aqarti?] šu-kut-ti [šûturti?]. Asurb vi 12 the jewels šu-kut-tu a-qar-tu (BA iii 236, 36 end) simat šarrûti, + 16 lubultu šu-kut (KB ii: tar)-tu *etc.* (Smith, *Asurb*, 199, 3); + 45. II 67, 28 šu-kut-ti xu-rāçi, *etc.*; see Hebr. viii 119 *ad* 81—6—7, 209, 22 šu-kut-ta-šu-nu (of the gods) ud-diš (I renewed); BA iii 262—3. Jastrow, Dibbara-*frg* see nabaṭu Š (635 *col* 2) shows that it is hardly a 'treasure'. Sm 954 (D 135) *O* 19—20 see šubû; D[H] 37; Br 7730. IV² 23 *no* 1 ii 27—8 (= GIL-SA-A, EME-SAL) see makkûru, 539 *col* 2; Br 1400 & K 2061 (H 203) ii 15 GIL-SA-A = šu-kut-tum (16 = da-ra-a-tum, ist das für die ferne Zukunft hingelegte). I 2 *no* ii 4*l*9 Ê(SAL)-GIL-SA. Creat.-*frg* V 13 newmoon (nannaru) is made šu-uk-nat mu-ši. Neb 414, 1—2: 8 shekel of gold a-na pit-qu ša šu-kut-tum were given to the goldsmith, KB iv 198—99. — T. A. (Ber) 25 *c* 58 (+ 61) šu-kut-tum an-ni-tum; 24, 27 = implement.

šallu *1.* captive, prisoner {Gefangener}. § 63. Z[Š] iv 34 šal-la u k[a-ma-a] lim-nu it-ti-ka-ma. K 3182 ii 16 (end) tu-kal-lam šal-la, AJSL xvii 139, thou makest the captive to see. Bu 88—5—12, 75 + 76 vii 5 ilâni mâtâti šal-lu-te, ... (9) [a-]na aš-ri-šu-nu u-tir, the captive gods of the countries, 24, 25 bûšâ-šu-nu šal-lu-te u-tir, BA iii 252—3; *cf* Sarg *Khors* 137 ilâni-šu-nu šal-lu-ti ... u-tir(-ra). II 65 *a* 42 (= Synchr. Hist. iv 18) nišê šal-lu-te ana ašrišu u-te-ra, AV 7876; *cf* K 2801 = K 221 + 2669 *O* 37 who nišê .... šal-lu-u-ti ana ašrišunu utirrû-ma. √šalalu, 1.

šallu *2.* so Zimmern-Jensen, KAT³ 577 *rm* 4 for çallu, NE X *col* 6, (= H[NE] 66) 33; Zimmern: der Neugeborene (Tlm שלילא); Jensen: Fehlgeburt (>< KB vi (1) 477—8). Perhaps here K 3182 iii 22 um-mi šal-la.

šal-la *3.* V 29 *g* 39; equivalent broken off.

šâlu(m), ask, AV 7857; Br 3303 see ša'alu.

šalû, šelû *1.* send; then also, throw, sling, shoot {senden; werfen, schleudern, schiessen}. L⁴ i 22 a-šal-lu ki-ma tar-ta-xi as-ma-ra-ni-e nurruṭûti, heavy lances I threw like javelins; Lehmann, ii 67. Asurb i 34 al-ma-ad ša-li-e qašti. See also K 3476 quoted in BA ii 434 *rm* *. K 382, 6 (the slave) who has been sent (še-lu-') to (the service of) Ninib in Kelach (KB iv 154: dedicated); Rm III 105 i *b* 19 ana libbi axâmeš kakkêšunu i-še-el-li, axâmeš u-ra-sa-a-bu (hurled the weapons against one another), Winckler, *Forsch.*, i 254, 255; JRAS '92, 350. — D[Pr] 34 & 182 *rm* 2; Nöldeke, ZDMG 40, 725; G § 90 = שלח; Barth, *Etym. Stud.*, 41 = سَرَحَ, he sent off, but *cf* Fränkel, BA iii 78 = סרח.

Perhaps here, also, Sm 1803, 2—3 še-lu-u; 4, šu-ul-lu-u (AV 8226; M[S] *pl* 19). S^c 6, 12 [BE] = še-lu-u (& še-gu-u). 83, 1—18, 1335 iv 27 TAR (su-lu) = še-li-tum ša DUN-GIŠ-GI.

ℑ = Q see above, and Smith, *Asurb*, 143 Teumman said to his son: šu-li-e (iç) qašti, shoot with the bow (KB ii

180, 181). According to ZA v 306 also Sn v 49; but see ša'alu, ℨ.

Der. — tešlītu, command, order.

šalû 2. sink in or, down; float, wade {eintauchen, versinken; waten}. Sn v 81 my chariot horses ina dâmêšunu gabšûti (211 *col* 2) i-šal-lu-u [(i1)] Nâri-iš (-iš perhaps = kīma). IV² 20* *b* 3 liš-la-ni-im-ma, they may sink down, M^S; but Johnston, *Johns Hopk. Circ.*, 114 *p* 118, may they drive off *etc.* (√šalû, 1?). II 39 *c-d* 62 A-[cuneiform]-RI = ša-lu-u (Br 11491), followed by ṭi-bu-u & na-pa-gu, AV 7854. Rm 345 *O* 6 ša-lu(?)-u prec. by na-pa-gu & ṭi-bu-u (M^S *pl* 22). Here perhaps also Xammurabi-*code* v 53 ša [(i1)] Nâram iš-li-a-am, he who threw himself into the river (ZA xviii 24); *ps* v 41 i-ša-al-li-a-am-ma; xxii 6 i-ša-al-li (Harper).

ℨ II 62 *no* 3, 68 A-[cuneiform] = šu-lu-u ša mê, Br 4822, 11489. Perhaps IV² 58 *a* 44, see šaxxû.

Derr. — šillân & perhaps these 2:

šulû 1. T.A. (Ber) 25 i 27: 1 ŠU du-ti-na-tum xurâçi ša da-ma šu-lu-u; ii 7 + 9; 26 i 20 + 25 (ta?-ma šu-u-lu-u; so also ii 8 + 15); 26 iv 18: 1 du-u-du siparri 1 ša me-e šu-u-li-i siparri.

šallû 1. IV² 30 *no* 2 i *R* 13 rab-bu-tu-šu ina e-bu-ri šal-lu [-u-ma çallum?], KAT³ 398 *rm* 1: Erwachsen liegt er in der untergetauchten (*i. e.* soviel wie abgemähten) Feldfrucht.

šallû 2. — *a*) some kind of vessel, ship *etc.* K 8239 *b-c* 12 GIŠ-MA-SAL-LA = ŠU-u. — *b*) some kind of peg or bolt. V 26 *c-d* 23 GIŠ-KAK-SAL-LA = ŠU-u. See also mašlû, mašla'u, mašla'tum (606).

šûlû 1. *ac* of Š of elû (41, 42); also II 62 *no* 3 (K 44, 10—13) 69—71 A-BU (Br 69), TAR (Br 382) & AN-AŠ-A-AN (Br 70) = šu-lu-u ša sûqi = direct, lead (*cf* Br 11575); Jensen, ZA xiv 182—3; KB vi (1) 496—7 = sulû. NE XII *col* iii *ll* 1 + 8 Eabani ša u-na šu-li-i(e) ummu [(i1)] NIN-A-ZU. P. N. Šu-la-a, AV 8446. Here belongs also II 107, 9 (112, 9—10; D 126, 10; V 11 *b* 9) IR | DU | šu-lu-u, preceded by li-ku-u & ta-ba-lu; S^r 84 (?). Br 4901, 4920, 5389.

šûlû 2. — *a*) *adj* √elû. Scheil, *Nabd* vi 33 (Marduk) i-na qi-rib ša-ma-me šu-lu-tu, see Messerschmidt, 48. — *b*) *noun*: a conjured shade {ein heraufbeschworener Schatten (oder Totengeist)}. D^Par 153; J^W 53 & 72; J^{I-N} 55 & *rm* 107; Z^B 39; KAT³ 641. V 47 *a* 66 šu-lum lim-nu it-ta-ça-a ap-tu-uš-šu. šu-lum explained by e-kim-mu; KB vi (1) 529. Also H 83, 25 šu-u-lu lim-nu (= U[*i. e.* ši + lu]-MU-UN-XUL) AV 8448, Br 9477. Or *no b*) from √alû, 1 (39 *col* 1)?

šulû 2. II 35 *a-b* 45 UB-LI-A = šu-lu-u ‖ ka-ar-mu. AV 8450; Br 5789.

šulû 3. see pûru, 2 (826 *col* 1, end of article) = Evil Mer. 20, 3. Nabd 768, 1 one alpu šu-ul mâr šatti; 797, 1; & *cf* 1071, 1.

šulû 4. Sm 1803, 10 šu-lu-u, M^S *pl* 19; see also ši-u.

šullu 1. KB iv 318 *no* 12, 1: 18 shekel of money šul-lu šarrâni; perh. a mistake for šul-šu, *q. v.*

šul-lu 2. II 48 *d* 14.

šêlu, šîlu 1. ruler, king; decider {Regent, König; Entscheider} Z^B 99 √ša'alu. V 36 *a-c* 15 (u) ⟨ = ši-lum (Br 8758), preceded by xa-si-su & li-ê-u & followed by i-lu, šar-rum, be-lum. K 4835 iv 25 še-e-lu ma-al(?)-ku. See šûlûtu.

šîlu 2. K 4191 *O* 4 ⟨ = ši-i-lu, preceded by u-ba-nu & followed by ba-'-u, AV 8225; Br 8763. Here perhaps V 37 *d-f* 7 (bu-ru) ⟨ = ši-lum ša šîri (Br 8760) & Sm 1803, 5—6 še-e-lu ša šîri.

šîlu 3. arbor, bower {Laube} or the like. KB vi (1) 361; Jensen, ZA xv 243 *rm* 1. Z^S viii 36 ši-lum u a-me, Jensen, KAT³ 636: eine Art Gemach oder Raum. V 37 *d-f* (i) 19 (ši-il) ⟨ = ši-lum ša NU-GIŠ-SAR (= ^{amêl} urqi) AV 8211, Br 8762, & see sillu, 1 (end) 760 *col* 1. V 37 *d-f* 8 (bu-ru) ⟨ = ši-lum ša iççuri, Br 8759.

ši'îlu 4. V 37 *d-f* 6 (bu-ru) ⟨ = ši-lum ša ṬU (= šiqli) Br 8761, where also II 62 *c-d* 64 is added (??).

ši-lum? Br 13864 reads II 30 (*c-*)*f* 9 u-ru-u ši-lum.

šillû' = שליה, AV 8233; see çillû, *p* 875 *col* 2. M^S 94 skin {Haut}. On V 26 *e-f*

48 see JENSEN, ZK ii 328; ZA i 54; MEISSNER, BA ii 561 = some skin-like covering. Br 14109—10. Also add Rm 346, 11—13 ... KU, ... MU, ... DU = š(s, ç)illu-u. 83, 1—18, 1335 iv 22 TAR = šil-lum ša sinništi; Sm 1803, 11 [š]illu ša sinništi = hymen of a woman; see PRINCE, AJP xv 112 & paṭaru, 708 *col* 2, below. Nabd 476, 8—9 (15 + 24) so & so many mašlxē ša šil-li-e (skins?); 739, 7.

šelû. K 4143 *R* 6 SI = še-lu-u(?), preceded by ur-ru-u, pi-tu-u, AV 8266; Br 3410. See ši-lum.

'š'illu; see sillu, 3 (760 *col* 1). II Rawl. reads ši instead of 'š'il.

šillû. Br 8555 *ad* IV^{2} 13 *b* 42, 43; but read ši-i lu-u, & see 864 *col* 1 *ll* 11—12 from below.

šulbu see šulpu.

šulbû, part of door or bolt {Teil einer Tür oder eines Riegels}. Z^{B} 39; AV 8459, 5620. II 23 *c-d* 37—39 šu-ul-bu-u ‖ midi-lu, pa-ar-ku, mar-kas dalti. mukil šu-ul-bi-i ‖ sik-ku-rum, 758 *col* 2, below. ⊕ 287 *R* 12 GIŠ-MUD-SAG-G(K)UL = šul-bu-u, Br 2282, AV 6655. HAUPT, AJSL xix 14 combines שלבים 1 Kings 7, 28 and suggests √לפה 'surround', protect with walls *etc.*

šēli(a)bu, *m* fox; jackal {Fuchs; Schakal}? §§ 27; 32*a* *γ*; 35. IV^{2} 11 *a* 45, 46 še-li-bu (= LUB-A, EME-SAL, Br 7283) zib-bat-su im-ta-na-aš-šir, JENSEN, 121. IV^{2} 30* *no* 3 *O* 16 âlu lim-nu ša kima še-lib (= LUB-A) âli ša-qu-meš ina mu-ši i-du-ul-lu atta, *Rev. Sém.*, '98, 148—9; JENSEN, KB vi (1) 334. ⊕ 51 i 49, 50 .....] LUB-A = še-li-bu; .....] 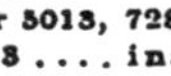 = š ša (amēl) çaxri. (šam) karan še-li-bi see karānu & AV 8218, Br 5013, 7283. K 2852 + K 9662 iv Margin 3 .... ina eš-šu-u-ti še-la-bu u pu-çu(?)-nu-nu (see 819 *col* 1), WINCKLER, *Forsch.*, ii 40 *fol.* H 40, 206; II 49 *no* 4, 42. H^{P} 16; BA i 5. In *c. t.* we have P. N. Še-el-li-bi, PINCHES, *Inscr. Tablets*, 23, *no* 9, 4; PEISER, *Vertr.*, 343 *col* 1; AV 8234; AJSL xviii 253. Connected with šēli(a)bu are these 2:

šēlabiš, *adv* III 15 ii 16 he fled še-la-biš, like a fox, § 80, 2*b*.

(amēl) **še-lib-pa-a-a**, a title of an official, K 4395 ii 2.

šelibb(pp)û. some worm; or, vermin {ein Wurm; oder, Ungeziefer} *etc.* AV 8219. S^{r} 15 [u-xu] | UX | še-lib-bu-u ‖ ublu; Br 8299. V 21 *a-b* 42 see bitrâmu, 207—8.

šalbabu, *adj* wise, prudent {weise, klug}? M^{S} 94; K^{M} mighty, courageous. AV 7860. IV^{2} 21* *no* 1 C *R* iii 3 šal-ba-bu, said of Marduk; K^{M} 53, 3; 9, 3 + 31 *etc.* ZA iv 227, 3; 237, 39 (242: explains it as 'anger', but??). V 29 *g-h* 23 [...]ZU = šal-ba-bu, Br 13868. K 8663 i 2 na-am-ru, šal-ba-bu, ra-šub-bu, na-'-du; Sm 2013.

šulbur, AV 8460 see labaru, 1 Š (472 *col* 1).

šallabittum see šallarittum.

šalgu. snow {Schnee} = שֶׁלֶג. K 3182 iv 13 .... ku-çu xal-pa-a šu-ri-pa (*var* bu) šal-gi. Sn iv 77 zunnē ša zunnē u šal-gu; I 43, 43 ša-mu-tum la-zi-iz-tum (477 *col* 2) il-lik-ma šal-gu. III 15 i 14, see kuççu (425 *col* 2). II 32 *a-b* 34 šal-gu ‖ šu-ri-b(p)u; V 12 *c-d* 42 IM-ŠEŠ = šal-gu, im-ba-ru, followed by šu-ri-b(p)u.

š'û'ludu. II 55 *d* 9 ša ana par-çi šu-lu-ku ana zu-un-ni šu-lu-du.

šalaxu 1. perh. tear out, or, flay {vielleicht ausreissen, oder schinden} D^{Pr} 182 *rm* 2; ZA v 45. NE VI 179 Êabani iš-lu-ux i-mit(bat, dil)-ti GUD-AN-NA-ma ana pāniša id-di. K 1220 *R* 1 ni-iš-lux-šu-nu ar-xiš, Hr^{L} 271.

šalxu. KNUDTZON, 55 *R* 9 inassaxū šu-u ša-al-xa u-maš-ša-ru ....

šalaxu 2. ip šu-lux IV^{2} 16 *b* 37 see salaxu (761) & KAT^{3} 602; ℑ pm; ZIMMERN, *Ritualtafeln* *no* 83, 16 šu-lux-xu šu-lux-xu, Besprengungen sind besprengt.

(iç) **šalxu.** especially in *c. t.* Nabd 115, 6: 1 (iç) šal-xu eš-ši; 1 (iç) šal-xu pi-tu-u; 2 (iç) kib-su eš-ši; + 7 + 8; 694, 5—6: 2 (iç) šal-xu eš-šu, *etc.*; 143, 2, 3, 4: 2 (iç) šal-xu eš-šu; 9 (iç) šal-xu la-bi-ri; 9 (iç) kib-su eš-šu; 146, 6: 2 (iç) kib-su (see 4, 5, 12) eš-šu; + 8: 8 kib-su 3 (iç) šal-xu; 179, 4: 2 (iç) šal-xi, 3 (iç) kib-su. Cyr 241, 10 + 18: 2 (iç) šal-xu. AJSL xv 75, 3: 2 (iç) šal-xu; & 13, without (iç). BA i 521 Binde,

Gurt; AJSL xv 75 & 77, some personal apparel; cord, girdle or the like. — V 32 *a-b* 43 ša šal-xu du-uš-ši ‖ pa-tin-nu (*q. v.*) Br 14237. Connected with this šalxu is probably:

šalxū *1.* II 22 *a-c* 17 GIŠ-SA-ŠI-GAL-GAL = šal-xu-u (AV 7863, Br 3150), + 20 GIŠ-SA-SAL-SAL = šal-xu-u ‖ še-e-tum, net ⟨Netz⟩ Br 3160.

šalxū *2.* the outer wall or rampart enclosing the inner wall (dūru) & the moat ⟨die äussere Mauer, der Wall⟩. § 65, 38 *rm.* AV 7863; Lyon, *Sargon*, 77; JBL xix 69 *rm* 42; √שלח extend ⟨sich erstrecken⟩? see dūru, 2 (267—8). Sarg *Cyl* 71 dūr-šu ‖ šal-xu-u-šu; *bull* 92; *Ann* XIV 86; Asb iv 130 (*cf* 120). I 7 F 15, 16 dūru u šal-xu-u (ZA iv 289); H 2 dūra u ša-al-xu ša (al) Kak-zi, Meissner & Rost, 104 *rm* 3 × KB ii 114. *Cf* K 1709 + DT 3 i 7. Neb viii 47 ša-al-xi-e Bābili; Sn *Bav* 5 dūri-šu u šal-xu-šu. II 50 *a-b* 26 [BAD] ni-mit (il) Bēl = šal-xu-u-šu (of Babylon); *ibid* 29—31 (Br 148, 2820, 5344, 5345, 10002); ZDMG 53, 659—60. I 49 *d* 19 + 20. II 32 *g* 10 = šal-xu-u, Br 9878; same id = qān ša-la-li. See also salxu, 761 *col* 2.

šuluxxu. *c. st.* šu-lux. meaning not clear. Zimmern, *Rituall.*, 1—20, 74 (end) & 99 (beg). šu-lux-xi ta-šal-lax, du sollst die Besprengungen ausführen; 54, 7 (u-çur-tu u-šak-lil) šu-lux (*var* -xi) gaç-çi al-me(*var* -mi)-šu-nu-ti, eine Gipsverschalung legte ich um sie (= IV² 24 *no* 1 B *O* 6, 7) AV 8451; Br 7185. Z^{B} ix 19 šu-lux šu-ul AN-EN-KI-GA-K[ID]. — 81—6—7, 209, 25 si-mu-u-ti iš-tak-ka-nu uš-te-ši-ru šu-lux-xu, Strong, Hebr. viii 119, originally, hand-washing; then perhaps: rites & ceremonies in general; BA iii 283: der die Culte recht leitete. Merodach-Balad.-stone i 7 Marduk ga-mir šu-lux-xi, BA ii 259 der vollkommenste Gebieter. Nabd *Grot* iii 41 pa-ra-ç šar-ru-ti šu-lu-ux be-lu-tim i-na li-ib-bi-ša u-ša-pa-am, KB iii (2) 88: *cf* iii 11 & see zuluxxū (282 *col* 1). KB iii (2) 76 i 9—10 Neriglissar mu-da-ax-xi-id sa-at-tu-uk-ku mu-uš-te-ši-ru šu-lu-ux-xi-šu-un; + ii 17 a-na ul-lu-lu šu-lu-ux-xu za-na-na-te, Bezold: Abgaben; Tempelabgaben. Scheil, *Nabd*, iii 19 šu-lux-xi-šu (uš-pi-el-lu), Messerschmidt, 45: Einkünfte. K^{M} 48, 17; 58, 15. T. A. (Ber) 25 ii 58; 26 ii 51; iv 22; IV² 59 *b* 1 (but??). Connected with šuluxxu may be muš(šu)-luxxu (606 *col* 2).

šulxū? K 8204, 3 ša šul(sul, dun)-xa-a u mi-ik-ti ab-bak (579 *col* 2).

šuluxtu. T. A. (Ber) 165, 7—8 u uš]-ši-ir šar-ru bēli-ja šu-lu-ux-ta. KB v 371: a present?

šilixtu? K 517 *R* 8, 9 um-ma: ši-li-ix-ti ša (nār) Banīti a-na Nipur^{ki} xi-ra-'-a; 12 liš-pu-ram-ma ši-li-ix-ti ša (nār) Banīti *etc.* (Hr^{L} 327). AV 8220. PSBA xxiii 66; M^{S} 94: canal (?). Artaxerxes 29, 17 (nār) *B.* ultu ba-bi-ša a-di ši-li-ix-ti-ša. See also mušlaxu, 606 *col* 2.

šalaṭu *1. ps* išallaṭ dispose of, have power over; claim, raise claim on, to ⟨verfügen, Macht haben über; Besitzansprüche erheben⟩ with ina muxxi, eli. AV 7840. Neb 198, 8 ša ina mux-xi-ša i-šal-la-ṭu, whosoever raises claim on her ⟨wer Besitzansprüche auf sie erhebt⟩; 283, 11; & see rašū, 2. Peiser, *Vertr.*, xxvii 7 (e-li); viii 11; xxviii 11 (ina eli ul i-šal-laṭ); Nabd 58, 6; 67, 7 *etc.*; T^{C} 135—6. Camb 373, 8 written i-šal-la-' (Meissner, 149); Neb 258, 7 i-ša-la-aṭ.

Q¹ pm *Rec. Trav.* xx 205 *no* XLI *col* i 18 šit-lu-ṭa-at be-lut-su. Asb ix 77 (Bēlit) ša it-ti A-nim u Bēl šit-lu-ṭa-at man-za-zu; *cf* K 11152, 4 (Ištar) ru-ba-tum ša it-ti (il) Bēl šit-lu-ṭa-at ṭa-ba-an (?).

ℑ¹ achieve victory, become victorious ⟨den Sieg gewinnen, Sieger werden⟩. TP iv 47 see mēšu(e)riš, 612 *col* 1.

NOTE. — 1. V 63 *a* 10 (KB iii (2) 114) reads ina paraç ili la ša-la-ṭi; Scheil, ZA v 401, 406 la-ša la ṬI (= šalimtu).

2 ša-laṭ = governor, read ša-kin, *c. st.* of šaknu, 2 (*q. v.*).

3. šil-ṭan-nu (AV 8230) read tar-tan-nu (*q. v.*).

Derr. šitluṭu, šitluṭiš & these 3:

šalṭu *1.* Sp II 265 *a* xxiii 9 u-ta (K 3452 dan, tan)-na-an (*var* -nu) šal-ṭu ša pu-xur-šu an..... or ŠAL-TU?, see Zimmern, *Ritualtafeln*, 1—20, 24.

šalṭiš & **šalṭāniš** (AV 7864, 7865), *adv.* — *a)* imperious; as king, ruler *etc.* ⟨gebieterisch, als König, Herrscher *etc.*}. V 61 vi 33—4 ša ina ēkalli šal-ṭiš iz-za-az-zu-ma. IV² 32 *a* 33 the king šal-ṭiš ul i-tam-me; *b* 18 + 44 (i-ta-me); 33 *b* 6 + 39; also see Bu 88, 5—12, 11 *l* 12 (end); PSBA xxiv 220 *foll.* Perhaps IV² 13 *no* 1 *R* 24, 25 (Br 345). — *b*) victoriously, as victor {siegreich, als Sieger}. TP ii 77 šal-ṭe-iš (*var* ṭiš) ētētiq (1 *sg*). at-ta(l)-lak šal-ṭiš Asb ii 129; v 40 + 125; viii 117; KB ii 240, 33. K 694, 5; K 695, 9 (THOMPSON, *Reports*, 166 & 169); K 1304 *O* 9; K 759 *R* 4 šal-ṭa-niš il-lakū *pl* (*ibid*, 89 & 82). Šalm, *Mon*, ii 7 see mēšariš; also KB vi (1) 100, 13. Esh iii 36 ina kir-bi-šu šal-ṭa-niš at-tal-lak; III 16 iv 18; *cf* III 58 *a* 5; K 2852 + K 9662 ii 1.

šulluṭu. victorious {siegreich}. Anp i 6 Ninib šu-ul-lu-ṭu git-ma-lu, AV 8465; ZDMG 34, 762; ZA v 5.

(mašak) **šalṭu** = שֶׁלֶט. T^C 136 shield {Schild} BA i 535 *no* 53, ein Lederschild. Nabd 1034, 1 ište-en (mašak) šal-ṭu ište-en (mašak) çal-lu; 661, 4; 702, 1.

šalaṭ(& t)u 2. *ps* išallaṭ, cut through, cut off {zerschneiden, abschneiden}. AV 7840; ZDMG 32, 21 *foll*; ZK i 302; ii 22 *rm* 4; Z^B 103 *rm* 1. IV² 22 *a* 30, 31 (= SIL-SIL-LA) see xinnu, 3 (325 *col* 2) & Br 387. II 39 *g-h* 14 (= Ⓗ 59 ii) SIL (si-la) LA = ša-la-ṭu šu . . . (*cf* nusuku, 701 *col* 2); H 9 & 204, 21. Perhaps = tear a hole in: K 620, 16—17 ma-a i-šal-laṭ ēkal bat-qu i-ka-çur (Hr^L 91). TP III (Zür. Mus. inscr.) 3 it-gu-ru-ti ki-ma ki-e i-šal-li-tu-ma (Z^B 103 *rm* 1, on *p* 104; PSBA xviii 158, 159). See also salatu, 2 (764 *col* 1. below).

ב = Ⓠ. IV² 3 *a* 7, 8 the muruç qaqqadi bu-a-ni-šu ki-ma Gl xi-ni u-šal-liṭ (= SIL-SIL-LA, Br 387, 395), ‖ ixtaççi (5, 6); H 204 *no* 21. Creat.-*frg* IV 102 kir-bi-ša (of Tiâmat) u-bat-ti-qa (subj. Marduk) u-šal-liṭ libba. Hymn to Ninib (ABEL & WINCKLER, 60 *fol*) *R* 13 (end) li-šal-liṭ-ka-ma (+ 19, end). IV² 17 *b* 17 Šamaš mu-šal-li-tum ki-e lum-ni, who cuts through the snare of the wicked; see also K^M 62, 11 (-tu).

š(s)al-ṭu *2.* II 39 *no* 7 *R* . . . . BE | šal-ṭu, AV 7866; Br 1534.

šûluku *1.* (*ac &*) pm of ש of alaku, 1. go {gehen} AV 8452 customary, adapted to, becoming, current {gangbar, angemessen, passend} *etc.* §§ 65, 33; 88 *b* & *rm*. ZA iii 296, 297. V 65 *a* 21, *b* 2; TP vii 88, 89; IV² 18* *no* 1 *O* 8, 9 see sīmtu (768 *col* 1); also KB iii (2) 92, 15—16. IV² 18* *no* 3 *R* iv 19, 20 ša kuzba u ulça mālāt ana tab-ra-a-ti (= ŠI-E-DI) šu-lu-kat; 18 *no* 3 i 31, 32 the lofty weapon ša a-na i-di šarrūti šu-lu-ku (= DU-MA). II 19 *no* 2 *O* 27 see rabíš; 55 *d* 9 see š'ū'ludu; Sm 954 *O* 11 (D 135) see bar-ba'ru (190 *col* 1). Sn *Bav* 6 ša i-na la ma-mi na-mu-ta šu-lu-ka; also I 49 *d* 30.

šûluku *2.* *adj. pl m* šu-lu-ku-tum II 30 *e-f* 63 + 67; AV 8453, Br 6891, 6892. K 7673, 10 . . . . ilâni-šu gur-ru-tu (√גרר) šu-lu-ku[-tu u-šu-lik?]. or *noun*?

ši-lu-ku. KB iii (2) 112 *ad* V 65 *b* 3 (end) read U(*i.e.* ŠI + LU)-KU = ib of ašûxu.

šulkatkâta (?). ZA iv 114 *no* 5, 1: III par-zillu šul-kat-ka-a-ta, followed by 1 xa-çi-in-ni, 1 ap-pa-tum, 2 ma-rat *pl*; text of Nabopolassar.

šalalu 1. *pr* išlul, 1 *sg* aš-lul, TP iii 63; *ps* išallal, 1 *sg* a-šal-lal, KB ii 266, 98. lead away captive, lead into captivity; loot, plunder {als Beute, Gefangene wegführen, in Gefangenschaft führen; plündern}. AV 7841. D^H 20. NÖLDEKE, ZDMG 40, 724: primitive meaning: extract, draw out = سل; see also ZDMG 30, 309. ZA ix 193, 20 compares Arab ثَلَّة, small cattle; Sab ثَلَل, gain as booty {erbeuten}. — Sn *Kui* 3, 14 such & such iš-lu-lu-ni (3 *pl*); SMITH, *Asurb*, 274, 27; 283, 6. Nabd-Cyr. Chronicle *B* 4 iš-lul-u-ma, they carried off; KB iii (2) 130. TP III *Ann* 44 šal-la-su aš-lu-la (*cf* 16; also 160, 162, 169, 174, 178; II 67, 9; Šalm, *Ob*, 90, 91. 101—2, 116, 124, 187); 207—8 . . . aš-lu-la; 750 šal-la-at (al) *K* | . . . . [šal-la-at] (al) *I*; 550 šal-la-at (al) *M* aš-lu-la (& 230—240); 142 šal-la-su-nu iš-lu-la; 135 šal-la-su-nu u-bi-lu-ni; 228 aš-lu-lu-ma. TP ii 80, 81 aš-lul; iii 9, 10; 62, 63 aš-lul (*var* lu-la, i 72; 115, 116; ii 18; iii 53); Anp i 48; ii 38 & 57. Asb vi 26, 47 aš-lu-la ana (mât) Aššur (+ vii 14; ix 18); Esh i 23; Sn iii

23 his cities ša aš-lu-la (*cf* i 36; ii 68); Sn *Kuj* 1, 22. — *ps* H 81 (K 133) *R* 25, 26 a-la-a-ni i-šal-lal-šu-nu-ti (= BA-AB-$\frac{DU}{DU}$-$\frac{DU}{DU}$, Br 4948). K 1282 *etc.* *O* 31 šal-lat-su ka-bit-tu ta-šal-lal (KB vi, 1, 70—1). K 2619 i 22 (*Dibbara*-legend) na-kam bu-še-e Bâbili ta-šal-lal at-ta; + 13 ki-i šal-lat na-ki-ri ana ša-la-la, *etc.* he sends his host. — *pc* IV^2 12 *R* 46, 47 ana mât na-ki-ri-šu liš-lu-lu[-šu] Br 4048. — *ip* S^P 158 + S^P II 962, 13 šu-ul-la-' šal-lat ê-kur, carry off the spoil of the temple, JTVI 29, 58. — *pm* Babyl. Chron. iv 3 šal-lat-su (of the king of Sidon) šal-lat, + 20 + 28 (KB ii 282—5; ZA ii 159). — *ag* V 55, 10 Nebukadrezzar ka-šid(?) $^{(mât)}$A-mur-ri-i ša-li-lu Kaš-ši-i (§ 131); *cf* ša-lil, Sargon *Pp* iv 19 & 33; *Cyl* 18 & 27. K 1282 *O* 10 ki-i ša-lil mâti. — *ac* V 65 *b* 40 ana ša-la-la; *a* 8; Sarg *Khors* 77 xi-pi-e Mu-ça-çir ša-lal Xal-di-a ili-šu iš-me-ma; *Ann* 581 (§ 95). H 80, 12 ana mât nukur-tim ša-la-li um-man-šu upaxxar (to despoil the land of his enemies) Br 4898. K 2852 + K 9662 ii 35 (end) iq-qa-bi ša-lal nišê-ka, Winckler, *Forsch*, ii 34—7. K 2675 *O* 8 to kill, xa-ba-a-te ša-la-a-li, to rob & to plunder (he sent his army); III 28, 11; Esh *Sendsch*, *R* 35 a-na xa-ba-ti ša-la-li mi-çir $^{(mât)}$ Aššur. II 27 *a-b* 14 IR (also = tabalu, liqû, laqatu) = ša-la-lum (Br 5388); followed by šalalu ša amêli (Br 4942), H 20, 362; 21, 390. II 48 *c-d* 58 (61); V 21 *c-d* 15 (Br 4948); 20 *e-f* 13 see šallatu, & *cf* xabatu (303, 304); II 39 *d* 79 ša-la[-lu?]. Sm 1803, 7—10 ša-la-lum, šal-la-tum, š ša-la-lum, šu-lu-u. Šalâlu, as P. N. *cf* D^{Pr} 200 *rm* 7.

ℵ¹ K 41 *a* 8 .... nak-ri iš-ta-lal, the enemy carried off. Šalm, *Ob*, 129 šal-la-su a-ša-la (> aštalla > aštalala), his booty I brought away. V 55, 43 i-iš-ta-lal makkûr-ša (of Elam) § 10. K 512, 11 a-na me-i-ni ta-ša-al-li (?) Hr^L 204. II 127 (K 257) *O* 31, 32 a-li aš-tal-lum, the city which I captured (§§ 25 *b*; 37 *b*; 97).

ℵ II 27 *a-b* 16 (K 2008 i 15) $\frac{du}{du}$ (lax-lax) $\frac{du}{du}$ = na-šal-lu-lu (II 20, 360) Br 4947; §§ 88 *b*; 98; Z^B 69 or rather ℵ³? Xammurabi-*code* xxii 8, 28, 38 iš-ša-li-il.

ℵ³ *ac* II 48 *c-d* 62, AV 7841, Br 4947; K 2008 iii 40 i-taš-lu[-lu]. *id* in both the same as K 2008 i 15.

NOTE. — H 87, 61 (end) some read šal-lat, let it be thrown out; but read rak-sat.

Derr. — aš-lu-lu (115 *col* 2); šallu, 1 (& 2?), šallatu, šallatiš, šallûtu, šillatu, 2.

šalalu 2. flow, slide along, or over something. II 36 *g-h* 70 IR = ša-la-lum, followed by (la-ax) $\frac{DU}{DU}$ = š ša a-la-ki, Br 4941; H 20, 358, 359.

ℑ make slide; engage {laufen lassen; frachten} Nabd 1019, 5 elippu ana idi ûmu šul-lul, T^C 136: das Schiff ist für Frachtgeld *pro* Tag gefrachtet; 1033, 5; Neb 402, 15; Camb 250, 2.

ℵ S^c 5 *a* 4 SUR = na-šal-lu-lu, Br 2980.

ℵ³ V 19 *c-d* 38 NUM-NUM = i-taš-lu-lum; *cf* II 36 *g-h* 72 (Br 9038); 27 *g-h* 21; 39 *g-h* 86 BI-IZ-BI-IZ = i-ta-a[š-lu-lu?], BA ii 292. IV^2 1 *a* 32, 33 ina dal-ti ki-ma çi-ri it-ta[-aš]-la-lu, Br 2980; BA ii 292 *rm*.

Derr. — mašallu (606 *col* 2); mušulilu (so Jensen), 607 *col* 1.

šalâlu *3.* in the name of a reed: IV^2 26 *no* 7 *b* 35, 36 qa-an ša-la-lu = GI-ŠUL-XI, Br 2522, 9877. 79, 7—8, 21, 3 GI?]-ŠUL-XI = qa-an ša-la-li, M^S *pl* 23; also Z^B viii 70; Scheil, *Notes d'épigraphie*, LX *O* 15 (*Rec. Trav.*, vol. xxiii).

šûlulu *1.* shining, brilliant {scheinend, glänzend}. √alalu, 4 (46—7); prop^y *pm* Š. IV^2 20 *no* 1, 15—16 see ni(a)perdû, 709 *col* 2. Br 7090; § 25 *rm*.

šûlulu *2.* √alalu, 5, *ac* Š. IV^2 20 *a* 13 xar-ra-an šu-lu-lu (IV^2-ku, Br 11422). ‖ urux rišâti; *cf* *Rec. Trav.*, xxiv *nos* 1/2.

šalaltu, šelaltu see šalaštu.

šalultu *cf* šalšu.

šalamu 1. *pr* išlim (la iš-lim-a, K 5464. 26 = Hr^L 198), *ps* i-šal-lim (Peiser, KAS 101, 11), *pl* i-šal-li-mu (ZK i 88 *no* 2, 8). AV 7845; *id* DI; *pm* DI-im, DI-mat, Knudtzon, 321; ša-lim (§ 89 i). Z^B 6 *rm* 2; 7 *rm* 1; PAOS '86 *p* cxlviii.

a) be whole, complete, correct; safe, intact {ganz, vollständig, richtig; unbeeintrāchtigt oder dergl. sein. — *a.* be or remain sound, well, healthy, or uninjured {wolbehalten, vollständig, gesund sein oder bleiben}. SCHEIL, *Nabd,* ii 39 iš-lim-ma. IV^2 57 *a* 66 from (= ina) the bad mouth *etc.* of people pānukka lu-uš-lim-ma; 21* *no* 1 C *R* iii 9; K 8522 (KB vi, 1, 38—9) *R* 27 šu-u lu šal-ma, and himself be well (but § 106 = lū šāl-ma, let him decide). Perh. II 51 *b* 13 ina ū-me an-ni-i liš-li-mu it-ti-šu. III 59 *a* 40 šarru ša-lim (is well); 66 *col* 10 *R* 23 *c* lu TI-LA (= baluṭ?) lu ša-lim (§ 93*b*, may he be safe; PSBA xxi 129, 130). V 31 *f* 22, 23 du-p-pu ul ša-lim ul al-si-eš, the document is not sound (well preserved), so that I cannot read it. II 9 *c-d* 3 maçartašu (*q. v.*) šal-ma-at, AV 7880; Br 9534. Bu 91—5—9, 183 *O* 11 (its seals) šal-mu, are perfect, not touched (Hr^L 340): *pl* šal-ma, ZIMMERN, *Ritualtafeln*, 98—99, 8; *cf* 100, 8. V 52 iv 25 (ana) šu-lam zēr-šu. ša-lam ZI-MEŠ (= napišta)-šu, KNUDTZON, 144 *O* 6. — *β.* in *c. t.* (with *acc*) in a financial meaning: not to suffer, lose, be indemnified, have one's money guaranteed, be paid {keinen Verlust erleiden, schadlos gehalten werden} *etc.* T^C 136; § 138. Nabd 103, 11 kaspa u xubullašu i-šal-lim; 67, 8 a-di (sal) Gu-gu-a kaspašu taš-li-mu; 356, 37 i-šal-lim (3 *m*); + 38 ta-šal-lim (3 *f*). Neb 42, 15 kaspašu i-šal-li-mu; 60, 8 a-di kaspašunu i-šal-li-mu; 350, 12 a-di kaspašu ta-šal-lim-mu (3 *f*); 91, 10 (end). Camb 81, 13 a-di-i .... i-šal-li-mu; 431, 8; 315, 11; 428, 8; i-šal-lim-mu (§ 53*c*) 292, 15; ta-šal-li-mu, 300, 10 (BA iii 451); ‖ ℑ of eṭeru (Camb 68, 15; 409, 14 *etc.*) see MEISSNER, 144 *rm* 2 on ša-la-am xarrānim; ina ša-la-am gi-ir-ri[-šu-nu]. — *γ.* be carried to completion, be completed, executed, perfected; be accepted, succeed {zur vollen Ausführung kommen, vollführt werden; sich vollziehen; gelingen}. K 618 *R* 15, 16 u ši-pir qātā ša ardi-šu i-šal-li-mu-u (Hr^L 9), shall succeed. Asb ii 117 ki-i ša a-na Aššur am-xu-ru(ra) iš-li(m)-ma, as I have prayed to Aššur, it came to pass, KB ii 177 (WINCKLER, *Forsch*, i 246, er bewilligte). K 8522 *R* 11 see kalū, 1 ℑt *p* 381; but KB vi (1) 36 suggests liš-ši-ma (let him take it away). SCHEIL, *Rec. Trav.*, xvi 189 *no* VIII 5—8 li-ba-al-li-ṭu-ka (= ℑ) lu-u ša-al-ma-a-ta a-na šu-ul-mi-ka aš-pur šu-lum-ka šu-up-ra-am. Nabd *Ann* i 5 iš-lim (or -ši, KB iii, 2, 128); ii 7 (+ 12 + 21 + 25) sacrifices were brought in Esag(g)il & Ezida to the gods ki šal-mu, as was right (PRINCE, *Diss*, 86 *foll*; BA ii 237, 238); iii 8 isinnu a-ki-tu ki šal-mu ep-šu. — *δ.* be renewed {erneut werden} Creat.-*frg* IV 24 see lubāšu (475 *col* 1); KB vi (1) 326: ganz da sein.

b) be completed and finished; have run its course; especially of the sun: go down, set {fertig sein, vollendet haben; von der Sonne: untergehen}. šalam(u) šamši = west {Westen} § 72*a rm.* TP vi 44 (a-di) tāmdi (= A-AB-BA) e-li-ni-te ša ša-la-mu (il) Šam-ši. Sarg *Khors* 16, 17 Cyprus ša qabal tam-dim ša-lam (il) Šam-ši (= e-reb (il) Šam-ši, 146); *Cyl* 13; *Ann* 252; Sn i 13 from the upper sea ša ša-lam (il) Šam-ši (*Kui* 1, 3: ša šul-mu (il) Šam-ši); ZIMMERN, *Ritualtafeln*, 1—20, 31; or a *noun*? — Complete one's life, die *etc.* perh. KNUDTZON, 75, 10 i-šal-li-m[u-u].

𝔔t Perhaps Bu 91—5—9, 210 *R* 2 (end) al-ta-lim (Hr^L 403). ZIMMERN, *Ritualtafeln*, 1—20, 121 iš-tal-mi (3 times); iš-tal-ma, *ibid ll* 36 + 113; *etc.* Xammurabi-*code* v 49 iš-ta-al-mu-am, (if) he come forth unharmed (HARPER).

ℑ *a*) keep safe, intact, preserve {unversehrt erhalten, bewahren} id G I, BA iii 388. I 69 *c* 33 Nabd. glories in having kept the old plan of the temple intact (u-çu-ra-ti-šu-nu u-šal-lim). V 65 *a* 24 (ana) u-çu-ra-at bīti-šu šu-ul-lu-mu (+ *b* 31) ‖ Neb *Bors* ii 7 a-ša-ar-ša la e-ni. V 34 *c* 46; KB iv 198, 7 see napištu (711 *cole* 1, 2). V 34 *c* 8 (mu-ša-al-li-ma-at) & KB iii (2) 50 *col* 3, 47 see pir'u (826 *col* 1, below). V 65 *a* 8 mu-šal-lim kāl šip-ri; *cf* 28 ša ša-la-mu šip-ri-ja. Esh v 44 the bull colossusses nāçiru kibsi mu-šal-li-mu tal-lak-ti šarri bānišunu. Merod.-Balad.-stone ii 24; V 62 *no* 2, 12 see ki-dudē, 372 *col* 2. KB vi (1) 294 *col* 3, 1 u re-ū-um la mu-šal-li-mu um-ma-ni-šu; vi (1) 298, 299 *l* 23 p(b)u-ut-ka šul-lim (= ip) ‖ u-çur; 300, 301 (*no* i) 11 a-na-ku šar-ru la mu-ša-lim [ma]-ti-šu, ZK xii 318. NE IX *col* i 12 šul-li-ma-in-ni ja-a-ti, preserve me intact; see also NE 20 *R* 1 + 5 aš-šu šul-lu-mu & perh. K 233, 5 (end). IV^2 29 *b* 7, 8 at-ta-ma mu-šal-li-im, thou art the preserver, *cf* Br 9534. K 762, 2 + 6 (Hr^L 446) & see tašlimtu. — keep in order: Winckler, *Sargon*, 191 (below) in order to: šul-li-ma çindišu; *cf* K 3600 *R* 22 šul-li-me murnisqe; K 2711 *R* 21; Pinches, *Texts*, 16 *no* 4 *R* 9; Merod.-Balad.-stone ii 10 see parçu, 2 (836 *col* 2). IV^2 8 iv 24 mu-šal-li-ma. Xammurabi-*code* xl 43 mu-ša-al-li-mu-um, guardian, protecting (Harper). — *b*) restore, renew }ersetzen, vergüten{ AV 5580. Sarg *Cyl* 4; ZA iii 397, 36; V 62 *no* 1, 14—15 *etc.* see xibiltu, 301 *col* 2. ZA v 146, 3 šu-ul-li-im-šu, restore it (the money). Neb 325, 7 u-šal-lam, he will restore; 365, 7 u-šal-lam-ka (will compensate thee). K 2467 + K 8122 *O* 24 ša ilu-šu itti-šu zi-nu-u tu-šal (King: šal)-lam, thou restorest to favor. — *c*) execute }ausführen{ V 64 *c* 23 (Anunītu) mu-šal-li-ma-at ki-bi-it Bêl a-bi-šu (*cf* 34). — *d*) grant success, make or let succeed, cause to prosper }gelingen, gedeihen lassen{. Merod.-Balad.-stone i 35, 36 ši-bir-tu mu-šal-lim nišē (BA ii 259 & 267; KB iii, 1, 185); KB iii (2) 64. 14 mu-ša-li-im ni-ši. Sarg *Cyl* 69 (il) Anu mu-šal-lim epšit qâtija; *Harem*, B 8 e-piš-tuš (his action) šul-li-ma (= ip). Su *Kui* 4, 10 see liptu, *c* (494 *col* 1). I 44, 94 ilu mu-šal-li-mu ur-xi, who guards my way. Asb x 72 see maštaku (614 *col* 1). K 4740, 20 lu TIN-TIR(ki) u-šal-la-mu. ZA iv 382 *R* 7 see muttaprišu (624 *col* 2). Perh. K 629, 32—4 (Hr^L 65, *R* 11—13) a-na bu-luṭ napša-a-te ša mâr šarri bêli-ja lu-šal-li-mu. — *e*) finish, in the meaning of to ruin }zerstören{. K 647 *R* 1 ina qâtâ-ka ki-i u-šal-li-mu-' (Hr^L 210). — *f*) complete, finish }fertig machen, vollführen{. Knudtzon, 29 *R* 8 u-šal-la-mu; 67, 6 u]-šal-la-a-ma. Sarg *Khors* 141 u-šal-li-ma u-ru-ux bît a-ki-ti (+ *Ann* 310); V 34 *c* 4 u-ša-al-la-am (1 *sg*) ši-bi-eršu. See also KB iv 316—7, 26 (end). — *g*) in astronomical reports, *e. g.* the day will complete (ušallam) Nisân. Thompson, *Reports*, ii *pref.* xxi *foll* arxu mušallimu, a full month. — *h*) in Xammurabi: convey safely, see King, *Hammurabi*. Xammurabi-letters 45, 7 u-ša-al-la-ma-aq-qu, + 12 li-ša-al-li-mu, BA iv 471 *foll*; 34, 24. In Xammurabi-*code* = make good, restore (Harper, *The Code of Hammurabi*, 185). — V 45 *col* vii 21 tu-šal-lam. See also Br 8228 on S 28, 28. P. N. Mu-šal-li-mu, often. Mu-šal-lim Aš-šur; *M*-Marduk, Cyr 242; Dar 37, 9 *foll*; KB iv 302, 303; *M*-Ninib (KB iv 100 i 11), AV 5581—4. Nabû-axê-šal-lim, AV 5707 (= ip?); Nabû-u-šal-lim, KB iv 304, 37. Eponym-list v 747: Sin-'š'al-lim-a(n)-ni, KB i 204, 205. Name of a canal: (nâr) Axê-šul-lim, Neb 135, 2.

3¹ KB iv 120, 121 *no* X 5: 4 minas of money xa-bu-li ..... *Š* u-sa-lim it-ti-din. Xammurabi-letters 9, 14—15 as soon as the sacrifices at Ur are completed (uš-ta-al-li-mu) BA iv 487. K 831 *R* 10, 11 šarrâni ki-lal-li-e it-ti a-xa-meš us-sa-al-lim-mu (Hr^L 214) ZK ii 78. — Xammurabi-*code* xxxv 2 uš-ta-li-im, (if) he heal (the broken limb).

T. A. — *Q* you know that šal-ma-ku u ša-lim mâti-ja, I am well and my land is flourishing, (Lo) 8, 3—4; 12, 6 šal-ma-at (al) Gub-lu, all is well with *G*; (Ber) 90, 11: but 79, 8 šal-ma-at Gub-la - is lost, + 80, 16; (Lo) 13, 14 šal-mu šu-nu, are lost; BA iv 395 See also (Ber) 104, 27, where some translate: they made an alliance; 103, 12 all countries ša-li-mu (are lost!, ZA vi 252—3). (Lo) 2ᵛ, 50 šalmu maxâzi-šu, šal-mu bîti-šu (is prosperous); 65, 19 the city šal-ma-at (is prosperous); (Ber) 92, 21 la-a šal-mu gab-bu ša taq-bu-u, all that you say is not true; 100, 13 and (the city) šal-ma-at a-na ja-ti-ja (surrendered to me?); 92, 22 šul-ma-a-da (that you have made peace) + 24; 76, 11 (and all the princes) šal-mu-šu (are favorable to him); 103, 12 let the king know that all the countries ša-li-mu (have declared) hostility against me. — 3 (Ber) 7 *R* 34 xi-bi-il-ta-šu li-ša-al-li-mu, that they make good his loss.

Derr. — tašlimu, tašlimtu & these 1e:

šalâmu *2.*, AV 7845 & **šalmu** *1.* ZDMG 32 ('78) 21 *foll*; Stade, *Morgenl. Forsch*, 181. — *a*) health }Gesundheit{. 83—1—18, 4 *R* 12 liš-al ša-lam šarri. — *b*) prosperity, peace }Wolstand, Glück; Friede{.

K 168, 18 name of a temple bīt rim-ki bīt ša-la-me-e; L⁵ 26 ana ša-lam xēri-ja. Scheil, *Rec. Trav.*, xvii 31/2 (bel) niqē ša-lam bīti GIŠ-BAR šu-ma-a-ta; *cf* Nabd 641, 4; 767, 2; 318, 5 ša-la-mu bīti ša (il) Adad; Cyr 229, 8. Asb iv 91 ina šal-me u-tir-ma u-kin; *cf* x 64 (end) çalūlašunu ša ša-la-me. Winckler, *Sargon*, 194 *no* 9 ša-lam (mât) Aššur ēpu-uš; KB iii (2) 92, 46 an-na ki-i-ni ša ša-la-mu ūmi. P. N. Ša-lam di-ni-in-nu, D^{Prol} 201 *rm* 2. — T. A. Lo 8, 23 i-na ša-la-a-mi, ZA v 157 *rm* 10 = בְּשָׁלוֹם, in safety, safely. Ber 188, 9—11 šal-mi-iš a-li-ik u i-na ša-la-mi ti-ir(-ma). Ber 8 *R* 18 ax[i-ja ja]-tu ša-al-ma lu ti-i-di, you ought to know of my health. Lo 16, 13 u ni-pu-uš šal-ma bi-ri-nu, that we may all have peace.

šalmu *2. adj f* šalimtu, AV 7882. — *a*) intact, whole, well; in connection with days, months *etc.*: lucky, favorable {unversehrt, heil; ganz; von Tag, Monat, *etc.*: glücklich, glückbringend}. Neb *Bors* ii 8 (Neb viii 59) i-na (in) arxu ša-al-mu i-na ūme šēmē; *cf* V 64 *a* 50; K 2801 *R* 46; BA iii 286, 287. Knudtzon, 25, 5 purussīka šal-mu. King, *Xammurabi*, *no* 56, 23 *foll*: ina (šīr) te-ri-e-tim ša-al-ma-a-t[im], owing to favorable predictions. K 2852 + K 9662 i 20 see surtu, 784, 785. — *b*) just, correct, reliable {recht, richtig, verlässig}. V 65 *a* 28 an-na ša-lim-ti; Smith, *Asurb*, 187 *j* a-mat-u ša-lim-tu ši-i, is that really so? (§ 79). K 2729 *R* 16 šum-ma a-bu-tu ša-li-im-tu ši-i, BA ii 566 *foll*: wenn es der vollkommene Wille ist; KB iv 145. Knudtzon, 29 *a* 7 dib-bi ki-nu-u-tu ša[-al]-mu-tu; 76, 4 written DI-MEŠ. H 66 ii 24—26 (id DI); 58, 68—9 see kēnu (403, *col* 2, end); also see balzu (161 *col* 1) & Br 9585. — *c*) of sacrificial animals: without blemish {fehlerlos} JBL xix 60 & *rm* 113; KAT³ 596; Zimmern, *Ritualtafeln*, *a* 1—20, 72 + 153; 11, 15; *pl* šal-ma-a-ti, 79—82 iv 6. — *d*) ZA x 208 *O* 13, 14 ina dup(-pu) ul ša-lim (ši?)-tum.

NOTE. — 1. On Ur(i)-šalim(mu) = Jerusalem, see Haupt in Cheyne, *Isaiah* (SBOT) 99—100; Brown-Gesenius, 436, 437.

2. KB iii (1) 192, 26 read la na-til ša-lim-ša; but BA ii 265 & 273 la na-ṭil ša pāni-ša (= einen Kurzsichtigen).

šalimtu *1.* (properly *f* of šalmu, 2) peace, prosperity {Friede. Zufriedenheit, Wolsein} AV 7852; BA i 160. V 35, 33—34 see muštaku (614 *col* 1) & 28 i-na ša-lim-tim. KB vi (1) 72—3, 25 (end) ša-lim-tu šak-na-as-su. K 1234 *R* 3 ina ša-lim-ti . . . it-tu-ši-ib; K 14, 7—9 ina šul-me it-tu-çi-u ina ša-li-in-ti e-tar-bu-u; K 609, 9 (Hr^{L} 134, 42, 126). Written DI-tim; Knudtzon, 75, 12. Perhaps ZA x 208 *O* 13, 14 (see above).

šalimtu *2.* some piece of furniture {ein Hausgerät}. See šašītum.

šalme(i)š, *adv* in peace, peacefully {in Frieden, wolbehalten} AV 7881. 8721 (ša-al-mi-iš). H^{V} 30; § 56*b*. Asb v 103 (nār) Id-id-e e-bi-ru (3 *pl*) šal-miš; *cf* ii 47; viii 80 the rivers Tigris & Euphrates šal-meš (*var* me-iš) lu-u e-bi-ru (3 *pl*); 118 šal-me-iš lu i-tu-ru-nim-ma (they returned); viii 86. TP viii 30; KB ii 242, 69 (a-tu-ra). KB iii (2) 68—9 *no* 13 ii 15 ša-al-mi-iš, ZA i 41, 85. II 36 colophon 25 šal-meš i-tal-lu-ku ma-xar-šu; Esh *Sendsch*, *R* 38 šal-meš lu at-tal-lak. K 2729 *O* 18 i-tal-la-ku šal-me[-iš] ‖ ina ki-na-a-ti (17). Pinches, *Texts*, 16 *no* 4 *R* 9 šal-meš lit-tal-lak-ma li-šal-lim par-çi-šu. See also salimiš (762 *col* 2, below).

šalmu *3. c. st.* šalam; usually **šalamtu**, corpse, body (= "with whom it is all over") {Leichnam}. *Johns Hopk. Circ.*, '84 (*vol* iii) *p* 51; H^{CV} 29, 30; Haupt. iii 187; ZA ii 266 *rm* 5; BA i 160 = Arm שְׁלַדָּא = שְׁלַנְדָּא. D^{Pr} 141 & *rm*; ZDMG 40, 732; ZA iii 342. Creat.-*frg* IV 104 ša-lam-ša id-da-a, he threw down her (Tiāmat's) corpse; IV 135 (end) ša-lam-tuš i-bar-ri, he examined her corpse. K 8586, 42 [u] ša-lam-ta-šu ana tu-ša-ri (NE 57) n[it-ta-di?], KB vi (1) 162. NE XII *col* vi 6 ša ša-lam-ta-šu ina çēri na-da-at. TP i 77 (iii 53; iv 91) šal-ma-at qu-ra-de-šu-nu; v 92 šal-mat (*var* ma-at) *etc.*; iii 78; ii 23; Šalm. *Mon*, *O* 46; *R* 98; IV² 20 *no* 1, 8 (= AMĒL-BE, Br 1533) see maçii ב (571 *col* 1). Šamš iv 29 šal-ma-ta qu-ra-di-šu-nu, the corpses of their warriors (§ 72*b*). Asurb iii 8 (amêl) ša-lam-ta-šu; iii 40 šal-ma-a-ti-šu-nu, their corpses; SMITH, *Asurb*, 129, 98 šal-ma-a-te-šu-nu (KB ii 254, 255). V 61 vi 54 lim-qut šal-mat-su. K 2867 *O* 29 ša-lam-tu $^{(amêl)}$ mitûte. II 19 *b* 62 ša-lam-ta, Br 1533. Xammurabi-*code* xliv 13 ša-al-ma-at.

šalamtaš, *adv.* V 35, 11 the inhabitants of Šumēr & Akkad ša i-mu-u ša-lam-ta-aš, which were like corpses. IV² 60* C 24 *a* im-mu-ça-ma im-mu-a ša-lam-taš. V 47 *a* 45 ša-lam-t[a-aš].

šalammu *1.* T^{C} 121 & BA i 502 read Nabd 214, 9: 1 gurru 90 QA ke-me a-na ša (STRASSM., ça)-lam-ma bi[t . . .] it-ta-din; a sacrifice by which the god is reconciled, made gracious; *cf* perhaps Hebr שְׁלָם. Nabd 799, 15 + 17 (*med*) ša BI-RIŠ (or ŠAG = šikaru reštû?) ša-la-me-e " sattukku. T^{C} 135 reads ša la mê, *i. e.*, not mixed with water. VATh 69, 5; 60, 4; 70, 4; also perhaps PEISER, *Vertr.*, 107, 5 see ça-lam-ma (*p* 878 *col* 2). Probably only a variant to šalâmu, 2. Are also:

ša-lu-me-e, Neb 160, 2 &:

ša-la-man-nu, Nabd 324, 2 (beg.).

šalmûtu, welfare, condition of being well {Wolbefinden} IV² 19 *b* 20, 21 šal-mu-us-su (Br 9536); Z^{B} vii 96; IV² 4 *col* 3, 48 šal-mu-su.

šulmu, *c. st.*, šulum. AV 8454 *foll*; 8469; § 65, 3. id DI, Br 9538; S^{b} 186 si-li-im | DI | šul-mu; II 30, 695; IV² 57 *b* 2. — *a*) welfare, safety, peace, prosperity {Wolbefinden, Wolergehen; Friede, Wolstand}. *del* 196 (216) li-tur ina šul-me. PINCHES, *Texts*, 16 *no* 4 *R* 8 kir-rit šu-lum u xu-ud libbi. Creat.-*frg* IV 34 u-ru-ux šu-ul-mu u taš-me-e; *cf* KB iii (2) 46, 4. IV² 54 *a* 48 ina qaq-qar šul-me (in the land of peace) maxraka littallak; & see šalimtu; 17 *a* 47, 48 šu-ru-ur šul-mi šu-kun-šum-ma, establish the perfection of his welfare. II 98/99, 54 šul-me ki-ma ki-e maš-ši lim-maš-šiš. KB iii (2) 6/8 *col* ii 14 kar šu-ul-mi-im; *cf* KB iii (1) 130 *col* ii 2 in šu-ul-mi-im. Xammurabi-*code* xl 17, 55 (HARPER). KB iii (2) 78, 8 see rê'u, 1 Q^{in}. — qabii šulma or šulum see ZA iii 40. K 82, 3—4 šu-lum ba-la-ţu *etc.* liq-bu-u, Hr^{L} 275; BA i 242; PSBA xxiii 53 *foll.* Dar 385, 3—4 Bêl u Nabû šu-lum u balaţ ša axi-a liq-bu-u. Nabd *Ann* iii 19 šu-lum ana âli ša-kin $^{(amêl)}$ Ku-raš šu-lum ana Bâbili gab-bi-šu qi-bi (= pm). BA ii 222, 223. K 501, 13 ma-çar (?) šul-mi ba-la-ţi; 83—1—18, 35 *O* 13 ma-çar šul-me u ba-la-ţi (Hr^{L} 113; 427). — especially in: šulmu, šulum šarri ša'alu, properly: inquire after the welfare of the king, with a wish that it may be well with him in every respect; then, ordinarily: greet, pay one's respects to. Asb iv 5 Tammaritu . . . . la iš-a-lu (*var* iš-al) šu-lum šarrûtija; 134 the inhabitants . . . . la iš(-'a)-a-lu(m) šu-lum šarru-ti-ja, did not greet me becomingly; viii 62—4 he that had never sent an ambassador la iš(-'a)-a-lu(m) šu-lum šarru-ti-šu-nu . . . . now iš(-'a)-a-lu šu-lum šarru-ti-ja. a-na ša-'a-al šul-me-in Asb ii 101, 120 (ZK ix 342): iii 85; vii 89; SMITH, *Asurb*, 484, 95; Sarg *Khors* 111; *Ann* 379 (*var* 391). K 477, 9 DI-mu ša šarri bêlija liš-'a-lu (Hr^{L} 514). šulmu jâši = šulmija, § 55*b*. Often also in the phrase: ana . . . . bê-lija *etc.* lu-u šul(& DI)-mu . . . . lik-ru-bu, 81—7—27, 199, 1—3; 83—1—18, 41, 3—4; K 486, 3—5 DI-mu a-a-ši lu DI-mu a-na ummi šarri; K 83, 3 lu-u šu-lum (Hr^{L} 862, 375. 303, 202). Also lu(-u) šul-mu *etc.* a-na; K 125 *O* 3, 4, 5. 6 (PSBA xvii 234 *foll*); K 501, 3; K 112, 3—5 (Hr^{L} 196, 113, 223); & lu šul-mu a-na šarri . . . a-dan-niš a-dan-niš, in letters. S 1064 (Hr^{L} 392) *etc.*; K 614, 4—5 šul-mu a-na ma-çar-a-te a-dan-niš; K 186, 10 ma-a šul-mu a-na $^{(al)}$ bir-a-te (the fortresses are all right); K 589 *R* 5—6 (Hr^{L} 175; 178, 187). šul-mu ina mâti, KB i 212—3 *ad* 758 (peace) >< sixu ina mâti (rebellion). IV² 58 *a* 6 a-na ki-bi-ti ša šul-mi, ZA xvi 165 *fol.* V 51 *a* 29, 30 see Br 7133. IV² 8? *a* 30 šu-lum šarrû-ti-šu. id DI, KNUDTZON, 56, 3; II 49 *b* 62 šul-mu ina list of stars (?); *ibid* 60 taš-mu-u. — *b*) oracle {Orakel} in K 2401 ii 8 an-ni-u šul-mu + 26; DT 83 (PINCHES. *Texts*, 15 *no* 4) 14 ba]-ru-ut šu-lum u purussê: MARTIN, *Textes rélig.*, '03, *pp* 90/1. — *c*) sunset {Sonnenuntergang} see šalamu

Q ✕ napax šamši. 83—1—18, 215 *R* 10 the people of the upper sea ša šul-mu šam-ši (of the west) WINCKLER, *Forsch.*, ii 3—4. II 67, 4; TP III *Ann* 131 tâ'm-tim ša šul-mi (il) Šam-ši. I 35 *no* 1, 13 a-di eli tam-tim rabīti ša DI-mu (il) Šam-ši; see *ibid* 6, 10, 11; *no* 3, 7 ša ša-lam šam-ši. Šalm, *Obel*, 27 a-na tam-di ša šul-me (il) Šam-ši, *cf* Šamš ii 21 *foll* (§ 30). See SCHRADER, *Die Namen der Meere*, 171 *foll.*

On compounds with šulmu (šulum) see AV 8470—75. KB iv 178 *col* iii 2. T. A. has these forms: Lo 6, 4 *foll.* u iš-tu šul-mu-qa u šu-lum-qa šu-lum bītika *etc.*, and in addition (?) to thy good health *etc.* ... danniš lu-u šul-mu. Ber 7, 29 ina šu-ul-mi-ka ... la iš-mu-u, concerning thy welfare (ZA v 16); Ber 8 *R* 21. Lo 8. 5 ana ja-ši šul-mu a-na ka-a-ša lu-u šul-mu. ZA v 154, 155 with me it is well, may it also be well with thee. šulmu šaparu = send greetings, *e. g.* Ber 7, 23 šu-ul-ma .... i-ša-ap-pa-ra-ak-ku, + 38. ana šul-mi šaparu, inquire after one's health, Ber 7, 30 a-na šu-ul-mi-ka la iš-pu-ra.

šullamu (?) K 1113 + K 1229 *O* 8 1 šul-lam bit-xal-li, Hr^{L} 71; see BA ii 46, 47.

šulmānu, *m* peace-offering, present }Geschenk}. Creat.-*frg* IV 134 igisū šul-ma-nu u-ša-bi-lu-šu-nu a-na ša-a-šu. Sargon *Asdod* 35 šul-man-na-šu-nu iššū (WINCKLER, *Sargon*, 188). Rm 69 *R* 5 šul-ma-nu e-ta-dan, + 9 šul-man-nu ta-ad-din (+ 15); K 183 *R* 17, 18 ša šul-ma-an-nu a-da-na-aš-šu-un-ni (Hr^{L} 429; 2). Neb 280. 2 (+ 7) šu-ul-lu-ma-an-na ša šarri; ZA vii 118 *O* 16 šul-ma-a-ni. P. N. Šul-ma-nu-ašaridu (§ 46) *etc.* see BEZOLD, *Catalogue*, v 2193—4; 83—1—18. 215 *R* 13; V 64 *b* 4; AV 7878—9 See KAT^{2} 474, 475. God Šul-mānu §§ 9, 22; 65, 85.

It occurs, especially, in T. A. = greeting, gift, present; with šemû = to hear one's greeting. Lo 1, 34 šu-ul-ma-ni ša a-xa-ti-ka; also 7, 8 + 10 + 16; 8, 73, 74. — Lo 2, 9 šu-ul-ma-na ba-na-a, a beautiful present (+ 7 + 11); a-na šu-ul-ma-ni-ka, as a present for thee, Lo 2, 36; 3, 40 + 44; Ber 9, 12 (šul-); 4 *R* 3 a-na šu-ul-ma-ni. šu-ul-ma-na ma-'-da ba-na-a, a rich, fine present, ZA v 142 (Ber 7 *R*) 9; Ber 1, 11 + 15 + 22; 7 *R* 11 šu-ul-ma-na ma-'-da ba-na-a ul uš-ē-bilakku; + 10 šu-ul-ma-an ga(= qa)-ti = a small present (literally: a present of the hand. ZA v 142). Lo 8, 69 šul-ma-an ša axija i-ri-šu lu-ut-ti-in, the present my brother desires I shall give, ZA v 162—3.

šulmāniš, *adv* safely }wolbehalten}. V 35, 24 see šadaxu Q. Xammurabi-*code* iv 44 šu-ul-ma-ni-iš, peacefully (HARPER, *The Code of Hammurabi*, 1904).

šulmat(t)u (?). K 646, 11 a-na šul-ma-na-a-ti (= *pl*); Hr^{L} 498; AV 8468.

šullundu (> šullumtu?). Nabd 1009. 2 ŠE-BAR ša šul-lu-un-du; 1010, 1 ŠE-BAR ša šu-lu-un-du. & perh. PEISER, *Vertr*, *no* cliii 9 (see *ibid.* 309); T^{C} 4 *ad* § 48.

šilmu *1.* *c. st.* ši-lim, defeat, overthrow: corpse }Niederlage; Erschlagener, Leiche} HINCKS; AMIAUD, ZK i 242 *rm* 2; HAUPT, BA i 17, 18 *rm* 22 thus read ŠI-ŠI, usually considered iD for abiktu. Sn i 21 aš-ta-kan ši-lim-šu (KB ii 82, 83); TP III *Nimr* 12 ši-lim-šu-nu amxaç-ma (KB ii 6—7). Synchr. History (II 65) i 27 ši-lim-šu im-xa-aç (*cf* 26: a-bi-ik-tam ša *N* iš-kun); iii 6. Šalm, *Mon.* *O* 22; Sarg *Khors* 26. Asb viii 34 (end) ši-lim-šu aš-kun; *cf* i 55; iv 69 (end); ix 18; Šamš iv 34; Anp iii 36. III 12, 24 ši-lim-šu aš-ta-kan; & see šakanu Q. — Šalm, *Mon.* *O* 39 ši-lim (almost = šal-mat; see 46, 47) qu-ra-di-šu çūru rap-šu u-mal-li; *Ob* 64. 89 *etc.*

šilmu *2.* II 41 *g-h* 29 .... XU-MEŠ = (šam) ši-lim ša eqli; 30 .... TAG-MEŠ = (šam) ši-niš (or man?) ša eqli. OEFELE. *Mittheilungen der Vorderasiatischen Gesellschaft*, '02, *no* 6, reads (šam) ši-ši; (šam) ši-niš, comparing Egyptian *šaša*, *šanš*. names for medical herbs }Arzneimittel}. See also ŠI-ŠI.

šulmū = Š of lamū (485 *col* 1). Creat.-*frg* IV 41 see sapāru. 2 (770).

šullummū, Asb v 41 see sulummū (763 *col* 1).

(šam) **ša-lam-bi** TUR-RA (= çixru) = (šam) a-ra-ru-u & (šam) aš-šu-ul-tu, II 42 *c-d* 15, 16; *cf* çallu, 2. V 29 *e-f* 27

U-ŠA (= LIB) $^{ša-lam-bi}$ ŠAR = el-meš[.... ??].

šulmudu see lamadu Š (486 *col* 2).

šilimtu (BA i 18 *rm* 22). M^{S}: perhaps womb, uterus {Gebärmutter}. II 47 *c-d* 34, 35 TE (*cf* V 40 *c-d* 17; ZA iv 276; Br 7707) & SAL-SAL (Br 10970) = ši-lim (or ši?)-tu. AV 7883. 83—1—18, 1330 *R* iv 11, 12 te-e | TE | ši-lim-tu & i-b(p)u (PSBA Dec. '88; *Cuneif. Texts*, pt XII *p* 11). V 31 *a-b* 40? II 37 *c-f* 58; II 40 *b-c* 8 ši-lim-tu(m) = i-ba-xu(xi) Br 13931. See also ZA ix 157 *ad* V 40 *g-h* 9; & *cf* silītu, 764 *col* 2.

šalummatu. splendor, brilliancy (of meteors, stars *etc.*); glory, renown; espec. ‖ melammu (*q. v.*): awful, majestic splendor {Glanz (von Meteoren, Steinen *etc.*); Ruhm, Glorie; namentlich auch ‖ melammu, schreckenerregender Glanz}. AV 7858. A form like namurratu, rašubbatu, šaqummatu, *etc.* id SU-ZI (= puluxtu) Br 187; SU-ŠI (Br 235; KB iii, 1, 146 *rm* 4); II 37, 5; ZK i 171; ZA ii 85—7; JENSEN, 155. IV^{2} 34 i *O* 23—25 ša-lum-mat-su eli [māti itbuk?]. V 33 v 37 KA-SU-ŠI = bāb šalummati; ii 54, 55 (a-gi-e) ša ša-lum-ma-ti ma-la-ti; IV^{2} 20 *no* 1, 19/20 (beg.). Anp i 20 *Anp.* a-pi-ir (*var* a-bir) ša-lum-ma-te, endowed with awe-inspiring splendor. III 4 *no* 8 (Anp *Stand*) 13. Anp i 26 ša-lum-ma-at kakkēšu melam[-me] bēlūtišu. Sarg *Ann* 185 ša-lum-mat kakkēja. V 65 *b* 8 the wall of the temple ša-lum-ma-at u-šal-biš; 39, zimē bēlūtu ša-lum-ma-at šarrūtu. ZA iv 228, 11 $^{(ilat)}$ NIM-MEN-NA ba-ni-tu ša-lum-ma-tu u-dam[-mi-iq]. K 3182 i 19 the mighty mountains are pregnant ša-lum-mat-ka (with thy glory). K 5418 iii 3 ša-lum-mat ni-ši, KB vi (1) 297 (& 555) Schreckensglanz der Menschen. id SU-ZI in IV^{2} 6 *b* 41, 42; 26 *a* 35, 36; 18 *no* 1 *O* 8, 9, see ramû, 1 (Q); where, also, K 2001, 5. IV^{2} 24 *no* 1, 18, 19 pu-lux-tu u ša-lum-ma-tu (= SU-ZI); 21, 22 ša-lum-ma-tu (= SU-ŠI) ez-zi-ta; 25 *b* 46, 47 ša-lum-ma-tu (= SU-ŠI) na-ši said of the azkaru; also 5 *c* 40, 41. II 49 *e-f* 21 ša-lum[-ma-tu?] a ‖ of ç(z)al (or ni) lummū & mešxu.

šulumatu (?). KB iii (1) 132 *col* 3, 19 šu-lu-ma-tim i-šid-si-na u-ki-in.

šalammu *2.* see šaqummu, 2.

šullānu. K 4195 *R* 13 šu-ul-la-nu = mu(?)-'-ru.

ši(l)lān. see çītan (*p* 900) west, *i. e.* the region where the sun disappears {Westen; Gegend, wo die Sonne hineingeht und verschwindet}. K^{M} setting: a point in heaven. Br 5729. HOMMEL, *Expos. Times*, July '97: šīlān presupposes šīlu (or šēlu) = deep, identical with שְׁאוֹל. JENSEN, *Kosmologie*, 15, & ZA v 131 (*ad* Gen 49, 10) šīlan, west, = Hebr שׁאול; also ZA xv 243 *rm* 1; ZIMMERN, ZA vii 163, 164; but, again, KAT^{3} 636. HÜSING, OLZ '03, *col* 370; '04 *cols* 88—9 Hebr שִׁילֹה > שִׁילֹן. Babyl. šilāni: Sum. šitlam, as xilāni: xitlāni.

šilēnu. M^{S} 95 but see AV 4810 reading li-li-e-nu II 32 *c* 4 (ZIMMERN).

šilingu. a bird {ein Vogel} see puridu, 2 (827 *col* 2, below) & pilingu (808 *col* 1); AV 8222; Br 7972.

šullundu, see above *p* 1045 *col* 2.

šulsi (= ip) & šul-si-e (= ac) see šasū, Š.

šalapu, pr išlup, ps išallu(a)p. draw, pull out (*e. g.*, the sword) *etc.* {herausziehen (z. B., das Schwert aus der Scheide)} *etc.* D^{H} 20; ZDMG 40, 725 = سَلَكَ. BARTH, *Etymolog. Studien*, 27: שלף = سلب; so also SCHWALLY, *Idiotikon*, 130. Sarg *Nimr* 6 (end) kakku la max-ri iš(l)-lu-pu i-du-uš-šu; SMITH, *Asurb*, 137, 77—8 (148, 3) see šaxaṭu, 2; 124, 55 ištar šal-pat (= pm) nam-ça-ru zaq-tu ša e-peš ta-xa-zi (§ 89 i; KB ii 250, 251). NE IX *col* i 16 iš-lu-up namçar šibbišu. IV^{2} 58 iii 34 i-šal-lup šer-ra ša ta-ra-a[-ti], ZA xvi 180, 181: sie (die labartu) reisst gewaltsam das Kind von den Schwangeren heraus. T^{M} vii 97 a-max-xaç li-it-ki a-šal-la-pa lišānki. IV^{2} 3 *b* 50, 51 li]-pit-ta-šu šalpat (has been torn out) elišu it-ta-din. Z^{S} viii 46 paṭru parzilli ša-la-pu. II 26 (⊕ 84) *c-d* 31 GID-DA = ša-la-p[u]; 32, GID $^{(gi-id)}$ GID = š ša .... (Br 7566, 7573); preceded by 29, $^{(su-uk)}$ ŠE = šul-pu (Br 10313) & 30, = š ša $^{(amēl)}$ ŠU (Br 7663 š ša nāri?).

ג V 45 vii 22 tu-šal-lap.

Derr. — mašlupu (607 *col* 1) & these 2?:

šulpu *1.* see above.

šilpu. Sarg *Khors* 151 ši-il-pu il-lik; ANN 374. WINCKLER, *Forsch.*, ii ('98) 133 *rm* 2: er hatte Einfälle gemacht.

šulpu *2.* in the phrase pi-i šul-pu, Camb 257, 6; 409, 11; KB iv 290—1: pasture }Weide{; PEISER, KAS 101. KB iv 94, 95 *ad* VA 208, 7: IV Gur zēru pi-i šu-ul-pi (+36) = 4 Gur Saatfeld (und zwar) Weide; Nabd 4, 12; 108, 8 pi-i-šu šul-pu (unbebautes Land; Brachfeld); 678, 9; see Artax 10, 5 where pi šulpu is given out ana ir-ri-šu-tu (for cultivation); also Nabd 108, 5; Dar 144, 8; Cyr 3, 1; 308, 1. Artax 8, 6 zēru pi šulpu has the explanatory addition bīt re-e-ti, Weide-land. MEISSNER, 141. AV 8458.

šulupu. so KB iii (2) 134, 26 ina šu-lu-pu uš-bi, but read with HAUEN, BA ii 218 *foll.* & PRINCE, *Diss*, 92: ina qāti dib-bu uš-bi.

šallapānu, AV 7868 see sallapānu (763 *col* 2).

šallapītum. V 28 *a-b* 70 šal-la-pi-tum ‖ un-qu, AV 7869.

šulputu, *adj* (√lapatu, as also the next 3) destroyed, broken, tumbled down }zer-stört, eingefallen{. Z^B 41, 42. K 4620 iv 30, 31 a-li šul-pu-tum (my ruined city) bikītum ublamma ‖ bi-ti ab-tu. IV^2 33* *d* 51 ina (arax) Araxsamna ultu mū I (KAN) adi ūm XXX (KAN) šarru lu ilašu lu ištaršu lu ilānišu šul-pu-tu-ti (his destroyed gods) uddiš; *cf* IV^2 33 iv 4/6. 81, 2—4, 188, 33 (ilāni *pl*) šul-pu-tu-ti ab-ni, ZA v 67 the statues of the gods, which had been tumbled down, I put up again. II 48 *c-d* 63 XUL = šul[-pu-tu] Br 9507; followed, 64 by UD-DA-GID-DA = šal[-pu-tum] & NAM-GIL-MA = ša[x-lu-uq-tu?].

šulputtu. destruction, ruin; corruption }Zerstörung, Vernichtung; Verderben{ § 65, 33*b*. K 782 *R* 4 (il) Sin māt šul-pu-ut-ti u-šeš-šib; *ibid* 6 māt nakri šal-pu-ut-ti immar. III 62 *a* 31 mātu šul-pu-ut-tum i[-baš-ši?].

šalputtu. fall, devastation, ruin }Fall, Ver-wüstung, Verderben{. IV^2 10 *b* 41, 42. H 116 *O* 17/18 (= XUL-A, EME-SAL, Br 9506) see çamadu, Q pm. SCHEIL, *Nabd*, i 35—38, the king of Aššur who .... ša-al-pu-ut-tim māti iš-ku-nu; x 14 ina šal-pu-ut-ti Ummān-man-du. Bu 88—5—12, 75 + 76 ii (K 192 *O*) 11 uš-ta-nak-la-mu ittāti šal-pu-ti; Bu 88—5—12, 77 vi 13 šal-pu-ut-ta-šu-nu lu-mu-un-tu, their utter ruin; BA iii 248, 249 *rm* *††. III 54 *a* 51 šal-pu-tim māti iššaka-an, the country will be ruined; 64 *a* 13 (-ti); 38 *no* 1 *O* 16 + *R* 10 (-tim).

šalaputtū dissolution }Auflösung{ see la-patu, 493 *col* 1, above.

šu-lu-uç da-al-tum. II 23 *c-d* 46 = e-di-lu, bolt }Riegel{. AV 8457. *Theolog. Litbl.*, '00, *no* 5 compares Hebr אלץ.

šalaqu, cut open; tear out, pluck out }auf-schlitzen; ausreissen, aufschneiden{ Proc. A. O. S. '80, *p* cxlix; HAUPT in PATERSON. *Numbers* (SBOT) 50. Asb iv 69 pi-i (*var* lišān)-šu-nu aš-lu-uq (see šalapu). 83, 1—18, 1332 iv 16 [DAR] = ša-la-qu. — ג cut up (or, open) }ausschneiden, aufschlitzen{. Asb ix 36 see rukūšu. T^M vii 99 u-ša-laq a-xi-ki. V 45 vii 23 tu-šal-laq. K 10094, 8 šul-lu-qu, M^S *pl* 16.

šiliqqu *1.* a bird }ein Vogel{. II 37 *a-c* 48 NAM-BER-XAM-XU = as(z)-ki-qu = ši-liq-qu. AV 8221, 8224; Br 2138.

šiliqqu *2.* Br 923 & 6958 *ad* II 44 *e-f* 33 a tree }ein Baum{. See siliqqu (?).

šelqu. V 33 viii (the great goddess, mistress of the great lands) 1/2: še-el-qa li-šak-lil-šu. See KB iii (1) 150, 151.

šilqu see silqu, 2 (764 *col* 2, *ll* 1—4) & KAT^3 598 & *rm* 3. MEISSNER, ZA xv 415 (šēr) šilqu = Arm שלק; *cf* Arab سلق cook, boil. K^M 40, 10 (šēr) KA-IZI si-il-qa.

šallaru, *pl* šallarē. AV 7870. MEISSNER, ZA ix 270/1 zuerst Topf oder Kessel. V 32 *a-c* 21 [IM]-ZI = šal-la-ru ‖ si-i-ru (hedge?) Br 8388; V 42 *g-h* 27 IM-ZI (= enclosure made of clay *etc.*) = šal-la-ru (*cf* 25/6). *f* šallarittum (*q. v.*). — Dann: in bautechnischer Beziehung oft ‖ kalakku & taraxxu, Asb x 84; V 64 *b* 6 (see maxaçu, 2 *p* 525 *col* 2, end) wol: ein unten gelegener Raum. § 65, 24 wall }Wand{. ZK ii 344; ZA vi 35, 36. D^{Pr} 70 *rm* 1: wol die aus Backsteinen gefügte Wand. BA iii 273; 283 "Grundmauer" = foundation wall (K 2801 *R* 46); but HOM-MEL, ZDMG 55, 524 = Topf, Kessel; und

Schwelle. Neb ii 40 ša-al-la-ru-uš-šu, its (the papaxu's) walls I had covered with gold (>< KB iii, 2, 15). *Bors* i 18 papaxa bēlūtišu xurāçi nam-ri ša-al-la-ri-iš aštakkan; *Grot* i 30 (KB iii, 2, 33: prächtig??); also *cf* 85, 4—30, 1 i 34. OPPERT, GGA '84, 335: in Kuppelform.

NOTE. — šal-la-ru, WINCKLER, *Sargon*, 74, 433 (*Ann*); 182, 170 (*Khors*) honey; but read lallaru.

(iç) **šiluru** (?) Bu 88—5—12, 103 ii 14; BA iii 273: eine Art Baugerät aus kostbarem Material; *cf* ZA iv 106 + 130, 42 (KB iii, 2, 4). I 49 *d* 12 (BA iii 222): einen *šilūru* aus Elfenbein.

šelūru. PSBA xxi 120, 121 *ad* III 66 *col* 4, 1 (al) Umbara še-lu-ru libittu (?); *col* 8 (after the break) 4, še-lu-ru libnat ēkalli.

šalluru. a tree }ein Baum{. Rm 367 + 83, 1—18, 461 *a* iii 11 (M^S *pl* 23) GIŠ-KIB = šal-lu-ru. Rm 346, 14 šal-lu-ru = [(šam) ri-ib]-xu; *ibid*, *pl* 12. Nabd 486, 2.

šal-la-rit-tum, V 45 *g-h* 29; Br 8391 same id as ba-aç-çu; BA iii 283.

šalašu 1. H 71, 20 i-šal-la-aš, see šankaku, 2. id points to identification with šalašu, 2. AV 7850; Br 6937. BERTIN, RP^2 iii 94: *i* a mistake for *u* (translates: he divided it into 3 parts); see, however, ZA i 409. IV^2 30 *no* 2 *O* 5 (= Sm 2148) lax-ra (479 *col* 1) u pu-xad-sa i-šal-la-š[u?]. KNUDTZON, 133, 4 [i]-šal-li-i-ši.

šalašu 2. a denominative of šalšu, = say a third time }zum dritten Mal sagen{. II 39 *e-f* 10 U-MU-UN-NI-KA-PIŠ = šul-lis-sum-ma, tell him a third time; (Rm 345 *O* 20 = M^S *pl* 22; K 2361 i 46 = ZA iv 226); preceded by s, qi-bi-šum-ma & u, šu-un-ni-šum-ma. V 63 *b* 5 u-šal-liš(-ma), KB iii (2) 116, 117. ZA iv 14 *col* 2, 15 šu-la(-aš)-šum-ma. See also šušlušu.

ša(l)laš(l)tu, three }drei{. §§ 34 b; 51; 75; AV 7842. S^c 124 pi-eš | PIŠ | ša-lal-ti (Br 6938; II 25, 52l; ZK ii 339; ZA iv 121 *no* 19; KB iv 178 *no* 3, 5). D 130, 133 = H 110, 36 DUM-MU-UŠ | III | ša-la-aš-ti, AV 7851; Br 11878; PINCHES, PSBA iv (Jan. 6, '82) 112; ZK ii 279 below. KB iii (1) 162, 27 ga-ba-ri-e ša-lal-ti = 3 copies. K 3182 ii 49 (end) one shekel a-na še[-lal-ti?], for three. IV^2 5 *a* 64, 65 ana še-lal-ti-šu-nu ilāni (= III-A-AN-NE-NE, *i. e.* Sin, Šamaš, Ištar; Br 11879); 15 *col* ii 7, 8; 54 *b* 32 še-lal-ti ū-me = 3 days (§ 128); K 6012 + K 10684, 5 še-la-[šit ūmu], 3^d day, PSBA xxvi opposite, *p* 56. V 34 *c* 14; *b* 5 & KB iii (2) 48 *col* 1, 42 (pa-nim še-lal-ti-šu-nu u-ša-at-ri-iç) & Bu 88—5—12, 212, 26 adi ša-la-ši-šu (GGA '98, 826 = zum dritten Male); V 34 *a* 27 ka-a-ri danna-a-ti še-la-ši-šu iš-ti-en i-ti ša-ni-i = their thirds, the first and the second = two thirds. *Rec. Trav.*, xix 62, 5: še-lal-šu-nu > šelaltišunu (?). Nabd 172, 4: III-it (= šalaš-it?) šanāti. V 37 *d-f* 51 (e-eš) ⟨⟨⟨ = ša-lal-ti, Br 9990.

ša(e)lāšā = 30. AV 7849, 8217; § 75. V 37 *d-f* 45 (ba-a) ⟨⟨⟨ = ša-la-ša-a; + 50, (u-šu); II 41, 249 (še-); ZA iv 483 (= K 2124, 14). II 42, 47. id II 15 *c-d* 40; K 155 *O* 18 (Br 9991); ZA i 182. D 88 vi 18 (*cf* II 46 *a-b* 18; 62 *g-h* 46) GIŠ-MA' XXX GUR = elip še-la-ša-a (*sc.* gurru). IV^2 23 *a* 3/4 Nusku mār ša-la-še-e (= UD XXX GAN) bubbulum, Nusku, the son of the 30th day, the rest-day (or 'day of desire'), PINCHES, PSBA xxvi 52; K 6012 + K 10684 *l* 17 UD XXX-GAN = (ūmu) še-la-ša-a (*ibid* 56), *cf* BA iii 417; JENSEN, 91, 92.

šalšu *c. st.* šaluš, *f* šaluš(l)tu the third; also one third }der, die, das dritte; ein Drittel{ AV 7885; § 76. KB vi (1) 78 *no* ii 2 i-na ša-al-ši, also 208 i 4; 112, 31 šal-ša KAS-PU. NE I *col* 2, 44 one day, a second day u šal-ša, and a third (*cf* VII *col* 6, 6 (23)); *col* 3, 47 ina šal-ši ūme (*cf* K 655 *R* 2 a-na III-ši ū-me; also see timāli, Hr^L 182); X *col* 3, 49; 4, 4 šana-a šal-ša u ri-ba-a; VI 142 (143); *del* 187 (144) šal-ša ūma. See also šašūmu. IV^2 5 *a* 17, 18 šal-šu(ši) = III G(K)AN-MA (Br 11881); id IV^2 31 *O* 48, *R* 41; H 41, 290. IV^2 56 *a* 3 (*add*) šal-šu. Sn ii 34 i-na šal-ši gir-ri-ja, on my third campaign, *Kuj* 1, 18; § 129. V 64 *a* 28 i-na ša-lu-ul-ti šatti i-na ka-ša-du, when the 3^d year approached; KB vi (1) 294, 27. VATh 796, 15 i-na ša-lu-uš-tim e-çi-dim. ana ša-lu-uš-tim šûçû (§ 77) = rent for 3 years; Meissner, *no* 72, 8; 75, 11; 63 *no* 77, 6 a-na ša-lu-uš, auf 3 Jahre. K 644 *R* 24 ša-lul-ti mârat-su, Hr^{L} 336; PSBA xxiii 338. Nabd 824, 18 šal-lul-tum; Knudtzon, *pp* 53 & 321 (ša-lul-ti). K 287 (III 47 *no* 10) 8 a-na III-su-šu i-rab-bi, a third {ein Drittel} KB iv 110; *i. e.* it will gain 33 1/3 %; also K 350 (III 47 *no* 5) 7—8 a-na III-su-šu-nu i-rab-bi-u. KB iv 126, 127. *del* 205 (225*b*) šalul-tum; 215 (237*b*) *var* ša-lul-tum (§ 77). III 59 *no* 15, 48 III-šu *var* ša-lul(?)-ta(tin?)-šu (ZA ix 120). Xamm.-*code* xiii 50 if a man have rented a field u lu a-na mi-iš-la-ni u lu a-na ša-lu-uš (for either one-half or one-third of the crop) ZA xviii 38; x 46 ša-lu-uš-ti eqlim (xvi 69 -tam) ZA xviii 2 *rm* 2. *f pl* šalšâtu (*sc.* înâ) K 56 ii 22—24 šal-ša-a-tu; a-na šal-ša-a-ti; ana šal-ša-a-ti u-še-çi; idd ŠI-III-GAL-LA Br 9404, 11880; AV 7884; § 77 = שְׁלִישִׁית. Bezold, RP² iii 95. H 68 *R* 4 = V 40 *c-d* 52 = šal-ša-a-ti. H 74, 4 miksu šal-ša-ti, toll of a third (AV 2398).

šal-šiš = thirdly {drittens} *adv* K 8522, 5 (KB vi (1) 34, 35).

šalšâa. third in rank, age, command *etc.* {dritter in Rang, Alter, Befehl *etc.*}. Asb iii 48 Tammaritu axu šal-ša-a-a (§ 77 × BA i 460), KB ii 182, 183; Smith, *Asurb*, 130, 1. KB iv 88 *col* 4, 32 mârišu šal-ša-a-a, preceded by mârišu rabi-i & mârišu kud-din-nu. K 287, 10 pân Arbêla (amêl) šal-šu (+ 11); followed by pân *N* (amêl) šanu-u; III 48 *no* 3, 4; = שָׁלִישׁ?, on which see Haupt, BA iv 586.

šalšiânu, *adv* for the 3d time {zum 3ten Mal} Smith, *Asurb*, 217, k; 244 g (§ 77) šal-ši-a-nu, JA '89, xiii, 311.

šalšênu. K 525, 17 ša šad-dag-ţiš ina šal-še-ni (= ina šalši-šeni = 3 times) ina ra-bu-še-ni (= 4 times) Hr^{L} 252; BA ii 55; ZA xvii 391 *no* 6.

šalašêrî = 13th {13ter}. KB vi (1) 78, 7 i-na ša-la-še-e-ri-i, im dreizehnten.

šulšu (?) KB iv 316, 317 *l* 1: 2/3 ma-na kaspi qa-lu-u šul-šu; *f* perh.:

šullultu (?). Neb 164, 27 šul-lul-ti = 1/3; Nabd 1033, 5; Nabd 776, 5 šul-lul-ta-a-ti; 652, 7 receipt from šul-lul-ta-a-tum. Peiser, *Vertr.*, 241; Oppert, ZA vi 273. KB vi (1) 204, 205 *l* 16 šit-ta-šu ilu-ma šul-lul-ta-šu a-me-lu-tu two (thirds) of him (is) god; and one third of him (is) human; also 118 *no* II 1 (šit-tin-šu *etc.*).

šallatu *f* (√šalalu); AV 7872; § 63. — *a*) leading away {Wegführung} Esh iii 42 šal-la-at ilâni-šu. — *b*) spoil, booty {Beute} ‖ kišittu; H^{F} 36. very often in the phrase šal-la-su-nu, šal-lat-su-nu (*Khors* 47, 48; § 51) or šal-la-at aš-lu-la see šalalu; Anp ii 30, 31 šal-la (ZA i 362)-su-nu aš-lul: ii 84, 111; iii 38. See also kabtu *b*) (370 *col* 1) & Sarg *Khors* 71 šal-la-tu ka-bit-tu; 133 šal-lat maxâzišu ka-bit-ti. I 44, 67 šal-la-at na-ki-ri ka-bit-tu. TP iv 3 šal-la-su-nu ušêçâ. S^{P} II 987 *O* 27 .... rabûti(?) ina šal-lat u-še-iç-bi [-it?] JTVI 29, 54. Asb vi 125 nišê u šal-lat (mât) Elamti. si-it-ti šal-la-ti, ZA iii 312 (= Sn *Rassam*) 60; + 59 ina šal-la-at; also I 7 *no* 1, 8. Often šal-la-su-nu in connection with bušû, šêšu, makkûru, namkurru, maršîtu *etc.* — *c*) prisoners (collectively) {Kriegsgefangene} just as kišittu, *q. v.* Anp i 108: 3000 šal-la-su-nu I burnt in fire; iii 112. TP III *Ann* 143: 600 šal-la-at (al) NN. *etc.* (148, 149). S 1028, 15—16 um-ma ša xu-ub-tu u šal-lat ša Bâbili u-tir-ri (Hr^{L} 418). Sn iii 5 such & such persons a-na šal-la-ti am-nu. I made prisoners; Sarg *Khors* 139. Perhaps also Synchr. Hist., iv 6 (end) šal-la-su-nu ma-'-du (KB i 202, 203). V 20 *e-f* 12, 13 NAM-RI = šal-la-tum (II 38, 66; Knudtzon, 43, 15 NAM-RA ka-bit-tu; 35, 9); NAM-RI-AG-A = *š* ša-la-lu; Br 2142, 2576; *cf* V 20 *g-h* 37, 38.

šallatiš, *adv* = ana šallati; AV 7871; § 80*b* usually with am-nu (§ 150) = I counted as; see manû, 1 (556 *col* 2, below) for Asb vi 8; K 2852 + K 9662 iii 26. Sn i 33 šal-la-ti-iš (*var* tiš) am-nu (Sarg *Ann* 75; *Khors* 78; *Bull* 23); iii 20 šal-la-tiš (Asb ii 133; v 10; KB ii 240, 42).

šallûtu. captivity {Gefangenschaft} §§ 63; 65, 34 ‖ kamûtu (*q. v.*, 390 *col* 1). TP v

(12 +) 24 (= as prisoners); II 60 *c* 23 ki-i ša-al-lu-ut-tu, AV 7877.

šālūtu. H 108, 11; V 11 ii 9; D 128, 59 NA-AM-[. . .] | NAM-LUGAL | ša-lu-tum, followed by be-lu-tum. AV 7859; Br 1618, 2173, 4265. Z[B] 99 √שאל; PRINCE, *Diss*, 98 √elū.

šūlūtu & šūlītu. garrison }Garnison{ √elū (עלה) Š = šūlū· PRINCE, *Diss*, 98. Sn iv 48 the cities which the Elamite had taken forcibly I captured and despoiled: (amēl) çābē šu-lu-ti-ja (*cf* Sarg *Ann* 240) ušērib qiribšun. Nabd *Ann* ii 17 šu-lit ša ram-ni-šu ina libbi u-še-li-ma (+ 18 šu-lit-su); BA ii 219.

(šam) **šu-ul-tu** (AV 8235; Br 13066, 13069) & (šam) **šu-lu-tu** (II 42 *c-d* 18) see si-lammu (763 *col* 1, below).

šillatu *1*. see sillatu, 1. (704 *col* 1); AV 8232.

NOTE. — Here perhaps the following passages in JOHNS, *Deeds & Documents*, šu šil-la-a-te (80¹, 25, 34, *R* 5, 14); šu šil-lat 969, 5; BI šil-la-ti (???, 4); BI šil-lat (999, 1 *etc*); BI šū šil-lat (1013, 17) or xašlatu? (JOHNS).

šillatu *2*. KNUDTZON, 321 ‖ šallatu (√ša-lalu). SCHEIL, *Nabd*, ii 33, 34 ši-pi-ir Marduk ša ši-il-la-ti, MESSERSCHMIDT, 26 & 44: Das Verhalten Marduks, welches in Plünderung bestand, ix 32: 2750 ši-il-la-ti nakri xu-me-e . . . . ušruq. See also KB vi (1) 374; & sillatu, 2 (704 *col* 2) Br 11293.

še-el-tum. V 32 *c* 3; in *col b* is preserved MA . . . . DU; some vessel }ein Gefäss{.

šilūtu. II 62 *c-d* 72 AN-ME-NU-ŠU-UL = ši-lu-tum, AV 8228, Br 10393.

šelūtu *1*. Šalm, *Mon*, *R* 42 (*O* 19) ki-ma še-lu-ut paṭri parzilli, like the point of a dagger, CRAIG, *Diss*, 26. ZDMG 48, 22 compares שְׁלָח & Gen 37, 32. *Cf* L⁴ ii 17 i-nu-xu ul-me-šu-un še-lu-u-ti, LEHMANN, ii 69 = *pl* of *adj* šelū (√עלה = elū) sharp, pointed.

šelūtu *2*. IV² 61 *b* 51 ša pî (ilu) Ištar-bēl-da-i-ni šu-lu-tu ša šarri: HARPER, AJSL xiv 275: from the mouth of *I* the seer of the king, √שאל. PINCHES, RP² v 139: the choice (?) of the king. See also JOHNS, *Doomsdaybook*, 55.

šammu & šamu, *m* plant, herb, grass, vegetation }Pflanze, Kraut; Gras, Vegetation{ AV 7940. iD U (= ŠAM) §§ 9, 4; 25. Br 6027. S° 75 u | U | šam-mu; V 27 *g-h* 56; H 81, 20 (KAT³ 409 *rm* 9); II 7 *e-f* 45. iD also serves as a determ. before names of plants, *etc.* see II R 41 *etc.* Z[B] 36 (meadow); ZA ii 93 (herb). 80—7—19, 130, 6 alpu na-ka-ri šam-me ik-[kal], the ox of an enemy eats weeds. NE 8, 39 with the gazelles ik-ka-la šam-mi (= *pl*); 11, 3 ik-ka-la U. Creat.-*frg* IV 62 šam-mi-im ta-m[i]-i, a herb used for incantations. *del* 254 (284); 256 (286) see šū, 2; on 253 (283) see KB vi (1) 250 *rm* 2; 260 (291) šu-u il-qi šam-ma-ma; 264 (295) šam-mu an-nu-u šam-mu ni-bit(?)-ti; 266 (297) šam-ma lib-tuq; 272 (304, 305), 278 (314, end); here used throughout of the magic plant, rejuvenating the old man. On CRAIG, *Rel. Texts*, 59, 5 šam-me ba-la-ṭi; U-TI(-LA). I 35 *no* 1, 2 = šammu balāṭi (✕ KB i 190, 191) = Lebenspflanze, see KAT³ 523, 524 & passages quoted; &, again, MEISSNER, GGA '04, 754 (K 61 *a* 61, 66). Bu 88—5—12, 75 + 76 viii 11 (BA iii 254, 255). šammu also = medicine, whence, Syr-Arab *samm*, poison, & Hebr סמים, KB vi (1) 574; KAT³ 595 *rm* 5; KÜCHLER, *Beitr. zur Assyr. Medizin*, *p* 16. id-nam-ma šam-ma ša a-la-di, *Etana*-legend (K 1547 *R*) 14 (+ 15), see KAT³ 564; KB vi (1) 108. 109. IV² 57 *b* 7 šammē u nap-šal-tu. II 7 (*e*-)*f* 45 i-riš-tu šam-mu; AV 7953. Br 6070. II 36 *e-f* 45 . . . TI-LA-TAG-GA = e-qu-u ša šam-me; see *g-h* 58 e-gu-u ša U. II 42 *e-f* 69 (šam) ša-mi XAR-MEŠ (= xarrū) = (šam) e-zi-zu; II 43 *a-b* 65 (šam) ša-mi ra-pa-di = (šam) ka-si çir. II 42 *c* 36 (šam) ša-mu tar-bu-u (?); or, mutarbū? See 623 *col* 1. II 41 *a-b* 63. Br 12128—34. Xammurabi-*code* xv 47 ša-am-mi. T. A. (Ber) 6 *R* 8 ša-am-mi ša çi-e-ri, fieldplants: 28 iv 3: 9 ša-am-mu ša šin-bi-ri pa-aš-lu.

šammu *2*. K 2801 (= K 221 + 2669) *R* 31 la ki-šit-ti šam-me, BA iii 236, 237.

šamū *1*. burn, boil, roast }brennen, kochen, rösten{, ZA iii 190, below. II 34 *a-b* 71 ŠU-RU-UZ = ša-mu-u | ša-ba-bu. Br 7106. V 19 *a-b* 26 + II 34 *c-d* 14 ŠU-XU-UZ = ša-mu-u ša ša-ba-a-bi, Br 7116 (JENSEN, ZK ii 53); V 19 *a-b* 25 + II 34 *c-d* 13 la-ax | LAX | ša-mu-u ša um-ma-ri, Br 7796; KB vi (1) 510 (einen Kochtopf) aufs Feuer setzen.

ℑ II 28 *d-e* 58 ŠU-XU-UZ = šu-um-mu-u, Br 7117, AV 8419, 8504 (HAUPT, ZA ii 280 & BA i 293/300; JÄGER, BA i 453 *rm* **; LEHMANN, i 15 *rm* 5 *no a*; ZIMMERN, ZA v 85, 86). V 28 *e-f* 88 šu-u-u = šum-mu-u, = شَوَى, KB vi (1) pref xi; & on the other hand PRINCE, *Diss*, 125.

Der. šamû, 1.

šamû *2.* *m* heaven, sky }Himmel, Firmament} *pl* šamê. Chief id AN (§§ 9, 60; 25). S^{b} 1 a-na AN šu-mu-u; H 1, 12; 10 & 205, 29; 28, 632; 186 (Sm 23) 3; 136 § 5*a*. JENSEN, 4—16. AV 7944; Br 417, 418, 437; AN-NA, Br 450; MU, Br 1282. Written mostly ideographic, with or without phonetic complement *-e* (§ 23); Hesych. *σαύη* (§§ 29; 44). NE 58, 15 šamu-u ≍ qaq-qa-ru, heaven & earth. VATh 663 *O* 5 (REISNER, *Hymnen*, 145) ša-ma-'. III 59 *a* 64 AN iznun (see zananu, 2; 287). V 56, 60 a-di šamê u erçitu (§ 27) ba-šu-u (= exist). TP i 7 Šamaš da'an šame-e u erçi-ti; *cf* V 51 *c* 34 (-tim); K 2606 *O* 24 (see parakku, 830 *col* 2, *med*); TP i 15 šame-e erçi-ti. V 33 vii 16, 17 šame-e rap-šu-ti. S^{P} III 586 + Rm III 1, 2 (11) Šamaš a-na ki-rib šame-e ina e-ri-bi-ka; 4, ši-gar ša-me-e el-lu-tim; 6, da-la-at ša-me-e, PSBA viii 167 *fol*; HOMMEL, *Sum. Lesest.*, 120 *fol.* IV^{2} 20 *no* 3 *O* 18, 19 thy command, o Nebo, ki-ma ša-me-e (= AN) ul ut-tak-kar; 28 *no* 2 *O* 10 be-lum ina a-ga-gi-šu ša-mu-u (≍ er-çi-tim, 12) i-ta-na-ar-ra-ru-šu (quake before him): 19, 20 ilâni ša ša-me-e (= AN-NA) a-na šame-e itelû (≍ ilâni ša erçitim), H 125, 14 (+ 16). S 954 *O* 16 + 18 + 20 + 22 u-su-ma (*var* um) šame-e, said of Ištar. V 44 *a-b* 17; D^{K} 70 & *rm* 4; ZA ii 87. V 34 *c* 50 before Marduk šar ša-mi-e u ir-zi-tim (§ 127); KB iii (2) 66, 45; Neb *Bors* ii 26 (*cf* 24); II 51 *b* 10. Br 492; 9680. BANKS, *Diss*, 1 *no* 4, 23 amatsu ša-me-e u[-rab?]; 24—25, 102 i-'š'it-tum ša-mu-e it-gu-ru-tum (-tu). Neb *Bors* i 13 Na-bi-um pa-ki-id ki-iš-ša-at ša-mi-e u er-çi-tim. KB vi (1) 96 *R* 1 xar-r]a-an [š]a-me-e, the road to heaven; 98 *R* 21/22 ša ša-me-e u er-çi-e-ti ... li-ib-ba, the secret places of heaven & earth (BA ii 418, 419); 584, 20 (12) i-na ša-ma-i (+ 22 (14) = from heaven), in heaven. KB iii (2) 4 *col* 2, 8 read ki-ma ti-iq sa(= ša)-me-e, & see HILPRECHT, OBI i 32/33 *col* 2, 5. Xammurabi-*code* ii 31 Ebabbara which is like (ša kî = kîma) šu-ba-at ša-ma-i (a heavenly dwelling), HARPER. nîru ša šamê see nîru, 2 *d*) (724 *col* 1). mul šamê see 544 *col* 2. nalbaš, qirib, šiṭir šamê, see these words. On ešid šamê (Br 479), elat šamê (Br 481, 6456; H 37, 35) & šupuk šamê see these words and KB vi (1) 347/8, 473. 576/8. *del* 108 (115) ana šame-e ša (11) A-nim = sky, JENSEN, 11 *fol.* TIR-AN-NA = šubat šamê = milky way, see JENSEN, *Theol. Litztg.*, '99 *no* 2 on BA iii 214.

II 50 *c-d* 17—33 (ZDMG 53, 658) ša-mu-u (*d*) = (17) AN (II 7 *a-b* 25; V 39 *e-f* 44); (18) NA (Br 1585; H 205 *no* 29); (19) ME (Br 10378); (21) (e-nu) EN (Br 2815); (22) (gi-eš) GIŠ (Br 5705; H 21, 407; II 50 *e-f* 47); (23) IM (Br 8371; S^{c} 288); (24) (e?-kil) SAR (Br 4335 reads gloss si-rim); (25) SI (Br 8407; JENSEN, 24); (26) (u?-di-eš-šu) AŠ (Br 6753); (27) (zi-ku-um) 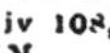 (Br 10219, 10221; AV 2948; ZA i 59; HOMMEL, *Semiten*, 501 note 263; *Semit. Lesest.*, 32, 879; JENSEN, 491, 492 and against the latter, JÄGER, BA ii 295 *rm*: read zi-ku-rit instead of zi-ku-um; ZA iv 108, 32, 33; H 41, 267); (28) zi-ka-ra IM/IM (Br 12241; AV 2942; V 19 *a-b* 22); (29) (e-nim) NUM (Br 9017; also = šaqû, 1; *cf* עָנָה); (30) (e(?)-k(d)im) BE (Br 1535; II 7 *a-b* 26; V 39 *e-f* 45; ZA i 59); (31) XAR-RA-AŠ (Br 8564; II 7 *a-b* 27; V 39 *e-f* 46; ZA i 59); (32) XI (Br 8233); (33) UR (Br 14441). II 48 *a-b* 26 ša-mu-u with gloss (zi-ga-rum) AV 2929; Br 12252; followed by erçi-tim with gloss (zi-ku-ra) Br 12253. II 34 *e-f* 10/11; V 19 *a-b* 23 AN-NA = šamû ša A-AN (= zunni) Br 449. II 59 *d-f* 47 MU (EME-SAL) | GIŠ | ša-mu-u, H 112, 22; D 127, 23; Br 5705; ZA i 184. S^{b} 1 ii 5 u-ta-ax | ⟨ + SA = tax, D 20 *rm* 1 ' ša-mu-u (H 28, 632; 186, 3; V 38 *c-d* 34; *e-f* 61; Br 9174). V 21 *c-d* 55 aš-ru = šu-mu-u, Br 6761. V 36 *d-f* 45 (bu-ru) ⟨

ša-mu-u, Br 8748; ZK ii 174; V 37 *a-c* 15 see Br 8803 & 3850 on NAP = šamû. V 37 *d-f* 4 ša-mu-u ru-qu-u-tum, the wide heavens; 5, ša-mu-u šap-lu-tum, the lower heavens. H 42, 22 BI-IR-RA | AN-NA | ša-me-e, Br 2486; & see Br 2441 on Sm 954 *O* 31, 32. T. A. written ša-mi(me)-e & ša-me, often. Berlin 24, 24 (+ 59) AN-KI, = šamê (u) erçitim.

The ‖ šamâmu see below.

NOTE. — 1. On the etymology of šamû see JENSEN, ZK ii 53 *rm* 3, & *Kosmologie* 6*foll*; HAUPT, ZA ii 268 & *rm* 1; JBL xix 78 *rm* 107. BARTH, ZDMG 42, 341*foll*; HOMMEL, *Südarab Chrest.*, 19 š of מים, water. HALÉVY, JA '97, Ja-Feb. -8*foll* √šamû, être élevé; ZA iii 196; a verb which according to HEBRAICA xi 102 is found in K 155, 15 uš-ta-mu-u = 3*pl* Ʒ¹; but K^M | amû

2. POGNON, *Wadi-Brissa*, 29 & 106 also = canopy ;; Baldachin, as Trg. אַמְּרָא. Neb 441, 6: 1 ša-me-e.

šamû 3. Camb 415, 9 içu ša dalti ša-me-e ša (il) Adad la-bi-ri, Holz für die Tür des alten šamû des Gottes Adad. See preceding NOTE 2.

šâmu (= שׂים) ***1.*** pr išim (§ 10); ps išâm, išammu & (in relative connection) išim-mu; ip šîm; ag šâimu. place, settle, fix {setzen, festsetzen}. AV 7943; id TAR, Br 381. 395; Z^B 37; GUYARD, ZK i 103; Hebr שׂוּם, שׂים, ZDMG 37 ('83) 532.

a) settle, decide, determine, decree, with šimtu, *pl* šîmâte as object. K 133, 23/4 (il) Ninib ..... šim-ta ina ša-a-mi-šu H 80: Br 381; § 92. Neb ii (55) parak ši-ma-a-ti ša .... (63*foll*) ši-ma-at û-um dâru-u-tim ši-ma-at ba-la-ṭi-ja i-ši-im-mu i-na ki-ir-bi (KB iii (2) 14/15). V 32 vii 37/8 (KB iii, 1, 150/1). Esh *Sendsch*, *R* 27/8 the great gods .... šarru-u-tam la ša-na-an ana šim-ti-ia i-ši-mu. KB vi (1) 582/3 *b* 13 (5) i-zi-nam a-na ni-ši i-ši-mu. KB vi (1) 100/101 (*Adapa*-legend) 11 ana ar-kat ûmê ana šu-pi-i šim-tu i-š[im]. V 64 *a* 4 anâku ša (il) Sin u (ilat) Nin-gal .... (5) a-na ši-ma-at šarrû-u-tu i-ši-mu ši-m[a-at-su] BA i 424. Asb x 44 Sarduri da-na-a-nu ep-še-e-tu ša ilâni rabûti i-ši-mu-in-ni iš-me-e-ma; x 73 ilâni rabûti ši-mat-su i-ši-mu a-na damiqtim (WINCKLER, *Forsch.*, i 252); iii 88 ša ilâni rabûti ši-mat damiqtim i-ši-mu-uš (*var* -šu). K 883, 10 (end) i-ši-mu-u-ni. S^P II 987 *O* 4+5 (beg) i-šim-šu-nu-tum. III 41 *b* 24, 25 Nebo su-gi-e u ar-ra-ti a-na ši-ma-ti-šu li-šim-šu (Asb ix 61 i-ši-mu-šu-nu-ti); KB iv 66/7, 18 *Gur*, *Ninâ* ... and *Êa* ši-mat balâṭi li-ši-ma-šu, V 62 *no* 1, 21 li-šim ši-ma-ti; Sarg *Ann* 452; ZK ii 260. Creat.-*frg* I 8 šu-ma la zuk-ku-ru ši-ma-tu la [ša-mu?] (NE 66, 37); II *c* 8 ep-šu pi-ja ki-ma ka-tu-nu-ma ši-ma-ta lu-ši-im, with my word instead of thine I will determine the lot; III 62 (+ 120) ši-ma-tu lu-šim-ma; 65 xu-um-ṭa-nim-ma ši-mat-ku-nu ar-xiš ši-ma-šu, hasten then & determine his lot for him speedily (+ 123); 138 a-na (il) Mar-duk .... i-šim-mu šim[-tu], + 10 li-ši-mu šim-ta; IV 33 i-ši-mu-ma ša (il) Bêl ši-ma-tu-uš (KB vi (1) 327 = *pl*) ilâni ab-bi-e-šu. *Cf* KB vi (1) 304, 315 & 318; KAT³ 493, 494. Hymn to Ninib (ABEL & WINCKLER, 60*fol*; HOMMEL, *Sum. Lesest*, 123) 1 (il) Nin-ib .... šim-tan i-ša-an-šu. ZA x 202, 16 it-ti (il) Bêl i-ša-mi ši-im-ta. K 44 *R* 14, 15 (H 70; D 133) mimma ša šu-ma na-bu-u šim-ta ta-ša-ma (= IV² 14 *b* 14; Br 5436, 8522; § 92 thou determinest fate); also IV² 9 *a* 34, 35 (Br 38[illegible]; WINCK-LER, *Sargon*, 192 B 7 an open ear .... ši-i-mi (= ip) ši-ma-tuš. K 3600 *R* 20 ba-laṭ û-me arkûti ši-i-me ši-ma-ki (hymn to Ninâ; CRAIG, *Rel. Texts*, i *pl* 54/55). KB vi (1) 582/3 *b* 9 (1) ru-bu-tum (il) Anunnaki ša-i-mu ši-im-tum.

b) buy, purchase, pay {kaufen, zahlen} T^C 133: calculate, fix a price; MEISSNER, 93 *rm* 5 pay the šîmu, purchase-price (Babylonian) = ina kaspi liqû (Assyrian). ZDMG 37, 274. *Lit. Or. Phil.* iii 111. KB iv 26, 1—5 šîmat .... (3) ša .... (5) i-ša-a-mu; + 13. Sarg *Cyl* 41 (end) i-na maxîri ša-a-mi. K 11571 viii 20 when somebody i-ša-am-ma a slave; KB iv 22 *no* II 2 ša *N* a-na kaspi i-ša-mu; 160, 37/8 i-šam šîmi-šu gam-ru-ti (ZA iii 220, 23). Neb 135, 18 i-šam a-na šîmi-šu gamrûtu; ZK i 48, 24/5; T^C 19; § 122; KB iv 90 *col* iv 41 i-na ša-a-me; see also maxîru, 538 *col* 2. Nabd 359, 5 i-ša-am-ma. la-ša-a-mu. I have acquired = lûšâm.

STRASSM., *Stockholm*, 6, 44/5 maxîru ... iš-ša-mu (𝔑?).

II 7 *a-b* 1—3, 5; = V 30 *e-f* 18—20, 22 TAR (H 9 + 202, 19; Br 881), GAR (Br 11976), SE (Br 4421) = ša-a-mu; NAM-TAR = šim-tum ša-a-mu (H 14, 168).

H 66, 35—7 ŠE-ŠAM (H 19, 339) = i šam; ŠE-ŠAM-E = i-ša-mi (*var* -mu); ŠE-ŠAM-E-MEŠ = i-šim-mu (*var* i-ša-mu-u), Br 4080.

𝔔^{t} *a*) with double *accus*, place something upon some one {etwas jemandem auferlegen} NE VI (= H^{NE} 44) 47 (54, 55, 56, 57) see bakû 𝔔^{t} (152 *col* 2, above); J^{I-M} 80 *rm* 55. — *b*) K 4832, 16 ši-ma-ta iš-ti-mu, KB vi (1) 8—9 sie bestimmten die Schicksale; *cf* Creat.-*frg* III 50; 108. ilu muš-ti-mi, BA i 269. — *c*) buy {kaufen} Xammurabi-*code* vi 52; xii 2 *etc.* iš-ta-am. — Rm 76 *R* 8 i-sa-a-mu (> ištâmu), Hr^{L} 358. BA iv 508 *foll*; PSBA xxiii 357.

𝔍 determine, fix {festsetzen, bestimmen} with šimâti, as object. pm IV^{2} 15* i y (end) la šum-mu. I 67 *a* 6 (Marduk) mu-ši-im ši-ma-a-ti, AV 5609. IV^{2} 23 *no* 1, i 30/31 the shepherd mu-šim ši-ma-a-ti (= NA-AM-TAR-TAR-RA, EME-SAL); perhaps also 21/22 (beg). I 27 *a* 11 ilâni rabûte mu-šim-mu ši-ma-at mâti. Šalm. *Ob*, 5 (*Mon*, *O* 1) Êa (& Bêl) mu-šim šimâte; *Ob* 14 ilâni rabûte mu-ši-mu šimâte; Creat.-*frg* III 130. Esh *Sendsch*, *O* 11 (mu-šim-mu šim-ti). K 3182 ii 33 i-na ū-um la ši-ma-ti u-ša[-a-mu ši-ma-ti]. K 56 (II 71) i 16 see Br 6614 & šamašu. — Also estimate {abschätzen} Nabd 103, 2 u-ši-ma.

ZA ix 109 (VATh 244 *O*) 5 tu-ša-am, lit^{y}: thou determinest, then: assumed, supposed (*i. e.* used as an *adv*); 6 tu-uš-ša-ma ki; 7 šu-uš-ša-ma, = 𝔖^{3} pr & pm. V 30 *e-f* 25 DIM = šu-um-mu (II 7 *a-b* 8 = šum-ma) Z^{B} 38, Br 9126.

Also *cf* šummu (> šujjumu) in P. N. Šum-ma (*var* BE-ma) ilâni; Šum-mu-ilâni; Šum-ma-Nabû.

𝔖^{3} see above.

𝔑 Bu 91—5—9, 418, 3 iš-ša-mu, was bought. Xammurabi-*code* vii 32.

NOTE. — 1. V 16 *e-f* 31 I]-GI-IN-ZU = tu[-uš]-ša-am, according to BOISSIER, PSBA xxii 107 from √ שׁ״ perceive, see, whence tašîmtu ‖ Einsehen.

2. JENSEN, ZA ix 80 *rm* 1; UNGNAD, ZA xvii 300 *rm* 1: šâmu, išâm, buy, is different verb from šâmu, išîm, put, fix, determine. See also HARPER's excellent edition of *The Code of Xammurabi* (Chicago, 1904) 186.

Derr. — šimtu, šâmânu (?), tašîmtu (?) & the following:

šîmu. AV 8246; § 64; H^{F} 8. — *a*) price, purchase price, value; properly: the fixed amount {Preis, Kaufpreis. Wert}. MEISSNER, 94 *rm* 3: *generis communis*; also ZK i 98 § 2. S^{b} 203 ša(*var* sa)-am | ⊨⟨ | še+a+an | ši-i-mu, AV 7886; Br 4681; H 19, 338; ZK i 103 § 12; also ŠU-GAR, Br 12105 on V 31 *a-b* 45. šîmu (lâ) gamru *etc.* see gamru (224) & Br 4681; BA iv 10 on šîmu gamrûtu & šîmu xarîç(u); for the latter also see xarîçu, 2 (340). Rm 609 *R* še-im ši-i-me (BA iii 215): Camb 153, 2 ši-i-mi nar-ma-ku ša siparri, written ši-i-mi, Nabd 85, 8 *etc.*; ši-me, 176, 7; ši-mi. 193, 14; ši-im, 829, 4; šim, 608, 7. II 33 *g-h* 13 (šeam) ši[-i-mi]; also see V 14 *c-d* 20 ša [ši-i-mi] Br 4683; V 32 *c-d* 17. Br 4682. — *b*) lot, portion, fate {Anteil, Loos}. K 3600 *R* 20, see above šâmu, 1 𝔔 *a*) end.

šummu. ZIMMERN, *Rituall.*. 1—20, 15 xi-im-mat šum-mi u mi-ša-ri. (Bestimmung und Recht).

šâmu 2. Bu 88—5—12, 75 + 76 vii 18 ša-u (*var* -a)-mu-te ša a-na ri-e-šu-te šu-zu-zu, which had fallen into misery, BA iii 252—3; 359.

šumu (§§ 27; 62, 2) *c. st.* šum (Šalm, *Mon*, ii 34, 35; šu-um, I 69 *c* 25; Sn vi 71; Merodach-Baladan-stone iv 53, 54; KB iv 104, 20); *pl* šumâte.

a) name {Name} AV 8483. שם BARTH, ZDMG 40, 635; BA i 378 *no* 59 on cognates; LEHMANN, i 11. ‖ mû, 2 (504 *col* 2). id MU, Br 1235; §§ 9, 52; 25; often in KNUDTZON; TP i 38 MU-šu; H 12, 114 mu-u | MU šu-mu. NA, JOHNS, *Deeds*, 812 *passim*; *pl* šu-ma-nu *ibid* 812, 15. — V 62 *no* 1, 24—27 šu-me, my name (§ 30); šumi(-ja)-a-ma, by my name {meines Namens} § 53*d*. V 61 *col* vi 50, 51; III 41 ii 37/9; TP viii 88; V 62 *no* 1, 29 see xalaqu, 317—18. *del* 266 (293) šum-ša, its name; on šumšu, by name {mit Namen} see BA i 430. Nabd 697, 2 whom Rimût šu-um-šu im-bu-u; + 5. V 33 *b* 42 (gems, *etc.*) ša šum(?)-šu na-as-qu, KB iii (1) 140—1. — Also šuššu > šumšu IV^{2} 12 *R* 32 šum-šu zēr-šu & *var* (K 8269) šu-uš-šu u zi-ra-šu; § 49*a*. V 21 *e-f* 47 (KB vi, 1, 357). Bu 89—4—26, 161 (Hr^{L} 435) 14 ilāni ša MU-šu-nu az-ku-ru, AJSL xiii 210; xiv 2.

kunuk šu-mi see qunuqqu. šaṭar šu-mi, šiṭir šumi(e), šumi šaṭru, see under שטר; V 64 *b* 43 šiṭir šu-um. Also see šaṭaru, 1, especially for colophons.

KB vi (1) 98, 23 (*Adapa*-legend) šu-u-[m]a i-te-pu-us-su; (158, 42) >< BA ii 438.

Call, or. mention (*i. e.*, nabû, zakaru) a person's or an object's name (MU = šu-mu; šu-mu; šum; šu-un-šu-nu; *pl* MU-MEŠ) see these verbs & Z^{B} 67; Jensen, 320 *fol* >< II^{F} 31 (= to be). II 67, 84 a-na šu-me-ši-in ab-bi; Nabd 697, 2 (end) šu-un-šu im-bu-u. II 43 *b* 5, 6 za-kar šu-mu; zikir šu-mi see zikru; II 40 *c-d* 47 šu-mu zak-ru, Br 1632; AV 6138.

mimma šum-šu, šu-um-šu (Br 1043, 11966. 12009, 12013—14) see mimma.

IV^{2} 19 (*no* 2) *a* 46 li-ša-nu mit-xar-ti ki-ma iš-ten šu-me tuš-te-šir, Lehmann, ii 66; ZA iii 352.

pl K 679 *O* 7 a-na šu-ma-a-ti a-ša-ṭar (Hr^{L} 212), concerning the names I will write; *cf* BA i 234. Written MU-MEŠ, K 1250, 14 (end). Hr^{L} 460; K 8522 *R* 21 his fifty MU-MEŠ (names).

b) reputation {Ruf}. See KB vi (1) 158, 42 (end) & 443 šu-mu iš-tak-nu. K 84, 12—13 šu-mu ša (amēl) TIN-TIR-KI-MEŠ .... lu-ba-iš; 20—22 šu-un-ku-nu ša ina pānija .... banû la tu-ba-'-a-ša (2 *pl*; Hr^{L} 301). šu-ma-am dūra-a-am ša šarrūtija lu aš-ta-ak-ka-an, ZA i 341. 11 + 12; ii 128 *b* 14. See also zikru; & Scheil, *Nabd*, x 36 a-na zi-ki-ir šumi-šu. šumu ṭābu, fair-named, § 73. V 27 *g-h* 42, Br 1209; 27 *g-h* 47, Br 1244; 21 *c-d* 61, Br 6781.

c) son {Sohn} *i. e.* he that continues, perpetuates a name. V 23 *b-d* 29—32 TUR-UŠ (Br 4120), TUR-ARAD (Br 4091), TUR-SAG (Br 4098), TUR-DIŠ (Br 4145) = ab-lu, ma-ru, šu-mu, ZK ii 309 & *rm* 1. KB vi (1) 108, 16 (& 418) šu-ma šuk-na-an-ni, create for me a son. Perhaps V 44 *c-d* 19 (ilat) Gu-la šu-me e-di lib-ši.

Especially note occurrence in P.N. Nabû-šu-um-u-ki-in, AV 5879, ZK i 70; Nabû-šum-iddina; Ê-anna-šum-iddina = zēr-banû in: Ésagil-zēr-ibni. Šu-ma(-a)-a Peiser, I, 1; § 18; BA ii 401. AV 8477; also *cf* AV 8485—91. Šamaš-šum-ukīn, Lehmann, i 9 *foll.* Marduk-šum-ibni, AV 5168; Šum-Adda (ZA v 156) in T. A. (Ber) 131, 3 Šu-mu-Addu; (Lo) 66, 3; (Ber) 8, 18 Šu-um-ad-da mār Ba-lum-me-e, + *R* 11. Šu-mu-um-li-çi.

K 2729, 19 (& *R* 20) ina šumi damqi irbû, Meissner, BA ii 569, they grow up in a happy state, condition.

šumû *1.* in šumê širi, roasted or broiled meat {geröstetes oder gebratenes Fleisch} KAT^{3} 598; JBL xix 60 & 78 *rm* 107. (šir) šumê (written KA-NE) Zimmern, *Rituall.* (1—20, 86 & 109 *etc.* (šir) šu-me-e), *p* 95 & *rm* 5; 171 *rm* 8, mentioned in connection with burnt-offerings; *ibid no* 56, 8/9 xi-in-ça u šu-me-e. NE 17, 44 šu-mi-e ši-i-ri; 10, 39 šu-me-e še-e-ri, KB vi (1) 188, 189; 402.

šumû *2.* D 89 vi *a-b* 64 GIŠ-GUL-ŠIM = šu-mu-u ša gi-sal-li (II 45, 18) Br 1667, 1681; AV 8484. II 22 *a-b* 6 sikkat (see 759 *col* 2) šu-me-e (Br 3417, 5276); Rm 353 *O* 3 (M^{S} *pl* 32). 82—5—22, 946 *O* 21 šu-mu-u mar[-ri], PSBA xxiii 200—1: marru = chariot, cart (in general).

šumû *3.* II 44 *g-h* 70 ..... GA = šu-mu-u, AV 8484, Br 14179, preceded by be-lu-u, na-šu-u, ma-xa-ru.

šûmu, *m* onion {Zwiebel}. id SE(= SUM)-SAR, often in *c. t.* see pītu, 2. = Hebr שום. AV 8482. II 7 *a-b* 24 (V 30 *e-f* 43) SE-SAR = šu(-u)-mu, Br 4435; H 38, 118. IV^{2} 7 *a* 46, 51; *b* 5; T^{M} v 57 see qalapu, 2. ZK i 320; ii 425. Perh. K 61, 14 šu-me (ZK ii 13, 14). D^{Pr} 84 *rm* 2; §§ 31; 62, 2 = garlic {Knoblauch}; but *cf* BA iii 401, 402. Z^{B} 37 *rm* 1; T^{C} 132; ZA vi 292 *no* 1.

šummu *1.* *m* mostly with determ. (šam), a plant {ein Gewächs} I 65 *a* 19 (see simtu, 768 *col* 2, *med*); *b* 29; *c* 13 (šam) šu-um-mu bi-e-la-a (*cf* 803, 1/2) *etc.* simat apparimi. add, also, Neb *Pognon* C vii 21 & *cf* A iv 37; vii 8 (išam) šum [-ma]. V 39 *e-f* 52 .... GIŠ-GI = (šam) šum-mu; II 7 *b* 34. Pognon read ušummu, see above, 116 *col* 1.

šummu 2. Sarg *Khors* 169 šu-um-me is-xi-it nūnē u iççūrāte xegal apsī; also *cf* *Ann* 432.

šummu 3. see šāmu, 1 ℑ.

šumma (& **šummu**). *conj* when, if {wenn} AV 8490; Z^B 99. §§ 79*a*; 82 > šū-ma = in case that; § 149 on syntax. BA i 415, 416; ZDGM 82, 714 *fol*; Pognon, *Wadi-Brissa*, 102. Zimmern, ZA ix 110, 111 = ℑ ac of šāmu, 1. IV² 31 *O* 16 šum-ma la tapattū bābu, when thou dost not open the door. šum-ma (la) na-ṭu-ma (see naṭū, 667 *col* 1). Sm 1034, 14 šum-ma šarru iqabbi (Hr^L 380). K 469 *R* 6/7 (Hr^L 138) ma-a a-ša-'-al šum-mu ina māti-ja. K 3466 *R* 17 (Hr^L 99); K 561 *R* 5 (Hr^L 101). Also written šu-ma, *e. g.* KB iv 52 *no* V 15 šu-ma la-ma ū-me-šu (if he *etc.*); but usually šum-ma la(-a), III 47 *no* 5 (K 350) 6. V 63 *b* 7 we have šum-ma, introducing an indirect question = אִם, BA iii 270 *rm* *.

It is found especially in the opening sentence of laws *etc.* V 25 *c-d* 23. 29, 34, 40; *a-b* 1, 8, 13 (id ŠU-GAR-TUR-LAL-BI); H 65 ii 6 preceded by ŠU-GAR-TUR-LAL = sur-ru (782 *col* 2); H^F 22. V 30 *c-f* 39—41 (= II 7 *a-b* 20—22) šum-ma = ŠU-GAR-TUR-LAL-BI (Br 7256); UD-DA (= ūmma, Br 7913); ZAG-GAR-RA (II 47 *c-d* 47, Br 6530); II 47 (*c*-)*d* 48 = AN-BE. II 47 *e-f* 64 ⊢⊣ (= šum)-ma see ZA i 182 *rm* 2.

šummū' ? *Rev. Sém.* ix 149 on K 4334 (II 60 *c* 26) ina šum-mi-ja, in my dreams.

šemu ‖ šumu. NE 60, 1—2 see māšu, 2 (595, 596) & add KB vi (1) 202; 467; 577—8; KAT³ 573, 574.

še-e-mu = še-me-tu, AV 8244, 8245. II 37 *e-f* 65. M^S 91: ein Körperteil. II 22 *no* 2 (*add*) = K 4248 .... NA = še-mi-e-tum.

šemū (§§ 32γ; 42; AV 8247) & very seldom **šamū** (§ 34β; but see ZA vi 306; AV 7945); *pr* iš-mi (§§ 80; 88. išmēma; 3 *pl* išmū, išmā); *ps* išemmi, išimi (§§ 32*a*γ; 34*a*; 39); *ip* šīmi — hear, listen; hearken, grant; obey {hören, vernehmen; erhören; gehorchen} § 138. IV² 10 *b* 1/2 I speak a plaint but none i-ši-man(an)-ni, has heard me, Br 1282. IV² 5 i 54 e-nu-šu (il) Bēl ṭe-e-ma šu-a-tum iš-me-ma; see H 76, 22 iš-me-ma (*var* -mi-e-ma); Br 5727 for other instances. Esh iii 42 iš-me-e-ma (§ 53*d*) (he) heard of; Asb ii 134; vii 92; viii 59; K 2675 *O* 15. I 43, 39; Sn iv 69; Asb v 70 iš-me-ma. P. N. (il) Iš-me ka-ra-bu III 66 *col* 5, 2 (Br 12658; § 65. 30 *rm*). IV² 31 *R* 53 ik-kil a-xi-ša taš-me, when she heard the lament of her brother. K 890 *O* 11 (ilat) be-lit ilāni [ta?]-aš-mu-ni, BA ii 634. KB iv 214, 215 *l* 13 taš-ma-e-me, heard and. P. N. (ilat) taš-me zi-ik-ri, III 68 *c* 31 (Br 13701). NE VI 75 at-ti taš-mi-ma an-na-a q[a-ba-a-šu] (KB vi, 1, 170); also see NE VI 178. Rm 76 *R* 5 end (Hr^L 358) aš-mu-u-ni, I heard (= I was told of). K 2852 + K 9662 i 33 çu]-ul-li-e-šu ul aš-me ‖ un-ni-ni-šu ul al-ki (√leqū). 81—11—3, 478 *col* iv 4 aš-me-e-ma; 7, ki-i aš-mu-u. Nabd 356, 29 the judge dib-bi-šu-nu iš-mu-u; Asb ix 94 iš-mu-u-ma (3 *pl*); IV² 47 *c* 19 ni-iš-mu-u, we heard; K 537 *R* 4 la ni-iš-me, we have not heard (= V 54 *c*); Rm 2, 1 *R* 21 (Hr^L 205; 408). — *ip del* 18 (22) ši-me ‖ xi-is-sa-as. K 2452 (T^M 148) ilī (my god) ši-ma-an-ni, ši-mi ik-ri-bi-e; see also šību, 1. K 4026, 13/14 ši-man-ni (H 180 IV; Br 1282). KB iii (2) 64, 18 should be ši-ma-a (Neb ix 61) for iš-ma-a. ZA x 203, 48 ši-mi-e-ma ta(e)s(ç)-li-tum. KB vi (1) 94/5, 12 ša pi-i (aban) nārā an-na-a ši-me-ma. — *pc* K 11 *R* 20 la-aš-me (Hr^L 186; BA i 222 on form; ii 26 on letter). III 66 *col* 8, 9 liš-me-u su-pi-e; 4, 5 liš-mu-u (6—8, lik-ru-bu); 6, 6 it-ti-ku (= ki) liš-me-u (PSBA xxi 126). TP viii 26 liš-me(mi)-u, may they hearken to (§ 38). II 65 iv 26 liš-me, let hear (KB i 202/3). Bu 89—4—26, 161 *O* 15 liš-mi-u (Hr^L 435; AJSL xiii 209; 3 *pl*); TP viii 26; V 64 *b* 42 li-iš-me-e-ma. — *ps* i-ša-me-e, Knudtzon, 66, 5; i-šim-me-šu-u, 2, 4.

še-mu-u i-šim-me-e, one hears (literally: one hearing hears) often in the prayers, published by KNUDTZON (*p* 24); *cf* the similar a-mi-ru i-ta-ma-ru, *no* 72, 7. II 54 *no* 4, 35 ša iš-šim ik-ri-bi, who hears prayers. $^{(il)}$ Ašur ik-ri-bi-šu i-šim-me, will hear his prayers, V 70, 23/4; IV² 39 *b* 14 ik-ri-be-šu i-še-me; V 62 *no* 1, 25/26 ik-ri-bi-šu Šamaš i-šem-me. Sarg *Ann* 458 ik-ri-bi-šu i-še-im-me. Sn vi 70 Ašur & Ištar ik-ri-bi-šu i-šem-mu-u; Esh vi 71; K 2729 *R* 38 (BA ii 566 *fol*). IV² 1* v 47/48 ik-ri-ba ta(e)s(ç)-li-ta ul i-šem-mu-u, prayer & supplication they hear not. I 27 *no* 2, 80 ša pi-i-šu i-še-im-mu-u (KB i 120). Šalm, *throne-inscr*. 5 i-še-im (§ 39). K 5291 *O* 8, 9 mi-i-nu ša a-ma-ru-ni ša a-šam-mu-ni, whatever I shall see and hear; K 84 *O* 14 (= IV² 45 *col* 1) u a-na-ku ul a-šim-me-ši (§ 32γ); 20, la ta-šim-ma-a (šu-un-ku-nu); K 617 *R* 1 (no one?) la i-ša-am-me, shall listen to him (Hr^L 317; 301; 208); K 3182 iii 15 + 18 ta-šim-me $^{(il)}$ Šamaš (su-up-pa-a, *etc*.). P. N. Sin ka-ra-bi i-šim-me Nabd 1032, 22; BA iii 398. Beh 7 these are the countries which anāku i-še-im-ma-'-in-ni, are subject to me; 48, the rebels, who la i-šim-mu-'-in-ni, do not obey me (§§ 84*a*; 56*b*). — *ag* šemû (§§ 32γ; 42). *Rec. Trav.*, xx 205 *no* XLI *col* 1, 4 še-ma-ti su-pi-e; 81—2—4, 188. 9 a-na še-ma-at (§ 30) ik-ri-bi, to her who hearkens to prayers (ZA v 66); II 66 *no* 1, 7. KB iv 102—3, 8 ilāni rabūti .... še-mu-u ta(e)s(ç)-li-ti-šu. — *ac del* 257 (?81) Gilgameš an-ni-ta ina še-me-šu, when G. heard this; Creat.-*frg* III 87 Ti-amat an-ni-ta i-na še-mi-šu; IV² 31 *R* 20. *Adapa-legend* (KB vi, 1, 94) 12 $^{(il)}$ A-nu a-ma-ta an-ni-ta i-na še-e-mi-šu; Z^B iii 55. II 7 *a-b* 7; V 39 *e-f* 24 ŠE-GA = še-mu-u (same id = magaru) Br 7477; and compare Sargon, *Magnesite* (*Antimony*)-*inscr*. 25, with *silver*-inscr. 48. V 19 *a-b* 24; + II 34 *c-d* 12 GIŠ-TUK = ša-mu-u ša ma-ga-ri (Br 3726), 'hear' in the meaning of 'obey'; also V 21 *g-h* 18, 19 (Br 2334).

$\mathfrak{Q}^{t}$ hear, listen {hören, vernehmen}. KNUDTZON, 24: šemu-u il-te-me-e (= *ps*). K 2852 + K 9662 i 29 (end) tal-te-me, did you hear?, followed by 30, la taš-ma-a zi-kir šap-ti-ja. K 635 *R* 14 liš-al šu 𒀀 i-si-me; K 194, 20 taš-ta-mi-u-šu-nu; S 456 *R* 1 taš-ta-am-me; K 5464, 20 a-si-me; K 84 *O* 5 al-te-me-šu-nu (*cf* 14), I heard them (§§ 84*a*; 42); K 595 *O* 15 as-si-me (BA iv 505) = Hr^L 132, 144, 456, 198, 301, 6). K 2401 ii 14 a-na-ku .... as-si-me. P. N. of god: $^{(il)}$ši-tam-me ka-ra-bu, III 66 *col* 5 *l* 6 (Br 13376; § 110). 83—1—18, 47 *R* 8 ša $^{(amēl)}$ M. il-te-me.

$\mathfrak{Q}^{tn}$ NE 8, 29 ta-zi-im-ta-ši-na iš-te-nim-me. K 4474 (NE 52) 50.

$\mathfrak{J}$ KB iv 22 *no* 2, 28 the former elders .... u-ša-mu, had listened to *N*. Perhaps: ZA iii 319, 94 li-šim-me.

$\mathfrak{J}^{t}$ 81—2—4, 104 *R* 4 u-sa-am-mu-'-in-ni um-ma, THOMPSON, *Reports*, 240.

$\mathfrak{S}$ announce, read {verkünden, lesen}. KB iii (1) 158, 35 u-še-eš-mi(-ma), he announced; K^M 33, 17 tu-ša-aš-mi-i ki-bit-su-nu; Nabd 837, 15 u-še-eš-me-ma: K 13 *R* 20 ul u-ša-aš-mu; K 525 *R* 2 u-ša-aš-mu-u-ni, BA ii 57: sie machen Mitteilung (Hr^L 281, 252).

$\mathfrak{S}^{t}$ make obedient, subject {sich gehorchen, untertan machen} Xammurabi *Louvre*, i 4 šarru mu-uš-te-eš-mi kibrātim arbaim (KB iii, 1, 122—3; Xamm.-*code* v 10); AV 2474, 5042; LEHMANN, BA ii 616, 617. K^M 33, 2 muš?]-te(?)-eš-ma-at a-mat-su.

$\mathfrak{Gt}$ K^M 8, 14 ki-bi-ma liš-še-mi zik-ri, speak & let the word be heard; K 753, 7; 80—7—19, 58 *R* 1 ul iš-šim-mi, THOMPSON, *Reports*, 22 B + 210.

$\mathfrak{Gt}^{t}$ Perhaps Nabd 682, 6—7 it-ti-šu it-te-še-mu-u, she hears from him; MEISSNER, *Diss*, 41; JOHNSTON, JAOS xix 82 on K 13, 30 ta(Hr^L 281 tal)-taš-ma-in-ni, ye heard me.

T. A. have forms like these: $\mathfrak{Q}$ *ps* (Ber) 45, 32 when thou hearest (tu-uš-mu-na) my words; (Ber) 49, 10 my requests u-ul tu-uš-mu-na, have not been listened to; '-uš-mu (3 *sg m*) Lo 14, 49; also the regular forms išmi, išmu: ta-aš-me (Lo) 37, 50 = 2 *sg m*. ki-i eš-mu-u, (Lo) 8, 26, when I heard (ZA v 156); iš-mi (6, 11; 29, 41); iš-ma-am (6, 14). — *ps* (Ber) 102, 54 la ta-ša-mi-u a-na ja-a-ši, if you do not listen to me (ZA vi 250); (Lo) 25, 9 te-še-im-me-e (2 *sg m*); (Lo) 6, 73; 9, 54 e-še-im-me; i-še-im-mi (35, 14); i-ši-me (22, 15 + 18). — ac (Ber) 90, 17 i-na ša-me, when I heard. — pm (Ber) 58, 98 šum-ma ša-mi šarru ana ardišu, if the king would hear his servant. — 𝔔^{t} (Lo) 1, 10 aš-te-me; (Ber) 82, 10 a-ma-ti-šu el-te-me, I have heard his message. — 𝔔^{tn} iš-te-nim-mu, Lo 75, 10. — 𝔍 Tel Hesy 15 (KB v 340—1) šum-ma-ni, grant me! — 𝔍^{t} (Lo) 8, 24 lu-ul-te-im-me, may I hear.

NOTE. — Here perhaps also T. A. (Ber) 71, 17 i-na ša-mi (al) Gub-la; + 49 if the troops march out u ša-mu; (Ber) 42, 8 ša-ni-tu (= furthermore) ša-mi amûlûti ina pân šarri.

Derr. — našmû, nišmû (739 *col* 2); tašmû, tašmêtum, &:

šemû *2.* properly ag 𝔔. § 32 *a β*. — *a*) hearing, intelligent {hörend, verständig}. Merodach-Baladan-stone v 26 see nâṭilu (668 *col* 2); III 43 *a* 31 la še-ma-a; for which I 70 *b* 22 gives ŠI-NU-GAL-LA; III 41 *b* 19 ŠI-NU-TUK-A (IV^{2} 38 *c* 12). — *b*) obedient, willing; then also, gracious, favorable {gehorsam, willig; günstig}. id ŠE-GA. KB iii (1) 120—1 no *f* 9 palxu še-mu-u (il) Šamaš. K 3600 (hymn to Ninâ) *R* 27 še-me-e-ki (il) Bêl magir-ki (il) TU-TU; K 2801 (= K 221 + 2669) *R* 15 ši-pir te-diš-ti it-ti a-melu-ti la še-me-ti (la mit-gar-ti), BA iii 284 *fol.* Sarg *Ann* 430 ina arxi še-mi-e (û-mu mit-ga-ri); *bull* 49. V 64 *a* 50 (še-mi-i; KB iii, 2, 100 & *rm* 1); see also Sn vi 40; id Esh v 27; Neb viii 59; *Bors* ii 8; Asb x 81 (*var* û-me še-me-e).

II 27 *a-b* 39 (.... bu-u-a)]-BAR = la še-mu-u (Br 13950) followed by la magi-ru (40), la sa-an-qu (41), la aš-ši-šu (42). Also see II 48 *a-b* 43—45 (Br 5727); II 60 *a*(-*b*) 33 (il) Še-mu-u, Br 13100.

šu-mi-di ša-na-tu-u-a: encrease my years. Š ip of ma'adu (505 *col* 1, below). V 34 iii 48 (KB iii, 2, 43/44).

šumdulu see šadalu, 𝔍.

šamaxu. thrive, grow luxuriantly; develop in pleasing, agreeable way; prosper {üppig wachsen, sich gedeihlich entwickeln, gedeihen}. akin to šîxu (שיח), KB vi (1) pref. xi. pr išmux, ps iša(m)mux(u). G §§ 67; 70 *rm* 2; D^{Pr} 171 *rm* 1; ZA iii 237 = xanabu; BARTH, *Etym. Stud.*, 38 perh. = שמח. Sn *Kui* 4, 37 wine, fruit *etc.* danniš iš-mu-xu (see *ibid* 11). K 2867, 25 kišâte MA-GAL (magal = danniš, 510 *col* 1) iš-mu-xa, the forests grew up luxuriantly (S. A. SMITH, *Asurb*, ii 1). K 2801 *R* 36 iš-mu-xu, sie gediehen, BA iii 236—7. — ps I 70 iv 13 see puquttu (823, 824, where also ‖ passages). Rm 76 *O* 14 šur-šu-ka li-iš-mu-xu (Hr^{L} 358); PSBA xxiii 355 *foll*; BA iv 508 *foll.* — ps K 2619 iv 3 see pirxu, 828 *col* 2. — pm NE 56, 26 see kimmatu (400 *col* 1 *b*, below). Rm 982 (end) šam-xat nabni-su, see DELITZSCH, *Weltschöpfungsepos*, 110; 111 *rm* 1.

𝔔^{t} T. A. (Ber) 26 iii 35: I (aban) ta-a-pa-tum SU (= mašku?) šit-mu-xu (or a n?).

𝔍 causative of 𝔔. K 3456 *O* 20 see miritu, 595 *col* 1, below. — ag V 55, 4 Nebuk. calls himself mu-šam-mi-xu niši-šu, he who makes his people prosperous, KB iii (1) 164, 165. Sarg *Cyl* 69 (59) name of a gate: (ilat) Ištar mu-šam-me-xat nišê-šu, AV 5587. POGNON, *Wadi-Brissa*, 33; *bull*-inscr. 87 (mu-šam-me-xa-at). K 2729 *O* 6 mu-šam-me-xu niši-šu (KB iv 142). — ac ZA iii 318 (Sn *Rassam*) 87 see bêrûtu, 2 (197 *col* 1); *Bell* 59; *Kui* 4, 33. — pm Asb i 50 see çippatu, 2 (*pp* 880, 887). Šamš i 21 Ninib .... ša šum-mu-xu meš-re-ti, & see mešrû, 611 *col* 1, *med.*

𝔍^{t} Neb ii 26, 27 mâtu uš-te-ši-ir-ma | ni-šim uš-ta-am-mi-ix (1 pr; KB iii, 2, 12—13). K 1550, 10 ina libbi axâmeš u-sa-am-ma-xu (WINCKLER, *Keilschr.*, 2, 30).

Derr. — these 3:

šamxu, *adj f* šamuxtu. growing luxuriantly, thriving {üppig wachsend, gedeihend} § 65, 8; RÉJ xiv 158 (below) = green, herb. ZA iii 314, 70 (& 330) appa-ri-šu-un šam-xu-ti. Perhaps Sp II 265 *a* xxi 11, see šarû. K 3456 *O* 22 idxu-ud kar-as-su-nu ša-mux-ta ri-i-ta. P. N. Ša-am-xu-um.

šumxu, *c. st.* šumux, luxuriousness, splendor {üppige Pracht, Glanz} Neb *Pognon* O VII 23 in-bi ru-uš-šu-tim šu-mu-ux çi-ip-pa-a-tim; A VII 12 in-ba ru-šu-tu šu-mux çip-pa[-a-ti]. POGNON, *Wadi-Brissa*, 65.

šummuxu, *adj* luxuriant, rich, grand {üppig, reich, grossartig} AV 8505; POGNON,

Wadi-Brissa, 33. Neb ii 36, 37 ip(b)ti kab'tti i-gi-sa-a šu-um-mu-xu, KB iii (2) 14, 15, a magnificent gift.

šamaxxu. IV^2 22 *a* 34, 35 see qatnu, & KB vi (1) 414; also see ZA xvii 267 *ad* Br 246.

šammaxu (?). V 47 *b* 14 šam(? U)-ma-xu ša ina un-çi it-tar-ru-u ki-ma pi-ir an-ni-ni (or AN-NI-NI?) rak-su.

šum-xu-ra-ta. T.A.(Lo) 23, 9; √maxaru? but KB v 176 suggests šum[-ma] xu-ra-ta.

šamxatu; so many for uxatu, *pl* u-xa-a-tu (see 31 *col* 2). § 65, 7 *rm* (√šamaxu); MEISSNER, 108 *rm* 7; KB vi (1) 375, 376 connecting it with ša-am-ku-tum & ša-mu-uk-tum, II 32 *c* 31, 32, AV 7954, 7947; mentioned together with xarmatum, xarimtum, kazratum, kizritum; the whole group = KAR-KIT (!) V 42 (*e-*)*f* 63. Also add K 2019 ii 6 (sal) ki-iz-re-ti šam(u?)-xa-a-tu u xa-rim-a-t[i]. On the other hand F. BURET, *Syphilis in Ancient & Prehistoric Times*, i 82 says: the name of the hierodule-*uxât* points very plainly to the *uchet*-disease, the *uxedu* or *uxeṭu*, that is the syphilis of the Ancient Egyptians.

šamaṭu 1. pluck, cut off {abpflücken, abschneiden} pr išmuṭ. AV 7888. II 67, 24 (šam) xi-nu-šu (*cf* xin(n)u, 2, *p* 325) aš-muṭ-ma umallâ qirbâti; ROST, 131; but PRINCE, AJPh xvi 119 reads uxinušu & translates, I cut off his revenue. K 625 *R* 3 liš-mu-ṭu liš-ši-u (Hr^L 131), WINCKLER, *Forsch*, ii 304, 305: abgeschnitten und festgenommen haben sie. ‖ qatapu (*q.v.*). II 29 *c-d* 28, Br 7574. Perhaps also KB ii 252, 70 (= SMITH, *Asurb*, 125) ul ta-šam-maṭ (instead of -kur) ZU (= li'û)-ut-ka ina qabal tam-xa-ri.
ℑ^1 IV^2 56 *b* 36 (see *add*) ul-tam-mi-iṭ (šam) xi-ni-ša, GGA '98, 818 & 826; ZA xvi 162, 163: schlägt sie ihre Früchte ab.

NOTE. — Against BARTH, *Etym. Stud.*, 10 (& ZA ix 193, 2); also AJPh xvi 119) comparing Hebr שׁמט see BA iii 67. — Der:

šamtu *1.* S 23 *O* 4 (ZA viii 201) ŠE-KAB-GAR-RA = šam-ṭ[u]; *cf* II 32 *g-h* 65 ša-an-ṭu, some sort of grain {eine Getreideart} perh. cut grain.

šamaṭu 2. jut {emporragen, in die Höhe starren}. pm šamṭu. AV 7958. TP iii 43, 44; iv 14, 15 see ziqpu (290, *col* 2) & translate: high mountains that jutted like the point of a dagger (HAUPT). KB vi (1) 580: šamaṭu von einem Berge wol eigentlich: grade einpflanzen. S^c 280 di-im | KIM | ša-ma-ṭu; H 29, 662; Br 9124. JENSEN, ZK ii 38 (= *Diss*, 69) = *alligare* ‖ rakasu; Syr שׁמטא, Arb سمط. See STRECK, ZA xviii 169, 170.

šamṭu *2.* Perhaps in K 9290 + K 3452 *var* to Sp II 265 *a* vi 4 see rîmu, thunder {Donner}.

šameṭu. K 4174 + K 4583 *O* 8 *c-d* ša-me-ṭu (7, qa-qu-lum; 6, man-gu); all three having the same id. M^S *pl* 8; HUSSEY, JAOS xxii 212.

šumuṭu. some kind or part of datepalm {eine Art oder Teil der Dattelpalme}. AV 8492. V 26 *g-h* 46 GIŠ-XI-BAD- = šu-mu-ṭu (Br 8345), preceded by sissinnu (775 *col* 1).

šumuk šamê, read šupuk šamê & *cf* šupku.

šu-ma-ki, *cf* sumâku (766 *col* 1), AV 8478. K 4338 *a* ii 68 (MS 95 *col* 2).

šamkatum, šamuktum. See šamxatu & ZA v 378.

šamallû. V 16 *g-h* 23 ŠAB-TUR = ša-ma-al-lu-u, AV 7889; Br 5674. BA i 635 suggests √שׁלמא. Same id = kaparru (423, 424); V 16 *g-h* 22 we have ŠAB-GAL = tam-ga-rum. KB iii (1) 123 *rm* * (*cf* ZA vii 205); KB vi (1) 490, 491: apprentice {Lehrling} comparing Talm-Mand שְׁוֹלְיָא, scholar, pupil, apprentice, journeyman. Also BA iv 83, 84. DT 81 vi 6 *foll* šum-ma tamkaru a-na ŠAKAN-LAL še'um šipâta šamna, *etc.* (12) i-sa-ad-dir-ma. 83, 1—18, 1330 i 5 *foll* ŠAKAN (*i. e.* id of S^b 366) = ŠA-KA-AN = šik-ka-tum & 6 ŠA-MAN = šap-pa-tum; thus ŠA-KAN-LAL = nâš šikkati, *etc.* id ŠAKAN-LAL-MEŠ, K 629 *R* 6 (Hr^L 65); K 3182 iii 27 (amêl) šamallû na-aš kîsi, AJSL xvii 140, 141, the tradesman, he who carries the weights (but see KB vi (1) 491); Z^Š ii 194 *var.* perh. Esh *Sendsch R* 36 ru-ub-bu-ti u(?) šam-mal-lu amêlu-ut-u-a (??). In Xammurabi-Code (*passim*) = agent, trader (see HARPER's edition, 186).

[11] ša-me-la-a, III 66 *col* 5, 1; *col* 2, 10 [11] Šam-la-a, PSBA xxi 118 *fol*. Also see V 44 *a-b* 86.

šumē(i)lu, left, left side {links, linke Seite} = שְׂמֹאל; AV 8480. §§ 30; 32 *a γ*; 65, 3. S^b 274 gu-bu | KAB | šu-mi-lu, H 2 + 178, 52; V 64 *b* 17; § 9, 120; Br 2684. IV² 20 *no* 1, 4 im-na u šu-me-la (= ID-KAB-BU, 3) pa-ni u ar-ku; V 65 *a* 31 im-nu u šu-me-lu pa-ni u ar-ku; I 69 *b* 54 im-nu šu-me-lu pa-ni u ar-ki; ZK ii 347; 398. H 130 *R* 44 im-na ana šu[-me-li]; 46, šu-me[-la] [ana] im-ni. Sn *Bav* 14 im-na u šu-me-li šadi-i, to the right & the left of the mountains. Also used in the meaning of round about. Sn vi 53 im-na u šu-me-la. ZIMMERN, *Ritualt*., 54 *O* 18, 19. Esh v 46 ZAG u KAB. IV² 18 *no* 3 i 20—1/22—3 ina im-ni-šu .... ina šu-me-li-šu. Creat.-*frg* V 10 šu-me-la u im-na. IV² 21* *no* 1 C *R* iii 12, 13 ina im-ni-ja ‖ ina šu-me-li-ia; IV² 30* *no* 3 *O* 36, 38. II 19 *no* 2, 54, 56. K^M 8, 13 ša im-nu-uk-ki ⨯ ša šu-me-lu[-uk-ki], that which is on thy right (left) side. H 90—1, 53 + 59 ina šu-me-li-šu (Br 6570); 92—3, 17. K 4349 KI-TA = šu-me-lu, Br 9676. iD 𒌋𒌋<<<, § 9, 275; IV² 61 *b* 24; Br 11315. NE II *col* 3 *b* 37 u-še-šib-ka šub-ta ni-ix-ta šu-bat šu-me-li. ⊕ 51 iv 18 ŠA-GIG-GA *i. e.*, all that is evil = šu-me-lu (LOTZ, *Tigl. Pil*., 87 *rm* 2; Z^B 40, *med*; Br 12145).

NOTE. — According to JÄGER, BA ii 291 ZI-DA = right, right side, a Semitic word; *cf* Hebr צַד; Targ סְטַר. GAB = left, left side, also Semitic; Arab جَنْب, Syr ܓܒܐ

šamlinnu, see ulinnu, 48 *col* 2.

šamamu 1. M^S 95 *col* 2 suggests: poison {vergiften} to K^M 53, 11, 12 ur-ka-ja ub-ba-lu šin^{pl}-ja i-šam-ma-mu, kal pag-ri-ia ub-ba-lu; a derivative would be šimmatu, *q. v.*

šamāmu 2. ‖ šamū, 2. AV 7890; Br 438. K 8522 *R* 7 (= KB vi, 1, 36—7); IV² 3 *a* 11, 12, see kakkabu (378 *col* 1). Nab iii 12 see kakkabiš (378, *cols* 1, 2). Neb *Bab* ii 2 ša-ma-mi an-nim, this heaven, § 57 *b*. SCHEIL, *Nabd*, vi 33 i-na qi-rib ša-ma-me šu-lu-tu; ZA iv 230, 4. III 38 *no* 1 *O* 19; I 49 *c* 13; V 64 *c* 18 see qaqqaru; L⁴ i 33 ba-ri-e ša-ma-me qaq-qar. I 69 *a* 24 i-na ša-ma-mu (+ *c* 54). Creat.-*frg* I 1 e-nu-ma e-liš la na-bu-u ša-ma-mu; V 11 ina ka-bit-ti ša-ma[-me] (ZIMMERN-GUNKEL, *Schöpfung & Chaos*: in der Mitte des Himmels; but see KB vi (1) 30 ina ka-b(p)it-ti-ša-ma, & *ibid* 347; ZK ii 35, 36); IV 138 see çalalu, 1 ג (876 *col* 2, below); 145, škalla Éšara ša ibnû ša-ma-mu. *Etana*-legend *b* 20 iç-çu-rat ša-ma-me (KB vi, 1, 106—7). NE 8, 19 ilāni ša-ma-mi; VI 81 (Ištar) a-na ša-ma-mi [i-te-la-a]. S 6 + S 2 *O* 6 ina ma-'-du-ti kakkabāni ša-ma-mi, *Rev. Sém*., '98, 1, *foll*. K 3459 *O* i 9 ina çir-rit ša-ma-mi (ZA iv 13) & *cf* V 33 vii 16, 17. ZA iv 228, 8 [11] Anim a-ši-bu ša-ma-mi. K 3182 i 3 [11] Šamaš mu-na-mir ...... ša-ma-mi (& 1); 29 the flood, the sea, the mountains, er-çi-ta ša-ma-mi (& 27); iii 42 (end) ša-ma-mu. K 11152 (hymn to Ištar) 7 Iš-tar kak-kabē nûr ša-ma-mi; *cf* K 3351, 19 (CRAIG, *Relig. Texts*, i 48); also PINCHES, *Texts*, 15 *no* 4, 4. IV² 15 ii 7, 8 ina kak-kab ša-ma-mi (*var* AN-e); 27 *no* 2 *a* 15—17 a mountain whose top ša-ma-mi (= AN) ša-an-na (rivals heaven; § 98); ZA iv 108, 38—9; KB iii (2) 4 *col* 1. ši-ţirti(m) ša-ma-mi ‖ šiţir šamê see šiţirtu. P. N. [11] Ba-al-'ā'a-mo-me, K 3500 + K 4444 + K 10235 i 10 (WINCKLER, *Forsch*, ii 10; KAT³ 357). — T. A. (Lo) 70, 16 a-na AN-e, with the gloss ša-me-ma; (Ber) 140, 17 AN, with gloss ša-mu-ma; also (Lo) 47, 10 ša-ma-mu (but see KB v *no* 202); KAT³ 652. An adverbial form is:

šamāmeš, heavenward, to heaven {himmelwärts, zum Himmel} = ana šamāmi. § 25. I 49 *b* 8 the gods & goddesses u-šib lib-bi-šu e-lu-u ša-ma-meš. S^P 158 + S^P II 962 *R* 13 me-xi-e šāru lim-nu il-ma-a ša-ma-mi-iš, the storm (and) the evil wind went around heavenward (?, or in heaven) *Jour. Trans. Vict. Inst*., xxix 61. Bu 88—5—12, 101 i 8 (& 103 ii 14) ša]-ma-meš.

šum'ā'mtum. II 32 *g-h* 68 ŠE]-ŠU-XU-UZ (Br 7118, see šamū, 1, šummû) = šu-ma-am-tum, a grain {eine Getreideart} AV 8479. Also S 23 *R* 2 (ZA viii 383 ⨯ 201: la-ma-am-tum).

šamnu *1. c. st.* šaman, *m* AV 7891. *a*) fat {Fett} id NI, § 9, 57. NE XII *col* 1, 16 see pūru, 1 (825 *col* 2, *med*). id also Zimmern, *Ritualtafeln*, 41—42, 18; IV² 58 *c* 27. Esh iii 59 see šuklulu & gumaxxu (220 *col* 2). NI-NUN-NA = ximêtu (824 *col* 2, below). — *b*) oil {Öl} id NI-GIŠ (or IÇ?) properly: fat of the tree; & NI; *pl* NI-MEŠ, TP viii 48; D^Pr 70; BA ii 280. See pašašu, anoint (846, 847); daxadu, duxxudu (243, 244). D 18, 148; *del* 64, 65, 66 (*var* šam-nu, H^NE 137, 70 & *rm* 2), 69 (= 68, 69, 70, 73); BA i 120 & *rm* *; KB vi (1) 490. IV² 26 *no* 7, 46—7 NI-GIŠ = ša-man; IV² 31 *b* 48. KB vi (1) 96—7, 32 (*Adapa*-legend) ša-am-na u-ku-lu-ni-ku-ma bi-iš-ša-aš; 98—99, 28—9 ša-am-na il-gu-ni-šu-um-ma it-ta-ap-ši-iš. K 2619 iv 7 the words which Išum spoke to him ki-i u-lu šam-ni eli-šu iṭ-ṭi-ib, were pleasing to him as finest oil (KB vi, 1, 66/7; 381). L⁴ ii 23 ki-ma u-lu šam-ni. IV² 23 *no* 2 *R* 12 u-lu NI-GIŠ; Sarg *Cyl* 55 ki-i u-lu šam-ni (*var* NI); I 65 *b* 33 u-ul ša-am-nim; *a* 20 du-mu-uq ša-am-nim. V 28 *a-b* 26, 27 u-lu, & u-ru = ša-man; V 21 *c-d* 58 RU(?) = šam(?)-ni, Br 1442; see also 5484. šamna gulē see gulū, 217 *col* 2. šaman ṭābi = שֶׁמֶן טוב, Zimmern, *Ritualt.*, 41—42, 18. Pinches, *Texts*, 16 *R* 12 NI-GIŠ reš-ti, finest oil; Esh vi 40 NI-SAG = šaman rēšti; see also I 49 *d* 7. II 58 *no* 6, 71 NI-GU-LA NI-GIŠ; 73, ša-man e-ri-ni [ana] diš-pi. — šamnuš xal-çu, Zimmern, *Ritualt.*, *no* 60 *O* 14 & *rm* 2 purified oil {gereinigtes Öl}; IV² 60 *a* 25 šamna xal-ça. Strassm., Cyr 279, 3 + 6 a-na šam-ni ša 2 xi-la-çu (BA i 524 *rm* 2: vielleicht ein Beleuchtungsapparat), (6) šam-ni ša nu-u-ru (Brennöl). Also perh. Nabd 737, 3. Cyr 290, 1: 11 ni-sip-pi (*q. v.*) ša šam-ni. ku-ut šam-ni (= NI) see kutū (456 *col* 2) & Br 5325, 8115. maçni šam-ni see maçnu (572 *col* 2, below) & Br 12064. ZA x 205 *R* 8 NI-KIL : ni-du-du : šam-ni nu-u-nu (650 *col* 2); 211 *R* 10 ša-man : si-li (& *ibid* 212). M^S 104 *col* 2 (med) *ad* K 126, 1 *fol*: NI-IL *i. e.* šamna ella-šu, instead of ni-il-šu (see nilu, 1. 678 *col* 1). bi-il-tum ša šam-ni, an oil-jug, Peiser, *Vertr.*, 287, 12.

On the ab-kal šamni, a name for the bārū, and the meaning of mē ana šamni nadū & šamni ina mē naṭalu, *etc.* see Zimmern, *Ritualtafeln*, *p* 85 & *rm* 6.

T^M vii 37 ap-šu-uš-ka šaman balāṭi, BA iv 160—2; KAT³ 526: Lebensöl.

šum(tak?)mannu. *a*) fetter; especially for the animal's feet {Fessel, Fussfessel eines Tieres} AV 8502. ‖ kurçu (440 *col* 2). V 39 *e-f* 48—50 ŠU-UD-NUN-KU-TU, Br 3226, 7214; ŠU-LAL, Br 7283; . . . . KA; Br 13886 = šum-man-nu ša alpi. Sn v 74 ki-ma šu-u-re ma-ru-ti ša na-du-u šum-man-nu, like fat oxen with shackles on their feet, Hebr. vii 64; Sn vi 39 šum-man-nu u bi-ri-tu parzilli ad-di-šu. — *b*) part of a cistern {Teil einer Cisterne, eines Brunnens} *etc.* V 39 *e-f* 51 (II 7 *b* 32, 33) [ ]-GAB-ZI-ER-KU (which last 3 signs = zirīqu) = šum-man-nu ša [<] (= būri) Br 8226; and, TIK-BA-RA = šam-man-nu, Br 14071.

ši-man. II 47 *g-h* 30 ^(šam) ši-man (?, or ŠI-MAN? GGA '04, 740, 741) ša eqli, see šilmu, 2.

šamnu *2.* = samnu (766 *col* 2; & § 76). K 146, 10 šam-na mu-šu (Hr^L 192), the eighth night (BA i 205 *fol*). Br 1030.

šāamānu, šajamānu (BA i 461). — *a*) Xammurabi-*code*: purchaser {Käufer}, xxxix 89 ša-a-a-ma-nu (vii 18 *etc.*, -um); xix 62 ša-a-a-ma-ni-šu-nu. — *b*) Sarg *Cyl* 51 the money (price) for the lands (estates) of that city I gave to the owners in silver and (or?) copper kī pī dup-pa-a-te ša-a-a-ma-nu-te(ti). KB iii (1) 158 *col* 3, 17 ku-ša-ad (449 *col* 1, below) ša-a-a-ma-a-ni, das als Preis genommene.

šum-ni-e see tak-ni-e (taknū).

šumassuxu. K 10094, 7 šu-mas-su-xu, see summasuxu, 767 *col* 1.

šamaçātum, a stone {ein Stein}. II 37 *g-h* 64 ^(aban) ša-ma-ça-a-tum; also II 40 *c-d* 18, Br 13040.

šum-çi-çi see taq-çi-çi.

šum-ça-tum, AV 8508 read tak-ça-tum.

šumqut(u), AV 8509. Š pm & ac of maqatu (578, 579).

šamaru 1. BA ii 252. MEISSNER & ROST, 35, perh. √שור, look around, inspect; BARTH, *Etym. Stud.*, 43 ثمر. Q^t — *a*) keep, guard, preserve {bewahren, aufbewahren}. Esh iv 58 a-na šit-mur sisē; III 16 v 6. AV 8358. — *b*) observe, pay attention to, be attentive; respect, revere {beobachten, Acht haben auf; achten, hochhalten, verehren}. V 35, 19 ṭābiš iktarrabūšu iš-tam-ma-ru zi-ki-ir-šu (& revered his name; or, obeyed his command) BA ii 210, 211; *cf* ZA iv 15, 7. ZA iv 241, 35 liš-tam-mar ilūtka; 1 *sg* lu-uš-tam-mar ilu-ut-ka IV^2 57 *b* 22; 21* *no* C *R* iii 9; 57 *b* 23 (qur-di[-ka]); K^M 21, 90 lul-tam-ma-ra, T^M vi 101.

D perh. V 28 *e-f* 9 šum-mu-ru ‖ bu-us-su-ru (181 *col* 1), AV 8506.

D^t K 8182 iii 53 uš-tam-ma-ra zik-ri-ka, (that) revere thy name; perh. ZIMMERN, *Ritualtafeln*, 66 *R* 6 ul-ta-mar GI.....

Š = Q^t *a*. I 44, 58 a-na šu-uš-mur sisē.

Derr. šitmaru &:

šimiru. watchman, guard {Aufseher, Wächter} T. A. (Ber) 41, 23 (amēl) rābiçu, with the gloss ši-mi-rum, KAT^3 653; &, again, see below, šomiru (šemir).

šamaru 2. ‖ ezezu. be or become violent, savage, wild {ungestüm, heftig, wild sein oder werden}, § 84. ZA ix 205 *no* 13 compares Hebr סמר, shudder; Arab شمور, excitement; Eth ሠምረ: be satisfied, contented. ip T^M v 28 ai-ki na-bal-kat-tum šu-um-ri na-bal-kat-tum. pm Rm 191 *R* 3 šam-ru, they rage, THOMPSON, *Reports*, 146. IV^2 55 *no* 1 *b* 6 + 7 the daughter of Anu ez-zi-it šam-rat (= 3 *sg f*); 58 *b* 59, 60; ZA xvi 173 *foll*; T^M v 139 ez-zi-tu-nu šam-ra-t[u-nu] — 2 *pl* — ZIMMERN, *Rituall.*, 26 v 75; *ibid* 62 *R* 14 [ma-rat?] ilu E-a dan-na-at šam-ra-at.

Q^t = Q (§ 88 *b*). K 3426 *O* 2 Nabukadnezzar sat in Babylon il-tam-mir ki-i nēši ki-i Adad išag[gum]; *Rev. Sém.*, ii 76. *Cf* P. N.: Ri-mut mūr Il-tam-mar (ilu) Adad, Camb 145, 8—9. TP iii 7 (11) i-na šit-mur (= ac) qar-du-ti-ja-ma, in my fierce valor (I marched a second time against the people of Qummux). IV^2 22 *R* 24 mu-ru-uç qaq-qa-di ša ki-ma zu-un-ni mu-ši šit-mu-ru (which rages).

D P. N. Adad-mu-šam-mir, KB i 206 *col* 3 (Eponym of 789 B. C.) = Adad, the bringer of tempest. AV 7505.

D^t P. N. Lul-tam-mar (ilu) Adad, ZA ii 200, 11. AV 4909; 3763. Also P. N. Lu-uš-tam-mar (ilu) Adad; KB iv 28 *no* 1, 18; 312, 2; 314, 16.

Š = Q (§§ 84; 88 *b*). Lay 44, 15 ina ti-ri-çi qāti-ja u šu-uš-mur libbi-ja, with outstretched arm and impetuous courage (I captured 15 mighty lions), KB i 124 NOTE. Asb vii 10 Ummanaldaš who šu-uš-mur kakkē (ilu) Ašur u (ilat) Ištar dan-nu-u-ti e-mu-ru. Anp i 82 ina gi-biš lib-bi-a u šu-uš-mur kakkē-ja, AV 8607.

Derr. — šitmarru, šitmuru, šitmuriš & these 4 (?):

šamru *1. adj* powerful, violent, wild, raging (especially of floods) {mächtig, ungestüm, heftig, wild, tosend} ‖ ezzu. IV^2 24 *no* 1, 33/34 gal-li-e šam-ru-ti, powerful demons (= SUR-RA. Br 6390). Šalm, *Bal* IV 2 Šul-ma-nu-ašaridu a-li-lu šam-ru; Sn v 64 kīma ti-ib me-xi-e šam-ri (‖ ez-zi), like the approach of a wild storm. Asb v 95 my army saw the river Idide a-gu-u šam-ru, a violent torrent (raging flood). *Cf* K 3500 + K 4444 + K 10235 i 18 šam-ru a-gu-u, WINCKLER, *Forsch*, ii 10 *foll*. Sn *Bav* 36 ki-i (iç) tar-ta-xi šam-ri I stormed against them. Šamš iv 22, 23 see namurratu (688 *col* 1, below). An *Adv* of šamru is:

šamriš, AV 7956. TP iii 57 (61) ana alāni ..... šam-riš lu as-niq; vi 2 šam-riš lu amdaxiç. POGNON, *Bavian*, 75. SMITH, *Asurb*, 38, 14 see xanṭiš (322 *col* 1).

šumru, *c. st.* šumur. rush, onslaught {Ungestüm, Angriff} ‖ uzzu. TP ii 63 i-na šu-mur kakkē-ja ezzūte; iv 87; also Br 4843 *ad* II 21 *c-d* 23. AV 8494.

šumurratu. violence, raging {Ungestüm, Toben} AV 7951, 8495. *del* 101 (106) ša (ilu) Adad šu-mur-ra-as-su i-ba-'-u šamē, KB vi (1) 236, 237 & *rm* 9; 496: Adad's Ungestüm kommt zum Himmel hin. See also šuxarratu.

šummuriš. II 28 *e* 58 šu-um-mu-riš.

šumurriš. III 38 *no* 2 (K 2660) *R* 13 (end) at-ta-šab šu-mur(xar?)-riš.

šamru 2. *c. st.* šamar. V 26 *a-b* 5 šamar za-'-i (sweet-smelling, fragrant plant or flower?), in a list of words, AV 7894. See 271 *col* 2, below. Perhaps from the same stem, from which the following 3:

šamrānu. II 42 *a-b* 40 U-XA (Br 11824) = šam-ra-nu; 41 U-XA (Br 11826) = šim-ra-nu = tam-šil (šam) ši-im-rum; 42 U-XA : U-XA-XI-A (= ZUN) = (šam) ši-im-rum (*cf* NAM = si-im, V 19 *c* 39); 43 U-XA = (šam) šim-rum; 45 .... al(or qul, gul?)]-la-a-nu-um = (šam) šam-ra-nu, Br 13909; also see *b* 48, 49. Br 12894; AV 7515. Rm 122, 32 when upon a field in a city šam-ra-nu is found, the field inna-di (will lie fallow); 34 šam-ra-a-nu : (šam) a-ra-an-tu : (šam) a-la-mu-u; 35 šam-me XA-ZUN. ‖ :

šimru. above, and II 44 *a-b* 44 (šam) pa-ri-e = U-XA (*i. e.* šam šimrum) ša šadi-i. (šam) ši-im-rum, AV 8254, Br 13379.

šimrānu, see šamrānu.

NOTE. — Haupt in *Johns Hopkins Circ.*, '03, 69 *col* 1: We have three plant-names derived from the stem שמר in Assyrian, viz: šamrānu, šimrānu & šimru. √שמר 'bristle' (Hebr) may be identical with Assyrian stem šamaru, 'be vehement, wild, enraged', the original meaning of which is probably 'to bristle up'. Hebr. שָׁמִיר perhaps a corruption for שמיר 'bristly', and perhaps a name for 'broom-corn'.

šemiru, *c. st.* šemir. bracelet, ring, or the like {Spange, Ring *etc.*} AV 8241, 2579; שָׁמִיר, Zech 7, 12. id XAR, Br 8540, 8528, 9015 *ad* V 19 *c-d* 12. D[S] 50, 121 *rm*; D[Pr] 69; Pognon, *Bavian*, 71. T. A. (Ber) 41, 22—24 place the ring (ši-mi-rum) on a *rabiç* in the presence of the king's feudal prince, BA iv 308; but see šimiru. — IV² 31 *O* 57 (58) XAR-MEŠ qātē-ša(-ja) u šēpē-ša(-ja); *R* 40 še-mir qātē-ša u šēpē-ša. KB vi (1) 84 *rm* 1 ‖ xalxallatu; Strеck, ZA xvii 242 compares سوار: Fussring. XAR-MEŠ often, *e. g.* Anp iii 62. 65; Sn v 72; vi 3; I 44, 52; Asb ii 11, 93; iii 92 (*var* XAR-ri perh. = šemir-ri). Nabd 61, 1; Neb 441, 4.

Šumēr(u). AV 8481. D[Par] 196 *foll*; II[OV] xxxi; § 9, 40. V 29 *c-f* 46 MA-DA KI-EN-GI = ma-a-tum Šu-me-ri, Br 6828; 6829 *ad* 47. Synchr-Hist. iv 28 the outrages ša (māt) Šu-me-ri (māt) Akka-di-i. S[P] 158 + S[P] II 962 *R* 20 xarrān Šu-me-ri-iš, the road to Šumer. ki-en-gi (Br 9662, 9679) = šu-me-ri, see kingu, 2; H 31, 713 ‖ ma-a-tum, 712; 81—11—3, 478 ii 1 (PSBA xviii, '96, 252), § 9, 223; KB iii (1) 80 *foll*: ki-en-gi[ki] Urdu = Šumer & Akkad (KAT³ 14, 15); 108 *O* 17; 122 i 11 when Anu & Bēl gave me to rule (māt) Šu-me-er-im u Ak-ka-di-im (+ 28, 29; ii 1, 2 *etc.*). K 2801 = K 221 + 2669, 23 šar (māt) Šu-me-ri u Akkadi[ki] (*var* Ak-ka-di-e). Xamm.-*code* v 7—9. TP III (Lay 17) 1 šar (māt) Aššur[ki] šar (māt) Šu-me-ri u Akkadi[ki]; also see KB iii (1) 184, 185 & BA ii 259, 260 *col* 2, 37. Sarg *Khors* 2, 3: king of Assur, šakkanak of Babylon *etc.* KB iii (2) 8 *no* 3 *col* 1, 4 šar (māt) Šu-me-er-im u Ak-ka-di-i; ZA iv 107, 11—12. V 35, 20 a-na-ku Kura-aš šar kiš-šat, šarru rabū, šarru dannu, šar Bābili, šar (māt) Šu-me-ri u Ak-ka-di-i, šar kib-ra-a-ti ir-bi-it-tim (also 10, 18, 33) BA ii 210, 211. On the title šar (māt) Šu-me-er-im u Ak-ka-di-i see Lehmann, BA ii 608 *foll*; 616: seit Hammurabi nur von denjenigen Herrschern geführt, die Babylon in der Gewalt hatten. See also Lehmann, *Šamaššumukîn*, i 57—173, & summary, ii 103 *col* 2; & the same author's *Zwei Probleme der Semitischen Zeitrechnung*. "Šumer (Sumerian kingi 'land' II 39, 9) = the southernmost part of Babylonia, the region about the ancient city of Ur; Akkadū = the country about & between the two rivers, or the real Babylonia" BA ii 589 *foll*; *ibid* 610 šar māt Šumēri u Akkadī durchaus nicht ‖ šar kibrat arba'i × Winckler, der beide als zwei einander beigeordnete Bestandteile des Zweistromlandes auffasst. On Sn *Bell* 13 see KAT³ 79, 80.

81—7—27, 130 (ZA iv 434) EME-KU = li-ša-an šu-me-ri tam-šil ak-k[a-di]-i? (see Weissbach, *Die Sumerische Frage*, 176); also on Sm 1538 (+ Sm 1290 + Sm 1409): Winckler, *Forsch*, i 206 & *rm* 1 (= nichtsemitische Mundarten); also KAT³ 10; Bezold: The Sumerian language; HALÉVY: The Sumerian race, people. BEZOLD, *Catalogue*, v 2194, 2195: South or Lower Babylonia. PRINCE, JAOS xxiv 104 EME-KU (Br 846) = Sumer, *i. e.* Babylonia; another ‖ for which is Kingi; also see HOMMEL, *Sum. Lesest.*, I *p* 3 *no* 21.

K 2167 (+K 11856) šap-liš ak-ka-da-a e-liš šu[-me-ri], below Akkadian, above Sumerian (of a certain text). See WEISSBACH, 174 *rm* 2; TIELE, JRAS, Apr. 1900, 344.

II 46 *no* 1 = D 80 v 1 GIŠ-MA-MA-URU, usually read elip šu-me-ri-tum (LENORMANT, OPPERT) or šu-rip-pak-tum (DELITZSCH) is elip ma-i-ri-tum, according to WEISSBACH, *Sum. Frage*, 10, 47 *etc.*; but BEZOLD, *Catalogue*, V 2195 reads again elip šu-me-ri-tum.

On O. T. שִׁנְעָר & *Šumer* (first compared by HAIGH) see §§ 46; 49 *a rm*. The two are still considered as of same origin, by HOMMEL, see PSBA xvi 209—212, & in HASTINGS, *Dictionary of the Bible*, i 224 *col* 2; PINCHES, *ibid* iv 503 suggests *Sin'ar* as modification of Kingi-Ura (which = Šumer & Akkad), through Šingi-Ura, because שנער always = the whole of Babylonia. — Against identification, see SAYCE, PSBA xviii (Jo '96) 173, 174; JENSEN, ZK ii 419 (would connect rather TIN-TIR & שנער). See also HALÉVY, *Revue critique*, '83 *no* 44; RÉJ xiii 15; *Mélanges de critique*, '83, 162 see Urû, 1 (92, 93). W. MAX MÜLLER, *Asien und Europa*, 278 connects שנער with Šanxar, in T. A. (Lo) 5 *R* 49 it-ti šar Xa-at-te u it-ti šar Ša-an-xa-ar it-ti-šu-nu la ta-ša-ki-in, *i. e.* with the king of *X* & the king of *S* have nothing in common; *ibid* 279 identifies Šanxar with Σιγγαρα, the modern *Sinjar*. But, WINCKLER, KAT³ 31 *rm* 1 (& 238): Šanxar = the Egyptian *Sankara* = the *Muçri* of the Assyrians.

šumruçu. sick, painful, filled with pain {krank, leidvoll} see maraçu, 2 (590), AV 8510. K 2493 *O* 13 šum-ru-çu. *Rec. Trav.* xxiv 103, 104. ZA v 67, 16. K 2452 ši-ma-an-ni ši-mi ik-ri-bi-e šum-ru-çu-u-ti, BEZOLD, *Catalogue*, 442.

šam-ri-mi, II 16 *c* 28; read perhaps u-ri-mi.

šam-ri-in-nu, see uri(n)nu, 103 *col* 2.

šamašu; pr išmuš. III 52 *a* 39, 40 (sal) XU ba-ki-tu ša ki-i TU-XU (=summatu) eli ali u na-me-e-šu it-mu-ru-ma iš-mu-šu. — Q^t P. N. Il-tam-meš-nûri, 82—3—23, 271, 1 & often as first component part of P. N., *Rec. Trav.*, xix 104, 105. Nabd 497, 4 Il-tam-meš-na-ta-nu; 554, 4 AN(=il?)-tam-meš, *Jour. Trans. Vict. Inst.*, xxvii 19, 20, & 36; perh. shortened to Tam-meš-na-ta-nu, K 961, 15 (Hr^L 454). See also Il-te-ri (under šêru, morning). — ℑ possibly H 71, 15—16 i-še-e(?)-ir u-ša-am [-maš?], BERTIN, RP² iii 94, he is at work from dawn till dusk (literally: he does (work) in the morning and at noon); but see Br 6614. The verb may be a denominative of:

šamšu. *c. st.* šamaš. *m* sun {Sonne}. mostly written ideographically & with determ. AN = ilu: AN-UD. AV 7959; Br 7795; §§ 9, 26 + 60 + 203; 23; 27; 46 *rm*; 65, 1. ZA i 390; BA i 2; ZDMG 41, 712.

çi-it šam-ši (& (il) Šam-ši; (il) UD-ši; (il) UD) = sunrise, see çîtu, 2 *e* (*p* 899), & Br 7794. Napâx(a) (il) Šam-ši, *etc.*; nipix šam-ši, see *pp* 705—707. VATh 4105 iv 11 far-off roads pi(=pa)-çi (il) Šam-ši, toward sunrise, *Mitth. Vorderas. Gesellsch.*, '02, *no* 1. e-reb šam-ši (Br 7830, 7954, 7958, 8675, 8037, 9250); ša-lam(u) (il) Šam-ši; šulmu(-me) & šulum (il) Šam-ši = sunset, see erebu, 2 (95, 96); šalamu, 1; šalâmu, 2; šulmu. çi-i šam-ši (Br 7931) see çî'u (857 *col* 1). In T. A. also mu-çi šam-ši ≍ ir-bi šam-ši, (Ber) 104, 6—7. OPPERT, ZA i 242: çît šamši = East; ereb šamši = West; nipix šamši = South; šalam šamši = North. On atalû šamaš & šamaš atalû see KUGLER, ZA xv, Heft 2; ZDMG 1900, Heft 1. Anp i 10 *Anp* is called (il) Šam-šu kiš-šat niši, ZA i 359; iv 306 *rm* 8. Šalm, *Ob* 16; *Mon* i 5. VATh 4105 i 13 i-na-ja ša-am-ša-am li-ip (mistake for it?)-tu-la-a-ma (נפל) na-pi-ir-tam.

II 5 *b* 45—48 mentions an animal kal-mat (il) Ša-maš; *col a* is mutilated; II 6 *b* 19 kalab] (il) Ša-maš. V 30 *g-h* 20 supplemented by H 214, 215: BAR = ša-am-šu, Br 1802; also H 27, 577. P. N. Ša-am-ši-ja, KB iv 18, 33 & *var* (il) Šamaš-mu-še-zi-ib. — The late Babylonian contracted form šaššu, & *adv* šaš-šiš & šaššâniš, see below.

(il) **Šamaš.** P.N. of god. AV 7895; JASTROW, *Religion*, 68—72; 143—144; 209 *foll.* MUSS-ARNOLT, *Assyro-Babyl. Months*, 25, 26. KAT³ 367—70 (& index, 670 *col* 1). IV² 3 *a* 34, 35 AN-UD = (il) Ša-maš (Σαώς; § 44); 19 *a* 47, 48 (end) see Br 7829. VATh 4105 i 5 (il) Šam-šu i-ta-šu-uš, became sad. *del* 72 (77) ina arx]i (il) Ša-maš ra(?)-bi-e, KB vi (1) 234—5. H 87, 41 AN-UD(-RA) = (il) Ša-maš; 193 *no* 158.

V 44 *c-d* 50 see ZK ii 271; 361; Br 1652; V 44 *d* 61 (il) Ša-maš ri-çu-u-a. V 36 *a-c* 7; 37 *d-f* 17 see Br 8747; V 37 *d-f* 27; 38—41 see Br 9960; on *d* 39 (ša-maš, Br 9948) see JENSEN, 101 *fol*; ZA ii 194. II 44 *a-b* 4, *cf* Br 10237; 48 *a-b* 34, Br 12218, 12219; 49 (III 69 *g* 67) Br 7296.

Son of Sin; sacred number: 20. He is the da'ān (the judge) of heaven & earth; see dānu, 2 (258 *col* 2) & I 27 *no* 1, 9 dān šamē u erçiti mu-ma-'-ri gi-im-ri (see 508 *cols* 1/2 *no b*); K 11152, 3 (il) Šamši da-i-na-a-a kib-ra-a-ti; bēl di-nim ZIMMERN, *Ritualt.*, 75—78, 56. The a-ša-rid ilāni, IV^2 4 iii 45; bēlu rabu-u, KB iii (2) 88, 50; called qar-ra-du, qu-radu *etc.* (see these). ed(t)la (il) Šamaš IV^2 5 *a* 75, 76; bēl e-la-ti u šap-la-ti V 62 *no* 1, 28 (ZK ii 357); V 65 *a* 10. Šamaš & Adad are the great oracle-gods; V 33 viii 32, 34 ilāni çirūti bēlū bīri; KB iii (1) 150, 151 & *rm* *†; 138, 139 & *rm* 4. ZIMMERN, *Ritualtafeln*, *pp* 89, 90. From him Xammurabi receives his famous code; see Frontispiece in R. F. HARPER's edition (Chicago, 1904). His chief seats of worship are Larsa (see 498 *col* 2) & Sippar (see 780 *cols* 1, 2). His consort A-a, KB iii (2) 88, 51 ilat A-a kal-la-tim na-ra-am-ti-šu. mār Šamaš, II 58 *a-b* 14 see Br 3434. See also PINCHES, *Jour. Trans. Vict. Inst.*, xxvii 16 *foll.* P. N. *e. g.* (il) Ša-maš u-pa-šar (xir?), Eponym of 875 B. C. (KB i 204/5 *col* 2); A-na (il) Šamaš-kal-la-ma KB iv 14, 22. On Šamši + compounds see AV 7957—7958; Šamaš + compounds *cf* BEZOLD, *Catalogue*, v 2177 *foll*; AV 7896—7936. — On *Šešbaçar* see KAT^3 286 (above) × E. MEYER, *Entstehung des Judentums*, 72 *foll* (> Sinbaluçur); also PRINCE, *Diss*, 118.

šamašu, 1. whence (MEISSNER, ZA viii 80) šutmaši, *q. v.*

šum-šu. V 22 *d* 60. PSBA x 224 = water course (??); Br 2890.

šum-šu-u V 37 (*f*) *b* 58, Br 9994 see mašu'u (597 *col* 2).

šumiš? T. A. (Lo) 5, 54, 55: your (my) messenger should come to me (you) šu-mi-iš.

šam(u?)-ma-šu, II 46 *a-b* 66, 67 = GIŠ-NER(= kurçu)-A-ŠA(= LIB)-GA, GIŠ-NER-ZAG-GE-A; + D 89 (K 4378) vi 55, 56. snare, pit? {Schlinge, Falle?} BP^2 i 96 *rm* 2 refers to Rm 204 i 22.

šimeššalū. a tree {ein Baum} KB vi (1) 444. AV 8242. Rm 367 + 83—1—18, 461 *a O* 12, 13 GIŠ-ŠIM-ŠAL, GIŠ-ŠIM-MEŠ-LA = ši-meš-ša-lu-u, M^S *pl* 28. *Cf* II 45 *g-h* 48; Br 5201.

šamaššammu. sesame; σήσαμον. id ŠE-GIŠ-NI, § 9, 87; AV 7937; 8182; often in *c. t.* T^C 138; Xammurabi-*code* (HARPER, 186); POGNON, *Bavian*, 58; D^S 81; II 5 *c-d* 32 UX-ŠE-GIŠ-NI = kalmat šamaš-šam-me, Br 7472, 8325. II 52 *g-h* 66 (H 68, 19) šu-ru-ub-tum ša-maš-šam-me.

šum-ši-ru, AV 2519, 8511 see tagširu.

šamatum *1.* SCHEIL, ZA x 211 ii *R* 4 aššum ša-ma-tum (AV 7939): ša-ši-gu.

šam'ātum *2.* II 7 *a-b* 18—19; V 39 *e-f* 35—38 NUM-MA-LAL (Br 9035); SUXUR-RI (= kimmatu, S^b 359; Br 8618); TIK-RI(-A) Br 3247, 3248; [ ]-GA (VR.: SI-TIK, Br 3429) = ša-ma(-a)-tum, AV 7939.

šamātum *3.* M^S 95 mentions K 4282 i 15 (II 37, 64) (aban) ša-ma-a-tum, AV 7939.

šam(u?)-ma-tu = [ ]BAB-BAB = GIŠ-DIM$^{(di-im)}$ see u-ma-tu (*p* 68 *col* 2) & add: ZK ii 280.

šamūtu. properly: anything that comes from above, ZA ii 434 & *note* 1 (*p* 435). JENSEN, 416 *fol*: rain {Regen}; BA i 130 & 67 *b*: the heavens {Himmel}. I 43, 43; Sn iv 76, 77 see laziztum, 477 *col* 2 (below); v 78 see gabšu, 211 *col* 2 (above). V 52 *b* 39, 40 (= *IM*, Br 8871); *del* 40 (47); 83 & 86 (88 & 91) see zananu, 2 Š (287 *col* 2); KB vi (1) 233, 235 translates: ša-mu-tu k(q)i-ba-a-ti (see kibtu, 371 *col* 2, below) by Schmutzregen (see *ibid* 480). REISNER, *Hymnen*, 38, 8 kima ša-mu-ti (= IM) ušpāli ‖ kima rādu.

šammutu (?). III 53 *a* 30 MUL-MAŠ-TAB-BA ana šam-mu-ti (il) Nergal.

šamuttu. See P. N. Sin-ša-mu-ut-te, KB iv 24 *no* 3, 17.

šu-ma-a-tum *etc.* see šu'âtu (*pl*); eqlu ši-ma-tim = šiâtim.

šumu(i)ttu *1.* a vegetable. gardenplant {Gartenpflanze} AV 8498. II 7 *a-b* 23 = V 39 *e-f* 42 U-$\frac{kil}{kil}$-ŠE-SAR = šu-mut-tu (tum) Br 14068, 6082. K 4174 + 4583 *O* 5 šu-mu-un-da | U-$\frac{dul}{dul}$-ŠE-SAR | u... mi-na-a-bi... šu-mut-tum; M[S] *pl* 8; JAOS xxii 214. šu-mit-tu SAR, ZA vi 291 ii 4. ZIMMERN, *Ritualt.*, (C) 11 *R* 27 šu-mut-tum & see *ibid* 115 *rm* η.

šumuttu *2.* KB vi (1) 58 (K 8571) 10 a-na šu-mut-ti = ac Š of mâtu, 2 (618 *col* 2).

šemêtu see šêmu.

šîmtu *1.* (§ 10) *f*; *c. st.* šîmat; properly *f* of ag šîmu; thus, that which is fixed, determined. id NAM(-TAR), Br 381. AV 8239, 8257. §§ 37*a*; 64; 68. — determination, both active: decision, as the expression of one's will; & passive: destiny, fate, lot, indicating the result of the decision. *pl* šîmâte(tu). Both meanings are represented by the passages quoted under šâmu, 1 Q & J. — *a*) determining, decision {Bestimmen, Bestimmung} Neb v 14 (ii 55) DU-AZAG, the KI-NAM-TAR-TAR-E-NE is called a pa-ra-ak (see 830 *col* 2, *med*) ši-ma-a-ti; ZA ii 41; KAT[3] 401*foll.* V 50 *a* 5, 6 DU-AZAG (= iš-tu ša-di-i) is called a-šar ši-ma-a-tum (Br 381, 9607; JENSEN, 237; but *cf* HOFFMANN, ZA xi 263 § 14: perh. horizon: als Ort der astronomischen Richtungen (= شام), der heliakalischen Auf- und Untergängen). I 27 *no* 2, 89—90 ([il] Ašur) bêl ši-ma-a-ti ši-ma(or im?)-ti-šu li-ru-ur. — *b*) destiny, fate, lot {Schicksal, Loos}. It is neuter in meaning; and qualified by an adjective or genetive, as *e.g.* šîmat balâṭi; damiqtim, Asurb iii 38; V 64 *a* 5 *etc.* Here perh. Creat.-*frg* I 8 (*b*) ši-ma-tu la [šâmu?] KB vi (1) 304; IV 4 (+ 6) ši-mat-ka la ša-na-an, + 21 ši-mat-ka be-lum lu-u max-ra-at ilâni-ma (KB vi, 1, 20—21; 324); II c 8 šuk-na-ma pu-ux-ra šu-te(ti)-ra-a-ba-a (√nabû?) šim-ti; III 62; IV 33; K 8522 *R* 21 (KB vi, 1, 38—39). TP i 24 *Tigl. Pil.* to whom ye (o gods) such & such ta-qi-ša-šu ši-ma-at bêlû-ti-šu. H 119 *b* 11 + *a* 13 ši-ma-tu-ša marça, her (the maiden's) fate is hard ‖ u-çurtu, KB vi (1) 405, 406. NE X *col* 6, 37 (ilat) Ma-am-me-tum ba-na-at šim-ti it-ti-šu-nu ši-ma-tu i-š[im-mu] KB vi (1) 228, 229; 479, 480. Creat.-*frg* III 123 ši-mat-ku-nu. K 5464 *O* 31 i-si-e-šu it-ti ši-ma-a-t[i?], Hr[L] 198; PSBA xvii 230*foll.* IV[2] 50 iii 2 see raggu; iv 13 see namaru, 1 J (685 *col* 2 *ll* 11/13). K 11152 (hymn to Ištar) 12 ši-mat la dum-qi. On Nebo as the naš dup(-pu) ši-mat ilâni see duppu (263 *col* 2, NOTE 2 & read: *Rec. Trav.*, xvi 177 = KB iv 102*fol*). — Sn v 2 ina û-um la ši-im-ti-šu ur-ru-xiš im-tu-ut (KB ii 104, 105); SCHEIL, *Nabd*, iv 35, 36 iç-ba-tu u-ru-ux ši-im-ti = they died. T. A. (Ber) 24, 55 and when my brother *N* a-na ši-i-im-ti-šu ki-i il-li-ku. VATh 1036, 6—8 a-bu-u-um a-na ši-im-tum it-tal-la-ku, PEISER, *Jurispr. Bab.*, 38. Salm, *Ob* 152 mu-ut šîmti-šu il-lik, he died a natural death. Rm 76 *R* 11 ina mu-ti šim-ti la-mu-ut, so may I die my appointed death (Hr[L] 358; BA iv 511; PSBA xxiii 357*foll*). šîmtu ûbilšu = שימה תובילתהו, DELITZSCH, *Koheleth*, 268 *rm* 1 (HAUPT). Cyr 332, 8 *N* šim-tum u-bil-lu-šu; Nabd 356, 23; 380, 5 (šim-tum); Neb 283, 17 on the day when she a-na ši-im-ti it-tal-ku; ZA iii 366, 16; probably for the more complete šîmat mûši, the nocturnal fate = death; Asurb ii 21 il-lik NAM (= šîmat) mu-ši-šu (see mûšu, 598 *cols* 1/2; & nammûšu, 690 *col* 1, *med*). Sp II 265 *a* i 9 šim(?)-tum (*var* ta, K 8463) ub-tel(*var* ti-il). Esh iii 19 šim-tu ûbilšuma, fate snatched him away; & often; see *Proc. Berl. Acad.*, '89, 826; HOMMEL, *Gesch*, 676 *rm* 2. K 2619 *R* iii 20 û-mu ub-be-la-an-ni ši-ma-ti, KB vi (1) 64, 65; KB iv 322 *col* 3, 35 u (= but) šim-ti ub-lu-uš. III 41 *b* 17 a-di û-mi šîmâti-šu a-a i-bi-ib (KB iv 76, 77); K 3182 ii 33 i-na û-um la ši-ma-ti u-ša[-mu? šimtu?] AJSL xvii 138, 139. — *c*) business {Geschäft}? T. A. (Ber) 8, 15 my merchants tarried in Kinaxxi a-na ši-ma-a-ti, on business; (Lo) 2, 34 they should not carry on ši-ma-a-ti mi-im-ma, any business. MEISSNER, 126 AZAG-ŠAM = šîmtu, property acquired by purchase.

S^c 58 na-am | NAM | ši-im-tum; H 14, 163; Br 2103; II 7 *a-b* 4; V 39 *c-f* 21 NAM = šim-tum, followed by šîmtum ša-a-mu, AJSL xix 208, 209. II 108 ii 8/9; V 11, 8/9; Br 1609. H 111, 54 na-am-tar | NAM-TAR | ši-im-tum, Br 381, 1611, 2112. V 29 *e-f* 68 NAM : SAG-AŠ = ši-im-tum : pi-ris-tum (see *p* 835 *col* 1), also AV 6029. V 42 *g-h* 12 (ši-mat) see Br 8443. — H 60, 20 ši-ma-tu (Br 9903) perhaps: prices; or, a by-form of šîmu. See also šitimtu.

šîmtu *2.* II 7 *b* 10—15 = V 39 *f* 27—34 ši-im-tu(m) for which *a* (*c*) has ZAG-ŠU (H 24, 488; Br 6522; K 44 *R* 14, 15; V 39, 27); ZIG-LU (Br 4695; V 39, 28; id also for emittum); GI (Br 2402; V 39, 30); NE-PA(= SIG)-GI (Br 4625; V 39, 31); ZIG (Br 4689; 6673; V 39, 33 with gloss (zi-ib); ŠE-ṬU (Br 7409; V 39, 34 with gloss (gi-in)); ZAG-LU V 39 *c* 29 (Br 6521); šim-tum, V 39 *e* 32 (ZK ii 258; Br 6673). See also šim-tan, below.

šimmatum. poison {Gift}? √šamamu. SCHEIL, Notes LX (Constant. 583) 10 šim-ma-tum  (ana?) šêri (*Rec. Trav.*, xxiv); Notes LIV (*Ibid*, vol. xxiii) 2 šim]-ma-tum ši-im-ma-tum (+ 3); 8 . . .] šim-ma-tum ki-ma ši-iz-bi ina tu-li-e; 12 çi-i im (perh. a *m* of imtu, poison?) šim-ma-tum ki-ma ši-iz-bi ina tu-li-e ir-ti-šu (+ 14). SCHEIL compares Hebr שׁמּמית; Arb سمام; and translates: lézard (lizard).

šimtan. II 7 *a-b* 28; V 39 *e-f* 47 ZIB = šim-tan, AV 8256; Br 8195.

šimêtan (*cf* ebirtan, *etc.*) properly *adv*; then *n*: dusk, evening, beginning of night, {Dämmerung, Abend, Beginn der Nacht}. id USAN & MUSUB, HOMMEL, *Sum. Les.*, 8 *no* 93; AV 8243; JENSEN, 118; ZK i 315 *rm* 1; ii 67 & 284 *rm* 3 on *p* 285; ZA v 131. S^b 371 u-sa-an | 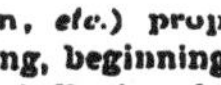 | ši-me[-tan]; H 24, 489 (*var* -ta); II 7 *a-b* 6 AN-USAN = ši-me-tan; Br 6346—48. 83, 1—18, 1330 ii 11 same id = ši-mi-tan : li-la-a-tum. Sm 954 *O* 37, 38 Ištar i-lat ši-me-tan (AN-USAN-NA, EME-SAL) ana-ku; 39, 40 i-lat še-ri-e-ti (= UD-ZAL-LA, EME-SAL) ana-ku; see KAT³ 424. K 44 *O* 26, 27 the whole country i-kam-mi (subj. god Nâru) ki-ma ši-me-tan e-la-a-ti (H 78). V 30 *e-f* 19 USAN+DU = ši-me-ta (20, = ra-xa-aç û-me) Br 6350. S^b 368 mu-su-ub |  | ši-me-tan; thus, in view of V 39 *e-f* 23; Br 8326. IV² 22 *b* 19 ina ši-me-tan pu-ru-'u-ma(= AN-MUSUB-AN-NA-TA. Br 8327). IV² 55 *no* 1 1 *R* (*b*) 24 KUR-RU (= napax, or nipix?) AN-NE (= qa-rêre) ši-me-tan, in the morning, noon, and evening, ZA xvi 184 *fol*; ZIMMERN, *Ritualtafeln*, *no* 67 *rm* 10 (*p* 184). See also šil(l)ân. Has šimêtan connection with šîmtu, 1?

ša-nu. AV 7977 read GAR(= šak)-nu & see šaknu, 2.

šânu. urinate {Urin lassen} Hebr שׁין. Q Z^Š iii 59 mâmit nâru ša-a-nu, Bann durch in den Fluss urinieren; *cf* II 52 (*a*-)*c* 57 a-xi nâri ša-a-nu (?) AV 7976.

Q^t MEISSNER & ROST, 85 quote K 8063 + K 8066 šumma kalbu ana eli amêli la mu-di-e-šu šinâta-šu iš-tin; K 10390 šumma UZU-DIR (= kamunu) ina nâar šînâti (id S^b 229) iš-tin-ma innamir, (both, Omen tablets) BEZOLD, *Catalogue*, 892; 1084.

ℑ^t NE II *col* iv *a* 7 . . . . . tur-ru-u lu-u uš-tin-ki, KB vi (1) 140/1; 436 möge (auf) dich pissen.

Der. šînâti (see below), & perh. maššanu (607 *col* 2).

šanû *1.* (= ثنى), a denominative of šina. two; šanû second, *etc.* = double, repeat. renew {doppeln, wiederholen, abermals tun} H^P 20 *rm* 3; BA i 33 *no* 23. *Etana*-legend (KB vi, 1, 106 & 416, 46) iš-ni-'ip-qid, he (the eagle) examined again, *i. e.* he renewed his examination. SCHEIL, *Nabd*, viii 10 aš-ni-ma; *cf* V 63 *b* 6 + 21 (aš-ni-e) = I visited a second time; KB iii (2) 92 *col* 2, 45. T. A. (Lo) 8, 46 ki-i-ni (faithfully?) a-naš-ni.

Q^t S^P 158 + S^P II 962 *R* 10 see šabrû. T. A. (Ber) 97, 10 aq-bi aš-ta-ni, I have said repeatedly; 71, 5 aš-tap-par aš-ta-ni; 76, 53; 79, 17—18 aš-ta-pa-ar [aš]-ta-ni, see BA iv 117/18 on this text; (Lo) 17, 5 iš(= aš)-ta-par u aš-ta-ni, I have written repeatedly; 10, 10—17 ša-ni-tu (further) šap-ra-ti .... u iš-ta-ni; 19, 21. (Rost) 3, 5 aq-ta-bi u aš-ta-ni; 14, ta-aš-ta-na(-ni, 27; 2 *sg*) a-ṣa-tu a-na ia-ši.

3 *a*) repeat something. II 39 *e-f* 9 U-MU-UN-NI-KA-TAB = šu-un-ni-šum-ma, Br 3770, between qibîšumma & šullissumma; tell him a second time. — *b*) communicate, report, announce something to someone {jem. etwas mitteilen, melden, verkünden}. Asb i 63 u-ša-an-na-a ia-a-ti (& -ši). SMITH, *Asurb*, 123, 52 the dream-vision u-ša-an-na-a ia-a-ti (*cf* Asurb ii 102); 37, 9; 65, 14; 119, 23 (ušannû, 3 *pl*); 125, 63 ši-i (*i. e.* Ištar) tu-ša-an-nak-ka umma (§ 56 *b*), KB ii 252—3. KB ii 268—9, 104 (his messenger) [la] u-ša-an-nu-u-šu ši-kin ṭe-e-me-ia; also *cf* Sarg *Ann* 379, 380; *Khors* 152 (see, above, 355 *col* 2, below). SCHEIL, *Nabd*, vi 21/23 šuttu ši-i ša iṭ-ṭu-lu lu-ša-an-ni-ka ka-a-šu. Creat.-*fry* III 12 šu-un-na-a ana ša-a-šu-un, announce to them! IV² 31 *O* 24 lullik šum-ki lu-ša-an-ni a-na šarrati (ilat) Ereš (Nin?)-ki-gal, I will go and announce thy name to the queen *E.* (§ 93, 1 *b*). *del* 17 (20) a-mat-su-nu u-ša-an-na-a, their (the gods') plan he announced to. H 76, 12 to god Ea in the apsû šu-un-ni-šum-ma, Br 7132. K 595 *O* 21 man-nu u-kin u-ša-an-na man-nu i-ša-na-an, Hr^L 6; BA iv 505. K 7599, 12 i-pu-lu-uš u-ša-an-n[a-a], he reported (to me). IV² 20 *no* 1, 23/24 their incomparable gifts ma-la šu-un-na-a(=KA-BAL-BAL-E, Br 558) li-ša-a-nu, as many as tongue can tell; *cf* K 3182 i 49 nap-xar mâtâte *pl* šu-par šu-un-na-a li-ša-nu. K 123, 13 see JENSEN, 472, 473. IV² 27 *a* 42, 43 a-ma-ti lu-ša-an-ni (= GA-MU-RA-AB-KA, Br 548) a-ma-ti ul ša šu-un-ni-e (= XAR-NU-GE-GE-A-NE, Br 8561). K 8522 *R* 24 li-ša-an-ni-ma a-bu u ma-ri li-ša-xi-iz, KB vi (1) 38/9 let father tell it and son learn it. KB vi (1) 286, 2 ....] u-šam (ša-am)-na-a, but?? S^P II 987 *O* 34 (end) u-ša-an-na-a, *Jour. Trans. Vict. Inst.*, xxix 52.

3t H 51 iii 50 IN-TAB = uš-te-ni (or √enû?) Br 8770.

Š t Xammurabi-*code* xxvi 58 uš-ta-ša-an-na-ma, he shall double; xvii 12 uš-ta-ša-na (HARPER, 187).

Der. šanîtu.

šanû 2. *f* šanû(i)tu second {zweiter, zweite} §§ 76; 77. K 3449 *a R* 7/8 iç-çu a-rik lu iš-te-nu-um-ma ša-nu [-um-ma] šal-šu šum-ša *etc.* Asurb ii 28 ina šani-e gir-ri-ia, Sn i 63; *Bav* 43; Šalm, *Bal* IV 5 ina ša-ni-e ta-lu-ki, on my second expedition. IV² 5 *a* 14/15 ša-nu[-u] = II KAN-MA (H 41, 274; Br 11219); 59 *no* 1 *b* 3 ina ša-ni-e û-me, on the second day. IV² 31 *O* 45; *R* 40 šana-a bâbu. *del* 136 (143) šana-a û-mu; also NE 9, 44; 70, 4; KB vi (1) 114, 30 ša-na-a KAS-BU, a second *k* (*Etana*-legend); šana-a, 112, 28; 298 i 2 i-na ša-ni-i II š[u]-š[i] li-mi (& 4), in the second place. K 2482, 2 (IV² 56 *add*, i) ša-nu-u. Bu 91—5—9, 418, 25 a-na ša-ni-i-im-ma, for a second time. *c. t.* ša-nu-u, II-u, II-i, ša-ni-e *etc* T. A. (Ber) 7 *R* 28 a-na ša]-ni-šu, or ŠU = šanîtu = twice. — *f* Šalm, *Ob*, 77 + 174 ša-nu-te-šu, secondly. *del* 205 (225) šanû-tum (*i. e.* kurummatu) muš-šu-k(q)at, § 77. NE I *col* 6, 21 I saw ša-ni-ta šu-na-ta (perh. mistake of *na* for *ut*), a second dreamvision (scarcely: another *i. e.* different), *cf* V *col* 3 (4) 13 I saw šalul-ta šu-ut-ta. ZIMMERN, *Rituall.*, 75—78, 68 II-te-šu, secondly, between (62) max-ri-ma, firstly; & (75) III-te-šu, thirdly. KB iv 54 *no* VII 13, 14 X ma-na kaspi a-na ša-ni-u-tim xa-ar-bi i-ša-qal, 10 minas of money he will pay on (or: after?) the second harvest. BOR iv 131, 28 ša-nu-u-tu. *c. t.* Nabd 178, 18 ša-ni-tum mi-ši-ix-tum; 203, 18 (-tim); Neb 101, 10; 164, 20; II-tum, Nabd 116, 20; 54, 4 (two-year old). — T^M i 44 (45) ištên-it .... ša-ni-tu, the first ... the second; also ša-ni-tum u-il-tim, AV 7975. — T. A. (Ber) 7 *R* 29 [iš]-te-it, the first time; 30, [u] ša-ni-ta, and the second time, ZA v 144 & *rm* 6; (Lo) 1, 74 ša-nu-ti (a second time) they came; 8, 58 i-na ša-nu-ut-ti-šu (or ŠU = šanîtu, ZA v

160, 161; see *ibid* 57 ana II-šu), in the second place >< ištēni-tum.

See also šinū, below. — *Adv* šaniš, 1 *q. v.*

(amēl) **šanū.** AV 7978. the second (in command, in the country, *etc.*) }der Zweite (als Befehlshaber; im Lande){. 81—7—27, 199 *O* 1 a-na (amēl) II-e bēlija (AJSL xiv 6, 7); 81, 7—27, 199 A *O* 1; K 514, 12 u ša-nu-u ša (al) Pu-qu-du; K 525, 12 (amēl) II-i-šu (BA ii 60); K 14 *R* 12 (amēl) šanu-u-šu; 82—5—22, 99 *O* 14 (Hr[L] 382, 268, 252, 42, 378). Neb 109, 18 (amēl) II-u ša māt tam-tim, preceded by (16) (amēl) ki-i-pi ša māt tam-tim; Neb 166, 14. KB iv 128 *no* VII 1; 140 *no* VIII 2. Perh. also V 55, 34 the brave charioteer did not see ša-na-a ša it-ti-šu & *cf* ZA v 148, 14; P. N. Nabd 158, 10 (amēl) ša-ni-e-šu. K 317, 38 (amēl) II-u ša (amēl) rab u-rat. N 187, 82—7—4 + N 17, 88—4—19 (ZA vi 234) 11 (amēl) rab u-qu (+ 34) šana-u. *pl* Rm 2, 8 *O* 5 (amēl) ša-nu-te (Hr[L] 380). See also T. A. (Ber) 189, 69 (amēl) ša-nu (BA iv 121 *foll* on KB v *no* 184) or = šak-nu, as also Rm 77, 10 (end)?

šanū 3. (שנה). be or become different, change }anders sein oder werden, sich verändern{ *cf* Philippi, ZDMG 32, 79 *foll*; Jensen, ZA vii 177. Cyr 376, 23/24 a-mat-ka it-ti-ja la ta-ša-an-na (= ps). šanū ṭēm(u) see 355 *col* 2; § 72*a*; KB ii 256, 53. P. N. III 47 *no* 8, 8 pūn La-taš-ni-ili (= pr); & see pulukku (807 *col* 2, *med*); pm K 183 *R* 5/6 ina bir-tu-šu-nu ik-ki-ni ku-ri(tal?) lib-bi-ni ša-ne, BA i 620—23; PSBA xxiii 351 *foll*; Hr[L] 2. *del* 3 mi-na-tu-ka ul ša-na-a (3 *f pl*); 4, u at-ta ul ša-na-ta (2 *m sg*) KB vi (1) 228—31.

Qt Perhaps V 47 *a* 44 ṭe-en-ši-na šit-ni; IV[2] 60* C *O* 23. Sp II 265 *a* xxi 1 i-na ad-na-a-ti ab-ri-e-ma šir-na-a i-da-a-tu. K 2846, 4 (end) iš-ta-ni mi-lik-šu-nu (Winckler, *Forschungen*, i 474—5).

J change }ändern{ Hehn. i 219, 2... šunnū ṭēmu see 355 *col* 2. K 2729 *R* 32 who pi-i dan-ni-te šu-a-tu u-ša-an-nu-u; *ibid* 7 ša la šu-un-ni-e (BA ii 572). IV[2] 48 *a* 30 (end) u]-ša-an-nu-u, I 70 *b* 13/14. III 65 *a* 61 (il) Bēl palā u-ša-an-ni. I 27 *no* 2, 73—4 who ana xulluq çalmija annē u ta-me-ti ana šu-un-ni-e. Sp II 265 *a* i 2 lu]-ša-an-ni-ka. III 41 *d* 1 *fol* Nebo .... li-še-en-ni, BA ii 242. Neb 125, 14 ša dib-bi an-nu-tu u-ša-an-nu-u ‖ en-nu(-u) Neb 198, 19 (368, 7). L[4] ii 33 ina piku elli ša la šu[-un-nu-u] = pm. T. A. (Ber) 24, 64 la u-še-i-nu-u, he will not change. KB iv 66/67 *no* 2, 21 mu-ša-nu an-ni-i. V 47 *b* 8 might be: e-ga-ti-ja u-ša-ne-im (??). K 4350 (= H 51) iii 59 (61) IN-KUR(-EŠ) = u-ša-an-ni (-nu-u); 63 (65) IN-KUR-RE(-NE) = u-ša-an-na (& -nu-u) Br 1148.

Jt = J III 43 *c* 20, 21 whosoever u-sa-mi-iç-ra u ku-dur-ra-šu u-sa-an-nu-u (§ 46). I 27 *no* 2, 47 & 56 see šiṭru *a*); 72 who pā-šu (*i. e.* of another man) a-na bar-ti uš-te-en-nu-u (or Št of enū?, see *pp* 67, 68). Creat.-*frg* III 135 ši-ri-sa mat-qu u-sa-an-ni (> uš-tanni) [çur-ra]-šu[-un].

Š change one's direction, course, *etc.* (of canal *etc*). I 28 *b* 22 ri-eš nāri ša-a-ti u-še-eš-ni-ma ax-ri.

Št ZA iii 315 (*Rass*) 75 uš-te-eš-na-a, I had changed (its course) § 110; see mā-lāku, 546 *cols* 1/2; Sn *Bell* 48. III 65 *b* 42 when the right kursinnu of a newborn filly šu-te-eš-na-at (= pm is changed); 43, when his 4 kursinnē šu-te-eš-na-a, § 110. K 2801 *O* = K 221 + 2669 *R* 4 the star Jupiter .... uš-taš-ni-ma, changed. *i. e.* rose later than the sun, BA iii 234, 4.

Derr. šaniš, 2; šunnūtu, &:

šanū 4. *f* šanītu (JA xiii, '89, 297). another, the other }ein anderer, der andere *etc.*{; šanumma, any other; šanamma, anything else, § 79. AV 7966. V 56, 5: li-bi-el ša-nu-um-ma. Xammurabi-*letters* 8 *R* 6 ri-it-tim-ma ša-nu-um[-ma]; 43, 29 ša-nu-tim-ma others }andere{. Asb i 126 not be among us ša-nu-um-ma (§ 53) be-lum; vi 4 nakru ša-nam-ma e-li (j)a-a-ši. K 2675 *O* 40. I 35 *no* 2, 12 trust not ana ili ša-ni-ma: K 2619 iii 22 ana ša-nim-ma (KB vi, 1. 64); ina aš-ri ša-nim-ma la ta-ša-kan, KB iv 104, 24; 20 a-na b(p)u-tuq-ti ša-ni-tim-ma la i-bat-taq. Camb

315, 12 a-šar ša-nam-ma (irgendwo anders hin); H 99, 40 (Br 1149); II 49 *c-f* 37 ša-nu-um-ma (51 *b* 71), name of a star: Mercury, JENSEN, 120; ZA v 126: the changing *i. e.*, morning & evening star. I 27 *no* 2, 31 ina ali ša-ni-e ēkallu ša-ni-te la i-ša-kan, in another city he shall not build another palace; + 40 ēkal-lum ša-ni-tu. Sm 61, 16 ina ali ša-nim-ma; AV 7980. V 64 *b* 55 ina bīti ša-nim-ma. Neb 101 (KB iv 186—7) 10 aššatu ša-ni-tu; often in Xammurabi-*code* (HARPER, 187). K 2852 + K 9662 iii 21 ana māti ša-ni-tim-ma, WINCKLER, *Forsch*, ii 36 *foll.* V 34 *a* 28 iš-te-en i-ti ša-ni-i, one after the other. 83—1—18, 37 *O* 16 ištēn a-na ša-ni-e (Hr^L 355). mam(m)a ša-nu-u, I 27 *no* 2, 77; *m* ša-nu-um-ma, V 56, 27; KB iv 104, 22; a-na *m* ša-nim-ma III 41 *b* 5; ma-ma ša-na-a IV^2 39 *b* 25. — rašū ša-nam-ma ina eli (muxxi) ul išallaṭ see rašū & ZA vi 332. — ištēn pūt šani-i našū: see pūtu, 849 *col* 1 *b*; & AV 7978. — *pl* see above; & perh. 83—1—18, 34 *O* 13 ša-ni-'-u-ti (Hr^L 364). Anp ii 8 mātāte ša-ni-a-te; Šalm, *Mon*, ii 33 (-ti) § 69. Achaemenian-inscr. H 7, 8 (15, 16) Persia, Media and mātāti ša-ni-ti-ma li-ša-nu ša-ni-tum (§ 09)

šanū 5. dip, dye {eintauchen, färben}? *cf* šinītu 1. H 108, 28 (112, 16); 114, 11; D 128, 71; V 11 *d-f* 23 A-]GE-A = A-GAR-RA = ša-nu-u (Br 11545, 11706). followed by mē raxaçu (same id). Perhaps originally identical with šanū, 3. AV 7979. Here according to GGA '98, 826 also IV^2 28* 4 *R* (*b*) 34 alu]m ša naqrum u ša-nu-u.

Derr. — šinītu, 1 & perhaps šanātum.

šanū ***6.*** perh. = šanū, 3 (T^C 188) in the specific meaning of: repair. KB iv 202, 9 u-ri i-ša-an-na; Cyr 177, 16 u-ri i-ša-ni (BA iii 397); 228, 7 ur-ru i-ša-an-ni (*cf* çabatu, Q *a e*; 861—2). PINCHES, *Inscr. Tablets*, 71, 9 ur-ri i-ša-an-nu, he shall renew the woodwork. Camb 306 *R* 2 u-ri ta-ša-an-ni. Q¹ Camb 182, 5 i-sa-an-nu (BA iii 399). — J Nabd 1030, 11 ūru u-ša-an-nu (= 3 *pl*). Here perhaps mušannītum, 608 *col* 1. — FEUCHTWANG, ZA vi 442: √שנן make smooth, polish {glätten, poliren, putzen}; but see MEISSNER & ROST, 107 *no* 23.

šanū 7. ‖ šananu? K 2852 + K 9662 i 27 ... la iš-nu-u qa-bal-šu šarru man-ma-an, whose onslaught no king can withstand; also perhaps Sp II 265 *a* xxi 10 li-'-u qar(-ra)-du ša ša-ni-i ni-bit-su.

šanū ***8.*** foal; the young of an ass {Füllen, Eselsfüllen} II 27 *c-d* 17 ša-nu-u, Br 4821; II 24, 28 (*no* 1, *add*, *R*; K 4204) IMĒR-TU-DU = ša-nu-u, with i-bi-lu. AV 7978, end; Br 4987. ZA iii 207 *no* 11; v 387. Also Rm 2, 588 *O* 30, 31 ša-nu-u, followed by is(ç)-pu ša ....; 37/8 (GGA '98, 826).

šanū ***9.*** V 29 *g-h* 5 GI = ša-nu-u, Br 2408.

-šunu (AV 8514), *f* **-šina**, 3 *pl* suff. to *nouns* & *adj*. — Also abbreviated to šun & šin (ši-in) II 67 *R* 86; Sarg *Cyl* 64; AV 8271; H 173 *no* 7; BEZOLD, *Diss*, 28. — ši-nu (V 66 ii 19 mandatti-ši-nu) & -šu-nim, KB iii (2) 92, 15 i-lu-ti-šu-nim. HAUPT-MOORE, *Judges* (SBOT) 65, 66 on origin.

šu-nu, added often for emphasis. See šū 1 & 2.

šunū ***1.*** V 26 *e-f* 28 GIŠ-ŠE-NA'(S^b 376)-A = šu-nu-u; perh. ‖ mā(u)nū (558 *col* 2) & tēnū; a couch {Bett}. But MEISSNER, GGA '04, 740: a plant. AV 8259, 8515. Also see II 35 *c-d* 8; read by AV 8522 SAL-UŠ-NA'-A = šu-un-ni, Br 10938.

šunū ***2.*** a plant {eine Pflanze} AV 8515. K 4845 *R* 29 (šam) šu-nu-u (Br 11425) ‖ (šam) a-mu-šu (AV 446). Perhaps also II 42 *no* 6, 76 (šam) a-uš-še = (šam) šu-nu; the former in *l* 77 also = (šam) e-na-nu (Br 11504; 13046, 13047).

šunū ***3.*** hump {Höcker, Buckel} HILPRECHT, *Assyriaca*, 59, 2 alap šu-nu-u, buffalo {Buckelochse}. Šalm, *Ob* (KB i 150) inscr. 1: gammālē (? udrāte?) ša šu-na-a-a çe-re-ši-na; LEHMANN, ZDMG 50, 317. See also gungulipu (227).

šu(i)nnu (√šananu, cut {schneiden}?). V 23 *g-h* 18 UD-KA-BAR (Br 7821) = šu(i)n[-nu] ‖ ebbu *etc.* thus = shining, & then, = copper {glänzend, und dann weiter, Kupfer}. JENSEN, *Deu. Litztg.*, 1900 *no* 47; KB vi (1) 556 *ad* 296 iv 8 & *cf* šuxtu. K 8676 *R* iii/iv 19 copper + ŠUN

= šu(i)n[-nu], following upon xa-çi-i[n-nu] ZA viii 77 & M^S *pl* 15. V 27 *e-f* 33 copper + ŠUN-DIL (AŠ, RUM) *etc.* = šu(i)n-nu (Br 254); same id in K 8676 *R* 21 = šu-un-nu & 29 = šu-ku (?). Perhaps here also K 133 *R* 28 (H 81) ina šadi-i šin-ni ku-ši-i a-ç(z)a-at-ma i-ta-nar-ra-ar.

šunnû, double {doppelt}. Zimmern (KB vi, 1, 458) *ad* NE vi 190 šun-nu-u ma (instead of ba)-ni-e, das Zweifache einer Mine.

(11) **Šin**, see (11) Sin (759 *cols* 1, 2).

šinâ (§§ 62, 1; 75) *f* šittâ, šittên, two {zwei}; ZDMG 32, 21*foll.* AV 8258; id § 9, 142; Br 11214*fol*, 11220. H 110, 35 (V 12, 33) II = ši-na, Br 1804. V 37 *d-f* 28 ma-an (ZA i 14) | ⟨⟨ | ši-na (Br 9962; § 9, 274); 34 mi-in | ⟨⟨ | ši-na, followed by ki-lal-la-an, both. Rm 2, 555, 7—10 ši-na = tu-'a-mu : ma-a-šu = ki-lal-la-an, ZA iv 436. KB vi 96*foll* = T. A. (Ber) 240 *O* 23 (24; *R* 8) i-lu ši (še)-na; *R* 7 (še-e-na). *Rec. Trav.* xvii 83 *no* XXIII *col* 2, 4 a-na še-na lu-u a-zu-uz; & see Creat.-*frg* IV 137 a-na šinâ-šu (KB vi, 1, 343). K 6012 + K 10684, 4 ši-na [ûmu], second day, PSBA xxvi opposite *p* 56. — A-di ši-na, often. literally: up to two, *i. e.* twice, repeated, *ditto*. IV² 7 *a* 21 a-di ši-na iq-bi-šu-(22 *a* 53 šum). Sm 10 a-di ši-na ina qa-bi-e. IV² 3 *b* 6, 7 ki-çir si-bit a-di ši-na ku-çur (see 745 *col* 1, above); also IV² 1* iv 61 [si-bit?] a-di ši-na-šu-nu; 2 v 58, 59.

f šit(t)ên. PSBA viii 240; JA xii ('89) 309. KB vi (1) 118 *ad* NE I ii 1 šit-ten-šu ilu-ma; 204 *ad* IX ii 16 šit-ta-šu ilu-ma, literally: two (-thirds), see *ibid* 424, 425. III 59 *no* 15, 48 ši-ten-šu gloss to II-šu, ZA v 105; Thompson, *Reports*, ii. ši-it-ti-in Xammurabi-*code* xvi 66 = two thirds, *cf* ZA xviii 2 *rm* 2. Pinches, Palest. Explor. Fund, *Quart. Stat.*, July '00 *p* 261 šit-ta kusêti = two robes. See also Br 4459.

Note. — From šinâ are derived šanû, 1; šanû, 2; šaniš, 1; (amêl) šanû; (ra-bu-) še-ni; šunnû; šanîânu; šanîtu; šinšerû. — An earlier form of šinâ, according to Hilprecht, *Assyriaca*, 69 is:

šinû *1.* Perhaps in *Rec. Trav.* xix 61, 62 ši-nu-u between BIŠ-TAN and še-lal-šu-nu. *f* V 34 *a* 26 a-ti ši-ni-su, KB iii (2) 40, 41 bis zu ihren 2 Dritteln; Nabd 258, 15 II-it gan-gan-an-nu; 12 II-it nam-za-tum. See also ZDMG 58, 199 *rm* 2. Xammurabi-*code* xxviii 82—4 ar-nam kab-tam a-na (!) ši-ni-šu it-ba-lam (for a second time); ZA xviii 38. *code* xxx 8 + 15 a-na ši-ni-šu (i-zu-uz-zu-ma).

šinû *2.* 88—1—18, 1866 *R col* vi 2, ... šekels of silver for a ši-nu-u (?) of UD-KA-BAR (copper).

šinnu, *f* (§ 71) tooth {Zahn} (√šananu? cut) *pl* šinnâti (§ 70*b*); *dual* šinnâ (perh. = the 2 rows of teeth?). id KA (§ 9, 39); *pl* KA-MEŠ-šu-nu, TP vi 74; I 27 *no* 2, 20 paššûrê KA-MEŠ a(u)x-xu-za-te; H 10 + 207, 42; II 39 *a-b* 44; AV 8282. IV² 27 *no* 6 *R* 10 mu-ru-uš šin-ni (= KA-GIG), toothache. Xammurabi-*code* xxxiii 67 ši-in-ni a-wi-lim (+ 70 + 74). Perh. K 532 (Hr^L 109) *R* 1, 2 ina eli bu-ul-ṭi ša šin-ni ša šarri (+ 5), concerning the abscess of the king's tooth, *Rec. Trav.* xxiii 162*fol.* Creat.-*frg* III 25 zaq-tu-ma šin-ni, sharp of tooth. šinni pîri see pîru (826 *col* 2, *med*). id KA-AM-SI, often mentioned together with SU-AM-SI = elephant's skin. Br 650; Sn iii 37; Esh i 20. Perh. Nabd 535, 10: III ši-in-nu bi[-i-ri?]; also šinnu alone: T. A. (Ber) 6 *R* 7 let wood ša šin-ni (with ivory) be inlaid; (Ber) 218 *R* 11; 14, 8: I ši-in-nu ša bi-ri; 13, 67; 25 iv 57; id 28 iii 75, 76; iv 1. — *dual*: III 65 *b* 18 when (of a newborn child) ši-in-na-a-šu a-çi-a (his teeth come out). Creat.-*frg* IV 53 šin-na-šu-nu (of the dragons) na-ša-a im-ta. Zim., *Ritualt.* 24 *O* 31 (end) xe-pu šinnâ = zahnlückig (see *ibid*, *p* 87). — *pl*: IV² 58 *d* (*col* 3) 38 qaqqad-sa qaqqad nêši šin-na-at imêri (§ 72*b*) šin-na[-a-ti?] but ZA xvi 180*foll* reads šin-na-at imêri šin-na[-as-sa] & translates: eine Eselsgestalt ist ihre Gestalt (see šinnatu). — ga-ça-çu ša šin-ni see קצץ & BA ii 570; xa-ma-šu ša šin-ni see xamašu (324 *col* 1) & Br 547; II 39 *a-b* 48.

Derr. šinnânu.

še-ni, in ra-bu-še-ni, four times {viermal}; perh. a *m* of šanîtu; or analogy of šal-še-ni *etc.*?? Compare also Xammurabi-*code* xxviii 33; xxx 3 + 15 a-di ši-ni-šu, a second time. Probably identical, originally, with šinū, 1 (??).

še-in-nu, see tibnu.

šēnu 1. NE XII (K 2774) i 22 (& dupl) perhaps: še-e-ni a-na (*var* ina) šēpē-ka la ta-še-ni. J^{I-N} 55 (see, above, 408, 1, *ll* 9, 10); KB vi (1) 256, 257 & *rm* 11 (>< BA i 72). 81, 7—1, 98 iii 4, 5 še-e-nu (= SU-E-SIR) ana še-pi-šu-nu še-in-ma (= ip). Pinches, *Jour. Trans. Vict. Inst.*, xxvi ('93) 154. The meaning of šēnu must be something like: put, bind the sandal on the foot.

šēnu *2. f* sandal, shoe {Sandale, Schuh}. id SU-E-SIR (or SER). Hebr סְאוֹן, Isa 9, 4. Hommel, *Zwei Jagdinschr.*, 38; VK 413 & 499 note 257; Pinches, ZK ii 324 *foll* (>< Z^B 6, 2 & 55; BA i 72: ring). K 41 b 6 [nakru šu-u ina šēpā-šu?] še-e-nu šak-nu, PSBA xvii 65 *foll.* K 246 (H 87) i 64 see mēsiru (568 *col* 2, below; Br 213). IV^2 56 *b* 53 lu-u šak-na-a-ti še-e-ni ša du-ur da-a-ri, ZA xvi 162, 163 sandals may be put on (thy feet) forever. Nabd 824, 13: II me-e še-e-nu; 566, 8 SU-me (= *pl*? for MEŠ, BA i 636) še-e-nu; Neb 178, 1 SU-me (?) še-en (or, rather, = mēšēnu, see mišēnu, 607 *col* 2). Nabd 673, 4 + 7: II ku-dur-ri ša še-e-nu. II 34 *no* 3, 46 še-nu mašak (or mašak?) parē, shoes of mule-leather | .... ša-tum, which in 44 = a-ša-tum. 83, 1—18, 1330 i 20 ŠU-KAT-ŠU-KAT (e-sir) = še-e-nu, PSBA xi, Dec. '88. II 25 *e-f* 54; V 28 *a-b* 82 še-e-nu | un-qu; *cf* KB vi (1) 392. [cuneiform] še-nu, K 61, 4 (ZK ii 12, 13). — T. A. (Lo) 28, 5 SU še-ni šarri bēli-ja, the sandals of my lord, the king; 30, 5; 31, 5 I am the dust iš-tu šu-pa-li SU še-ni, under the sandals of my lord, the king; (Ber) 231, 4 & 5; 162, 4; 88, 4. (Lo) 29, 4 & 5. See also me(i)šēnu.

šaniānu, *adv* a second time, for the second time {zum zweiten Mal} *cf* šalšiānu. § 77; AV 7972. From šanū, 2. Asb iv 18 ša-ni-ja (*var* 'a, BA i 478)-a-nu he said (ZA x 80 *rm* 1); viii 41 ša-ni(-ja)-a-nu (they bent him); v 34 ša-ni-ja-a-nu. Smith, *Asurb*, 215 *d* ša-ni-a-nu 1 assembled my army. K 94 *R* 4 u ša-ni-ja-'a-nu (PSBA xxiii 61 *fol*); K 145, 15 ša-ni-ja-' (BA i 590); = Hr^L 287, 436. T. A. (Ber) 92 *R* 12 ša-ni-ja-nu.

šinbu see sinbu, 2 (770 *col* 2) & add: perhaps V 14 *c-d* 9 ši-pat im-mir 'š'in-bi (*var* bu), AV 8271; ZK ii 264.

šunbuṭu see nabaṭu Š *ac* (635 *col* 2).

šunbultu *cf* šubultu, 1.

šangū, *m* priest {Priester} *pl* šangē. AV 6560, 7982. § 9, 160; ZA iv 264 id [cuneiform] = RIT; S^b 243 sa-an-gu (S^a ii 40) | RIT | ša-an-gu-u, Br 5980. *cf* S^b 1 ii 11 sa-an-ga = mullilu, Br 6155/6. id I 6 *no* v 2. II 31 *b* 60 (amēl) RIT dan-nu; 61 (amēl) RIT ša bīt kad-mu-ri. IV^2 39 *a* 13 Adad-Nirāri ša-an-gu-u çi-ru ša (il) Bēl (& 24). Salm, *Ob* 15 *Šalm.* rubu-u šangū (il) Ašur; + 17 son of Asurnaçipal šangu-u çi-i-ru ša šangū-su eli ilāni i-ṭi-bu. I 35 *no* 1, 8 Adad-Nirāri šangū ellu. Asb vi 46 (the Elamite gods & goddesses, their treasures) a-di (amēl) ša-an-gi-e (with the priests) and temple-servants aš-lu-lu ana (māt) Ašur (ki); also *cf* AV* 60 *col* 1, below. Bu 91—5—9, 704 (dedication of a temple) 10—14 Pī-ša-Šamaš-ma ša-gu-um bīti Nu-ur-i-li-šu a-na ša-gu-ti-im u-la i-ra-gu-um (will not bring action against the priesthood). Pinches, JRAS '99, 105: šagū: earlier form of šangū. √ apparently Akkadian saga = head. V 60 *b* 16 Ekuršumušabši RIT Sippar; *a* 22, 31; *b* 9; *c* 29; 61 *d* 52 Ekuršumušabši E-BAR Sippar; 60 *c* 27 Nabūnadinšum E-BAR Sippar; 61 *d* 44; *f* 12; *e* 8 + 36; see Jeremias, BA i 279 E-MAŠ = id for šangū, following Strassmaier-Pinches. Scheil, *Rec. Trav.* xvii 33 *no* XIV face ii 2, 3 Bēlbēlapli e-ba-ar (the priest).

id E-BAR, Nabd 165, 2; 293, 37; 299, 16; 309, 14; 395, 4, 15; 417, 21; 477, 37 *etc.* T^C 45 (E-MAŠ).

P. N. *e. g.* Šangū-Ašur-lil-bur, Eponym of 877/876 (AV 7983); Šangū-ili, II 63 viii 16 (AV 7984); Šangū-Ištar, K 10119.

Etymology: Hommel, *Sum. Les.*, 59 (below) √ sag (for dag) *i. e.* [cuneiform]; also see Hastings, *Dict. of Bible*, i 216. — Jensen, ZA vii 174 *rm* 1, šangû. Oberpriester = ša naqî, der Mann des Opferns; the priest as the one presiding over the sacrifice. WINCKLER, *Forsch*, ii 2 ('99) 314: bêl niqê, of secondary origin. — HAUPT, BA i 160 *rm* 2; 178 *rm* 3; JBL xix 60 *rm* 42: a Š-form; combines with נקי, sacrifice. — ZIMMERN, KAT³ 590 *rm* 7: perhaps > *šaggû, √שגע, thus properly: the raving, howler ‖ der "Rasende" oder "Heulende". — See also šangammaxu & šangûtu.

šingu. Nabd 1119, 3 ši-in-gu (?).

šingallu. V 32 *b* 66 šin-gal-lu ‖ ga-annu, preceded by un-qu, ring AV 8272. V 27 *e-f* 30 (erû) 'Š'IN-GAL-LA = maššit-tum (613 *col* 2, below). See also šagallatum.

šangammaxu. highpriest, chief-magician, or the like {Hohepriester, Obermagier} § 73 *rm*; ZA xv 42 *rm* 3; JENSEN, 490. id GA-ṬU 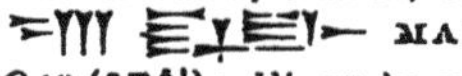 MAX. IV² 30' *no* 3 *O* 18 (amêl) a-š]i-pu ša-an-gam-[m]a-xu, *etc.*; also IV² 18* *no* 3 *R* iv 13; 8 *b* 51 (= Z^Š vi 173, 1; JENSEN, ZA iii 407: I am the high priest × JENSEN, ZK i 292; ii 51); BA i 291. II 58 *no* 6, 70—72 (il) AZAG-ŠUD (see ZIMMERN, *Ritualtafeln*, 142 *rm* β) ša-an-gam-ma-xu ša (il) Bêl (IV² 28* *no* 3, 12) id GA-ṬU (=EL)-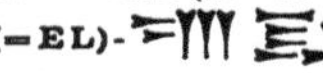-MAX *i. e.* EL + sur(ru)maxxu (784 *col* 1). See also II 51 *no* 1 *R* 14 (ZK ii 320 *foll*); III 68 *e-f* 12 AN-AZAG-ŠUD, the GA-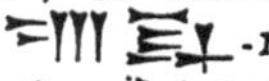-MAX of Bêl; II 32 *e-f* 9 where id + xu (= šangammaxu) occurs beetween ra-am-ku & maš-ma-šu.

šangûtu. *abstr. n* of šangû. priesthood {Priestertum} AV 7985. III 15 *a* 22 Ištar ra-'-i-mat ša-an-gu-ti-ja. Bu 88—5—12, 75 + 76 viii 6 zêr ša-an-gu-ti-ja (BA iii 254); TP i 25 zêr RIT (= šangû)-ti-šu (AV 3003 zer-RIT-tu); *cf* viii 34 zêr šangû-ti-ja; 36 (BA i 160 *rm* **; 323); vii 73 the great gods râ'imu šangû-ti-ja; *cf* Anp i 38, 99; I 28 *a* 1; Sn *Kui* 4, 10 Ašur u Ištar ra-'-i-mu (amêl) šangû-ti-ja; Esh *Sendsch*, *R* 28. Anp i 11 šangût-su; 25; Šalm, *Ob* 17. IV² 39 *a* 29 (Ašuruballiṭ) ša ša-an-gu-su ... šu-tu-rat. SMITH, *Asurb*, 11, 14 (amêl) ša-an-gu-ti. K 6303, 3 (end) šarrû(?)-su-un e-ki-im u ša-an-gu [-su-un]. KB ii 270 (K 1662) 6 ša-an-gu-tu gi-mir eš-rit. Bu 88—5—12, 75 + 76 viii 38 na-çir kussî ša-an-gu-ti-ja, BA iii 254. See SCHEIL, *Šalm*, 92; *Šamš*, 32 on bêlûtu, kiššûtu, šangûtu.

šandû. K 4560, 10 ....  | (šam) ša-an-du-u, Br 14116; AV 8415; M^S *pl* 12; or u-ša-an-du-u (?).

šanâdu. some sickness, disease, ulcer? {eine Krankheit; Geschwür?}. AV 7964. II 26 *b-c* 18 SA-AD-DIR = ša-na-du, Br 3105, preceded by nipištu (712 *col* 1) & followed by šaššaṭu.

šanûdu, šanundu. strong, powerful {stark, mächtig, gewaltig} ‖ qarradu (*q. v.*). Šamš i (I 29) 8/9 (il) Ninib al-lal-li ilâni šu-pi-i ša-nu-di kaš-ka-šu.

šindu *1.* V 32 *a-c* 30 + K 4602; V 27 *e-f* 6 (SU-ŠE-ṬU-GUŠKIN (or GI)) see šîbu, 3; Br 225; AV 8275. V 32 *a-c* 31 IM-ŠIM-TAQ-GIŠ = li-e]-ru = šin-di ni[-siq-ti? Z^B 45]; for ŠE-ṬU *cf* šimtu, 2. ZA iii 313, 62: ornament {Schmuck}. Nabd 416, 1—2: IV ma-na ši-in-du; Neb 222, 1: IV ma-na ši-in-du; 126, 1: XVI mana ši-in-di; Cyr 44, 2—3 ši-in-du; BA III 478. See also Br 1951 on K 4597, 11.

šindu *2.* PINCHES, JRAS '98, 444: "probably not 'spot', but certainly 'mark' *e. g.* on cattle to distinguish them from those of others." Camb 1, 1 imêru samânû sa-a-mu ša ši-in-du ina mux-xi-šu ja-a-nu, an eight-year old dark colored donkey, on whom there is no mark. KB iv 285; BA iii 478. Neb 360, 10 imêru šu-gu-ru-ru ša ina mux-xi (= eli) ap-pi-šu ši-in-du. See also mušindîtum, 807 *col* 2. It is used, likewise, of human beings: Cyr 307, 9 Ṭâbat-išxar will take ši-in-du ša amtu-u-tu, BA iv 10: das Zeichen der Magdschaft.

šandabakku. name or title of an official {ein Amtsname} AV 7712; 7986. Rm 338 *O* 11 E-ŠA (= LIB)-DUB = ša-ad-da-bak-ku, M^S *pl* 21. V 32 *a-c* 18, 19 (Br 8448) see kâniku (p3p). V 16 *e-f* 38 U]R-AN-XE-NUN-NA = ša-an-da-bak-ku, preceded by ša bâb êkalli & followed by ik-ka-rum. HOMMEL, PSBA xxi 115 > ŠA-DUB. MEISSNER & ROST 105, 9: Beamter, der mit dem Verschliessen zu tun hat. *Cf* also nadbaku,

NOTE, 1. (650 *cols* 1, 2), & see nukaribbu (677 *col* 2).

šundulu, AV 8521 see after šadalu.

šindilibbu (?) Br 3355/56 on V 23 *a-c* 11.

šan-du-tim see šadūtu.

šūnuxu, *adj* (√anaxu, 2; *pp* 69, 70) sighing, lamenting, moaning {seufzend, trauernd, wehklagend}. IV^2 54 *b* 1 naplisma (= ip) be-lum šu-nu-xu ardu-ka; 81—2—4, 188, 13 a-na at-mu-u-a šu-nu-xi lib-ša-a [u]-zu-un-ki, ZA v 66, 67. IV^2 29** *no* 5 *O* 5 anaku] arad-ki šu-nu-xu a-ša-as-si-ki (H 115). IV^2 20 *no* 1, 9—10 ik]-ri-bi-ia šu-nu-xu-ti. SMITH, *Asurb*, 123, 46 in-xe-ia šu-nu-xu(-u)-ti, my moaning lamentations (Ištar heard). *adv.*:

šūnuxiš. Sn iv 10 i-na ne-ri-bi-šu-un pi-qu-ti šu-nu-xi-iš (‖ marçiš, 1j) e-ru-um-ma.

šūnuxu *2.* (?). K 3182 i 45 ul i-ba-aš-ši ina gi-mir [11] Igigi ša šu-nu-xu ba-li-ka, AJSL xvii 187: among all the Igigi there is not one who gives rest besides thee. √anaxu, 1?

Sanxar see Šumēr(u).

šanṭu (> šamṭu?). II 32 *g-h* 65 [ŠE..].. KAB-GAR-RA = ša-an-ṭu, Br 14484; AV 7987. See šamṭu, 1.

šinṭu. some kind of fur or woolen stuff {Tierpelz oder Wollstoff}, or the like. AV 8276. V 28 *a-b* 19 ši-in-ṭu (& 20 nd or gir-du) ‖ ši-pat [sign] (kur?)-ri. V 14 *c-d* 30 SEG-GUŠUR = ši-in-ṭu (+ *b* 42) Br 5500; 12081 on K 4597, 10. STRECK, ZA xviii 171.

šinṭatu (?) K 4597, 12—17 ši-in-ṭa(?)-[tu], Br 10311, 119, 5885, 5350, 7177, 7078.

šanakku. See nikpakku (671 *col* 2) & add: K 626 *R* 6 (Hr^L 20); HOMMEL, PSBA xxi 115 √ŠA-NA; STRONG, JA '98, 382: encensoir. Also mentioned together with kinūnu (K 3821).

šunul(l)u. √na'alu (628, 629). II 60 *no* 1 *R* (14) 55 ... UZ (or, uz-?) qa-bi-e ša ina ba-çi šu-nu-lu (*Rev. Sém.* ix 186).

šunullu. Rm IV 97 (33,541) 7 *M* wept ša xa-lib-šu šu-nu-ul-lu, that her dress had been ruined. PSBA xxiii 195, 196.

šinamū. some official {ein Beamter}? Nabd 640, 3 (amēl) ši-na-mu-u. Camb 394, 4; AV 8260 on III 4, 14.

šinamtu (?). T. A. (Ber) 97, 25 i-na ši-nam-ti šarri šamši, KB v 100, 101.

šananu. *ps* iš(š)annan, *ag* šāninu, *pm* šanna. AV 7970 be like, equal, match, rival, come up (with s. o. or to s. t.), be equivalent to {einer Person oder Sache gleichkommen; erreichen, *etc.*}. On iš see § 25 — Creat.-*frg* IV 4 (+ 6) ši-mat-ka la ša-na-an (AV 7967). K 2619 iv 22 [11] sibitti-šunu qar-rad la ša-na-an (KB vi (1) 66, 67). Esh *Sendsch*, *R* 27 šarru-u-tam(-ut) la ša-na-an (ana šimtija išīmu) = unequalled. Sarg *Khors* 4; *Cyl* 8; Sn i 10; *Bell* 4; *Kui* 1, 2. I 35 *no* 1, 2; *no* 3, 4 mal-kut la ša-na-an. IV^2 38 *a* 26 Kurigalzu šarru la ša-na-an; I 35 *no* 3, 11; Anp i 10; Sn *Bell* 1; *Bass* 1. TP i 29 *Tigl. Pil.* šar kiššati la(-a) ša-na-an; vi 56. II 67, 11 ma-xa-zi la ša-na-an (said of Sippar, Nippur, *etc.*). Sarg *Harem-A* 7 e-mu-qan la ša-na-an. ZA iii 319, 91 ša-na-nu ‖ li-i-tu, victory. — *ps* K 2852 + K 9662 iv 15 Ašur-man-nu-i-ša-na-an, name of a city (+ 19 ša-ni-ni a-a ir-r[u-ub]), WINCKLER, *Forsch*, ii 40—43. IV^2 9 *b* 9—10 ka-a-tu a-mat-ka man-nu i-lam-mad man-nu i-ša-na-an, as for thee, who can learn thy word, who can rival thee?, PRINCE, AJSL xix 223; Br 6689. IV^2 20 *no* 3 *O* 5/6—13/14 to (= it-ti) thy power, thy house, thy city *etc.* ... a power, a house, a city *etc.* .... ul iš-ša-an-na-an, Br 6689 (= cannot come up = NU-MU-UN-DA-DI); H 40, 199 DA-DI = ša-na-nu. K 257 (H 126 *foll*) *O* 59/60 (63/64) be-ili-ku it-ti qa-ti-ia (še-pi-ia) qa-tu (še-pu) ša iš-ša-an-na-nu (H 128: nu-na; DI-A, EME-SAL, Br 9539) ul i-ba-aš-ši; see on this hymn especially PRINCE, JAOS xxiv ('03) *pp* 103—128. II 8 *a-b* 30 AN-DA-AB(P)-DI-A = (pi-ia it-ti amēlūti) iš-ša-na-an-ni (ZA iii 42), my mouth competes for me with other people. — *pm* T. A. (Ber) 44 *R* 9 ia-nu lib-bi ša-na-a-na, my heart has not changed. IV^2 27 *no* 2 *a* 15/17 (ša-an-na = DA-AB-DI-A) see šamānu; § 98. — *ag* šāninu, AV 7974 ‖ māxiru = one's equal, rival, *etc.* D^8 120 *foll*; ZDMG 29, 46; ZA ii 309, 10. H 40, 192 ZAG-DU = ša-ni-nu. TP iv 41 *Tigl. Pil.* ša-ni-nu gi-mir kāl šarrāni, a match for all the kings combined (Esh *Sendsch*, *R* 21); i 57 ša-ni-na ina qabli u ma-xi-ra ina taxâzi (B transposes & reads GAB-RI-A = mâxira Br 4505 & § 9, 143; or gab-ri-a (?) . . . ša-ni-na, thus indicating the equivalence of the two) la-a i-ša-a-ku; iv 48 (while I had no conqueror ina qabli) ša-ni-na i-na taxâzi. la i-šu-u; Sarg *Nimr* 4. Anp i 13 *Anp.* who among the princes of the four regions ša-nin-šu la išu-u (iii 115); *Bal O* 6 ša-nin(-in)-šu lā išu-u (written NU-TUK-u) = V 60, 6; § 23 *rm*; *Mon O* 10 (ii 126) ša-nin-šu la(-a) i-šu-u. Anp i 43 bad roads *etc.* I traversed and ša-nin (*var* ni-ni) ul ib-ši; IV² 29 *a* 18 ša ša-ni-na la i-šu-u (Br 6506); 34 i *O* 23 (Sargon) ša-ni-na GAB-RI NU-TUK-ši (mâxira lâ ibašši); Šalm, *Mon*, i 10 ša . . . ša-nin-šu la išu-u. ZA iv 228, 5 ul ti-i-ši ša-ni-na. Sn *Kui* 4, 32 Sennacherib's southwestpalace in Nineveh was called êkallu ša ša-ni-na la i-šu-u; *Bell* 56 êkallu ZAG-DI-NU-TUK-A; *Rm* 84. NE VI 21 parû-ka] ina ni-i-ri ša-ni-na a-a ir-ši, KB vi (1) 168—9. — *f* Scheil, ZA x 292, 27 ša-nin-tum (ilu) A-nu; K 3464, 26 ša-nin-ti ni-ši te-li-ti (ilat) Ištar (Craig, *Relig. Texts*, *pl* 60); Martin: rivale des hommes, auguste Ištar; see also PSBA xxiii 115 *foll.*

Q¹ originally: attempt to be equal to some one; then: rival, combat, fight. 83—3—23,131, 6 . . . ši]t-nu-nu-ma šit-nu-nu šadi-e (the subject!) zak-ru-ti Winckler, *Forsch*, ii (iii) 570 *foll.* NE 8, 32 liš-ta-an-na-nu-ma, may they combat one another. TP i 55 it-ti . . . . al-ta-na-an; 76 (la); iii 77; § 51. Xammurabi-*code* xliii 60 ba-la-ṭam ša it-ti mu-tim ši-ta-an-nu, a life like unto death, Harper, 106, 107; ZA xviii 36. H 80 (K 133) 19/20 it-ti (ilu) A-nim u (ilu) Bêl ina šit-nu-ni-šu, Br 6515. — with *acc.* Anp i 27 who nakrût Ašur . . . . . uliš u šapliš iš-ta-na-nu (iii 129). — KB iii (2) 4 *col* 1, 38—9 ri-e-ši-ša ša-ma-mi a-na ši-it-nu-ni (to make alike, equal) Marduk commanded me (ZA iv 108).

ℑ¹ (?) KB vi (1) 262—3 on NE XII *col* 3, 30 im-tal-li-ku uš-ta-an-na-an.

ℑℑ be equalled, reached {erreicht werden} *etc.* Anp i 1 Ninib ša ina taxâzi la iš-ša-na-nu ti-bu-šu; I 35 *no* 2, 6 Nebo ša la iš-ša-na-nu dan-nu-su; K^M 60, 10. *Rec. Trav.* xx 205 *foll* i 10 la iš-ša-an-na-nu be-lut-su ‖ la šit-lu-ṭa-at be-lut-su (13).

Derr. šinnatu, šitnuntu &:

šinintu. K 1349, 18 la bêl kussî la ši-nin-ti êkalli (Winckler, *Keilschrift-texte*, ii 1; *Forsch*, i 405) M^S 96 *col* 2.

-ši-na-ni verb suff. 3 *pl.* Anp iii 125 ša a-pi-lu-ši-na-ni, referring to mâtâti (see *ibid* 133). ‖ TP vii 2 ša a-pi-lu-ši-na-ti (+ 19); also K 112 (Hr^L 223) 7.

šinnânu (?). Sp III 6 *R* ii 3 GI-AŠ-DU-A = qa-nu-u šin-na-nu (PSBA xvi 308—9: the toothed cane?).

šanundu see šanûdu.

šu-nun-du see šu-gi-du & AV 8516. Also K 8665 *R* 6 (M^S *pl* 14).

šanunkat(u). 81—6—7, 209, 6, Ištar of Erech is called ša-nun-ka-at ad-na-a-ti, the princess of abodes (BA iii 260—1; 360—1); 81—4—28, 327 (dupl. of V 41 *no* 1 *a-b* 12) has ma-al-ka-tum & ša-nun-ka-tum explained by šar-ra-t[um]; Hebr. viii 118; M^S *pl* 26. Jensen, ZA xv 229 *rm* 1 compares early-Elamite (Alt-Elamitisch) *sunku(i)k*, kingdom, & *sunku*, king. See also Hommel, PSBA xxi 134 § 43.

šinunûtum. name of a star {Sternenname}. V 46 *a-b* 34 (kakkab) A-nu-ni-tum = (kakkab) ši-nu-nu-tum, ZA i 265 *rm* 1 & 2; *i. e.* the stars of the rivers Tigris & Euphrates, Br 13360. II 51 *a-b* 59 the star of the Euphrates-river is explained as (kakkab) ši-nun-tum; see *p* 771 *col* 1, above. KAT³ 431 *rm* 5.

šinipu = ²/₃ (two-thirds). *c. st.* šinipat; *pl* šinipâtu, AV 7962, 8266, 8267. ZDMG 27, 698. Tim [Hebrew]; § 77. ZA xviii 81. S^b 52 ša-na-bi | [cuneiform] | ši-i-ni-pu; §§ 34 *rm*; 35; Br 11225; H 35, 845; PSBA xxi 115. V 37 *a-c* 12, 13 ša-na-bi | [cuneiform] | ši-ni-pu & ši-ni-pa-a-tum (× BA ii 603) Br 10026—7. K 56 iii (= II 15 *c-d*) 45 ši-ni-pat suluppê. — V 40 *c-d* 57 [cuneiform]-bi = ši-ni-pa-tum, Br 11226. NE V i 12 . . . . ša-niš (?) ana ši-ni-pat [KAS-PU a-an]. KB vi (1) 160—161. *del* 76 (80) . . . .] li-ku ši-ni-pat-su.

HAUPT: the ship went (sank) into the water 2/3 of its height, AJP ix 428; BA i 127; KB vi (1) 491. On ŠA-NA-BI (= šînipat) = 40 in *c. t.*, see BA i 516, 517.

šinnipitum. some object made of reeds. Camb 417, 1: 700 (qan) ši-in-ni-pi-tum.

šanaçu pr išniç. blaspheme, slander {lästern, verläumden}. SMITH, *Asurb*, 247*j* KA (= lišân)-šu ša iš-ni-iç-çu ak-kis. — Q^t SCHEIL, *Rec. Trav.*, xxii, notes LIII, 1 i-ta-aš-ni-çi.

šannaçru. II 33 *a-b* 72 SAR-RA = ša-an-na-aç-ru, AV 7989; Br 14069. Could also be read ša AN (= ilu) na-aç-ru (pm of naçaru); but see *l* 71 SAR = xá-an-na (AV: -ba)-aç-ru.

šanaqu 1. pr aš-niq H 184 frg 5201 coloph. See sanaqu (771—2), the *aš* instead of *as*, probably a scribal error, owing to the preceding aš-ṭur.

šanāqu ***2.*** Nabd 10, 7 ša-na-qu; 119, 11 ša II ša-na-qu; Neb 23, 3; 457, 10: VI ša-na-qu. Perhaps = niknakku, *q. v.*

šu-nu-qa, AV 8517. II 16 *b* 51 see nâḳu (668 *col* 2, below).

'š'un-qu-u, Br 11420 *ad* II 48 *a-b* 41, but see ruqqû.

šunqut(u) see maqatu Š (end), 579 *col* 1; also used as a noun.

šaniš ***1.*** again, a second time; *ditto* {wiederum, *ditto*} *adv* to šanû, 2. IV^2 56 *b* 32 ša-niš uç-ça-am-ma; 83, 1—18, 1330 i 6 see šikkatu, 3. ZIMMERN, *Ritualt.*, 74, 41. Perhaps II 39 *d* 73; V 21 *c* 29; 28 *b* 26; K 2022 iii 12 + 20; II 29 *d* 11. NE V i 12 (= H^{NE} 24, 12) see šînipu.

šaniš ***2.*** *adv* to šanû, 4. somewhere else {anderwärts} III 54 *c* 32 ša-ni-iš ri-ig-mu GAR (= iššakn)-an, but?? (= K 712 *O* 6; THOMPSON. *Reports*, ii *no* 88).

šanašu. Q IV^2 56 ii 24 (end) paṭru ina libbi ta-ša-an-niš, ZA xvi 154*foll*: ein Schwert sollst du hineinstecken (in das Feuer); thus: put, place into s. t.; pierce *etc.* whence the ℶ. K 41 *c* 17 aq-bi-ma] çi-xa-ta-šu u-ša-na-aš-an-ni, its lamentation will make me sad, PINCHES, PSBA xvii 65*foll* (or √našašu?).

šanšu (?) KB iv 170—1 (below) 2: II ša-an-ša-nu pa-an raq-qa-a-ti ša (ilu) Malik; Nabd 591, 4: IV (??) ša-an-ša-nu ša (ilu) ....; also 98, 4 bit-qu ša ša-an-ša ša (ilu) ....

(šam) **ši-niš** see šilmu, 2.

šu-un-šu, his name, § 49*a* = šumšu see šumu, name.

-šunûši, -šinâši verb. suff. 3 *pl* (BA ii 564).

šanšala, AV 7990. II 32 *a-b* 20 ša(-)an-ša-la = iš-tu ΥΥ<ΥΥ-<< (?) = ša am-šala, *q. v.*

(a-na) **šu-na-šu-nu** K 525, 20 (Hr^L 252; BA ii 61) = šâšunu, *pl* of šuššu, šašu, *q. v.*

šinšēru, the twelfth {der Zwölfte} T. A. (Lo) 82, 6 (end) i-na ši-i-in-še-e-ri-i, im zwölften. iδ also KB vi (1) 192—3, 10 (26). Derived from šina, two.

šin-niš-tum, AV 8278 see sinništum, 773 *col* 1.

šanāti *pl* of šaṭṭu, year, *q. v.*

šanātum (?) V 14 (*a-*)*b* 24 ... ša-na-a-tum. √šanû, 5?

šanītu *f* repetition, time {Wiederholung, Mal} √šanû, 2. AV 7975; iδ ŠU ([cuneiform sign]) Br 10840; § 9, 88; H 7, 218; 34, 823; JENSEN, 407. See also KB ii 212 *ad* Asurb vii 54; III 5 *no* 6, 1; & ([cuneiform sign]) ZA v 18 *rm* 1; 144, 28 & *rm* 5. Šalm, *Mon*, ii 82 ša šanû-te šanītu, a second time (§ 77; SCHEIL, *Šalm*, 99). Lay 91, 77 ša-nu-te šanītu; *cf* Beh 55 ina ša-ni-ti KAS (= šanûti; HOMMEL); 51 ina ša-ni-tum III (= šalultum), a third time (+ 71); § 129. KNUDTZON, *no* 68, 4 ša-ni-ti = ša-niš, zweitens, oder, zum zweiten Mal. T. A. (Ber) 45, 21 ša-ni-tu, (and) again, furthermore; (Lo) 19, 31 & often. On Asurb vi 12 see KB ii 202—3, *rm* 12; & on *del* 58, 59 (61—63) consult KB vi (1) 232—4; 488.

šunāta(-tu) *pl* of šuttu, 1, dream, *q. v.*

šunūtu a plant {eine Pflanze, ein Gewächs}. ZA vi 291 *col* 2, 4 šu-nu-tu (SAR) see *ibid* 293, 294.

-šunūti(u) & šunûši, *m*; šinâti & šinâši, *f.* verb. suff. 3 *pl.* See *Johns Hopkins Circ.*, 114 *p* 118. TP vii 2 ša a-pi-lu-ši-na-ti (see -šinâni).

-šu-nu-ti for šu-nu, *e. g.* Asb i 120 libbašu-nu-ti (§ 56).

šunnūtu. *pl* in K 2801 = K 221 + 2669 *R* 17 li-in-ni-pu-uš ina la šu-un-na-a-te zi-kir šap-ti-ku-un, it shall be done without change of the words of your mouth {es soll gemacht werden ohne Abänderung eures Wortes} BA iii 234, 235. √šanū 8.

šinnatu. equality; form, figure {Gleichkommen, Ebenbürtigkeit; Figur, Gestalt}. √šananu. K 3351 (hymn to Ninib) *O* 11/12 be-lum ra-aš-bu ša ina puxur ilāni rabûti šin-na-as-su la ibba-šu-u, CRAIG, *Relig. Texts*, i *pl* 43. Sarg *Cyl* 38 *Sargon* šarru pi-it xa-si-si li-'i i-ni ka-la-ma šin-na-at abkalli; KB vi (1) 320: etwas einem ab-k(q)allu gleichkommendes. Lay 38, 4 to whom Êa gave .... šin-na-at NUN-ME (abkalli) A-da-pa, MEISSNER & ROST, 2; KAT³ 537, 538 & *rm* 2; AV 8277. IV² 58 *d* 38 see šinnu, tooth (end). Perhaps here also I 29 *a* 18 the goddess *Martu* bēlit ši-na-at (see KB i 174—5; JENSEN, 468—9 & *rm* 5).

šīnāti, *pl f* urine {Urin} — שֵׁינַיִם. ZK ii 11—12: ši-na-a-ti (K 61). S^b 229 ka-aš | [cuneiform] (*i. e.* [cuneiform], water, in [cuneiform], the penis) | ši-na-a-tu, H 20, 375; Br 5116; AV 8261. SCHEIL, Notes LIV text *l* 10 ki-ma ši-na-a-ti (*Rec. Trav.*, xxii), see purīdu (827 *col* 2). Here perhaps also V 47 *b* 3 ta-ba-aš-ta-nu explained as zu(-)u ši-na-tum (*cf* zū, 4; 271 *col* 2); both of which occur in Sn vi 20, 21 where read ši-na-te-šu-un u-za-ra-bu ..... u-maš-še-ru-ni zu-šu-un, rather than ni-zu-šu-un, as on *p* 656 *col* 2. Sn *Bav* (III 14) 39 ni-ša-a-šu-un, may be scribal error of *ša* for *zu* thus reading u-maš-še-ru-ni za-a-šu-un.

V 42 *a-b* 20, 21 DUK (ki-si) [cuneiform] (Br 5117), & DUK-A-ŠUR-RA (Br 11468) — kar-pat ši-na-a-ti, Br 5116.

šināti (AV 8261), šinātina see šū, 2.

šinītu *1.* dyed, colored stuff, garment {gefärbter, farbiger Kleiderstoff, Kleid} √šanū, 5. AV 8268. V 15 *e-f* 14 KU-A-GE-A (Br 11546) — ši-ni-tum, preceded by çi-bu-tum, 1 (see *p* 868 *col* 1) & followed by çirpu, 1 (see *p* 894 *col* 1). GGA '98, 826 & KAT³ 650 compares Hebr שָׁנִי.

šinītu *2.* K 8667, 11 ... [GA]-RAŠ-SAR — ši-ni-tu, a plant {eine Pflanze} M^5 *pl* 14.

še-na-tu (?). ZK ii 302, 8 la še-na-tu (— DA); an official {ein Beamter}.

šinnētum. II 46 *no* 5 (*d-*)*e* 78 ši-in-ne-tum, between šur-šu (77) & .... ra-tum (79); also see Br 14289 on II 48 *no* 4, *add*; AV 8279.

šasû. AV 7993. *pr* išsi, issi, ilsi; *ps* išas(s)i(u), išessi (§ 34 *a*); *ip* šisī. chief id KA-DE, Br 702. — *a*) call, cry to, invoke, call together; with *acc* {rufen, schreien, herbeirufen, zusammenrufen}. KB ii 250—1, 58 il-si-ka (ilat) Ištar ša-qu-ut ilāni i-šak-kan-ka ṭe-e-mu | um-ma. K 1282 *O* 24 is-si-ma (KB vi, 1. 70—1); NE V *col* i (ii) 43 (KB vi, 1, 162); 44 i-šes-si. Creat.-*frg* IV 89. SCHEIL, *Nabd*, vi 26 by my name il-sa-an-ni-me, he called me. NE VII *col* vi, 12 (28) il-si-ma (il) Gilgameš. H 76, 25, 26 Ea to his son Marduk is-si-ma a-ma-ta u-šax-xaz, spoke and addressed to him the word; IV² 18 *no* 3 *O* i 38, 39; 30,1 *R* 17, 18 (19, 20) ta-aš-si-ma (— KA-IZ-DE), thou didst speak. NE 58, 10 eb-ri ul tal-sa-an-ni (KB vi, 1, 164). IV² 17 *b* 8 al-si-ka Šamaš ina qirib šamê ellûti (I call to thee); 29* *no* 4 C *R* 12, 13 al-si-ki-na-ni al-ka-ni ul al-si-ki-na-ši; 60* B *O* 4 ili al-si-ma. K 8204, 5 al-si-ka (§ 51) Nabū, I called to thee, Nebo (PSBA xvii 138—9); *cf* II 64 *c* 46 (see 45) P. N. Nabū-al-si-ka nu-ur, AV 5710. II 51 *R* 17 ilāni ma-la al-su-u, ZK ii 328. K 2675 *O* 11 al-si-ma (amēl) tur-tan (amēl) paxāti adi çābē qātišunu, I called together (KB ii 236—7). Sn v 62 zar-biš u-me-iš al-sa-a (I shouted, cried out) ‖ kīma (il) Adad ašgum. — *pl* KB vi (1) 74 *no* ii 7 il-su-šu-ma; 96 *R* 4 (*Adapa*-legend) when they saw Adapa il-su-u: na-ra-ru (they shouted: help!), 11 (end) (il) A-nu il-si-ma. NE 58, 15 il-su-u šamû ‖ qaqqaru i-ram-mu-um; 8, 30 is-su-u. IV² 34 (K 3120) *R* 2 il-su-u. — *ps* NE VI 50 the eagle i-šes-si: kap-pi, cries out: my wing! *del* 110 (117) i-šes-si ilat Ištar. KB vi (1) 94, 8 Anu .... i-ša[-as]-si to his servant *Ilabrat*. K 3182 iii 20 from the depth of his mouth the feeble i-ša-as-si-ka, cries out to thee, AJSL xvii 140—1. IV² 3 *b* 35, 36 muruç qaqqadi iramum i-ša-as-si

(= KA-MU-UN-NA-AN-DE-E), howls; same id also 7 *a* 17, 18 Marduk a-na abišu (ilu) Êa ... i-šes-si; 15 ii 55, 56 (end) i-ša-as-si; 22 *a* '9, 50 (where DA-A is a *var* of DE-E, Br 694); 5 *b* 36, 37 (H 76, 6—7) bêlum ana sukkallišu Nusku i-šes-si (§ 34*a*), speaks to his servant *N*; 27 *a* 32—34 ana ilišu rêmênî ki-ma lit-ti i-ša-as-si (= KA-IM-ME, Br 754), I cried out; *cf* 26 *b* 58, 59 = inagag; 29** *no* 5 (H 115) 4 I, thy servant .... a-ša-as-si-ki; 14 i-ša-as-su-ki ka-a-ši, to thee they speak; 38 iii 42, 43 e-ma (when) (ilu) Šamaš u (ilu) Marduk i-ša-as-su-u they shall not hearken to him. K 257 (H 127) 41, 42 (43, 44) be-ili-ku ina qablu (& i-na qa-bal ša-di-i) a-ša-as-si-ma (= U-BA-NI-IN-DE). K 2674 i 18 naxlaptašu iš-ru-ṭu a-na abi ba-ni-šu i-ša-as-su-u, while he cried to the father, his begetter. Sarg *Khors* 162 ša ..... i-ša-as-su-šu, which they call so & so; *Ann* 423; *bull*-inscr. 69; BA i 403. Perhaps II 8 *a-b* 28 aš-ša-as-su a-mat (??). — pc NE 18, 22 eli]-ki lil-si; T^M iii 167 lil-sa-a; i 56 lil-sa-ki-ma; 58 lu-ul-si-ki-ma. — ip K^M 50, 10 šisi-ma, speak! — ag ZIMMERN, *Ritualt.*, *no* 89—90, 5 ša-sa-at ilâni rabûti ša-sa-at ilâni da'ânê, [the daughter of Anu] calling together, *etc.*; also 95 *O* 4, 5. — ac DT 67 (H 120) *R* 9, 10 be-el-tum is-si-ma ša-si-e ar-ni-im-ma, JÄGER, BA ii 300: die Herrin sprach und eine Erklärung der Schuld fürwahr! V 48 iv 16 the 12th of Tammuz ša-si-e šarri; 49 vii 28. K^M 11, 4 ša]-su-u u la a-pa-lu id-da-ça-an-ni. S^P 158 + S^P II 962 *R* 9 i-nu-um la ša-si mi-ša-ri, *Jour. Trans. Vict Inst.* xxix 60. V 31 *a-b* 54 ša-su-u ‖ šu-ta-mu-u; *c-d* 36 i-xa-az-zu ‖ i-ša-as-su (perh. to *b*). S^c 316 gu-u, KA ša-su-u (‖ rigmu *etc.*) Br 546; H 10 & 207, 46. H 10 & 212, 60 KA-DE = ša-su-u; *cf* K 2022 ii 18 = II 29 *c-d* 17 [KA-DE] = ša-su-u, followed by na-bu-u (18), xa-ba-bu (19); H 37, 55 KA-ME = ša-su-u, preceded by na-ga-gu. See also labû, 1 (467 *col* 1). — *b*) read aloud {laut lesen} *cf* קרא. JENSEN, KB vi (1) 556. Nabd 68, 2 u-il-tim ša ... (7) il-su-u-nu. 83—1—18, 2 *O* 15 ina pa-an šarri li-si-ja-u (Hr^L 391; *Rec. Trav.* xxiv 108), before the king let (the letter) be read. Anp *Bal* (V 70) *R* 14 naru ta-mar-ma ta-ša-su-u (ZA i 38) an-xu-su ud-diš (& 22), thou wilt find the tablet, read it and then rebuild its ruin; § 148; BA i 415. I 27 *no* 2, 64, 65 who ta-me-it šiṭ-ri-ja um-ma-na-te a-na a-ma-ri u ša-si-e i-kal-lu-u u ina pa-an musarija man-ma ki-i la-ma-a-ri u la ša-si-e i-pa-ar-ri-ku, KB i 120, 121. V 31 *f* 22, 23 see šalamu, 1 Q *aa*.

Q^1 ištasi, isasi. — *a*) call {nennen} TP ii 26 Kilianteru ..... ša (amêl) Ir(Sa?)-ru-pi i-sa-si-u-šu-ni, whom they also call *I*. NE I i 12 iš-ta]-as-sa šip-ta-šu, HAUPT, JAOS xxii pt. 1 × KB vi (1) 116, 117, see samâtu, 767 *col* 2. — *b*) read {lesen}. L^4 i 17 aš-ta-si, I read. K 2401 ii 32 ina pân šarri i-sa-as-si-u, before the king they shall read aloud (the document); BA ii 605 *foll* (Oracle to Esarhaddon). 83—1—18, 28 *O* 10 il-ta-su-šu, they read it, Hr^L 344. Nabd 356, 30 dup-pa-nu u rik-sa-a-tu .... iš-tas-su-ma; Cyr 332, 23 (riksa) ša .... ma-xar-šu-nu iš-ta-as-su-ma (they read before them). T. A. (Ber) 22, 10 dup-pa which he brought al-ta-ta-as-si (I have read) u a-ma-ti-šu el-te-me, + 35 (ZA v 20). Sarg *Stele* ii 59 (III *R* 11) my .... li-mur-ma lil-ta-si; Esh *Sendsch*, *R* 59 (lil-ta-su-ma); Xammurabi-*code* xli 11 na-ru-i ša-aṭ-ra-am li-iš-ta-aš-si-ma, let him read the inscription on my monument, HARPER, 100, 101.

Q^{tn} *a*) call to {zurufen} NE II *col* iii *b* 28 ul-tu ul-la-nu-um-ma iš-tu šame-e il-ta-na-sa-aš-šu, KB vi (1) 138, 139 rief ihm zu. K 8204 iii/iv 8 (16) al-ta-na-si ilâni-ma. — *b*) repeat {wiederholen} K 41 *c* 9 ar-ki[-ja] il-ta-na-as-si-a, PSBA xvii 65 *foll.* — *c*) read {lesen} Asb iii 121 (*var*) Nabû dupsar gim-ri ..... ušuzma iš-ta-na-sa-a malṭaru kigalli Sin (KB ii 186 *rm*). NE VII *col* v 48 (3) il-ta-na-as-si ina max-ri-šu, reads to her {liest ihr vor} KB vi (1) 190—1; 463. T. A. (Ber) 92 *R* 30 ša šu-u-pa-a-ru il-da-na-as, who is to read the despatch?

ג perhaps H 67, 14 .... ZI = u-ša-si .... T^{M} i 6 my god & my goddess u-šis (*var* ša-as)-su-u; iii 16 u-ša-as-si ili-MU (= ja) u ištari-MU (= ja) ina zumri-MU (= ja). K^{M} 13, 21 šêdu damqu u-še-is-sa.

ג^{t} ac V 37, 55 a-na ši-tas-si-šu, to read it. AV 8343; G §§ 45; 65. ZA iii 60. Often in colophons to tablets: I placed the tablet on record in my palace a-na ta-mar-ti ši-ta(-as)-si-ja, in order to see and read it, IV^{2} 56 coloph. 42; 50 coloph. 35; K 155 (= K^{M} *no* 1) *R* 24; T^{M} i 153. D 49, 41—43; II 21 *a* 33, 34; 23 *a* 67; V 16, 80; 30, 62; ZA v 69.

Š ac Sarg *Cyl* 36 šul-si-e a-la-la, KB ii 45 Jauchzen erklingen lassen. ip K 7599, 4 (end) ina mâtika šul-si, let it be proclaimed in thy country.

Derr. šisîtu & šassâitu.

šesâ. BA ii 636 (K 164) 29 mârtu še-sa-a tazarru; but read qalû (2) & see Zimmern, *Ritualtafeln*, 66 *rm* 21.

ša-sa-ga-te-šu, AV 7991, see sagîtu, 746 *col* 2.

šassukkat. Zimmern, *Ritualtafeln*, 24 *O* 36 (ilat) Bêlit-çêri ša-suk-kat šamê u erçitim (Craig, *Religious Texts*, 64); 87 i 7. Sm 802 irba (ilat) Bêlit-çêri ša-as-suk-kat ilâni rabûti, Bezold, *Catalogue*, 1438; M^{S} 96.

šusullu. Nabd 301, 8: šu-su-ul-lu.

šûsumu *1.* Š ptc of asamu; ססו, 75 *col* 2. IV^{2} 18 *no* 3 i 29, 30 kakku ša ana šarrûti šu-su-mu; 25 *b* 46, 47 e-til-lu-tu šu-su-um (= UL-A, in both cases). KB vi (1) 128 *col* 5, 10 (end) š]u-su-ma bi-nu-tu. Zimmern, *Ritualt.*, *no* 61, 7 šu-su-mat xi-ir-tu, + 62 *R* 4.

šûsumu *2.* *adj* of same √ asamu IV^{2} 20 *no* 1, 15—16 the inhabitants of the land saw la-an-šu e-la-a šu-su-mu (= GAN-UL) = his (Marduk's) lofty, fine appearance, or picture, statue; also see ZA v 67, 36.

šisinnu. Camb 56, 17 ši-sin-nu ul e-tir-ru-'u; see sissinnu, 775 *col* 1.

še-si-na-a-te, AV 8285; M^{S} 96 *col* 2; read qursinâte & see *p* 440 *col* 1; GGA '98, 826.

šusupp(bb)u. some garment or part of dress {ein Kleidungsstück}. AV 8527. V 15 *c-d* 30 KU-ŠU-SU-UB = šu-su-up-pu, Br 7076. ŠU-SU-UB = sûnu, 2 (V 15 *c-d* 43) see 770 *col* 1. T. A. (Ber) 26 iii 27 *fol*; perh. even 26 i 58, ii 48 (see subbu, 746 *col* 1).

šassûru *1.*,, šasûru. a kind or species of flies {eine Fliegenart}. II 5 *b* 12 ša-as-su-ru; ið to be supplemented from V 27 *g-h* 16 & II 31 *e-f* 77 (Br 9036) where = sa-su-ru. BA i 160 & *rm* 2. D^{S} 65; AV 7994. Also K 4152 + K 4183 *R* 9—18 na-pi-lu (?), ça-çi[-ru], bu-ka[-nu], ša-su[-ru], bu-ka-nu ... M^{S} *pl* 7; K 4378 *c* 6—10 (*ibid pl* 12).

šassûru *2.* V 16 *g-h* 36, 37 ÇU & ZAG-LAL = ša-as-su-rum.

šasurru. KB vi (1) 546 & 275 note: womb, uterus (?) {Mutterleib, Gebärmutter} *foetus?* IV^{2} 6 *a* 13, 14 ina ša-sur ni-ši çira (a serpent) u-kan-ni-nu (Br 2857); 18* *no* 6, 14 a-ta-nu a-lit-tu a-ta-nu mu-rap-pi-iš-tu ša-as-su-ru ša-as-sur-ši-na ul uš-te-šir, subj. the demon, evil spirit; ið ŠA(= LIB)-TUR (see šaturru) Br 8010, 10934. KB vi (1) 286—7, 9: [7] u 7 ša-su-ra-ti: 7 u-ba-na-a zikarê; 11, š]a-su-ru ba-na-at ši-im-tu; 292—3 (ZA xii 329 *foll*) i 16 (10) ša-sur-šu-un (ilat) Be-lit i-li u-ban-ni. Bu 91—5—9, 263 *O* 6—8 e-ri-iš-tu (il) Ma-mi at-ti-i-ma ša(?)-as-su-ru, ZA xiv, 281; KB vi (1) 275. V 29 *g-h* 68 (H 38, 98) AB-NAM (or SIM, which = abšânu; G § 55; ZA i 409) = ša-sur-rum (Br 3881), in one group with um-mu (65), ba-an-tum (66), a-ga-rin-nu (67), all words indicating mother; or the like. Also see Winckler, *Forsch*, ii 18 & *rm* 1, & KAT^{3} 403 & *rm* 4; Lay 38, 3 (Meissner & Rost, 2); Rm 284 *R* 8.

šasiš (?) Sarg *Cyl* 32 (Lyon, *Sargon* & KB ii 44, 45) ša-si-iš, shaking (?). I R reads da-si-iš šadi-e, while AV 6690 has ša si-mil-lat.

šisîtu. call, cry {Ruf, Geschrei} § 65, 9. √ šasû. Xammurabi-*code* viii 44, 45 a-na ši-si-it na-gi-ri-im, at the call of the commandant (Harper); ZA xviii 32 zum Befehle des Palastvogtes. Asb vi 102 ši-si-it a-la-la tâb(t?)a (written DUG-GA), a joyful shouting. IV^{2} 48 *a* 25 il-ki ši-si-it (amêl) na-gi-ri elišunu u-kan-nu; IV^{2} 30, 1 *R* 5, 6 ilâni ša erçi-tim ana ši-si-ti-ka uš-qa-ma-am-mu (Br 3225; H 125, 16) ‖ i-te-en-šu ‖ pa-ax-ru-ka; AJSL xix 210; KB vi (1) 355, schweigen still bei deinem Ruf. V 28 *no* 1, 1—2 (supplemented by 76, 4—13, M) ši-si-tum = ta-nu[-qa-tum]. 83—1—18, 1330 *O* i 18 $^{(ti-il)}$ ŠU-KAT-ŠU-KAT = ši-si-tum, followed by ta-nu-qa-tum, ZA xv 44. V 40 *g-h* 9 $^{(ma-ag-bi)}$ Ỵ = ši-s[i-tum], between ri[-ig-mu] & ta-nu[-qa-tum]. BEZOLD, *Diplomacy*, xxv gossip, rumor *ad* (Lo) 78, 20 ši-si-tum eli-ia, which KB v 379 translates: an insurrection against me.

šassāitu *adj f* (BA i 477) √šasū. IV^2 21* *no* 2 *R* 10, 11 ša-as-sa-i-tum (= KA-DE-DE, Br 702) $^{(ilat)}$ Bēlit Nippur. § 65, 9 speech {Rede}.

šappu. jug, pot, bowl, barrel {Krug, Fass} or the like. T^C 112 sappu; *f* šappatu, 1. see below. AV 7697. id ŠA(P)B (Cyr 319). S^b 218; Br 5671. Nabd 258, 12 išteen šap-pu ša dan-nu-tu; 600, 6 pu-ut šap-pu mur-çi, in case of a damaged barrel; 259, 1 šap-pi (BA i 538; 635—6). ZIMMERN, *Rituall.*, 75—78, 42 ^{karpat} ša]p-pu(pi) mē tumallī-ma; 43 & 44 (šap-pi), 45 (^{karpat} šap-pi ša mē). JOHNS, *Deeds & Documents*, 930 ii 11; 942, 5 (^{karpat} ŠAB); ŠAB alone 977 ii 6; ŠAB-MES 946 *R* 7. See also šabbu, 2.

šapū 1. be dense, thick, heavy {dicht, dick, schwer sein} ספע. KB vi (1) 355. K 196 *O* ii 10 when the gates of a house ša-pu-um, are heavy, that house will be destroyed (PINCHES, *Texts*, 11—13). NE 61, 11 ša-pat ek-li-tum-ma ul [i-ba-aš-ši nūru]; 62, 48; 63, 24 + 27 + 30 + 33 + 36 (KB vi (1) 206 *foll*). III 64 *a* 11 SER = ša-pu-u ša IM-DIR (= erpiti), be dense, said of the clouds; *l* 10 šamē ša-pu-u, JENSEN, 418 *rm* 2.

Derr. šapūtu &:

šapū *2.* — *a*) dense {dicht}. IV^2 5 *a* 33, 34 er-pi-tum ša-pi-tum (BU(= SIR)-RA, Br 7541), which causes darkness on heaven's expanse. — *b*) heavy {schwer}? of a garment. V 14 *c-d* 39 KU-BAR-LU-ŠA(= LIB)-BA-TUK = ša-pi-tum (*i. e.* ku-si-tum, 37); Br 1946; 7994 same id = xa-bi-i-tum; AV 8012.

šapū *3.* K 497 *R* 9/10 liš-pu-ra ša-pi-e ša $^{(māt)}$ Za-li-pa-a-a (Hr^L 165) = šabū, 2??

šupū 1. ac & pm Š √apū (יפע, 78). AV 8536; JENSEN, 328. KB vi (1) 100, 11 ana šu-pi-i, to magnify {zu verherrlichen}. — II 19 *b* 19, 20 ša ki-ma ū-me nu-ri šu-pu-u (= UD-DU, Br 7890), which like unto day streams forth light. IV^2 12 *O* 29, 30 ki-ma ū-mi šu-pat (= PA-UD-DU, Br 5638), said of the narkabtu; 2 vi 5, 6 ša ina zu-mur la šu-pu-u (= UD-DU). II 55 *d* 11 šu-pat, see qirbētu, 2. Sm 954 *R* 2 (Ištar) ša ina šu-pu-uk šamē nap-xat (*var* xa-tum) ina da-ad-mi zi-kir-ša šu-pu-u, Br 6518; H [illegible], 32 na-an (*var* -')-dur-šu ina šamē šu-pu-u (= BAR-TIG-QAR). TP vii 93 ša ki-ma kakkab šamē šu-pu-u. K 3182 ii 8 šu-pu-u zik-ru-ka, excellent is thy name (= ZA iv 9, 6). K 4874 see Br 2342. Sp III 586 + Rm III 1, 10 (end) çi-ru-ut-ka šu-u-pi, is glorious.

šupū *2.* *adj f* šupūtu. brilliant, shining, magnificent, strong {glänzend, leuchtend, herrlich, stark} D^{Pr} 84 *fol.* √יפע. V 65 *a* 6 lu-li-mu šu-pu-u. NE 1 *col* ii 26 (NE 8, 26) gaš-ru šu-pu-u mu-du-u (KB vi, 1, 118); ZIMMERN, *Rituall.*, *no* 53, 6; K 5268 *O* 1/2, 3/4 Nergal gaš-ru šu-pu-u (= UD-DU-A); IV^2 21* *no* 1 C *R* iii 1 (of Marduk) ga-aš-ru šu-pu-u. Rm III 105, 3 Nabū?] bēl gaš-ri, (4) . . . git-mal-li šu-pu-u (WINCKLER, *Forsch*, i 254 *foll*). Perhaps *Etana*-legend (Rm 2, 454 *etc.*) 15 eb-ri šu-pa-a, but see KB vi (1) 112, 113. I 67 *b* 31/32 (Marduk) bēlu rabū bēl ilāni šu-pu-u nu-ur ilāni; ZA v 59, 43; Samš i 8 (ana Ninib) šu-pi-i; JENSEN, 468 *rm* 1; K 128, 4. IV^2 9 *a* 13, 14 Nannar be-lum a-gi-e šu-pu-u (Br 1217); K^M 1, 1 Nannaru šu-pu-u (GGA '98, 825); 16 ^{il} Sin šu-pu-u. IV^2 25 *b* 50, 51 az-ka-ru el-liš šu-pu; id same as in S^b 273; H 13, 151 da-al-la | BAR-TIG-QAR | šu-p(b)u-u (or: [illegible]?) Br 1883; S^c 1 *b* 27; same id H 36, 874 = i-di-ik-lat: Tigris. ZIMMERN, *Rituall.*, 26 iii 53 $^{(il)}$ Sin as(z)karu šu-pu-u. — K 3464 *O* 22 ša-ku-tum šu-pu-tum qa-rit-tum Ištar (CRAIG, *Relig. Texts*, *p* 36; PSBA xxiii 115 *foll*). V 41 *a-b* 15 (+ 31 *no* 3, 15) šu-pu-u ‖ ra-bu-u (LOTZ, *Tigl. Pil.*, 89; ZK i 190 *ad* Rm 618, 5; ZA i 32; iii 302, 16). V 21 *g-h* 31 . . . DUL-DU (Br 9600) = šu-pu-u, together with ag(q)çu. V 40 *c-d* 4 TE = šu-pu-u preceded by si-im-tum, Br 7708. V 21 *a-b* 18; 23 *e-h* 41 šu[-pu-u??] Br 7890. — The *pl* is very doubtful. PINCHES, *Texts*, 16 *R* 12 šu-pu-u-ti ma-xa-zi-šu. STRONG, PSBA xvii 137 *fol*: the vats of the city. √שפע, *affluxit*; Job xxii 11 & see šappu. V 65 *b* 6 me-di-lu šu-pu-tu (or: šu[-ut?]-bu-tu? see KB iii (2) 112 *rm* 12). *Adv* šu-pēš, see below.

šupû *3.* *n*? brightness, splendor or the like. K 7592 *etc.* ii 34 (end) ina šu-pi-šu, (MARTIN).

šupû *4.* see šubû, 1.

šupû *5.* see šubû, 2.

šuppû. 83, 1—18, 1330 i 22 ZUR $^{(su-ur)}$ = šu-up-pu-u (?) √סוה?

ši-pa *del* 235 (262) see šību, 1, NOTE 1.

šippu. in namçar šip-pi-ja, see šibbu, 3.

šēpu (= שׁוּף) AV 8291. *f* (§ 71). id NER, NĒR (GIR, Br 9192); *pl* (*dual*? ZA v 38 *rm* 2) NER^{pl}, NER$^{2 \, (or \, II)}$, NER$^{2 \, pl}$ = šēpē, šēpā; § 9, 261; H 29, 666 gi-ir NER | še-(e-)pu; BARTH, *Etym. Stud.*, 31 = Arb شَوًى, foot; ZDMG 27, 697; G § 14 compared Arb أُثْفِيَة. — *a*) foot {Fuss}. TP iv 16 i-na šēpi-ja, afoot. V 65 *b* 32 xar-ran šullum *etc.* li-ša-aš-ki-na ana še-pi-ja; *b* 45 lik-ni (*var* nu)-šu a-na še-(e-)pi-ja. II 16 *b-c* 31 la(-)a(-)ni-xa še-pa-a-a, my feet (§§ 3; 41; 67, 4; 74, 2) BA ii 285—6; Z^B 96. V 47 *a* 59. IV^2 27 *no* 5 *b* 32 še-e-pu (= NER) ana erçi-tim ul .... ZA iv 230, 11 še-pu-uk-ka. IV^2 50 *b* 37 NER (= šēpā)-ki al-la-ka-a-ti. V 50 *a* 16 ša er-ba še-pa-a-šu = quadrupeds, Br 4840; & *cf* V 42 *a-b* 50. H 60 iv 10 see kurçu (440 *col* 2). Neb ii 20 far-off lands *etc.* a-šar .... še-e-pi la i-ba-aš-šu-u, where one could not get a foothold. H 121 (K 5332) *O* 4, 5 še-pu-šu ki-ma ṭi-ṭi e-ma (Z^B 69), his foot made like unto the dust. IV^2 8 *col* 3, 39 this man .... še-pi-šu u-rak-kis (see rakasu). III 43 iv (*c*) 6 likabbisā (366 *col* 1) še-pa-šu; I 70 *d* 15 NER$^{2 \, pl}$-šu. Asb ix 8 xar-ra-an $^{(māt \, var \, al)}$ Di-maš-qa u-ša-aš-ki-na še-pu-uš-šu-nu. — kanašu, in connection with šēpu: ana NER^2-ja, NER^{pl}-ja, še-pu-u-a, še-pu-'-u-a (§ 80*e*), ana še-pi-šu, see *pp* 409—411; 81—6—7, 209, 15 ša .... ina gi-mir ma-li-ku u-šak-ni-šu še-pu-uš-šu, BA iii 260, 261. — našaqu šēpē(ā), *etc.* kiss one's feet, see našaqu (740, 741); SCHEIL, *Nabd*, v 5 u-na-aš-ši-qu še-pa-a-a. — çabatu NER^{pl}, NER^{II}, NER$^{II \, pl}$, embrace one's feet, an indication of submission, see çabatu (860, 861). — šēpu parasu, *e. g.* ZIMMERN, *Rituali.*, 75—82 i 8 (100, 10 & *rm* 14) kī šēpu parsa-at, sobald der Schritt gehemmt ist; also *ibid p* 196 *rm a*; IV^2 55 *no* 2 *a* 14; Rm 99, 5 šēpu par-sat; K 8219, 3; & see parasu (832, 834). — raxaçu ša šēpi, *cf* raxaçu, 2. H 90—1, 69 NER-NE-NE NER-A-NI-TA = še-pi-šu-nu ana še-pi-šu (a-a iš-kunu) said of the evil powers; see also 81—7—1, 98 ii 5, 6, *Jour. Trans. Vict. Inst.*, xxvi 154. K 257 (H 126 *foll*) *O* 63, 64 see šananu & Br 10396. — šēpē(ā) in connection with qātē(ā) see qātu, hand. Rm 67, 6—7 (Hr^L 348) a-xi-ja še-pi-ja, my arms, my feet. K 1250 *R* 6 (Hr^L 460); IV^2 31 *O* 71, 72; III 65 *b* 44—46, MARTIN, *Rec. Trav.*, xxiv 230. — zuq šēpē see zu-ku, 289 *col* 1 & add: HAUPT, *Jour. Bib. Lit.*, xix 77 = infantry (literally: rush of feet); also BA iv 587. — $^{(is)}$ šupal šēpi, footstool, see šupalu. Perh. also without šupal; Ner 28, 9: 2 ši-pi ša ṭiṭi. — *c. st.* in P. N. še-ip Sin, MEISSNER, 46, 26 (= KB iv 26, 26); 32, 30; Xammurabi-*letter* 16, 5; BA ii 626 *rm* ***.

Name of a bird: še-ip (= NER) a-rik II 37 *a-c* 46 (long-foot? stork?) = çir-ku, 1 (893 *col* 2), Br 9219. — Neb iii 30 see šību, 3 & FLEMMING, *Neb*, 40. — *b*) foot or base of a mountain, a height *etc.* {Fuss eines Berges, einer Anhöhe, *etc.*}. Šn iii 71; iv 7 i-na NER^2 šadē; TP iii 59 (63); Šalm, *Ob* 38 the city *A* ša šēpā am-ma[-te] ša $^{(nār)}$ Purattu, KB i 132, 133. Anp iii 49, 50 I founded 2 cities on the Euphrates, one ina šēp an-na-te(ti) ša Puratti ... the other ina šēp am-ma-te(ti) ša Puratti, *i. e.* at the foot of the hills on the one side of the river's bank *etc.* Also iii 48, & *cf l* 1. TP ii 4 the cities ša šēp $^{(pl)}$ am-ma(-a)-te ša Diqlat. II 65 *O* i 30 the city Rapiqi ša šēp II am-ma[-ma]-te ša (nâr) Diqlat. — S^c 3, 20 [ŠI] = še-e-pu, Br 9283. — A f šēpîtu, see below.

NOTE. — HAUPT, *Johns Hopkins Circ*, 106 *pp* 107,8 suggests a denominative šêpu, crush, tread down, in IV² 19 *no* 3 *b* 46 nak-ru dan-nu ki-ma qa-ni-e i-di u-šip-pa-ni (× Z^D 57 udiššanni); also IV² 15 i 67 (*add*) nišē mâti u-šep-pu, they crushed the people of the land. See, however, ša(e)bû, 1 ℑ.

šapaxu = sapaxu (777); AV 7995. — Q IV² 31 *O* (*a*) 11 over door & bolt ša-pu-up ep-ru, dust has settled. SCHEIL, Notes LX (Constant. *no* 583) *R* 15 (+21) ta-ša-pa-ax (*Rec. Trav.* xxiii). — ℑ Xamm.-*code* xlii 63 li-ša-ab-bi-xa-aš-šum. DT 71 *R* 6 me-iq-šu šu-up-pu-ux, WINCKLER, *Forsch*, i 541 (= ip). — 𝔑 = *pass* of Q. IV² 39 *b* (*R*) 36 na-aš (𒋗; *var* in dupl. text ⟩—)-pu-ux mâti-šu xa-la-aq nišišu u kudûrišu; KB vi (1) 394. Xamm.-*code* xlii 73, 74 xa-la-aq ali-šu na-aš-pu-ux ni-ši-šu. — K 5157, 26 (H 181 XII) u-'š'ap-pi-ix; Asb vi 79; ZIMMERN, *Ritualt.*, *p* 101 *rm* δ.

šapxu = sapxu (777 *col* 2). Xamm.-*Louvre* ii 3 ni-ši-šu-nu ša-ap-xa-tim, Br 8508; KB iii (1) 122, 123.

šapaxûtu. K 6082 iii 13 ina ša-pa-xu-ti-ka ina libbi uznâka u-lax-xi-iš.

šapaṭu, **šipṭu** see šabaṭu, šibṭu.

šapaku, pr išpuk, AV 7996, 8648. pour out (a libation, *etc.*); heap up, store; construct {ausgiessen (ein Trankopfer, *etc.*); aufschütten, aufhäufen; errichten} ‖ tabaku. JENSEN, 41; ZA iv 311 *rm* 1; G § 15 = سفك; שפך; BA i 2. IV² 19 *b* 39, 40 (o Ištar) ina nap-xar ma-ta-ti-ki i-ša-tu id-di-ma tum-ri (= ŠE-MUR) iš-pu-uk (= BA-DUB. Br 3931), and like *t* he (the enemy) has poured (it) out. NE VI 59 (the shepherd) ša ka-a-a-nam-ma tu-um-ri iš-pu-kak-ki, KB vi (1) 171, der dir beständig Salz (?) hinschüttete; KB vi (1) 40, 18 e-pi-ri ib-ni-ma it-ti a-mi iš-pu-uk, baute Erde und schüttete sie neben dem Baldachin hin. TP vii 80 that place .... ina libnâti ki-ma ka-nu-ni aš-pu-uk (I overlaid). I 44, 72 erâ ki-rib-šu aš-pu-uk into the mould made of clay (see zi'pu, 272). — Often with šipik. I 28 *b* 13, 14 ši-pi-ik IŠ-MEŠ (= epirē) a-na li-me-ti-šu a-na e-li-nu aš-pu-uk. Sargon *Nimr* 16 eli (aban) pi-i-li dan-ni tem-mi-in-šu ki-ma ši-pik šadi-i zaq-ri aš-pu-uk. II 67, 71: XX great cubits šu-pul mê ez-zu-ti (aban) pi-lu-u dan-nu kîma ši-pik šadi-i aš-pu-uk. *pc* Rm 76 *R* 11, 12 ina mu-ti šim-ti la mu-ut šarru be-ili liš-pu-ka ki-li-a (Hr^L 358) BA iv 508 *foll*; PSBA xxiii 355 (reading KI-LI = rêšêti-a). — *ip* H 121 (K 5332) *O* 5, 6 kiš-šat da-ad-me-šu ti-la-niš šu-pu-uk, heap together all his dwellings like ruins, PRINCE, AJSL xix 214; Br 3408. — *pm* KB iii (2) 88, 43 ba-aç-ça ši-pi-ik e-pi-ru e-li maxâzi u bîti šu-a-tim ša-ap-ku ‖ I 69 *a* 53 ka-at-mu. KB vi (1) 140/141 on Nimr. Ep. II *col* iv *a* 8 (end) š(s)ap(b)-ku, ist hingegossen. — *ac* ša-pak šeim shall be ina NI-TE^{pl}, III 60, 62 + 79; ša-pa-ak šeim ina NI-TE^{pl}, 70; MEISSNER, 112: šapaku ša šeim = pay one's debt with grain. — *ag* III 58 *no* 7 *b* 43, 44 šamu-u DUB-ik, with gloss ša-mu-u ša-pi-ik (Br 3931; § 9, 137) zu-un-nu i-za-nun; 45 ina IM-DIR (= urpiti) ša-pi-ik-ti (THOMPSON, *no* 189: in rainclouds). — III 64 *a* 11 perhaps SER ša-pa-ku (?); 10 šamê ša-pi-ik, followed by šamê ša-pu-u. II 38 *a-b* 21 A-SI-GA = i-ku iš-pu-uk, preceded by a-tab-bu ix-ri, Br 1443. II 32 *a-b* 80 ša-pa-ki ša i-ki; 81, *š* ša epri, Br 3408, 3932. P. N. Šâpik-zêri, BA i 535 *no* 56. Ša-pi-ku, AV 8009. K^M 9, 37 e]-pi-rat en-še ša-pi-kat [zêru]. II 65 *b* 26 Marduk-ša-pi-ik-zêri (KB i 198 & AV 5163: -kul-lat); also V 68 *a* 15; 67 *a* 50; 68 *b* 44. — S^b 143 la-al | LAL | ša-pa-ku, H 32, 742; Br 10112; II 39 *f* 53 LAL = ša-pa-ku, together with ma-lu-u (*e*). H 17, 272; S^c 35 du-ub | DUB | ša-pa-ku, followed by ta-ba-ku, sa-ra-qu, Br 3931; DE = ša-pa-ku ša A (= mê) Br 6732. H 48, 45 (49, 56) IN-DUB (IN-SI) = iš-pu-uk; 49, 60 IN-SI-GI-EŠ = iš-pu-ku; 66 IN-NA-AN-SI = iš-pu-uk-šu; 68 IN-NA-AN-SI-GI-EŠ = iš-pu-ku-šu. H 55, 53—4 SE-GI-NIN & NE-IN-SE-GI = iš-pu-uk, Br 4425.

Q^t = Q Sn *Kui* 4, 24 e-ra-a ki-rib-šu aš-tap-pa-ka (see above). Neb vi 49, 50 ši-bi-ik e-pi-re aš-ta-ap-pa-ak-šu-nu-tim-ma, Flemming, *Neb*, 40; AV 8150; with an earthwall (a dam) I closed them (the waters) in. I 65 *b* 10, 11; 66 *c* 26 (ur[or ka?]-ri-e še-im .... aš-ta-pa-ak-šu); Pognon, *Wadi-Brissa*, Curs. Inscr. vi 25, 26 ši-pi-ik e-pi-ri dan-nu-tim aš-ta-ap-pa-ak-ma. ZA iii 360 *a* 26 lu aš-tap-pa-ak (KB iii, 1, 122—3); iv 110, 99 (*cf* 430 *col* 2, below). KB iii (2) 4 *col* 2, 21 see kirû, 1 (433); *l* 53 see šaplânu. H 55, 55 iš-ta-pa-ak (Br 4425). TP i 82 idât maxâzâni-šunu ki-ma ka-ri-e (see *pp* 430—1) lu-še-pi-ik (1 *sg*). H 48/9, 49 IN-DUB-DUB = u-ša-ap-pi-ik, 62 IN-SI-GI = u-šap-pa-ak, 64 IN-SI-GI-NE = u-šap-pa-ku.

ℑ^1 see karû, 3 (430 *col* 2, below); § 131; Br 3931 (DUB-DUB).

𝔑 be poured out. be stored {hingeschüttet, aufgespeichert werden}. I 51 *no* 2 *a* 15 ki-ir-bu-uš-šu ba-aç-ça iš-ša-ap-ku (> inšapku); *no* 1 *b* 4 (Neb *Bors*) li-bi-it ku-um-mi-ša iš-ša-pi-ik ti-la-ni-iš, KB iii, 2, 54—55: had fallen into heaps of ruins. I 69 *a* 47 iš-šap-ku-ma; KB iii 88, 36—7 ši-pi-ik e-pi-ru .... iš-ša-ap-ku-ma. Scheil, *Nabd*, v 3, 4 bi(M^S 97 kul)]-lat-zu-nu ana šêpê-ja iš-šap-ku-nim-ma (were heaped up); Xamm.-*letters* 28, 10 še-um a-šar iš-te[-en i]š-ša-bi-ik, BA iv 474 das Getreide wurde an einen Haufen aufgeschüttet. Xamm.-*code* xx 14 iš-ša-ap-ku, was stored.

𝔑^1 = 𝔑 IV^2 13 *b* 27/28 ina še-ip ni-ši-ka e ta-at-taš-pak (= BA-AN-SE-SE), at the foot of thy people be not poured out (addressed to the šadânu) >< Prince, AJSL xix 214.

NOTE. — H 129 (K 257) *R* 12 iššâtum napiz-tum (see 706 *cols* 1.2) šit-pu-kat ana-ku; Prince, JAOS xxiv 112; 125 reads šit-bu-tum (𝔔^1 √tebû): a glowing fire flaming forth I am.

Derr. našpaku, 1 & 2; našpakûtu, 1 & 2 (739, 740) & these 5 (6?):

šipku, *c. st.* šipik. pouring out, heaping up {Ausschüttung, Aufschüttung}; especially šipik epirê, sandheap {Erdaufwurf}; also a dam, made of earth; see šapaku; Sarg *Ann* 266. II 67, 16 see šubû, 1. K 2852 + K 9662 i 37 a-rum-mu ina ši-pik ip-ri-e u abnê, Winckler, *Forsch* ii, 34, 35. II 22 *no* 2, *add* (AV 8150); K 4335 i 7 .... SAL = ši-ip-ku, Br 11301; followed by tu-ra-am-an-ni. — founding, casting {Guss}. T. A. (Ber) 23, 25—6 your father also had the image cast (= a-na ši-ip-ki ut-te-e-ir-šu-nu); u ki-i ana ši-ip-ki du-ur-ru (= turru, *pm* ZA v 16, 17). — capacity. NE vi 189 še-lâšâ mana (ta)-a-an (aban) uq(k, g)ni ši-pi-ik (*var* -pik)-ši-na, KB vi (1) 177 (457; 577), their capacity; Z^B 105; ZK ii 315; also see NE 35, 22. — Sp II 265 *a* viii 5 ki-i ki-rib šamê šip-ki ilâni .... — In a medical text, Scheil, Notes LX (Constant. *no* 583) 12 ina SU (= zumri) ši-ip-ki te-tir-ri, *Rec. Trav.* xxiii.

šipiktu, *c. st.* šipkat. KB iv 48 *no* IV 1/2: 5 1/3 šiqlê 15 ŠE kaspi a-na ši-ip-ka-at e-bu-ri-im; Meissner, 106, 112. Zimmern, *Rituall.*, 100, 17 šip-kat bûli. hingeschüttet für das Getier.

šipkîtum. K 4606, 5 šip-ki-tum, & 4, šip-ku. So perhaps instead of me-ki-tum *etc.* (see 535 *col* 2, below). But šipkû, AV 8151; Br 11301 see mekû.

šapku. KB iv 102—3, 13 tim-me-en-šu kîma ša-pik šadi-e u-šar-šid, its foundation I had constructed like a mound {gleich einem Bergwall}.

šapku *adj c. st.* šapik, *f* šapiktu see above, šapaku, 𝔔 (III 58, 44—45).

šupku, *c. st.* šupuk. AV 8493. — *a*) heaping up {Aufschüttung}. ZA iii 316 (Sn *Rass*) 80 u-dan-ni-na šu-pu-uk-ša, I strengthened its (the terrace's) earthwork; also see tem(m)ênu. — *b*) firmament {Firmament, Himmelsveste}. Jensen, 37 *foll*; JA Jan-Febr. '97, 91. NE 60, 4—5 e-lu-šu-nu šu-pu-uk šamê-e .... ‖ šap-liš a-ra-li-e i-rat-su-nu kaš-da-at, KB vi (1) 204—5, 467—8, 576—8. IV^2 5 *a* 3, 4 merciless šêdê who ina šu-puk šame-e ib-ba-nu-u they are (the seven evil spirits); *a* 59—31; 70—72; id UL-KAN-A, Br 9150; H 40, 243. S 954 (D 136) *R* 2 Ištar ša ina šu-pu-uk šamê nap-xat. II 48 *c-d* 53 GER = šu-puk šamê (Br 310; >< AV 8493); 54 GER-KAN-A = š bu-ru-me (Br 317), in one group with elat šamê & qirib šamê. Winckler: supuk šamê. der Tierkreis; also Jeremias, *Das Alte Testament*, *etc.*, '04. 8—9; 52; 78 (Heb רקיע).

šapalu. *pr* išpil (?), *ps* išappil, *pm* ša-pil. lower one's self, be lowered; then, be low {sich senken, gesenkt sein oder werden; niedrig, unten sein} Br 10113; § 25. Perhaps I 69 *b* 44 (ix-ṭu-uṭ-ma, *cf* 311 *col* 1: xaṭaṭu) iš-pil-ma te-me-en-na Ê-ul-bar la ik-šu-ud; Camb 217, 9—10 (*cf* babbanû, 145 *col* 2) it-ti a-xa-meš i-šaq-qu(-?) u i-šap-pi-lu, together they will win or lose; literally: they will be high or low. 83—1—18, 184, 7 Sin ina tamarti-šu ša-pi-il, Thompson, *Reports*, ii *no* 77; perhaps also K 480, 19 (Hr^L vol. vii); Sp II 265 *a* xxii 8. V 36 *d-f* 26 (bu-ru) ⟨ = ša-pa-lum (Br 8749); II 39 *f* 53 ša-pa-la, Br 10113.

𝔔t Neb v 62 ša .... iš-ta-ap-pi-la ni-ri-ba-ši-in, their (*i. e.* Imgur-Bêl & Nimitti-Bêl's) entrance-gate was too low (owing to the filling in of the street of Babylon); see also BA i 393 (where, however, transliteration is wrong) × Flemming, *Neb*, 30. Neb vii 56 iš-ta-ap-pi-la bâbâni-ša (KB iii, 2, 20/1; 24/5). KB iii (2) 78, 14 iš-ta-ab-bi-lu-ma. K 8204 iii/iv 12 (6) al-ta-pil ina çûbê, PSBA xvii 138—9; Bezold, *Catalogue*, 905. See na'âlu, 3 (629 *cols* 1/2).

𝔓 — *a*) deepen, lower, make deep, dig down {tief machen, in die Tiefe gehen}. Sarg *Khors* 128: 21 cubits u-šap-pil (he lowered, sank) the moat; *Ann* 423. V 63 *a* 30: 18 cubits of earth (qaq-qar) u-ša-ap-pil (1 *sg*). Anp ii 132 a-di eli mê u-ša-pil, down to the underground water I dug (ZK ii 340); iii 136 (lu-); *Stand* 17 lu-u u-ša-pi(e)l; TP III *Ann* 116. — *b*) debase, humble, humiliate {erniedrigen}. V 21 *a-b* 26 KI-TA-MU = šup-pil-an-ni, bow me down, Br 9672; AJSL xix 205; *cf* qadadu, 𝔓. Sp II 265 *a* xxiii 4 u-šap-pal (*var* -pa-lu) dun-na-ma-a. K 3182 ii 52 (end) u-]šap-pal, (Šamaš) shall humiliate (him). — In astronomical texts: K 809 *R* 2 Sin ina tamartišu u-šap-pil-ma innamir. — V 36 *d f* 27 (bu-ru) ⟨ = šup-pu-lum, Br 8752. V 45 vi 33 tu-ša-ap-pal.

𝔓t In astron. texts: K 809 *O* 6 Sin ina tamartišu uš-tap-pil-ma innamir; 82—5—22, 58 *R* 1 (Thompson, *Reports*, ii 66; 60).

Š šušpulu see šaqû, 1 Š.

ℨ Sp II 265 *a* xxv 6 iš-ša-pil at-mu-u-a ‖ ri-ig-mu ul iš-ša-bu (√šebû, 2).

Derr. mušpalu (60? *col* 1) & the following 12:

šaplu *1.* *n. c. st.* šapal. ideogr. KI-TA, the lower part, bottom {der untere Teil, Boden}. *Etana*-legend iii *a* (KB vi, 1, 110) 11 ina šap-la (iç) kussî, below the throne. NE I iv 30 (H^{NE} 12) it-ta-šab ina ša-pal (sal) xa-rim-ti (KB vi (1) 126—7); VI 16 lik-me-šu ina šap-li-ka. *del* 150 (159) i-na (*var* ina) šap-li-šu-nu (underneath them) at-ta-bak qan(û) (iç) erinu u âsu (KB vi, 1, 240—1; 503). Nabd *Ann* iii 10. 11 ilâni ša (mât) Akkadê ša MUX(= eli)-im u KI-TA(= šapli)-im. II 51 *no* 1 *R* 7 ana šap-lu-ša lit-bal, ZK ii 322. K 616 *R* 2 ina šap-la(-)u-a (Hr^L 127). K^M 6, 46 ša-ap-la ... T. A. (Ber) 156, 21 iš-tu ša-pal [tap-pa-ti-ši]; 23 iš-tu ša-pal šêpi šarri bêlija (+ 28); (Lo) 19, 35—36 ri-šu-šu-nu i-na šap-li-šu-nu, and their sheiks are subject to them; also (Lo) 17, 48 + 50. — Used as a *prep.* šaplu & šapal, under, below, at the foot (feet) of {unter, unterhalb, zu Füssen von} § 81 *b*. Creat.-*frg* III 69 (Gaga ...) uš-ken-ma iš-šiq qaq-qa-ra ša-pal-šu-un, KB vi (1) 16—17. Asurb ii 119 the Gimirreans ša ša-pal-šu ik-bu-su. D 99 *R* 35 = Creat.-*frg* IV 118 see kabasu (365 *col* 2, below) and, again, KB vi (1) 28—9. Nabd 435, 6 šap-lu nâri × e-li nâri. See also kamasu (396, 397). A ‖ is:

šapâlu *2.* Zimmern, *Ritualt.*, *no* 60 *O* 19 ina ša-pa-lu-uš-šu, darunter.

šaplu *2.* *adj* šapiltu, AV 8010. *pl* šap-lûti, *f* šaplâti. — *a*) low {niedrig}. II 23 *a-b* 7, 8 ku-us-su-u ša-pil-tum = šu-šub-tum; see 414 *col* 1, & napal-suxtum, 708 *col* 1. III 4 *no* 7, 16 ša-di-i šap-lu-ti (× e-lu-ti), KB iii (1) 102. AV* 5 *col* 2 a-çi-tum ša-pil-tum. II 62 (K 64) *no* 3 *a-b* 65 ŠA (= LIB)-BIT-KU-MAL (= GA)-A-AN = šap-lu a-gi-ir, AV 8017; Br 7992, 8047. Low, in moral sense, perhaps II 62 *no* 3 *a-b* 70, 71 AMÊL-KA (+ inserted small ku)-DA-AN-KA-KA (Br 862); AMÊL-KA-ŠA (= LIB)-BU-1 = ša šap-la-ti i-ta-mu-u; 72—74 AMÊL-ŠE-LAL-

KI-TA; AMÊL-ŠE-KI-TA, AMÊL-ŠE-IM-GUB-BA (Br 7491, 9675; 7489, 9075; 7485) = ša ša-pil-ti. — *b*) lower, lower side, *etc.* {untere(r), untere Seite}. ✕ elītu, elūtu. II 30 *c-d* 3 AN-TA-BAL-RI = e-li-tum u ša-pil-tum (Br 281, 464, 9638). II 62 *no* 3 *a-b* 63, 64 KI-AN-BAL = šapiltum u e-li-tum (Br 281, 9654); TIK-KI-TIK-AN-TA-AN-AG-A = e-li-tu ša-pil-tu i-na-aṭ-ṭu (Br 3299, 9638), see *p* 667 *col* 1, below; & *cf* K 49 ii 19, 20 = II 62 *no* 1 *c-d* ša e-li-t[u] šap-li-tu i-na[-aṭ-ṭu] Br 3299. II 62 *a-b* 75, 76 IB(= TUM)-KID-ŠE = ša šapilti ša še-im (Br 4966); KI-TA-ŠI = ša šapilti ša i-nim (✕ e-lit i-nim, II 30 *c-d* 8—10), Br 9677. Sometimes also the inner side, inside, as compared to outside. II 62 *no* 3 *a-b* 66—68 KU-ŠA(= LIB)-GA = ša-pil-tu (Br 8045); KU-BAR-SI-ŠA(= LIB)-GA; KU-BUR-SUN-ŠA-GA = bar-si-ig šapiltu, Br 7992; 6952; ZA i 194 & parsigu (835, 836). AV 8010 reads II 30 *b-c* 78 ša-pi-il-ti, Br 459, 8961. See piriktu, 832 *col* 1. — *c*) deep; then, šapiltu = depth {tief; dann šapiltu = Tiefe}. II 38 *e-f* 4, 6 mu-š]e-lu-u (*l* 8 see 606 *col* 2 *c*) ša-pil-ti; da-lu-u (Br 265, 293, 9675; & see *l* 5) ša-pil-ti; *cf* *p* 247 *col* 2. — II 62 *a-b* 59—62 TAG-RU-TIK (= šapiltu?) [....]; TAG-AN-NA-GIŠ-TE-DA = *š* ša abni; BAR-TIK-GUB-BA & BAR-TIK-GAR-RA = *š* ša ba-ša-mi (*cf* e-lit ba-ša-mi, II 30 *c-d* 2). *adv.* to šaplu, 2 is:

šapliš. below {drunten} ✕ eliš (see 50 *col* 1). AV 8015. ša-ap-li-iš, POGNON, *Wadi-Brissa*, 100. IV² 6 *b* 45 šap-liš (Br 9674). BANKS. *Diss*, 12, 77 a-mat-su šap-liš ina a-la-ki-ša ✕ 75 e-liš ina ni-qil-pi-ša; also *ibid* 1, 18 & 15. Creat.-*frg* I *a* 1, 2 e-liš ✕ šap-liš; KB vi, 1, 276 *col* 2, 29—30; IV² 1 *col* i 9—11, 14—15 e-liš u šap-liš (Br 9674); K 3182 i, 2 + 4 + 26; IV² 21* 2 *O* 8—9, 10—11 e-liš, šap-liš; 12—13 e-liš u šap-liš (Br 9674); *dcl* 75 (79) end; NE 60, 4—5 see šupku. — Sm 954 *R* 3—4; IV² 3 *a* 3—4 (Br 11873). IV² 39 *O* 6 all the enemies e-liš u šap-liš; TP i 40; Anp i 27; iii 129 (Br 9784); Šamš i 42 the inhabitants of Assyria e-liš u šap-liš; *Khors* 138. V 20 *g-h* 42—43 AN-TA = e-liš; KI-TA = šap-liš; 44—45 AN-TA-KI-TA = e-liš u šap-liš, Br 9674. I 49 *b* 16, 17 e-liš a-na šap-liš uš-bal-kit. BA iii 271 = ganz Babylonien auf seine Seite bringen. T. A. (Ber) 26 ii 70; iii 8 ištu eliš u] iš-tu šap-liš(-li-iš).

šaplû, *adj f* šaplītu; *pl* šaplûti; šaplâti. AV 8016, 8017. § 65, 37. ideogr. KI-TA (✕ elû, ideogr. AN-TA) lower {unten befindlich, niedrig, untere(r)}. — II 50 *c-d* iv/v 2, 3 mâtu e[-li-tum], *u* šap[-li-tum], Br 9403; ZDMG 53, 657 *fol*; K 284 *R* 7 šar mâti e-li-tum u š[ap-li-tum]. WINCKLER, *Forsch.*, ii 12 *foll*: König des westlichen und östlichen Landes. Also T. A. (Ber) 92 *R* 35, 36. — Upper & Lower Zâb (see 272 *col* 2); Salm. *Bal*, IV 5, 6 (nâr) Za-ba AN-TA (*var* e-li-tu) u KI-TA (*var* šap-li-ta). See also šupalû. — Sarg *Ann* 72 xirītu šap-li-tu (✕ elītu) *etc.* — With tâmtu (sea, ocean) = the Persian Gulf (?). Sn i 13, 14 ul-tu A-AB-BA e-li-ni-ti ša ša-lam šam-ši (the Mediterranean Sea?) a-di tam-tim šap-li-ti ša çi-it šam-ši; D^Par 128. Neb ii 15, 16 iš-tu ti-a-am-ti e-li-ti a-di ti-a-am-ti ša-ap-li-ti. V 35, 29 iš-tu tam-tim e-li-tim a-di tam-tim šap-li-tim. TP III *Ann* 15 a-ax tam-tim šap-li-te, *etc.* Sn *Bav* 4 ul-tu tam-tim e-lit a-di tam-tim šap-lit; V 62, 2—3; SMITH, *Asurb*, 4, 18 ša tâmtim e-lit u šap-lit. — K 257 (H 130) *R* 68—70 ša u-ru e-lu-ti ✕ ša u-ru šap-lu[-ti]; JAOS xxiv 127. See also nukušû (677, 678), Br 2003, 9673; H 94/95, 56 see Br 9638; çirru (891 *col* 2); šiddu (ideogr. UŠ). — POGNON, *Wadi-Brissa*, 192 (below) ša-ap-lu-tim. II 62 *a-b* 69 TU-BAR = šap(b)-tu šap-li-tu, Br 11919; *cf* JENSEN, 386: Unterlippe ✕ J^I-N 5 judge of the terrestrial lands. II 62 *c-d* 19, 20 ša e-li-t[u] | šap-li-tu i-na .... — elâti u šaplâti, the things above and below; KAT³ 638 & *rm* 2. K 3182 i 31 šap-la-a-ti, 32 e-la-a-ti; 33 re-'-u šap-la-a-ti na-qi-du e-la-a-ti, the shepherd of what is below, leader of what is above (AJSL xvii 134, 135); iii 11 muš-tin-nu-u šap-la-a-ti. V 62, 28 Šamaš is called bêl e-lu-ti u šap-la-ti; also

IV² 56 *b* 12; 52 *b* 15 bêl AN-TA *pl* u KI-TA *pl*; see JENSEN, 1 *foll.* Merodach-Balad.-stone i 10, 11 bêl e-la-ti u šap-la-a-ti. — KNUDTZON, *p* 52 (& 322/23) written KI-TA & KI-tum. — ZA iv 234, 13 tak-zib (see 375 *col* 2) šap-la-a-ti-ka; K 2491 iii 20 še-'-i-tu šap-li-tu, CRAIG, *Relig. Texts*, i 78. — K 815, 12 (mât) Êlama (ki) e-la-a-ti (ilu) Sin >< Amurrû (ki) šap-la-a-ti (ilu) Sin, THOMPSON, *Reports*, no 268.

šaplitânu (?). 81—2—4, 80, 3 Šamšu elita-nu Sin šapli-ta-nu; also K 745, 1—2; THOMPSON, *Reports*, nos 176, 177.

šaplân(u) *adv* (>< elâniš) AV 8014; §§ 80 *b*; 81 *b*. — below, underneath {unten, unterhalb}. Sn *Rass* 81 (& *cf* 76) šap-la(-a)-nu ina uš-ši-ša (ZA iii 317); *Bell* 49 šap-la-a-nu qanâte e-la-niš aban šadî danni. KB iii (2) 4 *col* 2, 52—3 ša-ap-la-nim lib(p)itti lu aš-tap-pa-ak. — Asb iii 80, 81 e-liš (outwardly) ina šap-te-e-šu i-tam-ma-a ṭu-ub-ba-'a-ti šap-la-nu (inwardly) libba-šu ka-çir ni-ir-tu, KB ii 184, 185; § 152. *Cf* K 3364 *R* 25 šap-la-a-ti e ta-ta-me, DELITZSCH, *Weltschöpfungsepos*, 54 *fol.* K 3464 *R* 7 (end) ina šap-la-an xa-ri-e, CRAIG, *Relig. Texts*, 66; PSBA xxiii 115 *foll.* ZIMMERN, *Ritualtafeln*, no 54, 25 ina šap-la-an ir-ši; *ibid* 79—82 iii 7, 8 šap-la-nu >< e-la-nu. — Used as a *prep.* >< elân. I 44, 82 ina kisalli rabî šap-la-nu êkal (aban) pi-i-li. Neb iii 30 see šîbu, 3. Nabd *Ann* ii 16 šap-la-an (al) Ar-ba-'-il >< (nâr) Purattu el-la-nu Sip-par (13, end), KB iii (2) 130, 131. See also V 68 no 1, 3 (šap-la-nu). Camb 375, 15 ŠE-ZIR ša šap-la-a-ni nâri eš-šu; ZA i 47, 17; POGNON, *Wadi-Brissa*, 192 (below) ša-ap-la-an, en bas de.

šuplu, *c. st.* šupul, deep, depth {Tiefe, Vertiefung} also: the deep ocean. AV 8537, 8540. Often in the phrase: šu-pu-ul mê akšud, the deep waters I reached; Neb vii 60; I 67 *b* 24; POGNON, *Wadi-Brissa*, 69, 70; KB vi (1) 463, 464. Asb v 20 like a fish iç-baṭ šu-pul mê ru-qu-u-ti, he took to the deep waters. I 52 no 3 *b* 19 ina šu-pu-ul me-e bi-e-ru-tim, KB iii (2) 56, 57. II 29 *a-b* 68 (bu-ur) < = šup-lu, preceded by muš-palu (Br 8633, 8751; ZK ii 174 *rm* 2); H 28, 628. V 36 *d-f* 25 = šu-up-lum; V 20 *g-h* 49 < = šu-up-lum, Br 8751, together with šiddu, pûtum, mîlû, rupšu; K 4558, 4, see šiddu, 1. Also *cf* miqqu (577 *col* 1, above).

šupalu. AV 8528. — *a*) ‖ šaplu, 1. V 36 *d-f* 26 (bu-ru) < = šu-pa-lum (Br 8750). TP vii 81: 30 ti-ib-ki a-na šu-pa-li u-ṭe-bi (1 *sg*) LOTZ TP 117; RP² i 117 *rm* 3. Sargon, *Asdod*, 27; Neb 115, 21 ina šu-pa-lu. Camb 42, 9 šu-pal (iç) gi-šimmari, the ground around the date-palm (he shall water), KB iv 260—1. — As a *prep.* K 13 (Hr L 281) *O* 9 a-na šu-pal ša-a-ru, JOHNSTON, JAOS xix 82 southward (so also BA iv 527; or ša a-ru bei niederer Strömung?); see, however, ROST in OLZ ii no 5 *col* 157: vielmehr etwa: Unterlauf. K 145, 6 (Hr L 436) a-na šu-pa-lu. 83—1—18, 47 *R* 14 ša bît (amêl) rab-šâqê bêli-šu ki-i u-maš-ši-ru ina šu-pa-la (in the South? THOMPSON, *Reports*, no 90). Cyr 123, 17. 18 suluppu imittu ša šu-pa-lu nâr eš-šu e-li nâri u šu-pa-lu nâri (BA iii 404, 405). — T. A. (Ber) 160, 5—6 a-na šu-pa-li up-ri šep-bi šarri bêli-ja, in the dust of the feet of my Lord; 163, 4—5; 189, 4 thy servant ep-ri šu-p[a-a]l šêpê *pl*-bi šar-ri bêli-ja, the dust under the feet *etc.* (BA iv 121 on this letter); 214, 2 (end) šu-pa-a[-li], 3, [up-ri?] šêpê boli-ja; also 76, 2—3 a-na šupal šêpê bêli-ja. (Lo) 29, 4—5 a-na-ku ep-ru iš-tu šu-pa-li ši-ni šarri bêlija & see šênu, 2 (end). — *b*) foot-stool {Schemel} Nabd 990, 11 (iç) šu-pal NER II; 761, 2 (iç) šu-pa-li šêpi; 258, 14 ište-en šu-pal še-e-pu. T. A. (Ber) 28 ii 11 šu-ba-al šêpâ-šu; PEISER, *Babyl. Vertr.*, xcii 11; cxlviii 2 (šu-pa-lu šêpê); & see cxxi 9; cxxvii 9.

šupalû (‖ šaplû) >< elênû. AV 8529. the lower {unten befindlich, unterer}. Nabd 103, 6 eqlu šu-pa-lu-u (>< eqil-šu-nu e-li-e-nu-u, 5). PEISER, *Vertr.*, lxxvii 1: one çubât šu-pa-li-tum eš-še-tum, new undergarment; Neb 12, 3 (end) šu-pal-li-tum. — TP iii 94 (nâr) Za-ba šu-pa-la-a; III 5, 47 (nâr) Za-ba šu-pa-li-i; TP vi 40; Anp ii 129, 130 (>< iii

135). II 65 *O* ii 16 ina eli $^{(al)}$ Za-ban šu-ba-li-e (AV 8372; KB i 198, 199).

NOTE. — JOHNSTON, AJPh xix 386 reads Asp iii 83 iš-tu < < *i. e.* šupalu-u i-du-la-a-ni *etc.*

šupultu *1.*; **šupiltu** *1.* submission {Unterwerfung}. 82—5—22, 53 *R* 2 šu-pul-ti māti ru-uq-ti; 83—1—18, 184, 5 šu-pu-ul-ti māti rūqti; K 809 *R* 3 [šu]-pil-ti māti rūqti (THOMPSON, *Reports*, *nos* 60, 77, 86). Perhaps also T^{M} v 22 before Nusku & the firegod šu-pil-te šak-na-at.

ša(i)pulu *1.* a part of the human & animal body {Teil des menschlichen und Tierkörpers} M^{S} 97. BOISSIER, *Doc*, i 32 (*Rass* 2 III 149) 12 šumma aqrabu ša-pu-ul imittišu (& šumēlišu). Probably the same as 82, 9—18, 4156 (M^{S} *pl* 29) 11 ša-pu-lu, which BOISSIER, PSBA xxv 23 *fol*; ZA xvii 400 explains as organe excréteur (évacuation, urine, excrément); also K 2063. Perh. √שׁפל: some lower part of the body. See Br 3455 where SI-PU-UL (II 37 *c-f* 47) = bi-rit pu-ri-di; sipulu = šipulu = šapulu. K 191 ii 35.

šapulu *2.* II 30 *no* 5 *c-d* 66 ŠIM (with ša = gar inclosed) + UD(?)-DU-A = ša-pu-lu preceded by raṭbu (Br 5205); id ŠIM (+ ša inclosed) also IV^2 55 *b* 29; 56 *b* 55. AV 7693. JENSEN: trockener (Brotteig), connecting with it (KB vi, 1, 509—10) *del* 204 (224) iš-ta-at ša-pu-l(s,š,n)at kurummatsu; 214 (236); almost immediately followed by šalultum raṭ-bat; suggesting for šab(p)ulu the meaning = dry {trocken}; against his reading, KB vi (1) 244 ša-pu-šat, ist angerührt. He connects with it also na(ā)ba(ā)lu & ta(ā)ba(ā)lu = תֵּבֵל, dry land, *terra firma*, & su-bi-si II 30 *b* 30.

šupēlu, šu-pe-lu & šu-pel-tum (§ 65, 16) see pēlu (801, 802) Br 281, 288, 8535 & HAUPT in TOY, *Ezekiel* (SBOT) 67. To the same stem also:

šupēltu(m). exchange {Austausch}. BA i 495—6; 632. PEISER, KAS 22; 90; T^{C} xi & 113. Camb 375, 1 *fol* dup-pi šu-pil-tum ša eqlāte ša *I-N-E* exchange-document {Tauschvertrag über} *ibid* 7 it-ti a-xa-meš uš-pi-e-lu; BA iv 31 *foll.* PEISER, *Vertr.*, xlii 4; cvi 7 a-na šu-pil-tum a-na bīti ša *N*, zum Tausch gegen das Haus des *N*. Rm 609 *R* (II 32 *O* 2, *add* = ZA vii 18) 4 še-im šu-pil-tum, BA iii 215. II 28, 47 (*add*) šu-pil-tum ša ma-x[ir-ti?]. Nabd 205, 1; 448, 1; 616, 1 & 5, *etc.* See also Br 3383. According to some a ‖ is:

šupultum *2.* T^{C} 113 on Neb 72, 1 šu-pu-ul-tum; but see šubultu, 2.

šūpiltu *2.* answer {Antwort}. √אפל. K 2370 i 7 qi]-bi-i-šu-nu ki-ni šu-pil-tu u-pil-lu-ma, leur parole fidèle a fait une réponse (MARTIN). Also see Br 5716, 14142 on II 28 *c-d* 50 (*add*) = GIŠ-GIŠ = šu-pil-tum ša ki-bi-ti, AV 8535.

šupludu see paladu, 804 *col* 1.

šupalkū see פלכה, 807, 808 & ZA iii 303, 304; also K 3182 i 13 šu-pal-ki ba-a-bi ša ka-liš ...., wide open is the gate of all .... AJSL xvii 134, 135.

šapanu, AV 7998 see sapanu, 778 & Šalm, *Ob*, 158; also našpantu, 740 *col* 1.

šappināte (?). II 53 *d* 13, 14 II biltu $^{(al)}$ A-li-xu a-na ša-ap-pi-na-te, AV 8019; or ša appināte, and connected with appun(n)ama?

šap(b)a'šu, pr išp(b)u'š, KB vi (1) 383, 384 dig up, root up, burrow {aufwühlen}. IV^2 49 *b* 45 the witches who IŠ-ZUN (= epirē) šēpē-MU (= ja) iš-pu-šu = T^{M} i 133 (see *ibid*, *pp* 125, 126); & *cf* vi 55 iš-pu-šu epirē šēpē-ja. BOISSIER, *Rev. Sém.*, vii 51 *fol* = multiplier, rendre abondant, s'épaissir; the meaning of "wenden" (DELITZSCH) très problématique. He translates IV^2 49 *b* 45: ceux-qui ont multiplié la poussière de mes pieds. IV^2 57 *a* 55 IŠ (= epir) šēpē-MU (= ja) šap-su. *Dibbara*-legend (KB vi, 1, 66; 383—4) iv 23 i-šap-pi-su arki-šu (said of the seven), wühlen hinter ihm her (den Staub) auf. JENSEN, *loc. cit.*, suggests as belonging here also Rm 279 *O* 4 ša šu-mēli er-çi-ta ša-pi-is(ç, z), 6 ša tap-pi-šu ša-pi-is; 8 ša tap-pi-šu-ma ša-pi-is; perhaps meaning to touch {berühren} ZA ix 407. V 31 *a-b* 56 see AV 7999.

šip(b)su. KB iii (1) 100 *rm* 5 quotes K 4470 ii 5—7 iç-çu-ru qa(?)-be(?) ina ši-ip-si-šu il-lik.

šapūsu. exchange {Tausch}? III 46 *no* 3, 4—5 bēl amēlu a-na ša-pu-si ina libbi sinništi tada-a-ni, seller of a male (slave) in exchange for a female (slave).

šupūsu (?) Rm 69 *R* 10, 11 xurâçē šu-pu-us, Hr[L] 429.

šip-su-u. AV 8152 read mesū (& see 566—7).

šapapu 1. II 35 *e-f* 58 ša-pa-pu ‖ a-la-a-ku, AV 8000.

šapapu 2. whence šappu & šappatu, 1 (& 2?).

šupapitu, ‖ šasūru. K 3478 *d* 9 šu-pa-pi-tu; K 4152 *R* 12 (M[S] *pl* 12 + 7); GGA '98, 826.

šapaçu, be mighty, be strong {mächtig, stark sein}?, or the like; AV 8001. K 4386 i 23 (= II 48 *c-f* 13) ŠU (li-rum) KAL = ša-pa-çu (Br 7192; H 26, 541); for the gloss see II 33 *a-b* 1. *Cf* kirimmu (438 *col* 1) for id + gloss; Br 7188. L[TP] 224 (additions to 129).

Q[t] *ac* šit(rit?)-p(b)u-çu. K 4335 ii 23 (= II 22 *e-f* 46, Br 10741) = DIB-DIB-BI, which also = šit-pu-ru & šit (or git?)-mar-ru. AV 8360; ZA ix 108, 25 (VATh 244*b*) & 159.

Derr. these 3:

šapçu *1. n* might, highness, rule, government {Macht, Hoheit, Herrschaft}, AV 7703. V 20 *e-f* 14 NAM-EN-NA (& *g-h* 40) = šap-çu (Br 2147, 2814); same id in 18, 19 = bēlūtum, šarrūtum. AV 8153 reads šib-çu.

šapçu *2.* & **ši(e)pçu** *1. adj*; then *pl* šap-çūte, šipçūti also used as *n*: potentate, prince, ruler {Machthaber, Fürst, Regent} Hebr. ii 146. TP viii 32 mātāti šap-çu-te u mal-ki *pl* za-e-ri-ja, the countries of the mighty and the kings, my adversaries; ii 68, 69 the country Mildiš šap-çu-te la-a ma-gi-ri lu al-lik; + 89; iii 88, 89; v 35. Anp i 22 (Ninib) who šadā-ni šap-çu(*var* -zu)-te u malkē *pl* nakirē-šu kīma qānē a-bi u-xa-çi-çu (KB i 56, 57); iii 128 (KB i 116, 117). Sn i 16 mal-ki šip-çu-ti feared my battle. S[b] 331 di-ni-ig AMĒL-ME-EN | šap-çu; H 24, 482; Br 6428.

šipçu *2.* power, strength, dominion, majesty {Macht, Stärke, Hoheit, Majestät}. Anp ii 106, 107 ina šip-çi u da-na-ni (KB i 88 *foll*) my warriors came upon them like the divine stormbird. Šalm, *Balaw*, III 3 Axuni who from the days of my fathers šip(*var* ši-ip)-çu u da-na-nu il-ta-ka-na; Šalm, *Mon*, ii 66 (KB i 168, 169). DT 67 *R* 7, 8 (H 120) see meçū (571 *col* 2). K 4386 i 24 (= II 48 *e-f* 14) GIŠ-AD-UŠ = ši-ip-çu, Br 4180; AV 8295.

šipāçu (?). Nabd 337, 2: Two ši-pa-çu a-na ....

šaparu, *pr* išpur & išpar, *ps* išappar, AV 8002; Gesenius-Brown, 706, 707 (ספר). — *a)* send, charge with a mission, commission {schicken, senden}. Hebr ספר, = Arab سفر (III) travel (KB vi, 1, 440), not شفر (II) send on a journey. G §§ 16; 33; 102; Winckler, *Forsch*, iii 236. *pr* K 81, 7 whom the king my lord a-na bul-ṭi-ja iš-pu-ra (BA i 200); Bu 91—5—9, 210, 17 (duppu *etc.*) ša taš-pu-ra-a-ni; *R* 2 my servants and my friends iš-pa-ru-u-ni (have sent me; PSBA xxiii 348 *foll*); K 552 *O* 11 [ša] ... aš-pu-ru ul-tu Bābili at-ta-ša-a (WZKM xii 364; PSBA xxiii 191); K 94, 6 (amēl) Ru-u-a-a ša taš-pur-a-ni (PSBA xxiii 61); K 824 *R* 16 te-bu-ša-' ša taš-pur (PSBA xxiii 63); 82—5—22, 97 *R* 3/4 u siparri ša taš-pu-ra (Hr[L] 274; 408; 255; 287; 290; 400). Asb viii 61 his messenger la iš-pu-ra; Šalm, *Ob*, 143 aš-pur; II 67, 66; Creat.-*frg* III 53 (*ibid* 4 lu-uš-pur-ka); V 65 *a* 34 aš-pur-šu-nu-ti (I called them in); Smith, *Asurb*, 216*g* the favor (mercy) which I showed him ša (in as much as) aš-pu-ru nirā-rūt-su; II 65 *a* 10 (KB i 198, 199 iš-pu-ur). V 33 *b* 10 lu-u aš-pur-ma (I sent to *Xani*); KB vi (1) 44, 23 taš-pu-ra-an-ni, thou didst send me. Xammurabi-letters 8 *R* 5, 6 a-ḫa-tum ša ta-aš-pur-am. IV² 49 *a* 50 Anum & Antum iš-pu-ru-in-ni; 51 man-nu lu-uš-pur a-na (§ 93, 1). — *pc* Rm 77, 10 (amēl) ša-ni liš-pa-ru-u-ni; K 125, 18 niqa-būni ar-xiš liš-pa-ru-ni (PSBA xvii 234 *foll*); K 517 *R* 12 liš-pu-ram-ma (PSBA xxiii 66) = Hr[L] 414, 196, 327. Knudtzon, 17, 2; 33, 4 *etc.* liš-pur. S 6 + S 2 *O* 17 lu-uš-pur-ki (*Rev. Sém.* '98, 142 *foll*). — *ip* IV² 59 *no* 2 *R* 20, 21 it-ti-ka šup-ra-an-ni-ma (or Š barū, 3?). 82—3—23, 845, 10 šup-ra, *Rec. Trav.*

xix 106, 107; *ibid*, xvi 189 *no* VIII 5—7 lu-u ša-al-ma-a-ta a-na šu-ul-mi-ka aš-pur šu-lum-ka šu-up-ra-am; *no* IX 6—8; 14 (šu-up-ri-im-ma). KB vi (1) 74 *no* 1, 6 therefore šu-u-up-ri-im-ma (see Bezold, *Diplomacy*, xxiii § 18). Br. M. 23154, 29—30 šu-pur a-me-li-e šu-nu-ti li-it-ru-ni-ik-qu, send and let them bring to thee these men; also *cf Rec. Trav.*, xix 42, 10 (Constant., 1109). Also in Xammurabi-letters 12, 14 *foll* šu-pu-ur .... li-it-ru-ni-iq-qu; & šu-pur *etc.* 17, 18 *fol*; 19, 10; 39, 5, 11. = fetch {holen lassen}, BA iv 486. — pm KB vi (1) 76 *R* i 12 to Erešgkigal a-na-ku ša-ap-ra-ku (I have been sent) BA iv 131, 132. — *ps* K 528 *O* 10 warriors a-na eli (al) Gam-bu-lu ta-šap-par (thou shalt send, >< AV 7677); K 533 *R* 7 a-šap-pa-ra; K 647 *R* 18 (= IV² 45 *no* 3; Pinches, *Texts*, 4, 5) la i-šap-pa-ru-' (Hr^L 269, 304, 210). DT 42, 5 aš-ša-pa-rak-ka, I will send thee (= D 101), + 10 a-šap]-pa-rak-kam-ma. K 3500 + K 4444 + K 10235, 12 u e-gir-te ša a-šap-par-kan-ni (Winckler, *Forsch.*, ii 12 *foll*). IV² 15* i 25, 26 i-šap-par, Br 10765. — Especially note: send word, message, order, command, answer, *etc.* with or without introductory ma-a or um-ma. — pr K 483, 7—8 ina eli ša šarru bêli iš-pur-an-ni ma-a, in response to the message of the king, the Lord, thus; 83—1—18, 34, 8—10 (iš-pur-an-na-ši-ni; AJSL x 110; xiv 10); K 518, 9—10 (AJSL xiv 11, 12); K 555 *O* 8; 80—7—19, 20 *O* 7—9 ina eli (amêl) pu-u-xi ša šarru be-ili iš-pur-an-ni ma-a; K 542 *O* 9; K 512 *O* 10; K 167 *O* 8, 9; K 1220 *O* 8, 9; K 492, 7 (BA i 628); K 522 *O* 8, 9 (a question for information); K 592 *O* 4, 5 xa-an-nu-ti (= these, AJSL xiv 180) ša taš-pur-an-ni; K 95 *O* 6—8 ina eli (amêl) Pu-qu-di .... ša taš-pu-ra; 67, 4—2, 1 *l* 7; K 486 *O* 6, 7 (BA i 187 *foll*); K 647, 7—8 ša šarru bêl-a-ni iš-pur-an-na-a-šu (§ 56*b*) um-ma; K 528 *O* 18 ša šarru bêli-a iš-pu-ra um-ma (Hr^L 55, 364, 140, 76, 359, 193, 204, 1, 271, 3, 31, 305, 288, 399, 486, 210, 269). Creat.-*frg* IV 76 (to Tiâmat) .... ki-a-am iš-pur-ši, he sent this message. ZA ii 60, 16 a-di ba-ni ša taš-pu-ra (59, 8), until the coming about of what thou hast reported. K 2852 + K 9662 iii 25 iš-pur-šu-ma u(?)-tap-pa-lu, Winckler, *Forsch.*, ii 36 *foll*. Asb ii 12 (& 102) ina qâti (amêl) allaki-šu iš-pur-am-ma .... um-ma, BA i 14 *no* 8: שְׁלַח בְּיַד; see also Lehmann, ZA ii 214 *foll*; 356 *rm* 2; Jastrow, *ibid* 353 *foll*; Jensen, 258; Lehmann, i 121 *rm* 2; ZA ix 343 *rm* 1; Bezold in S. A. Smith, *Asurb*, ii 89. — *ps* K 622, 4—5 a-šap-ra-ku(??; or šu-ma??) ina pa-na-at amêl) X (PSBA xxiii 59); Bu 91—5—9, 183 *R* 1 i-šap-pa-ra to the king (Hr^L 306, 340). — See also šipru & mâr šipri. — *b*) rule, govern {regieren}. Winckler, *Forsch.*, iii 236 = Hebr שׁבר, Job 38, 10. Anp i 42 see kanašu Š (409 *col* 2, below); Sarg *Khors* 124 twelve years Bâbilu i-bil u iš-pur; perhaps KB iv 30, 31 *no* III *var* to iz-zi-zu-ma, 15: pân ši-bu-ut a-lim iš-pu-ru-nim-ma.

K 4470 *b* 12 ša-pa-ri (KB iii (1) 100 —101 *rm* 5); S^c 283; H 20, 354 gi-in DU | ša-pa-rum (Br 4899); V 29 *g-h* 3 GI = ša-pa-ru; H 15, 196; Br 2404.

Q¹ pr ištappar, iltapra, is(s)ap-par, is(s)apra (§51); iz-za-par, Xamm.-*code* xxxvi 17. — *a*) send {schicken, senden}. K 673 *R* 8 il-tap-raš-šu; K 181 *R* 25 i-sa-par-u-ni (JAOS xx 250—1; PSBA '95, 222 *foll*); K 610 *R* 13, 14 i-sa-pa-ru-u-ni ina muxxi (AJSL xiv 179); K 666 *R* 8 amâtu (a servant girl) ša šarri ultu bîti ta-sap-ra (BA i 627); K 312, 11—12 Bêl-ibni .... a-na a-lik pa-nu-ti ana eli-ku-nu al-tap-ra (I placed over you, ZA ii 62, 63); K 84 *R* 12 (PSBA xxiii 344 *foll*); K 831 *O* 17 —19 a-du-u (= until) ina qâtâ (amêl) mâr šipri-ka al-tap-ra[-ka]; 81—7, 27, 109 *O* 7—8 three e-gir-a-ti to the king, my lord, a-sa-par; *R* 2 + 4 (AJSL xiv 6, 7); S 760, 6—7 ina eli ṭi-e-me ša Akkada-a-a (amêl) da-a-a-li a-sa-par; *R* 13 a-sa-ap-ra-šu-nu; K 562 *R* 10; K 509 *O* 15, 16 a-na pa-an šarri bêlija al-tap-raš-šu-nu-ti; K 10 *O* 7: 500 men to (a-na) the city al-tap-ra (I sent) um-ma (with the order; Johnston, JAOS xviii 142); K 82, 19 (BA i 242 *foll*, PSBA xxiii 53 *foll*) = Hr^L 346, 197, 310, 12, 289, 301, 85, 214, 382, 424, 260, 259, 280, 275. K 114 *R* 9 e-muq al-taprak-ku-nu-ši (Hr^L vol. vi). Xammurabi-letters 28, 6 ša (whom) iš-ta-ap-ra-aq-qu-ma (= 1 *sg*). SMITH, *Asurb*, 145, 2 ša ir-xa-niš iš-tap-pa-raš-šu adi max-rija = S. A. SMITH, *Asurb*, iii 2, 32. III 15 *a* 8 šēr ta-kil-tu iš-tap-pa-ru-nim-ma. Sarg *Ann* 47 iš-tap-par, *var* to iš-pur. — Also K 3426, 14 ša du-un-qa al-ta-tap-pa-rak-ka (I send to thee). — send a message, communication, order, command; communicate. Cyr 311,4 amēl ša eli bit-a-nu il-tap-ra-an-ni um-ma, has given me this order. K 613 *R* 12 to the king my lord as-sa-pa-ra (= V 54 *a* 59; PSBA xxiii 61); K 181, 8, 9 is-sa-par ma-a; 21, 22 i-sa-ap-ra ma-a; *R* 6, 7; 9, 10; K 528 *R* 13 al-tap-ra; Rm 78 *O* 10 (I write); 80—7—19, 19, 2—3 X ina qātā Y il-tap-ra um-ma (THOMPSON, *Reports*, 267 A); K 1140 *O* 7; *R* 16; K 647 *R* 19 ni-il-tap-ra, we will send; K 678 *R* 13—15 ki-i an-ni-e a-na šarri bēli-ja a-sa-bar (= V 54 *col* 2) = Hr^L 85, 197, 269, 349, 416, 200, 506, *etc.* — pm K 2361 + S 389 ii 9 ša šit-pu-rat (ZA iv 15) *cf* kāru, 1 (429 *col* 1, *med*); Šamš i 13 the mighty of the gods ša nam-ri-ri šit-pu-ru. K 2675 *R* 23 (Mukallì) ša a-na šarrāni abē-ja kakkē šit-pu-ru (KB ii 170, 171). — ac II 22 *R* 47 DIB-DIB-BI = šit-pu-ru, AV 8361; Br 9061, 10740; same id = babalu, ta-balu, *etc.* — *b*) rule, govern {walten, regieren} Sarg *Khors* 190 im-mu u mu-ša ki-rib-šu-un (city & palace) liš-tap-ru-ma (3 *pl*); *Ann* 447; Pp iv 139.

(Q^tn *a*) send {schicken, senden}. K 114, 23 il-ta-nap-pa-ru, they sent (= IV² 47 *col* 1; Hr^L vol. vi). K 2801 *R* 14 šip-ru mar-çu taš-ta-nap-par-a-ni, BA iii 234, 235: zu einem schwierigen Werke habt ihr mich gesandt; 15 ši-pir te-diš-ti. Asb ii 111 his messenger whom ka-a-a-an iš-ta-nap-pa-ra (§ 53 *a*); x 42 (iš-ta-nap-par-u-ni); + 45 (KB ii 230, 231; ZA ix 345 *rm* 1). KB ii 248, 91 (+ 95) ^(amēl) rabē-šu iš-ta-nap-pa-ra a-na še-bu-li *etc.* — *b*) rule, govern {regieren} Sarg *Cyl* 45 ša . . . . il-ta-nap-pa-ru ba-'u-lat Bēl, who ruled; *Ann* XIV 67.

Š^t charge one self with, rule, govern {regieren} TP i 33 ša (*i. e. Tigl. Pil.*) ba-'u-lat Bēl ul-taš-pi-ru; Sarg [illegible] ag multašpiru = muštēširu = mu-mā'iru, see 552 *col* 1 (*med*).

NOTE. — 1. JOHNSTON, xix 63: "the primitive meaning of the stem šapāru may be *to be swift*, transit.: *to dispatch*; šapparu, *wild goat* (whence צָפִיר) may be *the swift one*; see *Proc. Am. Or. Soc.*, Oct. '95, *p* clxxv *n* 4; *Report of the U.-S.-Nat. Mus.* for '92, *pp* 437—450.

2. T. A. forms: (Ber) 56, 31 aš-pu-ur, I wrote; ti-eš-pu-ru-na (3 *sg f*); aš-pu-ra-ak-ku (Lo) 2, 32 (ZA v 152—3 I dit not write to thee). In some letters, says BA iv 372 *foll*, 𒋻 reads *taš*; (Ber) 3, 5; 92, 42 + 55 (= *R* 10). — pc axuja li-iš-pu-ra, let my brother write (ZA v 142, 15). — pm (Ber) 45, 21 ša-ap-ra-ti, I have written; also šap-ra-ti & ša-ap-ra-ti-šu-nu: 3 *sg* (Lo) 26, 18; 33, 15 ša-pa-ar; 40, 12 ša-par; *cf* Tel-Hesy 11 ša-par-mi (BA iv 153, × OLZ ii *no* 2 iš-par-mi); (Lo) 66, 7. — ip (Ber) 1, 8 šu-up-ra-am-ma; (Lo) 2, 18 (ZA v 132). — ps (Ber) 1, 9 formerly when my father sent to thee (i-ša-ap-ra-ak-ku um-ma) mār ši-ip-ri; + 13. — Q² (Lo) 28, 11 aš-tap-par dup-pa, I sent a letter; al-ta-ap-ra-ak-ku, I sent to thee, ZA v 146, 23; (Ber) 42, 58 aš-ta-par; 45, 29 aš-ta-pa-ru, I wrote; + 30—31 and thou didst say a-na mi-ni ti-eš-ta-pa-ru a-ya-te ša-ru-ta (BA iv 281); (Lo) 2, 20 to him el-ta-ap-ru-ni, they wrote (ZA v 153); (Ber) 65, 7 . . . pa-ni ti-iš-ta-pa-ru-na-šu-nu. On ta-šap-par-ta (Lo) 23, 10 see BEZOLD, *Diplomacy*, xxxi *rm* 4. — Q^tn il-ta-na-ap-pa-ru; ta-al-ta-na-ap-pa-ru; BEZOLD, *Dipl.*, xxxi; (Lo) 8, 75 ni-il-ta-nap-pa-ru, ZA v 163.

DERR. — išpar, ušparu (117 *col* 2), KB vi (1) 440; našparu, našpar(š)tu (740) & these 9 (or 12?):

šaprūtu. present, gift {Geschenk} *pl* šap-rāte. Anp ii 99 their property, their children ana (a-na) šap-ru(ra)-te am-xur-šu-nu, KB i 88, 89. III *R* 6 šap-rat, AV 8020.

šāpiru. AV 8011. — *a*) scribe; manager; agent {Schreiber; Geschäftsführer; Agent}. KB iii (1) 6—7. Hebr סֹפֵר, KAT³ 649 *rm* 3; Arm סָפְרָא, Ezra 4, 8. HOMMEL, *Aufsätze, etc.* ('92) 34; ZIMMERN in SCHWALLY, *Idiotikon*, 122; BARTH, *Etym. Studien*, 26, 27. Sarg *Ann* 95 far-off Bedouin tribes ša ^(amēl) ak-lu ^(amēl) ša-pi-ru la i-du-ma (concerning whom neither *a* nor *š* had any knowledge); *Khors* 178 ^(amēl) pa-xa-ti māti-ja ak-le ša-pi-re rubūti *etc.*; *Ann* 437; Pp III 40; also *Cyl* 74 (*cf* 2 Kings 17, 24 *foll*); *bull* 96—7; *bronze* 54 (see aklu, 2; 34 *col* 1). Esh *Sendsch*, *R* 49 ^(amēl) ša-pi-ri. WINCKLER, *Forsch.*, i

498 *R* 4 (end) (amēl) ša-kan u (amēl) ša-pi-ru of the land of Chaldea; ZŠ viii 53; K 7599, 3 (Winckler, *Forsch.*, i 530, 531). (amēl) ša-pir, Johns, *Doomsday-book*, *no* 1 *col* 1, 3 & *pp* 29; 35 (above) *ibid.* VATh 574, 14—16 šumma libbaki a-na ša-bi-ri-ja lu-uq-bi-ma, if thou desirest I will speak to my manager, BA ii 560, 561. ZK ii 300—2 on K 2012 *R* 14, 15 PA = ak-lu, ša-pi-ru; ZA i 302; 443 *rm* 2; M^S *pl* 4; Br 5590. Here belongs perhaps the (amēl) sipiru of *c. t.* (see above 779, 780). — *b*) ruler }Regent} whence *abstr. n.*:

šāpirūtu. government }Regierung}. Šalm, *Mon.* i 4 the great gods rā'imūt šarrū-ti-ja bēlū-ti kiš-šu-ti u ša-pi-ru-ti u-šar-bu, KB i 152, 153; Craig, *Diss*, 23.

šipru, *c. st.* šipir, AV 8206. id QI, KIN (Br 10753). S^b 273 ki-in | QI | šip-ru, which also = tērtu; H 34, 814; § 9, 74. — mission }Sendung} §§ 27; 65, 4. — *a*) communication, order, command, report, answer by messenger or letter, whence Hebr סֵפֶר, letter, book, KAT^3 649. IV^2 25 iii 63 ina ši-pir ili-šu-ma e-pu-uš, at the bidding of, or, through the revelation of (?), see below. Smith, *Asurb*, 134, 50—1 see mērixtu, 588 *col* 1. K 3445 + Rm 396 *R* 40 .... ma-na-ma šip-ri-ni ša-ni (Delitzsch, *Weltschöpfung*, 53). — Note especially the phrase **mār šipri** messenger }Bote} see māru, 582 *cols* 1, 2. It is variously written. — *α.* Nabd 562, 1 (amēl) mar šip-ri. KB vi (1) 74 i 3 ma-a-ar ši-i-ip-ri. — *β.* (amēl) A-QI (= KIN), Br 11682; Asb ii 102 (*cf* 111 amēl rak-bu-šu), also 122; viii 61; iii 21 (amēl) A-QI-ja; vii 25, 29, 43. Sarg *Khors* 152—3. (amēl) A-QI-ka K 831, 15 + 18; K 542, 11 & often (Hr^L 214, 193); *pl* Asb iv 20 (amēl) A-QI-MEŠ of Ašurbanipal; Neb 350, 21 (amēl) QI-GIL-A-MEŠ. — *γ.* (amēl) A šip-ri K 4395 iv 27; K 181, 49; K 523 *R* 5 [on which see KAT^3 456 *rm* 4] (= Hr^L 274, 324). Here also Rm 77 *R* 10 A-mi-li-'-ti TUR (= mār) A (= mār) šip-ri (× Zehnpfund, BA i 535 *no* 54; see Hr^L 414); Sarg *Khors* 31 a-na X iš-pu-ra (amēl) A šip-ri; Nabd 22, 13 *etc.* — *δ.* TUR šip-ri. Sarg *Khors* 119, *etc.* Br 10768 *ad* IV^2 5 *a* 27, 28 *etc.* II 39 *g-h* 47 RA-GAB *i. e.* ra-gab (see rakbu) = mār šip-ri, Br 6369. — *pl* K 574 *O* 9 (amēl) TUR šip-ra-ni-ja (Hr^L 123; Hebr. x 110); IV^2 1* iii 7/8 TUR-MEŠ šip-ri (= AMĒL-QI-GE-A, Br 10768).

K 4386 ii 27, 28 (= II 48 *g-h* 17, 18) U (muš) KU (Br 10552); KA (ki-im-mu) XI = šip-rum (Br 735), together with A-DU = alaktu. H 11 & 212, 61). II 27 *c-d* 44 & 47 QI = ter-tum; PA (ter-tum) SU = ter-tum ša (*i. e.* in the meaning of) šip-ri. mu-kil ši-ip-ri = p(b)usmu, *cf* KB vi (1) 440. kananu ša šipri see kananu, NOTE (408 *col* 1, above). D 80 i 1, 2 (Br 14310) .... ša šip-ri. — *b*) business, occupation, work, handicraft, construction }Geschäft, Beschäftigung, Beruf; Werk; Arbeit} G § 16. Xamm-letters 27, 6—7 ša .... ši-ib-ra-am i-te-ne-ip-šu çi-im-dam; see also Harper, *The Code of Hammurabi*, 187. 81—6—7, 209, 34 may Ištar graciously look upon ši-pir šu-a-tu (+ 36) BA iii 262, 263. ZA iii 314, 68 šip-ri šu-a-tu. Sn *Kui* 4, 20 I, Sennacherib mu-di-e šip-ri ka-la-ma; Sarg *Ann* 297. Merod.-Balad.-stone ii 49 mu-du-u kal šip-ri. *del* 166 (179) but Ea knows ka-la šip-ri (KB vi, 1, 242—3; 505: jegliche Verrichtung; or, perhaps: revelation?); 81—6—7, 209, 24. KB vi (1) 290, 17 ši-bi-ir-šu i-ba-aš-ši. — II 67, 77 abnē ši-pir (amēl) pur-kul-lu-ti (832 *col* 1) ab-ni-ma; AV 8289. I 44, 80 i-ši-ra šip-ru qa-ti-ia, my handiwork succeeded; Asb x 106 ši-pir ep-še-e-ti-šu. TP vii 94 i-na ši-pir (amēl) bānū-te, through the artists' skill; V 63 *b* 38 in šipir; V 61 iv 15 ina ši-pir; Esh vi 18 (*Lit. Centralbl.* '81, 735); V 65 *b* 10 ina ši-ip-ri des Ziegelgottes (81—6—7, 209, 38); *b* 38 i-na ši-ip-ri-ka šu-qu-ru. Asb iv 86 ina ši-pir i-šip-pu-ti. KB ii 252, 67 until I go šip-ru šu-a-tu ippušu (and execute this work). KB iii (2) 90 *col* 1, 53 çu-ux-xu-ru ši-pi-ir-šu, its execution. Neb viii 64—ix 1: in 15 days ši-bi-ir-ša (*i. e.* of the palace) u-ša-ak-li-il; iii 42 (-šu); iv 72 (-šu-un). V 34 *b* 38 ši-bi-ir-ši-in; AV 8133. I 51 *no* 1 *a* 22. S 769, 10 (see naggaru, 644 *col* 1). K 2801 *R* 51, 52 ina ši-pir um-ma-nu-ti. KB iii (2) 4 *col* 2, 39 i-na ši-bi-ir ašipuu-tu. Xammurabi-letters 4 *R* 2 ši-bi-ir nāri-im, the construction of the canal, BA iv 489 *foll.* IV^2 58 *a* 12 Marduk u-tam-mu-ki ši-pir limutti[-ki], ZA xvi 168 *foll:* soll dir beschwören dein böses Treiben. I 32, 32 who a-na šip-ri Ê-XAR-SAG-KUR-KUR-RA (with gloss E-KUR-MEŠ māti-šu) ušeškin libbašu. IV^2 7 *b* 21 + 41 a-na ši-pir çi-bu-ti. (ina) šipir nikilti *etc.* see nikiltu (670). V 20 *a-b* 4 perhaps šipru na-ak-li. mimma šip-ru šu-a-tu, such an art; often in colophons, D 49, 35; II 21*a* 30; 33, 71. K 5418 iv 16 ši-pir lu tēpu-uš (KB vi, 1, 298) see sûnu, 1 (770 *col* 1) & add: KB vi (1) 556. — *c*) decision {Entscheidung}. KB ii 252—3, 77 in the month of Elûl (the month of) ši-pir ištarāti; + 79; also perhaps *ibid* 95 ši-pir max-xi-e, KAT^3 427 & *rm* 3. — *d*) T. A. = number {Zahl}. (Lo) 8, 42 much gold ša ši-ip-ra la ip(b)-šu, without number; *ll* 50, 51; 59, ZA v 14, 15; 158, 159. — *e*) revelation {Offenbarung}. V 51 *R* 29, 30 šip-ru rabu-u ... ša $^{(ilu)}$ Êa; IV^2 48 *a* 7, 8; KAT^3 536, 537; 538 *rm* 2 on ši-]pir abk(q)alli Adapa, L^4 i 13. KB ii 186, 187 *rm* (*var* to Asb iii 121) Nabû dup-sar gim-ri ši-pir; *cf* Messerschmidt, *Nabuna'id*, 64, 24: ki-i šip-ri ilû-ti-ka ša taš-pu-ra; Winckler, *Forsch.*, i 493.

šipirtu, *pl* šiprēti. §§ 65, 4; 32*aa* & *rm*; D^{Pr} 140; AV 8200. *f* to šipru. — *a*) message, writing, letter {Botschaft, Nachricht, Schreiben, Brief}. V 32 *a-c* 5, 6 ši-pir-tum (Br 13861, 14081) followed by e-gir-tum. K 831, 12 šap-rak ši-pir-ti; *R* 7 ši-pir-ti liš-ša-'u, let him take the letter; 83—1—18, 28 *O* 7—9 ši-pir-ti (= a message) $^{(amēl)}$ māt tam-tim-u-a ... il-tap-ra-u-nu, they have sent; *R* 7—9 a-du-u a-na pa-ni šarri be-ili-i-ni ni-il-tap-raš-šu; K 83 *R* 14 ina ši-pir-ti ša šarri bēlija; K 13 *R* 4 ši-pir-ta-a pa-ši-rat-ti (Hr^L 214, 344, 202, 281). See also šibru, 1 & šibirtu, 2. 82—3—23, 925 *R* 12 gab-ri ši-pir-ti, an answer (to this) letter, JTVI xxvi 162. T. A. (Ber) 112, 46 ib-bu-šu ši-bi-ir-ti šar-ri (the command); (Ber) 111 *O* 8. — KB iv 94—5, 27 qunuq šarri ša šip-ri-e-ti, Verfügungssiegel des Königs; also *cf* V 61 vi 30, 31 gabri qunuq *š*; KB iii (1) 182, 183 & *rm* * & **; also KB iv 68, 69 (= I 66 *no* 2) i *b* 19. K 79 *R* 14, 15 ši-pir-e-ti a-ga-a ša ša-ra-a-ti ki-i ša šaṭ-ra (Hr^L 266); Johnston, JAOS xviii 147: (how) these treasonable letters were written. K 1107 *O* 11 ul-tu šad-da-giš ši-pir-e-ti ma-'-di-e-ti, many messages (PSBA xxiii pt. 2). — *b*) work, skill, *etc.* Knudtson, 1 *O* 10 ina mimma ši-pir-ti ni-kil-ti (see 670 *col* 1, end). K 2852 + K 9662 i 31 a-na ši-pir-ti-ja la ta-da-a li-it-ka. — T. A. (Ber) 208, 4 a-na ši-bi-ir-ti-šu (+ 6). — Scheil, Notes LX (*Rec. Trav.* xxiii), Constant. 583 *O* 19 ru-ub-çi ši-ip(or ib?)-ra-ti.

šupru. message {Botschaft?) Rm 2 II 9 šup-ru a-šap-ra, AV 8002.

šupāru, *c. st.* šu-par, AV 8531. Its ori-riginal meaning perhaps still seen in T. A. (Ber) 92 *R* 30 ša šu-u-pa-a-ra il-da-na-as, who is to rend the dispatch; V 31 *a* 37 ça-a-tum u šu-par pi-i (= command). The *c. st.* **su-par** in Creat.-*frg* I *c* 27 (III 41, 99) šu-par ta-am-xa-ru (ri) ∥ ra-ab šik-ka-tu(-u)-tu(ti); the command in battle, (to be) chief in authority. See also $^{(amēl)}$ šu-par-šāqû & $^{(amēl)}$ šaq-šup-par (see šāqû 3 & 5). — šu-par, in control of, intrusted with, charged with; then also, in the capacity of, & almost ∥ of ša. — Asb i 86 ilāni šu-par šamê erçitim, in control of heaven (&) earth; Neb ii 60 (so Ball, PSBA xi, referring to II 35 *a-b* 10 ši-pa-ri = pu-ux-ru. AV 8286); also compare Neb i 48 Nabû pa-ki-id kiššat šamê u erçitim. Scheil, *Nabd*, ix 6. V 46 *a* 15, 16 (end) šu-par Ê-KUR. Perhaps KB vi (1) 48, 24; BA iv 161 *ad* T^M vii 49. Babyl. Chron. iii 1 ilāni ša šu-par Uruk u nišê-šu; Šalm, *Balaw*, vi 1(+ 3) ilāni šu-par Êsagila u Bābili; KB iii (2) 130. 7; 132, 21 (Nabd-Cyr. Chron.). Rm 279, 12 (šuma-ša) apsî šu-par $^{(ilu)}$ Êa; K 2148 iii 3 Lu-ux-mi tāmti šu-par $^{(ilu)}$ Êa. K 3351, 18 ul-tu a-'š'ur-rak-ka bēlum ilāni šu-par da-ad-me, Craig, *Relig. Texts*. i 43. Thus *del* 118 (125) ilāni šu-par $^{(ilu)}$ A-nun-na-ki (Hrozny: the Black-cloud gods) ba-ku-u it-ti-ša, the gods controlling the Anunnaki wept with her, šu-par $^{(ilu)}$ *A* belonging to ilāni rather than bakū, which is construed with ana (= over), >< above, *p* 152 & literature referred to; KB vi (1) 497. — Concerning, with reference to: Merod.-Bal.-stone iii 13 ša . . . . šu-par ma-xa-zi ša (māt) Akkadī(ki) pi-šu ep(ib)-ši-ma. Asb vii 25 my messenger I sent šu-par še-bul Nabū-bēl-šume (*cf* 16, šu-par *N*), with reference to, concerning. the extradition of *N*; ‖ iš-ta-na-ap-pa-ra a-na še-bu-li (KB ii 248, 249). KB ii 250, 26 šu-par mi-ri-ix-ti an-ni-ti ša *T* iq-bu-u; šupar. instead of eli, perhaps with reference to the šipir mērixti, mentioned in the context. K 2652, 9 šu-par mi-ri-xi-e-ti Teumman iš-tap-pa-ra (& see 588 *col* 1). K 621 1, 2 (Hr[L] 515) šu-par a-di e-mu-qi-šu. DT 83 *R* 14 šu-par ep-še-tu-šu-nu ul-çi-iš, PINCHES, *Texts*, 16. Sarg *Khors* 158 šu-par it-xu-zu nin-da-an-šu-un (LYON, *Sargon*, 80 = eli, concerning). Perhaps even T. A. (Tel Hesy) 20 šu-par mu-ul-ka (KB v *no* 219; OLZ ii ('99) *nos* 1 & 2; BA iv 153, 154; 325 *foll*). — Asb vi 59 maççarē šu-par Ê-KUR ma-la ba-šu-u (charged with, intrusted with). II 67, 81 u ça-lam ab-ni ma-çar šu-par ilāni rabûti (574 *col* 1, *ll* 3—6) — for, as. IV² 48 *a* 38 mur-ni-is-ki šu-par im-ra-šu-nu i-ku-lu — as a relative pron. K 3182 i 49 nap-xar mātāte šu-par šu-un-na-a li-ša-nu, with which compare IV² 20 *no* 1, 23—24 qit-ru-ba-aš-šu šu-par la max-ra ma-la šu-un-na-a liššānu (see šanū, 1 ℶ) Br 4749. Also K 3182 I 25 (= as many as); iii 12, 13; 35 (= those who have prayed to thee); 51, 52; iv 1, 2. S[P] II 987, 5 nam-kur šu-par Bābili, the property of Babylon (or šupar = the handicraft? *Jour. Trans. Vict. Inst.*, xxix 51). — Merod.-Balad.-stone i 42 ina pu-xur šu-par (= ša) ma-al-ku. Creat.-*frg* I *c* 23 i-na ilāni bu-uk-ri-ša šu-par iš-ku-nu[-ši pu-ux-ru]; III 37, 95 šu-par, instead of ša, on account of puxru. A rather strange use we find in I 68 *no* 1, 8 Ur (il) UK šarri šu-par (KB iii, 2, 94 ša, but wrong!) max-ri, compared with the usual šar maxri. Sargon, *bull* 70, 8 ner(ur?)-gallē tu-'a-a-me šu-par (of = weighing) one šar, nēr, six šūš, fifty gunu; *Ann* 424. T. A. (Lo) 36, 7 e-nu-ma šu-par = ēnuma ša = since. — K 188 *O* 1 ana kakkabu zal-lum-mu-u[pl] ina šu-par (il) A(?)-nu(?) innamir (THOMPSON, *Reports*, ii 183). MUL šu-par Anim (JENSEN, 19); xarrān šu-par Anim; *x š* Bēl; *x š* Êa = controlled by. — With the help of, on: K 3600+DT 75 i 7 see šebītu. NE X *col* 2, 29 UR-NI-NIM (amēl) malaxu šaPir(?, UT?)-napištim ša šu-par abnē it-ti-šu, *col* 3, 38—9 tax(tux)-tap-pi šu-par abnē . . . .; šu-par abnē xu-up-pu-ma. Perhaps a ‖ of tamšil, or meaning: work, monument, idol of stone, which Gilgameš by accident breaks to pieces. šupar abnē a talisman, to guide Gilgameš safely across the ocean. *U*, it is assumed, intrusts the talisman to *G*. between *ll* 35 and 36 the original account contained probably this episode. *U* suggests another way for *G* to reach Pir-napištim. This is given in the lines following (KB vi (1) 220, 221).

NOTE. — 1. Šu- considered by many a non-Semitic word, read ŠU-UD(D); see KB ii *passim*. DELITZSCH, *Hwb*, 643 & 648 (& § 81 *b*) assumes 2 different words šud (*c. st.* of šudū or šūdu?) √šadū, be high, prominent; & šūtu, šūt, pronominal particle. See also ZK ii 187 *foll*; 239 *rm* 2. — JENSEN, 19 *rm* 2: šu-uṭ(d) deutet ganz im allgemeinen eine Beziehung an; 28, 29 *rm* 2 √šāṭu, bear, carry, ‖ çīr(u), over; metaphorically: concerning, with reference to; or if šud, then √šuddu, šadadu, pull, draw — WINCKLER, *Forsch.*, i 539 šu-par; KB iii (2) 14 *etc.* & *Sargon*, 231 šu-pur. — BEZOLD, ZA ix 116 šūt = *id est*, namely.

2. NE VII *col* 4, 39 (43) perh. . . . . šu-tam a-gi-e who since days of old have ruled the country; *c. st.* of šutammu, by-form of šatammu, just as tartānu & turtānu, targumānu & turgumānu; unless we read na-] šu-ut a-gi-e, suggested KB vi (1) 461, 462, proposed first by J[W].

3. Here perhaps also TP i 55 šu-par ku-u-riš al-ta-na-an; kūriš *c. st.* of kūrišu a noun like purīdu, purīmu, *etc.* √karašu, destroy, ruin; or qarašu, cut; unless we accept JENSEN's (KB vi, 1, 568) šutamkūriš > šutamxuriš = gegenübertretend; but why -ku-u-riš? STRECK, ZA xviii 166 nothing new.

4. See the author's article Šupar, (amēl) šuparšāq(ū), (amēl) šaqšupp(bb)ar in AJSL xx ('04) 186—93.

šiparu. assembly {Versammlung}. IV² 51 *b* 25 ina ši-pa-ri iz-za-ax-zu-ma lu šal-ma-a-te i-ta-mu-u (= Z[Š] ii 82; see *ibid*, *p* 54). Perh. ZA iii 315, 72 šipar-ša. II 35 *a-b* 10 ši-pa-ri ‖ pu-ux-ru, AV 8286.

šuppuru. K 1374 *R* 24, 25 u 2 (or 3) sisē šup-pu-ru-u-tu a-na bēl šarrāni bēli-a aš-pu-ram-ma, Hr^{L} 462.

šap(b)ru. S^{b} 198 xa-aš šap(b)-ru (*var* ri) skin {Fell} or the like. NE VI 63 u kalbē-šu u-na-aš-ša-ku š(s)ap(b)-ri-šu, KB vi (1) 171 and his dogs tear (bite) his skin (*i. e.* of the shepherd turned into a wild dog). Also see NE II *col* 4 *a* 3 li-i]m-xaç ša-p(b)ar-šu, KB vi (1) 140, 141; 435. 436. The *f* is:

šappartu. V 50 *b* 48, 49 the demon a-tu-da šap-par (= SIQQA-BAR-RA, Br 241) šadi-i šap-par-ta-šu-nu (= SU + MUNŠUB = skin + hair, see šārtu, hair) iççabat, grasps hold of the shaggy hair of the mountaingoat.

šapparu. wild mountaingoat {wilder Bergziegenbock} § 65, 24; see NOTE, 1 to šaparu. II 6 *c-d* 6 SIQQA (written ŠU-ŠE-KU-KAK = atūdu)-BAR = šap-pa-ru, preceded by atūdu, AV 8018, Br 10903. KB vi (1) 40/41 (& 368) 30 a-tu-du š(s)ap-pa-ri iz(ç)-x(ç)a-az(ç)-ru-šu. D^{Pr} 124 *rm* 2; ZIMMERN, ZA vii 168, 169. HOMMEL, *Expos. Times*, October 1900, a west-Semitic loanword.

šap(b)ru. KB iii (2) 116 *ad* V 63 *a* 43 ša-ap(b)-ru ra-šu-uš-šu, but see rēšu, rāšu, 1 *c*.

šappuru see pāqu, 2 (810 *col* 2).

šippirū, AV 8294 see sippirū (780 *col* 2).

šippuru see sippuru (780 *col* 2) & K 2148 iii 32; also Rm 422, 5 .... iš-tu ti-ki-šu (= tikku? neck) ana šip-pu[-ri-šu?]; 6 ... iš-tu šip-pu-ri-šu ana šēpā; 14 šip-pu-ra ra-ki[-is?]. ZA ix 407.

šipp(bb)uratu. a plant {eine Pflanze}. K 4152 + K 4183 *O* 44 (šam) šip-pur-ra-tu, M^{S} *pl* 6. Rm 356 *O* 9 [(šam) a-na-me?]-ru = (šam) šip-pur-ra-tu; followed by [.......]-tu = šippuratu; [...... KUR]-RA = *š* ša-di-e; also see AV 8146.

šupardū see ספרא. 827, 828 & KB vi (1) 462, 463.

šuparkū see פרכת, 831 *col* 1, below.

šuprusu, AV 8543 see parasu, Š, 884 *col* 1.

שפר, *pr* ušparir, *ac* šupar(r)uru, spread out {ausbreiten} D^{Pr} 127; but KB vi (1) 338 stretch forth, stretch out {ausstrecken}. Creat.-*frg* IV 95 uš-pa-ri-ir-ma be-lum sa-pa-ra-šu u-šal-mi(*var* me)-ši, KB vi (1) 26, 27. TP vii 58 see nubalu, 2 (637 *col* 2) & LOTZ, *Tigl. Pil.*, 175. V 50 *b* 42, 43 ana šame-e sa-par-šu uš-pa-ri-ir-ma, Br 5534, 10610. *pm* III 64 *O* 7 the moon like a mulmullu šu-par-ru-ur. S^{b} 237 ba-ra | PAR šu-par-ru-ru, Br 5534; H 39, 180. — **Der.:**

šuparruru (whence D^{Pr} 126 Hebr שַׁפְרִיר; on which see, however, HOFFMANN, ZATW ii 68; & BARTH, *Nominalbildung* § 144 β), *f* šuparrurtu. spread out or stretched forth {ausgebreitet; ausgestreckt}? III 64 *R* 13 su-pu-ru explained as tarbaçu šu-par-ru-ru; *cf* KB vi (1) 338 & 424. II 39 *e-f* 45 DIR (= urpatu?) šu-par-ru-rum; DIR = xa-la-pu, Br 3747. IV^{2} 26 *a* 22, 23 še-e-tu (net) šu-par-ru-ur-tu (both words = SA-PAR, Br 3127, 5534), KB vi (1) 338: gerade ausgestreckt; AV 8532. Perhaps also:

šuparruštu. II 22 *a-c* 20 GIŠ-SA-KAL-GA = šu-par-ru-uš-tum ‖ še-e-tum, *q. v.* Br 3134; AV 8533.

ša-par-ta, TP iv 1 see šabru, šabartu.

ša-par-tum. II 43 *a-b* 40 see mašla'tum, 606 *col* 2.

šupēš. *adv* SCHEIL, *Rec. Trav.*, xix *p* 46, 11 .... šu-pi-eš lu-ul-ta-šib.

šūpušu. Š of epešu (82, 83) *pm.* V 65 *b* 1 the temple of the sungod ša šu-pu-šu a-na bēlūtišu šūluku (*q. v.*) ana simat ilūtišu; also *a* 20 (KB iii, 2. 108—9); Sarg *Ann* XIV 68. SCHEIL, *Rec. Trav.*, XIX, *pp* 43, 44 (BA iv 91 *foll*) Xammurabi-text: tu-še-ip-pi-is-su-nu-ti šu-pu-šu-um-ma li-še-pi-šu, qu'on leur fasse faire ce qu'ils doivent faire (Constant. 1109, 9—10). *f* šu-pu-šat, Asb vi 20. See also Br 7442 *ad* II 30 *a-b* 76 ŠE-BA-SI-GA = šu-pu-š[u?]. — *ac* Sn *Kui* 3, 25 a-na šu-pu-uš elippē.

šupšuxu, *adj* AV 7657, 8544. Perhaps V 38 *a-c* 36 git(?)-ma-lu ‖ šup-šu-xu, AMIAUD, ZA iii 48; Br 7543. For *ac* & *pm* Š of pašaxu. see 842 *col* 1.

šipšiṭu. √pašaṭu. $Z^{\check{S}}$ vii 82 ina šip-šiṭ qa-ti-ša el-li-te; yet rather ina me-šid; see mešdu, 600 *col* 1 & ZIMMERN, *Ritualtafeln*, pref. xi.

šapšaqu, *n* need, trouble, tribulation {Not, Drangsal, Beschwerde} √pašaqu, 843, 844. § 65, 33*a*; AJP viii 267. Šalm, *Mon*, i 7 a-me-ru du-ur-gi u šap-ša-qi (KB i 153 Notsteg, Steige). Lay 43, 1 e-ta tiq šadê dannûte a-tam-mar du-rug šap-ša-qi ša kališina kib-râte, I traversed mighty mountains and opened for myself a way through difficulty in all directions. IV^2 54 *a* 26, 28 lu-u-çi ina šap-ša-qi, may he escape the tribulation. V 35, 17 his city Babylon i-ṭi-ir i-na šap-ša-ki, he saved from need, BA ii 210, 211. To the same stem belongs?

šupšuqu, *adj* hard, steep, laborious {arg, steil, mühselig} § 88 *rm*, ‖ pašqu. AV 8545. Sn i 69 aš-ru šup-šu-qu (steep, hard territory) ina šêpija rîmâniš at-tag-giš, *Kui* 1, 10; *Bell* 21; Sn iii 76, 77 see šaxaṭu, 1 (⟨Q⟩^{t}). Sargon, *Ann* 376; TP iv 54 see nêribu (725 *col* 2, end). — of people: reduced to misery, gotten into trouble. IV^2 26 *b* 56, 57 kîma summati idammum šu-up-šu-uq (= LA-RA-AX, Br 1003) mu-ši u ur-ri, full of trouble, by night and by day; also 27 *a* 30, 31. *adv.*:

šup-šu-qiš e-si-ir-šu, ZA iv 412 on WINCKLER, *Sargon*, Texts 55, 9 *foll.*

šaptu, *f* (§§ 62, 1; 71); *c. st.* šapat; *pl* šaptâ, šaptân, šaptê. BARTH, ZDMG 41. 631 √שפו; AV 7706, 8021. — *a*) lip {Lippe} id KA + inserted sa (§ 9, 221). Asb ii 51 zi-kir šap-te (*var* id)-ja, the word of my lips; K 2852 + K 9662 i 30 (*cf* siqir, seqar, 781 *col* 2). Sarg *Khors* 192, 193 ina šap-ti-šu el-li-tim li-ça-a; *Ann* 453 (KB ii 80, 81); *Ann* 239 liššakin šap-tu-uš-šu, his will, command, be done. Asb iii 80 see šaplânu & § 69 *rm*; iv 135 šaptê-šu-nu ap-ru-su. SMITH, *Asurb*, 247, *k*. KB ii 248, 249 *l* 12 see kabalu, 365 *col* 1, end; & WINCKLER, *Forsch.*, i 252. V 64 *b* 29 damiqtim of their city & house liš-ša-ki-in šap-tu-uk-ka (§ 80*e*; KB iii (2) 102, 103). I 51 *no* 2 *b* 21 li-iš-ša-ki-in ša-ap-tu-uk-ka; I 52 *no* 3 *b* 26. ZA i 41, 29. 81—6—7, 209, 34 a-mat damiqti-ja liš-ša-kin šap-tuš-šu, BA iii 262, 263. Creat.-*frg* IV 61 i-na šap-ti [....] u-k(q)al-lu; 72 i-na šap-t[i] ša lullâ ukâl sarrâti, KB vi, 1, 26—7. *del* 120 (127) their lips *etc.* see šababu; Creat.-*frg* IV 98 see katamu, ⟨Q⟩ *c* (458 *cols* 1/2). IV^2 58 iii 39 šap-ta-a-ša ziz-ziq-qu-um-ma, ZA xvi 180, 181 ihre (der labartu) Lippen und Spritzen. K 194, 11 (end) a-di $^{(amêl)}$ša šaptê (written KA + inserted sa + MEŠ; = interpreter?). — id KA + inserted zil, nun (Br 803). IV^2 5 *b* 54, 55 ša-pat-su (§ 74, 1) iššuk, he bit his lip (in anger) H 16, 23—4; Z^B 32. KB vi (1) 10, 20 ša]-pat-su it-taš-ka. H 84/5, 33 šap-tu li-mut-tu; IV^2 16 *b* 60, 61 šap-tan muççaprâtum (*cf* ça-paru, 1; 885 *col* 2). H 11 & 213, 69; V 41 *a-b* 65 see sanaqu (771 *col* 2, *med*) = close one's lips, be silent. III 64 *a* 24 id + AN-TA-KI-TA = šaptu elîtu šaplîtu; 25 id + MEŠ-šu-nu = šaptâ-šu-nu. — *b*) border, seam {Saum, Einfassung}. V 31 *a-b* 10 ša-pat bûri = šap-ti ša bûri, rim or edge of a well, Br 12189; see 186 *col* 2, end. II 62 *a-b* 69 see šaplû. Perhaps IV^2 31 *O* 30 ki-ma ša-p(b)at(d,ṭ) ku-ni-ni (see kunînu, 1; 408 *col* 2).

šapatu judge {richten}. V 28 *e-f* 39 ša-pa-tu ‖ da-a-nu; II 35 *e-f* 1 (see 258 *col* 2 & JENSEN, ZA iv 279, Hebr שפט); AV 1873; 8008. D^{II} 20; D^{Pr} 39 (see ZDMG 40, 724 on Arb سفط). K 2022 i 64 ša-pa-tu together with a-ba-ru. V 36 *a-c* 60 šu-u ⟩ ša-pa-tum Br 8753.

Der. nišpatu (740 *col* 2).

šapâtu. Nabd 1088, 1—2 twenty shekels .... a-na ša-pa-a-tum ša 60 lu-bu-uš-tum, BA i 533: für eine Lade zu 60 Kleidern. √'שפ, whence išpu, quiver {Köcher}.

šappatu *1.* *f* of šappu *c. t.* WZKM iv 116 *rm* 4; T^C 112; PEISER, *Vertr.*, 287; BA i 533; JOHNSTON, JAOS xix 83: better perhaps sappatu, *cf* Hebr ספות, basins, dishes. 83—1—18, 39 (Hr^L 345) 9—10 ta-šat-tu-u lu 41 $^{(karpat)}$ šap-pa-ti, PSBA xxiii 70, 71. K 154 *R* 2 (Hr^L 276). Nabd 247, 10—11 one hundred šap-pa-tum ša karâni el-lu (+8); 279, 8: 30 šap-pa-tum ša karâni el-li (*ibid* 10; 17—18); 334, 2 ištêni-it šap-pa-tum; 481, 10 šap-pat-MEŠ; 743, 14 (karpat) šap-pat; 779, 3 (karpat) šap-pa-tum; 1013, 6. Neb 441, 9 ište-en (karpat) šap-pa-a-tum (Krug zur Aufbewahrung des Weines). Camb 212, 1 ištēni-it šap-pa-tum [karâni]; 352, 1: 2-ta šap-pa-tum rabî-tum; Dar 91, 4 *foll*; 115, 1.

šappatu *2.* see pūru, 1 (825 *col* 2) & šikkatu, 3.

šapattum, AV 8004 see šabattum.

šapūtu. III 64 *a* 11 ina IM-DIR ša-pu-ti. Creat.-*frg* VII *O* 28 (KB vi, 1, 36/7 & *rm* 3; 355). malṭû ša(-)pu-ut(tu(m)) see malṭû (546 *col* 1).

šapītu (?). PEISER, *Vertr.*, *no* 148, 18 ištēni-it ša-pi-ti ša 6 ma-na parzilli, in a list of furniture belonging to Gimillu. See also šapātu. — Br 1850 ša-pi-ti i-nim, V 13 *a-b* 13 read ša pi-ti i-nim.

šiptu, *f c. st.* šipat, AV 8207; § 65, 4. √ašapu (§ 25) see 117 *col* 1; PRAETORIUS, *Lit. Or. Phil.*, i 197; Z^{H} 89; AJP v 79; KB vi (1) 462—3; JBL xix 64 *rm* 22 exorcism, incantation }Beschwörung{. ZIMMERN, *Ritualtafeln*, *p* 91 *fol*: the âšipu-priest acts through the šiptu-incantation; the šiptu is the prerogative of Êa & his son Marduk, emanating from the apsû, the abode of Êa, or from Eridu, the sacred city of Ea. KAT^3 373. — Pronounce an incantation, exorcism = šiptu nadû or manû, see *pp* 640—9; 556—7; also tamû; and, in addition, KB vi (1) 286 *col* 4, 3 [.... tam-n]u ši-ip-ta iš-tu-ma tam-nu-u ši-pa-sa. K 8522 *O* 12 be-el šip-tu elli-tim, KB vi (1) 34—5. K 2107 *O* 14 (ilu) ŠAR-AZAG ša ši-pat-su el-lit, one of Marduk's names, Br 4338. On the idd see ZK i 319; ii 423, 424. These idd are used more or less: NAM-RU, H 38, 70; Br 2130. IV^2 3 *b* 7/8 ši-pat ER-ṬI (= Eridi) i-di (ip of nadû); 4 *a* 29/30; 5 *c* 63/64; 15* iii 43/44 .... šip-ti ša E-ri-du, (16 *b* 33; 27 *b* 50 + 59); 6 *b* 42/43 šip-tum elli-tum ina na-di-e-a; 16 *b* 34/35, 25 *a* 52/53 = me-e šip-ti; 30* *no* 3 *O* 23/24 a-ši-pu (*var* šip) Êridu ša ši-pat-su nak-lat a-na-ku. — NAM-ŠIB-BA, Br 2315; § 9, 51; H 38, 72; IV^2 13 *b* 54 (me-e šip-ti; Br 10379 & *cf* S^c 4, 5); on S 28, 37 *R* see Br 2180. — KA + inserted li, Br 1781; H^F 69. IV^2 15* iii 12/13 ina šip-ti (= KA-KA-MA, Br 589; H 37, 50) çir-ti ši-pat (= KA + inserted li) E-ri-du ša te-lil-ti, with the lofty exorcism, the purifying exorcism of Eridu; 45/46 ši-pat ap-si-i (= ZU-AB) u E-ri-du çir-ti; 19 *b* 12/13 ina šip-ti-ka el-li-ti ša ba-la-ṭi (= recovery, KAT^3 373), o Marduk; 22 *b* 12 ši-pat-ka elli-ti; 29 *no* 1 *a* 35/36 ši-pat ba-la-ṭu (see balâtu, 163 *col* 2, end of § 1). — Twice KA + li (inserted) Br 785; IV^2 29* *no* 4 C *a* 21 ši-pat ap-si-i i-di. — Three times KA + li (inserted) for šip-tum ši-pat (ilu) Marduk, IV^2 21 *no* 1 B *O* 40/41. — Twice KA + li (inserted) followed by NAM-RU, IV^2 21 *no* 1 B *R* 1/2. — IV^2 22 *no* ii 14/15 a-ši-pu ina ši-[ip]-ti = KA-AZAG-GA. — V 21 *c-d* 37 KA + li (inserted) = šip-[tum]; *ibid* 48 id has gloss mu. V 23 *a-d* 50 me | ME šip-tum; H 11 & 213, 66; S^c 4, 5; H 33, 781. S^b 43 en | [illegible] | ši-ip-tum (Br 10857), an id serving often as superscription or heading of incantations, exorcisms, *etc.*; H^F 49 *rm* 2; ZA i 63, 64; *cf* K 626, 7 + 27; LEHMANN, ii *pl* XLIV; Z^Š *p* 67; K^M 149, 150; Br 10857; T^M 158. IV^2 55 *no* 1 *O* 35: III EN-MEŠ an-na-a-ti, these 3 incantations (thou shalt recite 3 times).

šipātu, *f pl* šipâte, AV 8288. hairy or woolly animal skin, fur; then, also, wool, woolen stuff }haariges (*cf* šârtum) oder wolliges Tierfell, Pelz; dann auch Wolle, Wollstoff} *cf* III 9 *no* 3, 55. id SEG, Br 10781, 10787, 10792. Z^B 6 *rm* 2; BA i 494; ii 561. IV^2 7 *b* 38 SEG enzi = *lana caprina*, ZK ii 28. it is used as a determinative before id(t)qu, çirpu, argamannu, takiltu, tabarru, *etc.* id SEG in IV^2 8 *b* 28/29 ši-pa-a-te pi-ça-a-te(ti) ši-pa-a-te çal-[ma-a-te], ZK ii 27, 28; H 190; Z^Š v/vi 151. H 90, 91 (K 246 ii) 55 & 58, see ṭamû, 356 *col* 2. II 27 *a-b* 61 [.....]-BAR = ba-ša-mu SEG (= šipâti), to dress a skin. SEG = šipâti also in V 14 *cols* 1 & 2; thus *b* 20 pi-ça-a-tum; 21 i-ša-ra-a-tum; 22, çal-ma-a-tum; 23 sa-ma-a-tum, *etc.* On the bēl šipâti (çalmâti) u ulinni aunī, see ZIMMERN, *Ritualtafeln*, *p* 191 *rm c.* — *pl* SEG-ZUN = wool {Wolle} in *c. t.* (BA i 494), Camb 24, 1; 367, 1, for which Cyr 157, 5: iste-en ši-pa-tum pa-tin-nu, BA i 534. V 28 *a-b* 19, 20 ši-pat -ri ‖ ši-in-ṭu (*q. v.*) & ad-du (or gir-du?); 21 ši-pat ruk-bi ‖ a-ru. V 14 *a-b* 14 SEG-ŠIT-MA (= id(t)qu) = ši-pat su-ti-i, Br 10788. A ‖ is:

šupātum *1.* S^b 1 iii 16 si-ig | SEG | šu-pa-a-tum, Br 10782; H 34, 816 (*var* ši-, followed by lu-bu-uš-tum); V 38 *e-f* 45; § 65, 13; AV 8534. V 15 (*c-*)*d* 32—36 šu-pa-tum; on *c* 32 see Br 14106. H 86, 87 i 72 šu-pa-tu, garment, dress.

šupātum *2.* K 6027, 13 šu-pa-a-tum, apparently in a list of animals (M^S *pl* 13).

šipittu (?). AV 8138. Nabd 130, 2 ina ši-pit(bit)-tum ša ....; 145, 6 kaspa ina ši-pit-ti-šu i-šal-lim; 160, 9—10.

šēpītu *1.* a *f* to šēpu. foot {Fussende}. IV² 55 *no* 1 *R* 15 ina ri-eš (see rēšu) erši u še-pi-ti erši. III 53 *a* 56 star called GUD-AN-UD (= sun-bull) še-pi-it tarbaçi šu-par ^il Ea. Perhaps Sarg *Nimr* 15 še-pit-su ip-pa-ṭir-ma, KB ii 38 suggests li-pit-su, foundation. See also rēštu. *pl* rūšēti.

šēpītu *2.* KB iii (1) 188 on Merod.-Balad.-stone iii 51 še-pi-it xu-'-uz-tu, but read 40 pi-it *etc.* (see 276 *col* 2, *med*).

šuptaqtu, see rušumtu.

šaçû. croak, caw {krächzen} AV 8022. II 62 *a-b* 50 SER-BUR-XU (= āribu, raven)-KA-DE (= šasū, call, cry) = ša-çu-u, Br 1661; JENSEN, 505 *ad* 153. IV² 61 *a* 54, 55 ki-i ū-mu i-ši-çu-u-ni, AJSL xiv 277, when the storm is raging. where belongs K 1523 + K 1436, 13 the lofty king iš-ša-aç, PSBA xxiii 220 *foll* (is despoiled?)?

šūçū *1.* *ac* ש of açū (84, 85). II 62 *a-b* 51 (= NUNUZ?)-IN-ŠA (= LIB)-ŠUD = šu-çu-u, AV 8546; D^Pr 140 *fol*; Arm שׁיצא. — pm Sarg *Cyl* 35 high banks ša ultu ullā ina qirbišun urqitu la šu-ça-at (= 3 *f sg*; *passive* in meaning). — ip šu-ça-a IV² 31 *R* 33; *O* 69 šu-ça-aš-ši, lead, bring (her) out. To the same stem belongs

šūçū *2.* *n* edict {Edikt} or the like. V 47 *R* 21 ki-ma na-kim-tum šu-çi-i. 22: (amēl) šu-çu-u; GGA '98, 815: Amtsname; referring also to ZA iv 237, 13 (which see *p* 671 *col* 2). *cf* V 27 *g-h* 24 ŠU^(si-im) SIM = šu-çu-u; V 19 *c-d* 41, Br 7119. S 1357, 5 ŠA ..... | šu-çu-u, AV 8546, Br 14261.

šaçūlum. V 40 *e-f* 1 U^(u)A = ša-çu-lum, Br 6092.

ši-çu-ti, Anp i 26 see širiqtu. AV 8298.

šaqqu *1.* AV 8032. šaq-qu ša še-im, grain-sack {Kornsack} ‖ alluxappu (48 *col* 2). Hebr שַׂק; Br 6528. K 4241 + 4556 *O* 7 GIŠ-SA-AL-XAP-PU = a[l-lu-xap]-pu = šaq-qu ša še-im, M^S *pl* 11.

šaqqu *2.* (or saqqu?, rišqu?). II 36 *c-d* 3 BAR-RA = šaq-qu, AV 8032, Br 6902, in one group with u-du-u & ba-ša-mu. KAT³ 603 & ZIMMERN, *Ritualtafeln*, *p* 99 *rm p*: Büssergewand = Hebr שַׂק. WINCKLER, *Forsch.*, ii 44; JENSEN. KB vi (1) 365, 400, (Trauertuch) ‖ sissiktu, ulinnu. Perhaps Nabd 624, 4 a-na šaq-qa.

ša-a-qu, II 29 *e-f* 9.

šūqu *1.* abundance, luxuriousness {Überfluss, Üppigkeit} AV 8551. AJSL xix 5. V 28 *g-h* 61 (*e-f* 41) šu-u-qu ‖ xe-gal-lum (see *p* 305). Hebr שׁוק, Arb شاق, BARTH, *Etym. Stud.*, 46.

šūqu *2.* (?) ‖ sūqu. K 963 *R* 3 šarru a-na šu-u-qu la uç-ça-a, THOMPSON, *Reports*, ii *no* 245. Also see ZA vi 440, 441 on ina šu-u-qa (*c. t.*). *Cf* Hebr שׁוק, Arm שׁוקא.

šīqu *1.* V 41 *c-d* 49 [ ]-ÇI-GIG = ši-i-qu, Br 14059, preceded by uq-qu. AV 8300.

šaqū *1.* be high, lofty, grand {hoch, erhaben sein} AV 8028; § 25. pr K^M 12, 54 iš[-qu-u] *var* to il-qu-u; perh. III 52, 49 (il) Šamaš iš-gam-ma kakkabu iç-ru-ur-ma, JENSEN 156, die Sonne stand hoch; Babyl. Chron. iii 40 ki-i iš-qa-a ina eli Uru (KB ii 282/3). ps K 86 *R* 5 i-ša-qa-am-ma; K 120 A 8 i-šaq-qa-ma, is high, THOMPSON, *Reports*, ii, *nos* 91, 94; JENSEN, 119. IV² 60* B *O* 5 u-s(ç)al-li (ilat) iš-tar-ri ul i-šaq-qa-a ri-ši-ša. KB vi (1) 186, 46 ūpu-uš-ki aš-ša-aq(g.k)-ki ina Nippur (but??, see KB vi, 1, 460), I have made thee, I am lofty in Nippur. K 685, 9—11 Sin on the 30th day i-ta-mar ša-qi-a (= pm) ša ūmu XXX ina pi-it-ti i-ša-qi-a, AV 8026. Camb 217, 10 see šapalu, 1 Q ps. — pm Anp ii 105 ša-qi, was high, see kirxu (486 *col* 2); K 1395, 3 Sin ina tamartišu ša-qu-ma innamir, THOMPSON, 59. K 44 *R* 6/7, 8/9 ša ina ma-a-ti ša-qu-u (= EL-LA); H 78; D 133; Br 6151. IV² 1* iv 11 šēdu ... ša e-mu-qa-šu ša-qa-a (= AN-NA-KID); 13 ša e-mu-qa-šu ša-qa-a tal-lak-ta-šu ša-qa-at, ZA ii 292—3. H 129 (K 257 *R*) 20 ša tal-lak-ta-šu ša-qa-tum (Br 6151), whose way is haughty. BANKS, *Diss*, 18 *no* 2, 68 be-lum [....]-na ša re-e-šu ša-qa-a-tu (*var* qa-at); 80 ⁽ⁱˡᵃᵗ⁾ Iš-tar ša-qa-at; 24, 86 qarrad ša la im-max-xar ina māti ša-qa-at. ZA iv 232, 71 ša-qa-at; 230, 2 (v 57, 2) ša ... ša-qu-u e-diš-ši-šu, who alone is exalted. Creat.-*frg* IV 15 lu-u ša-ga-ta a-mat-ka; K^M 18, 4 ša-qa-ta ina ša-ma-mi. V 39 *g-h* 68 e-ma i-red-du re-ša-a-šu ša-qa-a. TP III *Ann* 114 el-lit-ma ša-qa-at. III 9, 5 (= TP III *Ann* 106) .... la nibi ana šamē ša-qu-u (KB ii 26, 27). K 3351, 13 see parçu, 837 *col* 1, end. K 2487 + K 8122, 16 (end) ša-qa-a ri-ša-a-ka. *del* 55 (58) šaq-qa-a, were high (KB vi, 1, 487). — pc perhaps II 33 *c-d* 15 [mašdaxu] liš-qu-u (??). — ac II 30 *a-b* 1—5 SAG-UŠ (H 16, 249; Br 3585, 5043); SAG-ZI (Br 3554); SAG-EL (Br 3614, 6151); TIK-LI (Br 3243); TIK-EL-E (Br 3280, 6151) = ša-qu-u ša re-ši; 6, DIR (= atru) = ša-qu-u ša amēli, be high up, lofty (H 16, 243) Br 3746; 7, ŠI-AN-KU-MU-ŠIT = ša-qu-u ša i-ni (of the eye) Br 494, 9290; 8, GIŠ-MA'-RU-RU-TIK = ša-qu-u ša elippi, Br 1452; 9, A-RU-TIK-KU-GA' (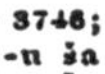)-GA' = šaqū ša ma-xir-ti, Br 1463, 11430 same id = maxaru ša maxirti; 18, see Br 280; 19—22 ša-qu-u = 19, AN-AN (Br 446); 20, AN-TA (Br 462); 21, 22 AN-TA-GAL (Br 468); also II 27 *e-f* 16 (& *cf* II 27 *e-f* 39). II 31 *h-i* 2 ša-qu-u, Br 6151; V 21 *c-d* 46 DA = ša-qu-u (Br 6654); V 36 *d-f* 10 ša-qu-u ša lu-ub-ši (Br 8746) see lubšu, 2 (475 *col* 2); also V 36 *a-c* 21 (Br 8745). S^b 356 ni-im | NIM | ša-qu-u, H 29, 651; Br 9016; S^c 3, 6 [ZI] = ša-qu-u. On ša-ku-u V 28 *h* 82 see ZA i 251 & again POGNON, *Wadi-Brissa*, 97.

Q^tn 81—2—4, 89 *O* 4 iš-ta-naq-qa-a, THOMPSON, *Reports*, *no* 226.

𝔍 make high, lift up, elevate, raise up, (of buildings, *etc.*) heighten {hoch machen, erheben, hoch heben, hoch aufführen}. BANKS, *Diss*, 18 *foll*. *no* 2, 72 Bēl u-šak-ki-ka, has raised thee. *Etana*-legend 23 one kaspu u-ša-qi[-šu-ma], +28 + 31 (KB vi (1) 112); *ibid* 114, 17 + 20 + 23. ZA v 68. 13—14 ul u-ša-qa-a (my eyes) a-na e-li-ni pa-an qaq-qa-ri. SMITH, *Asurb*, 9, 4 (Marduk) u-ša-qa-an-ni (L⁴ i 6) eli māre šarri (KB ii 236, 237). Sn vi 40: 200 ti-ib-ki a-na e-la-ni u-šak-ki ri-e-su; ZA iii 387, 82; *cf* I 44, 68 & 89; I 49 *d* 23/24, see rabū, 1 Š. TP vii 103 the ṣigurrāte of the temple a-na šamē u-še-qi (1 *sg*); Ṣarg *Cyl* 33 ina te-me-qi u-šaq-qi-ma (my hands). KB vi (1) 44, 13 u-še-iq-qi zi-im-bat-su, (the monster) raised high its tail; NE X *col* 1, 18 u-š(s)aq(k)-q(k)i zu-qat-su-ma (his head?) = H^NE 68. Asb x 80 see šikittu. T. A. (Ber) 90, 16 ju-ša-ki rēši-ja, I lifted up my head. IV² 31 *R* 18 šu-qi rēšo (or qaqqadē)-ka (ₐ uz-na šu-kun) KB vi (1) 88/89: lift high thy heads; but HROZNY, WZKM xvii 324 šu-kin!

Š = 𝔍. — pr Tiāmat among the gods u-ša-aš-qi ⁽ⁱˡ⁾ Kin-gu, Creat.-*frg* I *c* 24 (+ 35 en-na-nu .... šu-uš-qu-u = pm, with passive meaning; II 15; III 49, 107); II 4; III 38, 96. K 2487 + K 8122 (= K^M 2), 21 la li-'-a tu-ša-aš-qa (*var* tu-šaq-qa-ri, √eqeru?). Sp II 265 *a* xxiii 8 u-ša-aš-qu-u a-mat kab-tu. — pm ZA iv 231 (v 58 & 64) 25 šu-uš-qu-ma ana ti-di-ik bēlūtišu šurrux, it is exalted & for the dress of his lordship it is arranged. NE 25, 29 lu šu-uš-qat (or -šu?), KB vi (1) 160, 161. — ac ZA iii 317 (Sn *Rass*) 82 šu-uš-qu-u tam-li-i (AV 8609; § 72*a*, note), the raising of the terrace; Sn *Bell* 54. Creat.-*frg* IV 8 šu-uš-qu-u u šu-uš-pu-lu ši-i lu-u ga-at-ka.

Št II 44 *no* 9 *g-h* 73 .... BAR-RI = šu-ta-aš-qu-u (? Br 13957 šu-ta-qu-u).

Derr. ušku (?, EVETTS); mašqu (THOMPSON, *Reports*, ii *no* 234 *ad* 82—5—22, 46, 9 (kakkab)

DIL-GAN ina maš-qa-šu izziz, when Dilgan (= *virgo*) stands at its top, summit); šušqūtu & these 4:

šāqū *2.* (§ 65, 7 & 8), *f* šāqū(i)tu (§§ 37*a*; 76); *gen* šāqī, šāqē (§§ 30; 66). AV 8028. *a*) high }hoch}. Anp ii 105 kîma ubān (*var* u-ba-an) šadi-e ša-qi (or -kin) see KB ii 88/89. Lay 51 *no* 1, 2 ubān šadi-e ša-qi-tu iç-ba-tu; TP III *Ann* 33. TP iii 43 (47) šadē ša-qu-ti; ii 41 (iii 68) gisallat šadi-i ša-qu(-u)-ti, the peaks of the high mountains; iii 18 (22), 37 (42); I 28 *a* 12; SMITH, *Asurb*, 68, 61 (KB ii 170 *rm*); Asurb viii 52 see xuršu (341, 342). Sn iii 77 a-na zuq-ti (see *p* 292 *col* 2) ša-qu-te. — *b*) high, lofty, grand, exalted }hoch, erhaben, ausgezeichnet}. TP i 6 Sin .... ša-qu-u namrîri; Šalm, *Ob*, 6 (nam-ri-ri); SCHEIL, *Šalm*, 2/3; I 27 *no* 1, 4—5. Šalm, *Balaw*, V 5 ša-ki-e šûtu, KB i 136/7 *rm*. I 35 *no* 2, 1 to Nebo ṭa-pi-ni ša-ki-e; Rm III 105, 1 Nabû ša-ki-i e-til-l[am], WINCKLER, *Forsch.*, i 254. IV^2 54 *b* 31 o Bêl, be-lum ša-qu-u; L^5 1. H 80, 30 be-lum man-za-zu ša-qu-u (Br 436). BANKS, *Diss*, 24/6, 88 nap-tan(-nu) ša-qu (*var* ku)-u. ZIMMERN, *Ritualtafeln*, 68, 31 e-til-lum ša-qi ina šamê. — *f* of Ištar; ZA v 66 (81—2—4, 188) 5 [ilāni] ša-qu-tu; 19 ša-qu-tu malkat. KB ii 250, 27 am-xur [ša?]-qu-ti Iš-tar, ich ging die erhabene Ištar an; 58 il-si-ka Ištar ša-qu-ut (*var* qut) ilāni (§ 68), es sagte zu dir Ištar, die erhabene unter den Göttern; K 2652 *R* 53. K 7673, 14 te-li-tum-ma na-mir-tu šaq[-qu-tu]; 81—6—7, 209, 6 ša-qu-ti ilāni (BA iii 260, 261). H 129 (K 257) *R* 25 .... par(bir?)-ku ša-qu-tum ana-ku ša-qu-tum na-mir[-tum] ana-ku, the lofty .... I am, the lofty one, the glowing one, I am; 127 *O* 58 e-mu-qa-a-a ša-qa-tu, my exalted power; 62 [tal-lak-tum] ša-qu-tum er-çi-tam (= tu) gam-rat, my mighty pace fills the earth (BA i 463). See J.D.PRINCE, JAOS xxiv ('03) 103—28 on this text. S 6 + S 2 *O* 5 ... i-li bêltu ša-qu-ti, *Rev. Sém.* '98, 142 *foll* (a hymn to Ištar). K 3464, 22 ša-qu-tum .... Ištar, CRAIG, *Relig. Texts*, *pl* 66. *Rec. Trav.*, xx 205 *foll* (*no* XLI) i 8 i-lat i-la-a-ti ša-qut bêlêti. — *pl* V 51 *b* 32 ilāni ša-qu-tu ša šamê u erçitim, Br 436. ZIMMERN, *Ritualt.*, 26 iii 47 (ilat) Dam-ki-na belit ilāni ša-qu-tu. *f* BANKS, *Diss*, 18 *foll*, *no* 2, 76 i-dan ša-qa-a-tu. — *c*) loud, of voice }laut, von Stimme} ‖ elû. II 30 *a-b* 10 KA-SUD-GA = a-ma-tum ša-qu-tum, Br 728, 7606.

V 36 *d-f* 19 (u-mun) ⟨ = ša-qu-u, preceded by kab-tum (18) & ru-bu-u (17); V 37 *a-c* 29, 30 with gloss ga-ša-an (= id) for bêlu): ša-qu-u & ša-qu-tum. Br 6994, 6995.

NOTE. — NE 24, 4 (= V *col* 1) ša-qi (or -kin?) kib-su see KB vi (1) 160—1; 448.

šāqū *3.* *n* magnate, high dignitary }Magnat, hoher Würdenträger} Sm 61, 6 nadanu ša šarri tu-ub-bu (= ṭubbu) ša ša-ki-i (= ŠU-KA-GAB, Br 7008), D 134 C; D^H 26; HOMMEL, *Sum. Lesest.*, 118 secretary of state }Minister}; KING: ruler; KNUDTZON, a high officer in the army; § 9, 181. (amêl) SAG, KNUDTZON, 108, 15 & often; K 1359, 55 (amêl) SAG-MEŠ; *b* 48 (amêl) SAG; Nabd 170, 2 see šaku. — III 41 *a* 11 (end) (amêl) SAG-šarri, the king's general }der Königsoberste} AV 8033; K 686 *O* 5 (amêl) rab-SAG un-qi šarri (Hr^L 173), keeper of the (great) seal. — Another high officer is the (amêl) šaq-šup(b)-p(b)ar, written LU (or, AMÊL)-SAG-RU-MAŠ. I 66 *no* 2 *b* 10 *B* mâr *N* (amêl) šaq-šup-par (=⤚), mentioned together with the ša-kin of Išin (7); (amêl) šaq, Meru ša ṭe-mi & bêl paxâti (KB iv 66, 67). III 43 *a* 30 *E* (amêl) šaq-šup-par ša mātāti; *b* 6 *B* mâr (amêl) šaq-šup-par (KB iv 70, 71 a P. N.; but *cf* BELSER, BA ii) ša ṭe-mi ša mātāti; edge of *col* iv 4, *M* (amêl) šaq-šup-par ša bît A-da. KB iv 90, 48 *N* šaq-šub-bar, preceded by (amêl) šaq. The same component parts, only reversed in their order, are in the other title (amêl) šu-par-šaq = šupar šāqū, *pl* šuparšāqē (G § 33 high officer; connected with šaparu; WINCKLER, *Forsch.*, i 476); rendered usually: general, commander. IV^2 48 *b* 7 um-ma-an u šu-par-šaq, the army & the commander. KB ii 4, 7 (amêl) šu-par-šāqi-ja ina mux-xi aš-kun, my general I placed over (them). II 67, 30 (37) (amêl) šu-par-šâqi-ja bêl paxâti eli-šu-nu aš-kun, my general I placed over them as governor; 66 (amêl) šu-par-šâqi-ja (amêl) rab-šaq (= רַב־שָׁקֵה) I sent to Tyre, *i. e.*, my general, who was also the rab-šâqû. TP III *Ann* 50 (amêl) šu-par-šâqi-ja (amêl) bêl paxâti eli-šu-nu aš-kun. Sarg *Cyl* 16 (amêl) šu-par-šâqê-šu (amêl) šak-nu-ti eli-šu-nu iš-tak-ka-nu-ma, his general he placed over them as governors (KB ii 40, 41); *bronce* 28; *bull* 20; Pp i 20; iii 20; WINCKLER, *Sargon*, 231 *col* 2. K 2729, 7 *Asurb* who turns with favor to his (amêl) šu-par-šâqê *pl* man-za-az pâni-šu; Asurb i 128; ii 15. On the basis of this reading ANDREAS in MARTI, *Gramm. Bibl. Aram.*, *p* 53* emends Ezra 4, 9; 5, 6 אפרסכיא into אספרכיא; STRECK, ZA xv 394. See also šu-tam-šaq & šu-tum-šaq.

šâqiš, *adv* to šâqû, 2. KB vi (1) 98, 99 *l* 4 Anu ana ep-šit of Ea ša-qiš i-çi-ix-ma ..., was highly (greatly) astounded at the deed of Ea. Sn *Kui* 4, 16 cedars which ša-qiš na-an-zu-zu, were placed loftily, POGNON, *Wadi-Brissa*, 110. S 954 *O* 36 (= D 135) ana-ku ša-ki-iš al-lik, Br 436, AJSL xix 220. IV² 15 *b* 5, 6 ana šamê ša-qiš (*var* ki-eš) iš-du-du-u-ma, *etc.* Neb iv 34 such & such ša-qi-iš e-pu-uš; + 48; viii 57 (AV 4418, 7812).

šîqu *2.* highland {Hochland} ✕ lowland. MEISSNER, 48, 9 land ina ši-ki-im u iš-di-im. Also see K 5414 *a* (BEZOLD, *Catalogue*, 714) & *cf* šubultu, 2.

šaqû 4. pr išqi(u), ps išaqqi, ip šiqi water, give to drink {tränken} w. double *acc.* (§ 130). G § 103 (*p* 94). — ac šu-qi-e, KNUDTZON, 144, 7; 145, 2. II 30 *a-b* 11 NAG = ša-qu-u ša A (= mê) Br 548, 837; H 11 & 216, 79; II 30 *a-b* 12—15 TAG (Br 5281); (di-e) [illegible] (Br 6730, H 25, 510); A-DUG-GA (Br 11406); A-DE-A (Br 11565) = ša-qu-u ša eqli, irrigate a field. II 30 *a-b* 16, 17 [illegible]-SE & SE-BAL (Br 798, 799, 4424, 4432) = ša-qu-u ša im-ti, poison some one. — pr KB vi (1) 138—9, 31 (= NE II *col* 3 *b*) ku-ru-un-na iš-ku (*var* qu)-ka. T^M i 104 iš-qu-in-ni, did give me to drink. Sn *Bav* 8 Nineveh's pastures aš-qu-ma. KNUDTZON, 336 on *no* 146 (*pp* 263—4), 6 û-um iš-qa-a; 144 *R* 9 NAG (= išqâ)-ma. — pc Xammurabi-*code* xliv 11 da-mi-šu-nu er-çi-tam li-iš-qi, may he drench the ground with their blood. — ps K 492, 13 ni-ša-aq-qi (Hr^L 3) we will give water to ....; H 72, 33 eqla mê i-ša-aq-ki (id of II 30, 13); also 73, 11 (II 15 *c-d* 28), he irrigates the field. — ip IV² 26 *b* 39, 40 mê ellûti ši-ki-šu-ma, pure water give him to drink! (Br 872).

Q^t = Q KB vi (1) 188—9 (NE VII *col* 4) 40 (45) iš-taq-q[u-u] *var* it-taq-qu-u mê na-da-a-te. K 2401 iii 2 mê zar-za-ri ta-si-qi-šu-nu (also see çarçaru, 2; 896 *col* 2).

J drench, wet freely & thoroughly {reichlich tränken}. Esh vi 40 šaman rêšti ..... mux-xa-šu-nu (see *pp* 518, 519) u-ša-qi (1 *sg*) ‖ III 16 vi (*f*) 2 u-ša-aš-qi (I caused to drench). K 161, 14 tu-ša-qa, ZK ii 9.

Š causative of Q. Sn *Kui* 4, 42 (Lay 42, 51 & see dilûtu, 251 *col* 2) u-ša-aš-qa-a (1 *sg*) mux-xa-šin (*var* ši-in). Sarg *Cyl* 37 the city's commons kî gibiš edê mê nuxši šu-uš-qi-e (= ac), to irrigate with abundant water like the flood of the sea, LYON, *Sargon*, 67; KB ii 45. Xamm.-*code* iv 4 mu-še-eš-ki nu-ux-ši-im a-na Šidlam, who poured out abundance (HARPER, 6—7); ZA xviii 24.

Derr. — mašqû, mašqîtu (608 *col* 2) & these 7:

šâqû *5.* II 31 *u* 34 (amêl) rab šâqû (written LU-GAL-SAG, Br 12091); 35, (amêl) šâqê (written LU-SAG-MEŠ), explained by ZIMMERN, ZDMG 53, 118/19; KAT³ 273 *rm* 3; 651 as chief cup-bearer {Obermundschenk}. He also explains as š'â'qû the ŠU-QA-GAB, II 31 *u* 29. K 2729 *O* 11 (amêl) rab-šaq, + 28; *R* 19, 20 (KB iv 143, 145: general); K 7, 5; K 1359, 10 (amêl) rab-šâqê, Šamaš ii 17. II 52 *c-d* 19 (+ Rm 81); 83—1—18, 47 *R* 10 (Br 6860, 12992; AV 7446). 82—5—22, 169 *R* 9 ina mât (amêl) rab-ša-ki-e, AJSL xiii 211. See also K 11437 (KNUDTZON, *no* 118; see *ibid* 317). — D^H 13 general {Oberbefehlshaber}; §§ 9, 131; 46; 72*a*. JOHNS, *Doomsdaybook*, 53. STRECK, ZA xiii 61 *rm* 2:

rabšaq ein unter dem Turtan, dem assyrischen Generalissimus, stehender höherer Offizier.

šaqū, in (karpat) šaqū. Rm 113 *O* 9 ina eli (karpat) [or karpat?] ša-ku-u qāt-su liš-kun, & 11. V 42 *c* 27, 28 karpat ša-ku-u; karpat ša-ku-u TUR-RA (= çixru); perh. Neb 90, 15.

šuqqū. II 22 *c-d* 62 BU-BU-I = šu-uq-qu-u ‖ a-la-mi[-tum] & ni-ip-r[u?], Br 7581, AV 8553.

(amēl) **šaqqā**. Camb 197, 3/4 (amēl) ša-aq-qa-a-a, the irrigator {der Bewässerer} BA iii 488; perhaps also Nabd 237, 5 + 13 šaq-qa-a-a.

šīqu *3*. watering, irrigation {Tränkung, Bewässerung}. II 48 *e-f* 37 A-LAL-A-AK-DA = ši-qi na-a-ri; yet rather ši-kin, see šiknu *d*. Sn *Bav* 7 the inhabitants of Nineveh mē ši-qi la i-da-a, did not find water to drink.

šiqīnu, II 22 *d-f* 22 DUK ŠAP-TUR = ši-qi-nu ‖ xubunnu (302 *col* 1), AV 8195, Br 5677; BA i 635: niedrige, flache Schale, Napf.

šiqītum *1*. ‖ šīqu, 3. S^b 91 di-e (*var* -im)  | ši-ki-tum (§ 65, 9; Br 6731) *var* but not ‖ si-si-tum. II 47 *c-d* 14 ān ši-ki-tum ‖ zu-ri-qa-a-ti, AV 8197, Br 9380. Xamm.-*code* xv 33 if a man open his canal (a-tap-pa-šu) a-na ši-qi-tim (for irrigation purposes). H 25, 511.

šiqbu see šikbu.

šaqbītu see šaqqaštu & risbītu.

šaqalu. pr išqul, *pl* iš-ku(qu)-lu, § 19; ps išaq(q)al (§ 53a). id LAL, § 9, 205, Br 10110. hang up {aufhängen}, then: balance, weigh, weigh out, pay {wägen, darwägen, zahlen} whence, Hebr שָׁקַל, KAT³ 649; ‖ çamadu (*ibid* 339). Hincks, ZDMG 10, 517; Prätorius, *ibid*, 32, 21 *foll*; H^F 7; G § 98; Barth, ZA ii 377—87 (see also madadu). S^b 144 la-al LAL | ša-qa-lu. PSBA xix 280, 8 aš-ku-ul a-xa-a-ta kaspi, I have weighed the rest of the silver. II 16 *d* 40 kaspu ta-ša-qal; 9 *b* 46 [i]-šaq-qal; 15 *a-b* 33—35 see manaxtu (562, 563). V 25 *a-b* 12 half a mina of silver i-šaq-qal (= NI-LAL-E), he will pay. 82, 7—14, 804 *col* 3 *a-b* 14 see seššu (785 *col* 2, below). KB iv 50 *no* 2, 7—8 after 4 months i-ša-qal šu-ma la iš-qul (he will pay; but if he have not paid); *no* 3, 10—11 i-ša-qal šu-ma la iš-ku-ul; 54 *no* 7, 19: twenty minas of money i-ša-ku-lu-šu, they will pay him. Nabd 760, 9 i-šaq-qi-lu-ma (or isaqqilu > ištaqqilu?). — pm K 3182 i 22 kip-pat mātāte ina ki-rib šamē šaq-la-a-ta, thou art suspended, AJSL xvii 135. AV 8023.

H 64/65 (V 29, 21—26) 21—26: NI-LAL = iš-qul; NI-LAL-E = i-šaq-qal; NI-LAL-E-MEŠ = i-šaq-qa-lu; IN-NA-AN-LAL = iš-qul; IN-NA-AN-LAL-E = i-šaq-qal; IN-NA-AN-LAL-E-MEŠ = i-šaq-qa-lu(lum); 34—37: AZAG-LAL(-E) = kas-pu iš-qul (i-šaq-qal); AZAG-LAL-E-MEŠ = kaspu i-šaq-qa-lum; NU-AZAG-LAL = kaspu ul iš-qul. K 4158, 1 *foll*. H 59, 34 (i-ša-qal). H 47 ii 1—8 (= D 91, ii 1—8) iš-ku-ul; iš-ku-lu; i-ša-gal; i-ša-qa-lu; iš-ku-ul[-šu]; iš-ku-lu-šu; i-ša-gal-šu; i-ša-ga-lu-šu. Ungnad, ZA xviii 32 šaqalu ina = zahlen für was man erhalten resp. getan hat; šaqalu ana = zahlen um etwas zu erhalten.

Q^t balance, be equal {sich das Gleichgewicht halten} ZA i 456; Jensen, 68. III 51 *no* 1 (K 15) 1—3 (*no* 2, 3) on the sixth (& 15th) of Nisan ū-mu u mu-ši šit-qu-lu, were in balance (of equal length?). III 58, 5 see Thompson, *Reports*, ii *pref* xxvi & *p* 131 *col* 2. Scheil, *Rec. Trav.*, xviii 74 (Cappadocian text): 7½ minas of silver iš-ta-ki-el, he paid.

𝔍 K 625 (Hr^L 131) *R* 6 u-ša-qal-na-ši-ni (the king will pay us).

Š^t Xammurabi-*letters* 30, 14—15 ja-ti kaspu ga-am-ra-am ēkallu uš-tu-aš-ki-la-a[n-ni], but the palace(-authorities) made me pay the whole amount.

𝔑 perh. IV² 28* *no* 4 *b* 44 a-lum ša .... ud-di-tum (Thureau-Dangin, *Rec. Crit.*, '04, *no* 8: le sol, le fond) iš-šaq-lu-šu.

Derr. šitqultu & the following 6:

šaqīlu *1*. *n* ⊕ 287 *R* vi 10. 11 GIŠ-SAG(K)-G(K)UL-NUM-MA-KI (= mu-tir-ru), GIŠ-SAG(K)-G(K)UL-LAL = sikkur ša-ki-li, Br 9034, 10130; 3547—8; AV 6655. part of a door; bolt? in the shape of weights? {Riegel?}; compare the gloss ša-kil, H 26, 543 = me-di-lu ša dalti; II 33 *a-b* 9, 10.

šaqīlu *2. adj f* šaqīltu. paid {bezahlt} AV 7807; Br 9817; see šibru, 1.

šiqlu *1.* shekel {Sekel}. ið TU, often in *c. t.* § 9, 37; Br 11913; KAT³ 339; 649; ZA vii 20 gi-e | TU | ši-iq-li; MEISSNER, 93; LEHMANN, *Berliner Anthropol. Gesellschaft*, '91, 518 *rm* 1. See OPPERT, ZA iii 122 *no* 4 on šiqlu & its subdivisions. Rm 2, 588 *O* 26 *b-c* (di-e) TU = ši-iq-lam. Also in T. A.

šuqlu. PSBA xix 289, 10—11 šu-ku-ul XX ma-na-um, the payment of 20 minas, PINCHES. *cf* šu-qul D 87 i 51.

šuqultu. weight {Gewicht}? BA i 508; 633. V 41 *a-b* 58 KI-LAL = sanaqu ša šu-qul-ti, Br 9815; JASTROW, HEBR. iv 246; ZA iv 264; also LAL-KI *var* to šu-qul-tu, VATh 204, PEISER, KAS 92. ið KI-LAL & LAL-KI often in *c. t.*, see T^C 81; 89. KI-LAL-BI-šu-nu Cyr 161, 33 & 37; Nabd 116, 23 & 25; 490, 1 (šu-qul-tum); 948, 7; 1052, 3; Cyr 57, 1; Camb 331, 4 ša 7½ ma-na šu-qul-ta-šu-nu, whose weight was 7½ minas. Asb ii 42 (KB ii 168 *rm* 5); Šalm, *Mon*, ii 75 ša KI-LAL-šu; Anp iii 66; 75.

šaqallatum. Nabd 867, 3: three ša-qal-la-a-tum parzilli, KB iv 248, 249. See, also, šagallatum, 1010 *col* 1.

šaq-qul-lum, Br 8046 see sakkullu, 756 *col* 2 & add ZA i 191.

šiqlu *2.* 82—5—22, 63 *O* 4—6 ab-qal-lu ši-iq-la (il) Bēl ri-mi-nu-u qar-rad (il) Marduk ina mūši i-zu-uz-ma. THOMPSON, *Reports*, ii *no* 170 (*pref* lxii): the Abqallu šiqla 'Bēl-riminū-qar-rad-Marduk' stopped last night. *ibid pp* xviii, xix: abqallu šiqla means measure-governor, and it is probable that the words indicate the existence of a kind of clock. See also šiklu.

šuqalulu (a form like šuparruru, šu-gammumu). *pr* ušqalal; *pm* šuqa-lulu; AV 8390, 8547. § 117, 2 be suspended, hanging {hängen, schweben}. ZK ii 158; G § 23; BA i 159. S^b 145 la-al | LAL | šu-qa-lu-lu (preceded by šaqalu); H 32, 746, Br 10132. V 20 *a-b* 14 ID-DA-LAL = šu-qal-lu-lu, AV 8001, 8390. *pm* Anp iii 51 the city like a cloud from heaven šu-qa-lu-la; Šamš ii 48 (3 *pl f*); Šalm, *Mon*, ii 70 ubānu (a mountain-peak) which like a cloud from heaven šu-qal-lu-la-at, KB i 168, 169 (hung suspended). Anp i 62 šu-qa-lu-la & *var* šu-qu-lu-lat. K 2148 ii 16 ina pi-šu mu-u šu-q(g?)al-lu-lu-ni (or נגלל? see 219 *col* 1). Also KB vi (1) 104 *b* 6. *pr* uš-qa-lal III 65 *b* 44—46 see kursinnu (440 *col* 1) & MARTIN, *Rec. Trav.*, xxiv 230.

šuqullānu (?). Camb 330, 6—7 a-ra-an-nu qanu-u šu-qul-la-a-na (BA iii 463 *foll*); or, šu-qul-la a-na *etc.*

šaqaltu, šiqiltu, see below, after ša-qašu.

šaqummu, *adj* quiet, still; fixed, motionless {still, ruhig; starr, regungslos} JENSEN, KB vi (1) 354, 355; *f* šaqummatu, AV 8029, 8030 used as a *n*: quiet, sti(ll)ffness, torpidity} *etc.* § 65. 23 & others: miserable, in misery {leidvoll}; šaqummatu misery {Leid, Wehe}. HOMMEL, *Sum. Les.*, 3 *no* 127: properly: sand, sandstorm; ið SIG (which = pašaxu). IV² 1* v 23, 24 see nāgiru (644 *col* 2) & Br 5589, ið PA(=SIG)-GA; Z^B 27; 56 originally stormwind; then, mourning, anguish. II 21 *a-b* 17 su-qu ša-qu-um-mu, KB vi (1) 355: the quiet street in the kingdom of the dead, Br 14180; 15, 16 = ša-qu(&qum)-ma-tum, Br 14181, iðð ending in -GA, thus probably SIG-GA. H 11 & 217, 85, Br 825. IV² 20 *no* 1 (K 4444) 3, 4 the interior of the town, the surroundings of the town, field and heights ša-qu-um-ma-tu ušamlima (3 pr) ušālika namūeš (also *cf* H 39, 128). WINCKLER, *Forsch.*, i 537/9; MARTIN, *Rec. Trav.*, xxiv *pts* 1/2. 81—7—1, 98 i 5/6 et-lu ša ina šim-ti-šu ša-qu-um-ma-tu rak-sa-at, PINCHES, *Jour. Trans. Vict. Inst.*, xxvi 153. Asb iii 3 a distance of 15 days (in area) I devastated & ša-qu-um-ma-tu at-bu-uk (KB ii 178, 179; JENSEN, 424); SMITH, *Asurb*, 92, 51/2 (KB ii 242, 243) = III 19, 60. III 38 *no* 1, *O* 43 ša-qu-um-ma-tu u-mal-li (1 *sg*). KB vi (1) 36—7, 27 mu-šat[-bu-u ša-qum-ma-tu], der das Schweigen aufstehen lässt. II 38 *g-h* 24 (Br 5625) see šaxarratu; & also V 20 *e-f* 54. II 55, 20. S^b 284 še-ig | ið | ša-qu-um-ma-tu, Br 899. *Adv:*

šaqummeš. quietly, silently {leise, lautlos} JENSEN, KB vi (1) 334. IV^2 5 *b* 20, 21 Sin .... iddalixma ša-qu-um-meš (= PA-PA-GA-BI) i-me, Br 5589. IV^2 30* *no* 3 *O* 16 see šêlibu. ZA iv 231, 26 ša-qu-um-meš ramû ana. ZIMMERN, *Ritualt.*, *no* 11, 21 i-ra-muk .... ša-qu-um-meš. 81—7—1, 98 i 1/2 et-lu ša ina su-qu ša-qu-um-meš ..... pâni-šu it-ta-na-aš-ša-bu (√ašabu). A ‖ is:

šaqumme. ZIMMERN, *Ritualt.*, *no* 100, 10 i-ra-muk ..... ša-qu-um-me & *ibid* *rm* 2 + 13.

šuqamumu 1., ps ušqamam. IV^2 18 *no* 3 *b* 58 ina mu-ši ma-ši-il (see 605 *col* 2) bîtu ina šu-qa-mu[-mi?], KB vi (1) 354 at midnight when the house is dark (or, quiet?), Br 5591. IV^2 30 *no* 1 *R* 5, 6 see šisîtu (Br 8432, MU-UN-SI-SI-EŠ, EME-SAL) = H 125 *R* 15/16. REISNER, *Hymnen*, 49, 17 axulap bîtu utullašu uš-qa-am-ma-mu (= AL-SI) rê'ušu ušxarar, 80, 5 ša uš-qa-am-ma[-mu] = BA-SI-SI .... M^S 97 *col* 2. II 21 *a-b* 18 ..... ŠUR | šu-qam(or gam?)-mu-mu ša û-me (day? or, storm?), AV 8391, Br 2990. See also S^c 5 *a* 3.

šuqamumu *2.*, *adj*? II 44 *c-d* 8 SI-DI = šu-qa-mu-mu, Br 3465, AV 8548.

šaqummu *2.* V 28 *a-b* 5 ša-qum(lam?)-ma (*c-d* 54) ‖ of lamxuššu (486 *col* 2).

šuqamuna, in P. N. Šu-qa-mu-na-axi-iddin-na, III 48 *b* 23 (BA ii 116 *foll*; KB iv 68 *foll*). KB iv 60 *col* 4, 3; 81—11—3, 111 *O* 13 (il) Šu-qa-mu-nu = Marduk ša pi-sa-an-nu, *Jour. Trans. Vict. Inst.*, xxvii 8/9. V 33 *a* 4 Agumkakrine, the lofty offspring of (il) Šu-qa-mu-nu (JENSEN, KB iii (1) 136 *rm* ** = the Assyrian Nergal; D^K 25, 27 *fol*). Against SCHEFTELOWITZ etymology (KUHN's *Zeitschrift*, xxxviii 260 *foll*) see BLOOMFIELD, AJP xxv 4. V 44 *a-b* 35 ME-LI-ŠU-MU = amêl (il) Šu-qa-mu-na. Z^B ii 130.

šaqapu, set up, plant (AV 8024) whence išqup, ašqup, see zaqapu (289, 290).

šaqaçu. pm IV^2 56 *a* 5 & *add* xa-an-šu il-tum .... ša pa-nu-ša šaq-çu; ZA xvi 154 *foll*: whose countenance is terrible; see also šagaçu. K 12846, 6 ša-ka-çu, M^S *pl* 17, left column broken off; 82—9—18, 4156 *O* 21 ša-qa-çu, M^S *pl* 39; GGA '98, 826.

Derr. these 2:

šaqçu. *adj* K 2022 (II 29 *e-f*) i 7 šaq-çu, preceded by aq-çu. K 1349, 7.

šiqçu. *n* sickness, disease; impurity {Krankheit; Unreinigkeit} = שקץ, AV 8207; D^{Pr} 85. III 65 *b* 10, 11 see xalû, 2 (312 *col* 2). II 48 *d-e* 19 ši-iq-çu = mur-çu.

šaqaru 1. (ZDMG 40, 725) whence taš-qirtu, *q. v.*

šaqaru 2. AV 8025 whence apparently such forms as išqur, littašqar V 35, 35 (§ 142), & ušašqir (see also Br 9416) see saqaru (782 *col* 2) & zakaru (279, 280).

šûquru *1.* *ac & pm of* Š *of* aqaru, eqeru be precious *etc.* (90 *col* 1). IV^2 60* C *O* 10 šu-mi (ilat) Iš-tar šu-qu-ru; B *O* 30 šu-qur. I 7 *E* 5 the ašnan-stone which at the time of my ancestors .... šu-qu-ru (*var* aq-ru), was held precious. NE 57, 39 šu-ut-tum šu-qu-rat (3 *f*). A derivative of the same verb is:

šûquru *2.* *adj* valuable, weighty, costly, precious {wertvoll, kostbar} ‖ aqru, AV 8434, 8552. ZK ii 343. Neb ii 32 mi-im-ma šu-um-šu šu-ku-ru, all kind of costly things; viii 11; *Bab* i 26. Anp i 86 aban šade-e šu-qu-ru; iii 21; see also ZA v 67, 37 (& *p* 74 *ibid*). V 63 *a* 15 a-na šu-mi-šu-nu šu-qu-ru, for the sake of their lofty name. V 65 *b* 33 see šipru; *b* 21 li-pit(-ti) ga-ti-ja šu-qu-ru. Sp II 265 *a* xv 10 aš-ša-ru ša ṭe-en(?)-ga šu-qu-ru. K 3364 *O* 4 see DELITZSCH, *Weltschöpfungsepos*, 54. SCHEIL, *Nabd*, x 32, 33 (aban) aš-pu-u šu-qu-ru aban šarrû-tu. *pl* Neb *Bab* i 24 with silver, gold, ni-se-iq-tim TAG-TAG (= abnê) šu-qu-ru-u-tim. Neb ii 30 (šu-ku-ru-ti); *cf* V 64 *b* 1 & 62. V 62 *no* 2, 21 par-çi-šu-nu (836 *col* 2) šu-qu-ru-tu (= KAL-KAL, Br 7186). V 63 *a* 22 i-gi-si-e šu-qu-ru-ti. V 34 *b* 44 ka-la e-ep-še-e-ti-ja šu-qu-ra-a-tim, all my precious deeds. Xamm.-*code* xl 74 a-qa-ti-ja šu-ku-ra-tim, my weighty words (xli 13). See also ZA ii 140 *a* 18; 388, 30. V 40 *g-h* 10 (Br 8444). Here also šugurû, *q. v.*

šûqurûtu. treasure {Schatz}. √aqaru. 81—6—7, 209 (dupl. K 6346) 29 the offspring of Ašur šu-qu-ru-tim šarru-u-tu, the treasure of the kingdom, epithet of Esarh. BA iii 262—3.

šu-uq-qur, III 60, 84 see naqaru, $\overset{x}{\supset}$ (720 *col* 2).

šaq(g)ašu, pr išq(g)iš, *ps* išaqq(gg)iš, ip šiqiš, destroy, ruin, slay }zerstören, vernichten, erschlagen} AV 7713, 7806. BALL, PSBA xii 278. — pr aš-gi-iš za-ma-nu, KB iii (2) 76, 37. Šalm, *Balaw*, III 2 (mât) Ku-ti-e rapal-tu ki (11) Dibbar-ra aš-gi-iš(giš). aš-giš Sarg *Ann* XIV 8. NE 137, 72 & *rm* 14. *del* 68 (72) aš-gi-i[š], KB vi (1) 234; 490. — pc KB vi (1) 72—3, 24 liš-gi-šu (11) si-bittišunu; *del* 175 (194) end: liš-giš, BA i 139. KB iv 84 ii 5 (Nergal) i-na taxâzi-šu liš-gi-is-su. — ip Rm 673 *c* 37 ši-gi-iš la ma-gi-ri (KB iii, 2, 66). — *ps* ZIMMERN, *Ritualtafeln*, 67 *R* 2 i-ša-qi-ši šapta-ša i-na-šik(q?). IV² 54 *b* 7 see gamalu, ip (221 *col* 2). — *ag* TP i 11 Ninib ša-giš lim-ni u a-a-bi; Sarg *Cyl* 30 (Sargon) ša-a-giš niši (mât) Xar-xar; Pp iv 20; K^{M} 21, 43. Anp i 34 Anp ša-giš š(a)lâni u xuršâni; iii 131. Esh *Sendsch* 24 ša-giš da-ad-me na-ki-ri-e-šu. V 35, 7 (end) [ša]-qi-še a-šu-uš-šu, BA ii 208, 209. KB iii (1) 114, 115 *l* 7 (Xammurabi) ša-qi-iš a-a-bi, Br 386. — *ac* IV² 16 *no* 2 *O* (K 1283) 6, 8 e-k(d?)im-mu lim-nu ina çi-rim i-ku-uš-ma ša-ga-ša (Br 8071) ....; gal-lu-u lim-nu ina šli i-da-al a-na ša-ga-aš (= GAZ-AG-A, Br 4730) ni-ši ul .... (T^{M} 127, 128). P. N. ša-ga-še-A-šur-na-da, KB iv 52 (v) 14. V 17 *c-d* 35—40 ša-ka-šum (*d*; § 19; ZK i 124; H 169 § 13) = 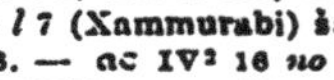-KIT, GIŠ-XAŠ-AG-A, GIŠ-GAZ, GIŠ-GAZ-AG-A, KA(gu-ug)KA, KA-KAK-KAK (Br 1220, 386, 4731, 661, 663).

 K 4335 i 23 ..... AB-TUK = šu-ug-gu-šu, AV 8398, Br 14035. SCHEIL, *Rec. Trav.*, xvii 84 lu-šag-giš, je saccagerai.

NOTE. — si-gi-še = ni-qu-u, S^{b} 165 perhaps from šaqašu.

Derr. mašqašu (608 *col* 2), šigûšu (?) & these 7 (?):

šaqšu. destoyer, slayer, murderer }Zerstörer, Totschläger}. V 50 *a* 31, 32 see xablu (301 *col* 1), Br 8080. A ‖ is:

šaggišu, § 65, 27. I 65 *b* 3 that no li-im-num u ša-ag-gi-šu approach Babylon. JAOS xvi 73—5, 8 li-im-nim u ša-ag-gi-šum, ZA i 339; KB iii (2) 64, 65.

š(s)ag-ga-ša-a NE I *col* iv 7 (KB vi, 1, 126); ZIMMERN, *Rituall.*, 45 i 11 lu šag-ga-šu (Hinschlachter, meaning the demon of pestilence) lu šib(p)-ṭu.

šiqšu. destruction }Zerstörung}. V 17 *c-d* 41—43 GIŠ-AD-UŠ, GIŠ-DIM-KAK-KAK (also = maxrašu), GIŠ-KA-LIBIT (Br 4179, 2755, 769) = ši-iq-šum, between ša-ka-šum & maš-ga-šu. AV 8210. A ‖ is:

šagaltu (> šaqaštu) AV 7710. TP iv 89—91 see rixiç(l)tu.

šaqqaštu (šaggaštu). murderess }Mörderin} Z^{Š} 58 "pestilence" personified. AV 7826. IV² 7 *a* 42, 43 lû arrat abišu lû arrat ummišu ... lû ar-rat šaq-qaš-te (*var* ti) ša amêlu lâ idû = Z^{Š} v/vi 47, 49; ideogr. KI-LUL, Br 9781 (šakbitu). II 36 *a-b* 4 ŠA-BIR (Br 8507, 12120) = šaq-qaš-tum, between d(ṭ)i-xu & mu-ta-nu. While JENSEN's reading ris-bîtu (*q. v.*) would suit all the passages quoted (see also ZA ii 293), we have, on the other hand, KB iv 60 *col* 4, 2 (11) Nergal i-na ša-ga-aš-ti & perhaps 83—1—18, 200, 4: when Jupiter stands in the "brilliance of Pabilsag", there will be destructions (šag-ga-ša-a-ti) in the land, THOMPSON, *Reports*, ii *no* 190.

šigiltu ‖ šaqaštu. Merod.-Balad.-stone iii 16, 17 ša çâbu nakru (the enemy) ina ši-qil-ti it-ba-lu-ma, KB iii (1) 188, 189; BA ii 262, 263; 269 shedding of blood }Blutvergiessen}. K 3615 *O* 1 ina še-qil-ti (?). — Perhaps also ZA iv 261, 15—16 & 264 eqil še-qil(KB iv 172 -rim)-ti (??).

šaqâtu. Esh iv 29 because the xazânâti ša-qa-a-tu id-ku-šu-nu-ti; ZA xvii 242, 243: absolut unverständlich!

šiqîtum *2.* a precious stone. II 40 *c-d* 10 + II 37 *g-h* 62 ši-qi[-tum]. AV 7080, Br 8108. See xandammu (326 *col* 1). Perh. √šaqû, 1.

šuqtu (§ 62, 1), šuqtiš see pattu, 1 & pattiš. ~ šuqtû see pattû. ~ šuqtâte TP vi 81 see pattu(û), *pl* pattûte, *p* 853 *cols* 1, 2. ~ šuquttu (G § 72) see šukuttu.

šîru, šēru *1.* (§ 47). meat, flesh {Fleisch} § 65, 2; AV 8312. Hebr שְׁאֵר, poetic for בָּשָׂר. D^H 20; ZDMG 40, 723; ZA ix 194, 28 compares Arb بَشَر. id UZU, § 9, 241; S^b 358; H 9 & 200, 13 ZU = ši-i-ru; Br 170, 4559; *pl* UZU-MEŠ, often in $Z^{\check{s}}$; H 13, 143 BAR = ši-i-ru, Br 1803. — *a*) meat, flesh {Fleisch}. id *pl* Asurb iv 14 (ix 59 without *pl*) see bûru, 4 (188 *col* 1); one might read šir-ri-šu-nu (> širišunu) instead of bu-ri-šu-nu, which rather requires ina instead of ana; see also ix 37; ix 105, 106 see xutnû (348 *col* 1), laxû, 1 (478 *col* 1) & meçu (570 *col* 1). NE 17, 44; 19, 39 see šumû, 1; 58, 12 am-mi-ni xa-mu-u šîru-u-a (KB vi, 1, 165). KB vi (1) 106—7, 24 (*Etana*-legend, K 2527 + K 1547) nu-ru-ub(p) šîri; 36 (end) ik-ka-la ši-i-ra (+ 36). IV^2 1* iv 27, 28 a-kil ši-i-ri, Br 170. V 61 *e* 15 diqâr A *pl* UZU = mē šîri, BA i 274, a pot of bouillon; 23 šēr alpi šēr LU-NITA. VAT2 4105 i 2 (end) i-ik-ka-al ši-ra-am. Bu 91—5—9, 269 *O* 24 i-na ši-ri-šu u da-mi-šu (*i. e.* of the slaughtered god), ZA xiv 181 & KB vi (1) 275 *rm*. ZA x 211, 14 . . . . ši-i-ri : šu-u. II 24 *c-d* 61; also T^M viii 86. — *b*) body, in *pl*: members of the body {Leib, Körper; Körperteile, Glieder}; hence šîr(u) also a determinative before names of parts or members of the human or animal body; see V 61 *e* 10 *foll*; xinçu (326 *col* 2; id perhaps ^(šir) ME-KAN, Zimmern, *Ritualt.*, *p* 95 & *rm* 4), *etc.*; II 40 *e* 5, 6. It also means well-being. Anp i 92 UZU *pl*-šu-nu u-bat-tiq, I cut off their members. Asb iv 74 see nukkusu (673 *col* 1, beg.). TP vii 33 UZU *pl* niši-ja u-ṭi-ib. Neb iv 53 Gula, the goddess, mu-ṭi-ba-at ši-ri-ja, *etc.*, see 380 *col* 1 *b*. KB iii (1) 117, 8; 119, 5 see ṭâbu, 1 (349 *col* 1 *b*); *ibid*, *col* 2 *d* see T. A. B 7 *O* 9; 12, 14 *etc*. Also Br. M. 12215 (Xammurabi-text) ii 5, 6 whose deeds a-na ši-ir ^(il) Šamaš u ^(il) Marduk ṭa-ba. IV^2 1* iii 43, 44 (id ZU, Br 170) see ṭâbu, 2 (351 *col* 1, *med*); also see IV^2 26 *b* 32 ša ana ši-ri (= ZU) la ṭa-ba; 28* *no* 3 *O* 12 lu-ba-di ša UZU *pl*-MU (= ja). III 66 *col* 10, 34—35 bul-ṭa (ip > bulliṭa) ši-ri-a. NE IX *col* 2, 14 he that cometh (to us) šîr ilâni zu-mur-šu (flesh of the gods is his body); X *col* 1, 7 (KB vi, 1, 204 & 210). NE 72, 29 ši-ir-a-ni-ja (my members) nissata um-dal-li, KB vi (1) 227: mein Fleisch. On šēr ku-pu see 421 *col* 1 & qûpu; KB vi (1) 31: Rumpf. On ^(šîr) imittu written ZAG & ZAG-LU, Fleischstück der rechten Seite & wol die rechte Keule, see Zimmern, *Ritualt.*, *p* 95 & *rm* 3; also see ^(šîr) 'š'ilqu (*p* 764 *col* 1) & šilqu. V 47 *a* 37 ^(ic) il-lu-ur-tum ši-ri-ja na-da-a i-da-a-a, & IV^2 60* B *R* 2. ina ṭûb šēri (written UZU) = welfare, health of body see *p* 350 *col* 1 *b*. ZA iv 240, 4 see xinçurru (326 *col* 2); nakasu ša ši-i-ri see 672 *col* 1, below; & naglabu ša šēri *cf* naglabu, 643 *col* 2, above. — *c*) flesh & blood, next of kin {Fleisch und Blut; Blutsverwandter} § 80. V 34 *c* 47 see pir'u (826 *col* 1, below). II 9 *c-d* (K 245 iii) 23 ši-ir-šu (= NU-NU-NE), between bîtu çît libbi & da-mu-šu, Br 1969. II 29 *e-f* 61 see bišru (202 *col* 1); possibly to šerru, *q. v.*

Here perhaps also P. N. Ax-še-e-ri (*var* -ra) Asb ii 126, 133; iii 4, 6 *etc*. ZA xiv 137; & again, *Johns Hopkins Circ.*, Je '84; ZK ii 290 *rm* 3. Also *cf* Knudtzon, *no* 24 *O* 4.

Identical with šîru, flesh is:

šîru *2.* oracle, oracular answer {Orakel, Orakelspruch}. Haupt, AJP xvii 489 *rm* 3: refers, perhaps, originally to the inspection of the intestines of sacrificial victims = *haruspicium*; hence id UZU. H 19, 358; S^b 358 u-zu | UZU | ši-i-ru, Br 4559 & see 4564, têrtu ša šîri; perhaps also H 13, 143, see šîru, 1. Zimmern, *Ritualtafeln*, 89 & *rm* 2. — Notice šîr dunqi: Neb iv 30 ^(il) Šamaš ša-kin šîr dumqi i-na te-ir-ti-ja; I 69 *b* 50, 51 šîr dum-ki u šîr šipri-ja (?) KB iii (2) 84; also KB iii (2) 90, 48. V 63 *b* 5 šîr šik(?)-nu iš-šak-na ina ter-ti-ja; 22/23 šîr dumqi ša e-peš agî (or, parakki?) šu-a-ti ki-ma la-bi-ri-im-ma iš-šak-na in te-ir-ti-ja. — šîr tukulti: I 49 *c* 19, 20 ina ma-kal-ti ^(amêl) XAL (= bâru)-u-ti šîr tu-kul-ti iš-šak-nu-nim-ma, BA iii 220, 221. — šîr tikilti: K 2801 (= K 221 + 2669) *R* 25 ina šîr ti-kil-ti, BA iii 236, 237. — šîr takiltu: III 15 *a* 7 the gods ina an-ni-šu-nu ki-nim šîr ta-kil-tu iš-tap-pa-ru-nim-ma. — IV^2 34 *no* 1 *a* 1 šīr an-ni-i, 7, 13, 36; *b* 5, 12, 16. II 37 *e-f* 67 ši-i-ru pu-ut-tu-u. See also tērtu.

šēru 2. morning, dawn {Morgen, Morgendämmerung} >< lilātu which see (483) for IV^2 54 *b* 32, 41, 50; L^4 iii 9. §§ 29; 32*aγ*; 42; 65, 1 = שַׁחַר. GGN '83, 94 & 102; BA iii 80. Asb x 71 ina ša (*i. e.*, mā'al ša) še-e-ri ba-nu-u e-gir-ru-u-a, Z^B 38; WZKM i 160. T^M vii 143 (*c*) še-e-ru; 144 še-ru-um-ma še[-e-ru amsi qātā]; vii *col* 4, 10 (suppl. by 81, 7—27, 152 *R*) ina še-rim (also viii 68/71) BA iv 162/7. Rm 201, 6 maçartu (H 38, 78) ša še-e-ri ša (mât) Êlamti, Pinches, *Texts*, 2 *no* 4; ZA i 436, 437; Thompson, *Reports*, ii *no* 181. KB vi (1) 238/9 ii 12 i-na še-ri di(??, so Scheil, *Rec. Trav.*, xx 55, 56)-ib-ba-ra li-ša-az-ni-in. III 55 *b* 49 ina še-rim, in the morning (>< ina urru, ina tam-xa-a-ti, 50), K 5641 *R* 4. Zimmern, *Ritualtafeln*, 112, *no* 11, 3 see napaxu Q (705 *col* 2, *med*), also *no* 75—78, 14; 45 iii 8 ina še-rim kîma (il) [Šamaš açē]; 49, 4; 52, 3 ina še-e-ri; 75—78, 65 nap-tan še-rim, Morgenmahlzeit (& 89—90, 17); L^4 iii 9 nap-tan še-e-ri li-la-a-ti. 82—5—22, 63 R 1 ina še-e-ri, Thompson, *Reports*, *no* 170. DT 57 *R* 1, 2 see çaparu, 1 (885 *col* 2) & ZK ii 6. *del* 41, 92 (= 48, 97); NE 75, 45; 74 *b* 23 *etc.* see mim(m)ū, 565 *col* 1 (*med*). NE (55) V (ii) iii 43 [i]-na ša še-e-ri a[....], KB vi (1) 162; 445. IV^2 3 *a* 38, 39 ina še-e-ri (= ID-TIK-ZI-GA) la-am (il) Šamaš a-çi-e, Br 6576; same id K 56 i 15 (H 71) = i-še-e-ir (Br 6610), whence Bertin translates (RP^2 iii 94 *foll*), he (works) in the morning. K 11152 (*frg* of hymn to Ištar), the goddess is called (8) še-e-ru ša ur-xa-ti u-pat-tu-u. If šēru occurs as a verb the name (il) Il-te-ri Cyr 177, 3, might be added here. See *Jour. Trans. Vict. Inst.*, xxvii 19; 36.

V 24 *e-f* 1 ti]-ib ūmi = mu-na-a[t-tum]; 2, še-e]-ri = še-xi-ri; 3, še-]e-ri = na-ma-ru; 4, še-e-ri = mu-šu-ma; also see V 28 *a-b* 37, 38; TSBA viii 230 *foll*; AV 8305; Br 14155; KB vi (1) 337—8; 336; Lotz, *Quaestiones*, 52 (end). K 2008 iv 31 = II 27 *e-f* 12 ID-TIK-ZI-GA = še-e-ru, AV 8311; Br 6576. fem. form šērtu 2, see below. Connected with šēru, 2. are also šeri'tu &:

ši'āru, šiāru, used as *prep.* ina ši'''āri, contracted to iššiāri = tomorrow, in the morning {Morgen}; then also: not long ago, &, as soon as possible. BA i 484; Hebr. x 109, 110. used especially in letter-literature. K 167 *R* 5 ina ši-'-a-ri al-lak (BA ii 24); K 618 *R* 7—8; K 983 *O* 8 (AJSL xiv 12, 13); K 572 *R* 2 iš-ši-a-ri (BA i 217 *foll*; PSBA xxiii 334); K 21 *O* 8, 9 ma-a a-na ši-ja-a-ri e-pu-uš (do it tomorrow); K 979 *O* 7 ina ši-a-ri ša-ba-a-ṭi (>< Hebr. x 196 *fol*); K 519, 18 (end) a-na ši-a-ri, *ibid* 5 ina ti-ma-li (*Rec. Trav.*, xxiii 160 *fol*); K 623 *O* 8; K 589 *R* 5; 83—1—18, 34 *R* 1 ina ši-a-ri; so also 83—1—18, 2 *R* 7; 83—1—18, 14 *R* 4; 83—1—18, 40 *R* 3 (AJSL xiii 211; xiv 10 & 179—80; xv 141; *Rec. Trav.*, xxiv 106, 107, *au plus vite*); K 493 *R* 1 = Hr^L 1, 9, 35, 33, 51, 47, 108, 191, 206, 364, 391, 406, 407, 440. K 774 *R* 4 ši-i-a-ri (tomorrow) I will inform the king my lord, Thompson, *Reports*, ii, *no* 68; III 66 *O* 10 *d* see nu-⊢-tu (641 *col* 1).

šeri'tu. V 61 v 44 (çubāt) še-ri-'-tu (+ 52 + 54; vi 3) in the list of festival robes furnished to Šamaš, Malkatu & Bunēne. KB iii (1) 180 a morning-garment {ein Morgenkleid}.

šāru 1. = שׁוּר, *pr* išūr, *ps* išurrū (= *pl*). wander, roam about, traverse {wandern, umherwandern, einherziehen}. IV^2 5 *a* 38, 39 with the evil wind i-šur-ru (= UL-UL, Br 9146) šu-nu, they wandered about; 70, 71 and when the evil seven ina šupuk šamē i-šur-ru (= UL-UL); 1 *a* 24, 25 u-ri e-lu-ti u-ri rap-šu-ti ki-ma a-gi-e (= A-MI) i-šur-rum (= UL-UL). possibly also IV^2 30 *no* 1 *R* 4 ilāni ša ša-me-e ta-šur (= MU-UN-DAX-DAX-GI-EŠ). — Q^1 K 41 *c* (iii) 4 (end) eš-te-ri, Pinches, I perch (or √šerū, 3?). see nigiççu, 648 *col* 2, below; M^8 97 *col* 2 √שׁאר. — ℑ — *a*) go somewhere, penetrate into {wohin seinen Weg nehmen, wohin dringen}. IV^2 26 *a* 45/46, 47/48, 49/50 thy mighty word (o Marduk) ana tam-ti (çūçē, a-gi-e Purāti) u-šar (= UM-MI-LAL, Br 10109). Zimmern, *Ritualt.*, 64, 11 še-ix-tu tu-šar-ra; perh. Asb vi 66 their secret forests ša mam-ma a-xu-u la u-šar-ru ina libbi, Meissner, ZA x 81, umhergehen (>< KB ii 206, 207 sich niederlassen); &, again, Jensen, ZA x 249, 250; see also Winckler, *Forsch.*, i 250 √šarū, betreten. pm Zimmern, *Ritualt.*, 1—20, 3 (end) ilāni šur (*var* šu)-ru-šu (& 75—78, 20). — *b*) in the sense of šaxaṭu; *cf* Cant. 4, 8 תָּשׁוּרִי. IV² 31 *R* 7 (*O* 77) imēru atâna ul u-ša-ra, KB vi (1) 87 legt sich der Esel nicht auf die Eselin; 8 (*O* 78) ar-da-tum ina sûqi ul u-ša-ra [et(d)-lu]; but Jensen, KB vi (1) 399 √ašaru (י"פ) see above, *pp* 119, 120. Perhaps IV² 50 *a* 55 ša la u-šar-ru man-ma, T^M iii 55.

Derr. would be mašāru, unless Berry's reading magarru (AJSL xvi 50) & etymology √gararu, is correct.

šāru 2. slander, be hostile {verleumden, feindselig sein} *cf* Hebr שׁוּר. ℑ T. A. (Ber) 102, 6 (someone) i-ka-lu ka-ar-zi-ja u-ša-a-ru before my lord the king; 21, & (for this reason) u-ša-ya-ru, they slander (me); 24; ZA vi 246 *rm* 5. — pm ℚ perh. (Lo) 23, 26 ti-di i-nu-ma gab-bu ša-ru, ye know that all are hostile.

Derr. these 2 & šārūtu:

šāru *3.* lie, slander {Lüge, Verleumdung}. K 84, 3 dib-bi ša ša-a-ri I have heard; 6, ša-a-ru la ta-qi-pa-šu, lies they are! do not believe them; Hr^L 301; PSBA xxiii 342—344.

šāru *4.* *adj* used also as *n.* T. A. (Ber) 189, 56—7 ^(amêl) ša-ri *pl*; 64 (end) ^(amêl) ša-ru = an enemy; 70 ^(amêl) ša-ru-ta *pl* (BA i 121 *foll*); (Lo) 42, 16 ^(amêl) ša-ri šar-ri, the king's enemy. (Ber) 71, 42 çâbū ša-ra, 48 ^(amêlūti) ša-ru-tu will abandon it (the city); (Lo (23, 32 ^(amêlūti) ša-ru-tum šu-nu, they are enemies; (Ber) 62 *R* 6 ^(amêlūti) ša-ru-tu (BA iv 118, 119 on this text); (Ber) 107, 21 ^(amêlūti) ša-ru-ta. (Ber) 78, 2 (KB v 412 *ad* 224 *no* 115) ^(amêlūti) ša]-a-ru[-ta]. Here, according to ZA vi 246 *rm* 5 also (Ber) 40, 22; 34*a*, 32; (Lo) 35, 7; (Ber) 35, 32 gab-bi-šu-nu sa-ar-ru-u-tum (KB v 408, below), variants simply to šāru, not connected with סרר be refractory {widerspenstig sein} see, above, *p* 782, 1/2. *pl f* probably K 84, 18—20 at-tu-nu ap-pit-tim-ma ša-ra-te-e-šu (*sc.* amâte) la ta-šim-ma-a (PSBA xxiii 344—48; Johnston, JAOS xix 83 = *pl f* of šāru, wind, comparing the German Windbeuteleien (?) >< D^Pr 152); K 79 *R* 19 see šipirtu.

šāru *5.* — *a*) wind {Wind} id IM § 9, 54; Br 8369; H^F 24 *foll*; Hebr. i 178; = שְׂעָרָה Job 9, 17; Neh 1, 3. AV 8052. III 4 *a* 37 ša-a-ru dan-nu. *del* 122 (129) il-lik ša-a-ru a-bu-bu me-xu-u. IV² 1 *b* 65, 66 ša-a-re (= IM) lim-nu-tum ‖ û-mu up-pu-tum; 3 *a* 50 [kîma] il-ti (like chaff) ša ša-a-ri ub-lu-šu (Br 8397); 9 *a* 61, 62 ki-ma ša-a-ri (= IM-EME-SAL); 10 *a* 41, 42 the sin I committed ša-a-ru lit-bal, let the wind carry away; 48 *b* 9 ar-kat-sun ša-a-ru i-tab-bal; 59 *no* 2 *b* 13 ta-ni-xi-ja lit-ba-lu sibit šārū (IM-XI-A). Creat.-*frg* IV 33 ša-a-ru da-mi-šu a-na pu-uz̧-ra-tum li-bil-lu-ni; 47 u-še-ça-am-ma IM-MEŠ; 132 ša-a-ru il-ta-nu (the northwind; *cf* ZA iii 316 (Sn *Bass*) 78 ša-a-ri a-mur-ri, the westwind). VATh 4105 i 4 never me-e i-ri-id-di ša-ri, *Mitth. d. Vorderasiat. Gesellsch.*, '02, *no* 1, does the wind drive along the waters. K 3445 + Rm 396 *O* te-bi ša-a-ri, Delitzsch, *Weltschöpf.*, 51 *fol.* K 747, 11 ina qabal ti-ib ša-a-ri (Thompson, *Reports*, ii *no* 235). H 86, 87 *l* 70 [ša?] ša-ar çi-rim la eṭ-pu, whom the blast of the desert carries not away. Banks, *Diss*, 14, 91 kab-tu ki-ma ša-a-ri (+ 93): ina me-xi-e : ki-ma ša-a-ri. K 161 *col* 3 šiptu: ša-ru um-mi ša-ru ša-ru am-ma ili at-tam ša-ru bi-rit zi-e, ZK ii 11, 12. ki-ma ša-a-ri, ša-a-ru, IM-MEŠ (= šārē) er-bit-ti, *etc.*; zi-iq ša-a-re see zāqu, 2, zîqu (288, 289); siba sibitti with šārū see 745 *col* 1, *med* & § 128. Br 8395. I 51 *no* 2 *a* 20 IM-TAB-TAB-BA (= šārū erbitti); I 69 *a* 52 it-bu-n]im-ma ša-a-ri er-bitti me-xi-e rabûti. iç-çur ša-a-ri *cf* naçaru, 715 *col* 1, *med.* K 4378 i 13—15 iç-çur ša-a-ri (Br 8130, 8453, 8454). V 16 *a-b* 33 ša(-a)-ru iš-ta-biṭ-su, Br 8369, 8380, see šabaṭu. a *pl* form we find in 83—1—18, 197, 8 IM-MEŠ (with the gloss ša-ra-a-ni) NU-DUG-GA-MEŠ (gloss: la ṭa-bu-u-ti) Thompson, *Reports*, ii 112. S^c 290 i-im | IM | ša-a-rum; II 31 *c-d* 6; H 6, 168; 28, 613; 109, 45 (= V 11 *d-f* 45; D 129, 93) ME-IR | IM | ša-a-rum, Br 10421, 10424. V 21 *g-h* 15 $^{(tu)}$ IM = ša-a-ri; H 28, 616; Br 8370. S^c 210 li-il | LIL | ša-a[-ru]; V 39 *e-f* 63 LIL-LA(L) = ša-a-ri, iD = zaqiqu, 290, 291; Br 5940; see also lil(l)ū (481 *col* 1); ZK i 196; 298; S^b 234. V 39 *e-f* 70 EL = ša-a-rum, Br 11176. II 38 *g-h* 21; V 20 *e-f* 51 PA-PA (= SIG-SIG) = ša-a-ru (see šaxurratu), Br 5622.

IM-XUL = šāru limnu, IV^2 30 *R* 40 & often (see limnu, 488 *col* 1 § 1); IV^2 5 *a* 38, 39 it-ti IM-XUL-li (see imxullu) ša-a-ri lim-ni i-šur-ru(-)šu-nu.

šarbillu see sarbillu (783 *col* 1) & below.

b) air, draft {Wind, Windzug}. K 519 *R* 15 ša-a-ru i-ka-si-ir (Hr^L 108), the air will be kept away, JOHNSTON, JAOS xviii 163, 164; MARTIN, *Rec. Trav.*, xxiii 160.

c) quarter, region of the heavens, the 4 cardinal points {Himmelsrichtung, Himmelsgegend} H 40, 229. Sarg *Khors* 164 a-na er-bit-ti ša-a-ri, *Ann* 427. *del* 147 (156) u-še-çi-ma (1 *sg*) a-na erbitti IM-MEŠ. Sarg *Cyl* 66 mi-ix-rit VIII (*bull* 82: IV) šārē VIII abullē ap-te-e-ma. K 13 *O* 9 a-na šu-pal ša-a-ru, Hr^L 281; BA iv 527 in südlicher Richtung (or, ša a-ru, bei niederer Strömung).

d) breath, favor {Hauch, Gunst} T. A. (Lo) 28, 23 e-nu-ma la-a it-ta-zi ša-a-ru ištu (šir) bi šarri bēlišu, unless the (life) breath goes forth from the mouth of his lord, the king; 42, 36 ša-ri šar-ri u-ul ti-na-mu-uš iš-tu mu-xi-nu, let the breath of the king not depart from us (+40+41); 26, 7 ša-ri balāṭija, the breath of my life (thus is the king called), +15—17; (Ber) 45, 55 tu-ça-na (√açū) ša-ri a-na ja-ši.

Creat.-*frg* VII (K 8522) *O* 6 Marduk is called il ša-a-ri ṭa-a-bi be-el taš-me-e u ma-ga-ri; 9 ni-çi-nu šāri-šu ṭa-a-bu, KB vi (1) 34—5; 351; KAT^3 526. Sp II 265 *a* xx 10 ša-a-ra ṭa-a-ba ša ilāni ši-te-'-e-ma, ZA x 10 M^S 91 *col* 1 = grace, favor. K 8204 iii/iv 8 ša-ar-ka ṭāba li-zi-qam-ma, PSBA xvii 138, 139.

NOTE. — 1. KB vi (1) 469 suggests as verb, belonging to šāru: NE IX *col* 5, 47 (KB vi, 1, 208) a-n[a?] ... KIM xi iç-çi [š]a ilāni ina a-ma-ri i-ši-ir, he hastened to ‖ er eilte hin, wie ein Sturm; also IV^2 19 *a* 22 e-li-šu i-ši-ru-ma (iD SI); V 50 *a* 42 upon whom the evil utukku i-ši-ru (= SI-GA) stormed, blew. also NE X *col* 1, 14 a-a-nu-um-ma i-ši-ra; IV^2 15 *b* 48 (*med*) ma-la pa-ni-ka i-ši-ru (= SI(G), Br 4422). Hm^2 130, 14 (?) see nazaqu, 1 (660 *col* 2).

2. On IM = šār breath, in P. N. see JENSEN, ZA vi 252.

3. NE 56, 23 ul ša-ru çululka (?). J^{I-N} 29, dein Schatten ist nicht kühl genug.

šāru *6.* (?) S^b 355 ša-ra | BAR | ša-a-ru, Br 6879. Same iD S^b 354 = pa-rak-ku. V 41 *a-b* 4 šar-ru ‖ pa-rak-ku; thus perh. šāru = šarru.

šāru *7.* = 3600 = ὁ σάρος. AV 8052. S^c 79 ša-ar | ŠAR | ša-ar; H 27, 604; Br 8234. iD Sarg *bull* 79; *Cyl* 65; *del* 62—66 (66—68); iD see Br 10072. § 75. šar = Zahlenperiode = Abschluss = 3600, die höchste Zahleneinheit der Babylonier; ZA xviii 84; 90. šu-uš-ša-ar II 45 *f* 28, 29, preceded by šu-uš]-ša-an. ZIMMERN, *Ritualt.*, 41—43 ii 12. See also literature quoted in the article nēr(u) 4, *p* 724 *col* 2. In its general meaning of quantity, superabundance {Übermass, Überschwang} we find šāru in II 19 *a* 7, 8 Anunnaki ilāni rabūti a-di ša-a-ri (= ŠAR-RA) i-tar-ru; *b* 45, 46 šadē zaqrūti a-di ša-a-ri i-xe-iš-šu; JENSEN, 2, 3: totality. AV 8034, Br 8235; § 25 (whence character sar; § 9, 34). See also REISNER, *Hymnen*, 71 *O* 14, 15, *R* 5, 6.

ša(gar?)-ru. K 4574, 18 (M^S *pl* 12) see nusxu (700 *col* 2) & šabnu.

šarru (§§ 27; 63) *c. st.* šar (V 34 *a* 23); *pl* šarrāni, king {König} de SAULCY (1849). AV 8075; √šararu, shine. D^H 20; 55; >< RÉJ x 302, 303; D^{Pr} 92 >< RÉJ xiv 150 bel.; Z^B 46; 104. S^b 333 lu-gal LUGAL | šar-ru; H 18, 293; § 9, 288; Br 4266. II 31 *no* 2 *c-d* 9, 17; TP iv 55; Beh 1 *etc.*; V 14 *c-d* 48 šar-ri. @ 252, 12 šar-ru-um, AV 8073, Br 14469. IV^2 5 *c* 37, 38 LUGAL-E = šar-ru. *Cf* Hebr שׂר. *pl* LUGAL-MEŠ Beh 3; LUGAL-LUGAL-MEŠ, NR 3, 4. Also TP i 3; § 9, 303; Anp i 19 & 32, Br 9061. — referring to gods. Anu: IV^2 5 *a* 28 si-bit-ti-šu-nu mâr šip-ri ša (il) A-nim šar-ri-šu-nu; *Adapa*-legend *R* 10 (end) a-na pa-ni (il) A-ni šar-ri, KB vi (1) 96. — Ašur šar (*var* <<) ilâni Esh iv 56; III 16 *c* 5 (<<); I 7 ix *E* 1; Asb viii 5; šar ilâni Ašur Asb iii 82; V 33 viii 41. — Êa šar ap-si-i, ZIMMERN, *Ritualt.*, 75—78, 39 & often. Sarg *Cyl* 47 (37) (il) šar apsî. — Marduk šar ilâni, V 35, 7; šar ilâni Marduk, Asb ix 11; V 55, 12. Often in *c. t.* as P. N. Marduk-šar-an-ni, Nabd 8, 8; *M*-šar-a-ni, 355, 2 *etc.* T^C 5; AV 5164; HILPRECHT, *Assyriaca*, 56 *rm* 1. On V 46 *a-b* 8 see JENSEN, 130; & HOMMEL, "Die Astronomie der alten Chaldaeer", *Ausland* 1891 *nos* 19, 20. — (il) Ninib šar-ru ma-ru ša (il) Bêl, II 80, 6 & 14. — Sin: šar ilâni ša šamê u erçitim ilâni ša ilâni I 68 *no* 1 *b* 4, 5; *a* 20. — *b*) of human beings. Often: šarru rabû šarru dannu šar kiššati (on which see 454 &, now, KAT³ 27 *rm* 1; 30; 84) šar (mât) Aššur, *etc.* TP; Anp; Asb; Sarg *Ann* XIV 1; Anp i 32 šar-ra (*var* šarra)-ku. V 66 i 1/2 & *cf* dannu; KB iii (1) 114, 115 *col* 4, 5—6 Xa-am-mu-ra-bi šar-ru-um qar-ra-du-um, da-an-nu-um; Nebukadrezzar, son of Nabopolassar, šar Ba-bi-lam^ki a-na-ku, 1 65 *a* 7 *etc.* Nabd-Cyr Chron. ii 18 šu-lit-su u šar-ri, garrison & king. H 67, 43—44 ni-iš šar-ri-šu-nu ana axâmeš iz-qu(*var* ku)-ru; K 257 (H 128) *R* 1, 2 šar-ra (= LUGAL-RA) a-ta-a u-ša-aš (Br 6152 pa?)-ši (PRINCE, JAOS xxiv 111; 123), verily, I will raise up the king. K 4223 iii 26, 27 a-na xar-ra-an šar-ri-im (BA iv 85—7). Often especially in letters: šarru bêlu; ana šarri bêlija, see HARPER's *Assyrian & Babylonian Letters.* — *pl* LUGAL-MEŠ-ni = šarrâ-ni Sn i 65; ii 55, 73; Esh *Sendsch*, *R* 21; D 49, 38; II 21 *a* 29; K 161 *a* 5 (ZK ii 2); <<-MEŠ, TP i 30; <<-MEŠ-ni, TP i 54. — T. A. (Ber) 7, 37 i-na ga-at šar-ra-ni, between us kings, ZA v 16; 140; (Lo) 1, 57 ša-ru-ti ra-bu-ti = great kings.

II 31 *no* 3, 1—5 (*d-e* 40 *foll*); V 41 *a-b* 1—5 šar-ru ‖ ma-al-ku, ma-li-ku, lu-li-mu, pa-rak-ku, e-til-lum. II 33 *no* 3 = V 30 *a-b* 1—31 LUGAL (= šarru) Br 4266 a ‖ of 1 mal]-ku, 2 ma]-li-ku, 3 m]a-lik, 4 SUD-DA (Br 7613), 5 YYY (iš-še-bu) <<< (Br 11886; H 36, 885), 6 (gi) Y (Br 10073; Z^B 46; H 32, 737), 7 SE Y (Br 7490), 8 & 9 (di-me-ir) AN (Br 438), 10 (Br 5526), 11 (Br 4707), 12 UN-GAL (Br 5917), 13 (Br 2148), 14 (Br 8016), 15 UD-DA-GAL (Br 7912; D^Pr 192), 16 KA-SAR (Br 645), 17 EN (Br 2816), 18 šar-ru (II 31 *f-g* 9, Br 10576), 19 EN-AN (Br 2823), 20 [sign]-DI-MA (Br 1212), 21 GIŠ-TUK (Br 5728), 22 (Br 2107), 23 (Br 1401), 24 (Br 7834), 25 MU (Br 1233), 26 (Br 4437), 27 (Br 6905), 28 ZAG-SAG (Br 6385), 29 LA-BA-UD-DU (= Ê) Br 988, 30 (Br 8604), 31 (Br 8605). — II 44 *c-d* 1 see Br 1169; 47 *a-b* 5, 7, 8 Br 3862. S^c 313 a-li-im | iD | šarru, Br 8887. II 38 *a-b* 67; V 16 *a-b* 7 NIR = šar-rum (Br 6286), H 28, 471 ‖ e-til-lu' (470). V 29 *g-h* 58 see Br 10451; 36 *a-c* 17 (u) šar (<); *d-f* 13 (u-mun) < = šar-rum, Br 8754; K 4567, 3 see Br 6407. V 16 *e-f* 52 bît šar-ru, Br 4254, 6247. — šarru also in connection with lubšu, 1 (474 *col* 2), lubûšu (475 *col* 1), lamxuššû (486 *col* 2), parçu, 2 (836, 837), paššûru (846), çubâtu (866, 867). — mâr šarru & mâr šarrûtu see mâru (581 *col* 2).

On šarru & malku see *p* 548 *cols* 1, 2. — On šarru & compounds, BEZOLD, *Catalogue*, v 2182, 2183; AV 8076—88. — On šar apsî = Serapis see LEHMANN, *Wochenschrift für klass. Philologie*, '98 *no* 1, *cols* 26 *foll*; accepted by PINCHES, JRAS '98, 445; also LEHMANN, ZA xii 396 *foll* × PRISER, *Or. Lit. Ztg.*, i *cols* 81, 82. — On Šarezer see HAUPT in CHEYNE, *Isaiah*, (SBOT) 113, 114; KAT³ 84; 428. — On Šarru-ukîn & Šarru-ki-i-nu see SCHRADER, ABK '72, 162 *fol*; WINCKLER, *Sargon*, pref. xiv *fol*; J^AT 340, 341; AV 8060, 8061. On Sargon II & šarru-ukîn, KAT³ 38 *rm* 3; 62. II 48 *a-b* 40 Šar-gi-na = šar ket-ti, Br 12234. — *adv* šarriš; *f* šarratu; *abstr. n.* šarrûtu, see below.

šarû 1. = שׁרא. germinate, grow luxuriantly, thrive {keimen, wachsen, (üppig) gedeihen} § 109; ZA v 9 *rm* 3. III 4 *no* 4, 37—8 great, wild vines ina libbi še-ru-'-u-ni ‖ ša-a-ru dan-nu ka-a-a-ma-nu i-na bir-tu-uš-šu-nu a-la-ku, AV 8314. *ps* K 710, 5 rag-gu ixaliq ket-tu ibašši dan-nu i-ša(e)r-ri mešrû. *pm* perh. T^M i 21 (iç) bînu . . . . ša kim-ma-tu ša-ru-u. — ℶ III 54 *c* 45 la šur-ru-u še-im (K 712 *R* 7); K 955, 16 la šur]-

ri-e bu-bul-ti, THOMPSON, ii 88 & 270; Nichtgedeihen, Misswachs des Getreides. Perhaps K 4995 (H 124) *O* 17 šur-ru-u : ina šur-ri-i xab-bu-ur-šu (D^{H} 34 *rm* 2; Br 7461, 3530); also II 16 *f-g* 30 xab-bur-ru la i-ša-r[u [= 𝔔 ps ïD SI = išaru]; 31, 32 še-ir-tum a-a u[-šar-ri], BA i 460 *rm* 2; ii 303, 304; JENSEN, ZA i 409 *foll.*

DERR. mašrû, mešrû (610, 611), šer'û, šir'û, growth; širûtu; še-ir-tum.

šer'û, šir'û. growth, luxurious growth, vegetation {Wachstum, üppiges Gedeihen, Pflanzenwuchs}. § 25; LYON, *Sargon*, 66; BA ii 143, 144. ïD AB-SIM, § 9, 141. III 43 *d* 6; I 70 *d* 13—15 see birû, 2 (189 *col* 2) & birîtu, 1 (197 *col* 1). Sarg *Cyl* 36 the desert land which had never been irrigated šer-'a šu-zu-zi-im-ma, to raise a rich vegetation (KB ii 45, after LYON). V 43 *a* 13 Simânu is called arax ši-ir-i ebûri. JENSEN, 311 (>< himself, ZA i 409) šer'û = grain in ears {Ähre}; thus V 43 *a* 13 = harvest month. H 71 (K 56 i) 6—7 (*cf* V 17 *b* 19, 20) ši-ir-a . . . . i-max-xa-aç; 8, 9 pi-i ši-ir-i-šu u-sa-ap i-ša-kan, Br 3832; AV 8301. 82—8—16, 1 iv 9 ab-si-in | KI-AŠ (*i. e.* ➤—)-AŠ di-li-min-na-bi AB-SIM še-ir-'u-u, S. A. SMITH, *Misc. Texts, p* 26; HOMMEL, *Sum. Lesest.*, 96; Br 9641, 9642. SCHEIL, ZA x 202, 6 še-ru-' : ša ir-ri aš-ta-pi-ru pul-lu[-uk-ku]?? 81—2—4, 206 *R* 5 ši-ir-'a-ša ibašši (ïD I-KU + Br 51) CRAIG, *Astronom. Texts*, 27. III 53 *a* 2 (kakkab) APIN a-na ABSIN (= šer'i) šur-ri-i, KAT³ 428: Ähre: Name des Sternbildes der Jungfrau in Arsacideninschriften; THOMPSON, *Reports*, ii, *pref.* xxiii. *abstr. n.*:

šir'ûtu. Esh *Negoub*, 13 ši-ir-'(u)-u-sa, BA iii 207 sein Halm (>< SCHEIL, *Rec. Trav.*, xvii 81, 82 ši-ir-' u-sa).

šarû 1. (? שרה) 𝔓 begin, open, dedicate {öffnen, beginnen, einweihen}. III 53 *a* 2, see above; 3 šur-ru-u ša la-pa-ti AB-SIN il-lap-pat-ma, with the gloss še ina û-me-šu u-šar-qa; ri-eš me-riš-te šur-ri, T^{M} 118. Anp ii 87 a palace in Tilu-u-li u-šar-ri (III 6 *O* 36 u-sa-ri = 𝔓¹); 101 êkal ina Tuš-xa(-an) u-ša(*var* sa)-ri. Asb x 107 (the bît ri-dûti) ina xidâti ri-ša-a-ti u-šar-ri-šu, I dedicated it, KB ii 235. Rm III 105 i *b* 14 šip-ri ša-a-ši u-šar-ri-i, WINCKLER, *Forsch.*, i 254 *foll*, JRAS '92, 350 *foll.* II 22 *a* 53 (K 4335 iv 24) ri-eš šur-ri-e. Here, according to WINCKLER, also Asb vi 66 (see šâru, 1.). 83—1—18, 287 *R* 3 lu-u la (arax) Addari u-šar-ri; K 2085, 4+7 a-šar u-šar(šir)-ru; a-šar u-še-ir-ru-u, where it began; THOMPSON, 264; 268. 82—5—22, 78 *R* 7 is-su-ri la u-ša-ru-ni la e-rab, unless they have begun I shall not come in (*ibid* 217). — 𝔓¹ u-sa-ri, see 𝔓.

DERR. tašrîtu, tišrîtu, šurru, & šurratu.

šerû 2. V 36 *d-f* 38 bu-ru | u | še-ru-u, Br 8757, preceded by na-qa-bu (718 *col* 2). ZK ii 373 refers to שער split (>< Z^{B} 56 *rm* 1), separate *etc.*; if so, then here perhaps, T. A. (Lo) 8, 27 even if all the friendly relations which we have had with one another šu-ur-ru-um-ma, had ceased (ZA v 156, 157 comp. שׁרה?). — 𝔖 ZA v 68 *R* 6 (& *p* 71) šu-uš-ra-ku, I unloosen (?). K 3600 *R* 12 (Ninâ) mu-ša-aš-ra-a-at (or √ašâru, 3; see *p* 120) ka-ti-e (ZA v 75); 23 šur-ru-u, CRAIG, *Rel. Texts*, i *pl* 54. BEZOLD, *Catal.*, 1457 dunnamâ u-ša-aš-ra, M^{S} 97, the weak he supports. P. N. Šu-uš-ra-an-ni, AV 8610. — All this is mere suggestion. It is more probable, that the 𝔖-forms, quoted here, belong to:

šerû 3. II 34 *a-b* 15 UŠ (?) = še-ru-u in a group with si'û, sanabu, sinbu. ïD usually = emedu (Br 5045); thus KB vi (1) 530 suggests: erect, put up {aufstellen}. K 56 iv (II 15 *a-b*) 15 gu-šu-ra dan-nu i-še-ir-ri (= BA-AB-GUŠUR-RI). — Here, perhaps, also ZIMMERN, *Ritualtafeln*, 1—20, 41 iš-tu kakkab ša-ma-mi uš-ta-ta-ši-ru-ni; but see KAT³ 421 *rm* 3. A Der. would be:

šerû (?) ***4.*** pedestal, base {Postament}. ZIMMERN, *Ritualt.*, *p* 140 *rm* γ on K 4174 iii 12 GI-KI-IT-MA-XA-A-KU = še-ru-u; thus *Ritualt.* 31—37 i 38 GI-KIT-MAX = šerû; ii 6; 41—42 i 3. — V 26 *g-h* 25 GIŠ-ŠE-KAK (= RU) = še-ru-u ‖ ziqpu; KB vi (1) 530; D^{Pr} 83 stalk, stem {Stengel}. Also see šurinnu.

šer'û 5. ïD BU of sanabu II 34 *a-b* 13 (Br

7535) is also used for še-ru-u, II 34 *no* 6 *add*, AV 8314; see also Br 2491, 5045, 7542, 9684, 10322, 11360 (compares V 22 *a-d* 54). Br 7576 quotes II 34 *no* 6, *add* BU (si-ir si-ir) BU = šu-ur-ru-u. II 34 *no* 6 *R* 20, 21 (sa-ar) SAR & SAR-AK-A = šu-ur-ru-u, Br 4342, 4357; also *cf* Br 5064.

šarū *2.* see lagin (477 *col* 1); it is preceded by mušarbidu ‖ sukallu. Perhaps here, also, II 29 *c-d* 5 (K 2022 iii *O*) TIK-TUK = ša-ru-u, AV 8053, Br 8314; if, indeed, *l* 6 SAG-TIK-TUK is = šar-xu. See also Rm 348 *R* 4 TIK-LAL = 'š'ur-rum, Br 3306 & see maqnqu, 577 *col* 2, below. Sp II 265 *a* xxi 11 i-na(-)a-ça-an-ni a-xu-ru-u ša-ru-u u u(šam?)-xu; *ibid* xxiv 6 see šarxiš.

šūru *1.* bull, ox {Stier, Ochs} §§ 31; 46; 64; D[II] 19; D[Pr] 43. = שׁוֹר. Sn v 74 see marū, 2 (554 *col* 2) & šummannu. V 28 *c-f* 8 šu-u-ru (7, lu-u) = al-pu, AV 8564; H 21, 411. 82—3—23, 131, 12 (end) šu-u-ri taš[-ri-ix-ti], Winckler, ***Forsch.***, ii (iii) 570 *foll*: tadellose Stiere. Against reading šu-u[-ru? = ox] in II 16 *c* 37 see BA ii 285, 286; iṣ GI-U-QI(KIN) in *b* suggesting rather šūru, 2. ZA iv 25, 5 šu-ra-ta.

šūru *2.* some kind of reed {ein gewisses Rohr}. Perh. > šur'u from √šerū, 1 or 3? AV 8564. V 32 *d-f* 66 (Br 2507) see ximmatu, 1 (324 *col* 2). III 4 (*no* 7, 5) 58 see quppu, 1. *var* reads šu-u[-ri], KB iii (1) 101 *rm* 9. 81—11—8, 154 *R* *col* 3, 14 (dupl. of preceding) reads ina qu-up-pi ša šu-u-šu, in a receptacle of wicker; see šūšu.

šūrum *3.* S[c] 5 *a* 7, 8 šur = šu-u-ru[m], Br 2991.

šurrū *1.* AV 8586. Here are classed some forms, whose meaning and etymology is yet unknown. S[c] 153 ta-ab | TAB | šur-ru-u; *cf* S[b] 69, Br 3778. II 33 *c-d* 72; 28 *b-c* 47 $\frac{du}{du}$-$\frac{du}{du}$ (= LAX-LAX) = šur-ru-u, Br 4949, between da-ru-u & pa-ak-da-ru-u. II 30 *g-h* 54 TAB = xa-ma-ṭu & šur-ru-u (ZA ii 89); *ibid* 56, 57 ix-mu-ma : šur-ru-u : ix-mu-ma ; ša-ka-nu, Br 8309.

šurrū *2.* priest, magician, see surrū, 1 (783 *col* 1) & Br 3714.

šurru *1.* (> šūru > šur'u) properly *ac* ג of šarū, begin, dedicate; *f* šurratu, AV 8584, 8585. beginning {Anfang}. TP i 62 (vii 71) i-na šur-ru šarrū-ti-ja, in the beginning of my reign = ina rēš šar-rūtija. Šalm, *Ob*, 22 ina šur-rat šarrū-ti-ja: ***Mon*** i 14; ii 66. Anp i 43 (end) see KB i 60 *rm* *: im ersten unserer Regierungsjahre.

šurru *2.* ZA vii 22 *etc.* for surru (782 *col* 2), issuri > ina šurri, AV 8585; and add 83—1—18, 2 *R* 1 + 14; Bu 91—5—9, 183 *O* 23 i-su-ri (Hr[L] 391, 340); *adv*:

šurriš. BA iii 271 for šurriš (see 782, 783). ZA iv 236, 29 inūx a-na 'š'ur-ri.

šur-rum see šarū, 2.

šu-ri-'-im-am-mu, make me to love Neb i 69 see ra'amu; AV 8561.

-šērī (= tenth {zehnter})? T. A. *e. g.* KB vi (1) 78—9 = (Lo) 82, 6 i-na il-te-en-še-e-ri-i, in the eleventh; see *ibid* i-na ši-i-in-še-e-ri-i; 7, i-na ša-la-še-e-ri-i, ina er-bi-še-e-ri-i (ba-a-bi).

šerru. small, weak; *n* child, infant {klein, schwach; Kind}. √šararu, 3? ZA viii 235 & *rm* 1. AV 8821. K 2619, 21 see šizbu. KB vi (1) 284, 51 (end) ja u-še-šir šer-ra, und möge kein Kindchen richtig werden lassen; + 61; 286, 19 šer-ri (& *rm* 16); *del* 52 (55) šer-ru followed by dan-nu, 53 (56), KB vi (1) 282; but Haupt, BA i 128 suggested šar-ru[-ru]. K 2148 ii 6 ina šumēli-ša še-ir-ra na-šat-me tulā (çirta?)-ša ikkal ina imittiša ikarrab, on her (its) left (arm) she carries a child which feeds on her breast, (and) with her right hand she blesses; description of a statue of Bēlit-ili, ZA ix 121; 417; KAT[3] 429. IV[2] 58 *b* 48 šer-ru ša ana xa-bu-ni-ja anaššū ana xa-bu-ni-ki tanašši, ZA xvi 176, 177; *c* 34 i-šal-lup šer-ru ša ta-ra-a-[ti], sie reisst gewaltsam das Kind von den schwangeren heraus (*ibid* 180, 181). Here according to KB vi (1) 154, 155 also NE 22, 42 ki-i šer-ri la-'-i, against, above, *p* 464 *col* 1 end. ZA iv 111, 123—6 Nabū-šulīšir ta-li-im-šu še-ir-ra-am zi-it lib-bi-ja = KB iii (2) 6 *col* 3, 6—9. V 47 *a* 24 šer-ru ki-ma a-tur a-na ri-e-ši. III 61 *a* 18 the people will sell their children (šir-ri-ši-na) for money. II 32 (*a-*)*b* 78 šer-ra mu-xur, an infant receive with compassion! V 28 *b-d* 33 TUR-DA = šer-ru (Br 4134) & çi-ix-ru; la-'-u, la-ku-u, 34. V 38 *a-c* 15 𒁹 (gi-na) TUR = šer-rum, followed by çi-i[x]-rum; la[-'-u?], la[-ku-u?], Br 4154 & see Br 4157 *ad* ⊕ 252 *R* 11. K 7331 iii 11 (še-ir-ru); JAOS xxii 210; II 36 *a-b* 54—56 ‖ daqqu (265 *col* 2) & lā'û (465 *col* 1); ⊕ 51 iv 11 še-ir-ru ‖ la-'u-u, la-ku-u, gu-dā-du (see qudādu). še-ir-rum ‖ ma-ar, see 581 *col* 1, *med* § 2; also *cf* bišru; & bandû, 179 *col* 1, *med* for S^{a} v 30 *foll.* *f* perhaps IV^{2} 51 *a* 39 a-na šer-ti it-ta-din ina ra-bi-ti im[. . . .].

(ilat) **Šērû'a** P. N. of goddess. AV 8315. K 2852 + K 9662 iii 7 (end) a-na Ašur Bēlit (= NIN-LIL) Še-ru-u-a, Winckler, *Forsch.*, ii 36 *foll.* K 252 i 9 (= III Rawl. 66) (ilat) Še-ru-ja ilâni rabûti; iv 31 (PSBA xxi 118 *foll*). Also K 501, 27 sal (ilat) Še-ru-u-a-eṭera-at, P. N. (Hr^{L} 113 *R* 8); id K 1619 B *R* 1 (Hr^{L} 309) ša (ilat) Šērû'a-e-ṭe-rat, mārtu rabītu ša bît ridû-te (Hr^{L} 309); see on this letter Hommel, *Gesch.*, 694 *rm* 4; Tiele, *Gesch.*, 406, 413; Amiaud, BOR ii 197 *foll*; Scheil, ZA xi 49; Winckler, *Forsch.*, ii 58—59 Johnston, JAOS xx 244—49. 83—1—18, 1847 *R* iv (sal) Am-ti (ilat) Šēru-u-a (PSPA xviii 256). L^{4} i 32 he prayed to NIN-LIL (= Bēlit) Še-ru-u-a ru-bat i-la-a-ti be-lit ištarâti. KB ii 6—7, 15 we have Ašur Še-ru-'-a, Bēl, Zēr-bani-ti, Nabû, Tašmêtum *etc.*: KAT^{3} 429 *rm* 2: ein Name der Ištar, speciell als Muttergöttin, der ursprünglich der Bêlit von Nippur zugehören wird. Lehmann, ii 34 *foll* connects Šērûa with Erûa (√הרה); but, Jensen, ZDMG 50, 258 would rather prefer a connection of Šērua (= Çarpan tu) with šēru, morning & morning-dawn.

širû (?). II 50 *c-d* 64 KUR-ŠI (*cf* ŠIR, 67)-RUM-KI = šad Ši-r[i-i], Br 9289; ZDMG 53, 656 *foll.*

šūrubu. √erebu (95, 96). — *a*) Š pm IV 55 (= IV^{2} 48) *a* 20 when the king the people of *N* a-na bît çi-bit-tim šu-ru-bu (+ 22); II 9 *d* 33 ina su-ki šu-ru-ub. — *b*) ac NE 22, 47 a-na šu-ru-bi, KB vi (1) 154, 155. K 2801 *R* 22 e-piš šip-ri u šu-ru-ub pi-ris-ti, BA iii 236, 237. V 55, 54 a-na libbi alâni la šu-ru-bi.

šūrib. Š ip of same verb. *q. v.* & KB vi (1) 298, 299 *l* 21. A deriv of this verb is:

šūrubtu *1. f* ingathering, produce {Einbringung, Feldertrag} ZA i 194; *cf* Job 39, 12. §§ 65, 33; 88 *b* & *rm*; BA i 289. II 15 *c-d* 42 -na šu-ru-ub-ti (id MU-UN-DU) su-lu-pi; thus also supplement II 33 *g-h* 19. H 68, 17—20 = II 52 *no* 3, 64—67; H 68, 13 a-na šu-ru-ub-ti ebûri, Br 1290. V 61 *e* 31—33 u mimma šu-ru-ub-ti Ê-BAR-RA, and all that is gathered into *E.* AV 8569; see also *Rec. Trav.*, xx 206 *col* 2, 11.

šurbû *1. adj f* šurbûtu (§§ 38; 39; 65, 33 *b*; ZA iv 70 *rm* 2) great, powerful, lofty, majestic, brilliant {gross, gewichtig, hehr, majestätisch, herrlich ‖ rubû *q. v.* AV 8575. used especially in connection with gods & goddessess; & demons. Marduk: ina kâl ilâni^{pl} šur-ba-ta i-lut-ka, great over all the gods is thy divinity; KB iii (2) 78, 5—6 ša ina I-gi-gi šu-ur-ba-tim a-ma-at-su i-na A-nun-na-ki šu-tu-ga-at be-lu-ut-su; 78, 28 bēlu šu-ur-bi-i ‖ e-te-el-lu çi-i-ri; 92, 48 be-lu šu-ur-bi-ja. — Ninib: dan-dan-nu çi-ru šur-bu-u, Šamš i 20; *ibid* 2 ša-ga-pi-ri šur-bi-i. — Bēl: Zimmern, *Ritualt.*, 26 iii 41 (il) Bēl šur-bu-u. — Nusku: T^{M} i 122 (il) Nusku šur-bu-u i-lit-ti (il) A-nim (i 144; ii 1; viii 1). — To Kingu Tiâmat says: lu-šu-ur-ba ta (m)a (§ 39) xa-'-i-ri e-du-u at-ta (or pm?) see KB vi (1) 6—7, 81; Creat.-*frg* III 103 (lu-u šur-ba-ta-ma xa-i-ri, *etc.*). — *f* Ištar šur-bu-ut ilâni, II 66 *no* 1, 4. K 3456 *R* 34 (ilat) Iš-tar šur-bu-ṭum, PSBA xxi 40 *foll*; K 11152, 2 Ištar šur-bu-tum e-til-lit axê-ša; K 3464 *O* 23 (Ištar) mu-tal-la-tum šur-bu-tum Ir-ni-ni bēltum (Craig, *Relig. Texts*, *p* 66). K 4931 *O* 13. 14 be-el-tum šur-bu tum (H 116—117; Br 11144); 81—6—7, 209, 1 a-na (ilat) Iš-tar bēlti šur-bu-ti; 34, (ilat) Ištar bēlit šur-bu-ti, & 41 (BA iii 260 *foll*). N 3554 *O* 3 bēltum šur-bu-tum al-si-ki, PSBA xxiii 120 *foll.* — Beltis of Nippur is called be-il-tim šu-ur-bu-tim, KB iii (2) 8 *col* 2, 12. IV^{2} 54 *b* 29 (Bēlit) il-tum šur-bu-tu.

Zimmern, *Ritualt.*, 26 iii 38 (ilat) Anatum .... šur-bu-tim; 51 (ilat) Gu-la bēltu šur-bu-tu. (ilat) Nanâ šur-bu-ti ilāni, *Rec. Trav.* xx 205 (*no* XLII) 2. — H 94—5, 66 la[-bar-tu] šur-bu-tu, Br 4974. *pl* IV² 52 *b* 49 ilāni šur-bu-tu (§ 67*b*). — Also *cf* ZA v 58, 41 šur-bu-u šumu-ka, great is thy name. — Of kings *etc.* Šalm, *Ob* 71 see çalmu, 2 (878 *col* 2). Zimmern, *Ritualtaf.*, 100, 28 (end) ina pu-ut šu'i šur-bi-i, vor dem grossen Schaf. Br 41; 2993 & AV 8575 quote ṭi-'u šur-bu-u. ZA v 59, 3 šur-bu-u na-'-du ar-mu. — S 28, 7 SAG-GAN-NA = šur-bu-u, Br 3597. V 13 *a-b* 46 UN-GAL = šur-bu-u (Br 5919; also = šarru). *abstr. n.* is:

šurbûtu. greatness, majesty, *etc.* {Grösse, Majestät, *etc.* IV² 30 *no* 1 *a* 20, 21 šur-bu-u (see K 4995 *R* 8—9 = H 125) ina šur-bu-ti-ka, Br 1166; Z^B 50; Flemming, *Neb*, 51.

šurubû *1.* II 31 (*e-*)*f* 4 šu-ru-bu-u, followed by ra-bu-u (5) & e-til-lu (6) AV 8567.

šarab(p)u ‖ alāku. II 35 *e-f* 54 ša-ra-bu = a-la-a-ku.

(amēl) **šar-ra-b(p)u**, K 2085, 16 + 26 (AV 8072).

šarrabu *1.* KAT³ 366; 412 *rm* 4 (Brenner = שָׁרָב Isa. 35, 7; 49, 10); 415: not = שָׂרָף. AV 8072. V 46 *c-d* 22 (il) šar-ra-bu (Br 12531), name for Nergal in the west-land (MAR-KI); *cf* II 54 *c-d* 76, Br 12557; III 68 *a* 66 (il) DAN (= KAL) šar-ra-bu EDIN; preceded by (il) DAN bi-ir-du EDIN, Br 12877, 12878. II 28 *no* 4, *add* (il) šar-ra-ab(p), AV 6606, Br 12555. — Sp II 265 *a* xxi 2 see parasu 833 *col* 1, *ll* 4—5. Martin, *Textes rélig.*, '03 also compares שָׁרָב: '*mirage*' = desert.

(amēl) **šurābu** an official {ein Beamter} KB iv 42, 14 ma-xar I-tab-bu-u (amēl) šu-ra-bi.

šarb(p)u, šurb(p)u *1.* frost, cold {Kälte, Frost} AV 8058, 8574. See sarbu, 2 (cold wind) 783 *col* 1. KB vi (1) 218, 6 (= NE 73, 6) š(s)ar-bi u tam-rim (& 13); 200, 18; frost & heat {Frost & Glut}. K 883, 16 .... nin mu-ma-a-te a-na š(s)ar-bi u-tar-ra, BA ii 633, 634; √שרף; = Craig, *Relig. Texts*, 26 *R* 2. V 22 *a-d* 34, 35 še-ig | A-AN | šur-bu & šar-bu (also = zunnu, zananu, nalšu, nalāšu) Br 11397—8. K 4219 *R* 6 (M^S *pl* 10) preceded by šal-gu, šu-ri-bu, na-la-šu. — See Jensen, *Theol. Litztg.*, '97 *no* 1; Idem, ZA i 250 *rm* 3 compared Tlm. שְׂרָף; Sayce, ZA ii 95—97. Z^B 27 & 46 √rapû; Delitzsch, *ibid* 116 √šarapu; KAT³ 366 perhaps = שָׁרָב, Isa. 49, 10 = Gluthitze. A ‖ is:

šurîb(p)u, AV 8559. I 28 *a* 14; IV² 55, 1 *R* 2 see xalpû; Br 3063; ZA xviii 192 *rm* 2; IV² 58 *a* 11 u-xal-laq um-mu kuççu xal-pa-a šu-ri-[b(p)]u, ZA xvi 165—9; Z^B 27; 42. K 3182 iv 13 (ZA iv 12) ... kuççu xal-pa-a šu-ri-pa (*var* bu) šal-gi, AJSL xvii 143 cold, frost, sleet, snow. NE VI 33 see KB vi, 1, 168—9; 449. III 61 *b* 2 in the month Ṭebet šu-ri-bu ibaš-ši, ZA i 250 *rm* 1. II 32 *a-b* 33 šu (II Rawl. lat)-ri-bu between tak-ça-a-tum (*cf* kuççu) & šal-gu. V 12 *c-d* 43 .... GE-A = šu-ri-bu (Br 14201) followed by um-ma-nu (44) & preceded by šal-gu, im-ba-ru (42). V 22 *a-d* 28 a-šu-gi | id, Br 11758 | šu-ri-bu, preceded by ma-am-mu-u & xal-pu. 83—1—18, 1330 iv 2 [cuneiform] A-DI [cuneiform] (a-ma-am) = šu-ri-bu; iii 10 GAB(du) = ka-ma-rum ša šu-ri-bu, ZA i 248 *foll.*

šurubtu *2.* *c. st.* šur(u)bat. shudder, fear {Schauer, Graus, Furcht}. K 3182 iii 24 [ina] šu-ru-bat çêri ri-'-u i-max-xar-ka, AJSL xvii 141, in the shudder (created) by the field (desert) the shepherd prays to thee. Anp ii 78 the terror of my majesty *etc.*, see namurratu (688 *col* 1, below) >< AV 8573. A ‖ is:

šurîbtu. Anp ii 119 (*var* III R 6 -ba-at) see namurratu, iii 24 šu-ri-bat kak-kê(-a) (māt) Kal-du u-sa-xi-ip ‖ pul-xat; AV 8558. Šalm, *Ob* (& Lay 91) 84 šu-ri-pat kakkê-ja a-di mar-ra-ti is-xu-up; KB i 138, 139.

šurubb(pp)û, § 65, 38. AV 8568. — *a*) shudder, shivers, fever *etc.* {Schüttelfrost, kaltes Fieber} Ball, PSBA xiii 103. IV² 15* i 37, 38 (id ŠA(=LIB)-GIG, Br 3065) see ṭi'û, 348 *col* 2; Z^B 26, 27. I *a* 1—3 see xarbašu (336 *col* 2, *med*) Br 11701. KB vi (1) 280 iii 9 šu-ru-bu-u lib-ši, Schüttelfieber möge entstehen; 282, 12, 13, 16 *etc.*; 541—2. T^M vii 39 (supplemented by BA iv 161) .... šu-ru-ub-bu-u ša zumrika. — *b*) ‖ ša(u)rbu. V 22 *a-d* 29 še-ig | A-ZA-AD | šu-ru-ub-bu[-u]. III 54 *a* 24, 25 šu-ru-bu-u. K 1395, 2 when the moon appears on the 30th day šu-ru-ub-bu-u, there will be frost. 82—5—22, 53, 5; 80—7—19, 54, 2; S 1974, 6 & 7 šu-ru-ub-bu-u ina mâti ibašši; K 774, 3 šu-ru-ub-bu-u ku-uç-çu; Bu 89—4—26, 27, 3; K 877 *R* 6 šu-ru-bu-u [ku-uç-çu] = Thompson, *Reports*, ii *nos* 59, 60, 61, 62, 68, 81 B, 84.

šurbû 2. K 4197, 2 A+DI = šur-b(p)u-u; D 73 *rm* 7; Br 8064.

širîbu (?) T. A. (Ber) 189, 69 (amêlu) ša-nu u la-a ši-ri-bu, BA iv 121 *foll.*

ši-ir-ba, KB v 178 on T. A. (Ber) 42, 15 ši-ir-ba, read ši-ir-ma, *q. v.*

šarbabu 1., whence according to some mu-šarbibu; but see rababu, 2. Amiaud, *Rev. d'Assyr.*, ii 12 derives mušarbibu √šababu.

šarbabu 2. *n?* Creat.-*frg* III 28, 29 (KB vi, 1, 16—17) & Sp II 265 *a* xxiv 11 see xar-mamu, 338.

šarabdû. II 32 *a* 56 XI (šar-ra-ab-du) (AV 8068, Br 8259), which Jensen, KB vi (1) 389 combines in meaning with âkil qarçê of *b* 58. Here, probably, belongs the name (il) Ša-ra-ab-da-a, one of the company of Nergal, KB vi (1) 76, 6; 78, 3; KAT[3] 461; J[AT] 330; also BA iv 131, 132 on T. A. (Ber) 236 + 239*a* + 234 + 237, 21.

šarbaṭu, whence muttašrab(b)iṭu, see *p* 626 *col* 2; according to Banks, *Diss*: blow {wehen} >< Br 7572. $\mathfrak{N}^{tn}$ Banks, 10, 30; 18, 38 qar-rad (il) Nergal it-ta-na-aš-rab-biṭ (webet und wehet) = Reisner, *Hymnen*, 7, 39; 95, 38.

šarbillu, AV 8057 see sarbillu (783 *col* 1); II 31 *d* 8; Br 6963, 10428. Hommel: Schwacher Wind.

(GIŠ) ŠIR-GAL, ZA xvii 196—7 *rm* 4, perh.: marble {Marmor}; see parûtu (840 *col* 1). OLZ '04 i *col* 3.

šar-ga-nu, AV 8060. See sarganu, 783 *col* 1. Oppert, ZA iii 124 (>< his former reading Bingânu, 179 footnote) derives the word from šaragu, be powerful, mighty; comparing שרג and connects with it the name Šar-ga-ni-šar-ali (or maxâzi; strong is the king of the city KB iii (1) 100 *nos* 1 & 2. Also see Hilprecht, *OBI*, i *p* 16; McCurdy, *History, Prophecy & the Monuments*, i 104. KAT[3] 17, 18. On Šargâni-šar-ali & Sargon I see Hommel, *Geschichte*, 301; Lehmann, BA ii 611 *foll.*

šurdu ša (il) **Šamaš,** a disease, illness {Krankheit}. K 10625, § 2. šumma amêlu šur-du ša (il) Šamaš mariç, Bezold, *Catalogue*, 1102.

šurdû. II 34 *a-b* 18; AV 8578 see ri(a)dû Š. From the same verb is derived probably:

šurdûtu. 83—1—18, 233, 3 šur-du-ut mâti, Thompson, *Reports*, ii *no* 236 A.

šûrudu. K[M] 2, 22 ša a-na a-ra-al[-li]-e šu-ru-du, KAT[3] 639 whosoever has been led to the realm of the dead {wer in das Totenreich hinabgeführt worden ist}. √aradu, 97, 98.

šar-din-nu, AV 8062 see sartennu, 785 *col* 2.

šurdunû *cf* surdunû, 783 *col* 2.

(il) **Še-ra-ax.** II 59 *a-b* 21 = (il) Çir, ZA iii 169; AV 8303; Br 7481.

šaraxu, AV 8037. — *a*) be powerful, strong, gigantic {gewaltig, stark, riesig sein} & *b*) be bright, shine {herrlich sein, glänzen}, KB vi (1) 357; 454. RÉJ xiv 159 compares Hebr סָרַח, Arb سرح = II 35 *g* 3 ša-ra-xu. — *pm* NE VI 201 (203) man-nu-um-ma ša-ru-ux (‖ banû) ina zik-karê, who is the most powerful among men (*cf* NE 36, 5); *ibid* 20 lu-u ša-ru-ux la-sa-mu, KB vi (1) 168, 169. K 3351, 12 i-na bu-ru-mi ellûti ša-ru-ux (is brilliant) ta-lu-uk-šu, Craig, *Relig. Texts*, i *pl* 43. K 155 *O* 6 šar-xat (‖ namrat) ṣi-pa-ra-ka kîma (il) BIL-GI, K[M] *no* 1: thy torch is brilliant; ZA iv 232, 11; Jensen, 424, AV 8063. I 44, 65 palaces which ma-diš šu-tu-ra raba-a u šar-xa. K 7592 + K 8717, DT 363 *R* 6 ša-ru-ux ilu, *etc.* T[M] v 89 (or *adj?*).

$\mathfrak{Q}^{t}$ ip KB vi (1) 50, 42; 52, 86 (*Zû*-legend) šit-ra-ax ina max-ri (ma-xar) ilâni, be brilliant above the gods. — *pm* Esh *Sendsch*, *R* 20 (end) šit-ra-xa-ku (or, *adj?*). — *ag* muš(l)tarxu, see 615 *col* 1.

$\mathfrak{Z}$ make great, powerful; splendid, brilliant: G §§ 17; 62. ZA iv 241, 44—46 ta-nit-ta-ka u-šar-ri-xa ana ça-a-ti. TP vii 101 see nama(e)ru, 1 (684 *col* 2, *med*). Anp i 27 šalummat (*q. v.*) kakkēšu mēlam(me) bēlūtišu eli šarrāni .... u-šar-ri-xu-šu, 3 *pl.* I 27 *no* 2, 15 ēkalla u-si-im (√asamu, 75 *col* 2) u-šar-rix (1 *sg pr*); Anp *Stand* 11 *b* u-si-im-ši u-šar-ri-ix (*var* rix)-ši; 20, u-šar-rix-ši; Anp ii 4, 85, 135 u-šar-ri-xi. V 70, 9 that same sanctuary u-si-im u-šar-rix; III 4, 34. Asb x 97 see rapašu, ℑ. Esh *Sendsch*, *R* 33 šarru-u-ti u-šar-ri-ix-ma. Sarg *Cyl* 31 Sargon who u-šar-ri-xu zi-kir-šu. I 44, 86; I 49 *d* 24 see rabū, 1 Š. Creat.-*frg* VII (K 8522) *R* 16 ma-a ša abē-šu (= AD-ME; not atmē, as on *p* 131 *col* 1) u-šar-ri-xu zik-ru-u-šu, KB vi (1) 38—9; 264, 19 u-šar-ri-ix-k[a], ich habe dir herrlich gemacht. Merodach-Balad.-stone ii 53, 54 whose birth the goddess NIN-EN-NA, the mother of the gods, u-šar-ri-xu, KB iii (1) 186. Zimmern, *Rituall.*, *no* 52, 15 tu]-šar-rax (18, [tu-ša-r]a-ax)-šu-nu-ti ‖ tu-ka(b)-ba-su-nu-ti. — pc ZA v 60, 18 lu-šar-ri-ix qur-di-ki, I will magnify thy might. Creat.-*frg* VII *O* 11 one of the names of Marduk is AN-AGA-AZAG explained as li-šar-ri-xu ab(p)-ra-a-te, KB vi (1) 35 (& 353) möge verherrlichen die Gesammtheit. — ac V 60 *c* 6 (ana) šur-ru-ux nindabē. 82, 9—18, 4154 + 4155 iv 10 [BAR] = šur-ru-xu ša Bl (= ši-kari). — ip K 3600 iv 14 see rabū Š. — pm Sarg *Cyl* 42 in order that ..... šu-ur-ru-ux (be supplied in great quantity), AV 8587. Šamš i 17 binūt Ēšarra mār šit-lu-ṭu ša ina bu-ru-mi elli šur-ru-xu, Jensen, 469 der .... erstrahlen lässt. Also ZA v 58, 25. Esh *Sendsch*, *R* 21 kab-ta-ku šur-ru-xa-ku (or, *adj?*; Anp i 32); L⁵ 4 šur-ru-xa-at ki-bit-su. — ag TP i 13, 14 Ištar reš-ti ilāni be-lit te-še-e mu-šar-ri-xat qablā-te. On šurruxu & kubbutu (of sacrifices) see IV² 25 *b* 35 šur-ri-ix kubbit & *cf* niqē tašrixti ‖ niqē takbitti; Zimmern, *Rituall.*, *p* 167.

ℑ¹ Smith, *Asurb*, 117, 1 kirib Elamti uš-tar-ra-ax ina puxur ummāni-šu, KB ii 249: and considered himself great in Elam, surrounded by his troops; × Winckler, *Forsch.*, i 252 (rüstete sich). NE VI 150 eb-ri nu-uš-tar-ri-ix, KB vi (1) 174; 454. ag muštarrixu, 615 *col* 1; perhaps also mul-ta-ri-xu, 552 *col* 1, unless √araxu, 2 (*p* 88 *col* 2) is preferred.

Š ZA iv 230, 6 u-ša-aš-ri-xu be-lu-us-su. u-ša-aš-ra-xu ba-nu-u Ē-sag-il, they build Ē in a splendid manner. ZA v 67, 29 attīma Ištar tu-ša-aš-ri-xi zik-ri. Sp II 265 a ii 7 na[.....]-šu [ ]-en-šu ul-te(?)-lu-u u-ša-aš-ri [-ix?]. — ZA v 59, 6 (K 7592 *etc.*) šu-uš-ru-xu qi-e, strong are the cords; see also rabū, 1 Š.

Derr. šitrāxu, šitruxu, (tašrixu), tašrixtu & these 3:

šarxu *1.* *n* K 155 (K^M *no* 1) *O* 8 šar-xa nišē ug-da-ša-ra a-na a-ma-ri-ka [-ma?], the brightness of the nation he gathers (uq-ṭa-ša-ra?) in thy sight (King). IV² 1* iv 31, 32 ina bīti ^{il} DU-AZAG-GA ša-rix(?)-šu, *var* on K 3121 reads du-uš-šu-u.

šarxu *2.* *adj f* šaruxtu. powerful, awe inspiring {riesig, übergewaltig, Schrecken erregend} AV 8063; G § 62. Anp i 1 Ninib qardu šar-xu git-ma-lu; 7 he is called ilu šar-xu, Jensen, 465: the shining. K 3452 *R* 10 šar-xu, also Sp II 265 *a* xxiv 2. IV² 57 *a* 18 Marduk šar-xu ed-diš-šu-u git-ma-lu = K^M 12, 18. D^K reads V 33 *a* 22 ša-xum ri-ē-u, but see KB iii (1) 186. P. N. Nabū-šar-xi-ilāni II 64 *a* 54, Nebo is mighty among the gods, AV 5668. Šalm, *Mon*, 10 šar mātāti šar-xu. K 3600 iv 15 ul-la-a ša-ru-ux-tu (addressed to Ninā). Craig, *Relig. Texts*, i 54/55 ša-ru-u[x-ti ma-rat ^{il} A-nim]; *cf* 95 *O* 4. IV² 55 (= IV 62) *no* 2 *O* 26 ša-ru-ux-tu(m) i-la-a-ti preceded by ka-nu-ut be-li-e-ti; Zimmern, *Ritualtafeln*, 89—90, 4. 81—6—7, 209, 1 (*b*) a-na ^{(ilat)} Iš-tar ..... ša-ru-ux-ti, BA iii 260, 261. — II 35 *e-f* 17 see rašubbu; II 29 *c-d* 6 *cf* šarū (Br 3564). — *pl* Sm 526, 14 a-na çēni çi-e-ni šar-xa-a-ti la tušeççā; Smith, *Misc. Texts*, *pl* xxiv. K 2396 at-tu-nu kakkabē šar-xu-tum (Bezold, *Catalogue*, 439) = K^M 8, 22.

šarxiš, *adv* Sp II 265 *a* xxiv 6 šar-xi-iš ša ša-ri-i i-dib-bu-bu dum-ki-šu.

šarraxu ‖ šarxu. P. N. $^{(ilu)}$ Šar-ra-xu II 60 *a-b* 6 Br 12554; $Z^{Š}$ ii 177; viii 15; AV 8070. Ball, *Genesis* (SBOT) 50: šarraxu, a title of Sin, the god of Ur-Casdim, whence Abraham migrated. Another ‖ is:

šurruxu, AV 8587. TP i 42 nab-lu šur-ru-xu (or פחז ‏ג?); Zimmern, *Rituall.*, *no* 68, 30. IV^2 20 *no* 1, 26—27 zi-i-bu šur-ru-xu, Br 2254. Sarg *Khors* 172—3; *Ann* 434 see qutrinnu.

šuruxtum, *n*? T. A. (Ber) 24 *R* 89: one šu-ru-ux-tum [xu]rāçi.

širraxu. II 32 *c* 5 ši-ir-ra-xu, powerful, mighty (??), AV 8321.

širīxu (?), bulky. siparri ši-ri-xu, Jastrow, Hebr. v 242 *ad* Lay 98 *no* 5, instead of the sipa-ar-ri, of KB i 150.

šerxānu (?) Ungnad, ZA xviii 18 *ad* Xamm.-*code* xxxv 8 še-ir-xa-nam, while Harper: še-ir xa-nam, diseased bowels.

šaraṭu, pr išruṭ, § 84. AV 8038. tear, rent (a garment *etc.*), cut, strip, make an incision {reissen, zerreissen, einschneiden} *etc.* Hebr שרט, Arb شرط; KAT^3 603. K 2674 i 17 see naxlaptu (664 *col* 1); Smith, *Asurb*, 142. Sarg *Ann* 294 [na-ax-lap]-tuš iš-ru-ṭa. S^p II 987 *O* 28 ša-ri-ṭi, ravaging *Jour. Trans. Vict. Inst.* 29, 54. Winckler, *Forsch.*, ii 144 reads V 55, 10 ša-riṭ (>< ka-šid) māt A-mur-ri-i. S^b 59 bi-ir | [cuneiform] | ša-ra-ṭu, Br 8094, 8095.

Q^1 ZA ix 108 (VATh 244 ii) 24 A-GIŠ-AK-A = šit-ru-ṭ(d)a-at; perh. V 21 (*c*-)*d* 32 šit(?)-ru-du.

ג III 4 *no* 4, 45—6 çu-ba-tu be-lu-ti-šu u-šar-riṭ (3 pr) his lordship's robe he rent. V 45 v 19 tu-šar-raṭ. K 3445 + Rm 396, 11 (Delitzsch, *Weltschöpfung*, 51 *fol*) kir-bu-uš-šu ma-xa-za-šu lu-šar-riṭ-ma.

$Ṭ^1$ Smith, *Asurb*, 127, 81 my warriors, the fighters, who at the behest of the gods it-ta-na-aš-ra-ṭu qabal tam-xa-ri (= in the battle), exposed themselves to tearing wounds, KB ii 252—3.

Derr. — these 5:

širṭu, *n* bandage {Binde} Johnston, JAOS xix 88; OLZ ii 5, *col* 158 (Rost) {Lappen, Fetzen}. V 15 *e-f* 9 KU-BAR (so Pinches, ZK ii 266)-MAN = ši-ir-ṭu, Br 493, AV 8818. Sm 1064 *R* 2, 3 ši-ir-ṭu ša ina lib-bi ça-bit-u-ni up-ta-ṭar, Hr^L 392. Perh. T. A. (Ber) 28 ii 55 ša še-ir-da i-ki-iz-zi-ru. A ‖ is:

šarūṭu. K 891 *R* 2 in order to commemorate the shades of my ancestors ša-ru-ṭu lu ar-ku-us (I put on a torn garment); *cf* Z^B 2 *rm* 2; J^W 54 *rm* 1. KB ii 262 reads ša šub-ṭu-lu *etc.* (see *p* 151 *col* 1, *med*).

širriṭu (?). Banks, AJSL xiv 277 reads IV^2 61 *a* 59 ši-ir-ri-ṭu ultu libbi ēkallija ušēça (the tattered garments).

šurruṭu, *adj* torn, in pieces {zerrissen, in Stücken}. V 15 *e-f* 8 KU-BIR-BIR-RA = (çubātu?) šur-ru-ṭu, AV 8588, Br 8512.

šarriṭu see niçu, 714 *col* 1.

šarku. Sp II 265 *a* xxii 8 see ligīmu (476, 477); *ibid.*, xxiv 9 šar-ku-uš (*var* šu) nu (or NU? = lā)-ul-la-tum i-qap-pu-du-šu nir-ti. Clay, 63 *rm* † & ‡ on šarku, širku, šišku.

šurkīnu see surqīnu, 784 *col* 2.

širk(q)upu, Creat.-*frg* IV 136 see KB vi (1) 30, 31 & qūpu.

šurrukūtu, K 4211 *O* 5 (M^S *pl* 10) šur-ru-ku-tu.

šaramu. cut off, blunt (? of horns) {abschneiden, stumpf machen} *etc.* S^b 219 ša-ab | ŠAB | ša-ra-mu; *cf* S^c 221; AV 8040. Br 5672; 2482; also V 17 *a-b* 33; & see baqamu, 182, 183. Perhaps V 31 *g-h* 21 la-am gišimmari ša-ra-mi *etc.* pr Sm 1032 sect. ii *col* 2, 8—9 i-ša-'-la šum-ma XAR-BE u šamnu iš-ri-mu.

ג V 45 v 20 tu-šar-ra-am. Xammurabi-*code* xxxvii 58 if a man have not protected (la u-šar-ri-im) his (the vicious bull's) horns, Harper, *The Code of Hammurabi*, 86—7. — $^{(amēl)}$ mu-ša-rim ZA iv 120 (Nabd 306, 3) read mu-ša-kil.

Derr. našramu, 742 *col* 1.

šarmu (?) Sp II 265 *a* xxiv 7 šar-ma(*var* adds -mi) meš(maš)-ru-u(*var* -šu) il-la-ku i-da-a-šu (Martin, *Textes Rélig.*, '03: ruin). T. A. (Ber) 25 i 45—54: one ma-ni-in-nu (563 *cols* 1, 2) šar(šer?)-mu; 26 ii 6: one ma-ni-i-in-ni šar-mu; also i 31 . . . gi ^{pl} šar-mu ba-nu-u.

širma. T. A. (Ber.) 42, 15 ši-ir-ma, BA iv 281 the širma people. Perhaps an

Egyptian word for charioteer (?) or, warrior fighting from a chariot. {Wagenlenker, Wagenkämpfer}?

(çubāt) **šir-a-am**, a by-form of siriam, 783 *col* 2.

ša(u)rmaxxu see sa(u)rmaxxu, 784 *col* 1,

šurmē(ī)nu (> šurmānu; §§ 32$a\gamma$; 44; 65,35 & *rm*) cypress, cypresswood {Cypresse, Cypressenholz}. id GIŠ-ŠUR-MAN (§ 34 *rm*); perh. NE 26, 3. I 44, 71 dalāti GIŠ-ŠUR-MAN, ZA ii 268; AV 8581. Scheil, *Notes d'epigr. LX* (Constant. 583 *O* 18) ina NI (= šamni) GIŠ-ŠUR-MAN, with oil of the cypress anoint (rub) him, *Rec. Trav.*, xxiii. ZA x 208 *O* 14 dup(-pu) ul ša-lim (or ši)-tum : GI ŠUR-MAN. Neb ix 6, 7 (iç) šu-ur-mi-ni ni-is-ki bi-e-ru-tim; also ii 34 šu-ur-me-ni; ZA iii 317 (Sn *Bass*) 84. Cyr 247, 2 ište-en (iç) šur-man-ni. In Gudea-inscr. written (iç) šu-ur-me (Cyl A *col* xii 5), Thureau-Dangin, ZA xvi 362 *rm* 1 = sorte de pin ou cyprès. V 65 *b* 4 (iç) šur-i-ni (§ 49*a*) iç-çi dam-qu-tu; *i. e.* šuruīnu, BA i 591 >< ZA ii 270 *foll*; BA i 98 *rm*; also *cf* ZA iii 298. It is often mentioned with da(u)prānu (264 *col* 1); AV 8582. V 26 *g-h* 17 GIŠ-TIR-GIŠ-ŠUR-MAN = kiš-tu šur-me-ni (H 39, 150), Br 3006, 7667. See also H^F 70, 71 (‖ burāšu); Hoffmann, *Abh. Gött. Akad.*, '89, *p* 27.

šerīmtu (?). KB iii (1) 172, 15: and 120 gur ŠE-ZIR eqil še-rim (ZA iv 261: qil??)-ti, als Stiftungsgut, *ibid* 178 *rm* * √rāmu, *c*, assign, allot.

šarānu *1.* an animal of a lower species {ein Tier niederer Ordnung}. K 4373 *a* 20 ša-ra-nu, between ša'il eqli & UR-MAX qaq-qa-ri, KB vi (1) 518. Compare also the gloss ša-ri-in in II 5 *c* 21 i-šid (miš??) bu-ka-ni (see 152, 153); *ibid* 20 gloss šu-ri-in, Br 5549; AV 8050, 8562. A derivative is probably:

šarānu *2.* 79, 7—8, 19 / 5 (šam) ša-ra-nu ‖ (šam) ku .... M^S *pl* 25; AJSL xiii 221. KB vi (1) 518 connects with šarānu, 1 also:

šūrānu, Sarg *Khors* 132 ki-ma šu-ra-ni ṭi-xi dūri-šu iç-bat-ma, KB ii 71 suggests: *pl* of šūru, bull; or a form like mīrānu > mī(š)ru.

šurinnu *1.* *m* column, pillar {Säule}?? AV 2399, 8562. *Jour. Bib. Lit.*, xix 4 perh. Š-form of רנא. K 891 *O* 5 (iç) šu-ri-in-ni bābi bīti Iš-tar .... az-qup, + 10, (iç) šu-ri-in-ni bīt Nergal ša (al) Tar-bi-çi .... azqup; Lehmann, ii 20, 21; KB ii 260; Pinches, *Texts*, 17. NE XII *col* vi ki-i šu-ri-in-ni dam-ki (K 2774), KB vi (1) 265 & 530, wie ein schöner Pfeiler. II 26 *no* 1 *add* (= 34 iv) 32 ŠU-NIR = šu-ri-in-nu in one group with (33) ZAG(u-suk)AN = eš-re-e-tum & (34) ZAG-GAR-RA = bītāti ilāni (Br 7198). II 32 *no* 7, 16 (*l* 77) šu-ri-in-nu, between na-as-xu (700 *col* 2) & še-im ....—ŠU-NIR often in Gudea-inscr. Cyl A *col* iv 22 *etc.* see Thureau-Dangin, ZA xvi 357 *rm* 7 for other passages. he translates: *emblème.* Also *cf* qatrinnu.

šurinnu *2.* BA ii 295, 296 suggests reading šurinnu in II 16 *c-d* 10 IM-ŠU-RIN-NA = (kīma) ti-nu-ri, derived from *šūru coal {Kohle}, Hebr שְׁחוֹר, √שחר be black; thus properly: Kohlenbecken. See also tinūru.

šarnupp(bb)u, AV 8065 see nuppu, 705 *col* 2 (K 13 = Hr^L 281); BA iv 527 *foll*: Elamitischer Amtsname.

širinnatu. T. A. (Ber) 26 i 45: one ŠU ši-ri-in-na-a-tum kaspi.

šires(u) see seraš (785 *col* 1).

šūrupu, šurip, šuruptu, 1 (√erebu); **šarapu**, 1; šarrapu, 1; **šarpu**, šurpu, 1; šuruptu, 2 *etc.* see šūrubu *etc.*

šarapu 2. *pr* išrup (§§ 27; 41), *ps* išarrap. id  § 9, 272; H 34, 827 = ša-ra-pu. AV 8041, Br 10874; D^H 20. Nöldeke, ZDMG 40, 722 & *rm* 1: שׂרף. — *a*) burn {verbrennen} with fire, written NE & NE *pl*; while with qamū we usually, but not always, find ina (il) GIŠ-BAR (see qamū, 2). See also nabalu, 1 (636) & TP III *Ann* 3, 52, 110, 160, 162, 164, 178, 183, 188, 189. TP vi 10 such & such city (cities) ina NE *pl* aš-ru-up; Šalm, *Mon*, *O* 20, 25 ina NE aš-ru-up. II 65 *b* 6 iš-ru-up; S..rg *Ann* 115 (& 31 *etc.*) ina i-ša-a-ti aš-ru-up. IV^2 8 iv 2/3, 5/6 išāti (*i. e.* NE) aš-ru-pu. II 51 *R* 19 (ZK ii 321). — K 257 *R* 13, 14 (H 129) i-ša-tum na-pi-ix-tum ša ina ki-rib šadi-i iš-šar-ra-pu ana-ku (Br 5654), a glowing fire which burns in the midst of the mountains I am (JAOS xxiv 115; *ibid* 125: probably Ifteal, but??). T. A. (Ber) 189, 60 read u i-š[a]-r[a-p]u-ni-ma i-na išāti (BA iv 121 *fol*); 76, 52 i-ša-ra-pu mātāti [i-n]a išāti; (Lo) 37, 39 i-na išāti i-š(s: Q^{t}?)ar-ri-ip-šu. Bu 88, 5—12, 11 *O* 32 ta-ša-rap; ZA iv 229, 16 ta-šar-rap; T^{M} ii 68 see qalū, 1 Q. I 70 *c* 4 whosoever this tablet i-na NE i-šar-ra-pu. Šalm, *Mon*, *O* 17 see maqlūtu (577 *col* 1). Zimmern, *Ritualt.*, 26 ii 25 (end) šu'u (?) ab-ri ta-šar-rap. K 164, 7 (beg.) (iç) er-nu ta-šar-rap (& 21 end); 16 ū-mu ša šar-up-tu i-šar-rap-u-ni, BA ii 635, 636. T^{M} iv 114 a-šar-rap-ši-na-ti; ii 68. — *b*) kindle {anbrennen} V 50 *b* 40, 41 ina lib-bi-šu i-ša-tu i-šar-rap, he kindles a fire (= NE-MU-UN-NE, Br 4595) nu-ni-šu u-šab-šal, ZK ii 54, above. II 35 *e-f* 14, 15 see qādu, 2.

Q^{t} Anp ii 21 the cities ina NE^{pl} a-sa-rap (§ 51); also see nabalu, Q^{t}. II 51 *R* 15 (*med*) al-ta-rap, ZK ii 328. — On Johns, *Deeds*, iii 346 see KAT^{3} 484 *rm* 3.

ℑ II 60 *a* 62 (end) u-šar-ri-pu.

Derr. — našraptu (?) see *p* 742 *col* 1 & these 4:

šurpu *2.* burning {Verbrennung}, name, especially, of a series of incantations, edited by Zimmern, Leipzig, 1896 = *Assyriologische Bibliothek*, vol. XII; see King's review in AJSL xiii ('97) 144—47, and Zimmern, *Ritualtafeln*, pref. xi, xii. T^{M} viii 53 šur-pu ta-šar[-rap!].

šarrapu *2.* II 28 *no* 4 (*add*) (KU?) šar-ra-ap, Br 12556, AV 6606.

šaruptu, see šarapu Q *a*.

šuruptu (?) *3.* Sp III 6 *O* ii 9 GI-BIL = qa-nu-u šu-ru-up-tum; & GI-BIL-LAL, PSBA xvi ('94) 308—9: cane of burning. *l* 13 = ṭi-pa-ri (torch). K 168 *O* 16 (Hr^{L} 437) šu-ru-up-tu šar-pat (× Lehmann, ii 66, 67).

Šurippak, name of a city. *del* 11 (al) šu(-u)-ri(-ip)-pak the city which thou knowest situate on the banks of the Euphrates, BA i 123 & 320; KB vi (1) 481, 579: perhaps part of the city of Eridu; *del* 22 (23) amēlu šu-ru-up(*var* ri-ip)-pa-ku-u; see also ZA i 3 *rm* 1; Jensen, 387. 82—8, 16, 1 i 2 (from below), see Jensen, ZA xv 210 *rm*. II 46 *c-d* 1 (D 88 *col* v) elippu šu-rip-pak-tum; so read by some (D^{Par} 224; KAT^{2} 520, 521) but see ma-i-ri-tum; while Bezold, *Catalogue*, v 2195 reads šu-me-ri-tum.

šaraçu. II 48 *e-f* 12 (K 4386 i 22) GUB-BA = ša-ra-çu, together with šapaçu (13) & šipçu (14). AV 8042; Br 4907. See also P. N. Ša-ru-çu, II 63, 5, AV 8054.

šaraqu 1. *pr* išruq, *ip* šurqa(m) § 94, *ps* išarraq; AV 8580. give, present, bestow; offer; loan {schenken, geben, leihen}. *id* GAR § 9, 84; H 36, 887; H^{F} 36; G § 5; Br 11982, 11983. TP ii 62 such & such a-na (il) Adad aš-ru-uq; iv 39 lu-u aš-ru-uq. Asurb vii 1 rēšāti . . . aš-ruq; Anp ii 26 the mighty weapons which Ašur is (*var* iš)-ru-ka (*var* ruq) a-na (ana) a-ja-ši (ja-a-ši), § 46; KB i 74 *rm* 15. Sarg *Nimr* 6 to whom Nugimmud (= Ēa) great power iš-ru-ku-uš. KB iii (1) 172 *no* 2, 40 a-na (il) Er-ja iš-ru-uq-šu-nu-ti. very often in colophons: to whom Nabū & Tašmētum uznu ra-paštum iš-ru-ku-uš (*var* -šu), D 49, 29; II 21 *a* 27; 28 *a* 45; 27, 24; 33 *e-f* 63. Smith, *Asurb*, 11, 7 uz-na ra-pa-aš-tu iš-ru-ku-u-ni. Sarg *Cyl* 75 the gods . . . . iš-ru-ku-in-ni a-na da-riš; *Rp* 28; *Khors* 13 (iš-ru-ku-nim-ma). TP i 47, 48 the gods who kiš-šu-ta u da-na-na a-na iš-qi-ja iš-ru-ku-ni; ii 64; Esh iv 57 (iš-ru-qa); Šalm, *Mon*, ii 97. — Scheil, *Nabd*, vii 32 taš-ri-ku (3 *f sg*) balaṭ ūmē ruqūtu, see Messerschmidt, 50; could not be from šaraqu, 2 see also — *pc* Bu 88—5—12, 11 *O* 19 qīšta liš-riq, PSBA xxiv 220, 221, which might be √šaraqu, 2. — Asb x 115 ki-ma ja-a-ti-ma liš-ru-ku-uš da-na-nu u li-i-tu. TP viii 29 this a-na palē^{pl}-ja liš-ru-ku (= 3 *pl*). — *ip* K 2801 (= K 221 + 2669) *R* 19 šur-qa-šu-nu-ti(-ma) BA iii 234—5; DT 363 *O* 39 ana dāriš ja-a-ti šur-qa (a hymn to Bēl-Marduk). K^{M} 30, 14 šur-qim-ma šumu u zēru. Neb i 72. K 2493 *O* 8 šur-qam-ma balāṭi; *Rec. Trav.*, xxiv 103—4. — *ps* Sp II 265 *a* xxi 8 see katū, 2 (455 *col* 1). Asb iii 124 mūtu limnu a-šar-raq-šu-nu-ti, I will let them have. V 61 *f* 38 whosoever annuls this gift by giving it to another (ana ša-nim-ma i-šar-ra-ku), see Hilprecht, *Assyriaca*,

42 × JEREMIAS, BA i 279. IV^2 48 *a* 18 Marduk his property ana nakrišu i-šar-raq; 32 GAR-ra-ki; & perh. 40 ni-šar(?)-ra-ku. 81—6—7, 209, 5 (end) i-šar-ra-ku-uš da-na-nu u li-i-ti; also see Esh *Sendsch*, *O* 12; L^5 8 (KB iii, 1, 104). III 43 *c* 18 whosoever eqla an-na-a ana ili i-šar-ra-ku; ZIMMERN, *Ritualt.*, 25, 19 i-šar-ra-ku-šu. I 27 *no* 2, 36 see killu, 1 (383 *col* 2) & translate: for a prison he shall not give it. K^M 31, 10 ta-šar-raq; see ZIMMERN, *Ritualt.*, 61, 1 + 3 ta-ša-raq (+ 6). — ag K 3182 iv 16 ša-ri-ku ba-la-ṭi, the giver of life. — ac V 21 *e-f* 2 .... RU = ša-ra-ku, AV 8039. II 62, 26 see salaqu, 763 *col* 2; AV 8043. H 109, 36 (= V 11 *d-f* 36; D 128, 84) MAR = GAR = ša-ra-qu (‖ qi-a-šu = qâšu), preceded by ša-ka-nu, Br 5821, 11982. H 47—48 (= D 91 *col* ii) 9 iš-ru-uq, 11 iš-ru-qu, 13 i-ša-ar-raq, 15 i-ša-ra-qu; 17 iš-ru-uq-šu, 19 iš-ru-qu-šu, 21 i-ša-raq-šu, 23 i-ša-ra-qu-šu; 25 i-ša-ar-raq, 27 i-ša-ar-ra-ku-šu, 29 i-ša-raq-šu, 31 i-ša-ra-ku-šu, Br 5438. — Q pr often in Xammurabi-*code*, see HARPER's edition, 188. See also širqu & širiqtu for other instances.

Q^t = Q WINCKLER, *Forsch.*, i 498 *R* 5 (end) iš-tar-ra-ku a-xa-nu, they had given (it) to others. Xammurabi-*code* xi 58 iš-ta-ra-aq. DT 83 (= PINCHES, *Texts*, 15 *no* 4) *O* 9 ar (STRONG, PSBA xvii, 95, 131 *foll* = *c. st.* of āru, ‖ māru) ri-'-i za-ni-ni-šu ba-laṭ ṭu-ub lib-bi liš-tar-raq.

3 = Q K 943, 8 ma-a im-ma-te u-ša-ra-qu (Hr^L 452), wann wird man lie-liefern, MEISSNER & ROST, *Bît-xillâni*, 15; BA iv 254 *foll*, 13 nu-ša-ra-qa; 17 u-ša-ra-qu[-u?]; & see širiqtu.

Š I 70 *b* 10 lu-u a-na ili u-ša-aš(!)-ra-ku. — Derr. — these 6:

šaraqtu. present, gift {Geschenk, Gabe}. SMITH, *Asurb*, 131, 9 the wagons & their spoil were brought joyfully from Elam & a-na gi-mir ummâni-ja ša-raq-tu šak-na-at, and were made a present to my whole army.

šarqu *1. adj* something donated, presented, given {etwas geschenktes, gegebenes}. *f* ša-riq-tu PEISER, *Vertr.*, lxxxviii, 11. Nabd 958, 2 P. N. (sal ilat) Bânî-tu-dan-na-at who was a (sal) šar-qat ša (il) Šamaš, given to Šamaš; Nabd 842, 3 (amêl) šar-ki; perhaps Sp II 265 *a* xxiv 4 šar-ku ana a-me-lut (*var* lu-ti) it-gu-ru da-ba-bu, ZA x 12.

širqu, present, gift {Geschenk, Gabe}, AV 8319. K 2801 *O* (= K 221 + 2669) 39 ša-riq šir-ki, BA iii 232, 288. PEISER, *Vertr.*, cxl 6 ši-riq (il) Marduk (see *ibid* 303: as a contribution for the temple of Marduk). NE III *col* 3 *b* 36 (= H^{NE} 23) it-ti ši-ir-q(k)i ša (il) Šamaš, KB vi (1) 151; 439. ZIMMERN, *Ritualt.*, *no* 61, 9 + 11 še-ir-qu ina maxar *D*... ta-ša-raq (+ 15); *no* 62, 14 & *R* 9 *etc.*; 64, 12, 15, 16, 17 ši-ir-qu ta-ša(r)-raq; 66 *R* 18. Nabd 929, 3 P. N. Ši-riq ša na-ši-šu, *Š* the cup-bearer, BA i 635. Dar 385, 3 a-na Ši-ir-ki my brother; also see AV 8306. Nabd 172, 2 (amêl) ši-riq (il) .....; 643, 3 (amêl) rab ši-ir-ku ša (il) Šamaš; KB iv 244, 245. Cyr 281, 1 (+ 4) (amêl) ši-riq ša (il) Šamaš, BA iii 433 servant of the sungod {Bedienstete der Sonnengottes}; also see *ibid* 420, 421. K 1541, 21 (M^S 98 *col* 2). CLAY, 63 *rm* † & ‡: širku (šišku) & šarku, in these passages = a certain class of temple officers.

širâqu (?) Nabd 234, 7 (1129, 7 *etc.*) (amêl) ši-ra-ku.

širiqtu ‖ of širqu. § 65, 4. AV 8307. TP viii 42 the victories of my prowess, which Anu & Adad a-na ši-riq(*i. e.* çu)-ti iš-ru-ku(-u)-ni. Anp i 26 the gods who their weapons a-na ši-riq-ti(-te) bê-lûtija iš-ru-ku. I 69 *c* 39, 40 a-na ši-riq-tu liš-ru-ki-i-ni. Samsuiluna (KB iii, 1, 132) iv 20 may such & such a-na ši-ri-iq-tim lu iš-ru-ku-nim. KB iii (2) 6 *col* 3, 17—18 a-na ši-ri-iq-tim lu aš-ru-uq-šum. K 2852 + K 9662 iii 9 (end) ana ši-riq-ti aš-ruq; K 418, 3 *foll* see AJSL xiv 175. K 382, 11 a-na ši-riq-ti is-sa-ar-ku, KB iv 154; 322 *col* 4, 15 šum-ma mu-ut-su ši-riq-tum iš[-ša]-raq-šu; 64 ii 20 (& HILPRECHT, *Assyriaca*, 18—19) a-na ši-riq-ti liš-ru-ka-šu. V 51 *b* 51, 52 balaṭ ṭûb libbi ana ši-riq-ti lu-ša-riq-šu (Br 3526, 5655; KB iii, 1, 53 *rm* *†); also see *ibid* *a* 22, 28; II 19 *a* 40, 41. JAOS xvi 74 (Nebuchad. text) ii 23 such & such a-na ši-ri-iq-tim šu-ur-qam; ZA i 342; ii 138 *b* 22 (-ti); = I 52 *no* 4 *b* 21, 22; I 51 *no* 1 *b* 22 (-tim; -qa-am). I 68 *no* 1 *b* 23 a-na ši-riq-ti šur-qam; V 63 *b* 45 a-na še-ri-iq-tim šu-ur-qam; V 66 *a* 30. — Often in Xammurabi-*code* (gift, betrothal present) see HARPER's edition, 188. — P. N. see AV 8304; 48—7—20, 116 (Hr^{L} 815) 2; Camb 379, 3 *etc.* Another ‖ is:

šurqu *1.* IV² 51 *b* 29 ina šur-ki iš-ru-qu it-ta-mi; + 19 ina šur-ki šum ili-šu i-me-šu; Z^{S} ii 76, 86; iii 54. Also perh. NE III *col* 2 *a* 9 iš-kun š(s)ur-q[u], KB vi (1) 146, 147.

šaraqu 2. pr išriq, steal {stehlen}. HAUPT, *Jour. Bib. Lit.*, xix 78 *rm* 107 perhaps Š of riqu, empty. Arb سرق. K 279, 7 the ox, ša .... ištu bît *N.N.* iš-ri-qu-u-ni, whom he has stolen from the house of *N.N.*, AV 843; + 10 the ox ša iš-riq-u-ni. Xamm.-*code* vi 34 *etc.* iš-ri-iq; xxxviii 71 ša iš-ri-qu, what he has stolen. — pm III 4 *no* 2, 4 ša-ri-iq ta-din, was stolen (&) taken; see 653 *col* 2, end; ZA xviii 160, 161; JOHNS, *Jour. Theol. Stud.*, '05, Jan., 294, 295 × KING, *Tukulti-Ninib*, i, 107.

Q¹ = Q KB vi (1) 283 *col* 2, 13 li-iš-ta-ar-ri-iq(k, g) i-na mu-ši. Xamm.-*code* viii 28 (xxxviii 13) iš-ta-ri-iq.

Derr. — these 4:

šarraqu. thief {Dieb} AV 8073. Xamm.-*code* vi 56 he shall be put to death šar-ra-aq, as a thief; vii 30 & 58. II 60 *c* 13 šar-ra-qu ik-ki-bu-u-a mim-mu-u a-ma-ru ul e-zib (KB vi (1) 375 ikkibû mimmû = unantastbares Eigentum) ☉ 252, 11 šar-ra-qu, Br 13872. K 7331 *O* 13 šar-ra-qu, M^{S} *pl* 13. K 3182 iii 31 (= K 8233 ii 31) mu-tax-li-lu šar-ra-qu mu-çal-lu-u ša (ilu) Šam-ši, AJSL xvii 141 the robber, the thief, is an enemy of Šamaš. See also šarraqu, 784 *col* 2. K 2852 + K 9662 i 15 šar-ra-qa-ku, I am a thief. A ‖ is:

šarrag(q)ânu. Xamm.-*code* vi 67 šar-ra-ga-nu-um (*cf* xxi 6).

šarraqiš, *adv* like a thief {wie ein Dieb}. Sargon *Ann* 164 nations, that had thrown off the yoke of Ašur and šadû u madbaru irtappudû šar-ra-qiš; *Ann* XIV 12 Yaman & Ašdod ..... šar-ra-qiš u-šib. Sp II 265 xxiv 8 see lamanu, 2 ג (487 *col* 2). WINCKLER, *Forsch.*, i 256 *foll*; ii 74 perhaps: like a Bedouin {wie ein Wüstenbewohner}. or: in the desert. not √šrq, steal, but √šrq be alone, lonely, deserted; *cf* Hebr שרקה desert {Einöde} Jer xxv 18; xxix 18; 2 Chron xxix 8. šarraqu (*fa''âl*), whence also Saracen = dweller of the desert; but šarraqu, thief, in Rm III 105 (= F. S. 256; STRONG, JRAS '92, 350 *foll*) ii 1 i-na šat mu-ši kima šar-ra-ki-iš, *etc.*

šurqu *2.* a thing stolen. Xamm.-*code* vi 37 ša šu-ur-ga-am i-na qa-ti-šu im-xu-ru, ZA xviii 63.

šarqu *2.* light-red blood, lymph, pus {hellrotes Blut, Eiter} Hebr שרק. GGA '77, 22. × adamatu (20 *col* 2); but also different from dâmu (251, 252). I 70 *d* 7 da-ma u šar-ka let him spill like water (Z^{B} 76); III 41 *b* 31 BE-UD u BE; III 43 *d* (iv) 17 ša-ar-ka u da-ma. 83—1—18, 2 *R* 8, 9 the sickness is i-na šar-ki-ma (in the blood), AJSL xv 141; *Rec. Trav.*, xxiv 106, 107. Sm 1064 *R* 5, 6 šar-ka ina eli ta-li-i-te b'aši, there was pus upon the dressing; JOHNSTON, JAOS xviii 162, 163. (Hr^{L} 391, 392). S^{b} 224 lu-gu-ud | BE-UD | šar-ku, H 13, 134, Br 1690, 1691. II 37 *e-f* 60 a-da-ma-tum & šar-ku, mentioned together, both meaning blood. V 41 *e-f* 58 BE-UD = šar-ku; 59 da-mu u šar-ku (= BE-UD) a-la-ku. AV 8061.

šurqînu ša šâ'ili (so ZEHNPFUND, *Theol. Litbl.* '00 *no* 5) see surqînu, 784 *col* 2. KAT³ 595 and × J^{AT} 266.

šar-qa-tum II 40 *e-f* 5 = UZU-KUN-A-ŠA(= LIB)-GA, Br 4562, AV 8066. ‖ ku-ku-ba-tum (378 *col* 2), a part of the body {ein Körperteil}.

šararu 1. pr išrur, ps išarrur, rise brilliantly, be brilliant, shine {strahlend aufgehen (von Gestirnen), erglänzen, scheinen}. G §§ 17; 18; 76 (advancer, s'élancer, on the basis of II 27 *a-b* 13 where he reads na-ša-ru-rum, but see gararu, גרר); 118. HAUPT, *Jour. Bib. Lit.*, xix 78 *rm* 107. II 29 *g-h* 7 (= K 2022 ii); H 38, 92; V 16 *c-d* 46 SAG-BU-I = ša-ra-ru, AV 8044, Br 3632 ‖ nikelmû. Z^{S} ii 79 iš-ru-ru-ma niš qa-ti ir-šu-u. K 6050 *O* 5 ina taxâz çêri i-šar-ru-ur-ma, BEZOLD, *Dipl.*, xxx *rm* 1.

$\mathfrak{Q}^1$ II 29 *g-h* 8; H 38, 93 SAG-BU-BU-I = ši-tar-ru-ru, Br 3635.

$\mathfrak{J}$ K 4195 *R* 7, SI = šu-ur-ru-ru, Br 3412, followed by (8) SI = ša-ru-ru, Br 3409. See also NOTE to purruru, 838 *col* 1, *ll* 1/2.

DERR. — šarru, šarratu, šarrûtu, šarûru, 1.

šararu 2. (denom. of šarru, king) be king {König sein}. pm = become king. ZA iv 230, 9 (Marduk) ina erçi-tim šar-ra-ta; T. A. (Lo) 30, 53 ša-ar-ra, he became king.

šararu 3. V 48 iv 36 šeu i-ša-ru-ur qât ili u šarri ikašad, the grain will decrease {das Getreide wird abnehmen}. pm u ša-ar-ru-um-ma, & when (the gold) is all gone, T. A. (Ber) 24, 49; (Lo) 18, 27.

$\mathfrak{J}$ V 63 *b* 32 mu-šar-ri-ir ummâni nakri; SCHEIL, *Nabd*, xi 34, 35.

$\mathfrak{A}^1$ II 9 *b* 10 ar-ka-nu it-taš-ra-ar.

DERR. — šerru & šarûru, 2 (?).

šarûru *1.* brightness of the rising stars, sun, *etc.*, shine, splendor, brilliance {Glanz der aufgehenden Gestirne, Sonne *etc.*; Schein, Glanz, Herrlichkeit}. AV 8055; § 63; G §§ 17; 18; 61; 76; 103; 113 (= شرّ); Z^B 46; 104; ZK ii 286. TP vii 99, 100 see çîtu, 2 (end) *p* 899 *col* 1. Neb vii 6 the temples of Esagila & Ezida ki-ma ša-ru-ru (il) Šam-šu u-še-bi. Neb *Bab* i 29 (I 52 *no* 3) ša-aš-ši-iš u-ša-pa-a ša-ru-ru-u-šu (its, Esagila's, splendor). IV² 17 *a* 47, 48 see šulmu, *a* & Br 7470; 27 *a* 21, 22 see nabaṭu $\mathfrak{A}^{tn}$ (635, 636). VATh 4105 i 15 (end) he may see ša-ru-ur (il) Šam-ši, *Mitth. d. Vorderas. Ges.*, '02 *no* 1. K 2619 (*Dibbara*-legend) iv 1 [ša] (il) ŠUL(= DUN)-PA-UD-DU (*i. e.* Ê) ša-ru-ru-šu lu-šam(?)-qit, KB vi (1) 66, 67. ZIMMERN, *Rituall.*, 66 *O* 2 ša-ru-ri (il) Šamaš. K 11152, 5 (*frg* of hymn to Ištar) ga-bu-tum ša šu-ru-ru-ša uš-nam-ma-ra ik-li-ti (686 *col* 1, above). K 3182 i 5 (end) ša]-ru-ru-ka; iv 6; ZA iv 230, 13 see birbirru (190 *col* 1, below). 83—1—18, 243 *R* 1 u ša-ru-ru-šu ma-aq[-tu], THOMPSON, *Reports*, ii *no* 33, & often. II 35 *e-f* 4—8 ša-ru-ru ‖ of id-di-šu-u, nam-ri-ir-ru, bir-bir-ru, me-lam-mu, ši-bu-bu; 9 ša-ru-ru = ni-ip-xu. K 2061 ii 3, 4 (H 203; Br 7470) ŠE-IR-ZI = ša-ru-ru & ba-ri-ru, see 194 *col* 1; also Rm 201 *O* 4 (PINCHES, *Texts*, 2 *no* 4); V 29 *g-h* 56 ŠE-IR = ša[-ru-ru] Br 7467; 57 ŠE-ZI = š nim[-ru], Z^B 46, Br 7445; ZK ii 196 *rm* 3. II 48 *c-d* 24 (ša) RI = ša-ru-rum, Br 2577. P. N. Nam-ra-am-ša-ru-ur, *Rec. Trav.*, xvii 35 *no* XVI.

šarûru *2.* a kind of cucumber {eine Art Gurke} see qiššû (985 *col* 2), & ZA i 52, 53.

'Šarrarû. 82—5—22, 946 *R* 6 GI-SAG-NU-TIL-LA = šar-ra-ru-u, PSBA xxiii 200, 201.

ša-riš, in (amêl) rab ša-riš, JENSEN, ZA vii 174, he who is the head, chief. whence Hebr רַב־סָרִים. ZIMMERN, ZDMG 53 ('99) 116 *rm* 2; KAT³ 649; WINCKLER, *Untersuch. z. Altor. Gesch.*, ('89) 138, excurs. v. ZIMMERN, *Rituall.*, *no* 57, 10 (amêl) ša-riš šarri, der Eunuch (?) des Königs. Anp i 92 ša (amêl) ša(= NIN)-riš *pl* ša (amêl) ša-riš šarrâ-ni bêl xi-i-ṭi šêrê-šu-nu u-bat-tiq; also PINCHES, London *Academy* '92, June 25, 618 rubû-ša-ri-e-šu. PINCHES, *ibid* maintains against WINCKLER that rab ša-riš is the Assyrian translation of the rab šâkê (Sumerian). See also MEINHOLD, *Jesaiaerzählungen* & PRINCE, *Daniel*, 196 *rm* 6. HALÉVY, RÉJ xx 6; HAUPT, *Kings* (SBOT) '04, 271 chief Eunuch; *cf* rêšu, 1 *b* (983 *col* 2).

šaršu, Br 3838 *ad* V 18 *d* 29 see xiršu, 841 *col* 2.

šarriš, *adv* like a king {wie ein König}? Sp II 265 *a* xxiv 10 šar-ri-iš (*var* eš) ka-la(-)mi(-)nu, *etc.*; ZA x 12.

šurriš see surriš, 782, 783.

širiš (?) KB iv 86, 87 *l* 12 la ši-ri-iš ki-mu-u.

šuršu *c. st.* šuruš *m.* — *a*) root of a plant, of a tree {Wurzel einer Pflanze, eines Baumes} *etc.* PRAETORIUS, *Litbl. Or. Phil.*, i 198 = Sab. שרש; D^H 20; 34 *rm* 2; D^{Pr} 35. K 2619 (*Dibbara*-legend) iv 2 ša iç-çi šu-ru-us-su lup-[ ]-ma, KB vi (1) 66. BANKS, *Diss*, 14 (= REISNER, *Hymnen*, 9) 105 šur-šu-u-a nu-us-su-xu. Rm 78 *O* 14 see šamaxu, $\mathfrak{Q}$. NE 56, 24 šur-šu-ka ul dun-nu-[nu?], J^{I-N} 28 deine Wurzel ist nicht stark genug. IV² 7 *a* 55 šur-šu-

šu (of the onion) la i-çab-ba-tu (IV 28 c 11); 3 a 41 su(& šu!)-ru-us-su li-qēma; K 161 *col* 3 šur-šu-šu, ZK ii 11. ZIMMERN, *Ritualtafeln*, 79—82 iii 7 šap-la-nu šur-ši-šu [11] Ē[-a] .... u-rab[-bi?], unten hat Ea seine Wurzel grossgezogen; 8 e-le-nu ar-ta-šu, *etc.* Esh *Sendsch*, *R* 46 šur-uš (the root *i. e.* all that reminded of Tarqû's lordship) (mât) Ku-u-si ul-tu (mât) Mu-çur as-sux-ma. Sarg *Cyl* 25 na-si-ix šur-uš (mât) A-ma-at-te, AV 8572. *Ann* 40 amēl (al) Sukkai ..... milik limutti ša nasax šur-še ma-ti imtalliku. Sm 2052 ii 16 šu-ur-šu = li[-tu?], M[S] *pl* 19. KB vi (1) 466. II 42 (*no* 5) *e-f* 39 (šam) šur-ši (šam il) Šamaš; 40 = (iç šam) GIR (= ašāgi), used as herbs (šammu) against KA-GIG-GA = simmu; 43 the same = GIŠ-NUM-BAB-BAR (= balti piçiti). II 46 *no* 5 *e* 77 šur-šu. — *b*) sprout, shoot, offshoot {Sprössling} *etc.* ‖ li-i-pu see 492 *col* 1, below. *adv.*:

šuršiš. Creat.-*frg* IV 90 see malmališ, 551 *col* 1; KB vi (1) 336.

šûriša(m). Creat.-*frg* IV 124 a-a-bu mut-ta-'i-du u-ša-pu-u šu-ri-šam, KB vi (1) 341, below.

šaršabiṭṭu (?). V 26 *e-f* 32 GIŠ-NE(=BIL)-DU-KU = šar-ša-b(p)iṭ(t)-ṭu, Br 4622, AV 8088. JOHNS, PSBA '05, 36 GIŠ-ṬE-DU-KU = urqu ša bîti.

šuršudu *1.* Š ac of rašadu (*q.v.*), AV 8590; K 2801 *O* (= K 221 + 2669 *R*) 8 šur-šu-di kussî šangû-ti-ja, BA iii 234, 235. II 36, 22, colophon (-du); Sarg *Cyl* 52.

šuršudu *2.* *adj* ZIMMERN, *Ritualt.*, *no* 53, 13 (il) LUGAL-GIR-RA šur-šu-du ilu ga-aš-ru.

šuršummu (§ 61, 3), from same root as ru-šumtu, AV 8591. KB vi (1) 476, 477, wol = Schlamm, oder ähnlich. NE 72, 42 ana lil-li šur-š(s)um-me, KB vi (1) 227 zu(m) ..... Hefe. V 32 *a-c* 25 see qadû, 6 (JENSEN, ZA i 309), where meaning Hefe, Satz des Weines is suggested by KÜCHLER; K 2611 *O* i 16. II 36 *g-h* 21, 22 ..... NAM = šur-šum-mu, & š BI (= šikari) preceded by tax(?)-ri-xu (20); M[S] 25 *col* 1 bi-ri-xu is only a guess. — SCHEIL, Notes LX, Constant. 583 *O* 11 (*Rec. Trav.*, xxiii) ina šur-šum-mi e-pu-ti, dans un pot à cuire; *R* 6 (+ 19 + 26) šur-šum-mi GEŠ la-bi-ru, dans un pot de vieux vin.

šur-šu-ru see xinçurru, 326 *col* 2.

šeršer(r)u. K 4152 *R* 17 ŠIM .... (Br 14113), 18 ŠIM-DIR (Br 5171), 19 ŠIM-GUG (Br 5203) = šer-šer-ru, AV 8139; 20 ŠIM-]DIR = šer-še-ru followed by šîbu (21—23), lêru (24—26), Br 5172; M[S] *pl* 7. JENSEN-ZIMMERN, KAT³ 649 compares Hebr שְׁשַׁר *, שָׁשַׁר, rote Paste.

ša(e)rša(e)rratu, chain, fetter {Kette, Fessel} or the like Z[B] 36, *med*; KAT³ 650, below. ZA iii 86 *foll*; MEISSNER, 6 *rm* 2. H 60, 11 šar-šar-ra-tu (= erû SAR-SAR Br 4366, Z[B] 37 *rm* 1) i-xad-su (see (xâdu. 2; 305, 306), fetters he puts around him. Hebr שַׁרְשְׁרָה. — Also **šaršarru** Br. M. 22446, 3 + 4 + 6—9 + 14 *etc.* ZA xviii 224: Ring, Ringgebilde. HEHN, OLZ vii 399 ('04, Oct.): Kette auf dem Wasser sich bildender Bläschen.

šârtu, *c. st.* šârat. hair on one's body ✕ pirtu (‖ muttatu) hair of the head {Haar am Körper} = שַׂעֲרָה, شَعْرَة. — *a*) hair, hairy skin of the human body. NE 8, 36 ud-d]u-ur (but see KB vi (1) 120, 121) šar-ta ka-lu zu-um-ri-šu. KB vi (1) 78 (= T. A. (Lo) 82, 30) ii 12 i-na ša-ar-ti-ša (by her hair) uqiddi-daššimma (√קדד) to his throne. K 246 i 6 (H 82, 83) ša-rat (id = compound of H 34, 816 + 28, 825) zu-um-ri šu-zu-uz-zu (✕ AV 8038; § 88); also IV² 6 *col* v 47—49. V 50 *a* 51, 52 ša ra-bi-]çu lim-nu ša-rat (id = V 42 *e-f* 59: ziq-na-tu, Br 10816) zu-um-ri-šu uš-xi-zu, one whom the evil demon has robbed of the hair of his body. S[h] 1 *O* iii 19 MU-UN-ŠU-UB | id, Br 10812 | šar-tum; same id = kimmatu, *b* (500 *col* 1, below). — *b*) hairy skin, fur *etc.* of an animal {Haarpelz, haariges Fell des Tieres} id SEG (= šipâtu, *q. v.*). IV² 5 *c* 33/34 ša-rat u-ni-ki (IV² 3 *a* 42, 43; *b* 3 *etc.*; Br 10779) & ša-rat pu(bu)-xat-ti; Z[B] 95; ZK ii 27 *rm* 2. K 2148 iii 11 (& 21, end) šar-tu iš-tu bi-rit qarnâ-ša, ZA ix 118; 419. — *c*) also barley = the bearded or 'hairy' cereal; thus šar-ti in a tablet publ. in *Palest. Explor. Fund*, Quarterly Statement, July 1900, 259, 260: X ma-na šar-ti *etc.* & 5 times more in different amounts; iD̃ ŠE-<.

šarratu (§§ 53; 63) *f* of šarru. queen {Königin} *c. st.* šar-rat, H^{CV} xxxvii NOTE 8. AV 8074; *pl* šar-ra-a-ti, § 69. iD̃ see Z^{B} 6 *rm* 2. — especially of goddesses. ilat) Damkina ka-ab-ta-at šar-rat, ZA v 59, 16. V 51 *b* 24 (ilat) Dam-ki-na šar-rat (= NIN-GAL, Br 11053; see *p* 695 *col* 1; KAT^{3} 362, 363) ap-si-i; II 57 *c* 9 šar-rat ap-si-i (*col d* broken off). On (ilat) šar-rat for the moon-goddess see JENSEN, ZA vi 242. KAT^{3} 364—5 on šarratu & P. N. שרה. Ištar: Esh *Sendsch*, *R* 22, 23 na-ra-mu šar-ra-ti (ilat) Iš-tar. II 66 *no* 1, 1 šar-rat kāl ilāni; V 62 *no* 2, 8 (Br 5918). 81—2—4, 188, 4 (prayer to Ištar of Nineveh) en-na šar-rat ilāni ^{pl}; Asb ii 128 (*etc.*) Ištar of Nineveh (ilat) (Br 6996; *var* šar-rat) kid-mu-ri (see 372 *col* 2 for other instances). KB ii 248, 17 i-sin-ni šar-ra-ti ka-bit-ti mārat (il) Bēl; & *rm* 4, *ibid.* TP III *Ann* 73 (ilat) [Ištar] (ilat) šar-rat (al) [Ninua]. NE 51, 19 [a-na (ilat) I]š-tar šar-ra-tum, KB vi (1) 372—3; HAUPT, JAOS xxii *pl* 1. On šarrat šamāmi u kakkabē, K 100 *O* 14; (Ištar) šar-rat šamē, Sm 954 *R* 3, 4 (Br 6851) = Ištar of Nineveh see KAT^{3} 425, 426. — Bēlit. K 11, 35—6 (Hr^{L} 186 *R* 12, 13) ilat Bēlit ša (ilat) šarrat (or bēlit?) ki-di-mu-ri. — K 3600 *R* 13 šar-ra-ti (ilat) Na-na-a, CRAIG, *Relig. Texts*, i 54, 55. — V 66 *a* 20, 21 (ilat) Ēru-u-a šar-rat pa-ti-qat nab-ni-ti. IV^{2} 13 *a* 10, 11 ina šar-ra-a-ti be-lum e-liš. ZA iv 232, 13 i-lat i-la-a-ti šar-rat šar[-ra-a-ti]. — IV^{2} 31 *O* 24 (25) a-na šar-ra-ti ilat E[reš-k]i-gal (*i. e.* the queen of ki-gal, or, the netherworld; V 28 *a-b* 31 e-ri-šu ‖ šar-ra-tum); KAT^{3} 583 *fol*; also NE 19, 46 šar-rat erçi-tum (ilat) Ereš-ki-gal. — of human beings. TP III *Ann* 154 (sal) Za-bi-bi-e šar-rat (māt) A-ri-bi; 210 (sal) Sa-am-si šar-rat (māt) A-ri-bi. K 1619 B 2 (Hr^{L} 308; III 16 *no* 2) (sal al) Aššur-šar-rat; JAOS xx 244—49. V 66 *b* 27 Stratonike, his wife, šar-ra-at, the queen. — šar-rat kib-ri = lallartu, Br 14457 see kibru *b* (end) 307 *col* 2. — II 31 *no* 3, 11—12; V 41 *a-b* 11—12 šar-ra-t[um] ‖ ma-al-ka-tum & ša-nun-ka-tum. II 31 *e-f* 7 šar-ra[-tum]. V 36 *d-f* 14 (u-mun) < = šar-ra-tum, Br 8755. V 37 *a-c* 32 gloss ga-ša-an, Br 6996. — Sp II 265 *a* xxiv 3 šar-ra-tum pa-ti-iq-ta-ši-na šu-e-tu šama(*var* ša-ma)(-ma)-mi, STRONG, PSBA xvii 141: (ilat) ma-ma, which would confirm ZDMG 43, 198 ><, above, 552 NOTE 2.

šarrūtu. royalty, sovereignty {Königswürde, Königsherrschaft}, AV 8087. šarrūtu epešu = rule, govern. Often written LUGAL(-u)-tu (ti, tam, *etc*) Br 4266. LUGAL-ti-šu-nu TP v 17; iD̃ <<-ut, TP i 21; 46 <<-ti-ja. II 16 *c-d* 18 šar-ru[-tu]. IV^{2} 9 *a* 15, 16 see Br 5513; *a* 34, 35 na-bu-u šar-ru-ti, Br 6880. K 133 *R* 19, 20 (H 81) ana šar-ru-ti-šu-nu (KAT^{3} 409 *rm* 9). Neb *Grot*, (I 66) iii 45 Sin na-ra-am šar-ru-ti-ja. II 67, 4 who the countries i-pi-lu-ma e-pu-šu šar-ru-us-si-in; 13 the wide land of Karduniaš a-pil-ma e-pu-ša (= 1 *sg*) šarru-u-sa. K 2729 *O* 14 ša ultu ri-du-ti a-di e-peš šarru-u-ti; 20 iç-ç]u-ru ma-çar-ti šarru-ti[-ja], KB iv 142, 143; BA ii 566 *fol*. KB iii (2) 46, 10 [mu-šar-bu]-u šar-ru-ti-šu; & thus perh. IV^{2} 12 *a* 6 ..... u šar-ru-ti-šu; TP i 17. Ner *a* 5 a-na e-pi-e-šu šarru-u-ti-šu da-ri-ti (KB iii, 2, 70). Nabopolassar (KB iii, 2, 4) ii 54 çalam šar-ru-ti-ja; 61, 62 lu-ba-ra(-am) te-di-iq šar-ru-ti-ja (HILPRECHT, *OBI*, I 32, 33 ii 64, 65); KB iii (2) 8 *no* 8 *col* ii 21 šar-ru-tim šu-ul-bi-ri-im, let my rule (kingdom) endure. Neb viii 36 šu-ba-at šar-ru-ti-ja; Sarg *Ann* 60 *etc.* maxaz šar-ru-ti-šu. V 52 iv 26 (= IV^{2} 53 *R* iv 43) ana kun-ni ešid kussi-e šar-ru-ti-šu; SCHEIL, *Nabd*, viii 40, 41 (-ja); IV^{2} 18 *no* 2 *R* 14 iš-di kussī šar-ru-ti-šu. See also kussû, 413, 414. Neb *Grot*, iii 27 the palace mu-ša-ab šar-ru-ti-ja; 41 pa-ra-aç šar-ru-ti; KB iii (2) 64 *col* 3, 15. V 51 iii 19 ni-šu-ut šar-ru-ti. See also našû (Q *a*) 732 *col* 1, end. šurru-u-ut la ša-na-an, Esh *Sendsch*, *R* 26 & often; Sarg *Ann* XIV 2; *Khors* 4. K 629 *R* 20, 21 šar-ru-ut-ka a-na ça-at ū-me lu-ša-li-ku (3 *pl*) = Hr^{L} 59. K 501, 8 (the gods) ra-i-mu-te šar-ru-ti-ka (Hr^{L} 113;

Lehmann, ii 74, 75). šarrût šamê IV^2 5 *a* 8 (KAT^3 426). — II 47 *c-f* 22 SAR-DA = a-gi-e šarru-ti, Br 4371; also V 28 *g-h* 22 (Br 2207, 9340); 20 *e-f* 17 NAM-LUGAL-LA (Br 2174) & 19 NAM-EN-NA (Br 2816) = šarru(-ru)-tum, in both instances preceded by be-lu-tum, with same ið H 42, 17. II 26 *e-f* 17 (⊕ 84 i 24) NAM-NIR-GAL (=IK) = šar-ru-tum, Br 2108, 6293. See also šurru, šurratu. rêš šarrûti, KAT^3 325 = Regierungsantritt; Zeit vom Antritt bis zum Jahresabschluss. — šarrût kiššati Winckler & Johns, *Doomsdaybook*, 7 = Harrau, claimed by the Assyrian kings since Adad-Nirâri, I. — mâr šarrûtu sec 581 *col* 3 & § 73. — arad-šarrûti & amat-šarrûti, see Johns, *Doomsdaybook*, 32 & 81; often in Peiser, *Vertr.*; BA iv 71; 428: Königsknechtschaft, *i. e.* Königssklaven waren unveräusserlich. — On mu-kin šarrû-ti TP i 2 see ZA xviii 162, 163.

šârûtu, *abstr. n.* to šâru, 2 (& 3) slander, lie {Verleumdung, Lüge}. T. A. (Ber) 45, 29 a-ųa-te ša-ru-ta aš-ta-pa-ru, 30/31; 42, 20—21 now they speak a-ųa-tu ša-ru-tu (see BA iv 281 *foll* on this letter); 58, 13 (aųâti) ša-a-ru-tu, BA iv 317.

šarîtu, *pl* šarište (?) Anp ii 75 ša(-a)-ri-MEŠ (*var* -a-te) among the tribute of Sipirmena, AV 8046; KB i 82—3; ZA i 368, some vessel or instrument.

šêrtu *1. c. st.* šêrit. ið NAM-TAG-GA = annu, arnu). ZK ii 21, 22; Jensen, KB vi (1) 340, 341. Perh. = שֵׂרְתָה. — *a*) anger, wrath {Zorn}; then also: anger in action, punishment. KB vi (1) 108—9 // 54, 55 (*Etana*-legend) še-rit-ka i-si(a)x-xu-ra a-na mux-xi-ja ša a-šak-ka-nu-ka a-na-ku še-er-ta, BA iii 366, 367. Creat.-*frg* IV 114 še-rit-su na-šu-u (3 *pl*). IV^2 54 *b* 3 lištapšix šer-ta-ka ka-bit-ta, may thy severe anger calm down; *a* 42 šu-ut-bi-ma šer-tuk-ka, let him escape from thy wrath; see also ZA iv 237, 46. NE I v 20 (= H^{NE} 6, 39; 13, 20) (il) Ea-bani nu-uk-ki-ra še-rit-ka (*var* -su). — punishment: KB ii 246—7, 63 e-me-is-su Marduk šar ilâni še-ir-ta-šu rabî-tu. Perhaps K^M 11, 19 (end) šer-ti pu-šur. — *b*) sin, misdeed, iniquity {Sünde, Missetat, Verbrechen}, *i. e.* the cause of anger & its subsequent punishment. IV^2 51 *a* 34 ul i-di šer-ti ili ul i-di en-nit ištari. IV^2 7 *a* 8 murçi ta-ni-xi ar-ni šer-ti ųil-la-ti xi-ṭe-ti (K 2868 *R* 26 = Smith, *Miscellaneous Texts*, 19); 8 *a* 5 & 11 še-rit-su lit-ta-bi-ik, his sin be carried away (√abaku); V 51 *c* 10. V 20 *e-f* 3 NAM-TAG-GA = šer-tu; Z^B 115; Br 2164 (× AV 3370, 8091 šar-tu). Xammurabi-*code* xliii 43 še-ri-zu. Here also T. A. (Lo) 61, 14 qa-ar-zi-ja : ši-ir-ti = slanders; & perhaps III 66 *O* 10 *d* ina û-me še-ir-ti nu-bat-te (× 641 *col* 1); this latter, possibly also to:

šêrtu *2.* a *f* of šêru, 2. Zimmern, *Ritualt.*, *no* 50, 4 [ina] šer-ti e-ma (il) Šamaš ittapxa. 80—7—19, 65, 7 (še-ir-ti); K 871 *O* 1 ina še-ir-ti (ik-tu-un); 82—5—22, 57, 1; K 742, 11; K 750 (edge) 1 = Thompson, *Reports*, ii *nos* 23, 185, 186, 190, 271; *ibid*, *no* 243 (K 761) *R* 3 ni-qu-u ina ši-ri-e-ti im-ba-ru, = *pl.* which also in Sm 954 *O* 39, 40 (Br 7907; KAT^3 424; *cf* šimêtan; ið UD-ZAL-LA, EME-SAL; for which compare also uddazallû, 19 *col* 2). III 52 *a* 50; 57 *no* 7, 15 (*b* 61) ina še-ri-e-ti, used as a *sg*, just as lilâti, ZA i 353 & *rm* 2: morning-dawn. III 67 *c-d* 57, 59, 60 Papsukkal is called (il) PAP-GAL, (il) GA-AN-DU & (il) GA-AN-GU as the god ša še-ir-ti, Br 13855 *ad* K 4349 *R col* 9, 58 (= II 54, 32), AV 6953. K 3182 iv 19 še-ri-e-ti.

šêrtu *3.* IV^2 25 *b* 50, 51 šer(šar?, šir?)-tu (= GIR-GAL, Br 319) ittananbiṭ az-ka-ru el-liš šu-pu; ið also = namçaru sword, scimetar (683 *col* 1; Br 318); perhaps here: the beams or rays of the early morning sun, shooting out, pointed like a sword. Xamm.-*code* xliii 43 May Sin, the lord of heaven, my divine creator, whose scimetar (ša še-ri-zu) shines (šu-pa-a-at) among the gods, Harper's edition, 104, 105.

šêrtu(m) *4.* growth? germ? {Wuchs?, Keim?} see šerû, 1 (end).

šerîtum (?). KB iv 38 *no* I 5 Še-ri-tum mâr Ibni-ilu, a female P. N.

šartennu see sartennu (785 *col* 2) & add: II 31 *c-d* 38, Br 12560.

šaššu *1.*, **šâšu** *1.* AV 8004. mentioned together with šallatu, Anp i 48, 65 *etc.*; with bušû, 1, see 200 *col* 2. Šamš iv 17 (21) šal-la-su-nu makkûr-šu-nu ša-šu-šu-nu. Sarg *Khors* 59, 75, 106, 133 himself & ša-šu makkûri ni-çir-ti êkalli-šu; 115; Sn iv 15, 16. IV² 48 *a* 18 ša-šu ŠA-GA (= makkûra)-šu *etc.* Marduk will give to his enemies. K 5418 iv 20 read ša-šu-ka (>< KB vi, 1, 298—99) namkurraka & see namkur(r)u, 681, 682; ZA xii 321 *foll.* D 101 *frg* 7 ša-šu(qat?)-ka >< KB vi (1) 254, 255; Sn i 29; Asb iv 65 ŠA-GA, *var* ša-šu. Perhaps I 7 *no* E 3 (end) ŠA(*i. e.* ŠI + LU)-šu *var* ŠA (= GAR *i. e.* šikin)-šu (Meissner & Rost, 58; Lotz, *Tigl. Pil.*, 179, 95); but ??; rather ša-šu, *no* 1 44, 72. Perhaps also Sn ii 56 igise-e šad-lu-ti ta-mar-ta-šu-nu ka-biṭ-tu a-di ša (-a)-šu they brought before me, ZA iii 253; BA i 314. Also *cf* ^(erû) šâšu in Zimmern, *Rituall.*. 31—37 i 45 ^(erû) pâšu ^(erû) šaš & *ibid*, *rm* 6. IV² 18 *no* 3 ii 1, 2 ina ša-aš ....; perhaps also additions to this text: Rm 2, 133. 11—12 ša]-aš ^(il) Šamaš pit-pa-nu šu-a-tu

Haupt, BA i 12 *rm* 2 jewel, Kleinod: 160 *rm* *; PAOS *vol* XV (May '90) xx; Hebr. vii 59. ZK ii 303—4, *no* 6.

NOTE. — Delitzsch, BA iv 486: ŠA-ŠU in Xammurabi-*letters* perh. = ŠA (*i. e.* AG)-gâti; or sometimes even ša gâti, rather than = bûšu.

šaššu *2.* Neb iv 5—6 u-ša-al-bi-šu ti-i-ri ša-aš-ši u abni, AV 8100. II 67, 83 a-na šu-bat šarrû-ti-ja ad-ma-an ša-aš-ši ni-siq-ti abni, *etc.* Pinches, Flemming, *Neb*, 35; Rost, 132; Ball, *Light from the East*. 177 compare Hebr שַׁיִשׁ, 1 Chron 29, 2. Lagarde, *Mittheilungen*, ii 20; white marble {weisser Marmor}.

šaššu *3.* > šanšu > šamšu, BA i 12 *rm* 2; 160. V 65 *b* 33 (end) a-šib sa-as-si; *var* a-ši-bi sa-as-su; ZA iii 309 meaning doubtful; Jensen, 109 perh.: sundisc {Sonnenscheibe}. KB iii (2) 8, 9—10 (Nabopolassar) mi-gi-ir ^(il) Ša-aš-šu; *l* 20 ša-aš-šu bêlu rabû: 64, 11 u-ga-a-am ša-aš-ši, I looked up to the sun; 13 u-sa-ap-pa ša-aš-ši. *adv* šaššâniš, šaššiš, see below.

šaššu *4.* KB ii 230—1, 59 Ištar commanded thee: ta-na-ṭa-la a-na e-piš ša-aš-ši (blicke hin darauf, dass du kämpfest?); thus = fight, battle, war? Probably a mistake by the scribe of *ši* (<Y—) for *me* (Y—); thus = ša-aš-me, see šašmu.

šâšu *2.*, **šâša**, **šâšunu**, *etc.* see šuâšu; AV 8095.

šašû *1.* NE V iv 8 (end) am-mi-ni ša-ša-ku, + 11 but šu-ut-ta ša a-mu-ru ka-liš ša-ša-at, the dream I saw was exceedingly frightful; KB vi (1) 164—5; 162, 32; 445.

šašû *2.* Q¹ Neb 101, 11 when *D* aššatu ša-ni-tu (another [a second?] woman) iš-ta-aš-šu-u; KB iv 186 *rm* 7 = Q¹ of rašû.

šûšu *1.* V 26 *e-f* 29 GIŠ-ŠE-RU(= KAK)-A = šu-u-šum, followed by su-pa-lu (778 *col* 1, beg.); id = ziqpu & šerû, 4. Br 7465, AV 8601; D^H 35 *rm* 1; also see V 26 *f* 60. II 45 *no* 4 *R* (*add*) ^(iç) šu-u-šu, Br 13056. 81—11, 154 *R col* 3, 14 see šûru, 2. GGA '04, 740 = Süssholz; *cf* سوس.

NOTE. — Scheil, Notes d'épigr. LX (Constant. *no* 543; *Rec. Trav.*, xxiii, reprint *p* 4 *rm* 7) šûšum pouvait (donc) être le nom d'une espèce de cèdre et idéogramme de Suse: Šûši, šûšum = ERIN-KI venir de ce jeu de mot. The name of Susa the capital of Elam occurs *e. g.* Z^B ii 162 Šu-u-ši^(ki); IV² 52 iii 46 lip-ṭu-ru ina Šu-u-ši^(ki), D^K 43 *rm* 1. II 48 (*a*-)*b* 50 a star is called Šu-ši^(ki), followed by another called Aš-šur^(ki), AV 8599; Bezold, *Catalogue*, v 2196; KAT³ *passim*. The form Šûšan: Asb vi 27 zi-q-qu-rat ^(al) Šu-ša-an, AV 8594 = שׁוּשַׁן; D^Par 326; Weissbach, *Anzanische Inschriften*, 136; Jensen, WZKM vi 54; Hagen, BA ii 233. II 60 *a-b* 9 ^(il) Ar-man-nu = ^(il) Šu-ša-an(-ki) AV 8600; Br 13074. ^(il) Šušinak, Asb vi 30, the God of the Susâans; KB ii 201 *rm* **; 83, 1—18, 1330 *R* 35. II 57 *c-d* 48 ^(il) Šu-ši-na-ak = ^(il) Ninib in Elam. KAT³ 485; 570 *rm* 8; V 35, 30 (BA ii 233). — ^(sal) Šu-ša-an-nu, often in *c. t.*, AV 8607. On the earliest mention of Susa see Hilprecht, *OBI*, I *p* 31 & *rm* 5.

šuššu *1.*; **šûšu** *2.* = *σῶσσος*, sixty {sechzig}; id Y. ZDMG 46, 570: properly ¹/₆ of 360 *i. e.* sixty; but see ZA xviii 82. AV 8598. 8614; idd also: UŠ § 9, 94; Br 5046, 10078; Sarg *Ann* 373; *Khors* 162; *Bull* 70; KU *e. g.* KU-U = 60 ammatu, Nabd 265, 12; 361, 9; 694, 27; Neb 318, 1; Cyr 230, 3. Delitzsch, *Ägypt. Zeitschr.*, '78, 56—70; § 75; Lehmann, i 130. *pl* šu-ši. K 4378 vi (D 88) 15 GIŠ-MA'-*I*-ŠU-GUR = elip šu-uš-še (*var* šu), a ship of 60 gur; II 46 *a-b* 15; H 110, 37—40 (= V 12 *e-f*

35—38) see nēru, 4 (724 *col* 2), Br 10075; ZK ii 268—79. TP i 54 against (= it-ti) one šu-ši šarrāni .... I fought; ii 49 (61; 51) 1 šu-ši ruq-qi erē *pl*; iii 103; ii 29 (3 šu-ši). IV^2 31 *O* 69 let loose upon her šu-ši murçi, 60 diseases, KB vi (1) 84—5; also *ibid* 298, 2 + 4 + 6. Xamm.-*letters* 46, 4: six šu-ši zābilē = 360 porters, + 6 + 8 (BA iv 471 *foll*). Also see T. A. (Ber) 218, 6; 28 iii 73: 99 šu-ši u 3; 25 ii 8: one šu-ši aban uknī banû; 26 i 30. II 55 (*a*)-*b* 21 be-lit šu-ši, Br 14420. Perh. V 35, 7 (end) šu-uš-šu. V 36 *d-f* 8 (šu-uš) ⟨ = šu-uš-šu, Br 8766.

Against Zimmern, *Ber. Sächs. Akad.*, 1901, 50: šuššu = 60 = ⅙ of the year = double-month, als Naturmass, see Lehmann, *Beitrr. z. Alten Gesch.*, i 483 & Kewitsch, ZA xviii 80, 81; *ibid* 82: das Tagessechstel (šuššu = ⅙ of a day = 4 hrs.) wurde verdrängt vom Tageszwölftel (kaspu) und dieses wiederum vom Tag 24 tel: der Stunde, während die Unterteilung zu je 60 (imdu) auch ferner eingehalten wurde. KB vi (1) 412 > šudšu = ⅙ of 360.

šuššu *2.* šu-uš-šu > šumšu, his (its) name, see šumu; also V 21 *g-h* 47 NE (= BIL) šu-uš-šu, Br 4596. *ll* 47—51 are a kind of glossary to K 8522 *R* 6; see Nibiru, 3 (639 *col* 2, end).

šuššû, AV 8615 see našû Š, 735 *col* 2.

(šam) **ši-ši** or ŠI-ŠI (GGA '04, 740, 741) see šilmu, 2. Also Zimmern, *Ritualt.*, *no* 11 *R* 4; 75—78, 15; K^M 12, 10; 51, 14.

šiššu *1.* V 19 *a-b* 10 SI (= qarnu) = ši-iš-šu, Br 3411; AV 8338, followed by šuxarruru, 2 (*q. v.*). — With this Meissner & Rost, 59 & BA iii 213; KB vi (1) 461 combine I 44, 83: IV dimmē siparri ša šeš-ša-šu-nu anāki bal-lum, translating šiššu by: Oberfläche, resp. Kapitäl, *i. e.* surface, capital. others (see above, 168 *col* 2 balulu pm) connect with šiššu, sixth.

šiššu *2.* (§§ 48; 75; 76). sixth {sechster} see seššu, 785 *col* 2; Br 12199. Xamm.-*code* xii 15 iš-tu ši-ši-im arxi-im, from the sixth month. KB iv 312, 313 *no* XI 2, 8 ši-iš-šu ša ūmu (the sixth part of a day?); napxar ši-iš-šu ina ū-mu *pl* šuāti; 314—5, 6 + 11 + 14 + 22. KB vi (1) 78, 8 ši-iš-ši. Scheil, *Rec. Trav.*, xix 61—2 *no* 3 *l* 8 šiš-šit-ti ūmi, sixth day. V 37 *a-c* 23 see Br 10047. Peiser, *Vertr.*, ixc, 9 (šiš-šu) = ⅙. § 32 *aβ*; ZA vii 20; xiv 182, 183. K 6012 + K 10684, 8 šiš(*var* 81—8—30, 789 še-eš)-šit [ūmu] = 6th day, PSBA xxvi (opposite *p* 56); but see Zimmern, ZDMG 58, 199 *rm* 2. KB vi (1) 412 > šidšu.

šûšib = ip Š of ašabu, 112 *col* 2; but not še-šib NE 15, 37 which KB vi (1) 138 reads u-še(*var* šeš)-šib-ka. IV^2 31 *R* 33 (end) šu-šib.

šûšub(u), *ac* Š of same verb. AV 8602. Sarg *Cyl* 34 a-na šu-šu-ub na-me-e na-du-te (49); 46 šu-šu-ub-šu ul i-di; *Bull*-inscr. 45, 46 (*Ann* XIV 67) šu-šu-ub-šu ul il-ma-du. BA iii 244, 10 ša šu-šu-ub āli ud-du-uš [eš-ri-e-ti] ušašṭira mu-xiš. V 60 *b* 30 (ša ana) ... šu-šub ma-xa-zi. Merod-Balad.-stone ii 20 (KB iii, 1, 186—7). I 35 *no* 2, 5 see šuddû, 2 & šûšupu.

Derr. of ašabu are also these 2:

šûšubu, *adj* garnished, trimmed {besetzt}, or pm? V 63 *b* 37 (aban) mux-digil šu-šu-bu in aban ni-siq-tim šuk-lu-lu, KB iii (2) 118.

šušubtu (*sc.* kussû), a small chair, foot-rest {ein kleiner Stuhl, Schemel}. II 23 *a-b* 7 šu-šu-ub-tum ‖ ku-us-su-u ša-pil-tum, § 88 NOTE.

šûššubû (?). II 45 *e-f* 62 GIŠ-GEŠTIN-ŠU-UŠ-ŠUB(=RU) = ŠU-u (Br 5017, 10845; AV 8603); some kind or species of vine or wine; perh. šušrû (?).

šaššûgu. V 26 *e-f* 31 GIŠ-ŠE-ŠEŠ = ša-aš-šu-gu, AV 8102; Br 7482. Sm 68, 5 ša-aš-šu[-gu]; K 165 *O* 14 (iç) ša-aš-šu-gu, M^S *pll* 18; 3. Johns, *Doomsday-book*, 22, 4; 29 *no* I *col* ii 42 & *p* 38: a plant. Jⅾ also ZA xvi 164. Zimmern, *Ritualt.*, *no* 41—42, 26 (beg.) translates Bitterkorn.

šašîgu (?) ZA x 211 ii *R* 4 (end) ša-ši-gu; see šamatum, 1.

šešgallum II 29 *a-b* 63 = šeš-gal-lu(m) = axu rabû, eldest brother. AV 8331; Br 1178; S^c 1 *b* 10 *foll*; ZA i 389; Prince, *Diss*, 96; but not certain. Synchr. Hist. i 27 read karas-su ‖ urigallē-šu (his flags, standards) i-pu-ga-šu. *Cf* pāgu, 1 790 *col* 1) D^K 7, 8; RP^2 iv 24 *foll*; Z^R 126 *rm* 9.

(šam) **ša-ša-da.** 79—7—8, 9 (M^S *pl* 25) = (šam) at (= gir) .... AJSL xiii 220.

šaššaṭu. mentioned in a list of ulcers, or the like, ZK ii 105. AV 8098. II 28 *b-c*

19—23 ša-aš-ša-ṭu = SA-AD(T)-DUGUD, SA-ME-EL-GAL, SA-AD(T)-GAL (= ra-pa-du, 2; maš-ka-du), SA-NUM-MAR-RA, SA-AD(T)-NU(I)M (= bennu, 3), Br 3112, 3158, 3109, 3144, 3111. V 21 *a-b* 7 SA-SAR-SA (Br 3117) = ša-aš-ša-ṭu in a group with maš-ka-du (= SA-SAR) & šu-'u-u, PSBA xxii 110. V 31 (*g-*)*h* 58 ša-aš-ša-ṭu, Br 3085. K 246 i 10 (H 82) iḌ SA-AD(T)-NUM (Br 3106) see maš-kadu, 603 *col* 2 & samānu, 766 *col* 2; between bu-a-nu la ṭa-bu-tu & bu-a-nu lim-nu.

šišku. (amēl) rab ši-iš-ku, Cyr 74, 8; 283, 7 (?); Nabd 102, 8 (sal) A-xat-abi-šu (sal) ši-iš-ka-tum of my queen (BA iii 427); often as P. N. Ši-iš-ku, AV 8332. BA iii 442 = Obergehülfe. M^S 98 *col* 2 = širk(q)u; Neb 253, 3. See širqu.

šuškallu. AV 8606, Br 3139, 3140. Lotz, *Tigl. Pil.*, 134 whip {Geissel}. ZK i 308 *rm* 2; § 73 NOTE: a species of snare or the like. Meissner, ZA ix 277—9: fisherman's net {Netz des Fischers} √שכל = شكل braid, weave {flechten}. IV² 17 *b* 13 sa-xi-ip šu-uš-kal-la-ka (o Šamaš) puxur mātāte; IV² 50 *col* 3, 48 kīma šu-uš-kal-li a-ša-rid-du i-bar-ru = T^M iii 163; *cf* K 3182 i 5; ii 27. K 133 (H 80) *O* 7—8 qar-ra-du ša šu-uš-kal-la-šu a-a-bu i-sax-xa-pu, iḌ GIŠ-SA-ŠU-UŠ-KAL-BI, Br 7166. II 19 *b* 3, 4 ša šadū ina qātišu la ipparšiddu šu-uš-kal (= ŠU-UŠ-KAL) ta-xa-zi — in a rather figurative sense we find it in IV² 27 *a* 59 ŠU(*i. e.* SA-ŠU-UŠ-GAL, 58)-ma sa-xi-ip māt nukurtim. TP iii 83 šu-uš-kal la(-a) ma-gi-re; Sarg *Nimr* 10 Sargon mal-ku pit-qu-du šu-uš-kal la-a ma-gi-re. K 4241 + 4556, *O* 6 GIŠ-SA-ŠU-UŠ-KAL = šu[-uš-kal-lu] = ša-tam(par?)(-)gal-lu ša (amēl) ŠU-XA(?) (= bā'iru?) M^S *pl* 11; also S 31, 52 *R* (end) GIŠ-SA-ŠU-UŠ-GAL & GIŠ-SA-ŠA (= GAR)-ŠA-RA = šu-uš-kal-lum, ZA ix 222.

šašallu, back {Rücken}?. K 2148 iii 11—12 šur-tu iš-tu bi-rit qarnā-ša ana ša-šal-li-ša na-da-at, + 22; K 8337, 15 šārtu qaqqadiša ana ša-šal-li-ša nadāt, ZA ix 121; 419; 125. T. A. (Lo) 60, 5 ka-ab-tum-ma u ša-ša-lu (upon my) breast and back; (Ber) 140, 5 u (šīr) ša-ša-lu-ma u (šīr) XAR (= kabittu?).

šušlušu (√šalašu, 2). K 8676 *R* 6 [URUDU?] .... U-BA = šu-uš-lu-šu. K 2034 i 12 bu-nu šu-uš-lu-šu (= PIŠ-A) M^S *pll* 15 & 4. IV² 4 iv 26 pi-til-ti šu-uš-lu[-uš-ti], KB vi (1) 486, 487 (= PIŠ-A). threefold {dreifach}.

šašmu. fight, battle {Kampf, Streit} AV 8097; G § 31; Lotz, *Tigl. Pil.*, 94. TP i 16 the great gods ša ti-bu-šu-nu GIŠ-LAL (= tuquntu) u ša-aš-mu, whose onset means fight & battle. Creat.-*frg* IV 86 I and thou i ni-pu-uš ša-aš-ma, we will fight. Esh *Sendsch*, *O* 22 Esarh calls himself la a-di-ru ša-aš-me(ma). KB iv 104, 27 ina ša-aš-me qabli u ta-xa-zu. K 3216, 8 ša-aš-mu ša iššti, ZA iv 227. K 2801 (= K 221 + 2669) *O* 1 (il) Sibi (?) .... ša ti-bu-šu-nu tam-xa-ru ša-aš-mu, see also šaššu, 4.

šašmeš = ana šašmi. Creat.-*frg* IV 94 see qarabu, Q¹ pm; & also KB vi (1) 26—7; 475.

šašūmu. Behrens, ZA xvii 389 *no* 1 > šalšu ūmu, third day = Hebr. שִׁלְשׁוֹם = day before yesterday. Hr^L 414 (Rm 77) *R* 7—9 (amēl) Ar-ba-a-a a-ki ša ti-ma-li ša-šu-me e-ru-bu u-çu-u (& BA iv 525); Hr^L 605, 7 i-ti-ma-li iš-ša-šu-me (> ina šaššūme) la u-na-ri-ṭi; *cf* Hr^L 709, 12 [ina] ti-ma-li ina šal-ši ū-me.

šuššama = šu-uš-ša-ma = I-GI-IN-ZU see šāmu 1, 3.

ši-šim read ši-riq & *cf* širqu.

šušmur(u) *1.* & *2.* see šamaru, 1 & 2.

šuššān(u), [*f* šuššāntu?]. a third {ein Drittel} iḌ 𒈫; § 77; AV 8612. TP iii 101 see napaxu, 705 *col* 2 (*med*) & translate perhaps: "until one third of the day had elapsed counting from the sun in his rise" (Haupt); see also Oppert, ZA i 235 (& JA '87, x 536, 3); Jensen, *ibid* 252 *rm* 1. But Streck, ZA xviii 172—3 reads šulul-ti. S^b 50 šu-uš-ša-na | iḌ | šu-uš-ša-an (*var* -nu) Br 11221, 11222; V 37 *d-f* 36 (Br 9950, 9963); H 35, 843; AV 8595. Oppert, ZA iii 123 = ¹/₆; vi 272 *foll* √šuššu. According to *Leyden Congress* ii, 1, 564 > šul-šānu; Feller, ZDMG 46, 570: properly *dual* of šuššu = ²/₆ *i. e.* ¹/₃. On šuššānu in *c. t.* meaning 20 (= 1/3 of 60) see BA i 516, 517. Also *cf* ZA xviii 81.

(amēl) **šušanūtu.** Dar 212, 9 pūt sixi paqirānu (amēl) Arad-šarrūtu (amēl) mār-bānūtu u (amēl) šu-ša-an-nu-tu ša ina muxxi (il) Nabû-silim-illa', BA iii 418. Also 83—1—18, 225 *R* 2 (amēl) šu-ša-nu; THOMPSON, *Reports*, ii *no* 158.

šišnu & šišānu names of two plants {Name zweier Pflanzen} AV 8334; 7868 see sallapānu, 763 *col* 2 (below), Br 12912. K 4354 i 5, 6; II 43 *d-e* 51, 52 (Br 1378, 10929) (šam) gu-ug GUG = (šam) ši-iš-nu, Br 13367. Bu 89, 4—26, 112, 3 (šam) ši-iš-nu, M^S *pl* 32.

šiššinnu, AV 8337. See sissinnu, 775 *col* 1; & add: Cyr 174, 2 (KB iv 271: Vorgewinn?).

ša-aš-ni-bi SAR, a plant {eine Pflanze} ZA vi 291 i 8.

šaššāniš, šāšāniš, **šaššiš,** like the sun {wie die Sonne}, AV 8099, 8101. *adv* to šaššu, 3. D^K 70 *rm* 6; PSBA x 294; PINCHES, TSBA '82 (Nov. 7, *p* 8 *rm* 1); J. OPPERT, GGA '84, 834; FLEMMING, *Neb*, 35, rather from šaššu, 2; while BA i 12 *rm* 2 from šaššu, 1 = like jewels; *cf* Hebr ששׁן. I 52 *no* 3 *a* 29 (Neb, *Bab*) see šarūru, 1. Neb ii 45 see nabaṭu Š (635 *col* 2); V 64 *b* 13 ša-aš-ša-ni-iš & *var* (ilu) šaš-ši-iš (KB iii, 2, 100); K 2801 *R* 38 where we have, in its stead; ušanbiṭu kīma (il) Šam-ši.

šu-šu-pu (√ašapu) see šušulū, 2; & KB vi (1) 462, 463.

šušpulu & šušqū see šaqū, 1 Š. A Der. of the same verb is:

šušqūtu. PINCHES, *Texts*, 16 (DT 83) *R* 11 šu-uš-qu-us-su (of Marduk) ina (iṣ) ZAG-SAL (*cf* šebītu; & see *p* 887 *col* 2, end, where read *sal* instead of *qal*) li-iz-za-mir-ma (*cf* 284 *cols* 1, 2) ‖ ta-nit-ta-šu, 11.

šuššar. II 45 (*e-*)*f* 28, 29 šu-uš-ša-ar, preceded by šu-uš]-ša-an. See šāru, 7. AV 8613.

šaššaru. K 8676 iv 11 [(erū) GAM or TAG-] GAM-MA = ša-aš-ša-ru, M^S *pl* 15. ZIMMERN, ZDMG 58, 953 saw {Säge}, also MEISSNER, MVAG, '04, 234—5. Neb 457, 9.

šašurru, Br 3831 see šasurru.

šušru *1.* AV 8611; a gloss, II 48 *a* 30, to (il) A-nu-um; ZA iv 388, 389 √ašaru, 2 (119, 120). Br 1170 šu-uš-šub. — II 48 *g-h* 38 šu-uš-ru = uš-šu-šu, preceded by a-ša-šu; & followed by ši-mu-ba (?)' šu-uš-ru = na-piš-ti šu-uš-rat.

šušr(ū) *2.* see šuššubū.

šu-ša-ru-u (?) PEISER, *Vertr.*, lxviii 9 (*ibid*, *p* 267; AV 806). See šuga(r)rū, 1011 *col* 2.

šūšuru *1.* *adj* (?). IV² 34 *b* 4 GIŠ-KU (= kakku) šu-šu-ru, overthrowing {niederwerfend}. √ašaru, 2. BOISSIER, *Rev. Sém.*, x (Apr. '02) 275 *foll* on this text (the id of *a* 30, 35 = ašaru, II 31 *g-h* 5). K 4335 i 37 (= II 44 *g-h* 74 TUM-TUM = šu-šu-ru, AV 8604, Br 9063; preceded by šutašqū.

šūšuru *2.* √ašaru, 3 (see *p* 120). K 2487 + K 8122 *O* 20 *O* 20 tuš-te-šir la šu-šu-ru, thou leadest him that is without a leader. K^M 2, 20; 3, 16.

šūšir = ip Š of ašaru, 3. Sp iii 586 + Rm III 1, 22 (il) Šamaš xar-ra-an-ka šu-šir; *etc.*

šūšurtu. overthrow {Niederwerfung, Niederlage} §§ 65, 33; 88 *b* & note. √ašaru, 2. Z^B 43; 96. LOTZ, *Tigl. Pil.*, 114, 115. II 43 *a-b* 4 šu-šur-tum ‖ sa-kap nakri (757 *col* 2, below). II 32 *g-h* 7 šu-šu-rat bīti, overthrow of the house, Br 5098; IV² 59 *no* 1 *O* 32 (end) šu-šu-ra-at bīti, GGA '98, 816. T^M ii 156 (167) ki-ma ša-šu-rat igāri, gleich dem Umsturz der Mauer. AV 8605.

šašītum *1.* some instrument or furniture {ein Werkzeug oder Möbel, Hausgerät}. PEISER, *Vertr.*, ci 5 ša-ši-tum siparri mu-šax-xi-nu siparri; cxxi 11 written ša-ši-i-tum siparri. If this latter is correct, then also Ner 28, 18 ištēnit šu-ši-tum ša parzilli ša xarrāni belongs here; Dar 301, 11.

šašītum *2.* ZA x 208 *O* 14 dup(pu) ul ša-ši-tum see šalmu, 2 *d*.

ši-ši-tum, AV 8330. See šilimtum.

šuštu (?) SCHEIL, *Nabd*, xi 29 šu-uš(nit?)-ti ummā-ni erçi-ti; see MESSERSCHMIDT, *Nabuna'id*, 69.

šātu, šāti, šātunu, šātina, AV 8111, see šuātu.

ša-ta, ZA x 211, 12 see tēlu.

ši-it pi-i II 39 *b* 6—7 see pit pī & *cf* 851 *col* 1 (Q), end.

šattu (> šantu), *c. st.* šanat (§ 68). *pl* šanâti. AV 8120. §§ 37*b*; 62, 1. שָׁנָה, ܫܰܢܬܳܐ, Arm שְׁנָא *c. st.* שְׁנַת. iᴅ MU (H 12, 118; Br 1234) & MU-AN-NA (§ 9, 52; Br 1247). H. C. Rawlinson (1846); see GGA '77, 1487 *rm* 4. D^H 9; G § 19; Barth, ZDMG 41, 621; Halévy, ZK i 180 § 8; ii 406 *fol*; RÉJ xi 64, 65. ZA i 94 *rm* 1. KAT³ 327 *foll.* II 40 *g-h* 41 (K 4317 *R* 4) ar-xu û-mu u šat-tu (= MU). Pinches, *Texts*, (DT 83) 15 *no* 4, *b* ar-xu u šat-tu. BA ii 293 šattu here = hour. ri-e-ša ša-at-ti I 67, 34; see rêšu, 1 *e* = the Babylonian Newyear. mišil šatti, the middle of the year, see 605 *col* 2, below. ina ki-it šatti Nabd 299, 7. pa-an šatti see 812 *col* 2 *β* & 81—2—4, 63 *O* 9 *foll* (*cf* qutru, 1, end). III 4 *no* 1 (*passim*) ina MU-ma ši-a-ti, in the same year. Šalm, *Ob*, 50; *Mon*, ii 75. T. A. (Ber) 6 *R* 14 ina libbi ša-at-ti an-ni-ti. Xammurabi-*letters* 14, 4 ša-at-tum ki-ri-ga-am i-šu, da das Jahr eine Lücke (?) hat; but Delitzsch, BA iv 490 reads ašru (= KI) ri-ga-am = rêqam. Anp i 99 see limu (485 *col* 1, below). K 10488 i (?) 4 [i]-na ša-at-tim šu-a-ti, that year; K 595 *R* 17 (end) ša-tim an-ni-ti, this year (Hr^L 6; BA iv 505 *fol*). K 4223 ii 10 *foll* šum-ma ša-at-tu | iš-te-a-at-at | ud-da-ab-bi-ir-ma, BA iii 495 wenn er es (das Feld) ein Jahr bewirtschaftet hat. Xamm.-*code* xii 10, 11 iš-tu ri-eš ša-at-tim a-di xa-am-ši-im arxi-im; 15, 16 iš-tu ši-ši-im arxi-im a-di ta-aq-ti-it ša-at-tim; ZA xviii 33. Xamm.-*code* xi 5 ša-at-tam iš-ti-a-at. ein Jahr lang, ZA xviii 25. H 55, 85 çi-bat ša-na-at (= MU-*I*-KAN), followed by çibat a-ra-ax. Sp II 18 MU-*I*(*i.e.* DIŠ)-KAN = ša-na-at, Br 1328 = V 29 *a-b* 14. III 60, 108; 62 *a* 20 xu-šax-xu šat-ti, but might be mat-ti (in the country). NE VI 47 šat-ta a-na šat-ti = year for year = always; KB vi (1) 380 jedenfalls aus ištu šatti ana šatti, von Jahr zu Jahr abgekürzt. V 65 *a* 26 a-na ša-at-ti. I 69 *c* 36; II 66 *no* 2, 14 a-na (ana) ša-at-ti, KB ii 266, 267 für die Zukunft (?). KB iii (2) 8 *no* 3 *col* 2, 11 a-na ša-at-tim, für ewig. IV² 5 *b* 16 ana ša-at-ti (= ŠI-UM-TA, 15); V 62 *b* 30 a-na ša]t-ti, Lehmann, ii 54. See BA i 385 *rm* *** (on *p* 386); ii 293 *rm* * >< Winckler's (ZA ii 146) ša at-ti = as for thee; ZA i 94 *rm* 1 = now. ina šatti, Meissner, 103 *no* 6 = alljährlich; if correct, then, here also I 52 *no* 4 *R* 14 AŠ (= ina) ša-at-ta, KB iii (2) 60, 61. Xamm.-*code* xx 27 i-na ša-na-at, yearly. KB ii 244, 55 ina šatti-šu, in the self-same year. — NAM-BI, Sm 48, 1 = ina ša-at-ti, Br 2186; GAN-U-ÇIR II 47 *e-f* 51 šat-tu, Br 3195. — *pl* V 34 *c* 43 šu-mi-di ša-na-tu-u-a, increase (o goddess) my years (§ 74, 2). V 66 *b* 12 li-mi-da MU-AN-NA-ti-ja. KB vi (1) 92, 5 ina û-me-šu-ma ina ša-na-a-ti ši-na-a-ti. MU *pl* da-ra-a-ti IV² 61 *c* 56; III 66 *col* 10, 12. MU-AN-NA *pl* da-ra(-a)-te IV² 61 *c* 20, 28; ma-'-da-ti. K 183, 23 (Hr^L 2); K 562 *O* 4; 509, 4 (Hr^L 260, 259); BA i 239 *foll.* TP i 64: 50 MU *pl*-te; vi 97, 98 MU *pl*-te dan-na-a-te. IV² 60* B *O* 10 u-a-i-te ep-še-e-ti ša-na-a-ti ma-ti-tan a-mur-ma; VATh 4105 i 12 ka-lu ša-na-tim lu-uš-bi, *Mittheil. d. Vorderas. Gesellsch.*, '02 *no* 1. *c. st.* TP viii 27 ša-na-at nuxše u mašrê (610 *col* 2, end); *Dibbara*-legend (K 1282) *R* 1 ša-na-at la ni-bu, countless years.

NOTE. — 1. On the connection between šattu & Sin see Jensen, ZA vii 177 *rm* 1; & *cf* *p* 769 *col* 1, end.

2. KB vi (1) 386: im Assyrischen existirt ebensowenig ein šattu, Weile, Dauer, Ewigkeit, wie ein šadû, hoch sein. (>< BA ii 293 *rm* *; Lehmann, ii 54, *etc.*)

Derr. — šattišu, šattišam.

šat mûši, see mûšu, 598 *col* 1 (*med*). K 2652, 25 ša-at mu-ši (KB ii 240, 241; S. A. Smith, *Asurb*, iii *p* 11); thus Asb iii 119 ina šat mu-ši; v 97 (end); Smith, *Asurb*, 98, 11 (= KB ii 180—1 *rm*); 123, 49 (= KB ii 250—1); Scheil, *Nabd*, vii 11. Sarg *Ann* 265. K 1282 *R* 6, KB vi (1) 71 (& 386) suggests: in the cool of the night; IV² 26 *a* 18, 19 butuqtum ša ina šat mu-ši (= MI-U [= ŠI + LU]-NA-KIT(D)) šur-da-at, Br 8947, 9467. iᴅ MI-U-NA = kaçâtu (see kaçû, 2; 425 *col* 1, end), which is from the same root as kuççu & takçâtum, cold {Kälte}.

šaturri. Jensen, KB vi (1) 386 suggests: the cool of the day {Tageskühle}; but Zimmern, *Ritualt.*, 1—20, 69 ina [11] šamaš ša-at-tu-ri, in der Morgenstunde, 149 (*var* -ur); see also MEISSNER, ZA xv 415*fol*: die Zeit (= šat) urri (des Lichtes) >< šat mūši, die Zeit der Nacht; name of the third (or last) nightwatch ‖ na-ma-ri-tum; see IV^2 49 *a* 3. II 39 (⊕ 59) *c-f* 18 EN-NUN (= maççartu)-UD-ZAL-LA = šat-túr-rum, Br 2856. id UD-ZAL, III 56 *no* 3, 32; UD-ZAL-LI, III 52 *b* 57 *etc.*; *cf* uddaza(i)llū (19 *col* 2), namaru (684 *col* 2, *med*) & šēru, šērtu morning. V 40 *d* 27 ša-at ur-ri, preceded by qab-li-tum & ba-ra-ri-tum (see 194 *cols* 1, 2); Rm 345 *O* 24 (M^8 *pl* 22); BEZOLD, *Catalogue*, 942 (K 8583 ii 5) ina ba-ra-ar-ti qab-li-ti šat-ur-ri. II 55 *a* 54 ša-t(d)ur-ri. KB ii 248 v 6 attalū šat ur-ri adi nūri (?).

NOTE. — D^{Pr} 39, 40; 96 (ZK ii 289*foll*) ša-ad mūši = das Heraufziehen der Nacht, der Anbruch der Nacht. *Handwörterbuch*, 632 *col* 1 √שׁעה(?) whence šattu, duration, time, hour. — Also HALÉVY, ZK i 180 § 3; ii 406, 407 = שָׁעָה, Arm שַׁעְתָּא, Arb سَاعَة; the same according to HALÉVY also in šat urri, during day-time (see also LENORMANT, *Rev. Trav.*, i '77, 62; DELITZSCH, ZK ii 284—7). D^{Pr} 96 compares šad (from šadū) urri = rising of the light; day-break with Hebr (P. N) [illegible].

satū 1. pr išti, ip šiti, ps išatti; drink {trinken} Hebr שׁתה. Z^B 43; § 110. AV 8113. Sn iii 80 lu aš-ti, see çummū, 881 *col* 1. Asb viii 119 see nišbū, 738 *col* 2; vi 21 ša .... ina libbi e-ku-lu iš-tu-u, out of which they eat (and) drank. IV^2 27, 4/5, 12/13 (3 *sg*) see musarū, 1 (569 *col* 1, beg.). IV^2 10 *a* 31 me-e .... [ul] aš-ti. K 517 *R* 14 A-MEŠ (= mē) it-ti-šu-nu ni-il-ti (Hr^L 327; PSBA xxiii 66); K 569 *R* 4 (Hr^L 78) la aš-ši (> ašti?). II 56 *c* 17 AN (or, an = ana?) mi-na-a iš-ti bēli (wr. ⟶-ni); preceded by AN mi-na-a i-kul bēli; JENSEN, ZK i 317; ZDMG 53, 118—19. KNUDTZON, 323 NAG-u & NAG either = ištū or aštū. — *pc* T^M iii 168 the firegod li-kul, the firegod liš-ti, the firegod liš-ta-bel. H 86—7, 17 ša-tam (or ša ū?)-ma lu-uš-ti, whenever I may drink; also see KAT^3 638 *rm* 2. — ip III 32, 65 see kurūnu, 439 *col* 1, end. S. A. SMITH, *Asurb*, iii 12, 34. IV^2 13 *a* 57, 58 mē el-lūti ši-ti (-NAG-AB); IV^2 21 *no* 1 B *R* 6, 7 (= IV 21 *a* 52, 53) ši-ta-a (2 *pl*; NAG) da-aš-pa = ZIMMERN, *Ritualt.*, 54 *R* 7, 8. — *ps* 83—1—18, 39 (Hr^L 345) 9, 10 ka-rānu ta-šat-tu-u, PSBA xxiii 70, 71. IV^2 61 *a* 63, 64 mē taq-nu-ti ta-ša-at-ti (2 *m sg*) AJSL xiv 277. IV^2 56 *a* 3 ṭi-du i-šat-tu-u; *cf* Sn *Bav* 7 ša-ta-a (pm?) ṭi-e-it-tu-ti (??), see ṭīṭu, *b* (355 *col* 1, *med*). NE 11, 4 (10, 50) i-šat-ti see mašqū, 608 *col* 2, beg.; XII *col* 6, 2 mē za-ku-ti i-šat-ti (3 *sg*). KB vi (1) 62—3, 32 ul i-šat-t[i] mē-šu; 96—7, 31 la ta-ša-at-ti; 98—99, 27 u-ul il-[t]i; 31 la ta-al-ti-ma; 33 (= *Adapa*-legend) 290 i 6 išattu-u. 81—7—1, 98 iv 7, 8 a-ka-lu la-a ta-kal mē la ta-šat-ta, *Jour. Trans. Vict. Inst.*, xxvi 155. K 3182 iii 45 tak-kal ta-šat-ti (49), ZA iv 12; AJSL xvii 142, 143. K 2401 iii 12 ta-šat-ti-a, ye shall drink, BA ii 628 *foll.* — *ac* IV^2 18 *b* 25, 26 see le'u, 2 (463 *col* 2, end). Creat.-*frg* III 136; V 30 *g-h* 26 see šikru, 1. H 86—7, 68 mu-u ša ina ša-te-e (Br 878) ri-e-xu (*q. v.*); K 583 *R* 16 la a-ka-lu la ša-tu-u (Hr^L 5). Z^Š iii 21 (end) ma-mit ina DUK-TIK-ZI (= kāsi?) la ça-rip-tum mē ša-tu-u (also iii 58, 119, 120, 123, 124). H 11 & 216, 78 NAG (*i. e.* KA + inserted small A) = ša-tu-u. — T. A. (Ber) 75, 34 a-na ša-te-šu-nu (33, a-na a-ka-li); 48, 54 mū a-na ša-te-šu; (Lo) 29, 65 a-na na-da-an me-e a-na šu-ta-ja, in order to give me water to drink; 30, 39 mē a-na ši-it-'u; 31, 10 mē (with gloss) mi-ma (= מים) a-na ši-te-šu (+ 25; *cf* Ber 99, 12; 162, 18). — ši-ta, gloss to rāṭu, perhaps from the Semitic; AV 8340.

Q^1 = Q Z^Š ii 104 ina DUK-TIK-ZI (= kāsi) ta-mi-i il-ta-t[i] = IV^2 51 *b* 47; IV^2 59 *no* 2 *a* 24, 25 kēm (= instead of) ku-ru-un-ni aš-ta-ti mē pušqi u kim-ri; [kēm maš-t]i(?)-ti aš-ta-ti mē marrūti. IV^2 31 *R* 19 mē ina libbi lu-ul-ta-ti (§ 93, 1 *b*) see HROZNÝ, WZKM xvii ('03) 323—331. Asb ix 37 see dāmu (252 *col* 1, beg.).

Q^{tn} perh. = intensive of Q. IV^2 56 *b* 39 (43 tal-ta-na-at-ti-i) subject: the daughter of Anu, see nišbūtu, 738 *col* 2, and add: ZA xvi 162—3 & *rm* 7. ZIMMERN, *Ritualt.*, 100, 18 (88) iš-ta-na-at-ti mē ma-xa-zi (wells?) ellūti.

Derr. — maš(l)tū, maš(l)tītu, meštū (613 *col* 2).

šatu 2. sweat {schwitzen} King, *First Steps in Assyrian*. NE VI (= H^{NE} 44) 56 da-la-xu u ša-ta-a tal-ti-meš-šu (= [illegible]¹ of šâmu); object is the horse.

šatû 3. some garment or stuff {ein Kleid}. V 15 *e-f* 5 KU-DUN-DUN = ša-tu-u (Br 9882, AV 8113) ‖ kandu, see 406 *col* 2, end. Or, perhaps, = שְׁתִי Lev 13, 48 *etc.*, PAOS '89, clxxviii. See šitûtu. Of similar meaning, perhaps is also:

šutû 1. V 14 *b* 43 šu-tu-u, AV 8638. See also xazaštu, 308 *col* 2.

šatû 4. see šadû, 3, end.

šittu 1. *f* sleep {Schlaf}. Hebr שֵׁנָה, *Jour. Bibl. Lit.*, xix 69 *rm* 42; mod. Hebr יָשֵׁן, Arb وَسِنَ, be sleepy, slumber {schlummern} *Rev. Et. Juiv.*, xi 65. *del* 190, 193 (210, 213) see napšâšu, 1 [illegible] (710 *cols* 1, 2) & also *del* 200 (231); & see nirṭu (728 *col* 2). KB vi (1) 100, 20 .... šit-tum ṭâbtum la i-ṣal-lal. IV² 20 *no* 1, 7—8 (= U-DI-NA-NAM?); K 3657 i 11; ii 11; NE 58, 8 see qatû, 1 [illegible]. NE 58, 7 ši]t-tum dal-xat niši eliša im-qut (KB vi, 1, 164). IV² 22 *a* 6, 7 the muruṣ qaqqadi ... ul u-ša-aṣ-lal š[it]-ta (= U) ul uš-ṭa-a-bi, his sleep is not healthy. IV² 15* iii 22, 23 ina šit-ti (= U-DI) ṭa-ab-ti (II 176; Br 9491; ZK i 299 *rm* 1; Z^B 93 *rm* 1). From the same stem is:

šuttu 1. *f* dream {Traum}; *pl* šunâtu. §§ 39; 65, 5. AV 8644. *Jour. Bibl. Lit.*, xix 69 *rm* 42, dream-vision; *cf* Daniel 2, 2 (Kamphausen, *Daniel* [SBOT] 15, 16). id [illegible]-MI (Br 2035; § 9, 230: Prince, AJSL xx 175 BIR-GI(G), = a beast of the night); K 2061, 15 (H 202) = šu-ut-tu, see biru, 4 (189 *col* 2, *med*); H 14, 157; Z^B iv 21 šuttu limut-tim. Asb v 102 e-li šutti an-ni-ti; id + *pl*, T^M vii 119 (& see *ibid*, *p* 147); IV² 57 *O* 64; 17 *R* 16; Asb x 69, 70 see damaqu, [illegible] 234 *col* 1, end. IV² 59 *no* 2 *b* 21 (= IV 66 *a* 55) šub(p)-ra-an-ni-ma šuttu da-miq-tu luṭṭul; *cf* naṭalu, 667—8, for // 22, 23. Also Asb iii 120; KB ii 250—1, 50; Scheil, *Nabd*, vi 21, 22; NE 6, 43 (13, 24); 14, 14 (6, 45); 50, 209 (210 see pašaru, 845 *col* 1, *b*); 55, 20; K^M 6, 116 *etc.* KB vi (1) 132 (NE I) *col* vi 19 .. šu-na-at-ka; 21 um-mi a-t]a-mar ša-ni-ta šu-na(mistake for ut?)-ta (& see KB vi (1) 162 ii (iii) 31, 32; // 38, 39, 49 see NE 57). *Cf* وَثَنٌ, idol, KB vi (1) 431. NE 58, 13—14 a-ta-mar šalul-ta šu-ut-ta; šu-ut-ta ša a-mu-ru; 22, Eabani šu-ut-ta-šu u-šam-xar-šu (KB vi (1) 164—5). NE IX *col* i 13 (= H^{NE} 59, 13) see קלתא; *del* 177 (196); V 64 *a* 16, 17 see barû, 3 [illegible] (184 *col* 2, *med*). H 84—5, 28 šu-ut-tu NU (*i. e.* lâ) da-me-iq-tu. IV² 22 *no* 2, 6—7 u ina šu-ut-ti. 83—1—18, 24, 34 (late Babylonian), 5 abli-šu ša Xa-na-da-a-a ina šu-ut-tum i-mu-ru; 17 i-na šu-ut-tum, in a dream, Pinches, *Rec. Trav.*, xix 101 *fol.* II 36 *f* 6—8 šu-ut-tum, e-gir-ru-u, bi-ru-tum. IV² 59 *no* 2 *b* 24 (ilu) MA-ŠAR (*cf* V 70, 1; Z^B 105: MA-XIR) ilu ša [illegible]-MI-MEŠ, the god of dreams; 24 *a* 48, 49 ki-ma šu-ut-ti (= MA-ŠAR, Br 6806). ZA xviii 197.

šittu 2. V 16 *g-h* 24 AL-LUB = ši-it-tum (√Z^B 92, 93 √šatatu) Br 5765; AV 8175. ZK i 298, 299; ‖ kûru, 1 (431, 432). Perhaps also K 3182 ii 4 i-ri-ix-xi-šu-ma šit-ta, ZA iv 9, 2; AJSL xvii 136, 137. oppression, distress, misery; sin {Unterdrückung, Drangsal, Elend; Sünde}. T^M iii 184 šiptu šit-tu-ma .... šit[-tu]; 185 šit]-tum dan[-na-tu] ša a-me-lu-ti; 187 ...... dan-na-ti šit-ta-ki; 191 .... šit-ta-ku-nu-ma, BA iv 160; also see T^M iii 158 *fol*; 165, 168; 191. Sp II 265 *a* xxii 8 see ligimu, 476, 477. K 583 *R* 3 ši-it-ta u-ma-ti (?), Hr^L 5. K^M 6, 8 še-it-ti; 12, 78 (itti) šit-tu (*var* -ta) qil-la-tu (*var* -lat) u xi-ṭi-tu lip-šu-ru. KB iii (2) 72, 20 ši-it-tim u xi-ṭe-tim ana la šu-ub-ši-i, to commit no sin nor error. Perh. IV² 29* C i 18 ši-it-ta lim-na. See also šittûtu.

šittu 3. V 14 *e-f* 54, 55 KU-ŠU-KUD (= TAR)-DA & KU-KUD-KUD-DA = šittum, in a list of clothing, garments. Br 7082, 397. Perhaps a torn (garment) see galbu, 218 *col* 1. ZA ii 331 *no* 14 compares שׂיט, but *cf* Z^B 55 *rm* 1. See šuttu, 3.

šittu 4. (?). V 19 *c-d* 30 RI = e-rum ša šit-ti (II 27 *g h* 13; V 16 *g-h* 38), followed by RI-RI = e-rum ša ŠI (= pâni?).

JENSEN, ZK ii 33 connects with šinâti (= שִׁנַּיִם), but see Z^{B} 88 *rm* 1.

šit-tu(m) *5*. see laqtu, 407 *col* 2, & rittu, 2.

ši-tu-u SAR, a plant {eine Pflanze} ZA vi 291 *col* 2, 1.

šitta ši(t)tûn see šinâ, two.

šuttu *2*. √*šaṭatu. — *a*) V 28 *a-b* 32; V 47 *a* 29, 30 see xaštu, 346, 1—2 & pirittum, 840 *col* 2. Z^{B} 55 *rm* 1; 92 *rm* 1; AV 8644. Rm 2 II 399 (NE 77) 15 šu-ut-tu (13, pi-rit-tum); 17 nissatu; thus ‖ šittu, 2. Here also V 21 *c-d* 31 AN-ZAG(?)-GAR-RA = ilu ša šu-ut-ti, Br 3810, AV 8096, 8676, preceded by ilu lim-nu. — *b*) V 38 *d-f* 53 buru < šu-ut-tu, hole, shaft {Loch, Schaft} *etc.* Br 8769.

šuttu *3*. V 16 *e-f* 24 KU-TI-DAX-DAX = šu-ut-tu, in a list of clothing, garments. See šittu, 3.

šu-ut. See šu-par.

šûtu *1*. *pron.* — *a*) = šû, 1. he, it {er, es} *etc.* K 181 *R* 13 šu-u-tu ix-tal-qu (Hr^{L} 197; JAOS xx 250, 251; PSBA xvii, '95, 222*foll*) *O* 24 ma-a šu-tu-u-ma (referring to ṭi-e-mu, 22) šu-u, my report is just as it is represented. T. A. (Ber) 38, 20 a-na-ku u šu-u-ut(?tum) ni-il-la-ak; (Lo) 12, 52 šu-tu ji-di, he knows about it; 36, 4 a-na-ku šu-u-ut, I am it. — *b*) = šû, 2. K 5464, 30 ma-a šu-u-tu e-mu-qi e-ça-te (& perh. 23) = Hr^{L} 198 (PSBA xvii, '95, 230*foll*). K 525, 9 nišê mâti šu-u-tu; *R* 8 a-na te-gir-te šu-u-tu (Hr^{L} 252; BA ii 55*foll*); also see K 691 *O* 11 (Hr^{L} 45; & see PSBA Je. '87). K 537 *R* 5 šane-e šarru liš-al šu-u-tu (Hr^{L} 205 = V 54 *no* 4, 22). K 2729 *R* 26 ša šarri bêli-šu šu-tu-ni (= it is, šûtu + ni, BA i 221; ii 566—7). K 483 *R* 2 a-a-u šu-tu-u-ni, wer der betreffende sein soll, Hr^{L} 55. T. A. (Ber) 73, 35 (amêlu) kal-bu šu-ut(tu), that cur! 74, 11 & 15; 63, 18. — See also KRAETZSCHMAR, BA i 383 *rm* ***.

šûtu *2*. south, southwind {Süden, Südwind} § 46. AV 8632; Br 896, 947. ID § 9, 54; D^{S} 24; 139, JENSEN, 462; G § 18 *rm* 1; Z^{B} 15; ZK i 8 (East-wind); ZA i 243; HOMMEL, *Semiten*, 452. *Cf* Hebr תֵּימָן. KB vi (1) 94, 1 *foll* šu-u-tu; 100, 13 kap-pi šu-u-ti; 94, 6 ša [šu-u]-ti ka-ap-pa-šu, BA iv 128*foll*. K 2022 ii 1 (= II 29 *g-h* 3) IM-MER-LU = šu-u-tu; together with il-ta-nu, ša-du-u, a-xur(mur)-ru; *ibid* i 60 . . . . . GAL = šu-u-tu, Br 14244. ID also I 70 *a* 11; III 43 *a* 16. In contract tablets we find IM-[illegible]-LU (*cf* H 40, 224; 183 *no* XVI), Nabd 116, 9; 178, 6; 193, 8 (T^{C} 132).

šûtu *3*. S^{b} 116 su-mu-ug | UM (= DUB with ša = lib inclosed) | = šu-u-tum, Br 3913, 3914, preceded by DUB = lamû & followed by umçatum. HOMMEL, *Sum. Lesest.*, 11 *no* 129 = Südwind, Sturm.

šûtu *4*. Nabd 795, 1—2 (amêl?) šu-u-tu ša ina eli giš(?)-par-ra u SA (= šêti?) (ilat) Gu-la.

šutû *2*. in: (amelûti) šutû, *cf* sutû, 786 *col* 1, beg. D^{Par} 237.

šêtu 1. (= שׁחת). *pr* & *ps* išêt, withdraw, leave, escape {sich entziehen, entrinnen} D^{Pr} 140. K 120 *b* + 144 + 3290 + 3265, 22 i-šit la ik-kud-ma (√כשׁד, or iq-qut? √קוט). K 1282 *R* 20 (*Dibbara*-legend) i-še-ti ina nak-ri i-kab-bit, KB vi (1) 72—3. V 64 *a* 38 la e-gi la a-še-it (I withdrew not) a-xi (= my arms) la ad-da. III 64 *b* 11 atalû ša ul i-še-it. Asb iv 60 the people who . . . . i-še-tu-u-ni, sought a refuge place; 94 the rest of the inhabitants ša . . . . i-še-tu-u-ni. K 525 *R* 4 (end) ina lib-bi i-šet-u-ni, had escaped thither, Hr^{L} 252; BA ii 56, 57.

Q^{t} perhaps T. A. (Ber) 236 + 239*a* + 234 + 237, 20 . . . us-sa-a il-te-e-it, BA iv 131, 132.

šêtu *2*. trap, net. snare {Falle, Fallstrick, Netz, Schlinge} AV 8353. D^{H} 20; D^{Pr} 118, 119 (*cf* שַׁחַת); ZK i 295; ii 152. ID SA. IV^{2} 6 *a* 16, 17 (= IV 6 *a* 12, 13) amêlu šu-u ina ni-ši qa-a e-ša-a ana še-e-ti (= SA) tar-çu, Br 3083. IV^{2} 26 *a* 22. 23 see šuparrurtu. IV^{2} 50 *d* (iii) 47 who kîma še-e-ti u-kat-ti-mu qar-ra-du (= T^{M} iii 162); *cf* T^{M} ii 163; 152 ki-ma še-e-ti ana ka-ta-me-ja; vii 82 ša ina sûqâta na-da-tu še-is-sa. K 1547 + K 2527 A 11 (*b*) še-e-tu ša (ilu) Šamaš i-ba[-ru-ka], soll das Netz des Šamaš dich fangen; B *O* 10 (BA iii 364, 365; KB vi, 1, 104) a-maš-ša (ilu) Šamaš še-it-ka er-çi[-tum rapaštum], because (?), o Šamaš, thy net is the wide world; 12 i-na še-ti-ka a-a-u u-[še-e-çi?]. K 2616 (*Dibbara*-legend) i 10 i-n]a še-e-ti tak-miš-šu-nu-ti-ma, KB vi (1) 60, 61 with the net thou doest capture them. K 3182 ii 31 tar-ça-at še-it-ka rap[-šu?], thy broad snare is spread, AJSL xvii 138, 139; ZA iv 9. K 257 (H 128) *R* 10 perhaps [šētu it-qur]-tum ša ina çi-rim[tar-ça?]-at ana-ku, PRINCE, JAOS xxiv 124. 82—3—23, 4344 + 4473 + 4593 see maxaru, Q[t], 527 *col* 2, *med*. II 22 *a-c* (K 242) 13 GIŠ-SA-PAR = sa-pa-ru = še-e-tum; 14 GIŠ-SA-XU-KAK (MUŠEN-DU) = a-xu = šē-tum ša (amel) XU-KAK (= bird catcher); *c* 15—23 še-e-tum ša XU-KAK = *a-b* 15 GIŠ-SA-XU-KAK = mu-tir-ru; 16 GIŠ-SA-du-du/du-du : mut-tab-bil-tum; 17 GIŠ-SA-ŠI-GAL-GAL = šal-xu-u; 18. 19 GIŠ-SA-P(B)AR-KAK (*i. e.* net to catch gazelles) = mu-sax-xi-ip-tum & pa-qa-tum, 20 GIŠ-SA-KAL-GA = šu-par-ru-uš-tum; 21 GIŠ-SA  = qa-rit(šit)-tum; 22 GIŠ-SA-SAL = pa-su-ut-tum; 23 GIŠ-SA-SAL-SAL = šal-xu-u; 24 GIŠ-SA-GIŠ-GI = sa-an-nu = še-e-tum ša (amêl) ŠU-XA (*i. e.* bâ'iri?). II 34 *no* 3 (*g-h* 29, 30) mu-tir-tum = SA ša iç-ç'ū'ri; a-xu = the same. S[c] 142 sa-a | SA | sa-gi-tu | še[-e-tu]; Br 3083; *cf* V 26 *c-d* 62; II 44 *c-d* 59 & *ibid* 62—65. — a by-form perhaps in S[b] 146 u-sar (√eseru?) | LAL-SAR | še-it-tum; H 32, 748; AV 8175; Br 10138, 10139; but BROWN-GESENIUS & others explain it as pasture-land (> šed-tum) connected with šadū, שדה. ZA x 207 ii *O* 4 .... ti-im-mu : ŠU-u (?); ka-mar-ri : še-e[-tum].

šētu *3*. side, wall? {Seite, Wand?}. Xamm.-*code* xliv 75 še-it bi-tim, the wall of the temple, HARPER, 108, 109.

še-ti, T. A. (Ber) 58, 77 gloss to ištu, since. ZA vi 157 *no* 11; KAT[3] 325; 652; *cf* שתה.

šutbū, see tebū, 1 Š.

šit-bu-u. K 2044, 5 = UL (du-du) UL, AV 7661, Br 9162.

šūtābulu, Š[t] of abalu, 2 (*pp* 7—8). — ac S[c] 73 ša-ar | XI | šu-ta-bu-lu, JAOS xxii 202, 220 on Br 8237, AV 8616. Sm 954, 24 (D 135) ana šu-ta-bu-ul te-ri-e-ti, also *ll* 26, 28, 30, 32. — *pm* Sn *Bell* 36; Rm (ZA iii 313) 63 Nineveh ša mimma šumšu šipir nikilti .... šu-ta-bu-lu (*var* -la) qiribšu, Z[B] 11. L[4] i 15 šu-ta-bu-la-ku, LEHMANN, ii 65; ZIMMERN, *Rituall.*, 24 *O* 18 šu-ta-bu-lu (3 *pl*); √אבל₁.

šutabrū, AV 8617. Š[t] of barū, 4 (185 *col* 2, end); K 2034 *R* NI-NI (or ZAL-ZAL)-LA = šu-tab[-ru-u] M[S] *pl* 5; V 29 *e-f* 26 NI-NI (= ZAL-ZAL) = šu-[-tab-ru-u].

šutabšu (√אבש, see 11 *col* 1) headgear, cover, turban {Kopfbinde, Kopfbedeckung, Turban}? V 28 *g-h* 18 šu-tab-šum ‖ a-gu-u, 1 (see *pp* 12, 13), AV 8618; BA i 343 *rm* 3.

šu-tu-ga-ta. (ša kīma šamē u erçitim šu-tu-ga-ta), IV[2] 30 *no* 1 *a* 6, 7 = Š *pm* 2 *sg* √etequ (132, 133); also KB iii (2) 78, 6 šu-tu-ga-at (3 *sg f*).

šu-ta-du-ra-ku, S 6 + S 2 *O* 13 (*Rev. Sém.* '98, 142 *foll*) = K 3927 (H 75) *R* 9, I am in fear, terrified; √adaru, 2 Š[t] (22, 23).

šataxu. 83, 1—18, 1330 iii 23 tu-ux GAB, ša-ta-xu. — AV 8107 reads Sm 456, 45 i-šat-ta-xu-u-ni, but read imattaxūni & see mataxu, 621.

šutaxu, šutamxu (> šutaxxu), √šīxu, 1. high, tall, lofty {hoch, hochgewachsen, hochragend}. Sarg *Khors* 163 four dimmē erini šu-ta-xu-ti; *Ann* 425; *Ann* XIV 75; Pp ii 34 (-te), iv 118 šu-ta- (= qut? thus √šaqū; *var* -xu)-ti; *bull* 72 šu-tam (*var* ta)-xu-te (*var* ti). K 2745 iii 2/3 (iç) dalāti (iç) šur-man šu-ta-xa-a-ti.

šutaxū. 81, 2—4, 206 *O* 9 šu-ta-xu-u, CRAIG, *Astron. & Astrol. Texts*, 27.

šitku, *c. st.* šitik, AV 8349. Neb v 44 li-bitti (aban) ši-ti-ik šadi-i, KB iii (2) 21 Backsteine aus Gebirgsgesteinschutt (??); ix 23—26 a great wall i-na aban dannū-tim ši-ti-ik šadē rabūti I built, KB iii (2) 29 dem Erzeugnis (?) der grossen Gebirge. II 40 *b-c* 25 ši-ti-ik sa (AV 8349)-tum, name for a part of the body. — From this stem, perhaps, also maštaku, maš(l)taktu (614) &:

šatiktu, AV 8112, Br 2114; ‖ natiktum, 743 *col* 1, beg.

šattukku, AV 8121 see sattukku, 786, 787.

šutukku *1.* some kind of reed, cane {ein Rohr} ‖ pattû, 853 *col* 2; AV 8634. KB vi (1) 361. II 22 (K 242 iv) *d-f* 7 GI-ŠU-A = šu-tuk-ku = GI (= qān) (amêl) UX-ME (= pāšišu), Br 2537. Rm 340 (dupl. K 4174) 3 nap-pa-xu; 4, 5 GI-PAD (= 'Š'UK)-KU-U = šu-tuk-ku followed by xa-an-du-u (see 326 *col* 1) & pu]-uk-ku; also see K 4174 + 4513 *R* iv 26—31; M[5] *pl* 9.

šutukku *2.* some place in a house, temple *etc.* V 51 *b* 69, 70 ina šu-tuk (= GI-PAD-UD [= LAX]) bīti r[im-ki], ein aus Rohr hergestelltes schattiges Gemach, z. B. Laube, Baldachin ‖ amu. id also Zimmern, *Rituall.*, *no* 26 iv 21; 31—37 ii 5, 8, 19. 81—7—1, 98 iii 21, 23 ku-šur-ra ša (il) Ē-a šu-tuk-ku .... ša (il) Marduk of Eridu, *Jour. Trans. Vict. Inst.*, xxvi 155. Thureau-Dangin, ZA xvii 196 *rm* 1: rather = corbeille ‖ bug(u)innu & pattû, un récipient.

šit(rit)-tu-ku, AV 8363 see ridû, 4.

šutkūriš see NOTE 3 to šupār(u).

šatalu. perhaps ℑ 82—7—4, 42 *O* 11 the god who over heaven & earth u-ša-til be-lu-ut-su i-na-a-du (√נאר) ilûtsu; G § 49; PSBA xx 155 *foll* or √אתל, whence etlu, etillu, *etc.* שתל probably the stem of altalû ‖ kištum, forest. — Der.:

šitlum (*cf* שְׁתִיל) sprout, germ *etc.* {Spross, Setzling. Keim}, AV 8355; ‖ pirxu, 828 *col* 2; D[Pr] 83 *rm* 2.

šitalū. V 30 *g-h* 41 NIR-NIR = ši-ta-lu-u, Br 6801, AV 8342.

ši-tu-lum, K 4606, 6; followed by git-ma-lum, 7. Perhaps √ša'alu, ZA iv 162.

šutelū, Š[t] of אלה curse, swear, see 39 *col* 1.

šitluṭu, victorious {siegreich, sieghaft} § 65, 40 *rm*; √šalaṭu. Pognon, *Wadi-Brissa*, 28, 87 ši-it-lu-du (= ṭu?). Neb *Bors* (I 51 *no* 1) ii 17 Nebo, ši-it-lu-ṭu na-ra-am (il) Marduk. Rm III 105, 8 šit-lu-ṭu naram (il) Marduk, ZA ii 138; Winckler, *Forsch.*, i 254 *foll.* L[4] iii 16 Nabû mār šit-lu-ṭu, Nebo his (Marduk's) victorious son; also Šamš i 17 (KB i 174, 175). *adv.*:

šitluṭiš. garg *Khors* 74 a-na (al) Muça-çiri šit-lu-ṭiš ērumma, victoriously.

šutlumu, AV 8640 see talamu, Š.

šitultu (> šit'ultu, form like mitgurtu) ‖ milku, § 65, 40; Z[B] 99; AV 8352; √ša'alu. — *a*) consultation, and the result thereof, decision, decree {Beratung; Entscheidung}. Sm 526, 19—20 be-lum (o Lord!) a-šar ši-tul-ti (= AŠ-TE-BA) la [ter-ru-ub], S. A. Smith, *Misc. Texts*, *pl* xxiv. IV[2] 58 *b* 17 Ub(p)-šu-k(g)in-na(ki) šu-bat ši-tul-ti ilāni rabûti, ZA xvi 154 *foll.* Rm III 105 i 5, 6 Ēa is called [bēl] ni-me-ki u ši-tul-ti muš-ta-bi-il(-li?) te-ri-e-ti, Winckler, *Forsch*, i 254 *foll.* Bu 88—5—12, 75 + 76 x 28 ina Ub(p)-šu-k(g)in-na[ki] ki-sal (see 415 *col* 2) puxur ilāni šu-bat ši-tul-ti, dem Orte der Entscheidung, BA iii 258, 259. K 3182 iv 18 ... ṭe-me mit-lu-ku ši-tul-ti (*var* ta) mil[-ku], AJSL xvii 144, 145. — *b*) intelligence, wisdom, advice {Einsicht, Weisheit, Rat}. Sn *Kui* 4, 21 (end) i-na uz-ni ni-kil-ti ša u-šat-li-ma rubû Bēl-nīmeqi i-na ši-tul-ti ram-ni-ja (& by his own wisdom). IV[2] 15 ii 17—8 see malaku Q[t] 547 *col* 2. Merod.-Balad.-stone ii 49, 50 see karšu, 1 *b* (441 *col* 2, end). K 7592 + K 8717 + DT 363, 27 mit-lu-uk mil-ki (see 623 *col* 2 & KB vi, 1, 584) ši-it[-al] šu-'i-i-ti ši-tul-tu (ana (il) Marduk). IV[2] 48 *a* 8 ina ši-tul-ti u tu-da-at mi-ša-ri uš-šib-šu. — V 17 *c-d* 6 (II 26 *a-b* 9) AD-MAR (Br 4182) = ši-tul-tum between milku (5) & ta-šim-tum (= ŠA [= LIB]-KI (mu) SAR). AD-GAR = malaku, 546, 547. V 16 (*a*-)*b* 1 ši-tul-tum followed by [ ] (ma) SAR = ta-šim-tu.

šatamma. so J. D. Prince, AJSL xix 214, 215 & xx 181 § 12 *ad* H 86—7, 15 *foll* for the usual ša ū-ma, = whensoever, for a time, deriving it from šattu, duration, time, hour, √שא; compare שָׁעָה. — From which, with Delitzsch & others ina šat mūši; *cf* Egypt.-Arab في مدة الليل *fi middet el leyl.*

šat(t)ammu, G § 27, title of an official {ein Berufsname} AV 8108. Lotz, *Tigl. Pil.*, 105, 217 judge; TP i 36 calls himself ša-tam-mu çi-i-ru ša A-šur kakkē-šu u-ša-xi-lu. See also ZK i 62; Oppert, ZA iii 179 *rm* 4; Rm 338 *O* 13—15 (šat-tam) LUB = šat-tam-mu; (me-na-ri) ŠA (= GAR), the same; ŠAT-TAM-E-ŠA-GI-NA (M[8] *pl* 21), Br 12114, 13209.

See also BA iii 359; ZIMMERN, *Rituall.*, *p* 93, *med.* id UT, 82, 9—18, 4159 *O* 45 *foll* = ša (= gar)-tam. Merod.-Balad.-stone v 8 (among the witnesses to the document) is mentioned *L* (amêl) ša-tam Ésaggil; v 20 see šaknu, 2. H^{NE} 93, 3 (KB vi, 1, 266; 531, 532) Gilgameš is called ša-tam erçi-tim, Verwalter der Erde. Usually written ša (= lib)-tam: V 56, 20 ša-tam bît u-na-ti; *cf* KB iv 88 *col* iv 9 (HOMMEL, *Geschichte*, 469: secretary of the treasury). I 66 *no* 2 ii 16 ša-tam bît u-na-a-ti (KB iv 66 *fol*). Nabd 43, 2 (amêl) ša-tam bît u-na[-a-ti]. Also IV² 48 *b* 14 (amêl) ša-tam E-KUR; & 15 (amêl) ša (= gar)-tam Ê-KUR. 48—7—20, 115 *O* 15 (amel) ša-tam ša Dûr-ilu ina pa-ni-ja (Hr[1] 412). Nabd 308. 2 (amêl) ša-tam ša Kiš(ki); 1024, 13; 192, 3 (amêl) ša-tam-mu Ê-ŠIT-LAM; Cyr 263, 1—4 Ri-mut (amêl) mâr šip-ri ša (amêl) ša-tam-mu ša Ê-sag-gil. Rm III 105 i *b* 21 (amêl) ša-tam Ê-zi-da. ša (= lib)-tam in Xammurabi-*letters*, ein höheres Tempelverwaltungsamt, BA iv 486. Perhaps KB iv 58 *col* 2, 4 u ša(?)-tam(?) Bît-gu-bi-na(?), und der Verwaltungsbeamte von *B.*; 172 *no* II 27 (amêl) ša-tam (amel) TU bît (il) Marduk; *cf* Ner 13, 1—2 (amêl) TU bît Nabû (amêl) ša-tam Ê-zi-da, KB iv 204 *no* II. See also PEISER, *Vertr.*, clv 1, *etc.* STRECK, ZA xviii 164, 165.

NOTE. — šu-[illegible] in šu-par-šaq is read šu-tam-šaq, ZK ii 62; *Rev. d'Assyr.* i 6, 7 šu-tammu assumed as a by-form of šatammu.

šatammûtu. K 168, 40 (= *R* 15) ki-i ša ina pa-ni-ti (amêl) sa-ak-lu a-na (amêl) ša (= lib)-tam-u-ti lu-u pa-qi-di, Hr[1] 437. Also K 4682, 19 (M^{R} 99 *col* 2).

šutummu & bît šutummu, perhaps: storehouse, warehouse, granary {Speicher, Vorratshaus, Kornkammer} ‖ bît niçirti. BA iii 486, 487. T^{C} 141; BA i 531 √שתם. NE I *col* i 10 Ê-a]n-na is called qud-du-ši šu-tum-mi el-lim, KB vi (1) 116; 424 dem leuchtenden, dem strahlenden Vorratshause; & see *ibid* 454 *ad* NE VI 109 *foll.* 81, 8—30, 9 ii 9 Babylon is called bît šu-tum-me, KB iii (1) 120, 121. PINCHES, *Texts*, 16 (DT 83) *R* 13 šu-tum-me ê-kur-ri-šu li-mal-la-a bušû la ni-bi a-qar-tu. Nabd 658, 12 so & so many mašîxu ša sattuk suluppi ina šu-tum-mu šarri (+ 14); 968, 2 ištu šu-tu-um-mu šarri; 550, 3; 546, 30 šu-tum-mu šarri; 1054, 1 (end) ultu šu-tu-um-mu šarri, KB iv 254. bît šu-tu-um šarri, Nabd 729, 3; bît šu-tum-mu šarri, 364, 9; 374, 2; 754, 4; 998, 19 bêl ša šu-tum šarri. Cyr 74, 1 suluppu ša ina bît šu-tum šarri. $Z^{Š}$ ii 146 E-ki-ur lip-ṭur šu-tum-mu xi-ir-ti, das Heiligtum der Frau.

NOTE. — šu-[illegible]-šaq might also be read šu-tum-šaq, = the chief-storehouse-keeper, an official similar in character to the rab-šaq, the chief-cup-bearer.

ša-tam-gal-lu ša bâ'iru see šuskallu.

šutêmudu, *adj* (√ emedu?). Esh v 48, 49 (iç) erini šu(?)-te-mu-du-ti, KB ii 137 hochragende (= lofty) Cedern.

šutamḍuxu, § 52. See šadaxu, Q^{t}.

šitmaxu, see šamaxu, Q^{t}.

šu-tam-ku-riš see NOTE 3 to šupâr(u).

šu-tam-mu-ul-ka, see mulka, 549 *col* 1; PEISER: soll dir übergeben werden. Perhaps to be read šu-par mu-ul-ka.

šu-tam-çi. V 16 *c-d* 1 (Br 5755) $Š^{t}$ of maçû, 1 or 2?

šutêmuqu, properly *ac* $Š^{t}$ of emequ (59 *col* 1), supplication, imploring, prayer {Flehen, Bitten, Gebet} ‖ têmequ. II 39 *c-d* 68 NAM-Ê-DUB-KIT = šu-te-mu-qu, together with suppû, teçbitu, teslitu. AV 8628. LOTZ, *Tigl. Pil.*, 182; H^{OV} xxxvi; Z^{B} 12; 14. S^{a} 74 ša-ar XI šu-te-mu-qu, Br 8232; AV 8627 šu-te-mu-u; but??). — *pm* ZA ii 138 *a* 18 šu-te-mu-ga-ak-šu, I implored him.

šitmaru, *adj* √ šamaru, 1. ZA iv 225 *ad* iv 12—13, 2 šit-ma-ra tam-tal-ku, thou takest careful counsel.

šitmarru ‖ šamru, 1. II 22 *d-e* 45 DIB-DIB-BI = šit-mar-ru, AV 8357, Br 10742. √ šamaru, 2 whence also the following 2:

šitmuru. violent, vehement, wild {heftig, ungestüm, wild}. Sn *Bell* 46; *Rass* 73 (ZA iii 315 & 331), the canal te-bil(ne?)-ti a-gu-u šit-mu-ru; *Kui* 3, 30. Anp i 107 ina gi-biš ummânâti-a taxâzi-a šit-mu-ri; ii 105; iii 46 (‖ 47 idâti-a git-ma-la-ti); iii 73. Sarg *Ann* 124:

1000 (imêr) bit-xal šêpā-ja šit-murti, 1000 Mann meiner schneidigen Gardereiterei. § 65, 40*b*; AV 8358.

šitmuriš, *adv* Creat.-*frg* IV 89 is-si-ma (√šasû) Ti-âmat šit-mu-riš e-li-ta, KB vi (1) 26, 27.

šitamrat(u), perh. name of a mountain. Šalm, *Mon*, ii 69 arki-šu ar-te-di (šad) ši-i-ta-am-rat uban šadi-e ša a-xat (nâr) Pu-rat; thus read also *Obel* 46 ši-tam-rat (not -gi, as KB i 132) uban šadi-e ša a-xat Puratti a-na dan-nu-ti-šu iš-kun. Šalm, *Balaw*, III 4.

šutmāšu, AV 8341; § 65, 40*b* & Meissner, ZA viii 80 √šamašu. TP ii 14 their warriors ina kirib xuršāni ki-ma šut-ma-ši(še) lu(-u)-mi(me)-çi, I spread out, I scattered like š; iii 79; iv 93. See maçû, 2 ג, 571 *col* 1. Feuchtwang, ZA v 91 reads šudmāši. like sheaves, comparing Hebr שְׁרֵמָה Isa 37, 27. Streck, ZA xviii 167: Gewimmel, Ameisenhaufen (so Hommel, *Aufsätze und Abh.*, 156 *rm* 4) *i. e.* Bezeichnung einer ausserordentlich grossen Heeresmacht.

šutmēšu, quoted in § 65, 40*b* & referred to IV^2 45 *b* 43 (end) = K 13 (Hr^L 281) is to be read ŠE-BAR šib-ši (Johnston, *etc.*); see also BA iv 527*foll*. Streck, ZA xviii 167 reads again šutmūši.

šitīmtu ‖ šīmtu, 1 *b*. Sn *Bav* 42 a-di û-um ši-tim-ti-šu-nu, Z^B 100; or error for ši-im-ti?

šūtu-ni (šu-tu-ni), it is; *cf* šûtu, + ni (emphatic).

šittē(i)n, *f* of šina, two, *q. v.*

šitīni (??) AV 8346. K 650 *R* 9, 12 mi-i-ni ši-ti-ni a-na šarri bêli-ja; ma-a: me-ni ši-ti-ni a-ta-a la ta-aš-pu-ra. K 910 *R* 4 mi-i-nu ša ši-ti-ni ša libbi e-gir-te an-ni-te ina êkalli la-aš-pur. S 456 *R* 9 mi-nu-u ša ši-ti-i-ni šarri bêli liš-pu-ra; DT 98 *R* 10 = Hr^L 128; 145; 467, 337.

šutānuxu. sighing, moaning {Seufzen, Stöhnen} √anaxu, 2 (69, 70). K 8426, 5 šu-ta-nu-xu, *Rev. Sém.* ii 76. V 47 *a* 31 û-mu šu-ta-nu-xu, by day moaning, Z^B 14.

šitnuntu. fight, battle {Kampf, Schlacht}? √šananu. AV 8359. TP i 56 li-i-ta šit-nun-ta elišunu altakan; also see Sarg *Ann* 33 šit-nun-tu id-bu-bu-u.

šitassû, AV 8343 see šasû, ג¹.

šatapu, surround, help {umgeben, helfen}? Xamm.-*code* iv 38 ša-ti-ip ni-ši-šu, who helps his people (in time of need) perh. = šaṭapu, *q. v.* Sm 896, 6/7 ša-ta-pu ši-ti-ip-ti, 8 la-qa-tum (see 497 *col* 1), 9 aš-lu-ka-tum, AV 8104. — **Der.:**

šetiptu ring {Ring}? V 28 *a-b* 81 = II 25 *e-f* 58 še-ti-ip-tum ‖ unqu. AV 8347.

šutapû. Meissner, 143 & ZA viii 82—5 companion, associate, √apû, 3 (78 *col* 2) combine, associate {sich vereinigen}, whence Arm שותף (שֻׁתָּפָא). Marx, BA iv 60 reads šutāpu, companion, partner, (= Mod. Hebr שֻׁתָּף). According to Prince, AJP xx 106, šutāpu is a cognate of šetiptu, both from √שתף, bind. Instead of Meissner's reading (ZA viii 82) of S^c 78 šu-ta-pu-u, read šu-ta-bu-lu; see JAOS xxii 220.

šutappû. 81—2—4, 107, 4 when (kakkab) UR-MAX šu-tap-pu-u, Thompson, *Reports*, ii *no* 189: shines. thus $Š^t$ of apû, 2. or √apû?, whence upû & uppû? (78 *col* 2).

šutāpulu. M^S 14 *col* 1 *ad* Boissier, *Doc. Ass*, 40, 16 šumma .... damqātiša u limnētiša šu-ta-pu-lu, $Š^t$ of apalu, correspond. *f* šutāpultu, *ibid* 37, 12; 45, 1.

šitpuçu & **šitpuru**, AV 8360, 8361; Br 10740, 10741 see šapaçu & šaparu, Q^t.

ši-tap-ru-šu, AV 8344 see parašu, 1 Q^t (838 *col* 1).

šuteçû, *n* edict {Edikt} or perhaps rather *ac*: pronounce an edict. AV 8629. II 62 *a-b* 53—56 (K 64 iv 14—17) šu-te-çu-u in *b* corresponding to (53) A-DA-MAN-DI, Br 11568; (54) A-DA-MAN-DUG-GA, Br 11562; (55) DI (sa-sa) DI, Br 9564; H 30, 698; (56) ...... KA, Br 13894; 14328. V 21 *a-b* 31 ... LAL-LAL = šu-te-çu-u, Br 14389 (× AV 8538 šu-pu-çu-u!); see also II 39 *c-d* 78, Br 11560. √açû, 1 (84, 85).

šataqu. 83, 11—18, 1332 iv 7 [DIR] = ša-ta-qu, M^S 99 *col* 2.

šutuqqu. V 29 *g-h* 11 DIR = šu-tuq-qu (10, = e-li) AV 8636, Br 3748; Z^B 114 *rm* 2.

šūtuqu *1.* ($Š$, etequ, 133 *cols* 1, 2). — *ac* i 44, 73 ri-ix-çu šu-tu-qi (name of a stone) advance, create confidence; but M^S 88 *col* 2, end = rixçu, 2: Regen kommen zu lassen. — pm IV² 24 *a* 48, 49 (Nergal) git-m]a-lu ša dan-nu-us-su šu-tu-qat (= LAL-BA, Br 6207) ki-ma šu-ut-ti (also Sm 954 *O* 5, 6). IV² 30 *no* 1 *a* 3, 4 kab-tum ša kīma šamē šu-tu-qu (or ru?); *ibid* 7 (end) ša ki-ma šamē u erçitim šu-tu-ga-ta (see above, šutugāta). Sarg *Harem*, A, 1 Ninib bēl a-ba-ri ša šu-tu-qat dan-nu-su. bu-ga-na šu-tu-uq see bu-kânu, 1 (152 *col* 2, end). From etequ also the following 4:

šūtiq. *Š* ip IV² 59 *no* 2 *b* 20 (= IV 66 *a* 54) šu-ti-qa-an-ni, remove me (from = it-ti).

šūtuqu *2. adj* renowned, magnificent, glorious }hochangesehen, berühmt{ *etc.* AV 8635; V 36 *d-f* 51 šu-tu-qu (Br 8767), followed by šu-te-tu-qu (Br 8768). K 11152, 1 (Ištar is called) in-nin-na-at ilāni šu-tu-qa-at be-li-e-ti.

šūtuqtu. *n* perhaps advance }Fort-, Vorrücken{ Knudtzon, *no* 52 *O* 5 (*p* 29) šu-tuq-ti.

šūtuqūtu. *n* K 1107 *R* 9 ša a-na šu-tu-qu-ti ša un-qa-a-ti. Hr^L 238; AV 8635.

šitqulu, see šaqalu, Q^t; from same verb:

šitqultu, *n* § 65, 40*b*. III 52 *a* 52 šit-qul-ti (il) Sin. 81—2—4, 135 *R* 9 ina šit-qul-ti (il) Sin, Thompson, *Reports*, ii *no* 242 balancing (in astronomy).

šu-ta-qut-ti (√šaqū, 1?) *var* to šu-ta-xu-ti, Sarg Pp iv 113.

šutaqtū (?). K 4225, 24 šu-taq-tu-u, H 185; Br 444; √qatū?

šataru. ravage, devastate }verwüsten, zerstören{. ZA x 211 *O* 11 ša-ta-ri : da-mu-u; K 883 *R* 2. ZDMG 32, 751, Hebr שׁתר, Arb شتر. — *3* Sn *Kui* 4, 34 šadē i-na ag(q)-g(q)ul-la-a-ti AN-BAR (= parzilli) u-šat-tir; *Rass* 87 (ZA iii 318; 331) šada-a u bi-ru-tu (see *p* 196 *col* 2, end) i-na ag(q)-g(q)ul-la(-a)-ti u-šat-tir; ‖ aq-qur, Anp ii 96; Šalm, *Mon*, ii 42. Does S^c 66 da-ar | DAR šu-ut-tu-ru (AV 8345, Br 3493) belong here or to ataru, 1 (see 133 *col* 2, end). — *Š* Meissner & Rost, 44 *no* 2 u-ša-aš-ti-ru. Connected with this stem may be these 2:

ša(= lib)-tur-ru, V 27 *g-h* 30 an animal = [ŠA (= LIB)]-[illegible] (*i. e.* TUR) = nam(zi?)-da ... AV 8115, Br 8011. id see šasurru. Compare also KB vi (1) 309—10; Zimmern, *Rituall.*, *no* 50, 2 on bašmu, salamander.

šetirtu. Dar 273, 16 še-tir-ti imaxaçu.

šatāru, garment }Kleid{. V 28 *c-d* 53 ša-ta-ru ‖ na-al-ba-ši, AV 8109; *cf* Arm סתרא cover, clothing }Umhüllung{. A ‖ is:

šatūru. V 28 *a-b* 6 ša-tu-ru = lam-xuš-šu-u, AV 8114; KB vi (1) 418. A ‖ of this is:

šutūru, or **šūturu** *1.* V 28 *c-d* 55 šu-tu-ru = la-ma-xuš-šu-u; *ibid* 57 šu-tu-ur, AV 8637, 8638. Either √šataru = סתר; or √ataru, 133, from which we have:

šūturu *2.* = *Š* pm (133 *col* 2) & III 38 *no* 2 *O* β1 (K 2660, 3) who eli abēšu ar-na šu-tu-ru šur-bu-u xi-ṭu-šu kab-tu. (Pognon, *Wadi-Brissa*, 198 *Š* pm of tāru = il est établi, considérable; but see KGF 136 *rm*; Lotz, *Tigl. Pil.*, 159; Flemming, *Neb*, 51). K 3182 i 46 (nor is there) ina ilāni *pl* napxar (*var* nap-xar) kiš-ša-ti ša šu-tu-ru ki-ma ka-a-ta, among the gods of all the regions one who excels like thee, AJSL xvii 137. Xamm.-*code* xl 80 šarru ša in šar + alim šu-tu-ru a-na-ku, the king, who is pre-eminent among city-kings, am I. IV² 30 *no* 1 *a* 3, 4 see šūtuqu, 1 (H 191, *med*). IV² 26 *a* 56 Marduk ina ilāni mala šu-um na-bu-u at-ta [šu-tu]-ra-at, thou art exalted. K 7592 + K 8717 + DT 363 *O* 28 šu-tur bi-nu-tum, ZA v 58; see kat-tum, 455 *col* 1. K^M 1, 10 šu-tu-rat urruka (of Sin); 60, 12 šu-tu-rat a-mat-ka. From the same verb ataru is derived also:

šūturu *3.* pre-eminent, mighty, glorious, prodigious }hervorragend, mächtig, herrlich{ *f* šūturtu. AV 8638. Šalm, *Obel* (Layard 87) 7 Adad giš-ru šu-tu-ru bēl xe-gal-li, KB i 130, 131. K 11152 (hymn to Ištar) 13 šu-tu-rum šu-me. K^M 12, 21 (il) Marduk kab-tu šu-tu-ru, M. the illustrious, the great; = IV² 57 *a* 21. — *f* Anp ii 6 ta-na-ti (? I Rawl. -na) kiš-šu-ti-ia šu-tur(*var* tu-ur)-te. II 66 *no* 1, 2 Ištar šu-tu-rat nab-ni-sa; 8 (Ištar) git-mal-tu šu-tu-ur-tu ša šamê erçitim. ZA x 293 the daughter of Nannar is called *l* 34 ul-la-a-tum šu-tu-rat [u] šar-rat. — *pl* TP vi 62: four male wild oxen dan-nu-te šu-tu-ru-te(ti). Also I 28 *a* 4.

šitru. ZA x 211 *col* 2 *R* 6 šu-bu-ul-tum : ši-it-ri. Scheil, *ibid* suggests = ŠE-TIR = ašnan.

šit-ru-du (?). V 21 *d* 32. AV 8362. Perhaps a mistake for qit-ru-du.

šitarxu ‖ of šarxu 2, as well as the two following. K[M] 11, 46 (Marduk) .... çi-i-ru git-ma-lu ši-tar-xu, the exalted, the perfect, the powerful.

šitrâxu. I 35 *no* 2, 1 to Nebo šit-ra-xu. Šamš i 6 to Ninib ma-am-li (553 *col* 1, end) šit-ra-xi. KB iii (2) 78, 29 (Marduk) ka-ab-ti ši-it-ra-xu (I call on thee)!

šitruxu. ZA v 60, 20 = Craig, *Relig. Texts*, i 31, 20 ut-nen-ka be-lum šit-ru-xu ezzu, I beseech thee (Marduk), powerful & mighty lord. — *f* Zimmern, *Ritualt.*, *no* 61, 7 šit-ru-ux-tu (ilat) Ištar, the glorious Ištar; 62, 13 šit-ru-ux-tu.

šitarruru, see Q[t] of šararu, 1.

šutartu, AV 8622 see šukuttu.

šu-ta-šu, V 36 (*d*-)*f* 8.

šattišu (§ 80*b*, note), *adj* yearly, annual {jährlich} BA ii 298 (below). derived from šattu. II 38 *e-f* 18 KA-SAR-MU 1 KAN = ki-çir šat-ti-šu, yearly rent, Br 1234; see 428 *col* 2, *med.* — Sn iii 27 na-dan šat-ti-šu-un, their yearly gift; *cf* III 12, 30; Asb ix 119; but KB ii 228 reads mâti (-ti)-šu-un.

šattišam, šattišamma (§ 80*b* & note), *adv* yearly, annually; then also: continuously, continually, always {jährlich; dann auch: fortwährend, immer} AV 7990, 8119. Merod.-Balad.-stone ii 14 who šat-ti-šam-ma *etc.*; Esh iv 37 biltu mandatu bêlûtija šat-ti-šam-ma ukîn çiru-šun. Smith, *Asurb*, 317*d*. TP v 40 MU (= šatti)-šam-ma ana lâ šuparkê, see 831 *col* 1, end; ii 94 (Lotz, *Tigl. Pil.*, 130). Sarg *Khors* 67 na-dan sisê šat-ti-šam elišunu uktîn. Sn ii 46 šat-ti-šam la ba-aṭ-lu. III 15 ii 25 šat-ti-šam-ma la na-par-ka-a. Esh vi 50; III 16 vi 10 šat-ti-šam; ZA iii 318 (šat-tu-šam) 65; Asb iv 109; K 2852 + K 9662 i 14; Esh *Sendsch*, *R* 50, 51. IV[2] 38 *b* 22, 23 ša-at-ti-šam la na-bar-ka-a, preceded by û-mi ... ar-xi ...; KB iv 62, 63. I 66 *c* 16 ša-at-ti-ša-am. V 63 *a* 45 šat-ti-ša-am-ma; *b* 48 ša-ti-ša-am-ma. Sn *Bav* 34 i-na MU-AN-NA-šam (= u)-ma, >< § 55*a*, Note. T. A. (Ber) 11, 11 ša-at-ta-ša-ta-ma, yearly.

šu-ut-šaq see šuparšaq under šâqû, 8.

šutêšur(u) *1.* *Š*[t] of ešeru, ašaru, 3 (see *p* 120). AV 8630 = extend, III 3, 13 a-na šu-te-šur mât Aš-šur; IV[2] 12 *O* 19, 20 xaṭ-ṭa-šu el kiš-šat ni-še šu-te-šu-ri (= SI-DI, Br 3463). — rule, IV[2] 5 *a* 59—61 šu-pak šamê ana šu-te-šu-ri (= SI-DI); Neb i 44 a-na šu-te-šu-ur ni-ši; V 34 *a* 12 mâta šu-te-šu-ru .... uma'iranni. — *pm* Asb i 50 šu-te-šur.

šutêšir = *ip* of the same verbform. Xammurabi-*letters* 4 *R* 12 šu-te-še-ir-ši, bring ihn (den Kanal) in Ordnung. Winckler, *Sargon*, 191 (below) murnisqi šu-te-ši-ra. IV[2] 28 *no* 1 *a* 4, 5 te-rit kiš-šat niši šu-te[-šir?] = rule! AV 8721 quotes ša-al-mi-iš šu-te-ši-ri ta-li-it-ti.

šutêšuru *2.* *n*? IV[2] 17 *b* 25, 26 mu-us-su (see 566 *col* 2) pi-ja šu-te-šu-ra qa-ta-a-a šu-te-ši-ra-am-ma, the cleansing of my mouth, the proper care of my hands take thou in charge.

šuttatu ‖ šuttu, 2, *b.* hole, trap, pit {Loch, Grube, Fallgrube}. Z[B] 93 *rm* 1: Bedrängnis, thus = šuttu, 2, *a.* K 2527 + K 1547 *O* 28 see baqamu, 182, 183 & KB vi (1) 106—7; 416. NE VI 52: 7 u 7 tu-ux-tar-ri-iš-šu šu-ut-ta-a-ti, KB vi (1) 171: grubst du ihm (dem Löwen) 7 u. 7 Fallgruben. KB vi (1) 584—5 *d* 1 (end) u-ši-te-ga šu-ut-ta[-tu], (dann) ging er wieder hin zu der Fallgrube. K 4341 i 25 (II 36 *e-f* 60) ŠA(?)-KI-XUŠ-A, see naxallu (663 *col* 2). K 2022 i 51 ŠA-XUŠ-A = šu-ut-ta-tu, together with naxbalu & xâštu, AV 3291, Br 12124. II 35 *a-b* 20 xa-aš-tu = šu-ut-ta-tu (K 4320 i 20). II 32 *g-h* 17 SI(du)DUG = šu-ut-ta-tum (Br 3419) followed by naxlum (663 *col* 2). V 16 *g-h* 12 SI-DUG = šu-ut-t[a-tum] = šu-xar-ru-ru, V 19 *a-b* 11.

šutatu (?). K 126, 18 zikaru itti sinništi ina šu-ta-ti-šu UŠ (= ridû)-šu ittanaplas, *Rev. Sém.* i 170, 171 or qattatu = qatattu (*q. v.*).

šutatû *1.* properly $\check{S}^t$ of atû (126 *col* 2), in astronomical texts: ana Sin u (il) Šamšu šu-ta-tu-u; often in THOMPSON, *Reports*, ii = be invisible (see index, 139, 140). *ibid* preface xxvi (end) THOMPSON says: "the astrologers noted: .... (3) whether the sun (or moon) had set and the moon (or sun) had not yet risen, both celestial bodies being, in consequence, below the horizon, that is to say, invisible (šutatû). The word 'invisible' represents as nearly as possible the meaning of šutatû, as we may see by the phrase ša mi-xi-is-su šu-ta-tu-u (= RI-A, Br 2578), *i. e.*, 'whose wound (or sickness) is invisible', which occurs in the hymn to Nergal (IV² 24 *no* 1 *a* 36, 37). The same view of the meaning of this word is also held by Dr. JASTROW, *Religion of Babylonia*, *p* 359. The word šutatû had probably another shade of meaning also, for the word ittintu, which means the gradual disappearance of the Moon as it draws near the Sun at the end of the month, is once used as its equivalent (see 82—5—22, 89 *O* 4; THOMPSON, *no* 124)." See also K 2902 *O* 10 (CRAIG, *Astron.-Astrol. Texts*, *p* 27).

šutatû *2.* originally same as *no* 1. BA ii 35; ZIMMERN, ZA ix 110 = indeed, forsooth, evidently {in der Tat, fürwahr, ersichtlich}. VATh 244 i 14 I-GI-IX-ZU = šu-ta-tu-u, M^S 21 *col* 2.

šitât. Xammurabi-*letters* 16, 4 ši-ta-at kaspi-im. DELITZSCH, BA iv 490, Geldeinkünfte, Geldsummen?

šitûtu. 82—5—22, 107 (Hr^L 870) *O* 8 KU ši-tu-tu tar-ta-kas *cf* Hebr שְׁתִי "warp in a loom"; perhaps: thou hast made fast the (threads of the) warp, *i. e.* thou hast formed a plot. JOHNSTON, JAOS xxv 79.

šittûtu. *abstr. n.* of šittu, 2. K^M 11, 16 anâ-ku šit-tu-tu (*var* -um) lu e-pu-uš, I have committed sin.

šûtêtuqu. V 36 *d-f* 52 see šûtuqu, 2. AV 8631. properly $\check{S}^t$ of etequ.

ת

Tû. *m & f* charm, magic formula, incantation {Beschwörung, Zauberformel}. H^CV xxxii; L^TP 97, 98. JENSEN, ZK i 319, 320 (√atû); ZA iii 305; on JENSEN, 302 see HOMMEL, *Sum. Lesest.*, 1 *no* 15. On Z^B 117 see HAUPT in TOY, *Ezekiel* (SBOT) 102. id KA + inserted li = MU´ (V 21 *c* 48; Br 782). nadû (Q & Q^{tn}) tû see nadû (647 *col* 2 *g*; 648 *col* 2); Creat.-*frg* III 43, 101; IV 91; VII *O* 19 ta-a-šu ella pa-ši-na lit-tab(p)-b(p)al, KB vi (1) 34; 353. K 2107 *O* 15 Marduk is written DINGIR-MU´-AZAG as ša tu-u-šu el-lit ‖ ša ši-pat-su el-lit (14), AV 8976. IV² 22 *no* 1 *R* 13 ina ti-e-ka el-li ul-lil-ma; V 51 *b* 73, 74 ina te-e-šu ša ba-la-ṭi. V 65 *b* 20 liš-mi ta-a ib-bi-ku (= ka). Rm 541 ta-a-ka el-la. K 4872 ii 64 tû (*var* ta-a) šipti elliti mu-nu-ma, T^M 149. id also T^M vii 44 ina tê ša (il) Ea ina šipat (il) Šilig-gal-šar (BA iv 161); v 147 tu-a ša pi-MU ta-a ša pi-ku-nu.

NOTE. — *del* 201 (213); 218 (242) read by J^{I-N} 33 i-te-kil (te-et-te-kil) ta-a (H^{NE} 144, 242 & *rm* 17); but see [illegible], where also *del* 185 (215). — MARTIN, *Textes relig.*, '03, 170—1 reads Sp II 265 *a* vii 10 gi-ir-ri an-nu tu-u *etc.* (see xašaxu, 344 *col* 2, end).

ta'au, tâu eat {essen} = תאה. V 28 *e-f* 84 ta-ar (*var* 'a, 'u)-u = a-ka[-lu], AV 8682. — **Der.:**

te'ûtu, ti''ûtu, victuals, nourishment, support; outfit {Speisen, Nahrung, Unterhalt; Zubehör}. ZK i 134 *rm* 1. Sarg *Cyl* 39 ti-'u-u-tu niš-bi-e (738 *col* 2) u bu-luṭ lib-bi ti-il-li-nu-u; AV 8871, LYON, *Sargon*, 91. SMITH, *Asurb*, 59 (KB ii 168, below) 88 *b* mê u te-'u-u-ta balaṭ napišti(-tim)-šu-nu a-na pi-i-šu-nu u-ša-qi-ir. Sp II 265 *a* xxi 8 see katû, 2 (455 *col* 1, end); xxiii 8 see pixnuqiš (792—3). T^M v 53 (šam) xaltappânu ti-'-ut ma-a-ti, T^M 154 √ תאר? = begehrenswertes, Zierde. II 48 *g-h* 46 ŠA (= GAR = akalu?)-NI-SI = ti-u (✕ AV 1568, 8969 šam)-tum, Br 12075, followed by ma-ka-lu-u (*p* 536) ‖ ip-tennu. Here also III 41 *a* 15 one nar-kabtu a-di ti-'u-u-ti-ša, with its equipment (literally: its provisions) {Zubehör} KB iv 74, 74; K 3456 *R* 10 edlu narkabtu šug(?)-mu-ra-ku (or narka-bat mu-ra-ku?) ti-'-u-ti (= harness? PSBA xxi 40 *foll*: accessoirs d'un char). BA ii 151.

te'û. II 29 *c-d* 35 ŠU-GUŠUR-RA = te-'u-u (Br 7176) followed by si-'e-ru (36), which, perhaps, identical with si-e-ru, 2 (744 *col* 2) AV 8871.

te'û. T^{M} v 160 šadu-u li-te-'-ku-nu-ši, der Berg erschüttere euch.

tu-u-ja. V 40 *f* 60 between tul-tu sa-am-tu & aqrab imēri, perhaps a worm; or the like, AV 9003.

tiālu. V 26 (*g-*)*h* 57—60 (Br 11518, 11417, 11416, 4637) = ti-a-a-lu, a tree {ein Baum}; also Sm 68, 8 *fol* (M^{S} *pl* 18) ti-ja-a[-lum], GGA '98, 826.

ti-'i-il-tu, D 77 *rm* 1 explaining sign for bāru, Br 1809. √ علق?

ta'amu ℑ, occurring in Achaemenian-inscr. (Bezold, *Achaem.*, 56) rule, govern {gebieten, regieren}. Xerxes who alone ana nap-xar mātāte gabbi u-ta-'-a-ma, C *a* 5, *b* 8; K 9; what Auramazda u-ta-'-a-ma (commands) NR 35. V 45 iv 15 tu-ta-'-am. ag muta'imu, mute'imu, see 621 *col* 1.

tu''āmu *f* **tu''āmtu.** twin {Zwilling} *pl* tu''āmē; *f* tu''āmāte (of doors). AV 8996; §§ 10; 65, 12. *Rec. Trav.* i ('80) 105 *rm* 5. Etym: Barth, *Nominalbildung*, § 182*b*, *rm* 1; *cf* תאומים; AJSL xix 3. below. — *a*) *cf* gods & goddesses, K 11152, 3 Ištar is called tu-am-ti (il) Šamaš; also K 13728 (Bezold, *Catal.*, 1335). — *b*) of animals. NE VI 18 (end) çēnē-ka tu-'-a-me li-li-da (√aladu), KB vi (1) 169 deine Schafe (sollen) Zwillinge werfen. — *c*) of ornaments, furniture *etc.* Sarg *Ann* 424 (*Khors* 162): 8 ner(ur, gir)gallē (see nergallû' 727, 728 & KAT^{3} 413, 414) tu-'a-me(-mi), 8 pair of *n.* *bull* 70 tu-'a-a-me; BA iv 254, 266. V 28 *c-d* 63 tu-'a-am-tu ‖ ku(KU? or d(t)ur?)-max-um. II 23 *c-d* 24 tu-'a-a-ma-ti (*sc.* dalāte) ‖ mu-tir-re-e-tum (see mu-tirru, 625 *col* 2); Rm 2, 555, 8; S^{c} 1 *a* 10 (Br 1811); II 7 *c-d* 28 (Br 1896), 29 (GIŠ-IK[=GAL]-MAŠ(?)-TAB-BA, Br 2259). V 33 *d* 38 (dalāti) tu-'a-a-ma-ti, KB iii (1) 144, 145 *i. e.* Türen, die sich um eine Axe in der Mitte drehen. II 67, 78 (dalāt) tu-'a-ma-te, KB ii 24. K 1014 (Bezold, *Catalogue*, 210) = Hr^{L} 457, 5 dalāte ta-'-u-ma-a-te = doublegates; *l* 3 (end) ta-'-ma-te. S^{c} 1 *b* 7 [MAŠ-MAŠ] = tu-a-mu, Br 1851; 20 tu-'-a-mu (19: m]a?-a-šu, see 596 *col* 1). K 107 *R* (II 32 *no* 2 *add*) 1 tu-a-mu, 3 ta-li-mu, AV 8978. 85—5—22, 946 *R* 15 DUK kisim MAŠ-TAB-BA = tu-ma-'-[tum], perhaps a mistake for tu'a-mātum, PSBA xxiii 200, 201; KB vi (1) 422. III 53 *a* 75 MUL tu-a-mu GAL-MEŠ a-na mul MAŠ-TAB-BA TUR-TUR i-qab-bi.

tiām(a)tu see tāmtu.

(amelūti) **ta-i-qa-ni-šu** T. A. (Lo) 9, 19, the murderers of (for dā'ikūti). Bezold, *Dipl.*, pref. xxiv § 19*a*; see dāku 245 *col* 1, *med.*

tajāru, tajārtu see tāru, 3, tārtu.

tuāru (√תור). a legal term, occurring especially in *c.t.* AV 8979. *e.g.* tu-a-ru di-e-nu da-ba-a-bu la-aš-šu, III 48 *no* 5, 8—9; *no* 2, 11—12; *no* 3, 19—20; 46 *no* 1 *a* 14, 15; *no* 6, 13; 49 *no* 1, 12—13; 5 *O* 9; 50 *no* 4, 12—13; 49 *no* 2, 11 GUR-ra; also tāru see tāru, 2. Jensen, *Deutsche Literat.-Ztg.*, '91, 1450.

tiāru. some kind of cedar-tree {eine Art von Cedern}. II 23 *e-f* 23 ti-ja-rum explained by GIŠ erinu, which in 22 is = su-pa-lum; 24 ti-ja-ar explained by GIŠ erinu piçu-u; Br 10806—7; H 34, 821. AV 8875 reads II 26 *b* 16 ti-ja-a-rum & suggests also V 16 *g-h* 9—10 ti-j[a-rum], Br 4345. K 4152 + 4183 *R* iv 18 (iç) ti-ja[-rum?], preceded by (šam) su-pa[-lum], M^{S} *pl* 7.

tiurāti (?) K 2608 + 2633 + 3101 *b* + 3435, 14 ina xi-miṭ urri ṭa-rid ti-u-ra-ti (il) Adad. Martin, *Textes relig.*, '03, 43/44.

tiatum. Pinches, JRAS '98, 444 name of a herb or gardenplant. K 191 ii 3 (šam) ti-ja-tu; K 249 ii 10, 43 (šam) ti-a-tu (+ *R* 15); *Rev. Sém.*, '94, 133 *foll.*

tab-ba (?) KB iv 42 *no* II 6 a-na tab-ba il-ki', haben zum Gesellschaftsgeschäft genommen. Nanm.-*letters* 7, 10—11 it-ti (amēl) mu-še-bi-ši tab-bi-šu li-še-bi-eš, mit dem Bauführer, seinem Kollegen, BA iv 439. See tappû.

ta-a-bu (3 *pl*, Q); la ta-bu-tu, šumma ta-bu-ut-ta pânu-ka; tub (§ 19); Neb *Grot*, ii 45 šu-bat tu-ub li-ib-bi; D 134, 9*foll*; KB iii (2) 4 *col* 2, 18—9 see ṭâbu, 1 & 2 (348—51).

tabû (?) *1.* ZA x 211 ii *R* 7 ta-bu-u : d(ṭ)a-bu-u .... ma-lu-u ša.

tabû *2.* Harper, *The Code of Ḫammurabi*, 189 sink, run aground (= ṭebû? see 353 *col* 1). — Q pm whose boat te(Ungnad, ZA xviii 61 ṭe)-bi-a-at (was sunk) xxxvi 72; ℑ u-te-ib-bi, xxxvi 58; u-te-ib-bu-u, *ibid* 51 + 78; ℑ[1] if a boat strike a ferryboat and sink it (= ut-te-ib-bi), xxxvi 71; *ibid* 47; 33 ut-te-bi. KAT^3 398 *rm* 1; 546—7 *rm* 7; 650. Perhaps Johns, *Deeds and Documents*, 916 i 3; 917 ii 7, 11, 14 (ṭa-bi-u); 917 ii 18 (ta-bi-u-te).

ti(e)bû 1. pr itbi, ps ita(e)bbi, pm tebi rise, rise against {aufstehen, sich erheben gegen} KB vi (1) 306. AV 8848; Br 2335, id ZI. Barth, ZA ii 207—9 and, against him, Haupt, BA i 9. IV^2 29* 4 C *R* 12 it-ba-ki-na-ši, there rose up for you (*Johns Hopk. Circ.*. 114 *p* 118). TP iv 87 to battle with me lu it-bu(-u)-ni (3 *pl*). Šalm, *Obel*, 98 a-na taxâzi it-ba-a (3 *sg*). Asb ii 120 it-bu-nim-ma (3 *pl*); iii 138 (Ummanigaš) it-ba-a a-na kit-ri-šu; vii 117 the Arabians, as many as were with him, it-bu-u-ni; viii 16 it-ba-am-ma a-na mit-xu-uç (*var* -çi) šarrâni (mât) Amurrê. NE 50 (= VI) 210 it-bi-e-ma Êabani (KB vi, 1, 178); 58 (= Sm 1040) 9 i]t-bi-e-ma KB vi (1) 165 er stand auf; also 6, 25 (= I *col* v); 71 (= X *col* v) 22 ul a-te-ib-ba-a du-ur [dûr?]; & KB vi (1) 200, 37. 75 (*no* 39) 7 it-ba-am-ma. IV^2 14 *no* 1 *R* 6 ul-tu qi-ni (il) Zi-i it-bi-ma (= BA-BA-ZI). I 69 *a* 52 [it-bu-n]im-ma ša-a-ri er-bit-ti. T. A. (W.-A.) 236 + 239*a* + 234 + 237, 37 (end) [i-na pa-ni]-ja la it-bu-u, BA iv 131, 132. K 533 (Hr^L 304) 14 la ta-at-bu-u-ma. — Z^b iv 52 ma-aq-tu l[it]-bi, let the lame rise up. *del* 172*foll* (188, 190, 194) lit-ba-am-ma. K 174 (Hr^L 58) 10 li-it-bi (9, lu-ši-ib). — K 145, 14—15 a-na eli alâni ša Bît-da-ku-ru ni-te-ib-bi (BA i 590); K 82, 11 a-na mux-xi alâni i-tib-bu-u, *R* 6 ki-i it-bu-u (BA i 242*foll*; PSBA xxiii 53*foll*); K 509, 11 (BA i 239*foll*) = Hr^L 436, 275, 259. Perhaps IV^2 61 *a* 27, 28 a-na-ku ina lib-bi 'u-u-a a-ta-ab-bi u-šab, Banks, AJSL xiv 270 but I, in the midst of the trouble will come & remain (>< 631 *col* 2 Q[1]). — *ip* IV^2 30* *no* 3 *R* 12 (14) a-lu-u lim-nu te(ti)-bi. T^M iii 34 perhaps e-ka-a-ma te-ba-ti-na 2 *pl f*, BA iv 157—8. *Dibbara*-legend (KB vi, 1, 58) 13 i-ta-mu-u (3 *pl*) a-na .... te-bi i-ziz-ma. — *pm* KB ii 252, 60 a-šar pa-nu-ki šak-nu te-ba-ku (§ 84*d*) a-na-ku, = Smith, *Asurb*, 124. Creat.-*frg* III 19 + 77 & ‖ passages i-du-uš Ti-âmat te-bu-u-ni; IV 48 ti-bu-u arki-šu, they rise up behind (? or after?) him. Banks, *Diss*, 10, 23 a-mat-su a-bu-bu te-bu-u ša ma-xi-ra la i-šu-u; also 10, 31; 18, 19 (= *ag*), 29. IV^2 51 (K 150) *O* 9 ar-ki limutti te-bu-u, he has risen up (followed) after the evil, bad. H 77, 37—8 (= IV^2 5 ii 68, 69 & 70/1) the seven evil spirits (gods) ša ki-ma a-bu-bi (*var* ba) ti(*var* te)-bu-ma; 40, ana ma-a-ti ki-ma me(mi)-xi-e ti(te)-bu-ni-šu-nu. Sn v 40 a-na Bâbili te-bu-ni (3 *pl*); 15 te-bu-u-ni. — *ag* L^4 iii 16 na-ki-ri ti-bu-te; Xamm.-*code* ii 2 the wise king ti-i-ib ki-ib-ra-at ir-bi-tim, who stormed the four quarters of the world. — *ac* Creat.-*frg* III 98 te-bu-u a-na-an-tu, to arise for the fight. V 21 *c-d* 42 IB (= TUM) = te-bu-u, Br 490. H 15, 189 ZI = te-bu-u. Ana (seldom ina) irti ...... tebû, see irtu, 108 *col* 2 (beg.) & Šalm, *Obel*, 145 (it-ba-a). — Here probably also (thy mighty weapons, *etc.*) ... lu-u ti-bu-u lu-u za-aq-tu, see 292 *col* 2 (beg.). — Knudtzon, 1 *R* 13 pm te-bi; written ZI-bi 29 *R* 16; *cf* V 50 *a* 30 (end) te-bi-u (?, 3 *pl*).

Q[1] *Adapa*-legend ii 13 he cried out: help! it-ti-bi ina ku-us-si-šu, & arose from his throne, KB vi (1) 94; IV^2 5 *b* 31 (end) it-te-bu-ni šu-nu; K 82, 14 (+ 18) a-na mux-xi ...... it-te-bu-u. Creat.-*frg* IV 94 see šašmeš & qarabu, Q[1] pm. H 129 *R* 12 (K 257) išâtum napixtum šit-bu-tum anaku, Prince, JAOS xxiv 112; 125 going forth hostilely.

On BA i 456 deriving a-si-bi, Anp i 82 *etc.* from tebū 𝔔[t], see šabū, šebū, 1 𝔔[t].

𝔔[tn] K 10 *O* 22, 23 a-na a-xi-šu-nu ul-li-i-it-te-ni-ib-bu-u (JAOS xviii 142*foll*; Hr[L] 290); K 145, 11—12 a-na eli ..... it-te-ni-ib-bu-u (Hr[L] 436). IV² 15* *b* 27, 28 ina ni-du-ti erçiti it-te-ni-en-bu-u ‖ 26 it-ta-na-aš-ša-bu (𝔔[tn] ašabu); see nidūtu & Br 11857.

ℑ Perhaps S 61, 10 tu-ub-bu, Br 2385; yet rather √ṭābu.

ℑ[t] 81—6—7, 209 *O* 32 te-me-en-šu u-ši-bi-ma, BA iii 262—3.

Š T[M] vii 40 u-šat-bi qu-lu ku-ru *etc.*, BA iv 161. IV² 1 *a* 38—9 ma-ru ina bir-ki amēli u-šat-bu-u (3 *pl*, they compel to rise). Xamm.-*code* vi 26 i-na (= from) (iç) kussê da-a-a-nu-ti-šu u-še-it-bu-u-šu-ma (ZA xviii 27), they shall remove him from his seat of judgment. I 51 *no* 2 *a* 20 Marduk šarre er-bitti u-ša-at (*var* šat)-ba-am-ma. V 64 *a* 29 the gods u-šat-bu-niš-šum-ma (§ 22) Kūraš šar Anzan; *a* 12 let the Umman-manda come (u-šat-ba-am-ma); *cf* III 56 *no* 3, 37 Umman-manda ZI (= itebbi) in an omen. Zimmern, *Ritualtaf.*, *no* 60, 26 (end) ištu eli (il) Ašur u-šat-ba-a, vor dem Ašur(bild) soll er ihn aufstehen lassen; 62, 7 tu-šat-ba-šu; 66, 13; 68 *R* 8. especially with kakkē. V 55, 13 a-na tur-ri gi-mil-li (māt) Akkadi u-šat-ba-a (iç) kakkē-šu. K 2675 *O* 60 eli ummānija kakkē-šu u-šat-ba-a, Smith, *Asurb*, 47. — Bu 88—5—12, 75 + 76 ix 6—7 kakkē-ja li-šat-bu-u-ma, BA iii 256—7. — K 3500 + K 4444 + K 10235 i 11 šāru lim-nu ina elippi-ku-nu lu-šat-ba, Winckler, *Forsch.*, ii 10. ip ZA iv 14 *b* 13 (& 226) šu-ut-bi-e. Xamm.-*letters* 4 *R* 11 xa-mi-ša (*i. e.* of the Euphrates) šu-ut-bi. Winckler, *Sargon*, 191 (below) kakkē-šu šu-ut-bi. IV² 54 *a* 42 šu-ut-bi-ma šer-tuk-ku, let him escape from thy wrath; ZA iv 287, 46 šu-ut-bi šērtuš. — pm KB vi (1) 118 *ad* NE 1 *col* ii 9 + 22 ina p(b)u-uk-ki šu-ut-bu-u, werden sie aufgescheucht. — ac Z[Š] iv 17 ma-aq-tu šu-ut-bu-u; *ibid* 78 ušatbū marçu, (dessen Beschwörung) dem Kranken aufhilft. Sarg *Cyl* 7 Sargon who a-na šumqut nakirē šu-ut-bu-u kakkē-šu (§ 89); *bull* 12; *Nimr* 3 (KB ii 36, 37). K 2801 *O* = K 221 + 2669, 44. — V 45 vii 30 tu-šat-ba.

Derr. — these 7:

tību (> tib'u), arising, advancing, advance {Aufstehen, Anrücken} *etc.* K 82 (Hr[L] 277) 6 (amēl) Pu-qu-du ina ti-bi ...... 7 (end) uq-te-it-tu-u. TP i 16 the great gods ša ti-bu-šu-nu tuqumtu u šanaš-mu. Anp i 1 see šananu 𝔑; i 7 ša ti-bu-šu a-bu-bu. Creat.-*frg* IV 78 (= D 98, 38) ti-bu-ka, KB vi (1) 27 dein Aufstehen. K 2801 = K 221 + 2669 *O* 12 (end) [ša] ti-bu-šu-nu tam-xa-ru ša-aš[-mu], BA iii 228, 229 whose advance means fight & battle. K 3351 *O* 11 see ša'irru. Perhaps K 3445 + Rm 396 *O* 32 te-bi ša-a-ri; *cf* K 747 *O* 11 ina qabal ti-ib ša-a-ri, Thompson, *no* 235. — *c. st.* TP III 14/15; 66/67 (= 18/19, 70/71) ti-ib taxāzi-ja dan-na(nu) (lu-u) e-du-ru; v 36; vi 25; Sn iii 54; v 65; Asb ii 36; iii 34 ki-ma ti-ib me-xi-e ez-zi aktum Êlamtu (Sn v 64; *Bav* 44; Sarg *Ann* 279); viii 72 a-na ti-ib limut-tim, KB ii 220, 221. III 52 *a* 9, 10 ul-tu ti-ib [iltāni] a-na ti-ib šūti, Jensen, 156, 157. V 25 *a-b* 35, 36 see munattu, 565 *col* 2; V 24 *col* 1 .... ti]-ib ūm = muna-a[t-tum], KB vi (1) 386. *abstr. n.* of tību is:

tibūtu. uprising, invasion {Aufstand, Einfall} AV 8849. Sn v 43, 44 see pānu *β*. (812 *col* 2, end); also Sarg *Ann* 60; KB ii 244, 43. Asb ix 90 ti-bu-ut (iç) kakkē (il) Ašur u (ilat) Ištar .... they heard; Sarg *Ann* 276. Smith, *Asurb*, 119, 20 (KB ii 248—9) aš-šu ti-bu-ut (amēl) Êlami-a ša ba-lu ilāni it-ba-a they brought me word. KB iii (2) 64 *col* 3, 17—18 i-na kakkē ez-zu-ti te-bu-ti ta-xa-za.

tebū *2. adj* KB iv 66 *ad* III 41 ii 16 iš-ru(šub?)-ba-a la te-ba-a, nicht weichender Aussatz. *f* te-bi-tum, K 4558 (S. A. Smith, *Asurb*, i 101) *O* 6 see malū, 3 (544 *col* 1) = K 4574 (M[S] *pl* 12). — *pl* IV² 5 *a* 35, 36 zi-iq ša-a-ru te-bu-tum. AV 8846.

tēbū (properly 𝔔 ag) *m* aggressor, enemy {Angreifer, Feind} AV 8848. ‖ 𝔓, KB vi

(1) 306. Asb iii 65 (amēl) Ur-bi (amēl) te-bi-e nišē (māt) Gam-bu-li. Neb v 46—8; POGNON, *Wadi-Brissa*, 77 *fol* see 758 *col* 1 *ll* 3—8. K 82 *O* 17 (+ *R* 12) (amēl) te-bi-e (= *pl*) .... it-te-bu-u. K 769 *O* 2 te-bi-e (al) kiš-ša-tu; K 712 *O* 2 (THOMPSON, *nos* 82, 88). V 16 *c-d* 49 SAG-ZI = te-bu-u; preceded by sa-ar-ru (1, see 782 *col* 1), Br 2335, 8555.

tēbānu. raid, incursion {Einfall} K 10, 9 ti-ba-a-nu ina (māt) Nim-ma-ki (= Êlamti) ti-ba-', make ye a raid into Elam (JOHNSTON). Hi^L 280.

tabū (= tebū, 3). KB vi (1) 306; KAT^3 370, 371; 388; 515; BROCKELMANN, ZA xvi 396. Neb vii 24 i-na i-si-num zag-mu-ku (at the newyear's festival) te-bi-e bēl ilāni Marduk, the resurrection of Marduk, the lord of the gods. Ner (1 67) *a* 35 ... a]-ki-ti ta-bi-e bēl ilāni Marduk. IV^2 20 *no* 3 *O* 3, 4 ta-bi ...(?). Perhaps also Nabd 696, 1 (end); 848, 3 a-na ta-bi-e ša (il) Šamaš u (il) ....

tu-bi. T. A. (Ber) 3 *R* 12 u at-ta i-na tu-bi xuráça .... šu-bi-la (send!), + 15 u i-na tu-bi a-na mi-ni-i tu-še-bi-la-am. JA xvi ('90), 310 √תבע (literally: dans la suite) = plus tard; later on.

tēbibtu. brightness, light, splendor {Helligkeit, Licht, Glanz} AV 8844. § 32 *aβ*.] ´ababu, ebebu, 5 *col* 1. KB iii (2) 108, 31—32 te-bi-ib-ti-šu u-qa-ad-diš-ma, PSBA xi 89. II 54 *b* 30 Šamaš is the god ša te-bi-ib-ti, 32 = (il) Šamaš ša šer-ti (morning? or, growth?). K 56 (H 74) iii 14 .... GAR (= ŠA) = te-bi-ib-tu (Br 12186); perhaps: the sprouting, green of the field; *cf* ereštu (3; 107 *col* 2 *ll* 15, 16); ebbu is also used in such meaning.

tab-xu V 27 *h* 24 | ib-xu (*g*) = UX-ZAG-LAL, some kind of vermin.

tabaku. *pr* itbuk, 1 *sg* atbuk (§ 18), *ip* tubuk, *ps* itabba(u)k, *ag* tābiku. AV 8648; id DUB (§ 9, 137; Br 3933). — pour out, heap up, pile up {ausgiessen, ausschütten, aufschütten}. V 47 *b* 23 it-bu-uk; H 48, 46 (= IN-DUB). Anp ii 83 pagrēšunu at-bu-uk, I heaped up; iii 82 grain & straw ina libbi DUB-uk; ii 118; 9 (*var* at-bu-uk). Šalm, *Mon*, *O* 46 the corpses of the slain enemy ina xi-ri-çi at-bu-uk-šu-nu. — *pc* IV^2 16 *a* 60 ki-ma me-e (= A) lit-bu-ku-šu (= XE-EN-BAL-E, Br 282). See also WINCKLER, *Forsch.*, ii 167 & *rm* 3 on BAL = tabaku in the *Gudea*-inscr. — *ip* Creat.-*frg* IV 18 (end) tu-bu-uk nap-šat-su; IV^2 16 *a* 52 (mē šunûti) ana re-bi-ti tu-bu-uk-ma (H 144); 26 *b* 40, 41 ša amēli šuatu me-e e-li-šu tu-bu-uk-ma, Br 6733. — *pm* Perhaps KB iii (1) 158, 20 (end) tab-ki — *ps* K 2846, 7 i-tab-ba-ku (= 3 *pl*) WINCKLER, *Forsch.*, i 474. K 164, 10—11 karānē ..... a-na qaq-ki-ri i-tab-bu-ku; also 24 (BA ii 635, 636). IV^2 50 iii 2 a-max-xa-ax a-tab-bak ana qaqqad raggati šim-ti-ki; 55 *no* 1 *R* (*b*) 28 ba-ax-ru ta-tab-bak-ši, *b*-fruits thou shalt pour out for her; 56 *a* 26 (end). 81, 2—4, 219 *R* i 14 šiu da-mu-šu-nu i-tab-ba-ku, *Rev. Sém.* vi 359, 361. SCHEIL, *Notes* LX (Constant. *no* 583: a medical text) 12 ŠIM ra-bi-ki TAB (= tatab)-bak (*R* 3); 22 ina ...... DUK nam-xar ta-tab-bak (+ 24), *Rec. Trav.* xxiii. — *ag* Sp. II 987 *O* 12 a-ri-bi (the raven) .... tab-bi-ik mar-tum; + 14 (end) ta-bi-ik, *Jour. Trans. Vict. Inst.*, xxix 52. IV^2 14 *no* 1, 30—31 Nergal ušumgallu çîru ta-bi-ik (= NI-DUB-DUB-BU) im-ti (= poison) e-li-šu-nu. ZA iv 301, 1—2 P.N. Marduk-ta-bi-ik-zi-ri-im, KB iii (1) 162; AV 8655. — *ac* S^c 30 du-ub | DUB | ta-ba-ku, between ša-paku & šaraqu, H 17, 273. H 37, 13 BAL = ta-ba-ku ‖ ni-qu-u, 12. T. A. (Lo) 6, 51 a-na ta-pa-ki a-na [qa-qa?]-di-ka. — figuratively: mēlammu (see *p* 550; Šalm. *Bal*, ii 3; Anp ii 112 *etc.*); namurratu (688), šaxarratu, šaxrar-tu & šaqummatu tabaku, see these words.

Q^t ‖ Q IV^2 51 *a* 52; Z$^{\acute{S}}$ ii 49 damē (da-mi) tap-pi-e-šu it-ta-bak(-ba-ak). *del* 62, 63 (66, 67) 6 šar ku-up-ri at-ta-bak a-na k(q)i-i-ri (KAT^3 548); 150 (159) see šaplu, 1.

ℑ intens. of Q. V 50 *a* 76 u-tab-bi-ku-šu, Br 10698. H 49, 50 IN-DUB-DUB = u-ta-ab-bi-ik. IV^2 58 *col* 3

tab-bu-u, tab-du-u, AV 8662, 8663 see tappū, tapdū. ~ tabxani see tapxu.

(*d*) 39 šap-ta-a-šu ..... u-tab-ba-ka q[a-a], ZA xvi 180 *fol*: ihre Lippen giessen (Speichel) aus.

𝔍^t V 65 *a* 22 i-na la a-dan-ni-šu ša bîti šu-a-ti ri-ša-a-šu iq-du-du ut-tab-bi-ka mi-la(-a)-šu, KB iii (2) 110, 111 & mêlu, *e* (545 *col* 1).

𝔔 — *a*) IV^2 16 *b* 55, 56 that ki-ma me-e lit-ta-bi-ik (Br 282). — *b*) metaphorically. Sarg *Khors* 111 it-ta-bi-ik-šu xa-at-tu, terror was cast over him. Sn *Bav* 41 xat-tu pu-lux-tu eli Êlamti kâlišun it-ta-bi-ik. — *c*) II 47 *d* 59, 60 $^{(iç)}$ qaššâti ul-ta-ma-la kakkê it-tab-ba-ku (= *ps*) D^{Pr} 155 *rm* compares הָרִיק, Exod 15, 9; *Ps* 35, 3.

𝔔^t KB vi (1) 48, 23 (*Zû*-legend) it-ta-at-bak ša-xar-ra-tum. K 6082 *c* 9 it-ta-at-ba-ku-ni (= 3 *pl*).

NOTE. — On nadbaku from tabaku see BA i 15 *no* 13: *d* may be the result of partial assimilation; but see nadbaku, 650. — Derr. these 3:

tabku *1. n.* — *a*) heaping up of grain, pouring out {Aufschüttung von Getreide, *etc.*} TP vi 102—4 ta-ab-ka ša še-im a-na ša abê-ja lu-ut(*var* -u)-tir lu(-u) at-bu-uk. — *b*) ta-ba-ak na-piš-ti-šu ki-ma me-e, Xamm.-*code* xlii 93 the pouring out of his life like water. A ‖ is:

tibku *1. c. st.* tibik. Neb *Grot* (I 66) *c* 15 ti-bi-ik se-ra-aš la ne-bi; Pognon, *Wadi-Brissa*, 18, 10—11 ti-bi-ik si-e-ra-aš ina la ni-ba & *p* 116 (*ibid*).

tabku *2. adj* poured out {ausgeschüttet}. IV^2 26 *b* 7 rimka tab-ka (= BAL) Br 282; IV^2 8 *b* 20 kîma [m]ê ri[xûti] tab-ku-ti (= BAL), GGA '98, 827.

tib(p)k(q)u *2.* some measure of length {ein Längenmass} AV 8851. TP vii 81 see šupalu, *a*. KB i 12, 10 fifteen ti-ib-ki lu ax[-ri-i]. III 3 (*no* 6) 21. Sn vi 39: 200 ti-ib-ki .... ušaqqi rêšu. I 44, 62: III šûš + XX = 3 × 60 + 20 = 200 ti-ib-ki; Sarg *Silver* 38 (Lyon, *Sargon*, 82); Asb x 76: fifty $^{(a-an)}$ ti-ib-ki maš-kan ši-kit-ti-šu. AV 8851 quotes TA. 38 eli III šûš(i) ta-a-an ti-ib-ki. Sn *Bell* 53, 54: 160 ti-ib-ki tam-li-i; later 20 ti-ib-ki çir maxrî uççipma 180 ti-ib-ki ušaqqi êlâniš; *Rass* 81, 82 (ZA iii 317). ZA iii 55 *no* 9. ID perh. I 28 *b* 27. K 8665 *a-b* 9, 10 (M^S *pl* 14) according to M^S 74 *col* 1 ti]-ib-qu = si-ip-pu & ri-kis sip-pi, see 776 *col* 2.

KB i 216 suggests a mistake on the part of the scribe in Anp ii 132: 120 tik-pi a-na muš-pa-li lu-ṭa-bi; also iii 136 but see Anp *Stand* 17; 11 *a* (tik-pi, *var* ti-ik-pi); Scheil, *Nabd*, xi 11 ti-gi-ib(?); K 1247, 13 (Hr^L vol vi) ti-ik-pi ša $^{(aban)}$ pûli. Also King, *Tukulti-Ninib* I, 91, 12—13: III šu-ši ti-ik-pi; e-li-en ti-ik-pi ša-tu-nu.

Oppert (KB i 12 *rm* 5) = Ziegelschicht; *ibid* 95 *rm** tiq-pi = Ziegelschicht (Winckler). — Fox Talbot, JRAS xviii 81: a measure of 9 inches.

tab(p)k(q)irtu. V 14 *e-f* 56 ša ina tab-kir (or piš?)-ti na-du-u. ZK i 320, 321; ZA ii 331 *no* 14 compares בקרת. Br 4377.

tabakbakku. Cyr 131, 4 çâbê ša itti alpê ana ta-bak-ba-ak-ka (or ta-bak ba-ak-ka?) illiku.

tabalu 1. *pr* itbal, *ps* itabbal, *ip* ta-ba-al, Rm 277 ii 5; vii 7 (BA iii 503, 504). AV 8651. Ungnad, WZKM xvii, 277 *foll*: tabalu a secondary formation from זבל = für sich nehmen; dann, wegnehmen. take away, appropriate, rob, abduct {wegnehmen, an sich reissen, berauben, entführen}. V 47 *b* 10 it-bal a-mer-ši-na, their deafness he has taken away; Merod.-Balad.-stone iii 16, 17 see šiqiltu. Esh ii 47 (who had carried away) see pariktu, 880 *col* 1 (beg.); also III 15 *c* 23 (it-ba-lu). Bu 91—5—9, 418, 7 it-ba-al-ma i-te-pu-uš, he took and acquired. IV^2 31 *O* 43 (46, 49, 52, 55, 58, 61) why, o porter, ta-at-bal, hast thou taken away (see 𝔔^t). T^M iii 9 + 12 (= IV^2 50) ša ar-datu damiq-tum i-ni-ib-ša it-bal KB vi (1) 448. IV^2 25 *a* 45/46; 47/48 $^{(il)}$ Êa ana a-šar te-lil-ti it-bal-ka (Br 4902); II 9 *c-d* 57. T. A. (Ber) 8 *R* 3 kaspa ša it-ba-lu, ZA v 17, the money he has (KB v they have) stolen. — IV^2 10 *b* 41, 42 an-na e-pu-uš ša-a-ru lit-bal (MU-UN-TUM, EME-SAL, Br 9062); 16 *b* 53, 54 ma-ru-uš-tu ša e-mu-qi i-na-aš-ša-ru re-bi-tu lit-bal (= XA-BA-AN-TUM); 59 *no* 2 *b* 15 i-dir-ti XA (= nûnu) lit-bal; 13 ta-ni-xi-ja lit-ba-lu sibit šârê (= IM-XI-A); Zimmern, *Rituall.*, *no* 45 vi 1 may

Ea, Šamaš, & Marduk (lit-ba-lu) take away. II 51 *no* 1 *R* 7 (end) lit-bal, ZK ii 322. — IV² 58 iv 41 whosoever the tablet i-tab-ba-lum, shall take away; V 51 *a* 67 man-nu ša i-tab-ba-lu; id TUM often, IV² 6 *a* 53; 17 *b* 57; 19 *b* (*R*) 31 (BA i 428); 50 *c* 37; 56 *a* 50; 57 *b* 67; V 33 viii 42 (KB iii, 1, 152 *rm* 3). IV² 48 *b* 9 ar-kat-sun ša-a-ru i-tab-bal; III 41 *a* 37 whosoever these lands (fields) i-tab-ba-lu u-šat-ba-lu; 38 *c* 4, 5 whosoever this field i-tab-ba[-lu] u-šat-ba[-lu]; K 4223 iii 33, 34 mu-na-gi-ir[-šu] bît-su i-tab-ba[-al]. — Xamm.-*code* xiv 27 e-si-ip ta-ba-al, harvest & take to thyself (HARPER). — I 70 *b* 7 whosoever a-na ta-bal eqli šu-a-tum ..... izzazzûma; III 41 *a* 35; Merod-Balad.-stone v 32 (BA ii 265; KB iii, 1, 192). — In astronomical texts: disappear {verschwinden}. K 752 *O* 4 (PINCHES, *Texts*, 1 *no* 2 = III 58 *no* 14) Sin i-tab-bal; K 124 *R* 8 ki-ma i-tab-bu-lu, (= ps THOMPSON, *Reports*, ii *nos* 85, 267. pr itbal, often. III 63 *a* 4; H 20, 349 tu-um | DU | ta-ba-lum; 107, 7 (112, 7; D 126, 7) 1R = DU = ta-ba-lu(m) xamṭu, Br 4903, 5390.

Q¹ = Q the porter it-ta-bal the crown on her head, *etc.* IV² 31 *O* 42, 45, 48, 51, 54, 57, 60 (see Q). IV² 51 *a* 53 çu-bat tap-pi-e-šu it-ta-bal = Z⁸ ii 50. Xamm.-*code* xl 56 at-tab-ba-al-ši-na-ti. H 61, 46 a-mat-su (*i. e.* his female slave) [it]-ta-bal, he can take away.

ℑ S^P 158 + S^P II 962 *R* 36 u-tab-ba-la E-lam-mat. (and) he carried off to Elam. V 45 *d* 48 tu-tab-bal. Perhaps ZIMMERN, *Ritualt.*. *no* 64 *R* 11 (end).

Š see Q; & KB iii (1) 160, 37; K 3456 *O* 15 xur-ru na-ad-ba-ku u-šat-ba-lum šadû, PSBA xxiv 87, 38. ZIMMERN, *Ritualtafeln*, *no* 41/43 ii 10 ... u-tab??-b]i-lu u-šat-ba-lum u-še-iç-çu-u; Z⁵ ii 61.

tabālu *2.* T. A. (Ber) 43, 42 u lu-ya-ši-ra XX ta-bal ša dum-ku sisē a-na ardi-šu, KB v 185 (may it seem good to my lord) to send 20 pair (?) of good horses to his servant; often in T. A. see KB v 33*.

tabālu *3.* T. A. (Lo) 8, 30 u-ma-ma lu ša ta-ba-li lu ša a-la, KB v *p* 405 water or air (??).

t'ā'b'ā'lu *4.* see kallû, 388 *col* 1, end & nabālu, nabāliš, 687. KB vi (1) 510 = תֵּבֵל, dry land, *terra firma*; also see JENSEN-BROCKELMANN, 392. ZA iv 265, 266. BROWN-GESENIUS, 385 *col* 2.

tabūlu, *m* shepherd {Hirte} ‖ utullu, KB vi (1) 575 *ad* 451. NE VI 58 ta-ra-mi-ma ^(amēl) SE(A)B (= rē'û) ta-b(p)u-la (*var* u-tul-la), thou didst love a shepherd (?? see KB vi, 1, 451), a herdsman.

tabbūlu, flock {Herde} *i. e.* subjects. III 66 x 24 such & such a-na tab-bu-li-šu di-na-ni-šu (to his flock & himself) lu TI-LA (= balîṭ) lu ša-lim, PSBA xxi 129, 130.

tabilu *1.* Nabd 239, 17 see sellu, 2 (760 *col* 1); BA iii 423—4: perh. = Bachschisch für den Hausmeister.

tabilu *2.* Neb 441, 2: one bît ta-bi(?)-lu, 1 bît ṭâbti, bît (bid-?)li-e, PEISER, *Vertr.*, *p* 287. T^C 142; WZKM iv 127 *no* 3; perhaps from Aram תְּבַל; תַּבְלָא, a spice, condiment, which passed into Arabic as تَابَل, FRÄNKEL, *Lehnwörter*, 37.

tabbilu. Asp ii 75 at that time I received as tribute siparri tab-bi-li siparri kam-ma-at (*var* -a-te) *etc.*, AV 8661.

tubalû. V 26 *g-h* 51 GIŠ-KU-LAL-[cuneiform] = tu-ba-lu[-u?], followed by 52 GIŠ-KID-DA-[cuneiform] = tu-xal-[lum?]. AV 8981, Br 10643. ZK i 307 *foll*; ii 26 compares תובלא & תחלא; Löw, *Aram. Pflanzennamen*, 109 *foll.* V 34 *c* 25, 26 mi-ši-il agurri tu-ba-lu (??, KB iii (2) 44, 45).

tub(p)lu, *c. st.* tubul, AV 8986, 8990; Br 1049. II 25 *a-b* 49 (K 4188 iv 1) MAX = tu-ub-lu, followed by (50) MAX = ti-iz-qa-ru, which in 51, 52 is = MAX-DI & GAL-DI. Šalm. Throne inscr. ii 3 tu-ub-lu nîqê-ia a-na ilâni maxâzê ša ^(mât) Akkadi aqqi. III 61 *b* 14 (62 *b* 11) when the gods of heaven & earth ep-šit a-me(mi)-lu-ti tu-bu-ul-šu-nu i-ši-im-mu. REISSNER, *Hymnen*, 92 *b* 25 tu-ub-lu-šu (= BIT-E-ŠIT-LAL-BI) itta'batum.

tubullû. K 4174 + 4583 iv 35 ..... lum-mar | KI-SAG ... | ... UN ... BU tu-bu-ul-lu-u, JAOS xxii 217.

tūbil, (√abalu, 2, *pp* 7, 8) in name of canal tu-bil nu-ux-ša, II 51 *a-b* 50, AV 8984, Br 3342.

tēbelu. III 4 *no* 7, 15 .... te]-e-be-li ša-di-i e-li[-u-ti]; + 23 te-be-li šadê ēlûti; compare 17 (+ 24) xi-çib]-ti ti-šmat. *l* 16 read perhaps at-ta tap-lak-ka-ta (√palakul?) ša-di-i šap-lu-ti.

tēbiltu (> tābiltu) in name of canal, river (nâr) te-bil(ne?)-ti a-gu-u šit-mu-ru, Sn *Bass* 78 (ZA iii 315; 330); MEISSNER & ROST, 4. D^Pr 124; AV 8845. Esh *Negoub* 6 nâr te-bil-ti max-ri-tu of Asurnaçirpal, BA iii 206, 207. Perhaps these two from same root as ablūtu.

taballallu (?). Br 3778 on II 35 *c-d* 5 KU-TAB-BAL = ta-b(pal-lal[-lu?] AV 8652.

tuballaç, AV 8982 see balluçitu, 167 *col* 2.

tabnū, properly: creature, offspring {Geschöpf, Spross} √banû, 1 (173—176); AV 8667, 8668; D^Pr 198; 215; in P. N. K 175, 2 ardu-ka Tab-ni-i (Hr^L 221). Nabd 348, 21 Tab-ni-e-a; KB iv 200 *no* i 16; Cyr 332, 9 Tab-ba-ni-e-a (see below). — But Tabni in P. N. Bêl-tab-ni-bul-liṭ, Nabū-tab-ni-uçur, = 2 *sg* Ⓠ pr of banû, 1 (M^S 24 *col* 2).

tabnītum *1.* Nabd 753, 27 fifty shekel of silver a-na tab-ni-tum ša ziq-ra-tum (see above 292 *col* 1, NOTE 4) or zik-ra-tum (??); Nabd 924, 5 UD-KA-BAR-MEŠ-ša tab-ba-ni-tum (see below). Sp II 265 *a* vii 5 il(-)tab-ni-i-te bêli (= EN)-šu; ZA x 6; while STRONG, PSBA xvii 142 *foll* il-tab-ni i-te-en-šu.

tabannu, handiwork {Machwerk} K^M 12, 31 ta-ba-an-na ša ilu u (ilat) iš-tar ba-nu-u, who createth the handiwork of god & goddess.

tabbanū *1.* *m* edifice, building {Gebäude} § 65, 32 *f*; BEZOLD, *Achaem.*, 50; *pl* tab-banūtu, § 67, 6. Achaem.-inscr. *D* 14, 15 tab-ba-nu-u[-tu?] (§ 57 *c*) ullūtu gab-bi (BA i 421); 13 šanūtima mādūtu tab-ba-nu-u-tu.

tabbanū *2.* *adj?* *f* tabbanītum, see tab-nītum.

tabnītu *2.* (√banû, 2; 176, 177). Cyr 290, 1—2: eleven ni-sip-pi ša šam-ni ša a-na tab-ni-tum (for lighting purposes {zur Beleuchtung bestimmt}). Nabd 957, 1—2: fifty ni-sip (character ME) ša šam-ni ... [a-na] tab-ni-tum.

tibnu *1.* straw {Stroh} תֶּבֶן, تِبْن. AV 8117, 8281; ZA ii 298. ꞉ IN-NU & ŠE-IN-NU, Br 7452. Nabd 231, 3: twelve minas of silver, the price for brick, cane, wood and ti-ib-ni ša e-piš ša bît (& straw for the building of the house). T. A. (Ber) 99, 33—34 for the bringing of içê a-na ti-ib-nu | a-na ti-i-ti (wood, straw & clay); 38 ia-nu mi ti-ib-nu, I have no straw. V 42 *g-h* 18 IM-IN-NU = di-id (rather than ṭi-iṭ) ti-ib-ni = a basket of straw (× 355 *col* 1 *c*). ZK ii 57; ZA i 67; Br 4231, 8418. še-am (or ŠE-AM?) *pl* ŠE-IN-NU *pl* Anp ii 9, 86, 118; iii 82 še-am *pl* u ŠE-IN-NU I harvested & stored. K 4289 *R* 9 see šabašu. K 678 (Hr^L 506) *R* 1 šu-ux ŠE-IN[-NU?]; *cf* *l* 6. K 515 (Hr^L 89) *R* 6. Sn *Kui* ii 22 še-im u ŠE-IN-NU; SMITH, *Sen*, 92, 68; III 57 *no* 7, 50. ⊕ 59 ii 22 xa-ba-šu ša IN-NU (= tibni?); puššušu ša IN-NU see pašašu, ב (847 *col* 1).

NOTE. — See LAGARDE, *Nominalübersicht*, 138, 139 against GESENIUS; HOMMEL, *Gesch. Assyr. & Babyl.*, 791.

tibnu *2.* name of a bird {Name eines Vogels}. II 37 *a-b* 52 KUR (*i. e.* kāšid) ti-ib-nu ‖ aš-ki-ki-tum çal-mu (AV 8117 reading šat-ti-ib-nu), Br 4814; D^S 102. BEZOLD, *Catalogue*, 570.

tibnu *3.* H 24, 497; V 30 *a-b* 47 (ga-ra-aš) MAL (+ inserted small KAB) = ti-ib-nu, AV 8852; Br 5477, 5478. HOMMEL-HASTINGS, *Dict. of the Bible*, i 219 = Babylonian weight of 10 shekels.

tabīnu *f* **tabīnatu.** V 40 *c-d* 33 IT-BAD (= dūru) = ta-bi-nu, KB vi (1) 463 = "side" of a wall, *i. e.* what is outside of the wall {"Seite" der Mauer; *d. i.*, das "ausserhalb der Mauer" befindliche}? NE VII *col* v *a* (*b*) 1 i-na a-mat (il) Šamaš ta-bi[-nu] KB vi (1) 190—1: *Mauer.* die ausserhalb der Stadtmauer befindliche Flur; K 5410 *a* tabīnu ‖ rītu, pasture. Also see IV² 20 *no* 3 *O* 4, 5, beg. II 19 *b* 41, 42 ta-bi-na-as-su-un (= IT-BAD-BI) lu-u il-li-ku. Z^B 17 √banû.

tab(p)-su-u, cover {Decke}. V 28 *g-h* 48, 49 = lid(t)-du (477 *col* 1) & ta-šab-šu.

AV 8669. Zimmern, *Ritualt.*, 31—37 ii 6 ila šuata ina eli GI-KIT-MAX ina tab-si-e kitē tūšēšabšu, sollst du selbigen Gott auf ein *Postament* mit einer Decke (?) von Leinwand setzen.

tabāqu. AV 8653. II 41 *c-d* 3 U-ŠIM = ta-ba-qu, Br 5164. powdered perfumes; Hebr אֲבָקָה, Gesenius[12] 7. same id = ur-ki-tum; H 39, 168; II 41 *c-d* 4.

tub(p)qu & tub(p)uqtu, AV 8985. — enclosed place, room, chamber; inner room; (world as a) room {umschlossener Raum, Gelass, Kammer; Innenraum; (Welt)raum}. AV 9043. 9044; H[F] 73; ZA v 2 *rm*; Jensen, 165; 183*foll*; 240; 255. IV[2] 1* iv 37, 38 (= UB, Br 5786) see šaxātu, 4. Neb iv 47 I built *E*, her temple, i-na tu-ub-ga (perh. a mistake for -ga-at) dūr Bābili, KB iii (2) 18, 19 & *rm* †. V 34 *b* 9, 10 where the same temple was built ša tu-ub-ga-at dūr i-na Ba-bi-lam (ki); also KB iii (2) 48 *col* 1, 49—50. Creat.-*frg* IV 113 (= D 99 *R* 30) ga?]-du tub-qa-a-ti ma-lu-u du-ma-mu, KB vi (1) 28—9; 340; also see *ibid*, 564; 586 (kibratu); IV[2] 56 ii 26 ina UB-DUR = tubqi dūri bury her; must be a burial place within the wall. IV[2] 30* *no* 3 *R* 18 ina tub-qat bīti (= E-A-UB-UB-TA); 22 ina tub-qa-a-ti lu-uz-ziz. K 41 *a* 15 .... ina tub-ki šu-uz-zu-zu. KB vi (1) 298, 22 [..... ra-k]u-us-ma tub(p)-qa-a-ti e-mid, und errichtete Innenkammern. On the seven tubuqāti of the Babylonians, see Jensen, 163*foll*; 255; KB vi (1) 340, 586; KAT[3] 615*fol*; &, again, Winckler, *Gesch. Israels*, i 108 *rm* 6; J[AT] 11 & *rm* 4. II 35 *a-b* 38, 39 UB-DUG-GA = tu-bu-qa-tum; UB-DA-ĒĒ = *t* ir-bit-ti (40 = kib-rat er-bitti) Br 5787; = H 39, 163, 164. S[b] 309 UB | ub | tu-ub-qu; H 4, 118; 22, 425 ‖ kib-ra-tum. S[b] 221 tu-bu-uq-tu. Pognon, *Wadi-Brissa*, 105, plateforme (?). 83, 1—18, 1330 iv 5 tubqu = tēlum, Jensen, 165 *rm* 2.

tub'ā'qu, name of a bird see marratu, 2 (594 *col* 2); AV 8983.

tubuqqu. II 24 *a-b* 78 SU-ŠU-DUR = tu-bu-uq-qu, AV 8988, Br 222.

tabrū, fulness {Fülle} √barū, 4; *pp* 185, 186. AV 8671. II 42 *g-h* 25 U-XI-A (= ZUN) = tab-ru-u followed by ab-lu-tum & ma-'a-du-tum; H 39, 172. Br 8627, 6069, 14068.

tabarru. perh. an *adj* from barū, 4: sated (with color, dye); dyed {gefärbt} then a piece, a garment dyed; usually explained as: light-purple, because found together with argamānu & takiltu. 81—11—28, 38, 7 one (çubāt) qarbītu (?) ta-bar-ra, one çubāt piçū; 15 one mut-ta-tum ša ta-bar-ri; 8 one-half mina five shekels ta-bar-ri xis-su (Jastrow, AJSL xv *no* 2). K 10050, 4 ta-bar-[ru]; 6 ar-ga-ma-nu, M[S] *pl* 16. V 61 v 47, 48 šipāt ta-bar-ru šipāt ta-kil-tu, KB iii (1) 180, 181. Nabd 664, 1—2: two minas for (of) šipāt ta-bar-ri, two minas for (of) šipāt ta-kil-tum (BA i 528); 467, 1 (& 3) so & so many shekels ta-bar-ri xis-su (BA i 525); 222, 11—12 forty minas ana (?) çu-pa-tum ša ta-bar-ri (BA i 508); 284, 3 (& 22) šipāt ta-bar-ri; 7 (& 9) šipāt ta-bar-ri u ta-kil-tum. ZA iv 120 *no* 18: two-hundred çubāti of šipāt ta-bar-ru; see also Nabd 1029, 6; Neb 240, 2 (çubāt) ta-bar-ra; 457, 6. Camb 267, 2 (BA i 633). Here perhaps also T. A. (Ber) 26 iii 27 .... ru-ba-at ša ku-zi-ti (= ku-sītu) tu-par-ra la a-din; 30 pa?]-ru-di ša ta-par-ri (?? so instead of XU).

tabiru (?). V 40 *e-f* 46 NUM-KA-R]A-AX = ta-bi-ru, AV 8657; same id (K 4373 ii 10) = gur-gur-ru; 11 = zumbu la-bi-e (M[S] *pl* 12); see 467 *col* 1, beg.

tēbiru, transgression {Überschreitung} √eberu, *p* 10. K 3182 iii 15 ta-šim-me te(*var* 83—1—18, 472 ta)-bir-ši-na-ti, AJSL xvii 140, 141, thou hearest their transgressions.

tabrītu *f pl* tabrāti; §§ 38; 65, 31*a*, 69. √barū, 3 (183, 184); AV 8774. — *a*) KB ii 250, 51 i-na(-aṭ)-ṭal šuttu i-gi-il-ti-ma tab-rit mu-ši (Haupt, *Jour. Bib. Lit.*, xix 69 *rm* 42) Ištar u-šab-ru-u-šu (a vision during the night = a dream

tibbaru see lubāru (473 *col* 2) & tippāru. ∾ tabrānu see daprānu.

‖ šuttu, 1); ZK ii 338. — *b*) sight, wonder, *pl* tabrâti, marvellous wonders {Ansehen, Bewundern} *etc.* FLEMMING, *Neb*, 42; Anp i 13 *Anp* calls himself rē'ū tabra-a-te, the guardian of marvellous wonders; iii 115 (rē'ū tab-ra-te). II 67 *R* 80 lion- & bull-colossusses *etc.* a-na tab-ra-a-te ušazziz. Sarg *Khors* 165 a-na tab-ra-a-ti u-ša-ziz(?); *Ann* 428 (*cf* BA iv 246); *Stele* 79. Esh *Sendsch*, *R* 53, 54 ana tab-rat kiš-ša na-ki-ri ana ça-at ū-mi ul-ziz. KB iii (2) 6, 29—30 ana ta-ab-ra (HILPRECHT, OBI *col* 1, 32—33 iii 36 *var* ri)-a-tim lu u-ša-az-zi-im-šu; Z^B 68; ZA iv 112, 146. Neb vii 36 the palace bît ta-ab-ra-a-ti ni-ši, the wonder for the people; ii 11 I made Babylon splendid a-na ta-ab-ra-a-tim; iii 63 a-na ta-ab-ra-a-ti, *etc.*; ix 29; vi 20 the gates a-na tab-ra-a-ti kiššāt nišē lul(l)ē ušmallam; V 65 *b* 9 (tab-ra(t)-a-ti, § 65. 23 *rm*); I 44, 86 ana tab-rat kiššat nišē; ZK ii 338 *rm* 2; 344 *rm* 1; ZA ii 94. KB iv 66, 15 (ilat) Ninā bēlit ta(?)-ab(?)-ra-a-tu (HILPRECHT, iš-ta-ra-a-tu); II 19 *b* 25—28 a-na tab-ra-a-ti (= ŠI + Ē-DI; Br 9360) iz-za-zu; DT 67 (H 119), 27 ana āli ana tab-ra-a-ti [ī nillikšu?]; id also IV^2 9 *b* 21; 23. II 8 *b* 35 ana tab-rat ma-a-ti (*col a* broken off); 36 ina ēli it-ta-çi. ana tabrâti šūluku see šūluku, 1 (Br 9360).

tabšū. V 15 *c-d* 13 KU-GAB-GAB = tab-šu-u, some headgear; AV 8672, Br 4512; 14 KU-GAB-GAB-ŠU-A = il-lu-ku; *cf* ZIMMERN, *Ritualt.*, *no* 70, 6 KU-GAB-GAB ina qaqqadi.

ta-bu-ša (*var* ši) ZIMMERN, *Ritualt.*, *no* 75—78 *R* 45.

tebušā (?). K 824 (Hr^L 290) *R* 16, 17 te-bu-ša-' ša taš-pur ba-an ša te-bu-ša-' . . . . . ša taš[-pur?].

tabaštānu. excrements {Excremente} ‍ב‌ba'ašu, 1 (140). AV 8654. IV^2 60* C *R* 9 ub-tal-lil ki-i immeri ina ta-ba-aš-ta-ni-ja. V 47 *b* 2; 3, ta-ba-aš-ta-nu explained as zu(-)u ši-na-tum. IV^2 22 *no* 2, 18—19 . ki-ma im-me-ri ina [ta-ba-aš]-ta-ni-šu bu-lul.

tab(p)ātu. salvebox {Salbenbüchschen} ? T. A. (Lo) 9, 44 one (aban) ta-ba-tum ša šamna ṭāba malū; 11, 65 (aban) ta-pa-tum ša šamna ta-a-pa ma-lu-u. (Ber) 25 iv 52—56 one (two) (aban) ta-pa-tum šamni mur-ri *etc.*; 26 iii 29 one (aban) ta-a-pa-te ša [šamni mur?]-ri.

NOTE. — HALÉVY, *Mém. de la Société de ling. de Paris*, xi 88: T. A. tapadu = Hebr פִּטְדָה = topaze = τοπάζιον. tapadu, no doubt, a Phoenician form.

te-bit (?). V 31 *a-b* 1 SA-T(D)UL-BI a-bur-ru : te-bit libitti.

tubbātu. KNUDTZON, 150 *R* 10 *etc.* tu-ub-ba-a-ti see ṭūbtu, 351 *col* 2. Also K 7000 *O* ina tu-ub-ba-a-ti āli, BEZOLD, *Catalogue*, 824.

tig(g)ū *1.* V 27 *e-f* 25 + 32 *a-b* 62 (erū) DUB (ti-gi) LUB(L) = ti-gu-u; also = ti-ig-gu-u ‖ xalxallatu (313 *col* 2, end). AV 8854, 8857; Br 7041. ZA xvii 242, 243 = röhrenartiges, bronzenes Musikinstrument, perh. = Flöte (*cf* חָלִיל). Also probably ‖ lilisu & uppu. REISNER, *Hymnen*, 109, 30 Ištar says of herself: kalû abrûtu ina ti-gi-i izzazūni, the assembled (?) priests are standing around me with flutes. The same word is probably found in:

tigū *2.* K 4239 *R* 2 ši-kar ti-gi-i = bi . . . .; ZA iv 157 *no* 4; vi 85 perhaps a circular bowl or dish; or a certain drink (*cf* the German: Bowle).

tugudū. II 23 *a-b* 20 mi-eš tu-gu-du-u ‖ paššūru (846 *col* 2). AV 8994.

tigilū. some plant, perhaps wild cucumber {eine Pflanze, vielleicht wilde Gurke}, AV 8855. ZK ii 211; ZA i 52, 53; iii 236; JENSEN, 231 *fol*; KB iii (1) 64 *rm* 4; vi (1) 492. II 44 *g-h* 6 XUL(?)-TI-GI-LU-SAR (Br 10895) = ti-gi-lu-u, preceded by u-ba-nu, 5; & qiš-šu-u, 4. II 28 *e-f* 16 (šam) xul-ti-gi-li KUR-RA = xi-il(-)bal-ti šadi-i (see 312 *col* 2); *cf* II 41 *a* 10, 11 XUL-LI-LI-GI-SAR followed by X. KUR-RA, Br 10896; 8, (šam) XUL-TI-GIL-LA = (šam) . . . . .; 9, (šam) XUL-TI-GIL-LA KUR-RA = ti[-gil-lu-u šadi-i?]. IV^2 3 *a* 32, 33 tigila-a ša ina çi-e-ri e-diš-ši-šu a-çu-u (& 36, 37). Sm 60 *O* 3 (šam) ti-

tiggalu (AV 8859), tiggallūtu see gugallu, gugallūtu (212, 213). ~ tagiabtu see takkaltu.

gi(?)-lu-u, preceded by (šam) pir(? [illegible])-tu (= [illegible]) xal-tap-pa-ni, & followed by (šam) meš(AV: me = šip, šib)-ru-u, (šam) ga-a-nu, (šam) mu(?)-bi-ir; M^S *pl* 18. Also see xultigilū, 319 *col* 2, end.

tug'ā'nu. V 41 *c-d* 47 [ ]-BAR = tu-ga-nu, AV 8902; Br 1812, 13951.

tagaru = tamkaru (?). AV 8674 quoting Neb 37, 25/7 a-ki-i ta-ga-ru.

tāgiru (?) protection {Schutz} (?) ZA iv 238, 46 ta-gir-šu ix-ši-ix.

tug'ā'rum. V 16 *g-h* 73 'Š'UR = tu-ga-rum (*cf* tuqārum); AV 8903, Br 2993.

tigaru = diquru. T. A. (Ber) 28 ii 39 one ti-ga-ru ra[-bu-u?]; see *l* 37 one kar-patu ra-bu-u; 48 one ti-ga-ru(-)a-ri eq-du.

tegurrū. II 23 *a-b* 19 mi-eš te-gur-ru-u ‖ paššūru, AV 8858.

tagrinnu. 80, 11—12, 9*fol* (JRAS '94, 831) NIGIN (+ inclosed AZAG) with gloss da-ag-rin = ta[-ag-rin-nu]; M^S 20 *col* 2, beg. Br 10283.

tēgirtu ‖ egirtu, 16 *col* 1. ZA vii 215 √agaru. AV 8856. K 525 (Hr^L 252) 15 a-na te-gir-te it-tal-ku-u-ni; 23, a-na te-gir-te-šu-nu i-sa-ak-nu, preceded by 21, 22 ina libbi e-gir-te^{pl} i-sa-ṭa-ru; *R* 11 la ki-e-tu ši-i te-e-gir-tu (BA ii 262 ši-i-te e-gir-tu) an-ni-tu; 8 ša il-lik-u-ni-ni a-na te-gir-te šu-u-tu, BA ii 60, wegen solcher Schutzgewährung; *ibid* 56 & 61: perh. = Schutzgenossenschaft. K 5464 *R* 1 ina te[-gir-te?].

tag(k, q)šū (?). NE VI 18 alpē-k]a tag-ši-i çēni-ka tu-'a-me li-li-da, KB vi (1) 168—9. V 37 i 53 tag(k,q)-šu-u preceded by ma-'-du-ti; or šum-šu-u (? see 1004 *col* 2 & 597 *col* 2).

tag(k)šīru *1.* support; properly: strengthening {Stütze; eigtl. Festigung} √gašaru 233, 234 (or kašaru?). S^c 6, 3 [BE] = tag-ši--ru, preceded by in-du, √עשר; AV 8511 šumširu.

tagšīru *2.* V 23 *b-d* 37 TUR-DA = tag-ši-ru, Br 4136.

ti-giš(is, iz, iç)-tum. BA iv 157, 158 *ad* T^M iii 44 dupl. reads qa-diš-tum ti-giš-tum, probably a phonetic spelling of SAL-ME = ašiptu. Reference to T^M v 83 ti-il-ti is wrong. See tilti.

ta-du. T. A. (Lo) 26, 33 may the troops of the king ... dash to pieces (šār) ta-du (amēl) a-ja-bi-šu, the breast (?) of his enemies, KB v 33* comparing רדד. See also Boissier, PSBA xxii 110; comparing Aram תדיך. (>< kan-ta-du, 411 *col* 1).

tudukū incantation {Beschwörung} Z^Š v/vi 51 ma-mit ina tuduki-e ša (il) Ea-a; & *ibid*, *p* 58 referring to IV^2 15* *b* 42, *var*.

tidūku. killing, fight, battle {Morden, Kampf, Schlacht} §§ 64 *rm*; 83 *rm*. id § 9, 146. AV 8869. √dāku, 244, 245. Rost, 100; BA ii 295, end. ‖ mitxuçu, 524 *col* 1, which see for Anp i 155; ii 55; so & so many çābē ti-du-ki-šu-nu (warriors) *ibid* i 52, 111, 115; ii 32, 89, 110; iii 20, 32*fol*. Šalm, *Obel*, 66; *Mon*. i 39; ii 97, 98; Sarg *Ann* 35. Anp iii 39, 40 one thousand çābē ti-du-ki-šu a-duk; iii 41: 172 çābē GAZ (Br 4728, 8172 *var* ti-du-ki)-šu-nu a-tuk (*var* duk); also i 47, 48; ii 57. TP III *Ann* 65 ina qabal ti-du-ki.

tadilibu (?). K 532 *R* 9 (Hr^L 109) ta-di-li-bi im-ma-te (or a verb form?). See *Rec. Trav.* xxiii 160*fol* on this text.

tadmiqtu, favor {Gunst} Xamm.-*code* xvii 17 a-na ta-ad-mi-iq-tim, as a favor. √damaqu.

Tidnu, tidānu, AV 8870. II 50 iii/iv 15 (*c-d* 58) (šad) ti-id-nu-um (ki) = (šad) A-mur-ri-e; 59 KUR-GIR-GIR-KI = (māt) A-mur-ri-e. II 48 *c-d* 12 (ti-id-nu) GIR-GIR = a-x(m)ur-ru-u, Br 9220. S^b 2, 15.

NOTE. — On Tidānu, Tidnu & Dedān see Zimmern, *Theol. Rundschau*, i 323 on Hommel, *Altisrael. Überlieferung*, 34; 339; also see KAT^3 15 & *rm* 5; 190; 141—2 against Hommel, *Sum. Lesestl.*, 29, 345 & Amiaud, RP^2 ii 41 *rm* 1. Jensen, ZA x 336—7; KB iii (1) 37 *rm* **: Tidnu was in Syria, probably name for the Lebanon-mountains, later = the whole of Syria. Also see PSBA '96, 251; *Jour. Trans. Vict. Inst.*, xxvi 133, 134, (Tidal(n)um of Gudea inscr. = a mountain of Phoenicia; Tidnu in Assyr.-Babyl. inscr.).

taddannu (> tandānu), tadānu; √nadanu, 650—654. AV 8680, 8681. — *a*) gift, present {Gabe, Geschenk}. K 618 (Hr^L 9) *R* 9—12 thousand & thousand years of joy of heart & health of body to the king, my lord, a-na ta-da-ni (= V 53 *no* 3; BA i 224*foll*; 232); P. N. Ta-ad-dan-nu, Nabd 306, 3; 711, 2 + 5 + 6; Cyr 292, 11. Nabū-ta-ad-dan-nu, AV 5885. Also *cf* Nabd 343, 8 Ta-at-ta-dan-nu. — *b*) sale {Verkauf}, especially in *c. t.* K 328, 3 *N* [bēl eqli] ta-da-a-ni, (KB iv 146 *no* XI); K 347, 3 (KB iv 134); III 49 *no* 2; 4 (46 *no* 7, 2) *N* bēl amēl nišē ta-da-a-ni. participants in a sale of people, slaves, *etc.* are written bēl (amēl) SE (= tada)-a-ni; III 49 *no* 5, 2; nišē SE-ni, 46 *no* 6, 2; 49 *no* 4, 5; bēl sinnišāti SE(-a)-ni, 46 *no* 1, 3; *no* 2, 7; bēl bīti SE-ni (of a house) 46 *no* 10, [1]; 48 *no* 2, 2 (be-ili); bīt SE (= tada)-an, 48 *no* 3, 5; bēl eqli SE-a(n)-ni, 50 *no* 3, 4; *no* 4, 2; bēl kirē eqlē nišē SE-an, 48 *no* 4, 4; K 317, 8 bēl kirē amēli ta-da-a-ni, KB iv 136 *no* VI. III 46 *no* 3, 4—5 see šapūsu. from nadanu is also derived:

tidintu, present {Geschenk} ‖ nidintu. Bu 91—5—9, 157 *O* 12, 13 (Hr^{L} 415) ti-din-tu ša šarri a-na be-li-ni id-di-nu-u-ni, AJSL xiv 13.

tē(ī)diqu, garment, dress, robe {Kleid, Robe} √עדק; § 65, 32 *d*, *rm*. *del* 238 (259) te-di-qa (*var* -qi) lu-u la-biš çu-bat bul (bal?)-ti-šu; 238 (262) te-di-qu ši-pa a-a id-di-ma e-de-šu li-diš; 239 (268), see KB vi (1) 246, 249; 397, 398. KB iii (2) 4 *col* 2, 61—63 lu-ba-ra-am te-di-iq šar-ru-ti-ja lu-ak-nu-un = ZA iv 111, 107—9; *cf* kananu, 407 *col* 1, end & lubāru, 478 *col* 2. IV² 9 *a* 17, 18 (id KU-KU) see rubūtu & Br 10647. ZA 231 & v 58, 25 see šaqū, 1 Š. Scheil, *Nabd*, iv 27 (Nergalšaruçur) te-di-iq ilu-u-ti ud-di-iq-šu (he covered him); viii 13—15 (for Ea, Nabū, Tašmētu) a-na te-di-qu ilu-u-ti-šu-nu rabū-ti as-mi-iš u-ša-lik (1 *sg*). V 28 *a-b* 7 see pa-li(j)āmu, 808 *col* 1, end; AV 8866. V 28 *a-b* 8 see lilū, 481 *col* 2 & taxabšu; 9 KU (= çubāt) SE (še?)-mu-u & Jensen, ZA x 332 who reads ku-li-lu-u = tēdiq be-ili = Gewand des Herrn.

tādirtu, sadness, mourning, lament(ation) {Trauer, Betrübnis, Wehklage} §§ 32 *aβ*; 65, 32 *b*. √adaru, 2 (22, 23). K 891 *O* 8 (= I 8 *no* 2) see bikitu (153 *col* 2) = L³ 8 (Lehmann, ii 20, 21). 83—1—18, 40 (Hr^{L} 407) 5 ūmu ša ta-di-ir-ti, AJSL xiv 179, 180.

ta-dur(ku)-ru, AV 8702 *ad* II 22 *no* 2 *add* (= II 44 *no* 9), Br 14449.

tidarum (?) II 26 *no* 1 *a-b* 16 ṬAR-ṬAR-NU = ti-id(-)a-rum, preceded by ti-iq-nu & zi-i-mu, Br 2499. AV reads ti-ja-a-rum, *q. v.*

tēdištu, restoration, renewal {Wiederherstellung, Erneuerung} √edešu, *p* 24. § 32 *aβ*; Latrille, ZK ii 259; Pognon, *Wadi-Brissa*, 195. V 34 *b* 40 te-di-iš-ti Ba-bi-lam (ki) Ba-ar-zi-pa (ki) ‖ 39 zi-in-na-a-at Ê-sag-ila Ê-zi-da. K 2801 (= K 221 + 2669) *R* 15 ši-pir te-diš-ti; BA 3, 235 zum Werk der Erneuerung.

tudātu *1.* (*pl* of tudtu?) decision {Entscheidung} §§ 62, 1; 65, 32 *a*; √ādū, 1 (ידה) 17 *col* 1, end see šitultu.

tudātu *2.* II 29 *e* 69, 70 tu-da-a-tu see lidātu, 477 *col* 2; AV 8995.

tūzu (?) ⊕ 252, 1 KU .... MAX = tu-u-zu, AV 9042, Br 14409; K 7331 ii 1; M^{S} *pl* 13.

tizkaram = ip Q¹ of zakaru; call, proclaim; see *p* 280 *col* 1, *med.*

tazkītu, dissolution of partnership {Lösung eines Kompagniegeschäftes} √zakū, 277, 278. Meissner, *no* 78, 4 (*pp* 143, 144). *M* & *M* tap-pu-ta-am i-pu-šu-u, had contracted a partnership-business; a-na ta-az-ki-tim da-a-a-ni ikšudūma, for a dissolution (of this partnership) they went to a judge. WZKM iv 304.

tazmērtu (√zamaru, 284) see tazzimtu.

tazzimtu. lament(ation) {Klage, Wehklage}; Jensen, KB vi (1) 525 Nörgeleien. §§ 36; 65, 32 *b*. Z^{B} 23 *rm* 1 *etc.* √נזם; see 660 *col* 2; Z^{Š} 62; KB v 33* *etc.* √אזם. V 35, 9 a-na ta-zi-im ti-ši-na bēl ilāni ez-zi-iš i-gu-ug(-ma), BA ii 208, 209. NE XII *col* i (K 2774) 28 ta(-az)-zi-im-ti (*var* -tum) erçi-tim i-[ç]ab-bat-ka; ii 19 ta-z[i-im]-ti erçi-tim iç-ça-bat-s[u], KB vi (1) 256—9. NE 8, 29 (18) ta-zi-im-ta-ši-na iš-te-nim-me (ilat) [A-ru-ru], KB vi (1) 120, 121. K 875 *R* 2 ta-az-zi-im-ti an-ni[-ti?], Thompson, *Reports*, *no* 236 B. III 60 *a* 21, 22 ta-zi-im-tum u ta-zu(= su)-ux-tum ina māti; Z^{Š} iv 8. T^{M} vii 129 (end) ta-zi-im-ti. V 22 *e-h* 7, 8 e-ir | A-ŠI | = tak-kal-tum; & ta-az-z[i-im-tum]; *h* 42 = ta-

tizmuru see tiçmuru.

ni-xu, 44 tak-kal-tum, 45 ta-zi-im-tum; AV 8683, Br 11620. II 47 *a-b* 29, 30 KA-AN-MU-GAL (Br 566) = ta-zi-im-tum, taz-me-ir-tum. Z[B] 23 *rm* 1 suggests also II 47 *c-d* 10 ta-su-ux-tu = ta-zim(? <⊏, = lit, rim?)-tu. T. A. (Ber) 24 *R* 67 u axi-ja] a-na ta-az-zi-i-im-ti u a-na mi-im-ma ma lu-u la u-ta-za-a[m-ma], KB v 62; vi (1) 548 (complaint).

tizqāru, high, exalted, lofty, noble {hoch, hochragend, erhaben, edel} √zaqaru, 291. for zitqāru?; §§ 65, 40*a*; 88 *rm*. AV 8948. FLEMMING, *Neb*, 26. Anp i 20 *Anp* tiz(KB i 56 taz *i. e.* 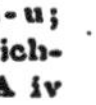)-qa-ru; iii 127; LHOTZKY, *Anp*, 30. K[M] 12, 19 tiz-qa-ru çīru (*var* ti-iz-qa-ru çi-ru; also see 27, 1; 29, 3; 9. 2). IV² 57 *a* 19 Marduk tiz-qa-ru çīru. IV² 21* *no* 1 C *R* iii 2 rubū ti-iz-ga (*var* qa)-ru. ZIMMERN. *Ritualtafeln*, *no* 26, 57 [il] Nabjū gaš-ru tiz-qa-ru. II 57 *c-d* 20 Na-a-bu-u | tiz (AV 2716 ur)-qa-ru e-lu-u; MEISSNER *apud* ROST, 103, 104: Oberrichter, an epithet of Ninib. See also ZA iv 113, 175. K 1279, 4 qar-rad tiz-qa-rum, AV 7357; Br 1061. — K 257 (H 128) *O* 73, 74 ti-iz[-qar]-tum a-bi-ja [(il)] Sin ana-ku, the noble heroine of my father Sin I am, Br 6867; JAOS xxiv 111, 114, 123. 81—6—7, 209 (dupl. K 6346) 4 ru-um-ti ti-iz-qar-ti, said of Ištar; BA iii 260, 261; HEBR. viii 114; PAOS May '91, cxxx. II 7 *g-h* 53, 54 MAX-DI (Br 1050), GAL-DI (Br 6867) = ti-iz--qa-rum. *cf* II 25 *a-b* 51, 52. II 25 *a-b* 50 MAX (= çīru) = ti-iz-qa-ru, Br 1048.

ti-zu-ru defendant, protector {Verteidiger}. T. A. (Lo) 17, 41 çābē narkabāti u ti-zu-ru [a-na] āl šarri bēli-ja; (Lo) 22, 13 & 14.

tazīru, an official's title {Beamtentitel}. K 469 *R* 11 (Hr[L] 138) [(amēl)] ta-zi-ru [(amel)] i-tu-'-u (another title).

taxū *1.* offspring, child, or the like {Sprössling, Kind, *etc.*} AV 8687. II 30 *c-d* 38 ta-xu-u ‖ ma-ar, AV 8687; ZA vii 213 √axū, from which also atxū.

taxū *2.* see ṭaxū, 353, 354. Here, perhaps. BOISSIER, *Doc.*, 2, 11 šumma eribē ina bit amēli ta-xi-e innamrū, or to 1?

taxxu. K 3456 *R* 29 im-ru-ka (thy food?) tax-xu qaq-qa-ri, the *t* of the soil, PSBA xxi 40 *foll.* *Berl. Congr.* ii, 1, 362 *col* 2 U Si-ni-Nanā tax-xu-šu-nu id-dan (?). 83, 1—18, 1330 iii 18 [(du-ud-da)] DAX = tax-xu ša nūni.

texū. K 168 *R* 12 (Hr[L] 437) u ištu du-ri atali (*i. e.* AN-MI) Sin te-xi-e (?) ilāni i-ba-aš-ši, LEHMANN, ii 76, 77; ZA xi 116 *rm* 1. HALÉVY, *Rev. Hist. Relig.*, '88, 50 = ṭexū; approach. II 48 *g-h* 49 TE = te-xu-u, between e-pu-u ša GAR (= akāli) & na-sa-xu, AV 8874, Br 7709; JENSEN, KB iii (1) 41 *rm* **† > ṭexū. III 65 *a* 6 when its right ear mu-diš-šu te-xa-a-at.

taxab(p?)šu, mat, matting, cover {Matte, Decke}. AV 8684; BA i 525, 526; ZEHNPFUND, *Theolog. Litbl.*, 1901 *col* 606. Ezek 27, 20, חֹפֶשׁ. V 15 *c-d* 16 KU-LIL-LA(L) *i. e.* [(çubāt)] lilū or kuli(l)lū? = ta-xab-šu, Br 5941; ZIMMERN, *Ritualt.*, *no* 70, 5. V 28 *a-b* 8 ku-(or KU? = [çubāt])li-lu-u = te-di-iq ta-xab-ši (AV 8699 ta-kil-lim); *d* 26 çu?]-bat ta-xab-ši. Nabd 494, 3 + 8 ta-xab-šu; 694, 11—15: one [(iç)] kib-su labiru a-na ta-xab-šu ana [(ilat)] Anunītum; 539, 4 a-na ta-xa-ab-šu ša [(araz)] Āri (Neb 392, 8); 948, 11 (end) one-half bilat a-na ta-xab-šu; 696, 10—11 šal-xi labiri a-na ta-xab-šu ana [il] Šamaš; 12—14; 15 *etc.*; Neb 312, 15 —17; 392, 8; Cyr 185, 7—8.

taxbatu. NE VI 190 šun-nu-u ma-ni-e a-an ta-ax(*var* xa)-ba-tu-ši-na (*i. e.* of the horns); perh. T. A. (Ber) 26 iii 26 ten-ŠU (= fold?) lubuštu (or [çubāt]) ta-ax-pa-tum ten-ŠU (= ten-fold?) ša E-SIR bat-ta-nu?

taxāzu or **tāxazu**, *m* fight, battle {Kampf, Schlacht} § 65, 11; S[b] 294 (H 16, 222) me-e | 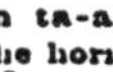 (§ 9, 222) | ta-xa-zu, Br 2804; & KA + inserted ÇAB, Br 829; TP i 58; iii 49 (58) *var* to ta-xa-zi; Anp i 1; Anp *Bal* (V 70) *R* 24. — Asb iii 111 (end) *var* ta-xa-zu; x 3. II 19 *b* 11, 12 a-bu-ub ta-xa-zi, said of Ninib's weapon; *ibid* 3, 4 šu-uš-kal ta-xa[-zi]; also 18 sa-kip ta-xa-zi ez-zi; 60 lit-ti ta-xa-zi. IV² 13 *a* 38, 39 a-na ta-xa-zi-ja; V 51 *a* 24, 25 a-šar ta-xa-zi, in battle (Ninib be thy helper). Sn i 16 ĕdurū ta-xa-zi; vi 7 ša lapān ta-xa-zi-ja iplaxū; v 56 narkabāt taxāzi-ja; iv 37 ina ta-xa-az çēri (KB ii 280 *col* 3, 4); iii 72 (amêlūti) çābē ta-xa-zi-ja la ga-me-lu-ti; iii 47 see xar-bašu (336 *col* 2) & § 72*a*, *n*. V 55, 38 i-na mi-xi-e ta-xa-zi-šu-nu. III 15 i 24 see raksu. K 2852 + K 9662 iii 10 e-peš qabli u ta-xa-zi, WINCKLER, *Forsch.*, ii 42, 43. Creat.-*frg* III 34 (= 92) la a-di-ru ta-xa-za(zi). K 2774 ii 26 = NE XII ii 26 (+ iii 4, 19) a-šar ta-xa-az zi-ka-re; vi 3 ša ina ta-xa-zi di-e-ku, KB vi 258*foll*. III 43 iv 23*fol* (il) Za-ma[-ma] šar ta-xa-zi i-na ta-xa-zi qātsu lā içabat; + 29 the goddess Iš-xara i-na ta-xa-zi da-an-ni lā i-še-mi-šu. lî' ta-xa-zi, Sarg *Ann* 125; 288. III 32, 52 = SMITH, *Asurb*, 124, 55 see zaqtu, 292 *col* 2. KB iv 104, 27 see šašmu; ZA iv 281, 6; v 58, 38 see mit-xuçu, 524 *col* 1, end. K 4995 *R* 14 (H 125; = IV² 30, 1 *R* 2 & 4) ina (a-na) ta-xa-zi; id = S^b 294. 81—11—8, 111, 5 ZA-GA-GA = Marduk ša ta-xa-zu, *Jour. Trans. Vict. Inst.*, xxvii 8—9; see above, = il Zamāma (?). I 7 *no* ix B 2 (= D 121 *no* 10 *h* 2) Ištar be-lit ta-xa-zi; bēlit taxāzi (id = S^b 204) A 2, E 1; also II 66 *no* 1, 5; ZIMMERN, *Ritualt.*, *no* 87 i 5; 95 *O* 14. SMITH, *Asurb*, 121, 35 Ištar i-lat qab-li be-lit ta-xa-zi, KB ii 250, 251; KAT³ 430 *rm* 5. Esh *Sendsch*, *R* 15 ta-xa-zi-šu dan-nu; Sarg *Ann* 285. T. A. (Ber) 189, 44—45 ni-pu[-uš]-mi ta-xa-za, KB v 284; BA iv 121; (Lo) 72, 18 ina taxāzi with added gloss ta-xa-zi. — u-nu-ut ta-xa-zi Sn *Rass* (ZA iii 312) 57. q(g)a-an ta-xa-zi Neb viii 42; ix 40; id vi 22 = spear {Speer} Br 2446; see also bēlu, 3 (159 *col* 1); ZA 339, 10. — kaçaru with taxāzu see kaçaru, 1 *b* (426 *col* 2, below). tīb taxāzi see tību. — V 28 *d* 80 lu-lu-un-tum = nax-laptu ta-xa-zi (*c*), which is also = da-ni-tum (81) & gu-lal-e (82); II 25 *g-h* 52—54. II 23 *a-b* 30 ta-xa-zu = zu-la-ta, see 282, footnotes; Br 146; V 28 *e-f* 83 where read zu-la-at, ZK ii 383*foll* >< Br 158; AV 3022.

NOTE. — D 147 √ תחר; others אחז; ZDMG 32, 181; SCHEIL, *Šalm*, 58; THOMPSON, *Reports*, ii 123 *col* 2 reads taxaçu, & connects with maxaçu.

taxāziš = to the fight, battle {zum Kampf, zur Schlacht} = ana taxāzi. Creat.-*frg* IV 94 see qarabu Q^t pm. K 2852 + K 9662 ii 9 ..... ta-xa-zi]-iš it-bu-šu-nu ma iš-ku-nu tax-ta-šu-un; also *ibid* 8 (end), WINCKLER, *Forsch.*, ii 34—7.

tāxizu (?) K 161 vii; ZK ii 4.

taxazū. II 23 *c-d* 31 ta-xa-zu-u ‖ ta-ri-mu, *q. v.* AV 8026.

taxūzatu, a creeper plant {eine Schling-pflanze} § 65, 32*e* √ אחז?. (šam) ta-xu-za-tu.

ta-xa(or ma?)-xu ‖ raxaxu. *q. v.*

tuxallu. some part of the datepalm. T^C 143 halbreife Dattel; JENSEN, ZK ii 26; FEUCHT-WANG, ZA vi 445, *cf* Arm תוחלא *palmula praematura*; PEISER, *Vertr.*, 240: unreif abgefallene Datteln. AV 9000; V 26 *g-h* 52 see tubalū, Br 5938. KB iv 298/99 *no* IV 9; 308/9 *no* IX 16/17 see man-gagu, 559. Camb 56, 8: one gur tu-xal-lu gi-pu-u man-ga-ga bil-tum ša xu-ça-bi (see xuçābu, 2; 332 *cols* 1, 2) ... inamdinnū; 319, 7; Nabd 623, 6; 973, 9; 1013; Cyr 123, 8 itti one gur tu-xal-la gi-pu-u *etc.* (BA iii 404, 405); AV^w 15 *col* 2 *etc.* — PEISER, *Vertr.*, cxlvii 7: fifteen tu-xal-lum lib-lib-bi man-ga-ga gi-pu-u, *etc.* With this compare HILPRECHT, *Inscr.* Ser A *vol* IX 62, 9: one gur tu-xal-lib-bi man-ga-ga bil-tum ša xu-ça-bi ina-an-din; KOTALLA, BA iv 573, 574 compares طُحْلُب = green moss {Grünes Moos}; perh. the green husk, cover, which covers the date-fruit; but *ibid*, 574 footnote * HAUPT, re-jects this and refers to [illegible], with BROCKEL-MANN.

tuxaltum. PEISER, *Vertr.*, *no* 75, 9—10 it-ti one gur bil-tum tu-xal-tum gi-pu-u man-ga-ga bil-tum ša xu-ça-bi; also AV^w 15 *col* 2 tu-xal-tu gi-pi-e. *f* to tuxallu?

taxlubu & taxlubtu (§ 65, 32*e*) literally: cover, covering, lining of a building with burnt brick {Bedeckung, Verschalung aus gebrannten Ziegeln}. AV 8691, 8692. KB vi (1) 397. especially in the phrase: ištu

tax-zu-u see gabzū, 209 *col* 2, end.

(ultu) uš-ši-šu(ša) adi tax-lu-bi-šu (ša), from the bottom, ground to the roofing (*i. e.* the including or lining with burnt brick), *i. e.* from start to finish. — of palaces: Anp ii 5: Esh vi 22, 23; Sarg *Nimr* 17; temples: TP vii 85; I 6 *no* vii 4; *cf* V 64 *b* 9 ul-tu te-me-en-šu a-di tax-lu-bi-šu; house: TP viii 5, 6; Asb x 96; wall: TP vi 29; a city: ul-tu uš-še-šu a-di tax-lu-bi-e[-šu], Lay 52 *no* 1; TP III *Ann* 9; SMITH, *Asurb*, 318*k*; KB iv 102, 11 ištu uššē-šu a-di tax-lu-bi-šu lu-u u-šak-lil. Sn *Bav* 51: city & houses I destroyed ultu uššē-šu a-di tax-lu-bi-šu, *i. e.* completely. *I* 28 *b* 27—31 tam-li-a ra-ba-a of the new palace . . . (31) iš-tu uš-še-šu a-di tax-lu-bi-šu ar-çi-ip. TP vii 103, 104 tax-lu-bi-šu i-na a-gur-ri u-re-ki-is (= mêsiru, 568 *col* 2), its lining I completed with (= I made of) agurru-brick. III 3 *no* 6, 21 iš-tu tax-lu-bi-šu-nu adi GUŠUR (= urū, 2) bīti ‖ naburru (639 *col* 1). taxlubtu: Neb *Bors* (I 51 *no* 1) ii 3 (9) a-gu-ur(*var* gur)-ri ta-ax-lu-ub-ti-ša (of the temple tower). Neb vi 12 dalāte erinu ta-ax-lu-ub-ti siparri (vi 37 tax-lu-ub-ti); ix 9—13 dalāte musukkana (iç) e-ri-nim (iç) šu-ur-mi-ni u-ša-a u šin pīri i-xi-iz ka-as-pa xu-ra-çu u ta-ax-lu-ub-ti siparri.

ta(u)xūmu, boundary, territory {Grenze, Gebiet} ZA ii 268; AV 8688. Whence Targ תְּחוּמָא, Arb تَخُومٌ, تَخُومَةٌ; ZA iv 315 >< D^{Pr} 42, DEL^{K} 7 *rm* 5. KNUDTZON, 19, 2 + *R* 8; 35, 8 ta-xu-mu; 72 *O* 2; *R* 2 tu-xu-mu. Synchr. Hist. = II 65 *O* i 6, 7; 23; 28; iv 14; 21 *etc.* see miçru, 1 (575 *col* 1, end). K 359, 14 niše i-ba-aš-ši bēl ta-xu-me-šu-nu. K 181 *R* 8 (7) (amēl) EN-NUN (al) bi-ra-a-te ša ina eli ta-xu-u-me ina eli ṭe-e-mu ša šarri, *etc.*; *R* 23, 24 (amēl) EN-NUN (al) bi-rat gab-bu ša ina eli ta-xu-me ṭe-e-mu *etc.* (Hr^{L} 197; IV^{2} 47 *col* 2) see JAOS xx 250, 251; PSBA xvii '95, 222*foll.* K 525 *O* 8 (end), Hr^{L} 252; BA ii 60.

NOTE. — KB i 194 agreement, compact, contract] Abmachung; from same √ as axāmeš. *cf* K 4444 u ina maxāzi ta-xu-me ša (māt) Aššur ša ši-di tam-tim, ein durch Abmachung hergestelltes Verhältniss; thus in II 65. See also ZA iv 315 *rm* 1. If so, then, here, perhaps also Nabd 160, 17—18 tax-mu-mu la ba-še-e.

taxanatu (?) Sp II 265 *a* iv 10 . . . . ša ta-xa-na-tu liš-ku [. . . .] ZA x 4.

taxxisu, taxsīstu, taxsītu, reminder {Mahnung}. PEISER, KAS 103; *Vertr.* 330: Abrechnung; OPPERT, ZA vii 69: 'acquiescement'. √xasasu, 328. T^{C} 143 √חסס? Nabd 741, 15—16 tax-sis-tum la ma-še-e see mašū (596 *col* 2); 68, 14—15 tax-sis-ti la ba-še-e, KB iv 212, 213; 557, 12 tax-sis-tum a-na la maš-še-e (PEISER, *Vertr.*, ix 17); Neb 338, 10 tax-si-is-tum la ba-še-e; 342, 13 tax-si [-isi, omitted by scribe]-ti la ba(?)-še-e. CRAIG, *Relig. Texts*, 32, 12 tax-sis-tu ana šamē arkūti. Nabd 466, 16 tax-xi-su la maš-ši; 1006, 11—12; 708, 13—14 tax-xi-is ana la ba(? ma?)-še-e; Neb 338, 10 tax-si-is-tum la ba-še-e. Dar 211, 1 tax-si-it-tum, M^{S} 40 *col* 1. IV^{2} 55 *R* coloph. 11 a-na tax-sis-ti, GGA '98, 818. Nabd 562, 15 tax-sis(?) la ma(? [sign])-še-e. See also rapadu, 1, Q & MARTIN, *Textes relig.*, '00, 12. K 25 *O* ii 5 tax-si-sat ilāni, *Rev. Sém.*, xii 274, 275, the designs of the gods.

taxapšu see taxabšu.

taxpatu see taxbatu.

(iç) t(d, ṭ)ax-ri. perhaps V 47 *a* 61 qi-na-zu (iç) tax(gab?)-ri.

tuxūru. Nabd 1020, 6 ana (il) Šamaš a-ba-ri ša tu-xu-ri (or TU-XU-ri?).

taxraxxu. § 65, 32*c*. V 48 iv 28 tax-ra-ax-xu; v 28, followed by (29) zi-nu-ut (tam) ax-xi-e, anger, strife among brothers? (but Z^{B} 24 das Zurückweichen des Feindes). Z^{B} 24 reads GAB (= maxra)-ra ax-xu (= axū) = Vorrücken des Feindes; HAUPT: competition of the brother.

tax-ri-xu see šuršummu.

taxšū, with determ. pref. SU = (mašak). CRAIG, *Diss*, 28; D^{Pr} 76*foll* = תַּחַשׁ wether {Hammel}; also DELITZSCH in B-D. *Ezek* xvii. NÖLDEKE, ZDMG xl 732 & *rm* 2: it is not certain that תחש means Hammel; see also SCHRADER, ZA i 460 bel. Z^{B} 16 *rm* 1: sea-lion {Seehund}; ZK i 314; ii 422. — VATh 208, 5 šēr tax-ši-e, KB iv 94, mutton {Hammelfleisch}. Anp iii 34 ina elippē ša e-pu-šu-ni elippē ša SU tax-ši-e . . . I crossed the Euphrates;

iii 64 tax(gab, *var* ga)-ši-e; BA i 391 on syntax. Šalm, *Mon*, *O* 86; *R* 77; 82 (KB i 156; 170). TP v 57 i-na elippi (mašak) tax-ši-a (AV 1479 gab-ši-a) I crossed the Euphrates. II 31 *b* 76 (amēl) ça-rip SU tax-ši-a. Nabd 928, 1: hundred (mašak) tax-šu-u pl = 100 sheep-skins, KB iv 250 *no* 58. Ner 55, 13 (mašak) du(?, or gab, tax)-še-e (?) see ni'āru, 680 *col* 1. — T. A. (Ber) 26 ii 23 one ŠU-E-SIR ša tax(gab)-ši-a u tar-ta-ra-ax-šu ša xurāçi; 25 iii 16 one ŠU tax (gab)-ša çēri qa-du na-ak-ta . . .; *ibid* 18 twenty-five ŠU tax-ša imēri qa-du na-ak-ta . . . . .; + 20; iv 1 mentions (aban) GAB(TAX)-ŠI-A?

JOHNSTON, AJPh xix 386 reads (mašak) gab-ši-e (ships of) inflated skins. gabšu ‖ nādu in (mašak) nādu, originally: inflated, swollen. Also see HAUPT, AJSL xx 170 √גבשׁ bulge, be bulky, grow large, swell; *cf Ezekiel* (SBOT) 65, 14 & *p* 125 of English translation. SCHRADER, KGF 192; 216 *rm* 2 *etc*. read kab-ši-e & compared כֶּבֶשׂ.

taxtū. defeat, overthrow, ruin {Niederlage, Zerstörung} √xatū, 346, 347. AV 8693. K 2674, 14 tax-te-e ummānišu (S. A. SMITH, *Asurb*, iii, 1 *foll*). Asb i 83 (Tarqū) iš-ma-a tax-te-e ummānāti-šu. taxtā šakanu = defeat, kill. murder. Sarg *Khors* 120, 121 Ni-bi-e a-di um-ma-an e-la-mi-i ri-çi-i-šu i-na *M* iš-ku-nu (3 *pl*) tax-ta-a-šu (& *Ann* 331); 130 (KB ii 68—71); *Cyl* 17 Sargon the valiant hero who iš-ku-nu tax-ta-a-šu (= TP III *Ann* 236); 19 ši-lim-u (māt) Muçri iškunu-nu-ma, perhaps a confusion on the part of the scribe of tax-tu-u & ši-lim; see šilmu, 2. In reverse manner we have Sarg *Nimr* 7 iš-ku-nu tax-ta-šu. Sarg *bull* 12 Sargon šākin tax-te-e Xumbanigaš; *cf Stele* 12; *Khors* 23 tax-tu(-a)-šu. Sn iii 82 aš-ta-kan tax-ta-šu-un; v 75 aš-ku-na tax-ta-šu-nu. K^{M} 46, 17 ša-kin tax-te[-e] ‖ mu-ša-aš-ki-nu li-i-ti. K 2852 + K 9662 ii 9 see taxāziš. V 31 *e-f* 27 . . . . . XUB-= tax-tu-u, followed by (28) tax-tu]-u = tap-du-ū, ZK ii 81; Br 2697, 7848.

tax-xi-e-ti, Cyr 381, 11.

ta-xa-a-tum, V 14 *c-d* 8; ZK ii 264; perh. *pl* of:

taxūtu. NE 16, 8; 18, 11 (= KB vi, 1, 186 *col* 3) (. . . . . ta]-ram(?)-mi-i . . . [. . . .] ša ta-xu-ti-ki.

texūtu. 83, 1—18. 1335 i 16 DUB with gloss di-ix = te-xu-tum.

taxtamu (?). T. A. (Lo) 61, 24—27 ap-pu-na-ma nu-bu-ul (BEZOLD, *Dipl.*, √abalu; see *p* 637 *col* 1) me ta-ax-ta-mu u ti-ma-xa-zu-ka. two nouns rather than two verbal forms.

taxtīpu. oppression {Bedrückung}. D^{Pr} 181 *rm* 2 & 4. K 4197 together with xa-lu-u, zur-bu libbi, umçatum; ZA ii 459 *rm* 8.

ti-xi-ta-ti. T. A. (Lo) 23, 13. KB v 16* perhaps √xatū > xi-ta-ti, as ta-šap-par-ta for šap-par-ta.

takū, BA i 197, 198 see dakū, 246, 247.

tak(šum?)-ku, KB vi (1) 58, 20.

ti-ik, ti-ki see תקן.

tikku neck {Nacken}, whence id TIK = ki-šadu; *pl* tikkāti. NE VI 169 ina bi-rit ti-ik-ki qarni, (tragen) zwischen dem Nacken die Hörner, KB vi (1) 177; 454, 455; 575. Rm 422 *R* 5 iš-tu ti-ki-šu ana 'šip(b)-pu[-ri-šu, ZA ix 118; K 1:07 *R* 17 (Hr^{L} 238). T. A. (Ber) 21, 35 *foll* may the ma-ni-in-nu (necklace, chain) for 100.000 years be suitable (fit; lu-u na-ti) a-na ti-ik-ki ša axi-ia × ZA v 19 *rm* 2. (Ber) 28 ii 2 nine BU is-si-xu ša ti-ik-ki ša xurāçu. Here, according to JENSEN's fine suggestion also Sn i 68 narkabāt šēpi-ja i-na ti-ik-ka-a-ti(te) u-ša-aš-ši, *Bell* 21 ti-ik-ka-a-te. KB vi (1) 575 explains also TP iii 49 labānī as: Nackenmuskeln, so that the passage means: the war-chariots are carried on the neck-muscles; also JENSEN *apud* SCHULTHESS, 90.

tu-ka, T. A. (Lo) 16, 28 gloss to DUG-GA (= ṭāba).

tukku shield, pavisse {Schild}. V 32 *b-c* 46 = II 32 *g-h* 35 see qabābu. Nabd-Cyr. *Chron.* iii 16 at the end of the month Tammuz (mašak) tuk-ku me ša (māt) Gu-ti-um surround the gates of Esaggil be-la ša mamma ina Ésaggil . . . . ul iššakin. PRINCE, *Diss*, 100 √takū ‖ našū, (BA i 198) × KB iii (2) 134, 135. See also HAUPT. AJSL xix 1 & tīru, 2.

tikbu, see tibku, 2.

takkab(p)u. hole {Loch}. KB vi (1) 262, 263; 528, 529 on NE XII *col* 3, 23 luman tak-ka-ab(p) [erçitim pi-ti-e-ma] = [öffne] alsbald das Loch [der Erde und]; 27. II 33 *a-b* 6 NAB (+ inserted A + LAL) = tak-ka-bu (Br 10320), preceded by qin-nu, hole = nest of birds. Rm 343, 5 (S. A. SMITH, *Misc. Texts, pl* 16); K 10472 (catchline) šumma ina takkab abul âli; K 9701, BEZOLD, *Catalogue*, 1091; 1031—2. A ‖ also of aptu, dovecot, or a hole in the wall through which the dove enters; & ‖ naplaštu. Perhaps II 34 *a* 74 .... lu-bil-šu takga-ab?

takbittu *1. adj* √כבד. Sarg *Pp* iii 36 (immer) niqê tak-bit-ti ellûti maxaršun aqqi. fat {fett, feist}.

takbittu *2.* see takpittu.

tikdu (& ṭuru) portions of the harness of an ass, PINCHES, JRAS '98, 444.

TIK-ZI. KB iv 252, 253 on Nabd 990, 24: 3-ta TIK-ZI, PEISER, *Vertr.*, *no* 92: some article of furniture, garment. Also *Vertr.*, *no* 130, 10 (end) ištên-it (erû) TIK-ZI, preceded by ištên (erû) mu-šax-xi-nu; 148, 7: two siparri (copper) TIK-ZI-MEŠ. ZIMMERN, *Ritualtafeln*, *no* 68 *O* 27 suggests (karpat) kâsu (ša mû) as the proper reading of the iḏ (see also, above, *p* 411 *col* 2). PEISER, *Vertr.*, *no* 101, 5—6 where mu-šax-xi-nu siparri is followed by 3-ta ka-a-su siparri & ba-ṭu-u siparri. Camb 331, 4: 7-ta TIK-ZI siparri u 3 ba-ṭu-u. IV^2 51 *b* 47 ina (karpat) TIK-ZI ta-mi-i il-ta-[ti] ZA ii 104 (109; iii 10, 21; viii 43).

TUK; *pl* TUK-ZUN, T^C 143, 144 = nab'âsu. see 638, 639.

takalu. pr itka(i)l, ps itakkil, pm takil, 1 *sg* taklak. be firm, strong; then, rest assured (eli, ina eli, ana, with respect to, on *etc.*), trust, have confidence in, rely upon {fest, stark sein; sicher sein; vertrauen. Vertrauen haben} Syr תְּכַל, Eth *takâla*; Hebr ii 5 *rm* 6, Arab وكل. AV 8698. D^H vi & 6; G § 68; ZDMG 40, 720. — TP i 69 a-na da-na-ni-šu-nu it-ka-lu, they trusted upon their might, power. Asb iii 127 at-kil a-na amât (il) Sin bêlija. KB ii 248 *col* 5, 2 at-kil a-na (ilat) Ištar ša u-tak-kil-an-ni, I trusted Ištar who strengthened me. I 40 *d* 2 a-na an-ni-šu-nu ki-[e-ni] at-kal-ma, § 96. KB iii (2) 92, 48—9 a-na a-mat ..... at-ka-al; V 63 *b* 35 a-na a-mat (il) Šamši u (il) Adad bêlê bi-ri at-kal-ma; also see V 65 *a* 30; III 38 *no* 1 *O* 23. Šalm, *Mon*, i 43 a-na ri-çu-ut a-xa-meš i-tak-lu(-ma), they relied upon mutual assistance. — IV^2 61 *b* 27 ina eli a-me-lu-ti la ta-tak-kil. I 35 *no* 2, 12 a-na (il) Nabû na-at-kil ana ili ša-ni-na la ta-tak-kil, trust in Nebo; do not trust in any other god; § 144. — *Creat.-fry* IV 17 be-lum ša tak-lu-ka, o Lord, he that trusteth in thee. IV^2 58 iv 32 ša a-na (il) Ašur u (ilat) Bêlit tak-lum; K 2675 *R* 7 tak-lu-ma (3 *pl*); KB iii (2) 78 *col* 2, 18. K 8204, (9) 18 dunnamû ša tak-lu-ka i-šib-bi duxdu. P. N. Šamaš-tak-lak, AV 7936; Bêl-xarrâni-tak-lak, K 78, 5 (KB iv 124; = III 46 *no* 6). On P. N. Tak-lak *etc.* see AV 8707—9. Perh. iḏ GI in V 33 viii 39 (KB iii, 1, 152/3 *rm* 1); K 5268 *O* 7, 8 GI-DI-A = ša ana e-mu-ki-šu tak-lu (iḏ also in takaltum, 1 *q. v.*). V 51 *col* iv 43 ša .... tak-lu; Sm 954 *R* 33; IV^2 4 *a* 37; 6 *a* 41; 49 *b* 58; 52 *a* 28; 57 *b* 58; ZIMMERN, *Ritualt.*, *no* 26, 55 (tak-lum).

ℑ — *a*) strengthen, fortify, *etc.* {stärken, stark machen, befestigen}. KB vi (1) 298 *col* 4, 17 dûrâni-ka tuk-kil, strengthen thy walls! Sm 2052 iii 15 tu(?)-uk-ku-lum ‖ du-un-nu-nu (see paqâlu, 3; 822 *col* 1, end). — make seaworthy: Xamm.-*code* xxxvi 14 u-tak-ki-il. — *b*) of persons: strengthen, encourage, fill with confidence {ermutigen, mit Vertrauen erfüllen}. Sn i 63 on my second campaign Ašur, my lord, u-tak-kil-an-ni(-ma); iii 42; iv 43. Sn *Bell* 20; also TP III *Ann* 26; 157. Asb viii 59 he heard of the power of Ašur ša u-tak-kil-a(n)-ni; SMITH, *Asurb*, 292, s; KB ii 240, 32 the great gods ša u-tak-ki-lu-in-ni, who had made me strong; 252, 94 Ašur & Marduk the gods ša u-tak-kil-u-in-ni; SMITH, *Asurb*, 289, 47; 217 k. K 512 *R* 2 ša u-tak-kil-ku-ni (Hr^L 204; LEHMANN, i 15, 16 *rm* >< BA i 196 *foll*). K 3364 *R* 27 šum-ma tu-tak-kil-ma, DE-

LITZSCH, *Weltsch. Epos*, 55. V 45 vii 19 tu-tak-kal. 𝔞𝔤 in P. N. Mu-tak-kil-Nusku, TP i 45. Mu-tak-kil (*var* ⊨𒐈) (il) Ašur, Epon. of 706 B. C.; K 682, 8 (Hr^L 218); K 342 (= III 47 *no* 6) 18 = KB iv 140. Mu-tak-kil (il) Marduk, Epon. of 799 B. C. K 287 (= III 47 *no* 10) 5 pān Ašur-mu-tak-kil šarri, KB iv 100 *no* 3. K 2107 *O* 10 Marduk is called DINGIR-RA-KA as mu-tak-kil ilāni. AV 5646—8; also *cf* BEZOLD, *Catalogue*, v 2146 on P. N. with Mutakkil.

Š V 45 vi 50 tu-ša-at-gal (or ad-dan?); vii 32 tu-šat-kal.

Št perhaps 80—7—19, 20 *O* 11 (il) Šamaš nu-us-sa-at(d)-k(g)il; or √da-galu? Hr^L 359.

𝔑 = 𝔔 properly: be made strong, confident, *etc.* Šalm, *Obel*, (the king of Damascus *etc.*) 61, 62 a-na idi a-xa-meš it-tak-lu; 144, 145 Siduri ..... a-na gi-biš um-ma-ni-šu ma-'-di it-ta-kil, put his trust in his vast army; Šamš iv 38; Sarg *Khors* 39, *Ann* 58; Esh i 39 (ana šadē marçūti). Asb i 56, 57 and Tarqū it-ta-kil a-na e-muq ra-man-i-šu; ii 118. K 2801 (= K 221 + 2669) *R* 27 an-na-šu-un ki-e-nu .... at-ta-kil(-ma), BA iii 236, 237. K 4225, 18 at-ta-kil-an[-ni]; see H 185. Esh i 44 anāku ana (il) Ašur bēlija at-ta-kil. 81—6—7, 209, 10—11 who ... a-na (il) Ašur ...... it-tak-lu-ma, BA iii 260, 261. Sarg *Cyl* 56 na-an-nu(ni)-uš-šu-un ..... at-ta-ki-il; *Khors* 73 who a-na Ursā it-tak-lu-ma; 122 eli (nār) [or nār(?)] mar-ra-ti gu-bu-uš e-di-i it-ta-kil(-ma); Esh ii 38; i 48. Anp i 114; ii 17, 27; iii 35, 52; 17 a-na um-mānāt (māt) Kaš-ši-i (D^K 13) rapšāti it-ti-kil; 39 (ZA i 370) eli ..... it-ta-kil; Sarg *Khors* 113; *Ann* 229, 300. K 84 (Hr^L 301) *O* 12 it-ti-kil; Rm 283, 8 .... i]t-tak-lum = 3 *pl*; WINCKLER, *Forsch*, ii 9, 10. Esh ii 13; III 15 *c* 6. — P. N. (il) Ašur-na-at-kil (= ip) Epon. of 871 (KB i 204); I 35 *no* 2, 12 see 𝔔.

DERR. — takaltu, 1; ta(i)kiltu, 1; tukultu and these 3:

taklu, *adj* trusty, trustworthy {verlässlich} SCHEIL, *Rec. Trav.*, xix 42/3 (Xammurabi-*text*) 11 iš-te-en (= *quidam*) ta-ki-il-ka, BA iv 94 *fol*: einen auf den du dich verlassen kannst. 83—1—18, 19 *R* 11 mūtir pu-tu tak-lu liš-pu-ra (Hr^L 339) a trusted vassal. K 2801 (= K 221 + 2669) *O* 34 .... ri-e-u tak-lum, BA iii 230—1. Xammurabi-*letters* 22, 7 itti amēlē ta-ak-lu-tum (BA iv 453; 492); 33, 29 ma-aç-ça]-ar-ka ta-ak-lum, thy trusty guard. II 63, 41 P. N. Ta-kil-šu-na-tu, AV 8700. *f* takiltu, 1 see below.

takkilu. in P. N. of Eponyms, Tak-kil a-na bēli-ja (888, B. C.); Sin-tak-kil (739, B. C.); Tak-kil ana šarri (848, B. C.); Ašur-tak-kil (806, B. C.). KB i 205—6.

tiklu, *pl* tiklē helper, help {Helfer, Hilfe} properly: the object of confidence. AV 8882. Anp i 104 ilāni ti-ik-le-(j)a; ii 65 tik-li-[a]; ZA i 361; Sarg *Ann* XIV, 2; D 121 *no* 10 (= I 7 *no* 9 D) C 8; Šamš ii 14 tik-le-a; iii 65 (-ja); Asb iv 101; ii 121 tik(*var* ti-ik)-le-ja; Sn v 51; III 38 *no* 1 *O* 36 (-a); Bu 88—5—12, 75 + 76 viii 1 (BA iii 254 *fol*). Anp i 22 ilāni tik-le-šu (✕ AV 1945 diq-le-šu); KB i 50 *no* 2, 6; V 62 *no* 1, 2 ti-ik-li-šu; 81—6—7, 209, 14 (BA iii 260); SMITH, *Asurb*, 4, 8; Asb i 9 ti-ik-le-e-šu; Esh *Sendsch*, *O* 22.

***takalu* 2.** bring about {verschaffen, zu Stande bringen} T. A. (Ber) 92, 16 am-me-ni la-a da-a-ku-ul-te a-zi-i-šu a-na pa-ni šarri bēli-ka, 23, akālu (u) šikaru (?) it-ti a-xa-mi-iš da-ag-ga-a-la, to deliver food & drink mutually; but better = dagalu, see 240 *col* 1 NOTE 3.

tak(q?)līmu. KB vi (1) 64 (K 2619) iii 27 (*Dibbara*-legend) mu-šax-miṭ tak-lim ili; see *ibid* 65 *rm* 12. JASTROW, *Dibb.-frg* 5 ša ana šu-ux-muṭ tak-li-mu (il) [A-nim?]. ZA iv 15, 12 tak-li-ma. CRAIG, *Relig. Texts*, 35, 6 (36, 1) nādin surqīni mušaxmiṭ tak-li-me, M^S 105 *col* 1. V 11 *d-f* 2; II 108 ii 2; 110 + 113,

ta-kil-lim, AV 8699 see taxabāu. ∼ tik-kal-lu see gu-gal-lu, 212, 213. ∼ tak-lab(lib)-tu, WINCKLER, *Sargon*; KB ii 192 *ad* Asb iv 89 see takkaltu.

48; D 127, 50 AM-PAT-AN-►ΨY (= Ištar) = PAT (*i. e.* kurmatu)-AN-►ΨY = tak-li-mu, same iδ in preceding line = ni(n)dabū (649, 650), Br 4774, 9933. AV 8710. usually √כלם, 387, 388; but JENSEN. KB vi (1) 388: nindabū (> nid(s)aba)-taqlīmu = bread, cake for Ištar }Brot, Backwerk der Ištar{ √qalū = Hebr קלה; KAT^3 441; 596: Röstbrot.

taklimtu. order, command }Weisung, Befehl{. V 20 *a-b* 22 [ID-AG]-GA' = tak-lim-tum, also = u-ur-tum (21); te-er-tum (20); Br 6581; AV 8714. II 35 *g-h* 45. K 983 (Hr^L 35) *O* 11 + *R* 1 . . . tak-lim-a-ti; *R* 8, 9 tak-lim-tu ina (al) Arba-ilu lu-u-kal-li-mu, AJSL xiv 12, 13. K 164, 18 tak-lim-tu u-kal-lam; also (1) tak-lim-tu u-kal-lu-mu, BA ii 635.

takaltu *1.* V 19 *a-b* 37; II 34 *c-d* 25 GI-DI = t[a-kal-tum]. Br 2520; AV 8697; T^C 144 an animal }ein Tier{.

takiltu *1.* (*f* of taklu) in šēr takiltu. Br 9431; also tikiltu & tukultu see šē(I)ru oracle }Orakel{. According to LEHMANN, ii 76, 77 here also K 168 (Hr^L 437) *O* 14 dum-mu-qu ka-an-nu-u tak-li-ta-šu-nu kal ipšat; iδ *l* 16 ŠI-DUB (iδ for ittu, 3)-MEŠ kali-ši-na; but??

tukultu, *f c. st.* tuklat, seldom used; usually in its stead tukulti. H^F 15—17; AV 9006. — *a*) strength, force, might }Stärke, Gewalt, Macht{ iδ KU, § 9, 31 & 41; iδ ŠI-UM (= DUB?) § 9, 265; = H 7, 214; 41, 254 ŠI-UM-ti (?) = tu-kul-tu. Br 9432, 9484. V 35, 19 see balaṭu, ב pr (162 *col* 2) & KAT^3 638 *foll.* 'ā'l (or maxaz) tukul (= KU)-ti ‖ 'ā'l dannūti, fortified town, fortress. Asb iii 1, 54, 68. K 2675 *O* 20 Memphis al šar-rūtišu a-šar tu-kul-ti-šu, KB ii 238; & *ibid* 30. *pl* tuklāte forces, army, troops }Streitkräfte, Truppen{ ‖ idāte, emūqē; § 65, 5. 82—3—23, 131, 4 (al) A-za-qa-a bīt tuk-la-te-šu, WINCKLER, ii (pt. iii) 570 *foll*: seinen Zufluchtsort. Sarg *bull* 33 maxaz (al) tuk-la-ti-šu rabā; *Ann* 266 Umliaš nār tuk-la-ti-šu-nu; *cf* 272, 375. Asb iv 124 the royal city maxaz or al tuk-la-a-te ša (māt) Elamti (KB ii 195**; *cf* SMITH, *Asurb*, 207, 56 = III 21, 56). Sn ii 42 Sidon, Sarepta, Akko *etc.* . . . . bīt tuk-la-ti-šu, his garrisons, barracks. III 15 *b* 30 Sidon maxaz tuk-la-ti-šu. KB ii 238, 18 çābē tuk-la-ti-šu. TP III *Ann* 136 tuk-la-te-e-šu i-du[-ku] ‖ 135 di-ik-ta-šu-nu i-du-ku, KB ii 28, 29. K 2675 *O* 18 see rasabu, ב & KB ii 238. — *b*) strength, power; assistance, help received therefrom; helper }Beistand; Hilfe; Helfer{ BA ii 252 (*never* confidence, reliance). iδ KU; GIŠ-KU; V 31 *b* 53 GIŠ-KU-tu. Šalm *Bal* IV 2 *Šalm* a-li-lu šam-ru ša tu-kul-ta-šu Ninib, KB ii 134. Sn v 25 tu-kul-ta-ni (§ 74, 1) lu at-ta, be thou our helper; v 71 Xumbanundaša tu-kul-ta-šu rabu-u. Šamš i 15 Ninib KU-ti ilāni za-ri-e-šu. IV^2 21* *no* 1 C iii 4 Marduk KU-ti Bābili. — ina tukulti, with the help of. Sarg *Khors* 138 ina tu-kul-ti ilāni rabūte; Esh iv 43; Merod.-Balad.-stone ii 26. I 7 *no* F 8 i-na tu-kul-ti-šu-un rabī-tim. Neb ii 12 i-na tu-ku-ul-ti-šu çir-ti. MESSERSCHMIDT, *Nabuna'id*, 63, 19 ina tu-kul-ti-šu = WINCKLER, *Forsch*, i 493. TP i 70 i-na GIŠ-KU-ti (il) A-šur, iv 45 (ša ilāni rabūti) ‖ ina ri-çu-ti (ša il Ašur) KB i 48 *no* 2, 1. Sn ii 78 i-na KU-ti (il) Ašur; Asb ix 6; D 121 *no* 10 R 2; Br 10558. Anp i 12 ina GIŠ-KU-ti (il) Ašur; iii 114; i 42; ii 25, 103; iii 46. V 69, 4; II 67, 1; Esh *Sendsch*, *R* 52; also *cf* Esh i 5 *foll*; Asb i 81 (-ti); KB ii 161 *rm* ††. Anp i 15; iii 116 (ilāni rabūti); i 22 (il Ašur u il Šamaš). In P. N. Tukulti(u) is often written GIŠ-KU-ti, ŠI-UM *etc.*; AV 9007 *foll*; BEZOLD, *Catalogue*, v 2202—3. Cyr 128, 21 Tu-kul-tum-Marduk; Neb 386, 3 (ilat) Ba-ni-tum-tuk-lat, name of a woman.

Xamm.-*letters* 28, 11 ina GIŠ-KU (= tukulti) ša ili, with priestly cooperation, assistance }mit priesterlicher Mitwirkung{. — Esh ii 20 see šīru, oracle.

tākaltu *2.* omen-tablet }Omentafel{ KAT^3 533, 534. ZIMMERN, *Rituall.*, *no* 24 *O* 7/8 (= II 52 coloph 32) d(t)up-pi ilāni ta-kal-ta pi-ri'š'-ti (see 835 *col* 1) šame-e [u erçitim]; also 13, 14; 16, 17 (where we have tup-pi ilāni (šir) ṬU [= tākaltu?] [= K 2486 + K 4364] preceded by šamnē ina mē na-ṭa-lu ni-çir-ti (il) A-nim [il Bēl u il Ea]. V 19 *a-b* 33

= II 34 *c-d* 21 QI-GE-A (Br 10767) = ta-kal-tum; ideogr. also = šaparu & (amêl) mâr šipri. AV 8697.

NOTE. — 1. √akalu, 4 (see aklu, 2 *pp* 34, 35) which KB (1) 572 explains as: to write ‖ schreiben, whence also mâkaltu; rather than √כלא, kâlu, 1 as stated above, *p* 380. ZIMMERN, *Rituait.*, 116, 117 translated it by (sacred) pouch ‖ die Ledertasche, & *ibid rm c* compared חשן the oracle-pouch of the high-priest, see also KB vi (1) 491: properly: Behälter. HAUPT. *Jour. Bib. Lit.*, xix 59 & 74 *rm* 64 & in *Kings* (SBOT) 293, 294: some kind of receptacle; not certain whether pouch, or bag, or case, or box! — J^AT 4, Schreibtafel. — MARTIN, *Textes Relig.*, '03, 238: le sachet de cuir. — On the other hand, MEISSNER, *Theol. Litztg.*, '04 *col* 69 & ZDMG 58, 247: takaltu gewiss Eingeweide, resp. einen Teil der Eingeweide; *cf* MVAG '04, 138; >< HUNGER, *Becherwahrsagung*. QUINCKE, ZA xviii 226, 227, Schwanz (wie eines Schafes).

2. It cannot be proven how many of the following, if any, belong here: V 27 *c-d* (2) SU-[ṬU] = t]a-kal-[tum], AV 8697; (3) SU-ṬU-ŠU = *t* qa[-ti]; (4) SU-ṬU-ŠU-I = *t* gal-l[a-bi]; *cf* V 19 *a-b* 34 = II 34 *c-d* 22; Br 10564, 11915; (5) SU-ṬU-APIN = *t* e-pi[-ni?]; (6) SU-ṬU-A-ZU = *t* a-s[i-i], of a physician; *cf* V 19 *a-b* 35 = II 32 *c-d* 23; Br 192; (7) SU-ṬU-GIR = *t* paṭ-[ri]; (8) SU-ṬU-GI-DUB-BA-A = *t* [dup-pi?]. The same with determ. GIŠ instead of SU in K 4378 i 28—34 (D 86). — S^b 1 *O* ii 14 ṭu-un | ṬU | ta-kal-tum (& = pâšu, 3 see 841 *col* 1) Br 11914; H 36, 884; 186, 12 = V 33 *no* 2, 43. — Also see ZIMMERN, *Rituait.*, 1—20 *ll* 24, 38. — V 16 *c-d* 52 . . . . . BAR = ta-kaltum, Br 1805, preceded by pa-da-nu. II 62 *no* 3 *R* 44 (?): AV 8697. — V 19 *a-b* 36 see Br 6617, 6620.

takkaltu (> ta'kaltu), weeping, lamentation; lament, elegy, dirge }Weinen, Wehklagen; Klage, Klagelied{ *cf* קִינָה, BROWN-GESENIUS, 884 *col* 1, § 65, 32*a*; √akalu, 3 (35 *col* 1). Z^B 1 & *rm* 3; 23 (taqribtu); 115; ZA ii 349 *rm* 5. V 22 *h* 44; *e-h* 7 (Br 11618; AV 8706) see taz(z)imtu. K 4623 *R* 7, 8 (H 123) i-li tak-kal-tam (= A-ŠI [= ER]-RA) iš-kun-ki libbaki li-nu-ux; 9. 10 (ilat) iš-ta-ri tesli-ti iq-bi-ki ka-bit-ta-ki lip-šax. IV² 21* *no* 2 *R* 3, 4 ilu-šu tak-kal-tu ub-lam; 28 *no* 2 *b* 15 (coloph.) ša Ašurbânpal û-me-šam šur-kan (= qam) tak-kal-ti. Asb iv 80 their angered gods u-ni-ix ina tak-kal-ti u A-ŠE-ŠA (= LIB)-KU-MAL (= GA); see ZIMMERN, *Ritualt.*, *no* 20, 7, 8.

tâkultu, feast, banquet }Fest, Schmauserei, Gastmahl{ √akalu, 1 (34, 35). Esh vi 35 see kirêtu (443 *col* 1). IV² 14 *no* 1 *a* 20 ZU ina ta-kul-ti (= KI-BI-GAR-RA, Br 9737) lu-še-ši-ib, I will invite to a feast, KB vi (1) 54, 55. OLZ '02, April ‖ simâtu = Prachtmahl.

takiltu, whence Hebr תְּכֵלֶת, Exod 25, 4; JENSEN, KAT³ 649; with determ. SEG = šipâtu, violet-purple wool. AV 8071. PINCHES, *Palest. Expl. Fund*, Quarterly Statement, July '00, 261, 1 SEG-KAN-ME-DA SEG ta-kil-ti (violet woolen-stuff). TP III *Ann* 156 winged fowls of heaven whose wings a-na ta-kil-te çarpu (= III 9, 56; KB ii 30, 31); *ibid* 155 (šipât) ta-kil-tu (šipât) ar-ga-mannu (among articles of tribute); Sarg *Khors* 142 (šipât) ta-kil-tu (šipât) ar-gaman-nu, + 182; *Ann* 397; 439; Su *Bass* 55 (ZA iii 312); Nabd 284, 4 (*cf* 23) TUK (= nabâsu?) ta-kil-tum; 751, 1—2: ½ ma-na (šipât) ta-kil-tum a-na a-di-la-nu ša ku-si-tum; ZK ii 326 *no* 2; KB iv 246 *no* XLVI. Nabd 664, 1—2; V 61 v 47, 48 see tabarru. ideogr. Anp i 88; iii 68; Šalm, *Mon*, ii 28 (see SCHEIL, *Šalm*, 94). — T. A. (Ber) 25 iii 75 . . . . ša taki-il-ti; iv 3 . . . lubuštu (?) šu-ubtum ša ta-kil-ti; 26 ii 18 ma-at-ru-u-šu (?) ša ta-kil-ti. Also see natkiltu, 743 *col* 1. — ZK ii 265; BA i 507; 530 darkblue. HAUPT, ZA ii 267 violet purple. PRINCE, *Daniel*, 227, lighter purple wool; also *cf* HOMMEL. *Expos. Times*, Aug. '98, 525. KING, purple wool. JENSEN, KB vi (1) 570 √akalu, be dark.

tukummu (?). IV² 30 *a* 12 tu-ku-um-mu (= AL-DI) allak.

taknû, *n* careful preparation; correctness; fitness }sorgsame Zubereitung; Herstellung; Richtigkeit, Gehörigkeit{. AV 8711. √kanû, 1 (405). ZA x 208—9; ii 91—2. Asb iii 90 (I gave them a banquet), Esh vi 36, II 23 *a-b* 28 see paššûru, 846. Asb x 108 see zarâtu, 2 (298 *col* 1). NE 15, 36 see ma'âlu, 507 *col* 2 & see II 23 *c-d* 62 tak-ni-tum ‖ ir-šu; ZA v 67, 35. 85, 4—30, 1 i 42 (KB iii, 2, 30) see maštaku, 614 *col* 1 & read ta-ak-ni-e. POGNON, *Wadi-Brissa*, 71; 106 & 107.

takmannu, Br 3226 see ummannu.

NOTE. — Here, perhaps, also Sarg *Khors* 176, 177 (*Ann* 437) the gods of Assyria returned (i-tu-ru) to their city i-na tam-gi-ti u mar(?-)tak-ni-e; mar may have been *c. st.* of ma-ru V 21 *g-h* 39 = GIŠ, thus designating the phrase as name for an instrument, furniture, or the like; or, possibly, it is an abbreviation for ammar, as we find in K 903 (Hr^L 124) 3, 4 apparäte mar (= ammar) i-ba-šu-ni; possibly also that after mar the character tak, šum has been omitted, thus lending itself either to mar-tak (> maštak) tak-ni-e or mar-šum (. ma'š-lu *etc.*) tak-ni-e. AJSL xx July, '04 *p* 225 *rm* 8.

taknītu, a *f* to taknū. AV 8712. ZA x 293, 29 the daughter of Nannar is called tak-ni-tum. IV² 25 *b* 60, 61 (as-ka-ru, 55) ina tak-ni-ti ke-niš (both = SAL-ZI-EŠ-DUG-GA, Br 533) šu-uk-lu-ul. K 1451 *R* 7 Nanā be-lit tak-ni-e-ti. K 257 *O* 75, 76 be-ili-ku [tak]-nit (= SAL-DUG-GA, 75) ^(ilu) Nu-dim-mud ana-ku (H 128); PRINCE, JAOS xxiv 111 = I am supreme. The duly appointed spouse (?) of Ēa I am; see *ibid* 123. II 35 *c-d* 46 see kanū, 3 (405 *col* 2). II 23 *c-d* 62 tak-ni-tum ‖ ir-šu, bed; AV 8883 reads also II 23, 27 ti-ik-ni-tim; see ^(iç) tanittu, 2. K 3351, 13 ina ē-kur bīt tak-na-a-ti ša-qu-u par-çu-u-šu, CRAIG, *Relig. Texts*, i *pl* 43.

takkannu. ZK ii 83, 10 KI ^(ta-kan) ... = tak(par?)-kan-ni; see perhaps par-kannu, 832 *col* 1.

tukkannu, leatherbag, pouch }Ledertasche{. iṣ SU-BIR, ZIMMERN, *Rituall.*, *no* 1—20, 39; 24 *R* 7; 75—78, 21 (& *p* 190 *rm* ζ). K 164, 40 (BA ii 636). II 44 *e-f* 61—63 [SU]-BIR-MUN (Br 230) = tuk-kan ṭa-ab-tum; SU-BIR-ELTEG = tuk-kan ^(šam) xu-l[i?]; or u-xu-li; SU-BIR-GI-DUB-BA-A = tuk-kan qa-an dup[-pi?]; see also tākaltu, 2, NOTE 2.

takkasū. PEISER, *Vertr.*, lxiii 2 tak-ka-su-u pān ilu ka-ri-bi ina Ē-sag-gil bīt Marduk; 10, six tak-ka-su-u daily, beginning with the first of Addar; lxx 1 arax 4 rab-bu-u ša tak-ka-su-u.

takap(b)u. IV² 58 *a* 37 ki-ma] .... nim-ri (panther) tuk-ku-pa ka-la-tu-ša, ZA xvi 168, 169; 170, 171. V 45 vii 18 tu-tak-kap(b). Perh. compare תקף, attack, overpower, NÖLDEKE, ZDMG 47, 102; also see BARTH, *Etym. Stud.*, 28; FRÄNKEL, BA iii 74.

tikpu *1. c. st.* tikip in tikip santakki, see 787 *col* 2. AV 8876, 8885; ZA xvi 166, 167 on IV² 50 coloph. 33; 56 coloph. 40. II 49 *c-d* 13 [....] VII | ti-ik-pi; also perhaps III 57 *a* 52 & see JENSEN, 57: a group of stars.

tik(q?)pu *2.* see tibku, 2 (end).

takpuru. Dar 379, 13 (35) six mana kaspi tak-pu[-ru].

takpirtu. purification }Sühnung(en){ √ka-paru, 2 (423 *col* 1); see ZIMMERN, *Rituall.*, *p* 92 *no* 1: die durch kuppuru bezeichnete Handlung des āšipu. Grundbedeutung von kaparu, 1 & 2 wol wegwischen. See also KAT³ 584; 597 *rm* 2; 601. IV² 13 *b* 50, 51 food place at his head, food for his body prepare tak-pir-ta-šu (= ŠU-GUŠUR-GUŠUR-RU-DA-KI, also = muššudu, Br 5497, 7173; ZK i 308 *rm* 2). K 80 (Hr^L 52) *O* 6—9 ina eli tak-pi-ir-ti ša ṭe-e-mu šak-na-ku-ni (1 *sg* pm) at-ta-lak tak-pi-ir-tu da-at-tu u-sa-aç-bit; PSBA Nov. '87. Perhaps also K 983 (Hr^L 35) *R* 2 .... [tak? ta-ak?]-pir-a-ti preceded by tak-lim-a-ti, AJSL xiv 12, 13. ZIMMERN, *Rituall.*, *no* 26 i 18, 19 arki[-šu tak-pi-ra-t]i eb-bi-ti šarra tu-kap-par kīma tak-p[i]-ra-a-ti tuq-te-tu-u a-na bābi tu-še-ça; ii 2, 3 (arki-šu) tak-pi-ra-ti eb-bi-e-ti šarra tu-kap-par kīma tak-pi-ra-a-ti tuq-te-it-tu-u ana bābi tu-še-ça; also *ibid* v 34; *no* 28, 4; 41—42 i 28 bīta tu-kap-par-ma tak-pi-rat bīti, *etc.*

takpuštu. PEISER, *Vertr.*, cxxvi 15 ta-ak-pu-uš-tum it-ti bīti-šu, das was bei einem Tauschgeschäft zur Ausgleichung dem geringeren Wertstück in baar zugefügt wird. Dar 265, 16: five mana kaspi ša ina 1 šiqlu pitqa nuxxutu tak-pu-uš-ti; Cyr 128, 14 adi 2 qānē tak-pu-uš-tum. The by-form takpuru, Dar 379, shows that the stem is kaparu not kapašu, ZATW xvii 350, 351.

takpittu (√כבד). Bu 88—5—12, 75 + 76 vii 40, 41 ip-pu-šu tak-pit-tu, BA iii 360 ‖ kipdu; BA iii 258 planning, thinking }Trachten, Sinnen{.

takçiçi, name of a bird }Name eines Vogels{, AV 8713. II 37 *a-c* 51 GIRI-XU = tak-çi-çi = aš-ki-ki-tum piçū (?), Br 4813.

takçâtum. cold, frost }Kälte, Frost}. √kaçû, 1 (425 *col* 1). II 32 *b* 32 see šurîbu. II 62 *no* 1 *R* (= K 49 iv) 2 takça-tum ‖ xal-p(b)u-u, 1. AV 8508; Br 10187. Perhaps also V 22 *a-d* 26 xalpu-u t[ak-ça-tum]? ZA i 248, 249; ii 96; 438 (taqçâtu).

tuktû. vengeance }Rache}. Winckler, *Forsch.*, i ('95) 252; Martin, *Textes rélig.*, '03, √קנא. Smith, *Asurb*, 172, 16—17 a-lik ul-tu (mât) Aššur ter-ra tukte-e abi ba-ni-ka, KB ii 264, 265: bring back the bones (= NER-PAD-DU ^{pl}) of the father, thy begetter; see *ibid rm* *; & KB ii 176 *rm* 5; on the other hand, see Winckler, *Forsch.*, i 246; 252, 258; 492 *rm* 1. K 528 *O* 20 (Hr[L] 269) tuk-te-e. K 120 *b* + 144 + 8298 + 8265. 17 a-na ša-kan gi-mil-li u tur-ri tuk-te-e = Messerschmidt, *Nabuna'id*, 63; 67: zu helfen und zu rächen Ašur, meinen Herrn. III 61 *no* 2, 22 after 30 years tuk-tu-u ut-tar-ru (they [the Babylonians] shall take vengeance), ilâni rabûti KI (= ašri)-šu-nu u-ter-ru. ‖ i-ri-ba tuk-te-e & utîr gimillu. See also Hommel, PSBA xix '97, 87—88 *no* 27, comparing Eth *tĕklō*, blood (of the woman). — P. N. Nabû tuk-ti-e ter-ri, Cyr 292, 16 (KB iv 280—1); also Nabû tukte-e er-ba. Scheil, *Nabd.* ii 13, 14 I-ri-ba (M[S] 15 √ארב) tuk-te-e šar Umman-ma-an-da, Hommel, *Rec. Trav.*, xviii 217: da nahm Rache der König der *U-M.*; also in PSBA xix 88 (√ריב, impf. of continuation); while Messerschmidt √ירב. Hommel, Hastings, *Dictionary*, i *col* 190 & *rm* *: allusion to, or play upon, Arbak, a Manda king = 'Αρβάκης; Lehmann, ZA xi 332—44.

tukuttu (?) Scheil, *Rec. Trav.*, xix 61 *no* 2, 10 Tabnit IM[ki] tu-kut-ti ....

tikkatu see tikku.

têkîtu. weakness, want }Schwäche, Mangel} √akû? V 37 *a-c* 36 te-ki-tum, AV 8877, Br 6997. K 4188 iii 61 [XAR ....]-LAL = te-ki[-tum] preceded by ik-ki [-tum?]. Bu 91—5—9, 183 *R* 8, 4 iç-çi-e-u-ni si-il-a-te-ši-na ina te-ki-ti šâ a-na (amêl) ša-ku ^{pl} iq-bu-u-ni (Hr[L] 340). IV² 55 *no* 1 *R*, *b* 39 (end) te-ki-e-te, perh. = *pl*, but??

taktîmu. a cover, covering, cloak }Decke, Umhüllung, Mantel} § 65, 32*b*; AV 8715; √katamu, 457—9. V 15 *c-d* 17, 18 KU-AN-DUL (Br 491); KU-AN-TA-DUL (Br 475) = tak-ti-mu. V 14 *e-f* 43, 44; V 28 *c-d* 43 tak]-ti-mu (42, ub-bu-nu) = up-pu-xu, see 79 *col* 1.

tallu *1.* S[c] 1 *a* 11; 1 *b* 3 ma-aš | MAŠ tal-lum, AV 8730; Br 1806; 2548; mentioned together with tu'âmu & çib(p)-tum, 1 (867); II 30 *e-f* 49, Br 1810. V 40 *g-h* 10 read (ta-al) ➤— | ri[-ig-mu] ✕ 247 *col* 2 (dallu, *b*), AV 8716; Br 25.

tallu *2.* a vessel }ein Gefäss}. II 22 *e-f* 18 DUK-RI (= TAL) = tal-lu = na-man[-du?], Br 2579; see nassabu, 698 *col* 2, beg. IV² 20* 4 C *R* 1 (M[S] 101 *col* 1) but?? Perhaps T. A. (Ber) 28 ii 45 one ta-lu ša kaspi. Also see talgiddû & talmaxxu.

tallu *3.* V 65 *b* 4 ana ši-i-bu (+ 25) (iç) tal-lu (iç) KAN-UL (= xittu) *etc.* ZA iii 300. Neb iii 49. (iç) tal-lum, Pognon, *Wadi-Brissa*, 38, 38 & *ibid*, *p* 42. Craig, *Relig. Texts*, ii 2, 22 anniu ša ina eli (iç) tal-li ša (il) Ningal (& 1, 19).

tâlu, 1. K 4334 ii 16 a-di (karpat) diš-pi u-ma-al-lu-u ul a-ta-al (?); preceded by a-pat-tan, = II 60 *no* 1. M[S] *p* 1 √אתל; reads a-di bâb diš-pi.

tâlu *2.* ZA xii 410, 411, 13 GIŠ-GIŠIM-MAR-TUR-TUR = ta-a-lu; same id 11—12 = su-xuš-šu; 14 = qi-nu: see also *Rev. Sém.*, x 248 *fol*. Sp II 111, 1 same id = ta-a-lum, followed by [tâlu] ša qin-nu. Halévy = le très jeune palmier; √אתל.

talû 1. hang up, suspend }aufhängen, herabhängen} or the like. Smith, *Asurb*, 124, 53 Ištar entered; right & left tu-ul (*var* tul)-la-a-ta iš-pa-a-ti tam-xa-at pitpânu ina idiša šalpat namçaru, she had quivers hanging; a bow she held by her side, from the sheath she drew the sharp sword of battle, § 80 i; KB ii 251; D[K] 26; 29 (*cf* Gen 27, 13). I 44. 51 their

---

ta-ku-ru, AV 8702 *cf* ta-dur-ru. ∾ takrîbtu, Br 11618 & others, see takkaltu. ∾ takšû see tagšû. ∾ tak-ši-tum, AV 8714 see taklimtu. ∾ ta-kut-tu, AV 8103 see tašiltu. ∾ taktamtu, Br 7173 see takpirtu.

magnates who .... as-ma-a-ti xurâçi tul-lu-u, had hanging down (from their shoulders) golden ornaments, Haupt, *Andover Rev.*, July '84, 96.

tulû *1.* a vessel, jar }ein Gefäss. Fass, Napf{ or the like. K 4378 iii 47 GIŠ-LIŠ-AT = tu-lu-u; 51 (GIŠ)-MA-ŠIR-ru (Br 6780, 7755) = tu-lu-u & (52) ta-an-nu (*var* tan-nu, = II 46, 34 & 38; D 87 iii 47, 51); KB vi (1) 437; 572. *pl* perhaps in TP III (small inscr.. Rost, 80, 81): eleven tu-la(?)-ni kišitti ilâniša .... ikimši; Rost, 133: Opferbecken; Winckler: altars.

tu(i)lû *2. m* female breast, *mamma* }weibliche Brust{ Oppert, 1868 (see GGA '78, 1044). AV 9016. S^b 249 u-bur | iò, Br 5555 | tu-lu-u, followed by çi-ir-tu (897 *col* 2, end); II 22, 416; 23, 449 iò GA which also = ši-iz-bu, 450. iò GA (Br 6115) also K 246 i 36—39 (H 84, 85) mušêniqtu ša tu-lu-ša ṭa-a-bu (saltish *not* sweet; see Haupt, AJSL xx 171, note *) Br 3340 (37, mar-ru; 38, max-çu); 39, ša ina mi-xi-iç tu-li-e i-mut. II 28 *d-e* 68 see parasu, 833 *col* 2, § 2. II 37 *e-f* 59 çir-tum ‖ tu-lu-u. Nabd 832, 2 (+ 9) his daughter and his son ša eli tilu-u (BA i 436 *rm* 1); Neb 67, 3 mârîšu ša eli tu-lu-u, ‖ Camb 365, 3 mârat-su-nu ša ši-zib. K 2148 ii 6 see šerru (or, çirtu instead of tulû?). — *Cf* Eth *talâ'ĕ* = *pectus*, *mamma*, Hommel, ZDMG 32 ('78) 708 *foll*; or Arab ﻃﻠﻊ, send, project; *cf* çirtu; but see D^{Pr} 41 *rm* 1. Haupt, AJSL xx 171 (JAOS xiii *p* cclili) çirtu 'breast' is the *f* to çîru, high exalted and its ‖ tu(i)lû is connected with tilu, tillu, hill.

tulû *3.* see tamlû, NOTE 1.

tul'u *f* **tultum.** (§ 65, 3), worm }Wurm{ or the like. II 5 *c-d* 43 UX-TU-RA = tul-'-u (Oppert, GGA '77, 25; ZK ii 298), followed by mu-bat-ti[-ru], Br 8307 (tul-lu). If tul'u is correct, then S^b 249, II 26, 416 might belong here instead of to tulû. breast. In either place it is mentioned with z(ç)irbabu, xa-ru-bu, kisi-im-mu, *etc.* V 41 *f* 59 tul-tu sa-am-tu, a dark-colored worm; D^{Pr} 113; AV 9023. VATh 4105 ii 9 (7 days & 7 nights) a-ki tu-ul-tu im-ku-ut i-na ab(p)-bi-šu, *Mitth. Vorderasiat. Gesellsch.* '02 *no* 1. II 25 *no* 4, *add* R 38 tu-ul-tum, preceded by tu-li-mu, AV 5544, 9015; Br 8543. 80, 11—12, 9, 5 (tu-ul) PU = tu-ul-tum, JRAS '94, 831. ZA x 202, 2 miq?]-ka-nu = tul-tum ça-xir[-tum?], le ver petit. — √תלע D^H 66; & see Praetorius, *Lit. Or. Phil.*, i 197—8.

til(l)u *1.* whence Hebr תֵּל (KAT³ 650), *pl* tilânu, § 67, 2. hill, heap, mound (of ruins) }Hügel, Ruinen-, Trümmerhügel, Schutthaufen{, KGF 194 *rm* 2. S^b 1 R iv 9 du-u | DUL | ti-lu; S^c 28; V 38, 9; Br 9591; § 9, 199. — Often in ana tili u karme târu, turru, see 437 *col* 2. til abûbiš, KAT³ 555 ein Sintflut-*tell*. TP ii 78 ki-ma til a-bu-biš aš-xu-up, like a mound from the time of the deluge; iii 75 (79) ki-ma til a-bu-be; v 100. TP III *Ann* 209 kîma til abûbi uabbit. Sarg *Ann* 165 see mašû, 2 (597 *col* 1). See also Ball, *Light from the East*, 178 *rm* †; = תל אביב, Ezek 3, 15, SBOT *Ezekiel*, Engl. Tr. 97 *l* 44. J^{AT} 350. *pl* III 66 R (*col* 9) 37 *d* ti-la-nu(-)ša, preceded by xar-bu-nu-ša, her ruins; PSBA xxi 126, 127. — Adv til(l)âniš see below.

NOTE. — 1. Jensen-Brockelmann, 397 tillu > tal'u, *cf* تَلع.

2. Often found in names of towns *etc.* Til-xamri, II 67, 10; Til-abnê Asp iii 55; I 29, 49. Til-ašurri, Esh ii 23. Til-Barsip, I 43, 24, capital of Bît-Adini; see Bezold, *Catalogue*, v 2200—1 for further instances; AV 8898—8906.

3. Here perhaps V 18 *a-b* 22 ni[-e]-rum ša til(or adr)-li, preceded by ša eqli; = cultivate a hillland.

tilu (?) *2.* II 60 *d* 17 a-na ti-li xa-aç-ba-ti. Connected with til(l)u, 1?

(ic) **til-li** (qa-ra-bi), Asb vi 17 read be-li = weapons (bêlu, 3; 159 *col* 1); but it may be the same as tillu, 2.

tillâ in aga-la (NU?) tillâ see agalu, 2 (14 *col* 1).

tillu *2. pl* tillâ. K 514 (Hr^L 268) 14 u ti-il-li-šu-nu ša kaspi (+ 16); some part of the harness of horses; AV 8914; *cf* Arab تَلّ, drag behind (?); & see tallultum & tullultum.

tulla. AV 2329, tilla, AV 8914, see dullu, 1 (247 *col* 1).

tillum *3.* so perhaps instead of bil-lum (see 160 *col* 1, end); Br 4581, 5012; & see tillatu.

tēlu, tēltu, tēlitu. √אאל. ZA x 211, 12 te-il-tum ša(-)ta(-)te-e-lu : te-lit um-mi-ja. Rm 2, II *O* 1—4 UB-AG-A = te-e-lum (Br 5795; AV 8907; V 39 *e* 53); UB-DUG-GA = *t* xa-an-ṭu; UB-AD-AG-A = *t* ma-ru-u; UB-DI-DI = *t* . . . .? (5) UB = te-el-tum. Also see II 35 *a-b* 31 U]B = te-el-tum followed by ta-na-ad(t)-tum (same id) & nu-'-u-du (Br 5785; AV 8917). Perhaps confusion with √علی. 83, 1—18, 1330 iv 5; Jensen, 165 *rm* 2. — The *f* tēlit(t)u probably = tax, duties }Auflage{. VATh 208 (KB iv 94; KAS 2) 4 ur-bu u te-li-tu, Eingangsabgabe und Auflage; Peiser, *Vertr.*, cliv 7; Nabd 815, 3 & 11. Cyr 94, 1 suluppu (KA-LUM-MA) te-lit ša šatti; 338, 1; Nabd 1058, 8 te-lit-tum a-na, *etc.*; AV 8893. K 3609, 4 te-li-tu ina eqli ibašši (an omen; ZA xvi 204: √علی or תאל). V 61 *c* (v) 49, 50 (çubât) qar-bit rabītu u te-lit ka-ri-bi. te-lit Ištar, Bēl *etc.*, Peiser, *Juris. Babyl.*, 40, 41.

tēlū *f* tēlītu, lofty, sublime }erhaben, hehr{ √علی Martin, *Textes relig.*, '03; PSBA xxiii 115 *foll*; rather than mighty, strong }mächtig, stark{ √le'ū, 2 (463, 464). BA iii 274, 275 *ad* K 2001, 4 te-li-tu (ilat) Ištar ša tu-qu-un-ti xal-pat, die mächtige Ištar, kampfgerüstet. ZA ix 270. K 3464 *O* 26 te-li-ti (ilat) Ištar, Craig, *Relig. Texts*, *pl* 66. II 59 *e-f* 16 AN-NIN-BAR (so AV 8896; Br 7357; 11055) explained by te-li-tum. K 7673, 14 . . . . ū-mu tu-çi-a (when thou didst go) te-li-tum-ma (na-mir-tu šaq[-qu-tu]) said of Ištar. Xamm.-*code* ii 48, 49 Xammurabi calls himself mi-gi-ir te-li-tim, the favorite of the sublime.

telē'u, intelligent, reasoning, wise }verständig, vernünftig, weise{ √la'u, 1; ‖ li'ū, 1 (463); Z^B 14. *f* telijātu. II 60 *c-d* 36 AN-NI-ZU-ZU = (il) Nabū ilu te-li-'u-u, AV 8894; *cf* V 43 *c-d* 35, preceded by il mu-du-u. K 2361 ii 5 ti-li-ē-u-um ina mi-in-ni ṭi-p[u . . .]; ZA iv 238, 27 (29). ZA x 293, 29 see rubūtu.

tulubu. KB iii (1) 34 *col* 5, 57 (iç) tu-lu-bu-um, Tulubu-bäume, Winckler, *Forsch.*, ii ('00) 399; *cf* דלב?, shingle; but queried by ZA xviii 199 *rm* 2. See also Hommel, *Gesch.*, 326; Amiaud, RP^2 ii 80, 57; Löw, *Aram. Pflanzennamen*, 73 (178) & Jensen, *platanus orientalis*; Pinches, *Jour. Trans. Vict. Inst.*, xxvi 133.

talbišu. dress, garment }Bekleidung, Kleid, √labašu. *Merod.-Balad.*-stone ii 39, 40 tal-bi-iš ina li-ti, Bekleidung mit Sieg. BA ii 261; 267. M^S 53 *col* 1, = *adj*: clothed with. A ‖ perh.:

talbuaštu. K 4525 *R* 1 tal-bu-aš-ti tu-lab-ba-šu, Winckler, *Forsch.*, ii 574 *foll.*

talgiddū. some object made of wood }ein Gegenstand aus Holz{. Zimmern, *Rituall.*, *no* 66 *R* 13 TAL-GID-DA šamnē. Reisner, *Hymnen*, 114, 18 axa (iç) tal-gid-di-e-šu (= GIŠ-TAL-GID-DA-BI) ittepxi; *cf* tallu, 2, & talmaxxu.

tallakku, way, entrance }Weg, Zugang{ § 65, 32*c*. V 65 *b* 28 ki-ib-su li-iç-çi-ru (*var* -çu-ur) liš-te-ši-ru tal-la-ak-ku (*var* ki). ZA iv 362 *R* 3 (6) ašur tal-la-ku (or kat) 7 kas-bu. √alaku, 1 (43—45) whence also the following 2 (3):

tallaktu. AV 8729; § 65, 32*a*. — *a*) walk, step, walking }Gang, Schritt, Einhergehen{. IV^2 1* iv 13 (= GIR-DU-NA, Br 9193, 9207); II 120 (K 257 *R*) 20 (= ME-RI, EME-SAL, Br 10397) see šaqû, 1 Q pm. H 128 *O* 62 see šaqū, 2. V 65 *b* 52 see sadaru, Q (748 *col* 1). Esh *Sendsch*, *R* 13 šarru ša tal-lak-ta-šu a-bu-bu-um-ma; *c. st.* ZA iv 110. 75 tal-ka-at (il) Šamaš. V 16 *a-b* 24 GIR = tal-lak[-tum]; H 30, 672. — *b*) road, way upon which one walks }Gang, Weg, Strasse{. T^M ii 110 ina ē-kur a-šar tal-lak-ti-ka; Neb iii 54 ta-al-la-ak-ti pa-pa-xa (ZA vii 124), the entrance to the sanctuary proper × mūlak bīti, the road leading to the whole temple; v 20 ta-al-lak-ti; v 54. KB iii (2) 92, 12 u-ba-an-na-a ta-al-la-ak-tu-uš.

taldu, AV 8728 see ri-du. ~ tilludū read billudū (160, 161). ~ taldūtu see ridūtu. ~ tul-lux-xu *cf* dulluxu, dalaxu, 219. ~ tulxānu, AV 9616 see dulxānu.

Esh v 45 tal-lak-ti šarri ‖ kib-si, 44; see BA iv 253. POGNON, *Wadi-Brissa*, 38, 37 ta-al-la-ak-tim (& *pp* 44; 53). — *c*) extent, surface }Strecke, Fläche{ also: yard. Esh vi 18; Asb x 75 see rapašu, 3. — *d*) entrance }Zugang{. KB iii (2) 90 i 52 ta-al-la-ak-tu-šu i-ça-at-ma, its entrance was too small. — *e*) II 48 *g-h* 16 A (a-ra) DU | [tal?]-lak[-tum], ZK i 312; Br 11499; followed by šip-ru.

tālūku. AV 8726; § 65, 32*a*. — *a*) road, way, walk, progress }Weg, Gang, Bahn{. III 57 *b* 25 it is said of the Venus-star ina ta-lu-ki-ša (= K 35, 2). 82—5—22, 67, 3 it is said of Mars ta-lu-ki-šu un-di-iṭ-ṭu (√maṭû?), THOMPSON, *Reports*, 236 E. K 3351, 12 i-na bu-ru-mi ellūti ša- u-ux ta-lu-uk-šu, CRAIG, *Relig. Texts*, i *pl* 43. BANKS, *Diss*, 18, 78 ina ta-lu-ke (*var* -uk) rabûte. mit hehren Schritten. — *b*) expedition }Zug{. Šalm. *Balaw* IV 5 ina ša-ni-e ta-lu-ki, TSBA vii 101; KB i 136—7; § 129. — *c*) course }Verlauf{. TP v 33 i-na ta-lu-uk gir-ri-ma šu-a-tu, in the course of this same campaign.

tālkūtu. way }Weg{ Xamm.-*code* xxxii 85 that son (u-ul it-ta-al-la-ak. ZA xviii 25) shall not go tal-ku-zu (his way) without money. But see riqûtu in *Supplement*.

tālukatu. Nabd 694, 6 three (iç) šal-xi eš-šu ana ta-lu-ka-tum; 696, 7: three (iç) šal-xi a-na ta-al-lu-ka-tum; Camb 148, 7: five (iç) šal-xu a-na ta-lu-ka-a-ta. Perhaps the same as illû'ku, 45 *col* 2.

talikkāti (?) Neb 247, 8 šîr ri-qi-ti šîr ta-lik-ka-ti šîr xi-li-da-mu (or XI-LI = kuzub?). PEISER, *Vertr.*, 289 *ad* cvii 9; TALLQVIST, *Schenkungsbriefe*, 21; 24.

talalu (?) K 4210 *R* 1 tu-lu-lu. M^S *pl* 10 ‖ upû clouds }Gewölk{ GGA '98, 827.

NOTE. — § 25 derives ta(l)-lu-tu in IV² 30 *no* 1 *a* 24 = H 125, 12 from √talalu, throw (Ps 137: 3); but see la'atu; also Br 1599; and, further, ZIMMERN, ZDMG 58, 952 √'-l-t(:, *d*).

tallalu. Bu 88, 5—12, 11 *O* 4 tal-lal, un vêtement, PSBA xxiv 220 *foll.* √alalu, 1?

tallultu. harness }Geschirr{ √alalu, 1 (46 *col* 1); see, however tillu, 2. K 527 (Hr^L 32) 13—15 ina eli sisî dan-ni ša tal-lul-tu ša (mât) Ku-u-si ri-šu-u-ni; HEBR. x 198; AJSL xiv 178. Asb vi 25 sisê parê rabûti ša tal-lul-ta-šu-nu xurâçu çarpu. A ‖ probably:

tullultum. 82—8—23, 646, 1—2 šalšet baru ([illegible]) ma-na xamšet šiqli (ṬU) tu-ul-lu-ul-tum ša alpi, *Rec. Trav.*, xix 107, 108.

tēliltu, splendor, purification }Glanz, Reinigung{. √alalu, elelu, 4 (46 *col* 2), but ZA iv 340 √eleçu. §§ 32 *a* β; 65, 33 *b*; AV 8895. V 33 v 7 te-lil-ta-šu-nu lu-u-ša-aš-ki-in-ma (KB iii (1) 145 ich liess dieselben erstrahlen = entsühnen; & *rm* †*); 17 iš-tu te-lil-ti bi-tim mit-xa-riš šak[-nat?]. K 1451 *R* 1 be-lit te-lil-ti bêltu a-li-kat su-li-e (MEISSNER & ROST, 108); K 157 *O* 9 ana mê tēlilti, T^M 133; ZIMMERN, *Ritualt.*, 142 *rm* β. IV^2 15* iii 12, 13 ši-pat E-ri-du ša te-lil-ti (= NA-RI-GA, Br 1602); 25 *a* 45, 46 (AZAG-GA, Br 9893); 47, 48 (EL-LA, Br 11177) = (a-na) a-šar te-lil-ti (it-bal-ka) = embalm }einbalsamieren{. V 61 *d* 22 ina te-lil-ti ša É-a u (il) Marduk. Creat.-*frg* VII *O* 5 (il) Marduk (il) ZI-AZAG šal-šiš im-bu-u mu-kir (KB vi, 1, 34 & *rm* 4; or -kil, see 379 *col* 2) te-lil-ti, der Reinigung bewirkt; see kârum, 3 (480 *col* 1). K 6012 + K 10684, 23 UD-EL-E-NE = ûm te-lil-tum, purification day, PSBA xxvi, opposite *p* 56. V 32 *d-e* 39 GI-EL-E-NE = qa-an te-li-il (*var* lil)-ti; II 24 *a-b* 7, Br 11177. K 4204, 72 (II 24 *no* 1 *add*) DUK-EL-E-NE = kar-pat te-lil-te = e[-gub-bu-u], = mullilu ZIMMERN, *Ritualt.*, *p* 220 *col* 1); & II 22 (*d*-)*e* 83 (-ti). See also natiktum, 748 *col* 1. 82—8—16, 1 *O* 12 te-lil-tum, HOMMEL, *Sum. Lesest.*, 96. V 21 *g-h* 13 AZAG = te-lil-tum (& el-lum, 12) Br 9893.

talamu. present, give }schenken, geben{ AV 8719; SCHRADER, ZDMG 28, 126 × PRAETORIUS, *ibid* 27, 512. Q KB vi (1) 108, 51

---

te-lak-ši-na, ZA iv 11 (*ad* K 3182 iii 17) read te-rit-ši-na, AJSL xvii, 140, 141. ~ tul-lu-lu V 20, 5: AV 9020 see dullulu (√dalalu). ~ tul-la-tu, AV 9019 *cf* dullatu.

rim(?)-an-ni-ma kīma e-ri-ši nu-dun-na-a lut-lim-ka (*Etana*-legend), erbarme dich mein! dann will ich dir wie einem Bräutigam ein Brautgeschenk geben. — Š perhaps originally: I brought to his side; give, bestow, offer, present, intrust {darbringen, zu teil werden lassen, verleihen, übergeben}. Sarg *Cyl* 8 Sargon to whom Ašur & Marduk a kingdom unrivalled u-šat-li-mu-šu(-ma); *bull* 4; also Merod.-Balad.-stone iii 7 (BA ii 261, 267; KB iii, 1, 187); Sn i 11 u-šat-li-ma-an-ni; *Ku* 1, 2; *Bell* 4; Sarg *Khors* 4 u-šat-li-mu-ni(-ma); *Ann* 380; u-šat-li-mu-in-ni; *Ann* 380; *Ann* XIV 2. Sn *Kui* 4, 4 u-šat-lim kat-ra-a-a (see 460 *col* 1) = I sacrificed; Sn v 59 the mighty bow ša (il) Ašur u-šat-li-ma. I 44, 67 šal-la-at na-ki-ri ka-bit-tu ša u-šat-li-ma (il) Ašur. ZA iv 228, 10 u-šat-lim-ka. Xamm.-*code* xl 25 u-ša-at-li-mu-nim. Smith, *Asurb*, 11, 12 the great gods dunnu zikrūtu . . . u-šat-lim-u-ni, §§ 17; 56*b*. I 7 ix A 1, 2 ša (il) Ašur (ilat) Bēlit e-mu-ki çi-ra-a-ti u-šat-li-mu-uš (= D 121 *no* 10); also I 7 viii F 6 u-šat-li-ma-an-ni-ma; see dupl. text, ZA iv 284 *foll.* — I 27 *no* 2, 52 ina is-qi-šu (BA i 228) lu-šat-li-mu, als seinen Anteil mögen sie geben. IV^2 57 *b* 16 (karpat) agubbū ša Marduk li-šat-lim-ma damēqta. — 81—2—4, 188, 4 Ištar a-na šar-rat ilāni^{pl} ša par-çe ilāni rabūti šu-ut-lu-mu (= pm) qa-tuš-ša (ZA v 66), into whose hands are given the commands of the great gods. — Xamm.-*letters* 1, 25 šu-ut-li[-ma-aš-šu??], BA iv 437 überweise ihn! Sarg *Harem*-A 7 šu-ut-lim-šu e-mu-qan la ša-na-an. — S^c 81 si-i SI | šu-ut-lu-mu, AV 8640; Br 4427; ZA vii 144.

talīmu, *f* talīmtu. AV 8723; § 65, 14. associate, companion {Genosse} Haupt. Lehmann, i 28—33 ‖ axu. NE 15, 34 Gilgameš ib-ri ta-li-me-ka; see KB vi (1) 138, 139; 434 thy friend (and) brother (× Jensen, KB iii (1) 197 *rm* * twin-brother; & Winckler, *Forsch.*, ii 193 *foll*). *c. st.* ta-li-im, Xamm.-*code* ii 56. S^1 12 ta-lim Ašur-ban-abli, + 27. K 891 *O* 14 (= I 8 *no* 2; Pinches, *Texts*. 17; Lehmann, ii 62) Šamaš-šumu-ukīn axi-MU (= ia) ta-li-me, KB ii 263 Š meinen Bruder (und) Genossen; *ibid rm* †: axu talimu, ein Bruder, der zusammen mit einem andern aufgewachsen ist (following Haupt); & again, see Lehmann, ii 107, 108. V 62 *no* 1, 11 Š axu ta-li-me (= P^1 14); 22 axi ta-lim-ia (P^1 24) = *gen* §§ 12; 17; Le Gac, ZA vi 201, 202; V 62, 26 šum ta-lim-ia (L^5 31); L^4 iii 5 axu ta-li-me. Sarg *Khors* 94 Aximiti axu ta-lim-šu; *Ann* 218; Nabop. (KB iii, 2, 6) iii 7 Na-bi-um-li-ši-ir ta-li-im-šu (of Nebukadrezzar) . . . . . tu-up-pu-su-um, Jensen, ZA viii 235 talīmu & tuppusu ‖ not ×, as Oppert, ZA vii 335. On talīmu la kēnu see Lehmann, i 32; ZDMG 49, 306—7 & × Jensen, *ibid* 50, 242 *foll.*

II 66 *no* 1, 3 of Ištar (Bēltis) ša kīma (il) Šamaš ta-li-me-ša; Smith, *Asurb*, 122, 40 ana Marduk axi ta-li-me-ki (of Ištar of Arbēla). Sarg *Cyl* 53 a-na (il) Dumqu u (il) Šar-ilāni (or ili) da-i-nu-te te-ni-še-te ta-li-ma-ni ina te-me-qi u-šaq-ki-ma; KB ii 47 the brothers. IV^2 13 *a* 53, 54 ilāni ta-li-mu-ka (= AN-AŠ-AŠ-E-NE, Br 33), the gods thy associates; H^{CV} xxxiv; *cf* V 27, 47 MU-AŠ-AŠ = šumu a-xu-u. Scheil, ZA x 292, 26 il-tum kun-nu-tum ru-ba-tum ta-li-me-ša *etc.*

K 101 *R* 3 (II 32 *no* 2, *add*) see tu'āmu. K 2061 (H 202) 19 (TAM? > TAB)-MA = ta-li-mu (Br 7921) preceded by ru-u-a; Rm 345 (M^B *pl* 22). P. N. (il) Nabū-ta-li-me (*var* TAM-MA)-uçur. II 64 *a* 17: 18 (il) Nabū-AŠ (= DIL)-uçur. AV 5833. Ta-lim, AV 8722; Ta-lim-mu, AV 8724. Perhaps V 19 *a-b* 53 TAB-A-ŠUR-RA = ta-lim i. e. d(ṭ)a-ni-b(p)u.

f Anūnit is called ta-lim-tu (il) Šamaš. ZA v 66 & 79, 6 Ištar of Nineveh the mārat (il) Sin is called ta-li-mat (il) Šam-ši (81—2—4, 188). Sm 954 *O* 21, 22 (Ištar) ta-lim-ti (= AK-U-AŠ, EME-SAL, Br 4762) (il) Šamši. ZA i 389, 392. *Rec. Trav.*, xx 205 *foll* i 6 (Nanā) ta-lim-mat (il) Šamši.

NOTE. — See also *Proc. Am. Or. Soc.*, '-6, *p* cxlviii. Tiele, ZA vii 76 *foll*; Nöldeke, ZDMG

80, 85 *rm* 2 (תלמיד אח, in Ecclus. 7, 16). Samaritan תלמיד = brother.

talimmutu (??) *abstr. n.* V 41 *a-b* 56 SAG-DU = sanaqu ša ta-lim-mu-tu(ut).

tulimu. II 40 *b* 28 tu-li-mu, preceded by xi-in-çu, *col a* broken off. AV 9015. II 25 *no* 4, *add* (AV 5544) *R* 37 (= K 4188 iii) NAR (Br 8542) = tu-li-mu. See tul'u.

tullummā'u, Johnston, JAOS xix 84 apparently a term of reproach. K 13 *R* 4 (Hr^{L} 281) šu-nu tul-lu-um-ma-'-u; also *cf* BA iv 527 *foll.*

talmēdu, K 46 iii 9 (= II 13 *c-d* 19; H 58, 9) KAR-ZU-ZU-NE = a-na tal-me-di, AV 8732; Br 7748. Meissner, ZA ix 272—4 borrowed from the Aram. whence Hebr תַּלְמִיד, pupil, scholar }Schüler{, 1 Chron. 25, 8. See also ZA ix 422. — Jensen, *Deu. Lit. Ztg.*, '90, 1456 proposed tilmedu for IZ-ZU (= document). S. A. Smith. *Asurb*, iii 3, 83.

tal(ri?)maxau. a large vessel }ein grosses Gefäss{ AV 8731, 8361. II 22 *d-f* 15 DUK-TAL-MAX = ŠU-xu, *i. e.* talmaxxu = d(t)an-n[u?] Br 2587; see dannu, 2 (255 *col* 1).

Tilmun, Tilmunū (AV 8915, 8916) see Dilmun (251 *col* 1) & Jensen, KB iii (1) 53 *rm* †*. AJP x 76, 77 = Τύλος. Br 11864 *ad* V 41 *g-h* 20. K 8240, 5—6 GIŠIMMAR] NI-TUK-KI = til-mu-nu-u & as(ç)-nu-u (M^{S} *pl* 14); ZA xii 409 *foll*: Tilmuner Datteln.

tillinū (tillēnū) the choicest, best }das Beste{. Sarg *Cyl* 39 see te'ūtu. tillīnū a *l*-formation of عنى, like terdē(n)nu, √ridū; d(ṭ)iqmēnu √qamū. AV 8913. Here perh. also T. A. (Ber) 26 iv 7 one ŠU te-la-a-an-nu ša (aban) giš-šir-gal.

til(l)āniš, *adv* (from tillu, 1) like a mound of ruins }wie ein Ruinenhügel{. D^{II} 16, 17. K 3352 (H 121) *O* 6, 7 all his dwellings ti-la-niš (= [DUL]-DUL-DA-AŠ. Br 28; 9591) šu-pu-uk; see šapaku & H 182. Hommel, *Semiten*, 320; 461 *rm* 191. I 51 *no* 1, 4 see šapaku, ℵ; *no* 2. 14 e-mu-u ti-la-ni-iš || emū kar-mi-iš, had fallen to ruins. IV^{2} 24 *no* 3, 6—7 til-la-niš (= DUL-DUL-AŠ) tam-nu (H 208 *no* 49; AJSL xix 217) || kima ṭīṭi tēmā. DT 71. 21 ti-la-niš tu-še[-me]; see also H 7 & 196, 197.

ta-li-tum. III 41 *b* 21 Ištar may afflict that man with ta-li-tum, perhaps √alū, curse; KB iv 79 *rm* * Unreinigkeit (Belser, BA ii 154) = tal'itu, *q. v.*; or = talittu, 1?

tal'itum (√לאי?). Johnston: a surgical dressing }ein (ärztlicher) Umschlag{. JAOS xviii 162, 168. S 1064 (Hr^{L} 392) *O* 12 ta-al-i-tu ina eli ur-ta-ki-is, I had applied a dressing; *R* 4—6 ta-al-i-tu ša ina eli u-tu-li šar-ku ina eli ta-al-i-te, I removed the dressing (and) there was pus upon the dressing.

talittu *1.* II 47 *c-d* 10 ta-su-ux-tu || ta-lit(zim?, rim?)-tu, AV 8721; Br 8960. breakdown, despair }Gebrochenheit, Verzweiflung{.

talittu *2.* birth; what is born; progeny, offspring, child; young }Geburt; das Geborene; Nachkommenschaft, Brut, Kinder{. AV 8721; § 65, 32*b*, *rm.* √aladu. Barth > littu. KB iii (2) 68, 16 šu-te-ši-ri ta-li-it-ti, may let prosper the progeny; K 2867 *O* 26 ta-lit-ti nēšē, S. A. Smith. *Asurb*, ii 1. Sarg *Cyl* 70; Sn *Kui* 4, 39 (ta-lit-tu); Sarg *Ann* XIV 83, 84 see rapašu, ℶ. K 183 (Hr^{L} 2) 20, 21 ta-lit-tu aš-rat, BA i 617 *fol*; PSBA xxiii 351 *fol.* Xamm.-*code* xxxviii 56 & 58 ta-li-it-tam, birth-rate. Sm 2052 *O* 27 ta-li[-tum?] M^{S} *pl* 19. S 875 *O* 11 see Thompson, *Reports*, ii *no* 103. Asb i 50 būlu šu-te-šur ina ta-lit-ti, the cattle is blessed with progeny. Perh. Rm 2, 1 (Hr^{L} 408) *O* 15 (al) Dūr-ta-li-ti.

tilti, nine }neun{ *f* to תשע. Schmidt., *Notes*, xxxviii *no* 3, 9 (10) til-ti ūmu, preceded by sa-man-ti ūmu, Hilprecht, *Assyriaca*, 69. T^{M} v 83 ti-il-ti ū-me im-ba-ru ša na-ad-na šit[-tum?], on the ninth day (lit^{y} nine days) a storm which will cause destruction (?). K 6012 + K 10, 684, 11 UD IX = ūmu til-ti, ZDMG 58, 200 *rm* 3 >< PSBA xxvi 53 (bat-ti). See ti-šit (§ 75).

tilla(i)tu. vine }Weinrebe, Rebe{ KB vi (1) 469; AV 3909. II 45 *no* 4, 69—71 (K 4346

---

talmūtu, Br 4367 see rimūtu. ∾ (bītu) tal-pi-tu Johns, *Doomsdaybook*, 15, 1 see ri-pi-tu. ∾ tilpānu *cf* pitpānu, 855 *col* 1. ∾ talqattum, Br 2728, 8095 read riššūtu.

i 23—25) GIŠ ka-ra-an GEŠTIN [or TIN] (Br 679, 688; also = xunnatu, 68), GIŠ-TIL-LA-GEŠTIN; GIŠ-PA-PA-AL-GEŠTIN (Br 5631 also = papallum, 72) = til-la-tum; 65, GIŠ-GEŠTIN-GAM-MA (Br 5014, 7316) = til-lat ka-ra-ni; also = ka-ra-an li-e & karan la-a-ni, 63, 64. So manifestly, instead of be-lat karāni, p 170 col 1, beg. l 60 perh. til (instead of bil)-lum, Br 5012. II 24 a-b 10; V 32 d-f 42 may be qa-an til(? instead of be)-la-ti; if so, then also V 13 c-d 36 çābē til-la-ti vintager, vine-dresser {Winzer}. Br 3700 foll, 6692, 8162, 8164. — (is) til-lit, JOHNS, *Doomsday-Book*, 20, 21 (no 4 iv 4); 29 ll 35, 47 etc. (is) til-lit, JOHNS, *Deeds*, 66, 7 & often; (is) til-lit-ti; 359, 4. Here, also, M^{8} p 22 col 1 s. v. be-lit; KB iv 116 (ii) 5; 139, 5.

tilītu? KB iv 18, 16 ša i-na ti-li-ti-šu a-na e-li-a-ti-šu il-ku-u, den er bei seinem Rechtsanspruch auf sein zu beansprechendes genommen hat.

tulātum. II 40 c 5 XA pl (= nūnē?) tu-la-a-tum.

taltallū, AV 8735 see daldallū (249 col 1), Br 2596; GGA '98, 827 prefers to read taltallū, comparing Cant 5, 11 תַּלְתַּלִּים.

tēmu. II 32 no 5 (add) E(ri-ib)RIB (Br 5875); LAL-A-BAR-RI (Br 10123) = mar ti-e-mi, AV 5193, ZA i 398. Also Br 11451 on II 29 c-d 48 A-RI = mar ti-e-mi, ZA i 396—7; evidently for ṭēmu, q. v.

tamū 1. pr itmū(ū). ps itam(m)u(i, e, ā), § 108, AV 8743. Secondary formation from amū; H^{F} 34; GGN '80, 587; G § 50 rm 2. HALÉVY, Hebr המה = תוה, be astonished. — a) talk, speak {reden, sprechen}. it-ma, KB iii (1) 156 col 1, 45. As a rule we find the ps used in a pr sense. Asb iii 80 e-liš ina šap-te-e-šu i-tam-ma-a ṭu-ub-ba-a-ti; KB ii 250, 56—7 ši-i ki-ma ummi a-lid-ti i-tam-ma-a it-ti-ka. V 64 a 19 Marduk i-ta-ma-a it-ti-ja. + 23 palxiš a-ta-ma-a ana bēl ili (il) Marduk. NE V col 3 (4) 9 i-ta-ma-a-a-na eb-ri-šu (KB vi, 1, 164). K 3364 R 9 'š'ur-riš ta-ta-mu-u, DELITZSCH, *Weltschöpfungsepos*, p 55 (& R 25 e ta-ta-me). Perhaps Sargon, *Ann* 409 ardūtu i-tam-ma (?), he promised (lit: he talked of) submission. IV^2 51 b 25 ($Z^{Š}$ ii 82) end: la šal-ma-a-te i-ta-mu-u, 3 sg. II 30 c-d 21 (e-la-a-tum) ki-i i-ta-mu-u. Br 862, 5127, 6112; Z^{B} 73. On l 22 & II 7 c-d 31 see Br 233. See also šaplū, šaplītu Br 578, 733. — ps 1 sg K^{M} 18, 17 la-ta-am nar-bi-ka ana nišē rapšāti, I will declare (show forth) thy majesty to the wide nations, § 93, 1 b. — pm del 16 (19) ta-me (šib?)-ma Ēa ittišunu, PINCHES, *Guide to the Nimroud Central Station*, London '86 p 86; HALÉVY, ZA iv 61; J^{1-N} 53 no 81; KB vi (1) 230, 231. — POGNON, *Wadi-Brissa*, 30, 10 a-ta-mu, 16 i-ta-ma-a. III 54 a 8 the son to his father ket-tu i-ta-ma; 58 b 2 (-me); 54 a 7 in the whole land ket-tu i-ta-mu-u (Br 578), truth shall be spoken. IV^2 32 a 38, b 18 + 44 etc. see šalṭiš; 54 a 33 i-ta-mu-ka (3 sg) ina un-nin-ni, he implores thee, H^{CV} xxxvi; Z^{B} 89. III 52, 40 ta-tam-mi, ZA i 237. — With (or without) libba(m) = think {denken} § 151. SCHEIL, *Nabd*, vi 3 a-ta-me ina libbi-ja, I meditated within myself. Sarg *Ann* 393 i-tam-ma. Neb *Bab.* i 23 whatever pleases Marduk i-ta-ma-am li-ib-ba-am, KB iii (2) 56. Neb iii 26 i-tam lib-bam, cf i 52; TSBA vii 219 a 11; SCHEIL, *Nabd*, i 2—2 (see libbu, 468 col 2 (end of § 1); also cf uš-tam-ma a-na lib-bi-ša (said of the sa-bi-tum) NE 65, 11 (12) & 70, 13 (14) uš-tam-ma-a = Št of amū. 1. — b) swear, take an oath, confirm on oath {schwören, beeidigen, durch Eid bekräftigen} II 65 a 6 Buçuraššur, king of Aššur, & Burnaburiaš, king of Karduniaš, it-mu-ma mi-iç-ri ta-xu-mu an-na-ma u-ki-nu; cf 4 ma-mi-tu ina eli mi-iç-ri an-na-ma a-na a-xa-meš id-di-nu. T. A. (Lo) 28, 59—60 it-mu-mi u iš-ta-ni ma-mi-ta i-na be-ri-šu-nu. ⊕ 116 ii 42, 43 (H 67) = II 40 no 4, 23—26; H 67, 1—5; 72, 47 = V 29, 47 see niš(u) 736; 737. BOISSIER,

---

tultabâl > tuštabšâl see bašū, Št (197—200); e. g. Nabū-tul-tab-ši-li-ši-ru, P. N. KB iv 190 no XIV (Neb 161) 5. ∾ tultēšera = tuštēšera thou rulest, IV^2 60 b 12, § 51, 3 See ešeru, ašaru, ישר.

Diss, 2; BA i 202; WZKM iv 302 *no* 1. V 20 *c-f* 9, 10 see mamītu, 554 *col* 1, beg.; Br 390, 2182, 2184. — *c*) conjure, exorcise, charm, bewitch, enchant }besprechen, beschwören, bannen{; thus niš šamê lu-u ta-mat niš erçiti lu-u ta-mat (= pm; § 93*b*; H 85, 34 *etc.*). see niš(u) *pp* 730, 737: the incantation-formula used most frequently. lū ta-ma-a-ta, IV^2 29 *b* 50; lū ta-ma-ti IV^2 7 *a* 50; ZK i 322; lu ta-ma-mat, H 85, 49; ZA ii 97. See especially Br 9418; AV 8730. H 78 *R* 4 o ma-mit! .... ta-ma-a-ti, 2*f*. IV^2 16 *R* 16 (ša i-ta-ma-a, Br 703) see çaparu, 1 (885 *col* 2, end). — II 7 *c-d* 22—25 PAD (H 78 *R* 3), PAD-DA Br 9417; KUD-DA, Br 390; SAB-BI, Br 3588 = [ta-mu]-u. H 9 & 201, 16 ku-tu | KUD | ta-mu-u; H 30, 681 pa-a | ŠI + RU | ta-mu-u. II 33 *c-f* 3, 4 it-mu, i-ta-mi. it-mu-u, see II 211, 5. K 4350 iii 20 (= II 11, 20; II 50, 20) it-ma (preceded by iš-qu-ur, u-tu); 23 it-mu-u; 26 i-tam-ma; 29 i-ta-mu-u, Br 9417.

$\mathfrak{Q}^1$ — *a*) speak }reden, sprechen{. V 35. 35 all the gods . . . ša a-ra-ku ūmêja li-ta-mu-u littaškaru (√סכר) amāta dunqija. — *b*) swear, swear by, confirm on (with an) oath }schwören, schwören bei{. Neb 42, 8 the debtor ina Bêl u šarri it-te-me kī (followed by the wording of the oath), 307, 7—8; Nabd 83, 3; 197. 7; 849. 4 & 13; 964, 14 (ina Bêl u Nabû); KB iv 206—7 *no* 3, 5. Neb 103, 18—19 ina Bêl it-te-mu-u ki-i (of two debtors), BOR ii 22. PEISER, *Vertr.*, xlvii 10 ina [šum?] šarri it-te-me, he confirms with (or in?) the name of the king. WZKM iv 307. Dar 358, 10—11 ki-i it-te-mu-u zak-ku-u. T. A. (Ber) 199, 22 u-ma-š[e]-i[r] [l]u-u [i]-te-mi šar-ri. BA iv 127.

$\mathfrak{I}$ — *a*) with double *accus*: have some one (or, something) cast a spell. charm, bewitch something (someone) }etwas jemanden besprechen, bannen lassen; jem. durch etwas beschwören lassen{. Sp II 265 *a* i 7 .... ni-is-sa-tum lu-u-ta-me-šu. IV^2 55 *no* 1 *R* (*b*) 18 šiptu: tum-mu[-u], sei beschworen!; 33 tu-tam-ma-ši. du sollst sie beschwören, ZA xvi 184*foll*; 56 *b* 7(—10) u-tam-me-ki (o witch) ilu A-num abu ilāni rabûti; *b* 57; 18 (end) tum-ma-ti (2*f* pm) ZA xvi 154*foll*. 58 *a* 12 Marduk u-tam-mu-ki ši-pir limutti-ki, soll dir beschwören; 48 tum-ma-ti lu-um-ma-ti, sei gebannt! sei umschlossen! ZA xvi 168*foll*. ZIMMERN, *Rituall.*, *no* 24 *O* 20/1 a-pil-šu ša i-ram-mu ina tup-pi u qān tup-pi ina ma-xar (il) Šamaš u (il) Adad u-tam-ma-šu-ma, lässt seinen Sohn, den er liebt, auf die Tafel und den Tafelstift vor *Š* & *A* schwören; *no* 70—82 ii 6 la tum-mi (??); see *rm* δ. IV^2 1 ii 3, 4 (5, 6) a-'š'ak-ku ma-mit (il) A-nun-na-ki u-tam-me-ka (I conjure thee, Br 9417); 1^* iv 37, 38 ma-mit (*q. v.*) tum-me-šu-nu-ti (= KUD, Br 390), H 201; 144 § 17; JENSEN, 285 on DT 122. IV^2 31 *R* 17 tum-me-ši(-ma) šūm ilāni rabûti, KB vi (1) 87 lass sie "aussprechen den Namen" der grossen Götter, *i. e.* let her swear by (so DELITZSCH, *Chald. Gen.*, 317) × LENORMANT, J^w, with whom now agrees D. H. MÜLLER, WZKM xvii 334 *rm*: banne sie mit dem Namen der grossen Götter. K 9417 (BEZOLD, *Catalogue*, 1010) u-tam-me-ku-nu-šim (I conjure you) AN-e (= šamê) u [cuneiform sign] (erçi??)-tum, HOMMEL, PSBA xviii, 18 § 14. — *b*) with mamītu, let someone swear, affirm by, an oath }jem. einen Eid schwören lassen{. TP v 14—16 (1 *sg*, I made them swear) see mamītu, 554 *col* 2. — II 7 *c-d* 32 KA-BAL-BAL-E = mu-ta-mu-u, = V 39 *c-d* 11; or √amû (see 623 *col* 2, end). V 45 vi 7 tu-tam-ma.

$\mathfrak{S}$ ip perh K 6172, 8 sibitti šanītu ana pān ereb (il) Šamši mamit šu-ut-me; see MARTIN, *Textes rélig.*, 1900, 28; but FOSSEY, JA Mr., '02, 364 *foll*: ū-me-šam mu-ru-uç.

$\mathfrak{N}$ perhaps IV^2 51 *b* 26—30; 32—36 = Z^b ii 83—87; 89—93 it-ta-mi (ZIMMERN, = $\mathfrak{Q}^1$, er ist gebannt).

$\mathfrak{N}^1$ perhaps Nabd 954, 10 i-te-it-me; 105, 16 it-te-te-mu.

Derr. tamī(ê)tu & these 3 (4):

tamû 2. *n* incantation, magic formula. spell }Beschwörung{ or the like. IV^2 58 *a* 54 Papsuk(k)al ša ta-mu-šu la i[-tur]-ra, dessen Beschwörung nicht zurückkehrt. ZIMMERN, *Rituall.*, *no* 16 *R* 14 . . . .

d]i-nim u măkaltu (√akalu, write) u ta-mu-u. Creat.-*frg* IV 62 šam-mi-im ta-m[i]-i ta-me-ix rit(laq)-tuš-šu, KB vi (1) 25 ein Kraut des Beschwörens. Perh. IV² 1 *b* 30 e-lip (?) ta-me-šu; NE 52 *no* 25 (K 8574) 5 a-na bît ta-me (šib, šip?).

tamû *3. adj* charmed {gebannt} ZŠ *p* 54. IV² 51 *b* 42, 43 (ZŠ ii 99, 100): a-na pa-an ta-mi-i i-te-šir ta-mu-u a-na pa-ni-šu i-te-šir, ob er einem Gebannten entgegengegangen, *etc.*, *ibid* 44—47 = ZŠ ii 101—104 ina erši (kussê, paššûri, kâsi) ta-mi-i it-ta-til (it-ta-šab, it-ta-kal, il-ta-t[i]).

tamma'u (?) enchanter, conjurer {Beschwörer} II 7 *c-d* 26 (27) amêl NAM-ERIM-KUD-DA = tam-ma[-'u], Br 2183.

tu-ma, V 28 *e-f* 17 = ki-ma, AV 9027.

tamû *4.* Br 11475 *ad* V 26 *e-f* 20 GIŠ-A-AB-BA = ta-mu[-u?].

temû = ṭamû (?) 356 *col* 2. T. A. (Ber) 25 iv 49 KU *pl* (= lubšâti) ša eliš u šapliš te-mu-tum; 26 iv 11 te-mu-u; perh. *adj.*

tu-mu (?). II 42 *d* 66 (šam) a-a-ar tu-mu (?), a plant {eine Pflanze}.

timmu, rope, cable {Seil, Tau} § 25, AV 8928; ZA i 191 *rm* 1; id DIM (= markasu & riksu). II 7 *c-d* 30 (tim-mu) §§ 9, 122; 25. Here also D 80 vi 72 GIŠ-IR-D(T)IM = tim-mu, Br 5400 (also = irkû see *p* 100 *col* 2 & maxrašu, 534 *col* 1); 33 DIM-MA' = tim-mu ša elippi (32, = markas elippi) Br 2747. Rm 353 *R* 5, 6 (MS *pl* 22). KB vi (1) 495—6 accepts only one word d(t)immu = Pfahl, Mastbaum; see dimmu. Very uncertain is ZA x 207 ii *O* 4 .... ti-im-mu = šu(ŠU?)-u.

tumbê (?) Nabd 784, 9—11: 2 parzillu (or parzillu) ba-ti-qa-nu ša xu-up-pu-u ša tu-um-bi-e a-na *NN.*

timbûbu (?). Br 7043, 7382 *ad* V 26 *c-d* 7; see above, 356 *col* 2.

tam(ma)bukku *1.* see pukku, 801 *col* 2; KB vi (1) 256 *col* 1.

tambukku *2.* II 5 *a-b* 27 (V 27 *g-i* 9) NUM-SAR = tam-bu-uk-ku = xa...., Br 9027; AV 8745. J*p* 50 *rm* 3 the insect which stings, between lallartum & nubtum. On II 5 *a-b* 26 see Br 14258.

timbuttu, see ṭimbû, 356 *col* 2, below. seal-ring, ring {Siegelring, Ring} ZŠ iii 37 (36) ma-mit ta-pa-li u tim-bu-ut-ti; & *p* 55 Bann durch Tünche und Siegel (löst er). ZIMMERN, *Ritualt.*, *no* 45 iii 4 tim-bu-ut-tu; 46—47 ii 16. S 578, 4 [ra-ga-mu] tim-bu-ut-ti (MS *pl* 19); K 12848, 3 (MS *pl* 17). KAT³ 653 reads timbu'êti = מצבעת in T. A. (Lo) 8, 42: one aban kišâdi ša ti-im-bu-e-ti; (Ber) 6 *R* 22; 25 ii 20, nine ti-im-bu-'-u aban uknû banû.

tumagu see niqqu, 718 *col* 2; AV 9028.

tamganû, vessel {Gefäss}. tam-ga-nu-u, JOHNS, *Deeds*, 1104 *R* 6.

tamgurtu. favor, present {Gunstbezeigung, Geschenk}. √magaru, 510, 511. § 65, 32*e*; AV 8748; Br 2204. II 40 *no* 4 *R* 52 (= K 4317 *R* 15) TAG-ŠID-NAM-ŠE-ŠE-GA = kunuk tam-gur-ti = the result of the šaṭaru ina mitgurtišunu. K 46 ii (H 57) 30 ŠU-GA-AN-NA-AB-DU = tam-gur-tu ‖ nam-xur(mur?)-tu 28; man-da-tu 29. = II 12 *c* 9; Br 7176.

tam-gu-u-tum. T. A. (Ber) 24 *R* 91.

tamgîtu Sarg *Khors* 176, 177. √nigû, = nu-ug libbi (641, 642) or √nagû (642) = ina ni(n)gûti. See taknû & AJSL xx ('04) *p* 225 *no* 5.

tâmdu see tâmtu.

Tammûz see Du'ûzu (235, 236); KB vi (1) 411; KAT³ 397 *foll*; Br 4092.

tam-zi-zi-iš, Sn v 69 or ûziziš (?; 26 footnote).

tamaxu, pr itmux, ps itammax, AV 8737. — *a*) take, grasp, capture, take prisoner {fassen, greifen, gefangen nehmen}. K 7592 *R* 8 (ZA v 59); Sn v 60; D 97, 27 (= Creat.-*frg* IV 62; see also tamû, 2) compare laqtu (497 *col* 2), for which read probably rittu. Creat.-*frg* IV 122 ir-[t]u-[u]š it-mu-ux, KB vi (1) 28. Sn vi 9 the rest alive, in battle, it-mu-xa qâtâ-a-a (‖ ikšuda qâtâa, i 25; ii 82). Asb vi 119 the hand of the great goddess at-mu-ux (or to *b*?). K 2674 iii 22 at-

---

timgullu see tarkullu. ~ tim-gal *cf* dimgallu (253 *col* 1, *beg.*) & timkallu. ~ tamgâniš see parganiš. ~ tamgaru *cf* tamkaru.

mu-xu (mašak) a-ša-a-ti Ištar (S. A. SMITH, *Asurb*, iii 3, 72). K 2652 *R* 44 the bow ina qātā-ja at-mu-[-ux]. V 47 *a* 18, 19 a-tam-max (ZA i 359); [ta]-ma-xu = ça-ba-tum, Z^B 25; ZK ii 401. K 2801 = K 221 + 2669 *O* 12 ta-me-xu pit-pa-nu, BA iii 228 — or rather to — *b*) hold {halten}. 82—7—4, 42 *O* 6 (& 18) see rittu, 1. L⁴ ii 19 tam-xa-ak pit-pa-nu. SMITH. *Asurb*, 124, 54 Ištar tam-xa-at (11) qašta ina i-di-ša, KB ii 250, 251. V 33 *a* 21 ta-mi-ix çir-ri-ti. KB iii (1) 136 & *rm* 7. K 13733, 7 see çirrîtu. 1 (898 *col* 1). K 2487 + K 8122 *O* (= K^M 2) 18 te-rit kul-lat ilāni *pl* qa-tuk-ka tam-xat. IV² 9 *a* 26, 27 Sin ša balaṭ napxar māti ga-tuš-šu tam-xu (= MU-UN-DIB-BA). TP vi 56 Tigl. Pil. ta-me-ix xaṭṭa la šanān; *cf* I 35 *no* 2, 4. — *c*) give {geben}. Anp i 18 when Ašur his merciless weapon ana i-da-at bêlūtia lu(-u) it-mux. KB iv 102, 1 Marduk is called ta-me-ix kip-pāt (written GAM) šame-e u erçi-tim; *cf* ZA iv 230, 8 ta-mi-ix kip-pat bu-ru-um-me. IV² 9 *a* 51 ta-me-ix (AN) gir-ri (usually read li'bu; Br 7247) u me-e, KB vi (1) 390—1: der da hält Feuer & Wasser; KAT³ 364 *rm* 2; 417 *rm* 5 perhaps = qirru (קרר); 30* *no* 8 *O* 36 ina im-ni-ja at-mu-ux, *Rev. Sém.*, vi 149. — S^c 82 si-i | SE | ta-ma[-xu], Br 4428; S^c 157 ta-ab | TAB | ta-ma [-xu], Br 3774. H 34, 807 di-ib | LU | ta-ma-xu, between ka-mu-u & e-te-qu. K 4350 iii 48 (II 51: II 11 *c-f*) IN-TAB = it-mu-xu (|| ēçip(b). uštēni, uraddi). See also raxaxu. HAUPT: תמך.

Q^t V 35, 12 Marduk . . . . it-ta-ma-ax qa-tu-uš-šu, seized his (the righteous ruler's) hand; BA ii 210, 211.

ℑ capture, take prisoner, *etc.*; especially, kill game, be successful in hunting {erbeuten; gefangen nehmen; Wild erlegen} *etc.* I 28 *a* 20 u-te-im-me-ix (3 *sg*; § 36); TP iv 96: 120 of their chariots in battle lu-te-me-ix; vii 9 u-tam-mi(me)-xu = 1 *sg*. Xamm.-*code* iii 47 Xammurabi calls himself mu-tam-me-ix a-a-bi. — *b*) hold fast, keep captive {festhalten, gefangen halten} Asb i 131 ina bi-ri-ti parzilli iš-qa-ti parzilli u-tam-me-xu (3 *pl*) qātā u šēpâ (of the kings). SMITH, *Asurb*, 44, 45 (KAT³ 371); Asb iii 59, 60; ii 109 (u-tam-me-ix, 3 pr; *cf* çiççu, 887 *col* 2). V 45 iv 9 tu-tam-max.

Š causative of Q. — *a*) with double *accus*. (qātā of someone). TP i 51 their powerful (mighty) weapons qa-a-ti lu-šat-me-xu (§ 36), they gave into my hand; ii 98 when Ašur kakka dan-na . . . . qa-ti u-šat-me-xu-ma. Esh *Sendsch*, *R* 29, 30; I 48, 6 (u-šat-me-ix); Bu 88—5—12, 75 + 76 ix 5 (BA iii 256); ZA iv 230, 10, see laqtu; also *cf* šibirru. Neb i 46 Nabū xaṭṭa išarti(m) u-ša-at-mi-ix ga-tu-u-a; *Bors* i 14. Ner i 11 Nerigl. ša . . . . Nabū . . . . xaṭṭa išarti u-ša-at-mi-xu qa-tu-uš-šu. Anp i 45 in the beginning of my reign when Šamaš . . . . . xaṭṭa . . . . ana (a-na) qāti-ja u-šat-me-xu, i 42 without qātu. Šalm, *Mon*, i 13 when Ašur the weapon . . . . u-šat-me-xa-ni-ma. V 64 *c* 20, 21 ši-bir-ri ki-i-nim ša tu-šat-mi-xu qa-tu-u-a (2 *sg*). ZIMMERN, *Rituall*.. *no* 24, 9 & 13 u-š[at-me-xu (3 *pl*) qāt-su] & qāt-su-nu u-šat[-me-ix, 3 *sg*). — *b*) 82—7—4, 42 *O* 18 see rittu, 1. POGNON, *Wadi-Brissa*, 29, 2 u-ša-at-mi-xa. V 65 *b* 5 u-šat(-mi)-ix-ma, Z^B 98; § 49*a*; BA i 591 ✕ HAUPT, ZA ii 270; BA i 98 *rm*; KB iii (2) 108, 24 I fastened = I placed doors into the gates. K 5419 *c R* 10 . . . . id-din DUB-NAM-MEŠ i-rat-šu u-šat-mi-ix; KB vi (1) 6 & 315, 33. V 45 vi 33 tu-šat-ma-ax.

Š^t Neb ii 27 (AV 8737) see šamaxu.

tamxū, tamxātu, evening, sunset, dusk {Abend, Sonnenuntergang, Abenddämmerung} AV 8748, 8750; D^S 51; GGN '80, 104 *rm* 1; ZA i 452. II 32 *a-b* 19; II 25 *a-b* 25 = V 28 *c-f* 23 see lilātu, 483 *cols* 1, 2 & AJSL xx *p* 223, *no* 1. V 16 *e-f* 45 UD-GIŠ-MI-LAL = çil-li (*cf* çillu, 1; 875 *col* 1 *a*) tam-xi-e = II 49 *a-b* 27, Br 7910, 7948. III 55 *b* 50 see šēru, 2.

timaxazu see taxtamu.

tamxuçu (√maxaçu, 1; 522—4) § 65, 32 *e*. IV² 13 *b* 9, 10 ina tam-xu-uç (= SIG-SIG [written PA-PA]-GA, Br 5626) kakki qar-ra-du ša ta-na-ru ra-biš šuk-li-la.

tamxiçu ‖ tarîmu, AV 8749. K 11185, 10 . . . . AJŠ | tam-xi-çu.

tamxaru. hostile meeting, combat, battle {feindliches Begegnen, Kampf, Schlacht} AV 8747; § 65, 32*a*; √maxaru, 525—29. Sarg *Cyl* 21 li-'(u) tam-xa-ri; TP i 50 kakkē-šu-nu dan-nu-ti a-bu-ub tam-xa-ri qa-a-ti lu-šat-me-xu (3 *pl*); v 43; viii 40 ir-nin-tu tam-xa-ri-ja; i 67 i-na tam-xa-ri; ii 27 (79; iv 95) i-na ki-rib tam-xa-ri ‖ ina mit-xu-uç kak-ki = e-peš ta-xa-zi; Šalm, *Mon*, ii 101 ina ki-rib tam-xa-ri šu-a-ti. Šalm, *Obel*, 11 Nergal šar tam-xa-ri, king of battle, D^K 53 *rm* 2. 1 44, 52 ki-rib *t.*; Sn i 22 i-na qabal *t.* (ii 82; vi 9; *Bell* 6); Asb ix 21. šu-par tam(ta-am)-xa(-a)-ri(ra) *etc.* see šu-pāru. K 2801 = K 221 + 2669 *O* 12 see tibû, 2. Creat.-*frg* III 21 na-šu-u (3 *pl* pm) tam-xa-ri; ZA iv 229, 15 ki-i a-gi-e tam-xa-ri. T. A. (Lo) 12, 2 šar ta-am-xa-ar; also 13. 2; 20, 4 (here perhaps in a more general meaning).

tamṭēru, rain {Regen}. √maṭaru, 525 *col* 1. Hebr. vii 64. Sn iv 75 see kuççu, 425 *col* 2, 4 *foll.*

tamaku (? = Hebr תמך). T^M iv 72 a-ta-am-ma-ak-šu-nu-ti, I will seize them.

tamēku. tribute {Tribut} or the like. T. A. (Ber) 99, 5 aš-šum ta-me-ku ša i-pa-aš-ši; KB v 412: W. Max Müller ta-me-ku: מסה, pay.

tumku. KB iii (2) 66, 47 ki-be tu-um-ku-u-a = qibē dumqû'a (§ 19) see dumqu.

timkallu (Hebr. vii 70) see dimgallu, 253 *col* 1. If Semitic, perh √כבל, a form like tizqaru (Hebr. vii 255).

tamkaru. merchant, trader, agent {Kaufmann, Händler, Agent}. id (amēl) DAM-Q(K)AR, often in Xamm.-*code*; see Harper's edition, *p* 190. T. A. (Lo) 6, 30 (amēl) tam-ga-ri-ja; 40 (-ru-ka). K 245 (H 69) ii 8 ka-sap tam-ka-ri (= DAM-QAR-RA, Br 11123). Rm 277 vii 9 tam-kar šu-u, ZA vii 17; BA iii 503 *fol.* II 7 *g-h* 34, 35; V 39 *g-h* 38, 39 KA (with kib inclosed) & gloss i-bi-ra; DAM-QAR = tam-ka-rum, Br 812, 813, 11122; H 11 & 214, 70; H 35, 837 dam(*var* tam)-ka-rum. V 16 *g-h* 22 see šamallû (Br 5679; ✕ BA i 635, 636). III 46 *no* 6, 15 (end) amēl tam-q(k)ar (KB iv 124, 125); III 48 *no* 2 (K 316) 7; (amēl) DAM-QAR *pl* bring foreign animals, I 28 *a* 26; K 4395 iv 18; K 1252, 4 (Hr^L 529), attend to the importation of horses. K 125 (Hr^L 196) 20 (amēl) tam-k(q)ar-MEŠ iq-ṭi-bu-u-ni; Nabd 612, 5 (amēl) DAM-QAR; 887, 2; II 31 *b* 72; DT 81 vi 13 (BA iii 351—3); Rm 2, 22, 10; K 381, 11 (KB iv 148). V 49 viii 18. III 67 *b* 19 (ilu) DAM-QAR. Also found in Cappad. tablets, see Delitzsch, *Kappad. Keilinschr.*, *p* 18. Camb 384, 11 (amēl) rab DAM-QAR-MEŠ.

√מכר (whence makkûru, 589); Guyard, ZK i 98; *Rev. crit.*, '82 ii 56; Hebr. vii 255; viii 184 (Pinches) Š^t 409, 2: cattle-keeper; Jensen, *Theol. Litztg.*, '95 *no* 10 *col* 251: urspr. der Kauf, speziell der Frauenkauf (H 69, 8 *foll*), *conjux* heisst im Sumerischen DAM; daher die Spielerei damqaru; also ZA vi 149, 349: the Syriac from the Assyrian. ZA vii 17; Meissner, 13 *rm* 2; H^F 35, 30 & *rm* 6 (field laborer) see also Oppert, ZA iii 22; BA ii 28 (> taggaru √agaru); Haupt, *Kings* (SBOT) 117; Bezold, *Diplomacy*, 97.

tamlû, tamlîu. AV 8751; √malû, 1; 540—43. § 65, 32*d*. — *a*) filling in, heaping up; terrace {Auffüllung, Aufschüttung; Terrasse}. tamlâ u(š)malli, I (he) raised an embankment, artificial terrace, see malû, 1 ℑ (542 *col* 1, *med*) & Š^3 *b* (543 *col* 1, *med*). I 44, 57 ša ēkalli ša-a-tu tam-ul-u-šu ul ib-ši; Sn vi 31; *Rass* 82; *Bell* 54 see šaqû, 1 Š. Esh v 28 e-li tam-li-e šu-a-tu. Asb x 79 tam-la-a šu-a-tu (ši-kit-ta-šu); 81 çir tam-li-e šu-a-tu uššē-šu ad-di (*t* ša-a-tu, Sn vi 41; I 44, 63). Neb v 60 i-na ta-am-li-e su-li-e Bâbili, on account of the filling in of the street of *B.* KB iii (2) 78, 13—14 (this building) i-na ta-am-li-e iš-ta-ab-bi-lu-ma i-ni-šu i-ga-ru-ša, had settled and its walls had gone to ruins. II 67, 72 tam(ut?)-li-ši-in (of the palaces) aš-kun-ma iš-di-šin u-kin-ma. I 28 *b* 4 tam-li-a (& 2) raba-a. Also *cf* xuzappu, 308 *col* 2. — *b*) ‖ tamlîtu border, embroidery; filling {Besatz, Einfassung; Füllung}. I 35 *no* 1, 20 a bed of ivory, a chair of ivory ix-zi tam-li-e. T. A. (Lo) 8, 80 one rabû xurâçi tam-lu-u (aban) uknû banū (in a list of presents); KB v 33*: massive. (Ber) 24, 26 four shekels xurâçi tam-lu-u; *R* 38 one u-çu xurâçi tam-lu-u; 28 i 12, 13, 20 *etc.*; often.

NOTE. — 1. R. F. HARPER suggests reading tam-la-a instead of tu-la-a, NE 69, 41—2; 46; see kaparu, 3 (423 *col* 1, end); KB vi (1) 473 tu-la-a.

2. tam-lu read ut(d)lu, 129, 130.

timāli > itimāli, 131 *col* 1, end. §§ 27; 39; 47; 78. Eth *temālĕm.* yesterday {gestern}. AV 8910; D^{H} 19; PRAETORIUS, *Lit. Or. Phil.*, i 19. K 519 (Hr^{L} 108) *R* 5 ina ti-ma-li; K 122 *O* 9 (Hr^{L} 43); K 1113+K 1229 *R* 3 (Hr^{L} 71; BA ii 46, 47) ša ina ti-ma-li; Sm 1064, 15 (Hr^{L} 392). Hr^{L} 595 *R* 5 (ina) ti-ma-li ina šal-ši û[-me] = all the time, always; 610 *R* 10 ki-i ša ina ti-ma-a-li šal-še û-me; see also šaššûmu. II 32 *a-b* 22 ûmu (?) ku-nu-ru-u (408 *col* 2) = ti-ma-li; 23 ti-ma-li = mu-šam-ma, Br 7951, 7952. K 2009, 15 UD-KU-NU-A-RI-A = ti-ma-la; 16 ŠA(=LIB)-KA-BA = mu-šam-ma; ZA iv 155; v 46, 47; Br 7953.

tamlīlu. shouting, jubilation {Jauchzen, Frohlocken}. KB iii (1) 113 *col* 2, 6—7 ina kibrat erbittim tam-li-li-ma šum-ka li-iz-za-ki-ir. √מלל.

tamlītu, *pl* tamlâti, *n f* to tamlû. AV 8752 embroidery; border of precious stones {Garnierung; Edelsteinbesatz} or the like. Anp iii 74, 75 chairs, beds ša tam-li-te (Lay 45, 32 & 35); iii 62 golden rings & bracelets ša tam-li-te (ga-gi xurâçi); 68 an ivory chair .... ša tam-li-te(ti) si-mat šarrū-ti-šu. III 16 *no* 3, 2 xarrê xurâçi tam-lit šinni, mit Elfenbeineinlegung, + 4 these jewels (?) ša tam-lit-su-nu (aban) UD-AŠ, *etc.*; WINCKLER, *Forsch.*, ii 56.

tamlittu (> taylittu?). Neb 266, 9: 100 çêni gi-iz-za-ti u tam-lit-tu; KB iv 195 & *rm* ††: das geborene. CLAY, *Murashû*, 23.

tumāmītu. spell, charm, ban {Bann} √תמא. Z^{B} iv 58, 59 d(t)up-pi ar-ni-šu xi-ṭa-ti-šu, qil-la-ti-šu, ma-ma-ti-šu tu-ma-ma-ti-šu (*i. e.* the *pl*) ana mê linnadû. BA ii 412.

tamanu. BA i 622, 623 *ad* K 183, 28 (Hr^{L} 2 *R* 2) ub-bu-lu-ti us-sa-at-mi-nu, the mourners have been comforted (> uštatminu); PSBA xxiii 351 *foll.*

(is) **tu-ma-a-nu,** II 23 *f* 19 = (is) gušūru; H 39, 143; AV 9080; Br 5502.

tim(m)ēn(n)u, *m. c. st.* temên, AV 8920, 8921, 8927. id TE. — *a*) foundation, basis, substructure {Fundament}; but KB vi (1) 424 *ad* NE I (1) 11 [id-di tim-me?]-na-šu, warf er seine Aufschüttung hin; also 254 on *del* 285 (323) te-me-en-na xi-i-ṭe-ma, besieh die Aufschüttung; 286 (324) u uš-ši-šu la id-du-u (sein Fundament); KB vi (1) 424. ‖ išdu & uššu. V 64 *b* 8, 9 ul-tu te-me-en-šu a-di tax-lu-bi-šu. I 44, 64 upon this terrace (tamlû) at-ta-di tem-me-en-šin (of the palaces). I 51 *no* 2 *b* 4, 5 e-li te-me-en-ni-šu la-bi-ri epiri el-lu-ti am-qu-uq. V 65 *a* 18 ub-bu-tu te-me-en-šu; 24 a-na šu-ur-šu-du te-me-en. 81—6—7, 209 *O* 32 te-me-en-šu u-si-bi-ma, BA iii 262, 263. K 2711 *O* 33 (end) at-ta-ad-di tim-me-en-šu (+ 39), ich legte seinen Grundstein, BA iii 264, 265; *cf R* 33; 40. KB iii (2) 92 *col* 3, 4 uš-te-ši-ir te-me-en-šu-un; 4 *col* 2, 45 (i-na ki-gal-e ri-iš-ti-im) u-ki-in TE(= temên)-en (= phonetic complement)-šu; 57 (çalam šarrūtija) i-na te-me-en-na lû aštakkan. Merod.-Balad.-stone ii 37 TE (= temênu) raš-b(p)u. Sarg *Khors* 134 te-me-en-šu (of the city of DUR-(or Dur-)Jakīn) as-su-xa. Sn *Bell* 35; *Rass* 62 (& 92; ZA iii 313) Nineveh tim-me-en-nu da-ru-u ça-a-ti; *Rass* 74 tim-me-en-ša (of the kutallu) e-niš-ma; I 44, 59. BA iii 246 (Bu 88—5—12, 75 + 76) iv 18 .... te-me-en-šu ki-ma šu-pu-uk šadi-i dan-ni u-dan-nin; K 192 *R* 22 (*ibid* 244 *rm* *). KB iv 102, 13 (= *Rec. Trav.*, xvi 178) tim-me-en-šu ki-ma ša-pik šadi-e u-šar-šid. Sarg *Nimr* 16, 17 eli (aban) pi-i-li dan-ni tim-mi-in-šu ki-ma ši-pik ša-di-i zaq-ri aš-pu-uk ištu uš-ši-šu a-di tax-lu-bi-šu, *etc.* KB vi (1) 424: der *t* (& uššu) eines Prachtbaues wird ... nicht aus Ziegelsteinen gebaut. Darnach der Teil eines Baues, der sich unter dem Ziegelbau befindet, wohl auch mit Einschluss des eigtl. Fundaments; jedenfalls auch die Aufschüttung unter dem eigtl. Bau. — In a more restricted sense, perhaps: — *b*) corner-stone {Eckstein}. I 69 *b* 50 ka-ša-du te-me-en-na Ê-UL-BAR; 52 a-na bu-'-i te-me-en-na šu-a-ti; 56; *c* 19 te-me-en Ê-UL-BAR; 45. I 65 *b* 56 te-me-en-na Ê-AN-NA la-be-ri a-xi-iṭ ab-ri-e-ma (& 58 e-li te-me-en-ša la-be-ri u-ki-in uš-šu-ša; *c* 35 u-ša-ar-ši-id te-me-en-ša). KB iii (2) 78 *col* 2, 21—23 te-im-me-en-ša la-bi-ri a-xi-iṭ ab-ri-e-ma e-li te-im-me-en-ni-šu la-be-ri u-ki-in uš-ši-šu; KB iii (2) 50, 43—44. V 63 *a* 31—33 te-im-mi-en-na la-bi-ru ša *N* ... ap-pa-li-is-ma, e-li te-me-en-na la-bi-ru ad-da-a libnat-su. KB iii (2) 92 *col* 2, 57; 3, 14 ri-tu-u te-me-en-šu. V 65 *a* 19 šarru ma-ax-ri te-me-en la-bi-ri u-ba-'-ma la i-mu-ru (+ 34, 36, 38, 40); see BA i 414 on *ll* 17—28; ZK ii 316. I 51 *no* 2, ii 2 te-me-en-šu la-bi-ri a-xi-iṭ ab-ri-e-ma. V 42 *g-h* 8 IM-TE-ME-EN = temen-nu. S^b 311 tem-me-en-na | TE | te-me-en-nu, Br 7710. 83—1—18, 1330 iv 18 te-me-en | TE | te-me-en-nu, H 21, 567. — *c*) foundation-cylinder inclosed in the corner-stone; mentioned together with narû = memorial cylinder, containing inscriptions. TP viii 43 such & such i-na (aban) narī-ja u tim-me-ni-ja al-ṭu-ur; *cf* Winckler, *Sarg*, i 183 *rm*: Gründungsurkunde; TP viii 56 may he cleanse with oil (*cf* pašašu, Q, 846 *col* 2, end) (aban) narê *pl*-ja u tem-me-ni-ja; see also 63.

tumsuxu (Hommel, *Geschichte*, 533 *rm* 6) see namsuxu, 682, 683; and, again, Streck, ZA xviii 193.

tēmequ. fervor, fervent entreaty {Inbrunst, inbrünstiges Bitten; Flehen} § 65, 32*d*, *rm*. AV 8923. √emequ, 59 *col* 1. TP viii 26 te-me-iq ik-ri-be-ja liš-me-u, H^{CV} xxxvi; L^{TP} 182, may they hearken to my fervent prayers. Also without ikrêbu. Sarg *Khors* 120 (*Ann* 315); V 63 *a* 12; 65 *a* 36 see suppû, 776 *col* 1. Sarg *Cyl* 53 (43) see talīmu; Sp II 265 *a* vii 7 see labanu, 1 (470 *col* 1). K 2852 + K 9662 i 5 ina te-me-ki çu-ul-li-e la-ban ap-pi ka-me-is e-li dûr maxâziśu. K 5418 iii 15 ina te-me-qi ša (il) E-a, KB vi (1) 297 in fervent prayer to Ea. K^M 11, 27 ina ik-ri-be tas(ç)-li-ti u te-me-ki da-riš lu-ziz-ka. H 115 (K 101) *O* 5, 6 te-liq-qi-e te-me-iq-šu (= IV^2 29** *no* 5; Br 720) thou accepts his prayer, Z^B 12; 14. BA i 428. IV^2 54 *a* 35, 36 see rêmu, ℶ.

tum-qu-ma-ti, Anp i 2, 6 *cf* tuqumtu.

tamqēti, Sarg *Khors* 178 tam-qi-ti la nar-ba-a-ti, √na(i)qû, offer, sacrifice; = unceasing sacrifices; preferable to pirqêti, 837 *col* 2. Also see IV^2 60* B *O* 12 ki-i ša tam-ki-tum a-na ili la uk-tin-nu, because they do not bring sacrifice unto god. AJSL xx 205, *no* 5 *rm* 7.

tamaru, pr itmur see šamašu; but M^S 24 *a* 1 reads id-mu-um-ma not it-mu-ru-ma. ℶ V 45 iv 8 tu-tam-mar. Perhaps the same as:

temeru 1. cover, hide {bedecken, verbergen}; but meaning not beyond doubt. AV 8924. II 34 *no* 6 (K 4362 *O*) 67 .... TUL = te-mi-ru ša IŠ (= epri), Br 5108, 9590; 68 ..... SUD-SUD = the same, Br 5106, 7621. KB vi (1) 425, 426 (✕ BA i 269: Rauchsäule); Haupt, AJSL xix, *p* 1: cover with dust; seems to be a denominative verb; √אמר, be high, ascend. — 69 & 70 GIŠ-GUŠUR-R]A(?)-DIB-DIB-BA (Br 240, 5504); KU-KU-NE(bi)-EB (= TUM)-BI (Br 10655) = *t* ša gušûri. Here, perhaps, but not necessarily, the forms quoted on *pp* 356, 357 under ṭamaru.

temeru 2. II 34 *no* 6, 71 NE?] ..... UŠ (= NIT?) Br 4623, 5047 = te-me-ru ša išâti. Ⓗ 51 iv 33 te-me-rum [ša išâti]? followed by na-pa-xu [ša išâti?] & ša-xa-nu. If synonyms, then = ascend (?) said of the fire; but need not be synonyms. Perh. = be bitter (smoky? *cf* tumru) said of the fire. *cf* nitmirtu, chimney (?), hole through which smoke escapes.

tumru. KB vi (1) 447 perh. salt {Salz}. KAT^3 442 *rm* 2 Salz oder wenigstens etwas Salzartiges. 82—8—16, 1 *R* (iv) 18—20 (ni-mu-ur) KI-NE = tu-um-ru ‖ ṭa-ab-tum (see 353 *col* 1) & id(t)-ra-nu; Br 9712; S. A. Smith, *Misc. Texts*, 26;

---

tamqēti see pirqēti, 836 *col* 2.

HOMMEL, *Sum. Lesest.*, 78: smoke {Rauch}. IV² 19 b 39, 40 (Br 7486); NE VI 59 see šapaku, ℚ. IV² 32 *a* 30 (*b* 15; 33 *c* 8 & 35) see bašalu, 201 *col* 1 & read: širu ša (ina) pi-en-ti ba-aš-lu ŠA (= akal) tum-ri he shall not eat. NE V iii (iv) 20 (= Sm 1040) qu-ut-ru] im-taq-qu-tu i-tu-ur ana tu-um-ri, KB vi (1) 165; 447—8: Rauch] (der) niederfiel, wandelte sich in Salz (?). = H^NE 38. Rm 79, 7—8 ŠA-NE-MUR-RA = a-kal tum-ri, ZIMMERN, *Rituall.*, 95 *rm* 2: gesäuertes Brot, >< akal mutqi. kamān tumri see KB vi (1) 447; 511 & KAT³ 442.

NOTE. — D⁸ 81 *rm* 2: a column of smoke; Z^H 76, 77: smoke; reads also V 12 *a-e* 7, 8 (= D 120, 105—6) ŠE-MUR = KI[-MUR] = tu-um-ru); ŠE-NE (= BIL) = KI-NE = ki-nu-nu; V 42 *a-b* 25. Br 7486; ZA i 184. — SCHRADER, KAT² 594 (= date) SAYCE, ZK ii 6 (a palm); PSBA xiii 371 *rm* 2 (& xx 11 *rm* *) combining with תָּמָר, palmtree, properly: the tall, lofty (tree); evidently wrong!

tamru (?) KB vi (1) 200, 18; 218 (= H^NE 78) J suggests š(s)ar-bi u *tam*-rim; & *p* 465 refers to tumru.

timru (?) II 34 *no* 6, 72, 73 ..... XA & XA-NE .... A = XA (= nūnu?) tim-ri, AV 8929.

tāmartu *1.* — *a*) seeing, observing, observation (esp. of stars) {Sehen, Beobachten (namentl. von Sternen}) AV 8738. III 51 *no* 6, 15 bi-it ta-mar-ti = observatory, (K 297, 15). — appearance {Erscheinen} iD ŠI-LAL (III 64 *a* 9), THOMPSON, *Reports*, ii *nos* 7 (K 900) 5; 10 (K 744) 5; 11 (K 1308) 6. 81—2—4, 109 *R* 5 ta-mar-tu ša MUL-LU-BAD; K 856 *R* 4 ta-mar-ti ^(il) Sin; K 1304 *O* 1 (THOMPSON, 244 C; 22 A; 89). III 64 *a* 1, 3, 5, 6 *etc.* when the moon ina ta-mar-ti-šu, when it is observed (is seen in the East); 10 Sin ina ta-mar-ti arax šamē ša-pi-ik šamē ša-pu-u (ZA i 437 *rm* = rību, quarter of the moon {Mondviertel}). *pl* K 1734 *R* 6 A-na eli ta-ma-ra-a-ti a-gan-na-a-ti ša ^(il) Šamaš, THOMPSON, 82. Ēnuma Sin ina ta-mar-ti-šu (& ŠI-GAB-A), name of a series of astrological forecasts, BEZOLD, *Catalogue*, v *pp* xxiv; 2117. — *b*) sight, inspection {Besichtigung, Beobachtung}. K 8182 i 7 a-na ta-mar-ti-ka ix-du[-u], AJSL xvii 134. Asb iv 136 a-na ta-mar-ti nišē māti-ja I brought them to Aššur. KB ii 258, 83 u-še-bil a-na ta-mar-ti ma-ti-tan. a-na (& ana) ta-mar-ti (*var* ŠI-GAB) (u) ši-ta(-as)-si-ja (qi-rib ēkallija ukīn), *etc.*; often in colophons see šasū, ℑ¹. — *c*) aim, goal, toward which one looks {Ziel}. IV² 20 *no* 1, 5—6 (= ŠI-GAB-A) see pāqu, ℑ¹, 819 *col* 2; Br 9329. MARTIN, *Rec. Trav.*, xxiv pts 1/2.

tamārtu (? tāmartu), *2.* & **tamirtu** *1.* AV 8738. payment, tribute, offering, present {Zahlung, Tribut, Geschenk}. KB ii 242, 69 it-ti xu-ub-ti ma-'-di ta-mir-ti ka-bit-ti šal-meš a-tu-ra. Esh iii 4 it-ti ta-mar-ti-šu ka-bit-te he came to Nineveh. III 15 *b* 25 I received ta-mar-ta-šu ka-bit-tu; *Bell* 17; Sn ii 56 ta-mar-ta-šu-nu ka-bit-tu; Sarg *Khors* 160; *Ann* 230 ta-mar-tuš. See also kabtu, 370 *col* 1 *b*; kalū, 1 ℚ *b*, 379 *col* 2, end.

√אמר SCHRADER, KAT²; LATRILLE, ZA i 37; M^S 10 *col* 1; & ZA x 399 = Schau-, Prunkstück; see also *p* 60 *col* 2. — √מחר S. A. SMITH, *Asurb*, ii 15; LYON, *Manual*¹ 116; § 65 *no* 32*d*; ZDMG 40, 154 (= a missive, a gift sent by messenger); ROST, 118; Z^B 54; HAUPT-KITTEL, *Chronicles* (SBOT) 80. — KAT³ 151 on irbu & tamārtu. — ZA i 368 reads Anp i 97 tam (instead of ud)-ra-a-te (= presents) ma-da-ta-šu am-xur.

tāme(a)rtu *2, 3.* vicinity, surrounding, outskirts of a town {Nachbarschaft, Umgebung, Weichbild}, *pl* tamī(ē)ratu. AV 8741; § 65, 32*b*. ZA iii 318 (Sn *Bass*) 86 to plant orchards I gave to the inhabitants of Nineveh eqil ta-mir-ti ēlēn ali, a piece of land in the vicinity, north of the city (*Bell* 58), followed by 87: ultu paṭi ^(al) Ki-si-ri a-di ta-mir-ti ^(al) Ninā, *var* *Kui* 4, 34 ta-mar-ti. Asb iii 41 with their corpses I filled the ta-mir-ti ^(al) Šūšan (*var* KB ii 254, 99 ta-mar-ti). Sn vi 36 qirubū ma'adu ultu kirib u-'š'al-li u ta-mir-ti ali .... lū aç-bata; Sarg *Khors* 128 (*Ann* 325) u-šar-da-a ta-mir-tuš u-'š'al-lum maxāzi .... mē u-mal-li-ma. Perhaps II 60 *col* 2, 25 (K 4334). Battles were fought: ina (& i-na) ta-mir-ti *e.g.* of Kiš, Sn i 21; *Bell* 5; *Kui* 1, 4; of Xalūlē, I 43,

47; Sn *Bav* 35 (HAUPT, *Andov. Rev.*, May '86, 542*foll*); Altaqū, Sn ii 76; *Kui* 1, 29. — Esh *Negoub* 7 ul-]tu šaplān (nâr) Za-ban êli ta-mar-ti (al) Kal-xi, BA iii 206, 207. — *pl* K 3456 *O* 14 ba-ma-a-tum ..... ta-me-ra-a-ti, + 16 i-na ta-me-ra-a-ti id-ni-nu in-gi (+ *O* 31 qi)-ru u-ga-ru, PSBA xxi 37, 38. III 14 (Sn *Bav*) 6 Nineveh's ta-me-ra-tu-šu (KB ii 177: reservoirs {Wasserbehälter}) ša i-na la ma-mi na-mu-ta šu-lu-ka-ma. III 43 iv (*d*) 4 may Adad nârâte sa-ki-ki li-mi-li u ta-mi-ra-ti-šu li-mi-la-a pu-qut-ta, BA ii 139. — Sn *Bav* 28, 29 see kuppu, 420 *col* 2, & translate: Êa, lord of the fountain, the whirlpool, & the pasture (rather than: reservoir). Sarg *Harem*-B 6 see makaru, Š (539 *col* 1); *Cyl* 37 in-ni ta-mir-ti-šu ku-up-pi ka-ra-at-tu pi-te-e-ma ki-i gi-biš e-di-i mê nu-ux-ši šu-uš-ki-e e-liš u šap-liš. — Br. Mus. Texts ii 23. 5; 32, 2; 34, 2—3 (Bu 91—5—9. 307) i-na ta-pi-ir-tim ša A-mu-ru-um, PINCHES, JRAS, July, '97, 597*foll*: in the district of the Amorites. ZA xvii 247 *rm* 3, √תור; also ZDMG 58, 248 >< DAICHES, *Altbabyl. Rechtsurkunden*, ('03) 31, 1. — √amaru, 3 (61 *col* 1); but DELITZSCH, *Lit. Centralbl.*, '82 *cols* 1192—3 √תמר.

tumurtu. BOISSIER, *Doc.*, 1, 6 šumma eribû ina bît amêli tu-mu-ur-ta-šu-nu ušôçûni.

tâmurtu. T. A. (Ber) 24, 75 ta-a-mu-ur-ti, KB v 57, exchange; *cf* תמורה?

tamašu, whence it-mu-šu. II 35 *e-f* 51 ‖ a-la-a-ku; but rather Q^1 of amašu.

timêšu, forgiving {vergebungsvoll} ZA iv 238, 28 (K 2361 ii 6) ti-mi-e-šu qil-la[-tu?], GGA '98, 820; see mâšu, 595 *col* 2.

tam-ša-xu, 82, 9—18, 4156 *R* 12; M^8 *pl* 29.

tam(n)šîlu. § 65, 32*b*, *rm*. HAUPT, Henn. i 219, 220. AV 8755; √mašalu, 604, 605. — *a*) likeness, evenness, similarity; image, picture {Gleichung, Gleichheit, Ebenbild; Bild}. KB ii 246—7, 71 ar-kâ(nu) Te-um-man tam-šil gallê (like a demon) sat upon the throne of Urtaku. Merod.-Balad.-stone ii 31—33 the lofty prince ša ina dun-ni u [ina šar?]-ru-ut la ib-šu-u tam-šil-šu, who has not his equal, KB iii (1) 186; BA ii 261 reads u [gaš?]-ru-tu & i-šu-u; ‖ ša la šanân. IV^2 49 *b* 35, 36 šiptu: (il) Nusku šur-bu-u i-lit-ti (il) A-nim tam-šil abi bu-kur (il) Bêl, = T^M i 122, 123; iii 140 šiptu: la tam (but 30, 426 a *var*-text reads ŠA)-šil *pl* (il) Nusku, BA iv 159. Creat.-*frg* IV 144 eš-k(g)al-la tam-ši-la-šu u-ki-in Êšara(-ra); V 2 kakkabê tam-šil-šu-nu (*i. e.* of the great gods), KB vi (1) 30, 31. Bu 88—5—12, 75 + 76 ii 13 (= K 192 *O*) mêlû kaš-šu tam-šil a-bu-bi; iv 16 tam-šil meš-ri-šu, BA iii 242/3; 246/7 ähnlich seiner Gestalt. V 35, 4 .... ta-am]-ši-li u-ša-aš-ki-na çi-ru-šu-un; (5) ta-am-ši-li Êšakkil i-te[-ni-ib-bu-uš]. — bît xi-la-an-ni ta-an (*var* tam)-ši-il êkal(li) (mât) Xatti, Sarg *Cyl* 64 (54); *bull* 67 (tam-šil); II 67, 68 bît xi-it-la-an-ni tam-šil êkal (mât) Xa-at-ti; see also I 44, 64. Sn *Kui* 4, 4 (625 *col* 2. end) see BA iv 243*foll* & especially *ibid* Note * on *p* 249. Sn *Rass* 85 see ZA iii 317. Esh vi 14 a great park tam-šil (šad) Xa-ma-nim. — On li-ša-an Šu-me-ri tam-šil Ak-k[a-di] see ZA iv 454; WINCKLER, *Forsch.*, iii 206 & *rm* 1; & Šumêru. — *b*) name of a bird {Name eines Vogels}. II 37 *d-f* 13 ....]-SAG-KU = ur(? tas?)-sa-nu = ta-am-ši-lu; same id in 12 = a-xar(xur)-sa-nu, Br 14020; D^8 107 compares Turg חֲסִילָא, & translates wild dove {Wildtaube}. KB vi (1) 491. — *c*) some vessel for wine {ein Weingefäss} II 44 *e-g* 49 [karpat?] tam-ši-lu | ..... | karpat ka-ra[-ni?].

tamšiltu. PINCHES, *Inscr. Tabl.*, *no* 8, 8 three shekel tam-ši-il-tum ša Par-šu-u, and an image from Paršu'u (PINCHES).

tamšâru. KB vi (1) 377; 450—1: whip (of leather, to punish a horse) {Peitsche (aus Leder, mit der das Pferd gequält wird)} √mašaru ‖ gullubu scratch {ritzen}. V 32 *b-c* 48 see dirratu, 269 *col* 1.

tâmt(d)u, tiâmtu (§§ 10; 48 >< ZA iii 187; § 37*a*). *f pl* t(i)âmâte; ta-ma-a-ti (§§ 30; 69), ocean {Meer}. § 65, 12. AV 8756, 8841. Chief id A-AB-BA, Br 11474; see *p* 2 *col* 2. V 69 *a* 7 a-di (šad) Lab-na-na u A-AB-BA (*var* tam-di) ZA i 361. IV^2 20 *no* 1 *a* 21, 22 tam-tum; 30

no 1 *a* 15, 16 ta-a-am-tum, H 41, 282. — IV² 9 *a* 29 tam-tim (28, A-AB-BA) ra-pa-aš-tam; also K 3182 i 35 tam-tim rap-ša-ti ša-dil-ta, & *var* K 3474 ta-ma-tum rapaš-tum ša-di-il-ta; AJSL xvii 136/7. — IV² 8 *a* 16 calm be A-AB-BA ta-ma-tu rapal-tum, *i. e.* the wide ocean of oceans, ZK i 294; 26 *no* 2, 24 (end) sa-pa-ru ša ana tam(! II 183 *no* XVII)-tim tar-çu; H 82—3, 3 u-tuk tam-tim (= A-AB-BA). KB vi (1) 92, 22 ina tam-ti ra-pa-aš-ti. — K 2675 *R* 29 eli tam-tim gal-la-ti (K 3351, 16) e-lu-u-ma; Neb vi 45 ki-ma e-bir ti-a-am-ti (§ 10) gal-la-ti (*f* of gallu, 2). Sn *Kui* (= III R 12 slab 2) ii 32 tam(?)-tim ga-lit-ti (*f* of galtu). Sp II 265 *a* iii 2 ku......... gi-biš tam-tim, ZA x 4. — II 67, 63 bi-nu-ut tam-tim; 81, bi-nu-ut ZU-AB (= apsī). II 19 *b* 17 çir-ruš (?; see 891 *col* 2) tam-tim (= A-AB-BA, 15). III 60, 116 a-gar-ga-ru-tum xi-çib A-AB-BA; 62 *a* 28; II 51 *b* 32. III 4 *no* 7, 17 xi-çib]-ti ti-âmat lu-u al-ma-a; Merodach-Balad.-stone i 15 xi-çib tam-tim. IV² 20 *no* 1, 22 tam-tum (21, A-AB-BA) mi-x(š)ir-ta-šu. V 27 *a-b* 10 see qadū, 6. 81—7—1, 98 iv 9/10 mē tam-tim mē ṭa-bu-tu | mē mar-ru-tu mē I-di-ik-la-at the waters of the ocean are saltish (? Pinches, *Jou. Trans. Vict. Inst.*, xxvi 155, sweet), but bitter are the waters of the Tigris. — Šalm, *Obel*, 28 ina tam-di; *Mon*, ii 58, 59 (ina libbi tam-di; *cf* בלב ים, Haupt, *Proverbs* (SBOT) 58, 2; AJSL xx 162). Asb i 69: twenty-two kings ša a-xi tam-tim (*cf* ix 116) qabal tam-tim u na-ba-li; Esh i 29; Sn iii 58; TP III *Ann* 126 a-ax t]am-tim. Šalm, *Obel*, 61 kings of (māt) Xat-te u a-xat tam-ti; II 52 *c* 61 see pītu, 1 (852, 853). TP III *Ann* 146 Sianna ša šid-di tam-tim; also see šiddu, 1. K 2675 *R* 27 a-šib ra-pa-aš-ti qa-bal tam-tim, KB ii 170; Smith, *Asurb*, 68, 60—61; Sn iii 57 *N* ša qa-bal tam-tim; ii 37 = into the ocean; Esh i 9 & 16 ina *q t*. Asb ii 95 Lydia na-gu-u ša ni-bir-ti tam-tim. Neb 329, 17 na-gi-i ni-su-tu ša ki-rib tam-tim; Esh i 12 ki-rib tam-tim (& 17). V 33 iii 33 ta-am-tu lu-aš-ku-nu, KB iii (1) 142, 143 & *rm* †. KB vi (1) 40, 10 & 11 nap-xar ma-ta-a-tu tam-tum-ma i-nu ša ki-rib tam-tim ra-ṭu-um-ma; 96 (*Adapa*-legend) *R* 14 i-na ga-a-ab-la-at ta-am-ti; 15 ta-am-ta i-na mi-še-li im-ši-il-ma; 112 (*Etana*-legend) 27 tam-tum i-tu-ra a-na me-e(-)[....]; 26; 33; 114, 20 u tam-tum rapaš-tum (23; 26 -tu). NE X ii 18 (end) A-AB-BA lu-bir; 22 (end) no one (la) ib-bi-ru tam-ta + 23 (tam-ti); 26 a-lum-ma (il) Gilgameš te-te-bir tam-ta; *del* 116 (124) ki-i mārē nūnē u-ma-al-la-a tam-ta-am-ma, (BA i 132; KB vi (1) 238—9); iD A-AB-BA 125 (132), 132 (139); 281 (256), 288 (265) li(& u)-bil tam-tim; 129 (133) ap-pa-al-sa-am-ma ū-mu (*var* ta-ma-ta) KB vi (1) 289; 498. Haupt, BA i 134, 135 perh. = ud-mu & PAOS Mr. '99 cv *rm*: reading ud-mu = Hebr אֲדָמָה. J^I-X 9 tāmtu in NE = Persian Gulf {persischer Meerbusen}. — Ba'alra'si ša rēš tam-di, III 5 *no* 6. 60/1; KAT³ 43, 190. Asb iii 98 (māt) A-ra (*var* ru)-mu (and) māt tam-tim from Aqaba to Bābsalimēti; iv 97 = the sea-country; Bezold, *Catalogue*, v: country on the Persian Gulf. II 67, 26 Merodach Baladan šar tam-tim; I 48, 8; Neb 109, 17 (amēl) ki-i-pi ša (māt) tam-tim, the prefect of the sea-country; KB vi (1) 66, 10 tam-tim tam-tim; Neb 109, 4, 16, 18; 116, 14; 166, 14; Hebr. i 221 *rm* 4. — K 312, 1 a-na (amēl) māt tam-tim-a-a; 83—1—18, 28, 7 ši-pir-ti (amēl) māt tam-tim-u-a (Hr^L 289; 344). — On Esh *B* i kings of (māt) Xatti u ebir tamdi see KAT³ 188 & *rm* 1.

pl II 66 *no* 1, 4 (Ištar) da-li-xat ta-ma-a-te. Neb ii 35 xi-iç-bi ta-ma-a-tim (§ 72*a*; Pognon, *Wadi-Brissa*, 31 *foll*); vi 42 great waters ki-ma gi-bi-iš ti-a-ma-ti māta u-ša-al-mi; I 65—66 ii 13 ki-ma gi-bi-iš ti-a-am-tim; iii 22 xi-çib ta-ma-a-tim; V 63 *b* 47 nu-xu-uš ta-ma-a-ti. NE X v (H^NE 71) 27 la?] e-te-te-bi-ra ka-li-ši-na ta-ma-a-tum, *cf* 25.

On the names of the seas & oceans see Schrader, *Die Namen der Meere, etc.* (*Abh. Berl. Akad.*, 1877, 177—81). tāmtu rapaštu perh. = Mediterranean sea. TP iv 50 to the countries of far-off kings ša a-ax tâmti e-li-ni-te (D^{Par} 185 Mediterranean sea); vi 43 as far as the land of the Xatti u tâmti (wr. A-AB-BA) e-li-ni-te ša ša-la-mu (il) Šam-ši. II 67, 4 tam-tim ša šul-mi šam-ši a-di (mât) Mu-uç-ri; Šalm, *Obel*, 27; Šamš ii 21. Sn i 13, 14 ul-tu tâmti e-li-ni-ti ša ša-lam šam-ši a-di tam-tim (*var* tâmti) šap-li-ti (D^{Par} 185, Persian Gulf) ša çi-it šam-ši. — Asb i 19 the kings ša tam-tim e-li-ti u šap-lit; V 35, 29 the kings iš-tu tam-tim e-li-tim a-di tam-tim šap-li-tim. Neb ii 15, 16 iš-tu ti-a-am-te e-li-te a-di ti-a-am-ti ša-ap-li-ti. Sarg *Khors* 153 a-na tam-tim ša çi-it Šamši (Esh i 32; 33); 146 Cypress ina qabal tam-tim e-reb šam-ši (148); Jensen, 248. I 35 *no* 1, 10—11 (13) a-di eli tam-tim rabî-ti ša na-pax (šul-mu) šam-ši; 13 a-di eli tam-tim rabî-ti ša šul-mu; & *cf no* 3, 5—7. III 4 *no* 6, 8/9 ištu tam-di rabî-te ša (mât) A mur(xur?)-ri a-di tam-di ša (mât) Na-i-ri. Šalm, *Mon*, i 26 a-na tam-di ša (mât) Na-i-ri; ii 58, 59. (Streck, ZA xiii 67).

Winckler, *Untersuch.*, 110 *rm* 3; *Forsch.*, i 104. tâmtu elînîtu (in general) = Mediterranean sea; šaplîtu = Persian Gulf; *t e* ša (mât) A-mur(xar, xur)-ri = Mediterr. sea (or gulf of Issus); *t š* ša (mât) *A* = sea of Antiochia. *t e* ša (mât) Nairi = Lake Van; *t š* ša (mât) *N* Lake Urumiah. — *t* ša napax šamši Caspian Sea. tâmtu ša çît šamši = Persian Gulf; *t* ša šulmu šamši, the Black Sea. *t* šaplîtu ša ereb šamši = the Red Sea. See, in addition, Streck, ZA xiii 67 *foll.*

II 5 *c-d* 4 e-reb (= grasshopper?) tam-tim (= A-AB BA). K 4418, 2/3 (šam) im-bu-u tam-tim (ocean-flora), Br 12138 ‖ (šam) ša-mi ki-rib tam-tim; (šam) KA-A-AB-BA (= nib tâmtim); 5/6 (šam) ku-sa A-AB-BA = (šam) mul (or MUL?) ta-am-tim; which latter also = (šam) ku-sa ia-a-me (see iâmu, 360 *col* 1; BA i 171 *rm* *) = II 41 *no* 10 *a-b* 41/42; 44/45. S^c 95 ab | AB | tam-tum. V 39 *c-d* 15, 16; V 21 *g-h* 43 (65) NE-RU = tam-tim, Br 4608.

Etymology: — L^{TP} 143 [illegible]; D^{H} 66; D^{Pr} 113; Jensen, 246; 307 *foll*; 542 √[illegible] desert; perhaps connected with [illegible]; so already Guyard, *RHRelig.*, i 340; AJP v 77 ZA ii 267 & *rm* 3; v 101. KB vi (1) 559, 560; & KB^{3} 493 √[illegible] (= [illegible]) stink ‖ stinken. JA '97 Ja 112 *foll.*

Note. — 1. V 19 *a-b* read xa-na-b(p)u ša pir-tim (Br 14796; see 339 *col* 2, end).

2. I 28 *a* 13, 14; KB 124 na âma-at; Oppert, tâm-at; ZA i 239; 437, 438; ii 230, 231.

3. Asp iii 31 TA (= ištu) pi-a-te (nâr) Xa-bur see pû, 1 (789 *col* 1, *med*), & *pl* of pîtu, (832, 853) read by Sayce, RP^{2} ii 165 *rm* 2: ta-pi(= ia ma a-te; this reading is supported perhaps by K 5296 A-AB-BA = ti-pi (= ia = a)-ma D 26 *rm* 1; ZA ii 74, 75; v 89. K 3473 (L^{TP} 113) ti-pi-pi (= a-ia = a-ma)-ti, BA i 453; Z^{B} 86 *rm* 1.

Tiâmat. a personification of t(i)âmtu, in Creat.-*frgg* mostly written Ti-âmat. Creat.-*frg* I *a* 4 (D 93, 4) mu-al-li-da-at gi-im-ri-šu-un. On kirbiš Tiâmat, IV 41 (kir-bi-iš); 48 (kir-biš) *etc.* see qirbiš. I *b* 6 a-na [Ti-a-ma-t]u; II *a* 26 Ti-a-ma]-tim; *b* 10 me-ku-uš Ti-pi-pi(= a-ma)-ti = ša *T.* mêkiša (D 97, 30; BA i 453); III (19) 77 i-du-uš *T.* *cf* I *c* 5 i-du-uš Ti-a-mat; IV 65 qab-lu-uš *T.*; 129 ša Ti-a-ma-tum i-šid-sa; III 15 um-ma *T.* KB vi (1) 292, 15 Ti-a-ma-tu u-ša niq-šu-nu-ti, es säugte sie *T.* See Delitzsch, *Chald. Gen.*, 293 *foll*; *Weltschöpfungsepos*, 127, 128. Hommel, *Gesch.*, 313 *rm* 1; Guyard § 106 *p* 98; on Guyard, ZK 103 see BA i 406. KAT^{3} 491; 498 on apsû (= sweet water) & Tiâmat (= salt water); also *ibid* 373; 391; 509, 511, 585; KB vi (1) 302—4. PAOS xv *pp* xiii *foll* ὕδωρ of Berosus; Jensen, 307 *foll.* Stucken, *Astralmythen*, 57 *rm* * Berosus: Θαμτε, ZA vi 339 Damascius Ταυθε (§ 44). On ummu xubur & Tiâmat see *p* 303; KB vi (1) 303; 307—8; 541; 561. — Tiâmat instead of tâmtim, also in historical texts, *e. g.* Asurb ii 58 (ti-âmat).

tamê(î)tu *f* § 108 (end); √tamû, 1. — *a*) speech, wording {Rede, Wortlaut}. I 27 *no* 2, 62—3 whosoever ta-me-it šiț-ri-ia um(I Rawl. ta)-ma-na-te a-na a-ma-ri u ša-si-e i-kal-lu-u; 55, 56 ta-me-it | [ša?] šiț-ri-ia; 74 ta-me-ti ana šu-un-ni, to change my wording (*i. e.* the inscription on top of the statue); see also šițru. Šamš i 42, 43 niše (mât) Aššur e-liš u šap-liš it-ti-šu u-šeš-kin-ma u-dan-ni-na ta-me-tu; perh.

‖ udannina riksāte, Asb i 22. — *b*) enquiry (properly address, speech) to a god concerning human affairs *etc.* {Anfrage (eigtl. Anrede); concerning documents of that kind see ZIMMERN, *Rituall.*, 191 *rm a* & *b*; see also *ibid*, *pp* 88, 89 & *rm* 6 on *p* 88; *ibid*, *no* 75—78, 10 + 61 + 74 ta-mit a-kar-ra-bu, die Anfrage die ich weihe; also *no* 79—82 iii 16; iv 9; 83 ii 2; 88 *O* 6; 95 *O* 1 + 19 + 24; *no* 16, 15 ta-mit ilāni rabūti (K^{M} 1, 16 + 17); 100, 30 ta-mit mār bārē. KNUDTZON, *Gebete*, *pp* 42; 47; 50; 324; answer; esp. oracular answer {Ausspruch, spez. Orakelausspruch}; 1 *R* 6 heed not that .... ta-mit ina pi-ja up-tar-ri-du (see paradu). tāmit piri'š'ti, geheimnisvoller Ausspruch; K 2486, 3? *etc.* = the divine oracle, revealed (pētū) to the bārû; JENSEN, *Theol. Litztg.*, '99 *no* 2, *col* 33. ZIMMERN, *Rituall.*, 1—20, 18 + 26 ta-mit pi-ri'š'-ti(te) bārūti; *l* 119 ta-mit pi-ri'š'-ti ul i-ta-mu-šu; *no* 24, 38 (39) ta-mit pi-ri'š'-ti ul i-pat-tu-šu. V 29 *a-b* 72 ZAG = ta-mi-tu & pi-ri'š'-tu, AV 8742; Br 6493. II 7 *c-d* 33, 34 ZAG = ta-me-tu; ZAG-KU = *t* ta-mu-u, Br 6493, 6510, 10555. — A ‖ may be:

tu-mu-tum. V 11 *a-c* (D 127) 34; H 113, 31; AV 9033.

tamtalku. Perhaps III 8 *no* 6, 15 ir-šu çi-i-ru qar-rad (*q. v.*) tam-tal[-ku]. √malaku.

ta-a-an, following or preceding terms of measurement, capacity, or cardinal numerals. = ta *i. e.* TA (= ina or ana) + a-an *c. st.*, of ānu, see 65 *col* 1. Also written ta-an, a-an, 'a, 'a-n. See for examples & further discussion, MUSS-ARNOLT, AJSL xx, 231, 232, *no* 24. Also IV^{2} 34 i *O* 27, 28 five ta-a-an mid-bak u-rap-pi-šu; Asb ix 66 ina eli VII (ta-a-an) mūšēniqūti ēniqûma.

ta-nu = dannu (?) T. A (Ber) 25 ii 36 ina pa-ra-ak-ka ta-nu xurāçu.

tannu. id GIŠ-LIŠ]-TUR. D 87 iii 43 *etc.* ‖ tulū, 1. AV 8765; Br 6787; id also = nalpatu, 679 *col* 1.

tanū, AV 8764 *ad* Anp i 83 see natanu, 743 *col* 2.

tēnu *1.* in u-ki-in te-en-šu, KB iii (2) 4 *col* 2, 45 *etc.* read TE (= temēn-en)-šu.

tēnu *2.* grind {mahlen} see ṭēnu, 357 *col* 1; KB iii (1) 41 (not 141) *rm* **†. Bu 91—5—9, 2176 A 26 maš(bar?)(-)šu-ši i-te-en-ma, her meal she shall grind, JRAS, July '97, 607—8. IV^{2} 3 *b* 61, 62 (end) XAR-XAR = te-en-ma pm, ZIMMERN, *Rituall.*, 149 *rm* *μ*; GGA '98, 826. SCHEIL, Notes LX: Constant. 588 *R* 20 te-ṭi-en, thou shalt cook; perh. *O* 8 te-ne-e-ti (?), might be *pl* of a *n* derived from the verb; or to tenū, 1? AV 8936.

tenū *1.* Nabd 78, 1 max]-çu te-nu-u; 694, 27; Cyr 232, 14 (iç) te-nu-u; 241, 1 mi-ix-çi te-nu-u, in a list of bands, ribbons, *etc.* {in einer Liste von Bändern}, see enū headgear, band, ribbon *etc.* Perhaps here V 28 *g-h* 58 te(?)-nu, BA i 533, end; & 81, 11—28, 33, 4 (çubāt) tin-nu; AJSL xv 77 translates: couch.

tenū *2.* resting place, couch, bed {Ruhelager, Bett} § 65, 32 *a*; √תנה$_{1}$; Z^{B} 44 *rm* 3; 117. AV 8937. II 28 *c-d* 60 (iç) te-nu-u ‖ ir-šu. V 63 *a* 45 la i-ba-aš-šu-u te-na-a-šu (of the foundation of the parakku of the sun-god); 46 te-ni-e parakki šu-a-ti, >< rāšu; ZA v 403, 408. — bedchamber, resting place {Schlafgemach} Asb x 51 te-ni-e ēkalli, in apposition to the bīt ridu-u-ti. — place, stead {Statt}? K 120 *b* + 144 + 3298 + 3265, 24 of Sandakšatra, his son, ša a-na te-ni-šu iš-ku-nu, whom they (the people) had put in his place, MESSERSCHMIDT, *Nabuna'id*, 64.

NOTE. — Does here also belong II 23 *c-d* 67 ki-it-b(p)ar-at-tum (√kaparu?, whence kapru, village, settlement) = tin-nu-u (see dinnū, 259 *col* 2), in a group with (iç) du-un-nu (64) = ma-a-a-al-tum, & ma-ra-šum (66); AV 8940. If so, then here, also, dinnūtu.

tenū *3.* II 30 *no* 4 *R* 13 (41) BAR = te-nu-u (Br 1808; AV 8937) = a-xu-u & a-xi-tu.

ta-an-ga-lu-u ? Nabd 84, 4.

tinida. T. A. (Ber) 28 ii 48 .... nu-ni ša kaspu ti-ni-da šum-ša, called *t.* BA iv 105, 106 on such words.

tānixu. § 65, 32 *b*; AV 8768; Z^{B} 30; HAUPT, *Sintfl. Ber.*, 25, 26. √anaxu, 2, 69—70. lamentation, sighing, sigh; pain {Wehklagen, Seufzen; Schmerz}. H 115—6 (K 101) *R* 9, 10 like a dove adammum ta-ni-xu (= A-ŠE-IR-RA, EME-SAL,

Br 11574) uš-ta[-bar-ri], I am full of sighs. ZK ii 281; Z^B 10 reads uš-ta[-na-ax]. Same id in IV² 26 *b* 50, 51 ina ta-ni-xi a(character pi)-ši-ib; see also H 180 iv (K 4926) 9—10; IV² 11 *a* 37, 38. V 52 *R* 40 ta-ni-xu (= A-ŠE-IR, 39) ina ma-a-tum ki-ma ša-mu-ti u-ša-az-nin; *O* 65 ša ka-ra-na im-lu-u in-na-ku-u ta-ni-xu it-ta-an-ki (= נקי √na(i)qū?), where wine is wont to be poured out, there he pours (or, are poured) out sighs. ZA iii 343, 344. IV² 26 *b* 54, 55 ina ta-ni-xi (= A-NIR-RA, Br 11541) lim-ni (‖ ina bikīti limutti; Z^B 85); 60, 61 ta-ni-xa (= A-NIR) mar-ça-am iš-ta-na-ka-an; AJSL xix 225 § 63. IV² 24 *no* 3, 20—21 ta-ni-xi ū-me-šam uš-ta-bar-ri (see H 208 *no* 49 on this text); IV² 7 *b* 3 *etc.* see xablatu (= qillatu) 301 *col* 1 = $Z^Š$ v/vi 68 *etc.*; IV² 54 *a* 14 murçu .... eli-šu ir-te-ix-xu-u im-ṭu-u ta-ni-xu; 57 *a* 51 a-lal di-xu(-?)u ta-ni-xu = K^M 12, 51 who reads A-LAL (= alū) di-xu u ta-ni-xu. Xamm.-*code* xliii 54, 55 i-na ta-ne-xi-im u di-im-ma-tim, ZA xviii 30. K 2660 *R* 15 see ma'ālu, 507 *col* 2; KB ii 244, 53 ina ta-ni-xi iq-tu-u. T^M vii 126 qu-lu k[u-ru ni-is]-sa-tu ni-ziq-tu im-ṭu-u ta-ni-xu; KB vi (1) 364; ZA iv 237 i 38; 252, 13 + 15. K 155, 45 (*b*) li-ta-kil (or -rid? Henn. xi 102, 103) ta-ni-xu ša šēri *pl* [-ja] ‖ li-in-ni-is-si murçu ša zumri-ja; 48 *b* perh. li-ta-kil ni[-is-sa-ti-ja]; K^M 33, 29; K 2866, 26 ($Z^Š$ viii) mu-ru-uç-ka ta-ni-ix-ka. $Z^Š$ iv 64 u-a a-a ūm la ça-lal-šu na-zaq-šu ni-is-sa-su ta-ni-ix-šu; 84; 86 may *Ninkarrag* ta-ni-xu ša zumri-šu lis-si; on *l* 36 see AJSL xiii 147; NE IX iv 35 ina ta-ni-xi preceded by ina ni-is-s[a(-a?)-ti?] & ina s(š)a(i)r-bi. — *pl* IV² 59 *no* 2 *b* 13 ta-ni-xe-ja lit-ba-lu sibit šārē. Asb iv 10 ta-ni-xe-ja im-xu-ru (*var* to un-nin-ni-ja il-qu-u) KB ii 158, 159. — V 22 *h* 42 ta-ni-xu = [A-ŠI (e-ir)]; & perh. *h* 11; un-ni-nu = ta[-ni-xu] see *ibid* 43; Br 11619. II 62 *c-d* 22 NIR = ta-ni-x[u], Br 6287. a *f* is:

tānixtu. K^M 15, 15 ina šu-bat ta-ni-ix-ti-ja. K 2711 *R* 37 šu-bat ta-ni-ix-ti ša .....; BA iii 260: the habitation of the quiet, rest, of; evidently assuming √nāxu?

tēnixu *1.*, **tēnixū**, bed, couch {Bett, Lager}; √nnaxu, 1. § 65, 32*b*; AV 8932. II 23 *d* 59 ir-šu = te-ni-xu (*c*); 61 = (*sic*) te-ni-xu-u. Lehmann, *Šamaššumukîn*, √נוח reading K 501, 16 (Hr^L 113) ina bīt te-niẋi (or irši?); Br 9000; Jensen, ZK ii 39.

tēnixu *2.* distaff {Spinnrocken}?? $Z^Š$ v/vi 149 sin-niš-tu e[t-peš-tu ina te-ni-]xa u-še-šib.

tinanū. V 26 *e-f* 24 GIŠ[-AT?, but see Johns, PSBA '05, 36]-GIŠ-MA = ti-na-nu-u, AV 8931; Br 14238. Zimmern, ZDMG 58, 952 fig {Feige}; *cf* GIŠ-MA = t[i-it-tu].

tenanū? T^M ii 133 (= K 2455, 21) e-peš bar-ti te-na-na-a ku-šu-ud lim-nu; seize the wicked, that rebels (against me); that resists me; *ibid* 133 √אנן₄; so also Martin, *Textes Relig.*, '03, 50.

tinīnu, grace, favor {Gnade} √a₃nanu, 2; Z^B 23; 86. AV 8933. V 21 *a-b* 66 ti-ni-nu = ri-e-mu. a *f* is:

tinīntu; *ibid* 67 *a* ti-ni]n-tum = ri-e-mu.

tēnīnu. sigh, sighing, imploring {Seufzer, Flehen} √ananu, 1 (70 *col* 1). IV² 54 *a* 22 dulūl(*b*?, see KB vi (1) 338, 475)šu iqabbi ina te-ni-ni; Z^B 28; 88; 95; Haupt-Cheyne, *Isaiah* (SBOT) 117 *rm* *.

tēnīntu. *f* imploring, prayer {Flehen, Gebet}. K 143 *O* 16 a-na te-nin-ti ni-iš qātija sux-xi-ra-ni pa-ni-ku-nu; see 752—3.

ta-an-ni-is in T. A. = danniš. ZA v 154 *rm* 5; T. A. (Lo) 8, 31; also ZA v 201 *foll*; Hilprecht, *Assyriaca*, 121 *rm*. Also ta-an-ni-iš, (Ber) 22 *R* 9.

tanpaxu. 82, 9—18, 4156 *R* 17 [UX] = ta-an-pa-xu, M^S *pl* 29. Same √as nappaxtu, 707 *col* 1.

tēniqu. baby, suckling {Säugling} √enequ, 72 *col* 1; § 65, 32*b*. AV 8935; Lhotzky, *Anp*, 27, 28. II 35 (K 4320) *a-b* 12 te-ni-qa (II Rawl. -tu) = li-pi-li-pi. $Z^Š$ iii 9 mūmit d(t)ar-ka-ti u te-ni-qi

---

ta-na-ca, App ii 5 (end); AV 8759; KB i 72 corrects to ta-na-ti, see tanattu. ~ tannīnu see dannīnu, 261 *col* 2.

(ki); T^{M} 138; Z^{Š} iii 163; Sm 787 + Sm 949 *O* 20; *ibid p* 55.

tanûqatum. howling, shouting {Geheul, Geschrei}. KB vi (1) 322. √nâqu. V 40 *g-h* 10 (ti-il) AŠ = ta-nu[-qa-tum], preceded by ši-si-tum & ri[-ig-mu] & followed by (ta-al) DIŠ = ik-ki[l-lum] ZA i 187. K 4219 *O* 10, 11. M^{S} *pl* 10. V 23 *no* 1, *d* 2 ta-nu[-qa-tum], preceded by ši[-si-tum] & followed by bit-t[a-ku-u?]; also see Babyl. dupl. 76, 4—13, M. 83, 1—18, 1330 i 10 (ta-al) ŠU-KAT-ŠU-KAT = ta-nu-qa-tum, preceded by ši-si-tum, ZA xv 44. *pl* Rm 3, 105 ii 8 ta-nu-qa-a-ti, JRAS '92, 350 *foll.*

tinûru. *m* oven {Ofen}. T^{M} ii 172 a-li-ku ti-nu-ru, a portable stove; ‖ iv 114 ana u-tu-ni a-lik-ti; iii 171 ki-ma ti-nu-ri ina xi(*var* xa)-ṭa-ti-ku-nu, followed by ki-ma di-qa-ri ina lu-xu-um-me-ku-na. Z^{Š} viii 58 itti ma-mit utûni la-ab-ti ti-nu-ri kinûni KI-UD-BA u nap-pa-xa-tu. II 16 *c-d* 10—13 ki-ma ti-nu-ri la-bi-ri, *etc.* see BA ii 294—6; ZK i 120. V 42 *a-b* 27 IM-ŠU-RIN-NA (see šurinnu, 2) = ti-nu-ru followed by same id + du-du = mut-tal-li-ku, a portable oven, Br 8372, 8459; 29 KA-PAR(TAM)-IM-ŠU-RIN-NA = ka-par(tam) ti-nu-ri, (Br 732; V 39 *a-b* 58); 30, ‹ IM-ŠU-RIN-NA = pi-k(q)al-lu-lum, see 801 *col* 2. S 28 NE(=BIL)-GAR = te-nu-u-ri (ZA viii 203).— ZK ii 52 on II 51 *b* 9.— See AV 8938; §§ 64, *rm*; 83 *rm*; D^{H} 42; D^{Pr} 146; Nöldeke, ZDMG 40, 742; Z^{B} 14; WZKM i 23; Haupt. i 182, 183; T^{M} 169 √נור (nûru); Hommel, ZDMG 44, 546; BA ii 294 *ad* § 83 *rm.* — On the other hand, Dvořák, ZK i 115—150 maintains Indo. Germ. origin. see also Fränkel, *Aram. Lehnwörter*, 26 (from the Persian); while Halévy, *Mém. de la Soc. de ling. de Paris*, xi 87 derives the Persian *tanûra* from the Semitic; he refers to Isa 30, 9: תַּנּוּר. See, also, JA, Ja.-Feb., '05, 141—3.

tênišêtum. — *a*) human beings, mankind {Menschen, Menschheit} in general. §§ 32 *aa*; 65, 32 *b*. AV 8934. √enešu, 1 (*p* 72). Merod.-Balad.-stone i 12, 13 (Marduk) muš-te-ši-ru te-ni-še-e-ti. Šalm, *Mon.* i 3 Šamaš muš-te-šir te[-ni]-še-e-ti, KB i 152, 153. Asb i 11 Êa bêl te-ni-še-e-ti; KB ii 236, 1; IV^{2} 33 iv coloph. (Winckler, *Forsch.*, ii, 3, 367); Z^{Š} iv 70. Neb x 10 ša ka-la te-ni-še-e-ti, of all mankind; Ner ii 38 (ka-al *etc.*); I 66 *c* 52 (te-ne-še-e-ti); 65 *a* 2 Nebuk. mu-ut-ta-ru-u te-ne-še-ti. KB iii (2) 88 *a* 32 (Šamaš) be-lu te-ni-še-e-tim; ZA ii 133 *a* 7. K 101 (H 115; IV^{2} 29**) *O* 9, 10 (be-lit) te-ni-še-e-ti = A-ZA-LU-LU, EME-SAL, Br 1335, 11703. K 4931 (H 116) *O* 7, 8. *del* 127 (134) kul-lat te-ni-še-e-ti. K 3182 i 51 .....]-nik-ka kul-lat-si-na te-ni-še-e-ti = ZA iv 8, 49. K 2001 *O* 10 Ištar called bânat tênišêti, KAT³ 428 *rm* 3. K 152 iv 61 = II 24 *e-g* 24 A-Z]A-LU-LU = te-ni-še-e-tum ‖ a-me-lu-tum, Br 11703; VATh 244 iii 25 *foll*; ZA ix 159 *foll. c. st.* TP vii 50, 51 mul-taš-pi-ru te-ni-šet (il) Bêl. See also Zimmern, *Rituall.*, 55, 9; Sarg *Cyl* 53 (43) see talîmu. K^{M} 2, 19 = K 2487 + K 81220 ta-dan di-in te-ni(*var* ne)-še-e-ti; 3, 16; 19, 13; 50, 9; te-ni-še-ti 9, 52; 12, 33 ir-šu bu-kur (il) Êa ba-nu-u te[-ni]-šit gim-ri. KB vi (1) 282, 23 (+25) ut-ta-z(ç)a-ma ta-ni-še-ti. — *b*) in a more restricted sense: the inhabitants of a country *etc.* Sarg *Ann* 428 te-ne-še-ti (373 te-ni-še-e-ti) ma-ti-tan ša .... ak-šud-du-ma; *Pp* II 43; while *Khors* 165 da-ad-me ma-ti-tan. Sn *Bell* 42 te-ne-šit of the lands of Chaldea, Aramea, *etc.* *Bass* 69 (ZA iii 314); *Kui* 3, 12 te-ne-šit (amêl) Kal-di.

tunšu (?), tunšânu, tuššu *1.* perh. turban, headgear, or the like {Turban}. BA i 519, 520 √נשׁו. Nabd 467, 4—5 a-na pit-qa tu-un-ša-nu (BA i 525); 415, 4 a-na pit-qa ša (çu-bat) tu-un-za(? = ša?)-a-nu .... ša (ilat) Anunîtum; 329, 4 written tu-un-ça-nu; Camb 4, 4 a-na pit-qa ša tun(-un)-ša-nu. BA i 519 quotes tunšu explained as lubuštum qaqqadi from VATh 266, an unedited (?) text at Berlin. If so, then also perhaps K 4152 + 4183 *R* 40 e-peš tu-un-ši = xu .... M^{S} *pl* 7. V 32 *d-f* 24 AMÊL U(=ŠAM)-TIR/TIR-TAG-GA = e-piš tu-uš-ši = xup-pu-u, Br 6065; 26 *d-e* (amêl) xup-pu (*e* 25 xup-pu-u) = xu-up-pu-u; II 51 *no* 2 *R* 13 AMÊL-TIR/TIR-TAG-GA = e-piš tu[-uš]-ši = xup

[-pu-u], Br 7747. BA i 520 explains KU-SAG, KB iv 272, 6 = cover of the head as tuššu.

tanattu, tanātu, *pl* tanadāte. loftiness, glory, fame, majesty }Erhabenheit, Ehre, Ruhm, Majestät}. § 65, 32*a*; AV 8758, 8760. √na'adu, nādu, 1 (527, 528) > tanādtu. Anp iii 25, 26 *Anp* ša ta-na-ta-šu (KGF 142; ZK i 160; ZA i 355) da-na-a-nu ka-ja-ma-nu; ii 5 ta-na-ti kiš-šu-ti-ja šu-tur(*var* tu-ur)-te u il-ka-kat (*var* ka-at) qur-di-ja (I wrote thereon); *cf* i 98, 99 li(-i)-ta u ta-na-ti (ina libbi) aš-ṭu-ur; ta-na-ti giš-ru-ti-a ina libbi alṭur. Šalm, *Mon*, ii 44 ta-na-ti (il) Ašur bēli rabē bēlija (I wrote on the statue); 55 (ša il A.); 59; 62; i 71. K 2729, 22 ta-na]-at-ta-šu ax-su-us, KB iv 142. V 34 *a* 16 Babylon ER-KI (= al) ta-na-da-a-tu-šu (*i. e.* of Marduk); KB iii (2) 48 *a* 55. V 65 *b* 12 to the gods my lords bīt ta (*var* da)-na-da-a-tu (*var* ti) ušēpiš. ZK ii 336; 346; ZA vii 174. Synchr. Hist. iv 27 ta-na-ti (māt) Aššūr lid-lu-lu (KB i 202); V 66, 18 Nebo . . . ša a-na ta-na-da-a-ti šit-ku-nu. Zimmern, *Ritualt.*, no 11 *R* 15 NAM-BUR-BI (= tapširti?) ta-na-at (*var* IM-TUK(?))-ti ba-ru-ti a-ma-ru. K 5332 (H 121) *R* 2 nar-bi ta-na-at-ti-ka . . . . lid-lu-la (Br 5794) see dalalu 250 *col* 1. — Sm 954 *O* 33/4 ta-na-da-tu-u-a (= UB-RI-MU, EME-SAL); 41/42 —*R* 7/8, the glory is mine! AJSL xix 207. IV² 60* C *R* 11 (B *O* 31) ta-na-da-a-ti šarri i-liš umaššil, see 605 *col* 1; 13 *b* 13, 14 (end) ana ta-na-da-a-te liš-kun-ka, may he make it unto thee for glory, AJSL xix 215, § 24. KB iii (1) 112/3 ii 12—14 ta-na-da-ti-ka ra-bi-a-tim li-iš-ta-ni-da. ZA v 66, 2 bēlit ta-na-da-a-ti (of Ištar). II 35 *a-b* 32 UB (= AR) = ta-na-at-tum, Br 5784, preceded by te-el-tum, *q. v.* 82, 8—16, 1 *O* 48 a-rat-ta | iD (Br 9054) ¦ ta-na-da-tum; same iD = kabtu & arattū. A ‖ is:

tanittu *1.* § 65, 32*b*; AV 8761. TP III *Ann* 222 ta-nit-]ti be-lu-ti-ja. Šalm, *Mon*, i 27 ta-nit-ti (il) Ašur bēli rabī bēlija u lītī kiššūtija I wrote thereon. Asb i 30 a-da-bu-ba ta-nit-ta-šu-un (*i. e.* of the great gods); viii 8 a-na kul-lum ta-nit-ti (il) Ašur *etc.*; ix 112 (H^F 29; Hebr. i 217*foll*; Z^B 69; KB ii 216). V 34 *b* 52 ta-ni-it-ti ilāni li-ix-ta-as-sa-as, let him remember the majesty of the gods. K 2852 + K 9662 i 7 qur-di (il) Ašur bēli-ja u ta-nit-ti qar-ra-du-ti-ja iq-ta-nab-ba-a (& 17 lu-ša-pa-a ta-nit-ti (il) Ašur). Esh *Sendsch*, *R* 51, 52; II 67, 39 qur-di ta-nit-ti ša (il) Ašur. K 192 *R* 23 (aban) ça-lam-ti (879 *col* 2) ta-nit-ti bēli rabi-e bēli-ja (il) Marduk. Pinches, *Texts*, 16 (DT 83) *R* 11 ta-nit-ta-šu le-i-ni(‼ šu-uš-qu-us-su). K 2801 *R* 49, 50 aš-šu . . . . kul-lu-mi-im-ma ta-nit-ti ilu-ti-šu; ZA iv 241, 44 see šaraxu 3. KB vi (1) 70 (*Dibbara*-legend) *R* 1 ta-nit-ti bēli rabī (il) . . . .; 72, 16 ša ta-nit-ti qar-ra-du-ti-ja i-dib-bu-bu. V 44 *c-d* 24 P. N. AN-EN-ZAQ-SAL = Ta-nit-ti Bēl (ZA iii 42: an ancient Babylonian ruler); (iç) zaq(g)-sal occurs together with tanittu in DT 83 *R* 11. KB iv 314, 16 P. N. Ta-nit-tum (il) Anum; AV 8762. II 35 *a-b* 36 UB(= AR)-RI = ta-ni-it-tum, Br 5793.

tanittu *2.* II 23 *e-f* 26 (iç) ta-ni-it-tim = ŠIM (= riqqu?) GIG (= marçu) H 30, 676. followed by (iç) ti-in(? sign is blurred; Br 5196 ik)-ni-tim = ŠIM-GIG.

tanittu *3.* JAOS xxii 210 ja = ta-ni-it-tum & ka-ka-si-ga.

tintu. K 4335 ii 21 (= II 22 *e-f* 44) DIB-DIB-BI = ti-in-tum, AV 8943; Br 10748. Hommel, *Geschichte*, 421; & in Hastings, *Dict. of Bible*, i 214 *col* 1, end = figtree & fig }Feigenbaum; Feige} > DIB. D^Pr 35. compare perhaps תְּאֵנָה, Lagarde, *Mittheilungen*, i 58; WZKM i 26; Halévy, *Mel. crit.*, 197 *fol.* II 23 *O* (*add*) 5 . . . ti-it-tu, preceded by GIŠ-NU-UR-MA (3 & 4) & followed by . . . . ti-ta (& GIŠ-AT-SU-KI), AV 8973, 8975. IV² 29* 4 C *b* 12 ša ti-it-tu ni-ik-qa-ša. S 896, 16 i(or kan?)-nu ša ti-it-ti. II 26 *b* 16 ti-it-a-rum, but see tiāru & Br 3499.

tinnūtu, Br 12854; see dinnūtu, 259 *col* 2 & tinnū, tenū, 2.

Camb 189, 15 (iç) ti-it-tum. II 45 *e-f* 75 GIŠ-MA = t[i-it-tu] ‖ tinānu, *q. v.*

TIN-TIR(-KI) id for Babylon (see 145 *col* 1 *c*); AV 8942. See also Šumēr(u), end of the article.

tesū. Sarg *Ann* 272 the rest of them who upon *M* & *Š* te-su-nu id-du; DT 71, 10 a-a te-su (?) id-da-a. T^{M} v 28 dajjānu te(or TE?)-sa li-tir amāt-sa ana pī-ša; vi 59 .... te-sa ter-ra amāt-sa ana pī[-ša]; or tētu?

tessi. Šalm, *Obel*, 121 see pissi, 815 *col* 1.

tasxiru, II 21 *c-d* 12—15 tas-xi-rum, Br 2451—53 *ad* 12—14; 5602 *ad* 15 (gloss zi-lu-lu) AV 2954, 8767.

tas(s)uxtu despair, mourning {Verzweiflung, Trauer} √esexu ‖ enešu, KB vi (1) 294, 28; 554; AV 8766 ‖ ta-zim(lid, t)-tu, Br 3960. III 60, 72 & 86 ta-as-su-ux-tum shall be in the country. Z^{B} 23 *rm* 1.

ti'š'-ku-u ‖ of pašširu, see 846 *col* 2; KB vi (1) 408, beg.

taslixu see, for the present, tašlixu.

te(a)slītum, imploring, supplication, prayer {Flehen, Gebet} so rather than ti(n)ç-litum, *pp* 760, 761. AV 8047. Z^{B} 41. K 806 *R* 3 ilāni ikribē max-ru tes-li-ti še-mu-u, Thompson, *Reports*, *no* 187. V 64 *c* 20 mu-gu-ur ta-as-li-ti. II 66 *no* 1, 7 Ištar le-qa-at un-ni-ni ma-xi-rat tas(= UR)-li-te; also *cf* 81—2—4, 188 (ZA v 66), 8. V 52 iv 27 [ana] ma-xa-ri tes-li-ti-šu; IV² 53 *R* iv 44. IV² 2 v 47, 48 ik-ri-ba ta(e)s-li-ta (.... RA) ul išemmū; KB iv 102, 8 the great gods .... še-mu-u tes-li-ti-šu. V 43 *c* 74 Nebo is the god ša tes-lit-tu i-ma-xa-rum; § 147 who heareth prayer. K 4623 *R* 9, 10 (H 123) (ilat) iš-ta-ri tes-li-ti iq-bi-ki (& 14, 15. end = A-RA-ZU, Br 11548). IV² 60* C *O* 4; V 47 *a* 43 see šakkū. ZA x 203, 48—9 ši-mi-e-ma tis-li-tum. II 39 *c-d* 67 A-RA-ZU = te-is-li-tu = su-up-pu[-u], 65; te-iç-bi-tu, 66; šu-te-mu-qu, 68. See K 5157, 10/11 & 14/15 (H 180 *no* XII). K 133, 21—22 (H 80); H 41, 283. V 21 *a-b* 51, 52 xas-si-tum = te-is-li-tum & su-ul-lu-u. — IV² 21* *no* 2 *O* 36, 37 te-eš(character AP)-li-ti (= A-RA-ZU-A); K 4931 (H 116) *O* 15, 16 te-eš-li-tim (= A-RA-ZU) luqbi; also see IV² 59 *a* 6 ina [ik-ri?]-bi u te-eš(AP)-li-ti is-za-aš(= az?)-ku, Z^{B} 28.

tassūmu. splendor {Pracht}? K 3351, 9 a-na .... ta-as-su-mi-šu id-dal-la-xu ap-su-u. Martin, *Textes rélig.*, '03, 158; √DD1.

tēsiru (?) *n.* 81—7—1, 98 iii 15—17 pa-ni-šu-nu a-na e-reb (il) Šamši ta-šak-kan-ma ki-ma te-si-ru (× *Jour. Trans. Vict. Inst.*, xxvi 155; 160.

tappū. companion, neighbor, colleague {Genosse, Nachbar, Kollege}. AV 8771; §§ 25; 65, 25. id TAB § 9, 133; Br 3775. Scheil, *Nabd*, ii 2, 3 ri-çu id-din[-šum-ma] tap-pa-a u-šar-ši-iš. K 8182 ii 32 ša a-na al-ti tap-pi-šu iš-šu[-u? ēnā-šu?]. may he die at a premature time. K 44 (H 79) *R* 20, 21 ša (ilat) Nin-ka-si (II 59 *a-c* 32) tap-pu-šu (= TAB-BA-BI) at-ta; D 133. L⁴ ii 19 bi-rit ali u bīti amēlu mim-mu-u (the property) tap-pi-e-šu ul e-kim ina da-na-ni. V 47 *a* 25 na-al-bu-bu tap-pi-e. V 35, 15 ki-ma eb-ri u tap-pi-e, as a friend & companion; KB ii 267, 78. K 3364 *R* 24 it-ti eb-ri u tap-pi-e e ta-ta-me ..., Delitzsch, *Weltschöpf.*, 55. IV² 50 *b* 56 eb-ru tap-pu-u; 51 *b* 34 eb-ri u tap-pi-e (*gen*) = $Z^{Š}$ iii 10; IV² 51 *a* 50—53 bīt, axāt, dāmē, çubāt tap-pi-e-šu. K 2148 iii 36 kin-za (> kimza? √?) ša tap-pi-e-šu, ZA ix 117, 119. NE I vi 34 Eabani dan-nu tap-pu-u; II iii *b* 33 (H^{NE} *pp* 9; 15; 87) u dam-qu (il) Gilgameš tap-pa-a u-šar-šu-ka ka-a-ša; iv *b* 44 paṭ-ri-ka tap-pi[-i ....]; (KB vi (1) 132; 138); IV vi 41 pa-gar-šu iç-çur (√naçaru) tap-pa-a li-šal-lim; III i *a* 8 (16). KB vi (1) 144; 158 × J^{I-X} 48 *rm* 38. T. A. (Ber) 63, 8 to the court ki-ma tab-bi-ja, as my companion; 85, 45; (Lo) 70, 22. K 3806, 8 *foll* šumma sisū iš-še-gu-ma lu tap-pa-a-šu .... u-na-šaš. V 44 *c-d* 21 (il) Marduk tap-pi-e e-di

tas-sa-nu see u r s a n u. ~ tasniqu, AV 11287 instead of u r - n i - q u (103 *col* 2); see kalū, 8 (381 *col* 1). ~ tisqāru *cf* t i s q ā r u. ~ ta-a-pa = ṭāba T. A. (Lo) 11 + Murch, 65 š a m n a t a - a - p a. ~ tappu see tappu (357 *col* 1). ~ ti-ip read tīb (& *cf* tību).

šub-ši (√bašû), Br 311. ⊕ 116 (H 66) ii 7—12 ka-sap tap-pi-e, capital of the partner; *k* tap-pi-e-šu; *k* tap-pi-e-šu-nu; tap-pu-u; tap-pu-u-šu; -šu-nu. II 30 *g-h* 40 see Br 1807; S[c] 158 ta-ab | TAB | tap-pu[-u]; H 17, 257. V 37 *d-f* 30 ma-an | MAN | tap-pu-u, followed by at-xu-u, Br 9964. V 31 *a-b* 22 tap-pu-u preceded by eb-ri, AV 8662; Br 14048. K 4219 *R* 11—14 (M[8] *pl* 10) tap-pu-u, ‖ *col* (partly broken off, perhaps:) it]-ba-rum (11); ib]-ru (13); ru-'-]a (14). — See Haupt, *Sintfluther.*, 27, 21; Delitzsch, *Chald. Gen.*, 271. — Meissner, ZA viii 82, 83 √חבו combine, unite, whence also šutapû. The following 2 belong to tappû:

tappattu (*cf* axattu = axâtu, 31 *col* 2) companion, concubine {Genossin, Kebse}. § 66 note 1. V 39 *c-d* 61, 62 DAM-TAB-BA = tap-pu-u, tap-pat-tum, followed by çir-ri-tum (897 *col* 1) & a-xat-tum.

tappûtu. partnership {Compagniegeschäft}. II 29 *e-f* 60 tap-pi-u-tum ‖ tap-pu-u-tum, AV 8772. Sm 2052 ii 1 tap-pu-u-tum. H 69, 20 kasap tap-pu-tu (= NAM-TAB-BA); 72, 40—3 eqil tap-pu-ti *etc.* see also tazkîtu. Whether V 24 *b* 48, 49 belong here, cannot be determined. See also ṭappûtu, 358 *col* 2.

tuppu, see duppu, 262, 263. K 883, 5 (end) see BA ii 633; 645. T. A. (W-A.) 235 + B 1617 + (W-A.) 239*β*, 7 a-]li-ik li-ga-a tu-up-pa-ti-ma i-[m]u-ur.

NOTE. — KB vi (1) 72, 23 reads tup-pu (ša-a-šu) referring to Kingu, ZA xi 53; Jensen also reads tupšarru (Br 3911; § 73; KAT[3] 400 *rm* 5; 651); tup-šimâti. See Zimmern, *Ritualt.*, *p* 100 *rm* c; *no* 24, 20: makes his son swear ina tup-pi u qân tup-pi; qa-an d(t)up-pi see qanû, 4 & Zehnpfund, *Stockholm. Orient. Congress*, i (2) B, 269. — tup-pi ilâni ta-kal-ta pi-ri'š'-ti; Zimmern, *Ritualt.*, *no* 24, 8 (14, 16); KAT[3] 541; *no* 26 iii 5 tup-pu ar-ni; Z[3] iv 58; KAT[3] 402. — KB vi (1) 78 (T. A. (Lo) 82; BA iv 130, 131) ii 17, 18 tu-up-pa (= *accus*) ša ni-mi-e-qi I will put into thy hand. — On the dup-šimâti see also AJSL xvi 207 *foll.*

tapdû. defeat, overthrow, destruction {Niederlage, Niederwerfung, Zerstörung} √padû, 791 *col* 2; AV 8663, 8768. TP iii 52 (+ 78) tap-da-šu-nu aš-kun, I accomplished their defeat; ii 67 mit-xu-uç (524 *col* 1) tap-di-e. I 28 *a* 36 tap-da-šu-nu iš-ku-un. Sarg *Khors* 149 a-di a-na-ku tap-di-e (mât) *B* . . . ašak-kanu, *Ann* 371; *bull* 38 šakin tap-di-e. K 2674 i 16 ša ina tap-di-e ip-par-ši-du, who had escaped the destruction; K 2867 *O* 29 ki-i tap-di-e Dibbar-ra tap-qid ša-lam-tu (amêl) mitûte, S. A. Smith, *Asurb*, iii *pl* 1; ii *pl* 1. Z[3] ii 94, 95 tap-da-a uk-ta-bi-is [ar]-ka tap-di-e it-ta-ta-al-lak. V 31 *g-h* 28 see taxtû (Br 14163); also ‖ kamâru, 2 (398 *col* 1). V 49 x 6 ša tap-di-e; xi 4 tap-du-u. KB vi (1) 298, 1 (3, 7) im-ta-xa-aç ta-ap-da-a (ra-bi-a). K 710, 6 tap-du bêl bîti šuatu, ruin for the master of the house, Thompson, *no* 200.

tapdîru fat {fett}. Neb 74, 5 immer tap-di-ri (& 1); 213, 3 one alpu šuk-lu-lu. one alpu tap-di-ri a-na (il) Bu-ne-ne; 182, 12 one alpu tap-di-ir. J[AT] 269, 270 tapṭiri (√פטר) Stier der Loslösung; *cf* Levit 4, 3.

tapzirtu hiding, concealment {Verbergung} Sarg *Ann* 273 a-šar ta-ap-zi-ir-ti-šu-nu, the place of their concealment.

tapxu, *pl* tapxâni. Anp i 84 tap-xa-a-ni siparri. Some vessel ‖ dûdu. AV 8664. Bezold, *Catalogue*, 615 (K 4297) mentions tap-xa-a-ni together with dûdê, aganâti, dalâni & maziš-ni, or √ṭabaxu?

tapxirtu *1.* S[c] 329 (colophon) = IV[2] 68, 68 dup-pu šu-a-tam(-ti) ina tap-xir-ti um-ma-a-ni aš-ṭur, *etc.*

ta-pa-ak-ka II 16 *c* 16, 17 √bakû, cry {weinen} *q. v.*, 152 *col* 1; Br 11630.

(niš) **tup-ki-na-ti** u . . . . IV[2] 58 *a* 56; ZA xvi 173 *foll.*

tapalu. K 4138 *O* 11 ta-pa-lu; M[8] *pl* 5. Z[3] iii 37 (85) see timbuttu. Perh. here also Nabd 66, 1: twenty (iç) gušurê ta-pa-lu; 441, 1 (or, a verb?).

taplakkata (√palaku?) see tûbelu.

---

tapxirtu 2. see tapširtu. ∾ tap-ṭir-tum Sp II 265 *a* (ZA x 3, 12) ii 1 read i-dir-tum. ∾ tipku see tibku. ∾ tapkirtu see tabkirtu. ∾ tuplu *cf* tublu & dublu (239 *col* 2). ∾ tabalû see tabalû. ∾ tupp(bb)usû *cf* duppusû, 263, 264.

tappaltum. Ner 28, 7 ištēnit tap-pal-tum.

tapalatum. II 29 *g* 67 a-pi-i[l-tum?]; 68, ap-la[-tum?]; 69, ta-pa-la[-tum], WZKM vi 209; ZA vii 218, 219: daughter {Tochter}.

(çubât) **tappinu** (K 164, 8 & 23) see dappinnu, 263 *col* 2; ṭappin(n)u, 358 *col* 1. ZIMMERN, *Rituall.*, 175 *rm* 6 reads tappinu & compares, *ibid*, *no* 66 *O* 8 VII akal tu-up-pi-ni (& *rm* 11): a kind of grain or flour {eine Getreide- oder Mehlart} JENSEN, KB vi (1) 485, 486. II 49 *no* 3 (*add*) = K 263 *O* 60 tap-pi-in-nu ku-uk-ku ellu; AV 8769.

tap-pi-in-ni V 50 *b* 57 see banū, 1 Ⓠ *ps* (173 *col* 2); AV 8770; Br 7436.

tappanni. T. A. (Ber) 26 i 18 tap(?)-pa-a-an-ni-šu-nu.

tappissu. some vessel, jar or the like {ein Gefäss, oder dergl.}. V 41 *g-h* 21, 22 IM-DUL; IM-ME-DUL = tap-pi-is-su, Br 8483, 8489.

tups(š)innu. KB vi (1) 296 (iv) 8 tup-'š'i(u)n-[n]a e-pu-uš-ka narā aš-ṭur-ka, or tuppi šinnu, tablet of ivory? or tuppa-šin, tuppa-[ši-n]a, their tablet; see *ibid* 556: perhaps a plate, tablet, of copper or bronce (see šu(i)nnu).

taparu. *Cf* P. N. III 43 *col* 2, 26 abulla ta-ta-par-a-a-u.

tipparu. clothing, garment, robe {Gewand, Robe} *etc.* perh. √eperu, אפר; KB vi (1) 186 *ad* NE II (ii) 6 tib-bar i-sin-na-ti-ia; so perh. PEISER, *Vertr.*, xciv 15; cxvii 20 tip(or lu?)-bar-ri; cxlvi 6 (çubât) tib-bar-ri. V 28 *a-b* 12 te-ip-p(b)ar = çu-bat (a-dir-tu) muq, Br 7733, 8850.

tapšaxu. resting place {Ruhestätte}; √pašaxu, 841, 842. § 65, 32*a*. See LYON, *Sargon* on *Cyl* 5. IV² 23 *no* 1 *b* 33, 34 tap-ša-xa (= KI-NA, Br 9799) el-lum, preceded by aš-ru el-lum, 32. H 31, 719. From the same stem:

tapšuxtu. quieting, calming down, rest, peace {Beruhigung, Ruhe, Frieden} § 65, 32*e*. KB iii (2) 8 *no* 3 *b* 8 E-EDIN-NA bīt ta-ap-šu-ux-te-šu, the temple where she (the goddess) rests peacefully. V 65 *a* 17 ki-iç-çi el-lu šu-bat tap-šu-ux-ti; *b* 16. V 35, 8 (*b*) nišē-šu i-na ap-ša-a-ni la ta-ap-šu-ux-tim u-xal-li-iq kul-lat-si-in, BA ii 208, 209. K 4931 *R* 5, 6 be-el-ti e-piš-ti tim-di tap-šu-ux-ti šuk-ni; H 163 § 6; Br 9796.

tapšūru. ransom {Lösegeld, Lösung}. K 13 *R* 7 tap-šu-ru a-na rubē-šu i-gam-mar-ma, he will pay a ransom to the nobles; Hr[L] 281; JAOS xviii 136—142; BA iv 527*foll.* √pašaru, whence also:

tapširtu salvation, redemption, delivery {Erlösung} Z[Š] ii 2 god & goddess (?) bēlē tap-šer-ti; 138 (il) Nergal bēl tap-šer-ti. II 24 *a-b* 6 GI-ŠU-DI-A = qa-an tap-šir-ti, followed by qa-an te-lil-ti; = V 32 *d-e* 38; ZK ii 323; AV 8775; Br 2506, 7228. ZIMMERN, *Rituall.*, *p* 113 *rm* *v* reads tapširtu for NAM-BUL(R)-BI = Sühneritus; see 680.

tapatu. ZIMMERN, *Rituall.*, *no* 79—82 iii 10 lit-pa-ta-ma (il) Šamaš u (il) Adad ilāni da-a-a-ni.

tappatu. T. A. (Lo) 57, 19 šu-pal tap-pa-ti-ši, from under its coping. Rostow. 1, 14 iš-tu šu-pal tap-pa-te-ši; perh. (Ber) 156, 20.

tu-pat (?) IV² 17 *b* 10 lušakna šēpēka ina eli tu-pat būrāši. HALÉVY, JA VIII (12) 516—17 (Dec. '88) compares Hebr תֹּפֶת.

taptū. *n* or *adj*? T[C] 118 ploughing, ploughed land {das Pflügen, Gepflügtes}. Merod.-Balad.-stone IV 33 ŠE-ZIR ..... tap-tu-u pa-na-at kirē i-li-ni-i; 44 five gur (bushel) ŠE-ZIR .... a-di tap-te-e ša pa-na-at kirī. Nabd 293, 1 ŠE-ZIR eqil tap-tu-u u gišimmarē suppuxūtu, BA ii 273; KB iii (1) 190, 191. undoubtedly a √petū: cultivate a field (see 850 *col* 2 *f*) & compare 81—11—3, 71 *O* 4 ina ū-me pa-an māti (or šatti?) it-tap-tu-u, when the surface of the land sprouts again. See also RP² iv 97; ZA vii 189. Nabd 440, 1 ŠE-ZIR eqli mi-ri-šu u tap-tu-u. Neb 135, 1; Cyr 90, 35; 225, 10; Camb 102, 1*foll.*

---

tupqu. tupuqtu see tubqu. ~ tuppuru, Br 4401 see daparu, 264 *col* 1. ~ tap(tup)rānu, AV 8773 see da(u)prānu, 264 *col* 1. ~ ta-pi-ir-tim see tamērtu. ~ taprāti, AV 8774 see tabrītu. ~ tupšikku see dupšikku, 261 *co's* 1, 2. ~ tapatum, (T. A.) *cf* tabātum.

taptū *2.* open, opened {geöffnet} T^{M} iv 37, 38 ina .... būri tap-ta-a, in an open ditch, hole {in einem offenen Graben}.

tepītum (?) KB iv 40 *no* 3, 14—15 for the first day te-ip[-i-tum]; for the first month bi-en-nu (has to be done) perh. some kind of tax, burden *etc*. See bennu. 1 in suppl. vol.

teptītu. KB iv 40 *no* 4, 10 eqlu a-na te-ip-ti-tim, KB iv: zur Halbpacht; adding: Grundbedeutung: Bepflügung; MEISSNER, 141, 142 zur Beackerung. Xamm.-*code* xiii 20 if a man rent an unreclaimed field for 3 years a-na te-ip-ti-tim, in order to develop it (R. F. HARPER).

tiçbū. V 30 *c-d* 67 SA-SAR-SAR-IR = ti-iç-bu[-u?]. √çibū, 2. AV 8946; Br 8121. meaning not clear.

ti-iç-bu-tu Creat.-*frg* I 26; IV 40 *etc*. see çabatu, Q^{t}, 864 *col* 1, beg. see also V 31 *c-d* 44 DIB-DIB-ta-ma = ti-iç-bu-ta-ma.

teçbītu. desire, wish, prayer {Begehren, Wunsch, Gebet} or the like. √çu(i)bū, 1. §§ 34δ; 65, 32*d*. II 39 *c-d* 66 te-iç-bi-tu = XI(= DUG)-AG-AG, Br 8249, AV 8945 see teslītu.

tiççulu. Rm 345 *O* 9 .... SAR-SAR = ti-iç-çu-lu; M^{8} *pl* 22.

taçliltu. K 7856 i 7 ^(aban)^ a-ra-nu a-šar ta-aç-lii-t[i] ina eri danni bāb-ša ak-nu-uk, where he lay, I have sealed up his door with strong bronce. √çalalu, 1 (876, 877). M^{8} 81 *col* 2.

tuçātum sprout, offspring {Spross, Nachkommenschaft}. Sm 2052 *O* 19 tu-ça-tum = zi[-rum]; √açū, 1 (84, 85); M^{8} *pl* 19. From the same verb also:

teçītu, edict {Edikt}. II 62 *a-b* 52 A-DA-MAN = te-çi-tu, AV 8949; Br 11561.

taqū, pr itqā (?). SMITH, *Senn*, 92, 68 see çidētu, 869 *col* 1. meaning very uncertain; III 15 *a* 13 suggests: pour out (& then: collect, heap up); JOHNS, *Doomsday-Book*, 56. Still more uncertain is Sarg *Cyl* 20; see innu & etequ. Q^{t} K 662 *O* 10 ṭabtū (the beverage) ša ^(amēl)^ a-ba ēkalli ina muxxi-ja te-te-qi, pours out (?) for me.

Derr. of this could be these 2:

tīq(k)u, *c. st.* tiq(k). pouring out, outpour (of water, rain, *etc*.) {Ausschüttung, Erguss}. AV 8950. IV^{2} 49 *b* 31 see nādu, 3 (645, 646). TP i 42 see rixçu, 2 & translate: like the outpouring of a flood. Sarg *Nimr* 15 see rādu. Sn *Bav* 7 see zunnu, 285 *col* 2. KB iii (2) 4 *col* 2, 8 read on the basis of HILPRECHT, *OBI*, i 32, 33 *col* 2, 5 ki-ma ti-iq sa-me-e la ma-nu-tim. Esh *Sendsch*, *R* 14 zi-bu na-ad-ru pa-nu-uš-šu er-um-ma ar-ki-i-šu ti-ku e-ru-ub; JENSEN ṭi-ku = Stoss.

tiqtum. S^{b} 1 *col* 2, 6 u-tu = di(*var* ti)-ik-tum, preceded by ša-mu-u; perh. *f* of tīqu. Also V 38 *no* 4, 62. Br 9174; AV 8886.

tiqū. ZIMMERN, *Rituall.*, *no* 100, 13 speaks of a young gazelle (for sacrificial purposes) ša ..... ti-qu-u pa-nu-šu im-nu su-up-pa-ar-šu; colored {farbig}. MARTIN, *Textes rělig.*, '03 = dont la face belle (?).

tiq (?) NE III *col* 3 *b* 38 in-di it-ta-di a-na ti-ik(q, g); KB vi (1) 150.

taqqaku. 82—8—16, 1 *O* NU-UM-ME = taq-qa-ku, JRAS xxii 207.

taqlīmu see taklīmu.

tuqum(n)tu, tuqmatu *pl* tu(m)q(u)-māte. AV 9046, 9047; G §§ 31; 46. √taqamu, perhaps an old *ta*-formation of qâmu (קום). § 65, 5 *rm*. — *a*) resistance {Widerstand}. Anp i 2 see xašalu, 2 (346 *col* 1); 6 ša tum-qu(*var* tuq)-ma-tu i-pe-lu. Creat.-*frg* IV 118 ga-du tuq-ma-ti-šu-nu ša-pal-šu [ik-bu?]-us, but see KB vi (1) 28 *rm* 2. L^{4} ii 18 powerless (?) were the mighty ša a-na la ma-gi-ri-šu-un tu-qu-un-tu tar[-çu?]. Esh *Sendsch*, *O* 23 Esarh. calls himself la pa-du-u tu-qu-un-tu; K 2801 = K 221 + 2669, 11 Agušea di-kat a-na-an-ti ki-nat tu-qu-un-t[i], BA iii 228. K 2001, 4 (Ištar) ša tu-qu-un-ti xal-pat (or to *b*). — *b*) attack, battle, fight {Angriff, Schlacht, Streit} id GIŠ-LAL, Br 10116; § 9, 31. H 39, 154 = tuq-ma-tum; S^{b} 320. TP i 16 GIŠ-LAL u ša-aš-mu; Anp i 51; Šalm, *Mon*, ii 71; Anp i 35 & *var*; iii 131. KB iii (1) 115 iv 8 a-bu-ub tu-qu-ma-tim (= GIŠ-GIŠ-LAL); 10 mu-bi-il-li tu-uq-ma-tim,

---

te(a)çlītu §§ 34 ζ; 65, 32*d* see teslītu. ∼ tiçmuru see çamaru Q^{t}, 842 *col* 2.

Br 7716. K 4832, 23 di-ku]-u tu-qu-un-tu, 6 di-ku-u] a-na-an-ti, KB vi (1) 8—10. Sarg *Khors* 79 tu-qu-un-tu ix-šu-ux, he longed for a fight. Sn v 44 a-na e-peš tuq-ma-ti. Creat.-*frg* IV 55 ra-aš-ba tu-qu-un-tum, are terrible in the fight. *Zū*-legend ii 16 ik-pu-ud-ma libba(-ba)-šu tu-qu-un-ta (= K 8454 + K 3935), KB vi (1) 48. Anp i 13 (20) *Anp* lā ādiru GIŠ-LAL; Sarg *Cyl* 25 *Sargon* la a-dir tuq-ma-te(ti); see Lyon, *Sargon*, 63. Craig, *Diss*, la ga-mil tu-qu-un-te = lā ādiru. *del* 5 gu-um-mur-ka libbi(bi) a-na e-peš tu-qu-un-ti, KB vi (1) 230; 480—1; but see Haupt, *Johns Hopk. Circ*, 69, 17 & JAOS xxv 72. II 29 *c-d* 54 tu-qu-un-tu, Br 297 between a-na-an-tu & aš-ga-gu. II 36 *a-b* 6 AMĒL-NE = tu-qu-un-tum ‖ çal-tum, 880 *col* 1; Br 6415.

NOTE. — On tukundi & tuqumtu, see Lehmann, i 110 *rm* 5.

tiqmēnu. (√qamū?) see diqmēnu, 247 *col* 1.

taqanu, be or become staple, firm, right, in order }fest, recht, richtig sein oder werden{ ‖ kānu; AV 8776. תקן; Arm תקן. — Q IV² 61 *a* 66 ina ēkalli-ka ta-taq-qu-un, within thy palace thou shalt be prosperous. — pm Rm 2 III 150 *R* 6 kīma mē *pl* būri lu-u taq-na-a-ta. L⁴ ii 23 ki]-ma u-lu šam-ni taq-na (= *pl*) kib-rat erbit-tim. — V 29 *g-h* 4 GI = ta-qa-nu, Br 2406. — ℑ causat. of Q: order, reduce to order, arrange, prepare, decorate }ordnen, arrangieren, vorbereiten, (aus)schmücken{. K 2801 *R* 37 ki-šad-su-un u-taq-qin-ma, I have ornamented their neck. Sarg *Khors* 121 (māt) El-li-pi da-li-ix-tu (*var* -tum) u-taq-qin; 52 u-taq-qi-na da-li-ix-tu māt-su, *Ann* 157; § 121: u-taq-qi-in, *Ann* 28. K 114, 20 (Hr^L vi) = IV² 46 *no* 1. 20 ša māta(?) la u-taq-qa-nu. V 45 vii 20 tu-taq-qa-an. K 226, 7 (il) Sin kussi-šu taq-qi-in (= ip). Sarg *Cyl* 31 Sargon mu-pa-xir (māt) Ma-an-na-a-a sa-ap-xi mu-ta-ki-in (māt) El-li-bi(pi) dal-xi. Lay 33 (= Sarg *Nimr*) 9 mu-ta-qi-in (māt) Man-na-a-a dal-xu-u-te, KB ii 36; 44; AV 5645.

Derr. these 3:

taqnu, *adj* IV² 61 *a* 62—4 ak-lu taq-nu ta-kal mē taq-nu-ti ta-ša-at-ti, well-prepared food shalt thou eat, well-prepared beverages shalt thou drink, AJSL xiv 277.

tiqnu. ornament, fineries }Schmuck, Putz{ = תִּקְנָא. Neb iii 6 xurāçi nam-ri ti-iq-nim me-lam-mi u-ša-al-bi-iš-su, Flemming, *Neb*, 38. K 2801 *R* 32 ti-iq-ni ilu-ti-šu-nu ma-'-diš uš-tar-si-ma (Š¹ rašū) BA iii 236; 281. V 63 *a* 44 ti-iq-nu tu-ug-gu-nu (ℑ pm), KB iii (1) 110; AJP xi 302 *rm* 3. ZA x 293, 35 (& 38) z(c?)i-im-ru-ša du-uš-šu-pu ra-bu[-u ti-iq-nu]; 44 a-šar ṭu-ub ka-bat-ti lu-u ti-iq-nu-ki. II 26 *a-b* 15 SUX (su-ux) SAR = ti-ik-nu, AV 8884, Br 3029. II 37 *g-h* 64 TAG-SUX-SAR = ti-iq-nu & KB vi (1) 397; Br 3031. See also II 16 *f* 11—12 ki-ma ku-us-si-e .... | ti-ik-ni .... | tu-tag-ga-a[n?], Br 3033. *pl* IV² 21* *no* 1 C *R* iii 26 ça-lam ti-iq-na-a-ti (= SUX-SAR-SAR-RI); Zimmern, *Ritualtafeln*, *p* 166 *rm* 7.

tuqunnu. IV² 61 *a* 43, 44 nāru ina tu-qu-un-ni | u-še-ba-ar-ka, I shall cause thee to cross the river in security, BOR iii 30; AJSL xiv 278.

taqappatu (?). Strassmaier, *Liverpool*, 12, 8 *fol* tu-xal-la gi-pi-e man-ga-ga bil-tum ša xu-ça-bi + ta-qa-ap-pa-tum + za-bi-la-nu + da-ri-ka-nu it-ti i-nam-di-nu. But rather 4-ta qa-ap-pa-tum (see 922 *col* 2).

tuqāru. V 28 *e-f* 81 tu-qa-a-rum ‖ iš (= mil) .... see tugāru; AV 9045.

taqrubtu. fight, battle }Kampf, Schlacht{ √qarabu. V 70, 24—5 ina taxāzi ša šarrāni a-šar taq-ru-ub-ṭe. § 65, 32*a*; Z^B 1 *rm* 3.

taqridu. V 41 *a-b* 27 taq-ri-du ‖ qit-ru-du, *q. v.* AV 8779.

ta-qiš (ilat) Gu-la, P. N. see qāšu; AV 8778; also Ta-qiš Ba-u, V 68 *b* 44; ta-qiša (ilāt) Ištar III 48 *b* 7, *etc.*

---

taq-su. Anp iii 110 (KB i 112 *rm* 4): kib-su [u me-tu-qu]. ∼ taqçātu *cf* takçātu. ∼ takribtu see takkaltu.

taqtītu, end {Ende}. Xamm.-*code* xii 15, 16 see šattu; Harper, 189; ZA xviii, 18 & 33. √qatū.

târu 1. pr itūr; *ps* itâr, iturru (in relat. connection; § 90*a*, note); 3 *f* ta-tar (§ 87); = תור. idd GI (Br 2405); GUR (Br 3367; § 9, 129); GE (Br 6331, 7199); AV 8792; D^{H} 20; Barth, *Etym. Stud.*, 67. — *a*) turn, turn around {wenden, umwenden}. — *α*. with ana arkišu, arkiš, *etc.* Creat.-*frg* II *b*, *R* 11 i-tu-ra ar-kiš, returned; III 54, 112; IV 128 ṣi-ri-iš Ti-āmat .... i-tu-ra ar-ki-iš. K 2852 + K 9662 ii 38 ul i-tu-ra ar-ka-niš, Winckler, *Forsch.*, ii 34 *foll.* IV^{2} 16 *b* 57, 58 kiš-pu .... ana a-·-ka-ti li-tu-ru, let the charm pass away! I 43, 30 i-tur ar-ka-niš. Sm *Asurb* 127, 86 Teumman ip-lax-ma arka-šu i-tur e-ru-ub [ki-rib] (al) Šu-ša-an. III 38 *no* 2 *R* 63 ana taxāzi ul a-ir a-tu-ra arkiš; 57 a-a a-tur a-na ar-ki-ja, *I* will not recede. — *β*. without arkiš(u). return, come back {zurück-, umkehren}. Sarg *Khors* 177 see taknū. V 65 *a* 37 i-tu-ru-nim-ma (they came back) & said to me; 55, 44 a-na (māt) Akkadā i-tu-ra. II 65 *O* ii 7 is-xur-ma (751 *col* 2) a-na māti-šu i-tur. Rm^{2} 139, 3 when a man i-tu-ur-ši, returns to her (his wife). K 13, 6 (Hr^{L} 281) ša .... i-tu-ra]-am-ma, JAOS xix 84. Asb ii 47 a-tu-ra a-na Ninā. Smith, *Asurb*, 94, 69 šal-meš a-tu-ra; 133 *š a* a-na Ninā (see šalmeš for further instances); 103, 49 i-tur a-na māti-šu, KB ii 242, 254, 244. K 84 *R* 4 5 a-na bil-ti-ni i-ta-ra, because of our taxes he returns, Hr^{L} 301; = IV^{2} 45 *col* 1; PSBA xxiii 344—48. II 16 *a-b* 58, 59 (i-tu-ru) see namū, 2 (679 *col* 2). *del* 140, 142 (148, 151) il-lik summatu (& sinuntu) XU i-tu (written pi)-ra-am-ma; 196, 197 (217, 218) li-tur ina šul-me (a-na ma-ti-šu); 246 (276) mi-na-a ta-ad-dan-na-ma i-ta-ar ana māti-šu; 251 (281) ta-ta-ar ana māti-ka. IV^{2} 1* iv 37, 38 see šaxatu, 4; 6 v 9 ana šub-ti-šu-nu li-tu-ru ‖ ana šamē li-lu-u (علی); 56 *O* i 20 ... an-ni-i ta-tur-rim-ma, return! Zimmern, *Ritualt.*, *no* 43, 8 ta-tar-ma, thou wilt return (& § 87). IV^{2} 58 *a* 54 see tamū, 2. ZA v 148, 7 i-tu-ur-ru-ma; Banks, *Diss*, 14 *foll*, 99 a-na ki-bi-ti-šu la i-tur-ra. KB iv 322 *col* 3, 37 her dower to the house of her father i-ta-a-ri, shall return. Xamm.-*code* i-ta-ar, he shall return (restore), vi 27 *etc.* Knudtzon, 71, 2 i-tur-ram-ma (= *ps*). Sn *Bav* 40 la i-tu-ru-ni ar-kiš, ZA ix 105 *rm* 1. — ana ašrišu târu, return (something) to its place. See the equivalent use of שוב; Haupt, *Kings* (SBOT) 199, 41—8. IV^{2} 10 *no* 1 *a* 1, 2 ana aš-ri-šu li-tu-ra (& 14, -rum = *pl*); II 51 *b* 4 ana KI (= ašri)-šu a-a i-tur, ZK ii 320. Also figuratively: restore something: V 64 *b* 27 god Sin without whom city & land cannot be founded nor i-tur-ru (= *ps*) aš-ru-uš-šu. — pm IV^{2} 31 *O* 6 to the land ša a-lak-ta-ša la ta-a-a[-rat], KB vi (1) 80—1; 188—9 on NE VII *col* 4, 31 (36) H^{NE} 17, 36; 19, 31. See also § 89 i; BA i 462 (below) & *rm* *** (= pm כ; by the side of the regular turru). V 65 *b* 35 ina a-la-ku u ta-a-ru, in going & coming. — On ana u-di-tim i-tu-ur of Hunger, *Becherwahrsagung*, see Thureau-Dangin, *Rev. Crit.*, '04 *no* 6 = si (huile) retourne au fond (du vase); and again, Boissier, OLZ '04, Nov., 454. — *b*) turn to some one, in the meaning of: take compassion on, favor *etc.* {sich jem. zuwenden}. See târu, 2. II 64 *a* 38 AN-PA (= Nabū)-GUR (= tūr)-an-ni, AV 5688. — *c*) become undone; change {ändern, sich verändern}. Creat.-*frg* II *c* 10 a-a i-tur a-a i-in-nin-na-a se-kar š[ap-ti-ja]; III 64. V 47 *a* 24 ki-ma a-tur (or from aṭ(t)urru, a *n*?) a-na ri-e-ši. — *d*) turn to or into; become {werden}. NE 58 (Sm 1040) 20 = V iii (iv) 20 see tumru. V 47 *a* 56 see kisukku, 414 *col* 2, end. a-na ṭīṭi târu see ṭīṭu, *b* (355 *col* 1); on *del* 112 (119), 127 (134) see KB vi (1) 238/9; 497, 498. ana til(l)i u karmē târu see 437 *col* 2. *Etana*-legend (KB vi (1) 112), 27 *b* tam-tum i-tu-ra a-na me-e(-)[....]; 33; 114, 22 it-tur (= Q^{t}) *var* i[-tu-ru] ma-a-tu a-na mu-sa-ri-e [....]; *del* 268 (299) lu-tur a-na ša ṣu-ux-ri-ja-ma. IV^{2} 7 *b* 20 ana sissinni qatpu la i-tur-ru. Asb v 26 (i-tu-ru, 3 *pl*) see mimmū, 565 *col* 1. K 11 *R* 1, 2 (Hr^{L} 186) maṣṣarē ša šarri a-ta-a tu-ra-am-me, will become guardians of the king, BA ii 26 *foll.* Beh 11 arkiša ana šarri atūru, after I had become king. Perh. Sp II 265 *a* iv 7 i-ta-ri ina .... — *c*) repeat {wiederholen}? Creat.-*frg* IV 24 tu-ur qi-bi-šum-ma, befiehl ihm wieder (+ 26 i-tu-ur iq-bi-šum-ma). Also see GGA 1904, 748 — *f*) turn over to some one {jemandem ausliefern, übergeben} H 61, 47—8 when the money is paid (the seller) aradsu i-tar-šu, will turn over to him (the buyer) his servant. — *g*) in legal terminology: perhaps = re-open a case {einen Fall wieder eröffnen}; MEISSNER 118 Ungültigkeitsklage stellen. T^C 142 einen Vertrag, Kauf *etc.*, rückgängig machen. PEISER, *Vertr.*, 94, 22 ul i-tur-ru-ma a-xa-meš ul i-rag-gu-mu. Bu 91—5—9, 2463, 11/12 they rejected their claim u-ul i-tu-ru-ma, and they shall not take action; see PINCHES, JRAS '97, July, 597 *foll*; Bu 91—5—9, 367. 12/13 u la i-ta-ar u la i-ra-ga-am; Bu 91—5—9. 511, 15/16 u-ul i-tu-ru u-ul i-ra-ga-mu. KB iv 24 *no* 3, 12/13 u-ul i-ta-a-ar u-ul i-gi-ir-ri; 36 *no* 3, 10 i-ta-a-ar & *rm* *; 54 *no* 6, 14 šu-ma .... i-du-a-ar. — S^b 209 gu-ur | GUR | ta-a-ru; II 16. 230; 23, 412/13 GE(-GE); 15, 195 GI = ta-a-ru; § 9, 251.

Q^t — *a*) turn {sich wenden} V 55, 21 see purīdu, 1 (827 *col* 2). — *b*) return, restore. Xamm.-*code* x 24, 65 *etc.* it-tu-ra-am; xix 78 it-ta-ru; xliii 6 li-it-ta-ar-ru-šu. — make returns: K 4223 ii 13 it-tu-ra-am, BA iii 495 *rm* **. — *c*) turn into. NE 51 (KB vi, 1, 272) 12 + 14 it-tu-ra a-na *etc.* — *d*) become. Beh 5 (& 7) šarru-ši-na at-tur, I became their king. — Sp II 265 *a* i 10 a-ga-riu-n[u] a-lit-ti it-ta-ar (or אר?) KUR-NU-GI. K 3456 *O* 17 aš-rat la me-riš-ti (ana) ..... lu-ti it-tur, PSBA xxi 37, 38.

Q^tn turn to, approach {sich zuwenden, nähern}. IV² 16 *a* 41, 42 the demon ša a-na bi-ti it-ta-nu-ur-ru (= GE-GE-E-A) ana biti pixē lišēribūšu. Perh. S 1981 + K 4355 (II 35 *no* 4) 1 ar-da-tu ša bit za-qi-qi ana ar-da-tu ina ap-ti it-ta-nu-ru, AV 8792; T^M 128, 129.

ℑ — *a*) turn, turn back, drive back {wenden, zurückwenden, zurücktreiben} Asb v 42 see niru, 2 (723—4). K 3182 ii 5 tu-tar-ra çal-pa. — On ūmu utarra = the day turns back, in astronomical reports, see THOMPSON, *Reports*, ii, pref. xxi; 82—5—22, 66, 3 (5, a-na tur-ru). S 1974 *R* 5 u-tir-ra, the moon will "draw back" the day in Nisan & Iyyār. 81—2—4, 79, 8 ut-tir-ir-ra (= ℑ^t?), THOMPSON, *no* 70. — IV² 48 *a* 16 see qalū, 2 Q. D 96, 30 (98, 36) = Creat.-*frg* IV 71 see kišadu, *a*) 449 *col* 2. — *b*) hold back, stop {zurückhalten} especially in mu-tir (= GI) ir-ti lem-ni, IV² 21 *no* 1 B *R* 15 = ZIMMERN, *Ritualt.*, *no* 54 *R* 15, stopping the advance of the enemy, JAOS xxiv 126. H 79 *R* 23 (K 44) ša lem-ni ina mu-ši mu-tir ir-ti-šu at-ta; 83 i 15 read la mu-[tir ir-ti]; 99, 37/8 ša-du-u it-gu-ru-ti i-rat-su-nu li-tir-ru. Esh v 48 šēdi u lamassi ša ..... irti lem-ni u-tar-ru. mutir pūtu see mutīru (625 *col* 2) & pūtu (848 *col* 2). IV² 1 i 29—31 šu-nu dal-tu ul i-kal-lu šu-nu-ti me-di-lu ul u-tar-šu-nu-ti, perh. = bolt {verriegeln}; for which see II 23 *c-d* 44 tu-ur-ru ‖ e-di-lu, AV 9062 & Neb 184, 17 bābu tu-ru, the gate is bolted. KB vi (1) 254, 6 (end) bāb ^(iç) elippi ter[-ra] ‖ ap-te-xi ba-a-bi, *del* 94. — — *c*) turn = lead away, take away {wegführen}. TP v 53 spoil from them (consisting of) their goods & herds, *etc.* u-te-ir(*var* ter)-ra. Anp ii 8 (40) u-te-ru-šu-nu, I lead them away; 42 GUR(*var* u-te)-ra; iii 40 ilā-ni-šu u-te-ra, I lead away their gods. II 65 *O* ii 12 forty of his warchariots .... u-te-ru-ni (= 3 *pl*). — *d*) return, bring back; restore, requite {zurückbringen; wiederbringen}. Z^N iv 11 amēlu tu-ur-ru (= *a*:). TP v 8 u-ter-ra, I brought back; u-te-ir-ra (53). S 1028 *R* 8 u-ter-ri (Hr^L 418; WINCKLER, *Forsch.*, ii, '99, 308; PSBA xxiii 335). Esh ii 49 these lands u-ter-ma (I turned back to their former owners); III 15 *c* 23. Sarg *Khors* 137 *etc.* see šallu, 1 & § 90*c*. Xamm.-*letters* 26, 21—22 ša te-el-ku-u te-ir-šum BA iv 456; IV² 31 *R* 46 (end) ter[-ra-ši], bring her back! Rm 76 *O* 28, 29 a-na bēl ṭābtišu ṭa-ab-tu u-tir-ru-u-ni (BA iv 508 *foll*; PSBA xxiii 355); K 528 *R* 11 nu-ter-ra-am-ma a-na šar bēli-ja (JAOS xix 84); K 824. 40 ša u-tar-rak-ka ana libbi ša ana mār mārē (PSBA xxiii 63 *fol*) = Hr^{L} 358; 269; 290. K 810, 5 an-ni-u nu-tar-ra (1 *pl*). Xamm.-*code* xiii 16 (31 *etc.*) u-ta-ar, he shall return; xvi 47, 52 u-ta-a-ar; viii 67 u-ta-ar-ru-šu; li-te-ir xliii 80, 106; tu-ur-ru x 17, 34; xi 17. Perhaps KB iv 318, 12 tur-ru u xalaqi. H 60, 6 a-na bēli-šu ul u-tir; 8 u-te-ru-šu, they bring him back. PEISER, *Vertr.*, xl 13 *X.* u-il-tim$^{(meš)}$ ki-i u-tir-ri; cxix 10 the document Kabtā ki-i tu-ter-ru; T^{C} 142. — Rm 215 *R* 9, 10 the people of Nadan "la i-xal-li-iq" lu-u-ter-ru-nu (brought word) = Hr^{L} 422; PINCHES, *Texts*, *p* 7; ṭēmu turru. report, bring word see ṭēmu, 350 *cols* 1, 2. — especially note ana ašrišu(nu) turru, return to its (their) place, restore (used literally or figuratively). V 35, 32 the gods a-na aš-ri-šu-nu u-tir; 81—6—7. 209, 23 (BA iii 262—3); V 33 ii 13—17 Marduk & Çarpānit to Esagila & Babylon lu-u-tir-šu-nu-ti (& 21). Merod.-Balad.-stone ii 30 who the scattered people u-ter-ru aš-ru-uš-šin. Bu 88—5—12, 75 & 76 vi 12, 13 (BA iii 246, 247). KB iii (2) 90, 7 *E.* a-na aš-ri-šu tu-ur-ru. IV^{2} 39 *b* 13 my tablet a-na aš-ri-šu lu-ti(*var* te)-ir; also TP viii 49 u-tir (1 *sg*; § 30); 58 lu(-u)-tir. Sn vi 69 lu-tir. V 44 *d* 50 ana aš-ri-šu te-ir (*c-d* 30); V 70, 15. I 69 *c* 34 u-te-ir e-bi-ri-šu-nu a-na aš-ri-šu-nu. IV^{2} 16 *b* 50, 51 me-e šu-nu-ti a-na kar-pa-ti ter-ma (ip); H 144 put into! SCHEIL, *Notes* xxi 7 a-na aš-ri-šu li-te-ir (pc); 12 te-ir (ip). Sarg *Khors* 137 (*Ann* 304) sattukkēšunu baṭlūti u-tir aš-ru-uš-šu-un, I restored. *del* 285 (328) when its brickwork la-a GUR(-rat) = turrat, is not restored (renewed), KB vi (1) 254, 255. I 49 iii 20, 21 aš-šu ep-še-e-te ši-na-ti a-na aš-ri-ši-na tur-ri, BA iii 220, 221. — H 45, 11—12 ana ittišu u-tar-šu, he brings him over to his side. — Of eating: vomit. K 246 (H 86—7) i 67 a-ka-lu ša ina a-ka-li tur-ru (= GUR-GUR-RI), see muššudu, 599 *col* 2.

PINCHES in S. A. SMITH, *Asurb*, ii 74. — L^{4} ii 30 ki-šad-ka ter-ra, turn thy neck (in favor); K 824 *R* 5 (end) u-tir ri-mu, I turn (to thee) in favor. — *e*) turn over, deliver {übergeben, ausliefern} PEISER, *Vertr.*, cxiii 6 three minas .... *B* u-te-ru-ma (has turned over); xxvii 5 *K.* Bēl-si-lim tu-ter-ri, has turned over *B.*; also cxiii 12 & 23 u-ta-ri-ma, 24 tu-ta[-ri-m]a .to her sons. Xamm.-*code* xiv 54, 55 the loan and its interest to the merchant u-ta-ar, he shall return; but if he have no money (57) a-na tu-ur-ri-im. VATh 800, 10 a-nu-um-ma kaspa u-te-ra-qu, BA ii 558. — *f*) bring, reduce to (in general); change (in)to; make {bringen; verwandeln; machen}. V 61 vi 41; Bu 91—5—9, 210, 9; III 15 *c* 23; K 2675 *O* 5; Sn iv 37; Sarg *Khors* 136 see ramānu (*i. e.* use for one's own purpose; bring into one's power). KB iv 64 *no* 2 (= HILPRECHT, *Assyriaca*, 12—13) 15 ana pixāti u-te-ir. ZA viii 221. II 67, 23 the countries a-na mi-çir$^{(mât)}$ Aššur u-tir-ra see miçru, 1 (575 *col* 1), reduced to a province of Assyria. KB ii 8. 28; 242, 81; BA ii 308, 310. KB iv 66 *no* 2 *R* 10 eqlu šu-a-tum a-na pil[-ki]-šu u-ter-ru (= 3 *pl*). Here also Asb iv 90; see pū, 789 *col* 1, 15—17. — K 8522 *O* 8 sa mim-ma-ni i-çu a-na ma-'-di-e u-ter-ru, KB vi (1) 34, 35; *ibid* 62 ii 10 (*Dibbara*-legend) u-te-ru, had changed into. K 8204 iii/iv 24 du-ur ab-ni aš-ṭu la tu-tar ti-id-du (= טרפו) PSBA xvii 138, 139; BEZOLD, *Catalogue*, 905. — Sn i 77 ṭi-ṭal-liš u-še-me u-ti: -ma; *Kui* 1, 11: *Bell* 24. Sn iii 20 u-tir-ma ‖ am-nu; but may also begin a new sentence, = I returned. Asb v 34 u-tir-ru-niš-š.: ša-ni-ja-a-nu, they repented it. ana tilli u karmē turru, see karmu, 437 *col* 2. Sarg *Ann* 165 see mašū, 2 (597 *col* 1). IV^{2} 10 *b* 40 xi-iṭ-ṭi ax-tu-u ana da-me-iq-ti te-ir (§ 28); 59 *no* 2 (K 254) *b* 23 šutta a-na-ṭa-lu ana damēq-ti ter-ra. — *g*) in legal language. Rm 157, 6—7 *A.* was paid tur-ru u da-ba-bu ja-'-nu, KB iv 124, 125. — *h*) note especially gimillu(i, a) turru, see 222 *cols* 1, 2. Br 11984 & Šalm, *Throne-inscr.*, 14 a-na tu-ur gi-mil-li. — On tuktū terri see tuktū. — Here, perhaps, also Sn iii 22, 23 u-tir-ra ik-ki-bu-uš, I punished his sin?.

Knudtzon has: tur-ri (= ac) 150, 9; pr u-tir-ru-uš 19, 3; ps u-ta-ru 48 *R* 10; u-GUR-ra, 150 *R* 11; pm GUR-ur, 116 *R* 19 = return, recapture, regain.

K 3182 iii 29 mu-tir-ru bûli, tender of herds of cattle, herder.

turn, come back {zurückkommen}. T^M i 28 tu-ur-rat amât-sa ana pî-ša; v 81 your own deeds tu(*var* tur)-ra-ni (*var* nik)-ku-nu-ši, have come back on you. — IV² 13 *a* 45 mu-du-ka ana me-e li-tir-ka, AJSL xix 223 may thy wise one turn for thee to the waters. — V 45 iv 14 tu-ta-a-ra; H 55, 51—2 (= D 91, 33—4) NE-IN-GUR = u-te-ir; BA-AB-GUR = ut-te-ir; H 65, 42—45 u-tir; u-ta-ra; u-ta(*var* tar)-ru-u (*var* omits; confusion of târu & tarû; or Š¹ of arû = ארה); ul u-tir (*var* -ta-ri). II 9 *b* 31 u-ter-šu.

Zimmern, *Rituall.*, 31—37 ii 9 te-ri GAM(= takammis)-ma; iii 12 (or, te-ri-qam-ma? √rêqu); see *ibid rm* λ.

ℑ¹ — *a*) return, give back {zurückgeben}. IV² 31 *R* 39—45 ut-te-ir-ši, he returned to her (Ištar). — *b*) return {zurückkehren} Bu 91—5—9, 210 *O* 9—10 ra-man-ku-nu a-na ^(amêl) *N* tu-ut-te-ra (*cf* 20) = Hr^L 403; PSBA xxiii 348 *foll.* Xamm.-*code* xviii 1; xxvii 18, 26. — *c*) call back {zurückrufen} K 81, 21 ut-ter-ra-an-ni + *R* 6 (Hr^L 274; BA i 200; 441). — *d*) report, bring news, see ṭêmu. — *e*) bring {bringen} Peiser, *Vertr.*, xcvii 9 Šillibi ut-ter(-ma), has brought (the money). — *f*) bring into one's power. H 77, 44 et-lu Šamaš Adad qar-du ana i-di-šu-nu ut-ter-ru = IV² 5 *a* 76; Lehmann, ii 111 *rm* 1 on *l* 43. — *g*) change, turn into {verwandeln} NE VI 61 ana barbari tu-ut-ter-ri-šu; *del* 102 (107) mim]-ma nam-ru ana e-ṭ[u-t]i ut-ter-ru. — *h*) prolong. K 3182 ii 44 (end) balâṭa ut-tar, he shall prolong his life (& 50). — *i*) gain; K 3182 ii 47 mi-na-a ut-tar, what does he gain? — *k*) claim. Bu 91—5—9, 511, 11 ut-te-er-ru-ši, they claimed for her.

T. A. (Bezold, *Diplomacy*, xxxvi) has these forms: Q pr i-tu-ur (Lo) 36 *R* 25; 16, 33 a-na-ku a-tu-ur, I returned; 9, 38 i-du-ru ja-nu, none have returned; (Ber) 18 *R* 7 i-tu-ru; 26 *R* 65 ki la i-du-ur-ra; 8 *R* 7 i-tu-ur-ru (= ps). — pc (Lo) 10, 23 li-du-u-ra, that she may return; (Ber) 24 *R* 54 Gilia li-du-ur-ra-aš-šu ought to return to him. — ps (?) (Lo) 41, 20 i-na xarrâ-ni i-ta-ar-ra-aš-šu. — pm (Ber) 48, 54 ta-ra a-na mâti-šu, he returned to his country; 71, 51 the city ta-ra-at to my lord. — ac (Ber) 9 *R* 4 a-nja? a-la-ki u ta-ri; 48, 70 iš-tu ta-ri a-bi-ka. — ℑ pr & ps (Lo) 8, 53 u a-na-ku II-šu a-na eli-ka u-te-ir-ru (I will return twofold); Tel H.sy 19 u a-di u-ti-ru-ši; (Lo) 11, 8 a-na mi-ni la-a tu-te-ru-na a-ya-tu a-na ja-a-ši (+ 48). — pc (Ber) 22 *R* 31 axi-ja li-i-te-ir-an-ni, let my brother return to me. 7 *R* 35 pi-dij-e-šu li-te-ir-ru-ni-iš-šu, that they may refund him his ransom. — ip (Ber) 8 *R* 5 kill them and da-mi-šu-nu te-e-ir, avenge their blood! (ZA v 146); 56, 139 i ti-ir-nu, bring us back (into our city)!; 106, 10—11 u i-na ša-la-mi ti-ir-ma bîti-ka, return to thy house! (Lo) 13, 25 te-ra-ni a-ya-tu, send me word! — ps (Ber) 3 *R* 19 u-ta-ar-ra-ak-ku, I would send it back; 24 *R* 54, 55; 18 *R* 8 u-da-a-ar-šu-nu-ti, I will return them. — ac (Ber) 92, 20 ša te-la-am-ma du-ru, whom you wished to bring. — ℑ¹ (Ber) 21, 53 a-ma-ti a-na la a-ma-ti la ut-te-e-ir; 23 *O* 56; + 25 a-na ši-ip-ki ut-te-e-ir-šu-nu, the images were cast; 26 u ki-i a-na ši-ip-ki du-ur-ru, and when the images were cast; ZA v 16; 144. (Lo) 22, 34 li-it-te-ir. — ℑ¹ (Ber) 100, 14 šu-te-ra-at ali-ia a-na ja-ti-ja, and my city has been restored to me. (Lo) 14, 22 šu-te-ra a-ya-tu a-na ja-ši, the return of an answer has not been granted to me. — ℑℑ (?) (Lo) 28, 13 la-a it-te-ir a-ma-tu a-na ja-ši (& 31).

Derr. mutirru, mutîru, 636 *col* 2; tušâru; tamêrtu (??; ZA xvii 247; ZDMG 58, 248) & these 10:

târu *2. n.* — *a*) return {Rückkehr}. V 33 i 50 ta]-ar-šu iq-bu-u, his return (to Babylon) they announced, KB iii (1) 138 *rm* 2. *del* 273 (306) ina ta-ri-šu, on his return (>< J^I-N 40 in seinem Schrecken). IV² 31 *O* 1 a-na erçit la târi (= KUR-NU-GI), KB vi (1) 80, & *rm* 2; KAT³ 636 & *rm* 3 >< H^F 56; J^W 65 *no* 11; Jeremias, *Hölle & Paradies*, 14 *fol*, Br 7406, 1973; AV 8694, 8788 târat; II 32 *g-h* 19; K 1451 *R* 3; BA i 462 *rm* **; AV 6396; Br 1996 >< 7406; see also Br 7407 on II 48 *e-f* 7. Perhaps K 1396 (Hr^L 185) 12—13 li-ix-xu-ra ta-a-a-ar-šu am-ra a-na xi-is-si-ti. K 629 (Hr^L 65) 10 (JAOS xix 84). — *b*) mercy, favor {Erbarmen, Gnade}. V 21 *a-b* 54—56 ta-a-ru ‖ ti-ra-nu, ša(written LIB)-gur-ru-u, kiš-šu, BA i 462 *rm* 1; ZK ii 338. KB vi (1) 96 *R* 18 (*Adapa*-legend) .... la ta-a-ar (see *rm* 4 *ibid*) ip-pa-lu, no mercy! they say. SCHEIL, *Nabd*, i 5; V 35, 11 (>< KB iii, 2, 122); V 64 *a* 15; K 8522 *O* 13 (KB vi, 1, 34) see rašû, 1 Q & Q¹. — *c*) in legal language: claim; *cf* tuâru. KB iv 168 ii 10 duppi la ta-ri u la da-bu-bu, *i. e.* he shall for ever renounce all claim to (JASTROW, *Papers of Philad. Or. Club*, i 121, 122); 200 i 11 ta-a-ri u da-ba-bu ina bi-ri-šu-nu ia-a-nu (Neb 116, 8; 122, 6 ta-ri). KB iii (1) 158 *col* 3, 30 abnu (?) la ta-a-ra u la ra-ga-mi; Br. M. 84, 2—11, 138 ta-a-ri u ru-gum-ma-a ul i-šu-u.

târu *3.*; **tajâru**, *adj* merciful, compassionate, gracious {erbarmend, barmherzig, gnädig} §§ 13; 14; 64. I 35 *no* 2, 7; IV² 9 *a* 26, 27 (= MAR-BA-NA, EME-SAL, Br 5822); 59 *no* 2, 8 see rêmênû. K^M 6, 63 ta-a-a-ra-ta (ilu) Sin; 27, 16 aš-šum ta-a-a-ra-ta (*var* -rat), since thou art compassionate. H 81 (K 133) *R* 16 be-lum ša ana a-li-šu ta-a-a-ru, ana um-mi-šu it-pe-šu, PSBA xvi 227 *foll.* KB iv 48 (iii) 9 Šamaš-ta-ja-ru; vi (1) 278 i 44 ta-ja-a[-ru].

(ilu) **te-ir**, god of mercy, JOHNS, *Doomsday-Book*, 82; but see (HILPRECHT-)CLAY, *Murashû*, pref. xvi *foll.*

turru *1.* ‖ e-di-lu, see târu, 1 ℶ. Here perhaps also Neb 134, 14 tu-ru bâbi lock {Thorschluss}. I 52 *no* 3 *b* 13 ina tu-ur-ri e-li-i ša abulli (ilat) Ištar. BEZOLD, *Achaem.*, 45 *no* xvii 9 combines with תור.

turru *2.* reduced? S^c 6, 13 BE = tur-rum; *f* perh. KNUDTZON, 33 *R* 9 tur-ri-tum, see *ibid p* 325.

tîru *1.* lock; cover {Verschluss, Überzug} AV 8958. Šalm, *Mon*, ii 101 see kasaru. 418 *col* 2. Neb iv 6 (iç) ka-ri-e-šu za-râti qirbišu ušalbišu ti-i-ri ša-aš-ši u abni; KB iii (2) 16. FLEMMING, *Neb*, 45 = row, especially of pearls & metal pieces. Ner i 28 the copper-serpents ti-i-ri kaspi e-ib-bi u-ša-al-bi-iš, KB iii (2) 72.

tîru *2.* guardian {Wächter} Z^B 46 *rm* 2. II 51 *d-f* 47 ti-i-rum = manzaz pâni, see 562 *col* 1; where also further instances. Br 0865. GGA '98, 826—7 *ad* IV² 55 *no* 2 *O* 4, 6, 21 & 10 (ti-ru). K 13583 (M^S *pl* 17) 4 GAL-T]E = ti-i-ru; 5 tîru ša tuk-ki; 8 ti-ir bi-ti. Rm 338 *R* 7 GAL-GAL with gloss ti-ru (M^S *pl* 21). K^M 9, 15 ti(-i)-ru u na-an-za-zu liq-bu[-u damiqtim]; 22, 16 ti-i-ru u man-za[-za]; KING translates as if têru = ip: return and be established! 18, 9 çab-ta-ku-ma ki-i ti-i-ri. THUREAU-DANGIN, *Rev. Hist. Lit. Rel.*, '91 Nov. 488 *rm* 4 = prefect.

tîrânu. mercy, compassion {Gnade, Erbarmen}. Z^B 102; AV 8952. V 21 *a-b* 62 ti-ra-nu = re-e-mu; 54 = ta-a-ru; 57 = mu-us-ta-ru. ZA iv 241, 30 see naqrûṭum, 720 *col* 2. K 13583 (M^S *pl* 17) 10 ti-ra-nu ša LU (= DIB?). K 3802 *O* 1; K 12484 (catchline) šumma ti-ra-nu ina qaqqad amêli.

târtu, tajârtu. §§ 13; 64; 65, 11 *rm* (properly *f* of Q ac of târu, 1); ZA iii 13, 14; vi 208; BA i 442; 432; AV 8694. return {Rückkehr}. Anp ii 15 ina ta-(j)a-ar-ti-(j)a, upon my return; Šalm, *Obel*, 41, 130, 140; *Mon*, i 27; Šamš ii 30 ina ta-a-a-ar-ti-šu; iii 37 ina ta-a-a-ar-ti-a, § 74, 1. Sn i 40 i-na ta-a-a-ar-ti-ja; ii 29; iii 68. I 43, 38 i-na ta-a-a-ar-ti-šu-nu; Sn *Bav* 40. Asb iii 52; v 41 & 126; ix 115; vi 112 ta-a-a-rat ilû(*var* bêlû)-ti-ša. On II 48 *e-f* 7 see Br 7407. II 43 *a-b* 15 a-lik-tum >< ta-a-a-ra-tum AV 8694.

târâtu. mercy, compassion ‖ tîrânu. K^M 6, 92 çu-lul-ki rap-šu ta-a-a-ra-tu-ki kab[-ta?]; 7, 30: broad is thy protection; mighty thy compassion; 46, 6 ta-a-a-ra-tu-ka kab-ta-a-tum; 22, 58.

tarû *1.* pr itarri croak {krächzen} JENSEN, 436; 517. *del* 146 (155) the raven ik-kal i-ša-ax-xi i-tar-ri ul is-sa(i)x-ra. BALL, *Genesis* (SBOT) 54 reads iq-rib išaxxi itarri, he made for it, waded about, croaking, (returned not); KB vi (1) 500, 501. others, ZA iii 420 *etc.*: he went off; √arû. ℶ ag see mutarritu, 626 *col* 1.

tarû *2.* protect {beschützen}. V 35, 14 Marduk, the great lord, ta-ru-u nišê-šu, the protector (?) of his nations, BA ii 210,

211; *ibid* 231 mentions ta-ru-u = na-šu-u. II 39 *f* 41 GI = ta-ra-u, AV 8782 id that of târu, 1. — Der.

tarânu. protection {Schutz, Schirm}? V 47 *a* 17 ta-ra-nu : çil-lu, 875 *col* 1. Sn *Kui* 4. 8 çu-lul ta-ra-a-ni ša qirib barakkâni e-ṭu-su-un u-šax-la-a ûmêš ušnammir. V 23 *a-d* 18 MI-MI (ku-uk-ku) = ta-ru[-nu] ‖ eṭûtum, eklitum, BA ii 231. Bu 88—5—12, 75 + 76 v 8, 9 u-šat-r]i-ça ta-ra-an]-šu. *cf* Bu 88—5—12, 77 vi 1 *foll.* BA iii 246, 247. Meissner & Rost, 27 roof {Dach}.

tarû 3. take, fetch {nehmen, holen}? II 9 *c-d* 61 see maruštu, 582 *col* 2; Br 2580. IV[2] 2 vi 1, 2 u-tuk-ku lim-nu i-ta-ru-nš (= MU-UN-DA-RU-UŠ, Br 1445); + *a* 22, 23 ul-tu ša-di-i i-ta-ra-a; could also be Q[t] of arû (see KB vi (1) 54; 371). K 3456 *O* 35 u sisû la-tur (> la itur; √tûru?, does not return) u-ga-ri i-tar-ri (goes away?). Scheil, Notes lx (Constant. 588) *O* 12 ina SU (= zumri) ši-ip-ki te-tir-ri; *R* 8, 11, 15, 21 (*Rec Trav.*, xxiii). Often in Xamm.-*letters*: šu-pu-ur .... li-it-ru-ni-iq-qu, BA iv 480 (√arû). Where belongs NE 11 *col* iv *a* 7 tur-ru-u lu-u uš-ten-ki? KB vi (1) 140.

tarru. so KB vi (1) 458, 476; AV 8816 for ṭarru, 358 *col* 2. Here, also, tarl(u)u-gallu = the king of the tar(DAR)-birds = the rooster. II 37 *a-c* 87 K]U-KU-RA-NU-XU = tar-lugal-lum; II 40 *no* 1 *R* 35. On the (kakkab) tar-lugal V 46 *a(-b)* 27 see KB vi (1) 458. Also see ZA vii 399 & viii 339.

tarru *2*. see darru, 268 *col* 2, end.

tar-ru, Br 4008 see qutru.

tûra (?) K 583 *R* 2 e-da-ar tu-u-ra, Hr[L] 5.

te-rum (so perhaps instead of kar-rum). V 28 *c-d* 64 = si-pu-u, 777 *col* 1; AV 8957.

tirru *1*. forest {Wald}. II 23 *e-f* 56 tir-rum ‖ ki-iš-tum; § 25; AV 8967; Br 7656. *cf* S[a] vi 20 te-ir (see value TIR; § 9, 179) = ki-iš-tum, AV 8951. tijâru (*q. v.*) may belong here also.

tirru *2*. (?) Neb 313, 2 ten ma-ši-xu ša AŠ-A-AN ten ma-ši-xu ti(?)-ir-ri.

tarabu. AV 8784, Br 8946; M[S] 101 *col* 1 *ad* V 23 *a-d* 18 see tarânu. AV 8784 also quotes S 896, 2 .... | tur-ru-bu; 3 .... xa-ba-šu. K 4195 *R* 6.

tarbû. sprout, offspring {Spross, Sprössling}. § 65, 32*a*; AV 8790. V 29 *g-h* 71 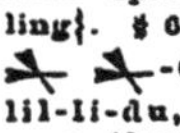-GA = tar-bu-u, followed by lil-li-du, Br 1167. II 42 *c* 36 could be read (šam) ša-mu (> šammu) tar-bu-u; see mutarbû, 626 *col* 1. √rabû, 1; whence also these 4:

tarbâtu. K 3182 iii 54 tar-ba-ti-ka i-dal-lal, he shall worship thy greatness. AJSL xvii 143; ZA iv 12. Pognon, *Wadi-Brissa*, 94 has ta-ar-ba-a-tim, (but??).

tarbîtu ‖ of turbû. AV 8798. Heur. i 176. Sn iii 64 tar-bit bir-ki-ja (Ball, *Genesis*, SBOT, 117 *ad* Gen 50, 23); vi 47 beams out from lofty cedars tar-bit (šad) Xa-ma-nim; Asb x 98; Smith, *Asurb*, 55, 3; KB iii (2) 198, 22. Esh iii 18 *T.* tar-bit êkalli-ja. K 2675 *R* 3 (III 29 *R*) see pagû, 790 *col* 2. K 4871 + K 3622 tar-bit ki-e-ši (*var* ki-is-sa). der Spross von *Kiš*, ZDMG 58, 659—60. K 133 (H 81) *R* 6—7 be-lum tar-bit a-bi ul i-di. T[M] i 124 Nusku is called tar-bit apsî bi-nu-ut (il) Êa. S[3] 59 er-nu u šur-man çi-ru-ut tar-bi-ti Xa-ma-nu u Lab-na-nu, Lehmann, ii 16, 17. V 64 *b* 10 (KB iii, 2, 100); I 69 *b* 12 (KB iii, 2, 82). Xamm.-*code* xxxii 37 (47, 62, 72) tar-bi-tum(-tim, *ll* 55, 83), Harper, 190: one brought up, foster-son, adopted son. II 9 *c-d* 67—72 NAM-ID-UD-DU = tar-bi-tu (Br 7885); id + A-NI = tar-bi-su (> t-šu); id + A-NI-KU = a-na tar-bi-ti-šu (ZA i 400 education; bringing up); -GA = tar-bi-tu; id + A-NI = tar-bi-is-su; id + A-NI-KU = a-na tar-bi-ti-šu; (*cf* II 33 *no* 2, *e-f* 16; -bu-). Z[B] 49, 50 on V 50 *b* 43.

tarbittu. Cyr 349, 10 & 12 tar-bit-tum. T[C] 126 compares תַּרְבִּית.

tarbûtu. abstr. noun. AV 8800. V 40 *d* 35 ID-UD-DU = tar-bu-tum (& li-qu-tum) Br 6613, 7885; *cf* 38 *b-c* 29  = tar-bu-tu (27, 28 = ra-bu-u; ru-ub-bu-u) Br 7437. Also see Br 2423 on ZK ii 81, 21.

turubu, turbu'u & turbûtu. dust, dust-cloud, cloud; multitude {Staub, Staubwolke, Wolke; Getümmel, (Menschen)-masse} or, at least, something the like. § 65, 31 *f*. D[8] 78; HAUPT-PATERSON, *Numbers*, (SBOT) 57: brood. KB iii (2) 88 *col* 1, 36 ba-aç-ça u tu-ru-ba ši-pi-ik e-pi-ru ra-bu-tim. Sn iv 12 and that *M.* saw tur-bu-' šēpē çābē-ja, KB ii 101 den Staub der Füsse meiner Krieger. V 55, 31 i-na tur-bu-'u-ti-šu-nu na-'a-du-ru pān [(il)] Šam-ši, through their dust was darkened the face of the sun. II 5 *c-d* 3 XU-BER?]-IŠ-RA = e-rib (*cf* eribū, 95 *col* 1) tur-bu-'u-ti, a cloud of grasshoppers (?) Br 5087. II 32 *g-h* 9 IŠ (= SAXAR = epru, dust) PIŠ-PIŠ (= rapašu, be wide, extend) = tur-bu-'u-tum, Br 5100. Perh. II 28 *no* 5, 64 tu-ru-bat išāti; Br 6101: tušub-batu.

turbal'ū' see nidūtu, 649 *col* 2 & II 52, 71 (AV 9053 tur-ba-ṭu-u), Br 9790.

tarbiānu an officer }ein Beamter}. K 616 *R* 4 [(amêl)] tar-bi-a-ni i-si-ja it-tal-ku-u-ni, Hr[L] 127. AV 8796 reads -*ça*- instead of -*a*-.

tarbaçu — *a*) sheepfold, stable, yard }Hürde, Stall, Hof}. √rabaçu. § 65, 32*a*; AV 8794. id S[b] 133 tu-ur | 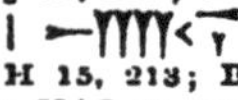 (= TUR) | tar-ba-çu; H 15, 213; Br 2864; GGN '83, 96; PEISER, KAS 85 properly: court, yard. JOHNS, *Doomsday-Book*, 24. id in Xamm.-*code* xiii 76; Anp ii 71. T. A. (Lo) 82, 8 i-na ta-ar-ba-ç[i]. KB vi (1) 78, 79; BA iv 130, 131; (Ber) 73. 18 Simyra tar-ba-aç bēli-ja u e[-kal]-lim, a court & a house. BANKS, *Diss.* 18 *no* 2, 4 ša be-lu(m) a-mat-su tar-ba-ça(-çi) maruštum i-pu-uš (inflicts misery upon the stable); 14, 103 tar-ba-ça i-a-ab-bat ‖ su-pu-ri i-na-as-sax. S 1708 *O* (= IV[2] 18[*] *no* 6) 5 u-tuk-ku lim-nu a-lu-u lim-nu ina çi-rim tar-ba-ça ib-ta-'-u; 7 tar-ba-ça ki-ma nu-še-e un-ni-iš; *R* 6 (+12) ina i-tal-lu-ki-šu tar-ba-çu šu-a-tu. IV[2] 4 *b* 28, 29 (K 3169 iii) xi-mētu ša iš-tu tar-ba-çi el-li ub-lūni. cream which some one (*i. e.*, they) brought from a clean stable, AJSL xix 136; 209. IV[2] 9 *b* 3, 4 thy word (o Sin) tar-ba-çu u su-pu-ru u-šam-ri(dal?); see marū, 1 (584 *col* 2; THOMPSON, *Reports*, ii pref. xxv). K 161 *col* 3 alpu ina tar-ba-si (? ZK ii 11). Sm 26 i (?) 16 see miqtu, 579 *col* 2, end, & translate: Niederlage des Hofes (*i. e.*, die geschädigten Tiere) BA iv 84 × BA iii 500. KB iv 160 (ii) 29 end: tar-ba-çu, garden. II 67, 18 [(al)] Tar-ba-çu, AV 8795. See also ZA vi 440: ein beim Hause gelegener Garten, especially in Anp ii 71. — id often in astronomical texts: halo, of 22°, both of the moon & the sun, THOMPSON, *Reports*, ii pref. xxiv *fol.* — *b*) womb, uterus }Mutterleib} see rubçu. Lay 38, 3; or ša-surru (?) as MEISSNER & ROST, 2 suggest. Also see II 55 *a* 15. — *c*) as ‖ of maçallu, ZA vi 440: des Hirten schattiger Ruheplatz (572 *col* 2), Br 2480.

NOTE. — [(1)] Bêl tarbaçi perhaps the lord (owner) of the court; the moon god, III 66 *col* 8, 17; BA ii 611, 8; PSBA xxi 126.

Tarbīçu. name of a town. I 48 *no* 5, 6 [(al)] Tar-bi-çi; 6, 4; I 7 D 4: AV 8797. KNUDTZON, *no* 124 left edge 2; L[3] 9 (LEHMANN, i 38, 39; ii 20, 21).

tērubtu. entry, entrance }Einzug, Eingang} AV 8959. √erebu. *c. st.* te-ru-bat, TP vi 90 the temples of the gods I finished te-ru-bat (some -be, assuming *pl* of *tērubu) bītātišunu aškun. KB v (index, 33* *col* 2, end) consecration (?) of a temple; (Ber) 1, 26 .... ti-ru-ba-at bīti-a.

te-ri-gu-u, II 23 *c-d* 11 ‖ daltum; AV 8954.

targigu. bad, evil, wicked; enemy }schlecht, böse; Feind}. √ragagu; AV 8801. TP iii 34 Tigl. Pil. sāpinu qa-bal tar-ge-ge; L[TP] 134, 135. Anp i 7 Ninib mu-šamqit tar-gi-ge. ZA ix 273 *rm* 3 √רגג or רגע (?).

tar-gul-lum, S[b] 284. *cf* ṭarkullu (359) & tarkullu.

ta(u)rgumān(n)u. dragoman, interpreter }Dolmetscher} √רגם; § 65, 32*e*. JENSEN, *Deu. Litztg.*, '95 *no* 26 *col* 808. K 2012

---

tur-ru-bi-e, POGNON, *Wadi-Brissa*, 108, V 12 *c-d* 45, Br 14359 read mār ra-bi-e & see KB iii (2) 124 *rm* 3 on V 66 ii 3. ∾ turbanūtu. REVILLOUT, *Mélanges Assyr.-Babyl.*, i 7/8 (1889) read mār banūtu & see *pp* 581, 582.

R 10 .... BAL = tur-gu-man-nu, ZK ii 300; 302; ZA i 68. ZK ii 509: Aramean loanword for Assyrian bēl lišāni. K 1260, 7 tar-gu-ma-nu ša (mât) Man-na-a-a (AV 8803). T. A. (Ber) 21, 25 and Xanī tar-gu-ma-an[-nu] of my brother. LAGARDE *Mitth.*, ii 177 תַּרְגְּמָן Indo-European; see also *Armen. Stud.*, *no* 847; FRÄNKEL, *Aram. Lehnwörter*, 280. On the other hand, see HAUPT, *Kings* (SBOT) 117.

taradu (?). Xammurabi-*letters* = send {senden}. AV 8785; BA iv 439 *foll*; 480. 33, 8 a-na Bāb-ili (ki) ta-ra[-di]-im-ma, to send to *B*. + 10 it-ti-šu-nu ta-ra-di-im; 41, 15 i-na ta-ra-di-ka, and when thou doest send. — pr 1, 15 (amēl) *G* ša ta-at-ru-da-aš-šu, whom thou hast sent; 43, 9 (end) and *Š* a-na ma-ax-ri-ja ta-at-ru-dam. — ip 41, 13 tu-ur-da-aš-šu-nu-ti, send them! + 19 tu-ur-dam (2, 15; 9, 20). — ps 41, 17 la [ta]-tar-ra-da-aš-šu-nu-ti. — Q[t] 1, 13; 22, 6; 34, 7 (end) at-tar-dam, I did send. *Cf* MEISSNER, BA ii 563, 564 (VATh 793) 13 at-tar-da-qu, ich schicke zu dir.

terdū, terdennu ‖ rid(d)u, child, offspring {Kind, Nachkomme} *etc.*; D^{S} 143. AV 8960, 8961; ‖ mār(u) 581 *col* 1, *med.* Sp II 265 *a* xxi 8 see katū, 2 (455 *col* 1). PRINCE, *Diss*, 96; & AJP xiv 113 *ad* BA i 505 *rm* †† would read tar (instead of quṭ)-d(ṭ)in-ni-e *etc.*

tirxu, a vessel {ein Gefäss}. II 22 *d-f* 17 (V 42 *c* 29) DUK-NAM-TAR = tirxu, Br 2115, T^{M} 144; ZA vi 216; AV 8963 compares also K 2061, 10 tir (xu-um) xum = ṭa-ab(p)-lum (353 *col* 2).

terxu in P. N. of female: (sal) te-ir(& ter)-xi li-ja 83—1—18, 1847 *R* iv (PSBA xviii 256); T^{M} vi 37 mārē tir-xi ša e-ni-ti.

NOTE. — Perhaps connected with תרח ZDMG 40, 167, 168; LAGARDE, *Übersicht*, 131; JENSEN, ZA vi 70 (Tarxu Gottes(?)name der Mitanni); SACHAU, ZA vii 90 *foll.* But see KAT³ 484 *rm* 2 against ZA vi 70. On תרח also WINCKLER, *Forsch.*, i 98—100.

taraxu. ℨ V 45 vii 47 tu-tar-rax; or ℨ[t] of araxu, 1? (see 98 *col* 2). ZK ii 216 nam-xar tur-ru-xu.

tarax(x)u. BA iii 223; 272—3: Grundmauer (?). V 64 *b* 6, 7 see šallaru & maxaçu, 2 (525 *col* 2, end). ‖ kalakku, Asb x 83 (ZK ii 344). I 49 *d* 9 with the finest of oil ab-lu-la t[a]-ra-xuš. Bu 88—5—12, 75 + 76 iv (K 192 *R*) 12 (end) ab-lu-la ta-ra-ax(*var* omits)-xuš. See also OPPERT, *Mélanges Renier*, 228 & *rm* 1. T. A. (Ber) 26 i 29 ta-ra-ax-šu ša xurāçi.

turāxu. ibex {Steinbock}? § 65, 13. TP vii 6 they (the gods) permitted me to hunt in the high mountains sugullāt na-a-le *pl* ajalē ar-mi *pl* tu-ra-(a-)xe *pl*. I 28 *a* 19 ar-me *pl* tu-ra-a-xe *pl* na-a-le *pl* ja-e-le *pl*. IV² 58 *a* 42 çab-t]i (= catch!) a-a-li u tu-ra-xu, ZA xvi 168 *foll.* NE 72, 31 nim-ri min-di-na a-a-la tu-ra-xa, KB vi (1) 227. V 50 *b* 47 tu-ra-xa (= DARA) ina qaq-qa-di-šu u qar-ni-šu iç-ça-bat. Šalm, *Mon*, ii 80 city: Til-ša-tur-a-xi, KB i 170 *rm* 4. II 6 *c-d* 10 DARA = tu-ra-xu (S^{b} 377 da-ra | ID | tu-ra-xu; H 15, 205; Br 2947; ZK ii 274; 313); followed by (11) DARA-BAR (= MAŠ) = a-a-lu; (12) DARA-BAR-KAK = na-a-a-lu. AV 9050. See also II 55, 27; 62 *a* 9; LOTZ, *Sabbat*, 78.

NOTE. — See GEORG HOFFMANN, *Auszüge*, *no* 124; NÖLDEKE, ZDMG 32, 33; DELITZSCH, *Lit. Centralbl.*, '85 *col* 384; ZK ii 153; 314—5. D^{Par} 90 *fol*; D^{Pr} 90 *rm* תרח = turāxu; BA i 224 *ad* 170.

tar-xab-ni see qutrinnu.

terxatu, *f* betrothal gift; marriage settlement, dowry, trousseau {Vermählungsgeschenk, Mitgift, Aussteuer} AV 8962. Asb ii 61 his daughter & the daughters of his brothers it-ti tir-xa-ti ma-'a-as-si I received from him; 70, 71 ‖ 78 nudunnē (654, 655) ma'adi; SMITH, *Asurb*, 70, 69. See also Xamm.-*code* edited by R. F. HARPER, 190. T. A. (Lo) 8, 48 a-na te-ir-xa-tim-ma li-še-e-bi-il (+ 58); (Ber) 24, 23—24; 28, 14. V 24 *c-d* 46—48 ŠA-SAL-UŠ(?)-DI-A-NI = tir-xa-az[-su]; AZAG-NIN-TUK = tir-xa[-tum]; AZAG-NIN-TUK-A-NI = tir-xa-az-su (ina? pa-aš-šu-ri iš-ku-un); H 217, 86; MEISSNER, 148 (er legte seine Morgengabe auf eine Schüssel); WZKM iv 305. Br 9920 on 47. V 11 *d-f* 7 AM-MU-LU-UŠ-SA (Br 4755; ZA ii 201) = ŠA-SAL-UŠ-SA (KB iii, 1, 50 *rm* 15: NIG-GAL-GIŠ-SA) = tir-xa-tum, Br 5062, 12174; H 108, 7; 111, 54; D 128, 55; KB iii (1) 58 *rm* 14; on ìòò see also ZK i 296; ZA iii 38, 39. K 245 (H 69) ii 10 = ka-sap [ti]r-xa-ti, ZK ii 273; ZA i 198. — See ZDMG 43, 193; MEISSNER, 13, 14; ZA i 395 (√rixû, verschwägern). AMIAUD, ZA iii 39. Also *cf* further in supplement. To the same stem, no doubt, belongs:

terxûtu. Nabd 1030, 14 ina lib-bi ip-pu-šu te-ir-xu-ti, WZKM iv 126 obligation {Verpflichtung}? ZIMMERN, *Ritualt.*, *no* 61 ii 10 t]er-xa-a-te ina mux-xi-šu tu-še-taq, die *Gaben* sollst du von ihm entfernen.

taraku. pr itruk; *ps* itarrak. — *a*) *trans.* beat, strike {schlagen, hauen}. V 19 *c-d* 26 ta-ar | TAR | ta-ra-ku (AV 8786, Br 391; H 9 & 202, 18); 27 du-ub | DUP ta-ra-ku ša qi-na-zi (Br 7032); H 25, 535; followed by ma-xa-çu. SCHEIL, Notes lx (Constant. 583) *O* 23 A-ŠA-ŠA (= mê têbibti) ta-tar-rak, *Rec. Trav.*, xxiii. K 3464 *O* 10 ka-li-šu-nu ta-tar (= xaš?)-rak (= šal?), PSBA xxiii 115 *fol*; see *ibid* 119. IV^2 22 *a* 27 which H 202, 18 reads i-tar-rak × the usual i-xaš-šal (Br 391); see puqlu (822 *col* 2). Perh. K 8204, 11 see PSBA xvii 138, 139. — *b*) *intr.* break asunder, burst. go to pieces, go to ruin {(zer)brechen, zu Grunde gehen}. *Etana*-legend (Rm 2, 454) *R* 30 našru i-tar-rak, KB vi (1) 114, 115; 421. Sarg *Khors* 148 lib-bu-šu-un it-ru-ku(-ma imqutsunûti xattu), their heart beat (with fright), KÜCHLER; *Ann* 256 it-ru-ku lib-bu-šu-un (ZA iv 412); *Stele* ii 38; Sn iii 48. Sn vi 19 ki-i ša at(d)-mi summati kuš-šu-di i-tar-ra-ku lib-bu-šu-un (Sn *Bav* 42, where *at-* is a mistake for *i-*). — K 770 *R* 1 GI : ta-ra-ki; 2 GI : ša-la-mu; 3 GI : ka-a-nu; K 874 *R* 5 GI : ta-ra-ku; GI : ka-a-nu, THOMPSON, *Reports*, 25; 27; *ibid* 87 A (K 1007 *R* 1). K 4241 + 4556 *R* 5 A?]N la ta-rak; *cf* II 59 *R* 22 (il) la ta-rak, Br 6410; P. N. of a god; III 69 *a* 66; IV^2 21, 1 B *O* 26 (Br 997); ZIMMERN, *Ritualt.*, 50 ii 7 two pictures of god la(-)ta-ra-ak; T^M vi 7. It is, of course, not certain whether this name has any connection with taraku.

$\mathfrak{Q}^t$ (?). K 3456 *O* 33 (amêl) naggaru mu-du-u it-ta-rak qi-e .... PSBA xxi 38—40.

$\mathfrak{J}$ IV^2 30* *no* 3 *R* 9, 10 see qinazu, 918 *col* 1. turruku see nasasu, 2 (703, 704) & T^M i 65, 66 tur-ru-uk e (la) tal-lik (lak), lässt ab (?), gehe nicht. V 45 vii 48 tu-tar(xaš?)-rak(šal?) (or $\mathfrak{J}^t$ of ארך?). In Astronomical Reports: K 770, 3 when at the moon's appearance its horns tur-ru-ka, point away from one another (THOMPSON, *Reports*, *no* 25; pref. xxxvii); K 874 *R* 1; K 1007 *O* 6 (*ibid* 27; 87 A).

$\mathfrak{N}$ *del* 123 (130) si-bu-u û-mu i-na ka-ša-a-di it-ta-rak (*tur* -rik?) me-xu-u, KB vi (1) 238, 239 & *rm* 11, wird der Orkan ... (nieder)geschlagen. IV^2 28 *no* 1 *a* 16 see qinazu. Cyr 370, 12 ta-at-ta-rak. — **Der.**:

tirku *1*. IV^2 49 *b* 32 (= T^M 1, 119) see qa-çaçu, $\mathfrak{J}^t$ (923 *col* 1). T^M 125; 157 *col* 2: perhaps √ארך, whence urraku.

tirku *2*. (?). PSBA xxiii 119: membre du corps humain (K 6473).

tarruku. some perfume {ein Parfüm}. M^S 101 *col* 2. Rm 367 + 83, 1—18, 461 *a* iii 7 GIŠ-ŠIM-TAR-RU-UK = tar-ru-ku, M^S *pl* 23.

tiriku (?). K 4152 + 4183 *R* 37 ti-ri-ku a-ga-lim(-ši)? = u (U?) .... (M^S *pl* 7) so DELITZSCH; while M^S 71 *col* 1 (end) reads su-xu-ur a-ga-lim; the text is badly preserved, and accurate reading quite impossible. — Nabd 693, 2 te-rik-šarru-ut-su, a P. N. (√ארך?).

ti(e)riktu. (√ארך?, be long); § 65, 32 *b*; thus length {Länge} K 4170 + K 4322 *R* 23 KI-UD = ti(te)-rik-tum (Br 9789); also ‖ ni-du-tum, *q. v.* & maš-ka-nu (H 31, 724 gloss ki-is-lax); 27 KI-KAL (Br 9761) = te-rik-tum (& kankal-lum, nidûtum). H 68, 21—27; AV 8955. See also Br 10456 *ad* II 22 *c-d* 39.

ti(a)rkatu see dirkatu, 268 *col* 2; & also têniqu. Br 11532. Some √ארך.

tirkatê (?). V 54 *O* 7 = Rm 2, 2 (Hr^L 409) tir-ka-te-e i-la(i)k.

tarik'â'tu. a *pl*? Nabd 206, 7 two ta-ri-ka-a-tu ša (ic) ma-ši-xu; 118, 3; 223, 1—2 twelve ma-na UD-KA-BAR a-na ta-ri-ik-a-ta(-)ša šu (?) ziq-gur-ra-tum; 591, 3 ta-ri-ka-tum ša (? or IV?) ša-an-ša-nu of a goddess.

tarkullu see ţarkullu (359) & add: ZIMMERN, GGA '98. 818 reads tarkullu in

IV^{2} 50 *d* 19 = T^{M} iii 134. K 3500 + K 4444 + K 10235 i 12 (iç) tar-kul-la-ši-na li-is-su-xu e-du-u dan-nu, Winckler, *Forsch.*, ii 10 *foll.* KB vi (1) 290 *col* 7, 21 (= *Rec. Trav.*, xx 57 *foll*) ta-ar-ku-ul-li pi-ir [. . . .], den Schiffspfahl; 493/96 on *del* 97 (102); on the other hand, Thureau-Dangin (ZA xvii 193 *rm* 6) = le mât; IV^{2} 25 *a* 20, the mast planted in the center-part of the ship. Pinches, PSBA xxiii 192 = rope.

tarāmu *1.* crop {Ernte} Johns. K 400 (KB iv 126, 127) 10, 11 qaqqad kaspi (= the original amount) ina eli ŠE ta-ra-me i-šak-kan (ZA xiii 139: wird er aus dem Getreide herausschlagen). See also KB iv 153 *rm* °° *ad* K 330, 23; id ÇAR; Johns, *Deeds & Documents*, 621 *R* 8; 623 *R* 13; also 69 *R* 1; 70 right edge 1 (ta-ra-me) & often.

Tarāmū *2.* in P. N. III 66 (K 252) ii 16 (il) Ša-la (il) Ta-ra-mu-u-a, PSBA xxi 118 *foll*; Bu 91—5—9, 2176 A 21 xi(or çe?)-ni Ta-ra-am-sag-ila, JRAS '97, 613.

tarīmu. part of a door {Teil einer Türe} AV 8790. II 23 *c-d* 26—31 mentions ta-ri-mu as ‖ of (iç) ṭ(d)a-ab-tu-u (353 *col* 2); ta-am-xi-çu, AV 8749; (iç) bur-rum (188 *col* 1; Br 6976); ṭi-it-bu-u (√[illegible]? 359 *col* 2); ik-lal-lu-u; ta-xa-zu-u.

tirīmu. I 67 (Ner) *a* 22 ti-ri-i-mu kaspi ša se-ip-pi-e (+31); see Johns, *Deeds & Documents*, 930 ii 13 ti-ri-ma-ti kaspi.

tarmazilu ‖ qaqū (923 *col* 2). AV 8810. Rm 66, 11: three tar-ma-zi-li (iççur), Bezold, *Catalogue*, 1577.

t(ṭ,d)ur-ma-xu ‖ šarru. II 31 *g-h* 3 & 8 (Br 10577, 4267); Br 5072 on II 32 *e-f* 16; KB iii (1) 67 *rm* **; Guyard, ZK i 100 § 8. AV 3514, 4532.

tur-max-um see Supplement *s. v.* dur-max-um.

tarmanu *1.* (Br 409) ‖ šaggilimut, a stone (*q. v.*).

tarmanu *2.* perh. V 41 *a-b* 8 + II 31 *no* 3, 8 ta-ar-ma-nu = be-lu.

tar-ma-çu (?). V 27 *g-h* 28 . . . . GAL tar(?)-ma-çu | reš (or ŠAG?) . . . .; AV 8811; Br 14244; in a list of vermin, D^{S} 90.

tarīmtu = תְּרוּמָה, KAT^{3} 596; 651 sacrifice, offering {Opfer, Weihegeschenk} BA i 281. √râmu (רום). V 33 vi 7 ta-ri-im-te çarpi (kaspi) ra-bi-ti, KB iii (1) 146, 147 & *rm* †† ‖ ki(= qi)-ša-a-ti (*l* 10). Here perhaps Nabd 823, 2 ta-ri-in-du kaspi ša (il) Šamaš. II 47 *c-d* 10 ta-rim(zim?)-tu.

tirīnu. Sarg *Khors* 132 (*Ann* 292) ti-ri-ni kišadi-šu, KB ii 71 his necklace {seine Halskette}. Delitzsch: *ri* mistake for *ik*; reads ti-iq-ni.

tirinnatu. part of earrings. T. A. (Ber) 25 iii 55 (59, 60) two ŠU in-ça-pa-tum xurāçi ti-ri-in-na-tu-šu-nu (aban) XI-LI-PA.

tarpi'u. some tree or wood {ein Baum oder eine Holzart} AV 8813. Anp *Stand* 18 ēkal (iç) bu-uṭ-ni (151 *col* 2) u (iç) tar-pi-'i I built there. I 28 *b* 15.

tarpašū (§ 66) √rapašu. width, expanse, extent {Weite, Ausdehnung}. Lay 38, 17 tar-pa-šu-u eli ša ūmē pāni u-šar-bi = Sn *Rass* 83 (ZA iii 317). Nabd 1128, 22 (und) itti tar-pa-šu-u. Meissner & Rost, 24 = nabālu, dry land.

taraçu, *pr* itruç, *ps* itar(r)aç. AV 8687. ZDMG 27, 517; ZK ii 106 *no* 1; PSBA xiii 12. id LAL, Br 10115; Zimmern, *Ritualt.*, 48, 13 (çubāt) andulla elišu tatarraç (spread out). — *a*) stretch, extend, spread (out) {strecken, ausstrecken, ausbreiten}. IV^{2} 16 *a* 13, 14 (= LAL-E) see suparu, 2 (779 *col* 1); IV^{2} 6 *a* 16, 17; K 257 (H 128) *R* 10; K 3182 ii 31 see šētu, 2. IV^{2} 26 *a* 22, 23 see šuparurtu & Br 7062. Asb x 64, 65; Sarg *Cyl* 6 *etc.* see çulūlu (877 *col* 2); also Sarg *Rp* 7; 81—6—7, 209, 12—18 (BA iii 260). Zimmern, *Ritualt.*, 54 (= IV^{2} 21 *no* 1 B) 2 ana ni-iš i-di-šu-nu çu-ba-tu sa-a-ma at-ru-uç; 52, 8 çubātē mi-iš-xu ina muxxi ta-tar-ra-aç; also 57, 12; 74, 35 & 39. II 10 *a* 6 a-na ni-iš i-di-ka çil-lu ta-ri-iç. Z^{Š} iii 16 ana nūri(?) qātā ta-ra-çu; 116 ta-mu-u (als Gebannter) qāt-su ana ili u (ilat) Ištar

tirinnu, see qutrinnu, 949/1. ∼ tar-si-tum AV 8812 see xaseltum, 329 *col* 2. ∼ tarpū, tarpūtu read tarbū, tarbūtu.

ta-ra-çu. IV² 15* *b* 55 zi-mu-ša uk-nu-u eb-bi ša a-na ap-si-i tar-çu (extends); 63 çil-lu tar-çu = pm. Rm 279 *O* 26 .... šu ša imitti tar-ça-at-ma, ZA ix 407. H 80, 10 see puluxtu, *b*. Xamm.-*code* xl 48 whose beneficent protection ta-ri-iç (is spread) over my city. — *b*) direct {richten, lenken}. KB iii (2) 4, 20 Nabû & Nin-sabê ... ša ta-ar-sa-an-ni, who direct me = ZA iv 109, 64—5. V 61 iv 42 eli *N* ... it-ru-ça bu-ni-šu, BA i 274. Anp iii 26 see xuribtu, 336 *col* 2; § 89 i; Lyon, *Sargon*, 60; AV 8793. II 64 *a* 40 Nabû-tur-ça-an-ni, direct me! AV 5889. — *c*) prepare {zurüsten}. IV² 58 *a* 28 ter-ça ta-tar-ra-aç; ZA xvi 154 *foll*: eine Zurüstung sollst du zurüsten. IV² 55 *no* 1 *R* (*b*) 21 ter-ça ta-tara-aç. — *d*) drive back {zurücktreiben} KB ii 244—5, 50 at-ru-us-su (> ç-šu) a-di mi-çir mâti-šu. — *e*) Xamm.-*letters* 43, 7 mârê-šu ta-ar-zu-ma, BA iv 471 *foll*: seine Söhne sind tauglich. — *f*) dissolve partnership {Compagniegeschäft auflösen} KB iv 52 *no* v 13, 16 šu-ma (= šum-ma) la-ma û-me-šu xa-ra-nam i-ta-ra-iç, when he dissolves partnership prematurely. — H 32, 743 LAL = ta-ra-çu; V 31 *e-f* 64 = NIR (Br 6288), preceded by NIR-NIR-aç = it-ta-in(= ar?)-ra-aç, 𝔗 or 𝔔¹? Knudtzon, *Gebete*, 325 pm LAL (*p* 52); ag *pl* (?) tar(?)-ça-a-te, 132, 6.

𝔔¹ Xamm.-*code* xxi 82 see below. Z^š ii 88 a-na ân dunâni ubân-šu it-ta-ra-aç, ob er nach einer Gestalt mit dem Finger deutete.

𝔍 Šalm, *Balaw*, vi 5 see bûnu (178 *col* 1); *Mon*, ii 72 kakkê (il) Ašur ina libbi-šu-nu u-tar-ri-çi (1 *sg*), KB i 169. K 1107, 7 mar šipri ša a-na pa-ni-šu aš-pu-ru ul u-tar-ri-iç-ma (did not go to him) it-ti-šu ul id-bu-ub. V 50 *a* 18 tur-ru-ça-ku, Br 4492, 10001. Sn *Bav* 7 see xunnu (285 *col* 2) & § 89.

Š extend, cover, protect {ausbreiten, bedecken, beschützen} Bu 88—5—12, 75 + 76 v 8, 9 see tarânu. V 60 *a* 17—19 ni-ib-xa ša pa-an (il) Šamaš u-šat-ri-ça-am-ma (see 635 *col* 1); 62 *no* 1, 15 e-li kul-lat ma-xa-zi u-šat-ri-çi an-dul-lum, (1 *sg*; § 92); 64 *b* 11 u-ša-at-ri-iç çi-ru-uš-šu; *c* 1 u-šat-ri-iç; also KB iii (2) 48 *col* 1, 42; V 34 *b* 5. Sn vi 48 u-šat-ri-ça e-li-šin; i 44, 70; Esh v 37; Asb x 99 (Winckler, *Forsch.*, i 252); Jensen, *Diss*, 35 (= ZK i 315); ZA iii 308 *rm* 1; vi 452. KB iii (2) 48 *a* 41; I 44, 84—5; L³ 15 (Lehmann) see çulûlu; Neb vi 9, 10 mighty cedarbeams a-na zu-lu-li-ši-na u-ša-at-ri-iç; viii 3, 4; I 67 *b* 30; Sarg *Khors* 160 gušûrê erini rabûtê e-li-šin (the palaces) u-šat-ri-ça = *Ann* 422; 442; *bull* 64; 56 pi-el-šu (802 *col* 2, end) u-šat-ri-ça; S² 61 (Lehmann). — Xamm-*code* xxi 28 if any one e-li NIN-AN (= êntim. priestess) ... u-ba-nam u-ša-at-ri-iç-ma (literally: has stretched out his finger = accuse {denunzieren} ZA xviii 83); xxi 82 it-ta-ri-iç = 𝔔¹?

𝔗 ZA iii 315 (*no* 9) 3 it-tar-ri-iç; iv 241, 7 lit-tar-ri-çu e-li-šu.

NOTE — On taraçu in astronomical observations see Oppert, ZA vi 447—54; PSBA xx 27. Strassm.-Epping, ZA iv 78. Schrader, *Proc. Berl. Akad.*, '90, 1228 *foll*.

T. A. (Ber) 24, 67 i-ta-ar-ra-aç a-ma-a-tum a-na pa-ni *N*. (Lo) 11 + Murch, 51 am-mi-n[im-me la]-a ta-at-ru-uç, why do you not bring them; + 52 a-na pa[-ni-š]u la ta-tar-ra-aç. (Lo) 12, 60 .... ma li-it-ri-iç i-na pa-ni šarri, may it seem good to my lord (ZA vi 248) (Ber) 43, 35 li-it-ri-iç (BA iv 305 *fol*); 102, 41 li-it-ru-uç i-na pa-ni šarri; 77, 40 li-it-ru-uç; 154, 22-3 — (Ber) 52 *R* 24 (amelûti) xa-za-nu-tu u ul tar(?)-ça it-ti-ia, are not friendly with me; 61, 26 u-ul ta-ri-iç (BA iv 308). — 𝔍 (Ber) 154, 6 tu-ur-ri-zu (are directed) to the son of the rebel; 143, 21 u a-mu-ta la nu-tar-ri-iç, but we do not know for certain; 71, 64 li(m)-ta-ri-iç lib-bi eli šarri beli-ia, let my lord, the king, take care. — Derr. these 6 (?):

tarçu *1.* *n* properly: direction {Richtung}. AV 8814. iš LAL, III 47 *b* 22 (al) Tariç-Ašur. — Used especially with *prep*. — *a*) ana tarçi, before. toward, against {vor, nach, gegen ... hin, wider}. K 250, 28 a(*rar* az)-zi-ma (√(u)azamu) a-na tar-çi-ša, I lamented before her ‖ akmi-is ša-pal-ša. Merod.-Balad.-stone iv 18 a-na tar-çi (al) Na-ba-ti, BA ii 263; KB iii (1) 190. K 82 *R* 15 a-na tar-çi ali ša aš-bu-u (amêl) qal-lu-u lu-še-te-qu-u (a question; Hr^L 275; BA i 242 *foll*; PSBA xxiii 53 *foll*); K 823 *R* 10 a-na tar-çi-šu-nu .... li-iz-zi; K 10 *R* 22 a-du-u ina eli nâri a-na tar-çi a-xa-meš na-du-u, they are encamped opposite one another (Hr^{L} 781; 280). K 1203, 10 a-na tar-çi-ku-nu, LEHMANN, ii 78 at your time. Beh 50 (54, 55) a-na tar-çi = against. Su *Bav* 49 the statues of the gods which *M* a-na tar-çi *T* il-qu-ma, which *M* (in the war?) against *T* had taken away, KB ii 118, 119. — *b*) ina tarçi: *a*. local }räumlich{ against, opposite }gegenüber{. II 65 ii 16 ina tar-çi (al) *A* he placed his battle-array. Asb ii 33 see KB ii 168; K 183, 15 ina tar-çi šarri bêli-ja, BA i 618; OPPERT, ZA xiii 268 in the presence of the king. — *β*. temporal }zeitlich{ at the time of, in the days of (§ 81 *b*). II 65 i 8, 18; ii 25, 29 (iii 1, 25 *etc.*) ina tar-çi of such & such a king. Šalm, *Balaw*, iv 1 ina tar-çi *M* (KB i 135); Sn iv 46 i-na tar-çi abi-ja; Esh iv 23 ina tar-çi šarrâni abê-ja. — *c*) ištu tarçi: *a*. local }räumlich{ from . . . . . on }von . . . an{ TP v 48, 49 iš-tu tar-çi (mât) Su-xi, from the direction of. II 65 i 29—31 iš-tu tar-çi (mât) P. . . . (31) a-di L. — *β*. temporal }zeitlich{: since the time of. TP vi 96, 97 iš-tu tar-çi abê-ja.

NOTE. — 1. On T. A. (Ber) 46, 82 see KB v 410 (*ad* 161).

2. Sarg *Cyl* 24 mu-tir tar-çi, AV 8814 read xal-çi, KB ii 12.

tarçu 2. *adj* Z^{Š} ii 55 pi-i-šu tar-çu (*var* ça) lib-ba-šu la ki-i-ni, war er mit dem Munde aufrichtig, im Herzen falsch.

tarçûtu. BANKS, *Diss*, 24—26, 82 ina ni-ri-bi tar-çu-tum(-ti) be-el-tum *etc.*

tir(i)çu, *c. st.* -iriç, AV 8965. — *a*) stretching out, extending (of one's hand: qâti) }Ausstrecken (der Hand){ *etc.* Anp i 37 ina bi-ib-lat lib-bi-ja u tir-çi (*var* ti-ri-iç) qâti-(j)a (ilat) Ištar lu(-u) tam-gu-ra-ni, KB i 58—9; ZA i 367. Lay 44, 15 see šamaru, 2 Š. — *b*) object of the extended, helping hand: favorite, darling }Begünstigter, Liebling{. 81—6—7, 209, 9 ti-ri-iç qâtâ (il) Ašur (BA iii 260, 261); Merod.-Balad.-stone i 26, 27 ti-ri-iç qa-ti-šu (*i. e.* of Marduk) BA ii 259; iii 185. Nabopol. ti-ri-iç qa-at Na-bi-um u Marduk, KB iii (2) 2 i 14; ZA iv 107. KB iii (2) 6 i 3 (ZA ii 73); 8 *no* 3 i 8. — *c*) direction, time }Richtung, Zeit{ ‖ tar-çu. Asb iii 23 ina tir-çi šarrâni abêa; KB ii 242, 53 & 74. Perhaps IV^2 34 *no* 1 *O* 21 u]-šak-ši-du-šu ana ti-ri[-iç?]. T. A. (Lo) 10, 18 i-na tir-çi a-bi-ja, in the time of my father. — *d*) preparation }Zurüstung{ see ta-raçu, 𝔔.

tirçîtu. T. A. (Lo) 4 & (Ber) 17, 15 ti-ir-zi-ti ša bîti-ka, KB v 13: necessaries for your house.

turçu in P. N. Turçu-Ištar.

tarqatu see darkatu & tarkatu.

tararu, pr itrur, *ps* itarrur. tremble, shake, quake; break down, break asunder }zittern, (er)beben, wanken, zusammenfallen{ Z^{B} 111; 118 & *rm* 1. Creat.-*frg* IV 90 (KB vi, 1, 337); V 63 *a* 27 see ṭa-raru, 350 *col* 2. I 44, 59 see rêšu, 1, *c*. K 5418 iv 14 (KB vi (1) 298) see pala-xu, 𝔔 *ps* (804 *col* 2). K 2852 + K 9662 i 2 (end) i-tar-ru-ra šur (KB vi, 1, 337: perh. mistake for *iš*)-da-a-šu, WINCKLER, *Forsch.*, ii 28: so dass er erschrack sie zu halten.

$\mathfrak{Q}^{t}$ = 𝔔 Creat.-*frg* IV 108 (= D 98 *R* 22) see palaxu 𝔔 pr. *Zû*-legend i *col* 3, 5 it-tar-ru, (die Götter) zitterten; § 97; KB vi (1) 54. *del* 87 (92) is read by KB vi (1) 236 at-ta-ṭal; see also *ibid* 220 on NE X *col* 3, 49. V 65 *b* 44 see nâšu (732 *col* 1 *ll* 1, 2). *Etana*-legend (Rm 2, 254 *etc.*) iii 13 see galatu (219 *col* 2) or קלתא (so KB vi, 1, 110). II 19 *a* 7, 8 a-di ša-a-ri i-tar-ru (Br 389) ‖ i-xe-ia-šu (*b* 45, 46) see 343 *col* 1.

$\mathfrak{Q}^{tn}$ IV^2 28 *no* 2 *a* 9, 10 ša-mu-u i-ta-na-ar-ra-ni-šu = MU-UN-DA-[cuneiform]-[cuneiform], EME-SAL (quake before him) see nâšu, 𝔔. K 133 (H 81) *R* 27, 28 (end) ina (= out of) šadi-i . . . . a-ça-at-ma (צאת) i-ta-na-ra-ar (might be $\mathfrak{Q}^{tn}$ of araru; but the id is the same as IV^2 28 *a* 9, 10). IV^2 5 *b* 26, 27 mukîl rêš limuttim . . . . it-ta-na-ar-ra-ru šûnu. II 28 *a* 12 i-ta-na-ra-ar (or √ארר?).

𝔍 IV^2 49 *b* 11 ki-ša-di-MU (= ja) u-tar-ri-ru, they make tremble, = T^{M} i 97.

tariru (?). BA iii 206—7, 8 . . . . ša nâri šu-a-tu i-na ia ta-ri-ri-šu; SCHEIL, *Rec. Trav.*, xvii 81 combines with tararu.

turârum. II 32 *c* 9 tu(= du?)-ra-a-rum

= dar[??-ru?] M^S 102 *col* 1; AV 9052.
followed by da(?)-ri-i-ru & a-na(-?)
da-ru (?).

ṭarašu, Br 2580 on II 9 *c-d* 61; see tarū, 3.

tārtu & **tārātu** see above after tāru, 1.

tārītu ‖ erītu (109 *col* 1, end) AV 8791.
woman with child, pregnant {schwanger}
§ 65, 32*a*; H^F 54; GGN '80, 521 *rm* 1; ZK
i 299 *rm* 1; ii 107; ZA i 393; 402. H 84
—5, 40—43 (K 246 i) ta-ri-tu (id UM-
ME-DA; S^b 119; H 23, 448; Br 3910;
DA = našū ša amēli) ša ki-rim-ma-
ša uš-šu-ru; paṭ-ru; ru-um-mu-u;
la i-ša-ru; *cf* the glossary in II 25 *h* 74
—77. V 52 *b* 14, 15 UM-ME-DA = ta-
ri-tum, Br 12434. K 883, 20 tāri-su-
nu > tārīt-šunu; 21 ma-a ki-i ta-
ri-ti ina eli gi-iš-ši-ja, BA ii 633.
Rm 982, 5 ta-ri-tu it-tar-[. . . .] Delitzsch, *Weltschöpf.-Epos*, 110/11 *rm* 1.
K 3456 *O* 22 id-xu-ud kar-as-su-nu
ša (= like as) eli ta-ri-i-ta, PSBA xxi
37, 38; but see šamxu, 1057 *col* 2. V
31 *g-h* 27 ta-ri-tum = mārat up-pi.
II 32 *c-d* 56, 57 (e-me) 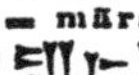 (Br 838;
6005—6) : ta-ri-tu | ŠIT-ME-DA . . .
‖ ŠIT-ME-GA (Br 3906 reads UM instead of ŠIT; but see Br 6004) : ta-ri-tu
| ŠIT-ME-GA (Br 3908: UM-ME-GA-
LAL). *pl* IV² 58 iii 34 šer-ru ša ta-
ra-a[-ti].

turtu *1.* $Z^Š$ *pp* 58; 78 pain {Pein}? Merod.-
Balad.-stone v 38 tur-ti ēnā sa-kak
uz-na ub-bur meš-ri-e-ti may befall
him who ruins my tablet, KB iii (1)
193: Blindheit. $Z^Š$ viii 39 tur-tu ma-
mit *etc.*; & 62; tur-ta, v/vi 67, 77, 87,
97 *etc.*

turtu *2.* a plant {eine Pflanze}. 79—7—18,
183, 6 . . . . bar-ti = šam-me tur-ti,
M^S *pl* 26. Perhaps a herb used for the
healing of the illness indicated by
turtu, 1. See also ZK ii 12, 13 (K 61
a 4); GGA '04, 753; Sm 796, 6 (BT xiv 33).

tērtu *f pl* tērēti. AV 8968. §§ 62, 1; 65,
32*a* by-form tūrtu. Z^B 68; Zimmern,
Ritualt., *pp* 88—9; 91; KAT³ 606 *rm* 3.
— *a*) command, order; law' {Befehl, Geheiss; Gesetz} ‖ urtu (108 *col* 1). Xamm.-
code iii 50, 51 mu-ša-ak-li-il te-ri-
tim, who put into execution the laws (of
Aleppo). V 52 *a* 16 šēdu] ša te-ri-tu-
šu çi-rum, whose commands are lofty.
V 20 *a-b* 20 ID-AG]-GA = te-ir-tum,
Br 6582. IV² 28 *no* 1 *a* 5, 6 te-rit (= ID-
AG-GA) kiš-šat ni-ši šu-te-šir. II
62 (K 49 i) 22, 23 (= V 20 *b* 23, 24) ID-
AG-GA-DUGUD & ID-AG-GA-UD-
DU = ter-tum ka-bit-tum, Br 6585/6
& ter-tum 'u-u-rum, send out an order.
II 22 *e-f* 38 ME-ME-A = ter-tum, Br
10380, 10457. Golenischeff 17, 17 e-na
te-ir-te-ga(= ka?) du(= ṭu)-ur-da,
Delitzsch, *Kappad. Keilschrifttaf.*, 45; 60.
II 27 *c-d* 45 AG (Br 4750) = ter-tum ša
ṭe-mi, *i. e.* tērtum in the meaning of
ṭēmu; 44 QIN = ter-tum, Br 10756.
Creat.-*frg* III 35 (= 93) gab-ša te-re-
tu, gewaltig "von Befehlen"; 14 (= 72)
te-rit libbi-šu. S 1371 *O* 10 ta-bar-
ri te-ri-ti-šu-nu, KB vi (1) 267 du
prüfest ihre Befehle (& 532). V 65 *a* 12
Šamaš . . . . ba-ru-u te-re-e-ti. K^M
2, 18 te-rit kul-lat ilāni *pl* qa-tuk-
ka tam-xat (addressed to Ninib). KB vi
(1) 48 (= K 3454 + K 3935 ii) 13 u te-
ri-e-ti ša ilāni ka-li-šu-nu lu-ux-
mu-um; 46, 1; 296 iii 18; 555. KB iii
(1) 194, 3 xa-mi-im] par-çi ša gu-um-
mu-ru te-ri-e-ti; see *ibid* 195 *rm* †.
81—6—7, 209 (dupl. K 6346) 3 (Ištar) ša
ri-kis te-ri-e-ti xa-am-mat, BA iii
260. ZA v 59, 11 (Marduk) mu-kin te-
rit ap-si-e, establisher of the laws of
the ocean. — *b*) mission {Schickung, Sendung} see šipru *a*) end; PSBA xiii 372. —
c) dispensation, divine ordinance, revelation; omen {Göttlicher Befehl, Offenbarung; Omen}. BA iii 271, 272 suggests
tūrtu as reading of UZU, in connection
with barū, see, decide. King, *Xammurabi*, 56, 26 *foll* ina (šir) te-ri-e-tim
ša-al-ma-a-t[im], auf günstige Vorzeichen hin. Zimmern: determ. šīru wol
zu erklären, dass tērtu in den meisten
Fällen aus einem Fleischstücke mittelst
Opferschau entnommen wurde. *Ritualt.*,
84, 85 *O* 2 ana (?) te-ir-te ši-ik-na-
a[t]; written XAR-BE 93, 2. V 63 *b* 4
i-na te-ir-ti-šu-nu ul-li i-tap-pa-
lu-in-ni; 21 ter-ti ap-lu; 20 du-um-
qu te-ir-ti an-ni-ti . . . . . a-mur, the
favor of this (= this favorable) omen I
perceived; 9 Šamaš & Adad an-na ki-nu
u-ša-aš-ki-nu in ter-ti-ja, had laid

a faithful promise (= Zusage) into the oracle (given me); 5; 23 iš-šak-na in te-ir-ti-ja; 34 ter-ti šu-a-ti ap-pa-lis-ma, *etc.* Neb iv 30 ša-kin šīr dumqi i-na te-ir-ti-ja. V 65 *a* 28, 29 (KB iii, 2, 110). K 3182 iii 39 te-rit-ši-na; 17 (*var* te-ri-te-ši-na) AJSL xvii 142; 140. *pl* te-re-ti-ja IV^2 60* C *R* 10; AV 8056. Šalm, *Obel*, 9 Marduk is called bēl te-ri-e-te, KB i 130; Lehmann, ii 41; *cf* I 27 *no* 1, 5 (end) bēl te-ri-te. IV^2 54 *b* 31 Bēl mukīn te-ri-e-ti. bēl ter-ti V 13 *a-b* 42 = NUN-ME-TAG (Br 2654), which is also = em-qu (37), mu-du-u (38), ep-pi-šu (39), xa-as-su (40), mār um-ma-ni (41); *cf* ZK ii 402—3 (82, 8—6, i 33 *etc.*). — S 954, 24 *etc.* Ištar stands there ana šu-ta-bu-ul te-ri-e-ti (Br 1287). to carry out (?) the omen. Rm 105 i Ēa is called muš-ta-bi-il (or li?) te-ri-e-ti. — On mu-di-e ter-ti (Br 10380, 10385, 10442, 10462) see 513 *col* 2 (end); 514 *col* 1 (beg.); KAT^3 533 *rm* 9. See also II 62 *a-b* 1 *foll*; 14 (Br 13919); 15 (Br 14128); 16 (Br 10380); 17 (& II 27 *c* 47) ZA i 191 *rm* 1; 195; 24f *rm* 1; Br 5642, 5663; 20 (Br 10457); 21 (Br 1457); 25—7 na-sa-xu ša ter-ti, Br 5610; Z^B 26.

II 25 *no* 4 *R* (*add*) = K 4188 iii 36 XAR = te-ir-tum AV 9015; Br 8541. II 27 *c-d* 46 XAR-BE (Br 1539, 8548; = BAD) = ter-tum ša xa-šo-e (see xašū, 2 *b*; 343 *col* 2, end; also Knudtzon, 47 *foll*). II 62 *a-b* 24 $^{(šir)}$ XAR $^{(ur-uš)}$ BE (Br 4564) = ter-tum ša šīri (see šīru, 2) Br 8547. KB iii (1) 32 *rm* 2; 41 *rm* ** reads UR (instead of XAR) = intellect {Verstand}; ZA i 195 *rm* 1; while PSBA xii 285: the bowels. Same id also K 2801 *R* 23 (BA iii 236); IV^2 57 (= IV 64) *a* 58 idātu-u-a $^{(šir)}$ XAR-BAD (= tērētu)-u-a, my signs & my omens.

Etymology: Haupt in Kittel, *Chronicles* (SBOT) 80 | [illegible] command; also *Jour. Bibl. Lit.*, xix 58 & *rmm* 44, 49 on *pp* 71, 72; Haupt in Guthe, *Ezra-Nehemiah* (SBOT) 31; 78; & in Cheyne, *Isaiah* (SBOT) 88 — L^{Pr} 47 √[illegible]; see also Nöldeke, ZDMG 40, 724 *rm* 1; Barth, *Etym. Stud.*, 13; Wellhausen, *Proleg.*, 418 *foll* √[illegible]; but see Idem, *Skizzen*, III 167. KB iii (1) 195 *rm* † & others [illegible]; Zimmern, *Rituall.*, 220 *col* 1 √[illegible]. — D^H 12 derives turtānu from by-form *turtu. See also ZA ii 74; iii 96, 97; JA VIII (2) 193.

tartaxu, *m* spear, javelin {Speer, Wurfspiess} Jensen, KB vi (1) 328 arrow {Pfeil}. AV 8818. Esh *Sendsch*, *R* (19) 29 $^{(iç)}$ qaštu dan-na-tu $^{(iç)}$ tar-ta-xu giš-ru; 41 and himself five times ina uç-çi $^{(iç)}$ tar-ta-xi I wounded mortally. Sn v 60 $^{(iç)}$ tar-ta-xu pa-ri-' nap-ša-te atmux laq(rit)tūa; *Bav* 36 see šamru, 1. L^4 i 22 I threw ki-ma tar-ta-xi as-ma-ra-ni-e nu-ur-ru-ṭu-u-ti, like (light?) spears the cumbersome (heavy) lances. Asb ix 84 BAR (NIN-IB) tar-ta-xu qar-ra-du, *etc.* (KB ii 226—7). KB vi (1) 202 on NE IX *col* 1, 17 ki-ma *tar-ta*[-xi ana b]e-ri-šu-nu im-qut; 216, 35. On tartaxu, as name of a star (Br 401; 5294) see šukudu; Jensen, 49 *foll*; 149, 150; ZA i 257; iii 251. II 57 *a-b* 32 MUL-BAR(= MAŠ)-RA-DI tar-ta-xu = $^{(il)}$ Nin-ib. — KAT^3 650 (below), following Barth § 183*c* compares Hebr תּוֹתָח, Job 41, 21. On Job 38, 36 see Cheyne, *Jew. Quart. Rev.*, x 570, 571 (reads תרתה instead of טֻחוֹת).

tartaxānu. AV 8817. III 66 *col* 7, 33 *fol* $^{(il)}$ tar-ta-xa-a-nu, Br 402; PSBA xxi 124, 125; Jensen, 150 = Lanzenträger.

ta(u)rtānu. commander in chief {Generalissimus} AV 8230, 9064 (šiltannu); § 65, 35. Perh. √retū; or a'aru (see 3 *col* 2, end). ZA v 302 *rm* 1; 304 *rm* 1; Winckler, *Untersuch.*, 93; KAT^3 273 *rm* 3. Sarg *Ann* 399 $^{(amēl)}$ tur-ta-nu bīt KAB (= šumēli?) aq-bi-šu-ma; *Khors* 25 (of a foreign army-commander) Seb-'-e $^{(amēl)}$ tar-tan-nu (*var* $^{(amēl)}$ tur-ta-nu) $^{(māt)}$ Muçūri; *Ann* 27 (KAT^3 146 *rm* 1). Šalm, *Obel*, 142 Dāin-Ašur tur-ta-a-nu rab ummānāti gabšāti; 149. TP III *Nimr* 33 (KB ii 8/9; ZA v 301, 302); *Ann* 17 ina pān pixat $^{(amēl)}$ tur-ta-ni. 82—5—22, 90 *O* 8 sisē ku-sa-a-a ša $^{(amēl)}$ tur-tan-ni (AJSL xiv 16); K 537 *R* 6—7 (= V 54 *no* 4; BA i 221) a-ki a-na $^{(amēl)}$ tur-tan ṭi-e-mu iš-kun-u-ni; K 181 *R* 1 a-na $^{(amēl)}$ tur-ta-nu-šu (JAOS xx 250—1; PSBA xvii, '95, 222 *foll*) = Hr^{L} 373, 205, 197. K 4395 i 1, 2 (= II 31 *no* 5, *a* 26, 27) $^{(amēl)}$ tur-ta-nu imnu (Br 12470; D^S 129); $^{(amēl)}$ tar-tan-nu šumēlu (Br 406). K 321 (KB iv 132) i 35 Mar-la-rim $^{(amēl)}$ tur-tan $^{(al)}$ Ku-mu-xi;

= III 2 *no* xxiv 2. Haupt, *Jour. Bib. Lit.*, xix 71 *rm* 48 connects with tērtu (for original *tărtu); see also KAT^3 606 *rm* 3; 651 (Hebr from Babyl.-Assyr.); D^H 12; ZDMG 32, 181. (amēl) tur-ta-nu occurs in KB i 208 *foll*; KB iii (2) 142 *foll*; & see Br 12469. Haupt, *Kings* (SBOT) 271.

tartaraxu. T. A. (Ber) 26 i 28 ta-ar-ta-ra-ax ša xurāçi; ii 23 tar-ta-ra-ax-šu ša xurāçi; 27.

tešū. ruin, rebellion, revolution; hurricane {Zerstörung; Revolution; Sturm} √ešū, 4 (111 *cols* 1/2). AV 8970. ‖ ešītu, 123 *col* 2; Z^B 71; ZK ii 308 *rm* 2. Xamm.-*code* xlii 59, 60 te-ši la šu-ub-bi-im (√šabū); Ungnad, ZA xviii 20 *rm* 1 = revolutions, not a revolution. TP i 13 Ištar bēlit te-še-e mušarrixat qablāte, L^{TP} 92; Jeremias, BA iii 103. K 3182 iii 25 ina te-še-e, in disaster; iv 17 ina te-še-e qabal (*var* qa-bal) mu-u-ti, in dissolution in the midst of death, AJSL xvii 140 *foll*. IV^2 39 *b* 40 te-šu-u (rebellion) ašamšūtu, *etc*. V 50 *b* 54, 55 amēlu šu-a-tum ina bît ram-ni-šu te-šu-u (= SA-AL-GUŠUR-RA, Br 8130; *cf* IV^2 5 *a* 40, 41 & rixiçtu) is-sa-xap-šu. H 187—8; L^{TP} 92; Hommel, *Semiten*, 307; 497: a female demon. S 31—52 *R* 20 te-šu-u. preceded by pu-u-gu & me-še-eš-tum (see 618 *col* 2). III 69 *no* 2 *e-f* 55 see Br 2619. V 49 viii 8 te-šu-[u] in a calendar, mentioned in a list of plagues. *etc*. Br 49 reads V 16 *h* 9 te-šu-u.

tušū. T. A. (Ber) 28 iii 69: one ša ri-e-ši (rēši) ša aban tu-še-e; = dušû? see 270 *col* 1.

tuššu *1.* see tunšu.

tuššu *2.* wickedness, vileness; strife {Bosheit, Roheit; Streit} or the like. *pl* tuššāti. AV 9068; Z^B 73; Z^Š 54; BA i 520. Xamm.-*code* viii 2 tu-uš-ša-am-ma id-ki, he has stirred up strife. IV^2 17 *b* 21 it-gur libba-šu-nu-ma ma-lu-u tuš-ša-a-t[i]. ZŠ ii 41 tuš-ša iq-ta-bi, preceded by la a-mer-ti iq-ta-bi; iv 32. II 36 *g-h* 6 (+ ⊕ 270) PAP-KUR-DUG-GA = tuš-šu ‖ sillatum, 764 *col* 2; V 21 *a-b* 22 ..... DUG-GA = tu-uš-šu, together with sillatu & bartu, Br 13887. II 35 *g-h* 47 tu-uš-šu ‖ mi-iq-tum (see 579 *col* 2, end).

tišū = תשע. ninth {neunter} NE 54, 8 sa-ma-na-a ti-ša-a; KB vi (1) 78 *R* ii 5 i-na ti-ši-i, followed by ina eš-ri-i & preceded by i-na sa-ma-ni-i. *f* ti-šit = nine {neun} § 75. Sm 669 ti-šit, Pinches. Haupt, BAL 103, 3 & *rm* 3. Also til-ti, *q. v.*

tišab. Nabd 380, 9 ti-ša-ab. irregular form for tūšab, √ašabu, 112 *col* 2, beg. NOTE 2. H^{CV} ix 5; Z^B 54; but ZA iii 366; vi 348 *etc*. √ישב. Creat.-*frg* II *c* 7 (end) when .... tiš-ba-ma (you sit with them). A **der.** of ašabu perhaps also:

tušubtu. K 97 (Hr^L 541) ultu pān tu-šub-te ša ku-tal-li.

tašabšu, AV 8820 see tabsū.

tušubbatu, Br 6101 *cf* turbūtu.

tiškū see tiskū.

tāšlu. T. A. (Ber) 26 i 25 ta-a-aš-li xurāçi.

tašl'i'xu. II 51 *no* 2 *R* 46 (amēl) ki-xu-u = taš-li-xu, see 375 *col* 2. G § 28 compares سلّح, faire prendre les armes.

tašlīmu. P. N. of female slave. V 67 *a* 41, 46 (sal) Taš-li-mu; √šalamu, to which belongs also:

tašlimtu, *pl* tašlimāti. K 762 (Hr^L 446) 1 e-gir-tu ša taš-li-ma-a-ti ša šarru be-li u-šal-lim-u-ni: 6 ina pu-u-ti taš-li-ma-a-ti lu-šal-lim, AJSL xiv 6. Br. M. 84, 2—11 (middle of text) Aplā a-na ta-ši-li-in-di ša xi-it-ti-šu ana *I-M.* i-nam-din, Kohler-Peiser, ii 61 wird A zur völligen Begleichung (= tašlimtu) seines Teiles an *I-M.* geben. II 35 *g(-h)* 45 ta'š'-lim(šit?)-tum. AV 8831.

tašīltu, *pl* tašīlāti. | שאל; AV 8821. — *a)* desire, pleasure; enjoyment {Wunsch, Wonne, Ergötzen}. *voluptas, deliciae*. TP vii 92 šu-bat xi-da-te (*var* -ti)-šu-nu (307 *col* 1, end) mu-šab ta-ši-il-ti-šu-nu, the habitation of their joys, the house of their delight. L^{TP} 178. Esh vi 35, 36 ina ta-kul-te u ki-ri-e-ti (*q. v.*) ina paššūri ta-ši-la-a-ti I made them sit down; BA i 323; *cf* Asb iii 90 ina paš-šūr taknē. V 34 *a* 47 Esagila .... šu-ba-at ta-ši-la-a-tim; see ZA iv 13, 28 = K 3182 iv 25 ... nam-ru šu-bat ta-ši-la-ti-ka. IV^2 14 *no* 1 *O* 30 ina ši-kar iz-za-xu ta-ši[-la-ti]; KB vi (1) 56. ZA iv 228, 12 see rēšu, 1 *a*. —

b) enjoyment; festival, feast, banquet {Ergötzung; Fest, Festmahl}. Anp iii 82 ta-ši-il-tu ina ēkallišu aškun-un. Šalm, *Mon*, ii 80; Sarg *bull* 99 (ta-šil-ta-ši-na); Scheil, *Šalm*, 98, 99. NE 51, 21 . . . . al ta-ši-la]-ti-ja Bābilu bīt xa-du-ti[-ja] KB vi (1) 272. K^{M} 2, 16 (3, 14) ina Ê-KUR bīt ta[-ši]-la-a-ti ša-qa-a ri-ša-a-ka; 1, 18 (K 155) the thirtieth day i-sin-na-ka ū-um ta-šil-ti ilū-ti[-ka]. I 69 *c* 32, 39 balāṭ ri-ša-a-ti | ta]-ši-la-a-ti, KB iii (2) 86. IV^{2} 20 *no* 1 *R* 33 ta-šil-ta šak-na-at, *Rec. Trav.*, xxiv 98, 99. ZA x 293, 47 ina bīt arax i-sin-ni ta-ši-la-ti ni-gu-u[-ti], *etc.* V 31 *e-f* 24 (ZK ii 81) see xidūtu (Br 14121); for *col e* . . . . NI see perhaps IV^{2} 13 *a* 26, 27 bīti ša ta-šil-ta (= KA-NI)-ma, Br 668; AV 8703.

tešlītu *1.* command, order {Befehl} § 65, 32*d*. √šalū. originally: mission, missive. II 22 *b-c* 64 BU-I = te-eš-li[-tum] (Br 7558) preceded by u-ur[-tum]. II 22 *e-f* 54 ŠIT-ŠIT = a-lak te-eš-li[-ti], Br 5991. ZA iv 241, 40 teš(taš)-lit-su.

tešlītu *2.* see taslītu.

tu-ša-am. V 16 *e-f* 31 see šāmu, 1 ג.

tašmū *1.* ‖ salīmu, *a* (762 *col* 1, end) which see for V 33 i 12 (Z^{B} 57; D^{K} 17); K 874 *R* 3—4. Thompson, *Reports*, ii = obedience *ad* K 770 *O* 5 a-rad maççarāti taš-mu-u [u sa-li]-mu; 83—1—18, 175, 8 taš-mu(-)u sa-li-mu. K^{M} 178: prosperity, success *ad* 4, 26 nap?]-lu-us-sa taš-mu-u ki-bit-sa šul[-mu?], whose regard is prosperity, whose word is peace; 6 . . . . . taš-me-e u sa-li-mu; 8, 2 (+ 9 taš-mu-u u ma-ga-ru); 33, 15, 16 taš-ma-a u sa-li-ma; also 61, 19. Pinches, *Texts*, 16 *no* 4 (DT 83) *R* 7 q(k)ir-ri-e dum-ki u taš-me-e li-tap-pa-lu-uš ū-mi-šam. Creat.-*frg* IV 34 u-ru-ux šu-ul-mu u taš-me-e. K 8522 *O* 6 (end) Marduk is called be-el taš-me-e u ma-ga-ri, KB vi (1) 35 Herr des Erhörens und Willfahrens. II 49 *b-c* 60 (star) taš-mu-u ina māti ibašši (≍ AV 2702); *ibid* 62 šul-mu; also Sm 1386, 14. The *f* to tašmū is:

tašmētum (§§ 32 *a γ*; 65, 32 *c*), properly an *abstr. n.* granting {Erhörung}; then used as P. N. of goddess, consort of Nabū, who was the ilu (ša) taš-me-tum. AV 8827, 8828. KAT^{3} 403, 404. See colophon to S^{a} vi *l* 28; also II 23 *b* 41; 48 *b* 39 (Br 10133); 43, 39; 59 *a-b* 58 (see 56/7). K 252 (= III Rawl. 66) i 10 $^{(ilat)}$ Taš-me-tum; iv 32 (Br 11296, 11258; PSBA xxi 118, 119). T^{M} i 148. K 501 (Hr^{L} 113) 5 $^{(il)}$ Nabū $^{(ilat)}$ Taš-me-tum, + 15, 16; *R* 12 (Lehmann, ii 74, 75); Rm 76, 4 (Hr^{L} 358; PSBA xxiii 355; BA iv 508 *foll*). Scheil, *Nabd*, viii 10 $^{(ilat)}$ Taš-me-tum bēlit na-çi-rat na-piš-ti-ja, mentioned together with Nabū. Also see Zimmern, *Rituall.*, 26 iii 57, 58. K 2711 *R* 6 (BA iii 266); K 2801 (= K 221 + 2669) 24 (BA iii 280). K 2801 *R* 39 written AN-LAL (*var* taš-me-tum) BA iii 282; Br 10138; Sm 954 *R* 33, 34. H 32, 747 KUR-NU-UN (?) = $^{(ilat)}$ Taš-me-tum. P. N. Taš-me-tum-dam-qat, ZA i 199, 2. *Berl. Orient. Congr.*, ii, 1, 367 has the form Taš-mi(*var* me)-tum.

NOTE — See Jastrow, *Religion*, 136 *foll*; 220: properly: god of revelation = Nabū; then, name of goddess, always with Nabū. — Halévy, *Rev. Hist. Rel.*, xvii 187; '96, *p* 20: tradition, oracle. Tiele, ZA xiv 187.

tašīmtu, *pl* tašīmāti. √šāmu, 1. AV 8822; Z^{B} 37; D^{K} 57; Haupt, *And. Rev.*, July '84, 96. properly: decision {Entscheidung}; then: intellect, intelligence, wisdom, prudence {Urteilskraft, Einsicht, Überlegung, Bedacht, Klugheit}. Xamm-*code* ii 22 šar ta-ši-im-tim, *cf* xli 76. V 33 *a* 11 (Agum) šar mil-ki u ta-šim-ti. Sarg *Cyl* 47 see mērišu, 1 (593 *cols* 1, 2); 38 see šīxu, 1. K^{M} 41, 3 šarru ni-me-ki ba-nu-u ta-šim-ti (Zimmern, *Rituall.*, 26 iii 45); KB iii (2) 46, 7 mu-di-e ta-ši-im-ti. KB vi (1) 92, 1 ta-š]im-tum ir-[š]a. Sp II 265 *a* xxii 1 (end) šu-e(-)ta(-)šim-ti. II 16 *b-c* 32 la ra-aš ta-šim-ti, Br 3592. V 17 *c-d* 7 (= II 26 *a-b* 10; ☉ 84 iv) ŠA(= LIB)-KI$^{(mu)}$ SAR = ta-šim-tum (Br 8063), with ṭēmu, milku, šitultum in one group. II 7 *a-b* 9; V 39 *e-f* 26 ta-šim(ši-im)-tu(tum). Also perhaps V 16 *a-b* 2. IV^{2} 2 *a* 9 ta-šim-tu (= TUR-DA) ul i-du-u (GGA '98, 825); if so,

Tiâmat, G § 106 (*p* 98) read Tiāmat, *q. v.*

then here also V 23 *a-d* 36 TUR-DA = [cuneiform]-du | ta-šim-tu, Br 4137. IV^2 60* C *O* 4; V 47 *a* 43 see šakkū.

tušēnu (?) Lay 43, 44 *l* 19 ni-im-ri si-en-kur-ri tu-še-ni u-ma-am çēri, *etc.*; KB i 124 *rm* 8; also I 28 *a* 26 b(p)ur-xi-iš ud-ra-a-te te-še-ni (*pl*) (amēl) tamkarrē ..... il-qi-u-ni; it must be a noun.

tiš-pak (or **-xu?**) Br 3013. 81—11—3. 111. (*Jour. Trav. Vict. Inst.*, xxviii 8*foll*) 11 Marduk ša um-ma-nu, list of names & titles of Marduk. See also gloss ti-iš-pak II 57 *c* 35 = ša ram-ku-ti. Z^B 5; 27. BA ii 294 *rm*. J^{AT} 58 = Ninib.

tašq(g)irtu. lie, calumny, slander }Lüge. Verleumdung} or the like. § 65, 32*b*. *cf* Hebr. שֶׁקֶר, שַׁקְרָ. D^{II} 20; D^{Pr} 35; 48; ZDMG 40, 725; ZA ix 200, 23. Sarg *Ann* 76 see tapalu, 857 *col* 2, beg. V 21 *a-b* 20 .... AN-GAR = taš-gi-ir-tu ‖ qar-çu (933 *col* 2) Br 13884, AV 8825.

ta-ši-ru (?) AV 8823 *ad* V 19 *a-b* 54.

tūšaru *1.* § 65, 32*a*; AV 9066; Z^B 98; √našaru, 2 (119, 120). — *a*) prostration, falling down (in worship), *etc.* }Niederfallen, das Sichniederwerfen} V 21 *a-b* 46 tu-ša-ru = la-ban ap-pi, KB vi (1) 399; 445. — *b*) defeat, overthrow }Niederlage}. TP i 78 see mitxuçu (524 *col* 1, *med*) ‖ ii 67 (mitxuç) tapdē; KB vi (1) 445 = Feldschlacht, & ‖ taxāz çēri, Streck. ZA xviii 166; thus = *c*) field }Feld, Gefilde}. KB vi (1) 162 (= H^{NB} 57) 42 [u] ša-lam-ta-šu ana tu-ša-ri n[i-it-ta-di], und seinen Leichnam auf das Gefilde werfen. V 21 *a-b* 45 tu-ša-ru = çi-e-ru.

Note. — qa-an tu-ša-ri; so some for li-ša-ri (see 499 *col* 2, end); others read pa (or, ma)-ša-ri.

tūšaru *2.* K 4256 *O* 2 tu-ša-ru, followed by ši-ip-pu, ç(z)a-mu-u in one group. M^S *pl* 11; GGA 98, 816.

t'ī'š'ā'ru. 82, 7—14, 631 i 29 (BA iii 557) a Nebuk.-text. KB vi (1) 445: etwas wie Trümmerhügel oder Wüstenei. See:

tišāriš. KB iii (2) 62 *no* 10 *col* 2, 1 *Ebarra* which e-mu-u ti-ša-ri-iš, was like a mound of ruins }einem Schutthaufen gleich}.

tašrixtu; properly *f* of *tašrixu; √ša-raxu. AV 8829. — *a*) immense; gigantic; great mass }riesig. gewaltig; grosse Masse}. ZK ii 347 (⨯ ZA ii 81 *rm* 3); BA i 284. Esh vi 29; Asb x 106 see naqū, 717 *col* 2, beg. Sn *Kui* 4, 41 (immer) niqē taš-ri-ix-ti aq-qi; V 64 *b* 22 ‖ takbittu, 1 (Zimmern, *Ritualt.*, 167 *rm* 2). Neb viii 16 see qurdu, *b* (931 *col* 2); 82—3—23, 151, 12 sea šūru, 1. K 2745 iii 16 see BA iii 208. — *b*) greatness, splendor, majesty }Riesigkeit, Glanz, Majestät} or the like. IV^2 32 *b* 2 e-nu-ma arxu (?) agā taš-ri-ix(*var* rix)-ti na-šu-u; o Sin agā taš-rix-ti ana māti na-šu-u. III 55 *no* 3, 6 agū taš-ri-ix(?)[-ti?]. K 555 *O* 13, 14 a-gi-e ... ta-aš-ri-ix-t[i], Hr^L 76; Jensen, WZKM ii 159. K 4386 ii 56 (= II 48 *e-f* 46) KA(si-lim)DI = taš-ri-ix-tum, Br 746; followed by muštarrixu, see 615 *col* 1. IV^2 34 (below) 11 dib-bi ša taš-ri-ix-ti i-dib-bu (?). Esh *Sendsch*, *R* 31, 32 aš-šu taš-ri-ix-ti da-na-an ep-še-ti-ja nišē kul-lu-mi-am-ma.

tašrītu *1.* — *a*) dedication, opening }Einweihung, Eröffnung} | šarū, 1. §§ 34δ; 65, 32*d*. Sn *Kui* 4. 42 ina (= at the) taš-ri-it ēkalli; *Bav* 27: Br 10556. — *b*) beginning }Anfang} Boissier, *Doc.*, 20, 5 (& 15) šumma ina taš-rit murçišu, M^S 98. The same noun is also:

Tašrītu (& **Tišrītu**) *2.* = *Tišri*, name of the seventh Babyl.-Assyr. month, *i. e.* the "beginning" of the second part of the year. § 46. D^{II} 15; Jensen, 238—9 (⨯ Jensen, ZA ii 210 *rm* 1); Muss-Arnolt, *Assyr.-Babyl. Months.* 24; KAT^3 380 & *rm* 2. ⊕ 116 i (= V 29 *a-b*; II 44 & 64; D 92) 7 (arax) DUL-AZAG = ta(i)š-ri-tu, Br 9608. iδ K 1118, 8 (Lehmann, ii 77, 78: Hr^L vol vi). II 60 *no* 2 (*add*) = V 43 *a-b* 34—39 (AV 8830; Br 1277 *on l* 37; 1010 on *l* 38). IV^2 33 *col* iv 11 & colophon, 7 (arax) DUL (Br 9589) ša (il) Šamaš qu-ra-du; Winckler, *Forsch.*, ii (3) 367—8.

tuš-mu-u, tašmū, 2. = atān nāri see kumū, 394 *cols* 1, 2. ~ tašmērtum. AV 8826 see tazmērtu. ~ ti-šam-tum, AV 8868 see ti'i'ātu. ~ taš-nu see urun, 1 (103 *col* 1) & Br 7650. ~ tu-ša-ru, 3 see tamšāru.

Lightning Source UK Ltd.
Milton Keynes UK
UKHW02f0309180818
327398UK00011B/394/P

9 781528 019644